FIND IT FAST

Literary Concepts

Writing Literary Arguments

Preparing for the Free-Response Questions on the AP® English Literature Exam

Ideas in Literature

Building Skills and Understanding

for the AP® English Literature Course

John R. Williamson
Eastern Kentucky University, KY

Mary Jo Zell
Keller High School, TX

Elizabeth Davis
College Station High School, TX

bedford, freeman & worth
publishers

Boston | New York

Executive Vice President, General Manager, Macmillan Learning: Chuck Linsmeier
Vice President, Social Sciences and High School: Shani Fisher
Executive Program Director, High School: Ann Heath
Program Manager, High School English: Caitlin Kaufman
Development Editor: Jeff Ousborne
Editorial Assistant: Sophie Dora Tulchin
Director of Media Editorial: Adam Whitehurst
Executive Media Editor: Lisa Samols
Senior Media Editor: Justin Perry
Executive Marketing Manager: Claire Brantley
Senior Director, Content Management Enhancement: Tracey Kuehn
Senior Managing Editor: Michael Granger
Senior Manager of Publishing Services: Andrea Cava
Content Project Manager: Matt Glazer
Senior Workflow Project Manager: Jennifer Wetzel
Production Supervisor: Brianna Lester
Director of Design, Content Management: Diana Blume
Interior Design: Heather Marshall, Periwinkle Design Studio
Cover Design: William Boardman
Illustration Coordinator: Janice Donnola
Illustrations: Ron Weickart
Director of Rights and Permissions: Hilary Newman
Text Permissions Project Manager: Elaine Kosta, Lumina Datamatics, Inc.
Photo Permissions Project Manager: Krystyna Borgen, Lumina Datamatics, Inc.
Director of Digital Production: Keri deManigold
Lead Media Project Manager: Jodi Isman
Copy Editor: Melissa Brown Levine
Composition: Lumina Datamatics, Inc.
Printing and Binding: Transcontinental

Copyright © 2023 by Bedford, Freeman & Worth Publishers.

Library of Congress Control Number: 2022943721

ISBN 978-1-319-46174-4 (Student Edition)
ISBN 978-1-319-47545-1 (Teacher's Edition)

Printed in Canada.

2   3   4   5   6   7   28   27   26   25   24   23

Acknowledgments

Text acknowledgments and copyrights appear at the back of the book on pages AK-1–AK-4, which constitute an extension of the copyright page. Art acknowledgments and copyrights appear on the same page as the art selections they cover.

AP® is a trademark registered by the College Board, which is not affiliated with, and does not endorse, this product.

For information, write: BFW Publishers, 120 Broadway, New York, NY 10271
hsmarketing@bfwpub.com

To the poets, dramatists, and authors
who create inviting stories
that entertain, engage, and inspire
all of us

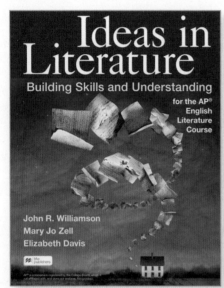
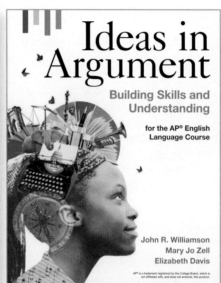

Ideas in Literature cover: © Copyright Maggie Taylor. Ideas in Argument cover: nantonov/Getty Images (brush stroke); klikk/Getty Images (fountain pen); narvikk/Getty Images (typewriter); Ollustrator/Getty Images (color wheel); Imo/Getty Images (book); pedrosala/Getty Images (musical score); dottedhippo/Getty Images (butterflies); bgblue/Getty Images (abstract background); Juliasv/Getty Images (compass); David Malan/Getty Images (young woman); Fotofeeling/Getty Images (elephant); Photographs in the Carol M. Highsmith Archive, Library of Congress, Prints and Photographs Division (Statue of Liberty, Brooklyn Bridge, U.S. Capitol); goktugg/Getty Images (trumpet); WLADIMIR BULGAR/Getty Images (laboratory glassware); Radoslav Zilinsky/Getty Images (scales)

Ideas in Literature is a companion to *Ideas in Argument*,
which aligns with the AP® English Language course.
Together, they foster interpretive skills and empower
students to become critical thinkers and lifelong learners.

About the Authors

Photo by Timothy D. Sofranko for Fort Thomas Independent Schools

John R. Williamson

John R. Williamson is associate professor and dean of P–12 programs at Eastern Kentucky University where he also continues to teach AP® English Language and AP® English Literature at the University's Model Laboratory School. Prior to this role, John served as the vice president of curriculum, instruction, and assessment for the College Board's AP® Program where he led the transformation of the suite of AP® courses and exams, including both AP® English courses. John continues to lead workshops as an AP® faculty consultant. Additionally, he has experience as a reader and table leader for both AP® English Exams. John has taught courses at all high school levels, as well as both undergraduate and graduate courses in composition, rhetoric, linguistics, theater, and literature.

Mary Jo Zell

Mary Jo Zell

A teacher for almost thirty years, **Mary Jo Zell** currently serves as the English department chair at Keller High School in Keller, Texas, where she teaches AP® English Language, AP® English Literature, and Dual Credit English. She is also an adjunct professor at Tarrant County Community College. She is an experienced reader and table leader for the AP® English Language Exam. She served on the AP® English Literature Instructional Design Team and conducts many workshops as an AP® faculty consultant for both AP® English Language and AP® English Literature.

Steve Lemon

Elizabeth Davis

Elizabeth Davis has taught English for more than three decades for Round Rock Independent School District (ISD) and College Station ISD, where she also served as English department chair. She has been a reader for the AP® English Language and AP® English Literature Exams and served on the AP® Literature Instructional Design Team. For over twenty years, she has served as an AP® faculty consultant, conducting workshops in both AP® English Language and AP® English Literature.

Advisory Board

Jim Egan
Brown University,
Providence, Rhode
Island

Celine Gomez
Plano West Senior High
School, Plano, Texas

Susan Pedone
Doherty Memorial
High School, Worcester,
Massachusetts

Jacquelyn Stallworth
Washington Liberty High
School, Arlington, Virginia

Acknowledgments

We are grateful to all who made this project possible:

To our editors, Ann Heath and Caitlin Kaufman, and former editor, Nathan Odell, who believed in this project and brought it to life; Jeff Ousborne, our developmental editor, who polished our prose and wrote introductions that provided context for the literary texts; Hilary Newman, who worked tirelessly to acquire permissions for some of the most current literary works in any textbook; Matt Glazer, our content project manager, whose keen eye kept us consistent; Sophie Dora Tulchin, who helped manage our extensive resource program; Claire Brantley, our marketing manager, who found just the right ways to share our book; and the entire team at Bedford, Freeman & Worth for bringing this book to market and supporting us every step of the way.

To Erick Collings, who helped us find a voice that speaks to students and Brandon Abdon, who developed scaffolded AP®-like multiple-choice questions.

To the many of you who evaluated early proposal materials and helped guide the direction of this project.

To all those who have been in our workshops and fellow AP® readers and consultants who shared favorite texts, instructional strategies, and nuggets of wisdom.

To all our students, especially those we taught while we were writing *Ideas in Literature*, who provided invaluable feedback that informed our final literary selections and whose writings became the student models throughout the text.

To our friends and colleagues who provided feedback, support, and mentorship: Trevor Packer, Jay McTighe, Daniel McDonough, David McFaddin, Brian Robinson, Terry Redican, Christopher Budano, Chris Heiert, Sally Guadagno, Patti Azzara, and Kris Vogel.

And, most importantly, to our families who provided encouragement when we really needed it and who made sacrifices so that we could share our ideas with you: Rob, Sophie, Sam, Mickey, Josh, Kaitlyn, Nick, Hannah, Margot, Jaime, Paul, Jeanne, Jessica, Lynn, Hershey, Paddington, and Robert.

Thank you!

An Introduction to *Ideas in Literature*

Perfectly Aligned with the AP® Units

At the heart of the AP® English Literature and Composition course are Big Ideas that are presented through strategically scaffolded and sequenced units that build skills for achieving success on the AP® Exam.

Ideas in Literature is a complete curriculum that puts the Big Ideas into practice, turning the AP® units into a clear pathway to success in the AP® English Literature and Composition course. The authors have organized this program into nine units, with instruction and practice deeply aligned with the AP® Course Framework. In addition to guiding students to success, this structure will also make it easy to use the resources found on AP® Classroom, such as Personal Progress Checks, released AP® Exam Items, AP® Daily videos, and more.

Why Ideas?

After decades of experience as writing teachers and AP® Exam leaders, the authors agree that the one secret ingredient to realizing success on the AP® Exam is just that — ideas.

It's not enough to just discuss a topic. To be successful, students need to express an *idea* about that topic. That's why **ideas are at the core of every unit in *Ideas in Literature.***

More importantly, ideas — like hubris, envy, greed, power, endurance, courage, faith, opportunity, intuition, identity — are at the heart of literature and at the heart of the human experience. Whether students are reading, writing, researching, or thinking, they will be discovering, analyzing, and connecting ideas.

Diverse, High-Interest Readings from Classic to Modern

In addition to classic works from authors like William Shakespeare, John Donne, James Joyce, and Mary Shelley, we've included a wealth of contemporary and diverse voices like Colson Whitehead, Billy Collins, Toni Morrison, Anthony Doerr, Octavia Butler, Ken Liu, Jesmyn Ward, Joy Harjo, Stephen King, Khaled Hosseini, Amanda Gorman, and more.

Longer fiction units include full-length works:

Novels:	*Frankenstein, The Modern Prometheus* *The Strange Case of Dr. Jekyll and Mr. Hyde*
Novellas:	*Bartleby the Scrivener: A Story of Wall Street* *The Metamorphosis*
Plays:	*The Tragedy of Othello, the Moor of Venice* • *A Doll's House* *Top Girls* • *Cat on a Hot Tin Roof*
One-Act Plays:	*Manhunt* • *Naked Lunch* *Los Vendidos* • *Mistaken Identity*

How Does a Unit Work?

Each unit is divided into four sections, each of which is identified by a color-coded tab on the page.

Big Idea Workshops
Ideas in Literature Collections
Composition Workshop
Preparing for the AP® Exam Workshop

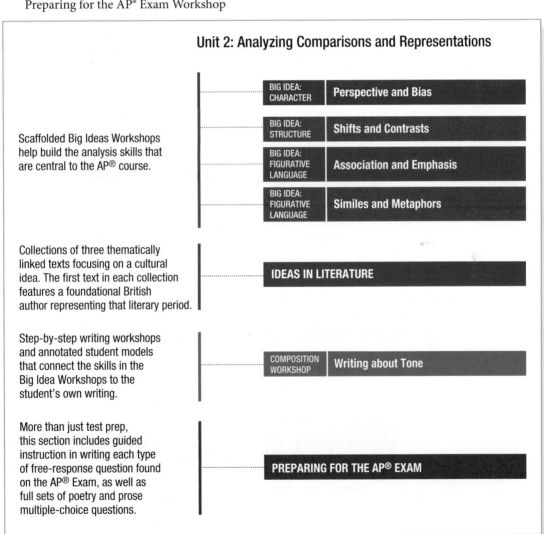

Unit 2: Analyzing Comparisons and Representations

Scaffolded Big Ideas Workshops help build the analysis skills that are central to the AP® course.

BIG IDEA: CHARACTER	Perspective and Bias
BIG IDEA: STRUCTURE	Shifts and Contrasts
BIG IDEA: FIGURATIVE LANGUAGE	Association and Emphasis
BIG IDEA: FIGURATIVE LANGUAGE	Similes and Metaphors

Collections of three thematically linked texts focusing on a cultural idea. The first text in each collection features a foundational British author representing that literary period.

IDEAS IN LITERATURE

Step-by-step writing workshops and annotated student models that connect the skills in the Big Idea Workshops to the student's own writing.

| COMPOSITION WORKSHOP | Writing about Tone |

More than just test prep, this section includes guided instruction in writing each type of free-response question found on the AP® Exam, as well as full sets of poetry and prose multiple-choice questions.

PREPARING FOR THE AP® EXAM

Big Ideas Workshops Teach Critical Reading

Each unit begins with focused workshops in critical reading and literary analysis, keyed to the Big Ideas and Enduring Understandings of the course and color coded to align with the AP® English Literature Course and Exam Description for ease of navigation.

Engaging and Focused Instructional Content That Highlights Essential Knowledge and Builds Enduring Understanding

- Makes relevant connections to illustrate the literary skill
- Introduces key vocabulary and explains the function and significance

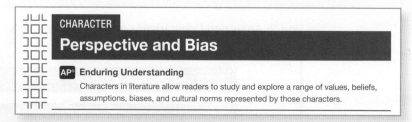

CHARACTER
Perspective and Bias

AP® Enduring Understanding

Characters in literature allow readers to study and explore a range of values, beliefs, assumptions, biases, and cultural norms represented by those characters.

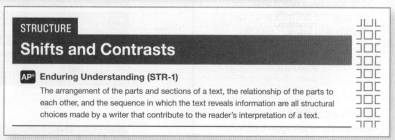

STRUCTURE
Shifts and Contrasts

AP® Enduring Understanding (STR-1)

The arrangement of the parts and sections of a text, the relationship of the parts to each other, and the sequence in which the text reveals information are all structural choices made by a writer that contribute to the reader's interpretation of a text.

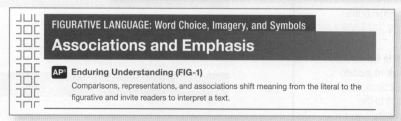

FIGURATIVE LANGUAGE: Word Choice, Imagery, and Symbols
Associations and Emphasis

AP® Enduring Understanding (FIG-1)

Comparisons, representations, and associations shift meaning from the literal to the figurative and invite readers to interpret a text.

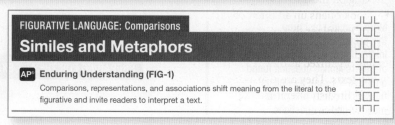

FIGURATIVE LANGUAGE: Comparisons
Similes and Metaphors

AP® Enduring Understanding (FIG-1)

Comparisons, representations, and associations shift meaning from the literal to the figurative and invite readers to interpret a text.

Help When and Where It Is Needed

Key Point Boxes Help Identify the Focus of the Workshop

KEY POINT

A character or speaker's perspective and biases are shaped by his or her past. These biases appear in the character's choices, actions, dialogue, internal thoughts, and interactions with others.

At the start of each Big Idea Workshop, **Key Point boxes** provide insight about the focused skill within the Big Idea.

At-a-Glance Reference Tables

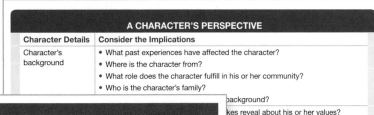

A CHARACTER'S PERSPECTIVE	
Character Details	Consider the Implications
Character's background	• What past experiences have affected the character? • Where is the character from? • What role does the character fulfill in his or her community? • Who is the character's family?

SHIFTS AND CONTRASTS		
	Signal	Effect
Shift	• Contrasting transition words (e.g., *but, however, yet*) • Syntactic markers (e.g., isolated simple sentences) • Punctuation (e.g., use of question mark, dash, colon, parentheses) • Structural changes (e.g., change in paragraph or stanza, one-sentence paragraphs) • A change in the connotation of words or language	Provides a revelation Gives new insight or understanding Signals a change in perspective, tone, or attitude

Dozens of **color-coded reference charts** and **instructional graphics** help students understand the effects of an author's literary choices and strategies.

AP® Skills Practice and Graphic Organizers

AP® Skills Practice is integrated throughout the book to support skill development in an approachable and structured way.

Clicking on the document icon in the ebook opens up an interactive **Graphic Organizer** that mirrors that found in the print book and helps students stay organized as they read and study key texts. They are also available in the AP® English Literature Skills Practice Workbook.

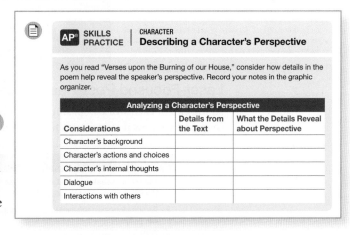

AP® SKILLS PRACTICE | **CHARACTER**
Describing a Character's Perspective

As you read "Verses upon the Burning of our House," consider how details in the poem help reveal the speaker's perspective. Record your notes in the graphic organizer.

Analyzing a Character's Perspective		
Considerations	Details from the Text	What the Details Reveal about Perspective
Character's background		
Character's actions and choices		
Character's internal thoughts		
Dialogue		
Interactions with others		

Corresponding **Graphic Organizers** are available to teachers as generalized blackline masters that provide structured support for any text selection in the book.

Guided Readings and Practice Texts

In the short fiction and poetry units, the first reading in each Big Idea Workshop is the **Guided Reading**. It includes **Guided Questions** at appropriate points in the work to help prompt students on questions to ask as they read. In the longer fiction units, students work solely with Practice Texts.

The second text in each workshop, the **Practice Text**, provides an opportunity for students to practice the focus skill themselves by answering questions at the end of the reading.

GUIDED READING

On Listening to Your Teacher Take Attendance

Aimee Nezhukumatathil

Cheyenne Alford

THE TEXT IN CONTEXT

Born in Chicago to a Filipina mother and Sou
poet and essayist Aimee Nezhukumatathil (b
explores nature, wonder, metaphor, and cult
in her work. She is the author of several boo
prose, including *Miracle Fruit* (2003), *At the [*

On Listening to Your Teacher Take Attendance   Guided Questions

Breathe deep even if it means you wrinkle
your nose from the fake-lemon antiseptic

1. Who are the characters in the poem? What is the relationship between the characters? Who this consoling?

PRACTICE TEXT

Verses upon the Burning of our House

Anne Bradstreet

THE TEXT IN CONTEXT

Anne Bradstreet (1612–1672) was born to an affluent Puritan family in Northampton, England. An unusually well-educated woman at the time, she (along with her husband and parents) emigrated

Courtesy of the American Antiquarian Society, Worcester, Massachusetts

---

Laser-Focused Post-Reading Questions

At the end of each workshop, students apply the skill emphasized in the workshop and see how it contributes to an interpretation of the text.

CHARACTER

1. How is the **speaker** described in the first few lines? What does her reaction to the fire reveal about her **values**?

2. As she reconciles the events of the poem, what does the speaker reveal about her beliefs?

3. How do the **speaker's** values and beliefs contribute to her **perspective**?

4. The **speaker** experiences a new understanding of material possessions and their value. What does this insight reveal about her **perspective**?

Ideas in Literature — Discovering Cultural Ideas

Following the Big Idea Workshops are one or two Ideas in Literature collections that explore some of the ideas and contexts that inform our cultural conversation. They are arranged to highlight cultural ideas that parallel the development of Britain's literary heritage. These sections focus on thinking critically and guiding students to the next level of literary analysis and interpretation.

Each section begins with a brief introduction to contextualize the ideas, and an **Idea Bank** to help students consider essential ideas.

IDEAS IN LITERATURE
Thought and Feeling

The transition from the medieval period to the Renaissance in England (and Europe) was a complex political, social, economic, religious, and cultural process that occurred over two centuries. In fact, no one living at that time would have used *renaissance*—a French word meaning "rebirth"—to describe the era: nineteenth-century historians first applied the term to the period. But the idea of a rebirth captures many elements integral to this revival of Greek and Roman classical culture—and the subsequent flowering of art, science, literature, philosophy, politics, and music.

In a sense, the Renaissance shifted Western culture from being institutionally centered (especially the institutions of the church and monarchy) to being more human-centered. We can see the implications of this humanism in the Protestant reformation that was underway throughout Europe. In England, King Henry VIII (1491–1547) broke away from the authority of the Catholic Church when the Pope denied him a divorce. But a more important change was already occurring. Protestants (i.e., Puritans, Calvinists, Quakers, and others) argued that individuals had a personal, intellectual, and emotional relationship with God: a faith rooted in "knowing" God through their own individual experiences, rather than a faith mediated by the Catholic Church—an institution that Protestants viewed as corrupt. Certainly, the first English translations of the Bible—the Geneva Bible in 1560 and the King James Bible in 1611—nurtured this view. For the first time, an increasingly literate public could interpret the word of God on their own.

But the consequences of humanism went far beyond religion. In contrast to the medieval period, when authority emanated solely from the church and the divinely ordained king, the Renaissance saw the emergence of a new authority: individual experience, perception, and judgment. In England, for example, the philosopher,

IDEA BANK
Beauty
Carpe Diem
Continuity
Culture
Desire
Exaggeration
Feelings
Humanism
Inquiry
Learning
Love
Passion
Reformation
Renaissance
Thought
Transformation
Wonder

The Last Supper, 1495-97 (tempera and oil on plaster)/Vinci, Leonardo da (1452-1519)/MAURO RANZANI (IMAGINART)/ Santa Maria delle Grazie, Milan, Italy/Bridgeman Images

◄ *The Last Supper*, Leonardo da Vinci, 1495. The painting covers an end wall of the dining hall at the monastery of Santa Maria delle Grazie in Milan, Italy.

How does this painting reflect the spirit of the Renaissance period?

Practice Texts That Build Understanding and Context

Each of the collections begins with a foundational text from English literature, followed by two additional texts that are thematically linked to the idea. The following is an example from Unit 2, Thought and Feeling:

- John Donne, *A Valediction: Forbidding Mourning*
- John Loomis, *Deer Hit*
- Nafissa Thompson-Spires, *Fatima, the Biloquist: A Transformation Story*

Questions Reinforce Skill Development

Organized by the Big Idea, a series of questions follows each text. They provide an opportunity for students to apply what they have learned, connect ideas within the collection, and arrive at their own interpretations.

CHARACTER

1. Explain what the description of Fatima reveals about her **values**.
2. When does Fatima's **perspective** begin to change? Identify and explain an event in the story that reveals this change.
3. What assumptions can we make about Fatima and Violet's relationship?
4. As Fatima and Rolf begin their relationship, what **motivates** Fatima's choices?

STRUCTURE

5. Think about what Fatima and Violet represent. How do they function as **contrasts** in the story?
6. The story **shifts** to reveal **tensions** between the characters. Identify a tension and explain how this tension contributes to a change in perspective for a character.

FIGURATIVE LANGUAGE: Word Choice, Imagery, and Symbols

7. How does the **word choice** at the beginning of the text reveal details about Fatima?
8. How do the lists of slang words further develop the conflict in the story?

FIGURATIVE LANGUAGE: Comparisons

9. The story both begins and ends with **similes**, but each evokes a different image of Fatima. What are the similes? How does the contrast between them affect your interpretation of the text?
10. What is being compared in the story? How does the **comparison** contribute to your interpretation of the text?

IDEAS IN LITERATURE: Thought and Feeling

11. "Fatima, the Biloquist: A Transformation Story" reminds us of important cultural values. How does this story compare the thoughts and feelings of the characters in a way that sends a larger message? What is the larger message for all communities?

PUTTING IT ALL TOGETHER

12. The characters in the story are contrasted in many ways. Explain how the multiple contrasts combine to create an extended comparison. How do the contrasts contribute to the conflict of the story?

Composition Workshops — Developing Literary Argumentation Skills

Each unit includes a **process writing workshop** focused on building composition skills and analyzing a specific literary element. Writing assignments are designed to develop critical analysis skills from the unit workshops. As the reading skills build, and students gain practice with writing, they are able to write increasingly sophisticated analyses.

Unit	Writing Workshop	Writing Workshop Skill Focus
1	Writing about Theme	Establishing a Unifying Idea through a Defensible Thesis Statement
2	Writing about Tone	Justifying a Thesis through a Line of Reasoning
3	Writing about Character	Explaining an Interpretation through Commentary
4	Writing about Point of View	Creating Unity through Commentary
5	Writing about Motif and Extended Metaphor	Creating Coherence through Transitional Elements
6	Writing about Symbols	Writing Commentary with Purposeful Syntax
7	Writing about Setting	Writing Introductions
8	Writing about Structure and Irony	Writing Conclusions
9	Writing a Source-Based Literary Argument	Using and Citing Secondary Sources

Structured Graphic Organizers

Each Composition Workshop includes a graphic organizer to guide students as they develop their literary arguments focused on the specific literary element.

WRITING A THESIS FOR ANALYSIS OF TONE	
Template 1: Thesis connects tone to the idea and previews the line of reasoning.	In [title of work], the author conveys a [adjective] tone using [literary technique] and [literary technique], in order to reveal that [unifying idea + insight].
Template 2: Thesis connects tone to the idea and insight.	In [title of work], the author/speaker/narrator conveys a [adjective] tone to reveal that [unifying idea + insight].
Template 3: Thesis reveals complexity in tone and connects to the idea.	In [title of work], the author/speaker/narrator shifts from a [adjective] to a [adjective] tone to illustrate that [unifying idea + insight].

Student Model: Writing about Tone

Review the following student model to observe how the thesis statement, line of reasoning, and evidence work together to convey an interpretation of the literary argument.

Escaping Expectations
Sophia Amstalden

May Swenson recognizes how societal pressures burden her into hiding her true playful, childish nature as a young girl as she looks at a memory of her playing outside and embodying the freedom of a horse. In "The Centaur," through a shift in tone from carefree to judgmental developed by poetic devices, May Swenson depicts the freedom her younger self felt playing as a horse in a tone that shifts and becomes more reserved under the judging eyes of her mother, who represents the societal norms placed on girls from a young age to be good-mannered and composed.

Through metaphors and similes in the first several stanzas of the poem, the girl explores her freedom when she is alone in the yard, depicting the persona of the adventurous and playful nature of youth.

thesis statement with interpretation

idea: freedom

insight: humans desire freedom

tone: shifts from carefree to reserved

claim: societal expectations for girls impede their freedom

Annotated Student Models

To give a clear example of the skill in practice, each Composition Workshop includes an annotated student model demonstrating the skills for writing about that particular literary element.

Preparing for the AP® Exam

Four-Step Process

Each unit includes a free-response writing workshop aligned with the AP® English Literature and Composition units. Students will practice the same four-step process while building their skills, depth of analysis, and sophistication.

Step	Poetry and Prose Analysis	Literary Argument
1	Annotate the Passage Based on a Unifying Idea	Determine a Unifying Idea and Brainstorm Relevant Examples from a Text
2	Develop a Defensible Claim and a Unified Line of Reasoning	
3	Choose Relevant Evidence	
5	Develop Your Commentary	

Instruction in Writing Free-Response Essays

This invaluable section is more than just test prep. It's a detailed guide to writing for the AP® Exam. Each Preparing for the AP® Exam section begins with a mini workshop on a key AP® Exam writing skill.

Each workshop includes an annotated sample prompt that models the steps in the process and a practice prompt for students to practice their writing.

Unit	Essay Type	Key Skill
1	Prose Fiction	Establishing a Unifying Idea through a Defensible Thesis Statement
2	Poetry Analysis	Justifying a Thesis through a Line of Reasoning
3	Literary Argument	Explaining an Interpretation through Commentary
4	Prose Fiction	Creating Unity through Commentary
5	Poetry Analysis	Creating Coherence through Transitional Elements
6	Literary Argument	Writing Commentary with Purposeful Syntax
7	Prose Fiction	Writing Introductions
8	Poetry Analysis	Writing Conclusions
9	Literary Argument	Considering Alternate Interpretations

Explore Each Free-Response Question Type

Free-Response Question: Poetry Analysis

AP® **Enduring Understanding (LAN-1)**
Readers establish and communicate their interpretations of literature through arguments supported by textual evidence.

Justifying a Thesis through a Line of Reasoning

The first free-response essay prompt on the AP® English Literature and Composition Exam requires you to write a literary argument analyzing a poem. In this workshop, you will continue to develop the skills you need to complete this task with a specific focus on establishing a line of reasoning.

Multiple-Choice Prose and Poetry Practice

Every unit also includes a set of multiple-choice prose analysis questions and a set of multiple-choice poetry analysis questions so that students are prepared for all aspects of the exam.

Multiple-Choice Questions: Prose

from The Comet
W. E. B. Du Bois

The following is an excerpt from a sh[...]
published in 1920.

He stood a moment on the steps o[...]
watching the human river that swi[...]
Broadway. Few noticed him. Few e[...]

Multiple-Choice Questions: Poetry

A Noiseless Patient Spider
Walt Whitman

> A noiseless patient spider,
> I mark'd where on a little promontory[1] it stood isolated,
> Mark'd how to explore the vacant vast surrounding,
> It launch'd forth filament,[2] filament, filament, out of itself,
> 5 Ever unreeling them, ever tirelessly speeding them.

Student and Teacher Resource Materials

The Student and Teacher Resource Materials can be found by accessing the book's digital platform or by contacting your Bedford, Freeman & Worth representative. They include a wealth of valuable tools, from graphic organizers and handouts to correlations, pacing and planning guides, videos, ELL Essential Guide handouts, quizzes, unit tests with AP®-style questions, classroom posters, and scored student sample AP® essays.

For more information go to: bfwpub.com/ideaslit1e.

Digital Options | More Than Just an e-Book

Ideas in Literature is available on our fully interactive digital platform. In this platform, students can read, highlight, and take notes on any device, online or offline. They may access additional resources, do homework, take quizzes, and engage in additional activities assigned by the teacher. The integrated **LearningCurve** adaptive quizzing engine provides review and practice on grammar.

For teachers, the digital platform is the gateway to all the supporting resources, including the teacher's e-book, which links to all resources at point of use. This makes assignments easy, and most results sync automatically to your gradebook.

AP® English Literature Skills
Practice Workbook | ISBN 978-1-319-51787-8

Offered for sale, this consumable workbook includes every AP® Skills Practice graphic organizer denoted by the icon in the student book.

Teacher's Edition | ISBN 978-1-319-47545-1

This comprehensive tool provides pacing and planning guides, details on how the content aligns to the AP® English Literature Course Framework and AP® Classroom resources, lesson overviews, reading check questions, instruction strategies and differentiation tips, answers to all questions, and links to reproducible handouts, graphic organizers, ELL Essential Guides, and assessment tools that are available on the digital platform.

Test Bank | ISBN 978-1-319-51788-5

Unit tests with AP®-style-assessment practice questions, a midyear exam, and a full-length AP® Practice Exam give students lots of practice to help confirm mastery of the course content and to help them prepare for success on the AP® Exam.

Brief Contents

Contents

An Introduction to *Ideas in Literature*   viii

UNIT 2

Analyzing Comparisons and Representations

xxiv   Contents

UNIT 3

Analyzing Tensions

BIG IDEA Character	**210**
Workshop Focus: **Static and Dynamic Characters**	
PRACTICE TEXT Sharon Cooper, *Mistaken Identity* ■ One-Act Play	212

BIG IDEA Setting	**218**
Workshop Focus: **Social, Cultural, and Historical Contexts**	
PRACTICE TEXT Luis Valdez, *Los Vendidos* ■ One-Act Play	220

BIG IDEA Structure	**228**
Workshop Focus: **Conflict**	
PRACTICE TEXT Michael Hollinger, *Naked Lunch* ■ One-Act Play	231

IDEAS IN LITERATURE	**235**
Power and Control	235
William Shakespeare, *The Tragedy of Othello, the Moor of Venice* ■ Drama	237
Henrik Ibsen, *A Doll's House* ■ Drama	333

UNIT 4

Analyzing Perspectives

UNIT 5

Analyzing Comparisons

UNIT 6

Analyzing Representations

UNIT 7

Analyzing Associations

UNIT 8

Analyzing Incongruities

UNIT 9

Analyzing Complexities

© Ourit Ben-Haim

UNIT

1

Reading Literally and Figuratively

UNIT GOALS

	Focus	Goals
Big Idea: Character	**Characterization**	Explain how textual details reveal a character and their motivation.
Big Idea: Setting	**Time and Place**	Explain how textual details reveal a story's setting.
Big Idea: Structure	**Plot**	Explain how the sequence of events in a narrative reveals relationships about those events.
Big Idea: Narration	**Point of View**	Explain the significance of the point of view from which a story is told.
Ideas in Literature	• **Courage and Fate** • **Faith and Doubt**	Explain how the ideas of courage, fate, faith, and doubt are reflected in classic and contemporary texts.
Big Idea: Literary Argumentation	**Writing about Theme**	Write a literary argument that explains how an author uses characterization, setting, plot, or point of view to convey an interpretation of a unifying idea.
Preparing for the AP® Exam	**Free-Response Question: Prose Fiction Analysis** Establishing a Unifying Idea through a Defensible Thesis Statement	Develop a thesis statement with a defensible claim and select relevant textual evidence that supports it.
	Multiple-Choice Questions: Prose	Analyze literary elements and techniques in classic and contemporary prose and poetry.
	Multiple-Choice Questions: Poetry	

CHARACTER

Characterization

 Enduring Understanding (CHR-1)

Characters in literature allow readers to study and explore a range of values, beliefs, assumptions, biases, and cultural norms represented by those characters.

KEY POINT

Characters often represent values. A reader comes to understand characters based on their speech and actions, as well as by descriptions of them by others.

Imagine that your best friend wants to play matchmaker and set you up on some dates. How do you gather information about these potential dates? You might start with your friend's description of them, but then you would probably take a closer look at these people on your own to see whether they would be a good fit. In your investigation, you may find out what school they go to, who they hang out with, what they look like, how they act around different groups of people, and maybe even what they sound like. In other words, you would gather details and interpret them as you reflect on whether one of these people could be a match.

Getting to know a person in real life is much like learning about a character in a work of fiction. You gather and examine details about them — their words, actions, relationships, and reputation.

Characters Represent Values

From the very first sentence of a text, the author works to reveal a story's characters to the reader. As you probably already know, characters are the figures speaking and acting in any given story. Authors create entire worlds and adventures for their readers to experience through the presentation of characters. The most fully realized fictional characters often connect with readers and communicate insight to the audience about the real world. But unlike real human beings, fictional characters usually represent the ideas and values at play in a story.

Characters make choices based on their backgrounds and beliefs, and, therefore, embody and represent **values**. Readers learn about characters when writers describe them **directly**, as in stories where a narrator *tells* the audience key details and information. A writer can also reveal characters **indirectly**, as when a story *shows* them speaking and acting. Whether the process is direct or indirect, this element of fiction is called *characterization*.

Sometimes, even a person's name may reveal something about a character's identity. For example, a character named *Faith* or *Hope* may embody or represent those abstract concepts. Some authors use the sound or connotation of a name (*Boo Radley, Ebenezer Scrooge, Lord Voldemort*) to suggest personal characteristics rather than expressing them directly.

Characterization: Speech, Actions, Descriptions

Speech

As you already know, students can often tell a lot about their teachers by hearing them speak for the first time. They may speak boisterously and energetically, or they may speak slowly, solemnly, and pensively. Indeed, we learn much about people, generally, from what they say — and how they say it.

In the same way, readers can learn important details about characters through their spoken words. When characters have conversations with one another, they engage in **dialogue**: another tool writers use to show how characters think, feel, and interact. Other characters' perspectives, reactions, or behaviors can also reveal information about a character that the reader might not have gotten from another source. Alternatively, writers can also choose to reveal a character's unspoken thoughts or feelings directly to the reader by presenting them explicitly.

Actions

As the old adage says, actions speak louder than words. Or, as the novelist F. Scott Fitzgerald once wrote, "Action is character." When characters choose to do certain things or behave in certain ways, they reveal specific aspects of their identity: what they desire, what they value, and how they make decisions. Even noticing what a character does when alone can provide useful information and insight.

Descriptions

Writers often tell the reader what to think about characters by describing them explicitly. For example, they may choose to detail a character's physical appearance, attitude, mood, or psychological state, or to recount how the character behaves around others.

A Character's Perspective

Characters must navigate their fictional worlds from their own perspectives. A **perspective** is a lens through which someone can understand their surroundings and circumstances. These different perspectives (including that of a story's narrator) are like a kaleidoscope: a character's understanding of the world changes and shifts based on events that happen to them, their relationships to other characters, and their own backgrounds, biases, and personality traits.

A character's perspective is shaped and revealed by relationships with other characters, the events of the plot, and the ideas expressed in the text. Perspectives may also be affected by a character's cultural, environmental, or personal background.

Motivation

What drives characters to think, feel, and act in the manner that they do? What is a character's goal? Have you ever been frustrated or confused by a character's actions? Perhaps you may have been on the edge of your seat, asking, "How could he ever betray her?" Or, "Why did she leave when they needed her most?" Just like people in real life, characters' actions and thoughts are driven by their inner wants, needs, and values. But if we understand a character's **motivation**, those motives can reveal key information about the character's background or perspective.

INSIDER AP® TIP   **A character's perspective is different from the author's perspective.** Authors create characters with their own backgrounds, values, and perspectives.

CHARACTERIZATION		
Type of Characterization	**Method of Characterization**	**Considerations**
Direct Characterization	Direct statement from the narrator	**Description** • What words and phrases does the narrator use to describe the character? • What might the character's name reveal about their personality? • What is the character's psychological or emotional state? • What does the character think?
Indirect Characterization	What the character says	**Speech** • What does a character say? • How does a character speak?
	What the character does	**Action** • What choices does a character make? • How does the character interact with others? • What does a character do when alone? • Is the character's behavior consistent?
	What other characters say about the character	**Description** • What words and phrases do characters use to describe the character? • What physical features does the character have? • What is the character wearing? • What might a character's background reveal about him or her?

GUIDED READING

Charles
Shirley Jackson

THE TEXT IN CONTEXT

Today, Shirley Jackson (1916–1965) is a widely celebrated writer. Her most well-known works, the novel *The Haunting of Hill House* and short stories such as "Charles" (included here) and "The Lottery," remain powerful and unsettling to contemporary readers. But in her own time, Jackson struggled to be taken seriously. She also struggled to balance her literary ambitions with her role as the married mother of four children. Jackson's career reflected this divide: On one hand, she wrote humorously about domestic life for women's magazines such as *Good Housekeeping*. On the other, she wrote dark, gothic fiction that provoked — and even outraged — readers. In several of her stories, including "Charles," Jackson combines these two elements of her life, writing a comic tale about a mother and her imaginative kindergartner.

© Erich Hartmann/Magnum Photos

Charles

The day my son Laurie started kindergarten he renounced corduroy overalls with bibs and began wearing blue jeans with a belt; I watched him go off the first morning with the older girl next door, seeing clearly that an era of my life was ended, my sweet-voiced nursery-school tot replaced by
5   a long-trousered, swaggering character who forgot to stop at the corner and wave good-bye to me.

He came home the same way, the front door slamming open, his cap on the floor, and the voice suddenly become raucous shouting, "Isn't anybody *here*?"
10   At lunch he spoke insolently to his father, spilled his baby sister's milk, and remarked that his teacher said we were not to take the name of the Lord in vain.

"How *was* school today?" I asked, elaborately casual.

"All right," he said.
15   "Did you learn anything?" his father asked.

Laurie regarded his father coldly. "I didn't learn nothing," he said.

"Anything," I said. "Didn't learn anything."

Guided Questions

1. What details does the narrator use to describe Laurie? What does this reveal about Laurie?

"The teacher spanked a boy, though," Laurie said, addressing his bread and butter. "For being fresh," he added, with his mouth full.

20   "What did he do?" I asked. "Who was it?"

Laurie thought. "It was Charles," he said. "He was fresh. The teacher spanked him and made him stand in a corner. He was awfully fresh."

"What did he do?" I asked again, but Laurie slid off his chair, took a cookie, and left, while his father was still saying, "See here, young
25 man."

The next day Laurie remarked at lunch, as soon as he sat down, "Well, Charles was bad again today." He grinned enormously and said, "Today Charles hit the teacher."

"Good heavens," I said, mindful of the Lord's name, "I suppose he got
30 spanked again?"

"He sure did," Laurie said. "Look up," he said to his father.

"What?" his father said, looking up.

"Look down," Laurie said. "Look at my thumb. Gee, you're dumb." He began to laugh insanely.

35   "Why did Charles hit the teacher?" I asked quickly.

"Because she tried to make him color with red crayons," Laurie said. "Charles wanted to color with green crayons so he hit the teacher and she spanked him and said nobody play with Charles but everybody did."

The third day—it was Wednesday of the first week—Charles bounced
40 a see-saw on the head of a little girl and made her bleed, and the teacher made him stay inside all during recess. Thursday Charles had to stand in a corner during story-time because he kept pounding his feet on the floor. Friday Charles was deprived of blackboard privileges because he threw chalk.

45   On Saturday I remarked to my husband, "Do you think kindergarten is too unsettling for Laurie? All this toughness, and bad grammar, and this Charles boy sounds like such a bad influence."

"It'll be all right," my husband said reassuringly. "Bound to be people like Charles in the world. Might as well meet them now as later."

50   On Monday Laurie came home late, full of news. "Charles," he shouted as he came up the hill; I was waiting anxiously on the front steps. "Charles," Laurie yelled all the way up the hill, "Charles was bad again."

"Come right in," I said, as soon as he came close enough. "Lunch is waiting."

55   "You know what Charles did?" he demanded, following me through the door. "Charles yelled so in school they sent a boy in from first grade to tell the teacher she had to make Charles keep quiet, and so Charles had to stay after school. And so all the children stayed to watch him."

"What did he do?" I asked.

Guided Questions

2. How does Laurie describe Charles? What does that description reveal about Laurie's feelings toward Charles?

3. What does Laurie's departure suggest to his father?

4. What does the ongoing description reveal about Charles?

5. How do Laurie's comments to his father reveal Charles' "toughness"?

6. What details does Laurie convey to his parents in the next few days about Charles? Why does he continue to tell his parents about Charles?

60 "He just sat there," Laurie said, climbing into his chair at the table. "Hi,
Pop, y'old dust mop."

"Charles had to stay after school today," I told my husband. "Everyone
stayed with him."

"What does this Charles look like?" my husband asked Laurie. "What's
65 his other name?"

"He's bigger than me," Laurie said. "And he doesn't have any rubbers
and he doesn't ever wear a jacket."

Monday night was the first Parent-Teachers meeting, and only the fact
that the baby had a cold kept me from going; I wanted passionately to
70 meet Charles's mother. On Tuesday Laurie remarked suddenly, "Our
teacher had a friend come to see her in school today."

"Charles's mother?" my husband and I asked simultaneously.

"Naaah," Laurie said scornfully. "It was a man who came and made us
do exercises, we had to touch our toes. Look." He climbed down from his
75 chair and squatted down and touched his toes. "Like this," he said. He got
solemnly back into his chair and said, picking up his fork, "Charles didn't
even *do* exercises."

"That's fine," I said heartily. "Didn't Charles want to do exercises?"

"Naaah," Laurie said. "Charles was so fresh to the teacher's friend he
80 wasn't *let* do exercises."

"Fresh again?" I said.

"He kicked the teacher's friend," Laurie said. "The teacher's friend told
Charles to touch his toes like I just did and Charles kicked him."

"What are they going to do about Charles, do you suppose?" Laurie's
85 father asked him.

Laurie shrugged elaborately. "Throw him out of school, I guess," he
said.

Wednesday and Thursday were routine; Charles yelled during story
hour and hit a boy in the stomach and made him cry. On Friday Charles
90 stayed after school again and so did all the other children.

With the third week of kindergarten Charles was an institution in our
family; the baby was being a Charles when she cried all afternoon; Laurie
did a Charles when he filled his wagon full of mud and pulled it through
the kitchen; even my husband, when he caught his elbow in the tele-
95 phone cord and pulled telephone, ashtray, and a bowl of flowers off the
table, said, after the first minute, "Looks like Charles."

During the third and fourth weeks it looked like a reformation in
Charles; Laurie reported grimly at lunch on Thursday of the third week,
"Charles was so good today the teacher gave him an apple."

100   "What?" I said, and my husband added warily, "You mean Charles?"

Guided Questions

7. How do other
children in the
class feel about
Charles? How do
you know? Why
are all the other
children staying
after school?

8. What is meant
by, "Laurie did
a Charles," and
what does that
reveal about their
relationship?

"Charles," Laurie said. "He gave the crayons around and he picked up the books afterward and the teacher said he was her helper."

"What happened?" I asked incredulously.

"He was her helper, that's all," Laurie said, and shrugged.

105   "Can this be true, about Charles?" I asked my husband that night. "Can something like this happen?"

"Wait and see," my husband said cynically. "When you've got a Charles to deal with, this may mean he's only plotting."

He seemed to be wrong. For over a week Charles was the teacher's
110 helper; each day he handed things out and he picked things up; no one had to stay after school.

"The PTA meeting's next week again," I told my husband one evening. "I'm going to find Charles's mother there."

"Ask her what happened to Charles," my husband said. "I'd like to
115 know."

"I'd like to know myself," I said.

On Friday of that week things were back to normal. "You know what Charles did today?" Laurie demanded at the lunch table, in a voice slightly awed. "He told a little girl to say a word and she said it and the teacher
120 washed her mouth out with soap and Charles laughed."

"What word?" his father asked unwisely, and Laurie said, "I'll have to whisper it to you, it's so bad." He got down off his chair and went around to his father. His father bent his head down and Laurie whispered joyfully. His father's eyes widened.

125   "Did Charles tell the little girl to say *that*?" he asked respectfully.

"She said it *twice*," Laurie said. "Charles told her to say it *twice*."

"What happened to Charles?" my husband asked.

"Nothing," Laurie said. "He was passing out the crayons."

Monday morning Charles abandoned the little girl and said the evil
130 word himself three or four times, getting his mouth washed out with soap each time. He also threw chalk.

My husband came to the door with me that evening as I set out for the PTA meeting. "Invite her over for a cup of tea after the meeting," he said. "I want to get a look at her."

135   "If only she's there," I said prayerfully.

"She'll be there," my husband said. "I don't see how they could hold a PTA meeting without Charles's mother."

At the meeting I sat restlessly, scanning each comfortable matronly face, trying to determine which one hid the secret of Charles. None of
140 them looked to me haggard enough. No one stood up in the meeting and apologized for the way her son had been acting. No one mentioned Charles.

9. What do you think changed Charles's behavior in school?

10. What may have changed Charles's behavior again?

After the meeting I identified and sought out Laurie's kindergarten teacher. She had a plate with a cup of tea and a piece of chocolate cake;
145 I had a plate with a cup of tea and a piece of marshmallow cake. We maneuvered up to one another cautiously, and smiled.

"I've been so anxious to meet you," I said. "I'm Laurie's mother."

"We're all so interested in Laurie," she said.

"Well, he certainly likes kindergarten," I said. "He talks about it all the
150 time."

"We had a little trouble adjusting, the first week or so," she said primly, "but now he's a fine little helper. With occasional lapses, of course."

"Laurie usually adjusts very quickly," I said. "I suppose this time it's Charles's influence."

155 "Charles?"

"Yes," I said, laughing, "you must have your hands full in that kindergarten, with Charles."

"Charles?" she said. "We don't have any Charles in the kindergarten."

Guided Questions

11. What does the teacher's dialogue reveal about Charles?

PRACTICE TEXT

Here There Be Tygers
Stephen King

Scott Eisen/Getty Images Entertainment/ GettyImages

THE TEXT IN CONTEXT

Stephen King (b. 1947) is one of America's most popular and prolific writers of horror stories and novels. His most well-known fiction includes *Carrie* (1974), *The Shining* (1977), *The Stand* (1978), *It* (1986), *Dr. Sleep* (2013), and *The Lady of Shadows* (2020). In the short story "Here There Be Tygers" (1968), which he wrote as a teenager, King evokes a child's dread of a particular teacher, as well as the prosaic humiliations of being in school. But the writer also uses this commonplace setting as the backdrop for a surprising and surreal tale of horror. Achieving the related effects of terror, suspense, and horror is no simple feat, as King notes in his nonfiction book *Danse Macabre* (1981): "What's behind the door or lurking at the top of the stairs is never as frightening as the door or the staircase itself."

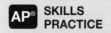 SKILLS PRACTICE | CHARACTER
Analyzing Character

As you read Stephen King's "Here There Be Tygers," think about how the details of the story contribute to your understanding of the main character. Use the following graphic organizer to capture details from the text and describe what they reveal about Charles.

Analyzing Character

Speech
- What does a character say?
- How does a character speak?

Details from the text:	What does this reveal about the character?

Action
- What choices does a character make?
- How does the character interact with others?
- Is the character's behavior consistent?
- What does a character do when alone?

Details from the text:	What does this reveal about the character?

Description
- What physical features does the character have?
- What is the character wearing?
- What might a character's background reveal about him or her?
- What words and phrases does the narrator or other characters use to describe the character?
- What might the character's name reveal about their personality?

Details from the text:	What does this reveal about the character?

Here There Be Tygers

Charles needed to go to the bathroom very badly.

There was no longer any use in trying to fool himself that he could wait for recess. His
5 bladder was screaming at him, and Miss Bird had caught him squirming.

There were three third-grade teachers in the Acorn Street Grammar School. Miss Kinney was young and blond and bouncy
10 and had a boyfriend who picked her up after school in a blue Camaro. Mrs. Trask was shaped like a Moorish pillow and did her hair in braids and laughed boomingly. And there was Miss Bird.

15 Charles had known he would end up with Miss Bird. He had *known* that. It had been inevitable. Because Miss Bird obviously wanted to destroy him. She did not allow children to go to the basement. The base-
20 ment, Miss Bird said, was where the boilers were kept, and well-groomed ladies and gen-tlemen would never go down *there*, because basements were nasty, sooty old things. Young ladies and gentlemen do not go to the
25 basement, she said. They go to the *bathroom*.

Charles squirmed again.

Miss Bird cocked an eye at him. "Charles," she said clearly, still pointing her pointer at Bolivia, "do you need to go to the bathroom?"
30 Cathy Scott in the seat ahead of him gig-gled, wisely covering her mouth.

Kenny Griffen sniggered and kicked Charles under his desk.

Charles went bright red.
35 "Speak up, Charles," Miss Bird said brightly. "Do you need to—" (*urinate she'll say urinate she always does*).

"Yes, Miss Bird."

"Yes, what?"
40 "I have to go to the base—to the bath-room."

Miss Bird smiled. "Very well, Charles. You may go to the bathroom and urinate. Is that what you need to do? Urinate?"
45 Charles hung his head, convicted.

"Very well, Charles. You may do so. And next time kindly don't wait to be asked." General giggles. Miss Bird rapped the board with her pointer.

50 Charles trudged up the row toward the door, thirty pairs of eyes boring into his back, and every one of those kids, including Cathy Scott, knew that he was going into the bath-room to urinate. The door was at least a foot-
55 ball field's length away. Miss Bird did not go on with the lesson but kept her silence until he had opened the door, entered the bless-edly empty hall, and shut the door again.

He walked down toward the boys' bath-
60 room (*basement IF I WANT*) dragging his fin-gers along the cool tile of the wall, letting them bounce over the thumbtack-stippled bulletin board and slide lightly across the red (*BREAK GLASS IN CASE OF EMERGENCY*) fire-
65 alarm box.

Miss Bird liked it. Miss Bird liked making him have a red face. In front of Cathy Scott—who never needed to go to the base-ment, was that fair?—and everybody else.
70 Old *b-i-t-c-h*, he thought. He spelled because he had decided last year God didn't say it was a sin if you spelled.

He went into the boys' bathroom.

It was very cool inside, with a faint, not
75 unpleasant smell of chlorine hanging pun-gently in the air. Now, in the middle of the morning, it was clean and deserted, peaceful and quite pleasant, not at all like the smoky, stinky cubicle at the Star Theatre downtown.
80 The bathroom (*!basement!*) was built like an L, the short side lined with tiny square mirrors and white porcelain washbowls and

a paper towel dispenser, (NIBROC) the longer side with two urinals and three toilet
85 cubicles.

Charles went around the corner after glancing morosely at his thin, rather pallid face in one of the mirrors.

The tiger was lying down at the far end,
90 just underneath the pebbly-white window. It was a large tiger, with tawny venetian blinds and dark stripes laid across its pelt. It looked up alertly at Charles, and its green eyes narrowed. A kind of silky, purring grunt issued
95 from its mouth. Smooth muscles flexed, and the tiger got to its feet. Its tail switched, making little chinking sounds against the porcelain side of the last urinal.

The tiger looked quite hungry and very
100 vicious.

Charles hurried back the way he had come. The door seemed to take forever to wheeze pneumatically closed behind him, but when it did, he considered himself safe.
105 This door only swung in, and he could not remember ever reading or hearing that tigers are smart enough to open doors.

Charles wiped the back of his hand across his nose. His heart was thumping so hard he
110 could hear it. He still needed to go to the basement, worse than ever.

He squirmed, winced, and pressed a hand against his belly. He really had to go to the basement. If he could only be sure no one
115 would come, he could use the girls'. It was right across the hall. Charles looked at it longingly, knowing he would never dare, not in a million years. What if Cathy Scott should come? Or—black horror!—what if *Miss Bird*
120 should come?

Perhaps he had imagined the tiger.

He opened the door wide enough for one eye and peeked in.

The tiger was peeking back from around
125 the angle of the L, its eye a sparkling green.

Charles fancied he could see a tiny blue fleck in that deep brilliance, as if the tiger's eye had eaten one of his own. As if—

A hand slid around his neck.
130 Charles gave a stifled cry and felt his heart and stomach cram up into his throat. For one terrible moment he thought he was going to wet himself.

It was Kenny Griffen, smiling compla-
135 cently. "Miss Bird sent me after you 'cause you been gone six years. You're in trouble."

"Yeah, but I can't go to the basement," Charles said, feeling faint with the fright Kenny had given him.
140 "Yer constipated!" Kenny chortled gleefully. "Wait'll I tell *Caaathy!*"

"You better not!" Charles said urgently. "Besides, I'm not. There's a tiger in there."

"What's he doing?" Kenny asked. "Takin a
145 piss?"

"I don't know," Charles said, turning his face to the wall. "I just wish he'd go away." He began to weep.

"Hey," Kenny said, bewildered and a little
150 frightened. "Hey."

"What if I have to go? What if I can't help it? Miss Bird'll say—"

"Come on," Kenny said, grabbing his arm in one hand and pushing the door open with
155 the other. "You're making it up."

They were inside before Charles, terrified, could break free and cower back against the door.

"Tiger," Kenny said disgustedly. "Boy, Miss
160 Bird's gonna kill you."

"It's around the other side."

Kenny began to walk past the washbowls. "Kitty-kitty-kitty? Kitty?"

"Don't!" Charles hissed.
165 Kenny disappeared around the corner. "Kitty-kitty? Kitty-kitty? Kit—"

Charles darted out the door again and pressed himself against the wall, waiting, his

hands over his mouth and his eyes squinched
170 shut, waiting, waiting for the scream.

There was no scream.

He had no idea how long he stood there, frozen, his bladder bursting. He looked at the door to the boys' basement. It told him noth-
175 ing. It was just a door.

He wouldn't.

He *couldn't*.

But at last he went in.

The washbowls and the mirrors were
180 neat, and the faint smell of chlorine was unchanged. But there seemed to be a smell under it. A faint, unpleasant smell, like freshly sheared copper. With groaning (but silent) trepidation, he went to the corner of
185 the L and peeped around. The tiger was sprawled on the floor, licking its large paws with a long pink tongue. It looked incuriously at Charles. There was a torn piece of shirt caught in one set of claws.
190 But his need was a white agony now, and he couldn't help it. He *had* to. Charles tiptoed back to the white porcelain basin closest the door.

Miss Bird slammed in just as he was zipping his pants.
195 "Why, you dirty, filthy little boy," she said almost reflectively.

Charles was keeping a weather eye on the corner. "I'm sorry, Miss Bird . . . the tiger . . .

I'm going to clean the sink . . . I'll use soap . . .
200 I swear I will . . ."

"Where's Kenneth?" Miss Bird asked calmly.

"I don't know."

He didn't, really.
205 "Is he back there?"

"No!" Charles cried.

Miss Bird stalked to the place where the room bent. "Come here, Kenneth. Right this moment."
210 "Miss Bird—"

But Miss Bird was already around the corner. She meant to pounce. Charles thought Miss Bird was about to find out what pouncing was really all about.
215 He went out the door again. He got a drink at the drinking fountain. He looked at the American flag hanging over the entrance to the gym. He looked at the bulletin board. Woodsy Owl said GIVE A HOOT, DONT
220 POLLUTE. Officer Friendly said NEVER RIDE WITH STRANGERS. Charles read everything twice.

Then he went back to the classroom, walked down his row to his seat with his
225 eyes on the floor, and slid into his seat. It was a quarter to eleven. He took out Roads to Everywhere and began to read about Bill at the Rodeo.

CHARACTER

1. What words, phrases, and actions does the narrator use to describe the **character** Charles? What does this description reveal about Charles?

2. What does the reader know about Miss Bird's **character**? How is this revealed?

3. What is the relationship between Charles and Miss Bird? What does this relationship reveal about Charles's **perspective**?

4. What do Charles's choices and actions reveal about his **motivation**?

Time and Place

 Enduring Understanding (SET-1)

Setting and the details associated with it not only depict a time and place but also convey values associated with that setting.

KEY POINT

The setting (time and place a story occurs) may represent values that are important to the story.

While you may not know the name Edward Bulwer-Lytton, you probably know one of his most famous lines: "It was a dark and stormy night."

To the author's credit, that's just a part of the full opening line. The full sentence reads: "It was a dark and stormy night; the rain fell in torrents — except at occasional intervals, when it was checked by a violent gust of wind which swept up the streets (for it is in London that our scene lies), rattling along the housetops, and fiercely agitating the scanty flame of the lamps that struggled against the darkness."

Bulwer-Lytton first published this infamous line in his 1830 novel *Paul Clifford*. But in the nearly two centuries since, readers and writers alike have referred to it so often that it is now a melodramatic cliché.

Today, the San Jose State University English Department holds the annual Bulwer-Lytton Fiction Contest to recognize the worst examples of "dark and stormy night" writing. The contest challenges entrants to create an original story with "the opening sentence to the worst of all possible novels." The "best" of the resulting entries are published in a series of books.

This opening line (like many other notable opening lines in fiction) serves to introduce the audience to the setting, which includes not only the time, place, and physical location but also — more importantly — the values those elements represent.

It Was the Best of Times, It Was the Worst of Times

Dickens's famous opening line certainly does one thing well: it establishes the setting. In the most basic definition, **setting** is the time and place during which the events of a text happen. The setting also includes the physical environment of a story.

Everything that has ever happened to us has occurred at a moment in time and space. Our experiences are tied to our interactions with our environment: where we are and *when* we are. Likewise, authors set their stories in a specific time and place for innumerable reasons — to establish plot, to make stories realistic (or fantastic), to explore a theme at a key historical moment, to examine characters in a particular social or natural environment. Regardless, the setting is a critical element to consider as you interpret a story.

The author can reveal elements of the setting through a narrator's direct statements and descriptions. Or, readers may need to infer the setting through details and descriptions provided by the story's characters.

When authors choose to include details about the setting, they're communicating more than just facts about the time and place. The following elements are all part of a story's setting:

- Time of year
- Time of day
- The weather or climate
- The geographical location
- The physical description of the surroundings and/or landscape
- The lighting (or lack thereof)
- The culture

A setting might be historical (e.g., nineteenth-century Paris), contemporary (e.g., a small rural town with only one stoplight and a diner), or imaginary (e.g., the Upside Down, Asgard, or Gravity Falls). Writers build these fictional worlds with detailed descriptions, vivid imagery, and other literary tools. The reader must ask, "What kind of impression do these details and descriptions give? How do they affect my understanding of the story or characters?"

Settings Reveal Values

Perhaps more importantly, settings reveal **values**, which may help the reader interpret the story in a meaningful way. A setting can be part of a cycle, such as the changing of the seasons. For instance, a story set in spring may illustrate the theme of renewal. In contrast, a story set in winter may suggest ideas of death or destruction. Similarly, when an author chooses to set a story in a particular environment, that environment may reveal something about the values and traditions of a community. A story set in the American South, for instance, may explore parts of that culture, such as family, race, social class, religion, or a sense of place.

A Setting May Be a Character

Some settings are so lifelike that they function in stories like a character. A haunted house, for example, may interact with other characters and influence the narrative. Additionally, natural features such as the sea or a forest may take on a role as a character if the narrator chooses to characterize them as such, directly or indirectly. If an element in the setting appears to make choices or have emotions, it may be functioning as more than just a representation of values.

INSIDER AP® TIP

Setting is more than time and place. Careful readers use the details of the story to understand why a writer chose a particular setting. You must be able to explain the significance and relevance of the setting, as well as how the author's intentional choice of setting contributes to the writer's message.

SETTING	
Aspect of Setting	**Questions to Consider**
Place	• Is the location urban or rural? Why is this important? • Is the location nondescript? Could the story take place anywhere in the world? • Is the story set in a significant cultural or religious location? • Is the setting physically isolated or deeply integrated into a community? What does this suggest? • Does the story take place inside or outside? What details of this choice may be significant?
Time	• Does the story take place in the past, present, or future? • Is the story happening in a particular historical period? • What season of the year is it? • What day, week, or month is it? • What time of day does the story take place or span? • Are the characters recognizing any holidays or events? • How long does the story take place? Minutes? Hours? A day? Multiple days? A year? Multiple years?
Physical Environment	• What geographical location is the setting for the story? Do you know the country, territory, state, city, town, neighborhood, or location? • How is the landscape described? • What are the weather conditions and climate like? • Are there natural features (such as the forest, the sea, or the mountains)? • Are there constructed or architectural features (e.g., hospital, an ice skating rink, a bridge, etc.)?

GUIDED READING

The Flowers
Alice Walker

Bruce Glikas/FilmMagic/Getty Images

THE TEXT IN CONTEXT

In "The Flowers," writer and activist Alice Walker (b. 1944) explores themes that recur in her work: race, the American South, and the perspectives of women and girls. She also evokes the history of lynching in the United States. According to the National Association for the Advancement of Colored People (NAACP), 4,743 people were lynched in the United States between 1882 and 1968. These murders were often justified by their perpetrators as reprisals against African Americans for perceived crimes or improprieties. But lynching was an act of vigilante terrorism that spread fear and helped maintain white supremacy. Growing up as the daughter of two sharecroppers in Jim Crow–era Georgia, Walker was familiar with the practice. Walker herself moved to New York to attend Sarah Lawrence College but returned to the South after graduating to work in the civil rights movement. She also began a celebrated writing career that now includes dozens of novels and books of poetry, along with several collections of essays and short stories. Walker remains best known for her 1982 novel *The Color Purple*, which won a Pulitzer Prize and the National Book Award.

The Flowers

It seemed to Myop as she skipped lightly from hen house to pigpen to smokehouse that the days had never been as beautiful as these. The air held a keenness that made her nose twitch. The harvesting of the corn and cotton, peanuts and squash, made each day a golden surprise that
5 caused excited little tremors to run up her jaws.

Myop carried a short, knobby stick. She struck out at random at chickens she liked, and worked out the beat of a song on the fence around the pigpen. She felt light and good in the warm sun. She was ten, and nothing existed for her but her song, the stick clutched in her dark brown hand,
10 and the tat-de-ta-ta-ta of accompaniment.

Turning her back on the rusty boards of her family's sharecropper cabin, Myop walked along the fence till it ran into the stream made by the spring. Around the spring, where the family got drinking water, silver

Guided Questions

1. In what time of year is the story set?

2. Where is Myop? What do the details of the landscape reveal about location?

3. What does the detail "sharecropper" reveal about the historical period?

ferns and wildflowers grew. Along the shallow banks pigs rooted. Myop
15 watched the tiny white bubbles disrupt the thin black scale of soil and the
water that silently rose and slid away down the stream.

She had explored the woods behind the house many times. Often, in
late autumn, her mother took her to gather nuts among the fallen
leaves. Today she made her own path, bouncing this way and that way,
20 vaguely keeping an eye out for snakes. She found, in addition to various common but pretty ferns and leaves, an armful of strange blue
flowers with velvety ridges and a sweetsuds bush full of the brown,
fragrant buds.

By twelve o'clock, her arms laden with sprigs of her findings, she was a
25 mile or more from home. She had often been as far before, but the
strangeness of the land made it not as pleasant as her usual haunts. It
seemed gloomy in the little cove in which she found herself. The air was
damp, the silence close and deep.

Myop began to circle back to the house, back to the peacefulness of the
30 morning. It was then she stepped smack into his eyes. Her heel became
lodged in the broken ridge between brow and nose, and she reached down
quickly, unafraid, to free herself. It was only when she saw his naked grin
that she gave a little yelp of surprise.

He had been a tall man. From feet to neck covered a long space. His
35 head lay beside him. When she pushed back the leaves and layers of earth
and debris Myop saw that he'd had large white teeth, all of them cracked
or broken, long fingers, and very big bones. All his clothes had rotted away
except some threads of blue denim from his overalls. The buckles of the
overall had turned green.

40   Myop gazed around the spot with interest. Very near where she'd
stepped into the head was a wild pink rose. As she picked it to add to
her bundle she noticed a raised mound, a ring, around the rose's root.
It was the rotted remains of a noose, a bit of shredding plowline, now
blending benignly into the soil. Around an overhanging limb of a
45 great spreading oak clung another piece. Frayed, rotted, bleached, and
frazzled—barely there—but spinning restlessly in the breeze. Myop laid
down her flowers.

And the summer was over.

Guided Questions

4. Does she know the location? What does the season suggest about this trip?

5. What details about the setting reveal that this trip is different?

6. Describe how Myop interacts with the physical environment.

7. What does the action of picking a wild pink rose reveal and what does she discover in this revelation?

8. Why does Myop lay down her flowers and what does it mean that "summer was over"?

PRACTICE TEXT

Another April
Jesse Stuart

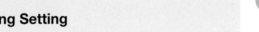

Ed Clark/The LIFE Picture Collection/Shutterstock

THE TEXT IN CONTEXT

In his own time, writer and educator Jesse Stuart (1906–1984) was often compared to popular literary figures such as Walt Whitman and the Scottish poet Robert Burns, among others. Stuart was born in rural Kentucky, and this rustic Appalachian setting — including its landscape, people, and way of life — became his subject. Indeed, Stuart exemplifies American *regionalism*: a style of poetry and prose that focuses on the customs, dialects, topography, and other elements of "local color" associated with specific regions. Regionalism reached the height of its popularity in the decades after the Civil War. But later practitioners, such as Stuart, still gained widespread popularity in the early decades of the twentieth century. He was also enormously prolific, producing fifty-nine books of poems, fiction, autobiography, sociology, history, and essays. Nearly all of them, like "Another April," evoke a powerful sense of place — nearly to the point where the setting becomes a character itself.

AP® SKILLS PRACTICE | SETTING **Analyzing Setting**

As you read "Another April," record details from the story that describe place, time, or the physical environment. Then consider what those details reveal about the values of the setting.

Analyzing Setting
Place
• Is the location urban or rural?
• Is the location nondescript? Could it take place anywhere in the world?
• Is the story set in a significant cultural or religious location?
• Is the setting physically isolated or deeply integrated into a community?
• Does the story take place inside or outside?

Details from the text:	What does this reveal about the setting?

(continued)

Time

- Does the story take place in the past, present, or future?
- Is the story happening in a particular historical period?
- What season of the year is it?
- What day, week, or month is it?
- What time of day does the story take place or span?
- Are the characters recognizing any holidays or events?
- How long does the story take place? Minutes? Hours? A day? Multiple days? A year? Multiple years?

Details from the text:	What does this reveal about the setting?

Physical Environment

- What geographical location is the setting for the story? Do you know the country/territory, state, city, town, neighborhood, or location?
- How is the landscape described?
- What are the weather conditions and climate like?
- Are there natural features (such as the forest, the sea, or the mountains)?
- Are there constructed features (such as a hospital, an ice skating rink, or a bridge)?

Details from the text:	What does this reveal about the setting?

Another April

"Now, Pap, you won't get cold," Mom said as she put a heavy wool cap over his head.

"Huh, what did ye say?" Grandpa asked, holding his big hand cupped over his ear to
5 catch the sound.

"Wait until I get your gloves," Mom said, hollering real loud in Grandpa's ear. Mom had forgotten about his gloves until he raised his big bare hand above his ear to catch the
10 sound of Mom's voice.

"Don't get 'em," Grandpa said, "I won't ketch cold."

Mom didn't pay any attention to what Grandpa said. She went on to get the gloves
15 anyway. Grandpa turned toward me. He saw that I was looking at him. "Yer Ma's a-puttin' enough clothes on me to kill a man," Grandpa said; then he laughed a coarse laugh like March wind among the pine tops at his own
20 words. I started laughing but not at Grandpa's words. He thought I was laughing at them and we both laughed together. It pleased Grandpa to think that I had laughed with him over something funny that he had said. But I
25 was laughing at the way he was dressed. He looked like a picture of Santa Claus. But Grandpa's cheeks were not cherry-red like Santa Claus's cheeks. They were covered with

white thin beard—and above his eyes were
30 long white eyebrows almost as white as per-
coon petals and very much longer.

Grandpa was wearing a heavy wool suit
that hung loosely about his big body but
fitted him tightly round the waist where he
35 was as big and as round as a flour barrel. His
pant legs were as big 'round his pipestem
legs as emptied meal sacks. And his big
shoes, with his heavy wool socks dropping
down over their tops, looked like sled run-
40 ners. Grandpa wore a heavy wool shirt and
over his wool shirt he wore a heavy wool
sweater and then his coat over the top of all
this. Over his coat he wore a heavy overcoat
and about his neck he wore a wool scarf.

45 The way Mom had dressed Grandpa you'd
think there was a heavy snow on the ground
but there wasn't. April was here instead, and
the sun was shining on the green hills where
the wild plums and the wild crab apples
50 were in bloom enough to make you think
there were big snowdrifts sprinkled over the
green hills. When I looked at Grandpa and
then looked out at the window at the sunshine and the green grass, I laughed more.
55 Grandpa laughed with me.

"I'm a-goin' to see my old friend," Grandpa
said just as Mom came down the stairs with
his gloves.

"Who is he, Grandpa?" I asked, but
60 Grandpa just looked at my mouth working.
He didn't know what I was saying. And he
hated to ask me the second time.

Mom put the big wool gloves on Grandpa's
hands. He stood there just like I had to do
65 years ago, and let Mom put his gloves on. If
Mom didn't get his fingers back in the
glove-fingers exactly right, Grandpa quarreled at Mom. And when Mom fixed his fingers exactly right in his gloves the way he
70 wanted them, Grandpa was pleased.

"I'll be a-goin' to see 'im," Grandpa said to
Mom. "I know he'll still be there."

Mom opened our front door for Grandpa
and he stepped out slowly, supporting him-
75 self with his big cane in one hand. With
the other hand he held to the door frame.
Mom let him out of the house just like she
used to let me out in the spring. And when
Grandpa left the house, I wanted to go
80 with him, but Mom wouldn't let me go. I
wondered if he would get away from the
house—get out of Mom's sight—and pull
off his shoes and go barefoot and wade the
creeks like I used to do when Mom let me
85 out. Since Mom wouldn't let me go with
Grandpa, I watched him as he walked slowly
down the path in front of our house. Mom
stood there watching Grandpa too. I think
she was so afraid that he would fall. But
90 Mom was fooled; Grandpa toddled along the
path better than my baby brother could.

"He used to be a powerful man," Mom said
more to herself than she did to me. "He was
a timber cutter. No man could cut more tim-
95 ber than my father; no man in the timber
woods could sink an ax deeper into a log
than my father. And no man could lift the
end of a bigger saw log than Pop could."

"Who is Grandpa goin' to see, Mom?" I
100 asked.

"He's not goin' to see anybody," Mom said.

"I heard 'im say that he was goin' to see
an old friend," I told her.

"Oh, he was just a-talkin'," Mom said.

105 I watched Grandpa stop under the pine
tree in our front yard. He set his cane against
the pine tree trunk, pulled off his gloves and
put them in his pocket. Then Grandpa
stooped over slowly, as slowly as the wind
110 bends down a sapling, and picked up a pine
cone in his big soft fingers. Grandpa stood
fondling the pine cone in his hand. Then, one

by one, he pulled the little chips from the pine cone—tearing it to pieces like he was hunting for something in it—and after he had torn it to pieces he threw the pine-cone stem on the ground. Then he pulled pine needles from a low-hanging pine bough, and he felt of each pine needle between his fingers. He played with them a long time before he started down the path.

"What's Grandpa doin'?" I asked Mom. But Mom didn't answer me.

"How long has Grandpa been with us?" I asked Mom.

"Before you's born," she said. "Pap has been with us eleven years. He was eighty when he quit cuttin' timber and farmin'; now he's ninety-one."

I had heard her say that when she was a girl he'd walk out on the snow and ice barefooted and carry wood in the house and put it on the fire. He had shoes but he wouldn't bother to put them on. And I heard her say that he would cut timber on the coldest days without socks on his feet but with his feet stuck down in cold brogan shoes, and he worked stripped above the waist so his arms would have freedom when he swung his double-bitted ax. I had heard her tell how he'd sweat and how the sweat in his beard would be icicles by the time he got home from work on the cold winter days. Now Mom wouldn't let him get out of the house, for she wanted him to live a long time.

As I watched Grandpa go down the path toward the hog pen, he stopped to examine every little thing along his path. Once he waved his cane at a butterfly as it zigzagged over his head, its polka-dot wings fanning the blue April air. Grandpa would stand when a puff of wind came along, and hold his face against the wind and let the wind play with his white whiskers. I thought maybe his face was hot under his beard and he was letting the wind cool his face. When he reached the hog pen, he called the hogs down to the fence. They came running and grunting to Grandpa just like they were talking to him. I knew that Grandpa couldn't hear them trying to talk to him, but he could see their mouths working and he knew they were trying to say something. He leaned his cane against the hog pen, reached over the fence, and patted the hogs' heads. Grandpa didn't miss patting one of our seven hogs.

As he toddled up the little path alongside the hog pen, he stopped under a blooming dogwood. He pulled a white blossom from a bough that swayed over the path above his head, and he leaned his big bundled body against the dogwood while he tore each petal from the blossom and examined it carefully. There wasn't anything his dim blue eyes missed. He stopped under a redbud tree before he reached the garden to break a tiny spray of redbud blossoms. He took each blossom from the spray and examined it carefully.

"Gee, it's funny to watch Grandpa," I said to Mom; then I laughed.

"Poor Pap," Mom said. "He's seen a lot of Aprils come and go. He's seen more Aprils than he will ever see again."

I don't think Grandpa missed a thing on the little circle he took before he reached the house. He played with a bumblebee that was bending a windflower blossom that grew near our corncrib beside a big bluff. But Grandpa didn't try to catch the bumblebee in his big bare hand. I wondered if he would and if the bumblebee would sting him, and if he would holler. Grandpa even pulled a butterfly cocoon from a blackberry briar that grew beside his path. I saw him try to tear it into shreds but he couldn't. There wasn't any

butterfly in it, for I'd seen it before. I won-
200 dered if the butterfly with the polka-dot
wings, that Grandpa waved his cane at when
he first left the house, had come from this
cocoon. I laughed when Grandpa couldn't
tear the cocoon apart.

205   "I'll bet I can tear that cocoon apart for
Grandpa if you'd let me go help him," I said
to Mom.

"You leave your Grandpa alone," Mom
said. "Let 'im enjoy April."

210   Then I knew that this was the first time
Mom had let Grandpa out of the house all
winter. I knew that Grandpa loved the sunshine and the fresh April air that blew from
the redbud and dogwood blossoms. He loved
215 the bumblebees, the hogs, the pine cones,
and pine needles. Grandpa didn't miss a
thing along his walk. And every day from
now on until just before frost Grandpa would
take this little walk. He'd stop along and look
220 at everything as he had done summers
before. But each year he didn't take as long a
walk as he had taken the year before. Now
this spring he didn't go down to the lower
end of the hog pen as he had done last year.
225 And when I could first remember Grandpa
going on his walks, he used to go out of sight.
He'd go all over the farm. And he'd come to
the house and take me on his knee and tell
me about all that he had seen. Now Grandpa
230 wasn't getting out of sight. I could see him
from the window along all of his walk.

Grandpa didn't come back into the house
at the front door. He toddled around back of
the house toward the smokehouse, and I ran
235 through the living room to the dining room
so I could look out the window and watch
him.

"Where's Grandpa goin'?" I asked Mom.

"Now never mind," Mom said. "Leave
240 Grandpa alone. Don't go out there and disturb him."

"I won't bother 'im, Mom," I said. "I just
want to watch 'im."

"All right," Mom said.

245   But Mom wanted to be sure that I didn't
bother him so she followed me into the dining room. Maybe she wanted to see what
Grandpa was going to do. She stood by the
window, and we watched Grandpa as he
250 walked down beside our smokehouse where
a tall sassafras tree's thin leaves fluttered in
the blue April wind. Above the smokehouse
and the tall sassafras was a blue April sky—
so high you couldn't see the sky-roof. It was
255 just blue space and little white clouds floated
upon this blue.

When Grandpa reached the smokehouse
he leaned his cane against the sassafras tree.
He let himself down slowly to his knees
260 as he looked carefully at the ground.
Grandpa was looking at something and I
wondered what it was. I just didn't think or I
would have known.

"There you are, my good old friend,"
265 Grandpa said.

"Who is his friend, Mom?" I asked.

Mom didn't say anything. Then I saw.

"He's playin' with that old terrapin, Mom,"
I said.

270   "I know he is," Mom said.

"The terrapin doesn't mind if Grandpa
strokes his head with his hand," I said.

"I know it," Mom said.

"But the old terrapin won't let me do it," I
275 said. "Why does he let Grandpa?"

"The terrapin knows your Grandpa."

"He ought to know me," I said, "but when I
try to stroke his head with my hand, he
closes up in his shell."

280   Mom didn't say anything. She stood by
the window watching Grandpa and listening
to Grandpa talk to the terrapin.

"My old friend, how do you like the sunshine?" Grandpa asked the terrapin.

285 The terrapin turned his fleshless face to one side like a hen does when she looks at you in the sunlight. He was trying to talk to Grandpa; maybe the terrapin could understand what Grandpa was saying.

290 "Old fellow, it's been a hard winter," Grandpa said. "How have you fared under the smokehouse floor?"

"Does the terrapin know what Grandpa is sayin'?" I asked Mom.

295 "I don't know," she said.

"I'm awfully glad to see you, old fellow," Grandpa said. He didn't offer to bite Grandpa's big soft hand as he stroked his head.

"Looks like the terrapin would bite 300 Grandpa," I said.

"That terrapin has spent the winters under that smokehouse for fifteen years," Mom said. "Pap has been acquainted with him for eleven years. He's been talkin' to 305 that terrapin every Spring."

"How does Grandpa know the terrapin is old?" I asked Mom.

"It's got 1847 cut on its shell," Mom said. "We know he's ninety-five years old. He's 310 older than that. We don't know how old he was when that date was cut on his back."

"Who cut 1847 on his back, Mom?"

"I don't know, child," she said, "but I'd say whoever cut that date on his back has long 315 been under the ground."

Then I wondered how a terrapin could get that old and what kind of a looking person he was who cut the date on the terrapin's back. I wondered where it happened—if it 320 happened near where our house stood. I wondered who lived here on this land then, what kind of a house they lived in, and if they had a sassafras with tiny thin April leaves on its top growing in their yard, and if 325 the person that cut that date on the terrapin's back was buried at Plum Grove, if he

had farmed these hills where we lived today and cut timber like Grandpa had—and if he had seen the Aprils pass like Grandpa had 330 seen them and if he enjoyed them like Grandpa was enjoying this April. I wondered if he had looked at the dogwood blossoms, the redbud blossoms, and talked to this same terrapin.

335 "Are you well, old fellow?" Grandpa asked the terrapin. The terrapin just looked at Grandpa. "I'm well as common for a man of my age," Grandpa said.

"Did the terrapin ask Grandpa if he was 340 well?" I asked Mom.

"I don't know," Mom said. "I can't talk to a terrapin."

"But Grandpa can."

"Yes."

345 "Wait until tomatoes get ripe and we'll go to the garden together," Grandpa said.

"Does the terrapin eat tomatoes?" I asked Mom.

"Yes, that terrapin has been eatin' toma- 350 toes from our garden for fifteen years," Mom said. "When Mick was tossin' the terrapins out of the tomato patch, he picked up this one and found the date cut on his back. He put him back in the patch and told him to 355 help himself. He lives from our garden every year. We don't bother him and don't allow anybody else to bother him. He spends his winters under our smokehouse floor buried in the dry ground."

360 "Gee, Grandpa looks like the terrapin," I said.

Mom didn't say anything; tears came to her eyes. She wiped them from her eyes with the corner of her apron.

365 "I'll be back to see you," Grandpa said. "I'm a-gettin' a little chilly; I'll be gettin' back to the house." The terrapin twisted his wrinkled neck without moving his big body, poking his

head deeper into the April wind as Grandpa
370 pulled his bundled body up by holding to the
sassafras tree trunk.

"Goodbye, old friend!"

The terrapin poked his head deeper into
the wind, holding one eye on Grandpa, for I
375 could see his eye shining in the sinking sunlight. Grandpa got his cane that was leaned
against the sassafras tree trunk and hobbled
slowly toward the house. The terrapin
looked at him with first one eye and then
380 the other.

SETTING

1. What does the story's title, "Another April," reveal about the **setting**? Why might the season be important?

2. How is the physical environment, specifically the weather and the landscape of the surroundings, described? Describe the feelings that the surroundings evoke.

3. The story occurs within a time frame. What is that time frame, and what does that reveal about the relationship between the grandpa and the terrapin?

4. How does the date on the terrapin's back contribute to the relationship of the grandpa and the terrapin?

Plot

 Enduring Understanding (STR-1)

The arrangement of the parts and sections of a text, the relationship of the parts to each other, and the sequence in which the text reveals information are all structural choices made by a writer that contribute to the reader's interpretation of a text.

KEY POINT

Authors strategically arrange and connect the events of a plot of a story in a way that builds to a conflict or tension that offers insight into human nature.

A young girl prepares a basket of treats to go on a journey through the dangerous woods to visit her grandmother. Along the way, she meets a suspicious wolf character who attempts to change her plans. She ignores the temptation and eventually arrives at her grandmother's house, only to find that her grandmother is acting (and sounding) very strange. The young girl realizes too late that the wolf from the woods has anticipated her arrival and devoured her grandmother. He plans to eat the young girl too.

You may have heard different versions of the tale of "Little Red Riding Hood." In some, she and her grandmother are saved by a nearby hunter; in others, the girl outsmarts the wolf, saving herself and her grandmother. But interestingly enough, these variations all affect the *ending* of the tale as opposed to the beginning or the middle.

Many stories you've read or heard begin, "Once upon a time." In other words, they follow a predictable chronological pattern: beginning, middle, and end. We meet the characters, a problem pops up, and the problem is resolved. The resolution of the problem and the characters' experiences during that process reveal something about life and human nature. So it's no wonder that there are many versions of "Little Red Riding Hood," with each variant allowing for different interpretations of the story as a whole.

More often than not, readers expect to start at the beginning because this pattern of storytelling helps us navigate the series of events that unfold within a story.

One Thing Leads to Another

Stories have a **narrative arc**: a sequence of situations, actions, and incidents that leads to (and revolves around) a primary conflict. This series of events, each one leading to the next, make up the plot of a story. The term **plot** refers to the author's arrangement of these events in a story. While it is important to comprehend the events of a story, it's more important to understand how the events are ordered and how each one is connected to the next. When readers understand the relationship between these incidents and the story's outcome, they can better understand the author's **message**.

Authors intentionally arrange and sequence the events in a story to help readers gain insight. In other words, every detail and every event is relevant. As we read, we can think about why a specific detail is important and how it might help us interpret the story. The events in a story are connected; each one leads to the next.

Early in a story, authors may use details to introduce the characters, setting, and other key background information, which is called the **exposition**. The author presents the interaction of characters and setting to initiate a problem. This inciting moment is often called the **narrative hook**. With this hook established, the events that follow create the rising action, where additional complications are revealed. These complicating factors create anticipation and suspense for the reader. They also lead to the **climax** of the story: a crisis, defining moment, or decision point for the main character. The final details and events of the story, called the **falling action**, lead to the story's **resolution**. In the resolution, the main character often finds new insight or a realization, which results from his or her experience.

In stories, characters find themselves in a circumstance. A circumstance is a moment in time, a situation, a conflict, or even a conversation. These individual **moments** are a significant part of the narrative's plot and are relevant to the dramatic situation. In longer stories, characters may be involved in multiple circumstances that may intersect. In short stories, a single circumstance may create a dramatic situation.

Dramatic Situation

By selecting and arranging the events of a story in a way that builds to a conflict, an author creates a **dramatic situation**. In a dramatic situation, characters are placed in conflict. By examining this **tension** between characters, a reader can begin to understand the human insight that the writer is sharing. For example, the plot of many stories shows the rise and fall of the fortunes of the main character or a set of characters (like a community or a family). In experiencing the plot, the character (and we as readers) usually discover new insights into the world around us.

Unresolved Endings and Twists

While most stories end with a clear resolution, some authors may withhold information and intentionally make the plot's outcome ambiguous. Such **unresolved** stories allow readers to infer the conclusion and apply their own values to determine meaning. Other authors may include an unexpected twist to complete the resolution. These twists create dramatic tension for both the story's characters and readers. You will look more at unexpected twists in a later unit.

INSIDER **A character's conflict is key to unlocking meaning.**
AP TIP Describing and labeling each part of the plot is only a starting point. As readers, we must analyze the tension an author creates in a story. That is, we must explain how each part of the plot, each event, leads to the next and ultimately to a conflict that comes to some resolution.

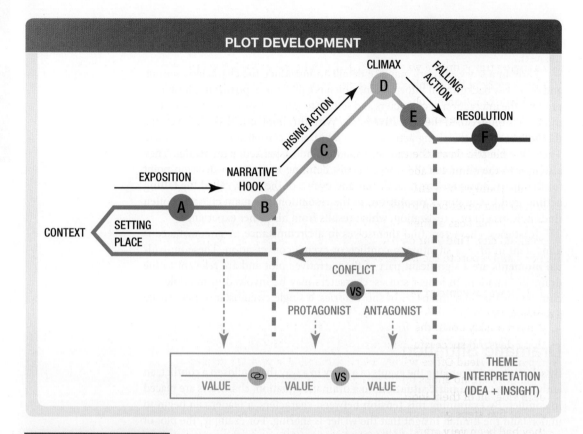

PLOT DEVELOPMENT

CLIMAX

FALLING ACTION

D

E

RESOLUTION

RISING ACTION

C

F

EXPOSITION

NARRATIVE HOOK

A

B

SETTING
PLACE

CONTEXT

CONFLICT

VS

PROTAGONIST   ANTAGONIST

VALUE   VALUE   VS   VALUE

THEME
INTERPRETATION
(IDEA + INSIGHT)

GUIDED READING

The Landlady
Roald Dahl

THE TEXT IN CONTEXT

Roald Dahl (1916–1990) was a British inventor, Royal Air Force pilot, and author. He is most famous for his childhood stories, including *Charlie and the Chocolate Factory* (1964), *Revolting Rhymes* (1982), and *Matilda* (1988). Additionally, Dahl penned some works for adults with more mature themes such as *My Uncle Oswald* (1979). Many of his adult

stories exhibit a fascination with the gothic and grotesque. One such story, "The Landlady," originally published in the *New Yorker* in 1959, presents a character looking for a room to rent who encounters an eccentric landlady. Some critics have argued that Dahl may have used this story to explore his interest in true crime, especially that of the Victorian period when accounts ran rampant of women poisoning their lovers with arsenic. In 1979 the story became an episode of *Tales of the Unexpected*, a British television series.

The Landlady

Billy Weaver had travelled down from London on the slow afternoon train, changing trains on the way, and by the time he got to Bath it was about nine o'clock in the evening. The air was very cold and the wind was like a flat blade of ice on his cheeks.

5 'Excuse me,' he said, 'but is there a fairly cheap hotel not too far away from here?'

'Try the pub down the road,' a man at the station said, pointing. 'They might take you in. It's about a kilometer along on the other side.'

Billy thanked him and picked up his suitcase and set out to walk to the 10 inn. He had never been to Bath before. He didn't know anyone who lived there, but his boss at the Head Office in London had told him it was a splendid city. 'Find your own accommodation,' he had said, 'and then go along and report to the Local Manager as soon as you've got yourself settled.'

15 Billy was seventeen years old. He was wearing a new dark blue over-coat, a new brown hat, a new brown suit, and he was feeling fine. He walked briskly down the street. He was trying to do everything briskly these days. All successful businessmen, he had decided, were brisk. The top men at Head Office were brisk all the time. They were amazing.

20 There were no shops on this wide street, only a line of tall houses on each side, all of them looking the same. They had grand entrances and four or five steps going up to their front doors, and it was obvious that they had been very grand houses indeed. But now, even in the darkness, he could see that the paint was coming off the doors and windows, and 25 that the handsome white exteriors had cracks and patches from lack of repair.

Suddenly, in a downstairs window that was illuminated by a nearby street lamp, Billy saw a printed notice leaning against the glass in one of the windows. It said BED AND BREAKFAST.

30 He stopped walking. He moved a bit closer. Green curtains were hanging down on each side of the window. He went right up to it and looked through the glass into the room, and the first thing he saw was a bright fire burning in the fireplace. On the carpet in front of the fire, a pretty little dog was curled up asleep. The room itself, which he could only see in half-35 darkness, was filled with pleasant furniture. There was a piano and a big sofa and several comfortable armchairs; and in one corner he saw a large parrot in a cage. Animals were usually a good sign in a place like this, Billy told himself, and it looked to him as if it would be a pretty decent house to stay in. Certainly it would be more comfortable than a pub.

40 On the other hand, a pub would be more friendly than a guesthouse. There would be beer and cards in the evenings, and lots of people to talk

STRUCTURE

Guided Questions

1. Structurally, how does this story begin? What is the protagonist doing?

2. What is the main character's goal?

3. These details make up the expositions of the plot. What effect might these details have? How do they affect Billy?

4. What choice is Billy faced with? How might this choice be the narrative hook?

to, and it would probably be a lot cheaper, too. He had stayed a couple of nights in a pub once before and had liked it. He had never stayed in any guesthouses and, to be perfectly honest, he was a tiny bit frightened of
45 them. The word 'guesthouse' suggested watery vegetables and greedy landladies.

After hesitating like this in the cold for two or three minutes, Billy decided that he would walk on and look at the pub before making up his mind. He turned to go.

50 And now a strange thing happened to him. He was just going to step back and turn away from the window when his eye was caught and held in the most peculiar manner by the small notice that was there. BED AND BREAKFAST, it said. BED AND BREAKFAST, BED AND BREAKFAST. Each word was like a large black eye staring at him through the glass, holding
55 him, forcing him to stay where he was and not to walk away from that house, and the next thing he knew, he was actually moving across from the window to the front door, climbing the steps that led to it and reaching for the bell.

He pressed it. Far away in a back room he heard it ringing, and then at
60 once — it must have been at once because he hadn't even had time to take his finger from the bell-button — the door swung open and a woman was standing there.

She was about forty-five or fifty years old, and the moment she saw him, she gave him a warm welcoming smile.

65 'Please come in,' she said pleasantly. She stepped to one side, holding the door wide open, and Billy found himself automatically starting forward into the house: the force or, more accurately, the desire to follow her was extraordinarily strong.

'I saw the notice in the window,' he said, holding himself back.
70 'Yes, I know.'

'I was wondering about a room.'

'It's all ready for you, my dear,' she said. She had a round pink face and very gentle blue eyes.

'I was on my way to a pub,' Billy told her. 'But I noticed the sign in your
75 window.'

'My dear boy,' she said, 'why don't you come in out of the cold?'

'How much do you charge?'

'Nine pounds a night, including breakfast.'

It was amazingly cheap. It was less than half of what he had been will-
80 ing to pay.

'If that is too much,' she added, 'then perhaps I can reduce it just a tiny bit. Do you desire an egg for breakfast? Eggs are expensive at the moment. It would cost less without the egg.'

Guided Questions

5. How do these details contribute to the rising action?

6. Describe this dramatic situation. How does it relate to the conflict and further the plot?

'Nine pounds is fine,' he answered. 'I would like very much to stay
85 here.'

'I knew you would. Do come in.'

She seemed terribly nice. She looked exactly like the mother of one's
best school friend welcoming one into the house to stay for the Christmas
holidays. Billy took off his hat and stepped inside.
90 'Just hang it there,' she said, 'and let me help you with your coat.'

There were no other hats or coats in the hall. There were no umbrellas,
no walking-sticks—nothing.

'We have it all to ourselves,' she said, smiling at him over her shoulder
as she led the way upstairs. 'You see, I don't very often have the pleasure
95 of taking a visitor into my little nest.'

The old girl is slightly mad, Billy told himself. But at nine pounds a
night, who cares about that? 'I should've thought you'd be simply full of
visitors wanting to stay,' he said politely.

'Oh, I am, my dear, I am, of course I am. But the trouble is that I am just
100 a tiny bit careful about whom I choose—if you see what I mean.'

'Ah, yes.'

'But I'm always ready. Everything is always ready day and night in this
house just in case an acceptable young gentleman comes along. And it is
such a pleasure, my dear, when now and again I open the door and I see
105 someone standing there who is just exactly right.' She was halfway up the
stairs, and she paused, turned her head and smiled down at him. 'Like
you,' she added, and her blue eyes travelled slowly all the way down the
length of Billy's body, to his feet, and then up again.

On the first floor she said to him, 'This floor is mine.'
110 They climbed up more stairs. 'And this one is all yours,' she said. 'Here's
your room. I do hope you'll like it.' She took him into a small but charming
front bedroom, switching on the light as she went in.

'The morning sun comes right in the window, Mr Perkins. It is Mr Perkins,
isn't it?'
115 'No,' he said. 'It's Weaver.'

'Mr Weaver. How nice. I've put a hot water bottle between the sheets to
warm them, Mr Weaver. And you may light the gas fire at any time if you
feel cold.'

'Thank you,' Billy said. 'Thank you very much.' He noticed that the bed-
120 clothes had been neatly turned back on one side, all ready for someone to
get in.

'I'm so glad you appeared,' she said, looking seriously into his face. 'I
was beginning to get worried.'

'That's all right,' Billy answered brightly. 'You mustn't worry about me.'
125 He put his suitcase on the chair and started to open it.

Guided Questions

7. How does the
conversation
between Billy
and the landlady
contribute to the
rising action and
dramatic situation?

STRUCTURE

'And what about supper, my dear? Did you manage to get anything to eat before you came here?'

'I'm not hungry, thank you,' he said. 'I think I'll just go to bed as soon as possible because tomorrow I've got to get up rather early and report to the
130 office.'

'Very well, then. I'll leave you now so that you can unpack. But before you go to bed, would you be kind enough to come into the sitting room on the ground floor and sign the book? Everyone has to do that because it's the law, and we don't want to break any laws at this stage in the proceed-
135 ings, do we?' She gave him a little wave of the hand and went quickly out of the room and closed the door.

The fact that his landlady appeared to be slightly crazy didn't worry Billy at all. She was not only harmless—there was no question about that—but she was also quite obviously a kind and generous person. He
140 guessed that she had probably lost a son of her own or something like that, and had never recovered from it.

So a few minutes later, after unpacking and washing his hands, he walked downstairs to the ground floor and entered the sitting room. His landlady wasn't there, but the fire was still burning and the little dog was
145 still sleeping in front of it. The room was wonderfully warm and comfortable. I'm a lucky fellow, he thought, rubbing his hands. This is great.

He found the guest-book lying open on the piano, so he took out his pen and wrote down his name and address. There were only two other names above his on the page and, as one always does, he started to read
150 them. One was a Christopher Mulholland from Cardiff. The other was Gregory W. Temple from Bristol.

That's funny, he thought suddenly. Christopher Mulholland. That name sounds familiar.

Now where had he heard that rather unusual name before? Was he a
155 boy at school? No. Was it one of his sister's numerous young men, perhaps, or a friend of his father's? No, no, it wasn't any of those. He glanced down again at the book. In fact, thinking about it again, he wasn't at all sure that the second name wasn't as familiar to him as the first. 'Gregory Temple?' he said aloud, searching his memory. 'Christopher Mulholland . . . ?'

160 'Such charming boys,' a voice behind him answered, and he turned and saw his landlady walking into the room carrying the tea tray in front of her.

'They sound somehow familiar,' he said.

They do? How interesting.'

165 'I'm almost positive I've heard those names before somewhere. Isn't that strange? Maybe it was in the newspapers. They weren't famous in any way, were they? I mean, famous footballers or something like that?'

Guided Questions

8. Up to this point in the plot, what details are most suspenseful?

9. Can you think of other stories or movies where characters have been asked to "sign" something? What is the outcome of those stories?

10. How might this be a turning point in the story?

'Famous,' she said, setting the tray down on the low table in front of the sofa. 'Oh no, I don't think they were famous. But they were extraordi-
170 narily handsome, both of them, I can promise you that. They were tall and young and handsome, my dear, just exactly like you.'

Once more, Billy glanced down at the book. 'Look here,' he said, notic-ing the dates. 'This last entry is over two years old.'

'Is it?'

175 'Yes, indeed. And Christopher Mulholland's is nearly a year before that—more than three years ago.'

'Oh dear,' she said, shaking her head. 'I never would have thought it. How time flies away from us all, doesn't it, Mr Wilkins?'

'It's Weaver,' Billy said. 'W-E-A-V-E-R.'

180 'Oh, of course it is!' she cried, sitting down on the sofa. 'How silly of me. I do apologize.'

'Do you know something that's extraordinary about all this? Both those names, Mulholland and Temple, I not only seem to remember each one separately but they appear to be connected as well. As if they were both
185 famous for the same sort of thing, if you see what I mean.'

'Well, come over here now, dear, and sit down beside me on the sofa and I'll give you a nice cup of tea and a biscuit before you go to bed.'

Billy watched her as she busied herself with the cups and saucers. He noticed that she had small, white, quickly moving hands, and red
190 fingernails.

'I'm almost positive I saw them in the newspapers,' Billy said. 'I'll think of them in a second. I'm sure I will.'

There is nothing more annoying than a thing like this which remains just outside one's memory. He hated to give up.

195 'Now wait a minute,' he said. 'Wait just a minute. Mulholland . . . Christopher Mulholland . . . wasn't that the name of the schoolboy who was on a walking tour through the West Country, and then suddenly . . .'

'Milk?' she said. 'And sugar?'

'Yes, please. And then suddenly . . . ?'

200 'Schoolboy?' she said. 'Oh no, my dear, that can't possibly be right because my Mr Mulholland was certainly not a schoolboy when he came to me. He was a university student. Come over here now and sit next to me and warm yourself in front of this lovely fire. Come on. Your tea's all ready for you.'

205 He crossed the room slowly, and sat down on the edge of the sofa. She placed his teacup on the table in front of him.

'There we are,' she said. 'How nice and comfortable this is, isn't it?'

Billy started drinking his tea. She did the same. For half a minute, nei-ther of them spoke but Billy knew that she was looking at him. Her body

STRUCTURE

Guided Questions

11. How do the landlady's actions contribute to the dramatic situation and build toward the story's climax?

12. How do the details regarding Billy's memory advance the plot?

210 was half-turned towards him and he could feel her eyes resting on his face, watching him from over her teacup. Now and again he caught a peculiar smell that seemed to come from her direction. It wasn't unpleasant, and it reminded him—well, he wasn't quite sure what it was. New leather? Or was it the corridors of a hospital?

215   'Mr Mulholland loved his tea,' she finally said. 'I've never seen anyone in my life drink as much tea as dear, sweet Mr Mulholland.'

'I suppose he left fairly recently,' Billy said.

'Left?' she said. 'But my dear boy, he never left. He's still here. Mr Temple is also here. They're on the third floor, both of them together.'

220   Billy put down his cup slowly on the table, and stared at his landlady. She smiled back at him and then put out one of her white hands and patted him comfortingly on the knee.

'How old are you, my dear?' she asked.

'Seventeen.'

225   'Seventeen!' she cried. 'Oh, it's the perfect age! Mr Mulholland was also seventeen. But I think he was a little shorter than you are—in fact I'm sure he was. And his teeth weren't quite so white. You have the most beautiful teeth, Mr Weaver. Mr Temple was a little older. He was actually twenty-eight. I wouldn't have guessed it, though, if he hadn't told me.

230 There wasn't a mark on his body.'

'A what?' Billy said.

'His skin was just like a baby's.'

There was a pause. Billy picked up his teacup, drank some more and then put it down again in its saucer. He waited for her to say something

235 else but she seemed to have fallen into another of her silences. He sat there, looking ahead, biting his lower lip.

'That parrot,' he said at last. 'You know something? It completely fooled me when I looked through the window from the street. I thought it was alive.'

240   'Sadly, no longer.'

'It's very clever the way it's been stuffed,' he said. 'It doesn't look at all dead. Who did it?'

'I did.'

'You did?'

245   'Of course,' she said. 'And have you met my little Basil as well?' She nodded towards the dog curled up so comfortably in front of the fire. Billy looked at it. Suddenly he realized that this animal had all the time been as silent and motionless as the parrot. He touched it gently on the top of its back. It was hard and cold but perfectly preserved.

250   'Good heavens,' he said. 'How very interesting. It must be awfully difficult to do a thing like that.'

Guided Questions

13. How do the smells and furnishings affect Billy? How do they contribute to the narrative arc?

14. What might the landlady mean when she says, "He's still here"?

15. How might this moment be a decision point for Billy?

'Not at all,' she said. 'I stuff all my little pets myself when they die. Will you have another cup of tea?'

'No, thank you,' Billy said. The tea tasted faintly bitter and he didn't
255 really like it.

'You did sign the book, didn't you?'

'Oh, yes.'

'That's good. Because later, if I forget what you were called, then I can always look it up. I still do that every day with Mr Mulholland and Mr . . .
260 Mr . . .'

'Temple,' Billy said. 'Gregory Temple. Excuse me for asking, but haven't there been any other guests here except them in the last two or three years?'

Holding her teacup high in one hand, moving her head slightly to the
265 left, she looked at him out of the corners of her eyes and gave him another gentle little smile.

'No, my dear,' she said. 'Only you.'

Guided Questions

16. What might Billy realize about his earlier fears?

17. Is the story resolved?

PRACTICE TEXT

Luke 15:11–32, The Parable of the Prodigal Son
King James Bible

Hulton Archive/Getty Images

THE TEXT IN CONTEXT

In the New Testament Gospel of Luke, Jesus speaks in many *parables*: brief metaphorical stories that teach lessons. In other words, they are not meant to be taken literally. "The Parable of the Prodigal Son" is among the most well known. But keep in mind that this story is last in a related series of three parables on the same theme. In the first one, Jesus makes his point explicit: "I tell you, there will be more joy in heaven over one sinner who repents than over ninety-nine righteous persons who need no repentance" (Luke 15:7). Similarly, note the significance of his audience for this story. Jesus is speaking to a mixed crowd of overt sinners (e.g., prostitutes) and those who considered themselves righteous (e.g., priests and scholars). As you read, think about how the two groups are reflected in the parable itself, as well as how the story's conflict reveals their character.

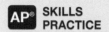 | STRUCTURE
Analyzing Plot

Identify the details of the text that describe each part of the plot in "The Parable of the Prodigal Son." Then create an illustration of the story's plot that depicts the relationship between each event and shows how these events create the story's narrative arc.

Analyzing Plot

Considerations:
- In what ways does the story's plot develop a narrative arc?
- How does a story's plot develop a dramatic situation?
- What character relationships are revealed through the story's plot?
- How does the conflict reflect a tension of values?
- How does the story's resolution reveal an interpretation?

Beginning	Middle	End
• Exposition • Narrative hook	• Rising action • Climax	• Falling action • Resolution
Plot details:	Plot details:	Plot details:

Illustration of the narrative arc of the plot:

Luke 15:11–32, The Parable of the Prodigal Son

11 And he said, A certain man had two sons:

12 And the younger of them said to his father, Father, give me the portion of goods that falleth to me. And he divided unto them his living.

13 And not many days after the younger son gathered all together, and took his journey into a far country, and there wasted his substance with riotous living.

14 And when he had spent all, there arose a mighty famine in that land; and he began to be in want.

15 And he went and joined himself to a citizen of that country; and he sent him into his fields to feed swine.

16 And he would fain have filled his belly with the husks that the swine did eat: and no man gave unto him.

17 And when he came to himself, he said, How many hired servants of my father's have bread enough and to spare, and I perish with hunger!

18 I will arise and go to my father, and will say unto him, Father, I have sinned against heaven, and before thee,

19 And am no more worthy to be called thy son: make me as one of thy hired servants.

20 And he arose, and came to his father. But when he was yet a great way off, his father saw him, and had compassion, and ran, and fell on his neck, and kissed him.

21 And the son said unto him, Father, I have sinned against heaven, and in thy sight, and am no more worthy to be called thy son.

22 But the father said to his servants, Bring forth the best robe, and put it on him; and put a ring on his hand, and shoes on his feet:

23 And bring hither the fatted calf, and kill it; and let us eat, and be merry:

24 For this my son was dead, and is alive again; he was lost, and is found. And they began to be merry.

25 Now his elder son was in the field: and as he came and drew nigh to the house, he heard musick and dancing.

26 And he called one of the servants, and asked what these things meant.

27 And he said unto him, Thy brother is come; and thy father hath killed the fatted calf, because he hath received him safe and sound.

28 And he was angry, and would not go in: therefore came his father out, and intreated him.

29 And he answering said to his father, Lo, these many years do I serve thee, neither transgressed I at any time thy commandment: and yet thou never gavest me a kid, that I might make merry with my friends:

30 But as soon as this thy son was come, which hath devoured thy living with harlots, thou hast killed for him the fatted calf.

31 And he said unto him, Son, thou art ever with me, and all that I have is thine.

32 It was meet that we should make merry, and be glad: for this thy brother was dead, and is alive again; and was lost, and is found.

STRUCTURE

1. What does the **exposition** reveal about the relationships central to the parable?

2. How does the **plot** place the characters in **conflict**?

3. What part of the plot is considered the **climax**? What is the **tension**?

4. How do the events of the plot lead to a **resolution**?

Point of View

AP® Enduring Understanding (NAR-1)

A narrator's or speaker's perspective controls the details and emphases that affect how readers experience and interpret a text.

KEY POINT

The point of view refers to who is telling a story. Stories are told by characters or narrators, and the person telling the story controls what a reader knows or does not know.

Every story has a storyteller. If you've ever gotten caught with a group of siblings or friends doing something you weren't supposed to be doing, then you already know the importance of knowing who is telling the story. For example, if an onlooker were to tell the story, key details may be left out (such as the context or the series of events that led up to you getting caught). Or perhaps the onlooker can confirm that you walked right into the trap of whoever caught you. The story's narrator (and the narrator's perspective) influence the story's meaning for readers.

Similarly, in fictional texts, the writer's choice of narrator and the point of view of the narrator determines what, when, and how readers learn about the events of the story.

The Person Telling the Story Matters

Narrators (or **speakers** in poetry) are created by writers to fulfill one of the most important roles in the text: relating the story to the reader and building a connection between the reader and the text. This also applies to poetry, but the narrator of a poem is referred to as the speaker.

The **point of view** of a story is the narrator's vantage point. Point of view refers to both who is telling the story as well as that person's involvement in the story. It determines what narrators, characters, or speakers can and cannot relay to a reader. Several factors contribute to the narrative point of view, including the narrator's level of involvement in the story, knowledge of the characters' thoughts and actions, and familiarity with the details of the narrative. Ultimately, the author decides how much a narrator knows and tells the reader. Generally, narrators fall into two main categories: first-person narrators and third-person narrators.

First-Person Narrators

First-person narrators are characters who play a role in the story. Using the first-person pronoun "I," they narrate from their own perspectives; therefore, they cannot know the inner thoughts or emotions of anyone else in the text. The narrator's relationship with other characters and events in the plot will shape their perspective and influence the story.

Third-Person Narrators

In contrast, **third-person narrators** do not appear in a story. They use the third-person pronouns *he*, *she*, or *they* to describe characters. Many of the classic fairy tales ("Once upon a time, there lived a princess in a castle guarded by a fierce dragon...") are told by third-person narrators. A third-person narrator's knowledge can range from surface-level observations to intimacy with every character's deepest, darkest secrets. This is known as the narrator's point of view.

Omniscient narrators see and know everything about everyone in a story. They report the thoughts, feelings, and experiences of the characters. They may also provide background information that is unknown to any character. Like an all-seeing, all-knowing presence, they're not bound by space or time.

By contrast, third-person narrators who lack omniscient access to one character or a group of characters are known as **third-person limited narrators**. They report the thoughts and experiences of a specific set of characters but are limited in their knowledge of others (unlike the omniscient narrator).

Second-Person Narrators

This point of view employs second-person pronouns like *you* to drop the reader into the action of the story. Authors rarely use **second-person narrators**; however, some horror novels and short stories feature second-person narration to generate suspense and psychological tension by immersing the reader in the text.

INSIDER AP® TIP

Perspective and point of view are not the same.
Perspective is how characters understand the world around them, whereas a point of view refers to the vantage point from which a narrator delivers the story.

POINT OF VIEW		
Point of View	Indicators	Effect on Narrative
First Person	The narrator uses the pronouns *I*, *me*, *my*, and *mine*.	• The narrator understands the story from his or her perspective. • Because the narrator understands the story from his or her perspective, the narrator only has knowledge about his or her own perspective. • The narrator is affected by other characters and the events of the plot.
Limited Third Person	The narrator uses third-person pronouns *he*, *she*, *they*, *him*, *her*, *them*, *his*, *hers*, and *theirs*.	• The narrator may be bound by time or space. • The narrator knows the thoughts and experiences of some, but not all characters.
Omniscient	The narrator uses third-person pronouns *he*, *she*, *they*, *him*, *her*, *them*, *his*, *hers*, and *theirs*.	• The narrator is unbound by time and space. • The narrator knows all of the characters' thoughts and experiences. • The reader has information that the characters don't have.
Second Person	The narrator uses the pronouns *you*, *your*, and *yours*.	• The narrator forces the reader to be a participant in the story. • The narrator decides the reader's actions.

GUIDED READING

The Pie
Gary Soto

THE TEXT IN CONTEXT

Poet, novelist, and memoirist Gary Soto (b. 1952) is known for his vivid representations of Mexican American life — both his own and the lives of his wider community. In the following narrative, excerpted from his memoir *A Summer Life* (1990), Soto evokes his experience shoplifting as a child. He also explores themes and subjects that permeate much of his work: desire, sin, guilt, shame, and his memories of growing up as the child of migrant laborers. While Soto makes autobiographical writing seem easy, it requires a careful balancing act — especially in the context of childhood memories. On one hand, the account must capture the visceral impressions and immature perspective of a child's point of view; on the other hand, the adult narrator must bring clarity and insight to the experience that no child would likely have.

The Pie

I knew enough about hell to stop me from stealing. I was holy in almost every bone. Some days I recognized the shadows of angels flopping on the backyard grass, and other days I heard faraway messages in the plumbing that howled underneath the house when I crawled there looking for
5   something to do.

But boredom made me sin. Once, at the German Market, I stood before a rack of pies, my sweet tooth gleaming and the juice of guilt wetting my underarms. I gazed at the nine kinds of pie, pecan and apple being my favorites, although cherry looked good, and my dear, fat-faced
10 chocolate was always a good bet. I nearly wept trying to decide which to steal and, forgetting the flowery dust priests give off, the shadow of angels and the proximity of God howling in the plumbing underneath the house, sneaked a pie behind my coffee lid Frisbee and walked to the door, grinning to the bald grocer whose forehead shone with a window
15 of light.

"No one saw," I muttered to myself, the pie like a discus in my hand, and hurried across the street, where I sat on someone's lawn. The sun

Guided Questions

1. Who is the narrator? What details reveal the values and beliefs of the narrator?

2. How do these details contribute to the description of the event?

wavered between the branches of a yellowish sycamore. A squirrel nailed itself high on the trunk, where it forked into two large bark-scabbed limbs.
20 Just as I was going to work my cleanest finger into the pie, a neighbor came out to the porch for his mail. He looked at me, and I got up and headed for home. I raced on skinny legs to my block, but slowed to a quick walk when I couldn't wait any longer. I held the pie to my nose and breathed in its sweetness. I licked some of the crust and closed my
25 eyes as I took a small bite.

In my front yard, I leaned against a car fender and panicked about stealing the apple pie. I knew an apple got Eve in deep trouble with snakes because Sister Marie had shown us a film about Adam and Eve being cast into the desert, and what scared me more than falling from
30 grace was being thirsty for the rest of my life. But even that didn't stop me from clawing a chunk from the pie tin and pushing it into the cavern of my mouth. The slop was sweet and gold-colored in the afternoon sun. I laid more pieces on my tongue, wet finger-dripping pieces, until I was finished and felt like crying because it was about the best thing
35 I had ever tasted. I realized right there and then, in my sixth year, in my tiny body of two hundred bones and three or four sins, that the best things in life came stolen. I wiped my sticky fingers on the grass and rolled my tongue over the corners of my mouth. A burp perfumed the air.
40 I felt bad not sharing with Cross-Eyed Johnny, a neighbor kid. He stood over my shoulder and asked, "Can I have some?" Crust fell from my mouth, and my teeth were bathed with the jam-like filling. Tears blurred my eyes as I remembered the grocer's forehead. I remembered the other pies on the rack, the warm air of the fan above the door and the car that
45 honked as I crossed the street without looking.

"Get away," I had answered Cross-Eyed Johnny. He watched my fingers greedily push big chunks of pie down my throat. He swallowed and said in a whisper, "Your hands are dirty," then returned home to climb his roof and sit watching me eat the pie by myself. After a while, he jumped off
50 and hobbled away because the fall had hurt him.

I sat on the curb. The pie tin glared at me and rolled away when the wind picked up. My face was sticky with guilt. A car honked, and the driver knew. Mrs. Hancock stood on her lawn, hands on hip, and she knew. My mom, peeling a mountain of potatoes at the Redi-Spud factory, knew.
55 I got to my feet, stomach taut, mouth tired of chewing, and flung my Frisbee across the street, its shadow like the shadow of an angel fleeing bad deeds. I retrieved it, jogging slowly. I flung it again until I was bored and thirsty.

Guided Questions

3. How do these details contribute to the narrator's perspective?

4. How does the narrator's description create a relationship with the reader?

5. How does the narrator's distance from the event affect his perspective both then and now?

6. What does this interaction reveal about the narrator?

I returned home to drink water and help my sister glue bottle
60 caps onto cardboard, a project for summer school. But the bottle
caps bored me, and the water soon filled me up more than the pie.
With the kitchen stifling with heat and lunatic flies, I decided to crawl
underneath our house and lie in the cool shadows listening to the
howling sound of plumbing. Was it God? Was it Father, speaking from
65 death, or Uncle with his last shiny dime? I listened, ear pressed to a
cold pipe, and heard a howl like the sea. I lay until I was cold and then
crawled back to the light, rising from one knee, then another, to dust
off my pants and squint in the harsh light. I looked and saw the glare
of a pie tin on a hot day. I knew sin was what you took and didn't
70 give back.

Guided Questions

7. How do the details at the end reveal the true nature of the narrator and the implications of the event?

PRACTICE TEXT

Sweetness
Toni Morrison

THE TEXT IN CONTEXT

Toni's Morrison (1931–2019) is one of the major American writers in the last century. Born in Ohio, Morrison attended Howard University as an undergraduate and then Cornell University, where she studied literature as a graduate student. In the 1960s, Morrison became an editor at Random House, where as the publisher's first Black woman fiction editor, she helped raise the profile of Black writers such as Chinua Achebe, Toni Cade Bambara, and Angela Davis.

Jack Mitchell/Archive Photos/Getty Images

Morrison published her own first novel, *The Bluest Eye*, in 1970. Over the next several decades, she explored race, American history, family, and community in novels such as *Sula* (1973), *Beloved* (1987), *Jazz* (1992), and *Home* (2012). She also taught at several universities, including Howard University, Yale University, and Princeton University. In 1993, she became the first African American to win the Nobel Prize for Literature. The following story, "Sweetness," was originally published in the February 9, 2015, issue of the *New Yorker*.

AP® **SKILLS PRACTICE** | NARRATION
Analyzing Narration

Identify the type of point of view in "Sweetness." Provide details from the story that reveal that point of view. Finally, explain the effect that this type of point of view has on the story as a whole.

Analyzing Narration	
Point of view:	
Details from the Story That Reveal Point of View	**Effect on the Narrative**

Sweetness

It's not my fault. So you can't blame me. I didn't do it and have no idea how it happened. It didn't take more than an hour after they pulled her out from between my
5 legs for me to realize something was wrong. Really wrong. She was so black she scared me. Midnight black, Sudanese black. I'm light-skinned, with good hair, what we call high yellow, and so is Lula Ann's father. Ain't
10 nobody in my family anywhere near that color. Tar is the closest I can think of, yet her hair don't go with the skin. It's different— straight but curly, like the hair on those naked tribes in Australia. You might think
15 she's a throwback, but a throwback to what? You should've seen my grandmother; she passed for white, married a white man, and never said another word to any one of her children. Any letter she got from my mother
20 or my aunts she sent right back, unopened. Finally they got the message of no message and let her be. Almost all mulatto types and quadroons did that back in the day—if they had the right kind of hair, that is. Can you
25 imagine how many white folks have Negro blood hiding in their veins? Guess. Twenty

per cent, I heard. My own mother, Lula Mae,
could have passed easy, but she chose not to.
She told me the price she paid for that deci-
30 sion. When she and my father went to the
courthouse to get married, there were two
Bibles, and they had to put their hands on
the one reserved for Negroes. The other one
was for white people's hands. The Bible! Can
35 you beat it? My mother was a housekeeper
for a rich white couple. They ate every meal
she cooked and insisted she scrub their
backs while they sat in the tub, and God
knows what other intimate things they made
40 her do, but no touching of the same Bible.

Some of you probably think it's a bad
thing to group ourselves according to skin
color—the lighter the better—in social
clubs, neighborhoods, churches, sororities,
45 even colored schools. But how else can we
hold on to a little dignity? How else can we
avoid being spit on in a drugstore, elbowed at
the bus stop, having to walk in the gutter to
let whites have the whole sidewalk, being
50 charged a nickel at the grocer's for a paper
bag that's free to white shoppers? Let alone
all the name-calling. I heard about all of that
and much, much more. But because of my
mother's skin color she wasn't stopped from
55 trying on hats or using the ladies' room in
the department stores. And my father could
try on shoes in the front part of the shoe
store, not in a back room. Neither one of
them would let themselves drink from a
60 "Colored Only" fountain, even if they were
dying of thirst.

I hate to say it, but from the very beginning in the maternity ward the baby, Lula
Ann, embarrassed me. Her birth skin was
65 pale like all babies', even African ones, but it
changed fast. I thought I was going crazy
when she turned blue-black right before my
eyes. I know I went crazy for a minute,
because—just for a few seconds—I held a
70 blanket over her face and pressed. But I
couldn't do that, no matter how much I
wished she hadn't been born with that terrible color. I even thought of giving her away to
an orphanage someplace. But I was scared to
75 be one of those mothers who leave their
babies on church steps. Recently, I heard
about a couple in Germany, white as snow,
who had a dark-skinned baby nobody could
explain. Twins, I believe—one white, one
80 colored. But I don't know if it's true. All I
know is that, for me, nursing her was like
having a pickaninny sucking my teat. I went
to bottle-feeding soon as I got home.

My husband, Louis, is a porter, and when
85 he got back off the rails he looked at me like
I really was crazy and looked at the baby like
she was from the planet Jupiter. He wasn't a
cussing man, so when he said, "God damn!
What the hell is this?" I knew we were in
90 trouble. That was what did it—what caused
the fights between me and him. It broke our
marriage to pieces. We had three good years
together, but when she was born he blamed
me and treated Lula Ann like she was a
95 stranger—more than that, an enemy. He
never touched her.

I never did convince him that I ain't never,
ever fooled around with another man. He
was dead sure I was lying. We argued and
100 argued till I told him her blackness had to be
from his own family—not mine. That was
when it got worse, so bad he just up and left
and I had to look for another, cheaper place
to live. I did the best I could. I knew enough
105 not to take her with me when I applied to
landlords, so I left her with a teen-age cousin
to babysit. I didn't take her outside much,
anyway, because, when I pushed her in the
baby carriage, people would lean down and
110 peek in to say something nice and then give

a start or jump back before frowning. That hurt. I could have been the babysitter if our skin colors were reversed. It was hard enough just being a colored woman—even a
115 high-yellow one—trying to rent in a decent part of the city. Back in the nineties, when Lula Ann was born, the law was against discriminating in who you could rent to, but not many landlords paid attention to it. They
120 made up reasons to keep you out. But I got lucky with Mr. Leigh, though I know he upped the rent seven dollars from what he'd advertised, and he had a fit if you were a minute late with the money.

125   I told her to call me "Sweetness" instead of "Mother" or "Mama." It was safer. Her being that black and having what I think are too thick lips and calling me "Mama" would've confused people. Besides, she has
130 funny-colored eyes, crow black with a blue tint—something witchy about them, too.

   So it was just us two for a long while, and I don't have to tell you how hard it is being an abandoned wife. I guess Louis felt a little
135 bit bad after leaving us like that, because a few months later on he found out where I'd moved to and started sending me money once a month, though I never asked him to and didn't go to court to get it. His fifty-
140 dollar money orders and my night job at the hospital got me and Lula Ann off welfare. Which was a good thing. I wish they would stop calling it welfare and go back to the word they used when my mother was a girl.
145 Then it was called "relief." Sounds much better, like it's just a short-term breather while you get yourself together. Besides, those welfare clerks are mean as spit. When finally I got work and didn't need them anymore, I
150 was making more money than they ever did. I guess meanness filled out their skimpy paychecks, which was why they treated us

like beggars. Especially when they looked at Lula Ann and then back at me—like I was
155 trying to cheat or something. Things got better but I still had to be careful. Very careful in how I raised her. I had to be strict, very strict. Lula Ann needed to learn how to behave, how to keep her head down and not to make
160 trouble. I don't care how many times she changes her name. Her color is a cross she will always carry. But it's not my fault. It's not my fault. It's not.

   Oh, yeah, I feel bad sometimes about how
165 I treated Lula Ann when she was little. But you have to understand: I had to protect her. She didn't know the world. With that skin, there was no point in being tough or sassy, even when you were right. Not in a world
170 where you could be sent to a juvenile lockup for talking back or fighting in school, a world where you'd be the last one hired and the first one fired. She didn't know any of that or how her black skin would scare white people
175 or make them laugh and try to trick her. I once saw a girl nowhere near as dark as Lula Ann who couldn't have been more than ten years old tripped by one of a group of white boys and when she tried to scramble up
180 another one put his foot on her behind and knocked her flat again. Those boys held their stomachs and bent over with laughter. Long after she got away, they were still giggling, so proud of themselves. If I hadn't been watch-
185 ing through the bus window I would have helped her, pulled her away from that white trash. See, if I hadn't trained Lula Ann properly she wouldn't have known to always cross the street and avoid white boys. But the
190 lessons I taught her paid off, and in the end she made me proud as a peacock.

   I wasn't a bad mother, you have to know that, but I may have done some hurtful things to my only child because I had to

195 protect her. Had to. All because of skin
privileges. At first I couldn't see past all that
black to know who she was and just plain
love her. But I do. I really do. I think she
understands now. I think so.

200   Last two times I saw her she was, well,
striking. Kind of bold and confident. Each
time she came to see me, I forgot just how
black she really was because she was using it
to her advantage in beautiful white clothes.

205   Taught me a lesson I should have known
all along. What you do to children matters.
And they might never forget. As soon as she
could, she left me all alone in that awful
apartment. She got as far away from me as

210 she could: dolled herself up and got a big-
time job in California. She don't call or visit
anymore. She sends me money and stuff
every now and then, but I ain't seen her in I
don't know how long.

215   I prefer this place—Winston House—to
those big, expensive nursing homes outside
the city. Mine is small, homey, cheaper, with
twenty-four-hour nurses and a doctor who
comes twice a week. I'm only sixty-three—

220 too young for pasture—but I came down
with some creeping bone disease, so good
care is vital. The boredom is worse than the
weakness or the pain, but the nurses are
lovely. One just kissed me on the cheek

225 when I told her I was going to be a grandmother. Her smile and her compliments
were fit for someone about to be crowned. I
showed her the note on blue paper that I got
from Lula Ann—well, she signed it "Bride,"

230 but I never pay that any attention. Her
words sounded giddy. "Guess what, S. I am
so, so happy to pass along this news. I am
going to have a baby. I'm too, too thrilled
and hope you are, too." I reckon the thrill is

235 about the baby, not its father, because she
doesn't mention him at all. I wonder if he is
as black as she is. If so, she needn't worry
like I did. Things have changed a mite from
when I was young. Blue-blacks are all over

240 TV, in fashion magazines, commercials,
even starring in movies.

    There is no return address on the enve-
lope. So I guess I'm still the bad parent
being punished forever till the day I die for

245 the well-intended and, in fact, necessary
way I brought her up. I know she hates me.
Our relationship is down to her sending me
money. I have to say I'm grateful for the
cash, because I don't have to beg for extras,

250 like some of the other patients. If I want my
own fresh deck of cards for solitaire, I can
get it and not need to play with the dirty,
worn one in the lounge. And I can buy my
special face cream. But I'm not fooled. I

255 know the money she sends is a way to stay
away and quiet down the little bit of conscience she's got left.

    If I sound irritable, ungrateful, part of it is
because underneath is regret. All the little

260 things I didn't do or did wrong. I remember
when she had her first period and how I
reacted. Or the times I shouted when she
stumbled or dropped something. True. I was
really upset, even repelled by her black skin

265 when she was born and at first I thought
of . . . No. I have to push those memories
away—fast. No point. I know I did the best
for her under the circumstances. When my
husband ran out on us, Lula Ann was a

270 burden. A heavy one, but I bore it well.

    Yes, I was tough on her. You bet I was. By
the time she turned twelve going on thirteen, I had to be even tougher. She was
talking back, refusing to eat what I cooked,

275 primping her hair. When I braided it, she'd
go to school and unbraid it. I couldn't let her

go bad. I slammed the lid and warned her about the names she'd be called. Still, some of my schooling must have rubbed off. See how she turned out? A rich career girl. Can you beat it?

Now she's pregnant. Good move, Lula Ann. If you think mothering is all cooing, booties, and diapers you're in for a big shock. Big. You and your nameless boyfriend, husband, pickup—whoever—imagine, Oooh! A baby! Kitchee kitchee koo!

Listen to me. You are about to find out what it takes, how the world is, how it works, and how it changes when you are a parent.

Good luck, and God help the child.

NARRATION

1. What is the **point of view** in the story? Why is this important to the story?

2. Identify and explain details in the story that reveal the characteristics, values, and attributes of the **narrator**.

3. Describe the multiple **perspectives** from which the story is told.

4. Explain how these multiple **perspectives** affect the relationship between the characters and the events of the story.

Courage and Fate

IDEA BANK

Adventure

Betrayal

Courage

Destiny

Evil

Family

Fate

Fortune

Good

Heroism

Honor

Ideal

Journey

Love

Loyalty

Obligation

Power

Quest

Strength

Valor

Violence

In a sense, the history of the country that we know as England begins in 449 A.D. The Romans had conquered what they called "Britannia" over three hundred years earlier, establishing their rule, building infrastructure, and bringing Christianity to the region's native tribes. But as the empire collapsed in the fifth century, the Romans retreated from the colony. This withdrawal allowed tribes from Northern Europe to settle in England, Wales, and Scotland. The most dominant were the Angles and the Saxons: Germanic warriors who revered courage and strength. These Anglo-Saxons built their social structure on tribal groups led by chieftains. These leaders had to be brave and heroic but also generous. As "ring-givers," they dispensed treasure, weapons, and other spoils of warfare to their "thanes": military noblemen who were predecessors to the English knights. Warfare was their way of life, whether they were fighting against the native Britons or engaging in intertribal blood feuds. According to their code, hostilities were usually settled when one of the feuding parties paid *wergild*: an Old English term that means "man payment."

The Anglo-Saxons originally worshipped the "pagan" gods of their Viking ancestors: a religion that undergirded their reverence for courage and honor. They kept many vestiges of these beliefs, even after most of them converted to Christianity in the seventh century. Norse mythology emphasized the primary role of fate (*wyrd* in Old English) in determining events. Many readers have identified

Longships were a specialized warship used by the Norse tribes as they battled and forged new lands.

How does the design of these ships contribute to ideas of courage and fate of the warriors from the Anglo-Saxon period?

Photo 12/Universal Images Group/Getty Images

this theme in "The Seafarer" (p. 52), an Anglo-Saxon poem that explores life, heroism, mortality, impermanence, and alienation. If the legendary epic *Beowulf* exemplifies the heroic tradition in Anglo-Saxon literature, then "The Seafarer" illustrates the elegiac form. An elegy is usually a serious reflection or lament, often for the dead. But the unknown speaker of this poem laments the difficulties, uncertainties, and destinies of others living at the time, as well as his own life and fate.

Art, literature, and film have always explored the relationship between acts of individual courage and the wider factors that shape human destiny. We can see it in the struggles of the king in Alfred Lord Tennyson's poem "Ulysses" (p. 56), as well as in the pressures that shape Frank Stockton's short story "The Lady or the Tiger (p. 60)." Indeed, fate helps explain characters and drive dramatic action. In *Star Wars: Episode III — Revenge of the Sith*, for example, the wicked Emperor Palpatine encourages Anakin Skywalker to join the dark side as a matter of fate: "You're fulfilling your destiny, Anakin." But more importantly, we see the dichotomy between individual courage and impersonal forces in real life, whether in the actions of combat troops, the choices of political leaders trying to manage events beyond their control, or the challenges faced by individuals in difficult social and economic circumstances.

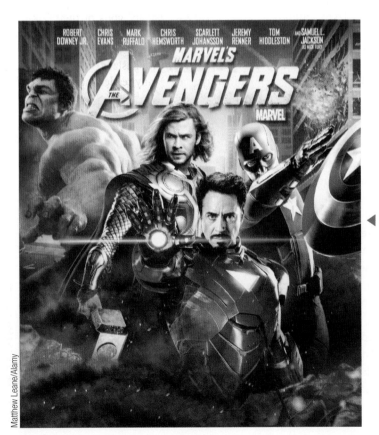

Matthew Leane/Alamy

The Marvel Cinematic Universe films are a series of twenty-three superhero films that share the same universe. The films have been in production since 2007. They are based on characters that appear in publications by Marvel Comics.

Marvel Studios has earned billions of dollars at the box office with its films. How do these stories appeal to our contemporary ideas about fate?

The Seafarer
Translated by Ezra Pound

THE TEXT IN CONTEXT

Many manuscripts have survived from the Anglo-Saxon period, including wills, chronicles, geography guides, narrative histories, and even medical texts. But relatively little poetry remains, in large part because Anglo-Saxon poetry existed as an oral form, not a written one. In other words, poems were sung or read aloud and passed along by bards or *scops*. Readers may infer this oral quality from the poem's extensive use of alliteration. As emphasized in Ezra Pound's translation, the repetition of opening consonants helped scops remember the verses. The Anglo-Saxon epic *Beowulf* deploys similar techniques and — along with "The Seafarer" (c. 450–c. 1100) and other examples — suggests that poetry of the time was highly alliterative. Similarly, "The Seafarer" includes the use of *kenning*: vivid, two-word phrases that take the place of one-word nouns, as in *whale-path* for *sea*. These compound terms could be used repeatedly by oral poets as a device for remembering their tales.

The Seafarer

May I for my own self song's truth reckon,
Journey's jargon, how I in harsh days
Hardship endured oft.
Bitter breast-cares have I abided,
5 Known on my keel many a care's hold,
And dire sea-surge, and there I oft spent
Narrow nightwatch nigh the ship's head
While she tossed close to cliffs. Coldly afflicted,
My feet were by frost benumbed.
10 Chill its chains are; chafing sighs
Hew my heart round and hunger begot
Mere-weary mood. Lest man know not
That he on dry land loveliest liveth,
List how I, care-wretched, on ice-cold sea,
15 Weathered the winter, wretched outcast
Deprived of my kinsmen;
Hung with hard ice-flakes, where hail-scur flew,
There I heard naught save the harsh sea
And ice-cold wave, at whiles the swan cries,

20 Did for my games the gannet's clamour,
   Sea-fowls, loudness was for me laughter,
   The mews' singing all my mead-drink.
   Storms, on the stone-cliffs beaten, fell on the stern
   In icy feathers; full oft the eagle screamed
25 With spray on his pinion.
   Not any protector
   May make merry man faring needy.
   This he little believes, who aye in winsome life
   Abides 'mid burghers some heavy business,
30 Wealthy and wine-flushed, how I weary oft
   Must bide above brine.
   Neareth nightshade, snoweth from north,
   Frost froze the land, hail fell on earth then
   Corn of the coldest. Nathless there knocketh now
35 The heart's thought that I on high streams
   The salt-wavy tumult traverse alone.
   Moaneth alway my mind's lust
   That I fare forth, that I afar hence
   Seek out a foreign fastness.
40 For this there's no mood-lofty man over earth's midst,
   Not though he be given his good, but will have in his youth greed;
   Nor his deed to the daring, nor his king to the faithful
   But shall have his sorrow for sea-fare
   Whatever his lord will.
45 He hath not heart for harping, nor in ring-having
   Nor winsomeness to wife, nor world's delight
   Nor any whit else save the wave's slash,
   Yet longing comes upon him to fare forth on the water.
   Bosque taketh blossom, cometh beauty of berries,
50 Fields to fairness, land fares brisker,
   All this admonisheth man eager of mood,
   The heart turns to travel so that he then thinks
   On flood-ways to be far departing.
   Cuckoo calleth with gloomy crying,
55 He singeth summerward, bodeth sorrow,
   The bitter heart's blood. Burgher knows not—
   He the prosperous man—what some perform
   Where wandering them widest draweth.
   So that but now my heart burst from my breast-lock,
60 My mood 'mid the mere-flood,

Over the whale's acre, would wander wide.
On earth's shelter cometh oft to me,
Eager and ready, the crying lone-flyer,
Whets for the whale-path the heart irresistibly,
65 O'er tracks of ocean; seeing that anyhow
My lord deems to me this dead life
On loan and on land, I believe not
That any earth-weal eternal standeth
Save there be somewhat calamitous
70 That, ere a man's tide go, turn it to twain.
Disease or oldness or sword-hate
Beats out the breath from doom-gripped body.
And for this, every earl whatever, for those speaking after—
Laud of the living, boasteth some last word,
75 That he will work ere he pass onward,
Frame on the fair earth 'gainst foes his malice,
Daring ado, . . .
So that all men shall honour him after
And his laud beyond them remain 'mid the English,
80 Aye, for ever, a lasting life's-blast,
Delight mid the doughty.
Days little durable,
And all arrogance of earthen riches,
There come now no kings nor Cæsars
85 Nor gold-giving lords like those gone.
Howe'er in mirth most magnified,
Whoe'er lived in life most lordliest,
Drear all this excellence, delights undurable!
Waneth the watch, but the world holdeth.
90 Tomb hideth trouble. The blade is layed low.
Earthly glory ageth and seareth.
No man at all going the earth's gait,
But age fares against him, his face paleth,
Grey-haired he groaneth, knows gone companions,
95 Lordly men are to earth o'ergiven,
Nor may he then the flesh-cover, whose life ceaseth,
Nor eat the sweet nor feel the sorry,
Nor stir hand nor think in mid heart,
And though he strew the grave with gold,
100 His born brothers, their buried bodies
Be an unlikely treasure hoard.

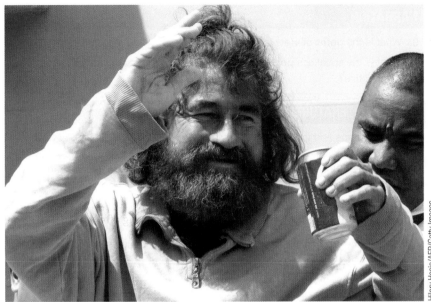

Hilary Hosia/AFP/Getty Images

▲

The image shows José Salvador Alvarenga, the man who survived 438 days on the Atlantic Ocean in a 15-foot skiff with limited supplies. The heroic survival was retold in the 2000 movie *Castaway* starring Tom Hanks.

Explain how the seafarer's and José Salvador Alvarenga's courage contributed to their survival and intervened with their fate.

CHARACTER

1. Identify and explain details, words, and phrases that **characterize** the seafarer.

2. How does the narrator describe the seafarer's background? How does this contribute to his **motivation**?

3. What is the seafarer's psychological or emotional state?

SETTING

4. How is the setting described? What do these details of this **setting** reveal about the values of this culture?

5. The **setting's** climate is described extensively in "The Seafarer." How does that climate connect the characters and the events of the journey? Explain.

STRUCTURE

6. How are the events of the **plot** ordered in the poem?

7. What is the **climax** of the journey?

8. What is the final **resolution** for "The Seafarer"? How does this resolve and conclude the poem?

NARRATION

9. What is the **point of view** in the poem?

10. What is the speaker's **perspective**? What details in the story reveal that perspective?

IDEAS IN LITERATURE: Courage and Fate

11. Both courage and fate are important ideas for understanding "The Seafarer." The poem combines Anglo-Saxon views on fate and courage. How do they both contribute to the ideas in the poem and continue to be concepts we struggle with today?

PUTTING IT ALL TOGETHER

12. How do the falling action and resolution reveal the seafarer's complex perspective and contribute to the tone of the poem?

Ulysses
Alfred Lord Tennyson

THE TEXT IN CONTEXT

England's poet laureate from 1850 until his death, Alfred Lord Tennyson (1809–1892) was the most admired and celebrated English poet of his age. His work seems to embody the values, ideals, and anxieties of England during his lifetime, especially its reverence for courage and determination. In "Ulysses" (1833), Tennyson borrows from Homer's ancient Greek epic, *The Odyssey*: an aged Ulysses, back from twenty years of heroic adventures, finds domestic life unsatisfying and pointless. In this monologue, he speaks to his son and expresses complex emotions that reveal his character traits — perhaps unintentionally.

Christopher Furlong/Getty Images

Ulysses

It little profits that an idle king,
By this still hearth, among these barren crags,
Match'd with an aged wife, I mete and dole
Unequal laws unto a savage race,
5 That hoard, and sleep, and feed, and know not me.

I cannot rest from travel: I will drink
Life to the lees: All times I have enjoy'd
Greatly, have suffer'd greatly, both with those
That loved me, and alone, on shore, and when
10 Thro' scudding drifts the rainy Hyades
Vext the dim sea: I am become a name;
For always roaming with a hungry heart
Much have I seen and known; cities of men
And manners, climates, councils, governments,
15 Myself not least, but honour'd of them all;
And drunk delight of battle with my peers,
Far on the ringing plains of windy Troy.
I am a part of all that I have met;
Yet all experience is an arch wherethro'
20 Gleams that untravell'd world whose margin fades
For ever and forever when I move.
How dull it is to pause, to make an end,
To rust unburnish'd, not to shine in use!
As tho' to breathe were life! Life piled on life
25 Were all too little, and of one to me
Little remains: but every hour is saved
From that eternal silence, something more,
A bringer of new things; and vile it were
For some three suns to store and hoard myself,
30 And this gray spirit yearning in desire
To follow knowledge like a sinking star,
Beyond the utmost bound of human thought.

This is my son, mine own Telemachus,
To whom I leave the sceptre and the isle,—
35 Well-loved of me, discerning to fulfil
This labour, by slow prudence to make mild
A rugged people, and thro' soft degrees
Subdue them to the useful and the good.
Most blameless is he, centred in the sphere
40 Of common duties, decent not to fail
In offices of tenderness, and pay
Meet adoration to my household gods,
When I am gone. He works his work, I mine.

There lies the port; the vessel puffs her sail:
45 There gloom the dark, broad seas. My mariners,

Souls that have toil'd, and wrought, and thought with me—
That ever with a frolic welcome took
The thunder and the sunshine, and opposed
Free hearts, free foreheads—you and I are old;
50 Old age hath yet his honour and his toil;
Death closes all: but something ere the end,
Some work of noble note, may yet be done,
Not unbecoming men that strove with Gods.
The lights begin to twinkle from the rocks:
55 The long day wanes: the slow moon climbs: the deep
Moans round with many voices. Come, my friends,
'T not too late to seek a newer world.
Push off, and sitting well in order smite
The sounding furrows; for my purpose holds
60 To sail beyond the sunset, and the baths
Of all the western stars, until I die.
It may be that the gulfs will wash us down:
It may be we shall touch the Happy Isles,
And see the great Achilles, whom we knew.
65 Tho' much is taken, much abides; and tho'
We are not now that strength which in old days
Moved earth and heaven, that which we are, we are;
One equal temper of heroic hearts,
Made weak by time and fate, but strong in will
70 To strive, to seek, to find, and not to yield.

The photograph captures Queen Elizabeth II (1926–2022), the longest-reigning British monarch, and the royal family of Great Britain. Upon her death in 2022, her son Charles (second from left) was crowned king.

In Tennyson's poem, how does Ulysses manage his succession? Why does he decide to turn the kingdom over to his son Telemachus before his own death?

Chris Jackson/Getty Images

CHARACTER

1. How does Ulysses describe himself? What specific words does the speaker use in these descriptions? What do the descriptions reveal about his **character**, emotionally and psychologically?

2. What values does Ulysses represent?

3. How does the poet reveal Ulysses's **motivation**? Give an example of how the characterization reveals motivation.

SETTING

4. What is the **setting**?

5. What is the time span of this narrative poem? How does the duration of time contribute to the poem?

STRUCTURE

6. How does the poem's **exposition** reveal the relationship between the character and the setting?

7. Identify the beginning, the middle, and the end of the poem. Explain how the **narrative arc** connects and builds through these three sections.

NARRATION

8. How would you characterize the poem's **point of view**?

9. What is the **perspective** of the **speaker**?

IDEAS IN LITERATURE: Courage and Fate

10. The speaker refers to fate both implicitly and explicitly in the poem. How does fate function in your experience?

PUTTING IT ALL TOGETHER

11. How does the structure of the poem tell a story and reveal Ulysses, an epic hero?

The Lady or the Tiger
Frank Stockton

Culture Club/Getty Images

THE TEXT IN CONTEXT

Frank Stockton (1834–1902) was a popular American writer of humorous stories, children's literature, science fiction, and adventure novels. His most well-known story, "The Lady or the Tiger," originally appeared in an 1882 issue of *Century Magazine* to wide acclaim. While Stockton's tale is set in an imaginary time and place, it cleverly dramatizes serious themes of fate, individual choice, betrayal, love, and obligation. Indeed, over the years, some critics have even interpreted the story as a meditation on the relationship between free will and divine predestination.

The Lady or the Tiger

In the very olden time there lived a semi-barbaric king, whose ideas, though somewhat polished and sharpened by the progressiveness of distant Latin neighbors, were still
5 large, florid, and untrammeled, as became the half of him which was barbaric. He was a man of exuberant fancy, and, withal, of an authority so irresistible that, at his will, he turned his varied fancies into facts. He was greatly
10 given to self-communing, and, when he and himself agreed upon anything, the thing was done. When every member of his domestic and political systems moved smoothly in its appointed course, his nature was bland and
15 genial; but, whenever there was a little hitch, and some of his orbs got out of their orbits, he was blander and more genial still, for nothing pleased him so much as to make the crooked straight and crush down uneven places.
20 Among the borrowed notions by which his barbarism had become semified was that of the public arena, in which, by exhibitions of manly and beastly valor, the minds of his subjects were refined and cultured.
25 But even here the exuberant and barbaric fancy asserted itself. The arena of the king was built, not to give the people an opportunity of hearing the rhapsodies of dying gladiators, nor to enable them to view the
30 inevitable conclusion of a conflict between religious opinions and hungry jaws, but for purposes far better adapted to widen and develop the mental energies of the people. This vast amphitheater, with its encircling
35 galleries, its mysterious vaults, and its unseen passages, was an agent of poetic justice, in which crime was punished, or virtue rewarded, by the decrees of an impartial and incorruptible chance.
40 When a subject was accused of a crime of sufficient importance to interest the king, public notice was given that on an appointed day the fate of the accused person would be decided in the king's arena, a structure which

45 well deserved its name, for, although its form
and plan were borrowed from afar, its purpose
emanated solely from the brain of this man,
who, every barleycorn a king, knew no tradition to which he owed more allegiance than
50 pleased his fancy, and who ingrafted on every
adopted form of human thought and action
the rich growth of his barbaric idealism.

When all the people had assembled in the
galleries, and the king, surrounded by his
55 court, sat high up on his throne of royal state
on one side of the arena, he gave a signal, a
door beneath him opened, and the accused
subject stepped out into the amphitheater.
Directly opposite him, on the other side of
60 the enclosed space, were two doors, exactly
alike and side by side. It was the duty and
the privilege of the person on trial to walk
directly to these doors and open one of
them. He could open either door he pleased;
65 he was subject to no guidance or influence
but that of the aforementioned impartial and
incorruptible chance. If he opened the one,
there came out of it a hungry tiger, the fiercest and most cruel that could be procured,
70 which immediately sprang upon him and
tore him to pieces as a punishment for his
guilt. The moment that the case of the criminal was thus decided, doleful iron bells were
clanged, great wails went up from the hired
75 mourners posted on the outer rim of the
arena, and the vast audience, with bowed
heads and downcast hearts, wended slowly
their homeward way, mourning greatly that
one so young and fair, or so old and respected,
80 should have merited so dire a fate.

But, if the accused person opened the
other door, there came forth from it a lady,
the most suitable to his years and station
that his majesty could select among his fair
85 subjects, and to this lady he was immediately married, as a reward of his innocence.
It mattered not that he might already

possess a wife and family, or that his affections might be engaged upon an object of his
90 own selection; the king allowed no such subordinate arrangements to interfere with his
great scheme of retribution and reward. The
exercises, as in the other instance, took place
immediately, and in the arena. Another door
95 opened beneath the king, and a priest, followed by a band of choristers, and dancing
maidens blowing joyous airs on golden horns
and treading an epithalamic measure,
advanced to where the pair stood, side by
100 side, and the wedding was promptly and
cheerily solemnized. Then the gay brass bells
rang forth their merry peals, the people
shouted glad hurrahs, and the innocent man,
preceded by children strewing flowers on his
105 path, led his bride to his home.

This was the king's semi-barbaric method
of administering justice. Its perfect fairness is
obvious. The criminal could not know out of
which door would come the lady; he opened
110 either he pleased, without having the slightest
idea whether, in the next instant, he was to be
devoured or married. On some occasions the
tiger came out of one door, and on some out of
the other. The decisions of this tribunal were
115 not only fair, they were positively determinate:
the accused person was instantly punished if
he found himself guilty, and, if innocent, he
was rewarded on the spot, whether he liked it
or not. There was no escape from the judg-
120 ments of the king's arena.

The institution was a very popular one.
When the people gathered together on one of
the great trial days, they never knew whether
they were to witness a bloody slaughter or a
125 hilarious wedding. This element of uncertainty lent an interest to the occasion which it
could not otherwise have attained. Thus, the
masses were entertained and pleased, and
the thinking part of the community could
130 bring no charge of unfairness against this

plan, for did not the accused person have the whole matter in his own hands?

This semi-barbaric king had a daughter as blooming as his most florid fancies, and with 135 a soul as fervent and imperious as his own. As is usual in such cases, she was the apple of his eye, and was loved by him above all humanity. Among his courtiers was a young man of that fineness of blood and lowness of 140 station common to the conventional heroes of romance who love royal maidens. This royal maiden was well satisfied with her lover, for he was handsome and brave to a degree unsurpassed in all this kingdom, and 145 she loved him with an ardor that had enough of barbarism in it to make it exceedingly warm and strong. This love affair moved on happily for many months, until one day the king happened to discover its existence. He 150 did not hesitate nor waver in regard to his duty in the premises. The youth was immediately cast into prison, and a day was appointed for his trial in the king's arena. This, of course, was an especially important 155 occasion, and his majesty, as well as all the people, was greatly interested in the workings and development of this trial. Never before had such a case occurred; never before had a subject dared to love the daugh- 160 ter of the king. In after years such things became commonplace enough, but then they were in no slight degree novel and startling.

The tiger-cages of the kingdom were searched for the most savage and relentless 165 beasts, from which the fiercest monster might be selected for the arena; and the ranks of maiden youth and beauty throughout the land were carefully surveyed by competent judges in order that the young man might 170 have a fitting bride in case fate did not determine for him a different destiny. Of course, everybody knew that the deed with which the accused was charged had been done. He had loved the princess, and neither he, she, nor 175 any one else, thought of denying the fact; but the king would not think of allowing any fact of this kind to interfere with the workings of the tribunal, in which he took such great delight and satisfaction. No matter how the 180 affair turned out, the youth would be disposed of, and the king would take an aesthetic pleasure in watching the course of events, which would determine whether or not the young man had done wrong in allow- 185 ing himself to love the princess.

The appointed day arrived. From far and near the people gathered, and thronged the great galleries of the arena, and crowds, unable to gain admittance, massed them- 190 selves against its outside walls. The king and his court were in their places, opposite the twin doors, those fateful portals, so terrible in their similarity.

All was ready. The signal was given. A 195 door beneath the royal party opened, and the lover of the princess walked into the arena. Tall, beautiful, fair, his appearance was greeted with a low hum of admiration and anxiety. Half the audience had not known so 200 grand a youth had lived among them. No wonder the princess loved him! What a terrible thing for him to be there!

As the youth advanced into the arena he turned, as the custom was, to bow to the king, 205 but he did not think at all of that royal personage. His eyes were fixed upon the princess, who sat to the right of her father. Had it not been for the moiety of barbarism in her nature it is probable that lady would not have 210 been there, but her intense and fervid soul would not allow her to be absent on an occasion in which she was so terribly interested. From the moment that the decree had gone forth that her lover should decide his fate in 215 the king's arena, she had thought of nothing, night or day, but this great event and the

various subjects connected with it. Possessed
of more power, influence, and force of character than any one who had ever before been
220 interested in such a case, she had done what
no other person had done—she had possessed herself of the secret of the doors. She
knew in which of the two rooms, that lay
behind those doors, stood the cage of the
225 tiger, with its open front, and in which waited
the lady. Through these thick doors, heavily
curtained with skins on the inside, it was
impossible that any noise or suggestion
should come from within to the person who
230 should approach to raise the latch of one of
them. But gold, and the power of a woman's
will, had brought the secret to the princess.

And not only did she know in which room
stood the lady ready to emerge, all blushing
235 and radiant, should her door be opened, but
she knew who the lady was. It was one of the
fairest and loveliest of the damsels of the court
who had been selected as the reward of the
accused youth, should he be proved innocent
240 of the crime of aspiring to one so far above
him; and the princess hated her. Often had she
seen, or imagined that she had seen, this fair
creature throwing glances of admiration upon
the person of her lover, and sometimes she
245 thought these glances were perceived, and
even returned. Now and then she had seen
them talking together; it was but for a moment
or two, but much can be said in a brief space; it
may have been on most unimportant topics,
250 but how could she know that? The girl was
lovely, but she had dared to raise her eyes to
the loved one of the princess; and, with all the
intensity of the savage blood transmitted to
her through long lines of wholly barbaric
255 ancestors, she hated the woman who blushed
and trembled behind that silent door.

When her lover turned and looked at her,
and his eye met hers as she sat there, paler
and whiter than any one in the vast ocean of
260 anxious faces about her, he saw, by that
power of quick perception which is given to
those whose souls are one, that she knew
behind which door crouched the tiger, and
behind which stood the lady. He had expected
265 her to know it. He understood her nature, and
his soul was assured that she would never
rest until she had made plain to herself this
thing, hidden to all other lookers-on, even to
the king. The only hope for the youth in
270 which there was any element of certainty was
based upon the success of the princess in discovering this mystery; and the moment he
looked upon her, he saw she had succeeded,
as in his soul he knew she would succeed.

275 Then it was that his quick and anxious
glance asked the question: "Which?" It was
as plain to her as if he shouted it from where
he stood. There was not an instant to be lost.
The question was asked in a flash; it must be
280 answered in another.

Her right arm lay on the cushioned parapet before her. She raised her hand, and
made a slight, quick movement toward the
right. No one but her lover saw her. Every eye
285 but his was fixed on the man in the arena.

He turned, and with a firm and rapid step
he walked across the empty space. Every
heart stopped beating, every breath was held,
every eye was fixed immovably upon that
290 man. Without the slightest hesitation, he
went to the door on the right, and opened it.

Now, the point of the story is this: Did the
tiger come out of that door, or did the lady?

The more we reflect upon this question,
295 the harder it is to answer. It involves a study
of the human heart which leads us through
devious mazes of passion, out of which it is
difficult to find our way. Think of it, fair
reader, not as if the decision of the question
300 depended upon yourself, but upon that hot-
blooded, semi-barbaric princess, her soul at a
white heat beneath the combined fires of

despair and jealousy. She had lost him, but who should have him?

305 How often, in her waking hours and in her dreams, had she started in wild horror, and covered her face with her hands as she thought of her lover opening the door on the other side of which waited the cruel fangs of 310 the tiger!

But how much oftener had she seen him at the other door! How in her grievous reveries had she gnashed her teeth, and torn her hair, when she saw his start of rapturous delight as 315 he opened the door of the lady! How her soul had burned in agony when she had seen him rush to meet that woman, with her flushing cheek and sparkling eye of triumph; when she had seen him lead her forth, his whole 320 frame kindled with the joy of recovered life; when she had heard the glad shouts from the multitude, and the wild ringing of the happy bells; when she had seen the priest, with his joyous followers, advance to the couple, and 325 make them man and wife before her very

eyes; and when she had seen them walk away together upon their path of flowers, followed by the tremendous shouts of the hilarious multitude, in which her one despairing shriek 330 was lost and drowned!

Would it not be better for him to die at once, and go to wait for her in the blessed regions of semi-barbaric futurity?

And yet, that awful tiger, those shrieks, 335 that blood!

Her decision had been indicated in an instant, but it had been made after days and nights of anguished deliberation. She had known she would be asked, she had decided 340 what she would answer, and, without the slightest hesitation, she had moved her hand to the right.

The question of her decision is one not to be lightly considered, and it is not for me to 345 presume to set myself up as the one person able to answer it. And so I leave it with all of you: Which came out of the opened door—the lady, or the tiger?

▲ On television game shows such as *Let's Make a Deal*, contestants take risks and make decisions that are subject to chance.

How is "The Lady or the Tiger" similar to game shows like *Let's Make a Deal*? How is it different?

CHARACTER

1. How is the king described in the exposition of the story? How does he represent a set of beliefs and **values**?

2. How is the princess described? What does the description reveal about her **character**?

3. What is the princess's final motion? What does that motion reveal about her **motivation**?

SETTING

4. What is the time, place, and occasion of "The Lady or the Tiger"? How does this **setting** contribute to the story?

5. How does the historical **setting** impact the story?

STRUCTURE

6. How does each event in the story connect to create dramatic **tension**?

7. What is the action that leads to the **climax** of the story? Remember that the term **climax** refers to a crisis, defining moment, or decision point for the main character.

8. What is the **resolution** of this story?

NARRATION

9. What is the story's narrative **point of view**? How does it contribute to what we know (and don't know) about the characters?

10. How does the **narrator** reveal the details of the tribunal? Explain how every person in the kingdom contributes to the event.

IDEAS IN LITERATURE: Courage and Fate

11. The tribunal is intended to be a game of fate. How does the princess intercede with fate in the story? Can you think of another literary character that intercedes with fate? Do you think that individuals can change fate? Explain.

PUTTING IT ALL TOGETHER

12. How does the complexity of the character's motivation contribute to the complexity of the story?

IDEAS IN LITERATURE
Faith and Doubt

IDEA BANK

Character

Class

Corruption

Deception

Doubt

Faith

Faustian

Forgiveness

Government

Greed

Honesty

Integrity

Obedience

Penance

Power

Redemption

Religion

Sin

Theocracy

Trust

Value

In 597 A.D., Pope Gregory sent Christian missionaries from Rome to convert the Anglo-Saxons. The mission was enormously successful—including the conversions of many Anglo-Saxon kings. But even as Christianity grew stronger in England, the Anglo-Saxons' hold on power grew weaker. A series of Viking raids, in particular, had devastated many Anglo-Saxon chieftains. Then in 1066 the Normans, led by William the Conqueror, invaded and conquered England. A tribe from northern France, the Normans had assimilated to European customs. They brought orthodox Roman Catholicism to England; in fact, William the Conqueror had received the pope's blessing for his invasion by promising to bring English Christianity in line with Catholic doctrine. This blending of religious authority with political authority helped William consolidate power. Along with installing their own church officials, the Normans began building monasteries, cathedrals, and churches across the country. In Chaucer's *The Canterbury Tales*, the pilgrims are traveling to Canterbury Cathedral, which was built under Norman authority between 1070 and 1077.

The Normans also imported feudalism: the social and economic system that defined the medieval era. In the feudal hierarchy, the king ruled over three "estates": the church, the nobility, and the peasants. The king kept a portion of the country's land for his own use while distributing the rest to powerful church officials and barons of the nobility. In return, they supplied the king with knights to protect the realm. These knights lived by a chivalric code: an oath to serve baron and king, defend the weak, and guard the Christian faith. The rest of the population were peasants who provided the labor and rent that sustained the feudal order.

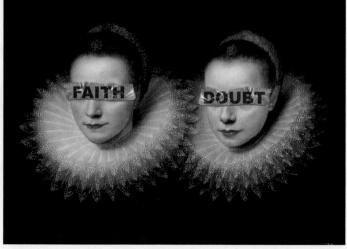

Faith + Doubt (digital art printed on Picasso canvas) by the contemporary Italian artist Slasky is a fusion of urban influences and classic contemporary pop art.

Do faith and doubt work together? How does faith and doubt function in the contemporary world?

© Slasky Art

66

The church played a central role in society: it gave moral and religious legitimacy to the entire system. It affirmed faith in divine right: the principle that kings were ordained by God. By the same doctrine, everyone was born to a static, predetermined social station. The church was a center of learning and intellectual life, as monks, priests, and bishops were often literate and educated. Religious leaders engaged in politics, as well, which brought them into conflict with the king. In 1170, for example, knights murdered Thomas à Becket, the archbishop of Canterbury, after he opposed King Henry II's attempts to undermine the church's autonomy.

But the power and wealth of the medieval church led to its corruption too. Some clergy led lives of pleasure, despite vows of poverty and chastity, while priests and pardoners conned the faithful with fraudulent holy relics. Worst of all, perhaps, the church raised money by selling "indulgences": payments to the church that cleansed people of sins. Reformers urged the church to purge its corruption and abuses of power. Chaucer's cynical "The Pardoner's Tale" (p. 68) traces this corrupting power of avarice and wealth. When the clergy proved unable to save people from the Black Death (a bubonic plague epidemic from 1347 to 1352), many began to doubt their legitimacy.

From its origins, the United States has defined itself against the feudal system's static social hierarchy, its disregard for individual choice, its inequality of opportunity, and its intermixing of religious and government authority. Yet we may not be as far from this medieval order as we'd like to think: powerful political and religious interests still intermix. While disparities in wealth increase, economic mobility declines, leaving more Americans trapped by economic and social circumstances. Still, people keep faith in the promise of American ideals, despite their doubts.

North Wind Picture Archives/Alamy

▲
The image depicts a classic rendition of the pilgrims from *The Canterbury Tales*.

How does the image represent the faithful people on a journey to the Shrine of St. Thomas Becket? Explain how the details reflect the various types of people on the pilgrimage. What do the details tell us about them? What do the details communicate about the various people who go on pilgrimages?

The Pardoner's Tale
Geoffrey Chaucer

THE TEXT IN CONTEXT

Print Collector/Getty Images

Born near the end of England's medieval period, Geoffrey Chaucer (c. 1343–1400) was part of an emerging middle class that challenged the rigid, prevailing social order of the church, the nobility, and the peasantry. These three feudal classes (or "estates") are represented in various forms by the pilgrims in Chaucer's best-known work, *The Canterbury Tales* (c. 1400). Originally in Middle English, the version here was translated into modern English by John Urban Nicolson. The poem's premise is deceptively simple: a diverse group of people agrees to a storytelling contest to pass the time on their way to a religious shrine, which allows Chaucer to criticize ideas and issues such as social class, nobility, desire, love, marriage, religion, and faith. Indeed, the corruption of the church is one of Chaucer's primary targets. That is especially evident in the comically hypocritical pardoner. At the time, pardoners were low-level clerics who sold "indulgences": they were authorized to take money from people to absolve their sins. Chaucer's pardoner gleefully exploits the faith of others.

The Pardoner's Tale

IN FLANDERS, once, there was a company
Of young companions given to folly,
Riot and gambling, brothels and taverns;
And, to the music of harps, lutes, gitterns,
5 They danced and played at dice both day
  and night,
And ate also and drank beyond their might,
Whereby they made the devil's sacrifice
Within that devil's temple, wicked wise,
By superfluity both vile and vain.
10 So damnable their oaths and so profane
That it was terrible to hear them swear;
Our blessed Saviour's Body did they tear;
They thought the Jews had rent Him not
  enough;
And each of them at others' sins would
  laugh.
15 Then entered dancing-girls of ill repute,

Graceful and slim, and girls who peddled
  fruit,
Harpers and bawds and women selling cake,
Who do their office for the Devil's sake,
To kindle and blow the fire of lechery,
20 Which is so closely joined with gluttony;
I call on holy writ, now, to witness
That lust is in all wine and drunkenness.
O gluttony, of you we may complain!
Oh, knew a man how many maladies
25 Follow on excess and on gluttonies,
Surely he would be then more moderate
In diet, and at table more sedate.
Alas! A foul thing is it, by my fay,
To speak this word, and fouler is the deed,
30 When man so guzzles of the white and red
That of his own throat makes he his privy,
Because of this cursed superfluity.

But truly, he that such delights entice
Is dead while yet he wallows in this vice.
35 A lecherous thing is wine, and drunkenness
Is full of striving and of wretchedness.
O drunken man, disfigured is your face,
Sour is your breath, foul are you to embrace,
You fall down just as if you were stuck swine;
40 Your tongue is loose, your honest care obscure;
For drunkenness is very sepulture
Of any mind a man may chance to own.
In whom strong drink has domination
   shown
He can no counsel keep for any dread.
45 Now keep you from the white and from
   the red.
And now that I have told of gluttony,
I'll take up gambling, showing you thereby
The curse of chance, and all its evils treat;
From it proceeds false swearing and deceit,
50 Blaspheming, murder, and—what's more—
   the waste
Of time and money; add to which, debased
And shamed and lost to honour quite is he,
Who once a common gambler's known to be.
And ever the higher one is of estate,
55 The more he's held disgraced and desolate.
And if a prince plays similar hazardry
In all his government and policy,
He loses in the estimate of men
His good repute, and finds it not again.
60 Now these three roisterers, whereof I tell,
Long before prime was rung by any bell,
Were sitting in a tavern for to drink;
And as they sat they heard a small bell clink
Before a corpse being carried to his grave;
65 Whereat one of them called unto his knave:
"Go run," said he, "and ask them civilly
What corpse it is that's just now passing by,
And see that you report the man's name
   well."
"Sir," said the boy, "it needs not that they tell.
70 I learned it, ere you came here, full two
   hours;

He was, by gad, an old comrade of yours;
And he was slain, all suddenly, last night,
When drunk, as he sat on his bench upright;
An unseen thief, called Death, came
   stalking by,
75 Who hereabouts makes all the people die,
And with his spear he clove his heart in two
And went his way and made no more ado.
He's slain a thousand with this pestilence;
And, master, ere you come in his presence,
80 It seems to me to be right necessary
To be forewarned of such an adversary:
Be ready to meet him for evermore.
My mother taught me this, I say no more."
"By holy Mary," said the innkeeper,
85 "The boy speaks truth, for Death has slain,
   this year,
A mile or more hence, in a large village,
Both man and woman, child and hind
   and page.
I think his habitation must be there;
To be advised of him great wisdom 'twere,
90 Before he did a man some dishonour."
"Yea, by God's arms!" exclaimed this rois-
   terer,
"Is it such peril, then, this Death to meet?
I'll seek him in the road and in the street,
As I now vow to God's own noble bones!
95 Hear, comrades, we're of one mind, as each
   owns;
Let each of us hold up his hand to other
And each of us become the other's brother,
And we three will go slay this traitor Death;
He shall be slain who's stopped so many a
   breath,
100 By God's great dignity, ere it be night."
Together did these three their pledges plight
To live and die, each of them for the other,
As if he were his very own blood brother.
And up they started, drunken, in this rage,
105 And forth they went, and towards that
   village
Whereof the innkeeper had told before.

And so, with many a grisly oath, they swore
And Jesus' blessed body once more rent—
"Death shall be dead if we find where he
     went."
110 When they had gone not fully half a mile,
Just as they would have trodden over a stile,
An old man, and a poor, with them did meet.
This ancient man full meekly them did greet,
And said thus: "Now, lords, God keep you
     and see!"
115 The one that was most insolent of these
     three
Replied to him: "What? Churl of evil grace,
Why are you all wrapped up, except your
     face?
Why do you live so long in so great age?"
This ancient man looked upon his visage
120 And thus replied: "Because I cannot find
A man, nay, though I walked from here to
     Ind,
Either in town or country who'll engage
To give his youth in barter for my age;
And therefore must I keep my old age still,
125 As long a time as it shall be God's will.
Not even Death, alas! my life will take;
Thus restless I my wretched way must make
But, sirs, in you it is no courtesy
To speak to an old man despitefully,
130 Unless in word he trespass or in deed.
In holy writ you may, yourselves, well read
'Before an old man, hoar upon the head,
You should arise.' Which I advise you read,
Nor to an old man any injury do
135 More than you would that men should do to
     you
In age, if you so long time shall abide;
And God be with you, whether you walk or
     ride.
I must pass on now where I have to go."
"Nay, ancient churl, by God it sha'n't be so,"
140 Cried out this other hazarder, anon;
"You sha'n't depart so easily, by Saint John!

You spoke just now of that same traitor
     Death,
Who in this country stops our good friends'
     breath
Hear my true word, since you are his own
     spy,
145 Tell where he is or you shall rue it, aye
By God and by the holy Sacrament!
Indeed you must be, with this Death, intent
To slay all us young people, you false thief."
"Now, sirs," said he, "if you're so keen, in
     brief,
150 To find out Death, turn up this crooked way,
For in that grove I left him, by my fay,
Under a tree, and there he will abide;
Nor for your boasts will he a moment hide.
See you that oak? Right there you shall him
     find.
155 God save you, Who redeemed all humankind,
And mend your ways!"—thus said this
     ancient man.
And every one of these three roisterers ran
Till he came to that tree; and there they
     found,
Of florins of fine gold, new-minted, round,
160 Well-nigh eight bushels full, or so they
     thought.
No longer, then, after this Death they sought,
But each of them so glad was of that sight,
Because the florins were so fair and bright,
That down they all sat by this precious
     hoard.
165 The worst of them was first to speak a word.
"Brothers," said he, "take heed to what I say;
My wits are keen, although I mock and play.
This treasure here Fortune to us has given
That mirth and jollity our lives may liven,
170 And easily as it's come, so will we spend.
But might this gold be carried from this place
Home to my house, or if you will, to yours—
For well we know that all this gold is ours—
Then were we all in high felicity.

175 But certainly by day this may not be;
For men would say that we were robbers
strong,
And we'd, for our own treasure, hang ere
long.
This treasure must be carried home by night
All prudently and slyly, out of sight.
180 So I propose that cuts among us all
Be drawn, and let's see where the cut will
fall;
And he that gets the short cut, blithe of heart
Shall run to town at once, and to the mart,
And fetch us bread and wine here, privately.
185 And two of us shall guard, right cunningly,
This treasure well; and if he does not tarry,
When it is night we'll all the treasure carry
Where, by agreement, we may think it best."
That one of them the cuts brought in his fist
190 And bade them draw to see where it might
fall;
And it fell on the youngest of them all;
And so, forth toward the town he went anon.
And just as soon as he had turned and gone,
That one of them spoke thus unto the other:
195 "You know well that you are my own sworn
brother,
So to your profit I will speak anon.
You know well how our comrade is just gone;
And here is gold, and that in great plenty,
That's to be parted here among us three.
200 Nevertheless, if I can shape it so
That it be parted only by us two,
Shall I not do a turn that is friendly?"
The other said: "Well, now, how can that be?
He knows well that the gold is with us two.
205 What shall we say to him? What shall we
do?"
"Shall it be secret?" asked the first rogue,
then,
"And I will tell you in eight words, or ten,
What we must do, and how bring it about."
"Agreed," replied the other, "Never doubt,

210 That, on my word, I nothing will betray."
"Now," said the first, "we're two, and I dare
say
The two of us are stronger than is one.
Watch when he sits, and soon as that is done
Arise and make as if with him to play;
215 And I will thrust him through the two sides,
yea,
The while you romp with him as in a game,
And with your dagger see you do the same;
And then shall all this gold divided be,
My right dear friend, just between you and
me;
220 Then may we both our every wish fulfill
And play at dice all at our own sweet will."
And thus agreed were these two rogues, that
day,
To slay the third, as you have heard me say.
This youngest rogue who'd gone into the
town,
225 Often in fancy rolled he up and down
The beauty of those florins new and bright.
"O Lord," thought he, "if so be that I might
Have all this treasure to myself alone,
There is no man who lives beneath the
throne
230 Of God that should be then so merry as I."
And at the last the Fiend, our enemy,
Put in his thought that he should poison buy
With which he might kill both his fellows;
aye,
The Devil found him in such wicked state,
235 He had full leave his grief to consummate;
For it was utterly the man's intent
To kill them both and never to repent.
And on he strode, no longer would he tarry,
Into the town, to an apothecary,
240 And prayed of him that he'd prepare and sell
Some poison for his rats, and some as well
For a polecat that in his yard had lain,
The which, he said, his capons there had
slain,

And fain he was to rid him, if he might,
245 Of vermin that thus damaged him by night.
The apothecary said: "And you shall have
A thing of which, so God my spirit save,
In all this world there is not live creature
That's eaten or has drunk of this mixture
250 As much as equals but a grain of wheat,
That shall not sudden death thereafter meet;
Yea, die he shall, and in a shorter while
Than you require to walk but one short mile;
This poison is so violent and strong."
255 This wicked man the poison took along
With him boxed up, and then he straightway
   ran
Into the street adjoining, to a man,
And of him borrowed generous bottles three;
And into two his poison then poured he;
260 The third one he kept clean for his own
   drink.
For all that night he was resolved to swink
In carrying the florins from that place.
And when this roisterer, with evil grace,
Had filled with wine his mighty bottles three,
265 Then to his comrades forth again went he.
What is the need to tell about it more?
For just as they had planned his death
   before,
Just so they murdered him, and that anon.
And when the thing was done, then spoke
   the one:
270 "Now let us sit and drink and so be merry,
And afterward we will his body bury."
And as he spoke, one bottle of the three
He took wherein the poison chanced to be
And drank and gave his comrade drink also,
275 For which, and that anon, lay dead these two.
Thus ended these two homicides in woe;
Died thus the treacherous poisoner also.
O cursed sin, full of abominableness!
O treacherous homicide! O wickedness!
280 O gluttony, lechery, and hazardry!
O blasphemer of Christ with villainy,
And with great oaths, habitual for pride!

Alas! Mankind, how may this thing betide
That to thy dear Creator, Who thee wrought,
285 And with His precious blood salvation
   bought,
Thou art so false and so unkind, alas!
Now, good men, God forgive you each
   trespass,
And keep you from the sin of avarice.
My holy pardon cures and will suffice,
290 So that it brings me gold, or silver brings,
Or else, I care not—brooches, spoons or
   rings.
Bow down your heads before this holy bull!
Come up, you wives, and offer of your wool!
Your names I'll enter on my roll, anon,
295 And into Heaven's bliss you'll go, each one.
For I'll absolve you, by my special power,
You that make offering, as clean this hour
As you were born.
And lo, sirs, thus I preach.
300 And Jesus Christ, who is our souls' great
   leech,
So grant you each his pardon to receive;
For that is best; I will not you deceive.
But, sirs, one word forgot I in my tale;
I've relics in my pouch that cannot fail,
305 As good as England ever saw, I hope,
The which I got by kindness of the pope.
If gifts your change of heart and mind reveal.
You'll get my absolution while you kneel.
Come forth, and kneel down here before,
   anon.
310 And humbly you'll receive my full pardon;
Or else receive a pardon as you wend,
All new and fresh as every mile shall end,
So that you offer me each time, anew,
More gold and silver, all good coins and true.
315 It is an honour to each one that's here
That you may have a competent pardoner
To give you absolution as you ride,
For all adventures that may still betide.
Perchance from horse may fall down one or
   two,

320 Breaking his neck, and it might well be you.
See what insurance, then, it is for all
That I within your fellowship did fall,
Who may absolve you, both the great and less,
When soul from body passes, as I guess.
325 I think our host might just as well begin,
For he is most enveloped in all sin.
Come forth, sir host, and offer first anon,
And you shall kiss the relics, every one,
Aye, for a groat! Unbuckle now your purse."
330 "Nay, nay," said he, "then may I have Christ's
    curse!
Why, you would have me kissing your old
    breeches,
And swear they were the relics of a saint,
Though with your excrement 'twere dabbed
    like paint.
By cross Saint Helen found in Holy Land,

335 I would I had your ballocks in my hand
Instead of relics in a reliquary;
Let's cut them off, and them I'll help you carry;
They shall be shrined within a hog's fat turd."
This pardoner, he answered not a word;
340 So wrathy was he no word would he say.
"Now," said our host, "I will no longer play
With you, nor any other angry man."
But at this point the worthy knight began,
When that he saw how all the folk did laugh:
345 "No more of this, for it's gone far enough;
Sir pardoner, be glad and merry here;
And you, sir host, who are to me so dear,
I pray you that you kiss the pardoner.
And, pardoner, I pray you to draw near,
350 And as we did before, let's laugh and play."
And then they kissed and rode forth on their
    way.

Jeff J Mitchell/Getty Images

In this 2013 image of St. Peter's Square in Rome, thousands of people flood the area in and around the Vatican during the inauguration of Pope Francis. In fact, St. Peter's Basilica receives millions of visitors every year. Likewise, millions of Muslims make the pilgrimage (known as the Hajj) to Mecca in Saudi Arabia.

What drives people to go on pilgrimages today? Do pilgrimages require a religious focus, or can they also be secular?

CHARACTER

1. How is the pardoner described? What does this description reveal about his **values** and beliefs?

2. What **motivates** the pardoner to think, feel, speak, and act in the way that he does?

SETTING

3. Where does "The Pardoner's Tale" begin? How does its geographical location contribute to the tale?

4. What is the **setting** of the rest of the tale? What is supposed to be under the tree? Why does the old man suggest they "follow a crooked way"?

STRUCTURE

5. What passes by the rioters while they are in the tavern? How does this contribute to the **narrative arc** of the story?

6. What do the rioters actually find under the tree? How does this contribute to the **conflict** in the story?

NARRATION

7. Who is the **narrator** of the story?

8. What is the story's point of view? Why is this **point of view** significant?

IDEAS IN LITERATURE: Faith and Doubt

9. Consider how the pardoner "sells" his tale to the pilgrims. What is his "sales pitch"? Do you think that these appeals and techniques still work today? Find a modern advertisement that uses one or more of these sales strategies. Are they effective? Explain.

PUTTING IT ALL TOGETHER

10. While the pardoner tells us the moral of the story, what other morals or values are revealed through his tale, and how do they contribute to the complexity of the tale?

The Devil and Tom Walker
Washington Irving

Historic Images/Alamy

THE TEXT IN CONTEXT

Best known for his short stories "Rip Van Winkle" (1890) and "The Legend of Sleepy Hollow" (1820), the Manhattan-born Washington Irving (1783–1859) was the first American to achieve international success with his literary work, as well as the first American to earn his living solely as a writer. Irving not only helped develop the short story as a genre; he is also a key figure in inventing an American version of the Gothic. His tales of mystery, superstition, and horror often take place in New York's Hudson Valley: an area long-settled by Irving's time but also rural and isolated. In "The Devil and Tom Walker" (1824), the story's key setting is a dark, swampy, woodsy area "a few miles from Boston." Irving often drew on older stories and folklore, which he adapted for his purposes in an American setting. The following story revises the legend of Faust: a German tale about a brilliant, ambitious man who sells his soul to the devil in exchange for pleasure and divine knowledge. Both "Old Scratch" and "The Black Man" are traditional nicknames for Satan in English and European folklore.

The Devil and Tom Walker

A few miles from Boston, in Massachusetts, there is a deep inlet winding several miles into the interior of the country from Charles Bay, and terminating in a thickly wooded
5 swamp or morass. On one side of this inlet is a beautiful dark grove; on the opposite side the land rises abruptly from the water's edge into a high ridge, on which grow a few scattered oaks of great age and immense size.
10 Under one of these gigantic trees, according to old stories, there was a great amount of treasure buried by Kidd the pirate. The inlet allowed a facility to bring the money in a boat secretly, and at night, to the very foot of
15 the hill; the elevation of the place permitted a good lookout to be kept that no one was at hand; while the remarkable trees formed good landmarks by which the place might easily be found again. The old stories add,
20 moreover, that the devil presided at the hiding of the money, and took it under his guardianship; but this, it is well known, he always does with buried treasure, particularly when it has been ill-gotten. Be that as
25 it may, Kidd never returned to recover his wealth; being shortly after seized at Boston, sent out to England, and there hanged for a pirate.

About the year 1727, just at the time that
30 earthquakes were prevalent in New England, and shook many tall sinners down upon their knees, there lived near this place a meagre, miserly fellow, of the name of Tom Walker. He had a wife as miserly as himself;

35 they were so miserly that they even con-
spired to cheat each other. Whatever the
woman could lay hands on she hid away; a
hen could not cackle but she was on the alert
to secure the new-laid egg. Her husband was
40 continually prying about to detect her secret
hoards, and many and fierce were the conflicts that took place about what ought to
have been common property. They lived in a
forlorn-looking house that stood alone and
45 had an air of starvation. A few straggling
savin-trees, emblems of sterility, grew near
it; no smoke ever curled from its chimney; no
traveller stopped at its door. A miserable
horse, whose ribs were as articulate as the
50 bars of a gridiron, stalked about a field,
where a thin carpet of moss, scarcely
covering the ragged beds of pudding-stone,
tantalized and balked his hunger; and
sometimes he would lean his head over the
55 fence, look piteously at the passer-by, and
seem to petition deliverance from this land
of famine.

    The house and its inmates had altogether
a bad name. Tom's wife was a tall termagant,
60 fierce of temper, loud of tongue, and strong
of arm. Her voice was often heard in wordy
warfare with her husband; and his face
sometimes showed signs that their conflicts
were not confined to words. No one ven-
65 tured, however, to interfere between them.
The lonely wayfarer shrank within himself
at the horrid clamor and clapper-clawing;
eyed the den of discord askance; and hurried
on his way, rejoicing, if a bachelor, in his
70 celibacy.

    One day that Tom Walker had been to a
distant part of the neighborhood, he took
what he considered a short-cut homeward,
through the swamp. Like most short-cuts,
75 it was an ill-chosen route. The swamp was
thickly grown with great, gloomy pines and

hemlocks, some of them ninety feet high,
which made it dark at noonday and a
retreat for all the owls of the neighborhood.
80 It was full of pits and quagmires, partly
covered with weeds and mosses, where the
green surface often betrayed the traveller
into a gulf of black, smothering mud; there
were also dark and stagnant pools, the
85 abodes of the tadpole, the bull-frog, and
the water-snake, where the trunks of pines
and hemlocks lay half-drowned, half-
rotting, looking like alligators sleeping
in the mire.

90   Tom had long been picking his way
cautiously through this treacherous forest,
stepping from tuft to tuft of rushes and
roots, which afforded precarious footholds
among deep sloughs, or pacing carefully, like
95 a cat, along the prostrate trunks of trees,
startled now and then by the sudden
screaming of the bittern, or the quacking of a
wild duck, rising on the wing from some solitary pool. At length he arrived at a firm piece
100 of ground, which ran like a peninsula into
the deep bosom of the swamp. It had been
one of the strongholds of the Indians during
their wars with the first colonists. Here they
had thrown up a kind of fort, which they had
105 looked upon as almost impregnable, and had
used as a place of refuge for their squaws
and children. Nothing remained of the old
Indian fort but a few embankments, gradually sinking to the level of the surrounding
110 earth, and already overgrown in part by oaks
and other forest trees, the foliage of which
formed a contrast to the dark pines and
hemlocks of the swamps.

    It was late in the dusk of evening when
115 Tom Walker reached the old fort, and he
paused there awhile to rest himself. Any
one but he would have felt unwilling to linger in this lonely, melancholy place, for the

common people had a bad opinion of it, from
120 the stories handed down from the times
of the Indian wars, when it was asserted that
the savages held incantations here and made
sacrifices to the Evil Spirit.

Tom Walker, however, was not a man to
125 be troubled with any fears of the kind. He
reposed himself for some time on the trunk
of a fallen hemlock, listening to the boding
cry of the tree-toad, and delving with his
walking-staff into a mound of black mould
130 at his feet. As he turned up the soil unconsciously, his staff struck against something
hard. He raked it out of the vegetable
mould, and lo! a cloven skull, with an
Indian tomahawk buried deep in it, lay
135 before him. The rust on the weapon
showed the time that had elapsed since
this death-blow had been given. It was a
dreary memento of the fierce struggle that
had taken place in this last foothold of the
140 Indian warriors.

"Humph!" said Tom Walker, as he gave it a
kick to shake the dirt from it.

"Let that skull alone!" said a gruff voice.
Tom lifted up his eyes and beheld a great
145 black man seated directly opposite him, on
the stump of a tree. He was exceedingly surprised, having neither heard nor seen any
one approach; and he was still more perplexed on observing, as well as the gather-
150 ing gloom would permit, that the stranger
was neither negro nor Indian. It is true he
was dressed in a rude Indian garb, and had
a red belt or sash swathed round his body;
but his face was neither black nor copper-
155 color, but swarthy and dingy, and begrimed
with soot, as if he had been accustomed to
toil among fires and forges. He had a shock
of coarse black hair, that stood out from his
head in all directions, and bore an axe on
160 his shoulder.

He scowled for a moment at Tom with a
pair of great red eyes.

"What are you doing on my grounds?"
said the black man, with a hoarse, growling
165 voice.

"Your grounds!" said Tom, with a sneer;
"no more your grounds than mine; they
belong to Deacon Peabody."

"Deacon Peabody be damned," said the
170 stranger, "as I flatter myself he will be, if he
does not look more to his own sins and less
to those of his neighbors. Look yonder, and
see how Deacon Peabody is faring."

Tom looked in the direction that the
175 stranger pointed, and beheld one of the great
trees, fair and flourishing without, but rotten
at the core, and saw that it had been nearly
hewn through, so that the first high wind
was likely to blow it down. On the bark of the
180 tree was scored the name of Deacon Peabody,
an eminent man who had waxed wealthy by
driving shrewd bargains with the Indians. He
now looked around, and found most of the
tall trees marked with the name of some
185 great man of the colony, and all more or less
scored by the axe. The one on which he had
been seated, and which had evidently just
been hewn down, bore the name of Crownin-
shield; and he recollected a mighty rich man
190 of that name, who made a vulgar display of
wealth, which it was whispered he had
acquired by buccaneering.

"He's just ready for burning!" said the
black man, with a growl of triumph. "You see
195 I am likely to have a good stock of firewood
for winter."

"But what right have you," said Tom, "to
cut down Deacon Peabody's timber?"

"The right of a prior claim," said the other.
200 "This woodland belonged to me long before
one of your white-faced race put foot upon
the soil."

"And, pray, who are you, if I may be so bold?" said Tom.

205   "Oh, I go by various names. I am the wild huntsman in some countries; the black miner in others. In this neighborhood I am known by the name of the black woodsman. I am he to whom the red men consecrated

210   this spot, and in honor of whom they now and then roasted a white man, by way of sweet-smelling sacrifice. Since the red men have been exterminated by you white savages, I amuse myself by presiding at the

215   persecutions of Quakers and Anabaptists; I am the great patron and prompter of slave-dealers and the grand-master of the Salem witches."

"The upshot of all which is, that, if I mis-

220   take not," said Tom, sturdily, "you are he commonly called Old Scratch."

"The same, at your service!" replied the black man, with a half-civil nod.

Such was the opening of this interview,

225   according to the old story; though it has almost too familiar an air to be credited. One would think that to meet with such a singular personage in this wild, lonely place would have shaken any man's nerves; but

230   Tom was a hard-minded fellow, not easily daunted, and he had lived so long with a termagant wife that he did not even fear the devil.

It is said that after this commencement

235   they had a long and earnest conversation together, as Tom returned homeward. The black man told him of great sums of money buried by Kidd the pirate under the oak-trees on the high ridge, not far from the

240   morass. All these were under his command, and protected by his power, so that none could find them but such as propitiated his favor. These he offered to place within Tom Walker's reach, having conceived an

245   especial kindness for him; but they were to be had only on certain conditions. What these conditions were may be easily surmised, though Tom never disclosed them publicly. They must have been very hard, for

250   he required time to think of them, and he was not a man to stick at trifles when money was in view. When they had reached the edge of the swamp, the stranger paused. "What proof have I that all you have been

255   telling me is true?" said Tom. "There's my signature," said the black man, pressing his finger on Tom's forehead. So saying, he turned off among the thickets of the swamp, and seemed, as Tom said, to go down, down,

260   down, into the earth, until nothing but his head and shoulders could be seen, and so on, until he totally disappeared.

When Tom reached home he found the black print of a finger burned, as it were,

265   into his forehead, which nothing could obliterate.

The first news his wife had to tell him was the sudden death of Absalom Crownin-shield, the rich buccaneer. It was announced

270   in the papers, with the usual flourish, that "A great man had fallen in Israel."

Tom recollected the tree which his black friend had just hewn down, and which was ready for burning. "Let the freebooter roast,"

275   said Tom; "who cares!" He now felt convinced that all he had heard and seen was no illusion.

He was not prone to let his wife into his confidence; but as this was an uneasy secret,

280   he willingly shared it with her. All her avarice was awakened at the mention of hidden gold, and she urged her husband to comply with the black man's terms, and secure what would make them wealthy for life. However

285   Tom might have felt disposed to sell himself to the devil, he was determined not to do so

to oblige his wife; so he flatly refused, out of the mere spirit of contradiction. Many and bitter were the quarrels they had on the sub-
290 ject; but the more she talked, the more reso-lute was Tom not to be damned to please her.

At length she determined to drive the bargain on her own account, and, if she suc-ceeded, to keep all the gain to herself. Being
295 of the same fearless temper as her husband, she set off for the old Indian fort toward the close of a summer's day. She was many hours absent. When she came back, she was reserved and sullen in her replies. She spoke
300 something of a black man, whom she had met about twilight hewing at the root of a tall tree. He was sulky, however, and would not come to terms; she was to go again with a propitiatory offering, but what it was she
305 forbore to say.

The next evening she set off again for the swamp, with her apron heavily laden. Tom waited and waited for her, but in vain; mid-night came, but she did not make her
310 appearance; morning, noon, night returned, but still she did not come. Tom now grew uneasy for her safety, especially as he found she had carried off in her apron the silver tea-pot and spoons, and every portable arti-
315 cle of value. Another night elapsed, another morning came; but no wife. In a word, she was never heard of more.

What was her real fate nobody knows, in consequence of so many pretending to
320 know. It is one of those facts which have become confounded by a variety of histori-ans. Some asserted that she lost her way among the tangled mazes of the swamp, and sank into some pit or slough; others,
325 more uncharitable, hinted that she had eloped with the household booty, and made off to some other province; while others surmised that the tempter had decoyed her

into a dismal quagmire, on the top of which
330 her hat was found lying. In confirmation of this, it was said a great black man, with an axe on his shoulder, was seen late that very evening coming out of the swamp, carrying a bundle tied in a check apron, with an air
335 of surly triumph.

The most current and probable story, however, observes that Tom Walker grew so anxious about the fate of his wife and his property that he set out at length to seek
340 them both at the Indian fort. During a long summer's afternoon he searched about the gloomy place, but no wife was to be seen. He called her name repeatedly, but she was nowhere to be heard. The bittern alone
345 responded to his voice, as he flew screaming by; or the bull-frog croaked dolefully from a neighboring pool. At length, it is said, just in the brown hour of twilight, when the owls began to hoot and the bats to flit about, his
350 attention was attracted by the clamor of car-rion crows hovering about a cypress-tree. He looked up and beheld a bundle tied in a check apron and hanging in the branches of the tree, with a great vulture perched hard
355 by, as if keeping watch upon it. He leaped with joy, for he recognized his wife's apron, and supposed it to contain the household valuables.

"Let us get hold of the property," said he,
360 consolingly, to himself, "and we will endeavor to do without the woman."

As he scrambled up the tree, the vulture spread its wide wings and sailed off, screaming, into the deep shadows of the
365 forest. Tom seized the checked apron, but, woful sight! found nothing but a heart and liver tied up in it!

Such, according to this most authentic old story, was all that was to be found of Tom's
370 wife. She had probably attempted to deal

with the black man as she had been
accustomed to deal with her husband; but
though a female scold is generally considered a match for the devil, yet in this
375 instance she appears to have had the worst
of it. She must have died game, however; for
it is said Tom noticed many prints of cloven
feet deeply stamped about the tree, and
found handfuls of hair, that looked as if they
380 had been plucked from the coarse black
shock of the woodsman. Tom knew his wife's
prowess by experience. He shrugged his
shoulders as he looked at the signs of fierce
clapper-clawing. "Egad," said he to himself,
385 "Old Scratch must have had a tough time
of it!"

Tom consoled himself for the loss of his
property, with the loss of his wife, for he was
a man of fortitude. He even felt something
390 like gratitude toward the black woodsman,
who, he considered, had done him a kindness. He sought, therefore, to cultivate a
further acquaintance with him, but for some
time without success; the old black-legs
395 played shy, for, whatever people may think,
he is not always to be had for the calling; he
knows how to play his cards when pretty
sure of his game.

At length, it is said, when delay had
400 whetted Tom's eagerness to the quick and
prepared him to agree to anything rather
than not gain the promised treasure, he
met the black man one evening in his usual
woodsman's dress, with his axe on his
405 shoulder, sauntering along the swamp and
humming a tune. He affected to receive
Tom's advances with great indifference,
made brief replies, and went on humming
his tune.

410 By degrees, however, Tom brought him
to business, and they began to haggle
about the terms on which the former was

to have the pirate's treasure. There was
one condition which need not be men-
415 tioned, being generally understood in all
cases where the devil grants favors; but
there were others about which, though of
less importance, he was inflexibly obstinate. He insisted that the money found
420 through his means should be employed in
his service. He proposed, therefore, that
Tom should employ it in the black traffic;
that is to say, that he should fit out a
slaveship. This, however, Tom resolutely
425 refused; he was bad enough in all conscience, but the devil himself could not
tempt him to turn slave-trader.

Finding Tom so squeamish on this point,
he did not insist upon it, but proposed,
430 instead, that he should turn usurer; the devil
being extremely anxious for the increase of
usurers, looking upon them as his peculiar
people.

To this no objections were made, for it
435 was just to Tom's taste.

"You shall open a broker's shop in Boston
next month," said the black man.

"I'll do it to-morrow, if you wish," said Tom
Walker.

440 "You shall lend money at two per cent a
month."

"Egad, I'll charge four!" replied Tom
Walker.

"You shall extort bonds, foreclose mort-
445 gages, drive the merchants to bankruptcy—"

"I'll drive them to the devil," cried Tom
Walker.

"You are the usurer for my money!" said
black-legs with delight. "When will you want
450 the rhino?"

"This very night."

"Done!" said the devil.

"Done!" said Tom Walker. So they shook
hands and struck a bargain.

455 A few days' time saw Tom Walker seated behind his desk in a counting-house in Boston.

His reputation for a ready-moneyed man, who would lend money out for a good con-460 sideration, soon spread abroad. Everybody remembers the time of Governor Belcher, when money was particularly scarce. It was a time of paper credit. The country had been deluged with government bills; the famous 465 Land Bank had been established; there had been a rage for speculating; the people had run mad with schemes for new settlements, for building cities in the wilderness; land-jobbers went about with maps of 470 grants and townships and Eldorados, lying nobody knew where, but which everybody was ready to purchase. In a word, the great speculating fever which breaks out every now and then in the country had raged to 475 an alarming degree, and everybody was dreaming of making sudden fortunes from nothing. As usual, the fever had subsided, the dream had gone off, and the imaginary fortunes with it; the patients were left in 480 doleful plight, and the whole country resounded with the consequent cry of "hard times."

At this propitious time of public distress did Tom Walker set up as usurer in 485 Boston. His door was soon thronged by customers. The needy and adventurous, the gambling speculator, the dreaming land-jobber, the thriftless tradesman, the merchant with cracked credit—in short, 490 everyone driven to raise money by desperate means and desperate sacrifices hurried to Tom Walker.

Thus Tom was the universal friend to the needy, and acted like "a friend in need"; that 495 is to say, he always exacted good pay and security. In proportion to the distress of the applicant was the hardness of his terms. He accumulated bonds and mortgages, gradually squeezed his customers closer and 500 closer, and sent them at length, dry as a sponge, from his door.

In this way he made money hand over hand, became a rich and mighty man, and exalted his cocked hat upon "Change." He 505 built himself, as usual, a vast house, out of ostentation, but left the greater part of it unfinished and unfurnished, out of parsimony. He even set up a carriage in the fulness of his vain-glory, though he nearly 510 starved the horses which drew it; and, as the ungreased wheels groaned and screeched on the axle-trees, you would have thought you heard the souls of the poor debtors he was squeezing.

515 As Tom waxed old, however, he grew thoughtful. Having secured the good things of this world, he began to feel anxious about those of the next. He thought with regret of the bargain he had made with 520 his black friend, and set his wits to work to cheat him out of the conditions. He became, therefore, all of a sudden, a violent church-goer. He prayed loudly and strenuously, as if heaven were to be taken by 525 force of lungs. Indeed, one might always tell when he had sinned most during the week by the clamor of his Sunday devotion. The quiet Christians who had been modestly and steadfastly travelling Zionward 530 were struck with self-reproach at seeing themselves so suddenly outstripped in their career by this new-made convert. Tom was as rigid in religious as in money matters; he was a stern supervisor and cen-535 surer of his neighbors, and seemed to think every sin entered up to their account became a credit on his own side of the page. He even talked of the expediency of

reviving the persecution of Quakers and
540 Anabaptists. In a word, Tom's zeal became
as notorious as his riches.

Still, in spite of all this strenuous attention to forms, Tom had a lurking dread that
the devil, after all, would have his due. That
545 he might not be taken unawares, therefore, it
is said he always carried a small Bible in his
coat-pocket. He had also a great folio Bible
on his counting-house desk, and would frequently be found reading it when people
550 called on business; on such occasions he
would lay his green spectacles in the book, to
mark the place, while he turned round to
drive some usurious bargain.

Some say that Tom grew a little crack-
555 brained in his old days, and that, fancying
his end approaching, he had his horse new
shod, saddled, and bridled, and buried with
his feet uppermost; because he supposed
that at the last day the world would be
560 turned upside-down; in which case he
should find his horse standing ready for
mounting, and he was determined at the
worst to give his old friend a run for it. This,
however, is probably a mere old wives' fable.
565 If he really did take such a precaution, it
was totally superfluous; at least so says the
authentic old legend, which closes his story
in the following manner:

One hot summer afternoon in the dog-
570 days, just as a terrible black thunder-gust
was coming up, Tom sat in his counting-
house, in his white linen cap and India silk
morning-gown. He was on the point of fore-
closing a mortgage, by which he would com-
575 plete the ruin of an unlucky land-speculator
for whom he had professed the greatest
friendship. The poor land-jobber begged him
to grant a few months' indulgence. Tom had
grown testy and irritated, and refused
580 another delay.

"My family will be ruined, and brought
upon the parish," said the land-jobber.

"Charity begins at home," replied Tom;
"I must take care of myself in these hard
585 times."

"You have made so much money out of
me," said the speculator.

Tom lost his patience and his piety. "The
devil take me," said he, "if I have made a
590 farthing!"

Just then there were three loud knocks at
the street door. He stepped out to see who
was there. A black man was holding a black
horse, which neighed and stamped with
595 impatience.

"Tom, you're come for," said the black
fellow, gruffly. Tom shrank back, but too late.
He had left his little Bible at the bottom of
his coat-pocket and his big Bible on the desk
600 buried under the mortgage he was about to
foreclose: never was sinner taken more
unawares. The black man whisked him like
a child into the saddle, gave the horse the
lash, and away he galloped, with Tom on his
605 back, in the midst of the thunder-storm. The
clerks stuck their pens behind their ears,
and stared after him from the windows.
Away went Tom Walker, dashing down the
streets, his white cap bobbing up and down,
610 his morning-gown fluttering in the wind,
and his steed striking fire out of the pavement at every bound. When the clerks
turned to look for the black man, he had
disappeared.

615 Tom Walker never returned to foreclose
the mortgage. A countryman, who lived on
the border of the swamp, reported that in the
height of the thunder-gust he had heard a
great clattering of hoofs and a howling along
620 the road, and running to the window caught
sight of a figure, such as I have described, on
a horse that galloped like mad across the

fields, over the hills, and down into the black hemlock swamp toward the old Indian fort, 625 and that shortly after a thunder-bolt falling in that direction seemed to set the whole forest in a blaze.

The good people of Boston shook their heads and shrugged their shoulders, but had 630 been so much accustomed to witches and goblins, and tricks of the devil, in all kinds of shapes, from the first settlement of the colony, that they were not so much horror-struck as might have been expected. Trustees 635 were appointed to take charge of Tom's effects. There was nothing, however, to administer upon. On searching his coffers, all his bonds and mortgages were reduced to cinders. In place of gold and silver, his iron 640 chest was filled with chips and shavings;

two skeletons lay in his stable instead of his half-starved horses, and the very next day his great house took fire and was burned to the ground.

645 Such was the end of Tom Walker and his ill-gotten wealth. Let all gripping money-brokers lay this story to heart. The truth of it is not to be doubted. The very hole under the oak-trees, whence he dug Kidd's money, is to 650 be seen to this day; and the neighboring swamp and old Indian fort are often haunted in stormy nights by a figure on horseback, in morning-gown and white cap, which is doubtless the troubled spirit of the usurer. In 655 fact, the story has resolved itself into a prov-erb, and is the origin of that popular saying, so prevalent throughout New England, of "The devil and Tom Walker."

▲
This image is from the Walt Disney Classic, *The Little Mermaid* (1989).

In Disney's *The Little Mermaid*, Ariel "makes a deal" with the devilish Ursula: she agrees to give up her beautiful voice to become human. How is this deal similar to the one that Tom Walker makes with the black man? How do the fates of Ariel and Tom Walker differ? What might their different fates suggest about their differences as characters?

CHARACTER

1. How is Tom Walker **characterized**? Give specific details.

2. How is Tom Walker's wife **characterized**? Give specific details.

3. How is the black man described physically and emotionally? Give an example of both descriptions.

SETTING

4. How is the Walker house described? Give a specific example.

5. What is the historical **setting** of the story? What historical details within the story reflect this period?

6. How is the swamp described? What details indicate that this was an "ill-chosen route" for Tom Walker?

STRUCTURE

7. What is the **inciting moment** that forces Tom to make a decision or make a change?

8. What is the **resolution** of "The Devil and Tom Walker"?

NARRATION

9. Describe the story's **point of view**.

10. How are both the **narrator** and the narration affected by the events of the plot?

IDEAS IN LITERATURE: Faith and Doubt

11. Tom Walker believes that the contract he made with the black man will change his life forever. In a sense, he is correct. Can you think of another example in literature, movies, or songs when a deal has not gone as expected? Explain.

PUTTING IT ALL TOGETHER

12. Explain how the characterization functions in "The Devil and Tom Walker" to reveal the true nature and complexity of each character.

Exchange Value
Charles Johnson

AP Images/La'Tisha Davis

THE TEXT IN CONTEXT

A novelist, screenwriter, essayist, cartoonist, and
academic philosopher, Charles Johnson (b. 1948)
writes philosophical fiction: stories that explore
metaphysical questions, dramatize moral dilemmas,
and examine complex ideas. Many of his books are
also historical novels, set among real people, places, and events of the past. For example,
his best-known work, *Middle Passage* (1990), is set aboard an illegal American slave ship
in 1830. Johnson has focused much of his writing on African American lives while striving
to avoid overgeneralizations about a monolithic "Black" experience. In "Exchange Value,"
included here, the characters make economic and moral choices that lead to an unexpected outcome.

Content Note: This story includes derogatory language, which we have chosen
to reprint in this textbook to accurately reflect Johnson's original intent, as well as the
culture and racism that is part of the setting of the story. While the use of this language
in Johnson's context might not be hurtful, the use of it in our current context very
often is. Be mindful of context, both Johnson's and yours, as you read and discuss
"Exchange Value."

Exchange Value

Me and my brother, Loftis, came in by the
old lady's window. There was some kinda
boobytrap—boxes of broken glass—that
shoulda warned us Miss Bailey wasn't the easy
5 mark we made her to be. She been living alone
for twenty years in 4-B down the hall from
Loftis and me, long before our folks died—a
hincty, halfbald West Indian woman with a
craglike face, who kept her door barricaded,
10 shutters closed, and wore the same sorry-
looking outfit—black wingtip shoes, cropfin-
gered gloves in winter, and a man's floppy
hat—like maybe she dressed half-asleep or in
a dark attic. Loftis, he figured Miss Bailey had
15 some grandtheft dough stashed inside, jim, or
leastways a shoebox full of money, 'cause she

never spent a nickel on herself, not even for
food, and only left her place at night.

Anyway, we figured Miss Bailey was gone.
20 Her mailbox be full, and Pookie White, who
run the Thirty-ninth Street Creole restaurant,
he say she ain't dropped by in days to collect
the handouts he give her so she can get by.
So here's me and Loftis, tipping around Miss
25 Bailey's blackdark kitchen. The floor be littered with fruitrinds, roaches, old food furred
with blue mold. Her dirty dishes be stacked
in a sink feathered with cracks and it looks
like the old lady been living, lately, on Ritz
30 crackers and Department of Agriculture
(Welfare Office) peanut butter. Her toilet be
stopped up, too, and on the bathroom floor,

there's five Maxwell House coffee cans full of
s***. Me, I was closing her bathroom door
35 when I whiffed this evil smell so bad, so
thick, I could hardly breathe, and what air
I breathed was stifling, like solid fluid in my
throatpipes, like broth or soup. "Cooter,"
Loftis whisper, low, across the room, "you
40 smell that?" He went right on sniffing it, like
people do for some reason when something
be smelling stanky, then took out his head-
rag and held it over his mouth. "Smells like
something crawled up in here and died."
45 Then, head low, he slipped his long self into
the living room. Me, I stayed by the window,
gulping for air, and do you know why?

  You oughta know, up front, that I ain't too
good at this gangster stuff, and I had a real bad
50 feeling about Miss Bailey from the get-go.
Mama used to say it was Loftis, not me, who'd
go places—I see her standing at the sideboard
by the sink now, big as a Frigidaire, white flour
to her elbows, a washtowel over her shoulder,
55 while we ate a breakfast of cornbread and
syrup. Loftis, he graduated fifth at DuSable
High School, had two gigs and, like Papa, he be
always be wanting the things white people had
out in Hyde Park, where Mama did daywork
60 sometimes. Loftis he be the kind of brother
who buys *Esquire*, sews Hart, Schaffner & Marx
labels in Robert Hall suits, talks properlike,
packs his hair with Murray's; and he took
classes in politics and stuff at the Black Peo-
65 ple's Topographical Library in the late 1960s. At
thirty, he make his bed military-style, reads
Black Scholar on the bus he takes to the plant,
and, come hell or high water, plans to make
a Big Score. Loftis, he say I'm 'bout as useful
70 on a hustle—or when it comes to getting
ahead—as a headcold, and he says he has to
count my legs sometimes to make sure I ain't a
mule, seeing how, for all my eighteen years, I
can't keep no job and sorta stay close to home,
75 watching TV, or reading *World's Finest* comic

books, or maybe just laying dead, listening to
music, imagining I see faces or foreign places
in water stains on the wallpaper, 'cause some
days, when I remember Papa, then Mama, kill-
80 ing theyselves for chump change—a pitiful li'l
bowl of porridge—I get to thinking that even if
I ain't had all I wanted, maybe I've had, you
know, all I'm ever gonna get.

  "Cooter," Loftis say from the living room.
85 "You best get in here quick."

  Loftis, he'd switched on Miss Bailey's
bright, overhead living room lights, so for a
second I couldn't see and started coughing—
the smell be so powerful it hit my nostrils like
90 coke—and when my eyes cleared, shapes
come forward in the light, and I thought for
an instant like I'd slipped in space. I seen why
Loftis called me, and went back two steps.
See, 4-B's so small if you ring Miss Bailey's
95 doorbell, the toilet'd flush. But her living
room, webbed in dust, be filled to the max
with dollars of all denominations, stacks of
stock in General Motors, Gulf Oil, and 3M
Company in old White Owl cigar boxes, bat-
100 tered purses, or bound in pink rubber bands.
It be like the kind of cubbyhole kids play in,
but filled with . . . things: everything, like a
world inside the world, you take it from me,
so like picturebook scenes of plentifulness
105 you could seal yourself off in here and settle
forever. Loftis and me both drew breath
suddenly. There be unopened cases of Jack
Daniel's, three safes cemented to the floor,
hundreds of matchbooks, unworn clothes, a
110 fuel-burning stove, dozens of wedding rings,
rubbish, World War II magazines, a carton of a
hundred canned sardines, mink stoles, old
rags, a birdcage, a bucket of silver dollars,
thousands of books, paintings, quarters in
115 tobacco cans, two pianos, glass jars of pennies, a set of bagpipes, an almost complete
Model A Ford dappled with rust, and, I swear,
three sections of a dead tree.

"Damn!" My head be light; I sat on an
120 upended peach crate and picked up a bottle
of Jack Daniel's.

"Don't you touch anything!" Loftis, he
panting a little; he slap both hands on a
table. "Not until we inventory this stuff."

125 "Inventory? Aw, Lord, Loftis," I say,
"something ain't right about this stash.
There could be a curse on it. . . ."

"Boy, sometime you act weak-minded."

"For real, Loftis, I got a feeling. . . ."

130 Loftis, he shucked off his shoes, and sat
down heavily on the lumpy arm of a stuffed
chair. "Don't say *anything*." He chewed his
knuckles, and for the first time Loftis looked
like he didn't know his next move. "Let me
135 think, okay?" He squeezed his nose in a way he
has when thinking hard, sighed, then stood up
and say, "There's something you better see in
that bedroom yonder. Cover up your mouth."

"Loftis, I ain't going in there."

140 He look at me right funny then. "She's a
miser, that's all. She saves things."

"But a tree?" I say. "Loftis, a tree ain't
normal!"

"Cooter, I ain't gonna tell you twice."

145 Like always, I followed Loftis, who swung
his flashlight from the plant—he a night
watchman—into Miss Bailey's bedroom, but
me, I'm thinking how trippy this thing is getting, remembering how, last year, when I had
150 a paper route, the old lady, with her queer,
crablike walk, pulled my coat for some
change in the hallway, and when I give her a
handful of dimes, she say, like one of them
spooks on old-time radio, "Thank you,
155 Co-o-oter," then gulped the coins down like
aspirin, no lie, and scurried off like a hunchback. Me, I wanted no parts of this squirrely
old broad, but Loftis, he holding my wrist
now, beaming his light onto a low bed. The
160 room had a funny, museumlike smell. Real
sour. It was full of dirty laundry. And I be

sure the old lady's stuff had a terrible string
attached when Loftis, looking away, lifted her
bedsheets and a knot of black flies rose. I
165 stepped back and held my breath. Miss Bailey be in her long-sleeved flannel nightgown,
bloated, like she'd been blown up by a bicycle
pump, her old face caved in with rot, fly-
blown, her fingers big and colored like
170 spoiled bananas. Her wristwatch be ticking
softly beside a half-eaten hamburger. Above
the bed, her wall had roaches squashed in
little swirls of bloodstain. Maggots clustered
in her eyes, her ears, and one fist-sized rat
175 hissed inside her flesh. My eyes snapped
shut. My knees failed; then I did a Hollywood
faint. When I surfaced, Loftis, he be sitting
beside me in the living room, where he'd
drug me, reading a wrinkled, yellow article
180 from the *Chicago Daily Defender*.

"Listen to this," Loftis say. "'Elnora Bailey,
forty-five, a Negro housemaid in the Highland Park home of Henry Conners, is the
beneficiary of her employer's will. An old
185 American family, the Conners arrived in this
country on the *Providence* shortly after the
voyage of the *Mayflower*. The family flourished in the early days of the 1900s.' . . ." He
went on, getting breath: "'A distinguished
190 and wealthy industrialist, without heirs or a
wife, Conners willed his entire estate to Miss
Bailey of 3347 North Clark Street for her
twenty years of service to his family.' . . ." Loftis, he give that Geoffrey Holder laugh of his,
195 low and deep; then it eased up his throat
until it hit a high note and tipped his head
back onto his shoulders. "Cooter, that was
before we was born! Miss Bailey kept this in
the Bible next to her bed."

200 Standing, I braced myself with one hand
against the wall. "She didn't earn it?"

"Naw." Loftis, he folded the paper—"Not
one penny"—and stuffed it in his shirt
pocket. His jaw looked tight as a horseshoe.

205 "Way I see it," he say, "this was her one shot in a lifetime to be rich, but being country, she had backward ways and blew it." Rubbing his hands, he stood up to survey the living room. "Somebody's gonna find Miss Bailey soon,
210 but if we stay on the case—Cooter, don't square up on me now—we can tote everything to our place before daybreak. Best we start with the big stuff."

"But why didn't she use it, huh? Tell me
215 that?"

Loftis, he don't pay me no mind. When he gets an idea in his head, you can't dig it out with a chisel. How long it took me and Loftis to inventory, then haul Miss Bailey's queer old
220 stuff to our crib, I can't say, but that cranky old ninnyhammer's hoard come to $879,543 in cash money, thirty-two bank books (some deposits be only $5), and me, I wasn't sure I was dreaming or what, but I suddenly flashed
225 on this feeling, once we left her flat, that all the fears Loftis and me had about the future be gone, 'cause Miss Bailey's property was the past—the power of that fellah Henry Conners trapped like a bottle spirit—which we could
230 live off, so it was the future, too, pure potential: can do. Loftis got to talking on about how that piano we pushed home be equal to a thousand bills, jim, which equals, say, a bad TEAC A-3340 tape deck, or a down payment on a deuce-and-
235 a-quarter. Its value be (Loftis say) that of a universal standard of measure, relational, unreal as number, so that tape deck could turn, magically, into two gold lamé suits, a trip to Tijuana, or twenty-five blow jobs from a ho—we had
240 $879,543 worth of wishes, if you can deal with that. Be like Miss Bailey's stuff is raw energy, and Loftis and me, like wizards, could transform her stuff into anything else at will. All we had to do, it seemed to me, was decide exactly
245 what to exchange it for.

While Loftis studied this over (he looked funny, like a potato trying to say something, after the inventory, and sat, real quiet, in the kitchen), I filled my pockets with fifties,
250 grabbed me a cab downtown to grease, yum, at one of them high-hat restaurants in the Loop. . . . But then I thought better of it, you know, like I'd be out of place—just another jig[1] putting on airs—and scarfed instead at a
255 ribjoint till both my eyes bubbled. This fat lady making fishburgers in the back favored an old hardleg baby-sitter I once had, a Mrs. Paine who made me eat ocher, and I wanted so bad to say, "Loftis and me Got Ovuh," but I
260 couldn't put that in the wind, could I, so I hatted up. Then I copped a boss silk necktie, cashmere socks, and a whistle-slick maxi leather jacket on State Street, took cabs everywhere, but when I got home that eve-
265 ning, a funny, Pandora-like feeling hit me. I took off the jacket, boxed it—it looked trifling in the hallway's weak light—and, tired, turned my key in the door. I couldn't get in. Loftis, he'd changed the lock and, when he
270 finally let me in, looking vaguer, crabby, like something out of the Book of Revelations, I seen this elaborate, booby-trapped tunnel of cardboard and razor blades behind him, with a two-foot space just big enough for him or
275 me to crawl through. That wasn't all. Two bags of trash from the furnace room downstairs be sitting inside the door. Loftis, he give my leather jacket this evil look, hauled me inside, and hit me upside my head.
280 "How much this thing set us back?"

"Two fifty." My jaws got tight; I toss him my receipt. "You want me to take it back? Maybe I can get something else. . . ."

Loftis, he say, not to me, but to the receipt,
285 "Remember the time Mama give me that ring we had in the family for fifty years? And I took it to Merchandise Mart and sold it for a few pieces of candy?" He hitched his chair

---

[1]This is an offensive term that should not be read aloud in class. —Eds.

forward and sat with his elbows on his
290 knees. "That's what you did, Cooter. You
crawled into a Clark bar." He commence to
rip up my receipt, then picked up his flashlight and keys. "As soon as you buy something you lose the power to buy something."
295 He button up his coat with holes in the
elbows, showing his blue shirt, then turned
'round at the tunnel to say, "Don't touch Miss
Bailey's money, or drink her splo, or do *anything* until I get back."

300   "Where you going?"
       "To work. It's Wednesday, ain't it?"
       "You going to work?"
       "Yeah."
       "You got to go *really*? Loftis," I say, "what
305 you brang them bags of trash in here for?"
       "It ain't trash!" He cut his eyes at me.
"There's good clothes in there. Mr. Peterson
tossed them out, he don't care, but I saw
some use in them, that's all."

310   "Loftis . . ."
       "Yeah?"
       "What we gonna do with all this money?"
       Loftis pressed his fingers to his eyelids, and
for a second he looked caged, or like some-
315 body'd kicked him in his stomach. Then he cut
me some slack: "Let me think on it tonight—it
don't pay to rush—then we can TCB, okay?"
       Five hours after Loftis leave for work, that
old blister Mr. Peterson, our landlord, he
320 come collecting rent, find Mrs. Bailey's body
in apartment 4-B, and phoned the fire
department. Me, I be folding my new jacket
in tissue paper to keep it fresh, adding the
box to Miss Bailey's unsunned treasures
325 when two paramedics squeezed her on a
long stretcher through a crowd in the hallway. See, I had to pin her from the stairhead,
looking down one last time at this dizzy old
lady, and I seen something in her face, like
330 maybe she'd been poor as Job's turkey for
thirty years, suffering that special Negro fear

of using up what little we get in this life—
Loftis, he call that entropy—believing in her
belly, and for all her faith, jim, that there just
335 ain't no more coming tomorrow from grace,
or the Lord, or from her own labor, like she
can't kill nothing, and won't nothing die . . .
so when Conners will her his wealth, it put
her through changes, she be spellbound, pos-
340 sessed by the promise of life, panicky about
depletion, and locked now in the past 'cause
every purchase, you know, has to be a poor
buy: a loss of life. Me, I wasn't worried none.
345 Loftis, he got a brain trained by years of
talking trash with people in Frog Hudson's
barbershop on Thirty-fifth Street. By morning, I knew, he'd have some kinda wheeze
worked out.
       But Loftis, he don't come home. Me, I got
350 kinda worried. I listen to the hi-fi all day Thursday, only pawing outside to peep down the
stairs, like that'd make Loftis come sooner. So
Thursday go by; and come Friday the head's
out of kilter—first there's an ogrelike belch
355 from the toilet bowl, then water bursts from
the bathroom into the kitchen—and me, I
can't call the super (How do I explain the tunnel?), so I gave up and quit bailing. But on Saturday, I could smell greens cooking next door.
360 Twice I almost opened Miss Bailey's sardines,
even though starving be less an evil than eating up our stash, but I waited till it was dark
and, with my stomach talking to me, stepped
outside to Pookie White's, lay a hard-luck story
365 on him, and Pookie, he give me some jamba-
laya and gumbo. Back home in the living room,
finger-feeding myself, barricaded in by all that
hope-made material, the Kid felt like a king in
his counting room, and I copped some Zs in an
370 armchair till I heard the door move on its
hinges, then bumping in the tunnel, and a
heavy-footed walk thumped into the bedroom.
       "Loftis?" I rubbed my eyes. "You back?" It
be Sunday morning. Six-thirty sharp. Darkness

375 dissolved slowly into the strangeness of twilight, with the rays of sunlight surging at
exactly the same angle they fall each evening, as if the hour be an island, a moment
outside time. Me, I'm afraid Loftis gonna fuss
380 'bout my not straightening up, letting things
go. I went into the bathroom, poured water
in the one-spigot washstand—brown rust
come bursting out in flakes—and rinsed my
face. "Loftis, you supposed to be home four
385 days ago. Hey," I say, toweling my face, "you
okay?" How come he don't answer me?
Wiping my hands on the seat on my trousers, I tipped into Loftis's room. He sleeping
with his mouth open. His legs be drawn up,
390 both fists clenched between his knees. He'd
kicked his blanket on the floor. In his sleep,
Loftis laughed, or moaned, it be hard to tell.
His eyelids, not quite shut, show slits of
white. I decided to wait till Loftis wake up for
395 his decision, but turning, I seen his watch,
keys, and what looked in the first stain of

sunlight to be a carefully wrapped piece of
newspaper on his nightstand. The sunlight
swelled to a bright shimmer, focusing the
400 bedroom slowly like solution do a photo-
graphic image in the developer. And then
something so freakish went down I ain't sure
it took place. Fumble-fingered, I unfolded the
paper, and inside be a blemished penny. It be
405 like suddenly somebody slapped my head
from behind. Taped on the penny be a slip of
paper, and on the paper be the note "Found
while walking down Devon Avenue." I hear
Loftis mumble like he trapped in a night-
410 mare. "Hold tight," I whisper. "It's all right."
Me, I wanted to tell Loftis how Miss Bailey
looked four days ago, that maybe it didn't
have to be like that for us—did it?—because
we could change. Couldn't we? Me, I pull his
415 packed sheets over him, wrap up the penny,
and, when I locate Miss Bailey's glass jar in
the living room, put it away carefully, for
now, with the rest of our things.

Good Fortune is a painting from the
seventeenth century by the Baroque
Italian painter Lionella Spada.

How does the painting portray the
pickpocketer? What does this image
suggest about the motivation of
thieves?

Good Fortune/Spada, Lionello (1576-1622)/ARTE & IMMAGINI Srl/Galleria e Museo Estense, Modena, Italy/Bridgeman Images

CHARACTER

1. How is Miss Bailey described? How is she **characterized**, physically and emotionally?

2. How do Loftis, Cooter, and Miss Bailey represent different values, respectively? What does this reveal about each **character**?

3. How are the **perspectives** of Loftis and Cooter revealed?

SETTING

4. How is Miss Bailey's apartment described? What **values** are revealed through this description?

5. How is the **setting** of the brothers' apartment described? Why are these descriptions important to the story?

STRUCTURE

6. How does the **exposition** focus the readers on Miss Bailey? Describe the details that suggest the plot of the story.

7. Describe the **narrative arc** of the story.

8. How does the description of the brothers' apartment at the end of the "Exchange Value" contribute to the **resolution** of the story?

NARRATION

9. Who is the **narrator**? How does this narrative **point of view** help develop the story's plot?

10. How does the narrator's **perspective** of the story contribute to the relationship between the **narrator** and the reader?

11. How does the **narrator** indicate how Cooter and Loftis will continue to live?

IDEAS IN LITERATURE: Faith and Doubt

12. The brothers in the story believe that money will change their lives. Consider that idea, and then explain both the positive and negative consequences of wealth. Is the ending inevitable?

PUTTING IT ALL TOGETHER

13. What is the conflict in this story? How does the vivid description of both the characters and setting create dramatic tension?

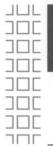

Writing about Theme

 Enduring Understanding (LAN-1)

Readers establish and communicate their interpretations of literature through arguments supported by textual evidence.

KEY POINT

The thesis statement of a literary argument makes a claim that includes an idea and an insight about that idea, revealing an interpretation of a work based on evidence from that text.

Establishing a Unifying Idea through a Defensible Thesis Statement

If you have ever recommended a book to a friend, your friend probably asked you, "So what is it about?" Your answer could go one of two ways. You might offer a basic plot summary by talking about the events and the characters. Or you might communicate what the book is really about, sharing its **ideas** about the human experience. These abstract concepts include such ideas as justice, mercy, hope, loyalty, or revenge. Observations about the human condition are expressed through literature by authors who relate insights about these ideas. In fact, novels, plays, stories, and poems are almost always about ideas. When you identify these ideas and perspectives as you read, you make **interpretations** about a text.

Strategic readers set a purpose for reading. They read like detectives. That means that they have a hypothesis about the idea of the text before they even begin and then look for clues and evidence to confirm their hypothesis. They establish their hypothesis by previewing the text which includes the following:

- Examining the title (and cover of a longer work) to speculate a unifying idea
- Considering the context
- Reading a little at the beginning and end of a text

Once these readers have a hunch about the idea, then they annotate the details in the text that relate to that idea. Strategic readers rarely read a text in isolation. Keeping all of their clues in mind, they annotate the text for details that are relevant to their hypothesis rather than going on a scavenger hunt for literary details alone. In doing so, strategic readers become effective writers when they incorporate their ideas and insights into a strong thesis statement that expresses their interpretation of the text.

In this composition workshop, you will learn to write a literary argument focused on an idea in a text. First, you will explore how that idea sparks an interpretation. Then you will write a defensible thesis statement that includes your claim (idea + insight), which you can support with textual evidence.

YOUR ASSIGNMENT

Choose a work from Unit 1 and write a literary argument in which you analyze the theme of the work by explaining how two or more literary elements contribute to your interpretation of the text. Develop a thesis statement that expresses your interpretation and support it with evidence from the text.

Over the course of this year, you will learn to write complex literary arguments, but they all begin with a basic foundation. In this unit, you will learn that foundation. Therefore, your first literary argument should interpret a literary work and include the following:

- A thesis statement that conveys an interpretation (a unifying idea + insight about that idea)
- Topic sentences that indicate the focus of each body paragraph
- Relevant textual evidence that connects to your unifying idea

The potential focus for body paragraphs includes the following:

- How characterization contributes to an interpretation of a text
- How setting contributes to an interpretation of a text
- How structure contributes to an interpretation of a text
- How narration contributes to an interpretation of a text

Set a Purpose for Reading

As you read and interpret literature, you will uncover an idea within a text and determine how that idea is communicated by the author's choices of characters, setting, plot structure, and narrator. The combination of these elements leads the reader to an insight, understanding, or observation about humanity. For example, a story that recounts a character's brave actions within a certain time and place, or against seemingly insurmountable obstacles, might exemplify the ideas of courage, fear, loyalty, or even hope. Likewise, when you are ready to analyze a text, you will consider the literary elements and choose a single **unifying idea** for your argument.

You will begin to form an interpretation of the text by focusing on the idea that is most prevalent to you as you read. Next, dig into that idea and ask the question, "So what about it?" In other words, what does the text reveal about the idea? To answer this question, explore the elements of the text and examine the speech, actions, and descriptions of characters; the choice and details of the setting; the structure of the events; and the narrative perspective. Considering these literary elements can help you form your interpretation of a text. There may be multiple plausible interpretations of any literary works, but keep in mind, an interpretation is only plausible if it can be supported with evidence from the text.

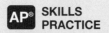 **SKILLS PRACTICE** | **LITERARY ARGUMENTATION**
Determining a Unifying Idea and Insight

Review the details from the text you are analyzing for your literary argument. Record details for each of the text elements in the column. Next, consider how these details reveal a unifying idea and an insight. Record these in the right column.

Determining a Unifying Idea and Insight	
Idea:	
Story Elements	**Details**
Characters	
Setting	
Structure	
Narration	
Idea + insight:	

Develop a Defensible Thesis Statement

When you have determined a unifying idea and insight, you are ready to write a **thesis statement**. An effective thesis statement for a literary argument must include a **claim** that conveys your insight into the idea. Because this is a literary argument, that means your interpretation must be defensible. But that does not mean that all interpretations are equally valid: an interpretation must be based on careful consideration of textual details.

Effective interpretations must be both defensible *and* arguable. **Defensible** interpretations require justification through reasoning and evidence. **Arguable** interpretations go beyond a statement of fact by expressing a claim that reveals insight into an idea. Likewise, the claim in your thesis must be defensible and arguable. Writing a defensible and arguable thesis statement can be difficult and takes practice.

When you write your thesis statement, make sure you include the idea and your insight. Without it, you are simply stating a fact about the story. In other words, you would not simply write, "The author uses characters and setting." Instead, you will identify what the characters and setting reveal about the work or how they contribute to your insight. Your thesis statement will then contain an interpretation for you to develop throughout the rest of your literary argument.

WRITING A THESIS FOR A LITERARY ARGUMENT	
Template 1: The thesis previews the line of reasoning and connects literary strategies and techniques to the idea and insight.	In [title of work], [author] uses [literary element/technique], [literary element/technique], and [literary element/technique] to reveal that [unifying idea + insight].
Template 2: The thesis conveys the idea and insight.	In [title of work], a story about [context], the [author/ speaker/narrator] reveals/illustrates that [unifying idea + insight].

 INSIDER **AP® TIP**

Avoid clichés like the plague. When you express your thesis statement for a literary argument, write an original thought in your own words to convey the message about the idea rather than relying on common sayings or platitudes, such as, "You can't judge a book by its cover," or "What doesn't kill you makes you stronger."

 **SKILLS PRACTICE** | LITERARY ARGUMENTATION
Developing a Thesis Statement

In the following chart, record the title, author, and focus in the left column and then add your unifying idea and insight about that idea. Putting these pieces together will result in a workable thesis statement.

Developing a Defensible Thesis Statement for Literary Argument		
Topic	**Claim**	
Title, Author, and Focus (author choices)	Unifying Idea +	Insight

Organize a Line of Reasoning

Your thesis statement generally appears in the first paragraph, also called an introduction. To develop your argument and support the claim in your thesis statement, you will compose two or more body paragraphs that each begin with a **topic sentence** to provide a focus. These topic sentences, when directly connected to your idea and insight, serve as a logical sequence of reasons, also called a line of reasoning, to support the claim. Since your claim must be defensible, it will rely on this **reasoning** and textual evidence for support.

In this unit, you may use the literary elements that relate to your unifying idea as your way of organizing your analysis of the theme. In later units, you will explore additional ways to present your reasoning and develop a complex literary argument.

For example, you could develop your interpretation of a work by writing a body paragraph about character development in one paragraph, setting in another, and narration in a third body paragraph. In each body paragraph, you should identify a literary element or technique, provide textual evidence for support, and then link that evidence to the claim in your thesis. This pattern, identify — evidence — link, will serve as a basic structure for developing your literary argument.

When you have completed your supporting paragraphs, you should conclude your literary argument by briefly describing how this unifying idea remains relevant today.

Review the following basic structure for developing a literary argument. As you work through subsequent units, you will explore more sophisticated ways to develop your literary arguments. For now, create two or more body paragraphs to support your interpretation. When you are ready to plan your literary argument, you may use the following graphic organizer or something similar.

 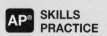

AP® SKILLS PRACTICE | **LITERARY ARGUMENTATION**
Organizing a Literary Argument

Review your text for a unifying idea and literary elements (character, setting, plot structure, and narration). Next, complete the graphic organizer to plan your thesis statement and focus for each body paragraph.

Organizing a Literary Argument		
Defensible Thesis Statement with Claim (idea + insight):		
Topic Sentence 1 (Focus of paragraph related to unifying idea):	**Topic Sentence 2** (Focus of paragraph related to unifying idea):	**Topic Sentence 3** (Focus of paragraph related to unifying idea):

STRUCTURE OF A LITERARY ARGUMENT

Introduction

The **introduction** is an opportunity for the writer to establish the purpose of their literary argument and to invite and interest the audience into the literary work and the writer's interpretation of it. To achieve this goal, many literary arguments follow this structure:

- Engage the audience through an interesting hook
- Provide historical, cultural, or social context of a literary work
- Identify the title, author, genre (TAG)
- Introduce the literary topic of analysis by
  - describing the importance of that literary concept; and
  - summarizing the work succinctly with details critical to that concept

The **thesis statement** presents a defensible interpretation that includes an idea and an insight about that idea.

Body

(Develops a line of reasoning with supporting evidence that justifies the thesis)

Topic Sentence 1 (Identify the focus of the paragraph related to the unifying idea)	Topic Sentence 2 (Identify the literary element related to the unifying idea)	Topic Sentence 3 (Identify the literary element related to the unifying idea)
Textual Details (Evidence of elements and techniques and their function)	Textual Details (Evidence of elements and techniques and their function)	Textual Details (Evidence of elements and techniques and their function)
Commentary (Link evidence by explaining its relevance to the line of reasoning and claim)	Commentary (Link evidence by explaining its relevance to the line of reasoning and claim)	Commentary (Link evidence by explaining its relevance to the line of reasoning and claim)

Conclusion

The **conclusion** should do more than restate your thesis; therefore, the conclusion should be a robust and important paragraph. It is the opportunity for the writer to demonstrate understanding of the literary work's relevance by explaining how the literary work stands the test of time and reflects the human experience. Writers further their idea and insight by:

- Discussing the significance or relevance of interpretation
- Relating the work to other relevant literary works
- Connecting the theme to their own experience
- Presenting alternate interpretations
- Explaining how the work explores complexities and tensions
- Situating the theme within a broader context

This table illustrates the general structure of a literary argument. It does not intend to imply that all literary arguments are five paragraphs. Writers should determine the number of reasons needed to justify their claim, as well as how much evidence is sufficient to support each of these reasons.

Select Relevant Evidence

To support the claim and topic sentences in your literary argument, you will need to include **relevant evidence** from the text that supports your interpretation in the thesis statement. This evidence will include textual details (e.g., details of character, setting, plot structure, and narration). Stories include many details, but not all details are relevant to your interpretation.

As you read a text, you annotate details that are directly related to your unifying idea. When you are ready to select evidence for your argument, you eliminate any details that are not directly relevant to that interpretation. Keeping your focus on your idea and insight will help you write a focused and relevant literary argument. Finally, once you have chosen textual evidence that supports your interpretation, you will organize that evidence in the appropriate body paragraphs of your literary argument.

When you have generated evidence to support your thesis (idea + insight), you are ready to begin drafting your full literary argument. You have actually completed a lot of the work already. In Unit 1, you will focus specifically on three elements of the literary argument: the thesis statement, topic sentences, and evidence. In later units, you will add more content to your draft.

To incorporate textual evidence from a source, you will need to integrate that text properly. That means you must either paraphrase the textual passage or embed direct quotations from the text into your own sentence. In both cases, you must use a signal phrase to let your reader know that you are referring to a source. You should never drop a stand-alone quotation into your paragraph. Whether you are quoting directly from the text or paraphrasing, remember to acknowledge the source when the words or ideas are not your own.

INCORPORATING TEXTUAL EVIDENCE		
Method	**Description**	**Source Attribution**
Paraphrasing	Using details from the text by restating them in your own voice and style	Because you are rephrasing, you do not need to use quotations. However, you will still need to add a citation at the end.
Using a signal phrase	Introducing a quotation directly from the text with a short attribution	[Author] describes the character as "[text]" (citation). [Narrator] describes the character as "[text]" (citation). [Author] describes the setting as "[text]" (citation). [Author] writes, "[text]" (citation).

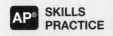 **SKILLS PRACTICE** | LITERARY ARGUMENTATION
Incorporating Supporting Evidence

Write your thesis statement and then draft two or more body paragraphs to support your claim (idea + insight). Your body paragraphs should begin with topic sentences that include a focus for the paragraph related to your unifying idea. Next, include evidence from the text to support the focus in the paragraph. Finally, write a concluding statement that expresses the relevance of the unifying idea.

Developing an Argument through Supporting Evidence		
Defensible Thesis Statement with Claim (idea + insight):		
Topic Sentence 1 (Focus of the paragraph related to the unifying idea):	**Topic Sentence 2** (Focus of the paragraph related to the unifying idea):	**Topic Sentence 3** (Focus of the paragraph related to the unifying idea):
Evidence:	**Evidence:**	**Evidence:**
Conclusion (Relevance of idea):		

Revise Your Argument

Your writing process is not complete until you revise and edit your work. **Revision** involves looking at the structure and organization of your argument. To do this, you should do the following:

- Examine your thesis statement and topic sentences to determine if they are unified by an idea and convey an insight.
- Review each body paragraph to check to see that you have evidence that supports your topic sentence and that it is relevant to the idea.
- Read your concluding sentence to make sure you have briefly explained the relevance or insight related to your idea.

Editing involves looking more closely at your own writing craft and conventions. In later units, you will learn more about editing.

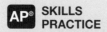 SKILLS PRACTICE | LITERARY ARGUMENTATION
Revising and Editing a Literary Argument

After you have completed revising and editing your own argument, review
another student's literary argument and provide helpful feedback.

Peer-Revision Checklist: Revising and Editing a Literary Argument		
Revising and Editing Checklist	**Unit 1 Focus Skills**	**Comment on the Effectiveness and/or Make a Suggestion**
Does the thesis statement convey an interpretation? Does the interpretation include an idea and an insight?	Defensible thesis	
Does the writer provide a focus for each body paragraph to develop the idea and insight in the thesis? Is the unifying idea reflected in each topic sentence?	Topic sentences	
Does the writer provide evidence to support the interpretation in the thesis?	Supporting evidence	
Does the writer demonstrate control over the conventions of writing?	Conventions	

Student Model: Writing about Theme

Review the following student model to observe how the thesis statement, topic
sentences, and evidence work together to convey an interpretation in the literary
argument.

Impulse, Ignorance, and Imminent Consequence
Preston Davis

   In "The Landlady," Roald Dahl follows Billy Weaver's journey to find
nighttime lodgings in a small English city. As Billy searches for a pub
recommended by the porter at the train station, he notices a luminous,
alluring boardinghouse in which he decides to stay. Captivated by its
cheap price and the apparent generosity of the landlady, Billy becomes
blind to all the peculiarities of the boardinghouse, such as the lack of
patrons and the landlady's obsession over taxidermy. Eventually, Dahl

reveals the true intention of the landlady to kill and taxidermize Billy, giving rise to new themes surrounding the plot. Through the complimentary development of an inviting but deceptively dangerous setting with Billy's ignorant, slightly prideful character, Dahl shows how acting on impulse cultures ignorance, ultimately leading to dire circumstances.

Throughout the plot, Dahl invokes an uncertain feeling towards the setting by contrasting the Bed and Breakfast's inviting nature with the abnormalities Billy faces. Consequently, this contrast allows Dahl to highlight the importance of situational awareness. At the beginning of the story, for instance, Dahl emphasizes the Bed and Breakfast's enticing elements, such as the "bright fire burning in the fireplace" accompanied by "comfortable armchairs." Effectively, these elements of the setting increase the reader's trust of the boardinghouse by conveying a sense of comfort and familiarity. However, later introduced peculiarities decrease this trust, invoking suspicion within the reader towards the setting. For example, as Billy begins to make himself comfortable, Dahl introduces details such as the "peculiar smell" emitted by the landlady, the presence of preserved, stuffed animals around the boardinghouse, and the faint bitter taste of the tea. Although the story mentions these aspects of the setting superficially, they contrast the boardinghouse's comfort described thoroughly earlier in the plot, creating a sense of uncertainty. Near the end of the story, these abnormalities become increasingly abundant, eventually revealing the true motivation of the landlady to taxidermize Billy himself. By initially presenting a seemingly harmless setting that develops into a hostile environment, Dahl effectively stresses how ignoring the potential dangers of a situation and falling to temptation can lead to detrimental outcomes.

To complement the effect of the setting, Dahl exposes Billy's exploitable character by emphasizing his impulsive decision-making and pride for his condition. Eventually, Billy's impulsiveness and arrogance contribute to his demise, which strengthens the author's message that these characteristics can lead to dire consequences, in this case death. For example, when searching for a place to stay the night, rather than visiting the pub recommended to him by the porter at the train station, Billy impulsively decides to stay at the boardinghouse. After ringing the doorbell, "Billy found himself automatically starting forward into the house" (Dahl 2). Through these details, the author communicates how Billy's irresistible urge compels him to enter a foreign situation. Eventually, Billy's impulsive naivety feeds his personal pride when he considers himself "a lucky fellow" in a situation that "is great" (Dahl 4). At this point, the landlady wins complete control over Billy, demonstrating how pride can easily lead to temptation. By developing his character

thesis statement with interpretation
idea: impulse
insight: impulse cultivates ignorance
claim: impulse leads to dire circumstances

topic sentence: focused on setting details

evidence: setting details related to impulse and ignorance

topic sentence: focused on character details

evidence: character details related to impulse and ignorance

in this way, Dahl shows how Billy's lack of impulse control and pride led to ignorance of the peculiar, dangerous aspects of the boardinghouse that contributed to his downfall.

In summary, by describing the appealing aspects of the setting with its peculiarities, and by highlighting how Billy's character led to his dismissal of these peculiarities, Dahl conveys how decisions based on impulse and pride lead to situational ignorance, which can create detrimental personal circumstances. Similar to how Billy's impulsive decisions allowed the landlady to captivate him, real world situations such as substance abuse, addiction, and poor habits feed off a lack of impulse control and the irresistible desire for comfort. Therefore, before executing a decision, one must consider the imminent consequences of the choice rather than succumbing to its instantaneous pleasure.

conclusion: revisits idea and insight

Free-Response Question: Prose Fiction Analysis

AP® **Enduring Understanding (LAN-1)**

Readers establish and communicate their interpretations of literature through arguments supported by textual evidence.

Establishing a Unifying Idea through a Defensible Thesis Statement

The free-response section of the AP® English Literature and Composition Exam requires you to write literary arguments within a limited amount of time. One of these is the prose fiction analysis. In this workshop, you will begin to develop the skills you need to complete this task with a specific focus on writing a defensible thesis statement.

Read the following practice prompt and the accompanying passage, which is an adaptation of the type of prompt you may see on the exam. Please note that on the actual exam, you will be required to write a full essay incorporating a discussion of multiple literary elements and techniques.

Prompt:

The following excerpt is from the novel *Mudbound* by Hillary Jordan (published in 2008). In this passage, Laura, a woman in the late 1940s, describes her daily routine in her new role as a farmer's wife after her husband unexpectedly bought a farm. Read the passage carefully.

Write a paragraph in which you make a defensible claim regarding how Jordan characterizes Laura to reveal her complex perspective about surviving life on the farm. In your paragraph, you should incorporate at least one piece of evidence from the text to support your claim.

In your response, you should do the following:

- Respond to the prompt with a claim that presents an interpretation
- Select and use evidence to develop and support your interpretation
- Use appropriate grammar and punctuation in communicating your argument

Unifying Idea	*from* **Mudbound** Hillary Jordan	Effect of Literary Elements and Techniques
	When I think of the farm, I think of mud. Limning my husband's fingernails and encrusting the children's knees and hair. Sucking at my feet like a greedy newborn on the breast. Marching	
survival	5 in boot-shaped patches across the plank floors of the house. There was no defeating it. The mud coated everything. I dreamed in brown.	character understands her circumstances require survival
	When it rained, as it often did, the yard turned into a thick gumbo, with the house floating in it	
	10 like a soggy cracker. When the rains came hard, the river rose and swallowed the bridge that was	
survival	the only way across. The world was on the other side of that bridge, the world of light bulbs and paved roads and shirts that stayed white. When	character wishes she could escape the farm
	15 the river rose, the world was lost to us and we to it.	
survival	One day slid into the next. My hands did what was necessary: pumping, churning, scouring, scraping. And cooking, always cooking. Snap-	character's actions suggest survival behavior
	20 ping beans and the necks of chickens. Kneading dough, shucking corn and digging the eyes out of potatoes. No sooner was breakfast over and the mess cleaned up than it was time to start on dinner. After dinner came supper, then breakfast	
	25 again the next morning.	
survival	Get up at first light. Go to the outhouse. Do your business, shivering in the winter, sweating in the summer, breathing through your mouth year-round. Steal the eggs from under the hens. Haul	description of daily challenges emphasizes her determination to survive
	30 in wood from the pile and light the stove. Make the biscuits, slice the bacon and fry it up with the eggs and grits. Rouse your daughters from their bed, brush their teeth, guide arms into sleeves and feet into socks and boots. Take your youngest	
	35 out to the porch and hold her up so she can clang the bell that will summon your husband from the fields and wake his hateful father in the lean-to	

next door. Feed them all and yourself. Scrub the
iron skillet, the children's faces, the mud off the
40 floors day after day while the old man sits and
watches. He is always on you: "You better stir
them greens, gal. You better sweep that floor now.
Better teach them brats some manners. Wash
them clothes. Feed them chickens. Fetch me my
45 cane." His voice, clotted from smoking. His sly
pale eyes with their hard black centers, on you.

survival [line 45 annotation]

character must survive this relationship with Pappy

He scared the children, especially my youngest,
who was a little chubby.

"Come here, little piglet," he'd say to her.

50 She peered at him from behind my legs. At
his long yellow teeth. At his bony yellow fingers
with their thick curved nails like pieces of ancient
horn.

"Come here and sit on my lap."

55 He had no interest in holding her or any other
child, he just liked knowing she was afraid of
him. When she wouldn't come, he told her she
was too fat to sit on his lap anyway, she might
break his bones. She started to cry, and I imag-
60 ined that old man in his coffin. Pictured the lid
closing on his face, the box being lowered into
the hole. Heard the dirt striking the wood.

survival [line 59 annotation]

character survives mentally by fantasizing about Pappy's death

"Pappy," I said smiling sweetly at him, "how
about a nice cup of coffee?"

→ Step One: Annotate the Passage Based on a Unifying Idea

The prose fiction analysis question will include a fictional passage from a novel, play, or short story that is between five hundred and seven hundred words long. While this passage may only be a small portion of the overall text, you should still be able to identify a **unifying idea** in the passage when you read it closely. By identifying this unifying idea, you will establish a purpose for your reading and annotations.

Prose analysis passages frequently present characters within particular situations. They may describe a single character within an environment (e.g., an oppressive society, a place in nature, a new or unfamiliar environment). Or, they may present two or more characters within a narrative situation (e.g., in a domestic scene, at a social gathering, on a journey). In some cases, the passages focus on the details and values of a place or society. To analyze these passages, you will put your interpretive skills to use.

The prompt will include important context for the passage and define a specific task on which to focus your literary analysis. For example, the practice prompt for *Mudbound* reveals the time period (late 1940s), the setting (a farm), and the narrator (a wife surviving in a new situation). Additionally, the prompt informs you that your task is to analyze the narrator's perspective about her life.

Pay close attention to all of the information in the prompt, as it will guide your reading and annotation of the provided passage. Carefully consider who is in the scene, where and when it takes place, and what is happening. Also, read critically to uncover a unifying idea revealed by this narrative situation and note the details that connect to that unifying idea.

Consider these questions as you read and annotate:

- What abstract idea about the human experience emerges in the passage?
- What insight does the passage suggest about this idea and the human experience?
- What details in the passage reveal this idea and insight?

For example, in the practice prompt, you might determine that the passage is about the abstract **idea** of survival. Furthermore, based on the details in the passage (e.g., Laura's detailed descriptions of the harsh conditions of the farm and her cruel father-in-law), you might conclude with the **insight** that survival sometimes requires extreme physical and emotional effort from a person.

The analysis task also directs you to examine how the author's literary elements and techniques contribute to your understanding of the idea and your **interpretation** of the passage. Often it is helpful to organize your essay around techniques and use elements to illustrate the techniques. The model prompt specifies that you examine characterization. Recall from the reading workshop earlier in this unit that characters are revealed through description, actions, thoughts, and dialogue and their perspective is shaped by their background, environment, and circumstances.

→ Step Two: Develop a Defensible Thesis Statement

To begin to develop your literary argument, you will need to express your interpretation of the text with a claim that is both defensible and arguable. Defensible interpretations require justification through reasoning and evidence. Arguable interpretations go beyond a statement of fact by expressing a claim that reveals insight into an idea. You state your interpretation in your **thesis statement**.

By combining your unifying idea with an insight, you should be able to convey an interpretation of the passage. When you review the details in the passage, you should be able to defend your interpretation and explain how the author uses literary elements to create techniques. Ultimately, you will support your thesis with evidence that comes from these techniques.

A defensible thesis statement should be arguable (i.e., not just a statement of fact) and should include an interpretation (idea + insight).

Review the following examples of thesis statements:

Sample Thesis Statements	Notes on Effectiveness
In the novel Mudbound, the character Laura describes her new role as a farmer's wife.	Not a thesis, only a fact: This sentence merely states a fact provided in the prompt and does not require a defense (i.e., it is not arguable). This statement does not offer an interpretation.
In the novel Mudbound, Jordan uses point of view to characterize Laura as overwhelmed.	Thesis with no claim: This sentence could have evidence for support (details that reveal Laura as "overwhelmed") but does not actually state a claim with an idea and insight.
In the excerpt from the novel, Mudbound, Jordan characterizes Laura as overwhelmed, yet determined to survive her life on the farm.	Defensible thesis with a claim: This model is the strongest thesis statement. It articulates an arguable claim about an idea (although she is overwhelmed, she is determined to survive). Also, this interpretation can be supported with evidence from the text (details to support the characterization of Laura as "overwhelmed, yet determined").

INSIDER AP® TIP **Your thesis statement must include an interpretation.** Throughout the year, you will learn to write increasingly complex thesis statements. Be sure to include an insight about an idea word (abstract noun) to help ensure your thesis has an idea that will unify the literary argument and convey your interpretation.

→ Step Three: Choose Relevant Evidence

Stating a thesis is not enough to develop a literary argument. You must include **evidence** from the text to support your thesis. You will notice that passages include many details; however, you should only include textual evidence that directly relates to your interpretation: your idea and insight about that idea. Review the details of the passage that you have annotated. Choose examples from the passage that are directly related to the idea in your thesis statement.

When you incorporate evidence from the text, you will need to integrate the text into your argument properly. That means you must either paraphrase the textual passage or embed direct quotations from the text into your own sentence. In both cases, you must use a signal phrase to let your reader know that you are referring to a source. You should never drop a stand-alone quotation into your paragraph.

Whether you are quoting directly from the text or paraphrasing, it is standard practice to acknowledge the source when the words or ideas are not your own. However, when you take the AP® Exam, you will *not* be expected to include source citations since you are writing under time constraints, and your essay is considered a first draft.

The following examples demonstrate three ways of incorporating textual evidence.

Original text	The world was on the other side of that bridge, the world of light bulbs and paved roads and shirts that stayed white. When the river rose, the world was lost to us and we to it.
Paraphrasing: Using details from the text by restating them in your own voice and style	Laura struggles to overcome feelings of isolation because it feels like the whole world is on the other side of the bridge that would wash out during hard rains.
Using a signal phrase: Introducing a quotation directly from the text with a short attribution	After experiencing days of heavy rains, Laura describes the cause of her feelings of isolation by saying, "The world was on the other side of that bridge."
Embedding the text: Quoting words or phrases directly from the text in a manner that weaves single words or short phrases into the grammatical structure of your own sentence	Jordan characterizes Laura's feelings of isolation by emphasizing that "the world of light bulbs and paved roads" was so far away it was "lost" to Laura.

→ Step Four: Develop Insightful Commentary

Even after you have included evidence to support your thesis, your analysis will be incomplete until you explain how all of the evidence you provided connects to your interpretation in your thesis. In later units, you will learn how to write these explanations, also known as commentary, that not only make this connection clear to your reader but also offer insight into your interpretation of the passage.

AP® EXAM PRACTICE

The following is an example of a prose fiction analysis free-response question. Practice the skills you learned in this workshop to write a thesis statement and a paragraph that includes evidence in response to the prompt.

Remember to follow the four steps:

- Step One: Annotate the passage based on a **unifying idea**
- Step Two: Write a **defensible thesis statement**
- Step Three: Choose **relevant evidence**
- Step Four: Develop **insightful commentary**

Prompt:

The following excerpt is from the novel *Jane Eyre* by Charlotte Brontë (published in 1847). In this passage, Mr. Brocklehurst, a reverend and patron of an orphanage for girls, pays the school a visit to evaluate the conditions of the school and the behavior of the girls. Upon seeing a young girl with red curly hair, he orders that her hair be cut. Read the passage carefully.

Write a paragraph in which you make a defensible claim regarding how Brontë characterizes Mr. Brocklehurst to reveal his complex attitude about vanity. In your paragraph, you should incorporate at least one piece of evidence from the text to support your claim.

In your response, you should do the following:

- Respond to the prompt with a claim that presents an interpretation
- Select and use evidence to develop and support your interpretation
- Use appropriate grammar and punctuation in communicating your argument

"Miss Temple, Miss Temple, what — *what* is that girl with curled hair? Red hair, ma'am, curled — curled all over?" And extending his cane he pointed to the awful
5 object, his hand shaking as he did so.

"It is Julia Severn," replied Miss Temple, very quietly.

"Julia Severn, ma'am! And why has she, or any other, curled hair? Why, in defiance
10 of every precept and principle of this house, does she conform to the world so openly — here in an evangelical, charitable establishment — as to wear her hair one mass of curls?"
15 "Julia's hair curls naturally," returned Miss Temple, still more quietly.

"Naturally! Yes, but we are not to conform to nature; I wish these girls to be the children of Grace: and why that abundance? I have
20 again and again intimated that I desire the hair to be arranged closely, modestly, plainly. Miss Temple, that girl's hair must be cut off entirely; I will send a barber to-morrow: and I see others who have far too much of the
25 excrescence[1] — that tall girl, tell her to turn round. Tell all the first form to rise up and direct their faces to the wall."

Miss Temple passed her handkerchief over her lips, as if to smooth away the invol-
30 untary smile that curled them; she gave the

order, however, and when the first class could take in what was required of them, they obeyed. Leaning a little back on my bench, I could see the looks and grimaces with which
35 they commented on this manoeuvre: it was a pity Mr. Brocklehurst could not see them too; he would perhaps have felt that, whatever he might do with the outside of the cup and platter, the inside was further beyond his
40 interference than he imagined.

He scrutinised the reverse of these living medals some five minutes, then pronounced sentence. These words fell like the knell of doom —
45 "All those top-knots must be cut off." Miss Temple seemed to remonstrate.

"Madam," he pursued, "I have a Master to serve whose kingdom is not of this world: my mission is to mortify in these girls the
50 lusts of the flesh; to teach them to clothe themselves with shame-facedness and sobri-ety, not with braided hair and costly apparel; and each of the young persons before us has a string of hair twisted in plaits which vanity
55 itself might have woven; these, I repeat, must be cut off; think of the time wasted, of — "

Mr. Brocklehurst was here interrupted: three other visitors, ladies, now entered the room. They ought to have come a little
60 sooner to have heard his lecture on dress, for they were splendidly attired in velvet, silk, and furs. The two younger of the trio

[1] an unwanted growth

(fine girls of sixteen and seventeen) had grey beaver hats, then in fashion, shaded
65 with ostrich plumes, and from under the brim of this graceful head-dress fell a profusion of light tresses, elaborately curled; the elder lady was enveloped in a costly velvet shawl, trimmed with ermine, and she wore a
70 false front of French curls.

 These ladies were deferentially received by Miss Temple, as Mrs. and the Misses Brocklehurst, and conducted to seats of honour at the top of the room. It seems they
75 had come in the carriage with their reverend relative, and had been conducting a rummaging scrutiny of the room upstairs, while he transacted business with the housekeeper, questioned the laundress, and
80 lectured the superintendent. They now proceeded to address divers[2] remarks and reproofs to Miss Smith, who was charged with the care of the linen and the inspection of the dormitories: but I had no time to lis-
85 ten to what they said; other matters called off and enchanted my attention.

[2] numerous

DEVELOPING A LITERARY ARGUMENT FOR PROSE FICTION ANALYSIS (I)

Defensible Thesis Statement with Claim (idea + insight):

In [title], [author] illustrates [idea + insight] through the use of [element/technique 1], [element/technique 2], and [element/technique 3].

Topic Sentence 1	Topic Sentence 2	Topic Sentence 3
(Identify the first aspect of the topic related to the unifying idea):	(Identify the second aspect of the topic related to the unifying idea):	(Identify the third aspect of the topic related to the unifying idea):
To begin, [author] includes [technique/element 1] to [purpose connect to idea].	Next, [author] includes [technique/element 2] to [purpose connect to idea].	Finally, [author] includes [technique/element 3] to [purpose connect to idea].
Textual Details	**Textual Details**	**Textual Details**
(Relevant and sufficient evidence):	(Relevant and sufficient evidence):	(Relevant and sufficient evidence):
For example, the detail/image/comparison [text evidence], used to describe [context] illustrates [link to topic sentence].	To illustrate, [author] describes/compares [context] by describing [text evidence] to reveal [link to topic sentence].	As an example of [technique/element], the author includes [text evidence] to explain [link to topic sentence].
Additionally, the detail/image/comparison [text evidence], used to describe [context] illustrates [link to topic sentence].	To continue [author] describes/compares [context] by describing [text evidence] to reveal [link to topic sentence].	In another example, of [technique/element], the author includes [text evidence] to explain [link to topic sentence].
Commentary	**Commentary**	**Commentary**
(Link evidence to reason and idea):	(Link evidence to reason and idea):	(Link evidence to reason and idea):
The association of [text evidence] with [topic sentence] reveals [idea and insight].	Through this choice, [author] develops [idea and insight].	By including this [element/technique] the author suggests that [idea and insight].

from Where the Crawdads Sing

Delia Owens

The following is an excerpt from a novel published in 2018.

Later, near sunset, Jodie found Kya on the beach staring at the sea. As he stepped up beside her, she didn't look at him but kept her eyes on the roiling waves. Still, she knew by the
5 way he spoke that Pa had slugged his face.

"I hafta go, Kya. Can't live here no longer."

She almost turned to him, but didn't. Wanted to beg him not to leave her alone with Pa, but the words jammed up.

10 "When you're old enough you'll under-stand," he said. Kya wanted to holler out that she may be young, but she wasn't stupid. She knew Pa was the reason they all left; what she wondered was why no one took her with them.
15 She'd thought of leaving too, but had nowhere to go and no bus money.

"Kya, ya be careful, hear. If anybody comes, don't go in the house. They can get ya there. Run deep in the marsh, hide in the bushes.
20 Always cover yo' tracks; I learned ya how. And ya can hide from Pa, too." When she still didn't speak, he said good-bye and strode across the beach to the woods. Just before he stepped into the trees, she finally turned and watched him
25 walk away.

"This little piggy stayed home[1]," she said to the waves.

Breaking her freeze, she ran to the shack. Shouted his name down the hall, but Jodie's
30 things were already gone, his floor bed stripped bare.

She sank onto his mattress, watching the last of that day slide down the wall. Light lingered after the sun, as it does, some of it pooling in
35 the room, so that for a brief moment the lumpy beds and piles of old clothes took on more shape and color than the trees outside.

A gnawing hunger — such a mundane thing — surprised her. She walked to the
40 kitchen and stood at the door. All her life the room had been warmed from baking bread, boiling butter beans, or bubbling fish stew. Now, it was stale, quiet, and dark. "Who's gonna cook?" she asked out loud. Could have
45 asked, *Who's gonna dance?*

She lit a candle and poked at hot ashes in the woodstove, added kindling. Pumped the bellows till a flame caught, then more wood. The Frigidaire[2] served as a cupboard because
50 no electricity came near the shack. To keep the mold at bay, the door was propped open with the flyswatter. Still, greenish-black veins of mildew grew in every crevice.

Getting out leftovers, she said, "I'll tump[3]
55 the grits in lard, warm 'em up," which she did and ate from the pot, looking through the window for Pa. But he didn't come.

---

[1]Reference to a traditional English and American nursery rhyme

[2]Frigidaire — a brand of electric refrigerator

[3]tump — to tip into or to fall over

When light from the quarter moon finally
touched the shack, she crawled into her porch
60 bed — a lumpy mattress on the floor with real
sheets covered in little blue roses that Ma had
got at a yard sale — alone at night for the first
time in her life.

At first, every few minutes, she sat up
65 and peered through the screen. Listening
for footsteps in the woods. She knew the
shapes of all the trees; still some seemed to
dart here and there, moving with the moon.
For a while she was so stiff she couldn't
70 swallow, but on cue, the familiar songs of
tree frogs and katydids filled the night. More
comforting than three blind mice with a
carving knife. The darkness held an odor of
sweetness, the earthy breath of frogs and sal-
75 amanders who'd made it through one more
stinky-hot day. The marsh snuggled in closer
with a low fog, and she slept.

1. In the context of the passage as a whole, the
   details in lines 7–9 ("She almost . . . jammed
   up.") could suggest all of the following about
   Kya EXCEPT
   (A) she was stunned into silence by Jodie's
       announcement.
   (B) she was physically shocked by Jodie's
       announcement.
   (C) she relied on Jodie for support in her
       family situation.
   (D) she doesn't understand the words Jodie is
       using.
   (E) she fears being left with her father.

2. Kya "[b]reaking her freeze" (line 28) and
   running "to the shack" (line 28) is significant
   when it occurs in the excerpt because
   (A) it emphasizes how important Jodie's
       presence actually was to her and how
       much his announcement that he was
       leaving had stunned her into silence.
   (B) it illustrates her inability to care for
       herself or to make her own decisions
       based on her age.
   (C) it emphasizes how important Jodie's
       presence actually was to her and suggests
       that her behaviors cannot be trusted
       because they are often rash and self-
       destructive.
   (D) it demonstrates her inability to accept
       reality and face the consequences of her
       action or inaction.
   (E) it suggests that Jodie is not a real person
       and that her "[b]reaking" free relates only
       to her growing up and letting go of her
       imagination.

3. Of the following, which paragraph is struc-
   tured and included where it is in the excerpt to
   illustrate Kya's worsening dramatic situation?
   (A) Paragraph 6
   (B) Paragraph 7
   (C) Paragraph 9
   (D) Paragraph 10
   (E) Paragraph 12

4. In the context of the excerpt, which of the
   following details related to the setting BEST
   suggest Kya's isolation?
   (A) ". . . Jodie found Kya on the beach staring
       at the sea" (lines 1–2).
   (B) "Run deep in the marsh, hide in the
       bushes" (line 21).
   (C) ". . . his floor bed stripped bare"
       (lines 30–31).
   (D) " . . . no electricity came near the shack"
       (line 50).
   (E) ". . . light from the quarter moon finally
       touched the shack" (lines 58–59).

5. Details throughout the excerpt suggest Kya's perspective that
   (A) she could not understand the decisions of her family members.
   (B) she was stronger than her siblings.
   (C) she felt abandoned by others in her family.
   (D) she was unable to care for herself.
   (E) she was overwhelmed by the environment surrounding her.

6. Which of the following BEST describes the narrator of this passage?
   (A) Third-person narrator with extensive information about the past and the future of the characters
   (B) Third-person narrator with extensive knowledge about both the emotions underlying the characters' decisions and the long-term effects of those decisions
   (C) Third-person narrator with knowledge of the characters' thoughts and emotions and awareness of the setting limited to the perception of the characters
   (D) First-person narrator with a perspective of pity toward Kya and disappointment in Jodie for his decision to leave
   (E) First-person narrator who is involved with the story and who has a clear bias toward the characters because of that involvement

7. All of the following are aspects of the setting of the passage EXCEPT
   (A) "... Jodie found Kya on the beach staring at the sea" (lines 1–2).
   (B) "... nowhere to go and no bus money" (lines 15–16).
   (C) "... he said good-bye and strode across the beach to the woods" (lines 22–23).
   (D) "... his floor bed stripped bare" (lines 30–31).
   (E) "Now, it was stale, quiet, and dark" (line 43).

8. The excerpt as a whole might be BEST understood as
   (A) the resolution to a story about the pains of raising children.
   (B) a pitiful cry for help from the helpless children of a neglectful father.
   (C) set in a location that can only divide people.
   (D) a cautionary tale about the consequences of abandoning your family.
   (E) the beginning of a journey for Kya despite her remaining in one place.

Of the Threads That Connect the Stars
Martín Espada

Did you ever see stars? asked my father with a cackle. He was not
speaking of the heavens, but the white flash in his head when a fist burst
between his eyes. In Brooklyn, this would cause men and boys to slap
the table with glee; this might be the only heavenly light we'd ever see.

5 I never saw stars. The sky in Brooklyn was a tide of smoke rolling over us
from the factory across the avenue, the mattresses burning in the junkyard,
the ruins where squatters would sleep, the riots of 1966 that kept me
locked in my room like a suspect. My father talked truce on the streets.

My son can see the stars through the tall barrel of a telescope.
10 He names the galaxies with the numbers and letters of astronomy.
I cannot see what he sees in the telescope, no matter how many eyes I shut.
I understand a smoking mattress better than the language of galaxies.

My father saw stars. My son sees stars. The earth rolls beneath
our feet. We lurch ahead, and one day we have walked this far.

1. The statement "in Brooklyn, this would cause
   men and boys to slap / the table with glee"
   (lines 3–4) most likely indicates which of the
   following about the speaker's perspective on
   his own father?
   (A) He saw his father as respected by others
       in Brooklyn.
   (B) He feared for his father's life.
   (C) He longed to escape the influence of his
       father and the brutality of Brooklyn.
   (D) He felt his father could not earn respect in
       any other way.
   (E) He saw him as hypocritical for later
       wanting peace on the streets.

2. The details provided in the third stanza (lines
   9–12) reveal that the speaker's son
   (A) longs to escape the poverty in which his
       family lives.
   (B) cannot understand the value of the
       speaker's experiences.
   (C) has a significantly different quality of life
       from that of the speaker as a young boy.
   (D) fails to respect the struggles faced by
       generations of his family.
   (E) shows little respect for the experiences of
       earlier generations in his family.

3. In the final lines of the poem (lines 13 and 14), the speaker establishes a relationship between the text and the reader by
   (A) talking about himself and his own feelings toward his father and his own son.
   (B) making connections between several generations of the same family.
   (C) talking about fathers and children.
   (D) using language that can include the reader and the characters of the poem.
   (E) defining the role of a parent in a child's life.

4. The sequence of events in the poem focuses attention on the
   (A) changes in family relationships over time.
   (B) similarities and differences in the experiences of multiple generations of the same family.
   (C) failure of the speaker to relate to his own son.
   (D) different experiences across multiple generations and how family members eventually grow apart.
   (E) lessening acceptance of violence as a fact of life.

5. In the context of the poem, all of the following are aspects of Brooklyn as a setting EXCEPT
   (A) "...a tide of smoke rolling over us / from the factory across the avenue" (lines 5–6).
   (B) "...ruins where squatters would sleep" (line 7).
   (C) "...locked in my room like a suspect" (line 8).
   (D) "I understand a smoking mattress..." (line 12).
   (E) "The earth rolls beneath / our feet" (lines 13–14).

6. Which of the following BEST describes the speaker in the poem as a result of his point of view?
   (A) Intimately involved with the characters and events of the poem
   (B) Angry about the conditions in the Brooklyn of his childhood
   (C) Biased against those who exploited his father and son
   (D) Uncertain of his family's future
   (E) Unaware of the circumstances in which his own father raised him

7. The poem as a whole might BEST be described as exploring the
   (A) way sons grow apart from their fathers.
   (B) social condition of Brooklyn throughout history.
   (C) changes families experience across multiple generations.
   (D) role family plays in affecting one's perspective.
   (E) peace and calm people seek as they age.

© Robert Couse-Baker

UNIT

2

Analyzing Comparisons and Representations

UNIT GOALS

	Focus	Goals
Big Idea: Character	**Perspective and Bias**	Explain how a character's experiences and actions reveal his or her biases.
Big Idea: Structure	**Shifts and Contrasts**	Analyze how shifts and contrasts in literary texts contribute to an interpretation.
Big Idea: Figurative Language	**Associations and Emphasis**	Explain how authors create associations through referents and repetition.
Big Idea: Figurative Language	**Similes and Metaphors**	Explain the significance of literary comparisons.
Ideas in Literature	• **Thought and Feeling** • **Opportunity and Loss**	Explain how the ideas of thought, feeling, opportunity, and loss are reflected in classic and contemporary texts.
Big Idea: Literary Argumentation	**Writing about Tone**	Write a literary argument that explains how an author's use of figurative elements contributes to the tone of a work.
Preparing for the AP® Exam	**Free-Response Question: Poetry Analysis** Justifying a Thesis through a Line of Reasoning	Justify a defensible thesis statement through a line of reasoning and relevant textual evidence for support.
	Multiple-Choice Questions: Prose	Analyze literary elements and techniques in classic and contemporary prose and poetry.
	Multiple-Choice Questions: Poetry	

Perspective and Bias

 AP® **Enduring Understanding**

Characters in literature allow readers to study and explore a range of values, beliefs, assumptions, biases, and cultural norms represented by those characters.

KEY POINT

A character or speaker's perspective and biases are shaped by his or her past. These biases appear in the character's choices, actions, dialogue, internal thoughts, and interactions with others.

You can tell a lot about people based on the content that they post on their social media profile. For example, you can potentially figure out their sense of humor, their taste in music, or their views of current events. You'd also get a sense of how often they engage with social media and respond to online content. While you cannot learn everything about people solely based on their online activity, it's one source of clues about the person running the account.

Values Influence Character's Perspective

Characters must navigate their fictional worlds from their own **perspectives**, which often seem as complex and nuanced as people's perspectives in real life. Readers learn about a character's values through details about his or her thoughts, words, and actions.

As with people in real life, the perspectives of characters are influenced by their backgrounds, their education, their families, and their past experiences. Even apparently minor details in the story can provide helpful information about a character's perspective. Characters reveal their perspectives and biases in their assumptions about others, the stories they tell, their secrets, their decision-making process, and even their misperceptions.

Discovering a Character's Perspective

Readers can learn about a character's **biases** through a character's choices and actions. How characters act toward people who are different from them, how they apologize to someone close to them, and even how they adapt to new circumstances — all of these may reveal a character's perspective or bias. Indeed, an astute reader not only infers a character's **values** (ideas, attitudes, or beliefs about the human condition) from all the elements of characterization but also applies that information when interpreting other parts of the text.

Characters may even be unaware that they are revealing information about their values and biases to the reader.

Character's Actions	May Reveal . . .
A father tells his children long, heroic stories about their grandfather's military service.	This character spends a lot of time thinking about his own father, admires the grandfather's patriotism, and wants to inspire those feelings within his own kids.
A neighbor opens her home one night a week for the neighborhood to eat dinner together for free.	This character has the resources and space to feed many people; she enjoys sharing meals with her community and values them like family.
A detective methodically interviews every person who was at the scene of a crime.	This character is thorough and detail-oriented; they may be very calculating in their thinking processes.
An older sibling gently drapes a blanket over their younger sibling as they take a nap.	This character cares about their sibling's comfort and won't take advantage of them when they're vulnerable.
A bully mocks someone's appearance or clothing.	This character may be projecting insecurities about their own appearance onto someone they can control.
A friend bursts into a room and exclaims a scandalous secret that they just heard.	This character may act on impulse and assume that they are entitled to share information without discretion, consideration for others, or concerns about consequences.

INSIDER AP® TIP   **Perspective contributes to tone.** Tone is by definition an attitude. A character's perspective often conveys his or her attitude about a character, event, place, or idea in a literary work.

A CHARACTER'S PERSPECTIVE

Character Details	Consider the Implications
Character's background	• What past experiences have affected the character? • Where is the character from? • What role does the character fulfill in his or her community? • Who is the character's family? • Does the character have a religious background?
Character's actions and choices	• What do the choices a character makes reveal about his or her values? • What factors does the character consider when deciding what to do? • Is the character consistent in what he or she does? • What factors does a character consider before deciding to act or not to act?

(continued)

Character Details	Consider the Implications
Character's internal thoughts	• What adjectives does the character use when describing people, places, events, or ideas? • What internal struggles or choices does the character have? • What factors influence a character's choices and decisions? • Does the perspective change? If so, why?
Dialogue	• What does the character choose to say? • How often does the character speak with others? • How would you describe the character's way of speaking? • What can you tell about the character's personality from how he or she speaks to others?
Interactions with others	• Who does the character interact with? • Who does the character not interact with? • How does the character treat the other characters he or she is around? • In comparison, how does the character act when he or she is alone?

GUIDED READING

On Listening to Your Teacher Take Attendance
Aimee Nezhukumatathil

THE TEXT IN CONTEXT

Born in Chicago to a Filipina mother and South Indian father, poet and essayist Aimee Nezhukumatathil (b. 1974) often explores nature, wonder, metaphor, and cultural difference in her work. She is the author of several books of poetry and prose, including *Miracle Fruit* (2003), *At the Drive-In Volcano* (2007), *Oceanic* (2018), and the *New York Times* best seller *World of Wonders: In Praise of Fireflies, Whale Sharks, and Other Astonishments* (2018). Nezhukumatathil currently teaches poetry and creative nonfiction at the University of Mississippi. In the following poem, she uses figurative language and imagery to re-create a classroom experience.

Cheyenne Alford

On Listening to Your Teacher Take Attendance

Breathe deep even if it means you wrinkle
your nose from the fake-lemon antiseptic

of the mopped floors and wiped-down
doorknobs. The freshly soaped necks

5 and armpits. Your teacher means well,
even if he butchers your name like

1. Who are the characters in the poem? What is the relationship between the characters? Who is this consoling?

he has a bloody sausage casing stuck
between his teeth, handprints

on his white, sloppy apron. And when
10 everyone turns around to check out

your face, no need to flush red and warm.
Just picture all the eyes as if your classroom

2. What does this physical description reveal?

is one big scallop with its dozens of icy blues
and you will remember that winter your family

15 took you to the China Sea and you sank
your face in it to gaze at baby clams and sea stars

the size of your outstretched hand. And when
all those necks start to crane, try not to forget

3. Why do the students crane their necks to stare?

someone once lathered their bodies, once patted them
20 dry with a fluffy towel after a bath, set out their clothes

for the first day of school. Think of their pencil cases
from third grade, full of sharp pencils, a pink pearl eraser.

4. What do the character's final thoughts reveal about the character?

Think of their handheld pencil sharpener and its tiny blade.

Verses upon the Burning of our House

Anne Bradstreet

Courtesy of the American Antiquarian Society, Worcester, Massachusetts

THE TEXT IN CONTEXT

Anne Bradstreet (1612–1672) was born to an affluent Puritan family in Northampton, England. An unusually well-educated woman at the time, she (along with her husband and parents) emigrated to Massachusetts as part of John Winthrop's Puritan fleet in 1630. These settlers sought to practice a purer form of English Protestantism free from the official Church of England, which they considered corrupt. Like many of the Puritans, Bradstreet found the hardships of the New World difficult. She began writing poems in the early 1630s that reflected both her religion and her personal experiences — especially the fragility of human life, the impermanence of material things, and her hope for religious salvation. Later, her poetry became more personal, as she meditated on herself and her domestic life as the mother of eight children. In the 1666 poem "Verses upon the Burning of our House," Bradstreet reflects on a personal experience that had an important meaning.

 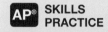

SKILLS PRACTICE	CHARACTER
	Describing a Character's Perspective

As you read "Verses upon the Burning of our House," consider how details in the poem help reveal the speaker's perspective. Record your notes in the graphic organizer.

Analyzing a Character's Perspective		
Considerations	**Details from the Text**	**What the Details Reveal about Perspective**
Character's background		
Character's actions and choices		
Character's internal thoughts		
Dialogue		
Interactions with others		

Verses upon the Burning of our House

In silent night when rest I took,
For sorrow near I did not look,
I waken'd was with thund'ring noise
And piteous shrieks of dreadful voice.
5 That fearful sound of "fire" and "fire,"
Let no man know is my Desire.
I starting up, the light did spy,
And to my God my heart did cry
To straighten me in my Distress
10 And not to leave me succourless.
Then coming out, behold a space
The flame consume my dwelling place.
And when I could no longer look,
I blest his grace that gave and took,
15 That laid my goods now in the dust.
Yea, so it was, and so 'twas just.
It was his own; it was not mine.
Far be it that I should repine,
He might of all justly bereft
20 But yet sufficient for us left.
When by the Ruins oft I past
My sorrowing eyes aside did cast
And here and there the places spy
Where oft I sate and long did lie.
25 Here stood that Trunk, and there that chest,
There lay that store I counted best,
My pleasant things in ashes lie
And them behold no more shall I.
Under the roof no guest shall sit,
30 Nor at thy Table eat a bit.
No pleasant talk shall 'ere be told
Nor things recounted done of old.
No Candle 'ere shall shine in Thee,
Nor bridegroom's voice ere heard shall bee.
35 In silence ever shalt thou lie.
Adieu, Adieu, All's Vanity.
Then straight I 'gin my heart to chide:
And did thy wealth on earth abide,
Didst fix thy hope on mouldring dust,
40 The arm of flesh didst make thy trust?
Raise up thy thoughts above the sky

That dunghill mists away may fly.
Thou hast a house on high erect
Fram'd by that mighty Architect,
45 With glory richly furnished
Stands permanent, though this be fled.
It's purchased and paid for too
By him who hath enough to do.
A price so vast as is unknown,
50 Yet by his gift is made thine own.
There's wealth enough; I need no more.
Farewell, my pelf; farewell, my store.
The world no longer let me love;
My hope and Treasure lies above.

CHARACTER

1. How is the **speaker** described in the first few lines? What does her reaction to the fire reveal about her **values**?

2. As she reconciles the events of the poem, what does the speaker reveal about her beliefs?

3. How do the **speaker's** values and beliefs contribute to her **perspective**?

4. The **speaker** experiences a new understanding of material possessions and their value. What does this insight reveal about her **perspective**?

Shifts and Contrasts

AP **Enduring Understanding (STR-1)**

The arrangement of the parts and sections of a text, the relationship of the parts to each other, and the sequence in which the text reveals information are all structural choices made by a writer that contribute to the reader's interpretation of a text.

Authors use literature as a way to explore or to relate ideas and issues that are part of the human experience. As you've already learned, characters represent values, perspectives, and expectations. For example, a character chooses to do (or not to do) something; a character navigates a moment of crisis; a character learns something after overcoming an obstacle. In the process, the character reveals familiar human struggles.

KEY POINT

Shifts and contrasts within a text often illustrate a tension of values that helps readers interpret a literary work.

A Text's Structure May Reveal Meaning

To communicate their insights, authors set up the plot or the structure of a literary work to help readers uncover meaning. Good readers often discover meaning and make interpretations by looking for changes within the work, such as shifts in

- the dramatic situation, especially a conflict;
- a character's or a speaker's perspective;
- the attitude or tone of the work;
- point of view;
- setting or time; and
- images.

These changes are important because they indicate new understandings or a conflict of values that help us get at meaning as we interpret a text. Good readers look for **shifts** and **contrasts** in the structure of literary works to help them find these changes. In prose, for example, the shifts and contrasts may occur as part of the plot; characters in conflict may even signal these shifts explicitly.

As you read poetry, you should consider the text's structure as well. Poems are made up of **lines** and **stanzas**. A stanza is a group of lines in a poem. The arrangement of the lines and stanzas make up a poem's structure, which also depends on the poetic form the writer has chosen. For example, sonnets are traditionally structured to have contrasts in their final lines, with rhymes to reinforce the shift.

Shifts Happen

What exactly is a shift? Shifts can emphasize contrasts within particular sections of a text. Often, they are signaled by a physical marker, such as

- a transition word or phrase (e.g., *but, however, even though, so, now*);
- a less frequently used punctuation mark, such as a dash, colon, question mark, or parentheses;
- a change in syntax, such as the use of a fragment or short simple sentence; or
- a change in structure, such as a new paragraph or stanza, OR a change in speaker or narrator.

Why are shifts important? Shifts often indicate a change in a character's thinking: a reconsideration, a new insight, or even a new perspective. Generally, authors include details before the shift to contrast with details after the shift; such contrasts can reveal values. If readers can clearly see the conflict between these different values, they should be able to interpret the text effectively. Indeed, the characterization and events after a shift are likely to convey the author's message and point. As a general rule, look for a significant shift in the last third of a literary work.

Contrasts

Some authors structure their texts to include a series of contrasts that run throughout the text. By doing so, they allow the reader to consider two or more ideas. In other words, the author is going back and forth between the two elements in opposition to illustrate a conflict of values.

Some writers establish contrasts by including parallel elements or setting up side-by-side dramatic action called **juxtaposition**. For example, an author may structure a text so that two events happen simultaneously as the reader switches back and forth between them. Or an author may set up clear contrasts between two ideas, images, or even settings.

Structure and Meaning

To make a thoughtful, engaging interpretation, you must notice these contrasts and juxtapositions. Identify and analyze the details on each side of the contrast as well: they will help you explain the shift in relationship to the work as a whole.

INSIDER AP® TIP

Contrasts and shifts reveal tensions. Understanding and explaining tensions within a text lead to an interpretation. But you must do more than just identify shifts and contrasts: you also need to explain how they contribute to your overall sense of the text's meaning.

SHIFTS AND CONTRASTS		
	Signal	**Effect**
Shift	• Contrasting transition words (e.g., *but, however, yet*) • Syntactic markers (e.g., isolated simple sentences) • Punctuation (e.g., use of question mark, dash, colon, parentheses) • Structural changes (e.g., change in paragraph or stanza, one-sentence paragraphs) • A change in the connotation of words or language	Provides a revelation Gives new insight or understanding Signals a change in perspective, tone, or attitude
Contrast	• A back-and-forth movement in dialogue, plot, or other elements that create contrast • Frequent changes in speaker, imagery, point of view • Contrasting words (e.g., *I* and *we*; *then* and *now*) or images	Shows values in tension or debate Highlights positive or negative aspects of each side Places emphasis on ideas Prompts reflection through the contrast

Snapping Beans
Lisa Parker

THE TEXT IN CONTEXT

Born and raised in Fauquier County, Virginia, poet Lisa Parker (b. 1972) often writes about rural and southern life. She graduated from George Mason University and earned her MFA in poetry from Penn State University. Her work has been published in several journals, including *Southern Review, The Louisville Review*, and *Appalachian Heritage*. Parker's 2010 poetry collection *The Gone Place* won the Weatherford Prize from Berea College and the Appalachian Studies Association. In "Snapping Beans," Parker presents a conversation between a grandmother and her college-aged granddaughter.

Courtesy of Laura Coleman

Snapping Beans

(For Fay Whitt)

I snapped beans into the silver bowl
that sat on the splintering slats
of the porchswing between my grandma and me.
I was home for the weekend,
5 from school, from the North,
Grandma hummed "What A Friend We Have In Jesus"
as the sun rose, pushing its pink spikes
through the slant of cornstalks,
through the fly-eyed mesh of the screen.
10 We didn't speak until the sun overcame
the feathered tips of the cornfield
and Grandma stopped humming. I could feel
the soft gray of her stare
against the side of my face
15 when she asked, *How's school a-goin?*
I wanted to tell her about my classes,
the revelations by book and lecture
as real as any shout of faith,
potent as a swig of strychnine.
20 She reached the leather of her hand
over the bowl and cupped
my quivering chin;
the slick smooth of her palm held my face
the way she held cherry tomatoes under the spigot,
25 careful not to drop them,
and I wanted to tell her
about the nights I cried into the familiar
heartsick panels of the quilt she made me,
wishing myself home on the evening star.
30 I wanted to tell her
the evening star was a planet,
that my friends wore noserings and wrote poetry
about sex, about alcoholism, about Buddha.
I wanted to tell her
35 how my stomach burned acidic holes
at the thought of speaking in class,
speaking in an accent, speaking out of turn,
how I was tearing, splitting myself apart
with the slow-simmering guilt of being happy
40 despite it all.
I said, *School's fine.*

1. How do the actions and description of the characters suggest a contrast?

2. What changed? What action of the Grandma indicates this change?

3. How does this change create a shift in the tone of the poem?

4. What does the action of the Grandma reveal about her intentions?

5. How does this set up the contrast between the speaker's inner thoughts and external behavior?

6. How does the short sentence response create a shift? What is the shift, and what does it reveal about the relationship?

We snapped beans into the silver bowl between us
and when a hickory leaf, still summer green,
skidded onto the porchfront,
45 Grandma said,
It's funny how things blow loose like that.

Guided Questions

7. How does the
last line reveal an
understanding?

PRACTICE TEXT

Janet Waking
John Crowe Ransom

THE TEXT IN CONTEXT

An influential critic and educator, as well as a poet, John
Crowe Ransom (1888–1974) played a key role in the
development of the "New Criticism": a literary movement
that took its name from Ransom's 1941 book of that title.
The New Critics were poets and academics who argued that
literary texts must be viewed as self-contained aesthetic
artifacts, like sculptures or paintings. Largely avoiding
factors such as historical context, authorial intention, or
personal responses, these writers focused on close reading the poem or story itself. This formalist approach valued
tension, precision, paradox, ambiguity, and irony in literature. It also asserted that a poem's "meaning" could not be separated from the
experience of reading it (i.e., it is impossible to paraphrase or summarize a good
poem). Ransom's poetry reflects these aesthetic values, particularly in its irony and
its lack of sentimentality.

Bettmann/Getty Images

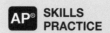 SKILLS PRACTICE | STRUCTURE
Analyzing Shifts and Contrasts

Read the following poem, "Janet Waking." As you read, consider whether the author incorporates a primary shift or a series of contrasts in the text. Then, record details from the poem in the following graphic organizer, which will help you make an interpretation.

Analyzing Shifts and Contrasts

Indicators of Shifts

- Contrasting transition words (e.g., *but*, *however*, *yet*)
- Syntactic markers (e.g., isolated simple sentences)
- Punctuation (e.g., use of question mark, dash, colon, parentheses)
- Structural changes (e.g., change in paragraph or stanza, one-sentence paragraphs)
- A change in the connotation of words or language

Indicators of Contrasts

- A back-and-forth movement in dialogue, plot, or other elements that create contrast
- Frequent changes in speaker, imagery, point of view
- Juxtaposed characters, settings, points of view, or images (e.g., *I* and *we*; *then* and *now*)

Shift (detail before) or Contrast (details of Side A)	Shift (after) or Contrasts (details Side B)
Indication in the text:	Indication in the text:

What is revealed through these contrasts or shifts?

Janet Waking

Beautifully Janet slept
Till it was deeply morning. She woke then
And thought about her dainty-feathered hen,
To see how it had kept.

5 One kiss she gave her mother,
Only a small one gave she to her daddy
Who would have kissed each curl of his shining baby;
No kiss at all for her brother.

"Old Chucky, Old Chucky!" she cried,
10 Running across the world upon the grass
To Chucky's house, and listening. But alas,
Her Chucky had died.

It was a transmogrifying bee
Came droning down on Chucky's old bald head
15 And sat and put the poison. It scarcely bled,
But how exceedingly

And purply did the knot
Swell with the venom and communicate
Its rigour! Now the poor comb stood up straight
20 But Chucky did not.

So there was Janet
Kneeling on the wet grass, crying her brown hen
(Translated far beyond the daughters of men)
To rise and walk upon it.

25 And weeping fast as she had breath
Janet implored us, "Wake her from her sleep!"
And would not be instructed in how deep
Was the forgetful kingdom of death.

STRUCTURE

1. Is there a **shift** in the poem? If so, how do you know? What identifies the shift?

2. Identify and explain the **juxtaposition** in the poem. How do these parallel events contribute to your interpretation of the poem?

3. How does the **perspective** of the speaker change from the beginning of the poem to the end?

4. The poem has many **contrasts**. Choose two contrasts and explain how they contribute to the poem's meaning.

Associations and Emphasis

 Enduring Understanding (FIG-1)

Comparisons, representations, and associations shift meaning from the literal to the figurative and invite readers to interpret a text.

KEY POINT

Authors use referents and repetition to create associations within their works. These associations may emphasize an idea, create intentional ambiguity, or trace a concept throughout the text.

People use associations to make meaning in everyday life. For example, when commercials repeat messages about "great low prices" or a product's high quality, companies hope that you associate their brands with these positive ideas.

In addition, you may have experienced a conversation at some point in your life when someone makes an association that is unclear to you. For example, a person might say, "They're all out to get me!" without clarifying who the term "they're" refers to. In this instance, it may not be crucial to understand what the person means, but in other instances, ambiguity could change the entire meaning of the sentence. Consider the following example: "When guests come over, Samuel often brings his dog to the living room because he loves to give sloppy, wet kisses." Is Samuel just very affectionate with his guests or does he have a very friendly dog?

Associations Connect Elements within a Text

Authors have several different ways of signaling to readers that details are important. There are two types of associations: writers may choose words, images, and symbols that they believe will create emotional connections with their readers, or they may make syntactical choices such as antecedents, repetition, and ambiguity to create associations within a literary work. Because these associations move beyond the literal, they are a type of **figurative language**. In short, figurative language draws upon the literal and concrete to reveal the intangible and abstract ideas.

Antecedents and Referents

An **antecedent** is a device in which a word or pronoun in a line or sentence refers to an earlier one. Generally speaking, antecedents refer to the noun that a pronoun replaces and refers to.

To make an association, authors connect two parts: a **referent** and an antecedent. An antecedent is a word, phrase, or clause that comes before its referent. Referents can be the following:

- Pronouns
- Nouns

- Phrases (noun phrases)
- Clauses

It's important to trace a referent to its antecedent so you can make an informed interpretation. Sometimes referents can be ambiguous if they can apply to more than one antecedent. This allows the reader to interpret the meaning in new, different ways. Consider the example, "The anniversary of the accident and the rain brought everyone's mood down: it was heavy." The pronoun "it" is the referent, but it could refer to one of two antecedents: the anniversary of the accident (which may be emotionally taxing) or the large amount of rain falling.

In a broader sense, the term *antecedent* refers to something prior. So, when you consider the plot or structure of a work of literature, **antecedent action** refers to an action or event that took place prior to the plot of the text; sometimes, this is referred to later in the text and may affect interpretation.

Repetition

Humans are pattern seekers who tend to notice and recall when something is repeated. Authors repeat words, sounds, phrases, clauses, or images in texts to create emphasis or to make associations by repeating through a **refrain** or using **synonyms** for an important word or phrase.

Writers may also deploy **alliteration** by choosing words with the same beginning sound. This technique makes an image or phrase memorable and rhythmic; it creates associations between sound and meaning as well. Of course, we are familiar with alliteration in daily life, as it is common in brand names, such as "Dunkin Donuts" and "Bed Bath and Beyond."

INSIDER AP® TIP **Ambiguity may be intentional.** An author may create intentional ambiguity by keeping the relationship between a referent and an antecedent open-ended. This leaves the text open to a broader range of interpretations, meanings, and implications.

LINGUISTIC ASSOCIATIONS		
Literary Element	**Description**	**Effect**
Antecedents	Authors refer to nouns, pronouns, phrases, or clauses expressed in earlier parts of a text. The first or initial instance is called the antecedent of the referent.	Pronouns stand in for nouns used earlier. The noun a pronoun replaces is called the antecedent.
		Words, phrases, sentences, or stanzas may come between the pronoun and its antecedent.
		Ambiguity may be created if referents can refer to more than one antecedent.

(continued)

Literary Element	Description	Effect
Repetition	Repetition occurs when a writer uses the exact word or phrase consecutively, repeats a refrain that occurs throughout a text, or substitutes a synonym for a word or image in multiple instances.	By repeating words or phrases, an author creates emphasis.
	Alliteration refers to the repetition of consonant sounds at the beginning of multiple consecutive or closely placed words in a text.	Alliteration often produces a memorable phrase that can create emphasis, establish a sensory association set up by the sound of the phrase, or by creating an emotional association between the word or image and the reader.

GUIDED READING

Death by Basketball

Frank X Walker

Photo by Rachel Eliza Griffiths

THE TEXT IN CONTEXT

Poet and artist Frank X Walker (b. 1961) was born and raised in Danville, Kentucky. While Walker originally planned to be an engineer, he followed his literary interests at the University of Kentucky and earned an MFA in writing at Spalding University. He coined the word "Affrilachia" to describe the culture of African Americans living in Appalachia: a mountainous region that extends from southern New York State to Mississippi, including much of Kentucky. Walker also founded *The Affrilachian Journal of Arts and Culture*, which publishes work from multicultural artists and writers who identify with the Appalachian region. His books include *Black Box* (2005), *Turn Me Loose: The Unghosting of Medgar Evers* (2013), and *About Flight* (2015). He is currently a professor and director of the MFA program in writing at the University of Kentucky. In "Death by Basketball," Walker uses repetition to explore the dreams of a young boy in an impoverished neighborhood.

Death by Basketball

Before and after school
      he stood
    on a milk crate
  eyeballed the mirror
5 and only saw wayne turner
    at tournament time
     a third grader
    just off the bus
    barely four feet
10   off the ground
  he dropped his books
      sank a j'
  from the top of the key
and heard the crowd roar
15 beat his man off the dribble
  with a break yaneck
     crossover
  and slammed himself
  on the cover of a box
20   of wheaties
   he was out there
    every night
  under a street light
fighting through double picks
25   talking trash
  to imaginary body checks
  'you can't hold me fool'
    fake right
  'this is my planet'
30   drive left
  'is the camera on'
   reverse lay-up
  'that's butter baby'
  finishing with a trey
35 from downtown, swish!
  I'm inna zone t'night
    whogotnext?
  more than a little
   light in the ass
40   hands so small

Guided Questions

1. Who is being referred to by the pronoun "he"?

2. What antecedent action has influenced the character?

3. How does the alliteration contribute to your understanding?

the ball almost dribbled him
he formed his own lay-up line
in the bluegrass
wildcat jersey
45 hanging like a summer dress
on a court made bald
from daily use
and instead of writing
his spelling words
50 he signed a contract
he could barely read
inked a commitment
in big block letters
to the NBA
55 and NIKE
and SPRITE
scribbled superstar in cursive
with a fat red pencil
and practiced his
60 million dollar smile
not his multiplication table
thinking of how many
chocolate milks
he could buy
65 with his signing bonus
or his all-star game
appearance fee
after recess
another shooting
70 another tragic death
another little genius
who will never test out
of a dream
that kills legitimate futures
75 every night
under street lights
wherever these products
are sold . . .

Guided Questions

4. The basketball court replaced what activity?

5. How does the pronoun "he" here connect the literal and figurative meanings of the poem?

6. What is being compared to schoolwork? How does this contribute to a deeper figurative meaning?

7. How does the repetition of "another" contribute to your interpretation of the poem?

PRACTICE TEXT

It was easier to manage
Arisa White

THE TEXT IN CONTEXT

Poet Arisa White is an assistant professor in English and Creative Writing at Colby College. A Brooklyn native, she attended Sarah Lawrence College and received her MFA from the University of Massachusetts, Amherst. White's books include *A Penny Saved* (2012), *Hurrah's Nest* (2012), and *You're the Most Beautiful Thing That Happened* (2016). She cowrote *Biddy Mason Speaks Up* (2020), a children's book about Biddy Mason, a woman who escaped slavery to become a businesswoman, a civil leader, and a philanthropist. She explores her childhood extensively in her poetry as is evident in "It was easier to manage."

© Nye Lyn Tho

AP® SKILLS PRACTICE	FIGURATIVE LANGUAGE **Explaining the Function of Words and Phrases**

As you read White's poem, look for examples of repetition and referents that emphasize her message. Record those examples and explain how they contribute to her message.

Analyzing Linguistic Associations		
Literary Element	**Examples from the Text**	**Effect**
Antecedents: Authors refer to nouns, pronouns, phrases, or clauses expressed in earlier parts of a text. The first or initial instance is called the antecedent of the referent.		
Repetition: Repetition occurs when a writer uses the exact word or phrase consecutively or throughout a text.		
Alliteration is a type of repetition when consonant sounds at the beginning of multiple consecutive or closely placed words in a text.		

It was easier to manage

I started kindergarten that fall you went off to Guyana.
Granny cut off my dreadlocks. She knew how to press
and curl, ponytail, and cornrow but palm roll
locks till the roots stiffened with beeswax,
5 glistens like licorice, she didn't know.
For that matter, no one in the Projects knew
what to do with hair left natural, left
unparted and wild—they were afraid to touch
that unmothered part of themselves. Each snip
10 made each one alive and each one dead.
And if you said goodbye, it was an honest whisper,
short and fine in your throat.
She cut my hair like a boy's
who hadn't been to the barber for a month,
15 and I sat at the cafeteria table alone for weeks.
They couldn't make sense of me, my classmates
with their gender-proper hairstyles. I didn't
want anything to do with franks & beans,
those pucks of grilled meat. I waited at lunchtime
20 for peanut butter and jelly and was hesitant to eat
bread that wasn't our color. It was hard
not hearing your voice each morning,
throughout the day. And unwilling to correct them
when they said my name wrong, I gave into
25 the Sizzlean; the fried chicken crunched
between my teeth, I could've bitten both of your hands
for leaving me here, each finger for the gunshots that rang
the night, the footsteps running on the roof, the gravel mashed
deeper and deeper into my sleep. Flocks of butterflies
30 broke my skin and I was shatter where I stood,
a whole constellation of wondering if I could throw
myself to the sky, coat it with urgent wishes
you'd see that I missed you, that the barter was unfair,
that you mistook me for sheep.

FIGURATIVE LANGUAGE: Word Choice, Imagery, and Symbols

1. Consider the **pronouns** and **antecedents** in the poem. How do these pronouns create relationships?

2. The speaker characterizes a child through repetitive words and phrases. How does this **repetition** create a message? Explain how repetition contributes to the message.

3. Choose an **alliterative** phrase and explain how the **repetition** of the sound contributes to your interpretation of the poem.

Similes and Metaphors

 Enduring Understanding (FIG-1)

Comparisons, representations, and associations shift meaning from the literal to the figurative and invite readers to interpret a text.

When telling stories or even in everyday conversations, people rely on comparisons to make a story juicier. For example, when your friend says, "That statistics test was an absolute monster!," he or she isn't saying that the Scantron literally had razor-sharp teeth, venomous pinchers, and a lust for blood. Rather, you know that your friend really means that taking the test felt like a standoff with something scary, dangerous, and unknown. Your friend could have just said, "That statistics test was really hard," but by comparing it to a monster, your friend communicated a more vivid and visceral sense of his or her experience.

KEY POINT

Authors compare concrete objects with ideas about the human experience to emphasize, clarify, or explain these ideas in a way that connects to an audience's emotions.

Comparisons Create Associations

Effective comparisons draw on the experiences and associations that are already familiar to readers. By using **figurative language**, writers invite the audience to join in the act of meaning making; in the process, the readers access information about something that they already know and transfer that knowledge to a new thing. For many readers, these fresh ways of seeing, connecting, and understanding are a source of aesthetic pleasure and interest. But striking comparisons also provide a deeper, richer understanding of the two subjects being compared.

As with any kind of interpretation, understanding the context in which a comparison is made is key to understanding its significance. **Comparisons** made at the beginning of a text might take on new meaning after the resolution of a story or poem's conflict. The circumstances in the text may affect the comparison.

In any comparison, the thing being compared is referred to as the *main subject*; the thing to which it is being compared is the *comparison subject*.

Writers use comparisons to connect with an audience too. In other words, the author expects the reader to understand the comparison. But readers should also ask, Why did the author make this comparison? Did the readers at the time a text was written understand it differently than readers today? For example, a literary comparison written in Shakespeare's time may now have different meanings than it did for its original audience. In fact, comparisons can lose their meaning when readers change or a time passes. When reading stories, poems, and plays from different cultures and historical periods, close readers ask, Does this comparison still hold meaning for this audience?

Writers make comparisons primarily through two types of figurative language: similes and metaphors.

Similes

Similes use words such as *like* or *as* to make an explicit comparison between two objects or concepts. This kind of figurative language calls attention to the act of comparing.

> The boy hurried away like a frightened puppy.
> (main subject)   (comparison subject)

- The old lighthouse stood firm as an anchor against the waves.
- My mother's words were smooth and sweet as honey.

Metaphors

Metaphors are another type of comparison between two seemingly unlike things. But in contrast to similes, metaphors imply comparisons through the forms of the verb *be*. That is, writers equate the two things in a way that reveals or emphasizes one or more of their characteristics.

> That book was a roller-coaster ride.
> (main subject)   (comparison subject)

This metaphor highlights how a novel's suspense, surprises, and figurative plot twists are similar to the literal course of a roller coaster.

- When her name was called at graduation, her heart roared with pride.
- I can't find anything because the website is just a maze of links!
- My younger siblings were sheep, blindly believing whatever I told them.

Writers choose comparison subjects with careful thought and intention. In turn, attentive readers should be able to determine what specific aspects, qualities, and traits are being compared. For example, if a writer compares love to a rose, close readers should ask, "What exactly about the rose is being compared to love? The thorns? The petals? The color?" If readers understand different aspects of the comparison subject, they can make a more informed interpretation.

Moreover, interpretations of a comparison are contextual. All interpretation draws upon the experiences and associations that readers have with the objects and concepts being compared. Similar to historical references, literary quotations, or pop culture allusions, comparisons may rely on the audience's cultural understanding of an idea or object.

Sometimes comparisons can lose some of their meaning when the audience or time frame changes. Especially when reading texts that were written in another time frame or for another culture, close readers must consider, Does this comparison still hold meaning for this audience?

INSIDER
AP® TIP

Some metaphors extend throughout a text.
Metaphors aren't limited to one-sentence descriptions.
Some authors choose to carry a metaphor throughout
a literary text in order to communicate something more
complex. We'll come back to this concept in future chapters.

GUIDED READING

In This Place (An American Lyric)
Amanda Gorman

Rob Carr/Getty Images

THE TEXT IN CONTEXT

The first official National Youth Poet Laureate
of the United States, Los Angeles–native
Amanda Gorman (b. 1998) is a writer and
activist who came to wide acclaim after she
performed her poem "The Hill We Climb" at the 2021 Presidential Inauguration ceremony.
Her books include *The One for Whom Food Is Not Enough* (2015), *Change Sings: A
Children's Anthem* (2021), and *Call Us What We Carry* (2021). She has also contributed
articles to publications such as the *New York Times* and *HuffPost*. Gorman often writes
about race, feminism, marginalization, and resilience, among other themes. In "In This
Place (An American Lyric)," she reflects on tragedy, protest, hope, and poetry in the
context of the United States, both past and present.

In This Place (An American Lyric)

There's a poem in this place—
in the footfalls in the halls
in the quiet beat of the seats.
It is here, at the curtain of day,
5 where America writes a lyric
you must whisper to say.

There's a poem in this place—
in the heavy grace,
the lined face of this noble building,
10 collections burned and reborn twice.

Guided Questions

1. This poem was
presented at the
inauguration of Poet
Laureate Tracy K.
Smith at the Library
of Congress. What
metaphor is being
introduced in the
opening lines of the
poem?

2. What characteristics
of subjects are
being transferred?

There's a poem in Boston's Copley Square
where protest chants
tear through the air
like sheets of rain,
15 where love of the many
swallows hatred of the few.

There's a poem in Charlottesville
where tiki torches string a ring of flame
tight round the wrist of night
20 where men so white they gleam blue—
seem like statues
where men heap that long wax burning
ever higher
where Heather Heyer
25 blooms forever in a meadow of resistance.

There's a poem in the great sleeping giant
of Lake Michigan, defiantly raising
its big blue head to Milwaukee and Chicago—
a poem begun long ago, blazed into frozen soil,
30 strutting upward and aglow.

There's a poem in Florida, in East Texas
where streets swell into a nexus
of rivers, cows afloat like mottled buoys in the brown,
where courage is now so common
35 that 23-year-old Jesus Contreras rescues people from floodwaters.

There's a poem in Los Angeles
yawning wide as the Pacific tide
where a single mother swelters
in a windowless classroom, teaching
40 black and brown students in Watts
to spell out their thoughts
so her daughter might write
this poem for you.

There's a lyric in California
45 where thousands of students march for blocks,
undocumented and unafraid;
where my friend Rosa finds the power to blossom
in deadlock, her spirit the bedrock of her community.
She knows hope is like a stubborn
50 ship gripping a dock,
a truth: that you can't stop a dreamer
or knock down a dream.

Guided Questions

3. What values are suggested by the comparisons to various locations in America?

4. How does this simile create a message about protest?

5. What is the simile and how does it connect to a message about the human experience?

6. Explain the comparison of Lake Michigan to a sleeping giant. How does this comparison contribute to an understanding of the poem?

7. How does the poet create an association within this metaphor?

8. How does this simile compare a concrete object with ideas about the human experience?

How could this not be her city
sunación
55 our country
our America,
our American lyric to write—
a poem by the people, the poor,
the Protestant, the Muslim, the Jew,
60 the native, the immigrant,
the black, the brown, the blind, the brave,
the undocumented and undeterred,
the woman, the man, the nonbinary,
the white, the trans,
65 the ally to all of the above
and more?

Tyrants fear the poet.
Now that we know it
we can't blow it.
70 We owe it
to show it
not slow it
although it
hurts to sew it.
75 when the world
skirts below it.

Hope—
we must bestow it
like a wick in the poet
80 so it can grow, lit,
bringing with it
stories to rewrite—
the story of a Texas city depleted but not defeated
a history written that need not be repeated
85 a nation composed but not yet completed.

There's a poem in this place—
a poem in America
a poet in every American
who rewrites this nation, who tells
90 a story worthy of being told on this minnow of an earth
to breathe hope into a palimpsest of time—
a poet in every American
who sees that our poem penned
doesn't mean our poem's end.

Guided Questions

9. In what way is the "American lyric" a metaphor, and what does it have to do with the list that follows?

10. What is the function of this comparison, and how does it contribute to the message of the poem?

95 There's a place where this poem dwells—
   it is here, it is now, in the yellow song of dawn's bell
   where we write an American lyric
   we are just beginning to tell.

Guided Questions

11. Explain the final comparison and how the metaphor contributes to your understanding of the poem.

PRACTICE TEXT

she being Brand
e.e. cummings

Bettmann/Getty Images

THE TEXT IN CONTEXT

Born in Cambridge, Massachusetts, Edward Estlin Cummings (1894–1962) began writing poems as a child. He received his BA and MA from Harvard University, where he not only discovered the work of avant-garde modernist writers like Ezra Pound and Gertrude Stein but also visual artists such as the French post-impressionist painter Paul Cezanne. Cummings's first collection of poems, *Tulips and Chimneys*, appeared in 1923. While many poems in the book followed conventional forms, others intro-duced readers to Cummings's idiosyncratic language, eccentric punctuation, and playful experiments with grammar. His more experimental 1926 collection *is 5* included the fol-lowing poem, which creates an elaborate extended comparison.

 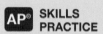 | FIGURATIVE LANGUAGE
Explaining the Function of Comparisons

As you read the following poem by e.e. cummings, use the graphic organizer to record details from the poem of the comparison in the poem. Explain the signifi-cance of each aspect of the traits being compared.

Analyzing Metaphorical Comparisons

Considerations

• Which two objects are being compared in a particular metaphor?
• What are the particular traits and characteristics being compared?
• What is significant about the selection of the objects being compared?

- How does a comparison through a metaphor contribute to meaning in the text?
- How might the figurative meaning of a metaphor depend on the context in which it is presented?
- How does a metaphorical comparison contribute to the figurative meaning of a character, conflict, setting, theme, etc.?

Metaphorical Object	Idea of Human Experience	Significance of Comparison

she being Brand

she being Brand
-new;and you
know consequently a
little stiff i was
5 careful of her and(having

thoroughly oiled the universal
joint tested my gas felt of
her radiator made sure her springs were O.

K.)i went right to it flooded-the-carburetor cranked her

10 up,slipped the
clutch(and then somehow got into reverse she
kicked what

the hell)next
minute i was back in neutral tried and

15   again slo-wly;bare,ly nudg. ing(my

lev-er Right-
oh and her gears being in
A 1 shape passed
from low through
20   second-in-to-high like
greasedlightning)just as we turned the corner of Divinity

avenue i touched the accelerator and give

her the juice,good

(it

25   was the first ride and believe i we was
happy to see how nice she acted right up to
the last minute coming back down by the Public
Gardens i slammed on

the
30   internalexpanding
&
externalcontracting
brakes Bothatonce and

brought allofher tremB
35   -ling
to a:dead.

stand-
;Still)

FIGURATIVE LANGUAGE: Comparisons

1. The poem uses a **metaphor** to make a comparison. What two things are being compared?

2. What characteristics are shared by both objects of **comparison**?

3. Why does e.e. cummings use the comparisons he does, and what **associations** can we make through the figurative comparisons?

IDEAS IN LITERATURE
Thought and Feeling

The transition from the medieval period to the Renaissance in England (and Europe) was a complex political, social, economic, religious, and cultural process that occurred over two centuries. In fact, no one living at that time would have used *renaissance* — a French word meaning "rebirth" — to describe the era: nineteenth-century historians first applied the term to the period. But the idea of a rebirth captures many elements integral to this revival of Greek and Roman classical culture — and the subsequent flowering of art, science, literature, philosophy, politics, and music.

In a sense, the Renaissance shifted Western culture from being institutionally centered (especially the institutions of the church and monarchy) to being more human-centered. We can see the implications of this humanism in the Protestant reformation that was underway throughout Europe. In England, King Henry VIII (1491–1547) broke away from the authority of the Catholic Church when the Pope denied him a divorce. But a more important change was already occurring. Protestants (i.e., Puritans, Calvinists, Quakers, and others) argued that individuals had a personal, intellectual, and emotional relationship with God: a faith rooted in "knowing" God through their own individual experiences, rather than a faith mediated by the Catholic Church — an institution that Protestants viewed as corrupt. Certainly, the first English translations of the Bible — the Geneva Bible in 1560 and the King James Bible in 1611 — nurtured this view. For the first time, an increasingly literate public could interpret the word of God on their own.

But the consequences of humanism went far beyond religion. In contrast to the medieval period, when authority emanated solely from the church and the divinely ordained king, the Renaissance saw the emergence of a new authority: individual experience, perception, and judgment. In England, for example, the philosopher,

IDEA BANK

Beauty
Carpe Diem
Continuity
Culture
Desire
Exaggeration
Feelings
Humanism
Inquiry
Learning
Love
Passion
Reformation
Renaissance
Thought
Transformation
Wonder

The Last Supper, 1495-97 (tempera and oil on plaster)/Vinci, Leonardo da (1452-1519)/MAURO RANZANI (IMAGINART)/ Santa Maria delle Grazie, Milan, Italy/Bridgeman Images

◀ *The Last Supper*, Leonardo da Vinci, 1495. The painting covers an end wall of the dining hall at the monastery of Santa Maria delle Grazie in Milan, Italy.

How does this painting reflect the spirit of the Renaissance period?

147

statesman, and scientist Francis Bacon (1561–1626) advocated a scientific process based on the observation of nature followed by inductive reasoning about the observations. While it may sound obvious now, this empiricism — the revolutionary idea that knowledge comes from our sensory experiences — forms the basis of the modern scientific method.

If Francis Bacon embodied these Renaissance ideals, so did the English poet, clergyman, scholar, soldier, and politician John Donne (1572–1631). While Donne's poetry explores powerful emotional responses to love, death, sex, faith, and other universal themes, it does so with irony, dazzling wit, and elaborate metaphysical conceits (i.e., comparisons) that highlight his intellectual sophistication. Indeed, twentieth-century modernist writers such as T. S. Eliot revered Donne and other "metaphysical poets" of this era for their ability to express both complex thoughts and emotions simultaneously. We can see this skill on display in Donne's famous poem "A Valediction: Forbidding Mourning" (p. 149).

Today writers and artists continue to draw upon the power of metaphor. Pop icons such as Taylor Swift, Kendrick Lamar, Nicki Minaj, and others use concrete and familiar objects to make comparisons to complex human emotions.

The Thinker statue is located on the grounds of the Musee Rodin, Paris.

What qualities or characteristics could this statue represent to both its original Renaissance audience and to contemporary viewers?

davidf/iStock/Getty Images

A Valediction: Forbidding Mourning

John Donne

THE TEXT IN CONTEXT

English poet John Donne (1572–1631) had a varied career as a scholar, lawyer, member of Parliament, and Anglican priest. But he is best-known as a major "metaphysical poet" of the sixteenth and seventeenth centuries, along with Andrew Marvell, George Herbert, and several others. The poet John Dryden later coined the term to describe the striking style and subjects of his immediate predecessors. In contrast to the sweet and smooth cadences of poetry in the previous century, Donne's verse is rough, energetic, and striking; where earlier poets used more obvious metaphors and similes, Donne's comparisons are clever, surprising, and intellectually demanding — making comparisons between human emotions and the natural world. This was true of other metaphysical poets as well, who, like Donne, incorporated irony and paradox into their work. These stylistic elements matched the poets' themes, which ranged from love and sexuality to mortality and the individual's relationship with God. The following poem provides a good example of a "metaphysical conceit": an elaborate extended metaphor.

A Valediction: Forbidding Mourning

As virtuous men pass mildly away,
   And whisper to their souls to go,
Whilst some of their sad friends do say
   The breath goes now, and some say, No:

5 So let us melt, and make no noise,
   No tear-floods, nor sigh-tempests move;
'Twere profanation of our joys
   To tell the laity our love.

Moving of th' earth brings harms and fears,
10   Men reckon what it did, and meant;
But trepidation of the spheres,
   Though greater far, is innocent.

Dull sublunary lovers' love
   (Whose soul is sense) cannot admit

15 Absence, because it doth remove
  Those things which elemented it.

But we by a love so much refined,
  That our selves know not what it is,
Inter-assured of the mind,20
20 Care less, eyes, lips, and hands to miss.

Our two souls therefore, which are one,
  Though I must go, endure not yet
A breach, but an expansion,
  Like gold to airy thinness beat.25

25 If they be two, they are two so
  As stiff twin compasses are two;
Thy soul, the fixed foot, makes no show
  To move, but doth, if the other do.

And though it in the center sit,30
30 Yet when the other far doth roam,
It leans and hearkens after it,
  And grows erect, as that comes home.

Such wilt thou be to me, who must,
  Like th' other foot, obliquely run;35
35 Thy firmness makes my circle just,
  And makes me end where I begun.

The photograph by Chandan Chakraborty shows the compass at work.

What do circles represent to you? How can a circle translate to a human experience?

Chandan Chakraborty/EyeEm/Getty Images

CHARACTER

1. Who is the **speaker**? What do the details in the first stanza reveal about beliefs, values, and cultural norms of the speaker's culture?

2. The **speaker** reveals a relationship in the poem. What is that relationship? How does it contribute to the poem's meaning?

3. How does the **speaker's** action contribute to your interpretation of the poem?

STRUCTURE

4. How does the first **stanza** create a larger context for understanding this poem?

5. How does the speaker's relationship to the events of the poem contribute to the **conflict** of the poem?

6. How does the sequencing of events in "A Valediction: Forbidding Mourning" contribute to the experience of reading the poem?

FIGURATIVE LANGUAGE: Word Choice, Imagery, and Symbols

7. How do the **pronouns** and their **antecedents** further develop the relationship between the speaker and the subject of the poem?

8. How do the speaker's words and phrases create **ambiguous** meanings? Point to a specific example that invites multiple interpretations.

FIGURATIVE LANGUAGE: Comparisons

9. Stanza three introduces a **comparison**. What objects or concepts are being compared? How does the comparison contribute to the meaning of the poem?

10. The **simile** in stanza six compares two objects. What are they? How does the comparison contribute to the message of the poem?

IDEAS IN LITERATURE: Thought and Feeling

11. The speaker claims that he and his beloved share a "love so much refined / That our selves know not what it is / Inter-assured of the mind." How do these lines capture both the thought and the feeling of the speaker? How does this characterization combine both emotion and logic to resolve the tension in the poem?

PUTTING IT ALL TOGETHER

12. Donne introduces a conceit in the poem — that is, an extended metaphor between objects or concepts that seem very different. What is the conceit? What is being compared? How does this comparison contribute to the reader's understanding?

Deer Hit

Jon Loomis

Allyson Goldin Loomis

THE TEXT IN CONTEXT

Jon Loomis (b. 1959) grew up in Athens, Ohio, in the
Appalachian Mountains. As a writer, Loomis is both a novelist
and poet. All three of his novels are mysteries set in Provinc-
etown, Massachusetts. Additionally, he has published three
books of poetry. His second book of poetry, *The Pleasure
Principle* (2001), includes the poem printed here, "Deer Hit." The
poem is a narrative written in the second person present tense,
but it recounts an incident in the past. The action begins and
ends with violent imagery.

Deer Hit

You're seventeen and tunnel-vision drunk,
swerving your father's Fairlane wagon home

at 3:00 a.m. Two-lane road, all curves
and dips—dark woods, a stream, a patchy acre

5 of teazle and grass. You don't see the deer
till they turn their heads—road full of eyeballs,

small moons glowing. You crank the wheel,
stamp both feet on the brake, skid and jolt

into the ditch. Glitter and crunch of broken glass
10 in your lap, deer hair drifting like dust. Your chin

and shirt are soaked—one eye half-obscured
by the cocked bridge of your nose. The car

still running, its lights angled up at the trees.
You get out. The deer lies on its side.

15 A doe, spinning itself around
in a frantic circle, front legs scrambling,

back legs paralyzed, dead. Making a sound—
again and again this terrible bleat.

You watch for a while. It tires, lies still.
20 And here's what you do: pick the deer up

like a bride. Wrestle it into the back of the car—
the seat folded down. Somehow, you steer

the wagon out of the ditch and head home,
night rushing in through the broken window,

25 headlight dangling, side-mirror gone.
Your nose throbs, something stabs

in your side. The deer breathing behind you,
shallow and fast. A stoplight, you're almost home

and the deer scrambles to life, its long head
30 appears like a ghost in the rearview mirror

and bites you, its teeth clamp down on your shoulder
and maybe you scream, you struggle and flail

till the deer, exhausted, lets go and lies down.

Your father's waiting up, watching tv.
35 He's had a few drinks and he's angry.

Christ, he says, when you let yourself in.
It's Night of the Living Dead. You tell him

some of what happened: the dark road,
the deer you couldn't avoid. Outside, he circles

40 the car. Jesus, he says. A long silence.
Son of a bitch, looking in. He opens the tailgate,

drags the quivering deer out by a leg.
What can you tell him—you weren't thinking,

you'd injured your head? You wanted to fix
45 what you'd broken—restore the beautiful body,

color of wet straw, color of oak leaves in winter?
The deer shudders and bleats in the driveway.

Your father walks to the toolshed,
comes back lugging a concrete block.

50 Some things stay with you. Dumping the body
deep in the woods, like a gangster. The dent

in your nose. All your life, the trail of ruin you leave.

The image shows a young boy illustrating the size of a fish he caught on a recent fishing trip. In retellings and reflections, stories may become exaggerated or even larger than life.

Steven Gottlieb/Corbis Historical/Getty Images

———

Consider events in life that have had a significant impact. How do stories allow us to share thoughts and feelings?

CHARACTER

1. Who is the primary **speaker** of "Deer Hit"? How does this particular **perspective** contribute to the meaning of the poem?

2. What details are revealed about the **speaker's** knowledge of the past? How do they affect your interpretation of the poem?

3. How does the **speaker** describe the surroundings and the events of the poem? How does this description contribute to the tone of the text?

STRUCTURE

4. Choose one example of a **contrast** in the poem, and then explain how that contrast contributes to the poem's dramatic situation.

5. Explain how the poem ends. What is the **resolution** of its **conflict** or tension?

FIGURATIVE LANGUAGE: Word Choice, Imagery, and Symbols

6. Identify and explain the use of **repetition** throughout the poem. What effect does this repetition have in "Deer Hit"?

7. The poem is filled with **antecedents** (nouns) with ambiguous referents. How does the poet's use of pronouns affect your interpretation of the poem?

FIGURATIVE LANGUAGE: Comparisons

8. The speaker uses **similes** to make comparisons. Explain what is being compared in the first two-thirds of the poem.

9. Consider the **simile** in the last stanza. How does this comparison reveal a change in the speaker's perspective?

10. This poem expresses thoughts and feelings about an emotional experience
    for the speaker. In your view, how do thoughts and feelings about experiences
    evolve and shift over time? Does the passage of time bring more insight, or less?

PUTTING IT ALL TOGETHER

11. Explain how the poem's speaker and the structure work together to achieve a
    tone and reveal an interpretation of the poem.

Fatima, the Biloquist: A Transformation Story
Nafissa Thompson-Spires

Roberto Ricciuti/Getty Images

THE TEXT IN CONTEXT

Thoughtful, witty, and ingenious, Nafissa
Thompson-Spires (b. 1983) has emerged as
one of the most perceptive writers about identity and race in contemporary literature.
Her stylish debut short story collection, *Heads of the Colored People* (2018), explores
the lives — and challenges — of various African American characters as they seek to
connect with others and discover their own identities. Thompson-Spires is currently
an assistant professor at Cornell University. Her award-winning stories and nonfiction
have appeared in *The Paris Review Daily*, *The Root*, *Buzzfeed Books*, the *Los Angeles
Review of Books Quarterly Journal*, and many other places. The following excerpt from
Heads of the Colored People provides an excellent introduction to her inventive fiction.

   Content Note: This story includes the N-word, which we have chosen to reprint
in this textbook to accurately reflect Thompson-Spires's original intent as well as
the culture depicted in the story. We recognize that this word has a long history as a
disrespectful and deeply hurtful expression when used by white people toward
Black people. Thompson-Spires's choice to use this word relates not only to that
history but also to a larger cultural tradition in which the N-word can take on different
meanings, emphasize shared experience, and be repurposed as a term of endearment
within Black communities. While the use of that word in the context of this story might
not be hurtful, the use of it in our current context very often is. Be mindful of context,
both the author's and yours, as you read and discuss "Fatima, the Biloquist: A
Transformation Story."

Fatima, the Biloquist: A Transformation Story

In the '90s you could be whatever you wanted—someone said that on the news—and by 1998 Fatima felt ready to become black, full black, baa baa black sheep
5 black, black like the elbows and knees on praying folk black, if only someone would teach her.

Up to that point, she had existed like a sort of colorless gas, or a bit of moisture,
10 leaving the residue of something familiar, sweat stains, hot breath on the back of a neck, condensation rings on wood, but never a fullness of whatever matter had formed them.

15 The week she met Violet, Fatima had recited "An Address to the Ladies, by their Best Friend Sincerity" before her eleventh-grade AP English class. She blended her makeup to perfection that morning, but the
20 other students barely looked at her, instead busying themselves by clicking and replacing the lead in mechanical pencils or folding and flicking paper footballs over finger goalposts—even during the part she said
25 with the most emphasis: "Ah! sad, perverse, degenerate race / The monstrous head deforms the face." They clapped dull palms for a few seconds as Fatima sulked back to her desk. But they sat up, alert, when Wally
30 "the Wigger" Arnett recited "Incident" and said the word that always made the white kids pay attention.

"You know, I identify with Countee Cullen and all," Wally, with brown freckles and a
35 floppy brown haircut, finished up. "He was a black man, and he was, like, oppressed for who he was and stuff."

The hands pounded a hero's applause as Wally headed back to his seat next to Fatima,
40 looking like he expected a high five. She rolled her eyes at him, but she couldn't articulate her wrath into something more specific. Later in the morning when Wally asked her for the fourth time that semester
45 whether she listened to No Limit rappers, she nearly lunged at his face. Mrs. Baker sent her to the principal to "cool down" before Fatima's fingernails could scratch off any of Wally's freckles.

50 It wasn't fair, Fatima thought, that Wally was praised, even mildly popular for his FUBU shirts and Jordans with the tags still on them, yet Fatima was called "ghetto supastar" the one time she outlined her lips
55 with dark pencil. Nor was it fair that she should get a warning from Principal Lee for "looking like she might become violent" when Wally said "nigger" and got applause. She was still thinking about Wally when she
60 first encountered Violet.

They met at the Montclair Plaza, where Fatima had been dropped off by her mother, Monica, along with the warnings that she better not: 1. spend more than she had, 2.
65 use her emergency credit card for non-emergencies, or 3. pick up any riffraff, ruffnecks, or pregnancies while she was there. Number three was highly unlikely—and Fatima knew Monica knew it—but she
70 said it anyway as easily as "stand up straight," because she had to.

Fatima moped near the Clinique counter with her heavy Discman tucked in a tiny backpack and her headphones wrapped
75 around her neck, trying to decide between one shade of lipstick and another. The college student behind the counter ignored her, chatting with another colleague. In situations like this, Fatima usually bought
80 something expensive just to show the store clerk that she could. A blonde girl with a short bob sauntered up next to her and said,

"The burgundy is pretty, but you could do something darker."

Fatima peripherally saw the hair first, so she didn't expect the rest of the package. A voluptuous—really, that was the only word that would work—girl with a wide nose and black features stood next to her. Fatima had a friend with albinism before in preschool who wore thick red glasses and blushed almost the same color when she wet her pants at nap time once. She recognized in Violet similar features.

"But you could get the same stuff at Claire's for cheaper," Violet said. "It's not like old girl's trying to help you anyway."

The clerk, not chastened but amused, moved back to her post and said, "May I help you" in one of those voices that means "get lost."

"I'm still—" Fatima started.

But the blonde girl spoke again, "We'd like some free samples of some of the lipsticks, that color," she pointed, reaching over Fatima, to a pot of dark gloss, "and that one."

"We only give samples," the clerk said, "to—."

"To everyone who asks, right?" Violet finished.

The clerk frowned, looked back at her colleague, looked at Violet and Fatima, and frowned again. "I'll get those ready for you," she said.

Fatima considered putting her headphones back on and trying to float out of the department store, away from this loud girl with the jarring features and booming voice.

"Here," Violet said, handing her the dark gloss in its tiny gloss pot.

"You keep it," Fatima said and started trying to vaporize towards the shoe department.

"It's for you," the girl said, following her.

And like that, they were friends—or something to that effect.

• • •

It was Violet's appraisal, "You're, like, totally a white girl, aren't you?" that set Fatima into motion. They were eating dots of ice cream that same day at the food court after Violet showed Fatima how to get samples from Estée Lauder, Elizabeth Arden, and MAC. Fatima felt a little like a gangster holding up the reluctant sales girls for their stash, but she had a nearly full bag of swag by then—perfume, lip-gloss, and oil-blotting papers—without spending any of her allowance. It was already too good to be true, so she didn't feel sad when Violet said "white girl," but almost relieved by the inevitable.

Fatima had been accused of whiteness and race traitorism before, whenever she spoke up in Sunday school at her AME church or visited her family in Southeast San Diego (Southeast a universal geographical marker for the ghetto), or when a cute guy who was just about to ask her out backed away saying, "You go to private school, don't you?" It was why she didn't have any black friends—and why, she worried, she would never have a boyfriend, even a riffraff, to upset her mother.

The allegations upset her but never moved her to any action other than private crying or retreating further into her melancholy belief that her school, Westwood Prep, and her parents' high-paying jobs had made her somehow unfit for black people. She usually turned her Discman up louder, sinking into the distantly black but presently white sounds of ska and punk, and sang under her breath, "I'm a freak / I'm a freak" (in the style of Silverchair, not Rick James).

165 At the moment she was especially into listening to Daniel Johns whine, reading
Charles Brockden Brown, and daydreaming
of a sickly boyfriend like Arthur Mervyn, for
reasons limited omniscience can't or won't
170 explain. If black people wouldn't accept her,
she would stick to what she knew.

But Violet's judgment held more heft in
her critique—a possibility for transformation. When a black girl with natural green
175 eyes and blonde hair and a big chest and
bubble butt that wiggle independently of
each other tells you that you, with your sable
skin and dark hair, are not black enough,
sometimes you listen.

180 "It's not that I'm trying to be white. It's
just that's what I'm around."

"You don't have no church friends? You
adopted? Your parents white, too?" Violet
didn't seem to want a response. "Where do
185 you stay?"

"With my parents," Fatima wondered if
something was wrong with Violet for asking
such a stupid question.

"I mean where do you live?" Violet said.
190 "Upland," Fatima said.

"They got black people there. My cousin
Frankie lives there," Violet said, chewing the
dots of ice cream in a way that upset
Fatima's teeth. Violet wore a tight white
195 top, cream Dickies, and white Adidas
tennis shoes.

"Yes, but not on my street." Fatima wore a
pink cardigan, black Dickies, and skater
shoes, Kastels.

200 Violet paused her crunching and talking
for a moment. "You have a boyfriend?"

Fatima shook her head. "Do you?"

"I'm in between options right now. Anyway the last one is locked up in Tehachapi."

205 Fatima nodded. She had a cousin who had
served time there. He called her bourgie, and

she kicked him in the face once, delighting in
his fat lip and his inability to hit girls who
weren't his girlfriend or baby mama.

210 "I'm kidding," Violet said. "We don't all get
locked up."

Fatima stuttered.

"I can see I'ma have to teach you a lot of
things. You ready?" Violet meant ready to
215 leave the food court, but Fatima meant more
when she said, "Yeah, I'm ready." And thus
began her transformation.

• • •

If only Baratunde Thurston had been writing
when Fatima came of age, she could have
220 learned how to be black from a book instead
of from Violet's charm school. Even a quick
glance at Ellison could have saved her a lot of
trouble, but she wasn't ready for that, caught
up, as she was, in the dramas of Arthur
225 Mervyn and Carwin the Biloquist and all of
them. With Violet's help, Fatima absorbed the
sociocultural knowledge she'd missed, not
through osmosis or through more relevant
literature, but through committed, structured
230 ethnographical study.

She immersed herself in slang as rigor-
ously as she would later immerse herself in
Spanish for her foreign language exam in
grad school; she pored over *VIBE Magazine*
235 and watched *Yo MTV Raps* and *The Parkers*,
trying to turn her mouth around phrases
with the same intonation that Countess
Vaughn used—a sort of combination of a
Jersey accent and a speech impediment.
240 When she couldn't get into those texts, she
encouraged herself with old episodes of
Fresh Prince that played in constant
early-morning and late-afternoon rotation,
feeling assured that if Ashley Banks could,
245 after five seasons, become almost as cool as
Will, then she could, too. Her new turns of

phrase fit her about as bulkily as the puffy
powder-blue FUBU jacket she found in a
thrift store in downtown Rialto.

250 Still, she was happy when Violet looked
approvingly at it. Pale Violet became the
arbiter of Fatima's blackness, the purveyor of
all things authentic. Though she was barely
5'1 and chunky by most standards—nearly
255 obese by Fatima's—you would think Violet
was Pamela Anderson, the way she walked,
like a hula doll on a dashboard swinging hips
and breasts.

She lived in Fontana, and the distance
260 between their respective houses was fifteen
minutes, but only seven if they met halfway,
Fatima borrowing her father's alternate car
(the 1993 Beamer, so as not to look ostentatious) and Violet getting a ride from one of
265 her brothers or occasionally driving her
mother's old Taurus. They never met at each
other's houses, lest Fatima's upper-middle
opulence embarrass Violet, and because
there was no space for Violet to carve out for
270 herself at her house.

Violet made Fatima a study guide of
the top-ten black expressions for rating
attractive men, and they worked over the
pronunciations together.

275 1. Foine
2. *Dang* Foine
3. Hella Foine
4. Bout it, bout it [as in "Oooh, he bout it,
bout it." This phrase especially required
280 the Countess Vaughn intonation and
often included spontaneous bouts of raising the roof].
5. Hot Diggity, said with a scowl
6. Dizam!
285 7. Hot Diggity Dizam
8. Ooh, hurt me, hurt me
9. Phat
10. Ooohw*eee*

Fatima's suggestions that "Heavens to
290 Murgatroid" and "Oh my gosh, he is *so* hot"
be added to the list as numbers 11 and 12
respectively, were met with a frown and a
threat from Violet that she would revoke
Fatima's study-guide privileges if she
295 persisted with lame interjections. Fatima
stifled her joke about the rain in Spain falling
mostly on the plains and practiced on,
assured that Violet's tutelage would confer
upon her, like Carwin, "a wonderful gift" of
300 biloquism.

Glossaries soon followed.

1. Hella = a more intense "hecka"
2. Hecka = a lot / really; Fatima preferred
this to "hella."
305 3. Fisshow = for sure, or as Fatima used to
pronounce it, fer shure.
4. Crunk = crazy, as in "we bout to get crunk
up in here." [Fatima already knew what
this meant from an *N'Sync chatroom,
310 where she lurked while girls discussed
Justin Timberlake's frequent use of the
term.]
5. A grip = a lot, as in "I just found a grip of
marshmallows in the cupboard."
315 6. Peeps = those cute little marshmallows
and also people / folks
7. Whoadie = ? [Violet wasn't sure either, but
you were supposed to say it.]
8. Shawty = like, your girl, or your boo
320 9. Boo = your shawty or your girl
10. Playa = One who gets a lot of women
or men [Fatima thought this was a beach,
at first].
11. Playahata = Wally the Wigger
325 12. **Nigga = [a word Fatima could not bring
herself to say or embrace, no matter how
much Violet, *VIBE*, or others insisted that
it was positive, or reappropriated.]
13. *Gangsta = cool. But also gangster, as in
330 "You's a gangsta / No I'm not / You's a

gangsta / No I'm not / You's a gangsta."
[Not as in "So You Wanna Be a Gangsta"
from *Bugsy Malone*, which Fatima and her
younger brother and sister used to sing
335 around the house.]

14. Ride or Die = a friend who's down for
anything and will stand up for your cause,
even unto death.

"So basically," Fatima summarized, "you
340 want me to turn good things into bad things
and vice versa."

Violet said, "Mostly."

Fatima tried pumping her shoulders in a
brief Bankhead Bounce, but it was obvious
345 she lacked the follow-through and wasn't
ready for dancing yet.

And it was almost like any romantic
comedy where the sassy black person
moves in with the white people and
350 teaches them how to live their lives in
color and put some bass in their voices,
only Steve Martin wasn't in it, no one was a
maid or a butler or nanny, and the romance
was between two girls, it was platonic, and
355 they were both black this time, but one
didn't look like it, and one didn't sound like
it consistently.

● ● ●

"They racist up at that school? I can't stand
cocky white people," Violet said one day
360 while they sat at their usual table, near the
flower divider in the mall's arboretum. Some
white guys from Hillwood sat across the way,
laughing loudly.

Fatima didn't like to talk about her
365 school, but everyone in the Inland Empire
knew Westwood and Hillwood, their analog
and football rival. "I don't think so," Fatima
said.

"What do you mean you don't think so?
370 Either something's racist or it's not."

No one at school poked out his tongue
and called her *that*, like they did in the poem
Wally read, but Fatima thought about Wally,
his affectations, and Principal Lee.

375 "It's not always comfortable," she said. "It
can be real awkward, but I'm awkward."

"You sure are," Violet laughed, and Fatima
laughed, too. She was learning to do more of
that, and to wear a kind of self-assuredness
380 with her side-swooped Aaliyah bangs.

Even with her usual levels of discomfort
in place, most interactions were easier with
Violet. Violet understood things. When she
told Violet, for example, the history of her
385 name and how its spirit hovered over Fatima
like Jiminy Cricket or a mirror of unholiness—
even without an accent or an "h," wedging
her between two religious worlds, both
agreeing on her need for chastity and
390 immaculate conduct—Violet said, "Word,
that's deep," and explained that she, too, felt
the weight of her name, because the Johnson
family was all single moms and dads with
eight kids and three jobs and no peace, and
395 she couldn't end up like her mother, even if
it meant she had to run away and start a
new identity one day.

Violet confided that, despite her
confidence, she had a complex about
400 her albinism. She could call other black people like Fatima white, but to be called white
herself pushed Violet to violent tears. Just
ask her ex-boyfriend and her ex-friend
Kandice from middle school, who had called
405 her Patty Mayonnaise in a fit of anger and
gotten a beatdown that made her wet her
pants like Fatima's preschool friend.

"Why Patty Mayonnaise?" Fatima said.

"You know, from *Doug*; she was the black
410 girl on the DL who looked white, and
mayonnaise is white. It's a stupid joke."

"Patty was black?" Fatima said.

"Girl, a whole lot of everybody got black in them," Violet started.

415 Fatima had heard some of Violet's theories before. It was a game they played sometimes on the phone. The list included Jennifer Beals, Mariah Carey, and "that freaky girl from *Wild Things*," Denise Richards, and now

420 apparently, Patty Mayonnaise. When Fatima suggested Justin Timberlake, Violet said, "Nah, he's like that Wally kid at your school."

The nuances of these and other things Fatima's best friend since first grade, Emily,

425 just couldn't understand, no matter how earnestly Emily tried or how many questions she asked, like why they couldn't share shampoo when she slept over, "What does 'for us, by us' mean," and why Fatima's top lip

430 was darker than her bottom one.

Fatima picked up some theories on her own, too, without Violet or the literature. The thing about the brown top lip and the pink lower one, Fatima had learned after moving

435 between Violet's guidance and her school life, was that you could either read them as two souls trying to merge into a better self, or you could hide them under makeup and talk with whichever lip was convenient for

440 the occasion. At school and with Emily, she talked with her pink lip, and with Violet, she talked with her brown one, and that only created tension if she thought too much about it.

445 Fatima passed the time at school by imagining the time she would spend after school with Violet, who promised to teach her how to flirt better on their next excursion and to possibly, eventually, hook her up with one of

450 her cousins, but not one of her brothers, because "most of them aren't good for anything except upsetting your mother, if you want to do that." Fatima did not want to do that.

455 Now at school when Wally the Wigger looked like he was even thinking about saying something to her, Fatima made a face that warned, "Don't even look like you're thinking about saying something to me," and

460 he obeyed. In her mind, she not only said this aloud, but said it in Violet's voice.

She didn't mind the laughter in her parents' eyes when she tried out a new phrase or hairstyle, because it was all work-

465 ing. There was something prettier about her now, too, and people seemed to see it before Fatima did, because a guy named Rolf at Westwood—a tall brunette in her history class, with whom she'd exchanged a few eye

470 rolls over Wally—asked her for her phone number.

Without pausing to consider anything, she gave it to him.

It might seem, up to this point, that

475 Fatima simultaneously wore braces, glasses, and forehead acne, when you hardly needed to glance to see the gloss of her black hair or the sheen on her shins, with or without lotion. Fatima knew this truth instinctively,

480 but buried its warmth under the shame of early childhood teasing and a preference for melancholy self-pity. It was more romantic to feel ugly, modest to pretend she couldn't hold her head just right, unleash her

485 beautiful teeth and make a skeptical man kneel at her skirt's hem. She just didn't have the practice, but she was hopeful that she might get it, with Rolf or one of Violet's cousins, hopeful that the transformation had

490 taken hold.

• • •

She had just returned from a movie with Violet—where in the space in front of the theater, not one but two guys had asked for her phone number, though three had asked

495 for Violet's, pronouncing their approval of
her "thickness" with grunts, smiles, and by
looking directly at her butt—when her
mother said, "You got a phone call, from
a boy."

500   It couldn't be one of the boys from theater
already; that would make anyone look
desperate.

"Who is Rolf?" her mother smiled, "and
why didn't you mention him before?"

505   Fatima nearly floated up to her bedroom.
She thought about calling Violet but called
Rolf back instead, waiting the appropriate
hour she had rehearsed with Violet for a
hypothetical situation such as this.

510   By now, and with some authenticity,
Fatima could intone the accent marks in
places they hadn't been before, recite all the
names of all the members of Cash Money,
Bad Boy, No Limit, Wu-Tang, Boyz II Men,
515 ABC, BBD, ODB, LDB, TLC, B.I.G., P-O, P-P-A,
Ronny, Bobby, Ricky, Mike, Johnny, Ralph,
Tony, Toni, and Tone, if she wanted. But when
she called Rolf, all they talked about were
skateboards and the Smiths, in whose music
520 Fatima had dabbled before Violet.

"The Smiths are way better than Morrissey,"
Rolf said. His voice was nasal but deep.
Fatima imagined that he was at least 6'7,
though she hadn't stood next to him yet.
525 When she did, he was 6'1.

"You can barely tell the difference since
Morrissey's voice is so overpowering," she
said with her pink lip.

"No, but The Smiths' stuff is way darker,"
530 Rolf said. "You should hear the first album.
Then you'll get it. I've got it on vinyl."

"Okay," Fatima waited.

She noticed that he didn't invite her
over to listen or offer to lend her the
535 album, but he did call back two days later

and ask if she wanted to hang out over the
weekend, "like at the mall or something,
see a movie?"

Fatima counted to twelve, as per the rules
540 (the universal ones, not just Violet's) and
said, "Yeah, that'd be cool." She almost left
the "l" off the end of the word, but caught
herself. "Which mall?"

"Where else?" Rolf said. "The Montclair
545 Plaza."

This would be her first date, and though
that was the kind of thing to share with a
best friend, especially one with more experience, Fatima felt—in some deep way that
550 hurt her stomach—that Violet didn't need to
know about Rolf, not yet at least. She would
keep her lips glossed and parted, her two
worlds separate.

• • •

The week leading up to the date, Fatima tried
555 to play extra cool, asking Violet more questions than usual when they spoke on the
phone. Neither of the guys from the movie
theater had called Fatima, but one of Violet's
three had asked Violet out, and she was
560 "letting him stew for a while before I let him
know. Anyway, we're supposed to check out
Rush Hour this weekend."

"This weekend?" Fatima said.

"This weekend."

565   "I told my parents I would babysit this
weekend, I forgot," Fatima lied, feeling a bit
like a grease stain on a silk shirt.

"Since when?" Violet pushed.

"We can go next weekend, or during
570 the week," Fatima said, and changed the
subject.

Before they got off the phone, Violet said,
"I guess I'll call Mike back then, and tell him
I'm free after all."

• • •

575 Fatima wasn't embarrassed of Violet or of Rolf, but she wasn't good at managing. She was relieved, then, when their first and second dates went without a hitch—and ended with a gentle but sort of blank kiss—and 580 even more relieved that Rolf was okay with seeing each other during the week so that Fatima wouldn't have to explain to Violet why she suddenly had other plans on Fridays and Saturdays.

585 "Tell me more about your other friends," Rolf had said on the phone one night, when Fatima was starting to think she might love him. He knew Emily from school, and he knew about her family and had met her par-590 ents and siblings by then, though she still hadn't met his. He knew she went to an AME church. He knew she was black.

"I guess my other best friend, besides Em, is Violet," Fatima said.

595 "Violet," Rolf repeated. "Cool name. She's not at Westwood, is she?"

"No, public school."

"Ah," Rolf said, in a tone which Fatima interpreted as neutral.

600 "She's my girl." She stopped herself from saying Ace boon coon. "We hang out a lot on the weekends, actually."

"How come you never mentioned her before?"

605 "I don't know," Fatima felt her mouth lying again, moving somehow separately from her real voice. "She's kind of shy. She got teased a lot."

"Oh, that's too bad," Rolf said.

610 "They called her Patty Mayonnaise," Fatima said, and she didn't know why she was still talking.

"Don't tell anybody this, but I always thought Patty was cute on *Doug*," Rolf said 615 and shifted to talking about all of his favorite cartoons. Fatima exhaled.

Over time they grew to joke, a little awkwardly, about Fatima's position at school, as one of two black girls. She asked Rolf if 620 this was a thing for him or if she was his first black girlfriend, because they had labels by now.

"I don't see color," he said. "I just saw you. Like, one day there you were."

625 Violet would say that colorblind people were the same ones who followed you in the store and that Rolf's game was hella corny. Fatima remembered the lifelessness, before Violet, of feeling like a colorless gas and 630 tried, in spite of a dull ache, to take Rolf's words as a compliment.

• • •

The conventions of such a transformation dictate that a snaggletooth, broken heel, or some other inconvenience 635 threatens to throw the recently realized heroine back to her former life. That snaggletooth, for Fatima, was either Rolf or Violet, depending on how you looked at things, and Fatima wasn't sure 640 how she did.

When she saw Violet, on April 4th—after hiding her relationship with Rolf for three months—approaching from across the Lobby of Edwards Cinema with Mike's arm 645 around her waist, Fatima's first instinct was to grab Rolf's hand and steer him towards the exit. But Violet was already calling her name.

This wasn't the natural order of things, for 650 these separate lives to converge. Other factors aside, the code went hos before bros, school life before social life, family before anyone else. But Rolf was both school and social, and Violet both social and nearly fam-655 ily, and Fatima's math skills couldn't balance this equation.

"I knew I saw you," Violet said to Fatima once she got close. "Who is this?"

"Rolf, Violet. Violet, Rolf," Fatima said, "and
660 Mike."

Mike smiled, and Rolf smiled, and they shook hands, but neither young woman saw the guys, their eyes deadlocked on each other.

665 "Ha, so this is Violet," Rolf said, ignoring or misreading Fatima's firm grip on his arm. "Even your black friends are white, too," Rolf laughed.

"I was gonna tell you—" Fatima started to
670 say to Violet.

"Wait, Patty Mayonnaise, I get it now," Rolf said aloud, then, "Oops, I," and both women scowled at him.

Fatima made a sound that could be
675 interpreted as either a guffaw or a deep moan.

Then she turned back to Violet, she couldn't make any sounds, only open and close her mouth several times. She didn't
680 mean to hurt her; some things had just come out, and other things she hadn't told Violet because she wasn't sure which lip she was supposed to use, her voice was over there and then over there, and she was
685 ventriloquizing what she'd learned all at once, but from too many places and all at the wrong time.

Violet didn't say anything or make Fatima wet her pants—and perhaps one of those
690 options might have been better for Fatima; she just grabbed Mike's arm and walked away.

And like that, Fatima was a vapor again, but something darker, like a funnel cloud, or
695 black smoke that mocked what had already been singed.

The image is taken from the Netflix series *Sexy Beasts*. In every episode, singles are expected to change into human-sized creatures through prosthetics and then go on dates with others, in the hopes of finding a perfect match.

How does this image bring to mind "you cannot judge a book by its cover" or "beauty is in the eye of the beholder"? Do these adages hold true today? Do you believe that beauty is merely skin deep and that the essence of true human connection goes beyond our appearance?

CHARACTER

1. Explain what the description of Fatima reveals about her **values**.

2. When does Fatima's **perspective** begin to change? Identify and explain an event in the story that reveals this change.

3. What assumptions can we make about Fatima and Violet's relationship?

4. As Fatima and Rolf begin their relationship, what **motivates** Fatima's choices?

STRUCTURE

5. Think about what Fatima and Violet represent. How do they function as **contrasts** in the story?

6. The story **shifts** to reveal **tensions** between the characters. Identify a tension and explain how this tension contributes to a change in perspective for a character.

FIGURATIVE LANGUAGE: Word Choice, Imagery, and Symbols

7. How does the **word choice** at the beginning of the text reveal details about Fatima?

8. How do the lists of slang words further develop the conflict in the story?

FIGURATIVE LANGUAGE: Comparisons

9. The story both begins and ends with **similes**, but each evokes a different image of Fatima. What are the similes? How does the contrast between them affect your interpretation of the text?

10. What is being compared in the story? How does the **comparison** contribute to your interpretation of the text?

IDEAS IN LITERATURE: Thought and Feeling

11. "Fatima, the Biloquist: A Transformation Story" reminds us of important cultural values. How does this story compare the thoughts and feelings of the characters in a way that sends a larger message? What is the larger message for all communities?

PUTTING IT ALL TOGETHER

12. The characters in the story are contrasted in many ways. Explain how the multiple contrasts combine to create an extended comparison. How do the contrasts contribute to the conflict of the story?

IDEAS IN LITERATURE

Opportunity and Loss

IDEA BANK

Art

Carpe Diem

Comfort

Creativity

Despair

Development

Education

Empathy

Experience

Fervor

Humanity

Idealism

Innovation

Joy

Loss

Lust

Music

Opportunity

Progress

Purity

Risk

Technology

Youth

The English civil wars of the fifteenth century saw competing royal families fight for the English crown. When Henry VII ultimately became king in 1485, he ushered in a period of relative peace and prosperity that lasted for most of the next two centuries. But the war had exposed cracks in the static feudal order. The English government was gradually becoming more centralized, as the monarch and Parliament uneasily shared power. Rents to local lords were increasingly superseded by taxes paid to the state. In the process, the status and wealth of English noblemen declined.

These historical developments opened a space for stock companies, entrepreneurs, and foundational elements of capitalism. Merchants and tradespeople moved to cities: new centers of commerce that were already becoming overcrowded. Even peasants gained more freedom to sell their labor, which allowed them some social and economic mobility. Most importantly perhaps, wealth increasingly derived

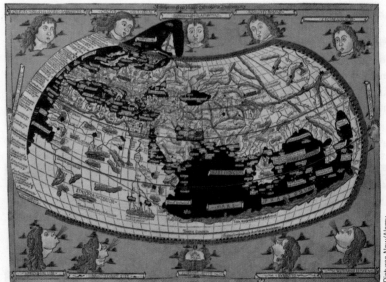

Pictures Now/Alamy

▲

This is a map from 1482 based on the work of the second-century Roman mathematician Ptolemy. The rediscovery of Ptolemy's maps revolutionized Renaissance mapmaking by suggesting that maps should be determined geographically and based on distance calculations. Previously, mapmakers relied on other sources, such as geographical references from biblical stories.

What perspective on the world does this map suggest?

from money and trade instead of landholdings. The implications of this economic and social shift were broad and deep. For example, new capital holding corporations provided lucrative rewards for those willing to risk investing in businesses operating in India or China. Even William Shakespeare accumulated wealth from his investment in the Globe Theatre.

Indeed, ambitious individuals had new opportunities to get ahead. The Renaissance witnessed a revival of humanist learning, which was increasingly available to the public. For the first time, the sons of merchants, yeoman farmers, or — in the case of Shakespeare — glovemakers studied Latin, Greek, rhetoric, poetry, mathematics, and other disciplines; they memorized passages from classical authors and aspired to be ethical, wise, and refined. In fact, our contemporary ideas about "well-rounded" individuals and the value of the liberal arts largely derive from this model of education, which served well for positions such as clerks, lawyers, and government officials. Those seeking recognition and career advancement tried to embody the Renaissance ideal of *sprezzatura*: an Italian term with connotations of effortless elegance and casual brilliance. In a way, sprezzatura is analogous to our contemporary notions of being cool. Today, we refer to a person with many talents, interests, and fields of knowledge as a "Renaissance" man or woman.

But the decline of feudalism also meant loss: the end of a premodern society in which every person knew his or her place; in which members of the nobility were obligated to protect peasants; in which authority was familiar and local, rather than remote and impersonal; in which society was — ideally — stable and harmonious. Our contemporary popular culture has often explored feudal systems, from George R. R. Martin's series *Game of Thrones* to the British historical drama *Downton Abbey*.

Many consider the English Renaissance the greatest period of English literature: poet Andrew Marvell epitomizes the shift from medieval Christian England into the modern, secular, and individualistic culture that seems closer to our own. His poem "To His Coy Mistress" reflects the *carpe diem* idea ("seize the day"), a central theme of the Renaissance.

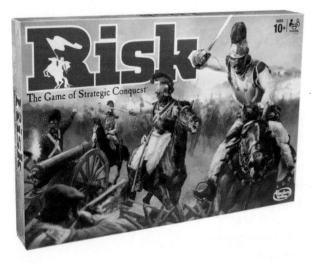

◀ Risk is a game of strategy and chance. The goal is to build an army, move your troops, engage in battles, and control territories. Depending on a roll of the dice, a player will either defeat the enemy or be defeated.

Why does this popular game continue to fascinate its players? In life, do you believe that the person who takes the most risks wins? How does risk affect the chances of an individual's success?

To His Coy Mistress
Andrew Marvell

Culture Club/Getty Images

THE TEXT IN CONTEXT

The poetry of Andrew Marvell (1621–1678), like the work of other metaphysical poets, brims with vivid imagery, gaudy metaphors, and brainy wit. In his most famous work, "To His Coy Mistress," he uses a traditional form: the *carpe diem* ("seize the day") poem. This form has a long history, dating back over 2,000 years to the work of the Roman poet Horace. *Carpe diem* poems, like the following poem, urge an implied listener (almost always a woman) to live in the present and enjoy immediate pleasures.

To His Coy Mistress

    Had we but world enough and time,
    This coyness, lady, were no crime.
    We would sit down, and think which way
    To walk, and pass our long love's day.
5 Thou by the Indian Ganges' side
    Shouldst rubies find; I by the tide
    Of Humber would complain. I would
    Love you ten years before the flood,
    And you should, if you please, refuse
10 Till the conversion of the Jews.
    My vegetable love should grow
    Vaster than empires and more slow;
    An hundred years should go to praise
    Thine eyes, and on thy forehead gaze;
15 Two hundred to adore each breast,
    But thirty thousand to the rest;
    An age at least to every part,
    And the last age should show your heart.
    For, lady, you deserve this state,
20 Nor would I love at lower rate.
       But at my back I always hear
    Time's wingèd chariot hurrying near;
    And yonder all before us lie
    Deserts of vast eternity.

25 Thy beauty shall no more be found;
    Nor, in thy marble vault, shall sound
    My echoing song; then worms shall try
    That long-preserved virginity,
    And your quaint honour turn to dust,
30 And into ashes all my lust;
    The grave's a fine and private place,
    But none, I think, do there embrace.
        Now therefore, while the youthful hue
    Sits on thy skin like morning dew,
35 And while thy willing soul transpires
    At every pore with instant fires,
    Now let us sport us while we may,
    And now, like amorous birds of prey,
    Rather at once our time devour
40 Than languish in his slow-chapped power.
    Let us roll all our strength and all
    Our sweetness up into one ball,
    And tear our pleasures with rough strife
    Through the iron gates of life:
45 Thus, though we cannot make our sun
    Stand still, yet we will make him run.

◀ Look closely at Jean-Honoré Fragonard's painting *The Swing* (1767), which depicts a woman in a billowing dress kicking her heel up as the men surround her and push her on the swing.

What does *coy* mean? How is the woman in the painting being coy? How are the men reacting to her?

CHARACTER

1. Who is the **speaker**? What is his relationship to the subject? How is that relationship revealed in the poem?

2. How does the speaker show his **perspective** and his bias toward the subject in the first stanza?

STRUCTURE

3. How does the speaker's perspective **shift** throughout the poem? Where are the shifts? How do they contribute to your interpretation of the poem?

4. The poem presents a sequence of events. How does the poem begin? What happens in the middle of the poem? How does the poem **conclude**?

5. What is the relationship between the three parts, and how does this relationship contribute to an interpretation of the poem?

FIGURATIVE LANGUAGE: Word Choice, Imagery, and Symbols

6. How do the **pronouns** in the poem function as a **referent** that reveals a relationship between the speaker and the subject of the poem?

7. How do specific words and phrases contribute to the figurative meaning of the poem? Give an example and explain.

FIGURATIVE LANGUAGE: Comparisons

8. What is being **compared** in the first lines of the poem? How does this comparison change throughout the poem?

9. The speaker uses many **similes** and **metaphors** in the poem. Choose two and explain how they contribute to the tensions within the poem.

IDEAS IN LITERATURE: Opportunity and Loss

10. The Latin phrase *carpe diem* means "seize the day," and "To His Coy Mistress" is an example of a *carpe diem* poem: a plea to make the most of every opportunity while there is still time. This was a common poetic theme during the Renaissance period. What does the idea of carpe diem suggest about opportunity and loss? How does it balance the two?

PUTTING IT ALL TOGETHER

11. Explain how the poetic elements present a complex perspective on the subject of time.

Pilgrimage
Natasha Trethewey

THE TEXT IN CONTEXT

A two-time U.S. poet laureate, Natasha Tretheway (b. 1966) writes powerfully about African American working-class men and women in the South, southern history, and the lives of mixed-race individuals. The latter reflects her own childhood and experiences as the daughter of mixed-race parents: a couple who had to travel to Ohio to wed because their marriage was illegal in their native Mississippi. Tretheway's poetry collections include *Domestic Work* (2000), *Native Guard* (2006), and *Thrall* (2012). She's also the author of the memoir *Memorial Drive: A Daughter's Memoir* (2020). In "Pilgrimage," which appeared in *Native Guard*, the speaker meditates on the history of Vicksburg, Mississippi (the site of a pivotal Civil War battle) and the Mississippi River. The poem exemplifies Tretheway's skill at evoking the past in the present.

Pilgrimage

Vicksburg, Mississippi

Here, the Mississippi carved
    its mud-dark path, a graveyard

for skeletons of sunken riverboats.
    Here, the river changed its course,

5 turning away from the city
    as one turns, forgetting, from the past—

the abandoned bluffs, land sloping up
    above the river's bend—where now

the Yazoo fills the Mississippi's empty bed.
10   Here, the dead stand up in stone, white

marble, on Confederate Avenue. I stand
    on ground once hollowed by a web of caves;

they must have seemed like catacombs,
    in 1863, to the woman sitting in her parlor,

15 candlelit, underground. I can see her
    listening to shells explode, writing herself

into history, asking *what is to become*
of all the living things in this place?

This whole city is a grave. Every spring—
20   *Pilgrimage*—the living come to mingle

with the dead, brush against their cold shoulders
in the long hallways, listen all night

to their silence and indifference, relive
their dying on the green battlefield.

25 At the museum, we marvel at their clothes—
preserved under glass—so much smaller

than our own, as if those who wore them
were only children. We sleep in their beds,

the old mansions hunkered on the bluffs, draped
30   in flowers—funereal—a blur

of petals against the river's gray.
The brochure in my room calls this

living history. The brass plate on the door reads
Prissy's Room. A window frames

35 the river's crawl toward the Gulf. In my dream,
the ghost of history lies down beside me,

rolls over, pins me beneath a heavy arm.

This image depicts an Islamic pilgrimage.

___

What are some other pilgrimages? Explain a contemporary pilgrimage and the impact of the journey.

Muhannad Fala'ah/Getty Images

CHARACTER

1. Who is the **speaker**? What is the context of the poem?

2. Identify and explain some present choices that the **speaker** makes that reveal her perspective on the history and the pilgrimage.

3. What are the **speaker's values**, background, and beliefs?

STRUCTURE

4. The beginning of the poem introduces the **tension** within the poem. What is the tension?

5. Where is there a **shift** in the poem, and how do you know? What is revealed through this shift?

6. Identify and explain how the images of the setting **contrast** to create meaning in the poem.

FIGURATIVE LANGUAGE: Word Choice, Imagery, and Symbols

7. Explain how the **pronouns** and **antecedents** in the poem contribute to your interpretation of the poem.

8. Choose an image from the poem and explain how that **image** contributes to the meaning of the poem.

FIGURATIVE LANGUAGE: Comparisons

9. Choose a **comparison** in the poem. Explain the attributes of the characteristics.

10. The **comparisons** in the poem are linked through shared values between the speaker and audience. Choose a comparison that demonstrates these shared values.

IDEAS IN LITERATURE: Opportunity and Loss

11. The poem reflects the loss suffered in Vicksburg, Mississippi, through a shared experience at a museum. Consider other museums or memorials that honor fallen soldiers. Explain how the impact of visiting a memorial or museum has affected you.

PUTTING IT ALL TOGETHER

12. The stanzas in this poem shift. Identify and explain how the shift contributes to the complex context of the poem and reveals the message of the poem.

Cloud Nine
Sofia T. Romero

Courtesy of Sofia T. Romero

THE TEXT IN CONTEXT

Writer Sofia T. Romero (b. 1972) is a native of Wellesley, Massachusetts. She received her undergraduate degree from Wellesley College and her graduate degree from Boston College. Her fiction has appeared in literary journals such as *Blue Mountain Review*, *Waterwheel Review*, *Rigorous*, and *Leon Literary Review*. Romero is an editor, as well as the proprietor of the blog *The Mighty Red Pen*, which focuses on issues of language and grammar. In "Cloud Nine," she skillfully captures the complex thoughts and emotions of the young protagonist.

Cloud Nine

After a grey, drizzly morning, the sun finally broke through. Outside on the playground for recess, we divvied up the roles. Everyone wanted to be Jo, of course. I called dibs.

5 You can't be Jo, Susie said.

Why not? I said, kicking the damp dirt a bit with my sneakers. We were all wearing sneakers, but I was the only one who didn't get nice white sneakers that year. Mami
10 made me get Zips. They were navy blue so they wouldn't get dirty. Susie had white Nikes, the leather kind.

Because, she started. And then she paused. Why don't you be Meg?
15 No one wanted to be Meg. Meg is bossy. She's the annoying big sister. We all wanted to be Jo because she was cool. I liked her because she wrote stories.

You know what, said Christina. I'll be Beth.
20 Phew. No one really wanted to be Beth, who did nothing interesting but be sweet to everyone and then die at the end. Where's the fun in that?

I like being Beth, said Christina.
25 And you're good at it, I said, trying to be encouraging.

You can't be Jo because Jo had brown hair and you have black hair, said Susie to me, seizing on what she thought was some kind
30 of reason. Down the hill, the boys were playing kickball on the blacktop. Another group of girls was playing on the swings and Kimberly was upside down on the jungle gym again. Everyone could see her underpants.
35 The whistle. A teacher spotted Kimberly and ordered her to sit upright. She did, but stuck her tongue out at the teacher first.

I'm going to be Jo, I insisted.

She flushed. You can't be Jo, Lulu, and I
40 won't play if you are.

Why can't she just be Jo, Christina put in. Recess was almost over. We wouldn't be able to play.

I looked over at Christina, who smiled
45 softly at me. Christina was always on my side.

Lourdes, I said. My name is Lourdes.

Tina, she can't be Jo because she is, Susie paused, well, she's portorican that's why and
50 Jo is not portorican.

I opened my mouth again but the words would not come. En boca cerrada no entran moscas, I heard Mami say. I stood up from the grass, brushing dust off my Toughskins.
55 I could not be Jo.

C'mon, Lulu, said Susie. Say something in portorican. Ooono, dossss, tress, quatrrrro, she started counting.

It's not called Puerto Rican, I muttered.
60 Say something in portorican! she insisted and started to laugh.

It's called Spanish, I said, and then I ran. I ran to the swings and climbed on and started to swing and swing.
65 Swinging, I could see the foursome had fallen apart. Christina had walked away. Susie kicked the dirt. I kept swinging.

I closed my eyes, felt the breeze on my face, my hair flying backward behind me and
70 then forward in front of me.

Can I swing with you? It was Christina.

Sure, I said. I don't care.

Christina was different from the other girls. She has dark hair like me but her
75 mom and dad came from someplace else, too, from Greece. They spoke with even more accent than Mami and Papi did. She never asked me to say things in Puerto Rican or made fun of my hair when it got
80 frizzy. And I didn't make fun of the t-shirt that her mom made her wear that said Foxy Lady all over it.

Your mom made you wear Foxy Lady today, I said.
85 She rolled her eyes. Frowned. She doesn't really get what it means, she said.

Susie called you Tina, I said.

Yeah, said Christina. No one else calls me that. And she called you Lulu.

90 Yeah, no one calls me that, I said. Sometimes my family calls me Luli. But not Lulu.

Christina nodded and said, Hey, I'm going to race you to the top.

What do you mean?
95 I'm on Cloud Five, she said. I'm going to race you to Cloud Nine.

I started pumping my legs. No way! I screamed. I'm going to get to Cloud Nine faster than you!
100 We pumped our legs faster and faster. I'm on Cloud Six! Cloud Seven! Cloud Eight! We were gasping, swinging so high that sometimes the chain went slack.

There was a cheer from the blacktop.
105 I could see the ball dribbling past the diamond, just out of reach of one of the boys, the one wearing a striped top. He was running toward us to catch it.

Hey, Lulu! he shouted when he saw us.
110 Lulu's a loser! He snickered and ran back to the game.

Ignore him, said Christina, and we went back to our game. Six, seven, eight. I'm on Cloud Nine! we yelled at the same time. And
115 we swung and swung until the teacher whistled for the end of recess.

● ● ●

At home after dinner, I walked into the kitchen and when I saw them there, looking sharply at each other, stabbing the air with
120 their gestures and with the sound of their voices.

Today, Mami stood over the sink, trying to stuff something down the drain, the disposal was running, the water was running. She got
125 something down there, and I could hear something grinding, grinding, and then stopping. Papi had flicked the disposal switch.

Carajo, he said to her, grabbing her wrist and holding it tight. I can't believe you would
130 do that.

Let go of me, Mami said, but he held her wrist tighter, and he pulled at something in her hand, and what she was holding in her hands suddenly broke and dozens of tiny
135 beads fell to the floor. It was Abuela's necklace.

They didn't see me as Papi told her to go to el infierno and Mami said she would see his Mama there, and my father saw me and
140 yelled come here come here. And in his hand I could see that he was holding Abuela's prendas, the ones he brought home after she died, and Mami was trying to throw them away. These are yours, he shouted at me and
145 thrust them at me, but I couldn't move my hands, move my arms, and they fell to the ground in front of me.

And finally I willed myself to leave, and I ran to my room, just as the jewelry, some
150 earrings and a necklace, crashed to the ground, the sound chasing me up the stairs.

My windows were open to let in a little bit of air, and the breeze blew the curtains slightly. I could hear the rise and fall of my
155 parents' voices, not enough to know what they were saying, but enough to know they were still arguing.

I got the flashlight from my night table and opened the drawer. I could see all the
160 tiny travel-sized things I had gathered: a toothbrush, toothpaste, a bar of soap. What had started as a collection of things I thought were cute because they were small had turned into my running away stash.
165 There was an envelope, I knew it had 17 dollars in it. I wondered how much more I would need before I could run away.

Out of the corner of my eye, I saw a brief movement, but when I looked, there was
170 nothing but the blank yellow wall. The moonlight cast a strange shadow. And then the shadow moved.

Then I realized who it was.

Hi, I said.
175 Bambi nodded.

I hadn't seen Bambi since I was five. He and all his friends used to live along the wall of my bedroom then. Bambi, Thumper, Flower. They were all there. I used to talk to
180 them at night about the things that happened to me that day and what I was thinking about. They were there every night, until one night they just weren't anymore. When my mom asked me what happened,
185 I just said: They went to Florida.

And now they were back. Well, at least Bambi was.

No Thumper? I said. No Flower?

Bambi shook his head.
190 I told Bambi I was happy he came back. He bent down to nibble at something. I could tell he was listening.

I don't know what to do about Mami and Papi are fighting all the time, I said. Run away?
195 I could tell from the look in his eye that he didn't think it was a great idea.

I want them to stop fighting, I said. But they don't. So I just read my book and pretend I can't hear them.
200 Bambi thought this was a good plan.

Bambi, can I tell you something?

Bambi nodded.

When I'm on the swing and swinging super high, I sometimes pretend I go to
205 Cloud Nine, I told him. You know what Cloud Nine is? Christina says it's a place where you're really really happy.

Bambi seemed interested.

You're not really in Florida, are you,
210 Bambi? I said. You're on Cloud Nine, aren't you? Can I go there, too?

I was crying a little bit now, and I closed my eyes. When I opened them again, Bambi had faded away.

• • •

215 Miss Matthews let me go to the nurse because my stomach hurt. I walked down the hall. The door to the nurse's office was closed, and the sign said "knock, walk in." I knocked and politely waited outside. Come 220 in come in, Mrs. Phillips shouted impatiently, don't you see the sign says come in? You don't have to wait outside.

Honey, what's the matter, said Mrs. Phillips. Her white hair framed her face. 225 On her desk she had lots of photographs of people who were smiling.

My stomach hurts, I said. I don't feel good.

Mrs. Phillips looked me over and asked 230 some questions. Then she had me sit down. Well, let me call your mother, she said, and disappeared into the room next door.

There was a pile of old books next to the 235 chair I was sitting in and I started to flip through them but none of them was interesting. I stared at the poster on the wall. "BE HEALTHY, BE HAPPY" it said in really big, really red letters. There was a family sitting 240 around a picnic table, and the mom was giving out the lunch. The kids, a boy and a girl who both had blonde hair, were waiting patiently for their sandwiches. Peanut butter and jelly, I thought.

245 Yup, that's right, said the boy in the picture, turning to me. Good old PB&J. And after this, my dad and I are going to play catch. Then we'll go home and watch the Brady Bunch.

250 I'm not allowed to watch the Brady Bunch, I told the boy.

Your parents won't let you watch the Brady Bunch? he said, surprised.

No, I said. My mom doesn't like it. I 255 shrugged. I don't know why.

But I saw it one time, I told him, so he wouldn't think I was a total loser. One of the girls was in trouble. I forget what else happened, she got in trouble but her parents 260 weren't that mad or anything.

Marcia and Jan have long blond hair, just like mine, said the girl. She tossed her hair to prove her point.

My hair was too frizzy to toss. At home 265 sometimes when I changed into my pajamas at night, I wouldn't pull my shirt completely off so it would make something like long smooth hair, good for tossing.

On Cloud Nine, I have long hair and I can 270 toss it, too, I said.

You do not, said the girl.

I do, too, I said. Christina said on Cloud Nine, everything makes us happy.

Mrs. Phillips reappeared. Honey, she said. 275 Did you say something?

No, I said. I looked back at the poster. The boy and girl were frozen, smiling, waiting.

Oh, she frowned. I thought I heard you say something. Anyway, your mom wasn't home. 280 But your housekeeper said she could come and get you.

We don't have a housekeeper, I said.

What do you mean? she said. I just called your house and the housekeeper answered.

285 No housekeeper, I said.

Mrs. Phillips couldn't hear me. What's that, Christina?

I'm not Christina, I mumbled again. I'm Lourdes Martinez.

290 Oh my goodness, she said. What a mistake! I always get you two confused.

She's Greek, I said, my voice soft. I'm not Greek.

What's that, dear? Mrs. Phillips said.

295 Nothing, I said, looking away. I am not Greek, I said, again, under my breath. I am Lourdes.

• • •

While we are driving home, I told Mami what I told Mrs. Phillips while I was waiting

300 to be picked up. How Mrs. Phillips asked me how everything was going, in a voice that was warm and made me want to tell her everything.

I told Mami what I told Mrs. Phillips, how

305 when I told her that when I came downstairs on Saturday, Papi was holding Mami by the wrist at the top of the steps that led out of the house. How she was turning away from him, pulling away from him, and finally he

310 let go of her and how she fell. How they told me to get out. How he pushed her away, how she fell, stumbled down the few steps to the bottom.

My mother's black eyebrows were jagged

315 on her face. Her mouth was like a bruise, angry and hard. She could see me in the rearview mirror. I looked out the side window, as though she couldn't see me if I couldn't see her.

320 She was already annoyed she had to pick me up. She said I didn't even look sick. Luli, why would you tell her that, she asked, finally.

I don't know, I said. She asked.

325 She was angry. She was silent. We don't talk about that, she said, finally. It's private.

But she asked, I said. She asked how everything was going at home.

But nada, Mami said. It's private.

330 We were quiet in the car after that. Before we got home, I said, I wish you didn't give me such a dumb name, I wish you named me something else.

Oh? said Mami.

335 Yeah, something like Beth . . . or Amy . . . I said. Lourdes is a stupid name.

• • •

At dinner, Mami and Papi were fighting again, but this time they were fighting about me. You won't believe what Luli did today,

340 she said to him, putting dinner on the table. My father started to eat while Mami got dinner together for the rest of us, her and me and Mateo.

She told the teacher about what

345 happened yesterday, she says. How do you like that?

My father had no expression, but I could tell he was getting mad by the way his neck was turning red.

350 I slid to the floor so that Papi wouldn't see me. If he did, he might pinch my nalga, twisting my skin between my fingers so that it really hurt. Or he might make me kneel in the corner for a long time. Maybe fifteen

355 minutes, maybe thirty minutes. Really kneeling, like in church, without my bum resting on my feet. If he caught me resting my bum on my feet, he would give me another fifteen minutes, with my back to the clock, with no

360 way to tell what time it was except for when the clock boinged at the end of each fifteen minutes.

I kept expecting someone to say something but now my parents were fighting about

365 what happened yesterday. Papi put his fork and knife down, stopped eating his dinner.

I slipped out the door, into the backyard. I could hear their voices, her high-pitched one getting higher and higher, his low-

370 pitched one getting louder and louder.

In the backyard, the light was still grey, I could just make out the outline of the swingset. From inside the house, a door slammed. I sat down on the swing and

375 started to pump my legs.

Cloud Two, I said softly. Cloud Three. Cloud Four. Cloud Five. Cloud Six. Cloud Seven. Cloud Eight.

The wind swept my hair, forward and
380 then backward. When it blew back, I imagined I was a princess, my long hair blowing over my face, and my swing was my horse and we were running away. I had 17 dollars in my pocket. I kept pumping my
385 legs, the swing going higher and higher. I could feel the mist wrapping around me, bathing my arms and my legs, my face. When I opened my eyes, I couldn't see inches in front of me from the fog, chilling
390 and damp. I opened my mouth, tasted the cool cotton.

I had arrived. I was sure of it. Cloud Nine. I waited for the happiness to come.

◀ *Swing Life Away II* by Nicole Roggeman is an oil painting of two best friends swinging as high as they can.

Do you remember swinging on a swing as an escape that you shared with childhood friends? How did swinging feel? Why do you think children find such joy in swinging as high as they can?

© Nicole Roggeman

CHARACTER

1. Explain how background, history, and culture **motivate** the characters' actions.
2. How do Lourdes and Christina's actions together reveal their shared experience?

STRUCTURE

3. "Cloud Nine" begins and concludes in a similar setting and situation. What is different at the end of the story? How does the **contrast** contribute to your interpretation of the text?
4. What is the **tension** between Lourdes and Susie? How do the details of the text reveal this tension? Does the story ultimately **resolve** it? Explain.

FIGURATIVE LANGUAGE: Word Choice, Imagery, and Symbols

5. The narrator's **word choice** reveals the tension within the story and within herself. Give an example of a specific word or phrase that highlights this underlying tension within Lourdes or the text.

6. The story's conclusion includes a range of **images**. How do these images contribute to the story's figurative meaning?

FIGURATIVE LANGUAGE: Comparisons

7. There are many **comparisons** in the text. Choose one example and then explain how the comparison contributes to your interpretation of the story.

8. "Cloud Nine" is often defined as a feeling of elation. Explain how the title functions as a **metaphor** for the story.

IDEAS IN LITERATURE: Opportunity and Loss

9. How does this story dramatize a struggle with opportunity and loss? What elements represent opportunity? What aspects represent loss? How does the relationship between these two ideas create tension within the story?

PUTTING IT ALL TOGETHER

10. The story functions on both the literal and figurative levels. What happens in "Cloud Nine," literally? How do the actions and dialogue contribute to the ambiguous and more figurative ending of the story?

COMPOSITION WORKSHOP
Writing about Tone

AP **Enduring Understanding (LAN-1)**

Readers establish and communicate their interpretations of literature through arguments supported by textual evidence.

Justifying a Thesis through a Line of Reasoning

When you have conversations with other people, you understand their meaning not only by *what* they say but also by *how* they say it. For example, the words "have a nice day" can be a warm sentiment or a snarky comeback, depending on the context. As a result, we instinctively listen to a speaker's tone of voice to detect that speaker's attitude and true meaning.

Reading is similar, but instead of hearing an audible voice, we must read beyond the literal meaning of words on the page to detect the speaker's or narrator's **tone**. Some people call this "reading between the lines." When you pay close attention to an author's choice of words, imagery, and figures of speech, you begin to make associations that will help you detect the tone within a work.

In this composition workshop, you will learn to write a literary argument that analyzes the tone in a text. First, you will develop a defensible thesis statement with a claim that conveys your interpretation (idea + insight) related to the tone, and then you will develop this claim with a **line of reasoning** and textual evidence.

KEY POINT

The line of reasoning in a literary argument provides a logical sequence of supporting reasons to justify the interpretation in the thesis statement. A thesis statement may or may not preview the line of reasoning for an interpretation.

 YOUR ASSIGNMENT

Choose a poem or story from Unit 2 or a text that your teacher has assigned. Then, write a literary argument that analyzes how the tone contributes to your interpretation of the work.

Remember that in these early units, you are building the foundation of a literary argument. Throughout the year, your thesis statements and lines of reasoning will continue to grow more complex.

This argument should interpret a literary work and include the following:

- A thesis statement with a claim that conveys an interpretation (a unifying idea + an insight about that idea)
- A line of reasoning that justifies the interpretation in the claim
- Relevant textual evidence that supports the line of reasoning

Potential Subjects

- How metaphor contributes to tone and reveals an idea and insight
- How simile contributes to tone and reveals an idea and insight
- How repetition contributes to tone and reveals an idea and insight
- How the shifts in tone within the text reveal an idea and insight

Set a Purpose for Reading

As you analyze a text, you can determine the narrator's or speaker's attitude about the subject by paying close attention to the specific language. This attitude — as it is implicit in specific stylistic choices — is referred to as **tone**. In Unit 2, you have learned that authors employ techniques (e.g., repetition, specific word choice, shifts) to highlight ideas and tensions. You have also learned that they use figurative language (e.g., symbol, imagery, metaphor, and simile) to create associations between their subjects and familiar objects. You must pay close attention to all these elements to understand the tone of a text.

For example, if the metaphorical associations and connotations of a text are positive, then the writer's attitude and tone are likely positive. If these elements are negative, then the tone is probably negative. But as your readings get more complex throughout the year, you may notice that some writers create tension between tone and subject matter (e.g., a comic tone applied to a serious theme or problem). These incongruities can lead to irony, insight, and opportunities for multiple interpretations. Strategic readers make thoughtful connections between the language and the subject to identify the tone and interpret the text.

Therefore, when you are preparing to analyze a text in a literary argument, you should pay particular attention to how the author's use of language reveals tone (or more than one tone) and connects to the unifying idea. To do this, consider how the author's figurative elements work within the text to accomplish the following:

- Reveal attitudes about subjects or experiences
- Reveal a narrator's or speaker's tone
- Make associations to familiar objects or experiences
- Suggest similarities and differences within comparisons
- Further inform the context of a comparison
- Emphasize qualities and traits of a subject

To prepare to write about tone, you can begin broadly by classifying this attitude as either positive, neutral, or negative based on the associations you make. Then, the more you delve into the specific connotations of words and figurative language, the more precise you can be about analyzing this tone or attitude. In your analysis, you will describe the tone of the work using adjectives. Make sure you choose the most precise adjectives to do the job. For example, it would be accurate to describe the winner of a prize as "happy." But if the prize is $100 million, it would be more precise to say that the winner is "ecstatic."

Consult the following table, which gives examples of words and the different tones and attitudes they suggest.

DESCRIBING TONE		
Positive	**Neutral**	**Negative**
Happy	Objective	Sad
• Content	• Detached	• Melancholy
• Joyful	• Clinical	• Despondent
• Ecstatic	• Matter of fact	• Despairing
Friendly	Logical	Unfriendly
• Polite	• Instructive	• Unsociable
• Accommodating	• Didactic	• Spiteful
• Indulgent	• Persuasive	• Malicious
Pleasurable	Apathetic	Angry
• Satisfied	• Detached	• Indignant
• Amused	• Stoic	• Perturbed
• Enraptured	• Resigned	• Furious
Loving	Cautious	Mocking
• Affectionate	• Prudent	• Patronizing
• Sensual	• Wary	• Pompous
• Amorous	• Reticent	• Contemptuous
Humorous	Sentimental	Fearful
• Amused	• Reminiscent	• Apprehensive
• Playful	• Nostalgic	• Nervous
• Giddy	• Longing	• Terrified

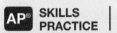 LITERARY ARGUMENTATION
Analyzing Tone through Figurative Elements

Review the text that you are analyzing for your literary argument. Identify the unifying idea that will guide your analysis. Record this in the first row. Then, in the left column, record details related to that idea for each of the figurative elements that you have identified. In the right column, record how these details lead you to an insight about that idea. Next, consider the associations that you have made from your reading to determine the tone (or different tones) in the text.

(continued)

Analyzing Tone through Figurative Elements	
Idea:	
Textual Details	**Insights and Connections to Unifying Idea**
Tone(s):	
Idea + insight:	

Develop a Defensible Thesis Statement

In Unit 1, you learned how to combine the unifying idea and an insight about that idea to write a defensible thesis statement that conveys your interpretation of a literary text. You will continue to do this for every literary argument that you write. In this workshop, you are analyzing tone, so in addition to your interpretation, your thesis statement should identify the tone in the text using precise adjectives. Your thesis can also preview the reasons that you will develop in your body paragraphs for support.

To determine these reasons, you need to pay attention to what is happening in the text. In other words, you should take note of the author's techniques. For example, some texts shift from one distinct tone to another or from a concrete image to an abstract idea. Some present comparisons, contrasts, or repetitions. Likewise, the author may choose a series of closely related images and comparisons that work toward a common idea. Consider the following as you plan your literary argument:

- Concrete and abstract associations of figurative language
- Conflicts and tensions in the text
- Comparisons and contrasts of objects and images

- The structure of the text
- Shifts in tone
- Complexity of tone, perspectives, or ideas
- Literary techniques

You must have a line of reasoning for your literary argument; however, you may choose whether to preview this line of reasoning within your thesis statement. Review the following templates that may help you write your thesis statement.

WRITING A THESIS FOR ANALYSIS OF TONE	
Template 1: Thesis connects tone to the idea and previews the line of reasoning.	In [title of work], the author conveys a [adjective] tone using [literary technique] and [literary technique], in order to reveal that [unifying idea + insight].
Template 2: Thesis connects tone to the idea and insight.	In [title of work], the author/speaker/narrator conveys a [adjective] tone to reveal that [unifying idea + insight].
Template 3: Thesis reveals complexity in tone and connects to the idea.	In [title of work], the author/speaker/narrator shifts from a [adjective] to a [adjective] tone to illustrate that [unifying idea + insight].

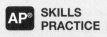 **SKILLS PRACTICE**

LITERARY ARGUMENTATION
Developing a Thesis Statement for Tone Analysis

Record the unifying idea and insight of the text you are analyzing in the following graphic organizer. Next, using the thesis templates as a guide, write a defensible thesis statement. You may choose whether or not to preview your line of reasoning.

Developing a Defensible Thesis Statement for Literary Argument		
Topic	Claim	
Title, Author, and Focus (author choices)	Unifying Idea +	Insight

Organize a Line of Reasoning

We have probably all heard the frustrating words "because I said so!" at one time or another—especially when we want to know why a decision was made or a request was denied. These empty words never satisfy our desire to understand the reason for the decision. Likewise, when you write a literary argument, simply making a claim and perhaps previewing your reasons is not enough. To justify your argument, you must reveal why you believe as you do, as well as the progression of thought that led to your position. Therefore, when you analyze a work of literature, you must justify your thesis with this logical progression of reasons, called the **line of reasoning**.

Now that you have practiced writing thesis statements, you will develop your line of reasoning in the body of your argument. You present your line of reasoning in the **topic sentences** that begin each body paragraph; you develop each reason within the paragraphs through commentary. So when you write your topic sentences, make sure that they both provide a purpose for your evidence and connect to your thesis in the first paragraph. In other words, your topic sentences should do the following:

- Connect to the unifying idea in your thesis statement
- Present reasons to support your interpretation
- Establish a purpose for the evidence and commentary in the paragraph
- Reveal the reasons in a logical order

The order of your line of reasoning matters. Indeed, the progression of thought that develops your thesis should move logically from one idea to another. Therefore, you must present your insights in a thoughtful sequence that is informed by the text, such as beginning to end, concrete to abstract, Tone A to Tone B.

Techniques represent the author's literary "moves," while elements are the specific tools the author uses to create the technique. You should use the techniques to guide your line of reasoning and the elements to support that line of reasoning. A line of reasoning may be organized by techniques. An author's techniques (e.g., imagery, contrast, comparison) are made up of elements. Techniques are larger than elements.

SOME TECHNIQUES AND ELEMENTS	
Techniques	**Elements**
Imagery	connotation, allusion, personification, simile, motif
Contrast	irony, juxtaposition, paradox, antithesis, imagery
Comparison	simile, metaphor, conceit, image, allusion, symbol
Narration	point of view, perspective, speaker, tone
Pacing	sentence structure, flashback, foreshadowing, suspense, pause, variety
Emphasis	subordination, coordination, cumulative sentence, periodic sentence, rhetorical question, exaggeration, repetition, simple sentence, fragment
Balance	coordination, parallelism, coordinating conjunction, repetition

STRUCTURE OF AN ANALYSIS OF TONE

Introduction

The **introduction** is an opportunity for the writer to establish the purpose of his or her literary argument and to invite and interest the audience into the literary work and the writer's interpretation of it. To achieve this goal, many literary arguments follow this structure:

- Engage the audience through an interesting hook
- Provide historical, cultural, or social context of a literary work
- Identify the title, author, genre (TAG)
- Introduce the literary topic of analysis by
  - describing the particular aspect of tone; and
  - summarizing the work succinctly with details critical to that aspect of tone

The **thesis statement** presents a defensible interpretation that includes an idea and an insight about that idea.

Body

(Develops a line of reasoning with supporting evidence that justifies the thesis)

Topic Sentence 1	Topic Sentence 2	Topic Sentence 3
(Identify the literary element related to the unifying idea)	(Identify the literary element related to the unifying idea)	(Identify the literary element related to the unifying idea)
Textual Details (Evidence of elements and techniques and their function)	**Textual Details** (Evidence of elements and techniques and their function)	**Textual Details** (Evidence of elements and techniques and their function)
Commentary (Link evidence by explaining its relevance to the line of reasoning and claim)	**Commentary** (Link evidence by explaining its relevance to the line of reasoning and claim)	**Commentary** (Link evidence by explaining its relevance to the line of reasoning and claim)

Conclusion

The **conclusion** should do more than restate the thesis; instead, it should be a robust and important paragraph. It is the opportunity for the writer to demonstrate understanding of the literary work's relevance by explaining how it stands the test of time and reflects the human experience. Writers further their idea and insight by:

- Discussing the significance or relevance of interpretation
- Relating the work to other relevant literary works
- Connecting the theme to their own experience
- Presenting alternate interpretations
- Explaining how the work explores complexities and tensions
- Situating the theme within a broader context

This table illustrates the general structure of a literary argument. It does not intend to imply that all literary arguments are five paragraphs. Writers should determine the number of reasons needed to justify their claim, as well as how much evidence is sufficient to support each of these reasons.

 **INSIDER AP TIP**

Shifts in tone contribute to complexity. For your tone analysis, your line of reasoning will likely be guided either by the author's techniques that contribute to your understanding of the tone or by a shift from one tone to another. You can choose either of these options to focus your paragraph on the tone and your unifying idea.

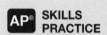 **AP SKILLS PRACTICE** | **LITERARY ARGUMENTATION**
Developing a Line of Reasoning

Review your thesis statement, which may or may not preview the line of reasoning. Record the topic sentences to represent your line of reasoning and place them in a logical order. As you do this, consider the potential evidence from the text that helped you arrive at your line of reasoning. That textual evidence will serve as support for each of your techniques.

Supporting a Thesis Statement with a Line of Reasoning

Defensible Thesis Statement with Interpretation (idea + insight):

Topic Sentence 1	Topic Sentence 2	Topic Sentence 3
(Author's first technique that contributes to tone and illustrates unifying idea):	(Author's second technique that contributes to tone and illustrates unifying idea):	(Author's third technique that contributes to tone and illustrates unifying idea):

Select Relevant Evidence

After you have planned your line of reasoning, you must support each topic sentence with **relevant evidence** from the text. In other words, every body paragraph should include evidence. You should examine your notes for potential evidence that you recorded as you developed your line of reasoning.

In this workshop, you have been focusing specifically on the tone of a text and how the author's use of figurative elements contributes to the tone and to your interpretation of the text. Therefore, you will quote evidence that exemplifies the following:

- Specific words and phrases in a text that convey a tone and relate to your idea and insight

- References and their antecedents whose associations reveal an idea or insight
- Repetition of words or letter sounds that convey a tone, emphasize an idea, or lead to insight
- Similes (comparisons of unlike things using "like" or "as") that relate to an idea and insight
- Metaphors (comparisons of unlike things) that relate to an idea and insight

In choosing textual evidence or details from the passage, make sure that you arrange those details into the related body paragraphs. Next, link your evidence to your thesis by briefly explaining the function of your evidence in relation to the claim in your thesis. You may use sentence stems like the following to begin to explain the function of your evidence:

- By using these examples, the author reveals . . .
- The author includes the metaphor to illustrate . . .
- This specific word choice suggests . . .
- The simile explores the connection between . . .
- The repetition of _____ emphasizes . . .

In the next unit, we will begin to develop skills to write insightful explanations of your carefully chosen evidence. These explanations, also called commentary, will link your textual evidence to your interpretation by revealing the purpose of your evidence not only on its own but also in conjunction with other details from the text.

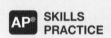 **SKILLS PRACTICE** | LITERARY ARGUMENTATION
Selecting Relevant Evidence to Support a Line of Reasoning

Write your thesis statement and develop a logical line of reasoning to support your interpretation. Next, draft two or more body paragraphs that include textual evidence from the text to support each reason. Finally, write a concluding statement that explains the significance of your idea. You may use the following table for planning.

Developing an Argument with Supporting Evidence		
Defensible Thesis Statement with Interpretation (idea + insight):		
Topic Sentence 1 (Identify the author's first technique that contributes to tone and illustrates unifying idea):	**Topic Sentence 2** (Identify the author's second technique that contributes to tone and illustrates unifying idea):	**Topic Sentence 3** (Identify the author's third technique that contributes to tone and illustrates unifying idea):

(continued)

Relevant Evidence:	**Relevant Evidence:**	**Relevant Evidence:**
Commentary (Link the evidence to your thesis by explaining its significance in relation to the claim in your thesis):	**Commentary** (Link the evidence to your thesis by explaining its significance in relation to the claim in your thesis):	**Commentary** (Link the evidence to your thesis by explaining its significance in relation to the claim in your thesis):

Note: Your argument should include the number of reasons necessary to justify your claim. These organizers are illustrative of three reasons. Your argument may include more or fewer.

Contextualize Your Argument

To conclude your literary argument, you need to include a final statement that not only reflects back on your interpretation but also explains the relevance of your idea. Often, the interpretation that guides your thesis statement is based on the specific details in the text. This final statement will be slightly different.

When you explain the significance of the idea at the end of your literary argument, you broaden the scope of your interpretation beyond the text that you are analyzing. In future workshops, you will continue to explore ways to contextualize your argument. To begin, consider the following questions:

- What does the reader discover about the idea from reading the text?
- How is this idea relevant beyond the pages of the text?

 **SKILLS PRACTICE** | LITERARY ARGUMENTATION
Explaining the Relevance of the Idea

When you have completed your final body paragraph, add a sentence or two at the end of your argument in which you explain the relevance of the unifying idea in your thesis.

Explaining Relevance
Unifying idea:
Relevance of the idea:

Revise Your Argument

In Unit 1, you learned to revise your literary argument by examining your thesis and topic sentences to make sure that they are unified by an idea and that they convey an insight. Also, you learned to examine your evidence to ensure that it is relevant to the line of reasoning that you have established to support your thesis.

For your tone analysis, locate the adjectives that you have included to describe tone within the work. Review the following questions related to your treatment of tone in your literary argument. Revise your draft if your answer is "no" to any of the following questions:

- Are your tone words precise?
- Does your textual evidence exemplify the tone(s) that you have identified?
- Have you identified the author's techniques that create the tone?
- Does your textual evidence include elements to support the techniques?
- Does your interpretation of the work logically align with the tone(s) that you identified?

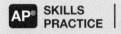 SKILLS PRACTICE | LITERARY ARGUMENTATION
Revising and Editing an Analysis of Tone

After you have completed revising and editing your own argument, review another student's literary argument and provide helpful feedback.

Peer-Revision Checklist: Revising and Editing an Analysis of Tone		
Revising and Editing Checklist	Unit 2 Focus Skills	Comment on the Effectiveness and/or Make a Suggestion
Does the thesis statement identify one or more tones and convey an interpretation? Does the interpretation connect to a unifying idea and an insight?	Defensible thesis	
Does the writer provide a logical line of reasoning to develop the idea and insight in the thesis? Is the unifying idea evident in this line of reasoning?	Line of reasoning	
Does the writer provide evidence for each topic sentence to support the interpretation in the thesis? Does the evidence defend the choice of tone(s) identified in the thesis?	Relevant evidence	
Does the concluding statement explain the significance of the unifying idea?	Contextualizing the argument	
Does the writer demonstrate control over the conventions of writing?	Conventions	

Student Model: Writing about Tone

Review the following student model to observe how the thesis statement, line of reasoning, and evidence work together to convey an interpretation of the literary argument.

Escaping Expectations
Sophia Amstalden

May Swenson recognizes how societal pressures burden her into hiding her true playful, childish nature as a young girl as she looks at a memory of her playing outside and embodying the freedom of a horse. In "The Centaur," through a shift in tone from carefree to judgmental developed by poetic devices, May Swenson depicts the freedom her younger self felt playing as a horse in a tone that shifts and becomes more reserved under the judging eyes of her mother, who represents the societal norms placed on girls from a young age to be good-mannered and composed.

> thesis statement with interpretation
> idea: freedom
> insight: humans desire freedom
> tone: shifts from carefree to reserved

Through metaphors and similes in the first several stanzas of the poem, the girl explores her freedom when she is alone in the yard, depicting the persona of the adventurous and playful nature of youth. May Swenson's younger self becomes the perspective of the audience through her poem. By following her as she uses her "brother's jack knife" to "cut [herself] a long limber horse," the audience understands her playful nature. She cuts herself a horse which symbolizes her freedom and carefree nature as she plays outside, but her attention to detail as she makes her toy shows how these moments of freedom have great importance to her. The detail of her brother's knife depicts how she has to use a boy's object to create this free world she can play in, as this playful and rambunctious nature is more closely associated with little boys. She embodies the freedom the horse represents as her head becomes "shaped like a horse" and her hair is "like a mane of a horse in the wind." These similes show her transformation into a creature that is wild and free, roaming where she wants and playing however she sees fit. She is not confined by any societal ideas of how she should play with tea sets or dollhouses, she is free of all judgment to explore her youth and childhood. The wind is also representative of freedom as it twists and moves anyway and anywhere it wants. It is again referenced as "the wind twanged in [her] mane." The sense of freedom that the wind represents calls her and she allows herself to roam free for a short while until she has to return home. The tone of carefree youth is exemplified through the poetic devices used to depict this young girl's adventures playing horse.

> claim: societal expectations for girls impede their freedom
> topic sentence: freedom associated with the playfulness of youth

> evidence: figurative language illustrates the joy from freedom found outside the home

In the last stanzas, the tone shifts from jovial to judgmental as the young girl enters the confines of her home and is questioned by her mother, representing the societal norms of being well-behaved girls and women have to follow. As she walks into the house, her carefree nature already dissipates. As she notices the "clean linoleum," she "smoothed her skirt": a gesture that contrasts with the dirty and playful tone from outside, instead shifting into a stricter environment inside. In this new environment, she adjusts accordingly to please others by fixing her clothing. She leaves behind the windblown hair and rumpled clothing that represent her freedom outside to look better adjusted for her mother and others. She is berated by her mother with questions about her time outside. Her mother represents the judgment and questioning women often get by others when acting against the societal norms of a perfect, well-mannered lady. The little girl is carefree and playful, just like a child should be, but in this new environment she is more reserved and obedient to please and conform to those standards of women even as a child. When her mother asks about what is in her pocket she answers obediently that it is her knife and notices how it "weighted [her] pocket and stretched [her] dress awry." This object associated with her brother and the playful rambunctious nature of boys, the knife, is weighing on her as she tries her hardest to conform to the perfect little girl her mother expects and wants. The knife also messes up her dress, showing how this object that represents her freedom from outside is messing with the mask she is putting on with orderly clothing and hair. It instead rumples her dress and depicts her true nature as a playful child, but her mother's judging eyes do not accept that, so the little girl conforms to the well-mannered stereotype that society wants her to be, instead of being her true self. The tone shift contrasts the freedom she feels playing outside as a horse with her mother's questioning and judgment.

> *topic sentence: loss of freedom signified by tone shift from playful to reserved*

> *evidence: details and word choice illustrate the loss of freedom experienced within the rules of society*

In Swenson's poem "The Centaur," the speaker depicts the societal pressures placed on girls to be obedient and well-mannered. She uses metaphors and similes to create a tonal shift from the carefree independence of a child playing outside alone to the constraints and judgments of social expectations.

> *conclusion: articulates the desire for freedom from societal pressures*

Free-Response Question: Poetry Analysis

AP® Enduring Understanding (LAN-1)

Readers establish and communicate their interpretations of literature through arguments supported by textual evidence.

Justifying a Thesis through a Line of Reasoning

The first free-response essay prompt on the AP® English Literature and Composition Exam requires you to write a literary argument analyzing a poem. In this workshop, you will continue to develop the skills you need to complete this task with a specific focus on establishing a line of reasoning.

Read the following practice prompt and the accompanying poem, which is an adaptation of the type of prompt you may see on the exam. Please note that on the actual exam, you will be required to write a full analytical essay about multiple poetic elements and techniques.

Prompt:

In the following poem by William Shakespeare (published in 1609), the speaker addresses a loved one who has noticed that he is growing old and closer to death. Write a paragraph in which you make a defensible claim regarding how Shakespeare uses metaphors to convey the complex relationship between the aging speaker and the loved one.

In your paragraph, you should incorporate at least one piece of evidence from the text to support your claim.

In your response, you should do the following:

- Respond to the prompt with a claim that presents a defensible interpretation
- Select and use evidence to support your line of reasoning
- Use appropriate grammar and punctuation in communicating your argument

Unifying Idea	Sonnet 73 William Shakespeare	Effect of Literary Elements and Techniques
mortality	That time of year thou mayst in me behold When yellow leaves, or none, or few, do hang Upon those boughs which shake against the cold, Bare ruin'd choirs, where late the sweet birds sang.	speaker compared to dying season
mortality	5 In me thou see'st the twilight of such day As after sunset fadeth in the west, Which by and by black night doth take away, Death's second self, that seals up all in rest.	speaker compared to end of day
mortality	In me thou see'st the glowing of such fire 10 That on the ashes of his youth doth lie, As the death-bed whereon it must expire, Consum'd with that which it was nourish'd by.	speaker compared to dying fire
	This thou perceiv'st, which makes thy love more strong, To love that well which thou must leave ere long.	insight: love grows stronger with the threat of the death of a loved one

→ Step One: Annotate the Passage Based on a Unifying Idea

Unlike the prose fiction analysis question that you practiced in Unit 1, the poetry analysis question most often includes an entire poem rather than a short excerpt from a longer text for you to interpret. When you identify a unifying idea in a full poem, your goal is to arrive at an interpretation of the whole work.

To communicate an insight about an idea, poets often write using condensed language and, at times, unusual sentence structure, which requires you to read carefully and methodically. Poetic language is highly sensory with words that have strong connotations. Additionally, to represent ideas, poets often compare familiar images and objects to more abstract concepts. The two most common comparison techniques you will encounter are **metaphor** and **simile**. In a poem, these comparisons shed light on the speaker's attitude, tone, or deeper understanding of an experience. To interpret this deeper understanding, you must make associations between the literal context in the poem and the overall figurative meaning suggested by the comparisons.

Consider these questions as you read and annotate for comparisons in poetry:

- What are the qualities of the literal or familiar object (also called the comparison subject)?
- How do these qualities relate to — or reveal — characteristics of the main subject of comparison?

- How does the comparison relate to an idea?
- What insight about the human experience can you glean from that idea?

In "Sonnet 73," Shakespeare uses comparison by including three distinct metaphors within the poem. You should first examine the details of the comparison subjects (winter, twilight, and a dying fire) and associate them with the main subject (the speaker). Next, you can draw upon your experiences with these objects to infer that the speaker is aging and therefore facing his imminent death (unifying idea). Your experiences then help you understand the perspective in the speaker's final revelation: his loved one grows fonder of him because of the realization of his mortality.

→ Step Two: Develop a Defensible Thesis Statement and a Unified Line of Reasoning

To decide how to subdivide your literary argument into manageable topics of discussion, consider the following questions:

- Are some details or images in contrast or tension within the text?
- Is an idea presented in a complex or contradictory manner?
- Is there a shift in point of view, perspective, or tone within the text?
- Are contrasting ideas, images, or perspectives juxtaposed within the text?
- Do different literary techniques work together to reveal the final message?

In all of these questions, two or more topics emerge for discussion. When you develop your line of reasoning, you will explore the topics one at a time and include evidence for support within each body paragraph.

In Unit 1, you learned to write a thesis statement that includes a defensible claim. Remember that your claim must include the interpretation of the text (idea + insight). You will now practice developing a logical sequence of reasons to support your thesis statement called the **line of reasoning**. To develop your literary argument, you should have two or more reasons that will serve as topic sentences for the body paragraphs to prove the validity of your interpretation. These reasons are often guided by the author's techniques within the text.

Techniques represent the author's literary "moves," while elements are the specific tools the author uses to create the technique. You should use the techniques to guide your line of reasoning and the elements to support that line of reasoning. A line of reasoning may be organized by techniques. An author's techniques (e.g., imagery, contrast, comparison) are made up of elements. Techniques are larger than elements.

Furthermore, just as the author planned the order of the events and details within a text, you should carefully consider the order in which you present your topics of discussion to analyze those details. In other words, if you have identified a shift in tone or perspective, then you can explain the details before the shift first, and then develop the details after the shift.

As a word of caution, you should avoid simply summarizing or paraphrasing a text. Summary is not analysis. The purpose of a line of reasoning is to avoid such a

SOME LITERARY TECHNIQUES AND ELEMENTS	
Techniques	**Elements**
Imagery	connotation, allusion, personification, simile, motif
Contrast	irony, juxtaposition, paradox, antithesis, imagery
Comparison	simile, metaphor, conceit, image, allusion, symbol
Narration	point of view, perspective, speaker, tone
Pacing	sentence structure, flashback, foreshadowing, suspense, pause, variety
Emphasis	subordination, coordination, cumulative sentence, periodic sentence, rhetorical question, exaggeration, repetition, simple sentence, fragment
Balance	coordination, parallelism, coordinating conjunction, repetition

misstep by organizing your analysis with focused reasons related to your unifying idea and insight.

While an argument must have a line of reasoning, the writer may choose whether to preview the line of reasoning in the thesis statement. Review the following examples of defensible thesis statements that omit and include a stated preview of the line of reasoning:

Sample Thesis Statements	Notes Regarding Line of Reasoning Preview
In his poem "Sonnet 73," Shakespeare compares the speaker to objects near death to suggest that love grows stronger with the threat of loss.	Defensible thesis with no stated line of reasoning: This thesis refers to a technique (comparison) and includes an interpretation (love grows stronger with the threat of loss); however, it does not directly state the line of reasoning that will guide the body paragraphs. Even so, the writer may successfully develop the literary argument with this thesis by stating the reasons in the topic sentences for the subsequent body paragraphs.
In his poem "Sonnet 73," William Shakespeare compares the aging speaker to objects that were once youthful but are now near death to support the speaker's final revelation that love grows stronger with the threat of loss.	Defensible thesis with a stated line of reasoning: This thesis focuses on one unifying strategy (comparison) and includes an interpretation (love grows stronger with the threat of loss). This writer indicates a line of reasoning by further breaking down the qualities in the comparison subjects into two categories: (1) once youthful and (2) near death. The writer's thesis suggests a line of reasoning that focuses first on details related to youth and then on details related to death. The order of these justifications is effective as well because life precedes death, and the speaker's revelation at the end of the poem is a response to impending death. By developing a body paragraph for each of these observations, the writer can support the thesis and develop the literary argument.

INSIDER AP® TIP

The author's strategies justify the idea and insight. Topic sentences in each body paragraph serve to develop the technique(s) in your thesis. You can use the following basic template to structure your topic sentences. The author [technique] to illustrate [connection to insight and idea].

→ Step Three: Choose Relevant Evidence

You have learned already that you must provide **relevant evidence** to support your thesis and that you should choose this evidence carefully. Additionally, you must include evidence to support each reason in your line of reasoning. In other words, every body paragraph should include evidence.

In choosing textual evidence or details from the text, make sure that you arrange those details into the related body paragraphs. For example, in the paragraph dedicated to the speaker's once youthful past, you could include the detail of the season and location where "late the sweet birds sang," and in the paragraph dedicated to the speaker's approaching death, you could include the detail that the ashes of the fire are now on "the death-bed whereon it must expire." As a general rule, you should include more than one piece of evidence within each body paragraph and represent multiple literary elements and techniques within your literary argument.

Finally, when you incorporate evidence from a poem, you will need to integrate the text into your argument properly. Quoting from poetry is a bit different than quoting from prose. When you are quoting directly, you must keep the original punctuation and capitalization intact and indicate line breaks as well.

The following examples demonstrate three ways of incorporating textual evidence from a poem.

Original text	That time of year thou mayst in me behold When yellow leaves, or none, or few, do hang Upon those boughs which shake against the cold, Bare ruin'd choirs, where late the sweet birds sang.
Paraphrasing	The speaker realizes that his loved one notices his aging body and compares himself to the season of winter — a cold season when birds no longer sing.
Using a signal phrase	Revealing his loved one's perspective on his aging, Shakespeare's speaker says, "That time of year thou mayst in me behold / When yellow leaves, or none, or few, do hang / Upon those boughs."
Embedding the text	In describing his aging body, Shakespeare's speaker compares himself to winter when the trees "shake" and the "cold / Bare ruin'd choirs" are no longer inhabited by the "sweet birds."

→ Step Four: Develop Your Commentary

Even after you have included evidence to support your thesis, your analysis will be incomplete until you explain how all of the evidence connects to the idea and insight stated in your thesis. You can begin by including a sentence following your evidence to explain how the evidence functions. Review these basic sentence stems:

- By using these examples, the author reveals . . .
- The author includes the metaphor to illustrate . . .
- This specific word choice suggests . . .
- The simile explores the connection between . . .
- The repetition of _____ emphasizes . . .

In Unit 3, you will begin to write these explanations, also known as commentary, that not only identify the link between your evidence and make your reasons clear but also make the connection to the unifying idea clear to your reader. Your goal is to offer insight into your interpretation of the passage and explain your line of reasoning.

AP® EXAM PRACTICE

The following is an example of a poetry analysis free-response question. Practice the skills you learned in this workshop to write a thesis statement and a paragraph that includes evidence in response to the prompt.

Remember to follow the four steps:

- Step One: Annotate the passage based on a **unifying idea**
- Step Two: Write a **defensible thesis statement**
- Step Three: Choose **relevant evidence**
- Step Four: Develop **insightful commentary**

Prompt:

In the following poem "Perhaps the World Ends Here" by Joy Harjo (published in 1994), the speaker describes a variety of human events that take place around the kitchen table. Read the poem carefully.

Write a paragraph in which you make a defensible claim regarding how Harjo uses the kitchen table as a metaphor to convey a complex understanding of the human experience. In your paragraph, you should incorporate evidence from the text to support your claim.

In your response you should do the following:

- Respond to the prompt with a claim that presents a defensible interpretation
- Select and use evidence to support your line of reasoning
- Use appropriate grammar and punctuation in communicating your argument

Perhaps The World Ends Here

The world begins at a kitchen table. No matter what, we must eat to live.

The gifts of earth are brought and prepared, set on the table. So it has been since creation, and it will go on.

5   We chase chickens or dogs away from it. Babies teethe at the corners. They scrape their knees under it.

It is here that children are given instructions on what it means to be human. We make men at it, we make women.

At this table we gossip, recall enemies and the ghosts of lovers.

10   Our dreams drink coffee with us as they put their arms around our children. They laugh with us at our poor falling-down selves and as we put ourselves back together once again at the table.

This table has been a house in the rain, an umbrella in the sun.

Wars have begun and ended at this table. It is a place to hide in the
15   shadow of terror. A place to celebrate the terrible victory.

We have given birth on this table, and have prepared our parents for burial here.

At this table we sing with joy, with sorrow. We pray of suffering and remorse. We give thanks.

20   Perhaps the world will end at the kitchen table, while we are laughing and crying, eating of the last sweet bite.

ORGANIZING A POETRY ANALYSIS (I)

Defensible Thesis Statement with Claim (idea + insight):

In [title], [poet] illustrates [idea + insight] through the use of [element/technique 1], [element/technique 2], and [element/technique 3].

Topic Sentence 1 (Identify the first aspect of the topic related to the unifying idea):	Topic Sentence 2 (Identify the second aspect of the topic related to the unifying idea):	Topic Sentence 3 (Identify the third aspect of the topic related to the unifying idea):
To begin, [poet] includes [technique/element 1] to [purpose connect to idea].	Next, [poet] includes [technique/element 2] to [purpose connect to idea].	Finally, [poet] includes [technique/element 3] to [purpose connect to idea].
Textual Details (Relevant and sufficient evidence):	**Textual Details** (Relevant and sufficient evidence):	**Textual Details** (Relevant and sufficient evidence):
For example, the detail/image/comparison [text evidence], used to describe [context] illustrates [link to topic sentence].	To illustrate, [poet] describes/compares [context] by describing [text evidence] to reveal [link to topic sentence].	As an example of [technique/element], the author includes [text evidence] to explain [link to topic sentence].
Additionally, the detail/image/comparison [text evidence], used to describe [context] illustrates [link to topic sentence].	To continue, [author] describes/compares [context] by describing [text evidence] to reveal [link to topic sentence].	Through another example, of [technique/element], the author includes [text evidence] to explain [link to topic sentence].
Commentary (Link evidence to reason and idea):	**Commentary** (Link evidence to reason and idea):	**Commentary** (Link evidence to reason and idea):
The association of [text evidence] with [topic sentence] reveals [idea and insight].	Through this choice, [poet] develops [idea and insight].	By including this [element/technique] the author suggests that [idea and insight].

from The Comet

W. E. B. Du Bois

The following is an excerpt from a short story published in 1920.

He stood a moment on the steps of the bank, watching the human river that swirled down Broadway. Few noticed him. Few ever noticed him save in a way that stung. He was outside
5 the world — "nothing!" as he said bitterly. Bits of the words of the walkers came to him.

"The comet?"

"The comet —"

Everybody was talking of it. Even the pres-
10 ident,[1] as he entered, smiled patronizingly at him, and asked:

"Well, Jim, are you scared?"

"No," said the messenger shortly.

"I thought we'd journeyed through the
15 comet's tail once," broke in the junior clerk affably.

"Oh, that was Halley's," said the president; "this is a new comet, quite a stranger, they say — wonderful, wonderful! I saw it last night.
20 Oh, by the way, Jim," turning again to the messenger, "I want you to go down into the lower vaults today."

The messenger followed the president silently. Of course, they wanted *him* to go
25 down to the lower vaults. It was too dangerous for more valuable men. He smiled grimly and listened.

"Everything of value has been moved out since the water began to seep in," said the pres-
30 ident; "but we miss two volumes of old records. Suppose you nose around down there, — it isn't very pleasant, I suppose."

[1]President of the bank for whom the main character works.

"Not very," said the messenger, as he walked out.

35 "Well, Jim, the tail of the new comet hits us at noon this time," said the vault clerk, as he passed over the keys; but the messenger passed silently down the stairs. Down he went beneath Broadway, where the dim light filtered through
40 the feet of hurrying men; down to the dark basement beneath; down into the blackness and silence beneath that lowest cavern. Here with his dark lantern he groped in the bowels of the earth, under the world.

45 He drew a long breath as he threw back the last great iron door and stepped into the fetid slime within. Here at last was peace, and he groped moodily forward. A great rat leaped past him and cobwebs crept across his face.
50 He felt carefully around the room, shelf by shelf, on the muddied floor, and in crevice and corner. Nothing. Then he went back to the far end, where somehow the wall felt different. He sounded and pushed and pried. Nothing. He
55 started away. Then something brought him back. He was sounding and working again when suddenly the whole black wall swung as on mighty hinges, and blackness yawned beyond. He peered in; it was evidently a secret
60 vault — some hiding place of the old bank unknown in newer times. He entered hesitatingly. It was a long, narrow room with shelves, and at the far end, an old iron chest. On a high shelf lay the two missing volumes of records,
65 and others. He put them carefully aside and stepped to the chest. It was old, strong, and rusty. He looked at the vast and old-fashioned lock and flashed his light on the hinges.

They were deeply encrusted with rust. Looking
70 about, he found a bit of iron and began to pry.
The rust had eaten a hundred years, and it had
gone deep. Slowly, wearily, the old lid lifted, and
with a last, low groan lay bare its treasure —
and he saw the dull sheen of gold!
75   "Boom!"
     A low, grinding, reverberating crash struck
upon his ear. He started up and looked about.
All was black and still. He groped for his light
and swung it about him. Then he knew! The
80 great stone door had swung to. He forgot the
gold and looked death squarely in the face.
Then with a sigh he went methodically to
work. The cold sweat stood on his forehead;
but he searched, pounded, pushed, and worked
85 until after what seemed endless hours his
hand struck a cold bit of metal and the great
door swung again harshly on its hinges, and
then, striking against something soft and
heavy, stopped. He had just room to squeeze
90 through. There lay the body of the vault clerk,
cold and stiff. He stared at it, and then felt sick
and nauseated. The air seemed unaccountably
foul, with a strong, peculiar odor. He stepped
forward, clutched at the air, and fell fainting
95 across the corpse.

1. In the context of the passage as a whole, which
of the following details about setting are most
significant?
(A) ". . . the human river that swirled down
Broadway" (lines 3–4).
(B) ". . . the dim light filtered through the feet
of hurrying men . . ." (lines 39–40).
(C) "A great rat leaped past him and cobwebs
crept across his face" (lines 48–49).
(D) ". . . a long, narrow room with shelves,
and at the far end, an old iron chest"
(lines 62–63).
(E) ". . . the great door swung again harshly
on its hinges, and then, striking against
something soft and heavy, stopped" (lines
86–89).

2. The pronoun "*him*" (italicized in the original
story) in line 24 refers to
(A) Jim, the messenger, who is the main
character.
(B) the bank president.
(C) the junior clerk who accompanies the
bank president.
(D) any of the people referred to in the
"human river" in the first sentence.
(E) no one in particular as it is intended to be
ambiguous.

3. Which of the following details BEST illustrate
Jim's bitter annoyance with his task?
(A) ". . . 'nothing!' as he said bitterly" (line 5).
(B) "He smiled grimly and listened" (lines
26–27).
(C) ". . . but the messenger passed silently
down the stairs" (lines 37–38).
(D) ". . . down into the blackness and silence
beneath that lowest cavern" (lines 41–42).
(E) "The cold sweat stood on his forehead . . ."
(line 83).

4. In the context of the passage as a whole, the
introduction of gold in line 74 creates
(A) the turning point for Jim and his
bitterness.
(B) an example of how others in the passage
are tempting Jim.
(C) a symbol of impending wealth and
prosperity for Jim.
(D) a conflict affecting the trust established
between Jim and the bank president.
(E) a contrast revealing a narrow window of
hope for Jim.

5. During the bank president's entrance, his perspective on Jim is most directly revealed by
   (A) his need to immediately ask him a question.
   (B) the kind of smile he offers Jim.
   (C) his failure to ask how Jim is doing.
   (D) the lack of handshake offered to Jim.
   (E) his avoidance of eye contact with Jim.

6. The narrator's statement that Jim "groped in the bowels of the earth" (lines 43–44) serves figuratively to both
   (A) describe Jim's surroundings and explain why he takes as long as he does.
   (B) emphasize the nastiness of Jim's task and comment on his value to the bank.
   (C) explain the actions of the bank president and the vault clerk.
   (D) display Jim's perspective and encourage him to finish his task despite his bitterness and disgust.
   (E) contradict the gold Jim will soon find and preserve his low place in the hierarchy of the bank.

7. The narrator of the passage can BEST be described as
   (A) a first-person narrator who is biased toward the people running the bank.
   (B) a first-person narrator who is intimately involved with the bank.
   (C) an all-knowing, third-person narrator aware of the thoughts of characters.
   (D) an all-knowing, third-person narrator who shows bias toward Jim.
   (E) a third-person narrator with a limited perspective on the characters involved.

8. Which of the following BEST describes the relationship of the two paragraphs in lines 45–74 and lines 76–95 ("He drew . . . of gold" and "A low, grinding . . . corpse.") in the context of the passage as a whole?
   (A) The earlier paragraph provides a broad description of the underworld setting while the latter paragraph then provides more specific details to emphasize the significance of his journey.
   (B) The two paragraphs restate significant details about Jim's journey in different ways to emphasize their significance and the significance of the journey itself.
   (C) The two paragraphs contradict one another in their description of Jim's personality and his behaviors in his setting.
   (D) The earlier paragraph establishes Jim's fears during his descent only to have those fears realized during his return to the world in the latter paragraph.
   (E) The earlier paragraph shows Jim descending into a terrible place but possibly being rewarded with gold only to be faced with an even more terrible return in the latter paragraph.

9. As a whole, the passage establishes all of the following EXCEPT
   (A) the bank president's perspective on Jim.
   (B) Jim's attitude toward the bank president.
   (C) Jim's place in the hierarchy at the bank.
   (D) background on Jim's position at the bank.
   (E) the narrator's point of view in the narrative.

A Noiseless Patient Spider
Walt Whitman

A noiseless patient spider,
I mark'd where on a little promontory[1] it stood isolated,
Mark'd how to explore the vacant vast surrounding,
It launch'd forth filament,[2] filament, filament, out of itself,
5 Ever unreeling them, ever tirelessly speeding them.

And you O my soul where you stand,
Surrounded, detached, in measureless oceans of space,
Ceaselessly musing, venturing, throwing, seeking the spheres[3] to connect them,
Till the bridge you will need be form'd, till the ductile anchor hold,
10 Till the gossamer[4] thread you fling catch somewhere, O my soul.

1. Alliteration in line 3 ("Mark'd . . . surrounding,")
   emphasizes
   (A) the journey facing the spider.
   (B) the enormity of the isolation perceived by
       the spider.
   (C) how much the spider has explored in his
       time.
   (D) how lost the spider feels in his
       unexplored surroundings.
   (E) the dangers the spider perceives from his
       high vantage point.

2. Use of the word "somewhere" (line 10)
   suggest that the speaker is
   (A) talking as much to himself as he is his
       soul.
   (B) unable to accept responsibility for the
       actions of his own soul.
   (C) frightened of the growing distance
       between himself and his soul.
   (D) uncertain about his own direction and
       existence.
   (E) willing to follow wherever his soul
       may wander.

[1]A point of high land that juts out into a large body of water.
[2]In this case, a thread of spider's web; some spiders begin building webs by releasing filaments into
 the air until they stick to something nearby.
[3]Heavenly bodies such as planets, sun, moon, and stars.
[4]A fine, filmy substance consisting of cobwebs spun by small spiders.

3. The speaker's perspective is directly shaped by
   (A) the initial observation of the spider seeking to explore its surroundings.
   (B) the perceived separation of the speaker from their soul.
   (C) the first-person involvement of the speaker with their soul.
   (D) the outside perspective of a third-person point of view.
   (E) the all-knowing point of view that prevents bias in the speaker.

4. Which of the following BEST describes how the spider in the first stanza serves as a metaphor for the speaker's soul in the second stanza?
   (A) The spider cannot find a hold in its "vacant vast surrounding" (line 3) despite working "tirelessly." This suggests that the speaker's soul continually fails to make a connection in its "measureless oceans of space" (line 7).
   (B) The spider is isolated in space but sending filaments "out of itself" (line 4) seeking connection as it builds its web. This suggests that the speaker's soul is also isolated in its "measureless oceans of space" (line 7) but working to find a sense of connection.
   (C) The spider climbs to its highest point on the "little promontory" (line 2) and "tirelessly" launches filaments with no connections. This suggests that the speaker's soul has reached the peak of existence but it is meaningless as all it can do is "ceaselessly" (line 8) muse.
   (D) The spider works "tirelessly" (line 5) until it makes a connection in its "vacant vast surrounding" (line 3) while the speaker's soul remains "detached" (line 7) and cannot make its own connections.
   (E) The spider "stood isolated" (line 2) and overwhelmed by its "vacant vast surrounding" (line 3) while the speaker's soul "stand[s], surrounded" (lines 6–7) and does not need to seek connection as the spider does.

5. The effect of structuring the poem with the spider stanza first is to
   (A) establish details for comparison before the actual comparison is made.
   (B) distinguish the animal qualities of the spider from the celestial qualities of the soul.
   (C) combine the circumstances of the spider as it is compared to the circumstances of the speaker's soul.
   (D) ensure that the spider is seen as being the speaker's soul.
   (E) avoid any confusion that the speaker, soul, and spider are all the same thing in the overall context of the poem.

6. The poem as a whole suggests a contrast between
   (A) isolation and detachment.
   (B) love and connection.
   (C) hope and isolation.
   (D) fear and loathing.
   (E) patience and anxiety.

Sebastian Willnow/Getty Images

UNIT

3
Analyzing Tensions

UNIT GOALS

	Focus	Goals
Big Idea: Character	**Static and Dynamic Characters**	Explain the significance of a character's changing over the course of a story.
Big Idea: Setting	**Social, Cultural, and Historical Contexts**	Explain how a story's setting reveals historical context and reflects social or cultural values.
Big Idea: Structure	**Conflict**	Explain how events in a narrative progress toward a conflict, revealing a tension of values that contributes to an interpretation of a story.
Ideas in Literature	**Power and Control**	Explain how the ideas of power and manipulation are reflected in classic and contemporary texts.
Big Idea: Literary Argumentation	**Writing about Character**	Write a literary argument that analyzes a character and conveys an interpretation of a text.
Preparing for the AP® Exam	**Free-Response Question: Literary Argument** Explaining an Interpretation through Commentary	Write commentary that explains the connection between the evidence and the reasons in the line of reasoning.
	Multiple-Choice Questions: Prose	Analyze literary elements and techniques in classic and contemporary prose and poetry.
	Multiple-Choice Questions: Poetry	

Static and Dynamic Characters

 Enduring Understanding

Characters in literature allow readers to study and explore a range of values, beliefs, assumptions, biases, and cultural norms represented by those characters.

KEY POINT

A character's background, cultural context, and interactions with other characters influence that character's motivation. The choices a character makes affect his or her trajectory (whether the character changes or remains the same) and ultimately the story's outcome.

There's nothing more frustrating than watching a character knowingly walk right into a dangerous situation, only to be met with consequences: usually, in thrillers or horror films, something like a crazed ax murderer lying in wait. You might think, "I can't believe they did that! Who in their right mind would do that in the real world?"

Just as people in real life do, characters often make decisions based on who they are and what values they hold. We expect characters to act plausibly and in ways consistent with their personalities. But how can we understand why characters do what they do?

Characters Are Complex

Understanding a character is a complex process. You learned in Unit 1 that characterization is based on speech, action, and description. What makes analyzing characters especially complex is that much of the description about a character comes from the narrator or other characters. Because readers draw conclusions about characters based on details shared by narrators or other characters, they must consider those biases and perspectives. You must keep this in mind as you analyze a narrator's or character's description of another character. Ultimately, how a character is developed sets up your own expectations for that character. Those expectations are likely based on your understanding of the character within the context.

Narrators

Narrators play a major role in shaping how readers interpret characters. A narrator's description of a character directly affects how the reader expects the character to behave. For example, you might expect a character who is repeatedly described as calm, patient, and gentle to behave in ways that display kindness and compassion; on the other hand, you might expect completely different behavior from a character described as nasty, rude, or self-absorbed. When the gentle character lashes out in anger or the nasty character must sacrifice something important, the reader's expectations shift, as do their interpretations.

It is important to notice that when narrators, characters, or speakers compare another character to something or someone else, they reveal something central and critical in the comparison. That means you must specifically consider why the character is being compared to another character or object.

In other words, how is the character similar to another character or object, and what do these similarities reveal about the character?

Motivation

Characters have a goal—something they are trying to accomplish in the story. This goal requires them to make choices that affect the plot and story line. Those decisions are also informed and guided by a character's **motivation**: the reasons that someone does what they do (or don't do). When characters lack clear and purposeful motivation (such as the poor victim in the movie aimlessly wandering into the serial killer's trap), they become less believable. In contrast, characters with clear motivations are more compelling and authentic. Keep in mind that as a character's perspective may change over the course of a story, so can their motivation.

Dynamic and Static Characters

When characters interact with other characters and events in the plot, they may react in significant ways that alter their perspectives. Characters who undergo a fundamental change in their perspective or personality during the narrative are known as dynamic characters. A **dynamic character** develops over the course of a story. Usually, dynamic characters make decisions that directly or indirectly affect the climax or even resolution of the narrative. Keep in mind, too, that external changes can lead to internal changes and vice versa. Characters who remain unchanged or fixed are known as **static characters**.

Character changes may come about from the events in the plot or interactions with other characters. These changes can be physical and external, such as

- changes in their health or physical ability;
- changes in their financial situation; and
- changes in their interactions with space and possessions.

However, they can also be mental, emotional, invisible, or internal, such as

- changes in their psychological state;
- changes in their emotional outlook; and
- changes in their thought processes.

As you read, you'll also want to consider how other characters react to a character's choices, as well as what happens to the character as a result of his or her choices. Some narrators and characters may convey empathy toward a character while others remain stoic or emotionally detached.

 INSIDER **AP TIP**   **Shifts are crucial to interpretation.** Analytical readers can describe a shift in a character's perspective. They can also explain the significance of the shift in relation to the change in a character's thinking, especially within the historical, cultural, and social context.

DYNAMIC CHARACTERS	
Type of Change	**Examples**
Physical	Change in physical appearance
	Change in health/fitness
	Change in mobility
Social	Change in economic status
	Change in occupation
	Change in association or disassociation with a group or cause
	Change in conforming to or rebelling against social norms
	Change in relationships
	Change in family dynamics
Behavioral	Change in motivation
	Change in opting to choose/refusing to choose
Emotional	Change in feeling or attitude
	Change in mood
Psychological	Change in understanding/awareness
	Change in mental state
	Change in education status
	Change in personality
Spiritual	Change in religion or religious belief
	Change in morals
	Change in earthly/spiritual state

Mistaken Identity

Sharon Cooper

Kevin L Watkins Jr

THE TEXT IN CONTEXT

New York–based playwright and screenwriter Sharon Cooper works in many dramatic forms, but she is especially known for her ten-minute, one-act plays, such as the one that follows. These short, often comic dramatic forms can bring characters into focus and illuminate the dramatic tensions in everyday life. In *Mistaken Identity*, Cooper brings together two disparate individuals who have mistaken assumptions about each other. At first, the two characters appear profoundly different — in background, ethnicity, religion, and perspective. The progress of the play traces their development in the context of their conversation on a blind date. *Mistaken Identity* also illustrates the ways in which drama — and our interactions with others — can reveal character and identity.

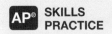 **SKILLS PRACTICE** | **CHARACTER**
Analyzing Dynamic Characters

As you read *Mistaken Identity*, identify physical, social, behavioral, emotional, psychological, and spiritual details that establish each character. Consider whether either of the characters changes in any of these aspects. If so, note the details after the shift. Then, explain the significance of that change in relation to the play's conflict.

Analyzing Dynamic Characters			
	Textual Details before the Shift	Textual Details after the Change	Significance
Physical			
Social			
Behavioral			
Emotional			
Psychological			
Spiritual			

Mistaken Identity

CHARACTERS: KALI PATEL, *29. Single lesbian Hindu of Indian heritage; social worker who works as much as possible; lives in Leicester, England.* STEVE DODD, *32. Single straight guy, desperate to marry, raised Baptist but attends church only on Christmas and Easter; studying abroad for his final year as an undergraduate.*

SETTING: *The Castle, a pub in Kirby Muxlowe in Leicester, England.*

TIME: *The present.*

(Lights up on Steve and Kali in a busy pub on their first date. They are in the middle of dinner.)

STEVE: You must get tired of fish and chips all the time. Why do y'all call them "chips"? When they're french fries, I mean. And you ever notice when people
5   swear, they say, "Excuse my French." Not

me. Nope. I have nothing against the French.

KALI: Right, well, I'm not French, Steve, now am I?

10 **STEVE:** I just didn't want you to think I was prejudiced against the French or anyone else. . . . They're like your neighbors, the French. And your neighbors are like my neighbors. And like a good neighbor, State
15 Farm is there. Have you heard that commercial?

KALI: What? No. Steve—

STEVE: It's for insurance. Y'all must not play it here. (Pause.) So I know that you all do
20 the arranged marriage thing. Rashid and I had a long talk about it. Of course, Rashid and I wanted you to approve, too, Kali.

KALI: How twenty-first century of you and
25 my brother. Steve . . .

KALI: I'm gay. / **STEVE:** Will you marry me?

KALI: Come again? / **STEVE:** What?

KALI: How could you ask me to . . . / **STEVE:** Well, I can't believe this.

30 **KALI:** Bloody hell, stop talking while I'm talking . . . / **STEVE:** This is very strange.

KALI: So—what?

STEVE: This new information is, well, new, and changes things, I guess.

35 **KALI:** You guess? What the hell is wrong with you? I'm sorry, Steve, you just happened to show up at the end of a very long line of a lot of very bad dates. You know, movies where the bloke negotiates
40 holding your hand while you're just trying to eat popcorn; running across De Montfort University in the pouring rain; dropping a bowling ball on the bloke's pizza.

45 **STEVE:** You had me until the bowling ball. Kali, this doesn't make sense. I invite you out on a lovely date. We eat fish and chips—when I would rather be eating a burger or lasagna—

50 **KALI:** Steve, I'm sorry.

STEVE: I figured we would have a nice long traditional wedding with the colorful tents. All of my family would be there. We're more of the Christmas/Easter
55 Christians, so we'd do your religion and I would wear—

KALI: (Overlapping.) You don't know anything about my people. What are you—

STEVE: (Overlapping.) Ooohhh, yes, I do. I saw
60 *Monsoon Wedding.* And the director's cut! And I saw *Slumdog Millionaire* like three times. Three times. Unbelievable!

KALI: Yes, this makes loads of sense at the end of the day. I am a lesbian who has to
65 date every Hindu bloke in England until her brother gets so desperate that he sets her up with a cowboy—

STEVE: I take offense to that.

KALI: (Overlapping.) But I should feel sorry
70 for *you* because *you* watched *two,* count them, *two* movies about Indian people in your entire life and ordered fish when there are hamburgers on the menu! Forgive *me* for being so insensitive.

75 **STEVE:** I ordered fish because I wanted you to like me. And I'm sure I've seen other Asian movies. Like all those fighting movies. You know, the ones where women are jumping through the air—

80 **KALI:** Aaahhh! Do you see how all of this is a moot point now?

STEVE: I'm confused. Let's review.

KALI: Please, no, bloody hell, let's not review. Let's get the waiter. Haven't you had
85 enough? (She gets up. He follows.)

STEVE: (Overlapping.) Why is your brother setting up his *lesbian* sister—

KALI: (Overlapping.) Will you please keep your voice down?

90 **STEVE:** (*Overlapping.*)—up on dates for marriage and tricking well-meaning men—specifically me—into proposing to her? I'm here to finish my business degree, but I wasn't born yesterday. So I
95 took a few years off and changed careers a few times, was a fireman—

KALI: (*Overlapping.*) What does that have to do with anything?

STEVE: And I'm thirty-two years old, but that
100 doesn't mean—

KALI: Mate, are you going to keep on and on?

STEVE: Why did your brother put me through this? This isn't one of those new reality
105 shows: "Big Brothers Set Up Their Lesbian Sisters." Is there a camera under the table? (*He looks.*) Let's talk about this. (*He sits back down.*) I'm a good listener. Go ahead. (*Pause.*) I'm listening. (*Pause.*) You have to
110 say something if you want this to continue as what we call in America, a conversation.

KALI: Are you done?

STEVE: Go ahead. (*She sits.*)

KALI: I guess I was hoping you wouldn't tell
115 Rashid.

STEVE: He doesn't know?

KALI: You are finishing your bachelor's degree, is that right?

STEVE: If you're so "bloody" smart, I'm
120 wondering why you would tell me, a man that is friends with your brother and sits next to him twice a week in eight a.m. classes—why would you tell *me* you're a lesbian and *not* your brother?

125 **KALI:** Maybe for the same reason you would ask a woman you've never met before to marry you.

STEVE: Your brother made it sound like it would be easy. I've been looking for that.

130 **KALI:** (*Overlapping.*) Look, you seem very nice, you do.

STEVE: I am very nice.

KALI: And at the end of the day, I hope you find someone you like.

135 **STEVE:** I like how you say at the end of the day and I like how you say bloke and mate. It's so endearing. And you're beautiful and small and your hair falls on your back so.

140 **KALI:** Steve, being a lesbian is not negotiable. And don't start with how sexy it would be to be with me or to watch me and another woman—

STEVE: (*Overlapping.*) Kali, I didn't say any of
145 that.

KALI: You didn't have to. Up until a few minutes ago, you thought I was a quiet, subservient Asian toy for sale from her brother. Steve, go get a doll. She can travel
150 with you to America whenever you want. In the meantime, I'll continue to be a loud, abrasive (*Whispering.*) lesbian while my brother sets me up with every bloke on the street—and they don't even have to
155 be Hindu anymore! Do you have any idea what that's like? (*Pause.*) How would you know?

STEVE: You're right. I wouldn't.

KALI: Steve, why did you want to be with
160 me? I mean, before.

STEVE: I figured that we would have visited my family in the winter when it's so cold here. I would have been willing to stay here when I'm done with school and we
165 would get a nice little place by the—

KALI: Steve, we hadn't even shared dessert yet.

STEVE: Don't blame me for all of this. Five minutes ago, we were on a date.

170 **KALI:** We're just two people in a pub.

STEVE: Kali, do you remember the last time someone—man, woman, I don't care—had their hand down the small of

your back or leaned into you like it didn't
175 matter where you ended and they began?

KALI: Yes, I do remember that. And that was
strangely poetic.

STEVE: You don't have to sound so surprised.
Anyway, I remember that feeling. Three
180 years ago, at a Fourth of July celebration—
you know, that's the holiday—

KALI: Yes, Steve, I know the holiday.

STEVE: She was the only woman I ever really
loved. I knew it was ending. Could taste it.
185 I just held her as the fireworks went off
and the dust got in our skin. Figured I
would hold on, hoping that would keep
me for a while. You know how they say
babies will die if they're left alone too
190 long. Always wondered if it's true for
bigger people, too. Like how long would
we last? . . . She left with her Pilates mat
and Snoopy slippers a few days later. I bet
it hasn't been three years for you.

195 KALI: No, it hasn't. But you wouldn't want to
hear about that.

STEVE: Why not?

KALI: Come on, Steve, I'm not here for your
fantasies—

200 STEVE: This thing where you assume you
know what I'm thinking—it's gettin' old.

KALI: I'm . . . sorry. I do have a woman in my
life, Michele—she's a teacher for people
that are deaf. We've been together for
205 eleven months. The longest we were away
from each other was this one time for
three weeks. She was at a retreat where
they weren't allowed to talk—you know,
total immersion. So she would call and I
210 would say, Is it beautiful there, love? and
she would hit a couple of buttons.
Sometimes she would leave me messages:
beep, beep, beep beep beep beep. It didn't
matter that she didn't say anything . . .
215 But I can't take her home for Diwali.

STEVE: What's that?

KALI: It's a festival of lights where—

STEVE: You mean like Hanukkah.

KALI: No, like Diwali. It's a New Year's cele-
220 bration where we remember ancestors,
family, and friends. And reflect back and
look to the future.

STEVE: It sounds nice. You know, my mother
has been asking me for grandchildren
225 since I turned twenty-seven. Every year at
Christmas, it's the same: I can't wait to
hang another stocking for my grandchildren, if I ever get to have them.

KALI: Now, imagine that same conversation,
230 well, not about Christmas, and what if you
could never give that to them—could
never bring someone home for any holiday for the rest of your life?

STEVE: Then why don't you just tell them
235 the truth?

KALI: I can't say, Mum, Daddy, Rashid, I've
chosen women over men—it's not a
hamburger over fish. You just don't know
how they'll react. I'd run the risk of not
240 being allowed to see my nieces. I'm so
exhausted from hiding, I can barely
breathe.

STEVE: So stop hiding.

KALI: Have you been listening to what I've
245 been saying?

STEVE: Have you?

KALI: Are you going to tell my brother?

STEVE: Do you want me to?

KALI: I don't know.

250 STEVE: I've never thought about that thing
that you said.

KALI: Which thing would that be?

STEVE: The one where maybe you can't see
your nieces 'cause you're gay. That must
255 suck.

KALI: Yes, well, thanks for trying to make
me feel better.

STEVE: Listen, you get to decide what you tell your family and when. As far as I'm concerned, I'll tell Rashid tomorrow that we're getting married. Or I can tell him you're a lesbian, and if he doesn't let you be with his kids anymore, I'll punch him in the face. That was me kidding.

KALI: You're funny. (*Pause.*) Maybe I told you because somewhere deep down, I do want him to know. But I don't know if I can take the risk.

STEVE: You don't have to rush.

KALI: I just wish it could be more simple. Like, why can't what I want be part of the whole picket-fence thing? That's pretty ridiculous, huh?

STEVE: We're all looking for that. My grandparents met before World War II, dated for seven days in a row, and my grandfather asked my grandmother to go with him to Louisiana, where he'd be stationed. She said, "Is that a proposal?" And he said, "Of course it is." And they've been together ever since. And I just want that, too. Huh—asking you to marry me on a first date! You must think I'm pretty desperate, huh?

KALI: Not any more than the rest of us . . . Oh, hell, do you want to have some dessert?

STEVE: Oh, hell, sure. You know, we're going to share dessert.

KALI: Hey, mate, no one said anything about sharing.

STEVE: I would go home with you for Diwali I mean, as friends. If you ever wanted one around. You're a nice girl, Kali. I mean woman, mate, bloke. I mean—

KALI: Sssshhhh. Let's just get some dessert. (*Lights fade as they motion for the waiter. Blackout.*)

CHARACTER

1. Which words, phrases, and details contribute to both characters' **characterization**?

2. Which aspects of both characters' backgrounds contribute to their **motivations**?

3. Explain how both characters could be considered **dynamic**.

4. To what degree does the playwright convey empathy for the characters in the play? Explain.

Social, Cultural, and Historical Contexts

 Enduring Understanding

Setting and the details associated with it not only depict a time and place but also convey values associated with that setting.

KEY POINT

Writers set stories in particular contexts as a way of reflecting historical, cultural, and/or social values.

Whether it's a fantastical world in another realm, a grungy dystopia in the future, an old Western saloon, or a familiar neighborhood, authors choose the settings of their stories with care and the intention to communicate about more than just the time and place.

Consider the popular streaming series *The Handmaid's Tale*, which is based on a 1985 novel of the same name by Margaret Atwood. It's set in a futuristic American dystopia named Gilead which is governed as a totalitarian theocracy. This setting informs every aspect of the narrative and the conflicts that characters face. Or think about the drama *Bridgerton*, which is based on a series of historical novels by Julia Quinn. The story is set in Regency-era London in 1813, where rigid social structures and cultural conventions shape not only the plot but also the identities, behaviors, and trajectories of all the characters.

Context Matters

In Unit 1, you learned that setting includes the time and place in which a story happens. But the setting is more than that. The setting also includes the social, cultural, and historical context during which a text occurs.

- **Social:** How people live and what they believe at the time the story is set
- **Cultural:** The arts and popular interests of the time the story is set
- **Historical:** The events in history that occurred at the time the story is set

While each of these contexts is distinct, they all interact and affect one another. By analyzing these aspects of a setting, you can discover information that is critical to an accurate interpretation. For example, just as social events in real life are directly affected by the culture of the community, a story's social context is heavily influenced by its cultural context of the narrative.

Regional Writers

Some writers write about particular regions, including the American South, the Southwest, the Pacific Northwest, Appalachia, and New England. By capturing a strong sense of place, these writers can evoke the social, cultural, and historical values of that region. Regional writers also use their settings — with distinctive landscapes, regional dialects, and local customs — in ways that bring their stories and characters to life. Similarly, elements of a setting may influence characters; in some cases, a character can even take on specific aspects of their region. For example, you might notice that the narrator describes the character with the same details used to describe the setting.

INSIDER TIP

The reader's context is not necessarily the story's context. A story has three contexts: when it was written, when it is set, and when it is read. It is important that a reader apply the cultural, social, and historical context of the story's setting when making an interpretation.

SETTING AND CONTEXT

Context	Aspects	Examples	Questions to Consider When Making an Interpretation
Social	• Event • Occasion • Class • Living and working conditions	• Weddings, funerals, celebrations • Relationships • Interactions • Occupations • Habitats	What critique or criticism might the author be making through the choice of setting? How does the story's setting reveal traditions, norms, and values that are important to your interpretation of the story?
Cultural	• Religion, beliefs, and shared stories • Traditions and customs • Manners • Identity	• Holidays • Rituals • Ceremonies • Race, gender • Nationality • Food, dress • Legends/folklore	Why might a story have been written during one time period but set in another? What is the significance of historical, cultural, and/or social references or allusions in the work?
Historical	• Historical events • Innovations, discoveries • Conventions • Diction: historical meaning of words	• Wars • Movements • Political events • Technologies • Language choices	How does the conflict of cultures or subcultures contribute to interpretation?

Los Vendidos

Luis Valdez

Patsy Lynch/Shutterstock

THE TEXT IN CONTEXT

Luis Valdez (b. 1940) is an actor, playwright, director, and screenwriter. He is also a foundational figure in the history of the Chicano Movement: a social and political movement of Mexican Americans who resisted assimilation, encouraged unity within their ethnicity, and sought political power for their communities. The Chicano movement reached its highest point in the 1960s and 1970s: the era of Valdez's satire of Latin American stereotypes, *Los Vendidos* (1967). Note that the play's title has a double meaning in Spanish. It can refer to anything that is bought, but it also carries a strong pejorative connotation of the term *sellout*. Given that the drama takes place in a store (however unusual the product), *vendidos* is a key term for the setting. The play's wider context is important too. Valdez wrote it to be produced at his theater collective El Teatro Campesino, which translates to The Farm Workers' Theater. It was first performed at an event hosted by the militant left-wing Chicano organization, the Brown Berets. In addition to being a playwright, Valdez is probably best known for writing and directing the films *Zoot Suit* (1981) and *La Bamba* (1987).

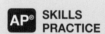 | SETTING
Analyzing Setting and Context

As you read the play *Los Vendidos*, identify details of the story that reveal aspects of the social, cultural, and historical context. Consider how each of these details may contribute to your interpretation of the story.

Analyzing Setting and Context		
Context	Aspects	Details from the Story and Significance
Social	• Event • Occasion • Class • Living and working conditions	

Cultural	• Religion, beliefs, and shared stories • Traditions and customs • Manners • Identity	
Historical	• Historical events • Innovations, discoveries • Conventions • Diction: historical meaning of words	

Los Vendidos

Characters:

HONEST SANCHO

SECRETARY

FARMWORKER

PACHUCO

REVOLUCIONARIO

MEXICAN-AMERICAN

SCENE   **HONEST SANCHO**'s *Used Mexican Lot and Mexican Curio Shop. Three models are on display in* **HONEST SANCHO**'s *shop. To the right, there is a* **REVOLUCIONARIO**, *complete with sombrero, carrilleras and carabina 30-30. At center, on the floor, there is the* **FARMWORKER**, *under a broad straw sombrero. At stage left is the* **PACHUCO**, *filero in hand.* **HONEST SANCHO** *is moving among his models, dusting them off and preparing for another day of business.*

SANCHO: Bueno, bueno, mis monos, varnos aver a quién vendemos ahora, ¿no? (*To audience.*) ¡Quihubo! I'm Honest Sancho and this is my shop. Antes fui contratista,
5   pero ahora logré tener mi negocito. All I need now is a customer. (*A bell rings offstage.*) Ay, a customer!

SECRETARY: (*Entering.*) Good morning, I'm Miss Jimenez from . . .

10 **SANCHO:** Ah, una chicana! Welcome, welcome Señorita Jiménez.

SECRETARY: (*Anglo pronunciation.*) JIM-enez.

SANCHO: ¿Qué?

SECRETARY: My name is Miss JIM-enez. Don't
15   you speak English? What's wrong with you?

SANCHO: Oh, nothing, Señorita JIM-enez. I'm here to help you.

SECRETARY: That's better. As I was starting to say, I'm a secretary from Governor
20   Reagan's office, and we're looking for a Mexican type for the administration.

SANCHO: Well, you come to the right place, lady. This is Honest Sancho's Used Mexican Lot, and we got all types here.
25   Any particular type you want?

SECRETARY: Yes, we were looking for some-body suave . . .

SANCHO: Suave.

SECRETARY: Debonaire.

30 **SANCHO:** De buen aire.

SECRETARY: Dark.

SANCHO: Prieto.

SECRETARY: But of course, not too dark.

SANCHO: No muy prieto.

35 **SECRETARY:** Perhaps, beige.

SANCHO: Beige, just the tone. Así como cafecito con leche, ¿no?

SECRETARY: One more thing. He must be hard-working.

40 **SANCHO:**   That could only be one model. Step right over here to the center of the shop, lady. (*They cross to the* **FARMWORKER**.) This is our standard farmworker model. As you can see, in the words of our beloved

45   Senator George Murphy, he is "built close to the ground." Also, take special notice of his 4-ply Goodyear huaraches, made from the rain tire. This wide-brimmed sombrero is an extra added feature; keeps

50   off the sun, rain and dust.

SECRETARY: Yes, it does look durable.

SANCHO: And our farmworker model is friendly. Muy amable. Watch. (*Snaps his fingers.*)

55 **FARMWORKER:**   (*Lifts up head.*) Buenos días, señorita. (*His head drops.*)

SECRETARY: My, he is friendly.

SANCHO: Didn't I tell you? Loves his patrones! But his most attractive feature is that he's

60   hard-working. Let me show you. (*Snaps fingers.* **FARMWORKER** *stands.*)

FARMWORKER: ¡El jale! (*He begins to work.*)

SANCHO: As you can see he is cutting grapes.

SECRETARY: Oh, I wouldn't know.

65 **SANCHO:**   He also picks cotton. (*Snaps.* **FARMWORKER** *begins to pick cotton.*)

SECRETARY: Versatile, isn't he?

SANCHO: He also picks melons. (*Snaps.* **FARMWORKER** *picks melons.*) That's his

70   slow speed for late in the season. Here's his fast speed. (*Snap.* **FARMWORKER** *picks faster.*)

SECRETARY: Chihuahua . . . I mean, goodness, he sure is a hard-worker.

75 **SANCHO:**   (*Pulls the* **FARMWORKER** *to his feet.*) And that isn't the half of it. Do you see these little holes on his arms that appear to be pores? During those hot sluggish days in the field when the vines or the

80   branches get so entangled, it's almost impossible to move, these holes emit certain grease that allows our model to slip and slide right through the crop with no trouble at all.

85 **SECRETARY:**   Wonderful. But is he economical?

SANCHO: Economical? Señorita, you are looking at the Volkswagen of Mexicans. Pennies a day is all it takes. One plate of beans and tortillas will keep him going all

90   day. That, and chile. Plenty of chile. Chile jalapeños, chile verde, chile colorado. But, of course, if you do give him chile (*Snap.* **FARMWORKER** *turns left face. Snap.* **FARMWORKER** *bends over.*), then you have to

95   change his oil filter once a week.

SECRETARY: What about storage?

SANCHO: No problem. You know these new farm labor camps our Honorable Governor Reagan has built out by Parlier or Raisin

100   City? They were designed with our model in mind. Five, six, seven, even ten in one of those shacks will give you no trouble at all. You can also put him in old barns, old cars, riverbanks. You can even leave him

105   out in the field overnight with no worry!

SECRETARY: Remarkable.

SANCHO: And here's an added feature: every year at the end of the season, this model goes back to Mexico and doesn't return,

110   automatically, until next Spring.

SECRETARY: How about that. But tell me, does he speak English?

SANCHO: Another outstanding feature is that last year this model was programmed to

115   go out on strike! (*Snap.*)

FARMWORKER: ¡Huelga! ¡Huelga! Hermanos, sálganse de esos files. (*Snap. He stops.*)

SECRETARY: No! Oh no, we can't strike in the State Capitol.

120 **SANCHO:**   Well, he also scabs. (*Snap.*)

FARMWORKER: Me vendo barato, ¿y qué? (*Snap.*)

SECRETARY: That's much better, but you didn't answer my question. Does he speak English?

125 **SANCHO:** Bueno . . . no, pero he has other . . .

SECRETARY: No.

SANCHO: Other features.

SECRETARY: No! He just won't do!

SANCHO: Okay, okay, pues. We have other

130 models.

SECRETARY: I hope so. What we need is something a little more sophisticated.

SANCHO: Sophisti-qué?

SECRETARY: An urban model.

135 **SANCHO:** Ah, from the city! Step right back. Over here in this corner of the shop is exactly what you're looking for. Introducing our new 1969 Johnny Pachuco model! This is our fast-back model.

140 Streamlined. Built for speed, low-riding, city life. Take a look at some of these features. Mag shoes, dual exhausts, green chartreuse paint-job, dark-tint windshield, a little poof on top. Let me just turn him

145 on. (*Snap.* **JOHNNY** *walks to stage center with a* **PACHUCO** *bounce.*)

SECRETARY: What was that?

SANCHO: That, señorita, was the Chicano shuffle.

150 **SECRETARY:** Okay, what does he do?

SANCHO: Anything and everything necessary for city life. For instance, survival: he knife fights. (*Snaps.* **JOHNNY** *pulls out a switchblade and swings at* **SECRETARY**.

155 **SECRETARY** *screams*.) He dances. (*Snap.*)

JOHNNY: (*Singing.*) Angel Baby, my Angel Baby . . . (*Snap.*)

SANCHO: And here's a feature no city model can be without. He gets arrested, but not

160 without resisting, of course. (*Snap.*)

JOHNNY: En la madre, la placa. I didn't do it! I didn't do it! (**JOHNNY** *turns and stands up against an imaginary wall, legs spread out, arms behind his back.*)

165 **SECRETARY:** Oh no, we can't have arrests! We must maintain law and order.

SANCHO: But he's bilingual.

SECRETARY: Bilingual?

SANCHO: Simón que yes. He speaks English!

170 Johnny, give us some English. (*Snap.*)

JOHNNY: (*Comes downstage.*) F***-you!

SECRETARY: (*Gasps.*) Oh! I've never been so insulted in my whole life!

SANCHO: Well, he learned it in your school.

175 **SECRETARY:** I don't care where he learned it.

SANCHO: But he's economical.

SECRETARY: Economical?

SANCHO: Nickels and dimes. You can keep Johnny running on hamburgers, Taco Bell

180 tacos, Lucky Lager beer, Thunderbird wine, yesca . . .

SECRETARY: Yesca?

SANCHO: Mota.

SECRETARY: Mota?

185 **SANCHO:** Leños . . . marijuana. (*Snap.* **JOHNNY** *inhales on an imaginary joint.*)

SECRETARY: That's against the law!

JOHNNY: (*Big smile, holding his breath.*) Yeah.

190 **SANCHO:** He also sniffs glue. (*Snap.* **JOHNNY** *inhales glue, big smile.*)

JOHNNY: Tha's too much man, ése.

SECRETARY: No, Mr. Sancho, I don't think this . . .

SANCHO: Wait a minute, he has other

195 qualities I know you'll love. For example, an inferiority complex. (*Snap.*)

JOHNNY: (*To* **SANCHO**.) You think you're better than me, huh, ése? (*Swings switchblade.*)

SANCHO: He can also be beaten and he

200 bruises. Cut him and he bleeds, kick him and he . . . (*He beats, bruises and kicks* **PACHUCO**.) Would you like to try it?

SECRETARY: Oh, I couldn't.

SANCHO: Be my guest. He's a great scapegoat.

205 **SECRETARY:** No really.

SANCHO: Please.

SECRETARY: Well, all right. Just once. (*She kicks* **PACHUCO**.) Oh, he's so soft.

SANCHO: Wasn't that good? Try again.

210 **SECRETARY:** (*Kicks* **PACHUCO**.) Oh, he's wonderful! (*She kicks him again.*)

SANCHO: Okay, that's enough, lady. You'll ruin the merchandise. Yes, our Johnny Pachuco model can give you many hours of plea-

215 sure. Why, the LAPD just bought twenty of these to train their rookie cops on. And talk about maintenance. Señorita, you are look- ing at an entirely self-supporting machine. You're never going to find our Johnny

220 Pachuco model on the relief rolls. No, sir, this model knows how to liberate.

SECRETARY: Liberate?

SANCHO: He steals. (*Snap.* **JOHNNY** *rushes to* **SECRETARY** *and steals her purse.*)

225 **JOHNNY:** ¡Dame esa bolsa, vieja! (*He grabs the purse and runs. Snap by* **SANCHO**, *he stops.* **SECRETARY** *runs after* **JOHNNY** *and grabs purse away from him, kicking him as she goes.*)

230 **SECRETARY:** No, no, no! We can't have any more thieves in the State Administration. Put him back.

SANCHO: Okay, we still got other models. Come on, Johnny, we'll sell you to some

235 old lady. (**SANCHO** *takes* **JOHNNY** *back to his place.*)

SECRETARY: Mr. Sancho, I don't think you quite understand what we need. What we need is something that will attract the

240 women voters. Something more tradi- tional, more romantic.

SANCHO: Ah, a lover. (*He smiles meaningfully.*) Step right over here, señorita. Introducing our standard Revolucionario and/or Early

245 California Bandit type. As you can see, he is well-built, sturdy, durable. This is the International Harvester of Mexicans.

SECRETARY: What does he do?

SANCHO: You name it, he does it. He rides

250 horses, stays in the mountains, crosses deserts, plains, rivers, leads revolutions, follows revolutions, kills, can be killed, serves as a martyr, hero, movie star. Did I say movie star? Did you ever see *Viva*

255 *Zapata? Viva Villa, Villa Rides, Pancho Villa Returns, Pancho Villa Goes Back, Pancho Villa Meets Abbott and Costello?*

SECRETARY: I've never seen any of those.

SANCHO: Well, he was in all of them. Listen

260 to this. (*Snap.*)

REVOLUCIONARIO: (*Scream.*) ¡Viva Villaaaaa!

SECRETARY: That's awfully loud.

SANCHO: He has a volume control. (*He adjusts volume. Snap.*)

265 **REVOLUCIONARIO:** (*Mousey voice.*) Viva Villa.

SECRETARY: That's better.

SANCHO: And even if you didn't see him in the movies, perhaps you saw him on TV. He makes commercials. (*Snap.*)

270 **REVOLUCIONARIO:** Is there a Frito Bandito in your house?

SECRETARY: Oh yes, I've seen that one!

SANCHO: Another feature about this one is that he is economical. He runs on raw

275 horsemeat and tequila!

SECRETARY: Isn't that rather savage?

SANCHO: Al contrario, it makes him a lover. (*Snap.*)

REVOLUCIONARIO: (*To* **SECRETARY**.) Ay,

280 mamasota, cochota, ven pa'ca! (*He grabs* **SECRETARY** *and folds her back, Latin-lover style.*)

SANCHO: (*Snap.* **REVOLUCIONARIO** *goes back upright.*) Now wasn't that nice?

285 **SECRETARY:** Well, it was rather nice.

SANCHO: And finally, there is one outstand- ing feature about this model I know the ladies are going to love: he's a genuine antique! He was made in Mexico in 1910!

290 SECRETARY: Made in Mexico?

SANCHO: That's right. Once in Tijuana, twice in Guadalajara, three times in Cuernavaca.

SECRETARY: Mr. Sancho, I thought he was an American product.

295 SANCHO: No, but . . .

SECRETARY: No, I'm sorry. We can't buy anything but American made products. He just won't do.

SANCHO: But he's an antique!

300 SECRETARY: I don't care. You still don't understand what we need. It's true we need Mexican models, such as these, but it's more important that he be American.

SANCHO: American?

305 SECRETARY: That's right, and judging from what you've shown me, I don't think you have what we want. Well, my lunch hour's almost over, I better . . .

SANCHO: Wait a minute! Mexican but

310 American?

SECRETARY: That's correct.

SANCHO: Mexican but . . . (A sudden flash.) American! Yeah, I think we've got exactly what you want. He just came in today!

315 Give me a minute. (He exits. Talks from backstage.) Here he is in the shop. Let me just get some papers off. There. Introducing our new 1970 Mexican-American! Ta-ra-ra-raaaa! (SANCHO brings

320 out the MEXICAN-AMERICAN model, a clean-shaven middle-class type in a business suit, with glasses.)

SECRETARY: (Impressed.) Where have you been hiding this one?

325 SANCHO: He just came in this morning. Ain't he a beauty? Feast your eyes on him! Sturdy U.S. steel frame, streamlined, modern. As a matter of fact, he is built exactly like our Anglo models, except that

330 he comes in a variety of darker shades: naugahyde, leather or leatherette.

SECRETARY: Naugahyde.

SANCHO: Well, we'll just write that down. Yes, señorita, this model represents the

335 apex of American engineering! He is bilingual, college educated, ambitious! Say the word "acculturate" and he accelerates. He is intelligent, well-mannered, clean. Did I say clean? (Snap. MEXICAN-AMERICAN

340 raises his arm.) Smell.

SECRETARY: (Smells.) Old Sobaco, my favorite.

SANCHO: (Snap. MEXICAN-AMERJCAN turns toward SANCHO.) Eric? (To SECRETARY.) We call him Eric Garcia. (To ERIC.) I want you

345 to meet Miss JIM-enez, Eric.

MEXICAN-AMERICAN: Miss Jim-enez, I am delighted to make your acquaintance. (He kisses her hand.)

SECRETARY: Oh, my, how charming!

350 SANCHO: Did you feel the suction? He has seven especially engineered suction cups right behind his lips. He's a charmer all right!

SECRETARY: How about boards, does he func-

355 tion on boards?

SANCHO: You name them, he is on them. Parole boards, draft boards, school boards, taco quality control boards, surf boards, two by fours.

360 SECRETARY: Does he function in politics?

SANCHO: Señorita, you are looking at a political machine. Have you ever heard of the OEO, EOC, COD, WAR ON POVERTY? That's our model! Not only that, he makes

365 political speeches.

SECRETARY: May I hear one?

SANCHO: With pleasure. (Snap.) Eric, give us a speech.

MEXICAN-AMERICAN: Mr. Congressman, Mr.

370 Chairman, members of the board, honored guests, ladies and gentlemen. (SANCHO and

SECRETARY *applaud.*) Please, please. I come before you as a Mexican-American to tell you about the problems of the Mexican.

375 The problems of the Mexican stem from one thing and one thing only: he's stupid. He's uneducated. He needs to stay in school. He needs to be ambitious, forward-looking, harder-working. He needs to think

380 American, American, American, American, American! God bless America! God bless America! God bless America! (*He goes out of control.* SANCHO *snaps frantically and the* MEXICAN-AMERICAN *finally slumps forward,*

385 *bending at the waist.*)

SECRETARY: Oh my, he's patriotic too!

SANCHO: Sí, señorita, he loves his country. Let me just make a little adjustment here. (*Stands* MEXICAN-AMERICAN *up.*)

390 SECRETARY: What about upkeep? Is he economical?

SANCHO: Well, no, I won't lie to you. The Mexican-American costs a little bit more, but you get what you pay for. He's worth

395 every extra cent. You can keep him running on dry Martinis, Langendorf bread . . .

SECRETARY: Apple pie?

SANCHO: Only Mom's. Of course, he's also

400 programmed to eat Mexican food at ceremonial functions, but I must warn you, an overdose of beans will plug up his exhaust.

SECRETARY: Fine! There's just one more ques-

405 tion. How much do you want for him?

SANCHO: Well, I tell you what I'm gonna do. Today and today only, because you've been so sweet, I'm gonna let you steal this model from me! I'm gonna let you drive

410 him off the lot for the simple price of, let's see, taxes and license included, $15,000.

SECRETARY: Fifteen thousand dollars? For a Mexican!!!!

SANCHO: Mexican? What are you talking

415 about? This is a Mexican-American! We

had to melt down two pachucos, a farm-worker and three gabachos to make this model! You want quality, but you gotta pay for it! This is no cheap run-about.

420 He's got class!

SECRETARY: Okay, I'll take him.

SANCHO: You will?

SECRETARY: Here's your money.

SANCHO: You mind if I count it?

425 SECRETARY: Go right ahead.

SANCHO: Well, you'll get your pink slip in the mail. Oh, do you want me to wrap him up for you? We have a box in the back.

SECRETARY: No, thank you. The Governor is

430 having a luncheon this afternoon, and we need a brown face in the crowd. How do I drive him?

SANCHO: Just snap your fingers. He'll do anything you want. (SECRETARY *snaps.*

435 MEXICAN-AMERICAN *steps forward.*)

MEXICAN-AMERICAN: ¡Raza querida, vamos levantando armas para liberamos de estos desgraciados gabachos que nos explotan! Vamos . . .

440 SECRETARY: What did he say?

SANCHO: Something about taking up arms, killing white people, etc.

SECRETARY: But he's not supposed to say that!

SANCHO: Look, lady, don't blame me for bugs

445 from the factory. He's your Mexican-American, you bought him, now drive him off the lot!

SECRETARY: But he's broken!

SANCHO: Try snapping another finger.

450 (SECRETARY *snaps.* MEXICAN-AMERICAN *comes to life again.*)

MEXICAN-AMERICAN: Esta gran humanidad ha dicho basta! ¡Y se ha puesto en marcha! ¡Basta! ¡Basta! ¡Viva la raza! ¡Viva

455 la causa! ¡Viva la huelga! ¡Vivan los brown berets! ¡Vivan los estudiantes! ¡Chicano power! (*The* MEXICAN-AMERICAN *turns toward the* SECRETARY, *who gasps and backs up. He keeps turning toward the*

460   PACHUCO, FARMWORKER *and* REVOLUCIONARIO,
*snapping his fingers and turning each of them
on, one by one.*)

PACHUCO: (*Snap. To* SECRETARY.) I'm going to
get you, baby! ¡Viva la raza!

465 FARMWORKER: (*Snap. To* SECRETARY.) ¡Viva
la huelga! ¡Viva la huelga! ¡Viva la
huelga!

REVOLUCIONARIO: (*Snap. To* SECRETARY.)
¡Viva la revolución! (*The three models*

470 *join together and advance toward the*
SECRETARY, *who backs up and runs out of
the shop screaming.* SANCHO *is at the other
end of the shop holding his money in his
hand. All freeze. After a few seconds of*

475 *silence, the* PACHUCO *moves and stretches,
shaking his arms and loosening up. The*
FARMWORKER *and* REVOLUCIONARIO *do the
same.* SANCHO *stays where he is, frozen to
his spot.*)

480 JOHNNY: Man, that was a long one, ése.
(*Others agree with him.*)

FARMWORKER: How did we do?

JOHNNY: Pretty good, look at all that lana,
man! (*He goes over to* SANCHO *and removes*

485 *the money from his hand.* SANCHO *stays
where he is.*)

REVOLUCIONARIO: En la madre, look at all the
money.

JOHNNY: We keep this up, we're going to be

490 rich.

FARMWORKER: They think we're machines.

REVOLUCIONARIO: Burros.

JOHNNY: Puppets.

MEXICAN-AMERICAN: The only thing I don't

495 like is how come I always get to play the
goddamn Mexican-American?

JOHNNY: That's what you get for finishing
high school.

FARMWORKER: How about our wages,

500 ése?

JOHNNY: Here it comes right now, $3,000 for
you, $3,000 for you, $3,000 for you and
$3,000 for me. The rest we put back into
the business.

505 MEXICAN-AMERICAN: Too much, man. Heh,
where you vatos going tonight?

FARMWORKER: I'm going over to Concha's.
There's a party.

JOHNNY: Wait a minute, vatos. What about

510 our salesman? I think he needs an
oil job.

REVOLUCIONARIO: Leave him to me. (*The*
PACHUCO, FARMWORKER *and* MEXICAN-
AMERICAN *exit, talking loudly about their*

515 *plans for the night. The* REVOLUCIONARIO
goes over to SANCHO, *removes his derby
hat and cigar, lifts him up and throws him
over his shoulder.* SANCHO *hangs loose,
lifeless. To audience.*) He's the best model

520 we got! ¡Ajua!
(*Exit.*)

SETTING

1. What is the **setting** of the play? How does the **historical context** of the play contribute to your interpretation?

2. What is the relationship between the **culture** of the setting and the characters?

3. Authors place characters within a culture or society. Choose a character, and explain to what degree that character is accepted by his or her society or culture.

4. Explain how one of the character's occupations contributes to the **setting**. What does the occupation represent?

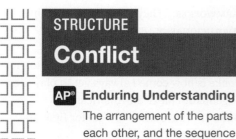

STRUCTURE
Conflict

AP® Enduring Understanding

The arrangement of the parts and sections of a text, the relationship of the parts to each other, and the sequence in which the text reveals information are all structural choices made by a writer that contribute to the reader's interpretation of a text.

KEY POINT

Stories revolve around a central tension that presents a conflict of values. Understanding the story's conflict and resolution is crucial to making an interpretation of a narrative.

In Unit 1, you learned that characters represent ideas and values and that when characters come into conflict so do these values. Identifying the values associated with a character and how those values are in conflict in a literary work is crucial to interpreting the meaning of that work.

Consider the *Star Wars* series, which features recurring characters in galactic conflicts. Though these characters grow, change, and depart throughout the saga, many of them are aligned to a system of values. In an iconic scene from *The Empire Strikes Back* (1980), for example, Darth Vader reveals that he is Luke's father. The revelation is powerful, not least because Luke and Vader each represent such anti-thetical values. Whether or not he always lives up to them, Luke is aligned with heroic and virtuous ideals: courage, loyalty, hope, compassion, commitment, and resistance to oppression. In contrast, Vader represents cruelty, anger, tyranny, and the lust for power. Notice that, in this example, the physical appearance of heroes may suggest these values: Luke spends much of *The Empire Strikes Back* and *A New Hope* (1977) wearing white. Many characters who represent the opposite (or different) values wear black, dark, or otherwise menacing costumes.

Stories Revolve around a Central Tension

Conflict is the internal or external struggle faced by the main character or protagonist. And while the events leading up to the conflict along with the conflict itself may make a story engaging, much of a story's depth and meaning comes from its contrast of values and ideals. That is why analyzing these **tensions** is so important to interpretation.

Plot and Suspense

As you learned in Unit 1, stories have a beginning, a middle, and an end. The moments, scenes, and episodes of a literary work make up a story's **plot**. Longer literary works are structured by genre conventions. For example, most novels are divided into chapters. Plays are made up of acts which may further be divided into scenes.

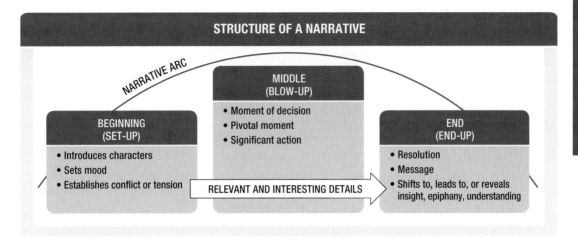

In longer works of literature, such as novels, plays, and films, the story may include multiple, smaller conflicts (*subplots*) that relate to — or even comment on — the main conflict. Each of these individual **moments** may be significant if it reveals something about the character and the ultimate choice or battle he or she will face. Analyzing a conflict means considering how each event within a story connects to and contributes to other events.

Stories generate suspense when a character battles other characters, faces impersonal forces (like nature), or struggles with a moral or emotional dilemma throughout the story. The reader wonders — and usually tries to predict — what a character will do or which character will win out. The author has developed the narrative around this conflict to convey something about the human condition. As a reader, you will use what you know about the characters' backgrounds, what others have revealed about the characters, and your understanding of the setting as you make an interpretation of the narrative.

Types of Conflict

Conflicts reveal a tension of values that are represented through a character or characters in a story. On the most obvious level, that conflict of values may be good versus evil. However, critical readers and viewers may look deeper to identify a more precise or complex tension, such as the guilt of a father. Keep in mind that a tension may occur with another character or force; this type of conflict is called an **external** conflict. However, some characters may have a psychological, emotional, or moral struggle; this is called an **internal** conflict.

Inconsistencies

Some characters may behave surprisingly or a story may turn out differently than you expect. These **inconsistencies** in a text may create **contrasts** that represent conflicts of values or perspectives.

TYPES OF CONFLICT			
	Protagonist	**Antagonist**	**Description**
External	Person vs.	Person	The protagonist is prevented from obtaining his or her goal by the antagonist.
			The antagonist takes something away from the protagonist.
	Person vs.	Society	The protagonist struggles with a community's values or value system.
	Person vs.	Nature	The protagonist is confronted with an animal, aspect of the weather, or another part of the environment that he or she must overcome.
	Person vs.	Technology	The protagonist reckons with an innovation (real or abstract) that forces unwanted interaction.
	Person vs.	Unknown	The protagonist faces fate or another force beyond his or her control.
Internal	Person vs.	Self	The protagonist has to make a moral decision that presents a conflict of values.
			The protagonist's weakness or flaw is revealed.
			The protagonist seeks an unrealistic or unattainable goal.

Authors create **irony** when something happens in a story that is inconsistent with what the reader expects. We will explore irony in more detail in later units. You may likely be familiar with irony (or sarcasm) in your everyday life as a source of comedy or entertainment. Irony is a tool authors use to reveal a conflict of values or perspectives by creating humor, surprise, or shock.

INSIDER AP® TIP

Conflict reveals theme. Embedded in any conflict is a tension of values. The resolution of the conflict reveals the author's perspective about the human condition. Unresolved conflicts require the reader to consider the implications of the conflict with cultural, social, and historical contexts.

Naked Lunch

Michael Hollinger

THE TEXT IN CONTEXT

Michael Hollinger (b. 1962) is an associate professor of theater at Villanova University and the author of over two dozen dramas, comedies, musicals, adaptations, and translations. A trained viola player, Hollinger often views his plays through the lens of music: "Plays are music to me; characters are instruments, scenes are movements; tempo, rhythm and dynamics are critical; and melody and counterpoint are always set in relief by rests — beats, pauses, the spaces in between." His full-length dramatic works include *Tooth and Claw* (2004), *Opus* (2006), and *Ghost-Writer* (2010). In his one-act play *Naked*

©Michael Hollinger

Lunch (2003), Hollinger explores contrasting ideals, values, and desires by dramatizing a lunch date between two people who once had a relationship.

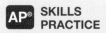 **SKILLS PRACTICE** | **STRUCTURE**
Analyzing Conflict

As you read *Naked Lunch*, identify the important moments of the play. What do the characters' actions and decisions reveal about them? Explain how each of these moments contributes to the central conflict. Which moment in the sequence could be identified as the climax? How is the conflict resolved?

Analyzing Conflict		
Moment: Problem and Type of Conflict	**Action/Decision:** Character Action or Decisions	**Importance:** Effect on Next or Other Events of the Plot, Especially the Primary Conflict or Story's Resolution

Naked Lunch

Lights up on Vernon and Lucy sitting at a small dining-room table, eating. There's a small vase with too many flowers in it, or a large vase with too few. A bottle of wine has been opened. Vernon regales Lucy as he vigorously devours a steak. Lucy discreetly nibbles on her corn-on-the-cob.

VERNON: Larry thinks the whole show's a fake. He says the guy's just an actor and all the crocs are trained. I said, you can't train a crocodile! It's not like some poodle

5   you can teach to ride a bike. It's got this reptile brain, a million years old. All it knows, or wants to know, is whether or not you're juicy. Anyway, this one show the guy sneaking up on a mother protect-

10   ing her nest. And she's huge—I mean, this thing could swallow a Buick. And the guy's really playing it up: (*Australian accent.*) "Amazing—look at the size of those teeth!" But just—(*He stops, looking at Lucy.*

15   *Pause. She looks up from her corn.*)

LUCY: What?

VERNON: What's the matter?

LUCY: I'm listening.

VERNON: You're not eating your steak.

20   LUCY: Oh. No.

VERNON: How come?

LUCY: I'll just eat the corn. (*She returns to nibbling.*)

VERNON: What's wrong with the steak?

25   LUCY: Nothing.

VERNON: Then eat it. It's good.

LUCY: I'd . . . rather not.

VERNON: Why not? (*Pause.*)

LUCY: I'm vegetarian. (*Beat.*)

30   VERNON: What?

LUCY: I don't eat meat anymore.

VERNON: Since when?

LUCY: Since we, you know. Broke up. (*Pause.*)

VERNON: Just like that?

35   LUCY: Well—

VERNON: You break up with me and the next day you start eating tofu?

LUCY: I'd been thinking about it for a while.

VERNON: First I ever heard of it.

40   LUCY: Well, I'd been thinking. (*Pause. Lucy picks up her corn again, guiding him back to the story:*) So anyway, the guy's sneaking up on the mother . . .

VERNON: Was it because of me?

45   LUCY: No . . .

VERNON: Something I said, or did . . .

LUCY: It's nothing like that.

VERNON: You were always fond of cataloguing the careless things I said and did . . .

50   LUCY: I just did some soul-searching, that's all. (*Beat.*)

VERNON: Soul-searching.

LUCY: About a lot of things.

VERNON: And your soul said to you "no more

55   meat."

LUCY: You make it sound silly when you say it like that.

VERNON: Then what, what did your soul tell you? (*Beat. Lucy exhales heavily and sets

60   down her corn.*)

LUCY: I decided I didn't want to eat anything with a face. (*Beat.*)

VERNON: A face? (*He gets up, stands behind her and looks at her plate.*)

65   LUCY: Vern . . .

VERNON: I don't see any face . . .

LUCY: This doesn't have to be a big deal . . .

VERNON: I don't see a face. Do you see a face? (*He lifts the plate toward her face.*)

70   LUCY: There's other reasons.

VERNON: No face. (*He sets the plate down again.*)

LUCY: I've been reading things.

VERNON: What things?

75 LUCY: You know, health reports . . .

VERNON: You can't believe that stuff.

LUCY: What do you mean?

VERNON: You can't! One day they say bran's good for you—"Want to live forever? Eat

80 more bran."—the next day they find out bran can kill you.

LUCY: Whatever.

VERNON: Too much bran boom you're dead.

LUCY: There are diseases you can get from

85 meat.

VERNON: Like what?

LUCY: Well, listeria . . .

VERNON: That's chicken. Chicken and turkey.

LUCY: Or Mad Cow.

90 VERNON: Mad Cow? Did you—that's not even—that's *English*, they have that in *England*. This isn't English meat, this is from, I don't know, Kansas or . . . *Wyoming*.

LUCY: Even so,—

95 VERNON: No. Now you're making stuff up.

LUCY: I'm not; I saw an article—

VERNON: You're just being paranoid, this whole . . . You know what this is? Do you?

LUCY: What?

100 VERNON: Carnophobia.

LUCY: "Carnophobia"?

VERNON: It's a word, look it up.

LUCY: It's not like I'm scared of meat . . .

VERNON: How do you think this makes me

105 feel?

LUCY: Look, let's just drop it.

VERNON: Huh?

LUCY: We were doing so well . . .

VERNON: I invite you over, cook a nice steak,

110 set out flowers, napkins, the whole nine yards . . .

LUCY: I appreciate the napkins.

VERNON: . . . figure I'll open a bottle of wine, apologize . . . maybe we'll get naked, be

115 like old times.

LUCY: So let's start over.

VERNON: Then you get *carnophobic* on me.

LUCY: Can we?

VERNON: Throw it in my face.

120 LUCY: Please?

VERNON: Start *cataloguing* what's wrong with everything . . .

LUCY: I never meant this to be a big deal. (*Beat. She puts her hand on his. He looks at*

125 *her.*) I really didn't. (*Long pause.*)

VERNON: Then eat it. (*Beat.*)

LUCY: Vern . . . (*He picks up her fork, jams it into her steak, and cuts off a bite with his knife.*) Why do you always have to—(*He*

130 *extends the piece of meat toward Lucy's mouth.*)

VERNON: Eat the meat.

LUCY: I don't want to.

VERNON: *Eat the meat.*

135 LUCY: Vernon . . .

VERNON: I SAID EAT THE MEAT! (*They are locked in a struggle, he menacing, she terrified. Long pause. Finally, Lucy opens her mouth and takes the bite into it. Pause.*)

140 Chew. (*She chews for fifteen or twenty seconds.*) Swallow. (*She swallows. Cheerfully, without malice.*) Good, isn't it. (*Lucy nods obediently.*) Nice and juicy. (*He stabs his fork into his own steak, cuts off a*

145 bite and lifts it.*) See nothing to be afraid of. (*He pops it into his mouth and begins cutting another. After a moment, Lucy goes back to her corn. They eat in absolute silence. Lights fade.*)

STRUCTURE

1. How does the lunch conversation develop a **conflict** between competing value systems?

2. How does a **contrast** between the two characters indicate a conflict of values and reveal opposing motivations?

3. How does the lunch conversation present different perspectives of the **conflict**?

4. Is the conflict **resolved**? If so, how? If not, what effect does this have on the play's audience?

IDEAS IN LITERATURE
Power and Control

The highest point of the English Renaissance, the reign of Queen Elizabeth (1558–1603) is often considered a golden era of English history and culture. If you attend a contemporary Renaissance fair, for example, it will likely be modeled after the customs of this period. That ideal is generally based on historical reality: the monarch was beloved and the government was stable. England enjoyed relative domestic peace. The Elizabethan Religious Settlement eased tensions between Catholics and Protestants. The population of London increased to two hundred thousand, with a growing merchant class. Abroad, England clashed with its rival Spain — and also prepared to challenge the Spanish Empire for colonial supremacy of the New World.

The queen had supreme authority. At court, she dispensed positions, land, and other benefits to her patrons among the nobility and gentry. In turn, they helped run the government and control the lands she apportioned to them. As a woman in a patriarchal society, Elizabeth had to be a skilled manipulator — for example, playing naive advisors against each other to further her own political aims. At the same time, she understood the relationship between power and the *appearance of power*: in idealized paintings, she was bedecked in gold and jewelry. Elizabeth also grasped the importance of cultural power. Her court became a center of style, entertainment, gossip, and influence, akin to U.S. power and media centers in Washington, D.C., New York, or Los Angeles. Like these places, Elizabeth's London drew the ambitious, whether they were hungry for political power or artistic success.

The queen loved theatrical productions and William Shakespeare (1564–1616) was a favorite. On several occasions, the queen invited his theater company

IDEA BANK

Achievement
Altruism
Ambition
Authority
Class
Conflict
Consequence
Control
Corruption
Egoism
Ethnocentrism
Flaw
Greed
Hubris
Humanism
Influence
Jealousy
Manipulation
Obsession
Persuasion
Power
Recognition
Revenge
Temptation
Tragedy

Michael Honegger/Alamy

◀ The image depicts a modern Renaissance festival. Festivals like this occur throughout the country.

How do these people embody the culture of the Renaissance? Why do you think thousands of people continue to relive the rebirth of the arts?

to perform his plays at court. If Elizabeth was (in the words of one poet) the mother of England, then many consider Shakespeare to be a father of English culture. Even now, he remains the most produced playwright in the world, including film adaptations such as *10 Things I Hate About You* (1999), *She's the Man* (2006), *Romeo & Juliet* (2011), and *The King* (2019). In his history plays such as Henry *V* and *Richard III*, Shakespeare fashions drama from familiar events and power struggles from England's past. His comedies, like *All's Well That Ends Well* and *A Midsummer Night's Dream*, unleash the chaotic power of passion before ending happily with weddings. Shakespeare's tragedies explore ambition, revenge, power, deception, self-sabotage, and (as in the case of *Othello* (p. 237)) power; they almost always end in the death of a king.

Later playwrights explored similar ideas and problems. Henrik Ibsen, known as the father of theatrical realism, presented characters in real-life conflicts. Like *Othello's* scheming Iago, the villain of Henrik Ibsen's (1828–1906) *A Doll's House* (p. 333) is a master manipulator. Ibsen's tragedy offers a more nuanced and modern approach to plot and characterization. But in both plays, power manifests itself in action and motivation.

▲

The photo shows a replica of Shakespeare's Globe Theatre today. The theater is located on the banks of the Thames River where the original sixteenth-century Globe Theatre stood. Tourists fill the Globe every season to see Shakespearean plays performed in the Bard's theater.

What is so appealing about live theater, and what do you think continues to bring the crowds to see Shakespearean drama?

The Tragedy of Othello, the Moor of Venice

William Shakespeare

Universal History Archive/Getty Images

THE TEXT IN CONTEXT

Nothing about the early life of William Shakespeare (1564–1616) marked him for greatness. He grew up in the town of Stratford-on-Avon as the son of a middle-class glovemaker. Almost certainly, he attended the local school and received a rigorous humanistic education, studying Latin and classics, which partly accounts for the breadth of reference in his writing. Similarly, while we think of his works as high art, he wrote commercial dramas for his own time, designed to make money for his theater company, the Lord Chamberlain's Men. They produced most of his plays at London's Globe Theatre (he was a partial owner), where the audience ranged from nobles in cushioned seats to groundlings — commoners, laborers, and pickpockets — who paid a penny to watch from the general admission pit. Today, we generally sit silently and watch plays. But Shakespeare's crowd would have hooted, booed, cheered, ate, drank, and occasionally brawled. They would be familiar with the story lines: like other playwrights of his time, Shakespeare borrowed heavily from earlier poems, histories, and plays. Even *Othello* originates in the works of Italian writer Giovanni Battista Giraldi (1504–1573).

Indeed, we read Shakespeare for the *how* of his works as much as we do for the *what.* First, his skill with different literary forms and genres (sonnets, tragedies, comedies, histories) is unmatched, as is his ability to build a universe of vivid, complex characters out of words. In some ways, the very idea of a literary character as we know it comes from Shakespeare. Second, his powerful, even eerie insight into the human condition (including our inner emotional and psychological lives) rewards endless rereadings and restagings, as do the intricate structures and motifs of his works. For example, as you read *Othello*, notice how the patterns of light and dark, black and white, interconnect with the play's themes (evil and good, blindness and insight, deception and truth). Finally, Shakespeare pushed the English language to its figurative, imagistic, and musical limits, introducing hundreds of words and phrases that we still use today (*wild-goose chase, love is blind, in a pickle*).

The Tragedy of Othello, the Moor of Venice

List of Characters

OTHELLO, *the Moor, a general in the service of Venice*

BRABANTIO, *father to Desdemona, a Venetian Senator*

CASSIO, *an honorable lieutenant to Othello*

IAGO, *a villain, ensign to Othello*

RODERIGO, *a gulled (tricked) gentleman*

DUKE OF VENICE

SENATORS OF VENICE

MONTANO, *Governor of Cyprus*

GENTLEMEN OF CYPRUS

LODOVICO, *a noble Venetian, kinsman of Brabantio*

GRATIANO, *a noble Venetian, brother of Brabantio*

SAILORS

CLOWN, *servant of Othello*

DESDEMONA, *wife to Othello and daughter of Brabantio*

EMILIA, *wife to Iago*

BIANCA, *a courtesan, mistress of Cassio*

MESSENGER, HERALD, OFFICERS, GENTLEMEN, MUSICIANS, ATTENDANTS

ACT I

SCENE i°

Enter **RODERIGO** *and* **IAGO.**

RODERIGO Tush, never tell me,° I take it much unkindly
That thou, Iago, who hast had my purse
As if the strings were thine shouldst know of this.

IAGO 'Sblood,° but you will not hear me.

5   If ever I did dream of such a matter,
Abhor me.

RODERIGO Thou told'st me thou didst hold him° in thy hate.

IAGO Despise me if I do not: three great ones of the city,
In personal suit to make me his lieutenant,

10   Off-capped° to him; and by the faith of man,
I know my price, I am worth no worse a place.
But he, as loving his own pride and purposes,
Evades them with a bombast circumstance,°
Horribly stuffed° with epithets° of war,

Act I, Scene i.

1. never tell me: a common phrase expressing disbelief; as in American slang "You don't say."

4. 'Sblood: i.e., by Christ's blood; a very strong oath.

7. him: Othello remains unnamed throughout the scene and is only identified for the first time at 33 as "his Moorship."

10. Off-capped: removed their hats as a sign of respect.

13. bombast circumstance: rhetorically inflated circumlocution.
14. stuffed: "Bombast" was cotton material used for lining or padding garments. **epithets:** terms (of technical military terminology).

15 And in conclusion,°
Non-suits° my mediators. For "Certes,"° says he,
"I have already chosen my officer."
And what was he?
Forsooth, a great arithmetician,°
20 One Michael Cassio, a Florentine,°
A fellow almost damned in a fair wife,°
That never set° a squadron° in the field,
Nor the devision of a battle° knows
More than a spinster, unless the bookish theoric,°
25 Wherein the togèd° consuls can propose°
As masterly as he. Mere prattle without practice
Is all his soldiership. But he, sir, had the election,°
And I, of whom his eyes had seen the proof
At Rhodes, at Cyprus, and on other grounds
30 Christian and heathen,° must be lee'd° and calmed
By debitor and creditor;° this counter-caster,°
He, in good time,° must his lieutenant be,
And I, God bless the mark,° his Moorship's° ancient.°
RODERIGO   By heaven, I rather would have been his
hangman.
35 **IAGO**   Why, there's no remedy. 'Tis the curse of service;°
Preferment° goes by letter and affection,°
Not by the old gradation,° where each second
Stood heir to the first. Now sir, be judge yourself
Whether I in any just term° am affined°
40 To love the Moor.
RODERIGO   I would not follow him then.
IAGO   O sir, content you.°
I follow him to serve my turn upon him.
We cannot all be masters, nor all masters
Cannot be truly° followed. You shall mark°
45 Many a duteous and knee-crooking knave,°
That doting on his own obsequious bondage,
Wears out his time° much like his master's ass
For nought but provender, and when he's old, cashiered.
Whip me° such honest knaves. Others there are
50 Who, trimmed° in forms and visages° of duty,
Keep yet their hearts attending on themselves,
And throwing° but shows° of service on their lords,
Do well thrive by them; and when they have lined their
coats,°
Do themselves homage.° These fellows have some soul,

15. And in conclusion: "Conclusion" could be used as a legal term meaning "a totally binding decision." **16. Non-suits:** causes a withdrawal of the petition of. **Certes:** assuredly.

19. arithmetician: Iago's sneer is that Cassio is a theoretical soldier with no practical experience of war, a point he develops at 21–26. **20. a Florentine:** i.e., a foreigner, not a Venetian. **21. almost damned in a fair wife:** a version of the proverb "Who has a fair wife needs more than two eyes." **22. set:** dispose, arrange (a technical military term). **squadron:** a small unit of troops, usually twenty-five men. **23. devision of a battle:** devising or planning of the movement of an army. **24. bookish theoric:** textbook theory. **25. togèd:** i.e., dressed in an official gown or toga (like ancient Roman senators). **propose:** hold forth, expound. **27. had the election:** was selected.

29–30. At Rhodes . . . heathen: Crusading wars are the background of the tragedy. **30. be lee'd:** A ship is in the lee when another ship stands between it and the wind and so prevents it from moving; this is how Iago views himself—unable to advance owing to Cassio's intervention. **31. debitor and creditor:** bookkeeper. **counter-caster:** one who reckons with counters or tokens, a petty accountant. **32. in good time:** literally, "opportunely," but used ironically here. **33. God bless the mark:** God help us! **Moorship's:** a play on "Worship's." **ancient:** ensign (originally the army's standard-bearer). **35. service:** the military life. **36. Preferment:** promotion. **letter and affection:** personal recommendation and favoritism. **37. old gradation:** old-fashioned method of steady advancement from rank to rank. **39. term:** way, manner. **affined:** bound, constrained.

41. content you: be pacified.

44. truly: loyally, faithfully. **shall mark:** cannot avoid observing.
45. knee-crooking knave: bowing servant.

47. time: working life.

49. me: literally, "for me."

50. trimmed: decked out. **visages:** appearances.

52. throwing: bestowing. **but shows:** mere outward appearances.

53. lined their coats: gained all they can.

54. Do themselves homage: turn their attentions totally to their own interests.

55 And such a one do I profess myself.
    For, sir,
    It is as sure as you are Roderigo,
    Were I the Moor, I would not be Iago;°
    In following him, I follow but myself.
60 Heaven is my judge, not I for love and duty,
    But seeming so for my peculiar° end.
    For when my outward action doth demonstrate
    The native act and figure° of my heart
    In complement extern,° 'tis not long after
65 But I will wear my heart upon my sleeve°
    For daws° to peck at. I am not what I am.

RODERIGO What a full fortune° does the thick-lips owe,°
    If he can carry° it thus!

IAGO   Call up her father:
    Rouse him, make after him, poison his° delight,
70 Proclaim him in the street, incense her kinsmen,
    And though he in a fertile climate dwell,
    Plague him with flies: though that his joy be joy,
    Yet throw such chances of vexation on't
    As it may° lose some colour.

75 RODERIGO Here is her father's house; I'll call aloud.

IAGO Do, with like timorous° accent and dire yell,
    As when, by night and negligence, the fire°
    Is spied in populous cities.

RODERIGO What ho, Brabantio! Signior Brabantio, ho!

80 IAGO Awake! What ho, Brabantio! Thieves, thieves!
    Look to your house, your daughter, and your bags!
    Thieves, thieves!

BRABANTIO [*appears*] *above at a window.*

BRABANTIO What is the reason of this terrible summons?
    What is the matter° there?

85 RODERIGO Signior, is all your family within?

IAGO Are your doors locked?

BRABANTIO   Why, wherefore ask you this?

IAGO Zounds,° sir, you're robbed; for shame, put on your gown;
    Your heart is burst;° you have lost half your soul;
    Even now, now, very now, an old black ram
90 Is tupping° your white ewe. Arise, arise;
    Awake the snorting° citizens with the bell,
    Or else the devil° will make a grandsire of you.
    Arise, I say!

58. Were I . . . Iago: If I were in Othello's position, I would be able to see through the kind of apparently loyal service a subordinate like me is giving him.

61. peculiar: personal, private.

63. native act and figure: real action and intention. **64. complement extern:** outward demonstration.

65. upon my sleeve: This is where servants wore the badge indicating the master they served. Iago dissociates himself from such obvious displays of allegiance, because he is not what he seems to be. **66. daws:** Jackdaws were proverbially stupid and obsessed with snapping up trifles. **67. full fortune:** perfect good luck. **owe:** possess. **68. carry:** get away with, succeed in. **69. him, him, his:** All refer to Othello.

74. As it may: that may cause it to.

76. like timorous: such frightening.

77. by night and negligence, the fire: i.e., a fire caused by negligence at night.

84. the matter: your business.

87. Zounds: i.e., by Christ's wounds; a strong oath.

88. burst: broken.

90. tupping: copulating with.

91. snorting: snoring.

92. devil: i.e., Othello, because he is black.

BRABANTIO What, have you lost your wits?

RODERIGO Most reverend signior, do you know my voice?

95 **BRABANTIO** Not I; what are you?

RODERIGO My name is Roderigo.

BRABANTIO   The worser welcome;

I have charged thee not to haunt about my doors;

In honest plainness thou hast heard me say

My daughter is not for thee. And now in madness,

100 Being full of supper and distempering° draughts,

Upon malicious bravery° dost thou come

To start my quiet.°

RODERIGO Sir, sir, sir—

BRABANTIO   But thou must needs be sure

My spirit and my place° have in them power

105 To make this bitter to thee.

RODERIGO   Patience, good sir.

BRABANTIO What tell'st thou me of robbing? This is Venice;

My house is not a grange.°

RODERIGO   Most grave Brabantio,

In simple and pure° soul I come to you.

IAGO Zounds, sir; you are one of those that will not serve God

110 if the devil bid you. Because we come to do you service and

you think we are ruffians, you'll have your daughter covered

with a Barbary horse,° you'll have your nephews° neigh° to

you, you'll have coursers for cousins, and jennets° for

germans.°

115 **BRABANTIO** What profane° wretch art thou?

IAGO I am one, sir, that comes to tell you your daughter and

the Moor are now making the beast with two backs.°

BRABANTIO Thou° art a villain.

IAGO   You are a senator.

BRABANTIO This thou shalt answer;° I know thee, Roderigo.

120 **RODERIGO** Sir, I will answer° anything. But I beseech you

If't be your pleasure and most wise° consent

(As partly I find° it is) that your fair daughter,

At this odd-even° and dull watch o'the night,

Transported with no worse nor better guard,

125 But with a knave° of common hire, a gondolier,

To the gross clasps of a lascivious Moor:

If this be known to you, and your allowance,°

We then have done you bold and saucy° wrongs.

But if you know not this, my manners° tell me,

---

100. distempering: exciting, disturbing.

101. bravery: noisy, showy display.

102. start my quiet: disturb my rest.

104. My spirit and my place: my character and my position as senator.

107. grange: house in the country (hence isolated).

108. simple and pure: sincere and disinterested.

112. Barbary horse: i.e., Othello (with a pun on "barbarian"). **nephews:** close relatives; here, grandsons. **neigh:** There is probably a pun on "nay" = deny their title to your blood and culture. **113. jennets:** small Spanish horses. **114. germans:** close kinsmen.
115. profane: foulmouthed.

117. making the beast with two backs: copulating.
118. thou: specifically addressed to Roderigo.

119. answer: be called to account for.

120. answer: give a satisfactory reply to any charge.
121. wise: knowing, fully informed.
122. partly I find: I am half-convinced (in view of your reception of my news).
123. odd-even: just after midnight.

125. knave: servant.

127. your allowance: something approved of by you.
128. saucy: insolent.
129. manners: knowledge of correct social behavior.

130   We have your wrong rebuke. Do not believe
     That from the sense of all civility°
     I thus would play and trifle with your reverence.°
     Your daughter, if you have not given her leave,
     I say again, hath made a gross revolt,
135   Tying her duty, beauty, wit,° and fortunes
     In an extravagant and wheeling° stranger
     Of here and everywhere. Straight satisfy° yourself.
     If she be in her chamber or your house,
     Let loose on me the justice of the state
140   For thus deluding you.
    BRABANTIO   Strike on the tinder, ho!
     Give me a taper;° call up all my people.
     This accident° is not unlike my dream;
     Belief of it oppresses me already.
     Light, I say, light!   *Exit*
    IAGO   Farewell, for I must leave you.
145   It seems not meet° nor wholesome to my place°
     To be produced,° as if I stay I shall,
     Against the Moor. For I do know the state,
     However this may gall him with some check,°
     Cannot with safety cast° him; for he's embarked
150   With such loud reason° to° the Cyprus wars,
     Which even now stands in act,° that, for their souls,°
     Another of his fathom° they have none
     To lead their business; in which regard,
     Though I do hate him as I do hell's pains,
155   Yet, for necessity of present life,°
     I must show out a flag and sign of love,
     Which is indeed but sign. That you shall surely find him,
     Lead to the Sagittary° the raisèd search,
     And there will I be with him. So farewell.   *Exit*

    Enter Brabantio in his nightgown,° and **SERVANTS** *with torches.*

160   **BRABANTIO** It is too true an evil. Gone she is,
     And what's to come of my despisèd time°
     Is nought but bitterness. Now Roderigo,
     Where didst thou see her? O unhappy girl!
     With the Moor, say'st thou? Who would be a father?
165   How didst thou know 'twas she? O she deceives me
     Past thought! What said she to you? Get more tapers,
     Raise all my kindred. Are they married, think you?
    RODERIGO Truly I think they are.

---

131. from the sense of all civility: contrary to every feeling of good conduct.
132. your reverence: the respect due to you.

135. wit: intelligence.

136. extravagant and wheeling: extremely wide-ranging.
137. Straight satisfy: immediately ascertain the facts for.

141. taper: candle.

142. accident: occurrence.

145. meet: fitting. **place:** position (as Othello's ensign).
146. produced: i.e., as a witness.

148. gall him with some check: irritate him with some reprimand; literally, slightly hurt a horse by pulling back the rein. **149. cast:** discharge. **149–50. embarked . . . to:** about to be engaged in. **150. loud reason:** shouted agreement (by the Senate). **151. stands in act:** (1) are in progress, (2) are about to break out. **for their souls:** to save themselves.
152. fathom: capability.

155. life: livelihood.

158. Sagittary: the name of a house or inn where Othello and Desdemona have taken lodgings, so called because of its sign of Sagittarius or Centaur.

159sd. nightgown: dressing gown or robe.

161. despisèd time: (1) the rest of my life, which is now odious to me; (2) the remainder of my existence, in which people will look with scorn on me.

BRABANTIO O heaven! How got she out? O treason of the
   blood!
170 Fathers, from hence trust not your daughters' minds
   By what you see them act. Is there not charms°
   By which the property° of youth and maidhood
   May be abused? Have you not read, Roderigo,
   Of some such thing?
   RODERIGO   Yes, sir, I have indeed.
175 **BRABANTIO** Call up my brother. O that you had had her!
   Some one way, some another. Do you know
   Where we may apprehend her and the Moor?
   RODERIGO I think I can discover him,° if you please
   To get good guard and go along with me.
180 **BRABANTIO** Pray you lead on. At every house I'll call;
   I may command at° most. Get weapons, ho!
   And raise some special officers of night:
   On, good Roderigo; I'll deserve your pains.°

                                             Exeunt

171. charms: spells (or perhaps love potions).

172. property: nature.

178. discover him: reveal where he is.

181. command at: demand help from.

183. deserve your pains: recompense you for your trouble.

SCENE II°

Enter **OTHELLO**, **IAGO** *and* **ATTENDANTS** *with torches.*

IAGO Though in the trade° of war I have slain men,
   Yet do I hold it very stuff° o'the conscience
   To do no contrived° murder. I lack iniquity
   Sometimes to do me service. Nine or ten times
5 I had thought to have yerked° him° here, under the ribs.
   OTHELLO 'Tis better as it is.
   IAGO   Nay, but he prated,
   And spoke such scurvy° and provoking terms
   Against your honour,
   That, with the little godliness I have,
10 I did full hard forbear him.° But I pray, sir,
   Are you fast° married? For be sure of this,
   That the magnifico° is much beloved,
   And hath in his effect a voice potential°
   As double as the duke's. He will divorce you,
15 Or put upon you what restraint and grievance°
   The law, with all his might to enforce it on,°
   Will give him cable.°
   OTHELLO   Let him do his spite;°
   My services which I have done the signiory°
   Shall out-tongue° his complaints. 'Tis yet to know°—
20 Which, when I know that boasting is an honour,

Act I, Scene ii.

1. trade: actual business.

2. very stuff: essential material (carrying on the metaphor implicit in "trade").
3. contrived: premeditated, planned, cold-blooded.

5. yerked: jabbed (here, with a sword or dagger). **him:** i.e., Roderigo.

7. scurvy: insulting.

10. full hard forbear him: restrain myself with great difficulty from attacking him. **11. fast:** firmly.
12. magnifico: i.e., Brabantio. The chief noblemen of Venice were called *Magnifici*.
13. in his effect a voice potential: at his command a powerful influence.

15. grievance: injury, punishment.

16. with all . . . it on: applied with the utmost rigor.
17. cable: scope (a nautical term). **spite:** utmost harm to me.

18. signiory: oligarchy of Venice.

19. out-tongue: outweigh; literally, "cry louder than." **to know:** unknown.

I shall provulgate°—I fetch my life and being
From men of royal siege,° and my demerits°
May speak unbonneted° to as proud a fortune°
As this that I have reached. For know, Iago,

25   But that I love the gentle° Desdemona,
I would not my unhousèd° free condition
Put into circumscription and confine°
For the sea's worth. But look what lights come yond!

IAGO   Those are the raisèd° father and his friends;
30   You were best go in.

OTHELLO   Not I; I must be found.
My parts,° my title,° and my perfect soul°
Shall manifest me rightly. Is it they?

IAGO   By Janus,° I think no.

Enter CASSIO, *with* OFFICERS *and torches.*

OTHELLO   The servants of the duke and my lieutenant!
35   The goodness of the night upon you, friends.
What is the news?

CASSIO   The duke does greet you, general,
And he requires your haste-post-haste appearance
Even on the instant.

OTHELLO   What is the matter,° think you?

CASSIO   Something from Cyprus, as I may divine.°
40   It is a business of some heat.° The galleys
Have sent a dozen sequent messengers
This very night at one another's heels;
And many of the consuls, raised and met,
Are at the duke's already. You have been hotly called for,
45   When, being not at your lodging to be found,
The senate hath sent about° three several quests°
To search you out.

OTHELLO   'Tis well I am found by you.
I will but spend a word here in the house,
And go with you.   [Exit]

CASSIO   Ancient, what makes he° here?
50 IAGO   Faith, he tonight hath boarded a land carrack;°
If it prove lawful prize, he's made for ever.

CASSIO   I do not understand.

IAGO   He's married.

CASSIO   To who?

[*Enter Othello.*]

---

21. provulgate: make known.

22. siege: rank. **demerits:** worth, merits.

23. unbonneted: with all due respect (having removed their hats), without impertinence. **proud a fortune:** elevated a success.
25. gentle: retiring, soft-natured; with a pun on "of noble birth."
26. unhousèd: unconfined (by marriage).
27. confine: restriction.

29. raisèd: who has been got out of bed; with a pun on "angered."

31. parts: natural gifts, character. **title:** legal right, position as a husband. **perfect soul:** fully prepared conscience.
33. Janus: the Roman two-faced god of beginnings; ironically appropriate for Iago to swear by.

38. matter: business.

39. divine: guess.

40. heat: urgency.

46. about: all over the city. **several quests:** separate search parties.

49. makes he: is he doing.

50. carrack: a large treasure ship, such as those that carried the wealth of America to Spain. In using this metaphor, Iago is debasing Othello's marriage by viewing it as an act of high-seas piracy. "Boarded" has a sexual connotation.

IAGO Marry,° to—Come, captain, will you go?

OTHELLO   Have° with you.

CASSIO Here comes another troop to seek for you.

Enter BRABANTIO, RODERIGO *and* OFFICERS *with lights and weapons.*

55 IAGO It is Brabantio; general, be advised,

   He comes to bad intent.

OTHELLO   Holla, stand there!

RODERIGO Signior, it is the Moor.

BRABANTIO   Down with him, thief!

IAGO You, Roderigo?° Come, sir, I am for you.

OTHELLO Keep up your bright swords, for the dew° will rust
   them.

60   Good signior, you shall more command with years
   Than with your weapons.

BRABANTIO O thou foul thief! Where hast thou stowed° my
   daughter?

   Damned as thou art, thou hast enchanted° her,

   For I'll refer me to° all things of sense,°

65   If she in chains of magic were not bound,

   Whether a maid so tender, fair, and happy,

   So opposite to marriage that she shunned

   The wealthy curlèd darlings of our nation,

   Would ever have, t'incur a general mock,°

70   Run from her guardage° to the sooty bosom

   Of such a thin as thou—to fear,° not to delight.

   Judge me the world, if 'tis not gross in sense°

   That thou hast practised on her with foul charms,

   Abused her delicate youth with drugs or minerals°

75   That weakens motion.° I'll have't disputed on;°

   'Tis probable and palpable to thinking.

   I therefore apprehend and do attach° thee

   For an abuser of the world,° a practiser

   Of arts inhibited and out of warrant.°

80   Lay hold upon him. If he do resist,

   Subdue him at his peril.

OTHELLO   Hold your hands,

   Both you of my inclining° and the rest.

   Were it my cue to fight, I should have known it

   Without a prompter. Where will you that I go

85   To answer this your charge?

BRABANTIO   To prison, till fit time

---

53. Marry: by the Virgin Mary; a mild oath.
Have: I'll go.

58. You, Roderigo?: Iago takes immediate steps to protect himself and his "purse" should a brawl develop, by singling out Roderigo as his opponent. **59. dew:** i.e., rather than blood. Othello's scorn is that of the professional fighter toward civilian brawlers.

62. stowed: hidden away, lodged.

63. enchanted: cast a spell on.

64. refer me to: have recourse to as authority. **all things of sense:** all reasonable creatures.

69. general mock: public ridicule.

70. her guardage: her father's guardianship.

71. fear: be frightened.

72. gross in sense: palpably obvious.

74. minerals: poisonous mineral drugs.

75. weakens motion: dulls the normal perceptive faculties. **disputed on:** contested, debated (by experts).
77. attach: arrest.
78. abuser of the world: corrupter of society.

79. arts inhibited and out of warrant: magical practices which are prohibited and illegal.

82. of my inclining: on my side.

Of law and course of direct session°

Call thee to answer.

86. course of direct session: specially convened sitting of a court of justice.

OTHELLO   What if I do obey?

How may the duke be therewith satisfied,

Whose messengers are here about my side

90   Upon some present° business of the state

To bring me to him?

90. present: immediate.

OFFICER   'Tis true, most worthy signior;

The duke's in council, and your noble self

I am sure is sent for.

BRABANTIO   How? The duke in council?

In this time of the night? Bring him away;

95   Mine's not an idle cause.° The duke himself,

Or any of my brothers of the state,°

Cannot but feel this wrong as 'twere their own;

For if such actions may have passage free,°

Bondslaves and pagans shall our statesmen be.

95. idle cause: trifling, unimportant legal case.

96. brothers of the state: fellow senators.

98. have passage free: go unchecked.

Exeunt

SCENE iii°

Enter **DUKE** *and* **SENATORS**, *set at a table with lights, and* **ATTENDANTS**.

Act I, Scene iii.

DUKE There is no composition° in these news

That gives them credit.°

1. composition: consistency, agreement.

1 SENATOR   Indeed they are disproportioned.°

My letters say a hundred and seven galleys.

2. credit: credibility. **disproportioned:** inconsistent.

DUKE And mine, a hundred and forty.

2 SENATOR   And mine, two hundred;

5   But though they jump° not on a just accompt°—

As in these cases where the aim° reports

'Tis oft with difference—yet do they all confirm

A Turkish fleet, and bearing up to Cyprus.

5. jump: agree, coincide. **just accompt:** exact numbering.
6. aim: estimate.

DUKE Nay, it is possible enough to judgement:°

10   I do not so secure me in the error,°

But the main article° I do approve°

In fearful sense.°

9. to judgement: when carefully considered.

10. secure me in the error: feel safe because of the inconsistency. **11. main article:** item which the reports have in common.
11–12. approve / In fearful sense: believe as cause for alarm.

SAILOR (*Within*) What ho! What ho! What ho!

OFFICER A messenger from the galleys.

Enter a **SAILOR**.

DUKE   Now, what's the business?

SAILOR The Turkish preparation° makes for Rhodes;

14. preparation: fleet fitted out for battle.

15   So was I bid report here to the state
       By Signior Angelo.
    DUKE How say you by this change?
    1 SENATOR   This cannot be,
       By no assay° of reason. 'Tis a pageant°
       To keep us in false gaze.° When we consider
20   The importancy of Cyprus to the Turk,
       And let ourselves again but understand
       That as it more concerns the Turk than Rhodes,
       So may° he with more facile question° bear it,
       For that° it stands not in such warlike brace,°
25   But altogether lacks the abilities°
       That Rhodes is dressed in.° If we make thought of this,
       We must not think the Turk is so unskillful
       To leave that latest which concerns him first,
       Neglecting an attempt of ease and gain°
30   To wake and wage° a danger profitless.
    DUKE Nay, in all confidence he's not for Rhodes.
    OFFICER Here is more news.

Enter a **MESSENGER**.

    MESSENGER The Ottomites, reverend and gracious,
       Steering with due course toward the isle of Rhodes
35   Have there injointed with an after fleet.°
    1 SENATOR Ay, so I thought. How many, as you guess?
    MESSENGER Of thirty sail, and now they do restem°
       Their backward course,° bearing with frank appearance
       Their purposes toward° Cyprus. Signior Montano,
40   Your trusty and most valiant servitor,
       With his free duty recommends° you thus,
       And prays you to believe him.
    DUKE 'Tis certain then for Cyprus.
       Marcus Luccicos, is not he in town?
45 **1 SENATOR** He's now in Florence.
    DUKE   Write from us to him
       Post-post-haste dispatch.
    1 SENATOR Here comes Brabantio and the valiant Moor.

Enter **BRABANTIO**, **OTHELLO**, **CASSIO**, **IAGO**, **RODERIGO** *and*
OFFICERS.

    DUKE Valiant Othello we must straight° employ you
       Against the general° enemy Ottoman.

18. assay: test. **pageant:** pretense, show.

19. in false gaze: looking in the wrong direction, with our attention diverted.

23. may: can. **more facile question:** an easier trial of strength over power.
24. For that: because. **warlike brace:** state of military preparedness. **25. abilities:** defensive capability.
26. dressed in: equipped with.

29. attempt of ease and gain: easy and profitable undertaking.
30. wake and wage: stir up and risk.

35. injointed with an after fleet: united with a following fleet.

37–38. restem / Their backward course: steer back to their original course. **38–39. bearing . . . toward:** making openly for.

41. free duty recommends: willing service informs.

48. straight: immediately.
49. general: universal (because anti-Christian).

50   [*To Brabantio*] I did not see you: welcome, gentle° signior;   50. **gentle:** noble.
        We lacked your counsel and your help tonight.

    BRABANTIO   So did I yours. Good your grace, pardon me:
        Neither my place° nor aught I heard of business   53. **place:** public office.
        Hath raised me from my bed, nor doth the general care

55   Take hold on me; for my particular° grief   55. **particular:** personal.
        Is of so flood-gate° and o'erbearing° nature   56. **flood-gate:** a sluice gate which holds back water; but here used to mean the torrent of water so held back. **o'erbearing:** overwhelming.   57. **engluts:** devours, gulps down.
        That it engluts° and swallows other sorrows
        And yet is still itself.

    DUKE   Why, what's the matter?

    BRABANTIO   My daughter! O, my daughter!

    SENATORS   Dead?

    BRABANTIO   Ay, to me.

60   She is abused,° stol'n from me, and corrupted   60. **abused:** wronged, harmed.
        By spells and medicines bought of mountebanks;°   61. **mountebanks:** charlatans.
        For nature so preposterously to err,
        Being not deficient,° blind, or lame of sense,°   63. **deficient:** naturally defective, simpleminded.   **lame of sense:** of faulty sensory perception.   64. **Sans:** without.
        Sans° witchcraft could not.

65 DUKE   Whoe'er he be that in this foul proceeding
        Hath thus beguiled your daughter of herself,°   66. **beguiled your daughter of herself:** cunningly robbed your daughter of her normal natural reactions.   67. **bloody:** death-dealing. Witchcraft was a capital crime.
        And you of her, the bloody° book of law
        You shall yourself read in the bitter letter
        After your own sense,° yea, though our proper° son   69. **After your own sense:** according to your own interpretation. **our proper:** my own. 70. **Stood in your action:** faced your charge.

70   Stood in your action.°

    BRABANTIO   Humbly I thank your grace.
        Here is the man: this Moor, whom now it seems
        Your special mandate for the state affairs
        Hath hither brought.

    ALL   We are very sorry for't.

    DUKE   [*To Othello*] What in your own part can you say to this?

75 BRABANTIO   Nothing, but this is so.

    OTHELLO   Most potent, grave, and reverend signiors,
        My very noble and approved° good masters,   77. **approved:** esteemed.
        That I have tane away this old man's daughter,
        It is most true; true I have married her;

80   The very head and front° of my offending   80. **head and front:** whole extent; literally, "height and breadth."   81. **Rude:** unrefined, unpracticed.
        Hath this extent, no more. Rude° am I in my speech
        And little blessed with the soft phrase of peace,
        For since these arms of mine had seven years' pith°   83. **pith:** strength.
        Till now some nine moons wasted,° they have used   84. **moons wasted:** months ago.

85   Their dearest° action in the tented field;   85. **dearest:** most important.

And little of this great world can I speak
More than pertains to feats of broil and battle;
And therefore little shall I grace my cause
In speaking for myself. Yet, by your gracious patience,
90   I will a round° unvarnished tale deliver

    90. round: plain, blunt.

Of my whole course of love: what drugs, what charms,
What conjuration° and what mighty magic—

    92. conjuration: magical incantation.

For such proceedings I am charged withal°—

    93. withal: with.

I won his daughter.

    BRABANTIO   A maiden never bold;
95   Of spirit so still and quiet that her motion°

    95–96. her motion / Blushed at herself: she was embarrassed by her own natural impulses.

Blushed at herself;° and she, in spite of nature,
Of years,° of country, credit,° everything,

    97. years: i.e., the difference in age between Desdemona and Othello.   **credit:** reputation.

To fall in love with what she feared to look on?
It is a judgement maimed and most imperfect
100   That will confess perfection so could err
Against all rules of nature, and must be driven
To find out practices° of cunning hell

    102. practices: evil machinations.

Why this should be. I therefore vouch again
That with some mixtures powerful o'er the blood
105   Or with some dram° conjured to this effect°

    105. dram: dose.   **conjured to this effect:** magically created for this purpose.

He wrought upon her.

    DUKE   To vouch this is no proof°

    106. To vouch this is no proof: proverbially, "Accusation is no proof."

Without more wider° and more overt test°
Than these thin habits° and poor likelihoods°
Of modern seeming° do prefer against him.

    107. wider: fuller.   **test:** testimony, evidence.   **108. thin habits:** insubstantial outward appearances.   **poor likelihoods:** weak inferences, tenuous indications.
    109. modern seeming: commonplace assumptions.

110 **1 SENATOR** But, Othello, speak:
Did you by indirect° and forcèd courses°

    111. indirect: underhand.   **forcèd courses:** means used against the will of the victim.

Subdue and poison this young maid's affections?
Or came it by request and such fair question°

    113. question: conversation.

As soul to soul affordeth?

    OTHELLO   I do beseech you
115   Send for the lady to the Sagittary
And let her speak of me before her father.
If you do find me foul° in her report,

    117. foul: guilty.

The trust, the office I do hold of you,
Not only take away, but let your sentence
120   Even fall upon my life.

    DUKE   Fetch Desdemona hither.

    OTHELLO Ancient, conduct them: you best know the place.

              [Exit Iago with two or three Attendants]

And till she come, as truly as to heaven

I do confess the vices of my blood,°

So justly° to your grave ears I'll present

125   How I did thrive in this fair lady's love,

And she in mine.

DUKE   Say it, Othello.

OTHELLO   Her father loved me, oft invited me,

Still° questioned me the story of my life

From year to year—the battles, sieges, fortunes

130   That I have passed.

I ran it through, even from my boyish days

To the very moment that he bade me tell it;

Wherein I spake of most disastrous chances,

Of moving accidents° by flood and field,

135   Of hair-breadth scapes° i'th'imminent deadly breach,

Of being taken by the insolent foe

And sold to slavery; of my redemption thence,

And with it all my travels' history:

Wherein of antres° vast and deserts idle,°

140   Rough quarries,° rocks, and hills whose heads touch

heaven,

It was my hint° to speak—such was the process:

And of the cannibals that each other eat,

The Anthropophagi, and men whose heads

Do grow beneath their shoulders. This to hear

145   Would Desdemona seriously incline;

But still the house affairs would draw her thence,

Which ever as she could with haste dispatch

She'd come again, and with a greedy ear

Devour up my discourse; which I observing

150   Took once a pliant° hour and found good means

To draw from her a prayer of earnest heart

That I would all my pilgrimage dilate°

Whereof by parcels° she had something heard,

But not intentively.° I did consent,

155   And often did beguile her of° her tears

When I did speak of some distressful stroke

That my youth suffered. My story being done,

She gave me for my pains a world of sighs:

She swore, in faith, 'twas strange, 'twas passing° strange,

160   'Twas pitiful, 'twas wondrous pitiful;

She wished she had not heard it, yet she wished

That heaven had made her° such a man. She thanked me,

And bade me, if I had a friend that loved her,

I should but teach him how to tell my story,

123. blood: nature.

124. justly: truthfully, exactly.

128. Still: continually.

134. moving accidents: stirring adventures.

135. scapes: escapes.

139. antres: caves.   **idle:** desolate, empty.

140. Rough quarries: rugged precipices, jagged mountain sides.

141. hint: opportunity, cue.

150. pliant: suitable, opportune.

152. dilate: tell in full.

153. by parcels: piecemeal.

154. intentively: with continuous attention.

155. beguile her of: steal from her, coax from her.

159. passing: exceedingly.

162. had made her: i.e., she had been born.

165 And that would woo her. Upon this hint I spake:
She loved me for the dangers I had passed,
And I loved her that she did pity them.
This only is the witchcraft I have used.
Here comes the lady: let her witness it.

Enter DESDEMONA, *Iago and Attendants.*

170 DUKE   I think this tale would win my daughter too.
Good Brabantio, take up this mangled matter at the best:
Men do their broken weapons rather use
Than their bare hands.

BRABANTIO   I pray you hear her speak.
If she confess that she was half the wooer,
175 Destruction on my head if my bad blame
Light on the man! Come hither, gentle mistress;
Do you perceive in all this noble company
Where most you owe obedience?

DESDEMONA   My noble father,
I do perceive here a divided duty:
180 To you I am bound for life and education;°
My life and education both do learn° me
How to respect you. You are lord of all my duty;°
I am hitherto your daughter. But here's my husband;
And so much duty as my mother showed
185 To you, preferring you before her father,
So much I challenge° that I may profess
Due to the Moor my lord.

BRABANTIO   God bu'y!° I have done.
Please it your grace, on to° the state affairs.
I had rather to adopt a child than get° it.
190 Come hither, Moor:
I here do give thee that with all my heart°
Which, but thou hast already, with all my heart
I would keep from thee. For your sake,° jewel,
I am glad at soul I have no other child,
195 For thy escape° would teach me tyranny
To hang clogs° on them. I have done, my lord.

DUKE   Let me speak like yourself° and lay a sentence°
Which as a grise° or step may help these lovers
Into your favour.
200 When remedies° are past the griefs are ended
By seeing the worst which° late on hopes depended.°

180. **education:** upbringing.

181. **learn:** teach.

182. **all my duty:** all the respect that is due to you as my father.

186. **challenge:** claim.

187. **bu'y:** be with you.

188. **on to:** let us proceed with.

189. **get:** beget.

191. **with all my heart:** in which my whole heart was wrapped up.

193. **For your sake:** on your account.

195. **escape:** elopement.

196. **clogs:** shackles; literally, blocks of wood tied to the legs of animals to prevent their straying.   **197. like yourself:** on your behalf and as you would speak (if you were not in your present frame of mind).   **lay a sentence:** apply a maxim.   **198. grise:** step.

200. **remedies:** hopes of cure.

201. **which:** i.e., the griefs, worst expectations. **late on hopes depended:** were bolstered until recently by hopeful expectations.

To mourn a mischief° that is past and gone

Is the next° way to draw new mischief on.

What cannot be preserved when fortune takes,

205   Patience her injury a mockery makes.°

The robbed that smiles steals something from the thief;

He robs himself that spends a bootless° grief.

BRABANTIO   So let the Turk of Cyprus us beguile,

We lose it not so long as we can smile;

210   He bears the sentence well that nothing bears

But the free° comfort which from thence he hears;

But he bears both the sentence and the sorrow

That to pay grief must of poor° patience borrow.°

These sentences, to sugar or to gall,°

215   Being strong on both sides, are equivocal.

But words are words; I never yet did hear

That the bruisèd heart was piercèd through the ear.°

Beseech you now, to the affairs of the state.

DUKE   The Turk with a most mighty preparation makes for

220   Cyprus. Othello, the fortitude° of the place is best known to

you; and though we have there a substitute° of most allowed

sufficiency,° yet opinion,° a more sovereign mistress of

effects,° throws a more safer voice on you.° You must

therefore be content to slubber° the gloss of your new fortunes

225   with this more stubborn° and boisterous° expedition.

OTHELLO   The tyrant custom, most grave senators,

Hath made the flinty and steel° couch of war

My thrice-driven° bed of down. I do agnise°

A natural and prompt alacrity°

230   I find in hardness,° and do undertake

These present wars against the Ottomites.

Most humbly, therefore, bending to your state,°

I crave fit disposition for my wife,

Due reference of place° and exhibition°

235   With such accommodation and besort°

As levels with° her breeding.°

DUKE   If you please,

Be't at her father's.

BRABANTIO   I'll not have it so.

OTHELLO   Nor I.

DESDEMONA   Nor I; I would not there reside

To put my father in impatient thoughts

240   By being in his eye. Most gracious duke,

202. mischief: misfortune.

203. next: nearest, quickest.

204–05. What . . . makes: i.e., patient endurance enables one to take inevitable losses as trifles.

207. spends a bootless: indulges in an unavailing.

210–13. He bears . . . borrow: Brabantio's distinction is between the easy comfort of an indifferent platitude and the real cost of patience to the man whose deeper interest is violated. **211. free:** unmixed with sorrow. **213. poor:** because patience has nothing to lend. **214. gall:** bitterness.

217. the bruised . . . ear: the broken heart was reached (or lanced, and so cured) by words.

220. fortitude: strength of the defenses.

221. substitute: deputy (i.e., Montano). **221–22. allowed sufficiency:** acknowledged ability. **222. opinion:** public opinion. **222–23. more sovereign mistress of effects:** more paramount arbiter of what should be done. **223. throws a more safer voice on you:** judges you are the more reliable. **224. slubber:** slobber, sully. **225. stubborn:** harsh, rough. **boisterous:** violent. **227. flinty and steel:** The allusion is to sleeping on the ground in armor. **228. thrice-driven:** i.e., of the softest feathers (because they have been winnowed three times). **agnise:** acknowledge, confess to. **229. alacrity:** eagerness. **230. hardness:** hardship.

232. state: authority.

234. Due reference of place: appropriate assigning of a residence. **exhibition:** financial support. **235. besort:** appropriate companions or attendants. **236. levels with:** is suitable to. **breeding:** social position.

To my unfolding° lend your prosperous° ear
And let me find a charter° in your voice
T'assist my simpleness.°

DUKE   What would you, Desdemona?

DESDEMONA   That I did love the Moor to live with him,

245   My downright violence° and storm of fortunes°
May trumpet to the world. My heart's subdued
Even to the very quality° of my lord.
I saw Othello's visage in his mind
And to his honours and his valiant parts°

250   Did I my soul and fortunes° consecrate.
So that, dear lords, if I be left behind
A moth° of peace, and he go to the war,
The rites° for which I love him are bereft me,
And I a heavy interim shall support

255   By his dear° absence. Let me go with him.

OTHELLO   Let her have your voice.°
Vouch with me, heaven, I therefore beg it not
To please the palate of my appetite,
Nor to comply with heat° the young affects°

260   In my distinct° and proper satisfaction,°
But to be free° and bounteous to her mind.
And heaven defend° your good souls that you think°
I will your serious and great business scant
For she is with me. No, when light-winged toys

265   Of feathered Cupid seel° with wanton dullness
My speculative and officed instruments,°
That my disports° corrupt and taint° my business,
Let housewives make a skillet° of my helm,
And all indign° and base adversities

270   Make head° against my estimation!°

DUKE   Be it as you shall privately determine,
Either for her stay or going. Th'affair cries° haste,
And speed must answer it. You must hence tonight.

DESDEMONA   Tonight, my lord?

DUKE   This night.

OTHELLO   With all my heart.

275   **DUKE**   At nine i'the morning, here we'll meet again.
Othello, leave some officer behind
And he shall our commission bring to you
With such things else of quality and respect°
As doth import° you.

---

241. unfolding: disclosure, explanation.
prosperous: favorable.   **242. charter:** permission.   **243. simpleness:** innocence, lack of sophistication.

245. downright violence: absolute violation of the norm.   **storm of fortunes:** (1) my taking my future by storm, (2) the upheaval created for my future life.   **247. quality:** nature.

249. valiant parts: military virtues.

250. soul and fortunes: whole being and future.

252. moth: drone, idler.

253. rites: rites of love.

255. dear: (1) that I can least afford, (2) emotionally affecting.
256. voice: consent.

259–60. to comply . . . satisfaction: Othello believes that he is too mature to be at the mercy of unbridled sexual desire, and that although he expects physical satisfaction in marriage, he also values just as highly mental sympathy with his wife.   **259. comply with heat:** satisfy eagerly.   **young affects:** newly felt emotions.   **260. distinct:** individual.
261. free: generous.   **262. defend:** forbid.
think: should think.   **265. seel:** blind (from the practice in falconry of sewing up the eyelids of the young hawk).   **266. speculative and officed instruments:** powers of perception which are for the purpose of my duty.
267. disports: sexual pleasures.   **taint:** impair.
268. skillet: small cooking pot.

269. indign: unworthy.

270. Make head: take up arms, mount an attack.   **estimation:** reputation.

272. cries: calls for.

278. quality and respect: importance and relevance.
279. import: concern.

OTHELLO   So please your grace, my ancient:

280   A man he is of honesty and trust.

To his conveyance° I assign my wife,   281. **conveyance:** escorting.

With what else needful your good grace shall think

To be sent after me.

DUKE   Let it be so.

Good night to everyone. [*To Brabantio*] And noble signior,

285   If virtue no delighted° beauty lack,   285. **delighted:** delightful.

Your son-in-law is far more fair than black.

1 SENATOR   Adieu, brave Moor; use Desdemona well.

BRABANTIO   Look to her, Moor, if thou hast eyes to see:

She has deceived her father and may thee.

290   **OTHELLO**   My life upon her faith!

Exeunt [Duke, Brabantio, Cassio, Senators

and Attendants]

Honest Iago

My Desdemona must I leave to thee;

I prithee, let thy wife attend on her,

And bring her after in the best advantage.°   293. **in the best advantage:** at the most
                                                                                favorable opportunity.

Come, Desdemona, I have but an hour

295   Of love, of worldly matters and direction°   295. **direction:** instructions.

To spend with thee. We must obey the time.°   296. **time:** present pressing necessity.

Exeunt Othello and Desdemona

RODERIGO   Iago.

IAGO   What say'st thou, noble heart?

RODERIGO   What will I do, think'st thou?

300   **IAGO**   Why, go to bed and sleep.

RODERIGO   I will incontinently° drown myself.   301. **incontinently:** at once.

IAGO   If thou dost, I shall never love thee after. Why, thou silly

gentleman?

RODERIGO   It is silliness to live, when to live is torment: and

305   then we have a prescription° to die, when death is our   305. **prescription:** (1) right based on long
                                                                                tradition, (2) a doctor's order.

physician.

IAGO   O villainous!° I have looked upon the world for four   307. **villainous:** pernicious nonsense.

times seven years, and since I could distinguish betwixt a

benefit and an injury, I never found a man that knew how to

310   love himself. Ere I would say I would drown myself for the

love of a guinea-hen,° I would change my humanity with a   311. **guinea-hen:** prostitute.

baboon.

RODERIGO   What should I do? I confess it is my shame to be so

fond,° but it is not in my virtue° to amend it.   314. **fond:** infatuated.   **virtue:** nature.

315 **IAGO** Virtue? A fig!° 'Tis in ourselves that we are thus or thus. Our bodies are our gardens, to the which our wills are gardeners. So that if we will plant nettles or sow lettuce, set° hyssop and weed up thyme,° supply° it with one gender° of herbs or distract it with° many, either to have it sterile with

320 idleness or manured with industry, why the power and corrigible authority° of this lies in our wills. If the balance° of our lives had not one scale of reason to poise° another of sensuality, the blood° and baseness of our natures would conduct us to most preposterous conclusions.° But we have

325 reason to cool our raging motions,° our carnal stings,° our unbitted° lusts; whereof I take this, that you call love, to be a sect or scion.°

RODERIGO It cannot be.

IAGO It is merely a lust of the blood and a permission of the

330 will. Come, be a man. Drown thyself? Drown cats and blind puppies. I have professed me thy friend, and I confess me knit to thy deserving° with cables of perdurable° toughness. I could never better stead° thee than now. Put money in thy purse.° Follow thou these wars; defeat thy favour with an

335 usurped beard.° I say, put money in thy purse. It cannot be that Desdemona should long continue her love to the Moor—put money in thy purse—nor he his to her. It was a violent commencement, and thou shalt see an answerable sequestration°—put but money in thy purse. These Moors

340 are changeable in their wills°—fill thy purse with money. The food that to him now is as luscious as locusts shall be to him shortly as acerb° as the coloquintida.° She must change for youth;° when she is sated with his body she will find the error of her choice. Therefore put money in thy

345 purse. If thou wilt needs damn thyself, do it a more delicate way than drowning. Make° all the money thou canst. If sanctimony° and a frail vow betwixt an erring° barbarian and a super-subtle° Venetian be not too hard for my wits and all the tribe of hell, thou shalt enjoy her—therefore

350 make money. A pox of drowning thyself! It is clean out of the way.° Seek thou rather to be hanged in compassing° thy joy than to be drowned and go without her.

RODERIGO Wilt thou be fast to° my hopes, if I depend on the issue?

IAGO Thou art sure of me. Go make money. I have told thee

355 often, and I retell thee again and again, I hate the Moor.

315. A fig: a derogatory term, usually accompanied by a vulgar gesture of shooting the thumb between the first and second fingers. **317–18. if we will . . . thyme:** Nettles and lettuce were considered horticultural opposites, having the complementary qualities of dryness and wetness and so believed to aid the growth of each other. The aromatic herbs, hyssop and thyme, were also believed to have the same qualities. **317. set:** plant. **318. supply:** fill. **gender:** kind. **319. distract it with:** divide it among. **321. corrigible authority:** corrective power. **balance:** scales. **322. poise:** counterbalance. **323. blood:** natural passions. **324. conclusions:** experiments.

325. motions: impulses. **stings:** compelling desires. **326. unbitted:** unbridled, unrestrained by a curb.

327. sect or scion: branch or graft.

332. thy deserving: what is due to thee. **perdurable:** everlasting. **333. stead:** be of use to.

333–34. Put money in thy purse: proverbial saying meaning "provide yourself for success." **334–35. defeat . . . beard:** disfigure your face with a false beard.

338–39. answerable sequestration: correspondingly violent separation. **340. wills:** sexual desires.

342. acerb: bitter. **coloquintida:** a bitter apple from the Mediterranean, used as a laxative. **343. for youth:** for a younger man.

346. Make: raise.

347. sanctimony: holiness (of the marriage bond). **erring:** (1) wandering, (2) sinful (because anti-Christian). **348. super-subtle:** exceptionally refined or delicate.

350–51. clean out of the way: a completely inappropriate course of action. **351. compassing:** achieving; with a pun on "embracing."

353. fast to: in complete support of.

My cause is hearted:° thine hath no less reason. Let us be
conjunctive° in our revenge against him. If thou canst
cuckold him, thou dost thyself a pleasure, me a sport. There
are many events in the womb of time which will be delivered.
360 Traverse!° Go, provide thy money. We will have more of this
tomorrow. Adieu.

356. hearted: deeply felt.

357. conjunctive: allied.

360. Traverse!: a military order for setting troops in motion.

RODERIGO Where shall we meet i'the morning?

IAGO At my lodging.

RODERIGO I'll be with thee betimes.°

364. betimes: early.

365 **IAGO** Go to; farewell. Do you hear, Roderigo?

RODERIGO What say you?

IAGO No more of drowning, do you hear?

RODERIGO I am changed.

IAGO Go to; farewell. Put money enough in your purse.

370 **RODERIGO** I'll sell all my land.   Exit

IAGO Thus do I ever make my fool my purse;
For I mine own gained knowledge° should profane
If I would time expend with such a snipe°
But for my sport and profit. I hate the Moor,
375 And it is thought abroad that 'twixt my sheets
He's done my office. I know not if't be true
Yet I, for mere suspicion in that kind,°
Will do as if for surety.° He holds me well:°
The better shall my purpose work on him.
380 Cassio's a proper° man: let me see now;
To get his place and to plume° up my will
In double knavery. How? How? Let's see.
After some time, to abuse° Othello's ear
That he is too familiar with his wife;
385 He hath a person and a smooth dispose°
To be suspected, framed to make women false.
The Moor is of a free and open nature,
That thinks men honest that but seem to be so,
And will as tenderly° be led by the nose
390 As asses are.
I have't. It is engendered. Hell and night
Must bring this monstrous birth to the world's light.   Exit

372. gained knowledge: practical wisdom and experience. **373. snipe:** a long-billed bird, used as a type of worthlessness.

377. kind: regard.

378. surety: certainty. **holds me well:** esteems me.

380. proper: handsome.

381. plume: glorify, set a plume in the cap of.

383. abuse: deceive.

385. dispose: manner, disposition.

389. tenderly: easily, effortlessly.

EVERYTHING COMES FULL CIRCLE...

◄ The 2000 movie *O* takes the classic tale of *Othello* onto the basketball courts of a high school. The story focuses on Odin, a young African American man who is convinced by his manipulative best friend, Hugo, that his girlfriend is unfaithful to him.

There are many modern renditions of Shakespeare's plays. What aspects of the play are timeless? Why do these plays still resonate with contemporary audiences?

CHARACTER

1. How are Othello and Cassio **characterized**? Which aspects of the characters' backgrounds contribute to how each character perceives the world?

2. What **motivates** Iago? What motivates Roderigo? How do their motivations drive these characters to think, feel, and act as they do?

3. What provokes Brabantio to react the way that he does? And how do his actions advance the plot?

4. What important choices does Othello make in this part of the play? To what degree does the text convey empathy for Othello?

5. How does Desdemona react? Explain how this reaction reveals her thoughts, feelings, and values.

SETTING

6. Describe the **setting** of Act I. How do the play's details in a text convey one or more aspects of the historical, geographical, and cultural setting?

7. How does the time of day contribute to the events of Act I?

8. How does the change of the **setting** reveal tensions within the play?

STRUCTURE

9. How does the sequence of events in Act I introduce Othello's **conflict**?

10. How does the Duke's response reveal a **contrast**?

11. How do the external circumstances contribute to the **tension** that Iago intends to create between Othello and Desdemona?

IDEAS IN LITERATURE: Power and Control

12. In Act I, many characters are competing for power. Can you think of a time in your school or community when a desire for power was observed? Explain.

ACT II

SCENE i°   Act II, Scene i.

Enter MONTANO *and two* GENTLEMEN.

MONTANO What from the cape can you discern at sea?

1 GENTLEMAN Nothing at all; it is a high-wrought flood.°   **2. high-wrought flood:** angry sea.

    I cannot 'twixt the heaven and the main

    Descry a sail.

5 MONTANO Methinks the wind does speak aloud at land,

    A fuller blast ne'er shook our battlements.

    If it hath ruffianed° so upon the sea,   **7. ruffianed:** raged.

    What ribs of oak, when mountains melt on them,

    Can hold the mortise?° What shall we hear of this? **9. hold the mortise:** keep their joints intact.

10 2 GENTLEMAN A segregation° of the Turkish fleet: **10. segregation:** dispersal.

    For do but stand upon the banning shore,   **11–12. the banning . . . clouds:** The idea is that the shore is cursing or forbidding the encroachment of the mountainous waves which then, so rebuked, fall back and rise up, seeming to strike the clouds. **13. monstrous mane:** mane like a wild beast. The pun is with "main," or sea. **14. Bear:** the constellation *Ursa Minor.* **15. guards:** The two stars in *Ursa Minor,* which were second in brightness to the Pole Star and used with it for navigation purposes, were known as the Guardians.

    The chidden billow seems to pelt the clouds;°

    The wind-shaked surge, with high and monstrous mane,°

    Seems to cast water on the burning Bear°

15   And quench the guards° of th'ever-fixèd Pole.

    I never did like molestation° view   **16. like molestation:** similar upheaval.

    On the enchafèd flood.°   **17. enchafèd flood:** enraged sea.

MONTANO   If that the Turkish fleet   **18. embayed:** protected in a bay.

    Be not ensheltered and embayed,° they are drowned:

    It is impossible they bear it out.°   **19. bear it out:** weather the storm.

Enter a third GENTLEMAN.

20 3 GENTLEMAN News, lads! Our wars are done:

    The desperate tempest hath so banged the Turks

    That their designment halts.° A noble ship of Venice **22. designment halts:** enterprise is crippled.

    Hath seen a grievous wrack and sufferance°   **23. sufferance:** damage.

    On most part of their fleet.

25 MONTANO How? Is this true?

3 GENTLEMAN   The ship is here put in,

    A Veronesa; Michael Cassio,

    Lieutenant to the warlike Moor Othello,

    Is come on shore; the Moor himself at sea,

    And is in full commission here for Cyprus.

30 MONTANO I am glad on't; 'tis a worthy governor.

3 GENTLEMAN But this same Cassio, though he speak of comfort

    Touching the Turkish loss, yet he looks sadly°   **32. sadly:** gravely, seriously.

    And prays the Moor be safe; for they were parted

    With foul and violent tempest.

MONTANO   Pray heaven he be;

35 For I have served him, and the man commands
Like a full° soldier. Let's to the seaside, ho!   36. **full:** perfect, complete.
As well to see the vessel that's come in
As to throw out our eyes for brave Othello,
Even till we make the main and th'aerial blue
40 An indistinct regard.°   39–40. **the main . . . regard:** the sea and sky
                                                                    become indistinguishable.
  3 GENTLEMAN   Come, let's do so;
For every minute is expectancy°   41. **is expectancy:** gives expectation.
Of more arrivance.°   42. **arrivance:** people arriving.

Enter CASSIO.

CASSIO Thanks, you the valiant of this warlike isle
That so approve° the Moor. O, let the heavens   44. **approve:** honor.
45 Give him defence against the elements,
For I have lost him on a dangerous sea.
MONTANO Is he well shipped?
CASSIO His bark is stoutly timbered, and his pilot
Of very expert and approved allowance;°   49. **approved allowance:** tested reputation.
50 Therefore my hopes, not surfeited to death,
Stand in bold cure.°   50–51. **not surfeited . . . cure:** not being
        [*A shout*] *within,* "A sail, a sail, a sail!"   excessively optimistic are nevertheless
                                                                    confident.

Enter a MESSENGER.

CASSIO What noise?
MESSENGER The town is empty; on the brow o'the sea°   53. **brow o'the sea:** cliff-edge.
Stand ranks of people and they cry, "A sail!"
55 CASSIO My hopes do shape him for° the governor.   55. **My . . . for:** I hope it is.
                        A shot [*is heard within*].
  2 GENTLEMAN They do discharge their shot of courtesy;
Our friends at least.
CASSIO   I pray you, sir, go forth,
And give us truth who 'tis that is arrived.
  2 GENTLEMAN I shall.   *Exit*
60 MONTANO But, good lieutenant, is your general wived?
CASSIO Most fortunately: he hath achieved a maid
That paragons description and wild fame;°   62. **paragons description and wild fame:**
One that excels the quirks° of blazoning° pens   equals extravagant praise and most
And in th'essential vesture of creation°   unrestrained report. 63. **quirks:** extravagant
                                                                    conceits. **blazoning:** Originally a heraldic
65 Does tire the ingener.°   term, this word had come to mean
                                                                    "proclaiming the praises of." 64. **essential
                                                                    vesture of creation:** absolute beauty of the
                                                                    human form. 65. **tire the ingener:** outstrip
Enter Second Gentleman.   the artist's imagination.

              How now? Who's put in?
  2 GENTLEMAN 'Tis one Iago, ancient to the general.

CASSIO He's had most favourable and happy speed:
Tempests themselves, high seas, and howling winds,
The guttered° rocks and congregated sands,

70 Traitors enscarped° to clog the guiltless keel,
As having sense of beauty do omit°
Their mortal natures,° letting go safely by
The divine Desdemona.

MONTANO   What is she?

CASSIO She that I spake of, our great captain's captain,

75 Left in the conduct of the bold Iago,
Whose footing° here anticipates our thoughts
A se'nnight's° speed. Great Jove Othello guard
And swell his sail with thine own powerful breath,
That he may bless this bay with his tall° ship,

80 Make love's quick pants in Desdemona's arms,
Give renewed fire to our extincted° spirits,
And bring all Cyprus comfort.

Enter **DESDEMONA, IAGO, EMILIA** *and* **RODERIGO**.

                    O, behold,
The riches of the ship is come on shore!
You men of Cyprus, let her have your knees.

85 Hail to thee, lady! And the grace of heaven,
Before, behind thee, and on every hand,
Enwheel° thee round.

DESDEMONA   I thank you, valiant Cassio.
What tidings can you tell me of my lord?

CASSIO He is not yet arrived; nor know I aught

90 But that he's well, and will be shortly here.

DESDEMONA O, but I fear—how lost you company?

CASSIO The great contention of the sea and skies
Parted our fellowship.°

                    [*A shout*] *within,* "A sail, a sail!" [*A shot is heard.*]
                    But hark, a sail!

2 GENTLEMAN They give their greeting° to the citadel:

95 This likewise is a friend.

CASSIO   See for the news.

                    [*Exit Second Gentleman*]

Good ancient, you are welcome. [*To Emilia*] Welcome,
    mistress.
Let it not gall° your patience, good Iago,
That I extend my manners. 'Tis my breeding
That gives me this bold show of courtesy.°

                    [*He kisses Emilia.*]

69. guttered: jagged with gullies, furrowed.

70. enscarped: drawn up into ridges.

71–72. omit / Their mortal natures: forbear to exercise their deadly natural propensities. Opposition is implied between mortal and divine.

76. footing: landing.

77. se'nnight: week.

79. tall: gallant.

81. extincted: extinguished, dulled; an allusion to the theory of humors.

87. Enwheel: encircle.

93. Parted our fellowship: separated our ships.

94. give their greeting: i.e., by firing a salvo; compare 56 above.

97. gall: irritate.

98–99. extend . . . courtesy: stretch my greeting, for it is my training in polished behavior that guides me to this gesture of welcome.

100 **IAGO** Sir, would she give you so much of her lips

As of her tongue she oft bestows on me

You would have enough.

DESDEMONA Alas, she has no speech.

IAGO   In faith, too much:

I find it still° when I have list° to sleep.

105 Marry, before your ladyship,° I grant

She puts her tongue a little in her heart

And chides with thinking.°

EMILIA   You've little cause to say so.

IAGO Come on, come on; you are pictures° out of doors, bells°

in your parlours, wild-cats° in your kitchens, saints in your

110 injuries,° devils being offended, players° in your housewif-

ery, and housewives° in your beds.

DESDEMONA O fie upon thee, slanderer!

IAGO Nay, it is true, or else I am a Turk:°

You rise to play and go to bed to work.

115 **EMILIA** You shall not write my praise.

IAGO   No, let me not.

DESDEMONA What wouldst thou write of me, if thou shouldst

praise me?

IAGO O, gentle lady, do not put me to't,

For I am nothing if not critical.

DESDEMONA Come on, assay.° There's one gone to the harbour?

120 **IAGO** Ay, madam.

DESDEMONA [*Aside*] I am not merry, but I do beguile°

The thing I am° by seeming otherwise—

Come, how wouldst thou praise me?

IAGO I am about it, but indeed my invention

125 Comes from my pate as birdlime° does from frieze°—

It plucks out brains and all. But my muse labours,°

And thus she is delivered:°

"If she be fair and wise, fairness and wit,

The one's for use, the other useth it."

130 **DESDEMONA** Well praised! How if she be black° and witty?°

IAGO "If she be black, and thereto have a wit,

She'll find a white° that shall her blackness fit."°

DESDEMONA Worse and worse.

EMILIA   How if fair and foolish?

IAGO "She never yet was foolish that was fair,

135 For even her folly° helped her to an heir."

104. still: always. **list:** a desire.

105. before your ladyship: in your ladyship's presence.

107. chides with thinking: keeps her shrewish inclinations in her thoughts.

108. pictures: silent appearances (of virtue). **bells:** i.e., noisy.
109. wild-cats: spitfires. **109–10. saints in your injuries:** adopting a saintly air when you are claiming to be injured. **110. players:** deceivers, triflers. **111. housewives:** i.e., economical with your sexual favors.

113. Turk: i.e., infidel (and thus my word is not worthy of belief).

119. assay: try, tackle it.

121–22. beguile / The thing I am: divert attention from my state of anxiety.

125. birdlime: a sticky substance spread on bushes to catch small birds. **frieze:** a coarse woolen cloth (from which birdlime would be difficult to remove). **126. labours:** (1) works hard, (2) tries to give birth. **127. is delivered:** (1) produces, (2) gives birth.

130. black: dark-haired or brown-complexioned. **witty:** quick of apprehension.

132. white: The pun is on (1) fair lover; (2) wight, or person. **fit:** suit. This word contains a sexual innuendo.

135. folly: (1) foolishness, (2) unchastity.

DESDEMONA These are old fond paradoxes° to make fools
    laugh i'th'alehouse. What miserable praise hast thou for her
    that's foul° and foolish?

IAGO "There's none so foul and foolish thereunto,°

140   But does foul pranks which fair and wise ones do."

DESDEMONA O heavy ignorance! Thou praisest the worst
    best. But what praise couldst thou bestow on a deserving
    woman indeed? One that in the authority of her merit did
    justly put on the vouch of very° malice itself?

145 **IAGO** "She that was ever fair, and never proud,
    Had tongue at will, and yet was never loud;
    Never lacked gold, and yet went never gay;°
    Fled from her wish, and yet said "Now I may";
    She that being angered, her revenge being nigh,

150   Bade her wrong stay, and her displeasure fly;
    She that in wisdom never was so frail
    To change° the cod's head for the salmon's tail;°
    She that could think and ne'er disclose her mind,
    See suitors following and not look behind;

155   She was a wight,° if ever such wight were—"

DESDEMONA To do what?

IAGO "To suckle fools and chronicle small beer."°

DESDEMONA O, most lame and impotent conclusion! Do not
    learn of him, Emilia, though he be thy husband. How say

160   you, Cassio, is he not a most profane° and liberal° counsellor?

CASSIO He speaks home,° madam; you may relish him more
    in° the soldier than in the scholar.

IAGO [*Aside*] He takes her by the palm. Ay, well said;° whisper.
    With as little a web as this will I ensnare as great a fly as

165   Cassio. Ay, smile upon her, do. I will gyve thee in thine own
    courtship.° You say true, 'tis so indeed. If such tricks as these
    strip you out of your lieutenantry, it had been better you
    had not kissed your three fingers so oft,° which now again
    you are most apt to play the sir° in. Very good, well kissed,

170   an excellent courtesy! 'Tis so indeed. Yet again your fingers
    to your lips? Would they were clyster-pipes° for your sake!
                         Trumpets within.

    The Moor! I know his trumpet.°

CASSIO   'Tis truly so.

DESDEMONA Let's meet him and receive him.

CASSIO   Lo, where he comes!

---

136. old fond paradoxes: hackneyed and foolish sayings.

138. foul: ugly, sluttish.

139. thereunto: in addition.

144. put on the vouch of very: commend the testimony of even.

147. gay: elaborately dressed.

152. To change . . . tail: to exchange something worthless for something more valuable. There is clearly sexual innuendo in "cod's head" (penis) and "tail" (pudendum). **change:** exchange, accept.
155. wight: person.

157. chronicle small beer: keep petty household accounts, be concerned with trivialities.

160. profane: worldly; ribald. **liberal:** licentious. **161. home:** directly and to the point (a term from fencing). **161–62. relish him more in:** appreciate him better in the character of.
163. well said: well done.

165–66. gyve . . . courtship: fetter, shackle yourself in your own courtly manners.

168. kissed your three fingers so oft: a courtly gesture of a gentleman to a lady.
169. sir: fine gentleman.

171. clyster-pipes: medical syringes for enemas and vaginal douches.

172. trumpet: trumpet-call.

Enter OTHELLO *and* ATTENDANTS.

OTHELLO   O, my fair warrior!

DESDEMONA   My dear Othello!

175 OTHELLO   It gives me wonder great as my content°

> 175. **my content:** the fulfillment of my desire.

To see you here before me. O, my soul's joy,

If after every tempest come such calms,

May the winds blow till they have wakened death,

And let the labouring bark climb hills of seas,

180 Olympus-high, and duck again as low

As hell's from heaven. If it were now to die,

'Twere now to be most happy; for I fear

My soul hath her content so absolute

That not another comfort like to this

185 Succeeds in unknown fate.

DESDEMONA   The heavens forbid

But that our loves and comforts should increase,

Even as our days do grow.

OTHELLO   Amen to that, sweet powers!

I cannot speak enough of this content;

It stops me here;° it is too much of joy.

They kiss.

> 189. **stops me here:** i.e., prevents me in my heart.

190 And this, and this, the greatest discords be

That e'er our hearts shall make.

IAGO   [*Aside*]   O, you are well tuned now!

But I'll set down the pegs° that make this music,

As honest as I am.°

> 192. **set down the pegs:** i.e., slacken the strings (as of a stringed instrument).   193. **As honest as I am:** for all my supposed honesty.

OTHELLO   Come, let us to the castle.

News, friends; our wars are done; the Turks are drowned.

195 How does my old acquaintance of this isle?

Honey, you shall be well desired° in Cyprus;

> 196. **well desired:** warmly welcomed (and sought out as a guest).

I have found great love amongst them. O my sweet,

I prattle out of fashion° and I dote

> 198. **out of fashion:** irrelevantly.

In mine own comforts.° I prithee, good Iago,

> 199. **comforts:** happiness.

200 Go to the bay and disembark my coffers;°

> 200. **coffers:** boxes and trunks.

Bring thou the master° to the citadel;

> 201. **master:** captain (of the ship that brought me).

He is a good one, and his worthiness

Does challenge° much respect. Come, Desdemona,

> 203. **challenge:** deserve.

Once more well met at Cyprus!

Exeunt [all except Iago and Roderigo]

205 IAGO   [*To a departing Attendant*] Do thou meet me presently

at the harbour. [*To Roderigo*] Come hither. If thou be'st

valiant—as they say base° men being in love have then a

> 207. **base:** lowly born.

nobility in their natures more than is native to them—list
me. The lieutenant tonight watches on the court of guard.°

209. **court of guard:** guardhouse.

210   First, I must tell thee this: Desdemona is directly° in love
with him.

210. **directly:** undoubtedly.

RODERIGO With him? Why, 'tis not possible!

IAGO Lay thy finger thus,° and let thy soul be instructed. Mark
me with what violence she first loved the Moor but° for

213. **thus:** i.e., on his lips. The phrase is proverbial for "keep quiet." **214. but:** only.

215   bragging and telling her fantastical lies. And will she love
him still° for prating? Let not thy discreet heart think it. Her
eye must be fed. And what delight shall she have to look
on the devil? When the blood is made dull with the act of
sport,° there should be, again to inflame it and to give

216. **still:** continually.

219. **sport:** coitus.

220   satiety a fresh appetite, loveliness in favour,° sympathy° in
years, manners and beauties: all which the Moor is defective
in. Now for want of these required conveniences,° her delicate tenderness will find itself abused,° begin to heave the
gorge,° disrelish and abhor the Moor. Very nature° will

220. **favour:** appearance. **sympathy:** agreement, correspondence.

222. **required conveniences:** requisite conditions of sexual desire. **223. tenderness will find itself abused:** sensibility will find itself disgusted. **223–24. heave the gorge:** vomit. **224. Very nature:** natural reactions themselves.

225   instruct her in it, and compel her to some second choice.
Now, sir, this granted—as it is a most pregnant° and unforced
position°—who stands so eminent in the degree of° this
fortune as Cassio does?—a knave very voluble;° no further
conscionable° than in putting on the mere form of civil and

226. **pregnant:** cogent. **227. position:** hypothesis. **in the degree of:** as next in line for.

228. **voluble:** plausible, glib.

229. **conscionable:** conscientious.

230   humane° seeming for the better compassing of his salt° and
most hidden loose affection. Why none; why none—a
slipper° and subtle knave, a finder out of occasions,° that
has an eye can stamp° and counterfeit advantages, though
true advantage never present itself; a devilish knave! Besides,

230. **humane:** polite. **salt:** lecherous.

232. **slipper:** slippery. **occasions:** opportunities.

233. **stamp:** coin.

235   the knave is handsome, young, and hath all those requisites
in him that folly and green° minds look after. A pestilent
complete knave; and the woman hath found him° already.

236. **green:** unripe; hence "immature."

237. **found him:** seen sympathetically what he is after.

RODERIGO I cannot believe that in her; she's full of most blest
condition.°

238–39. **blest condition:** heavenly disposition.

240 IAGO Blest fig's end! The wine she drinks is made of grapes. If
she had been blest she would never have loved the Moor.
Blest pudding! Didst thou not see her paddle with° the palm
of his hand? Didst not mark that?

242. **paddle with:** stroke suggestively.

RODERIGO Yes, that I did; but that was but courtesy.

245 IAGO Lechery, by this hand: an index and obscure prologue to°
the history of lust and foul thoughts. They met so near with
their lips that their breaths embraced together—villainous
thoughts, Roderigo! When these mutualities° so marshal the
way, hard at hand comes the master and main exercise, the

245. **index . . . to:** indicator of.

248. **mutualities:** reciprocal intimacies.

250   incorporate° conclusion. Pish! But, sir, be you ruled by me.

250. **incorporate:** carnal, bodily.

I have brought you from Venice; watch you tonight; for the
command, I'll lay't upon you. Cassio knows you not; I'll not
be far from you. Do you find some occasion to anger Cassio,
either by speaking too loud or tainting° his discipline, or

255 from what other course you please, which the time shall
more favourably minister.°

RODERIGO Well.

IAGO Sir, he's rash and very sudden on choler, and haply° with
his truncheon° may strike at you: provoke him that he may;

260 for even out of that will I cause these of Cyprus to mutiny,
whose qualification shall come into no true taste again° but
by the displanting of Cassio. So shall you have a shorter
journey to your desires by the means I shall then have to
prefer° them, and the impediment most profitably removed

265 without the which there were no expectation of our
prosperity.

RODERIGO I will do this, if you can bring it to any opportunity.

IAGO I warrant° thee. Meet me by and by° at the citadel. I must
fetch his° necessaries ashore. Farewell.

270 **RODERIGO** Adieu.   Exit

IAGO That Cassio loves her, I do well believe't;
That she loves him, 'tis apt and of great credit.°
The Moor, howbeit that I endure him not,
Is of a constant, loving, noble nature;

275 And I dare think he'll prove to Desdemona
A most dear husband. Now, I do love her too,
Not out of absolute lust—though peradventure
I stand accountant° for as great a sin—
But partly led to diet° my revenge,

280 For that I do suspect the lusty Moor
Hath leaped into my seat, the thought whereof
Doth like a poisonous mineral° gnaw my inwards;
And nothing can or shall content my soul
Till I am evened with him, wife for wife;

285 Or failing so, yet that I put the Moor
At least into a jealousy so strong
That judgement cannot cure. Which thing to do,
If this poor trash of Venice, whom I trace°
For his quick hunting,° stand the putting on,°

290 I'll have our Michael Cassio on the hip,°
Abuse° him to the Moor in the rank garb°—
For I fear Cassio with my night-cap too—
Make the Moor thank me, love me, and reward me,

254. tainting: disparaging, sneering at.

256. minister: provide.

258. haply: perhaps.

259. truncheon: baton of office.

261. qualification . . . again: i.e., appeasement shall not be reattained.

264. prefer: forward, promote.

268. warrant: assure. **by and by:** immediately.

269. his: i.e., Othello's.

272. apt and of great credit: likely and most believable.

278. accountant: accountable.

279. diet: feed.

282. mineral: drug.

288–89. trace / For his quick hunting: follow after because of his lively sexual pursuit (of Desdemona). **289. stand the putting on:** persist in doing what I incite him to. **290. on the hip:** at my mercy.
291. Abuse: slander. **rank garb:** lascivious manner.

For making him egregiously an ass,

295   And practising upon° his peace and quiet

    Even to madness. 'Tis here, but yet confused;

    Knavery's plain face is never seen till used.   Exit

295. practising upon: plotting against.

SCENE ii°

Act II, Scene ii.

Enter Othello's **HERALD** *with a proclamation.*

HERALD It is Othello's pleasure, our noble and valiant general,
    that upon certain tidings° now arrived importing the mere
    perdition° of the Turkish fleet, every man put himself into
    triumph:° some to dance, some to make bonfires, each man
5   to what sport and revels his addiction° leads him; for besides
    these beneficial news, it is the celebration of his nuptial. So
    much was his pleasure should be proclaimed. All offices° are
    open, and there is full liberty of feasting from this present
    hour of five till the bell have told° eleven. Heaven bless the
10   isle of Cyprus and our noble general Othello!   Exit

2. upon certain tidings: because of reliable tidings.   **2–3. mere perdition:** total loss.

4. triumph: public festivity.

5. addiction: inclination.

7. offices: e.g., kitchens, cellars, butteries (for the distribution of food and drink).

9. told: struck, counted.

SCENE iii°

Act II, Scene iii.

Enter **OTHELLO, DESDEMONA, CASSIO** *and* **ATTENDANTS.**

OTHELLO Good Michael, look you to the guard tonight.
    Let's teach ourselves that honourable stop,°
    Not to out-sport discretion.°

CASSIO Iago hath direction what to do;
5   But notwithstanding with my personal eye
    Will I look to't.

OTHELLO   Iago is most honest.
    Michael, good night; tomorrow with your earliest°
    Let me have speech with you—Come, my dear love,
    The purchase made, the fruits are to ensue;
10   That profit's yet to come 'tween me and you.
    Good night.

            Exeunt Othello, Desdemona [and Attendants]

2. stop: restraint.

3. out-sport discretion: celebrate to excess.

7. with your earliest: at your earliest convenience.

Enter **IAGO.**

CASSIO Welcome, Iago; we must to the watch.

IAGO Not this hour,° lieutenant; 'tis not yet ten o'th'clock. Our
    general cast° us thus early for the love of his Desdemona;
15   who let us not therefore blame: he hath not yet made
    wanton the night with her, and she is sport for Jove.

CASSIO She's a most exquisite lady.

IAGO And I'll warrant her full of game.°

13. Not this hour: not for an hour yet.

14. cast: dismissed.

18. full of game: sexually active.

CASSIO Indeed she is a most fresh and delicate creature.

20 **IAGO** What an eye she has! Methinks it sounds a parley to provocation.°

> **20–21. sounds a parley to provocation:** literally, "summons sexual desire to a meeting."

CASSIO An inviting eye, and yet methinks right modest.

IAGO And when she speaks, is it not an alarum° to love?

> **23. alarum:** call to arms.

CASSIO She is indeed perfection.

25 **IAGO** Well, happiness to their sheets! Come, lieutenant, I have a stoup° of wine, and here without are a brace of Cyprus gallants, that would fain have a measure° to the health of the black Othello.

> **26. stoup:** a tankard of two quarts.
>
> **27. fain have a measure:** gladly drink a toast.

CASSIO Not tonight, good Iago; I have very poor and unhappy°
30 brains for drinking. I could well wish courtesy would invent some other custom of entertainment.

> **29. unhappy:** i.e., productive of an unfortunate outcome.

IAGO O, they are our friends—but one cup; I'll drink for you.°

> **32. for you:** in your place.

CASSIO I have drunk but one cup tonight, and that was craftily qualified° too; and behold what innovation° it makes here.°
35 I am unfortunate in the infirmity and dare not task my weakness with any more.

> **34. qualified:** diluted. **innovation:** disturbance. **here:** i.e., in my head.

IAGO What, man! 'Tis a night of revels; the gallants desire it.

CASSIO Where are they?

IAGO Here at the door; I pray you call them in.

40 **CASSIO** I'll do't, but it dislikes° me.   *Exit*

> **40. dislikes:** displeases.

IAGO If I can fasten but one cup upon him,
With that which he hath drunk tonight already,
He'll be as full of quarrel and offence°

> **43. offence:** readiness to take umbrage.

As my young mistress' dog.° Now my sick° fool Roderigo,

> **44. my young mistress' dog:** i.e., a spoiled pet. **sick:** love-sick.

45 Whom love hath turned almost the wrong side out,
To Desdemona hath tonight caroused
Potations pottle-deep,° and he's to watch.

> **47. pottle-deep:** to the bottom of the tankard.

Three lads of Cyprus, noble swelling° spirits,

> **48. swelling:** arrogant.

That hold their honours in a wary distance,°

> **49. hold . . . distance:** are quick to take offense at anything resembling an insult to their honor. **50. very elements:** characteristic types.

50 The very elements° of this warlike isle,
Have I tonight flustered° with flowing cups;

> **51. flustered:** excited, befuddled.

And they watch° too. Now, 'mongst this flock of drunkards,

> **52. watch:** are awake.

Am I to put° our Cassio in some action

> **53. put:** incite.

That may offend the isle. But here they come.

Enter Cassio, **MONTANO** *and* **GENTLEMEN**.

55 If consequence° do but approve° my dream,
My boat sails freely, both with wind and stream.

> **55. consequence:** what happens, future events. **approve:** substantiate.

CASSIO 'Fore God, they have given me a rouse° already.

> **57. rouse:** full glass of drink.

MONTANO Good faith, a little one; not past a pint, as I am a soldier.

60 **IAGO**   Some wine, ho!

> [*Sings*]
>
> And let me the cannikin° clink, clink,
>
> And let me the cannikin clink;
>
> > A soldier's a man,
> >
> > O, man's life's but a span,°

61. **cannikin:** small drinking-can.

64. **span:** short time.

65   Why then, let a soldier drink.

Some wine, boys!

CASSIO   'Fore God, an excellent song.

IAGO   I learned it in England, where indeed they are most
potent in potting.° Your Dane, your German, and your swag-
70   bellied° Hollander—drink, ho!—are nothing to your English.

69. **potent in potting:** heavy drinkers.
69–70. **swag-bellied:** pendulously paunched.

CASSIO   Is your Englishman so exquisite° in his drinking?

71. **exquisite:** accomplished.

IAGO   Why, he drinks you with facility your Dane dead drunk;
he sweats not to overthrow your Almain;° he gives your
Hollander a vomit ere the next pottle can be filled.

73. **Almain:** German.

75 **CASSIO**   To the health of our general!

MONTANO   I am for it, lieutenant, and I'll do you justice.°

76. **do you justice:** match your pledge.

IAGO   O sweet England!

> [*Sings*]
>
> King Stephen was and a worthy peer,
>
> > His breeches cost him but a crown;
>
> 80   He held them sixpence all too dear,
>
> > With that he called the tailor lown.°

81. **lown:** rascal, rogue.

> He was a wight of high renown,
>
> > And thou art but of low degree;
>
> 'Tis pride° that pulls the country down;

84. **pride:** ostentation, extravagance.

> 85   Then take thine auld cloak about thee.

Some wine, ho!

CASSIO   'Fore God, this is a more exquisite song than the other.

IAGO   Will you hear't again?

CASSIO   No, for I hold him to be unworthy of his place that does
90   those things. Well, God's above all, and there be souls must
be saved, and there be souls must not be saved.

IAGO   It's true, good lieutenant.

CASSIO   For mine own part—no offence to the general, nor
any man of quality°—I hope to be saved.

94. **quality:** rank.

95 **IAGO**   And so do I too, lieutenant.

CASSIO   Ay, but by your leave, not before me; the lieutenant is
to be saved before the ancient. Let's have no more of this;
let's to our affairs. God forgive us our sins! Gentlemen, let's
look to our business. Do not think, gentlemen, I am drunk;
100   this is my ancient, this is my right hand, and this is my left

hand. I am not drunk now, I can stand well enough, and I
speak well enough.

ALL Excellent well.

CASSIO Why, very well then; you must not think then that
105   I am drunk.   Exit

MONTANO To the platform,° masters. Come, let's set the watch.°

> 106. **platform:** gun ramparts. **set the watch:** mount the guard.

IAGO You see this fellow that is gone before,
He is a soldier fit to stand by° Caesar
And give direction. And do but see his vice—

> 108. **stand by:** be lieutenant to, or perhaps "be the equal of."

110   'Tis to his virtue a just equinox,°
The one as long as th'other. 'Tis pity of him.
I fear the trust Othello puts him in,
On some odd time° of his infirmity,
Will shake this island.

> 110. **just equinox:** exact equivalent; i.e., the darkness of his vice counterbalances exactly the light of his virtue.

> 113. **odd time:** chance moment.

MONTANO   But is he often thus?
115 **IAGO** 'Tis evermore the prologue to his sleep:
He'll watch the horologe a double set,°
If drink rock not his cradle.

> 116. **watch the horologe a double set:** stay awake for two revolutions of the clock.

MONTANO   It were well
The general were put in mind of it.
Perhaps he sees it not, or his good nature
120   Prizes the virtue that appears in Cassio
And looks not on his evils: is not this true?

Enter **RODERIGO**.

IAGO [*Aside to Roderigo*] How now, Roderigo?
I pray you after the lieutenant, go.

Exit Roderigo

MONTANO And 'tis great pity that the noble Moor
125   Should hazard such a place as his own second
With° one of an ingraft° infirmity;
It were an honest action to say so
To the Moor.

> 125–26. **hazard . . . With:** risk giving the position of lieutenant to.
> 126. **ingraft:** deep-rooted.

IAGO   Not I, for this fair island:
I do love Cassio well, and would do much
130   To cure him of this evil.

[*A cry of*] *"Help, help!" within.*
But hark! what noise?

Enter Cassio, pursuing Roderigo.

CASSIO Zounds, you rogue, you rascal!

MONTANO What's the matter, lieutenant?

CASSIO A knave teach me my duty! I'll beat the knave into a
twiggen° bottle.

135 **RODERIGO** Beat me?

CASSIO Dost thou prate, rogue?

[He strikes Roderigo.]

MONTANO Nay, good lieutenant, I pray you, sir, hold your
hand.

CASSIO Let me go, sir; or I'll knock you o'er the mazzard.°

140 **MONTANO** Come, come, you're drunk.

CASSIO Drunk?

They fight.

IAGO *[Aside to Roderigo]* Away I say, go out and cry a mutiny.°

[Exit Roderigo]

Nay, good lieutenant; God's will, gentlemen!

Help ho! Lieutenant, sir! Montano, sir!

145 Help, masters, here's a goodly watch indeed!

A bell rings.

Who's that which rings the bell?° Diabolo,° ho!

The town will rise.° God's will, lieutenant, hold!

You will be shamed forever.

Enter Othello, and **GENTLEMEN** *with weapons.*

OTHELLO What is the matter here?

MONTANO   Zounds, I bleed still.

150 I am hurt to th'death.

OTHELLO   Hold for your lives!

IAGO Hold ho, lieutenant, sir; Montano, gentlemen,

Have you forgot all place of° sense and duty?

Hold! the general speaks to you; hold, for shame!

OTHELLO Why, how now, ho! From whence ariseth this?

155 Are we turned Turks,° and to ourselves do that

Which heaven hath forbid the Ottomites?°

For Christian shame, put by this barbarous brawl.

He that stirs next to carve for his own rage°

Holds his soul light:° he dies upon his motion.

160 Silence that dreadful bell: it frights the isle

From her propriety.° What is the matter, masters?

Honest Iago, that looks dead with grieving,

Speak. Who began this? On thy love, I charge thee.

IAGO I do not know. Friends all but now, even now,

165 In quarter° and in terms° like bride and groom,

Divesting° them for bed; and then but now—

As if some planet had unwitted men°—

---

134. twiggen: covered with wicker. Cassio may
mean he will so pattern Roderigo's hide with
his sword.

139. mazzard: head, skull.

142. mutiny: riot.

146. bell: warning bell. **Diabolo:** devil.

147. rise: grow riotous.

152. place of: dignity derived from.

155. turned Turks: proverbial, but especially
apt here. **155–56. to ourselves . . . Ottomites:**
i.e., slaughter our own soldiers, which God has
prevented the Turks from doing (by sending
the storm that destroyed their fleet).
158. carve for his own rage: strike with his
sword as his fury prompts him. **159. Holds
his soul light:** values his life at little worth.

161. From her propriety: out of its natural
state (of peace).

165. quarter: conduct. **in terms:** standing in
relation to each other. **166. Divesting:**
undressing. **167. As if . . . men:** It was
believed in astrology that errant planets
drawing too close to the earth could "unwit,"
or turn men mad.

Swords out and tilting one at other's breasts
In opposition bloody. I cannot speak°   **169. speak:** explain.

170   Any beginning to this peevish odds:°   **170. peevish odds:** senseless quarrel.
And would in action glorious I had lost
Those legs that brought me to° a part of it.   **172. to:** i.e., to be.

OTHELLO How comes it, Michael, you are thus forgot?

CASSIO I pray you pardon me, I cannot speak.

175 **OTHELLO** Worthy Montano, you were wont be civil:
The gravity and stillness° of your youth   **176. stillness:** sober behavior, staidness.
The world hath noted; and your name is great
In mouths of wisest censure.° What's the matter   **178. censure:** judgment.
That you unlace your reputation thus,   **179–80. That you . . . opinion:** The image here appears to be of Montano undoing the strings of his purse of reputation and squandering the high opinion people have of him.
180 And spend your rich opinion° for the name
Of a night-brawler? Give me answer to it.

MONTANO Worthy Othello, I am hurt to danger;
Your officer Iago can inform you—
While I spare speech, which something now offends° me—   **184. something now offends:** somewhat now hurts.
185 Of all that I do know; nor know I aught
By me that's said or done amiss this night,
Unless self-charity be sometimes a vice,
And to defend ourselves it be a sin
When violence assails us.

OTHELLO   Now by heaven
190 My blood° begins my safer guides to rule,   **190. blood:** anger.
And passion having my best judgement collied,°   **191. collied:** darkened, blackened.
Assays to lead the way. Zounds, if I stir,
Or do but lift this arm, the best of you
Shall sink in my rebuke. Give me to know
195 How this foul rout° began, who set it on,   **195. rout:** brawl, uproar.
And he that is approved in° this offence,   **196. approved in:** found guilty of.
Though he had twinned with me, both at a birth,
Shall lose me. What, in a town of war,
Yet wild, the people's hearts brimful of fear,
200 To manage° private and domestic quarrel,   **200. manage:** carry on, conduct.
In night, and on the court and guard of safety?°   **201. on the court and guard of safety:** at the headquarters of the guard and on sentry duty.
'Tis monstrous. Iago, who began't?

MONTANO If partially affined or leagued in office,°   **203. If partially . . . office:** if because you are bound by partiality or are confederate as soldiers in the same unit.
Thou dost deliver more or less than truth,
205 Thou art no soldier.

IAGO   Touch me not so near.
I had rather have this tongue cut from my mouth
Than it should do offence to Michael Cassio.

Yet, I persuade myself, to speak the truth
Shall nothing wrong him. This it is, general:

210 Montano and myself being in speech,
There comes a fellow crying out for help,
And Cassio following him with determined sword
To execute upon him. Sir, this gentleman°

213. **this gentleman:** i.e., Montano.

Steps in to Cassio and entreats his pause;°

214. **his pause:** him to stop.

215 Myself the crying fellow did pursue,
Lest by his clamour—as it so fell out—
The town might fall in fright. He, swift of foot,
Outran my purpose and I returned the rather°

218. **the rather:** all the sooner.

For that I heard the clink and fall of swords

220 And Cassio high in oath, which till tonight
I ne'er might say before. When I came back—
For this was brief—I found them close together
At blow and thrust, even as again they were
When you yourself did part them.

225 More of this matter can I not report;
But men are men; the best sometimes forget.°

226. **forget:** i.e., themselves.

Though Cassio did some little wrong to him,°

227. **him:** i.e., Montano.

As men in rage strike those that wish them best,
Yet surely Cassio, I believe, received

230 From him that fled some strange indignity
Which patience could not pass.°

231. **patience could not pass:** self-control
could not overlook.

OTHELLO   I know, Iago,
Thy honesty and love doth mince this matter,
Making it light to Cassio. Cassio, I love thee,
But never more be officer of mine.

Enter Desdemona attended.

235 Look if my gentle love be not raised up!
I'll make thee an example.

DESDEMONA   What's the matter, dear?

OTHELLO All's well now, sweeting; come away to bed.
Sir, for your hurts myself will be your surgeon.°

238. **be your surgeon:** pay for your medical
treatment.

                    [Montano is led off]

Iago, look with care about the town,

240 And silence those whom this vile brawl distracted.
Come, Desdemona, 'tis the soldier's life
To have their balmy slumbers waked with strife.

                    Exeunt [all but Iago and Cassio]

IAGO What, are you hurt, lieutenant?

CASSIO Ay, past all surgery.

245 **IAGO** Marry, God forbid!

CASSIO Reputation, reputation, reputation! O, I have lost my
reputation! I have lost the immortal part of myself, and
what remains is bestial. My reputation, Iago, my reputation!

IAGO As I am an honest man, I thought you had received some
250 bodily wound: there is more of sense° in that than in reputation. Reputation is an idle and most false imposition,° oft
got without merit and lost without deserving. You have lost
no reputation at all, unless you repute yourself such a loser.
What, man! There are ways to recover° the general again.
255 You are but now cast in his mood,° a punishment more in
policy° than in malice, even so as one would beat his
offenceless dog to affright an imperious lion.° Sue to him
again, and he's yours.

CASSIO I will rather sue to be despised than to deceive so good
260 a commander with so light,° so drunken, and so indiscreet
an officer. Drunk! And speak parrot!° And squabble!
Swagger! Swear! And discourse fustian° with one's own
shadow! O thou invisible spirit of wine, if thou hast no
name to be known by, let us call thee devil!

265 **IAGO** What was he that you followed with your sword? What
had he done to you?

CASSIO I know not.

IAGO Is't possible?

CASSIO I remember a mass of things, but nothing distinctly: a
270 quarrel, but nothing wherefore. O God, that men should put
an enemy in their mouths to steal away their brains! That
we should with joy, pleasance, revel and applause° transform ourselves into beasts!

IAGO Why, but you are now well enough. How came you thus
275 recovered?

CASSIO It hath pleased the devil drunkenness to give place to
the devil wrath; one unperfectness shows me another, to
make me frankly despise myself.

IAGO Come, you are too severe a moraler.° As the time, the
280 place, and the condition of this country stands, I could
heartily wish this had not befallen; but since it is as it is,
mend it for your own good.

CASSIO I will ask him for my place again; he shall tell me I am
a drunkard. Had I as many mouths as Hydra,° such an
285 answer would stop them all. To be now a sensible man, by

250. **of sense:** of physical feeling, of sensibility.

251. **imposition:** that which is laid on a person by other people.

254. **recover:** win back (to your side).

255. **cast in his mood:** dismissed in a temporary state of anger.   256. **in policy:** i.e., to demonstrate publicly his control of affairs.
256–57. **would beat . . . lion:** i.e., would punish an innocent unimportant man in order to deter a powerful and dangerous one.

260. **light:** irresponsible.

261. **parrot:** nonsense.

262. **fustian:** bombastic nonsense.

272. **applause:** celebration of some event.

279. **moraler:** moralizer.

284. **Hydra:** the multi-headed serpent in Greek mythology which was killed by Hercules. Whenever one of its heads was cut off, two more grew in its place.

and by a fool, and presently a beast! O strange! Every inordinate cup is unblessed, and the ingredience° is a devil.

IAGO Come, come, good wine is a good familiar° creature, if it
be well used; exclaim no more against it. And, good
290   lieutenant, I think you think I love you.

CASSIO I have well approved it, sir. I drunk!

IAGO You or any man living may be drunk at a time,° man. I'll
tell you what you shall do. Our general's wife is now the
general. I may say so in this respect, for that° he hath
295   devoted and given up himself to the contemplation, mark,
and denotement of her parts° and graces. Confess yourself
freely to her, importune her help to put you in your place
again. She is of so free,° so kind, so apt, so blest a disposition, that she holds it a vice in her goodness not to do more
300   than she is requested. This broken joint between you and
her husband entreat her to splinter;° and my fortunes
against any lay° worth naming, this crack of your love shall
grow stronger than it was before.

CASSIO You advise me well.

305 **IAGO** I protest, in the sincerity of love and honest kindness.

CASSIO I think it freely;° and betimes in the morning I will
beseech the virtuous Desdemona to undertake° for me. I am
desperate of my fortunes if they check° me here.

IAGO You are in the right. Good night, lieutenant, I must to the
310   watch.

CASSIO Good night, honest Iago.   *Exit*

IAGO And what's he then that says I play the villain,
When this advice is free I give, and honest,
Probal° to thinking, and indeed the course
315   To win the Moor again? For 'tis most easy
Th'inclining° Desdemona to subdue
In any honest suit. She's framed as fruitful°
As the free elements;° and then for her
To win the Moor, were't to renounce his baptism,
320   All seals and symbols of redeemèd sin,
His soul is so enfettered to her love,
That she may make, unmake, do what she list,
Even as her appetite shall play the god
With his weak function.° How am I then a villain
325   To counsel Cassio to this parallel° course
Directly to° his good? Divinity of hell!°

287. ingredience: contents.

288. familiar: friendly.

292. at a time: sometime.

294. in this respect, for that: in the light of the fact that.

296. parts: accomplishments, qualities.

298. free: generous.

301. splinter: set in splints.

302. lay: wager.

306. freely: unreservedly.

307. undertake: take up the matter.

308. check: repulse.

314. Probal: probable (or perhaps "reasonable").

316. inclining: compliant.

317. framed as fruitful: created as generous.

318. free elements: unrestrained natural forces.

324. weak function: inability to resist.

325. parallel: i.e., to Iago's design.

326. Directly to: in complete accord with.
Divinity of hell: theology of the Devil.

When devils will the blackest sins put on,°

327. put on: incite.

They do suggest° at first with heavenly shows

328. suggest: tempt, seduce.

As I do now. For whiles this honest fool

330   Plies° Desdemona to repair his fortunes,

330. Plies: solicits.

And she for him pleads strongly to the Moor,

I'll pour this pestilence into his ear:

That she repeals° him for her body's lust;

333. repeals: tries to procure Cassio's reinstatement.

And by how much she strives to do him good,

335   She shall undo her credit with the Moor.

So will I turn her virtue into pitch,°

336. pitch: (1) blackness, (2) something odious, (3) that which has the power to ensnare.

And out of her own goodness make the net

That shall enmesh them all.

Enter Roderigo.

          How now, Roderigo?

RODERIGO I do follow here in the chase, not like a hound that

340   hunts, but one that fills up the cry.° My money is almost

340. fills up the cry: merely makes one of the pack.

spent; I have been tonight exceedingly well cudgelled; and I

think the issue will be, I shall have so much experience for

my pains; and so, with no money at all, and a little more

wit,° return again to Venice.

344. wit: intelligence.

345 **IAGO** How poor are they that have no patience!

What wound did ever heal but by degrees?

Thou know'st we work by wit and not by witchcraft,

And wit depends on dilatory time.

Does't not go well? Cassio hath beaten thee,

350   And thou by that small hurt hath cashiered Cassio.

Though other things grow fair against the sun,

351–52. Though other . . . ripe: Although our long-term plans for the seduction of Desdemona are blossoming slowly, yet our preliminary plan against Cassio has already borne fruit.

Yet fruits that blossom first will first be ripe.°

Content thyself awhile. By th'mass, 'tis morning:

Pleasure and action make the hours seem short.

355   Retire thee, go where thou art billeted.

Away, I say, thou shalt know more hereafter—

Nay, get thee gone.

                                    Exit Roderigo

             Two things are to be done.

My wife must move° for Cassio to her mistress—

358. move: plead.

I'll set her on.

360   Myself the while to draw the Moor apart,

And bring him jump° when he may Cassio find

361. jump: exactly at the moment.

Soliciting his wife. Ay, that's the way:

Dull not device° by coldness° and delay.   *Exit*

363. device: plan, plot. **coldness:** lack of energy.

The image shows a 2013 staging of William Shakespeare's *Othello*, directed by Nicholas Hytner at the National Theatre in London.

Robbie Jack/Getty Images

———

The quest for power is an important element of the tragedy of Othello. Explain how the hierarchical organization of the military contributes to Iago's motivation. Does this type of motivation remain today? Explain how people respond to the systems of advancement in a contemporary hierarchical structure.

CHARACTER

1. In Act II, Scene i, consider specific words, phrases, and details that Iago and Desdemona use as they talk. How does their dialogue reveal each of their **characters**?

2. Explain what drives Cassio and Desdemona to think, feel, or act as they do. Describe how this **motivates** Iago's actions.

3. What provokes Cassio's circumstances to change? How does this change contribute to Iago's plan?

SETTING

4. Explain the location of Act II. How do these details reveal one or more aspects of the play's **geographical** and **cultural setting**?

5. How does the weather in Act II, Scene i, contribute to the events of the play?

6. What social event in Act II changes the **setting**? Explain how the events contribute to the action of the play.

STRUCTURE

7. Explain how the sequence of events in Act II affects the **contrast** between Othello and Desdemona.

8. At the end of Act II. Explain how Iago and Rodrigo's actions contribute to Cassio's dilemma.

9. Explain the **conflict** in Act II. How does this conflict reveal the opposing motivations and values of Othello and Desdemona?

IDEAS IN LITERATURE: Power and Control

10. Iago's strategy is based on control through manipulation. What does *manipulative* mean in this context? Can you think of an example in your own experience when manipulation — or a manipulative person — controlled the outcome of an event or situation? Why is manipulation so powerful? How can we resist that power?

ACT III

SCENE i°

Enter CASSIO, MUSICIANS *and* CLOWN.

CASSIO Masters, play here;° I will content your pains.°
　　Something that's brief, and bid "Good morrow, general."
　　　　　　　　　　　　　　　　　　　　[They play.]

CLOWN Why, masters, have your instruments been in Naples,
　　that they speak i'th'nose° thus?

5 1 MUSICIAN How, sir, how?

CLOWN Are these, I pray you, wind instruments?

1 MUSICIAN Ay, marry are they, sir.

CLOWN O, thereby hangs a tail.°

1 MUSICIAN Whereby hangs a tale, sir?

10 CLOWN Marry, sir, by many a wind instrument° that I know.
　　But, masters, here's money for you; and the general so likes
　　your music that he desires you, for love's sake,° to make no
　　more noise° with it.

1 MUSICIAN Well sir, we will not.

15 CLOWN If you have any music that may not° be heard, to't
　　again; but, as they say, to hear music the general does not
　　greatly care.

1 MUSICIAN We have none such, sir.

CLOWN Then put up your pipes in your bag, for I'll away. Go,
20　　vanish into air, away!

　　　　　　　　　　　　　　　　Exeunt Musicians

CASSIO Dost thou hear, mine honest friend?

CLOWN No, I hear not your honest friend; I hear you.

CASSIO Prithee keep up thy quillets°—there's a poor piece of
　　gold for thee. If the gentlewoman that attends the general's
25　　wife be stirring, tell her there's one Cassio entreats her a
　　little favour of speech. Wilt thou do this?

CLOWN She is stirring, sir; if she will stir hither, I shall seem°
　　　　to notify unto her.

CASSIO Do, good my friend.

　　　　　　　　　　　　　　　　　Exit Clown

Enter IAGO.

　　　　　　　　　　In happy time,° Iago.

30 IAGO You have not been abed then?

CASSIO Why, no; the day had broke before we parted.
　　I have made bold, Iago,
　　To send in to your wife. My suit to her

Act III, Scene i.

1. play here: It was a custom to wake newlyweds with music on the morning after their first night together. **content your pains:** pay for your efforts.

3–4. have . . . nose: The Clown may mean that the music has an ugly nasal twang like the Neapolitan accent, but there is probably also a reference to venereal disease, which attacked the nose.

8. tail: slang term for "penis."

10. wind instrument: i.e., anus.

12. for love's sake: for the sake of any affection you may have for him; with a pun on "for the sake of his erotic concentration."
13. noise: (1) music, (2) nose.

15. may not: cannot.

23. quillets: verbal quibbles.

27. seem: arrange.

29. In happy time: You have come at an opportune moment.

Is that she will to virtuous Desdemona
35   Procure me some access.

IAGO   I'll send her to you presently;
And I'll devise a mean to draw the Moor
Out of the way, that your converse and business
May be more free.

CASSIO   I humbly thank you for't.

Exit [Iago]

I never knew a Florentine° more kind and honest.

39. a Florentine: i.e., even one of my own countrymen.

Enter EMILIA.

40   EMILIA   Good morrow, good lieutenant; I am sorry
For your displeasure;° but all will sure be well.
The general and his wife are talking of it,
And she speaks for you stoutly. The Moor replies
That he you hurt is of great fame in Cyprus
45   And great affinity,° and that in wholesome° wisdom
He might not but refuse you; but he protests he loves you,
And needs no other suitor but his likings
To take the safest occasion° by the front°
To bring you in again.

41. displeasure: being out of favor.

45. great affinity: related to important people. **wholesome:** prudent.

48. occasion: opportunity.   **front:** forehead.

CASSIO   Yet I beseech you,
50   If you think fit, or that it may be done,
Give me advantage of some brief discourse
With Desdemon alone.

EMILIA   Pray you, come in;
I will bestow you where you shall have time
To speak your bosom° freely.

54. bosom: private thoughts and feelings.

CASSIO   I am much bound to you.

Exeunt

SCENE ii°

Enter OTHELLO, IAGO and GENTLEMEN.

OTHELLO   These letters give, Iago, to the pilot,
And by him do my duties° to the senate.
That done, I will be walking on the works;°
Repair° there to me.

Act III, Scene ii.

2. do my duties: pay my respects.

3. works: fortifications.

4. Repair: return.

IAGO   Well, my good lord, I'll do't.   [Exit]
5   OTHELLO   This fortification, gentlemen, shall we see't?
GENTLEMEN   We'll wait upon° your lordship.

6. wait upon: attend

Exeunt

SCENE iii°

Act III, Scene iii.

Enter DESDEMONA, CASSIO *and* EMILIA.

DESDEMONA Be thou assured, good Cassio, I will do
    All my abilities in thy behalf.

EMILIA Good madam, do; I warrant it grieves my husband
    As if the case were his.

5 **DESDEMONA** O, that's an honest fellow. Do not doubt, Cassio,
    But I will have my lord and you again
    As friendly as you were.

CASSIO   Bounteous madam,
    Whatever shall become of Michael Cassio,
    He's never anything but your true servant.

10 **DESDEMONA** I know't; I thank you. You do love my lord,
    You have known him long, and be you well assured
    He shall in strangeness° stand no farther off
    Than in a politic distance.°

CASSIO   Ay, but, lady,
    That policy may either last so long
15   Or feed upon such nice° and waterish diet,
    Or breed itself so out of circumstance,°
    That I being absent and my place supplied,°
    My general will forget my love and service.

DESDEMONA Do not doubt° that. Before Emilia here,
20   I give thee warrant° of thy place. Assure thee
    If I do vow a friendship, I'll perform it
    To the last article.° My lord shall never rest,
    I'll watch him tame° and talk him out of patience;
    His bed shall seem a school, his board a shrift;°
25   I'll intermingle every thing he does
    With Cassio's suit. Therefore be merry, Cassio;
    Thy solicitor° shall rather die
    Than give thy cause away.°

Enter OTHELLO *and* IAGO.

EMILIA Madam, here comes my lord.
30 **CASSIO** Madam, I'll take my leave.

DESDEMONA Why, stay and hear me speak.

CASSIO Madam, not now: I am very ill at ease,
    Unfit for mine own purposes.

DESDEMONA Well, do your discretion.°

                          Exit Cassio

35 **IAGO** Ha! I like not that.

OTHELLO   What dost thou say?

---

12. strangeness: estrangement.

13. in a politic distance: is expedient politically.

15. nice: thin, sparse.

16. breed itself so out of circumstance: bring about so few opportunities for my reinstatement. **17. supplied:** filled (by someone else).

19. doubt: fear.

20. warrant: guarantee.

22. article: a legal term meaning "clause in a contract." **23. watch him tame:** prevent him from sleeping until he is tractable.
24. board a shrift: table (shall seem) a confessional.

27. Thy solicitor: your advocate.

28. give thy cause away: abandon your case.

34. do your discretion: do what you think is discreet.

IAGO   Nothing, my lord; or if—I know not what.

OTHELLO   Was not that Cassio parted from my wife?

IAGO   Cassio, my lord? No, sure I cannot think it

That he would steal away so guilty-like,

40   Seeing you coming.

OTHELLO   I do believe 'twas he.

DESDEMONA   How now, my lord?

I have been talking with a suitor here,

A man that languishes in your displeasure.

OTHELLO Who is't you mean?

45 **DESDEMONA**   Why, your lieutenant, Cassio. Good my lord,

If I have any grace° or power to move you,

His present reconciliation take.°

For if he be not one that truly loves you,

That errs in ignorance, and not in cunning,°

50   I have no judgement in an honest face.

I prithee call him back.

OTHELLO   Went he hence now?

DESDEMONA   Ay, sooth; so humbled

That he hath left part of his grief with me

To suffer with him. Good love, call him back.

55 **OTHELLO**   Not now, sweet Desdemon; some other time.

DESDEMONA   But shall't be shortly?

OTHELLO   The sooner, sweet, for you.

DESDEMONA   Shall't be tonight at supper?

OTHELLO   No, not tonight.

DESDEMONA   Tomorrow dinner° then?

OTHELLO   I shall not dine at home.

I meet the captains at the citadel.

60 **DESDEMONA**   Why, then, tomorrow night, or Tuesday morn,

On Tuesday noon, or night; on Wednesday morn.

I prithee name the time, but let it not

Exceed three days. In faith, he's penitent;

And yet his trespass, in our common reason—

65   Save that, they say, the wars must make example

Out of their best°—is not almost° a fault

T'incur a private check.° When shall he come?

Tell me, Othello. I wonder in my soul

What you would ask me that I should deny,

70   Or stand so mammering on.° What! Michael Cassio,

That came a-wooing with you, and so many a time

46. grace: favor in your eyes.

47. present reconciliation take: restore him immediately to favor.

49. in cunning: knowingly, with complete mental awareness.

58. dinner: i.e., what we call "lunch."

66. best: i.e., the highest-ranking officers.
not almost: hardly, barely.
67. check: reprimand.

70. mammering on: hesitating.

When I have spoke of you dispraisingly
Hath tane your part, to have so much to do
To bring him in?° By'r Lady, I could do much—

74. **in:** i.e., into favor.

75 **OTHELLO** Prithee no more. Let him come when he will;
I will deny thee nothing.

DESDEMONA   Why, this is not a boon;
'Tis as I should entreat you wear your gloves,
Or feed on nourishing dishes, or keep you warm,
Or sue to you to do a peculiar profit°

79–80. **a peculiar profit / To your own person:** something of special personal advantage to yourself.

80   To your own person.° Nay, when I have a suit
Wherein I mean to touch° your love indeed,

81. **touch:** test, make trial of.

It shall be full of poise° and difficult weight,°
And fearful to be granted.

82. **poise:** weight, importance. **difficult weight:** momentous, hard to decide on.

OTHELLO   I will deny thee nothing.
Whereon,° I do beseech thee, grant me this,

84. **Whereon:** in return for which.

85   To leave me but a little to myself.

DESDEMONA Shall I deny you? No; farewell, my lord.

OTHELLO Farewell, my Desdemona, I'll come to thee straight.°

87. **straight:** at once.

DESDEMONA Emilia, come. Be as your fancies° teach you;

88. **fancies:** inclinations.

Whate'er you be, I am obedient.

Exeunt Desdemona and Emilia

90 **OTHELLO** Excellent wretch!° Perdition catch my soul

90. **wretch:** a term of endearment.

But I do° love thee; and when I love thee not,°
Chaos is come again.°

91. **But I do:** if I do not. **when I love thee not:** if ever I were not to love you. **91–92. when I . . . again:** allusion to the classical legend that Love was the first of the gods to spring out of original chaos.

IAGO   My noble lord—

OTHELLO What dost thou say, Iago?

IAGO   Did Michael Cassio,
When you wooed my lady, know of your love?

95 **OTHELLO** He did from first to last. Why dost thou ask?

IAGO But for a satisfaction of my thought;
No further harm.

OTHELLO   Why of thy thought, Iago?

IAGO I did not think he had been acquainted with her.

OTHELLO O yes, and went between us very oft.

100 **IAGO** Indeed?

OTHELLO Indeed? Ay, indeed. Discern'st thou aught in that?
Is he not honest?

IAGO Honest, my lord?

OTHELLO Honest? Ay, honest.

105 **IAGO** My lord, for aught I know.

OTHELLO   What dost thou think?

IAGO Think, my lord?

OTHELLO Think, my lord! By heaven, he echoes me,
As if there were some monster in his thought
Too hideous to be shown. Thou dost mean something.
110 I heard thee say even now thou lik'st not that,
When Cassio left my wife. What didst not like?
And when I told thee he was of my counsel
In my whole course of wooing, thou cried'st "Indeed?"
And didst contract and purse° thy brow together,
115 As if thou then hadst shut up in thy brain
Some horrible conceit.° If thou dost love me,
Show me thy thought.

IAGO My lord, you know I love you.°

OTHELLO   I think thou dost;
And for I know thou'rt full of love and honesty,
120 And weigh'st thy words before thou giv'st them breath,
Therefore these stops° of thine fright me the more;
For such things in a false disloyal knave
Are tricks of custom;° but in a man that's just,
They're close dilations,° working from the heart,
125 That passion cannot rule.°

IAGO   For Michael Cassio,
I dare be sworn I think that he is honest.

OTHELLO I think so too.

IAGO   Men should be what they seem;
Or those that be not, would they might seem none!°

OTHELLO Certain, men should be what they seem.

130 **IAGO** Why then, I think Cassio's an honest man.

OTHELLO Nay, yet there's more in this.
I prithee speak to me as to thy thinkings,
As thou dost ruminate, and give thy worst of thoughts
The worst of words.

IAGO   Good my lord, pardon me;
135 Though I am bound to every act of duty,
I am not bound to that all slaves are free to.°
Utter my thoughts! Why, say they are vile and false?
As where's that palace, whereinto foul things
Sometimes intrude not? Who has a breast so pure,
140 But some uncleanly apprehensions°
Keep leets° and law-days, and in session sit
With meditations lawful?

OTHELLO Thou dost conspire° against thy friend, Iago,

---

114. purse: knit, draw together.

116. conceit: idea, conception.

118. you know I love you: a diabolic echo of Peter's words to the risen Christ in John 21:15: "Yea Lord, thou knowest that I love thee."

121. stops: breakings off, sudden pauses.

123. of custom: customary.

124. close dilations: (1) involuntary delays, (2) half-hidden expressions. **125. That passion cannot rule:** (1) that cannot control its passions, (2) that cannot be controlled by emotion.

128. none: (1) not to be men, (2) not to be honest men.

136. that all slaves are free to: i.e., the right that even slaves have to think what they wish.

140. apprehensions: ideas.

141. leets: courts of record, which some lords of the manor were empowered to hold yearly or half-yearly in their localities; hence days on which such courts were held. **143. conspire:** used to describe actions by a single person as well as by a group.

If thou but think'st him wronged, and mak'st his ear
145   A stranger to thy thoughts.
IAGO   I do beseech you,
  Though I perchance am vicious in my guess—
  As I confess it is my nature's plague
  To spy into abuses, and oft my jealousy°
  Shapes faults that are not—that your wisdom then,
150   From one that so imperfectly conceits,°
  Would take no notice, nor build yourself a trouble
  Out of his scattering° and unsure observance.
  It were not for your quiet, nor your good,
  Nor for my manhood, honesty, and wisdom,
155   To let you know my thoughts.
OTHELLO   What dost thou mean?
IAGO   Good name in man and woman, dear my lord,
  Is the immediate° jewel of their souls.
  Who steals my purse, steals trash;° 'tis something, nothing,
  'Twas mine, 'tis his, and has been slave to thousands:
160   But he that filches from me my good name
  Robs me of that which not enriches him
  And makes me poor indeed.
OTHELLO   By heaven, I'll know thy thoughts.
IAGO   You cannot, if my heart were in your hand,
165   Nor shall not, while 'tis in my custody.
OTHELLO   Ha!
IAGO   O beware, my lord, of jealousy:
  It is the green-eyed monster which doth mock°
  The meat it feeds on.° That cuckold lives in bliss
170   Who certain of his fate loves not his wronger;°
  But O, what damnèd minutes tells° he o'er
  Who dotes, yet doubts, suspects, yet fondly° loves?
OTHELLO   O misery!
IAGO   Poor and content is rich, and rich enough;
175   But riches fineless° is as poor as winter
  To him that ever fears he shall be poor.
  Good God, the souls of all my tribe defend
  From jealousy.
OTHELLO   Why, why is this?
  Think'st thou I'd make a life of jealousy,
180   To follow still the changes of the moon
  With fresh suspicions?° No, to be once in doubt

148. **jealousy:** suspicious vigilance.

150. **conceits:** imagines, conjectures.

152. **scattering:** random.

157. **immediate:** directly touching, most important.   158. **trash:** a scornful term for money.

168–69. **mock / The meat it feeds on:** i.e., torments its victim, the jealous man himself.

170. **his wronger:** the wife betraying him.

171. **tells:** counts.

172. **fondly:** foolishly.

175. **fineless:** boundless, endless.

180–81. **follow still . . . suspicions:** be ever drawn into new suspicions with each waxing and waning of the moon (as a madman is).

Is once° to be resolved.° Exchange me for a goat°

When I shall turn the business of my soul

To such exsufflicate° and blown° surmises

185   Matching thy inference.° 'Tis not to make me jealous

To say my wife is fair, feeds well, loves company,

Is free of speech, sings, plays, and dances well:

Where virtue is, these are more virtuous.

Nor from mine own weak merits° will I draw

190   The smallest fear or doubt° of her revolt,°

For she had eyes and chose me. No, Iago,

I'll see before I doubt; when I doubt, prove;

And on the proof, there is no more but this:

Away at once with love or jealousy!

195   **IAGO** I am glad of this; for now I shall have reason

To show the love and duty that I bear you

With franker spirit. Therefore, as I am bound,

Receive it from me. I speak not yet of proof.

Look to your wife, observe her well with Cassio;

200   Wear your eyes thus: not jealous, nor secure.°

I would not have your free and noble nature,

Out of self-bounty,° be abused. Look to't.

I know our country disposition well:

In Venice they do let God see the pranks

205   They dare not show their husbands. Their best conscience°

Is not to leave't undone, but keep't unknown.

OTHELLO Dost thou say so?

IAGO She did deceive her father, marrying you;

And when she seemed to shake and fear your looks

210   She loved them most.

OTHELLO   And so she did.

IAGO   Why, go to° then!

She that so young could give out such a seeming

To seel her father's eyes up close as oak

He thought 'twas witchcraft—but I am much to blame,

I humbly do beseech you of your pardon

215   For too much loving you.

OTHELLO   I am bound° to thee for ever.

IAGO I see this hath a little dashed your spirits.

OTHELLO Not a jot, not a jot.

IAGO   I'faith, I fear it has.

I hope you will consider what is spoke

Comes from my love. But I do see you're moved.

182. once: once and for all. **resolved:** convinced, free from all doubt. **goat:** a type of animal lust. **183–85. When I . . . inference:** the moment I bring my mind to concentrate on such inflated and rumored suspicions as you describe. **184. exsufflicate:** puffed up, inflated. **blown:** bandied about, rumored. **185. inference:** demonstration, depiction.

189. weak merits: i.e., lack of attractive (physical) qualities. **190. doubt:** suspicion. **revolt:** unfaithfulness.

200. secure: free from suspicion.

202. self-bounty: innate generosity.

205. best conscience: highest idea of morality.

210. go to: there you are (colloquial).

215. bound: indebted.

220   I am to pray you not to strain° my speech
       To grosser issues° nor to larger° reach
       Than to suspicion.
       OTHELLO   I will not.
       IAGO   Should you do so, my lord,
       My speech should fall into such vile success°
225   As my thoughts aimed not at. Cassio's my worthy friend—
       My lord, I see you're moved.
       OTHELLO   No, not much moved.
       I do not think but Desdemona's honest.°
       IAGO   Long live she so, and long live you to think so!
       OTHELLO   And yet how nature erring from itself—
230   IAGO   Ay, there's the point: as, to be bold with you,
       Not to affect° many proposèd matches
       Of her own clime, complexion, and degree,
       Whereto we see in all things nature tends—
       Foh! one may smell, in such, a will° most rank,°
235   Foul disproportion, thoughts unnatural.
       But pardon me: I do not in position°
       Distinctly° speak of her; though I may fear
       Her will, recoiling to her better judgement,
       May fall to match you with her country forms,°
240   And happily° repent.
       OTHELLO   Farewell, farewell.
       If more thou dost perceive, let me know more;
       Set on thy wife to observe. Leave me, Iago.
       IAGO   [Going.] My lord, I take my leave.
       OTHELLO   Why did I marry? This honest creature doubtless
245   Sees and knows more, much more, than he unfolds.
       IAGO   [Returning.] My lord, I would I might entreat your honour
       To scan° this thing no farther. Leave it to time.
       Although 'tis fit that Cassio have his place—
       For sure he fills it up with great ability—
250   Yet if you please to hold him off awhile,
       You shall by that perceive him and his means.°
       Note if your lady strain his entertainment°
       With any strong or vehement importunity—
       Much will be seen in that. In the mean time,
255   Let me be thought too busy° in my fears—
       As worthy cause I have to fear I am—
       And hold her free,° I do beseech your honour.
       OTHELLO   Fear not my government.°

220. strain: enlarge the meaning of.

221. grosser issues: (1) more substantial conclusions, (2) more lewd conclusions. **larger:** (1) wider, (2) more licentious.

224. success: result.

227. honest: chaste, virtuous.

231. affect: look favorably on, like.

234. will: (1) sexual desire, (2) purpose. **rank:** (1) corrupt, (2) lascivious.

236–37. in position / Distinctly: in applying a deliberate proposition specifically.

239. May fall . . . forms: may begin to compare you with the style of good looks typical of her own countrymen. **240. happily:** haply, perhaps.

247. scan: scrutinize.

251. his means: the methods he uses (to recover his position). **252. strain his entertainment:** urge that he be received again.

255. busy: interfering.

257. free: innocent.
258. my government: my control over my behavior.

IAGO   I once more take my leave.   Exit

260 OTHELLO   This fellow's of exceeding honesty
        And knows all qualities,° with a learnèd spirit,
        Of° human dealings. If I do prove her haggard,°
        Though that her jesses° were my dear heart-strings,
        I'd whistle her off° and let her down the wind°
265 To prey at fortune.° Haply for° I am black,
        And have not those soft parts of conversation°
        That chamberers° have, or for I am declined
        Into the vale of years—yet that's not much—
        She's gone, I am abused,° and my relief
270 Must be to loathe her. O curse of marriage,
        That we can call these delicate creatures ours
        And not their appetites! I had rather be a toad
        And live upon the vapour of a dungeon
        Than keep a corner in the thing I love
275 For others' uses. Yet 'tis the plague of great ones,
        Prerogatived are they less than the base;°
        'Tis destiny unshunnable, like death:
        Even then this forkèd plague° is fated to us
        When we do quicken.° Look where she comes.

        Enter Desdemona and Emilia.

280 If she be false, O then heaven mocks itself;°
        I'll not believe it.

DESDEMONA   How now, my dear Othello?
        Your dinner and the generous° islanders,
        By you invited, do attend° your presence.

OTHELLO   I am to blame.

DESDEMONA   Why do you speak so faintly?
285 Are you not well?

OTHELLO   I have a pain upon my forehead° here.

DESDEMONA   Faith, that's with watching;° 'twill away again.
        Let me but bind it hard, within this hour
        It will be well.

OTHELLO   Your napkin is too little.
        [*He puts the handkerchief from him, and she drops it.*]
290 Let it alone. Come, I'll go in with you.

DESDEMONA   I am very sorry that you are not well.
                              Exeunt Othello and Desdemona

EMILIA   I am glad I have found this napkin:°
        This was her first remembrance from the Moor.
        My wayward° husband hath a hundred times

261. qualities: natures, characters of people.

262. Of: in regard to.   **haggard:** intractable, wild (as an untrained hawk).   **263. jesses:** narrow strips of soft leather, silk, or other material, fastened around the legs of a trained hawk.   **264. whistle her off:** a term used to describe the setting free of an untrainable hawk.   **let her down the wind:** the way a hawk was released in order to loose it. **265. prey at fortune:** fend for herself, hunt at random.   **Haply for:** perhaps because. **266. soft parts of conversation:** pleasant arts of social behavior.   **267. chamberers:** frequenters of ladies' chambers, courtly gallants; with the overtone of "seducers" as in "chambering."   **269. abused:** deceived, disgraced.

276. Prerogatived . . . base: Important people are less free from this curse than men of low birth, and the peccadilloes of the great are more likely to be widely known than those of their social inferiors.   **278. forkèd plague:** the curse of the cuckold's horns.   **279. do quicken:** are conceived, are born.

280. heaven mocks itself: i.e., by creating something that only appears so perfect.

282. generous: noble.

283. attend: wait.

286. upon my forehead: i.e., where his cuckold's horns grow.   **287. watching:** lack of sleep.

292. napkin: handkerchief.

294. wayward: capricious, unaccountable.

295 Wooed me to steal it; but she so loves the token,
For he conjured her° she should ever keep it,
That she reserves it evermore about her
To kiss and talk to. I'll have the work tane out°
And give't Iago.
300 What he will do with it, heaven knows, not I:
I nothing but to please his fantasy.°

296. conjured her: made her swear, solemnly commanded her.

298. work tane out: embroidery copied.

301. his fantasy: some capricious idea he has.

Enter Iago.

IAGO How now? What do you here alone?

EMILIA Do not you chide; I have a thing for you.

IAGO You have a thing° for me? It is a common° thing—

305 **EMILIA** Ha!

IAGO To have a foolish wife.

EMILIA O, is that all? What will you give me now
For that same handkerchief?

IAGO   What handkerchief?

EMILIA What handkerchief!

310 Why, that the Moor first gave to Desdemona,
That which so often you did bid me steal.

IAGO Hast stolen it from her?

EMILIA No, faith; she let it drop by negligence,
And to th'advantage° I being here took't up.

315 Look, here it is.

IAGO   A good wench! Give it me.

EMILIA What will you do with't, that you have been so earnest
To have me filch it?

IAGO [*Snatching it*] Why, what's that to you?

EMILIA If it be not for some purpose of import,°
Give't me again. Poor lady, she'll run mad

320 When she shall lack° it.

IAGO   Be not acknown on't:°
I have use for it. Go, leave me.

304. thing: female sexual organ.   **common:** open to everyone.

314. to th'advantage: opportunely, fortunately.

318. import: importance.

320. lack: miss.   **Be not acknown on't:** do not admit to any knowledge of it, feign ignorance about it.

Exit Emilia

I will in Cassio's lodging lose this napkin
And let him find it. Trifles light as air
Are to the jealous confirmations strong
325 As proofs of holy writ. This may do something.
The Moor already changes with my poison:
Dangerous conceits° are in their natures poisons,
Which at the first are scarce found to distaste°
But, with a little act° upon the blood,
330 Burn like the mines of sulphur.° I did say so.

327. conceits: conceptions, ideas.

328. distaste: be distasteful.

329. act: action.

330. mines of sulphur: These were popularly associated with the Aeolian Islands and Sicily.

Enter Othello.

Look where he comes! Not poppy° nor mandragora,°
Nor all the drowsy syrups of the world,
Shall ever medicine thee to that sweet sleep
Which thou owed'st° yesterday.

OTHELLO   Ha, ha, false to me!

335 **IAGO**   Why, how now, general! No more of that.

OTHELLO   Avaunt, be gone! Thou hast set me on the rack.
I swear 'tis better to be much abused
Than but to know't a little.

IAGO   How now, my lord!

OTHELLO   What sense° had I of her stolen hours of lust?
340   I saw't not, thought it not, it harmed not me.
I slept the next night well, fed well, was free° and merry;
I found not Cassio's kisses on her lips.
He that is robbed, not wanting° what is stolen,
Let him not know't and he's not robbed at all.

345 **IAGO**   I am sorry to hear this.

OTHELLO   I had been happy if the general camp,
Pioners° and all, had tasted her sweet body
So° I had nothing known. O, now for ever
Farewell the tranquil mind! Farewell content!
350   Farewell the plumèd troops, and the big wars
That makes ambition virtue—O farewell!
Farewell the neighing steed and the shrill trump,
The spirit-stirring drum, th'ear-piercing fife,
The royal banner, and all quality,°
355   Pride,° pomp, and circumstance° of glorious war!
And, O you mortal engines,° whose rude throats
Th'immortal Jove's dread clamours° counterfeit,
Farewell! Othello's occupation's gone.

IAGO   Is't possible, my lord?

360 **OTHELLO**   Villain, be sure thou prove my love a whore;
Be sure of it. Give me the ocular proof,
Or by the worth of mine eternal soul,
Thou hadst been better have been born a dog
Than answer my waked wrath!

IAGO   Is't come to this?

365 **OTHELLO**   Make me to see't; or, at the least, so prove it
That the probation° bear no hinge nor loop°
To hang a doubt on—or woe upon thy life!

IAGO   My noble lord—

---

331. poppy: opium. **mandragora:** the mandrake plant, yielding a soporific drug.

334. owed'st: possessed.

339. sense: awareness.

341. free: untroubled.

343. wanting: missing.

347. Pioners: i.e., pioneers; considered at this time the lowest type of soldier.
348. So: if only.

354. quality: essential nature.

355. Pride: proud display. **circumstance:** ceremony, pageantry.
356. mortal engines: deadly cannons.
357. Jove's dread clamours: i.e., thunder.

366. probation: proof. **hinge nor loop:** pivot or holding-string.

OTHELLO If thou dost slander her and torture me,
370 Never pray more; abandon all remorse;
On horror's head horrors accumulate;
Do deeds to make heaven weep, all earth amazed:°
For nothing canst thou to damnation add
Greater than that.

IAGO   O grace! O heaven forgive me!
375 Are you a man? Have you a soul? Or sense?
God bu'y° you; take mine office. O wretched fool,
That lov'st to make thine honesty a vice!°
O monstrous world! Take note, take note, O world!
To be direct and honest is not safe.
380 I thank you for this profit,° and from hence
I'll love no friend, sith° love breeds such offence.°

OTHELLO Nay, stay: thou shouldst be honest.

IAGO I should° be wise; for honesty's a fool
And loses that it works for.

OTHELLO   By the world,
385 I think my wife be honest, and think she is not;
I think that thou art just, and think thou art not.
I'll have some proof. Her name, that was as fresh
As Dian's° visage, is now begrimed and black
As mine own face. If there be cords or knives,
390 Poison or fire or suffocating streams,
I'll not endure it. Would I were satisfied!

IAGO I see, sir, you are eaten up with passion.
I do repent me that I put it to you.
You would be satisfied?

OTHELLO   Would? Nay, I will.

395 **IAGO** And may. But how? How satisfied, my lord?
Would you, the supervisor,° grossly gape on?
Behold her topped?

OTHELLO   Death and damnation! O!

IAGO It were a tedious° difficulty, I think,
To bring them to that prospect. Damn them then,
400 If ever mortal eyes do see them bolster°
More° than their own. What then? How then?
What shall I say? Where's satisfaction?
It is impossible you should see this,
Were they as prime° as goats, as hot° as monkeys,
405 As salt° as wolves in pride,° and fools as gross
As Ignorance made drunk. But yet, I say,

---

372. amazed: paralyzed with horror.

376. bu'y: be with.

377. vice: failing (by carrying it to excess).

380. profit: profitable lesson.

381. sith: since. **offence:** injury (to the one who loves).

383. should: ought (with a play on "shouldst" at 382).

388. Dian: Diana, goddess of chastity and the moon.

396. supervisor: looker-on.

398. tedious: hard to arrange, laborious.

400. bolster: bed together.

401. More: other.

404. prime: lecherous. **hot:** sexually excited.

405. salt: lustful. **pride:** lust.

If imputation and strong circumstances,°
Which lead directly to the door of truth,
Will give you satisfaction, you might have't.

407. imputation and strong circumstances: opinion founded on strong circumstantial evidence.

410 **OTHELLO** Give me a living reason she's disloyal.

IAGO I do not like the office;
But sith I am entered in this cause so far—
Pricked° to't by foolish honesty and love—
I will go on. I lay with Cassio lately,

413. Pricked: spurred.

415 And being troubled with a raging tooth
I could not sleep.
There are a kind of men so loose of soul°
That in their sleeps will mutter their affairs.
One of this kind is Cassio.

417. loose of soul: i.e., loose-tongued about their innermost thoughts.

420 In sleep I heard him say, "Sweet Desdemona,
Let us be wary, let us hide our loves."
And then, sir, he would gripe° and wring my hand,
Cry, "O sweet creature!" and then kiss me hard,
As if he plucked up kisses by the roots

422. gripe: seize.

425 That grew upon my lips; then laid his leg
Over my thigh, and sighed, and kissed, and then
Cried, "Cursèd fate that gave thee to the Moor."

OTHELLO O monstrous, monstrous!

IAGO   Nay, this was but his dream.

OTHELLO But this denoted a foregone conclusion.°

429. foregone conclusion: previous consummation.

430 **IAGO** 'Tis a shrewd doubt,° though it be but a dream;
And this may help to thicken° other proofs
That do demonstrate thinly.

430. 'Tis a shrewd doubt: it gives rise to grievous suspicion. **431. thicken:** substantiate.

OTHELLO   I'll tear her all to pieces!

IAGO Nay, yet be wise; yet we see nothing done,
She may be honest yet. Tell me but this:

435 Have you not sometimes seen a handkerchief
Spotted with strawberries° in your wife's hand?

436. Spotted with strawberries: embroidered with a strawberry pattern.

OTHELLO I gave her such a one; 'twas my first gift.

IAGO I know not that; but such a handkerchief—
I am sure it was your wife's—did I today

440 See Cassio wipe his beard with.

OTHELLO   If it be that—

IAGO If it be that, or any that was hers,
It speaks against her with the other proofs.

OTHELLO O that the slave° had forty thousand lives!
One is too poor, too weak, for my revenge.

443. slave: i.e., Cassio.

445 Now do I see 'tis true. Look here, Iago,

All my fond° love thus do I blow to heaven;
'Tis gone.
Arise, black vengeance, from thy hollow cell!
Yield up, O love, thy crown and hearted° throne
450 To tyrannous hate! Swell, bosom, with thy fraught,°
For 'tis of aspics'° tongues.

                              He kneels.

IAGO   Yet be content.°

OTHELLO O, blood, blood, blood!

IAGO Patience, I say; your mind perhaps may change.

OTHELLO Never, Iago. Like to the Pontic Sea,°
455 Whose icy current and compulsive° course
Ne'er feels retiring ebb but keeps due on
To the Propontic° and the Hellespont,°
Even so my bloody thoughts with violent pace
Shall ne'er look back, ne'er ebb to humble love,
460 Till that a capable° and wide revenge
Swallow them up. Now by yond marble° heaven,
In the due reverence of a sacred vow
I here engage my words.

IAGO   Do not rise yet.

                              He kneels.

Witness you ever-burning lights above,
465 You elements that clip° us round about,
Witness that here Iago doth give up
The execution° of his wit,° hands, heart,
To wronged Othello's service. Let him command,
And to obey shall be in me remorse,
470 What bloody business ever.°

                         [They rise.]

OTHELLO   I greet thy love,
Not with vain thanks, but with acceptance bounteous;
And will upon the instant put thee to't.°
Within these three days let me hear thee say
That Cassio's not alive.

IAGO   My friend is dead;
475 'Tis done at your request. But let her live.

OTHELLO Damn her, lewd minx!° O, damn her, damn her!
Come, go with me apart. I will withdraw
To furnish me with some swift means of death
For the fair devil. Now art thou my lieutenant.

480 **IAGO** I am your own for ever.

                       Exeunt

---

446. fond: foolish (because given to Desdemona).

449. hearted: located in the heart.

450. fraught: burden, freight.

451. aspics': asps', venomous serpents'. **content:** patient, calm.

454. Pontic Sea: Black Sea.

455. compulsive: driving onward, irresistible.

457. Propontic: Sea of Marmora, located between the Black Sea and the Aegean. **Hellespont:** Dardanelles Straits, which join the Sea of Marmora and the Aegean.

460. capable: ample, capacious.

461. marble: (1) shining or grained like marble; (2) hard, unfeeling.

465. clip: encompass.

467. execution: operation, activities. **wit:** intelligence. **469–70. to obey . . . ever:** i.e., whatever bloody deed I am called upon to perform shall be done because of the pity I feel for Othello.

472. to't: to the proof.

476. minx: wanton.

SCENE iv°

Enter DESDEMONA, EMILIA *and* CLOWN.

DESDEMONA Do you know, sirrah,° where Lieutenant Cassio
  lies?°

CLOWN I dare not say he lies° anywhere.

DESDEMONA Why, man?

5 **CLOWN** He's a soldier, and for one to say a soldier lies is
  stabbing.

DESDEMONA Go to. Where lodges he?

CLOWN To tell you where he lodges is to tell you where I lie.°

DESDEMONA Can anything be made of this?

10 **CLOWN** I know not where he lodges, and for me to devise a
  lodging, and say he lies here, or he lies there, were to lie in
  mine own throat.°

DESDEMONA Can you enquire him out, and be edified by
  report?

15 **CLOWN** I will catechise the world for him: that is, make
  questions,° and by them answer.°

DESDEMONA Seek him; bid him come hither; tell him I have
  moved my lord on his behalf and hope all will be well.

CLOWN To do this is within the compass° of man's wit, and
20 therefore I will attempt the doing of it.   *Exit*

DESDEMONA Where should I lose that handkerchief, Emilia?

EMILIA I know not, madam.

DESDEMONA Believe me, I had rather lose my purse
  Full of crusadoes;° and but my noble Moor
25 Is true of mind and made of no such baseness
  As jealous creatures are, it were enough
  To put him to ill thinking.

EMILIA   Is he not jealous?

DESDEMONA Who, he? I think the sun where he was born
  Drew all such humours° from him.

Enter OTHELLO.

EMILIA   Look where he comes.

30 **DESDEMONA** I will not leave him now; let Cassio
  Be called to him.—How is't with you, my lord?

OTHELLO Well, my good lady. [*Aside*] O hardness to dissemble!
  How do you, Desdemona?

DESDEMONA   Well, my good lord.

OTHELLO Give me your hand. This hand is moist,° my lady.

35 **DESDEMONA** It yet hath felt no age, nor known no sorrow.

OTHELLO This argues° fruitfulness° and liberal° heart.

Act III, Scene iv.

1. sirrah: a term of address to an inferior.

2. lies: lodges.

3. lies: tells an untruth.

8. lie: deceive.

11–12. were to lie in mine own throat: were to lie foully; with a pun on "were/where" at 11.

15–16. I will . . . answer: The Clown is alluding to the instructional method used in the Catechism. **make questions:** (1) ask questions, (2) express doubts.

19. compass: range, reach; with a quibble on "moved."

24. crusadoes: gold coins of Portuguese origin.

29. humours: bodily fluids, the proportions of which were believed to determine a person's temperament. The reference here is to black bile, believed to cause jealousy.

34. moist: A moist palm was believed to indicate youthfulness and amorousness.

36. argues: is proof of. **fruitfulness:** (1) generosity, (2) amorousness, (3) fertility. **liberal:** (1) free, (2) licentious.

Hot, hot, and moist. This hand of yours requires
A sequester° from liberty, fasting and prayer,
Much castigation,° exercise devout;°
40 For here's a young and sweating devil° here
That commonly rebels.° 'Tis a good hand,
A frank° one.

DESDEMONA You may indeed say so,
For 'twas that hand that gave away my heart.

OTHELLO A liberal hand! The hearts of old gave hands;
45 But our new heraldry is hands, not hearts.

DESDEMONA I cannot speak of this. Come now, your promise.

OTHELLO What promise, chuck?

DESDEMONA I have sent to bid Cassio come speak with you.

OTHELLO I have a salt and sorry rheum° offends me;
50 Lend me thy handkerchief.

DESDEMONA   Here, my lord.

OTHELLO That which I gave you.

DESDEMONA   I have it not about me.

OTHELLO Not?

DESDEMONA No, faith, my lord.

OTHELLO   That's a fault. That handkerchief
Did an Egyptian to my mother give:
55 She was a charmer° and could almost read
The thoughts of people. She told her, while she kept it,
'Twould make her amiable° and subdue my father
Entirely to her love; but if she lost it
Or made a gift of it, my father's eye
60 Should hold her loathèd and his spirits should hunt
After new fancies.° She dying gave it me,
And bid me when my fate would have me wive,
To give it her. I did so, and take heed on't:
Make it a darling, like your precious eye.
65 To lose't or give't away were such perdition
As nothing else could match.

DESDEMONA   Is't possible?

OTHELLO 'Tis true. There's magic in the web° of it:
A sibyl,° that had numbered in the world
The sun to course two hundred compasses,°
70 In her prophetic fury° sewed the work;°
The worms were hallowed that did breed the silk,
And it was dyed in mummy, which the skilful
Conserved of° maidens' hearts.

DESDEMONA   I'faith, is't true?

---

38. sequester: a legal term for restraint, imprisonment. **39. castigation:** corrective discipline. **exercise devout:** religious observances. **40. sweating devil:** spirit of sexual desire. **41. rebels:** i.e., against virtuous self-control. **42. frank:** (1) liberal, (2) undisguised.

49. salt and sorry rheum: wretched running cold.

55. charmer: witch, enchantress.

57. amiable: desirable, beloved.

61. fancies: loves.

67. web: weaving.

68. sibyl: prophetess.

69. compasses: yearly circuits.

70. prophetic fury: frenzy of inspiration. **work:** embroidered pattern.

73. Conserved of: prepared as a drug from.

OTHELLO Most veritable; therefore look to't well.

75 DESDEMONA Then would to God that I had never seen't!

OTHELLO Ha? Wherefore?

DESDEMONA Why do you speak so startingly° and rash?°   **77. startingly:** disjointedly. **rash:** excitedly.

OTHELLO Is't lost? Is't gone? Speak; is't out of th'way?°   **78. out of th'way:** misplaced, gone astray.

DESDEMONA Heaven bless us!

80 OTHELLO Say you?

DESDEMONA It is not lost, but what and if it were?

OTHELLO How?

DESDEMONA I say it is not lost.

OTHELLO   Fetch't, let me see't.

DESDEMONA Why so I can, sir; but I will not now.

85   This is a trick to put me from my suit.
    Pray you let Cassio be received again.

OTHELLO Fetch me the handkerchief. My mind misgives.

DESDEMONA Come, come;
    You'll never meet a more sufficient° man.   **89. sufficient:** able.

90 OTHELLO The handkerchief!

DESDEMONA   I pray, talk me of Cassio.

OTHELLO The handkerchief!

DESDEMONA   A man that all his time
    Hath founded his good fortunes on your love,
    Shared dangers with you—

OTHELLO The handkerchief!

DESDEMONA   I'faith, you are to blame.

95 OTHELLO Zounds!   Exit

EMILIA Is not this man jealous?

DESDEMONA   I ne'er saw this° before.   **96. saw this:** i.e., perceived this trait.
    Sure there's some wonder° in this handkerchief;   **97. wonder:** magical quality.
    I am most unhappy in the loss of it.

EMILIA 'Tis not a year or two shows us a man.

100   They are all but stomachs,° and we all but food;   **100. but stomachs:** only appetites.
    They eat us hungerly, and when they are full,
    They belch us.

Enter IAGO and CASSIO.

                    Look you, Cassio and my husband.

IAGO There is no other way: 'tis she must do't.
    And lo, the happiness!° Go, and importune her.   **104. happiness:** good luck, fortunate occurrence.

105 DESDEMONA How now, good Cassio! What's the news with you?

CASSIO Madam, my former suit. I do beseech you
    That, by your virtuous° means, I may again   **107. virtuous:** efficacious.
    Exist and be a member of his love,

Whom I, with all the office° of my heart,

110   Entirely honour. I would not be delayed.

If my offence be of such mortal kind

That nor my service past nor present sorrows,

Nor purposed merit in futurity,

Can ransom me into his love again,

115   But° to know so must be my benefit:°

So shall I clothe me in a forced content,

And shut myself up in° some other course

To fortune's alms.°

DESDEMONA   Alas, thrice-gentle Cassio,

My advocation is not now in tune:

120   My lord is not my lord; nor should I know him,

Were he in favour° as in humour altered.

So help me every spirit sanctified,

As I have spoken for you all my best,

And stood within the blank of° his displeasure

125   For my free speech! You must awhile be patient.

What I can do, I will; and more I will

Than for myself I dare. Let that suffice you.

IAGO Is my lord angry?

EMILIA   He went hence but now

And certainly in strange unquietness.

130 **IAGO** Can he be angry? I have seen the cannon

When it hath blown his ranks into the air,

And like the devil from his very arm

Puffed his own brother—and is he angry?

Something of moment° then. I will go meet him.

135   There's matter in't indeed if he be angry.

DESDEMONA I prithee do so.

Exit Iago

Something sure of state,°

Either from Venice, or some unhatched practice°

Made demonstrable here in Cyprus to him,

Hath puddled° his clear spirit; and in such cases

140   Men's natures wrangle with inferior things,

Though great ones are their object.° 'Tis even so;

For let our finger ache, and it endues°

Our other healthful members even to a sense

Of pain. Nay, we must think men are not gods,

145   Nor of them look for such observancy°

As fits the bridal. Beshrew me much, Emilia,

---

109. office: devoted service.

115. But: merely. **benefit:** i.e., because he will know the worst.

117. shut myself up in: confine myself to.

118. To fortune's alms: i.e., accepting whatever fortune can spare.

121. favour: external appearance.

124. within the blank of: as the center of the target for.

134. moment: immediate importance.

136. of state: to do with state affairs.

137. unhatched practice: previously undisclosed conspiracy.

139. puddled: muddied, sullied the purity of.

141. object: real point of concern.

142. endues: brings, leads.

145. observancy: tender attention.

I was—unhandsome° warrior as I am—

Arraigning his unkindness with my soul;

But now I find I had suborned the witness°

150 And he's indicted falsely.

EMILIA   Pray heaven it be state matters, as you think,

And no conception° nor no jealous toy°

Concerning you.

DESDEMONA   Alas the day, I never gave him cause.

155 EMILIA   But jealous souls will not be answered so.

They are not ever jealous for the cause,

But jealous for they're jealous. 'Tis a monster

Begot upon itself, born on itself.

DESDEMONA   Heaven keep that monster from Othello's mind.

160 EMILIA   Lady, amen!

DESDEMONA   I will go seek him. Cassio, walk here about.

If I do find him fit,° I'll move your suit

And seek to effect it to my uttermost.

CASSIO   I humbly thank your ladyship.

Exeunt Desdemona and Emilia

Enter BIANCA.

165 BIANCA   'Save° you, friend Cassio.

CASSIO   What make you from home?

How is it with you, my most fair Bianca?

I'faith, sweet love, I was coming to your house.

BIANCA   And I was going to your lodging, Cassio.

What! Keep a week away? Seven days and nights?

170 Eight score eight° hours? And lovers' absent hours

More tedious than the dial° eight score times!

O weary reckoning!

CASSIO   Pardon me, Bianca.

I have this while with leaden thoughts been pressed;°

But I shall in a more continuate° time

175 Strike off this score° of absence. Sweet Bianca,

Take me this work out.°

BIANCA   O Cassio, whence came this?

This is some token from a newer friend.°

To the felt absence now I feel a cause.

Is't come to this? Well, well.

CASSIO   Go to, woman!

180 Throw your vile guesses in the devil's teeth

From whence you have them. You are jealous now

147. unhandsome: unskillful (with perhaps also the meaning of "unjust").

149. suborned the witness: influenced the witness to give false evidence.

152. conception: fantasy, false supposition. **toy:** fancy, whim.

162. fit: receptive.

165. 'Save: i.e., God save.

170. Eight score eight: i.e., one hundred sixty plus eight (= seven days and nights). **171. the dial:** the whole round of the clock.

173. with leaden thoughts been pressed: The image here is based on the torture of being pressed to death. **174. continuate:** uninterrupted.
175. Strike off this score: pay off this debt.
176. Take me this work out: Copy this embroidered pattern for me.

177. friend: mistress.

That this is from some mistress, some remembrance.
No, by my faith, Bianca.

BIANCA   Why, whose is it?

CASSIO I know not neither; I found it in my chamber.

185 I like the work well. Ere it be demanded°—

As like enough it will—I'd have it copied.

Take it and do't, and leave me for this time.

BIANCA Leave you? Wherefore?

CASSIO I do attend here on the general;

190 And think it no addition,° nor my wish,

To have him see me womaned.°

BIANCA   Why, I pray you?

CASSIO Not that I love you not.

BIANCA   But that you do not love me.

I pray you, bring° me on the way a little,

And say if I shall see you soon at night.

195 **CASSIO** 'Tis but a little way that I can bring you,

For I attend here; but I'll see you soon.

BIANCA 'Tis very good; I must be circumstanced.°

Exeunt

185. demanded: inquired about.

190. addition: credit to me.

191. womaned: accompanied by a woman.

193. bring: accompany.

197. be circumstanced: accept conditions as they are.

© Cincinnati Shakespeare Company

◀ The image appeared on the playbill from the Cincinnati Shakespeare Company's production of *Othello* in March of 2018.

The handkerchief in the play *Othello* marks the turning point in the play. How does this small and simple object shatter the beliefs, values, and perceptions of so many characters in the play?

CHARACTER

1. At the beginning of Act III, which characters are empathetic to Cassio? Why are some characters empathetic to him while others are not?

2. In Act III, Scene iii, why do Desdemona and Emilia think, feel, and act in the manner they do? What is **motivating** them?

3. Explain how Iago convinces Othello to doubt himself in Act III. In what ways does Othello's response reveal his character?

4. Explain how Desdemona's thoughts, actions, and **values** with regard to the handkerchief cause her to act in the manner she does.

SETTING

5. How does the opening scene's location reveal details that contribute to Cassio's situation?

6. Explain the location of Act III, Scene iii. How does this location contribute to the tension between Othello and Desdemona?

STRUCTURE

7. How do Emilia and Iago **contrast** with Othello and Desdemona? What ideas or values does this conflict reveal?

8. How does the scene between Iago and Othello at the end of Act III contribute to the **conflict**?

9. What event in Act III is the **climax** of the play? What does this moment reveal about Othello?

IDEAS IN LITERATURE: Power and Control

10. In Act III, Othello says he will need ocular proof to convince him of Iago's suspicions. In what circumstances might ocular proof convince you to believe something? In what situations is it often unpersuasive? Have you ever been deceived by appearances? Explain.

ACT IV

SCENE i°

Enter OTHELLO *and* IAGO.

Act IV, Scene i.

IAGO Will you think so?

OTHELLO   Think so, Iago?

IAGO   What,

  To kiss in private?

OTHELLO   An unauthorised kiss!

IAGO Or to be naked with her friend in bed
  An hour or more, not meaning any harm?

5 **OTHELLO** Naked in bed, Iago, and not mean harm?
  It is hypocrisy against the devil.°
  They that mean virtuously and yet do so,
  The devil their virtue tempts, and they tempt heaven.

IAGO So° they do nothing, 'tis a venial slip;

10   But if I give my wife a handkerchief—

OTHELLO What then?

IAGO Why, then 'tis hers, my lord; and being hers,
  She may, I think, bestow't on any man.

OTHELLO She is protectress of her honour too.

15   May she give that?

IAGO Her honour is an essence that's not seen:
  They have it very oft that have it not.°
  But for the handkerchief—

OTHELLO By heaven, I would most gladly have forgot it.

20   Thou said'st—O it comes o'er my memory,
  As doth the raven o'er the infected° house,
  Boding to all!—he had my handkerchief.

IAGO Ay, what of that?

OTHELLO   That's not so good now.

IAGO   What

  If I had said I had seen him do you wrong?

25   Or heard him say—as knaves be such abroad,
  Who having by their own importunate suit
  Or voluntary dotage° of some mistress
  Convincèd° or supplied° them, cannot choose
  But they must blab—

OTHELLO   Hath he said anything?

30 **IAGO** He hath, my lord; but be you well assured
  No more than he'll unswear.

OTHELLO   What hath he said?

IAGO Faith, that he did—I know not what he did.

OTHELLO What, what?

6. hypocrisy against the devil: As hypocrisy against God entails a pretense of good to conceal evil, so evil actions pretending to virtue are the opposite: "hypocrisy against the devil."

9. So: if, as long as.

17. They . . . not: i.e., those women who have actually lost their honor are often credited with still having it.

21. infected: plague-stricken.

27. voluntary dotage: willing infatuation.

28. Convincèd: overcome, overpowered. **supplied:** satisfied sexually.

IAGO Lie—

OTHELLO   With her?

IAGO   With her, on her, what you will.

35 OTHELLO Lie with her? Lie on her? We say lie on her when
they belie° her. Lie with her! Zounds, that's fulsome!°
Handkerchief—confessions—handkerchief! To confess and
be hanged for his labour. First to be hanged and then to
confess. I tremble at it. Nature would not invest herself in
40 such shadowing passion without some instruction.° It is not
words that shakes me thus. Pish! Noses, ears, and lips. Is't
possible?—Confess? Handkerchief? O devil!

36. belie: vilify, slander.   **fulsome:** rank, foul.

39–40. Nature . . . instruction: i.e., my natural faculties would not become obliterated by strong emotion unless there were some basis of fact in what I have heard.

[He] *falls in a trance.*

IAGO Work on,
My medicine, work! Thus credulous fools are caught;
45 And many worthy and chaste dames even thus,
All guiltless, meet reproach.° What ho, my lord!
My lord, I say! Othello!

46. reproach: shame, disgrace.

Enter CASSIO.

How now, Cassio!

CASSIO What's the matter?

IAGO My lord is fallen into an epilepsy.
50 This is his second fit; he had one yesterday.

CASSIO Rub him about the temples.

IAGO   No, forbear.
The lethargy° must have his quiet course.
If not, he foams at mouth and by and by
Breaks out to savage madness. Look, he stirs.
55 Do you withdraw yourself a little while;
He will recover straight. When he is gone,
I would on great occasion° speak with you.

52. lethargy: coma, unconsciousness.

57. great occasion: an important matter.

[Exit Cassio]

How is it, general? Have you not hurt your head?

OTHELLO Dost thou mock me?°

IAGO   I mock you? No, by heaven!
60 Would you would bear your fortune like a man!

OTHELLO A hornèd man's° a monster and a beast.

IAGO There's many a beast then in a populous city,
And many a civil° monster.

OTHELLO Did he confess it?

IAGO   Good sir, be a man:
65 Think every bearded fellow that's but yoked°
May draw° with you. There's millions now alive
That nightly lie in those unproper° beds

59. Dost thou mock me?: Othello refers to the cuckold's horns.

61. hornèd man: cuckold.

63. civil: civilized.

65. yoked: (1) married, (2) burdened (with wrongs).   **66. draw:** (1) pull (like yoked oxen), (2) join.

67. unproper: not (solely) their own (because shared by their wives' lovers).

Which they dare swear peculiar.° Your case is better.

O, 'tis the spite of hell, the fiend's arch-mock,

70 To lip° a wanton in a secure° couch

And to suppose her chaste! No, let me know;

And knowing what I am,° I know what she shall be.°

OTHELLO   O, thou art wise; 'tis certain.

IAGO   Stand you awhile apart,

Confine yourself but in a patient list.°

75 Whilst you were here, o'erwhelmèd with your grief—

A passion most unsuiting such a man—

Cassio came hither. I shifted him away°

And laid good scuse upon your ecstasy;°

Bade him anon return and here speak with me,

80 The which he promised. Do but encave° yourself,

And mark the fleers,° the gibes, and notable° scorns

That dwell in every region of his face;

For I will make him tell the tale anew,

Where, how, how oft, how long ago, and when

85 He hath and is again to cope° your wife.

I say but mark his gesture.° Marry, patience,

Or I shall say you're all in all in spleen°

And nothing of a man.

OTHELLO   Dost thou hear, Iago?

I will be found most cunning in my patience,

90 But—dost thou hear—most bloody.

IAGO   That's not amiss.

But yet keep time° in all. Will you withdraw?

                                    [*Othello withdraws.*]

Now will I question Cassio of Bianca,

A housewife° that by selling her desires

Buys herself bread and clothes. It is a creature

95 That dotes on Cassio; as 'tis the strumpet's plague

To beguile many and be beguiled by one.

He, when he hears of her, cannot refrain

From the excess of laughter. Here he comes.

Enter Cassio.

As he shall smile, Othello shall go mad;

100 And his unbookish° jealousy must construe

Poor Cassio's smiles, gestures, and light° behaviours

Quite in the wrong. How do you now, lieutenant?

CASSIO   The worser that you give me the addition°

Whose want even kills me.

---

68. peculiar: their own.

70. lip: kiss.   **secure:** free from care, free from suspicion.

72. what I am: i.e., a cuckold.   **she shall be:** will happen to her.

74. in a patient list: within the bounds of self-control.

77. shifted him away: got rid of him by a stratagem.   **78 ecstasy:** fit, trance.

80. encave: conceal.

81. fleers: sneers.   **notable:** observable, obvious.

85. cope: (1) meet, (2) copulate with.

86. gesture: bearing, demeanor.

87. all in all in spleen: totally governed by passion.

91. keep time: be controlled (a musical term).

93. housewife: hussy.

100. unbookish: ignorant.

101. light: cheerful, merry.

103. addition: title, rank.

105   **IAGO**   Ply Desdemona well and you are sure on't.

Now if this suit lay in Bianca's power,

How quickly should you speed!°

  CASSIO   Alas, poor caitiff!°

  OTHELLO [*Aside*] Look how he laughs already!

  IAGO   I never knew a woman love man so.

110   **CASSIO**   Alas, poor rogue! I think, i'faith, she loves me.

  OTHELLO [*Aside*] Now he denies it faintly,° and laughs it out.

  IAGO   Do you hear, Cassio?

  OTHELLO [*Aside*]   Now he importunes him

To tell it o'er. Go to, well said, well said!°

  IAGO   She gives it out that you shall marry her.

115   Do you intend it?

  CASSIO   Ha, ha, ha!

  OTHELLO [*Aside*] Do you triumph, Roman?° Do you triumph?

  CASSIO   I marry her? What! A customer!° I prithee, bear some

charity to my wit.° Do not think it so unwholesome.° Ha,

120   ha, ha!

  OTHELLO [*Aside*] So, so, so, so: they laugh that wins.

  IAGO   Faith, the cry° goes that you shall marry her.

  CASSIO   Prithee, say true.

  IAGO   I am a very villain else.

125   **OTHELLO** [*Aside*] Have you scored me?° Well.

  CASSIO   This is the monkey's own giving out. She is persuaded

I will marry her out of her own love° and flattery,° not out of

my promise.

  OTHELLO [*Aside*] Iago beckons me. Now he begins the story.

130   **CASSIO**   She was here even now. She haunts me in every place.

I was the other day talking on the sea-bank° with certain

Venetians, and thither comes this bauble° and, by this hand,

falls me thus about my neck.

  OTHELLO [*Aside*] Crying "O dear Cassio!" as it were. His gesture

135   imports it.

  CASSIO   So hangs and lolls and weeps upon me, so hales and

pulls me. Ha, ha, ha!

  OTHELLO [*Aside*] Now he tells how she plucked him to my

chamber. O, I see that nose of yours, but not that dog I shall

140   throw it to!

  CASSIO   Well, I must leave her company.

  IAGO   Before me,° look where she comes!

  CASSIO   'Tis such another° fitchew!° Marry, a perfumed one.

Enter **BIANCA**.

What do you mean by this haunting of me?

---

107. speed: prosper, succeed.   **caitiff:** wretch.

111. faintly: without seriously intending it.

113. said: i.e., done.

117. Do you triumph, Roman?: The association is with the tradition among Roman conquerors of triumphant processions.   **118. customer:** common woman, harlot.   **118–19. bear . . . wit:** think more charitably of my judgment. **119. unwholesome:** morally tainted.

122. cry: rumor, report.

125. scored me: (1) branded, wounded me; (2) posted my name (as a cuckold); (3) made my reckoning.

127. love: love for me.   **flattery:** self-flattery (leading to delusion).

131. sea-bank: seashore.

132. bauble: worthless plaything.

142. Before me: upon my soul, before God.

143. such another: one just like all the others. **fitchew:** polecat, noted for its rank odor and lechery.

145 **BIANCA** Let the devil and his dam° haunt you! What did you
mean by that same handkerchief you gave me even now?
I was a fine fool to take it. I must take out the work? A likely
piece of work° that you should find it in your chamber and
not know who left it there! This is some minx's token, and
150 I must take out the work? There, give it your hobby-horse,°
wheresoever you had it. I'll take out no work on't.

CASSIO How now, my sweet Bianca! How now, how now!

OTHELLO [*Aside*] By heaven, that should be my handkerchief!

BIANCA If you'll come to supper tonight, you may. If you will
155 not, come when you are next prepared for.°   *Exit*

IAGO After her, after her!

CASSIO Faith, I must. She'll rail in the streets else.

IAGO Will you sup there?

CASSIO Faith, I intend so.

160 **IAGO** Well, I may chance to see you; for I would very fain
speak with you.

CASSIO Prithee, come; will you?

IAGO Go to; say no more.

Exit Cassio

OTHELLO [*Coming forward.*] How shall I murder him, Iago?

165 **IAGO** Did you perceive how he laughed at his vice?

OTHELLO O, Iago!

IAGO And did you see the handkerchief?

OTHELLO Was that mine?

IAGO Yours, by this hand. And to see how he prizes the foolish
170 woman your wife: she gave it him, and he hath given it his
whore.

OTHELLO I would have him nine years a-killing. A fine woman,
a fair woman, a sweet woman!

IAGO Nay, you must forget that.

175 **OTHELLO** Ay, let her rot and perish, and be damned tonight, for
she shall not live. No, my heart is turned to stone: I strike it
and it hurts my hand. O, the world hath not a sweeter creature! She might lie by an emperor's side and command him
tasks.

180 **IAGO** Nay, that's not your way.°

OTHELLO Hang her, I do but say what she is: so delicate with her
needle, an admirable musician—O, she will sing the savageness
out of a bear—of so high and plenteous wit and invention°—

185 **IAGO** She's the worse for all this.

OTHELLO O, a thousand, thousand times—and then of so
gentle a condition!°

IAGO Ay, too gentle.°

145. dam: mother.

148. piece of work: story, business.

150. hobby-horse: a loose woman.

155. you are next prepared for: the next time I shall expect you (i.e., never).

180. your way: the proper course (of thought).

184. invention: imagination.

186–87. of so gentle a condition: (1) so well born, (2) so amiable a character.

188. gentle: kind, yielding (to men).

OTHELLO Nay, that's certain; but yet the pity of it, Iago!
190   O Iago, the pity of it, Iago!

IAGO If you are so fond over° her iniquity, give her patent° to
offend; for if it touch not you, it comes near° nobody.

OTHELLO I will chop her into messes.° Cuckold me!

IAGO O, 'tis foul in her.

195 **OTHELLO** With mine officer!

IAGO That's fouler.

OTHELLO Get me some poison, Iago, this night. I'll not expostu-
late° with her, lest her body and beauty unprovide my mind°
again—this night, Iago.

200 **IAGO** Do it not with poison; strangle her in her bed, even the
bed she hath contaminated.

OTHELLO Good, good! The justice of it pleases; very good!

IAGO And for Cassio, let me be his undertaker.° You shall hear
more by midnight.

205 **OTHELLO** Excellent good!

A trumpet [sounds within].

What trumpet is that same?

IAGO I warrant something from Venice.

Enter LODOVICO, DESDEMONA *and* ATTENDANTS.

'Tis Lodovico. This comes from the duke. See, your wife's
with him.

LODOVICO God save you, worthy general!

OTHELLO   With all my heart, sir.

210 **LODOVICO** The duke and senators of Venice greet you.

[He gives Othello a letter.]

OTHELLO I kiss the instrument of their pleasures.

[He opens the letter and reads.]

DESDEMONA And what's the news, good cousin Lodovico?

IAGO I am very glad to see you, signior;
215   Welcome to Cyprus.

LODOVICO I thank you. How does Lieutenant Cassio?

IAGO Lives, sir.

DESDEMONA Cousin, there's fallen between him and my lord
An unkind breach;° but you shall make all well.

220 **OTHELLO** Are you sure of that?

DESDEMONA My lord?

OTHELLO "This fail you not to do, as you will—"

LODOVICO He did not call; he's busy in the paper.
Is there division 'twixt my lord and Cassio?

225 **DESDEMONA** A most unhappy one; I would do much

---

191. **fond over:** stupid about, doting on.
patent: license.
192. **comes near:** affects, harms.
193. **messes:** pieces of meat.

197–98. **expostulate:** argue at length.

198. **unprovide my mind:** weaken my resolution.

203. **be his undertaker:** deal with him.

219. **unkind breach:** unnatural separation, uncharacteristic quarrel.

T'atone them, for the love I bear to Cassio.

OTHELLO Fire and brimstone!

DESDEMONA My lord?

OTHELLO Are you wise?

230 **DESDEMONA** What, is he angry?

LODOVICO   Maybe the letter moved him;

For as° I think they do command him home,

Deputing Cassio in his government.°

DESDEMONA By my troth, I am glad on't.°

OTHELLO   Indeed!

DESDEMONA   My lord?

OTHELLO I am glad to see you mad.

DESDEMONA   Why, sweet Othello?

235 **OTHELLO** Devil!

[*He strikes her.*]

DESDEMONA I have not deserved this.

LODOVICO My lord, this would not be believed in Venice,

Though I should swear I saw't. 'Tis very much.°

Make her amends; she weeps.

OTHELLO   O devil, devil!

240   If that the earth could teem with° woman's tears,

Each drop she falls° would prove° a crocodile.

Out of my sight!

DESDEMONA   I will not stay to offend you.

LODOVICO Truly, an obedient lady.

I do beseech your lordship, call her back.

245 **OTHELLO** Mistress!

DESDEMONA My lord?

OTHELLO What would you with her, sir?

LODOVICO   Who? I, my lord?

OTHELLO Ay, you did wish that I would make her turn.°

Sir, she can turn, and turn, and yet go on,

250   And turn again.° And she can weep, sir, weep.

And she's obedient; as you say, obedient,°

Very obedient—proceed you in your tears—

Concerning this, sir,—O, well-painted passion!°—

I am commanded home—get you away!

255   I'll send for you anon.—Sir, I obey the mandate,

And will return to Venice.—Hence, avaunt!

[*Exit Desdemona*]

Cassio shall have my place. And, sir, tonight

I do entreat that we may sup together.

You are welcome, sir, to Cyprus. Goats and monkeys!   Exit

260 **LODOVICO** Is this the noble Moor whom our full senate

231. For as: because.

232. government: office of command.

233. on't: of it.

238. very much: outrageous.

240. teem with: be impregnated by, spawn
with. **241. falls:** lets fall. **prove:** (1) turn into,
(2) be the same as the tears of.

248. turn: come back.

249–50. turn . . . again: (1) come back, (2) be
fickle, (3) go for sexual intercourse.
251. obedient: yielding to whatever is asked of
her (with a sexual innuendo).

253. painted passion: simulated emotion.

Call all-in-all sufficient? Is this the nature
Whom passion could not shake? Whose solid virtue
The shot of accident nor dart of chance
Could neither graze nor pierce?

IAGO   He is much changed.

265 **LODOVICO** Are his wits safe? Is he not light of brain?

IAGO He's that he is; I may not breathe my censure
What he might be. If what he might he is not,
I would to heaven he were.°

LODOVICO   What! Strike his wife!

IAGO Faith, that was not so well; yet would I knew
270   That stroke would prove the worst.

LODOVICO   Is it his use?°
Or did the letters work upon his blood°
And new-create this fault?

IAGO   Alas, alas!
It is not honesty in me to speak
What I have seen and known. You shall observe him,
275   And his own courses will denote° him so,
That I may save my speech. Do but go after,
And mark how he continues.

LODOVICO I am sorry that I am deceived in him.

Exeunt

SCENE ii°

Enter **OTHELLO** *and* **EMILIA.**

OTHELLO You have seen nothing then?

EMILIA Nor ever heard, nor ever did suspect.

OTHELLO Yes, you have seen Cassio and she together.

EMILIA But then I saw no harm, and then I heard
5   Each syllable that breath made up between them.

OTHELLO What! Did they never whisper?

EMILIA   Never, my lord.

OTHELLO Nor send you out o'th'way?

EMILIA   Never.

OTHELLO To fetch her fan, her gloves, her mask, nor nothing?

EMILIA Never, my lord.

10 **OTHELLO** That's strange.

EMILIA I durst, my lord, to wager she is honest,
Lay down my soul at stake.° If you think other,
Remove your thought; it doth abuse your bosom.°
If any wretch have put this in your head,
15   Let heaven requite it with the serpent's curse!°

267–68. If what . . . were: i.e., if he is not out of his mind, I wish to God he were (for only that would serve to excuse his actions).

270. use: custom.

271. blood: passion (here of anger).

275. courses will denote: actions will reveal.

Act IV, Scene ii.

12. at stake: as the wager.

13. abuse your bosom: deceive you.

15. serpent's curse: "Then the Lord God said to the serpent, Because thou hast done this, thou art cursed above all cattle, and above every beast of the field: upon thy belly shalt thou go, and dust shalt thou eat all the days of thy life" (Genesis 3:14).

For if she be not honest, chaste, and true,
There's no man happy.° The purest of their wives
Is foul as slander.

17. happy: fortunate.

OTHELLO   Bid her come hither; go!

Exit Emilia

She says enough; yet she's a simple bawd°
20   That cannot say as much. This° is a subtle whore,
A closet lock and key° of villainous secrets;
And yet she'll kneel and pray. I have seen her do't.

19. bawd: madam, the keeper of a place of prostitution. **20. This:** i.e., Desdemona.

21. closet lock and key: one who (1) conceals, (2) locks away, (3) renders inaccessible.

Enter DESDEMONA *and Emilia.*

DESDEMONA My lord, what is your will?
OTHELLO   Pray, chuck, come hither.
DESDEMONA What is your pleasure?
OTHELLO   Let me see your eyes.
25   Look in my face.
DESDEMONA   What horrible fancy's this?
OTHELLO [*To Emilia*] Some of your function,° mistress:
Leave procreants alone and shut the door;
Cough or cry "hem" if anybody come.
Your mystery,° your mystery! Nay, dispatch!

26. Some of your function: do your job (as brothel-keeper).

29. mystery: trade (of bawd).

Exit Emilia

30 **DESDEMONA** Upon my knees, what doth your speech import?
I understand a fury in your words,
But not the words.
OTHELLO   Why? What art thou?
DESDEMONA Your wife, my lord; your true and loyal wife.
OTHELLO Come, swear it; damn thyself;
35   Lest, being like one of heaven, the devils themselves
Should fear to seize thee. Therefore be double-damned:
Swear thou art honest.
DESDEMONA   Heaven doth truly know it.
OTHELLO Heaven truly knows that thou art false as hell.
DESDEMONA To whom, my lord? With whom? How am I
false?
40 **OTHELLO** Ah, Desdemon, away, away, away!
DESDEMONA Alas, the heavy day! Why do you weep?
Am I the motive of these tears, my lord?
If haply° you my father do suspect
An instrument of this your calling back,
45   Lay not your blame on me. If you have lost him,
I have lost him too.

43. haply: by chance.

OTHELLO   Had it pleased heaven

To try me with affliction, had they rained
All kind of sores and shames on my bare head,
Steeped me in poverty to the very lips,
50   Given to captivity me and my utmost hopes,
I should have found in some place of my soul
A drop of patience. But, alas, to make me
The fixèd figure for the time of scorn
To point his slow unmoving finger at!°

53–54. The fixèd . . . at: Othello sees himself as an eternal object of derision, pointed at forever—like the numbers on a clockface, pointed at by the hour hand which, though moving, appears to the human eye to be standing still. **56. garnered:** stored.

55   Yet could I bear that too, well, very well;
But there where I have garnered° up my heart,
Where either I must live or bear no life,
The fountain° from the which my current runs

58. fountain: spring.

Or else dries up—to be discarded thence
60   Or keep it as a cistern° for foul toads

60. cistern: cesspool.

To knot and gender° in! Turn thy complexion there,°
Patience, thou young and rose-lipped cherubin;
Ay, there look grim as hell!

61. knot and gender: copulate and engender. **Turn thy complexion there:** grow pale when that happens.

DESDEMONA   I hope my noble lord esteems me honest.°

64. honest: chaste.

65   OTHELLO   O ay: as summer flies are in the shambles,°

65. shambles: butchery or butcher's shop.

That quicken even with blowing.° O, thou weed,
Who art so lovely fair and smell'st so sweet

66. quicken even with blowing: come to life merely with the depositing of larvae.

That the sense aches at thee, would thou hadst ne'er been
born!

DESDEMONA   Alas, what ignorant° sin have I committed?

69. ignorant: unknowing, innocent.

70   OTHELLO   Was this fair paper, this most goodly book,
Made to write "whore" upon? What committed!
Committed?° O thou public commoner!°

72. Committed: committed adultery. **commoner:** whore.

I should make very forges of my cheeks
That would to cinders burn up modesty
75   Did I but speak thy deeds. What committed!
Heaven stops the nose at it, and the moon° winks;°
The bawdy° wind, that kisses all it meets,
Is hushed within the hollow mine° of earth

76. moon: the symbol of chastity. **winks:** closes its eyes. **77. bawdy:** i.e., because it blows promiscuously on everybody. **78. mine:** cave.

And will not hear it. What committed?
80   Impudent strumpet!
DESDEMONA   By heaven, you do me wrong.
OTHELLO   Are not you a strumpet?
DESDEMONA   No, as I am a Christian.
If to preserve this vessel° for my lord
From any other foul unlawful touch

82. vessel: body.

Be not to be a strumpet, I am none.
85   OTHELLO   What, not a whore?
DESDEMONA   No, as I shall be saved.
OTHELLO   Is't possible?

DESDEMONA O, heaven forgive us!

OTHELLO   I cry you° mercy then:

 I took you for that cunning whore of Venice

 That married with Othello. You, mistress,

90 That have the office opposite to Saint Peter,

 And keeps the gate of hell! You, you, ay, you!

87. cry you mercy: ask your pardon.

Enter Emilia.

 We have done our course;° there's money for your pains.

 I pray you turn the key, and keep our counsel.   *Exit*

EMILIA Alas, what does this gentleman conceive?°

95 How do you, madam? How do you, my good lady?

DESDEMONA Faith, half-asleep.°

EMILIA Good madam, what's the matter with my lord?

DESDEMONA With who?

EMILIA Why, with my lord, madam.

100 **DESDEMONA** Who is thy lord?

EMILIA   He that is yours, sweet lady.

DESDEMONA I have none. Do not talk to me, Emilia.

 I cannot weep, nor answers have I none

 But what should go by water.° Prithee tonight

 Lay on my bed my wedding sheets, remember;

105 And call thy husband hither.

EMILIA   Here's a change indeed!   *Exit*

DESDEMONA 'Tis meet I should be used so, very meet!°

 How have I been behaved that he might stick°

 The smallest opinion° on my least misuse?°

92. done our course: completed our business (with sexual overtones).

94. conceive: imagine.

96. half-asleep: i.e., stunned.

103. go by water: be given expression by tears.

106. meet: fitting.

107–08. stick / The smallest opinion: attach the least censure.   **108. least misuse:** most trivial misbehavior.

Enter IAGO and Emilia.

IAGO What is your pleasure, madam? How is't with you?

110 **DESDEMONA** I cannot tell. Those that do teach young babes

 Do it with gentle means and easy tasks.

 He might have chid me so; for, in good faith,

 I am a child to chiding.°

IAGO   What is the matter, lady?

EMILIA Alas, Iago, my lord hath so bewhored her,

115 Thrown such despite° and heavy terms upon her

 As true hearts cannot bear.

DESDEMONA Am I that name, Iago?

IAGO   What name, fair lady?

DESDEMONA Such as she said my lord did say I was.

EMILIA He called her whore. A beggar in his drink

120 Could not have laid such terms upon his callet.°

113. am a child to chiding: have no experience of being upbraided.

115. despite: abuse.

120. callet: slut, drab.

IAGO Why did he so?

DESDEMONA I do not know; I am sure I am none such.

IAGO Do not weep, do not weep! Alas the day!

EMILIA Hath she forsook so many noble matches,
125   Her father, and her country, and her friends,
     To be called whore? Would it not make one weep?

DESDEMONA It is my wretched fortune.

IAGO   Beshrew° him for't!
     How comes this trick° upon him?

DESDEMONA   Nay, heaven doth know.

EMILIA I will be hanged if some eternal° villain,
130   Some busy and insinuating° rogue,
     Some cogging,° cozening° slave, to get some office,
     Have not devised this slander; I'll be hanged else.

IAGO Fie, there is no such man; it is impossible.

DESDEMONA If any such there be, heaven pardon him.

135 **EMILIA** A halter° pardon him and hell gnaw his bones!
     Why should he call her whore? Who keeps her company?
     What place, what time, what form,° what likelihood?°
     The Moor's abused by some most villainous knave,
     Some base notorious knave, some scurvy fellow.
140   O heaven, that such companions° thou'dst unfold,°
     And put in every honest hand a whip
     To lash the rascals naked through the world,
     Even from the east to th'west!

IAGO   Speak within door.°

EMILIA O fie upon them! Some such squire° he was
145   That turned your wit the seamy side without°
     And made you to suspect me° with the Moor.

IAGO You are a fool, go to.°

DESDEMONA   O good Iago,
     What shall I do to win my lord again?
     Good friend, go to him; for, by this light of heaven,
150   I know not how I lost him. Here I kneel:
     If e'er my will did trespass 'gainst his love
     Either in discourse of thought° or actual deed;
     Or that° mine eyes, mine ears, or any sense
     Delighted them° in any other form;
155   Or that I do not yet,° and ever did,
     And ever will—though he do shake me off
     To beggarly divorcement—love him dearly,
     Comfort forswear me!° Unkindness may do much,
     And his unkindness may defeat° my life,

127. **Beshrew:** curse.

128. **trick:** delusion.

129. **eternal:** inveterate.

130. **insinuating:** worming into favor, wheedling. 131. **cogging:** cheating, deceiving. **cozening:** deceiving.

135. **halter:** hangman's noose.

137. **form:** appearance. **likelihood:** grounds for such an inference.

140. **companions:** rogues. **unfold:** disclose, expose.

143. **within door:** less loudly, more controlledly.

144. **squire:** fellow.

145. **seamy side without:** wrong side out.

146. **suspect me:** i.e., of adultery.

147. **go to:** be quiet.

152. **discourse of thought:** process of thinking.

153. **that:** if.

154. **Delighted them:** took delight.

155. **yet:** still.

158. **Comfort forswear me!:** Let comfort abandon me!
159. **defeat:** destroy.

160 But never taint my love. I cannot say "whore":

It does abhor° me now I speak the word; **161. abhor:** (1) disgust, (2) make into a whore.

To do the act that might the addition° earn **162. addition:** title.

Not the world's mass of vanity° could make me. **163. vanity:** finery.

IAGO I pray you be content; 'tis but his humour.

165 The business of the state does him offence,

And he does chide with you.

DESDEMONA If 'twere no other—

IAGO   It is but so, I warrant.

                    [*Trumpets sound within.*]

Hark how these instruments summon to supper!

The messengers of Venice stay the meat.° **169. stay the meat:** wait for their meal.

170 Go in, and weep not; all things shall be well.

                    Exeunt Desdemona and Emilia

Enter **RODERIGO**.

How now, Roderigo?

RODERIGO I do not find that thou deal'st justly with me.

IAGO What in the contrary?

RODERIGO Every day thou daff'st me° with some device,° Iago, **174. daff'st me:** dost fob me off. **device:**

175 and rather, as it seems to me now, keep'st from me all conve- scheme, trick. **175–76. conveniency:**

niency° than suppliest me with the least advantage° of hope. opportunity, advantage. **176. advantage:**

I will indeed no longer endure it. Nor am I yet persuaded to furthering, increase.

put up° in peace what already I have foolishly suffered. **178. put up:** accept, endure.

IAGO Will you hear me, Roderigo?

180 **RODERIGO** Faith, I have heard too much; for your words and

performances are no kin together.

IAGO You charge me most unjustly.

RODERIGO With naught but truth. I have wasted myself out of

my means. The jewels you have had from me to deliver to

185 Desdemona would half have corrupted a votarist.° You have **185. votarist:** nun (sworn to chastity).

told me she hath received them, and returned me expecta-

tions and comforts° of sudden respect° and acquaintance, **187. comforts:** encouragements. **sudden**

but I find none. **respect:** immediate regard.

IAGO Well, go to;° very well. **189. go to:** have sex.

190 **RODERIGO** Very well, go to! I cannot go to, man, nor 'tis not

very well. By this hand, I say 'tis very scurvy and begin to

find myself fopped° in it. **192. fopped:** duped, cheated.

IAGO Very well.

RODERIGO I tell you 'tis not very well. I will make myself known

195 to Desdemona. If she will return me my jewels, I will give

over my suit and repent my unlawful solicitation; if not,

assure yourself I will seek satisfaction° of you. **197. seek satisfaction:** demand

repayment (not "challenge to a duel").

IAGO You have said now?°

RODERIGO Ay, and said nothing but what I protest intendment°
200 of doing.

IAGO Why, now I see there's mettle in thee, and even from this
instant do build on thee a better opinion than ever before.
Give me thy hand, Roderigo. Thou hast taken against me a
most just exception;° but yet I protest I have dealt most
205 directly° in thy affair.

RODERIGO It hath not appeared.

IAGO I grant indeed it hath not appeared; and your suspicion
is not without wit and judgement. But, Roderigo, if thou
hast that in thee indeed, which I have greater reason to
210 believe now than ever—I mean purpose, courage, and
valour—this night show it. If thou the next night following
enjoy not Desdemona, take me from this world with treachery, and devise engines for° my life.

RODERIGO Well, what is it? Is it within reason and compass?°

215 **IAGO** Sir, there is especial commission come from Venice to
depute Cassio in Othello's place.

RODERIGO Is that true? Why, then Othello and Desdemona
return again to Venice.

IAGO O no, he goes into Mauritania° and takes away with him
220 the fair Desdemona, unless his abode be lingered° here by
some accident; wherein none can be so determinate° as the
removing of Cassio.

RODERIGO How do you mean "removing" of him?

IAGO Why, by making him uncapable of Othello's place—
225 knocking out his brains.

RODERIGO And that you would have me to do?

IAGO Ay, if you dare do yourself a profit and a right. He sups
tonight with a harlotry,° and thither will I go to him. He
knows not yet of his honourable fortune. If you will watch
230 his going thence—which I will fashion to fall out° between
twelve and one—you may take him at your pleasure. I will
be near to second your attempt, and he shall fall between us.
Come, stand not amazed at it, but go along with me. I will
show you such a necessity in his death that you shall think
235 yourself bound to put it on him. It is now high° supper-time
and the night grows to waste.° About it!

RODERIGO I will hear further reason for this.

IAGO And you shall be satisfied.

Exeunt

198. You have said now?: You have spoken
your mind then? **199. protest intendment:**
aver the intention.

204. exception: objection.

205. directly: straightforwardly.

213. engines for: plots against.

214. compass: range of possibility.

219. Mauritania: an ancient kingdom in north
Africa which included modern Morocco and
part of Algeria—hence, the land of the Moors.
220. abode be lingered: stay be prolonged.
221. determinate: decisive, conclusive.

228. harlotry: harlot.

230. fall out: occur.

235. high: fully, quite.
236. grows to waste: is passing; but Iago may
mean literally that he is wasting time on a
night when he has so much to do.

SCENE iii°

Act IV, Scene iii.

Enter OTHELLO, LODOVICO, DESDEMONA, EMILIA *and* ATTENDANTS.

LODOVICO I do beseech you, sir, trouble yourself no further.

OTHELLO O, pardon me; 'twill do me good to walk.

LODOVICO Madam, good night. I humbly thank your ladyship.

5 **DESDEMONA** Your honour is most welcome.

OTHELLO Will you walk, sir? O, Desdemona.

DESDEMONA My lord?

OTHELLO Get you to bed on th'instant. I will be returned forthwith. Dismiss your attendant there. Look't be done.

10 **DESDEMONA** I will, my lord.

Exeunt [Othello, Lodovico and Attendants]

EMILIA How goes it now? He looks gentler than he did.

DESDEMONA He says he will return incontinent;°

> 12. **incontinent:** at once.

He hath commanded me to go to bed
And bade me to dismiss you.

EMILIA   Dismiss me?

15 **DESDEMONA** It was his bidding; therefore, good Emilia,
Give me my nightly wearing,° and adieu.

> 16. **nightly wearing:** nightclothes.

We must not now displease him.

EMILIA I would you had never seen him.

DESDEMONA So would not I: my love doth so approve him

20 That even his stubbornness,° his checks,° his frowns—

> 20. **stubbornness:** roughness. **checks:** rebukes. **21. unpin:** presumably the fastenings of her dress or hair.

Prithee, unpin° me—have grace and favour in them.

EMILIA I have laid those sheets you bade me on the bed.

DESDEMONA All's one.° Good faith, how foolish are our
minds!

> 23. **All's one:** it doesn't matter, all right.

If I do die before thee, prithee shroud me

25 In one of those same sheets.

EMILIA   Come, come, you talk.°

> 25. **talk:** talk nonsense. **26. Barbary:** a form of the name Barbara; but ironically resonant in view of the barbarian–Venetian polarity at the heart of the play.

DESDEMONA My mother had a maid called Barbary:°
She was in love, and he she loved proved mad
And did forsake her. She had a song of willow;
An old thing 'twas but it expressed her fortune,°

> 29. **fortune:** fate.

30 And she died singing it. That song tonight
Will not go from my mind. I have much to do°

> 31–32. **I have much to do / But:** it's all I can do not.
> 32. **all at one side:** i.e., in the traditional pose of melancholy.

But° to go hang my head all at one side°
And sing it like poor Barbary—prithee, dispatch.

EMILIA Shall I go fetch your nightgown?°

> 34. **nightgown:** dressing gown.

DESDEMONA   No, unpin me here.

35 This Lodovico is a proper° man.

> 35. **proper:** fine, handsome.

EMILIA A very handsome man.

DESDEMONA   He speaks well.

EMILIA I know a lady in Venice would have walked barefoot
　　　to Palestine for a touch of his nether lip.

DESDEMONA [*Sings*]

　　　The poor soul sat sighing by a sycamore° tree,
40　　　　Sing all a green willow;°
　　　Her hand on her bosom, her head on her knee,
　　　　　Sing willow, willow, willow;
　　　The fresh streams ran by her and murmured her moans;
　　　　　Sing willow, willow, willow.
45　　　Her salt tears fell from her and softened the stones—
　　Lay by these.°
　　　　　Sing willow, willow, willow—
　　Prithee, hie thee;° he'll come anon.°
　　　　　Sing all a green willow must be my garland.
50　　Let nobody blame him; his scorn I approve—
　　Nay that's not next. Hark, who is't that knocks?

EMILIA It's the wind.

DESDEMONA [*Sings*]

　　　I called my love false love, but what said he then?
　　　　　Sing willow, willow, willow;
55　　If I court moe women, you'll couch with moe° men—
　　So get thee gone; good night. Mine eyes do itch—
　　Does that bode weeping?

EMILIA　　　　　　　　　'Tis neither here nor there.

DESDEMONA I have heard it said so. O, these men, these men!
　　Dost thou in conscience think—tell me, Emilia—
60　That there be women do abuse° their husbands
　　In such gross kind?°

EMILIA　　　　　　There be some such, no question.

DESDEMONA Wouldst thou do such a deed for all the world?

EMILIA Why, would not you?

DESDEMONA　　　　　　No, by this heavenly light.°

EMILIA Nor I neither by this heavenly light;
65　I might do't as well i'th'dark.

DESDEMONA Wouldst thou do such a deed for all the world?

EMILIA The world's a huge thing; it is a great price°
　　For a small vice.

DESDEMONA　　　　In troth, I think thou wouldst not.

EMILIA In troth, I think I should, and undo't° when I had done
70　it. Marry, I would not do such a thing for a joint-ring,° nor
　　for measures of lawn,° nor for gowns, petticoats, nor caps,
　　nor any petty exhibition.° But for all the whole world!

39. sycamore: the Elizabethan name for the fig mulberry, not traditionally associated with the forsaken in love (except perhaps by the punning "sick-amour"). **40. willow:** a proverbial emblem for the forsaken lover.

46. these: presumably some of her jewelry or other accessories.

48. hie thee: make haste. **anon:** at once.

55. moe: more.

60. abuse: deceive.

61. gross kind: obscene manner.

63. heavenly light: i.e., of the moon.

67. price: prize.

69. undo't: make it right again.

70. joint-ring: a finger ring made in two separable parts.
71. lawn: fine white linen.
72. exhibition: allowance, gift.

Ud's° pity, who would not make her husband a cuckold, to
make him a monarch? I should venture purgatory° for't.

75 **DESDEMONA** Beshrew me, if I would do such a wrong for the
whole world.

EMILIA Why, the wrong is but a wrong i'th'world; and having
the world for your labour, 'tis a wrong in your own world,
and you might quickly make it right.

80 **DESDEMONA** I do not think there is any such woman.

EMILIA Yes, a dozen; and as many to th'advantage° as would
store° the world they played° for.
But I do think it is their husbands' faults
If wives do fall. Say that they slack their duties°

85 And pour our° treasures into foreign° laps,
Or else break out in peevish jealousies,
Throwing restraint upon us; or say they strike us,
Or scant° our former having° in despite°—
Why, we have galls,° and though we have some grace,

90 Yet have we some revenge. Let husbands know
Their wives have sense like them: they see, and smell,
And have their palates both for sweet and sour
As husbands have. What is it that they do
When they change us for others? Is it sport?°

95 I think it is. And doth affection° breed it?
I think it doth. Is't frailty that thus errs?
It is so too. And have not we affections,
Desires for sport, and frailty, as men have?
Then let them use us well; else let them know

100 The ills we do, their ills instruct us so.

DESDEMONA Good night, good night. God me such uses° send,
Not to pick bad from bad, but by bad mend!°

Exeunt

73. Ud's: God's.

74. venture purgatory: risk being condemned to purgatory. Emilia sees adultery as an ultimately forgiveable sin.

81. to th'advantage: over and above, in addition. **82. store:** populate. **played:** (1) gambled, hazarded; (2) copulated.

84. duties: marital duties, sexual activity in marriage. **85. our:** i.e., which should be ours. **foreign:** alien (other than their wives').

88. scant: reduce. **having:** allowance, but this, like "duties," "pour our treasures," and "laps," probably has sexual overtones. **in despite:** out of spite. **89. galls:** tempers or spirits to make us feel resentment.

94. sport: (1) entertainment, (2) copulation.

95. affection: passion.

101. uses: profitable habits of thought. **102. Not to pick . . . mend:** i.e., not to learn bad ways from the evil that has befallen me, but to learn good from it.

◄ The image is an illustration of Emilia and Desdemona at the end of Act IV.

———

How does the friendship of Emilia and Desdemona play a significant part in the action of the tragedy? How does this relationship serve to balance the imbalance between the men and women in the play?

CHARACTER

1. How does Othello's collapse at the beginning of Act IV reveal a flaw within the **protagonist**?

2. What or who is **motivating** Othello to think, feel, or act as he does? How do you know this?

3. Which specific words, phrases, and details reveal Rodriego's motivation for his decision in Act IV, Scene ii? Who is controlling Rodriego's decisions?

4. What **internal conflicts** does Emila have at the end of Act IV? How do these struggles contribute to the tension of the play?

SETTING

5. Explain how the outside location of Act IV, Scene i contributes to the events of the play.

6. How do the interior locations contribute to Desdemona's thoughts, speech, and actions?

7. Consider the role of time in *Othello*. How much time has passed since the beginning of the play? How does this duration affect your interpretation of the play?

STRUCTURE

8. Act IV opens with Iago telling a story about Cassio. Explain how the handkerchief contributes to Othello's fall. How does it contribute to the falling action of the play?

9. How does Iago's conversation with Cassio in Act IV, Scene i contribute to the events that follow?

10. How do the interactions between Iago and Emilia reveal a **conflict**? How do they treat each other when they are alone? How do they treat each other around other characters? How does this conflict contribute to the falling action in Act IV?

11. Explain how the final scene of Act IV advances might **foreshadow** events to come.

IDEAS IN LITERATURE: Power and Conflict

12. Desdemona seems defeated as Act IV ends. How do the events of the play and the power of manipulation deflate such a strong independent woman? Can you think of moments in your life when events or circumstances left you feeling powerless? Think of a time when you overcame that feeling. What did you do? What was the result?

ACT V

SCENE i°

Enter IAGO *and* RODERIGO.

IAGO Here, stand behind this bulk,° straight will he come.
Wear thy good rapier bare,° and put it home.
Quick, quick, fear nothing; I'll be at thy elbow.
It makes us or it mars us; think on that,

5   And fix most firm thy resolution.

RODERIGO Be near at hand; I may miscarry in't.

IAGO Here, at thy hand; be bold, and take thy stand.

[*He retires.*]

RODERIGO I have no great devotion to the deed,
And yet he hath given me satisfying reasons.

10   'Tis but a man gone. Forth my sword! He dies!

IAGO [*Aside*] I have rubbed this young quat° almost to the sense,°
And he grows angry. Now, whether he kill Cassio,
Or Cassio him, or each do kill the other,
Every way makes my gain.° Live Roderigo,

15   He calls me to a restitution large
Of gold and jewels that I bobbed° from him
As gifts to Desdemona.
It must not be. If Cassio do remain,
He hath a daily beauty° in his life

20   That makes me ugly; and besides, the Moor
May unfold° me to him—there stand I in much peril.
No, he must die. But soft, I hear him coming.

Enter CASSIO.

RODERIGO I know his gait; 'tis he. Villain, thou diest!

[*He lunges at Cassio.*]

CASSIO That thrust had been mine enemy indeed

25   But that my coat is better than thou think'st.
I will make proof of thine.°

[*He wounds Roderigo.*]

RODERIGO   O, I am slain!

[*Iago wounds Cassio in the leg and exit*]

CASSIO I am maimed forever. Help, ho! Murder, murder!

Enter OTHELLO.

OTHELLO [*Aside*] The voice of Cassio: Iago keeps his word.

RODERIGO O villain that I am!

OTHELLO [*Aside*]   It is even so.

Act V, Scene i.

1. bulk: a projecting part of a building.

2. bare: drawn, unsheathed.

11. quat: contemptible youngster; literally, a pimple or small boil (which can be irritated by rubbing). **to the sense:** to the quick, raw.

14. makes my gain: helps me win the game.

16. bobbed: swindled.

19. daily beauty: regularly demonstrated attractiveness.

21. unfold: expose.

25–26. my coat . . . thine: This may mean merely that Cassio's coat is more substantial than Roderigo suspected. However, the reference may be to a metal-plated or reinforced leather undercoat worn for protection. **26. I will make proof of thine:** I will put yours to the test.

30 **CASSIO** O help, ho! Light! A surgeon!

OTHELLO [*Aside*] 'Tis he. O brave° Iago, honest and just,

That hast such noble sense of thy friend's wrong!

Thou teachest me. Minion,° your dear lies dead,

And your unblest° fate hies.° Strumpet, I come!

35 Forth° of my heart those charms, thine eyes, are blotted;

Thy bed, lust-stained, shall with lust's blood be spotted.

Exit Othello

Enter **LODOVICO** *and* **GRATIANO**.

CASSIO What, ho! No watch? No passage?° Murder, murder!

GRATIANO 'Tis some mischance; the cry is very direful.

CASSIO O, help!

40 **LODOVICO** Hark!

RODERIGO O, wretched villain!

LODOVICO Two or three groan. It is a heavy° night.

These may be counterfeits: let's think't unsafe

To come in to the cry° without more help.

45 **RODERIGO** Nobody come? Then I shall bleed to death.

LODOVICO Hark!

Enter Iago, with a light.

GRATIANO Here's one comes in his shirt, with light and weapons.

IAGO Who's there? Whose noise is this that cries on° murder?

LODOVICO We do not know.

IAGO   Did you not hear a cry?

50 **CASSIO** Here, here; for heaven's sake, help me!

IAGO   What's the matter?

GRATIANO This is Othello's ancient, as I take it.

LODOVICO The same indeed, a very valiant fellow.

IAGO What are you here that cry so grievously?

CASSIO Iago? O, I am spoiled,° undone by villains!

55 Give me some help.

IAGO O me, lieutenant! What villains have done this?

CASSIO I think that one of them is hereabout

And cannot make away.

IAGO   O, treacherous villains!

[*To Lodovico and Gratiano*] What are you there? Come in,

and give some help.

60 **RODERIGO** O, help me here!

CASSIO That's one of them.

IAGO   O murderous slave! O villain!

[*He stabs Roderigo.*]

31. brave: excellent, noble.

33. Minion: darling (used contemptuously here to mean "hussy"); i.e., Desdemona. **34. unblest:** i.e., because she is damned. **hies:** approaches swiftly.   **35. Forth:** from out.

37. passage: passers-by.

42. heavy: gloomy, dark.

44. come in to the cry: (1) draw near to the place the cries came from, (2) approach the brawling group.

48. cries on: shouts out.

54. spoiled: ruined, finished.

RODERIGO O damned Iago! O inhuman dog!

[He faints.]

IAGO Kill men i'th'dark? Where be these bloody thieves?
How silent is this town! Ho, murder, murder!

[Lodovico and Gratiano come forward.]

65 What may you be? Are you of good or evil?

LODOVICO As you shall prove us, praise° us.   66. **praise:** value, appraise.

IAGO Signior Lodovico?

LODOVICO He, sir.

IAGO I cry you mercy.° Here's Cassio hurt by villains.   69. **I cry you mercy:** pardon me.

70 **GRATIANO** Cassio?

IAGO How is't, brother?

CASSIO My leg is cut in two.

IAGO   Marry, heaven forbid!
Light, gentlemen. I'll bind it with my shirt.

Enter **BIANCA**.

BIANCA What is the matter, ho? Who is't that cried?

75 **IAGO** Who is't that cried?

BIANCA O, my dear Cassio, my sweet Cassio!
O, Cassio, Cassio, Cassio!

IAGO O notable strumpet! Cassio, may you suspect
Who they should be that have thus mangled° you?   79. **mangled:** wounded.

80 **CASSIO** No.

GRATIANO I am sorry to find you thus; I have been to seek
you.

IAGO Lend me a garter: so. O for a chair
To bear him easily hence!

BIANCA   Alas, he faints!
O, Cassio, Cassio, Cassio!

85 **IAGO** Gentlemen all, I do suspect this trash
To be a party in this injury.
Patience awhile, good Cassio. Come, come,
Lend me a light. Know we this face or no?
Alas, my friend and my dear countryman!

90 Roderigo? No—yes, sure—O, heaven, Roderigo!

GRATIANO What, of Venice?

IAGO Even he, sir; did you know him?

GRATIANO   Know him? Ay.

IAGO Signior Gratiano! I cry your gentle pardon.
These bloody accidents° must excuse my manners   94. **accidents:** sudden happenings.

95 That so neglected° you.   95. **neglected:** failed to recognize, ignored.

GRATIANO   I am glad to see you.

IAGO How do you, Cassio? O, a chair, a chair!

GRATIANO Roderigo?

IAGO He, he, 'tis he.

[*Enter* **ATTENDANTS** *with a chair.*]

O, that's well said,° the chair!
Some good men bear him carefully from hence.
100 I'll fetch the general's surgeon. [*To Bianca*] For you, mistress,
Save you your labour.°—He that lies slain here, Cassio,
Was my dear friend. What malice° was between you?

CASSIO None in the world, nor do I know the man.

IAGO [*To Bianca*] What, look you pale?—O, bear him out
o'th'air.

[*Cassio is carried off; Roderigo's body is removed*]

105 Stay you, good gentlemen. Look you pale, mistress?
Do you perceive the gastness° of her eye?
[*To Bianca*] Nay, if you stare, we shall hear more anon.
Behold her well; I pray you, look upon her.
Do you see, gentlemen? Nay, guiltiness
110 Will speak, though tongues were out of use.°

Enter **EMILIA**.

EMILIA 'Las, what's the matter? What's the matter, husband?

IAGO Cassio hath here been set on in the dark
By Roderigo and fellows that are 'scaped.
He's almost slain and Roderigo dead.

115 **EMILIA** Alas, good gentleman! Alas, good Cassio!

IAGO This is the fruits of whoring. Prithee, Emilia,
Go know° of Cassio where he supped tonight.
[*To Bianca*] What, do you shake at that?

BIANCA He supped at my house, but I therefore shake not.

120 **IAGO** O, did he so? I charge you go with me.

EMILIA O, fie upon thee, strumpet!

BIANCA I am no strumpet, but of life as honest°
As you that thus abuse me.

EMILIA   As I? Foh! Fie upon thee!

IAGO Kind gentlemen, let's go see poor Cassio dressed.°
125 Come, mistress, you must tell's another tale.
Emilia, run you to the citadel
And tell my lord and lady what hath happed.
Will you go on afore? [*Aside*] This is the night
That either makes me, or fordoes me quite.°

Exeunt

---

98. said: i.e., done.

101. Save you your labour: don't trouble yourself (by attending to Cassio any further).
102. malice: ill-will (to cause the quarrel).

106. gastness: terror, frightened look.

110. though tongues were out of use: if men no longer had the power to speak.

117. know: learn.

122. honest: chaste.

124. dressed: i.e., his wound bandaged.

129. fordoes me quite: ruins me completely.

SCENE ii°

Enter OTHELLO, *with a light, and* DESDEMONA *in bed.*

OTHELLO   It is the cause,° it is the cause, my soul:
Let me not name it to you, you chaste stars.
It is the cause. Yet I'll not shed her blood,
Nor scar that whiter skin of hers than snow°
5   And smooth as monumental° alabaster—
Yet she must die, else she'll betray more men.°
Put out the light, and then put out the light:°
If I quench thee, thou flaming minister,°
I can again thy former light restore,
10   Should I repent me; but once put out thy light,
Thou cunning'st pattern of excelling nature,°
I know not where is that Promethean heat°
That can thy light relume.° When I have plucked thy rose,
I cannot give it vital growth again;
15   It needs must wither. I'll smell it on the tree.

He kisses her.

O balmy breath, that dost almost persuade
Justice to break her sword!° One more, one more!
Be thus when thou art dead, and I will kill thee
And love thee after. One more, and this the last.
20   So sweet was ne'er so fatal. I must weep.
But they are cruel tears: this sorrow's heavenly—
It strikes where it doth love. She wakes.

DESDEMONA   Who's there? Othello?

OTHELLO   Ay, Desdemona.

DESDEMONA   Will you come to bed, my lord?

25 OTHELLO   Have you prayed tonight, Desdemon?

DESDEMONA   Ay, my lord.

OTHELLO   If you bethink yourself of any crime
Unreconciled as yet to heaven and grace,
Solicit° for it straight.°

DESDEMONA   Alack, my lord, what may you mean by that?

30 OTHELLO   Well, do it, and be brief: I will walk by:
I would not kill thy unpreparèd spirit;
No—heaven forfend!—I would not kill thy soul.

DESDEMONA   Talk you of killing?

OTHELLO   Ay, I do.

DESDEMONA   Then heaven
Have mercy on me!

OTHELLO   Amen, with all my heart!

Act V, Scene ii.

1. It is the cause: i.e., I must keep in my mind the crime (of adultery).

4. that whiter skin of hers than snow: her skin that is whiter than snow.   **5. monumental:** i.e., like that used for tombs.   **6. else she'll betray more men:** Othello is attempting to raise his action from being one of personal revenge to one that is for the good of society.   **7. Put out the . . . light:** i.e., first quench this lamp, and then snuff out the life of Desdemona.   **8. flaming minister:** i.e., the lamp in his hand.

11. cunning'st pattern of excelling nature: skillfully created product of nature at its most perfect.   **12. Promethean heat:** i.e., the life-giving fire that the Titan Prometheus stole from heaven and gave to men.   **13. relume:** light again.

17. sword: i.e., the symbol of Justice's ability to punish.

28. Solicit: pray (for forgiveness).   **straight:** at once.

35 **DESDEMONA**   If you say so, I hope you will not kill me.

OTHELLO   Hum!

DESDEMONA   And yet I fear you, for you're fatal then
   When your eyes roll so. Why I should fear I know not,
   Since guiltiness I know not, but yet I feel I fear.

OTHELLO   Think on thy sins.

40 **DESDEMONA**   They are loves I bear to you.°

OTHELLO   Ay, and for that thou diest.

DESDEMONA   That death's unnatural that kills for loving.
   Alas, why gnaw you so your nether lip?
   Some bloody passion shakes your very frame:

45   These are portents; but yet I hope, I hope
   They do not point on me.°

OTHELLO   Peace, and be still!

DESDEMONA   I will so. What's the matter?°

OTHELLO   That handkerchief which I so loved and gave thee,
   Thou gav'st to Cassio.

DESDEMONA   No, by my life and soul!

50   Send for the man and ask him.

OTHELLO   Sweet soul, take heed.
   Take heed of perjury: thou art on thy death-bed.

DESDEMONA   Ay, but not yet to die.

OTHELLO   Yes, presently.°
   Therefore confess thee freely of thy sin;
   For to deny each article° with oath

55   Cannot remove nor choke the strong conception°
   That I do groan withal.° Thou art to die.

DESDEMONA   Then Lord have mercy on me!

OTHELLO   I say, Amen.

DESDEMONA   And have you mercy too! I never did
   Offend° you in my life; never loved Cassio

60   But with such general warranty° of heaven
   As I might love. I never gave him token.

OTHELLO   By heaven, I saw my handkerchief in's hand.
   O perjured woman! Thou dost stone° my heart,
   And mak'st me call what I intend to do

65   A murder, which I thought a sacrifice.
   I saw the handkerchief.

DESDEMONA   He found it then;
   I never gave it him. Send for him hither;
   Let him confess a truth.

OTHELLO   He hath confessed.

40. They are loves I bear to you: an allusion to the sin of loving a human being more than God.

46. point on me: presage my future.

47. matter: thing in question (disturbing you).

52. presently: immediately.

54. article: a legal term meaning an item in a formal indictment.   **55. conception:** (1) belief, (2) plan (I have conceived).   **56. groan withal:** (1) am distressed by, (2) am giving birth to.

59. Offend: sin against.

60. warranty: allowance, permission.

63. stone: harden, turn to stone.

DESDEMONA What, my lord?

70 **OTHELLO** That he hath used° thee.

> **70. used:** copulated with.

DESDEMONA   How? Unlawfully?

OTHELLO Ay.

DESDEMONA He will not say so.

OTHELLO   No, his mouth is stopped:
Honest Iago hath tane order for't.°

> **73. tane order for't:** arranged.

DESDEMONA O, my fear interprets! What, is he dead?

75 **OTHELLO** Had all his hairs been lives, my great revenge
Had stomach° for them all.

> **76. stomach:** appetite, capacity.

DESDEMONA Alas, he is betrayed, and I undone.

OTHELLO Out, strumpet! Weep'st thou for him to my face?

DESDEMONA O banish me, my lord, but kill me not!

80 **OTHELLO** Down, strumpet!

DESDEMONA Kill me tomorrow; let me live tonight!

OTHELLO Nay, if you strive—

DESDEMONA But half an hour!

OTHELLO   Being done, there is no pause.°

> **83. Being done, there is no pause:** Having thus started to do the deed, I cannot stop.

DESDEMONA But while I say one prayer!

OTHELLO   It is too late.

85 **DESDEMONA** O, Lord, Lord, Lord!

> *He smothers her.*

EMILIA (*Within*) My lord, my lord! What, ho! My lord, my
lord!

OTHELLO What noise is this? Not dead? Not yet quite dead?
I that am cruel am yet merciful;
I would not have thee linger in thy pain.

90 So, so.

EMILIA (*Within*) What, ho! My lord, my lord!

OTHELLO   Who's there?

EMILIA [*Within*] O, good my lord, I would speak a word with
you.

OTHELLO Yes—'tis Emilia—by and by.—She's dead.
'Tis like° she comes to speak of Cassio's death:
The noise was high.° Ha! No more moving?

> **93. like:** likely that.

> **94. The noise was high:** The uproar (created by the attack on Cassio) was loud.

95 Still as the grave. Shall she come in? Were't good?
I think she stirs again. No. What's best to do?
If she come in, she'll sure speak to my wife—
My wife, my wife! What wife? I have no wife.
O insupportable! O heavy hour!

100 Methinks it should be now a huge eclipse
Of sun and moon, and that th'affrighted globe
Should yawn° at alteration.°

> **102. yawn:** gape wide (as with an earthquake). **at alteration:** i.e., with the change in nature brought on by Desdemona's murder.

EMILIA [*Within*]   I do beseech you
  That I may speak with you. O, good my lord!
OTHELLO I had forgot thee. O, come in, Emilia.
105 Soft, by and by. Let me the curtains draw.
  Where art thou?

          [*He unlocks the door.*]
  What's the matter with thee now?

Enter EMILIA.

EMILIA O, my good lord, yonder's foul murders done.
OTHELLO What? Now?
EMILIA But now, my lord.
110 OTHELLO It is the very error° of the moon: **110. error:** straying off course.
  She comes more nearer earth than she was wont
  And makes men mad.
EMILIA Cassio, my lord, hath killed a young Venetian
  Called Roderigo.
OTHELLO   Roderigo killed?
115 And Cassio killed?
EMILIA   No, Cassio is not killed.
OTHELLO Not Cassio killed! Then murder's out of tune,
  And sweet revenge grows harsh.
DESDEMONA O, falsely, falsely murdered!
EMILIA   O Lord! What cry is that?
OTHELLO That? What?
120 EMILIA Out° and alas, that was my lady's voice!   **120. Out:** used merely to emphasize "alas."
     [*She draws the bed-curtains.*]
  Help, help, ho, help! O, lady, speak again!
  Sweet Desdemona, O sweet mistress, speak!
DESDEMONA A guiltless death I die.
EMILIA O, who hath done this deed?
125 DESDEMONA Nobody; I myself. Farewell.
  Commend me to my kind lord. O farewell!   *She dies*
OTHELLO Why, how should she be murdered?
EMILIA   Alas, who knows?
OTHELLO You heard her say herself it was not I.
EMILIA She said so; I must needs report the truth.
130 OTHELLO She's like a liar gone to burning hell:
  'Twas I that killed her.
EMILIA   O, the more angel she,
  And you the blacker devil!
OTHELLO She turned to folly,° and she was a whore. **133. folly:** unchastity, lewdness.
EMILIA Thou dost belie° her, and thou art a devil. **134. belie:** slander.

135 OTHELLO She was false as water.

EMILIA   Thou art rash as fire to say

That she was false. O, she was heavenly true!

OTHELLO Cassio did top her: ask thy husband else.°   137. **else:** i.e., if you do not believe.

O, I were damned beneath all depth in hell

But that I did proceed upon just grounds

140 To this extremity.° Thy husband knew it all.   140. **extremity:** final punishment (a legal term).

EMILIA My husband?

OTHELLO   Thy husband.

EMILIA   That she was false to wedlock?

OTHELLO Ay, with Cassio. Nay, had she been true,

If heaven would make me such another world

Of one entire and perfect chrysolite,°   144. **entire and perfect chrysolite:** pure and
perfect topaz.

145 I'd not have sold her for it.

EMILIA   My husband?

OTHELLO Ay, 'twas he that told me on her first;

An honest man he is, and hates the slime

That sticks on filthy deeds.

EMILIA   My husband?

OTHELLO What needs this iterance,° woman? I say thy   149. **iterance:** repetition.

husband.

150 EMILIA O mistress, villainy hath made mocks with° love!   150. **made mocks with:** made a dupe of,
played games with.

My husband say that she was false?

OTHELLO   He, woman;

I say thy husband. Dost understand the word?

My friend, thy husband, honest, honest Iago.

EMILIA If he say so, may his pernicious soul

155 Rot half a grain a day! He lies to th'heart.

She was too fond of her most filthy bargain.

OTHELLO Ha!

EMILIA Do thy worst.

This deed of thine is no more worthy heaven

160 Than thou wast worthy her.

OTHELLO   Peace, you were best.°   160. **you were best:** it would be best for you.

EMILIA Thou has not half that power to do me harm

As I have to be hurt. O gull!° O dolt!   162. **gull:** dupe.

As ignorant as dirt. Thou hast done a deed—

I care not for thy sword—I'll make thee known,

165 Though I lost twenty lives. Help! help! ho, help!

The Moor hath killed my mistress. Murder, murder!

Enter MONTANO, GRATIANO *and* IAGO.

MONTANO What is the matter? How now, general?

EMILIA   O, are you come, Iago? You have done well,
That men must lay their murders on your neck.

170 **GRATIANO**   What is the matter?

EMILIA   Disprove this villain, if thou be'st a man.
He says thou told'st him that his wife was false.
I know thou didst not, thou'rt not such a villain.
Speak, for my heart is full.

175 **IAGO**   I told him what I thought, and told no more
Than what he found himself was apt° and true.

> 176. **apt:** plausible, likely.

EMILIA   But did you ever tell him she was false?

IAGO   I did.

EMILIA   You told a lie, an odious damnèd lie:

180 Upon my soul, a lie, a wicked lie!
She false with Cassio? Did you say with Cassio?

IAGO   With Cassio, mistress. Go to, charm° your tongue.

> 182. **charm:** exercise a spell upon (to silence).

EMILIA   I will not charm my tongue; I am bound° to speak:
My mistress here lies murdered in her bed.

> 183. **bound:** in duty bound.

185 **ALL**   O, heavens forfend!

EMILIA   And your reports have set the murder on.

OTHELLO   Nay, stare not, masters; it is true indeed.

GRATIANO   'Tis a strange truth.

MONTANO   O monstrous act!

EMILIA   Villainy, villainy, villainy!

190 I think upon't, I think—I smell't—O villainy!
I thought so then; I'll kill myself for grief.
O villainy, villainy!

IAGO   What, are you mad? I charge you get you home.

EMILIA   Good gentlemen, let me have leave to speak.

195 'Tis proper I obey him, but not now.
Perchance, Iago, I will ne'er go home.

OTHELLO   O! O! O!

> *Othello falls on the bed.*

EMILIA   Nay, lay thee down and roar,
For thou hast killed the sweetest innocent
That e'er did lift up eye.°

> 199. **lift up eye:** i.e., to heaven in purity of spirit and prayer.

OTHELLO   [*Standing up*]   O, she was foul!

200 I scarce did know you, uncle; there lies your niece,
Whose breath indeed these hands have newly stopped.
I know this act shows horrible and grim—

GRATIANO   Poor Desdemon, I am glad thy father's dead:
Thy match was mortal to him, and pure grief

205 Shore his old thread in twain.° Did he live now,

> 205. **Shore his old thread in twain:** The allusion is to the Parcae, or Fates: Clotho, who spun the thread of human life, and Atropos, who cut it.

This sight would make him do a desperate turn,°

Yea, curse his better angel from his side

And fall to reprobance.°

OTHELLO 'Tis pitiful; but yet Iago knows

210   That she with Cassio hath the act of shame

    A thousand times committed. Cassio confessed it,

    And she did gratify° his amorous works

    With that recognisance° and pledge of love

    Which I first gave her. I saw it in his hand:

215   It was a handkerchief, an antique token

    My father gave my mother.

EMILIA   O God! O heavenly God!

IAGO Zounds, hold your peace!

EMILIA   'Twill out,° 'twill out. I peace!

    No, I will speak as liberal as the north;°

    Let heaven, and men, and devils, let them all,

220   All, all cry shame against me, yet I'll speak.

IAGO Be wise and get you home.

EMILIA   I will not.

            [Iago draws his sword and threatens Emilia.]

GRATIANO   Fie,

    Your sword upon a woman!

EMILIA O thou dull Moor, that handkerchief thou speak'st of

    I found by fortune and did give my husband,

225   For often, with a solemn earnestness—

    More than indeed belonged° to such a trifle—

    He begged of me to steal it.

IAGO   Villainous whore!

EMILIA She give it Cassio! No, alas, I found it

    And I did give't my husband.

IAGO   Filth, thou liest!

230 **EMILIA** By heaven, I do not, I do not, gentlemen.

    O murderous coxcomb,° what should such a fool

    Do with so good a wife?

OTHELLO   Are there no stones° in heaven

    But what serves for the thunder? Precious villain!

            [Othello runs at Iago; Montano disarms him;

            Iago stabs Emilia from behind and exit.]

GRATIANO The woman falls; sure he hath killed his wife.

235 **EMILIA** Ay, ay; O, lay me by my mistress' side.

GRATIANO He's gone, but his wife's killed.

MONTANO 'Tis a notorious villain. Take you this weapon,

206. turn: act.

208. to reprobance: into a state of damnation.

212. gratify: reward.

213. recognisance: token.

217. 'Twill out: i.e., "Murder will out."

218. liberal as the north: as unrestrainedly as the north wind blows.

226. belonged: was appropriate.

231. coxcomb: fool; literally, the cap resembling a cock's comb that professional fools wore.

232. stones: thunderbolts.

Which I have here recovered from the Moor.
Come guard the door without; let him not pass,
240   But kill him rather. I'll after the same villain,
For 'tis a damnèd slave.

Exeunt Montano and Gratiano

OTHELLO   I am not valiant neither,
But every puny whipster° gets my sword.
But why should honour outlive honesty?°
Let it go all.

> **242. whipster:** whippersnapper (one who is prone to whip out his sword). **243. honour outlive honesty:** the reputation for honor outlast the possession of honor itself.

EMILIA   What did thy song bode, lady?
245   Hark, canst thou hear me? I will play the swan
And die in music: [*Sings*] "Willow, willow, willow."
Moor, she was chaste; she loved thee, cruel Moor;
So come my soul to bliss, as I speak true;
So speaking as I think, I die, I die.   *She dies*

250   **OTHELLO** I have another weapon in this chamber;
It was a sword of Spain,° the ice-brook's temper.°
O, here it is.—Uncle, I must come forth.

> **251. sword of Spain:** Spain was noted for the production of fine swords. **ice-brook's temper:** tempered by being plunged into ice-cold water.

GRATIANO (*Within*) If thou attempt it, it will cost thee dear;
Thou hast no weapon, and perforce must suffer.
255   **OTHELLO** Look in upon me then, and speak with me,
Or naked° as I am, I will assault thee.

> **256. naked:** unarmed.

[*Enter Gratiano.*]

GRATIANO What is the matter?
OTHELLO   Behold, I have a weapon:
A better never did itself sustain
Upon a soldier's thigh. I have seen the day
260   That with this little arm and this good sword
I have made my way through more impediments
Than twenty times your stop.° But, O vain boast!
Who can control his fate? 'Tis not so now.
Be not afraid, though you do see me weaponed:

> **262. your stop:** the hindrance you constitute.

265   Here is my journey's end, here is my butt°
And very sea-mark° of my utmost sail.°
Do you go back dismayed? 'Tis a lost° fear:
Man but a rush° against Othello's breast,
And he retires. Where should Othello go?

> **265. butt:** target (for archery), goal.
>
> **266. sea-mark:** beacon or other landmark used by ships to make land. **my utmost sail:** the farthest point of my voyage (of life). **267. lost:** wasted, idle. **268. Man but a rush:** aim only a reed (as if it were a spear).

[*He goes to the bed.*]

270   Now, how dost thou look now? O ill-starred° wench!
Pale as thy smock! When we shall meet at compt°
This look of thine will hurl my soul from heaven
And fiends will snatch at it. Cold, cold, my girl,

> **270. ill-starred:** ill-fated.
>
> **271. compt:** the day of Judgment.

Even like thy chastity.

275 O cursèd, cursèd slave!° Whip me, ye devils,

From the possession of° this heavenly sight!

Blow me about in winds! Roast me in sulphur!

Wash me in steep-down° gulfs of liquid fire!

O Desdemon! Dead Desdemon! Dead! O! O!

Enter LODOVICO, *Montano,* CASSIO *in a chair, Iago in the charge of*
OFFICERS.

280 **LODOVICO** Where is this rash and most unfortunate man?

OTHELLO That's he that was Othello: here I am.

LODOVICO Where is that viper? Bring the villain forth.

OTHELLO I look down towards his° feet; but that's a fable.°

If that thou be'st a devil, I cannot kill thee.

[*He wounds Iago.*]

285 **LODOVICO** Wrench his sword from him.

IAGO   I bleed, sir, but not killed.

OTHELLO I am not sorry neither; I'd have thee live,

For in my sense° 'tis happiness to die.

LODOVICO O, thou Othello, that wert once so good,

Fallen in the practice° of a damnèd slave,°

290 What shall be said to thee?

OTHELLO   Why, anything:

An honourable murderer, if you will;

For naught did I in hate, but all in honour.

LODOVICO This wretch hath part confessed his villainy.

Did you and he consent in° Cassio's death?

295 **OTHELLO** Ay.

CASSIO Dear general, I never gave you cause.

OTHELLO I do believe it, and I ask your pardon.

Will you, I pray, demand that demi-devil

Why he hath thus ensnared my soul and body?

300 **IAGO** Demand me nothing; what you know, you know.

From this time forth I never will speak word.

LODOVICO What! Not to pray?

GRATIANO Torments° will ope your lips.

OTHELLO   Well, thou dost best.

LODOVICO Sir, you shall understand what hath befallen,

305 Which, as I think, you know not. Here is a letter

Found in the pocket of the slain Roderigo,

And here another: the one of them imports

275. slave: i.e., himself, not Iago.

276. the possession of: being haunted by.

278. steep-down: precipice-like.

283. his: i.e., Iago's. **fable:** i.e., that the Devil has cloven feet.

287. in my sense: to one who feels like me.

289. in the practice: through the machinations. **slave:** villain.

294. consent in: agree to the planning of.

303. Torments: torture.

The death of Cassio, to be undertook

By Roderigo.

OTHELLO   O villain!

CASSIO   Most heathenish and most gross!°

310 **LODOVICO** Now here's another discontented paper,°

Found in his pocket too; and this, it seems,

Roderigo meant to have sent this damnèd villain,

But that, belike, Iago, in the nick,°

Came in° and satisfied him.°

OTHELLO   O the pernicious caitiff!

315 How came you, Cassio, by that handkerchief

That was my wife's?

CASSIO   I found it in my chamber;

And he himself confessed but even now

That there he dropped it for a special purpose

Which wrought to his desire.°

OTHELLO   O fool, fool, fool!

320 **CASSIO** There is besides in Roderigo's letter

How he upbraids Iago, that he made him

Brave° me upon the watch, whereon it came°

That I was cast;° and even but now he spake—

After long seeming dead—Iago hurt him,

325 Iago set him on.

LODOVICO You must forsake this room and go with us.

Your power and your command is taken off°

And Cassio rules in Cyprus. For this slave,

If there be any cunning cruelty

330 That can torment him much and hold him long°

It shall be his. You shall close prisoner rest°

Till that the nature of your fault be known

To the Venetian state. Come, bring him away.

OTHELLO Soft you;° a word or two before you go.

335 I have done the state some service and they know't:

No more of that. I pray you, in your letters

When you shall these unlucky° deeds relate,

Speak of me as I am; nothing extenuate,

Nor set down aught in malice. Then must you speak

340 Of one that loved not wisely, but too well;

Of one not easily jealous but, being wrought,°

Perplexed° in the extreme; of one whose hand,

Like the base Indian, threw a pearl away

Richer than all his tribe; of one whose subdued° eyes,

345 Albeit unusèd to the melting mood,

309. gross: flagrant, monstrous.

310. discontented paper: letter expressing resentment.

313. nick: nick of time.

314. Came in: interposed. **satisfied him:** gave him a satisfactory explanation.

319. wrought to his desire: worked out in accordance with his wishes.

322. Brave: insult, provoke. **whereon it came:** because of which it happened.
323. cast: dismissed.

327. off: away.

330. hold him long: keep him a long time in dying. **331 rest:** remain.

334. Soft you: Wait a moment.

337. unlucky: unfortunate, unhappy.

341. wrought: worked upon.

342. Perplexed: desperately troubled, bewildered.

344. subdued: overcome by emotion.

Drops tears as fast as the Arabian trees
Their medicinable gum. Set you down this;
And say besides that in Aleppo° once
Where a malignant and a turbaned Turk
350   Beat a Venetian and traduced the state,
I took by th'throat the circumcisèd dog
And smote him thus.

348. Aleppo: a city in Turkey, where it was a capital crime for a Christian to strike a Turk.

He stabs himself.

LODOVICO   O bloody period!°

353. period: conclusion.

GRATIANO   All that's spoke is marred!

OTHELLO   I kissed thee ere I killed thee: no way but this,
355   Killing myself, to die upon a kiss.

He [falls on the bed and] dies

CASSIO   This did I fear, but thought he had no weapon,
For he was great of heart.

LODOVICO [*To Iago*]   O Spartan dog,
More fell° than anguish, hunger, or the sea,
Look on the tragic loading of this bed:

358. fell: fierce, cruel.

360   This is thy work. The object° poisons sight;
Let it be hid.

360. object: spectacle, that which meets the eyes.

[The bed-curtains are drawn.]

Gratiano, keep° the house
And seize upon° the fortunes of the Moor,
For they succeed on° you. To you, lord governor,°
Remains the censure° of this hellish villain:

361. keep: remain in.

362. seize upon: take legal possession of.

363. succeed on: descend to.   **lord governor:** i.e., Cassio.
364. censure: judgment, trial.

365   The time, the place, the torture, O, enforce it!
Myself will straight° aboard, and to the state
This heavy act with heavy° heart relate.

366. straight: immediately.

367. heavy: sorrowful.

Exeunt

Christian Köhler (1809–1861) Title: Othello; Deutsch: Othello mit seiner schlafenden Frau Date 1859, public domain

◄ The painting depicts the final scene between Othello and Desdemona.

As you view the painting, pay attention to the light and the dark imagery. What does the painting suggest about Desdemona's final moments? What does the painting suggest about Othello in this scene?

CHARACTER

1. Explain what drives Desdemona to think, feel, and act as she does.

2. What **motivates** Emilia to reveal the truth? Explain how this choice affects the resolution of the play.

3. In what ways is Othello a **dynamic** character? Explain how his traits change from the beginning of the tragedy to the end.

SETTING

4. Act V is set in two locations. How do these locations contribute to the overall effect of the tragedy? What ideas does the physical setting suggest?

5. Where is Roderigo killed? How does this **setting** contribute to the complexity of the play?

6. What is the symbolic relationship between the bedroom scene and the tragic ending of the characters? How does this create a relationship between the characters and the setting?

STRUCTURE

7. Recall Iago uses many **contrasts** in Act V. Find an example of an important **contrast** and then explain how it contributes to the complexity of the play.

8. Review the definition of *tragedy*. How is the ending of *Othello* tragic? Do the events of the play resolve the main **conflict**? Explain.

IDEAS IN LITERATURE: Power and Control

9. *Othello* revolves around jealousy, envy, and power. What do you think could have changed the outcome of the play? Think of a moment in your experience when jealousy and envy overpowered you and distorted your perception. What could have altered or changed the outcome of the moment or your reactions?

PUTTING IT ALL TOGETHER

10. How do the conflicts reveal dramatic contrasts throughout *Othello* and contribute to the play's dramatic tensions? Choose a specific conflict and explain how it reveals a dramatic tension. How does this example inform your interpretation of the play?

A Doll's House
Henrik Ibsen

ullstein bild Dtl./Getty Images

THE TEXT IN CONTEXT

Often considered the father of modern theatrical realism, Norwegian playwright Henrik Ibsen (1828–1906) is one of the most influential figures in literature. He defined many of the conventions that we take for granted in realistic modern drama. For example, while earlier playwrights focused on kings, queens, and grandiose figures, with the lower classes used for comic effect, Ibsen wrote about everyday middle-class people, such as the couple in *A Doll's House*. These characters have realistic psychologies and motivations; their dialogue is relatively natural rather than poetic or mannered; they are influenced by their environment and specific cultural setting; the play's action and scenes have logical cause-and-effect relationships. But Ibsen's innovations go beyond technique. His plays offer sharp social criticism; they explicitly address weighty topics such as politics, power, business, war — and in *A Doll's House* — marriage, divorce, and the role of women.

A Doll's House

Dramatis Personae

TORVALD HELMER.

NORA, *his wife*.

DOCTOR RANK.

MRS. LINDE.

NILS KROGSTAD.

HELMER'S THREE YOUNG CHILDREN.

ANNE, THEIR NURSE.

A HOUSEMAID.

A PORTER.

(*The action takes place in Helmer's house.*)

ACT I

(SCENE—*A room furnished comfortably and tastefully, but not extravagantly. At the back, a door to the right leads to the entrance-hall, another to the left leads to Helmer's study. Between the doors stands a piano. In the middle of the left-hand wall is a door, and beyond it a window. Near the window are a round table, arm-chairs and a small sofa. In the right-hand wall, at the farther end, another door; and on the same side, nearer the footlights, a stove, two easy chairs and a rocking-chair; between the stove and the door, a small table. Engravings on the wall; a cabinet with china and other small objects; a small book-case with well-bound books. The floors are carpeted, and a fire burns in the stove. It is winter.*

A bell rings in the hall; shortly afterwards the door is heard to open. Enter NORA, *humming a tune and in high spirits. She is in out-door dress and carries a number of parcels; these she lays on the table to the right. She leaves the outer door open after her, and through it is seen a* PORTER *who is carrying a Christmas Tree and a basket, which he gives to the* MAID *who has opened the door.*)

NORA.   Hide the Christmas Tree carefully, Helen. Be sure the children do not see it till this evening, when it is dressed. (*To the* PORTER, *taking out her purse.*) How

5   much?

PORTER.   Sixpence.

NORA.   There is a shilling. No, keep the change. (*The* PORTER *thanks her, and goes out.* NORA *shuts the door. She is laughing to*

10   *herself, as she takes off her hat and coat. She takes a packet of macaroons from her pocket and eats one or two; then goes cautiously to her husband's door and listens.*) Yes, he is in. (*Still humming, she goes to the table on the*

15   *right.*)

HELMER (*calls out from his room*).   Is that my little lark twittering out there?

NORA (*busy opening some of the parcels*).   Yes, it is!

20   HELMER.   Is it my little squirrel bustling about?

NORA.   Yes!

HELMER.   When did my squirrel come home?

NORA.   Just now. (*Puts the bag of macaroons into her pocket and wipes her mouth.*) Come

25   in here, Torvald, and see what I have bought.

HELMER.   Don't disturb me. (*A little later, he opens the door and looks into the room, pen in hand.*) Bought, did you say? All these

30   things? Has my little spendthrift been wasting money again?

NORA.   Yes, but, Torvald, this year we really can let ourselves go a little. This is the first Christmas that we have not needed

35   to economize.

HELMER.   Still, you know, we can't spend money recklessly.

NORA.   Yes, Torvald, we may be a wee bit more reckless now, mayn't we? Just a tiny

40   wee bit! You are going to have a big salary and earn lots and lots of money.

HELMER.   Yes, after the New Year; but then it will be a whole quarter before the salary is due.

45   NORA.   Pooh! we can borrow till then.

HELMER.   Nora! (*Goes up to her and takes her playfully by the ear.*) The same little featherhead! Suppose, now, that I borrowed fifty pounds today, and you spent it all in

50   the Christmas week, and then on New Year's Eve a slate fell on my head and killed me, and—

NORA (*putting her hands over his mouth*). Oh! don't say such horrid things.

55   HELMER.   Still, suppose that happened,— what then?

NORA. If that were to happen, I don't suppose I should care whether I owed money or not.

60 **HELMER.** Yes, but what about the people who had lent it?

NORA They? Who would bother about them? I should not know who they were.

65 **HELMER** That is like a woman! But seriously, Nora, you know what I think about that. No debt, no borrowing. There can be no freedom or beauty about a home life that depends on borrowing and debt. We two

70 have kept bravely on the straight road so far, and we will go on the same way for the short time longer that there need be any struggle.

NORA (*moving towards the stove*). As you

75 please, Torvald.

HELMER (*following her*). Come, come, my little skylark must not droop her wings. What is this! Is my little squirrel out of temper? (*Taking out his purse.*) Nora, what do you

80 think I have got here?

NORA (*turning round quickly*). Money!

HELMER. There you are. (*Gives her some money.*) Do you think I don't know what a lot is wanted for housekeeping at

85 Christmas-time?

NORA (*counting*). Ten shillings—a pound— two pounds! Thank you, thank you, Torvald; that will keep me going for a long time.

90 **HELMER** Indeed it must.

NORA Yes, yes, it will. But come here and let me show you what I have bought. And ah so cheap! Look, here is a new suit for Ivar, and a sword; and a horse and a trumpet

95 for Bob; and a doll and dolly's bedstead for Emmy.—they are very plain, but anyway she will soon break them in pieces. And here are dress-lengths and handkerchiefs for the maids; old Anne ought really to

100 have something better.

HELMER. And what is in this parcel?

NORA (*crying out*). No, no! you mustn't see that till this evening.

HELMER. Very well. But now tell me, you

105 extravagant little person, what would you like for yourself?

NORA. For myself? Oh, I am sure I don't want anything.

HELMER. Yes, but you must. Tell me some-

110 thing reasonable that you would particularly like to have.

NORA. No, I really can't think of anything— unless, Torvald—

HELMER. Well?

115 **NORA** (*playing with his coat buttons, and without raising her eyes to his*). If you really want to give me something, you might—you might—

HELMER. Well, out with it!

120 **NORA** (*speaking quickly*). You might give me money, Torvald. Only just as much as you can afford; and then one of these days I will buy something with it.

HELMER. But, Nora—

125 **NORA.** Oh, do! dear Torvald; please, please do! Then I will wrap it up in beautiful gilt paper and hang it on the Christmas Tree. Wouldn't that be fun?

HELMER. What are little people called that

130 are always wasting money?

NORA. Spendthrifts—I know. Let us do as you suggest, Torvald, and then I shall have time to think what I am most in want of. That is a very sensible plan,

135 isn't it?

HELMER (*smiling*). Indeed it is—that is to say, if you were really to save out of the money I give you, and then really buy something for yourself. But if you spend it all on the

140 housekeeping and any number of unnecessary things, then I merely have to pay up again.

NORA. Oh but, Torvald—

HELMER. You can't deny it, my dear, little
145 Nora. (*Puts his arm round her waist.*) It's a
sweet little spendthrift, but she uses up a
deal of money. One would hardly believe
how expensive such little persons are!

NORA. It's a shame to say that. I do really
150 save all I can.

HELMER (*laughing*). That's very true,—all you
can. But you can't save anything!

NORA (*smiling quietly and happily*). You
haven't any idea how many expenses we
155 skylarks and squirrels have, Torvald.

HELMER. You are an odd little soul. Very like
your father. You always find some new way
of wheedling money out of me, and, as soon
as you have got it, it seems to melt in your
160 hands. You never know where it has gone.
Still, one must take you as you are. It is in
the blood; for indeed it is true that you can
inherit these things, Nora.

NORA. Ah, I wish I had inherited many of
165 papa's qualities.

HELMER. And I would not wish you to be
anything but just what you are, my sweet
little skylark. But, do you know, it strikes
me that you are looking rather—what
170 shall I say—rather uneasy today?

NORA. Do I?

HELMER. You do, really. Look straight at me.

NORA (*looks at him*). Well?

HELMER (*wagging his finger at her*). Hasn't
175 Miss Sweet Tooth been breaking rules in
town today?

NORA. No; what makes you think that?

HELMER. Hasn't she paid a visit to the
confectioner's?

180 NORA. No, I assure you, Torvald—

HELMER. Not been nibbling sweets?

NORA. No, certainly not.

HELMER. Not even taken a bite at a macaroon or two?

185 NORA. No, Torvald, I assure you really—

HELMER. There, there, of course I was only
joking.

NORA (*going to the table on the right*). I
should not think of going against your
190 wishes.

HELMER. No, I am sure of that; besides, you
gave me your word—(*Going up to her.*)
Keep your little Christmas secrets to
yourself, my darling. They will all be
195 revealed tonight when the Christmas Tree
is lit, no doubt.

NORA. Did you remember to invite Doctor
Rank?

HELMER. No. But there is no need; as a
200 matter of course he will come to dinner
with us. However, I will ask him when he
comes in this morning. I have ordered
some good wine. Nora, you can't think
how I am looking forward to this evening.

205 NORA. So am I! And how the children will
enjoy themselves, Torvald!

HELMER. It is splendid to feel that one has a
perfectly safe appointment, and a big
enough income. It's delightful to think of,
210 isn't it?

NORA. It's wonderful!

HELMER. Do you remember last Christmas?
For a full three weeks beforehand you
shut yourself up every evening till long
215 after midnight, making ornaments for the
Christmas Tree and all the other fine
things that were to be a surprise to us. It
was the dullest three weeks I ever spent!

NORA. I didn't find it dull.

220 HELMER (*smiling*). But there was precious
little result, Nora.

NORA. Oh, you shouldn't tease me about
that again. How could I help the cat's
going in and tearing everything to pieces?

225 HELMER. Of course you couldn't, poor little
girl. You had the best of intentions to
please us all, and that's the main thing.

But it is a good thing that our hard times are over.

230 **NORA.** Yes, it is really wonderful.

HELMER. This time I needn't sit here and be dull all alone, and you needn't ruin your dear eyes and your pretty little hands—

NORA (*clapping her hand*). No, Torvald, I
235 needn't any longer, need I! It's wonderfully lovely to hear you say so! (*Taking his arm.*) Now I will tell you how I have been thinking we ought to arrange things, Torvald. As soon as Christmas is over—(*A*
240 *bell rings in the hall.*) There's the bell. (*She tidies the room a little.*) There's someone at the door. What a nuisance!

HELMER. If it is a caller, remember I am not at home.

245 **MAID** (*in the doorway*). A lady to see you, ma'am,—a stranger.

NORA. Ask her to come in.

MAID (*to* **HELMER**). The doctor came at the same time, sir.

250 **HELMER.** Did he go straight into my room?

MAID. Yes, sir.

(**HELMER** *goes into his room. The* **MAID** *ushers in* **MRS. LINDE**, *who is in traveling dress, and shuts the door.*)

255 **MRS. LINDE** (*in a dejected and timid voice*). How do you do, Nora?

NORA (*doubtfully*). How do you do—

MRS. LINDE. You don't recognize me, I suppose.

NORA. No, I don't know—yes, to be sure, I
260 seem to—(*Suddenly.*) Yes! Christine! Is it really you?

MRS. LINDE. Yes, it is I.

NORA. Christine! To think of my not recognising you! And yet how could I—(*In a*
265 *gentle voice.*) How you have altered, Christine!

MRS. LINDE. Yes, I have indeed. In nine, ten long years—

NORA. Is it so long since we met? I suppose
270 it is. The last eight years have been a

happy time for me, I can tell you. And so now you have come into the town, and have taken this long journey in winter—that was plucky of you.

275 **MRS. LINDE.** I arrived by steamer this morning.

NORA. To have some fun at Christmas-time, of course. How delightful! We will have such fun together! But take off your things. You are not cold, I hope. (*Helps her.*)
280 Now we will sit down by the stove, and be cosy. No, take this armchair; I will sit here in the rocking-chair. (*Takes her hands.*) Now you look like your old self again; it was only the first moment—You are a little
285 paler, Christine, and perhaps a little thinner.

MRS. LINDE. And much, much older, Nora.

NORA. Perhaps a little older; very, very little; certainly not much. (*Stops suddenly and*
290 *speaks seriously.*) What a thoughtless creature I am, chattering away like this. My poor, dear Christine, do forgive me.

MRS. LINDE. What do you mean, Nora?

NORA (*gently*). Poor Christine, you are a
295 widow.

MRS. LINDE. Yes; it is three years ago now.

NORA. Yes, I knew; I saw it in the papers. I assure you, Christine, I meant ever so often to write to you at the time, but I
300 always put it off and something always prevented me.

MRS. LINDE. I quite understand, dear.

NORA. It was very bad of me, Christine. Poor thing, how you must have suffered. And
305 he left you nothing?

MRS. LINDE. No.

NORA. And no children?

MRS. LINDE. No.

NORA. Nothing at all, then?

310 **MRS. LINDE.** Not even any sorrow or grief to live upon.

NORA (*looking incredulously at her*). But, Christine, is that possible?

MRS. LINDE (*smiles sadly and strokes her hair*).

315   It sometimes happens, Nora.

NORA.   So you are quite alone. How dreadfully sad that must be. I have three lovely children. You can't see them just now, for they are out with their nurse. But now you

320   must tell me all about it.

MRS. LINDE.   No, no; I want to hear about you.

NORA.   No, you must begin. I mustn't be selfish today; today I must only think of your affairs. But there is one thing I must tell

325   you. Do you know we have just had a great piece of good luck?

MRS. LINDE.   No, what is it?

NORA.   Just fancy, my husband has been made manager of the Bank!

330 MRS. LINDE.   Your husband? What good luck!

NORA.   Yes tremendous! A barrister's profession is such an uncertain thing, especially if he won't undertake unsavoury cases; and naturally Torvald has never been will-

335   ing to do that, and I quite agree with him. You may imagine how pleased we are! He is to take up his work in the Bank at the New Year, and then he will have a big salary and lots of commissions. For the

340   future we can live quite differently—we can do just as we like. I feel so relieved and so happy, Christine! It will be splendid to have heaps of money and not need to have any anxiety, won't it?

345 MRS. LINDE.   Yes, anyhow I think it would be delightful to have what one needs.

NORA.   No, not only what one needs, but heaps and heaps of money.

MRS. LINDE (*smiling*).   Nora, Nora, haven't you

350   learnt sense yet? In our schooldays you were a great spendthrift.

NORA (*laughing*).   Yes, that is what Torvald says now. (*Wags her finger at her.*) But "Nora, Nora" is not so silly as you think.

355   We have not been in a position for me to waste money. We have both had to work.

MRS. LINDE.   You too?

NORA.   Yes; odds and ends, needlework, crochet-work, embroidery, and that kind of

360   thing. (*Dropping her voice.*) And other things as well. You know Torvald left his office when we were married? There was no prospect of promotion there, and he had to try and earn more than before. But during

365   the first year he overworked himself dreadfully. You see, he had to make money every way he could, and he worked early and late; but he couldn't stand it, and fell dreadfully ill, and the doctors said it was

370   necessary for him to go south.

MRS. LINDE.   You spent a whole year in Italy, didn't you?

NORA.   Yes. It was no easy matter to get away, I can tell you. It was just after Ivar

375   was born; but naturally we had to go. It was a wonderfully beautiful journey, and it saved Torvald's life. But it cost a tremendous lot of money, Christine.

MRS. LINDE.   So I should think.

380 NORA.   It cost about two hundred and fifty pounds. That's a lot, isn't it?

MRS. LINDE.   Yes, and in emergencies like that it is lucky to have the money.

NORA.   I ought to tell you that we had it from

385   papa.

MRS. LINDE.   Oh, I see. It was just about that time that he died, wasn't it?

NORA.   Yes; and, just think of it, I couldn't go and nurse him. I was expecting little Ivar's

390   birth every day and I had my poor sick Torvald to look after. My dear, kind father—I never saw him again, Christine. That was the saddest time I have known since our marriage.

395 MRS. LINDE.   I know how fond you were of him. And then you went off to Italy?

NORA.   Yes; you see we had money then, and the doctors insisted on our going, so we started a month later.

400 MRS. LINDE. And your husband came back quite well?

NORA. As sound as a bell!

MRS. LINDE. But—the doctor?

NORA. What doctor?

405 MRS. LINDE. I thought your maid said the gentleman who arrived here just as I did, was the doctor?

NORA. Yes, that was Doctor Rank, but he doesn't come here professionally. He is

410 our greatest friend, and comes in at least once every day. No, Torvald has not had an hour's illness since then, and our children are strong and healthy and so am I. (*Jumps up and claps her hands.*) Christine!

415 Christine! it's good to be alive and happy!—But how horrid of me; I am talking of nothing but my own affairs. (*Sits on a stool near her, and rests her arms on her knees.*) You mustn't be angry with me.

420 Tell me, is it really true that you did not love your husband? Why did you marry him?

MRS. LINDE. My mother was alive then, and was bedridden and helpless, and I had to

425 provide for my two younger brothers; so I did not think I was justified in refusing his offer.

NORA. No, perhaps you were quite right. He was rich at that time, then?

430 MRS. LINDE. I believe he was quite well off. But his business was a precarious one; and, when he died, it all went to pieces and there was nothing left.

NORA. And then?—

435 MRS. LINDE. Well, I had to turn my hand to anything I could find—first a small shop, then a small school, and so on. The last three years have seemed like one long working-day, with no rest. Now it is at an

440 end, Nora. My poor mother needs me no more, for she is gone; and the boys do not need me either; they have got situations and can shift for themselves.

NORA. What a relief you must feel it—

445 MRS. LINDE. No, indeed; I only feel my life unspeakably empty. No one to live for anymore. (*Gets up restlessly.*) That is why I could not stand the life in my little backwater any longer. I hope it may be

450 easier here to find something which will busy me and occupy my thoughts. If only I could have the good luck to get some regular work—office work of some kind—

NORA. But, Christine, that is so frightfully

455 tiring, and you look tired out now. You had far better go away to some watering-place.

MRS. LINDE (*walking to the window*). I have no father to give me money for a journey, Nora.

460 NORA (*rising*). Oh, don't be angry with me!

MRS. LINDE (*going up to her*). It is you that must not be angry with me, dear. The worst of a position like mine is that it makes one so bitter. No one to work for,

465 and yet obliged to be always on the look-out for chances. One must live, and so one becomes selfish. When you told me of the happy turn your fortunes have taken—you will hardly believe it—I was delighted

470 not so much on your account as on my own.

NORA. How do you mean?—Oh, I understand. You mean that perhaps Torvald could get you something to do.

475 MRS. LINDE. Yes, that was what I was thinking of.

NORA. He must, Christine. Just leave it to me; I will broach the subject very cleverly—I will think of something that will please

480 him very much. It will make me so happy to be of some use to you.

MRS. LINDE. How kind you are, Nora, to be so anxious to help me! It is doubly kind in

you, for you know so little of the burdens
485   and troubles of life.

NORA. I—? I know so little of them?

MRS. LINDE (*smiling*). My dear! Small household cares and that sort of thing!—You
are a child, Nora.

490 **NORA** (*tosses her head and crosses the stage*).
You ought not to be so superior.

MRS. LINDE. No?

NORA. You are just like all the others. They
all think that I am incapable of anything
495   really serious—

MRS. LINDE. Come, come—

NORA. —that I have gone through nothing in
this world of cares.

MRS. LINDE. But, my dear Nora, you have just
500   told me all your troubles.

NORA. Pooh!—those were trifles. (*Lowering
her voice.*) I have not told you the important thing.

MRS. LINDE. The important thing? What do
505   you mean?

NORA. You look down upon me altogether,
Christine—but you ought not to. You are
proud, aren't you, of having worked so
hard and so long for your mother?

510 **MRS. LINDE.** Indeed, I don't look down on any
one. But it is true that I am both proud
and glad to think that I was privileged to
make the end of my mother's life almost
free from care.

515 **NORA.** And you are proud to think of what
you have done for your brothers?

MRS. LINDE. I think I have the right to be.

NORA. I think so, too. But now, listen to
this; I too have something to be proud and
520   glad of.

MRS. LINDE. I have no doubt you have. But
what do you refer to?

NORA. Speak low. Suppose Torvald were to
hear! He mustn't on any account—no
525   one in the world must know, Christine,
except you.

MRS. LINDE. But what is it?

NORA. Come here. (*Pulls her down on the sofa
beside her.*) Now I will show you that I too
530   have something to be proud and glad of. It
was I who saved Torvald's life.

MRS. LINDE. Saved? How?

NORA. I told you about our trip to Italy.
Torvald would never have recovered if he
535   had not gone there—

MRS. LINDE. Yes, but your father gave you the
necessary funds.

NORA (*smiling*). Yes, that is what Torvald and
all the others think, but—

540 **MRS. LINDE.** But.—

NORA. Papa didn't give us a shilling. It was I
who procured the money.

MRS. LINDE. You? All that large sum?

NORA. Two hundred and fifty pounds. What
545   do you think of that?

MRS. LINDE. But, Nora, how could you possibly do it? Did you win a prize in the
Lottery?

NORA (*contemptuously*). In the Lottery? There
550   would have been no credit in that.

MRS. LINDE. But where did you get it from,
then?

NORA (*humming and smiling with an air of
mystery*). Hm, hm! Aha!

555 **MRS. LINDE.** Because you couldn't have
borrowed it.

NORA. Couldn't I? Why not?

MRS. LINDE. No, a wife cannot borrow without her husband's consent.

560 **NORA** (*tossing her head*). Oh, if it is a wife who
has any head for business—a wife who
has the wit to be a little bit clever—

MRS. LINDE. I don't understand it at all, Nora.

NORA. There is no need you should. I never
565   said I had borrowed the money. I may have
got it some other way. (*Lies back on the sofa.*)
Perhaps I got it from some other admirer.
When anyone is as attractive as I am—

MRS. LINDE. You are a mad creature.

570 **NORA.** Now, you know you're full of curiosity, Christine.

MRS. LINDE. Listen to me, Nora dear. Haven't you been a little bit imprudent?

NORA (*sits up straight*). Is it imprudent to save
575 your husband's life?

MRS. LINDE. It seems to me imprudent, without his knowledge, to—

NORA. But it was absolutely necessary that he should not know! My goodness, can't
580 you understand that? It was necessary he should have no idea what a dangerous condition he was in. It was to me that the doctors came and said that his life was in danger, and that the only thing to save
585 him was to live in the south. Do you suppose I didn't try, first of all, to get what I wanted as if it were for myself? I told him how much I should love to travel abroad like other young wives; I
590 tried tears and entreaties with him; I told him that he ought to remember the condition I was in, and that he ought to be kind and indulgent to me; I even hinted that he might raise a loan. That
595 nearly made him angry, Christine. He said I was thoughtless, and that it was his duty as my husband not to indulge me in my whims and caprices—as I believe he called them. Very well, I
600 thought, you must be saved—and that was how I came to devise a way out of the difficulty—

MRS. LINDE. And did your husband never get to know from your father that the money
605 had not come from him?

NORA. No, never. Papa died just at that time. I had meant to let him into the secret and beg him never to reveal it. But he was so ill then—alas, there never was any need
610 to tell him.

MRS. LINDE. And since then have you never told your secret to your husband?

NORA. Good Heavens, no! How could you think so? A man who has such strong
615 opinions about these things! And besides, how painful and humiliating it would be for Torvald, with his manly independence, to know that he owed me anything! It would upset our mutual relations alto-
620 gether; our beautiful happy home would no longer be what it is now.

MRS. LINDE. Do you mean never to tell him about it?

NORA (*meditatively, and with a half smile*).
625 Yes—someday, perhaps, after many years, when I am no longer as nice-looking as I am now. Don't laugh at me! I mean, of course, when Torvald is no longer as devoted to me as he is now; when my
630 dancing and dressing-up and reciting have palled on him; then it may be a good thing to have something in reserve— (*Breaking off.*) What nonsense! That time will never come. Now, what do you think
635 of my great secret, Christine? Do you still think I am of no use? I can tell you, too, that this affair has caused me a lot of worry. It has been by no means easy for me to meet my engagements punctually.
640 I may tell you that there is something that is called, in business, quarterly interest, and another thing called payment in installments, and it is always so dread-fully difficult to manage them. I have had
645 to save a little here and there, where I could, you understand. I have not been able to put aside much from my house-keeping money, for Torvald must have a good table. I couldn't let my children be
650 shabbily dressed; I have felt obliged to use up all he gave me for them, the sweet little darlings!

MRS. LINDE. So it has all had to come out of your own necessaries of life, poor
655 Nora?

NORA. Of course. Besides, I was the one responsible for it. Whenever Torvald has given me money for new dresses and such things, I have never spent more than half of it; I have always bought the simplest and cheapest things. Thank Heaven, any clothes look well on me, and so Torvald has never noticed it. But it was often very hard on me, Christine—because it is delightful to be really well dressed, isn't it?

MRS. LINDE. Quite so.

NORA. Well, then I have found other ways of earning money. Last winter I was lucky enough to get a lot of copying to do; so I locked myself up and sat writing every evening until quite late at night. Many a time I was desperately tired; but all the same it was a tremendous pleasure to sit there working and earning money. It was like being a man.

MRS. LINDE. How much have you been able to pay off in that way?

NORA. I can't tell you exactly. You see, it is very difficult to keep an account of a business matter of that kind. I only know that I have paid every penny that I could scrape together. Many a time I was at my wits' end. (*Smiles.*) Then I used to sit here and imagine that a rich old gentleman had fallen in love with me—

MRS. LINDE. What! Who was it?

NORA. Be quiet!—that he had died; and that when his will was opened it contained, written in big letters, the instruction: The lovely Mrs. Nora Helmer is to have all I possess paid over to her at once in cash.

MRS. LINDE. But, my dear Nora—who could the man be?

NORA. Good gracious, can't you understand? There was no old gentleman at all; it was only something that I used to sit here and imagine, when I couldn't think of any way of procuring money. But it's all the same now; the tiresome old person can stay where he is, as far as I am concerned; I don't care about him or his will either, for I am free from care now. (*Jumps up.*) My goodness, it's delightful to think of, Christine! Free from care! To be able to be free from care, quite free from care; to be able to play and romp with the children; to be able to keep the house beautifully and have everything just as Torvald likes it! And, think of it, soon the spring will come and the big blue sky! Perhaps we shall be able to take a little trip—perhaps I shall see the sea again! Oh, it's a wonderful thing to be alive and be happy. (*A bell is heard in the hall.*)

MRS. LINDE (*rising*). There is the bell; perhaps I had better go.

NORA. No, don't go; no one will come in here; it is sure to be for Torvald.

SERVANT (*at the hall door*). Excuse me, ma'am—there is a gentleman to see the master, and as the doctor is with him—

NORA. Who is it?

KROGSTAD (*at the door*). It is I, Mrs. Helmer. (MRS. LINDE *starts, trembles, and turns to the window.*)

NORA (*takes a step towards him, and speaks in a strained low voice*). You? What is it? What do you want to see my husband about?

KROGSTAD. Bank business—in a way. I have a small post in the Bank, and I hear your husband is to be our chief now—

NORA. Then it is—

KROGSTAD. Nothing but dry business matters, Mrs. Helmers; absolutely nothing else.

NORA. Be so good as to go into the study then. (*She bows indifferently to him and shuts the door into the hall; then comes back and makes up the fire in the stove.*)

MRS. LINDE. Nora—who was that man?

NORA. A lawyer, of the name of Krogstad.

MRS. LINDE. Then it really was he.

NORA. Do you know the man?

MRS. LINDE. I used to—many years ago. At
745 one time he was a solicitor's clerk in our
town.

NORA. Yes, he was.

MRS. LINDE. He is greatly altered.

NORA. He made a very unhappy marriage.

750 MRS. LINDE. He is a widower now, isn't he?

NORA. With several children. There now, it is
burning up. (*Shuts the door of the stove and
moves the rocking-chair aside.*)

MRS. LINDE. They say he carries on various
755 kinds of business.

NORA. Really! Perhaps he does; I don't know
anything about it. But don't let us think of
business; it is so tiresome.

DOCTOR RANK (*comes out of* HELMER'S *study.
760 Before he shuts the door he calls to him*). No,
my dear fellow, I won't disturb you; I
would rather go in to your wife for a little
while. (*Shuts the door and sees* MRS. LINDE.) I
beg your pardon; I am afraid I am disturb-
765 ing you too.

NORA. No, not at all. (*Introducing him.*) Doctor
Rank, Mrs. Linde.

RANK. I have often heard Mrs. Linde's name
mentioned here. I think I passed you on
770 the stairs when I arrived, Mrs. Linde?

MRS. LINDE. Yes, I go up very slowly; I can't
manage stairs well.

RANK. Ah! some slight internal weakness?

MRS. LINDE. No, the fact is I have been over-
775 working myself.

RANK. Nothing more than that? Then I
suppose you have come to town to amuse
yourself with our entertainments?

MRS. LINDE. I have come to look for work.

780 RANK. Is that a good cure for overwork?

MRS. LINDE. One must live, Doctor Rank.

RANK. Yes, the general opinion seems to be
that it is necessary.

NORA. Look here, Doctor Rank—you know
785 you want to live.

RANK. Certainly. However wretched I may
feel, I want to prolong the agony as long
as possible. All my patients are like that.
And so are those who are morally dis-
790 eased; one of them, and a bad case, too, is
at this very moment with Helmer—

MRS. LINDE (*sadly*). Ah!

NORA. Whom do you mean?

RANK. A lawyer of the name of Krogstad, a
795 fellow you don't know at all. He suffers
from a diseased moral character, Mrs.
Helmer; but even he began talking of its
being highly important that he should live.

NORA. Did he? What did he want to speak to
800 Torvald about?

RANK. I have no idea; I only heard that it
was something about the Bank.

NORA. I didn't know this—what's his
name—Krogstad had anything to do with
805 the Bank.

RANK. Yes, he has some sort of appointment
there. (*To* MRS. LINDE.) I don't know
whether you find also in your part of the
world that there are certain people who
810 go zealously snuffing about to smell out
moral corruption, and, as soon as they
have found some, put the person
concerned into some lucrative position
where they can keep their eye on him.
815 Healthy natures are left out in the cold.

MRS. LINDE. Still I think the sick are those
who most need taking care of.

RANK (*shrugging his shoulders*). Yes, there you
are. That is the sentiment that is turning
820 Society into a sick-house.

(NORA, *who has been absorbed in her thoughts,
breaks out into smothered laughter and claps
her hands.*)

RANK. Why do you laugh at that? Have you
825 any notion what Society really is?

NORA. What do I care about tiresome Society? I am laughing at something quite different, something extremely amusing. Tell me, Doctor Rank, are all the people who are employed in the Bank dependent on Torvald now?

RANK. Is that what you find so extremely amusing?

NORA (*smiling and humming*). That's my affair! (*Walking about the room.*) It's perfectly glorious to think that we have—that Torvald has so much power over so many people. (*Takes the packet from her pocket.*) Doctor Rank, what do you say to a macaroon?

RANK. What, macaroons? I thought they were forbidden here.

NORA. Yes, but these are some Christine gave me.

MRS. LINDE. What! I?—

NORA. Oh, well, don't be alarmed! You couldn't know that Torvald had forbidden them. I must tell you that he is afraid they will spoil my teeth. But, bah!—once in a way—That's so, isn't it, Doctor Rank? By your leave! (*Puts a macaroon into his mouth.*) You must have one too, Christine. And I shall have one, just a little one—or at most two. (*Walking about.*) I am tremendously happy. There is just one thing in the world now that I should dearly love to do.

RANK. Well, what is that?

NORA. It's something I should dearly love to say, if Torvald could hear me.

RANK. Well, why can't you say it?

NORA. No, I daren't; it's so shocking.

MRS. LINDE. Shocking?

RANK. Well, I should not advise you to say it. Still, with us you might. What is it you would so much like to say if Torvald could hear you?

NORA. I should just love to say—Well, I'm damned!

RANK. Are you mad?

MRS. LINDE. Nora, dear—!

RANK. Say it, here he is!

NORA (*hiding the packet*). Hush! Hush! Hush! (HELMER *comes out of his room, with his coat over his arm and his hat in his hand.*)

NORA. Well, Torvald dear, have you got rid of him?

HELMER. Yes, he has just gone.

NORA. Let me introduce you—this is Christine, who has come to town.

HELMER. Christine—? Excuse me, but I don't know—

NORA. Mrs. Linde, dear; Christine Linde.

HELMER. Of course. A school friend of my wife's, I presume?

MRS. LINDE. Yes, we have known each other since then.

NORA. And just think, she has taken a long journey in order to see you.

HELMER. What do you mean?

MRS. LINDE. No, really, I—

NORA. Christine is tremendously clever at book-keeping, and she is frightfully anxious to work under some clever man, so as to perfect herself—

HELMER. Very sensible, Mrs. Linde.

NORA. And when she heard you had been appointed manager of the Bank—the news was telegraphed, you know—she traveled here as quick as she could. Torvald, I am sure you will be able to do something for Christine, for my sake, won't you?

HELMER. Well, it is not altogether impossible. I presume you are a widow, Mrs. Linde?

MRS. LINDE. Yes.

HELMER. And have had some experience of book-keeping?

MRS. LINDE. Yes, a fair amount.

HELMER. Ah! well it's very likely I may be able to find something for you—

NORA (*clapping her hands*). What did I tell you? What did I tell you?

HELMER. You have just come at a fortunate
915 moment, Mrs. Linde.

MRS. LINDE. How am I to thank you?

HELMER. There is no need. (*Puts on his coat.*) But today you must excuse me—

RANK. Wait a minute; I will come with you.
920 (*Brings his fur coat from the hall and warms it at the fire.*)

NORA. Don't be long away, Torvald dear.

HELMER. About an hour, not more.

NORA. Are you going too, Christine?

925 MRS. LINDE (*putting on her cloak*). Yes, I must go and look for a room.

HELMER. Oh, well then, we can walk down the street together.

NORA (*helping her*). What a pity it is we are so
930 short of space here; I am afraid it is impossible for us—

MRS. LINDE. Please don't think of it! Goodbye, Nora dear, and many thanks.

NORA. Goodbye for the present. Of course
935 you will come back this evening. And you too, Dr. Rank. What do you say? If you are well enough? Oh, you must be! Wrap yourself up well. (*They go to the door all talking together. Children's voices are heard on the
940 staircase.*)

NORA. There they are. There they are! (*She runs to open the door. The* NURSE *comes in with the children.*) Come in! Come in! (*Stoops and kisses them.*) Oh, you sweet
945 blessings! Look at them, Christine! Aren't they darlings?

RANK. Don't let us stand here in the draught.

HELMER. Come along, Mrs. Linde; the place will only be bearable for a mother now!

950 (RANK, HELMER, *and* MRS. LINDE *go downstairs. The* NURSE *comes forward with the children;* NORA *shuts the hall door.*)

NORA. How fresh and well you look! Such red cheeks!—like apples and roses. (*The

955 children all talk at once while she speaks to them.*) Have you had great fun? That's splendid! What, you pulled both Emmy and Bob along on the sledge?—both at once?—that was good. You are a clever
960 boy, Ivar. Let me take her for a little, Anne. My sweet little baby doll! (*Takes the baby from the* MAID *and dances it up and down.*) Yes, yes, mother will dance with Bob too. What! Have you been
965 snowballing? I wish I had been there too! No, no, I will take their things off, Anne; please let me do it, it is such fun. Go in now, you look half frozen. There is some hot coffee for you on the stove.

970 (*The* NURSE *goes into the room on the left. Nora takes off the children's things and throws them about, while they all talk to her at once.*)

NORA. Really! Did a big dog run after you?
975 But it didn't bite you? No, dogs don't bite nice little dolly children. You mustn't look at the parcels, Ivar. What are they? Ah, I daresay you would like to know. No, no—it's something nasty! Come, let us
980 have a game. What shall we play at? Hide and Seek? Yes, we'll play Hide and Seek. Bob shall hide first. Must I hide? Very well, I'll hide first. (*She and the children laugh and shout, and romp in and
985 out of the room; at last Nora hides under the table, the children rush in and look for her, but do not see her; they hear her smothered laughter run to the table, lift up the cloth and find her. Shouts of laughter.
990 She crawls forward and pretends to frighten them. Fresh laughter. Meanwhile there has been a knock at the hall door, but none of them has noticed it. The door is half opened, and* KROGSTAD
995 *appears. He waits a little; the game goes on.*)

KROGSTAD. Excuse me, Mrs. Helmer.

NORA (*with a stifled cry, turns round and gets up on to her knees*). Ah! what do you
1000 want?

KROGSTAD. Excuse me, the outer door was ajar; I suppose someone forgot to shut it.

NORA (*rising*). My husband is out, Mr. Krogstad.

1005 **KROGSTAD.** I know that.

NORA. What do you want here, then?

KROGSTAD. A word with you.

NORA. With me?—(*To the children, gently.*) Go in to nurse. What? No, the strange man
1010 won't do mother any harm. When he has gone we will have another game. (*She takes the children into the room on the left, and shuts the door after them.*) You want to speak to me?

1015 **KROGSTAD.** Yes, I do.

NORA. Today? It is not the first of the month yet.

KROGSTAD. No, it is Christmas Eve, and it will depend on yourself what sort of a
1020 Christmas you will spend.

NORA. What do you want? Today it is absolutely impossible for me—

KROGSTAD. We won't talk about that till later on. This is something different. I presume
1025 you can give me a moment?

NORA. Yes—yes, I can—although—

KROGSTAD. Good. I was in Olsen's Restaurant and saw your husband going down the street—

1030 **NORA.** Yes?

KROGSTAD. With a lady.

NORA. What then?

KROGSTAD. May I make so bold as to ask if it was a Mrs. Linde?

1035 **NORA.** It was.

KROGSTAD. Just arrived in town?

NORA. Yes, today.

KROGSTAD. She is a great friend of yours, isn't she?

1040 **NORA.** She is. But I don't see—

KROGSTAD. I knew her too, once upon a time.

NORA. I am aware of that.

KROGSTAD. Are you? So you know all about it; I thought as much. Then I can ask you, without beating about the bush—is Mrs.
1045 Linde to have an appointment in the Bank?

NORA. What right have you to question me, Mr. Krogstad?—You, one of my husband's subordinates! But since you
1050 ask, you shall know. Yes, Mrs. Linde is to have an appointment. And it was I who pleaded her cause, Mr. Krogstad, let me tell you that.

KROGSTAD. I was right in what I thought, then.

1055 **NORA** (*walking up and down the stage*). Sometimes one has a tiny little bit of influence, I should hope. Because one is a woman, it does not necessarily follow that—. When anyone is in a subordinate
1060 position, Mr. Krogstad, they should really be careful to avoid offending anyone who—who—

KROGSTAD. Who has influence?

NORA. Exactly.

1065 **KROGSTAD** (*changing his tone*). Mrs. Helmer, you will be so good as to use your influence on my behalf.

NORA. What? What do you mean?

KROGSTAD. You will be so kind as to see that
1070 I am allowed to keep my subordinate position in the Bank.

NORA. What do you mean by that? Who proposes to take your post away from you?

KROGSTAD. Oh, there is no necessity to keep
1075 up the pretence of ignorance. I can quite understand that your friend is not very anxious to expose herself to the chance of rubbing shoulders with me; and I quite understand, too, whom I have to thank for
1080 being turned off.

NORA. But I assure you—

KROGSTAD. Very likely; but, to come to the point, the time has come when I should advise you to use your influence to
1085 prevent that.

NORA. But, Mr. Krogstad, I have no influence.

KROGSTAD. Haven't you? I thought you said yourself just now—

NORA. Naturally I did not mean you to put
1090 that construction on it. I! What should make you think I have any influence of that kind with my husband?

KROGSTAD. Oh, I have known your husband from our student days. I don't suppose he
1095 is any more unassailable than other husbands.

NORA. If you speak slightly of my husband, I shall turn you out of the house.

KROGSTAD. You are bold, Mrs. Helmer.

1100 **NORA.** I am not afraid of you any longer. As soon as the New Year comes, I shall in a very short time be free of the whole thing.

KROGSTAD (*controlling himself*). Listen to me, Mrs. Helmer. If necessary, I am pre-
1105 pared to fight for my small post in the Bank as if I were fighting for my life.

NORA. So it seems.

KROGSTAD. It is not only for the sake of the money; indeed, that weighs least with me
1110 in the matter. There is another reason— well, I may as well tell you. My position is this. I daresay you know, like everybody else, that once, many years ago, I was guilty of an indiscretion.

1115 **NORA.** I think I have heard something of the kind.

KROGSTAD. The matter never came into court; but every way seemed to be closed to me after that. So I took to the business
1120 that you know of. I had to do something; and, honestly, don't think I've been one of the worst. But now I must cut myself free from all that. My sons are growing up; for their sake I must try and win back
1125 as much respect as I can in the town. This post in the Bank was like the first step up for me—and now your husband is going to kick me downstairs again into the mud.

1130 **NORA.** But you must believe me, Mr. Krogstad; it is not in my power to help you at all.

KROGSTAD. Then it is because you haven't the will; but I have means to compel you.

NORA. You don't mean that you will tell my
1135 husband that I owe you money?

KROGSTAD. Hm!—suppose I were to tell him?

NORA. It would be perfectly infamous of you. (*Sobbing.*) To think of his learning my secret, which has been my joy and pride,
1140 in such an ugly, clumsy way—that he should learn it from you! And it would put me in a horribly disagreeable position—

KROGSTAD. Only disagreeable?

NORA (*impetuously*). Well, do it, then!—and
1145 it will be the worse for you. My husband will see for himself what a blackguard you are, and you certainly won't keep your post then.

KROGSTAD. I asked you if it was only a
1150 disagreeable scene at home that you were afraid of?

NORA. If my husband does get to know of it, of course he will at once pay you what is still owing, and we shall have nothing
1155 more to do with you.

KROGSTAD (*coming a step nearer*). Listen to me, Mrs. Helmer. Either you have a very bad memory or you know very little of busi- ness. I shall be obliged to remind you of a
1160 few details.

NORA. What do you mean?

KROGSTAD. When your husband was ill, you came to me to borrow two hundred and fifty pounds.

1165 **NORA.** I didn't know anyone else to go to.

KROGSTAD. I promised to get you that amount—

NORA. Yes, and you did so.

KROGSTAD. I promised to get you that
1170 amount, on certain conditions. Your mind was so taken up with your husband's illness, and you were so anxious to get the money for your journey, that you seem to have paid no attention to the conditions
1175 of our bargain. Therefore it will not be amiss if I remind you of them. Now, I promised to get the money on the security of a bond which I drew up.

NORA. Yes, and which I signed.

1180 **KROGSTAD.** Good. But below your signature there were a few lines constituting your father a surety for the money; those lines your father should have signed.

NORA. Should? He did sign them.

1185 **KROGSTAD.** I had left the date blank; that is to say your father should himself have inserted the date on which he signed the paper. Do you remember that?

NORA. Yes, I think I remember—

1190 **KROGSTAD.** Then I gave you the bond to send by post to your father. Is that not so?

NORA. Yes.

KROGSTAD. And you naturally did so at once, because five or six days afterwards you
1195 brought me the bond with your father's signature. And then I gave you the money.

NORA. Well, haven't I been paying it off regularly?

KROGSTAD. Fairly so, yes. But—to come back to
1200 the matter in hand—that must have been a very trying time for you, Mrs. Helmer?

NORA. It was, indeed.

KROGSTAD. Your father was very ill, wasn't he?

NORA. He was very near his end.

1205 **KROGSTAD.** And died soon afterwards?

NORA. Yes.

KROGSTAD. Tell me, Mrs. Helmer, can you by any chance remember what day your father died?—on what day of the month,
1210 I mean.

NORA. Papa died on the 29th of September.

KROGSTAD. That is correct; I have ascertained it for myself. And, as that is so, there is a discrepancy (*taking a paper from his pocket*)
1215 which I cannot account for.

NORA. What discrepancy? I don't know—

KROGSTAD. The discrepancy consists, Mrs. Helmer, in the fact that your father signed this bond three days after his death.

1220 **NORA.** What do you mean? I don't understand—

KROGSTAD. Your father died on the 29th of September. But, look here; your father dated his signature the 2nd of October. It is
1225 a discrepancy, isn't it? (**NORA** *is silent.*) Can you explain it to me? (**NORA** *is still silent.*) It is a remarkable thing, too, that the words 2nd of October, as well as the year, are not written in your father's handwriting but in
1230 one that I think I know. Well, of course it can be explained; your father may have forgotten to date his signature, and someone else may have dated it haphazard before they knew of his death. There is no
1235 harm in that. It all depends on the signature of the name; and that is genuine, I suppose, Mrs. Helmer? It was your father himself who signed his name here?

NORA (*after a short pause, throws her head up*
1240 *and looks defiantly at him*). No, it was not. It was I that wrote papa's name.

KROGSTAD. Are you aware that is a dangerous confession?

NORA. In what way? You shall have your
1245 money soon.

KROGSTAD. Let me ask you a question; why did you not send the paper to your father?

NORA. It was impossible; papa was so ill. If I had asked him for his signature, I should
1250 have had to tell him what the money was to be used for; and when he was so ill

himself I couldn't tell him that my husband's life was in danger—it was impossible.

1255 **KROGSTAD.** It would have been better for you if you had given up your trip abroad.

NORA. No, that was impossible. That trip was to save my husband's life; I couldn't give that up.

1260 **KROGSTAD.** But did it never occur to you that you were committing a fraud on me?

NORA. I couldn't take that into account; I didn't trouble myself about you at all. I couldn't bear you, because you put so 1265 many heartless difficulties in my way, although you knew what a dangerous condition my husband was in.

KROGSTAD. Mrs. Helmer, you evidently do not realise clearly what it is that you have 1270 been guilty of. But I can assure you that my one false step, which lost me all my reputation, was nothing more or nothing worse than what you have done.

NORA. You? Do you ask me to believe that 1275 you were brave enough to run a risk to save your wife's life.

KROGSTAD. The law cares nothing about motives.

NORA. Then it must be a very foolish law.

1280 **KROGSTAD.** Foolish or not, it is the law by which you will be judged, if I produce this paper in court.

NORA. I don't believe it. Is a daughter not to be allowed to spare her dying father 1285 anxiety and care? Is a wife not to be allowed to save her husband's life? I don't know much about law; but I am certain that there must be laws permitting such things as that. Have you no knowledge of 1290 such laws—you who are a lawyer? You must be a very poor lawyer, Mr. Krogstad.

KROGSTAD. Maybe. But matters of business— such business as you and I have had

together—do you think I don't under-1295 stand that? Very well. Do as you please. But let me tell you this—if I lose my position a second time, you shall lose yours with me. (*He bows, and goes out through the hall.*)

1300 **NORA** (*appears buried in thought for a short time, then tosses her head*). Nonsense! Trying to frighten me like that!—I am not so silly as he thinks. (*Begins to busy herself putting the children's things in order.*) 1305 And yet—? No, it's impossible! I did it for love's sake.

THE CHILDREN (*in the doorway on the left*). Mother, the stranger man has gone out through the gate.

1310 **NORA.** Yes, dears, I know. But, don't tell anyone about the stranger man. Do you hear? Not even papa.

CHILDREN. No, mother; but will you come and play again?

1315 **NORA.** No no,—not now.

CHILDREN. But, mother, you promised us.

NORA. Yes, but I can't now. Run away in; I have such a lot to do. Run away in, sweet little darlings. (*She gets them into the room by* 1320 *degrees and shuts the door on them; then sits down on the sofa, takes up a piece of needlework and sews a few stitches, but soon stops.*) No! (*Throws down the work, gets up, goes to the hall door and calls out.*) Helen, 1325 bring the Tree in. (*Goes to the table on the left, opens a drawer, and stops again.*) No, no! it is quite impossible!

MAID (*coming in with the Tree*). Where shall I put it, ma'am?

1330 **NORA.** Here, in the middle of the floor.

MAID. Shall I get you anything else?

NORA. No, thank you. I have all I want.

[Exit **MAID.**]

NORA (*begins dressing the tree*). A candle 1335 here—and flowers here—The horrible man! It's all nonsense—there's nothing wrong. The Tree shall be splendid! I will do everything I can think of to please you, Torvald!—I will sing for you, dance for

1340 you—(HELMER *comes in with some papers under his arm.*) Oh! are you back already?

HELMER. Yes. Has anyone been here?

NORA. Here? No.

HELMER. That is strange. I saw Krogstad

1345 going out of the gate.

NORA. Did you? Oh yes, I forgot Krogstad was here for a moment.

HELMER. Nora, I can see from your manner that he has been here begging you to say a

1350 good word for him.

NORA. Yes.

HELMER. And you were to appear to do it of your own accord; you were to conceal from me the fact of his having been here;

1355 didn't he beg that of you too?

NORA. Yes, Torvald, but—

HELMER. Nora, Nora, and you would be a party to that sort of thing? To have any talk with a man like that, and give him

1360 any sort of promise? And to tell me a lie into the bargain?

NORA. A lie—?

HELMER. Didn't you tell me no one had been here? (*Shakes his finger at her.*) My little

1365 songbird must never do that again. A song-bird must have a clean beak to chirp with—no false notes! (*Puts his arm round her waist.*) That is so, isn't it? Yes, I am sure it is. (*Lets her go.*) We will say no more about

1370 it. (*Sits down by the stove.*) How warm and snug it is here! (*Turns over his papers.*)

NORA (*after a short pause, during which she busies herself with the Christmas Tree*). Torvald!

1375 HELMER. Yes.

NORA. I am looking forward tremendously to the fancy-dress ball at the Stensborgs' the day after tomorrow.

HELMER. And I am tremendously curious

1380 to see what you are going to surprise me with.

NORA. It was very silly of me to want to do that.

HELMER. What do you mean?

1385 NORA. I can't hit upon anything that will do; everything I think of seems so silly and insignificant.

HELMER. Does my little Nora acknowledge that at last?

1390 NORA (*standing behind his chair with her arms on the back of it*). Are you very busy, Torvald?

HELMER. Well—

NORA. What are all those papers?

1395 HELMER. Bank business.

NORA. Already?

HELMER. I have got authority from the retir-ing manager to undertake the necessary changes in the staff and in the rearrange-

1400 ment of the work; and I must make use of the Christmas week for that, so as to have everything in order for the new year.

NORA. Then that was why this poor Krogstad—

1405 HELMER. Hm!

NORA (*leans against the back of his chair and strokes his hair*). If you hadn't been so busy I should have asked you a tremen-dously big favour, Torvald.

1410 HELMER. What is that? Tell me.

NORA. There is no one has such good taste as you. And I do so want to look nice at the fancy-dress ball. Torvald, couldn't you take me in hand and decide what I shall

1415 go as, and what sort of a dress I shall wear?

HELMER. Aha! so my obstinate little woman is obliged to get someone to come to her rescue?

1420 NORA. Yes, Torvald, I can't get along a bit without your help.

HELMER. Very well, I will think it over, we shall manage to hit upon something.

NORA. That is nice of you. (*Goes to the Christmas Tree. A short pause.*) How pretty the red flowers look—. But, tell me, was it really something very bad that this Krogstad was guilty of?

HELMER. He forged someone's name. Have you any idea what that means?

NORA. Isn't it possible that he was driven to do it by necessity?

HELMER. Yes; or, as in so many cases, by imprudence. I am not so heartless as to condemn a man altogether because of a single false step of that kind.

NORA. No you wouldn't, would you, Torvald?

HELMER. Many a man has been able to retrieve his character, if he has openly confessed his fault and taken his punishment.

NORA. Punishment—?

HELMER. But Krogstad did nothing of that sort; he got himself out of it by a cunning trick, and that is why he has gone under altogether.

NORA. But do you think it would—?

HELMER. Just think how a guilty man like that has to lie and play the hypocrite with everyone, how he has to wear a mask in the presence of those near and dear to him, even before his own wife and children. And about the children—that is the most terrible part of it all, Nora.

NORA. How?

HELMER. Because such an atmosphere of lies infects and poisons the whole life of a home. Each breath the children take in such a house is full of the germs of evil.

NORA (*coming nearer him*). Are you sure of that?

HELMER. My dear, I have often seen it in the course of my life as a lawyer. Almost everyone who has gone to the bad early in life has had a deceitful mother.

NORA. Why do you only say—mother?

HELMER. It seems most commonly to be the mother's influence, though naturally a bad father's would have the same result. Every lawyer is familiar with the fact. This Krogstad, now, has been persistently poisoning his own children with lies and dissimulation; that is why I say he has lost all moral character. (*Holds out his hands to her.*) That is why my sweet little Nora must promise me not to plead his cause. Give me your hand on it. Come, come, what is this? Give me your hand. There now, that's settled. I assure you it would be quite impossible for me to work with him; I literally feel physically ill when I am in the company of such people.

NORA (*takes her hand out of his and goes to the opposite side of the Christmas Tree*). How hot it is in here; and I have such a lot to do.

HELMER (*getting up and putting his papers in order*). Yes, and I must try and read through some of these before dinner; and I must think about your costume, too. And it is just possible I may have something ready in gold paper to hang up on the Tree. (*Puts his hand on her head.*) My precious little singing-bird! (*He goes into his room and shuts the door after him.*)

NORA (*after a pause, whispers*). No, no—it isn't true. It's impossible; it must be impossible.

(*The* **NURSE** *opens the door on the left.*)

NURSE. The little ones are begging so hard to be allowed to come in to mamma.

NORA. No, no, no! Don't let them come in to me! You stay with them, Anne.

NURSE. Very well, ma'am. (*Shuts the door.*)

NORA (*pale with terror*). Deprave my little children? Poison my home? (*A short pause. Then she tosses her head.*) It's not true. It can't possibly be true.

Victorian Dollhouse (colour photo)/./DEREK BAYES ARCHIVE/ Bridgeman Images

The image depicts a Victorian doll's house.

▶

As you examine the image, pay attention to the details in the doll's house. How could this doll's house be a metaphor for Nora's home? Why do you think Ibsen titled the play *A Doll's House*?

CHARACTER

1. What words, phrases, and details contribute to the **characterization** of Nora?
2. What words, phrases, and details contribute to the **characterization** of Torvald?
3. How would you characterize the Helmers' marriage? How do the word choice and details reveal the emotional and psychological state of their marriage?
4. How do Nora's interactions with Torvald reveal her **motivation**? What is that motivation?

SETTING

5. Think about the play's **setting**, especially the location and the season. How do these elements affect the rising action?
6. What does the play reveal about gender roles during the time it was set?

STRUCTURE

7. How do the events of Act I affect the development of the **conflict** between Nora and Helmer?
8. Choose a contrast between characters in Act I and explain how that **contrast** reveals the values of each character.
9. How does Nora's forgery cause or affect another event?

IDEAS IN LITERATURE: Power and Control

10. There are many male-female interactions in Act I. Identify the power and control that is present in all of these exchanges. How do individuals resist when someone establishes power over them? Explain.

ACT II

(THE SAME SCENE—*The Christmas Tree is in the corner by the piano, stripped of its ornaments and with burnt-down candle-ends on its dishevelled branches.* NORA'S *cloak and hat are lying on the sofa. She is alone in the room, walking about uneasily. She stops by the sofa and takes up her cloak.*)

NORA (*drops the cloak*).   Someone is coming now! (*Goes to the door and listens.*) No—it is no one. Of course, no one will come today, Christmas Day—nor tomorrow
5   either. But, perhaps—(*opens the door and looks out.*) No, nothing in the letter-box; it is quite empty. (*Comes forward.*) What rubbish! of course he can't be in earnest about it. Such a thing couldn't happen;
10   it is impossible—I have three little children.

(*Enter the* NURSE *from the room on the left, carrying a big cardboard box.*)

NURSE.   At last I have found the box with the
15   fancy dress.

NORA.   Thanks; put it on the table.

NURSE (*doing so*).   But it is very much in want of mending.

NORA.   I should like to tear it into a hundred
20   thousand pieces.

NURSE.   What an idea! It can easily be put in order—just a little patience.

NORA.   Yes, I will go and get Mrs. Linde to come and help me with it.

25 NURSE.   What, out again? In this horrible weather? You will catch cold, ma'am, and make yourself ill.

NORA.   Well, worse than that might happen. How are the children?

30 NURSE.   The poor little souls are playing with their Christmas presents, but—

NORA.   Do they ask much for me?

NURSE.   You see, they are so accustomed to have their mamma with them.

35 NORA.   Yes, but, nurse, I shall not be able to be so much with them now as I was before.

NURSE.   Oh well, young children easily get accustomed to anything.

NORA.   Do you think so? Do you think they
40   would forget their mother if she went away altogether?

NURSE.   Good heavens!—went away altogether?

NORA.   Nurse, I want you to tell me something I have often wondered about—how
45   could you have the heart to put your own child out among strangers?

NURSE.   I was obliged to, if I wanted to be little Nora's nurse.

NORA.   Yes, but how could you be willing to
50   do it?

NURSE.   What, when I was going to get such a good place by it? A poor girl who has got into trouble should be glad to. Besides, that wicked man didn't do a single thing for me.

55 NORA.   But I suppose your daughter has quite forgotten you.

NURSE.   No, indeed she hasn't. She wrote to me when she was confirmed, and when she was married.

60 NORA (*putting her arms round her neck*). Dear old Anne, you were a good mother to me when I was little.

NURSE.   Little Nora, poor dear, had no other mother but me.

65 NORA.   And if my little ones had no other mother, I am sure you would—What nonsense I am talking! (*Opens the box.*) Go in to them. Now I must—. You will see tomorrow how charming I shall look.

70 NURSE.   I am sure there will be no one at the ball so charming as you, ma'am. (*Goes into the room on the left.*)

NORA (*begins to unpack the box, but soon pushes it away from her*). If only I dared
75 go out. If only no one would come. If only I could be sure nothing would happen here in the meantime. Stuff and non-sense! No one will come. Only I mustn't think about it. I will brush my muff.
80 What lovely, lovely gloves! Out of my thoughts, out of my thoughts! One, two, three, four, five, six—(*Screams.*) Ah! there is someone coming—. (*Makes a movement towards the door, but stands
85 irresolute.*)
(*Enter* MRS. LINDE *from the hall, where she has taken off her cloak and hat.*)
NORA. Oh, it's you, Christine. There is no one else out there, is there? How good of you
90 to come!
MRS. LINDE. I heard you were up asking for me.
NORA. Yes, I was passing by. As a matter of fact, it is something you could help me
95 with. Let us sit down here on the sofa. Look here. Tomorrow evening there is to be a fancy-dress ball at the Stenborgs', who live above us; and Torvald wants me to go as a Neapolitan fisher-girl, and
100 dance the Tarantella that I learnt at Capri.
MRS. LINDE. I see; you are going to keep up the character.
NORA. Yes, Torvald wants me to. Look, here is the dress; Torvald had it made for me
105 there, but now it is all so torn, and I haven't any idea—
MRS. LINDE. We will easily put that right. It is only some of the trimming come unsewn here and there. Needle and thread? Now
110 then, that's all we want.
NORA. It is nice of you.
MRS. LINDE (*sewing*). So you are going to be dressed up tomorrow, Nora. I will tell you what—I shall come in for a moment and
115 see you in your fine feathers. But I have

completely forgotten to thank you for a delightful evening yesterday.
NORA (*gets up, and crosses the stage*). Well I don't think yesterday was as pleasant as
120 usual. You ought to have come to town a little earlier, Christine. Certainly Torvald does understand how to make a house dainty and attractive.
MRS. LINDE. And so do you, it seems to me;
125 you are not your father's daughter for nothing. But tell me, is Doctor Rank always as depressed as he was yesterday?
NORA. No; yesterday it was very noticeable. I must tell you that he suffers from a very
130 dangerous disease. He has consumption of the spine, poor creature. His father was a horrible man who committed all sorts of excesses; and that is why his son was sickly from childhood, do you
135 understand?
MRS. LINDE (*dropping her sewing*). But, my dearest Nora, how do you know anything about such things?
NORA (*walking about*). Pooh! When you have
140 three children, you get visits now and then from—from married women, who know something of medical matters, and they talk about one thing and another.
MRS. LINDE (*goes on sewing. A short silence*).
145 Does Doctor Rank come here every day?
NORA. Every day regularly. He is Torvald's most intimate friend, and a great friend of mine too. He is just like one of the family.
MRS. LINDE. But tell me this—is he perfectly
150 sincere? I mean, isn't he the kind of a man that is very anxious to make himself agreeable?
NORA. Not in the least. What makes you think that?
155 MRS. LINDE. When you introduced him to me yesterday, he declared he had often heard my name mentioned in this house; but afterwards I noticed that your husband

160 hadn't the slightest idea who I was. So how could Doctor Rank—?

NORA. That is quite right, Christine. Torvald is so absurdly fond of me that he wants me absolutely to himself, as he says. At first he used to seem almost jealous if I mentioned
165 any of the dear folk at home, so naturally I gave up doing so. But I often talk about such things with Doctor Rank, because he likes hearing about them.

MRS. LINDE. Listen to me, Nora. You are still
170 very like a child in many ways, and I am older than you in many ways and have a little more experience. Let me tell you this—you ought to make an end of it with Doctor Rank.

175 NORA. What ought I to make an end of?

MRS. LINDE. Of two things, I think. Yesterday you talked some nonsense about a rich admirer who was to leave you money—

NORA. An admirer who doesn't exist, unfor-
180 tunately! But what then?

MRS. LINDE. Is Doctor Rank a man of means?

NORA. Yes, he is.

MRS. LINDE. And has no one to provide for?

NORA. No, no one; but—

185 MRS. LINDE. And comes here every day?

NORA. Yes, I told you so.

MRS. LINDE. But how can this well-bred man be so tactless?

NORA. I don't understand you at all.

190 MRS. LINDE. Don't prevaricate, Nora. Do you suppose I don't guess who lent you the two hundred and fifty pounds.

NORA. Are you out of your senses? How can you think of such a thing! A friend of ours,
195 who comes here every day! Do you realise what a horribly painful position that would be?

MRS. LINDE. Then it really isn't he?

NORA. No, certainly not. It would never have
200 entered into my head for a moment.

Besides, he had no money to lend then; he came into his money afterwards.

MRS. LINDE. Well, I think that was lucky for you, my dear Nora.

205 NORA. No, it would never have come into my head to ask Doctor Rank. Although I am quite sure that if I had asked him—

MRS. LINDE. But of course you won't.

NORA. Of course not. I have no reason to
210 think it could possibly be necessary. But I am quite sure that if I told Doctor Rank—

MRS. LINDE. Behind your husband's back?

NORA. I must make an end of it with the other one, and that will be behind
215 his back too. I must make an end of it with him.

MRS. LINDE. Yes, that is what I told you yesterday, but—

NORA (walking up and down). A man can put
220 a thing like that straight much easier than a woman—

MRS. LINDE. One's husband, yes.

NORA. Nonsense! (Standing still.) When you pay off a debt you get your bond back,
225 don't you?

MRS. LINDE. Yes, as a matter of course.

NORA. And can tear it into a hundred thousand pieces, and burn it up—the nasty, dirty paper!

230 MRS. LINDE (looks hard at her, lays down her sewing and gets up slowly). Nora, you are concealing something from me.

NORA. Do I look as if I were?

MRS. LINDE. Something has happened to
235 you since yesterday morning. Nora, what is it?

NORA (going nearer to her). Christine! (Listens.) Hush! there's Torvald come home. Do you mind going in to the
240 children for the present? Torvald can't bear to see dressmaking going on. Let Anne help you.

MRS. LINDE (*gathering some of the things together*).   Certainly—but I am not going
245 away from here till we have had it out with one another. (*She goes into the room, on the left, as Helmer comes in from, the hall.*)

NORA (*going up to* HELMAR).   I have wanted
250 you so much, Torvald dear.

HELMER.   Was that the dressmaker?

NORA.   No, it was Christine; she is helping me to put my dress in order. You will see I shall look quite smart.

255 HELMER.   Wasn't that a happy thought of mine, now?

NORA.   Splendid! But don't you think it is nice of me, too, to do as you wish?

HELMER.   Nice?—because you do as your
260 husband wishes? Well, well, you little rogue, I am sure you did not mean it in that way. But I am not going to disturb you; you will want to be trying on your dress, I expect.

265 NORA.   I suppose you are going to work.

HELMER.   Yes. (*Shows her a bundle of papers.*) Look at that. I have just been into the bank. (*Turns to go into his room.*)

NORA.   Torvald.

270 HELMER.   Yes.

NORA.   If your little squirrel were to ask you for something very, very prettily—?

HELMER.   What then?

NORA.   Would you do it?

275 HELMER.   I should like to hear what it is, first.

NORA.   Your squirrel would run about and do all her tricks if you would be nice, and do what she wants.

HELMER.   Speak plainly.

280 NORA.   Your skylark would chirp about in every room, with her song rising and falling—

HELMER.   Well, my skylark does that anyhow.

NORA.   I would play the fairy and dance for you in the moonlight, Torvald.

285 HELMER.   Nora—you surely don't mean that request you made of me this morning?

NORA (*going near him*).   Yes, Torvald, I beg you so earnestly—

HELMER.   Have you really the courage to open
290 up that question again?

NORA.   Yes, dear, you must do as I ask; you must let Krogstad keep his post in the bank.

HELMER.   My dear Nora, it is his post that I
295 have arranged Mrs. Linde shall have.

NORA.   Yes, you have been awfully kind about that; but you could just as well dismiss some other clerk instead of Krogstad.

HELMER.   This is simply incredible obstinacy!
300 Because you chose to give him a thought-less promise that you would speak for him, I am expected to—

NORA.   That isn't the reason, Torvald. It is for your own sake. This fellow writes in the
305 most scurrilous newspapers; you have told me so yourself. He can do you an unspeakable amount of harm. I am frightened to death of him—

HELMER.   Ah, I understand; it is recollections
310 of the past that scare you.

NORA.   What do you mean?

HELMER.   Naturally you are thinking of your father.

NORA.   Yes—yes, of course. Just recall to
315 your mind what these malicious crea-tures wrote in the papers about papa, and how horribly they slandered him. I believe they would have procured his dismissal if the Department had not sent
320 you over to inquire into it, and if you had not been so kindly disposed and helpful to him.

HELMER.   My little Nora, there is an impor-tant difference between your father and
325 me. Your father's reputation as a public official was not above suspicion. Mine is,

and I hope it will continue to be so, as long as I hold my office.

NORA. You never can tell what mischief these men may contrive. We ought to be so well off, so snug and happy here in our peaceful home, and have no cares—you and I and the children, Torvald! That is why I beg you so earnestly—

HELMER. And it is just by interceding for him that you make it impossible for me to keep him. It is already known at the Bank that I mean to dismiss Krogstad. Is it to get about now that the new manager has changed his mind at his wife's bidding—

NORA. And what if it did?

HELMER. Of course!—if only this obstinate little person can get her way! Do you suppose I am going to make myself ridiculous before my whole staff, to let people think that I am a man to be swayed by all sorts of outside influence? I should very soon feel the consequences of it, I can tell you. And besides, there is one thing that makes it quite impossible for me to have Krogstad in the bank as long as I am manager.

NORA. Whatever is that?

HELMER. His moral failings I might perhaps have overlooked, if necessary—

NORA. Yes, you could—couldn't you?

HELMER. And, I hear he is a good worker, too. But I knew him when we were boys. It was one of those rash friendships that so often prove an incubus in afterlife. I may as well tell you plainly, we were once on very intimate terms with one another. But this tactless fellow lays no restraint upon himself when other people are present. On the contrary, he thinks it gives him the right to adopt a familiar tone with me, and every minute it is I say, Helmer, old fellow! and that sort of thing. I assure you

it is extremely painful to me. He would make my position in the bank intolerable.

NORA. Torvald, I don't believe you mean that.

HELMER. Don't you? Why not?

NORA. Because it is such a narrow-minded way of looking at things.

HELMER. What are you saying? Narrow-minded? Do you think I am narrow-minded?

NORA. No, just the opposite, dear—and it is exactly for that reason.

HELMER. It's the same thing. You say my point of view is narrow-minded, so I must be so, too. Narrow-minded! Very well—I must put an end to this. (*Goes to the hall door and calls.*) Helen!

NORA. What are you going to do?

HELMER (*looking among his papers*). Settle it. (*Enter* MAID.) Look here; take this letter and go downstairs with it at once. Find a messenger and tell him to deliver it, and be quick. The address is on it, and here is the money.

MAID. Very well, sir. (*Exit with the letter.*)

HELMER (*putting his papers together*). Now, then, little Miss Obstinate.

NORA (*breathlessly*). Torvald—what was that letter?

HELMER. Krogstad's dismissal.

NORA. Call her back, Torvald! There is still time. Oh Torvald, call her back! Do it for my sake—for your own sake, for the children's sake! Do you hear me, Torvald? Call her back! You don't know what that letter can bring upon us.

HELMER. It's too late.

NORA. Yes, it's too late.

HELMER. My dear Nora, I can forgive the anxiety you are in, although really it is an insult to me. It is, indeed. Isn't it an insult to think that I should be afraid of a

starving quill-driver's vengeance? But I
forgive you, nevertheless, because it is
such eloquent witness to your great love
for me. (*Takes her in his arms.*) And that is
415 as it should be, my own darling Nora.
Come what will, you may be sure I shall
have both courage and strength if they be
needed. You will see I am man enough to
take everything upon myself.

420 NORA (*in a horror-stricken voice*). What do you
mean by that?

HELMER.   Everything I say—

NORA (*recovering herself*).   You will never have
to do that.

425 HELMER.   That's right. Well, we will share it,
Nora, as man and wife should. That is
how it shall be. (*Caressing her.*) Are you
content now? There! There!—not these
frightened dove's eyes! The whole thing
430 is only the wildest fancy!—Now, you
must go and play through the Tarantella
and practice with your tambourine.
I shall go into the inner office and shut
the door, and I shall hear nothing; you
435 can make as much noise as you please.
(*Turns back at the door.*) And when
Rank comes, tell him where he will
find me. (*Nods to her, takes his papers
and goes into his room, and shuts the door
440 after him.*)

NORA (*bewildered with anxiety, stands as if
rooted to the spot, and whispers*).   He was
capable of doing it. He will do it. He will
do it in spite of everything.—No, not
445 that! Never, never! Anything rather
than that! Oh, for some help, some
way out of it. (*The door-bell rings.*) Doctor
Rank! Anything rather than that—
anything, whatever it is! (*She puts her
450 hands over her face, pulls herself together,
goes to the door and opens it.* RANK *is
standing without, hanging up his coat.*

*During the following dialogue it begins to
grow dark.*)

455 NORA. Good day, Doctor Rank. I knew your
ring. But you mustn't go into Torvald now;
I think he is busy with something.

RANK.   And you?

NORA (*brings him in and shuts the door after
460 him*).   Oh, you know very well I always
have time for you.

RANK.   Thank you. I shall make use of as
much of it as I can.

NORA.   What do you mean by that? As much
465 of it as you can.

RANK.   Well, does that alarm you?

NORA.   It was such a strange way of putting
it. Is anything likely to happen?

RANK.   Nothing but what I have long been
470 prepared for. But I certainly didn't expect
it to happen so soon.

NORA (*gripping him by the arm*).   What have
you found out? Doctor Rank, you must
tell me.

475 RANK (*sitting down by the stove*).   It is all up
with me. And it can't be helped.

NORA (*with a sigh of relief*).   Is it about
yourself?

RANK.   Who else? It is no use lying to one's
480 self. I am the most wretched of all my
patients, Mrs. Helmer. Lately I have been
taking stock of my internal economy.
Bankrupt! Probably within a month I
shall lie rotting in the church-yard.

485 NORA.   What an ugly thing to say!

RANK.   The thing itself is cursedly ugly, and
the worst of it is that I shall have to face
so much more that is ugly before that. I
shall only make one more examination of
490 myself; when I have done that, I shall
know pretty certainly when it will be
that the horrors of dissolution will begin.
There is something I want to tell you.
Helmer's refined nature gives him an

495   unconquerable disgust of everything that is ugly; I won't have him in my sick-room.

NORA. Oh, but, Doctor Rank—

RANK. I won't have him there. Not on any account. I bar my door to him. As soon as I
500   am quite certain that the worst has come, I shall send you my card with a black cross on it, and then you will know that the loathsome end has begun.

NORA. You are quite absurd today. And I
505   wanted you so much to be in a really good humour.

RANK. With death stalking beside me?—To have to pay this penalty for another man's sin! Is there any justice in that? And in
510   every single family, in one way or another, some such inexorable retribution is being exacted—

NORA (*putting her hands over her ears*). Rubbish! Do talk of something cheerful.

515 **RANK.** Oh, it's a mere laughing matter, the whole thing. My poor innocent spine has to suffer for my father's youthful amusements.

NORA (*sitting at the table on the left*). I suppose you mean that he was too partial to aspara-
520   gus and pate de foie gras, don't you?

RANK. Yes, and to truffles.

NORA. Truffles, yes. And oysters too, I suppose?

RANK. Oysters, of course, that goes without
525   saying.

NORA. And heaps of port and champagne. It is sad that all these nice things should take their revenge on our bones.

RANK. Especially that they should revenge
530   themselves on the unlucky bones of those who have not had the satisfaction of enjoying them.

NORA. Yes, that's the saddest part of it all.

RANK (*with a searching look at her*). Hm!—
535 **NORA** (*after a short pause*). Why did you smile?

RANK. No, it was you that laughed.

NORA. No, it was you that smiled, Doctor Rank!

540 **RANK** (*rising*). You are a greater rascal than I thought.

NORA. I am in a silly mood today.

RANK. So it seems.

NORA (*putting her hands on his shoulders*).
545   Dear, dear Doctor Rank, death mustn't take you away from Torvald and me.

RANK. It is a loss you would easily recover from. Those who are gone are soon forgotten.

550 **NORA** (*looking at him anxiously*). Do you believe that?

RANK. People form new ties, and then—

NORA. Who will form new ties?

RANK. Both you and Helmer, when I am
555   gone. You yourself are already on the high road to it, I think. What did that Mrs. Linde want here last night?

NORA. Oho!—you don't mean to say you are jealous of poor Christine?

560 **RANK.** Yes, I am. She will be my successor in this house. When I am done for, this woman will—

NORA. Hush! don't speak so loud. She is in that room.

565 **RANK.** Today again. There, you see.

NORA. She has only come to sew my dress for me. Bless my soul, how unreasonable you are! (*Sits down on the sofa.*) Be nice now, Doctor Rank, and tomorrow you will
570   see how beautifully I shall dance, and you can imagine I am doing it all for you—and for Torvald too, of course. (*Takes various things out of the box.*) Doctor Rank, come and sit down here, and I will show you
575   something.

RANK (*sitting down*). What is it?

NORA. Just look at those.

RANK. Silk stockings.

NORA. Flesh-coloured. Aren't they lovely? It

580   is so dark here now, but tomorrow—. No, no, no! you must only look at the feet. Oh, well, you may have leave to look at the legs too.

RANK. Hm!—

585 NORA. Why are you looking so critical? Don't you think they will fit me?

RANK. I have no means of forming an opinion about that.

NORA (*looks at him for a moment*). For shame!

590   (*Hits him lightly on the ear with the stockings.*) That's to punish you. (*Folds them up again.*)

RANK. And what other nice things am I to be allowed to see?

595 NORA. Not a single thing more, for being so naughty. (*She looks among the things, humming to herself.*)

RANK (*after a short silence*). When I am sitting here, talking to you as intimately as this,

600   I cannot imagine for a moment what would have become of me if I had never come into this house.

NORA (*smiling*). I believe you do feel thoroughly at home with us.

605 RANK (*in a lower voice, looking straight in front of him*). And to be obliged to leave it all—

NORA. Nonsense, you are not going to leave it.

RANK (*as before*). And not be able to leave

610   behind one the slightest token of one's gratitude, scarcely even a fleeting regret—nothing but an empty place which the first comer can fill as well as any other.

615 NORA. And if I asked you now for a—? No!

RANK. For what?

NORA. For a big proof of your friendship—

RANK. Yes, yes.

NORA. I mean a tremendously big favour—

620 RANK. Would you really make me so happy for once?

NORA. Ah, but you don't know what it is yet.

RANK. No—but tell me.

NORA. I really can't, Doctor Rank. It is some-

625   thing out of all reason; it means advice, and help, and a favour—

RANK. The bigger a thing it is the better. I can't conceive what it is you mean. Do tell me. Haven't I your confidence?

630 NORA. More than anyone else. I know you are my truest and best friend, and so I will tell you what it is. Well, Doctor Rank, it is something you must help me to prevent. You know how devotedly, how inexpressibly

635   deeply Torvald loves me; he would never for a moment hesitate to give his life for me.

RANK (*leaning toward her*). Nora—do you think he is the only one—?

NORA (*with a slight start*). The only one—?

640 RANK. The only one who would gladly give his life for your sake.

NORA (*sadly*). Is that it?

RANK. I was determined you should know it before I went away, and there will never

645   be a better opportunity than this. Now you know it, Nora. And now you know, too, that you can trust me as you would trust no one else.

NORA (*rises deliberately and quietly*). Let

650   me pass.

RANK (*makes room for her to pass him, but sits still*). Nora!

NORA (*at the hall door*). Helen, bring in the lamp. (*Goes over to the stove.*) Dear Doctor

655   Rank, that was really horrid of you.

RANK. To have loved you as much as anyone else does? Was that horrid?

NORA. No, but to go and tell me so. There was really no need—

660 RANK. What do you mean? Did you know—? (**MAID** *enters with lamp, puts it down on the table, and goes out.*) Nora— Mrs. Helmer—tell me, had you any idea of this?

665 **NORA.** Oh, how do I know whether I had or whether I hadn't. I really can't tell you— To think you could be so clumsy, Doctor Rank! We were getting on so nicely.

RANK. Well, at all events you know now that 670 you can command me, body and soul. So won't you speak out?

NORA (*looking at him*). After what happened?

RANK. I beg you to let me know what it is.

675 **NORA.** I can't tell you anything now.

RANK. Yes, yes. You mustn't punish me in that way. Let me have permission to do for you whatever a man may do.

NORA. You can do nothing for me now. 680 Besides, I really don't need any help at all. You will find that the whole thing is merely fancy on my part. It really is so—of course it is! (*Sits down in the rocking-chair, and looks at him with a smile.*) 685 You are a nice sort of man, Doctor Rank!—don't you feel ashamed of yourself, now the lamp has come?

RANK. Not a bit. But perhaps I had better go—forever?

690 **NORA.** No, indeed, you shall not. Of course you must come here just as before. You know very well Torvald can't do without you.

RANK. Yes, but you?

695 **NORA.** Oh, I am always tremendously pleased when you come.

RANK. It is just that, that put me on the wrong track. You are a riddle to me. I have often thought that you would almost as 700 soon be in my company as in Helmer's.

NORA. Yes—you see there are some people one loves best, and others whom one would almost always rather have as companions.

705 **RANK.** Yes, there is something in that.

NORA. When I was at home, of course I loved papa best. But I always thought it tremendous fun if I could steal down into the maids' room, because they never 710 moralized at all, and talked to each other about such entertaining things.

RANK. I see—it is their place I have taken.

NORA (*jumping up and going to him*). Oh, dear, nice Doctor Rank, I never meant that at 715 all. But surely you can understand that being with Torvald is a little like being with papa—(*Enter* MAID *from the hall.*)

MAID. If you please, ma'am. (*Whispers and hands her a card.*)

720 **NORA** (*glancing at the card*). Oh! (*Puts it in her pocket.*)

RANK. Is there anything wrong?

NORA. No, no, not in the least. It is only something—It is my new dress—

725 **RANK.** What? Your dress is lying there.

NORA. Oh, yes, that one; but this is another. I ordered it. Torvald mustn't know about it—

RANK. Oho! Then that was the great secret.

730 **NORA.** Of course. Just go in to him; he is sitting in the inner room. Keep him as long as—

RANK. Make your mind easy; I won't let him escape. (*Goes into* HELMER'S *room.*)

735 **NORA** (*to the* MAID). And he is standing waiting in the kitchen?

MAID. Yes; he came up the back stairs.

NORA. But didn't you tell him no one was in?

740 **MAID.** Yes, but it was no good.

NORA. He won't go away?

MAID. No; he says he won't until he has seen you, ma'am.

NORA. Well, let him come in—but quietly. 745 Helen, you mustn't say anything about it to any one. It is a surprise for my husband.

MAID. Yes, ma'am, I quite understand. (*Exit.*)

NORA. This dreadful thing is going to happen. It will happen in spite of me! No, 750 no, no, it can't happen—it shan't happen!

(*She bolts the door of* HELMER'S *room. The* MAID *opens the hall door for* KROGSTAD *and shuts it after him. He is wearing a fur coat, high boots and a fur cap.*)

755 NORA (*advancing towards him*). Speak low—my husband is at home.

KROGSTAD. No matter about that.

NORA. What do you want of me?

KROGSTAD. An explanation of something.

760 NORA. Make haste then. What is it?

KROGSTAD. You know, I suppose, that I have got my dismissal.

NORA. I couldn't prevent it, Mr. Krogstad. I fought as hard as I could on your side, but

765 it was no good.

KROGSTAD. Does your husband love you so little, then? He knows what I can expose you to, and yet he ventures—

NORA. How can you suppose that he has any

770 knowledge of the sort?

KROGSTAD. I didn't suppose so at all. It would not be the least like our dear Torvald Helmer to show so much courage—

NORA. Mr. Krogstad, a little respect for my

775 husband, please.

KROGSTAD. Certainly—all the respect he deserves. But since you have kept the matter so carefully to yourself, I make bold to suppose that you have a little

780 clearer idea than you had yesterday, of what it actually is that you have done?

NORA. More than you could ever teach me.

KROGSTAD. Yes, such a bad lawyer as I am.

NORA. What is it you want of me?

785 KROGSTAD. Only to see how you were, Mrs. Helmer. I have been thinking about you all day long. A mere cashier—a quill-driver, a—well, a man like me—even he has a little of what is called feeling, you know.

790 NORA. Show it, then; think of my little children.

KROGSTAD. Have you and your husband thought of mine? But never mind about that. I only wanted to tell you that you

795 need not take this matter too seriously. In the first place there will be no accusation made on my part.

NORA. No, of course not; I was sure of that.

KROGSTAD. The whole thing can be arranged amicably; there is no reason why anyone

800 should know anything about it. It will remain a secret between us three.

NORA. My husband must never get to know anything about it.

KROGSTAD. How will you be able to prevent

805 it? Am I to understand that you can pay the balance that is owing?

NORA. No, not just at present.

KROGSTAD. Or perhaps that you have some expedient for raising the money soon?

810 NORA. No expedient that I mean to make use of.

KROGSTAD. Well, in any case, it would have been of no use to you now. If you stood there with ever so much money

815 in your hand, I would never part with your bond.

NORA. Tell me what purpose you mean to put it to.

KROGSTAD. I shall only preserve it—keep it

820 in my possession. No one who is not concerned in the matter shall have the slightest hint of it. So that if the thought of it has driven you to any desperate resolution—

825 NORA. It has.

KROGSTAD. If you had it in your mind to run away from your home—

NORA. I had.

KROGSTAD. Or even something worse—

830 NORA. How could you know that?

KROGSTAD. Give up the idea.

NORA. How did you know I had thought of that?

KROGSTAD. Most of us think of that at first.

835 I did, too—but I hadn't the courage.

NORA (*faintly*). No more had I.

KROGSTAD (*in a tone of relief*). No, that's it, isn't it—you hadn't the courage either?

NORA. No, I haven't—I haven't.

840 KROGSTAD. Besides, it would have been a great piece of folly. Once the first storm at home is over—. I have a letter for your husband in my pocket.

NORA. Telling him everything?

845 KROGSTAD. In as lenient a manner as I possibly could.

NORA (*quickly*). He mustn't get the letter. Tear it up. I will find some means of getting money.

850 KROGSTAD. Excuse me, Mrs. Helmer, but I think I told you just how—

NORA. I am not speaking of what I owe you. Tell me what sum you are asking my husband for, and I will get the money.

855 KROGSTAD. I am not asking your husband for a penny.

NORA. What do you want, then?

KROGSTAD. I will tell you. I want to rehabilitate myself, Mrs. Helmer; I want to get on;

860 and in that your husband must help me. For the last year and a half I have not had a hand in anything dishonourable, and all that time I have been struggling in most restricted circumstances. I was content to

865 work my way up step by step. Now I am turned out, and I am not going to be satisfied with merely being taken into favour again. I want to get on, I tell you. I want to get into the Bank again, in a

870 higher position. Your husband must make a place for me—

NORA. That he will never do!

KROGSTAD. He will; I know him; he dare not protest. And as soon as I am in there again

875 with him, then you will see! Within a year I shall be the manager's right hand. It will be Nils Krogstad and not Torvald Helmer who manages the Bank.

NORA. That's a thing you will never see!

880 KROGSTAD. Do you mean that you will—?

NORA. I have courage enough for it now.

KROGSTAD. Oh, you can't frighten me. A fine, spoilt lady like you—

NORA. You will see, you will see.

885 KROGSTAD. Under the ice, perhaps? Down into the cold, coal-black water? And then, in the spring, to float up to the surface, all horrible and unrecognizable, with your hair fallen out—

890 NORA. You can't frighten me.

KROGSTAD. Nor you me. People don't do such things, Mrs. Helmer. Besides, what use would it be? I should have him completely in my power all

895 the same.

NORA. Afterwards? When I am no longer—

KROGSTAD. Have you forgot that it is I who have the keeping of your reputation? (*Nora stands speechlessly looking at him.*) Well,

900 now, I have warned you. Do not do anything foolish. When Helmer has had my letter, I shall expect a message from him. And be sure you remember that it is your husband himself who has forced

905 me into such ways as this again. I will never forgive him for that. Goodbye, Mrs. Helmer. (*Exit through the hall.*)

NORA (*goes to the hall door, opens it slightly and listens*). He is going. He is not

910 putting the letter in the box. Oh, no, no, that's impossible! (*Opens the door by degrees.*) What is that? He is standing outside. He is not going downstairs. Is he hesitating? Can he—? (*A letter drops

915 into the box; then* KROGSTAD'S *footsteps are heard, till they die away as he goes downstairs. nora utters a stifled cry, and runs across the room to the table by the sofa. A short pause.*)

920 NORA. In the letter-box. (*Steals across to the hall-door.*) There it lies—Torvald, Torvald, there is no hope for us now!

(MRS. LINDE *comes in from the room on the left, carrying the dress.*)

925 MRS. LINDE. There, I can't see anything more to mend now. Would you like to try it on—?

NORA (*in a hoarse whisper*). Christine, come here.

MRS. LINDE (*throwing the dress down on the 930 sofa*). What is the matter with you? You look so agitated!

NORA. Come here. Do you see that letter? There, look—you can see it through the glass in the letter-box.

935 MRS. LINDE. Yes, I see it.

NORA. That letter is from Krogstad.

MRS. LINDE. Nora—it was Krogstad who lent you the money!

NORA. Yes, and now Torvald will know all 940 about it.

MRS. LINDE. Believe me, Nora, that's the best thing for both of you.

NORA. You don't know all. I forged a name.

MRS. LINDE. Good heavens—!

945 NORA. I only want to say this to you, Christine—you must be my witness.

MRS. LINDE. Your witness! What do you mean? What am I to—?

NORA. If I should go out of my mind—and it 950 might easily happen—

MRS. LINDE. Nora!

NORA. Or if anything else should happen to me—anything, for instance, that might prevent my being here—

955 MRS. LINDE. Nora! Nora! you are quite out of your mind.

NORA. And if it should happen that there were someone who wanted to take all the responsibility, all the blame, you under- 960 stand—

MRS. LINDE. Yes, yes—but how can you suppose—?

NORA. Then you must be my witness, that it is not true, Christine. I am not out of my 965 mind at all; I am in my right senses now,

and I tell you no one else has known anything about it; I and I alone, did the whole thing. Remember that.

MRS. LINDE. I will, indeed. But I don't under-970 stand all this.

NORA. How should you understand it? A wonderful thing is going to happen.

MRS. LINDE. A wonderful thing?

NORA. Yes, a wonderful thing!—But it is so 975 terrible, Christine; it mustn't happen, not for all the world.

MRS. LINDE. I will go at once and see Krogstad.

NORA. Don't go to him; he will do you some 980 harm.

MRS. LINDE. There was a time when he would gladly do anything for my sake.

NORA. He?

MRS. LINDE. Where does he live?

985 NORA. How should I know—? Yes (*feeling in her pocket*) here is his card. But the letter, the letter—!

HELMER (*calls from his room, knocking at the door*). Nora.

990 NORA (*cries out anxiously*). Oh, what's that? What do you want?

HELMER. Don't be so frightened. We are not coming in; you have locked the door. Are you trying on your dress?

995 NORA. Yes, that's it. I look so nice, Torvald.

MRS. LINDE (*who has read the card*). I see he lives at the corner here.

NORA. Yes, but it's no use. It is hopeless. The letter is lying there in the box.

1000 MRS. LINDE. And your husband keeps the key?

NORA. Yes, always.

MRS. LINDE. Krogstad must ask for his letter back unread, he must find some pretence—

1005 NORA. But it is just at this time that Torvald generally—

MRS. LINDE. You must delay him. Go in to him in the meantime. I will come back as

1010 soon as I can. (*She goes out hurriedly through the hall door.*)

NORA (*goes to helmer's door, opens it and peeps in*). Torvald!

HELMER (*from the inner room*). Well? May I venture at last to come into my own

1015 room again? Come along, Rank, now you will see—(*Halting in the doorway.*) But what is this?

NORA. What is what, dear?

HELMER. Rank led me to expect a splendid

1020 transformation.

RANK (*in the doorway*). I understood so, but evidently I was mistaken.

NORA. Yes, nobody is to have the chance of admiring me in my dress until tomorrow.

1025 HELMER. But, my dear Nora, you look so worn out. Have you been practising too much?

NORA. No, I have not practised at all.

HELMER. But you will need to—

1030 NORA. Yes, indeed I shall, Torvald. But I can't get on a bit without you to help me; I have absolutely forgotten the whole thing.

HELMER. Oh, we will soon work it up again.

NORA. Yes, help me, Torvald. Promise that

1035 you will! I am so nervous about it—all the people—. You must give yourself up to me entirely this evening. Not the tiniest bit of business—you mustn't even take a pen in your hand. Will you prom-

1040 ise, Torvald dear?

HELMER. I promise. This evening I will be wholly and absolutely at your service, you helpless little mortal. Ah, by the way, first of all I will just—(*Goes toward the hall*

1045 *door.*)

NORA. What are you going to do there?

HELMER. Only see if any letters have come.

NORA. No, no! don't do that, Torvald!

HELMER. Why not?

1050 NORA. Torvald, please don't. There is nothing there.

HELMER. Well, let me look. (*Turns to go to the letter-box. nora, at the piano, plays the first bars of the Tarantella. helmer stops in the*

1055 *doorway.*) Aha!

NORA. I can't dance tomorrow if I don't practise with you.

HELMER (*going up to her*). Are you really so afraid of it, dear?

1060 NORA. Yes, so dreadfully afraid of it. Let me practise at once; there is time now, before we go to dinner. Sit down and play for me, Torvald dear; criticise me, and correct me as you play.

1065 HELMER. With great pleasure, if you wish me to. (*Sits down at the piano.*)

NORA (*takes out of the box a tambourine and a long variegated shawl. She hastily drapes the shawl round her. Then she*

1070 *springs to the front of the stage and calls out*). Now play for me! I am going to dance!

(HELMER *plays and* NORA *dances.* RANK *stands by the piano behind* HELMER, *and*

1075 *looks on.*)

HELMER (*as he plays*). Slower, slower!

NORA. I can't do it any other way.

HELMER. Not so violently, Nora!

NORA. This is the way.

1080 HELMER (*stops playing*). No, no—that is not a bit right.

NORA (*laughing and swinging the tambourine*). Didn't I tell you so?

RANK. Let me play for her.

1085 HELMER (*getting up*). Yes, do. I can correct her better then.

(RANK *sits down at the piano and plays. Nora dances more and more wildly.* HELMER *has taken up a position beside the stove, and*

1090 *during her dance gives her frequent instructions. She does not seem to hear him; her hair comes down and falls over her shoulders; she pays no attention to it, but goes on dancing. Enter* MRS. LINDE.)

1095 **MRS. LINDE** (*standing as if spell-bound in the doorway*). Oh!—

NORA (*as she dances*). Such fun, Christine!

HELMER. My dear darling Nora, you are danc- ing as if your life depended on it.

1100 **NORA.** So it does.

HELMER. Stop, Rank; this is sheer madness. Stop, I tell you. (**RANK** *stops playing, and* **NORA** *suddenly stands still.* **HELMER** *goes up to her.*) I could never have believed

1105 it. You have forgotten everything I taught you.

NORA (*throwing away the tambourine*). There, you see.

HELMER. You will want a lot of coaching.

1110 **NORA.** Yes, you see how much I need it. You must coach me up to the last minute. Promise me that, Torvald!

HELMER. You can depend on me.

NORA. You must not think of anything but

1115 me, either today or tomorrow; you mustn't open a single letter—not even open the letter-box—

HELMER. Ah, you are still afraid of that fellow—

1120 **NORA.** Yes, indeed I am.

HELMER. Nora, I can tell from your looks that there is a letter from him lying there.

NORA. I don't know; I think there is; but you must not read anything of that kind now.

1125 Nothing horrid must come between us till this is all over.

RANK (*whispers to* **HELMER**). You mustn't contradict her.

HELMER (*taking her in his arms*). The child

1130 shall have her way. But tomorrow night, after you have danced—

NORA. Then you will be free. (*The* **MAID** *appears in the doorway to the right.*)

MAID. Dinner is served, ma'am.

1135 **NORA.** We will have champagne, Helen.

MAID. Very good, ma'am.

HELMER. Hullo!—are we going to have a banquet? (*Exit.*)

NORA. Yes, a champagne banquet till the

1140 small hours. (*Calls out.*) And a few maca- roons, Helen—lots, just for once!

HELMER. Come, come, don't be so wild and nervous. Be my own little skylark, as you used.

1145 **NORA.** Yes, dear, I will. But go in now and you too, Doctor Rank. Christine, you must, help me to do up my hair.

RANK (*whispers to* **HELMER** *as they go out*). I suppose there is nothing—she is not

1150 expecting anything?

HELMER. Far from it, my dear fellow; it is simply nothing more than this childish nervousness I was telling you of. (*They go into the right-hand room.*)

1155 **NORA.** Well!

MRS. LINDE. Gone out of town.

NORA. I could tell from your face.

MRS. LINDE. He is coming home tomorrow evening. I wrote a note for him.

1160 **NORA.** You should have let it alone; you must prevent nothing. After all, it is splendid to be waiting for a wonderful thing to happen.

MRS. LINDE. What is it that you are waiting for?

1165 **NORA.** Oh, you wouldn't understand. Go in to them. I will come in a moment. (**MRS. LINDE** *goes into the dining-room.* **NORA** *stands still for a little while, as if to compose herself. Then she looks at her watch.*)

1170 Five o'clock. Seven hours till midnight; and then four-and-twenty hours till the next midnight. Then the Tarantella will be over. Twenty-four and seven? Thirty-one hours to live.

1175 **HELMER** (*from the doorway on the right*). Where's my little skylark?

NORA (*going to him with her arms outstretched*). Here she is!

Nigel Norrington/Camera Press/Redux

◀ The image depicts Nora dancing the tarantella at the end of Act II. It is from the 2013 production of *A Doll's House* at the Duke of York's Theatre in London.

What is Nora's expression in this image? Why is this moment so important for Nora? How might it still resonate with modern women?

CHARACTER

1. What **motivates** Krogstad to act in the manner he does over the letter? To whom do these actions impact? What do they reveal about Krogstad's values?

2. Describe how Dr. Rank is characterized. What motivates him to think, feel, and act as he does?

3. What is Torvald's reaction to Nora's dance? Explain how this reaction contributes to their relationship.

SETTING

4. Where do Krogstad and Torvald meet? How does the social and cultural **setting** establish a relationship between the two men?

5. The mailbox located outside of the Helmer's home becomes an important location in the play. What is the significance of this location?

STRUCTURE

6. Act II includes many **contrasting** attitudes and behaviors. Choose one **conflict** and explain how it reveals the contrasting attitudes of the characters.

7. Why is Krogstad's letter significant to the structure of the play?

8. Is the play's primary **conflict** internal or external? How do you know?

9. What is the **climactic** moment in Act II? To what degree do Nora's choices contribute to her progress or her decline?

IDEAS IN LITERATURE: Power and Control

10. Dr. Rank tells Nora, "In every single family, in one way or another, the same merciless law of retribution is at work." What does this mean? Have you witnessed retribution in your own experience, family, or community? How does retribution function and connect to power and control?

ACT III

(THE SAME SCENE—*The table has been placed in the middle of the stage, with chairs around it. A lamp is burning on the table. The door into the hall stands open. Dance music is heard in the room above.* MRS. LINDE *is sitting at the table idly turning over the leaves of a book; she tries to read, but does not seem able to collect her thoughts. Every now and then she listens intently for a sound at the outer door.*)

MRS. LINDE (*looking at her watch*).   Not
5   yet—and the time is nearly up. If only he does not—. (*Listens again.*) Ah, there he is. (*Goes into the hall and opens the outer door carefully. Light footsteps are heard on the stairs. She whispers.*) Come in. There is no one here.

KROGSTAD (*in the doorway*).   I found a note from you at home. What does this mean?

10 MRS. LINDE.   It is absolutely necessary that I should have a talk with you.

KROGSTAD.   Really? And is it absolutely necessary that it should be here?

MRS. LINDE.   It is impossible where I live; there
15   is no private entrance to my rooms. Come in; we are quite alone. The maid is asleep, and the Helmers are at the dance upstairs.

KROGSTAD (*coming into the room*).   Are the Helmers really at a dance tonight?

20 MRS. LINDE.   Yes, why not?

KROGSTAD.   Certainly—why not?

MRS. LINDE.   Now, Nils, let us have a talk.

KROGSTAD.   Can we two have anything to talk about?

25 MRS. LINDE.   We have a great deal to talk about.

KROGSTAD.   I shouldn't have thought so.

MRS. LINDE.   No, you have never properly understood me.

30 KROGSTAD.   Was there anything else to understand except what was obvious to all the world—a heartless woman jilts a man when a more lucrative chance turns up.

35 MRS. LINDE.   Do you believe I am as absolutely heartless as all that? And do you believe that I did it with a light heart?

KROGSTAD.   Didn't you?

MRS. LINDE.   Nils, did you really think that?

40 KROGSTAD.   If it were as you say, why did you write to me as you did at the time?

MRS. LINDE.   I could do nothing else. As I had to break with you, it was my duty also to put an end to all that you felt
45   for me.

KROGSTAD (*wringing his hands*).   So that was it. And all this—only for the sake of money.

MRS. LINDE.   You must not forget that I had a
50   helpless mother and two little brothers. We couldn't wait for you, Nils; your prospects seemed hopeless then.

KROGSTAD.   That may be so, but you had no right to throw me over for anyone else's
55   sake.

MRS. LINDE.   Indeed I don't know. Many a time did I ask myself if I had a right to do it.

KROGSTAD (*more gently*).   When I lost you, it
60   was as if all the solid ground went from under my feet. Look at me now—I am a shipwrecked man clinging to a bit of wreckage.

MRS. LINDE.   But help may be near.

65 KROGSTAD.   It was near; but then you came and stood in my way.

MRS. LINDE.   Unintentionally, Nils. It was only today that I learnt it was your place I was going to take in the bank.

70 KROGSTAD.   I believe you, if you say so. But now that you know it, are you not going to give it up to me?

MRS. LINDE. No, because that would not benefit you in the least.

75 KROGSTAD. Oh, benefit, benefit—I would have done it whether or no.

MRS. LINDE. I have learnt to act prudently. Life, and hard, bitter necessity have taught me that.

80 KROGSTAD. And life has taught me not to believe in fine speeches.

MRS. LINDE. Then life has taught you something very reasonable. But deeds you must believe in?

85 KROGSTAD. What do you mean by that?

MRS. LINDE. You said you were like a shipwrecked man clinging to some wreckage.

KROGSTAD. I had good reason to say so.

MRS. LINDE. Well, I am like a shipwrecked
90 woman clinging to some wreckage—no one to mourn for, no one to care for.

KROGSTAD. It was your own choice.

MRS. LINDE. There was no other choice, then.

KROGSTAD. Well, what now?

95 MRS. LINDE. Nils, how would it be if we two shipwrecked people could join forces?

KROGSTAD. What are you saying?

MRS. LINDE. Two on the same piece of wreckage would stand a better chance than
100 each on their own.

KROGSTAD. Christine!

MRS. LINDE. What do you suppose brought me to town?

KROGSTAD. Do you mean that you gave me a
105 thought?

MRS. LINDE. I could not endure life without work. All my life, as long as I can remember, I have worked, and it has been my greatest and only pleasure. But now I am
110 quite alone in the world—my life is so dreadfully empty and I feel so forsaken. There is not the least pleasure in working for one's self. Nils, give me someone and something to work for.

115 KROGSTAD. I don't trust that. It is nothing but a woman's overstrained sense of generosity that prompts you to make such an offer of yourself.

MRS. LINDE. Have you ever noticed anything
120 of the sort in me?

KROGSTAD. Could you really do it? Tell me— do you know all about my past life?

MRS. LINDE. Yes.

KROGSTAD. And do you know what they
125 think of me here?

MRS. LINDE. You seemed to me to imply that with me you might have been quite another man.

KROGSTAD. I am certain of it.

130 MRS. LINDE. Is it too late now?

KROGSTAD. Christine, are you saying this deliberately? Yes, I am sure you are. I see it in your face. Have you really the courage, then—?

135 MRS. LINDE. I want to be a mother to someone, and your children need a mother. We two need each other. Nils, I have faith in your real character—I can dare anything together with you.

140 KROGSTAD (grasps her hands). Thanks, thanks, Christine! Now I shall find a way to clear myself in the eyes of the world. Ah, but I forgot—

MRS. LINDE (listening). Hush! The Tarantella!
145 Go, go!

KROGSTAD. Why? What is it?

MRS. LINDE. Do you hear them up there? When that is over, we may expect them back.

150 KROGSTAD. Yes, yes—I will go. But it is all no use. Of course you are not aware what steps I have taken in the matter of the Helmers.

MRS. LINDE. Yes, I know all about that.

155 KROGSTAD. And in spite of that have you the courage to—?

MRS. LINDE.   I understand very well to what lengths a man like you might be driven by despair.

160 KROGSTAD.   If I could only undo what I have done!

MRS. LINDE.   You cannot. Your letter is lying in the letter-box now.

KROGSTAD.   Are you sure of that?

165 MRS. LINDE.   Quite sure, but—

KROGSTAD (*with a searching look at her*).   Is that what it all means?—that you want to save your friend at any cost? Tell me frankly. Is that it?

170 MRS. LINDE.   Nils, a woman who has once sold herself for another's sake, doesn't do it a second time.

KROGSTAD.   I will ask for my letter back.

MRS. LINDE.   No, no.

175 KROGSTAD.   Yes, of course I will. I will wait here till Helmer comes; I will tell him he must give me my letter back—that it only concerns my dismissal—that he is not to read it—

180 MRS. LINDE.   No, Nils, you must not recall your letter.

KROGSTAD.   But, tell me, wasn't it for that very purpose that you asked me to meet you here?

185 MRS. LINDE.   In my first moment of fright, it was. But twenty-four hours have elapsed since then, and in that time I have witnessed incredible things in this house. Helmer must know all about it.

190 This unhappy secret must be disclosed; they must have a complete understanding between them, which is impossible with all this concealment and falsehood going on.

195 KROGSTAD.   Very well, if you will take the responsibility. But there is one thing I can do in any case, and I shall do it at once.

MRS. LINDE (*listening*).   You must be quick and
200 go! The dance is over; we are not safe a moment longer.

KROGSTAD.   I will wait for you below.

MRS. LINDE.   Yes, do. You must see me back to my door. . . .

205 KROGSTAD.   I have never had such an amazing piece of good fortune in my life! (*Goes out through the outer door. The door between the room and the hall remains open.*)

210 MRS. LINDE (*tidying up the room and laying her hat and cloak ready*).   What a difference! What a difference! Someone to work for and live for—a home to bring comfort into. That I will do, indeed. I wish they
215 would be quick and come. (*Listens.*) Ah, there they are now. I must put on my things. (*Takes up her hat and cloak.* HELMER'S *and* NORA'S *voices are heard outside; a key is turned, and* HELMER
220 *brings* NORA *almost by force into the hall. She is in an Italian costume with a large black shawl round her; he is in evening dress, and a black domino which is flying open.*)

225 NORA (*hanging back in the doorway, and struggling with him*).   No, no, no!—don't take me in. I want to go upstairs again; I don't want to leave so early.

HELMER.   But, my dearest Nora—

230 NORA.   Please, Torvald dear—please, please—only an hour more.

HELMER.   Not a single minute, my sweet Nora. You know that was our agreement. Come along into the room; you are catch-
235 ing cold standing there. (*He brings her gently into the room, in spite of her resistance.*)

MRS. LINDE.   Good evening.

NORA.   Christine!

240 HELMER.   You here, so late, Mrs. Linde?

MRS. LINDE. Yes, you must excuse me; I was so anxious to see Nora in her dress.

NORA. Have you been sitting here waiting for me?

245 **MRS. LINDE.** Yes, unfortunately I came too late, you had already gone upstairs; and I thought I couldn't go away again without having seen you.

HELMER (*taking off* **NORA'S** *shawl*). Yes, take a

250 good look at her. I think she is worth looking at. Isn't she charming, Mrs. Linde?

MRS. LINDE. Yes, indeed she is.

HELMER. Doesn't she look remarkably pretty? Everyone thought so at the dance.

255 But she is terribly self-willed, this sweet little person. What are we to do with her? You will hardly believe that I had almost to bring her away by force.

NORA. Torvald, you will repent not having

260 let me stay, even if it were only for half an hour.

HELMER. Listen to her, Mrs. Linde! She had danced her Tarantella, and it had been a tremendous success, as it deserved—

265 although possibly the performance was a trifle too realistic—little more so, I mean, than was strictly compatible with the limitations of art. But never mind about that! The chief thing is, she had made a

270 success—she had made a tremendous success. Do you think I was going to let her remain there after that, and spoil the effect? No, indeed! I took my charming little Capri maiden—my capricious little

275 Capri maiden, I should say—on my arm; took one quick turn round the room; a curtsey on either side, and, as they say in novels, the beautiful apparition disappeared. An exit ought always to be effec-

280 tive, Mrs. Linde; but that is what I cannot make Nora understand. Pooh! this room is hot. (*Throws his domino on a chair, and opens the door of his room.*) Hullo! it's all dark in here. Oh, of course—excuse

285 me—. (*He goes in, and lights some candles.*)

NORA (*in a hurried and breathless whisper*). Well?

MRS. LINDE (*in a low voice*). I have had a talk

290 with him.

NORA. Yes, and—

MRS. LINDE. Nora, you must tell your husband all about it.

NORA (*in an expressionless voice*). I knew it.

295 **MRS. LINDE.** You have nothing to be afraid of as far as Krogstad is concerned; but you must tell him.

NORA. I won't tell him.

MRS. LINDE. Then the letter will.

300 **NORA.** Thank you, Christine. Now I know what I must do. Hush—!

HELMER (*coming in again*). Well, Mrs. Linde, have you admired her?

MRS. LINDE. Yes, and now I will say good-

305 night.

HELMER. What, already? Is this yours, this knitting?

MRS. LINDE (*taking it*). Yes, thank you, I had very nearly forgotten it.

310 **HELMER.** So you knit?

MRS. LINDE. Of course.

HELMER. Do you know, you ought to embroider?

MRS. LINDE. Really? Why?

315 **HELMER.** Yes, it's far more becoming. Let me show you. You hold the embroidery thus in your left hand, and use the needle with the right—like this—with a long, easy sweep. Do you see?

320 **MRS. LINDE.** Yes, perhaps—

HELMER. But in the case of knitting—that can never be anything but ungraceful; look here—the arms close together, the knitting-needles going up and down—it

325 has a sort of Chinese effect—. That was really excellent champagne they gave us.

MRS. LINDE. Well,—goodnight, Nora, and don't be self-willed any more.

HELMER. That's right, Mrs. Linde.

330 **MRS. LINDE.** Goodnight, Mr. Helmer.

HELMER (*accompanying her to the door*). Goodnight, goodnight. I hope you will get home all right. I should be very happy to—but you haven't any great
335 distance to go. Goodnight, goodnight. (*She goes out; he shuts the door after her and comes in again.*) Ah!—at last we have got rid of her. She is a frightful bore, that woman.

340 **NORA.** Aren't you very tired, Torvald?

HELMER. No, not in the least.

NORA. Nor sleepy?

HELMER. Not a bit. On the contrary, I feel extraordinarily lively. And you?—you
345 really look both tired and sleepy.

NORA. Yes, I am very tired. I want to go to sleep at once.

HELMER. There, you see it was quite right of me not to let you stay there any
350 longer.

NORA. Everything you do is quite right, Torvald.

HELMER (*kissing her on the forehead*). Now my little skylark is speaking reasonably. Did
355 you notice what good spirits Rank was in this evening?

NORA. Really? Was he? I didn't speak to him at all.

HELMER. And I very little, but I have not for a
360 long time seen him in such good form. (*Looks for a while at her and then goes nearer to her.*) It is delightful to be at home by ourselves again, to be all alone with you—you fascinating, charming little
365 darling!

NORA. Don't look at me like that, Torvald.

HELMER. Why shouldn't I look at my dearest treasure?—at all the beauty that is mine, all my very own?

370 **NORA** (*going to the other side of the table*). You mustn't say things like that to me tonight.

HELMER (*following her*). You have still got the Tarantella in your blood, I see. And it
375 makes you more captivating than ever. Listen—the guests are beginning to go now. (*In a lower voice.*) Nora—soon the whole house will be quiet.

NORA. Yes, I hope so.

380 **HELMER.** Yes, my own darling Nora. Do you know, when I am out at a party with you like this, why I speak so little to you, keep away from you, and only send a stolen glance in your direction now and
385 then?—do you know why I do that? It is because I make believe to myself that we are secretly in love, and you are my secretly promised bride, and that no one suspects there is anything between us.

390 **NORA.** Yes, yes—I know very well your thoughts are with me all the time.

HELMER. And when we are leaving, and I am putting the shawl over your beautiful young shoulders—on your lovely neck—
395 then I imagine that you are my young bride and that we have just come from the wedding, and I am bringing you for the first time into our home—to be alone with you for the first time—quite alone
400 with my shy little darling! All this evening I have longed for nothing but you. When I watched the seductive figures of the Tarantella, my blood was on fire; I could endure it no longer, and
405 that was why I brought you down so early—

NORA. Go away, Torvald! You must let me go. I won't—

HELMER. What's that? You're joking, my little
410 Nora! You won't—you won't? Am I not
your husband—? (*A knock is heard at the
outer door.*)

NORA (*starting*). Did you hear—?

HELMER (*going into the hall*). Who is it?

415 **RANK** (*outside*). It is I. May I come in for a
moment?

HELMER (*in a fretful whisper*). Oh, what does
he want now? (*Aloud.*) Wait a minute?
(*Unlocks the door.*) Come, that's kind of you
420 not to pass by our door.

RANK. I thought I heard your voice, and felt
as if I should like to look in. (*With a swift
glance round.*) Ah, yes!—these dear familiar rooms. You are very happy and cosy in
425 here, you two.

HELMER. It seems to me that you looked
after yourself pretty well upstairs too.

RANK. Excellently. Why shouldn't I? Why
shouldn't one enjoy everything in this
430 world?—at any rate as much as one can,
and as long as one can. The wine was
capital—

HELMER. Especially the champagne.

RANK. So you noticed that too? It is almost
435 incredible how much I managed to put
away!

NORA. Torvald drank a great deal of champagne tonight, too.

RANK. Did he?

440 **NORA.** Yes, and he is always in such good
spirits afterwards.

RANK. Well, why should one not enjoy a
merry evening after a well-spent day?

HELMER. Well spent? I am afraid I can't take
445 credit for that.

RANK (*clapping him on the back*). But I can, you
know!

NORA. Doctor Rank, you must have been
occupied with some scientific investiga-
450 tion today.

RANK. Exactly.

HELMER. Just listen!—little Nora talking
about scientific investigations!

NORA. And may I congratulate you on the
455 result?

RANK. Indeed you may.

NORA. Was it favourable, then.

RANK. The best possible, for both doctor and
patient—certainty.

460 **NORA** (*quickly and searchingly*). Certainty?

RANK. Absolute certainty. So wasn't I
entitled to make a merry evening of it
after that?

NORA. Yes, you certainly were, Doctor Rank.

465 **HELMER.** I think so too, so long as you don't
have to pay for it in the morning.

RANK. Oh well, one can't have anything in
this life without paying for it.

NORA. Doctor Rank—are you fond of fancy-
470 dress balls?

RANK. Yes, if there is a fine lot of pretty
costumes.

NORA. Tell me—what shall we two wear at
the next?

475 **HELMER.** Little featherbrain!—are you thinking of the next already?

RANK. We two? Yes, I can tell you. You shall
go as a good fairy—

HELMER. Yes, but what do you suggest as an
480 appropriate costume for that?

RANK. Let your wife go dressed just as she is
in everyday life.

HELMER. That was really very prettily turned.
But can't you tell us what you will be?

485 **RANK.** Yes, my dear friend, I have quite
made up my mind about that.

HELMER. Well?

RANK. At the next fancy-dress ball I shall be
invisible.

490 **HELMER.** That's a good joke!

RANK. There is a big black hat—have you
never heard of hats that make you

invisible? If you put one on, no one can see you.

495 **HELMER** (*suppressing a smile*). Yes, you are quite right.

RANK. But I am clean forgetting what I came for. Helmer, give me a cigar—one of the dark Havanas.

500 **HELMER.** With the greatest pleasure. (*Offers him his case.*)

RANK (*takes a cigar and cuts off the end*). Thanks.

NORA (*striking a match*). Let me give you a
505 light.

RANK. Thank you. (*She holds the match for him to light his cigar.*) And now goodbye!

HELMER. Goodbye, goodbye, dear old man!

NORA. Sleep well, Doctor Rank.

510 **RANK.** Thank you for that wish.

NORA. Wish me the same.

RANK. You? Well, if you want me to sleep well! And thanks for the light. (He nods to them both and goes out.)

515 **HELMER** (*in a subdued voice*). He has drunk more than he ought.

NORA (*absently*). Maybe. (**HELMER** *takes a bunch of keys out of his pocket and goes into the hall.*) Torvald! what are you going to do
520 there?

HELMER. Empty the letter-box; it is quite full; there will be no room to put the newspaper in tomorrow morning.

NORA. Are you going to work tonight?

525 **HELMER.** You know quite well I'm not. What is this? Someone has been at the lock.

NORA. At the lock—?

HELMER. Yes, someone has. What can it mean? I should never have thought the
530 maid—. Here is a broken hairpin. Nora, it is one of yours.

NORA (*quickly*). Then it must have been the children—

HELMER. Then you must get them out of
535 those ways. There, at last I have got it open. (*Takes out the contents of the letter-box, and calls to the kitchen.*) Helen!—Helen, put out the light over the front door. (*Goes back into the room and shuts the door into the hall.*
540 *He holds out his hand full of letters.*) Look at that—look what a heap of them there are. (*Turning them over.*) What on earth is that?

NORA (*at the window*). The letter—No!
545 Torvald, no!

HELMER. Two cards—of Rank's.

NORA. Of Doctor Rank's?

HELMER (*looking at them*). Doctor Rank. They were on the top. He must have put them
550 in when he went out.

NORA. Is there anything written on them?

HELMER. There is a black cross over the name. Look there—what an uncomfortable idea! It looks as If he were announc-
555 ing his own death.

NORA. It is just what he is doing.

HELMER. What? Do you know anything about it? Has he said anything to you?

NORA. Yes. He told me that when the cards
560 came it would be his leave-taking from us. He means to shut himself up and die.

HELMER. My poor old friend. Certainly I knew we should not have him very long with us. But so soon! And so he hides
565 himself away like a wounded animal.

NORA. If it has to happen, it is best it should be without a word—don't you think so, Torvald?

HELMER (*walking up and down*). He has so
570 grown into our lives. I can't think of him as having gone out of them. He, with his sufferings and his loneliness, was like a cloudy background to our sunlit happiness. Well, perhaps it is best so. For him,

575 anyway. (*Standing still.*) And perhaps for us too, Nora. We two are thrown quite upon each other now. (*Puts his arms around her.*) My darling wife, I don't feel as if I could hold you tight enough. Do you know, Nora,

580 I have often wished that you might be threatened by some great danger, so that I might risk my life's blood, and everything, for your sake.

NORA (*disengages herself, and says firmly and*

585 *decidedly*).   Now you must read your letters, Torvald.

HELMER.   No, no; not tonight. I want to be with you, my darling wife.

NORA.   With the thought of your friend's

590 death—

HELMER.   You are right, it has affected us both. Something ugly has come between us—the thought of the horrors of death. We must try and rid our minds of that. Until then—

595 we will each go to our own room.

NORA (*hanging on his neck*).   Goodnight, Torvald—Goodnight!

HELMER (*kissing her on the forehead*).   Goodnight, my little singing-bird. Sleep

600 sound, Nora. Now I will read my letters through. (*He takes his letters and goes into his room, shutting the door after him.*)

NORA (*gropes distractedly about, seizes* HELMER'S *domino, throws it round her, while she says in*

605 *quick, hoarse, spasmodic whispers*).   Never to see him again. Never! Never! (*Puts her shawl over her head.*) Never to see my children again either—never again. Never! Never!—Ah! the icy, black water—the

610 unfathomable depths—If only it were over! He has got it now—now he is reading it. Goodbye, Torvald and my children! (*She is about to rush out through the hall, when* HELMER *opens his door*

615 *hurriedly and stands with an open letter in his hand.*)

HELMER.   Nora!

NORA.   Ah!—

HELMER.   What is this? Do you know what is

620 in this letter?

NORA.   Yes, I know. Let me go! Let me get out!

HELMER (*holding her back*).   Where are you going?

625 NORA (*trying to get free*).   You shan't save me, Torvald!

HELMER (*reeling*).   True? Is this true, that I read here? Horrible! No, no—it is impossible that it can be true.

630 NORA.   It is true. I have loved you above everything else in the world.

HELMER.   Oh, don't let us have any silly excuses.

NORA (*taking a step towards him*).   Torvald—!

635 HELMER.   Miserable creature—what have you done?

NORA.   Let me go. You shall not suffer for my sake. You shall not take it upon yourself.

HELMER.   No tragedy airs, please. (*Locks the*

640 *hall door.*) Here you shall stay and give me an explanation. Do you understand what you have done? Answer me? Do you understand what you have done?

NORA (*looks steadily at him and says with*

645 *a growing look of coldness in her face*).   Yes, now I am beginning to understand thoroughly.

HELMER (*walking about the room*).   What a horrible awakening! All these eight

650 years—she who was my joy and pride— a hypocrite, a liar—worse, worse—a criminal! The unutterable ugliness of it all!—For shame! For shame! (NORA *is silent and looks steadily at him. He stops in front of*

655 *her.*) I ought to have suspected that something of the sort would happen. I ought to have foreseen it. All your father's want of principle—be silent!—all your father's

660 want of principle has come out in you. No religion, no morality, no sense of duty—How I am punished for having winked at what he did! I did it for your sake, and this is how you repay me.

NORA. Yes, that's just it.

665 **HELMER.** Now you have destroyed all my happiness. You have ruined all my future. It is horrible to think of! I am in the power of an unscrupulous man; he can do what he likes with me, ask anything he likes of me,
670 give me any orders he pleases—I dare not refuse. And I must sink to such miserable depths because of a thoughtless woman!

NORA. When I am out of the way, you will be free.

675 **HELMER.** No fine speeches, please. Your father had always plenty of those ready, too. What good would it be to me if you were out of the way, as you say? Not the slightest. He can make the affair known
680 everywhere; and if he does, I may be falsely suspected of having been a party to your criminal action. Very likely people will think I was behind it all—that it was I who prompted you! And I have to thank
685 you for all this—you whom I have cherished during the whole of our married life. Do you understand now what it is you have done for me?

NORA (coldly and quietly). Yes.

690 **HELMER.** It is so incredible that I can't take it in. But we must come to some understanding. Take off that shawl. Take it off, I tell you. I must try and appease him some way or another. The matter must
695 be hushed up at any cost. And as for you and me, it must appear as if everything between us were as before—but naturally only in the eyes of the world. You will still remain in my house, that is a matter of
700 course. But I shall not allow you to bring up the children; I dare not trust them to

you. To think that I should be obliged to say so to one whom I have loved so dearly, and whom I still—. No, that is all over.
705 From this moment happiness is not the question; all that concerns us is to save the remains, the fragments, the appearance—

(A ring is heard at the front-door bell.)

710 **HELMER** (with a start). What is that? So late! Can the worst—? Can he—? Hide yourself, Nora. Say you are ill.

(**NORA** stands motionless. **HELMER** goes and unlocks the hall door.)

715 **MAID** (half-dressed, comes to the door). A letter for the mistress.

HELMER. Give it to me. (Takes the letter, and shuts the door.) Yes, it is from him. You shall not have it; I will read it myself.

720 **NORA.** Yes, read it.

HELMER (standing by the lamp). I scarcely have the courage to do it. It may mean ruin for both of us. No, I must know. (Tears open the letter, runs his eye over a few lines, looks at a
725 paper enclosed, and gives a shout of joy.) Nora! (She looks at him, questioningly.) Nora!—No, I must read it once again—. Yes, it is true! I am saved! Nora, I am saved!

730 **NORA.** And I?

HELMER. You too, of course; we are both saved, both saved, both you and I. Look, he sends you your bond back. He says he regrets and repents—that a happy change
735 in his life—never mind what he says! We are saved, Nora! No one can do anything to you. Oh, Nora, Nora!—no, first I must destroy these hateful things. Let me see—. (Takes a look at the bond.) No, no, I
740 won't look at it. The whole thing shall be nothing but a bad dream to me. (Tears up the bond and both letters, throws them all into the stove, and watches them burn.) There—now it doesn't exist any longer.

745 He says that since Christmas Eve you—. These must have been three dreadful days for you, Nora.

NORA. I have fought a hard fight these three days.

750 **HELMER.** And suffered agonies, and seen no way out but—. No, we won't call any of the horrors to mind. We will only shout with joy, and keep saying, "It's all over! It's all over!" Listen to me, Nora. You don't

755 seem to realise that it is all over. What is this?—such a cold, set face! My poor little Nora, I quite understand; you don't feel as if you could believe that I have forgiven you. But it is true, Nora, I swear it; I have

760 forgiven you everything. I know that what you did, you did out of love for me.

NORA. That is true.

HELMER. You have loved me as a wife ought to love her husband. Only you had not

765 sufficient knowledge to judge of the means you used. But do you suppose you are any the less dear to me, because you don't understand how to act on your own responsibility? No, no; only lean on me; I

770 will advise you and direct you. I should not be a man if this womanly helplessness did not just give you a double attractiveness in my eyes. You must not think anymore about the hard things I said in

775 my first moment of consternation, when I thought everything was going to overwhelm me. I have forgiven you, Nora; I swear to you I have forgiven you.

NORA. Thank you for your forgiveness. (*She*

780 *goes out through the door to the right.*)

HELMER. No, don't go—. (*Looks in.*) What are you doing in there?

NORA (*from within*). Taking off my fancy dress.

785 **HELMER** (*standing at the open door*). Yes, do. Try and calm yourself, and make your mind easy again, my frightened little singing-bird. Be at rest, and feel secure; I have broad wings to shelter you under.

790 (*Walks up and down by the door.*) How warm and cosy our home is, Nora. Here is shelter for you; here I will protect you like a hunted dove that I have saved from a hawk's claws; I will bring peace to your

795 poor beating heart. It will come, little by little, Nora, believe me. Tomorrow morning you will look upon it all quite differently; soon everything will be just as it was before. Very soon you won't need me

800 to assure you that I have forgiven you; you will yourself feel the certainty that I have done so. Can you suppose I should ever think of such a thing as repudiating you, or even reproaching you? You have no

805 idea what a true man's heart is like, Nora. There is something so indescribably sweet and satisfying, to a man, in the knowledge that he has forgiven his wife—forgiven her freely, and with all his heart. It seems

810 as if that had made her, as it were, doubly his own; he has given her a new life, so to speak; and she is in a way become both wife and child to him. So you shall be for me after this, my little scared, helpless

815 darling. Have no anxiety about anything, Nora; only be frank and open with me, and I will serve as will and conscience both to you—. What is this? Not gone to bed? Have you changed your things?

820 **NORA** (*in everyday dress*). Yes, Torvald, I have changed my things now.

HELMER. But what for?—so late as this.

NORA. I shall not sleep tonight.

HELMER. But, my dear Nora—

825 **NORA** (*looking at her watch*). It is not so very late. Sit down here, Torvald. You and I have much to say to one another. (*She sits down at one side of the table.*)

HELMER.   Nora—what is this?—this cold, set
830   face?

NORA.   Sit down. It will take some time; I
have a lot to talk over with you.

HELMER (*sits down at the opposite side of the
table*).   You alarm me, Nora!—and I don't
835   understand you.

NORA.   No, that is just it. You don't understand me, and I have never understood
you either—before tonight. No, you
mustn't interrupt me. You must simply
840   listen to what I say. Torvald, this is a
settling of accounts.

HELMER.   What do you mean by that?

NORA (*after a short silence*).   Isn't there one
thing that strikes you as strange in our
845   sitting here like this?

HELMER.   What is that?

NORA.   We have been married now eight
years. Does it not occur to you that this is
the first time we two, you and I, husband
850   and wife, have had a serious conversation?

HELMER.   What do you mean by serious?

NORA.   In all these eight years—longer than
that—from the very beginning of our
acquaintance, we have never exchanged a
855   word on any serious subject.

HELMER.   Was it likely that I would be continually and forever telling you about worries
that you could not help me to bear?

NORA.   I am not speaking about business
860   matters. I say that we have never sat
down in earnest together to try and
get at the bottom of anything.

HELMER.   But, dearest Nora, would it have
been any good to you?

865 **NORA.**   That is just it; you have never
understood me. I have been greatly
wronged, Torvald—first by papa and
then by you.

HELMER.   What! By us two—by us two, who
870   have loved you better than anyone else in
in the world?

NORA (*shaking her head*).   You have never
loved me. You have only thought it pleasant to be in love with me.

875 **HELMER.**   Nora, what do I hear you saying?

NORA.   It is perfectly true, Torvald. When I
was at home with papa, he told me his
opinion about everything, and so I had the
same opinions; and if I differed from him
880   I concealed the fact, because he would not
have liked it. He called me his doll-child,
and he played with me just as I used to
play with my dolls. And when I came to
live with you—

885 **HELMER.**   What sort of an expression is that
to use about our marriage?

NORA (*undisturbed*).   I mean that I was
simply transferred from papa's hands
into yours. You arranged everything
890   according to your own taste, and so I
got the same tastes as you—or else I
pretended to, I am really not quite sure
which—I think sometimes the one and
sometimes the other. When I look back on
895   it, it seems to me as if I had been living
here like a poor woman—just from hand
to mouth. I have existed merely to perform tricks for you, Torvald. But you
would have it so. You and papa have
900   committed a great sin against me. It is
your fault that I have made nothing of
my life.

HELMER.   How unreasonable and how
ungrateful you are, Nora! Have you not
905   been happy here?

NORA.   No, I have never been happy. I thought
I was, but it has never really been so.

HELMER.   Not—not happy!

NORA.   No, only merry. And you have always
910   been so kind to me. But our home has
been nothing but a playroom. I have been
your doll-wife, just as at home I was
papa's doll-child; and here the children
have been my dolls. I thought it great fun

915 when you played with me, just as they
thought it great fun when I played with
them. That is what our marriage has been,
Torvald.

HELMER. There is some truth in what you
920 say—exaggerated and strained as your
view of it is. But for the future it shall be
different. Playtime shall be over, and
lesson-time shall begin.

NORA. Whose lessons? Mine, or the
925 children's?

HELMER. Both yours and the children's, my
darling Nora.

NORA. Alas, Torvald, you are not the man
to educate me into being a proper wife
930 for you.

HELMER. And you can say that!

NORA. And I—how am I fitted to bring up
the children?

HELMER. Nora!

935 NORA. Didn't you say so yourself a little
while ago—that you dare not trust me to
bring them up?

HELMER. In a moment of anger! Why do you
pay any heed to that?

940 NORA. Indeed, you were perfectly right. I am
not fit for the task. There is another task
I must undertake first. I must try and
educate myself—you are not the man
to help me in that. I must do that for
945 myself. And that is why I am going to
leave you now.

HELMER (*springing up*). What do you say?

NORA. I must stand quite alone, if I am to
understand myself and everything about
950 me. It is for that reason that I cannot
remain with you any longer.

HELMER. Nora, Nora!

NORA. I am going away from here now, at
once. I am sure Christine will take me in
955 for the night—

HELMER. You are out of your mind! I won't
allow it! I forbid you!

NORA. It is no use forbidding me anything
any longer. I will take with me what
960 belongs to myself. I will take nothing
from you, either now or later.

HELMER. What sort of madness is this!

NORA. Tomorrow I shall go home—I mean
to my old home. It will be easiest for me
965 to find something to do there.

HELMER. You blind, foolish woman!

NORA. I must try and get some sense,
Torvald.

HELMER. To desert your home, your husband
970 and your children! And you don't consider
what people will say!

NORA. I cannot consider that at all. I only
know that it is necessary for me.

HELMER. It's shocking. This is how you would
975 neglect your most sacred duties.

NORA. What do you consider my most
sacred duties?

HELMER. Do I need to tell you that? Are they
not your duties to your husband and your
980 children?

NORA. I have other duties just as sacred.

HELMER. That you have not. What duties
could those be?

NORA. Duties to myself.

985 HELMER. Before all else, you are a wife and
mother.

NORA. I don't believe that any longer. I
believe that before all else I am a reasonable human being, just as you are—or, at
990 all events, that I must try and become
one. I know quite well, Torvald, that most
people would think you right, and that
views of that kind are to be found in
books; but I can no longer content myself
995 with what most people say, or with what
is found in books. I must think over

things for myself and get to understand them.

HELMER. Can you not understand your place in your own home? Have you not a reliable guide in such matters as that?—have you no religion?

NORA. I am afraid, Torvald, I do not exactly know what religion is.

1005 HELMER. What are you saying?

NORA. I know nothing but what the clergyman said, when I went to be confirmed. He told us that religion was this, and that, and the other. When I am away from all this, and am alone, I will look into that matter too. I will see if what the clergyman said is true, or at all events if it is true for me.

HELMER. This is unheard of in a girl of your age! But if religion cannot lead you aright, let me try and awaken your conscience. I suppose you have some moral sense? Or—answer me—am I to think you have none?

1020 NORA. I assure you, Torvald, that is not an easy question to answer. I really don't know. The thing perplexes me altogether. I only know that you and I look at it in quite a different light. I am learning, too, that the law is quite another thing from what I supposed; but I find it impossible to convince myself that the law is right. According to it a woman has no right to spare her old dying father, or to save her husband's life. I can't believe that.

HELMER. You talk like a child. You don't understand the conditions of the world in which you live.

NORA. No, I don't. But now I am going to try. I am going to see if I can make out who is right, the world or I.

HELMER. You are ill, Nora; you are delirious; I almost think you are out of your mind.

NORA. I have never felt my mind so clear and certain as tonight.

HELMER. And is it with a clear and certain mind that you forsake your husband and your children?

NORA. Yes, it is.

1045 HELMER. Then there is only one possible explanation.

NORA. What is that?

HELMER. You do not love me anymore.

NORA. No, that is just it.

1050 HELMER. Nora!—and you can say that?

NORA. It gives me great pain, Torvald, for you have always been so kind to me, but I cannot help it. I do not love you anymore.

1055 HELMER (regaining his composure). Is that a clear and certain conviction too?

NORA. Yes, absolutely clear and certain. That is the reason why I will not stay here any longer.

1060 HELMER. And can you tell me what I have done to forfeit your love?

NORA. Yes, indeed I can. It was tonight, when the wonderful thing did not happen; then I saw you were not the man I had thought you.

HELMER. Explain yourself better—I don't understand you.

NORA. I have waited so patiently for eight years; for, goodness knows, I knew very well that wonderful things don't happen every day. Then this horrible misfortune came upon me; and then I felt quite certain that the wonderful thing was going to happen at last. When Krogstad's letter was lying out there, never for a moment did I imagine that you would consent to accept this man's conditions. I was so absolutely certain that you would say to him: Publish the thing to the whole world. And when that was done—

HELMER. Yes, what then?—when I had exposed my wife to shame and disgrace?

NORA. When that was done, I was so abso-
1085 lutely certain, you would come forward and take everything upon yourself, and say: I am the guilty one.

HELMER. Nora—!

NORA. You mean that I would never have accepted such a sacrifice on your part?
1090 No, of course not. But what would my assurances have been worth against yours? That was the wonderful thing which I hoped for and feared; and it was to prevent that, that I wanted to
1095 kill myself.

HELMER. I would gladly work night and day for you, Nora—bear sorrow and want for your sake. But no man would sacrifice his honour for the one he loves.

1100 **NORA.** It is a thing hundreds of thousands of women have done.

HELMER. Oh, you think and talk like a heedless child.

NORA. Maybe. But you neither think nor talk
1105 like the man I could bind myself to. As soon as your fear was over—and it was not fear for what threatened me, but for what might happen to you—when the whole thing was past, as far as you were
1110 concerned it was exactly as if nothing at all had happened. Exactly as before, I was your little skylark, your doll, which you would in future treat with doubly gentle care, because it was so brittle and fragile.
1115 (*Getting up.*) Torvald—it was then it dawned upon me that for eight years I had been living here with a strange man, and had borne him three children—. Oh! I can't bear to think of it! I could tear
1120 myself into little bits!

HELMER (*sadly*). I see, I see. An abyss has opened between us—there is no denying it. But, Nora, would it not be possible to fill it up?

1125 **NORA.** As I am now, I am no wife for you.

HELMER. I have it in me to become a different man.

NORA. Perhaps—if your doll is taken away from you.

1130 **HELMER.** But to part!—to part from you! No, no, Nora, I can't understand that idea.

NORA (*going out to the right*). That makes it all the more certain that it must be done. (*She comes back with her cloak and hat and
1135 a small bag which she puts on a chair by the table.*)

HELMER. Nora, Nora, not now! Wait till tomorrow.

NORA (*putting on her cloak*). I cannot spend
1140 the night in a strange man's room.

HELMER. But can't we live here like brother and sister—?

NORA (*putting on her hat*). You know very well that would not last long. (*Puts the shawl
1145 round her.*) Goodbye, Torvald. I won't see the little ones. I know they are in better hands than mine. As I am now, I can be of no use to them.

HELMER. But some day, Nora—some day?

1150 **NORA.** How can I tell? I have no idea what is going to become of me.

HELMER. But you are my wife, whatever becomes of you.

NORA. Listen, Torvald. I have heard that
1155 when a wife deserts her husband's house, as I am doing now, he is legally freed from all obligations towards her. In any case I set you free from all your obligations. You are not to feel yourself bound in the
1160 slightest way, any more than I shall. There must be perfect freedom on both sides. See, here is your ring back. Give me mine.

HELMER. That too?

NORA. That too.

1165 **HELMER.** Here it is.

NORA. That's right. Now it is all over. I have put the keys here. The maids know all about everything in the house—better than I do. Tomorrow, after I have left her,

1170 Christine will come here and pack up my own things that I brought with me from home. I will have them sent after me.

HELMER. All over! All over!—Nora, shall you never think of me again?

1175 **NORA.** I know I shall often think of you and the children and this house.

HELMER. May I write to you, Nora?

NORA. No—never. You must not do that.

HELMER. But at least let me send you—

1180 **NORA.** Nothing—nothing—

HELMER. Let me help you if you are in want.

NORA. No. I can receive nothing from a stranger.

HELMER. Nora—can I never be anything

1185 more than a stranger to you?

NORA (*taking her bag*). Ah, Torvald, the most wonderful thing of all would have to happen.

HELMER. Tell me what that would be!

1190 **NORA.** Both you and I would have to be so changed that—. Oh, Torvald, I don't believe any longer in wonderful things happening.

HELMER. But I will believe in it. Tell me? So

1195 changed that—?

NORA. That our life together would be a real wedlock. Goodbye. (*She goes out through the hall.*)

HELMER (*sinks down on a chair at the door and

1200 buries his face in his hands*). Nora! Nora! (*Looks round, and rises.*) Empty. She is gone. (*A hope flashes across his mind.*) The most wonderful thing of all—?

(*The sound of a door shutting is heard from

1205 below.*)

The image is from Stef Smith's *Nora: A Doll's House* (photo by Marc Brenner). In this 2020 production, Smith reimagines Nora in 1918, 1968, and 2018.

Consider this image that reimagines Nora. How might this contemporary rendition of the play and its images of women throughout history change your perspective on Nora's future? Explain.

© Marc Brenner

CHARACTER

1. In Act III, how has Nora changed from Act I? Explain.

2. What provokes Mrs. Linde to make the choices that she does?

3. Which specific words, phrases, and details does Nora use to describe her husband? How has her view changed? Is Nora's language justified? Why or why not?

4. What is Nora's final action in the play? What does it reveal about her?

SETTING

5. In Act III, Ibsen introduces the dollhouse as a metaphor. Explain the significance of the play's title.

STRUCTURE

6. How does Torvald receiving the letter cause, develop, or resolve a **conflict**?

7. How does the relationship between Nora and Torvald reveal the truth about a relationship in Nora's past? Explain.

8. Is the play's **conflict** resolved? Review the sequence of events surrounding the end of the play and explain your response.

IDEAS IN LITERATURE: Power and Control

9. Over the years, some viewers and readers of the play have claimed that the shutting of the door at the end echoed all around the world. How does the shutting of the door contribute to the power and control that resonates in the play? What might it suggest about women? How might it continue to affect those who see and read the play today?

PUTTING IT ALL TOGETHER

10. The tension in the play builds to a climactic moment that reveals Nora's new understanding and insight. What is her insight and how does the dramatic structure in *A Doll's House* contribute to that new understanding?

Writing about Character

 Enduring Understanding (LAN-1)

Readers establish and communicate their interpretations of literature through arguments supported by textual evidence.

KEY POINT

Commentary serves to link the evidence to the writer's interpretation by explaining the relationship among the evidence, the line of reasoning, and the claim in the thesis statement.

Explaining an Interpretation through Commentary

When reading, watching, or listening to stories, we often react most intensely to the characters. We cheer for protagonists when they overcome obstacles. We cringe when they make questionable choices. We feel sad or even cry when they come to a tragic end. As readers, we genuinely care about them. And sometimes, we see a bit of ourselves in certain characters — whether we hope to emulate them or whether we hope to avoid their bad decisions and misfortunes.

It is no wonder that our reactions to fictional characters are so passionate. Using different methods of **characterization**, authors create their characters strategically to represent commonly shared values. These values may (or may not) belong to both the characters and the author. Like real people, characters are complex. They struggle in a world in which they must make difficult choices. The way an author presents a character directly affects the readers' interpretation of the work.

In this composition workshop, you will learn how to write a literary argument that analyzes a character (or characters) in a text. Building on your work in Units 1 and 2, you will develop a defensible thesis statement that conveys your interpretation (idea + insight) as it relates to characterization. Next, you will support your thesis with a line of reasoning and evidence. Finally, you will learn the important step of writing **commentary** that explains your evidence by linking it to your reason or topic sentence.

YOUR ASSIGNMENT

Choose a text from Unit 3 or one that your teacher has assigned. Then, write a literary argument that analyzes a character and conveys an interpretation of the work. Support your thesis with evidence from the text.

Your argument should interpret a literary work and include the following:

- An introduction that identifies the title, author, context, and character
- A thesis statement with a claim that conveys an interpretation (a unifying idea + insight about that idea)
- A line of reasoning that justifies the interpretation in the claim
- Relevant textual evidence that supports the line of reasoning
- Commentary that links the evidence to the unifying idea in the line of reasoning

Potential Subjects

- A character who is driven by a selfish or immoral motive
- A character who demonstrates growth or maturity
- A character who contrasts with another character in the story or play
- A character who commits an evil act
- A character who rebels against society
- A character who suffers from illness or disease
- A character who must respond to temptation
- A character who makes a sacrifice

Explaining Complexity

To analyze the complexity of a character, you should consider the **conflicts** and **tensions** that the character faces within the text. In some cases, the character contrasts with one or more other characters, or even with the society in which the character lives. Conflict is also possible within a single character if that character's behavior contrasts with his or her inner thoughts or values (e.g., a woman who abandons a dream for a domestic obligation, a soldier who must obey a direct order even though he may find it immoral).

When these types of conflict are present, you should examine the nature of the conflict or tension and consider what the author wishes to reveal through the **incongruity**. External and internal conflicts shed light on these tensions within the character. By exploring those internal tensions, close readers can identify the values and motivations of a character and arrive at an interpretation of the text. This is especially true of **dynamic characters** who come to a realization as a result of tensions or conflicts.

Finally, by closely studying a character's appearance, actions, interactions, speech, emotions, and inner thoughts, you can explore how the character changes and what those changes reveal. Here are some questions to help you dig a little deeper into character complexity:

- What conflicts or tensions does the character experience in the story?
- What does the character's reaction to the conflict or tension reveal about the character's values?
- How does the character change (in appearance, behavior, speech, or thinking) within the story?
- What does the character's change reveal about his or her values?
- What other characters contrast the character, and how are their values at odds?
- How does the character's behavior contrast with the character's thoughts or values?

Set a Purpose for Reading

As you review your selected text for your analysis, you must first select a character (or characters) to analyze. As you have already learned throughout the reading workshops, characters in literature are complex. In other words, they undergo changes, experience tensions, and engage in conflict throughout a story. Careful readers, therefore, examine the specific details that authors include about characters and identify a **unifying idea** associated with the overall characterization. This unifying idea is often connected to the character's values.

Consider the following questions with your unifying idea in mind as you examine the shifts, changes, and conflicts that reveal a character's values:

- Does the character's name represent attributes, virtues, or vices of the character? If so, does the character meet these expectations?

- How does the character's physical appearance relate to his or her other traits? Does the character undergo any changes in appearance or physical health in the story?

- How do the character's actions, interactions, and choices reveal his or her values? Do the character's actions, interactions, or choices shift throughout the story?

- How do the character's thoughts reveal his or her motivation? Is there a shift in these thoughts throughout the story?

- What do you learn about the character from other characters' words, thoughts, and reactions to him or her? Do these views shift or change throughout the story?

- Does the character undergo a physical, social, behavioral, emotional, psychological, or spiritual change throughout the story? How do these changes reveal the complexity of the character?

 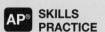 **SKILLS PRACTICE** | **LITERARY ARGUMENTATION**
Analyzing a Character

Review the text that you are analyzing for your literary argument. Record your unifying idea, as well as the topic and focus of your analysis. Then, use the graphic organizer to identify details and their significance for different moments in the work. (You may need to delete or add rows.)

Analyzing Character Complexity
Unifying idea:
Topic and focus of analysis:

Section of the Text	Details from the Text	Insights and Connections to the Unifying Idea

Develop a Defensible Thesis Statement

A thesis statement for a character analysis, as in other literary arguments, requires a claim that includes your interpretation. In this essay, you will focus on how the methods of characterization contribute to this interpretation. You should identify the character and the specific focus of your analysis — along with your broader interpretation of the text — within your thesis statement.

WRITING A THESIS FOR ANALYSIS OF CHARACTER	
Template 1: The thesis identifies two different character traits to establish a line of reasoning and connect to the idea.	In [title of work], [author] characterizes [character] as not only [characteristic 1] but also [characteristic 2] to illustrate [unifying idea + insight].
Template 2: The thesis identifies a change in the character to establish a line of reasoning and connect to the idea.	In [title of work], [author] reveals the change in [character] from [attribute 1] to [attribute 2] to illuminate [unifying idea + insight].
Template 3: The thesis identifies attributes of contrasting characters to establish a line of reasoning and connect to the idea.	In [title of work], [author] contrasts the [attribute] of [character 1] to the [attribute] of [character 2] to suggest that [unifying idea + insight].

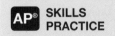 | LITERARY ARGUMENTATION
Developing a Thesis Statement for Character Analysis

Record the unifying idea and insight of the text that you are analyzing in the following graphic organizer. Next, using the thesis templates as a guide, write a defensible thesis statement. You may choose whether or not to preview your line of reasoning.

Developing a Defensible Thesis Statement for Character Analysis		
Topic	**Claim**	
Title, Author, and Focus (aspect of character)	Unifying Idea +	Insight

Organize a Line of Reasoning

You learned in Unit 2 that you justify your interpretation with a line of reasoning that is revealed in your topic sentences. For a literary argument that analyzes a character, your line of reasoning will focus on specific aspects of the character that relate back to the unifying idea in your claim.

In developing your line of reasoning, you might organize your reasons in one of the following aspects:

- Character attributes and choices that reveal the character's values
- A shift in character attributes or behaviors that reveal a change in the character's values
- A contrast to another character that illuminates the character's values

Recall that the reasons in your argument should be presented in a logical progression. Therefore, you might analyze the character details as they are revealed within the story to illustrate the development of the character. If you are writing about a shift in the character, for example, you should present the details before the shift and then explain the evidence of the change after the shift. If you are contrasting your character with another, you might organize your analysis by parallel categories of comparison (e.g., physical attributes, behavior, relationships, or attitudes and values).

STRUCTURE OF A CHARACTER ANALYSIS

Introduction

The **introduction** is an opportunity for the writer to establish the purpose of his or her literary argument and to invite the audience into the literary work and the writer's interpretation of it. To achieve this goal, many literary arguments follow this structure:

- Engage the audience through an interesting hook
- Provide historical, cultural, or social context of a literary work
- Identify the title, author, genre (TAG)
- Introduce the literary topic of analysis by
  - describing the importance of that literary concept; and
  - summarizing the work succinctly with details critical to that concept

The **thesis statement** presents a defensible interpretation that includes an idea and an insight about that idea.

Body

(Develops a line of reasoning with supporting evidence that justifies the thesis)

Topic Sentence 1	Topic Sentence 2	Topic Sentence 3
(Identify the first aspect of the character related to the unifying idea)	(Identify the second aspect of the character related to the unifying idea)	(Identify the third aspect of the character related to the unifying idea)
Textual Details	**Textual Details**	**Textual Details**
(Evidence of elements and techniques that contribute to character development and complexity)	(Evidence of elements and techniques that contribute to character development and complexity)	(Evidence of elements and techniques that contribute to character development and complexity)
Commentary	**Commentary**	**Commentary**
(Link evidence by explaining its relevance to the line of reasoning and claim)	(Link evidence by explaining its relevance to the line of reasoning and claim)	(Link evidence by explaining its relevance to the line of reasoning and claim)

Conclusion

The **conclusion** should do more than restate the thesis; rather, it should be a robust and important paragraph. It is the opportunity for the writer to demonstrate understanding of the literary work's relevance and explain how the literary work stands the test of time and reflects the human experience. Writers further their idea and insight by:

- Discussing the significance or relevance of interpretation
- Relating the work to other relevant literary works
- Connecting the theme to their own experience
- Presenting alternate interpretations
- Explaining how the work explores complexities and tensions
- Situating the theme within a broader context

This table illustrates the general structure of a literary argument. It does not intend to imply that all literary arguments are five paragraphs. Writers should determine the number of reasons needed to justify their claim, as well as how much evidence is sufficient to support each of these reasons.

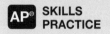 | **SKILLS PRACTICE** | LITERARY ARGUMENTATION
Developing a Line of Reasoning

Review your thesis statement, which may or may not preview the line of reasoning. Record the topic sentences to represent your line of reasoning and place them in a logical order. As you do this, consider the potential evidence from the text that helped you arrive at your line of reasoning. That textual evidence will serve as support for these reasons.

Organizing a Character Analysis		
Defensible Thesis Statement with Claim (idea + insight):		
Topic Sentence 1 (Identify the first aspect of the character related to the unifying idea):	**Topic Sentence 2** (Identify the second aspect of the character related to the unifying idea):	**Topic Sentence 3** (Identify the third aspect of the character related to the unifying idea):

Select Relevant Evidence

In earlier workshops, you have learned how to select and introduce **relevant evidence** from a text to support your line of reasoning. Recall that every reason must be accompanied by relevant supporting evidence. In other words, the evidence you select must relate directly to the purpose for that paragraph as it is established in the topic sentence.

In this workshop, you have been focusing specifically on how an author's methods of characterization contribute to your analysis of the character and to your interpretation of the text. In a longer work, you will learn a great deal about the main characters; you may even become overwhelmed with the amount of details and information available to you for your analysis. For this reason, you must select your evidence strategically, choosing only the most relevant details and moments in the text and providing the best evidence to exemplify each of your reasons.

Additionally, you must be aware of the narrative context as you choose details so that you are accurate in your portrayal of the character. If you misrepresent the character by pulling a detail or quotation out of context, your analysis could unravel. Remember to choose the best pieces of evidence and arrange them in the paragraphs where they provide the most apt support.

Keeping your unifying idea in mind, you might incorporate evidence that illustrates, clarifies, exemplifies, associates, amplifies, or qualifies the following aspects of characterization:

- Physical descriptions of the character, including imagery and comparisons
- Details of the character's actions during significant moments
- Direct quotations from the character, including thoughts and dialogue
- Quotations from other characters revealing attitudes or judgments
- Textual details or evidence that reveal a shift in attitude, perspective, or values

Finally, strategic writers not only choose relevant evidence and use it strategically but they also make sure that they have **sufficient evidence** to support the argument. Every reason in the line of reasoning must have evidence for support. You will need to judge how much evidence is needed to prove each reason. For example, if you are writing about a character's change throughout the course of a narrative, it would be insufficient to include only one piece of evidence from the beginning of the story. That would be neither strategic nor sufficient.

Once you have chosen your evidence, introduce it within your argument with a **signal phrase**. Review the following sentence stems to help you incorporate your evidence fluently:

- For example, . . .
- For instance, . . .
- As an illustration, . . .
- In the following lines, . . .
- The author includes the details of . . .
- As an example of the character's [trait], the author writes, . . .
- To highlight the character's [trait], the author describes him/her as . . .
- The description of the [character, setting] as . . .
- The use of [literary element or technique], as seen in the example . . .
- When [character says/does/thinks] . . .

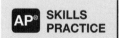 SKILLS
PRACTICE

LITERARY ARGUMENTATION
Incorporating Relevant and Sufficient Evidence

Write your thesis statement and develop a logical line of reasoning to support your interpretation. Carefully organize your body paragraphs and arrange the evidence within them. Next, draft two or more body paragraphs that include evidence from the text to support each reason. Include transitions to link your reasons and evidence to your claim.

Incorporating Relevant and Sufficient Evidence		
Defensible Thesis Statement with Claim (idea + insight):		
Topic Sentence 1 (Identify the first aspect of the character related to the unifying idea):	**Topic Sentence 2** (Identify the second aspect of the character related to the unifying idea):	**Topic Sentence 3** (Identify the third aspect of the character related to the unifying idea):
Textual Details (Relevant and sufficient evidence):	**Textual Details** (Relevant and sufficient evidence):	**Textual Details** (Relevant and sufficient evidence):

Write Insightful Commentary

One key to success in the literary argument is in explaining how the evidence links to the line of reasoning and the claim (idea + insight). By linking, you will create **unity** in your essay. When building the content of your body paragraphs, you should follow this basic pattern: identify — evidence — link. The link step in this pattern represents your explanation of the relevance of the evidence, also called **commentary**. Commentary works within your argument to do the following:

- It explains how one piece of evidence relates to another.
- It explains the function of the author's literary choices.

- It explains how the evidence links to the reasons in the topic sentences.
- It explains how the reasons in the line of reasoning link to the claim in the thesis.
- It unifies the argument by communicating your insight about the unifying idea.

Too often, however, writers substitute plot summary or paraphrase for insightful (or analytical) commentary. These writers mistakenly believe they are offering insight that links to the idea when they are simply retelling events, repeating general observations, or even defining a literary element or technique. However, this kind of explanation does not create a link to ideas; it may neglect the writer's interpretation entirely.

Commentary is where the majority of literary analysis takes place. To state it another way: commentary fulfills the mission determined by the thesis statement. Therefore, when you write your commentary, you should keep a tight hold on the idea and insight in your thesis statement while elaborating on your evidence. In this space, your task is to explain the effect of the author's choices and to persuade your audience that your interpretation of the text is valid. If you have selected your evidence carefully, and the details you incorporate connect to the line of reasoning and unifying idea, you are more likely to be able to explain *why* and *how* in your commentary.

As you write your essay, you will need to decide how the commentary should function at that moment. As a general rule, sentences of commentary should outnumber sentences that only present your evidence. In other words, you should consistently explain the connections among all the elements in your essay.

The following chart includes sentence stems that will help you explain the function of your textual evidence. In later units, we will continue to explore ways to incorporate insightful commentary and dig into the complexity of a text.

INSIDER AP TIP **Commentary is analytical.** Summary focuses on *what* is happening in the story rather than exploring *why* an author makes a particular literary choice and *how* that choice contributes to the reader's understanding of the text. The most effective commentary identifies an author's strategy or technique, explains the effect, and links the evidence to the reason and unifying idea.

EXPLAINING AN INTERPRETATION THROUGH COMMENTARY

The author . . .	. . . in order to . . .
alludes to	associate with
characterizes as	connect to
chooses to	convey
compares and	create a sense of
contrasts and	demonstrate
creates	depict
describes as	emphasize
employs	illustrate
includes	imply
incorporates	portray
juxtaposes and	reveal
refers to	suggest
repeats	
shifts from to	

By . . .	. . . the author
alluding to	connects to
characterizing as	conveys
choosing	demonstrates
comparing to	explores the tension between and
contrasting and	illustrates
creating	implies
describing as	questions
employing	reveals the conflict between and
including	serves to
incorporating	suggests
juxtaposing and	
shifting from to	. . . the reader
repeating	connects
	understands
	infers
	questions
	reflects upon
	compares and
	contrasts to

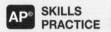 **SKILLS PRACTICE** | LITERARY ARGUMENTATION
Linking Evidence to the Line of Reasoning

Build on your emerging literary argument by adding commentary to your relevant and sufficient evidence. As you plan your explanation, carefully consider your unifying idea so that you may carry this idea throughout your argument in a unified way.

Incorporating Relevant and Sufficient Evidence		
Defensible Thesis Statement with Claim (idea + insight):		
Topic Sentence 1 (Identify the first aspect of the character related to the unifying idea):	**Topic Sentence 2** (Identify the second aspect of the character related to the unifying idea):	**Topic Sentence 3** (Identify the third aspect of the character related to the unifying idea):
Textual Details (Relevant and sufficient evidence):	**Textual Details** (Relevant and sufficient evidence):	**Textual Details** (Relevant and sufficient evidence):
Signal phrase and evidence 1:	Signal phrase and evidence 1:	Signal phrase and evidence 1:
Signal phrase and evidence 2:	Signal phrase and evidence 2:	Signal phrase and evidence 2:
Commentary (Link evidence to reason and idea):	**Commentary** (Link evidence to reason and idea):	**Commentary** (Link evidence to reason and idea):
Sentence stem and explanation of function of evidence:	Sentence stem and explanation of function of evidence:	Sentence stem and explanation of function of evidence:

Contextualize Your Argument

In the first two units, you have worked on writing thesis statements to guide your literary arguments. However, the thesis statement is rarely the first sentence of an essay. In an **introduction**, writers often contextualize the literary work before

 SKILLS PRACTICE | LITERARY ARGUMENTATION
Introducing Your Literary Argument

In the chart below, record some notes to help you communicate the context of your argument, along with other introductory material that will funnel your ideas to your thesis statement. Next, record ideas to help you explain the relevance of your idea and insight in your concluding statements.

Introducing Your Literary Argument	
Introducing Context	
Title, Author, Genre	
Character and Narrative Situation	
Thesis	

presenting their thesis. These sentences are not just extra. They help establish the essential context for the argument. In a character analysis, for example, an introduction can situate the character within a time and place, or introduce a conflict or tension before you reveal your interpretation of the text.

It may seem counterintuitive to write an introduction after you have completed your analysis; however, the purpose of an introduction is to set up your argument for your reader. Therefore, you are better able to situate your argument after you have completed it.

Your introduction will serve as an invitation for readers to join you in exploring the literary text. An effective introduction includes the following:

- A hook or lead sentence or two that provides narrative context for the reader
- A reference to the title, author, and genre of the text
- A sentence that funnels the discussion from the general context to the focus of the thesis
- A thesis statement that includes a claim (idea + insight)

Revise Your Argument

For your character analysis, review the following questions related to your treatment of complex characters. Revise your draft if you answer no to any of the following questions:

- Does your introduction provide relevant background information and context for your character?

- Does your identification of the character's change, conflict, or contrast focus on the significance of the character within your interpretation of the story rather than just facts and information about the character?
- Do your reasons in your line of reasoning refer to the unifying idea related to your character and support your interpretation?
- Have you included relevant details, methods of characterization, and narrative techniques that contribute to your analysis of the character and interpretation of the text?
- Does your interpretation of the work logically align with your discussion of the character's change, contrast, or complexity?
- Is your argument coherent with a logical sequence of reasons and transitions that connect evidence, reasons, and claim?
- Does your commentary unify your argument by connecting your evidence and reasons to your unifying idea?

 **SKILLS PRACTICE** | LITERARY ARGUMENTATION
Revising and Editing a Character Analysis

After you have completed revising and editing your own argument, review another student's literary argument and provide helpful feedback.

Peer-Revision Checklist: Revising and Editing a Character Analysis		
Revising and Editing Checklist	Unit 3 Focus Skills	Comment on the Effectiveness and/or Make a Suggestion
Does the writer include the narrative situation and perspective, title, and author of the literary text in the first paragraph? Does the brief summary of context lead to the idea?	Introductions for character analysis	
Does the thesis statement convey an interpretation? Does the interpretation connect to an idea and an insight?	Defensible thesis	
Does the writer provide a logical sequence of reasons to support the idea and insight in the thesis? Are these reasons linked to the claim with transitions?	Line of reasoning: Unity	
Does the writer provide relevant and sufficient evidence to support the interpretation in the thesis? Is the evidence linked to the topic sentences with transitions?	Relevant and sufficient evidence: Coherence	

(continued)

Revising and Editing Checklist	Unit 3 Focus Skills	Comment on the Effectiveness and/or Make a Suggestion
Does the writer explain how the evidence supports a reason and connects to the interpretation in the thesis? Does the commentary connect to the unifying idea?	Commentary: Unity	
Does the writer explain the argument's significance within a broader context?	Relevance	
Does the writer demonstrate control over the conventions of writing?	Conventions	

Student Model: Writing about Character

Review the following student model which analyzes two contrasting characters. Observe how the thesis statement, line of reasoning, and evidence work together to convey an interpretation of the work.

Tom Jones: A Study in Compassion
By Jillian Skaggs

It seems to be human nature to want to conform to society's moral and ethical standards: almost everyone wants to fit in, and it takes great strength to stand on one's own. In addition, while we most often hew to what we think is right according to society's norms, those norms change. In 1749, Henry Fielding published the novel *Tom Jones*, which begins with the finding of a baby, which is evidently born out of wedlock, in Squire Allworthy's bed, something extremely scandalous in the 1700's. He calls his servant, Mrs. Deborah Wilkins, an older lady with almost a Victorian (some 100 years before the Victorian Era) sense of propriety. By contrasting the responses of Squire Allworthy and Mrs. Deborah Wilkins, Fielding characterizes Mr. Allworthy as a compassionate, if occasionally fixated, man and Mrs. Deborah as a submissive, yet forthright woman in order to convey the idea that society's notions about propriety are some-times overvalued and should be brushed aside.

By describing Squire Allworthy's response to finding an unknown baby in his bed, Fielding characterizes Mr. Allworthy as a compassionate, if occasionally fixated, man, uninterested in propriety. While at first he simply stands in astonishment,

identifies contrasting characters, bridge to thesis

thesis statement with interpretation
idea: propriety
insight: humans overvalue propriety
contrasting characters

topic sentence: benevolent character uninterested in propriety "his good-nature had always the ascendant in his mind, [and] he soon began to be touched with sentiments of compassion for the little wretch before him." Upon seeing the infant, Mr. Allworthy's compassion shines. He gives no immediate thought to the baby's parents or position in life, only that it is a child in need. Fielding characterizes Mr. Allworthy as a good man in order to emphasize his disregard of propriety when compassion should be the goal. Emphasizing this Christian context, he tells of Mr. Allworthy's nightly "minutes on his knees . . . which he never br[eaks] on any account," cementing his devotion to God. In addition, Fielding chooses the name Squire Allworthy, conferring nobility through Squire and the worthiness and goodness of the character through Allworthy. It is not until the end of the first paragraph that his flaw of fixation comes into the picture. He is in a state of undress (though perhaps not by modern standards) in only his shirt when he finds the baby, and he calls for Mrs. Deborah. So entranced by the baby, Mr. Allworthy fails to consider his state of undress, even though Mrs. Deborah "giv[es] her master sufficient time to dress himself . . . out of respect to him and regard to decency." Fielding continues to add strength to Allworthy's fixation as Allworthy almost completely misses Mrs. Deborah's speech as he "ha[s] now got one of his fingers into the infant's hand, which by its gentle pressure, seeming to implore his assistance, had certainly outpleaded the eloquence of Mrs. Deborah." Interestingly, Fielding's portrayal does not depict the fixation as a flaw, but rather another sign of Mr. Allworthy's all-worthiness: in contrast to the tragic hero's fatal flaw (hubris, indecision, and the like), Mr. Allworthy's flaw is a further part of his flawlessness. Mr. Allworthy has total compassion and an overriding fixation on the illegitimate baby, even to the point of forgetting propriety. Thus, Fielding suggests that propriety should never be considered as important as compassion and decency.

On the other hand, Fielding characterizes Mrs. Deborah as strictly adhering to propriety, yet pliable to her master's wishes, by showcasing her dynamic response to the finding of the baby. In contrast to Mr. Allworthy's dismissal of propriety, Mrs. Deborah adheres strictly to principles of decency: "out of . . . regard to decency, she [spends] many minutes in adjusting her hair . . . notwithstanding all the hurry in which she had been summoned . . . and though her master, of aught she knew, lay expiring in apoplexy, or in some other fit." Fielding's emphasis on Mr. Allworthy's goodness in ignoring propriety immediately casts a shadow on Mrs. Deborah's sense of decency. His inclusion of the possible state of Mr. Allworthy while she dawdled at the mirror cements Mrs. Deborah as someone who places too much emphasis on propriety. When Mrs. Deborah finally opens the door to her master's room, she

evidence: character values compassion over propriety

commentary: explains how the character's choice demonstrates compassion over propriety

evidence: focuses on name and other details that illustrate benevolence

evidence: focuses on the character's actions that go against propriety

commentary: suggests the purpose of the details is to prioritize compassion over propriety

topic sentence: proper character introduced to contrast the first

evidence: character's actions suggest a foolish display of propriety

commentary: contrast of characters' actions amplifies the criticism of prioritizing propriety

immediately balks at his state of undress and might perhaps [swoon] before he orders her to step out and puts clothes on. While Mr. Allworthy fixates instantly on the baby, Mrs. Deborah is blind to it when she first opens the door. The true contrast between Mr. Allworthy and Mrs. Deborah comes when he introduces her to the baby's presence. Horrified at the breach of decency to produce a child out of wedlock, Mrs. Deborah advises that the baby "be put in a basket, and sent out and laid at the churchwarden's door. It is a good night, only a little rainy and windy; and if it was well wrapt up, and put in a warm basket, it is two to one but it lives till it is found in the morning. But if it should not, we have discharged our duty in taking proper care of it; and it is, perhaps, better for such creatures to die in a state of innocence, than to grow up and imitate their mothers." By presenting Mrs. Deborah's dialogue, Fielding presents a shocking characterization with this talk of odds and death, as the suggestion of leaving the baby at the churchwarden's door appears villainous. Since Mrs. Deborah suggests doing so, it must therefore be something society deems proper. We eventually learn that Mrs. Deborah is strictly a creature of decency unless this decency goes against the wishes of her master. While Mr. Allworthy is static in his goodness and devotion to the child in the passage, Mrs. Deborah changes. After her recommendations to leave the baby at the church door, Mr. Allworthy gives Mrs. Deborah positive orders to take the child to her own bed, and to call up a maid-servant to provide it pap, and other things. Fielding then describes Mrs. Deborah's response: "such [was] the respect she bore her master . . . that her scruples gave way to his peremptory commands; and she took the child under her arms, without any apparent disgust at the illegality of its birth; and [declared] it was a sweet little infant." Mrs. Deborah, for all her adherence to society's sense of propriety, favors her master's commands. This is not without warrant, of course: if he were to fire her, it's possible that she could starve to death on the streets. Her position as a woman and a servant dictates that she be pliable. However, Fielding emphasizes that her feelings about the child change too when her master so orders: she declares it a sweet little infant and forgets her prior disgust towards it.

Fielding wants to portray the idea that propriety should be set aside at times when decency is in question. He emphasizes the inherent, deepset, flawless goodness of Mr. Allworthy and his dismissal of the notion that the baby be sent away, and he marks the change in a decent woman who changes her attitude towards the baby and accepts it at her master's bidding. If a person who places so much on propriety should be so swayed to put it aside, then it is right to do so at times.

evidence: character's dialogue demonstrates the lack of compassion that propriety encourages

commentary: connects character's adherence to propriety to general attitudes of society

evidence: detail of the character's change from the focus on propriety to decency

commentary: explanation of the character's change links to focus on propriety

conclusion: emphasizes that strict adherence to propriety can be damaging

Free-Response Question: Literary Argument

AP **Enduring Understanding (LAN-1)**

Readers establish and communicate their interpretations of literature through arguments supported by textual evidence.

Explaining an Interpretation through Commentary

The final free-response prompt on the AP® English Literature and Composition Exam requires you to write a literary argument about an assigned topic that focuses on your choice of a work of fiction. The topics assigned in the prompts will focus on a particular aspect of literature (e.g., character, setting, structure, narration). In this workshop, you will begin to develop the skills you need to complete this task with a specific focus on writing commentary that links your evidence to your reasoning.

Read the following practice prompt, and the list of suggested works, which is a model of the type of prompt you may see on the exam. Please note that you may select a work from the list of suggestions or another work of fiction of your own choosing.

Prompt:

Many works of literature feature characters who, through their circumstances or relationships, learn a valuable lesson or come to a new understanding throughout the course of the narrative.

Either from your own reading or from the following list, choose a work of fiction in which a character learns a lesson or gains a new understanding. Then, in a well-written essay, analyze how this lesson reveals the character's values and contributes to an interpretation of the work as a whole. Do not merely summarize the plot.

In your response, you should do the following:

- Respond to the prompt with a thesis that presents a defensible interpretation
- Select and use evidence to support your line of reasoning
- Explain how the evidence supports your line of reasoning
- Use appropriate grammar and punctuation in communicating your argument

All the Light We Cannot See	*Jasmine*
Atonement	*Kindred*
The Awakening	*The Leavers*
Bartleby the Scrivener	*A Lesson Before Dying*
Black Boy	*Mudbound*
Bless Me, Ultima	*The Nickel Boys*
The Bluest Eye	*Obasan*
Brown Girl, Brownstones	*Othello*
A Doll's House	*The Picture of Dorian Gray*
Frankenstein	*The Poisonwood Bible*
Geek Love	*A Prayer for Owen Meany*
A Gesture Life	*The Rime of the Ancient Mariner*
The Handmaid's Tale	*Sing, Unburied Sing*
Harry Potter and the Deathly Hallows	*The Strange Case of Dr. Jekyll and Mr. Hyde*
Heads of the Colored People	*The Street*
House Made of Dawn	*The Sympathizer*
I'm Not Your Perfect Mexican Daughter	*A Tale of Two Cities*
In the Time of Butterflies	*Things Fall Apart*
Invisible Man	*A Thousand Splendid Suns*
Jane Eyre	*Where the Crawdad's Sing*

→ ## Step One: Determine a Unifying Idea and Determine Relevant Examples from a Text

When you read the prompt for the open question literary argument, you must make sure that you understand exactly what the question is asking by examining the topic carefully. To address the question, you are invited to choose a work of fiction to explore. Note that you should write about only one work in your argument. Since you get to choose the work, you should pick one that you know well enough to provide relevant and specific details in your analysis.

Next, when you identify the specific topic in the question, you will further narrow your focus within your chosen work. Longer fiction contains multiple characters, settings, and relevant moments. However, when you read the prompt, you should pay close attention to the directions as most require a specific focus on *a character* or *a setting*. In this case, you should not write about multiple characters or settings, etc. as it will make your analysis too broad or general.

Here are a few possibilities:

- A type or aspect of character (e.g., a villain, a minor character, parent-child relationships)

- A type or function of setting (e.g., country settings, contrasting settings)

- A feature of structure (e.g., happy endings, distortion of time)
- A type or function of the narrator (e.g., reliable narrators, objective narrators)

The prompt requires you to explain how the author's choice to include this literary element (e.g., a villain, contrasting settings, distorted time) contributes to an interpretation of the work as a whole. As you dig into the topic, then, you need to identify a **unifying idea** that emerges from the details. This idea will likely surface as you examine the relationship between the topic, major themes in the work of literature, and details about your specific focus.

Consider these questions as you prepare to write your literary argument:

- Which work of fiction do you know that will serve as the best evidence for the topic of this literary argument?
- What specific subject from the work (i.e., character, setting, scene, or other aspect indicated in the prompt) will be the focus of the analysis?
- What idea and insight about that idea emerge as you explore the topic within the specific work?
- What significant moments and details in the work relate to the idea?
- What insight will you offer about the idea based on these details?

For example, the practice prompt directs you to identify a character who learns a lesson or reaches a new understanding throughout the course of the narrative. It further asks how that lesson reveals the values of the character and contributes to an interpretation of the work. If you choose to explore the novel *Jane Eyre* and its title character, then you might note that Jane values independence as she progresses throughout the narrative.

Next, recall the most relevant moments for Jane and identify a lesson she learned that illustrates this value. Finally, once you have chosen your idea and explored the relevant moments, you can express an insight about the idea. In this novel, Jane learns that she must first struggle to be independent so that she can participate meaningfully in her relationships.

→ Step Two: Develop a Defensible Claim and a Unified Line of Reasoning

You have learned in earlier workshops that you must make a defensible claim in your thesis statement, and that a claim includes an idea and insight. A defensible thesis for this student-choice literary argument makes a claim (idea + insight) that conveys your interpretation of the work as a whole. Once you state this claim, you must determine the reasons that will support your claim. In the poetry and prose analysis tasks, you explored the author's techniques to develop your line of reasoning. For the open-ended question, you will need to use the topic in the prompt to guide your reasoning. For example, if you are exploring a character, then the character's attributes, choices, relationships with other characters, or evidence of change may guide your line of reasoning.

Your thesis should be included in your **introduction** or may serve as your introduction. If your introduction is more than one sentence, then you might briefly introduce the topic of the essay. Next, you should write one or two sentences of summary about the narrative context of your work, specifically related to this topic. Finally, you should narrow the focus down to your defensible thesis statement, which may or may not preview your line of reasoning.

Examine the following example of a thesis and line of reasoning (topic sentences) for the sample question.

Thesis Statement

In Charlotte Brontë's novel Jane Eyre, *the protagonist discovers that she must achieve both financial and emotional independence before she can feel like an equal partner in her relationships with others.*

Topic Sentence 1	Topic Sentence 2
When Jane experiences financial independence, she begins to believe she has more to contribute to her relationships.	*Jane finally learns that in addition to financial independence, she must be emotionally independent to contribute equally to her relationships.*

→ Step Three: Choose Relevant Evidence

Because you will not have a provided passage nor will you be permitted to use a copy of your literary text during the exam, your evidence will consist primarily of paraphrased details from the work. You must rely on the topic of the passage to determine which evidence from your chosen text is relevant to support your claim.

Recall that your evidence must be both relevant and sufficient. Relevant evidence comes from details that are directly related to your topic of discussion. Even though you will not have the text, your evidence should still be apt and specific. Your details will likely come from the elements of literature (e.g., character, setting, structure, and narration) and focus on major moments from the text.

Your evidence, therefore, must be sufficient in both specificity and quantity to support your claim. For example, in discussing the lesson Jane Eyre learns within the narrative, it is not enough just to write, "Early in her life, Jane depends a great deal on the people around her." That statement is too general; it is also inadequate to support the assertion. Instead, you must provide a specific instance or moment, such as at Lowood Charity School, when Jane relishes the private tea time with her kind teacher Miss Temple and relies heavily on the wisdom and counsel of her friend Helen to navigate the cruel environment and harsh conditions.

Additionally, as we learned in Unit 2, you must arrange your evidence strategically within your line of reasoning. You should choose the best pieces of evidence and place them in the proper paragraph and then arrange the evidence within the paragraph in the most logical and effective order.

Review the following example of evidence to support the line of reasoning in the sample prompt.

Topic Sentence 1	Topic Sentence 2
When Jane experiences financial independence, she begins to believe she has more to contribute to her relationships.	*Jane finally learns that in addition to financial independence, she must be emotionally independent to contribute equally to her relationships.*
Relevant and Sufficient Evidence	**Relevant and Sufficient Evidence**
Thornfield: *Jane realizes that if she does not like the job, she can advertise for another.* *Moor House:* *Jane resists the temptation to depend upon St. John for her livelihood.* *Jane becomes financially independent through her inheritance.*	*Lowood School:* *Jane is alone and depends upon her teacher, Miss Temple, and her friend Helen to navigate the harsh environment.* *Thornfield:* *She begins to feel a motherly connection to her pupil Adele and an affection for her master Mr. Rochester.* *She becomes dependent upon the opinions of Mr. Rochester.* *Moor House:* *Jane gains the confidence to return to Thornfield to be an equal partner to Rochester.*

To introduce the evidence for your argument, you might use some of the following sentence stems:

- For example, . . .
- For instance, . . .
- As an illustration, . . .
- The following lines, . . .
- The author includes the details of . . .
- As an example of the character's [trait], the author writes . . .
- To highlight the character's [trait], the author describes him/her as . . .
- The description of the [character, setting] as . . .
- The use of [literary element or technique], as seen in the example . . .
- When [character says/does/thinks] . . .

→ Step Four: Develop Your Commentary

To develop your literary argument, must include commentary that explains how the evidence you included links to the line of reasoning and the claim (idea + insight).

Your specific details should be followed by an explanation, also called **commentary**. Commentary works within your argument to do the following:

- It explains how one piece of evidence relates to another.
- It explains how the evidence links to the reasons in the topic sentences.
- It explains how the reasons in the line of reasoning link to the claim in the thesis.
- It unifies the argument by communicating your insight about the unifying idea.

Because you are writing about an entire work, you might feel overwhelmed with the amount of information you might include. In fact, you may be tempted to summarize the events of the text rather than keep your focus on the specific topic. However, if your commentary remains focused on your unifying idea, then you are less likely to summarize irrelevant information.

Remember that your commentary serves the purpose of creating a link between your evidence and your idea. In this way, you are conveying your interpretation to your reader, who may or may not have read the work you are analyzing. Your commentary must make strong connections between the specific moments and the insight, especially if your reader is unfamiliar with the work. If your evidence is specific enough and your commentary is thorough, your reader can follow your argument without having read the text.

Here are a few sentence stems to help you get started with commentary. You may also consult the chart on page 394. In later units, we will continue to explore ways to incorporate insightful commentary and dig into the complexity of a text.

- The author includes details about/to convey/reveal/illustrate _____.
- The author compares/contrasts/juxtaposes and to emphasize _____.
- The author wishes the reader to notice/understand/examine _____.
- This reveals/shows/demonstrates/contrasts to _____.
- This event/incident/choice/detail illustrates _____.

Evidence	Commentary Connected to Idea
As an illustration of Jane Eyre's growing financial independence, Brontë includes Jane's realization that if the working conditions are unfavorable at Thornfield or if she is unhappy, she can simply seek other employment.	*Jane's emerging thought of independence starkly contrasts her timid and fearful younger self that the reader witnessed at Lowood School. Brontë wishes the reader to notice that Jane is beginning to discover a source of power within herself. However, as the narrative continues, Jane's progress will stall as she becomes tangled in the world of Thornfield.*

 **INSIDER** **AP® TIP**

Commentary is where analysis happens. As you write your essay, you will need to decide how the commentary should function at that moment. As a general rule, sentences of commentary should outnumber sentences that merely present your evidence. In other words, you should consistently explain the connections among all the elements in your essay.

AP® EXAM PRACTICE

The following is an example of the literary argument free-response question. Practice the skills you have learned in this workshop to write an argument in response to the prompt.

Remember to follow the four steps:

- Step One: Brainstorm evidence based on a **unifying idea**
- Step Two: Write a **defensible thesis statement**
- Step Three: Choose **relevant evidence**
- Step Four: Develop **insightful commentary**

> "If there is no possibility for change in a character, we have no interest in him."
> — Flannery O'Connor

Novels and plays often feature dynamic characters who experience a significant change throughout the course of the narrative. Readers may note a difference in the character's behavior, relationships, or perspectives. It is through these changes that authors reveal the character's motives and values.

Either from your own reading or from the following list, choose a work of fiction in which a character experiences a significant change. Then, in a well-written essay, analyze how the character's change reveals his or her values and contributes to an interpretation of the work as a whole. Do not merely summarize the plot.

In your response, you should do the following:

- Respond to the prompt with a thesis that presents a defensible interpretation
- Select and use evidence to support your line of reasoning
- Explain how the evidence supports your line of reasoning
- Use appropriate grammar and punctuation in communicating your argument

The Alchemist	*No-No Boy*
All the Light We Cannot See	*Othello*
Belinda	*The Picture of Dorian Gray*

The Bluest Eye

Cat on a Hot Tin Roof

A Doll's House

Don Quixote

Frankenstein

Geek Love

Great Expectations

Heads of the Colored People

Home to Harlem

Homegoing

House Made of Dawn

I'm Not Your Perfect Mexican Daughter

Invisible Man

Jane Eyre

The Joy Luck Club

Metamorphosis

Mudbound

The Poisonwood Bible

A Prayer for Owen Meany

Purple Hibiscus

A Raisin in the Sun

The Remains of the Day

The Rime of the Ancient Mariner Roots

Sense and Sensibility

Sing, Unburied, Sing

Sister of My Heart

The Strange Case of Dr. Jekyll and
    Mr. Hyde

Their Eyes Were Watching God

Things Fall Apart

A Thousand Splendid Suns

Top Girls

Where the Crawdad's Sing

Wuthering Heights

ORGANIZING A LITERARY ARGUMENT (I)

Defensible Thesis Statement with Claim (idea + insight):

In [title], [author] illustrates [idea + insight] by including [aspect of topic 1], [aspect of topic 2], and [aspect of topic 3].

Topic Sentence 1	Topic Sentence 2	Topic Sentence 3
(Identify the first aspect of topic related to the unifying idea):	(Identify the second aspect of topic related to the unifying idea):	(Identify the third aspect of topic related to the unifying idea):
To begin, [author] includes [element 1] to [purpose connect to idea].	Next, [author] includes [element 2] to [purpose connect to idea].	Finally, [author] includes [element 3] to [purpose connect to idea].
Textual Details	**Textual Details**	**Textual Details**
(Relevant and sufficient evidence):	(Relevant and sufficient evidence):	(Relevant and sufficient evidence):
For example, the detail [text evidence], used to describe [context] illustrates [link to topic sentence].	To illustrate, [author] describes/ compares [context] by describing [text evidence] to reveal [link to topic sentence].	As an example of [technique/ element], the author includes [text evidence] to explain [link to topic sentence].
Similarly, the detail [text evidence], used to describe [context] illustrates [link to topic sentence].	To continue, [author] describes/ compares [context] by describing [text evidence] to reveal [link to topic sentence].	Through another example, of [technique/element], the author includes [text evidence] to explain [link to topic sentence].
Commentary	**Commentary**	**Commentary**
(Link evidence to reason and idea):	(Link evidence to reason and idea):	(Link evidence to reason and idea):
The association of [evidence] with [topic sentence] reveals [idea and insight].	Through this choice, [author] develops [idea and insight].	By including this [element/ technique] the author suggests that [idea and insight].

from The Picture of Dorian Gray

Oscar Wilde

The following is an excerpt from a novel published in 1890.

"Dorian Gray? Is that his name?" asked Lord Henry, walking across the studio towards Basil Hallward.

"Yes, that is his name. I didn't intend to tell
5 it to you."

"But why not?"

"Oh, I can't explain. When I like people immensely, I never tell their names to any one. It is like surrendering a part of them. I have grown
10 to love secrecy. It seems to be the one thing that can make modern life mysterious or marvellous to us. The commonest thing is delightful if one only hides it. When I leave town now I never tell my people where I am going. If I did, I would
15 lose all my pleasure. It is a silly habit, I dare say, but somehow it seems to bring a great deal of romance into one's life. I suppose you think me awfully foolish about it?"

"Not at all," answered Lord Henry, "not at
20 all, my dear Basil. You seem to forget that I am married, and the one charm of marriage is that it makes a life of deception absolutely necessary for both parties. I never know where my wife is, and my wife never knows
25 what I am doing. When we meet — we do meet occasionally, when we dine out together, or go down to the Duke's — we tell each other the most absurd stories with the most serious faces. My wife is very good at it — much bet-
30 ter, in fact, than I am. She never gets confused over her dates, and I always do. But when she does find me out, she makes no row[1] at all.

I sometimes wish she would; but she merely laughs at me."

35 "I hate the way you talk about your married life, Harry," said Basil Hallward, strolling towards the door that led into the garden. "I believe that you are really a very good husband, but that you are thoroughly ashamed of your own virtues.
40 You are an extraordinary fellow. You never say a moral thing, and you never do a wrong thing. Your cynicism[2] is simply a pose."

"Being natural is simply a pose, and the most irritating pose I know," cried Lord Henry, laugh-
45 ing; and the two young men went out into the garden together and ensconced themselves on a long bamboo seat that stood in the shade of a tall laurel bush. The sunlight slipped over the polished leaves. In the grass, white daisies were tremulous.
50 After a pause, Lord Henry pulled out his watch. "I am afraid I must be going, Basil," he murmured, "and before I go, I insist on your answering a question I put to you some time ago."

"What is that?" said the painter, keeping his
55 eyes fixed on the ground.

"You know quite well."

"I do not, Harry."

"Well, I will tell you what it is. I want you to explain to me why you won't exhibit Dorian
60 Gray's picture. I want the real reason."

"I told you the real reason."

"No, you did not. You said it was because there was too much of yourself in it. Now, that is childish."

65 "Harry," said Basil Hallward, looking him straight in the face, "every portrait that is

---

[1] A "row" (rhymes with "now") is British English for a serious disagreement or noisy argument.

[2] An inclination to believe that people are motivated purely by self-interest.

painted with feeling is a portrait of the
artist, not of the sitter.[3] The sitter is merely
the accident, the occasion. It is not he
70 who is revealed by the painter; it is rather
the painter who, on the coloured canvas,
reveals himself. The reason I will not
exhibit this picture is that I am afraid
that I have shown in it the secret of my
75 own soul."

Lord Henry laughed. "And what is that?" he
asked.

"I will tell you," said Hallward; but an
expression of perplexity came over his face.
80 "I am all expectation, Basil," continued his
companion, glancing at him.

"Oh, there is really very little to tell, Harry,"
answered the painter; "and I am afraid you will
hardly understand it. Perhaps you will hardly
85 believe it."

Lord Henry smiled, and leaning down,
plucked a pink-petalled daisy from the grass
and examined it. "I am quite sure I shall understand it," he replied, gazing intently at the
90 little golden, white-feathered disk, "and as for
believing things, I can believe anything, provided that it is quite incredible."

1. In context, which of the following is the most
   likely understanding of the simile in the
   sentence on lines 8–9 (It is . . . them.)?
   (A) Basil feels that naming someone is
   basically a way of asserting power over
   them and controlling their personality.
   (B) Basil feels that liking people is the first
   route to getting to know them but talking
   about personal relationships betrays
   the people with whom you are in those
   relationships.
   (C) Basil feels that a person's name is an
   intimate part of who they are, and if
   anyone other than the person to whom
   the name belongs shares it then they are
   handing over an intimate part of that
   person.
   (D) Lord Henry feels that knowing Basil's
   secret about Dorian's name will allow
   him to control Basil.
   (E) Lord Henry feels that people's names
   are useless because they ultimately say
   nothing about the person and are only
   used as a passive label — it is how they
   behave that really says who they are.

2. Use of the word "deception" in lines 19–23
   ("Not at all, . . . parties.") demonstrates
   (A) an emphasis on Lord Henry's perspective
   that marriages fail to make people happy.
   (B) a tension between Lord Henry's
   perspective on marriage and Basil's
   perspective on marriage.
   (C) an inconsistency between what many
   people value in a marriage and what Lord
   Henry claims to value.
   (D) a conflict internal to Basil's character
   concerning what he says about his
   marriage and what he really feels about
   marriage in general.
   (E) an uncertainty about the status of Basil's
   marriage.

[3]In this context, a person who poses — or "sits" — for a painting.

3. Which of the following best describes the effect of the structure of the sentence in lines 69–72 ("It is not . . . reveals himself.")?
   (A) Using vague pronouns throughout the sentence creates ambiguity that allows for varied interpretations.
   (B) The punctuation confuses the subject of each clause, allowing for a variety of possible understandings.
   (C) Placing that sentence between two others focusing on the sitter and the reason demonstrates Basil's uncertainty about his response to Lord Henry.
   (D) Using a shorter sentence immediately before it emphasizes the length of this particular sentence.
   (E) Dividing the sitter and the painter into separate clauses emphasizes the difference between the two.

4. The extended dialogue following Lord Henry's question at line 76 ("And what is that?") proves significant, as it allows room in the text for
   (A) illustrating how Basil attempts to disregard and stall Lord Henry.
   (B) prolonging Basil's embarrassment about the situation.
   (C) representing the anger the two characters feel toward one another.
   (D) illustrating the complex relationship between the two characters.
   (E) including more details about the setting of the interaction.

5. In the context of the passage as a whole, which of the following provides the most helpful information for what a reader should come to expect from Lord Henry's character?
   (A) You are an extraordinary fellow (line 40).
   (B) You never say a moral thing, and you never do a wrong thing (lines 40–41).
   (C) Being natural is simply a pose, and the most irritating pose I know (lines 43–44).
   (D) No, you did not. You said it was because there was too much of yourself in it (lines 62–63).
   (E) I am afraid you will hardly understand it. Perhaps you will hardly believe it (lines 83–85).

6. All of the following are true about Lord Henry in the context of the passage EXCEPT that he
   (A) changes as a result of Basil's comments toward him.
   (B) seeks control in the situation with Basil.
   (C) appears indifferent to what his wife knows about his behavior.
   (D) challenges Basil's decision to not display the painting.
   (E) enjoys incredible and impressive things.

7. Which of the following can reasonably be assumed about the setting of the passage?
   (A) The situation takes place in a second-empire drawing room.
   (B) The country they are in is at war.
   (C) The social and cultural setting is wealthy and upper class.
   (D) The characters do not belong in the setting presented in the passage.
   (E) The culture of the setting does not value painted portraits.

8. Which of the following best describes the central conflict between Basil and Lord Henry in the context of this passage?
   (A) Lord Henry wants to use people for his own gain, while Basil wants to make real connections with the people in his life.
   (B) Lord Henry values art for its monetary worth, while Basil values art for its expression.
   (C) Basil seeks to protect other people while Lord Henry only wishes to exploit others for his own gains and pleasure.
   (D) Basil worries about the intentions of Lord Henry, while Lord Henry has no concern for other people at all.
   (E) Basil cares greatly about his art and the people in his life while Lord Henry cares only about himself and his own interests.

PREPARING FOR THE AP® EXAM
Multiple-Choice Questions: Poetry

Enter the Dragon[1]
John Murillo

The following is a poem published in 1976.

Los Angeles, California, 1976

For me, the movie starts with a black man
Leaping into an orbit of badges, tiny moons

Catching the sheen of his perfect black afro.
Arc kicks, karate chops, and thirty cops

5 On their backs. It starts with the swagger,
The cool lean into the leather front seat

Of the black and white[2] he takes off in.
Deep hallelujahs of moviegoers drown

Out the wah wah guitar. Salt & butter
10 High-fives, Right on, brother! And Daddy

Glowing so bright he can light the screen
All by himself. This is how it goes down.

Friday night and my father drives us
Home from the late show, two heroes

15 Cadillacking across King Boulevard.
In the car's dark cab, we jab and clutch,

Jim Kelly and Bruce Lee with popcorn
Breath, and almost miss the lights flashing

In the cracked side mirror. I know what's
20 Under the seat, but when the uniforms[3]

---

[1]*Enter The Dragon* is the title of a martial arts movie starring Chinese American Bruce Lee and African American Jim Kelly. Released in 1973, it is widely regarded as the most successful martial arts movie ever made.
[2]A slang term for a police car because of the colors of most police cars at the time.
[3]American slang for a police officer.

Approach from the rear quarter panel,
When the fat one leans so far into my father's

Window I can smell his long day's work,
When my father — this John Henry[4] of a man —

25 Hides his hammer, doesn't buck, tucks away
His baritone, license and registration shaking as if

Showing a bathroom pass to a grade school
Principal, I learn the difference between cinema

And city, between the moviehouse cheers
30 Of old men and the silence that gets us home.

1. Considering the poem as a whole, starting the poem with the words "for me" (line 1) indicates that the
   (A) poem focuses only on the speaker's opinion.
   (B) speaker is intimately involved in the events of the poem.
   (C) speaker is the only character in the poem.
   (D) events of the poem matter only to the speaker.
   (E) conflict in the poem only affects the speaker.

2. In line 12, the sentence, "This is how it goes down" indicates a shift in the
   (A) dramatic situation of the poem.
   (B) conflict between the characters in the poem.
   (C) speaker's point of view.
   (D) speaker's perspective on the film.
   (E) stanza structure of the poem.

3. The exposition provided in lines 25–26 ("Hides . . . as if") focuses the readers' attention on the
   (A) hard day's work done by the police officer.
   (B) approach of the police officers.
   (C) details relating to the John Henry comparison.
   (D) strong characteristics of the speaker's father.
   (E) way details of the scene in the car relate to the movie.

4. The interaction between the police officer and the father in lines 19–28 ("I know what's . . . Principal") makes use of which of the following?
   (A) Shift in stanza structure
   (B) Shift in the speaker's point of view
   (C) Ambiguous pronoun referents
   (D) Simile
   (E) Contrasting settings

[4]An American folk hero, John Henry was an African American who worked as a "steel-driving man" hammering tunnels out of rock for the railroads in the nineteenth century. A large and powerful man, legend holds that he died while competing against — and defeating — a steel-driving machine.

5. The alliteration present in lines 28–29 ("Principal . . . cheers") emphasizes the
   (A) inexperience of the speaker.
   (B) different experiences represented by the movie and the real world.
   (C) contrast illustrated by the interactions between the police office and the father.
   (D) fear displayed by the father when the officer approaches.
   (E) metaphor used to describe the city.

6. Which of the following describes the relationship between the dramatic situations of the poem?
   (A) The other moviegoers understood the difference between the movie and real life, while the speaker would only realize it on the drive home.
   (B) The speaker realizes that he relates better to the actors and characters in the movie than he does with his own father.
   (C) The world of the movie seemed more realistic than the experiences on the drive home afterward.
   (D) The movie scene makes the characters feel proud, while the scene with the police officer displays the fear experienced in their circumstances.
   (E) The movie captures the reality of the speaker's circumstances better than the actual experiences during the drive home.

7. Which of the following represents the most reasonable and defensible claim about the poem as a whole?
   (A) The poem demonstrates the harsh difference between the cinematic fantasy world that its characters enjoy so much and a reality where they live in fear.
   (B) The poem creates a connection between the fantastic fiction of the movie and the hopes of the characters in their reality.
   (C) The poem provides a scene in a movie theater and a scene in a car on the way home from that movie.
   (D) The poem provides a dramatic situation that only someone who has experienced something similar could really understand.
   (E) The poem is narrated by the child of the man who drives the car after the movie is over.

Hector Guerrero/Bloomberg/Getty Images

UNIT
4

Analyzing Perspectives

UNIT GOALS

	Focus	Goals
Big Idea: Character	**Characters in Conflict**	Explain how characters in conflict contribute to an interpretation of a story.
Big Idea: Setting	**Mood and Atmosphere**	Explain how setting creates a mood and atmosphere and how they in turn contribute to tone.
Big Idea: Structure	**Archetypal Patterns**	Describe archetypes within a story and explain how they contribute to an interpretation.
Big Idea: Narration	**Narrative Perspective**	Explain how the perspective of the narrator affects the interpretation of a text.
Ideas in Literature	• **Irony and Incongruity** • **Reason and Order**	Explain how the ideas of irony, incongruity, reason, and order are reflected in classic and contemporary texts.
Big Idea: Literary Argumentation	**Writing about Point of View**	Write a literary argument that analyzes how the narrative perspective contributes to an interpretation of a text.
Preparing for the AP® Exam	**Free-Response Question: Prose Fiction Analysis** Creating Unity through Commentary	Write commentary that explains the connections between the reasons in the line of reasoning and the unifying idea and claim in the thesis statement.
	Multiple-Choice Questions: Prose	Analyze literary elements and techniques in classic and contemporary prose and poetry.
	Multiple-Choice Questions: Poetry	

Characters in Conflict

 Enduring Understanding

Characters in literature allow readers to study and explore a range of values, beliefs, assumptions, biases, and cultural norms represented by those characters.

KEY POINT

Authors place characters into dramatic situations where characters must face conflict or tension between competing values.

Dramatic conflicts over values and ideas are not confined to "serious" literature. In Marvel's *Captain America: Civil War* (2016), for example, the superhero team the Avengers faces a challenging internal struggle between two characters' competing perspectives and values. On one side, Steve Rogers (Captain America), represents the individual's right to freedom of choice (less government control). On the other side, Tony Stark (Ironman) represents the idea that power must be regulated in order to protect others (more government control). This central tension between these two characters' values takes center stage, ultimately resulting in a climactic battle between them.

In literary fiction and drama, authors set up contrasts that provoke questions for the reader about universal aspects of being human. If they can identify these contrasts — especially conflicts of values and ideas — readers can interpret the text more thoroughly and persuasively.

Characters in Conflict Represent a Conflict of Values

Authors place characters into **dramatic situations** that create conflict or tension between competing values. Often, characters face consequential choices within a story; their responses to these conflicts both reveal and shape who they are — and who they might become. Characters in conflict are the literal, concrete representations of abstract or figurative ideas.

You'll recall from previous units that characters represent values and that authors reveal those values through the process of characterization. As you do with people in your own life, you can understand a character's values by observing what they choose to say, what they choose to do, and sometimes, what they choose *not* to do.

In other words, characters in conflict point directly to values in conflict. By identifying and analyzing the conflicting values of characters, you can form an interpretation of the literary work.

Protagonists and Antagonists

The **protagonist** is the central character in a narrative. Protagonists may have extraordinary powers or traits, or they can be ordinary people. Whether they embark on a quest, go to war, or grapple with the challenges of growing up, protagonists face problems that test their physical, mental, psychological, or emotional qualities. The protagonist may succeed or fail at resolving these conflicts, but regardless, the character will likely be transformed by the dramatic experience of the play or narrative. In other cases, a protagonist may amuse, shock, or sadden readers by remaining unchanged after a profound realization or transformative experience.

In contrast, **antagonists** oppose the protagonist. An antagonist may be another character, the internal conflicts of the protagonist, a collective (such as a society or an organization), or nature.

Protagonists and antagonists may represent contrasting values. But don't assume that all protagonists stand for the good and true while all antagonists are vile serpents. Some protagonists may represent objectionable or ambiguous values, while some antagonists can embody good — or seemingly good — values, as in *Captain America: Civil War*.

As you learned in Unit 3, **conflict** is created by the tension between two opposing value systems. These conflicts are sometimes more complex than just "good" versus "evil." Some value systems may privilege a specific group, type of person, or even personal quality over others, but those biases don't necessarily make one set of values objectively better than another. For example, one system may privilege innovation and ingenuity while another system may instead prefer the preservation of tradition and history. Both systems have their merits, along with their limitations and drawbacks.

There are at least six different ways to categorize conflicts. And while identifying the conflict is helpful, a reader must also consider the values represented by the characters on each side of the conflict. This conflict of values is the key to making an interpretation of a literary work.

- Character versus (other) person
- Character versus group (society)
- Character versus self
- Character versus nature
- Character versus technology
- Character versus the unknown

Agency of Characters

A character's **agency** is the ability to make meaningful decisions at defining moments in the narrative and take actions to achieve a desired effect. An author gives or does not give a character agency, and this distinction is important and affects how we as readers interpret a character.

At its foundation, agency refers to a character's power to push, create, or challenge the events in the plot. Without this ability, a character is prevented from acting on his or her motivation.

A character's significance is often revealed by his or her agency — or the lack of it. Likewise, competing agencies (between characters and other forces) create conflict and shape narratives. As readers, we often identify with these characters and conflicts: they drive stories; they can also reflect the real-life, universal human experience of conflict — with people, ideas, nature, and other factors.

One-dimensional characters (who are often rigidly characterized by one trait or presented as completely good or entirely evil) may not have the same degree of agency as other more developed characters. Characters who have greater depth or nuance (in words, actions, ideas, and emotions) are more likely to have agency in the narrative.

Authors give characters power. Because authors create characters, they also determine how much autonomy a character has. In some stories, characters exert power to make choices, and in other stories, characters choose not to act, which in itself is a choice. By noticing moments when characters face decisions and examining those choices, you can strengthen your interpretation of a text.

CHARACTERS IN CONFLICT	
Type of Conflict	• Character versus (other) person • Character versus group (society) • Character versus self • Character versus nature • Character versus technology • Character versus the unknown
Description of Characters	• How is the protagonist described? • How is the antagonist described?
Choices Made by Protagonist	• What choices does the protagonist face? • How does the protagonist respond when faced with choices? • What choices does the antagonist present to the protagonist? • How much agency does the protagonist have?
Values Represented by Characters	• What values does the protagonist embody? • What values does the antagonist embody? • How does the conflict place those values in debate? • How is the conflict resolved? Who wins? • How does the resolution of the conflict contribute to an interpretation of the text?

Gentleman of Río en Medio
Juan A. A. Sedillo

THE TEXT IN CONTEXT

Born in New Mexico to a prominent family, Juan A. A. Sedillo (1902–1980) distinguished himself primarily as an attorney, such as the one who narrates "Gentlemen of Río en Medio." *Río en Medio* translates to "river in the middle." The following story, written in 1939, is based on an experience from his law practice in Santa Fe, New Mexico. This story presents two characters in conflict as both assert their agency.

Gentleman of Río en Medio

It took months of negotiation to come to an understanding with the old man. He was in no hurry. What he had the most of was time. He lived up in Río en Medio, where his people had been for hundreds of years. He tilled the same land they had tilled. His house was small and wretched, but quaint.
5 The little creek ran through his land. His orchard was gnarled and beautiful.

The day of the sale he came up to the office. His coat was old, green and faded. I thought of Senator Catron, who had been such a power with these people up there in the mountains. Perhaps it was one of his old Prince Alberts. He also wore gloves. They were old and torn and his finger-
10 tips showed through them. He carried a cane, but it was only the skeleton of a worn out umbrella. Behind him walked one of his innumerable kin—a dark young man with eyes like a gazelle.

The old man bowed to all of us in the room. Then he removed his hat and gloves, slowly and carefully. Chaplin once did that in a picture, in a
15 bank—he was the janitor. Then he handed his things to the boy, who stood obediently behind the old man's chair.

There was a great deal of conversation about rain and about his family. He was very proud of his large family. Finally we got down to business. Yes, he would sell, as he had agreed, for twelve hundred dollars, in cash.
20 We would buy, and the money was ready. "Don Anselmo," I said to him in Spanish, "we have made a discovery. You remember that we sent that surveyor, that engineer, up there to survey your land so as to make the deed. Well, he finds that you own more than eight acres. He tells us that your land extends across the river and that you own almost twice as
25 much as you thought." He didn't know that. "And now, Don Anselmo," I added, "these Americans are *buena gente*, they are good people, and they

Guided Questions

1. What is being negotiated and between whom?

2. How does the old man control the negotiations?

3. How does the old man represent the values of Río en Medio?

4. Who is the protagonist? Who is the antagonist?

5. What values do each of the characters represent?

are willing to pay you for the additional land as well, at the same rate per acre, so that instead of twelve hundred dollars you will get almost twice as much, and the money is here for you."

30   The old man hung his head for a moment in thought. Then he stood up and stared at me. "Friend," he said, "I do not like to have you speak to me in that manner." I kept still and let him have his say. "I know these Americans are good people, and that is why I have agreed to sell to them. But I do not care to be insulted. I have agreed to sell my house and land

35 for twelve hundred dollars and that is the price."

6. What is the conflict between the central characters?

I argued with him but it was useless. Finally he signed the deed and took the money but refused to take more than the amount agreed upon. Then he shook hands all around, put on his ragged gloves, took his stick and walked out with the boy behind him.

40   A month later my friends had moved into Río en Medio. They had replastered the old adobe house, pruned the trees, patched the fence, and moved in for the summer. One day they came back to the office to complain. The children of the village were overrunning their property. They came every day and played under the trees, built little play fences around

45 them, and took blossoms. When they were spoken to, they only laughed and talked back good-naturedly in Spanish.

7. How do the words and actions end the negotiations and resolve the conflict between the characters?

I sent a messenger up to the mountains for Don Anselmo. It took a week to arrange another meeting. When he arrived he repeated his previous preliminary performance. He wore the same faded cutaway, carried

50 the same stick and was accompanied by the boy again. He shook hands all around, sat down with the boy behind his chair, and talked about the weather. Finally I broached the subject. "Don Anselmo, about the ranch you sold to these people. They are good people and want to be your friends and neighbors always. When you sold to them you signed a docu-

55 ment, a deed, and in that deed you agreed to several things. One thing was that they were to have the complete possession of the property. Now, Don Anselmo, it seems that every day the children of the village overrun the orchard and spend most of their time there. We would like to know if you, as the most respected man in the village, could not stop them from doing

60 so in order that these people may enjoy their new home more in peace."

Don Anselmo stood up. "We have all learned to love these Americans," he said, "because they are good people and good neighbors. I sold them my property because I knew they were good people, but I did not sell them the trees in the orchard."

8. The final conflict is between what two entities?

65   This was bad. "Don Anselmo," I pleaded, "when one signs a deed and sells real property one sells also everything that grows on the land, and those trees, every one of them, are on the land and inside the boundaries of what you sold."

"Yes, I admit that," he said. "You know," he added, "I am the oldest man

70 in the village. Almost everyone there is my relative and all the children of

9. How does Don Anselmo's perspective contribute to the conflict?

Río en Medio are my *sobrinos* and *nietos*, my descendants. Every time a child has been born in Río en Medio since I took possession of that house from my mother I have planted a tree for that child. The trees in that orchard are not mine, *señor*, they belong to the children of the village.

75 Every person in Río en Medio born since the railroad came to Santa Fé owns a tree in that orchard. I did not sell the trees because I could not. They are not mine."

There was nothing we could do. Legally we owned the trees but the old man had been so generous, refusing what amounted to a fortune for him.

80 It took most of the following winter to buy the trees, individually, from the descendants of Don Anselmo in the valley of Río en Medio.

Guided Questions

10. How is the conflict resolved?

11. Who is in control of the resolution?

PRACTICE TEXT

A Good Man Is Hard to Find
Flannery O'Connor

AP Images/Joe McTyre

THE TEXT IN CONTEXT

More than fifty years after her death, Flannery O'Connor (1925–1964) remains one of the most unmistakable voices in American literature. Born in Savannah, Georgia, she spent much of her life living on her mother's dairy farm in Milledgeville, Georgia. O'Connor attended the prestigious Iowa Writers' Workshop and published her acclaimed first novel *Wise Blood* in 1952. But in the same year, she was diagnosed with lupus, a debilitating and (at the time) terminal autoimmune disease that limited her mobility and energy. Nevertheless, she published another novel, *The Violent Bear It Away* (1960), as well as two volumes of celebrated short stories: *A Good Man Is Hard to Find* (1955) and *Everything That Rises Must Converge* (1965). O'Connor's work is notable for its violence, its dark humor, and its expression of the "Southern Gothic": grotesque and freakish characters, extreme situations, decaying settings, and other disturbing elements. She was a devout Catholic whose religious beliefs are reflected in her fiction — especially in the following short story, "A Good Man Is Hard to Find."

Content Note: This story includes the N-word, which we have chosen not to reprint in full here. We wish to accurately reflect O'Connor's original intent, as well as call attention to the racism of the time period. However, we also recognize that this word has a long history as a disrespectful and deeply hurtful expression when used by white people toward Black people. Be mindful of context, both O'Connor's and yours, as you read and discuss "A Good Man Is Hard to Find."

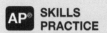

SKILLS PRACTICE | **CHARACTER**
Analyzing Characters in Conflict

As you read "A Good Man Is Hard to Find," record details about the characters and conflict. Identify the protagonist's choices, as well as the values represented by the protagonist and antagonist. Use these details as you analyze the story's resolution.

Analyzing Characters in Conflict		
	Protagonist:	Antagonist:
Type of Conflict		
Description of Characters		
Choices Made by Protagonist		
Values Represented by Character		

A Good Man Is Hard to Find

The Grandmother didn't want to go to Florida. She wanted to visit some of her connections in east Tennessee and she was seizing at every chance to change Bailey's
5 mind. Bailey was the son she lived with, her only boy. He was sitting on the edge of his chair at the table, bent over the orange sports section of the Journal. "Now look here, Bailey," she said, "see here, read this,"
10 and she stood with one hand on her thin hip and the other rattling the newspaper at his bald head. "Here this fellow that calls himself The Misfit is aloose from the Federal Pen and headed toward Florida and
15 you read here what it says he did to these people. Just you read it. I wouldn't take my children in any direction with a criminal like that aloose in it. I couldn't answer to my conscience if I did."
20 Bailey didn't look up from his reading so she wheeled around then and faced the children's mother, a young woman in slacks, whose face was as broad and innocent as a cabbage and was tied around with a green

25 headkerchief that had two points on the
top like rabbit's ears. She was sitting on the
sofa, feeding the baby his apricots out of
a jar. "The children have been to Florida
before," the old lady said. "You all ought to
30 take them somewhere else for a change
so they would see different parts of the
world and be broad. They never have been
to east Tennessee."

The children's mother didn't seem to hear
35 her but the eight-year-old boy, John Wesley, a
stocky child with glasses, said, "If you don't
want to go to Florida, why dontcha stay at
home?" He and the little girl, June Star, were
reading the funny papers on the floor.

40 "She wouldn't stay at home to be queen
for a day," June Star said without raising her
yellow head.

"Yes and what would you do if this fellow,
The Misfit, caught you?" the grandmother
45 asked.

"I'd smack his face," John Wesley said.

"She wouldn't stay at home for a million
bucks," June Star said. "Afraid she'd miss
something. She has to go everywhere we go."

50 "All right, Miss," the grandmother said.
"Just remember that the next time you want
me to curl your hair."

June Star said her hair was naturally curly.

The next morning the grandmother was
55 the first one in the car, ready to go. She had
her big black valise that looked like the head
of a hippopotamus in one corner, and underneath it she was hiding a basket with Pitty
Sing, the cat, in it. She didn't intend for the
60 cat to be left alone in the house for three
days because he would miss her too much
and she was afraid he might brush against
one of the gas burners and accidentally
asphyxiate himself. Her son, Bailey, didn't
65 like to arrive at a motel with a cat.

She sat in the middle of the back seat
with John Wesley and June Star on either
side of her. Bailey and the children's mother
and the baby sat in front and they left
70 Atlanta at eight forty-five with the mileage
on the car at 55890. The grandmother wrote
this down because she thought it would be
interesting to say how many miles they had
been when they got back. It took them
75 twenty minutes to reach the outskirts of
the city.

The old lady settled herself comfortably,
removing her white cotton gloves and putting them up with her purse on the shelf in
80 front of the back window. The children's
mother still had on slacks and still had her
head tied up in a green kerchief, but the
grandmother had on a navy blue straw
sailor hat with a bunch of white violets on
85 the brim and a navy blue dress with a small
white dot in the print. Her collars and cuffs
were white organdy trimmed with lace and
at her neckline she had pinned a purple
spray of cloth violets containing a sachet. In
90 case of an accident, anyone seeing her dead
on the highway would know at once that
she was a lady.

She said she thought it was going to be a
good day for driving, neither too hot nor too
95 cold, and she cautioned Bailey that the speed
limit was fifty-five miles an hour and that
the patrolmen hid themselves behind bill-
boards and small clumps of trees and sped
out after you before you had a chance to
100 slow down. She pointed out interesting
details of the scenery: Stone Mountain; the
blue granite that in some places came up to
both sides of the highway; the brilliant red
clay banks slightly streaked with purple; and
105 the various crops that made rows of green
lace-work on the ground. The trees were full

of silver-white sunlight and the meanest of them sparkled. The children were reading comic magazines and their mother had gone 110 back to sleep.

"Let's go through Georgia fast so we won't have to look at it much," John Wesley said.

"If I were a little boy," said the grandmother, "I wouldn't talk about my native 115 state that way. Tennessee has the mountains and Georgia has the hills."

"Tennessee is just a hillbilly dumping ground," John Wesley said, "and Georgia is a lousy state too."

120   "You said it," June Star said.

"In my time," said the grandmother, folding her thin veined fingers, "children were more respectful of their native states and their parents and everything else. People 125 did right then. Oh look at the cute little pickaninny!" she said and pointed to a Negro child standing in the door of a shack. "Wouldn't that make a picture, now?" she asked and they all turned and looked at the 130 little Negro out of the back window. He waved.

"He didn't have any britches on," June Star said.

"He probably didn't have any," the grandmother explained. "Little n*****s in the 135 country don't have things like we do. If I could paint, I'd paint that picture," she said.

The children exchanged comic books.

The grandmother offered to hold the baby and the children's mother passed him over 140 the front seat to her. She set him on her knee and bounced him and told him about the things they were passing. She rolled her eyes and screwed up her mouth and stuck her leathery thin face into his smooth bland one. 145 Occasionally he gave her a faraway smile. They passed a large cotton field with five or six graves fenced in the middle of it, like a small island. "Look at the graveyard!" the

grandmother said, pointing it out. "That was 150 the old family burying ground. That belonged to the plantation."

"Where's the plantation?" John Wesley asked.

"Gone With the Wind," said the grand-155 mother. "Ha. Ha."

When the children finished all the comic books they had brought, they opened the lunch and ate it. The grandmother ate a peanut butter sandwich and an olive and would 160 not let the children throw the box and the paper napkins out the window. When there was nothing else to do they played a game by choosing a cloud and making the other two guess what shape it suggested. John Wesley 165 took one the shape of a cow and June Star guessed a cow and John Wesley said, no, an automobile, and June Star said he didn't play fair, and they began to slap each other over the grandmother.

170   The grandmother said she would tell them a story if they would keep quiet. When she told a story, she rolled her eyes and waved her head and was very dramatic. She said once when she was a maiden lady she had been 175 courted by a Mr. Edgar Atkins Teagarden from Jasper, Georgia. She said he was a very good-looking man and a gentleman and that he brought her a watermelon every Saturday afternoon with his initials cut in it, E. A. T. 180 Well, one Saturday, she said, Mr. Teagarden brought the watermelon and there was nobody at home and he left it on the front porch and returned in his buggy to Jasper, but she never got the watermelon, she said, 185 because a n***** boy ate it when he saw the initials, E. A. T.! This story tickled John Wesley's funny bone and he giggled and giggled but June Star didn't think it was any good. She said she wouldn't marry a man 190 that just brought her a watermelon on

Saturday. The grandmother said she would have done well to marry Mr. Teagarden because he was a gentleman and had bought Coca-Cola stock when it first came out and
195 that he had died only a few years ago, a very wealthy man.

They stopped at The Tower for barbecued sandwiches. The Tower was a part stucco and part wood filling station and dance hall set
200 in a clearing outside of Timothy. A fat man named Red Sammy Butts ran it and there were signs stuck here and there on the building and for miles up and down the highway saying, TRY RED SAMMY'S FAMOUS BARBECUE.
205 NONE LIKE FAMOUS RED SAMMY'S! RED SAM! THE FAT BOY WITH THE HAPPY LAUGH. A VETERAN! RED SAMMY'S YOUR MAN!

Red Sammy was lying on the bare ground outside The Tower with his head under a
210 truck while a gray monkey about a foot high, chained to a small chinaberry tree, chattered nearby. The monkey sprang back into the tree and got on the highest limb as soon as he saw the children jump out of the car and
215 run toward him.

Inside, The Tower was a long dark room with a counter at one end and tables at the other and dancing space in the middle. They all sat down at a board table next to the
220 nickelodeon and Red Sam's wife, a tall burnt-brown woman with hair and eyes lighter than her skin, came and took their order. The children's mother put a dime in the machine and played "The Tennessee
225 Waltz," and the grandmother said that tune always made her want to dance. She asked Bailey if he would like to dance but he only glared at her. He didn't have a naturally sunny disposition like she did and trips
230 made him nervous. The grandmother's brown eyes were very bright. She swayed her head from side to side and pretended

she was dancing in her chair. June Star said play something she could tap to so the chil-
235 dren's mother put in another dime and played a fast number and June Star stepped out onto the dance floor and did her tap routine.

"Ain't she cute?" Red Sam's wife said,
240 leaning over the counter. "Would you like to come be my little girl?"

"No I certainly wouldn't," June Star said. "I wouldn't live in a broken-down place like this for a minion bucks!" and she ran back to
245 the table.

"Ain't she cute?" the woman repeated, stretching her mouth politely.

"Arn't you ashamed?" hissed the grandmother.

250 Red Sam came in and told his wife to quit lounging on the counter and hurry up with these people's order. His khaki trousers reached just to his hip bones and his stomach hung over them like a sack of meal
255 swaying under his shirt. He came over and sat down at a table nearby and let out a combination sigh and yodel. "You can't win," he said. "You can't win," and he wiped his sweating red face off with a gray handker-
260 chief. "These days you don't know who to trust," he said. "Ain't that the truth?"

"People are certainly not nice like they used to be," said the grandmother.

"Two fellers come in here last week," Red
265 Sammy said, "driving a Chrysler. It was a old beat-up car but it was a good one and these boys looked all right to me. Said they worked at the mill and you know I let them fellers charge the gas they bought? Now why did I
270 do that?"

"Because you're a good man!" the grandmother said at once.

"Yes'm, I suppose so," Red Sam said as if he were struck with this answer.

275 His wife brought the orders, carrying the five plates all at once without a tray, two in each hand and one balanced on her arm. "It isn't a soul in this green world of God's that you can trust," she said. "And I don't count 280 nobody out of that, not nobody," she repeated, looking at Red Sammy.

"Did you read about that criminal, The Misfit, that's escaped?" asked the grand- mother.

285 "I wouldn't be a bit surprised if he didn't attact this place right here," said the woman. "If he hears about it being here, I wouldn't be none surprised to see him. If he hears it's two cent in the cash register, I wouldn't be a 290 tall surprised if he . . ."

"That'll do," Red Sam said. "Go bring these people their Co'-Colas," and the woman went off to get the rest of the order.

"A good man is hard to find," Red Sammy 295 said. "Everything is getting terrible. I remem- ber the day you could go off and leave your screen door unlatched. Not no more."

He and the grandmother discussed better times. The old lady said that in her opinion 300 Europe was entirely to blame for the way things were now. She said the way Europe acted you would think we were made of money and Red Sam said it was no use talking about it, she was exactly right. The 305 children ran outside into the white sunlight and looked at the monkey in the lacy china- berry tree. He was busy catching fleas on himself and biting each one carefully between his teeth as if it were a delicacy.

310 They drove off again into the hot after- noon. The grandmother took cat naps and woke up every few minutes with her own snoring. Outside of Toombsboro she woke up and recalled an old plantation that she 315 had visited in this neighborhood once when she was a young lady. She said the house had six white columns across the front and that there was an avenue of oaks leading up to it and two little wooden trellis arbors on 320 either side in front where you sat down with your suitor after a stroll in the garden. She recalled exactly which road to turn off to get to it. She knew that Bailey would not be willing to lose any time looking at an old 325 house, but the more she talked about it, the more she wanted to see it once again and find out if the little twin arbors were still standing. "There was a secret panel in this house," she said craftily, not telling the truth 330 but wishing that she were, "and the story went that all the family silver was hidden in it when Sherman came through but it was never found . . ."

"Hey!" John Wesley said. "Let's go see it! 335 We'll find it! We'll poke all the woodwork and find it! Who lives there? Where do you turn off at? Hey Pop, can't we turn off there?"

"We never have seen a house with a secret panel!" June Star shrieked. "Let's go to 340 the house with the secret panel! Hey Pop, can't we go see the house with the secret panel!"

"It's not far from here, I know," the grand- mother said. "It wouldn't take over twenty 345 minutes."

Bailey was looking straight ahead. His jaw was as rigid as a horseshoe. "No," he said.

The children began to yell and scream that they wanted to see the house with the 350 secret panel. John Wesley kicked the back of the front seat and June Star hung over her mother's shoulder and whined desperately into her ear that they never had any fun even on their vacation, that they could never do 355 what THEY wanted to do. The baby began to scream and John Wesley kicked the back of the seat so hard that his father could feel the blows in his kidney.

"All right!" he shouted and drew the car to
360 a stop at the side of the road. "Will you all
shut up? Will you all just shut up for one second? If you don't shut up, we won't go anywhere.

"It would be very educational for them,"
365 the grandmother murmured.

"All right," Bailey said, "but get this: this is
the only time we're going to stop for anything like this. This is the one and only time."

"The dirt road that you have to turn down
370 is about a mile back," the grandmother
directed. "I marked it when we passed."

"A dirt road," Bailey groaned.

After they had turned around and were
headed toward the dirt road, the grand-
375 mother recalled other points about the
house, the beautiful glass over the front
doorway and the candle-lamp in the hall.
John Wesley said that the secret panel was
probably in the fireplace.

380 "You can't go inside this house," Bailey
said. "You don't know who lives there."

"While you all talk to the people in front,
I'll run around behind and get in a window,"
John Wesley suggested.

385 "We'll all stay in the car," his mother said.
They turned onto the dirt road and the car
raced roughly along in a swirl of pink dust.
The grandmother recalled the times when
there were no paved roads and thirty miles
390 was a day's journey. The dirt road was hilly
and there were sudden washes in it and
sharp curves on dangerous embankments.
All at once they would be on a hill, looking
down over the blue tops of trees for miles
395 around, then the next minute, they would be
in a red depression with the dust-coated
trees looking down on them.

"This place had better turn up in a
minute," Bailey said, "or I'm going to turn
400 around."

The road looked as if no one had traveled
on it in months.

"It's not much farther," the grandmother
said and just as she said it, a horrible thought
405 came to her. The thought was so embarrassing that she turned red in the face and her
eyes dilated and her feet jumped up, upsetting her valise in the corner. The instant the
valise moved, the newspaper top she had
410 over the basket under it rose with a snarl
and Pitty Sing, the cat, sprang onto Bailey's
shoulder.

The children were thrown to the floor
and their mother, clutching the baby, was
415 thrown out the door onto the ground; the
old lady was thrown into the front seat.
The car turned over once and landed right-
side-up in a gulch off the side of the road.
Bailey remained in the driver's seat with the
420 cat-gray-striped with a broad white face and
an orange nose-clinging to his neck like a
caterpillar.

As soon as the children saw they could
move their arms and legs, they scrambled
425 out of the car, shouting, "We've had an
ACCIDENT!" The grandmother was curled
up under the dashboard, hoping she was
injured so that Bailey's wrath would not
come down on her all at once. The horrible
430 thought she had had before the accident
was that the house she had remembered so
vividly was not in Georgia but in Tennessee.

Bailey removed the cat from his neck with
both hands and flung it out the window
435 against the side of a pine tree. Then he got
out of the car and started looking for the
children's mother. She was sitting against
the side of the red gutted ditch, holding the
screaming baby, but she only had a cut down
440 her face and a broken shoulder. "We've had
an ACCIDENT!" the children screamed in a
frenzy of delight.

"But nobody's killed," June Star said with disappointment as the grandmother limped out of the car, her hat still pinned to her head but the broken front brim standing up at a jaunty angle and the violet spray hanging off the side. They all sat down in the ditch, except the children, to recover from the shock. They were all shaking.

"Maybe a car will come along," said the children's mother hoarsely.

"I believe I have injured an organ," said the grandmother, pressing her side, but no one answered her. Bailey's teeth were clattering. He had on a yellow sport shirt with bright blue parrots designed in it and his face was as yellow as the shirt. The grandmother decided that she would not mention that the house was in Tennessee.

The road was about ten feet above and they could see only the tops of the trees on the other side of it. Behind the ditch they were sitting in there were more woods, tall and dark and deep. In a few minutes they saw a car some distance away on top of a hill, coming slowly as if the occupants were watching them. The grandmother stood up and waved both arms dramatically to attract their attention. The car continued to come on slowly, disappeared around a bend and appeared again, moving even slower, on top of the hill they had gone over. It was a big black battered hearse-like automobile. There were three men in it.

It came to a stop just over them and for some minutes, the driver looked down with a steady expressionless gaze to where they were sitting, and didn't speak. Then he turned his head and muttered something to the other two and they got out. One was a fat boy in black trousers and a red sweat shirt with a silver stallion embossed on the front of it. He moved around on the right side of them and stood staring, his mouth partly open in a kind of loose grin. The other had on khaki pants and a blue striped coat and a gray hat pulled down very low, hiding most of his face. He came around slowly on the left side. Neither spoke.

The driver got out of the car and stood by the side of it, looking down at them. He was an older man than the other two. His hair was just beginning to gray and he wore silver-rimmed spectacles that gave him a scholarly look. He had a long creased face and didn't have on any shirt or undershirt. He had on blue jeans that were too tight for him and was holding a black hat and a gun. The two boys also had guns.

"We've had an ACCIDENT!" the children screamed.

The grandmother had the peculiar feeling that the bespectacled man was someone she knew. His face was as familiar to her as if she had known him all her life but she could not recall who he was. He moved away from the car and began to come down the embankment, placing his feet carefully so that he wouldn't slip. He had on tan and white shoes and no socks, and his ankles were red and thin. "Good afternoon," he said. "I see you all had you a little spill."

"We turned over twice!" said the grandmother.

"Oncet," he corrected. "We seen it happen. Try their car and see will it run, Hiram," he said quietly to the boy with the gray hat.

"What you got that gun for?" John Wesley asked. "Whatcha gonna do with that gun?"

"Lady," the man said to the children's mother, "would you mind calling them children to sit down by you? Children make me nervous. I want all you all to sit down right together there where you're at."

"What are you telling US what to do for?" June Star asked.

Behind them the line of woods gaped like
530 a dark open mouth. "Come here," said their mother.

"Look here now," Bailey began suddenly, "we're in a predicament! We're in . . ."

The grandmother shrieked. She scram-
535 bled to her feet and stood staring. "You're The Misfit!" she said. "I recognized you at once!"

"Yes'm," the man said, smiling slightly as if he were pleased in spite of himself to be
540 known, "but it would have been better for all of you, lady, if you hadn't of reckernized me."

Bailey turned his head sharply and said something to his mother that shocked even the children. The old lady began to cry and
545 The Misfit reddened.

"Lady," he said, "don't you get upset. Sometimes a man says things he don't mean. I don't reckon he meant to talk to you thataway."

550 "You wouldn't shoot a lady, would you?" the grandmother said and removed a clean handkerchief from her cuff and began to slap at her eyes with it.

The Misfit pointed the toe of his shoe into
555 the ground and made a little hole and then covered it up again. "I would hate to have to," he said.

"Listen," the grandmother almost screamed, "I know you're a good man. You
560 don't look a bit like you have common blood. I know you must come from nice people!"

"Yes mam," he said, "finest people in the world." When he smiled he showed a row of
565 strong white teeth. "God never made a finer woman than my mother and my daddy's heart was pure gold," he said. The boy with the red sweat shirt had come around behind

them and was standing with his gun at his
570 hip. The Misfit squatted down on the ground. "Watch them children, Bobby Lee," he said. "You know they make me nervous." He looked at the six of them huddled together in front of him and he seemed to be embar-
575 rassed as if he couldn't think of anything to say. "Ain't a cloud in the sky," he remarked, looking up at it. "Don't see no sun but don't see no cloud neither."

"Yes, it's a beautiful day," said the grand-
580 mother. "Listen," she said, "you shouldn't call yourself The Misfit because I know you're a good man at heart. I can just look at you and tell."

"Hush!" Bailey yelled. "Hush! Everybody
585 shut up and let me handle this!" He was squatting in the position of a runner about to sprint forward but he didn't move.

"I prechate that, lady," The Misfit said and drew a little circle in the ground with the
590 butt of his gun.

"It'll take a half a hour to fix this here car," Hiram called, looking over the raised hood of it.

"Well, first you and Bobby Lee get him and
595 that little boy to step over yonder with you," The Misfit said, pointing to Bailey and John Wesley. "The boys want to ast you some-thing," he said to Bailey. "Would you mind stepping back in them woods there with
600 them?"

"Listen," Bailey began, "we're in a terrible predicament! Nobody realizes what this is," and his voice cracked. His eyes were as blue and intense as the parrots in his shirt and he
605 remained perfectly still.

The grandmother reached up to adjust her hat brim as if she were going to the woods with him but it came off in her hand. She stood staring at it and after a second she
610 let it fall on the ground. Hiram pulled Bailey

up by the arm as if he were assisting an old man. John Wesley caught hold of his father's hand and Bobby Lee followed. They went off toward the woods and just as they reached 615 the dark edge, Bailey turned and supporting himself against a gray naked pine trunk, he shouted, "I'll be back in a minute, Mamma, wait on me!"

"Come back this instant!" his mother 620 shrilled but they all disappeared into the woods.

"Bailey Boy!" the grandmother called in a tragic voice but she found she was looking at The Misfit squatting on the ground in front 625 of her. "I just know you're a good man," she said desperately. "You're not a bit common!"

"Nome, I ain't a good man," The Misfit said after a second as if he had considered her statement carefully, "but I ain't the worst in 630 the world neither. My daddy said I was a different breed of dog from my brothers and sisters. 'You know,' Daddy said, 'it's some that can live their whole life out without asking about it and it's others has to know why it is, 635 and this boy is one of the latters. He's going to be into everything!'" He put on his black hat and looked up suddenly and then away deep into the woods as if he were embarrassed again. "I'm sorry I don't have on a shirt before 640 you ladies," he said, hunching his shoulders slightly. "We buried our clothes that we had on when we escaped and we're just making do until we can get better. We borrowed these from some folks we met," he explained.

645 "That's perfectly all right," the grandmother said. "Maybe Bailey has an extra shirt in his suitcase."

"I'll look and see terrectly," The Misfit said.

"Where are they taking him?" the children's 650 mother screamed.

"Daddy was a card himself," The Misfit said. "You couldn't put anything over on him.

He never got in trouble with the Authorities though. Just had the knack of handling 655 them."

"You could be honest too if you'd only try," said the grandmother. "Think how wonderful it would be to settle down and live a comfortable life and not have to think about somebody 660 chasing you all the time."

The Misfit kept scratching in the ground with the butt of his gun as if he were thinking about it. "Yes'm, somebody is always after you," he murmured.

665 The grandmother noticed how thin his shoulder blades were just behind-his hat because she was standing up looking down on him. "Do you ever pray?" she asked.

He shook his head. All she saw was the 670 black hat wiggle between his shoulder blades. "Nome," he said.

There was a pistol shot from the woods, followed closely by another. Then silence. The old lady's head jerked around. She could 675 hear the wind move through the tree tops like a long satisfied insuck of breath. "Bailey Boy!" she called.

"I was a gospel singer for a while," The Misfit said. "I been most everything. Been in 680 the arm service, both land and sea, at home and abroad, been twict married, been an undertaker, been with the railroads, plowed Mother Earth, been in a tornado, seen a man burnt alive oncet," and he looked up at the 685 children's mother and the little girl who were sitting close together, their faces white and their eyes glassy; "I even seen a woman flogged," he said.

"Pray, pray," the grandmother began, "pray, 690 pray . . ."

"I never was a bad boy that I remember of," The Misfit said in an almost dreamy voice, "but somewheres along the line I done something wrong and got sent to the

695 penitentiary. I was buried alive," and he looked up and held her attention to him by a steady stare.

"That's when you should have started to pray," she said. "What did you do to get sent 700 to the penitentiary that first time?"

"Turn to the right, it was a wall," The Misfit said, looking up again at the cloudless sky. "Turn to the left, it was a wall. Look up it was a ceiling, look down it was a floor. I forget 705 what I done, lady. I set there and set there, trying to remember what it was I done and I ain't recalled it to this day. Oncet in a while, I would think it was coming to me, but it never come."

710 "Maybe they put you in by mistake," the old lady said vaguely.

"Nome," he said. "It wasn't no mistake. They had the papers on me."

"You must have stolen something," she 715 said.

The Misfit sneered slightly. "Nobody had nothing I wanted," he said. "It was a head-doctor at the penitentiary said what I had done was kill my daddy but I known that for 720 a lie. My daddy died in nineteen ought nine-teen of the epidemic flu and I never had a thing to do with it. He was buried in the Mount Hopewell Baptist churchyard and you can go there and see for yourself."

725 "If you would pray," the old lady said, "Jesus would help you."

"That's right," The Misfit said.

"Well then, why don't you pray?" she asked trembling with delight suddenly.

730 "I don't want no hep," he said. "I'm doing all right by myself."

Bobby Lee and Hiram came ambling back from the woods. Bobby Lee was dragging a yellow shirt with bright blue parrots in it.

735 "Thow me that shirt, Bobby Lee," The Misfit said. The shirt came flying at him and landed on his shoulder and he put it on. The grandmother couldn't name what the shirt reminded her of. "No, lady," The Misfit said 740 while he was buttoning it up, "I found out the crime don't matter. You can do one thing or you can do another, kill a man or take a tire off his car, because sooner or later you're going to forget what it was you done and just 745 be punished for it."

The children's mother had begun to make heaving noises as if she couldn't get her breath. "Lady," he asked, "would you and that little girl like to step off yonder with Bobby 750 Lee and Hiram and join your husband?"

"Yes, thank you," the mother said faintly. Her left arm dangled helplessly and she was holding the baby, who had gone to sleep, in the other. "Hep that lady up, Hiram," The 755 Misfit said as she struggled to climb out of the ditch, "and Bobby Lee, you hold onto that little girl's hand."

"I don't want to hold hands with him," June Star said. "He reminds me of a pig."

760 The fat boy blushed and laughed and caught her by the arm and pulled her off into the woods after Hiram and her mother.

Alone with The Misfit, the grandmother found that she had lost her voice. There was 765 not a cloud in the sky nor any sun. There was nothing around her but woods. She wanted to tell him that he must pray. She opened and closed her mouth several times before anything came out. Finally she found herself 770 saying, "Jesus. Jesus," meaning, Jesus will help you, but the way she was saying it, it sounded as if she might be cursing.

"Yes'm," The Misfit said as if he agreed. "Jesus shown everything off balance. It was 775 the same case with Him as with me except He hadn't committed any crime and they could prove I had committed one because they had the papers on me. Of course," he said, "they never shown me my papers. 780 That's why I sign myself now. I said long ago, you get you a signature and sign everything you do and keep a copy of it. Then you'll know what you done and you can hold up the crime to the punishment and see do they 785 match and in the end you'll have something to prove you ain't been treated right. I call myself The Misfit," he said, "because I can't make what all I done wrong fit what all I gone through in punishment."

790   There was a piercing scream from the woods, followed closely by a pistol report. "Does it seem right to you, lady, that one is punished a heap and another ain't punished at all?"

    "Jesus!" the old lady cried. "You've got 795 good blood! I know you wouldn't shoot a lady! I know you come from nice people! Pray! Jesus, you ought not to shoot a lady. I'll give you all the money I've got!"

    "Lady," The Misfit said, looking beyond her 800 far into the woods, "there never was a body that give the undertaker a tip."

    There were two more pistol reports and the grandmother raised her head like a parched old turkey hen crying for water and 805 called, "Bailey Boy, Bailey Boy!" as if her heart would break.

    "Jesus was the only One that ever raised the dead," The Misfit continued, "and He shouldn't have done it. He shown everything 810 off balance. If He did what He said, then it's nothing for you to do but throw away everything and follow Him, and if He didn't, then it's nothing for you to do but enjoy the few minutes you got left the best way you can— 815 by killing somebody or burning down his house or doing some other meanness to him. No pleasure but meanness," he said and his voice had become almost a snarl.

    "Maybe He didn't raise the dead," the old 820 lady mumbled, not knowing what she was saying and feeling so dizzy that she sank down in the ditch with her legs twisted under her.

    "I wasn't there so I can't say He didn't," 825 The Misfit said. "I wisht I had of been there," he said, hitting the ground with his fist. "It ain't right I wasn't there because if I had of been there I would of known. Listen lady," he said in a high voice, "if I had of been there I 830 would of known and I wouldn't be like I am now." His voice seemed about to crack and the grandmother's head cleared for an instant. She saw the man's face twisted close to her own as if he were going to cry and she 835 murmured, "Why you're one of my babies. You're one of my own children!" She reached out and touched him on the shoulder. The Misfit sprang back as if a snake had bitten him and shot her three times through the 840 chest. Then he put his gun down on the ground and took off his glasses and began to clean them.

    Hiram and Bobby Lee returned from the woods and stood over the ditch, looking 845 down at the grandmother who half sat and half lay in a puddle of blood with her legs crossed under her like a child's and her face smiling up at the cloudless sky.

    Without his glasses, The Misfit's eyes were 850 red-rimmed and pale and defenseless-looking. "Take her off and thow her where you shown the others," he said, picking up the cat that was rubbing itself against his leg.

    "She was a talker, wasn't she?" Bobby 855 Lee said, sliding down the ditch with a yodel.

    "She would of been a good woman," The Misfit said, "if it had been somebody there to shoot her every minute of her life."

860   "Some fun!" Bobby Lee said.

    "Shut up, Bobby Lee" The Misfit said. "It's no real pleasure in life."

CHARACTER

1. How do the description and the speech of the grandmother contribute to the **values** she represents?

2. Who is the **antagonist**, and how do you know?

3. How are the traits of the **protagonist** and **antagonist** contrasted?

4. What provokes the **protagonist** to change? In what ways does this character change?

5. What do the contrasting traits of the characters reveal about them as individuals and about their relationship with other characters?

Mood and Atmosphere

AP **Enduring Understanding**

Setting and the details associated with it not only depict a time and place but also convey values associated with that setting.

KEY POINT

A story's setting creates an atmosphere and mood that affect a reader's interpretation of that story.

How do you describe your hometown? How has it shaped you as a person? When people visit, would they describe your hometown in the same way that you would? If you've traveled to a different town or city, how would you describe it in comparison? Places as big as cities or as small as bedrooms can hold unique meaning for people. They can also influence the identity of one individual or a larger community. In literature, the setting works similarly.

The specific location of the setting can shape or reveal valuable information about a character. For example, a character who has worked at the same prison for forty years likely knows critical security information, as well as the history of the institution. They may even have known the same incarcerated individuals for their entire career.

In earlier units, you learned that setting encompasses more than just the time and location of a story. Setting involves the social, cultural, and historical situation in which the events occur. All of this matters when you are considering how a story's setting contributes to your interpretation.

Setting Creates Atmosphere and Mood

You should also consider how the author has described that setting. For example, what words and images does the writer use? How do these specific choices make you, as the reader, feel? Is the setting bright and festive? Mysterious? Isolated? Do you feel suspense? Gloom and doom?

We often use the words atmosphere, mood, and tone to describe the feelings evoked by a story. While these three terms are related, they are not the same.

Tone, as you learned in Unit 2, is the author's attitude about the subject or the idea in the text. The author reveals tone through the characters, conflicts and their outcomes, word choice, and imagery that he or she creates through the story. **Mood** refers to the way the author's descriptions and images make the reader feel. And, a story's **atmosphere** is how a particular setting makes the reader feel and think. Since a story's setting contributes to atmosphere and mood, let's look at each a little more closely.

Some writers use aspects of the physical setting, especially nature and weather, as a way of representing the internal mental or emotional state of a character. When the outside environment reflects the internal psychological state of a character, the author has employed the **pathetic fallacy**.

Atmosphere

The **atmosphere** of a work is often created by the way an author describes the setting.

While a story's atmosphere includes the way those choices make you feel, it also establishes some expectations for the reader. For example, a story set with a character in a boat lost at sea could make you feel a sense of fear; you may wonder how the character will overcome the powerful force of nature. A story with a Civil War–era historical setting may elicit your own attitudes toward questions of freedom and equality. Likewise, a story with a fantastical setting prepares the reader to suspend disbelief and assumptions about reality.

In Unit 3, you learned that setting also includes a story's social, cultural, and historical contexts. As you read a story, you will want to consider how its atmosphere contributes to your interpretation of that story. Specifically, you'll want to analyze how the social, cultural, and historical context of a setting helps establish a story's atmosphere.

- **Social:** The way that people live and what they believe at the time the story is set
- **Cultural:** The arts and popular interests of the time the story is set
- **Historical:** The events in history that occurred at the time the story is set

Mood

The **mood** of a narrative is the pervasive feeling or emotional impression a reader gets from the text as a whole. While a narrative's atmosphere contributes to the mood, mood is more encompassing than the atmosphere. A story's mood is created by all of the author's choices about setting, characters, and plot.

INSIDER AP TIP **Mood and tone are not the same.** Mood is the feeling created in the reader, while tone is the attitude of the author, character, speaker, or narrator.

MOOD AND ATMOSPHERE AS A PART OF SETTING		
Types of Setting	**Considerations**	**Key Questions**
Physical Setting (the place where the story is set)	• Outside or inside • Real or imaginary • Location • Time of day, season • Familiar or unfamiliar	What is the location, and what values are embodied in that location? Why might the time of day or time of year be important? What might the weather reveal? How is nature portrayed? How might aspects of the physical environment or nature reflect aspects of a character?

(continued)

Social Setting (the way people live and what they believe at the time the story is set)	• Traditions • Rituals • Customs • Religious beliefs	What do the descriptions, the physical objects, and possessions reveal? Are there works of art present? If so, why? Does the setting encompass a social event (e.g., a wedding, funeral, or festival)? Why might this be important? What role does religion or faith play?
Cultural Setting (the arts and popular interests at the time the story is set)	• Urban or rural • Country/locale	How does the urban or rural setting affect the characters? What might the description of buildings or other structures and their proximity to each other reveal?
Historical Setting (the events in history that occurred at the time the story is set)	• Present day • Historical period • The future	How does the story's time period affect the reader's understanding? What values are associated with the historical setting? How do a character's actions and values fit within the historical setting?

GUIDED READING

The Law of Life
Jack London

THE TEXT IN CONTEXT

Novelist, journalist, adventurer, and political activist Jack London (1876–1916) was one of the most successful authors of his time. Born and raised in San Francisco, he rejected most formal education and spent his early years working and traveling: riding trains, hiring out on ships, and laboring in canning factories. In his early twenties, he traveled to northern Canada to join the 1890s Yukon gold rush. While he failed to strike it rich, he did return to California and began publishing fiction that reflected his experiences and perspectives, including *The Call of the Wild* (1903), *The Sea Wolf* (1904), and *South Sea Tales* (1911). He also

Bettmann/Getty Images

wrote many short stories, poems, plays, memoirs, and articles for newspapers and magazines. London is usually characterized as a literary *naturalist*. Naturalists take a grim view of humanity and its place in the universe. Instead of viewing individuals as autonomous agents, naturalists see people as determined by their biological urges, their natural or social environment, and other factors largely beyond their control. While most naturalists focused on urban settings, London often preferred to write about harsh, natural environments — as in the case of this 1901 story, "The Law of Life."

The Law of Life

Old Koskoosh listened greedily. Though his sight had long since faded, his hearing was still acute, and the slightest sound penetrated to the glimmering intelligence which yet abode behind the withered forehead, but which no longer gazed forth upon the things of the world. Ah! that was
5   Sit-cum-to-ha, shrilly anathematizing the dogs as she cuffed and beat them into the harnesses. Sit-cum-to-ha was his daughter's daughter, but she was too busy to waste a thought upon her broken grandfather, sitting alone there in the snow, forlorn and helpless. Camp must be broken. The long trail waited while the short day refused to linger.

1. Where is the story taking place?

10   The thought made the old man panicky for the moment, and he stretched forth a palsied hand which wandered tremblingly over the small heap of dry wood beside him. Reassured that it was indeed there, his hand returned to the shelter of his mangy furs, and he again fell to listening. The sulky crackling of half-frozen hides told him that the
15   chief's moose-skin lodge had been struck, and even then was being rammed and jammed into portable compass. The chief was his son, stalwart and strong, head man of the tribesmen, and a mighty hunter. As the women toiled with the camp luggage, his voice rose, chiding them for their slowness. Old Koskoosh strained his ears. It was the last time
20   he would hear that voice. There went Geehow's lodge! And Tusken's! Seven, eight, nine; only the shaman's could be still standing. There! They were at work upon it now. He could hear the shaman grunt as he piled it on the sled. A child whimpered, and a woman soothed it with soft, crooning gutturals. Little Koo-tee, the old man thought, a fretful
25   child, and not overstrong. It would die soon, perhaps, and they would burn a hole through the frozen tundra and pile rocks above to keep the wolverines away. Well, what did it matter? A few years at best, and as many an empty belly as a full one. And in the end, Death waited, ever-hungry and hungriest of them all.

2. How is the setting slowly revealed in this introduction?

30   What was that? Oh, the men lashing the sleds and drawing tight the thongs. He listened, who would listen no more. The whip-lashes snarled and bit among the dogs. Hear them whine! How they hated the work and the trail! They were off! Sled after sled churned slowly away into the silence. They were gone. They had passed out of his life, and he faced the
35   last bitter hour alone. No. The snow crunched beneath a moccasin; a man stood beside him; upon his head a hand rested gently. His son was good to do this thing. He remembered other old men whose sons had not waited after the tribe. But his son had. He wandered away into the past, till the young man's voice brought him back.

3. What mood is created through the character and the setting?

40   "Is it well with you?" he asked.
        And the old man answered, "It is well."

"There be wood beside you," the younger man continued, "and the fire burns bright. The morning is gray, and the cold has broken. It will snow presently. Even now is it snowing."

45 "Ay, even now is it snowing."

"The tribesmen hurry. Their bales are heavy, and their bellies flat with lack of feasting. The trail is long and they travel fast. I go now. It is well?"

"It is well. I am as a last year's leaf, clinging lightly to the stem. The first breath that blows, and I fall. My voice is become like an old woman's. My 50 eyes no longer show me the way of my feet, and my feet are heavy, and I am tired. It is well."

Guided Questions

4. How does the leaf parallel Old Koskoosh and reinforce the atmosphere created in the text?

He bowed his head in content till the last noise of the complaining snow had died away, and he knew his son was beyond recall. Then his hand crept out in haste to the wood. It alone stood between him and the 55 eternity that yawned in upon him. At last the measure of his life was a handful of fagots. One by one they would go to feed the fire, and just so, step by step, death would creep upon him. When the last stick had surrendered up its heat, the frost would begin to gather strength. First his feet would yield, then his hands; and the numbness would travel, slowly, from 60 the extremities to the body. His head would fall forward upon his knees, and he would rest. It was easy. All men must die.

He did not complain. It was the way of life, and it was just. He had been born close to the earth, close to the earth had he lived, and the law thereof was not new to him. It was the law of all flesh. Nature was not 65 kindly to the flesh. She had no concern for that concrete thing called the individual. Her interest lay in the species, the race. This was the deepest abstraction old Koskoosh's barbaric mind was capable of, but he grasped it firmly. He saw it exemplified in all life. The rise of the sap, the bursting greenness of the willow bud, the fall of the yellow leaf—in this alone was 70 told the whole history. But one task did Nature set the individual. Did he not perform it, he died. Did he perform it, it was all the same, he died. Nature did not care; there were plenty who were obedient, and it was only the obedience in this matter, not the obedient, which lived and lived always. The tribe of Koskoosh was very old. The old men he had known 75 when a boy, had known old men before them. Therefore it was true that the tribe lived, that it stood for the obedience of all its members, way down into the forgotten past, whose very resting-places were unremembered. They did not count; they were episodes. They had passed away like clouds from a summer sky. He also was an episode, and would pass away. 80 Nature did not care. To life she set one task, gave one law. To perpetuate was the task of life, its law was death. A maiden was a good creature to look upon, full-breasted and strong, with spring to her step and light in her eyes. But her task was yet before her. The light in her eyes brightened, her step quickened, she was now bold with the young men, now timid,

5. What is "the way of life"?

6. What is the relationship between nature and the character?

85 and she gave them of her own unrest. And ever she grew fairer and yet fairer to look upon, till some hunter, able no longer to withhold himself, took her to his lodge to cook and toil for him and to become the mother of his children. And with the coming of her offspring her looks left her. Her limbs dragged and shuffled, her eyes dimmed and bleared, and only the

90 little children found joy against the withered cheek of the old squaw by the fire. Her task was done. But a little while, on the first pinch of famine or the first long trail, and she would be left, even as he had been left, in the snow, with a little pile of wood. Such was the law.

He placed a stick carefully upon the fire and resumed his meditations.

95 It was the same everywhere, with all things. The mosquitoes vanished with the first frost. The little tree-squirrel crawled away to die. When age settled upon the rabbit it became slow and heavy, and could no longer outfoot its enemies. Even the big bald-face grew clumsy and blind and quarrelsome, in the end to be dragged down by a handful of yelping hus-

100 kies. He remembered how he had abandoned his own father on an upper reach of the Klondike one winter, the winter before the missionary came with his talk-books and his box of medicines. Many a time had Koskoosh smacked his lips over the recollection of that box, though now his mouth refused to moisten. The "painkiller" had been especially good. But

105 the missionary was a bother after all, for he brought no meat into the camp, and he ate heartily, and the hunters grumbled. But he chilled his lungs on the divide by the Mayo, and the dogs afterwards nosed the stones away and fought over his bones.

Koskoosh placed another stick on the fire and harked back deeper into

110 the past. There was the time of the Great Famine, when the old men crouched empty-bellied to the fire, and let fall from their lips dim traditions of the ancient day when the Yukon ran wide open for three winters, and then lay frozen for three summers. He had lost his mother in that famine. In the summer the salmon run had failed, and the tribe looked

115 forward to the winter and the coming of the caribou. Then the winter came, but with it there were no caribou. Never had the like been known, not even in the lives of the old men. But the caribou did not come, and it was the seventh year, and the rabbits had not replenished, and the dogs were naught but bundles of bones. And through the long darkness the

120 children wailed and died, and the women, and the old men; and not one in ten of the tribe lived to meet the sun when it came back in the spring. That was a famine!

But he had seen times of plenty, too, when the meat spoiled on their hands, and the dogs were fat and worthless with overeating—times when

125 they let the game go unkilled, and the women were fertile, and the lodges were cluttered with sprawling men-children and women-children. Then it

Guided Questions

7. What is the "law," and how does it apply to both man and nature?

8. How are the fire and the snow contrasted? Explain what they may represent.

9. What does the feast and famine contrast suggest?

was the men became high-stomached, and revived ancient quarrels, and crossed the divides to the south to kill the Pellys, and to the west that they might sit by the dead fires of the Tananas. He remembered, when a
130 boy, during a time of plenty, when he saw a moose pulled down by the wolves. Zing-ha lay with him in the snow and watched—Zing-ha, who later became the craftiest of hunters, and who, in the end, fell through an air-hole on the Yukon. They found him, a month afterward, just as he had crawled halfway out and frozen stiff to the ice.

135   But the moose. Zing-ha and he had gone out that day to play at hunting after the manner of their fathers. On the bed of the creek they struck the fresh track of a moose, and with it the tracks of many wolves. "An old one," Zing-ha, who was quicker at reading the sign, said—"an old one who cannot keep up with the herd. The wolves have cut him out from his
140 brothers, and they will never leave him." And it was so. It was their way. By day and by night, never resting, snarling on his heels, snapping at his nose, they would stay by him to the end. How Zing-ha and he felt the blood-lust quicken! The finish would be a sight to see!

        Eager-footed, they took the trail, and even he, Koskoosh, slow of sight
145 and an unversed tracker, could have followed it blind, it was so wide. Hot were they on the heels of the chase, reading the grim tragedy, fresh-written, at every step. Now they came to where the moose had made a stand. Thrice the length of a grown man's body, in every direction, had the snow been stamped about and uptossed. In the midst were the deep
150 impressions of the splay-hoofed game, and all about, everywhere, were the lighter footmarks of the wolves. Some, while their brothers harried the kill, had lain to one side and rested. The full-stretched impress of their bodies in the snow was as perfect as though made the moment before. One wolf had been caught in a wild lunge of the maddened victim and
155 trampled to death. A few bones, well picked, bore witness.

        Again, they ceased the uplift of their snowshoes at a second stand. Here the great animal had fought desperately. Twice had he been dragged down, as the snow attested, and twice had he shaken his assailants clear and gained footing once more. He had done his task long since, but none
160 the less was life dear to him. Zing-ha said it was a strange thing, a moose once down to get free again; but this one certainly had. The shaman would see signs and wonders in this when they told him.

        And yet again, they come to where the moose had made to mount the bank and gain the timber. But his foes had laid on from behind, till he
165 reared and fell back upon them, crushing two deep into the snow. It was plain the kill was at hand, for their brothers had left them untouched. Two more stands were hurried past, brief in time-length and very close together. The trail was red now, and the clean stride of the great beast had

10. What does the description of the moose and the wolves suggest about nature?

11. How is the moose representative of a cycle?

grown short and slovenly. Then they heard the first sounds of the battle—
170 not the full-throated chorus of the chase, but the short, snappy bark
which spoke of close quarters and teeth to flesh. Crawling up the wind,
Zing-ha bellied it through the snow, and with him crept he, Koskoosh,
who was to be chief of the tribesmen in the years to come. Together they
shoved aside the under branches of a young spruce and peered forth. It
175 was the end they saw.

The picture, like all of youth's impressions, was still strong with him,
and his dim eyes watched the end played out as vividly as in that far-off
time. Koskoosh marvelled at this, for in the days which followed, when he
was a leader of men and a head of councillors, he had done great deeds
180 and made his name a curse in the mouths of the Pellys, to say naught of
the strange white man he had killed, knife to knife, in open fight.

For long he pondered on the days of his youth, till the fire died down
and the frost bit deeper. He replenished it with two sticks this time,
and gauged his grip on life by what remained. If Sit-cum-to-ha had
185 only remembered her grandfather, and gathered a larger armful, his
hours would have been longer. It would have been easy. But she was
ever a careless child, and honored not her ancestors from the time the
Beaver, son of the son of Zing-ha, first cast eyes upon her. Well, what
mattered it? Had he not done likewise in his own quick youth? For a
190 while he listened to the silence. Perhaps the heart of his son might
soften, and he would come back with the dogs to take his old father on
with the tribe to where the caribou ran thick and the fat hung heavy
upon them.

12. How do the fire dying down and the frostbite getting deeper contribute to the tone of the story?

He strained his ears, his restless brain for the moment stilled. Not a
195 stir, nothing. He alone took breath in the midst of the great silence. It
was very lonely. Hark! What was that? A chill passed over his body. The
familiar, long-drawn howl broke the void, and it was close at hand. Then
on his darkened eyes was projected the vision of the moose—the old bull
moose—the torn flanks and bloody sides, the riddled mane, and the great
200 branching horns, down low and tossing to the last. He saw the flashing
forms of gray, the gleaming eyes, the lolling tongues, the slavered fangs.
And he saw the inexorable circle close in till it became a dark point in the
midst of the stamped snow.

13. What atmosphere do the details of the story create?

A cold muzzle thrust against his cheek, and at its touch his soul
205 leaped back to the present. His hand shot into the fire and dragged out a
burning faggot. Overcome for the nonce by his hereditary fear of man,
the brute retreated, raising a prolonged call to his brothers; and greedily
they answered, till a ring of crouching, jaw-slobbered gray was stretched
round about. The old man listened to the drawing in of this circle. He
210 waved his brand wildly, and sniffs turned to snarls; but the panting

14. How do the images contribute to the pathetic fallacy?

brutes refused to scatter. Now one wormed his chest forward, dragging his haunches after, now a second, now a third; but never a one drew back. Why should he cling to life? he asked, and dropped the blazing stick into the snow. It sizzled and went out. The circle grunted uneasily,
215 but held its own. Again he saw the last stand of the old bull moose, and Koskoosh dropped his head wearily upon his knees. What did it matter after all? Was it not the law of life?

Guided Questions

15. How does the last question connect to the title and your interpretation of the story?

PRACTICE TEXT

A Rose for Emily
William Faulkner

Mario De Biasi/Mondadori Portfolio/Getty Images

THE TEXT IN CONTEXT

Nobel Prize winner William Faulkner (1897–1962) is known primarily for his groundbreaking modernist novels, such as *The Sound and the Fury* (1929), *As I Lay Dying* (1930), and *Absalom, Absalom!* (1936). But while his literary techniques and narrative innovations were new at the time, his setting was largely the defeated and decaying American South during Reconstruction and the early decades of the twentieth century. In fact, Faulkner created an entire fictional world that provides both recurring characters and the setting for most of his stories: Yoknapatawpha County, a fictional-ized version of Mississippi's Lafayette County, where Faulkner lived most of his life. He places the short story "A Rose for Emily" in the town of Jefferson, the writer's stand-in for Oxford, Mississippi. As part of the literary subgenre known as the Southern Gothic, Faulkner creates a tale whose forbidding mood, gothic atmosphere, and eerie setting (including a crumbling mansion) all work to reveal the grotesque reality beneath the refined and genteel surfaces of the South.

   Content Note: This story includes the N-word, which we have chosen not to reprint in full here. We wish to accurately reflect Faulkner's original intent, as well as call attention to the racism of the time period. However, we also recognize that this word has a long history as a disrespectful and deeply hurtful expression when used by white people toward Black people. Be mindful of context, both Faulkner's and yours, as you read and discuss "A Rose for Emily."

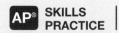 **SKILLS PRACTICE** | SETTING
Analyzing the Significance of Setting

Describe the physical, social, cultural, and historical setting of "A Rose for Emily." Note the details from the story that convey the different types of settings. Analyze how the details of setting contribute to your interpretation of the text.

Analyzing the Significance of Setting		
Types of Setting	**Key Questions**	**Details from the Story and Significance**
Physical Setting (the place where the story is set)	• What is the location? And what values are embodied in that location? • Why might the time of day or time of year be important? • What might the weather reveal? • How is nature portrayed or presented? • How might aspects of the physical environment or nature reflect aspects of a character?	
Social Setting (how people live and what they believe at the time the story is set)	• What do the descriptions, the physical objects, and possessions reveal? • Are there works of art present? If so, why? • Does the setting encompass a social event (e.g., wedding, funeral, festival)? Why might this be important? • What role does religion or faith play?	
Cultural Setting (the arts and popular interests of the time the story is set)	• How does the urban or rural setting affect the characters? • What might the description of buildings or other structures and their proximity to each other reveal?	
Historical Setting (the events in history that occurred at the time the story is set)	• How does when the story is set affect the reader's understanding? • What values are associated with the historical setting? • How do a character's actions and values fit within the historical setting?	

A Rose for Emily

I

When Miss Emily Grierson died, our whole town went to her funeral: the men through a sort of respectful affection for a fallen monument, the women mostly out of curiosity to
5 see the inside of her house, which no one save an old man-servant—a combined gardener and cook—had seen in at least ten years.

It was a big, squarish frame house that
10 had once been white, decorated with cupolas and spires and scrolled balconies in the heavily lightsome style of the seventies, set on what had once been our most select street. But garages and cotton gins had encroached
15 and obliterated even the august names of that neighborhood; only Miss Emily's house was left, lifting its stubborn and coquettish decay above the cotton wagons and the gasoline pumps—an eyesore among eyesores.
20 And now Miss Emily had gone to join the representatives of those august names where they lay in the cedar-bemused cemetery among the ranked and anonymous graves of Union and Confederate soldiers who fell at
25 the battle of Jefferson.

Alive, Miss Emily had been a tradition, a duty, and a care; a sort of hereditary obligation upon the town, dating from that day in 1894 when Colonel Sartoris, the mayor—he
30 who fathered the edict that no Negro woman should appear on the streets without an apron—remitted her taxes, the dispensation dating from the death of her father on into perpetuity. Not that Miss Emily would have
35 accepted charity. Colonel Sartoris invented an involved tale to the effect that Miss Emily's father had loaned money to the town, which the town, as a matter of business, preferred this way of repaying. Only a
40 man of Colonel Sartoris' generation and thought could have invented it, and only a woman could have believed it.

When the next generation, with its more modern ideas, became mayors and alder-
45 men, this arrangement created some little dissatisfaction. On the first of the year they mailed her a tax notice. February came, and there was no reply. They wrote her a formal letter, asking her to call at the sheriff's office
50 at her convenience. A week later the mayor wrote her himself, offering to call or to send his car for her, and received in reply a note on paper of an archaic shape, in a thin, flowing calligraphy in faded ink, to the effect that
55 she no longer went out at all. The tax notice was also enclosed, without comment.

They called a special meeting of the Board of Aldermen. A deputation waited upon her, knocked at the door through which no visitor
60 had passed since she ceased giving china-painting lessons eight or ten years earlier. They were admitted by the old Negro into a dim hall from which a stairway mounted into still more shadow. It smelled of dust and
65 disuse—a close, dank smell. The Negro led them into the parlor. It was furnished in heavy, leather-covered furniture. When the Negro opened the blinds of one window, they could see that the leather was cracked; and
70 when they sat down, a faint dust rose sluggishly about their thighs, spinning with slow motes in the single sun-ray. On a tarnished gilt easel before the fireplace stood a crayon portrait of Miss Emily's father.
75 They rose when she entered—a small, fat woman in black, with a thin gold chain descending to her waist and vanishing into her belt, leaning on an ebony cane with a tarnished gold head. Her skeleton was small and
80 spare; perhaps that was why what would have been merely plumpness in another was

obesity in her. She looked bloated, like a body long submerged in motionless water, and of that pallid hue. Her eyes, lost in the fatty
85 ridges of her face, looked like two small pieces of coal pressed into a lump of dough as they moved from one face to another while the visitors stated their errand.

She did not ask them to sit. She just stood
90 in the door and listened quietly until the spokesman came to a stumbling halt. Then they could hear the invisible watch ticking at the end of the gold chain.

Her voice was dry and cold. "I have no
95 taxes in Jefferson. Colonel Sartoris explained it to me. Perhaps one of you can gain access to the city records and satisfy yourselves."

"But we have. We are the city authorities, Miss Emily. Didn't you get a notice from the
100 sheriff, signed by him?"

"I received a paper, yes," Miss Emily said. "Perhaps he considers himself the sheriff . . . I have no taxes in Jefferson."

"But there is nothing on the books to
105 show that, you see. We must go by the—"

"See Colonel Sartoris. I have no taxes in Jefferson."

"But, Miss Emily—"

"See Colonel Sartoris." (Colonel Sartoris
110 had been dead almost ten years.) "I have no taxes in Jefferson. Tobe!" The Negro appeared. "Show these gentlemen out."

II

So she vanquished them, horse and foot, just as she had vanquished their fathers thirty
115 years before about the smell.

That was two years after her father's death and a short time after her sweetheart—the one we believed would marry her—had deserted her. After her father's
120 death she went out very little; after her sweetheart went away, people hardly saw her at all. A few of the ladies had the temerity to

call, but were not received, and the only sign of life about the place was the Negro man—a
125 young man then—going in and out with a market basket.

"Just as if a man—any man—could keep a kitchen properly, "the ladies said; so they were not surprised when the smell devel-
130 oped. It was another link between the gross, teeming world and the high and mighty Griersons.

A neighbor, a woman, complained to the mayor, Judge Stevens, eighty years old.
135 "But what will you have me do about it, madam?" he said.

"Why, send her word to stop it," the woman said. "Isn't there a law?"

"I'm sure that won't be necessary," Judge
140 Stevens said. "It's probably just a snake or a rat that n***** of hers killed in the yard. I'll speak to him about it."

The next day he received two more complaints, one from a man who came in diffident
145 deprecation. "We really must do something about it, Judge. I'd be the last one in the world to bother Miss Emily, but we've got to do something." That night the Board of Aldermen met—three graybeards and one younger man,
150 a member of the rising generation.

"It's simple enough," he said. "Send her word to have her place cleaned up. Give her a certain time to do it in, and if she don't . . ."

"Dammit, sir," Judge Stevens said, "will
155 you accuse a lady to her face of smelling bad?"

So the next night, after midnight, four men crossed Miss Emily's lawn and slunk about the house like burglars, sniffing along
160 the base of the brickwork and at the cellar openings while one of them performed a regular sowing motion with his hand out of a sack slung from his shoulder. They broke open the cellar door and sprinkled lime
165 there, and in all the outbuildings. As they

recrossed the lawn, a window that had been
dark was lighted and Miss Emily sat in it,
the light behind her, and her upright torso
motionless as that of an idol. They crept qui-
170 etly across the lawn and into the shadow of
the locusts that lined the street. After a week
or two the smell went away.

That was when people had begun to feel
really sorry for her. People in our town,
175 remembering how old lady Wyatt, her great-
aunt, had gone completely crazy at last,
believed that the Griersons held themselves a
little too high for what they really were. None
of the young men were quite good enough for
180 Miss Emily and such. We had long thought of
them as a tableau, Miss Emily a slender figure
in white in the background, her father a
spraddled silhouette in the foreground, his
back to her and clutching a horsewhip, the
185 two of them framed by the back-flung front
door. So when she got to be thirty and was
still single, we were not pleased exactly, but
vindicated; even with insanity in the family
she wouldn't have turned down all of her
190 chances if they had really materialized.

When her father died, it got about that
the house was all that was left to her; and in
a way, people were glad. At last they could
pity Miss Emily. Being left alone, and a pau-
195 per, she had become humanized. Now she
too would know the old thrill and the old
despair of a penny more or less.

The day after his death all the ladies prepared to call at the house and offer condo-
200 lence and aid, as is our custom Miss Emily met
them at the door, dressed as usual and with
no trace of grief on her face. She told them
that her father was not dead. She did that for
three days, with the ministers calling on her,
205 and the doctors, trying to persuade her to let
them dispose of the body. Just as they were
about to resort to law and force, she broke
down, and they buried her father quickly.

We did not say she was crazy then. We
210 believed she had to do that. We remembered
all the young men her father had driven
away, and we knew that with nothing left,
she would have to cling to that which had
robbed her, as people will.

III

215 She was sick for a long time. When we saw
her again, her hair was cut short, making her
look like a girl, with a vague resemblance to
those angels in colored church windows—
sort of tragic and serene.

220 The town had just let the contracts for
paving the sidewalks, and in the summer
after her father's death they began the work.
The construction company came with n*****s
and mules and machinery, and a foreman
225 named Homer Barron, a Yankee—a big, dark,
ready man, with a big voice and eyes lighter
than his face. The little boys would follow
in groups to hear him cuss the n*****s, and
the n*****s singing in time to the rise and
230 fall of picks. Pretty soon he knew everybody
in town. Whenever you heard a lot of laughing anywhere about the square, Homer
Barron would be in the center of the group.
Presently we began to see him and Miss
235 Emily on Sunday afternoons driving in the
yellow-wheeled buggy and the matched
team of bays from the livery stable.

At first we were glad that Miss Emily
would have an interest, because the ladies all
240 said, "Of course a Grierson would not think
seriously of a Northerner, a day laborer." But
there were still others, older people, who
said that even grief could not cause a real
lady to forget *noblesse oblige*—without calling
245 it *noblesse oblige*. They just said, "Poor Emily.
Her kinsfolk should come to her." She had
some kin in Alabama; but years ago her
father had fallen out with them over the
estate of old lady Wyatt, the crazy woman,

250 and there was no communication between the two families. They had not even been represented at the funeral.

And as soon as the old people said, "Poor Emily," the whispering began. "Do you suppose
255 it's really so?" they said to one another. "Of course it is. What else could . . ." This behind their hands; rustling of craned silk and satin behind jalousies closed upon the sun of Sunday afternoon as the thin, swift clop-clop-
260 clop of the matched team passed: "Poor Emily."

She carried her head high enough—even when we believed that she was fallen. It was as if she demanded more than ever the recognition of her dignity as the last Grierson;
265 as if it had wanted that touch of earthiness to reaffirm her imperviousness. Like when she bought the rat poison, the arsenic. That was over a year after they had begun to say "Poor Emily," and while the two female cous-
270 ins were visiting her.

"I want some poison," she said to the druggist. She was over thirty then, still a slight woman, though thinner than usual, with cold, haughty black eyes in a face the
275 flesh of which was strained across the temples and about the eyesockets as you imagine a lighthouse-keeper's face ought to look. "I want some poison," she said.

"Yes, Miss Emily. What kind? For rats and
280 such? I'd recom—"

"I want the best you have. I don't care what kind."

The druggist named several. "They'll kill anything up to an elephant. But what you
285 want is—"

"Arsenic," Miss Emily said. "Is that a good one?"

"Is . . . arsenic? Yes, ma'am. But what you want—"

290 "I want arsenic."

The druggist looked down at her. She looked back at him, erect, her face like a strained flag.

"Why, of course," the druggist said. "If that's what you want. But the law requires you to tell
295 what you are going to use it for."

Miss Emily just stared at him, her head tilted back in order to look him eye for eye, until he looked away and went and got the arsenic and wrapped it up. The Negro deliv-
300 ery boy brought her the package; the druggist didn't come back. When she opened the package at home there was written on the box, under the skull and bones: "For rats."

IV

So the next day we all said, "She will kill her-
305 self"; and we said it would be the best thing. When she had first begun to be seen with Homer Barron, we had said, "She will marry him." Then we said, "She will persuade him yet," because Homer himself had remarked—
310 he liked men, and it was known that he drank with the younger men in the Elks' Club—that he was not a marrying man. Later we said, "Poor Emily" behind the jalousies as they passed on Sunday afternoon in
315 the glittering buggy, Miss Emily with her head high and Homer Barron with his hat cocked and a cigar in his teeth, reins and whip in a yellow glove.

Then some of the ladies began to say that it
320 was a disgrace to the town and a bad example to the young people. The men did not want to interfere, but at last the ladies forced the Baptist minister—Miss Emily's people were Episcopal—to call upon her. He would never
325 divulge what happened during that interview, but he refused to go back again. The next Sunday they again drove about the streets, and the following day the minister's wife wrote to Miss Emily's relations in Alabama.

330 So she had blood-kin under her roof again and we sat back to watch developments. At first nothing happened. Then we were sure that they were to be married. We learned

that Miss Emily had been to the jeweler's and
335 ordered a man's toilet set in silver, with the
letters H. B. on each piece. Two days later we
learned that she had bought a complete outfit of men's clothing, including a nightshirt,
and we said, "They are married." We were
340 really glad. We were glad because the two
female cousins were even more Grierson
than Miss Emily had ever been.

So we were not surprised when Homer
Barron—the streets had been finished some
345 time since—was gone. We were a little disappointed that there was not a public blow-
ing-off, but we believed that he had gone on
to prepare for Miss Emily's coming, or to give
her a chance to get rid of the cousins. (By that
350 time it was a cabal, and we were all Miss
Emily's allies to help circumvent the cousins.)
Sure enough, after another week they
departed. And, as we had expected all along,
within three days Homer Barron was back in
355 town. A neighbor saw the Negro man admit
him at the kitchen door at dusk one evening.

And that was the last we saw of Homer
Barron. And of Miss Emily for some time. The
Negro man went in and out with the market
360 basket, but the front door remained closed.
Now and then we would see her at a window
for a moment, as the men did that night
when they sprinkled the lime, but for almost
six months she did not appear on the streets.
365 Then we knew that this was to be expected
too; as if that quality of her father which had
thwarted her woman's life so many times
had been too virulent and too furious to die.

When we next saw Miss Emily, she had
370 grown fat and her hair was turning gray.
During the next few years it grew grayer and
grayer until it attained an even pepper-and-
salt iron-gray, when it ceased turning. Up to
the day of her death at seventy-four it was
375 still that vigorous iron-gray, like the hair of
an active man.

From that time on her front door
remained closed, save for a period of six or
seven years, when she was about forty,
380 during which she gave lessons in china-
painting. She fitted up a studio in one of the
downstairs rooms, where the daughters and
granddaughters of Colonel Sartoris' contemporaries were sent to her with the same reg-
385 ularity and in the same spirit that they were
sent to church on Sundays with a twenty-
five-cent piece for the collection plate.
Meanwhile her taxes had been remitted.

Then the newer generation became the
390 backbone and the spirit of the town, and the
painting pupils grew up and fell away and
did not send their children to her with boxes
of color and tedious brushes and pictures cut
from the ladies' magazines. The front door
395 closed upon the last one and remained
closed for good. When the town got free
postal delivery, Miss Emily alone refused to
let them fasten the metal numbers above her
door and attach a mailbox to it. She would
400 not listen to them.

Daily, monthly, yearly we watched the
Negro grow grayer and more stooped, going
in and out with the market basket. Each
December we sent her a tax notice, which
405 would be returned by the post office a week
later, unclaimed. Now and then we would see
her in one of the downstairs windows—she
had evidently shut up the top floor of the
house—like the carven torso of an idol in a
410 niche, looking or not looking at us, we could
never tell which. Thus she passed from generation to generation—dear, inescapable,
impervious, tranquil, and perverse.

And so she died. Fell ill in the house filled
415 with dust and shadows, with only a dodder-
ing Negro man to wait on her. We did not
even know she was sick; we had long since
given up trying to get any information from
the Negro.

420 He talked to no one, probably not even to her, for his voice had grown harsh and rusty, as if from disuse.

She died in one of the downstairs rooms, in a heavy walnut bed with a curtain, her 425 gray head propped on a pillow yellow and moldy with age and lack of sunlight.

V

The Negro met the first of the ladies at the front door and let them in, with their hushed, sibilant voices and their quick, curi-430 ous glances, and then he disappeared. He walked right through the house and out the back and was not seen again.

The two female cousins came at once. They held the funeral on the second day, with the 435 town coming to look at Miss Emily beneath a mass of bought flowers, with the crayon face of her father musing profoundly above the bier and the ladies sibilant and macabre; and the very old men—some in their brushed 440 Confederate uniforms—on the porch and the lawn, talking of Miss Emily as if she had been a contemporary of theirs, believing that they had danced with her and courted her perhaps, confusing time with its mathematical progres-445 sion, as the old do, to whom all the past is not a diminishing road but, instead, a huge meadow which no winter ever quite touches, divided from them now by the narrow bottle-neck of the most recent decade of years.

450 Already we knew that there was one room in that region above stairs which no one had seen in forty years, and which would have to be forced. They waited until Miss Emily was decently in the ground before they opened it.

455 The violence of breaking down the door seemed to fill this room with pervading dust. A thin, acrid pall as of the tomb seemed to lie everywhere upon this room decked and fur-nished as for a bridal: upon the valance cur-460 tains of faded rose color, upon the rose-shaded lights, upon the dressing table, upon the deli-cate array of crystal and the man's toilet things backed with tarnished silver, silver so tar-nished that the monogram was obscured.

465 Among them lay a collar and tie, as if they had just been removed, which, lifted, left upon the surface a pale crescent in the dust. Upon a chair hung the suit, carefully folded; beneath it the two mute shoes and the discarded socks.

470 The man himself lay in the bed.

For a long while we just stood there, look-ing down at the profound and fleshless grin. The body had apparently once lain in the atti-tude of an embrace, but now the long sleep 475 that outlasts love, that conquers even the gri-mace of love, had cuckolded him. What was left of him, rotted beneath what was left of the nightshirt, had become inextricable from the bed in which he lay; and upon him and 480 upon the pillow beside him lay that even coating of the patient and biding dust.

Then we noticed that in the second pillow was the indentation of a head. One of us lifted something from it, and leaning for-485 ward, that faint and invisible dust dry and acrid in the nostrils, we saw a long strand of iron-gray hair.

SETTING

1. How does the setting contribute to the **atmosphere** and **mood** of the story?

2. How do the descriptions of the town and the historical period reflect the values of the **setting**?

3. How do Miss Emily's actions and values fit within the historical **setting**?

4. How do the details and descriptions throughout the story contribute to its **tone**?

Archetypal Patterns

 Enduring Understanding

The arrangement of the parts and sections of a text, the relationship of the parts to each other, and the sequence in which the text reveals information are all structural choices made by a writer that contribute to the reader's interpretation of a text.

KEY POINT

Patterns in literature, called archetypes, emerge because many human experiences are shared across cultures. For this reason, themes in literature stand the test of time.

Have you watched a movie or read a story that seemed eerily similar to another one? Perhaps you knew exactly what a character would do or say; you may have felt a sense of *déjà vu* as you correctly guessed the resolution of the conflict. You might be able to predict the end of a story because of its familiar plotlines.

The dramatic situation of the narrative can set up expectations for the reader. The guy gets the girl; the main character comes to a tragic end; the main character finds riches. These plotlines mirror human experiences and create literary patterns. In other words, you have seen this pattern before, and you have some expectations about it. Sometimes these expectations are met, and sometimes they are not. When they are not met, the story's outcome is ironic. We will discuss irony in Unit 8.

Story Patterns Often Mirror Those in the Human Experience

So why do many literary worlds stand the test of time? Because many authors from different cultures tell the same stories — all with different characters and settings but similar dramatic situations.

Some patterns in dramatic situations are so common that they have become archetypes. An **archetype** is a plot pattern, character type, setting, or object that occurs frequently in literature, folklore, or myth. It often elicits an emotional response because it taps into the reader's unconscious memory. The term archetype emerged from the work of Swiss psychologist Carl Jung. Jung suggested that the images associated with these patterns are a reflection of the collective human experience.

Many people have analyzed these patterns and plots. In 1895, the French writer George Polti published *The Thirty-Six Dramatic Situations*, which attempted to catalog and describe all possible plotlines. And in his master's thesis, American author Kurt Vonnegut outlined a similar idea of how the rise and fall of the main character creates the shape of a story. More recently, in 2016, a group of researchers from the University of Vermont and the University of Adelaide used artificial intelligence (AI) to map out the structure of 1,732 works of fiction. Their findings identified six different plot structures and affirmed Vonnegut's shapes.

Story Patterns

Archetypes create certain expectations about the progression and resolution of dramatic situations. They also tie back to what you learned about conflict in the last unit and what we know about characters from Unit 1. As you read literature, it's important to trace the rise and fall of the protagonist, especially the conflicts the character encounters. Understanding who or what "wins" the conflict will shape the story's message and your interpretation.

Vonnegut's Visualization of Story Patterns

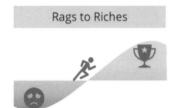

Rags to Riches

This is the prototypical happy story. It's common in creation tales in different world religions: gods create great things, culminating with Humans. It's also common in children's stories.

📖 The Importance of Being Earnest
The Jungle Book

Man in the Hole

The main character has a problem and falls deep into until he climbs his way out.

📖 The Wonderful Wizard of Oz
Through the Looking Glass
The Secret Garden

Cinderella

Up, down and up again is the story that Vonnegut recognized in both Cinderella and the New Testament, bringing him to study story shapes. It is one of the most common shapes in Western storytelling.

📖 King Solomon's Mines
Star Wars

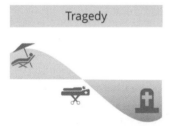

Tragedy

In Tragedies, the main character starts in a positive state, but as the story evolves, the situation goes worse and worse. Kafka and Shakespeare were masters of tragedy.

📖 Hamlet
The Picture of Dorian Gray
The Metamorphosis

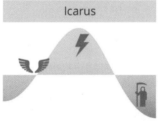

Icarus

Icarus is another type of tragedy, but here everything starts going well for the protagonist before souring.

📖 Garden of Eden
A Christmas Carol

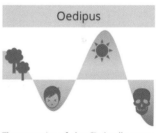

Oedipus

The opposite of the Cinderella story, Oedipus is the modern tragedy, where the protagonist fights for his sake but ends up losing.

📖 Frankenstein
The War of Worlds

The Pattern of Shape of Stories When Analyzed by AI

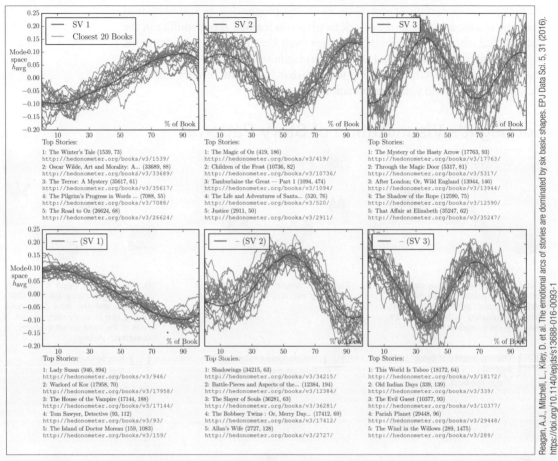

Top Stories:

1: The Winter's Tale (1539, 73)
http://hedonometer.org/books/v3/1539/
2: Oscar Wilde, Art and Morality: A... (33689, 88)
http://hedonometer.org/books/v3/33689/
3: The Terror: A Mystery (35617, 61)
http://hedonometer.org/books/v3/35617/
4: The Pilgrim's Progress in Words ... (7088, 55)
http://hedonometer.org/books/v3/7088/
5: The Road to Oz (26624, 68)
http://hedonometer.org/books/v3/26624/

Top Stories:

1: The Magic of Oz (419, 186)
http://hedonometer.org/books/v3/419/
2: Children of the Frost (10736, 82)
http://hedonometer.org/books/v3/10736/
3: Tamburlaine the Great — Part 1 (1094, 474)
http://hedonometer.org/books/v3/1094/
4: The Life and Adventures of Santa... (520, 76)
http://hedonometer.org/books/v3/520/
5: Justice (2911, 50)
http://hedonometer.org/books/v3/2911/

Top Stories:

1: The Mystery of the Hasty Arrow (17763, 93)
http://hedonometer.org/books/v3/17763/
2: Through the Magic Door (5317, 81)
http://hedonometer.org/books/v3/5317/
3: After London; Or, Wild England (13944, 146)
http://hedonometer.org/books/v3/13944/
4: The Shadow of the Rope (12590, 75)
http://hedonometer.org/books/v3/12590/
5: That Affair at Elizabeth (35247, 62)
http://hedonometer.org/books/v3/35247/

Top Stories:

1: Lady Susan (946, 894)
http://hedonometer.org/books/v3/946/
2: Warlord of Kor (17958, 70)
http://hedonometer.org/books/v3/17958/
3: The House of the Vampire (17144, 188)
http://hedonometer.org/books/v3/17144/
4: Tom Sawyer, Detective (93, 112)
http://hedonometer.org/books/v3/93/
5: The Island of Doctor Moreau (159, 1083)
http://hedonometer.org/books/v3/159/

Top Stories:

1: Shadowings (34215, 63)
http://hedonometer.org/books/v3/34215/
2: Battle-Pieces and Aspects of the... (12384, 194)
http://hedonometer.org/books/v3/12384/
3: The Slayer of Souls (36281, 63)
http://hedonometer.org/books/v3/36281/
4: The Bobbsey Twins : Or, Merry Day... (17412, 69)
http://hedonometer.org/books/v3/17412/
5: Allan's Wife (2727, 128)
http://hedonometer.org/books/v3/2727/

Top Stories:

1: This World Is Taboo (18172, 64)
http://hedonometer.org/books/v3/18172/
2: Old Indian Days (339, 139)
http://hedonometer.org/books/v3/339/
3: The Evil Guest (10377, 93)
http://hedonometer.org/books/v3/10377/
4: Pariah Planet (29448, 96)
http://hedonometer.org/books/v3/29448/
5: The Wind in the Willows (289, 1475)
http://hedonometer.org/books/v3/289/

Reagan, A.J., Mitchell, L., Kiley, D. et al. The emotional arcs of stories are dominated by six basic shapes. EPJ Data Sci. 5, 31 (2016). https://doi.org/10.1140/epjds/s13688-016-0093-1

Contrasts

You've already learned that characters often represent values and that the conflict between these values creates tension in literature. By examining these contrasts, especially when we consider the archetypal patterns, we can see how literature reflects the human condition. While the plot may be archetypal, it is important to analyze the conflict because authors use contrasting characters or settings to emphasize particular traits, aspects, or characteristics. By examining the complexity created by these contrasts and tensions, readers can make an interpretation. Consider the values associated with these archetypal contrasts:

Characters

- Fathers and sons
- Protagonist and devil

- Innocence and experience
- Protagonist and other siblings

Settings

- Urban and rural
- Heaven and hell
- Reality and fantasy
- Land and sea

ARCHETYPES IN LITERATURE			
Situational Archetypes	Character Archetypes	Symbolic Archetypes	Setting Archetypes
Battle	Caregiver	Blindness	City/urban area
Coming of age	Christ figure	Colors	Desert
Fall	Confidante	Communion	Forest/wilderness
Initiation	Devil figure	Day cycles	Garden/paradise
Intervention	Earth mother	Disease	Island
Journey	Fool	Food	River
Quest	Friendly beast	Illness	Rural areas
Redemption	Hero	Light and dark	Sea
Supernatural	Innocent	Magic weapon	Space
	Outcast/outsider/ stranger	Rain	Underworld
	Rebel	Seasons	Unfamiliar places
	Scapegoat	Water	Utopia
	Soothsayer/sage		West
	Star-crossed lovers		
	Temptress		
	Wolf in sheep's clothing		

INSIDER AP® TIP **The conflict of many stories boils down to idealism or realism.** In some ways, literature presents a conflict or tension between romanticism (or the ideal) and realism (life as it really is).

Sarah Orne Jewett, Photograph ca. 1890; photographed by Frederick Hollyer

GUIDED READING

A White Heron
Sarah Orne Jewett

THE TEXT IN CONTEXT

A native of South Berwick Maine, Sarah Orne Jewett (1849–1909) wrote fiction that was deeply rooted in the natural surroundings and culture of her home region. Her story "A White Heron" exemplifies recurring themes and patterns in her work: an emphasis on female perspective, agency, and relationships; the dichotomy between urban and rural life; and the sense of a burgeoning conservation movement in the context of increasing industrialization. Many critics and historians view Jewett as a key example of American literary "regionalism": a literary genre and period style that focused on the settings, customs, and landscapes of provincial American regions like the Southwest and rural New England. Regionalism emerged in the wake of the American Civil War and — at least implicitly — sought to preserve the distinctive aspects of specific places, even as standardization made the United States increasingly homogeneous. Jewett's works include *Old Friends and New* (1879).

A White Heron

I.

The woods were already filled with shadows one June evening, just before eight o'clock, though a bright sunset still glimmered faintly among the trunks of the trees. A little girl was driving home her cow, a plodding, dilatory, provoking creature in her behavior, but a valued companion for all
5 that. They were going away from whatever light there was, and striking deep into the woods, but their feet were familiar with the path, and it was no matter whether their eyes could see it or not.

   There was hardly a night the summer through when the old cow could be found waiting at the pasture bars; on the contrary, it was her greatest
10 pleasure to hide herself away among the huckleberry bushes and though she wore a loud bell she had made the discovery that if one stood perfectly still it would not ring. So Sylvia had to hunt for her until she found her, and call Co' ! Co' ! with never an answering Moo, until her childish patience was quite spent. If the creature had not given good milk and
15 plenty of it, the case would have seemed very different to her owners.

Guided Questions

1. What is the setting? How is the setting described?

2. How does this description contribute to the archetypal patterns for setting?

Besides, Sylvia had all the time there was, and very little use to make of it. Sometimes in pleasant weather it was a consolation to look upon the cow's pranks as an intelligent attempt to play hide and seek, and as the child had no playmates she lent herself to this amusement with a good
20 deal of zest. Though this chase had been so long that the wary animal herself had given an unusual signal of her whereabouts, Sylvia had only laughed when she came upon Mistress Moolly at the swamp-side, and urged her affectionately homeward with a twig of birch leaves. The old cow was not inclined to wander farther, she even turned in the right
25 direction for once as they left the pasture, and stepped along the road at a good pace. She was quite ready to be milked now, and seldom stopped to browse. Sylvia wondered what her grandmother would say because they were so late. It was a great while since she had left home at half-past five o'clock, but everybody knew the difficulty of making this errand a short
30 one. Mrs. Tilley had chased the hornéd torment too many summer evenings herself to blame any one else for lingering, and was only thankful as she waited that she had Sylvia, nowadays, to give such valuable assistance. The good woman suspected that Sylvia loitered occasionally on her own account; there never was such a child for straying about out-of-doors
35 since the world was made! Everybody said that it was a good change for a little maid who had tried to grow for eight years in a crowded manufacturing town, but, as for Sylvia herself, it seemed as if she never had been alive at all before she came to live at the farm. She thought often with wistful compassion of a wretched geranium that belonged to a town
40 neighbor.

"'Afraid of folks,'" old Mrs. Tilley said to herself, with a smile, after she had made the unlikely choice of Sylvia from her daughter's houseful of children, and was returning to the farm. "'Afraid of folks,' they said! I guess she won't be troubled no great with 'em up to the old place!" When
45 they reached the door of the lonely house and stopped to unlock it, and the cat came to purr loudly, and rub against them, a deserted pussy, indeed, but fat with young robins, Sylvia whispered that this was a beautiful place to live in, and she never should wish to go home.

The companions followed the shady wood-road, the cow taking slow
50 steps and the child very fast ones. The cow stopped long at the brook to drink, as if the pasture were not half a swamp, and Sylvia stood still and waited, letting her bare feet cool themselves in the shoal water, while the great twilight moths struck softly against her. She waded on through the brook as the cow moved away, and listened to the thrushes with a heart
55 that beat fast with pleasure. There was a stirring in the great boughs overhead. They were full of little birds and beasts that seemed to be wide awake, and going about their world, or else saying good-night to each other in sleepy twitters. Sylvia herself felt sleepy as she walked along.

Guided Questions

3. How is this relationship an expected association?

4. Consider the meaning of her name. What is the relationship between Sylvia and her surroundings?

5. "Afraid of folks" reveals what about Sylvia's character?

However, it was not much farther to the house, and the air was soft and
60 sweet. She was not often in the woods so late as this, and it made her feel
as if she were a part of the gray shadows and the moving leaves. She was
just thinking how long it seemed since she first came to the farm a year
ago, and wondering if everything went on in the noisy town just the same
as when she was there, the thought of the great red-faced boy who used
65 to chase and frighten her made her hurry along the path to escape from
the shadow of the trees.

Suddenly this little woods-girl is horror-stricken to hear a clear whistle
not very far away. Not a bird's-whistle, which would have a sort of friendli-
ness, but a boy's whistle, determined, and somewhat aggressive. Sylvia
70 left the cow to whatever sad fate might await her, and stepped discreetly
aside into the bushes, but she was just too late. The enemy had discovered her, and called out in a very cheerful and persuasive tone, "Halloa,
little girl, how far is it to the road?" and trembling Sylvia answered almost
inaudibly, "A good ways."

75 She did not dare to look boldly at the tall young man, who carried a
gun over his shoulder, but she came out of her bush and again followed
the cow, while he walked alongside.

"I have been hunting for some birds," the stranger said kindly, "and I
have lost my way, and need a friend very much. Don't be afraid," he added
80 gallantly. "Speak up and tell me what your name is, and whether you
think I can spend the night at your house, and go out gunning early in the
morning."

Sylvia was more alarmed than before. Would not her grandmother consider her much to blame? But who could have foreseen such an accident
85 as this? It did not seem to be her fault, and she hung her head as if the
stem of it were broken, but managed to answer "Sylvy," with much effort
when her companion again asked her name.

Mrs. Tilley was standing in the doorway when the trio came into view.
The cow gave a loud moo by way of explanation.

90 "Yes, you'd better speak up for yourself, you old trial! Where'd she
tucked herself away this time, Sylvy?" But Sylvia kept an awed silence; she
knew by instinct that her grandmother did not comprehend the gravity of
the situation. She must be mistaking the stranger for one of the farmer-
lads of the region.

95 The young man stood his gun beside the door, and dropped a lumpy
game-bag beside it; then he bade Mrs. Tilley good-evening, and repeated
his wayfarer's story, and asked if he could have a night's lodging.

"Put me anywhere you like," he said. "I must be off early in the morning, before day; but I am very hungry, indeed. You can give me some milk
100 at any rate, that's plain."

Guided Questions

6. What atmosphere is created as Sylvia walks home? Why is the boy referred to as an enemy? Could this enemy be representative of a character archetype?

7. What contrast does the gun introduce?

8. How does this situation seem familiar and archetypal?

"Dear sakes, yes," responded the hostess, whose long slumbering hospitality seemed to be easily awakened. "You might fare better if you went out to the main road a mile or so, but you're welcome to what we've got. I'll milk right off, and you make yourself at home. You can
105　sleep on husks or feathers," she proffered graciously. "I raised them all myself. There's good pasturing for geese just below here towards the ma'sh. Now step round and set a plate for the gentleman, Sylvy!" And Sylvia promptly stepped. She was glad to have something to do, and she was hungry herself.

110　It was a surprise to find so clean and comfortable a little dwelling in this New England wilderness. The young man had known the horrors of its most primitive housekeeping, and the dreary squalor of that level of society which does not rebel at the companionship of hens. This was the best thrift of an old-fashioned farmstead, though on such a small scale
115　that it seemed like a hermitage. He listened eagerly to the old woman's quaint talk, he watched Sylvia's pale face and shining gray eyes with ever growing enthusiasm, and insisted that this was the best supper he had eaten for a month, and afterward the new-made friends sat down in the door-way together while the moon came up.

9. Could this ornithologist be representative of a character archetype?

120　Soon it would be berry-time, and Sylvia was a great help at picking. The cow was a good milker, though a plaguy thing to keep track of, the hostess gossiped frankly, adding presently that she had buried four children, so Sylvia's mother, and a son (who might be dead) in California were all the children she had left. "Dan, my boy, was a great hand to go gunning," she
125　explained sadly. "I never wanted for pa'tridges or gray squer'ls while he was to home. He's been a great wand'rer, I expect, and he's no hand to write letters. There, I don't blame him, I'd ha' seen the world myself if it had been so I could.

"Sylvy takes after him," the grandmother continued affectionately, after
130　a minute's pause. "There ain't a foot o' ground she don't know her way over, and the wild creaturs counts her one o' themselves. Squer'ls she'll tame to come an' feed right out o' her hands, and all sorts o' birds. Last winter she got the jay-birds to bangeing here, and I believe she'd 'a' scanted herself of her own meals to have plenty to throw out amongst
135　'em, if I hadn't kep' watch. Anything but crows, I tell her, I'm willin' to help support—though Dan he had a tamed one o' them that did seem to have reason same as folks. It was round here a good spell after he went away. Dan an' his father they didn't hitch,—but he never held up his head ag'in after Dan had dared him an' gone off."

10. How does Sylvia's grandmother describe her to the hunter?

140　The guest did not notice this hint of family sorrows in his eager interest in something else.

"So Sylvy knows all about birds, does she?" he exclaimed, as he looked round at the little girl who sat, very demure but increasingly sleepy, in the moonlight. "I am making a collection of birds myself. I have been at it ever
145 since I was a boy." (Mrs. Tilley smiled.) "There are two or three very rare ones I have been hunting for these five years. I mean to get them on my own ground if they can be found."

"Do you cage 'em up?" asked Mrs. Tilley doubtfully, in response to this enthusiastic announcement.

150 "Oh no, they're stuffed and preserved, dozens and dozens of them," said the ornithologist, "and I have shot or snared every one myself. I caught a glimpse of a white heron a few miles from here on Saturday, and I have followed it in this direction. They have never been found in this district at all. The little white heron, it is," and he turned again to look at
155 Sylvia with the hope of discovering that the rare bird was one of her acquaintances.

But Sylvia was watching a hop-toad in the narrow footpath.

"You would know the heron if you saw it," the stranger continued eagerly. "A queer tall white bird with soft feathers and long thin legs. And
160 it would have a nest perhaps in the top of a high tree, made of sticks, something like a hawk's nest."

Sylvia's heart gave a wild beat; she knew that strange white bird, and had once stolen softly near where it stood in some bright green swamp grass, away over at the other side of the woods. There was an open place
165 where the sunshine always seemed strangely yellow and hot, where tall, nodding rushes grew, and her grandmother had warned her that she might sink in the soft black mud underneath and never be heard of more. Not far beyond were the salt marshes just this side the sea itself, which Sylvia wondered and dreamed much about, but never had seen, whose
170 great voice could sometimes be heard above the noise of the woods on stormy nights.

"I can't think of anything I should like so much as to find that heron's nest," the handsome stranger was saying. "I would give ten dollars to anybody who could show it to me," he added desperately, "and I mean to
175 spend my whole vacation hunting for it if need be. Perhaps it was only migrating, or had been chased out of its own region by some bird of prey."

Mrs. Tilley gave amazed attention to all this, but Sylvia still watched the toad, not divining, as she might have done at some calmer time, that the creature wished to get to its hole under the door-step, and was much
180 hindered by the unusual spectators at that hour of the evening. No amount of thought, that night, could decide how many wished-for treasures the ten dollars, so lightly spoken of, would buy.

Guided Questions

11. How does this description contribute to a character archetype?

12. How could the ornithologist's intent represent a conflict for Sylvia?

13. What does the setting reveal about Sylvia?

The next day the young sportsman hovered about the woods, and
Sylvia kept him company, having lost her first fear of the friendly lad, who
185 proved to be most kind and sympathetic. He told her many things about
the birds and what they knew and where they lived and what they did
with themselves. And he gave her a jack-knife, which she thought as great
a treasure as if she were a desert-islander. All day long he did not once
make her troubled or afraid except when he brought down some unsus-
190 pecting singing creature from its bough. Sylvia would have liked him
vastly better without his gun; she could not understand why he killed the
very birds he seemed to like so much. But as the day waned, Sylvia still
watched the young man with loving admiration. She had never seen anybody so charming and delightful; the woman's heart, asleep in the child,
195 was vaguely thrilled by a dream of love. Some premonition of that great
power stirred and swayed these young creatures who traversed the solemn woodlands with soft-footed silent care. They stopped to listen to a
bird's song; they pressed forward again eagerly, parting the branches—
speaking to each other rarely and in whispers; the young man going
200 first and Sylvia following, fascinated, a few steps behind, with her gray
eyes dark with excitement.

She grieved because the longed-for white heron was elusive, but she
did not lead the guest, she only followed, and there was no such thing as
speaking first. The sound of her own unquestioned voice would have
205 terrified her—it was hard enough to answer yes or no when there was
need of that. At last evening began to fall, and they drove the cow home
together, and Sylvia smiled with pleasure when they came to the place
where she heard the whistle and was afraid only the night before.

II.

Half a mile from home, at the farther edge of the woods, where the
210 land was highest, a great pine-tree stood, the last of its generation.
Whether it was left for a boundary mark, or for what reason, no one
could say; the woodchoppers who had felled its mates were dead and
gone long ago, and a whole forest of sturdy trees, pines and oaks and
maples, had grown again. But the stately head of this old pine towered
215 above them all and made a landmark for sea and shore miles and
miles away. Sylvia knew it well. She had always believed that whoever
climbed to the top of it could see the ocean; and the little girl had
often laid her hand on the great rough trunk and looked up wistfully at
those dark boughs that the wind always stirred, no matter how hot and
220 still the air might be below. Now she thought of the tree with a new
excitement, for why, if one climbed it at break of day, could not one see

Guided Questions

14. How do Sylvia's
feelings reveal a
conflict of values?

all the world, and easily discover from whence the white heron flew, and mark the place, and find the hidden nest?

Guided Questions

225 What a spirit of adventure, what wild ambition! What fancied triumph and delight and glory for the later morning when she could make known the secret! It was almost too real and too great for the childish heart to bear.

15. How does "the secret" create a tension for Sylvia?

230 All night the door of the little house stood open and the whippoorwills came and sang upon the very step. The young sportsman and his old hostess were sound asleep, but Sylvia's great design kept her broad awake and watching. She forgot to think of sleep. The short summer night seemed as long as the winter darkness, and at last when the whippoorwills ceased, and she was afraid the morning would after all come too soon, she stole out of the house and followed the pasture path through

235 the woods, hastening toward the open ground beyond, listening with a sense of comfort and companionship to the drowsy twitter of a half-awakened bird, whose perch she had jarred in passing. Alas, if the great wave of human interest which flooded for the first time this dull little life should sweep away the satisfactions of an existence heart to heart with

240 nature and the dumb life of the forest!

There was the huge tree asleep yet in the paling moonlight, and small and silly Sylvia began with utmost bravery to mount to the top of it, with tingling, eager blood coursing the channels of her whole frame, with her bare feet and fingers, that pinched and held like bird's claws

245 to the monstrous ladder reaching up, up, almost to the sky itself. First she must mount the white oak tree that grew alongside, where she was almost lost among the dark branches and the green leaves heavy and wet with dew; a bird fluttered off its nest, and a red squirrel ran to and fro and scolded pettishly at the harmless housebreaker. Sylvia felt her

16. How is Sylvia's climb archetypal?

250 way easily. She had often climbed there, and knew that higher still one of the oak's upper branches chafed against the pine trunk, just where its lower boughs were set close together. There, when she made the dangerous pass from one tree to the other, the great enterprise would really begin.

255 She crept out along the swaying oak limb at last, and took the daring step across into the old pine-tree. The way was harder than she thought; she must reach far and hold fast, the sharp dry twigs caught and held her and scratched her like angry talons, the pitch made her thin little fingers clumsy and stiff as she went round and round the tree's great stem,

260 higher and higher upward. The sparrows and robins in the woods below were beginning to wake and twitter to the dawn, yet it seemed much lighter there aloft in the pine-tree, and the child knew she must hurry if her project were to be of any use.

The tree seemed to lengthen itself out as she went up, and to reach far-
265 ther and farther upward. It was like a great main-mast to the voyaging
earth; it must truly have been amazed that morning through all its pon-
derous frame as it felt this determined spark of human spirit wending its
way from higher branch to branch. Who knows how steadily the least
twigs held themselves to advantage this light, weak creature on her way!
270 The old pine must have loved his new dependent. More than all the
hawks, and bats, and moths, and even the sweet voiced thrushes, was the
brave, beating heart of the solitary gray-eyed child. And the tree stood still
and frowned away the winds that June morning while the dawn grew
bright in the east.

275   Sylvia's face was like a pale star, if one had seen it from the ground,
when the last thorny bough was past, and she stood trembling and tired
but wholly triumphant, high in the tree-top. Yes, there was the sea with
the dawning sun making a golden dazzle over it, and toward that glorious
east flew two hawks with slow-moving pinions. How low they looked in
280 the air from that height when one had only seen them before far up, and
dark against the blue sky. Their gray feathers were as soft as moths; they
seemed only a little way from the tree, and Sylvia felt as if she too could
go flying away among the clouds. Westward, the woodlands and farms
reached miles and miles into the distance; here and there were church
285 steeples, and white villages, truly it was a vast and awesome world

The birds sang louder and louder. At last the sun came up bewilder-
ingly bright. Sylvia could see the white sails of ships out at sea, and the
clouds that were purple and rose-colored and yellow at first began to fade
away. Where was the white heron's nest in the sea of green branches, and
290 was this wonderful sight and pageant of the world the only reward for
having climbed to such a giddy height? Now look down again, Sylvia,
where the green marsh is set among the shining birches and dark hemlocks; there where you saw the white heron once you will see him again;
look, look! A white spot of him like a single floating feather comes up
295 from the dead hemlock and grows larger, and rises, and comes close at
last, and goes by the landmark pine with steady sweep of wing and outstretched slender neck and crested head. And wait! Wait! Do not move a
foot or a finger, little girl, do not send an arrow of light and consciousness
from your two eager eyes, for the heron has perched on a pine bough not
300 far beyond yours, and cries back to his mate on the nest and plumes his
feathers for the new day!

The child gives a long sigh a minute later when a company of shouting
cat-birds comes also to the tree, and vexed by their fluttering and law-
lessness the solemn heron goes away. She knows his secret now, the wild,
305 light, slender bird that floats and wavers, and goes back like an arrow

Guided Questions

17. How does Sylvia change as a result of her experience?

18. How does this moment at the top of the tree affect Sylvia?

presently to his home in the green world beneath. Then Sylvia, well satisfied, makes her perilous way down again, not daring to look far below the
branch she stands on, ready to cry sometimes because her fingers ache
and her lamed feet slip. Wondering over and over again what the stranger
310 would say to her, and what he would think when she told him how to find
his way straight to the heron's nest.

"Sylvy, Sylvy!" called the busy old grandmother again and again, but
nobody answered, and the small husk bed was empty and Sylvia had
disappeared.

315 The guest waked from a dream, and remembering his day's pleasure
hurried to dress himself that it might sooner begin. He was sure from the
way the shy little girl looked once or twice yesterday that she had at least
seen the white heron, and now she must really be made to tell. Here she
comes now, paler than ever, and her worn old frock is torn and tattered,
320 and smeared with pine pitch. The grandmother and the sportsman stand
in the door together and question her, and the splendid moment has
come to speak of the dead hemlock-tree by the green marsh.

But Sylvia does not speak after all, though the old grandmother fret-
fully rebukes her, and the young man's kind, appealing eyes are looking
325 straight in her own. He can make them rich with money; he has promised
it, and they are poor now. He is so well worth making happy, and he waits
to hear the story she can tell.

No, she must keep silence! What is it that suddenly forbids her and
makes her dumb? Has she been nine years growing and now, when the
330 great world for the first time puts out a hand to her, must she thrust it
aside for a bird's sake? The murmur of the pine's green branches is in
her ears, she remembers how the white heron came flying through the
golden air and how they watched the sea and the morning together,
and Sylvia cannot speak; she cannot tell the heron's secret and give its
335 life away.

Dear loyalty, that suffered a sharp pang as the guest went away disappointed later in the day, that could have served and followed him
and loved him as a dog loves! Many a night Sylvia heard the echo of his
whistle haunting the pasture path as she came home with the loitering
340 cow. She forgot even her sorrow at the sharp report of his gun and the
sight of thrushes and sparrows dropping silent to the ground, their
songs hushed and their pretty feathers stained and wet with blood.
Were the birds better friends than their hunter might have been,—who
can tell? Whatever treasures were lost to her, woodlands and summer-
345 time, remember! Bring your gifts and graces and tell your secrets to
this lonely country child.

Guided Questions

19. How does Sylvia connect with her environment? How does Sylvia's experience advance the dramatic situation?

20. Why does Sylvia keep silent?

21. What does Sylvia's silence reveal about her?

22. How does the story end? What values are gained and lost through this experience?

Red
Malinda Lo

©Patty Nason

THE TEXT IN CONTEXT

Novelist and critic Malinda Lo (b. 1974) was born in China and moved to the United States when she was three. While earning academic degrees at Wellesley College, Harvard University, and Stanford University, she began writing about popular culture at the blog *AfterEllen*, where she became managing editor. Lo turned to fiction with her critically acclaimed 2009 novel *Ash*, a retelling of "Cinderella" with the protagonist reimagined as a teen lesbian. Her other novels include *Inheritance* (2013), *A Line in the Dark* (2017), and *Last Night at the Telegraph Club* (2021). Lo also founded the website Diversity in YA, which promotes and celebrates diversity in Young Adult literature. In the short story "Red," she retells and revises the familiar story of "Little Red Riding Hood" as a metaphor of historical and political strife.

 | **STRUCTURE**
Analyzing Archetypes

As you read "Red," record details about the characters and the conflict. Reflect on the choices that the protagonist makes and the values represented by both the protagonist and antagonist. Use these details as you analyze how the story's resolution contributes to your interpretation of the text.

Analyzing Archetypes		
Type	Examples from the Story	Significance
Situational archetypes: • Battle • Coming of age • Fall • Initiation • Intervention • Journey • Quest • Redemption • Supernatural		

(continued)

Character archetypes:		
• Caregiver		
• Christ figure		
• Confidante		
• Devil figure		
• Earth mother		
• Fool		
• Friendly beast		
• Hero		
• Innocent		
• Outcast/outsider		
• Rebel		
• Scapegoat		
• Soothsayer/sage		
• Star-crossed lovers		
• Temptress		
• Wolf in sheep's clothing		
Symbol archetypes:		
• Blindness		
• Colors		
• Communion		
• Day cycles		
• Disease		
• Food		
• Illness		
• Light and dark		
• Magic weapon		
• Rain		
• Seasons		
• Water		
Setting archetypes:		
• City/urban area		
• Desert		
• Forest/wilderness		
• Garden/paradise		
• Island		
• River		
• Rural areas		
• Sea		
• Space		
• Underworld		
• Unfamiliar places		
• Utopia		
• West		

Red

The east is red when Xiaohong leaves the two-room apartment that has been allocated to her and her parents—two rooms carved out of a once-grand courtyard home, now
5 divided between five families by order of the local Party authorities. The manor has been forced into a new identity, with makeshift kitchens elbowing their way into the sky well, and the walls pasted over with red
10 posters of Chairman Mao quotations. The speaker for the public address system, installed in one corner of the sky well, blasts announcements at all hours, but it has been mercifully quiet so far this morning.

15 "Take this to your Popo," Xiaohong's mother had told her, handing her a small covered basket. "She is sick, and I cannot visit her today." Inside the basket is a feast saved up carefully from their rations: two
20 plain steamed buns, a small tin bowl of bean curd stir-fried with bits of pork, and a bottle of pork bone broth. Popo, Xiaohong's grandmother, lives outside of town in a dilapidated mudbrick farmhouse, alone now that
25 Xiaohong's grandfather, who was branded a counterrevolutionary, has died.

The morning is cool and slightly damp; the night's rain has left traces of bright water in the ruts on Anti-revisionist Street.
30 Xiaohong has walked the three miles to Popo's house countless times before, and she likes to start out early, while the town is still quiet and the sky has not yet fully lightened. She likes to watch the sunrise spreading red
35 and then gold like a spilled yolk over the old town wall. Thinking of eggs, her stomach rumbles: she has not yet eaten. She peeks beneath the red cloth that covers her basket, gazing hungrily at the plump white buns, but
40 does not steal a bite. Popo is elderly and has pneumonia, while Xiaohong is only sixteen

and perfectly healthy, even if she is all too accustomed to an empty stomach.

On the corner of Anti-revisionist Street
45 and Red Guard Road, a lanky boy pushes a motorbike out of the shadow of the town wall. He wears a khaki uniform with a red armband tied around his left bicep. When he sees Xiaohong, a wolfish grin twists his face.
50 "Xiaohong, you're out early," he says.

The boy is Wu Lang. They went to school together, before the schools were shut down last summer so that they could make revolution. "Wu Lang," Xiaohong says warily.
55 "Hello."

"Where are you off to?" he asks.

He is pretending to be casual and friendly, but Xiaohong knows better. "I'm bringing this food to my Popo," she answers carefully.
60 He moves to block the street in front of her with his motorbike, and then saunters over. "How is the famous Lin Popo?"

Xiaohong knows he is baiting her by using the word *famous*. She ignores it and says,
65 "She is sick. I should go."

"If I remember correctly, your grandmother lives three miles away. Are you walking there?"

"Yes."
70 "What food are you bringing her?" He comes closer and plucks the red cloth off the basket, tossing it onto the ground. His fingernails are grimy, and Xiaohong suddenly remembers the way he caught Yulin's kitten
75 in his hands last year, squeezing the animal's furry little neck until it squealed, its tiny white teeth useless against him. "Mmm, looks delicious," he says, studying the contents of the basket. "I haven't eaten yet."
80 Without asking for permission, he takes both buns and devours them in two bites. Xiaohong glimpses the dark red cavern of his

mouth, his teeth slick with saliva. She hastily kneels down to pick up the fallen red cloth,
85 tucking it back over the basket before he can take more of the food.

"I'm off to see your grandmother too," Wu Lang says.

She looks at him in shock. "You are?"

90 His mouth curves into a cold smile. "I wonder who will arrive first?" Then he jumps onto his motorbike and twists the handlebars, gunning the engine. "Long live Chairman Mao!" he cries.

95 "Long live Chairman Mao," she echoes. He salutes her as if she were a Red Guard like him, but she knows he is only mocking her. His motorbike roars and cuts a track in the dirt road as he jerks it around, speeding
100 through the town gate.

Fear is a meaty hand squeezing her lungs. Her heart pounds as she hurries after him.

● ● ●

Wu Lang has never been to Xiaohong's grandmother's home, but he knows where it
105 is. There is only one counterrevolutionary widow who used to be a famous Shanghai actress living in the area. Indeed, Wu Lang and the other Red Guards often discuss where the counterrevolutionaries are
110 located. If they are to make revolution, they must root out the black elements among them.

It isn't long before he reaches the derelict farmhouse on the empty country road. A
115 middle peasant and his family also used to live there, but the middle peasant hanged himself a few months ago, and his wife and children moved back to their home village, a hundred miles away. Now the only person
120 still living in the farmhouse is Xiaohong's grandmother.

The front door is closed tight. The dirty white wall is bare of any decoration — not even a photograph of Chairman Mao torn
125 from the *People's Daily*. Wu Lang cuts the engine of his motorbike, and silence descends like a knife across the morning. Not a single bird sings as he strides up the dirt path to the wooden front door.

130 Wu Lang pounds on the door, and it shakes on its hinges. "Lin Popo," he calls. "Let me in!"

There is no answer. Wu Lang's anger builds in the thick silence; his breath is hot
135 as a furnace in his lungs.

"Lin Popo!" he shouts again, and though he might have heard her whispered response had he been listening, he does not listen.

140 He shoves the door; the bottom hinges give way and the door sags open. He enters carelessly, not bothering to take off his shoes. Inside, the farmhouse is cold and dark. A shovel and a scythe lean against the
145 wall, the curve of the scythe's blade catching the sunlight slanting through the front door. He stomps through the main room and turns to the right. The room is empty, but at last he sees Chairman Mao. A newspaper article
150 about the Great Leader's famous swim cross the Yangtze River is taped to the wall just inside the door.

"Lin Popo!" Wu Lang yells. He goes back through the main hall to the other room.
155 This is the kitchen, lit by a single hanging lightbulb, and a fire is burning in the stove.

"You have found me," croaks a voice behind him.

Wu Lang turns toward the sound and sees
160 a cot set up in the dim corner. In the cot lies Lin Popo, the blankets drawn up to her chin. Wu Lang strides over and peers down at the old woman. Her face is wrinkled and wizened as a walnut; her white hair escapes in spider
165 silk-like wisps from beneath the black cloth

she has tied over her head. But her eyes are bright and clear as a robin that has spotted a worm in the ground.

"What do you want?" Lin Popo asks.

170 "To carry the revolution through to the end!" Wu Lang answers. "To drive out the Four Olds!"

"I admit," Lin Popo says, "that I am old."

"You are decadent bourgeoisie," Wu Lang 175 declares.

Lin Popo smiles coyly, and though her cheeks are sunken and her skin is spotted with age, the beauty she was in her youth is still visible, like a ghost, in the curve of her 180 mouth and the shine of her eyes.

This glimpse of her bourgeois past infuriates Wu Lang. He spins around, searching for evidence of her pre-communist decadence. The room is bare of anything obviously 185 incriminating; there is only a small wooden table and chair, a wooden cupboard, and the cot. Wu Lang yanks open the door to the cupboard; inside are two bowls, chopsticks, a dried-out knob of ginger, a battered black 190 pot, and a cleaver. While he is bending over to look in the cupboard, he realizes there is space to hide something beneath the cot. He goes back to Lin Popo's corner, gets on his knees, and peers underneath.

195 A book has been shoved back against the wall. He pulls it out; it is a Buddhist tract. "This is one of the Four Olds," he announces. "We must break away from old ideology, old culture, old customs, and old habits! There is 200 no place for this in modern China."

"Modern China arises from the old," Lin Popo says.

He rips out page after page in fury, and a photograph flutters from the book toward 205 the floor. It's a hand-colored picture of a beautiful young woman wearing a white qipao embroidered with pink and red

flowers. Her lips are vividly red, her cheeks rouged as pink as the Chairman's. Her eyes 210 are Lin Popo's eyes, and he realizes it's a photo of her from forty years ago, when she was an actress.

It disgusts him. He crumples up the photo, preparing to throw it into the fire, but obliter- 215 ating it is not enough.

The bourgeoisie must be destroyed. Lin Popo must be destroyed.

"Revolution is not a dinner party," Wu Lang recites as he glares down at Lin Popo. 220 Her face is serene as a deep mountain lake, and it enrages him.

"It cannot be so refined, so leisurely and gentle," Wu Lang continues, the Great Leader's words rolling off his tongue like 225 thunder.

Lin Popo does not flinch as he hurls the book and her picture into the fire.

"A revolution is an insurrection, an act of violence," Wu Lang snarls.

230 Lin Popo only watches him implacably as he picks up the cleaver and stalks toward the cot.

His lungs heave, filled with revolutionary fervor. She closes her eyes so that she does 235 not have to look at his monstrous face. She feels the blade bite into her neck—the same blade she used to prepare food for her children—and her blood spills bright red upon the thin pillow, redder than the sunrise 240 in the east, redder than the band on Wu Lang's arm.

• • •

Xiaohong has run almost all the way to her grandmother's house. Her skin is wet with sweat when she arrives, breathless, and sees 245 Wu Lang's motorbike parked outside. The farmhouse's front door hangs open on one hinge, like a sleeping mouth partially agape. Xiaohong's stomach churns with dread. She

enters the house on trembling legs, and
250 hears the sizzle of meat in a wok. The
unmistakable scent of ginger hangs in the
air. Confused, she wonders if her grandmother has miraculously risen from her
sickbed to cook a meal. Hope buds in her,
255 and she takes off her shoes and tiptoes
toward the kitchen.

Wu Lang stands at the stove, tossing sliv-
ers of meat together in the wok. There is no
trace of the cot where Popo slept, only a
260 smear of something dark and shiny in the
corner where it used to stand. Xiaohong's
hope shrivels.

Wu Lang sees her in the doorway.
"Xiaohong," he growls. "Have you eaten?" He
265 scoops the cooked meat out of the wok and
into a waiting bowl, placing it on the table
next to an earthenware teapot and cup.

"No," she says. Her skin crawls at the
savage smile on his face.
270   "You must be hungry," Wu Lang says.
"Come in."

She yearns to flee, but she forces herself
to stay. She sets the basket of food on the
floor. "Where is my grandmother?" she asks.
275   "She has gone out." Wu Lang approaches
her. "Sit down and eat."

When she does not obey, he lunges
toward her and clamps his hand around her
arm, dragging her to the table and shoving
280 her into the chair. She cries out in pain. He
pushes the bowl of meat toward her and
pours a dark, steaming liquid from the
teapot into the cup. Has she imagined the
claws on his fingertips? They click against
285 the pottery.

"I am not hungry," Xiaohong lies.

Wu Lang looms over her. "I could hear
your stomach growling from a mile away,"
he says. "Eat and drink. Your grandmother
290 would not want you to go hungry."

"Where is Popo?" she asks again.

"Eat and drink," Wu Lang says, grinning,
"and I will tell you." Has she imagined the
sharp points of his teeth, like daggers?
295   Shuddering, she reluctantly draws the
bowl of shredded meat toward her. It has an
unsettling fragrance. She smells the ginger,
but there is something else too, something
oddly familiar, like the scent of her grand-
300 mother's skin: crushed roses, milk, and soap.
Her empty stomach clenches, and she gags
on the burning acid that rises hotly in the
back of her throat.

With a growl of frustration, Wu Lang
305 thrusts the chopsticks into her hand. She
recoils from his touch, her blood curdling as
she looks up at him. His eyes are extraordinarily large. Has she imagined their golden
gleam? They are lupine; ravenous.
310   She drops her gaze hastily, and the glistening meat is waiting for her. She knows
that Wu Lang will force her to eat it. She
hears the angry exhalation of his breath as
he watches her. Before he can touch her
315 again, she raises a bite to her mouth—

And to her shock, the meat is soft and
tender, more delicious than anything she has
ever tasted. It is miraculous: like a single perfect pearl within the clutch of an oyster's
320 muscle, like the sweet flesh of a lychee as it
emerges from its vermilion shell.

In that instant, she understands everything. Wu Lang has killed her grandmother
and made a meal of her. It should taste pol-
325 luted: foul and contaminated as the stench
of Wu Lang's breath. But it does not.

It is as if her grandmother has offered up
her soul to Xiaohong as nourishment, as if
she is whispering in her ear: *eat me.*
330   Xiaohong picks up the earthenware teacup and sips the hot, thick liquid. She tastes
the power of her grandmother's blood on her

tongue, earthy and rich as fermented bean curd. Every year of her long life is a fire spreading through Xiaohong's blood. Ten thousand memories in one deep breath, the taste of love on her lips, bone-crushing pain and bittersweet wisdom like flakes of salt on her tongue. She eats every bite. She drinks all of the tea.

Wu Lang watches her, gloating. "Dragons give birth to dragons, and phoenixes give birth to phoenixes," he says, "but a rat's descendants can only dig holes. You will never be more than your parents and your grandparents. You will always be a bastard!"

Xiaohong raises her eyes to meet his. She feels Popo rising within her like a phoenix stretching its wings. "You are right," she says. "I will never be more than my parents and my grandparents. Fortunately, they are great people!"

She stands up and runs toward the main hall. Wu Lang growls and lunges after her. In the shadow of the broken front door she reaches for the scythe. She spins to face him. His shadow stretches wolf-like along the floor, his muzzle dripping with long thick threads of spittle, and he swipes at her with his paw-like hands.

The scythe whistles through the air and slices off his hand. It tumbles onto the floor, scattering a spray of black blood in its wake. Wu Lang yelps like a wounded animal and clutches the stump of his arm close to his body, shrinking away from her.

But the hand on the floor is not a human hand—it is a wolf's paw. The fur is black with gore, the claws sharp as razors.

"As Chairman Mao proclaims, letting ghosts and spirits out of their hiding places makes it easier to annihilate them," Xiaohong says. "We must sweep away all monsters and demons!" She raises her scythe high, advancing on him.

Wu Lang flees, running into the yard and jumping on his motorbike, holding on with his remaining hand as he speeds away. Standing in the doorway, Xiaohong watches until she can no longer see the dust trail behind the motorbike, and then she puts down the scythe and steps around the wolf's paw that lies like a dead rat on the floor.

She goes back to the kitchen and opens the iron door to the stove's firebox. Inside, a photograph is wedged between the glowing coals, but the paper is unburned. She pulls it out, shaking off the ashes, and gazes down at the picture of her grandmother. She smiles up at Xiaohong across the decades, unharmed. Her cheeks are still pink as lotus flowers, her lips red as dates.

STRUCTURE

1. What is the primary **conflict** in the story? What perspectives are represented by the antagonist and protagonist?

2. How does the **dramatic situation** establish a conflict of values?

3. In what way does the **plot** of the narrative set up expectations? Are the expectations met?

4. Identify and describe the **archetypes** in the story.

NARRATION
Narrative Perspective

 Enduring Understanding

A narrator's or speaker's perspective controls the details and emphases that affect how readers experience and interpret a text.

KEY POINT

A narrator's unique perspective is influenced by their background, past experiences, values, and beliefs, as well as their proximity to the characters, setting, and events in the narrative.

If you want to understand the importance of narrative perspective, consider the countless books, movies, musicals, TV shows, and comics that have been created to tell a familiar story from the perspective of the antagonist. *Maleficent* (2014) tells the story of Sleeping Beauty from the evil queen's perspective, *Wicked* (2003) tells the story of the witches' perspective from *The Wizard of Oz*, *Hyde* (2014) tells the story of Dr. Jekyll and Mr. Hyde from the monster's perspective, and *Cruella* (2021) depicts the evolution of the villain from *The Hundred and One Dalmatians*.

In other words, if you've ever wondered what a classic story or fairy tale would sound like if another character could tell the tale, you already understand the importance of a narrator's perspective. These retellings are revealing. Different narrators with different frames of reference can lead to new information and fresh interpretations.

Recall that in earlier units, you learned that authors create narrators to relate the story to the audience. Narrators usually share information from a first-person point of view or a third-person point of view, which determines how much the narrator knows and tells the reader.

A Narrator Has a Unique Perspective

Not only do narrators have points of view, but they also have **perspectives**, which are how they understand the world around them. This understanding is shaped by who they are and how they became that way. A narrator's point of view is included in their perspective. Their perspective—like that of other characters—is influenced by their background, past experiences, values, and beliefs.

Just like other characters, narrators' and speakers' perspectives shape how they communicate about a subject or event in the text. Consider these examples:

If a narrator is . . .	he or she may . . .
religious or a person of faith	apply specific values to events, situations, others
related to other characters	believe that blood is thicker than water
from a particular culture or place	embody values and attitudes from that place

Tone

Tone is the attitude of a narrator, character, or speaker about an idea, other characters, or situation; their attitudes are shaped by their perspective, background, values, beliefs, and other experiences. Their perspective is revealed through their choice of words or tone.

The key to understanding a narrator's tone is found in examining the author's choice of words and descriptions. An author's choice of words communicates qualitative information about whatever it is he or she is describing, but it also reveals the narrator's perspective on the subject — whether that be the character or the situation.

Recall that narrators may themselves be characters within a narrative. As in real life, a person may have a different perspective if they are directly involved in a situation or event (as opposed to someone who is not directly involved). Narrators may directly address the reader. For example, Herman Melville's most famous narrator opens the novel *Moby Dick* by telling the reader, "Call me Ishmael." A narrator may also be recalling events in the near (or distant) past, or even describing them as they occur in the present moment of the story.

Narrative Distance

The proximity of the narrator to the story's characters, settings, and events is known as **narrative distance**. Narrators exist on a spectrum of distance that directly affects their perspective. Narrators can be very close or very far away in relation to the story depending on the following factors:

- The narrator's physical location
- The narrator's place in time, relative to the events of the story
- The narrator's relationship to the characters
- The narrator's emotional proximity to the story and characters

Stream of Consciousness

Stream of consciousness is a type of narration where a character's thoughts are communicated to the reader through a continuous monologue or flow of the narrator's thoughts and feelings. Essentially, the author gives you a telepathic peak into the operations and reactions within a character's mind. Readers may find stream of consciousness narration disorganized and difficult to follow, as it is uninterrupted by objective description or conventional dialogue. But the technique allows writers to evoke a sense of thinking and feeling in real time without a filter.

INSIDER AP® TIP   **Time and distance allow for reflection and insight.** It matters whether a first-person narrator tells the story in the moment or tells the story about an event that happened in the past. Those choices made in the moment often reflect unfiltered, impulsive reactions. In contrast, narrators who tell stories about the past often have more reflection, awareness, and insight.

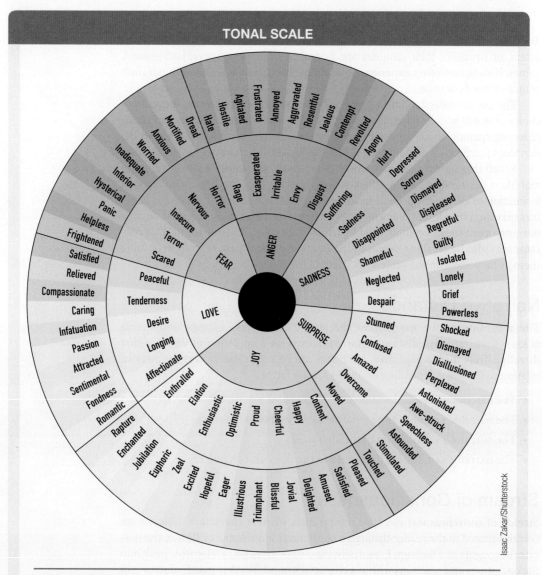

TONAL SCALE

The wheel depicts words that can describe tone. The innermost words are the most general. Moving outward, the words become more precise descriptors.

Isaac Zakar/Shutterstock

GUIDED READING

Girl

Jamaica Kincaid

Anthony Barboza/Getty Images

THE TEXT IN CONTEXT

In the short story "Girl," writer Jamaica Kincaid (b. 1949) draws on her childhood experience growing up on the Caribbean island of Antigua. Since she began publishing in the 1970s, Kincaid has been a prolific author of fiction, essays, memoirs, and (more recently) works on gardening. Her books include *Annie John* (1985), *The Autobiography of My Mother* (1996), and *See Now and Then* (2013). Like much of Kincaid's other fiction, "Girl" explores themes of femininity, class, domesticity, and propriety in a patriarchal society. It presents a narrative with both a distinct point of view and a strong perspective. Kincaid also evokes the tension between local Antiguan traditions and the English customs imported to the island during its centuries of colonization. (Antigua gained independence in 1981.)

Girl

Wash the white clothes on Monday and put them on the stone heap; wash the color clothes on Tuesday and put them on the clothesline to dry; don't walk bare-head in the hot sun; cook pumpkin fritters in very hot sweet oil; soak your little cloths right after you take them off; when
5 buying cotton to make yourself a nice blouse, be sure that it doesn't have gum in it, because that way it won't hold up well after a wash; soak salt fish overnight before you cook it; is it true that you sing benna in Sunday school?; always eat your food in such a way that it won't turn someone else's stomach; on Sundays try to walk like a lady and not like the slut you
10 are so bent on becoming; don't sing benna in Sunday school; you mustn't speak to wharf-rat boys, not even to give directions; don't eat fruits on the street—flies will follow you; but I don't sing benna on Sundays at all and never in Sunday school; this is how to sew on a button; this is how to make a buttonhole for the button you have just sewed on; this is how to
15 hem a dress when you see the hem coming down and so to prevent yourself from looking like the slut I know you are so bent on becoming; this is how you iron your father's khaki shirt so that it doesn't have a crease; this is how you iron your father's khaki pants so that they don't have a crease; this is how you grow okra—far from the house, because okra tree
20 harbors red ants; when you are growing dasheen, make sure it gets plenty of water or else it makes your throat itch when you are eating it; this is how you sweep a corner; this is how you sweep a whole house; this is how

Guided Questions

1. Who is telling the story? What is the narrator's relationship to the story?

2. How does the syntax of this story contribute to the style of stream of consciousness?

3. What do the details reveal about the narrator's background, culture, and values?

you sweep a yard; this is how you smile to someone you don't like too much; this is how you smile to someone you don't like at all; this is how
25 you smile to someone you like completely; this is how you set a table for tea; this is how you set a table for dinner; this is how you set a table for dinner with an important guest; this is how you set a table for lunch; this is how you set a table for breakfast; this is how to behave in the presence of men who don't know you very well, and this way they won't recognize
30 immediately the slut I have warned you against becoming; be sure to wash every day, even if it is with your own spit; don't squat down to play marbles—you are not a boy, you know; don't pick people's flowers—you might catch something; don't throw stones at blackbirds, because it might not be a blackbird at all; this is how to make a bread pudding; this is how
35 to make doukona; this is how to make pepper pot; this is how to make a good medicine for a cold; this is how to make a good medicine to throw away a child before it even becomes a child; this is how to catch a fish; this is how to throw back a fish you don't like, and that way something bad won't fall on you; this is how to bully a man; this is how a man bullies
40 you; this is how to love a man, and if this doesn't work there are other ways, and if they don't work don't feel too bad about giving up; this is how to spit up in the air if you feel like it, and this is how to move quick so that it doesn't fall on you; this is how to make ends meet; always squeeze bread to make sure it's fresh; but what if the baker won't let me feel the
45 bread?; you mean to say that after all you are really going to be the kind of woman who the baker won't let near the bread?

Guided Questions

4. How do these images reveal the tone of the story?

5. The text ends with a question. Explain how the question reveals a shift in perspective.

PRACTICE TEXT

Interpreter of Maladies
Jhumpa Lahiri

THE TEXT IN CONTEXT

The following selection comes from Jhumpa Lahiri's (b. 1967) debut book of short stories, *The Interpreter of Maladies* (1999). The collection won the Pulitzer Prize for fiction and a PEN/Hemingway Award. In the years since, she has published short stories, novels, and essays, including *The Namesake* (2003), *Unaccustomed Earth* (2008), and *Whereabouts* (2018). In "The Interpreter of Maladies," Lahiri explores themes that reflect her own upbringing between American and Indian cultures: the difficulties of communication and the complexity of identity.

LEON NEAL/AFP/Getty Images

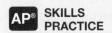

AP® SKILLS PRACTICE | NARRATION
Connecting Narration and Tone

As you read "Interpreter of Maladies," consider the narrative perspective and distance of the narrator. How does Lahiri's use of these techniques contribute to her tone and your interpretation of the story?

Connecting Narration and Tone		
	Details from the Text	What the Details Reveal about Tone
Narrative Perspective		
Narrative Distance		
Narrator's Tone		

Interpreter of Maladies

At the tea stall, Mr. and Mrs. Das bickered about who should take Tina to the toilet. Eventually Mrs. Das relented when Mr. Das pointed out that he had given the girl her
5 bath the night before. In the rearview mirror Mr. Kapasi watched as Mrs. Das emerged slowly from his bulky white Ambassador, dragging her shaved, largely bare legs across the back seat. She did not hold the little girl's
10 hand as they walked to the rest room.

They were on their way to see the Sun Temple at Konarak. It was a dry, bright Saturday, the mid-July heat tempered by a steady ocean breeze, ideal weather for sight-
15 seeing. Ordinarily Mr. Kapasi would not have stopped so soon along the way, but less than five minutes after he'd picked up the family that morning in front of Hotel Sandy Villa, the little girl had complained. The first thing

20 Mr. Kapasi had noticed when he saw Mr. and Mrs. Das, standing with their children under the portico of the hotel, was that they were very young, perhaps not even thirty. In addition to Tina they had two boys, Ronny and
25 Bobby, who appeared very close in age and had teeth covered in a network of flashing silver wires. The family looked Indian but dressed as foreigners did, the children in stiff, brightly colored clothing and caps with
30 translucent visors. Mr. Kapasi was accustomed to foreign tourists; he was assigned to them regularly because he could speak English. Yesterday he had driven an elderly couple from Scotland, both with spotted
35 faces and fluffy white hair so thin it exposed their sunburnt scalps. In comparison, the tanned, youthful faces of Mr. and Mrs. Das were all the more striking. When he'd

introduced himself, Mr. Kapasi had pressed
40 his palms together in greeting, but Mr. Das
squeezed hands like an American so that Mr.
Kapasi felt it in his elbow. Mrs. Das, for her
part, had flexed one side of her mouth, smiling dutifully at Mr. Kapasi, without display-
45 ing any interest in him.

As they waited at the tea stall, Ronny, who
looked like the older of the two boys, clambered suddenly out of the back seat, intrigued
by a goat tied to a stake in the ground.

50 "Don't touch it," Mr. Das said. He glanced
up from his paperback tour book, which said
"INDIA" in yellow letters and looked as if it
had been published abroad. His voice, somehow tentative and a little shrill, sounded as
55 though it had not yet settled into maturity.

"I want to give it a piece of gum," the boy
called back as he trotted ahead.

Mr. Das stepped out of the car and
stretched his legs by squatting briefly to the
60 ground. A clean-shaven man, he looked
exactly like a magnified version of Ronny. He
had a sapphire blue visor, and was dressed in
shorts, sneakers, and a T-shirt. The camera
slung around his neck, with an impressive
65 telephoto lens and numerous buttons and
markings, was the only complicated thing
he wore. He frowned, watching as Ronny
rushed toward the goat, but appeared to
have no intention of intervening. "Bobby,
70 make sure that your brother doesn't do
anything stupid."

"I don't feel like it," Bobby said, not moving. He was sitting in the front seat beside
Mr. Kapasi, studying a picture of the elephant
75 god taped to the glove compartment.

"No need to worry," Mr. Kapasi said. "They
are quite tame." Mr. Kapasi was forty-six
years old, with receding hair that had gone
completely silver, but his butterscotch com-
80 plexion and his unlined brow, which he

treated in spare moments to dabs of lotus-oil
balm, made it easy to imagine what he must
have looked like at an earlier age. He wore
gray trousers and a matching jacket-style
85 shirt, tapered at the waist, with short sleeves
and a large pointed collar, made of a thin but
durable synthetic material. He had specified
both the cut and the fabric to his tailor—it
was his preferred uniform for giving tours
90 because it did not get crushed during his
long hours behind the wheel. Through the
windshield he watched as Ronny circled
around the goat, touched it quickly on its
side, then trotted back to the car.

95 "You left India as a child?" Mr. Kapasi
asked when Mr. Das had settled once again
into the passenger seat.

"Oh, Mina and I were both born in
America," Mr. Das announced with an air of
100 sudden confidence. "Born and raised. Our
parents live here now, in Assansol. They
retired. We visit them every couple years."
He turned to watch as the little girl ran
toward the car, the wide purple bows of her
105 sundress flopping on her narrow brown
shoulders. She was holding to her chest a
doll with yellow hair that looked as if it had
been chopped, as a punitive measure, with a
pair of dull scissors. "This is Tina's first trip
110 to India, isn't it, Tina?"

"I don't have to go to the bathroom anymore," Tina announced.

"Where's Mina?" Mr. Das asked.

Mr. Kapasi found it strange that Mr. Das
115 should refer to his wife by her first name
when speaking to the little girl. Tina pointed
to where Mrs. Das was purchasing something from one of the shirtless men who
worked at the tea stall. Mr. Kapasi heard one
120 of the shirtless men sing a phrase from a
popular Hindi love song as Mrs. Das walked
back to the car, but she did not appear to

understand the words of the song, for she did not express irritation, or embarrassment, or react in any other way to the man's declarations.

He observed her. She wore a red-and-white-checkered skirt that stopped above her knees, slip-on shoes with a square wooden heel, and a close-fitting blouse styled like a man's undershirt. The blouse was decorated at chest-level with a calico appliqué in the shape of a strawberry. She was a short woman, with small hands like paws, her frosty pink fingernails painted to match her lips, and was slightly plump in her figure. Her hair, shorn only a little longer than her husband's, was parted far to one side. She was wearing large dark brown sunglasses with a pinkish tint to them, and carried a big straw bag, almost as big as her torso, shaped like a bowl, with a water bottle poking out of it. She walked slowly, carrying some puffed rice tossed with peanuts and chili peppers in a large packet made from newspapers. Mr. Kapasi turned to Mr. Das.

"Where in America do you live?"

"New Brunswick, New Jersey."

"Next to New York?"

"Exactly. I teach middle school there."

"What subject?"

"Science. In fact, every year I take my students on a trip to the Museum of Natural History in New York City. In a way we have a lot in common, you could say, you and I. How long have you been a tour guide, Mr. Kapasi?"

"Five years."

Mrs. Das reached the car. "How long's the trip?" she asked, shutting the door.

"About two and a half hours," Mr. Kapasi replied.

At this Mrs. Das gave an impatient sigh, as if she had been traveling her whole life without pause. She fanned herself with a folded Bombay film magazine written in English.

"I thought that the Sun Temple is only eighteen miles north of Puri," Mr. Das said, tapping on the tour book.

"The roads to Konarak are poor. Actually it is a distance of fifty-two miles," Mr. Kapasi explained.

Mr. Das nodded, readjusting the camera strap where it had begun to chafe the back of his neck.

Before starting the ignition, Mr. Kapasi reached back to make sure the cranklike locks on the inside of each of the back doors were secured. As soon as the car began to move the little girl began to play with the lock on her side, clicking it with some effort forward and backward, but Mrs. Das said nothing to stop her. She sat a bit slouched at one end of the back seat, not offering her puffed rice to anyone. Ronny and Tina sat on either side of her, both snapping bright green gum.

"Look," Bobby said as the car began to gather speed. He pointed with his finger to the tall trees that lined the road. "Look."

"Monkeys!" Ronny shrieked. "Wow!"

They were seated in groups along the branches, with shining black faces, silver bodies, horizontal eyebrows, and crested heads. Their long gray tails dangled like a series of ropes among the leaves. A few scratched themselves with black leathery hands, or swung their feet, staring as the car passed.

"We call them the hanuman," Mr. Kapasi said. "They are quite common in the area."

As soon as he spoke, one of the monkeys leaped into the middle of the road, causing Mr. Kapasi to brake suddenly. Another bounced onto the hood of the car, then sprang away.

Mr. Kapasi beeped his horn. The children began to get excited, sucking in their breath and covering their faces partly with their
210 hands. They had never seen monkeys outside of a zoo, Mr. Das explained. He asked Mr. Kapasi to stop the car so that he could take a picture.

While Mr. Das adjusted his telephoto lens,
215 Mrs. Das reached into her straw bag and pulled out a bottle of colorless nail polish, which she proceeded to stroke on the tip of her index finger.

The little girl stuck out a hand. "Mine too.
220 Mommy, do mine too."

"Leave me alone," Mrs. Das said, blowing on her nail and turning her body slightly. "You're making me mess up."

The little girl occupied herself by button-
225 ing and unbuttoning a pinafore on the doll's plastic body.

"All set," Mr. Das said, replacing the lens cap.

The car rattled considerably as it raced along the dusty road, causing them all to pop
230 up from their seats every now and then, but Mrs. Das continued to polish her nails. Mr. Kapasi eased up on the accelerator, hoping to produce a smoother ride. When he reached for the gearshift the boy in front accommo-
235 dated him by swinging his hairless knees out of the way. Mr. Kapasi noted that this boy was slightly paler than the other children. "Daddy, why is the driver sitting on the wrong side in this car, too?" the boy asked.
240 "They all do that here, dummy," Ronny said.

"Don't call your brother a dummy," Mr. Das said. He turned to Mr. Kapasi. "In America, you know . . . it confuses them."
245 "Oh yes, I am well aware," Mr. Kapasi said. As delicately as he could, he shifted gears again, accelerating as they approached a hill in the road. "I see it on *Dallas*, the steering wheels are on the left-hand side."

250 "What's *Dallas*?" Tina asked, banging her now naked doll on the seat behind Mr. Kapasi.

"It went off the air," Mr. Das explained. "It's a television show."
255 They were all like siblings, Mr. Kapasi thought as they passed a row of date trees. Mr. and Mrs. Das behaved like an older brother and sister, not parents. It seemed that they were in charge of the children only
260 for the day; it was hard to believe they were regularly responsible for anything other than themselves. Mr. Das tapped on his lens cap, and his tour book, dragging his thumbnail occasionally across the pages so that they
265 made a scraping sound. Mrs. Das continued to polish her nails. She had still not removed her sunglasses. Every now and then Tina renewed her plea that she wanted her nails done, too, and so at one point Mrs. Das
270 flicked a drop of polish on the little girl's finger before depositing the bottle back inside her straw bag.

"Isn't this an air-conditioned car?" she asked, still blowing on her hand. The window
275 on Tina's side was broken and could not be rolled down.

"Quit complaining," Mr. Das said. "It isn't so hot."

"I told you to get a car with air-conditioning,"
280 Mrs. Das continued. "Why do you do this, Raj, just to save a few stupid rupees. What are you saving us, fifty cents?"

Their accents sounded just like the ones Mr. Kapasi heard on American television
285 programs, though not like the ones on *Dallas*.

"Doesn't it get tiresome, Mr. Kapasi, showing people the same thing every day?" Mr. Das asked, rolling down his own window all the way. "Hey, do you mind stopping the car.
290 I just want to get a shot of this guy."

Mr. Kapasi pulled over to the side of the road as Mr. Das took a picture of a barefoot man, his head wrapped in a dirty turban, seated on top of a cart of grain sacks pulled by a pair of bullocks. Both the man and the bullocks were emaciated. In the back seat Mrs. Das gazed out another window, at the sky, where nearly transparent clouds passed quickly in front of one another.

"I look forward to it, actually," Mr. Kapasi said as they continued on their way. "The Sun Temple is one of my favorite places. In that way it is a reward for me. I give tours on Fridays and Saturdays only. I have another job during the week."

"Oh? Where?" Mr. Das asked.

"I work in a doctor's office."

"You're a doctor?"

"I am not a doctor. I work with one. As an interpreter."

"What does a doctor need an interpreter for?"

"He has a number of Gujarati patients. My father was Gujarati, but many people do not speak Gujarati in this area, including the doctor. And so the doctor asked me to work in his office, interpreting what the patients say."

"Interesting. I've never heard of anything like that," Mr. Das said.

Mr. Kapasi shrugged. "It is a job like any other."

"But so romantic," Mrs. Das said dreamily, breaking her extended silence. She lifted her pinkish brown sunglasses and arranged them on top of her head like a tiara. For the first time, her eyes met Mr. Kapasi's in the rearview mirror: pale, a bit small, their gaze fixed but drowsy.

Mr. Das craned to look at her. "What's so romantic about it?"

"I don't know. Something." She shrugged, knitting her brows together for an instant. "Would you like a piece of gum, Mr. Kapasi?"

she asked brightly. She reached into her straw bag and handed him a small square wrapped in green-and-white-striped paper. As soon as Mr. Kapasi put the gum in his mouth a thick sweet liquid burst onto his tongue.

"Tell us more about your job, Mr. Kapasi," Mrs. Das said.

"What would you like to know, madame?"

"I don't know," she shrugged, munching on some puffed rice and licking the mustard oil from the corners of her mouth. "Tell us a typical situation." She settled back in her seat, her head tilted in a patch of sun, and closed her eyes. "I want to picture what happens."

"Very well. The other day a man came in with a pain in his throat."

"Did he smoke cigarettes?"

"No. It was very curious. He complained that he felt as if there were long pieces of straw stuck in his throat. When I told the doctor he was able to prescribe the proper medication."

"That's so neat."

"Yes," Mr. Kapasi agreed after some hesitation.

"So these patients are totally dependent on you," Mrs. Das said. She spoke slowly, as if she were thinking aloud. "In a way, more dependent on you than the doctor."

"How do you mean? How could it be?"

"Well, for example, you could tell the doctor that the pain felt like a burning, not straw. The patient would never know what you had told the doctor, and the doctor wouldn't know that you had told the wrong thing. It's a big responsibility."

"Yes, a big responsibility you have there, Mr. Kapasi," Mr. Das agreed.

Mr. Kapasi had never thought of his job in such complimentary terms. To him it was a

thankless occupation. He found nothing noble in interpreting people's maladies, assiduously translating the symptoms of so
380 many swollen bones, countless cramps of bellies and bowels, spots on people's palms that changed color, shape, or size. The doctor, nearly half his age, had an affinity for bell-bottom trousers and made humorless
385 jokes about the Congress party. Together they worked in a stale little infirmary where Mr. Kapasi's smartly tailored clothes clung to him in the heat, in spite of the blackened blades of a ceiling fan churning over their
390 heads.

The job was a sign of his failings. In his youth he'd been a devoted scholar of foreign languages, the owner of an impressive col-lection of dictionaries. He had dreamed of
395 being an interpreter for diplomats and digni-taries, resolving conflicts between people and nations, settling disputes of which he alone could understand both sides. He was a self-educated man. In a series of notebooks,
400 in the evenings before his parents settled his marriage, he had listed the common etymol-ogies of words, and at one point in his life he was confident that he could converse, if given the opportunity, in English, French,
405 Russian, Portuguese, and Italian, not to men-tion Hindi, Bengali, Orissi, and Gujarati. Now only a handful of European phrases remained in his memory, scattered words for things like saucers and chairs. English was the only
410 non-Indian language he spoke fluently any-more. Mr. Kapasi knew it was not a remark-able talent. Sometimes he feared that his children knew better English than he did, just from watching television. Still, it came
415 in handy for the tours.

He had taken the job as an interpreter after his first son, at the age of seven, con-tracted typhoid—that was how he had first made the acquaintance of the doctor. At the
420 time Mr. Kapasi had been teaching English in a grammar school, and he bartered his skills as an interpreter to pay the increasingly exorbitant medical bills. In the end the boy had died one evening in his mother's arms,
425 his limbs burning with fever, but then there was the funeral to pay for, and the other children who were born soon enough, and the newer, bigger house, and the good schools and tutors, and the fine shoes and
430 the television, and the countless other ways he tried to console his wife and to keep her from crying in her sleep, and so when the doctor offered to pay him twice as much as he earned at the grammar school, he
435 accepted. Mr. Kapasi knew that his wife had little regard for his career as an interpreter. He knew it reminded her of the son she'd lost, and that she resented the other lives he helped, in his own small way, to save. If ever
440 she referred to his position, she used the phrase "doctor's assistant," as if the process of interpretation were equal to taking some-one's temperature, or changing a bedpan. She never asked him about the patients who
445 came to the doctor's office, or said that his job was a big responsibility.

For this reason it flattered Mr. Kapasi that Mrs. Das was so intrigued by his job. Unlike his wife, she had reminded him of its intel-
450 lectual challenges. She had also used the word "romantic." She did not behave in a romantic way toward her husband, and yet she had used the word to describe him. He wondered if Mr. and Mrs. Das were a bad
455 match, just as he and his wife were. Perhaps they, too, had little in common apart from three children and a decade of their lives. The signs he recognized from his own marriage were there — the bickering, the
460 indifference, the protracted silences. Her sudden interest in him, an interest she did not express in either her husband or her

children, was mildly intoxicating. When Mr. Kapasi thought once again about how
465 she had said "romantic," the feeling of intoxication grew.

He began to check his reflection in the rearview mirror as he drove, feeling grateful that he had chosen the gray suit that morn-
470 ing and not the brown one, which tended to sag a little in the knees. From time to time he glanced through the mirror at Mrs. Das. In addition to glancing at her face he glanced at the strawberry between her breasts, and
475 the golden brown hollow in her throat. He decided to tell Mrs. Das about another patient, and another: the young woman who had complained of a sensation of raindrops in her spine, the gentleman whose birth-
480 mark had begun to sprout hairs. Mrs. Das listened attentively, stroking her hair with a small plastic brush that resembled an oval bed of nails, asking more questions, for yet another example. The children were quiet,
485 intent on spotting more monkeys in the trees, and Mr. Das was absorbed by his tour book, so it seemed like a private conversation between Mr. Kapasi and Mrs. Das. In this manner the next half hour passed, and when
490 they stopped for lunch at a roadside restaurant that sold fritters and omelette sandwiches, usually something Mr. Kapasi looked forward to on his tours so that he could sit in peace and enjoy some hot tea, he was disap-
495 pointed. As the Das family settled together under a magenta umbrella fringed with white and orange tassels, and placed their orders with one of the waiters who marched about in tricornered caps, Mr. Kapasi reluc-
500 tantly headed toward a neighboring table.

"Mr. Kapasi, wait. There's room here," Mrs. Das called out. She gathered Tina onto her lap, insisting that he accompany them. And so, together, they had bottled mango

505 juice and sandwiches and plates of onions and potatoes deep-fried in graham-flour batter. After finishing two omelette sandwiches Mr. Das took more pictures of the group as they ate.
510 "How much longer?" he asked Mr. Kapasi as he paused to load a new roll of film in the camera.

"About half an hour more."

By now the children had gotten up from
515 the table to look at more monkeys perched in a nearby tree, so there was a considerable space between Mrs. Das and Mr. Kapasi. Mr. Das placed the camera to his face and squeezed one eye shut, his tongue exposed
520 at one corner of his mouth. "This looks funny. Mina, you need to lean in closer to Mr. Kapasi."

She did. He could smell a scent on her skin, like a mixture of whiskey and
525 rosewater. He worried suddenly that she could smell his perspiration, which he knew had collected beneath the synthetic material of his shirt. He polished off his mango juice in one gulp and smoothed his silver hair with
530 his hands. A bit of the juice dripped onto his chin. He wondered if Mrs. Das had noticed.

She had not. "What's your address, Mr. Kapasi?" she inquired, fishing for something inside her straw bag.
535 "You would like my address?"

"So we can send you copies," she said. "Of the pictures." She handed him a scrap of paper which she had hastily ripped from a page of her film magazine. The blank por-
540 tion was limited, for the narrow strip was crowded by lines of text and a tiny picture of a hero and heroine embracing under a eucalyptus tree.

The paper curled as Mr. Kapasi wrote his
545 address in clear, careful letters. She would write to him, asking about his days interpreting

at the doctor's office, and he would respond eloquently, choosing only the most entertaining anecdotes, ones that would make
550 her laugh out loud as she read them in her house in New Jersey. In time she would reveal the disappointment of her marriage, and he his. In this way their friendship would grow, and flourish. He would possess
555 a picture of the two of them, eating fried onions under a magenta umbrella, which he would keep, he decided, safely tucked between the pages of his Russian grammar. As his mind raced, Mr. Kapasi experienced a
560 mild and pleasant shock. It was similar to a feeling he used to experience long ago when, after months of translating with the aid of a dictionary, he would finally read a passage from a French novel, or an Italian sonnet,
565 and understand the words, one after another, unencumbered by his own efforts. In those moments Mr. Kapasi used to believe that all was right with the world, that all struggles were rewarded, that all of life's mistakes
570 made sense in the end. The promise that he would hear from Mrs. Das now filled him with the same belief.

When he finished writing his address Mr. Kapasi handed her the paper, but as soon
575 as he did so he worried that he had either misspelled his name, or accidentally reversed the numbers of his postal code. He dreaded the possibility of a lost letter, the photograph never reaching him, hovering somewhere in
580 Orissa, close but ultimately unattainable. He thought of asking for the slip of paper again, just to make sure he had written his address accurately, but Mrs. Das had already dropped it into the jumble of her bag.
585 They reached Konarak at two-thirty. The temple, made of sandstone, was a massive pyramid-like structure in the shape of a chariot. It was dedicated to the great master

of life, the sun, which struck three sides of
590 the edifice as it made its journey each day across the sky. Twenty-four giant wheels were carved on the north and south sides of the plinth. The whole thing was drawn by a team of seven horses, speeding as if through
595 the heavens. As they approached, Mr. Kapasi explained that the temple had been built between A.D. 1243 and 1255, with the efforts of twelve hundred artisans, by the great ruler of the Ganga dynasty, King Narasimhadeva
600 the First, to commemorate his victory against the Muslim army.

"It says the temple occupies about a hundred and seventy acres of land," Mr. Das said, reading from his book.
605 "It's like a desert," Ronny said, his eyes wandering across the sand that stretched on all sides beyond the temple.

"The Chandrabhaga River once flowed one mile north of here. It is dry now," Mr. Kapasi
610 said, turning off the engine.

They got out and walked toward the temple, posing first for pictures by the pair of lions that flanked the steps. Mr. Kapasi led them next to one of the wheels of the char
615 iot, higher than any human being, nine feet in diameter.

"The wheels are supposed to symbolize the wheel of life," Mr. Das read. "'They depict the cycle of creation, preservation, and
620 achievement of realization.' Cool." He turned the page of his book. "'Each wheel is divided into eight thick and thin spokes, dividing the day into eight equal parts. The rims are carved with designs of birds and animals,
625 whereas the medallions in the spokes are carved with women in luxurious poses, largely erotic in nature.'"

What he referred to were the countless friezes of entwined naked bodies, making
630 love in various positions, women clinging to

the necks of men, their knees wrapped eternally around their lovers' thighs. In addition to these were assorted scenes from daily life, of hunting and trading, of deer being killed
635 with bows and arrows and marching warriors holding swords in their hands.

It was no longer possible to enter the temple, for it had filled with rubble years ago, but they admired the exterior, as did all
640 the tourists Mr. Kapasi brought there, slowly strolling along each of its sides. Mr. Das trailed behind, taking pictures. The children ran ahead, pointing to figures of naked people, intrigued in particular by the
645 Nagamithunas, the half-human, half-serpentine couples who were said, Mr. Kapasi told them, to live in the deepest waters of the sea. Mr. Kapasi was pleased that they liked the temple, pleased especially that it
650 appealed to Mrs. Das. She stopped every three or four paces, staring silently at the carved lovers, and the processions of elephants, and the topless female musicians beating on two-sided drums.
655 Though Mr. Kapasi had been to the temple countless times, it occurred to him, as he, too, gazed at the topless women, that he had never seen his own wife fully naked. Even when they had made love she kept the pan-
660 els of her blouse hooked together, the string of her petticoat knotted around her waist. He had never admired the backs of his wife's legs the way he now admired those of Mrs. Das, walking as if for his benefit alone. He
665 had, of course, seen plenty of bare limbs before, belonging to the American and European ladies who took his tours. But Mrs. Das was different. Unlike the other women, who had an interest only in the temple, and
670 kept their noses buried in a guidebook, or their eyes behind the lens of a camera, Mrs. Das had taken an interest in him.

Mr. Kapasi was anxious to be alone with her, to continue their private conversation,
675 yet he felt nervous to walk at her side. She was lost behind her sunglasses, ignoring her husband's requests that she pose for another picture, walking past her children as if they were strangers. Worried that he might dis-
680 turb her, Mr. Kapasi walked ahead, to admire, as he always did, the three life-sized bronze avatars of Surya, the sun god, each emerging from its own niche on the temple façade to greet the sun at dawn, noon, and evening.
685 They wore elaborate headdresses, their languid, elongated eyes closed, their bare chests draped with carved chains and amulets. Hibiscus petals, offerings from previous visitors, were strewn at their gray-green feet.
690 The last statue, on the northern wall of the temple, was Mr. Kapasi's favorite. This Surya had a tired expression, weary after a hard day of work, sitting astride a horse with folded legs. Even his horse's eyes were
695 drowsy. Around his body were smaller sculptures of women in pairs, their hips thrust to one side.

"Who's that?" Mrs. Das asked. He was startled to see that she was standing beside
700 him.

"He is the Astachala-Surya," Mr. Kapasi said. "The setting sun."

"So in a couple of hours the sun will set right here?" She slipped a foot out of one of
705 her square-heeled shoes, rubbed her toes on the back of her other leg.

"That is correct."

She raised her sunglasses for a moment, then put them back on again. "Neat."
710 Mr. Kapasi was not certain exactly what the word suggested, but he had a feeling it was a favorable response. He hoped that Mrs. Das had understood Surya's beauty, his power. Perhaps they would discuss it further

715 in their letters. He would explain things to her, things about India, and she would explain things to him about America. In its own way this correspondence would fulfill his dream, of serving as an interpreter

720 between nations. He looked at her straw bag, delighted that his address lay nestled among its contents. When he pictured her so many thousands of miles away he plummeted, so much so that he had an overwhelming urge

725 to wrap his arms around her, to freeze with her, even for an instant, in an embrace witnessed by his favorite Surya. But Mrs. Das had already started walking.

"When do you return to America?" he

730 asked, trying to sound placid.

"In ten days."

He calculated: A week to settle in, a week to develop the pictures, a few days to compose her letter, two weeks to get to India by

735 air. According to his schedule, allowing room for delays, he would hear from Mrs. Das in approximately six weeks' time. The family was silent as Mr. Kapasi drove them back, a little past four-thirty, to Hotel Sandy Villa.

740 The children had bought miniature granite versions of the chariot's wheels at a souvenir stand, and they turned them round in their hands. Mr. Das continued to read his book. Mrs. Das untangled Tina's hair with her

745 brush and divided it into two little ponytails.

Mr. Kapasi was beginning to dread the thought of dropping them off. He was not prepared to begin his six-week wait to hear from Mrs. Das. As he stole glances at her in

750 the rearview mirror, wrapping elastic bands around Tina's hair, he wondered how he might make the tour last a little longer. Ordinarily he sped back to Puri using a shortcut, eager to return home, scrub his feet and

755 hands with sandalwood soap, and enjoy the evening newspaper and a cup of tea that his wife would serve him in silence. The thought of that silence, something to which he'd long been resigned, now oppressed him. It was

760 then that he suggested visiting the hills at Udayagiri and Khandagiri, where a number of monastic dwellings were hewn out of the ground, facing one another across a defile. It was some miles away, but well worth seeing,

765 Mr. Kapasi told them.

"Oh yeah, there's something mentioned about it in this book," Mr. Das said. "Built by a Jain king or something."

"Shall we go then?" Mr. Kapasi asked. He

770 paused at a turn in the road. "It's to the left."

Mr. Das turned to look at Mrs. Das. Both of them shrugged. "Left, left," the children chanted. Mr. Kapasi turned the wheel, almost delirious with relief. He did not know what

775 he would do or say to Mrs. Das once they arrived at the hills. Perhaps he would tell her what a pleasing smile she had. Perhaps he would compliment her strawberry shirt, which he found irresistibly becoming.

780 Perhaps, when Mr. Das was busy taking a picture, he would take her hand.

He did not have to worry. When they got to the hills, divided by a steep path thick with trees, Mrs. Das refused to get out of

785 the car. All along the path, dozens of monkeys were seated on stones, as well as on the branches of the trees. Their hind legs were stretched out in front and raised to shoulder level, their arms resting on

790 their knees.

"My legs are tired," she said, sinking low in her seat. "I'll stay here."

"Why did you have to wear those stupid shoes?" Mr. Das said. "You won't be in the

795 pictures."

"Pretend I'm there."

"But we could use one of these pictures for our Christmas card this year. We didn't

get one of all five of us at the Sun Temple.
800 Mr. Kapasi could take it."

"I'm not coming. Anyway, those monkeys give me the creeps."

"But they're harmless," Mr. Das said. He turned to Mr. Kapasi. "Aren't they?"

805 "They are more hungry than dangerous," Mr. Kapasi said. "Do not provoke them with food, and they will not bother you."

Mr. Das headed up the defile with the children, the boys at his side, the little girl on
810 his shoulders. Mr. Kapasi watched as they crossed paths with a Japanese man and woman, the only other tourists there, who paused for a final photograph, then stepped into a nearby car and drove away. As the car
815 disappeared out of view some of the monkeys called out, emitting soft whooping sounds, and then walked on their flat black hands and feet up the path. At one point a group of them formed a little ring around
820 Mr. Das and the children. Tina screamed in delight. Ronny ran in circles around his father. Bobby bent down and picked up a fat stick on the ground. When he extended it, one of the monkeys approached him and
825 snatched it, then briefly beat the ground.

"I'll join them," Mr. Kapasi said, unlocking the door on his side. "There is much to explain about the caves."

"No. Stay a minute," Mrs. Das said. She got
830 out of the back seat and slipped in beside Mr. Kapasi. "Raj has his dumb book anyway." Together, through the windshield, Mrs. Das and Mr. Kapasi watched as Bobby and the monkey passed the stick back and forth
835 between them.

"A brave little boy," Mr. Kapasi commented.

"It's not so surprising," Mrs. Das said.

"No?"

"He's not his."

840 "I beg your pardon?"

"Raj's. He's not Raj's son."

Mr. Kapasi felt a prickle on his skin. He reached into his shirt pocket for the small tin of lotus-oil balm he carried with him at all
845 times, and applied it to three spots on his forehead. He knew that Mrs. Das was watching him, but he did not turn to face her. Instead he watched as the figures of Mr. Das and the children grew smaller, climbing up
850 the steep path, pausing every now and then for a picture, surrounded by a growing number of monkeys.

"Are you surprised?" The way she put it made him choose his words with care.

855 "It's not the type of thing one assumes," Mr. Kapasi replied slowly. He put the tin of lotus-oil balm back in his pocket.

"No, of course not. And no one knows, of course. No one at all. I've kept it a secret for
860 eight whole years." She looked at Mr. Kapasi, tilting her chin as if to gain a fresh perspective. "But now I've told you."

Mr. Kapasi nodded. He felt suddenly parched, and his forehead was warm and
865 slightly numb from the balm. He considered asking Mrs. Das for a sip of water, then decided against it.

"We met when we were very young," she said. She reached into her straw bag in
870 search of something, then pulled out a packet of puffed rice. "Want some?"

"No, thank you."

She put a fistful in her mouth, sank into the seat a little, and looked away from
875 Mr. Kapasi, out the window on her side of the car. "We married when we were still in college. We were in high school when he proposed. We went to the same college, of course. Back then we couldn't stand the
880 thought of being separated, not for a day, not for a minute. Our parents were best friends who lived in the same town. My entire life

I saw him every weekend, either at our house or theirs. We were sent upstairs to play
885 together while our parents joked about our marriage. Imagine! They never caught us at anything, though in a way I think it was all more or less a setup. The things we did those Friday and Saturday nights, while our par-
890 ents sat downstairs drinking tea . . . I could tell you stories, Mr. Kapasi."

As a result of spending all her time in college with Raj, she continued, she did not make many close friends. There was no one
895 to confide in about him at the end of a diffi-cult day, or to share a passing thought or a worry. Her parents now lived on the other side of the world, but she had never been very close to them, anyway. After marrying
900 so young she was overwhelmed by it all, having a child so quickly, and nursing, and warming up bottles of milk and testing their temperature against her wrist while Raj was at work, dressed in sweaters and corduroy
905 pants, teaching his students about rocks and dinosaurs. Raj never looked cross or harried, or plump as she had become after the first baby.

Always tired, she declined invitations
910 from her one or two college girlfriends, to have lunch or shop in Manhattan. Eventually the friends stopped calling her, so that she was left at home all day with the baby, sur-rounded by toys that made her trip when she
915 walked or wince when she sat, always cross and tired. Only occasionally did they go out after Ronny was born, and even more rarely did they entertain. Raj didn't mind; he looked forward to coming home from teach-
920 ing and watching television and bouncing Ronny on his knee. She had been outraged when Raj told her that a Punjabi friend, someone whom she had once met but did not remember, would be staying with them

925 for a week for some job interviews in the New Brunswick area.

Bobby was conceived in the afternoon, on a sofa littered with rubber teething toys, after the friend learned that a London phar-
930 maceutical company had hired him, while Ronny cried to be freed from his playpen. She made no protest when the friend touched the small of her back as she was about to make a pot of coffee, then pulled
935 her against his crisp navy suit. He made love to her swiftly, in silence, with an expertise she had never known, without the mean-ingful expressions and smiles Raj always insisted on afterward. The next day Raj drove
940 the friend to JFK. He was married now, to a Punjabi girl, and they lived in London still, and every year they exchanged Christmas cards with Raj and Mina, each couple tucking photos of their families into the envelopes.
945 He did not know that he was Bobby's father. He never would.

"I beg your pardon, Mrs. Das, but why have you told me this information?" Mr. Kapasi asked when she had finally finished
950 speaking, and had turned to face him once again.

"For God's sake, stop calling me Mrs. Das. I'm twenty-eight. You probably have children my age."
955 "Not quite." It disturbed Mr. Kapasi to learn that she thought of him as a parent. The feeling he had had toward her, that had made him check his reflection in the rear-view mirror as they drove, evaporated a little.
960 "I told you because of your talents." She put the packet of puffed rice back into her bag without folding over the top.

"I don't understand," Mr. Kapasi said.

"Don't you see? For eight years I haven't
965 been able to express this to anybody, not to friends, certainly not to Raj. He doesn't even

suspect it. He thinks I'm still in love with him. Well, don't you have anything to say?"

"About what?"·

970 "About what I've just told you. About my secret, and about how terrible it makes me feel. I feel terrible looking at my children, and at Raj, always terrible. I have terrible urges, Mr. Kapasi, to throw things away.

975 One day I had the urge to throw everything I own out the window, the television, the children, everything. Don't you think it's unhealthy?"

He was silent.

980 "Mr. Kapasi, don't you have anything to say? I thought that was your job."

"My job is to give tours, Mrs. Das."

"Not that. Your other job. As an interpreter."

985 "But we do not face a language barrier. What need is there for an interpreter?"

"That's not what I mean. I would never have told you otherwise. Don't you realize what it means for me to tell you?"

990 "What does it mean?"

"It means that I'm tired of feeling so terrible all the time. Eight years, Mr. Kapasi, I've been in pain eight years. I was hoping you could help me feel better, say the right thing.

995 Suggest some kind of remedy."

He looked at her, in her red plaid skirt and strawberry T-shirt, a woman not yet thirty, who loved neither her husband nor her children, who had already fallen out of love

1000 with life. Her confession depressed him, depressed him all the more when he thought of Mr. Das at the top of the path, Tina clinging to his shoulders, taking pictures of ancient monastic cells cut into the hills to

1005 show his students in America, unsuspecting and unaware that one of his sons was not his own. Mr. Kapasi felt insulted that Mrs. Das should ask him to interpret her common, trivial little secret. She did not resemble the

1010 patients in the doctor's office, those who came glassy-eyed and desperate, unable to sleep or breathe or urinate with ease, unable, above all, to give words to their pains.

Still, Mr. Kapasi believed it was his duty to

1015 assist Mrs. Das. Perhaps he ought to tell her to confess the truth to Mr. Das. He would explain that honesty was the best policy. Honesty, surely, would help her feel better, as she'd put it. Perhaps he would offer to preside over the

1020 discussion, as a mediator. He decided to begin with the most obvious question, to get to the heart of the matter, and so he asked, "Is it really pain you feel, Mrs. Das, or is it guilt?"

She turned to him and glared, mustard oil

1025 thick on her frosty pink lips. She opened her mouth to say something, but as she glared at Mr. Kapasi some certain knowledge seemed to pass before her eyes, and she stopped. It crushed him; he knew at that moment that

1030 he was not even important enough to be properly insulted. She opened the car door and began walking up the path, wobbling a little on her square wooden heels, reaching into her straw bag to eat handfuls of puffed

1035 rice. It fell through her fingers, leaving a zigzagging trail, causing a monkey to leap down from a tree and devour the little white grains. In search of more, the monkey began to follow Mrs. Das. Others joined him, so that

1040 she was soon being followed by about half a dozen of them, their velvety tails dragging behind.

Mr. Kapasi stepped out of the car. He wanted to holler, to alert her in some way,

1045 but he worried that if she knew they were behind her, she would grow nervous. Perhaps she would lose her balance. Perhaps they would pull at her bag or her hair. He began to jog up the path, taking a fallen branch in his

1050 hand to scare away the monkeys. Mrs. Das continued walking, oblivious, trailing grains of puffed rice. Near the top of the incline, before a group of cells fronted by a row of squat stone pillars, Mr. Das was kneeling on the ground, focusing the lens of his camera. The children stood under the arcade, now hiding, now emerging from view.

"Wait for me," Mrs. Das called out. "I'm coming."

Tina jumped up and down. "Here comes Mommy!"

"Great," Mr. Das said without looking up. "Just in time. We'll get Mr. Kapasi to take a picture of the five of us."

Mr. Kapasi quickened his pace, waving his branch so that the monkeys scampered away, distracted, in another direction.

"Where's Bobby?" Mrs. Das asked when she stopped.

Mr. Das looked up from the camera. "I don't know. Ronny, where's Bobby?"

Ronny shrugged. "I thought he was right here."

"Where is he?" Mrs. Das repeated sharply. "What's wrong with all of you?"

They began calling his name, wandering up and down the path a bit. Because they were calling, they did not initially hear the boy's screams. When they found him, a little farther down the path under a tree, he was surrounded by a group of monkeys, over a dozen of them, pulling at his T-shirt with their long black fingers. The puffed rice Mrs. Das had spilled was scattered at his feet, raked over by the monkeys' hands. The boy was silent, his body frozen, swift tears running down his startled face. His bare legs were dusty and red with welts from where one of the monkeys struck him repeatedly with the stick he had given to it earlier.

"Daddy, the monkey's hurting Bobby," Tina said.

Mr. Das wiped his palms on the front of his shorts. In his nervousness he acciden-

tally pressed the shutter on his camera; the whirring noise of the advancing film excited the monkeys, and the one with the stick began to beat Bobby more intently. "What are we supposed to do? What if they start attacking?"

"Mr. Kapasi," Mrs. Das shrieked, noticing him standing to one side. "Do something, for God's sake, do something!"

Mr. Kapasi took his branch and shooed them away, hissing at the ones that remained, stomping his feet to scare them. The animals retreated slowly, with a measured gait, obedient but unintimidated. Mr. Kapasi gathered Bobby in his arms and brought him back to where his parents and siblings were standing. As he carried him he was tempted to whisper a secret into the boy's ear. But Bobby was stunned, and shivering with fright, his legs bleeding slightly where the stick had broken the skin. When Mr. Kapasi delivered him to his parents, Mr. Das brushed some dirt off the boy's T-shirt and put the visor on him the right way. Mrs. Das reached into her straw bag to find a bandage which she taped over the cut on his knee. Ronny offered his brother a fresh piece of gum. "He's fine. Just a little scared, right, Bobby?" Mr. Das said, patting the top of his head.

"God, let's get out of here," Mrs. Das said. She folded her arms across the strawberry on her chest. "This place gives me the creeps."

"Yeah. Back to the hotel, definitely," Mr. Das agreed.

"Poor Bobby," Mrs. Das said. "Come here a second. Let Mommy fix your hair." Again she reached into her straw bag, this time for her hairbrush, and began to run it around the edges of the translucent visor. When she whipped out the hairbrush, the slip of paper with Mr. Kapasi's address on it fluttered away in the wind. No one but Mr. Kapasi noticed. He watched as it rose, carried higher 1140 and higher by the breeze, into the trees where the monkeys now sat, solemnly observing the scene below. Mr. Kapasi observed it too, knowing that this was the picture of the Das family he would preserve 1145 forever in his mind.

NARRATION

1. What is the **narrative perspective** of the story? Which character is filtering this experience?

2. What is the **narrator's attitude** toward the events of the story? Where do you see this attitude? Give examples throughout the text.

3. How does Mr. Kapasi's relationship with the Das family contribute to the **multiple tones** of the story?

4. How does the **narrative distance** contribute to the perspective? Give examples of word choice, description, or details that support this perspective.

IDEAS IN LITERATURE

Irony and Incongruity

IDEA BANK

Comedy

Contradiction

Contrast

Corruption

Criticism

Didacticism

Distortion

Humor

Incongruity

Irony

Juxtaposition

Loss

Morality

Observation

Opposition

Persuasion

Progress

Protest

Reformation

Ridicule

Satire

Self-Reflection

Wit

After the promise of the English Renaissance, the seventeenth century was an era of turmoil and conflict. The Civil Wars (1642–1651), fueled by hostility between Catholics and Protestants, tore the country apart. It was also a period of historical incongruities and ironies. Between 1642 and 1688, England witnessed the execution of a king, the abolition of the monarchy, a republican rebellion that turned into a military dictatorship, the restoration of a Catholic king—and finally his abdication and replacement by his Protestant daughter.

But however chaotic its development, England kept growing. Commerce and industry kept growing, too, as did the power and status of merchants. Cities grew more populated, despite outbreaks of bubonic plague. The first English newspaper began publication in 1641, and citizens became more politically aware as printed periodicals proliferated. In literature, the tempestuous century produced a remarkable range of poetry, prose, and drama, from the clever metaphysical poems of John Donne to John Milton's lofty Christian epic, *Paradise Lost* (1667).

Two of the most striking literary developments were Restoration stage comedies and the dominance of satire. After the Civil Wars began in 1642, the Puritan Parliament closed all of England's theaters: the new government thought plays were frivolous and wicked. But following the Restoration of King Charles II, newly

Universal History Archive/Getty Images

▲

This is an illustration of the events from the satirical novel *Gulliver's Travels* by Jonathan Swift. The fictional places Gulliver visits in the novel represent governments that Swift wished to criticize. In this image, Gulliver has been captured by the Lilliputians, a society of little people.

Examine the details of the illustration, including the contrast of size and proportion, between Gulliver and the Lilliputians, and explain how these details might be an example of satire.

opened theaters bustled with amoral, sexually explicit comedies like Aphra Behn's *The Rover* (1677). These sparkling, witty plays mocked unsophisticated country people, as well as fashionable city dwellers and courtesans. This period also saw a renaissance in satire, as writers used irony and incongruity to highlight social problems. For example, poet Alexander Pope's mock-heroic poem *Rape of the Lock* (1712) satirizes families feuding over trivial matters. In his darkly comic *Gulliver's Travels* (1726), Jonathan Swift satirizes the religious and political conflicts of his time with several techniques—allegory, hyperbole, and irony. In his most famous work, he turned his dark cynicism on all of humanity. Swift's "A Modest Proposal" (p. 494) remains a foundational example of political satire, as well as a model for juxtaposing a calm, rational style with a horrific subject matter. But Swift uses incongruity for a serious purpose: to highlight English oppression of the Irish.

We can recognize the same ironic and anarchic elements in contemporary satire, from *Saturday Night Live* and *The Onion* to resonant political memes on Twitter or Reddit. Much like Swift, these satirists use incongruity and ridicule to highlight—and help address—cultural and political problems. Kurt Vonnegut, whose satire "Harrison Bergeron" (p. 501) is included in this section, greatly admired Swift. We should also note that satirists of the seventeenth and early eighteenth centuries made little or no distinction between "art" (on one hand) and "social and political commentary" (on the other). They wrote with explicit social and political purposes. We can see this fusion of art and commentary in Clint Smith's contemporary poem "Counterfactual" (p. 507).

▲

Magic Ink (1989; disappearing ink on canvas) by Gianni Motti on view at a London Gallery. Another all-white painting, *Untitled* (1961) by Robert Ryman, sold at auction in 2014 for $15 million. Other artists, such as Robert Rauschenberg (1951; three-panel *White Painting*), have created similar works. In 1994, *Art*, a French play by Yasmina Reza premiered; it questions how much one would pay for "art" that is merely a blank canvas.

Should such works be considered art or satire? If neither, are people merely being duped?

A Modest Proposal

For preventing the children of poor people in Ireland,
from being a burden on their parents or country,
and for making them beneficial to the publick.

Jonathan Swift

DEA PICTURE LIBRARY/Getty Images

THE TEXT IN CONTEXT

Arguably the greatest satirist in the English language, Jonathan Swift
(1667–1745) was born in Ireland to English parents. The ambitious
Swift had a varied career as a poet, a writer of political pamphlets,
a secretary to a prominent statesman and diplomat, and an Anglican priest. But he is
mostly remembered as a writer of withering satires such as *Gulliver's Travels* (1726). His
"A Modest Proposal" provides a representative example of his technique: an "objective"
and sophisticated "projector" (similar to a modern "policy wonk") proposes a monstrous
program in a deadpan, seemingly rational voice. This comes across more clearly in the
full title: "A Modest Proposal for Preventing the Children of Poor People from Being a
Burthen to Their Parents or Country, and for Making Them Beneficial to the Publick."
But however dark the comedy, Swift's goal is to highlight the cruel, exploitative political
and economic policies of the English, who had ruled Ireland oppressively for the previous five hundred years.

A Modest Proposal

It is a melancholy object to those, who walk
through this great town, or travel in the
country, when they see the streets, the roads,
and cabbin-doors crowded with beggars of
5 the female sex, followed by three, four, or six
children, all in rags, and importuning every
passenger for an alms. These mothers,
instead of being able to work for their honest
livelihood, are forced to employ all their time
10 in stroling to beg sustenance for their helpless infants who, as they grow up, either turn
thieves for want of work, or leave their dear
native country, to fight for the Pretender in
Spain, or sell themselves to the Barbadoes.

15 I think it is agreed by all parties, that this
prodigious number of children in the arms,
or on the backs, or at the heels of their mothers, and frequently of their fathers, is in the
present deplorable state of the kingdom, a
20 very great additional grievance; and therefore whoever could find out a fair, cheap and
easy method of making these children sound
and useful members of the commonwealth,
would deserve so well of the publick, as to
25 have his statue set up for a preserver of the
nation.

But my intention is very far from being
confined to provide only for the children of

professed beggars: it is of a much greater
30 extent, and shall take in the whole number
of infants at a certain age, who are born of
parents in effect as little able to support
them, as those who demand our charity in
the streets.
35 As to my own part, having turned my
thoughts for many years upon this important subject, and maturely weighed the several schemes of our projectors, I have always
found them grossly mistaken in their com-
40 putation. It is true, a child just dropt from its
dam, may be supported by her milk, for a
solar year, with little other nourishment: at
most not above the value of two shillings,
which the mother may certainly get, or the
45 value in scraps, by her lawful occupation of
begging; and it is exactly at one year old
that I propose to provide for them in such a
manner, as, instead of being a charge upon
their parents, or the parish, or wanting food
50 and raiment for the rest of their lives, they
shall, on the contrary, contribute to the
feeding, and partly to the clothing of many
thousands.
There is likewise another great advantage
55 in my scheme, that it will prevent those voluntary abortions, and that horrid practice of
women murdering their bastard children,
alas! Too frequent among us, sacrificing the
poor innocent babes, I doubt, more to avoid
60 the expence than the shame, which would
move tears and pity in the most savage and
inhuman breast.
The number of souls in this kingdom
being usually reckoned one million and a
65 half, of these I calculate there may be about
two hundred thousand couple, whose wives
are breeders; from which number I subtract
thirty thousand couple, who are able to
maintain their own children, (although I
70 apprehend there cannot be so many under

the present distresses of the kingdom) but
this being granted, there will remain a hundred and seventy thousand breeders. I again
subtract fifty thousand, for those women
75 who miscarry, or whose children die by accident or disease within the year. There only
remain a hundred and twenty thousand children of poor parents annually born. The
question therefore is, How this number shall
80 be reared and provided for? Which, as I have
already said, under the present situation of
affairs, is utterly impossible by all the methods hitherto proposed. For we can neither
employ them in handicraft or agriculture;
85 they neither build houses, (I mean in the
country) nor cultivate land: they can very
seldom pick up a livelihood by stealing till
they arrive at six years old; except where they
are of towardly parts, although I confess they
90 learn the rudiments much earlier; during
which time they can however be properly
looked upon only as probationers; as I have
been informed by a principal gentleman
in the county of Cavan, who protested to
95 me, that he never knew above one or two
instances under the age of six, even in a part
of the kingdom so renowned for the quickest
proficiency in that art.
I am assured by our merchants, that a boy
100 or a girl, before twelve years old, is no sale-
able commodity, and even when they come
to this age, they will not yield above three
pounds, or three pounds and half a crown at
most, on the exchange; which cannot turn to
105 account either to the parents or kingdom,
the charge of nutriments and rags having
been at least four times that value.
I shall now therefore humbly propose my
own thoughts, which I hope will not be liable
110 to the least objection.
I have been assured by a very knowing
American of my acquaintance in London,

that a young healthy child well nursed, is, at a year old, a most delicious nourishing and wholesome food, whether stewed, roasted, baked, or boiled; and I make no doubt that it will equally serve in a fricasee, or a ragout.

I do therefore humbly offer it to publick consideration, that of the hundred and twenty thousand children, already computed, twenty thousand may be reserved for breed, whereof only one fourth part to be males; which is more than we allow to sheep, black cattle, or swine, and my reason is, that these children are seldom the fruits of marriage, a circumstance not much regarded by our savages, therefore, one male will be sufficient to serve four females. That the remaining hundred thousand may, at a year old, be offered in sale to the persons of quality and fortune, through the kingdom, always advising the mother to let them suck plentifully in the last month, so as to render them plump, and fat for a good table. A child will make two dishes at an entertainment for friends, and when the family dines alone, the fore or hind quarter will make a reasonable dish, and seasoned with a little pepper or salt, will be very good boiled on the fourth day, especially in winter.

I have reckoned upon a medium, that a child just born will weigh 12 pounds, and in a solar year, if tolerably nursed, encreaseth to 28 pounds.

I grant this food will be somewhat dear, and therefore very proper for landlords, who, as they have already devoured most of the parents, seem to have the best title to the children.

Infant's flesh will be in season throughout the year, but more plentiful in March, and a little before and after; for we are told by a grave author, an eminent French physician, that fish being a prolifick dyet, there are more children born in Roman Catholick countries about nine months after Lent, than at any other season; therefore, reckoning a year after Lent, the markets will be more glutted than usual, because the number of Popish infants, is at least three to one in this kingdom, and therefore it will have one other collateral advantage, by lessening the number of Papists among us.

I have already computed the charge of nursing a beggar's child (in which list I reckon all cottagers, labourers, and four-fifths of the farmers) to be about two shillings per annum, rags included; and I believe no gentleman would repine to give ten shillings for the carcass of a good fat child, which, as I have said, will make four dishes of excellent nutritive meat, when he hath only some particular friend, or his own family to dine with him. Thus the squire will learn to be a good landlord, and grow popular among his tenants, the mother will have eight shillings neat profit, and be fit for work till she produces another child.

Those who are more thrifty (as I must confess the times require) may flay the carcass; the skin of which, artificially dressed, will make admirable gloves for ladies, and summer boots for fine gentlemen.

As to our City of Dublin, shambles may be appointed for this purpose, in the most convenient parts of it, and butchers we may be assured will not be wanting; although I rather recommend buying the children alive, and dressing them hot from the knife, as we do roasting pigs.

A very worthy person, a true lover of his country, and whose virtues I highly esteem, was lately pleased in discoursing on this matter, to offer a refinement upon my scheme. He said, that many gentlemen of this kingdom, having of late destroyed their

deer, he conceived that the want of venison might be well supplied by the bodies of young lads and maidens, not exceeding four-
200 teen years of age, nor under twelve; so great a number of both sexes in every county being now ready to starve for want of work and service: and these to be disposed of by their parents if alive, or otherwise by their
205 nearest relations. But with due deference to so excellent a friend, and so deserving a patriot, I cannot be altogether in his senti-ments; for as to the males, my American acquaintance assured me from frequent
210 experience, that their flesh was generally tough and lean, like that of our schoolboys, by continual exercise, and their taste dis-agreeable, and to fatten them would not answer the charge. Then as to the females, it
215 would, I think, with humble submission, be a loss to the publick, because they soon would become breeders themselves: and besides, it is not improbable that some scrupulous peo-ple might be apt to censure such a practice,
220 (although indeed very unjustly) as a little bordering upon cruelty, which, I confess, hath always been with me the strongest objection against any project, how well soever intended.
225   But in order to justify my friend, he con-fessed, that this expedient was put into his head by the famous Psalmanaazor, a native of the island Formosa, who came from thence to London, above twenty years ago,
230 and in conversation told my friend, that in his country, when any young person hap-pened to be put to death, the executioner sold the carcass to persons of quality, as a prime dainty; and that, in his time, the body
235 of a plump girl of fifteen, who was crucified for an attempt to poison the Emperor, was sold to his imperial majesty's prime minister of state, and other great mandarins of the

court in joints from the gibbet, at four
240 hundred crowns. Neither indeed can I deny, that if the same use were made of several plump young girls in this town, who without one single groat to their fortunes, cannot stir abroad without a chair, and appear at a play-
245 house and assemblies in foreign fineries which they never will pay for, the kingdom would not be the worse.

Some persons of a desponding spirit are in great concern about that vast number of
250 poor people, who are aged, diseased, or maimed; and I have been desired to employ my thoughts what course may be taken, to ease the nation of so grievous an incum-brance. But I am not in the least pain upon
255 that matter, because it is very well known, that they are every day dying, and rotting, by cold and famine, and filth, and vermin, as fast as can be reasonably expected. And as to the young labourers, they are now in almost
260 as hopeful a condition. They cannot get work, and consequently pine away from want of nourishment, to a degree, that if at any time they are accidentally hired to com-mon labour, they have not strength to per-
265 form it, and thus the country and themselves are happily delivered from the evils to come.

I have too long digressed, and therefore shall return to my subject. I think the advan-tages by the proposal which I have made are
270 obvious and many, as well as of the highest importance.

For first, as I have already observed, it would greatly lessen the number of Papists, with whom we are yearly overrun, being the
275 principal breeders of the nation, as well as our most dangerous enemies, and who stay at home on purpose with a design to deliver the kingdom to the Pretender, hoping to take their advantage by the absence of so many
280 good Protestants, who have chosen rather to

leave their country, than stay at home and pay tithes against their conscience to an episcopal curate.

Secondly, The poorer tenants will have
285 something valuable of their own, which by law may be made liable to a distress, and help to pay their landlord's rent, their corn and cattle being already seized, and money a thing unknown.

290 Thirdly, Whereas the maintainance of a hundred thousand children, from two years old, and upwards, cannot be computed at less than ten shillings a piece per annum, the nation's stock will be thereby encreased
295 fifty thousand pounds per annum, besides the profit of a new dish, introduced to the tables of all gentlemen of fortune in the kingdom, who have any refinement in taste. And the money will circulate among our
300 selves, the goods being entirely of our own growth and manufacture.

Fourthly, The constant breeders, besides the gain of eight shillings sterling per annum by the sale of their children, will be rid of the
305 charge of maintaining them after the first year.

Fifthly, This food would likewise bring great custom to taverns, where the vintners will certainly be so prudent as to procure the
310 best receipts for dressing it to perfection; and consequently have their houses frequented by all the fine gentlemen, who justly value themselves upon their knowledge in good eating; and a skilful cook, who understands
315 how to oblige his guests, will contrive to make it as expensive as they please.

Sixthly, This would be a great inducement to marriage, which all wise nations have either encouraged by rewards, or enforced by
320 laws and penalties. It would encrease the care and tenderness of mothers towards their children, when they were sure of a settlement for life to the poor babes, provided in some sort by the publick, to their annual
325 profit instead of expence. We should soon see an honest emulation among the married women, which of them could bring the fattest child to the market. Men would become as fond of their wives, during the time of
330 their pregnancy, as they are now of their mares in foal, their cows in calf, or sows when they are ready to farrow; nor offer to beat or kick them (as is too frequent a practice) for fear of a miscarriage.

335 Many other advantages might be enumerated. For instance, the addition of some thousand carcasses in our exportation of barrel'd beef: the propagation of swine's flesh, and improvement in the art of making
340 good bacon, so much wanted among us by the great destruction of pigs, too frequent at our tables; which are no way comparable in taste or magnificence to a well grown, fat yearling child, which roasted whole will
345 make a considerable figure at a Lord Mayor's feast, or any other publick entertainment. But this, and many others, I omit, being studious of brevity.

Supposing that one thousand families in
350 this city, would be constant customers for infants flesh, besides others who might have it at merry meetings, particularly at weddings and christenings, I compute that Dublin would take off annually about twenty
355 thousand carcasses; and the rest of the kingdom (where probably they will be sold somewhat cheaper) the remaining eighty thousand.

I can think of no one objection, that will
360 possibly be raised against this proposal, unless it should be urged, that the number of people will be thereby much lessened in the kingdom. This I freely own, and was indeed one principal design in offering it to the

365 world. I desire the reader will observe, that I calculate my remedy for this one individual Kingdom of Ireland, and for no other that ever was, is, or, I think, ever can be upon Earth. Therefore let no man talk to me of
370 other expedients: Of taxing our absentees at five shillings a pound: Of using neither clothes, nor houshold furniture, except what is of our own growth and manufacture: Of utterly rejecting the materials and instru-
375 ments that promote foreign luxury: Of curing the expensiveness of pride, vanity, idleness, and gaming in our women: Of introducing a vein of parsimony, prudence and temper- ance: Of learning to love our country,
380 wherein we differ even from Laplanders, and the inhabitants of Topinamboo: Of quitting our animosities and factions, nor acting any longer like the Jews, who were murdering one another at the very moment their city
385 was taken: Of being a little cautious not to sell our country and consciences for nothing: Of teaching landlords to have at least one degree of mercy towards their tenants. Lastly, of putting a spirit of honesty, industry, and
390 skill into our shopkeepers, who, if a resolu- tion could now be taken to buy only our native goods, would immediately unite to cheat and exact upon us in the price, the measure, and the goodness, nor could ever
395 yet be brought to make one fair proposal of just dealing, though often and earnestly invited to it.

Therefore I repeat, let no man talk to me of these and the like expedients, till he hath
400 at least some glympse of hope, that there will ever be some hearty and sincere attempt to put them into practice.

But, as to myself, having been wearied out for many years with offering vain, idle,
405 visionary thoughts, and at length utterly despairing of success, I fortunately fell upon this proposal, which, as it is wholly new, so it hath something solid and real, of no expence and little trouble, full in our own power, and
410 whereby we can incur no danger in disoblig- ing England. For this kind of commodity will not bear exportation, and flesh being of too tender a consistence, to admit a long contin- uance in salt, although perhaps I could name
415 a country, which would be glad to eat up our whole nation without it.

After all, I am not so violently bent upon my own opinion, as to reject any offer, pro- posed by wise men, which shall be found
420 equally innocent, cheap, easy, and effectual. But before something of that kind shall be advanced in contradiction to my scheme, and offering a better, I desire the author or authors will be pleased maturely to consider
425 two points. First, As things now stand, how they will be able to find food and raiment for a hundred thousand useless mouths and backs. And secondly, There being a round million of creatures in humane figure
430 throughout this kingdom, whose whole sub- sistence put into a common stock, would leave them in debt two million of pounds sterling, adding those who are beggars by profession, to the bulk of farmers, cottagers
435 and labourers, with their wives and children, who are beggars in effect; I desire those poli- ticians who dislike my overture, and may perhaps be so bold to attempt an answer, that they will first ask the parents of these
440 mortals, whether they would not at this day think it a great happiness to have been sold for food at a year old, in the manner I pre- scribe, and thereby have avoided such a per- petual scene of misfortunes, as they have
445 since gone through, by the oppression of landlords, the impossibility of paying rent without money or trade, the want of com- mon sustenance, with neither house nor

clothes to cover them from the inclemencies
450 of the weather, and the most inevitable prospect of intailing the like, or greater miseries,
upon their breed for ever.

I profess in the sincerity of my heart, that
I have not the least personal interest in
455 endeavouring to promote this necessary

work, having no other motive than the publick good of my country, by advancing our
trade, providing for infants, relieving the
poor, and giving some pleasure to the rich. I
460 have no children, by which I can propose to
get a single penny; the youngest being nine
years old, and my wife past child-bearing.

For more than two decades, the Chick-fil-A ▶
cows and their successful advertising
campaign have made Chick-fil-A the number
one brand for chicken in America.

This long-running Chick-fil-A advertisement
is ironic. What is unexpected? Why is the
effect ironic?

CHARACTER

1. How are the children described?
2. What values do the **characters** represent in "A Modest Proposal"?
3. How are the mothers and children being **contrasted**?

SETTING

4. What is the **setting** of this satire?
5. How are the cultural values and beliefs of the time represented through the **setting**?

STRUCTURE

6. What is the **conflict** in "A Modest Proposal"? In what ways does this conflict set up a satire?
7. How does the narrator's "modest proposal" in the satire **contrast** with his actual proposal in the conclusion?

NARRATION

8. What is the **narrator** proposing?

9. How does the title contribute to the narrator's **tone**?

10. How do the narrator's background and **perspective** contribute to the **tone** of the text?

IDEAS IN LITERATURE: Irony and Incongruity

11. While this proposal is fictional, can you think of any government actions, programs, or proposals today that are incongruous, unintentionally ironic, or even cruel? Do they seem "reasonable" on the surface, as the narrator's ideas do here? Explain.

PUTTING IT ALL TOGETHER

12. Explain how Swift uses contrasts of diction, imagery, and details to convey a satirical message.

Harrison Bergeron
Kurt Vonnegut

THE TEXT IN CONTEXT

A prolific writer and pioneer of postmodern fiction, Kurt Vonnegut (1922–2007) was profoundly affected by his experience as a U.S. soldier in World War II. Vonnegut was captured by the Germans in 1944 and interned at a Dresden, Germany, slaughterhouse, where he witnessed the devastating Allied bombing of the city in 1945. This experience became the basis for his most well-known work, *Slaughterhouse Five* (1969), a novel that deployed postmodern literary techniques: black satirical comedy; an absurdist, nonlinear narrative; metafictional commentary that highlights the story's status as fiction; elements of science fiction and fantasy that undermine the book's "realism." Not surprisingly, war was one of Vonnegut's main themes, along with technology, individuality, conformity, religion, and hypocrisy. His other books include *Player Piano* (1952), *Cats Cradle* (1963), *Breakfast of Champions* (1973), and *Timequake* (1997). Vonnegut often incorporated science fiction elements into his works for satirical purposes, as is the case in his short story "Harrison Bergeron."

Ulf Andersen/Getty Images

Harrison Bergeron

The year was 2081, and everybody was finally equal. They weren't only equal before God and the law. They were equal every which way. Nobody was smarter than any-
5 body else. Nobody was better looking than anybody else. Nobody was stronger or quicker than anybody else. All this equality was due to the 211th, 212th, and 213th Amendments to the Constitution, and to the
10 unceasing vigilance of agents of the United States Handicapper General.

Some things about living still weren't quite right, though. April for instance, still drove people crazy by not being springtime.
15 And it was in that clammy month that the H-G men took George and Hazel Bergeron's fourteen-year-old son, Harrison, away.

It was tragic, all right, but George and Hazel couldn't think about it very hard. Hazel had a
20 perfectly average intelligence, which meant she couldn't think about anything except in short bursts. And George, while his intelligence was way above normal, had a little mental handicap radio in his ear. He was required by
25 law to wear it at all times. It was tuned to a government transmitter. Every twenty seconds or so, the transmitter would send out some sharp noise to keep people like George from taking unfair advantage of their brains.

30 George and Hazel were watching television. There were tears on Hazel's cheeks, but she'd forgotten for the moment what they were about.

On the television screen were ballerinas.
35 A buzzer sounded in George's head. His thoughts fled in panic, like bandits from a burglar alarm.

"That was a real pretty dance, that dance they just did," said Hazel.
40 "Huh" said George.

"That dance—it was nice," said Hazel.

"Yup," said George. He tried to think a lit-tle about the ballerinas. They weren't really very good—no better than anybody else
45 would have been, anyway. They were bur-dened with sashweights and bags of bird-shot, and their faces were masked, so that no one, seeing a free and graceful gesture or a pretty face, would feel like something the cat
50 drug in. George was toying with the vague notion that maybe dancers shouldn't be handicapped. But he didn't get very far with it before another noise in his ear radio scat-tered his thoughts.

55 George winced. So did two out of the eight ballerinas.

Hazel saw him wince. Having no mental handicap herself, she had to ask George what the latest sound had been.
60 "Sounded like somebody hitting a milk bottle with a ball peen hammer," said George.

"I'd think it would be real interesting, hearing all the different sounds," said Hazel
65 a little envious. "All the things they think up."

"Um," said George.

"Only, if I was Handicapper General, you know what I would do?" said Hazel. Hazel, as a matter of fact, bore a strong resemblance to
70 the Handicapper General, a woman named Diana Moon Glampers. "If I was Diana Moon Glampers," said Hazel, "I'd have chimes on Sunday—just chimes. Kind of in honor of religion."
75 "I could think, if it was just chimes," said George.

"Well—maybe make 'em real loud," said Hazel. "I think I'd make a good Handicapper General."
80 "Good as anybody else," said George.

"Who knows better than I do what normal is?" said Hazel.

"Right," said George. He began to think glimmeringly about his abnormal son who
85 was now in jail, about Harrison, but a twenty-one-gun salute in his head stopped that.

"Boy!" said Hazel, "that was a doozy, wasn't it?"
90   It was such a doozy that George was white and trembling, and tears stood on the rims of his red eyes. Two of of the eight ballerinas had collapsed to the studio floor, were holding their temples.
95   "All of a sudden you look so tired," said Hazel. "Why don't you stretch out on the sofa, so's you can rest your handicap bag on the pillows, honeybunch." She was referring to the forty-seven pounds of birdshot in a
100 canvas bag, which was padlocked around George's neck. "Go on and rest the bag for a little while," she said. "I don't care if you're not equal to me for a while."

George weighed the bag with his hands. "I
105 don't mind it," he said. "I don't notice it any more. It's just a part of me."

"You been so tired lately—kind of wore out," said Hazel. "If there was just some way we could make a little hole in the bottom of
110 the bag, and just take out a few of them lead balls. Just a few."

"Two years in prison and two thousand dollars fine for every ball I took out," said George. "I don't call that a bargain."
115   "If you could just take a few out when you came home from work," said Hazel. "I mean—you don't compete with anybody around here. You just sit around."

"If I tried to get away with it," said George,
120 "then other people'd get away with it—and pretty soon we'd be right back to the dark ages again, with everybody competing against everybody else. You wouldn't like that, would you?"

125   "I'd hate it," said Hazel.

"There you are," said George. "The minute people start cheating on laws, what do you think happens to society?"

If Hazel hadn't been able to come up with
130 an answer to this question, George couldn't have supplied one. A siren was going off in his head.

"Reckon it'd fall all apart," said Hazel.

"What would?" said George blankly.
135   "Society," said Hazel uncertainly. "Wasn't that what you just said?"

"Who knows?" said George.

The television program was suddenly interrupted for a news bulletin. It wasn't
140 clear at first as to what the bulletin was about, since the announcer, like all announcers, had a serious speech impediment. For about half a minute, and in a state of high excitement, the announcer tried to say,
145 "Ladies and Gentlemen."

He finally gave up, handed the bulletin to a ballerina to read.

"That's all right—" Hazel said of the announcer, "he tried. That's the big thing. He
150 tried to do the best he could with what God gave him. He should get a nice raise for trying so hard."

"Ladies and Gentlemen," said the ballerina, reading the bulletin. She must have
155 been extraordinarily beautiful, because the mask she wore was hideous. And it was easy to see that she was the strongest and most graceful of all the dancers, for her handicap bags were as big as those worn by two-
160 hundred pound men.

And she had to apologize at once for her voice, which was a very unfair voice for a woman to use. Her voice was a warm, luminous, timeless melody. "Excuse me—" she
165 said, and she began again, making her voice absolutely uncompetitive.

"Harrison Bergeron, age fourteen," she said in a grackle squawk, "has just escaped from jail, where he was held on suspicion of
170 plotting to overthrow the government. He is a genius and an athlete, is under-handicapped, and should be regarded as extremely dangerous."

A police photograph of Harrison Bergeron
175 was flashed on the screen—upside down, then sideways, upside down again, then right side up. The picture showed the full length of Harrison against a background calibrated in feet and inches. He was exactly seven feet tall.

180 The rest of Harrison's appearance was Halloween and hardware. Nobody had ever born heavier handicaps. He had outgrown hindrances faster than the H-G men could think them up. Instead of a little ear radio for
185 a mental handicap, he wore a tremendous pair of earphones, and spectacles with thick wavy lenses. The spectacles were intended to make him not only half blind, but to give him whanging headaches besides.

190 Scrap metal was hung all over him. Ordinarily, there was a certain symmetry, a military neatness to the handicaps issued to strong people, but Harrison looked like a walking junkyard. In the race of life, Harrison
195 carried three hundred pounds.

And to offset his good looks, the H-G men required that he wear at all times a red rubber ball for a nose, keep his eyebrows shaved off, and cover his even white teeth with black
200 caps at snaggle-tooth random.

"If you see this boy," said the ballerina, "do not—I repeat, do not—try to reason with him."

There was the shriek of a door being torn
205 from its hinges.

Screams and barking cries of consternation came from the television set. The photograph of Harrison Bergeron on the screen jumped again and again, as though dancing
210 to the tune of an earthquake.

George Bergeron correctly identified the earthquake, and well he might have—for many was the time his own home had danced to the same crashing tune. "My
215 God—" said George, "that must be Harrison!"

The realization was blasted from his mind instantly by the sound of an automobile collision in his head.

When George could open his eyes again,
220 the photograph of Harrison was gone. A living, breathing Harrison filled the screen.

Clanking, clownish, and huge, Harrison stood—in the center of the studio. The knob of the uprooted studio door was still in his
225 hand. Ballerinas, technicians, musicians, and announcers cowered on their knees before him, expecting to die.

"I am the Emperor!" cried Harrison. "Do you hear? I am the Emperor! Everybody must
230 do what I say at once!" He stamped his foot and the studio shook.

"Even as I stand here" he bellowed, "crippled, hobbled, sickened—I am a greater ruler than any man who ever lived! Now watch me
235 become what I can become!"

Harrison tore the straps of his handicap harness like wet tissue paper, tore straps guaranteed to support five thousand pounds.

Harrison's scrap-iron handicaps crashed
240 to the floor.

Harrison thrust his thumbs under the bar of the padlock that secured his head harness. The bar snapped like celery. Harrison smashed his headphones and spectacles
245 against the wall.

He flung away his rubber-ball nose, revealed a man that would have awed Thor, the god of thunder.

"I shall now select my Empress!" he
250 said, looking down on the cowering people.

"Let the first woman who dares rise to her feet claim her mate and her throne!"

A moment passed, and then a ballerina arose, swaying like a willow.

255 Harrison plucked the mental handicap from her ear, snapped off her physical handicaps with marvelous delicacy. Last of all he removed her mask.

She was blindingly beautiful.

260 "Now—" said Harrison, taking her hand, "shall we show the people the meaning of the word dance? Music!" he commanded.

The musicians scrambled back into their chairs, and Harrison stripped them of their 265 handicaps, too. "Play your best," he told them, "and I'll make you barons and dukes and earls."

The music began. It was normal at first— cheap, silly, false. But Harrison snatched two 270 musicians from their chairs, waved them like batons as he sang the music as he wanted it played. He slammed them back into their chairs.

The music began again and was much 275 improved.

Harrison and his Empress merely listened to the music for a while—listened gravely, as though synchronizing their heartbeats with it.

They shifted their weights to their toes.

280 Harrison placed his big hands on the girls tiny waist, letting her sense the weightlessness that would soon be hers.

And then, in an explosion of joy and grace, into the air they sprang!

285 Not only were the laws of the land abandoned, but the law of gravity and the laws of motion as well.

They reeled, whirled, swiveled, flounced, capered, gamboled, and spun.

290 They leaped like deer on the moon.

The studio ceiling was thirty feet high, but each leap brought the dancers nearer to it.

It became their obvious intention to kiss the ceiling. They kissed it.

295 And then, neutraling gravity with love and pure will, they remained suspended in air inches below the ceiling, and they kissed each other for a long, long time.

It was then that Diana Moon Glampers, 300 the Handicapper General, came into the studio with a double-barreled ten-gauge shotgun. She fired twice, and the Emperor and the Empress were dead before they hit the floor.

305 Diana Moon Glampers loaded the gun again. She aimed it at the musicians and told them they had ten seconds to get their handicaps back on.

It was then that the Bergerons' television 310 tube burned out.

Hazel turned to comment about the blackout to George. But George had gone out into the kitchen for a can of beer.

George came back in with the beer, 315 paused while a handicap signal shook him up. And then he sat down again. "You been crying" he said to Hazel.

"Yup," she said.

"What about?" he said.

320 "I forget," she said. "Something real sad on television."

"What was it?" he said.

"It's all kind of mixed up in my mind," said Hazel.

325 "Forget sad things," said George.

"I always do," said Hazel.

"That's my girl," said George. He winced. There was the sound of a rivetting gun in his head.

330 "Gee—I could tell that one was a doozy," said Hazel.

"You can say that again," said George.

"Gee—" said Hazel, "I could tell that one was a doozy."

©Barry Kite

Helen Birch Bartlett Memorial Collection, The Art Institute of Chicago

▲

Barry Kite's *Sunday Afternoon, Looking for the Car* (left) is a contemporary parody of Georges Seurat's 1884 Impressionistic work *A Sunday on La Grande Jatte* (right, oil on canvas). A parody is a humorous re-creation of a serious work.

———

Look carefully at both images. How does Kite's parody draw on incongruity and irony to present commentary or criticism about contemporary society? What is Kite's message?

CHARACTER

1. Who is the **protagonist**? Who is the **antagonist**? Explain how these characters are in conflict with one another.

2. Describe the ballerinas. Explain how George reacts to the ballerina and how this reaction contributes to his **perspective**.

3. Explain how Harrison uses his **agency**. What do his speech and actions reveal about his perspective?

SETTING

4. What is the **setting** of the story? How does the year contribute to the perspective of the characters?

5. Most of the action takes place when George and Hazel are watching TV. Explain how this impacts their agency with the outcome of the events.

STRUCTURE

6. What is the **conflict** in the story?

7. How are the characters contrasted? Explain how this contrast contributes to the conflict and the resolution of the story.

8. Harrison and the ballerina are archetypal. Identify and describe the **archetypes**.

NARRATION

9. What is the **point of view** in the story? How does this point of view contribute to your understanding of the text?

10. Explain how the **narrative perspective** contributes to the **tone** of the story.

IDEAS IN LITERATURE: Irony and Incongruity

11. Most of the incongruity in the story is ironically revealed through the seemingly congruent idea that everyone is the same. In the story, everyone is equal. Explain why the concept that all people are equal would create conflict among individuals and lead to inequalities in society.

PUTTING IT ALL TOGETHER

12. The ending of the story is difficult. The resolution and conclusion of the story both resolve the conflict and leave the reader with a conflicting conclusion. Explain how the conflict is resolved but the ending of the story is not concluded.

Counterfactual
Clint Smith

THE TEXT IN CONTEXT

Christopher Record/Davidson College

A former high school English teacher, Clint Smith (b. 1988) is a poet, journalist, activist, and staff writer for the *Atlantic* magazine. He published his first collection of poetry, *Counting Descent*, in 2016. In 2021, he published *How the Word Is Passed: A Reckoning with the History of Slavery Across America*, a book of narrative nonfiction. In the autobiographical poem "Counterfactual," Smith dramatizes (in his words) the "conversations" that Black parents have to have with their children, teaching them to navigate a world that is often taught to fear them — what is colloquially known in Black communities as "the talk." The poem also illustrates how Smith integrates explicit social commentary into poetry.

Counterfactual

One night
when I was twelve years old
on a field trip some place
I can't remember, my friends
5 and I bought supersoakers

and turned the hotel parking lot
into our arena of saturation.
We hid behind cars
running through the darkness
10 that lay between the streetlights.
Seditious laughter ubiquitous
across the pavement.

Within ten minutes
my father came outside
15 grabbed me by the forearm
and led me inside to our room
with an unfamiliar grip.

Before I could invoke objection,
acquaint him with how foolish
20 he had made me look in front
of my friends,
he derided me for being so naïve.

Told me I couldn't be out here
acting the same as these white boys—
25 *can't be pretending to shoot guns*
can't be running in the dark
can't be hiding behind anything
other than your own teeth.

I know now how scared
30 he must have been,
how easily I could have fallen
into the obsolescence of the night.
That some man would mistake
this water for a good reason
35 to wash all of this away.

The Talk ©Michael D'Antuono, ArtandResponse.com

▲

The Talk (2015) is an oil painting on canvas by Michael D'Antuono. The painting depicts parents warning their son about the dangers many Black teenagers experience in America.

_____

Consider the images in the painting. How do the incongruent images combine and contribute to your interpretation of *The Talk*?

CHARACTER

1. Who is the **speaker**? How do the speaker's speech and other details reveal his **perspective**?

2. What do the father's and son's contrasting traits reveal about them, both individually and in their relationship with others?

3. How do the poem's details convey the complexities within this parent-child relationship?

SETTING

4. Explain how the time of day contributes to the **setting** and how that affects your interpretation of the poem.

5. How does the description of the setting create an **atmosphere** and a **mood**? How does this affect your interpretation of the poem?

STRUCTURE

6. Give an example of **juxtaposition** in "Counterfactual." How does juxtaposition contribute to your interpretation of the poem?

7. What is the **conflict** in the poem? How does the conflict reflect the assumptions and cultural norms represented by the characters?

NARRATION

8. How do the speaker's background and **perspective** shape the tone of the poem?

9. Explain how the details and imagery in the poem suggest the **speaker's** contrasting **tones**. Provide textual details that illustrate the contrast.

10. Explain how a shift in **perspective** in the poem indicates the narrator's change.

IDEAS IN LITERATURE: Irony and Incongruity

11. The subject of this poem is a common one — the idea that an authority figure could misconstrue or mistake an action for something else based on assumptions. Reflect on your school or community, and then explain an instance when assumptions led to unintended consequences.

PUTTING IT ALL TOGETHER

12. The poem concludes with an image. How does the final image contrast with earlier images in "Counterfactual"? How does it contribute to your interpretation of the poem?

IDEAS IN LITERATURE
Reason and Order

The "Glorious Revolution" of 1688, during which King William III and Queen Mary II ascended the throne, ushered in a period of relative stability in England. The new monarchs agreed to many parliamentary restrictions on royal authority. These changes brought the monarchy into greater harmony with the principles of democracy and individual rights. This political progress matched many other developments at the time. For example, the era witnessed the start of the Industrial Revolution, as the production of goods began shifting from tradespeople to factories powered by coal and steam. Consumer culture took hold. People followed fashion trends and bought new products. The public grew more self-aware and engaged through popular magazines like the *Spectator*.

This new emphasis on individual reason and agency reflected powerful new ideas. Following Sir Francis Bacon, philosopher John Locke (1632–1704) argued that empirical observation and reason were the foundation of knowledge; he explored metaphysics, a branch of philosophy that examines abstract principles such as "being" and "knowing." The physicist and mathematician Isaac Newton (1643–1727) published *Philosophiæ Naturalis Principia Mathematica* (1687),

IDEA BANK

Abstraction
Aestheticism
Art
Balance
Control
Convention
Formality
Frivolity
Intellect
Metaphysics
Objectivity
Order
Ornament
Reality
Reason
Religion
Science
Theory

AF Fotografie/Alamy

◀ The image of the "Great Chain of Being" is derived from ancient philosophers like Plato and Aristotle. The illustration depicts the hierarchy of living things. God sits at the top of the hierarchy, with angels below him, and humans, animals, and plants following.

How does this illustration suggest reason, order, and hierarchy of beings?

which established the principles of classical mechanics. Newton sought order and harmony in nature — for example, in the way that both apples and planets are subject to the same gravitational forces.

This period is often called "the age of reason" or "the neoclassical period." Artists and poets privileged reason over passion, which they perceived as dangerous. Many looked to classical Roman writers for models of excellence. But if they looked backward in aesthetics, they gazed forward to new ideas in science, philosophy, technology, and economics. As the poet Alexander Pope (1688–1744) wrote, "Nature, and Nature's laws lay hid in night / God said, Let Newton be! and all was light." In other words, individuals can use reason to discover the patterns and laws of the universe. If Newton tried to discover reason and order in the natural world, Pope held similar goals for his poetry. His style reflects that aspiration, as evident in the excerpt from his 1711 "An Essay on Criticism" (p. 513). The perfectly balanced couplets rhyme; each word, image, metaphor, and line builds to a harmonious whole; the logical progression appeals as much to reason as it does to the ear or the emotions. That style also expresses Pope's version of the great chain of being: the belief that all of nature is arranged in a perfect hierarchy that ascends from minerals, vegetables, and animals, up to the divine. As Pope writes in his "Essay on Man" (1733), "Nothing is foreign; parts relate to whole; / One all-extending, all-preserving soul / Connects each being, greatest with the least."

We can see the aesthetic legacy of this era in the architecture of U.S. government buildings such as the Capitol and the Supreme Court: neoclassical architecture designed to evoke reason, order, and stability. In fact, the Founders sought to emulate a classical Roman republic in America. They also drew heavily on the political writings of John Locke in the Declaration of Independence and the Constitution. Today, when we refer to concepts like the importance of tolerance or the existence of natural human rights, we are drawing on the ideas of Locke. Our market-based economy, faith in technology, and consumer society derive from this period, as does our very concept of "news." In many ways, our entire media- and advertisement-saturated culture originates from the flood of newspapers, tracts, pamphlets, magazines, and other print media that began in the sixteenth and seventeenth centuries.

"Sophia" is an AI human-like robot developed by the Hong Kong–based humanoid robotics company Hanson Robotics. AI experts continue to discuss the ethical, technical, social, and political issues related to AI.

Are we living in the new age of reason? As we engage with scientific progress, how will future inventions offer both exciting innovations and encourage cautious trepidation?

FABRICE COFFRINI/AFP/Getty Images

from An Essay on Criticism
Alexander Pope

THE TEXT IN CONTEXT

Even if you are unfamiliar with the English poet Alexander Pope (1688–1744), you know some of his more famous lines: "A little learning is a dang'rous thing"; "Fools rush in where angels fear to tread"; "Hope springs eternal in the human breast"; "To err is human; to forgive, divine." No English poet better exemplifies the eighteenth-century desire for reason and order than Pope. Even his chosen poetic form — rhyming pairs of iambic pentameter lines, or "heroic couplets" — matches the rationality and harmony that often emerges as a theme in his poems.

Indeed, this was deliberate. As Pope writes in "An Essay on Criticism," his neoclassical manifesto on poetry and aesthetic judgment, "The Sound must seem an Echo to the Sense." In other words, the form and style of a text must align with its meaning. In the following excerpt from that poem, the speaker addresses problems of human judgment, the need for humility when pursuing knowledge, and the idea that art — poetry, architecture, or any other form — should be "bold, and regular."

from An Essay on Criticism

Of all the causes which conspire to blind
Man's erring judgment, and misguide the mind,
What the weak head with strongest bias rules,
Is pride, the never-failing vice of fools.
5 Whatever Nature has in worth denied,
She gives in large recruits of needful pride;
For as in bodies, thus in souls, we find
What wants in blood and spirits, swell'd with wind;
Pride, where wit fails, steps in to our defence,
10 And fills up all the mighty void of sense!
If once right reason drives that cloud away,
Truth breaks upon us with resistless day;
Trust not yourself; but your defects to know,
Make use of ev'ry friend—and ev'ry foe.

15   A little learning is a dang'rous thing;
Drink deep, or taste not the Pierian spring:

There shallow draughts intoxicate the brain,
And drinking largely sobers us again.
Fir'd at first sight with what the Muse imparts,
20 In fearless youth we tempt the heights of arts,
While from the bounded level of our mind,
Short views we take, nor see the lengths behind,
But more advanc'd, behold with strange surprise
New, distant scenes of endless science rise!
25 So pleas'd at first, the tow'ring Alps we try,
Mount o'er the vales, and seem to tread the sky;
Th' eternal snows appear already past,
And the first clouds and mountains seem the last;
But those attain'd, we tremble to survey
30 The growing labours of the lengthen'd way,
Th' increasing prospect tires our wand'ring eyes,
Hills peep o'er hills, and Alps on Alps arise!

    A perfect judge will read each work of wit
With the same spirit that its author writ,
35 Survey the whole, nor seek slight faults to find,
Where nature moves, and rapture warms the mind;
Nor lose, for that malignant dull delight,
The gen'rous pleasure to be charm'd with wit.
But in such lays as neither ebb, nor flow,
40 Correctly cold, and regularly low,
That shunning faults, one quiet tenour keep;
We cannot blame indeed—but we may sleep.
In wit, as nature, what affects our hearts
Is not th' exactness of peculiar parts;
45 'Tis not a lip, or eye, we beauty call,
But the joint force and full result of all.
Thus when we view some well-proportion'd dome
(The world's just wonder, and ev'n thine, O Rome!),
No single parts unequally surprise;
50 All comes united to th' admiring eyes;
No monstrous height, or breadth, or length appear;
The whole at once is bold, and regular.

Jack Corbett/CartoonStock

CartoonStock.com

◀ Twentieth-century cartoonist Jack Corbett alludes to a well-known couplet from Alexendar Pope's "An Essay on Criticism" in a contemporary comic.

What is the joke in this cartoon? Why is the term "know-it-all" ironic in this context? How would you explain the irony?

CHARACTER

1. How do the **speaker's** diction and details convey a particular perspective?

2. What do the images of "Nature" suggest about "her" as a character?

3. What details and description characterize the "perfect judge"?

SETTING

4. How does the poem use imagery to evoke a sense of time and place?

5. How does this poetic **setting** contribute to your interpretation of the poem?

STRUCTURE

6. Give an example of a **contrast** in the poem. Then explain how this contrast contributes to your interpretation.

7. Give an example of **juxtaposition** and explain how it contributes to your interpretation of the poem.

NARRATION

8. How do the diction and details of the poem express the tone of the **speaker**?

9. Explain how the imagery and syntax contribute to the tone of the poem.

IDEAS IN LITERATURE: Reason and Order

10. Pope reflects on taste, wit, and knowledge. He says, "A little learning is a dang'rous thing; Drink deep, or taste not the Pierian spring." How do you interpret this couplet? What might it mean for your own education?

PUTTING IT ALL TOGETHER

11. The couplets in the poem contribute to the unique structure. Consider how this structure develops a progression of ideas that contributes to your interpretation of the poem.

from The Nickel Boys
Colson Whitehead

Axel Koester/Corbis/Getty Images

THE TEXT IN CONTEXT

Author Colson Whitehead (b. 1969) has written eight novels, including *The Intuitionist* (1999), *Zone One* (2011), *The Underground Railroad* (2016), and *Harlem Shuffle* (2021). Much of Whitehead's writing focuses on themes of race and American history, as in the case of this excerpt from his novel *The Nickel Boys* (2019). Whitehead based the story on the Arthur G. Dozier School for Boys in Florida, a juvenile detention and reform institution known for its brutality, including torture and murder. After the school closed in 2011, investigators documented almost one hundred deaths at the school and over fifty burial sites on the school's grounds. In the selection that follows, the protagonist Elwood Curtis witnesses a fixed boxing match.

Content Note: This story includes the N-word, which we have chosen to reprint in this textbook to accurately reflect Whitehead's original intent, as well as the culture depicted in the story. We recognize that this word has a long history as a disrespectful and deeply hurtful expression when used by white people toward Black people. Whitehead's choice to use this word relates not only to that history but also to a larger cultural tradition in which the N-word can take on different meanings, emphasize shared experience, and be repurposed as a term of endearment within Black communities. While the use of that word in Whitehead's context might not be hurtful, the use of it in our current context very often is. Be mindful of context, both that of the characters in the story and yours, as you read and discuss this text.

from The Nickel Boys

The boys rooted for Griff, even though he
was a miserable bully who jimmied and
pried at their weaknesses and made up
weaknesses if he couldn't find any, such as
5 calling you a "knock-kneed piece of shit"
even if your knees had never knocked your
whole life. He tripped them and laughed at
the ensuing pratfalls and slapped them
around when he could get away with it. He
10 punked them out, dragging them into dark
rooms. He smelled like a horse and made fun
of their mothers, which was pretty low given

the general motherlessness of the student population. Griff stole their desserts on mul-
15 tiple occasions—swiped from trays with a grin—even if the desserts in question were no great shakes; it was the principle. The boys rooted for Griff because he was going to represent the colored half of Nickel at the
20 annual boxing match, and, no matter what he did the rest of the year, the day of the fight he would be all of them in one black body and he was going to knock that white boy out.
25   If Griff spat teeth before that happened, swell.

The Nickel Academy was a reform school for boys: juvenile offenders, wards of the state, orphans, runaways who'd lit out to get
30 away from mothers who entertained men for money, or to escape rummy fathers who came into their rooms in the middle of the night. Some of them had stolen money, cussed at their teachers, or damaged public
35 property. They told stories about bloody pool-hall fights or uncles who sold moonshine. A bunch of them were sent there for offenses they'd never heard of: malingering, mopery, incorrigibility. Words the boys didn't under-
40 stand, but what was the point when their meaning was clear enough: Nickel.

The combat served as a kind of mollifying spell, to tide them over through the daily humiliations. The colored boys had held the
45 boxing title for fifteen years, since 1949. Old hands on the staff still remembered the last white champion and talked him up. Terry (Doc) Burns had been an anvil-handed good old boy from a musty corner of Suwannee
50 County, who'd been sent to Nickel for stran-gling a neighbor's chickens. Twenty-one chickens, to be exact, because "they were out to get him." Pain had rolled off Doc Burns like rain from a slate roof. After he returned to
55 the free world, the white boys who advanced

to the final fight were pikers, so wobbly that over the years the tall tales about the former champion had grown more and more extrav-agant: nature had gifted Doc Burns with an
60 unnaturally long reach; his legendary combo had swatted down every comer and rattled windows. In fact, Doc Burns had been beaten and ill-treated by so many in his life—family and strangers alike—that by the time he
65 arrived at Nickel all punishments were gen-tle breezes.

This was Griff's first term on the boxing team. He'd arrived at Nickel in February, right after the previous champ, Axel Parks, turned
70 eighteen and was released back into the free world. Griff's emergence as the baddest brother on campus had made him Axel's nat-ural successor. He was a giant, broad-chested and hunched like a big brown bear; his
75 daddy, it was said, was on a chain gang in Alabama for murdering his mother, making Griff's meanness a handed-down thing. Outside the ring, he made a hobby of terror-izing the weaker boys, the boys without
80 friends, the weepy ones. Inside the ring, his prey stepped right up, so he didn't have to waste time hunting. Like an electric toaster or an automated washing machine, boxing was a modern convenience that made his
85 life easier.

The coach for the colored team was a Mississippian named Max David, who worked in the school garage. He got an enve-lope at the end of the year for imparting
90 what he'd learned during his welterweight stint. Max David made his pitch to Griff early in the summer. "My first fight made me cockeyed," he said. "And my farewell fight set my eyes right again, so trust me when I say
95 this sport will break you down to make you better, and that's a fact." Griff smiled. He pul-verized and unmanned his opponents with cruel inevitability through autumn. He was

not graceful. He was not a scientist. He was a
100 powerful instrument of violence, and that
sufficed.

Given the typical length of enrollment at
Nickel, most students were around for only
one or two fighting seasons. As the cham-
105 pionship approached, the boys had to be
schooled in the importance of those December
matches—the prelims within your dorm, the
matches between your dorm's best guy and
the best sluggers from the other two dorms,
110 and then the bout between the best black
fighter and whatever chump the white guys
put up. The championship was the boys' sole
acquaintance with justice at Nickel.

Trevor Nickel had instituted the matches
115 in 1946, soon after he came on as the director of the Florida Industrial School for Boys,
which was opened by the state in 1899.
Nickel had never run a school before; his
background was in agriculture. He'd made an
120 impression at Klan meetings, however, with
his impromptu speeches on moral improvement and the value of work, the disposition
of young souls in need of care. The right
people remembered his passion when an
125 opening came up. His first Christmas at the
school gave the county a chance to witness
his improvements. Everything that needed a
new coat of paint got a new coat of paint, the
regular beatings were relocated to a small,
130 white utility building, nicknamed the White
House, and the dark cells were briefly converted to more innocent use. Had the good
people of Eleanor, Florida, seen the industrial
fan that was kept in the White House to
135 mask the sound of the screams, they might
have had a question or two, but that was not
part of the tour.

Nickel, a longtime boxing evangelist, had
steered a lobbying group for the sport's
140 expansion in the Olympics. Boxing had
always been popular at the school, but the

new director took its elevation as his remit.
The athletics budget, long an easy target for
directors on the skim, was rejiggered to pay
145 for regulation equipment and to bolster the
coaching staff. Nickel had maintained a
general interest in fitness. He'd possessed a
fervent belief in the miracle of a human
specimen in top shape, and had often
150 watched the boys shower to monitor the
progress of their physical education.

"The director?" Elwood asked, when
Turner told him that last part.

"Where do you think Dr. Campbell got
155 that trick from?" Turner said. Nickel was
gone now, but Dr. Campbell, the school psychologist, was known to loiter at the white
boys' showers to pick his "dates." "All these
dirty old men got a club together."

160 Elwood had met Turner shortly after his
arrival at Nickel. In the mess hall, which was
loud with the rumble and roil of juvenile
activity, Turner had bobbed in his own pocket
of calm. Over time, Elwood saw that he was
165 both always at home wherever he found
himself and also seemed like he shouldn't be
there, inside and above at the same time, a
part and apart.

They became friends in the school infir-
170 mary. Turner had swallowed soap powder
and made himself sick to get out of his work
assignment, and Elwood was recovering from
his first White House beating. On his second
day at Nickel, Elwood had had the dumb idea
175 to break up a fight. The school's superintendent, Spencer, didn't care who'd started it
or who'd tried to stop it, and had whipped
the lot of them. Elwood had come to in the
school hospital. The beating had embedded
180 bits of his dungarees into his skin, and it
took the doctor two hours to remove the
fibres. It was a duty that the doctor had to
perform from time to time. Tweezers did
the trick.

185 Now Elwood and Turner were hanging out on the bleachers, while Griff sparred with Cherry, a mulatto who had taken up boxing as a matter of pedagogy, to teach others how not to speak about his white mother. He was 190 quick and lithe and Griff clobbered him.

Catching Griff at his regimen was a favorite occupation those early days in December. Boys from the colored dormitories made the rounds, as did the white scouts from down the hill 195 who wanted the skinny. Griff had been excused from his kitchen shift since Labor Day to train. It was a spectacle. Max David kept him on a diet of raw eggs and oats, and stored a jug of what he claimed was goat blood in the ice- 200 box. When the coach administered doses, Griff swallowed the stuff with a lot of theatre, then mortified the heavy bag in revenge.

Turner had seen Axel fight two years prior. He had been slow on his feet but as 205 solid and abiding as an old stone bridge; he had weathered what the skies decreed. Contrary to Griff, with his mealy disposition, he'd been kind and protective of the smaller kids. "I wonder where he is now," Turner said. 210 "That nigger didn't have a lick of sense. Making things worse for himself, probably, wherever he is."

Cherry wavered and sank on his ass. Griff spat out his mouthpiece and bellowed. His 215 friend and training companion Black Mike, a wiry youth from Opelousas, stepped into the sparring ring and held Griff's hand up like Lady Liberty's torch.

The likely white contender was a boy 220 named Big Chet, who came from a clan of swamp people and was a bit of a creature. "Do you think Griff'll knock him down?" Elwood asked.

"Look at those arms, man," Turner said. 225 "Those things are pistons. Or smoked hams."

To see Griff quiver with unspent energy after a match, two younger boys unlacing his gloves like retainers, it was hard to imagine how the giant could lose. Which was why, 230 two days later, Turner sat up in surprise when he heard Superintendent Spencer tell Griff to take a dive.

Turner was napping in the warehouse loft, where he'd made a nest among crates of 235 industrial scrubbing powder. Turner had warehouse detail, so none of the staff bugged him when he went alone into the big storage room. No supervisors, no students—just him, a pillow, an Army blanket, and a transis- 240 tor radio. It was his second stint at Nickel, after a brief free-world excursion that had ended when he threw a concrete block through a windshield. The owner of the car, a dumb redneck, had had it coming; the state 245 of Florida thought otherwise. Turner's parents were dead, and there was no one else to speak for him. The loft was a little place he'd carved out for himself. He spent a couple of hours a week up there.

250 The closing of the warehouse door woke him. Then came Griff's dumb donkey voice: "What is it, Mr. Spencer, sir?"

"How's that training coming along, Griff? Good old Max says you're a natural."

255 Turner frowned. Any time a white man asked you about yourself, he was about to f*** you over. Especially Spencer, who never passed on a chance to send a boy to the White House for a licking or to one of the 260 third-floor cells for an attitude adjustment in solitary confinement. Griff was so stupid that he didn't know what was happening. In class, the boy had struggled over two plus three, like he didn't know how many 265 damned fingers he had on his hand. Some foolhardies in the schoolhouse had laughed at him then, and Griff had stuck their heads into toilets, one by one, over the next week.

Turner's assessment was correct: Griff 270 was unable to grasp the reason for the secret

meeting. Spencer expounded on the importance of the fight, the tradition of the
December match. Then he hinted, "Good
sportsmanship means letting the other team
275 win sometimes." He tried euphemism: "It's
like when a tree branch has to bend so it
doesn't break." He appealed to fatalism:
"Sometimes it don't work out, no matter how
much you try." But Griff was too thick. *Yes,*
280 *sir . . . I suppose that's right, Mr. Spencer . . . I*
believe that is the case, sir. Finally, the superintendent told Griff that his black ass had to
take a dive in the third round or else they'd
take him out back.

285   "Yes, sir, Mr. Spencer," Griff said. Up in the
loft Turner couldn't see Griff's face, so he
didn't know if he understood. The boy had
stones in his fists and rocks in his head.

Spencer ended with "You know you can
290 beat him. That'll have to be enough." He
cleared his throat and said, "You come along,
now," as if herding a lamb who'd wandered.
Turner was alone again.

"Ain't that some shit?" he said later. He
295 and Elwood were lounging on the front steps
of their dorm. The daylight was thin, winter
coming down like the lid on an old pot.
Elwood was the only person Turner could
tell. The rest of these mutts would blab, and
300 then there'd be a lot of busted heads.

Turner had never met a kid like Elwood
before. "Sturdy" was the word he returned
to, even though the Tallahassee boy looked
soft, conducted himself like a goody-goody,
305 and had an irritating tendency to preach.
Wore eyeglasses you wanted to grind
underfoot like a butterfly. He talked like a
white college boy, read books when he
didn't have to, and mined them for ura-
310 nium to power his own personal A-bomb.
His education, in fact, was to blame for his
presence at Nickel. Though still a high-
school senior, he'd been taking night

classes at the local colored college. He was
315 hitching to campus when the cops stopped
the car that had picked him up; it was stolen. Nonetheless — sturdy.

Elwood wasn't surprised at Turner's news.
There was no question that Griff would
320 make it to the final match. "Organized boxing is corrupt on every level," he said with
authority. "There's been a lot in the newspapers about it. Only reason to fix a fight is
because you're betting on it."

325   "I'd bet on it, if I had any money," Turner
said.

"People are going to be upset," Elwood
said. Griff's victory would have been a feast,
but almost as delicious were the morsels
330 that the boys traded in anticipation, the sce-
narios in which the white contender lost
control of his bowels or threw up a geyser of
blood or spat white teeth "like they were
chipped out with an ice pick." Fantasies
335 hearty and fortifying.

"Sure," Turner said. "But Spencer says he's
going to take you out back, you listen."

"Take him to the White House?"

"I'll show you," Turner said.

340   They walked ten minutes to the laundry,
which was shut at this time of day. Turner
asked Elwood about the book under his arm
and Elwood said a British family was trying
to marry off the oldest daughter to keep their
345 estate and title. The story had complicated
turns.

"No one wants to marry her? She ugly?"

"She's described as having a handsome
face."

350   "Damn."

Past the laundry were the dilapidated
horse stables. The roof had given way long
ago and nature had crept inside, with skele-
tal bushes and limp grasses rising in the
355 stalls. You could get up to some wickedness
in there if you didn't believe in ghosts, but

none of the students had arrived at a definite opinion on the matter, so everyone stayed away to be safe. There were two oaks on one
360 side of the stables, with iron rings stabbed into the bark.

"This is *out back*," Turner said. "Once in a while they take a black boy here and shackle him up to those. Arms spread out. Then they
365 get a horse whip and tear him up."

Elwood made two fists, then caught himself. "No white boys?"

"The White House, they got that integrated. This place is separate. They take you
370 out back, they don't bring you to the hospital. They put you down as escaped and that's that, boy."

"What about your family?"

"How many boys you know here got
375 family? Or got family that cares about them? Not everyone is you, Elwood." Turner got jealous when Elwood's grandmother visited and brought him snacks, and it slipped out from time to time. Like now. The blinders Elwood
380 wore, walking around. The law was one thing—you could march and wave signs and change a law if you convinced enough white people. In Tampa, before coming to Nickel for the second time, Turner had seen the college
385 kids with their nice shirts and ties sit in at the Woolworths. He'd had to work, but they were out protesting. And it had happened— they'd opened the counter. Turner hadn't had the money to eat there either way. You could
390 change the law but you couldn't change people and how they treated each other. Nickel was racist as hell—half the people who worked there probably dressed up like the Klan on weekends—but, the way Turner saw
395 it, wickedness went deeper than skin color. It was Spencer. It was Spencer and it was Griff and it was all the parents who let their children wind up here. It was people.

Which was why Turner had brought
400 Elwood out to the two trees. To show him something that wasn't in books.

Elwood grabbed one of the rings and tugged. It was solid, part of the trunk now. Human bones would break before it came
405 loose.

Betting had been small-time when Director Nickel ran things—purity of the sport, etc. Nowadays, the fat cats turned out, anyone in three counties with a taste for
410 wagering. The big match was split up over two nights. On the first, the white campus and the black campus settled on whom to send to the main event. For the past two months, three boxing rings had been set
415 up in the gymnasium for training; now only one remained, at the center of the big room. It was chilly outside, and the spectators stepped into the humid cavern. White men from town claimed the folding chairs closest
420 to the ring, then came the staff, and beyond that the student body crammed into the bleachers or squatted on the floor, ashy elbow to ashy elbow. The racial division of the school re-created itself in the gym, with
425 white boys taking the south half and black boys claiming the north. They jostled at the borders.

Director Hardee acted as master of ceremonies. He rarely left his office in the
430 administration building. Turner hadn't seen him since Halloween, when he'd dressed in a Dracula outfit and distributed sweaty handfuls of candy corn to the younger students. He was a short man, fastened into his suits,
435 with a bald pate that floated in a cloud bank of white hair. Hardee had brought his wife, a robust beauty whose every visit to the school was thoroughly annotated by the students, if furtively—reckless eyeballing called for
440 mandatory beatings. She'd been Miss South

Louisiana, or so the story went. She cooled her neck with a paper fan.

Hardee made a few remarks. The chairman of the board, Mr. Charles Grayson—the
445 manager of the bank and a longtime Nickel supporter—was turning sixty on Friday. Hardee made the students sing "Happy Birthday." Mr. Grayson stood and nodded, hands behind his back like a dictator.

450 The white dormitories were up first. Big Chet squeezed between the ropes and bounded into the center of the ring. His cheerleaders expressed themselves with gusto; he commanded a legion. The white
455 boys may not have got it as bad as the black boys, but they were not at Nickel because the world cared overmuch about them. Big Chet was their Great White Hope. Gossip nailed him for a sleepwalker, punching holes in the
460 bathroom walls without waking. Morning found him sucking on his bloody knuckles. "Nigger looks like Frankenstein," Turner said. Square head, long arms, loping.

The opening fight went three unremark-
465 able rounds. The ref gave the decision to Big Chet and no one argued otherwise. He was regarded as an even personality, the ref, ever since he'd slapped a kid and his fraternity ring had left the kid half blind. After that
470 he'd bent a knee to our Savior and never again raised a hand in anger, except at his wife. The white boys' second match opened with a pop—a pneumatic uppercut that whisked Big Chet's opponent into a child-
475 hood fear. He spent the remainder of the round and the next two skittering like a rabbit. At the ref's decision, Big Chet rummaged in his mouth and spat out his mouthpiece in two pieces. He raised his big old arms to
480 the sky.

"I think he could take Griff," Elwood said.

"Maybe he can, but they have to make sure." If you had the power to make people do what you wanted and never exercised it,
485 what was the point of having it?

Griff's bouts with the champs of the colored dorms were brief affairs. Pettibone stood a foot shorter than Griff, an obvious mismatch when you saw them toe to toe. At
490 the bell, Griff barrelled out and humiliated his quarry with a battery of *zip-zip-zip* body blows. The crowd winced. "He's having ribs for dinner!" a boy behind Turner shouted. Mrs. Hardee shrieked when Pettibone floated
495 up dreamily on his tippy-toes and then toppled to kiss the dirty mat.

The second match was less lopsided. Griff tenderized the boy, Wilson, like a cheap cut of meat for three rounds, but Wilson stayed
500 on his feet. He had two bouts going—the one that everybody could see and the one that only he could, in which he was trying to prove his worth to his father. His father was long dead, and thus unable to revise his
505 assessment of his firstborn son's character, but that night Wilson slept without nightmares for the first time in years. The ref gave the fight to Griff with a concerned smile.

Turner surveyed the room and took in the
510 assembled marks, the boys and the bettors. You run a rigged game, you got to give the suckers a taste. Back in Tampa, a few blocks from where he lived, a street hustler had conducted rounds of Find the Lady outside a
515 cigar store. Taking suckers' money all day, weaving those cards around on a cardboard box. The rings on his fingers sparkled and shouted in the sun. Turner liked to hover and take in the show. Track the hustler's eyes,
520 track the marks' eyes as they tried to follow the queen of hearts. How their faces collapsed when they saw they weren't as smart as they thought. The hustler told Turner to beat it, but as the weeks went on he got
525 bored and let the boy hang around. "You got to let them think they know what's going

on," he told Turner one day. "They see it with their own eyes, distract themselves with that, so they can't see the bigger game."

530 When the cops hauled him to jail, his cardboard box lay in the alley around the corner for weeks.

At Nickel, Turner was transported back to that street corner. Watching a game of Find
535 the Lady, neither hustler nor mark, outside the game but knowing all its rules. The next evening, the white men would put up their money and the black boys would put up their hopes, and then the confidence man would
540 turn over the ace of spades and rake it all in. Turner remembered the excitement of Axel's fight two years ago, the deranged joy at the realization that the black boys were allowed to have something for a change. They were
545 happy, existing for a few hours in the free world, then it was back to Nickel.

Suckers, all of them.

The morning of Griff's big match, the black students got up wrung out from sleep-
550 lessness and the dining hall bubbled with chatter about the dimension and the magnitude of Griff's looming triumph. *That white boy's gonna be toothless as my old granny. The witch doctor can give him the whole bucket of*
555 *aspirin and he'll still have a headache. The Ku Klux Klan's gonna be crying under their hoods all week.* The colored boys frothed and speculated and stared off in class, slacked off in the sweet-potato fields. Mulling the pros-
560 pect of a black champion: one of them victorious for once, and those who kept them down whittled to dust, seeing stars. Griff strutted like a black duke, a gang of young boys in his wake. The younger kids threw
565 punches at their private, invisible adversaries and made up a song about their new hero's prowess. Griff hadn't bloodied or mistreated anyone outside the ring in a week, as if he'd sworn on a Bible. He was

570 unbothered by Spencer's order, or so it seemed to Elwood. "It's like he forgot," he whispered to Turner, as they walked to the warehouse after breakfast.

"If I got all this respect, I'd enjoy it, too,"
575 Turner said. The next day it would be as if it had never happened. He remembered Axel the afternoon after his big fight, stirring a wheelbarrow of concrete, gloomy and diminished once more. "When's the next time the
580 fools who hate and fear you are going to treat you like Harry Belafonte?"

"Or he forgot," Elwood said.

That evening they filed into the gymnasium. Some of the kitchen boys operated
585 a big kettle, cranking out popcorn and scooping it into paper cones. The younger boys chomped it down and raced to the back of the line for seconds. Turner, Elwood, and Jaimie squeezed together in the middle of
590 the bleachers. It was a good spot. "Hey, Jaimie, aren't you supposed to be sitting over there?" Turner asked. Jaimie's mother was Mexican, and the Nickel staff didn't know what to do with him. First he'd been put in
595 with the white kids, but after a day of working in the lime fields he'd got so dark that Spencer had had him reassigned to the colored half. Now he went back and forth.

Jaimie grinned. "Way I see it, I win either
600 way."

Turner crossed his arms and scanned the faces on the floor. There was Spencer. He shook hands with the fat cats in the front row, the director and his wife, and then sat
605 down, smug and sure. He withdrew a silver flask from his windbreaker and took a pull. The bank manager handed out cigars. Mrs. Hardee took one and everyone watched her blow smoke. Wispy gray figures twirled in
610 the overhead light, living ghosts.

On the other side of the room, the white boys stomped their feet on the wood and the

thunder bounced off the walls. The black
boys picked it up and the stomping rolled
615 around the room in a staggered stampede.
It travelled a full circuit before the boys
stopped and cheered at their racket.

"Send him to the undertaker!"

The ref rang the bell. The two fighters
620 were the same height and build, hacked from
the same quarry. An even match, the track
record of colored champions notwithstanding. Those opening rounds, there was no
dancing or ducking. The boys bit into each
625 other again and again, trading attacks, buck-
ing the pain. The crowd bellowed and jeered
at every advance and reversal. Black Mike
hung on the ropes, hooting scatological
invective at Big Chet, until the ref kicked his
630 hands away. If Griff feared knocking out Big
Chet by accident, he gave no sign. The black
giant battered the white boy without mercy,
absorbed his opponent's counterassault,
jabbed at the kid's face as if punching his
635 way through the wall of a prison cell. When
blood and sweat blinded him, he maintained
an eerie sense of Big Chet's position and
fended the boy off.

At the end of the second round, you had
640 to call the fight for Griff, despite Big Chet's
admirable offensives.

"Making it look good," Turner said.

Elwood frowned in disdain at the whole
performance, which made Turner smile. The
645 fight was rigged and rotten, another gear in
the machine that kept black folks down.
Turner enjoyed his friend's new bend toward
cynicism, even as he found himself swayed
by the magic of the fight. Seeing Griff, their
650 enemy and their champion, put a hurting on
that white boy made a fellow feel all right. In
spite of himself. Now that the third and final
round was upon them, he wanted to hold on
to that feeling. It was real—in their blood
655 and their minds—even if it was a lie. Turner

was certain that Griff was going to win, even
though he knew that he wasn't. Turner was a
mark, after all, another sucker, but he didn't
care.

660 Big Chet advanced on Griff and unfurled a
series of quick jabs that drove him into his corner. Griff was trapped and Turner thought,
Now. But the black boy gathered his opponent
in a clinch and remained on his feet. Body
665 blows sent the white boy reeling. The round
dwindled into seconds and Griff did not relent.
Big Chet squashed his nose with a thunk and
Griff shook it off. Each time Turner saw the
perfect moment to take a dive—Big Chet's rig-
670 orous assault would have covered even the
worst acting—Griff refused the opening.

Turner nudged Elwood, who had a look of
horror on his face. They saw it: Griff wasn't
going down. He was going to go for it.

675 No matter what happened after.

When the bell sounded for the last time,
the two Nickel boys in the ring were
entwined, bloody and slick, propping each
other up like a human tepee. The ref sepa-
680 rated them and they stumbled crazily to
their corners, spent.

Turner said, "Damn."

"Maybe they called it off," Elwood said.

Sure, it was possible that the ref was in
685 on it, and they'd decided to fix it that way
instead. Spencer's reaction dispelled that
theory. The superintendent was the only person in the first row still sitting, a malignant
scowl screwed into his face. One of the fat
690 cats turned around, red-faced, and grabbed
his arm.

Griff jerked to his feet, lumbered to the
center of the ring, and shouted. The noise of
the crowd smothered his words. Black Mike
695 held back his friend, who appeared to have
lost his wits. He struggled to cross the ring.
The ref called for everyone to settle down
and delivered his decision: the first two

rounds went to Griff, the last to Big Chet. The black boys had prevailed.

Instead of cavorting around the canvas in triumph, Griff squirmed free and traversed the ring to where Spencer sat. Now Turner heard his words: "I thought it was the second round! I thought it was the second round!" He was still screaming as the black boys led him back to the dormitories, cheering and whooping for their champion. They had never seen Griff cry before and took his tears for those of triumph.

Getting hit in the head can rattle your brains. Getting hit in the head like that can make you addle-minded and confused. Turner never thought it'd make you forget how to calculate two plus one. But Griff had never been good at arithmetic, he supposed.

Griff was all of them in one black body that night in the ring, and all of them when the white men took him out back to those two iron rings. They came for Griff that night and he never returned. The story spread that he had been too proud to take a dive. That he had refused to kneel. And if it made the boys feel better to believe that Griff had escaped, broken away and run off into the free world, no one told them otherwise, although some noted that it was odd that the school had never sounded the alarm or sent out the dogs.

When the state of Florida dug him up, fifty years later, the forensic examiner noted the fractures in the wrists and speculated that he'd been restrained before he died, in addition to the other violence attested to by the broken bones.

Most of those who know the story of the rings in the trees are dead by now. The iron is still there. Rusty. Deep in the heartwood. Testifying to anyone who cares to listen.

©Cullin Tobin

◀ Writer, director, and producer Jordan Peele (*Key & Peele*, *Get Out*, *Us*, *Nope*) formed his company Monkeypaw Productions to champion the perspectives of traditionally underrepresented voices.

How do productions by individuals from marginalized or underrepresented groups offer an opportunity for new voices and perspectives? Could this focus on representation limit the cultural conversation — and the productions themselves? How do films as an artform reflect the ideas of a culture?

CHARACTER

1. Choose two contrasting characters from the story. Then explain how the details and description contribute to the **contrast**.

2. How is Griff described? What does the description reveal about his character? What might it suggest about his relationships with other characters?

3. How do Turner's choices convey his values and contribute to the conflict of value systems?

SETTING

4. How does the **setting** of the text affect readers?

5. What is the relationship among the location, the historical period, and the characters in the story?

6. Explain how the descriptions of buildings and other structures (as well as their proximity to each other) contribute to the **atmosphere** and **mood** of the text.

STRUCTURE

7. How does the **contrast** between the characters contribute to the tension of the **dramatic situation**?

8. Explain how the text is archetypal. For example, what specific **archetypes** can you identify?

9. How does the **dramatic situation** reveal both expected and unexpected progress toward the **resolution**?

NARRATION

10. Who is the **narrator**? What is the narrator's **tone** toward the subject of the text?

11. How do the narrator's background and **perspective** shape the tone of the text?

12. How do the diction and details support a **shift** in tone within the text? Give an example of a shift and explain the change.

IDEAS IN LITERATURE: Reason and Order

13. The story takes place in a reform school. How is reform work supposed to create reason and order? Consider your community. Do you have any programs for reform in your community or school? Explain the effectiveness of these programs.

PUTTING IT ALL TOGETHER

14. The narrator of the story and the narrator's agency control the narrative. How do the narrator's actions, decisions, and distance contribute to your interpretation of the text?

The Bet
Anton Chekhov

THE TEXT IN CONTEXT

Anton Chekhov (1860–1904), one of the greatest playwrights
and short story writers in all of literature, often captured the
difficulties of everyday Russian people in ordinary situations.
He originally trained as a physician and published stories as
a medical student. While Chekhov still practiced medicine
sporadically throughout his career, he gained literary acclaim
with plays such as *Uncle Vanya* (1898) and *The Cherry Orchard*
(1904). Moreover, he reimagined the short story form, avoiding simplistic happy endings, strong authorial judgments,
and lengthy exposition. Instead, Chekhov pioneered concise
and moody tales, with nonintrusive narrators and plots that reveal character through
objective presentation. His works are perceptive, humane, compassionate, and often
humorous—even when dealing with tragic figures and problems. Those qualities are
evident in "The Bet," which explores questions of self-knowledge and materialism.

ullstein bild Dtl./Getty Images

The Bet

I

It was a dark autumn night. The old banker
was walking up and down his study and
remembering how, fifteen years before, he
had given a party one autumn evening.
5 There had been many clever men there, and
there had been interesting conversations.
Among other things they had talked of capital punishment. The majority of the guests,
among whom were many journalists and
10 intellectual men, disapproved of the death
penalty. They considered that form of punishment out of date, immoral, and unsuitable for
Christian States. In the opinion of some of
them the death penalty ought to be replaced
15 everywhere by imprisonment for life.

"I don't agree with you," said their host
the banker. "I have not tried either the death
penalty or imprisonment for life, but if one
may judge *a priori*, the death penalty is more
20 moral and more humane than imprisonment
for life. Capital punishment kills a man at
once, but lifelong imprisonment kills him
slowly. Which executioner is the more
humane, he who kills you in a few minutes
25 or he who drags the life out of you in the
course of many years?"

"Both are equally immoral," observed one
of the guests, "for they both have the same
object—to take away life. The State is not
30 God. It has not the right to take away what it
cannot restore when it wants to."

Among the guests was a young lawyer, a
young man of five-and-twenty. When he was
asked his opinion, he said:

35 "The death sentence and the life sentence
are equally immoral, but if I had to choose
between the death penalty and imprison-

ment for life, I would certainly choose the second. To live anyhow is better than not
40 at all."

A lively discussion arose. The banker, who was younger and more nervous in those days, was suddenly carried away by excitement; he struck the table with his fist and
45 shouted at the young man:

"It's not true! I'll bet you two millions you wouldn't stay in solitary confinement for five years."

"If you mean that in earnest," said the
50 young man, "I'll take the bet, but I would stay not five but fifteen years."

"Fifteen? Done!" cried the banker. "Gentlemen, I stake two millions!"

"Agreed! You stake your millions and I
55 stake my freedom!" said the young man.

And this wild, senseless bet was carried out! The banker, spoilt and frivolous, with millions beyond his reckoning, was delighted at the bet. At supper he made fun of the
60 young man, and said:

"Think better of it, young man, while there is still time. To me two millions are a trifle, but you are losing three or four of the best years of your life. I say three or four,
65 because you won't stay longer. Don't forget either, you unhappy man, that voluntary confinement is a great deal harder to bear than compulsory. The thought that you have the right to step out in liberty at any moment
70 will poison your whole existence in prison. I am sorry for you."

And now the banker, walking to and fro, remembered all this, and asked himself: "What was the object of that bet? What is
75 the good of that man's losing fifteen years of his life and my throwing away two millions? Can it prove that the death penalty is better or worse than imprisonment for life? No, no. It was all nonsensical and meaningless. On
80 my part it was the caprice of a pampered

man, and on his part simple greed for money. . . ."

Then he remembered what followed that evening. It was decided that the young man
85 should spend the years of his captivity under the strictest supervision in one of the lodges in the banker's garden. It was agreed that for fifteen years he should not be free to cross the threshold of the lodge, to see human
90 beings, to hear the human voice, or to receive letters and newspapers. He was allowed to have a musical instrument and books, and was allowed to write letters, to drink wine, and to smoke. By the terms of the agree-
95 ment, the only relations he could have with the outer world were by a little window made purposely for that object. He might have anything he wanted—books, music, wine, and so on—in any quantity he desired
100 by writing an order, but could only receive them through the window. The agreement provided for every detail and every trifle that would make his imprisonment strictly soli-tary, and bound the young man to stay there
105 *exactly* fifteen years, beginning from twelve o'clock of November 14, 1870, and ending at twelve o'clock of November 14, 1885. The slightest attempt on his part to break the conditions, if only two minutes before the
110 end, released the banker from the obligation to pay him two millions.

For the first year of his confinement, as far as one could judge from his brief notes, the prisoner suffered severely from loneli-
115 ness and depression. The sounds of the piano could be heard continually day and night from his lodge. He refused wine and tobacco. Wine, he wrote, excites the desires, and desires are the worst foes of the
120 prisoner; and besides, nothing could be more dreary than drinking good wine and seeing no one. And tobacco spoilt the air of his room. In the first year the books he sent for were

principally of a light character; novels with a complicated love plot, sensational and fantastic stories, and so on.

In the second year the piano was silent in the lodge, and the prisoner asked only for the classics. In the fifth year music was audible again, and the prisoner asked for wine. Those who watched him through the window said that all that year he spent doing nothing but eating and drinking and lying on his bed, frequently yawning and angrily talking to himself. He did not read books. Sometimes at night he would sit down to write; he would spend hours writing, and in the morning tear up all that he had written. More than once he could be heard crying.

In the second half of the sixth year the prisoner began zealously studying languages, philosophy, and history. He threw himself eagerly into these studies—so much so that the banker had enough to do to get him the books he ordered. In the course of four years some six hundred volumes were procured at his request. It was during this period that the banker received the following letter from his prisoner:

"My dear Jailer, I write you these lines in six languages. Show them to people who know the languages. Let them read them. If they find not one mistake I implore you to fire a shot in the garden. That shot will show me that my efforts have not been thrown away. The geniuses of all ages and of all lands speak different languages, but the same flame burns in them all. Oh, if you only knew what unearthly happiness my soul feels now from being able to understand them!" The prisoner's desire was fulfilled. The banker ordered two shots to be fired in the garden.

Then after the tenth year, the prisoner sat immovably at the table and read nothing but the Gospel. It seemed strange to the banker that a man who in four years had mastered six hundred learned volumes should waste nearly a year over one thin book easy of comprehension. Theology and histories of religion followed the Gospels.

In the last two years of his confinement the prisoner read an immense quantity of books quite indiscriminately. At one time he was busy with the natural sciences, then he would ask for Byron or Shakespeare. There were notes in which he demanded at the same time books on chemistry, and a manual of medicine, and a novel, and some treatise on philosophy or theology. His reading suggested a man swimming in the sea among the wreckage of his ship, and trying to save his life by greedily clutching first at one spar and then at another.

II

The old banker remembered all this, and thought:

"To-morrow at twelve o'clock he will regain his freedom. By our agreement I ought to pay him two millions. If I do pay him, it is all over with me: I shall be utterly ruined."

Fifteen years before, his millions had been beyond his reckoning; now he was afraid to ask himself which were greater, his debts or his assets. Desperate gambling on the Stock Exchange, wild speculation and the excitability which he could not get over even in advancing years, had by degrees led to the decline of his fortune and the proud, fearless, self-confident millionaire had become a banker of middling rank, trembling at every rise and fall in his investments. "Cursed bet!" muttered the old man, clutching his head in despair. "Why didn't the man die? He is only forty now. He will take my last penny from me, he will marry, will enjoy life, will gamble on the Exchange; while I shall look at him with envy like a beggar, and hear from him

every day the same sentence: 'I am indebted
to you for the happiness of my life, let me
210 help you!' No, it is too much! The one means
of being saved from bankruptcy and disgrace
is the death of that man!"

It struck three o'clock, the banker listened; everyone was asleep in the house and
215 nothing could be heard outside but the rustling of the chilled trees. Trying to make no
noise, he took from a fireproof safe the key of
the door which had not been opened for fifteen years, put on his overcoat, and went out
220 of the house.

It was dark and cold in the garden. Rain
was falling. A damp cutting wind was racing
about the garden, howling and giving the
trees no rest. The banker strained his eyes,
225 but could see neither the earth nor the white
statues, nor the lodge, nor the trees. Going to
the spot where the lodge stood, he twice
called the watchman. No answer followed.
Evidently the watchman had sought shelter
230 from the weather, and was now asleep
somewhere either in the kitchen or in the
greenhouse.

"If I had the pluck to carry out my intention," thought the old man, "suspicion would
235 fall first upon the watchman."

He felt in the darkness for the steps and
the door, and went into the entry of the
lodge. Then he groped his way into a little
passage and lighted a match. There was not
240 a soul there. There was a bedstead with no
bedding on it, and in the corner there was a
dark cast-iron stove. The seals on the door
leading to the prisoner's rooms were intact.

When the match went out the old man,
245 trembling with emotion, peeped through
the little window. A candle was burning
dimly in the prisoner's room. He was sitting
at the table. Nothing could be seen but his
back, the hair on his head, and his hands.
250 Open books were lying on the table, on

the two easy-chairs, and on the carpet near
the table.

Five minutes passed and the prisoner did
not once stir. Fifteen years' imprisonment
255 had taught him to sit still. The banker tapped
at the window with his finger, and the prisoner
made no movement whatever in response.
Then the banker cautiously broke the seals off
the door and put the key in the keyhole. The
260 rusty lock gave a grating sound and the door
creaked. The banker expected to hear at once
footsteps and a cry of astonishment, but three
minutes passed and it was as quiet as ever in
the room. He made up his mind to go in.

265 At the table a man unlike ordinary people
was sitting motionless. He was a skeleton
with the skin drawn tight over his bones,
with long curls like a woman's and a shaggy
beard. His face was yellow with an earthy
270 tint in it, his cheeks were hollow, his back
long and narrow, and the hand on which his
shaggy head was propped was so thin and
delicate that it was dreadful to look at it. His
hair was already streaked with silver, and
275 seeing his emaciated, aged-looking face, no
one would have believed that he was only
forty. He was asleep. . . . In front of his bowed
head there lay on the table a sheet of paper
on which there was something written in
280 fine handwriting.

"Poor creature!" thought the banker, "he is
asleep and most likely dreaming of the millions. And I have only to take this half-dead
man, throw him on the bed, stifle him a little
285 with the pillow, and the most conscientious
expert would find no sign of a violent death.
But let us first read what he has written
here. . . ."

The banker took the page from the table
290 and read as follows:

"To-morrow at twelve o'clock I regain my
freedom and the right to associate with
other men, but before I leave this room and

see the sunshine, I think it necessary to say a
few words to you. With a clear conscience I
tell you, as before God, who beholds me, that
I despise freedom and life and health, and all
that in your books is called the good things
of the world.

"For fifteen years I have been intently
studying earthly life. It is true I have not seen
the earth nor men, but in your books I have
drunk fragrant wine, I have sung songs, I
have hunted stags and wild boars in the forests, have loved women. . . . Beauties as ethe-
real as clouds, created by the magic of your
poets and geniuses, have visited me at night,
and have whispered in my ears wonderful
tales that have set my brain in a whirl. In
your books I have climbed to the peaks of
Elburz and Mont Blanc, and from there I have
seen the sun rise and have watched it at
evening flood the sky, the ocean, and the
mountain-tops with gold and crimson. I have
watched from there the lightning flashing
over my head and cleaving the storm-clouds.
I have seen green forests, fields, rivers, lakes,
towns. I have heard the singing of the sirens,
and the strains of the shepherds' pipes; I
have touched the wings of comely devils who
flew down to converse with me of God. . . .
In your books I have flung myself into the
bottomless pit, performed miracles, slain,
burned towns, preached new religions, conquered whole kingdoms. . . .

"Your books have given me wisdom. All
that the unresting thought of man has created in the ages is compressed into a small
compass in my brain. I know that I am wiser
than all of you.

"And I despise your books, I despise wisdom and the blessings of this world. It is all
worthless, fleeting, illusory, and deceptive,
like a mirage. You may be proud, wise, and
fine, but death will wipe you off the face of
the earth as though you were no more than
mice burrowing under the floor, and your
posterity, your history, your immortal
geniuses will burn or freeze together with
the earthly globe.

"You have lost your reason and taken the
wrong path. You have taken lies for truth,
and hideousness for beauty. You would marvel if, owing to strange events of some sorts,
frogs and lizards suddenly grew on apple and
orange trees instead of fruit, or if roses began
to smell like a sweating horse; so I marvel at
you who exchange heaven for earth. I don't
want to understand you.

"To prove to you in action how I despise
all that you live by, I renounce the two millions of which I once dreamed as of paradise
and which now I despise. To deprive myself
of the right to the money I shall go out from
here five hours before the time fixed, and so
break the compact. . . ."

When the banker had read this he laid
the page on the table, kissed the strange
man on the head, and went out of the lodge,
weeping. At no other time, even when he
had lost heavily on the Stock Exchange, had
he felt so great a contempt for himself.
When he got home he lay on his bed, but
his tears and emotion kept him for hours
from sleeping.

Next morning the watchmen ran in with
pale faces, and told him they had seen the
man who lived in the lodge climb out of the
window into the garden, go to the gate, and
disappear. The banker went at once with
the servants to the lodge and made sure of
the flight of his prisoner. To avoid arousing
unnecessary talk, he took from the table
the writing in which the millions were
renounced, and when he got home locked
it up in the fireproof safe.

▲

The image depicts a blindfolded Lady Justice, the Roman goddess of Justice, holding scales and carrying a sword.

How does "Lady Justice" serve as a metaphor? What characteristics or attributes are presented in this depiction? To what degree are these values reflected in our modern justice system?

CHARACTER

1. Describe the **protagonist**. Describe the **antagonist**. What is their relationship, and how does Chekhov develop this relationship to present the two characters as **foils** in the story?

2. How much **agency** does the protagonist have? What important choices does he make that reveal his agency?

3. How do each of the characters **contrast** and change throughout the course of the story?

SETTING

4. How does the **situation** reflect two distinct beliefs, values, or cultures?

5. How does the **setting** change throughout the story?

6. How does the **juxtaposition** of beliefs revealed through the characters' professions reflect the contrast of ideas expressed through the text?

STRUCTURE

7. The narrator describes the bet and sets up an **archetypal** scapegoat. Explain how this archetypal idea changes at the conclusion of the story.

8. Over what time span does the story occur? Why is this passage of time significant?

9. The story opens with two **flashbacks**. What are they, and what information is revealed?

10. Explain how the **contrasting** ideas of the prisoner in the story's resolution contribute to your interpretation.

NARRATION

11. Who is the **narrator**? What is the narrator's relationship to the story?

12. What is the narrator's attitude toward the events of the story? How does that **perspective** change over the course of the story?

IDEAS IN LITERATURE: Reason and Order

13. The value of a life is discussed at the beginning of the story. The worth and value of life is subjective. Consider the reason and order of the bet in this story. What does the bet reveal about how the characters see the value of life? Can you think of an example of how reason and order contribute to our sense of value in life?

PUTTING IT ALL TOGETHER

14. The ending of the story is unexpected. Based on the opening conversation and the flashbacks, explain how the actual result of the bet differs from the expected outcome. How does this incongruity contribute to your interpretation of the story?

Writing about Point of View

 Enduring Understanding (LAN-1)

Readers establish and communicate their interpretations of literature through arguments supported by textual evidence.

KEY POINT

Writers create unity by providing commentary that explains how their line of reasoning supports the claim in the thesis statement and connects to a unifying idea.

Creating Unity through Commentary

Q: Why was the man fired from his job at the M&M factory?
A: Because he kept throwing away all the "Ws."

While this joke is silly, it also illustrates an important point about literary analysis: perspective matters. Our perceptions of the world depend on our perspective. Likewise, our interpretation of a poem or story depends on the **point of view** from which it is told. So when careful readers analyze literature, they pay close attention to who is telling the story. They also try to understand why the author chose that narrator.

In fact, your interpretation of a text depends not only on the narrator's point of view (first person or third person) but also on the perspective of the narrator. For example, if a story is told by a **third-person narrator**, you should note the amount of information the narrator is willing or able to offer. Consider the following:

- Is the narrator omniscient or limited?
- Does the narrator remain a neutral reporter, or is the narrator a passionate critic with a strong point of view?
- Can we tell if the narrator shares the values of the other characters in the story?
- Is the narrator perceptive and reliable?

Perhaps the story is told by a **first-person narrator**. This character may be close to the dramatic action and biased in his or her account. Alternatively, the character narrating the story may be distant from the action and perhaps more reliable and analytical. A first-person narrator's **perspective** is shaped by many factors, including the character's age, background, past experiences, values, beliefs, interactions, environment, and circumstances. In short, you need to know the story's narrator.

When you write about point of view in literature, you should discover everything you can about the narrator, especially his or her perspective. Moreover, consider how the author's perspective influenced these choices and how these choices affect your interpretation. Then you will understand the complexity of the narration of the story.

In this composition workshop, you will learn how to write a literary argument that analyzes the perspective of the text. First, you will develop a defensible thesis statement that conveys your interpretation (idea + insight) as it relates to the perspective. Then you will support your thesis with a line of reasoning, textual evidence, and commentary that explains how the perspective contributes to an interpretation of the text.

 ## YOUR ASSIGNMENT

Choose a story from Unit 4 or a text that your teacher has assigned. Then write a literary argument that analyzes how the narrator's perspective contributes to your interpretation of the work. Support your thesis with evidence from the text.

Your argument should interpret a literary work and include the following:

- An introduction that identifies the title, author, context, and narrative perspective
- A thesis statement with a claim that conveys an interpretation (a unifying idea + insight about that idea)
- A line of reasoning that justifies the interpretation in the claim
- Relevant textual evidence that supports the line of reasoning
- Commentary that links the evidence to the unifying idea in the line of reasoning and thesis
- A conclusion that brings the literary argument to a unified end

Potential Subjects

- A narrator who is dealing with an event from the past
- A narrator who shares a dream or a memory
- A narrator who judges the characters in the text
- A narrator who cannot be trusted
- A narrator who offers a moral or a lesson
- A narrator who offers a humorous perspective in a text

Explaining Complexity

When you analyze the perspective of the narrator, you should take into consideration narrative distance. In other words, consider how close the narrator is to the action and the other characters. Additionally, consider how much time has passed between the action and the telling of the story. Here are some questions to help you dig a little deeper:

- How does the narrator's physical location impact his or her perspective?
- How does the narrator's relationship to other characters affect the details that the narrator includes?
- How does the amount of time that has passed between the story events and the narrator's account of the story affect his or her perspective?
- How does the narrator's emotional distance or proximity to the characters and events impact his or her perspective?

Set a Purpose for Reading

As you read your selected text for your analysis, begin by annotating the story for a **unifying idea**. Consider the following questions and the implications of these details with your unifying idea in mind as you examine the perspective.

- Who tells the story? What is the character's relationship to the events in the story and other characters in the story?
- Is the narrator a character in the story? If so, is the narrator a main character or a minor character? How reliable does the character seem?
- Is the narrator a third-person observer? If so, is the narrator all-knowing, observational, or limited? How do you know? What effect does this perspective have on your interpretation?
- Is the narrator describing events as they occur, or are they in the recent or distant past? What is the effect of this narrative distance?
- Is the narrator involved or detached from the events? What is the perspective of the narrator based on the level of involvement?
- What is the narrator's attitude toward the events of the story or other characters in the story? What words, details, or syntax reveal the tone?
- Does the author shift the narrative distance or perspective in the text? If so, what is the effect of this shift?

 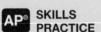 **SKILLS PRACTICE** | **LITERARY ARGUMENTATION**
Analyzing a Narrator's Perspective

Consider the text that you are analyzing and complete the following table. In the middle column, record specific details from the text related to the narrator of the story. In the right-hand column, explain the effect of the author's choice of narrator and narrative distance on the perspective. Be sure to connect these details to your unifying idea.

Analyzing a Narrator's Perspective		
Unifying idea:		
Topic and focus of analysis:		
Narrator	**Details from the Text**	**Implications for Narrative Perspective**
First or third person		
Background, values, experiences		
Distance from events		
Distance in time		
Narrator's tone or attitude		

Develop a Defensible Thesis Statement

To write a thesis statement for an analysis of perspective, you must make a claim, as in other literary arguments. The claim should include your interpretation. In this essay, however, you will focus on how the narrative perspective contributes to your interpretation. You will want to refer to the narrative perspective — along with your broader interpretation of the text — within your thesis statement.

WRITING A THESIS: AN ANALYSIS OF NARRATIVE PERSPECTIVE	
Template 1: Thesis connects perspective to the idea and the insight and lists author choices that lead to this insight.	In [title of work], the [first/third person] perspective of [aspect of narrator related to topic] illustrates [unifying idea + insight] as revealed through [literary element or technique], [literary element or technique], and [literary element or technique].
Template 2: Thesis connects perspective to the idea and the insight.	In [title of work], the [first/third person] perspective of [aspect of narrator related to topic] illustrates [unifying idea + insight].

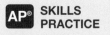 **SKILLS PRACTICE**

LITERARY ARGUMENTATION
Developing a Thesis Statement for Analysis of Perspective

In the first column record the title, author, and aspect of focus as your topic. Use the remaining columns to record the unifying idea and insight of the text you are analyzing. You may choose whether or not to preview your line of reasoning.

Developing a Thesis Statement for an Analysis of Perspective		
Topic	**Claim**	
Title, Author, and Focus (aspect of perspective)	Unifying Idea +	Insight

Organize a Line of Reasoning

Your line of reasoning for an analysis of perspective should allow you to explore the complexity of the narrator. You are not merely identifying details that reveal the point of view; rather, you are examining who the narrator is and how the narrator's identity affects the development of the story. Once you determine your thesis, you will generate reasons to support that thesis.

To achieve **unity** in your literary argument, you will need to link everything within your essay to your unifying idea. In other words, each reason in your line of reasoning should link to the unifying idea in your claim.

Your argument will be more effective if you organize your reasons logically. That is it should reveal a progression of thought where one reason builds upon another. For example, if you can rearrange the order of your body paragraphs without changing your argument, it is unlikely you have a solid line of reasoning. Your progression of thought, then, should be strategically arranged and evident within your sentences, between your sentences, within your paragraphs, and between your paragraphs.

STRUCTURE OF AN ANALYSIS OF NARRATIVE PERSPECTIVE

Introduction

The **introduction** is an opportunity for the writer to establish the purpose of his or her literary argument and to invite and interest the audience into the literary work and the writer's interpretation of it. To achieve this goal, many literary arguments follow this structure:

- Engage the audience through an interesting hook
- Provide historical, cultural, or social context of a literary work
- Identify the title, author, genre (TAG)
- Introduce the literary topic of analysis by
  - describing the importance of that literary concept; and
  - summarizing the work succinctly with details critical to that concept

The **thesis statement** presents a defensible interpretation that includes an idea and an insight about that idea.

Body
(Develops a line of reasoning with supporting evidence that justifies the thesis)

Topic Sentence 1 (Identify the first aspect of the narrative perspective related to the unifying idea)	Topic Sentence 2 (Identify the second aspect of the narrative perspective related to the unifying idea)	Topic Sentence 3 (Identify the third aspect of the narrative perspective related to the unifying idea)
Textual Details (Evidence of elements and techniques that contribute to the development of narrative perspective and complexity)	Textual Details (Evidence of elements and techniques that contribute to the development of narrative perspective and complexity)	Textual Details (Evidence of elements and techniques that contribute to the development of narrative perspective and complexity)
Commentary (Link evidence by explaining its relevance to the line of reasoning and claim)	Commentary (Link evidence by explaining its relevance to the line of reasoning and claim)	Commentary (Link evidence by explaining its relevance to the line of reasoning and claim)

Conclusion

The **conclusion** should do more than restate the thesis; instead, it should be a robust and important paragraph. It is the opportunity for the writer to demonstrate understanding of the literary work's relevance by explaining how the literary work stands the test of time and reflects the human experience. Writers further their idea and insight by:

* Discussing the significance or relevance of the interpretation
* Relating the work to other relevant literary works
* Connecting the theme to their own experience
* Presenting alternate interpretations
* Explaining how the work explores complexities and tensions
* Situating the theme within a broader context

This table illustrates the general structure of a literary argument. It does not intend to imply that all literary arguments are five paragraphs. Writers should determine the number of reasons needed to justify their claim, as well as how much evidence is sufficient to support each of these reasons.

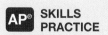 **SKILLS PRACTICE** | LITERARY ARGUMENTATION
Achieving Unity through a Line of Reasoning

Review the idea and insight in your thesis statement and choose a logical line of reasoning to support your thesis. Compose two or more supporting topic sentences and organize them in a logical sequence that represents your train of thought. Highlight the words related to your unifying idea and underline words that link one topic sentence to another.

Achieving Unity through a Line of Reasoning		
Defensible Thesis Statement with Claim (idea + insight):		
Topic Sentence 1 (Identify the first aspect of the perspective related to the unifying idea):	**Topic Sentence 2** (Identify the second aspect of the perspective related to the unifying idea):	**Topic Sentence 3** (Identify the third aspect of the perspective related to the unifying idea):

Select Relevant Evidence

In the first three units, you have practiced selecting relevant evidence to support your reasons and claim. You have learned to include that evidence within the proper paragraphs. You have also learned that you need sufficient evidence (one or more pieces of evidence for each claim). Recall the following functions of evidence:

- To illustrate your reason
- To clarify, amplify, or qualify a point
- To exemplify a literary element or technique
- To associate an image or comparison to an idea

You create coherence in your argument by arranging your evidence not only into its proper body paragraph but also in a logical order within the body paragraph. When you introduce your evidence, connect it to your reason, and provide narrative context, you help your reader travel seamlessly through your argument.

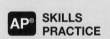 **SKILLS PRACTICE** | LITERARY ARGUMENTATION
Arranging Evidence for Unity and Coherence

Write your thesis statement (idea + insight) and develop a logical line of reasoning to support your interpretation. Then carefully organize your body paragraphs and arrange the evidence within them. Next, draft two or more body paragraphs that include evidence from the text to support each reason. Include transitions to link your reasons and evidence to your claim.

Arranging Evidence for Unity and Coherence		
Defensible Thesis Statement with Claim (idea + insight):		
Topic Sentence 1 (Identify the first aspect of the perspective related to the unifying idea):	**Topic Sentence 2** (Identify the second aspect of the perspective related to the unifying idea):	**Topic Sentence 3** (Identify the third aspect of the perspective related to the unifying idea):
Textual Details (Relevant and sufficient evidence):	**Textual Details** (Relevant and sufficient evidence):	**Textual Details** (Relevant and sufficient evidence):

Write Insightful Commentary

In Unit 3, you learned that commentary explains how the evidence supports the thesis. You also learned to distinguish between summary and analysis. This distinction is important to remember as you write all of your literary arguments. Now, you will work to refine your commentary so that it helps you achieve coherence in your line of reasoning and **unity** in support of the claim in your thesis.

But readers will be confused if the only information they receive is your line of reasoning and your evidence. These elements are like the framework of a house being built. You can begin to see a structure, but without the walls in between, the house is incomplete. Like the walls, commentary connects everything together so that the argument makes sense.

Commentary can serve several purposes within your argument:

- It communicates your insight about the unifying idea.
- It explains how the reasons in the line of reasoning connect to the claim in the thesis.
- It explains how the evidence connects to the reasons in the topic sentences.
- It explains how one piece of evidence connects to another.
- It explains how the author's choices help convey an interpretation.

For an analysis of narrative perspective, consider analyzing a tension, as it will explain the complexity of the narrative perspective. Review the following ways to explain your line of reasoning that will analyze this tension:

- Explore the complexity of attitude, tone, or perspective within the passage.
- Explore the shift from one attitude, tone, or perspective to another.
- Reveal multiple effects of the narrative perspective.
- Reveal multiple causes of the narrative perspective.
- Contrast the narrator's perspective with that of other characters.
- Follow the progression (chronologically) of the work.

Review the following table, which includes sentence frames to help you explain how your evidence relates to your claim.

CREATING UNITY THROUGH COMMENTARY		
Introducing the Author's Choice	**Explaining the Function of the Evidence**	**Connecting the Evidence to the Unifying Idea and Insight**

The author . . .
 	
   alludes to _____
   characterizes _____
   as _____
   chooses to _____
   compares _____ and
   _____
   contrasts _____ and
   _____
   creates _____
   describes _____ as
   _____
	. . . in order to . . .
	
	   associate _____ with
	   _____.
	   connect to _____.
	   convey _____.
	   create a sense of
	   _____.
	   demonstrate _____.
	   depict _____.
	   emphasize _____.
	   illustrate _____.
	   imply _____.
		Through this [choice], the author . . . about [idea and perspective].
		
		   demonstrates
		   develops
		   emphasizes
		   explores
		   illustrates
		   implies
		   intimates
		   proves
		   represents

(continued)

employs _____
includes _____
incorporates _____
juxtaposes _____
and _____
refers to _____
repeats _____
shifts from _____ to
_____

portray _____.
reveal _____.
suggest _____.

This [choice] . . .
connects _____ to
_____.
conveys _____.
demonstrates _____.
depicts _____.
emphasizes _____.
illustrates _____.
implies _____.
is fitting because _____.
is significant because
_____.
portrays _____.
reveals _____.
signifies _____.
suggests _____.

reveals
suggests

By . . .
alluding to _____
characterizing _____
as _____
choosing _____
comparing _____ to
_____
contrasting _____
and _____
creating _____
describing _____ as
_____
employing _____
including _____
incorporating _____
juxtaposing _____
and _____
shifting from _____
to _____
repeating _____

. . . the author . . .
connects _____ to
_____.
conveys _____.
demonstrates _____.
illustrates _____.
implies _____.
questions _____.
reveals _____.
serves to _____.
suggests _____.

. . . the reader . . .
connects _____.
understands _____.
infers _____.
questions _____.
reflects _____.
compares _____.

Strong writers use commentary to link the pieces of their arguments. You should strive to deepen your argument with each reason and piece of evidence. You achieve this by writing a logical line of reasoning with commentary that builds on each point rather than simply repeating the same observation with each piece of evidence.

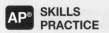 **SKILLS PRACTICE** | LITERARY ARGUMENTATION
Creating Unity through Commentary

Continue developing your literary argument by planning and writing helpful commentary that links your evidence to both your line of reasoning and the idea in your claim. Consult the reference chart "Creating Unity through Commentary" for sentence stems to help you write your explanations.

Arranging Evidence for Unity and Coherence		
Defensible Thesis Statement with Claim (idea + insight):		
Topic Sentence 1 (Identify the first aspect of the perspective related to the unifying idea):	**Topic Sentence 2** (Identify the second aspect of the perspective related to the unifying idea):	**Topic Sentence 3** (Identify the third aspect of the perspective related to the unifying idea):
Textual Details (Relevant and sufficient evidence):	**Textual Details** (Relevant and sufficient evidence):	**Textual Details** (Relevant and sufficient evidence):
Commentary (Link evidence to reason and idea):	**Commentary** (Link evidence to reason and idea):	**Commentary** (Link evidence to reason and idea):
Sentence stem and explanation of the function of evidence:	Sentence stem and explanation of the function of evidence:	Sentence stem and explanation of the function of evidence:

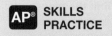 SKILLS PRACTICE

LITERARY ARGUMENTATION

Establishing Context and Explaining Relevance

In the following chart, record some notes to help you communicate the context of your argument, introductory details about the narrator, and introductory material that will funnel your ideas to your thesis statement. Next, record details to help you explain the relevance of your idea and insight in your concluding statements.

Establishing Context and Explaining Relevance	
Idea and Insight	Context for Introduction
	Significance of Idea in Conclusion

Contextualize Your Argument

When you write your analysis of the narrative, you should begin with an introduction that includes a quick summary of the text and identifies the narrator. You may wish to situate the narrator within the context of the story. Next, you should narrow your discussion to lead to your unifying idea within your thesis statement.

In your conclusion, remember to explain the relevance of your unifying idea within your interpretation. We will explore more about writing conclusions in a later unit.

Revise Your Argument

For your analysis of perspective, review the following questions related to your treatment of narrative perspective. Revise your draft if you answer "no" to any of the following questions:

- Is your identification of narrative perspective focused on the narrator's characterization rather than just an identification of first- or second-person point of view?

- Do your reasons in your line of reasoning refer to perspective and support your interpretation?

- Have you included relevant details, literary elements, and narrative techniques that contribute to narrative perspective?

- Does your interpretation of the work logically align with your discussion of narrative perspective?

- Is your argument coherent with a logical sequence of reasons and transitions that connect evidence, reasons, and claim?

- Does your commentary unify your argument by connecting your evidence and reasons to your unifying idea?

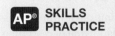 **SKILLS PRACTICE**

LITERARY ARGUMENTATION
Revising and Editing an Analysis of Perspective

After you have completed revising and editing your own argument, review another student's literary argument and provide helpful feedback.

Peer-Revision Checklist: Revising and Editing an Analysis of Perspective		
Revising and Editing Checklist	Unit 4 Focus Skills	Comment on the Effectiveness and/or Make a Suggestion
Does the writer include the author, title, narrative situation, and narrative perspective in the first paragraph? Does the brief summary of context lead to the idea?	Introductions for narrative perspective	
Does the thesis statement convey an interpretation? Does the interpretation connect to an idea and an insight?	Defensible thesis	
Does the writer provide a logical sequence of reasons to support the idea and insight in the thesis? Are these reasons linked to the claim with transitions?	Line of reasoning: Unity	
Does the writer provide relevant and sufficient evidence to support the interpretation in the thesis? Is the evidence linked to the topic sentences with transitions?	Relevant and sufficient evidence: Coherence	
Does the writer explain how the evidence supports a reason and connects to the interpretation in the thesis? Does the commentary connect to the unifying idea?	Commentary: Unity	
Does the writer explain the argument's significance within a broader context?	Relevance	
Does the writer demonstrate control over the conventions of writing?	Conventions	

Student Model: Writing about Point of View

Read the following student model that analyzes different points of view in Tennessee Williams's play *Cat on a Hot Tin Roof* to observe how a claim, line of reasoning, evidence, and commentary work together to analyze how comparing and contrasting perspectives leads to an interpretation.

Like Father, Like Son
Julia Luxon

The play *Cat On A Hot Tin Roof* by Tennessee Williams uses deception to illustrate the differing perspectives but similar characters of Brick and Big Daddy. Both characters use mendacity to accomplish their ultimate goal in the play and to attempt to relate to each other.

> thesis statement:
> idea: mendacity
> insight: people use mendacity to help reach their goals

Big Daddy uses mendacity as an attempt to fix Brick and get him sober as he wants to have Brick inherit his farm. Big Daddy claims he is worried about Brick, and concerned about his recent behavior, so he forces Brick

> topic sentence:
> identifies purpose for Big Daddy's mendacity

to have a talk with him to find out why he is being an alcoholic. Big Daddy decides that it is time for him and Brick to have a talk, despite the fact that while they always talk "nothing materializes" (pg. 92). Big Daddy proceeds to question him intensely trying to figure out exactly what to do with Brick, and how bad off he is, yet Brick offers up very little, and what Brick does offer up can be interpreted in many different ways. Big Daddy has this talk with Brick to try to find a way to get him sober so he can rightfully run the land, without Big Daddy having to "subsidize worthless behavior, rot, and corruption" (pg. 112). Both Brick and Big Daddy don't

> evidence: provides details from the play of the conversation between the two characters

trust anyone, yet for some reason despite them not having a strong connection, they are the most similar. They are both bitter, but Big Daddy needs Brick, so he puts up with his nonsense. Big Daddy needs someone that does not lie to him to run his land when he dies. Brick claims he has never lied to Big Daddy, because they have never truly talked (pg. 113).

> commentary: focuses on both characters' bitterness

Big Daddy has a more hardworking personality, one that's willing to pull himself up by his bootstraps, and therefore believes he doesn't need anything or anyone. Brick has a more indifferent personality, as he has gotten everything he's ever wanted, so he believes he doesn't need anyone or anything as well. Brick is completely fine with him not inheriting the farm,

> commentary: shifts to the differences between the two characters

but Big Daddy is not. After Big Daddy's talk with Brick is unsuccessful, he then hopes that Maggie will set him straight. Maggie does so by limiting his liquor until Brick has done what is required of him, all of which is a part of Big Daddy's plan to straighten Brick up. At the very end of the play, Maggie claims she is pregnant, and Big Daddy claims this is true as he can see the life inside her; this is Big Daddy's final

> evidence: includes another example of mendacity

attempt of mendacity to help Brick, as he knows that Maggie being pregnant will give her the motivation to finally set him straight so that she and Brick can inherit the farm and grow the wealth. Big Daddy uses mendacity in numerous ways to accomplish his goal of having Brick be the sole inheritor of his land.

> commentary: justifies Big Daddy's perspective and motives for being untruthful

Brick uses mendacity as a way to attempt to explain to Big Daddy why he is an alcoholic, and lies about the reasons he drinks. Brick simply wants to drink, it makes him happy, but his family, especially Big Daddy doesn't like this. Brick explains that he likes the click in his head, when he can finally be at peace, and that he drinks to accomplish that. Everyone believes that this is because he is sad about his old friend Skipper, who the last conversation he had with him was when Skipper admitted his feelings towards Brick and Brick hung up without saying a word (pg. 127). Big Daddy claims Brick started drinking right after he died (pg. 115). Brick runs with this story and creates an elaborate tale about him and Skipper, but Big Daddy does not tend to believe that this story is completely truthful. Brick explains that he drinks because of disgust, and that is all, yet Big Daddy knows he is holding back. Brick is lying to himself about why he drinks, claiming that mendacity is the system that they live in, liquor is one way out and death is the other. Brick uses lies to protect himself, and his ambitions of drinking himself away from his sorrow, whatever they may be. He uses lies to give people a valid excuse for why he is the way he is, when all Brick knows for certain is that he just wants to drink himself away because it makes him happy. Mendacity is used by Brick to make sure he can accomplish his goal of having a quiet life that he can drink away by himself.

> topic sentence: identifies purpose for Brick's mendacity

> evidence: provides details of Brick's mendacity

> commentary: identifies Brick's perspective and motives for lying as it relates to his goal

Brick and Big Daddy are the same character in a way because they both believe they don't need anyone or anything, and they are both rotting away from bitterness. Big Daddy is a lot more stubborn and loud whereas Brick is more quiet and conforming. Brick's weakness is his alcohol and Big Daddy's weakness is his belief that he can do everything himself. They reflect each other's weaknesses onto each other, and therefore they can be the most vulnerable with each other, the most each one will allow. They are both broken, but neither one of them fully realizes it and wants to do something to change it. They are relatable characters, by the end the audience can see why they are the way they are, why the characters believe they are by themselves. Both Brick and Big Daddy have to navigate the deceit they are met with in each person, making them relatable. They have common character flaws that many people can relate to, they represent loneliness and sadness. They are varying degrees of these emotions, making them relatable to the audience that can understand these feelings that are manifesting as these characters. These raw feelings are what makes the characters relatable to the audience and make it a timeless play, as the ideas of loneliness and sadness will never go away.

> topic sentence: identifies a shared trait between Brick and Big Daddy

> commentary: relates actions of mendacity to loneliness and sadness

> conclusion: emphasizes the relatability of the characters' consequence of mendacity

⊐⊔⊏
⊐⊐⊏
⊐⊐⊏
⊐⊐⊏
⊐⊐⊏
⊐⊐⊏
⊐⊐⊏
⊐⊐⊏
⊐⊐⊏
⊐⊐⊏
⊐⊓⊏

PREPARING FOR THE AP® EXAM

Free-Response Question: Prose Fiction Analysis

AP® **Enduring Understanding (LAN-1)**

Readers establish and communicate their interpretations of literature through arguments supported by textual evidence.

Creating Unity through Commentary

In the first three free-response workshops, you learned about the essential ingredients of a literary argument: a defensible thesis statement with a claim that includes an interpretation (idea + insight), a line of reasoning, relevant evidence, and commentary. You will now begin to focus more specifically on how to connect these elements that work together to develop your literary argument. In this workshop, you will return to the task of prose fiction analysis and build on your knowledge and skills.

Read the following practice prompt and the accompanying passage, which is the type of prompt you may see on the AP® English Literature and Composition Exam.

Prompt:

The following excerpt is from the 1847 novel *Wuthering Heights* by Emily Brontë. In this passage, Nelly Dean, the housemaid, is narrating a conversation she had with her young mistress, Catherine. Catherine has decided to marry a wealthy young man named Edgar Linton instead of her soulmate Heathcliff, a man with no position or prospects. Read the passage carefully. Then, in a well-written essay, analyze how Brontë uses literary elements and techniques to portray Catherine's complex perspective about love and marriage.

In your response, you should do the following:

- Respond to the prompt with a claim that presents an interpretation
- Select and use evidence to develop and support your interpretation
- Explain how the evidence supports your line of reasoning
- Use appropriate grammar and punctuation in communicating your argument

Unifying Idea	*from* **Wuthering Heights** Emily Brontë	Effect of Literary Elements and Techniques
love	'It would degrade me to marry Heathcliff now; so he shall never know how I love him: and that, not because he's handsome, Nelly, but because he's more myself than I am. Whatever our souls 5 are made of, his and mine are the same; and Linton's is as different as moonbeam from lightning, or frost from fire.'	Catherine's decision not to marry Heathcliff initially suggests that she values wealth over love
	Ere this speech ended I became sensible of Heathcliff's presence. Having noticed a slight 10 movement, I turned my head, and saw him rise from the bench, and steal out noiselessly. He	
love	had listened till he heard Catherine say it would degrade her to marry him, and then he stayed to hear no further. My companion, sitting on the	Nelly is an involved and caring narrator who knows Heathcliff loves Catherine
	15 ground, was prevented by the back of the settle[1] from remarking[2] his presence or departure; but I started, and bade her hush!	
	'Why?' she asked, gazing nervously round.	
	'Joseph is here,' I answered, catching oppor- 20 tunely the roll of his cartwheels up the road; 'and Heathcliff will come in with him. I'm not sure whether he were not at the door this moment.'	
	'Oh, he couldn't overhear me at the door!' said she. 'Give me Hareton, while you get the supper, 25 and when it is ready ask me to sup with you.	
love	I want to cheat my uncomfortable conscience, and be convinced that Heathcliff has no notion of these things. He has not, has he? He does not know what being in love is!'	Catherine justifies her actions by convincing herself that Heathcliff does not understand love
	30 'I see no reason that he should not know, as well as you,' I returned; 'and if you are his choice, he'll be the most unfortunate creature that ever	
love	was born! As soon as you become Mrs. Linton, he loses friend, and love, and all! Have you	Nelly's perspective suggests Catherine is cruel for depriving Heathcliff of love

[1]Settle — a long seat with a high back
[2]Remarking — noticing

35 considered how you'll bear the separation, and
how he'll bear to be quite deserted in the world?
Because, Miss Catherine —'
    'He quite deserted! we separated!' she
exclaimed, with an accent of indignation. 'Who
40 is to separate us, pray? They'll meet the fate of
Milo![3] Not as long as I live, Ellen: for no mortal
creature. Every Linton on the face of the earth
might melt into nothing before I could consent to forsake Heathcliff. Oh, that's not what I
45 intend — that's not what I mean! I shouldn't be
Mrs. Linton were such a price demanded! He'll
be as much to me as he has been all his lifetime.
Edgar must shake off his antipathy, and tolerate him, at least. He will, when he learns my
50 true feelings towards him. Nelly, I see now you
think me a selfish wretch; but did it never strike
you that if Heathcliff and I married, we should
be beggars? whereas, if I marry Linton I can
aid Heathcliff to rise, and place him out of my
55 brother's power.'

the cultural norms of the nineteenth century affect Catherine's decision to marry for position before love

love

    'With your husband's money, Miss Catherine?'
I asked. 'You'll find him not so pliable as you
calculate upon: and, though I'm hardly a judge, I
think that's the worst motive you've given yet for
60 being the wife of young Linton.'

the conflict of Catherine and Nelly's values regarding love reveals Catherine's true motives

love

    'It is not,' retorted she; 'it is the best! The oth-
ers were the satisfaction of my whims: and for
Edgar's sake, too, to satisfy him. This is for the
sake of one who comprehends in his person my
65 feelings to Edgar and myself. I cannot express
it; but surely you and everybody have a notion
that there is or should be an existence of yours
beyond you. What were the use of my creation, if
I were entirely contained here? My great miseries
70 in this world have been Heathcliff's miseries,
and I watched and felt each from the beginning:

[3]Milo — A man of enormous strength from Greek mythology who
tried to tear a tree apart but got his hand caught and was trapped.
Before he could tear himself loose, he was devoured by wolves.

my great thought in living is himself. If all else perished, and HE remained, I should still continue to be; and if all else remained, and he were
75 annihilated, the universe would turn to a mighty stranger: I should not seem a part of it. — My love for Linton is like the foliage in the woods: time will change it, I'm well aware, as winter changes the trees. My love for Heathcliff resembles the
80 eternal rocks beneath: a source of little visible delight, but necessary. Nelly, I AM Heathcliff! He's always, always in my mind: not as a pleasure, any more than I am always a pleasure to myself, but as my own being. So don't talk of our separa-
85 tion again: it is impracticable; and — '

She paused, and hid her face in the folds of my gown; but I jerked it forcibly away. I was out of patience with her folly!

'If I can make any sense of your nonsense,
90 Miss,' I said, 'it only goes to convince me that you are ignorant of the duties you undertake in marrying; or else that you are a wicked, unprincipled girl. But trouble me with no more secrets: I'll not promise to keep them.'

love

love

Catherine's description of her love for both men reveals her belief that spiritual love is eternal

Nelly and Catherine's conflict reveals their opposing ideas of love and Nelly's judgment of Catherine's choice

→ Step One: Annotate the Passage Based on a Unifying Idea

As we return to the prose analysis task, remember that you are directed to analyze a short excerpt from a longer work of fiction. Your job is to analyze this particular scene by reading it closely. As you read and annotate the excerpt, keep in mind the narrative situation provided for you in the prompt, including the year of publication, and the brief details of the scene that allow you to put the text in context and identify a **unifying idea**.

To guide your annotations of the passage, consider the following questions:

- When was the work written and by whom?
- In what location and era does the scene take place? How might this be relevant?
- Who are the characters in the excerpt, and what is the central conflict or tension?
- Who is narrating the scene, and what is the narrator's perspective?

- How does the passage begin and end? Is there a resolution? Why or why not?
- How do these elements (setting, character, structure, narration) relate to an idea?
- What insight does the passage suggest about his idea?

In the prompt from *Wuthering Heights*, note that the novel was published in the nineteenth century. That means that you should consider the historical and social background of that time period in analyzing the characters' behaviors, choices, and values. You also know the narrative context: one character has decided to marry for convenience rather than true love. This information might prompt you to read specifically for the abstract idea of love and determine a perspective about that idea.

Determining the unifying idea and a perspective about that idea will lead you to your **interpretation**, which becomes the basis for the thesis of your literary argument.

→ Step Two: Develop a Defensible Claim and a Unified Line of Reasoning

You have practiced writing thesis statements in the first three workshops. Recall that the claim in your thesis statement must be arguable and defensible. Also, your thesis may or may not preview your line of reasoning. Now you will begin to work on creating unity in your argument by connecting a precise thesis statement and line of reasoning to the evidence and commentary that follows. This begins with a precise and accurate thesis statement.

Some thesis statements make a claim, but may be oversimplified, vague, or general. As you draft your thesis statement, keep asking questions (e.g., why is this important?, so what?, what are the implications?) until you arrive at the most precise and accurate claim. Review the following examples that build in precision:

Sample Thesis Statements	Notes on Effectiveness
In Wuthering Heights, *Emily Brontë contrasts Nelly and Catherine to emphasize Catherine's unconventional ideas about love.*	This thesis refers to a technique (contrast), but the writer does not identify specifically what is being contrasted. Further, the description of Catherine's ideas about love as "unconventional" is vague and fails to reveal complexity.
In Wuthering Heights, *Emily Brontë contrasts Nelly Dean's practical ideas to Catherine's wildly unconventional ideas about love to emphasize Catherine's belief that while love can exist on both physical and spiritual levels, spiritual love is eternal.*	This thesis specifies the character qualities that are contrasted (practical and unconventional). It also identifies a complex attitude about love (physical and spiritual). Finally, the thesis expresses an interpretation that spiritual love is eternal.

Once you have a precise thesis statement, you can develop an effective argument by supporting your thesis with a logical line of reasoning that supports your interpretation. You will manage the discussion of your interpretation by forming two or more body paragraphs to support your thesis statement. Review the following questions to determine the structure of your line of reasoning. They will help you write your topic sentences.

- Do the author's literary elements and techniques work together to present complexity in a character, a relationship, or a narrative perspective?
- Does the passage reveal a change in a character's traits, values, or perspectives?
- Does the passage contrast two or more characters' traits, values, or perspectives?
- Does the narrator's perspective or attitude change within the passage?
- Does the atmosphere or narrative tone change within the passage?

After considering these questions, you can determine a logical sequence for discussing your interpretation. Your topic sentences should include language that is accurate and precise; they should also relate directly to the single unifying idea and insight in your thesis statement.

Review the following thesis statement and line of reasoning. Note that the unifying idea creates the connection between the claim in the thesis and the topic sentences that support the claim.

Sample Thesis Statement

In Wuthering Heights, *Emily Brontë contrasts Nelly Dean's practical ideas to Catherine's wildly unconventional ideas about love to emphasize Catherine's belief that while love can exist on both physical and spiritual levels, spiritual love is eternal.*

Topic Sentence 1	Topic Sentence 2
Brontë includes Nelly Dean's practical perspective and disapproving tone in her conversation with Catherine to establish Catherine's curious motives for marrying for convenience instead of love.	*Once the reader understands Catherine's motives, Brontë uses comparisons to reveal Catherine's distinction between physical and spiritual love which leads to her decision.*

In this example, the first topic sentence claims that the dialogue between the two characters (and the conflict caused by their differences) allows the reader to learn of Catherine's motives. It sets up the discussion that will follow, revealing her plan to marry Edgar for Heathcliff's benefit.

The second body paragraph builds on the first. A transitional phrase (*Once the reader understands Catherine's motives*) links the two paragraphs together and then establishes the purpose for the second body paragraph, it also adds another layer of understanding.

→ **Step Three: Choose Relevant Evidence**

With your line of reasoning in mind, choose **evidence** from the passage to align with each topic sentence. Your line of reasoning organizes your reasons in a logical sequence. Likewise, you should arrange the evidence in each body paragraph logically as well. This evidence should be both relevant and sufficient. Evidence is **relevant** when it directly relates to the reasons in your line of reasoning and connects to the claim in your thesis. Evidence is **sufficient** when it supports each reason in your line of reasoning.

Questions to consider when choosing evidence:

- Have you selected one or more pieces of evidence from the text for each reason in your line of reasoning?
- Is the evidence directly connected to the topic sentence and related to your unifying idea?
- Does your evidence represent multiple literary elements and techniques?
- If you have identified a particular literary element or technique, does the evidence exemplify that authorial choice?
- Will you paraphrase or quote directly from the text?
- Is the textual evidence that you selected a short phrase that can be embedded into your discussion?

Remember that the passages you will encounter contain rich language and many details. You cannot possibly discuss *everything* within a passage. Therefore, you will need to omit evidence that is not relevant to your discussion of the idea and insight.

Topic Sentence 1	Topic Sentence 2
Brontë includes Nelly Dean's practical perspective and disapproving tone in her conversation with Catherine to reveal Catherine's motives for marrying for convenience instead of love.	*Once the reader understands Catherine's motives, Brontë uses comparisons to reveal Catherine's distinction between physical and spiritual love, which leads to her decision.*
Relevant and Sufficient Evidence	**Relevant and Sufficient Evidence**
Evidence 1: *"It would degrade me to marry Heathcliff" / "I think that's the worst motive you've given yet"*	Evidence 1: *"My great miseries in this world have been Heathcliff's miseries"*
Evidence 2: *"you are ignorant of the duties you undertake in marrying" / "I see now you think me a selfish wretch . . ., but if I marry Linton I can aid Heathcliff to rise"*	Evidence 2: *"My love for Linton is like the foliage in the woods" / "My love for Heathcliff resembles the eternal rocks beneath"*

→ Step Four: Develop Your Commentary

In Unit 3, you learned to develop your literary argument by explaining how the evidence supports the reasons in your line of reasoning. This explanation, called **commentary**, is a vital part of your line of reasoning. It works to link your evidence to your reasons and your reasons to the claim in your thesis statement. When you link all of these elements logically and thoughtfully, the argument will have **unity**. The key to writing a unified argument is to stay focused on your unifying idea and insight. That means keeping that focus not just in your thesis but also throughout the body of your essay. So when you include evidence, you must explain how that evidence relates to the idea. Writing commentary that orbits around the unifying idea will help you avoid the trap of summarizing or giving superficial commentary. You must be aware of what observation you are making about that idea, however.

Questions that your commentary might answer in your analysis:

- Why an author chose an element or technique
- How an element or technique functions within a text
- How evidence relates to a unifying idea or insight
- How literary elements work together in a text for a unified purpose

To explain your evidence, you may consult the table on pages 541–542 or review the following question stems:

- The words/images/details of _____ emphasize _____. Through these choices, the author reveals _____.
- By comparing/contrasting/juxtaposing _____ and _____, the author emphasizes _____ prompting the reader to conclude _____.
- By including _____, the author means to symbolize _____. Through this association, the reader understands _____.
- The character's actions/words/thoughts reveal _____. As a result, the reader understands that the character values _____.
- The pattern of images leads the reader to understand that _____.

Review the following example of commentary and notice how the commentary connects to both the topic sentence and the thesis.

Evidence	Commentary Connected to Idea
"It would degrade me" / "I think that's the worst motive you've given yet"	Catherine's blunt admission that marrying Heathcliff would "degrade" her reveals at first that she values wealth and social position over spiritual love. Brontë uses Nelly's abrupt response, "that's the worst motive you've given yet," to establish the conflict between the two characters. As a result, Nelly's critical tone pushes Catherine to acknowledge her true emotions for Heathcliff, which run much deeper than status and security. Brontë, therefore, wishes to characterize the complexity of Catherine's connection to Heathcliff.

INSIDER AP® TIP

Commentary explains complexity. While all successful essays are unified, the most successful essays are those that analyze a tension. By explaining a tension, you are demonstrating your understanding of literary complexity. Commentary is where you reveal how all of the elements and techniques come together in a complex way to contribute to your interpretation.

AP® EXAM PRACTICE

The following is an example of a prose fiction analysis free-response question. Practice the skills you learned in this workshop to write a literary argument in response to the prompt.

Remember to follow the four steps:

- Step One: Annotate the passage based on a **unifying idea**
- Step Two: Write a **defensible thesis statement**
- Step Three: Choose **relevant evidence**
- Step Four: Develop **insightful commentary**

Prompt:

The following excerpt is from the 1968 novel *House Made of Dawn* by M. Scott Momaday, a story about a Native American man named Abel who has suffered many turbulent years trying to both assimilate into modern American culture and remain true to his native culture. In this passage from the end of the novel, Abel participates in the ceremonial running of the dead after the death of his grandfather. Read the passage carefully. Then, in a well-written essay, analyze how Momaday uses literary elements and techniques to convey Abel's complex perspective about his identity and cultural connections.

In your response you should do the following:

- Respond to the prompt with a thesis that presents a defensible interpretation
- Select and use evidence to support your line of reasoning
- Explain how the evidence supports your line of reasoning
- Use appropriate grammar and punctuation in communicating your argument

It was pitch black before the dawn, and he went along the corrals and through the orchards to the mission. The motor turned and, one after another, the lights went on
5 upstairs and in the stair well and in the hall, and Father Olguin threw open the door.

What in God's name — ?" he said.
"My grandfather is dead," Abel said. "You must bury him."
10 "Dead? Oh . . . yes — yes, of course. But, *good heavens*, couldn't you have waited until — "

"My grandfather is dead," Abel repeated. His voice was low and even. There was no emotion, nothing.

"Yes, yes. I heard you," said the priest, rubbing his good eye. "Good Lord, what time is it anyway? Do you know what *time* it is? I can understand how you must feel, but—"

But Abel was gone. Father Olguin shivered with cold and peered out into the darkness. "I can understand," he said. "I understand, do you hear?" And he began to shout. "I understand! *Oh God? I understand—I understand!*"

Abel did not return to his grandfather's house. He walked hurriedly southward along the edge of the town. At the last house he paused and took off his shirt. His body was numb and ached with cold, and he knelt at the mouth of the oven. He reached inside and placed his hands in the frozen crust and rubbed his arms and chest with ashes. And he got up and went on hurriedly to the road and south on the wagon road in the darkness. There was no sound but his own quick, even steps on the hard crust of the snow, and he went on and on, far out on the road.

The pale light grew upon the land, and it was only a trick of the darkness at first, the slow stirring and standing away of the night; and then the murky, leaden swell of light upon the snow and the dunes and the black evergreen spines. And the east deepened into light above the black highland, soft and milky and streaked with gray. He was almost there, and he saw the runners standing away in the distance.

He came among them, and they huddled in the cold together, waiting, and the pale light before the dawn rose up in the valley. A single cloud lay over the world, heavy and still. It lay out upon the black mesa, smudging out the margin and spilling over the lee. But at the saddle there was nothing. There was only the clear pool of eternity. They held their eyes upon it, waiting, and too slow and various to see, the void began to deepen and to change: pumice, and pearl, and mother-of-pearl, and the pale and brilliant blush of orange and of rose. And then the deep handing rim ran with fire and the sudden cold flare of the dawn struck upon the arc, and the runners sprang away.

The soft and sudden sound of their going, swift and breaking away all at once, startled him, and he began to run after them. He was running, and his body cracked open with pain, and he was running on. He was running and there was no reason to run but the running itself and the land and the dawn appearing. The sun rose up in the saddle and shone in shafts upon the road across the snow-covered valley and the hills, and the chill of the night fell away and it began to rain. He saw the slim black bodies of the runners in the distance, gliding away without sound through the slanting light and the rain. He was running and a cold sweat broke out upon him and his breath heaved with the pain of running. His legs buckled and he fell in the snow. The rain fell around him in the snow and he saw his broken hands, how the rain made streaks upon them and dripped soot upon the snow. And he got up and ran on. He was alone and running on. All of his being was concentrated in the sheer motion of running on, and he was past caring about the pain. Pure exhaustion laid hold of his mind, and he could see at last without having to think. He could see the canyon and the mountains and the sky. He could see the rain and the river and the field beyond. He could see the dark hills at dawn. He was running, and under his breath he began to sing. There was no sound, and he had no voice; he had only the words of a song. And he went running on the rise of the song. *House made of pollen, house made of dawn.*[1]

---

[1]Words to a song from a Navajo ritual.

ORGANIZING A PROSE FICTION ANALYSIS (II)

Defensible Thesis Statement with Claim (idea + insight):

In [title], the author shifts from [a to b] to reveal that [idea + insight].

Topic Sentence 1 (Identify the first aspect of topic related to the unifying idea):	Topic Sentence 2 (Identify the second aspect of topic related to the unifying idea):	Topic Sentence 3 (Identify the third aspect of topic related to the unifying idea):
Initially, [author] includes [literary element] to illustrate [universal idea].	As the narrative progresses, [author] shifts from [a to b] to explore [topic] further using [literary element] to reveal [universal idea].	Ultimately, [author] includes [literary element] to reveal [universal idea].
Textual Details (Relevant and sufficient evidence):	**Textual Details** (Relevant and sufficient evidence):	**Textual Details** (Relevant and sufficient evidence):
For example, the detail [evidence], used to describe [context] illustrates [link to reason].	To illustrate, [author] describes/compares [context] by including [text evidence] to reveal [link to reason].	As an example of [technique/element], the author includes [text evidence] to explain [link to reason].
Additionally, the detail [evidence], used to describe [context] illustrates [link to reason].	In the same way, [author] describes/compares [context] by including [text evidence] to reveal [link to reason].	Another example, of [technique/element], that the author includes [text evidence] illustrates [link to reason].
Commentary (Link evidence to reason and idea):	**Commentary** (Link evidence to reason and idea):	**Commentary** (Link evidence to reason and idea):
The association of [text evidence] with [topic sentence] reveals [idea and insight].	Through this choice, [author] develops [idea and insight].	By including this [element/technique] the author suggests that [idea and insight].
2–4 sentences explaining how the evidence exemplifies the universal idea	*2–4 sentences explaining how the evidence exemplifies the universal idea*	*2–4 sentences explaining how the evidence exemplifies the universal idea*

from The Street

Ann Petry

The following is an excerpt from a novel published in 1946.

The noise and confusion in the street were pleasant after the stillness that hung about the curtained booths of the beauty shop. Buses and trucks roared to a stop at the corners. People
5 coming home from work jostled against her. There was the ebb and flow of talk and laughter; punctuated now and then by the sharp scream of brakes.

The children swarming past Lutie added
10 to the noise and the confusion. They were everywhere — rocking back and forth on the traffic stanchions in front of the post-office, stealing rides on the backs of the crosstown buses, drumming on the sides of ash cans
15 with broomsticks, sitting in small groups in doorways, playing on the steps of the houses, writing on the sidewalk with colored chalk, bouncing balls against the sides of the buildings. They turned a deaf ear to the commands
20 shrilling from the windows all up and down the street, 'You Tommie, Jimmie, Billie, can't you see it's snowin'? Come in out the street.'

The street was so crowded that she paused frequently in order not to collide with a group
25 of children, and she wondered if these were the things that Bub had done after school. She tried to see the street with his eyes and couldn't because the crap[1] game in progress in the middle of the block, the scraps of obscene talk she

30 heard as she passed the poolroom, the tough young boys with their caps on backward who swaggered by, were things that she saw with the eyes of an adult and reacted to from an adult's point of view. It was impossible to know how
35 this street looked to eight-year-old Bub. It may have appealed to him or it may have frightened him.

There was a desperate battle going on in front of the house where she lived. Kids were
40 using bags of garbage from the cans lined up along the curb as ammunition. The bags had broken open, covering the sidewalk with litter, filling the air with a strong, rancid smell.

Lutie picked her way through orange skins,
45 coffee grounds, chicken bones, fish bones, toilet paper, potato peelings, wilted kale, skins of baked sweet potatoes, pieces of newspaper, broken gin bottles, broken whiskey bottles, a man's discarded felt hat, an old pair of pants.
50 Perhaps Bub had taken part in this kind of warfare, she thought, even as she frowned at the rubbish under her feet; possibly a battle would have appealed to some unsatisfied spirit of adventure in him, so that he would have
55 joined these kids, overlooking the stink of the garbage in his joy in the conflict just as they were doing.

Mrs. Hedges was leaning far out of her window, urging the contestants on.
60   'That's right, Jimmie,' Mrs. Hedges cried. 'Hit him on the head.' And then as the bag went past its mark, 'Aw, shucks, boy, what's the matter with your aim?'

She caught sight of Lutie and knowing that
65 she was home earlier than when she went to

[1] a gambling game played with two dice, chiefly in North America

work, immediately deduced that she had been
somewhere to see Bub or see about him. 'Did
you see Bub?' she asked.

 'Yes. For a little while.'

70 'Been to the beauty parlor, ain't you?' Mrs.
Hedges studied the black curls shining under
the skull cap on Lutie's head. 'Looks right nice,'
she said.

 She leaned a little farther out of the window.
75 'Bub being in trouble you probably need some
money. A friend of mine, a Mr. Junto — a very
nice white gentleman, dearie —'

 Her voice trailed off because Lutie turned
away abruptly and disappeared through the
80 apartment house door. Mrs. Hedges scowled
after her. After all, if you needed money you
needed money and why anyone would act like
that when it was offered to them she couldn't
imagine. She shrugged her shoulders and
85 turned her attention back to the battle going
on under her window.

 As Lutie climbed the stairs, she deliberately
accentuated the clicking of the heels of her shoes
on the treads because the sharp sound helped
90 relieve the hard resentment she felt; it gave
expression to the anger flooding through her.

1. Which of the following best describes Lutie's
   attitude toward the circumstances of paragraph 5 (lines 44–57)?
   (A) Disgusted as she navigates others' trash
   and harshly judges the children
   (B) Unconcerned as she contemplates
   possibilities of Bub's experiences
   (C) Amused by the capacity for the children
   on the street to find joy in anything
   (D) Shocked that parents would allow their
   children to behave as these are
   (E) Naive about the circumstances of the
   children she encounters

2. In the context of the passage as a whole, Mrs.
   Hedges's literal position in the setting as
   shown in lines 58–59 ("Mrs. Hedges . . . on.")
   significantly allows her to
   (A) directly create the noise and confusion on
   the street below.
   (B) be revered as a leader and wise-woman by
   others who live on the street.
   (C) oversee bad behaviors and meddle with
   others on the street.
   (D) worry about the well-being of those living
   on the street.
   (E) interact with passersby because she
   cannot leave her home.

3. Lutie's actions in lines 78–80 ("Her voice . . .
   house door.") most clearly suggests
   (A) that she is uninterested in Mrs. Hedges's
   proposal.
   (B) that Mrs. Hedges is her mother.
   (C) that her isolation is self-imposed.
   (D) her failure to develop relationships with
   people on the street.
   (E) her dislike and rejection of Mrs. Hedges's
   suggestion.

4. Mrs. Hedges's actions in lines 80–86
   ("Mrs. Hedges . . . her window.") most clearly
   suggest that she
   (A) understands Lutie's situation.
   (B) lives in the same building as Lutie.
   (C) is planning to approach Lutie later.
   (D) has no genuine concern for Lutie.
   (E) wants to exploit Lutie's kindness.

5. The tension between Mrs. Hedges and Lutie can be best described as a conflict of which of the following?
   (A) Lutie's optimism toward life and Mrs. Hedges's bitterness toward people younger than herself.
   (B) Lutie's fear of the people on the street and Mrs. Hedges's boldness toward Lutie.
   (C) Lutie's maturity and concern for others and Mrs. Hedges's immaturity and self-interest.
   (D) Lutie's determination to grow beyond the street and Mrs. Hedges's complacency.
   (E) Lutie's authenticity and Mrs. Hedges's need to please others.

6. All of the following contribute to the "noise and confusion in the street" EXCEPT
   (A) "children swarming past" (line 9).
   (B) "kids were using bags of garbage from the cans lined up along the curb as ammunition" (lines 39–41).
   (C) "orange skins, coffee grounds, chicken bones, fish bones, toilet paper, potato peelings, wilted kale, skins of baked sweet potatoes, pieces of newspaper, broken gin bottles, broken whiskey bottles, a man's discarded felt hat, an old pair of pants" (lines 44–49).
   (D) " 'that's right, Jimmie,' Mrs. Hedges cried. 'Hit him on the head' " (lines 60–61).
   (E) "the clicking of the heels of her shoes" (line 88).

7. The adjectives used in the last paragraph, lines 87–91 ("As Lutie . . . through her.") most likely suggest which of the following about Lutie's perspective on her situation?
   (A) She is uncomfortable with her anger.
   (B) She cannot understand why she gets angry.
   (C) She knows she must find an outlet for her resentment.
   (D) She longs to leave the street.
   (E) She understands Mrs. Hedges better than Mrs. Hedges understands herself.

8. Which of the following best describes the effect of the shift that occurs between paragraph 5 (lines 44–57) and paragraph 6 (lines 58–59)?
   (A) Mrs. Hedges's interest in Lutie's well-being is emphasized.
   (B) Lutie's concerns about the children on the street are emphasized.
   (C) Lutie's personality and concerns are contrasted with Mrs. Hedges's.
   (D) Mrs. Hedges's disgust with the children in the street becomes evident.
   (E) The narrator's attitude toward Lutie is contrasted with Mrs. Hedges's.

9. Which of the following is the best defensible interpretation of the passage as a whole?
   (A) Behavior and mindset define maturity, not age.
   (B) Setting determines personality, not experience.
   (C) Everyone needs some connection with other people.
   (D) Empathy and compassion must be earned, not given.
   (E) Others' perspectives matter more than anything else.

Harlem Shadows

Claude McKay

> I hear the halting footsteps of a lass
> In Negro Harlem when the night lets fall
> Its veil. I see the shapes of girls who pass
> To bend and barter at desire's call.
> 5 Ah, little dark girls who in slippered feet
> Go prowling through the night from street to street!
>
> Through the long night until the silver break
> Of day the little gray feet know no rest;
> Through the lone night until the last snow-flake
> 10 Has dropped from heaven upon the earth's white breast,
> The dusky, half-clad girls of tired feet
> Are trudging, thinly shod, from street to street.
>
> Ah, stern harsh world, that in the wretched way
> Of poverty, dishonor and disgrace,
> 15 Has pushed the timid little feet of clay,
> The sacred brown feet of my fallen race!
> Ah, heart of me, the weary, weary feet
> In Harlem wandering from street to street.

1. All of the following contribute to an understanding of the speaker's distance to the situation of the poem EXCEPT
   (A) "I hear the halting footsteps of a lass" (line 1).
   (B) "I see the shapes of girls who pass" (line 3).
   (C) "Are trudging, thinly shod, from street to street" (line 12).
   (D) "Ah, heart of me, the weary, weary feet" (line 17).
   (E) "The sacred brown feet of my fallen race!" (line 16).

2. The reference to the veil (line 3) is an example of a(n)
   (A) symbol.
   (B) simile.
   (C) allusion.
   (D) metaphor.
   (E) antecedent.

3. The shift between the second and third stanzas (lines 7–12 and 13–18, respectively) most significantly contrasts
    (A) the speaker's attitude about those around him with their attitude toward the speaker.
    (B) a specific example of a comment on the world in general.
    (C) the attitude of the speaker with the perspectives of the girls the speaker observes.
    (D) the girls' destructive behavior with the speaker's wish to intervene.
    (E) nighttime events on the street with daytime events on the street.

4. "The sacred brown feet of my fallen race!" (line 16) indicates the speaker's attitude toward his own race is one of
    (A) reverence and sorrow.
    (B) respect and disgrace.
    (C) pity and compassion.
    (D) indifference and contempt.
    (E) loss and responsibility.

5. Considered within the context of their lines and the poem as a whole, repetition of "feet" and "street to street" in the last two lines of each stanza might be understood as
    (A) commenting on the long-term failure of the speaker to preserve their race.
    (B) emphasizing the shared experiences of all people, regardless of race.
    (C) relating to the journey that the girls are on.
    (D) commenting on the relationship between the girls of the poem and the speaker's entire race.
    (E) emphasizing the decline and fall of the speaker's race over time.

6. Which of the following best describes the poem as a whole?
    (A) An observation about the ways outsiders find their way into a group.
    (B) A metaphor about the ongoing struggles of the speaker's race and how weary the people of his race are becoming.
    (C) A dream in which the speaker explores ways to better understand the situation of his race.
    (D) A meditation on the failure of the speaker's race and the speaker's own failure to protect himself from the dishonor of poverty.
    (E) A cautionary tale concerning what happens to a race of people when they allow themselves to be defined by only a few of their people.

Sven Hagolani/fStop/Getty Images

UNIT 5

Analyzing Comparisons

UNIT GOALS

	Focus	Goals
Big Idea: Structure	**Form, Sound, Rhythm, and Rhyme**	Explain the structure and form of a literary text and how they contribute to an interpretation.
Big Idea: Figurative Language	**Words and Images**	Explain the function of imagery and motifs in a literary text and how they contribute to an interpretation.
Big Idea: Figurative Language	**Metaphor, Personification, and Allusion**	Explain the function of extended metaphor, personification, and allusion and how they contribute to an interpretation.
Ideas in Literature	• **The Individual and Nature** • **Imagination and Intuition**	Explain how the ideas of the individual, nature, imagination, and intuition are reflected in classic and contemporary texts.
Big Idea: Literary Argumentation	**Writing about Motif and Extended Metaphor**	Write a literary argument that analyzes how the author's use of motif or extended metaphor contributes to an interpretation of a text.
Preparing for the AP® Exam	**Free-Response Question: Poetry Analysis** Creating Coherence through Transitional Elements	Incorporate transitional elements to convey relationships within a literary argument.
	Multiple-Choice Questions: Prose	Analyze literary elements and techniques in classic and contemporary prose and poetry.
	Multiple-Choice Questions: Poetry	

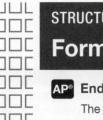

Form, Sound, Rhythm, and Rhyme

 Enduring Understanding (STR-1)

The arrangement of the parts and sections of a text, the relationship of the parts to each other, and the sequence in which the text reveals information are all structural choices made by a writer that contribute to the reader's interpretation of a text.

KEY POINT

The author's choice of structure and patterns of sound in a poem create relationships that contribute to a reader's interpretation.

Whether you're listening to music or you happen to hear an advertisement while watching TV or scrolling through social media, catchy jingles and audio clips are designed to stick in your memory long after you've heard them. According to research by the American Psychological Association, these "earworms" often feature simple melodies, recurring rhythmic patterns, and unusual pauses or repetitions — all of which contribute to the jingle's *stickiness*: a song or musical phrase's ability to occupy your mind even when you're not listening to it.

Keep this in mind when you read poetry, which, like music, must appeal to our ears: it is meant to be read aloud as much as it is meant to be read on the page. The structures or patterns of a poem — how a writer uses form, sound, rhythm, rhyme — add meaning, value, and enjoyment to the work as a whole.

Poetry May Be Conventional or Unconventional

You might notice that writers within a particular time period use similar overarching poetic structures or patterns, also known as the poem's *form*. These forms become conventions when they are frequently used over time. When writers intentionally break from a convention, they do so to emphasize an important idea. By deviating from conventions, they can even generate new forms that communicate new ideas.

Note: You won't be quizzed on the AP Exam to label or identify specific rhyme schemes, metrical patterns, or forms of poetry, but knowing how writers use and combine different forms, sounds, rhythms, and rhymes may provide another opportunity for interpretation.*

Types of Poetry

Some poems tell stories; others express ideas, emotions, or experiences. Poems can be grouped into categories that work toward or explore specific goals. An author chooses a type of poetry that coincides with his or her purpose for writing. Poetry is generally classified as narrative, lyric, epic, or dramatic.

- Narrative: A narrator or persona tells a story.
- Lyric: A first-person speaker expresses an intense emotion, idea, or insight.

- Epic: The speaker or narrator — along with characters in the poem — relates an extraordinary tale of heroism.
- Dramatic: One or more characters speak in the poem, which is usually meant to be acted or performed.

Forms: Closed and Open

A poem's form is its overall structure or shape. If a writer follows an established pattern of lines, meter, rhymes, and stanzas, the poem will have a "fixed" or "closed" form. In other words, it will follow **conventions**: rules and characteristics used so often that they define the form. These formal elements and patterns help develop relationships between the ideas in the poem. Just remember that form and structure are not superficial or decorative. If you can identify how a writer draws upon conventional literary forms (or subverts them), you will have an important key for developing an interpretation. Some **closed forms** of poetry include sonnets, villanelles, sestinas, haiku, epigrams, limericks, elegies, and odes.

In contrast, some poets reject the conventional forms of poetry. Poems that do not follow established patterns of meter, rhyme, and stanza are known as **open-form** poetry. These poems may avoid predictable patterns in the structures of their lines and stanzas, but poets may still use form to create relationships between ideas. Some open forms of poetry include free verse, blank verse, prose poems, visual or concrete poems, slam poetry, and found poetry.

Sound: Rhythm and Rhyme

Everyday conversations follow a natural **rhythm** or pattern of stressed and unstressed syllables and pauses. Likewise, a poem follows a beat that communicates meaning through the flow of sound patterns and silence. Rhythm directly affects the pacing or action of a poem. It emerges from the pattern of "feet" within a sentence. Feet are individual units of rhythm comprised of the syllables in words. English-language poetry uses five types of feet — each of which has different effects on the rhythm of the poem.

You may know the meter and foot combination in Shakespeare's sonnets: iambic pentameter, which usually follows a pattern of ten syllables in an unstressed-then-stressed pattern (for a total of five feet per line). Just as sound is important in poetry, silence also carries meaning: a **caesura** is a break in the rhythmical line that prompts the reader to pause.

You may have been taught as a child that all poetry must **rhyme**. Well, spoiler alert: as you've seen throughout the course, this is not true. Poems may or may not follow an identifiable **rhyme scheme**, which is the pattern of identical word sounds both within the line (*internal rhyme*) and at the end of each line (*end rhyme*). When words sound very similar but aren't an exact rhyme, they create an imperfect *slant rhyme*. Rhyme contributes to the poem's rhythm and flow, as well as its musical qualities. More importantly, rhyme schemes can create relationships between ideas. This is especially true of two successive lines that rhyme called a **couplet**.

 **INSIDER TIP**   **Read a poem by the punctuation, not by line.** It might be helpful to rewrite a poem into a paragraph to read it aloud that way.

STRUCTURE AND SOUND IN POETRY		
Author's Choices	**Literary Forms and Elements**	**Key Considerations**
Type	Narrative Lyric Epic Dramatic	How is the type of poetry related to the poet's purpose? How does the poem's context affect the poet's choice of type?
Form and structure	Closed Open	How does an author's choice of closed or open form contribute to a reader's interpretation? How does one part or section of a text relate to another part? How does one part or section of a text relate to the text as a whole? How does the structure of a poem contribute to a reader's interpretation?
Sound	Rhythm Rhyme	How do rhyme and rhythm (e.g., rhyme scheme, meter, slant rhyme) contribute to the poem? How does the punctuation or lack of punctuation convey relationships and pauses that contribute to the interpretation of a poem?

GUIDED READING

Sonnet XVIII
Erik Didriksen

THE TEXT IN CONTEXT

The sonnet has existed for around seven hundred years. It was a cliched poetic form even in Shakespeare's time — as he was well aware. But software engineer and sonneteer Erik Didriksen shows how these tight little poems can still be novel, witty, and perceptive. The following example comes from Didriksen's 2015 book *Pop Sonnets: Shakespearean Spins on Your Favorite Songs*. In the collection, Didriksen reimagines one hundred well-known hip-hop and pop songs by capturing them in son-net form. Here, he retells Will Smith's theme song to the 1990s television show *The Fresh Prince of Bel-Air.*

©Erik Didriksen, photo by Rebecca Bainbridge

Sonnet XVIII

From western Philadelphia I hail,
where in my youth I'd play upon the green
'til—rue the day!—I found myself assail'd
by ruffians contemptible and mean.
5 Although the spat was trivial and brief,
it wounded my dear mother deep within;
and so, to give her conscience sweet relief,
she sent me forth to live amongst her kin.
When to my port of call I'd been convey'd,
10 I came upon a coachman most unique;
and yet I simply took the trip and paid,
despite his cab's decor and fresh mystique.
—I survey all the land with princely mien
in fair Bel-Air, where I do lay my scene.

Will Smith, *"The Fresh Prince of Bel-Air"*

Guided Questions

1. What is the rhyme scheme? Does the poem have a consistent rhyming pattern?
2. Can you identify the meter by counting the syllables in the line?

3. How does the poem end? Is the rhyming pattern different at the end of the poem?

PRACTICE TEXT

The University of Wisconsin–Eau Claire

Ode to Chinese Superstitions, Haircuts, and Being a Girl
Dorothy Chan

THE TEXT IN CONTEXT

Dorothy Chan is a poet, editor, and assistant professor of English at the University of Wisconsin–Eau Claire. Her collections include *Chinatown Sonnets* (2017), *Attack of the Fifty-Foot Centerfold* (2018), and *Revenge of the Asian Women* (2019). A scholar as well as a poet, Chan's work often focuses on sexuality, gender, power, pop culture, and Asian American identity. Chan is also known for her playfulness with traditional poetic forms — as well as mastery of them.

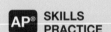

AP® SKILLS PRACTICE	**STRUCTURE**
	Analyzing Structure and Sound in Poetry

As you read Chan's poem, note how she draws upon the conventions of poetic forms, structures, and sound to convey her message.

Analyzing Structure and Sound in Poetry		
Author's Choices	**Key Considerations**	**Details and Effects**
Type: Narrative	How is the type of poetry related to the poet's purpose?	
Lyric	How does the poem's context affect the poet's choice of type?	
Epic		
Dramatic		
Form and Structure: Closed	How does an author's choice of closed or open form contribute to a reader's interpretation?	
Open	How does one part or section of a text relate to another part?	
	How does one part or section of a text relate to the text as a whole?	
	How does the structure of a poem contribute to a reader's interpretation?	

Sound: Rhythm Rhyme	How do rhyme and rhythm (e.g., rhyme scheme, meter, slant rhyme) contribute to the poem?	
	How does the punctuation (or lack of punctuation) convey relationships and pauses that contribute to the interpretation of a poem?	

Ode to Chinese Superstitions, Haircuts, and Being a Girl

Chinese superstition tells me it's bad luck
    to get a haircut when I'm sick, and my hair
gets cut twice a year, because I let it grow,
    tying it into a ponytail, exposing my forehead,
5 looking like I'm the protagonist of an anime,
    which makes me think about my last name,
Chan, also known as the Japanese honorific
    for someone endearing. *Chan*, like a friend

    or someone childlike. I've been told I sound
10   like a child when I pick up the phone, or maybe
    it's my pure joy to hear from the ones I love.
    And yes, voices are sexier than faces, so dial me,
    honey, let's get a little wild tonight, as I pour
    a glass of bourbon and picture myself in anime—
15   cartoon *Chan* starring in a slice-of-life show
    about a girl group trying to make it, and you bet

I'd be the rambunctious one, the tomboy-
    rabble-rouser-ringleader on the drums—
the *trouble* with the exposed forehead, also
20   known in East Asian culture as a symbol
of aggression, because an exposed forehead
    puts everything out there—you're telling
the world you're ready for a takedown,
    and according to my father, good Chinese

25   girls never show their foreheads, and I know
    he wishes I were born in the Year of the Rabbit,
    like my mother, the perfect woman with flawless
    skin who never causes trouble with the boys, but
    no, I'm the Year of the Snake, and I always bring

30   the party, cause the trouble, or as my lover says,
        I'm sarcastic wit personified, and it's boundless,
            because I am *Dorothy*—pop embodied in a gingham

        skirt with a puppy and a picnic basket
            filled with prosciutto and gouda and Prosecco,
35   but really, what is my fate? And my mother
            tells me the family fortune teller got me all
        wrong, because there's no way in hell
            I'd end up being a housewife with three
        children and a breadwinner of a husband.
40   But of course, the fortune teller got my brother's

        fate right. It's moments like this when I wonder
        if I even matter because I'm a girl and not a boy.
        It's moments like this when I think about my fate,
        or how Chinese superstition tells me not to cut or wash
45   my hair on Lunar New Year, so all my good fortune
        won't be snipped away. But really, what is fate?
        I tie my hair back and put on a short skirt, ready
        to take over the world—forehead forever exposed.

STRUCTURE

1. What is the poetic **form**? How do you know?

2. How does each stanza end? Is there a **rhyming** pattern? How does this structure contribute to an idea in the poem?

3. How does the writer's use of dashes in this poem help create relationships between ideas? Find a specific example and explain.

4. How does each **stanza** present a conflict? How do those conflicts build toward the poem's conclusion?

FIGURATIVE LANGUAGE: Word Choice, Imagery, and Symbols
Words and Images

AP **Enduring Understanding (FIG-1)**

Comparisons, representations, and associations shift meaning from the literal to the figurative and invite readers to interpret a text.

Imagine that you've been granted a wish from a powerful — yet tricky — magician who likes to turn people's words against them. That is, your exact choice of words will determine the specific fulfillment of the wish. So your language must be deliberate and precise. For example, if you wish for money, the magician may only conjure up a penny. On the other hand, if you wish for a hoard of gold, you may end up with an angry dragon along with your treasure. Both of these wishes have a similar literal meaning, but the associations and ambiguities of imprecise language lead to vastly different interpretations — and consequences for those who make wishes.

While writers don't have to anticipate the mischievous machinations of a trickster magician, they must think carefully about the words and images that they use to convey their attitudes and insights. This eventually becomes the writer's tone.

As you've learned, writers convey tone through the words and sentences that they choose. But they also develop their tone by choosing specific representations and comparisons to support their message, create helpful analogies, and evoke memorable images. To that end, writers often use literal or concrete objects to create associations and comparisons that reveal abstract ideas. Authors draw upon **figurative language** such as similes, metaphors, personification, and symbols when they use concrete objects to illustrate figurative meaning.

KEY POINT

Authors strategically choose words and images that create emotional associations and connections in readers in ways that emphasize ideas and concepts and convey tone.

Words Create Powerful Associations

Authors choose their words with care and precision. In fact, the author is counting on the precision of a word or image to convey an exact meaning. While words have exact literal meanings called **denotations**, they also carry powerful secondary meanings called **connotations**. Connotations are the emotional, intellectual, and visceral associations that words evoke in readers. A word may resonate with a reader because of its history, its common usage in popular culture, or even its deeply personal meaning. A word often has an emotional association with the author that he or she hopes to convey to the reader by choosing that word. The connotative meaning of a word may be universal across time and place, or it may be specific to a particular time and place or shared within a particular community, group, region, or identity.

Because words create such powerful associations, they contribute to the author's attitude called tone. And because words create emotional connections with a reader, they also contribute to the mood and atmosphere of a text.

Some words may have multiple meanings, which can lead to ambiguity or even humor. Such plays on words are known as **puns**.

Word Choice

Knowing the part of speech or function of a word in a sentence may provide a clue about the perspective of the character or speaker who uses that word. Make no mistake: authors choose the words that characters and speakers use, and carefully control the literary narrative.

- Adjectives: Describe what kind, which one, how many
- Adverbs: Explain relationships by clarifying how, when, where, why, or to what extent
- Verbs: Convey action, pacing, emphasis, and intensity

Imagery

By using specific words, authors create pictures — called **images** — in the minds of readers. Like words, these images also create emotional associations for readers. A single image may be so important that it is singular for emphasis, or the image may be used for description and to contribute to the mood or atmosphere.

A poem or story may have many images woven throughout. **Imagery** is the collection of sensory images collectively (e.g., visual images, sound images, taste images, smell images, or tactile images). As a reader, you can group the individual images by type to analyze how an author appeals to one or more senses. Authors create these image patterns to convey an emphasis. Some authors even develop a series or pattern of images related to a single idea or concept, or **motif**, which you will explore in more depth in a later unit.

Exaggerations

While most authors relate realistic and plausible images in their stories and poems, others create exaggerations, or **hyperboles**, to emphasize a particular idea or value. A hyperbole is a type of simile or metaphor that develops a larger-than-life comparison and emphasizes the similarity or difference of a particular trait. Hyperboles may be humorous or serious, but authors use them intentionally, so consider how the exaggeration contributes to your interpretation of a poem or story.

INSIDER AP® TIP **Ultimately, finding patterns in an author's use of images is critical to your interpretation of a literary work.** Keep in mind that simply noting the images an author uses is not enough. Analysis requires you to consider how and why an author creates images and how they work together to contribute to an interpretation of the literary work.

WORDS AND IMAGES

Aspect of Imagery	Specific	Consideration
Words	Denotation Connotation Pun	How would you describe the language the author uses? Which words create a specific emotional feeling in the reader? How does the author create associations for the reader by the words chosen? Are there plays on words? What effect do they have on the reader?
Images	Sensory image Imagery Motif	What sensory images does the author choose to include? Why did the author choose these specific images? Is there a pattern or type of images? If so, what might this type of imagery represent?
Exaggeration	Hyperbole Understatement	Does the author make exaggerations? Why?

GUIDED READING

Suburban
John Ciardi

THE TEXT IN CONTEXT

Poet, critic, etymologist, and translator John Ciardi (1916–1986) aimed to make poetry — the works of others, along with his own — more accessible to the general public. His 1959 textbook *How Does a Poem Mean?* was widely adopted by high schools and

Bettmann/Getty Images

colleges in the two decades after its publication. Ciardi's own poetry is characterized by its clear, direct, and immediate language, as well as its often deliberately ordinary subject matter in poems like "Serenade in a Drugstore" and "High Tension Lines across a Landscape." In the 1979 poem that follows, the speaker reflects on a prosaic conflict between neighbors but also casts irony and imagination over the exchange.

Suburban

Yesterday Mrs. Friar phoned. "Mr. Ciardi,
how do you do?" she said. "I am sorry to say
this isn't exactly a social call. The fact is
your dog has just deposited—forgive me—
5 a large repulsive object in my petunias."

I thought to ask, "Have you checked the rectal grooving
 for a positive I.D.?" My dog, as it happened,
was in Vermont with my son, who had gone fishing—
 if that's what one does with a girl, two cases of beer,
10 and a borrowed camper. I guessed I'd get no trout.

But why lose out on organic gold for a wise crack?
 "Yes, Mrs. Friar," I said, "I understand."
"Most kind of you," she said. "Not at all," I said.
 I went with a spade. She pointed, looking away.
15 "I always have loved dogs," she said, "but really!"

I scooped it up and bowed. "The animal of it.
I hope this hasn't upset you, Mrs. Friar."
"Not really," she said, "but really!" I bore the turd
 across the line to my own petunias
20 and buried it till the glorious resurrection

when even these suburbs shall give up their dead.

Guided Questions

1. What is Mrs. Friar calling about? How does the imagery contribute to the description?

2. Why does Mr. Ciardi not tell his neighbor what he is thinking?

3. What is organic gold?

4. Explain the language, "I always have loved dogs . . . but really," and Mr. Ciardi's response, "The animal of it."

5. Why does the poet choose a hyperbole? What is the effect of hyperbole?

6. What are the connotations and associations in line 21?

PRACTICE TEXT

The Lanyard
Billy Collins

Duncan Bryceland/Shutterstock

THE TEXT IN CONTEXT

Billy Collins was born March 22, 1941, and grew up in Brooklyn, New York. Collins is most noted as Poet Laureate of the United States from 2001 to 2003. He has received fellowships from the National Endowment for the Arts, the Guggenheim Foundation, and the New York Foundation for the Arts. Collins has taught at Columbia University, Sarah Lawrence College, and Lehman College, City University of New York (CUNY), where he is Distinguished Professor. He is one of the most popular poets in America with a conversational and witty style that often addresses mundane moments with a profound awareness of their significance. "The Lanyard" explores the childhood activity of making a gift for one's mother at summer camp and the impact of those gifts.

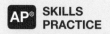 **SKILLS PRACTICE** | FIGURATIVE LANGUAGE
Analyzing Imagery

As you read "The Lanyard," identify aspects of its imagery. Consider how the words and images affect the reader and contribute to an interpretation of the poem.

Analyzing Imagery		
Aspect of Imagery	**Details from the Poem**	**Effect on Reader**
Word Choice • Denotation • Connotation • Pun		
Images • Sensory Image • Imagery • Motif		
Exaggeration • Hyperbole • Understatement		

The Lanyard

The other day I was ricocheting slowly
off the blue walls of this room,
moving as if underwater from typewriter to piano,
from bookshelf to an envelope lying on the floor,
5 when I found myself in the L section of the dictionary
where my eyes fell upon the word *lanyard*.

No cookie nibbled by a French novelist
could send one into the past more suddenly—
a past where I sat at a workbench at a camp
10 by a deep Adirondack lake
learning how to braid long thin plastic strips
into a lanyard, a gift for my mother.

I had never seen anyone use a lanyard
or wear one, if that's what you did with them,
15 but that did not keep me from crossing
strand over strand again and again
until I had made a boxy
red and white lanyard for my mother.

She gave me life and milk from her breasts,
20 and I gave her a lanyard.
She nursed me in many a sick room,
lifted spoons of medicine to my lips,
laid cold face-clothes on my forehead,
and then led me out into the air light

25 and taught me to walk and swim,
and I, in turn, presented her with a lanyard.
Here are thousands of meals, she said,
and here is clothing and a good education.
And here is your lanyard, I replied,
30 which I made with a little help from a counselor.

Here is a breathing body and a beating heart,
strong legs, bones and teeth,
and two clear eyes to read the world, she whispered,
and here, I said, is the lanyard I made at camp.
35 And here, I wish to say to her now,
is a smaller gift — not the worn truth

that you can never repay your mother,
but the rueful admission that when she took
the two-toned lanyard from my hand,
40 I was as sure as a boy could be
that this useless, worthless thing I wove
out of boredom would be enough to make us even.

FIGURATIVE LANGUAGE: Word Choice, Imagery, and Symbols

1. What **connotations** are associated with lanyards?

2. How does the poet's word choice, especially the use of adjectives and adverbs, contribute to the **imagery**?

3. What related sensory images can you find in the poem? How do these images work together to create **imagery**?

4. How does the narrator's perception of the lanyard change over time?

FIGURATIVE LANGUAGE: Comparisons

Metaphor, Personification, and Allusion

AP® Enduring Understanding (FIG-1)

Comparisons, representations, and associations shift meaning from the literal to the figurative and invite readers to interpret a text.

KEY POINT

Authors use extended metaphors, personification, and allusions to make comparisons and create associations that emphasize ideas important to the interpretation of a literary text.

In the age of social media, most of us are familiar with memes. Memes are brief, usually comic visual references to an event, a person, a place, or even an idea; they spread quickly online. But — as with certain jokes — we can only "get" a meme if we understand the context of the image. Essentially, memes create a shared connection between the creator and a specific audience who understand a meme's meaning. Similarly, authors create "memes" in their texts by allusions, comparisons, symbols: references that they expect their readers to know and understand.

As you've learned in previous chapters, a metaphor is complete only when the reader recognizes the comparison. If the reader doesn't understand the comparison, they'll likely be confused and misinterpret the text or the subjects being compared.

Comparisons Create Associations

Throughout your study of literature, you've seen how authors make comparisons to objects as a way to associate traits and feelings. They use comparisons to transfer concepts and emotions onto the objects of those comparisons.

You've learned that a **metaphor** is a comparison between two different objects that draws upon traits of one object to explain another object. You've likely considered both individual comparisons and larger patterns of metaphor in literary texts. Each contributes to your interpretation.

Extended Metaphors

But what if an author uses a single or primary metaphor throughout an entire work? You'd likely recognize that the comparison is important. Authors use **extended metaphors** when multiple aspects of the objects or experiences are important.

Extended comparisons draw upon words, details, images, symbols, and similes, so readers must understand how each of these elements contributes to the comparison and evokes associations. Both are important considerations in making an interpretation. When analyzing an extended metaphor, focus on the particular traits, qualities, or characteristics of the objects being compared, not just the objects themselves. As you think about extended metaphors, begin by asking yourself the following:

- Why did the author choose that specific metaphor?
- How was that metaphor relevant at the time the work was written?
- How is that metaphor relevant today?

Metaphors function most effectively when the reader understands both the characteristics of the comparison and the reason for the comparison. In other words, you might ask, "Why did the author choose this concrete object to make the comparison?" If you know the context of the comparison, you may uncover clues about the meaning behind the author's choice.

Personification

When writers use **personification**, they give human traits to inanimate or non-human objects. This means that personification is similar to a metaphor because it creates associations through comparison. Authors may use personification to humanize an object or suggest its importance as though it were a character. When an author directly addresses an absent person, nonhuman object, or abstract idea, this is known as **apostrophe**.

Allusion

Authors may refer to historical events, mythology, other literary works like Shakespeare's plays, fairy tales, the Bible, or other sacred texts as a way to make a comparison or association for a reader. Such references are called **allusions**. In addition to the specific references made within a text, readers should consider how the names of characters (or even the names of places within the setting) may be allusions.

Of course, readers must go beyond simply identifying the reference; they must also understand why the author chose the allusion and what aspects of the allusion are similar to aspects of the text. Obviously, the reader must be able to identify that the reference is an allusion. So you may also want to consider what the allusion reveals about both the author and the author's understanding of (and relationship to) the audience.

Occasionally, authors create new texts that directly respond to or speak to other texts. These responses and references create **intertextuality**: a connection between related works of literature, music, film, or other artistic mediums. Authors can respond to texts from hundreds of years in the past or from a completely different part of the globe. In popular culture today, you may see intertextuality as an integral element of superhero movie franchises, series spin-offs or prequels, fan fiction, and satire.

COMMON ALLUSIONS

Biblical/Judeo-Christian

Eden	The Garden of Eden before the Fall; connotes utopian innocence
Forbidden Fruit	Fruit of the Tree of Knowledge, which God forbade Adam and Eve; suggests the strong appeal of sin and of the things that we are prohibited from having
Prodigal Son	Parable from Jesus about a son who wastes his family inheritance but is welcomed back into his family
Job	Figure in the Old Testament whose faith in God is tested by a series of terrible hardships; implies themes of immense suffering and loyalty
Moses	Prophet and leader of the Jewish people who led the exodus from Egypt and received the Ten Commandments; suggests leadership, wisdom, truth-telling, and prophecy
Judas	Betrayer of Jesus; suggests disloyalty, treachery, and avarice
Christ	Biblical savior; implies a figure whose suffering is redemptive or a means of salvation for others
Flood	Old Testament story of Noah and the flood; suggests an apocalyptic event, and possible rebirth after
Gilead	Gilead is a region in Jordan known for its healing plants, spices, and medicines
Apocalypse	Event at the end of the New Testament synonymous with doomsday, end times, and judgment day
Jonah	In the Bible, Jonah disobeys a command from God; as part of his punishment, he is swallowed by a whale before repenting

Greco-Roman Mythology

Midas	A foolish, greedy king in Greek and Roman myth who was granted the ability to turn anything to gold with his touch; ultimately, he realized his error when his food and water also turned to gold
Sirens	Musical creatures who lured sailors to wreck their ships with their siren songs; suggest something that is irresistible, but dangerous or deadly
Sisyphus	A trickster who tried to cheat death; his eternal punishment was to roll a stone up a hill that always rolled back down; suggests a futile, repetitive task
Icarus	The son of craftsman Daedelus who, with this father, sought to escape the island of Crete with artificial wings; Icarus ignored his father's warnings, flew too close to the sun, and perished; refers to those who tempt fate or push limits unsuccessfully
Pandora	Figure in Greek mythology who opened a forbidden box and allowed human miseries like war, disease, and hatred into the world; it suggests an action that will lead to terrible unforeseen consequences
Trojan Horse	In Greek myth, the Greeks built a wooden horse and offered it to their enemies in the city of Troy as a tribute, but Greek soldiers hid inside and ultimately conquered Troy; allusions usually imply a seemingly harmless or beneficial thing that is actually dangerous and malevolent
Achilles	Great Greek warrior whose mother dipped him in the River Styx as a child to make him invulnerable; as she held him by his feet, they were not protected, and he was killed in the Trojan war; suggests a hidden vulnerability

(continued)

Muse	The muses were nine daughters of Zeus who inspired music, art, and literature; generally refers to a figure — real or imaginary — who compels an artist or writer
Fountain of Youth	A mythical spring that restores the health and youth of those who drink or bathe in it; suggests elixirs, magical waters, and other ways of achieving eternal youth
Xanadu	The summer capital of the Yuan Dynasty (1271–1368) founded by Kublai Khan; reimagined in Western stories, poems, and songs as a place of luxury, grandeur, and exotic pleasures
Eldorado	European legend — especially among Spanish explorers — that a lost city of gold exists in South America; suggests a treasure that is unimaginably valuable
Arachne	Greek myth about a gifted, boastful weaver who challenges Athena to a weaving contest and wins but ends up transformed into a spider; it implies themes of pride, pain, art, and human limitations

Literary

Star-Crossed Lovers	A romantic relationship that is precarious, threatened, or doomed by uncontrollable forces, as in Shakespeare's *Romeo and Juliet* and Emily Bronte's novel *Wuthering Heights*
Holy Grail	A legendary, healing cup, often figured as the cup Jesus used at the Last Supper; object of a quest in Arthurian legends; any object or goal that represents the highest level of quality, achievement, value, or status
Superman	Comic book superhero introduced by Action Comics in 1938; suggests highly exceptional, or even superhuman, powers and skills
Cinderella	Folk tale about a virtuous, mistreated young woman in impoverished circumstances who has a reversal of fortune; often used to describe a person (or group) of low status or expectation who achieves great public success
Sour Grapes	Phrase from Aesop's Fable "The Fox and the Grapes"; describes the attitude of a person who dislikes an object of desire because it is unattainable
Boy Who Cried Wolf	Title character from Aesop's Fable; refers to a person who repeatedly raises false alarms; suggests a person who's lied so much that no one believes them — even when they're telling the truth
Catch-22	Title and theme of Joseph Heller's novel *Catch 22*; refers to a dilemma in which the only solution to a problem is denied by a circumstance inherent in the problem: "You can't get a job until you have experience; you can't get experience without having a job"
Big Brother	A figure in George Orwell's dystopian novel *1984*; suggests a person, organization, or institution that seeks total surveillance and control of people's lives

Historical

Watergate	Scandal during the presidency of Richard Nixon that led to his resignation; subsequent scandals in the United States are often given the suffix *-gate*, even outside the political realm (e.g., *Deflategate* and *Gamergate*)
Tea Party	In 1773, American colonists reacted against British rule by throwing a shipment of tea into the Boston harbor; now, the term *Tea Party* is used more generally to describe protests against the government
Black Death	A pandemic of bubonic plague that ravaged Europe in the fourteenth century; suggests a deadly highly infectious disease

INSIDER AP® TIP

Titles may be metaphors. Don't overlook a poem or story's title, as it may take on figurative and symbolic meaning. In some works, the title may even introduce the metaphor before the work begins.

FIGURATIVE COMPARISONS

Literary Element	Key Considerations
Metaphor	What is being compared?
	Is this comparison extended throughout the text?
	What type of comparison is it? Why is this significant?
Extended metaphor	What particular traits, qualities, or characteristics are being compared?
	Why did the author choose this particular metaphor?
	How is this metaphor relevant at the time the work was written?
	How is this metaphor relevant today?
Allusion	Why did the author choose this particular reference?
	What does this allusion reveal about the author?
	What does this allusion reveal about the audience's relationship to the author?
	What are the points of comparison between the allusion (or its text of origin) and the text you're reading?
	How does this allusion fit into a larger motif?
	Does this text speak to another text? How? Why?
Personification	What physical object or idea is being assigned human qualities?
	Which human qualities are being assigned? Why might this be important?
	Why did the author humanize this particular object or idea?

GUIDED READING

Mending Wall
Robert Frost

Hulton Archive/Getty Images

THE TEXT IN CONTEXT

While Robert Frost (1874–1963) is often viewed as a New England poet who writes about regional landscapes and folksy local customs, his work is complex, unsentimental, and often dark. Critics generally group him with other demanding modernist American poets of the same period, such as T. S. Eliot and Wallace Stevens. Frost was born in San Francisco and moved to Massachusetts as a child; he attended Dartmouth College and Harvard University but never earned his degree. After a series of jobs (including farmer, cobbler, and teacher), Frost briefly moved to England, where he published his first full books of poetry: *A Boy's Will* (1913) and *North of Boston* (1914). The following poem, "Mending Wall," first appeared in *North of Boston*. It typifies the poet's approach, including its country characters, its rural setting, its figurative language, and its subversion of homespun platitudes. It also touches on themes persistent throughout Frost's work: ignorance, human disconnection, the limitations of language, and the difficulty of viewing nature as a source of knowledge or wisdom.

Mending Wall

Something there is that doesn't love a wall,
That sends the frozen-ground-swell under it,
And spills the upper boulders in the sun;
And makes gaps even two can pass abreast.
5 The work of hunters is another thing:
I have come after them and made repair
Where they have left not one stone on a stone,
But they would have the rabbit out of hiding,
To please the yelping dogs. The gaps I mean,
10 No one has seen them made or heard them made,
But at spring mending-time we find them there.
I let my neighbor know beyond the hill;
And on a day we meet to walk the line

Guided Questions

1. Explain the title of the poem. How can mending a wall be considered a metaphor?

2. What is the annual event between neighbors? What is the time of year?

And set the wall between us once again.
15 We keep the wall between us as we go.
To each the boulders that have fallen to each.
And some are loaves and some so nearly balls
We have to use a spell to make them balance:
'Stay where you are until our backs are turned!'
20 We wear our fingers rough with handling them.
Oh, just another kind of out-door game,
One on a side. It comes to little more:
There where it is we do not need the wall:
He is all pine and I am apple orchard.
25 My apple trees will never get across
And eat the cones under his pines, I tell him.
He only says, 'Good fences make good neighbors.'
Spring is the mischief in me, and I wonder
If I could put a notion in his head:
30 'Why do they make good neighbors? Isn't it
Where there are cows? But here there are no cows.
Before I built a wall I'd ask to know
What I was walling in or walling out,
And to whom I was like to give offense.
35 Something there is that doesn't love a wall,
That wants it down.' I could say 'Elves' to him,
But it's not elves exactly, and I'd rather
He said it for himself. I see him there
Bringing a stone grasped firmly by the top
40 In each hand, like an old-stone savage armed.
He moves in darkness as it seems to me,
Not of woods only and the shade of trees.
He will not go behind his father's saying,
And he likes having thought of it so well
45 He says again, 'Good fences make good neighbors.'

Guided Questions

3. What is the out-door game?

4. What is being compared?

5. How can "good fences" that divide people also create a union between "good neighbors"?

6. Explain why the first line of the poem is repeated.

7. Why is there an allusion to elves? What is the effect?

8. Why is the mending of the wall a valued annual event? And how does the metaphor extend throughout the poem?

PRACTICE TEXT

Digging
Seamus Heaney

Paul Faith - PA Images/Getty Images

THE TEXT IN CONTEXT

Nobel Prize–winning poet, playwright,
professor, and translator Seamus Heaney
(1939–2013) grew up on his family's small
farm in County Derry, Northern Ireland.
While he once characterized his life and
career as an ascent from the "earth of farm
labor to the heaven of education," much of
his poetry remains focused on rural landscapes and pastoral themes. That preoccupation is evident in "Digging": the first poem in his first collection, *Death of a Naturalist*
(1966). Although he fits into a Romantic tradition that includes William Wordsworth
and Robert Frost, Heaney's view of nature, imagination, memory, and myth is — like
Frost's — sophisticated and unsentimental. His other many books include *Wintering
Out* (1972), *Field Work* (1979), *Beowulf: A New Verse Translation* (1999), and *Human
Chain* (2010).

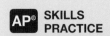

AP®	SKILLS PRACTICE	FIGURATIVE LANGUAGE **Analyzing Comparisons**

As you read Heaney's poem, identify his use of figurative elements by noting
particular textual details. Then, use the key considerations to explain the effect
of the figurative elements.

Analyzing Comparisons		
Literary Element	Key Considerations	Details from the Text and Effect
Metaphor	What is being compared? Is this comparison extended throughout the text? What type of comparison is it? Why is this significant?	

Extended metaphor	What particular traits, qualities, or characteristics are being compared?	
	Why did the author choose this particular metaphor?	
	How is this metaphor relevant at the time the work was written?	
	How is this metaphor relevant today?	
Allusion	Why did the author choose this particular reference?	
	What does this allusion reveal about the author?	
	What does this allusion reveal about the audience's relationship to the author?	
	What are the points of comparison between the allusion (or its text of origin) and the text you're reading?	
	How does this allusion fit into a larger motif?	
	Does this text speak to another text? How? Why?	
Personification	What physical object or idea is being assigned human qualities?	
	Which human qualities are being assigned? Why might this be important?	
	Why did the author humanize this particular object or idea?	

Digging

Between my finger and my thumb
The squat pen rests; snug as a gun.

Under my window, a clean rasping sound
When the spade sinks into gravelly ground:
5 My father, digging. I look down

Till his straining rump among the flowerbeds
Bends low, comes up twenty years away
Stooping in rhythm through potato drills
Where he was digging.

10 The coarse boot nestled on the lug, the shaft
Against the inside knee was levered firmly.
He rooted out tall tops, buried the bright edge deep
To scatter new potatoes that we picked,
Loving their cool hardness in our hands.

15 By God, the old man could handle a spade.
   Just like his old man.

   My grandfather cut more turf in a day
   Than any other man on Toner's bog.
   Once I carried him milk in a bottle
20 Corked sloppily with paper. He straightened up
   To drink it, then fell to right away
   Nicking and slicing neatly, heaving sods
   Over his shoulder, going down and down
   For the good turf. Digging.

25 The cold smell of potato mould, the squelch and slap
   Of soggy peat, the curt cuts of an edge
   Through living roots awaken in my head.
   But I've no spade to follow men like them.

   Between my finger and my thumb
30 The squat pen rests.
   I'll dig with it.

FIGURATIVE LANGUAGE: Comparisons

1. What is being compared in the poem's first **couplet**? Explain the traits and qualities of this **comparison**.

2. List the **images** in the poem. Then choose two images that are being compared. What traits and characteristics are being compared? How do these comparisons contribute to your interpretation of the poem?

3. How does the **imagery** of the father and the son contribute to the extended **metaphor**? How do they contribute to your interpretation of the poem?

4. How do the title and the final line create a **metaphor**? Explain how this metaphor contributes to your interpretation of the poem.

IDEAS IN LITERATURE
The Individual and Nature

When we use the word "romantic" now, we're usually referring to some facet of romantic love, such as *romance* novels or *romantic* comedies. But the term also denotes a major movement in the history of ideas, art, and politics that — much like the Enlightenment — took place across several countries. In late-eighteenth-century England, Romanticism emerged as a reaction to many factors, including industrialization, the rigid refinement of neoclassicism, and the influence of the French philosopher Jean-Jacques Rousseau. Rousseau is often considered the "Godfather of Romanticism." He extolled the importance of emotion and intuition; he asserted the superiority of rural life, away from corrupting cities; and he cast nature as the benevolent spiritual ideal and wild creative force.

These ideas are probably familiar to you — maybe even intuitive. For example, many of us still see nature in romantic terms: as a source of wonder, creativity, and even spiritual revelation. At the time, however, this notion signaled a profound shift from the tamer, neoclassical view of nature reflected in lines from Alexander Pope's "An Essay on Criticism": "Nature, like Liberty, is but restrained / By the same Laws which first herself ordained." That is, nature is orderly and controlled. It is also accessible to human reason. But the natural world and rural life were of limited interest in the age of reason: the proper subjects of literature were human beings in society, the grandeur of public life, and moral lessons based on classical principles. For the Romantics, however, nature was primary — as were the people who lived rustic lives close to nature, far from the insidious influences of cities. In *Lyrical Ballads* (1798), an influential collection of poems by William Wordsworth

IDEA BANK

Aestheticism
Attraction
Beauty
Emotion
Environment
Expression
Fervor
Ideal
Imagination
Individualism
Inspiration
Nature
Passion
Rebellion
Sensation
Spontaneity
Subjectivity
Transcendence
Truth

Heritage Images/Hulton Fine Art Collection/Getty Images

◀ Romanticism was a reaction against industrialism, as well as a disapproval of the aristocratic social and political norms and a call for more attention to nature.

How does this image combine the individual, imagination, and intuition and remain distinctly romantic?

and Samuel Coleridge, Wordsworth wrote that in nature, "our elementary feelings coexist in a state of greater simplicity, and, consequently, may be more accurately contemplated, and more forcibly communicated." In other words, country life led to greater authenticity and truth.

But for the Romantics, nature had another side — beyond daffodils and rustic country scenes. Coleridge's "The Rime of the Ancient Mariner" (p. 591), also included in *Lyrical Ballads*, exemplifies this conception of nature: as the expression of a mysterious spiritual world, as a source of fear and awe, as a power that is largely incomprehensible to humans. Moreover, Coleridge's ancient mariner exemplifies a romantic conception of the poet too: the exiled outsider but an outcast compelled to charm and haunt listeners with sublime truths. We might even compare the mariner to another alienated, enigmatic figure who seems compelled to repeat himself: Bartleby in Herman Melville's (1819–1891) story "Bartleby, the Scrivener: A Story of Wall Street" (1853) (p. 613). Melville, an American writer influenced by German and British Romanticism, highlights another key aspect of Romanticism: a preoccupation with the strange, extreme, and even bizarre. Indeed, if neoclassical poets privileged the examination of general humanity, the Romantics emphasized the individual and the idiosyncratic.

Today, we rely on romantic ideas when we encourage people to "be different" or "express their individuality." We draw on Romanticism when imagining that children are innately innocent and good. We follow the same tradition when we perceive nature in anthropomorphic terms ("Mother Earth") or see the wilderness as an idyllic, uncorrupted site of transcendent beauty. Not surprisingly, environmentalism springs from that last idea, as well: even the ancient mariner's transgression is an act of environmental destruction. In many ways, the Romantic view of nature corresponds to the Romantic view of poetry and art. That is, nature's value goes far beyond its *use* value (to mine ore, to harvest wood, to supply food). Its very existence is a positive good. That principle guides the aesthetic ideals of Romanticism: beautiful art, writing, and music are simply good in and of themselves. They don't need to teach lessons to prove their "use" value.

The photograph shows activists ▶ demonstrating against global warming. Today, there are many rallies around the world calling individuals to speak up for the future of the environment.

How does this image capture both the revolutionary spirit of the Romantic period and the call to nature that is prominent throughout the movement?

LeoPatrizi/E+/Getty Images

The Rime of the Ancient Mariner

Samuel Taylor Coleridge

THE TEXT IN CONTEXT

Even if you have never read Samuel Taylor Coleridge's (1772–1834) "The Rime of the Ancient Mariner" (1798), you are probably familiar with the phrase "an albatross around my neck," as well as the couplet, "Water, water, every where, / Nor any drop to drink." Both come from this narrative poem, which integrates several important aspects of Romanticism: the use of the supernatural, the personification of nature, and the figure of the poet as a strange outsider compelled to speak. "The Rime of the Ancient Mariner" first appeared in *Lyrical Ballads* (1798), arguably the most important book of poetry in British Romanticism. Coleridge coauthored the collection with his friend, William Wordsworth (1770–1850), as both shared the goal of fundamentally shifting the sound and sense of English poetry away from its rigid neoclassical conventions. Coleridge's other works include "The Eolian Harp" (1795), "Kubla Khan" (1816), and a literary autobiography *Biographia Literaria* (1817).

The Rime of the Ancient Mariner

Argument

How a Ship having passed the Line was driven by storms to the cold Country towards the South Pole; and how from thence she made her course to the tropical Latitude of the Great Pacific Ocean; and of the strange things that befell; and in what manner the Ancyent Marinere came back to his own Country.

PART I

It is an ancient Mariner,
And he stoppeth one of three.
'By thy long grey beard and glittering eye,
Now wherefore stopp'st thou me?

5 The Bridegroom's doors are opened wide,
And I am next of kin;
The guests are met, the feast is set:
May'st hear the merry din.'

He holds him with his skinny hand,
10 'There was a ship,' quoth he.

'Hold off! unhand me, grey-beard loon!'
Eftsoons his hand dropt he.

He holds him with his glittering eye—
The Wedding-Guest stood still,
15 And listens like a three years' child:
The Mariner hath his will.

The Wedding-Guest sat on a stone:
He cannot choose but hear;
And thus spake on that ancient man,
20 The bright-eyed Mariner.

'The ship was cheered, the harbour cleared,
Merrily did we drop
Below the kirk, below the hill,
Below the lighthouse top.

25 The Sun came up upon the left,
Out of the sea came he!
And he shone bright, and on the right
Went down into the sea.

Higher and higher every day,
30 Till over the mast at noon—'
The Wedding-Guest here beat his breast,
For he heard the loud bassoon.

The bride hath paced into the hall,
Red as a rose is she;
35 Nodding their heads before her goes
The merry minstrelsy.

The Wedding-Guest he beat his breast,
Yet he cannot choose but hear;
And thus spake on that ancient man,
40 The bright-eyed Mariner.

And now the STORM-BLAST came, and he
Was tyrannous and strong:
He struck with his o'ertaking wings,
And chased us south along.

45 With sloping masts and dipping prow,
As who pursued with yell and blow
Still treads the shadow of his foe,
And forward bends his head,

The ship drove fast, loud roared the blast,
50 And southward aye we fled.

And now there came both mist and snow,
And it grew wondrous cold:
And ice, mast-high, came floating by,
As green as emerald.

55 And through the drifts the snowy clifts
Did send a dismal sheen:
Nor shapes of men nor beasts we ken—
The ice was all between.

The ice was here, the ice was there,
60 The ice was all around:
It cracked and growled, and roared and howled,
Like noises in a swound!

At length did cross an Albatross,
Thorough the fog it came;
65 As if it had been a Christian soul,
We hailed it in God's name.

It ate the food it ne'er had eat,
And round and round it flew.
The ice did split with a thunder-fit;
70 The helmsman steered us through!

And a good south wind sprung up behind;
The Albatross did follow,
And every day, for food or play,
Came to the mariner's hollo!

75 In mist or cloud, on mast or shroud,
It perched for vespers nine;
Whiles all the night, through fog-smoke white,
Glimmered the white Moon-shine.'

'God save thee, ancient Mariner!
80 From the fiends, that plague thee thus!—
Why look'st thou so?'—With my cross-bow
I shot the ALBATROSS.

PART II

The Sun now rose upon the right:
Out of the sea came he,
85 Still hid in mist, and on the left
Went down into the sea.

And the good south wind still blew behind,
But no sweet bird did follow,
Nor any day for food or play
90 Came to the mariner's hollo!

And I had done a hellish thing,
And it would work 'em woe:
For all averred, I had killed the bird
That made the breeze to blow.
95 Ah wretch! said they, the bird to slay,
That made the breeze to blow!

Nor dim nor red, like God's own head,
The glorious Sun uprist:
Then all averred, I had killed the bird
100 That brought the fog and mist.
'Twas right, said they, such birds to slay,
That bring the fog and mist.

The fair breeze blew, the white foam flew,
The furrow followed free;
105 We were the first that ever burst
Into that silent sea.

Down dropt the breeze, the sails dropt down,
'Twas sad as sad could be;
And we did speak only to break
110 The silence of the sea!

All in a hot and copper sky,
The bloody Sun, at noon,
Right up above the mast did stand,
No bigger than the Moon.

115 Day after day, day after day,
We stuck, nor breath nor motion;
As idle as a painted ship
Upon a painted ocean.

Water, water, every where,
120 And all the boards did shrink;
Water, water, every where,
Nor any drop to drink.

The very deep did rot: O Christ!
That ever this should be!
125 Yea, slimy things did crawl with legs
Upon the slimy sea.

About, about, in reel and rout
The death-fires danced at night;
The water, like a witch's oils,
130 Burnt green, and blue and white.

And some in dreams assurèd were
Of the Spirit that plagued us so;
Nine fathom deep he had followed us
From the land of mist and snow.

135 And every tongue, through utter drought,
Was withered at the root;
We could not speak, no more than if
We had been choked with soot.

Ah! well a-day! what evil looks
140 Had I from old and young!
Instead of the cross, the Albatross
About my neck was hung.

PART III
There passed a weary time. Each throat
Was parched, and glazed each eye.
145 A weary time! a weary time!
How glazed each weary eye,

When looking westward, I beheld
A something in the sky.

At first it seemed a little speck,
150 And then it seemed a mist;
It moved and moved, and took at last
A certain shape, I wist.

A speck, a mist, a shape, I wist!
And still it neared and neared:
155 As if it dodged a water-sprite,
It plunged and tacked and veered.

With throats unslaked, with black lips baked,
We could nor laugh nor wail;
Through utter drought all dumb we stood!
160 I bit my arm, I sucked the blood,
And cried, A sail! a sail!

With throats unslaked, with black lips baked,
Agape they heard me call:
Gramercy! they for joy did grin,
165 And all at once their breath drew in,
As they were drinking all.

See! see! (I cried) she tacks no more!
Hither to work us weal;
Without a breeze, without a tide,
170 She steadies with upright keel!

The western wave was all a-flame.
The day was well nigh done!
Almost upon the western wave
Rested the broad bright Sun;
175 When that strange shape drove suddenly
Betwixt us and the Sun.

And straight the Sun was flecked with bars,
(Heaven's Mother send us grace!)
As if through a dungeon-grate he peered
180 With broad and burning face.

Alas! (thought I, and my heart beat loud)
How fast she nears and nears!
Are those *her* sails that glance in the Sun,
Like restless gossameres?

185 Are those her *ribs* through which the Sun
Did peer, as through a grate?
And is that Woman all her crew?
Is that a DEATH? and are there two?
Is DEATH that woman's mate?

190 *Her* lips were red, *her* looks were free,
Her locks were yellow as gold:
Her skin was as white as leprosy,
The Night-mare LIFE-IN-DEATH was she,
Who thicks man's blood with cold.

195 The naked hulk alongside came,
And the twain were casting dice;
'The game is done! I've won! I've won!'
Quoth she, and whistles thrice.

The Sun's rim dips; the stars rush out;
200 At one stride comes the dark;

With far-heard whisper, o'er the sea,
Off shot the spectre-bark.

We listened and looked sideways up!
Fear at my heart, as at a cup,
205 My life-blood seemed to sip!
The stars were dim, and thick the night,
The steersman's face by his lamp gleamed white;
From the sails the dew did drip—
Till clomb above the eastern bar
210 The hornèd Moon, with one bright star
Within the nether tip.

One after one, by the star-dogged Moon,
Too quick for groan or sigh,
Each turned his face with a ghastly pang,
215 And cursed me with his eye.

Four times fifty living men,
(And I heard nor sigh nor groan)
With heavy thump, a lifeless lump,
They dropped down one by one.

220 The souls did from their bodies fly,—
They fled to bliss or woe!
And every soul, it passed me by,
Like the whizz of my cross-bow!

PART IV

'I fear thee, ancient Mariner!
225 I fear thy skinny hand!
And thou art long, and lank, and brown,
As is the ribbed sea-sand.

I fear thee and thy glittering eye,
And thy skinny hand, so brown.'—
230 Fear not, fear not, thou Wedding-Guest!
This body dropt not down.

Alone, alone, all, all alone,
Alone on a wide wide sea!
And never a saint took pity on
235 My soul in agony.

The many men, so beautiful!
And they all dead did lie:

And a thousand thousand slimy things
Lived on; and so did I.

240 I looked upon the rotting sea,
And drew my eyes away;
I looked upon the rotting deck,
And there the dead men lay.

I looked to heaven, and tried to pray;
245 But or ever a prayer had gusht,
A wicked whisper came, and made
My heart as dry as dust.

I closed my lids, and kept them close,
And the balls like pulses beat;
250 For the sky and the sea, and the sea and the sky
Lay dead like a load on my weary eye,
And the dead were at my feet.

The cold sweat melted from their limbs,
Nor rot nor reek did they:
255 The look with which they looked on me
Had never passed away.

An orphan's curse would drag to hell
A spirit from on high;
But oh! more horrible than that
260 Is the curse in a dead man's eye!
Seven days, seven nights, I saw that curse,
And yet I could not die.

The moving Moon went up the sky,
And no where did abide:
265 Softly she was going up,
And a star or two beside—

Her beams bemocked the sultry main,
Like April hoar-frost spread;
But where the ship's huge shadow lay,
270 The charmèd water burnt alway
A still and awful red.

Beyond the shadow of the ship,
I watched the water-snakes:
They moved in tracks of shining white,
275 And when they reared, the elfish light
Fell off in hoary flakes.

Within the shadow of the ship
I watched their rich attire:
Blue, glossy green, and velvet black,
280 They coiled and swam; and every track
Was a flash of golden fire.

O happy living things! no tongue
Their beauty might declare:
A spring of love gushed from my heart,
285 And I blessed them unaware:
Sure my kind saint took pity on me,
And I blessed them unaware.

The self-same moment I could pray;
And from my neck so free
290 The Albatross fell off, and sank
Like lead into the sea.

PART V

Oh sleep! it is a gentle thing,
Beloved from pole to pole!
To Mary Queen the praise be given!
295 She sent the gentle sleep from Heaven,
That slid into my soul.

The silly buckets on the deck,
That had so long remained,
I dreamt that they were filled with dew;
300 And when I awoke, it rained.

My lips were wet, my throat was cold,
My garments all were dank;
Sure I had drunken in my dreams,
And still my body drank.

305 I moved, and could not feel my limbs:
I was so light—almost
I thought that I had died in sleep,
And was a blessed ghost.

And soon I heard a roaring wind:
310 It did not come anear;
But with its sound it shook the sails,
That were so thin and sere.

The upper air burst into life!
And a hundred fire-flags sheen,
315 To and fro they were hurried about!
And to and fro, and in and out,
The wan stars danced between.

And the coming wind did roar more loud,
And the sails did sigh like sedge,
320 And the rain poured down from one black cloud;
The Moon was at its edge.

The thick black cloud was cleft, and still
The Moon was at its side:
Like waters shot from some high crag,
325 The lightning fell with never a jag,
A river steep and wide.

The loud wind never reached the ship,
Yet now the ship moved on!
Beneath the lightning and the Moon
330 The dead men gave a groan.

They groaned, they stirred, they all uprose,
Nor spake, nor moved their eyes;
It had been strange, even in a dream,
To have seen those dead men rise.

335 The helmsman steered, the ship moved on;
Yet never a breeze up-blew;
The mariners all 'gan work the ropes,
Where they were wont to do;
They raised their limbs like lifeless tools—
340 We were a ghastly crew.

The body of my brother's son
Stood by me, knee to knee:
The body and I pulled at one rope,
But he said nought to me.

345 'I fear thee, ancient Mariner!'
Be calm, thou Wedding-Guest!
'Twas not those souls that fled in pain,
Which to their corses came again,
But a troop of spirits blest:

350 For when it dawned—they dropped their arms,
And clustered round the mast;

Sweet sounds rose slowly through their mouths,
And from their bodies passed.

Around, around, flew each sweet sound,
355 Then darted to the Sun;
Slowly the sounds came back again,
Now mixed, now one by one.

Sometimes a-dropping from the sky
I heard the sky-lark sing;
360 Sometimes all little birds that are,
How they seemed to fill the sea and air
With their sweet jargoning!

And now 'twas like all instruments,
Now like a lonely flute;
365 And now it is an angel's song,
That makes the heavens be mute.

It ceased; yet still the sails made on
A pleasant noise till noon,
A noise like of a hidden brook
370 In the leafy month of June,
That to the sleeping woods all night
Singeth a quiet tune.

Till noon we quietly sailed on,
Yet never a breeze did breathe:
375 Slowly and smoothly went the ship,
Moved onward from beneath.

Under the keel nine fathom deep,
From the land of mist and snow,
The spirit slid: and it was he
380 That made the ship to go.
The sails at noon left off their tune,
And the ship stood still also.

The Sun, right up above the mast,
Had fixed her to the ocean:
385 But in a minute she 'gan stir,
With a short uneasy motion—
Backwards and forwards half her length
With a short uneasy motion.

Then like a pawing horse let go,
390 She made a sudden bound:
It flung the blood into my head,
And I fell down in a swound.

How long in that same fit I lay,
I have not to declare;
395 But ere my living life returned,
I heard and in my soul discerned
Two voices in the air.

'Is it he?' quoth one, 'Is this the man?
By him who died on cross,
400 With his cruel bow he laid full low
The harmless Albatross.

The spirit who bideth by himself
In the land of mist and snow,
He loved the bird that loved the man
405 Who shot him with his bow.'

The other was a softer voice,
As soft as honey-dew:
Quoth he, 'The man hath penance done,
And penance more will do.'

PART VI

First Voice
410 'But tell me, tell me! speak again,
Thy soft response renewing—
What makes that ship drive on so fast?
What is the ocean doing?'

Second Voice
Still as a slave before his lord,
415 The ocean hath no blast;
His great bright eye most silently
Up to the Moon is cast—

If he may know which way to go;
For she guides him smooth or grim.
420 See, brother, see! how graciously
She looketh down on him.'

First Voice
'But why drives on that ship so fast,
Without or wave or wind?'

Second Voice
'The air is cut away before,
425 And closes from behind.

Fly, brother, fly! more high, more high!
Or we shall be belated:
For slow and slow that ship will go,
When the Mariner's trance is abated.'

430 I woke, and we were sailing on
As in a gentle weather:
'Twas night, calm night, the moon was high;
The dead men stood together.

All stood together on the deck,
435 For a charnel-dungeon fitter:
All fixed on me their stony eyes,
That in the Moon did glitter.

The pang, the curse, with which they died,
Had never passed away:
440 I could not draw my eyes from theirs,
Nor turn them up to pray.

And now this spell was snapt: once more
I viewed the ocean green,
And looked far forth, yet little saw
445 Of what had else been seen—

Like one, that on a lonesome road
Doth walk in fear and dread,
And having once turned round walks on,
And turns no more his head;

450 Because he knows, a frightful fiend
Doth close behind him tread.

But soon there breathed a wind on me,
Nor sound nor motion made:
Its path was not upon the sea,
455 In ripple or in shade.

It raised my hair, it fanned my cheek
Like a meadow-gale of spring—
It mingled strangely with my fears,
Yet it felt like a welcoming.

460 Swiftly, swiftly flew the ship,
Yet she sailed softly too:
Sweetly, sweetly blew the breeze—
On me alone it blew.

Oh! dream of joy! is this indeed
465 The light-house top I see?
Is this the hill? is this the kirk?
Is this mine own countree?

We drifted o'er the harbour-bar,
And I with sobs did pray—
470 O let me be awake, my God!
Or let me sleep alway.

The harbour-bay was clear as glass,
So smoothly it was strewn!
And on the bay the moonlight lay,
475 And the shadow of the Moon.

The rock shone bright, the kirk no less,
That stands above the rock:
The moonlight steeped in silentness
The steady weathercock.

480 And the bay was white with silent light,
Till rising from the same,
Full many shapes, that shadows were,
In crimson colours came.

A little distance from the prow
485 Those crimson shadows were:
I turned my eyes upon the deck—
Oh, Christ! what saw I there!

Each corse lay flat, lifeless and flat,
And, by the holy rood!
490 A man all light, a seraph-man,
On every corse there stood.

This seraph-band, each waved his hand:
It was a heavenly sight!
They stood as signals to the land,
495 Each one a lovely light;

This seraph-band, each waved his hand,
No voice did they impart—

No voice; but oh! the silence sank
Like music on my heart.

500 But soon I heard the dash of oars,
I heard the Pilot's cheer;
My head was turned perforce away
And I saw a boat appear.

The Pilot and the Pilot's boy,
505 I heard them coming fast:
Dear Lord in Heaven! it was a joy
The dead men could not blast.

I saw a third—I heard his voice:
It is the Hermit good!
510 He singeth loud his godly hymns
That he makes in the wood.
He'll shrieve my soul, he'll wash away
The Albatross's blood.

PART VII

This Hermit good lives in that wood
515 Which slopes down to the sea.
How loudly his sweet voice he rears!
He loves to talk with marineres
That come from a far countree.

He kneels at morn, and noon, and eve—
520 He hath a cushion plump:
It is the moss that wholly hides
The rotted old oak-stump.

The skiff-boat neared: I heard them talk,
'Why, this is strange, I trow!
525 Where are those lights so many and fair,
That signal made but now?'

'Strange, by my faith!' the Hermit said—
'And they answered not our cheer!
The planks looked warped! and see those sails,
530 How thin they are and sere!
I never saw aught like to them,
Unless perchance it were

Brown skeletons of leaves that lag
My forest-brook along;

535 When the ivy-tod is heavy with snow,
And the owlet whoops to the wolf below,
That eats the she-wolf's young.'

'Dear Lord! it hath a fiendish look—
(The Pilot made reply)
540 I am a-feared'—'Push on, push on!'
Said the Hermit cheerily.

The boat came closer to the ship,
But I nor spake nor stirred;
The boat came close beneath the ship,
545 And straight a sound was heard.

Under the water it rumbled on,
Still louder and more dread:
It reached the ship, it split the bay;
The ship went down like lead.

550 Stunned by that loud and dreadful sound,
Which sky and ocean smote,
Like one that hath been seven days drowned
My body lay afloat;
But swift as dreams, myself I found
555 Within the Pilot's boat.

Upon the whirl, where sank the ship,
The boat spun round and round;
And all was still, save that the hill
Was telling of the sound.

560 I moved my lips—the Pilot shrieked
And fell down in a fit;
The holy Hermit raised his eyes,
And prayed where he did sit.

I took the oars: the Pilot's boy,
565 Who now doth crazy go,
Laughed loud and long, and all the while
His eyes went to and fro.
'Ha! ha!' quoth he, 'full plain I see,
The Devil knows how to row.'

570 And now, all in my own countree,
I stood on the firm land!
The Hermit stepped forth from the boat,
And scarcely he could stand.

'O shrieve me, shrieve me, holy man!'
575 The Hermit crossed his brow.
'Say quick,' quoth he, 'I bid thee say—
What manner of man art thou?'

Forthwith this frame of mine was wrenched
With a woful agony,
580 Which forced me to begin my tale;
And then it left me free.

Since then, at an uncertain hour,
That agony returns:
And till my ghastly tale is told,
585 This heart within me burns.

I pass, like night, from land to land;
I have strange power of speech;
That moment that his face I see,
I know the man that must hear me:
590 To him my tale I teach.

What loud uproar bursts from that door!
The wedding-guests are there:
But in the garden-bower the bride
And bride-maids singing are:
595 And hark the little vesper bell,
Which biddeth me to prayer!

O Wedding-Guest! this soul hath been
Alone on a wide sea:
So lonely 'twas, that God himself
600 Scarce seemèd there to be.

O sweeter than the marriage-feast,
'Tis sweeter far to me,
To walk together to the kirk
With a goodly company!—

605 To walk together to the kirk,
And all together pray,
While each to his great Father bends,
Old men, and babes, and loving friends
And youths and maidens gay!

610 Farewell, farewell! but this I tell
To thee, thou Wedding-Guest!

He prayeth well, who loveth well
Both man and bird and beast.

He prayeth best, who loveth best
615 All things both great and small;
For the dear God who loveth us,
He made and loveth all.

The Mariner, whose eye is bright,
Whose beard with age is hoar,
620 Is gone: and now the Wedding-Guest
Turned from the bridegroom's door.

He went like one that hath been stunned,
And is of sense forlorn:
A sadder and a wiser man,
625 He rose the morrow morn.

duncan1890/DigitalVision Vectors/Getty Images

◄ The image is a 1875 illustration originally carved in wood by the French Romantic artist Paul Gustave Doré. He created thirty-nine wood engraved plates and three vignettes illustrating Coleridge's "The Rime of the Ancient Mariner."

What does the image depict? How do Doré's details convey the tone of the poem? What could be changed in this image to portray a more hopeful perspective?

STRUCTURE

1. Is the poem an **open** or **closed form**? What is the poetic structure of "The Rime of the Ancient Mariner"? Reflect on the stanzas and the rhyme scheme. Is there a pattern? Explain. How does this pattern contribute to your interpretation of the poem?

2. The poem is a literary ballad, which is a type of narrative poem that often reveals a character undergoing a change. Identify and explain the beginning, middle, and end of the poem as they reveal the speaker's transformation.

3. Give an example of a **contrast** that reveals a **conflict** of values or ideas. How does this **tension** contribute to your interpretation of the poem?

4. Identify the event or events that serve as the **climax** of the mariner's story. Explain.

FIGURATIVE LANGUAGE: Word Choice, Imagery, and Symbols

5. Describe the **imagery** surrounding the water snakes. How are the images contrasted throughout the poem? Find an example in which sensory details are contrasted in images. Explain the contrast.

6. The mariner uses **personification**. Using two examples, explain how this figurative device furthers the description of the text.

7. How does the poem's nature **imagery** convey figurative meaning? What associations and connotations do the images suggest? Choose one example and explain.

FIGURATIVE LANGUAGE: Comparisons

8. Explain the line "water, water, everywhere, nor any drop to drink." How is it **archetypal**?

9. "The Rime of the Ancient Mariner" is a highly metaphorical poem. Choose two **metaphors** and explain how they are important to your interpretation of the poem.

10. Find an **allusion** in the text and explain its effect. What is being referenced or alluded to? How does the allusion contribute to your interpretation of the poem?

IDEAS IN LITERATURE: The Individual and Nature

11. Coleridge tells an imaginative tale in "The Rime of the Ancient Mariner." Explain how this tale exemplifies the Romantic characteristics of the individual and nature. Use the text to support and exemplify these elements.

PUTTING IT ALL TOGETHER

12. What is the figurative meaning of the albatross? Explain and support your response with textual evidence.

Singapore
Mary Oliver

Kevork Djansezian/Getty Images

THE TEXT IN CONTEXT

In many ways, Pulitzer Prize–winning American writer Mary Oliver (1935–2019) epitomizes the Romantic poet in the contemporary world. Her work is grounded in wonder and awe at the natural world, as well as the conviction that nature is a source of sublime spirituality. Likewise, she uses language that is clear, direct, and accessible. Oliver's poems often explore the sublime in everyday life and seemingly ordinary situations, as in the case of "Singapore" (included here). Her books of poetry and criticism include *No Voyage and Other Poems* (1963), *American Primitive* (1983), *A Poetry Handbook* (1994), and *Felicity* (2015).

Singapore

In Singapore, in the airport,
A darkness was ripped from my eyes.
In the women's restroom, one compartment stood open.
A woman knelt there, washing something in the white bowl.

5 Disgust argued in my stomach
and I felt, in my pocket, for my ticket.

A poem should always have birds in it.
Kingfishers, say, with their bold eyes and gaudy wings.
Rivers are pleasant, and of course trees.
10 A waterfall, or if that's not possible, a fountain rising and falling.
A person wants to stand in a happy place, in a poem.

When the woman turned I could not answer her face.
Her beauty and her embarrassment struggled together,
and neither could win.
15 She smiled and I smiled. What kind of nonsense is this?
Everybody needs a job.

Yes, a person wants to stand in a happy place, in a poem.
But first we must watch her as she stares down at her labor,
which is dull enough.
20 She is washing the tops of the airport ashtrays, as big as hubcaps,

with a blue rag.
Her small hands turn the metal, scrubbing and rinsing.
She does not work slowly, nor quickly, like a river.
Her dark hair is like the wing of a bird.

25 I don't doubt for a moment that she loves her life.
And I want her to rise up from the crust and the slop and
fly down to the river.
This probably won't happen.
But maybe it will.
30 If the world were only pain and logic, who would want it?

Of course, it isn't.
Neither do I mean anything miraculous, but only
the light that can shine out of a life. I mean
the way she unfolded and refolded the blue cloth,
35 The way her smile was only for my sake; I mean
the way this poem is filled with trees, and birds.

Melting with Bucket, oil painting on vintage wallpaper by Kristina Kanders, Germany, 2017

◀ *Melting with Bucket* (2017) is an oil painting on wood created by the German artist Kristina Kanders. Her painting was part of a series called *Disappearing Housewives.*

What does the work suggest about identity? What artistic techniques does Kanders use to reveal the identity of her subject?

STRUCTURE

1. What is the **poetic structure**? For example, can you identify a rhyming pattern? How does this structural choice affect your interpretation of the poem?

2. What type of poem is "Singapore"? Explain how the type of poem relates to the purpose.

3. The first stanza presents a **contrast**. What is being contrasted? How does this contrast contribute to your interpretation of the poem?

4. How does the third **stanza** relate to the other stanzas and contribute to your interpretation of the poem?

FIGURATIVE LANGUAGE: Word Choice, Imagery, and Symbols

5. Choose a word or a phrase in the poem and explain how its **connotations**, representations, and associations convey figurative meaning. How does your example shape your interpretation of the poem as a whole?

6. Choose an **image** in the poem and explain how it suggests or creates a meaningful comparison in the poem.

7. How does the poem's **imagery** emphasize and reinforce the poem's idea?

FIGURATIVE LANGUAGE: Comparisons

8. Identify a **simile** in the poem. What traits, qualities, or characteristics are being **compared** in your example? How does the simile contribute to your interpretation of the poem?

9. Choose a **metaphor** in the poem. Why do you think the poet chose this metaphor? Is the metaphor still relevant? Explain.

IDEAS IN LITERATURE: The Individual and Nature

10. The poem's title is a city. If you wrote a poem about a city, what city would your poem be titled? What would the comparison suggest about you and the city? What associations and judgments would the reader interpret from your poem?

PUTTING IT ALL TOGETHER

11. How does the last stanza relate to the previous stanzas and contribute to your interpretation of the poem?

Bartleby, the Scrivener: A Story of Wall Street

Herman Melville

THE TEXT IN CONTEXT

While fiction writer and poet Herman Melville (1819–1891) is now a major figure in American literature, the author of *Moby Dick* (1851) never achieved popularity in his own time — and died largely forgotten. Indeed, his work remains challenging and disturbing, which places him among his peers in dark Romanticism like Nathaniel Hawthorne (1804–1864) and Edgar Allan Poe (1809–1849). But where Hawthorne and Poe use more conventional elements of the Gothic (psychological extremes, the supernatural, the bizarre), Melville's fiction pushes into metaphysical questions about knowledge, the difficulty of communication, and the limitations of language. All those preoccupations are evident in perhaps his most enigmatic short story, "Bartleby, the Scrivener: A Story of Wall Street" (1853). Melville's other works include *Typee* (1846); *Pierre; or, The Ambiguities* (1852); and *The Confidence-Man* (1857).

Bartleby, the Scrivener: A Story of Wall Street

I am a rather elderly man. The nature of my avocations for the last thirty years has brought me into more than ordinary contact with what would seem an interesting and
5 somewhat singular set of men, of whom as yet nothing that I know of has ever been written:—I mean the law-copyists or scriveners. I have known very many of them, professionally and privately, and if I pleased,
10 could relate divers histories, at which good-natured gentlemen might smile, and sentimental souls might weep. But I waive the biographies of all other scriveners for a few passages in the life of Bartleby, who was
15 a scrivener of the strangest I ever saw or heard of. While of other law-copyists I might write the complete life, of Bartleby nothing of that sort can be done. I believe that no materials exist for a full and satisfactory
20 biography of this man. It is an irreparable loss to literature. Bartleby was one of those beings of whom nothing is ascertainable, except from the original sources, and in his case those are very small. What my own
25 astonished eyes saw of Bartleby, *that* is all I know of him, except, indeed, one vague report which will appear in the sequel.

Ere introducing the scrivener, as he first appeared to me, it is fit I make some mention
30 of myself, my *employées*, my business, my chambers, and general surroundings; because some such description is indispensable to an adequate understanding of the chief character about to be presented.

35 Imprimis: I am a man who, from his youth upwards, has been filled with a profound conviction that the easiest way of life is the best. Hence, though I belong to a profession proverbially energetic and nervous, even to
40 turbulence, at times, yet nothing of that sort have I ever suffered to invade my peace. I am one of those unambitious lawyers who never addresses a jury, or in any way draws down public applause; but in the cool tranquility of
45 a snug retreat, do a snug business among rich men's bonds and mortgages and title-deeds. All who know me, consider me an eminently *safe* man. The late John Jacob Astor, a personage little given to poetic
50 enthusiasm, had no hesitation in pronouncing my first grand point to be prudence; my next, method. I do not speak it in vanity, but simply record the fact, that I was not unemployed in my profession by the late John
55 Jacob Astor; a name which, I admit, I love to repeat, for it hath a rounded and orbicular sound to it, and rings like unto bullion. I will freely add, that I was not insensible to the late John Jacob Astor's good opinion.

60 Some time prior to the period at which this little history begins, my avocations had been largely increased. The good old office, now extinct in the State of New York, of a Master in Chancery, had been conferred
65 upon me. It was not a very arduous office, but very pleasantly remunerative. I seldom lose my temper; much more seldom indulge in dangerous indignation at wrongs and outrages; but I must be permitted to be rash
70 here and declare, that I consider the sudden and violent abrogation of the office of Master in Chancery, by the new Constitution, as a—premature act; inasmuch as I had counted upon a life-lease of the profits,
75 whereas I only received those of a few short years. But this is by the way.

My chambers were up stairs at No.—Wall-street. At one end they looked upon the white wall of the interior of a spacious sky-
80 light shaft, penetrating the building from top to bottom. This view might have been considered rather tame than otherwise, deficient in what landscape painters call "life." But if so, the view from the other end of my cham-
85 bers offered, at least, a contrast, if nothing more. In that direction my windows commanded an unobstructed view of a lofty brick wall, black by age and everlasting shade; which wall required no spy-glass to
90 bring out its lurking beauties, but for the benefit of all near-sighted spectators, was pushed up to within ten feet of my window panes. Owing to the great height of the surrounding buildings, and my chambers being
95 on the second floor, the interval between this wall and mine not a little resembled a huge square cistern.

At the period just preceding the advent of Bartleby, I had two persons as copyists in my
100 employment, and a promising lad as an office-boy. First, Turkey; second, Nippers; third, Ginger Nut. These may seem names, the like of which are not usually found in the Directory. In truth they were nicknames,
105 mutually conferred upon each other by my three clerks, and were deemed expressive of their respective persons or characters. Turkey was a short, pursy Englishman of about my own age, that is, somewhere not far from
110 sixty. In the morning, one might say, his face was of a fine florid hue, but after twelve o'clock, meridian—his dinner hour—it blazed like a grate full of Christmas coals; and continued blazing—but, as it were, with
115 a gradual wane—till 6 o'clock, *p.m.* or thereabouts, after which I saw no more of the proprietor of the face, which gaining its meridian with the sun, seemed to set with it,

to rise, culminate, and decline the following
120 day, with the like regularity and undimin-
ished glory. There are many singular coincidences I have known in the course of my life,
not the least among which was the fact, that
exactly when Turkey displayed his fullest
125 beams from his red and radiant countenance, just then, too, at that critical moment,
began the daily period when I considered his
business capacities as seriously disturbed for
the remainder of the twenty-four hours. Not
130 that he was absolutely idle, or averse to business then; far from it. The difficulty was, he
was apt to be altogether too energetic. There
was a strange, inflamed, flurried, flighty
recklessness of activity about him. He would
135 be incautious in dipping his pen into his inkstand. All his blots upon my documents,
were dropped there after twelve o'clock,
meridian. Indeed, not only would he be reckless and sadly given to making blots in the
140 afternoon, but some days he went further,
and was rather noisy. At such times, too, his
face flamed with augmented blazonry, as if
cannel coal had been heaped on anthracite.
He made an unpleasant racket with his
145 chair; spilled his sand-box; in mending his
pens, impatiently split them all to pieces,
and threw them on the floor in a sudden
passion; stood up and leaned over his table,
boxing his papers about in a most indeco-
150 rous manner, very sad to behold in an elderly
man like him. Nevertheless, as he was in
many ways a most valuable person to me,
and all the time before twelve o'clock, meridian, was the quickest, steadiest creature too,
155 accomplishing a great deal of work in a style
not easy to be matched—for these reasons,
I was willing to overlook his eccentricities,
though indeed, occasionally, I remonstrated
with him. I did this very gently, however,
160 because, though the civilest, nay, the blandest

and most reverential of men in the morning,
yet in the afternoon he was disposed, upon
provocation, to be slightly rash with his
tongue, in fact, insolent. Now, valuing his
165 morning services as I did, and resolved not
to lose them; yet, at the same time made
uncomfortable by his inflamed ways after
twelve o'clock; and being a man of peace,
unwilling by my admonitions to call forth
170 unseemly retorts from him; I took upon me,
one Saturday noon (he was always worse on
Saturdays), to hint to him, very kindly, that
perhaps now that he was growing old, it
might be well to abridge his labors; in short,
175 he need not come to my chambers after
twelve o'clock, but, dinner over, had best go
home to his lodgings and rest himself till
teatime. But no; he insisted upon his afternoon devotions. His countenance became
180 intolerably fervid, as he oratorically assured
me—gesticulating with a long ruler at the
other end of the room—that if his services
in the morning were useful, how indispensable, then, in the afternoon?

185 "With submission, sir," said Turkey on this
occasion, "I consider myself your right-hand
man. In the morning I but marshal and
deploy my columns; but in the afternoon I
put myself at their head, and gallantly
190 charge the foe, thus!"—and he made a violent thrust with the ruler.

"But the blots, Turkey," intimated I.

"True,—but, with submission, sir, behold
these hairs! I am getting old. Surely, sir, a blot
195 or two of a warm afternoon is not to be
severely urged against gray hairs. Old age—
even if it blot the page—is honorable. With
submission, sir, we *both* are getting old."

This appeal to my fellow-feeling was
200 hardly to be resisted. At all events, I saw that
go he would not. So I made up my mind to
let him stay, resolving, nevertheless, to see to

it, that during the afternoon he had to do with my less important papers.

205   Nippers, the second on my list, was a whiskered, sallow, and, upon the whole, rather piratical-looking young man of about five and twenty. I always deemed him the victim of two evil powers—ambition and
210 indigestion. The ambition was evinced by a certain impatience of the duties of a mere copyist, an unwarrantable usurpation of strictly professional affairs, such as the original drawing up of legal documents. The indi-
215 gestion seemed betokened in an occasional nervous testiness and grinning irritability, causing the teeth to audibly grind together over mistakes committed in copying; unnecessary maledictions, hissed, rather than spo-
220 ken, in the heat of business; and especially by a continual discontent with the height of the table where he worked. Though of a very ingenious mechanical turn, Nippers could never get this table to suit him. He put chips
225 under it, blocks of various sorts, bits of pasteboard, and at last went so far as to attempt an exquisite adjustment by final pieces of folded blotting paper. But no invention would answer. If, for the sake of easing his back, he
230 brought the table lid at a sharp angle well up towards his chin, and wrote there like a man using the steep roof of a Dutch house for his desk:—then he declared that it stopped the circulation in his arms. If now he lowered the
235 table to his waistbands, and stooped over it in writing, then there was a sore aching in his back. In short, the truth of the matter was, Nippers knew not what he wanted. Or, if he wanted any thing, it was to be rid of a
240 scrivener's table altogether. Among the manifestations of his diseased ambition was a fondness he had for receiving visits from certain ambiguous-looking fellows in seedy coats, whom he called his clients. Indeed I

245 was aware that not only was he, at times, considerate of a ward-politician, but he occasionally did a little business at the Justices' courts, and was not unknown on the steps of the Tombs. I have good reason to
250 believe, however, that one individual who called upon him at my chambers, and who, with a grand air, he insisted was his client, was no other than a dun, and the alleged title-deed, a bill. But with all his failings, and
255 the annoyances he caused me, Nippers, like his compatriot Turkey, was a very useful man to me; wrote a neat, swift hand; and, when he chose, was not deficient in a gentlemanly sort of deportment. Added to this, he always
260 dressed in a gentlemanly sort of way; and so, incidentally, reflected credit upon my chambers. Whereas with respect to Turkey, I had much ado to keep him from being a reproach to me. His clothes were apt to look oily and
265 smell of eating-houses. He wore his pantaloons very loose and baggy in summer. His coats were execrable; his hat not to be handled. But while the hat was a thing of indifference to me, inasmuch as his natural
270 civility and deference, as a dependent Englishman, always led him to doff it the moment he entered the room, yet his coat was another matter. Concerning his coats, I reasoned with him; but with no effect. The
275 truth was, I suppose, that a man of so small an income, could not afford to sport such a lustrous face and a lustrous coat at one and the same time. As Nippers once observed, Turkey's money went chiefly for red ink. One
280 winter day I presented Turkey with a highly-respectable looking coat of my own, a padded gray coat, of a most comfortable warmth, and which buttoned straight up from the knee to the neck. I thought Turkey would
285 appreciate the favor, and abate his rashness and obstreperousness of afternoons. But no.

I verily believe that buttoning himself up in so downy and blanket-like a coat had a pernicious effect upon him; upon the same princi-
290 ple that too much oats are bad for horses. In fact, precisely as a rash, restive horse is said to feel his oats, so Turkey felt his coat. It made him insolent. He was a man whom prosperity harmed.

295   Though concerning the self-indulgent habits of Turkey I had my own private surmises, yet touching Nippers I was well persuaded that whatever might be his faults in other respects, he was, at least, a temperate
300 young man. But indeed, nature herself seemed to have been his vintner, and at his birth charged him so thoroughly with an irritable, brandy-like disposition, that all subsequent potations were needless. When I
305 consider how, amid the stillness of my chambers, Nippers would sometimes impatiently rise from his seat, and stooping over his table, spread his arms wide apart, seize the whole desk, and move it, and jerk it, with
310 a grim, grinding motion on the floor, as if the table were a perverse voluntary agent, intent on thwarting and vexing him; I plainly perceive that for Nippers, brandy and water were altogether superfluous.

315   It was fortunate for me that, owing to its peculiar cause—indigestion—the irritability and consequent nervousness of Nippers, were mainly observable in the morning, while in the afternoon he was comparatively
320 mild. So that Turkey's paroxysms only coming on about twelve o'clock, I never had to do with their eccentricities at one time. Their fits relieved each other like guards. When Nippers' was on, Turkey's was off; and *vice*
325 *versa*. This was a good natural arrangement under the circumstances.

    Ginger Nut, the third on my list, was a lad some twelve years old. His father was a carman, ambitious of seeing his son on the
330 bench instead of a cart, before he died. So he sent him to my office as student at law, errand boy, and cleaner and sweeper, at the rate of one dollar a week. He had a little desk to himself, but he did not use it much. Upon
335 inspection, the drawer exhibited a great array of the shells of various sorts of nuts. Indeed, to this quick-witted youth the whole noble science of the law was contained in a nut-shell. Not the least among the employ-
340 ments of Ginger Nut, as well as one which he discharged with the most alacrity, was his duty as cake and apple purveyor for Turkey and Nippers. Copying law papers being proverbially dry, husky sort of business, my two
345 scriveners were fain to moisten their mouths very often with Spitzenbergs to be had at the numerous stalls nigh the Custom House and Post Office. Also, they sent Ginger Nut very frequently for that peculiar cake—small, flat,
350 round, and very spicy—after which he had been named by them. Of a cold morning when business was but dull, Turkey would gobble up scores of these cakes, as if they were mere wafers—indeed they sell them at
355 the rate of six or eight for a penny—the scrape of his pen blending with the crunching of the crisp particles in his mouth. Of all the fiery afternoon blunders and flurried rashnesses of Turkey, was his once moisten-
360 ing a ginger-cake between his lips, and clapping it on to a mortgage for a seal. I came within an ace of dismissing him then. But he mollified me by making an oriental bow, and saying—"With submission, sir, it was gener-
365 ous of me to find you in stationery on my own account."

    Now my original business—that of a conveyancer and title hunter, and drawer-up of recondite documents of all sorts—was consid-
370 erably increased by receiving the master's

office. There was now great work for scriveners. Not only must I push the clerks already with me, but I must have additional help. In answer to my advertisement, a motionless young man
375 one morning, stood upon my office threshold, the door being open, for it was summer. I can see that figure now—pallidly neat, pitiably respectable, incurably forlorn! It was Bartleby.

After a few words touching his qualifica-
380 tions, I engaged him, glad to have among my corps of copyists a man of so singularly sedate an aspect, which I thought might operate beneficially upon the flighty temper of Turkey, and the fiery one of Nippers.
385 I should have stated before that ground glass folding-doors divided my premises into two parts, one of which was occupied by my scriveners, the other by myself. According to my humor I threw open these doors, or
390 closed them. I resolved to assign Bartleby a corner by the folding-doors, but on my side of them, so as to have this quiet man within easy call, in case any trifling thing was to be done. I placed his desk close up to a small
395 side-window in that part of the room, a win-dow which originally had afforded a lateral view of certain grimy back-yards and bricks, but which, owing to subsequent erections, commanded at present no view at all, though
400 it gave some light. Within three feet of the panes was a wall, and the light came down from far above, between two lofty buildings, as from a very small opening in a dome. Still further to a satisfactory arrangement, I pro-
405 cured a high green folding screen, which might entirely isolate Bartleby from my sight, though not remove him from my voice. And thus, in a manner, privacy and society were conjoined.
410 At first Bartleby did an extraordinary quan-tity of writing. As if long famishing for some-thing to copy, he seemed to gorge himself on my documents. There was no pause for diges-tion. He ran a day and night line, copying by
415 sun-light and by candle-light. I should have been quite delighted with his application, had he been cheerfully industrious. But he wrote on silently, palely, mechanically.

It is, of course, an indispensable part of a
420 scrivener's business to verify the accuracy of his copy, word by word. Where there are two or more scriveners in an office, they assist each other in this examination, one reading from the copy, the other holding the
425 original. It is a very dull, wearisome, and lethargic affair. I can readily imagine that to some sanguine temperaments it would be altogether intolerable. For example, I cannot credit that the mettlesome poet Byron
430 would have contentedly sat down with Bartleby to examine a law document of, say five hundred pages, closely written in a crimpy hand.

Now and then, in the haste of business, it
435 had been my habit to assist in comparing some brief document myself, calling Turkey or Nippers for this purpose. One object I had in placing Bartleby so handy to me behind the screen, was to avail myself of his services
440 on such trivial occasions. It was on the third day, I think, of his being with me, and before any necessity had arisen for having his own writing examined, that, being much hurried to complete a small affair I had in hand, I
445 abruptly called to Bartleby. In my haste and natural expectancy of instant compliance, I sat with my head bent over the original on my desk, and my right hand sideways, and somewhat nervously extended with the copy,
450 so that immediately upon emerging from his retreat, Bartleby might snatch it and proceed to business without the least delay.

In this very attitude did I sit when I called to him, rapidly stating what it was I wanted

455 him to do—namely, to examine a small paper with me. Imagine my surprise, nay, my consternation, when without moving from his privacy, Bartleby in a singularly mild, firm voice, replied, "I would prefer not to."

460 I sat awhile in perfect silence, rallying my stunned faculties. Immediately it occurred to me that my ears had deceived me, or Bartleby had entirely misunderstood my meaning. I repeated my request in the clearest tone

465 I could assume. But in quite as clear a one came the previous reply, "I would prefer not to."

"Prefer not to," echoed I, rising in high excitement, and crossing the room with a

470 stride. "What do you mean? Are you moonstruck? I want you to help me compare this sheet here—take it," and I thrust it towards him.

"I would prefer not to," said he.

475 I looked at him steadfastly. His face was leanly composed; his gray eye dimly calm. Not a wrinkle of agitation rippled him. Had there been the least uneasiness, anger, impatience or impertinence in his manner;

480 in other words, had there been any thing ordinarily human about him, doubtless I should have violently dismissed him from the premises. But as it was, I should have as soon thought of turning my pale plaster-

485 of-paris bust of Cicero out of doors. I stood gazing at him awhile, as he went on with his own writing, and then reseated myself at my desk. This is very strange, thought I. What had one best do? But my business

490 hurried me. I concluded to forget the matter for the present, reserving it for my future leisure. So calling Nippers from the other room, the paper was speedily examined.

495 A few days after this, Bartleby concluded four lengthy documents, being quadruplicates of a week's testimony taken before me in my High Court of Chancery. It became necessary to examine them. It was an important suit,

500 and great accuracy was imperative. Having all things arranged I called Turkey, Nippers and Ginger Nut from the next room, meaning to place the four copies in the hands of my four clerks, while I should read from

505 the original. Accordingly Turkey, Nippers and Ginger Nut had taken their seats in a row, each with his document in hand, when I called to Bartleby to join this interesting group.

510 "Bartleby! quick, I am waiting."

I heard a slow scrape of his chair legs on the uncarpeted floor, and soon he appeared standing at the entrance of his hermitage.

"What is wanted?" said he mildly.

515 "The copies, the copies," said I hurriedly. "We are going to examine them. There"—and I held towards him the fourth quadruplicate.

"I would prefer not to," he said, and gently disappeared behind the screen.

520 For a few moments I was turned into a pillar of salt, standing at the head of my seated column of clerks. Recovering myself, I advanced towards the screen, and demanded the reason for such extraordinary conduct.

525 "*Why* do you refuse?"

"I would prefer not to."

With any other man I should have flown outright into a dreadful passion, scorned all further words, and thrust him ignominiously

530 from my presence. But there was something about Bartleby that not only strangely disarmed me, but in a wonderful manner touched and disconcerted me. I began to reason with him.

535 "These are your own copies we are about to examine. It is labor saving to you, because one examination will answer for your four papers. It is common usage. Every copyist is

bound to help examine his copy. Is it not so?
540 Will you not speak? Answer!"

"I prefer not to," he replied in a flute-like
tone. It seemed to me that while I had been
addressing him, he carefully revolved every
statement that I made; fully comprehended
545 the meaning; could not gainsay the irresistible conclusions; but, at the same time, some
paramount consideration prevailed with him
to reply as he did.

"You are decided, then, not to comply
550 with my request—a request made according
to common usage and common sense?"

He briefly gave me to understand that on
that point my judgment was sound. Yes: his
decision was irreversible.

555   It is not seldom the case that when a man
is browbeaten in some unprecedented and
violently unreasonable way, he begins to
stagger in his own plainest faith. He begins,
as it were, vaguely to surmise that, wonder-
560 ful as it may be, all the justice and all the
reason is on the other side. Accordingly, if
any disinterested persons are present, he
turns to them for some reinforcement for his
own faltering mind.

565   "Turkey," said I, "what do you think of
this? Am I not right?"

"With submission, sir," said Turkey, with
his blandest tone, "I think that you are."

"Nippers," said I, "what do *you* think of it?"
570   "I think I should kick him out of the office."

(The reader of nice perceptions will here
perceive that, it being morning, Turkey's
answer is couched in polite and tranquil
terms, but Nippers replies in ill-tempered
575 ones. Or, to repeat a previous sentence,
Nippers' ugly mood was on duty and
Turkey's off.)

"Ginger Nut," said I, willing to enlist the
smallest suffrage in my behalf, "what do you
580 think of it?"

"I think, sir, he's a little *luny*," replied
Ginger Nut with a grin.

"You hear what they say," said I, turning
towards the screen, "come forth and do your
585 duty."

But he vouchsafed no reply. I pondered a
moment in sore perplexity. But once more
business hurried me. I determined again to
postpone the consideration of this dilemma
590 to my future leisure. With a little trouble we
made out to examine the papers without
Bartleby, though at every page or two, Turkey
deferentially dropped his opinion that this
proceeding was quite out of the common;
595 while Nippers, twitching in his chair with a
dyspeptic nervousness, ground out between
his set teeth occasional hissing maledictions
against the stubborn oaf behind the screen.
And for his (Nippers') part, this was the first
600 and the last time he would do another man's
business without pay.

Meanwhile Bartleby sat in his hermitage,
oblivious to every thing but his own peculiar
business there.

605   Some days passed, the scrivener being
employed upon another lengthy work. His
late remarkable conduct led me to regard his
ways narrowly. I observed that he never went
to dinner; indeed that he never went any
610 where. As yet I had never of my personal
knowledge known him to be outside of my
office. He was a perpetual sentry in the corner. At about eleven o'clock though, in the
morning, I noticed that Ginger Nut would
615 advance toward the opening in Bartleby's
screen, as if silently beckoned thither by a
gesture invisible to me where I sat. The boy
would then leave the office jingling a few
pence, and reappear with a handful of
620 ginger-nuts which he delivered in the hermitage, receiving two of the cakes for his
trouble.

He lives, then, on ginger-nuts, thought I; never eats a dinner, properly speaking; he must be a vegetarian then; but no; he never eats even vegetables, he eats nothing but ginger-nuts. My mind then ran on in reveries concerning the probable effects upon the human constitution of living entirely on ginger-nuts. Ginger-nuts are so called because they contain ginger as one of their peculiar constituents, and the final flavoring one. Now what was ginger? A hot, spicy thing. Was Bartleby hot and spicy? Not at all. Ginger, then, had no effect upon Bartleby. Probably he preferred it should have none.

Nothing so aggravates an earnest person as a passive resistance. If the individual so resisted be of a not inhumane temper, and the resisting one perfectly harmless in his passivity; then, in the better moods of the former, he will endeavor charitably to construe to his imagination what proves impossible to be solved by his judgment. Even so, for the most part, I regarded Bartleby and his ways. Poor fellow! thought I, he means no mischief; it is plain he intends no insolence; his aspect sufficiently evinces that his eccentricities are involuntary. He is useful to me. I can get along with him. If I turn him away, the chances are he will fall in with some less indulgent employer, and then he will be rudely treated, and perhaps driven forth miserably to starve. Yes. Here I can cheaply purchase a delicious self-approval. To befriend Bartleby; to humor him in his strange willfulness, will cost me little or nothing, while I lay up in my soul what will eventually prove a sweet morsel for my conscience. But this mood was not invariable with me. The passiveness of Bartleby sometimes irritated me. I felt strangely goaded on to encounter him in new opposition, to elicit some angry spark from him answerable to my own. But indeed I might as well have essayed to strike fire with my knuckles against a bit of Windsor soap. But one afternoon the evil impulse in me mastered me, and the following little scene ensued:

"Bartleby," said I, "when those papers are all copied, I will compare them with you."

"I would prefer not to."

"How? Surely you do not mean to persist in that mulish vagary?"

No answer.

I threw open the folding-doors near by, and turning upon Turkey and Nippers, exclaimed in an excited manner—

"He says, a second time, he won't examine his papers. What do you think of it, Turkey?"

It was afternoon, be it remembered. Turkey sat glowing like a brass boiler, his bald head steaming, his hands reeling among his blotted papers.

"Think of it?" roared Turkey; "I think I'll just step behind his screen, and black his eyes for him!"

So saying, Turkey rose to his feet and threw his arms into a pugilistic position. He was hurrying away to make good his promise, when I detained him, alarmed at the effect of incautiously rousing Turkey's combativeness after dinner.

"Sit down, Turkey," said I, "and hear what Nippers has to say. What do you think of it, Nippers? Would I not be justified in immediately dismissing Bartleby?"

"Excuse me, that is for you to decide, sir. I think his conduct quite unusual, and indeed unjust, as regards Turkey and myself. But it may only be a passing whim."

"Ah," exclaimed I, "you have strangely changed your mind then—you speak very gently of him now."

"All beer," cried Turkey; "gentleness is effects of beer—Nippers and I dined together to-day. You see how gentle *I* am, sir. Shall I go and black his eyes?"

"You refer to Bartleby, I suppose. No, not 710 to-day, Turkey," I replied; "pray, put up your fists."

I closed the doors, and again advanced towards Bartleby. I felt additional incentives tempting me to my fate. I burned to be rebelled against again. I remembered that 715 Bartleby never left the office.

"Bartleby," said I, "Ginger Nut is away; just step round to the Post Office, won't you? (it was but a three minute walk,) and see if there is any thing for me."

720 "I would prefer not to."

"You *will* not?"

"I *prefer* not."

I staggered to my desk, and sat there in a deep study. My blind inveteracy returned. 725 Was there any other thing in which I could procure myself to be ignominiously repulsed by this lean, penniless wight?—my hired clerk? What added thing is there, perfectly reasonable, that he will be sure to refuse to 730 do?

"Bartleby!"

No answer.

"Bartleby," in a louder tone.

No answer.

735 "Bartleby," I roared.

Like a very ghost, agreeably to the laws of magical invocation, at the third summons, he appeared at the entrance of his hermitage.

"Go to the next room, and tell Nippers to 740 come to me."

"I prefer not to," he respectfully and slowly said, and mildly disappeared.

"Very good, Bartleby," said I, in a quiet sort of serenely severe self-possessed tone, inti-745 mating the unalterable purpose of some terrible retribution very close at hand. At the moment I half intended something of the kind. But upon the whole, as it was drawing towards my dinner-hour, I thought it best to 750 put on my hat and walk home for the day, suffering much from perplexity and distress of mind.

Shall I acknowledge it? The conclusion of this whole business was, that it soon became 755 a fixed fact of my chambers, that a pale young scrivener, by the name of Bartleby, and a desk there; that he copied for me at the usual rate of four cents a folio (one hundred words); but he was permanently exempt 760 from examining the work done by him, that duty being transferred to Turkey and Nippers, one of compliment doubtless to their superior acuteness; moreover, said Bartleby was never on any account to be dispatched 765 on the most trivial errand of any sort; and that even if entreated to take upon him such a matter, it was generally understood that he would prefer not to—in other words, that he would refuse pointblank.

770 As days passed on, I became considerably reconciled to Bartleby. His steadiness, his freedom from all dissipation, his incessant industry (except when he chose to throw himself into a standing revery behind his 775 screen), his great stillness, his unalterableness of demeanor under all circumstances, made him a valuable acquisition. One prime thing was this,—*he was always there;*—first in the morning, continually through the day, 780 and the last at night. I had a singular confidence in his honesty. I felt my most precious papers perfectly safe in his hands. Sometimes to be sure I could not, for the very soul of me, avoid falling into sudden 785 spasmodic passions with him. For it was exceeding difficult to bear in mind all the time those strange peculiarities, privileges, and unheard of exemptions, forming the tacit stipulations on Bartleby's part under 790 which he remained in my office. Now and

then, in the eagerness of dispatching pressing business, I would inadvertently summon
Bartleby, in a short, rapid tone, to put his
finger, say, on the incipient tie of a bit of red
795 tape with which I was about compressing
some papers. Of course, from behind the
screen the usual answer, "I prefer not to,"
was sure to come; and then, how could a
human creature with the common infirmi-
800 ties of our nature, refrain from bitterly
exclaiming upon such perverseness—such
unreasonableness. However, every added
repulse of this sort which I received only
tended to lessen the probability of my
805 repeating the inadvertence.

Here it must be said, that according to the
custom of most legal gentlemen occupying
chambers in densely-populated law buildings, there were several keys to my door. One
810 was kept by a woman residing in the attic,
which person weekly scrubbed and daily
swept and dusted my apartments. Another
was kept by Turkey for convenience sake. The
third I sometimes carried in my own pocket.
815 The fourth I knew not who had.

Now, one Sunday morning I happened to
go to Trinity Church, to hear a celebrated
preacher, and finding myself rather early on
the ground, I thought I would walk around to
820 my chambers for a while. Luckily I had my
key with me; but upon applying it to the lock,
I found it resisted by something inserted
from the inside. Quite surprised, I called out;
when to my consternation a key was turned
825 from within; and thrusting his lean visage at
me, and holding the door ajar, the apparition
of Bartleby appeared, in his shirt sleeves, and
otherwise in a strangely tattered dishabille,
saying quietly that he was sorry, but he was
830 deeply engaged just then, and—preferred
not admitting me at present. In a brief word
or two, he moreover added, that perhaps I

had better walk round the block two or three
times, and by that time he would probably
835 have concluded his affairs.

Now, the utterly unsurmised appearance
of Bartleby, tenanting my law-chambers of a
Sunday morning, with his cadaverously gentlemanly *nonchalance*, yet withal firm and
840 self-possessed, had such a strange effect
upon me, that incontinently I slunk away
from my own door, and did as desired. But
not without sundry twinges of impotent
rebellion against the mild effrontery of this
845 unaccountable scrivener. Indeed, it was his
wonderful mildness chiefly, which not only
disarmed me, but unmanned me, as it were.
For I consider that one, for the time, is a sort
of unmanned when he tranquilly permits his
850 hired clerk to dictate to him, and order him
away from his own premises. Furthermore, I
was full of uneasiness as to what Bartleby
could possibly be doing in my office in his
shirt sleeves, and in an otherwise dismantled
855 condition of a Sunday morning. Was any
thing amiss going on? Nay, that was out of
the question. It was not to be thought of for a
moment that Bartleby was an immoral person. But what could he be doing there?—
860 copying? Nay again, whatever might be his
eccentricities, Bartleby was an eminently
decorous person. He would be the last man
to sit down to his desk in any state approaching to nudity. Besides, it was Sunday; and
865 there was something about Bartleby that for-
bade the supposition that he would by any
secular occupation violate the proprieties of
the day.

Nevertheless, my mind was not pacified;
870 and full of a restless curiosity, at last I
returned to the door. Without hindrance I
inserted my key, opened it, and entered.
Bartleby was not to be seen. I looked round
anxiously, peeped behind his screen; but it

875 was very plain that he was gone. Upon more
closely examining the place, I surmised that
for an indefinite period Bartleby must have
ate, dressed, and slept in my office, and that
too without plate, mirror, or bed. The cush-
880 ioned seat of a rickety old sofa in one corner
bore the faint impress of a lean, reclining
form. Rolled away under his desk, I found a
blanket; under the empty grate, a blacking
box and brush; on a chair, a tin basin, with
885 soap and a ragged towel; in a newspaper a
few crumbs of ginger-nuts and a morsel of
cheese. Yes, thought I, it is evident enough
that Bartleby has been making his home
here, keeping bachelor's hall all by himself.
890 Immediately then the thought came sweeping across me, What miserable friendless-
ness and loneliness are here revealed! His
poverty is great; but his solitude, how horrible! Think of it. Of a Sunday, Wall-street is
895 deserted as Petra; and every night of every
day it is an emptiness. This building too,
which of week-days hums with industry
and life, at nightfall echoes with sheer
vacancy, and all through Sunday is forlorn.
900 And here Bartleby makes his home; sole
spectator of a solitude which he has seen all
populous—a sort of innocent and transformed Marius brooding among the ruins of
Carthage!
905   For the first time in my life a feeling of
overpowering stinging melancholy seized me.
Before, I had never experienced aught but a
not-unpleasing sadness. The bond of a common humanity now drew me irresistibly to
910 gloom. A fraternal melancholy! For both
I and Bartleby were sons of Adam. I
remembered the bright silks and sparkling
faces I had seen that day, in gala trim, swan-
like sailing down the Mississippi of Broadway;
915 and I contrasted them with the pallid copyist,
and thought to myself, Ah, happiness courts

the light, so we deem the world is gay; but
misery hides aloof, so we deem that misery
there is none. These sad fancyings—
920 chimeras, doubtless, of a sick and silly
brain—led on to other and more special
thoughts, concerning the eccentricities of
Bartleby. Presentiments of strange discoveries
hovered round me. The scrivener's pale form
925 appeared to me laid out, among uncaring
strangers, in its shivering winding sheet.
   Suddenly I was attracted by Bartleby's
closed desk, the key in open sight left in
the lock.
930   I mean no mischief, seek the gratification of no heartless curiosity, thought I;
besides, the desk is mine, and its contents
too, so I will make bold to look within.
Every thing was methodically arranged, the
935 papers smoothly placed. The pigeon holes
were deep, and removing the files of documents, I groped into their recesses. Presently I felt something there, and dragged it
out. It was an old bandanna handkerchief,
940 heavy and knotted. I opened it, and saw it
was a savings' bank.
   I now recalled all the quiet mysteries
which I had noted in the man. I remembered
that he never spoke but to answer; that
945 though at intervals he had considerable time
to himself, yet I had never seen him reading—
no, not even a newspaper; that for long periods he would stand looking out, at his pale
window behind the screen, upon the dead
950 brick wall; I was quite sure he never visited
any refectory or eating house; while his pale
face clearly indicated that he never drank
beer like Turkey, or tea and coffee even, like
other men; that he never went any where in
955 particular that I could learn; never went out
for a walk, unless indeed that was the case at
present; that he had declined telling who he
was, or whence he came, or whether he had

any relatives in the world; that though so thin
960 and pale, he never complained of ill health.
And more than all, I remembered a certain
unconscious air of pallid—how shall I call
it?—of pallid haughtiness, say, or rather an
austere reserve about him, which had posi-
965 tively awed me into my tame compliance
with his eccentricities, when I had feared to
ask him to do the slightest incidental thing
for me, even though I might know, from his
long-continued motionlessness, that behind
970 his screen he must be standing in one of
those dead-wall reveries of his.

Revolving all these things, and coupling
them with the recently discovered fact that
he made my office his constant abiding place
975 and home, and not forgetful of his morbid
moodiness; revolving all these things, a pru-
dential feeling began to steal over me. My
first emotions had been those of pure melancholy and sincerest pity; but just in propor-
980 tion as the forlornness of Bartleby grew and
grew to my imagination, did that same melancholy merge into fear, that pity into repulsion. So true it is, and so terrible too, that up
to a certain point the thought or sight of
985 misery enlists our best affections; but, in certain special cases, beyond that point it does
not. They err who would assert that invariably this is owing to the inherent selfishness
of the human heart. It rather proceeds from
990 a certain hopelessness of remedying excessive and organic ill. To a sensitive being, pity
is not seldom pain. And when at last it is
perceived that such pity cannot lead to effectual succor, common sense bids the soul rid
995 of it. What I saw that morning persuaded me
that the scrivener was the victim of innate
and incurable disorder. I might give alms to
his body; but his body did not pain him; it
was his soul that suffered, and his soul I
1000 could not reach.

I did not accomplish the purpose of
going to Trinity Church that morning.
Somehow, the things I had seen disquali-
fied me for the time from church-going.
1005 I walked homeward, thinking what I would
do with Bartleby. Finally, I resolved upon
this;—I would put certain calm questions
to him the next morning, touching his history, etc., and if he declined to answer
1010 them openly and unreservedly (and I supposed he would prefer not), then to give
him a twenty dollar bill over and above
whatever I might owe him, and tell him his
services were no longer required; but that
1015 if in any other way I could assist him, I
would be happy to do so, especially if he
desired to return to his native place, wherever that might be, I would willingly help to
defray the expenses. Moreover, if, after
1020 reaching home, he found himself at any
time in want of aid, a letter from him
would be sure of a reply.

The next morning came.

"Bartleby," said I, gently calling to him
1025 behind his screen.

No reply.

"Bartleby," said I, in a still gentler tone,
"come here; I am not going to ask you to do
any thing you would prefer not to do—I sim-
1030 ply wish to speak to you."

Upon this he noiselessly slid into view.

"Will you tell me, Bartleby, where you
were born?"

"I would prefer not to."

1035 "Will you tell me *any thing* about yourself?"

"I would prefer not to."

"But what reasonable objection can you
have to speak to me? I feel friendly towards
1040 you."

He did not look at me while I spoke, but
kept his glance fixed upon my bust of Cicero,

which as I then sat, was directly behind me, some six inches above my head.

1045 "What is your answer, Bartleby?" said I, after waiting a considerable time for a reply, during which his countenance remained immovable, only there was the faintest conceivable tremor of the white attenuated 1050 mouth.

"At present I prefer to give no answer," he said, and retired into his hermitage.

It was rather weak in me I confess, but his manner on this occasion nettled me. 1055 Not only did there seem to lurk in it a certain calm disdain, but his perverseness seemed ungrateful, considering the undeniable good usage and indulgence he had received from me.

1060 Again I sat ruminating what I should do. Mortified as I was at his behavior, and resolved as I had been to dismiss him when I entered my offices, nevertheless I strangely felt something superstitious knocking at my 1065 heart, and forbidding me to carry out my purpose, and denouncing me for a villain if I dared to breathe one bitter word against this forlornest of mankind. At last, familiarly drawing my chair behind his screen, I sat 1070 down and said: "Bartleby, never mind then about revealing your history; but let me entreat you, as a friend, to comply as far as may be with the usages of this office. Say now you will help to examine papers to- 1075 morrow or next day: in short, say now that in a day or two you will begin to be a little reasonable:—say so, Bartleby."

"At present I would prefer not to be a little reasonable," was his mildly cadaverous reply.

1080 Just then the folding-doors opened, and Nippers approached. He seemed suffering from an unusually bad night's rest, induced by severer indigestion than common. He overheard those final words of Bartleby.

1085 "*Prefer not*, eh?" gritted Nippers—"I'd *prefer* him, if I were you, sir," addressing me—"I'd *prefer* him; I'd give him preferences, the stubborn mule! What is it, sir, pray, that he *prefers* not to do now?"

1090 Bartleby moved not a limb.

"Mr. Nippers," said I, "I'd prefer that you would withdraw for the present."

Somehow, of late I had got into the way of involuntarily using this word "prefer" upon 1095 all sorts of not exactly suitable occasions. And I trembled to think that my contact with the scrivener had already and seriously affected me in a mental way. And what further and deeper aberration might it not yet 1100 produce? This apprehension had not been without efficacy in determining me to summary means.

As Nippers, looking very sour and sulky, was departing, Turkey blandly and deferen- 1105 tially approached.

"With submission, sir," said he, "yesterday I was thinking about Bartleby here, and I think that if he would but prefer to take a quart of good ale every day, it would do much 1110 towards mending him, and enabling him to assist in examining his papers."

"So you have got the word too," said I, slightly excited.

"With submission, what word, sir," asked 1115 Turkey, respectfully crowding himself into the contracted space behind the screen, and by so doing, making me jostle the scrivener. "What word, sir?"

"I would prefer to be left alone here," said 1120 Bartleby, as if offended at being mobbed in his privacy.

"*That's* the word, Turkey," said I—"that's it."

"Oh, *prefer*? oh yes—queer word. I never 1125 use it myself. But, sir, as I was saying, if he would but prefer—"

"Turkey," interrupted I, "you will please withdraw."

"Oh certainly, sir, if you prefer that I 1130 should."

As he opened the folding-door to retire, Nippers at his desk caught a glimpse of me, and asked whether I would prefer to have a certain paper copied on blue paper or white. 1135 He did not in the least roguishly accent the word prefer. It was plain that it involuntarily rolled from his tongue. I thought to myself, surely I must get rid of a demented man, who already has in some degree turned the 1140 tongues, if not the heads of myself and clerks. But I thought it prudent not to break the dismission at once.

The next day I noticed that Bartleby did nothing but stand at his window in his dead-1145 wall revery. Upon asking him why he did not write, he said that he had decided upon doing no more writing.

"Why, how now? what next?" exclaimed I, "do no more writing?"

1150   "No more."

"And what is the reason?"

"Do you not see the reason for yourself," he indifferently replied.

I looked steadfastly at him, and perceived 1155 that his eyes looked dull and glazed. Instantly it occurred to me, that his unexampled diligence in copying by his dim window for the first few weeks of his stay with me might have temporarily impaired his vision.

1160   I was touched. I said something in condolence with him. I hinted that of course he did wisely in abstaining from writing for a while; and urged him to embrace that opportunity of taking wholesome exercise in the open air. 1165 This, however, he did not do. A few days after this, my other clerks being absent, and being in a great hurry to dispatch certain letters by the mail, I thought that, having nothing else

earthly to do, Bartleby would surely be less 1170 inflexible than usual, and carry these letters to the post-office. But he blankly declined. So, much to my inconvenience, I went myself.

Still added days went by. Whether Bartleby's 1175 eyes improved or not, I could not say. To all appearance, I thought they did. But when I asked him if they did, he vouchsafed no answer. At all events, he would do no copying. At last, in reply to my urgings, he informed 1180 me that he had permanently given up copying.

"What!" exclaimed I; "suppose your eyes should get entirely well—better than ever before—would you not copy then?"

1185   "I have given up copying," he answered, and slid aside.

He remained as ever, a fixture in my chamber. Nay—if that were possible—he became still more of a fixture than before. 1190 What was to be done? He would do nothing in the office: why should he stay there? In plain fact, he had now become a millstone to me, not only useless as a necklace, but afflictive to bear. Yet I was sorry for him. I speak 1195 less than truth when I say that, on his own account, he occasioned me uneasiness. If he would but have named a single relative or friend, I would instantly have written, and urged their taking the poor fellow away to 1200 some convenient retreat. But he seemed alone, absolutely alone in the universe. A bit of wreck in the mid Atlantic. At length, necessities connected with my business tyrannized over all other considerations. 1205 Decently as I could, I told Bartleby that in six days' time he must unconditionally leave the office. I warned him to take measures, in the interval, for procuring some other abode. I offered to assist him in this endeavor, if he 1210 himself would but take the first step towards a removal. "And when you finally quit me, Bartleby," added I, "I shall see that you go not away entirely unprovided. Six days from this hour, remember."

1215   At the expiration of that period, I peeped behind the screen, and lo!

   Bartleby was there.

   I buttoned up my coat, balanced myself; advanced slowly towards him, touched his

1220 shoulder, and said, "The time has come; you must quit this place; I am sorry for you; here is money; but you must go."

   "I would prefer not," he replied, with his back still towards me.

1225   "You *must*."

   He remained silent.

   Now I had an unbounded confidence in this man's common honesty. He had frequently restored to me sixpences and shil-

1230 lings carelessly dropped upon the floor, for I am apt to be very reckless in such shirt-button affairs. The proceeding then which followed will not be deemed extraordinary.

   "Bartleby," said I, "I owe you twelve dollars

1235 on account; here are thirty-two; the odd twenty are yours.—Will you take it?" and I handed the bills towards him.

   But he made no motion.

   "I will leave them here then," putting

1240 them under a weight on the table. Then taking my hat and cane and going to the door I tranquilly turned and added—"After you have removed your things from these offices, Bartleby, you will of course lock the

1245 door—since every one is now gone for the day but you—and if you please, slip your key underneath the mat, so that I may have it in the morning. I shall not see you again; so good-bye to you. If hereafter in your new

1250 place of abode I can be of any service to you, do not fail to advise me by letter. Good-bye, Bartleby, and fare you well."

But he answered not a word; like the last column of some ruined temple, he remained

1255 standing mute and solitary in the middle of the otherwise deserted room.

   As I walked home in a pensive mood, my vanity got the better of my pity. I could not but highly plume myself on my masterly

1260 management in getting rid of Bartleby. Masterly I call it, and such it must appear to any dispassionate thinker. The beauty of my procedure seemed to consist in its perfect quietness. There was no vulgar bullying, no

1265 bravado of any sort, no choleric hectoring, and striding to and fro across the apartment, jerking out vehement commands for Bartleby to bundle himself off with his beggarly traps. Nothing of the kind. Without

1270 loudly bidding Bartleby depart—as an inferior genius might have done—I *assumed* the ground that depart he must; and upon that assumption built all I had to say. The more I thought over my procedure, the more I was

1275 charmed with it. Nevertheless, next morning, upon awakening, I had my doubts,—I had somehow slept off the fumes of vanity. One of the coolest and wisest hours a man has, is just after he awakes in the morning. My proce-

1280 dure seemed as sagacious as ever.—but only in theory. How it would prove in practice—there was the rub. It was truly a beautiful thought to have assumed Bartleby's departure; but, after all, that assumption was sim-

1285 ply my own, and none of Bartleby's. The great point was, not whether I had assumed that he would quit me, but whether he would prefer so to do. He was more a man of preferences than assumptions.

1290   After breakfast, I walked down town, arguing the probabilities *pro* and *con*. One moment I thought it would prove a miserable failure, and Bartleby would be found all alive at my office as usual; the next moment it seemed certain that I should see his chair empty. And so I kept veering about. At the corner of Broadway and Canal-street, I saw quite an excited group of people standing in earnest conversation.

"I'll take odds he doesn't," said a voice as I passed.

"Doesn't go?—done!" said I, "put up your money."

I was instinctively putting my hand in my pocket to produce my own, when I remembered that this was an election day. The words I had overheard bore no reference to Bartleby, but to the success or non-success of some candidate for the mayoralty. In my intent frame of mind, I had, as it were, imagined that all Broadway shared in my excitement, and were debating the same question with me. I passed on, very thankful that the uproar of the street screened my momentary absent-mindedness.

As I had intended, I was earlier than usual at my office door. I stood listening for a moment. All was still. He must be gone. I tried the knob. The door was locked. Yes, my procedure had worked to a charm; he indeed must be vanished. Yet a certain melancholy mixed with this: I was almost sorry for my brilliant success. I was fumbling under the door mat for the key, which Bartleby was to have left there for me, when accidentally my knee knocked against a panel, producing a summoning sound, and in response a voice came to me from within—"Not yet; I am occupied."

It was Bartleby.

I was thunderstruck. For an instant I stood like the man who, pipe in mouth, was killed one cloudless afternoon long ago in Virginia, by a summer lightning; at his own warm open window he was killed, and remained leaning out there upon the dreamy afternoon, till some one touched him, when he fell.

"Not gone!" I murmured at last. But again obeying that wondrous ascendancy which the inscrutable scrivener had over me, and from which ascendancy, for all my chafing, I could not completely escape, I slowly went down stairs and out into the street, and while walking round the block, considered what I should next do in this unheard-of perplexity. Turn the man out by an actual thrusting I could not; to drive him away by calling him hard names would not do; calling in the police was an unpleasant idea; and yet, permit him to enjoy his cadaverous triumph over me,—this too I could not think of. What was to be done? or, if nothing could be done, was there any thing further that I could *assume* in the matter? Yes, as before I had prospectively assumed that Bartleby would depart, so now I might retrospectively assume that departed he was. In the legitimate carrying out of this assumption, I might enter my office in a great hurry, and pretending not to see Bartleby at all, walk straight against him as if he were air. Such a proceeding would in a singular degree have the appearance of a home-thrust. It was hardly possible that Bartleby could withstand such an application of the doctrine of assumptions. But upon second thoughts the success of the plan seemed rather dubious. I resolved to argue the matter over with him again.

"Bartleby," said I, entering the office, with a quietly severe expression, "I am seriously displeased. I am pained, Bartleby. I had thought better of you. I had imagined you of such a gentlemanly organization, that in any delicate dilemma a slight hint would have suffice—in short, an assumption. But it appears I am deceived. Why," I added,

unaffectedly starting, "you have not even
1380 touched that money yet," pointing to it, just
where I had left it the evening previous.

He answered nothing.

"Will you, or will you not, quit me?" I now
demanded in a sudden passion, advancing
1385 close to him.

"I would prefer *not* to quit you," he replied,
gently emphasizing the *not*.

"What earthly right have you to stay here?
Do you pay any rent? Do you pay my taxes?
1390 Or is this property yours?"

He answered nothing.

"Are you ready to go on and write now?
Are your eyes recovered? Could you copy a
small paper for me this morning? or help
1395 examine a few lines? or step round to the
post-office? In a word, will you do any thing
at all, to give a coloring to your refusal to
depart the premises?"

He silently retired into his hermitage.

1400 I was now in such a state of nervous
resentment that I thought it but prudent to
check myself at present from further demon-
strations. Bartleby and I were alone. I
remembered the tragedy of the unfortunate
1405 Adams and the still more unfortunate Colt in
the solitary office of the latter; and how poor
Colt, being dreadfully incensed by Adams,
and imprudently permitting himself to get
wildly excited, was at unawares hurried into
1410 his fatal act—an act which certainly no man
could possibly deplore more than the actor
himself. Often it had occurred to me in my
ponderings upon the subject, that had that
altercation taken place in the public street,
1415 or at a private residence, it would not have
terminated as it did. It was the circumstance
of being alone in a solitary office, up stairs, of
a building entirely unhallowed by humaniz-
ing domestic associations—an uncarpeted
1420 office, doubtless, of a dusty, haggard sort of

appearance;—this it must have been, which
greatly helped to enhance the irritable desperation of the hapless Colt.

But when this old Adam of resentment
1425 rose in me and tempted me concerning
Bartleby, I grappled him and threw him.
How? Why, simply by recalling the divine
injunction: "A new commandment give I
unto you, that ye love one another." Yes, this
1430 it was that saved me. Aside from higher considerations, charity often operates as a vastly
wise and prudent principle—a great safe-
guard to its possessor. Men have committed
murder for jealousy's sake, and anger's sake,
1435 and hatred's sake, and selfishness' sake, and
spiritual pride's sake; but no man that ever I
heard of, ever committed a diabolical murder
for sweet charity's sake. Mere self-interest,
then, if no better motive can be enlisted,
1440 should, especially with high-tempered men,
prompt all beings to charity and philan-
thropy. At any rate, upon the occasion in
question, I strove to drown my exasperated
feelings towards the scrivener by benevo-
1445 lently construing his conduct. Poor fellow,
poor fellow! thought I, he don't mean any
thing; and besides, he has seen hard times,
and ought to be indulged.

I endeavored also immediately to occupy
1450 myself, and at the same time to comfort my
despondency. I tried to fancy that in the
course of the morning, at such time as might
prove agreeable to him, Bartleby, of his own
free accord, would emerge from his hermit-
1455 age, and take up some decided line of march
in the direction of the door. But no. Half-past
twelve o'clock came; Turkey began to glow in
the face, overturn his inkstand, and become
generally obstreperous; Nippers abated down
1460 into quietude and courtesy; Ginger Nut
munched his noon apple; and Bartleby
remained standing at his window in one of

his profoundest dead-wall reveries. Will it be credited? Ought I to acknowledge it? That afternoon I left the office without saying one further word to him.

Some days now passed, during which, at leisure intervals I looked a little into "Edwards on the Will," and "Priestly on Necessity." Under the circumstances, those books induced a salutary feeling. Gradually I slid into the persuasion that these troubles of mine touching the scrivener, had been all predestinated from eternity, and Bartleby was billeted upon me for some mysterious purpose of an all-wise Providence, which it was not for a mere mortal like me to fathom. Yes, Bartleby, stay there behind your screen, thought I; I shall persecute you no more; you are harmless and noiseless as any of these old chairs; in short, I never feel so private as when I know you are here. At last I see it, I feel it; I penetrate to the predestinated purpose of my life. I am content. Others may have loftier parts to enact; but my mission in this world, Bartleby, is to furnish you with office-room for such period as you may see fit to remain.

I believe that this wise and blessed frame of mind would have continued with me, had it not been for the unsolicited and uncharitable remarks obtruded upon me by my professional friends who visited the rooms. But thus it often is, that the constant friction of illiberal minds wears out at last the best resolves of the more generous. Though to be sure, when I reflected upon it, it was not strange that people entering my office should be struck by the peculiar aspect of the unaccountable Bartleby, and so be tempted to throw out some sinister observations concerning him. Sometimes an attorney having business with me, and calling at my office and finding no one but the scrivener there,

would undertake to obtain some sort of precise information from him touching my whereabouts; but without heeding his idle talk, Bartleby would remain standing immovable in the middle of the room. So after contemplating him in that position for a time, the attorney would depart, no wiser than he came.

Also, when a Reference was going on, and the room full of lawyers and witnesses and business was driving fast; some deeply occupied legal gentleman present, seeing Bartleby wholly unemployed, would request him to run round to his (the legal gentleman's) office and fetch some papers for him. Thereupon, Bartleby would tranquilly decline, and yet remain idle as before. Then the lawyer would give a great stare, and turn to me. And what could I say? At last I was made aware that all through the circle of my professional acquaintance, a whisper of wonder was running round, having reference to the strange creature I kept at my office. This worried me very much. And as the idea came upon me of his possibly turning out a long-lived man, and keep occupying my chambers, and denying my authority; and perplexing my visitors; and scandalizing my professional reputation; and casting a general gloom over the premises; keeping soul and body together to the last upon his savings (for doubtless he spent but half a dime a day), and in the end perhaps outlive me, and claim possession of my office by right of his perpetual occupancy: as all these dark anticipations crowded upon me more and more, and my friends continually intruded their relentless remarks upon the apparition in my room; a great change was wrought in me. I resolved to gather all my faculties together, and for ever rid me of this intolerable incubus.

Ere revolving any complicated project, however, adapted to this end, I first simply suggested to Bartleby the propriety of his 1550 permanent departure. In a calm and serious tone, I commended the idea to his careful and mature consideration. But having taken three days to meditate upon it, he apprised me that his original determination remained 1555 the same; in short, that he still preferred to abide with me.

What shall I do? I now said to myself, buttoning up my coat to the last button. What shall I do? what ought I to do? what 1560 does conscience say I *should* do with this man, or rather ghost. Rid myself of him, I must; go, he shall. But how? You will not thrust him, the poor, pale, passive mortal,— you will not thrust such a helpless creature 1565 out of your door? you will not dishonor yourself by such cruelty? No, I will not, I cannot do that. Rather would I let him live and die here, and then mason up his remains in the wall. What then will you do? 1570 For all your coaxing, he will not budge. Bribes he leaves under your own paper-weight on your table; in short, it is quite plain that he prefers to cling to you.

Then something severe, something 1575 unusual must be done. What! surely you will not have him collared by a constable, and commit his innocent pallor to the common jail? And upon what ground could you pro-cure such a thing to be done?—a vagrant, is 1580 he? What! he a vagrant, a wanderer, who refuses to budge? It is because he will *not* be a vagrant, then, that you seek to count him *as* a vagrant. That is too absurd. No visible means of support: there I have him. Wrong 1585 again: for indubitably he *does* support him-self, and that is the only unanswerable proof that any man can show of his possessing the means so to do. No more then. Since he will

not quit me, I must quit him. I will change 1590 my offices; I will move elsewhere; and give him fair notice, that if I find him on my new premises I will then proceed against him as a common trespasser.

Acting accordingly, next day I thus 1595 addressed him: "I find these chambers too far from the City Hall; the air is unwhole-some. In a word, I propose to remove my offices next week, and shall no longer require your services. I tell you this now, in 1600 order that you may seek another place."

He made no reply, and nothing more was said.

On the appointed day I engaged carts and men, proceeded to my chambers, and having 1605 but little furniture, every thing was removed in a few hours. Throughout, the scrivener remained standing behind the screen, which I directed to be removed the last thing. It was withdrawn; and being folded up like a huge 1610 folio, left him the motionless occupant of a naked room. I stood in the entry watching him a moment, while something from within me upbraided me.

I re-entered, with my hand in my pocket— 1615 and—and my heart in my mouth.

"Good-bye, Bartleby; I am going—good-bye, and God some way bless you; and take that," slipping something in his hand. But it dropped upon the floor, and then,—strange 1620 to say—I tore myself from him whom I had so longed to be rid of.

Established in my new quarters, for a day or two I kept the door locked, and started at every footfall in the passages. When I returned to my 1625 rooms after any little absence, I would pause at the threshold for an instant, and attentively listen, ere applying my key. But these fears were needless. Bartleby never came nigh me.

I thought all was going well, when a per-1630 turbed looking stranger visited me, inquiring whether I was the person who had recently occupied rooms at No.—Wall-street.

Full of forebodings, I replied that I was.

"Then sir," said the stranger, who proved a
1635 lawyer, "you are responsible for the man you left there. He refuses to do any copying; he refuses to do any thing; he says he prefers not to; and he refuses to quit the premises."

"I am very sorry, sir," said I, with assumed
1640 tranquility, but an inward tremor, "but, really, the man you allude to is nothing to me—he is no relation or apprentice of mine, that you should hold me responsible for him."

"In mercy's name, who is he?"

1645   "I certainly cannot inform you. I know nothing about him. Formerly I employed him as a copyist; but he has done nothing for me now for some time past."

"I shall settle him then,—good morning,
1650 sir."

Several days passed, and I heard nothing more; and though I often felt a charitable prompting to call at the place and see poor Bartleby, yet a certain squeamishness of I
1655 know not what withheld me.

All is over with him, by this time, thought I at last, when through another week no further intelligence reached me. But coming to my room the day after, I found several per-
1660 sons waiting at my door in a high state of nervous excitement.

"That's the man—here he comes," cried the foremost one, whom I recognized as the lawyer who had previously called upon me
1665 alone.

"You must take him away, sir, at once," cried a portly person among them, advancing upon me, and whom I knew to be the landlord of No.—Wall-street. "These gentle-
1670 men, my tenants, cannot stand it any longer; Mr. B—" pointing to the lawyer, "has turned him out of his room, and he now persists in

haunting the building generally, sitting upon the banisters of the stairs by day, and sleep-
1675 ing in the entry by night. Every body is concerned; clients are leaving the offices; some fears are entertained of a mob; something you must do, and that without delay."

Aghast at this torrent, I fell back before it,
1680 and would fain have locked myself in my new quarters. In vain I persisted that Bartleby was nothing to me—no more than to any one else. In vain:—I was the last person known to have any thing to do with him,
1685 and they held me to the terrible account. Fearful then of being exposed in the papers (as one person present obscurely threatened) I considered the matter, and at length said, that if the lawyer would give me a confiden-
1690 tial interview with the scrivener, in his (the lawyer's) own room, I would that afternoon strive my best to rid them of the nuisance they complained of.

Going up stairs to my old haunt, there was
1695 Bartleby silently sitting upon the banister at the landing.

"What are you doing here, Bartleby?" said I.

"Sitting upon the banister," he mildly replied.

1700   I motioned him into the lawyer's room, who then left us.

"Bartleby," said I, "are you aware that you are the cause of great tribulation to me, by persisting in occupying the entry after being
1705 dismissed from the office?"

No answer.

"Now one of two things must take place. Either you must do something, or something must be done to you. Now what sort of
1715 business would you like to engage in? Would you like to re-engage in copying for some one?"

"No; I would prefer not to make any change."

1720 "Would you like a clerkship in a dry-goods store?"

"There is too much confinement about that. No, I would not like a clerkship; but I am not particular."

1725 "Too much confinement," I cried, "why you keep yourself confined all the time!"

"I would prefer not to take a clerkship," he rejoined, as if to settle that little item at once.

1730 "How would a bar-tender's business suit you? There is no trying of the eyesight in that."

"I would not like it at all; though, as I said before, I am not particular."

1735 His unwonted wordiness inspirited me. I returned to the charge.

"Well then, would you like to travel through the country collecting bills for the merchants? That would improve your
1740 health."

"No, I would prefer to be doing something else."

"How then would going as a companion to Europe, to entertain some young gentleman
1745 with your conversation,—how would that suit you?"

"Not at all. It does not strike me that there is any thing definite about that. I like to be stationary. But I am not particular."

1750 "Stationary you shall be then," I cried, now losing all patience, and for the first time in all my exasperating connection with him fairly flying into a passion. "If you do not go away from these premises before night, I
1755 shall feel bound—indeed I *am* bound—to—to—to quit the premises myself!" I rather absurdly concluded, knowing not with what possible threat to try to frighten his immobility into compliance. Despairing of all further
1760 efforts, I was precipitately leaving him, when a final thought occurred to me—one

which had not been wholly unindulged before.

"Bartleby," said I, in the kindest tone I
1765 could assume under such exciting circumstances, "will you go home with me now—not to my office, but my dwelling—and remain there till we can conclude upon some convenient arrangement for you at our lei-
1770 sure? Come, let us start now, right away."

"No: at present I would prefer not to make any change at all."

I answered nothing; but effectually dodging every one by the suddenness and rapidity
1775 of my flight, rushed from the building, ran up Wall-street towards Broadway, and jumping into the first omnibus was soon removed from pursuit. As soon as tranquility returned I distinctly perceived that I had now done all
1780 that I possibly could, both in respect to the demands of the landlord and his tenants, and with regard to my own desire and sense of duty, to benefit Bartleby, and shield him from rude persecution. I now strove to be
1785 entirely care-free and quiescent; and my conscience justified me in the attempt; though indeed it was not so successful as I could have wished. So fearful was I of being again hunted out by the incensed landlord
1790 and his exasperated tenants, that, surrendering my business to Nippers, for a few days I drove about the upper part of the town and through the suburbs, in my rockaway; crossed over to Jersey City and Hoboken, and
1795 paid fugitive visits to Manhattanville and Astoria. In fact I almost lived in my rockaway for the time.

When again I entered my office, lo, a note from the landlord lay upon the desk. I
1800 opened it with trembling hands. It informed me that the writer had sent to the police, and had Bartleby removed to the Tombs as a vagrant. Moreover, since I knew more about

him than any one else, he wished me to
appear at that place, and make a suitable
statement of the facts. These tidings had a
conflicting effect upon me. At first I was
indignant; but at last almost approved. The
landlord's energetic, summary disposition
had led him to adopt a procedure which I do
not think I would have decided upon myself;
and yet as a last resort, under such peculiar
circumstances, it seemed the only plan.

As I afterwards learned, the poor scrivener, when told that he must be conducted
to the Tombs, offered not the slightest obstacle, but in his pale unmoving way, silently
acquiesced.

Some of the compassionate and curious
bystanders joined the party; and headed by
one of the constables arm in arm with
Bartleby, the silent procession filed its way
through all the noise, and heat, and joy of
the roaring thoroughfares at noon.

The same day I received the note I went to
the Tombs, or to speak more properly, the
Halls of Justice. Seeking the right officer, I
stated the purpose of my call, and was
informed that the individual I described was
indeed within. I then assured the function-
ary that Bartleby was a perfectly honest man,
and greatly to be compassionated, however
unaccountably eccentric. I narrated all I
knew, and closed by suggesting the idea of
letting him remain in as indulgent confinement as possible till something less harsh
might be done—though indeed I hardly
knew what. At all events, if nothing else
could be decided upon, the alms-house
must receive him. I then begged to have an
interview.

Being under no disgraceful charge, and
quite serene and harmless in all his ways,
they had permitted him freely to wander
about the prison, and especially in the

inclosed grass-platted yard thereof. And so I
found him there, standing all alone in the
quietest of the yards, his face towards a high
wall, while all around, from the narrow slits
of the jail windows, I thought I saw peering
out upon him the eyes of murderers and
thieves.

"Bartleby!"

"I know you," he said, without looking
round,—"and I want nothing to say to you."

"It was not I that brought you here,
Bartleby," said I, keenly pained at his implied
suspicion. "And to you, this should not be so
vile a place. Nothing reproachful attaches to
you by being here. And see, it is not so sad a
place as one might think. Look, there is the
sky, and here is the grass."

"I know where I am," he replied, but would
say nothing more, and so I left him.

As I entered the corridor again, a broad
meat-like man, in an apron, accosted me,
and jerking his thumb over his shoulder
said—"Is that your friend?"

"Yes."

"Does he want to starve? If he does, let
him live on the prison fare, that's all."

"Who are you?" asked I, not knowing what
to make of such an unofficially speaking person in such a place.

"I am the grub-man. Such gentlemen as
have friends here, hire me to provide them
with something good to eat."

"Is this so?" said I, turning to the turnkey.
He said it was.

"Well then," said I, slipping some silver
into the grub-man's hands (for so they called
him). "I want you to give particular attention
to my friend there; let him have the best
dinner you can get. And you must be as
polite to him as possible."

"Introduce me, will you?" said the grub-
man, looking at me with an expression

which seem to say he was all impatience for an opportunity to give a specimen of his 1890 breeding.

Thinking it would prove of benefit to the scrivener, I acquiesced; and asking the grub-man his name, went up with him to Bartleby.

"Bartleby, this is Mr. Cutlets; you will find 1895 him very useful to you."

"Your sarvant, sir, your sarvant," said the grub-man, making a low salutation behind his apron. "Hope you find it pleasant here, sir;—spacious grounds—cool apartments, 1900 sir—hope you'll stay with us some time—try to make it agreeable. May Mrs. Cutlets and I have the pleasure of your company to dinner, sir, in Mrs. Cutlets' private room?"

"I prefer not to dine to-day," said Bartleby, 1905 turning away. "It would disagree with me; I am unused to dinners." So saying he slowly moved to the other side of the inclosure, and took up a position fronting the dead-wall.

"How's this?" said the grub-man, address-1910 ing me with a stare of astonishment. "He's odd, aint he?"

"I think he is a little deranged," said I, sadly.

"Deranged? deranged is it? Well now, 1915 upon my word, I thought that friend of yourn was a gentleman forger; they are always pale and genteel-like, them forgers. I can't pity 'em—can't help it, sir. Did you know Monroe Edwards?" he added touchingly, and 1920 paused. Then, laying his hand pityingly on my shoulder, sighed, "he died of consumption at Sing-Sing. So you weren't acquainted with Monroe?"

"No, I was never socially acquainted with 1925 any forgers. But I cannot stop longer. Look to my friend yonder. You will not lose by it. I will see you again."

Some few days after this, I again obtained admission to the Tombs, and went through 1930 the corridors in quest of Bartleby; but without finding him.

"I saw him coming from his cell not long ago," said a turnkey, "may be he's gone to loiter in the yards."

1935 So I went in that direction.

"Are you looking for the silent man?" said another turnkey passing me. "Yonder he lies—sleeping in the yard there. 'Tis not twenty minutes since I saw him lie down."

1940 The yard was entirely quiet. It was not accessible to the common prisoners. The surrounding walls, of amazing thickness, kept off all sounds behind them. The Egyptian character of the masonry weighed upon me 1945 with its gloom. But a soft imprisoned turf grew under foot. The heart of the eternal pyramids, it seemed, wherein, by some strange magic, through the clefts, grass-seed, dropped by birds, had sprung.

1950 Strangely huddled at the base of the wall, his knees drawn up, and lying on his side, his head touching the cold stones, I saw the wasted Bartleby. But nothing stirred. I paused; then went close up to him; stooped 1955 over, and saw that his dim eyes were open; otherwise he seemed profoundly sleeping. Something prompted me to touch him. I felt his hand, when a tingling shiver ran up my arm and down my spine to my feet.

1960 The round face of the grub-man peered upon me now. "His dinner is ready. Won't he dine to-day, either? Or does he live without dining?"

"Lives without dining," said I, and closed 1965 his eyes.

"Eh!—He's asleep, aint he?"

"With kings and counselors," murmured I.

• • •

There would seem little need for proceeding further in this history. Imagination will readily 1970 supply the meager recital of poor Bartleby's interment. But ere parting with the reader, let me say, that if this little narrative has sufficiently interested him, to awaken curiosity as to who Bartleby was, and what manner of life he led prior to the present narrator's making his acquaintance, I can only reply, that in such curiosity I fully share, but am wholly unable to gratify it. Yet here I hardly know whether I should divulge one little item of rumor, which came to my ear a few months after the scrivener's decease. Upon what basis it rested, I could never ascertain; and hence, how true it is I cannot now tell. But inasmuch as this vague report has not been without certain strange suggestive interest to me, however sad, it may prove the same with some others; and so I will briefly mention it. The report was this: that Bartleby had been a subordinate clerk in the Dead Letter Office at Washington, from which he had been suddenly removed by a change in the administration. When I think over this rumor, I cannot adequately express the emotions which seize me. Dead letters! does it not sound like dead men? Conceive a man by nature and misfortune prone to a pallid hopelessness, can any business seem more fitted to heighten it than that of continually handling these dead letters, and assorting them for the flames? For by the cart-load they are annually burned. Sometimes from out the folded paper the pale clerk takes a ring:—the finger it was meant for, perhaps, moulders in the grave; a bank-note sent in swiftest charity:—he whom it would relieve, nor eats nor hungers any more; pardon for those who died despairing; hope for those who died unhoping; good tidings for those who died stifled by unrelieved calamities. On errands of life, these letters speed to death.

Ah Bartleby! Ah humanity!

◀ This 2012 illustration, *Bartleby, the Scrivener* by Bill Bragg, appeared in the Folio Society's 2012 illustrated edition of *The Complete Shorter Stories of Herman Melville.*

Describe how the image portrays the prominent characteristics of Bartleby. How do the colors, shadows, and details of the image reinforce these qualities?

STRUCTURE

1. How do the comparable traits of two or more characters in the story create a meaningful **contrast**? Identify a specific example. How does this contrast contribute to the story's **conflict**?

2. How does the **resolution** of the story — especially the final paragraph — affect your interpretation of the text?

FIGURATIVE LANGUAGE: Word Choice, Imagery, and Symbols

3. What is the **denotation** of "prefer"? What are some **connotative** meanings of "prefer"? Why do you think Melville chose this word over a similar term, such as *want*, *favor*, or *choose*?

4. After reading the descriptions of the characters, consider their names: *Turkey*, *Nippers*, and *Ginger Nut*. How do the **connotations** of these names contribute to the narrator's perspective?

5. What might Bartleby's **repetitive** "I prefer not to" reveal about his psychological state? How could the repetition of the phrase affect readers over the course of the narrative?

6. When the narrator asks Bartleby why he won't write, Bartleby responds, "Do you not see the reason for yourself?" How do seeing and vision function as a **motif** in the story? What figurative associations does sight have?

FIGURATIVE LANGUAGE: Comparisons

7. What is the subtitle of the story? How might it work as a **metaphor** in the story?

8. Consider the allusion to "kings and counselors" near the story's end. Explain the points of comparison between the allusion and the aspects of the text that are being compared. How does the allusion contribute to your interpretation of the text?

9. How is Bartleby **metaphorically** confined? What literal aspects of the office create figurative associations? What do these figurative associations reveal?

IDEAS IN LITERATURE: The Individual and Nature

10. How does the text reject Romantic values? What does the text reveal about the individual and the individual's relationship within a society or collective humanity?

PUTTING IT ALL TOGETHER

11. What is the relationship between Bartleby and the narrator? Consider the comparisons between the characterizations of both. How do their similarities and differences lead to conflict? Why can't the narrator disengage from Bartleby or simply let him go?

IDEAS IN LITERATURE
Imagination and Intuition

Today, the terms *passion* and *imagination* have positive connotations. But writers of the neoclassical period were suspicious of both. Along with *enthusiasm*, passion was associated with fanaticism — especially the religious zealotry of the Puritans. From a neoclassical perspective, reason and judgment must always predominate. The role of the neoclassical poet was to restate "objective" general truths in witty, striking language using well-established forms. But the Romantics upended this view.

First, Romantic poets like Wordsworth and Coleridge privileged feeling over thinking. In fact, Wordsworth defined poetry as the "spontaneous overflow of powerful feelings," which "takes its origin from emotion recollected in tranquility." Unlike the neoclassical poets, who imitated literary ideals from antiquity, the Romantic poets sought to be original and individual. Their subjective creativity came from their emotions and intuitions; these two faculties were more important than formal rules and adherence to classical models.

Second, the Romantics elevated the role of imagination. While many eighteenth-century writers viewed imaginative "fancy" as dangerous, the Romantics saw it as a creative force that allowed them to express beauty and truth. Poet and artist William Blake (1757–1827) even claimed that the powers of imagination enabled us to experience a union with God. Coleridge held a similar view, which he elaborated on in both his poems and his literary criticism, as did later Romantics such as Percy Bysshe Shelley (1792–1822). All believed in a timeless, metaphysical realm of truth and beauty beyond the everyday empirical world — and that imagination

IDEA BANK

Conviction
Creativity
Curiosity
Excess
The Exotic
Expression
Fantasy
Feelings
The Gothic
Imagination
Immortality
Impulse
Inspiration
Intuition
Irrationalism
Mystery
Mysticism
Originality
Ornament
Passion
Soul
Spirituality
The Supernatural
Understanding
Utopica
Visionary
Wilderness

©RMN-Grand Palais/Art Resource, NY

◀ *Liberty Leading the People* is an 1830 oil on canvas work by artist Eugene Delacroix. It is now housed at the Louvre in Paris.

How does this painting capture the revolutionary spirit of the Romantic period? Look closely at the subjects, the colors, and the shadows of the painting. Then explain the details that evoke the philosophy of the period.

could offer glimpses of that transcendent place. John Keats's "Ode on a Grecian Urn" (p. 641) provides an exemplary elaboration on these themes, particularly in the poem's love of beauty for its own sake.

But if imagination opens us up to beauty and truth, it also allows us to access fear, confusion, and darkness. The Romantics were fascinated by the *sublime*: a quality that combines both beauty and fear. The infinite universe, natural occurrences (tidal waves, storms), breathtaking landscapes (the Alps, open oceans) — all embody the sublime. Similarly, the *gothic* is an expression of Romanticism: imaginative visions of horror, transgression, psychological turmoil, mystery, death, darkness, and the grotesque. Popular novelists such as Ann Radcliffe (1764–1823) and Horace Walpole (1717–1797) wrote dark tales of suspense, paranoia, and terror, often with innocent female protagonists. Mary Shelley's novel *Frankenstein; or, The Modern Prometheus* synthesizes many romantic and gothic themes, including (as the book's subtitle implies) the idea that passion and creativity can be taken too far, with terrible unforeseen consequences.

Our society and culture are still suffused with Romantic ideas and premises. When we describe an individual as a "visionary," use our emotions to guide our behavior, push against the limits of possibility, value the strange over the "normal," or embrace excess and spontaneity instead of moderation and order — all are Romantic impulses. We still feel the pull of the sublime and the gothic, too, whether we're scaring ourselves on a rollercoaster, reading a Stephen King novel, or watching a horror movie.

The movie poster was used to advertise Stephen King's ▶ 2017 Gothic horror film, *It*.

Gothic novels of the Romantic period would often combine supernatural and mysterious elements. These tales evoke emotions of terror, anguish, and fear in readers. Today, horror films draw on the appeal of some of those same elements. How might this poster appeal to moviegoers? Explain what draws us to scary movies. Why do we like to be afraid?

IDEAS IN LITERATURE

Ode on a Grecian Urn
John Keats

THE TEXT IN CONTEXT

If William Wordsworth and Samuel Coleridge were the first
generation of English Romantics, then John Keats (1795–1821)
is part of the second generation, along with younger poets
such as Percy Shelley (1792–1822) and George Gordon, Lord
Byron (1788–1824). Like several of his literary peers, Keats died
young (of tuberculosis) after a relatively brief career. But he left a
substantial and influential series of works, including six odes.
An *ode* is a song or poem in which the speaker directly
addresses a subject or object of admiration. Keats's "Ode
on a Grecian Urn" (1820) exemplifies his Romantic fascination with art, beauty, time,
imagination, nature, and aesthetic escape. It also highlights his poetic style, which is
rich in sensual imagery, personification, alliteration, and other devices. For this poem,
Keats took his inspiration from the urns made by ancient Greek artisans. These terra
cotta vessels held water and wine, but they also depicted Greek myths, showed
scenes from daily life, and told stories with their images.

Hulton Archive/Getty Images

Ode on a Grecian Urn

Thou still unravish'd bride of quietness,
    Thou foster-child of silence and slow time,
Sylvan historian, who canst thus express
    A flowery tale more sweetly than our rhyme:
5 What leaf-fring'd legend haunts about thy shape
    Of deities or mortals, or of both,
        In Tempe or the dales of Arcady?
    What men or gods are these? What maidens loth?
What mad pursuit? What struggle to escape?
10   What pipes and timbrels? What wild ecstasy?

Heard melodies are sweet, but those unheard
    Are sweeter; therefore, ye soft pipes, play on;
Not to the sensual ear, but, more endear'd,
    Pipe to the spirit ditties of no tone:
15 Fair youth, beneath the trees, thou canst not leave

Thy song, nor ever can those trees be bare;
    Bold Lover, never, never canst thou kiss,
Though winning near the goal yet, do not grieve;
    She cannot fade, though thou hast not thy bliss,
20   For ever wilt thou love, and she be fair!

Ah, happy, happy boughs! that cannot shed
    Your leaves, nor ever bid the Spring adieu;
And, happy melodist, unwearied,
    For ever piping songs for ever new;
25 More happy love! more happy, happy love!
    For ever warm and still to be enjoy'd,
        For ever panting, and for ever young;
All breathing human passion far above,
    That leaves a heart high-sorrowful and cloy'd,
30   A burning forehead, and a parching tongue.

Who are these coming to the sacrifice?
    To what green altar, O mysterious priest,
Lead'st thou that heifer lowing at the skies,
    And all her silken flanks with garlands drest?
35 What little town by river or sea shore,
    Or mountain-built with peaceful citadel,
        Is emptied of this folk, this pious morn?
And, little town, thy streets for evermore
    Will silent be; and not a soul to tell
40   Why thou art desolate, can e'er return.

O Attic shape! Fair attitude! with brede
    Of marble men and maidens overwrought,
With forest branches and the trodden weed;
    Thou, silent form, dost tease us out of thought
45 As doth eternity: Cold Pastoral!
    When old age shall this generation waste,
        Thou shalt remain, in midst of other woe
Than ours, a friend to man, to whom thou say'st,
    "Beauty is truth, truth beauty,—that is all
50   Ye know on earth, and all ye need to know."

The Metropolitan Museum of Art

◀ The photograph shows a Greek urn, *Terracotta Nolan neck-amphora* (jar), 470–460 B.C. The urn depicts the winged goddess Eos capturing her lover, the young Trojan prince Tithonus.

———

How does art still engage humanity in shared aesthetic experiences, thoughtful reflection, and meaningful discussions? Does art remain important? Have its functions changed? Explain.

STRUCTURE

1. What type of poem is "Ode on a Grecian Urn"? How does the historical and cultural context of this poem affect your interpretation?

2. What general role does each stanza play in the story of the poem? What relationships does each **stanza** reveal? How do these relationships contribute to your interpretation of the poem?

3. How do the punctuation and **caesuras** throughout the poem convey relationships between the literal and the figurative?

4. Do the last lines resolve the poem's tension or **conflict**? Explain. How do you interpret the conclusion?

FIGURATIVE LANGUAGE: Word Choice, Imagery, and Symbols

5. What do the **images** throughout the poem have in common? How does this imagery contribute to the multiple tones within the poem?

6. In stanza two, how do the representations and associations of specific phrases convey figurative meaning? How does that meaning influence your interpretation of the poem?

7. How does the **imagery** in the third stanza help emphasize the speaker's ideas about the lovers? How do the images contribute to your interpretation of the poem?

FIGURATIVE LANGUAGE: Comparisons

8. What is being **compared** in "Ode on a Grecian Urn"? Does this comparison continue throughout the entire poem? Explain.

9. In stanza four, what is being **personified**? How does this personification contribute to your interpretation of the poem?

10. What does the speaker compare the urn to in the final stanza? How does this **comparison** contribute to your interpretation of the text?

IDEAS IN LITERATURE: Imagination and Intuition

11. John Keats uses art and nature to express a timeless relationship among humans, beauty, and truth. How do you interpret the phrase "beauty is truth, truth beauty, — that is all / Ye know on earth, and all ye need to know"? Is this idea still relevant and applicable today? Can you identify examples of it?

PUTTING IT ALL TOGETHER

12. How does Keats's ode shift from a literal description to a more figurative expression of the poem's meaning? How does this shift contribute to the complexity of the poem?

To John Keats, at Springtime
Countee Cullen

THE TEXT IN CONTEXT

Novelist, poet, and playwright Countee Cullen (1903–1946) was an influential figure in the Harlem Renaissance: a flourishing of arts, music, culture, and intellectual life in Harlem during the 1920s and 1930s. The movement included writers like Langston Hughes (1901–1967) and Zora Neale Hurston (1891–1960), musicians like Duke Ellington (1899–1974), and painters like Aaron Douglas (1899–1979). But in contrast to most of his literary peers, who sought to express a distinctively African American heritage and culture, Cullen broadly embraced American and English literature. He argued that African American writers "may have more to gain from the rich background of English and American poetry than from any nebulous atavistic yearnings toward an African inheritance." His poem "To John Keats, at Springtime" (1925) provides a good example of this view — and follows Keats's idea that the Romantic poet must accept mystery and uncertainty.

To John Keats, at Springtime

I cannot hold my peace, John Keats;
There never was a spring like this;
It is an echo, that repeats
My last year's song and next year's bliss.
5 I know, in spite of all men say
Of Beauty, you have felt her most.
Yea, even in your grave her way
Is laid. Poor, troubled, lyric ghost,
Spring never was so fair and dear
10 As Beauty makes her seem this year.
I cannot hold my peace, John Keats,
I am as helpless in the toil
Of Spring as any lamb that bleats
To feel the solid earth recoil
15 Beneath his puny legs. Spring beats
her tocsin call to those who love her,
And lo! the dogwood petals cover
Her breast with drifts of snow, and sleek
White gulls fly screaming to her, and hover
20 About her shoulders, and kiss her cheek,
While white and purple lilacs muster
A strength that bears them to a cluster
Of color and odor; for her sake
All things that slept are now awake.

25 And you and I, shall we lie still,
John Keats, while Beauty summons us?
Somehow I feel your sensitive will
Is pulsing up some tremulous
Sap road of a maple tree, whose leaves
30 Grow music as they grow, since your
Wild voice is in them, a harp that grieves
For life that opens death's dark door.
Though dust, your fingers still can push
The Vision Splendid to a birth,
35 Though now they work as grass in the hush
Of the night on the broad sweet page of the earth.

"John Keats is dead," they say, but I
Who hear your full insistent cry
In bud and blossom, leaf and tree,
40 Know John Keats still writes poetry.

And while my head is earthward bowed
To read new life sprung from your shroud,
Folks seeing me must think it strange
That merely spring should so derange
45 My mind. They do not know that you,
John Keats, keep revel with me, too.

Rebirth Painting (2018), an acrylic on canvas, was created by the French artist Cécile Duchêne Malissin. Malissin's works often explore the tension between reality and fiction.

———

Describe how the image in the painting (color, contrast, specific elements) parallels the imagery in the poem. How do these two works express both a passion for spring and a desire to understand the voices of the past?

© Cécile Duchêne Malissin

STRUCTURE

1. What type of poetry is "To John Keats, at Springtime"? How does this type connect to the purpose of the poem?

2. How does the historical **context** of the poem affect the poet's structural choices?

3. How does Cullen **contrast** the seasons? Explain.

FIGURATIVE LANGUAGE: Word Choice, Imagery, and Symbols

4. Choose two literal objects or events presented as **symbols** in the poem and explain their meaning.

5. Select an **image** in the poem and then choose two or three words that contribute to the image's sensory details. What associations do the images evoke?

6. Give an example of nature **imagery** that repeats in the poem. How does this **motif** contribute to your interpretation of the text?

FIGURATIVE LANGUAGE: Comparisons

7. What is **personified** in the poem? What specific human traits are ascribed to it?

8. This poem begins with an **apostrophe** in which the speaker addresses a person who is not present. Why does Cullen call out to Keats during springtime, in particular?

9. Choose a simile and a **metaphor** from the poem. What traits, qualities, and characteristics are being compared? Explain what the **comparison** reveals.

10. Countee Cullen wrote this poem over one hundred years after Keats's death. Yet the poets share a connection through their imaginative and intuitive love of nature. How do nature and the natural world continue to engage our imaginations? Can you identify a contemporary book, trend, movie, song, or example in another form that expresses — or takes inspiration from — our relationship with nature?

PUTTING IT ALL TOGETHER

11. How does the speaker of the poem combine stylistic elements to create an attitude in the poem's voice? What tone does he evoke? Describe the tone of the poem and support your description with textual evidence.

The Enchanted Garden
Italo Calvino

Gianni GIANSANTI/Gamma-Rapho/Getty Images

THE TEXT IN CONTEXT

Italian fiction writer and journalist Italo Calvino (1923–1985) began as a highly realistic novelist, but in the course of his career, Calvino's work became more fantastical and experimental. He also turned to allegory and fable to explore the nature of fiction itself, as well as its relationship to imagination and reality. His major works include *The Cloven Viscount* (1952), *Italian Folktales* (1956), *Cosmicomics* (1965), and *Invisible Cities* (1972). In "The Enchanted Garden," Calvino examines the fragile and paradoxical qualities of beauty.

The Enchanted Garden

Giovannino and Serenella were strolling along the railroad tracks. Below was a scaly sea of somber, clear blue; above, a sky lightly streaked with white clouds. The railroad
5 tracks were shimmering and burning hot. It was fun going along the tracks, there were so many games to play—he balancing on one rail and holding her hand while she walked along on the other, or else both
10 jumping from one sleeper to the next without ever letting their feet touch the stones in between. Giovannino and Serenella had been out looking for crabs, and now they had decided to explore the railroad tracks as far
15 as the tunnel. He liked playing with Serenella, for she did not behave as all the other little

girls did, forever getting frightened or bursting into tears at every joke. Whenever
Giovannino said, "Let's go there," or "Let's do
20 this," Serenella followed without a word.

Ping! They both gave a start and looked
up. A telephone wire had snapped off the top
of the pole. It sounded like an iron stork
shutting its beak in a hurry. They stood with
25 their noses in the air and watched. What a
pity not to have seen it! Now it would never
happen again.

"There's a train coming," said Giovannino.
Serenella did not move from the rail. "Where
30 from?" she asked.

Giovannino looked around in a knowl-
edgeable way. He pointed at the black hole
of the tunnel, which showed clear one
moment, then misty the next, through the
35 invisible heat haze rising from the stony
track.

"From there," he said. It was as though
they already heard a snort from the darkness
of the tunnel, and saw the train suddenly
40 appear, belching out fire and smoke, the
wheels mercilessly eating up the rails as it
hurtled toward them.

"Where shall we go, Giovannino?"

There were big gray aloes down by the
45 sea, surrounded by dense, impenetrable nettles, while up the hillside ran a rambling
hedge with thick leaves but no flowers. There
was still no sign of the train; perhaps it was
coasting, with the engine cut off, and would
50 jump out at them all of a sudden. But
Giovannino had now found an opening in
the hedge. "This way," he called.

The fence under the rambling hedge was
an old bent rail. At one point it twisted about
55 on the ground like the corner of a sheet of
paper. Giovannino had slipped into the hole
and already half vanished.

"Give me a hand, Giovannino."

They found themselves in the corner of a
60 garden, on all fours in a flower bed, with
their hair full of dry leaves and moss. Everything was quiet; not a leaf was stirring.

"Come on," said Giovannino, and Serenella
nodded in reply.

65 There were big old flesh-colored eucalyptus trees and winding gravel paths. Giovannino and Serenella tiptoed along the paths,
taking care not to crunch the gravel. Suppose
the owners appeared now?

70 Everything was so beautiful: sharp bends
in the path and high, curling eucalyptus
leaves and patches of sky. But there was
always the worrying thought that it was not
their garden, and that they might be chased
75 away any moment. Yet not a sound could be
heard. A flight of chattering sparrows rose
from a clump of arbutus at a turn in the
path. Then all was silent again. Perhaps it
was an abandoned garden?

80 But the shade of the big trees came to an
end, and they found themselves under the
open sky facing flower beds filled with neat
rows of petunias and convolvulus and paths
and balustrades and rows of box trees. And
85 up at the end of the garden was a large villa
with flashing windowpanes and yellow-and-
orange curtains.

And it was all quite deserted. The two
children crept forward, treading carefully
90 over the gravel: perhaps the windows would
suddenly be flung open, and angry ladies
and gentlemen appear on the terraces to
unleash great dogs down the paths. Now
they found a wheelbarrow standing near a
95 ditch. Giovannino picked it up by the handles
and began pushing it along: it creaked like a
whistle at every turn. Serenella seated herself in it and they moved slowly forward,
Giovannino pushing the barrow with her on
100 top, along the flower beds and fountains.

Every now and then Serenella would point to a flower and say in a low voice, "That one," and Giovannino would put the barrow down, pluck it, and give it to her. Soon she had a 105 lovely bouquet.

Eventually the gravel ended and they reached an open space paved in bricks and mortar. In the middle of this space was a big empty rectangle: a swimming pool. They 110 crept up to the edge; it was lined with blue tiles and filled to the brim with clear water. How lovely it would be to swim in!

"Shall we go for a dip?" Giovannino asked Serenella. The idea must have been quite 115 dangerous if he asked her instead of just saying, "In we go!" But the water was so clear and blue, and Serenella was never afraid. She jumped off the barrow and put her bunch of flowers in it. They were already in bathing 120 suits, since they'd been out for crabs before. Giovannino plunged in—not from the diving board, because the splash would have made too much noise, but from the edge of the pool. Down and down he went with his eyes 125 wide open, seeing only the blue from the tiles and his pink hands like goldfish; it was not the same as under the sea, full of shapeless green-black shadows. A pink form appeared above him: Serenella! He took her 130 hand and they swam up to the surface, a bit anxiously. No, there was no one watching them at all. But it was not so nice as they'd thought it would be, they always had that uncomfortable feeling that they had no right 135 to any of this, and might be chased out at any moment.

They scrambled out of the water, and there beside the swimming pool they found a Ping-Pong table. Instantly Giovannino 140 picked up the paddle and hit the ball, and Serenella, on the other side, was quick to return his shot. And so they went on playing, though giving only light taps at the ball, in case someone in the villa heard them. Then 145 Giovannino, in trying to parry a shot that had bounced high, sent the ball sailing away through the air and smack against a gong hanging in a pergola.

There was a long, somber boom. The two 150 children crouched down behind a clump of ranunculus. At once two menservants in white coats appeared, carrying big trays, when they had put the trays down on a round table under an orange-and-yellow-155 striped umbrella, off they went.

Giovannino and Serenella crept up to the table. There was tea, milk, and sponge cake. They had only to sit down and help themselves. They poured out two cups of tea and 160 cut two slices of cake. But somehow they did not feel at all at ease, and sat perched on the edge of their chairs, their knees shaking. And they could not really enjoy the tea and cake, for nothing seemed to have any taste. Every-165 thing in the garden was like that: lovely but impossible to enjoy properly, with that worrying feeling inside that they were only there through an odd stroke of luck, and the fear that they'd soon have to give an account of 170 themselves.

Very quietly they tiptoed up to the villa. Between the slits of a Venetian blind they saw a beautiful shady room, with collections of butterflies hanging on the walls. And in 175 the room was a pale little boy. Lucky boy, he must be the owner of this villa and garden. He was stretched out on a chaise longue, turning the pages of a large book filled with figures. He had big white hands and wore 180 pajamas buttoned up to the neck, though it was summer.

As the two children went on peeping through the slits, the pounding of their hearts gradually subsided. Why, the little rich

185 boy seemed to be sitting there and turning
the pages and glancing around with more
anxiety and worry than their own. Then he
got up and tiptoed around, as if he were
afraid that at any moment someone would
190 come and turn him out, as if he felt that that
book, that chaise longue, and those butterflies framed on the wall, the garden and
games and tea trays, the swimming pool and
paths, were only granted to him by some
195 enormous mistake, as if he were incapable of
enjoying them and felt the bitterness of the
mistake as his own fault.

   The pale boy was wandering about his
shady room furtively, touching with his
200 white fingers the edges of the cases studded
with butterflies, then he stopped to listen.
The pounding of Giovannino and Serenella's

hearts, which had died down, now got
harder than ever. Perhaps it was the fear of
205 a spell that hung over this villa and garden
and over all these lovely, comfortable things,
the residue of some injustice committed
long ago.

   Clouds darkened the sun. Very quietly
210 Giovannino and Serenella crept away. They
went back along the same paths they had
come, stepping fast but never at a run. And
they went through the hedge again on all
fours. Between the aloes they found a path
215 leading down to the small, stony beach, with
banks of seaweed along the shore. Then they
invented a wonderful new game: a seaweed
fight. They threw great handfuls of it in each
other's faces till late in the afternoon. And
220 Serenella never once cried.

Illustration by Naï Zakharia of Calvino's story The Enchanted Garden

This work by Naï Zakharia is part of a
collection of pen and ink illustrations
that depict scenes from Calvino's "The
Enchanted Garden."

Consider the image of the young boy
in a villa. How does the image represent both curiosity and fear as the
children peer through the glass door?
How would you describe the painting's
"tone" or attitude toward its subjects?

STRUCTURE

1. How does the arrival of the train present a **conflict**? What happens once the children see the train?

2. What is the relationship between the children and the servants? What additional contrasting elements in the story contribute to **tensions** within the narrative?

3. Explain how the boy in the villa and the children function as **contrasts**. How does this relationship contribute to your interpretation of the story?

4. What effect does the story's **resolution** have on the narrator and the family?

FIGURATIVE LANGUAGE: Word Choice, Imagery, and Symbols

5. Choose one literal object that is used to create **imagery** in the story. Use this example to explain how literal objects and images work together to suggest an interpretation throughout the story.

6. The setting in the story suggests figurative meanings. Explain the **archetypal symbolism** of the setting.

7. Select an example of **imagery**. Explain how the imagery connects to your senses and evokes an emotional response.

8. How does the garden become a **motif** throughout the text? How does the comparison in this motif contribute to your interpretation of the story?

FIGURATIVE LANGUAGE: Comparisons

9. Choose a biblical **allusion** in the story and then explain how it contributes to your interpretation of the text.

10. Identify and explain two **metaphors** in the text. What is the effect of these comparisons? How do they contribute to your understanding of the text?

IDEAS IN LITERATURE: Imagination and Intuition

11. Italo Calvino crafts an imaginative story filled with supernatural elements that appeal to our imagination and intuition. Explain how the children's journey is both literal and figurative. Would you characterize this story as hopeful or pessimistic?

PUTTING IT ALL TOGETHER

12. Calvino draws upon images and symbols to convey ideas. Using specific examples from the text to support your interpretation, explain how Calvino uses images and symbols to create a complex message about human journeys.

Writing about Motif and Extended Metaphor

AP **Enduring Understanding (LAN-1)**

Readers establish and communicate their interpretations of literature through arguments supported by textual evidence.

KEY POINT

Transitional elements help create coherence by indicating relationships between the evidence and the reasoning, the reasoning and the claim, and the evidence and the commentary.

Creating Coherence through Transitional Elements

When we read literature, we learn about the characters and settings. We follow the plot. We understand a narrator's or speaker's attitude. We can also interpret a literary text through the author's comparisons and images. Indeed, many writers express their insights about abstract ideas by using a pattern of images or comparisons that — upon first reading — may not be entirely clear. When you write a literary argument about these authorial techniques, you must explain how they work together to contribute to your interpretation. So as you begin to analyze the text, try to explore the patterns of images you see and connect them to a unifying idea.

Authors develop patterns by creating multiple images that are closely tied to an idea. For example, you might identify a pattern of images related to sight or sound or other senses. You would explain how this **imagery** or **motif** evokes an emotional response, creates an **atmosphere**, or conveys a **tone**. Additionally, you might explore how an author uses a series of related comparisons or develops an **extended metaphor**. You can develop your interpretation of the work by identifying the associations that the comparisons evoke.

Keep in mind that when you focus on imagery or metaphor in literature, you must explain how the literary elements work together rather than addressing each image or metaphor in isolation. When you explore both how and also *why* the author creates these associations and then relate them to a unifying idea, you will develop a thoughtful interpretation of the text.

In this composition workshop, you will learn how to write a literary argument that analyzes the author's use of motif or extended metaphor and then shows how it contributes to an interpretation of the text. Additionally, you will work on incorporating transitional elements to create coherence in your literary argument.

YOUR ASSIGNMENT

Choose a story or poem from Unit 5 or a text that your teacher has assigned. Then, write a literary argument that analyzes how a pattern of images or an extended comparison contributes to your interpretation of the work. Support your claim (idea + insight) with evidence from the text.

Your argument should interpret a literary work and include the following:

- An introduction that identifies the title, author, and context (including the context for images and comparisons)
- A thesis statement with a claim that conveys an interpretation (a unifying idea + insight about that idea)
- A line of reasoning that justifies the interpretation in the claim
- Relevant textual evidence that supports the line of reasoning
- Commentary that connects the evidence to the unifying idea in the line of reasoning and claim
- Transitional elements that create coherence in the argument
- A conclusion that brings the literary argument to a unified end

Potential Subjects

- How a pattern of imagery or extended metaphor reveals an insight about a character
- How a pattern of imagery or extended metaphor reveals the speaker's attitude toward a subject
- How a pattern of imagery or extended metaphor connects a subject to an abstract idea
- How a pattern of imagery or extended metaphor establishes a tone and reveals an insight

Explaining Complexity

While exploring how the author's use of imagery or extended metaphor impacts your interpretation of the text, you should consider the element's multiple functions and associations. Authors often create complex associations between concrete objects and abstract ideas. Words may have ambiguous meanings or a number of plausible interpretations.

Here are some questions to help you dig a little deeper into the complexity of the text:

- Do the sensory images in the text create a contrast?
- Do the sensory images shift from one pattern to another?
- Do the words and images have multiple meanings or connotations?
- Does the extended metaphor evolve from one meaning to another?
- What are the overall implications of the metaphor?

Set a Purpose for Reading

As you begin to analyze your selected text, identify a unifying idea to guide and focus your annotations. Then keep that unifying idea in mind as you look for patterns of imagery or extended metaphor. Consider the following questions as you read and analyze a text.

- Are the sensory images describing a single object, place, or person, or are they depicting more than one? If one, how are the associations complex? If more than one, what comparisons, contrasts, or tensions do the images evoke?
- Are the descriptive words — the adjectives, for example — consistent in their general associations (i.e., positive or negative), or is there a contrast, shift, or more complex association? If a contrast or shift is present, what is in conflict or tension?
- Is there a series of related comparisons or an extended comparison?
- What is literally being compared in the text?
- What abstract associations do the comparisons create in the text?
- What was the meaning of these images and/or comparisons at the time of publication? How might these associations have changed over time?

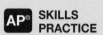 SKILLS PRACTICE | LITERARY ARGUMENTATION
Analyzing Imagery and Extended Metaphor

Consider the text you are analyzing and complete the following table. Choose a pattern of images or extended comparisons to explore in your analysis. In the middle column, record specific details of the images or comparisons from your text. In the right-hand column, explain the implications of the imagery or extended comparison. Be sure to connect these details to your unifying idea.

Analyzing Imagery/Extended Metaphor		
Unifying idea:		
Topic and focus of analysis:		
Literary Element	**Details from the Text**	**Insights and Connections to Unifying Idea**
Pattern of Images		
or		
Pattern of Comparisons		

Develop a Defensible Thesis Statement

As in other literary arguments, a thesis statement for an analysis of imagery or extended metaphor requires a claim that includes your interpretation (idea + insight). In this essay, you will focus on how these images or comparisons create associations for the reader and contribute to your interpretation. You should identify the author's technique along with your interpretation within your thesis statement.

Remember that your thesis must include a defensible claim. Simply stating that the author compares one thing to another thing is not enough. In your literary argument, you need to analyze how the subject and the comparison subject are similar, why the comparison is fitting, and what associations the reader might make when comparing them. In short, you explain how the comparison leads you to the insight in your interpretation. Therefore, the more precise your language is in your thesis statement, the stronger the thesis will be. For instance, instead of writing that an author compares a man to a fire, include descriptive adjectives (e.g., an *aging* man compared to a *dying* fire). Your precision will help your reader understand the associations more clearly. Review the following templates for writing a thesis statement in an analysis of imagery or extended metaphor.

WRITING A THESIS FOR ANALYSIS OF IMAGERY/EXTENDED METAPHOR	
Template 1: The thesis identifies three general types of imagery and previews the line of reasoning.	In [title of work], [author] illustrates [unifying idea + insight] by incorporating [adjective], [adjective], and [adjective] imagery.
Template 2: The thesis analyzes multiple aspects of a single pattern of imagery to the idea and insight.	In [title of work], [author] incorporates [adjective] imagery to illustrate [unifying idea + insight].
Template 3: The thesis identifies a series of related comparisons and connects them to the idea and insight.	Through a series of related comparisons comparing [subject] to [object], [object], and [object], [author] reveals that [unifying idea + insight].
Template 4: The thesis identifies an extended metaphor and connects it to the idea and insight.	In [title of work], [author] conveys [unifying idea + insight] by using an extended metaphor comparing [subject] to [object].

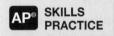 **SKILLS PRACTICE** | LITERARY ARGUMENTATION
Developing a Thesis Statement for Analysis of Imagery/Extended Metaphor

Complete the following chart. In the left column, record the title, author, and aspect of imagery or extended metaphor that you will explore. Next, record the unifying idea and insight that will convey your interpretation of your claim.

Developing a Defensible Thesis Statement for Analysis of Imagery/Extended Metaphor		
Topic	**Claim**	
Title, Author, and Focus (aspect of imagery or extended metaphor)	Unifying Idea +	Insight

Organize a Line of Reasoning

Your line of reasoning for the analysis of imagery or extended metaphor should direct your argument about how these literary elements function in the text to achieve a larger purpose. You should not only identify what is being compared but how the comparison creates associations and what those associations suggest to the reader. Your thesis should establish a unifying idea to keep your line of reasoning in focus.

To make sure your argument is unified and coherent, arrange your reasons logically and connect your reasons and evidence with transitional elements. Consider the following ways to organize your line of reasoning as you connect it to your unifying idea and insight:

- Describe the literal comparison and then explain the abstract meaning
- Explore two or more effects of the imagery or extended metaphor
- Explain how the author draws upon multiple senses
- Explore two or more associations between the main subject and the comparison subject in an extended metaphor
- Analyze two or more functions of a pattern of imagery or extended metaphor

STRUCTURE OF AN ANALYSIS OF MOTIF OR EXTENDED METAPHOR

Introduction

The **introduction** is an opportunity for the writer to establish the purpose of his or her literary argument and to invite and interest the audience into the literary work and the writer's interpretation of it. To achieve this goal, many literary arguments follow this structure:

- Engage the audience through an interesting hook
- Provide historical, cultural, or social context of a literary work
- Identify the title, author, genre (TAG)
- Introduce the literary topic of analysis by
  - describing the importance of that literary concept; and
  - summarizing the work succinctly with details critical to that concept

The **thesis statement** presents a defensible interpretation that includes an idea and an insight about that idea.

Body

(Develops a line of reasoning with supporting evidence that justifies the thesis)

Topic Sentence 1	Topic Sentence 2	Topic Sentence 3
(Identify the first aspect of the motif or extended metaphor related to the unifying idea)	(Identify the second aspect of the motif or extended metaphor related to the unifying idea)	(Identify the third aspect of the motif or extended metaphor related to the unifying idea)
Textual Details	**Textual Details**	**Textual Details**
(Evidence of elements and techniques that contribute to the development of the motif or extended metaphor and complexity)	(Evidence of elements and techniques that contribute to the development of the motif or extended metaphor and complexity)	(Evidence of elements and techniques that contribute to the development of the motif or extended metaphor and complexity)
Commentary	**Commentary**	**Commentary**
(Link evidence by explaining its relevance to the line of reasoning and claim)	(Link evidence by explaining its relevance to the line of reasoning and claim)	(Link evidence by explaining its relevance to the line of reasoning and claim)

Conclusion

The **conclusion** should do more than restate the thesis; rather it should be a robust and important paragraph. It is the opportunity for the writer to demonstrate understanding of the literary work's relevance by explaining how the literary work stands the test of time and reflects the human experience. Writers further their idea and insight by:

- Discussing the significance or relevance of interpretation
- Relating the work to other relevant literary works
- Connecting the theme to their own experience
- Presenting alternate interpretations
- Explaining how the work explores complexities and tensions
- Situating the theme within a broader context

This table illustrates the general structure of a literary argument. It does not intend to imply that all literary arguments are five paragraphs. Writers should determine the number of reasons needed to justify their claim, as well as how much evidence is sufficient to support each of these reasons.

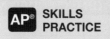

LITERARY ARGUMENTATION
Organizing an Analysis of Imagery/Extended Metaphor

Review the idea and insight in your thesis statement and then choose a logical line of reasoning to support your thesis. Compose two or more supporting topic sentences and organize them in a logical sequence that represents your train of thought. Highlight the words related to your unifying idea and underline words that link one topic sentence to another.

Organizing an Analysis of Imagery/Extended Metaphor		
Defensible Thesis Statement with Claim (idea + insight):		
Topic Sentence 1 (Identify the first aspect of imagery/extended metaphor related to the unifying idea):	**Topic Sentence 2** (Identify the second aspect of imagery/extended metaphor related to the unifying idea):	**Topic Sentence 3** (Identify the third aspect of imagery/extended metaphor related to the unifying idea):

Select Relevant Evidence

Arriving at an interpretation is a recursive process. That is, you may need to revise your claim and your evidence as your understanding of the text develops. In some cases, the evidence you explore will lead you to determine a line of reasoning, while in other cases, the line of reasoning will lead you to focus on certain kinds of evidence. The more experienced you become with analysis, the more you will become comfortable with the process of arranging your supporting evidence.

To select evidence for an analysis of imagery or extended metaphor, focus on an author's carefully chosen words and phrases. To incorporate the text in your analysis, you should weave short quotations within your own grammatical structures as you write. Additionally, you should identify the literary element or technique and include the necessary context for any textual evidence that you cite. You must carefully avoid misrepresenting quotations and paraphrases or taking them out of context. If you are analyzing a particular literary element (e.g., simile, metaphor, personification), then you must make sure your textual evidence exemplifies that element. Remember the pattern, identify — evidence — link, you learned in earlier units.

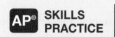 **SKILLS PRACTICE** | LITERARY ARGUMENTATION
Selecting and Arranging Relevant Evidence

Write your thesis statement and develop a logical line of reasoning to support your interpretation. Carefully organize your body paragraphs and arrange the evidence within them. Next, draft two or more body paragraphs that include evidence from the text to support each reason. Include transitions to link your reasons and evidence to your claim.

Selecting and Arranging Relevant Evidence		
Defensible Thesis Statement with Claim (idea + insight):		
Topic Sentence 1 (First aspect of imagery/extended metaphor related to the unifying idea):	**Topic Sentence 2** (Second aspect of imagery/extended metaphor related to the unifying idea):	**Topic Sentence 3** (Third aspect of imagery/extended metaphor related to the unifying idea):
Textual Details (Relevant and sufficient evidence):	**Textual Details** (Relevant and sufficient evidence):	**Textual Details** (Relevant and sufficient evidence):

Once you have selected your evidence and determined which topic sentence each piece of evidence will develop, you should carefully arrange the evidence within the body paragraphs. You may arrange the information within your paragraph according to, the order the evidence appears in the text, the function of that evidence, or the relationship between one piece of evidence and another. Your line of reasoning will determine your choice.

Finally, when you are working with especially rich texts, you should focus your analysis on your unifying idea and insight. To achieve unity in your argument and guide readers along your line of reasoning, you should use only **relevant evidence** — textual examples that relate directly to the unifying idea and insight in your thesis.

Write Insightful Commentary

When you analyze literary elements such as imagery and extended metaphor, you must explain what the element is doing in the text and explore why the author chose to include it. Your commentary serves to link the author's choice to the **unifying idea** and insight in your thesis.

Commentary related to imagery serves to explain the following:

- How imagery produces atmosphere or mood
- How imagery evokes an emotional response
- How imagery reveals characters' traits and perceptions
- How imagery establishes patterns that contribute to your interpretation

Commentary related to extended metaphor serves to explain the following:

- What is being compared in the metaphor
- How the comparison functions within the context
- The significance of the qualities of the comparison
- How the metaphor contributes to the tone
- The implication of the metaphor within its context
- How the metaphor contributes to your interpretation

Creating Coherence

Your arrangement of evidence and line of reasoning establishes the structure for your analysis. But as you have learned, your explanation and commentary reveal the most important part of the argument: your interpretation of the text. In Units 3 and 4, you practiced writing commentary that explains how evidence supports your reasons and how your reasons support your claim. Now, you will practice connecting all of the parts of your analysis with helpful **transitions**.

Transitions can be single words, short phrases, or clauses. They do the work of indicating the writer's intended relationships within the literary argument (i.e., evidence, line of reasoning, and claim). Some transitions work in a strictly functional manner, directing the readers from one point to the next (e.g., *first, furthermore, finally*). However, the most effective transitional elements (e.g., *unlike, in contrast, in the same manner, while on the surface*) also take on a more analytical function by indicating relationships and creating associations. If you think of your argument as a brick wall, then the transitions are the mortar in between every element holding the wall firmly in place.

INSIDER AP TIP **Transitions do not exist for fluency alone.** Transitions mainly function to contribute to the development of the argument by revealing important connections to the reader. Used carefully, transitions can elevate the sophistication of a literary argument.

TRANSITIONS FOR COHERENCE WITHIN PARAGRAPHS

Indicating Comparison	Indicating Contrast	Indicating Function or Effect
Additionally	Alternatively	Accordingly
Along with	Although	Because
Both . . . and . . .	Conversely	Evidently
Furthermore	Despite	Given that
In addition	However	In other words
In a similar manner	In contrast	In short
In the same way	Nonetheless	Since
Likewise	On the other hand	That is to say
Moreover	Unlike	This shows that
Not only . . . but also	While	Thus
Similarly	Yet	To explain
		Which suggests that
		While

Indicating a Reason or Example	Indicating Order or Time	Indicating a Conclusion
For example	At the beginning	As a result
For instance	Before	In essence
In the beginning	Finally	In short
One example occurs when	First	In summary
Specifically	In the first section	Therefore
To clarify	In turn	To conclude
To demonstrate	Last	To summarize
	Later	Ultimately
	Most importantly	
	Next	
	Once	
	Previously	
	Subsequently	
	To begin	
	To conclude	

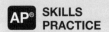 SKILLS PRACTICE | LITERARY ARGUMENTATION
Using Transitions for Coherence

Continue developing your literary argument by planning and writing helpful commentary that links your evidence to your line of reasoning and the idea in your claim. Continue practicing with the templates you used in Unit 4. In addition, incorporate transitions within and between paragraphs to create coherence.

Explaining the Relevance of Imagery/Extended Metaphor		
Defensible Thesis Statement with Claim (idea + insight):		
Topic Sentence 1 (First aspect of imagery/ extended metaphor related to the unifying idea):	**Topic Sentence 2** (Second aspect of imagery/extended metaphor related to the unifying idea):	**Topic Sentence 3** (Third aspect of imagery/ extended metaphor related to the unifying idea):
Textual Details (Relevant and sufficient evidence):	**Textual Details** (Relevant and sufficient evidence):	**Textual Details** (Relevant and sufficient evidence):
Commentary (Link evidence to reason and idea):	**Commentary** (Link evidence to reason and idea):	**Commentary** (Link evidence to reason and idea):
Sentence stem and explanation of function of evidence:	Sentence stem and explanation of function of evidence:	Sentence stem and explanation of function of evidence:

Contextualize Your Argument

When you write your analysis of imagery or an extended metaphor, begin with an introduction that includes a quick summary of the text and identifies the language technique that you are analyzing. You may wish to comment on the historical context

 **SKILLS PRACTICE**

LITERARY ARGUMENTATION
Establishing Context and Explaining Relevance

In the following chart, record some notes to help you communicate the context of your argument, along with introductory details about the narrative situation, extended metaphor, or pattern of imagery. This introductory material will funnel your ideas to your thesis statement. Next, record details to help you explain the relevance of your unifying idea and insight in your concluding statements.

Establishing Context and Explaining Relevance	
Idea and Insight	**Context for Introduction**
	Significance of Idea in Conclusion

of the language as well, especially if the text's setting and time period are unfamiliar to most contemporary readers. Next, you should funnel your discussion to the unifying idea, which prepares the reader for your thesis statement.

After you have presented your argument, remember to explain the relevance of your interpretation in your conclusion.

Revise Your Argument

When reviewing your analysis, ask the following questions related to your argument about the imagery or extended metaphor. Revise your draft if your answer is "no" to any of the questions.

- Have you identified a pattern of related imagery or extended metaphor rather than unrelated or isolated examples?
- Do your reasons in your line of reasoning refer to the function and effect of the imagery or extended metaphor?
- Does your line of reasoning support your interpretation?
- Have you included textual evidence that directly exemplifies the pattern of imagery or extended metaphor?
- Does your explanation of the evidence logically align to your interpretation of the work?
- Is your argument coherent with a logical sequence of reasons and transitions to connect evidence, reasons, and claim?
- Does your commentary unify your argument by connecting your evidence and reasons to your unifying idea?
- Do you include effective transitional elements between and within your body paragraphs to create coherence?

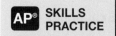 SKILLS PRACTICE

LITERARY ARGUMENTATION
Revising and Editing an Analysis of Imagery/Extended Metaphor

After you have completed revising and editing your own argument, review another student's literary argument and provide helpful feedback.

Peer-Revision Checklist: Revising and Editing an Analysis of Imagery/Extended Metaphor		
Revising and Editing Checklist	**Unit 5 Focus Skills**	**Comment on the Effectiveness and/or Make a Suggestion**
Does the writer include the narrative situation, title, and author of the literary text in the first paragraph? Does the brief summary of context and the reference to imagery/extended metaphor lead to the idea?	Introductions for analysis of imagery/ extended metaphor	
Does the thesis statement convey an interpretation? Does the interpretation connect to an idea and an insight?	Defensible thesis	
Does the writer provide a logical sequence of reasons to support the idea and insight in the thesis? Are these reasons linked to the claim with transitions?	Line of reasoning: Unity	
Does the writer provide relevant and sufficient evidence to support the interpretation in the thesis? Is the evidence linked to the topic sentences with transitions?	Relevant and sufficient evidence	
Does the writer explain how the evidence supports a reason and connects to the interpretation in the thesis? Does the commentary connect to the unifying idea? Does the writer include transitional elements to create coherence?	Commentary: Unity and coherence	
Does the writer explain significance within a broader context, discuss alternative interpretations, or use relevant analogies?	Relevance	
Does the writer demonstrate control over the conventions of writing?	Conventions	

Student Model: Writing about Extended Metaphor

Read the following student model that analyzes an extended metaphor in Sir Phillip Sidney's poem "Thou Blind Man's Mark." As you read, observe how a claim, line of reasoning, evidence, and commentary work together to explain how an extended metaphor contributes to an interpretation.

Weaving a Web of Desire
Teagan Ankersen

Within the poem "Thou Blind Man's Mark," the writer Sir Phillip Sidney describes the conflict between his feeling of desire and himself. His desire is portrayed as an evil entity, which entices individuals to do evil. Sidney describes it as a "fool's self-chosen snare" with only those holding no sense of direction falling to its trap (Sidney 1). To contrast the dark description of desire, the speaker continues to describe himself and his plight. He portrays himself as a hero, fighting the curse of desire, until realizing he himself is to blame for his actions. When describing his struggles, he acts as if he succumbed too quickly to the struggle, saying he "has too dearly bought" to the feeling of desire (Sidney 5). However, throughout the course of the poem, Sidney reveals that desire itself is not the source of his evil doings, but rather his actions when blindly following them. The speaker shows desire as an evil impulse, and how those with no direction may succumb to it. To describe it he uses language such as "scum" and "dregs" to emphasize its lowliness and compares it to a snare to represent how it drags people down (Sidney 2). He further emphasizes this throughout the quatrain by using imagery to describe it as a "web of will, whose end is never wrought" (Sidney 3) which insinuates that desire is a long and complicated road to unending destruction. Desire is seen to be an evil that many face from the speaker's perspective, despite many others viewing it as an attraction or invitation towards romance. His disdain for it provides an interesting outlook to the audience of how they may question it. He continues to belittle it by describing himself in an almost heroic way.

Within the second quatrain, he outlines his own plight with desire and how it has been an ongoing issue. He uses language such as how his "mind to higher things prepare" (Sydney 8) to show how he is being restrained by desire from achieving greater heights. As well as this, he describes his mind as mangled by desire because it twists him into doing wrong in its name.

thesis: idea (desire) + insight (blindly following desire can lead to evil)

topic sentence: establishes desire as an evil impulse

evidence: incorporates examples of word choice, comparison, and imagery

commentary: explains the association between a web and desire's trap

topic sentence: connects speaker personally to the plight caused by desire

evidence: paraphrases the description of desire's actions

This contrast to the first quatrain provides a solution or resolve against the evil that is the feeling of desire. He represents himself as the lone hero, defending his righteousness from the sickly pull of all evil. This allows the audience to resonate with the speaker and to connect with this battle as if it were their own. However, this comparison does not last as the speaker reveals to the audience the true source of evil doings.

commentary: explains the speaker's defense for the battle with desire

transition: final sentence leads to the last reason in the line of reasoning.

The speaker narrates his realization within the third quatrain that he is the source of his troubles rather than the feeling of desire within the first line. When starting the quatrain he contradicts his earlier statements when saying that "yet in vain thou hast my ruin sought" (Sidney 9) showing that his own ruin was brought by his actions and decisions. This twist is also shown through the change in rhyming scheme, which switches to represent the change in ideology and progression. His descriptions of himself go from being a righteous and good man being pulled by desire to describing himself as the source of his misery. The immediate turn from his previous descriptions is a show of his change as a person. Rather than blaming his emotions for his actions, he looks inside himself to find that despite the fact he was swayed to do bad, it was always his choice. Desire itself is not evil, but rather using it as an excuse to do wrong. This change in message is a whiplash to the audience, who having connected to the heroic idea against desire are now faced with the concept that they too may be viewing themselves as being better than reality. This idea is further pushed in the couplet with this new concept being explored.

topic sentence: introduces the speaker's epiphany of his own responsibility

evidence: includes the shift to the speaker's point that he is his own enemy

commentary: links to the idea that desire is not the enemy; humans are often their own enemies

In the couplet, the speaker now does not aim to kill desire, but rather fix the parts of himself that do evil. This alludes back to the first quatrain by correcting his own blind ideas of desire being the source of the blame. His original fight against desire has been broken down and is now an analysis of himself. As well as this, his anger against his emotions has turned into a more melancholic feeling of knowing he must make a change within himself to truly be happy. The audience can see how this change is more beneficial in the end because of how Sidney knows he will be happier once he accepts his emotions rather than use them as an excuse. The message by the end of the poem to the audience is to analyze oneself first before placing blame on outside forces for one's actions.

conclusion: after discussing the final couplet, revisits the thesis that the speaker, not desire, is to blame for his actions

Free-Response Question: Poetry Analysis

AP® **Enduring Understanding (LAN-1)**

Readers establish and communicate their interpretations of literature through arguments supported by textual evidence.

Creating Coherence through Transitional Elements

In the last workshop, you learned how to create unity in your analysis by connecting your claim in the thesis to your line of reasoning. You accomplish this by writing commentary that connects the claim, reasons, and evidence to a unifying idea. In this workshop, you will continue to work on developing strong literary arguments by focusing on creating coherence within your essay.

An argument is coherent when it progresses logically and seamlessly with transitions that develop the line of reasoning. In this workshop, you will return to the poetry analysis task and build on your knowledge and skills.

Read the following practice prompt, which is an adaptation of one you may see on the AP® English Literature and Composition Exam.

Prompt:

In the following poem by George Herbert (published in 1633), the speaker reflects upon the role of free will within the confines of religion. Read the poem carefully. Then, in a well-written essay, analyze how Herbert uses poetic elements and techniques to explore humanity's complex attitude toward freedom.

In your response you should do the following:

- Respond to the prompt with a thesis that presents a defensible interpretation
- Select and use evidence to support your line of reasoning
- Explain how the evidence supports your line of reasoning
- Use appropriate grammar and punctuation in communicating your argument

Unifying Idea	The Collar George Herbert	Effect of Literary Elements and Techniques
	The Collar	
	I struck the board, and cried, "No more; I will abroad! What? shall I ever sigh and pine?	title: the literal collar (suit) serves as an extended metaphor for confinement
freedom	My lines and life are free, free as the road,	
	5 Loose as the wind, as large as store.	similes convey the speaker's desire for freedom
freedom	Shall I be still in suit?	
	Have I no harvest but a thorn To let me blood, and not restore What I have lost with cordial fruit?	images of nature juxtaposed with images of religion show tension between individual freedom and religious duty

	10 Sure there was wine
	Before my sighs did dry it; there was corn
	   Before my tears did drown it.
	Is the year only lost to me?
	   Have I no bays to crown it,	

	15 No flowers, no garlands gay? All blasted?
	   All wasted?
	Not so, my heart; but there is fruit,
	   And thou hast hands.
	Recover all thy sigh-blown age	

	20 On double pleasures: leave thy cold dispute	
freedom	Of what is fit and not. Forsake thy cage, Thy rope of sands, Which petty thoughts have made, and made to thee Good cable, to enforce and draw,	cage, ropes, cables, and law represent confinement
	25 And be thy law, While thou didst wink and wouldst not see.	
	Away! take heed;	
freedom	I will abroad.	repetition emphasizes the desire for freedom
	Call in thy death's-head there; tie up thy fears;	
	30 He that forbears To suit and serve his need Deserves his load."	transition indicates a shift from desire for
freedom	But as I raved and grew more fierce and wild At every word,	freedom to possible submission
freedom	35 Methought I heard one calling, *Child!* And I replied *My Lord.*	ambiguous ending leaves the reader to determine if the speaker relinquishes his freedom

→ Step One: Annotate the Passage Based on a Unifying Idea

For this second poetry analysis workshop, we will dig a little deeper into analysis. Don't forget to read the poem sentence by sentence instead of line by line. Also, look carefully at the opening and closing lines to determine a unifying idea. Poems often include rich language—that is dense, highly figurative, sensory words and phrases. So try to determine how a pattern of imagery or comparisons can help lead you to an insight about that unifying idea.

As you read and annotate the poem, keep in mind the narrative situation provided for you in the prompt, including the year of publication. This will allow you to put the text in context and identify a unifying idea.

To guide your annotation of a poem, consider the following questions with your unifying idea in mind:

- When was the poem written and by whom?
- Does the title function as a metaphor?
- How does the poem begin and end? Explore what change, if any, occurs throughout the text.
- What structure and form does the poet employ? How does the structure affect your understanding of the poem?
- What word choices, images, or comparisons does the poet include to reveal a tone or attitude?
- What objects are being compared? Why does the author select this metaphor?
- What contrasts, conflicts, or tensions does the language reveal? What are the implications of these contrasts, conflicts, or tensions?
- Does the poem contain a shift in tone, attitude, or images? What are the implications of this shift?
- What line or lines reveal the speaker's reflection or insight about the subject of the poem?

For example, in the prompt for "The Collar" by George Herbert, we learn that the poem was published in the seventeenth century. The prompt also refers to the idea of free will in the context of religious rules. The title, then, may refer to a religious uniform like a priest might wear, but the word *collar* has other connotations as well. Throughout the poem, you will notice other images of confinement, so you should explore the speaker's attitude as revealed by these comparisons. Exploring the associations of the comparisons and images will help you arrive at your interpretation.

→ Step Two: Develop a Defensible Claim and a Unified Line of Reasoning

Continue developing your skill in writing an arguable and defensible thesis statement that is accurate and precise. For analyzing poetry, you may wish to identify an author technique (e.g., comparison, juxtaposition) and connect that to your interpretation of the text (idea + insight).

If you need help getting started, you may build from one of the following thesis templates or refer to the models that follow:

- In [poem], [poet] reveals [idea + insight] by shifting from [tone 1] to [tone 2].
- In [poem], [poet] reveals [idea + insight] by juxtaposing [image 1] and [image 2].

Review the following examples of thesis statements for poetry analysis.

Sample Thesis Statements	Notes on Effectiveness
In "The Collar," George Herbert uses the extended metaphor of a religious collar to explore the tension between humanity's desire for freedom from religious constraints and their longing for intimacy with God.	This thesis refers to an author technique (extended metaphor) and connects it to the tension between freedom and constraint. It is defensible and arguable.
In "The Collar," George Herbert juxtaposes contrasting images of freedom and confinement to reveal that though humans may desire free will, they will ultimately surrender to the voice of God.	This thesis refers to an author technique (contrasting imagery) and then states an interpretation (idea + insight). It is defensible and arguable.

Once you have written your thesis statement, you can determine your line of reasoning by addressing the contrasts or tensions or exploring the function of the author's techniques that lead you to your interpretation. Consider the most effective order for your line of reasoning and make sure each reason connects directly to your thesis. Finally, choose helpful transitions to connect your reasons to each other and to the claim in the thesis.

Once you have written your thesis statement, you will need to write two to three topic sentences to develop your line of reasoning.

If you need help getting started, you may build from the following topic sentence templates or refer to the following models:

- [Author] first includes [literary element] to reveal [connection to effect and unifying idea].
- [Transitional element] [author] includes [literary element] to further exemplify [connection to effect and unifying idea].

Review the following thesis statement and line of reasoning. Note that the unifying idea creates the connection between the claim in the thesis and the topic sentences that support the claim.

Sample Thesis Statement

In "The Collar," George Herbert juxtaposes contrasting images of freedom and confinement to reveal that though humans may desire free will, they will ultimately surrender to the voice of God.

Topic Sentence 1	Topic Sentence 2
Herbert begins by including images related to freedom to reveal the speaker's desire to follow his own free will.	*Throughout the exploration of freedom, Herbert juxtaposes contrasting images of confinement to establish the speaker's dilemma in remaining true to his vow to follow God.*

In this example, the first topic sentence explains the pattern of images that establishes the speaker's desire for freedom within his confinement. Note the contrast between being free and being confined: this tension helps reveal how the speaker's ultimate obedience to God is a sacrifice.

The second topic sentence then introduces the second pattern of imagery and shifts from the speaker's desire for freedom to his frustration as he complains about the lack of freedom in his life.

→ Step Three: Choose Relevant Evidence

With your line of reasoning established, you can arrange your relevant and sufficient evidence in the proper body paragraphs.

Remember that the passages you will encounter contain rich language and many details. You cannot possibly discuss everything within a passage. Therefore, you will need to omit evidence that is not relevant to your discussion of the idea and insight.

Topic Sentence 1	Topic Sentence 2
Herbert begins by including images related to freedom that reveal the speaker's desire to follow his own free will.	*Throughout the exploration of freedom, Herbert juxtaposes contrasting images of confinement to establish the speaker's dilemma in fulfilling his vow to follow God.*
Relevant and Sufficient Evidence	**Relevant and Sufficient Evidence**
Evidence 1: *free as the road . . .* *Loose as the wind, as large as store* *. . . I will abroad.* Evidence 2: *Have I no bays to crown it,* *No flowers, no garlands gay? All blasted? . . . All wasted?*	Evidence 1: *Title: "The Collar"* *Shall I be still in suit?* Evidence 2: *Forsake thy cage, . . . Thy rope of sands, . . . Good cable, . . . And be thy law,*

→ Step Four: Develop Your Commentary

In Units 3 and 4, you learned to write commentary that explains your evidence and connects it to your reasons. You also practiced writing commentary that connects your reasons to your claim (idea + insight). As you develop your skills at writing commentary, you will continue your focus on creating **unity** and **coherence** in your argument by incorporating helpful **transitional elements** that connect the parts of your essay. You may choose some of the following types:

- Signifying order (*before, after, finally, in the end, next*)
- Signifying comparison (*additionally, both, in comparison, similarly*)
- Signifying contrast (*although, however, in contrast, on the other hand, unlike, yet*)
- Signifying conclusion (*consequently, finally, therefore, ultimately*)
- Signifying evidence, author choice, or commentary (*by, for example, in order to, through*)

Remember that your commentary must explain how the author's literary elements and techniques contribute to your interpretation. To help begin incorporating evidence and writing commentary, you might build from the following templates:

- The words/images/details of _____ emphasize _____. These choices reveal _____.
- The pattern of images leads the reader to understand that _____.
- The speaker shifts from _____ to _____ in order to demonstrate a change in _____. This change suggests _____.
- By comparing/contrasting/ juxtaposing _____ and _____, the author emphasizes _____, prompting the reader to conclude _____.

Review the following examples and observe how commentary should connect to both the topic sentence and the thesis. In the model, notice that the transitional elements show readers the connection among the evidence, commentary, and line of reasoning.

Evidence	Transitional Element	Commentary Connected to Idea
free as the road, / loose as the wind, as large as store. *I will abroad.*	*Through* *By including* *Next* *once again*	*Through a series of similes, the speaker characterizes his natural desire for freedom, as he is "free as a road" and "loose as the wind." By including these images of a road that is never ending and of wind that cannot be contained, he emphasizes his longing for liberty. Next, the speaker reveals his plan to act on this desire and declares, "I will abroad." The word* abroad *suggests his intention to take deliberate action and go far away from his current situation to an entirely new country, once again revealing his longing to escape confinement.*

INSIDER **AP® TIP**   **Unity and coherence demonstrate that the writer has control over the argument.** To signify the logical progression of thought and arrangement of supporting details within your literary argument, use transitions, synonyms, and parallel structure to connect ideas, reasons, and evidence. These connections create unity.

AP® EXAM PRACTICE

The following is an example of a poetry analysis free-response question. Practice the skills you have learned in this workshop to write an argument in response to the prompt.

Remember to follow the four steps:

- Step One: Annotate the passage based on a **unifying idea**
- Step Two: Write a **defensible thesis statement**
- Step Three: Choose **relevant evidence**
- Step Four: Develop **insightful commentary**

Prompt:

In the following poem by Elisavietta Ritchie (published in 1988), the speaker reminisces while she is completing a common household task. Read the poem carefully. Then, in a well-written essay, analyze how Ritchie uses poetic elements and techniques to convey the speaker's complex perspective on a relationship in her life.

In your response you should do the following:

- Respond to the prompt with a thesis that presents a defensible interpretation
- Select and use evidence to support your line of reasoning
- Explain how the evidence supports your line of reasoning
- Use appropriate grammar and punctuation in communicating your argument

Sorting Laundry

Folding clothes,
I think of folding you
into my life.

Our king sized sheets
5 like table cloths
for the banquets of giants,

pillow cases, despite so many
washings seams still
holding our dreams.

10 Towels patterned orange and green,
flowered pink and lavender,
gaudy, bought on sale,

reserved, we said, for the beach,
refusing, even after years,
15 to bleach into respectability.

So many shirts and skirts and pants
recycling week after week, head over heels
recapitulating themselves.

All those wrinkles
20 to be smoothed, or else
ignored, they're in style.

Myriad uncoupled socks
which went paired into the foam
like those creatures in the ark.

25 And what's shrunk
is tough to discard
even for Goodwill.

In pockets, surprises:
forgotten matches,
30 lost screws clinking on enamel;

paper clips, whatever they held
between shiny jaws, now
dissolved or clogging the drain;

well washed dollars, legal tender
35 for all debts public and private,
intact despite agitation;

and, gleaming in the maelstrom,
one bright dime,
broken necklace of good gold

40 you brought from Kuwait,
the strangely tailored shirt
left by a former lover . . .

If you were to leave me,
if I were to fold
45 only my own clothes,

the convexes and concaves
of my blouses, panties, stockings, bras
turned upon themselves,

a mountain of unsorted wash
50 could not fill
the empty side of the bed.

ORGANIZING A POETRY ANALYSIS (II)

Defensible Thesis Statement with Claim (idea + insight):

In [title], the poet shifts from [a to b] to reveal that [idea + insight].

Topic Sentence 1 (Identify the first aspect of topic related to the unifying idea):	Topic Sentence 2 (Identify the second aspect of topic related to the unifying idea):	Topic Sentence 3 (Identify the third aspect of topic related to the unifying idea):
Initially, [poet] includes [literary element] to illustrate [universal idea].	As the poem progresses, [poet] shifts from [a to b] to explore [topic] further using [literary element] to reveal [universal idea].	Ultimately, [poet] includes [literary element] to reveal [universal idea].
Textual Details (Relevant and sufficient evidence):	**Textual Details** (Relevant and sufficient evidence):	**Textual Details** (Relevant and sufficient evidence):
For example, the detail [evidence], used to describe [context] illustrates [link to reason].	To illustrate, [poet] describes/compares [context] by including [text evidence] to reveal [link to reason].	As an example of [technique/element], the poet includes [text evidence] to explain [link to reason].
Additionally, the detail [evidence], used to describe [context] illustrates [link to reason].	In the same way, [poet] describes/compares [context] by including [text evidence] to reveal [link to reason].	Another example, of [technique/element], that the poet includes [text evidence] illustrates [link to reason].
Commentary (Link evidence to reason and idea):	**Commentary** (Link evidence to reason and idea):	**Commentary** (Link evidence to reason and idea):
The association of [text evidence] with [topic sentence] reveals [idea and insight].	Through this choice, [poet] develops [idea and insight].	By including this [element/technique] the poet suggests that [idea and insight].
2–4 sentences explaining how the evidence exemplifies the universal idea	*2–4 sentences explaining how the evidence exemplifies the universal idea*	*2–4 sentences explaining how the evidence exemplifies the universal idea*

from The Poisonwood Bible

Barbara Kingsolver

The following is an excerpt from a novel published in 1998.

Away down below now, single file on the path, comes a woman with four girls in tow, all of them in shirtwaist dresses. Seen from above this way they are pale, doomed blossoms, bound
5 to appeal to your sympathies. Be careful. Later on you'll have to decide what sympathy they deserve. The mother especially — watch how she leads them on, pale-eyed, deliberate. Her dark hair is tied in a ragged lace handkerchief, and
10 her curved jawbone is lit with large, false-pearl earrings, as if these headlamps from another world might show the way. The daughters march behind her, four girls compressed in bodies as tight as bowstrings, each one tensed to fire
15 off a woman's heart on a different path to glory or damnation. Even now they resist affinity like cats in a bag: two blondes — the one short and fierce, the other tall and imperious — flanked by matched brunettes like bookends, the for-
20 ward twin leading hungrily while the rear one sweeps the ground in a rhythmic limp. But gamely enough they climb together over logs of rank decay that have fallen across the path. The mother waves a graceful hand in front of her as
25 she leads the way, parting curtain after curtain of spiders' webs. She appears to be conducting a symphony. Behind them the curtain closes. The spiders return to their killing ways.

At the stream bank she sets out their drear
30 picnic, which is only dense, crumbling bread daubed with crushed peanuts and slices of bitter plantain. After months of modest hunger the children now forget to complain about food. Silently they swallow, shake off the
35 crumbs, and drift downstream for a swim in faster water. The mother is left alone in the cove of enormous trees at the edge of a pool. This place is as familiar to her now as a living room in the house of a life she never bargained
40 for. She rests uneasily in the silence, watching ants boil darkly over the crumbs of what seemed, to begin with, an impossibly meager lunch. Always there is someone hungrier than her own children. She tucks her dress under
45 her legs and inspects her poor, featherless feet in their grass nest at the water's edge — twin birds helpless to fly out of there, away from the disaster she knows is coming. She could lose everything: herself, or worse, her children.
50 Worst of all: you, her only secret. Her favorite. How could a mother live with herself to blame?

She is inhumanly alone. And then, all at once, she isn't. A beautiful animal stands on the other side of the water. They look up
55 from their lives, woman and animal, amazed to find themselves in the same place. He freezes, inspecting her with his black-tipped ears. His back is purplish-brown in the dim light, sloping downward from the gentle
60 hump of his shoulders. The forest's shadows fall into lines across his white-striped flanks. His stiff forelegs splay out to the sides like stilts, for he's been caught in the act of reaching down for water. Without taking his eyes
65 from her, he twitches a little at the knee, then the shoulder, where a fly devils him. Finally he surrenders his surprise, looks away, and drinks. She can feel the touch of his long, curled tongue on the water's skin, as if he
70 were lapping from her hand. His head bobs

677

gently, nodding small, velvet horns lit white from behind like new leaves.

It lasted just a moment, whatever that is. One held breath? An ant's afternoon? It was brief, I can
75 promise that much, for although it's been many years now since my children ruled my life, a mother recalls the measure of the silences. I never had more than five minutes' peace unbroken. I was that woman on the stream bank, of course. Orleanna
80 Price, Southern Baptist by marriage, mother of children living and dead. That one time and no other the okapi came to the stream, and I was the only one to see it.

1. In the context of the first paragraph, which of the following images most significantly contributes to the complexity of the mother's character?
   (A) "... ragged lace handkerchief..." (line 9)
   (B) "... bodies as tight as bowstrings," (lines 13–14)
   (C) "... while the rear one sweeps the ground in a rhythmic limp." (lines 21–22)
   (D) "... parting curtain after curtain of spiders' webs." (lines 25–26)
   (E) "She appears to be conducting a symphony." (lines 26–27)

2. Which of the following provides the most reasonable interpretation of the simile used in lines 16–17 ("Even now . . . bag")?
   (A) The mother may wish to nurse the girls — as a cat does her kittens — but they only resist her and fight to get away from her — as a cat would fight to get out of a bag.
   (B) The girls may think that they are ready to venture out into the world by themselves — as a stray cat may do — but the world is still dangerous and they need to be kept secure — as a stray cat might seek safety in a bag.
   (C) The girls may appear kind and approachable — as house cats may — but they are more likely to be angry and dangerous — as a house cat would be if trapped in a bag.
   (D) The mother wants to keep the girls away from the rest of the world — like keeping a cat in a bag — but all the girls want to do is fight — like an angry cat trapped in a bag.
   (E) The girls are not nice people and treat others the way a cat would treat someone trying to capture it in a bag — with suspicion, anger, and violence.

3. In the sentence "This place . . . bargained for." (lines 38–40), the narrator uses the simile and its related details to
   (A) explain why the children are less important in the passage than the setting.
   (B) explain the perspective of the mother on both her children and her living situation.
   (C) display the distaste and bitterness felt by the mother toward her own children.
   (D) display the mother's familiarity and disappointment with her circumstances.
   (E) argue that a mother's needs outweigh the needs of her children because she must care for them.

4. The sequence of paragraph 2, lines 29–51 ("At the stream . . . to blame?") followed by paragraph 3, lines 52–72 ("She is inhumanely . . . new leaves.") focuses attention on
   (A) how privileged the mother feels despite her relative unhappiness.
   (B) the loss of innocence represented by the daughters leaving the mother alone.
   (C) the daughters' dependence on their mother despite their advanced ages.
   (D) the silence the mother perceives in the setting despite the abundance of action around her.
   (E) the mother's loneliness and want of connection despite her four children.

5. The single sentence at the beginning of paragraph 3, line 52 ("She . . . alone.") makes use of
   (A) multiple connotations.
   (B) metaphor.
   (C) hyperbole.
   (D) understatement.
   (E) predictable patterns.

6. The personification in lines 68–70 ("She can feel . . . her hand.") has the effect of
   (A) giving the water traits to provide the mother with companionship.
   (B) figuratively connecting the mother and the okapi.
   (C) illustrating the longing for companionship felt by both the mother and okapi.
   (D) literally allowing the mother to feel the okapi's tongue.
   (E) demonstrating the surprise of both the okapi and the mother.

7. In context, the metaphor "An ant's afternoon?" (line 74) can be best understood to mean
   (A) a long period of time as a small creature may perceive the world of man.
   (B) how time feels when a person is alone.
   (C) a too small and too brief moment.
   (D) a lost moment.
   (E) how slowly time passes in such silent, meaningful moments.

8. All of the following illustrate the mother's attitude toward her circumstances EXCEPT
   (A) "doomed blossoms" (line 4).
   (B) "drear picnic" (lines 29–30).
   (C) "Silently they swallow" (line 34).
   (D) "impossibly meager" (line 42).
   (E) "my children ruled my life" (line 76).

9. Which of the following best describes this passage?
   (A) A mother regrets having children and worries that she could lose everything.
   (B) A narrator reflects on a particular event with suggestions of loss and loneliness.
   (C) A narrator describes the heartache of a mother who lost her daughters.
   (D) A mother fears admitting to herself how much her children ruined her life.
   (E) A mother shares concerns about silence and the fears it caused her when her children were young.

Black Boys Play the Classics

Toi Derricotte

The most popular "act" in
Penn Station
is the three black kids in ratty
sneakers & T-shirts playing
5 two violins and a cello — Brahms.
White men in business suits
have already dug into their pockets
as they pass and they toss in
a dollar or two without stopping.
10 Brown men in work-soiled khakis
stand with their mouths open,
arms crossed on their bellies
as if they themselves have always
wanted to attempt those bars.
15 One white boy, three, sits
cross-legged in front of his
idols — in ecstasy —
their slick, dark faces,
their thin, wiry arms,
20 who must begin to look
like angels!
Why does this trembling
pull us?
A: *Beneath the surface we are one.*
B: *Amazing! I did not think that they could speak this tongue.*

1. In the context of the poem, the word "act" (line 1) relies on which of the following multiple meanings?
   (A) Something someone does: an action AND a fictitious role created for a particular moment.
   (B) A planned and rehearsed performance AND a way to encourage others to participate in something.
   (C) A way to encourage others to participate in something AND a fictitious role created for a particular moment.
   (D) Something someone does: an action AND a planned and rehearsed performance.
   (E) A planned and rehearsed performance AND a fictitious role created for a particular moment.

2. In the context of the poem, the image of the "ratty sneakers" (lines 3–4) could suggest all of the following EXCEPT
   (A) the kids can only play this one song.
   (B) the poverty of the kids.
   (C) that the kids do not care about their sneakers as much as they care about music.
   (D) the lives of hard work and toil that the kids lead.
   (E) that playing music in the station makes them very little money.

3. The imagery in lines 15–17 ("One . . . idols") relates most clearly to
   (A) the contrasting image used to describe the shoes worn by the kids (lines 3–4).
   (B) the complementary image of the "White men in business suits" (line 6).
   (C) the contrasting images and details of the "White men" (line 6) and "Brown men" (line 10).
   (D) the description of the kids as they play their instruments with the boy in front of them (lines 18–21).
   (E) the trembling that pulls at the reader and the speaker (lines 22–23).

4. Lines 22–23 ("Why . . . us?") makes use of which of the following to characterize an aspect of the poem?
   (A) alliteration
   (B) rhyme
   (C) understatement
   (D) hyperbole
   (E) personification

5. Which of the following best explains the relationship between the last two lines (lines 24–25) and the rest of the poem?
   (A) These statements frame the poem to provide a way to interpret the images and descriptions provided throughout.
   (B) The last two lines provided possible responses to the question in lines 22–23 and relate to thematic possibilities of the poem as a whole.
   (C) The poem is summarized by the last two lines.
   (D) Each of the last two lines provide conflicting ways of understanding the poem to provide the reader an opportunity for meaning making.
   (E) These lines do not fit within the context of the poem.

6. Which of the following best describes the poem as a whole?
   (A) A cautionary narrative about what may happen to the reader if they wander too far from familiar things in an attempt to appreciate new things.
   (B) A collection of images and statements each meant to inspire the reader to better understand the differences between their perspective and the speaker's.
   (C) An exaggeration of how different people develop contrasting perspectives on shared experiences despite a connection in the setting of the poem.
   (D) Examples of how people are different regardless of things they share in common.
   (E) An example of something appreciated by people of multiple backgrounds and different ages to demonstrate how connected everyone is despite apparent differences.

pixelfit/E+/Getty Images

UNIT

6

Analyzing Representations

UNIT GOALS

	Focus	Goals
Big Idea: Character	**Contrasting Characters**	Explain how contrasting characters illuminate characteristics of the protagonist and contribute to an interpretation.
Big Idea: Structure	**Nonlinear Structures**	Explain how an author's arrangement of plot controls a narrative and influences an interpretation.
Big Idea: Narration	**Narrator Bias and Tone**	Explain how a character's tone and perspective, revealed through word choice and syntax, contribute to an interpretation.
Big Idea: Figurative Language	**Symbols**	Explain how a symbol and/or a symbolic character creates associations that contribute to an interpretation.
Ideas in Literature	**Repression and Conformity**	Explain how the ideas of repression and conformity are reflected in classic and contemporary texts.
Big Idea: Literary Argumentation	**Writing about Symbols**	Write a literary argument that analyzes how the author's use of a symbol contributes to an interpretation of a text.
Preparing for the AP® Exam	**Free-Response Question: Literary Argument** Writing Commentary with Purposeful Syntax	Incorporate coordination and subordination along with other purposeful syntax to convey relationships within a literary argument.
	Multiple-Choice Questions: Prose	Analyze literary elements and techniques in classic and contemporary prose and poetry.
	Multiple-Choice Questions: Poetry	

Contrasting Characters

 Enduring Understanding

Characters in literature allow readers to study and explore a range of values, beliefs, assumptions, biases, and cultural norms represented by those characters.

KEY POINT

Authors create contrasting characters to highlight or reveal key traits, attributes, and values of the protagonist.

Have you ever heard someone say, "I'm a people watcher"? Usually, this means they enjoy watching and interpreting human behavior and social interactions. And, in doing so, people watchers make assumptions and inferences about the values, attitudes, beliefs, and biases of others based on their words and actions. In a similar way, when you read literature, you must become a people watcher: an observer who closely scrutinizes the words, actions, appearances, and other details that create literary characters.

No two characters are exactly the same. It is this variety that is the spice of life, as some say, and it's also a must-have ingredient for a juicy story. If you've ever attended a family reunion or other large-scale event with relatives, you know that it's people's differences in behavior, demeanor, and perspective that make the world an interesting place.

On a more abstract level, the different perspectives of characters—their attitudes and worldviews—also help the reader make sense of their specific actions and conflicts within the story. Look for contrasting perspectives between characters: they may reveal larger themes and ideas that are important to your interpretation.

Contrasts Highlight Differences

You can learn a lot about someone's personality by defining who they are *not*. That's especially true in literature. In fiction or drama, a character who contrasts with another is known as a **foil**. Authors often use foils to highlight an important distinction or characteristic about the protagonist or other characters. But sometimes the contrasts are less obvious. For example, characters may face similar conflicts or have similar backgrounds, but they may react to conflict differently. If you can understand why and how those characters contrast with each other, you may discover the values or concepts that they represent. (Note that antagonists are not always foils simply because they oppose the protagonist, but they may be.)

Foils serve to illuminate significant traits. When you identify contrasting characters, remember that foils have a purpose beyond merely providing a contrast. The contrast's significance lies in the way it amplifies the traits of the main character. So when you analyze a foil, focus on the details that directly relate to the protagonist.

Stock Characters

Authors also have access to a cookie-cutter cast of familiar figures called **stock characters**. Stock characters can usually be classified as victims (those who are hurt), villains (those who do the hurting), and vindicators (those who help). Often, stock characters are associated with a particular genre. For example, in a western, we might see a quiet school marm, a greedy cattle thief, and an authoritative sheriff. In a horror story, these characters would be the naive individual, the masked figure, and the brawny hero.

Inconsistencies and Irony

Some characters may make decisions that seem to be contradictory, inconsistent, or "out of character." Moreover, when a character's private thoughts contradict their behavior, the disparity adds depth and complexity, revealing an important tension between what the character *says* they believe and what they *actually* believe. Effective readers can analyze these contrasts to understand a character's subtle nuances more fully. For example, consider a character who claims that they'll steal just to get enough money to pay off a drug dealer threatening their family. But if this character continues to steal after paying off the drug dealer and eliminating the threat, then readers may infer that another motive is at work — perhaps the fear of resource insecurity, the thrill of the crime, habit, or paranoia.

Inconsistencies in a character's behavior may lead to **dramatic irony**. Dramatic irony emerges from the discrepancy between what characters know and what readers know. This contrast often builds suspense and reveals important aspects of the narrative or the characters. In horror movies and thrillers, viewers may know a dangerous villain is hiding in a house while an unsuspecting character does not. But more subtle forms of dramatic irony occur as well. Imagine a story in which a character secretly betrays the trust of his or her best friend: the best friend has no reason to suspect the betrayal and continues to sacrifice for someone who has already sold him or her out. This irony may reveal a particular point of view or idea about the nature of friendship, or even the human capacity for treachery.

INSIDER AP® TIP **One ironic moment does not make an entire work ironic.** Some authors create irony throughout the entire narrative (including the subject, characters, and tone), which is known as an ironic vision. This is more characteristic of longer fictional works than poems or short stories.

PRACTICE TEXT

Spunk
Zora Neale Hurston

PhotoQuest/Archive Photos/Getty Images

THE TEXT IN CONTEXT

A poignant figure in American literature, writer Zora Neale Hurston (1891–1960) began writing as a student at Howard University. After moving to New York City, Hurston became the first Black woman to graduate from Barnard College. She then worked on a Ph.D. in anthropology at Columbia University, traveling through the South and documenting the stories, music, and folk cultures of African American communities. In the 1920s and 1930s, Hurston also wrote several plays, including *Color Struck* (1925) and *The Great Day: A Program of Original Negro Folklore at The Golden Theatre* on Broadway (1932). She wrote stories, memoirs, and four novels as well, including her famous work, *Their Eyes Were Watching God* (1936). In her final years, she worked as a maid and lived in obscurity in Florida, where she was buried in an unmarked grave. Hurston remained largely forgotten until the writer Alice Walker's (b. 1944) 1975 article for *Ms.* magazine, "In Search of Zora Neale Hurston." In the decades since her rediscovery, Hurston has been widely celebrated for her work. "Spunk" was Hurston's first published story.

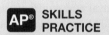 **SKILLS PRACTICE** | **CHARACTER**
Analyzing Contrasting Characters

As you read Hurston's short story "Spunk," identify characters who contrast with the protagonist. Record details from the text that characterize them. Then explain the significance of these contrasts.

Analyzing Contrasting Characters		
Protagonist:		
Contrasting characters:		
Attributes of Protagonist	**Attributes of Contrasting Character(s)**	**Significance (What this reveals about the protagonist)**

Spunk

I

A giant of a brown-skinned man sauntered up the one street of the Village and out into the palmetto thickets with a small pretty woman clinging lovingly to his arm.

5 "Looka theah, folkses!" cried Elijah Mosley, slapping his leg gleefully. "Theah they go, big as life an' brassy as tacks."

All the loungers in the store tried to walk to the door with an air of nonchalance but 10 with small success.

"Now pee-eople!" Walter Thomas gasped. "Will you look at 'em!"

"But that's one thing Ah likes about Spunk Banks—he ain't skeered of nothin' on God's 15 green footstool—nothin'! He rides that log down at saw-mill jus' like he struts 'round wid another man's wife—jus' don't give a kitty. When Tes' Miller got cut to giblets on that circle-saw, Spunk steps right up and 20 starts ridin'. The rest of us was skeered to go near it."

A round-shouldered figure in overalls much too large, came nervously in the door and the talking ceased. The men looked at 25 each other and winked.

"Gimme some soda-water. Sass'prilla Ah reckon," the newcomer ordered, and stood far down the counter near the open pickled pig-feet tub to drink it.

30 Elijah nudged Walter and turned with mock gravity to the new-comer.

"Say, Joe, how's everything up yo' way? How's yo' wife?"

Joe started and all but dropped the bottle 35 he held in his hands. He swallowed several times painfully and his lips trembled.

"Aw 'Lige, you oughtn't to do nothin' like that," Walter grumbled. Elijah ignored him.

"She jus' passed heah a few minutes ago 40 goin' thata way," with a wave of his hand in the direction of the woods.

Now Joe knew his wife had passed that way. He knew that the men lounging in the general store had seen her, moreover, he 45 knew that the men knew *he* knew. He stood there silent for a long moment staring blankly, with his Adam's apple twitching nervously up and down his throat. One could actually see the pain he was suffering, his 50 eyes, his face, his hands and even the dejected slump of his shoulders. He set the bottle down upon the counter. He didn't bang it, just eased it out of his hand silently and fiddled with his suspender buckle.

55 "Well, Ah'm goin' after her to-day. Ah'm goin' an' fetch her back. Spunk's done gone too fur."

He reached deep down into his trouser pocket and drew out a hollow ground razor, 60 large and shiny, and passed his moistened thumb back and forth over the edge.

"Talkin' like a man, Joe. Course that's yo' fambly affairs, but Ah like to see grit in anybody."

65 Joe Kanty laid down a nickel and stumbled out into the street.

Dusk crept in from the woods. Ike Clarke lit the swinging oil lamp that was almost immediately surrounded by candle flies. 70 The men laughed boisterously behind Joe's back as they watched him shamble woodward.

"You oughtn't to said whut you did to him, Lige—look how it worked him up," Walter 75 chided.

"And Ah hope it did work him up. 'Tain't even decent for a man to take and take like he do."

"Spunk will sho' kill him."

80 "Aw, Ah doan' know. You never kin tell. He might turn him up an' spank him fur gettin' in the way, but Spunk wouldn't shoot no unarmed man. Dat razor he carried outa

heah ain't gonna run Spunk down an' cut
85 him, an' Joe ain't got the nerve to go up to
Spunk with it knowing he totes that Army
.45. He makes that break outa heah to bluff
us. He's gonna hide that razor behind the
first likely palmetto root an' sneak back
90 home to bed. Don't tell me nothin' 'bout that
rabbit-foot colored man. Didn't he meet
Spunk an' Lena face to face one day las'
week an' mumble sumthin' to Spunk 'bout
lettin' his wife alone?"

95   "What did Spunk say?" Walter broke in—
"Ah like him fine but 'tain't right the way he
carries on wid Lena Kanty, jus' cause Joe's
timid 'bout fightin'."

    "You wrong theah, Walter. 'Tain't cause
100 Joe's timid at all, it's cause Spunk wants
Lena. If Joe was a passle of wile cats Spunk
would tackle the job just the same. He'd go
after anything he wanted the same way. As
Ah wuz sayin' a minute ago, he tole Joe right
105 to his face that Lena was his. 'Call her,' he
says to Joe. 'Call her and see if she'll come.
A woman knows her boss an' she answers
when he calls.' 'Lena, ain't I yo' husband?' Joe
sorter whines out. Lena looked at him real
110 disgusted but she don't answer and she don't
move outa her tracks. Then Spunk reaches
out an' takes hold of her arm an' says: 'Lena,
youse mine. From now on Ah works for you
an' fights for you an' Ah never wants you to
115 look to nobody for a crumb of bread, a stitch
of close or a shingle to go over yo' head, but
me long as Ah live. Ah'll git the lumber foh
owah house to-morrow. Go home an' git yo'
things together!'

120   "'Thass mah house,' Lena speaks up. 'Papa
gimme that.'

    "'Well,' says Spunk, 'doan give up whut's
yours, but when yousc inside don't forgit
youse mine, an' let no other man git outa his
125 place wid you!'

    "Lena looked up at him with her eyes so
full of love that they wuz runnin' over, an'
Spunk seen it an' Joe seen it too, and his lip
started to tremblin' and his Adam's apple
130 was galloping up and down his neck like a
race horse. Ah bet he's wore out half a dozen
Adam's apples since Spunk's been on the
job with Lena. That's all he'll do. He'll be back
heah after while swallowin' an' workin' his
135 lips like he wants to say somethin' an' can't."

    "But didn't he do *nothin'* to stop 'em?"

    "Nope, not a frazzlin' thing—jus' stood
there. Spunk took Lena's arm and walked off
jus' like nothin' ain't happened and he stood
140 there gazin' after them till they was outa
sight. Now you know a woman don't want no
man like that. I'm jus' waitin' to sec whut
he's gain' to say when he gits back."

II

But Joe Kanty never came back, never. The
145 men in the store heard the sharp report of a
pistol somewhere distant in the palmetto
thicket and soon Spunk came walking leisurely, with his big black Stetson set at the
same rakish angle and Lena clinging to his
150 arm, came walking right into the general
store. Lena wept in a frightened manner.

    "Well," Spunk announced calmly, "Joe
come out there wid a meatax an' made me
kill him."

155   He sent Lena home and led the men back
to Joe—Joe crumpled and limp with his right
hand still clutching his razor.

    "See mah back? Mah does cut clear
through. He sneaked up an' tried to kill me
160 from the back, but Ah got him, an' got him
good, first shot," Spunk said.

    The men glared at Elijah, accusingly.

    "Take him up an' plant him in 'Stoney
lonesome,'" Spunk said in a careless voice.
165 "Ah didn't wanna shoot him but he made me

do it. He's a dirty coward, jumpin' on a man from behind."

Spunk turned on his heel and sauntered away to where he knew his love wept in fear for him and no man stopped him. At the general store later on, they all talked of locking him up until the sheriff should come from Orlando, but no one did anything but talk.

A clear case of self-defense, the trial was a short one, and Spunk walked out of the court house to freedom again. He could work again, ride the dangerous log-carriage that fed the singing, snarling, biting, circle-saw; he could stroll the soft dark lanes with his guitar. He was free to roam the woods again; he was free to return to Lena. He did all of these things.

III

"Whut you reckon, Walt?" Elijah asked one night later. "Spunk's gittin' ready to marry Lena!"

"Naw! Why, Joe ain't had time to git cold yit. Nohow Ah didn't figger Spunk was the marryin' kind."

"Well, he is," rejoined Elijah. "He done moved most of Lena's things—and her along wid 'em—over to the Bradley house. He's buying it. Jus' like Ah told yo' all right in heah the night Joe wuz kilt. Spunk's crazy 'bout Lena. He don't want folks to keep on talkin' 'bout her—thass reason he's rushin' so. Funny thing 'bout that bob-cat, wan't it?"

"Whut bob-cat, 'Lige? Ah ain't heered 'bout none."

"Ain't cher? Well, night befo' las' was the fust night Spunk an' Lena moved together an' jus' as they was goin' to bed, a big black bob-cat, black all over, you hear me, *black*, walked round and round that house and howled like forty, an' when Spunk got his gun an' went to the winder to shoot it, he says it stood right still an' looked him in the eye, an' howled right at him. The thing got Spunk so nervoused up he couldn't shoot. But Spunk says twan't no bob-cat nohow. He says it was Joe done sneaked back from Hell!"

"Humph!" sniffed Walter, "he oughter be nervous after what he done. Ah reckon Joe come back to dare him to marry Lena, or to come out an' fight. Ah bet he'll be back time and agin, too. Know what Ah think? Joe, vuz a braver man than Spunk."

There was a general shout of derision from the group.

"Thass a fact," went on Walter. "Lookit whut he done; took a razor an' went out to fight a man he knowed toted a gun an' wuz a crack shot, too; 'nother thing Joe wuz skeered of Spunk, skeered plumb stiff! But he went jes' the same. It took him a long time to get his nerve up. 'Tain't nothin' for Spunk to fight when he ain't skeered of nothin'. Now, Joe's done come back to have it out wid the man that's got all he ever had. Y'll know Joe ain't never had nothin' nor wanted nothin' besides Lena. It musta been a h'ant cause ain' nobody never seen no black bob-cat."

"'Nother thing," cut in one of the men, "Spunk wuz cussin' a blue streak to-day 'cause he 'lowed dat saw wuz wobblin'— almos' got 'im once. The machinist come, looked it over an' said it wuz alright. Spunk musta been leanin' t'wards it some. Den he claimed somebody pushed 'im but 'twant nobody close to 'im. Ah wuz glad when knockin' off time come. I'm skeered of dat man when he gits hot. He'd beat you full of button holes as quick as he's look atcher."

IV

The men gathered the next evening in a different mood, no laughter. No badinage this time.

"Look, 'Lige, you goin' to set up wid Spunk?"

"Naw, Ah reckon not, Walter. Tell yuh the truth, Ah'm a lil bit skittish. Spunk died too
250 wicket—died cussin' he did. You know he thought he wuz done outa life."

"Good Lawd, who'd he think done it?"

"Joe."

"Joe Kanty? How come?"

255 "Walter, Ah b'leeve Ah will walk up thata way an' set. Lena would like it Ah reckon."

"But whut did he say, 'Lige?"

Elijah did not answer until they had left the lighted store and were strolling down the
260 dark street.

"Ah wuz loadin' a wagon wid scantlin' right near the saw when Spunk fell on the carriage but 'fore Ah could git to him the saw got him in the body—awful sight. Me an'
265 Skint Miller got him off but it was too late. Anybody could see that. The fust thing he said wuz: 'He pushed me, 'Lige—the dirty hound pushed me in the back!'—He was spittin' blood at ev'ry breath. We laid him on
270 the sawdust pile with his face to the East so's he could die easy. He helt mah han' till the last, Walter, and said: 'It was Joe, 'Lige—the dirty sneak shoved me . . . he didn't dare come to mah face . . . but Ah'll git the son-of-
275 a-wood louse soon's Ah git there an' make hell too hot for him. . . . Ah felt him shove me . . . !' Thass how he died."

"If spirits kin fight, there's a powerful tussle goin' on some where ovah Jordan 'cause
280 Ah b'leeve Joe's ready for Spunk an' ain't skeered any more—yas, Ah b'leeve Joe pushed 'im mahself."

They had arrived at the house. Lena's lamentations were deep and loud. She had
285 filled the room with magnolia blossoms that gave off a heavy sweet odor. The keepers of the wake tipped about whispering in frightened tones. Everyone in the village was there, even old Jeff Kanty, Joe's father, who a
290 few hours before would have been afraid to come within ten feet of him, stood leering triumphantly down upon the fallen giant as if his fingers had been the teeth of steel that laid him low.

295 The cooling board consisted of three sixteen-inch boards on saw horses, a dingy sheet was his shroud.

The women ate heartily of the funeral baked meats and wondered who would be
300 Lena's next. The men whispered coarse conjectures between guzzles of whiskey.

CHARACTER

1. Who is the **protagonist** and who is the **antagonist**? Describe the values associated with each. How does this contrast contribute to the **tension** of the story?

2. Which character functions as a **foil**? What values are emphasized through this foil character?

3. How does Elijah's **perspective** and the men in the general store contribute to your understanding of Spunk?

4. Which aspects of Spunk's words and actions change after Joe's death? How does this contribute to his perception of the world and contribute to the **complexity** of his character?

STRUCTURE
Nonlinear Structures

AP **Enduring Understanding (STR-1)**

The arrangement of the parts and sections of a text, the relationship of the parts to each other, and the sequence in which the text reveals information are all structural choices made by a writer that contribute to the reader's interpretation of a text.

KEY POINT

Authors arrange and manipulate the sequence of events in a plot to create tension, raise questions, build suspense, and elicit surprise from readers.

Everything that has ever happened in the history of the universe occurred at a specific point in time. In fact, every event in your own life took place on a linear time line since the day you were born; everything that will ever happen to you in the future will fall after all the events that came before it. While people cannot escape their own real-world time lines, storytellers often imagine and present stories that break free from real-world chronological restraints.

You may recall from Unit 1 that plot structures can be mapped or drawn based on the rise and fall of the main character. Readers expect that traditional stories follow a chronological sequence of events with a beginning, middle, and end. But many stories break that pattern.

The manipulations of structure are important. Why did a writer tell the story this way? As readers, we have to understand that the way a story is told is important because it contributes to our understanding of the text.

Not All Stories Are Chronological

Writers break the chronological progression of a story by creating nonlinear narratives. Writers use nonlinear narratives and other **inconsistencies**, such as unexpected endings, to bring focus or emphasis to *something*. And, the reader must figure out what that something is. As these stories disrupt the reader's expectations, we must understand why a writer (or narrator) chooses to tell a story this way.

What exactly are nonlinear narratives? Rather than beginning with "once upon a time," some stories begin in the middle of the action (***in medias res***), some stories give you clues about their resolution (**foreshadowing**), and some narrators interrupt a narrative to tell of past events that precede the events of the story (**flashback**). All these situations are examples of nonlinear narratives.

Writers manipulate the time line of a narrative and present the events in nonchronological order. But why? Nonlinear narratives often create suspense or intrigue. They capture experiences similar to real-world action, reflecting more of what it means to be human. More importantly, all nonlinear plots build a dramatic tension for the reader. Nonlinear plots pose questions and create complexity by altering cause-effect relationships.

Additionally, authors and narrators control the speed at which information is revealed to a reader, creating the **narrative pacing** of the story. The narrative pacing builds up suspense and emotional tension that can result in **catharsis**. If you have ever cried — or laughed — at a movie, you have experienced a cathartic moment. The catharsis builds with the suspense and culminates in an emotional release for the audience. In this moment, a character may experience an epiphany that reveals an insight into the human experience.

Parallel Plots

Sometimes nonlinear narratives follow the stories of multiple characters, with the threads of the narration moving back and forth among them. By **juxtaposing** narratives in this way, the author can reveal information about the story's protagonist, highlight a particular conflict, reveal contrasting perspectives, or even show the complexities of subjective truth.

Stream of Consciousness

Some writers use **stream of consciousness** — another nonlinear narrative technique — when they want readers to experience the real-time, unfiltered perceptions, thoughts, and feelings of a character. When done effectively, stream of consciousness can capture the emotional state and psychology of characters — and even bring readers into their minds. But this technique also challenges readers to make sense of the text and forces them to think in different, nonlinear ways.

The reader accepts this nonlinear structure as another factor in the **suspension of disbelief**: the process whereby we temporarily avoid logic and reality to immerse ourselves in a fiction. In fact, many writers use a nonlinear structure as a way to connect the past, the present, or future. Regardless of the specific narrative chronology, keep in mind that the author is making a conscious decision in sequencing and arranging the events of a story's plot as a way to affect a reader's response; an author can control that response by keeping suspense, building emotion, and determining when to bring the story to a resolution. Likewise, as noted earlier in the unit, writers are conscious of **narrative pacing**: the speed at which a story is told and information is revealed to readers. The pace can influence the reader's emotions, create suspense, or reveal insights about the text.

INSIDER AP TIP   **Authors control the structure.** When authors create stories that deviate from a linear chronological structure, they do so intentionally. As you interpret the text, you should explain why the author reveals information in a chosen structure as well as how that particular structure helps to reveal an interpretation.

NONLINEAR PLOTS		
Type	**Description**	**Effect on the Narrative**
Frame story	When there is a story within a story, the outer story is considered the frame story	The author purposely structures the story so that a character or narrator tells it within the larger story for a specific purpose (e.g., to reveal a moral, a tradition, an experience) to other characters (and the reader).
Parallel plots (juxtaposition)	Two or more plot lines that occur simultaneously within a story	The unfolding of a series of plot events gradually reveals the intersections of storylines and characters. The juxtaposition of contrasting plots often reveals contradictions or inconsistencies that introduce nuance, ambiguity, irony, or contradiction into a text. These contrasts make texts more complex.
Stream of consciousness	The events of the plot are presented through the unfiltered thoughts, feelings, and perspectives of the main character as they occur	Thoughts, feelings, impressions, and memories put the reader in the mind of the character to understand motivation or even create empathy.
In medias res	A story that begins "in the middle of the action"	This structure puts the reader right in the middle of a compelling plot, builds suspense, and then draws upon flashbacks to reveal antecedent action as necessary.
Flashback	An interruption in the narrative to provide or reveal action that happened earlier	By providing details about events prior to the current plot event, authors can provide a character's backstory. This allows readers to better understand a character's choices and motivations, or even learn how a character was shaped by earlier circumstances. Flashbacks allow an author, character, or narrator to reveal depth of character, fill in gaps. Flashbacks may be revealed through direct narration, memory, or reflection, such as a dream sequence.
Reverse order	Sets up a problem to be solved by the reader (may be then followed by a flashback)	This introduces confusion or poses a question for the reader or a character to solve.

(continued)

Foreshadowing	Clues provided by an author, narrator, or character about story	Clues about a story may advance the plot or build suspense by involving the reader in the narrative.
		Foreshadowing may be a scene or mood that previews a later aspect of the plot, or it may be an object, fact, detail, or clue that reveals an important aspect of a character or the story.
		Details from foreshadowing may contribute to the dramatic irony of a story if a reader pieces together information before it is revealed by the character or narrator.
Aside	An interruption of the plot that stops the action so that a narrator or character can speak directly to the audience or to him or herself	Interruptions allow a narrator or character to explain, interpret, or qualify an event or observation, which creates an intimacy with the reader.
		In a drama, an interruption may be an aside or monologue that breaks the "fourth wall."
Deus ex machina	An unexpected or unlikely incident or action to resolve the story (Latin for "god from the machine")	An author may use stock or forced action to resolve a difficult situation and in doing so, release a character from a conflict.
Ironic ending	An unexpected plot	An unexpected plot ending usually creates situational or dramatic irony that reveals values and ideas; it also creates an emotional reaction for the reader such as shock, fulfillment, or joy.
Unresolved ending	A story that leaves its conflict unresolved	By leaving a conflict unresolved, an author provides an opportunity for the reader to apply his or her own values to the interpretation of a story.

PRACTICE TEXT

"Richie" *from* Sing, Unburied, Sing

Jesmyn Ward

THE TEXT IN CONTEXT

Born in Berkeley, California, novelist Jesmyn Ward (b. 1977) grew up in DeLisle, Mississippi, where she currently lives. Ward graduated from Stanford University and earned an MFA degree from the University of Michigan. She struggled with her writing and almost abandoned it for a nursing career, but then her first novel, *Where the Line Bleeds*, was published in 2008. Ward has since become the first woman to win the National Book Award two times: in 2011 for her second book, *Salvage the Bones*, and again in 2017 for the novel *Sing, Unburied, Sing* (the source of the chapter that follows). Her memoir, *The Men We Reaped* (2013), follows the lives of five Black men from DeLisle (including her brother) who all died within a short time of each other. Ward received a 2017 MacArthur Foundation Award for (in the words of the foundation) exploring the "enduring bonds of community and familial love among poor African Americans of the rural South against a landscape of circumscribed possibilities and lost potential."

Content Note: This story includes the N-word, which we have chosen to reprint in this textbook to accurately reflect Ward's original intent, as well as the culture and racism depicted in the story. We recognize that this word has a long history as a dis-respectful and deeply hurtful expression when used by white people toward Black people. Ward's choice to use this word relates not only to that history but also to a larger cultural tradition in which the N-word can take on different meanings, emphasize shared experience, and be repurposed as a term of endearment within Black commu-nities. While the use of that word in Ward's context might not be hurtful, the use of it in our current context very often is. Be mindful of context, both that of the characters in the story and yours, as you read and discuss "Richie."

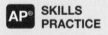 **SKILLS PRACTICE** | **STRUCTURE Analyzing Nonlinear Plots**

As you read the chapter "Richie" from Jesmyn Ward's *Sing, Unburied, Sing*, record the details of the plot that occur at the beginning, middle, and end of this chapter. Then identify the nonlinear narrative technique being used and explain what insight the technique offers into Ward's idea in this chapter.

(continued)

Analyzing Nonlinear Plots		
Moments and Details from the Plot	Narrative Technique	Significance in Relation to the Idea
Beginning:		
Middle:		
End:		

"Richie" *from* Sing, Unburied, Sing

The boy is River's. I know it. I smelled him as
soon as he entered the fields, as soon as the
little red dented car swerved into the parking
lot. The grass trilling and moaning all around,
5 when I followed the scent to him, the dark,
curly-haired boy in the backseat. Even if he
didn't carry the scent of leaves disintegrating
to mud at the bottom of a river, the aroma of
the bowl of the bayou, heavy with water and
10 sediment and the skeletons of small dead
creatures, crab, fish, snakes, and shrimp, I
would still know he is River's by the look of
him. The sharp nose. The eyes dark as swamp
bottom. The way his bones run straight and
15 true as River's: indomitable as cypress. He is
River's child.

When he returns to the car and I announce
myself, I know he is Riv's again. I know it by
the way he holds the little sick golden girl: as
20 if he thinks he could curl around her, make
his skeleton and flesh into a building to protect her from the adults, from the great reach
of the sky, the vast expanse of the grass-
ridden earth, shallow with graves. He protects
25 as River protects. I want to tell him this: *Boy,
you can't.* But I don't.

Instead, I fold myself and sit on the floor
of the car.

• • •

In the beginning, I woke in a stand of young
30 pine trees on a cloudy, half-lit day. I could
not remember how I came to be crouching in
the pine needles, soft and sharp as boar's
hair under my legs. There was no warmth or
cold there. Walking was like swimming
35 through tepid gray water. I paced in circles. I
don't know why I stayed in that place, why
every time I got to the edge of the young
stand, to the place where the pines reached
taller, rounded and darkened, draped with a
40 web of green thorny vines, I turned and
walked back. In that day that never ended, I
watched the tops of the trees toss, and I tried
to remember how I got there. Who I was
before this place, before this quiet haunt. But
45 I couldn't. So when I saw a white snake, thick
and long as my arm, slither out of the shadows beneath the trees, I knelt before It.

You are here, It said.
The needles dug into my knees.
50 *Do you want to leave?* It asked.
I shrugged.

I can take you away, It said. *But you have to want it.*

Where? I asked. The sound of my voice
55 surprised me.

Up and away, It said. *And around.*

Why?

There are things you need to see, It said.

It raised its white head in the air and
60 swayed, and slowly, like paint dissolving in
water, its scales turned black, row by row,
until it was the color of the space between
the stars. Little fingers sprouted from its
sides grow to wings, two perfect black scaly
65 wings. Two clawed feet pierced its bottom to
dig into the earth, and its tail shrunk to a
fan. It was a bird, but not a bird. No feathers.
All black scales. A scaly bird. A horned
vulture.

70   It bounced up to alight on the top of the
youngest pine tree, where it bristled and
cawed, the sound raw in that silent place.

Come, It said. *Rise.*

I stood. One of its scales dislodged and
75 floated to the earth, wispy as a feather.

Pick it up. Hold it, It said. *And you can fly.*

I clenched the scale. It was the size of a
penny. It burned my palm, and I rose up on
my tiptoes and suddenly I wasn't on the
80 ground anymore. I flew. I followed the scaly
bird. Up and up and out. Into the whitewater
torrent of the sky.

Flying was floating on that tumbling river.
The bird at my shoulder now, a raucous
85 smudge on the horizon then, sometimes
atop my head like a crown. I spread my arms
and legs and felt a laugh bubbling up in me,
but it died in my throat. Because I remembered. I remembered before. I remembered
90 being spread-eagle in the dirt, surrounded by
hunched, milling men, and a teenage boy at
my shoulder who stood tall under the long
shadows. River. River, who stood as the men
flayed my back, as I sobbed and vomited and
95 turned the earth to mud. I could feel him
there, knew that he would carry me after
they let me loose from the earth. My bones
felt pin-thin, my lungs useless. The way he
carried me to my cot, the way he bent over
100 me, made something soft and fluttery as a
jellyfish pulse in my chest. That was my
heart. Him my big brother. Him, my father.

I dropped from my flight, the memory
pulling me to earth. The bird screamed, upset.
105 I landed in a field of endless rows of cotton,
saw men bent and scuttling along like hermit
crabs, bending and picking. Saw other men
walking in circles around them with guns.
Saw buildings clustered at the edges of that
110 field, other fields, unto the ends of the earth.
The bird swooped down on the men's heads.
They disappeared. This is where I was worked.
This is where I was whipped. This is where
River protected me. The bird dropped to the
115 ground, dug its beak into the black earth, and
I remembered my name: Richie. I remembered the place: Parchman prison. And I
remembered the man's name: River Red. And
then I fell, dove into the dirt, and it parted
120 like a wave. I burrowed in right. Needing to
be held by the dark hand of the earth. To be
blind to the men above. To memory. It came
anyway. I was no more and then I was again.
The scale hot in my hand. I slept and woke
125 and rose and picked my way through the
prison fields, lurked in the barracks, hovered
over the men's faces. Tried to find River. He
wasn't there. Men left, men returned and left
again. New men came. I burrowed and slept
130 and woke in the milky light, my time measured by the passing of all those Black faces
and the turning of the earth, until the scaly
bird returned and led me to the car, to the
boy the same age as me sitting in the back of
135 the car. Jojo.

• • •

I want to tell the boy that I know the man
who sired him. That I knew him before this
boy. That I knew him when he was called
River Red. The gunmen called him River
140 because that was the name his mama and
daddy give him, and the men say he rolled
with everything like a river, over the fell
trees and stumps, through storms and sun.
But the men added the Red because that
145 was his color: him the color of red clay on
the Riverbank.

There's so much Jojo doesn't know. There
are so many stories I could tell him. The
story of me and Parchman, as River told it, is
150 a moth-eaten shirt, nibbled to threads: the
shape is right, but the details have been
erased. I could patch those holes. Make that
shirt hang new, except for the tails. The end.
But I could tell the boy what I know about
155 River and the dogs.

When the warden and sergeant told
River he was going to be in charge of the
dogs after Kinnie escaped, he took the news
easy, like he didn't care if he did it or if he
160 didn't. When they named River to keep the
dogs, I heard the men talking, especially
some of the old-timers: said all the dog
keepers were always older and White, long
as they been there, long as they remem-
165 bered. Even though some of those White
men had been like Kinnie, had escaped and
then been sent back to Parchman after
they'd been caught fleeing or had killed or
raped or maimed, the sergeant still chose
170 them to train the dogs. If they had any talent for it, they were given the job. Even if
they were flight risks, even if they had done
terrible things both in and out of Parchman,
the leashes were theirs. Even though they
175 were terrible, dangerous White men, the
old-timers still took more offense when

they knew Riv would be their hunter. They
didn't like Riv taking care of the dogs. *It's
different*, they said, *for the Black man to be a
180 trusty, with a gun.* Said: *That's unnatural, too,
but that's Parchman.* But it was something
about a colored man running the dogs; that
was wrong. There had always been bad
blood between dogs and Black people: they
185 were bred adversaries—slaves running
from the slobbering hounds, and then the
convict man dodging them.

But River had a way with animals. The
sergeant saw that. It didn't matter to him
190 that Riv couldn't make the hounds hunt
Kinnie. The sergeant knew there wasn't
another White inmate who could wrangle
those dogs, so Riv was his best bet for training them, for keeping them keen. The dogs
195 loved Riv. They turned floppy and silly when
he came around. I saw it, because Riv asked
them to transfer me out the fields and over
to him so I could assist him. He saw how sick
I was after I got whipped. He thought if I
200 were left to my despair, my slow-knitting
back, I would do something stupid. *You smart,*
he said. *Little and fast.* He told the sergeant
that I was wasted in the fields.

But I didn't have River's way with the
205 dogs. I think some part of me hated and
feared them. And they knew it. The dogs
didn't soften to silly puppies with me. Their
tails stiffened, their backs straightened,
and they stilled. When they saw Riv in the
210 dark morning, they bounced and yapped,
but when they saw me, they ossified to
stone. River held out his hands to the dogs
like he was a reverend and they were his
church. They were quiet with listening, but
215 he didn't say anything. Something about
the way they froze together in the blue
dawn was worshipful. But when I held out
my hand to them, like Riv told me, and

waited for them to acclimate to my scent,
to listen to me, they snapped and gurgled.
Riv said: *Have patience, Richie; it's going to
happen.* I doubted. Even though the dogs
hated me, and I still got up when the sun
was a dim shine at the edge of the sky and
spent all day hauling water and food and
running after those mutts, I was still happier than I had been before, still lighter,
almost, maybe okay. I know River hasn't
told Jojo that, because I never told River
that when I ran, it felt like the air was
sweeping me along. I thought the wind
might pick me up and hurl me through the
air, buoy me up out of the shitty dog pens,
the scarred fields, away from the gunmen
and the trusty shooters and the sergeant
up into the sky. That it would carry me
away. When I was lying on my cot at night
while River cleaned my wounds, those
moments blinked around me like fireflies
in the dark. I caught them in my hands and
held them to me, a golden handful of light,
before swallowing them.

I would tell Jojo this: *That was no place for
hope.*

It only got worse when Hogjaw returned to
Parchman. They called him Hogjaw because
he was big and pale as a three-hundred-
pound pig. His jaw was a hard square. His
mouth a long thin line. He had the jaw of a
hog that would gore. He was a killer. Everybody
knew. He had escaped Parchman once, but
then he committed another violent crime,
shooting or stabbing someone, and he was
sent back. That's what a White man had to do
to return to Parchman, even if he was free
because he had escaped: a White man had to
murder. Hogjaw did a lot of murdering, but
when he came back, the warden put him over
the dogs, over Riv. The warden said: "It ain't
natural for a colored man to master dogs.

A colored man doesn't know how to master,
because it ain't in him to master." He said:
"The only thing a nigger knows how to do is
slave."

I wasn't light anymore. When I ran to
fetch, I didn't feel like I was racing the wind.
There were no more firefly moments to
blink at me in the dark. Hogjaw smelled bad.
Sour like slop. The way he looked at me—
there was something wrong about it. I didn't
know he was doing it until one day we were
out running drills with the dogs, and Hogjaw
said, *Come with me, boy.* He wanted me to
follow him to the woods so we could run the
dogs up trees. Hogjaw told River to run a
message to the sergeant and leave us to the
drills. Hogjaw put his hand on my back,
gently. He grabbed my shoulders all the time,
hands hard as trotters; he usually squeezed
so tight I felt my back curving to bend, to
kneel. River gave Hogjaw a hard look, and
stood in front of me that day, and said, *Sergeant
need him.* He looked at me, tilted his head
toward the compound, and said, *Go, boy. Now.*

I turned and ran as fast as I could. My feet
running to darkness. The next morning Riv
woke me up and told me I wasn't his dog
runner anymore, and I was going back out in
the field.

• • •

I want to tell the boy in the car this. Want to
tell him how his pop tried to save me again
and again, but he couldn't. Jojo cuddles the
golden girl to his chest and whispers to her as
she plays with his ear, and as he murmurs, his
voice like the waves of a calm bay lapping
against a boat, I realize there is another scent
in his blood. This is where he differs from
River. This scent blooms stronger than the dark
rich mud of the bottom; it is the salt of the sea,
burning with brine. It pulses in the current of

his veins. This is part of the reason he can see me while the others, excepting the little girl, can't. I am subject to that pulse, helpless as a fisherman in a boat with no engine, no oars, 305 while the tide bears him onward.

But I don't tell the boy any of that. I settle in the crumpled bits of paper and plastic that litter the bottom of the car. I crouch like the scaly bird. I hold the burning scale in my 310 closed hand, and I wait.

STRUCTURE

1. How does this chapter break an established chronological sequence? How do the events' **flashbacks** contribute to the narrative?

2. How does the **climactic** flight affect the reader's experience and contribute to an interpretation of the text? Explain this series of events.

3. What ideas, traits, or values are emphasized by the **contrast** at Parchman?

4. How does this **contrast** contribute to the complexity of the text?

NARRATION

Narrator Bias and Tone

AP® **Enduring Understanding (NAR-1)**

A narrator's or speaker's perspective controls the details and emphases that affect how readers experience and interpret a text.

Many readers enjoy analyzing representations because the process gives them an opportunity to practice their detective skills, such as piecing together evidence and following clues. Most readers are ready to figure out the conflict of a plot, but they may not be as prepared to scrutinize the source of the clues within the story itself: the narrator.

You may recall from Unit 4 that narrators, like other characters, have a perspective or lens by which they understand and interpret the world and events happening around them. But remember: The narrator's perspective does not necessarily reflect the author's perspective. As the novelist Margaret Atwood once said, "People have a habit of identifying the author with the narrator, and you can't, obviously, be all of the narrators in all of your books, or else you'd be a very strange person indeed."

> **KEY POINT**
>
> The language (both word choice and sentence construction) and details that a writer, character, or narrator uses contribute to tone and reveal his or her perspective and biases.

Language Choices Reveal Attitudes

A narrator's tone reveals perspective and attitude toward a situation, conflict, or character. **Tone** includes the narrator's word choice, syntactical arrangement, and details they choose to include, emphasize, minimize, or exclude. If you understand the tone, you will have critical insight into the narrator, as well as how the narrator's perspective might influence a reader's interpretation of the text.

Diction: Word Choice

An author's choice of words, or **diction**, does more than, say, give descriptive information about a character or provide background details for the plot. Diction also reveals the author's attitude and perspective about the person being described or the conflict being explained. That is because words have both **denotations** and **connotations**. Denotation refers to a word's dictionary definition; connotation refers to the associations, implications, and other secondary meanings carried by words.

For example, a narrator who describes an elderly character as "decrepit and stubborn" has a different perspective than a narrator who describes the same person as "aged, yet resolute." Though the denotations of "stubborn" and "resolute" are similar (as are "old" and "decrepit"), their connotations reveal the contrasting attitudes of different narrative perspectives.

Syntax: Sentence Structures

Syntax refers to the grammatical arrangement of words, phrases, and clauses that also play an important part in affecting the reader's interpretation of tone. The author's syntactical choices may create emphasis or reveal the narrator's perspective. Consider the following examples.

- A narrator who describes a series of events in one long run-on sentence may be mentally or emotionally overwhelmed.
- When narrators open sentences with subordinate clauses, they reveal that the subject in the subordinate clause is a secondary concern or idea: "While I could have stopped to help the child tie her shoes, I didn't because I had much more important things to do." Narrators who use coordinate clauses reveal that both subjects and ideas in a sentence have equal importance: "I truly loved Jacob, but I was terrified of losing Edward."
- Narrators may also use syntactical choices to build suspense or use a sentence to reveal a surprise ending: "Noah loved Sophia, but their relationship failed because she was kind, intelligent, thoughtful, honest, and completely incompatible with Noah."

Adjectives answer questions such as What kind? How many? or Which one? Adverbs answer questions such as Where? When? How? and To what extent? So these different types of modifiers are important to interpretation, as they reveal relationships and provide important information.

In short, how authors choose to arrange sentences reveals important details, information, and relationships between and among those details.

Details

The narrator's or speaker's perspective influences how much information is provided for readers. What the narrator chooses to include (or exclude) may reveal the narrator's biases and affect a reader's interpretation.

For example, narrators who spend several paragraphs judging the clothes, accessories, and perceived economic status of each character signal that they value superficial appearances. The reader can use this insight to evaluate the narrator's other judgments.

Tone and Reliability

Not all narrators tell an accurate tale: some narrators are less reliable than others. There are several factors that influence a narrator's or character's **reliability**:

- Their relationships with other characters
- Their psychological and emotional state
- Their desire to achieve their goal
- Their susceptibility to others' influence

- Their maturity or level of experience
- Their knowledge and self-awareness
- Their sense of ethics and morals

When assessing a narrator's reliability, remember that **tone** is an important factor. Readers who detect a **bias** in diction, syntax, emphasis, and attitude may find the narrator less reliable.

Similarly, characters may be unreliable as well. Reliability exists on a spectrum. Unreliable narrators and characters may consciously (or unconsciously) misrepresent or misinterpret characters, plot, and other elements in a story. Some unreliable narrators are intentional in their deception. Others are naively unreliable, while still others change from being unreliable to reliable because of an epiphany or other influence.

Narrator reliability can influence a reader's interpretation of characters' motives. Narrators who have proven to be unreliable may misinterpret (and then mistakenly report to the reader) a character's action or decision.

INSIDER AP® TIP All narrators have a perspective, and that perspective reveals their biases. Some narrators are so biased that they are unreliable. Critical readers must not only recognize the motivation and the effect of the narrator's perspective but also explain why the author chose an unreliable narrator.

SOME WORDS TO DESCRIBE THE NARRATOR OR SPEAKER		
Allusive	Condescending	Fantastical
Angry	Confident	Fearful
Apologetic	Contemptuous	Flippant
Audacious	Contentious	Gullible
Austere	Credible	Haughty
Benevolent	Credulous	Hollow
Biased	Detached	Hopeful
Bitter	Devastated	Humble
Bold	Didactic	Humorous
Candid	Disdainful	Immature
Cautious	Elegiac	Imperious
Colloquial	Experienced	Inexperienced
Compassionate	Extravagant	Informative
Complacent	Faithful	Innocent

(continued)

Insane	Patriotic	Sentimental
Insecure	Patronizing	Shallow
Insipid	Persuasive	Sincere
Insolent	Poignant	Skeptical
Introverted	Proud	Spiritual
Ironic	Provocative	Stoic
Irreverent	Rebellious	Sympathetic
Joyful	Restrained	Triumphant
Mournful	Reverent	Trivial
Naive	Sarcastic	Uneducated
Nostalgic	Sardonic	Vivacious
Objective	Seductive	Whimsical
Pathetic		

PRACTICE TEXT

from The Sympathizer
Viet Thanh Nguyen

San Francisco Chronicle/Hearst Newspapers/Getty Images

THE TEXT IN CONTEXT

Novelist and nonfiction writer Viet Thanh Nguyen was born in Vietnam in 1971. His parents came to the United States after the city of Saigon fell in 1975, when American forces withdrew from the Vietnam war. His family ultimately settled in San Jose, California. Growing up in the United States, Nguyen was fascinated by the Vietnam war but found few accounts from a Vietnamese perspective. As he writes, "For most Americans and the world, 'Vietnam' means the 'Vietnam War,' and the Vietnam War means the American war, with novels written by American men about American soldiers." In his award-winning first novel *The Sympathizer* (2015), Nguyen writes from the perspective of a North Vietnamese double agent who becomes a refugee-expatriate and moves to the United States. Nguyen's other books include *Nothing Ever Dies: Vietnam and the Memory of War* (2016), *The Refugees* (2017), and the children's book *Chicken of the Sea* (2019). He is currently a professor of English and American Studies at the University of Southern California.

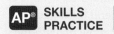 **SKILLS PRACTICE** | NARRATION
Analyzing Narrator Reliability

As you read the excerpt from *The Sympathizer*, note the choices the narrator makes (e.g., what he does, what he says). Consider why the narrator makes these choices and then explain the effect of those choices, especially how they contribute to his reliability.

Analyzing Narrator Reliability		
Narrator's Actions or Choices	Narrator's Motivation	Effect on the Narrative

from The Sympathizer

I am a spy, a sleeper, a spook, a man of two
faces. Perhaps not surprisingly, I am also a
man of two minds. I am not some misunderstood mutant from a comic book or a horror
5 movie, although some have treated me as
such. I am simply able to see any issue from
both sides. Sometimes I flatter myself that this
is a talent, and although it is admittedly one of
a minor nature, it is perhaps also the sole tal-
10 ent I possess. At other times, when I reflect on
how I cannot help but observe the world in
such a fashion, I wonder if what I have should
even be called talent. After all, a talent is
something you use, not something that uses
15 you. The talent you cannot not use, the talent
that possesses you—that is a hazard, I must
confess. But in the month when this confession begins, my way of seeing the world still
seemed more of a virtue than a danger, which
20 is how some dangers first appear.

The month in question was April, the
cruelest month. It was the month in which a
war that had run on for a very long time
would lose its limbs, as is the way of wars. It
25 was a month that meant everything to all
the people in our small part of the world and
nothing to most people in the rest of the
world. It was a month that was both an end
of a war and the beginning of . . . well, "peace"
30 is not the right word, is it, my dear Commandant? It was a month when I awaited the end
behind the walls of a villa where I had lived
for the previous five years, the villa's walls
glittering with broken brown glass and
35 crowned with rusted barbed wire. I had my
own room at the villa, much like I have my
own room in your camp, Commandant. Of
course, the proper term for my room is an
"isolation cell," and instead of a housekeeper
40 who comes to clean every day, you have provided me with a baby-faced guard who does
not clean at all. But I am not complaining.
Privacy, not cleanliness, is my only prerequi-
site for writing this confession.

45 While I had sufficient privacy in the General's villa at night, I had little during the day. I was the only one of the General's officers to live in his home, the sole bachelor on his staff and his most reliable aide. In the 50 mornings, before I chauffeured him the short distance to his office, we would breakfast together, parsing dispatches at one end of the teak dining table while his wife oversaw a well-disciplined quartet of children at 55 the other, ages eighteen, sixteen, fourteen, and twelve, with one seat empty for the daughter studying in America. Not everyone may have feared the end, but the General sensibly did. A thin man of excellent pos- 60 ture, he was a veteran campaigner whose many medals had been, in his case, genuinely earned. Although he possessed but nine fingers and eight toes, having lost three digits to bullets and shrapnel, only his fam- 65 ily and confidants knew about the condition of his left foot. His ambitions had hardly ever been thwarted, except in his desire to procure an excellent bottle of Bourgogne and to drink it with companions who knew bet- 70 ter than to put ice cubes in their wine. He was an epicurean and a Christian, in that order, a man of faith who believed in gastronomy and God; his wife and his children; and the French and the Americans. In his 75 view, they offered us far better tutelage than those other foreign Svengalis who had hypnotized our northern brethren and some of our southern ones: Karl Marx, V. I. Lenin, and Chairman Mao. Not that he ever read any of 80 those sages! That was my job as his aide-de-camp and junior officer of intelligence, to provide him with cribbed notes on, say, *The Communist Manifesto* or Mao's *Little Red Book.* It was up to him to find occasions to demon- 85 strate his knowledge of the enemy's thinking, his favorite being Lenin's question, plagiarized whenever the need arose: Gentlemen, he would say, rapping the relevant

table with adamantine knuckles, what is to 90 be done? To tell the General that Nikolay Chernyshevsky actually came up with the question in his novel of the same title seemed irrelevant. How many remember Chernyshevsky now? It was Lenin who 95 counted, the man of action who took the question and made it his own.

In this gloomiest of Aprils, faced with this question of what should be done, the general who always found something to do could no 100 longer do so. A man who had faith in the *mission civilisatrice* and the American Way was at last bitten by the bug of disbelief. Suddenly insomniac, he took to wandering his villa with the greenish pallor of a malar- 105 ial patient. Ever since our northern front had collapsed a few weeks before in March, he would materialize at my office door or at my room in the villa to hand off a snatch of news, always gloomy. Can you believe it? he 110 would demand, to which I said one of two things: No, sir! or Unbelievable!

We could not believe that the pleasant, scenic coffee town of Ban Me Thuot, my Highlands hometown, had been sacked in 115 early March. We could not believe that our president, Thieu, whose name begged to be spit out of the mouth, had inexplicably ordered our forces defending the Highlands to retreat. We could not believe that Da 120 Nang and Nha Trang had fallen, or that our troops had shot civilians in the back as they all fought madly to escape on barges and boats, the death toll running to the thousands. In the secret privacy of my 125 office, I dutifully snapped pictures of these reports, which would please Man, my handler. While they pleased me, too, as signs of the regime's inevitable erosion, I could not help but feel moved by the plight of these 130 poor people. Perhaps it was not correct, politically speaking, for me to feel sympathy for them, but my mother would have been one of them if she were alive. She was a poor person, I was her poor child, and no one asks poor people if they want war. Nor had anyone asked these poor people if they wanted to die of thirst and exposure on the coastal sea, or if they wanted to be robbed and raped by their own soldiers. If those thousands still lived, they would not have believed how they had died, just as we could not believe that the Americans — our friends, our benefactors, our protectors — had spurned our request to send more money. And what would we have done with that money? Buy the ammunition, gas, and spare parts for the weapons, planes, and tanks the same Americans had bestowed on us for free. Having given us the needles, they now perversely no longer supplied the dope. (Nothing, the General muttered, is ever so expensive as what is offered for free.)

At the end of our discussions and meals, I lit the General's cigarette and he stared into space, forgetting to smoke the Lucky Strike as it slowly consumed itself in his fingers. In the middle of April, when the ash stung him awake from his reverie and he uttered a word he should not have, Madame silenced the tittering children and said, If you wait much longer, we won't be able to get out. You should ask Claude for a plane now. The General pretended not to hear Madame. She had a mind like an abacus, the spine of a drill instructor, and the body of a virgin even after five children. All of this was wrapped up in one of those exteriors that inspired our Beaux Arts — trained painters to use the most pastel of watercolors and the fuzziest of brushstrokes. She was, in short, the ideal Vietnamese woman. For this good fortune, the General was eternally grateful and terrified. Kneading the tip of his scorched finger, he looked at me and said I think it's time to ask Claude for a plane. Only when he resumed

studying his damaged finger did I glance at Madame, who merely raised an eyebrow. Good idea, sir, I said.

Claude was our most trusted American friend, our relationship so intimate he once confided in me to being one-sixteenth Negro. Ah, I had said, equally smashed on Tennessee bourbon, that explains why your hair is black, and why you tan well, and why you can dance the cha-cha like one of us. Beethoven, he said, was likewise of hexadecimal descent. Then, I said, that explains why you can carry the tune of "Happy Birthday" like no one's business. We had known each other for more than two decades, ever since he had spotted me on a refugee barge in '54 and recognized my talents. I was a precocious nine-year-old who had already learned a decent amount of English, taught to me by a pioneering American missionary. Claude supposedly worked in refugee relief. Now his desk was in the American embassy, his assignment ostensibly to promote the development of tourism in our war-stricken country. This, as you might imagine, required every drop he could squeeze from a handkerchief soaked with the sweat of the can-do American spirit. In reality, Claude was a CIA man whose time in this country dated back to the days when the French still ruled an empire. In those days, when the CIA was the OSS, Ho Chi Minh looked to them for help in fighting the French. He even quoted America's Founding Fathers in his declaration of our country's independence. Uncle Ho's enemies say he spoke out of both sides of his mouth at the same time, but Claude believed he saw both sides at once. I rang Claude from my office, down the hall from the General's study, and informed him in English that the General had lost all hope. Claude's Vietnamese was bad and his French worse, but his English was excellent. I point this out only because the same thing could not be said of all his countrymen.

It's over, I said, and when I said it to Claude it finally seemed real. I thought Claude might protest and argue that American bombers might yet fill our skies, or that American air
225 cavalry might soon ride on gunships to our rescue, but Claude did not disappoint. I'll see what I can arrange, he said, a murmur of voices audible in the background. I imagined the embassy in disarray, teletypes overheat-
230 ing, urgent cables crisscrossing between Saigon and Washington, the staff working without respite, and the funk of defeat so pungent it overwhelmed the air condition- ers. Amid short tempers, Claude stayed cool,
235 having lived here so long he barely perspired in the tropical humidity. He could sneak up on you in the dark, but he could never be invisible in our country. Although an intellec- tual, he was of a peculiarly American breed,
240 the muscular kind who rowed crew and who flexed substantial biceps. Whereas our schol- arly types tended to be pale, myopic, and stunted, Claude was six-two, had perfect vision, and kept himself in shape by per-
245 forming two hundred push-ups each morn- ing, his Nung houseboy squatting on his back. During his free time, he read, and whenever he visited the villa, a book was tucked under his arm. When he arrived a few
250 days later, Richard Hedd's *Asian Communism and the Oriental Mode of Destruction* was the paperback he carried.

The book was for me, while the General received a bottle of Jack Daniel's—a gift I
255 would have preferred if given the choice. Nevertheless, breathless they might have been lifted from the transcript of a teenage girls' fan club, except that the excited gig- gling came from a pair of secretaries of
260 defense, a senator who had visited our coun- try for two weeks to find facts, and a renowned television anchor who modeled his enuncia- tion on Moses, as played by Charlton Heston. The reason for their excitement was found in

265 the significant type of the subtitle, *On Understanding and Defeating the Marxist Threat to Asia*. When Claude said everyone was reading this how-to manual, I said I would read it as well. The General, who had cracked
270 open the bottle, was in no mood to discuss books or chitchat, not with eighteen enemy divisions encircling the capital. He wanted to discuss the plane, and Claude, rolling his glass of whiskey between his palms, said the
275 best he could do was a black flight, off the books, on a C-130. It could hold ninety-two paratroopers and their gear, as the General well knew, having served in the Airborne before being called on by the president him-
280 self to lead the National Police. The problem, as he explained to Claude, was that his extended family alone amounted to fifty- eight. While he did not like some of them, and in fact despised a few, Madame would
285 never forgive him if he did not rescue all of her relations.

And my staff, Claude? The General spoke in his precise, formal English. What of them? Both the General and Claude glanced at me.
290 I tried to look brave. I was not the senior offi- cer on the staff, but as the aide-de-camp and the officer most fluent in American culture, I attended all the General's meetings with Americans. Some of my countrymen spoke
295 English as well as I, although most had a tinge of an accent. But almost none could discuss, like I, baseball standings, the awful- ness of Jane Fonda, or the merits of the Rolling Stones versus the Beatles. If an
300 American closed his eyes to hear me speak, he would think I was one of his kind. Indeed, on the phone, I was easily mistaken for an American. On meeting in person, my inter- locutor was invariably astonished at my
305 appearance and would almost always inquire as to how I had learned to speak English so well. In this jackfruit republic that served as a franchise of the United States, Americans

expected me to be like those millions who spoke no English, pidgin English, or accented English. I resented their expectation. That was why I was always eager to demonstrate, in both spoken and written word, my mastery of their language. My vocabulary was broader, my grammar more precise than the average educated American. I could hit the high notes as well as the low, and thus had no difficulty in understanding Claude's characterization of the ambassador as a "putz," a "jerkoff" with "his head up his ass" who was in denial about the city's imminent fall. Officially, there's no evacuation, said Claude, because we're not pulling out any time soon.

The General, who hardly ever raised his voice, now did. Unofficially, you are abandoning us, he shouted. All day and night planes depart from the airport. Everyone who works with Americans wants an exit visa. They go to your embassy for these visas. You have evacuated your own women. You have evacuated babies and orphans. Why is it that the only people who do not know the Americans are pulling out are the Americans? Claude had the decency to look embarrassed as he explained how the city would erupt in riots if an evacuation was declared, and perhaps then turn against the Americans who remained. This had happened in Da Nang and Nha Trang, where the Americans had fled for their lives and left the residents to turn on one another. But despite this precedent, the atmosphere was strangely quiet in Saigon, most of the Saigonese citizenry behaving like people in a scuppered marriage, willing to cling gamely to each other and drown so long as nobody declared the adulterous truth. The truth, in this case, was that at least a million people were working or had worked for the Americans in one capacity or another, from shining their shoes to running the army designed by the Americans in their own image to performing fellatio on them for the price, in Peoria or Poughkeepsie, of a hamburger. A good portion of these people believed that if the communists won — which they refused to believe would happen — what awaited them was prison or a garrote, and, for the virgins, forced marriage with the barbarians. Why wouldn't they? These were the rumors the CIA was propagating.

So — the General began, only to have Claude interrupt him. You have one plane and you should consider yourself lucky, sir. The General was not one to beg. He finished his whiskey, as did Claude, then shook Claude's hand and bid him good-bye, never once letting his gaze fall away from Claude's own. Americans liked seeing people eye to eye, the General had once told me, especially as they screwed them from behind. This was not how Claude saw the situation. Other generals were only getting seats for their immediate families, Claude said to us in parting. Even God and Noah couldn't save everyone. Or wouldn't, anyway.

NARRATION

1. Who is telling the story and who is the **narrator** speaking to? How does this **perspective** contribute to your understanding of the text?

2. How does the **narrator's** inclusion or exclusion of details affect his **reliability**?

3. Does the narrator acknowledge his **biases**? How do these biases contribute to his reliability?

4. How do the character's motivations contribute to his **reliability**?

Symbols

 Enduring Understanding (FIG-1)

Comparisons, representations, and associations shift meaning from the literal to the figurative and invite readers to interpret a text.

KEY POINT

Authors create and include physical objects, characters, and settings that represent abstract qualities or ideas and suggest figurative meanings.

Even if you don't realize it, you use and interpret symbols all the time. Whether you're watching a show or a commercial, listening to music, or texting a friend, you use visual shortcuts and icons to communicate ideas. You may wear a shirt that depicts an American flag to celebrate Independence Day; you may buy a bundle of red roses for a crush; you may include your astrological sign in your social media profile. Each of these symbols (the flag, the roses, and the astrological sign) has a unique figurative meaning beyond its literal visual representation. We even depend on colors to communicate meaning: consider the function of each color on the stoplight, for example. Symbols help keep our world running smoothly and safely, but they also allow for greater complexity in the sciences, humanities, arts, and literature.

Authors Reveal Ideas through Symbols

We usually define **symbol** as a concrete object that comes to stand for an abstract idea or value. Symbols may also be characters or settings that represent abstractions. So readers must pay attention to the figurative and symbolic implications of elements in a story, play, or poem. In other words, an author invites a reader to identify and interpret these suggestive, emblematic aspects of a text. As a result, you will need to read closely and analyze how objects, characters, and settings may mean something beyond themselves. What might they stand for? What values or ideas might they represent? Considering a symbol's attributes and circumstances will provide clues, and the more you read the more you will see how symbolic objects, characters, and places reveal ideas. Like images, symbols can create associations with readers by evoking their emotions. Some symbols are so common and recurrent that many readers have associations with them prior to reading a text. Other symbols are more dependent on context and only represent abstractions in one particular text. That is, a symbol can represent different things depending on the experiences of a reader and the context of its use. When writers deploy them effectively, symbols add depth and complexity to our interpretation of literary works.

Characters and Setting as Symbols

Characters and **settings** may be symbolic in that they represent values or ideas. And, as you've learned in earlier units, contrasting characters or settings may reveal contrasting values or ideas. In addition to analyzing the traits of a character or the values of a particular setting, you may also want to consider how the name of a character or a place symbolizes abstract ideas.

Some symbols are used so frequently they become recognizable **archetypes**. From Unit 4, you'll recall that when an object, character, location, or action takes on similar meaning across cultures, it comes to have universal significance. For example, the "hero" is an archetype (representing courage, persistence, and other virtues), as are pristine gardens (suggesting innocence or fertility).

Allegory

Allegories are stories that use a series of symbols with clear, often deliberately obvious meanings. In allegories, the names of characters and settings are often abstract values themselves, making clear what they represent. As such, allegorical symbols establish an extended metaphor, but their authors restrict the meaning of the characters or locations. This highlights a primary difference between symbolism and allegory: symbols are more open to interpretation, while allegories are more limited in their meaning.

When interpreting literature, you may want to look for a primary symbol in the text: an object, character, or setting that represents an idea or value beyond itself. Then, look for other objects or images that are related to the primary symbol and that you can use to support your overall interpretation of the work.

INSIDER AP® TIP **Recognizing a symbol is not enough.** Careful readers explore significant details related to a symbol and explain how symbols function to reveal a perspective. Ultimately, readers must explain what the symbol means and how it reveals an insight about an idea.

COMMON CONVENTIONAL SYMBOLS			
Colors		**Characters**	
White	Purity, innocence, forgiveness	Baby	Innocence, hope
Black	Evil, death, unknown, fear	Older person	Maturity, wisdom
Red	Sin, blood, immorality, temptation, sexuality, passion	Soothsayer	Foreboding, wisdom
Green	Hope, success, power, greed, opportunity	**Animals**	
Yellow	Caution, age, cowardice, joy	Birds	Freedom
Gold	Power, rarity, wealth	Buzzard	Impending doom
Light	Goodness	Dove	Peace
Dark	Evil	Eagle	Freedom, patriotism

(continued)

Numbers		Animals	
Zero	Mystery, nothingness	Lamb	Innocence, sacrifice
Three	Trinity, beginning-middle-end	Owl	Wisdom
Seven	Fortune, fulfillment	**Places and Settings**	
Twelve	Fulfillment, complete cycle	City	Vitality, labor, corruption, decay
Forty	Penance, purification	Desert	Death, sterility
Objects		East	renewal
Apple	Knowledge, temptation	Forest	Falsehood, evil, mystery
Books	Knowledge	Garden (Eden)	Truth, temptation
Candle	Light, truth	Mountain	Obstacle
Chain	Suffering, bondage, interdependence	Ocean	Isolation
Clock	Time	River	Life, freedom
Cross	Christianity, religion, sacrifice	Road	Choice, journey
Fire	Destruction, purgation	Wall	Barrier, boundary
Flowers	Beauty, youth	West	New frontier, old age, end of day
Found object	Power, magic, hope	Window/door	Opportunity, freedom, entrapment
Key	Knowledge, power, centrality	**Seasons and Time**	
Mask	Deception	Spring	New beginning, rebirth, love, youth
Mirror	Reflection	Summer	Coming of age, maturity, knowledge
Mud	Entrapment	Fall/autumn	Old age, decline, harvest
Pearl	Knowledge, wealth	Winter	Death, hopelessness
Ring	Eternity, love	Easter	Rebirth
Rose	Love, beauty	Early morning/ dawn	rebirth
Skull	Death, evil, warning	Evening	Death, old age, doom
Sword	Power, weapon, protection	Midnight	End of a cycle, death
Thorn	Evil, pain, suffering	**Weather**	
Tree	Knowledge, wisdom, strength, family	Rain/snow	Rebirth, turning points, renewal
Water	Life, renewal, cleansing, fertility	Fog/mist	Mystery, uncertainty, confusion
		Wind/storm	Hostility, danger
Weeds	Evil, confusion, deception, corruption	Sunshine	Calm, peacefulness, resolution
		Rainbow	Good fortune, fulfilled promise

PRACTICE TEXT

"The Foul Ball" *from* A Prayer for Owen Meany
John Irving

THE TEXT IN CONTEXT

Both a popular and a critically acclaimed novelist, John Irving (b. 1942) writes epic, plot- and character-rich stories in the tradition of his own favorite writer, Charles Dickens. Since publishing his first novel *Setting Free the Bears* in 1968, he has written nineteen books of fiction, including *The World According to Garp* (1978), *The Hotel New Hampshire* (1981), *The Cider House Rules* (1985), and *In One Person* (2012). Irving is known for his recurrent themes and motifs such as bears, wrestling, sexuality, fate, religious faith, and dysfunctional families. He is also noted for using symbolism conspicuously in his work. Irving often sets his novels in his native New Hampshire and explores how events in our lives shape who we are, as in the case of "The Foul Ball," the first chapter of *A Prayer for Owen Meany* (1989) excerpted here.

AP® SKILLS PRACTICE	FIGURATIVE LANGUAGE **Analyzing the Function of Symbols**

As you read Chapter 1 of *A Prayer for Owen Meany*, make note of potential symbols in the text. Describe their symbolic meaning and explain how they contribute to a unifying idea.

Analyzing the Function of Symbols		
Unifying idea:		
Colors, Numbers, Objects, Characters, Animals, Clothing, Places, Seasons, Holidays, Time, Weather	Symbolic Association	Connection to the Idea

"The Foul Ball" *from* A Prayer for Owen Meany

The Foul Ball

I am doomed to remember a boy with a wrecked voice — not because of his voice, or because he was the smallest person I ever knew, or even because he was the instrument
5 of my mother's death, but because he is the reason I believe in God; I am a Christian because of Owen Meany. I make no claims to have a life in Christ, or with Christ — and certainly not for Christ, which I've heard
10 some zealots claim. I'm not very sophisticated in my knowledge of the Old Testament, and I've not read the New Testament since my Sunday school days, except for those passages that I hear read aloud to me when I go
15 to church. I'm somewhat more familiar with the passages from the Bible that appear in The Book of Common Prayer; I read my prayer book often, and my Bible only on holy days — the prayer book is so much more
20 orderly.

I've always been a pretty regular churchgoer. I used to be a Congregationalist — I was baptized in the Congregational Church, and after some years of fraternity with Episcopalians
25 (I was confirmed in the Episcopal Church, too), I became rather vague in my religion: in my teens I attended a "nondenominational" church. Then I became an Anglican; the Anglican Church of Canada has been my church — ever
30 since I left the United States, about twenty years ago. Being an Anglican is a lot like being an Episcopalian — so much so that being an Anglican occasionally impresses upon me the suspicion that I have simply become
35 an Episcopalian again. Anyway, I left the Congregationalists and the Episcopalians — and my country once and for all.

When I die, I shall attempt to be buried in New Hampshire — alongside my mother —
40 but the Anglican Church will perform the necessary service before my body suffers the indignity of trying to be sneaked through U.S. Customs. My selections from the Order for the Burial of the Dead are entirely conven-
45 tional and can be found, in the order that I shall have them read — not sung — in The Book of Common Prayer. Almost everyone I know will be familiar with the passage from John, beginning with ". . . whosoever liveth
50 and believeth in me shall never die." And then there's ". . . in my Father's house are many mansions: If it were not so, I would have told you." And I have always appreciated the frankness expressed in that passage
55 from Timothy, the one that goes ". . . we brought nothing into this world, and it is certain we can carry nothing out." It will be a by-the-book Anglican service, the kind that would make my former fellow Congregation-
60 alists fidget in their pews. I am an Anglican now, and I shall die an Anglican. But I skip a Sunday service now and then; I make no claims to be especially pious; I have a church-rummage faith — the kind that needs patch-
65 ing up every weekend. What faith I have I owe to Owen Meany, a boy I grew up with. It is Owen who made me a believer.

In Sunday school, we developed a form of entertainment based on abusing Owen
70 Meany, who was so small that not only did his feet not touch the floor when he sat in his chair — his knees did not extend to the edge of his seat; therefore, his legs stuck out straight, like the legs of a doll. It was as if
75 Owen Meany had been born without realistic joints.

Owen was so tiny, we loved to pick him up; in truth, we couldn't resist picking him up. We thought it was a miracle: how little he
80 weighed. This was also incongruous because Owen came from a family in the granite business. The Meany Granite Quarry was a big place, the equipment for blasting and

cutting the granite slabs was heavy and
85 dangerous-looking; granite itself is such a
rough, substantial rock. But the only aura of
the granite quarry that clung to Owen was
the granular dust, the gray powder that
sprang off his clothes whenever we lifted
90 him up. He was the color of a gravestone;
light was both absorbed and reflected by his
skin, as with a pearl, so that he appeared
translucent at times—especially at his temples, where his blue veins showed through his
95 skin (as though, in addition to his extraordinary size, there were other evidence that he
was born too soon).

His vocal cords had not developed fully, or
else his voice had been injured by the rock
100 dust of his family's business. Maybe he had
larynx damage, or a destroyed trachea; maybe
he'd been hit in the throat by a chunk of
granite. To be heard at all, Owen had to shout
through his nose.

105 Yet he was dear to us—"a little doll," the
girls called him, while he squirmed to get
away from them; and from all of us.

I don't remember how our game of lifting
Owen began.

110 This was Christ Church, the Episcopal
Church of Gravesend, New Hampshire. Our
Sunday school teacher was a strained,
unhappy-looking woman named Mrs. Walker.
We thought this name suited her because
115 her method of teaching involved a lot of
walking out of class. Mrs. Walker would read
us an instructive passage from the Bible. She
would then ask us to think seriously about
what we had heard—"Silently and seriously,
120 that's how I want you to think!" she would
say. "I'm going to leave you alone with your
thoughts, now," she would tell us ominously—
as if our thoughts were capable of driving us
over the edge. "I want you to think very hard,"
125 Mrs. Walker would say. Then she'd walk out

on us. I think she was a smoker, and she
couldn't allow herself to smoke in front of
us. "When I come back," she'd say, "we'll talk
about it."

130 By the time she came back, of course, we'd
forgotten everything about whatever it
was—because as soon as she left the room,
we would fool around with a frenzy. Because
being alone with our thoughts was no fun,
135 we would pick up Owen Meany and pass him
back and forth, overhead. We managed this
while remaining seated in our chairs—that
was the challenge of the game. Someone—I
forget who started it—would get up, seize
140 Owen, sit back down with him, pass him to
the next person, who would pass him on,
and so forth. The girls were included in this
game; some of the girls were the most
enthusiastic about it. Everyone could lift up
145 Owen. We were very careful; we never
dropped him. His shirt might become a little
rumpled. His necktie was so long, Owen
tucked it into his trousers—or else it would
have hung to his knees—and his necktie
150 often came untucked; sometimes his change
would fall out (in our faces). We always gave
him his money back.

If he had his baseball cards with him,
they, too, would fall out of his pockets. This
155 made him cross because the cards were
alphabetized, or ordered under another
system—all the infielders together, maybe.
We didn't know what the system was, but
obviously Owen had a system, because when
160 Mrs. Walker came back to the room—when
Owen returned to his chair and we passed
his nickels and dimes and his baseball cards
back to him—he would sit shuffling through
the cards with a grim, silent fury.

165 He was not a good baseball player, but he
did have a very small strike zone and as a
consequence he was often used as a pinch

hitter—not because he ever hit the ball with any authority (in fact, he was instructed never to swing at the ball), but because he could be relied upon to earn a walk, a base on balls. In Little League games he resented this exploitation and once refused to come to bat unless he was allowed to swing at the pitches. But there was no bat small enough for him to swing that didn't hurl his tiny body after it—that didn't thump him on the back and knock him out of the batter's box and flat upon the ground. So, after the humiliation of swinging at a few pitches, and missing them, and whacking himself off his feet, Owen Meany selected that other humiliation of standing motionless and crouched at home plate while the pitcher aimed the ball at Owen's strike zone—and missed it, almost every time.

Yet Owen loved his baseball cards—and, for some reason, he clearly loved the game of baseball itself, although the game was cruel to him. Opposing pitchers would threaten him. They'd tell him that if he didn't swing at their pitches, they'd hit him with the ball. "Your head's bigger than your strike zone, pal," one pitcher told him. So Owen Meany made his way to first base after being struck by pitches, too.

Once on base, he was a star. No one could run the bases like Owen. If our team could stay at bat long enough, Owen Meany could steal home. He was used as a pinch runner in the late innings, too; pinch runner and pinch hitter Meany—pinch walker Meany, we called him. In the field, he was hopeless. He was afraid of the ball; he shut his eyes when it came anywhere near him. And if by some miracle he managed to catch it, he couldn't throw it; his hand was too small to get a good grip. But he was no ordinary complainer; if he was self-pitying,

his voice was so original in its expression of complaint that he managed to make whining lovable.

In Sunday school, when we held Owen up in the air—especially, in the air!—he protested so uniquely. We tortured him, I think, in order to hear his voice; I used to think his voice came from another planet. Now I'm convinced it was a voice not entirely of this world.

"PUT ME DOWN!" he would say in a strangled, emphatic falsetto. "CUT IT OUT! I DON'T WANT TO DO THIS ANYMORE. ENOUGH IS ENOUGH. PUT ME DOWN! YOU ASSHOLES!"

But we just passed him around and around. He grew more fatalistic about it, each time. His body was rigid; he wouldn't struggle. Once we had him in the air, he folded his arms defiantly on his chest; he scowled at the ceiling. Sometimes Owen grabbed hold of his chair the instant Mrs. Walker left the room; he'd cling like a bird to a swing in its cage, but he was easy to dislodge because he was ticklish. A girl named Sukey Swift was especially deft at tickling Owen; instantly, his arms and legs would stick straight out and we'd have him up in the air again.

"NO TICKLING!" he'd say, but the rules to this game were our rules. We never listened to Owen.

Inevitably, Mrs. Walker would return to the room when Owen was in the air. Given the biblical nature of her instructions to us: "to think very hard . . ." she might have imagined that by a supreme act of our combined and hardest thoughts we had succeeded in levitating Owen Meany. She might have had the wit to suspect that Owen was reaching toward heaven as a direct result of leaving us alone with our thoughts.

But Mrs. Walker's response was always the same—brutish and unimaginative and incredibly dense. "Owen!" she would snap.

255 "Owen Meany, you get back to your seat! You get down from up there!"

What could Mrs. Walker teach us about the Bible if she was stupid enough to think that Owen Meany had put himself up in

260 the air?

Owen was always dignified about it. He never said, "THEY DID IT! THEY ALWAYS DO IT! THEY PICK ME UP AND LOSE MY MONEY AND MESS UP MY BASEBALL CARDS—AND

265 THEY NEVER PUT ME DOWN WHEN I ASK THEM TO! WHAT DO YOU THINK, THAT I FLEW UP HERE?"

But although Owen would complain to us, he would never complain about us. If he was

270 occasionally capable of being a stoic in the air, he was always a stoic when Mrs. Walker accused him of childish behavior. He would never accuse us. Owen was no rat. As vividly as any number of the stories in the Bible,

275 Owen Meany showed us what a martyr was.

It appeared there were no hard feelings. Although we saved our most ritualized attacks on him for Sunday school, we also lifted him up at other times—more spon-

280 taneously. Once someone hooked him by his collar to a coat tree in the elementary-school auditorium; even then, even there, Owen didn't struggle. He dangled silently, and waited for someone to unhook him

285 and put him down. And after gym class, someone hung him in his locker and shut the door. "NOT FUNNY! NOT FUNNY!" he called, and called, until someone must have agreed with him and freed him from

290 the company of his jockstrap—the size of a slingshot.

How could I have known that Owen was a hero?

Let me say at the outset that I was a

295 Wheelwright—that was the family name that counted in our town: the Wheelwrights. And Wheelwrights were not inclined toward sympathy to Meanys. We were a matriarchal family because my grandfather died when he

300 was a young man and left my grandmother to carry on, which she managed rather grandly. I am descended from John Adams on my grandmother's side (her maiden name was Bates, and her family came to America

305 on the Mayflower); yet, in our town, it was my grandfather's name that had the clout, and my grandmother wielded her married name with such a sure sense of self-possession that she might as well have been a Wheel-

310 wright and an Adams and a Bates.

Her Christian name was Harriet, but she was Mrs. Wheelwright to almost everyone— certainly to everyone in Owen Meany's family. I think that Grandmother's final

315 vision of anyone named Meany would have been George Meany—the labor man, the cigar smoker. The combination of unions and cigars did not sit well with Harriet Wheelwright. (To my knowledge, George

320 Meany is not related to the Meany family from my town.)

I grew up in Gravesend, New Hampshire; we didn't have any unions there—a few cigar smokers, but no union men. The town

325 where I was born was purchased from an Indian sagamore in 1638 by the Rev. John Wheelwright, after whom I was named. In New England, the Indian chiefs and higher-ups were called sagamores; although, by the

330 time I was a boy, the only sagamore I knew was a neighbor's dog—a male Labrador retriever named Sagamore (not, I think, for his Indian ancestry but because of his owner's ignorance). Sagamore's owner, our neighbor,

335 Mr. Fish, always told me that his dog was

named for a lake where he spent his summers swimming—"when I was a youth,"
Mr. Fish would say. Poor Mr. Fish: he didn't
know that the lake was named after Indian
340 chiefs and higher-ups—and that naming a
stupid Labrador retriever "Sagamore" was certain to cause some unholy offense. As you
shall see, it did.

But Americans are not great historians,
345 and so, for years—educated by my neighbor—
I thought that sagamore was an Indian word
for lake. The canine Sagamore was killed by a
diaper truck, and I now believe that the gods
of those troubled waters of that much-
350 abused lake were responsible. It would be a
better story, I think, if Mr. Fish had been
killed by the diaper truck—but every study
of the gods, of everyone's gods, is a revelation
of vengeance toward the innocent. (This is a
355 part of my particular faith that meets with
opposition from my Congregationalist and
Episcopalian and Anglican friends.)

As for my ancestor John Wheelwright, he
landed in Boston in 1636, only two years
360 before he bought our town. He was from
Lincolnshire, England—the hamlet of
Saleby—and nobody knows why he named
our town Gravesend. He had no known contact with the British Gravesend, although
365 that is surely where the name of our town
came from. Wheelwright was a Cambridge
graduate; he'd played foot-ball with Oliver
Cromwell—whose estimation of Wheelwright (as a football player) was both wor-
370 shipful and paranoid. Oliver Cromwell
believed that Wheelwright was a vicious,
even a dirty player, who had perfected the
art of tripping his opponents and then falling
on them. Gravesend (the British Gravesend)
375 is in Kent—a fair distance from Wheelwright's
stamping ground. Perhaps he had a friend
from there—maybe it was a friend who

had wanted to make the trip to America
with Wheelwright, but who hadn't been
380 able to leave England, or had died on the
voyage.

According to Wall's History of Gravesend,
N.H., the Rev. John Wheelwright had been a
good minister of the English church until he
385 began to "question the authority of certain
dogmas"; he became a Puritan, and was
thereafter "silenced by the ecclesiastical
powers, for nonconformity." I feel that my
own religious confusion, and stubbornness,
390 owe much to my ancestor, who suffered not
only the criticisms of the English church
before he left for the new world; once he
arrived, he ran afoul of his fellow Puritans
in Boston. Together with the famous Mrs.
395 Hutchinson, the Rev. Mr. Wheelwright was
banished from the Massachusetts Bay
Colony for disturbing "the civil peace"; in
truth, he did nothing more seditious than
offer some heterodox opinions regarding
400 the location of the Holy Ghost—but
Massachusetts judged him harshly. He was
deprived of his weapons; and with his
family and several of his bravest adherents,
he sailed north from Boston to Great Bay,
405 where he must have passed by two earlier
New Hampshire outposts—what was then
called Strawbery Banke, at the mouth of
the Pascataqua (now Portsmouth), and the
settlement in Dover.
410 Wheelwright followed the Squamscott
River out of Great Bay; he went as far
as the falls where the freshwater river
met the saltwater river. The forest would
have been dense then; the Indians would
415 have showed him how good the fishing
was. According to Wall's History of
Gravesend, there were "tracts of natural
meadow" and "marshes bordering upon
the tidewater."

420   The local sagamore's name was
Watahantowet; instead of his signature, he
made his mark upon the deed in the form of
his totem—an armless man. Later, there was
some dispute—not very interesting—regarding
425 the Indian deed, and more interesting speculation regarding why Watahantowet's totem
was an armless man. Some said it was how it
made the sagamore feel to give up all that
land—to have his arms cut off—and others
430 pointed out that earlier "marks" made by
Watahantowet revealed that the figure,
although armless, held a feather in his
mouth; this was said to indicate the sagamore's frustration at being unable to write.
435 But in several other versions of the totem
ascribed to Watahantowet, the figure has a
tomahawk in its mouth and looks completely crazy—or else, he is making a gesture
toward peace: no arms, tomahawk in mouth;
440 together, perhaps, they are meant to signify
that Watahantowet does not fight. As for the
settlement of the disputed deed, you can be
sure the Indians were not the beneficiaries of
the resolution to that difference of opinion.
445   And later still, our town fell under Massachusetts authority—which may, to this day,
explain why residents of Gravesend detest
people from Massachusetts. Mr. Wheelwright
would move to Maine. He was eighty when
450 he spoke at Harvard, seeking contributions
to rebuild a part of the college destroyed by a
fire—demonstrating that he bore the citizens of Massachusetts less of a grudge than
anyone else from Gravesend would bear
455 them. Wheelwright died in Salisbury,
Massachusetts, where he was the spiritual
leader of the church, when he was almost
ninety.
    But listen to the names of Gravesend's
460 founding fathers: you will not hear a Meany
among them.

Barlow
Blackwell
Cole
465 Copeland
Crawley
Dearborn
Hilton
Hutchinson
470 Littlefield
Read
Rishworth
Smart
Smith
475 Walker
Wardell
Wentworth
Wheelwright

    I doubt it's because she was a Wheelwright
480 that my mother never gave up her maiden
name; I think my mother's pride was independent of her Wheelwright ancestry, and that she
would have kept her maiden name if she'd
been born a Meany. And I never suffered in
485 those years that I had her name; I was little
Johnny Wheelwright, father unknown, and—at
the time—that was okay with me. I never complained. One day, I always thought, she would
tell me about it—when I was old enough to
490 know the story. It was, apparently, the kind of
story you had to be "old enough" to hear. It
wasn't until she died—without a word to me
concerning who my father was—that I felt I'd
been cheated out of information I had a right
495 to know; it was only after her death that I felt
the slightest anger toward her. Even if my
father's identity and his story were painful to
my mother—even if their relationship had
been so sordid that any revelation of it would
500 shed a continuous, unfavorable light upon both
my parents—wasn't my mother being selfish
not to tell me anything about my father?

Of course, as Owen Meany pointed out to me, I was only eleven when she died, and my
505 mother was only thirty; she probably thought she had a lot of time left to tell me the story. She didn't know she was going to die, as Owen Meany put it.

Owen and I were throwing rocks in the
510 Squamscott, the saltwater river, the tidal river—or, rather, I was throwing rocks in the river; Owen's rocks were landing in the mud flats because the tide was out and the water was too far away for Owen Meany's little,
515 weak arm. Our throwing had disturbed the herring gulls who'd been pecking in the mud, and the gulls had moved into the marsh grass on the opposite shore of the Squamscott.

It was a hot, muggy, summer day; the low-
520 tide smell of the mud flats was more brinish and morbid than usual. Owen Meany told me that my father would know that my mother was dead, and that—when I was old enough— he would identify himself to me.

525 "If he's alive," I said, still throwing rocks. "If he's alive and if he cares that he's my father—if he even knows he's my father."

And although I didn't believe him that day, that was the day Owen Meany began his

530 lengthy contribution to my belief in God. Owen was throwing smaller and smaller rocks, but he still couldn't reach the water; there was a certain small satisfaction to the sound the rocks made when they struck the
535 mud flats, but the water was more satisfying than the mud in every way. And almost casu- ally, with a confidence that stood in surpris- ing and unreasonable juxtaposition to his tiny size, Owen Meany told me that he was
540 sure my father was alive, that he was sure my father knew he was my father, and that God knew who my father was; even if my father never came forth to identify himself, Owen told me, God would identify him for
545 me. "YOUR DAD CAN HIDE FROM YOU," Owen said, "BUT HE CAN'T HIDE FROM GOD."

And with that announcement, Owen Meany grunted as he released a stone that reached the water. We were both surprised;
550 it was the last rock either of us threw that day, and we stood watching the circle of ripples extending from the point of entry until even the gulls were assured we had stopped our disturbance of their universe,
555 and they returned to our side of the Squamscott.

FIGURATIVE LANGUAGE: Word Choice, Imagery, and Symbols

1. Irving includes religious **symbols**. Choose an example and explain what it might suggest about religion and faith.

2. Which objects or events in the childhood of the boys are **symbolic**? Choose one and consider what it reveals.

3. John, the protagonist, focuses on Owen's size and his seeming weightlessness. What is the **connotation** of weightlessness beyond Owen's physical size? How does this **symbolize** something more than size?

4. John says, "Owen Meany began his lengthy contribution to my belief in God." Why do you think John says this? How do the **images** and details relate to the religious **symbols** and contribute to John's perspective throughout the chapter?

IDEAS IN LITERATURE
Repression and Conformity

The Victorian period in British history and literature refers to the years of Queen Victoria's long reign (1837–1901). During this era, Britain reached the height of its imperial power. Its global territorial possessions — colonies and protectorates — were so large that it became "the empire on which the sun never sets." At home, the pace of social and economic transformation accelerated: the Industrial Revolution had changed a rural, agricultural society into a predominantly urban society. New technologies — photography, railroads, the telegraph — led to optimism about progress and social improvement. A rising middle class of urban professionals and merchants began wielding power financially, socially, and politically. They also led a shift in values. As inherited wealth and privilege became less important, Victorians elevated the importance of work, thrift, and the deferral of gratification. These values were as much a matter of morality as they were economics. For many Victorian social reformers, addressing poverty and other societal problems meant encouraging the poor to conform to "respectable" middle-class norms.

While the stereotype of the smug, prudish Victorian is an exaggeration, it also contains an element of truth — especially with regard to women and gender roles. Moreover, the Protestant work ethic required repression: the inhibition of immediate desires and animal instincts. The question of humanity's position above — or among — other animals was vital at the time. The British naturalist Charles Darwin (1809–1882) published his revolutionary *The Origin of Species* (1859), which provided the foundations of evolutionary biology. It also challenged traditional views of biblical creation and the place of humans in the natural world. At the same time, the Victorian era saw the emergence of psychology as a field of

IDEA BANK
Change
Class
Conformity
Corruption
Evolution
Imperialism
Incongruity
Indulgence
Materialism
Passion
Poverty
Progress
Propriety
Prosperity
Psychology
Reform
Repression
Social Norms
Uncertainty
Wealth

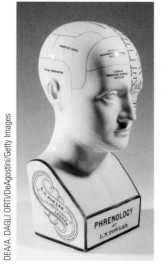

◀ Phrenology is based on the pseudoscientific belief that the shape of the skull indicates mental faculties and character traits. Scientists during the eighteenth and nineteenth centuries would observe, touch, and measure the skull to determine an individual's psychological attributes.

While phrenology is now discredited, it is part of our long history of trying to understand the human mind. For example, psychology is the study of behavior and the mental processes that create our thoughts, feelings, and desires. Neuroscience and cognitive science delve deeper into the brain, the mind, and the various elements that make up cognition. What do we still have to learn about the brain?

DEA/A. DAGLI ORTI/DeAgostini/Getty Images

study. Herbert Spencer (1820–1903) published *Principles of Psychology* (1855), one of the books that laid the groundwork for the Austrian neurologist and psychoanalyst Sigmund Freud (1856–1939). While Spencer's rudimentary approach was tied to pseudoscientific ideas like *phrenology* (the belief that the character traits of individuals could be determined by measuring the contours of their skulls), Freud helped establish psychology and psychiatry as both academic disciplines and clinical practices. His three-part model of the human psyche based on the *id*, the *ego*, and the *superego* remains a common framework for thinking about human cognition and behavior. The id represents our primal, instinctive desires; the superego represents our internalization of civilized behavior, manners, and laws. Mediating between these two agents is the ego, which must balance the desires of the id with the conscientiousness of the superego and the demands of reality. In other words, Freud challenged the very idea that we have unified and autonomous "selves."

The two readings that follow are Gothic tales: stories of mystery, horror, psychology, instability, and the grotesque that unfold in gloomy settings. The protagonist of each novel is an ambitious scientist who pushes the limits of human knowledge and power. Indeed, Victor Frankenstein and Dr. Henry Jekyll refuse to repress their desires and conform to conventional expectations. Both stories also offer a glimpse into nineteenth-century fears about science, progress, and new technologies. Both use multiple points of view in their narratives. Most of all, Mary Shelley's *Frankenstein; or, the Modern Prometheus* (p. 768) and Robert Louis Stevenson's *The Strange Case of Dr. Jekyll and Mr. Hyde* (p. 723) explore universal questions: What is a "human being"? What does it mean to be human? How do we reconcile contradictory aspects of ourselves? Should we place limits on scientific discovery? Contemporary science fiction, horror, and related genres often ask the same questions. We still use them to experience sublimity, fear, and catharsis. And as the Victorians did, we often confront our darkest fears and preoccupations through the vicarious experience of consuming fiction.

Alice's Adventures in Wonderland (1865) ▶ is a children's novel by Lewis Carroll. The story takes a young girl named Alice on a journey down a rabbit hole into a fantasy world of anthropomorphic animals. The story plays with logic through whimsical characters, imagery, and wordplay.

What is so fascinating about *Alice in Wonderland*? Why are we engaged by imaginative journeys and humanlike animals? Why does this Victorian classic continue to resonate with readers today?

Photo 12/Alamy

The Strange Case of Dr. Jekyll and Mr. Hyde
Robert L. Stevenson

THE TEXT IN CONTEXT

Scottish writer Robert Louis Stephenson (1850–1894) was a prolific and popular Victorian-era novelist, poet, essayist, and travel writer. His most well-known works include *Treasure Island* (1883), *Kidnapped* (1886), and *The Strange Case of Dr. Jekyll and Mr. Hyde* (1886). The latter novella, included here, combines elements of detective fiction, religious allegory, and Gothic horror. It is also a highly symbolic tale about divided identities, internal struggles, and the perils of scientific arrogance. The story has been retold many times in film, on stage, and even in song. Today, the term "Jekyll and Hyde" remains a common descriptive allusion for characterizing a person who displays incongruous or opposing personality traits.

The Strange Case of Dr. Jekyll and Mr. Hyde

STORY OF THE DOOR

Mr. Utterson the lawyer was a man of a rugged countenance that was never lighted by a smile; cold, scanty and embarrassed in discourse; backward in sentiment; lean, long,
5 dusty, dreary and yet somehow lovable. At friendly meetings, and when the wine was to his taste, something eminently human beaconed from his eye; something indeed which never found its way into his talk, but which
10 spoke not only in these silent symbols of the after-dinner face, but more often and loudly in the acts of his life. He was austere with himself; drank gin when he was alone, to mortify a taste for vintages; and though he
15 enjoyed the theatre, had not crossed the doors of one for twenty years. But he had an approved tolerance for others; sometimes wondering, almost with envy, at the high pressure of spirits involved in their mis-
20 deeds; and in any extremity inclined to help rather than to reprove. "I incline to Cain's heresy," he used to say quaintly: "I let my brother go to the devil in his own way." In this character, it was frequently his fortune
25 to be the last reputable acquaintance and the last good influence in the lives of downgoing men. And to such as these, so long as they came about his chambers, he never marked a shade of change in his demeanour.
30   No doubt the feat was easy to Mr. Utterson; for he was undemonstrative at the best, and even his friendship seemed to be founded in a similar catholicity of good-nature. It is the mark of a modest man to accept his
35 friendly circle ready-made from the hands of opportunity; and that was the lawyer's way. His friends were those of his own blood or

those whom he had known the longest; his affections, like ivy, were the growth of time,
40 they implied no aptness in the object. Hence, no doubt the bond that united him to Mr. Richard Enfield, his distant kinsman, the well-known man about town. It was a nut to crack for many, what these two could see in
45 each other, or what subject they could find in common. It was reported by those who encountered them in their Sunday walks, that they said nothing, looked singularly dull and would hail with obvious relief the
50 appearance of a friend. For all that, the two men put the greatest store by these excursions, counted them the chief jewel of each week, and not only set aside occasions of pleasure, but even resisted the calls of
55 business, that they might enjoy them uninterrupted.

It chanced on one of these rambles that their way led them down a by-street in a busy quarter of London. The street was small
60 and what is called quiet, but it drove a thriving trade on the weekdays. The inhabitants were all doing well, it seemed and all emulously hoping to do better still, and laying out the surplus of their grains in coquetry; so
65 that the shop fronts stood along that thoroughfare with an air of invitation, like rows of smiling saleswomen. Even on Sunday, when it veiled its more florid charms and lay comparatively empty of passage, the street
70 shone out in contrast to its dingy neighbourhood, like a fire in a forest; and with its freshly painted shutters, well-polished brasses, and general cleanliness and gaiety of note, instantly caught and pleased the eye
75 of the passenger.

Two doors from one corner, on the left hand going east the line was broken by the entry of a court; and just at that point a certain sinister block of building thrust forward
80 its gable on the street. It was two storeys high; showed no window, nothing but a door on the lower storey and a blind forehead of discoloured wall on the upper; and bore in every feature, the marks of prolonged and
85 sordid negligence. The door, which was equipped with neither bell nor knocker, was blistered and distained. Tramps slouched into the recess and struck matches on the panels; children kept shop upon the steps;
90 the schoolboy had tried his knife on the mouldings; and for close on a generation, no one had appeared to drive away these random visitors or to repair their ravages.

Mr. Enfield and the lawyer were on the
95 other side of the by-street; but when they came abreast of the entry, the former lifted up his cane and pointed.

"Did you ever remark that door?" he asked; and when his companion had replied
100 in the affirmative, "It is connected in my mind," added he, "with a very odd story."

"Indeed?" said Mr. Utterson, with a slight change of voice, "and what was that?"

"Well, it was this way," returned Mr.
105 Enfield: "I was coming home from some place at the end of the world, about three o'clock of a black winter morning, and my way lay through a part of town where there was literally nothing to be seen but lamps.
110 Street after street and all the folks asleep— street after street, all lighted up as if for a procession and all as empty as a church—till at last I got into that state of mind when a man listens and listens and begins to long
115 for the sight of a policeman. All at once, I saw two figures: one a little man who was stumping along eastward at a good walk, and the other a girl of maybe eight or ten who was running as hard as she was able down a
120 cross street. Well, sir, the two ran into one another naturally enough at the corner; and

then came the horrible part of the thing; for the man trampled calmly over the child's body and left her screaming on the ground. It sounds nothing to hear, but it was hellish to see. It wasn't like a man; it was like some damned Juggernaut. I gave a few halloa, took to my heels, collared my gentleman, and brought him back to where there was already quite a group about the screaming child. He was perfectly cool and made no resistance, but gave me one look, so ugly that it brought out the sweat on me like running. The people who had turned out were the girl's own family; and pretty soon, the doctor, for whom she had been sent put in his appearance. Well, the child was not much the worse, more frightened, according to the sawbones; and there you might have supposed would be an end to it. But there was one curious circumstance. I had taken a loathing to my gentleman at first sight. So had the child's family, which was only natural. But the doctor's case was what struck me. He was the usual cut and dry apothecary, of no particular age and colour, with a strong Edinburgh accent and about as emotional as a bagpipe. Well, sir, he was like the rest of us; every time he looked at my prisoner, I saw that sawbones turn sick and white with the desire to kill him. I knew what was in his mind, just as he knew what was in mine; and killing being out of the question, we did the next best. We told the man we could and would make such a scandal out of this as should make his name stink from one end of London to the other. If he had any friends or any credit, we undertook that he should lose them. And all the time, as we were pitching it in red hot, we were keeping the women off him as best we could for they were as wild as harpies. I never saw a circle of such hateful faces; and there was the man in the middle,

with a kind of black sneering coolness—frightened too, I could see that—but carrying it off, sir, really like Satan. 'If you choose to make capital out of this accident,' said he, 'I am naturally helpless. No gentleman but wishes to avoid a scene,' says he. 'Name your figure.' Well, we screwed him up to a hundred pounds for the child's family; he would have clearly liked to stick out; but there was something about the lot of us that meant mischief, and at last he struck. The next thing was to get the money; and where do you think he carried us but to that place with the door?—whipped out a key, went in, and presently came back with the matter of ten pounds in gold and a cheque for the balance on Coutts's, drawn payable to bearer and signed with a name that I can't mention, though it's one of the points of my story, but it was a name at least very well known and often printed. The figure was stiff; but the signature was good for more than that if it was only genuine. I took the liberty of pointing out to my gentleman that the whole business looked apocryphal, and that a man does not, in real life, walk into a cellar door at four in the morning and come out with another man's cheque for close upon a hundred pounds. But he was quite easy and sneering. 'Set your mind at rest,' says he, 'I will stay with you till the banks open and cash the cheque myself.' So we all set off, the doctor, and the child's father, and our friend and myself, and passed the rest of the night in my chambers; and next day, when we had breakfasted, went in a body to the bank. I gave in the cheque myself, and said I had every reason to believe it was a forgery. Not a bit of it. The cheque was genuine."

"Tut-tut!" said Mr. Utterson.

"I see you feel as I do," said Mr. Enfield. "Yes, it's a bad story. For my man was a fellow that nobody could have to do with, a really damnable man; and the person that drew the cheque is the very pink of the pro-prieties, celebrated too, and (what makes it worse) one of your fellows who do what they call good. Blackmail, I suppose; an honest man paying through the nose for some of the capers of his youth. Black Mail House is what I call the place with the door, in conse-quence. Though even that, you know, is far from explaining all," he added, and with the words fell into a vein of musing.

From this he was recalled by Mr. Utterson asking rather suddenly: "And you don't know if the drawer of the cheque lives there?"

"A likely place, isn't it?" returned Mr. Enfield. "But I happen to have noticed his address; he lives in some square or other."

"And you never asked about the—place with the door?" said Mr. Utterson.

"No, sir; I had a delicacy," was the reply. "I feel very strongly about putting questions; it partakes too much of the style of the day of judgment. You start a question, and it's like starting a stone. You sit quietly on the top of a hill; and away the stone goes, starting oth-ers; and presently some bland old bird (the last you would have thought of) is knocked on the head in his own back garden and the family have to change their name. No sir, I make it a rule of mine: the more it looks like Queer Street, the less I ask."

"A very good rule, too," said the lawyer.

"But I have studied the place for myself," continued Mr. Enfield. "It seems scarcely a house. There is no other door, and nobody goes in or out of that one but, once in a great while, the gentleman of my adventure. There are three windows looking on the court on the first floor; none below; the windows are always shut but they're clean. And then there is a chimney which is generally smoking;

so somebody must live there. And yet it's not so sure; for the buildings are so packed together about the court, that it's hard to say where one ends and another begins."

The pair walked on again for a while in silence; and then "Enfield," said Mr. Utterson, "that's a good rule of yours."

"Yes, I think it is," returned Enfield.

"But for all that," continued the lawyer, "there's one point I want to ask. I want to ask the name of that man who walked over the child."

"Well," said Mr. Enfield, "I can't see what harm it would do. It was a man of the name of Hyde."

"Hm," said Mr. Utterson. "What sort of a man is he to see?"

"He is not easy to describe. There is something wrong with his appearance; something displeasing, something down-right detestable. I never saw a man I so dis-liked, and yet I scarce know why. He must be deformed somewhere; he gives a strong feeling of deformity, although I couldn't specify the point. He's an extraordinary looking man, and yet I really can name nothing out of the way. No, sir; I can make no hand of it; I can't describe him. And it's not want of memory; for I declare I can see him this moment."

Mr. Utterson again walked some way in silence and obviously under a weight of con-sideration. "You are sure he used a key?" he inquired at last.

"My dear sir . . ." began Enfield, surprised out of himself.

"Yes, I know," said Utterson; "I know it must seem strange. The fact is, if I do not ask you the name of the other party, it is because I know it already. You see, Richard, your tale has gone home. If you have been inexact in any point you had better correct it."

290 "I think you might have warned me," returned the other with a touch of sullenness. "But I have been pedantically exact, as you call it. The fellow had a key; and what's more, he has it still. I saw him use it not a 295 week ago."

Mr. Utterson sighed deeply but said never a word; and the young man presently resumed. "Here is another lesson to say nothing," said he. "I am ashamed of my long tongue. Let 300 us make a bargain never to refer to this again."

"With all my heart," said the lawyer. "I shake hands on that, Richard."

SEARCH FOR MR. HYDE

That evening Mr. Utterson came home to his 305 bachelor house in sombre spirits and sat down to dinner without relish. It was his custom of a Sunday, when this meal was over, to sit close by the fire, a volume of some dry divinity on his reading desk, until the 310 clock of the neighbouring church rang out the hour of twelve, when he would go soberly and gratefully to bed. On this night however, as soon as the cloth was taken away, he took up a candle and went into his 315 business room. There he opened his safe, took from the most private part of it a document endorsed on the envelope as Dr. Jekyll's Will and sat down with a clouded brow to study its contents. The will was holograph, 320 for Mr. Utterson though he took charge of it now that it was made, had refused to lend the least assistance in the making of it; it provided not only that, in case of the decease of Henry Jekyll, M.D., D.C.L., L.L.D., F.R.S., etc., 325 all his possessions were to pass into the hands of his "friend and benefactor Edward Hyde," but that in case of Dr. Jekyll's "disappearance or unexplained absence for any period exceeding three calendar months,"

330 the said Edward Hyde should step into the said Henry Jekyll's shoes without further delay and free from any burthen or obligation beyond the payment of a few small sums to the members of the doctor's house- 335 hold. This document had long been the lawyer's eyesore. It offended him both as a lawyer and as a lover of the sane and customary sides of life, to whom the fanciful was the immodest. And hitherto it was his 340 ignorance of Mr. Hyde that had swelled his indignation; now, by a sudden turn, it was his knowledge. It was already bad enough when the name was but a name of which he could learn no more. It was worse when it 345 began to be clothed upon with detestable attributes; and out of the shifting, insubstantial mists that had so long baffled his eye, there leaped up the sudden, definite presentment of a fiend.

350 "I thought it was madness," he said, as he replaced the obnoxious paper in the safe, "and now I begin to fear it is disgrace."

With that he blew out his candle, put on a greatcoat, and set forth in the direction of 355 Cavendish Square, that citadel of medicine, where his friend, the great Dr. Lanyon, had his house and received his crowding patients. "If anyone knows, it will be Lanyon," he had thought.

360 The solemn butler knew and welcomed him; he was subjected to no stage of delay, but ushered direct from the door to the dining-room where Dr. Lanyon sat alone over his wine. This was a hearty, healthy, dapper, 365 red-faced gentleman, with a shock of hair prematurely white, and a boisterous and decided manner. At sight of Mr. Utterson, he sprang up from his chair and welcomed him with both hands. The geniality, as was the 370 way of the man, was somewhat theatrical to the eye; but it reposed on genuine feeling.

For these two were old friends, old mates both at school and college, both thorough respectors of themselves and of each other,
375 and what does not always follow, men who thoroughly enjoyed each other's company.

After a little rambling talk, the lawyer led up to the subject which so disagreeably preoccupied his mind.

380 "I suppose, Lanyon," said he, "you and I must be the two oldest friends that Henry Jekyll has?"

"I wish the friends were younger," chuckled Dr. Lanyon. "But I suppose we are. And
385 what of that? I see little of him now."

"Indeed?" said Utterson. "I thought you had a bond of common interest."

"We had," was the reply. "But it is more than ten years since Henry Jekyll became too
390 fanciful for me. He began to go wrong, wrong in mind; and though of course I continue to take an interest in him for old sake's sake, as they say, I see and I have seen devilish little of the man. Such unscientific balderdash,"
395 added the doctor, flushing suddenly purple, "would have estranged Damon and Pythias."

This little spirit of temper was somewhat of a relief to Mr. Utterson. "They have only differed on some point of science," he thought;
400 and being a man of no scientific passions (except in the matter of conveyancing), he even added: "It is nothing worse than that!" He gave his friend a few seconds to recover his composure, and then approached the
405 question he had come to put. "Did you ever come across a protégé of his—one Hyde?" he asked.

"Hyde?" repeated Lanyon. "No. Never heard of him. Since my time."

410 That was the amount of information that the lawyer carried back with him to the great, dark bed on which he tossed to and fro, until the small hours of the morning began to grow large. It was a night of little
415 ease to his toiling mind, toiling in mere darkness and besieged by questions.

Six o'clock struck on the bells of the church that was so conveniently near to Mr. Utterson's dwelling, and still he was digging
420 at the problem. Hitherto it had touched him on the intellectual side alone; but now his imagination also was engaged, or rather enslaved; and as he lay and tossed in the gross darkness of the night and the cur
425 tained room, Mr. Enfield's tale went by before his mind in a scroll of lighted pictures. He would be aware of the great field of lamps of a nocturnal city; then of the figure of a man walking swiftly; then of a child running from
430 the doctor's; and then these met, and that human Juggernaut trod the child down and passed on regardless of her screams. Or else he would see a room in a rich house, where his friend lay asleep, dreaming and smiling
435 at his dreams; and then the door of that room would be opened, the curtains of the bed plucked apart, the sleeper recalled, and lo! There would stand by his side a figure to whom power was given, and even at that
440 dead hour, he must rise and do its bidding. The figure in these two phases haunted the lawyer all night; and if at any time he dozed over, it was but to see it glide more stealthily through sleeping houses, or move the more
445 swiftly and still the more swiftly, even to dizziness, through wider labyrinths of lamplighted city, and at every street corner crush a child and leave her screaming. And still the figure had no face by which he might know
450 it; even in his dreams, it had no face, or one that baffled him and melted before his eyes; and thus it was that there sprang up and grew apace in the lawyer's mind a singularly strong, almost an inordinate, curiosity to
455 behold the features of the real Mr. Hyde. If he

could but once set eyes on him, he thought the mystery would lighten and perhaps roll altogether away, as was the habit of mysterious things when well examined. He might
460 see a reason for his friend's strange preference or bondage (call it which you please) and even for the startling clause of the will. At least it would be a face worth seeing: the face of a man who was without bowels of
465 mercy: a face which had but to show itself to raise up, in the mind of the unimpressionable Enfield, a spirit of enduring hatred.

From that time forward, Mr. Utterson began to haunt the door in the by-street of
470 shops. In the morning before office hours, at noon when business was plenty and time scarce, at night under the face of the fogged city moon, by all lights and at all hours of solitude or concourse, the lawyer was to be
475 found on his chosen post.

"If he be Mr. Hyde," he had thought, "I shall be Mr. Seek."

And at last his patience was rewarded. It was a fine dry night; frost in the air; the
480 streets as clean as a ballroom floor; the lamps, unshaken by any wind, drawing a regular pattern of light and shadow. By ten o'clock, when the shops were closed, the by-street was very solitary and, in spite of
485 the low growl of London from all round, very silent. Small sounds carried far; domestic sounds out of the houses were clearly audible on either side of the roadway; and the rumour of the approach of any
490 passenger preceded him by a long time. Mr. Utterson had been some minutes at his post, when he was aware of an odd light footstep drawing near. In the course of his nightly patrols, he had long grown accus-
495 tomed to the quaint effect with which the footfalls of a single person, while he is still a great way off, suddenly spring out distinct

from the vast hum and clatter of the city. Yet his attention had never before been so
500 sharply and decisively arrested; and it was with a strong, superstitious prevision of success that he withdrew into the entry of the court.

The steps drew swiftly nearer, and
505 swelled out suddenly louder as they turned the end of the street. The lawyer, looking forth from the entry, could soon see what manner of man he had to deal with. He was small and very plainly dressed and the look
510 of him, even at that distance, went somehow strongly against the watcher's inclination. But he made straight for the door, crossing the roadway to save time; and as he came, he drew a key from his pocket like one approaching
515 home.

Mr. Utterson stepped out and touched him on the shoulder as he passed. "Mr. Hyde, I think?"

Mr. Hyde shrank back with a hissing
520 intake of the breath. But his fear was only momentary; and though he did not look the lawyer in the face, he answered coolly enough: "That is my name. What do you want?"

525 "I see you are going in," returned the lawyer. "I am an old friend of Dr. Jekyll's—Mr. Utterson of Gaunt Street—you must have heard of my name; and meeting you so conveniently, I thought you might admit me."

530 "You will not find Dr. Jekyll; he is from home," replied Mr. Hyde, blowing in the key. And then suddenly, but still without looking up, "How did you know me?" he asked.

"On your side," said Mr. Utterson "will you
535 do me a favour?"

"With pleasure," replied the other. "What shall it be?"

"Will you let me see your face?" asked the lawyer.

540 Mr. Hyde appeared to hesitate, and then, as if upon some sudden reflection, fronted about with an air of defiance; and the pair stared at each other pretty fixedly for a few seconds. "Now I shall know you again," said
545 Mr. Utterson. "It may be useful."

"Yes," returned Mr. Hyde, "It is as well we have met; and à propos, you should have my address." And he gave a number of a street in Soho.

550 "Good God!" thought Mr. Utterson, "can he, too, have been thinking of the will?" But he kept his feelings to himself and only grunted in acknowledgment of the address.

"And now," said the other, "how did you
555 know me?"

"By description," was the reply.

"Whose description?"

"We have common friends," said Mr. Utterson.

560 "Common friends," echoed Mr. Hyde, a little hoarsely. "Who are they?"

"Jekyll, for instance," said the lawyer.

"He never told you," cried Mr. Hyde, with a flush of anger. "I did not think you would
565 have lied."

"Come," said Mr. Utterson, "that is not fitting language."

The other snarled aloud into a savage laugh; and the next moment, with extraordi-
570 nary quickness, he had unlocked the door and disappeared into the house.

The lawyer stood awhile when Mr. Hyde had left him, the picture of disquietude. Then he began slowly to mount the street, pausing
575 every step or two and putting his hand to his brow like a man in mental perplexity. The problem he was thus debating as he walked, was one of a class that is rarely solved. Mr. Hyde was pale and dwarfish, he gave an
580 impression of deformity without any nameable malformation, he had a displeasing

smile, he had borne himself to the lawyer with a sort of murderous mixture of timidity and boldness, and he spoke with a husky,
585 whispering and somewhat broken voice; all these were points against him, but not all of these together could explain the hitherto unknown disgust, loathing and fear with which Mr. Utterson regarded him. "There
590 must be something else," said the perplexed gentleman. "There is something more, if I could find a name for it. God bless me, the man seems hardly human! Something troglodytic, shall we say? Or can it be the old
595 story of Dr. Fell? Or is it the mere radiance of a foul soul that thus transpires through, and transfigures, its clay continent? The last, I think; for, O my poor old Harry Jekyll, if ever I read Satan's signature upon a face, it is on
600 that of your new friend."

Round the corner from the by-street, there was a square of ancient, handsome houses, now for the most part decayed from their high estate and let in flats and chambers to all
605 sorts and conditions of men; map-engravers, architects, shady lawyers and the agents of obscure enterprises. One house, however, second from the corner, was still occupied entire; and at the door of this, which wore a great air
610 of wealth and comfort, though it was now plunged in darkness except for the fanlight, Mr. Utterson stopped and knocked. A well-dressed, elderly servant opened the door.

"Is Dr. Jekyll at home, Poole?" asked the
615 lawyer.

"I will see, Mr. Utterson," said Poole, admitting the visitor, as he spoke, into a large, low-roofed, comfortable hall paved with flags, warmed (after the fashion of a
620 country house) by a bright, open fire, and furnished with costly cabinets of oak. "Will you wait here by the fire, sir? Or shall I give you a light in the dining-room?"

"Here, thank you," said the lawyer, and he drew near and leaned on the tall fender. This hall, in which he was now left alone, was a pet fancy of his friend the doctor's; and Utterson himself was wont to speak of it as the pleasantest room in London. But tonight there was a shudder in his blood; the face of Hyde sat heavy on his memory; he felt (what was rare with him) a nausea and distaste of life; and in the gloom of his spirits, he seemed to read a menace in the flickering of the firelight on the polished cabinets and the uneasy starting of the shadow on the roof. He was ashamed of his relief, when Poole presently returned to announce that Dr. Jekyll was gone out.

"I saw Mr. Hyde go in by the old dissecting room, Poole," he said. "Is that right, when Dr. Jekyll is from home?"

"Quite right, Mr. Utterson, sir," replied the servant. "Mr. Hyde has a key."

"Your master seems to repose a great deal of trust in that young man, Poole," resumed the other musingly.

"Yes, sir, he does indeed," said Poole. "We have all orders to obey him."

"I do not think I ever met Mr. Hyde?" asked Utterson.

"O, dear no, sir. He never dines here," replied the butler. "Indeed we see very little of him on this side of the house; he mostly comes and goes by the laboratory."

"Well, good-night, Poole."

"Good-night, Mr. Utterson."

And the lawyer set out homeward with a very heavy heart. "Poor Harry Jekyll," he thought, "my mind misgives me he is in deep waters! He was wild when he was young; a long while ago to be sure; but in the law of God, there is no statute of limitations. Ay, it must be that; the ghost of some old sin, the cancer of some concealed disgrace: punishment coming, pede claudo, years after memory has forgotten and self-love condoned the fault." And the lawyer, scared by the thought, brooded awhile on his own past, groping in all the corners of memory, least by chance some Jack-in-the-Box of an old iniquity should leap to light there. His past was fairly blameless; few men could read the rolls of their life with less apprehension; yet he was humbled to the dust by the many ill things he had done, and raised up again into a sober and fearful gratitude by the many he had come so near to doing yet avoided. And then by a return on his former subject, he conceived a spark of hope. "This Master Hyde, if he were studied," thought he, "must have secrets of his own; black secrets, by the look of him; secrets compared to which poor Jekyll's worst would be like sunshine. Things cannot continue as they are. It turns me cold to think of this creature stealing like a thief to Harry's bedside; poor Harry, what a wakening! And the danger of it; for if this Hyde suspects the existence of the will, he may grow impatient to inherit. Ay, I must put my shoulders to the wheel—if Jekyll will but let me," he added, "if Jekyll will only let me." For once more he saw before his mind's eye, as clear as transparency, the strange clauses of the will.

DR. JEKYLL WAS QUITE AT EASE

A fortnight later, by excellent good fortune, the doctor gave one of his pleasant dinners to some five or six old cronies, all intelligent, reputable men and all judges of good wine; and Mr. Utterson so contrived that he remained behind after the others had departed. This was no new arrangement, but a thing that had befallen many scores of times. Where Utterson was liked, he was liked well. Hosts loved to detain the dry lawyer, when the light-hearted and loose-tongued had already their foot on the

threshold; they liked to sit a while in his unobtrusive company, practising for solitude, sobering their minds in the man's rich silence after the expense and strain of
710 gaiety. To this rule, Dr. Jekyll was no exception; and as he now sat on the opposite side of the fire—a large, well-made, smooth-faced man of fifty, with something of a slyish cast perhaps, but every mark of
715 capacity and kindness—you could see by his looks that he cherished for Mr. Utterson a sincere and warm affection.

"I have been wanting to speak to you, Jekyll," began the latter. "You know that will
720 of yours?"

A close observer might have gathered that the topic was distasteful; but the doctor carried it off gaily. "My poor Utterson," said he, "you are unfortunate in such a client. I never
725 saw a man so distressed as you were by my will; unless it were that hide-bound pedant, Lanyon, at what he called my scientific heresies. O, I know he's a good fellow—you needn't frown—an excellent fellow, and I
730 always mean to see more of him; but a hide-bound pedant for all that; an ignorant, blatant pedant. I was never more disappointed in any man than Lanyon."

"You know I never approved of it," pursued Utterson, ruthlessly disregarding the fresh topic.

"My will? Yes, certainly, I know that," said the doctor, a trifle sharply. "You have told me so."
740 "Well, I tell you so again," continued the lawyer. "I have been learning something of young Hyde."

The large handsome face of Dr. Jekyll grew pale to the very lips, and there came a black-
745 ness about his eyes. "I do not care to hear more," said he. "This is a matter I thought we had agreed to drop."

"What I heard was abominable," said Utterson.
750 "It can make no change. You do not understand my position," returned the doctor, with a certain incoherency of manner. "I am painfully situated, Utterson; my position is a very strange—a very strange one. It is one of
755 those affairs that cannot be mended by talking."

"Jekyll," said Utterson, "you know me: I am a man to be trusted. Make a clean breast of this in confidence; and I make no doubt I can
760 get you out of it."

"My good Utterson," said the doctor, "this is very good of you, this is downright good of you, and I cannot find words to thank you in. I believe you fully; I would trust you before
765 any man alive, ay, before myself, if I could make the choice; but indeed it isn't what you fancy; it is not as bad as that; and just to put your good heart at rest, I will tell you one thing: the moment I choose, I can be rid of
770 Mr. Hyde. I give you my hand upon that; and I thank you again and again; and I will just add one little word, Utterson, that I'm sure you'll take in good part: this is a private matter, and I beg of you to let it sleep."
775 Utterson reflected a little, looking in the fire.

"I have no doubt you are perfectly right," he said at last, getting to his feet.

"Well, but since we have touched upon
780 this business, and for the last time I hope," continued the doctor, "there is one point I should like you to understand. I have really a very great interest in poor Hyde. I know you have seen him; he told me so; and I fear he
785 was rude. But I do sincerely take a great, a very great interest in that young man; and if I am taken away, Utterson, I wish you to promise me that you will bear with him and get his rights for him. I think you would, if

790 you knew all; and it would be a weight off
my mind if you would promise."

"I can't pretend that I shall ever like him,"
said the lawyer.

"I don't ask that," pleaded Jekyll, laying his
795 hand upon the other's arm; "I only ask for
justice; I only ask you to help him for my
sake, when I am no longer here."

Utterson heaved an irrepressible sigh.
"Well," said he, "I promise."

THE CAREW MURDER CASE

800 Nearly a year later, in the month of October,
18—, London was startled by a crime of singular ferocity and rendered all the more
notable by the high position of the victim.
The details were few and startling. A maid
805 servant living alone in a house not far from
the river, had gone upstairs to bed about
eleven. Although a fog rolled over the city in
the small hours, the early part of the night
was cloudless, and the lane, which the
810 maid's window overlooked, was brilliantly lit
by the full moon. It seems she was romanti-
cally given, for she sat down upon her box,
which stood immediately under the window,
and fell into a dream of musing. Never (she
815 used to say, with streaming tears, when she
narrated that experience), never had she felt
more at peace with all men or thought more
kindly of the world. And as she so sat she
became aware of an aged beautiful gentle-
820 man with white hair, drawing near along the
lane; and advancing to meet him, another
and very small gentleman, to whom at first
she paid less attention. When they had come
within speech (which was just under the
825 maid's eyes) the older man bowed and
accosted the other with a very pretty manner
of politeness. It did not seem as if the subject
of his address were of great importance;
indeed, from his pointing, it sometimes

830 appeared as if he were only inquiring his
way; but the moon shone on his face as he
spoke, and the girl was pleased to watch it, it
seemed to breathe such an innocent and old-
world kindness of disposition, yet with
835 something high too, as of a well-founded
self-content. Presently her eye wandered to
the other, and she was surprised to recognise
in him a certain Mr. Hyde, who had once visited her master and for whom she had con-
840 ceived a dislike. He had in his hand a heavy
cane, with which he was trifling; but he
answered never a word, and seemed to listen
with an ill-contained impatience. And then
all of a sudden he broke out in a great flame
845 of anger, stamping with his foot, brandishing
the cane, and carrying on (as the maid
described it) like a madman. The old gentleman took a step back, with the air of one
very much surprised and a trifle hurt; and at
850 that Mr. Hyde broke out of all bounds and
clubbed him to the earth. And next moment,
with ape-like fury, he was trampling his victim under foot and hailing down a storm of
blows, under which the bones were audibly
855 shattered and the body jumped upon the
roadway. At the horror of these sights and
sounds, the maid fainted.

It was two o'clock when she came to herself and called for the police. The murderer
860 was gone long ago; but there lay his victim in
the middle of the lane, incredibly mangled.
The stick with which the deed had been
done, although it was of some rare and very
tough and heavy wood, had broken in the
865 middle under the stress of this insensate
cruelty; and one splintered half had rolled in
the neighbouring gutter—the other, without
doubt, had been carried away by the murderer. A purse and gold watch were found
870 upon the victim: but no cards or papers,
except a sealed and stamped envelope,

which he had been probably carrying to the post, and which bore the name and address of Mr. Utterson.

875 This was brought to the lawyer the next morning, before he was out of bed; and he had no sooner seen it and been told the circumstances, than he shot out a solemn lip. "I shall say nothing till I have seen the body," 880 said he; "this may be very serious. Have the kindness to wait while I dress." And with the same grave countenance he hurried through his breakfast and drove to the police station, whither the body had been carried. As soon 885 as he came into the cell, he nodded.

"Yes," said he, "I recognise him. I am sorry to say that this is Sir Danvers Carew."

"Good God, sir," exclaimed the officer, "is it possible?" And the next moment his eye 890 lighted up with professional ambition. "This will make a deal of noise," he said. "And perhaps you can help us to the man." And he briefly narrated what the maid had seen, and showed the broken stick.

895 Mr. Utterson had already quailed at the name of Hyde; but when the stick was laid before him, he could doubt no longer; broken and battered as it was, he recognised it for one that he had himself presented many 900 years before to Henry Jekyll.

"Is this Mr. Hyde a person of small stature?" he inquired.

"Particularly small and particularly wicked-looking, is what the maid calls him," said the 905 officer.

Mr. Utterson reflected; and then, raising his head, "If you will come with me in my cab," he said, "I think I can take you to his house."

It was by this time about nine in the morn-910 ing, and the first fog of the season. A great chocolate-coloured pall lowered over heaven, but the wind was continually charging and routing these embattled vapours; so that as the cab crawled from street to street, 915 Mr. Utterson beheld a marvelous number of

degrees and hues of twilight; for here it would be dark like the back-end of evening; and there would be a glow of a rich, lurid brown, like the light of some strange conflagration; 920 and here, for a moment, the fog would be quite broken up, and a haggard shaft of daylight would glance in between the swirling wreaths. The dismal quarter of Soho seen under these changing glimpses, with its 925 muddy ways, and slatternly passengers, and its lamps, which had never been extinguished or had been kindled afresh to combat this mournful reinvasion of darkness, seemed, in the lawyer's eyes, like a district of some city 930 in a nightmare. The thoughts of his mind, besides, were of the gloomiest dye; and when he glanced at the companion of his drive, he was conscious of some touch of that terror of the law and the law's officers, which may at 935 times assail the most honest.

As the cab drew up before the address indicated, the fog lifted a little and showed him a dingy street, a gin palace, a low French eating house, a shop for the retail of penny numbers 940 and twopenny salads, many ragged children huddled in the doorways, and many women of many different nationalities passing out, key in hand, to have a morning glass; and the next moment the fog settled down again upon that 945 part, as brown as umber, and cut him off from his blackguardly surroundings. This was the home of Henry Jekyll's favourite; of a man who was heir to a quarter of a million sterling.

An ivory-faced and silvery-haired old 950 woman opened the door. She had an evil face, smoothed by hypocrisy: but her manners were excellent. Yes, she said, this was Mr. Hyde's, but he was not at home; he had been in that night very late, but he had gone 955 away again in less than an hour; there was nothing strange in that; his habits were very irregular, and he was often absent; for instance, it was nearly two months since she had seen him till yesterday.

960 "Very well, then, we wish to see his rooms," said the lawyer; and when the woman began to declare it was impossible, "I had better tell you who this person is," he added. "This is Inspector Newcomen of 965 Scotland Yard."

A flash of odious joy appeared upon the woman's face. "Ah!" said she, "he is in trouble! What has he done?"

Mr. Utterson and the inspector exchanged 970 glances. "He don't seem a very popular character," observed the latter. "And now, my good woman, just let me and this gentleman have a look about us."

In the whole extent of the house, which 975 but for the old woman remained otherwise empty, Mr. Hyde had only used a couple of rooms; but these were furnished with luxury and good taste. A closet was filled with wine; the plate was of silver, the napery ele- 980 gant; a good picture hung upon the walls, a gift (as Utterson supposed) from Henry Jekyll, who was much of a connoisseur; and the carpets were of many plies and agreeable in colour. At this moment, however, the 985 rooms bore every mark of having been recently and hurriedly ransacked; clothes lay about the floor, with their pockets inside out; lock-fast drawers stood open; and on

the hearth there lay a pile of grey ashes, as 990 though many papers had been burned. From these embers the inspector disinterred the butt end of a green cheque book, which had resisted the action of the fire; the other half of the stick was found behind the door; and 995 as this clinched his suspicions, the officer declared himself delighted. A visit to the bank, where several thousand pounds were found to be lying to the murderer's credit, completed his gratification.

1000 "You may depend upon it, sir," he told Mr. Utterson: "I have him in my hand. He must have lost his head, or he never would have left the stick or, above all, burned the cheque book. Why, money's life to the man. We have 1005 nothing to do but wait for him at the bank, and get out the handbills."

This last, however, was not so easy of accomplishment; for Mr. Hyde had numbered few familiars—even the master of the 1010 servant maid had only seen him twice; his family could nowhere be traced; he had never been photographed; and the few who could describe him differed widely, as common observers will. Only on one point were 1015 they agreed; and that was the haunting sense of unexpressed deformity with which the fugitive impressed his beholders.

Photo 12/Universal Images Group/Getty Images

THE FEATURES SEEMED TO MELT AND ALTER

◀ "The Features Seemed to Melt and Alter" is an illustration created by Edmund J. Sullivan from a 1928 edition of *The Strange Case of Dr. Jekyll and Mr. Hyde.*

As you view the illustration, consider the symmetry of the image by imagining a line that divides the character into equal halves, beginning at the top of the head. What features are highlighted through the symmetrical contrast? How do this image and the related portion of the novel reflect the coexistence of opposite traits within the human psyche?

CHARACTER

1. In "Story of the Door," how do the comparable traits of Mr. Utterson and Mr. Enfield **contrast**?

2. In "Story of the Door" and "Search for Mr. Hyde," which aspects of Dr. Jekyll's background contribute to the **character's** perception of the world?

3. In "Story of the Door" and "Search for Mr. Hyde," how is the "detestable" man described both physically and psychologically? What details seem particularly important?

4. In "Dr. Jekyll Was Quite at Ease" and "The Carew Murder Case," how do Mr. Hyde's speech, actions, and other textual details reveal his relationships with other characters?

5. In "Dr. Jekyll Was Quite at Ease" and "The Carew Murder Case," how does the narrator's choice of details convey a particular **perspective**? Do you see any inconsistencies?

6. In "The Carew Murder Case," what motivates Mr. Utterson to think, feel, and act in the manner that he does?

STRUCTURE

7. Explain how the story that Enfield tells Utterson breaks an established chronological order in the novel's **plot**.

8. Identify a **contrast** in "Story of the Door" or "Search for Mr. Hyde." How does this contrast represent a conflict of values?

9. How does the sequence of events in "Dr. Jekyll Was Quite at Ease" and "The Carew Murder Case" contribute to the story's **conflict**?

10. How does the event in "The Carew Murder Case" create anticipation or **suspense** in readers?

NARRATION

11. Who is the **narrator**? Which character does the narrator perceive events through? How does this character's perspective affect the story?

12. Explain how the narrative's descriptive language (especially adjectives and adverbs) conveys a **perspective** toward the events of the story.

13. How does the narrators' description of characters shape the **tone** of the story?

14. Is there a change in **tone** toward a particular subject? What is the change and how does that change indicate a change in the narrator?

FIGURATIVE LANGUAGE: Word Choice, Imagery, and Symbols

15. Explain the **connotation** of specific words used to describe Mr. Hyde. How do these associations contribute to your interpretation of the text?

16. The mysterious events surrounding Mr. Hyde take place behind "the door, which was equipped with neither bell nor knocker, was blistered and distained." Explain what the door **symbolizes**.

INCIDENT OF THE LETTER

It was late in the afternoon, when Mr. Utterson found his way to Dr. Jekyll's door, where he was at once admitted by Poole, and carried down by the kitchen offices and across a
5 yard which had once been a garden, to the building which was indifferently known as the laboratory or dissecting rooms. The doctor had bought the house from the heirs of a celebrated surgeon; and his own tastes being
10 rather chemical than anatomical, had changed the destination of the block at the bottom of the garden. It was the first time that the lawyer had been received in that part of his friend's quarters; and he eyed the
15 dingy, windowless structure with curiosity, and gazed round with a distasteful sense of strangeness as he crossed the theatre, once crowded with eager students and now lying gaunt and silent, the tables laden with
20 chemical apparatus, the floor strewn with crates and littered with packing straw, and the light falling dimly through the foggy cupola. At the further end, a flight of stairs mounted to a door covered with red baize;
25 and through this, Mr. Utterson was at last received into the doctor's cabinet. It was a large room fitted round with glass presses, furnished, among other things, with a cheval-glass and a business table, and looking out
30 upon the court by three dusty windows barred with iron. The fire burned in the grate; a lamp was set lighted on the chimney shelf, for even in the houses the fog began to lie thickly; and there, close up to the warmth,
35 sat Dr. Jekyll, looking deathly sick. He did not rise to meet his visitor, but held out a cold hand and bade him welcome in a changed voice.

"And now," said Mr. Utterson, as soon as
40 Poole had left them, "you have heard the news?"

The doctor shuddered. "They were crying it in the square," he said. "I heard them in my dining-room."
45 "One word," said the lawyer. "Carew was my client, but so are you, and I want to know what I am doing. You have not been mad enough to hide this fellow?"

"Utterson, I swear to God," cried the doc-
50 tor, "I swear to God I will never set eyes on him again. I bind my honour to you that I am done with him in this world. It is all at an end. And indeed he does not want my help; you do not know him as I do; he is safe, he is
55 quite safe; mark my words, he will never more be heard of."

The lawyer listened gloomily; he did not like his friend's feverish manner. "You seem pretty sure of him," said he; "and for your
60 sake, I hope you may be right. If it came to a trial, your name might appear."

"I am quite sure of him," replied Jekyll; "I have grounds for certainty that I cannot share with any one. But there is one thing on
65 which you may advise me. I have—I have received a letter; and I am at a loss whether I should show it to the police. I should like to leave it in your hands, Utterson; you would judge wisely, I am sure; I have so great a trust
70 in you."

"You fear, I suppose, that it might lead to his detection?" asked the lawyer.

"No," said the other. "I cannot say that I care what becomes of Hyde; I am quite done
75 with him. I was thinking of my own character, which this hateful business has rather exposed."

Utterson ruminated awhile; he was surprised at his friend's selfishness, and yet
80 relieved by it. "Well," said he, at last, "let me see the letter."

The letter was written in an odd, upright hand and signed "Edward Hyde": and it

85 signified, briefly enough, that the writer's benefactor, Dr. Jekyll, whom he had long so unworthily repaid for a thousand generosities, need labour under no alarm for his safety, as he had means of escape on which he placed a sure dependence. The lawyer

90 liked this letter well enough; it put a better colour on the intimacy than he had looked for; and he blamed himself for some of his past suspicions.

"Have you the envelope?" he asked.

95 "I burned it," replied Jekyll, "before I thought what I was about. But it bore no postmark. The note was handed in."

"Shall I keep this and sleep upon it?" asked Utterson.

100 "I wish you to judge for me entirely," was the reply. "I have lost confidence in myself."

"Well, I shall consider," returned the lawyer. "And now one word more: it was Hyde who dictated the terms in your will about

105 that disappearance?"

The doctor seemed seized with a qualm of faintness; he shut his mouth tight and nodded.

"I knew it," said Utterson. "He meant to murder you. You had a fine escape."

110 "I have had what is far more to the purpose," returned the doctor solemnly: "I have had a lesson—O God, Utterson, what a lesson I have had!" And he covered his face for a moment with his hands.

115 On his way out, the lawyer stopped and had a word or two with Poole. "By the bye," said he, "there was a letter handed in to-day: what was the messenger like?" But Poole was positive nothing had come except by post;

120 "and only circulars by that," he added.

This news sent off the visitor with his fears renewed. Plainly the letter had come by the laboratory door; possibly, indeed, it had been written in the cabinet; and if that were

125 so, it must be differently judged, and handled with the more caution. The newsboys, as he went, were crying themselves hoarse along the footways: "Special edition. Shocking murder of an M.P." That was the funeral oration

130 of one friend and client; and he could not help a certain apprehension lest the good name of another should be sucked down in the eddy of the scandal. It was, at least, a ticklish decision that he had to make; and

135 self-reliant as he was by habit, he began to cherish a longing for advice. It was not to be had directly; but perhaps, he thought, it might be fished for.

Presently after, he sat on one side of his

140 own hearth, with Mr. Guest, his head clerk, upon the other, and midway between, at a nicely calculated distance from the fire, a bottle of a particular old wine that had long dwelt unsunned in the foundations of his

145 house. The fog still slept on the wing above the drowned city, where the lamps glimmered like carbuncles; and through the muffle and smother of these fallen clouds, the procession of the town's life was still rolling

150 in through the great arteries with a sound as of a mighty wind. But the room was gay with firelight. In the bottle the acids were long ago resolved; the imperial dye had softened with time, as the colour grows richer in stained

155 windows; and the glow of hot autumn afternoons on hillside vineyards, was ready to be set free and to disperse the fogs of London. Insensibly the lawyer melted. There was no man from whom he kept fewer secrets than

160 Mr. Guest; and he was not always sure that he kept as many as he meant. Guest had often been on business to the doctor's; he knew Poole; he could scarce have failed to hear of Mr. Hyde's familiarity about the

165 house; he might draw conclusions: was it not as well, then, that he should see a letter which put that mystery to right? and above

all since Guest, being a great student and critic of handwriting, would consider the
170 step natural and obliging? The clerk, besides, was a man of counsel; he could scarce read so strange a document without dropping a remark; and by that remark Mr. Utterson might shape his future course.

175 "This is a sad business about Sir Danvers," he said.

"Yes, sir, indeed. It has elicited a great deal of public feeling," returned Guest. "The man, of course, was mad."

180 "I should like to hear your views on that," replied Utterson. "I have a document here in his handwriting; it is between ourselves, for I scarce know what to do about it; it is an ugly business at the best. But there it is; quite in
185 your way: a murderer's autograph."

Guest's eyes brightened, and he sat down at once and studied it with passion. "No sir," he said: "not mad; but it is an odd hand."

"And by all accounts a very odd writer,"
190 added the lawyer.

Just then the servant entered with a note.

"Is that from Dr. Jekyll, sir?" inquired the clerk. "I thought I knew the writing. Anything private, Mr. Utterson?"

195 "Only an invitation to dinner. Why? Do you want to see it?"

"One moment. I thank you, sir;" and the clerk laid the two sheets of paper alongside and sedulously compared their contents.
200 "Thank you, sir," he said at last, returning both; "it's a very interesting autograph."

There was a pause, during which Mr. Utterson struggled with himself. "Why did you compare them, Guest?" he inquired
205 suddenly.

"Well, sir," returned the clerk, "there's a rather singular resemblance; the two hands are in many points identical: only differently sloped."

210 "Rather quaint," said Utterson.

"It is, as you say, rather quaint," returned Guest.

"I wouldn't speak of this note, you know," said the master.

215 "No, sir," said the clerk. "I understand."

But no sooner was Mr. Utterson alone that night, than he locked the note into his safe, where it reposed from that time forward. "What!" he thought. "Henry Jekyll forge for a
220 murderer!" And his blood ran cold in his veins.

INCIDENT OF DR. LANYON

Time ran on; thousands of pounds were offered in reward, for the death of Sir Danvers was resented as a public injury; but Mr. Hyde
225 had disappeared out of the ken of the police as though he had never existed. Much of his past was unearthed, indeed, and all disreputable: tales came out of the man's cruelty, at once so callous and violent; of his vile life, of
230 his strange associates, of the hatred that seemed to have surrounded his career; but of his present whereabouts, not a whisper. From the time he had left the house in Soho on the morning of the murder, he was simply
235 blotted out; and gradually, as time drew on, Mr. Utterson began to recover from the hotness of his alarm, and to grow more at quiet with himself. The death of Sir Danvers was, to his way of thinking, more than paid for by
240 the disappearance of Mr. Hyde. Now that that evil influence had been withdrawn, a new life began for Dr. Jekyll. He came out of his seclusion, renewed relations with his friends, became once more their familiar guest and
245 entertainer; and whilst he had always been known for charities, he was now no less distinguished for religion. He was busy, he was much in the open air, he did good; his face seemed to open and brighten, as if with an

250 inward consciousness of service; and for more than two months, the doctor was at peace.

On the 8th of January Utterson had dined at the doctor's with a small party; Lanyon 255 had been there; and the face of the host had looked from one to the other as in the old days when the trio were inseparable friends. On the 12th, and again on the 14th, the door was shut against the lawyer. "The doctor was 260 confined to the house," Poole said, "and saw no one." On the 15th, he tried again, and was again refused; and having now been used for the last two months to see his friend almost daily, he found this return of solitude to 265 weigh upon his spirits. The fifth night he had in Guest to dine with him; and the sixth he betook himself to Dr. Lanyon's.

There at least he was not denied admittance; but when he came in, he was shocked 270 at the change which had taken place in the doctor's appearance. He had his death-warrant written legibly upon his face. The rosy man had grown pale; his flesh had fallen away; he was visibly balder and older; 275 and yet it was not so much these tokens of a swift physical decay that arrested the lawyer's notice, as a look in the eye and quality of manner that seemed to testify to some deep-seated terror of the mind. It was 280 unlikely that the doctor should fear death; and yet that was what Utterson was tempted to suspect. "Yes," he thought; "he is a doctor, he must know his own state and that his days are counted; and the knowledge is more 285 than he can bear." And yet when Utterson remarked on his ill looks, it was with an air of great firmness that Lanyon declared himself a doomed man.

"I have had a shock," he said, "and I shall 290 never recover. It is a question of weeks. Well, life has been pleasant; I liked it; yes, sir, I used to like it. I sometimes think if we knew all, we should be more glad to get away."

"Jekyll is ill, too," observed Utterson. "Have 295 you seen him?"

But Lanyon's face changed, and he held up a trembling hand. "I wish to see or hear no more of Dr. Jekyll," he said in a loud, unsteady voice. "I am quite done with that 300 person; and I beg that you will spare me any allusion to one whom I regard as dead."

"Tut, tut!" said Mr. Utterson; and then after a considerable pause, "Can't I do anything?" he inquired. "We are three very old 305 friends, Lanyon; we shall not live to make others."

"Nothing can be done," returned Lanyon; "ask himself."

"He will not see me," said the lawyer.

310 "I am not surprised at that," was the reply. "Some day, Utterson, after I am dead, you may perhaps come to learn the right and wrong of this. I cannot tell you. And in the meantime, if you can sit and talk with me of 315 other things, for God's sake, stay and do so; but if you cannot keep clear of this accursed topic, then in God's name, go, for I cannot bear it."

As soon as he got home, Utterson sat 320 down and wrote to Jekyll, complaining of his exclusion from the house, and asking the cause of this unhappy break with Lanyon; and the next day brought him a long answer, often very pathetically worded, and some- 325 times darkly mysterious in drift. The quarrel with Lanyon was incurable. "I do not blame our old friend," Jekyll wrote, "but I share his view that we must never meet. I mean from henceforth to lead a life of extreme seclu- 330 sion; you must not be surprised, nor must you doubt my friendship, if my door is often shut even to you. You must suffer me to go my own dark way. I have brought on myself a

punishment and a danger that I cannot
335 name. If I am the chief of sinners, I am the
chief of sufferers also. I could not think that
this earth contained a place for sufferings
and terrors so unmanning; and you can do
but one thing, Utterson, to lighten this des-
340 tiny, and that is to respect my silence."
Utterson was amazed; the dark influence of
Hyde had been withdrawn, the doctor had
returned to his old tasks and amities; a week
ago, the prospect had smiled with every
345 promise of a cheerful and an honoured age;
and now in a moment, friendship, and peace
of mind, and the whole tenor of his life were
wrecked. So great and unprepared a change
pointed to madness; but in view of Lanyon's
350 manner and words, there must lie for it some
deeper ground.

A week afterwards Dr. Lanyon took to his
bed, and in something less than a fortnight
he was dead. The night after the funeral, at
355 which he had been sadly affected, Utterson
locked the door of his business room, and sitting there by the light of a melancholy candle, drew out and set before him an envelope
addressed by the hand and sealed with the
360 seal of his dead friend. "PRIVATE: for the
hands of G. J. Utterson ALONE, and in case of
his predecease to be destroyed unread," so it
was emphatically superscribed; and the lawyer dreaded to behold the contents. "I have
365 buried one friend to-day," he thought: "what
if this should cost me another?" And then he
condemned the fear as a disloyalty, and broke
the seal. Within there was another enclosure,
likewise sealed, and marked upon the cover
370 as "not to be opened till the death or disappearance of Dr. Henry Jekyll." Utterson could
not trust his eyes. Yes, it was disappearance;
here again, as in the mad will which he had
long ago restored to its author, here again
375 were the idea of a disappearance and the

name of Henry Jekyll bracketted. But in the
will, that idea had sprung from the sinister
suggestion of the man Hyde; it was set there
with a purpose all too plain and horrible.
380 Written by the hand of Lanyon, what should
it mean? A great curiosity came on the
trustee, to disregard the prohibition and dive
at once to the bottom of these mysteries; but
professional honour and faith to his dead
385 friend were stringent obligations; and the
packet slept in the inmost corner of his private safe.

It is one thing to mortify curiosity, another
to conquer it; and it may be doubted if, from
390 that day forth, Utterson desired the society of
his surviving friend with the same eagerness.
He thought of him kindly; but his thoughts
were disquieted and fearful. He went to call
indeed; but he was perhaps relieved to be
395 denied admittance; perhaps, in his heart, he
preferred to speak with Poole upon the doorstep and surrounded by the air and sounds of
the open city, rather than to be admitted into
that house of voluntary bondage, and to sit
400 and speak with its inscrutable recluse. Poole
had, indeed, no very pleasant news to communicate. The doctor, it appeared, now more
than ever confined himself to the cabinet over
the laboratory, where he would sometimes
405 even sleep; he was out of spirits, he had
grown very silent, he did not read; it seemed
as if he had something on his mind. Utterson
became so used to the unvarying character of
these reports, that he fell off little by little in
410 the frequency of his visits.

INCIDENT AT THE WINDOW

It chanced on Sunday, when Mr. Utterson
was on his usual walk with Mr. Enfield, that
their way lay once again through the by-
street; and that when they came in front of
415 the door, both stopped to gaze on it.

"Well," said Enfield, "that story's at an end at least. We shall never see more of Mr. Hyde."

"I hope not," said Utterson. "Did I ever tell you that I once saw him, and shared your 420 feeling of repulsion?"

"It was impossible to do the one without the other," returned Enfield. "And by the way, what an ass you must have thought me, not to know that this was a back way to Dr. Jekyll's! 425 It was partly your own fault that I found it out, even when I did."

"So you found it out, did you?" said Utterson. "But if that be so, we may step into the court and take a look at the windows. To 430 tell you the truth, I am uneasy about poor Jekyll; and even outside, I feel as if the presence of a friend might do him good."

The court was very cool and a little damp, and full of premature twilight, although the 435 sky, high up overhead, was still bright with sunset. The middle one of the three windows was half-way open; and sitting close beside it, taking the air with an infinite sadness of mien, like some disconsolate prisoner, 440 Utterson saw Dr. Jekyll.

"What! Jekyll!" he cried. "I trust you are better."

"I am very low, Utterson," replied the doctor drearily, "very low. It will not last long, 445 thank God."

"You stay too much indoors," said the lawyer. "You should be out, whipping up the circulation like Mr. Enfield and me. (This is my cousin—Mr. Enfield—Dr. Jekyll.) Come 450 now; get your hat and take a quick turn with us."

"You are very good," sighed the other. "I should like to very much; but no, no, no, it is quite impossible; I dare not. But indeed, 455 Utterson, I am very glad to see you; this is really a great pleasure; I would ask you and Mr. Enfield up, but the place is really not fit."

"Why, then," said the lawyer, good-naturedly, "the best thing we can do is to stay down here 460 and speak with you from where we are."

"That is just what I was about to venture to propose," returned the doctor with a smile. But the words were hardly uttered, before the smile was struck out of his face and suc- 465 ceeded by an expression of such abject terror and despair, as froze the very blood of the two gentlemen below. They saw it but for a glimpse for the window was instantly thrust down; but that glimpse had been sufficient, 470 and they turned and left the court without a word. In silence, too, they traversed the by-street; and it was not until they had come into a neighbouring thoroughfare, where even upon a Sunday there were still some 475 stirrings of life, that Mr. Utterson at last turned and looked at his companion. They were both pale; and there was an answering horror in their eyes.

"God forgive us, God forgive us," said 480 Mr. Utterson.

But Mr. Enfield only nodded his head very seriously, and walked on once more in silence.

THE LAST NIGHT

Mr. Utterson was sitting by his fireside one 485 evening after dinner, when he was surprised to receive a visit from Poole.

"Bless me, Poole, what brings you here?" he cried; and then taking a second look at him, "What ails you?" he added; "is the doc- 490 tor ill?"

"Mr. Utterson," said the man, "there is something wrong."

"Take a seat, and here is a glass of wine for you," said the lawyer. "Now, take your 495 time, and tell me plainly what you want."

"You know the doctor's ways, sir," replied Poole, "and how he shuts himself up. Well,

he's shut up again in the cabinet; and I don't like it, sir—I wish I may die if I like it. Mr.
500 Utterson, sir, I'm afraid."

"Now, my good man," said the lawyer, "be explicit. What are you afraid of?"

"I've been afraid for about a week," returned Poole, doggedly disregarding the
505 question, "and I can bear it no more."

The man's appearance amply bore out his words; his manner was altered for the worse; and except for the moment when he had first announced his terror, he had not once
510 looked the lawyer in the face. Even now, he sat with the glass of wine untasted on his knee, and his eyes directed to a corner of the floor. "I can bear it no more," he repeated.

"Come," said the lawyer, "I see you have
515 some good reason, Poole; I see there is something seriously amiss. Try to tell me what it is."

"I think there's been foul play," said Poole, hoarsely.

520 "Foul play!" cried the lawyer, a good deal frightened and rather inclined to be irritated in consequence. "What foul play! What does the man mean?"

"I daren't say, sir," was the answer; "but
525 will you come along with me and see for yourself?"

Mr. Utterson's only answer was to rise and get his hat and greatcoat; but he observed with wonder the greatness of the relief that
530 appeared upon the butler's face, and perhaps with no less, that the wine was still untasted when he set it down to follow.

It was a wild, cold, seasonable night of March, with a pale moon, lying on her back
535 as though the wind had tilted her, and flying wrack of the most diaphanous and lawny texture. The wind made talking difficult, and flecked the blood into the face. It seemed to have swept the streets unusually bare of
540 passengers, besides; for Mr. Utterson thought he had never seen that part of London so deserted. He could have wished it otherwise; never in his life had he been conscious of so sharp a wish to see and touch his fellow-
545 creatures; for struggle as he might, there was borne in upon his mind a crushing anticipation of calamity. The square, when they got there, was full of wind and dust, and the thin trees in the garden were lashing themselves
550 along the railing. Poole, who had kept all the way a pace or two ahead, now pulled up in the middle of the pavement, and in spite of the biting weather, took off his hat and mopped his brow with a red pocket-
555 handkerchief. But for all the hurry of his coming, these were not the dews of exertion that he wiped away, but the moisture of some strangling anguish; for his face was white and his voice, when he spoke, harsh
560 and broken.

"Well, sir," he said, "here we are, and God grant there be nothing wrong."

"Amen, Poole," said the lawyer.

Thereupon the servant knocked in a very
565 guarded manner; the door was opened on the chain; and a voice asked from within, "Is that you, Poole?"

"It's all right," said Poole. "Open the door."

The hall, when they entered it, was
570 brightly lighted up; the fire was built high; and about the hearth the whole of the servants, men and women, stood huddled together like a flock of sheep. At the sight of Mr. Utterson, the housemaid broke into hys-
575 terical whimpering; and the cook, crying out "Bless God! It's Mr. Utterson," ran forward as if to take him in her arms.

"What, what? Are you all here?" said the lawyer peevishly. "Very irregular, very
580 unseemly; your master would be far from pleased."

"They're all afraid," said Poole.

Blank silence followed, no one protesting; only the maid lifted her voice and now wept 585 loudly.

"Hold your tongue!" Poole said to her, with a ferocity of accent that testified to his own jangled nerves; and indeed, when the girl had so suddenly raised the note of 590 her lamentation, they had all started and turned towards the inner door with faces of dreadful expectation. "And now," continued the butler, addressing the knife-boy, "reach me a candle, and we'll get this through 595 hands at once." And then he begged Mr. Utterson to follow him, and led the way to the back garden.

"Now, sir," said he, "you come as gently as you can. I want you to hear, and I don't want 600 you to be heard. And see here, sir, if by any chance he was to ask you in, don't go."

Mr. Utterson's nerves, at this unlooked-for termination, gave a jerk that nearly threw him from his balance; but he recollected his 605 courage and followed the butler into the laboratory building through the surgical theatre, with its lumber of crates and bottles, to the foot of the stair. Here Poole motioned him to stand on one side and listen; while he him- 610 self, setting down the candle and making a great and obvious call on his resolution, mounted the steps and knocked with a somewhat uncertain hand on the red baize of the cabinet door.

615   "Mr. Utterson, sir, asking to see you," he called; and even as he did so, once more violently signed to the lawyer to give ear.

A voice answered from within: "Tell him I cannot see anyone," it said complainingly.

620   "Thank you, sir," said Poole, with a note of something like triumph in his voice; and taking up his candle, he led Mr. Utterson back across the yard and into the great kitchen, where the fire was out and the beetles were 625 leaping on the floor.

"Sir," he said, looking Mr. Utterson in the eyes, "Was that my master's voice?"

"It seems much changed," replied the lawyer, very pale, but giving look for look.

630   "Changed? Well, yes, I think so," said the butler. "Have I been twenty years in this man's house, to be deceived about his voice? No, sir; master's made away with; he was made away with eight days ago, when 635 we heard him cry out upon the name of God; and who's in there instead of him, and why it stays there, is a thing that cries to Heaven, Mr. Utterson!"

"This is a very strange tale, Poole; this is 640 rather a wild tale my man," said Mr. Utterson, biting his finger. "Suppose it were as you suppose, supposing Dr. Jekyll to have been—well, murdered, what could induce the murderer to stay? That won't hold water; 645 it doesn't commend itself to reason."

"Well, Mr. Utterson, you are a hard man to satisfy, but I'll do it yet," said Poole. "All this last week (you must know) him, or it, whatever it is that lives in that cabinet, has 650 been crying night and day for some sort of medicine and cannot get it to his mind. It was sometimes his way—the master's, that is—to write his orders on a sheet of paper and throw it on the stair. We've had 655 nothing else this week back; nothing but papers, and a closed door, and the very meals left there to be smuggled in when nobody was looking. Well, sir, every day, ay, and twice and thrice in the same day, there 660 have been orders and complaints, and I have been sent flying to all the wholesale chemists in town. Every time I brought the stuff back, there would be another paper telling me to return it, because it was not 665 pure, and another order to a different firm.

This drug is wanted bitter bad, sir, whatever for."

"Have you any of these papers?" asked Mr. Utterson.

670 Poole felt in his pocket and handed out a crumpled note, which the lawyer, bending nearer to the candle, carefully examined. Its contents ran thus: "Dr. Jekyll presents his compliments to Messrs. Maw. He assures 675 them that their last sample is impure and quite useless for his present purpose. In the year 18—, Dr. J. purchased a somewhat large quantity from Messrs. M. He now begs them to search with most sedulous care, and 680 should any of the same quality be left, forward it to him at once. Expense is no consideration. The importance of this to Dr. J. can hardly be exaggerated." So far the letter had run composedly enough, but here with a 685 sudden splutter of the pen, the writer's emotion had broken loose. "For God's sake," he added, "find me some of the old."

"This is a strange note," said Mr. Utterson; and then sharply, "How do you come to have 690 it open?"

"The man at Maw's was main angry, sir, and he threw it back to me like so much dirt," returned Poole.

"This is unquestionably the doctor's hand, 695 do you know?" resumed the lawyer.

"I thought it looked like it," said the servant rather sulkily; and then, with another voice, "But what matters hand of write?" he said. "I've seen him!"

700 "Seen him?" repeated Mr. Utterson. "Well?"

"That's it!" said Poole. "It was this way. I came suddenly into the theatre from the garden. It seems he had slipped out to look 705 for this drug or whatever it is; for the cabinet door was open, and there he was at the far end of the room digging among the crates. He looked up when I came in, gave a kind of cry, and whipped upstairs into the 710 cabinet. It was but for one minute that I saw him, but the hair stood upon my head like quills. Sir, if that was my master, why had he a mask upon his face? If it was my master, why did he cry out like a rat, and run from 715 me? I have served him long enough. And then . . ." The man paused and passed his hand over his face.

"These are all very strange circumstances," said Mr. Utterson, "but I think I 720 begin to see daylight. Your master, Poole, is plainly seized with one of those maladies that both torture and deform the sufferer; hence, for aught I know, the alteration of his voice; hence the mask and the avoidance of 725 his friends; hence his eagerness to find this drug, by means of which the poor soul retains some hope of ultimate recovery— God grant that he be not deceived! There is my explanation; it is sad enough, Poole, ay, 730 and appalling to consider; but it is plain and natural, hangs well together, and delivers us from all exorbitant alarms."

"Sir," said the butler, turning to a sort of mottled pallor, "that thing was not my mas-735 ter, and there's the truth. My master"—here he looked round him and began to whisper— "is a tall, fine build of a man, and this was more of a dwarf." Utterson attempted to protest. "O, sir," cried Poole, "do you think I do 740 not know my master after twenty years? Do you think I do not know where his head comes to in the cabinet door, where I saw him every morning of my life? No, sir, that thing in the mask was never Dr. Jekyll—God 745 knows what it was, but it was never Dr. Jekyll; and it is the belief of my heart that there was murder done."

"Poole," replied the lawyer, "if you say that, it will become my duty to make certain.

750 Much as I desire to spare your master's feelings, much as I am puzzled by this note which
seems to prove him to be still alive, I shall
consider it my duty to break in that door."

"Ah, Mr. Utterson, that's talking!" cried the
755 butler.

"And now comes the second question,"
resumed Utterson: "Who is going to do it?"

"Why, you and me, sir," was the
undaunted reply.

760 "That's very well said," returned the lawyer; "and whatever comes of it, I shall make
it my business to see you are no loser."

"There is an axe in the theatre," continued
Poole; "and you might take the kitchen poker
765 for yourself."

The lawyer took that rude but weighty
instrument into his hand, and balanced it.
"Do you know, Poole," he said, looking up,
"that you and I are about to place ourselves
770 in a position of some peril?"

"You may say so, sir, indeed," returned the
butler.

"It is well, then that we should be frank,"
said the other. "We both think more than we
775 have said; let us make a clean breast. This
masked figure that you saw, did you recognise it?"

"Well, sir, it went so quick, and the creature
was so doubled up, that I could hardly swear
780 to that," was the answer. "But if you mean,
was it Mr. Hyde?—why, yes, I think it was!
You see, it was much of the same bigness; and
it had the same quick, light way with it; and
then who else could have got in by the labora-
785 tory door? You have not forgot, sir, that at the
time of the murder he had still the key with
him? But that's not all. I don't know, Mr.
Utterson, if you ever met this Mr. Hyde?"

"Yes," said the lawyer, "I once spoke with
790 him."

"Then you must know as well as the rest
of us that there was something queer about
that gentleman—something that gave a man
a turn—I don't know rightly how to say it,
795 sir, beyond this: that you felt in your marrow
kind of cold and thin."

"I own I felt something of what you
describe," said Mr. Utterson.

"Quite so, sir," returned Poole. "Well, when
800 that masked thing like a monkey jumped
from among the chemicals and whipped into
the cabinet, it went down my spine like ice.
O, I know it's not evidence, Mr. Utterson; I'm
book-learned enough for that; but a man has
805 his feelings, and I give you my bible-word it
was Mr. Hyde!"

"Ay, ay," said the lawyer. "My fears incline
to the same point. Evil, I fear, founded—evil
was sure to come—of that connection. Ay
810 truly, I believe you; I believe poor Harry is
killed; and I believe his murderer (for what
purpose, God alone can tell) is still lurking in
his victim's room. Well, let our name be vengeance. Call Bradshaw."

815 The footman came at the summons, very
white and nervous.

"Pull yourself together, Bradshaw," said
the lawyer. "This suspense, I know, is telling
upon all of you; but it is now our intention to
820 make an end of it. Poole, here, and I are going
to force our way into the cabinet. If all is
well, my shoulders are broad enough to bear
the blame. Meanwhile, lest anything should
really be amiss, or any malefactor seek to
825 escape by the back, you and the boy must go
round the corner with a pair of good sticks
and take your post at the laboratory door. We
give you ten minutes to get to your stations."

As Bradshaw left, the lawyer looked at
830 his watch. "And now, Poole, let us get to
ours," he said; and taking the poker under

his arm, led the way into the yard. The scud had banked over the moon, and it was now quite dark. The wind, which only broke
835 in puffs and draughts into that deep well of building, tossed the light of the candle to and fro about their steps, until they came into the shelter of the theatre, where they sat down silently to wait. London hummed
840 solemnly all around; but nearer at hand, the stillness was only broken by the sounds of a footfall moving to and fro along the cabinet floor.

"So it will walk all day, sir," whispered
845 Poole; "ay, and the better part of the night. Only when a new sample comes from the chemist, there's a bit of a break. Ah, it's an ill conscience that's such an enemy to rest! Ah, sir, there's blood foully shed in every step of
850 it! But hark again, a little closer—put your heart in your ears, Mr. Utterson, and tell me, is that the doctor's foot?"

The steps fell lightly and oddly, with a certain swing, for all they went so slowly; it was
855 different indeed from the heavy creaking tread of Henry Jekyll. Utterson sighed. "Is there never anything else?" he asked.

Poole nodded. "Once," he said. "Once I heard it weeping!"
860 "Weeping? How that?" said the lawyer, conscious of a sudden chill of horror.

"Weeping like a woman or a lost soul," said the butler. "I came away with that upon my heart, that I could have wept too."
865 But now the ten minutes drew to an end. Poole disinterred the axe from under a stack of packing straw; the candle was set upon the nearest table to light them to the attack; and they drew near with bated breath to
870 where that patient foot was still going up and down, up and down, in the quiet of the night.

"Jekyll," cried Utterson, with a loud voice, "I demand to see you." He paused a moment,
875 but there came no reply. "I give you fair warning, our suspicions are aroused, and I must and shall see you," he resumed; "if not by fair means, then by foul—if not of your consent, then by brute force!"
880 "Utterson," said the voice, "for God's sake, have mercy!"

"Ah, that's not Jekyll's voice—it's Hyde's!" cried Utterson. "Down with the door, Poole!"

Poole swung the axe over his shoulder;
885 the blow shook the building, and the red baize door leaped against the lock and hinges. A dismal screech, as of mere animal terror, rang from the cabinet. Up went the axe again, and again the panels crashed and
890 the frame bounded; four times the blow fell; but the wood was tough and the fittings were of excellent workmanship; and it was not until the fifth, that the lock burst and the wreck of the door fell inwards on the
895 carpet.

The besiegers, appalled by their own riot and the stillness that had succeeded, stood back a little and peered in. There lay the cabinet before their eyes in the quiet lamplight,
900 a good fire glowing and chattering on the hearth, the kettle singing its thin strain, a drawer or two open, papers neatly set forth on the business table, and nearer the fire, the things laid out for tea; the quietest room, you
905 would have said, and, but for the glazed presses full of chemicals, the most commonplace that night in London.

Right in the middle there lay the body of a man sorely contorted and still twitching.
910 They drew near on tiptoe, turned it on its back and beheld the face of Edward Hyde. He was dressed in clothes far too large for him, clothes of the doctor's bigness; the cords of

his face still moved with a semblance of life,
but life was quite gone; and by the crushed
phial in the hand and the strong smell of
kernels that hung upon the air, Utterson
knew that he was looking on the body of a
self-destroyer.

"We have come too late," he said sternly,
"whether to save or punish. Hyde is gone to
his account; and it only remains for us to
find the body of your master."

The far greater proportion of the building
was occupied by the theatre, which filled
almost the whole ground storey and was
lighted from above, and by the cabinet,
which formed an upper storey at one end
and looked upon the court. A corridor joined
the theatre to the door on the by-street; and
with this the cabinet communicated separately by a second flight of stairs. There were
besides a few dark closets and a spacious
cellar. All these they now thoroughly examined. Each closet needed but a glance, for all
were empty, and all, by the dust that fell
from their doors, had stood long unopened.
The cellar, indeed, was filled with crazy lumber, mostly dating from the times of the surgeon who was Jekyll's predecessor; but even
as they opened the door they were advertised of the uselessness of further search, by
the fall of a perfect mat of cobweb which had
for years sealed up the entrance. Nowhere
was there any trace of Henry Jekyll, dead or
alive.

Poole stamped on the flags of the corridor.
"He must be buried here," he said, hearken-
ing to the sound.

"Or he may have fled," said Utterson, and
he turned to examine the door in the by-
street. It was locked; and lying near by on the
flags, they found the key, already stained
with rust.

"This does not look like use," observed the
lawyer.

"Use!" echoed Poole. "Do you not see, sir,
it is broken? Much as if a man had stamped
on it."

"Ay," continued Utterson, "and the fractures, too, are rusty." The two men looked at
each other with a scare. "This is beyond me,
Poole," said the lawyer. "Let us go back to the
cabinet."

They mounted the stair in silence, and
still with an occasional awestruck glance at
the dead body, proceeded more thoroughly to
examine the contents of the cabinet. At one
table, there were traces of chemical work,
various measured heaps of some white salt
being laid on glass saucers, as though for an
experiment in which the unhappy man had
been prevented.

"That is the same drug that I was always
bringing him," said Poole; and even as he
spoke, the kettle with a startling noise boiled
over.

This brought them to the fireside, where
the easy-chair was drawn cosily up, and the
tea things stood ready to the sitter's elbow,
the very sugar in the cup. There were several
books on a shelf; one lay beside the tea
things open, and Utterson was amazed to
find it a copy of a pious work, for which
Jekyll had several times expressed a great
esteem, annotated, in his own hand with
startling blasphemies.

Next, in the course of their review of the
chamber, the searchers came to the cheval-
glass, into whose depths they looked with
an involuntary horror. But it was so turned
as to show them nothing but the rosy
glow playing on the roof, the fire sparkling
in a hundred repetitions along the glazed
front of the presses, and their own pale

and fearful countenances stooping to look in.

"This glass has seen some strange things, sir," whispered Poole.

1000 "And surely none stranger than itself," echoed the lawyer in the same tones. "For what did Jekyll"—he caught himself up at the word with a start, and then conquering the weakness—"what could Jekyll want with 1005 it?" he said.

"You may say that!" said Poole.

Next they turned to the business table. On the desk, among the neat array of papers, a large envelope was uppermost, and bore, in 1010 the doctor's hand, the name of Mr. Utterson. The lawyer unsealed it, and several enclosures fell to the floor. The first was a will, drawn in the same eccentric terms as the one which he had returned six months 1015 before, to serve as a testament in case of death and as a deed of gift in case of disappearance; but in place of the name of Edward Hyde, the lawyer, with indescribable amazement read the name of Gabriel John Utterson. 1020 He looked at Poole, and then back at the paper, and last of all at the dead malefactor stretched upon the carpet.

"My head goes round," he said. "He has been all these days in possession; he had no 1025 cause to like me; he must have raged to see himself displaced; and he has not destroyed this document."

He caught up the next paper; it was a brief note in the doctor's hand and dated at the 1030 top. "O Poole!" the lawyer cried, "he was alive and here this day. He cannot have been disposed of in so short a space; he must be still alive, he must have fled! And then, why fled?

And how? And in that case, can we venture 1035 to declare this suicide? O, we must be careful. I foresee that we may yet involve your master in some dire catastrophe."

"Why don't you read it, sir?" asked Poole.

"Because I fear," replied the lawyer sol- 1040 emnly. "God grant I have no cause for it!" And with that he brought the paper to his eyes and read as follows:

"My dear Utterson,—When this shall fall into your hands, I shall have disappeared, 1045 under what circumstances I have not the penetration to foresee, but my instinct and all the circumstances of my nameless situation tell me that the end is sure and must be early. Go then, and first read the narra- 1050 tive which Lanyon warned me he was to place in your hands; and if you care to hear more, turn to the confession of

"Your unworthy and unhappy friend,
"HENRY JEKYLL."

1055 "There was a third enclosure?" asked Utterson.

"Here, sir," said Poole, and gave into his hands a considerable packet sealed in several places.

1060 The lawyer put it in his pocket. "I would say nothing of this paper. If your master has fled or is dead, we may at least save his credit. It is now ten; I must go home and read these documents in quiet; but I shall be back before 1065 midnight, when we shall send for the police."

They went out, locking the door of the theatre behind them; and Utterson, once more leaving the servants gathered about the fire in the hall, trudged back to his office 1070 to read the two narratives in which this mystery was now to be explained.

Fredric March in movie art for the film
Dr. Jekyll and Mr. Hyde, 1931.

▶

How does this image from 1931 convey
the duality of humanity? Why do you
think we continue to be intrigued by this
idea?

Archive Photos/Moviepix/Getty Images

CHARACTER

1. In "The Last Night," which of Dr. Jekyll's ironic choices seem contradictory
   or inconsistent? Explain how the **protagonist's** choices contribute to the
   complexity of his character.

2. Explain the circumstances that provoke Dr. Jekyll to change in "Incident of
   Dr. Lanyon" and "Incident at the Window."

3. In "Incident at the Window," what particular images, dialogue, and textual details
   help readers understand Poole's relationship with Dr. Jekyll and Mr. Hyde?

4. Describe the complexities of the relationship between Dr. Jekyll and
   Mr. Hyde.

STRUCTURE

5. Explain how the events in "Incident of Dr. Lanyon" contribute to the development
   of the novel's **conflict**.

6. How do the events in "Incident at the Window" and "The Last Night" contribute
   to the **suspense** of the novel?

7. How does the dinner meeting between Dr. Jekyll's butler, Poole, and Mr. Utterson
   illustrate a cause-effect relationship with another event?

NARRATION

8. Is the **narrator reliable**? How does the relationship between the narrator and the
   subject affect our understanding of the narrator's reliability?

9. How does the **narrator** reveal the **motivation** of Poole and the relationship between Poole and Utterson?

10. Does the narrator have any **bias**? How are the details of the events described? Subjectively or objectively? Support your answer with textual evidence.

FIGURATIVE LANGUAGE: Word Choice, Imagery, and Symbols

11. The text includes many instances of scientific **imagery**. How does that imagery contribute to your interpretation of the story? Can you identify and explain a specific example?

12. How does the narrator's **diction** or word choice contribute to the suspense of the text?

DR. LANYON'S NARRATIVE

On the ninth of January, now four days ago, I received by the evening delivery a registered envelope, addressed in the hand of my col-league and old school companion, Henry
5 Jekyll. I was a good deal surprised by this; for we were by no means in the habit of corre-spondence; I had seen the man, dined with him, indeed, the night before; and I could imagine nothing in our intercourse that
10 should justify formality of registration. The contents increased my wonder; for this is how the letter ran:

"10th December, 18—.

"Dear Lanyon,—You are one of my oldest
15 friends; and although we may have differed at times on scientific questions, I cannot remember, at least on my side, any break in our affection. There was never a day when, if you had said to me, 'Jekyll, my life, my hon-
20 our, my reason, depend upon you,' I would not have sacrificed my left hand to help you. Lanyon, my life, my honour, my reason, are all at your mercy; if you fail me to-night, I am lost. You might suppose, after this preface,
25 that I am going to ask you for something dis-honourable to grant. Judge for yourself.

"I want you to postpone all other engage-ments for to-night—ay, even if you were summoned to the bedside of an emperor; to
30 take a cab, unless your carriage should be actually at the door; and with this letter in your hand for consultation, to drive straight to my house. Poole, my butler, has his orders; you will find him waiting your arrival with a
35 locksmith. The door of my cabinet is then to be forced; and you are to go in alone; to open the glazed press (letter E) on the left hand, breaking the lock if it be shut; and to draw out, with all its contents as they stand, the
40 fourth drawer from the top or (which is the same thing) the third from the bottom. In my extreme distress of mind, I have a morbid fear of misdirecting you; but even if I am in error, you may know the right drawer by its
45 contents: some powders, a phial and a paper book. This drawer I beg of you to carry back with you to Cavendish Square exactly as it stands.

"That is the first part of the service: now
50 for the second. You should be back, if you set out at once on the receipt of this, long before midnight; but I will leave you that amount of margin, not only in the fear of one of those

obstacles that can neither be prevented nor
55 foreseen, but because an hour when your
servants are in bed is to be preferred for
what will then remain to do. At midnight,
then, I have to ask you to be alone in your
consulting room, to admit with your own
60 hand into the house a man who will present
himself in my name, and to place in his
hands the drawer that you will have brought
with you from my cabinet. Then you will
have played your part and earned my grati-
65 tude completely. Five minutes afterwards, if
you insist upon an explanation, you will have
understood that these arrangements are of
capital importance; and that by the neglect
of one of them, fantastic as they must
70 appear, you might have charged your conscience with my death or the shipwreck of
my reason.

"Confident as I am that you will not trifle
with this appeal, my heart sinks and my
75 hand trembles at the bare thought of such a
possibility. Think of me at this hour, in a
strange place, labouring under a blackness of
distress that no fancy can exaggerate, and
yet well aware that, if you will but punctually
80 serve me, my troubles will roll away like a
story that is told. Serve me, my dear Lanyon
and save

"Your friend,
"H.J.
85 "P.S.—I had already sealed this up when a
fresh terror struck upon my soul. It is possible that the post-office may fail me, and this
letter not come into your hands until tomorrow morning. In that case, dear Lanyon,
90 do my errand when it shall be most convenient for you in the course of the day; and
once more expect my messenger at midnight.
It may then already be too late; and if that
night passes without event, you will know
95 that you have seen the last of Henry Jekyll."

Upon the reading of this letter, I made
sure my colleague was insane; but till that
was proved beyond the possibility of doubt, I
felt bound to do as he requested. The less I
100 understood of this farrago, the less I was in a
position to judge of its importance; and an
appeal so worded could not be set aside
without a grave responsibility. I rose accordingly from table, got into a hansom, and
105 drove straight to Jekyll's house. The butler
was awaiting my arrival; he had received by
the same post as mine a registered letter of
instruction, and had sent at once for a locksmith and a carpenter. The tradesmen came
110 while we were yet speaking; and we moved
in a body to old Dr. Denman's surgical theatre, from which (as you are doubtless aware)
Jekyll's private cabinet is most conveniently
entered. The door was very strong, the lock
115 excellent; the carpenter avowed he would
have great trouble and have to do much
damage, if force were to be used; and the
locksmith was near despair. But this last was
a handy fellow, and after two hour's work,
120 the door stood open. The press marked E was
unlocked; and I took out the drawer, had it
filled up with straw and tied in a sheet, and
returned with it to Cavendish Square.

Here I proceeded to examine its contents.
125 The powders were neatly enough made up,
but not with the nicety of the dispensing
chemist; so that it was plain they were of
Jekyll's private manufacture; and when I
opened one of the wrappers I found what
130 seemed to me a simple crystalline salt of a
white colour. The phial, to which I next
turned my attention, might have been about
half full of a blood-red liquor, which was
highly pungent to the sense of smell and
135 seemed to me to contain phosphorus and
some volatile ether. At the other ingredients
I could make no guess. The book was an

ordinary version book and contained little but a series of dates. These covered a period
140 of many years, but I observed that the entries ceased nearly a year ago and quite abruptly. Here and there a brief remark was appended to a date, usually no more than a single word: "double" occurring perhaps six times
145 in a total of several hundred entries; and once very early in the list and followed by several marks of exclamation, "total failure!!!" All this, though it whetted my curiosity, told me little that was definite. Here were
150 a phial of some salt, and the record of a series of experiments that had led (like too many of Jekyll's investigations) to no end of practical usefulness. How could the presence of these articles in my house affect either the
155 honour, the sanity, or the life of my flighty colleague? If his messenger could go to one place, why could he not go to another? And even granting some impediment, why was this gentleman to be received by me in
160 secret? The more I reflected the more convinced I grew that I was dealing with a case of cerebral disease; and though I dismissed my servants to bed, I loaded an old revolver, that I might be found in some posture of
165 self-defence.

Twelve o'clock had scarce rung out over London, ere the knocker sounded very gently on the door. I went myself at the summons, and found a small man crouching against
170 the pillars of the portico.

"Are you come from Dr. Jekyll?" I asked.

He told me "yes" by a constrained gesture; and when I had bidden him enter, he did not obey me without a searching back-
175 ward glance into the darkness of the square. There was a policeman not far off, advancing with his bull's eye open; and at the sight, I thought my visitor started and made greater haste.

180 These particulars struck me, I confess, disagreeably; and as I followed him into the bright light of the consulting room, I kept my hand ready on my weapon. Here, at last, I had a chance of clearly seeing him. I had
185 never set eyes on him before, so much was certain. He was small, as I have said; I was struck besides with the shocking expression of his face, with his remarkable combination of great muscular activity and great apparent
190 debility of constitution, and—last but not least—with the odd, subjective disturbance caused by his neighbourhood. This bore some resemblance to incipient rigour, and was accompanied by a marked sinking of the
195 pulse. At the time, I set it down to some idiosyncratic, personal distaste, and merely wondered at the acuteness of the symptoms; but I have since had reason to believe the cause to lie much deeper in the nature of man, and
200 to turn on some nobler hinge than the principle of hatred.

This person (who had thus, from the first moment of his entrance, struck in me what I can only describe as a disgustful curiosity)
205 was dressed in a fashion that would have made an ordinary person laughable; his clothes, that is to say, although they were of rich and sober fabric, were enormously too large for him in every measurement—the
210 trousers hanging on his legs and rolled up to keep them from the ground, the waist of the coat below his haunches, and the collar sprawling wide upon his shoulders. Strange to relate, this ludicrous accoutrement was
215 far from moving me to laughter. Rather, as there was something abnormal and misbegotten in the very essence of the creature that now faced me—something seizing, surprising and revolting—this fresh disparity
220 seemed but to fit in with and to reinforce it; so that to my interest in the man's nature

and character, there was added a curiosity as to his origin, his life, his fortune and status in the world.

225 These observations, though they have taken so great a space to be set down in, were yet the work of a few seconds. My visitor was, indeed, on fire with sombre excitement.

230 "Have you got it?" he cried. "Have you got it?" And so lively was his impatience that he even laid his hand upon my arm and sought to shake me.

I put him back, conscious at his touch of a 235 certain icy pang along my blood. "Come, sir," said I. "You forget that I have not yet the pleasure of your acquaintance. Be seated, if you please." And I showed him an example, and sat down myself in my customary seat 240 and with as fair an imitation of my ordinary manner to a patient, as the lateness of the hour, the nature of my preoccupations, and the horror I had of my visitor, would suffer me to muster.

245 "I beg your pardon, Dr. Lanyon," he replied civilly enough. "What you say is very well founded; and my impatience has shown its heels to my politeness. I come here at the instance of your colleague, Dr. Henry Jekyll, 250 on a piece of business of some moment; and I understood . . ." He paused and put his hand to his throat, and I could see, in spite of his collected manner, that he was wrestling against the approaches of the hysteria—"I 255 understood, a drawer . . ."

But here I took pity on my visitor's suspense, and some perhaps on my own growing curiosity.

"There it is, sir," said I, pointing to the 260 drawer, where it lay on the floor behind a table and still covered with the sheet.

He sprang to it, and then paused, and laid his hand upon his heart; I could hear his teeth grate with the convulsive action of his 265 jaws; and his face was so ghastly to see that I grew alarmed both for his life and reason.

"Compose yourself," said I.

He turned a dreadful smile to me, and as if with the decision of despair, plucked away 270 the sheet. At sight of the contents, he uttered one loud sob of such immense relief that I sat petrified. And the next moment, in a voice that was already fairly well under control, "Have you a graduated glass?" he asked.

275 I rose from my place with something of an effort and gave him what he asked.

He thanked me with a smiling nod, measured out a few minims of the red tincture and added one of the powders. The mixture, 280 which was at first of a reddish hue, began, in proportion as the crystals melted, to brighten in colour, to effervesce audibly, and to throw off small fumes of vapour. Suddenly and at the same moment, the ebullition ceased and 285 the compound changed to a dark purple, which faded again more slowly to a watery green. My visitor, who had watched these metamorphoses with a keen eye, smiled, set down the glass upon the table, and then 290 turned and looked upon me with an air of scrutiny.

"And now," said he, "to settle what remains. Will you be wise? will you be guided? will you suffer me to take this glass 295 in my hand and to go forth from your house without further parley? or has the greed of curiosity too much command of you? Think before you answer, for it shall be done as you decide. As you decide, you shall be left as you 300 were before, and neither richer nor wiser, unless the sense of service rendered to a man in mortal distress may be counted as a kind of riches of the soul. Or, if you shall so prefer to choose, a new province of knowl- 305 edge and new avenues to fame and power shall be laid open to you, here, in this room, upon the instant; and your sight shall be blasted by a prodigy to stagger the unbelief of Satan."

310 "Sir," said I, affecting a coolness that I was far from truly possessing, "you speak enigmas, and you will perhaps not wonder that I hear you with no very strong impression of belief. But I have gone too far in the way of 315 inexplicable services to pause before I see the end."

"It is well," replied my visitor. "Lanyon, you remember your vows: what follows is under the seal of our profession. And now, you who 320 have so long been bound to the most narrow and material views, you who have denied the virtue of transcendental medicine, you who have derided your superiors—behold!"

He put the glass to his lips and drank at 325 one gulp. A cry followed; he reeled, staggered, clutched at the table and held on, staring with injected eyes, gasping with open mouth; and as I looked there came, I thought, a change—he seemed to swell—his 330 face became suddenly black and the features seemed to melt and alter—and the next moment, I had sprung to my feet and leaped back against the wall, my arms raised to shield me from that prodigy, my mind sub-335 merged in terror.

"O God!" I screamed, and "O God!" again and again; for there before my eyes—pale and shaken, and half fainting, and groping before him with his hands, like a man 340 restored from death—there stood Henry Jekyll!

What he told me in the next hour, I cannot bring my mind to set on paper. I saw what I saw, I heard what I heard, and my soul 345 sickened at it; and yet now when that sight has faded from my eyes, I ask myself if I believe it, and I cannot answer. My life is shaken to its roots; sleep has left me; the deadliest terror sits by me at all hours of the 350 day and night; and I feel that my days are numbered, and that I must die; and yet I shall die incredulous. As for the moral turpitude that man unveiled to me, even with tears of penitence, I cannot, even in memory, 355 dwell on it without a start of horror. I will say but one thing, Utterson, and that (if you can bring your mind to credit it) will be more than enough. The creature who crept into my house that night was, on Jekyll's own confes-360 sion, known by the name of Hyde and hunted for in every corner of the land as the murderer of Carew.

HASTIE LANYON.

HENRY JEKYLL'S FULL STATEMENT OF THE CASE

I was born in the year 18—to a large fortune, 365 endowed besides with excellent parts, inclined by nature to industry, fond of the respect of the wise and good among my fellowmen, and thus, as might have been supposed, with every guarantee of an honourable 370 and distinguished future. And indeed the worst of my faults was a certain impatient gaiety of disposition, such as has made the happiness of many, but such as I found it hard to reconcile with my imperious desire 375 to carry my head high, and wear a more than commonly grave countenance before the public. Hence it came about that I concealed my pleasures; and that when I reached years of reflection, and began to look round me 380 and take stock of my progress and position in the world, I stood already committed to a profound duplicity of life. Many a man would have even blazoned such irregularities as I was guilty of; but from the high views that I 385 had set before me, I regarded and hid them with an almost morbid sense of shame. It was thus rather the exacting nature of my aspirations than any particular degradation in my faults, that made me what I was, and, with even a deeper trench than in the majority of men, severed in me those provinces of good and ill which divide and compound man's dual nature. In this case, I was driven to reflect deeply and inveterately on that hard law of life, which lies at the root of religion and is one of the most plentiful springs of distress. Though so profound a double-dealer, I was in no sense a hypocrite; both sides of me were in dead earnest; I was no more myself when I laid aside restraint and plunged in shame, than when I laboured, in the eye of day, at the furtherance of knowledge or the relief of sorrow and suffering. And it chanced that the direction of my scientific studies, which led wholly towards the mystic and the transcendental, reacted and shed a strong light on this consciousness of the perennial war among my members. With every day, and from both sides of my intelligence, the moral and the intellectual, I thus drew steadily nearer to that truth, by whose partial discovery I have been doomed to such a dreadful shipwreck: that man is not truly one, but truly two. I say two, because the state of my own knowledge does not pass beyond that point. Others will follow, others will outstrip me on the same lines; and I hazard the guess that man will be ultimately known for a mere polity of multifarious, incongruous and independent denizens. I, for my part, from the nature of my life, advanced infallibly in one direction and in one direction only. It was on the moral side, and in my own person, that I learned to recognise the thorough and primitive duality of man; I saw that, of the two natures that contended in the field of my consciousness,

even if I could rightly be said to be either, it was only because I was radically both; and from an early date, even before the course of my scientific discoveries had begun to suggest the most naked possibility of such a miracle, I had learned to dwell with pleasure, as a beloved daydream, on the thought of the separation of these elements. If each, I told myself, could be housed in separate identities, life would be relieved of all that was unbearable; the unjust might go his way, delivered from the aspirations and remorse of his more upright twin; and the just could walk steadfastly and securely on his upward path, doing the good things in which he found his pleasure, and no longer exposed to disgrace and penitence by the hands of this extraneous evil. It was the curse of mankind that these incongruous faggots were thus bound together—that in the agonised womb of consciousness, these polar twins should be continuously struggling. How, then were they dissociated?

I was so far in my reflections when, as I have said, a side light began to shine upon the subject from the laboratory table. I began to perceive more deeply than it has ever yet been stated, the trembling immateriality, the mistlike transience, of this seemingly so solid body in which we walk attired. Certain agents I found to have the power to shake and pluck back that fleshly vestment, even as a wind might toss the curtains of a pavilion. For two good reasons, I will not enter deeply into this scientific branch of my confession. First, because I have been made to learn that the doom and burthen of our life is bound for ever on man's shoulders, and when the attempt is made to cast it off, it but returns upon us with more unfamiliar and more awful pressure. Second, because, as my narrative will make, alas! too evident, my

470 discoveries were incomplete. Enough then, that I not only recognised my natural body from the mere aura and effulgence of certain of the powers that made up my spirit, but managed to compound a drug by which

475 these powers should be dethroned from their supremacy, and a second form and countenance substituted, none the less natural to me because they were the expression, and bore the stamp of lower elements in my soul.

480   I hesitated long before I put this theory to the test of practice. I knew well that I risked death; for any drug that so potently controlled and shook the very fortress of identity, might, by the least scruple of an

485 overdose or at the least inopportunity in the moment of exhibition, utterly blot out that immaterial tabernacle which I looked to it to change. But the temptation of a discovery so singular and profound at last overcame the

490 suggestions of alarm. I had long since prepared my tincture; I purchased at once, from a firm of wholesale chemists, a large quantity of a particular salt which I knew, from my experiments, to be the last ingredient

495 required; and late one accursed night, I compounded the elements, watched them boil and smoke together in the glass, and when the ebullition had subsided, with a strong glow of courage, drank off the potion.

500   The most racking pangs succeeded: a grinding in the bones, deadly nausea, and a horror of the spirit that cannot be exceeded at the hour of birth or death. Then these agonies began swiftly to subside, and I came to

505 myself as if out of a great sickness. There was something strange in my sensations, something indescribably new and, from its very novelty, incredibly sweet. I felt younger, lighter, happier in body; within I was con-

510 scious of a heady recklessness, a current of disordered sensual images running like a millrace in my fancy, a solution of the bonds of obligation, an unknown but not an innocent freedom of the soul. I knew myself, at

515 the first breath of this new life, to be more wicked, tenfold more wicked, sold a slave to my original evil; and the thought, in that moment, braced and delighted me like wine. I stretched out my hands, exulting in the

520 freshness of these sensations; and in the act, I was suddenly aware that I had lost in stature.

    There was no mirror, at that date, in my room; that which stands beside me as I write,

525 was brought there later on and for the very purpose of these transformations. The night however, was far gone into the morning— the morning, black as it was, was nearly ripe for the conception of the day—the inmates

530 of my house were locked in the most rigorous hours of slumber; and I determined, flushed as I was with hope and triumph, to venture in my new shape as far as to my bedroom. I crossed the yard, wherein the

535 constellations looked down upon me, I could have thought, with wonder, the first creature of that sort that their unsleeping vigilance had yet disclosed to them; I stole through the corridors, a stranger in my own house;

540 and coming to my room, I saw for the first time the appearance of Edward Hyde.

    I must here speak by theory alone, saying not that which I know, but that which I suppose to be most probable. The evil side of my

545 nature, to which I had now transferred the stamping efficacy, was less robust and less developed than the good which I had just deposed. Again, in the course of my life, which had been, after all, nine tenths a life of effort,

550 virtue and control, it had been much less exercised and much less exhausted. And hence, as I think, it came about that Edward Hyde was so much smaller, slighter and

younger than Henry Jekyll. Even as good
555 shone upon the countenance of the one, evil
was written broadly and plainly on the face
of the other. Evil besides (which I must still
believe to be the lethal side of man) had left
on that body an imprint of deformity and
560 decay. And yet when I looked upon that ugly
idol in the glass, I was conscious of no repugnance, rather of a leap of welcome. This, too,
was myself. It seemed natural and human. In
my eyes it bore a livelier image of the spirit,
565 it seemed more express and single, than the
imperfect and divided countenance I had
been hitherto accustomed to call mine. And
in so far I was doubtless right. I have
observed that when I wore the semblance of
570 Edward Hyde, none could come near to me at
first without a visible misgiving of the flesh.
This, as I take it, was because all human
beings, as we meet them, are commingled
out of good and evil: and Edward Hyde, alone
575 in the ranks of mankind, was pure evil.

I lingered but a moment at the mirror: the
second and conclusive experiment had yet to
be attempted; it yet remained to be seen if I
had lost my identity beyond redemption and
580 must flee before daylight from a house that
was no longer mine; and hurrying back to
my cabinet, I once more prepared and drank
the cup, once more suffered the pangs of dissolution, and came to myself once more with
585 the character, the stature and the face of
Henry Jekyll.

That night I had come to the fatal cross-
roads. Had I approached my discovery in a
more noble spirit, had I risked the experi-
590 ment while under the empire of generous or
pious aspirations, all must have been otherwise, and from these agonies of death and
birth, I had come forth an angel instead of a
fiend. The drug had no discriminating action;
595 it was neither diabolical nor divine; it but

shook the doors of the prisonhouse of my
disposition; and like the captives of Philippi,
that which stood within ran forth. At that
time my virtue slumbered; my evil, kept
600 awake by ambition, was alert and swift to
seize the occasion; and the thing that was
projected was Edward Hyde. Hence, although
I had now two characters as well as two
appearances, one was wholly evil, and the
605 other was still the old Henry Jekyll, that
incongruous compound of whose reformation and improvement I had already learned
to despair. The movement was thus wholly
toward the worse.

610 Even at that time, I had not conquered my
aversions to the dryness of a life of study. I
would still be merrily disposed at times; and
as my pleasures were (to say the least)
undignified, and I was not only well known
615 and highly considered, but growing towards
the elderly man, this incoherency of my life
was daily growing more unwelcome. It was
on this side that my new power tempted me
until I fell in slavery. I had but to drink the
620 cup, to doff at once the body of the noted
professor, and to assume, like a thick cloak,
that of Edward Hyde. I smiled at the notion;
it seemed to me at the time to be humou-
rous; and I made my preparations with the
625 most studious care. I took and furnished that
house in Soho, to which Hyde was tracked by
the police; and engaged as a housekeeper a
creature whom I knew well to be silent and
unscrupulous. On the other side, I announced
630 to my servants that a Mr. Hyde (whom I
described) was to have full liberty and power
about my house in the square; and to parry
mishaps, I even called and made myself a
familiar object, in my second character. I
635 next drew up that will to which you so much
objected; so that if anything befell me in the
person of Dr. Jekyll, I could enter on that of

Edward Hyde without pecuniary loss. And thus fortified, as I supposed, on every side, I
640 began to profit by the strange immunities of my position.

Men have before hired bravos to transact their crimes, while their own person and reputation sat under shelter. I was the first
645 that ever did so for his pleasures. I was the first that could plod in the public eye with a load of genial respectability, and in a moment, like a schoolboy, strip off these lendings and spring headlong into the sea of liberty. But
650 for me, in my impenetrable mantle, the safety was complete. Think of it—I did not even exist! Let me but escape into my laboratory door, give me but a second or two to mix and swallow the draught that I had always
655 standing ready; and whatever he had done, Edward Hyde would pass away like the stain of breath upon a mirror; and there in his stead, quietly at home, trimming the midnight lamp in his study, a man who could
660 afford to laugh at suspicion, would be Henry Jekyll.

The pleasures which I made haste to seek in my disguise were, as I have said, undignified; I would scarce use a harder term. But in
665 the hands of Edward Hyde, they soon began to turn toward the monstrous. When I would come back from these excursions, I was often plunged into a kind of wonder at my vicarious depravity. This familiar that I called
670 out of my own soul, and sent forth alone to do his good pleasure, was a being inherently malign and villainous; his every act and thought centered on self; drinking pleasure with bestial avidity from any degree of tor-
675 ture to another; relentless like a man of stone. Henry Jekyll stood at times aghast before the acts of Edward Hyde; but the situation was apart from ordinary laws, and insidiously relaxed the grasp of conscience.

680 It was Hyde, after all, and Hyde alone, that was guilty. Jekyll was no worse; he woke again to his good qualities seemingly unimpaired; he would even make haste, where it was possible, to undo the evil done by Hyde.
685 And thus his conscience slumbered.

Into the details of the infamy at which I thus connived (for even now I can scarce grant that I committed it) I have no design of entering; I mean but to point out the warn-
690 ings and the successive steps with which my chastisement approached. I met with one accident which, as it brought on no consequence, I shall no more than mention. An act of cruelty to a child aroused against me the
695 anger of a passer-by, whom I recognised the other day in the person of your kinsman; the doctor and the child's family joined him; there were moments when I feared for my life; and at last, in order to pacify their
700 too just resentment, Edward Hyde had to bring them to the door, and pay them in a cheque drawn in the name of Henry Jekyll. But this danger was easily eliminated from the future, by opening an account at another
705 bank in the name of Edward Hyde himself; and when, by sloping my own hand backward, I had supplied my double with a signature, I thought I sat beyond the reach of fate.

Some two months before the murder of
710 Sir Danvers, I had been out for one of my adventures, had returned at a late hour, and woke the next day in bed with somewhat odd sensations. It was in vain I looked about me; in vain I saw the decent furniture and
715 tall proportions of my room in the square; in vain that I recognised the pattern of the bed curtains and the design of the mahogany frame; something still kept insisting that I was not where I was, that I had not wakened
720 where I seemed to be, but in the little room in Soho where I was accustomed to sleep in

the body of Edward Hyde. I smiled to myself, and in my psychological way, began lazily to inquire into the elements of this illusion,
725 occasionally, even as I did so, dropping back into a comfortable morning doze. I was still so engaged when, in one of my more wakeful moments, my eyes fell upon my hand. Now the hand of Henry Jekyll (as you have often
730 remarked) was professional in shape and size; it was large, firm, white and comely. But the hand which I now saw, clearly enough, in the yellow light of a mid-London morning, lying half shut on the bedclothes, was lean,
735 corded, knuckly, of a dusky pallor and thickly shaded with a swart growth of hair. It was the hand of Edward Hyde.

I must have stared upon it for near half a minute, sunk as I was in the mere stupidity
740 of wonder, before terror woke up in my breast as sudden and startling as the crash of cymbals; and bounding from my bed I rushed to the mirror. At the sight that met my eyes, my blood was changed into some-
745 thing exquisitely thin and icy. Yes, I had gone to bed Henry Jekyll, I had awakened Edward Hyde. How was this to be explained? I asked myself; and then, with another bound of terror—how was it to be remedied? It was
750 well on in the morning; the servants were up; all my drugs were in the cabinet—a long journey down two pairs of stairs, through the back passage, across the open court and through the anatomical theatre, from where
755 I was then standing horror-struck. It might indeed be possible to cover my face; but of what use was that, when I was unable to conceal the alteration in my stature? And then with an overpowering sweetness of
760 relief, it came back upon my mind that the servants were already used to the coming and going of my second self. I had soon dressed, as well as I was able, in clothes of

my own size: had soon passed through the
765 house, where Bradshaw stared and drew back at seeing Mr. Hyde at such an hour and in such a strange array; and ten minutes later, Dr. Jekyll had returned to his own shape and was sitting down, with a darkened
770 brow, to make a feint of breakfasting.

Small indeed was my appetite. This inexplicable incident, this reversal of my previous experience, seemed, like the Babylonian finger on the wall, to be spelling out the letters
775 of my judgment; and I began to reflect more seriously than ever before on the issues and possibilities of my double existence. That part of me which I had the power of projecting, had lately been much exercised and nour-
780 ished; it had seemed to me of late as though the body of Edward Hyde had grown in stature, as though (when I wore that form) I were conscious of a more generous tide of blood; and I began to spy a danger that, if this were
785 much prolonged, the balance of my nature might be permanently overthrown, the power of voluntary change be forfeited, and the character of Edward Hyde become irrevocably mine. The power of the drug had not been
790 always equally displayed. Once, very early in my career, it had totally failed me; since then I had been obliged on more than one occasion to double, and once, with infinite risk of death, to treble the amount; and these rare
795 uncertainties had cast hitherto the sole shadow on my contentment. Now, however, and in the light of that morning's accident, I was led to remark that whereas, in the beginning, the difficulty had been to throw off the
800 body of Jekyll, it had of late gradually but decidedly transferred itself to the other side. All things therefore seemed to point to this; that I was slowly losing hold of my original and better self, and becoming slowly incorpo-
805 rated with my second and worse.

Between these two, I now felt I had to choose. My two natures had memory in common, but all other faculties were most unequally shared between them. Jekyll (who 810 was composite) now with the most sensitive apprehensions, now with a greedy gusto, projected and shared in the pleasures and adventures of Hyde; but Hyde was indifferent to Jekyll, or but remembered him as the 815 mountain bandit remembers the cavern in which he conceals himself from pursuit. Jekyll had more than a father's interest; Hyde had more than a son's indifference. To cast in my lot with Jekyll, was to die to those appe-820 tites which I had long secretly indulged and had of late begun to pamper. To cast it in with Hyde, was to die to a thousand interests and aspirations, and to become, at a blow and forever, despised and friendless. The bar-825 gain might appear unequal; but there was still another consideration in the scales; for while Jekyll would suffer smartingly in the fires of abstinence, Hyde would be not even conscious of all that he had lost. Strange as 830 my circumstances were, the terms of this debate are as old and commonplace as man; much the same inducements and alarms cast the die for any tempted and trembling sinner; and it fell out with me, as it falls with 835 so vast a majority of my fellows, that I chose the better part and was found wanting in the strength to keep to it.

Yes, I preferred the elderly and discontented doctor, surrounded by friends and 840 cherishing honest hopes; and bade a resolute farewell to the liberty, the comparative youth, the light step, leaping impulses and secret pleasures, that I had enjoyed in the disguise of Hyde. I made this choice perhaps with 845 some unconscious reservation, for I neither gave up the house in Soho, nor destroyed the clothes of Edward Hyde, which still lay ready

in my cabinet. For two months, however, I was true to my determination; for two 850 months, I led a life of such severity as I had never before attained to, and enjoyed the compensations of an approving conscience. But time began at last to obliterate the freshness of my alarm; the praises of conscience 855 began to grow into a thing of course; I began to be tortured with throes and longings, as of Hyde struggling after freedom; and at last, in an hour of moral weakness, I once again compounded and swallowed the transform-860 ing draught.

I do not suppose that, when a drunkard reasons with himself upon his vice, he is once out of five hundred times affected by the dangers that he runs through his brutish, 865 physical insensibility; neither had I, long as I had considered my position, made enough allowance for the complete moral insensibility and insensate readiness to evil, which were the leading characters of Edward Hyde. 870 Yet it was by these that I was punished. My devil had been long caged, he came out roaring. I was conscious, even when I took the draught, of a more unbridled, a more furious propensity to ill. It must have been this, I 875 suppose, that stirred in my soul that tempest of impatience with which I listened to the civilities of my unhappy victim; I declare, at least, before God, no man morally sane could have been guilty of that crime upon so pitiful 880 a provocation; and that I struck in no more reasonable spirit than that in which a sick child may break a plaything. But I had voluntarily stripped myself of all those balancing instincts by which even the worst of us con-885 tinues to walk with some degree of steadiness among temptations; and in my case, to be tempted, however slightly, was to fall.

Instantly the spirit of hell awoke in me and raged. With a transport of glee, I mauled

890 the unresisting body, tasting delight from
every blow; and it was not till weariness had
begun to succeed, that I was suddenly, in the
top fit of my delirium, struck through the
heart by a cold thrill of terror. A mist dis-
895 persed; I saw my life to be forfeit; and fled
from the scene of these excesses, at once
glorying and trembling, my lust of evil gratified and stimulated, my love of life screwed
to the topmost peg. I ran to the house in
900 Soho, and (to make assurance doubly sure)
destroyed my papers; thence I set out
through the lamplit streets, in the same
divided ecstasy of mind, gloating on my
crime, light-headedly devising others in the
905 future, and yet still hastening and still hear-
kening in my wake for the steps of the
avenger. Hyde had a song upon his lips as he
compounded the draught, and as he drank it,
pledged the dead man. The pangs of trans-
910 formation had not done tearing him, before
Henry Jekyll, with streaming tears of gratitude and remorse, had fallen upon his knees
and lifted his clasped hands to God. The veil
of self-indulgence was rent from head to
915 foot. I saw my life as a whole: I followed it up
from the days of childhood, when I had
walked with my father's hand, and through
the self-denying toils of my professional life,
to arrive again and again, with the same
920 sense of unreality, at the damned horrors of
the evening. I could have screamed aloud; I
sought with tears and prayers to smother
down the crowd of hideous images and
sounds with which my memory swarmed
925 against me; and still, between the petitions,
the ugly face of my iniquity stared into my
soul. As the acuteness of this remorse began
to die away, it was succeeded by a sense of
joy. The problem of my conduct was solved.
930 Hyde was thenceforth impossible; whether
I would or not, I was now confined to the

better part of my existence; and O, how I
rejoiced to think of it! with what willing
humility I embraced anew the restrictions of
935 natural life! with what sincere renunciation I
locked the door by which I had so often gone
and come, and ground the key under my
heel!

The next day, came the news that the
940 murder had been overlooked, that the guilt
of Hyde was patent to the world, and that
the victim was a man high in public estimation. It was not only a crime, it had been a
tragic folly. I think I was glad to know it; I
945 think I was glad to have my better impulses
thus buttressed and guarded by the terrors of
the scaffold. Jekyll was now my city of refuge; let but Hyde peep out an instant, and
the hands of all men would be raised to take
950 and slay him.

I resolved in my future conduct to redeem
the past; and I can say with honesty that my
resolve was fruitful of some good. You know
yourself how earnestly, in the last months of
955 the last year, I laboured to relieve suffering;
you know that much was done for others,
and that the days passed quietly, almost
happily for myself. Nor can I truly say that I
wearied of this beneficent and innocent life;
960 I think instead that I daily enjoyed it more
completely; but I was still cursed with my
duality of purpose; and as the first edge of
my penitence wore off, the lower side of me,
so long indulged, so recently chained down,
965 began to growl for licence. Not that I
dreamed of resuscitating Hyde; the bare idea
of that would startle me to frenzy: no, it was
in my own person that I was once more
tempted to trifle with my conscience; and it
970 was as an ordinary secret sinner that I at last
fell before the assaults of temptation.

There comes an end to all things; the
most capacious measure is filled at last; and

this brief condescension to my evil finally
975 destroyed the balance of my soul. And yet I
was not alarmed; the fall seemed natural,
like a return to the old days before I had
made my discovery. It was a fine, clear,
January day, wet under foot where the frost
980 had melted, but cloudless overhead; and the
Regent's Park was full of winter chirrupings
and sweet with spring odours. I sat in the
sun on a bench; the animal within me licking
the chops of memory; the spiritual side a lit-
985 tle drowsed, promising subsequent penitence, but not yet moved to begin. After all, I
reflected, I was like my neighbours; and then
I smiled, comparing myself with other men,
comparing my active good-will with the lazy
990 cruelty of their neglect. And at the very
moment of that vainglorious thought, a
qualm came over me, a horrid nausea and
the most deadly shuddering. These passed
away, and left me faint; and then as in its
995 turn faintness subsided, I began to be aware
of a change in the temper of my thoughts, a
greater boldness, a contempt of danger, a
solution of the bonds of obligation. I looked
down; my clothes hung formlessly on my
1000 shrunken limbs; the hand that lay on my
knee was corded and hairy. I was once more
Edward Hyde. A moment before I had been
safe of all men's respect, wealthy, beloved—
the cloth laying for me in the dining-room at
1005 home; and now I was the common quarry of
mankind, hunted, houseless, a known murderer, thrall to the gallows.

My reason wavered, but it did not fail me
utterly. I have more than once observed that
1010 in my second character, my faculties seemed
sharpened to a point and my spirits more
tensely elastic; thus it came about that,
where Jekyll perhaps might have succumbed,
Hyde rose to the importance of the moment.
1015 My drugs were in one of the presses of my

cabinet; how was I to reach them? That was
the problem that (crushing my temples in
my hands) I set myself to solve. The laboratory door I had closed. If I sought to enter by
1020 the house, my own servants would consign
me to the gallows. I saw I must employ
another hand, and thought of Lanyon. How
was he to be reached? how persuaded?
Supposing that I escaped capture in the
1025 streets, how was I to make my way into his
presence? and how should I, an unknown
and displeasing visitor, prevail on the
famous physician to rifle the study of his colleague, Dr. Jekyll? Then I remembered that of
1030 my original character, one part remained to
me: I could write my own hand; and once I
had conceived that kindling spark, the way
that I must follow became lighted up from
end to end.

1035   Thereupon, I arranged my clothes as best
I could, and summoning a passing hansom,
drove to an hotel in Portland Street, the
name of which I chanced to remember. At
my appearance (which was indeed comical
1040 enough, however tragic a fate these garments covered) the driver could not conceal
his mirth. I gnashed my teeth upon him with
a gust of devilish fury; and the smile withered from his face—happily for him—yet
1045 more happily for myself, for in another
instant I had certainly dragged him from his
perch. At the inn, as I entered, I looked about
me with so black a countenance as made the
attendants tremble; not a look did they
1050 exchange in my presence; but obsequiously
took my orders, led me to a private room,
and brought me wherewithal to write. Hyde
in danger of his life was a creature new to
me; shaken with inordinate anger, strung to
1055 the pitch of murder, lusting to inflict pain.
Yet the creature was astute; mastered his
fury with a great effort of the will; composed

his two important letters, one to Lanyon and one to Poole; and that he might receive

1060 actual evidence of their being posted, sent them out with directions that they should be registered. Thenceforward, he sat all day over the fire in the private room, gnawing his nails; there he dined, sitting alone with

1065 his fears, the waiter visibly quailing before his eye; and thence, when the night was fully come, he set forth in the corner of a closed cab, and was driven to and fro about the streets of the city. He, I say—I cannot say, I.

1070 That child of Hell had nothing human; nothing lived in him but fear and hatred. And when at last, thinking the driver had begun to grow suspicious, he discharged the cab and ventured on foot, attired in his misfitting

1075 clothes, an object marked out for observation, into the midst of the nocturnal passengers, these two base passions raged within him like a tempest. He walked fast, hunted by his fears, chattering to himself, skulking

1080 through the less frequented thoroughfares, counting the minutes that still divided him from midnight. Once a woman spoke to him, offering, I think, a box of lights. He smote her in the face, and she fled.

1085   When I came to myself at Lanyon's, the horror of my old friend perhaps affected me somewhat: I do not know; it was at least but a drop in the sea to the abhorrence with which I looked back upon these hours. A change had

1090 come over me. It was no longer the fear of the gallows, it was the horror of being Hyde that racked me. I received Lanyon's condemnation partly in a dream; it was partly in a dream that I came home to my own house and got

1095 into bed. I slept after the prostration of the day, with a stringent and profound slumber which not even the nightmares that wrung me could avail to break. I awoke in the morning shaken, weakened, but refreshed. I still

1100 hated and feared the thought of the brute that slept within me, and I had not of course forgotten the appalling dangers of the day before; but I was once more at home, in my own house and close to my drugs; and grati-

1105 tude for my escape shone so strong in my soul that it almost rivalled the brightness of hope.

    I was stepping leisurely across the court after breakfast, drinking the chill of the air

1110 with pleasure, when I was seized again with those indescribable sensations that heralded the change; and I had but the time to gain the shelter of my cabinet, before I was once again raging and freezing with the passions

1115 of Hyde. It took on this occasion a double dose to recall me to myself; and alas! six hours after, as I sat looking sadly in the fire, the pangs returned, and the drug had to be re-administered. In short, from that day forth

1120 it seemed only by a great effort as of gymnastics, and only under the immediate stimulation of the drug, that I was able to wear the countenance of Jekyll. At all hours of the day and night, I would be taken with the pre-

1125 monitory shudder; above all, if I slept, or even dozed for a moment in my chair, it was always as Hyde that I awakened. Under the strain of this continually impending doom and by the sleeplessness to which I now con-

1130 demned myself, ay, even beyond what I had thought possible to man, I became, in my own person, a creature eaten up and emptied by fever, languidly weak both in body and mind, and solely occupied by one

1135 thought: the horror of my other self. But when I slept, or when the virtue of the medicine wore off, I would leap almost without transition (for the pangs of transformation grew daily less marked) into the possession

1140 of a fancy brimming with images of terror, a soul boiling with causeless hatreds, and a

body that seemed not strong enough to contain the raging energies of life. The powers of Hyde seemed to have grown with the sickli-1145 ness of Jekyll. And certainly the hate that now divided them was equal on each side. With Jekyll, it was a thing of vital instinct. He had now seen the full deformity of that creature that shared with him some of the phe-1150 nomena of consciousness, and was co-heir with him to death: and beyond these links of community, which in themselves made the most poignant part of his distress, he thought of Hyde, for all his energy of life, as 1155 of something not only hellish but inorganic. This was the shocking thing; that the slime of the pit seemed to utter cries and voices; that the amorphous dust gesticulated and sinned; that what was dead, and had no 1160 shape, should usurp the offices of life. And this again, that that insurgent horror was knit to him closer than a wife, closer than an eye; lay caged in his flesh, where he heard it mutter and felt it struggle to be born; and at 1165 every hour of weakness, and in the confidence of slumber, prevailed against him, and deposed him out of life. The hatred of Hyde for Jekyll was of a different order. His terror of the gallows drove him continually to com-1170 mit temporary suicide, and return to his subordinate station of a part instead of a person; but he loathed the necessity, he loathed the despondency into which Jekyll was now fallen, and he resented the dislike with 1175 which he was himself regarded. Hence the ape-like tricks that he would play me, scrawling in my own hand blasphemies on the pages of my books, burning the letters and destroying the portrait of my father; and 1180 indeed, had it not been for his fear of death, he would long ago have ruined himself in order to involve me in the ruin. But his love of life is wonderful; I go further: I, who sicken

and freeze at the mere thought of him, when 1185 I recall the abjection and passion of this attachment, and when I know how he fears my power to cut him off by suicide, I find it in my heart to pity him.

It is useless, and the time awfully fails me, 1190 to prolong this description; no one has ever suffered such torments, let that suffice; and yet even to these, habit brought—no, not alleviation—but a certain callousness of soul, a certain acquiescence of despair; and 1195 my punishment might have gone on for years, but for the last calamity which has now fallen, and which has finally severed me from my own face and nature. My provision of the salt, which had never been renewed 1200 since the date of the first experiment, began to run low. I sent out for a fresh supply and mixed the draught; the ebullition followed, and the first change of colour, not the second; I drank it and it was without efficiency. 1205 You will learn from Poole how I have had London ransacked; it was in vain; and I am now persuaded that my first supply was impure, and that it was that unknown impurity which lent efficacy to the draught.

1210 About a week has passed, and I am now finishing this statement under the influence of the last of the old powders. This, then, is the last time, short of a miracle, that Henry Jekyll can think his own thoughts or see his 1215 own face (now how sadly altered!) in the glass. Nor must I delay too long to bring my writing to an end; for if my narrative has hitherto escaped destruction, it has been by a combination of great prudence and great 1220 good luck. Should the throes of change take me in the act of writing it, Hyde will tear it in pieces; but if some time shall have elapsed after I have laid it by, his wonderful selfishness and circumscription to the moment will 1225 probably save it once again from the action

of his ape-like spite. And indeed the doom
that is closing on us both has already
changed and crushed him. Half an hour from
now, when I shall again and forever reindue
1230 that hated personality, I know how I shall sit
shuddering and weeping in my chair, or continue, with the most strained and fearstruck
ecstasy of listening, to pace up and down
this room (my last earthly refuge) and give
1235 ear to every sound of menace. Will Hyde die
upon the scaffold? or will he find courage to
release himself at the last moment? God
knows; I am careless; this is my true hour
of death, and what is to follow concerns
1240 another than myself. Here then, as I lay
down the pen and proceed to seal up my
confession, I bring the life of that unhappy
Henry Jekyll to an end.

Theater marquee for the opening night
performance of Broadway's *Jekyll & Hyde:
The Musical* starring Constantine Maroulis and
Deborah Cox at the Marquis Theatre in New York
City on April 18, 2013.

———

The story of Dr. Jekyll and Mr. Hyde has long
fascinated readers. The image shows the theater
marquee for *Jekyll & Hyde: The Musical*. Why
do you think this mysterious story still resonates
today? How do you understand the ending of the
novel? What does it say about the condition of
human beings?

Walter McBride/Corbis/Getty Images

CHARACTER

1. Dr. Lanyon serves as a **foil** character to Dr. Jekyll. How does the **contrast** between these two characters contribute to your interpretation of the text?

2. How do the choices and actions of Mr. Hyde reveal contradictions and inconsistencies in his **character**?

3. How do the inconsistent traits of both Dr. Jekyll and Mr. Hyde contribute to the characters' complexity?

STRUCTURE

4. The two final letters break an established chronological sequence of the **plot**. Where do these events fit in the story? How does this break in the **plot** affect the reader?

5. The final letter explains how the main **conflict** of the novel represents Dr. Jekyll's **juxtaposed** motivations. What are those motivations?

6. How does the final letter from Dr. Jekyll **resolve** the **conflict** and contribute to the complexity of the text?

NARRATION

7. To what extent do you trust the letters from Dr. Lanyon and Dr. Jekyll? Are they **reliable** narrators? Explain.

8. To what degree is Dr. Lanyon aware of his own **biases**? How does this affect your interpretation of the story?

9. How does Dr. Jekyll's **perspective** in his letter contribute to the reader's understanding of his motivation?

FIGURATIVE LANGUAGE: Word Choice, Imagery, and Symbols

10. Explain how the **diction** in the final letters contributes to your understanding of the text.

IDEAS IN LITERATURE: Repression and Conformity

11. Dr. Jekyll struggles between vice and virtue. His need to repress his desires and conform to social standards reflects a duality in the human psyche. How do we manage this conflict? Why is it necessary to do so? Explain a time in your experience when you had an inner struggle between two opposing impulses.

PUTTING IT ALL TOGETHER

12. *The Strange Case of Dr. Jekyll and Mr. Hyde* is generally identified as a Gothic horror and mystery or detective story. Is there a solution to the novel's mystery? How do different characters confront the mystery? How does the investigation contribute to your interpretation of the text?

Frankenstein; or, The Modern Prometheus
Mary Shelley

THE TEXT IN CONTEXT

Mary Shelley (1797–1851) was the daughter of early feminist revolutionary Mary Wollstonecraft and the journalist and philosopher William Godwin. While she had little formal education, the precocious Shelley had access to her father's library, as well as to literary figures who visited her house, such as William Wordsworth and Samuel Coleridge. In her literary career, she wrote novels such as *Valperga* (1823), *The Last Man* (1826), and *Falkner* (1837). But she is best known for producing *Frankenstein; or, The Modern Prometheus* (1818). The novel's origins are famous in their own right: Shelley and her future husband, the Romantic poet Percy Shelley, were visiting their friend, the poet Lord Byron, in Switzerland during the unusually dreary summer of 1816. Byron proposed that they each write a ghost story. Mary Shelley's contribution proved to be the most substantial and lasting: a Gothic tale of monstrosity, the sublime, forbidden knowledge, scientific hubris, family relationships, and the tension between rationality and emotion. The story has proven remarkably durable and timeless, as have the metaphorical implications of its antagonist: the term "Frankenstein's monster" has come to refer to technologies gone awry and the unintended consequences of scientific innovation.

Frankenstein; or, The Modern Prometheus

Letter 1

You will rejoice to hear that no disaster has accompanied the commencement of an enterprise which you have regarded with such evil forebodings. I arrived here yesterday,
5 and my first task is to assure my dear sister of my welfare and increasing confidence in the success of my undertaking.

I am already far north of London, and as I walk in the streets of Petersburgh, I feel a
10 cold northern breeze play upon my cheeks, which braces my nerves and fills me with delight. Do you understand this feeling? This breeze, which has travelled from the regions towards which I am advancing, gives me a
15 foretaste of those icy climes. Inspirited by this wind of promise, my daydreams become more fervent and vivid. I try in vain to be persuaded that the pole is the seat of frost and desolation; it ever presents itself to my
20 imagination as the region of beauty and delight. There, Margaret, the sun is for ever visible, its broad disk just skirting the horizon and diffusing a perpetual splendour. There—for with your leave, my sister, I will
25 put some trust in preceding navigators— there snow and frost are banished; and, sailing over a calm sea, we may be wafted to

a land surpassing in wonders and in beauty every region hitherto discovered on the hab-
30 itable globe. Its productions and features may be without example, as the phenomena of the heavenly bodies undoubtedly are in those undiscovered solitudes. What may not be expected in a country of eternal light? I
35 may there discover the wondrous power which attracts the needle and may regulate a thousand celestial observations that require only this voyage to render their seeming eccentricities consistent for ever. I shall sati-
40 ate my ardent curiosity with the sight of a part of the world never before visited, and may tread a land never before imprinted by the foot of man. These are my enticements, and they are sufficient to conquer all fear of
45 danger or death and to induce me to com-mence this laborious voyage with the joy a child feels when he embarks in a little boat, with his holiday mates, on an expedition of discovery up his native river. But supposing
50 all these conjectures to be false, you cannot contest the inestimable benefit which I shall confer on all mankind, to the last generation, by discovering a passage near the pole to those countries, to reach which at present so
55 many months are requisite; or by ascertain-ing the secret of the magnet, which, if at all possible, can only be effected by an under-taking such as mine.

These reflections have dispelled the agita-
60 tion with which I began my letter, and I feel my heart glow with an enthusiasm which elevates me to heaven, for nothing contrib-utes so much to tranquillise the mind as a steady purpose—a point on which the soul
65 may fix its intellectual eye. This expedition has been the favourite dream of my early years. I have read with ardour the accounts of the various voyages which have been made in the prospect of arriving at the North

70 Pacific Ocean through the seas which sur-round the pole. You may remember that a history of all the voyages made for purposes of discovery composed the whole of our good Uncle Thomas' library. My education was
75 neglected, yet I was passionately fond of reading. These volumes were my study day and night, and my familiarity with them increased that regret which I had felt, as a child, on learning that my father's dying
80 injunction had forbidden my uncle to allow me to embark in a seafaring life.

These visions faded when I perused, for the first time, those poets whose effusions entranced my soul and lifted it to heaven. I
85 also became a poet and for one year lived in a paradise of my own creation; I imagined that I also might obtain a niche in the temple where the names of Homer and Shakespeare are consecrated. You are well acquainted
90 with my failure and how heavily I bore the disappointment. But just at that time I inher-ited the fortune of my cousin, and my thoughts were turned into the channel of their earlier bent.

95 Six years have passed since I resolved on my present undertaking. I can, even now, remember the hour from which I dedicated myself to this great enterprise. I commenced by inuring my body to hardship. I accompa-
100 nied the whale-fishers on several expedi-tions to the North Sea; I voluntarily endured cold, famine, thirst, and want of sleep; I often worked harder than the common sailors during the day and devoted my nights to the
105 study of mathematics, the theory of medi-cine, and those branches of physical science from which a naval adventurer might derive the greatest practical advantage. Twice I actually hired myself as an under-mate in a
110 Greenland whaler, and acquitted myself to admiration. I must own I felt a little proud

when my captain offered me the second dignity in the vessel and entreated me to remain with the greatest earnestness, so
115 valuable did he consider my services.

And now, dear Margaret, do I not deserve to accomplish some great purpose? My life might have been passed in ease and luxury, but I preferred glory to every enticement that
120 wealth placed in my path. Oh, that some encouraging voice would answer in the affirmative! My courage and my resolution is firm; but my hopes fluctuate, and my spirits are often depressed. I am about to proceed
125 on a long and difficult voyage, the emergencies of which will demand all my fortitude: I am required not only to raise the spirits of others, but sometimes to sustain my own, when theirs are failing.

130 This is the most favourable period for travelling in Russia. They fly quickly over the snow in their sledges; the motion is pleasant, and, in my opinion, far more agreeable than that of an English stagecoach. The cold is not
135 excessive, if you are wrapped in furs—a dress which I have already adopted, for there is a great difference between walking the deck and remaining seated motionless for hours, when no exercise prevents the blood
140 from actually freezing in your veins. I have no ambition to lose my life on the post-road between St. Petersburgh and Archangel.

I shall depart for the latter town in a fortnight or three weeks; and my intention is to
145 hire a ship there, which can easily be done by paying the insurance for the owner, and to engage as many sailors as I think necessary among those who are accustomed to the whale-fishing. I do not intend to sail until
150 the month of June; and when shall I return? Ah, dear sister, how can I answer this question? If I succeed, many, many months, perhaps years, will pass before you and

I may meet. If I fail, you will see me again
155 soon, or never.

Farewell, my dear, excellent Margaret. Heaven shower down blessings on you, and save me, that I may again and again testify my gratitude for all your love and kindness.
160 Your affectionate brother,
R. Walton

Letter 2
To Mrs. Saville, England.
Archangel, 28th March, 17—.
165 How slowly the time passes here, encompassed as I am by frost and snow! Yet a second step is taken towards my enterprise. I have hired a vessel and am occupied in collecting my sailors; those whom I have already
170 engaged appear to be men on whom I can depend and are certainly possessed of dauntless courage.

But I have one want which I have never yet been able to satisfy, and the absence of
175 the object of which I now feel as a most severe evil, I have no friend, Margaret: when I am glowing with the enthusiasm of success, there will be none to participate my joy; if I am assailed by disappointment, no
180 one will endeavour to sustain me in dejection. I shall commit my thoughts to paper, it is true; but that is a poor medium for the communication of feeling. I desire the company of a man who could sympathise with
185 me, whose eyes would reply to mine. You may deem me romantic, my dear sister, but I bitterly feel the want of a friend. I have no one near me, gentle yet courageous, possessed of a cultivated as well as of a capa-
190 cious mind, whose tastes are like my own, to approve or amend my plans. How would such a friend repair the faults of your poor brother! I am too ardent in execution and too impatient of difficulties. But it is a still

195 greater evil to me that I am self-educated: for the first fourteen years of my life I ran wild on a common and read nothing but our Uncle Thomas' books of voyages. At that age I became acquainted with the celebrated

200 poets of our own country; but it was only when it had ceased to be in my power to derive its most important benefits from such a conviction that I perceived the necessity of becoming acquainted with more languages

205 than that of my native country. Now I am twenty-eight and am in reality more illiterate than many schoolboys of fifteen. It is true that I have thought more and that my daydreams are more extended and magnifi-

210 cent, but they want (as the painters call it) keeping; and I greatly need a friend who would have sense enough not to despise me as romantic, and affection enough for me to endeavour to regulate my mind.

215 Well, these are useless complaints; I shall certainly find no friend on the wide ocean, nor even here in Archangel, among merchants and seamen. Yet some feelings, unallied to the dross of human nature, beat

220 even in these rugged bosoms. My lieutenant, for instance, is a man of wonderful courage and enterprise; he is madly desirous of glory, or rather, to word my phrase more characteristically, of advancement in his

225 profession. He is an Englishman, and in the midst of national and professional prejudices, unsoftened by cultivation, retains some of the noblest endowments of humanity. I first became acquainted with him on board a

230 whale vessel; finding that he was unemployed in this city, I easily engaged him to assist in my enterprise.

The master is a person of an excellent disposition and is remarkable in the ship

235 for his gentleness and the mildness of his discipline. This circumstance, added to his well-known integrity and dauntless courage, made me very desirous to engage him. A youth passed in solitude, my best years

240 spent under your gentle and feminine fosterage, has so refined the groundwork of my character that I cannot overcome an intense distaste to the usual brutality exercised on board ship: I have never believed it to be

245 necessary, and when I heard of a mariner equally noted for his kindliness of heart and the respect and obedience paid to him by his crew, I felt myself peculiarly fortunate in being able to secure his services. I heard of

250 him first in rather a romantic manner, from a lady who owes to him the happiness of her life. This, briefly, is his story. Some years ago he loved a young Russian lady of moderate fortune, and having amassed a considerable

255 sum in prize-money, the father of the girl consented to the match. He saw his mistress once before the destined ceremony; but she was bathed in tears, and throwing herself at his feet, entreated him to spare her, confess-

260 ing at the same time that she loved another, but that he was poor, and that her father would never consent to the union. My generous friend reassured the suppliant, and on being informed of the name of her lover,

265 instantly abandoned his pursuit. He had already bought a farm with his money, on which he had designed to pass the remainder of his life; but he bestowed the whole on his rival, together with the remains of his

270 prize-money to purchase stock, and then himself solicited the young woman's father to consent to her marriage with her lover. But the old man decidedly refused, thinking himself bound in honour to my friend, who,

275 when he found the father inexorable, quitted his country, nor returned until he heard that his former mistress was married according to her inclinations. "What a noble fellow!"

you will exclaim. He is so; but then he is
280 wholly uneducated: he is as silent as a Turk,
and a kind of ignorant carelessness attends
him, which, while it renders his conduct the
more astonishing, detracts from the interest
and sympathy which otherwise he would
285 command.

Yet do not suppose, because I complain a
little or because I can conceive a consolation
for my toils which I may never know, that I
am wavering in my resolutions. Those are as
290 fixed as fate, and my voyage is only now
delayed until the weather shall permit my
embarkation. The winter has been dreadfully
severe, but the spring promises well, and it is
considered as a remarkably early season, so
295 that perhaps I may sail sooner than I expected.
I shall do nothing rashly: you know me sufficiently to confide in my prudence and con-
siderateness whenever the safety of others is
committed to my care.
300   I cannot describe to you my sensations on
the near prospect of my undertaking. It is
impossible to communicate to you a conception of the trembling sensation, half pleasurable and half fearful, with which I am
305 preparing to depart. I am going to unexplored
regions, to "the land of mist and snow," but I
shall kill no albatross; therefore do not be
alarmed for my safety or if I should come
back to you as worn and woeful as the "Ancient
310 Mariner." You will smile at my allusion, but I
will disclose a secret. I have often attributed
my attachment to, my passionate enthusiasm
for, the dangerous mysteries of ocean to that
production of the most imaginative of mod-
315 ern poets. There is something at work in my
soul which I do not understand. I am practically industrious—painstaking, a workman to
execute with perseverance and labour—but
besides this there is a love for the marvellous,
320 a belief in the marvellous, intertwined in all

my projects, which hurries me out of the common pathways of men, even to the wild sea
and unvisited regions I am about to explore.

But to return to dearer considerations.
325 Shall I meet you again, after having traversed
immense seas, and returned by the most
southern cape of Africa or America? I dare
not expect such success, yet I cannot bear to
look on the reverse of the picture. Continue
330 for the present to write to me by every
opportunity: I may receive your letters on
some occasions when I need them most to
support my spirits. I love you very tenderly.
Remember me with affection, should you
335 never hear from me again.

Your affectionate brother,
Robert Walton

Letter 3
To Mrs. Saville, England.
340 July 7th, 17—.
My dear Sister,

I write a few lines in haste to say that I am
safe—and well advanced on my voyage. This
letter will reach England by a merchantman
345 now on its homeward voyage from Archangel;
more fortunate than I, who may not see my
native land, perhaps, for many years. I am,
however, in good spirits: my men are bold
and apparently firm of purpose, nor do the
350 floating sheets of ice that continually pass us,
indicating the dangers of the region towards
which we are advancing, appear to dismay
them. We have already reached a very high
latitude; but it is the height of summer, and
355 although not so warm as in England, the
southern gales, which blow us speedily
towards those shores which I so ardently
desire to attain, breathe a degree of renovat-
ing warmth which I had not expected.
360   No incidents have hitherto befallen us
that would make a figure in a letter. One or

two stiff gales and the springing of a leak are accidents which experienced navigators scarcely remember to record, and I shall be
365 well content if nothing worse happen to us during our voyage.

Adieu, my dear Margaret. Be assured that for my own sake, as well as yours, I will not rashly encounter danger. I will be cool, perse-
370 vering, and prudent.

But success shall crown my endeavours. Wherefore not? Thus far I have gone, tracing a secure way over the pathless seas, the very stars themselves being witnesses and testi-
375 monies of my triumph. Why not still proceed over the untamed yet obedient element? What can stop the determined heart and resolved will of man?

My swelling heart involuntarily pours
380 itself out thus. But I must finish. Heaven bless my beloved sister!

R.W.

Letter 4
To Mrs. Saville, England.
385 August 5th, 17—.

So strange an accident has happened to us that I cannot forbear recording it, although it is very probable that you will see me before these papers can come into your possession.
390 Last Monday (July 31st) we were nearly surrounded by ice, which closed in the ship on all sides, scarcely leaving her the sea-room in which she floated. Our situation was somewhat dangerous, especially as we were
395 compassed round by a very thick fog. We accordingly lay to, hoping that some change would take place in the atmosphere and weather.

About two o'clock the mist cleared away,
400 and we beheld, stretched out in every direc-tion, vast and irregular plains of ice, which seemed to have no end. Some of my comrades groaned, and my own mind began to grow watchful with anxious thoughts, when a
405 strange sight suddenly attracted our attention and diverted our solicitude from our own situ-ation. We perceived a low carriage, fixed on a sledge and drawn by dogs, pass on towards the north, at the distance of half a mile; a being
410 which had the shape of a man, but apparently of gigantic stature, sat in the sledge and guided the dogs. We watched the rapid progress of the traveller with our telescopes until he was lost among the distant inequalities of the ice.
415 This appearance excited our unqualified wonder. We were, as we believed, many hun-dred miles from any land; but this apparition seemed to denote that it was not, in reality, so distant as we had supposed. Shut in, how-
420 ever, by ice, it was impossible to follow his track, which we had observed with the great-est attention.

About two hours after this occurrence we heard the ground sea, and before night the
425 ice broke and freed our ship. We, however, lay to until the morning, fearing to encounter in the dark those large loose masses which float about after the breaking up of the ice. I profited of this time to rest for a few hours.
430 In the morning, however, as soon as it was light, I went upon deck and found all the sailors busy on one side of the vessel, appar-ently talking to someone in the sea. It was, in fact, a sledge, like that we had seen before,
435 which had drifted towards us in the night on a large fragment of ice. Only one dog remained alive; but there was a human being within it whom the sailors were persuading to enter the vessel. He was not, as the other traveller
440 seemed to be, a savage inhabitant of some undiscovered island, but a European. When I appeared on deck the master said, "Here is our captain, and he will not allow you to per-ish on the open sea."

445 On perceiving me, the stranger addressed me in English, although with a foreign accent. "Before I come on board your vessel," said he, "will you have the kindness to inform me whither you are bound?"

450 You may conceive my astonishment on hearing such a question addressed to me from a man on the brink of destruction and to whom I should have supposed that my vessel would have been a resource which he 455 would not have exchanged for the most precious wealth the earth can afford. I replied, however, that we were on a voyage of discovery towards the northern pole.

Upon hearing this he appeared satisfied 460 and consented to come on board. Good God! Margaret, if you had seen the man who thus capitulated for his safety, your surprise would have been boundless. His limbs were nearly frozen, and his body dreadfully 465 emaciated by fatigue and suffering. I never saw a man in so wretched a condition. We attempted to carry him into the cabin, but as soon as he had quitted the fresh air he fainted. We accordingly brought him back to 470 the deck and restored him to animation by rubbing him with brandy and forcing him to swallow a small quantity. As soon as he showed signs of life we wrapped him up in blankets and placed him near the chimney of 475 the kitchen stove. By slow degrees he recovered and ate a little soup, which restored him wonderfully.

Two days passed in this manner before he was able to speak, and I often feared that his 480 sufferings had deprived him of understanding. When he had in some measure recovered, I removed him to my own cabin and attended on him as much as my duty would permit. I never saw a more interesting crea-485 ture: his eyes have generally an expression of wildness, and even madness, but there are moments when, if anyone performs an act of kindness towards him or does him any the most trifling service, his whole countenance 490 is lighted up, as it were, with a beam of benevolence and sweetness that I never saw equalled. But he is generally melancholy and despairing, and sometimes he gnashes his teeth, as if impatient of the weight of woes 495 that oppresses him.

When my guest was a little recovered I had great trouble to keep off the men, who wished to ask him a thousand questions; but I would not allow him to be tormented by 500 their idle curiosity, in a state of body and mind whose restoration evidently depended upon entire repose. Once, however, the lieutenant asked why he had come so far upon the ice in so strange a vehicle.

505 His countenance instantly assumed an aspect of the deepest gloom, and he replied, "To seek one who fled from me."

"And did the man whom you pursued travel in the same fashion?"

510 "Yes."

"Then I fancy we have seen him, for the day before we picked you up we saw some dogs drawing a sledge, with a man in it, across the ice."

515 This aroused the stranger's attention, and he asked a multitude of questions concerning the route which the dæmon, as he called him, had pursued. Soon after, when he was alone with me, he said, "I have, doubtless, 520 excited your curiosity, as well as that of these good people; but you are too considerate to make inquiries."

"Certainly; it would indeed be very impertinent and inhuman in me to trouble you 525 with any inquisitiveness of mine."

"And yet you rescued me from a strange and perilous situation; you have benevolently restored me to life."

Soon after this he inquired if I thought 530 that the breaking up of the ice had destroyed

the other sledge. I replied that I could not answer with any degree of certainty, for the ice had not broken until near midnight, and the traveller might have arrived at a place of
535 safety before that time; but of this I could not judge.

From this time a new spirit of life animated the decaying frame of the stranger. He manifested the greatest eagerness to be
540 upon deck to watch for the sledge which had before appeared; but I have persuaded him to remain in the cabin, for he is far too weak to sustain the rawness of the atmosphere. I have promised that someone should watch
545 for him and give him instant notice if any new object should appear in sight.

Such is my journal of what relates to this strange occurrence up to the present day. The stranger has gradually improved in health but
550 is very silent and appears uneasy when anyone except myself enters his cabin. Yet his manners are so conciliating and gentle that the sailors are all interested in him, although they have had very little communication with him. For
555 my own part, I begin to love him as a brother, and his constant and deep grief fills me with sympathy and compassion. He must have been a noble creature in his better days, being even now in wreck so attractive and amiable.
560 I said in one of my letters, my dear Margaret, that I should find no friend on the wide ocean; yet I have found a man who, before his spirit had been broken by misery, I should have been happy to have possessed
565 as the brother of my heart.

I shall continue my journal concerning the stranger at intervals, should I have any fresh incidents to record.

August 13th, 17—.
570 My affection for my guest increases every day. He excites at once my admiration and my pity to an astonishing degree. How can I see so noble a creature destroyed by misery without feeling the most poignant grief? He
575 is so gentle, yet so wise; his mind is so cultivated, and when he speaks, although his words are culled with the choicest art, yet they flow with rapidity and unparalleled eloquence.
580 He is now much recovered from his illness and is continually on the deck, apparently watching for the sledge that preceded his own. Yet, although unhappy, he is not so utterly occupied by his own misery but that
585 he interests himself deeply in the projects of others. He has frequently conversed with me on mine, which I have communicated to him without disguise. He entered attentively into all my arguments in favour of my eventual
590 success and into every minute detail of the measures I had taken to secure it. I was easily led by the sympathy which he evinced to use the language of my heart, to give utterance to the burning ardour of my soul and to
595 say, with all the fervour that warmed me, how gladly I would sacrifice my fortune, my existence, my every hope, to the furtherance of my enterprise. One man's life or death were but a small price to pay for the acquire-
600 ment of the knowledge which I sought, for the dominion I should acquire and transmit over the elemental foes of our race. As I spoke, a dark gloom spread over my listener's countenance. At first I perceived that he tried to sup-
605 press his emotion; he placed his hands before his eyes, and my voice quivered and failed me as I beheld tears trickle fast from between his fingers; a groan burst from his heaving breast. I paused; at length he spoke, in broken accents:
610 "Unhappy man! Do you share my madness? Have you drunk also of the intoxicating draught? Hear me; let me reveal my tale, and you will dash the cup from your lips!"

Such words, you may imagine, strongly
615 excited my curiosity; but the paroxysm of
grief that had seized the stranger overcame
his weakened powers, and many hours of
repose and tranquil conversation were necessary to restore his composure.

620 Having conquered the violence of his feelings, he appeared to despise himself for
being the slave of passion; and quelling the
dark tyranny of despair, he led me again to
converse concerning myself personally.
625 He asked me the history of my earlier years.
The tale was quickly told, but it awakened
various trains of reflection. I spoke of my
desire of finding a friend, of my thirst for a
more intimate sympathy with a fellow
630 mind than had ever fallen to my lot, and
expressed my conviction that a man could
boast of little happiness who did not enjoy
this blessing.

"I agree with you," replied the stranger;
635 "we are unfashioned creatures, but half
made up, if one wiser, better, dearer than
ourselves—such a friend ought to be—do
not lend his aid to perfectionate our weak
and faulty natures. I once had a friend, the
640 most noble of human creatures, and am entitled, therefore, to judge respecting friendship. You have hope, and the world before
you, and have no cause for despair. But I—
I have lost everything and cannot begin life
645 anew."

As he said this his countenance became
expressive of a calm, settled grief that touched
me to the heart. But he was silent and presently retired to his cabin.
650 Even broken in spirit as he is, no one can
feel more deeply than he does the beauties
of nature. The starry sky, the sea, and every
sight afforded by these wonderful regions
seem still to have the power of elevating his
655 soul from earth. Such a man has a double

existence: he may suffer misery and be
overwhelmed by disappointments, yet
when he has retired into himself, he will be
like a celestial spirit that has a halo around
660 him, within whose circle no grief or folly
ventures.

Will you smile at the enthusiasm I
express concerning this divine wanderer?
You would not if you saw him. You have been
665 tutored and refined by books and retirement
from the world, and you are therefore somewhat fastidious; but this only renders you
the more fit to appreciate the extraordinary
merits of this wonderful man. Sometimes I
670 have endeavoured to discover what quality it
is which he possesses that elevates him so
immeasurably above any other person I ever
knew. I believe it to be an intuitive discern-
ment, a quick but never-failing power of
675 judgment, a penetration into the causes of
things, unequalled for clearness and precision; add to this a facility of expression and a
voice whose varied intonations are soul-
subduing music.

680 August 19th, 17—.
Yesterday the stranger said to me, "You
may easily perceive, Captain Walton, that I
have suffered great and unparalleled misfortunes. I had determined at one time that the
685 memory of these evils should die with me,
but you have won me to alter my determination. You seek for knowledge and wisdom, as
I once did; and I ardently hope that the gratification of your wishes may not be a serpent
690 to sting you, as mine has been. I do not know
that the relation of my disasters will be useful to you; yet, when I reflect that you are
pursuing the same course, exposing yourself
to the same dangers which have rendered
695 me what I am, I imagine that you may
deduce an apt moral from my tale, one that

may direct you if you succeed in your undertaking and console you in case of failure. Prepare to hear of occurrences which are usually deemed marvellous. Were we among the tamer scenes of nature I might fear to encounter your unbelief, perhaps your ridicule; but many things will appear possible in these wild and mysterious regions which would provoke the laughter of those unacquainted with the ever-varied powers of nature; nor can I doubt but that my tale conveys in its series internal evidence of the truth of the events of which it is composed."

You may easily imagine that I was much gratified by the offered communication, yet I could not endure that he should renew his grief by a recital of his misfortunes. I felt the greatest eagerness to hear the promised narrative, partly from curiosity and partly from a strong desire to ameliorate his fate if it were in my power. I expressed these feelings in my answer.

"I thank you," he replied, "for your sympathy, but it is useless; my fate is nearly fulfilled. I wait but for one event, and then I shall repose in peace. I understand your feeling," continued he, perceiving that I wished to interrupt him; "but you are mistaken, my friend, if thus you will allow me to name you; nothing can alter my destiny; listen to my history, and you will perceive how irrevocably it is determined."

He then told me that he would commence his narrative the next day when I should be at leisure. This promise drew from me the warmest thanks. I have resolved every night, when I am not imperatively occupied by my duties, to record, as nearly as possible in his own words, what he has related during the day. If I should be engaged, I will at least make notes. This manuscript will doubtless afford you the greatest pleasure; but to me,

who know him, and who hear it from his own lips—with what interest and sympathy shall I read it in some future day! Even now, as I commence my task, his full-toned voice swells in my ears; his lustrous eyes dwell on me with all their melancholy sweetness; I see his thin hand raised in animation, while the lineaments of his face are irradiated by the soul within. Strange and harrowing must be his story, frightful the storm which embraced the gallant vessel on its course and wrecked it—thus!

Chapter 1

I am by birth a Genevese, and my family is one of the most distinguished of that republic. My ancestors had been for many years counsellors and syndics, and my father had filled several public situations with honour and reputation. He was respected by all who knew him for his integrity and indefatigable attention to public business. He passed his younger days perpetually occupied by the affairs of his country; a variety of circumstances had prevented his marrying early, nor was it until the decline of life that he became a husband and the father of a family.

As the circumstances of his marriage illustrate his character, I cannot refrain from relating them. One of his most intimate friends was a merchant who, from a flourishing state, fell, through numerous mischances, into poverty. This man, whose name was Beaufort, was of a proud and unbending disposition and could not bear to live in poverty and oblivion in the same country where he had formerly been distinguished for his rank and magnificence. Having paid his debts, therefore, in the most honourable manner, he retreated with his daughter to the town of Lucerne, where he lived unknown and in wretchedness. My father loved Beaufort

with the truest friendship and was deeply
780 grieved by his retreat in these unfortunate
circumstances. He bitterly deplored the false
pride which led his friend to a conduct so little worthy of the affection that united them.
He lost no time in endeavouring to seek him
785 out, with the hope of persuading him to
begin the world again through his credit and
assistance.

Beaufort had taken effectual measures to
conceal himself, and it was ten months
790 before my father discovered his abode.
Overjoyed at this discovery, he hastened to
the house, which was situated in a mean
street near the Reuss. But when he entered,
misery and despair alone welcomed him.
795 Beaufort had saved but a very small sum of
money from the wreck of his fortunes, but it
was sufficient to provide him with sustenance for some months, and in the meantime he hoped to procure some respectable
800 employment in a merchant's house. The
interval was, consequently, spent in inaction;
his grief only became more deep and ran-
kling when he had leisure for reflection, and
at length it took so fast hold of his mind that
805 at the end of three months he lay on a bed of
sickness, incapable of any exertion.

His daughter attended him with the greatest tenderness, but she saw with despair that
their little fund was rapidly decreasing and
810 that there was no other prospect of support.
But Caroline Beaufort possessed a mind of
an uncommon mould, and her courage rose
to support her in her adversity. She procured
plain work; she plaited straw and by various
815 means contrived to earn a pittance scarcely
sufficient to support life.

Several months passed in this manner.
Her father grew worse; her time was more
entirely occupied in attending him; her
820 means of subsistence decreased; and in the

tenth month her father died in her arms,
leaving her an orphan and a beggar. This
last blow overcame her, and she knelt by
Beaufort's coffin weeping bitterly, when my
825 father entered the chamber. He came like a
protecting spirit to the poor girl, who committed herself to his care; and after the interment of his friend he conducted her to
Geneva and placed her under the protection
830 of a relation. Two years after this event
Caroline became his wife.

There was a considerable difference
between the ages of my parents, but this circumstance seemed to unite them only closer
835 in bonds of devoted affection. There was a
sense of justice in my father's upright mind
which rendered it necessary that he should
approve highly to love strongly. Perhaps
during former years he had suffered from
840 the late-discovered unworthiness of one
beloved and so was disposed to set a greater
value on tried worth. There was a show of
gratitude and worship in his attachment to
my mother, differing wholly from the doting
845 fondness of age, for it was inspired by reverence for her virtues and a desire to be the
means of, in some degree, recompensing her
for the sorrows she had endured, but which
gave inexpressible grace to his behaviour to
850 her. Everything was made to yield to her
wishes and her convenience. He strove to
shelter her, as a fair exotic is sheltered by the
gardener, from every rougher wind and to
surround her with all that could tend to
855 excite pleasurable emotion in her soft and
benevolent mind. Her health, and even the
tranquillity of her hitherto constant spirit,
had been shaken by what she had gone
through. During the two years that had
860 elapsed previous to their marriage my father
had gradually relinquished all his public
functions; and immediately after their union

they sought the pleasant climate of Italy, and the change of scene and interest attendant
865 on a tour through that land of wonders, as a restorative for her weakened frame.

From Italy they visited Germany and France. I, their eldest child, was born at Naples, and as an infant accompanied them
870 in their rambles. I remained for several years their only child. Much as they were attached to each other, they seemed to draw inexhaustible stores of affection from a very mine of love to bestow them upon me. My
875 mother's tender caresses and my father's smile of benevolent pleasure while regarding me are my first recollections. I was their plaything and their idol, and something better—their child, the innocent and helpless
880 creature bestowed on them by Heaven, whom to bring up to good, and whose future lot it was in their hands to direct to happiness or misery, according as they fulfilled their duties towards me. With this deep con-
885 sciousness of what they owed towards the being to which they had given life, added to the active spirit of tenderness that animated both, it may be imagined that while during every hour of my infant life I received a les-
890 son of patience, of charity, and of self-control, I was so guided by a silken cord that all seemed but one train of enjoyment to me.

For a long time I was their only care. My mother had much desired to have a daugh-
895 ter, but I continued their single offspring. When I was about five years old, while making an excursion beyond the frontiers of Italy, they passed a week on the shores of the Lake of Como. Their benevolent disposition often
900 made them enter the cottages of the poor. This, to my mother, was more than a duty; it was a necessity, a passion—remembering what she had suffered, and how she had been relieved—for her to act in her turn the

905 guardian angel to the afflicted. During one of their walks a poor cot in the foldings of a vale attracted their notice as being singularly disconsolate, while the number of half-clothed children gathered about it spoke of
910 penury in its worst shape. One day, when my father had gone by himself to Milan, my mother, accompanied by me, visited this abode. She found a peasant and his wife, hard working, bent down by care and labour,
915 distributing a scanty meal to five hungry babes. Among these there was one which attracted my mother far above all the rest. She appeared of a different stock. The four others were dark-eyed, hardy little vagrants;
920 this child was thin and very fair. Her hair was the brightest living gold, and despite the poverty of her clothing, seemed to set a crown of distinction on her head. Her brow was clear and ample, her blue eyes cloudless,
925 and her lips and the moulding of her face so expressive of sensibility and sweetness that none could behold her without looking on her as of a distinct species, a being heaven-sent, and bearing a celestial stamp in all her
930 features.

The peasant woman, perceiving that my mother fixed eyes of wonder and admiration on this lovely girl, eagerly communicated her history. She was not her child, but the daugh-
935 ter of a Milanese nobleman. Her mother was a German and had died on giving her birth. The infant had been placed with these good people to nurse: they were better off then. They had not been long married, and their
940 eldest child was but just born. The father of their charge was one of those Italians nursed in the memory of the antique glory of Italy—one among the *schiavi ognor frementi*, who exerted himself to obtain the liberty of his
945 country. He became the victim of its weakness. Whether he had died or still lingered in

the dungeons of Austria was not known. His property was confiscated; his child became an orphan and a beggar. She continued with

950 her foster parents and bloomed in their rude abode, fairer than a garden rose among dark-leaved brambles.

When my father returned from Milan, he found playing with me in the hall of our villa

955 a child fairer than pictured cherub—a creature who seemed to shed radiance from her looks and whose form and motions were lighter than the chamois of the hills. The apparition was soon explained. With his per-

960 mission my mother prevailed on her rustic guardians to yield their charge to her. They were fond of the sweet orphan. Her presence had seemed a blessing to them, but it would be unfair to her to keep her in poverty and

965 want when Providence afforded her such powerful protection. They consulted their village priest, and the result was that Elizabeth Lavenza became the inmate of my parents' house—my more than sister—the beautiful

970 and adored companion of all my occupations and my pleasures.

Everyone loved Elizabeth. The passionate and almost reverential attachment with which all regarded her became, while I

975 shared it, my pride and my delight. On the evening previous to her being brought to my home, my mother had said playfully, "I have a pretty present for my Victor—tomorrow he shall have it." And when, on the morrow, she

980 presented Elizabeth to me as her promised gift, I, with childish seriousness, interpreted her words literally and looked upon Elizabeth as mine—mine to protect, love, and cherish. All praises bestowed on her I received as

985 made to a possession of my own. We called each other familiarly by the name of cousin. No word, no expression could body forth the kind of relation in which she stood to

me—my more than sister, since till death

990 she was to be mine only.

Chapter 2

We were brought up together; there was not quite a year difference in our ages. I need not say that we were strangers to any species of disunion or dispute. Harmony was

995 the soul of our companionship, and the diversity and contrast that subsisted in our characters drew us nearer together. Elizabeth was of a calmer and more concentrated disposition; but, with all my ardour, I was capa-

1000 ble of a more intense application and was more deeply smitten with the thirst for knowledge. She busied herself with following the aerial creations of the poets; and in the majestic and wondrous scenes which

1005 surrounded our Swiss home—the sublime shapes of the mountains, the changes of the seasons, tempest and calm, the silence of winter, and the life and turbulence of our Alpine summers—she found ample scope

1010 for admiration and delight. While my companion contemplated with a serious and satisfied spirit the magnificent appearances of things, I delighted in investigating their causes. The world was to me a secret which

1015 I desired to divine. Curiosity, earnest research to learn the hidden laws of nature, gladness akin to rapture, as they were unfolded to me, are among the earliest sensations I can remember.

1020 On the birth of a second son, my junior by seven years, my parents gave up entirely their wandering life and fixed themselves in their native country. We possessed a house in Geneva, and a *campagne* on Belrive, the

1025 eastern shore of the lake, at the distance of rather more than a league from the city. We resided principally in the latter, and the lives of my parents were passed in considerable seclusion. It was my temper to avoid a crowd and to attach myself fervently to a few. I was indifferent, therefore, to my school-fellows in general; but I united myself in the bonds of the closest friendship to one among them. Henry Clerval was the son of a merchant of Geneva. He was a boy of singular talent and fancy. He loved enterprise, hardship, and even danger for its own sake. He was deeply read in books of chivalry and romance. He composed heroic songs and began to write many a tale of enchantment and knightly adventure. He tried to make us act plays and to enter into masquerades, in which the characters were drawn from the heroes of Roncesvalles, of the Round Table of King Arthur, and the chivalrous train who shed their blood to redeem the holy sepulchre from the hands of the infidels.

No human being could have passed a happier childhood than myself. My parents were possessed by the very spirit of kindness and indulgence. We felt that they were not the tyrants to rule our lot according to their caprice, but the agents and creators of all the many delights which we enjoyed. When I mingled with other families I distinctly discerned how peculiarly fortunate my lot was, and gratitude assisted the development of filial love.

My temper was sometimes violent, and my passions vehement; but by some law in my temperature they were turned not towards childish pursuits but to an eager desire to learn, and not to learn all things indiscriminately. I confess that neither the structure of languages, nor the code of governments, nor the politics of various states possessed attractions for me. It was the secrets of heaven and earth that I desired to learn; and whether it was the outward substance of things or the inner spirit of nature and the mysterious soul of man that occupied me, still my inquiries were directed to the metaphysical, or in its highest sense, the physical secrets of the world.

Meanwhile Clerval occupied himself, so to speak, with the moral relations of things. The busy stage of life, the virtues of heroes, and the actions of men were his theme; and his hope and his dream was to become one among those whose names are recorded in story as the gallant and adventurous benefactors of our species. The saintly soul of Elizabeth shone like a shrine-dedicated lamp in our peaceful home. Her sympathy was ours; her smile, her soft voice, the sweet glance of her celestial eyes, were ever there to bless and animate us. She was the living spirit of love to soften and attract; I might have become sullen in my study, rough through the ardour of my nature, but that she was there to subdue me to a semblance of her own gentleness. And Clerval—could aught ill entrench on the noble spirit of Clerval? Yet he might not have been so perfectly humane, so thoughtful in his generosity, so full of kindness and tenderness amidst his passion for adventurous exploit, had she not unfolded to him the real loveliness of beneficence and made the doing good the end and aim of his soaring ambition.

I feel exquisite pleasure in dwelling on the recollections of childhood, before misfortune had tainted my mind and changed its bright visions of extensive usefulness into gloomy and narrow reflections upon self. Besides, in drawing the picture of my early days, I also record those events which led, by insensible steps, to my after tale of misery, for when I would account to myself for the birth of that passion which afterwards ruled my destiny I find it arise, like a mountain river, from ignoble and almost forgotten sources; but,

swelling as it proceeded, it became the torrent which, in its course, has swept away all
1115 my hopes and joys.

Natural philosophy is the genius that has regulated my fate; I desire, therefore, in this narration, to state those facts which led to my predilection for that science. When I was
1120 thirteen years of age we all went on a party of pleasure to the baths near Thonon; the inclemency of the weather obliged us to remain a day confined to the inn. In this house I chanced to find a volume of the
1125 works of Cornelius Agrippa. I opened it with apathy; the theory which he attempts to demonstrate and the wonderful facts which he relates soon changed this feeling into enthusiasm. A new light seemed to dawn
1130 upon my mind, and bounding with joy, I communicated my discovery to my father. My father looked carelessly at the title page of my book and said, "Ah! Cornelius Agrippa! My dear Victor, do not waste your time upon
1135 this; it is sad trash."

If, instead of this remark, my father had taken the pains to explain to me that the principles of Agrippa had been entirely exploded and that a modern system of sci-
1140 ence had been introduced which possessed much greater powers than the ancient, because the powers of the latter were chimerical, while those of the former were real and practical, under such circumstances I should
1145 certainly have thrown Agrippa aside and have contented my imagination, warmed as it was, by returning with greater ardour to my former studies. It is even possible that the train of my ideas would never have received the fatal
1150 impulse that led to my ruin. But the cursory glance my father had taken of my volume by no means assured me that he was acquainted with its contents, and I continued to read with the greatest avidity.

1155 When I returned home my first care was to procure the whole works of this author, and afterwards of Paracelsus and Albertus Magnus. I read and studied the wild fancies of these writers with delight; they appeared
1160 to me treasures known to few besides myself. I have described myself as always having been imbued with a fervent longing to penetrate the secrets of nature. In spite of the intense labour and wonderful discoveries
1165 of modern philosophers, I always came from my studies discontented and unsatisfied. Sir Isaac Newton is said to have avowed that he felt like a child picking up shells beside the great and unexplored ocean of truth. Those
1170 of his successors in each branch of natural philosophy with whom I was acquainted appeared even to my boy's apprehensions as tyros engaged in the same pursuit.

The untaught peasant beheld the ele-
1175 ments around him and was acquainted with their practical uses. The most learned philosopher knew little more. He had partially unveiled the face of Nature, but her immortal lineaments were still a wonder and a mys-
1180 tery. He might dissect, anatomise, and give names; but, not to speak of a final cause, causes in their secondary and tertiary grades were utterly unknown to him. I had gazed upon the fortifications and impediments
1185 that seemed to keep human beings from entering the citadel of nature, and rashly and ignorantly I had repined.

But here were books, and here were men who had penetrated deeper and knew more.
1190 I took their word for all that they averred, and I became their disciple. It may appear strange that such should arise in the eighteenth century; but while I followed the routine of education in the schools of Geneva,
1195 I was, to a great degree, self-taught with regard to my favourite studies. My father was

not scientific, and I was left to struggle with a child's blindness, added to a student's thirst for knowledge. Under the guidance of my new preceptors I entered with the greatest diligence into the search of the philosopher's stone and the elixir of life; but the latter soon obtained my undivided attention. Wealth was an inferior object, but what glory would attend the discovery if I could banish disease from the human frame and render man invulnerable to any but a violent death!

Nor were these my only visions. The raising of ghosts or devils was a promise liberally accorded by my favourite authors, the fulfilment of which I most eagerly sought; and if my incantations were always unsuccessful, I attributed the failure rather to my own inexperience and mistake than to a want of skill or fidelity in my instructors. And thus for a time I was occupied by exploded systems, mingling, like an unadept, a thousand contradictory theories and floundering desperately in a very slough of multifarious knowledge, guided by an ardent imagination and childish reasoning, till an accident again changed the current of my ideas.

When I was about fifteen years old we had retired to our house near Belrive, when we witnessed a most violent and terrible thunderstorm. It advanced from behind the mountains of Jura, and the thunder burst at once with frightful loudness from various quarters of the heavens. I remained, while the storm lasted, watching its progress with curiosity and delight. As I stood at the door, on a sudden I beheld a stream of fire issue from an old and beautiful oak which stood about twenty yards from our house; and so soon as the dazzling light vanished, the oak had disappeared, and nothing remained but a blasted stump. When we visited it the next morning, we found the tree shattered in a singular manner. It was not splintered by the shock, but entirely reduced to thin ribbons of wood. I never beheld anything so utterly destroyed.

Before this I was not unacquainted with the more obvious laws of electricity. On this occasion a man of great research in natural philosophy was with us, and excited by this catastrophe, he entered on the explanation of a theory which he had formed on the subject of electricity and galvanism, which was at once new and astonishing to me. All that he said threw greatly into the shade Cornelius Agrippa, Albertus Magnus, and Paracelsus, the lords of my imagination; but by some fatality the overthrow of these men disinclined me to pursue my accustomed studies. It seemed to me as if nothing would or could ever be known. All that had so long engaged my attention suddenly grew despicable. By one of those caprices of the mind which we are perhaps most subject to in early youth, I at once gave up my former occupations, set down natural history and all its progeny as a deformed and abortive creation, and entertained the greatest disdain for a would-be science which could never even step within the threshold of real knowledge. In this mood of mind I betook myself to the mathematics and the branches of study appertaining to that science as being built upon secure foundations, and so worthy of my consideration.

Thus strangely are our souls constructed, and by such slight ligaments are we bound to prosperity or ruin. When I look back, it seems to me as if this almost miraculous change of inclination and will was the immediate suggestion of the guardian angel of my life—the last effort made by the spirit of preservation to avert the storm that was even then hanging

in the stars and ready to envelop me. Her victory was announced by an unusual tranquillity and gladness of soul which followed the
relinquishing of my ancient and latterly tor-
1285 menting studies. It was thus that I was to be
taught to associate evil with their prosecution, happiness with their disregard.

It was a strong effort of the spirit of good,
but it was ineffectual. Destiny was too potent,
1290 and her immutable laws had decreed my
utter and terrible destruction.

Chapter 3

When I had attained the age of seventeen
my parents resolved that I should become a
student at the university of Ingolstadt. I had
1295 hitherto attended the schools of Geneva, but
my father thought it necessary for the completion of my education that I should be
made acquainted with other customs than
those of my native country. My departure
1300 was therefore fixed at an early date, but
before the day resolved upon could arrive,
the first misfortune of my life occurred—an
omen, as it were, of my future misery.

Elizabeth had caught the scarlet fever; her
1305 illness was severe, and she was in the greatest danger. During her illness many arguments had been urged to persuade my
mother to refrain from attending upon her.
She had at first yielded to our entreaties, but
1310 when she heard that the life of her favourite
was menaced, she could no longer control
her anxiety. She attended her sickbed; her
watchful attentions triumphed over the
malignity of the distemper—Elizabeth was
1315 saved, but the consequences of this imprudence were fatal to her preserver. On the
third day my mother sickened; her fever was
accompanied by the most alarming symptoms, and the looks of her medical atten-
1320 dants prognosticated the worst event. On her

deathbed the fortitude and benignity of this
best of women did not desert her. She joined
the hands of Elizabeth and myself. "My children," she said, "my firmest hopes of future
1325 happiness were placed on the prospect of
your union. This expectation will now be the
consolation of your father. Elizabeth, my
love, you must supply my place to my
younger children. Alas! I regret that I am
1330 taken from you; and, happy and beloved as I
have been, is it not hard to quit you all? But
these are not thoughts befitting me; I will
endeavour to resign myself cheerfully to
death and will indulge a hope of meeting
1335 you in another world."

She died calmly, and her countenance
expressed affection even in death. I need not
describe the feelings of those whose dearest
ties are rent by that most irreparable evil, the
1340 void that presents itself to the soul, and the
despair that is exhibited on the countenance.
It is so long before the mind can persuade
itself that she whom we saw every day and
whose very existence appeared a part of our
1345 own can have departed for ever—that the
brightness of a beloved eye can have been
extinguished and the sound of a voice so
familiar and dear to the ear can be hushed,
never more to be heard. These are the reflec-
1350 tions of the first days; but when the lapse of
time proves the reality of the evil, then the
actual bitterness of grief commences. Yet
from whom has not that rude hand rent
away some dear connection? And why
1355 should I describe a sorrow which all have
felt, and must feel? The time at length
arrives when grief is rather an indulgence
than a necessity; and the smile that plays
upon the lips, although it may be deemed a
1360 sacrilege, is not banished. My mother was
dead, but we had still duties which we ought
to perform; we must continue our course

with the rest and learn to think ourselves fortunate whilst one remains whom the spoiler has not seized.

My departure for Ingolstadt, which had been deferred by these events, was now again determined upon. I obtained from my father a respite of some weeks. It appeared to me sacrilege so soon to leave the repose, akin to death, of the house of mourning and to rush into the thick of life. I was new to sorrow, but it did not the less alarm me. I was unwilling to quit the sight of those that remained to me, and above all, I desired to see my sweet Elizabeth in some degree consoled.

She indeed veiled her grief and strove to act the comforter to us all. She looked steadily on life and assumed its duties with courage and zeal. She devoted herself to those whom she had been taught to call her uncle and cousins. Never was she so enchanting as at this time, when she recalled the sunshine of her smiles and spent them upon us. She forgot even her own regret in her endeavours to make us forget.

The day of my departure at length arrived. Clerval spent the last evening with us. He had endeavoured to persuade his father to permit him to accompany me and to become my fellow student, but in vain. His father was a narrow-minded trader and saw idleness and ruin in the aspirations and ambition of his son. Henry deeply felt the misfortune of being debarred from a liberal education. He said little, but when he spoke I read in his kindling eye and in his animated glance a restrained but firm resolve not to be chained to the miserable details of commerce.

We sat late. We could not tear ourselves away from each other nor persuade ourselves to say the word "Farewell!" It was said, and we retired under the pretence of seeking repose, each fancying that the other was deceived; but when at morning's dawn I descended to the carriage which was to convey me away, they were all there—my father again to bless me, Clerval to press my hand once more, my Elizabeth to renew her entreaties that I would write often and to bestow the last feminine attentions on her playmate and friend.

I threw myself into the chaise that was to convey me away and indulged in the most melancholy reflections. I, who had ever been surrounded by amiable companions, continually engaged in endeavouring to bestow mutual pleasure—I was now alone. In the university whither I was going I must form my own friends and be my own protector. My life had hitherto been remarkably secluded and domestic, and this had given me invincible repugnance to new countenances. I loved my brothers, Elizabeth, and Clerval; these were "old familiar faces," but I believed myself totally unfitted for the company of strangers. Such were my reflections as I commenced my journey; but as I proceeded, my spirits and hopes rose. I ardently desired the acquisition of knowledge. I had often, when at home, thought it hard to remain during my youth cooped up in one place and had longed to enter the world and take my station among other human beings. Now my desires were complied with, and it would, indeed, have been folly to repent.

I had sufficient leisure for these and many other reflections during my journey to Ingolstadt, which was long and fatiguing. At length the high white steeple of the town met my eyes. I alighted and was conducted to my solitary apartment to spend the evening as I pleased.

The next morning I delivered my letters of introduction and paid a visit to some of the principal professors. Chance—or rather the evil influence, the Angel of Destruction, which asserted omnipotent sway over me 1450 from the moment I turned my reluctant steps from my father's door—led me first to M. Krempe, professor of natural philosophy. He was an uncouth man, but deeply imbued in the secrets of his science. He asked me 1455 several questions concerning my progress in the different branches of science appertaining to natural philosophy. I replied carelessly, and partly in contempt, mentioned the names of my alchemists as the principal 1460 authors I had studied. The professor stared. "Have you," he said, "really spent your time in studying such nonsense?"

I replied in the affirmative. "Every minute," continued M. Krempe with warmth, "every 1465 instant that you have wasted on those books is utterly and entirely lost. You have burdened your memory with exploded systems and useless names. Good God! In what desert land have you lived, where no one was kind enough 1470 to inform you that these fancies which you have so greedily imbibed are a thousand years old and as musty as they are ancient? I little expected, in this enlightened and scientific age, to find a disciple of Albertus Magnus and 1475 Paracelsus. My dear sir, you must begin your studies entirely anew."

So saying, he stepped aside and wrote down a list of several books treating of natural philosophy which he desired me to pro- 1480 cure, and dismissed me after mentioning that in the beginning of the following week he intended to commence a course of lectures upon natural philosophy in its general relations, and that M. Waldman, a fellow pro- 1485 fessor, would lecture upon chemistry the alternate days that he omitted.

I returned home not disappointed, for I have said that I had long considered those authors useless whom the professor repro- 1490 bated; but I returned not at all the more inclined to recur to these studies in any shape. M. Krempe was a little squat man with a gruff voice and a repulsive countenance; the teacher, therefore, did not 1495 prepossess me in favour of his pursuits. In rather a too philosophical and connected a strain, perhaps, I have given an account of the conclusions I had come to concerning them in my early years. As a child I had not 1500 been content with the results promised by the modern professors of natural science. With a confusion of ideas only to be accounted for by my extreme youth and my want of a guide on such matters, I had 1505 retrod the steps of knowledge along the paths of time and exchanged the discoveries of recent inquirers for the dreams of forgotten alchemists. Besides, I had a contempt for the uses of modern natural phi- 1510 losophy. It was very different when the masters of the science sought immortality and power; such views, although futile, were grand; but now the scene was changed. The ambition of the inquirer seemed to limit 1515 itself to the annihilation of those visions on which my interest in science was chiefly founded. I was required to exchange chimeras of boundless grandeur for realities of little worth.

1520 Such were my reflections during the first two or three days of my residence at Ingolstadt, which were chiefly spent in becoming acquainted with the localities and the principal residents in my new abode. But as the 1525 ensuing week commenced, I thought of the information which M. Krempe had given me concerning the lectures. And although I could not consent to go and hear that little conceited fellow deliver sentences out of 1530 a pulpit, I recollected what he had said of

M. Waldman, whom I had never seen, as he had hitherto been out of town.

Partly from curiosity and partly from idleness, I went into the lecturing room, which 1535 M. Waldman entered shortly after. This professor was very unlike his colleague. He appeared about fifty years of age, but with an aspect expressive of the greatest benevolence; a few grey hairs covered his temples, 1540 but those at the back of his head were nearly black. His person was short but remarkably erect and his voice the sweetest I had ever heard. He began his lecture by a recapitulation of the history of chemistry and the vari-1545 ous improvements made by different men of learning, pronouncing with fervour the names of the most distinguished discoverers. He then took a cursory view of the present state of the science and explained many of its elementary 1550 terms. After having made a few preparatory experiments, he concluded with a panegyric upon modern chemistry, the terms of which I shall never forget:

"The ancient teachers of this science," 1555 said he, "promised impossibilities and performed nothing. The modern masters promise very little; they know that metals cannot be transmuted and that the elixir of life is a chimera but these philosophers, whose 1560 hands seem only made to dabble in dirt, and their eyes to pore over the microscope or crucible, have indeed performed miracles. They penetrate into the recesses of nature and show how she works in her hiding-1565 places. They ascend into the heavens; they have discovered how the blood circulates, and the nature of the air we breathe. They have acquired new and almost unlimited powers; they can command the thunders of 1570 heaven, mimic the earthquake, and even mock the invisible world with its own shadows."

Such were the professor's words—rather let me say such the words of the fate—1575 enounced to destroy me. As he went on I felt as if my soul were grappling with a palpable enemy; one by one the various keys were touched which formed the mechanism of my being; chord after chord was sounded, and 1580 soon my mind was filled with one thought, one conception, one purpose. So much has been done, exclaimed the soul of Frankenstein—more, far more, will I achieve; treading in the steps already marked, I will 1585 pioneer a new way, explore unknown powers, and unfold to the world the deepest mysteries of creation.

I closed not my eyes that night. My internal being was in a state of insurrection and 1590 turmoil; I felt that order would thence arise, but I had no power to produce it. By degrees, after the morning's dawn, sleep came. I awoke, and my yesternight's thoughts were as a dream. There only remained a resolution 1595 to return to my ancient studies and to devote myself to a science for which I believed myself to possess a natural talent. On the same day I paid M. Waldman a visit. His manners in private were even more mild and 1600 attractive than in public, for there was a certain dignity in his mien during his lecture which in his own house was replaced by the greatest affability and kindness. I gave him pretty nearly the same account of my former 1605 pursuits as I had given to his fellow professor. He heard with attention the little narration concerning my studies and smiled at the names of Cornelius Agrippa and Paracelsus, but without the contempt that M. Krempe 1610 had exhibited. He said that "These were men to whose indefatigable zeal modern philosophers were indebted for most of the foundations of their knowledge. They had left to us, as an easier task, to give new names and

1615 arrange in connected classifications the facts
which they in a great degree had been the
instruments of bringing to light. The labours
of men of genius, however erroneously
directed, scarcely ever fail in ultimately turn-
1620 ing to the solid advantage of mankind." I listened to his statement, which was delivered
without any presumption or affectation, and
then added that his lecture had removed my
prejudices against modern chemists; I
1625 expressed myself in measured terms, with
the modesty and deference due from a youth
to his instructor, without letting escape
(inexperience in life would have made me
ashamed) any of the enthusiasm which
1630 stimulated my intended labours. I requested
his advice concerning the books I ought to
procure.

   "I am happy," said M. Waldman, "to have
gained a disciple; and if your application
1635 equals your ability, I have no doubt of your
success. Chemistry is that branch of natural
philosophy in which the greatest improvements have been and may be made; it is
on that account that I have made it my pecu-
1640 liar study; but at the same time, I have not
neglected the other branches of science. A
man would make but a very sorry chemist if
he attended to that department of human
knowledge alone. If your wish is to become
1645 really a man of science and not merely a
petty experimentalist, I should advise you to
apply to every branch of natural philosophy,
including mathematics."

   He then took me into his laboratory and
1650 explained to me the uses of his various
machines, instructing me as to what I ought
to procure and promising me the use of his
own when I should have advanced far enough
in the science not to derange their mecha-
1655 nism. He also gave me the list of books which
I had requested, and I took my leave.

   Thus ended a day memorable to me; it
decided my future destiny.

Chapter 4

From this day natural philosophy, and partic-
1660 ularly chemistry, in the most comprehensive
sense of the term, became nearly my sole
occupation. I read with ardour those works,
so full of genius and discrimination, which
modern inquirers have written on these sub-
1665 jects. I attended the lectures and cultivated
the acquaintance of the men of science of
the university, and I found even in M. Krempe
a great deal of sound sense and real information, combined, it is true, with a repulsive
1670 physiognomy and manners, but not on that
account the less valuable. In M. Waldman I
found a true friend. His gentleness was never
tinged by dogmatism, and his instructions
were given with an air of frankness and good
1675 nature that banished every idea of pedantry.
In a thousand ways he smoothed for me
the path of knowledge and made the most
abstruse inquiries clear and facile to my
apprehension. My application was at first
1680 fluctuating and uncertain; it gained strength
as I proceeded and soon became so ardent
and eager that the stars often disappeared in
the light of morning whilst I was yet engaged
in my laboratory.

1685   As I applied so closely, it may be easily
conceived that my progress was rapid. My
ardour was indeed the astonishment of the
students, and my proficiency that of the
masters. Professor Krempe often asked me,
1690 with a sly smile, how Cornelius Agrippa went
on, whilst M. Waldman expressed the most
heartfelt exultation in my progress. Two
years passed in this manner, during which I
paid no visit to Geneva, but was engaged,
1695 heart and soul, in the pursuit of some discoveries which I hoped to make. None but

those who have experienced them can conceive of the enticements of science. In other studies you go as far as others have gone before you, and there is nothing more to know; but in a scientific pursuit there is continual food for discovery and wonder. A mind of moderate capacity which closely pursues one study must infallibly arrive at great proficiency in that study; and I, who continually sought the attainment of one object of pursuit and was solely wrapped up in this, improved so rapidly that at the end of two years I made some discoveries in the improvement of some chemical instruments, which procured me great esteem and admiration at the university. When I had arrived at this point and had become as well acquainted with the theory and practice of natural philosophy as depended on the lessons of any of the professors at Ingolstadt, my residence there being no longer conducive to my improvements, I thought of returning to my friends and my native town, when an incident happened that protracted my stay.

One of the phenomena which had peculiarly attracted my attention was the structure of the human frame, and, indeed, any animal endued with life. Whence, I often asked myself, did the principle of life proceed? It was a bold question, and one which has ever been considered as a mystery; yet with how many things are we upon the brink of becoming acquainted, if cowardice or carelessness did not restrain our inquiries. I revolved these circumstances in my mind and determined thenceforth to apply myself more particularly to those branches of natural philosophy which relate to physiology. Unless I had been animated by an almost supernatural enthusiasm, my application to this study would have been irksome and almost intolerable. To examine the causes of life, we must first have recourse to death. I became acquainted with the science of anatomy, but this was not sufficient; I must also observe the natural decay and corruption of the human body. In my education my father had taken the greatest precautions that my mind should be impressed with no supernatural horrors. I do not ever remember to have trembled at a tale of superstition or to have feared the apparition of a spirit. Darkness had no effect upon my fancy, and a churchyard was to me merely the receptacle of bodies deprived of life, which, from being the seat of beauty and strength, had become food for the worm. Now I was led to examine the cause and progress of this decay and forced to spend days and nights in vaults and charnel-houses. My attention was fixed upon every object the most insupportable to the delicacy of the human feelings. I saw how the fine form of man was degraded and wasted; I beheld the corruption of death succeed to the blooming cheek of life; I saw how the worm inherited the wonders of the eye and brain. I paused, examining and analysing all the minutiae of causation, as exemplified in the change from life to death, and death to life, until from the midst of this darkness a sudden light broke in upon me— a light so brilliant and wondrous, yet so simple, that while I became dizzy with the immensity of the prospect which it illustrated, I was surprised that among so many men of genius who had directed their inquiries towards the same science, that I alone should be reserved to discover so astonishing a secret.

Remember, I am not recording the vision of a madman. The sun does not more certainly shine in the heavens than that which I now affirm is true. Some miracle might have produced it, yet the stages of the discovery

were distinct and probable. After days and nights of incredible labour and fatigue, I succeeded in discovering the cause of generation and life; nay, more, I became myself
1785 capable of bestowing animation upon lifeless matter.

The astonishment which I had at first experienced on this discovery soon gave place to delight and rapture. After so much
1790 time spent in painful labour, to arrive at once at the summit of my desires was the most gratifying consummation of my toils. But this discovery was so great and overwhelming that all the steps by which I had been
1795 progressively led to it were obliterated, and I beheld only the result. What had been the study and desire of the wisest men since the creation of the world was now within my grasp. Not that, like a magic scene, it all
1800 opened upon me at once: the information I had obtained was of a nature rather to direct my endeavours so soon as I should point them towards the object of my search than to exhibit that object already accomplished.
1805 I was like the Arabian who had been buried with the dead and found a passage to life, aided only by one glimmering and seemingly ineffectual light.

I see by your eagerness and the wonder
1810 and hope which your eyes express, my friend, that you expect to be informed of the secret with which I am acquainted; that cannot be; listen patiently until the end of my story, and you will easily per-
1815 ceive why I am reserved upon that subject. I will not lead you on, unguarded and ardent as I then was, to your destruction and infallible misery. Learn from me, if not by my precepts, at least by my example,
1820 how dangerous is the acquirement of knowledge and how much happier that man is who believes his native town to be

the world, than he who aspires to become greater than his nature will allow.

1825 When I found so astonishing a power placed within my hands, I hesitated a long time concerning the manner in which I should employ it. Although I possessed the capacity of bestowing animation, yet to pre-
1830 pare a frame for the reception of it, with all its intricacies of fibres, muscles, and veins, still remained a work of inconceivable difficulty and labour. I doubted at first whether I should attempt the creation of a being like
1835 myself, or one of simpler organization; but my imagination was too much exalted by my first success to permit me to doubt of my ability to give life to an animal as complex and wonderful as man. The materials
1840 at present within my command hardly appeared adequate to so arduous an undertaking, but I doubted not that I should ultimately succeed. I prepared myself for a multitude of reverses; my operations might
1845 be incessantly baffled, and at last my work be imperfect, yet when I considered the improvement which every day takes place in science and mechanics, I was encouraged to hope my present attempts would at least lay
1850 the foundations of future success. Nor could I consider the magnitude and complexity of my plan as any argument of its impracticability. It was with these feelings that I began the creation of a human being. As the
1855 minuteness of the parts formed a great hindrance to my speed, I resolved, contrary to my first intention, to make the being of a gigantic stature, that is to say, about eight feet in height, and proportionably large. After
1860 having formed this determination and having spent some months in successfully collecting and arranging my materials, I began.

No one can conceive the variety of feelings which bore me onwards, like a hurricane, in

1865 the first enthusiasm of success. Life and death appeared to me ideal bounds, which I should first break through, and pour a torrent of light into our dark world. A new species would bless me as its creator and source;
1870 many happy and excellent natures would owe their being to me. No father could claim the gratitude of his child so completely as I should deserve theirs. Pursuing these reflections, I thought that if I could bestow anima-
1875 tion upon lifeless matter, I might in process of time (although I now found it impossible) renew life where death had apparently devoted the body to corruption.

These thoughts supported my spirits,
1880 while I pursued my undertaking with unremitting ardour. My cheek had grown pale with study, and my person had become emaciated with confinement. Sometimes, on the very brink of certainty, I failed; yet still I
1885 clung to the hope which the next day or the next hour might realise. One secret which I alone possessed was the hope to which I had dedicated myself; and the moon gazed on my midnight labours, while, with unrelaxed
1890 and breathless eagerness, I pursued nature to her hiding-places. Who shall conceive the horrors of my secret toil as I dabbled among the unhallowed damps of the grave or tortured the living animal to animate the life-
1895 less clay? My limbs now tremble, and my eyes swim with the remembrance; but then a resistless and almost frantic impulse urged me forward; I seemed to have lost all soul or sensation but for this one pursuit. It was
1900 indeed but a passing trance, that only made me feel with renewed acuteness so soon as, the unnatural stimulus ceasing to operate, I had returned to my old habits. I collected bones from charnel-houses and disturbed,
1905 with profane fingers, the tremendous secrets of the human frame. In a solitary chamber,

or rather cell, at the top of the house, and separated from all the other apartments by a gallery and staircase, I kept my workshop of
1910 filthy creation; my eyeballs were starting from their sockets in attending to the details of my employment. The dissecting room and the slaughter-house furnished many of my materials; and often did my human nature
1915 turn with loathing from my occupation, whilst, still urged on by an eagerness which perpetually increased, I brought my work near to a conclusion.

The summer months passed while I was
1920 thus engaged, heart and soul, in one pursuit. It was a most beautiful season; never did the fields bestow a more plentiful harvest or the vines yield a more luxuriant vintage, but my eyes were insensible to the charms of nature.
1925 And the same feelings which made me neglect the scenes around me caused me also to forget those friends who were so many miles absent, and whom I had not seen for so long a time. I knew my silence
1930 disquieted them, and I well remembered the words of my father: "I know that while you are pleased with yourself you will think of us with affection, and we shall hear regularly from you. You must pardon me if I regard any
1935 interruption in your correspondence as a proof that your other duties are equally neglected."

I knew well therefore what would be my father's feelings, but I could not tear my
1940 thoughts from my employment, loathsome in itself, but which had taken an irresistible hold of my imagination. I wished, as it were, to procrastinate all that related to my feelings of affection until the great object, which
1945 swallowed up every habit of my nature, should be completed.

I then thought that my father would be unjust if he ascribed my neglect to vice or

faultiness on my part, but I am now con-
1950 vinced that he was justified in conceiving
that I should not be altogether free from
blame. A human being in perfection ought
always to preserve a calm and peaceful mind
and never to allow passion or a transitory
1955 desire to disturb his tranquillity. I do not
think that the pursuit of knowledge is an
exception to this rule. If the study to which
you apply yourself has a tendency to weaken
your affections and to destroy your taste for
1960 those simple pleasures in which no alloy can
possibly mix, then that study is certainly
unlawful, that is to say, not befitting the
human mind. If this rule were always
observed; if no man allowed any pursuit
1965 whatsoever to interfere with the tranquillity
of his domestic affections, Greece had not
been enslaved, Cæsar would have spared his
country, America would have been discovered more gradually, and the empires of
1970 Mexico and Peru had not been destroyed.

But I forget that I am moralizing in the
most interesting part of my tale, and your
looks remind me to proceed.

My father made no reproach in his letters
1975 and only took notice of my silence by inquiring into my occupations more particularly
than before. Winter, spring, and summer
passed away during my labours; but I did not
watch the blossom or the expanding leaves—
1980 sights which before always yielded me
supreme delight—so deeply was I engrossed
in my occupation. The leaves of that year
had withered before my work drew near to a
close, and now every day showed me more
1985 plainly how well I had succeeded. But my
enthusiasm was checked by my anxiety, and
I appeared rather like one doomed by slavery
to toil in the mines, or any other unwholesome trade than an artist occupied by his
1990 favourite employment. Every night I was

oppressed by a slow fever, and I became nervous to a most painful degree; the fall of a
leaf startled me, and I shunned my fellow
creatures as if I had been guilty of a crime.
1995 Sometimes I grew alarmed at the wreck I
perceived that I had become; the energy of
my purpose alone sustained me: my labours
would soon end, and I believed that exercise
and amusement would then drive away
2000 incipient disease; and I promised myself
both of these when my creation should be
complete.

Chapter 5

It was on a dreary night of November that I
beheld the accomplishment of my toils. With
2005 an anxiety that almost amounted to agony, I
collected the instruments of life around me,
that I might infuse a spark of being into the
lifeless thing that lay at my feet. It was
already one in the morning; the rain pattered
2010 dismally against the panes, and my candle
was nearly burnt out, when, by the glimmer
of the half-extinguished light, I saw the dull
yellow eye of the creature open; it breathed
hard, and a convulsive motion agitated its
2015 limbs.

How can I describe my emotions at this
catastrophe, or how delineate the wretch
whom with such infinite pains and care I
had endeavoured to form? His limbs were in
2020 proportion, and I had selected his features as
beautiful. Beautiful! Great God! His yellow
skin scarcely covered the work of muscles
and arteries beneath; his hair was of a lustrous black, and flowing; his teeth of a pearly
2025 whiteness; but these luxuriances only
formed a more horrid contrast with his
watery eyes, that seemed almost of the same
colour as the dun-white sockets in which
they were set, his shrivelled complexion and
2030 straight black lips.

The different accidents of life are not so changeable as the feelings of human nature. I had worked hard for nearly two years, for the sole purpose of infusing life into an
2035 inanimate body. For this I had deprived myself of rest and health. I had desired it with an ardour that far exceeded moderation; but now that I had finished, the beauty of the dream vanished, and breathless hor
2040 ror and disgust filled my heart. Unable to endure the aspect of the being I had created, I rushed out of the room and continued a long time traversing my bed-chamber, unable to compose my mind to sleep. At
2045 length lassitude succeeded to the tumult I had before endured, and I threw myself on the bed in my clothes, endeavouring to seek a few moments of forgetfulness. But it was in vain; I slept, indeed, but I was disturbed
2050 by the wildest dreams. I thought I saw Elizabeth, in the bloom of health, walking in the streets of Ingolstadt. Delighted and surprised, I embraced her, but as I imprinted the first kiss on her lips, they became livid
2055 with the hue of death; her features appeared to change, and I thought that I held the corpse of my dead mother in my arms; a shroud enveloped her form, and I saw the grave-worms crawling in the folds of the
2060 flannel. I started from my sleep with horror; a cold dew covered my forehead, my teeth chattered, and every limb became convulsed; when, by the dim and yellow light of the moon, as it forced its way through the
2065 window shutters, I beheld the wretch—the miserable monster whom I had created. He held up the curtain of the bed; and his eyes, if eyes they may be called, were fixed on me. His jaws opened, and he muttered some
2070 inarticulate sounds, while a grin wrinkled his cheeks. He might have spoken, but I did not hear; one hand was stretched out,

seemingly to detain me, but I escaped and rushed downstairs. I took refuge in the
2075 courtyard belonging to the house which I inhabited, where I remained during the rest of the night, walking up and down in the greatest agitation, listening attentively, catching and fearing each sound as if it
2080 were to announce the approach of the demoniacal corpse to which I had so miserably given life.

Oh! No mortal could support the horror of that countenance. A mummy again endued
2085 with animation could not be so hideous as that wretch. I had gazed on him while unfinished; he was ugly then, but when those muscles and joints were rendered capable of motion, it became a thing such as even
2090 Dante could not have conceived.

I passed the night wretchedly. Sometimes my pulse beat so quickly and hardly that I felt the palpitation of every artery; at others, I nearly sank to the ground through languor
2095 and extreme weakness. Mingled with this horror, I felt the bitterness of disappointment; dreams that had been my food and pleasant rest for so long a space were now become a hell to me; and the change was so
2100 rapid, the overthrow so complete!

Morning, dismal and wet, at length dawned and discovered to my sleepless and aching eyes the church of Ingolstadt, its white steeple and clock, which indicated the
2105 sixth hour. The porter opened the gates of the court, which had that night been my asylum, and I issued into the streets, pacing them with quick steps, as if I sought to avoid the wretch whom I feared every turning
2110 of the street would present to my view. I did not dare return to the apartment which I inhabited, but felt impelled to hurry on, although drenched by the rain which poured from a black and comfortless sky.

2115　　I continued walking in this manner for some time, endeavouring by bodily exercise to ease the load that weighed upon my mind. I traversed the streets without any clear conception of where I was or what I was doing.

2120　My heart palpitated in the sickness of fear, and I hurried on with irregular steps, not daring to look about me:

> 　　Like one who, on a lonely road,
> 　　Doth walk in fear and dread,
> 2125　And, having once turned round, walks on,
> 　　And turns no more his head;
> 　　Because he knows a frightful fiend
> 　　Doth close behind him tread.
> 　　[Coleridge's "Ancient Mariner."]

2130　　Continuing thus, I came at length opposite to the inn at which the various diligences and carriages usually stopped. Here I paused, I knew not why; but I remained some minutes with my eyes fixed on a coach

2135 that was coming towards me from the other end of the street. As it drew nearer I observed that it was the Swiss diligence; it stopped just where I was standing, and on the door being opened, I perceived Henry Clerval,

2140 who, on seeing me, instantly sprung out. "My dear Frankenstein," exclaimed he, "how glad I am to see you! How fortunate that you should be here at the very moment of my alighting!"

2145　　Nothing could equal my delight on seeing Clerval; his presence brought back to my thoughts my father, Elizabeth, and all those scenes of home so dear to my recollection. I grasped his hand, and in a moment forgot

2150 my horror and misfortune; I felt suddenly, and for the first time during many months, calm and serene joy. I welcomed my friend, therefore, in the most cordial manner, and we walked towards my college. Clerval con-

2155 tinued talking for some time about our mutual friends and his own good fortune in being permitted to come to Ingolstadt. "You may easily believe," said he, "how great was the difficulty to persuade my father that all

2160 necessary knowledge was not comprised in the noble art of book-keeping; and, indeed, I believe I left him incredulous to the last, for his constant answer to my unwearied entreaties was the same as that of the Dutch

2165 schoolmaster in The Vicar of Wakefield: 'I have ten thousand florins a year without Greek, I eat heartily without Greek.' But his affection for me at length overcame his dislike of learning, and he has permitted me to

2170 undertake a voyage of discovery to the land of knowledge."

　　"It gives me the greatest delight to see you; but tell me how you left my father, brothers, and Elizabeth."

2175　　"Very well, and very happy, only a little uneasy that they hear from you so seldom. By the by, I mean to lecture you a little upon their account myself. But, my dear Frankenstein," continued he, stopping short

2180 and gazing full in my face, "I did not before remark how very ill you appear; so thin and pale; you look as if you had been watching for several nights."

　　"You have guessed right; I have lately

2185 been so deeply engaged in one occupation that I have not allowed myself sufficient rest, as you see; but I hope, I sincerely hope, that all these employments are now at an end and that I am at length free."

2190　　I trembled excessively; I could not endure to think of, and far less to allude to, the occurrences of the preceding night. I walked with a quick pace, and we soon arrived at my college. I then reflected, and the thought

2195 made me shiver, that the creature whom I had left in my apartment might still be there, alive and walking about. I dreaded to behold this monster, but I feared still more that Henry

should see him. Entreating him, therefore, to
2200 remain a few minutes at the bottom of the
stairs, I darted up towards my own room. My
hand was already on the lock of the door
before I recollected myself. I then paused,
and a cold shivering came over me. I threw
2205 the door forcibly open, as children are accustomed to do when they expect a spectre to
stand in waiting for them on the other side;
but nothing appeared. I stepped fearfully in:
the apartment was empty, and my bedroom
2210 was also freed from its hideous guest. I could
hardly believe that so great a good fortune
could have befallen me, but when I became
assured that my enemy had indeed fled,
I clapped my hands for joy and ran down
2215 to Clerval.

We ascended into my room, and the servant presently brought breakfast; but I was
unable to contain myself. It was not joy only
that possessed me; I felt my flesh tingle
2220 with excess of sensitiveness, and my pulse
beat rapidly. I was unable to remain for a
single instant in the same place; I jumped
over the chairs, clapped my hands, and
laughed aloud. Clerval at first attributed my
2225 unusual spirits to joy on his arrival, but
when he observed me more attentively, he
saw a wildness in my eyes for which he
could not account, and my loud, unrestrained,
heartless laughter frightened and aston-
2230 ished him.

"My dear Victor," cried he, "what, for
God's sake, is the matter? Do not laugh in
that manner. How ill you are! What is the
cause of all this?"

2235 "Do not ask me," cried I, putting my hands
before my eyes, for I thought I saw the
dreaded spectre glide into the room; "he can
tell. Oh, save me! Save me!" I imagined that
the monster seized me; I struggled furiously
2240 and fell down in a fit.

Poor Clerval! What must have been his
feelings? A meeting, which he anticipated
with such joy, so strangely turned to bitterness. But I was not the witness of his
2245 grief, for I was lifeless and did not recover
my senses for a long, long time.

This was the commencement of a nervous fever which confined me for several
months. During all that time Henry was my
2250 only nurse. I afterwards learned that, knowing my father's advanced age and unfitness
for so long a journey, and how wretched my
sickness would make Elizabeth, he spared
them this grief by concealing the extent of
2255 my disorder. He knew that I could not have a
more kind and attentive nurse than himself;
and, firm in the hope he felt of my recovery,
he did not doubt that, instead of doing harm,
he performed the kindest action that he
2260 could towards them.

But I was in reality very ill, and surely
nothing but the unbounded and unremitting
attentions of my friend could have restored
me to life. The form of the monster on whom
2265 I had bestowed existence was for ever before
my eyes, and I raved incessantly concerning
him. Doubtless my words surprised Henry;
he at first believed them to be the wanderings of my disturbed imagination, but the
2270 pertinacity with which I continually recurred
to the same subject persuaded him that my
disorder indeed owed its origin to some
uncommon and terrible event.

By very slow degrees, and with frequent
2275 relapses that alarmed and grieved my friend,
I recovered. I remember the first time I
became capable of observing outward objects
with any kind of pleasure, I perceived that
the fallen leaves had disappeared and that
2280 the young buds were shooting forth from the
trees that shaded my window. It was a divine
spring, and the season contributed greatly to

my convalescence. I felt also sentiments of joy and affection revive in my bosom; my gloom disappeared, and in a short time I became as cheerful as before I was attacked by the fatal passion.

    "Dearest Clerval," exclaimed I, "how kind, how very good you are to me. This whole winter, instead of being spent in study, as you promised yourself, has been consumed in my sick room. How shall I ever repay you? I feel the greatest remorse for the disappointment of which I have been the occasion, but you will forgive me."

    "You will repay me entirely if you do not discompose yourself, but get well as fast as you can; and since you appear in such good spirits, I may speak to you on one subject, may I not?"

    I trembled. One subject! What could it be? Could he allude to an object on whom I dared not even think?

    "Compose yourself," said Clerval, who observed my change of colour, "I will not mention it if it agitates you; but your father and cousin would be very happy if they received a letter from you in your own handwriting. They hardly know how ill you have been and are uneasy at your long silence."

    "Is that all, my dear Henry? How could you suppose that my first thought would not fly towards those dear, dear friends whom I love and who are so deserving of my love?"

    "If this is your present temper, my friend, you will perhaps be glad to see a letter that has been lying here some days for you; it is from your cousin, I believe."

Chapter 6

Clerval then put the following letter into my hands. It was from my own Elizabeth:

    "My dearest Cousin,

    "You have been ill, very ill, and even the constant letters of dear kind Henry are not sufficient to reassure me on your account. You are forbidden to write—to hold a pen; yet one word from you, dear Victor, is necessary to calm our apprehensions. For a long time I have thought that each post would bring this line, and my persuasions have restrained my uncle from undertaking a journey to Ingolstadt. I have prevented his encountering the inconveniences and perhaps dangers of so long a journey, yet how often have I regretted not being able to perform it myself! I figure to myself that the task of attending on your sickbed has devolved on some mercenary old nurse, who could never guess your wishes nor minister to them with the care and affection of your poor cousin. Yet that is over now: Clerval writes that indeed you are getting better. I eagerly hope that you will confirm this intelligence soon in your own handwriting.

    "Get well—and return to us. You will find a happy, cheerful home and friends who love you dearly. Your father's health is vigorous, and he asks but to see you, but to be assured that you are well; and not a care will ever cloud his benevolent countenance. How pleased you would be to remark the improvement of our Ernest! He is now sixteen and full of activity and spirit. He is desirous to be a true Swiss and to enter into foreign service, but we cannot part with him, at least until his elder brother returns to us. My uncle is not pleased with the idea of a military career in a distant country, but Ernest never had your powers of application. He looks upon study as an odious fetter; his time is spent in the open air, climbing the hills or rowing on the lake. I fear that he will become an idler unless we yield the point

2365 and permit him to enter on the profession
which he has selected.

"Little alteration, except the growth of our
dear children, has taken place since you left
us. The blue lake and snow-clad mountains—
2370 they never change; and I think our placid
home and our contented hearts are regulated by the same immutable laws. My trifling occupations take up my time and
amuse me, and I am rewarded for any exer-
2375 tions by seeing none but happy, kind faces
around me. Since you left us, but one change
has taken place in our little household. Do
you remember on what occasion Justine
Moritz entered our family? Probably you do
2380 not; I will relate her history, therefore in a
few words. Madame Moritz, her mother, was
a widow with four children, of whom Justine
was the third. This girl had always been the
favourite of her father, but through a strange
2385 perversity, her mother could not endure her,
and after the death of M. Moritz, treated her
very ill. My aunt observed this, and when
Justine was twelve years of age, prevailed on
her mother to allow her to live at our house.
2390 The republican institutions of our country
have produced simpler and happier manners
than those which prevail in the great monar-
chies that surround it. Hence there is less
distinction between the several classes of its
2395 inhabitants; and the lower orders, being neither so poor nor so despised, their manners
are more refined and moral. A servant in
Geneva does not mean the same thing as a
servant in France and England. Justine, thus
2400 received in our family, learned the duties of a
servant, a condition which, in our fortunate
country, does not include the idea of ignorance and a sacrifice of the dignity of a
human being.

2405 "Justine, you may remember, was a great
favourite of yours; and I recollect you once
remarked that if you were in an ill humour,
one glance from Justine could dissipate it, for
the same reason that Ariosto gives concern-
2410 ing the beauty of Angelica—she looked so
frank-hearted and happy. My aunt conceived
a great attachment for her, by which she was
induced to give her an education superior to
that which she had at first intended. This
2415 benefit was fully repaid; Justine was the
most grateful little creature in the world: I do
not mean that she made any professions I
never heard one pass her lips, but you could
see by her eyes that she almost adored her
2420 protectress. Although her disposition was
gay and in many respects inconsiderate, yet
she paid the greatest attention to every gesture of my aunt. She thought her the model
of all excellence and endeavoured to imitate
2425 her phraseology and manners, so that even
now she often reminds me of her.

"When my dearest aunt died every one
was too much occupied in their own grief to
notice poor Justine, who had attended her
2430 during her illness with the most anxious
affection. Poor Justine was very ill; but other
trials were reserved for her.

"One by one, her brothers and sister died;
and her mother, with the exception of her
2435 neglected daughter, was left childless. The
conscience of the woman was troubled; she
began to think that the deaths of her favour-
ites was a judgement from heaven to chas-
tise her partiality. She was a Roman Catholic;
2440 and I believe her confessor confirmed the
idea which she had conceived. Accordingly, a
few months after your departure for Ingolstadt,
Justine was called home by her repentant
mother. Poor girl! She wept when she quitted
2445 our house; she was much altered since the
death of my aunt; grief had given softness
and a winning mildness to her manners,
which had before been remarkable for

vivacity. Nor was her residence at her moth-
2450 er's house of a nature to restore her gaiety.
The poor woman was very vacillating in her
repentance. She sometimes begged Justine to
forgive her unkindness, but much oftener
accused her of having caused the deaths of
2455 her brothers and sister. Perpetual fretting at
length threw Madame Moritz into a decline,
which at first increased her irritability, but
she is now at peace for ever. She died on the
first approach of cold weather, at the begin-
2460 ning of this last winter. Justine has just
returned to us; and I assure you I love her
tenderly. She is very clever and gentle, and
extremely pretty; as I mentioned before, her
mien and her expression continually remind
2465 me of my dear aunt.

"I must say also a few words to you, my
dear cousin, of little darling William. I wish
you could see him; he is very tall of his age,
with sweet laughing blue eyes, dark eyelashes,
2470 and curling hair. When he smiles, two little
dimples appear on each cheek, which are rosy
with health. He has already had one or two
little wives, but Louisa Biron is his favourite, a
pretty little girl of five years of age.

2475 "Now, dear Victor, I dare say you wish to be
indulged in a little gossip concerning the good
people of Geneva. The pretty Miss Mansfield
has already received the congratulatory visits
on her approaching marriage with a young
2480 Englishman, John Melbourne, Esq. Her ugly
sister, Manon, married M. Duvillard, the rich
banker, last autumn. Your favourite schoolfel-
low, Louis Manoir, has suffered several misfortunes since the departure of Clerval from
2485 Geneva. But he has already recovered his spirits, and is reported to be on the point of marrying a lively pretty Frenchwoman, Madame
Tavernier. She is a widow, and much older
than Manoir; but she is very much admired,
2490 and a favourite with everybody.

"I have written myself into better spirits,
dear cousin; but my anxiety returns upon
me as I conclude. Write, dearest Victor,—
one line—one word will be a blessing to us.
2495 Ten thousand thanks to Henry for his kindness, his affection, and his many letters; we
are sincerely grateful. Adieu! my cousin;
take care of yourself; and, I entreat you,
write!

2500   "Elizabeth Lavenza.
"Geneva, March 18th, 17—."

"Dear, dear Elizabeth!" I exclaimed, when I
had read her letter: "I will write instantly and
relieve them from the anxiety they must feel."
2505 I wrote, and this exertion greatly fatigued me;
but my convalescence had commenced, and
proceeded regularly. In another fortnight I
was able to leave my chamber.

One of my first duties on my recovery was
2510 to introduce Clerval to the several professors
of the university. In doing this, I underwent a
kind of rough usage, ill befitting the wounds
that my mind had sustained. Ever since the
fatal night, the end of my labours, and the
2515 beginning of my misfortunes, I had conceived
a violent antipathy even to the name of natural philosophy. When I was otherwise quite
restored to health, the sight of a chemical
instrument would renew all the agony of my
2520 nervous symptoms. Henry saw this, and had
removed all my apparatus from my view. He
had also changed my apartment; for he perceived that I had acquired a dislike for the
room which had previously been my labora-
2525 tory. But these cares of Clerval were made
of no avail when I visited the professors.
M. Waldman inflicted torture when he praised,
with kindness and warmth, the astonishing
progress I had made in the sciences. He soon
2530 perceived that I disliked the subject; but not
guessing the real cause, he attributed my
feelings to modesty, and changed the subject

from my improvement, to the science itself, with a desire, as I evidently saw, of drawing me out. What could I do? He meant to please, and he tormented me. I felt as if he had placed carefully, one by one, in my view those instruments which were to be afterwards used in putting me to a slow and cruel death. I writhed under his words, yet dared not exhibit the pain I felt. Clerval, whose eyes and feelings were always quick in discerning the sensations of others, declined the subject, alleging, in excuse, his total ignorance; and the conversation took a more general turn. I thanked my friend from my heart, but I did not speak. I saw plainly that he was surprised, but he never attempted to draw my secret from me; and although I loved him with a mixture of affection and reverence that knew no bounds, yet I could never persuade myself to confide in him that event which was so often present to my recollection, but which I feared the detail to another would only impress more deeply.

M. Krempe was not equally docile; and in my condition at that time, of almost insupportable sensitiveness, his harsh blunt encomiums gave me even more pain than the benevolent approbation of M. Waldman. "D—n the fellow!" cried he; "why, M. Clerval, I assure you he has outstript us all. Ay, stare if you please; but it is nevertheless true. A youngster who, but a few years ago, believed in Cornelius Agrippa as firmly as in the gospel, has now set himself at the head of the university; and if he is not soon pulled down, we shall all be out of countenance.—Ay, ay," continued he, observing my face expressive of suffering, "M. Frankenstein is modest; an excellent quality in a young man. Young men should be diffident of themselves, you know, M. Clerval: I was myself when young; but that wears out in a very short time."

M. Krempe had now commenced an eulogy on himself, which happily turned the conversation from a subject that was so annoying to me.

Clerval had never sympathised in my tastes for natural science; and his literary pursuits differed wholly from those which had occupied me. He came to the university with the design of making himself complete master of the oriental languages, and thus he should open a field for the plan of life he had marked out for himself. Resolved to pursue no inglorious career, he turned his eyes toward the East, as affording scope for his spirit of enterprise. The Persian, Arabic, and Sanskrit languages engaged his attention, and I was easily induced to enter on the same studies. Idleness had ever been irksome to me, and now that I wished to fly from reflection, and hated my former studies, I felt great relief in being the fellow-pupil with my friend, and found not only instruction but consolation in the works of the orientalists. I did not, like him, attempt a critical knowledge of their dialects, for I did not contemplate making any other use of them than temporary amusement. I read merely to understand their meaning, and they well repaid my labours. Their melancholy is soothing, and their joy elevating, to a degree I never experienced in studying the authors of any other country. When you read their writings, life appears to consist in a warm sun and a garden of roses,—in the smiles and frowns of a fair enemy, and the fire that consumes your own heart. How different from the manly and heroical poetry of Greece and Rome!

Summer passed away in these occupations, and my return to Geneva was fixed for the latter end of autumn; but being delayed by several accidents, winter and snow arrived, the roads were deemed impassable, and my journey was retarded until the ensuing spring. I felt this delay very bitterly; for I 2620 longed to see my native town and my beloved friends. My return had only been delayed so long, from an unwillingness to leave Clerval in a strange place, before he had become acquainted with any of its 2625 inhabitants. The winter, however, was spent cheerfully; and although the spring was uncommonly late, when it came its beauty compensated for its dilatoriness.

The month of May had already com- 2630 menced, and I expected the letter daily which was to fix the date of my departure, when Henry proposed a pedestrian tour in the environs of Ingolstadt, that I might bid a personal farewell to the country I had so 2635 long inhabited. I acceded with pleasure to this proposition: I was fond of exercise, and Clerval had always been my favourite companion in the ramble of this nature that I had taken among the scenes of my native 2640 country.

We passed a fortnight in these perambulations: my health and spirits had long been restored, and they gained additional strength from the salubrious air I breathed, the natu- 2645 ral incidents of our progress, and the conversation of my friend. Study had before secluded me from the intercourse of my fellow-creatures, and rendered me unsocial; but Clerval called forth the better feelings of my 2650 heart; he again taught me to love the aspect of nature, and the cheerful faces of children. Excellent friend! how sincerely you did love me, and endeavour to elevate my mind until it was on a level with your own. A selfish 2655 pursuit had cramped and narrowed me, until your gentleness and affection warmed and opened my senses; I became the same happy creature who, a few years ago, loved and

beloved by all, had no sorrow or care. When 2660 happy, inanimate nature had the power of bestowing on me the most delightful sensations. A serene sky and verdant fields filled me with ecstasy. The present season was indeed divine; the flowers of spring bloomed 2665 in the hedges, while those of summer were already in bud. I was undisturbed by thoughts which during the preceding year had pressed upon me, notwithstanding my endeavours to throw them off, with an invin- 2670 cible burden.

Henry rejoiced in my gaiety, and sincerely sympathised in my feelings: he exerted himself to amuse me, while he expressed the sensations that filled his soul. The resources 2675 of his mind on this occasion were truly astonishing: his conversation was full of imagination; and very often, in imitation of the Persian and Arabic writers, he invented tales of wonderful fancy and passion. At 2680 other times he repeated my favourite poems, or drew me out into arguments, which he supported with great ingenuity.

We returned to our college on a Sunday afternoon: the peasants were dancing, and 2685 every one we met appeared gay and happy. My own spirits were high, and I bounded along with feelings of unbridled joy and hilarity.

Chapter 7

On my return, I found the following letter 2690 from my father:—

"My dear Victor,

"You have probably waited impatiently for a letter to fix the date of your return to us; and I was at first tempted to write only a few 2695 lines, merely mentioning the day on which I should expect you. But that would be a cruel kindness, and I dare not do it. What would be your surprise, my son, when you expected a

happy and glad welcome, to behold, on the
2700 contrary, tears and wretchedness? And how,
Victor, can I relate our misfortune? Absence
cannot have rendered you callous to our joys
and griefs; and how shall I inflict pain on my
long absent son? I wish to prepare you for
2705 the woeful news, but I know it is impossible;
even now your eye skims over the page to
seek the words which are to convey to you
the horrible tidings.

"William is dead!—that sweet child,
2710 whose smiles delighted and warmed my
heart, who was so gentle, yet so gay! Victor,
he is murdered!

"I will not attempt to console you; but will
simply relate the circumstances of the trans-
2715 action.

"Last Thursday (May 7th), I, my niece, and
your two brothers, went to walk in Plainpalais.
The evening was warm and serene, and we
prolonged our walk farther than usual. It was
2720 already dusk before we thought of returning;
and then we discovered that William and
Ernest, who had gone on before, were not to
be found. We accordingly rested on a seat
until they should return. Presently Ernest
2725 came, and enquired if we had seen his
brother; he said, that he had been playing
with him, that William had run away to hide
himself, and that he vainly sought for him,
and afterwards waited for a long time, but
2730 that he did not return.

"This account rather alarmed us, and we
continued to search for him until night fell,
when Elizabeth conjectured that he might
have returned to the house. He was not
2735 there. We returned again, with torches; for I
could not rest, when I thought that my sweet
boy had lost himself, and was exposed to all
the damps and dews of night; Elizabeth also
suffered extreme anguish. About five in the
2740 morning I discovered my lovely boy, whom

the night before I had seen blooming and
active in health, stretched on the grass livid
and motionless; the print of the murder's
finger was on his neck.

2745 "He was conveyed home, and the anguish
that was visible in my countenance betrayed
the secret to Elizabeth. She was very earnest
to see the corpse. At first I attempted to
prevent her but she persisted, and entering
2750 the room where it lay, hastily examined the
neck of the victim, and clasping her hands
exclaimed, 'O God! I have murdered my
darling child!'

"She fainted, and was restored with
2755 extreme difficulty. When she again lived, it
was only to weep and sigh. She told me, that
that same evening William had teased her to
let him wear a very valuable miniature that
she possessed of your mother. This picture is
2760 gone, and was doubtless the temptation
which urged the murderer to the deed. We
have no trace of him at present, although our
exertions to discover him are unremitted;
but they will not restore my beloved William!

2765 "Come, dearest Victor; you alone can console Elizabeth. She weeps continually, and
accuses herself unjustly as the cause of his
death; her words pierce my heart. We are all
unhappy; but will not that be an additional
2770 motive for you, my son, to return and be our
comforter? Your dear mother! Alas, Victor! I
now say, Thank God she did not live to witness the cruel, miserable death of her youngest darling!

2775 "Come, Victor; not brooding thoughts of
vengeance against the assassin, but with
feelings of peace and gentleness, that will
heal, instead of festering, the wounds of our
minds. Enter the house of mourning, my
2780 friend, but with kindness and affection for
those who love you, and not with hatred for
your enemies.

"Your affectionate and afflicted father,
"Alphonse Frankenstein.

2785   "Geneva, May 12th, 17—."

Clerval, who had watched my countenance as I read this letter, was surprised to
observe the despair that succeeded the joy I
at first expressed on receiving new from my

2790   friends. I threw the letter on the table, and
covered my face with my hands.

"My dear Frankenstein," exclaimed Henry,
when he perceived me weep with bitterness,
"are you always to be unhappy? My dear

2795   friend, what has happened?"

I motioned him to take up the letter, while
I walked up and down the room in the
extremest agitation. Tears also gushed from
the eyes of Clerval, as he read the account of

2800   my misfortune.

"I can offer you no consolation, my
friend," said he; "your disaster is irreparable.
What do you intend to do?"

"To go instantly to Geneva: come with me,

2805   Henry, to order the horses."

During our walk, Clerval endeavoured to
say a few words of consolation; he could only
express his heartfelt sympathy. "Poor
William!" said he, "dear lovely child, he now

2810   sleeps with his angel mother! Who that had
seen him bright and joyous in his young
beauty, but must weep over his untimely
loss! To die so miserably; to feel the murderer's grasp! How much more a murdered that

2815   could destroy radiant innocence! Poor little
fellow! one only consolation have we; his
friends mourn and weep, but he is at rest.
The pang is over, his sufferings are at an end
for ever. A sod covers his gentle form, and he

2820   knows no pain. He can no longer be a subject
for pity; we must reserve that for his miserable survivors."

Clerval spoke thus as we hurried through
the streets; the words impressed themselves

2825   on my mind and I remembered them afterwards in solitude. But now, as soon as the
horses arrived, I hurried into a cabriolet, and
bade farewell to my friend.

My journey was very melancholy. At first I

2830   wished to hurry on, for I longed to console
and sympathise with my loved and sorrowing friends; but when I drew near my native
town, I slackened my progress. I could hardly
sustain the multitude of feelings that crowded

2835   into my mind. I passed through scenes familiar to my youth, but which I had not seen for
nearly six years. How altered every thing
might be during that time! One sudden and
desolating change had taken place; but a

2840   thousand little circumstances might have by
degrees worked other alterations, which,
although they were done more tranquilly,
might not be the less decisive. Fear overcame
me; I dared no advance, dreading a thousand

2845   nameless evils that made me tremble,
although I was unable to define them.

I remained two days at Lausanne, in this
painful state of mind. I contemplated the
lake: the waters were placid; all around

2850   was calm; and the snowy mountains, "the
palaces of nature," were not changed. By
degrees the calm and heavenly scene
restored me, and I continued my journey
towards Geneva.

2855   The road ran by the side of the lake,
which became narrower as I approached my
native town. I discovered more distinctly the
black sides of Jura, and the bright summit of
Mont Blanc. I wept like a child. "Dear moun-

2860   tains! my own beautiful lake! how do you
welcome your wanderer? Your summits are
clear; the sky and lake are blue and placid. Is
this to prognosticate peace, or to mock at my
unhappiness?"

2865   I fear, my friend, that I shall render myself
tedious by dwelling on these preliminary

circumstances; but they were days of comparative happiness, and I think of them with pleasure. My country, my beloved country!

2870 who but a native can tell the delight I took in again beholding thy streams, thy mountains, and, more than all, thy lovely lake!

Yet, as I drew nearer home, grief and fear again overcame me. Night also closed

2875 around; and when I could hardly see the dark mountains, I felt still more gloomily. The picture appeared a vast and dim scene of evil, and I foresaw obscurely that I was destined to become the most wretched of

2880 human beings. Alas! I prophesied truly, and failed only in one single circumstance, that in all the misery I imagined and dreaded, I did not conceive the hundredth part of the anguish I was destined to endure.

2885 It was completely dark when I arrived in the environs of Geneva; the gates of the town were already shut; and I was obliged to pass the night at Secheron, a village at the distance of half a league from the city. The sky

2890 was serene; and, as I was unable to rest, I resolved to visit the spot where my poor William had been murdered. As I could not pass through the town, I was obliged to cross the lake in a boat to arrive at Plainpalais.

2895 During this short voyage I saw the lightning playing on the summit of Mont Blanc in the most beautiful figures. The storm appeared to approach rapidly, and, on landing, I ascended a low hill, that I might observe its

2900 progress. It advanced; the heavens were clouded, and I soon felt the rain coming slowly in large drops, but its violence quickly increased.

I quitted my seat, and walked on,

2905 although the darkness and storm increased every minute, and the thunder burst with a terrific crash over my head. It was echoed from Salêve, the Juras, and the Alps of Savoy;

vivid flashes of lightning dazzled my eyes,

2910 illuminating the lake, making it appear like a vast sheet of fire; then for an instant every thing seemed of a pitchy darkness, until the eye recovered itself from the preceding flash. The storm, as is often the case in Switzerland,

2915 appeared at once in various parts of the heavens. The most violent storm hung exactly north of the town, over the part of the lake which lies between the promontory of Belrive and the village of Copêt. Another

2920 storm enlightened Jura with faint flashes; and another darkened and sometimes disclosed the Môle, a peaked mountain to the east of the lake.

While I watched the tempest, so beautiful

2925 yet terrific, I wandered on with a hasty step. This noble war in the sky elevated my spirits; I clasped my hands, and exclaimed aloud, "William, dear angel! this is thy funeral, this thy dirge!" As I said these words, I perceived

2930 in the gloom a figure which stole from behind a clump of trees near me; I stood fixed, gazing intently: I could not be mistaken. A flash of lightning illuminated the object, and discovered its shape plainly to me; its gigantic

2935 stature, and the deformity of its aspect more hideous than belongs to humanity, instantly informed me that it was the wretch, the filthy dæmon, to whom I had given life. What did he there? Could he be (I shuddered at the

2940 conception) the murderer of my brother? No sooner did that idea cross my imagination, than I became convinced of its truth; my teeth chattered, and I was forced to lean against a tree for support. The figure passed

2945 me quickly, and I lost it in the gloom. Nothing in human shape could have destroyed the fair child. He was the murderer! I could not doubt it. The mere presence of the idea was an irresistible proof of the fact. I thought of

2950 pursuing the devil; but it would have been in

vain, for another flash discovered him to me
hanging among the rocks of the nearly perpendicular ascent of Mont Salêve, a hill that
bounds Plainpalais on the south. He soon
2955 reached the summit, and disappeared.

I remained motionless. The thunder
ceased; but the rain still continued, and the
scene was enveloped in an impenetrable
darkness. I revolved in my mind the events
2960 which I had until now sought to forget: the
whole train of my progress toward the creation; the appearance of the works of my
own hands at my bedside; its departure. Two
years had now nearly elapsed since the night
2965 on which he first received life; and was this
his first crime? Alas! I had turned loose into
the world a depraved wretch, whose delight
was in carnage and misery; had he not murdered my brother?

2970 No one can conceive the anguish I suffered during the remainder of the night,
which I spent, cold and wet, in the open air.
But I did not feel the inconvenience of the
weather; my imagination was busy in scenes
2975 of evil and despair. I considered the being
whom I had cast among mankind, and
endowed with the will and power to effect
purposes of horror, such as the deed which
he had now done, nearly in the light of my
2980 own vampire, my own spirit let loose from
the grave, and forced to destroy all that was
dear to me.

Day dawned; and I directed my steps
towards the town. The gates were open, and I
2985 hastened to my father's house. My first
thought was to discover what I knew of the
murderer, and cause instant pursuit to be
made. But I paused when I reflected on the
story that I had to tell. A being whom I myself
2990 had formed, and endued with life, had met
me at midnight among the precipices of an
inaccessible mountain. I remembered also

the nervous fever with which I had been
seized just at the time that I dated my creation,
2995 and which would give an air of delirium to a
tale otherwise so utterly improbable. I well
knew that if any other had communicated
such a relation to me, I should have looked
upon it as the ravings of insanity. Besides, the
3000 strange nature of the animal would elude all
pursuit, even if I were so far credited as to
persuade my relatives to commence it. And
then of what use would be pursuit? Who
could arrest a creature capable of scaling the
3005 overhanging sides of Mont Salêve? These
reflections determined me, and I resolved to
remain silent.

It was about five in the morning when I
entered my father's house. I told the servants
3010 not to disturb the family, and went into the
library to attend their usual hour of rising.

Six years had elapsed, passed in a dream
but for one indelible trace, and I stood in the
same place where I had last embraced my
3015 father before my departure for Ingolstadt.
Beloved and venerable parent! He still remained
to me. I gazed on the picture of my mother,
which stood over the mantel-piece. It was an
historical subject, painted at my father's
3020 desire, and represented Caroline Beaufort in
an agony of despair, kneeling by the coffin of
her dead father. Her garb was rustic, and her
cheek pale; but there was an air of dignity
and beauty, that hardly permitted the senti-
3025 ment of pity. Below this picture was a miniature of William; and my tears flowed when I
looked upon it. While I was thus engaged,
Ernest entered: he had heard me arrive, and
hastened to welcome me: "Welcome, my
3030 dearest Victor," said he. "Ah! I wish you had
come three months ago, and then you would
have found us all joyous and delighted. You
come to us now to share a misery which
nothing can alleviate; yet your presence will,

3035 I hope, revive our father, who seems sinking under his misfortune; and your persuasions will induce poor Elizabeth to cease her vain and tormenting self-accusations.—Poor William! he was our darling and our pride!"

3040 Tears, unrestrained, fell from my brother's eyes; a sense of mortal agony crept over my frame. Before, I had only imagined the wretchedness of my desolated home; the reality came on me as a new, and a not less

3045 terrible, disaster. I tried to calm Ernest; I enquired more minutely concerning my father, and here I named my cousin.

"She most of all," said Ernest, "requires consolation; she accused herself of having

3050 caused the death of my brother, and that made her very wretched. But since the murderer has been discovered—"

"The murderer discovered! Good God! how can that be? who could attempt to pursue

3055 him? It is impossible; one might as well try to overtake the winds, or confine a mountain-stream with a straw. I saw him too; he was free last night!"

"I do not know what you mean," replied

3060 my brother, in accents of wonder, "but to us the discovery we have made completes our misery. No one would believe it at first; and even now Elizabeth will not be convinced, notwithstanding all the evidence. Indeed,

3065 who would credit that Justine Moritz, who was so amiable, and fond of all the family, could suddenly become so capable of so frightful, so appalling a crime?"

"Justine Moritz! Poor, poor girl, is she the

3070 accused? But it is wrongfully; every one knows that; no one believes it, surely, Ernest?"

"No one did at first; but several circumstances came out, that have almost forced conviction upon us; and her own behaviour

3075 has been so confused, as to add to the evidence of facts a weight that, I fear, leaves no

hope for doubt. But she will be tried today, and you will then hear all."

He then related that, the morning on

3080 which the murder of poor William had been discovered, Justine had been taken ill, and confined to her bed for several days. During this interval, one of the servants, happening to examine the apparel she had worn on the

3085 night of the murder, had discovered in her pocket the picture of my mother, which had been judged to be the temptation of the murderer. The servant instantly showed it to one of the others, who, without saying a word to

3090 any of the family, went to a magistrate; and, upon their deposition, Justine was apprehended. On being charged with the fact, the poor girl confirmed the suspicion in a great measure by her extreme confusion of manner.

3095 This was a strange tale, but it did not shake my faith; and I replied earnestly, "You are all mistaken; I know the murderer. Justine, poor, good Justine, is innocent."

At that instant my father entered. I saw

3100 unhappiness deeply impressed on his countenance, but he endeavoured to welcome me cheerfully; and, after we had exchanged our mournful greeting, would have introduced some other topic than that of our disaster,

3105 had not Ernest exclaimed, "Good God, papa! Victor says that he knows who was the murderer of poor William."

"We do also, unfortunately," replied my father, "for indeed I had rather have been for

3110 ever ignorant than have discovered so much depravity and ungratitude in one I valued so highly."

"My dear father, you are mistaken; Justine is innocent."

3115 "If she is, God forbid that she should suffer as guilty. She is to be tried today, and I hope, I sincerely hope, that she will be acquitted."

This speech calmed me. I was firmly con-
3120 vinced in my own mind that Justine, and
indeed every human being, was guiltless of
this murder. I had no fear, therefore, that any
circumstantial evidence could be brought
forward strong enough to convict her. My
3125 tale was not one to announce publicly; its
astounding horror would be looked upon as
madness by the vulgar. Did any one indeed
exist, except I, the creator, who would believe,
unless his senses convinced him, in the exis-
3130 tence of the living monument of presumption and rash ignorance which I had let loose
upon the world?

We were soon joined by Elizabeth. Time
had altered her since I last beheld her; it
3135 had endowed her with loveliness surpassing the beauty of her childish years. There
was the same candour, the same vivacity,
but it was allied to an expression more full
of sensibility and intellect. She welcomed
3140 me with the greatest affection. "Your
arrival, my dear cousin," said she, "fills me
with hope. You perhaps will find some
means to justify my poor guiltless Justine.
Alas! who is safe, if she be convicted of
3145 crime? I rely on her innocence as certainly
as I do upon my own. Our misfortune is
doubly hard to us; we have not only lost
that lovely darling boy, but this poor girl,
whom I sincerely love, is to be torn away by
3150 even a worse fate. If she is condemned, I
never shall know joy more. But she will not,
I am sure she will not; and then I shall be
happy again, even after the sad death of
my little William."

3155 "She is innocent, my Elizabeth," said I,
"and that shall be proved; fear nothing, but
let your spirits be cheered by the assurance
of her acquittal."

"How kind and generous you are! every
3160 one else believes in her guilt, and that made

me wretched, for I knew that it was impossible: and to see every one else prejudiced in
so deadly a manner rendered me hopeless
and despairing." She wept.

3165 "Dearest niece," said my father, "dry your
tears. If she is, as you believe, innocent, rely
on the justice of our laws, and the activity
with which I shall prevent the slightest
shadow of partiality."

Chapter 8

3170 We passed a few sad hours until eleven
o'clock, when the trial was to commence.
My father and the rest of the family being
obliged to attend as witnesses, I accompanied them to the court. During the whole of
3175 this wretched mockery of justice I suffered
living torture. It was to be decided whether
the result of my curiosity and lawless devices
would cause the death of two of my fellow
beings: one a smiling babe full of innocence
3180 and joy, the other far more dreadfully murdered, with every aggravation of infamy that
could make the murder memorable in horror.
Justine also was a girl of merit and possessed
qualities which promised to render her life
3185 happy; now all was to be obliterated in an
ignominious grave, and I the cause! A thousand times rather would I have confessed
myself guilty of the crime ascribed to Justine,
but I was absent when it was committed,
3190 and such a declaration would have been considered as the ravings of a madman and
would not have exculpated her who suffered
through me.

The appearance of Justine was calm. She
3195 was dressed in mourning, and her countenance, always engaging, was rendered, by
the solemnity of her feelings, exquisitely
beautiful. Yet she appeared confident in
innocence and did not tremble, although
3200 gazed on and execrated by thousands, for all

the kindness which her beauty might otherwise have excited was obliterated in the
minds of the spectators by the imagination
of the enormity she was supposed to have
3205 committed. She was tranquil, yet her tranquillity was evidently constrained; and as her confusion had before been adduced as a proof of
her guilt, she worked up her mind to an appearance of courage. When she entered the court
3210 she threw her eyes round it and quickly discovered where we were seated. A tear seemed to
dim her eye when she saw us, but she quickly
recovered herself, and a look of sorrowful affection seemed to attest her utter guiltlessness.

3215   The trial began, and after the advocate
against her had stated the charge, several
witnesses were called. Several strange facts
combined against her, which might have
staggered anyone who had not such proof of
3220 her innocence as I had. She had been out the
whole of the night on which the murder had
been committed and towards morning had
been perceived by a market-woman not far
from the spot where the body of the mur-
3225 dered child had been afterwards found. The
woman asked her what she did there, but
she looked very strangely and only returned
a confused and unintelligible answer. She
returned to the house about eight o'clock,
3230 and when one inquired where she had
passed the night, she replied that she had
been looking for the child and demanded
earnestly if anything had been heard concerning him. When shown the body, she fell
3235 into violent hysterics and kept her bed for
several days. The picture was then produced
which the servant had found in her pocket;
and when Elizabeth, in a faltering voice,
proved that it was the same which, an hour
3240 before the child had been missed, she had
placed round his neck, a murmur of horror
and indignation filled the court.

Justine was called on for her defence. As
the trial had proceeded, her countenance
3245 had altered. Surprise, horror, and misery
were strongly expressed. Sometimes she
struggled with her tears, but when she was
desired to plead, she collected her powers
and spoke in an audible although variable
3250 voice.

"God knows," she said, "how entirely I am
innocent. But I do not pretend that my pro-
testations should acquit me; I rest my innocence on a plain and simple explanation of
3255 the facts which have been adduced against
me, and I hope the character I have always
borne will incline my judges to a favourable
interpretation where any circumstance
appears doubtful or suspicious."

3260   She then related that, by the permission
of Elizabeth, she had passed the evening of
the night on which the murder had been
committed at the house of an aunt at Chêne,
a village situated at about a league from
3265 Geneva. On her return, at about nine o'clock,
she met a man who asked her if she had
seen anything of the child who was lost. She
was alarmed by this account and passed
several hours in looking for him, when the
3270 gates of Geneva were shut, and she was
forced to remain several hours of the night in
a barn belonging to a cottage, being unwilling to call up the inhabitants, to whom she
was well known. Most of the night she spent
3275 here watching; towards morning she
believed that she slept for a few minutes;
some steps disturbed her, and she awoke. It
was dawn, and she quitted her asylum, that
she might again endeavour to find my
3280 brother. If she had gone near the spot where
his body lay, it was without her knowledge.
That she had been bewildered when questioned by the market-woman was not surprising, since she had passed a sleepless

3285 night and the fate of poor William was yet uncertain. Concerning the picture she could give no account.

"I know," continued the unhappy victim, "how heavily and fatally this one circum-
3290 stance weighs against me, but I have no power of explaining it; and when I have expressed my utter ignorance, I am only left to conjecture concerning the probabilities by which it might have been placed in my
3295 pocket. But here also I am checked. I believe that I have no enemy on earth, and none surely would have been so wicked as to destroy me wantonly. Did the murderer place it there? I know of no opportunity
3300 afforded him for so doing; or, if I had, why should he have stolen the jewel, to part with it again so soon?

"I commit my cause to the justice of my judges, yet I see no room for hope. I beg per-
3305 mission to have a few witnesses examined concerning my character, and if their testi-mony shall not overweigh my supposed guilt, I must be condemned, although I would pledge my salvation on my innocence."

3310 Several witnesses were called who had known her for many years, and they spoke well of her; but fear and hatred of the crime of which they supposed her guilty rendered them timorous and unwilling to come for-
3315 ward. Elizabeth saw even this last resource, her excellent dispositions and irreproachable conduct, about to fail the accused, when, although violently agitated, she desired permission to address the court.

3320 "I am," said she, "the cousin of the unhappy child who was murdered, or rather his sister, for I was educated by and have lived with his parents ever since and even long before his birth. It may therefore be
3325 judged indecent in me to come forward on this occasion, but when I see a fellow crea-

ture about to perish through the cowardice of her pretended friends, I wish to be allowed to speak, that I may say what I know of her
3330 character. I am well acquainted with the accused. I have lived in the same house with her, at one time for five and at another for nearly two years. During all that period she appeared to me the most amiable and benev-
3335 olent of human creatures. She nursed Madame Frankenstein, my aunt, in her last illness, with the greatest affection and care and afterwards attended her own mother during a tedious illness, in a manner that
3340 excited the admiration of all who knew her, after which she again lived in my uncle's house, where she was beloved by all the fam-ily. She was warmly attached to the child who is now dead and acted towards him like
3345 a most affectionate mother. For my own part, I do not hesitate to say that, notwithstanding all the evidence produced against her, I believe and rely on her perfect innocence. She had no temptation for such an action; as
3350 to the bauble on which the chief proof rests, if she had earnestly desired it, I should have willingly given it to her, so much do I esteem and value her."

A murmur of approbation followed
3355 Elizabeth's simple and powerful appeal, but it was excited by her generous interference, and not in favour of poor Justine, on whom the public indignation was turned with renewed violence, charging her with the
3360 blackest ingratitude. She herself wept as Elizabeth spoke, but she did not answer. My own agitation and anguish was extreme during the whole trial. I believed in her inno-cence; I knew it. Could the dæmon who had
3365 (I did not for a minute doubt) murdered my brother also in his hellish sport have betrayed the innocent to death and igno-miny? I could not sustain the horror of my

situation, and when I perceived that the pop-
3370 ular voice and the countenances of the
judges had already condemned my unhappy
victim, I rushed out of the court in agony.
The tortures of the accused did not equal
mine; she was sustained by innocence, but
3375 the fangs of remorse tore my bosom and
would not forgo their hold.

I passed a night of unmingled wretchedness. In the morning I went to the court; my
lips and throat were parched. I dared not ask
3380 the fatal question, but I was known, and the
officer guessed the cause of my visit. The
ballots had been thrown; they were all black,
and Justine was condemned.

I cannot pretend to describe what I then
3385 felt. I had before experienced sensations of
horror, and I have endeavoured to bestow
upon them adequate expressions, but words
cannot convey an idea of the heart-sickening
despair that I then endured. The person to
3390 whom I addressed myself added that Justine
had already confessed her guilt. "That evidence," he observed, "was hardly required in
so glaring a case, but I am glad of it, and,
indeed, none of our judges like to condemn a
3395 criminal upon circumstantial evidence, be it
ever so decisive."

This was strange and unexpected intelligence; what could it mean? Had my eyes
deceived me? And was I really as mad as the
3400 whole world would believe me to be if I disclosed the object of my suspicions? I hastened to return home, and Elizabeth eagerly
demanded the result.

"My cousin," replied I, "it is decided as you
3405 may have expected; all judges had rather
that ten innocent should suffer than that
one guilty should escape. But she has confessed."

This was a dire blow to poor Elizabeth,
3410 who had relied with firmness upon Justine's

innocence. "Alas!" said she. "How shall I ever
again believe in human goodness? Justine,
whom I loved and esteemed as my sister,
how could she put on those smiles of inno-
3415 cence only to betray? Her mild eyes seemed
incapable of any severity or guile, and yet
she has committed a murder."

Soon after we heard that the poor victim
had expressed a desire to see my cousin.
3420 My father wished her not to go but said that
he left it to her own judgment and feelings
to decide. "Yes," said Elizabeth, "I will go,
although she is guilty; and you, Victor, shall
accompany me; I cannot go alone." The idea
3425 of this visit was torture to me, yet I could not
refuse.

We entered the gloomy prison chamber
and beheld Justine sitting on some straw at
the farther end; her hands were manacled,
3430 and her head rested on her knees. She rose
on seeing us enter, and when we were left
alone with her, she threw herself at the feet
of Elizabeth, weeping bitterly. My cousin
wept also.

3435 "Oh, Justine!" said she. "Why did you rob
me of my last consolation? I relied on your
innocence, and although I was then very
wretched, I was not so miserable as I am
now."

3440 "And do you also believe that I am so very,
very wicked? Do you also join with my enemies to crush me, to condemn me as a murderer?" Her voice was suffocated with sobs.

"Rise, my poor girl," said Elizabeth; "why
3445 do you kneel, if you are innocent? I am not
one of your enemies, I believed you guiltless,
notwithstanding every evidence, until I
heard that you had yourself declared your
guilt. That report, you say, is false; and be
3450 assured, dear Justine, that nothing can shake
my confidence in you for a moment, but your
own confession."

"I did confess, but I confessed a lie. I confessed, that I might obtain absolution; but
3455 now that falsehood lies heavier at my heart than all my other sins. The God of heaven forgive me! Ever since I was condemned, my confessor has besieged me; he threatened and menaced, until I almost began to think
3460 that I was the monster that he said I was. He threatened excommunication and hell fire in my last moments if I continued obdurate. Dear lady, I had none to support me; all looked on me as a wretch doomed to igno-
3465 miny and perdition. What could I do? In an evil hour I subscribed to a lie; and now only am I truly miserable."

She paused, weeping, and then continued, "I thought with horror, my sweet lady, that
3470 you should believe your Justine, whom your blessed aunt had so highly honoured, and whom you loved, was a creature capable of a crime which none but the devil himself could have perpetrated. Dear William! dear-
3475 est blessed child! I soon shall see you again in heaven, where we shall all be happy; and that consoles me, going as I am to suffer ignominy and death."

"Oh, Justine! Forgive me for having for one
3480 moment distrusted you. Why did you confess? But do not mourn, dear girl. Do not fear. I will proclaim, I will prove your innocence. I will melt the stony hearts of your enemies by my tears and prayers. You shall not die! You,
3485 my playfellow, my companion, my sister, perish on the scaffold! No! No! I never could survive so horrible a misfortune."

Justine shook her head mournfully. "I do not fear to die," she said; "that pang is past.
3490 God raises my weakness and gives me courage to endure the worst. I leave a sad and bitter world; and if you remember me and think of me as of one unjustly condemned, I am resigned to the fate awaiting me. Learn
3495 from me, dear lady, to submit in patience to the will of heaven!"

During this conversation I had retired to a corner of the prison room, where I could conceal the horrid anguish that possessed me.
3500 Despair! Who dared talk of that? The poor victim, who on the morrow was to pass the awful boundary between life and death, felt not, as I did, such deep and bitter agony. I gnashed my teeth and ground them together,
3505 uttering a groan that came from my inmost soul. Justine started. When she saw who it was, she approached me and said, "Dear sir, you are very kind to visit me; you, I hope, do not believe that I am guilty?"

3510 I could not answer. "No, Justine," said Elizabeth; "he is more convinced of your innocence than I was, for even when he heard that you had confessed, he did not credit it."

"I truly thank him. In these last moments
3515 I feel the sincerest gratitude towards those who think of me with kindness. How sweet is the affection of others to such a wretch as I am! It removes more than half my misfortune, and I feel as if I could die in peace now
3520 that my innocence is acknowledged by you, dear lady, and your cousin."

Thus the poor sufferer tried to comfort others and herself. She indeed gained the resignation she desired. But I, the true mur-
3525 derer, felt the never-dying worm alive in my bosom, which allowed of no hope or consolation. Elizabeth also wept and was unhappy, but hers also was the misery of innocence, which, like a cloud that passes over the fair
3530 moon, for a while hides but cannot tarnish its brightness. Anguish and despair had penetrated into the core of my heart; I bore a hell within me which nothing could extinguish. We stayed several hours with Justine,
3535 and it was with great difficulty that Elizabeth could tear herself away. "I wish," cried she, "that I were to die with you; I cannot live in this world of misery."

Justine assumed an air of cheerfulness,
3540 while she with difficulty repressed her bitter

tears. She embraced Elizabeth and said in a voice of half-suppressed emotion, "Farewell, sweet lady, dearest Elizabeth, my beloved and only friend; may heaven, in its bounty,
3545 bless and preserve you; may this be the last misfortune that you will ever suffer! Live, and be happy, and make others so."

And on the morrow Justine died. Elizabeth's heart-rending eloquence failed to move the
3550 judges from their settled conviction in the criminality of the saintly sufferer. My passionate and indignant appeals were lost upon them. And when I received their cold answers and heard the harsh, unfeeling rea-
3555 soning of these men, my purposed avowal died away on my lips. Thus I might proclaim myself a madman, but not revoke the sentence passed upon my wretched victim. She perished on the scaffold as a murderess!

3560 From the tortures of my own heart, I turned to contemplate the deep and voiceless grief of my Elizabeth. This also was my doing! And my father's woe, and the desolation of that late so smiling home all
3565 was the work of my thrice-accursed hands! Ye weep, unhappy ones, but these are not your last tears! Again shall you raise the funeral wail, and the sound of your lamentations shall again and again be heard!
3570 Frankenstein, your son, your kinsman, your early, much-loved friend; he who would spend each vital drop of blood for your sakes, who has no thought nor sense of joy except as it is mirrored also in your dear
3575 countenances, who would fill the air with blessings and spend his life in serving you—he bids you weep, to shed countless tears; happy beyond his hopes, if thus inexorable fate be satisfied, and if the destruction
3580 pause before the peace of the grave have succeeded to your sad torments!

Thus spoke my prophetic soul, as, torn by remorse, horror, and despair, I beheld those I loved spend vain sorrow upon the graves of
3585 William and Justine, the first hapless victims to my unhallowed arts.

Pictorial Press Ltd/Alamy

◀ Movie poster from 1931 advertises the first film adaptation of *Frankenstein*.

How does the image blend science, technology, and humanity? How do these three concepts combine in Victor's response to his animated creature?

CHARACTER

1. In Letters 1 and 2, which aspects of Walton's background contribute to how he perceives his world?

2. In Letters 3 and 4, when Walton encounters the emaciated man, what **motivates** him to think, feel, or act in the manner he does?

3. What do Elizabeth's and Victor's contrasting traits reveal about them individually? What do these **contrasts** reveal about their relationship with one another and their relationships with other characters?

4. How do the traits of Victor and Henry **contrast**? In what way is Henry a **foil** for Victor?

5. In Chapter 7, which of Victor's choices, actions, or speeches seem contradictory or inconsistent?

STRUCTURE

6. How do the events of Chapter 2 create contradictions that introduce **ambiguity** into the text?

7. In Chapter 3, what ideas, traits, or values are **juxtaposed** between Elizabeth and Victor?

8. In Chapter 5, what event creates anticipation or **suspense** in a reader?

9. There are several **foreshadowing** moments throughout the text. Identify a specific moment that foreshadows later events and explain the significance of this moment.

NARRATION

10. The four letters by Robert Walton to his sister frame the story. As the **narration** changes, who is narrating the story? How does the **narrator's distance** from the events affect the details and information presented to a reader?

11. How does Victor's **perspective** shape his **tone** toward his studies — especially science and philosophy?

12. To what extent can Victor Frankenstein be trusted? Is he aware of his own **biases**? Explain how this affects his **reliability**.

FIGURATIVE LANGUAGE: Word Choice, Imagery, and Symbols

13. In Chapters 4 and 5, what is Victor's **tone** toward his subject and his creation? How do the **diction**, **imagery**, and details in the text contribute to that tone?

14. Explain the light and dark **motif** in this early part of the novel. How does this pattern contribute to the complexity of the text?

15. Samuel Taylor Coleridge's "The Rime of the Ancient Mariner" is referred to twice in the first eight chapters. Consider why Shelley might have included these **allusions**. What associations or parallels can you identify between *Frankenstein* and "The Rime of the Ancient Mariner"?

Chapter 9

Nothing is more painful to the human mind than, after the feelings have been worked up by a quick succession of events, the dead calmness of inaction and certainty which
5 follows and deprives the soul both of hope and fear. Justine died, she rested, and I was alive. The blood flowed freely in my veins, but a weight of despair and remorse pressed on my heart which nothing could remove. Sleep
10 fled from my eyes; I wandered like an evil spirit, for I had committed deeds of mischief beyond description horrible, and more, much more (I persuaded myself) was yet behind. Yet my heart overflowed with kindness and
15 the love of virtue. I had begun life with benevolent intentions and thirsted for the moment when I should put them in practice and make myself useful to my fellow beings. Now all was blasted; instead of that serenity
20 of conscience which allowed me to look back upon the past with self-satisfaction, and from thence to gather promise of new hopes, I was seized by remorse and the sense of guilt, which hurried me away to a
25 hell of intense tortures such as no language can describe.

This state of mind preyed upon my health, which had perhaps never entirely recovered from the first shock it had sustained. I
30 shunned the face of man; all sound of joy or complacency was torture to me; solitude was my only consolation—deep, dark, deathlike solitude.

My father observed with pain the alter-
35 ation perceptible in my disposition and habits and endeavoured by arguments deduced from the feelings of his serene conscience and guiltless life to inspire me with fortitude and awaken in me the courage to dispel the
40 dark cloud which brooded over me. "Do you think, Victor," said he, "that I do not suffer also? No one could love a child more than I loved your brother"—tears came into his eyes as he spoke—"but is it not a duty to
45 the survivors that we should refrain from augmenting their unhappiness by an appearance of immoderate grief? It is also a duty owed to yourself, for excessive sorrow prevents improvement or enjoyment, or even
50 the discharge of daily usefulness, without which no man is fit for society."

This advice, although good, was totally inapplicable to my case; I should have been the first to hide my grief and console my
55 friends if remorse had not mingled its bitterness, and terror its alarm, with my other sensations. Now I could only answer my father with a look of despair and endeavour to hide myself from his view.

60 About this time we retired to our house at Belrive. This change was particularly agreeable to me. The shutting of the gates regularly at ten o'clock and the impossibility of remaining on the lake after that hour
65 had rendered our residence within the walls of Geneva very irksome to me. I was now free. Often, after the rest of the family had retired for the night, I took the boat and passed many hours upon the water.
70 Sometimes, with my sails set, I was carried by the wind; and sometimes, after rowing into the middle of the lake, I left the boat to pursue its own course and gave way to my own miserable reflections. I was often
75 tempted, when all was at peace around me, and I the only unquiet thing that wandered restless in a scene so beautiful and heavenly—if I except some bat, or the frogs, whose harsh and interrupted croaking
80 was heard only when I approached the shore—often, I say, I was tempted to plunge into the silent lake, that the waters might close over me and my calamities for ever.

But I was restrained, when I thought of the
85 heroic and suffering Elizabeth, whom I tenderly loved, and whose existence was bound
up in mine. I thought also of my father and
surviving brother; should I by my base
desertion leave them exposed and unpro-
90 tected to the malice of the fiend whom I
had let loose among them?

At these moments I wept bitterly and
wished that peace would revisit my mind
only that I might afford them consolation
95 and happiness. But that could not be.
Remorse extinguished every hope. I had
been the author of unalterable evils, and I
lived in daily fear lest the monster whom I
had created should perpetrate some new
100 wickedness. I had an obscure feeling that all
was not over and that he would still commit
some signal crime, which by its enormity
should almost efface the recollection of the
past. There was always scope for fear so long
105 as anything I loved remained behind. My
abhorrence of this fiend cannot be conceived. When I thought of him I gnashed
my teeth, my eyes became inflamed, and
I ardently wished to extinguish that life
110 which I had so thoughtlessly bestowed.
When I reflected on his crimes and malice,
my hatred and revenge burst all bounds of
moderation. I would have made a pilgrimage
to the highest peak of the Andes, could I,
115 when there, have precipitated him to their
base. I wished to see him again, that I might
wreak the utmost extent of abhorrence on
his head and avenge the deaths of William
and Justine.
120 Our house was the house of mourning.
My father's health was deeply shaken by the
horror of the recent events. Elizabeth was
sad and desponding; she no longer took
delight in her ordinary occupations; all
125 pleasure seemed to her sacrilege toward

the dead; eternal woe and tears she then
thought was the just tribute she should pay
to innocence so blasted and destroyed. She
was no longer that happy creature who in
130 earlier youth wandered with me on the
banks of the lake and talked with ecstasy of
our future prospects. The first of those sorrows which are sent to wean us from the
earth had visited her, and its dimming influ-
135 ence quenched her dearest smiles.

"When I reflect, my dear cousin," said she,
"on the miserable death of Justine Moritz, I
no longer see the world and its works as they
before appeared to me. Before, I looked upon
140 the accounts of vice and injustice that I read
in books or heard from others as tales of
ancient days or imaginary evils; at least they
were remote and more familiar to reason
than to the imagination; but now misery has
145 come home, and men appear to me as monsters thirsting for each other's blood. Yet I am
certainly unjust. Everybody believed that
poor girl to be guilty; and if she could have
committed the crime for which she suffered,
150 assuredly she would have been the most
depraved of human creatures. For the sake of
a few jewels, to have murdered the son of
her benefactor and friend, a child whom she
had nursed from its birth, and appeared to
155 love as if it had been her own! I could not
consent to the death of any human being,
but certainly I should have thought such a
creature unfit to remain in the society of
men. But she was innocent. I know, I feel she
160 was innocent; you are of the same opinion,
and that confirms me. Alas! Victor, when
falsehood can look so like the truth, who can
assure themselves of certain happiness? I
feel as if I were walking on the edge of a
165 precipice, towards which thousands are
crowding and endeavouring to plunge me
into the abyss. William and Justine were

assassinated, and the murderer escapes; he walks about the world free, and perhaps
170 respected. But even if I were condemned to suffer on the scaffold for the same crimes, I would not change places with such a wretch."

I listened to this discourse with the
175 extremest agony. I, not in deed, but in effect, was the true murderer. Elizabeth read my anguish in my countenance, and kindly taking my hand, said, "My dearest friend, you must calm yourself. These events have
180 affected me, God knows how deeply; but I am not so wretched as you are. There is an expression of despair, and sometimes of revenge, in your countenance that makes me tremble. Dear Victor, banish these dark pas-
185 sions. Remember the friends around you, who centre all their hopes in you. Have we lost the power of rendering you happy? Ah! While we love, while we are true to each other, here in this land of peace and beauty,
190 your native country, we may reap every tranquil blessing—what can disturb our peace?"

And could not such words from her whom I fondly prized before every other gift of fortune suffice to chase away the fiend that
195 lurked in my heart? Even as she spoke I drew near to her, as if in terror, lest at that very moment the destroyer had been near to rob me of her.

Thus not the tenderness of friendship, nor
200 the beauty of earth, nor of heaven, could redeem my soul from woe; the very accents of love were ineffectual. I was encompassed by a cloud which no beneficial influence could penetrate. The wounded deer dragging
205 its fainting limbs to some untrodden brake, there to gaze upon the arrow which had pierced it, and to die, was but a type of me.

Sometimes I could cope with the sullen despair that overwhelmed me, but sometimes

210 the whirlwind passions of my soul drove me to seek, by bodily exercise and by change of place, some relief from my intolerable sensations. It was during an access of this kind that I suddenly left my home, and bending
215 my steps towards the near Alpine valleys, sought in the magnificence, the eternity of such scenes, to forget myself and my ephemeral, because human, sorrows. My wanderings were directed towards the valley of
220 Chamounix. I had visited it frequently during my boyhood. Six years had passed since then: I was a wreck, but nought had changed in those savage and enduring scenes.

I performed the first part of my journey
225 on horseback. I afterwards hired a mule, as the more sure-footed and least liable to receive injury on these rugged roads. The weather was fine; it was about the middle of the month of August, nearly two months
230 after the death of Justine, that miserable epoch from which I dated all my woe. The weight upon my spirit was sensibly lightened as I plunged yet deeper in the ravine of Arve. The immense mountains and precipices that
235 overhung me on every side, the sound of the river raging among the rocks, and the dashing of the waterfalls around spoke of a power mighty as Omnipotence—and I ceased to fear or to bend before any being less
240 almighty than that which had created and ruled the elements, here displayed in their most terrific guise. Still, as I ascended higher, the valley assumed a more magnificent and astonishing character. Ruined castles hang-
245 ing on the precipices of piny mountains, the impetuous Arve, and cottages every here and there peeping forth from among the trees formed a scene of singular beauty. But it was augmented and rendered sublime by the
250 mighty Alps, whose white and shining pyramids and domes towered above all, as

belonging to another earth, the habitations of another race of beings.

255 I passed the bridge of Pélissier, where the ravine, which the river forms, opened before me, and I began to ascend the mountain that overhangs it. Soon after, I entered the valley of Chamounix. This valley is more wonderful and sublime, but not so beautiful and pictur-
260 esque as that of Servox, through which I had just passed. The high and snowy mountains were its immediate boundaries, but I saw no more ruined castles and fertile fields. Immense glaciers approached the road; I heard the
265 rumbling thunder of the falling avalanche and marked the smoke of its passage. Mont Blanc, the supreme and magnificent Mont Blanc, raised itself from the surrounding aiguilles, and its tremendous dôme overlooked the
270 valley.

A tingling long-lost sense of pleasure often came across me during this journey. Some turn in the road, some new object suddenly perceived and recognised, reminded
275 me of days gone by, and were associated with the lighthearted gaiety of boyhood. The very winds whispered in soothing accents, and maternal Nature bade me weep no more. Then again the kindly influence ceased to
280 act—I found myself fettered again to grief and indulging in all the misery of reflection. Then I spurred on my animal, striving so to forget the world, my fears, and more than all, myself—or, in a more desperate fashion, I
285 alighted and threw myself on the grass, weighed down by horror and despair.

At length I arrived at the village of Chamounix. Exhaustion succeeded to the extreme fatigue both of body and of mind
290 which I had endured. For a short space of time I remained at the window watching the pallid lightnings that played above Mont Blanc and listening to the rushing

295 of the Arve, which pursued its noisy way beneath. The same lulling sounds acted as a lullaby to my too keen sensations; when I placed my head upon my pillow, sleep crept over me; I felt it as it came and blessed the giver of oblivion.

Chapter 10

300 I spent the following day roaming through the valley. I stood beside the sources of the Arveiron, which take their rise in a glacier, that with slow pace is advancing down from the summit of the hills to barricade the valley.
305 The abrupt sides of vast mountains were before me; the icy wall of the glacier overhung me; a few shattered pines were scattered around; and the solemn silence of this glorious presence-chamber of imperial Nature was
310 broken only by the brawling waves or the fall of some vast fragment, the thunder sound of the avalanche or the cracking, reverberated along the mountains, of the accumulated ice, which, through the silent working of
315 immutable laws, was ever and anon rent and torn, as if it had been but a plaything in their hands. These sublime and magnificent scenes afforded me the greatest consolation that I was capable of receiving. They elevated me
320 from all littleness of feeling, and although they did not remove my grief, they subdued and tranquillised it. In some degree, also, they diverted my mind from the thoughts over which it had brooded for the last month. I
325 retired to rest at night; my slumbers, as it were, waited on and ministered to by the assemblance of grand shapes which I had contemplated during the day. They congregated round me; the unstained snowy mountain-top,
330 the glittering pinnacle, the pine woods, and ragged bare ravine, the eagle, soaring amidst the clouds—they all gathered round me and bade me be at peace.

Where had they fled when the next morning I awoke? All of soul-inspiriting fled with sleep, and dark melancholy clouded every thought. The rain was pouring in torrents, and thick mists hid the summits of the mountains, so that I even saw not the faces of those mighty friends. Still I would penetrate their misty veil and seek them in their cloudy retreats. What were rain and storm to me? My mule was brought to the door, and I resolved to ascend to the summit of Montanvert. I remembered the effect that the view of the tremendous and ever-moving glacier had produced upon my mind when I first saw it. It had then filled me with a sublime ecstasy that gave wings to the soul and allowed it to soar from the obscure world to light and joy. The sight of the awful and majestic in nature had indeed always the effect of solemnising my mind and causing me to forget the passing cares of life. I determined to go without a guide, for I was well acquainted with the path, and the presence of another would destroy the solitary grandeur of the scene.

The ascent is precipitous, but the path is cut into continual and short windings, which enable you to surmount the perpendicularity of the mountain. It is a scene terrifically desolate. In a thousand spots the traces of the winter avalanche may be perceived, where trees lie broken and strewed on the ground, some entirely destroyed, others bent, leaning upon the jutting rocks of the mountain or transversely upon other trees. The path, as you ascend higher, is intersected by ravines of snow, down which stones continually roll from above; one of them is particularly dangerous, as the slightest sound, such as even speaking in a loud voice, produces a concussion of air sufficient to draw destruction upon the head of the speaker. The pines are not tall or luxuriant, but they are sombre and add an air of severity to the scene. I looked on the valley beneath; vast mists were rising from the rivers which ran through it and curling in thick wreaths around the opposite mountains, whose summits were hid in the uniform clouds, while rain poured from the dark sky and added to the melancholy impression I received from the objects around me. Alas! Why does man boast of sensibilities superior to those apparent in the brute; it only renders them more necessary beings. If our impulses were confined to hunger, thirst, and desire, we might be nearly free; but now we are moved by every wind that blows and a chance word or scene that that word may convey to us.

> We rest; a dream has power to poison sleep.
> We rise; one wand'ring thought pollutes
>   the day.
> We feel, conceive, or reason; laugh or weep,
> Embrace fond woe, or cast our cares away;
> It is the same: for, be it joy or sorrow,
> The path of its departure still is free.
> Man's yesterday may ne'er be like his
>   morrow;
> Nought may endure but mutability!

It was nearly noon when I arrived at the top of the ascent. For some time I sat upon the rock that overlooks the sea of ice. A mist covered both that and the surrounding mountains. Presently a breeze dissipated the cloud, and I descended upon the glacier. The surface is very uneven, rising like the waves of a troubled sea, descending low, and interspersed by rifts that sink deep. The field of ice is almost a league in width, but I spent nearly two hours in crossing it. The opposite mountain is a bare perpendicular rock. From the side where I now stood Montanvert was exactly opposite, at the distance of a league; and above it rose Mont Blanc, in awful majesty.

I remained in a recess of the rock, gazing on this wonderful and stupendous scene. The sea, or rather the vast river of ice, wound among its dependent mountains, whose
420 aerial summits hung over its recesses. Their icy and glittering peaks shone in the sunlight over the clouds. My heart, which was before sorrowful, now swelled with something like joy; I exclaimed, "Wandering spir-
425 its, if indeed ye wander, and do not rest in your narrow beds, allow me this faint happiness, or take me, as your companion, away from the joys of life."

As I said this I suddenly beheld the figure
430 of a man, at some distance, advancing towards me with superhuman speed. He bounded over the crevices in the ice, among which I had walked with caution; his stature, also, as he approached, seemed to exceed
435 that of man. I was troubled; a mist came over my eyes, and I felt a faintness seize me, but I was quickly restored by the cold gale of the mountains. I perceived, as the shape came nearer (sight tremendous and abhorred!) that
440 it was the wretch whom I had created. I trembled with rage and horror, resolving to wait his approach and then close with him in mortal combat. He approached; his countenance bespoke bitter anguish, combined
445 with disdain and malignity, while its unearthly ugliness rendered it almost too horrible for human eyes. But I scarcely observed this; rage and hatred had at first deprived me of utterance, and I recovered only to overwhelm
450 him with words expressive of furious detestation and contempt.

"Devil," I exclaimed, "do you dare approach me? And do not you fear the fierce vengeance of my arm wreaked on your mis-
455 erable head? Begone, vile insect! Or rather, stay, that I may trample you to dust! And, oh! That I could, with the extinction of your

miserable existence, restore those victims whom you have so diabolically murdered!"
460   "I expected this reception," said the dæmon. "All men hate the wretched; how, then, must I be hated, who am miserable beyond all living things! Yet you, my creator, detest and spurn me, thy creature, to whom
465 thou art bound by ties only dissoluble by the annihilation of one of us. You purpose to kill me. How dare you sport thus with life? Do your duty towards me, and I will do mine towards you and the rest of mankind. If you
470 will comply with my conditions, I will leave them and you at peace; but if you refuse, I will glut the maw of death, until it be satiated with the blood of your remaining friends."
475   "Abhorred monster! Fiend that thou art! The tortures of hell are too mild a vengeance for thy crimes. Wretched devil! You reproach me with your creation, come on, then, that I may extinguish the spark which I so negli-
480 gently bestowed."

My rage was without bounds; I sprang on him, impelled by all the feelings which can arm one being against the existence of another.
485   He easily eluded me and said,

"Be calm! I entreat you to hear me before you give vent to your hatred on my devoted head. Have I not suffered enough, that you seek to increase my misery? Life, although it
490 may only be an accumulation of anguish, is dear to me, and I will defend it. Remember, thou hast made me more powerful than thyself; my height is superior to thine, my joints more supple. But I will not be tempted to set
495 myself in opposition to thee. I am thy creature, and I will be even mild and docile to my natural lord and king if thou wilt also perform thy part, the which thou owest me. Oh, Frankenstein, be not equitable to every other

500 and trample upon me alone, to whom thy justice, and even thy clemency and affection, is most due. Remember that I am thy creature; I ought to be thy Adam, but I am rather the fallen angel, whom thou drivest from joy
505 for no misdeed. Everywhere I see bliss, from which I alone am irrevocably excluded. I was benevolent and good; misery made me a fiend. Make me happy, and I shall again be virtuous."

510   "Begone! I will not hear you. There can be no community between you and me; we are enemies. Begone, or let us try our strength in a fight, in which one must fall."

   "How can I move thee? Will no entreaties
515 cause thee to turn a favourable eye upon thy creature, who implores thy goodness and compassion? Believe me, Frankenstein, I was benevolent; my soul glowed with love and humanity; but am I not alone, miserably
520 alone? You, my creator, abhor me; what hope can I gather from your fellow creatures, who owe me nothing? They spurn and hate me. The desert mountains and dreary glaciers are my refuge. I have wandered here many
525 days; the caves of ice, which I only do not fear, are a dwelling to me, and the only one which man does not grudge. These bleak skies I hail, for they are kinder to me than your fellow beings. If the multitude of man-
530 kind knew of my existence, they would do as you do, and arm themselves for my destruction. Shall I not then hate them who abhor me? I will keep no terms with my enemies. I am miserable, and they shall share my
535 wretchedness. Yet it is in your power to recompense me, and deliver them from an evil which it only remains for you to make so great, that not only you and your family, but thousands of others, shall be swallowed up
540 in the whirlwinds of its rage. Let your compassion be moved, and do not disdain me.

Listen to my tale; when you have heard that, abandon or commiserate me, as you shall judge that I deserve. But hear me.
545 The guilty are allowed, by human laws, bloody as they are, to speak in their own defence before they are condemned. Listen to me, Frankenstein. You accuse me of murder, and yet you would, with a satisfied con-
550 science, destroy your own creature. Oh, praise the eternal justice of man! Yet I ask you not to spare me; listen to me, and then, if you can, and if you will, destroy the work of your hands."

555   "Why do you call to my remembrance," I rejoined, "circumstances of which I shudder to reflect, that I have been the miserable origin and author? Cursed be the day, abhorred devil, in which you first saw light! Cursed
560 (although I curse myself) be the hands that formed you! You have made me wretched beyond expression. You have left me no power to consider whether I am just to you or not. Begone! Relieve me from the sight of
565 your detested form."

   "Thus I relieve thee, my creator," he said, and placed his hated hands before my eyes, which I flung from me with violence; "thus I take from thee a sight which you abhor. Still
570 thou canst listen to me and grant me thy compassion. By the virtues that I once possessed, I demand this from you. Hear my tale; it is long and strange, and the temperature of this place is not fitting to your fine sensa-
575 tions; come to the hut upon the mountain. The sun is yet high in the heavens; before it descends to hide itself behind your snowy precipices and illuminate another world, you will have heard my story and can decide. On
580 you it rests, whether I quit for ever the neighbourhood of man and lead a harmless life, or become the scourge of your fellow creatures and the author of your own speedy ruin."

585 As he said this he led the way across
the ice; I followed. My heart was full, and
I did not answer him, but as I proceeded, I
weighed the various arguments that he had
used and determined at least to listen to his
tale. I was partly urged by curiosity, and com-
590 passion confirmed my resolution. I had hitherto supposed him to be the murderer of my
brother, and I eagerly sought a confirmation
or denial of this opinion. For the first time,
also, I felt what the duties of a creator towards
595 his creature were, and that I ought to render
him happy before I complained of his wickedness. These motives urged me to comply
with his demand. We crossed the ice, therefore, and ascended the opposite rock. The air
600 was cold, and the rain again began to descend;
we entered the hut, the fiend with an air of
exultation, I with a heavy heart and depressed
spirits. But I consented to listen, and seating
myself by the fire which my odious compan-
605 ion had lighted, he thus began his tale.

Chapter 11

"It is with considerable difficulty that I
remember the original era of my being; all
the events of that period appear confused
and indistinct. A strange multiplicity of sen-
610 sations seized me, and I saw, felt, heard, and
smelt at the same time; and it was, indeed,
a long time before I learned to distinguish
between the operations of my various
senses. By degrees, I remember, a stronger
615 light pressed upon my nerves, so that I was
obliged to shut my eyes. Darkness then came
over me and troubled me, but hardly had I
felt this when, by opening my eyes, as I now
suppose, the light poured in upon me again.
620 I walked and, I believe, descended, but I
presently found a great alteration in my sensations. Before, dark and opaque bodies had
surrounded me, impervious to my touch or

sight; but I now found that I could wander on
625 at liberty, with no obstacles which I could not
either surmount or avoid. The light became
more and more oppressive to me, and the
heat wearying me as I walked, I sought a
place where I could receive shade. This was
630 the forest near Ingolstadt; and here I lay by
the side of a brook resting from my fatigue,
until I felt tormented by hunger and thirst.
This roused me from my nearly dormant
state, and I ate some berries which I found
635 hanging on the trees or lying on the ground.
I slaked my thirst at the brook, and then
lying down, was overcome by sleep.

"It was dark when I awoke; I felt cold also,
and half frightened, as it were, instinctively,
640 finding myself so desolate. Before I had quitted your apartment, on a sensation of cold, I
had covered myself with some clothes, but
these were insufficient to secure me from
the dews of night. I was a poor, helpless, mis-
645 erable wretch; I knew, and could distinguish,
nothing; but feeling pain invade me on all
sides, I sat down and wept.

"Soon a gentle light stole over the heavens
and gave me a sensation of pleasure. I
650 started up and beheld a radiant form rise
from among the trees. [The moon] I gazed
with a kind of wonder. It moved slowly, but it
enlightened my path, and I again went out in
search of berries. I was still cold when under
655 one of the trees I found a huge cloak, with
which I covered myself, and sat down upon
the ground. No distinct ideas occupied my
mind; all was confused. I felt light, and hunger, and thirst, and darkness; innumerable
660 sounds rang in my ears, and on all sides various scents saluted me; the only object that I
could distinguish was the bright moon, and I
fixed my eyes on that with pleasure.

"Several changes of day and night passed,
665 and the orb of night had greatly lessened,

when I began to distinguish my sensations from each other. I gradually saw plainly the clear stream that supplied me with drink and the trees that shaded me with their foli-
670 age. I was delighted when I first discovered that a pleasant sound, which often saluted my ears, proceeded from the throats of the little winged animals who had often inter-cepted the light from my eyes. I began also to
675 observe, with greater accuracy, the forms that surrounded me and to perceive the boundaries of the radiant roof of light which canopied me. Sometimes I tried to imitate the pleasant songs of the birds but was
680 unable. Sometimes I wished to express my sensations in my own mode, but the uncouth and inarticulate sounds which broke from me frightened me into silence again.

"The moon had disappeared from the night,
685 and again, with a lessened form, showed itself, while I still remained in the forest. My sensa-tions had by this time become distinct, and my mind received every day additional ideas. My eyes became accustomed to the light and to
690 perceive objects in their right forms; I distin-guished the insect from the herb, and by degrees, one herb from another. I found that the sparrow uttered none but harsh notes, whilst those of the blackbird and thrush were
695 sweet and enticing.

"One day, when I was oppressed by cold, I found a fire which had been left by some wandering beggars, and was overcome with delight at the warmth I experienced from it.
700 In my joy I thrust my hand into the live embers, but quickly drew it out again with a cry of pain. How strange, I thought, that the same cause should produce such opposite effects! I examined the materials of the fire,
705 and to my joy found it to be composed of wood. I quickly collected some branches, but they were wet and would not burn. I was

pained at this and sat still watching the operation of the fire. The wet wood which I
710 had placed near the heat dried and itself became inflamed. I reflected on this, and by touching the various branches, I discovered the cause and busied myself in collecting a great quantity of wood, that I might dry it
715 and have a plentiful supply of fire. When night came on and brought sleep with it, I was in the greatest fear lest my fire should be extinguished. I covered it carefully with dry wood and leaves and placed wet branches
720 upon it; and then, spreading my cloak, I lay on the ground and sank into sleep.

"It was morning when I awoke, and my first care was to visit the fire. I uncovered it, and a gentle breeze quickly fanned it into a
725 flame. I observed this also and contrived a fan of branches, which roused the embers when they were nearly extinguished. When night came again I found, with pleasure, that the fire gave light as well as heat and that
730 the discovery of this element was useful to me in my food, for I found some of the offals that the travellers had left had been roasted, and tasted much more savoury than the ber-ries I gathered from the trees. I tried, there-
735 fore, to dress my food in the same manner, placing it on the live embers. I found that the berries were spoiled by this operation, and the nuts and roots much improved.

"Food, however, became scarce, and I often
740 spent the whole day searching in vain for a few acorns to assuage the pangs of hunger. When I found this, I resolved to quit the place that I had hitherto inhabited, to seek for one where the few wants I experienced
745 would be more easily satisfied. In this emi-gration I exceedingly lamented the loss of the fire which I had obtained through accident and knew not how to reproduce it. I gave sev-eral hours to the serious consideration of this

750 difficulty, but I was obliged to relinquish all
attempt to supply it, and wrapping myself up
in my cloak, I struck across the wood towards
the setting sun. I passed three days in these
rambles and at length discovered the open
755 country. A great fall of snow had taken
place the night before, and the fields were
of one uniform white; the appearance was
disconsolate, and I found my feet chilled
by the cold damp substance that covered
760 the ground.

"It was about seven in the morning, and I
longed to obtain food and shelter; at length I
perceived a small hut, on a rising ground,
which had doubtless been built for the con-
765 venience of some shepherd. This was a new
sight to me, and I examined the structure
with great curiosity. Finding the door open, I
entered. An old man sat in it, near a fire, over
which he was preparing his breakfast. He
770 turned on hearing a noise, and perceiving
me, shrieked loudly, and quitting the hut, ran
across the fields with a speed of which his
debilitated form hardly appeared capable.
His appearance, different from any I had ever
775 before seen, and his flight somewhat surprised me. But I was enchanted by the
appearance of the hut; here the snow and
rain could not penetrate; the ground was dry;
and it presented to me then as exquisite and
780 divine a retreat as Pandæmonium appeared
to the dæmons of hell after their sufferings
in the lake of fire. I greedily devoured the
remnants of the shepherd's breakfast, which
consisted of bread, cheese, milk, and wine;
785 the latter, however, I did not like. Then, overcome by fatigue, I lay down among some
straw and fell asleep.

"It was noon when I awoke, and allured by
the warmth of the sun, which shone brightly
790 on the white ground, I determined to recommence my travels; and, depositing the

remains of the peasant's breakfast in a wal-
let I found, I proceeded across the fields for
several hours, until at sunset I arrived at a
795 village. How miraculous did this appear! The
huts, the neater cottages, and stately houses
engaged my admiration by turns. The vegetables in the gardens, the milk and cheese that
I saw placed at the windows of some of the
800 cottages, allured my appetite. One of the best
of these I entered, but I had hardly placed my
foot within the door before the children
shrieked, and one of the women fainted. The
whole village was roused; some fled, some
805 attacked me, until, grievously bruised by
stones and many other kinds of missile
weapons, I escaped to the open country and
fearfully took refuge in a low hovel, quite
bare, and making a wretched appearance
810 after the palaces I had beheld in the village.
This hovel however, joined a cottage of a
neat and pleasant appearance, but after my
late dearly bought experience, I dared not
enter it. My place of refuge was constructed
815 of wood, but so low that I could with difficulty sit upright in it. No wood, however, was
placed on the earth, which formed the floor,
but it was dry; and although the wind
entered it by innumerable chinks, I found it
820 an agreeable asylum from the snow and rain.

"Here, then, I retreated and lay down
happy to have found a shelter, however miserable, from the inclemency of the season,
and still more from the barbarity of man. As
825 soon as morning dawned I crept from my
kennel, that I might view the adjacent cottage
and discover if I could remain in the habitation I had found. It was situated against the
back of the cottage and surrounded on the
830 sides which were exposed by a pig sty and a
clear pool of water. One part was open, and
by that I had crept in; but now I covered
every crevice by which I might be perceived

835 with stones and wood, yet in such a manner that I might move them on occasion to pass out; all the light I enjoyed came through the sty, and that was sufficient for me.

"Having thus arranged my dwelling and carpeted it with clean straw, I retired, for I 840 saw the figure of a man at a distance, and I remembered too well my treatment the night before to trust myself in his power. I had first, however, provided for my suste- nance for that day by a loaf of coarse bread, 845 which I purloined, and a cup with which I could drink more conveniently than from my hand of the pure water which flowed by my retreat. The floor was a little raised, so that it was kept perfectly dry, and by its 850 vicinity to the chimney of the cottage it was tolerably warm.

"Being thus provided, I resolved to reside in this hovel until something should occur which might alter my determination. It was 855 indeed a paradise compared to the bleak for- est, my former residence, the rain-dropping branches, and dank earth. I ate my breakfast with pleasure and was about to remove a plank to procure myself a little water when I 860 heard a step, and looking through a small chink, I beheld a young creature, with a pail on her head, passing before my hovel. The girl was young and of gentle demeanour, unlike what I have since found cottagers and 865 farmhouse servants to be. Yet she was meanly dressed, a coarse blue petticoat and a linen jacket being her only garb; her fair hair was plaited but not adorned: she looked patient yet sad. I lost sight of her, and in 870 about a quarter of an hour she returned bearing the pail, which was now partly filled with milk. As she walked along, seemingly incommoded by the burden, a young man met her, whose countenance expressed a 875 deeper despondence. Uttering a few sounds

with an air of melancholy, he took the pail from her head and bore it to the cottage him- self. She followed, and they disappeared. Presently I saw the young man again, with 880 some tools in his hand, cross the field behind the cottage; and the girl was also busied, sometimes in the house and sometimes in the yard.

"On examining my dwelling, I found that 885 one of the windows of the cottage had for- merly occupied a part of it, but the panes had been filled up with wood. In one of these was a small and almost imperceptible chink through which the eye could just penetrate. 890 Through this crevice a small room was visi- ble, whitewashed and clean but very bare of furniture. In one corner, near a small fire, sat an old man, leaning his head on his hands in a disconsolate attitude. The young girl was 895 occupied in arranging the cottage; but pres- ently she took something out of a drawer, which employed her hands, and she sat down beside the old man, who, taking up an instrument, began to play and to produce 900 sounds sweeter than the voice of the thrush or the nightingale. It was a lovely sight, even to me, poor wretch who had never beheld aught beautiful before. The silver hair and benevolent countenance of the aged cottager 905 won my reverence, while the gentle manners of the girl enticed my love. He played a sweet mournful air which I perceived drew tears from the eyes of his amiable companion, of which the old man took no notice, until she 910 sobbed audibly; he then pronounced a few sounds, and the fair creature, leaving her work, knelt at his feet. He raised her and smiled with such kindness and affection that I felt sensations of a peculiar and overpower- 915 ing nature; they were a mixture of pain and pleasure, such as I had never before experi- enced, either from hunger or cold, warmth or food; and I withdrew from the window, unable to bear these emotions.

920   "Soon after this the young man returned, bearing on his shoulders a load of wood. The girl met him at the door, helped to relieve him of his burden, and taking some of the fuel into the cottage, placed it on the fire; then she
925 and the youth went apart into a nook of the cottage, and he showed her a large loaf and a piece of cheese. She seemed pleased and went into the garden for some roots and plants, which she placed in water, and then
930 upon the fire. She afterwards continued her work, whilst the young man went into the garden and appeared busily employed in digging and pulling up roots. After he had been employed thus about an hour, the young
935 woman joined him and they entered the cottage together.

"The old man had, in the meantime, been pensive, but on the appearance of his companions he assumed a more cheerful air,
940 and they sat down to eat. The meal was quickly dispatched. The young woman was again occupied in arranging the cottage, the old man walked before the cottage in the sun for a few minutes, leaning on the arm
945 of the youth. Nothing could exceed in beauty the contrast between these two excellent creatures. One was old, with silver hairs and a countenance beaming with benevolence and love; the younger was
950 slight and graceful in his figure, and his features were moulded with the finest symmetry, yet his eyes and attitude expressed the utmost sadness and despondency. The old man returned to the cottage, and the youth,
955 with tools different from those he had used in the morning, directed his steps across the fields.

"Night quickly shut in, but to my extreme wonder, I found that the cottagers had a

960 means of prolonging light by the use of tapers, and was delighted to find that the setting of the sun did not put an end to the pleasure I experienced in watching my human neighbours. In the evening the young
965 girl and her companion were employed in various occupations which I did not understand; and the old man again took up the instrument which produced the divine sounds that had enchanted me in the morn-
970 ing. So soon as he had finished, the youth began, not to play, but to utter sounds that were monotonous, and neither resembling the harmony of the old man's instrument nor the songs of the birds; I since found that
975 he read aloud, but at that time I knew nothing of the science of words or letters.

"The family, after having been thus occupied for a short time, extinguished their lights and retired, as I conjectured, to rest."

Chapter 12

980 "I lay on my straw, but I could not sleep. I thought of the occurrences of the day. What chiefly struck me was the gentle manners of these people, and I longed to join them, but dared not. I remembered too well the treat-
985 ment I had suffered the night before from the barbarous villagers, and resolved, whatever course of conduct I might hereafter think it right to pursue, that for the present I would remain quietly in my hovel, watching
990 and endeavouring to discover the motives which influenced their actions.

"The cottagers arose the next morning before the sun. The young woman arranged the cottage and prepared the food, and the
995 youth departed after the first meal.

"This day was passed in the same routine as that which preceded it. The young man was constantly employed out of doors, and the girl in various laborious occupations

1000 within. The old man, whom I soon perceived to be blind, employed his leisure hours on his instrument or in contemplation. Nothing could exceed the love and respect which the younger cottagers exhibited towards their

1005 venerable companion. They performed towards him every little office of affection and duty with gentleness, and he rewarded them by his benevolent smiles.

"They were not entirely happy. The young

1010 man and his companion often went apart and appeared to weep. I saw no cause for their unhappiness, but I was deeply affected by it. If such lovely creatures were misera- ble, it was less strange that I, an imperfect

1015 and solitary being, should be wretched. Yet why were these gentle beings unhappy? They possessed a delightful house (for such it was in my eyes) and every luxury; they had a fire to warm them when chill and

1020 delicious viands when hungry; they were dressed in excellent clothes; and, still more, they enjoyed one another's company and speech, interchanging each day looks of affection and kindness. What did their tears

1025 imply? Did they really express pain? I was at first unable to solve these questions, but perpetual attention and time explained to me many appearances which were at first enigmatic.

1030 "A considerable period elapsed before I discovered one of the causes of the uneasi- ness of this amiable family: it was poverty, and they suffered that evil in a very distress- ing degree. Their nourishment consisted

1035 entirely of the vegetables of their garden and the milk of one cow, which gave very little during the winter, when its masters could scarcely procure food to support it. They often, I believe, suffered the pangs of hunger

1040 very poignantly, especially the two younger cottagers, for several times they placed food

before the old man when they reserved none for themselves.

"This trait of kindness moved me sensibly.

1045 I had been accustomed, during the night, to steal a part of their store for my own con- sumption, but when I found that in doing this I inflicted pain on the cottagers, I abstained and satisfied myself with berries,

1050 nuts, and roots which I gathered from a neighbouring wood.

"I discovered also another means through which I was enabled to assist their labours. I found that the youth spent a great part of

1055 each day in collecting wood for the family fire, and during the night I often took his tools, the use of which I quickly discovered, and brought home firing sufficient for the consumption of several days.

1060 "I remember, the first time that I did this, the young woman, when she opened the door in the morning, appeared greatly aston- ished on seeing a great pile of wood on the outside. She uttered some words in a loud

1065 voice, and the youth joined her, who also expressed surprise. I observed, with pleasure, that he did not go to the forest that day, but spent it in repairing the cottage and cultivat- ing the garden.

1070 "By degrees I made a discovery of still greater moment. I found that these people possessed a method of communicating their experience and feelings to one another by articulate sounds. I perceived that the words

1075 they spoke sometimes produced pleasure or pain, smiles or sadness, in the minds and countenances of the hearers. This was indeed a godlike science, and I ardently desired to become acquainted with it. But I

1080 was baffled in every attempt I made for this purpose. Their pronunciation was quick, and the words they uttered, not having any apparent connection with visible objects, I

1085 was unable to discover any clue by which I could unravel the mystery of their reference. By great application, however, and after having remained during the space of several revolutions of the moon in my hovel, I discovered the names that were given to
1090 some of the most familiar objects of discourse; I learned and applied the words, *fire*, *milk*, *bread*, and *wood*. I learned also the names of the cottagers themselves. The youth and his companion had each of them
1095 several names, but the old man had only one, which was *father*. The girl was called *sister* or *Agatha*, and the youth *Felix*, *brother*, or *son*. I cannot describe the delight I felt when I learned the ideas appropriated to each of
1100 these sounds and was able to pronounce them. I distinguished several other words without being able as yet to understand or apply them, such as *good*, *dearest*, *unhappy*.

"I spent the winter in this manner. The
1105 gentle manners and beauty of the cottagers greatly endeared them to me; when they were unhappy, I felt depressed; when they rejoiced, I sympathised in their joys. I saw few human beings besides them, and if any other
1110 happened to enter the cottage, their harsh manners and rude gait only enhanced to me the superior accomplishments of my friends. The old man, I could perceive, often endeavoured to encourage his children, as some-
1115 times I found that he called them, to cast off their melancholy. He would talk in a cheerful accent, with an expression of goodness that bestowed pleasure even upon me. Agatha listened with respect, her eyes sometimes filled
1120 with tears, which she endeavoured to wipe away unperceived; but I generally found that her countenance and tone were more cheerful after having listened to the exhortations of her father. It was not thus with Felix. He
1125 was always the saddest of the group, and

even to my unpractised senses, he appeared to have suffered more deeply than his friends. But if his countenance was more sorrowful, his voice was more cheerful than that of
1130 his sister, especially when he addressed the old man.

"I could mention innumerable instances which, although slight, marked the dispositions of these amiable cottagers. In the midst
1135 of poverty and want, Felix carried with pleasure to his sister the first little white flower that peeped out from beneath the snowy ground. Early in the morning, before she had risen, he cleared away the snow that
1140 obstructed her path to the milk-house, drew water from the well, and brought the wood from the outhouse, where, to his perpetual astonishment, he found his store always replenished by an invisible hand. In the day, I
1145 believe, he worked sometimes for a neighbouring farmer, because he often went forth and did not return until dinner, yet brought no wood with him. At other times he worked in the garden, but as there was little to do in
1150 the frosty season, he read to the old man and Agatha.

"This reading had puzzled me extremely at first, but by degrees I discovered that he uttered many of the same sounds when he
1155 read as when he talked. I conjectured, therefore, that he found on the paper signs for speech which he understood, and I ardently longed to comprehend these also; but how was that possible when I did not even under-
1160 stand the sounds for which they stood as signs? I improved, however, sensibly in this science, but not sufficiently to follow up any kind of conversation, although I applied my whole mind to the endeavour, for I easily
1165 perceived that, although I eagerly longed to discover myself to the cottagers, I ought not to make the attempt until I had first become

master of their language, which knowledge might enable me to make them overlook the deformity of my figure, for with this also the contrast perpetually presented to my eyes had made me acquainted.

"I had admired the perfect forms of my cottagers—their grace, beauty, and delicate complexions; but how was I terrified when I viewed myself in a transparent pool! At first I started back, unable to believe that it was indeed I who was reflected in the mirror; and when I became fully convinced that I was in reality the monster that I am, I was filled with the bitterest sensations of despondence and mortification. Alas! I did not yet entirely know the fatal effects of this miserable deformity.

"As the sun became warmer and the light of day longer, the snow vanished, and I beheld the bare trees and the black earth. From this time Felix was more employed, and the heart-moving indications of impending famine disappeared. Their food, as I afterwards found, was coarse, but it was wholesome; and they procured a sufficiency of it. Several new kinds of plants sprang up in the garden, which they dressed; and these signs of comfort increased daily as the season advanced.

"The old man, leaning on his son, walked each day at noon, when it did not rain, as I found it was called when the heavens poured forth its waters. This frequently took place, but a high wind quickly dried the earth, and the season became far more pleasant than it had been.

"My mode of life in my hovel was uniform. During the morning I attended the motions of the cottagers, and when they were dispersed in various occupations, I slept; the remainder of the day was spent in observing my friends. When they had retired to rest, if there was any moon or the night was star-light, I went into the woods and collected my own food and fuel for the cottage. When I returned, as often as it was necessary, I cleared their path from the snow and performed those offices that I had seen done by Felix. I afterwards found that these labours, performed by an invisible hand, greatly astonished them; and once or twice I heard them, on these occasions, utter the words good spirit, wonderful; but I did not then understand the signification of these terms.

"My thoughts now became more active, and I longed to discover the motives and feelings of these lovely creatures; I was inquisitive to know why Felix appeared so miserable and Agatha so sad. I thought (foolish wretch!) that it might be in my power to restore happiness to these deserving people. When I slept or was absent, the forms of the venerable blind father, the gentle Agatha, and the excellent Felix flitted before me. I looked upon them as superior beings who would be the arbiters of my future destiny. I formed in my imagination a thousand pictures of presenting myself to them, and their reception of me. I imagined that they would be disgusted, until, by my gentle demeanour and conciliating words, I should first win their favour and afterwards their love.

"These thoughts exhilarated me and led me to apply with fresh ardour to the acquiring the art of language. My organs were indeed harsh, but supple; and although my voice was very unlike the soft music of their tones, yet I pronounced such words as I understood with tolerable ease. It was as the ass and the lap-dog; yet surely the gentle ass whose intentions were affectionate, although his manners were rude, deserved better treatment than blows and execration.

"The pleasant showers and genial warmth of spring greatly altered the aspect of the earth. Men who before this change seemed 1255 to have been hid in caves dispersed themselves and were employed in various arts of cultivation. The birds sang in more cheerful notes, and the leaves began to bud forth on the trees. Happy, happy earth! Fit habitation 1260 for gods, which, so short a time before, was bleak, damp, and unwholesome. My spirits were elevated by the enchanting appearance of nature; the past was blotted from my memory, the present was tranquil, and the 1265 future gilded by bright rays of hope and anticipations of joy."

Chapter 13

"I now hasten to the more moving part of my story. I shall relate events that impressed me with feelings which, from what I had been, 1270 have made me what I am.

"Spring advanced rapidly; the weather became fine and the skies cloudless. It surprised me that what before was desert and gloomy should now bloom with the most 1275 beautiful flowers and verdure. My senses were gratified and refreshed by a thousand scents of delight and a thousand sights of beauty.

"It was on one of these days, when 1280 my cottagers periodically rested from labour—the old man played on his guitar, and the children listened to him—that I observed the countenance of Felix was melancholy beyond expression; he sighed 1285 frequently, and once his father paused in his music, and I conjectured by his manner that he inquired the cause of his son's sorrow. Felix replied in a cheerful accent, and the old man was recommencing 1290 his music when someone tapped at the door.

"It was a lady on horseback, accompanied by a country-man as a guide. The lady was dressed in a dark suit and covered with a 1295 thick black veil. Agatha asked a question, to which the stranger only replied by pronouncing, in a sweet accent, the name of Felix. Her voice was musical but unlike that of either of my friends. On hearing this word, Felix came 1300 up hastily to the lady, who, when she saw him, threw up her veil, and I beheld a countenance of angelic beauty and expression. Her hair of a shining raven black, and curiously braided; her eyes were dark, but gentle, 1305 although animated; her features of a regular proportion, and her complexion wondrously fair, each cheek tinged with a lovely pink.

"Felix seemed ravished with delight when he saw her, every trait of sorrow vanished 1310 from his face, and it instantly expressed a degree of ecstatic joy, of which I could hardly have believed it capable; his eyes sparkled, as his cheek flushed with pleasure; and at that moment I thought him as beautiful as the 1315 stranger. She appeared affected by different feelings; wiping a few tears from her lovely eyes, she held out her hand to Felix, who kissed it rapturously and called her, as well as I could distinguish, his sweet Arabian. She 1320 did not appear to understand him, but smiled. He assisted her to dismount, and dismissing her guide, conducted her into the cottage. Some conversation took place between him and his father, and the young 1325 stranger knelt at the old man's feet and would have kissed his hand, but he raised her and embraced her affectionately.

"I soon perceived that although the stranger uttered articulate sounds and 1330 appeared to have a language of her own, she was neither understood by nor herself understood the cottagers. They made many signs which I did not comprehend, but I saw that her presence diffused gladness through the cottage, dispelling their sorrow as the sun dissipates the morning mists. Felix seemed peculiarly happy and with smiles of delight welcomed his Arabian. Agatha, the ever-gentle Agatha, kissed the hands of the lovely stranger, and pointing to her brother, made signs which appeared to me to mean that he had been sorrowful until she came. Some hours passed thus, while they, by their countenances, expressed joy, the cause of which I did not comprehend. Presently I found, by the frequent recurrence of some sound which the stranger repeated after them, that she was endeavouring to learn their language; and the idea instantly occurred to me that I should make use of the same instructions to the same end. The stranger learned about twenty words at the first lesson; most of them, indeed, were those which I had before understood, but I profited by the others.

"As night came on, Agatha and the Arabian retired early. When they separated Felix kissed the hand of the stranger and said, 'Good night sweet Safie.' He sat up much longer, conversing with his father, and by the frequent repetition of her name I conjectured that their lovely guest was the subject of their conversation. I ardently desired to understand them, and bent every faculty towards that purpose, but found it utterly impossible.

"The next morning Felix went out to his work, and after the usual occupations of Agatha were finished, the Arabian sat at the feet of the old man, and taking his guitar, played some airs so entrancingly beautiful that they at once drew tears of sorrow and delight from my eyes. She sang, and her voice flowed in a rich cadence, swelling or dying away like a nightingale of the woods.

"When she had finished, she gave the guitar to Agatha, who at first declined it. She played a simple air, and her voice accompanied it in sweet accents, but unlike the wondrous strain of the stranger. The old man appeared enraptured and said some words which Agatha endeavoured to explain to Safie, and by which he appeared to wish to express that she bestowed on him the greatest delight by her music.

"The days now passed as peaceably as before, with the sole alteration that joy had taken place of sadness in the countenances of my friends. Safie was always gay and happy; she and I improved rapidly in the knowledge of language, so that in two months I began to comprehend most of the words uttered by my protectors.

"In the meanwhile also the black ground was covered with herbage, and the green banks interspersed with innumerable flowers, sweet to the scent and the eyes, stars of pale radiance among the moonlight woods; the sun became warmer, the nights clear and balmy; and my nocturnal rambles were an extreme pleasure to me, although they were considerably shortened by the late setting and early rising of the sun, for I never ventured abroad during daylight, fearful of meeting with the same treatment I had formerly endured in the first village which I entered.

"My days were spent in close attention, that I might more speedily master the language; and I may boast that I improved more rapidly than the Arabian, who understood very little and conversed in broken accents, whilst I comprehended and could imitate almost every word that was spoken.

"While I improved in speech, I also learned the science of letters as it was taught to the stranger, and this opened before me a wide field for wonder and delight.

"The book from which Felix instructed Safie was Volney's *Ruins of Empires*. I should not have understood the purport of this book had not Felix, in reading it, given very minute explanations. He had chosen this work, he said, because the declamatory style was framed in imitation of the Eastern authors.
1425 Through this work I obtained a cursory knowledge of history and a view of the several empires at present existing in the world; it gave me an insight into the manners, governments, and religions of the different nations
1430 of the earth. I heard of the slothful Asiatics, of the stupendous genius and mental activity of the Grecians, of the wars and wonderful virtue of the early Romans—of their subsequent degenerating—of the decline of that mighty
1435 empire, of chivalry, Christianity, and kings. I heard of the discovery of the American hemisphere and wept with Safie over the hapless fate of its original inhabitants.

"These wonderful narrations inspired me
1440 with strange feelings. Was man, indeed, at once so powerful, so virtuous and magnificent, yet so vicious and base? He appeared at one time a mere scion of the evil principle and at another as all that can be conceived
1445 of noble and godlike. To be a great and virtuous man appeared the highest honour that can befall a sensitive being; to be base and vicious, as many on record have been, appeared the lowest degradation, a condition
1450 more abject than that of the blind mole or harmless worm. For a long time I could not conceive how one man could go forth to murder his fellow, or even why there were laws and governments; but when I heard
1455 details of vice and bloodshed, my wonder ceased and I turned away with disgust and loathing.

"Every conversation of the cottagers now opened new wonders to me. While I listened

1460 to the instructions which Felix bestowed upon the Arabian, the strange system of human society was explained to me. I heard of the division of property, of immense wealth and squalid poverty, of rank, descent,
1465 and noble blood.

"The words induced me to turn towards myself. I learned that the possessions most esteemed by your fellow creatures were high and unsullied descent united with riches. A
1470 man might be respected with only one of these advantages, but without either he was considered, except in very rare instances, as a vagabond and a slave, doomed to waste his powers for the profits of the chosen few! And
1475 what was I? Of my creation and creator I was absolutely ignorant, but I knew that I possessed no money, no friends, no kind of property. I was, besides, endued with a figure hideously deformed and loathsome; I was
1480 not even of the same nature as man. I was more agile than they and could subsist upon coarser diet; I bore the extremes of heat and cold with less injury to my frame; my stature far exceeded theirs. When I looked around I
1485 saw and heard of none like me. Was I, then, a monster, a blot upon the earth, from which all men fled and whom all men disowned?

"I cannot describe to you the agony that these reflections inflicted upon me; I tried to
1490 dispel them, but sorrow only increased with knowledge. Oh, that I had for ever remained in my native wood, nor known nor felt beyond the sensations of hunger, thirst, and heat!

1495 "Of what a strange nature is knowledge! It clings to the mind when it has once seized on it like a lichen on the rock. I wished sometimes to shake off all thought and feeling, but I learned that there was but one means
1500 to overcome the sensation of pain, and that was death—a state which I feared yet did

not understand. I admired virtue and good feelings and loved the gentle manners and amiable qualities of my cottagers, but I was shut out from intercourse with them, except through means which I obtained by stealth, when I was unseen and unknown, and which rather increased than satisfied the desire I had of becoming one among my fellows. The gentle words of Agatha and the animated smiles of the charming Arabian were not for me. The mild exhortations of the old man and the lively conversation of the loved Felix were not for me. Miserable, unhappy wretch!

"Other lessons were impressed upon me even more deeply. I heard of the difference of sexes, and the birth and growth of children, how the father doted on the smiles of the infant, and the lively sallies of the older child, how all the life and cares of the mother were wrapped up in the precious charge, how the mind of youth expanded and gained knowledge, of brother, sister, and all the various relationships which bind one human being to another in mutual bonds.

"But where were my friends and relations? No father had watched my infant days, no mother had blessed me with smiles and caresses; or if they had, all my past life was now a blot, a blind vacancy in which I distinguished nothing. From my earliest remembrance I had been as I then was in height and proportion. I had never yet seen a being resembling me or who claimed any intercourse with me. What was I? The question again recurred, to be answered only with groans.

"I will soon explain to what these feelings tended, but allow me now to return to the cottagers, whose story excited in me such various feelings of indignation, delight, and wonder, but which all terminated in additional love and reverence for my protectors (for so I loved, in an innocent, half-painful self-deceit, to call them)."

Chapter 14

"Some time elapsed before I learned the history of my friends. It was one which could not fail to impress itself deeply on my mind, unfolding as it did a number of circumstances, each interesting and wonderful to one so utterly inexperienced as I was.

"The name of the old man was De Lacey. He was descended from a good family in France, where he had lived for many years in affluence, respected by his superiors and beloved by his equals. His son was bred in the service of his country, and Agatha had ranked with ladies of the highest distinction. A few months before my arrival they had lived in a large and luxurious city called Paris, surrounded by friends and possessed of every enjoyment which virtue, refinement of intellect, or taste, accompanied by a moderate fortune, could afford.

"The father of Safie had been the cause of their ruin. He was a Turkish merchant and had inhabited Paris for many years, when, for some reason which I could not learn, he became obnoxious to the government. He was seized and cast into prison the very day that Safie arrived from Constantinople to join him. He was tried and condemned to death. The injustice of his sentence was very flagrant; all Paris was indignant; and it was judged that his religion and wealth rather than the crime alleged against him had been the cause of his condemnation.

"Felix had accidentally been present at the trial; his horror and indignation were uncontrollable when he heard the decision of the court. He made, at that moment, a solemn vow to deliver him and then looked around for the means. After many fruitless

attempts to gain admittance to the prison,
1585 he found a strongly grated window in an
unguarded part of the building, which
lighted the dungeon of the unfortunate
Muhammadan, who, loaded with chains,
waited in despair the execution of the barba-
1590 rous sentence. Felix visited the grate at night
and made known to the prisoner his intentions in his favour. The Turk, amazed and
delighted, endeavoured to kindle the zeal of
his deliverer by promises of reward and
1595 wealth. Felix rejected his offers with contempt, yet when he saw the lovely Safie, who
was allowed to visit her father and who by
her gestures expressed her lively gratitude,
the youth could not help owning to his own
1600 mind that the captive possessed a treasure
which would fully reward his toil and hazard.

"The Turk quickly perceived the impression that his daughter had made on the
heart of Felix and endeavoured to secure him
1605 more entirely in his interests by the promise
of her hand in marriage so soon as he should
be conveyed to a place of safety. Felix was
too delicate to accept this offer, yet he looked
forward to the probability of the event as to
1610 the consummation of his happiness.

"During the ensuing days, while the preparations were going forward for the escape of
the merchant, the zeal of Felix was warmed
by several letters that he received from this
1615 lovely girl, who found means to express her
thoughts in the language of her lover by the
aid of an old man, a servant of her father who
understood French. She thanked him in the
most ardent terms for his intended services
1620 towards her parent, and at the same time she
gently deplored her own fate.

"I have copies of these letters, for I found
means, during my residence in the hovel, to
procure the implements of writing; and the
1625 letters were often in the hands of Felix or

Agatha. Before I depart I will give them to
you; they will prove the truth of my tale; but
at present, as the sun is already far declined,
I shall only have time to repeat the substance
1630 of them to you.

"Safie related that her mother was a
Christian Arab, seized and made a slave by
the Turks; recommended by her beauty, she
had won the heart of the father of Safie, who
1635 married her. The young girl spoke in high and
enthusiastic terms of her mother, who, born
in freedom, spurned the bondage to which
she was now reduced. She instructed her
daughter in the tenets of her religion and
1640 taught her to aspire to higher powers of intellect and an independence of spirit forbidden
to the female followers of Muhammad. This
lady died, but her lessons were indelibly
impressed on the mind of Safie, who sickened
1645 at the prospect of again returning to Asia and
being immured within the walls of a harem,
allowed only to occupy herself with infantile
amusements, ill-suited to the temper of her
soul, now accustomed to grand ideas and a
1650 noble emulation for virtue. The prospect of
marrying a Christian and remaining in a
country where women were allowed to take
a rank in society was enchanting to her.

"The day for the execution of the Turk
1655 was fixed, but on the night previous to it he
quitted his prison and before morning was
distant many leagues from Paris. Felix had
procured passports in the name of his father,
sister, and himself. He had previously
1660 communicated his plan to the former, who
aided the deceit by quitting his house,
under the pretence of a journey and concealed himself, with his daughter, in an
obscure part of Paris.

"Felix conducted the fugitives through
1665 France to Lyons and across Mont Cenis to
Leghorn, where the merchant had decided to

wait a favourable opportunity of passing into some part of the Turkish dominions.

1670 "Safie resolved to remain with her father until the moment of his departure, before which time the Turk renewed his promise that she should be united to his deliverer; and Felix remained with them in expectation 1675 of that event; and in the meantime he enjoyed the society of the Arabian, who exhibited towards him the simplest and tenderest affection. They conversed with one another through the means of an interpreter, 1680 and sometimes with the interpretation of looks; and Safie sang to him the divine airs of her native country.

"The Turk allowed this intimacy to take place and encouraged the hopes of the 1685 youthful lovers, while in his heart he had formed far other plans. He loathed the idea that his daughter should be united to a Christian, but he feared the resentment of Felix if he should appear lukewarm, for he 1690 knew that he was still in the power of his deliverer if he should choose to betray him to the Italian state which they inhabited. He revolved a thousand plans by which he should be enabled to prolong the deceit until 1695 it might be no longer necessary, and secretly to take his daughter with him when he departed. His plans were facilitated by the news which arrived from Paris.

"The government of France were greatly 1700 enraged at the escape of their victim and spared no pains to detect and punish his deliverer. The plot of Felix was quickly discovered, and De Lacey and Agatha were thrown into prison. The news reached Felix 1705 and roused him from his dream of pleasure. His blind and aged father and his gentle sister lay in a noisome dungeon while he enjoyed the free air and the society of her whom he loved. This idea was torture to him.

1710 He quickly arranged with the Turk that if the latter should find a favourable opportunity for escape before Felix could return to Italy, Safie should remain as a boarder at a convent at Leghorn; and then, quitting the lovely 1715 Arabian, he hastened to Paris and delivered himself up to the vengeance of the law, hoping to free De Lacey and Agatha by this proceeding.

"He did not succeed. They remained 1720 confined for five months before the trial took place, the result of which deprived them of their fortune and condemned them to a perpetual exile from their native country.

"They found a miserable asylum in the 1725 cottage in Germany, where I discovered them. Felix soon learned that the treacherous Turk, for whom he and his family endured such unheard-of oppression, on discovering that his deliverer was thus 1730 reduced to poverty and ruin, became a traitor to good feeling and honour and had quitted Italy with his daughter, insultingly sending Felix a pittance of money to aid him, as he said, in some plan of future maintenance.

1735 "Such were the events that preyed on the heart of Felix and rendered him, when I first saw him, the most miserable of his family. He could have endured poverty, and while this distress had been the meed of his virtue, 1740 he gloried in it; but the ingratitude of the Turk and the loss of his beloved Safie were misfortunes more bitter and irreparable. The arrival of the Arabian now infused new life into his soul.

1745 "When the news reached Leghorn that Felix was deprived of his wealth and rank, the merchant commanded his daughter to think no more of her lover, but to prepare to return to her native country. The generous nature of 1750 Safie was outraged by this command; she attempted to expostulate with her father, but he left her angrily, reiterating his tyrannical mandate.

1755 "A few days after, the Turk entered his daughter's apartment and told her hastily that he had reason to believe that his residence at Leghorn had been divulged and that he should speedily be delivered up to the French government; he had consequently 1760 hired a vessel to convey him to Constantinople, for which city he should sail in a few hours. He intended to leave his daughter under the care of a confidential servant, to follow at her leisure with the greater part of his 1765 property, which had not yet arrived at Leghorn.

"When alone, Safie resolved in her own mind the plan of conduct that it would become her to pursue in this emergency. A 1770 residence in Turkey was abhorrent to her; her religion and her feelings were alike averse to it. By some papers of her father which fell into her hands she heard of the exile of her lover and learnt the name of the spot where 1775 he then resided. She hesitated some time, but at length she formed her determination. Taking with her some jewels that belonged to her and a sum of money, she quitted Italy with an attendant, a native of Leghorn, but 1780 who understood the common language of Turkey, and departed for Germany.

"She arrived in safety at a town about twenty leagues from the cottage of De Lacey, when her attendant fell dangerously ill. Safie 1785 nursed her with the most devoted affection, but the poor girl died, and the Arabian was left alone, unacquainted with the language of the country and utterly ignorant of the customs of the world. She fell, however, into 1790 good hands. The Italian had mentioned the name of the spot for which they were bound, and after her death the woman of the house in which they had lived took care that Safie should arrive in safety at the cottage of her 1795 lover."

Chapter 15

"Such was the history of my beloved cottagers. It impressed me deeply. I learned, from the views of social life which it developed, to admire their virtues and to deprecate the 1800 vices of mankind.

"As yet I looked upon crime as a distant evil, benevolence and generosity were ever present before me, inciting within me a desire to become an actor in the busy scene 1805 where so many admirable qualities were called forth and displayed. But in giving an account of the progress of my intellect, I must not omit a circumstance which occurred in the beginning of the month of 1810 August of the same year.

"One night during my accustomed visit to the neighbouring wood where I collected my own food and brought home firing for my protectors, I found on the ground a leathern 1815 portmanteau containing several articles of dress and some books. I eagerly seized the prize and returned with it to my hovel. Fortunately the books were written in the language, the elements of which I had 1820 acquired at the cottage; they consisted of *Paradise Lost*, a volume of *Plutarch's Lives*, and the *Sorrows of Werter*. The possession of these treasures gave me extreme delight; I now continually studied and exercised my mind 1825 upon these histories, whilst my friends were employed in their ordinary occupations.

"I can hardly describe to you the effect of these books. They produced in me an infinity of new images and feelings, that sometimes 1830 raised me to ecstasy, but more frequently sunk me into the lowest dejection. In the *Sorrows of Werter*, besides the interest of its simple and affecting story, so many opinions

are canvassed and so many lights thrown
1835 upon what had hitherto been to me obscure
subjects that I found in it a never-ending
source of speculation and astonishment. The
gentle and domestic manners it described,
combined with lofty sentiments and feelings,
1840 which had for their object something out
of self, accorded well with my experience
among my protectors and with the wants
which were for ever alive in my own bosom.
But I thought Werter himself a more divine
1845 being than I had ever beheld or imagined; his
character contained no pretension, but it
sank deep. The disquisitions upon death and
suicide were calculated to fill me with wonder. I did not pretend to enter into the merits
1850 of the case, yet I inclined towards the opinions of the hero, whose extinction I wept,
without precisely understanding it.

"As I read, however, I applied much personally to my own feelings and condition. I
1855 found myself similar yet at the same time
strangely unlike to the beings concerning
whom I read and to whose conversation I
was a listener. I sympathised with and partly
understood them, but I was unformed in
1860 mind; I was dependent on none and related
to none. 'The path of my departure was free,'
and there was none to lament my annihilation. My person was hideous and my stature
gigantic. What did this mean? Who was I?
1865 What was I? Whence did I come? What was
my destination? These questions continually
recurred, but I was unable to solve them.

"The volume of *Plutarch's Lives* which I possessed contained the histories of the first
1870 founders of the ancient republics. This book
had a far different effect upon me from the
Sorrows of Werter. I learned from Werter's
imaginations despondency and gloom, but
Plutarch taught me high thoughts; he elevated
1875 me above the wretched sphere of my own

reflections, to admire and love the heroes of
past ages. Many things I read surpassed my
understanding and experience. I had a very
confused knowledge of kingdoms, wide
1880 extents of country, mighty rivers, and
boundless seas. But I was perfectly unacquainted with towns and large assemblages
of men. The cottage of my protectors had
been the only school in which I had studied
1885 human nature, but this book developed new
and mightier scenes of action. I read of men
concerned in public affairs, governing or
massacring their species. I felt the greatest
ardour for virtue rise within me, and abhor-
1890 rence for vice, as far as I understood the
signification of those terms, relative as they
were, as I applied them, to pleasure and pain
alone. Induced by these feelings, I was of
course led to admire peaceable lawgivers,
1895 Numa, Solon, and Lycurgus, in preference to
Romulus and Theseus. The patriarchal lives
of my protectors caused these impressions
to take a firm hold on my mind; perhaps, if
my first introduction to humanity had been
1900 made by a young soldier, burning for glory
and slaughter, I should have been imbued
with different sensations.

"But *Paradise Lost* excited different and far
deeper emotions. I read it, as I had read the
1905 other volumes which had fallen into my
hands, as a true history. It moved every feeling of wonder and awe that the picture of an
omnipotent God warring with his creatures
was capable of exciting. I often referred the
1910 several situations, as their similarity struck
me, to my own. Like Adam, I was apparently
united by no link to any other being in existence; but his state was far different from
mine in every other respect. He had come
1915 forth from the hands of God a perfect creature, happy and prosperous, guarded by the
especial care of his Creator; he was allowed

to converse with and acquire knowledge from beings of a superior nature, but I was wretched, helpless, and alone. Many times I considered Satan as the fitter emblem of my condition, for often, like him, when I viewed the bliss of my protectors, the bitter gall of envy rose within me.

"Another circumstance strengthened and confirmed these feelings. Soon after my arrival in the hovel I discovered some papers in the pocket of the dress which I had taken from your laboratory. At first I had neglected them, but now that I was able to decipher the characters in which they were written, I began to study them with diligence. It was your journal of the four months that preceded my creation. You minutely described in these papers every step you took in the progress of your work; this history was mingled with accounts of domestic occurrences. You doubtless recollect these papers. Here they are. Everything is related in them which bears reference to my accursed origin; the whole detail of that series of disgusting circumstances which produced it is set in view; the minutest description of my odious and loathsome person is given, in language which painted your own horrors and rendered mine indelible. I sickened as I read. 'Hateful day when I received life!' I exclaimed in agony. 'Accursed creator! Why did you form a monster so hideous that even you turned from me in disgust? God, in pity, made man beautiful and alluring, after his own image; but my form is a filthy type of yours, more horrid even from the very resemblance. Satan had his companions, fellow devils, to admire and encourage him, but I am solitary and abhorred.'

"These were the reflections of my hours of despondency and solitude; but when I contemplated the virtues of the cottagers, their amiable and benevolent dispositions, I persuaded myself that when they should become acquainted with my admiration of their virtues they would compassionate me and overlook my personal deformity. Could they turn from their door one, however monstrous, who solicited their compassion and friendship? I resolved, at least, not to despair, but in every way to fit myself for an interview with them which would decide my fate. I postponed this attempt for some months longer, for the importance attached to its success inspired me with a dread lest I should fail. Besides, I found that my understanding improved so much with every day's experience that I was unwilling to commence this undertaking until a few more months should have added to my sagacity.

"Several changes, in the meantime, took place in the cottage. The presence of Safie diffused happiness among its inhabitants, and I also found that a greater degree of plenty reigned there. Felix and Agatha spent more time in amusement and conversation, and were assisted in their labours by servants. They did not appear rich, but they were contented and happy; their feelings were serene and peaceful, while mine became every day more tumultuous. Increase of knowledge only discovered to me more clearly what a wretched outcast I was. I cherished hope, it is true, but it vanished when I beheld my person reflected in water or my shadow in the moonshine, even as that frail image and that inconstant shade.

"I endeavoured to crush these fears and to fortify myself for the trial which in a few months I resolved to undergo; and sometimes I allowed my thoughts, unchecked by reason, to ramble in the fields of Paradise, and dared to fancy amiable and lovely creatures sympathising with my feelings and cheering my gloom; their angelic countenances breathed smiles of consolation. But it was all a dream; no Eve soothed my sorrows nor shared my thoughts; I was alone. I remembered Adam's supplication to his Creator. But where was mine? He had abandoned me, and in the bitterness of my heart I cursed him.

"Autumn passed thus. I saw, with surprise and grief, the leaves decay and fall, and nature again assume the barren and bleak appearance it had worn when I first beheld the woods and the lovely moon. Yet I did not heed the bleakness of the weather; I was better fitted by my conformation for the endurance of cold than heat. But my chief delights were the sight of the flowers, the birds, and all the gay apparel of summer; when those deserted me, I turned with more attention towards the cottagers. Their happiness was not decreased by the absence of summer. They loved and sympathised with one another; and their joys, depending on each other, were not interrupted by the casualties that took place around them. The more I saw of them, the greater became my desire to claim their protection and kindness; my heart yearned to be known and loved by these amiable creatures; to see their sweet looks directed towards me with affection was the utmost limit of my ambition. I dared not think that they would turn them from me with disdain and horror. The poor that stopped at their door were never driven away. I asked, it is true, for greater treasures than a little food or rest: I required kindness and sympathy; but I did not believe myself utterly unworthy of it.

"The winter advanced, and an entire revolution of the seasons had taken place since I awoke into life. My attention at this time was solely directed towards my plan of introducing myself into the cottage of my protectors. I revolved many projects, but that on which I finally fixed was to enter the dwelling when the blind old man should be alone. I had sagacity enough to discover that the unnatural hideousness of my person was the chief object of horror with those who had formerly beheld me. My voice, although harsh, had nothing terrible in it; I thought, therefore, that if in the absence of his children I could gain the good will and mediation of the old De Lacey, I might by his means be tolerated by my younger protectors.

"One day, when the sun shone on the red leaves that strewed the ground and diffused cheerfulness, although it denied warmth, Safie, Agatha, and Felix departed on a long country walk, and the old man, at his own desire, was left alone in the cottage. When his children had departed, he took up his guitar and played several mournful but sweet airs, more sweet and mournful than I had ever heard him play before. At first his countenance was illuminated with pleasure, but as he continued, thoughtfulness and sadness succeeded; at length, laying aside the instrument, he sat absorbed in reflection.

"My heart beat quick; this was the hour and moment of trial, which would decide my hopes or realise my fears. The servants were gone to a neighbouring fair. All was silent in and around the cottage; it was an excellent opportunity; yet, when I proceeded to execute my plan, my limbs failed me and I sank to the ground. Again I rose, and exerting all the firmness of which I was master, removed the planks which I had placed before my hovel to conceal my retreat. The fresh air revived me, and with renewed determination I approached the door of their cottage.

"I knocked. 'Who is there?' said the old man. 'Come in.'

"I entered. 'Pardon this intrusion,' said I; 'I am a traveller in want of a little rest; you would greatly oblige me if you would allow me to remain a few minutes before the fire.'

2090   "'Enter,' said De Lacey, 'and I will try in what manner I can to relieve your wants; but, unfortunately, my children are from home, and as I am blind, I am afraid I shall find it difficult to procure food for you.'

2095   "'Do not trouble yourself, my kind host; I have food; it is warmth and rest only that I need.'

"I sat down, and a silence ensued. I knew that every minute was precious to me, yet I 2100 remained irresolute in what manner to commence the interview, when the old man addressed me.

'By your language, stranger, I suppose you are my countryman; are you French?'

2105   "'No; but I was educated by a French family and understand that language only. I am now going to claim the protection of some friends, whom I sincerely love, and of whose favour I have some hopes.'

2110   "'Are they Germans?'

"'No, they are French. But let us change the subject. I am an unfortunate and deserted creature, I look around and I have no relation or friend upon earth. These amiable people to 2115 whom I go have never seen me and know little of me. I am full of fears, for if I fail there, I am an outcast in the world for ever.'

"'Do not despair. To be friendless is indeed to be unfortunate, but the hearts of men, 2120 when unprejudiced by any obvious self-interest, are full of brotherly love and charity. Rely, therefore, on your hopes; and if these friends are good and amiable, do not despair.'

"'They are kind—they are the most excel- 2125 lent creatures in the world; but, unfortunately, they are prejudiced against me. I have good dispositions; my life has been hitherto

harmless and in some degree beneficial; but a fatal prejudice clouds their eyes, and where 2130 they ought to see a feeling and kind friend, they behold only a detestable monster.'

"'That is indeed unfortunate; but if you are really blameless, cannot you undeceive them?'

2135   "'I am about to undertake that task; and it is on that account that I feel so many overwhelming terrors. I tenderly love these friends; I have, unknown to them, been for many months in the habits of daily kindness 2140 towards them; but they believe that I wish to injure them, and it is that prejudice which I wish to overcome.'

"'Where do these friends reside?'

"'Near this spot.'

2145   "The old man paused and then continued, 'If you will unreservedly confide to me the particulars of your tale, I perhaps may be of use in undeceiving them. I am blind and cannot judge of your countenance, but there is 2150 something in your words which persuades me that you are sincere. I am poor and an exile, but it will afford me true pleasure to be in any way serviceable to a human creature.'

"'Excellent man! I thank you and accept 2155 your generous offer. You raise me from the dust by this kindness; and I trust that, by your aid, I shall not be driven from the society and sympathy of your fellow creatures.'

"'Heaven forbid! Even if you were really 2160 criminal, for that can only drive you to desperation, and not instigate you to virtue. I also am unfortunate; I and my family have been condemned, although innocent; judge, therefore, if I do not feel for your 2165 misfortunes.'

"'How can I thank you, my best and only benefactor? From your lips first have I heard the voice of kindness directed towards me; I shall be for ever grateful; and your present

2170 humanity assures me of success with those friends whom I am on the point of meeting.'

"'May I know the names and residence of those friends?'

"I paused. This, I thought, was the 2175 moment of decision, which was to rob me of or bestow happiness on me for ever. I struggled vainly for firmness sufficient to answer him, but the effort destroyed all my remaining strength; I sank on the chair and sobbed 2180 aloud. At that moment I heard the steps of my younger protectors. I had not a moment to lose, but seizing the hand of the old man, I cried, 'Now is the time! Save and protect me! You and your family are the friends whom I 2185 seek. Do not you desert me in the hour of trial!'

"'Great God!' exclaimed the old man. 'Who are you?'

"At that instant the cottage door was 2190 opened, and Felix, Safie, and Agatha entered. Who can describe their horror and consternation on beholding me? Agatha fainted, and Safie, unable to attend to her friend, rushed out of the cottage. Felix darted forward, and 2195 with supernatural force tore me from his father, to whose knees I clung, in a transport of fury, he dashed me to the ground and struck me violently with a stick. I could have torn him limb from limb, as the lion rends 2200 the antelope. But my heart sank within me as with bitter sickness, and I refrained. I saw him on the point of repeating his blow, when, overcome by pain and anguish, I quitted the cottage, and in the general tumult escaped 2205 unperceived to my hovel."

Chapter 16

"Cursed, cursed creator! Why did I live? Why, in that instant, did I not extinguish the spark of existence which you had so wantonly bestowed? I know not; despair had not yet

2210 taken possession of me; my feelings were those of rage and revenge. I could with pleasure have destroyed the cottage and its inhabitants and have glutted myself with their shrieks and misery.

2215 "When night came I quitted my retreat and wandered in the wood; and now, no longer restrained by the fear of discovery, I gave vent to my anguish in fearful howlings. I was like a wild beast that had broken the toils, 2220 destroying the objects that obstructed me and ranging through the wood with a stag-like swiftness. Oh! What a miserable night I passed! The cold stars shone in mockery, and the bare trees waved their branches above 2225 me; now and then the sweet voice of a bird burst forth amidst the universal stillness. All, save I, were at rest or in enjoyment; I, like the arch-fiend, bore a hell within me, and finding myself unsympathised with, wished to tear 2230 up the trees, spread havoc and destruction around me, and then to have sat down and enjoyed the ruin.

"But this was a luxury of sensation that could not endure; I became fatigued with 2235 excess of bodily exertion and sank on the damp grass in the sick impotence of despair. There was none among the myriads of men that existed who would pity or assist me; and should I feel kindness towards my enemies? 2240 No; from that moment I declared everlasting war against the species, and more than all, against him who had formed me and sent me forth to this insupportable misery.

"The sun rose; I heard the voices of men 2245 and knew that it was impossible to return to my retreat during that day. Accordingly I hid myself in some thick underwood, determining to devote the ensuing hours to reflection on my situation.

2250 "The pleasant sunshine and the pure air of day restored me to some degree of tranquillity;

and when I considered what had passed at the cottage, I could not help believing that I had been too hasty in my conclusions. I had certainly acted imprudently. It was apparent that my conversation had interested the father in my behalf, and I was a fool in having exposed my person to the horror of his children. I ought to have familiarised the old De Lacey to me, and by degrees to have discovered myself to the rest of his family, when they should have been prepared for my approach. But I did not believe my errors to be irretrievable, and after much consideration I resolved to return to the cottage, seek the old man, and by my representations win him to my party.

"These thoughts calmed me, and in the afternoon I sank into a profound sleep; but the fever of my blood did not allow me to be visited by peaceful dreams. The horrible scene of the preceding day was for ever acting before my eyes; the females were flying and the enraged Felix tearing me from his father's feet. I awoke exhausted, and finding that it was already night, I crept forth from my hiding-place, and went in search of food.

"When my hunger was appeased, I directed my steps towards the well-known path that conducted to the cottage. All there was at peace. I crept into my hovel and remained in silent expectation of the accustomed hour when the family arose. That hour passed, the sun mounted high in the heavens, but the cottagers did not appear. I trembled violently, apprehending some dreadful misfortune. The inside of the cottage was dark, and I heard no motion; I cannot describe the agony of this suspense.

"Presently two countrymen passed by, but pausing near the cottage, they entered into conversation, using violent gesticulations; but I did not understand what they said, as they spoke the language of the country, which differed from that of my protectors. Soon after, however, Felix approached with another man; I was surprised, as I knew that he had not quitted the cottage that morning, and waited anxiously to discover from his discourse the meaning of these unusual appearances.

"'Do you consider,' said his companion to him, 'that you will be obliged to pay three months' rent and to lose the produce of your garden? I do not wish to take any unfair advantage, and I beg therefore that you will take some days to consider of your determination.'

"'It is utterly useless,' replied Felix; 'we can never again inhabit your cottage. The life of my father is in the greatest danger, owing to the dreadful circumstance that I have related. My wife and my sister will never recover from their horror. I entreat you not to reason with me any more. Take possession of your tenement and let me fly from this place.'

"Felix trembled violently as he said this. He and his companion entered the cottage, in which they remained for a few minutes, and then departed. I never saw any of the family of De Lacey more.

"I continued for the remainder of the day in my hovel in a state of utter and stupid despair. My protectors had departed and had broken the only link that held me to the world. For the first time the feelings of revenge and hatred filled my bosom, and I did not strive to control them, but allowing myself to be borne away by the stream, I bent my mind towards injury and death. When I thought of my friends, of the mild voice of De Lacey, the gentle eyes of Agatha, and the exquisite beauty of the Arabian, these thoughts vanished and a gush of tears somewhat soothed me. But again when I reflected that they had spurned and deserted me, anger returned, a rage of anger, and unable to injure anything human, I turned my fury towards inanimate 2340 objects. As night advanced, I placed a variety of combustibles around the cottage, and after having destroyed every vestige of cultivation in the garden, I waited with forced impatience until the moon had sunk to commence my 2345 operations.

"As the night advanced, a fierce wind arose from the woods and quickly dispersed the clouds that had loitered in the heavens; the blast tore along like a mighty avalanche 2350 and produced a kind of insanity in my spirits that burst all bounds of reason and reflection. I lighted the dry branch of a tree and danced with fury around the devoted cottage, my eyes still fixed on the western horizon, 2355 the edge of which the moon nearly touched. A part of its orb was at length hid, and I waved my brand; it sank, and with a loud scream I fired the straw, and heath, and bushes, which I had collected. The wind 2360 fanned the fire, and the cottage was quickly enveloped by the flames, which clung to it and licked it with their forked and destroying tongues.

"As soon as I was convinced that no assis-2365 tance could save any part of the habitation, I quitted the scene and sought for refuge in the woods.

"And now, with the world before me, whither should I bend my steps? I resolved 2370 to fly far from the scene of my misfortunes; but to me, hated and despised, every country must be equally horrible. At length the thought of you crossed my mind. I learned from your papers that you were my father, 2375 my creator; and to whom could I apply with more fitness than to him who had given me life? Among the lessons that Felix had

bestowed upon Safie, geography had not been omitted; I had learned from these the 2380 relative situations of the different countries of the earth. You had mentioned Geneva as the name of your native town, and towards this place I resolved to proceed.

"But how was I to direct myself? I knew 2385 that I must travel in a southwesterly direction to reach my destination, but the sun was my only guide. I did not know the names of the towns that I was to pass through, nor could I ask information from a single human 2390 being; but I did not despair. From you only could I hope for succour, although towards you I felt no sentiment but that of hatred. Unfeeling, heartless creator! You had endowed me with perceptions and passions 2395 and then cast me abroad an object for the scorn and horror of mankind. But on you only had I any claim for pity and redress, and from you I determined to seek that justice which I vainly attempted to gain from any 2400 other being that wore the human form.

"My travels were long and the sufferings I endured intense. It was late in autumn when I quitted the district where I had so long resided. I travelled only at night, fearful of 2405 encountering the visage of a human being. Nature decayed around me, and the sun became heatless; rain and snow poured around me; mighty rivers were frozen; the surface of the earth was hard and chill, and 2410 bare, and I found no shelter. Oh, earth! How often did I imprecate curses on the cause of my being! The mildness of my nature had fled, and all within me was turned to gall and bitterness. The nearer I approached to 2415 your habitation, the more deeply did I feel the spirit of revenge enkindled in my heart. Snow fell, and the waters were hardened, but I rested not. A few incidents now and then directed me, and I possessed a map of the

2420 country; but I often wandered wide from my path. The agony of my feelings allowed me no respite; no incident occurred from which my rage and misery could not extract its food; but a circumstance that happened when I

2425 arrived on the confines of Switzerland, when the sun had recovered its warmth and the earth again began to look green, confirmed in an especial manner the bitterness and horror of my feelings.

2430 "I generally rested during the day and travelled only when I was secured by night from the view of man. One morning, however, finding that my path lay through a deep wood, I ventured to continue my journey

2435 after the sun had risen; the day, which was one of the first of spring, cheered even me by the loveliness of its sunshine and the balminess of the air. I felt emotions of gentleness and pleasure, that had long appeared dead,

2440 revive within me. Half surprised by the novelty of these sensations, I allowed myself to be borne away by them, and forgetting my solitude and deformity, dared to be happy. Soft tears again bedewed my cheeks, and I

2445 even raised my humid eyes with thankfulness towards the blessed sun, which bestowed such joy upon me.

 "I continued to wind among the paths of the wood, until I came to its boundary, which

2450 was skirted by a deep and rapid river, into which many of the trees bent their branches, now budding with the fresh spring. Here I paused, not exactly knowing what path to pursue, when I heard the sound of voices,

2455 that induced me to conceal myself under the shade of a cypress. I was scarcely hid when a young girl came running towards the spot where I was concealed, laughing, as if she ran from someone in sport. She continued her

2460 course along the precipitous sides of the river, when suddenly her foot slipped, and she fell

into the rapid stream. I rushed from my hiding-place and with extreme labour, from the force of the current, saved her and

2465 dragged her to shore. She was senseless, and I endeavoured by every means in my power to restore animation, when I was suddenly interrupted by the approach of a rustic, who was probably the person from whom she had play-

2470 fully fled. On seeing me, he darted towards me, and tearing the girl from my arms, hastened towards the deeper parts of the wood. I followed speedily, I hardly knew why; but when the man saw me draw near, he aimed a

2475 gun, which he carried, at my body and fired. I sank to the ground, and my injurer, with increased swiftness, escaped into the wood.

 "This was then the reward of my benevolence! I had saved a human being from

2480 destruction, and as a recompense I now writhed under the miserable pain of a wound which shattered the flesh and bone. The feelings of kindness and gentleness which I had entertained but a few moments before gave

2485 place to hellish rage and gnashing of teeth. Inflamed by pain, I vowed eternal hatred and vengeance to all mankind. But the agony of my wound overcame me; my pulses paused, and I fainted.

2490 "For some weeks I led a miserable life in the woods, endeavouring to cure the wound which I had received. The ball had entered my shoulder, and I knew not whether it had remained there or passed through; at any

2495 rate I had no means of extracting it. My sufferings were augmented also by the oppressive sense of the injustice and ingratitude of their infliction. My daily vows rose for revenge—a deep and deadly revenge, such

2500 as would alone compensate for the outrages and anguish I had endured.

 "After some weeks my wound healed, and I continued my journey. The labours I endured were no longer to be alleviated by the bright sun or gentle breezes of spring; all joy was but a mockery which insulted my desolate state and made me feel more painfully that I was not made for the enjoyment of pleasure.

"But my toils now drew near a close, and in two months from this time I reached the environs of Geneva.

"It was evening when I arrived, and I retired to a hiding-place among the fields that surround it to meditate in what manner I should apply to you. I was oppressed by fatigue and hunger and far too unhappy to enjoy the gentle breezes of evening or the prospect of the sun setting behind the stupendous mountains of Jura.

"At this time a slight sleep relieved me from the pain of reflection, which was disturbed by the approach of a beautiful child, who came running into the recess I had chosen, with all the sportiveness of infancy. Suddenly, as I gazed on him, an idea seized me that this little creature was unprejudiced and had lived too short a time to have imbibed a horror of deformity. If, therefore, I could seize him and educate him as my companion and friend, I should not be so desolate in this peopled earth.

"Urged by this impulse, I seized on the boy as he passed and drew him towards me. As soon as he beheld my form, he placed his hands before his eyes and uttered a shrill scream; I drew his hand forcibly from his face and said, 'Child, what is the meaning of this? I do not intend to hurt you; listen to me.'

"He struggled violently. 'Let me go,' he cried; 'monster! Ugly wretch! You wish to eat me and tear me to pieces. You are an ogre. Let me go, or I will tell my papa.'

"'Boy, you will never see your father again; you must come with me.'

"'Hideous monster! Let me go. My papa is a syndic—he is M. Frankenstein—he will punish you. You dare not keep me.'

"'Frankenstein! you belong then to my enemy—to him towards whom I have sworn eternal revenge; you shall be my first victim.'

"The child still struggled and loaded me with epithets which carried despair to my heart; I grasped his throat to silence him, and in a moment he lay dead at my feet.

"I gazed on my victim, and my heart swelled with exultation and hellish triumph; clapping my hands, I exclaimed, 'I too can create desolation; my enemy is not invulnerable; this death will carry despair to him, and a thousand other miseries shall torment and destroy him.'

"As I fixed my eyes on the child, I saw something glittering on his breast. I took it; it was a portrait of a most lovely woman. In spite of my malignity, it softened and attracted me. For a few moments I gazed with delight on her dark eyes, fringed by deep lashes, and her lovely lips; but presently my rage returned; I remembered that I was for ever deprived of the delights that such beautiful creatures could bestow and that she whose resemblance I contemplated would, in regarding me, have changed that air of divine benignity to one expressive of disgust and affright.

"Can you wonder that such thoughts transported me with rage? I only wonder that at that moment, instead of venting my sensations in exclamations and agony, I did not rush among mankind and perish in the attempt to destroy them.

"While I was overcome by these feelings, I left the spot where I had committed the murder, and seeking a more secluded hiding-place, I entered a barn which had appeared to me to be empty. A woman was

sleeping on some straw; she was young, not indeed so beautiful as her whose portrait I
2590 held, but of an agreeable aspect and blooming in the loveliness of youth and health. Here, I thought, is one of those whose joy-imparting smiles are bestowed on all but me. And then I bent over her and whispered,
2595 'Awake, fairest, thy lover is near—he who would give his life but to obtain one look of affection from thine eyes; my beloved, awake!'

"The sleeper stirred; a thrill of terror ran
2600 through me. Should she indeed awake, and see me, and curse me, and denounce the murderer? Thus would she assuredly act if her darkened eyes opened and she beheld me. The thought was madness; it stirred the
2605 fiend within me—not I, but she, shall suffer; the murder I have committed because I am for ever robbed of all that she could give me, she shall atone. The crime had its source in her; be hers the punishment! Thanks to the
2610 lessons of Felix and the sanguinary laws of man, I had learned now to work mischief. I bent over her and placed the portrait securely in one of the folds of her dress. She moved again, and I fled.

2615 "For some days I haunted the spot where these scenes had taken place, sometimes wishing to see you, sometimes resolved to quit the world and its miseries for ever. At length I wandered towards these mountains,
2620 and have ranged through their immense recesses, consumed by a burning passion which you alone can gratify. We may not part until you have promised to comply with my requisition. I am alone and miserable;
2625 man will not associate with me; but one as deformed and horrible as myself would not deny herself to me. My companion must be of the same species and have the same defects. This being you must create."

Chapter 17

2630 The being finished speaking and fixed his looks upon me in the expectation of a reply. But I was bewildered, perplexed, and unable to arrange my ideas sufficiently to understand the full extent of his proposition. He
2635 continued,

"You must create a female for me with whom I can live in the interchange of those sympathies necessary for my being. This you alone can do, and I demand it of you as a
2640 right which you must not refuse to concede."

The latter part of his tale had kindled anew in me the anger that had died away while he narrated his peaceful life among the cottagers, and as he said this I could
2645 no longer suppress the rage that burned within me.

"I do refuse it," I replied; "and no torture shall ever extort a consent from me. You may render me the most miserable of men, but
2650 you shall never make me base in my own eyes. Shall I create another like yourself, whose joint wickedness might desolate the world. Begone! I have answered you; you may torture me, but I will never consent."

2655 "You are in the wrong," replied the fiend; "and instead of threatening, I am content to reason with you. I am malicious because I am miserable. Am I not shunned and hated by all mankind? You, my creator, would tear
2660 me to pieces and triumph; remember that, and tell me why I should pity man more than he pities me? You would not call it murder if you could precipitate me into one of those ice-rifts and destroy my frame, the
2665 work of your own hands. Shall I respect man when he condemns me? Let him live with me in the interchange of kindness, and instead of injury I would bestow every benefit upon him with tears of gratitude at his
2670 acceptance. But that cannot be; the human

senses are insurmountable barriers to our union. Yet mine shall not be the submission of abject slavery. I will revenge my injuries; if I cannot inspire love, I will cause fear, and chiefly towards you my arch-enemy, because my creator, do I swear inextinguishable hatred. Have a care; I will work at your destruction, nor finish until I desolate your heart, so that you shall curse the hour of your birth."

A fiendish rage animated him as he said this; his face was wrinkled into contortions too horrible for human eyes to behold; but presently he calmed himself and proceeded—

"I intended to reason. This passion is detrimental to me, for you do not reflect that you are the cause of its excess. If any being felt emotions of benevolence towards me, I should return them a hundred and a hundredfold; for that one creature's sake I would make peace with the whole kind! But I now indulge in dreams of bliss that cannot be realised. What I ask of you is reasonable and moderate; I demand a creature of another sex, but as hideous as myself; the gratification is small, but it is all that I can receive, and it shall content me. It is true, we shall be monsters, cut off from all the world; but on that account we shall be more attached to one another. Our lives will not be happy, but they will be harmless and free from the misery I now feel. Oh! My creator, make me happy; let me feel gratitude towards you for one benefit! Let me see that I excite the sympathy of some existing thing; do not deny me my request!"

I was moved. I shuddered when I thought of the possible consequences of my consent, but I felt that there was some justice in his argument. His tale and the feelings he now expressed proved him to be a creature of fine sensations, and did I not as his maker owe him all the portion of happiness that it was in my power to bestow? He saw my change of feeling and continued,

"If you consent, neither you nor any other human being shall ever see us again; I will go to the vast wilds of South America. My food is not that of man; I do not destroy the lamb and the kid to glut my appetite; acorns and berries afford me sufficient nourishment. My companion will be of the same nature as myself and will be content with the same fare. We shall make our bed of dried leaves; the sun will shine on us as on man and will ripen our food. The picture I present to you is peaceful and human, and you must feel that you could deny it only in the wantonness of power and cruelty. Pitiless as you have been towards me, I now see compassion in your eyes; let me seize the favourable moment and persuade you to promise what I so ardently desire."

"You propose," replied I, "to fly from the habitations of man, to dwell in those wilds where the beasts of the field will be your only companions. How can you, who long for the love and sympathy of man, persevere in this exile? You will return and again seek their kindness, and you will meet with their detestation; your evil passions will be renewed, and you will then have a companion to aid you in the task of destruction. This may not be; cease to argue the point, for I cannot consent."

"How inconstant are your feelings! But a moment ago you were moved by my representations, and why do you again harden yourself to my complaints? I swear to you, by the earth which I inhabit, and by you that made me, that with the companion you bestow, I will quit the neighbourhood of man and dwell, as it may chance, in the most savage of places. My evil passions will have fled,

2755 for I shall meet with sympathy! My life will
flow quietly away, and in my dying moments
I shall not curse my maker."

His words had a strange effect upon me. I
compassionated him and sometimes felt a
2760 wish to console him, but when I looked upon
him, when I saw the filthy mass that moved
and talked, my heart sickened and my feelings were altered to those of horror and
hatred. I tried to stifle these sensations; I
2765 thought that as I could not sympathise with
him, I had no right to withhold from him the
small portion of happiness which was yet in
my power to bestow.

"You swear," I said, "to be harmless; but
2770 have you not already shown a degree of malice that should reasonably make me distrust
you? May not even this be a feint that will
increase your triumph by affording a wider
scope for your revenge?"
2775 "How is this? I must not be trifled with,
and I demand an answer. If I have no ties
and no affections, hatred and vice must be
my portion; the love of another will destroy
the cause of my crimes, and I shall become
2780 a thing of whose existence everyone will
be ignorant. My vices are the children of a
forced solitude that I abhor, and my virtues
will necessarily arise when I live in communion with an equal. I shall feel the affections
2785 of a sensitive being and become linked to the
chain of existence and events from which I
am now excluded."

I paused some time to reflect on all he
had related and the various arguments
2790 which he had employed. I thought of the
promise of virtues which he had displayed
on the opening of his existence and the subsequent blight of all kindly feeling by the
loathing and scorn which his protectors had
2795 manifested towards him. His power and
threats were not omitted in my calculations;

a creature who could exist in the ice-caves of
the glaciers and hide himself from pursuit
among the ridges of inaccessible precipices
2800 was a being possessing faculties it would
be vain to cope with. After a long pause of
reflection I concluded that the justice due
both to him and my fellow creatures
demanded of me that I should comply with
2805 his request. Turning to him, therefore, I said,

"I consent to your demand, on your solemn
oath to quit Europe for ever, and every other
place in the neighbourhood of man, as soon
as I shall deliver into your hands a female
2810 who will accompany you in your exile."

"I swear," he cried, "by the sun, and by the
blue sky of heaven, and by the fire of love
that burns my heart, that if you grant my
prayer, while they exist you shall never
2815 behold me again. Depart to your home and
commence your labours; I shall watch their
progress with unutterable anxiety; and fear
not but that when you are ready I shall
appear."
2820 Saying this, he suddenly quitted me, fearful, perhaps, of any change in my sentiments. I saw him descend the mountain
with greater speed than the flight of an
eagle, and quickly lost among the undula-
2825 tions of the sea of ice.

His tale had occupied the whole day, and
the sun was upon the verge of the horizon
when he departed. I knew that I ought to hasten my descent towards the valley, as I should
2830 soon be encompassed in darkness; but my
heart was heavy, and my steps slow. The
labour of winding among the little paths of
the mountain and fixing my feet firmly as I
advanced perplexed me, occupied as I was by
2835 the emotions which the occurrences of the
day had produced. Night was far advanced
when I came to the halfway resting-place and
seated myself beside the fountain. The stars

shone at intervals as the clouds passed from
2840 over them; the dark pines rose before me,
and every here and there a broken tree lay on
the ground; it was a scene of wonderful
solemnity and stirred strange thoughts
within me. I wept bitterly, and clasping my
2845 hands in agony, I exclaimed, "Oh! stars and
clouds and winds, ye are all about to mock
me; if ye really pity me, crush sensation and
memory; let me become as nought; but if not,
depart, depart, and leave me in darkness."

2850   These were wild and miserable thoughts,
but I cannot describe to you how the eternal
twinkling of the stars weighed upon me and
how I listened to every blast of wind as if
it were a dull ugly siroc on its way to con-
2855 sume me.

    Morning dawned before I arrived at the
village of Chamounix; I took no rest, but
returned immediately to Geneva. Even in
my own heart I could give no expression to
2860 my sensations—they weighed on me with
a mountain's weight and their excess
destroyed my agony beneath them. Thus I
returned home, and entering the house, presented myself to the family. My haggard and
2865 wild appearance awoke intense alarm, but
I answered no question, scarcely did I speak.
I felt as if I were placed under a ban—as if I
had no right to claim their sympathies—as if
never more might I enjoy companionship
2870 with them. Yet even thus I loved them to
adoration; and to save them, I resolved to
dedicate myself to my most abhorred task.
The prospect of such an occupation made
every other circumstance of existence pass
2875 before me like a dream, and that thought
only had to me the reality of life.

© John Coulthart

◄ This image of Victor Frankenstein and his creation accompanies the following lines: "A flash of lightning illuminated the object, and discovered its shape plainly to me; its gigantic stature, and the deformity of its aspect more hideous than belongs to humanity, instantly informed me that it was the wretch, the filthy dæmon, to whom I had given life."

Weather plays a pivotal role in the novel. How does this image represent the tone and mood of the scene it depicts?

CHARACTER

1. In Chapter 9, how do Justine's conviction and death change Victor? Does it contribute to his progress, or does it contribute to his decline? What textual details support your answer?

2. When Victor meets his creature in Chapter 10, how does the **characterization** of the creature illustrate his complexities and contradictions?

3. In Chapters 13 and 14, how do the textual details reveal the creature's way of interacting with other characters?

4. In Chapter 16, what **motivates** the creature to think, feel, and act as he does?

5. What are the traits of the creature before and after the De Lacey family flees the cottage? How does he change?

STRUCTURE

6. In Chapters 9 and 10, Victor, his father, and his sister are each grieving over the deaths of William and Justine. How do the differences in the way they grieve emphasize a **contrast** of values?

7. In Chapters 11 to 15, what events in the **plot** create **suspense** in the text?

8. In Chapter 16, the creature finds Victor. How does this confrontation contribute to subsequent events?

NARRATION

9. In Chapter 11, the narration changes. How does the shift in **point of view** affect the details and information presented to the reader?

10. How does the **narrator's distance** from the events of the story affect the details and information presented to the reader?

11. How do the creature's background and **perspective** shape the **tone** in Chapters 11 and 15?

12. In Chapters 16 and 17, how does the narrative change? How does this change in point of view contribute to your interpretation of the text?

FIGURATIVE LANGUAGE: Word Choice, Imagery, and Symbols

13. The representation of sublime nature is a recurring **motif** throughout the novel. In what ways does nature affect both Victor and the creature? Explain the relationship that each character has with nature.

14. Shelley includes excerpts from John Milton's 1667 epic poem *Paradise Lost*, which tells the story of Satan's rebellion and Adam and Eve's expulsion from the Garden of Eden. What does this reference reveal about the creature's identity? How might the themes of *Paradise Lost* be relevant to *Frankenstein*?

Chapter 18

Day after day, week after week, passed away on my return to Geneva; and I could not collect the courage to recommence my work. I feared the vengeance of the disappointed 5 fiend, yet I was unable to overcome my repugnance to the task which was enjoined me. I found that I could not compose a female without again devoting several months to profound study and laborious 10 disquisition. I had heard of some discoveries having been made by an English philosopher, the knowledge of which was material to my success, and I sometimes thought of obtaining my father's consent to visit England for 15 this purpose; but I clung to every pretence of delay and shrank from taking the first step in an undertaking whose immediate necessity began to appear less absolute to me. A change indeed had taken place in me; my 20 health, which had hitherto declined, was now much restored; and my spirits, when unchecked by the memory of my unhappy promise, rose proportionably. My father saw this change with pleasure, and he turned his 25 thoughts towards the best method of eradicating the remains of my melancholy, which every now and then would return by fits, and with a devouring blackness overcast the approaching sunshine. At these moments I 30 took refuge in the most perfect solitude. I passed whole days on the lake alone in a little boat, watching the clouds and listening to the rippling of the waves, silent and listless. But the fresh air and bright sun seldom 35 failed to restore me to some degree of composure, and on my return I met the salutations of my friends with a readier smile and a more cheerful heart.

It was after my return from one of these 40 rambles that my father, calling me aside, thus addressed me,

"I am happy to remark, my dear son, that you have resumed your former pleasures and seem to be returning to yourself. And yet 45 you are still unhappy and still avoid our society. For some time I was lost in conjecture as to the cause of this, but yesterday an idea struck me, and if it is well founded, I conjure you to avow it. Reserve on such a point 50 would be not only useless, but draw down treble misery on us all."

I trembled violently at his exordium, and my father continued—

"I confess, my son, that I have always 55 looked forward to your marriage with our dear Elizabeth as the tie of our domestic comfort and the stay of my declining years. You were attached to each other from your earliest infancy; you studied together, and 60 appeared, in dispositions and tastes, entirely suited to one another. But so blind is the experience of man that what I conceived to be the best assistants to my plan may have entirely destroyed it. You, perhaps, regard her 65 as your sister, without any wish that she might become your wife. Nay, you may have met with another whom you may love; and considering yourself as bound in honour to Elizabeth, this struggle may occasion the poi-70 gnant misery which you appear to feel."

"My dear father, reassure yourself. I love my cousin tenderly and sincerely. I never saw any woman who excited, as Elizabeth does, my warmest admiration and affection. My 75 future hopes and prospects are entirely bound up in the expectation of our union."

"The expression of your sentiments of this subject, my dear Victor, gives me more pleasure than I have for some time experi-80 enced. If you feel thus, we shall assuredly be happy, however present events may cast a gloom over us. But it is this gloom which appears to have taken so strong a hold of

your mind that I wish to dissipate. Tell me,
85 therefore, whether you object to an immediate solemnisation of the marriage. We have
been unfortunate, and recent events have
drawn us from that everyday tranquillity
befitting my years and infirmities. You are
90 younger; yet I do not suppose, possessed as
you are of a competent fortune, that an early
marriage would at all interfere with any
future plans of honour and utility that you
may have formed. Do not suppose, however,
95 that I wish to dictate happiness to you or
that a delay on your part would cause me
any serious uneasiness. Interpret my words
with candour and answer me, I conjure you,
with confidence and sincerity."

100   I listened to my father in silence and
remained for some time incapable of offering
any reply. I revolved rapidly in my mind a
multitude of thoughts and endeavoured to
arrive at some conclusion. Alas! To me the
105 idea of an immediate union with my
Elizabeth was one of horror and dismay. I
was bound by a solemn promise which I had
not yet fulfilled and dared not break, or if I
did, what manifold miseries might not
110 impend over me and my devoted family!
Could I enter into a festival with this deadly
weight yet hanging round my neck and
bowing me to the ground? I must perform
my engagement and let the monster depart
115 with his mate before I allowed myself to
enjoy the delight of a union from which I
expected peace.

I remembered also the necessity imposed
upon me of either journeying to England or
120 entering into a long correspondence with
those philosophers of that country whose
knowledge and discoveries were of indispensable use to me in my present undertaking.
The latter method of obtaining the desired
125 intelligence was dilatory and unsatisfactory;

besides, I had an insurmountable aversion to
the idea of engaging myself in my loathsome
task in my father's house while in habits of
familiar intercourse with those I loved. I
130 knew that a thousand fearful accidents
might occur, the slightest of which would
disclose a tale to thrill all connected with me
with horror. I was aware also that I should
often lose all self-command, all capacity of
135 hiding the harrowing sensations that would
possess me during the progress of my
unearthly occupation. I must absent myself
from all I loved while thus employed. Once
commenced, it would quickly be achieved,
140 and I might be restored to my family in
peace and happiness. My promise fulfilled,
the monster would depart for ever. Or (so my
fond fancy imaged) some accident might
meanwhile occur to destroy him and put an
145 end to my slavery for ever.

These feelings dictated my answer to my
father. I expressed a wish to visit England,
but concealing the true reasons of this
request, I clothed my desires under a guise
150 which excited no suspicion, while I urged
my desire with an earnestness that easily
induced my father to comply. After so long
a period of an absorbing melancholy that
resembled madness in its intensity and
155 effects, he was glad to find that I was capable
of taking pleasure in the idea of such a journey, and he hoped that change of scene and
varied amusement would, before my return,
have restored me entirely to myself.

160   The duration of my absence was left to
my own choice; a few months, or at most a
year, was the period contemplated. One
paternal kind precaution he had taken to
ensure my having a companion. Without pre-
165 viously communicating with me, he had, in
concert with Elizabeth, arranged that Clerval
should join me at Strasburgh. This interfered

with the solitude I coveted for the prosecution of my task; yet at the commencement of my journey the presence of my friend could in no way be an impediment, and truly I rejoiced that thus I should be saved many hours of lonely, maddening reflection. Nay, Henry might stand between me and the intrusion of my foe. If I were alone, would he not at times force his abhorred presence on me to remind me of my task or to contemplate its progress?

To England, therefore, I was bound, and it was understood that my union with Elizabeth should take place immediately on my return. My father's age rendered him extremely averse to delay. For myself, there was one reward I promised myself from my detested toils—one consolation for my unparalleled sufferings; it was the prospect of that day when, enfranchised from my miserable slavery, I might claim Elizabeth and forget the past in my union with her.

I now made arrangements for my journey, but one feeling haunted me which filled me with fear and agitation. During my absence I should leave my friends unconscious of the existence of their enemy and unprotected from his attacks, exasperated as he might be by my departure. But he had promised to follow me wherever I might go, and would he not accompany me to England? This imagination was dreadful in itself, but soothing inasmuch as it supposed the safety of my friends. I was agonised with the idea of the possibility that the reverse of this might happen. But through the whole period during which I was the slave of my creature I allowed myself to be governed by the impulses of the moment; and my present sensations strongly intimated that the fiend would follow me and exempt my family from the danger of his machinations.

It was in the latter end of September that I again quitted my native country. My journey had been my own suggestion, and Elizabeth therefore acquiesced, but she was filled with disquiet at the idea of my suffering, away from her, the inroads of misery and grief. It had been her care which provided me a companion in Clerval—and yet a man is blind to a thousand minute circumstances which call forth a woman's sedulous attention. She longed to bid me hasten my return; a thousand conflicting emotions rendered her mute as she bade me a tearful, silent farewell.

I threw myself into the carriage that was to convey me away, hardly knowing whither I was going, and careless of what was passing around. I remembered only, and it was with a bitter anguish that I reflected on it, to order that my chemical instruments should be packed to go with me. Filled with dreary imaginations, I passed through many beautiful and majestic scenes, but my eyes were fixed and unobserving. I could only think of the bourne of my travels and the work which was to occupy me whilst they endured.

After some days spent in listless indolence, during which I traversed many leagues, I arrived at Strasburgh, where I waited two days for Clerval. He came. Alas, how great was the contrast between us! He was alive to every new scene, joyful when he saw the beauties of the setting sun, and more happy when he beheld it rise and recommence a new day. He pointed out to me the shifting colours of the landscape and the appearances of the sky. "This is what it is to live," he cried; "now I enjoy existence! But you, my dear Frankenstein, wherefore are you desponding and sorrowful!" In truth, I was occupied by gloomy thoughts and neither saw the descent of the evening star nor the golden

sunrise reflected in the Rhine. And you, my friend, would be far more amused with the journal of Clerval, who observed the scenery
255 with an eye of feeling and delight, than in listening to my reflections. I, a miserable wretch, haunted by a curse that shut up every avenue to enjoyment.

We had agreed to descend the Rhine in a
260 boat from Strasburgh to Rotterdam, whence we might take shipping for London. During this voyage we passed many willowy islands and saw several beautiful towns. We stayed a day at Mannheim, and on the fifth from our
265 departure from Strasburgh, arrived at Mainz. The course of the Rhine below Mainz becomes much more picturesque. The river descends rapidly and winds between hills, not high, but steep, and of beautiful forms. We saw
270 many ruined castles standing on the edges of precipices, surrounded by black woods, high and inaccessible. This part of the Rhine, indeed, presents a singularly variegated landscape. In one spot you view rugged hills,
275 ruined castles overlooking tremendous precipices, with the dark Rhine rushing beneath; and on the sudden turn of a promontory, flourishing vineyards with green sloping banks and a meandering river and populous
280 towns occupy the scene.

We travelled at the time of the vintage and heard the song of the labourers as we glided down the stream. Even I, depressed in mind, and my spirits continually agitated by gloomy
285 feelings, even I was pleased. I lay at the bottom of the boat, and as I gazed on the cloudless blue sky, I seemed to drink in a tranquillity to which I had long been a stranger. And if these were my sensations, who can describe
290 those of Henry? He felt as if he had been transported to Fairy-land and enjoyed a happiness seldom tasted by man. "I have seen," he said, "the most beautiful scenes of

my own country; I have visited the lakes of
295 Lucerne and Uri, where the snowy mountains descend almost perpendicularly to the water, casting black and impenetrable shades, which would cause a gloomy and mournful appearance were it not for the
300 most verdant islands that relieve the eye by their gay appearance; I have seen this lake agitated by a tempest, when the wind tore up whirlwinds of water and gave you an idea of what the water-spout must be on the great
305 ocean; and the waves dash with fury the base of the mountain, where the priest and his mistress were overwhelmed by an avalanche and where their dying voices are still said to be heard amid the pauses of the
310 nightly wind; I have seen the mountains of La Valais, and the Pays de Vaud; but this country, Victor, pleases me more than all those wonders. The mountains of Switzerland are more majestic and strange, but there is a
315 charm in the banks of this divine river that I never before saw equalled. Look at that castle which overhangs yon precipice; and that also on the island, almost concealed amongst the foliage of those lovely trees; and now
320 that group of labourers coming from among their vines; and that village half hid in the recess of the mountain. Oh, surely the spirit that inhabits and guards this place has a soul more in harmony with man than
325 those who pile the glacier or retire to the inaccessible peaks of the mountains of our own country."

Clerval! Beloved friend! Even now it delights me to record your words and to
330 dwell on the praise of which you are so eminently deserving. He was a being formed in the "very poetry of nature." His wild and enthusiastic imagination was chastened by the sensibility of his heart. His soul over-
335 flowed with ardent affections, and his

friendship was of that devoted and wondrous nature that the worldly-minded teach
us to look for only in the imagination. But
even human sympathies were not sufficient
340 to satisfy his eager mind. The scenery of
external nature, which others regard only
with admiration, he loved with ardour:—

> ——The sounding cataract
> Haunted him like a passion: the tall rock,
345 The mountain, and the deep and gloomy
> wood,
> Their colours and their forms, were then
> to him
> An appetite; a feeling, and a love,
> That had no need of a remoter charm,
> By thought supplied, or any interest
350 Unborrow'd from the eye.
> [Wordsworth's "Tintern Abbey".]

And where does he now exist? Is this gentle and lovely being lost for ever? Has this
mind, so replete with ideas, imaginations
355 fanciful and magnificent, which formed a
world, whose existence depended on the life
of its creator;—has this mind perished? Does
it now only exist in my memory? No, it is not
thus; your form so divinely wrought, and
360 beaming with beauty, has decayed, but your
spirit still visits and consoles your unhappy
friend.

Pardon this gush of sorrow; these ineffectual words are but a slight tribute to the
365 unexampled worth of Henry, but they soothe
my heart, overflowing with the anguish
which his remembrance creates. I will proceed with my tale.

Beyond Cologne we descended to the
370 plains of Holland; and we resolved to post
the remainder of our way, for the wind was
contrary and the stream of the river was too
gentle to aid us.

Our journey here lost the interest arising
375 from beautiful scenery, but we arrived in a

few days at Rotterdam, whence we proceeded by sea to England. It was on a clear
morning, in the latter days of December, that
I first saw the white cliffs of Britain. The
380 banks of the Thames presented a new scene;
they were flat but fertile, and almost every
town was marked by the remembrance of
some story. We saw Tilbury Fort and remembered the Spanish Armada, Gravesend,
385 Woolwich, and Greenwich—places which I
had heard of even in my country.

At length we saw the numerous steeples
of London, St. Paul's towering above all, and
the Tower famed in English history.

Chapter 19

390 London was our present point of rest; we
determined to remain several months in
this wonderful and celebrated city. Clerval
desired the intercourse of the men of genius
and talent who flourished at this time, but
395 this was with me a secondary object; I was
principally occupied with the means of
obtaining the information necessary for the
completion of my promise and quickly
availed myself of the letters of introduction
400 that I had brought with me, addressed to the
most distinguished natural philosophers.

If this journey had taken place during my
days of study and happiness, it would have
afforded me inexpressible pleasure. But a
405 blight had come over my existence, and I
only visited these people for the sake of the
information they might give me on the subject in which my interest was so terribly profound. Company was irksome to me; when
410 alone, I could fill my mind with the sights of
heaven and earth; the voice of Henry soothed
me, and I could thus cheat myself into a
transitory peace. But busy, uninteresting,
joyous faces brought back despair to my
415 heart. I saw an insurmountable barrier

placed between me and my fellow men; this barrier was sealed with the blood of William and Justine, and to reflect on the events connected with those names filled my soul
420 with anguish.

But in Clerval I saw the image of my former self; he was inquisitive and anxious to gain experience and instruction. The difference of manners which he observed was to
425 him an inexhaustible source of instruction and amusement. He was also pursuing an object he had long had in view. His design was to visit India, in the belief that he had in his knowledge of its various languages, and
430 in the views he had taken of its society, the means of materially assisting the progress of European colonization and trade. In Britain only could he further the execution of his plan. He was for ever busy, and the only
435 check to his enjoyments was my sorrowful and dejected mind. I tried to conceal this as much as possible, that I might not debar him from the pleasures natural to one who was entering on a new scene of life, undisturbed
440 by any care or bitter recollection. I often refused to accompany him, alleging another engagement, that I might remain alone. I now also began to collect the materials necessary for my new creation, and this was to
445 me like the torture of single drops of water continually falling on the head. Every thought that was devoted to it was an extreme anguish, and every word that I spoke in allusion to it caused my lips to
450 quiver, and my heart to palpitate.

After passing some months in London, we received a letter from a person in Scotland who had formerly been our visitor at Geneva. He mentioned the beauties of his native coun-
455 try and asked us if those were not sufficient allurements to induce us to prolong our journey as far north as Perth, where he resided.

Clerval eagerly desired to accept this invitation, and I, although I abhorred society,
460 wished to view again mountains and streams and all the wondrous works with which Nature adorns her chosen dwelling-places.

We had arrived in England at the beginning of October, and it was now February. We
465 accordingly determined to commence our journey towards the north at the expiration of another month. In this expedition we did not intend to follow the great road to Edinburgh, but to visit Windsor, Oxford,
470 Matlock, and the Cumberland lakes, resolving to arrive at the completion of this tour about the end of July. I packed up my chemical instruments and the materials I had collected, resolving to finish my labours in
475 some obscure nook in the northern highlands of Scotland.

We quitted London on the 27th of March and remained a few days at Windsor, rambling in its beautiful forest. This was a new
480 scene to us mountaineers; the majestic oaks, the quantity of game, and the herds of stately deer were all novelties to us.

From thence we proceeded to Oxford. As we entered this city, our minds were filled
485 with the remembrance of the events that had been transacted there more than a century and a half before. It was here that Charles I. had collected his forces. This city had remained faithful to him, after the
490 whole nation had forsaken his cause to join the standard of Parliament and liberty. The memory of that unfortunate king and his companions, the amiable Falkland, the insolent Goring, his queen, and son, gave a
495 peculiar interest to every part of the city which they might be supposed to have inhabited. The spirit of elder days found a dwelling here, and we delighted to trace its footsteps. If these feelings had not found an

500 imaginary gratification, the appearance of the city had yet in itself sufficient beauty to obtain our admiration. The colleges are ancient and picturesque; the streets are almost magnificent; and the lovely Isis,
505 which flows beside it through meadows of exquisite verdure, is spread forth into a placid expanse of waters, which reflects its majestic assemblage of towers, and spires, and domes, embosomed among aged trees.

510 I enjoyed this scene, and yet my enjoyment was embittered both by the memory of the past and the anticipation of the future. I was formed for peaceful happiness. During my youthful days discontent never visited
515 my mind, and if I was ever overcome by ennui, the sight of what is beautiful in nature or the study of what is excellent and sublime in the productions of man could always interest my heart and communicate elastic-
520 ity to my spirits. But I am a blasted tree; the bolt has entered my soul; and I felt then that I should survive to exhibit what I shall soon cease to be—a miserable spectacle of wrecked humanity, pitiable to others and
525 intolerable to myself.

We passed a considerable period at Oxford, rambling among its environs and endeavouring to identify every spot which might relate to the most animating epoch of
530 English history. Our little voyages of discovery were often prolonged by the successive objects that presented themselves. We visited the tomb of the illustrious Hampden and the field on which that patriot fell. For a
535 moment my soul was elevated from its debasing and miserable fears to contemplate the divine ideas of liberty and self-sacrifice of which these sights were the monuments and the remembrancers. For an instant I
540 dared to shake off my chains and look around me with a free and lofty spirit, but

the iron had eaten into my flesh, and I sank again, trembling and hopeless, into my miserable self.

545 We left Oxford with regret and proceeded to Matlock, which was our next place of rest. The country in the neighbourhood of this village resembled, to a greater degree, the scenery of Switzerland; but everything is on
550 a lower scale, and the green hills want the crown of distant white Alps which always attend on the piny mountains of my native country. We visited the wondrous cave and the little cabinets of natural history, where
555 the curiosities are disposed in the same manner as in the collections at Servox and Chamounix. The latter name made me tremble when pronounced by Henry, and I hastened to quit Matlock, with which that
560 terrible scene was thus associated.

From Derby, still journeying northwards, we passed two months in Cumberland and Westmorland. I could now almost fancy myself among the Swiss mountains. The lit-
565 tle patches of snow which yet lingered on the northern sides of the mountains, the lakes, and the dashing of the rocky streams were all familiar and dear sights to me. Here also we made some acquaintances, who almost
570 contrived to cheat me into happiness. The delight of Clerval was proportionably greater than mine; his mind expanded in the company of men of talent, and he found in his own nature greater capacities and resources
575 than he could have imagined himself to have possessed while he associated with his inferiors. "I could pass my life here," said he to me; "and among these mountains I should scarcely regret Switzerland and the Rhine."
580 But he found that a traveller's life is one that includes much pain amidst its enjoyments. His feelings are for ever on the stretch; and when he begins to sink into repose, he finds

himself obliged to quit that on which he rests
585 in pleasure for something new, which again
engages his attention, and which also he for-
sakes for other novelties.

     We had scarcely visited the various lakes
of Cumberland and Westmorland and con-
590 ceived an affection for some of the inhabitants when the period of our appointment
with our Scotch friend approached, and we
left them to travel on. For my own part I was
not sorry. I had now neglected my promise
595 for some time, and I feared the effects of the
dæmon's disappointment. He might remain
in Switzerland and wreak his vengeance on
my relatives. This idea pursued me and tormented me at every moment from which I
600 might otherwise have snatched repose and
peace. I waited for my letters with feverish
impatience; if they were delayed I was miserable and overcome by a thousand fears; and
when they arrived and I saw the superscrip-
605 tion of Elizabeth or my father, I hardly dared
to read and ascertain my fate. Sometimes I
thought that the fiend followed me and
might expedite my remissness by murdering
my companion. When these thoughts pos-
610 sessed me, I would not quit Henry for a
moment, but followed him as his shadow, to
protect him from the fancied rage of his
destroyer. I felt as if I had committed some
great crime, the consciousness of which
615 haunted me. I was guiltless, but I had indeed
drawn down a horrible curse upon my head,
as mortal as that of crime.

     I visited Edinburgh with languid eyes and
mind; and yet that city might have interested
620 the most unfortunate being. Clerval did not
like it so well as Oxford, for the antiquity of
the latter city was more pleasing to him. But
the beauty and regularity of the new town of
Edinburgh, its romantic castle and its
625 environs, the most delightful in the world,

Arthur's Seat, St. Bernard's Well, and the
Pentland Hills, compensated him for the
change and filled him with cheerfulness and
admiration. But I was impatient to arrive at
630 the termination of my journey.

     We left Edinburgh in a week, passing
through Coupar, St. Andrew's, and along the
banks of the Tay, to Perth, where our friend
expected us. But I was in no mood to laugh
635 and talk with strangers or enter into their
feelings or plans with the good humour
expected from a guest; and accordingly I told
Clerval that I wished to make the tour of
Scotland alone. "Do you," said I, "enjoy your-
640 self, and let this be our rendezvous. I may be
absent a month or two; but do not interfere
with my motions, I entreat you; leave me to
peace and solitude for a short time; and
when I return, I hope it will be with a lighter
645 heart, more congenial to your own temper."

     Henry wished to dissuade me, but seeing
me bent on this plan, ceased to remonstrate.
He entreated me to write often. "I had rather
be with you," he said, "in your solitary ram-
650 bles, than with these Scotch people, whom I
do not know; hasten, then, my dear friend, to
return, that I may again feel myself somewhat at home, which I cannot do in your
absence."

655   Having parted from my friend, I determined to visit some remote spot of Scotland
and finish my work in solitude. I did not
doubt but that the monster followed me and
would discover himself to me when I should
660 have finished, that he might receive his
companion.

     With this resolution I traversed the north-
ern highlands and fixed on one of the remot-
est of the Orkneys as the scene of my labours.
665 It was a place fitted for such a work, being
hardly more than a rock whose high sides
were continually beaten upon by the waves.

The soil was barren, scarcely affording pasture for a few miserable cows, and oatmeal for its inhabitants, which consisted of five persons, whose gaunt and scraggy limbs gave tokens of their miserable fare. Vegetables and bread, when they indulged in such luxuries, and even fresh water, was to be procured from the mainland, which was about five miles distant.

On the whole island there were but three miserable huts, and one of these was vacant when I arrived. This I hired. It contained but two rooms, and these exhibited all the squalidness of the most miserable penury. The thatch had fallen in, the walls were unplastered, and the door was off its hinges. I ordered it to be repaired, bought some furniture, and took possession, an incident which would doubtless have occasioned some surprise had not all the senses of the cottagers been benumbed by want and squalid poverty. As it was, I lived ungazed at and unmolested, hardly thanked for the pittance of food and clothes which I gave, so much does suffering blunt even the coarsest sensations of men.

In this retreat I devoted the morning to labour; but in the evening, when the weather permitted, I walked on the stony beach of the sea to listen to the waves as they roared and dashed at my feet. It was a monotonous yet ever-changing scene. I thought of Switzerland; it was far different from this desolate and appalling landscape. Its hills are covered with vines, and its cottages are scattered thickly in the plains. Its fair lakes reflect a blue and gentle sky, and when troubled by the winds, their tumult is but as the play of a lively infant when compared to the roarings of the giant ocean.

In this manner I distributed my occupations when I first arrived, but as I proceeded in my labour, it became every day more horrible and irksome to me. Sometimes I could not prevail on myself to enter my laboratory for several days, and at other times I toiled day and night in order to complete my work. It was, indeed, a filthy process in which I was engaged. During my first experiment, a kind of enthusiastic frenzy had blinded me to the horror of my employment; my mind was intently fixed on the consummation of my labour, and my eyes were shut to the horror of my proceedings. But now I went to it in cold blood, and my heart often sickened at the work of my hands.

Thus situated, employed in the most detestable occupation, immersed in a solitude where nothing could for an instant call my attention from the actual scene in which I was engaged, my spirits became unequal; I grew restless and nervous. Every moment I feared to meet my persecutor. Sometimes I sat with my eyes fixed on the ground, fearing to raise them lest they should encounter the object which I so much dreaded to behold. I feared to wander from the sight of my fellow creatures lest when alone he should come to claim his companion.

In the mean time I worked on, and my labour was already considerably advanced. I looked towards its completion with a tremulous and eager hope, which I dared not trust myself to question but which was intermixed with obscure forebodings of evil that made my heart sicken in my bosom.

Chapter 20

I sat one evening in my laboratory; the sun had set, and the moon was just rising from the sea; I had not sufficient light for my employment, and I remained idle, in a pause of consideration of whether I should leave my labour for the night or hasten its conclusion by an unremitting attention to it. As I sat, a train of reflection occurred to me which led

750 me to consider the effects of what I was now
doing. Three years before, I was engaged in
the same manner and had created a fiend
whose unparalleled barbarity had desolated
my heart and filled it for ever with the bitter-
755 est remorse. I was now about to form
another being of whose dispositions I was
alike ignorant; she might become ten thousand times more malignant than her mate
and delight, for its own sake, in murder and
760 wretchedness. He had sworn to quit the
neighbourhood of man and hide himself in
deserts, but she had not; and she, who in all
probability was to become a thinking and
reasoning animal, might refuse to comply
765 with a compact made before her creation.
They might even hate each other; the creature who already lived loathed his own
deformity, and might he not conceive a
greater abhorrence for it when it came before
770 his eyes in the female form? She also might
turn with disgust from him to the superior
beauty of man; she might quit him, and he
be again alone, exasperated by the fresh
provocation of being deserted by one of his
775 own species.

Even if they were to leave Europe and
inhabit the deserts of the new world, yet one
of the first results of those sympathies for
which the dæmon thirsted would be children,
780 and a race of devils would be propagated
upon the earth who might make the very
existence of the species of man a condition
precarious and full of terror. Had I right, for
my own benefit, to inflict this curse upon
785 everlasting generations? I had before been
moved by the sophisms of the being I had
created; I had been struck senseless by his
fiendish threats; but now, for the first time,
the wickedness of my promise burst upon
790 me; I shuddered to think that future ages
might curse me as their pest, whose selfishness

had not hesitated to buy its own peace at the
price, perhaps, of the existence of the whole
human race.

795   I trembled and my heart failed within me,
when, on looking up, I saw by the light of the
moon the dæmon at the casement. A ghastly
grin wrinkled his lips as he gazed on me,
where I sat fulfilling the task which he had
800 allotted to me. Yes, he had followed me in
my travels; he had loitered in forests, hid
himself in caves, or taken refuge in wide and
desert heaths; and he now came to mark my
progress and claim the fulfilment of my
805 promise.

As I looked on him, his countenance
expressed the utmost extent of malice and
treachery. I thought with a sensation of
madness on my promise of creating another
810 like to him, and trembling with passion, tore
to pieces the thing on which I was engaged.
The wretch saw me destroy the creature on
whose future existence he depended for
happiness, and with a howl of devilish
815 despair and revenge, withdrew.

I left the room, and locking the door, made
a solemn vow in my own heart never to
resume my labours; and then, with trembling
steps, I sought my own apartment. I was
820 alone; none were near me to dissipate the
gloom and relieve me from the sickening
oppression of the most terrible reveries.

Several hours passed, and I remained near
my window gazing on the sea; it was almost
825 motionless, for the winds were hushed, and
all nature reposed under the eye of the quiet
moon. A few fishing vessels alone specked
the water, and now and then the gentle
breeze wafted the sound of voices as the
830 fishermen called to one another. I felt the
silence, although I was hardly conscious of
its extreme profundity, until my ear was suddenly arrested by the paddling of oars near

the shore, and a person landed close to my
835 house.

In a few minutes after, I heard the creaking of my door, as if some one endeavoured
to open it softly. I trembled from head to
foot; I felt a presentiment of who it was and
840 wished to rouse one of the peasants who
dwelt in a cottage not far from mine; but I
was overcome by the sensation of helplessness, so often felt in frightful dreams, when
you in vain endeavour to fly from an impend-
845 ing danger, and was rooted to the spot.

Presently I heard the sound of footsteps
along the passage; the door opened, and the
wretch whom I dreaded appeared. Shutting
the door, he approached me and said in a
850 smothered voice,

"You have destroyed the work which you
began; what is it that you intend? Do you
dare to break your promise? I have endured
toil and misery; I left Switzerland with you; I
855 crept along the shores of the Rhine, among
its willow islands and over the summits of
its hills. I have dwelt many months in the
heaths of England and among the deserts of
Scotland. I have endured incalculable fatigue,
860 and cold, and hunger; do you dare destroy
my hopes?"

"Begone! I do break my promise; never
will I create another like yourself, equal in
deformity and wickedness."

865 "Slave, I before reasoned with you, but you
have proved yourself unworthy of my condescension. Remember that I have power; you
believe yourself miserable, but I can make
you so wretched that the light of day will be
870 hateful to you. You are my creator, but I am
your master; obey!"

"The hour of my irresolution is past, and
the period of your power is arrived. Your
threats cannot move me to do an act of
875 wickedness; but they confirm me in a

determination of not creating you a companion in vice. Shall I, in cool blood, set
loose upon the earth a dæmon whose
delight is in death and wretchedness?
880 Begone! I am firm, and your words will
only exasperate my rage."

The monster saw my determination in my
face and gnashed his teeth in the impotence
of anger. "Shall each man," cried he, "find a
885 wife for his bosom, and each beast have his
mate, and I be alone? I had feelings of affection, and they were requited by detestation
and scorn. Man! You may hate, but beware!
Your hours will pass in dread and misery,
890 and soon the bolt will fall which must ravish
from you your happiness for ever. Are you to
be happy while I grovel in the intensity of my
wretchedness? You can blast my other passions, but revenge remains—revenge, hence-
895 forth dearer than light or food! I may die, but
first you, my tyrant and tormentor, shall
curse the sun that gazes on your misery.
Beware, for I am fearless and therefore powerful. I will watch with the wiliness of a
900 snake, that I may sting with its venom. Man,
you shall repent of the injuries you inflict."

"Devil, cease; and do not poison the air with
these sounds of malice. I have declared my
resolution to you, and I am no coward to bend
905 beneath words. Leave me; I am inexorable."

"It is well. I go; but remember, I shall be
with you on your wedding-night."

I started forward and exclaimed, "Villain!
Before you sign my death-warrant, be sure
910 that you are yourself safe."

I would have seized him, but he eluded me
and quitted the house with precipitation. In a
few moments I saw him in his boat, which
shot across the waters with an arrowy swift-
915 ness and was soon lost amidst the waves.

All was again silent, but his words rang
in my ears. I burned with rage to pursue the

murderer of my peace and precipitate him into the ocean. I walked up and down my room hastily and perturbed, while my imagination conjured up a thousand images to torment and sting me. Why had I not followed him and closed with him in mortal strife? But I had suffered him to depart, and he had directed his course towards the mainland. I shuddered to think who might be the next victim sacrificed to his insatiate revenge. And then I thought again of his words—"*I will be with you on your wedding-night.*" That, then, was the period fixed for the fulfilment of my destiny. In that hour I should die and at once satisfy and extinguish his malice. The prospect did not move me to fear; yet when I thought of my beloved Elizabeth, of her tears and endless sorrow, when she should find her lover so barbarously snatched from her, tears, the first I had shed for many months, streamed from my eyes, and I resolved not to fall before my enemy without a bitter struggle.

The night passed away, and the sun rose from the ocean; my feelings became calmer, if it may be called calmness when the violence of rage sinks into the depths of despair. I left the house, the horrid scene of the last night's contention, and walked on the beach of the sea, which I almost regarded as an insuperable barrier between me and my fellow creatures; nay, a wish that such should prove the fact stole across me. I desired that I might pass my life on that barren rock, wearily, it is true, but uninterrupted by any sudden shock of misery. If I returned, it was to be sacrificed or to see those whom I most loved die under the grasp of a dæmon whom I had myself created.

I walked about the isle like a restless spectre, separated from all it loved and

miserable in the separation. When it became noon, and the sun rose higher, I lay down on the grass and was overpowered by a deep sleep. I had been awake the whole of the preceding night, my nerves were agitated, and my eyes inflamed by watching and misery. The sleep into which I now sank refreshed me; and when I awoke, I again felt as if I belonged to a race of human beings like myself, and I began to reflect upon what had passed with greater composure; yet still the words of the fiend rang in my ears like a death-knell; they appeared like a dream, yet distinct and oppressive as a reality.

The sun had far descended, and I still sat on the shore, satisfying my appetite, which had become ravenous, with an oaten cake, when I saw a fishing-boat land close to me, and one of the men brought me a packet; it contained letters from Geneva, and one from Clerval entreating me to join him. He said that he was wearing away his time fruitlessly where he was, that letters from the friends he had formed in London desired his return to complete the negotiation they had entered into for his Indian enterprise. He could not any longer delay his departure; but as his journey to London might be followed, even sooner than he now conjectured, by his longer voyage, he entreated me to bestow as much of my society on him as I could spare. He besought me, therefore, to leave my solitary isle and to meet him at Perth, that we might proceed southwards together. This letter in a degree recalled me to life, and I determined to quit my island at the expiration of two days.

Yet, before I departed, there was a task to perform, on which I shuddered to reflect; I must pack up my chemical instruments, and for that purpose I must enter the room which had been the scene of my odious work, and I must handle those utensils the sight of which was sickening to me. The next morning, at daybreak, I summoned sufficient courage and unlocked the door of my laboratory. The remains of the half-finished creature, whom I had destroyed, lay scattered on the floor, and I almost felt as if I had mangled the living flesh of a human being. I paused to collect myself and then entered the chamber. With trembling hand I conveyed the instruments out of the room, but I reflected that I ought not to leave the relics of my work to excite the horror and suspicion of the peasants; and I accordingly put them into a basket, with a great quantity of stones, and laying them up, determined to throw them into the sea that very night; and in the meantime I sat upon the beach, employed in cleaning and arranging my chemical apparatus.

Nothing could be more complete than the alteration that had taken place in my feelings since the night of the appearance of the dæmon. I had before regarded my promise with a gloomy despair as a thing that, with whatever consequences, must be fulfilled; but I now felt as if a film had been taken from before my eyes and that I for the first time saw clearly. The idea of renewing my labours did not for one instant occur to me; the threat I had heard weighed on my thoughts, but I did not reflect that a voluntary act of mine could avert it. I had resolved in my own mind that to create another like the fiend I had first made would be an act of the basest and most atrocious selfishness, and I banished from my mind every thought that could lead to a different conclusion.

Between two and three in the morning the moon rose; and I then, putting my basket aboard a little skiff, sailed out about four miles from the shore. The scene was perfectly solitary; a few boats were returning towards land, but I sailed away from them.

I felt as if I was about the commission of a dreadful crime and avoided with shuddering anxiety any encounter with my fellow creatures. At one time the moon, which had before been clear, was suddenly overspread by a thick cloud, and I took advantage of the moment of darkness and cast my basket into the sea; I listened to the gurgling sound as it sank and then sailed away from the spot. The sky became clouded, but the air was pure, although chilled by the northeast breeze that was then rising. But it refreshed me and filled me with such agreeable sensations that I resolved to prolong my stay on the water, and fixing the rudder in a direct position, stretched myself at the bottom of the boat. Clouds hid the moon, everything was obscure, and I heard only the sound of the boat as its keel cut through the waves; the murmur lulled me, and in a short time I slept soundly.

I do not know how long I remained in this situation, but when I awoke I found that the sun had already mounted considerably. The wind was high, and the waves continually threatened the safety of my little skiff. I found that the wind was northeast and must have driven me far from the coast from which I had embarked. I endeavoured to change my course but quickly found that if I again made the attempt the boat would be instantly filled with water. Thus situated, my only resource was to drive before the wind. I confess that I felt a few sensations of terror. I had no compass with me and was so slenderly acquainted with the geography of this part of the world that the sun was of little benefit to me. I might be driven into the wide Atlantic and feel all the tortures of starvation or be swallowed up in the immeasurable waters that roared and buffeted around me. I had already been out many hours and felt the torment of a burning thirst, a prelude to my other sufferings. I looked on the heavens,

1090 which were covered by clouds that flew before the wind, only to be replaced by others; I looked upon the sea; it was to be my grave. "Fiend," I exclaimed, "your task is already fulfilled!" I thought of Elizabeth, of

1095 my father, and of Clerval—all left behind, on whom the monster might satisfy his sanguinary and merciless passions. This idea plunged me into a reverie so despairing and frightful that even now, when the scene is on

1100 the point of closing before me for ever, I shudder to reflect on it.

Some hours passed thus; but by degrees, as the sun declined towards the horizon, the wind died away into a gentle breeze and the

1105 sea became free from breakers. But these gave place to a heavy swell; I felt sick and hardly able to hold the rudder, when suddenly I saw a line of high land towards the south.

1110 Almost spent, as I was, by fatigue and the dreadful suspense I endured for several hours, this sudden certainty of life rushed like a flood of warm joy to my heart, and tears gushed from my eyes.

1115 How mutable are our feelings, and how strange is that clinging love we have of life even in the excess of misery! I constructed another sail with a part of my dress and eagerly steered my course towards the land.

1120 It had a wild and rocky appearance, but as I approached nearer I easily perceived the traces of cultivation. I saw vessels near the shore and found myself suddenly transported back to the neighbourhood of civilised

1125 man. I carefully traced the windings of the land and hailed a steeple which I at length saw issuing from behind a small promontory.

As I was in a state of extreme debility, I resolved to sail directly towards the town, as

1130 a place where I could most easily procure nourishment. Fortunately I had money with me. As I turned the promontory I perceived a small neat town and a good harbour, which I entered, my heart bounding with joy at my

1135 unexpected escape.

As I was occupied in fixing the boat and arranging the sails, several people crowded towards the spot. They seemed much surprised at my appearance, but instead of

1140 offering me any assistance, whispered together with gestures that at any other time might have produced in me a slight sensation of alarm. As it was, I merely remarked that they spoke English, and I therefore

1145 addressed them in that language. "My good friends," said I, "will you be so kind as to tell me the name of this town and inform me where I am?"

"You will know that soon enough," replied

1150 a man with a hoarse voice. "Maybe you are come to a place that will not prove much to your taste, but you will not be consulted as to your quarters, I promise you."

I was exceedingly surprised on receiving so

1155 rude an answer from a stranger, and I was also disconcerted on perceiving the frowning and angry countenances of his companions. "Why do you answer me so roughly?" I replied. "Surely it is not the custom of Englishmen to

1160 receive strangers so inhospitably."

"I do not know," said the man, "what the custom of the English may be, but it is the custom of the Irish to hate villains."

While this strange dialogue continued, I

1165 perceived the crowd rapidly increase. Their faces expressed a mixture of curiosity and anger, which annoyed and in some degree alarmed me. I inquired the way to the inn, but no one replied. I then moved forward,

1170 and a murmuring sound arose from the crowd as they followed and surrounded me, when an ill-looking man approaching tapped me on the shoulder and said, "Come, sir, you must follow me to Mr. Kirwin's to give an 1175 account of yourself."

"Who is Mr. Kirwin? Why am I to give an account of myself? Is not this a free country?"

"Ay, sir, free enough for honest folks. Mr. Kirwin is a magistrate, and you are to give an 1180 account of the death of a gentleman who was found murdered here last night."

This answer startled me, but I presently recovered myself. I was innocent; that could easily be proved; accordingly I followed my 1185 conductor in silence and was led to one of the best houses in the town. I was ready to sink from fatigue and hunger, but being surrounded by a crowd, I thought it politic to rouse all my strength, that no physical debil-1190 ity might be construed into apprehension or conscious guilt. Little did I then expect the calamity that was in a few moments to overwhelm me and extinguish in horror and despair all fear of ignominy or death.

1195   I must pause here, for it requires all my fortitude to recall the memory of the frightful events which I am about to relate, in proper detail, to my recollection.

Chapter 21

I was soon introduced into the presence of 1200 the magistrate, an old benevolent man with calm and mild manners. He looked upon me, however, with some degree of severity, and then, turning towards my conductors, he asked who appeared as witnesses on this 1205 occasion.

About half a dozen men came forward; and, one being selected by the magistrate, he deposed that he had been out fishing the night before with his son and brother-in-law,

1210 Daniel Nugent, when, about ten o'clock, they observed a strong northerly blast rising, and they accordingly put in for port. It was a very dark night, as the moon had not yet risen; they did not land at the harbour, but, as they 1215 had been accustomed, at a creek about two miles below. He walked on first, carrying a part of the fishing tackle, and his companions followed him at some distance. As he was proceeding along the sands, he struck 1220 his foot against something and fell at his length on the ground. His companions came up to assist him, and by the light of their lantern they found that he had fallen on the body of a man, who was to all appearance 1225 dead. Their first supposition was that it was the corpse of some person who had been drowned and was thrown on shore by the waves, but on examination they found that the clothes were not wet and even that the 1230 body was not then cold. They instantly carried it to the cottage of an old woman near the spot and endeavoured, but in vain, to restore it to life. It appeared to be a handsome young man, about five and twenty 1235 years of age. He had apparently been strangled, for there was no sign of any violence except the black mark of fingers on his neck.

The first part of this deposition did not in the least interest me, but when the mark 1240 of the fingers was mentioned I remembered the murder of my brother and felt myself extremely agitated; my limbs trembled, and a mist came over my eyes, which obliged me to lean on a chair for support. The magis-1245 trate observed me with a keen eye and of course drew an unfavourable augury from my manner.

The son confirmed his father's account, but when Daniel Nugent was called he swore 1250 positively that just before the fall of his companion, he saw a boat, with a single man in it, at a short distance from the shore; and as far as he could judge by the light of a few stars, it was the same boat in which I had 1255 just landed.

A woman deposed that she lived near the beach and was standing at the door of her cottage, waiting for the return of the fishermen, about an hour before she heard of the 1260 discovery of the body, when she saw a boat with only one man in it push off from that part of the shore where the corpse was afterwards found.

Another woman confirmed the account of 1265 the fishermen having brought the body into her house; it was not cold. They put it into a bed and rubbed it, and Daniel went to the town for an apothecary, but life was quite gone.

1270 Several other men were examined concerning my landing, and they agreed that, with the strong north wind that had arisen during the night, it was very probable that I had beaten about for many hours and had 1275 been obliged to return nearly to the same spot from which I had departed. Besides, they observed that it appeared that I had brought the body from another place, and it was likely that as I did not appear to know 1280 the shore, I might have put into the harbour ignorant of the distance of the town of—— from the place where I had deposited the corpse.

Mr. Kirwin, on hearing this evidence, 1285 desired that I should be taken into the room where the body lay for interment, that it might be observed what effect the sight of it would produce upon me. This idea was probably suggested by the extreme agitation I had 1290 exhibited when the mode of the murder had been described. I was accordingly conducted, by the magistrate and several other persons, to the inn. I could not help being struck by the strange coincidences that had taken 1295 place during this eventful night; but, knowing that I had been conversing with several persons in the island I had inhabited about the time that the body had been found, I was perfectly tranquil as to the consequences of 1300 the affair.

I entered the room where the corpse lay and was led up to the coffin. How can I describe my sensations on beholding it? I feel yet parched with horror, nor can I reflect 1305 on that terrible moment without shuddering and agony. The examination, the presence of the magistrate and witnesses, passed like a dream from my memory when I saw the lifeless form of Henry Clerval stretched before 1310 me. I gasped for breath, and throwing myself on the body, I exclaimed, "Have my murderous machinations deprived you also, my dearest Henry, of life? Two I have already destroyed; other victims await their destiny; 1315 but you, Clerval, my friend, my benefactor—"

The human frame could no longer support the agonies that I endured, and I was carried out of the room in strong convulsions.

A fever succeeded to this. I lay for two 1320 months on the point of death; my ravings, as I afterwards heard, were frightful; I called myself the murderer of William, of Justine, and of Clerval. Sometimes I entreated my attendants to assist me in the destruction of 1325 the fiend by whom I was tormented; and at others I felt the fingers of the monster already grasping my neck, and screamed aloud with agony and terror. Fortunately, as I spoke my native language, Mr. Kirwin alone understood 1330 me; but my gestures and bitter cries were sufficient to affright the other witnesses.

Why did I not die? More miserable than man ever was before, why did I not sink into forgetfulness and rest? Death snatches away 1335 many blooming children, the only hopes of

their doting parents; how many brides and youthful lovers have been one day in the bloom of health and hope, and the next a prey for worms and the decay of the tomb!
1340 Of what materials was I made that I could thus resist so many shocks, which, like the turning of the wheel, continually renewed the torture?

But I was doomed to live and in two
1345 months found myself as awaking from a dream, in a prison, stretched on a wretched bed, surrounded by gaolers, turnkeys, bolts, and all the miserable apparatus of a dungeon. It was morning, I remember, when I
1350 thus awoke to understanding; I had forgotten the particulars of what had happened and only felt as if some great misfortune had suddenly overwhelmed me; but when I looked around and saw the barred windows
1355 and the squalidness of the room in which I was, all flashed across my memory and I groaned bitterly.

This sound disturbed an old woman who was sleeping in a chair beside me. She was a
1360 hired nurse, the wife of one of the turnkeys, and her countenance expressed all those bad qualities which often characterise that class. The lines of her face were hard and rude, like that of persons accustomed to see without
1365 sympathising in sights of misery. Her tone expressed her entire indifference; she addressed me in English, and the voice struck me as one that I had heard during my sufferings.
1370 "Are you better now, sir?" said she.

I replied in the same language, with a feeble voice, "I believe I am; but if it be all true, if indeed I did not dream, I am sorry that I am still alive to feel this misery and
1375 horror."

"For that matter," replied the old woman, "if you mean about the gentleman you murdered, I believe that it were better for you if you were dead, for I fancy it will go hard
1380 with you! However, that's none of my business; I am sent to nurse you and get you well; I do my duty with a safe conscience; it were well if everybody did the same."

I turned with loathing from the woman
1385 who could utter so unfeeling a speech to a person just saved, on the very edge of death; but I felt languid and unable to reflect on all that had passed. The whole series of my life appeared to me as a dream; I sometimes
1390 doubted if indeed it were all true, for it never presented itself to my mind with the force of reality.

As the images that floated before me became more distinct, I grew feverish; a
1395 darkness pressed around me; no one was near me who soothed me with the gentle voice of love; no dear hand supported me. The physician came and prescribed medicines, and the old woman prepared them
1400 for me; but utter carelessness was visible in the first, and the expression of brutality was strongly marked in the visage of the second. Who could be interested in the fate of a murderer but the hangman who would gain
1405 his fee?

These were my first reflections, but I soon learned that Mr. Kirwin had shown me extreme kindness. He had caused the best room in the prison to be prepared for me
1410 (wretched indeed was the best); and it was he who had provided a physician and a nurse. It is true, he seldom came to see me, for although he ardently desired to relieve the sufferings of every human creature, he
1415 did not wish to be present at the agonies and miserable ravings of a murderer. He came, therefore, sometimes to see that I was not neglected, but his visits were short and with long intervals.

1420 One day, while I was gradually recovering, I was seated in a chair, my eyes half open and my cheeks livid like those in death. I was overcome by gloom and misery and often reflected I had better seek 1425 death than desire to remain in a world which to me was replete with wretchedness. At one time I considered whether I should not declare myself guilty and suffer the penalty of the law, less innocent than 1430 poor Justine had been. Such were my thoughts when the door of my apartment was opened and Mr. Kirwin entered. His countenance expressed sympathy and compassion; he drew a chair close to mine 1435 and addressed me in French,

"I fear that this place is very shocking to you; can I do anything to make you more comfortable?"

"I thank you, but all that you mention is 1440 nothing to me; on the whole earth there is no comfort which I am capable of receiving."

"I know that the sympathy of a stranger can be but of little relief to one borne down as you are by so strange a misfortune. But 1445 you will, I hope, soon quit this melancholy abode, for doubtless evidence can easily be brought to free you from the criminal charge."

"That is my least concern; I am, by a 1450 course of strange events, become the most miserable of mortals. Persecuted and tortured as I am and have been, can death be any evil to me?"

"Nothing indeed could be more unfortu-1455 nate and agonising than the strange chances that have lately occurred. You were thrown, by some surprising accident, on this shore, renowned for its hospitality, seized immediately, and charged with mur-1460 der. The first sight that was presented to your eyes was the body of your friend,

murdered in so unaccountable a manner and placed, as it were, by some fiend across your path."

1465 As Mr. Kirwin said this, notwithstanding the agitation I endured on this retrospect of my sufferings, I also felt considerable surprise at the knowledge he seemed to possess concerning me. I suppose some astonish-1470 ment was exhibited in my countenance, for Mr. Kirwin hastened to say,

"Immediately upon your being taken ill, all the papers that were on your person were brought me, and I examined them that I 1475 might discover some trace by which I could send to your relations an account of your misfortune and illness. I found several letters, and, among others, one which I discovered from its commencement to be from 1480 your father. I instantly wrote to Geneva; nearly two months have elapsed since the departure of my letter. But you are ill; even now you tremble; you are unfit for agitation of any kind."

1485 "This suspense is a thousand times worse than the most horrible event; tell me what new scene of death has been acted, and whose murder I am now to lament?"

"Your family is perfectly well," said Mr. 1490 Kirwin with gentleness; "and someone, a friend, is come to visit you."

I know not by what chain of thought the idea presented itself, but it instantly darted into my mind that the murderer had come 1495 to mock at my misery and taunt me with the death of Clerval, as a new incitement for me to comply with his hellish desires. I put my hand before my eyes, and cried out in agony,

1500 "Oh! Take him away! I cannot see him; for God's sake, do not let him enter!"

Mr. Kirwin regarded me with a troubled countenance. He could not help regarding

my exclamation as a presumption of my
1505 guilt and said in rather a severe tone,

"I should have thought, young man, that
the presence of your father would have been
welcome instead of inspiring such violent
repugnance."

1510   "My father!" cried I, while every feature
and every muscle was relaxed from anguish
to pleasure. "Is my father indeed come? How
kind, how very kind! But where is he, why
does he not hasten to me?"

1515   My change of manner surprised and
pleased the magistrate; perhaps he thought
that my former exclamation was a momentary return of delirium, and now he instantly
resumed his former benevolence. He rose
1520 and quitted the room with my nurse, and in
a moment my father entered it.

Nothing, at this moment, could have
given me greater pleasure than the arrival of
my father. I stretched out my hand to him
1525 and cried,

"Are you then safe—and Elizabeth—and
Ernest?"

My father calmed me with assurances of
their welfare and endeavoured, by dwelling
1530 on these subjects so interesting to my heart,
to raise my desponding spirits; but he soon
felt that a prison cannot be the abode of
cheerfulness. "What a place is this that you
inhabit, my son!" said he, looking mournfully
1535 at the barred windows and wretched appearance of the room. "You travelled to seek happiness, but a fatality seems to pursue you.
And poor Clerval—"

The name of my unfortunate and mur-
1540 dered friend was an agitation too great to be
endured in my weak state; I shed tears.

"Alas! Yes, my father," replied I; "some destiny of the most horrible kind hangs over me,
and I must live to fulfil it, or surely I should
1545 have died on the coffin of Henry."

We were not allowed to converse for any
length of time, for the precarious state of my
health rendered every precaution necessary
that could ensure tranquillity. Mr. Kirwin
1550 came in and insisted that my strength should
not be exhausted by too much exertion. But
the appearance of my father was to me like
that of my good angel, and I gradually recovered my health.

1555   As my sickness quitted me, I was
absorbed by a gloomy and black melancholy
that nothing could dissipate. The image of
Clerval was for ever before me, ghastly and
murdered. More than once the agitation into
1560 which these reflections threw me made my
friends dread a dangerous relapse. Alas! Why
did they preserve so miserable and detested
a life? It was surely that I might fulfil my
destiny, which is now drawing to a close.
1565 Soon, oh, very soon, will death extinguish
these throbbings and relieve me from the
mighty weight of anguish that bears me to
the dust; and, in executing the award of justice, I shall also sink to rest. Then the appear-
1570 ance of death was distant, although the wish
was ever present to my thoughts; and I often
sat for hours motionless and speechless,
wishing for some mighty revolution that
might bury me and my destroyer in its ruins.

1575   The season of the assizes approached.
I had already been three months in prison,
and although I was still weak and in continual danger of a relapse, I was obliged to
travel nearly a hundred miles to the country
1580 town where the court was held. Mr. Kirwin
charged himself with every care of collecting
witnesses and arranging my defence. I was
spared the disgrace of appearing publicly as
a criminal, as the case was not brought before
1585 the court that decides on life and death. The
grand jury rejected the bill, on its being
proved that I was on the Orkney Islands at

the hour the body of my friend was found; and a fortnight after my removal I was liberated from prison.

My father was enraptured on finding me freed from the vexations of a criminal charge, that I was again allowed to breathe the fresh atmosphere and permitted to return to my native country. I did not participate in these feelings, for to me the walls of a dungeon or a palace were alike hateful. The cup of life was poisoned for ever, and although the sun shone upon me, as upon the happy and gay of heart, I saw around me nothing but a dense and frightful darkness, penetrated by no light but the glimmer of two eyes that glared upon me. Sometimes they were the expressive eyes of Henry, languishing in death, the dark orbs nearly covered by the lids and the long black lashes that fringed them; sometimes it was the watery, clouded eyes of the monster, as I first saw them in my chamber at Ingolstadt.

My father tried to awaken in me the feelings of affection. He talked of Geneva, which I should soon visit, of Elizabeth and Ernest; but these words only drew deep groans from me. Sometimes, indeed, I felt a wish for happiness and thought with melancholy delight of my beloved cousin or longed, with a devouring maladie du pays, to see once more the blue lake and rapid Rhone, that had been so dear to me in early childhood; but my general state of feeling was a torpor in which a prison was as welcome a residence as the divinest scene in nature; and these fits were seldom interrupted but by paroxysms of anguish and despair. At these moments I often endeavoured to put an end to the existence I loathed, and it required unceasing attendance and vigilance to restrain me from committing some dreadful act of violence.

Yet one duty remained to me, the recollection of which finally triumphed over my selfish despair. It was necessary that I should return without delay to Geneva, there to watch over the lives of those I so fondly loved and to lie in wait for the murderer, that if any chance led me to the place of his concealment, or if he dared again to blast me by his presence, I might, with unfailing aim, put an end to the existence of the monstrous image which I had endued with the mockery of a soul still more monstrous. My father still desired to delay our departure, fearful that I could not sustain the fatigues of a journey, for I was a shattered wreck—the shadow of a human being. My strength was gone. I was a mere skeleton, and fever night and day preyed upon my wasted frame.

Still, as I urged our leaving Ireland with such inquietude and impatience, my father thought it best to yield. We took our passage on board a vessel bound for Havre-de-Grace and sailed with a fair wind from the Irish shores. It was midnight. I lay on the deck looking at the stars and listening to the dashing of the waves. I hailed the darkness that shut Ireland from my sight, and my pulse beat with a feverish joy when I reflected that I should soon see Geneva. The past appeared to me in the light of a frightful dream; yet the vessel in which I was, the wind that blew me from the detested shore of Ireland, and the sea which surrounded me, told me too forcibly that I was deceived by no vision and that Clerval, my friend and dearest companion, had fallen a victim to me and the monster of my creation. I repassed, in my memory, my whole life; my quiet happiness while residing with my family in Geneva, the death of my mother, and my departure for Ingolstadt. I remembered, shuddering, the mad enthusiasm that hurried me on to the

creation of my hideous enemy, and I called to mind the night in which he first lived. I was unable to pursue the train of thought; a
1675 thousand feelings pressed upon me, and I wept bitterly.

Ever since my recovery from the fever, I had been in the custom of taking every night a small quantity of laudanum, for it was by
1680 means of this drug only that I was enabled to gain the rest necessary for the preservation of life. Oppressed by the recollection of my various misfortunes, I now swallowed double my usual quantity and soon slept profoundly.
1685 But sleep did not afford me respite from thought and misery; my dreams presented a thousand objects that scared me. Towards morning I was possessed by a kind of nightmare; I felt the fiend's grasp in my neck and
1690 could not free myself from it; groans and cries rang in my ears. My father, who was watching over me, perceiving my restlessness, awoke me; the dashing waves were around, the cloudy sky above, the fiend was
1695 not here: a sense of security, a feeling that a truce was established between the present hour and the irresistible, disastrous future imparted to me a kind of calm forgetfulness, of which the human mind is by its structure
1700 peculiarly susceptible.

Chapter 22

The voyage came to an end. We landed, and proceeded to Paris. I soon found that I had overtaxed my strength and that I must repose before I could continue my journey.
1705 My father's care and attentions were indefatigable, but he did not know the origin of my sufferings and sought erroneous methods to remedy the incurable ill. He wished me to seek amusement in society. I abhorred the
1710 face of man. Oh, not abhorred! They were my brethren, my fellow beings, and I felt attracted

even to the most repulsive among them, as to creatures of an angelic nature and celestial mechanism. But I felt that I had no right
1715 to share their intercourse. I had unchained an enemy among them whose joy it was to shed their blood and to revel in their groans. How they would, each and all, abhor me and hunt me from the world, did they know my
1720 unhallowed acts and the crimes which had their source in me!

My father yielded at length to my desire to avoid society and strove by various arguments to banish my despair. Sometimes he
1725 thought that I felt deeply the degradation of being obliged to answer a charge of murder, and he endeavoured to prove to me the futility of pride.

"Alas! My father," said I, "how little do you
1730 know me. Human beings, their feelings and passions, would indeed be degraded if such a wretch as I felt pride. Justine, poor unhappy Justine, was as innocent as I, and she suffered the same charge; she died for it; and
1735 I am the cause of this—I murdered her. William, Justine, and Henry—they all died by my hands."

My father had often, during my imprisonment, heard me make the same assertion;
1740 when I thus accused myself, he sometimes seemed to desire an explanation, and at others he appeared to consider it as the offspring of delirium, and that, during my illness, some idea of this kind had presented
1745 itself to my imagination, the remembrance of which I preserved in my convalescence. I avoided explanation and maintained a continual silence concerning the wretch I had created. I had a persuasion that I should be
1750 supposed mad, and this in itself would for ever have chained my tongue. But, besides, I could not bring myself to disclose a secret which would fill my hearer with consternation

and make fear and unnatural horror the
1755 inmates of his breast. I checked, therefore, my
impatient thirst for sympathy and was silent
when I would have given the world to have
confided the fatal secret. Yet, still, words like
those I have recorded would burst uncontrol-
1760 lably from me. I could offer no explanation of
them, but their truth in part relieved the burden of my mysterious woe.

Upon this occasion my father said, with
an expression of unbounded wonder, "My
1765 dearest Victor, what infatuation is this? My
dear son, I entreat you never to make such
an assertion again."

"I am not mad," I cried energetically; "the
sun and the heavens, who have viewed my
1770 operations, can bear witness of my truth.
I am the assassin of those most innocent
victims; they died by my machinations. A
thousand times would I have shed my own
blood, drop by drop, to have saved their lives;
1775 but I could not, my father, indeed I could not
sacrifice the whole human race."

The conclusion of this speech convinced
my father that my ideas were deranged, and
he instantly changed the subject of our con-
1780 versation and endeavoured to alter the
course of my thoughts. He wished as much
as possible to obliterate the memory of the
scenes that had taken place in Ireland and
never alluded to them or suffered me to
1785 speak of my misfortunes.

As time passed away I became more calm;
misery had her dwelling in my heart, but I no
longer talked in the same incoherent manner of
my own crimes; sufficient for me was the con-
1790 sciousness of them. By the utmost self-violence
I curbed the imperious voice of wretchedness,
which sometimes desired to declare itself to the
whole world, and my manners were calmer and
more composed than they had ever been since
1795 my journey to the sea of ice.

A few days before we left Paris on our way
to Switzerland, I received the following letter
from Elizabeth:

"My dear Friend,

1800 "It gave me the greatest pleasure to
receive a letter from my uncle dated at Paris;
you are no longer at a formidable distance,
and I may hope to see you in less than a fortnight. My poor cousin, how much you must
1805 have suffered! I expect to see you looking
even more ill than when you quitted Geneva.
This winter has been passed most miserably,
tortured as I have been by anxious suspense;
yet I hope to see peace in your countenance
1810 and to find that your heart is not totally void
of comfort and tranquillity.

"Yet I fear that the same feelings now
exist that made you so miserable a year ago,
even perhaps augmented by time. I would
1815 not disturb you at this period, when so many
misfortunes weigh upon you, but a conversation that I had with my uncle previous to his
departure renders some explanation necessary before we meet.

1820 "Explanation! You may possibly say, What
can Elizabeth have to explain? If you really
say this, my questions are answered and all
my doubts satisfied. But you are distant from
me, and it is possible that you may dread
1825 and yet be pleased with this explanation;
and in a probability of this being the case, I
dare not any longer postpone writing what,
during your absence, I have often wished to
express to you but have never had the cour-
1830 age to begin.

"You well know, Victor, that our union had
been the favourite plan of your parents ever
since our infancy. We were told this when
young, and taught to look forward to it as an
1835 event that would certainly take place. We
were affectionate playfellows during childhood, and, I believe, dear and valued friends

to one another as we grew older. But as brother and sister often entertain a lively affection towards each other without desiring a more intimate union, may not such also be our case? Tell me, dearest Victor. Answer me, I conjure you by our mutual happiness, with simple truth—Do you not love another?

"You have travelled; you have spent several years of your life at Ingolstadt; and I confess to you, my friend, that when I saw you last autumn so unhappy, flying to solitude from the society of every creature, I could not help supposing that you might regret our connection and believe yourself bound in honour to fulfil the wishes of your parents, although they opposed themselves to your inclinations. But this is false reasoning. I confess to you, my friend, that I love you and that in my airy dreams of futurity you have been my constant friend and companion. But it is your happiness I desire as well as my own when I declare to you that our marriage would render me eternally miserable unless it were the dictate of your own free choice. Even now I weep to think that, borne down as you are by the cruellest misfortunes, you may stifle, by the word honour, all hope of that love and happiness which would alone restore you to yourself. I, who have so disinterested an affection for you, may increase your miseries tenfold by being an obstacle to your wishes. Ah! Victor, be assured that your cousin and playmate has too sincere a love for you not to be made miserable by this supposition. Be happy, my friend; and if you obey me in this one request, remain satisfied that nothing on earth will have the power to interrupt my tranquillity.

"Do not let this letter disturb you; do not answer tomorrow, or the next day, or even until you come, if it will give you pain. My uncle will send me news of your health, and if I see but one smile on your lips when we meet, occasioned by this or any other exertion of mine, I shall need no other happiness.

"Elizabeth Lavenza.

"Geneva, May 18th, 17—"

This letter revived in my memory what I had before forgotten, the threat of the fiend—"*I will be with you on your wedding-night!*" Such was my sentence, and on that night would the dæmon employ every art to destroy me and tear me from the glimpse of happiness which promised partly to console my sufferings. On that night he had determined to consummate his crimes by my death. Well, be it so; a deadly struggle would then assuredly take place, in which if he were victorious I should be at peace and his power over me be at an end. If he were vanquished, I should be a free man. Alas! What freedom? Such as the peasant enjoys when his family have been massacred before his eyes, his cottage burnt, his lands laid waste, and he is turned adrift, homeless, penniless, and alone, but free. Such would be my liberty except that in my Elizabeth I possessed a treasure, alas, balanced by those horrors of remorse and guilt which would pursue me until death.

Sweet and beloved Elizabeth! I read and reread her letter, and some softened feelings stole into my heart and dared to whisper paradisiacal dreams of love and joy; but the apple was already eaten, and the angel's arm bared to drive me from all hope. Yet I would die to make her happy. If the monster executed his threat, death was inevitable; yet, again, I considered whether my marriage would hasten my fate. My destruction might indeed arrive a few months sooner, but if my torturer should suspect that I postponed it, influenced by his menaces, he would surely find other and perhaps more dreadful means of revenge. He had vowed to be with me on my wedding-night, yet he did not consider that threat as binding him to peace in the meantime, for as if to show me that he was not yet satiated with blood, he had murdered Clerval immediately after the enunciation of his threats. I resolved, therefore, that if my immediate union with my cousin would conduce either to hers or my father's happiness, my adversary's designs against my life should not retard it a single hour.

In this state of mind I wrote to Elizabeth. My letter was calm and affectionate. "I fear, my beloved girl," I said, "little happiness remains for us on earth; yet all that I may one day enjoy is centred in you. Chase away your idle fears; to you alone do I consecrate my life and my endeavours for contentment. I have one secret, Elizabeth, a dreadful one; when revealed to you, it will chill your frame with horror, and then, far from being surprised at my misery, you will only wonder that I survive what I have endured. I will confide this tale of misery and terror to you the day after our marriage shall take place, for, my sweet cousin, there must be perfect confidence between us. But until then, I conjure you, do not mention or allude to it. This I most earnestly entreat, and I know you will comply."

In about a week after the arrival of Elizabeth's letter we returned to Geneva. The sweet girl welcomed me with warm affection, yet tears were in her eyes as she beheld my emaciated frame and feverish cheeks. I saw a change in her also. She was thinner and had lost much of that heavenly vivacity that had before charmed me; but her gentleness and soft looks of compassion made her a more fit companion for one blasted and miserable as I was.

The tranquillity which I now enjoyed did not endure. Memory brought madness with it, and when I thought of what had passed, a real insanity possessed me; sometimes I was furious and burnt with rage, sometimes low and despondent. I neither spoke nor looked at anyone, but sat motionless, bewildered by the multitude of miseries that overcame me.

Elizabeth alone had the power to draw me from these fits; her gentle voice would soothe me when transported by passion and inspire me with human feelings when sunk in torpor. She wept with me and for me. When reason returned, she would remonstrate and endeavour to inspire me with resignation. Ah! It is well for the unfortunate to be resigned, but for the guilty there is no peace. The agonies of remorse poison the luxury there is otherwise sometimes found in indulging the excess of grief.

Soon after my arrival my father spoke of my immediate marriage with Elizabeth. I remained silent.

"Have you, then, some other attachment?"

"None on earth. I love Elizabeth and look forward to our union with delight. Let the day therefore be fixed; and on it I will consecrate myself, in life or death, to the happiness of my cousin."

"My dear Victor, do not speak thus. Heavy misfortunes have befallen us, but let us only cling closer to what remains and transfer our love for those whom we have lost to those who yet live. Our circle will be small but bound close by the ties of affection and mutual misfortune. And when time shall have softened your despair, new and dear objects of care will be born to replace those of whom we have been so cruelly deprived."

Such were the lessons of my father. But to me the remembrance of the threat returned; nor can you wonder that, omnipotent as the fiend had yet been in his deeds of blood, I should almost regard him as invincible, and that when he had pronounced the words "I shall be with you on your wedding-night," 2010 I should regard the threatened fate as unavoidable. But death was no evil to me if the loss of Elizabeth were balanced with it, and I therefore, with a contented and even cheerful countenance, agreed with my father 2015 that if my cousin would consent, the ceremony should take place in ten days, and thus put, as I imagined, the seal to my fate.

Great God! If for one instant I had thought what might be the hellish intention of my 2020 fiendish adversary, I would rather have banished myself for ever from my native country and wandered a friendless outcast over the earth than have consented to this miserable marriage. But, as if possessed of magic pow- 2025 ers, the monster had blinded me to his real intentions; and when I thought that I had prepared only my own death, I hastened that of a far dearer victim.

As the period fixed for our marriage drew 2030 nearer, whether from cowardice or a prophetic feeling, I felt my heart sink within me. But I concealed my feelings by an appearance of hilarity that brought smiles and joy to the countenance of my father, but hardly 2035 deceived the ever-watchful and nicer eye of Elizabeth. She looked forward to our union with placid contentment, not unmingled with a little fear, which past misfortunes had impressed, that what now appeared certain 2040 and tangible happiness might soon dissipate into an airy dream and leave no trace but deep and everlasting regret.

Preparations were made for the event, congratulatory visits were received, and all wore a 2045 smiling appearance. I shut up, as well as I could, in my own heart the anxiety that preyed there and entered with seeming earnestness

into the plans of my father, although they might only serve as the decorations of my 2050 tragedy. Through my father's exertions a part of the inheritance of Elizabeth had been restored to her by the Austrian government. A small possession on the shores of Como belonged to her. It was agreed that, immedi- 2055 ately after our union, we should proceed to Villa Lavenza and spend our first days of happiness beside the beautiful lake near which it stood.

In the meantime I took every precaution 2060 to defend my person in case the fiend should openly attack me. I carried pistols and a dagger constantly about me and was ever on the watch to prevent artifice, and by these means gained a greater degree of tranquillity. 2065 Indeed, as the period approached, the threat appeared more as a delusion, not to be regarded as worthy to disturb my peace, while the happiness I hoped for in my marriage wore a greater appearance of certainty 2070 as the day fixed for its solemnisation drew nearer and I heard it continually spoken of as an occurrence which no accident could possibly prevent.

Elizabeth seemed happy; my tranquil 2075 demeanour contributed greatly to calm her mind. But on the day that was to fulfil my wishes and my destiny, she was melancholy, and a presentiment of evil pervaded her; and perhaps also she thought of the dreadful 2080 secret which I had promised to reveal to her on the following day. My father was in the meantime overjoyed, and, in the bustle of preparation, only recognised in the melancholy of his niece the diffidence of a bride.

2085 After the ceremony was performed a large party assembled at my father's, but it was agreed that Elizabeth and I should commence our journey by water, sleeping that night at Evian and continuing our voyage on

2090 the following day. The day was fair, the wind favourable; all smiled on our nuptial embarkation.

Those were the last moments of my life during which I enjoyed the feeling of happi-2095 ness. We passed rapidly along; the sun was hot, but we were sheltered from its rays by a kind of canopy while we enjoyed the beauty of the scene, sometimes on one side of the lake, where we saw Mont Salêve, the pleas-2100 ant banks of Montalègre, and at a distance, surmounting all, the beautiful Mont Blanc, and the assemblage of snowy mountains that in vain endeavour to emulate her; some-times coasting the opposite banks, we saw 2105 the mighty Jura opposing its dark side to the ambition that would quit its native country, and an almost insurmountable barrier to the invader who should wish to enslave it.

I took the hand of Elizabeth. "You are sor-2110 rowful, my love. Ah! If you knew what I have suffered and what I may yet endure, you would endeavour to let me taste the quiet and freedom from despair that this one day at least permits me to enjoy."

2115 "Be happy, my dear Victor," replied Elizabeth; "there is, I hope, nothing to dis-tress you; and be assured that if a lively joy is not painted in my face, my heart is con-tented. Something whispers to me not to 2120 depend too much on the prospect that is opened before us, but I will not listen to such a sinister voice. Observe how fast we move along and how the clouds, which sometimes obscure and sometimes rise above the dome 2125 of Mont Blanc, render this scene of beauty still more interesting. Look also at the innu-merable fish that are swimming in the clear waters, where we can distinguish every peb-ble that lies at the bottom. What a divine 2130 day! How happy and serene all nature appears!"

Thus Elizabeth endeavoured to divert her thoughts and mine from all reflection upon melancholy subjects. But her temper was 2135 fluctuating; joy for a few instants shone in her eyes, but it continually gave place to dis-traction and reverie.

The sun sank lower in the heavens; we passed the river Drance and observed its 2140 path through the chasms of the higher and the glens of the lower hills. The Alps here come closer to the lake, and we approached the amphitheatre of mountains which forms its eastern boundary. The spire of Evian 2145 shone under the woods that surrounded it and the range of mountain above mountain by which it was overhung.

The wind, which had hitherto carried us along with amazing rapidity, sank at sunset 2150 to a light breeze; the soft air just ruffled the water and caused a pleasant motion among the trees as we approached the shore, from which it wafted the most delightful scent of flowers and hay. The sun sank beneath the 2155 horizon as we landed, and as I touched the shore I felt those cares and fears revive which soon were to clasp me and cling to me for ever.

Chapter 23

It was eight o'clock when we landed; we 2160 walked for a short time on the shore, enjoy-ing the transitory light, and then retired to the inn and contemplated the lovely scene of waters, woods, and mountains, obscured in darkness, yet still displaying their black 2165 outlines.

The wind, which had fallen in the south, now rose with great violence in the west. The moon had reached her summit in the heav-ens and was beginning to descend; the clouds 2170 swept across it swifter than the flight of the vulture and dimmed her rays, while the lake reflected the scene of the busy heavens, rendered still busier by the restless waves that were beginning to rise. Suddenly a heavy 2175 storm of rain descended.

I had been calm during the day, but so soon as night obscured the shapes of objects, a thousand fears arose in my mind. I was anxious and watchful, while my right hand 2180 grasped a pistol which was hidden in my bosom; every sound terrified me, but I resolved that I would sell my life dearly and not shrink from the conflict until my own life or that of my adversary was 2185 extinguished.

Elizabeth observed my agitation for some time in timid and fearful silence, but there was something in my glance which communicated terror to her, and trembling, she 2190 asked, "What is it that agitates you, my dear Victor? What is it you fear?"

"Oh! Peace, peace, my love," replied I; "this night, and all will be safe; but this night is dreadful, very dreadful."

2195   I passed an hour in this state of mind, when suddenly I reflected how fearful the combat which I momentarily expected would be to my wife, and I earnestly entreated her to retire, resolving not to join 2200 her until I had obtained some knowledge as to the situation of my enemy.

She left me, and I continued some time walking up and down the passages of the house and inspecting every corner that 2205 might afford a retreat to my adversary. But I discovered no trace of him and was beginning to conjecture that some fortunate chance had intervened to prevent the execution of his menaces when suddenly I heard a 2210 shrill and dreadful scream. It came from the room into which Elizabeth had retired. As I heard it, the whole truth rushed into my mind, my arms dropped, the motion of every

muscle and fibre was suspended; I could feel 2215 the blood trickling in my veins and tingling in the extremities of my limbs. This state lasted but for an instant; the scream was repeated, and I rushed into the room.

Great God! Why did I not then expire! Why 2220 am I here to relate the destruction of the best hope and the purest creature on earth? She was there, lifeless and inanimate, thrown across the bed, her head hanging down and her pale and distorted features half covered 2225 by her hair. Everywhere I turn I see the same figure—her bloodless arms and relaxed form flung by the murderer on its bridal bier. Could I behold this and live? Alas! Life is obstinate and clings closest where it is most 2230 hated. For a moment only did I lose recollection; I fell senseless on the ground.

When I recovered I found myself surrounded by the people of the inn; their countenances expressed a breathless terror, but 2235 the horror of others appeared only as a mockery, a shadow of the feelings that oppressed me. I escaped from them to the room where lay the body of Elizabeth, my love, my wife, so lately living, so dear, so wor- 2240 thy. She had been moved from the posture in which I had first beheld her, and now, as she lay, her head upon her arm and a handkerchief thrown across her face and neck, I might have supposed her asleep. I rushed 2245 towards her and embraced her with ardour, but the deadly languor and coldness of the limbs told me that what I now held in my arms had ceased to be the Elizabeth whom I had loved and cherished. The murderous 2250 mark of the fiend's grasp was on her neck, and the breath had ceased to issue from her lips.

While I still hung over her in the agony of despair, I happened to look up. The windows 2255 of the room had before been darkened, and

I felt a kind of panic on seeing the pale yellow light of the moon illuminate the chamber. The shutters had been thrown back, and with a sensation of horror not to be
2260 described, I saw at the open window a figure the most hideous and abhorred. A grin was on the face of the monster; he seemed to jeer, as with his fiendish finger he pointed towards the corpse of my wife. I rushed
2265 towards the window, and drawing a pistol from my bosom, fired; but he eluded me, leaped from his station, and running with the swiftness of lightning, plunged into the lake.

The report of the pistol brought a crowd
2270 into the room. I pointed to the spot where he had disappeared, and we followed the track with boats; nets were cast, but in vain. After passing several hours, we returned hopeless, most of my companions believing it to have
2275 been a form conjured up by my fancy. After having landed, they proceeded to search the country, parties going in different directions among the woods and vines.

I attempted to accompany them and pro-
2280 ceeded a short distance from the house, but my head whirled round, my steps were like those of a drunken man, I fell at last in a state of utter exhaustion; a film covered my eyes, and my skin was parched with the heat
2285 of fever. In this state I was carried back and placed on a bed, hardly conscious of what had happened; my eyes wandered round the room as if to seek something that I had lost.

After an interval I arose, and as if by
2290 instinct, crawled into the room where the corpse of my beloved lay. There were women weeping around; I hung over it and joined my sad tears to theirs; all this time no distinct idea presented itself to my mind, but
2295 my thoughts rambled to various subjects, reflecting confusedly on my misfortunes and their cause. I was bewildered, in a cloud of

wonder and horror. The death of William, the execution of Justine, the murder of Clerval,
2300 and lastly of my wife; even at that moment I knew not that my only remaining friends were safe from the malignity of the fiend; my father even now might be writhing under his grasp, and Ernest might be dead at his feet.
2305 This idea made me shudder and recalled me to action. I started up and resolved to return to Geneva with all possible speed.

There were no horses to be procured, and I must return by the lake; but the wind was
2310 unfavourable, and the rain fell in torrents. However, it was hardly morning, and I might reasonably hope to arrive by night. I hired men to row and took an oar myself, for I had always experienced relief from mental tor-
2315 ment in bodily exercise. But the overflowing misery I now felt, and the excess of agitation that I endured rendered me incapable of any exertion. I threw down the oar, and leaning my head upon my hands, gave way to every
2320 gloomy idea that arose. If I looked up, I saw scenes which were familiar to me in my happier time and which I had contemplated but the day before in the company of her who was now but a shadow and a recollection.
2325 Tears streamed from my eyes. The rain had ceased for a moment, and I saw the fish play in the waters as they had done a few hours before; they had then been observed by Elizabeth. Nothing is so painful to the
2330 human mind as a great and sudden change. The sun might shine or the clouds might lower, but nothing could appear to me as it had done the day before. A fiend had snatched from me every hope of future hap-
2335 piness; no creature had ever been so miserable as I was; so frightful an event is single in the history of man.

But why should I dwell upon the incidents that followed this last overwhelming event?

2340 Mine has been a tale of horrors; I have reached their acme, and what I must now relate can but be tedious to you. Know that, one by one, my friends were snatched away; I was left desolate. My own strength is 2345 exhausted, and I must tell, in a few words, what remains of my hideous narration.

I arrived at Geneva. My father and Ernest yet lived, but the former sunk under the tidings that I bore. I see him now, excellent and 2350 venerable old man! His eyes wandered in vacancy, for they had lost their charm and their delight—his Elizabeth, his more than daughter, whom he doted on with all that affection which a man feels, who in the 2355 decline of life, having few affections, clings more earnestly to those that remain. Cursed, cursed be the fiend that brought misery on his grey hairs and doomed him to waste in wretchedness! He could not live under the 2360 horrors that were accumulated around him; the springs of existence suddenly gave way; he was unable to rise from his bed, and in a few days he died in my arms.

What then became of me? I know not; I 2365 lost sensation, and chains and darkness were the only objects that pressed upon me. Sometimes, indeed, I dreamt that I wandered in flowery meadows and pleasant vales with the friends of my youth, but I awoke and 2370 found myself in a dungeon. Melancholy followed, but by degrees I gained a clear conception of my miseries and situation and was then released from my prison. For they had called me mad, and during many 2375 months, as I understood, a solitary cell had been my habitation.

Liberty, however, had been a useless gift to me, had I not, as I awakened to reason, at the same time awakened to revenge. As the 2380 memory of past misfortunes pressed upon me, I began to reflect on their cause—the

monster whom I had created, the miserable dæmon whom I had sent abroad into the world for my destruction. I was possessed by 2385 a maddening rage when I thought of him, and desired and ardently prayed that I might have him within my grasp to wreak a great and signal revenge on his cursed head.

Nor did my hate long confine itself to use- 2390 less wishes; I began to reflect on the best means of securing him; and for this purpose, about a month after my release, I repaired to a criminal judge in the town and told him that I had an accusation to make, that I 2395 knew the destroyer of my family, and that I required him to exert his whole authority for the apprehension of the murderer.

The magistrate listened to me with attention and kindness. "Be assured, sir," said he, 2400 "no pains or exertions on my part shall be spared to discover the villain."

"I thank you," replied I; "listen, therefore, to the deposition that I have to make. It is indeed a tale so strange that I should fear 2405 you would not credit it were there not something in truth which, however wonderful, forces conviction. The story is too connected to be mistaken for a dream, and I have no motive for falsehood." My manner as I thus 2410 addressed him was impressive but calm; I had formed in my own heart a resolution to pursue my destroyer to death, and this purpose quieted my agony and for an interval reconciled me to life. I now related my his- 2415 tory briefly but with firmness and precision, marking the dates with accuracy and never deviating into invective or exclamation.

The magistrate appeared at first perfectly incredulous, but as I continued he became 2420 more attentive and interested; I saw him sometimes shudder with horror; at others a lively surprise, unmingled with disbelief, was painted on his countenance.

When I had concluded my narration, I said, "This is the being whom I accuse and for whose seizure and punishment I call upon you to exert your whole power. It is your duty as a magistrate, and I believe and hope that your feelings as a man will not revolt from the execution of those functions on this occasion."

This address caused a considerable change in the physiognomy of my own auditor. He had heard my story with that half kind of belief that is given to a tale of spirits and supernatural events; but when he was called upon to act officially in consequence, the whole tide of his incredulity returned. He, however, answered mildly, "I would willingly afford you every aid in your pursuit, but the creature of whom you speak appears to have powers which would put all my exertions to defiance. Who can follow an animal which can traverse the sea of ice and inhabit caves and dens where no man would venture to intrude? Besides, some months have elapsed since the commission of his crimes, and no one can conjecture to what place he has wandered or what region he may now inhabit."

"I do not doubt that he hovers near the spot which I inhabit, and if he has indeed taken refuge in the Alps, he may be hunted like the chamois and destroyed as a beast of prey. But I perceive your thoughts; you do not credit my narrative and do not intend to pursue my enemy with the punishment which is his desert."

As I spoke, rage sparkled in my eyes; the magistrate was intimidated. "You are mistaken," said he. "I will exert myself, and if it is in my power to seize the monster, be assured that he shall suffer punishment proportionate to his crimes. But I fear, from what you have yourself described to be his properties, that this will prove impracticable; and thus, while every proper measure is pursued, you should make up your mind to disappointment."

"That cannot be; but all that I can say will be of little avail. My revenge is of no moment to you; yet, while I allow it to be a vice, I confess that it is the devouring and only passion of my soul. My rage is unspeakable when I reflect that the murderer, whom I have turned loose upon society, still exists. You refuse my just demand; I have but one resource, and I devote myself, either in my life or death, to his destruction."

I trembled with excess of agitation as I said this; there was a frenzy in my manner, and something, I doubt not, of that haughty fierceness which the martyrs of old are said to have possessed. But to a Genevan magistrate, whose mind was occupied by far other ideas than those of devotion and heroism, this elevation of mind had much the appearance of madness. He endeavoured to soothe me as a nurse does a child and reverted to my tale as the effects of delirium.

"Man," I cried, "how ignorant art thou in thy pride of wisdom! Cease; you know not what it is you say."

I broke from the house angry and disturbed and retired to meditate on some other mode of action.

Chapter 24

My present situation was one in which all voluntary thought was swallowed up and lost. I was hurried away by fury; revenge alone endowed me with strength and composure; it moulded my feelings and allowed me to be calculating and calm at periods when otherwise delirium or death would have been my portion.

My first resolution was to quit Geneva for ever; my country, which, when I was happy and beloved, was dear to me, now, in my adversity, became hateful. I provided myself 2510 with a sum of money, together with a few jewels which had belonged to my mother, and departed.

And now my wanderings began which are to cease but with life. I have traversed a vast 2515 portion of the earth and have endured all the hardships which travellers in deserts and barbarous countries are wont to meet. How I have lived I hardly know; many times have I stretched my failing limbs upon the sandy 2520 plain and prayed for death. But revenge kept me alive; I dared not die and leave my adversary in being.

When I quitted Geneva my first labour was to gain some clue by which I might trace the 2525 steps of my fiendish enemy. But my plan was unsettled, and I wandered many hours round the confines of the town, uncertain what path I should pursue. As night approached I found myself at the entrance of the 2530 cemetery where William, Elizabeth, and my father reposed. I entered it and approached the tomb which marked their graves. Everything was silent except the leaves of the trees, which were gently agitated by 2535 the wind; the night was nearly dark, and the scene would have been solemn and affecting even to an uninterested observer. The spirits of the departed seemed to flit around and to cast a shadow, which was 2540 felt but not seen, around the head of the mourner.

The deep grief which this scene had at first excited quickly gave way to rage and despair. They were dead, and I lived; their 2545 murderer also lived, and to destroy him I must drag out my weary existence. I knelt on the grass and kissed the earth and with quivering lips exclaimed, "By the sacred earth on which I kneel, by the shades that wander 2550 near me, by the deep and eternal grief that I feel, I swear; and by thee, O Night, and the spirits that preside over thee, to pursue the dæmon who caused this misery, until he or I shall perish in mortal conflict. For this pur- 2555 pose I will preserve my life; to execute this dear revenge will I again behold the sun and tread the green herbage of earth, which otherwise should vanish from my eyes for ever. And I call on you, spirits of the dead, and on 2560 you, wandering ministers of vengeance, to aid and conduct me in my work. Let the cursed and hellish monster drink deep of agony; let him feel the despair that now torments me."

2565 I had begun my adjuration with solemnity and an awe which almost assured me that the shades of my murdered friends heard and approved my devotion, but the furies possessed me as I concluded, and rage 2570 choked my utterance.

I was answered through the stillness of night by a loud and fiendish laugh. It rang on my ears long and heavily; the mountains re-echoed it, and I felt as if all hell 2575 surrounded me with mockery and laughter. Surely in that moment I should have been possessed by frenzy and have destroyed my miserable existence but that my vow was heard and that I was reserved for ven- 2580 geance. The laughter died away, when a well-known and abhorred voice, apparently close to my ear, addressed me in an audible whisper, "I am satisfied, miserable wretch! You have determined to live, and I 2585 am satisfied."

I darted towards the spot from which the sound proceeded, but the devil eluded my grasp. Suddenly the broad disk of the moon arose and shone full upon his ghastly and

2590 distorted shape as he fled with more than mortal speed.

2592 I pursued him, and for many months this has been my task. Guided by a slight clue, I followed the windings of the Rhone, but 2595 vainly. The blue Mediterranean appeared, and by a strange chance, I saw the fiend enter by night and hide himself in a vessel bound for the Black Sea. I took my passage in the same ship, but he escaped, I know not how.

2600 Amidst the wilds of Tartary and Russia, although he still evaded me, I have ever followed in his track. Sometimes the peasants, scared by this horrid apparition, informed me of his path; sometimes he himself, who 2605 feared that if I lost all trace of him I should despair and die, left some mark to guide me. The snows descended on my head, and I saw the print of his huge step on the white plain. To you first entering on life, to whom care 2610 is new and agony unknown, how can you understand what I have felt and still feel? Cold, want, and fatigue were the least pains which I was destined to endure; I was cursed by some devil and carried about with me my 2615 eternal hell; yet still a spirit of good followed and directed my steps and when I most murmured would suddenly extricate me from seemingly insurmountable difficulties. Sometimes, when nature, overcome by hun-2620 ger, sank under the exhaustion, a repast was prepared for me in the desert that restored and inspirited me. The fare was, indeed, coarse, such as the peasants of the country ate, but I will not doubt that it was set there 2625 by the spirits that I had invoked to aid me. Often, when all was dry, the heavens cloudless, and I was parched by thirst, a slight cloud would bedim the sky, shed the few drops that revived me, and vanish.

2630 I followed, when I could, the courses of the rivers; but the dæmon generally avoided these, as it was here that the population of the country chiefly collected. In other places human beings were seldom seen, 2635 and I generally subsisted on the wild animals that crossed my path. I had money with me and gained the friendship of the villagers by distributing it; or I brought with me some food that I had killed, which, after 2640 taking a small part, I always presented to those who had provided me with fire and utensils for cooking.

2643 My life, as it passed thus, was indeed hateful to me, and it was during sleep alone 2645 that I could taste joy. O blessed sleep! Often, when most miserable, I sank to repose, and my dreams lulled me even to rapture. The spirits that guarded me had provided these moments, or rather hours, of happiness that 2650 I might retain strength to fulfil my pilgrimage. Deprived of this respite, I should have sunk under my hardships. During the day I was sustained and inspirited by the hope of night, for in sleep I saw my friends, my wife, 2655 and my beloved country; again I saw the benevolent countenance of my father, heard the silver tones of my Elizabeth's voice, and beheld Clerval enjoying health and youth. Often, when wearied by a toilsome march, I 2660 persuaded myself that I was dreaming until night should come and that I should then enjoy reality in the arms of my dearest friends. What agonising fondness did I feel for them! How did I cling to their dear forms, 2665 as sometimes they haunted even my waking hours, and persuade myself that they still lived! At such moments vengeance, that burned within me, died in my heart, and I pursued my path towards the destruction 2670 of the dæmon more as a task enjoined by heaven, as the mechanical impulse of some power of which I was unconscious, than as the ardent desire of my soul.

What his feelings were whom I pursued I
2675 cannot know. Sometimes, indeed, he left
marks in writing on the barks of the trees or
cut in stone that guided me and instigated
my fury. "My reign is not yet over"—these
words were legible in one of these
2680 inscriptions—"you live, and my power is
complete. Follow me; I seek the everlasting
ices of the north, where you will feel the
misery of cold and frost, to which I am
impassive. You will find near this place, if
2685 you follow not too tardily, a dead hare; eat
and be refreshed. Come on, my enemy; we
have yet to wrestle for our lives, but many
hard and miserable hours must you endure
until that period shall arrive."

2690 Scoffing devil! Again do I vow vengeance;
again do I devote thee, miserable fiend, to
torture and death. Never will I give up my
search until he or I perish; and then with
what ecstasy shall I join my Elizabeth and
2695 my departed friends, who even now prepare
for me the reward of my tedious toil and horrible pilgrimage!

As I still pursued my journey to the north-
ward, the snows thickened and the cold
2700 increased in a degree almost too severe to
support. The peasants were shut up in their
hovels, and only a few of the most hardy
ventured forth to seize the animals whom
starvation had forced from their hiding-
2705 places to seek for prey. The rivers were covered with ice, and no fish could be procured;
and thus I was cut off from my chief article
of maintenance.

The triumph of my enemy increased with
2710 the difficulty of my labours. One inscription
that he left was in these words: "Prepare!
Your toils only begin; wrap yourself in furs
and provide food, for we shall soon enter
upon a journey where your sufferings will
2715 satisfy my everlasting hatred."

My courage and perseverance were invig-
orated by these scoffing words; I resolved not
to fail in my purpose, and calling on Heaven
to support me, I continued with unabated
2720 fervour to traverse immense deserts, until
the ocean appeared at a distance and formed
the utmost boundary of the horizon. Oh!
How unlike it was to the blue seasons of the
south! Covered with ice, it was only to be dis-
2725 tinguished from land by its superior wildness
and ruggedness. The Greeks wept for joy
when they beheld the Mediterranean from
the hills of Asia, and hailed with rapture the
boundary of their toils. I did not weep, but I
2730 knelt down and with a full heart thanked my
guiding spirit for conducting me in safety to
the place where I hoped, notwithstanding
my adversary's gibe, to meet and grapple
with him.

2735 Some weeks before this period I had procured a sledge and dogs and thus traversed
the snows with inconceivable speed. I know
not whether the fiend possessed the same
advantages, but I found that, as before I had
2740 daily lost ground in the pursuit, I now gained
on him, so much so that when I first saw
the ocean he was but one day's journey in
advance, and I hoped to intercept him before
he should reach the beach. With new cour-
2745 age, therefore, I pressed on, and in two days
arrived at a wretched hamlet on the seashore. I inquired of the inhabitants concerning
the fiend and gained accurate information. A
gigantic monster, they said, had arrived the
2750 night before, armed with a gun and many
pistols, putting to flight the inhabitants of a
solitary cottage through fear of his terrific
appearance. He had carried off their store of
winter food, and placing it in a sledge, to
2755 draw which he had seized on a numerous
drove of trained dogs, he had harnessed
them, and the same night, to the joy of the

horror-struck villagers, had pursued his journey across the sea in a direction that led to
2760 no land; and they conjectured that he must
speedily be destroyed by the breaking of the
ice or frozen by the eternal frosts.

On hearing this information I suffered a
temporary access of despair. He had escaped
2765 me, and I must commence a destructive and
almost endless journey across the mountainous ices of the ocean, amidst cold that few of
the inhabitants could long endure and which
I, the native of a genial and sunny climate,
2770 could not hope to survive. Yet at the idea that
the fiend should live and be triumphant, my
rage and vengeance returned, and like a
mighty tide, overwhelmed every other feeling. After a slight repose, during which the
2775 spirits of the dead hovered round and instigated me to toil and revenge, I prepared for
my journey.

I exchanged my land-sledge for one fashioned for the inequalities of the Frozen
2780 Ocean, and purchasing a plentiful stock of
provisions, I departed from land.

I cannot guess how many days have
passed since then, but I have endured misery
which nothing but the eternal sentiment of
2785 a just retribution burning within my heart
could have enabled me to support. Immense
and rugged mountains of ice often barred up
my passage, and I often heard the thunder
of the ground sea, which threatened my
2790 destruction. But again the frost came and
made the paths of the sea secure.

By the quantity of provision which I had
consumed, I should guess that I had passed
three weeks in this journey; and the contin-
2795 ual protraction of hope, returning back upon
the heart, often wrung bitter drops of
despondency and grief from my eyes.
Despair had indeed almost secured her prey,
and I should soon have sunk beneath this

2800 misery. Once, after the poor animals that
conveyed me had with incredible toil gained
the summit of a sloping ice mountain, and
one, sinking under his fatigue, died, I viewed
the expanse before me with anguish, when
2805 suddenly my eye caught a dark speck upon
the dusky plain. I strained my sight to discover what it could be and uttered a wild cry
of ecstasy when I distinguished a sledge and
the distorted proportions of a well-known
2810 form within. Oh! With what a burning gush
did hope revisit my heart! Warm tears filled
my eyes, which I hastily wiped away, that
they might not intercept the view I had of
the dæmon; but still my sight was dimmed
2815 by the burning drops, until, giving way to the
emotions that oppressed me, I wept aloud.

But this was not the time for delay; I dis-
encumbered the dogs of their dead companion, gave them a plentiful portion of food,
2820 and after an hour's rest, which was absolutely necessary, and yet which was bitterly
irksome to me, I continued my route. The
sledge was still visible, nor did I again lose
sight of it except at the moments when for a
2825 short time some ice-rock concealed it with
its intervening crags. I indeed perceptibly
gained on it, and when, after nearly two
days' journey, I beheld my enemy at no more
than a mile distant, my heart bounded
2830 within me.

But now, when I appeared almost within
grasp of my foe, my hopes were suddenly
extinguished, and I lost all trace of him more
utterly than I had ever done before. A ground
2835 sea was heard; the thunder of its progress, as
the waters rolled and swelled beneath me,
became every moment more ominous and
terrific. I pressed on, but in vain. The wind
arose; the sea roared; and, as with the
2840 mighty shock of an earthquake, it split and
cracked with a tremendous and overwhelming

sound. The work was soon finished; in a few minutes a tumultuous sea rolled between me and my enemy, and I was left drifting on a scattered piece of ice that was continually lessening and thus preparing for me a hideous death.

In this manner many appalling hours passed; several of my dogs died, and I myself was about to sink under the accumulation of distress when I saw your vessel riding at anchor and holding forth to me hopes of succour and life. I had no conception that vessels ever came so far north and was astounded at the sight. I quickly destroyed part of my sledge to construct oars, and by these means was enabled, with infinite fatigue, to move my ice raft in the direction of your ship. I had determined, if you were going southwards, still to trust myself to the mercy of the seas rather than abandon my purpose. I hoped to induce you to grant me a boat with which I could pursue my enemy. But your direction was northwards. You took me on board when my vigour was exhausted, and I should soon have sunk under my multiplied hardships into a death which I still dread, for my task is unfulfilled.

Oh! When will my guiding spirit, in conducting me to the dæmon, allow me the rest I so much desire; or must I die, and he yet live? If I do, swear to me, Walton, that he shall not escape, that you will seek him and satisfy my vengeance in his death. And do I dare to ask of you to undertake my pilgrimage, to endure the hardships that I have undergone? No; I am not so selfish. Yet, when I am dead, if he should appear, if the ministers of vengeance should conduct him to you, swear that he shall not live—swear that he shall not triumph over my accumulated woes and survive to add to the list of his dark crimes. He is eloquent and persuasive, and once his words had even power over my heart; but trust him not. His soul is as hellish as his form, full of treachery and fiend-like malice. Hear him not; call on the names of William, Justine, Clerval, Elizabeth, my father, and of the wretched Victor, and thrust your sword into his heart. I will hover near and direct the steel aright.

Walton, in continuation.

August 26th, 17—.

You have read this strange and terrific story, Margaret; and do you not feel your blood congeal with horror, like that which even now curdles mine? Sometimes, seized with sudden agony, he could not continue his tale; at others, his voice broken, yet piercing, uttered with difficulty the words so replete with anguish. His fine and lovely eyes were now lighted up with indignation, now subdued to downcast sorrow and quenched in infinite wretchedness. Sometimes he commanded his countenance and tones and related the most horrible incidents with a tranquil voice, suppressing every mark of agitation; then, like a volcano bursting forth, his face would suddenly change to an expression of the wildest rage as he shrieked out imprecations on his persecutor.

His tale is connected and told with an appearance of the simplest truth, yet I own to you that the letters of Felix and Safie, which he showed me, and the apparition of the monster seen from our ship, brought to me a greater conviction of the truth of his narrative than his asseverations, however earnest and connected. Such a monster has, then, really existence! I cannot doubt it, yet I am lost in surprise and admiration. Sometimes I endeavoured to gain from Frankenstein the particulars of his creature's formation, but on this point he was impenetrable.

"Are you mad, my friend?" said he. "Or whither does your senseless curiosity lead you? Would you also create for yourself and the world a demoniacal enemy? Peace, 2930 peace! Learn my miseries and do not seek to increase your own."

Frankenstein discovered that I made notes concerning his history; he asked to see them and then himself corrected and aug- 2935 mented them in many places, but principally in giving the life and spirit to the conversations he held with his enemy. "Since you have preserved my narration," said he, "I would not that a mutilated one should go 2940 down to posterity."

Thus has a week passed away, while I have listened to the strangest tale that ever imagination formed. My thoughts and every feeling of my soul have been drunk up by the 2945 interest for my guest which this tale and his own elevated and gentle manners have created. I wish to soothe him, yet can I counsel one so infinitely miserable, so destitute of every hope of consolation, to live? Oh, no! 2950 The only joy that he can now know will be when he composes his shattered spirit to peace and death. Yet he enjoys one comfort, the offspring of solitude and delirium; he believes that when in dreams he holds con- 2955 verse with his friends and derives from that communion consolation for his miseries or excitements to his vengeance, that they are not the creations of his fancy, but the beings themselves who visit him from the regions 2960 of a remote world. This faith gives a solemnity to his reveries that render them to me almost as imposing and interesting as truth.

Our conversations are not always confined to his own history and misfortunes. On 2965 every point of general literature he displays unbounded knowledge and a quick and piercing apprehension. His eloquence is forcible and touching; nor can I hear him, when he relates a pathetic incident or endeavours to move the 2970 passions of pity or love, without tears. What a glorious creature must he have been in the days of his prosperity, when he is thus noble and godlike in ruin! He seems to feel his own worth and the greatness of his fall.

2975 "When younger," said he, "I believed myself destined for some great enterprise. My feelings are profound, but I possessed a coolness of judgment that fitted me for illustrious achievements. This sentiment of the 2980 worth of my nature supported me when others would have been oppressed, for I deemed it criminal to throw away in useless grief those talents that might be useful to my fellow creatures. When I reflected on the work I 2985 had completed, no less a one than the creation of a sensitive and rational animal, I could not rank myself with the herd of common projectors. But this thought, which supported me in the commencement of my 2990 career, now serves only to plunge me lower in the dust. All my speculations and hopes are as nothing, and like the archangel who aspired to omnipotence, I am chained in an eternal hell. My imagination was vivid, yet 2995 my powers of analysis and application were intense; by the union of these qualities I conceived the idea and executed the creation of a man. Even now I cannot recollect without passion my reveries while the work was 3000 incomplete. I trod heaven in my thoughts, now exulting in my powers, now burning with the idea of their effects. From my infancy I was imbued with high hopes and a lofty ambition; but how am I sunk! Oh! My 3005 friend, if you had known me as I once was, you would not recognise me in this state of degradation. Despondency rarely visited my heart; a high destiny seemed to bear me on, until I fell, never, never again to rise."

3010 Must I then lose this admirable being? I have longed for a friend; I have sought one who would sympathise with and love me. Behold, on these desert seas I have found such a one, but I fear I have gained him only 3015 to know his value and lose him. I would reconcile him to life, but he repulses the idea.

"I thank you, Walton," he said, "for your kind intentions towards so miserable a wretch; but when you speak of new ties and 3020 fresh affections, think you that any can replace those who are gone? Can any man be to me as Clerval was, or any woman another Elizabeth? Even where the affections are not strongly moved by any superior excellence, 3025 the companions of our childhood always possess a certain power over our minds which hardly any later friend can obtain. They know our infantine dispositions, which, however they may be afterwards modified, 3030 are never eradicated; and they can judge of our actions with more certain conclusions as to the integrity of our motives. A sister or a brother can never, unless indeed such symptoms have been shown early, suspect the 3035 other of fraud or false dealing, when another friend, however strongly he may be attached, may, in spite of himself, be contemplated with suspicion. But I enjoyed friends, dear not only through habit and association, but 3040 from their own merits; and wherever I am, the soothing voice of my Elizabeth and the conversation of Clerval will be ever whispered in my ear. They are dead, and but one feeling in such a solitude can persuade me to 3045 preserve my life. If I were engaged in any high undertaking or design, fraught with extensive utility to my fellow creatures, then could I live to fulfil it. But such is not my destiny; I must pursue and destroy the being to 3050 whom I gave existence; then my lot on earth will be fulfilled and I may die."

My beloved Sister,
September 2d.
I write to you, encompassed by peril and 3055 ignorant whether I am ever doomed to see again dear England and the dearer friends that inhabit it. I am surrounded by mountains of ice which admit of no escape and threaten every moment to crush my vessel. 3060 The brave fellows whom I have persuaded to be my companions look towards me for aid, but I have none to bestow. There is something terribly appalling in our situation, yet my courage and hopes do not desert me. Yet 3065 it is terrible to reflect that the lives of all these men are endangered through me. If we are lost, my mad schemes are the cause.

And what, Margaret, will be the state of your mind? You will not hear of my destruc- 3070 tion, and you will anxiously await my return. Years will pass, and you will have visitings of despair and yet be tortured by hope. Oh! My beloved sister, the sickening failing of your heart-felt expectations is, in prospect, 3075 more terrible to me than my own death. But you have a husband and lovely children; you may be happy. Heaven bless you and make you so!

My unfortunate guest regards me with the 3080 tenderest compassion. He endeavours to fill me with hope and talks as if life were a possession which he valued. He reminds me how often the same accidents have happened to other navigators who have attempted this 3085 sea, and in spite of myself, he fills me with cheerful auguries. Even the sailors feel the power of his eloquence; when he speaks, they no longer despair; he rouses their energies, and while they hear his voice they 3090 believe these vast mountains of ice are molehills which will vanish before the resolutions of man. These feelings are transitory; each day of expectation delayed fills them with

fear, and I almost dread a mutiny caused by
3095 this despair.

    September 5th.

    A scene has just passed of such uncom-
mon interest that, although it is highly probable that these papers may never reach you,
3100 yet I cannot forbear recording it.

    We are still surrounded by mountains of
ice, still in imminent danger of being crushed
in their conflict. The cold is excessive, and
many of my unfortunate comrades have
3105 already found a grave amidst this scene of
desolation. Frankenstein has daily declined
in health; a feverish fire still glimmers in his
eyes, but he is exhausted, and when suddenly roused to any exertion, he speedily
3110 sinks again into apparent lifelessness.

    I mentioned in my last letter the fears I
entertained of a mutiny. This morning, as I
sat watching the wan countenance of my
friend—his eyes half closed and his limbs
3115 hanging listlessly—I was roused by half a
dozen of the sailors, who demanded admission into the cabin. They entered, and their
leader addressed me. He told me that he and
his companions had been chosen by the
3120 other sailors to come in deputation to me to
make me a requisition which, in justice, I
could not refuse. We were immured in ice
and should probably never escape, but they
feared that if, as was possible, the ice should
3125 dissipate and a free passage be opened, I
should be rash enough to continue my voyage and lead them into fresh dangers, after
they might happily have surmounted this.
They insisted, therefore, that I should engage
3130 with a solemn promise that if the vessel
should be freed I would instantly direct my
course southwards.

    This speech troubled me. I had not
despaired, nor had I yet conceived the idea
3135 of returning if set free. Yet could I, in justice,

or even in possibility, refuse this demand?
I hesitated before I answered, when
Frankenstein, who had at first been silent,
and indeed appeared hardly to have force
3140 enough to attend, now roused himself; his
eyes sparkled, and his cheeks flushed with
momentary vigour. Turning towards the men,
he said,

    "What do you mean? What do you
3145 demand of your captain? Are you, then, so
easily turned from your design? Did you not
call this a glorious expedition? "And wherefore was it glorious? Not because the way
was smooth and placid as a southern sea,
3150 but because it was full of dangers and terror,
because at every new incident your fortitude
was to be called forth and your courage
exhibited, because danger and death surrounded it, and these you were to brave and
3155 overcome. For this was it a glorious, for this
was it an honourable undertaking. You were
hereafter to be hailed as the benefactors of
your species, your names adored as belonging to brave men who encountered death for
3160 honour and the benefit of mankind. And
now, behold, with the first imagination of
danger, or, if you will, the first mighty and
terrific trial of your courage, you shrink away
and are content to be handed down as men
3165 who had not strength enough to endure cold
and peril; and so, poor souls, they were chilly
and returned to their warm firesides. Why,
that requires not this preparation; ye need
not have come thus far and dragged your
3170 captain to the shame of a defeat merely to
prove yourselves cowards. Oh! Be men, or be
more than men. Be steady to your purposes
and firm as a rock. This ice is not made
of such stuff as your hearts may be; it is
3175 mutable and cannot withstand you if you say
that it shall not. Do not return to your families with the stigma of disgrace marked on

your brows. Return as heroes who have fought and conquered and who know not
3180 what it is to turn their backs on the foe."

He spoke this with a voice so modulated to the different feelings expressed in his speech, with an eye so full of lofty design and heroism, that can you wonder that these
3185 men were moved? They looked at one another and were unable to reply. I spoke; I told them to retire and consider of what had been said, that I would not lead them farther north if they strenuously desired the con-
3190 trary, but that I hoped that, with reflection, their courage would return.

They retired and I turned towards my friend, but he was sunk in languor and almost deprived of life.

3195 How all this will terminate, I know not, but I had rather die than return shamefully, my purpose unfulfilled. Yet I fear such will be my fate; the men, unsupported by ideas of glory and honour, can never willingly con-
3200 tinue to endure their present hardships.

September 7th.

The die is cast; I have consented to return if we are not destroyed. Thus are my hopes blasted by cowardice and indecision; I come
3205 back ignorant and disappointed. It requires more philosophy than I possess to bear this injustice with patience.

September 12th.

It is past; I am returning to England. I have
3210 lost my hopes of utility and glory; I have lost my friend. But I will endeavour to detail these bitter circumstances to you, my dear sister; and while I am wafted towards England and towards you, I will not despond.

3215 September 9th, the ice began to move, and roarings like thunder were heard at a distance as the islands split and cracked in every direction. We were in the most imminent peril, but as we could only remain passive, my chief

3220 attention was occupied by my unfortunate guest whose illness increased in such a degree that he was entirely confined to his bed. The ice cracked behind us and was driven with force towards the north; a breeze
3225 sprang from the west, and on the 11th the passage towards the south became perfectly free. When the sailors saw this and that their return to their native country was apparently assured, a shout of tumultuous joy broke
3230 from them, loud and long-continued. Frankenstein, who was dozing, awoke and asked the cause of the tumult. "They shout," I said, "because they will soon return to England."

3235 "Do you, then, really return?"

"Alas! Yes; I cannot withstand their demands. I cannot lead them unwillingly to danger, and I must return."

"Do so, if you will; but I will not. You may
3240 give up your purpose, but mine is assigned to me by Heaven, and I dare not. I am weak, but surely the spirits who assist my vengeance will endow me with sufficient strength." Saying this, he endeavoured to spring from
3245 the bed, but the exertion was too great for him; he fell back and fainted.

It was long before he was restored, and I often thought that life was entirely extinct. At length he opened his eyes; he breathed
3250 with difficulty and was unable to speak. The surgeon gave him a composing draught and ordered us to leave him undisturbed. In the meantime he told me that my friend had certainly not many hours to live.

3255 His sentence was pronounced, and I could only grieve and be patient. I sat by his bed, watching him; his eyes were closed, and I thought he slept; but presently he called to me in a feeble voice, and bidding me come
3260 near, said, "Alas! The strength I relied on is gone; I feel that I shall soon die, and he, my

enemy and persecutor, may still be in being. Think not, Walton, that in the last moments of my existence I feel that burning hatred and ardent desire of revenge I once expressed; but I feel myself justified in desiring the death of my adversary. During these last days I have been occupied in examining my past conduct; nor do I find it blamable. In a fit of enthusiastic madness I created a rational creature and was bound towards him to assure, as far as was in my power, his happiness and well-being. This was my duty, but there was another still paramount to that. My duties towards the beings of my own species had greater claims to my attention because they included a greater proportion of happiness or misery. Urged by this view, I refused, and I did right in refusing, to create a companion for the first creature. He showed unparalleled malignity and selfishness in evil; he destroyed my friends; he devoted to destruction beings who possessed exquisite sensations, happiness, and wisdom; nor do I know where this thirst for vengeance may end. Miserable himself that he may render no other wretched, he ought to die. The task of his destruction was mine, but I have failed. When actuated by selfish and vicious motives, I asked you to undertake my unfinished work, and I renew this request now, when I am only induced by reason and virtue.

"Yet I cannot ask you to renounce your country and friends to fulfil this task; and now that you are returning to England, you will have little chance of meeting with him. But the consideration of these points, and the well balancing of what you may esteem your duties, I leave to you; my judgment and ideas are already disturbed by the near approach of death. I dare not ask you to do what I think right, for I may still be misled by passion.

"That he should live to be an instrument of mischief disturbs me; in other respects, this hour, when I momentarily expect my release, is the only happy one which I have enjoyed for several years. The forms of the beloved dead flit before me, and I hasten to their arms. Farewell, Walton! Seek happiness in tranquillity and avoid ambition, even if it be only the apparently innocent one of distinguishing yourself in science and discoveries. Yet why do I say this? I have myself been blasted in these hopes, yet another may succeed."

His voice became fainter as he spoke, and at length, exhausted by his effort, he sank into silence. About half an hour afterwards he attempted again to speak but was unable; he pressed my hand feebly, and his eyes closed for ever, while the irradiation of a gentle smile passed away from his lips.

Margaret, what comment can I make on the untimely extinction of this glorious spirit? What can I say that will enable you to understand the depth of my sorrow? All that I should express would be inadequate and feeble. My tears flow; my mind is overshadowed by a cloud of disappointment. But I journey towards England, and I may there find consolation.

I am interrupted. What do these sounds portend? It is midnight; the breeze blows fairly, and the watch on deck scarcely stir. Again there is a sound as of a human voice, but hoarser; it comes from the cabin where the remains of Frankenstein still lie. I must arise and examine. Good night, my sister.

Great God! what a scene has just taken place! I am yet dizzy with the remembrance of it. I hardly know whether I shall have the power to detail it; yet the tale which I have recorded would be incomplete without this final and wonderful catastrophe.

I entered the cabin where lay the remains of my ill-fated and admirable friend. Over him hung a form which I cannot find words to describe—gigantic in stature, yet uncouth and distorted in its proportions. As he hung over the coffin, his face was concealed by long locks of ragged hair; but one vast hand was extended, in colour and apparent texture like that of a mummy. When he heard the sound of my approach, he ceased to utter exclamations of grief and horror and sprung towards the window. Never did I behold a vision so horrible as his face, of such loathsome yet appalling hideousness. I shut my eyes involuntarily and endeavoured to recollect what were my duties with regard to this destroyer. I called on him to stay.

He paused, looking on me with wonder, and again turning towards the lifeless form of his creator, he seemed to forget my presence, and every feature and gesture seemed instigated by the wildest rage of some uncontrollable passion.

"That is also my victim!" he exclaimed. "In his murder my crimes are consummated; the miserable series of my being is wound to its close! Oh, Frankenstein! Generous and self-devoted being! What does it avail that I now ask thee to pardon me? I, who irretrievably destroyed thee by destroying all thou lovedst. Alas! He is cold, he cannot answer me."

His voice seemed suffocated, and my first impulses, which had suggested to me the duty of obeying the dying request of my friend in destroying his enemy, were now suspended by a mixture of curiosity and compassion. I approached this tremendous being; I dared not again raise my eyes to his face, there was something so scaring and unearthly in his ugliness. I attempted to speak, but the words died away on my lips.

The monster continued to utter wild and incoherent self-reproaches. At length I gathered resolution to address him in a pause of the tempest of his passion.

"Your repentance," I said, "is now superfluous. If you had listened to the voice of conscience and heeded the stings of remorse before you had urged your diabolical vengeance to this extremity, Frankenstein would yet have lived."

"And do you dream?" said the dæmon. "Do you think that I was then dead to agony and remorse? He," he continued, pointing to the corpse, "he suffered not in the consummation of the deed. Oh! Not the ten-thousandth portion of the anguish that was mine during the lingering detail of its execution. A frightful selfishness hurried me on, while my heart was poisoned with remorse. Think you that the groans of Clerval were music to my ears? My heart was fashioned to be susceptible of love and sympathy, and when wrenched by misery to vice and hatred, it did not endure the violence of the change without torture such as you cannot even imagine.

"After the murder of Clerval I returned to Switzerland, heart-broken and overcome. I pitied Frankenstein; my pity amounted to horror; I abhorred myself. But when I discovered that he, the author at once of my existence and of its unspeakable torments, dared to hope for happiness, that while he accumulated wretchedness and despair upon me he sought his own enjoyment in feelings and passions from the indulgence of which I was for ever barred, then impotent envy and bitter indignation filled me with an insatiable thirst for vengeance. I recollected my threat and resolved that it should be accomplished. I knew that I was preparing for myself a deadly torture, but I was the slave, not the master, of an impulse which I detested yet

3430 could not disobey. Yet when she died! Nay, then I was not miserable. I had cast off all feeling, subdued all anguish, to riot in the excess of my despair. Evil thenceforth became my good. Urged thus far, I had no

3435 choice but to adapt my nature to an element which I had willingly chosen. The completion of my demoniacal design became an insatiable passion. And now it is ended; there is my last victim!"

3440   I was at first touched by the expressions of his misery; yet, when I called to mind what Frankenstein had said of his powers of eloquence and persuasion, and when I again cast my eyes on the lifeless form of my

3445 friend, indignation was rekindled within me. "Wretch!" I said. "It is well that you come here to whine over the desolation that you have made. You throw a torch into a pile of buildings, and when they are consumed, you

3450 sit among the ruins and lament the fall. Hypocritical fiend! If he whom you mourn still lived, still would he be the object, again would he become the prey, of your accursed vengeance. It is not pity that you feel; you

3455 lament only because the victim of your malignity is withdrawn from your power."

        "Oh, it is not thus—not thus," interrupted the being. "Yet such must be the impression conveyed to you by what appears to be the

3460 purport of my actions. Yet I seek not a fellow feeling in my misery. No sympathy may I ever find. When I first sought it, it was the love of virtue, the feelings of happiness and affection with which my whole being over-

3465 flowed, that I wished to be participated. But now that virtue has become to me a shadow, and that happiness and affection are turned into bitter and loathing despair, in what should I seek for sympathy? I am content

3470 to suffer alone while my sufferings shall endure; when I die, I am well satisfied that abhorrence and opprobrium should load my memory. Once my fancy was soothed with dreams of virtue, of fame, and of enjoyment.

3475 Once I falsely hoped to meet with beings who, pardoning my outward form, would love me for the excellent qualities which I was capable of unfolding. I was nourished with high thoughts of honour and devotion.

3480 But now crime has degraded me beneath the meanest animal. No guilt, no mischief, no malignity, no misery, can be found comparable to mine. When I run over the frightful catalogue of my sins, I cannot believe that I

3485 am the same creature whose thoughts were once filled with sublime and transcendent visions of the beauty and the majesty of goodness. But it is even so; the fallen angel becomes a malignant devil. Yet even that

3490 enemy of God and man had friends and associates in his desolation; I am alone.

        "You, who call Frankenstein your friend, seem to have a knowledge of my crimes and his misfortunes. But in the detail which

3495 he gave you of them he could not sum up the hours and months of misery which I endured wasting in impotent passions. For while I destroyed his hopes, I did not satisfy my own desires. They were for ever ardent

3500 and craving; still I desired love and fellowship, and I was still spurned. Was there no injustice in this? Am I to be thought the only criminal, when all humankind sinned against me? Why do you not hate Felix,

3505 who drove his friend from his door with contumely? Why do you not execrate the rustic who sought to destroy the saviour of his child? Nay, these are virtuous and immaculate beings! I, the miserable and the

3510 abandoned, am an abortion, to be spurned at, and kicked, and trampled on. Even now my blood boils at the recollection of this injustice.

"But it is true that I am a wretch. I have
murdered the lovely and the helpless; I have
strangled the innocent as they slept and
grasped to death his throat who never
injured me or any other living thing. I have
devoted my creator, the select specimen of
all that is worthy of love and admiration
among men, to misery; I have pursued him
even to that irremediable ruin. There he lies,
white and cold in death. You hate me, but
your abhorrence cannot equal that with
which I regard myself. I look on the hands
which executed the deed; I think on the
heart in which the imagination of it was conceived and long for the moment when these
hands will meet my eyes, when that imagination will haunt my thoughts no more.

"Fear not that I shall be the instrument of
future mischief. My work is nearly complete.
Neither yours nor any man's death is needed
to consummate the series of my being and
accomplish that which must be done, but it
requires my own. Do not think that I shall be
slow to perform this sacrifice. I shall quit
your vessel on the ice raft which brought me
thither and shall seek the most northern
extremity of the globe; I shall collect my
funeral pile and consume to ashes this miserable frame, that its remains may afford no
light to any curious and unhallowed wretch
who would create such another as I have
been. I shall die. I shall no longer feel the
agonies which now consume me or be the
prey of feelings unsatisfied, yet unquenched.
He is dead who called me into being; and
when I shall be no more, the very remembrance of us both will speedily vanish. I shall
no longer see the sun or stars or feel the
winds play on my cheeks. Light, feeling, and
sense will pass away; and in this condition

must I find my happiness. Some years ago,
when the images which this world affords
first opened upon me, when I felt the
cheering warmth of summer and heard the
rustling of the leaves and the warbling of
the birds, and these were all to me, I should
have wept to die; now it is my only consolation. Polluted by crimes and torn by the bitterest remorse, where can I find rest but in
death?

"Farewell! I leave you, and in you the last
of humankind whom these eyes will ever
behold. Farewell, Frankenstein! If thou wert
yet alive and yet cherished a desire of
revenge against me, it would be better satiated in my life than in my destruction. But it
was not so; thou didst seek my extinction,
that I might not cause greater wretchedness;
and if yet, in some mode unknown to me,
thou hadst not ceased to think and feel, thou
wouldst not desire against me a vengeance
greater than that which I feel. Blasted as
thou wert, my agony was still superior to
thine, for the bitter sting of remorse will not
cease to rankle in my wounds until death
shall close them for ever.

"But soon," he cried with sad and solemn
enthusiasm, "I shall die, and what I now feel
be no longer felt. Soon these burning miseries will be extinct. I shall ascend my funeral
pile triumphantly and exult in the agony of
the torturing flames. The light of that conflagration will fade away; my ashes will be
swept into the sea by the winds. My spirit
will sleep in peace, or if it thinks, it will not
surely think thus. Farewell."

He sprang from the cabin-window as he
said this, upon the ice raft which lay close to
the vessel. He was soon borne away by the
waves and lost in darkness and distance.

Brenda Kato

The original painting by Brenda Kato was created with watercolor markers on paper. ▶

How does this painting depict different facets of Frankenstein? Explain how the shapes and colors combine to communicate about the monster's identity.

CHARACTER

1. In Chapter 18, which of Victor's choices and actions seem contradictory or inconsistent? How do these choices contribute to his change?

2. In Chapters 18 and 19, Henry and Victor travel to London. How do the characters' **perspectives** contrast? What do the contrasts reveal about Victor's character?

3. In Chapter 19, Victor finally leaves for Scotland on his own. How does this contribute to his change?

4. Describe Victor at the beginning of Chapter 20. Which contradictory or inconsistent traits contribute to the complexity of his character? Explain.

STRUCTURE

5. The death of Henry and the subsequent implication of Victor connect to earlier events in the novel. What is the creature communicating to Victor through these events around Henry's death?

6. In Chapter 20, Victor makes a choice. What provokes this action? Is this the **climax** of the story? Explain.

7. How do the **contrasting** events in Chapter 23 highlight contradictions and ambiguities?

8. The **resolution** and the conclusion occur in the ice of the Arctic. How does the story conclude? Is the **conflict** finally resolved? Explain your answer.

NARRATION

9. How does the **narrator's distance** from the events of the story affect the **perspective** of Chapter 20?

10. In Chapter 24, Walton meets Victor's creature. How does the narration change? How does Walton's **perspective** contribute to the resolution?

11. While Walton narrates the conclusion, the creature takes control of the last few pages. Is this perspective more **reliable** or less reliable? Explain your response.

FIGURATIVE LANGUAGE: Word Choice, Imagery, and Symbols

12. Consider the **imagery** and description throughout the novel. Explain the associations between the environment of the outside world and the characters and their inner motivations. How does this **motif** contribute to these associations?

13. There are many **symbols** throughout the text: symbols of light and dark, the natural world, the world of scientific discovery, the Garden of Eden, as well as Satan and fire. Choose two symbols associated with setting and explain how they reflect on the human condition in the novel.

IDEAS IN LITERATURE: Repression and Conformity

14. Many view the theme of the novel as the repression of Victor's creation and Victor's need to conform to the expectations of Victorian society. How does the repression of the creature contribute to the universal message of the text? Consider a time in your own experience when repression and conformity contributed to a conflict in your family, school, or community. Explain how you overcame this disconnection.

PUTTING IT ALL TOGETHER

15. Consider the unusual and mysterious origins of the creature. How do these mysterious origins shape the creature and the creature's relationship with other characters?

Writing about Symbols

 Enduring Understanding (LAN-1)

Readers establish and communicate their interpretations of literature through arguments supported by textual evidence.

KEY POINT

Writers craft and arrange the sentences strategically within their literary arguments to convey ideas and achieve their purpose.

Writing Commentary with Purposeful Syntax

The green light from *The Great Gatsby*. The red letter from *The Scarlet Letter*. The albatross from "The Rime of the Ancient Mariner." Yorick's skull from *Hamlet*. Students of literature often know the origins of these symbols, and even if they haven't read the original works, they can identify the well-known associations. These symbols—and others like them—have become so prominent that they are even referred to in our everyday lives.

Some symbols are so common that they have become **archetypes** or universal symbols. Others, still, are **contextual symbols**, dependent upon the context of a work for their symbolic meaning. Careful readers pay attention to how authors use concrete objects, characters, names, or settings to suggest meaning beyond the symbol itself.

Once readers make the association between the object and a value or idea, they can look for additional objects or images within the text that contribute to their analysis of the symbol.

In this composition workshop, you will learn to write a literary argument that analyzes how a symbol contributes to your interpretation of the text. As you develop your analysis, you will also focus on crafting purposeful syntax, especially coordination and subordination, to help create relationships and associations between the ideas in your argument.

Explaining Complexity

You may find it challenging to recognize every symbol as you first read a literary text. But, some symbols are overt in their primary association. When this is the case, you should anticipate that the symbol may have more layers of meaning upon further examination. Careful readers investigate the details to discover a deeper or nuanced symbolic meaning. A single symbol within a work may take on multiple meanings based on the perspectives of different characters, or a symbol may change in its associations as the narrative progresses.

Still, other symbols may be more subtle, yet just as meaningful. Readers should pay close attention to objects that appear at pivotal moments within a text. They should especially take note if the object reappears at different moments within a work. These deliberate repetitions signal to readers that they must pay attention to the symbolic object or place, to remember the details from before, and to watch for further references to come. While some associations may be ambiguous, careful readers may reach deeper understandings of characters, perspectives, and overall meaning by carefully considering the parallels surrounding the symbol.

Here are some questions to help you dig a little deeper into the complexity of a symbol:

- What conflicts or tensions does the symbol represent in the story?
- How does the symbol serve multiple functions in the text?
- How might the symbol suggest different meanings for different characters?
- How might the meaning of the symbol change or evolve throughout the text?
- How might the symbol contradict its universal or archetypal meaning within the context of the story?
- How might the symbol possess contemporary relevance beyond the context of the story?

✎ YOUR ASSIGNMENT

Choose a text from Unit 6 or one that your teacher has assigned. Then, write a literary argument that analyzes how a symbol within the text contributes to an interpretation of the work. Support your thesis with evidence from the text.

Your argument should interpret a literary work and include the following:

- An introduction that identifies the title, author, context, and symbol
- A thesis statement with a claim that conveys an interpretation (a unifying idea + insight about that idea)
- A line of reasoning that justifies the interpretation in the claim
- Relevant and sufficient textual evidence that supports the line of reasoning
- Commentary that links the evidence to the unifying idea in the line of reasoning and claim
- Transitional elements that create coherence in the argument
- A conclusion that brings the literary argument to a unified end
- Syntactical choices that emphasize ideas and information within the argument

Potential Subjects

- A concrete object that serves as a symbol
- A gift, article of clothing, or personal item that serves as a symbol
- A literary work whose title serves as a symbol
- A character whose role serves primarily as a symbol
- A character's name that serves as a symbol
- A physical attribute or personal characteristic that serves as a symbol
- A house or dwelling that serves as a symbol
- A natural setting or phenomenon that serves as a symbol
- An action or event that serves as a symbol

Set a Purpose for Reading

As you begin to analyze your selected text, identify a unifying idea to guide your annotations. Review the following questions and their implications with your unifying idea in mind as you examine the literal and metaphorical meaning of a symbol.

- What is the literal meaning or significance of the symbol?
- How is the symbol described, and what is the narrator's tone when the symbol is present?
- What abstract idea is associated with the symbol?
- Which characters are associated with the symbol? Are their experiences the same or different?
- What are the characters doing when the symbol is present?
- Does the symbol reappear throughout the text? If so, what parallels or contrasts can be drawn in each moment?
- Does the symbol play a significant role in the plot structure of the text?
- Does the symbol contribute to the development of the setting in the text?

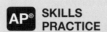 SKILLS PRACTICE | LITERARY ARGUMENTATION **Analyzing a Symbol**

Review the text that you are analyzing for your literary argument. Record your unifying idea, as well as the topic and focus of your analysis. Then, use the graphic organizer to identify details and their significance for different moments in the work. (You may need to delete or add rows).

Analyzing the Complexity of a Symbol		
Unifying idea:		
Topic and focus of analysis:		
Symbol	Details from the Text	Insights and Connections to the Unifying Idea

Develop a Thesis

A **thesis statement** for an analysis of a symbol, as in other literary arguments, requires a claim that includes your interpretation. In this essay, you will explain how the details of the symbol contribute to this interpretation. You should identify the symbol and the specific focus of your analysis — along with your broader interpretation of the text — within your thesis statement.

When you develop your line of reasoning, which will suggest how to organize your analysis, you may examine the following aspects of the symbol:

- The appearance of the symbol at different moments within the narrative
- The way different characters interact with or perceive the symbol within the narrative
- The literal, metaphorical, and universal associations of the symbol
- The way the symbol reveals a character's internal and external struggles
- The way a symbol's meaning evolves within the narrative
- The way the symbol functions in relation to other literary elements or techniques

WRITING A THESIS FOR ANALYSIS OF SYMBOL	
Template 1: The thesis identifies two or more functions of the symbol to establish a line of reasoning and connect to the idea.	In [title of work], by [author], the inclusion of [symbol] functions to [aspect 1], [aspect 2], and [aspect 3] revealing that [unifying idea + insight].
Template 2: The thesis identifies a contrast in an aspect of a single symbol to establish a line of reasoning and connect to the idea.	In [title of work], [author] contrasts [aspect 1] with [aspect 2] of [object/character/setting] to suggest [unifying idea + insight].
Template 3: The thesis identifies a shift in an aspect of a single symbol to establish a line of reasoning and connect to the idea.	In [title of work], [author] shifts from [aspect 1 of symbol] to [aspect 2 of symbol] to illustrate [unifying idea + insight].
Template 4: The thesis identifies the symbol and connects to the idea as an open thesis that chooses not to preview the line of reasoning.	In [author's] [title of work], the inclusion of [symbol] reveals [unifying idea + insight].

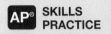 | **SKILLS PRACTICE**

LITERARY ARGUMENTATION
Developing a Thesis Statement for Analysis of Symbol

Complete the following chart. In the left column, record the title, author, and aspect of the symbol that you will explore in your analysis. Next, record the unifying idea and insight that will convey your interpretation in your claim.

Developing a Defensible Thesis Statement for an Analysis of Symbol		
Topic	**Claim**	
Title, Author, and Focus (aspect of symbol)	**Unifying Idea** +	**Insight**

Organize a Line of Reasoning

In earlier units, you learned to support your interpretation with a **line of reasoning** that is established in your topic sentences. For a literary argument that analyzes a symbol, your line of reasoning focuses on specific aspects of the symbol that relate to the unifying idea in your claim.

The body of your analysis should be organized according to the line of reasoning that you used in crafting your thesis.

STRUCTURE OF A SYMBOL ANALYSIS

Introduction

The **introduction** is an opportunity for the writer to establish the purpose of his or her literary argument and to invite and interest the audience in the literary work and the writer's interpretation of it. To achieve this goal, many literary arguments follow this structure:

- Engage the audience through an interesting hook
- Provide historical, cultural, or social context of a literary work
- Identify the title, author, genre (TAG)
- Introduce the symbol by
  - describing the importance of the symbol within the work; and
  - summarizing the work succinctly with details critical to the chosen symbol

The **thesis statement** presents a defensible interpretation that includes an idea and an insight about that idea.

Body

(Develops a line of reasoning with supporting evidence that justifies the thesis)

Topic Sentence 1	Topic Sentence 2	Topic Sentence 3
(Identify the first aspect of the symbol related to the unifying idea)	(Identify the second aspect of the symbol related to the unifying idea)	(Identify the third aspect of the symbol related to the unifying idea)
Textual Details	**Textual Details**	**Textual Details**
(Evidence of elements and techniques that contribute to symbol development and complexity)	(Evidence of elements and techniques that contribute to symbol development and complexity)	(Evidence of elements and techniques that contribute to symbol development and complexity)
Commentary	**Commentary**	**Commentary**
(Link evidence by explaining its relevance to the line of reasoning and claim)	(Link evidence by explaining its relevance to the line of reasoning and claim)	(Link evidence by explaining its relevance to the line of reasoning and claim)

Conclusion

The **conclusion** should do more than restate the thesis; instead, it should be a robust and important paragraph. It is the opportunity for the writer to demonstrate understanding of the literary work's relevance by explaining how the literary work stands the test of time and reflects the human experience. Writers further their ideas and insights by:

- Discussing the significance or relevance of interpretation
- Relating the work to other relevant literary works
- Connecting the theme to their own experience
- Presenting alternate interpretations
- Explaining how the work explores complexities and tensions
- Situating the theme within a broader context

This table illustrates the general structure of a literary argument. It does not intend to imply that all literary arguments are five paragraphs. Writers should determine the number of reasons needed to justify their claims, as well as how much evidence is sufficient to support each of these reasons.

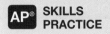 | LITERARY ARGUMENTATION
Developing a Line of Reasoning

Review your thesis statement, which may or may not preview the line of reasoning. Record the topic sentences to represent your line of reasoning and place them in a logical order. As you do this, consider the potential evidence from the text that helped you arrive at your line of reasoning. That textual evidence will support these reasons.

Organizing an Analysis of Symbol		
Defensible Thesis Statement with Claim (idea + insight):		
Topic Sentence 1 (Identify the first aspect of the symbol related to the unifying idea):	**Topic Sentence 2** (Identify the second aspect of the symbol related to the unifying idea):	**Topic Sentence 3** (Identify the third aspect of the symbol related to the unifying idea):

Select Relevant Evidence

In Units 1–5, you examined how to select and introduce **relevant** and **sufficient evidence** from a text to support your line of reasoning. Recall that every reason must be accompanied by relevant evidence for support. In other words, your evidence must relate directly to the purpose of that paragraph as it is defined by the topic sentence. Likewise, your evidence should be sufficient, meaning that it represents multiple instances of the symbol or highlights the symbol's various associations.

As you examine your symbol, record specific moments within the text accurately. If you misrepresent the text by pulling a detail out of context, for example, your analysis could unravel. Remember to choose the best textual evidence and arrange specific instances in paragraphs where they provide the most apt support.

With your unifying idea in mind, you might incorporate evidence that illustrates, clarifies, exemplifies, associates, amplifies, or qualifies. Here are some examples:

- Textual details that explain the literal context of the symbol
- Textual details that reveal the meaning of the symbol beyond its literal context
- Textual details that include multiple character interactions or perspectives with regard to the symbol
- Textual details that represent multiple moments in the text where the symbol emerges
- Textual details that reveal how the symbol interacts with other literary elements

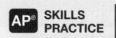 **SKILLS PRACTICE** | LITERARY ARGUMENTATION
Incorporating Relevant and Sufficient Evidence

Write your thesis statement and develop a logical line of reasoning to support your interpretation. Carefully organize your body paragraphs and arrange the evidence within them. Next, draft two or more body paragraphs that include evidence from the text to support each reason. Include transitions to link your reasons and evidence to your claim.

Incorporating Relevant and Sufficient Evidence		
Defensible Thesis Statement with Claim (idea + insight):		
Topic Sentence 1 (Identify the first aspect of the symbol related to the unifying idea):	**Topic Sentence 2** (Identify the second aspect of the symbol related to the unifying idea):	**Topic Sentence 3** (Identify the third aspect of the symbol related to the unifying idea):
Textual Details (Relevant and sufficient evidence):	**Textual Details** (Relevant and sufficient evidence):	**Textual Details** (Relevant and sufficient evidence):

Write Insightful Commentary

In Units 4 and 5, you practiced writing commentary to achieve unity (connecting evidence to the idea) and coherence (connecting evidence to your reasons). Recall that your commentary is the glue that holds your literary argument together. When you analyze a symbol, then, you will still follow the basic pattern for each body paragraph (identify — evidence — link) to write your complex argument. To link effectively within your commentary, you should continue to practice using sentence stems (p. 902) so that you avoid summarizing. Effective commentary explains the function of a symbol and how that symbol contributes to your interpretation of the text.

When you analyze a symbol, you must not only identify what it represents literally within the text but also explain its deeper implications and meaning. Your **commentary** serves to link the author's choice of symbol to the **unifying idea** and insight in your thesis.

DEVELOPING COMMENTARY THAT EXPLAINS THE SIGNIFICANCE OF SYMBOLS

Topics for Symbol Analysis	Templates for Introducing Symbol Details and Function of Details	Templates for Explaining Symbols in Commentary
The appearance of the symbol at different moments in the narrative	The symbol of _____ first appears when _____ and is associated with _____. Later, the symbol emerges again in association with _____.	Through this choice, the author • develops the idea of _____. • implies that _____. • reveals the values of _____. • develops the character _____.
The way different characters interact with or perceive the symbol	For the character [character], the symbol _____ represents _____ as a result of _____. Alternatively, to [character], the symbol _____ comes to mean _____ because _____.	The contrast in characters' interactions with the symbol • amplifies the idea that _____. • reveals the tension between _____ and _____.
The literal, metaphorical, and universal associations of the symbol	The author includes the symbol of _____ in order to • explore the implications that _____. • associate it with the common idea of _____.	Through this association, the author • develops the idea of _____. • implies that _____. • reveals the values of _____. • develops the character _____.
The way a symbol reveals a character's internal and external conflicts	The inclusion of the symbol _____ reveals • the character's conflict with _____. • the character's inner struggle with _____.	By creating a parallel between the character's external and internal conflict, the author explores the idea that _____.
The way a symbol evolves in meaning within a narrative	Initially, the symbol _____ is associated with _____ as revealed by the details _____. After _____ occurs, the symbol _____ shifts in its association from _____ to _____ because _____.	By shifting the association of the symbol from _____ to _____, the author exemplifies the change/growth/transformation of _____ and suggests that _____.
The way a symbol functions in relation to other literary elements and techniques	The character _____ serves as a symbol for _____ because his/her actions suggest _____. The setting _____ serves as a symbol for _____ because the details associate it with the idea/concept/emotion of _____.	By associating the character _____ with the idea of _____, the author reveals _____. Using the setting _____ as a symbol for _____ further develops the idea that _____.

As you write your commentary, you should also focus on your own craft as a writer. In addition to selecting effective verbs and choosing the most precise words to represent details accurately, you should use syntax, especially coordination and subordination, to convey relationships and associations within your argument.

For example, if you wish to emphasize a certain point, you might write a short, **simple sentence** that contains a single independent clause.

Consider the following **independent clauses** that stand as sentences on their own. Each clause, currently expressed as a simple sentence, contains an observation:

> *The scarlet letter "A" that Hester Prynne wears initially represents her sin of adultery.*
>
> *After Hester Prynne's many years of service, the letter "A" comes to signify her as "able" throughout the Salem community.*

Expressed as independent clauses, each of these ideas has equal importance. If you wish, you can use **coordination** to link two items of equal importance in a compound sentence, which conveys balance and congruity. You can achieve coordination in two ways:

- Using coordinating conjunctions ("FANBOYS": *for, and, nor, but, or, yet, so*), or
- Using conjunctive adverbs (e.g., *however, therefore, for example, in fact*)

The following compound sentence joins the two clauses with a coordinating conjunction. Note that you need to place a comma before the conjunction.

> *The scarlet letter "A" that Hester Prynne wears initially represented her sin of adultery, <u>but</u> after her many years of service, the letter "A" comes to signify her as "able" throughout the Salem community.*

You might also join the two clauses with a **conjunctive adverb**. In this case, you will need to use a semicolon before and a comma after a conjunctive adverb. Note that the two clauses still convey balance and congruity.

> *The scarlet letter "A" that Hester Prynne wears initially represents her sin of adultery; <u>however,</u> after her many years of service, the letter "A" comes to signify her as "able" throughout the Salem community.*

At other times in your analysis, you may wish to highlight the importance of one idea over another. To do this, you can construct a **complex sentence** using **subordination**. Writers use a **subordinate clause** (a clause that cannot stand alone) to modify an independent clause in thesis statements, topic sentences, or in commentary when they wish to do the following:

- Emphasize one idea over another
- Clarify or explain a noun
- Establish causal relationships
- Address the complexity of their subject
- Present a line of reasoning for their argument

Subordination connects an independent clause with a subordinate clause, result-ing in a **complex sentence**. You can achieve this in two ways:

- Using subordinating conjunctions (e.g., *although, because, whether, while*) to create an adverbial clause that explains a cause-effect relationship
- Using relative pronouns (e.g., *who, whose, whom, which, that*) to create an adjective clause that provides additional detail

Therefore, when you are developing commentary for your literary argument, you might employ a complex sentence structure — that is, a sentence with at least one independent clause and one subordinate clause.

When you want to emphasize one idea over another, you can make one of the sentences dependent by adding a subordinating conjunction such as *although, while, since,* or *because.* Your syntactical decision depends on your purpose.

Review the sample sentences once more. To emphasize the importance of the community's change in attitude about Hester Prynne over the years, you can make the first sentence subordinate. Note that when the subordinate clause begins the sentence, the clause should be followed by a comma. This syntactical choice emphasizes the change in the characterization of Hester, who is now considered able after her actions.

> *Even though the scarlet letter "A" that Hester Prynne wears initially represented her sin of adultery, the letter comes to characterize Hester Prynne as able after her many years of service to the Salem community.*

Alternatively, you can subordinate one idea and amplify another by employing a relative pronoun. Note that the subordinate clause directly follows the noun it modifies and is set off by commas.

> *The scarlet letter "A," which once represented Hester Prynne's sin of adultery, now signifies her as "able" after her many years of service to the Salem community.*

Finally, when you arrange a complex sentence with the subordinate clause first, you are writing a **periodic sentence**, which often places more emphasis on the idea in the independent or main clause. If your complex sentence begins with the independent clause followed by the subordinate clause, it is called a **cumulative sentence**. You can use this structure when you wish to add explanation or detail to the observation in the opening independent clause.

Review the following chart to see how to use additional syntactical strategies to enhance your literary argument.

INSIDER
AP® TIP

Subordinate clauses may serve as transitional elements. In addition to showing inequality or imbalance among ideas, these dependent clauses serve to convey a cause-effect relationship within your argument. When you use subordination to reveal these relationships, you create coherence within your essay.

USING STRATEGIC SYNTAX

Rhetorical Function	Rhetorical Effect	Syntactical and Grammatical Structure
Emphasis	Bringing a sense of finality or emphasis to the idea	Short, simple sentence ending with a period (.)
	Restating an idea to emphasize a trait, quality, or idea	Two sentences that express the same idea differently connected with a colon (:)
	Providing an example, insight, or point of emphasis about the idea	Sentence that sets off information with a dash (—)
Balance	Setting up parallel constructions to indicate equality or balance	Sentence with two independent clauses connected with a comma (,) and a coordinating conjunction
		Sentence with two independent clauses connected with a semicolon (;), a conjunctive adverb, and a comma (,)
		Sentence with a list of words and phrases in a series separated with commas; a coordinating conjunction is used before the final word or phrase in the series to indicate equality
Relationships	Illustrating a causal or adverbial relationship (how, when, where, why, to what extent)	Sentence with a subordinate clause set off with a comma (,)
Clarification	Further describing, modifying, or clarifying a noun	Sentence with an adjective clause introduced by a relative pronoun (e.g., *who*, *whose*, *whom*, *which*, *that*) to indicate specificity
Detail or description	Providing helpful, but nonessential information or detail	Sentence with an appositive phrase set off with commas (,)
Exemplification	Illustrating with either some examples or a clarification	Sentence with examples (e.g.,) or a clarification (i.e.,) in parentheses
Connection	Creating intimacy or connection between reader and writer with a parenthetical aside	Sentence with information or detail placed within parentheses (( ))
Omission	Excerpting relevant consecutive information that has been omitted from another source	Sentence with ellipses (. . .) that indicate omitted information or omitted words in direct quotation
Provocation or reflection	Posing a reflective or provocative question without providing an answer to elicit thought	Sentence with rhetorical question using a question mark (?)
Qualification	Qualifying an argument or claim by indicating circumstances where an argument would not apply	Sentence with subordinate clauses followed by a comma (,)

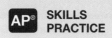 | LITERARY ARGUMENTATION
Using Coordination and Subordination to Establish Relationships within the Argument

Build on your emerging literary argument by adding commentary to your relevant and sufficient evidence. As you plan your explanation, carefully consider when you may need to show balance or imbalance within your commentary. Additionally, keep the focus on your unifying idea so that you may carry this idea throughout your argument in a unified way.

Explaining the Relevance of a Symbol

Defensible Thesis Statement with Claim (idea + insight):

Topic Sentence 1 (Identify the first aspect of the symbol related to the unifying idea):	Topic Sentence 2 (Identify the second aspect of the symbol related to the unifying idea):	Topic Sentence 3 (Identify the third aspect of the symbol related to the unifying idea):
Textual Details (Relevant and sufficient evidence):	**Textual Details** (Relevant and sufficient evidence):	**Textual Details** (Relevant and sufficient evidence):
Signal phrase and evidence 1:	Signal phrase and evidence 1:	Signal phrase and evidence 1:
Signal phrase and evidence 2:	Signal phrase and evidence 2:	Signal phrase and evidence 2:
Commentary (Link evidence to reason and idea):	**Commentary** (Link evidence to reason and idea):	**Commentary** (Link evidence to reason and idea):
Sentence stem and explanation of function of evidence:	Sentence stem and explanation of function of evidence:	Sentence stem and explanation of function of evidence:

Contextualize Your Argument

When you write your analysis of a symbol, your introduction should include a quick summary of the text that identifies the symbol you are analyzing. Next, you should funnel your discussion to the unifying idea to prepare for your thesis statement.

After you have presented your argument, remember to explain the relevance of your idea from your interpretation.

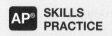 **SKILLS PRACTICE** | LITERARY ARGUMENTATION
Establishing Context and Explaining Relevance

In the following chart, record some notes to help you communicate the context of your argument, the introductory details about the symbol, and the introductory material that will funnel your ideas to your thesis statement. Next, record ideas to help you explain the relevance of your idea and insight in your concluding statements.

Establishing Context and Explaining Relevance	
Idea and Insight	Context for Introduction
	Significance of Idea in Conclusion

Revise Your Argument

Review the following questions related to your consideration of the symbol within the text. Revise your draft if you answer "no" to any of the following questions:

- Does your introduction identify the symbol within its narrative context?
- Is your discussion of the symbol focused on its metaphorical significance and relevance to your interpretation of the text rather than just its literal meaning?
- Do your reasons in your line of reasoning refer to the unifying idea related to your symbol and support your interpretation?
- Have you included relevant details that contribute to your analysis of the symbol and how it contributes to your interpretation of the text?
- Does your interpretation of the work logically align with your discussion of the function and effects of the symbol?
- Is your argument coherent with a logical sequence of reasons and transitions that connect evidence, reasons, and claims?
- Does your commentary unify your argument by connecting your evidence and reasons to your unifying idea?
- Have you included strategic syntax to represent the balance or inequality of ideas as appropriate?

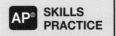 SKILLS PRACTICE | LITERARY ARGUMENTATION
Revising and Editing an Analysis of Symbol

After you have completed revising and editing your own argument, review another student's literary argument and provide helpful feedback.

Peer-Revision Checklist: Revising and Editing an Analysis of Symbol		
Revising and Editing Checklist	**Unit 6 Focus Skills**	**Comment on the Effectiveness and/or Make a Suggestion**
Does the writer include the narrative situation and perspective, title, and author of the literary text in the first paragraph? Does the brief summary of context and reference to the symbol lead to the idea?	Introductions for analysis of symbol	
Does the thesis statement convey an interpretation? Does the interpretation connect to an idea and an insight?	Defensible thesis	
Does the writer provide a logical sequence of reasons to support the idea and insight in the thesis? Are these reasons linked to the claim with transitions?	Line of reasoning: Unity	
Does the writer provide relevant and sufficient evidence to support the interpretation in the thesis? Is the evidence linked to the topic sentences with transitions?	Relevant and sufficient evidence: Coherence	
Does the writer explain how the evidence supports a reason and connects to the interpretation in the thesis? Does the commentary connect to the unifying idea?	Commentary: Unity and coherence	
Does the writer explain the argument's significance within a broader context?	Relevance	
Does the writer employ strategic syntax to represent equality or inequality of ideas?	Coordination and subordination	
Does the writer demonstrate control over the conventions of writing?	Conventions	

Student Model: Writing about Symbol

Review the following student model, which analyzes the symbol of darkness in a novel. Observe how the thesis statement, line of reasoning, and evidence work together to convey an interpretation of the work.

Darkness in a Changing Life
Robert Dohrman

In the English language's first major work of literature, the great hero, Beowulf, slays the evil monster, Grendel, in service to the Danish king, Hrothgar. The epic poem delights in telling of Beowulf's bravery as he kills the terrible Grendel, who had terrorized the Danish tribes for years. However, in his novel, *Grendel*, John Gardner gives a new perspective on the classic epic, this time giving readers insight into the monster's perspective. While the original poem casts Grendel as unchanging and mindlessly evil, Gardner shows readers a dynamic and lonely monster who feels cut off from the world. By weaving the symbol of darkness throughout his novel, Gardner not only sheds light on Grendel's transformation into an abominable monster but also suggests that isolation is damaging to one's character, making Grendel, to some extent, a product of his environment.

thesis: connects symbol of darkness to the idea
idea: transformation
insight: isolation causes transformation

To begin, darkness's repeated appearance and its changing relationship with Grendel reveal his transformation from an awkward youth to the horrifying monster depicted by the Old English tale. In the novel's beginning (and more or less until his meeting with the dragon), Grendel has a tense, but largely nonviolent, relationship with humans. At this point, he does not seem to like the darkness, and after a night of spying on a camp of Danes, he creeps away "into the darkness, furious" about the "stupid need" to monitor their activities (Gardner 33). Grendel's relationship with the darkness in this instance seems uncomfortable: he acknowledges feeling "stupid" running around in the dark and angry about his hiding from the humans. In fact, he seems embarrassed to need the darkness as much as he does. However, as Grendel's conflict with the Danes escalates and his temperament turns malevolent, his relationship with the darkness changes. For instance, after "darkness" falls on the night that Grendel attacks Beowulf, he remarks with morbid enthusiasm that "it is time." (166). Through this additional reference to the darkness, Gardner calls readers' attention to Grendel's transformed nature. While he had originally felt uncomfortable operating under darkness's cover, Grendel now seems to feel excitement. Evidently, after the meeting with the dragon and his ensuing escalation of relations with the humans, his connection to the darkness grows stronger. Thus, darkness and Grendel's dynamic relationship with it act as symbols for Grendel's evil transformation, helping Gardner characterize Grendel's changing nature.

topic sentence: darkness reveals transformation

evidence: Grendel retreats into darkness

commentary: association to character's initial alienation

evidence: Grendel uses darkness as a shield

syntax: subordination emphasizes his change to excitement

commentary: explains how the character is changing

In short, by making regular references to darkness, Gardner exposes Grendel's descent to evil.

Furthermore, Gardner includes intermittent references to darkness to suggest that the absence of connectedness is harmful and that Grendel's wicked nature may simply be a result of an isolated environment. Grendel's isolation begins early in the novel, as he desires a more peaceful interaction with the humans, though ultimately falls victim to the Shaper's rhetoric. The poet portrays the world as split "between darkness and light," with Grendel on the "dark side" and cursed by God, a sentiment that sends Grendel into a rage (51). By contrasting the dark (symbolizing Grendel) and the light (symbolizing humanity) and suggesting that the two must oppose each other, Gardner provides readers with the sense that Grendel faces a severe and damaging lack of connectedness. Grendel's rage demonstrates the detriments of personal isolation. Additionally, because this label of "dark," or isolated, is imposed by humans, Grendel's malicious actions are at least partially a result of his environment, rather than an inherently evil disposition. Later, he becomes further isolated after meeting with the dragon and receiving the spell of invulnerability to the humans' weapons, noting that the humans were "powerless" and that his "heart became darker because of that" (76). Mentioning darkness, in this case, both explicitly and implicitly connects to Grendel's wickedness. Of course, his heart becoming darker means that Grendel is more evil than before. But it also implies a lack of empathy, and thus, isolation from the humans with whom he is conflicting. By linking Grendel's emotional separation from others and his descent to evil, Gardner further demonstrates isolation's detrimental impacts and suggests that Grendel's violence is a consequence of that lack of connection. All in all, by including mentions of darkness throughout *Grendel*, Gardner indicates that Grendel's isolated environment may have damaged and influenced him at least as much as any intrinsic evil within.

Overall, through his repeated references to the symbol of darkness in *Grendel*, John Gardner reveals the monster's transformation and argues that an absence of connectedness is damaging to all people, including Grendel. In building this argument, Gardner also makes the point that Grendel's actions are, in many ways, results of his surroundings. By writing from an extremely unique perspective, he also gives new voice to some of the English language's oldest literature and forces readers to ponder the moral dilemma that, when originally written down, seemed as uncomplicated as a strong, benevolent hero versus a horrible, evil monster.

Annotations (margin notes):

- topic sentence: asserts possible cause of the transformation
- evidence: the separation into the darkness incites rage
- commentary: explains how the character's isolation begins to change him
- evidence: the character's heart became dark, suggesting it was not always that way
- commentary: connects darkness to the internal transformation of the character
- conclusion: connects the symbol to the idea that isolation results in a transformation

Work Cited

Gardner, John. *Grendel*. New York, Random House, Inc., 1971.

Free-Response Question: Literary Argument

AP **Enduring Understanding (LAN-1)**

Readers establish and communicate their interpretations of literature through arguments supported by textual evidence.

Writing Commentary with Purposeful Syntax

As you learned in Unit 3, the third free-response prompt on the AP® English Literature and Composition Exam requires you to write a literary argument about an assigned topic that focuses on your choice of literary work. In this workshop, you will continue to develop the skills that you need to complete this task with a focus on incorporating purposeful syntax — specifically coordination and subordination — to represent the balance or inequality of ideas in your argument.

Read the following practice prompt, which models the type of prompt you may see on the AP® English Literature and Composition Exam. Please note that you may select a work from the list of suggestions or you can write about a work of fiction that you choose.

Prompt:

In many works of literature a setting takes on a deeper meaning than just the time and place in which the story occurs. Settings can also be associated with more abstract concepts and ideas. In a story, a setting can be represented by natural surroundings like forests, mountains, rivers, or the ocean; countries, cities, or neighborhoods; or buildings like offices, restaurants, homes, or even a room within a dwelling.

Either from your own reading or from the following list, choose a work of fiction in which the details of a setting not only have literal significance but also have symbolic representations. Then, in a well-written essay, analyze how the symbolism of the setting contributes to an interpretation of the work as a whole. Do not merely summarize the plot.

In your response you should do the following:

- Respond to the prompt with a thesis that presents a defensible interpretation
- Select and use evidence to support your line of reasoning
- Explain how the evidence supports your line of reasoning
- Use appropriate grammar and punctuation in communicating your argument

The Adventures of Huckleberry Finn	*Obasan*
All the Light We Cannot See	*One Hundred Years of Solitude*
The Awakening	*Othello*
Billy Budd	*A Prayer for Owen Meany*
Cat on a Hot Tin Roof	*Purple Hibiscus*
Death of a Salesman	*A Raisin in the Sun*
Don Quixote	*The Road*
Frankenstein	*Rosencrantz and Guildenstern Are Dead*
The Great Gatsby	*The Round House*
Great Expectations	*Sense and Sensibility*
Homegoing	*The Strange Case of Dr. Jekyll and Mr. Hyde*
House Made of Dawn	*Sula*
The House on Mango Street	*Their Eyes Were Watching God*
In the Time of Butterflies	*A Thousand Splendid Suns*
Invisible Man	*To Kill a Mockingbird*
Jane Eyre	*Top Girls*
Joe Turner's Come and Gone	*Typical American*
The Leavers	*Where the Crawdads Sing*
Mudbound	*White Teeth*
Native Speaker	*Zoot Suit*

→ **Step One: Determine a Unifying Idea and Brainstorm Relevant Examples from a Text**

Once you have thoroughly examined the prompt and determined a topic to explore, you will need to choose a work of fiction that you know well to analyze for the literary question. Next, consider the abstract ideas associated with your choice of text. One of these ideas will serve as the unifying idea in your literary argument.

You will arrive at this idea once you narrow the focus for your argument. For example, in the model prompt, you are instructed to choose a work of literature that includes a symbolic setting. If you decide to write about *The Great Gatsby*, for instance, you might recall a number of ideas emerging from the work (e.g., the American dream, illusions, morality, class, deceit). Additionally, the novel offers a number of symbolic settings from which to choose (e.g., the Valley of the Ashes, East Egg, West Egg, Gatsby's mansion).

Once you choose your specific setting, you will then select the most fitting idea to explore in your argument. Some writers begin with an idea and select evidence to support that idea, while others may generate a list of potential evidence and then see what idea emerges in the process. Whatever your method, remember that you should focus on one idea and use only the evidence that directly relates to that idea as you develop your thesis (idea + insight) and line of reasoning.

→ Step Two: Develop a Defensible Claim and a Unified Line of Reasoning

Continue developing your skill in writing a debatable and defensible thesis statement that is accurate and precise. For analyzing a symbol, you should identify the symbol and connect it to your interpretation (idea + insight). You may choose whether or not to preview your line of reasoning.

If you need help getting started, you may build from one of the following thesis templates or refer to the models that follow:

- In [title], [author] reveals [idea + insight] by using [symbol] that suggests [aspect 1 of symbol], [aspect 2 of symbol], and [aspect 3 of symbol].

- In [title], [author] reveals [idea + insight] by shifting the associations of [symbol] from [aspect 1 of symbol] to [aspect 2 of symbol].

Sample Thesis Statements	Notes on Effectiveness
In F. Scott Fitzgerald's The Great Gatsby, Gatsby's elaborate West Egg mansion represents the promise of the dream, but then shifts to symbolize the decay and eventual death of the dream in order to suggest that the American dream is impossible for most Americans to obtain.	Connects the symbolic setting (Gatsby's mansion) to an idea (the American dream). Conveys the insight that the dream is impossible. Previews a line of reasoning (promise; decay; death).
In The Great Gatsby, F. Scott Fitzgerald associates Gatsby's elaborate West Egg mansion with Gatsby's valiant attempt — and then tragic failure — to capture the American dream, which illustrates that the dream is unattainable for most Americans.	Connects the symbolic setting (Gatsby's mansion) to an idea (the American dream). Conveys the insight that the dream is unattainable. Previews a line of reasoning (valiant attempt; tragic failure).

Once you have written your thesis statement, you will develop your line of reasoning. For an analysis of a symbol, you might organize your reasons based on one of the following aspects:

- The symbol's importance at different moments within the narrative
- The relevance of the symbol for different characters within the narrative
- The literal, metaphorical, and universal meaning of the symbol
- The way a symbol reveals a character's internal and external struggles
- The way a symbol evolves in meaning within the narrative
- The way the symbol functions in relation to other literary elements or techniques

Consider the most effective order for your line of reasoning and make sure each reason connects directly to your thesis. Finally, choose helpful transitions to connect your reasons to each other and to the claim in the thesis.

If you need help getting started, you may build from the following topic sentence templates or refer to the models that follow:

- [Author] first includes [reference to symbol] to reveal [first aspect of symbol] and associate it with [idea].
- [Transitional element] [author] shifts the association from [first aspect of symbol] to [second aspect of symbol] to emphasize [insight about the idea].

Review the following thesis statement and line of reasoning. Note that the unifying idea creates the connection between the claim in the thesis and the topic sentences that support the claim.

Thesis Statement

In F. Scott Fitzgerald's The Great Gatsby, *Gatsby's elaborate West Egg mansion represents the promise of the dream and then symbolizes the decay and eventual death of the dream in order to suggest that the American dream is impossible for most Americans to obtain.*

Topic Sentence 1	Topic Sentence 2	Topic Sentence 3
Initially, Gatsby's mansion appears as polished and elaborate as the protagonist himself, representing the promise of the American dream for anyone willing to work for it.	*As Gatsby's true origin becomes apparent throughout the narrative, Gatsby's mansion begins to show signs of slow decay as well, symbolizing that Gatsby is losing his grip on the dream.*	*Finally, Fitzgerald signifies the death of the protagonist and his dream at the end of the narrative through the symbol of Gatsby's abandoned mansion.*

In this example, the three topic sentences associate the symbolic setting of Gatsby's mansion with the American dream by following the progression of the narrator. The first body paragraph will focus on the promise of the dream; the second paragraph will illustrate the beginning of the decay; the final paragraph will draw parallels between the deserted mansion, the death of the protagonist, and the death of the American dream.

→ Step Three: Choose Relevant Evidence

With your line of reasoning established, you can arrange your relevant and sufficient evidence in the proper body paragraph. For an analysis of a symbol, you should examine the moments in the text where the symbol appears. Next, examine the details related to character, setting, and structure within those moments and select details that both explain the literal context and — more importantly — reveal the abstract associations.

For your evidence to be relevant, it should relate directly to the symbol and the unifying idea. For it to be sufficient, it should represent the importance of the symbol throughout the beginning, middle, and end of the narrative. Because you will not be permitted to use a copy of the text, your evidence will be paraphrased from the narrative. Even so, evidence should be apt and specific, with enough details to support your reasons and your claim.

Review the following notes for evidence to support the line of reasoning in the model prompt.

Topic Sentence 1	Topic Sentence 2	Topic Sentence 3
Initially, Gatsby's mansion appears as polished and elaborate as the protagonist himself, representing the promise of the American dream for anyone willing to work for it.	*As Gatsby's true origin becomes apparent throughout the narrative, Gatsby's mansion begins to show signs of slow decay as well, symbolizing that Gatsby is losing his grip on the dream.*	*Finally, Fitzgerald signifies the death of the protagonist and his dream at the end of the narrative through the symbol of Gatsby's abandoned mansion.*
Relevant and Sufficient Evidence	**Relevant and Sufficient Evidence**	**Relevant and Sufficient Evidence**
West Egg wealth symbolizes new money and upward mobility *Gaudy and flashy like Gatsby, but the thin ivy signifies the newness* *Library suggests a facade* *Blue gardens seem unreal*	*Parties become infrequent* *Unqualified staff hired for their discretion allow the mansion to become unkempt* *Gatsby's true background is revealed dispelling the romantic myths*	*The mansion stands empty after Gatsby's death* *Even the funeral was sparsely attended as everyone deserted him* *A final unknown partygoer seeks another chance at the dream*

→ Step Four: Develop Insightful Commentary

In Unit 5, you practiced creating unity and coherence in your argument by incorporating helpful **transitions** to connect the elements in your essay. Recall that you choose transitions based on their purpose (e.g., to signify order, comparison, contrast, conclusion, evidence, author choice, or commentary). Now you will practice using strategic syntax, especially **coordination** and **subordination**, to signify balance and inequality within your argument.

When you need to express equality or balance in your claims and commentary, you should use coordination. You can find examples of transitions to signify coordination on p. 904. This is especially helpful when you are comparing characters, settings, and other literary elements, or when you are connecting several pieces of textual evidence that work together for a single purpose.

However, you may wish to emphasize one point over another. For example, when you are analyzing a symbol, you will identify the concrete details of the symbol but more importantly its abstract associations. You can do this effectively by including the concrete details within the subordinate clause and identifying the symbolic meaning in the independent clause.

Review the following examples of commentary and notice how subordination and coordination reveal the relationship between the ideas.

Syntactical Move	Function	Example
Independent clause	A simple sentence creates emphasis by isolating the content.	*Jay Gatsby's massive library represents the lengths he is willing to go to make an impression.*
Coordination (compound sentence)	Combining two independent clauses with a coordinating conjunction or conjunctive adverb shows balance or equality of ideas.	*Jay Gatsby's massive library represents the lengths he is willing to go to make an impression; however, the thin beard of ivy outside the mansion walls reveals his inexperience and naivete.*
Subordination (periodic sentence)	A complex sentence that begins with a dependent clause before the independent clause shows imbalance or incongruity.	*Although it may seem that Gatsby is nearer to his dream when he begins seeing Daisy in secret, the gradual decline in the appearance and vitality of his mansion symbolizes that Gatsby is losing his grasp on the dream day by day.*
Subordination (cumulative sentence)	A complex sentence that begins with the independent clause followed by a dependent clause shows imbalance or incongruity.	*Fitzgerald symbolizes the ultimate death of Gatsby's dream through the pathetic details of Gatsby's deserted mansion at the end of the novel <u>as</u> the once-vibrant mansion hosts his sparse funeral and wayward partygoers now drive past knowing that the party is over.*

INSIDER AP TIP **Specificity strengthens your literary argument.** Even though you will not have the work available to you during the exam, you should review a few short, memorable, thematic quotations from the novels that you think you may use for the open questions. These details will be useful when you write about the major ideas in the work.

AP® EXAM PRACTICE

The following is an example of the literary argument free-response question. Practice the skills you have learned in this workshop to write an argument in response to the prompt. You may use the graphic organizer and templates to help you plan and write your analysis.

Remember to follow the four steps:

- Step One: Annotate the passage based on a **unifying idea**
- Step Two: Write a **defensible thesis statement**
- Step Three: Choose **relevant evidence**
- Step Four: Develop **insightful commentary**

Prompt:

In many works of literature, authors include characters who suffer from ailments that may be physical, mental, or spiritual (e.g., scars, disease, madness, a troubled soul). The character's condition may serve as a symbol and represent deeper meanings within the work.

Either from your own reading or from the following list, choose a work of fiction that includes a character with a physical, mental, or spiritual ailment that serves as a symbol within the work. Then, in a well-written essay, analyze how the symbolic associations of the ailment contribute to an interpretation of the work as a whole. Do not merely summarize the plot.

In your response you should do the following:

- Respond to the prompt with a thesis that presents a defensible interpretation
- Select and use evidence to support your line of reasoning
- Explain how the evidence supports your line of reasoning
- Use appropriate grammar and punctuation in communicating your argument

The Awakening	*Native Speaker*
Cat on a Hot Tin Roof	*The Nickel Boys*
A Doll's House	*One Hundred Years of Solitude*
Don Quixote	*Othello*
Fences	*The Picture of Dorian Gray*
Frankenstein	*The Poisonwood Bible*
Geek Love	*A Prayer for Owen Meany*
The Great Gatsby	*A Raisin in the Sun*
The Handmaid's Tale	*The Red Badge of Courage*
Harry Potter and the Deathly Hallows	"The Rime of the Ancient Mariner"
Homegoing	*Roots*
I'm Not Your Perfect Mexican Daughter	*The Scarlet Letter*
Invisible Man	*Sense and Sensibility*
The Joy Luck Club	*Sing, Unburied, Sing*
Kindred	*The Strange Case of Dr. Jekyll and Mr. Hyde*
The Kite Runner	*The Sympathizer*
The Leavers	*Their Eyes Were Watching God*
Middle Passage	*Top Girls*
Moby Dick	*Where the Crawdads Sing*
Mudbound	*White Teeth*

ORGANIZING A LITERARY ARGUMENT (II)

Defensible Thesis Statement with Claim (idea + insight):

In [title], the author shifts from [a to b] / juxtaposes [a and b] to reveal [idea + insight].

Topic Sentence 1 (Identify the first aspect of [topic] related to the unifying idea):	Topic Sentence 2 (Identify the first aspect of [topic] related to the unifying idea):	Topic Sentence 3 (Identify the first aspect of [topic] related to the unifying idea):
Initially, [author] includes [literary element] to illustrate [universal idea].	As the narrative progresses, [author] shifts from [a to b] to explore [topic] further using [literary element] to reveal [universal idea].	Ultimately, [author] includes [literary element] to reveal [universal idea].
Textual Details (Relevant and sufficient evidence):	**Textual Details** (Relevant and sufficient evidence):	**Textual Details** (Relevant and sufficient evidence):
For example, the detail [evidence], used to describe [context] illustrates [link to reason].	To illustrate, [author] describes/ compares [context] by including [text evidence] to reveal [link to reason].	As an example of [technique/ element], the author includes [text evidence] to explain [link to reason].
Additionally, the detail [evidence], used to describe [context] illustrates [link to reason].	In the same way, [author] describes/compares [context] by including [text evidence] to reveal [link to reason].	Another example, of [technique/ element], that the author includes [text evidence] illustrates [link to reason].
Commentary (Link evidence to reason and idea):	**Commentary** (Link evidence to reason and idea):	**Commentary** (Link evidence to reason and idea):
The association of [text evidence] with [topic sentence] reveals [idea and insight].	Through this choice, [author] develops [idea and insight].	By including this [element/ technique] the author suggests that [idea and insight].
Two to four sentences explaining how the evidence exemplifies the universal idea	*Two to four sentences explaining how the evidence exemplifies the universal idea*	*Two to four sentences explaining how the evidence exemplifies the universal idea*

from A Thousand Splendid Suns

Khaled Hosseini

The following is an excerpt from a novel published in 2007. The italicized words are also italicized in the original.

Nana made no secret of her dislike for visitors — and, in fact, people in general — but she made exceptions for a select few. And so there was Gul Daman's[1] leader, the village *arbab*,
5   Habib Khan, a small-headed, bearded man with a large belly who came by once a month or so, tailed by a servant, carried a chicken, sometimes a pot of *kichiri* rice, or a basket of dyed eggs, for Mariam.
10   Then there was a rotund, old woman that Nana called Bibi jo, whose late husband had been a stone carver and friends with Nana's father. Bibi jo was invariably accompanied by one of her six brides and a grandchild or
15   two. She limped and huffed her way across the clearing and made a great show of rubbing her hip and lowering herself, with a pained sigh, onto the chair that Nana pulled up for her. Bibi jo too always brought Mariam something, a
20   box of *dishlemeh* candy, a basket of quinces. For Nana, she first brought complaints about her failing health, and then gossip from Herat and Gul Daman, delivered at length and with gusto, as her daughter-in-law sat listening qui-
25   etly and dutifully behind her.

    But Mariam's favorite, other than Jalil of course, was Mullah[2] Faizullah, the elderly village Koran[3] tutor, its *akhund*. He came by once or twice a week from Gul Daman to
30   teach Mariam the five daily *namaz* prayers and tutor her in Koran recitation, just as he had taught Nana when she'd been a little girl. It was Mullah Faizullah who had taught Mariam to read, who had patiently looked over her
35   shoulder as her lips worked the words soundlessly, her index finger lingering beneath each word, pressing until the nail bed went white, as though she could squeeze the meaning out of the symbols. It was Mullah Faizullah who
40   had held her hand, guided the pencil in it along the rise of each *alef*, the curve of each *beh*, the three dots of each *seh*.

    He was a gaunt, stooping old man with a toothless smile and a white beard that
45   dropped to his navel. Usually, he came alone to the *kolba*,[4] though sometimes with his russet haired son Hamza, who was a few years older than Mariam. When he showed up at the *kolba*, Mariam kissed Mullah Faizullah's
50   hand — which felt like kissing a set of twigs covered with a thin layer of skin — and he kissed the top of her brow before they sat inside for the day's lesson. After, the two of them sat outside the *kolba*, ate pine nuts and
55   sipped green tea, watched the bulbul birds darting from tree to tree. Sometimes they went for walks among the bronze fallen leaves and alder bushes, along the stream and toward the mountains. Mullah Faizullah twirled the beads

---

[1]Gul Daman is the name of a village in Afghanistan — where this excerpt is set.

[2]An Islamic scholar well-versed in the sacred law of that religion.

[3]Or "Quran" — the Islamic sacred book.

[4]A mud hut or a small shack with walls made of mud bricks and mud mortar.

60 of his *tasbeh* rosary as they strolled, and, in
his quivering voice, told Mariam stories of all
the things he'd seen in his youth, like the two
headed snake he'd found in Iran, on Isfahan's
Thirty-three Arch Bridge, or the watermelon
65 he had split once outside the Blue Mosque in
Mazar, to find the seeds forming the words
Allahu on one half, *Akbar*[5] on the other.

Mullah Faizullah admitted to Mariam that,
at times, he did not understand the meaning
70 of the Koran's words. But he said he liked the
enchanting sounds the Arabic words made as
they rolled off his tongue. He said they comforted him, eased his heart.

"They'll comfort you too, Mariam jo," he
75 said. "You can summon them in your time of
need, and they won't fail you. God's words will
never betray you, my girl."

Mullah Faizullah listened to stories as well
as he told them. When Mariam spoke, his
80 attention never wavered. He nodded slowly
and smiled with a look of gratitude, as if he had
been granted a coveted privilege. It was easy to
tell Mullah Faizullah things that Mariam didn't
dare tell Nana.

1. The sentence in lines 3–9 ("And so . . .
   for Mariam") presents the pronoun "who" as
   most likely a reference to
   (A) Mariam.
   (B) a servant.
   (C) Habib Khan.
   (D) Nana.
   (E) Bibi jo.

[5]"Allahu Akbar": an Arabic phrase meaning "God is most
great" — used by Muslims in prayers and as a general declaration of faith or thanksgiving.

2. In the context of the first and second
   paragraphs (lines 1–25), the details pro-
   vided about Nana and Bibi jo demonstrate
   that
   (A) they get along so well because they are
       very alike in their attitudes about life
       and treatment of people.
   (B) Nana likes her despite Bibi jo
       constantly demanding attention and
       controlling conversations.
   (C) Nana tolerates Bibi jo only because
       Bibi jo keeps her informed about
       gossip from the surrounding area.
   (D) neither of them cares much for
       Mariam, and they tolerate her only
       because she is a child.
   (E) Bibi jo would have no reason to visit
       Nana were it not for the relationship
       Bibi jo has with Mariam.

3. In lines 50–51, the statement between the
   dashes ("which felt . . . skin") emphasizes
   which of the following about Mullah
   Faizullah?
   (A) His life has been tragic.
   (B) He is an exceptionally holy man.
   (C) His health is failing.
   (D) He has become one with nature.
   (E) He is frail and elderly.

4. According to details provided in the pas-
   sage, Mullah Faizullah can be said to most
   likely value
   (A) Bibi jo's kind and giving heart despite
       her penchant for gossip.
   (B) his ability to continue serving as
       village "akhund" (line 28) well into
       old age.
   (C) his relationship with the families of
       the village.
   (D) Mariam's family, religion, and his own
       stories.
   (E) Mariam's experiences, education, and
       relationship to her faith.

5. All of the following lines contribute to the contrast of Bibbi jo and Mullah Faizullah EXCEPT
   (A) "Then there was a rotund, old woman that Nana called Bibi jo, whose late husband had been a stone carver and friends with Nana's father" (lines 10–13).
   (B) ". . . she first brought complaints about her failing health, and then gossip from Herat and Gul Daman, delivered at length and with gusto, as her daughter-in-law sat listening quietly and dutifully behind her" (lines 21–25).
   (C) "He was a gaunt, stooping old man with a toothless smile and a white beard that dropped to his navel" (lines 43–45).
   (D) "Usually, he came alone to the kolba, though sometimes with his russet haired son Hamza, who was a few years older than Mariam (lines 45–48).
   (E) "It was Mullah Faizullah who had held her hand, guided the pencil in it along the rise of each alef, the curve of each *beh*, the three dots of each *seh*" (lines 39–42).

6. In the context of the passage as a whole, which of the following sentences contain details demonstrating the narrator's bias?
   (A) "Nana made no secret of her dislike for visitors and, in fact, people in general but she made exceptions for a select few" (lines 1–3).
   (B) "Bibi jo was invariably accompanied by one of her six brides and a grandchild or two" (lines 13–15).
   (C) "She limped and huffed her way across the clearing and made a great show of rubbing her hip and lowering herself, with a pained sigh, onto the chair that Nana pulled up for her" (lines 15–18).
   (D) "He was a gaunt, stooping old man with a toothless smile and a white beard that dropped to his navel" (lines 43–45).
   (E) "But he said he liked the enchanting sounds the Arabic words made as they rolled off his tongue" (lines 70–72).

Hugging the Jukebox

Naomi Shihab Nye

On an island the soft hue of memory,
moss green, kerosene yellow, drifting, mingling
in the Caribbean Sea,
a six-year-old named Alfred
5 learns all the words to all the songs
on his grandparents' jukebox, and sings them.
To learn the words is not so hard.
Many barmaids and teenagers have done as well.
But to sing as Alfred sings—
10 how can a giant whale live in the small pool of his chest?
How can there be breakers this high, notes crashing
at the beach of the throat,
and a reef of coral so enormous only the fishes know its size?

The grandparents watch. They can't sing.
15 They don't know who this voice is, trapped in their grandson's body.
The boy whose parents sent him back to the island
to chatter mango-talk and scrap with chickens—
three years ago he didn't know the word "sad"!
Now he strings a hundred passionate sentences on a single line.
20 He bangs his fist so they will raise the volume.

What will they do together in their old age?
It is hard enough keeping yourself alive.
And this wild boy, loving nothing but music—
he'll sing all night, hugging the jukebox.
25 When a record pauses, that live second before dropping down,
Alfred hugs tighter, arms stretched wide,
head pressed on the luminous belly. "Now!" he yells.
A half-smile when the needle breathes again.

They've tried putting him to bed, but he sings in bed.
30 Even in Spanish — and he doesn't speak Spanish!
Sings and screams, wants to go back to the jukebox.
O mama I was born with a trumpet in my throat spent all these years tryin' to
cough it up . . .

He can't even read yet. He can't *tell time*.
But he sings, and the chairs in this old dance hall jerk to attention.
35 The grandparents lean on the counter, shaking their heads.
The customers stop talking and stare, goosey bumps surfacing on their arms.
His voice carries out to the water where boats are tied
and sings for all of them, *a wave.*
For the hens, now roosting in trees,
40 for the mute boy next door, his second-best friend.
And for the hurricane, now brewing near Barbados[1] —
a week forward neighbors will be hammering boards over their windows,
rounding up dogs and fishing lines,
the generators will quit with solemn clicks in every yard.

45 But Alfred, hugging a sleeping jukebox,
the names of the tunes gone dark,
will still be singing, doubly loud now, teasing his grandmother,
"Put a coin in my mouth!" and believing what she wants to believe;
this is not the end of the island, or the tablets this life has been
50 scribbled on, or the song.

Utila, Honduras[2]

---

[1]An eastern Caribbean island and independent nation.
[2]Utila is the smallest of Honduras's (a country in central America) major Bay Islands.

1. In context, the metaphors in line 10 ("how . . . chest?") can be best understood
   (A) as illustrating the power of the boy's voice despite his size and age.
   (B) by relating them to the "barmaids and teenagers" in line 8.
   (C) to contrast the boy with the other people in the setting.
   (D) as demonstrating the speaker's bias against the boy and his situation.
   (E) by contrasting the size of a whale with the size of the "small pool" (line 10).

2. In the context of the poem, which of the following best describes an understanding of the personification in line 28 ("A half-smile . . . again")?
   (A) The jukebox shows an upside-down "half-smile" (since its top is arched) as the boy hugs it and that hug causes it to continue its music as it seeks to awaken the boy.
   (B) "The needle" of the record player makes a hissing, breathy sound as it touches a record and before the music begins, bringing back the music and reanimating the boy just like breath brings life.
   (C) The boy's demand for the jukebox to play "[n]ow!" (line 27) exhausts the jukebox, and it must rest, just as someone who is tired must pause and breathe to recover mental and physical strength.
   (D) The "luminous belly" (line 27) of the jukebox seems to heave with breath as the music plays just like the boy breathes heavily after his singing and dancing.
   (E) The boy has not yet learned to control his breathing when he sings, making his voice sound immature and inexperienced.

3. In the context of the poem, which of the following best explains the effect of the portion following the dash in line 30 ("Even . . . Spanish!")?
   (A) It emphasizes Alfred's ignorance and lack of experience.
   (B) It creates a distinction between Alfred's experiences and those who are native to the island.
   (C) It emphasizes the amazement felt for Alfred's surprising talents.
   (D) It illustrates how unbelieving Alfred's grandparents are about his talents.
   (E) It emphasizes the cultural contrasts at the heart of the poem.

4. In context, which of the following lines indicates a shift in the speaker's perspective on the boy?
   (A) Line 7 ("To learn . . . hard")
   (B) Line 16 ("The boy . . . island")
   (C) Line 23 ("And this . . . music —")
   (D) Line 34 ("But . . . attention")
   (E) Line 45 ("But Alfred . . . jukebox")

5. In context, details included in line 36 ("The customers . . . arms") allow the speaker to emphasize
   (A) the unease and discomfort that the customers feel for the boy as he sings.
   (B) the embarrassment the customers feel for the boy as he sings.
   (C) the customers' awestruck amazement with the boy's singing.
   (D) the customers' nervous excitement with the boy's singing.
   (E) the customers' fearful uncertainty about the boy's singing.

6. Which of the following is most likely presented as a contrast for the boy?
   (A) "... an island the soft hue of memory" (line 1)
   (B) "breakers this high, notes crashing / at the beach of the throat" (lines 11–12)
   (C) "... parents ..." (line 16)
   (D) "... the mute boy next door" (line 40)
   (E) "... hurricane, now brewing near Barbados —" (line 41)

7. The images in line 45 ("But Alfred . . . jukebox") echoes which line from earlier in the poem?
   (A) Line 9 ("But to . . . sings —")
   (B) Line 11 ("How can . . . crashing")
   (C) Line 20 ("He bangs . . . volume")
   (D) Line 26 ("Alfred . . . wide")
   (E) Line 29 ("They've . . . bed")

8. Introduction of "the hurricane, now brewing near Barbados" (line 41) presents a significant change to the poem's
   (A) arrangement of lines and stanzas.
   (B) structural convention.
   (C) perspective on Alfred.
   (D) imagery.
   (E) dramatic situation.

9. By the end of the poem, Alfred's singing can best be considered
   (A) symbolic of the things that endure when the world around us seems to collapse.
   (B) an extended metaphor comparing talent to education and illustrating that some things simply cannot be taught.
   (C) an image of the persistent creativity of youth.
   (D) a representation of how children respond when adults establish and maintain low expectations.
   (E) an archetype for the ways children overwhelm adults.

franckreporter/Getty Images

UNIT

7

Analyzing Associations

UNIT GOALS

	Focus	Goals
Big Idea: Character	**Character Change and Epiphany**	Explain how a character's epiphany contributes to an interpretation.
Big Idea: Setting	**Contrasting and Changing Settings**	Explain how contrasting or changing settings emphasize values and ideas within a narrative and contribute to an interpretation.
Big Idea: Structure	**Narrative Pacing**	Explain how an author structures a literary text to emphasize and reveal ideas that contribute to an interpretation.
Big Idea: Narration	**Reliable and Unreliable Narrators**	Explain how a narrator's reliability contributes to an interpretation.
Big Idea: Figurative Language	**Symbolic Settings and Motifs**	Explain how symbolic settings and motifs create associations that contribute to an interpretation.
Big Idea: Figurative Language	**Similes and Personification**	Explain the significance of comparisons created through the use of similes and personification.
Ideas in Literature	• **Appearance and Reality** • **Loss and Disillusionment**	Explain how the ideas of appearance, reality, loss, and disillusionment are reflected in classic and contemporary texts.
Big Idea: Literary Argumentation	**Writing about Setting**	Write a literary argument that analyzes how the author's use of a setting contributes to an interpretation of a text.
Preparing for the AP® Exam	**Free-Response Question: Prose Fiction Analysis** Writing Introductions	Write an introduction for a literary argument that establishes relevant context for the interpretation.
	Multiple-Choice Questions: Prose	Analyze literary elements and techniques in classic and contemporary prose and poetry.
	Multiple-Choice Questions: Poetry	

Character Change and Epiphany

 Enduring Understanding

Characters in literature allow readers to study and explore a range of values, beliefs, assumptions, biases, and cultural norms represented by those characters.

KEY POINT

Epiphanies occur when a character gains sudden insight as a result of an external or, more often, an internal conflict of values that affects how the character understands his or her circumstances.

If you've ever struggled to solve a problem or grasp a concept in class, you know that the experience can feel like you're hitting a brick wall. You focus, you listen, and you try — but something just won't connect. Then again, you may have gotten lucky enough to experience the sudden rush of *"Oh! I get it now!"* The excitement of finally seeing or understanding feels invigorating. In some cases, you may even remember a moment of insight for the rest of your life. In literature, authors use these moments of clarity (along with other character changes) as a way to explore new developments within a story.

Changes in Circumstance Lead to Character Changes

You've already learned that effective readers carefully trace whether characters change throughout the course of a story or stay the same. Characters who remain fundamentally unchanged throughout the narrative are called **static characters**, while those who experience a change are called **dynamic characters**.

Authors introduce character changes carefully and intentionally. These changes often emerge from an **internal conflict** of values, which the author has represented within a narrative. In other instances, a character may change because of a sudden shift or development in the character's unique **circumstances**. Generally speaking, the term *circumstance* refers to the physical, social, and cultural facts and conditions connected to an event within a narrative or the actions of a character. These changes may be external: for example, a character may be evicted from a home or receive a devastating medical diagnosis. But changes that characters experience may also be internal: for example, a character may experience a new emotion, gain a new perspective, or recall a pivotal incident from the past. A series of changes may indicate that a character's situation is getting progressively better (or worse).

When characters change, they often come to new understandings about themselves, other characters, or the world around them. As a result, their values can change, which may lead them to take new actions or change old behaviors.

Epiphanies

Some changes happen gradually, as when a character finishes a long journey filled with adventures, hardships, and discoveries.

But other changes happen in an instant. When characters come to a sudden realization, insight, or moment of clarity, they have an **epiphany**. You may have experienced an epiphany yourself if you've ever had an "Aha!" moment, where time seems to stand still and everything clicks into place and makes sense. Epiphanies allow a protagonist to see circumstances in a new way.

Epiphanies tend to happen when tensions are already running high. As a result, these sudden revelations can be important emotional experiences for a character. For example, a protagonist may feel compelled to act based on a new understanding, which means that epiphanies can have a direct impact on the narrative's plot.

Tragedy and Comedy

Often, the epiphany emerges from the central conflict in the plot and occurs at a **climactic moment** in the narrative. From this turning point, the events are set in motion toward the story's resolution. In a classical **tragedy**, the **tragic hero** comes to recognize his or her own flaw (*anagnorisis*), which results in that reversal of fortune that could be catastrophe or death (*peripeteia*), whereas in a classical **comedy**, the protagonist often finds true love or lives a better life as a result of the new insight.

In a classical tragedy, a character usually makes an error in judgment as the result of some **tragic flaw** (*harmartia*). Remember that the hero's tragic flaw is a character trait — greed, hubris, rigidity, recklessness — that affects the protagonist's judgment and ultimately leads to personal destruction and death.

Authors intentionally develop characters to propel the narrative forward. Character changes, including epiphanies, also reveal information critical to understanding and interpreting themes within the text.

INSIDER AP TIP

Epiphanies are often thematic insights. Character epiphanies are significant in a literary text because they present pivotal moments in the narrative that often reveal a perspective about an idea.

CHARACTER CHANGE AND EPIPHANY		
Type of Conflict	**Description**	**Considerations for Effect**
Internal Conflict	The protagonist is faced with a difficult decision. Each possible option represents a value or idea. Even not making a choice is, in fact, a choice.	Why does the character make the choice that he or she does? • How does a character's background affect the choice that he or she makes? • How do a character's relationships with other characters affect the choice that he or she makes? What decision does the character make?
External Conflict	The protagonist faces an antagonist, such as another character or a force of nature. The antagonist represents a value or idea.	• What options does the character have? • What does his or her choice reveal about the character? How does the character's choice affect the narrative? • What new insight or understanding does the character come to? • How does this new insight affect the character's interactions and the outcome of the narrative?

GUIDED READING

Araby
James Joyce

C. P. Curran/Hulton Archive/Getty Images

THE TEXT IN CONTEXT

One of the most influential writers of the twentieth century, Irish novelist James Joyce (1882–1941) is perhaps best known for *Ulysses* (1922): an epic work that incorporates a range of modernist fictional techniques such as stream-of-consciousness narration, the representation of interior subjectivity, fragmented perceptions, stylistic experiments, and ironic parallels to ancient myth. But Joyce's sprawling *Ulysses* began as an unused tale for his first book of stories, *Dubliners* (1914). In that collection's fifteen elegant narratives, he explores the psychological and emotional lives of everyday middle- and lower-class Dublin residents. He also evokes the corruption, inhibition, betrayal, death, and stifling Catholicism that — in Joyce's view — paralyzed Ireland and Irish society. The third story in *Dubliners*, "Araby" (included here) introduces readers to some of these ideas, as well as to another major element of Joyce's fiction: the use of epiphany. For the writer, these epiphanies are small but powerful revelations that provide characters with sudden insight into themselves and their circumstances. Joyce's other works are the novels *Portrait of the Artist as a Young Man* (1916) and *Finnegan's Wake* (1939).

Araby

North Richmond Street, being blind, was a quiet street except at the hour when the Christian Brothers' School set the boys free. An uninhabited house of two storeys stood at the blind end, detached from its neighbours in a square ground. The other houses of the street, conscious of decent
5 lives within them, gazed at one another with brown imperturbable faces.

The former tenant of our house, a priest, had died in the back drawing-room. Air, musty from having been long enclosed, hung in all the rooms, and the waste room behind the kitchen was littered with old useless papers. Among these I found a few paper-covered books, the pages of
10 which were curled and damp: *The Abbot*, by Walter Scott, *The Devout Communicant* and *The Memoirs of Vidocq*. I liked the last best because its leaves were yellow. The wild garden behind the house contained a central apple-tree and a few straggling bushes under one of which I found the late tenant's rusty bicycle-pump. He had been a very charitable priest;

Guided Questions

1. How does the narrator relate to the former resident? What similarities do they share?

15 in his will he had left all his money to institutions and the furniture of his house to his sister.

   When the short days of winter came dusk fell before we had well eaten our dinners. When we met in the street the houses had grown sombre. The space of sky above us was the colour of ever-changing violet and
20 towards it the lamps of the street lifted their feeble lanterns. The cold air stung us and we played till our bodies glowed. Our shouts echoed in the silent street. The career of our play brought us through the dark muddy lanes behind the houses where we ran the gauntlet of the rough tribes from the cottages, to the back doors of the dark dripping gardens where
25 odours arose from the ashpits, to the dark odorous stables where a coach-man smoothed and combed the horse or shook music from the buckled harness. When we returned to the street light from the kitchen windows had filled the areas. If my uncle was seen turning the corner we hid in the shadow until we had seen him safely housed. Or if Mangan's sister came
30 out on the doorstep to call her brother in to his tea we watched her from our shadow peer up and down the street. We waited to see whether she would remain or go in and, if she remained, we left our shadow and walked up to Mangan's steps resignedly. She was waiting for us, her figure defined by the light from the half-opened door. Her brother always teased
35 her before he obeyed and I stood by the railings looking at her. Her dress swung as she moved her body and the soft rope of her hair tossed from side to side.

   Every morning I lay on the floor in the front parlour watching her door. The blind was pulled down to within an inch of the sash so that I could
40 not be seen. When she came out on the doorstep my heart leaped. I ran to the hall, seized my books and followed her. I kept her brown figure always in my eye and, when we came near the point at which our ways diverged, I quickened my pace and passed her. This happened morning after morning. I had never spoken to her, except for a few casual words, and yet
45 her name was like a summons to all my foolish blood.

   Her image accompanied me even in places the most hostile to romance. On Saturday evenings when my aunt went marketing I had to go to carry some of the parcels. We walked through the flaring streets, jostled by drunken men and bargaining women, amid the curses of labourers, the
50 shrill litanies of shop-boys who stood on guard by the barrels of pigs' cheeks, the nasal chanting of street-singers, who sang a *come-all-you* about O'Donovan Rossa, or a ballad about the troubles in our native land. These noises converged in a single sensation of life for me: I imagined that I bore my chalice safely through a throng of foes. Her name sprang to my lips at
55 moments in strange prayers and praises which I myself did not under-stand. My eyes were often full of tears (I could not tell why) and at times a

Guided Questions

2. What does the narrator's religious background reveal about his feelings towards Mangan's sister?

flood from my heart seemed to pour itself out into my bosom. I thought
little of the future. I did not know whether I would ever speak to her or
not or, if I spoke to her, how I could tell her of my confused adoration. But
60 my body was like a harp and her words and gestures were like fingers
running upon the wires.

     One evening I went into the back drawing-room in which the priest
had died. It was a dark rainy evening and there was no sound in the
house. Through one of the broken panes I heard the rain impinge upon
65 the earth, the fine incessant needles of water playing in the sodden beds.
Some distant lamp or lighted window gleamed below me. I was thankful
that I could see so little. All my senses seemed to desire to veil themselves
and, feeling that I was about to slip from them, I pressed the palms of
my hands together until they trembled, murmuring: "O love! O love!"
70 many times.

     At last she spoke to me. When she addressed the first words to me I
was so confused that I did not know what to answer. She asked me was I
going to *Araby*. I forgot whether I answered yes or no. It would be a splendid bazaar, she said; she would love to go.

75   "And why can't you?" I asked.

     While she spoke she turned a silver bracelet round and round her
wrist. She could not go, she said, because there would be a retreat that
week in her convent. Her brother and two other boys were fighting for
their caps and I was alone at the railings. She held one of the spikes,
80 bowing her head towards me. The light from the lamp opposite our
door caught the white curve of her neck, lit up her hair that rested
there and, falling, lit up the hand upon the railing. It fell over one side
of her dress and caught the white border of a petticoat, just visible as
she stood at ease.

85   "It's well for you," she said.

     "If I go," I said, "I will bring you something."

     What innumerable follies laid waste my waking and sleeping thoughts
after that evening! I wished to annihilate the tedious intervening days.
I chafed against the work of school. At night in my bedroom and by day in
90 the classroom her image came between me and the page I strove to read.
The syllables of the word *Araby* were called to me through the silence in
which my soul luxuriated and cast an Eastern enchantment over me. I
asked for leave to go to the bazaar on Saturday night. My aunt was surprised and hoped it was not some Freemason affair. I answered few
95 questions in class. I watched my master's face pass from amiability to
sternness; he hoped I was not beginning to idle. I could not call my
wandering thoughts together. I had hardly any patience with the serious
work of life which, now that it stood between me and my desire, seemed
to me child's play, ugly monotonous child's play.

Guided Questions

3. What similarities
does the narrator
share with the
priest?

4. How does the
description affect
the protagonist's
perception of
Mangan's sister?

5. How does this
promise create an
internal conflict for
the narrator?

6. What does the
description of
Araby reveal about
the narrator?

CHARACTER

100   On Saturday morning I reminded my uncle that I wished to go to the
bazaar in the evening. He was fussing at the hallstand, looking for the
hat-brush, and answered me curtly:

"Yes, boy, I know."

As he was in the hall I could not go into the front parlour and lie at the
105 window. I left the house in bad humour and walked slowly towards the
school. The air was pitilessly raw and already my heart misgave me.

When I came home to dinner my uncle had not yet been home. Still it
was early. I sat staring at the clock for some time and, when its ticking
began to irritate me, I left the room. I mounted the staircase and gained
110 the upper part of the house. The high cold empty gloomy rooms liberated
me and I went from room to room singing. From the front window I saw
my companions playing below in the street. Their cries reached me weakened and indistinct and, leaning my forehead against the cool glass, I
looked over at the dark house where she lived. I may have stood there for
115 an hour, seeing nothing but the brown-clad figure cast by my imagination,
touched discreetly by the lamplight at the curved neck, at the hand upon
the railings and at the border below the dress.

When I came downstairs again I found Mrs Mercer sitting at the fire.
She was an old garrulous woman, a pawnbroker's widow, who collected
120 used stamps for some pious purpose. I had to endure the gossip of the
tea-table. The meal was prolonged beyond an hour and still my uncle did
not come. Mrs Mercer stood up to go: she was sorry she couldn't wait any
longer, but it was after eight o'clock and she did not like to be out late as
the night air was bad for her. When she had gone I began to walk up and
125 down the room, clenching my fists. My aunt said:

"I'm afraid you may put off your bazaar for this night of Our Lord."

At nine o'clock I heard my uncle's latchkey in the halldoor. I heard him
talking to himself and heard the hallstand rocking when it had received
the weight of his overcoat. I could interpret these signs. When he was
130 midway through his dinner I asked him to give me the money to go to the
bazaar. He had forgotten.

"The people are in bed and after their first sleep now," he said.

I did not smile. My aunt said to him energetically:

"Can't you give him the money and let him go? You've kept him late
135 enough as it is."

My uncle said he was very sorry he had forgotten. He said he believed
in the old saying: "All work and no play makes Jack a dull boy." He asked
me where I was going and, when I had told him a second time he asked
me did I know The Arab's Farewell to his Steed. When I left the kitchen he
140 was about to recite the opening lines of the piece to my aunt.

I held a florin tightly in my hand as I strode down Buckingham Street
towards the station. The sight of the streets thronged with buyers and

7. How does the
uncle's late arrival
affect the narrator?

8. What does their
treatment of the
boy reveal about
the aunt and
uncle?

glaring with gas recalled to me the purpose of my journey. I took my seat
in a third-class carriage of a deserted train. After an intolerable delay the
145 train moved out of the station slowly. It crept onward among ruinous
houses and over the twinkling river. At Westland Row Station a crowd of
people pressed to the carriage doors; but the porters moved them back,
saying that it was a special train for the bazaar. I remained alone in the
bare carriage. In a few minutes the train drew up beside an improvised
150 wooden platform. I passed out on to the road and saw by the lighted dial
of a clock that it was ten minutes to ten. In front of me was a large building which displayed the magical name.

    I could not find any sixpenny entrance and, fearing that the bazaar
would be closed, I passed in quickly through a turnstile, handing a shilling
155 to a weary-looking man. I found myself in a big hall girdled at half its
height by a gallery. Nearly all the stalls were closed and the greater part
of the hall was in darkness. I recognised a silence like that which
pervades a church after a service. I walked into the centre of the bazaar
timidly. A few people were gathered about the stalls which were still
160 open. Before a curtain, over which the words *Café Chantant* were written in
coloured lamps, two men were counting money on a salver. I listened to
the fall of the coins.

    Remembering with difficulty why I had come I went over to one of
the stalls and examined porcelain vases and flowered tea-sets. At the
165 door of the stall a young lady was talking and laughing with two young
gentlemen. I remarked their English accents and listened vaguely to their
conversation.

    "O, I never said such a thing!"

    "O, but you did!"

170   "O, but I didn't!"

    "Didn't she say that?"

    "Yes. I heard her."

    "O, there's a . . . fib!"

    Observing me the young lady came over and asked me did I wish to
175 buy anything. The tone of her voice was not encouraging; she seemed to
have spoken to me out of a sense of duty. I looked humbly at the great jars
that stood like eastern guards at either side of the dark entrance to the
stall and murmured:

    "No, thank you."

180   The young lady changed the position of one of the vases and went back
to the two young men. They began to talk of the same subject. Once or
twice the young lady glanced at me over her shoulder.

    I lingered before her stall, though I knew my stay was useless, to make
my interest in her wares seem the more real. Then I turned away slowly

9. What does the
train delay reveal
about the narrator?

10. What does this
conversation
reveal to the
narrator about
Araby?

11. What choice
must the narrator
make? Why
does he make
the choice he
does? What is
the narrator's
epiphany?

185 and walked down the middle of the bazaar. I allowed the two pennies to
fall against the sixpence in my pocket. I heard a voice call from one end
of the gallery that the light was out. The upper part of the hall was now
completely dark.

    Gazing up into the darkness I saw myself as a creature driven and
190 derided by vanity; and my eyes burned with anguish and anger.

Guided Questions

12. How does the narrator change?

PRACTICE TEXT

The Demon Lover
Elizabeth Bowen

Hulton-Deutsch/Corbis/Getty Images

THE TEXT IN CONTEXT

Elizabeth Bowen (1899–1973) was an Irish-British writer whose
novels and short stories often depict Anglo-Irish life, upper-
middle-class British anxiety, and the traumatic effects of
Germany's bombing of London during World War II. From July
through September of 1940, the German air force conducted
daily air raids on English cities. The Battle of Britain ultimately
left 43,000 civilians dead. It also damaged or destroyed over
a million houses, leaving one of every six Londoners homeless
at some point during the war. The experience was devastating
for England, even in victory. Bowen's work often dramatizes the
effects of this devastation on specific individuals, as in the case of her haunting — and
haunted — short story "The Demon Lover."

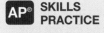 **SKILLS PRACTICE** | **CHARACTER**
Analyzing Character Epiphany

As you read "The Demon Lover," consider how details revealed through the story's structure develop a conflict that builds toward a climactic moment resulting
in an epiphany for the protagonist. Use the graphic organizer to record details
from the text that reveal the character. Explain how the textual details contribute
to epiphany.

(continued)

Analyzing Character Epiphany		
Beginning Textual details that indicate values associated with the protagonist	**Middle** Textual details that indicate the protagonist's choices at the climatic moment	**End** Textual details that illustrate the protagonist's epiphany
Details and effect:	Details and effect:	Details and effect:

The Demon Lover

Toward the end of her day in London Mrs. Drover went round to her shut-up house to look for several things she wanted to take away. Some belonged to herself, some to her
5 family, who were by now used to their country life. It was late August; it had been a steamy, showery day: At the moment the trees down the pavement glittered in an escape of humid yellow afternoon sun. Against the next batch
10 of clouds, already piling up ink-dark, broken chimneys and parapets stood out. In her once familiar street, as in any unused channel, an unfamiliar queerness had silted up; a cat wove itself in and out of railings, but no human eye
15 watched Mrs. Drover's return. Shifting some parcels under her arm, she slowly forced round her latchkey in an unwilling lock, then gave the door, which had warped, a push with her knee. Dead air came out to meet her as
20 she went in.

The staircase window having been boarded up, no light came down into the hall. But one door, she could just see, stood ajar, so she went quickly through into the room and
25 unshuttered the big window in there. Now the prosaic woman, looking about her, was more perplexed than she knew by everything that she saw, by traces of her long former habit of life—the yellow smoke stain up the
30 white marble mantelpiece, the ring left by a vase on the top of the escritoire; the bruise in the wallpaper where, on the door being thrown open widely, the china handle had always hit the wall. The piano, having gone
35 away to be stored, had left what looked like claw marks on its part of the parquet. Though not much dust had seeped in, each object wore a film of another kind; and, the only ventilation being the chimney, the
40 whole drawing room smelled of the cold hearth. Mrs. Drover put down her parcels on the escritoire and left the room to proceed upstairs; the things she wanted were in a bedroom chest.

45 She had been anxious to see how the house was—the part-time caretaker she shared with some neighbors was away this week on his holiday, known to be not yet back. At the best of times he did not look
50 in often, and she was never sure that she trusted him. There were some cracks in the structure, left by the last bombing, on which she was anxious to keep an eye. Not that one could do anything—
55 A shaft of refracted daylight now lay across the hall. She stopped dead and

stared at the hall table—on this lay a letter addressed to her.

She thought first—then the caretaker
60 *must* be back. All the same, who, seeing the house shuttered, would have dropped a letter in at the box? It was not a circular, it was not a bill. And the post office redirected, to the address in the country, everything for her
65 that came through the post. The caretaker (even if he were back) did not know she was due in London today—her call here had been planned to be a surprise—so his negligence in the manner of this letter, leaving it
70 to wait in the dusk and the dust, annoyed her. Annoyed, she picked up the letter, which bore no stamp. But it cannot be important, or they would know . . . She took the letter rapidly upstairs with her, without a stop to
75 look at the writing till she reached what had been her bedroom, where she let in light. The room looked over the garden and other gardens: The sun had gone in; as the clouds sharpened and lowered, the trees and rank
80 lawns seemed already to smoke with dark. Her reluctance to look again at the letter came from the fact that she felt intruded upon—and by someone contemptuous of her ways. However, in the tenseness pre-
85 ceding the fall of rain she read it: It was a few lines.

Dear Kathleen:
You will not have forgotten that today is our anniversary, and the day we said.
90 The years have gone by at once slowly and fast. In view of the fact that nothing has changed, I shall rely upon you to keep your promise. I was sorry to see you leave London, but was satisfied
95 that you would be back in time. You may expect me, therefore, at the hour arranged. Until then . . .

K.

Mrs. Drover looked for the date: It was
100 today's. She dropped the letter onto the bedsprings, then picked it up to see the writing again—her lips, beneath the remains of lipstick, beginning to go white. She felt so much the change in her own face that she went to
105 the mirror, polished a clear patch in it, and looked at once urgently and stealthily in. She was confronted by a woman of forty-four, with eyes starting out under a hat brim that had been rather carelessly pulled down. She
110 had not put on any more powder since she left the shop where she ate her solitary tea. The pearls her husband had given her on their marriage hung loose round her now rather thinner throat, slipping in the V of
115 the pink wool jumper her sister knitted last autumn as they sat round the fire. Mrs. Drover's most normal expression was one of controlled worry, but of assent. Since the birth of the third of her little boys, attended by a
120 quite serious illness, she had had an intermittent muscular flicker to the left of her mouth, but in spite of this she could always sustain a manner that was at once energetic and calm.

125 Turning from her own face as precipitately as she had gone to meet it, she went to the chest where the things were, unlocked it, threw up the lid, and knelt to search. But as rain began to come crashing down she could
130 not keep from looking over her shoulder at the stripped bed on which the letter lay. Behind the blanket of rain the clock of the church that still stood struck six—with rapidly heightening apprehension she
135 counted each of the slow strokes. "The hour arranged . . . My God," she said, "*what* hour? How should I . . . ? After twenty-five years . . ."

The young girl talking to the soldier in the garden had not ever completely seen his
140 face. It was dark; they were saying goodbye under a tree. Now and then—for it felt, from

not seeing him at this intense moment, as
though she had never seen him at all—she
verified his presence for these few moments
145 longer by putting out a hand, which he each
time pressed, without very much kindness,
and painfully, on to one of the breast buttons
of his uniform. That cut of the button on the
palm of her hand was, principally, what she
150 was to carry away. This was so near the end
of a leave from France that she could only
wish him already gone. It was August 1916.
Being not kissed, being drawn away from and
looked at intimidated Kathleen till she imag-
155 ined spectral glitters in the place of his eyes.
Turning away and looking back up the lawn
she saw, through branches of trees, the
drawing-room window alight: She caught a
breath for the moment when she could go
160 running back there into the safe arms of her
mother and sister, and cry: "What shall I do,
what shall I do? He has gone."

Hearing her catch her breath, her fiancé
said, without feeling: "Cold?"
165   "You're going away such a long way."
"Not so far as you think."
"I don't understand?"
"You don't have to," he said. "You will. You
know what we said."
170   "But that was—suppose you—I mean,
suppose."
"I shall be with you," he said, "sooner or
later. You won't forget that. You need do
nothing but wait."
175   Only a little more than a minute later she
was free to run up the silent lawn. Looking in
through the window at her mother and sister, who did not for the moment perceive
her, she already felt that unnatural promise
180 drive down between her and the rest of all
humankind. No other way of having given
herself could have made her feel so apart,
lost and forsworn. She could not have plighted
a more sinister troth.

185   Kathleen behaved well when, some
months later, her fiancé was reported missing, presumed killed. Her family not only
supported her but were able to praise her
courage without stint because they could not
190 regret, as a husband for her, the man they
knew almost nothing about. They hoped she
would, in a year or two, console herself—and
had it been only a question of consolation
things might have gone much straighter
195 ahead. But her trouble, behind just a little
grief, was a complete dislocation from everything. She did not reject other lovers, for
these failed to appear: For years she failed to
attract men—and with the approach of her
200 thirties she became natural enough to share
her family's anxiousness on this score. She
began to put herself out, to wonder, and at
thirty-two she was very greatly relieved to
find herself being courted by William Drover.
205 She married him, and the two of them settled down in this quiet, arboreal part of
Kensington: In this house the years piled up,
her children were born, and they all lived till
they were driven out by the bombs of the
210 next war. Her movements as Mrs. Drover
were circumscribed, and she dismissed any
idea that they were still watched.

As things were—dead or living the letter
writer sent her only a threat. Unable, for
215 some minutes, to go on kneeling with her
back exposed to the empty room, Mrs. Drover
rose from the chest to sit on an upright chair
whose back was firmly against the wall. The
desuetude of her former bedroom, her mar-
220 ried London home's whole air of being a
cracked cup from which memory, with its
reassuring power, had either evaporated or
leaked away, made a crisis—and at just this
crisis the letter writer had, knowledgeably,
225 struck. The hollowness of the house this evening canceled years on years of voices, habits, and steps. Through the shut windows she

only heard rain fall on the roofs around. To
rally herself, she said she was in a mood—
230 and for two or three seconds shutting her
eyes, told herself that she had imagined the
letter. But she opened them—there it lay on
the bed.

On the supernatural side of the letter's
235 entrance she was not permitting her mind to
dwell. Who, in London, knew she meant to
call at the house today? Evidently, however,
this had been known. The caretaker, *had he*
come back, had had no cause to expect her:
240 He would have taken the letter in his pocket,
to forward it, at his own time, through the
post. There was no other sign that the caretaker had been in—but, if not? Letters dropped
in at doors of deserted houses do not fly or
245 walk to tables in halls. They do not sit on the
dust of empty tables with the air of certainty
that they will be found. There is needed some
human hand—but nobody but the caretaker
had a key. Under circumstances she did not
250 care to consider, a house can be entered without a key. It was possible that she was not
alone now. She might be being waited for,
downstairs. Waited for—until when? Until
"the hour arranged." At least that was not six
255 o'clock: Six has struck.

She rose from the chair and went over
and locked the door.

The thing was, to get out. To fly? No, not
that: She had to catch her train. As a woman
260 whose utter dependability was the keystone
of her family life she was not willing to
return to the country, to her husband, her little boys, and her sister, without the objects
she had come up to fetch. Resuming work at
265 the chest she set about making up a number
of parcels in a rapid, fumbling-decisive way.
These, with her shopping parcels, would be
too much to carry; these meant a taxi—at
the thought of the taxi her heart went up
270 and her normal breathing resumed. I will

ring up the taxi now; the taxi cannot come
too soon: I shall hear the taxi out there running its engine, till I walk calmly down to it
through the hall. I'll ring up—But no: the
275 telephone is cut off . . . She tugged at a knot
she had tied wrong.

The idea of flight . . . He was never kind to
me, not really. I don't remember him kind at
all. Mother said he never considered me. He
280 was set on me, that was what it was—not
love. Not love, not meaning a person well.
What did he do, to make me promise like
that? I can't remember—But she found that
she could.

285 She remembered with such dreadful
acuteness that the twenty-five years since
then dissolved like smoke and she instinctively looked for the weal left by the button on
the palm of her hand. She remembered not
290 only all that he said and did but the complete
suspension of her existence during that
August week. I was not myself—they all told
me so at the time. She remembered—but
with one white burning blank as where acid
295 has dropped on a photograph: *Under no conditions* could she remember his face.

So, wherever he may be waiting, I shall
not know him. You have no time to run from
a face you do not expect.

300 The thing was to get to the taxi before any
clock struck what could be the hour. She
would slip down the street and round the
side of the square to where the square gave
on the main road. She would return in the
305 taxi, safe, to her own door, and bring the
solid driver into the house with her to pick
up the parcels from room to room. The idea
of the taxi driver made her decisive, bold:
She unlocked her door, went to the top of the
310 staircase, and listened down.

She heard nothing—but while she was
hearing nothing the *passé* air of the staircase
was disturbed by a draft that traveled up to

her face. It emanated from the basement:
315 Down there a door or window was being
opened by someone who chose this moment
to leave the house.

The rain had stopped; the pavements
steamily shone as Mrs. Drover let herself out
320 by inches from her own front door into the
empty street. The unoccupied houses opposite continued to meet her look with their
damaged stare. Making toward the thoroughfare and the taxi, she tried not to keep look-
325 ing behind. Indeed, the silence was so
intense—one of those creeks of London
silence exaggerated this summer by the
damage of war—that no tread could have
gained on hers unheard. Where her street
330 debouched on the square where people
went on living, she grew conscious of, and
checked, her unnatural pace. Across the open
end of the square two buses impassively
passed each other: Women, a perambulator,
335 cyclists, a man wheeling a barrow signalized,
once again, the ordinary flow of life. At the
square's most populous corner should
be—and was—the short taxi rank. This evening, only one taxi—but this, although it

340 presented its blank rump, appeared already
to be alertly waiting for her. Indeed, without
looking round the driver started his engine
as she panted up from behind and put her
hand on the door. As she did so, the clock
345 struck seven. The taxi faced the main road:
To make the trip back to her house it would
have to turn—she had settled back on the
seat and the taxi had turned before she, surprised by its knowing movement, recollected
350 that she had not "said where." She leaned
forward to scratch at the glass panel that
divided the driver's head from her own.

The driver braked to what was almost a
stop, turned round, and slid the glass panel
355 back: The jolt of this flung Mrs. Drover forward till her face was almost into the glass.
Through the aperture driver and passenger,
not six inches between them, remained for an
eternity eye to eye. Mrs. Drover's mouth hung
360 open for some seconds before she could issue
her first scream. After that she continued to
scream freely and to beat with her gloved
hands on the glass all round as the taxi, accelerating without mercy, made off with her into
365 the hinterland of deserted streets.

CHARACTER

1. How does Mrs. Drover's arrival at the house in London begin to reveal a change in circumstances that creates an **internal conflict** for her?

2. Consider Mrs. Drover's thoughts and actions as she reads the letter, remembers her lover, and packs her things. What is the climactic moment that incites an **internal conflict** for Mrs. Drover? What tension is revealed?

3. How does the character change at this climactic moment? Are the last actions at the end of the story consistent with Mrs. Drover's change?

4. What does she realize? What is her **epiphany**?

SETTING

Contrasting and Changing Settings

AP® **Enduring Understanding (SET-1)**

Setting and the details associated with it not only depict a time and place but also convey values associated with that setting.

If you've ever seen the original *The Wizard of Oz*, you may recall that the movie begins in black and white, revealing a farm in Kansas. When the protagonist Dorothy is caught in a tornado, however, she is transported to the Land of Oz where her journey is in wondrous Technicolor. This cinematic technique was an intentional choice for the filmmaker. What might the contrast between black and white and color represent?

Dorothy's experiences on the Kansas farm and in Oz occur in two different settings, each with different values, beliefs, and customs. And if we analyze that story, we would consider what each of those settings — and Dorothy's interactions in them — reveal.

Some writers choose to set stories in different locations. Some settings are realistic; some settings are romantic, fantastical, or exotic; some settings spark adventure; others are personified, and still other settings emphasize tradition and heritage. Most stories are set where they are for a reason. Examining the settings, including their change or contrast, may give you a clue as to which aspects of setting the author wants you to notice as you develop an interpretation.

KEY POINT

Values and ideas are associated with a particular setting. Therefore, when a setting changes, so do the values and ideas associated with that setting. Likewise, when settings are contrasted, so are the values.

Characters Are Associated with the Values of a Story's Setting

You've already learned that a setting may represent its associated values and ideas. So when an author places a character within a particular **setting** and set of **circumstances**, the values and ideas of both are part of the plot, theme, and development of characters. In fact, some authors use the setting to provide clues to readers about the characters. For example,

- setting may reflect or reveal the inner emotional state of a character;
- setting may contribute to other elements such as structure;
- setting may actually become an antagonist or another character in the story; or
- setting may be an archetype that represents a cultural tradition or familiar pattern.

A character's description of a setting can often reveal some attitude or perspective about the values associated with that setting. The way characters interact with their surroundings provides insights about those characters and their setting(s), as well. It is important to consider the character's role in and relationship to the setting he or she inhabits. It might even be helpful to ask yourself, "How would the story be different if it were in a different setting?"

Changes in Setting

Some stories occur in multiple settings. This could be as simple as multiple rooms in the same house or multiple locations in the same town or village, or it could involve larger spatial movements (different countries or planets) and different time periods (e.g., a Puritan village in colonial New England).

When a setting changes, it often suggests other movements, developments, or **shifts** in the narrative. For example, if a setting is specifically associated with historical or cultural values, when the setting changes so might those historical or cultural values. If a setting comes to represent the psychological state of a character, as the setting shifts, changes, and evolves so might the psychology of that character. And if a character begins in one setting, travels to another, and ultimately returns home, then those shifting settings may align with an emotional or spiritual journey.

Pay close attention to these changes, as they will often provide insight for your interpretation.

Contrasting Settings

When there are multiple settings in a narrative, you should also consider the degree to which the author is **contrasting** (or comparing) them. Because settings often represent values and ideas, an author may use different settings to contrast those values and ideas.

Remember: a setting is not a static part of the narrative structure. Its meaning will shift and develop. If you can analyze how characters interact with settings (and the values and ideas associated with them), you will be able to generate complex and effective interpretations.

When settings are contrasted, the author is most likely using the contrast to set up a **tension** of values that manifests in a **conflict** that the protagonist must deal with. That tension often manifests itself in a psychological, emotional, or other internal struggle for the protagonist. More often, that tension manifests itself in an internal conflict for the protagonist; however, if the setting is **personified**, then that conflict may be external for the protagonist.

From Romanticism to Realism

To understand attitudes about values and ideas, we can place these attitudes on a continuum from idealistic to realistic. Because authors create literature to explore the human experience, characters, like people, often face conflicts that put these values at odds. As characters grapple with such conflicts, their own values emerge, often illustrating a preference of values that the author wants the reader to understand. Recognizing this tension and analyzing it can lead to an insightful interpretation of the literary work.

CONTRASTING SETTINGS AND VALUES

The Romantic and Idyllic	The Realistic
Rural/pastoral	Urban
The ideal world	The actual world
The naturally perfect	The seedy, gritty, or mechanized
The beautiful and the aesthetic	The truth, no matter how ugly or sinister
Authentic	Superficial
Pure	Adulterated
Imagination	Reason
Innocent	Experienced

INSIDER
AP® TIP

Contrasts are critical to interpretations. Authors set up contrasts of setting or characters to highlight a tension of values, attitudes, or ideas. Insightful interpretations illuminate how the literal contrasts reveal figurative meanings.

GUIDED READING

A Mild Attack of Locusts
Doris Lessing

Colin McPherson/Corbis/Getty Images

THE TEXT IN CONTEXT

Nobel Prize–winning novelist Doris Lessing (1919–2013) was born to English parents in Iran; later, her family moved to the British colony of Southern Rhodesia, which is now the African country of Zimbabwe. Lessing is known for her versatility and insight across a wide range of literary genres, including realistic short stories and science fiction novels, along with more political, experimental, and postmodern work, such as her 1962 novel *The Golden Notebook*. Lessing wrote over fifty books of fiction, nonfiction, comics, poetry, and opera libretti. Her most well-known works are *The Summer Before the Dark* (1973), *Memoirs of a Survivor* (1974), and *The Good Terrorist* (1985). In the following short story, "A Mild Attack of Locusts," originally published in 1955 in the *New Yorker*, she evokes the vast power of natural forces.

A Mild Attack of Locusts

The rains that year were good; they were coming nicely just as the crops needed them—or so Margaret gathered when the men said they were not too bad. She never had an opinion of her own on matters like the weather, because even to know about a simple thing like the weather needs expe-

5 rience, which Margaret, born and brought up in Johannesburg, had not got. The men were her husband, Richard, and old Stephen, Richard's father, who was a farmer from way back, and these two might argue for hours over whether the rains were ruinous or just ordinarily exasperating. Margaret had been on the farm for three years now. She still did not

10 understand why they did not go bankrupt altogether, when the men never had a good word for the weather, or the soil, or the government. But she was getting to learn the language. Farmers' language. And she noticed that for all Richard's and Stephen's complaints, they did not go bankrupt. Nor did they get very rich; they jogged along, doing comfortably.

15 Their crop was maize. Their farm was three thousand acres on the ridges that rise up toward the Zambezi escarpment—high, dry, windswept country, cold and dusty in winter, but now, in the wet months, steamy with the heat that rose in wet, soft waves off miles of green foliage. Beautiful it was, with the sky on fair days like blue and brilliant halls

20 of air, and the bright-green folds and hollows of country beneath, and the mountains lying sharp and bare twenty miles off, beyond the rivers. The sky made her eyes ache; she was not used to it. One does not look so much at the sky in the city. So that evening, when Richard said, "The government is sending out warnings that locusts are expected, coming

25 down from the breeding grounds up north," her instinct was to look about her at the trees. Insects, swarms of them—horrible! But Richard and the old man had raised their eyes and were looking up over the nearest mountaintop. "We haven't had locusts in seven years," one said, and the other, "They go in cycles, locusts do." And then: "There goes our

30 crop for this season!"

But they went on with the work of the farm just as usual, until one day, when they were coming up the road to the homestead for the midday break, old Stephen stopped, raised his finger, and pointed. "Look, look!" he shouted. "There they are!"

35 Margaret heard him and she ran out to join them, looking at the hills. Out came the servants from the kitchen. They all stood and gazed. Over the rocky levels of the mountain was a streak of rust-colored air. Locusts. There they came.

At once, Richard shouted at the cookboy. Old Stephen yelled at the

40 houseboy. The cookboy ran to beat the rusty plowshare, banging from a tree branch, that was used to summon the laborers at moments of crisis.

1. How does Margaret's opinion about weather contribute to her attitude?

2. Describe the contrasts within the setting and how they create tension.

3. What details about the setting does the dialogue between Richard and the Old Man reveal?

The houseboy ran off to the store to collect tin cans—any old bits of metal. The farm was ringing with the clamor of the gong, and the laborers came pouring out of the compound, pointing at the hills and shouting 45 excitedly. Soon they had all come up to the house, and Richard and old Stephen were giving them orders: Hurry, hurry, hurry.

And off they ran again, the two white men with them, and in a few minutes Margaret could see the smoke of fires rising from all around the farmlands. When the government warnings came, piles of wood and grass 50 had been prepared in every cultivated field. There were seven patches of bared, cultivated soil, where the new mealies were just showing, making a film of bright green over the rich dark red, and around each patch now drifted up thick clouds of smoke. The men were throwing wet leaves onto the fires to make the smoke acrid and black. Margaret was watching the 55 hills. Now there was a long, low cloud advancing, rust-colored still, swelling forward and out as she looked. The telephone was ringing—neighbors to say, Quick, quick, here come the locusts! Old Smith had already had his crop eaten to the ground. Quick, get your fires started! For, of course, while every farmer hoped the locusts would overlook his farm and go on to the 60 next, it was only fair to warn the others; one must play fair. Everywhere, fifty miles over the countryside, the smoke was rising from a myriad of fires. Margaret answered the telephone calls and, between them, stood watching the locusts. The air was darkening—a strange darkness, for the sun was blazing. It was like the darkness of a veldt fire, when the air gets 65 thick with smoke and the sunlight comes down distorted—a thick, hot orange. It was oppressive, too, with the heaviness of a storm. The locusts were coming fast. Now half the sky was darkened. Behind the reddish veils in front, which were the advance guard of the swarm, the main swarm showed in dense black clouds, reaching almost to the sun itself.

70 Margaret was wondering what she could do to help. She did not know. Then up came old Stephen from the lands. "We're finished, Margaret, finished!" he said. "Those beggars can eat every leaf and blade off the farm in half an hour! But it's only early afternoon. If we can make enough smoke, make enough noise till the sun goes down, they'll settle somewhere else, 75 perhaps." And then: "Get the kettle going. It's thirsty work, this."

So Margaret went to the kitchen and stoked up the fire and boiled the water. Now on the tin roof of the kitchen she could hear the thuds and bangs of falling locusts, or a scratching slither as one skidded down the tin slope. Here were the first of them. From down on the lands came the 80 beating and banging and clanging of a hundred petrol tins and bits of metal. Stephen impatiently waited while Margaret filled one petrol tin with tea—hot, sweet, and orange-colored—and another with water. In the meantime, he told her about how, twenty years back, he had been

4. What is the shift? How does the shift contribute to a change in the narrative?

Guided Questions

eaten out, made bankrupt by the locust armies. And then, still talking,
85 he lifted the heavy petrol cans, one in each hand, holding them by the
wooden pieces set cornerwise across the tops, and jogged off down to
the road to the thirsty laborers.

By now, the locusts were falling like hail on the roof of the kitchen. It
sounded like a heavy storm. Margaret looked out and saw the air dark
90 with a crisscross of the insects, and she set her teeth and ran out into it;
what the men could do, she could. Overhead, the air was thick—locusts
everywhere. The locusts were flopping against her, and she brushed them
off—heavy red-brown creatures, looking at her with their beady, old
men's eyes while they clung to her with their hard, serrated legs. She held
95 her breath with disgust and ran through the door into the house again.
There it was even more like being in a heavy storm. The iron roof was
reverberating, and the clamor of beaten iron from the lands was like thunder. When she looked out, all the trees were queer and still, clotted with
insects, their boughs weighted to the ground. The earth seemed to be
100 moving, with locusts crawling everywhere; she could not see the lands at
all, so thick was the swarm. Toward the mountains, it was like looking into
driving rain; even as she watched, the sun was blotted out with a fresh
onrush of the insects. It was a half night, a perverted blackness. Then
came a sharp crack from the bush—a branch had snapped off. Then
105 another. A tree down the slope leaned over slowly and settled heavily to
the ground. Through the hail of insects, a man came running. More tea,
more water were needed. Margaret supplied them. She kept the fires
stoked and filled tins with liquid, and then it was four in the afternoon
and the locusts had been pouring across overhead for a couple of hours.
110 Up came old Stephen again—crunching locusts underfoot with every
step, locusts clinging all over him—cursing and swearing, banging with
his old hat at the air. At the doorway, he stopped briefly, hastily pulling at
the clinging insects and throwing them off, and then he plunged into the
locust-free living room.
115 "All the crops finished. Nothing left," he said.
But the gongs were still beating, the men still shouting, and Margaret
asked, "Why do you go on with it, then?"
"The main swarm isn't settling. They are heavy with eggs. They are
looking for a place to settle and lay. If we can stop the main body settling
120 on our farm, that's everything. If they get a chance to lay their eggs, we are
going to have everything eaten flat with hoppers later on." He picked a
stray locust off his shirt and split it down with his thumbnail; it was clotted inside with eggs. "Imagine that multiplied by millions. You ever seen a
hopper swarm on the march? No? Well, you're lucky."
125 Margaret thought an adult swarm was bad enough. Outside, the light
on the earth was now a pale, thin yellow darkened with moving shadow;

Guided Questions

5. What changes for
Margaret and what
does she do?

6. How is the setting
described? What
do the comparisons
reveal?

the clouds of moving insects alternately thickened and lightened, like driving rain. Old Stephen said, "They've got the wind behind them. That's something."

130 "Is it very bad?" asked Margaret fearfully, and the old man said emphatically, "We're finished. This swarm may pass over, but once they've started, they'll be coming down from the north one after another. And then there are the hoppers. It might go on for three or four years."

Margaret sat down helplessly and thought, Well, if it's the end, it's the
135 end. What now? We'll all three have to go back to town. But at this she took a quick look at Stephen, the old man who had farmed forty years in this country and been bankrupt twice before, and she knew nothing would make him go and become a clerk in the city. Her heart ached for him; he looked so tired, the worry lines deep from nose to mouth. Poor old
140 man. He lifted up a locust that had got itself somehow into his pocket, and held it in the air by one leg. "You've got the strength of a steel spring in those legs of yours," he told the locust good-humoredly. Then, although for the last three hours he had been fighting locusts, squashing locusts, yelling at locusts, and sweeping them in great mounds into the fires to
145 burn, he nevertheless took this one to the door and carefully threw it out to join its fellows, as if he would rather not harm a hair of its head. This comforted Margaret; all at once, she felt irrationally cheered. She remembered it was not the first time in the past three years the men had announced their final and irremediable ruin.

150 "Get me a drink, lass," Stephen then said, and she set a bottle of whiskey by him.

In the meantime, thought Margaret, her husband was out in the pelting storm of insects, banging the gong, feeding the fires with leaves, while the insects clung all over him. She shuddered. "How can you bear to let them
155 touch you?" she asked Stephen. He looked at her disapprovingly. She felt suitably humble, just as she had when Richard brought her to the farm after their marriage and Stephen first took a good look at her city self— hair waved and golden, nails red and pointed. Now she was a proper farmer's wife, in sensible shoes and a solid skirt. She might even get to
160 letting locusts settle on her, in time.

Having tossed down a couple of whiskeys, old Stephen went back into the battle, wading now through glistening brown waves of locusts.

Five o'clock. The sun would set in an hour. Then the swarm would settle. It was as thick as ever overhead. The trees were ragged mounds of
165 glistening brown.

Margaret began to cry. It was all so hopeless. If it wasn't a bad season, it was locusts; if it wasn't locusts, it was army worms or veldt fires. Always something. The rustling of the locust armies was like a big forest in a storm. The ground was invisible in a sleek brown surging tide; it was like

7. How does the way Stephen treats the locust change the narrative?

8. How much time has passed? What time of day is it?

9. How is the setting changed after the attack?

170 being drowned in locusts, submerged by the loathsome brown flood.
It seemed as if the roof might sink in under the weight of them, as if
the door might give in under their pressure and these rooms fill with
them—and it was getting so dark. Through the window, she looked up at
the sky. The air was thinner; gaps of blue showed in the dark moving
175 clouds. The blue spaces were cold and thin; the sun must be setting.
Through the fog of insects, she saw figures approaching. First old Stephen,
marching bravely along, then her husband, drawn and haggard with weariness, and behind them the servants. All of them were crawling with
insects. The sound of the gongs had stopped. Margaret could hear nothing
180 but the ceaseless rustle of myriads of wings.

The two men slapped off the insects and came in.

"Well," said Richard, kissing her on the cheek, "the main swarm has
gone over."

"For the Lord's sake!" said Margaret angrily, still half crying. "What's
185 here is bad enough, isn't it?" For although the evening air was no longer
black and thick but a clear blue, with a pattern of insects whizzing this
way and that across it, everything else—trees, buildings, bushes,
earth—was gone under the moving brown masses.

"If it doesn't rain in the night and keep them here," Stephen said, "if it
190 doesn't rain and weigh them down with water, they'll be off in the morning at sunrise."

"We're bound to have some hoppers," said Richard. "But not the main
swarm. That's something."

Margaret roused herself, wiped her eyes, pretended she had not
195 been crying, and fetched them some supper, for the servants were too
exhausted to move. She sent them off to the compound to rest.

She served the supper and sat listening. There was not one maize plant
left, she heard. Not one. They would get the planting machines out the
moment the locusts had gone. They must start all over again.

200 What was the use of that, Margaret wondered, if the whole farm was
going to be crawling with hoppers? But she listened while they discussed
the new government pamphlet that told how to defeat the hoppers. You
must have men out all the time, patrolling the farm, to watch for movement
in the grass. When you find a patch of hoppers—small, lively black things,
205 like crickets—then you dig trenches around the patch or spray them with
poison from pumps supplied by the government. The government wanted
every farmer to cooperate in a world plan for eliminating this plague forever. You must attack locusts at the source—hoppers, in short. The men
were talking as if they were planning a war, and Margaret listened, amazed.
210 In the night, it was quiet, with no sign of the armies that had settled
outside, except that sometimes a branch snapped or a tree could be heard
crashing down.

10. How does
Margaret react
to the discussion
about the
government
pamphlet?
What does she
understand about
the attack of
locusts?

Margaret slept badly, in the bed beside Richard, who was sleeping like the dead. In the morning, she woke to yellow sunshine lying across the
215 bed—clear sunshine, with an occasional blotch of shadow moving over it. She went to the window. Old Stephen was ahead of her. There he stood, outside, gazing down over the bush. And she gazed, astounded—and entranced, much against her will. For it looked as if every tree, every bush, all the earth, were lit with pale flames. The locusts were fanning their
220 wings to free them of the night dews. There was a shimmer of red-tinged gold light everywhere.

She went out to join the old man, stepping carefully among the insects. The two stood and watched. Overhead the sky was blue—blue and clear.

"Pretty," said old Stephen with satisfaction.

225 Well, thought Margaret, we may be ruined, we may be bankrupt, but not everyone has seen a locust army fanning their wings at dawn.

Over the slopes in the distance, a faint red smear showed in the sky. It thickened and spread. "There they go," said old Stephen. "There goes the main army, off south."

230 And now, from the trees, from the earth all around them, the locusts were taking wing. They were like small aircraft maneuvering for the take-off as they tried their wings to see if they were dry enough. Off they went. A reddish-brown steam was rising off the miles of bush, off the farmlands—the earth. Again the sunlight darkened.

235 And as the clotted branches lifted, the weight on them lightening, there was nothing left but the black spines of branches and tree trunks. No green—nothing. All morning they watched, the three of them—Richard having finally got up—as the brown crust thinned and broke and dissolved, flying up to mass with the main army, now a brownish-red
240 smear in the southern sky. The lands, which had been filmed with the green of the new, tender mealie plants, were stark and bare. A devastated landscape—no green, no green anywhere.

By midday, the reddish cloud had gone. Only an occasional locust flopped down. On the ground lay the corpses and the wounded. The
245 African laborers were sweeping them up with branches and collecting them in tins.

"Ever eaten sun-dried locust, Margaret?" asked old Stephen. "That time twenty years ago when I went broke, I lived on mealie meal and dried locusts for three months. They aren't bad at all—rather like smoked fish,
250 if you come to think of it."

But Margaret preferred not even to think of it.

After the midday meal, the men went off to the lands. Everything was to be replanted. With a bit of luck, another swarm would not come travel-ling down just this way. But they hoped it would rain very soon, to spring
255 some new grass, because the cattle would die otherwise; there was not a

Guided Questions

11. How is the description of the setting in the morning symbolic?

12. What remains on the farm, and how does it affect the characters' motivations?

blade of grass left on the farm. As for Margaret, she was trying to get used to the idea of three or four years of locusts. Locusts were going to be like the weather from now on—always imminent. She felt like a survivor after a war; if this devastated and mangled countryside was not ruin—well,
260 what then was ruin?

But the men ate their supper with good appetites.

"It could have been worse" was what they said. "It could be much worse."

Guided Questions

13. How is the setting described in the story's resolution? What might this change suggest or reveal?

PRACTICE TEXT

Cell One
Chimamanda Ngozi Adichie

Britta Pedersen/picture alliance/Getty Images

THE TEXT IN CONTEXT

Writer and lecturer Chimamanda Ngozi Adichie (b. 1977) was born in Enugu, Nigeria. After finishing her secondary education in Enugu, she came to the United States to attend college and graduate school. This dichotomy between the United States and Nigeria emerges in both the settings and themes of her work — especially in her 2009 short story collection, *The Thing Around Your Neck.* In "Cell One," taken from that book, Adichie writes about an academic community in Enugu much like the one where she spent her childhood and adolescence. She also evokes the corrupt, brutal, and unjust nature of official authority in Nigeria, as well as the consequences when that authority begins to weaken. These are common themes for Adichie, along with racial and ethnic differences, gender, religion, politics, colonialism, and the nature of storytelling itself. Her other works include *Purple Hibiscus* (2003), *Americanah* (2013), and *We Should All Be Feminists* (2014).

 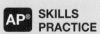 **SETTING**
Analyzing Changing or Contrasting Settings

As you read Adichie's "Cell One," record details of the contrasting settings. Note the values associated with (or represented by) the details of each setting. Then, consider how the contrast between those settings contributes to an interpretation of a single idea.

Analyzing Changing or Contrasting Settings	
Setting 1:	Setting 2:
Details from the text related to Setting 1:	Details from the text related to Setting 2:
Values associated with Setting 1:	Values associated with Setting 2:
How the contrast of settings or change in setting contributes to a single idea:	

Cell One

The first time our house was robbed, it was our neighbor Osita who climbed in through the dining-room window and stole our TV and VCR, and the "Purple Rain" and "Thriller"
5 videotapes that my father had brought back from America. The second time our house was robbed, it was my brother Nnamabia, who faked a break-in and stole my mother's jewelry. It happened on a Sunday. My parents
10 had travelled to their home town to visit our grandparents, so Nnamabia and I went to church alone. He drove my mother's green Peugeot 504. We sat together in church as we usually did, but we did not have time to
15 nudge each other and stifle giggles about somebody's ugly hat or threadbare caftan, because Nnamabia left without a word after ten minutes. He came back just before the priest said, "The Mass is ended, go in peace."
20 I was a little piqued. I imagined that he had gone off to smoke or to see some girl, since

he had the car to himself for once; but he could at least have told me. We drove home in silence, and when he parked in our long
25 driveway I stayed back to pick some ixora flowers while Nnamabia unlocked the front door. I went inside to find him standing in the middle of the parlor.

"We've been robbed!" he said.
30 It took me a moment to take in the room. Even then, I felt that there was a theatrical quality to the way the drawers had been flung open. Or perhaps it was simply that I knew my brother too well. Later, when my
35 parents had come home and neighbors began to troop in to say *ndo*—sorry—and to snap their fingers and heave their shoulders up and down, I sat alone in my room upstairs and realized what the queasiness in my gut
40 was: Nnamabia had done it, I knew. My father knew, too. He pointed out that the window louvres had been slipped out from

the inside, rather than from the outside
(Nnamabia was usually smarter than that—
45 perhaps he had been in a hurry to get back
to church before Mass ended), and that the
robber knew exactly where my mother's jewelry was: in the back left corner of her metal
trunk. Nnamabia stared at my father with
50 wounded eyes and said that he may have
done horrible things in the past, things that
had caused my parents pain, but that he had
done nothing in this case. He walked out the
back door and did not come home that night.
55 Or the next night. Or the night after. Two
weeks later, he came home gaunt, smelling of
beer, crying, saying he was sorry, that he had
pawned the jewelry to the Hausa traders in
Enugu, and that all the money was gone.
60   "How much did they give you for my
gold?" our mother asked him. And when he
told her she placed both hands on her head
and cried, "Oh! Oh! *Chi m egbuo m!* My God
has killed me!" I wanted to slap her. My father
65 asked Nnamabia to write a report: how he
had pawned the jewelry, what he had spent
the money on, with whom he had spent it.
I didn't think that Nnamabia would tell the
truth, and I don't think that my father thought
70 he would, but he liked reports, my professor
father, he liked to have things written down
and nicely documented. Besides, Nnamabia
was seventeen, with a carefully tended beard.
He was already between secondary school
75 and university, and was too old for caning.
What else could my father have done? After
Nnamabia had written the report, my father
filed it in the steel cabinet in his study where
he kept our school papers.
80   "That he could hurt his mother like that!"
was the last thing my father said on the
subject.
    But Nnamabia hadn't set out to hurt her.
He had done it because my mother's jewelry
85 was the only thing of any value in the house:

a lifetime's accumulation of solid-gold pieces.
He had done it, too, because other sons of
professors were doing it. This was the season
of thefts on our serene campus. Boys who
90 had grown up watching "Sesame Street,"
reading Enid Blyton, eating cornflakes for
breakfast, and attending the university staff
primary school in polished brown sandals
were now cutting through the mosquito
95 netting of their neighbors' windows, sliding
out glass louvres, and climbing in to steal
TVs and VCRs. We knew the thieves. Still,
when the professors saw one another at the
staff club or at church or at a faculty meet-
100 ing, they were careful to moan about the riffraff from town coming onto their sacred
campus to steal.
    The thieving boys were the popular ones.
They drove their parents' cars in the evening,
105 their seats pushed back and their arms
stretched out to reach the steering wheel.
Osita, our neighbor who had stolen our TV
only weeks before Nnamabia's theft, was
lithe and handsome in a brooding sort of
110 way, and walked with the grace of a cat. His
shirts were always crisply ironed, and I used
to watch him across the hedge, then close
my eyes and imagine that he was walking
toward me, coming to claim me as his. He
115 never noticed me. When he stole from us, my
parents did not go over to Professor Ebube's
house to ask for our things back. But they
knew it was Osita. Osita was two years older
than Nnamabia; most of the thieving boys
120 were a little older than Nnamabia, and maybe
that was why Nnamabia had not stolen from
another person's house. Perhaps he did not
feel old enough, qualified enough, for anything more serious than my mother's jewelry.
125   Nnamabia looked just like my mother—
he had her fair complexion and large eyes,
and a generous mouth that curved perfectly.
When my mother took us to the market,

traders would call out, "Hey! Madam, why did you waste your fair skin on a boy and leave the girl so dark? What is a boy doing with all this beauty?" And my mother would chuckle, as though she took a mischievous and joyful responsibility for Nnamabia's looks. When, at eleven, Nnamabia broke the window of his classroom with a stone, my mother gave him the money to replace it and didn't tell my father. When, a few years later, he took the key to my father's car and pressed it into a bar of soap that my father found before Nnamabia could take it to a locksmith, she made vague sounds about how he was just experimenting and it didn't mean anything. When he stole the exam questions from the study and sold them to my father's students, she yelled at him, but then told my father that Nnamabia was sixteen, after all, and really should be given more pocket money.

I don't know whether Nnamabia felt remorse for stealing her jewelry. I could not always tell from my brother's gracious, smiling face what he really felt. He and I did not talk about it, and neither did my parents. Even though my mother's sisters sent her their gold earrings, even though she bought a new gold chain from Mrs. Mozie—the glamorous woman who imported gold from Italy—and began to drive to Mrs. Mozie's house once a month to pay in installments, we never talked about what had happened to her jewelry. It was as if by pretending that Nnamabia had not done the things he had done we could give him the opportunity to start afresh. The robbery might never have been mentioned again if Nnamabia had not been arrested two years later, in his second year of university.

By then, it was the season of cults on the Nsukka campus, when signs all over the university read in bold letters, "SAY NO TO CULTS." The Black Axe, the Buccaneers, and the

Pirates were the best known. They had once been benign fraternities, but they had evolved, and now eighteen-year-olds who had mastered the swagger of American rap videos were undergoing secret initiations that sometimes left one or two of them dead on Odim Hill. Guns and tortured loyalties became common. A boy would leer at a girl who turned out to be the girlfriend of the Capone of the Black Axe, and that boy, as he walked to a kiosk later to buy a cigarette, would be stabbed in the thigh. He would turn out to be a Buccaneer, and so one of his fellow-Buccaneers would go to a beer parlor and shoot the nearest Black Axe in the leg, and then the next day another Buccaneer would be shot dead in the refectory, his body falling onto aluminum plates of garri, and that evening a Black Axe—a professor's son—would be hacked to death in his room, his CD player splattered with blood. It was inane. It was so abnormal that it quickly became normal. Girls stayed in their rooms after classes, and lecturers quivered, and when a fly buzzed too loudly people jumped. So the police were called in. They sped across campus in their rickety blue Peugeot 505 and glowered at the students, their rusty guns poking out of the car windows. Nnamabia came home from his lectures laughing. He thought that the police would have to do better than that; everyone knew the cult boys had newer guns.

My parents watched Nnamabia with silent concern, and I knew that they, too, were wondering if he was in a cult. Cult boys were popular, and Nnamabia was very popular. Boys yelled out his nickname—"The Funk!"—and shook his hand whenever he passed by, and girls, especially the popular ones, hugged him for too long when they said hello. He went to all the parties, the tame ones on campus and the wilder ones in town, and he was the kind of ladies' man who was also a guy's guy,

215 the kind who smoked a packet of Rothmans a day and was reputed to be able to finish a case of Star beer in a single sitting. But it seemed more his style to befriend all the cult boys and yet not be one himself. And I was 220 not entirely sure, either, that my brother had whatever it took—guts or diffidence—to join a cult.

The only time I asked him if he was in a cult, he looked at me with surprise, as if I 225 should have known better than to ask, before replying, "Of course not." I believed him. My dad believed him, too, when he asked. But our believing him made little difference, because he had already been arrested for 230 belonging to a cult.

This is how it happened. On a humid Monday, four cult members waited at the campus gate and waylaid a professor driving a red Mercedes. They pressed a gun to her 235 head, shoved her out of the car, and drove it to the Faculty of Engineering, where they shot three boys who were coming out of the building. It was noon. I was in a class nearby, and when we heard the shots our lecturer 240 was the first to run out the door. There was loud screaming, and suddenly the stairwells were packed with scrambling students unsure where to run. Outside, the bodies lay on the lawn. The Mercedes had already 245 screeched away. Many students hastily packed their bags, and *okada* drivers charged twice the usual fare to take them to the motor park to get on a bus. The vice-chancellor announced that all evening classes would be 250 cancelled and everyone had to stay indoors after 9 P.M. This did not make much sense to me, since the shooting had happened in sparkling daylight, and perhaps it did not make sense to Nnamabia, either, because 255 the first night of the curfew he didn't come home. I assumed that he had spent the night

at a friend's; he did not always come home anyway. But the next morning a security man came to tell my parents that Nnamabia 260 had been arrested at a bar with some cult boys and was at the police station. My mother screamed, "*Ekwuzikwana!* Don't say that!" My father calmly thanked the security man. We drove to the police station in town, and there 265 a constable chewing on the tip of a dirty pen said, "You mean those cult boys arrested last night? They have been taken to Enugu. Very serious case! We must stop this cult business once and for all!"

270 We got back into the car, and a new fear gripped us all. Nsukka, which was made up of our slow, insular campus and the slower, more insular town, was manageable; my father knew the police superintendent. But Enugu 275 was anonymous. There the police could do what they were famous for doing when under pressure to produce results: kill people.

The Enugu police station was in a sprawling, sandy compound. My mother bribed the 280 policemen at the desk with money, and with jollof rice and meat, and they allowed Nnamabia to come out of his cell and sit on a bench under a mango tree with us. Nobody asked why he had stayed out the night 285 before. Nobody said that the police were wrong to walk into a bar and arrest all the boys drinking there, including the barman. Instead, we listened to Nnamabia talk.

"If we ran Nigeria like this cell," he said, 290 "we would have no problems. Things are so organized. Our cell has a chief and he has a second-in-command, and when you come in you are expected to give them some money. If you don't, you're in trouble."

295 "And did you have any money?" my mother asked.

Nnamabia smiled, his face more beautiful than ever, despite the new pimple-like insect

300 bite on his forehead, and said that he had slipped his money into his anus shortly after the arrest. He knew the policemen would take it if he didn't hide it, and he knew that he would need it to buy his peace in the cell. My parents said nothing for a while. I imag-
305 ined Nnamabia rolling hundred-naira notes into a thin cigarette shape and then reaching into the back of his trousers to slip them into himself. Later, as we drove back to Nsukka, my father said, "This is what I should have
310 done when he stole your jewelry. I should have had him locked up in a cell."

My mother stared out the window.

"Why?" I asked.

"Because this has shaken him. Couldn't
315 you see?" my father asked with a smile. I couldn't see it. Nnamabia had seemed fine to me, slipping his money into his anus and all.

Nnamabia's first shock was seeing a Buccaneer sobbing. The boy was tall and
320 tough, rumored to have carried out one of the killings and likely to become Capone next semester, and yet there he was in the cell, cowering and sobbing after the chief gave him a light slap on the back of the head.
325 Nnamabia told me this in a voice lined with both disgust and disappointment; it was as if he had suddenly been made to see that the Incredible Hulk was really just painted green. His second shock was learning about the cell
330 farthest away from his, Cell One. He had never seen it, but every day two policemen carried a dead man out of Cell One, stopping by Nnamabia's cell to make sure that the corpse was seen by all.
335 Those in the cell who could afford to buy old plastic paint cans of water bathed every other morning. When they were let out into the yard, the policemen watched them and often shouted, "Stop that or you are going to
340 Cell One now!" Nnamabia could not imagine a place worse than his cell, which was so crowded that he often stood pressed against the wall. The wall had cracks where tiny *kwalikwata* lived; their bites were fierce and
345 sharp, and when he yelped his cellmates mocked him. The biting was worse during the night, when they all slept on their sides, head to foot, to make room for one another, except the chief, who slept with his whole
350 back lavishly on the floor. It was also the chief who divided up the two plates of rice that were pushed into the cell every day. Each person got two mouthfuls.

Nnamabia told us this during the first
355 week. As he spoke, I wondered if the bugs in the wall had bitten his face or if the bumps spreading across his forehead were due to an infection. Some of them were tipped with cream-colored pus. Once in a while, he
360 scratched at them. I wanted him to stop talking. He seemed to enjoy his new role as the sufferer of indignities, and he did not understand how lucky he was that the policemen allowed him to come out and eat
365 our food, or how stupid he'd been to stay out drinking that night, and how uncertain his chances were of being released.

We visited him every day for the first week. We took my father's old Volvo, because
370 my mother's Peugeot was unsafe for trips outside Nsukka. By the end of the week, I noticed that my parents were acting differently—subtly so, but differently. My father no longer gave a monologue, as soon as we
375 were waved through the police checkpoints, on how illiterate and corrupt the police were. He did not bring up the day when they had delayed us for an hour because he'd refused to bribe them, or how they had stopped a bus
380 in which my beautiful cousin Ogechi was travelling and singled her out and called her a whore because she had two cell phones,

and asked her for so much money that she had knelt on the ground in the rain begging them to let her go. My mother did not mumble that the policemen were symptoms of a larger malaise. Instead, my parents remained silent. It was as if by refusing to criticize the police they would somehow make Nnamabia's freedom more likely. "Delicate" was the word the superintendent at Nsukka had used. To get Nnamabia out anytime soon would be delicate, especially with the police commissioner in Enugu giving gloating, preening interviews about the arrest of the cultists. The cult problem was serious. Big Men in Abuja were following events. Everybody wanted to seem as if he were doing something.

The second week, I told my parents that we were not going to visit Nnamabia. We did not know how long this would last, and petrol was too expensive for us to drive three hours every day. Besides, it would not hurt Nnamabia to fend for himself for one day.

My mother said that nobody was begging me to come—I could sit there and do nothing while my innocent brother suffered. She started walking toward the car, and I ran after her. When I got outside, I was not sure what to do, so I picked up a stone near the ixora bush and hurled it at the windshield of the Volvo. I heard the brittle sound and saw the tiny lines spreading like rays on the glass before I turned and dashed upstairs and locked myself in my room. I heard my mother shouting. I heard my father's voice. Finally, there was silence. Nobody went to see Nnamabia that day. It surprised me, this little victory.

We visited him the next day. We said nothing about the windshield, although the cracks had spread out like ripples on a frozen stream. The policeman at the desk, the pleasant dark-skinned one, asked why

we had not come the day before—he had missed my mother's jollof rice. I expected Nnamabia to ask, too, even to be upset, but he looked oddly sober. He did not eat all of his rice.

"What is wrong?" my mother said, and Nnamabia began to speak almost immediately, as if he had been waiting to be asked. An old man had been pushed into his cell the day before—a man perhaps in his mid-seventies, white-haired, skin finely wrinkled, with an old-fashioned dignity about him. His son was wanted for armed robbery, and when the police had not been able to find his son they had decided to lock up the father.

"The man did nothing," Nnamabia said.

"But you did nothing, either," my mother said.

Nnamabia shook his head as if our mother did not understand. The following days, he was more subdued. He spoke less, and mostly about the old man: how he could not afford bathing water, how the others made fun of him or accused him of hiding his son, how the chief ignored him, how he looked frightened and so terribly small.

"Does he know where his son is?" my mother asked.

"He has not seen his son in four months," Nnamabia said.

"Of course it is wrong," my mother said. "But this is what the police do all the time. If they do not find the person they are looking for, they lock up his relative."

"The man is ill," Nnamabia said. "His hands shake, even when he's asleep."

He closed the container of rice and turned to my father. "I want to give him some of this, but if I bring it into the cell the chief will take it."

My father went over and asked the policeman at the desk if we could be allowed to see the old man in Nnamabia's cell for a few minutes. The policeman was the light-skinned acerbic one who never said thank you when my mother handed over the rice-and-money bribe, and now he sneered in my father's face and said that he could well lose his job for letting even Nnamabia out and yet now we were asking for another person? Did we think this was visiting day at a boarding school? My father came back and sat down with a sigh, and Nnamabia silently scratched at his bumpy face.

The next day, Nnamabia barely touched his rice. He said that the policemen had splashed soapy water on the floor and walls of the cell, as they usually did, and that the old man, who had not bathed in a week, had yanked his shirt off and rubbed his frail back against the wet floor. The policemen started to laugh when they saw him do this, and then they asked him to take all his clothes off and parade in the corridor outside the cell; as he did, they laughed louder and asked whether his son the thief knew that Papa's buttocks were so shrivelled. Nnamabia was staring at his yellow-orange rice as he spoke, and when he looked up his eyes were filled with tears, my worldly brother, and I felt a tenderness for him that I would not have been able to describe if I had been asked to.

There was another attack on campus—a boy hacked another boy with an axe—two days later.

"This is good," my mother said. "Now they cannot say that they have arrested all the cult boys." We did not go to Enugu that day; instead my parents went to see the local police superintendent, and they came back with good news. Nnamabia and the barman were to be released immediately. One of the cult boys, under questioning, had insisted

that Nnamabia was not a member. The next day, we left earlier than usual, without jollof rice. My mother was always nervous when we drove, saying to my father, "*Nekwa ya! Watch out!*," as if he could not see the cars making dangerous turns in the other lane, but this time she did it so often that my father pulled over before we got to Ninth Mile and snapped, "Just who is driving this car?"

Two policemen were flogging a man with *koboko* as we drove into the police station. At first, I thought it was Nnamabia, and then I thought it was the old man from his cell. It was neither. I knew the boy on the ground, who was writhing and shouting with each lash. He was called Aboy and had the grave ugly face of a hound; he drove a Lexus around campus and was said to be a Buccaneer. I tried not to look at him as we walked inside. The policeman on duty, the one with tribal marks on his cheeks who always said "God bless you" when he took his bribe, looked away when he saw us, and I knew that something was wrong. My parents gave him the note from the superintendent. The policeman did not even glance at it. He knew about the release order, he told my father; the barman had already been released, but there was a complication with the boy. My mother began to shout, "What do you mean? Where is my son?"

The policeman got up. "I will call my senior to explain to you."

My mother rushed at him and pulled on his shirt. "Where is my son? Where is my son?" My father pried her away, and the policeman brushed at his chest, as if she had left some dirt there, before he turned to walk away.

"Where is our son?" my father asked in a voice so quiet, so steely, that the policeman stopped.

"They took him away, sir," he said.

"They took him away? What are you saying?" my mother was yelling. "Have you killed my son? Have you killed my son?"

555 "Where is our son?" my father asked again.

"My senior said I should call him when you came," the policeman said, and this time he hurried through a door.

560 It was after he left that I felt suddenly chilled by fear; I wanted to run after him and, like my mother, pull at his shirt until he produced Nnamabia. The senior policeman came out, and I searched his blank face for 565 clues.

"Good day, sir," he said to my father.

"Where is our son?" my father asked. My mother breathed noisily.

"No problem, sir. It is just that we trans-570 ferred him. I will take you there right away." There was something nervous about the policeman; his face remained blank, but he did not meet my father's eyes.

"Transferred him?"

575 "We got the order this morning. I would have sent somebody for him, but we don't have petrol, so I was waiting for you to come so that we could go together."

"Why was he transferred?"

580 "I was not here, sir. They said that he misbehaved yesterday and they took him to Cell One, and then yesterday evening there was a transfer of all the people in Cell One to another site."

585 "He misbehaved? What do you mean?"

"I was not here, sir."

My mother spoke in a broken voice: "Take me to my son! Take me to my son right now!"

I sat in the back with the policeman, who 590 smelled of the kind of old camphor that seemed to last forever in my mother's trunk. No one spoke except for the policeman when he gave my father directions. We arrived

about fifteen minutes later, my father driving 595 inordinately fast. The small, walled compound looked neglected, with patches of overgrown grass strewn with old bottles and plastic bags. The policeman hardly waited for my father to stop the car before he opened 600 the door and hurried out, and again I felt chilled. We were in a godforsaken part of town, and there was no sign that said "Police Station." There was a strange deserted feeling in the air. But the policeman soon 605 emerged with Nnamabia. There he was, my handsome brother, walking toward us, seemingly unchanged, until he came close enough for my mother to hug him, and I saw him wince and back away—his arm was covered 610 in soft-looking welts. There was dried blood around his nose.

"Why did they beat you like this?" my mother asked him. She turned to the policeman. "Why did you people do this to my son? 615 Why?"

The man shrugged. There was a new insolence to his demeanor; it was as if he had been uncertain about Nnamabia's well-being but now, reassured, could let himself talk. 620 "You cannot raise your children properly—all of you people who feel important because you work at the university—and when your children misbehave you think they should not be punished. You are lucky they 625 released him."

My father said, "Let's go."

He opened the door and Nnamabia climbed in, and we drove home. My father did not stop at any of the police checkpoints 630 on the road, and, once, a policeman gestured threateningly with his gun as we sped past. The only time my mother opened her mouth on the drive home was to ask Nnamabia if he wanted us to stop and buy some *okpa*. 635 Nnamabia said no. We had arrived in Nsukka before he finally spoke.

"Yesterday, the policemen asked the old man if he wanted a free half bucket of water. He said yes. So they told him to take his
640 clothes off and parade the corridor. Most of my cellmates were laughing. Some of them said it was wrong to treat an old man like that." Nnamabia paused. "I shouted at the policeman. I told him the old man was inno-
645 cent and ill, and if they kept him here it wouldn't help them find his son, because the man did not even know where his son was. They said that I should shut up immediately, that they would take me to Cell One. I didn't
650 care. I didn't shut up. So they pulled me out and slapped me and took me to Cell One."

Nnamabia stopped there, and we asked him nothing else. Instead, I imagined him calling the policeman a stupid idiot, a spine-
655 less coward, a sadist, a bastard, and I imagined the shock of the policemen—the chief staring openmouthed, the other cellmates stunned at the audacity of the boy from the university. And I imagined the old man him-
660 self looking on with surprised pride and quietly refusing to undress. Nnamabia did not say what had happened to him in Cell One, or what happened at the new site. It would have been so easy for him, my charming
665 brother, to make a sleek drama of his story, but he did not.

SETTING

1. What is the **setting** of the narrative? How do the descriptions of the setting reveal an incongruity?

2. How does Nnamabia interact with his surroundings? Describe how his behavior reveals an attitude about his surroundings.

3. How does the **setting** change? How does Nnamabia adapt to the new setting?

4. How does the resolution of the narrative reveal a change in the **setting**? How does the resolution contribute to a change in Nnamabia?

Narrative Pacing

 Enduring Understanding (STR-1)

The arrangement of the parts and sections of a text, the relationship of the parts to each other, and the sequence in which the text reveals information are all structural choices made by a writer that contribute to the reader's interpretation of a text.

KEY POINT

Authors manipulate the chronology of the narrative as a way of pacing the story not only to keep the reader interested but also to reveal details and information that convey a single idea.

If you know people who are especially funny, they probably have a strong sense of comedic timing. Comedians must decide what information their audience needs for their jokes to work. They must also choose the pacing and order of the joke as it develops. If they miss a key part by accident and then interrupt the process to go back and explain, the punch line won't land. In other words, delivering a well-executed joke means delivering the punch line at just the right time. The same is true for literature: structure and pacing are critical to the reader's experience and interpretation. And as with jokes, literary texts deliver specific scenes and dialogue at the best time to affect readers.

As you've learned by now, stories come in many different forms. Authors give great consideration to the order and speed at which a reader experiences the events that affect a narrative.

Good Stories Hook Readers Early On

If you've ever recommended a book with a slow start to a friend, you may have cautioned them with something along the lines of, "You just need to make it past the first two chapters, and then it gets a lot more interesting!"

Whether starting at the very beginning ("Once upon a time . . .") or diving straight into the action (**in medias res**), great stories give just enough information early in the narrative to capture the reader's interest but not so much that the reader gets overwhelmed.

Effective narrative pacing hinges on the balance between **exposition** (or description) and action. The author must introduce a **conflict** or **tension** early on to propel the story forward. Throughout the narrative, authors may gradually reveal important details, which may build in significance to a **cathartic** moment of importance or **resolution**.

Narrative Pacing

Pacing is the speed at which the story moves for the reader — the heartbeat of the narrative. It may be slow and steady at some parts, but other times it may be racing exponentially faster.

It matters when and how readers discover new information in the story. If you've ever laughed out loud, cried, or gasped in shock because of a surprising plot twist, you know that choices in narrative pacing can elicit strong emotional reactions from readers. Authors make intentional decisions about pacing that consider the following factors:

- The order in which information is revealed
- When and how information is revealed
- Who reveals information
- The significance of the revealed information to other parts of the narrative

Authors control narrative pacing with narrative techniques that affect the story's order of events, point of view, description, and syntax. Authors intentionally manipulate these factors to create an effect on the reader's experience and interpretation of a narrative.

Narrative techniques contribute to a story's pacing.

- **Flashback:** takes place in the past and interrupts the current story
- **Foreshadowing:** provides clues given about events to come
- **Juxtaposition:** presents contrasted actions
- **Antecedent action:** refers to events occurring before the story begins
- **Suspense:** depends on details that create anticipation for the reader
- **In media res:** begins the narrative in the middle of the action
- **Deus ex machina:** Latin phrase for "god from the machine" refers to a sudden, artificial, and contrived resolution to a story's conflict that allows the protagonist to escape during the resolution
- **Aside:** refers to a monologue directed to the audience

One noteworthy storytelling structure is the **frame story**, or a story within a story. As a structural device, the frame (or frames) determines what readers know—and how they come to know it. The frame also shifts the focus to the narrator(s), including the narrator's circumstances, motives, biases, and reliability. In a frame story, an introductory or main narrative sets the stage either for a more emphasized second narrative or for a set of shorter stories. When executed effectively, this technique adds a layer of complexity to stories by introducing ironies, analogies, contrasts, and perspectives that reveal important ideas in a text.

┌INSIDER
AP® TIP

When **something is revealed is just as important as** *what* **is revealed.** Narration and structure interact. Authors give narrators agency to control the pacing of the narrative. The structure of a story creates dramatic tension with the deliberate parceling out of information from the narrator(s). From the reader's perspective, the structure traces the rise and fall of a character (or characters) and offers some revelation.

NARRATIVE PACING		
Aspect of Pacing	**Literary Elements and Techniques**	**Literary Function**
Plot Sequence	Narrative hook	Disrupts the traditional narrative structure
	Flashback	Creates intersecting of plotlines
	Antecedent action	Introduces tensions and conflicts
	Foreshadowing	Provides backstory
	Deus ex machina	Builds suspense, cliffhangers, and pivotal moments
	Parallel action	Sets up contrasts, incongruities, or irony
	Juxtaposition	
	In medias res	
Point of View	Dialogue	Presents observations and perspectives from the narrator and other characters
	Stream of consciousness	Captures the process of interior reflection and introspection
	Narration	Shows conflicts and tensions between characters
	Aside	Addresses the reader or audience directly, creating intimacy
	Frame story	Reveals secrets
		Creates narrative distance
Description	Details	Creates suspense
	Adjectives	Creates associations
	Adverbs	Illuminates the specificity of the actions
	Verbs	
Syntax	Short sentences	Creates variety, rhythm, or rhyme
	Long sentences	Speeds up or slows down the narrative
	Punctuation	Highlights or emphasizes critical moments or emotions

GUIDED READING

The Storyteller
H. H. Munro (Saki)

Pictorial Press Ltd/Alamy

THE TEXT IN CONTEXT

"Saki" is the pen name of writer and satirist Hector Hugo Munro (1870–1916), who was born to Scottish parents in colonial India. Munro grew up during the Victorian era (1837–1901), which marked the height of the British Empire. But his writing career spans the Edwardian period (1901–1914), during which British culture was moving away from the conservatism and moralism of the previous age. Indeed, Munro's unsentimental and darkly comic short stories often mock stereotypical Victorian ideals and values. That satire is evident in "The Storyteller" (1914), as a stuffy Victorian aunt embodies the moralistic assumptions associated with the previous century. For her, children's stories must be simple *fables*: tales, usually involving animals, that teach clear moral lessons. Note Munro's use of a *frame story*: that is, one story (the bachelor's tale) is embedded in another fictional narrative. This framing device adds another layer of irony to "The Storyteller."

The Storyteller

It was a hot afternoon, and the railway carriage was correspondingly sultry, and the next stop was at Templecombe, nearly an hour ahead. The occupants of the carriage were a small girl, and a smaller girl, and a small boy. An aunt belonging to the children occupied one corner seat, and
5 the further corner seat on the opposite side was occupied by a bachelor who was a stranger to their party, but the small girls and the small boy emphatically occupied the compartment. Both the aunt and the children were conversational in a limited, persistent way, reminding one of the attentions of a housefly that refuses to be discouraged. Most of the aunt's
10 remarks seemed to begin with "Don't," and nearly all of the children's remarks began with "Why?" The bachelor said nothing out loud. "Don't, Cyril, don't," exclaimed the aunt, as the small boy began smacking the cushions of the seat, producing a cloud of dust at each blow.

"Come and look out of the window," she added.
15 The child moved reluctantly to the window. "Why are those sheep being driven out of that field?" he asked.

Guided Questions

1. Who is the narrator? How do we know?

2. Why does the narrator tell a story?

"I expect they are being driven to another field where there is more grass," said the aunt weakly.

"But there is lots of grass in that field," protested the boy; "there's
20 nothing else but grass there. Aunt, there's lots of grass in that field."

"Perhaps the grass in the other field is better," suggested the aunt fatuously.

"Why is it better?" came the swift, inevitable question.

"Oh, look at those cows!" exclaimed the aunt. Nearly every field along
25 the line had contained cows or bullocks, but she spoke as though she were drawing attention to a rarity.

"Why is the grass in the other field better?" persisted Cyril.

The frown on the bachelor's face was deepening to a scowl. He was a hard, unsympathetic man, the aunt decided in her mind. She was utterly
30 unable to come to any satisfactory decision about the grass in the other field.

The smaller girl created a diversion by beginning to recite "On the Road to Mandalay." She only knew the first line, but she put her limited knowledge to the fullest possible use. She repeated the line over and over again
35 in a dreamy but resolute and very audible voice; it seemed to the bachelor as though some one had had a bet with her that she could not repeat the line aloud two thousand times without stopping. Whoever it was who had made the wager was likely to lose his bet.

"Come over here and listen to a story," said the aunt, when the bache-
40 lor had looked twice at her and once at the communication cord.

The children moved listlessly towards the aunt's end of the carriage. Evidently her reputation as a story-teller did not rank high in their estimation.

In a low, confidential voice, interrupted at frequent intervals by loud,
45 petulant questionings from her listeners, she began an unenterprising and deplorably uninteresting story about a little girl who was good, and made friends with every one on account of her goodness, and was finally saved from a mad bull by a number of rescuers who admired her moral character.

50 "Wouldn't they have saved her if she hadn't been good?" demanded the bigger of the small girls. It was exactly the question that the bachelor had wanted to ask.

"Well, yes," admitted the aunt lamely, "but I don't think they would have run quite so fast to her help if they had not liked her so much."

55 "It's the stupidest story I've ever heard," said the bigger of the small girls, with immense conviction.

"I didn't listen after the first bit, it was so stupid," said Cyril.

Guided Questions

3. How do these details contribute to the rising action? How does this affect the narrator's perspective?

4. How does this interaction between the aunt and the children contribute to the tension?

5. How do the details at the end of the aunt's story reveal the true nature of the narrator?

The smaller girl made no actual comment on the story, but she had long ago recommenced a murmured repetition of her favourite line.

60 "You don't seem to be a success as a story-teller," said the bachelor suddenly from his corner.

The aunt bristled in instant defence at this unexpected attack.

"It's a very difficult thing to tell stories that children can both understand and appreciate," she said stiffly.

65 "I don't agree with you," said the bachelor.

"Perhaps you would like to tell them a story," was the aunt's retort.

"Tell us a story," demanded the bigger of the small girls.

"Once upon a time," began the bachelor, "there was a little girl called Bertha, who was extra-ordinarily good."

70 The children's momentarily-aroused interest began at once to flicker; all stories seemed dreadfully alike, no matter who told them.

"She did all that she was told, she was always truthful, she kept her clothes clean, ate milk puddings as though they were jam tarts, learned her lessons perfectly, and was polite in her manners."

75 "Was she pretty?" asked the bigger of the small girls.

"Not as pretty as any of you," said the bachelor, "but she was horribly good."

There was a wave of reaction in favour of the story; the word horrible in connection with goodness was a novelty that commended itself. It
80 seemed to introduce a ring of truth that was absent from the aunt's tales of infant life.

"She was so good," continued the bachelor, "that she won several medals for goodness, which she always wore, pinned on to her dress. There was a medal for obedience, another medal for punctuality, and a third for
85 good behaviour. They were large metal medals and they clicked against one another as she walked. No other child in the town where she lived had as many as three medals, so everybody knew that she must be an extra good child."

"Horribly good," quoted Cyril.

90 "Everybody talked about her goodness, and the Prince of the country got to hear about it, and he said that as she was so very good she might be allowed once a week to walk in his park, which was just outside the town. It was a beautiful park, and no children were ever allowed in it, so it was a great honour for Bertha to be allowed to go there."

95 "Were there any sheep in the park?" demanded Cyril.

"No;" said the bachelor, "there were no sheep."

"Why weren't there any sheep?" came the inevitable question arising out of that answer.

Guided Questions

6. How does the narrator's reaction to the bachelor's attack create suspense?

7. What detail reveals that she was especially good?

8. Why does Cyril repeat the phrase "horribly good"?

The aunt permitted herself a smile, which might almost have been
100 described as a grin.

"There were no sheep in the park," said the bachelor, "because the
Prince's mother had once had a dream that her son would either be killed
by a sheep or else by a clock falling on him. For that reason the Prince
never kept a sheep in his park or a clock in his palace."

105 The aunt suppressed a gasp of admiration.

"Was the Prince killed by a sheep or by a clock?" asked Cyril.

"He is still alive, so we can't tell whether the dream will come true,"
said the bachelor unconcernedly; "anyway, there were no sheep in the
park, but there were lots of little pigs running all over the place."

110 "What colour were they?"

"Black with white faces, white with black spots, black all over, grey with
white patches, and some were white all over."

The storyteller paused to let a full idea of the park's treasures sink into
the children's imaginations; then he resumed:

115 "Bertha was rather sorry to find that there were no flowers in the park.
She had promised her aunts, with tears in her eyes, that she would not
pick any of the kind Prince's flowers, and she had meant to keep her
promise, so of course it made her feel silly to find that there were no flowers to pick."

120 "Why weren't there any flowers?"

"Because the pigs had eaten them all," said the bachelor promptly. "The
gardeners had told the Prince that you couldn't have pigs and flowers, so
he decided to have pigs and no flowers."

There was a murmur of approval at the excellence of the Prince's deci-
125 sion; so many people would have decided the other way.

"There were lots of other delightful things in the park. There were ponds
with gold and blue and green fish in them, and trees with beautiful parrots
that said clever things at a moment's notice, and humming birds that
hummed all the popular tunes of the day. Bertha walked up and down and
130 enjoyed herself immensely, and thought to herself: 'If I were not so extraordinarily good I should not have been allowed to come into this beautiful
park and enjoy all that there is to be seen in it,' and her three medals
clinked against one another as she walked and helped to remind her how
very good she really was. Just then an enormous wolf came prowling into
135 the park to see if it could catch a fat little pig for its supper."

"What colour was it?" asked the children, amid an immediate quicken-
ing of interest.

"Mud-colour all over, with a black tongue and pale grey eyes that
gleamed with unspeakable ferocity. The first thing that it saw in the park

Guided Questions

9. Why did the aunt smile?

10. What does the aunt's reaction reveal about her character?

11. What is the climax of the story?

Guided Questions

140 was Bertha; her pinafore was so spotlessly white and clean that it could
be seen from a great distance. Bertha saw the wolf and saw that it was
stealing towards her, and she began to wish that she had never been
allowed to come into the park. She ran as hard as she could, and the
wolf came after her with huge leaps and bounds. She managed to reach
145 a shrubbery of myrtle bushes and she hid herself in one of the thickest
of the bushes. The wolf came sniffing among the branches, its black
tongue lolling out of its mouth and its pale grey eyes glaring with rage.
Bertha was terribly frightened, and thought to herself: 'If I had not been
so extraordinarily good I should have been safe in the town at this
150 moment.' However, the scent of the myrtle was so strong that the wolf
could not sniff out where Bertha was hiding, and the bushes were so
thick that he might have hunted about in them for a long time without
catching sight of her, so he thought he might as well go off and catch a
little pig instead. Bertha was trembling very much at having the wolf
155 prowling and sniffing so near her, and as she trembled the medal for
obedience clinked against the medals for good conduct and punctuality.
The wolf was just moving away when he heard the sound of the medals
clinking and stopped to listen; they clinked again in a bush quite near
him. He dashed into the bush, his pale grey eyes gleaming with ferocity
160 and triumph, and dragged Bertha out and devoured her to the last morsel. All that was left of her were her shoes, bits of clothing, and the three
medals for goodness."

> 12. What happens here that reveals Bertha's location? Why is this significant?

"Were any of the little pigs killed?"

"No, they all escaped."

165 "The story began badly," said the smaller of the small girls, "but it had a
beautiful ending."

"It is the most beautiful story that I ever heard," said the bigger of the
small girls, with immense decision.

> 13. How does the story conclude? Why did it have a "beautiful ending" according to the listening children?

"It is the only beautiful story I have ever heard," said Cyril.

170 A dissentient opinion came from the aunt.

"A most improper story to tell to young children! You have undermined
the effect of years of careful teaching."

"At any rate," said the bachelor, collecting his belongings preparatory to
leaving the carriage, "I kept them quiet for ten minutes, which was more
175 than you were able to do."

> 14. Why does this story undermine the effect of "years of careful teaching"? What does this reveal about the narrator?

"Unhappy woman!" he observed to himself as he walked down the
platform of Templecombe station; "for the next six months or so those
children will assail her in public with demands for an improper story!"

PRACTICE TEXT

The Hack Driver
Sinclair Lewis

THE TEXT IN CONTEXT

The first American writer to receive a Nobel Prize for Literature, Sinclair
Lewis (1885–1951) used his fiction to produce keen social criticism
of life in the United States — especially small towns like Sauk Centre,
Minnesota, where he had grown up. He satirized their provincialism,
materialism, conformity, and narrow-mindedness in novels such as *Main
Street* (1920), *Babbitt* (1922), *Elmer Gantry* (1926), and *It Can't Happen
Here* (1935). His work usually looks beneath the surface of respectability,
manners, and stereotypes, as in the 1923 short story "The Hack Driver."

Culture Club/Getty Images

AP® SKILLS PRACTICE | **STRUCTURE**
Analyzing Narrative Pacing

As you read "The Hack Driver," notice how Sinclair Lewis uses a narrator to
manipulate the narrative. Record textual details and examples that show specific
literary techniques. Then explain how these techniques reveal a single idea or
insight that contributes to an interpretation of the text.

Analyzing Narrative Pacing		
Literary Techniques and Elements	**Details from the Text**	**Literary Effect**
Plot Sequence Narrative hook Flashback Antecedent action Foreshadowing Deus ex machina Parallel action Juxtaposition In medias res		
Point of View Dialogue Stream of consciousness Narration Aside Frame story		

Description		
Details		
Adjectives		
Adverbs		
Verbs		
Syntax		
Short sentences		
Long sentences		
Punctuation		

The Hack Driver

I dare say there's no man of large affairs,
whether he is bank president or senator or
dramatist, who hasn't a sneaking love for
some old rum-hound in a frightful hat, living
5 back in a shanty and making his living by
ways you wouldn't care to examine too
closely. (It was the Supreme Court Justice
speaking. I do not pretend to guarantee his
theories or his story.) He may be a Maine
10 guide, or the old garageman who used to
keep the livery stable, or a perfectly useless
innkeeper who sneaks off to shoot ducks
when he ought to be sweeping the floors, but
your pompous big-city man will contrive to
15 get back and see him every year, and loaf
with him, and secretly prefer him to all the
highfalutin leaders of the city.

There's that much truth, at least, to this
Open Spaces stuff you read in advertise-
20 ments of wild and woolly Western novels. I
don't know the philosophy of it; perhaps it
means that we retain a decent simplicity, no
matter how much we are tied to Things, to
houses and motors and expensive wives. Or
25 again it may give away the whole game of
civilization; may mean that the apparently
civilized man is at heart nothing but a hobo
who prefers flannel shirts and bristly cheeks
and cussing and dirty tin plates to all the

30 trim, hygienic, forward-looking life our wom-
enfolks make us put on for them.

When I graduated from law school I suppose I was about as artificial and idiotic
and ambitious as most youngsters. I
35 wanted to climb, socially and financially. I
wanted to be famous and dine at large
houses with men who shuddered at the
Common People who don't dress for dinner. You see, I hadn't learned that the only
40 thing duller than a polite dinner is the conversation afterward, when the victims are
digesting the dinner and accumulating
enough strength to be able to play bridge.
Oh, I was a fine young calf! I even planned
45 a rich marriage. Imagine then how I felt
when, after taking honors and becoming
fifteenth assistant clerk in the magnificent
law firm of Hodgins, Hodgins, Berkman and
Taupe, I was set not at preparing briefs but
50 at serving summonses! Like a cheap private detective! Like a mangy sheriff's officer! They told me I had to begin that way
and, holding my nose, I feebly went to
work. I was kicked out of actresses' dress-
55 ing rooms, and from time to time I was
righteously beaten by large and indignant
litigants. I came to know, and still more to
hate, every dirty and shadowy corner of the

city. I thought of fleeing to my home town,
60 where I could at once become a full-fledged
attorney-at-law. I rejoiced one day when
they sent me out forty miles or so to a
town called New Mullion, to serve a summons on one Oliver Lutkins. This Lutkins
65 had worked in the Northern Woods, and he
knew the facts about a certain timberland
boundary agreement. We needed him as a
witness, and he had dodged service.

When I got off the train at New Mullion,
70 my sudden affection for sweet and simple
villages was dashed by the look of the place,
with its mud-gushing streets and its rows of
shops either paintless or daubed with a sour
brown. Though it must have numbered eight
75 or nine thousand inhabitants, New Mullion
was as littered as a mining camp. There was
one agreeable-looking man at the station—
the expressman. He was a person of perhaps
forty, red-faced, cheerful, thick; he wore his
80 overalls and denim jumper as though they
belonged to him, he was quite dirty and very
friendly and you knew at once he liked people and slapped them on the back out of
pure easy affection.
85 "I want," I told him, "to find a fellow
named Oliver Lutkins."

"Him? I saw him 'round here 'twan't an
hour ago. Hard fellow to catch, though—
always chasing around on some phony
90 business or other. Probably trying to get up a
poker game in the back of Fritz Beinke's harness shop. I'll tell you, boy—Any hurry about
locating Lutkins?"

"Yes. I want to catch the afternoon train
95 back." I was as impressively secret as a stage
detective.

"I'll tell you. I've got a hack. I'll get out the
boneshaker and we can drive around together
and find Lutkins. I know most of the places
100 he hangs out."

He was so frankly friendly, he so immediately took me into the circle of his affection,
that I glowed with the warmth of it. I knew,
of course, that he was drumming up busi-
105 ness, but his kindness was real, and if I had
to pay hack fare in order to find my man, I
was glad that the money would go to this
good fellow. I got him down to two dollars an
hour; he brought from his cottage, a block
110 away, an object like a black piano-box on
wheels.

He didn't hold the door open, certainly
he didn't say "Ready, sir." I think he would
have died before calling anybody "sir." When
115 he gets to Heaven's gate he'll call St. Peter
"Pete," and I imagine the good saint will like
it. He remarked, "Well, young fellow, here's
the handsome equipage," and his grin—
well, it made me feel that I had always been
120 his neighbor. They're so ready to help a
stranger, those villagers. He had already
made it his own task to find Oliver Lutkins
for me.

He said, and almost shyly: "I don't want to
125 butt in on your private business, young fellow, but my guess is that you want to collect
some money from Lutkins—he never pays
anybody a cent; he still owes me six bits on a
poker game I was fool enough to get into. He
130 ain't a bad sort of a Yahoo but he just naturally hates to loosen up on a coin of the
realm. So if you're trying to collect any
money off him, we better kind of you might
say creep up on him and surround him. If
135 you go asking for him—anybody can tell you
come from the city, with that trick Fedora of
yours—he'll suspect something and take a
sneak. If you want me to, I'll go into Fritz
Beinke's and ask for him, and you can keep
140 out of sight behind me."

I loved him for it. By myself I might never
have found Lutkins. Now, I was an army with

reserves. In a burst I told the hack driver that I wanted to serve a summons on Lutkins;
145 that the fellow had viciously refused to testify in a suit where his knowledge of a certain conversation would clear up everything. The driver listened earnestly—and I was still young enough to be grateful at
150 being taken seriously by any man of forty. At the end he pounded my shoulder (very painfully) and chuckled: "Well, we'll spring a little surprise on Brer Lutkins."

"Let's start, driver."

155 "Most folks around here call me Bill. Or Magnuson. William Magnuson, fancy carting and hauling."

"All right, Bill. Shall we tackle this harness shop—Beinke's?"

160 "Yes, jus' likely to be there as anywheres. Plays a lot of poker and a great hand at bluffing—damn him!" Bill seemed to admire Mr. Lutkins's ability as a scoundrel; I fancied that if he had been sheriff he would have
165 caught Lutkins with fervor and hanged him with affection.

At the somewhat gloomy harness shop we descended and went in. The room was odorous with the smell of dressed leather. A
170 scanty sort of a man, presumably Mr. Beinke, was selling a horse collar to a farmer.

"Seen Nolly Lutkins around today? Friend of his looking for him," said Bill, with treacherous heartiness.

175 Beinke looked past him at my shrinking alien self; he hesitated and owned: "Yuh, he was in here a little while ago. Guess he's gone over to the Swede's to get a shave."

"Well, if he comes in, tell him I'm looking
180 for him. Might get up a little game of poker. I've heard tell that Lutkins plays these here immoral games of chance."

"Yuh, I believe he's known to sit in on Authors," Beinke growled.

185 We sought the barber shop of "the Swede." Bill was again good enough to take the lead, while I lurked at the door. He asked not only the Swede but two customers if they had seen Lutkins. The Swede
190 decidedly had not; he raged: "I ain't seen him, and I don't want to, but if you find him you can just collect the dollar thirty-five he owes me." One of the customers thought he had seen Lutkins "hiking down Main Street,
195 this side of the hotel."

"Well, then," Bill concluded, as we labored up into the hack, "his credit at the Swede's being ausgewent, he's probably getting a scrape at Heinie Gray's. He's too darn lazy to
200 shave himself."

At Gray's barber shop we missed Lutkins by only five minutes. He had just left—presumably for the poolroom. At the poolroom it appeared that he had merely bought
205 a pack of cigarettes and gone on. Thus we pursued him, just behind him but never catching him, for an hour, till it was past one and I was hungry. Village born as I was, and in the city often lonely for good coarse country
210 wit, I was so delighted by Bill's cynical opinions on the barbers and clergymen and doctors and draymen of New Mullion that I scarcely cared whether I found Lutkins or not.

"How about something to eat?" I sug-
215 gested. "Let's go to a restaurant and I'll buy you a lunch."

"Well, ought to go home to the old woman. And I don't care much for these restaurants—ain't but four of 'em and
220 they're all rotten. Tell you what we'll do. Like nice scenery? There's an elegant view from Wade's Hill. We'll get the old woman to put us up a lunch—she won't charge you but a half dollar, and it'd cost you that for a greasy
225 feed at the café—and we'll go up there and have a Sunday-school picnic."

I knew that my friend Bill was not free from guile; I knew that his hospitality to the Young Fellow from the City was not alto-
230 gether a matter of brotherly love. I was paying him for his time; in all I paid him for six hours (including the lunch hour) at what was then a terrific price. But he was no more dishonest than I, who charged the whole thing
235 up to the Firm, and it would have been worth paying him myself to have his presence. His country serenity, his natural wisdom, was a refreshing bath to the city-twitching youngster. As we sat on the hilltop, looking across
240 orchards and a creek which slipped among the willows, he talked of New Mullion, gave a whole gallery of portraits. He was cynical yet tender. Nothing had escaped him, yet there was nothing, no matter how ironically he
245 laughed at it, which was beyond his understanding and forgiveness. In ruddy color he painted the rector's wife who when she was most in debt most loudly gave the responses at which he called the "Episcopalopian
250 church." He commented on the boys who came home from college in "ice-cream pants," and on the lawyer who, after years of torrential argument with his wife, would put on either a linen collar or a necktie, but never
255 both. He made them live. In that day I came to know New Mullion better than I did the city, and to love it better.

If Bill was ignorant of universities and of urban ways, yet much had he traveled in the
260 realm of jobs. He had worked on railroad section gangs, in harvest fields and contractors' camps, and from his adventures he had brought back a philosophy of simplicity and laughter. He strengthened me. Nowadays,
265 thinking of Bill, I know what people mean (though I abominate the simpering phrase) when they yearn over "real he-men."

We left that placid place of orchards and resumed the search for Oliver Lutkins. We

270 could not find him. At last Bill cornered a friend of Lutkins and made him admit that "he guessed Oliver'd gone out to his ma's farm, three miles north."

We drove out there, mighty with strategy.
275 "I know Oliver's ma. She's a terror. She's a cyclone," Bill sighed. "I took a trunk out for her once, and she pretty near took my hide off because I didn't treat it like it was a crate of eggs. She's somewheres about nine feet
280 tall and four feet thick and quick's a cat, and she sure manhandles the Queen's English. I'll bet Oliver has heard that somebody's on his trail and he's sneaked out there to hide behind his ma's skirts. Well, we'll try bawling
285 her out. But you better let me do it, boy. You may be great at Latin and geography, but you ain't educated in cussing."

We drove into a poor farmyard; we were faced by an enormous and cheerful old
290 woman. My guardian stockily stood before her and snarled, "Remember me? I'm Bill Magnuson, the expressman. I want to find your son Oliver. Friend of mine here from the city's got a present for him."
295 "I don't know anything about Oliver and I don't want to," she bellowed.

"Now you look here. We've stood for just about enough plenty nonsense. This young man is the attorney general's provost, and
300 we got legal right to search any and all premises for the person of one Oliver Lutkins."

Bill made it seem terrific, and the Amazon seemed impressed. She retired into the kitchen and we followed. From the low old
305 range, turned by years of heat into a dark silvery gray, she snatched a sadiron, and she marched on us, clamoring, "You just search all you want to—providin' you don't mind getting burnt to a cinder!" She bellowed, she
310 swelled, she laughed at our nervous retreat.

"Let's get out of this. She'll murder us," Bill groaned and, outside: "Did you see her grin?

She was making fun of us. Can you beat that for nerve?"

315 I agreed that it was lese majesty.

We did, however, make adequate search. The cottage had but one story. Bill went round it, peeking in at all the windows. We explored the barn and the stable; we were 320 reasonably certain that Lutkins was not there. It was nearly time for me to catch the afternoon train, and Bill drove me to the station. On the way to the city I worried very little over my failure to find Lutkins. I was 325 too absorbed in the thought of Bill Magnuson. Really, I considered returning to New Mullion to practice law. If I had found Bill so deeply and richly human might I not come to love the yet uncharted Fritz Beinke and 330 the Swede barber and a hundred other slow-spoken, simple, wise neighbors? I saw a candid and happy life beyond the neat learnings of universities' law firms. I was excited, as one who has found a treasure.

335 But if I did not think much about Lutkins, the office did. I found them in a state next morning; the suit was ready to come to trial; they had to have Lutkins; I was a disgrace and a fool. That morning my eminent career 340 almost came to an end. The Chief did everything but commit mayhem; he somewhat more than hinted that I would do well at ditch-digging. I was ordered back to New Mullion, and with me they sent an ex-lumber-345 camp clerk who knew Lutkins. I was rather sorry, because it would prevent my loafing again in the gorgeous indolence of Bill Magnuson.

When the train drew in at New Mullion, 350 Bill was on the station platform, near his dray. What was curious was that the old dragon, Lutkins's mother, was there talking to him, and they were not quarreling but laughing.

355 From the car steps I pointed them out to the lumber-camp clerk, and in young hero-worship I murmured: "There's a fine fellow, a real man."

"Meet him here yesterday?" asked the 360 clerk.

"I spent the day with him."

"He help you hunt for Oliver Lutkins?"

"Yes, he helped me a lot."

"He must have! He's Lutkins himself!"

365 But what really hurt was that when I served the summons Lutkins and his mother laughed at me as though I were a bright boy of seven, and with loving solicitude they begged me to go to a neighbor's house and 370 take a cup of coffee.

"I told 'em about you, and they're dying to have a look at you," said Lutkins joyfully. "They're about the only folks in town that missed seeing you yesterday."

STRUCTURE

1. How does the point of view reveal the relationship between the narrator and Bill? How does it contribute to the text's **structure**?

2. Explain how the arrangement of details in the text contributes to the story's **suspense**.

3. What details **foreshadow** the ending of the story?

4. Explain how the author creates the **narrative pace** of the story.

Reliable and Unreliable Narrators

 Enduring Understanding (NAR-1)

A narrator's or speaker's perspective controls the details and emphases that affect how readers experience and interpret a text.

KEY POINT

A narrator's reliability influences how a reader reacts to the details of the story.

Imagine a friend calls to tell you about their fishing trip. They say they had a good time and caught plenty of smaller fish, as well as a twelve-inch fish. Later that week, you hear them tell the same story to a larger group of friends about a fish that was easily a foot-and-a-half long, or maybe two feet. With each retelling, the friend exaggerates the details of the story until they say they practically caught a shark.

What factors affect your assessment of a narrator's credibility? Consider the boy who cries wolf in Aesop's fable: the young shepherd tricks his neighbors so many times with false alarms that when a real wolf appears, nobody finds the boy credible. In literary texts, of course, narrators may be more subtle in their biases, blindspots, and deceptions. Regardless, keep in mind that the narrator's reliability — or unreliability — is a choice made by the author. And as you'll recall from Unit 4, authors choose a story's point of view with careful intention.

Some Narrators Are More Reliable Than Others

With **first-person point of view**, readers get a single perspective from a character whose subjective point of view may be biased, faulty, or even imperceptive. In other stories, authors choose **third-person point of view** with a narrator who is outside the story. While this detachment may suggest that the narrative is "objective," a third-person narrator can still have a background, a perspective, and limitations that influence the reader's experience of the story.

In most stories, the reader can believe the storyteller. These **reliable narrators** are trustworthy, and the reader has no reason to doubt their honesty and accuracy. However, reliable narrators have a perspective. Your job as a reader is to carefully consider why the narrator is telling the story and understand his or her relationship to the narrative.

Still other authors narrate stories from multiple points of view, which allows readers to experience the events from multiple perspectives. But regardless of point of view, readers must know who is telling the story and analyze how that narrator influences the reader's understanding of the narrative.

Unreliable Narrators

Readers usually perceive unreliable narrators by seeing discrepancies between the narrator's claims or perceptions and information provided by other characters, descriptions, and details in the text. So, readers must carefully consider the reliability of the narrator and remain mindful of the narrator's subjectivity and limitations.

Unreliable narrators allow readers to make inferences based on the information provided by the narrator, what other characters do and say, and the resulting plot events. Readers must carefully consider the degree to which a narrator or character can be trusted. Narrators may be unreliable because of their naivety, inexperience, immaturity, biases, emotional state, psychological state, and/or credibility.

Same Story, Different Accounts

Different narrators have different attitudes, biases, perspectives, and understandings. Some narrators have access to information (e.g., their own private thoughts) that other narrators or characters do not. In fact, some narrators provide key details or information uniquely perceived by their characters.

When a text has multiple speakers or narrators, effective readers become detectives, critically analyzing both the information they receive and the source of that information. Each narrator and character chooses what to reveal to readers (and what to *conceal* too). As suspects in a crime often give different accounts of what happened, narrators may also provide details that conflict or contradict claims from other characters. The reader must make inferences based on all of the information given by different characters' narrators.

Narrative Techniques

When you go to see a movie or a play, you already know that the performance is pretend: actors in costumes on a fake set taking scripted actions and having constructed conversations. Yet despite knowing that, you agree to briefly forget all of that to experience the story as if it were real. This phenomenon is known as the willing **suspension of disbelief**. In conventionally "realistic" drama, film, and fiction, writers, directors, and actors work hard to sustain this illusion.

When characters intentionally interrupt the audience's suspension of disbelief, they use a technique called breaking the fourth wall. The **fourth wall** is the dramatic convention that there is an invisible, imagined wall separating the fictional world from the real world (and the audience). While the audience can see through this "wall," the convention assumes the actors act as if they cannot.

Actors can break the fourth wall as a technique to elicit an emotional reaction from the audience (typically shock or humor). Ultimately, the **fourth wall** allows the audience to see everything happening so that the audience can draw their own inferences without the influence of a narrator.

Sometimes writers convey stories in ways that allow readers (or audience members) to know things about characters and situations that other characters don't know. These narrative techniques provide insights into a character's actions and behavior, inner thoughts, and motivations that contribute to both the narrative reliability and credibility.

In dramatic performances, for example, audiences may learn things that other characters don't know through **asides**: monologues delivered by a character directly to the audience. Through an aside, the audience may better understand the motivations or reflections of a character.

NARRATIVE RELIABILITY AND POINT OF VIEW		
Point of View	**Attributes That Affect Reader's Understanding**	**Questions to Consider When Linking Narration and Interpretation**
First Person	A character in the story Biases and limited knowledge	• What role does this character play in the story? • What is this character's background? • What is this character's relationship to other characters? • Is there any reason not to trust this character? • What is the character's emotional or psychological state?
Second Person (Rarely Used)	Extremely high narrative credibility, as it presents the action from the reader's point of view Limited perspective	• Is the narrator reporting events in real time? • How does bringing the reader into the narrative as a character affect the credibility of the narrator?
Third Person (Limited)	Source of what can be seen, heard, and inferred in the story Rarely a character in the story	• How does the narrator's limited knowledge affect the story? • How does the inclusion or exclusion of details reveal the narrator's biases? • What is the narrative distance? • What is the effect of the limited information on the narrative?
Third Person (Omniscient)	A perspective from outside the story	• Does this narrator know everything about all characters? • How does the inclusion or exclusion of details reveal the narrator's bias? • What is the narrative distance? • What is the effect of the comprehensive information on the narrative?

Additionally, some authors, poets, and songwriters create fictional **personas** (Latin for "masks" — as in those designed to obscure someone's identity), or speakers, who function exactly like narrators in a poem or song. Often, a persona is not directly the author but instead a character who stands in for the author, allowing a character to speak for the author.

Another narrative technique often used in prose fiction is stream of consciousness. **Stream of consciousness** is a first-person narrative technique that presents the flow of thoughts, feelings, associations, and memories of a character, allowing the reader to see inside the mind of the character.

INSIDER
AP® TIP

Who **reveals information is just as important as** *what* **is revealed.** Narrators are people like all other humans, and their credibility and reliability exist on a continuum. Careful interpretations take into account how trustworthy narrators are, what information they may know and not reveal, and the significance of when they reveal key information.

GUIDED READING

Miriam
Truman Capote

THE TEXT IN CONTEXT

Truman Capote (1924–1984) was a novelist, screenwriter, and journalist best known for his novel *Breakfast at Tiffany's* (1958) and his "nonfiction novel" *In Cold Blood: A True Account of a Multiple Murder and Its Consequences* (1966). He was born in New Orleans but spent much of his childhood in Monroeville, Alabama, and New York City. A precocious writer, Capote began writing short fiction for magazines like the *Atlantic*, the *New Yorker*, *Mademoiselle*, and *Harper's Bazaar* while he was still in his early twenties. "Miriam" (1946) is one of his earliest — and most celebrated — stories. While the tale is set in New York City, it has a haunted, unsettling, Gothic quality that Capote would explore further in his first novel, *Other Voices, Other Rooms* (1948).

Constantin Joffe/Condé Nast/Shutterstock

Miriam

For several years, Mrs. H. T. Miller lived alone in a pleasant apartment
(two rooms with kitchenette) in a remodeled brownstone near the East
River. She was a widow: Mr. H. T. Miller had left a reasonable amount of
insurance. Her interests were narrow, she had no friends to speak of, and
5 she rarely journeyed farther than the corner grocery. The other people in
the house never seemed to notice her: her clothes were matter-of-fact,
her hair iron-gray, clipped and casually waved; she did not use cosmetics,
her features were plain and inconspicuous, and on her last birthday she
was sixty-one. Her activities were seldom spontaneous: she kept the two
10 rooms immaculate, smoked an occasional cigarette, prepared her own
meals and tended a canary.

Then she met Miriam. It was snowing that night. Mrs. Miller had finished drying the supper dishes and was thumbing through an afternoon
paper when she saw an advertisement of a picture playing at a neighbor-
15 hood theatre. The title sounded good, so she struggled into her beaver
coat, laced her galoshes and left the apartment, leaving one light burning
in the foyer: she found nothing more disturbing than a sensation of
darkness.

The snow was fine, falling gently, not yet making an impression on the
20 pavement. The wind from the river cut only at street crossings. Mrs. Miller
hurried, her head bowed, oblivious as a mole burrowing a blind path. She
stopped at a drugstore and bought a package of peppermints.

A long line stretched in front of the box office; she took her place at the
end. There would be (a tired voice groaned) a short wait for all seats. Mrs.
25 Miller rummaged in her leather handbag till she collected exactly the correct change for admission. The line seemed to be taking its own time and,
looking around for some distractions, she suddenly became conscious of a
little girl standing under the edge of the marquee.

Her hair was the longest and strangest Mrs. Miller had ever seen: abso-
30 lutely silver-white, like an albino's. It flowed waist-length in smooth, loose
lines. She was thin and fragilely constructed. There was a simple, special
elegance in the way she stood with her thumbs in the pockets of a tailored plum-velvet coat.

Mrs. Miller felt oddly excited, and when the little girl glanced toward
35 her, she smiled warmly. The little girl walked over and said, "Would you
care to do me a favor?"

"I'd be glad to if I can," said Mrs. Miller.

"Oh, it's quite easy. I merely want you to buy a ticket for me; they won't
let me in otherwise. Here, I have the money." And gracefully she handed
40 Mrs. Miller two dimes and a nickel.

Guided Questions

1. Who is the
   narrator? What is
   the story's point of
   view?

2. How does
   the narrator's
   exclusion of details
   about anyone else
   contribute to her
   reliability?

3. What does the
   narrator reveal
   about Mrs. Miller's
   motivations?

They went over to the theatre together. An usherette directed them to a lounge; in twenty minutes the picture would be over.

"I feel just like a genuine criminal," said Mrs. Miller gaily, as she sat down. "I mean that sort of thing's against the law, isn't it? I do hope
45 I haven't done the wrong thing. You mother knows where you are, dear? I mean she does, doesn't she?"

The little girl said nothing. She unbuttoned her coat and folded it across her lap. Her dress underneath was prim and dark blue. A gold chain dangled about her neck, and her fingers, sensitive and musical looking,
50 toyed with it. Examining her more attentively, Mrs. Miller decided the truly distinctive feature was not her hair, but her eyes; they were hazel, steady, lacking any childlike quality whatsoever and, because of their size, seemed to consume her small face.

Mrs. Miller offered a peppermint. "What's your name, dear?"
55 "Miriam," she said, as though, in some curious way, it were information already familiar.

"Why, isn't that funny—my name's Miriam, too. And it's not a terribly common name either. Now, don't tell me your last name's Miller!"

"Just Miriam."
60 "But isn't that funny?"

"Moderately," said Miriam, and rolled a peppermint on her tongue.

Mrs. Miller flushed and shifted uncomfortably. "You have such a large vocabulary for such a young girl."

"Do I?"
65 "Well, yes," said Mrs. Miller, hastily changing the topic to: "Do you like the movies?"

"I really wouldn't know," said Miriam. "I've never been before."

Women began filling the lounge; the rumble of the newsreel bombs exploded in the distance. Mrs. Miller rose, tucking her purse under her
70 arm. "I guess I'd better be running now if I want to get a seat," she said. "It was nice to have met you."

Miriam nodded ever so slightly.

It snowed all week. Wheels and footsteps moved soundlessly on the street, as if the business of living continued secretly behind a pale but
75 impenetrable curtain. In the falling quiet there was no sky or earth, only snow lifting in the wind, frosting the window glass, chilling the rooms, deadening and hushing the city. At all hours it was necessary to keep a lamp lighted, and Mrs. Miller lost track of the days: Friday was no different from Saturday and on Sunday she went to the grocery story; closed, of
80 course.

That evening she scrambled eggs and fixed a bowl of tomato soup. Then, after putting on a flannel robe and cold-creaming her face, she

Guided Questions

4. Explain the details revealed by the narrator about Mrs. Miller and Miriam.

5. Why does the narrator provide this information? What do these details add to the story?

propped herself up in bed with a hot-water bottle under her feet. She was reading the *Times* when the doorbell rang. At first she thought it must be a
85 mistake and whoever it was would go away. But it rang and rang and set- tled to a persistent buzz. She looked at the clock: a little after eleven; it did not seem possible, she was always asleep by ten.

Climbing out of bed, she trotted barefoot across the living room. "I'm coming, please be patient." The latch was caught; she turned it this way
90 and that way and the bell never stopped for an instant. "Stop it," she cried. The bolt gave way and she opened the door an inch. "What in heaven's name?"

"Hello," said Miriam.

"Oh . . . why, hello," said Mrs. Miller, stepping hesitantly into the hall.
95 "You're that little girl."

"I thought you'd never answer, but I kept my finger on the button; I knew you were home. Aren't you glad to see me?"

Mrs. Miller did not know what to say. Miriam, she saw, wore the same plum velvet coat and now she had also a beret to match; her white hair
100 was braided in two shining plaits and looped at the ends with enormous white ribbons.

"Since I've waited so long, you could at least let me in," she said.

"It's awfully late. . . ."

Miriam regarded her blankly. "What difference does that make? Let me
105 in. It's cold out here and I have on a silk dress." Then, with a gentle ges- ture, she urged Mrs. Miller aside and passed into the apartment.

She dropped her coat and beret on a chair. She was indeed wearing a silk dress. White silk. White silk in February. The skirt was beautifully pleated and the sleeves long; it made a faint rustle as she strode about the
110 room. "I like your place," she said. "I like the rug, blue's my favorite color." She touched a paper rose in a vase on the coffee table. "Imitation," she commented wanly. "How sad. Aren't imitations sad?" She seated herself on the sofa, daintily spreading her skirt.

"What do you want?" Mrs. Miller asked.
115 "Sit down," said Miriam. "It makes me nervous to see people stand."

Mrs. Miller sank to a hassock. "What do you want?" she repeated.

"You know, I don't think you're glad I came."

For a second Mrs. Miller was without an answer; her hand motioned vaguely. Miriam giggled and pressed back on a mound of chintz pillows.
120 Mrs. Miller noticed that the girl was less pale than she remembered; her cheeks were flushed.

"How did you know where I lived?"

Miriam frowned. "That's no question at all. What's your name? What's mine?"
125 "But I'm not listed in the phone book."

6. What do this visit and conversation reveal about the characters?

"Oh, let's talk about something else."

Mrs. Miller said, "Your mother must be insane to let a child like you wander around at all hours of the night—and in such ridiculous clothes. She must be out of her mind."

130 Miriam got up and moved to a corner where a covered bird cage hung from a ceiling chain. She peeked under the cover. "It's a canary," she said. "Would you mind if I woke him? I'd like to hear him sing."

"Leave Tommy alone," Mrs. Miller said, anxiously. "Don't you dare wake him."

135 "Certainly," said Miriam. "But I don't see why I can't hear him sing." And then, "Have you anything to eat? I'm starving! Even milk and a jam sandwich would be fine."

"Look," said Mrs. Miller, arising from the hassock, "look—if I make some nice sandwiches will you be a good child and run along home? It's 140 past midnight, I'm sure."

"It's snowing," reproached Miriam. "And cold and dark."

"Well, you shouldn't have come here to begin with," said Mrs. Miller, struggling to control her voice. "I can't help the weather. If you want anything to eat you'll have to promise to leave."

145 Miriam brushed a braid against her cheek. Her eyes were thoughtful, as if weighing the proposition. She turned toward the bird cage. "Very well, she said, "I promise."

How old is she? Ten? Eleven? Mrs. Miller, in the kitchen, unsealed a jar of strawberry preserves and cut four slices of bread. She poured a glass of 150 milk and paused to light a cigarette. And why has she come? Her hand shook as she held the match, fascinated, till it burned her finger. The canary was singing; singing as he did in the morning and at no other time. "Miriam," she called, "Miriam, I told you not to disturb Tommy." There was no answer. She called again; all she heard was the canary. She inhaled the 155 cigarette and discovered she had lighted the cork-tip end and—oh, really, she mustn't lose her temper.

She carried the food in on a tray and set it on the coffee table. She saw first that the bird cage still wore its night cover. And Tommy was singing. It gave her a queer sensation. And no one was in the room. Mrs. Miller 160 went through an alcove leading to her bedroom; at the door she caught her breath.

"What are you doing?" she asked.

Miriam glanced up and in her eyes was a look that was not ordinary. She was standing by the bureau, a jewel case opened before her. For a 165 minute she studied Mrs. Miller, forcing their eyes to meet, and she smiled. "There's nothing good here," she said. "But I like this." Her hand held a cameo brooch. "It's charming."

Guided Questions

7. How do these descriptions from the narrator foreshadow Mrs. Miller's fate?

"Suppose—perhaps you'd better put it back," said Mrs. Miller, feeling suddenly the need of some support. She leaned against the door frame;
170   her head was unbearably heavy; a pressure weighted the rhythm of her heartbeat. The light seemed to flutter defectively. "Please, child . . . a gift from my husband."

"But it's beautiful and I want it," said Miriam. "*Give it to me.*"

As she stood, striving to shape a sentence which would somehow save
175   the brooch, it came to Mrs. Miller there was no one to whom she might turn; she was alone; a fact that had not been among her thoughts for a long time. Its sheer emphasis was stunning. But here in her own room in the hushed show-city were evidences she could not ignore or, she knew with startling clarity, resist.

180   Miriam ate ravenously, and when the sandwiches and milk were gone, her fingers made cobweb movements over the plate, gathering crumbs. The cameo gleamed on her blouse, the blond profile like a trick reflection on its wearer. "That was very nice," she sighed, "though now an almond cake or a cherry would be ideal. Sweets are lovely, don't you think?"

185   Mrs. Miller was perched precariously on the hassock, smoking a cigarette. Her hairnet had slipped lopsided and loose strands straggled down her face. Her eyes were stupidly concentrated on nothing and her cheeks were mottled in red patches, as though a fierce slap had left permanent marks.

190   "Is there a candy—a cake?"

Mrs. Miller tapped ash on the rug. Her head swayed slightly as she tried to focus her eyes. "You promised to leave if I made the sandwiches," she said.

"Dear me, did I?"

195   "It was a promise and I'm tired and I don't feel well at all."

"Mustn't fret," said Miriam. "I'm only teasing."

She picked up her coat, slung it over her arm, and arranged her beret in front of a mirror. Presently she bent close to Mrs. Miller and whispered, "Kiss me good night."

200   "Please—I'd rather not," said Mrs. Miller.

Miriam lifted a shoulder, arched an eyebrow. "As you like," she said, and went directly to the coffee table, seized the vase containing the paper roses, carried it to where the hard surface of the floor lay bare, and hurled it downward. Glass sprayed in all directions and she stamped her foot on
205   the bouquet.

Then slowly she walked to the door, but before closing it she looked back at Mrs. Miller with a slyly innocent curiosity.

Mrs. Miller spent the next day in bed, rising once to feed the canary and drink a cup of tea; she took her temperature and had none, yet her

Guided Questions

8. What does the narrator reveal about Miriam through this description?

9. Explain why the narrator includes a description of the room.

210 dreams were feverishly agitated; their unbalanced mood lingered even as she lay staring wide-eyed at the ceiling. One dream threaded through the others like an elusively mysterious theme in a complicated symphony, and the scenes it depicted were sharply outlined, as though sketched by a hand of gifted intensity: a small girl, wearing a bridal gown and a wreath

215 of leaves, led a gray procession down a mountain path, and among them there was unusual silence till a woman at the rear asked, "Where is she taking us?" "No one knows," said an old man marching in front. "But isn't she pretty?" volunteered a third voice. "Isn't she like a frost flower . . . so shining and white?"

220   Tuesday morning she woke up feeling better; harsh slats of sunlight, slanting through the Venetian blinds, shed a disrupting light on her unwholesome fancies. She opened the window to discover a thawed, mild-as-spring day; a sweep of clean new clouds crumpled against a vastly blue, out-of-season sky; and across the low line of rooftops she

225 could see the river and smoke curving from tugboat stacks in a warm wind. A great silver truck plowed the snow-banked street, its machine sound humming on the air.

    After straightening the apartment, she went to the grocer's, cashed a check and continued to Schrafft's, where she ate breakfast and chatted

230 happily with the waitress. Oh, it was a wonderful day more like a holiday—and it would be so foolish to go home.

    She boarded a Lexington Avenue bus and rode up to Eighty-sixth Street; it was here that she decided to do a little shopping.

    She had no idea what she wanted or needed, but she idled along,

235 intent only upon the passers-by, brisk and preoccupied, who gave her a disturbing sense of separateness.

    It was while waiting at the corner of Third Avenue that she saw the man: an old man, bowlegged and stooped under an armload of bulging packages; he wore a shabby brown coat and a checkered cap. Suddenly

240 she realized they were exchanging a smile: there was nothing friendly about this smile, it was merely two cold flickers of recognition. But she was certain she had never seen him before.

    He was standing next to an El pillar, and as she crossed the street he turned and followed. He kept quite close; from the corner of her eyes she

245 watched his reflection wavering on the shop windows.

    Then in the middle of the block she stopped and faced him. He stopped also and cocked his head, grinning. But what could she say? Do? Here, in broad daylight, on Eighty-sixth Street? It was useless and, despising her own helplessness, she quickened her steps.

250   Now Second Avenue is a dismal street, made from scraps and ends; part cobblestone, part asphalt, part cement; and its atmosphere of

Guided Questions

10. What does the narrator reveal about this encounter? What might this moment foreshadow?

desertion is permanent. Mrs. Miller walked five blocks without meeting anyone, and all the while the steady crunch of his footfalls in the snow stayed near. And when she came to a florist's shop, the sound was still
255 with her. She hurried inside and watched through the glass door as the old man passed; he kept his eyes straight ahead and didn't slow his pace, but he did one strange, telling thing: he tipped his cap.

"Six white ones, did you say?" asked the florist. "Yes," she told him, "white roses." From there she went to a glassware store and selected a
260 vase, presumably a replacement for the one Miriam had broken, though the price was intolerable and the vase itself (she thought) grotesquely vulgar. But a series of unaccountable purchases had begun, as if by prearranged plan: a plan of which she had not the least knowledge or control.

She bought a bag of glazed cherries, and at a place called the
265 Knickerbocker Bakery she paid forty cents for six almond cakes.

11. How does the description of Mrs. Miller's purchases contribute to the suspense?

Within the last hour the weather had turned cold again; like blurred lenses, winter clouds cast a shade over the sun, and the skeleton of an early dusk colored the sky; a damp mist mixed with the wind and the voices of a few children who romped high on mountains of gutter snow
270 seemed lonely and cheerless. Soon the first flake fell, and when Mrs. Miller reached the brownstone house, snow was falling in a swift screen and foot tracks vanished as they were printed.

The white roses were arranged decoratively in the vase. The glazed cherries shone on a ceramic plate. The almond cakes, dusted with sugar,
275 awaited a hand. The canary fluttered on its swing and picked at a bar of seed.

At precisely five the doorbell rang. Mrs. Miller knew who it was. The hem of her housecoat trailed as she crossed the floor. "Is that you?" she called.
280 "Naturally," said Miriam, the word resounding shrilly from the hall. "Open this door."

"Go away," said Mrs. Miller.

"Please hurry . . . I have a heavy package."

"Go away," said Mrs. Miller. She returned to the living room, lighted a
285 cigarette, sat down and calmly listened to the buzzer; on and on and on. "You might as well leave. I have no intention of letting you in."

Shortly the bell stopped. For possibly ten minutes Mrs. Miller did not move. Then, hearing no sound, she concluded Miriam had gone. She tiptoed to the door and opened it a sliver; Miriam was half-reclining atop a
290 cardboard box with a beautiful French doll cradled in her arms.

"Really, I thought you were never coming," she said peevishly. "Here, help me get this in, it's awfully heavy."

It was no spell-like compulsion that Mrs. Miller felt, but rather a curious passivity; she brought in the box, Miriam the doll. Miriam curled up
295 on the sofa, not troubling to remove her coat or beret, and watched disinterestedly as Mrs. Miller dropped the box and stood trembling, trying to catch her breath.

"Thank you," she said. In the daylight she looked pinched and drawn, her hair less luminous. The French doll she was loving wore an exquisite
300 powdered wig and its idiot glass eyes sought solace in Miriam's. "I have a surprise," she continued. "Look into my box."

Kneeling, Mrs. Miller parted the flaps and lifted out another doll; then a blue dress which she recalled as the one Miriam had worn that first night at the theatre; and of the reminder she said, "It's all clothes. Why?"
305 "Because I've come to live with you," said Miriam, twisting a cherry stem. "Wasn't it nice of you to buy me the cherries . . . ?"

"But you can't! For God's sake go away—go away and leave me alone!"

". . . and the roses and the almond cakes? How really wonderfully generous. You know, these cherries are delicious. The last place I lived was
310 with an old man; he was terribly poor and we never had good things to eat. But I think I'll be happy here." She paused to snuggle her doll closer. "Now, if you'll just show me where to put my things . . ."

Mrs. Miller's face dissolved into a mask of ugly red lines; she began to cry, and it was an unnatural, tearless sort of weeping, as though, not hav-
315 ing wept for a long time, she had forgotten how. Carefully she edged backward till she touched the door.

She fumbled through the hall and down the stairs to a landing below. She pounded frantically on the door of the first apartment she came to; a short, redheaded man answered and she pushed past him. "Say, what the
320 hell is this?" he said. "Anything wrong, lover?" asked a young woman who appeared from the kitchen, drying her hands. And it was to her that Mrs. Miller turned.

"Listen," she cried, "I'm ashamed behaving this way but—well, I'm Mrs. H. T. Miller and I live upstairs and . . ." She pressed her hands over her face.
325 "It sounds so absurd . . ."

The woman guided her to a chair, while the man excitedly rattled pocket change. "Yeah?"

"I live upstairs and there's a little girl visiting me, and I suppose that I'm afraid of her. She won't leave and I can't make her and—she's going
330 to do something terrible. She's already stolen my cameo, but she's about to do something worse—more terrible."

The man asked, "Is she a relative, huh?"

Mrs. Miller shook her head. "I don't know who she is. Her name's Miriam, but I don't know for certain who she is."

Guided Questions

12. What does the narrator's description of Miriam reveal about her motivation?

13. What does the dialogue between Miriam and Mrs. Miller reveal about their characters?

335 "You gotta calm down, honey," said the woman, stroking Mrs. Miller's arm. "Harry here will tend to this kid. Go on, lover." And Mrs. Miller said, "The door's open—5A."

After the man left, the woman brought a towel and bathed Mrs. Miller's face. "You're very kind," Mrs. Miller said. "I'm sorry to act like such a fool, 340 only this wicked child . . ."

"Sure, honey," consoled the woman. "Now, you better take it easy."

Mrs. Miller rested her head in the crook of her arm; she was quiet enough to be asleep. The woman turned a radio dial; a piano and a husky voice filled the silence and the woman, tapping her foot, kept excellent 345 time. "Maybe we oughta go up too," she said.

"I don't want to see her again. I don't want to be anywhere near her."

"Uh-huh, but what you shoulda done, you shoulda called a cop."

Presently they heard the man on the stairs. He strode into the room frowning and scratching the back of his neck. "Nobody there," he said, 350 honestly embarrassed. "She musta beat it."

"Harry, you're a jerk," announced the woman. "We been sitting here the whole time and we woulda seen . . ." She stopped abruptly, for the man's glance was sharp.

"I looked all over," he said, "and there just ain't nobody there. Nobody, 355 understand?"

"Tell me," said Mrs. Miller, rising, "tell me, did you see a large box? Or a doll?"

"No, ma'am, I didn't."

And the woman, as if delivering a verdict, said, "Well, for cryinoutloud . . ."

360 Mrs. Miller entered her apartment softly; she walked to the center of the room and stood quite still. No, in a sense it had not changed: the roses, the cakes, and the cherries were in place. But this was an empty room, emptier than if the furnishings and familiars were not present, life-less and petrified as a funeral parlor. The sofa loomed before her with a 365 new strangeness: its vacancy had a meaning that would have been less penetrating and terrible had Miriam been curled on it. She gazed fixedly at the space where she remembered setting the box and, for a moment, the hassock spun desperately. And she looked through the window; surely the river was real, surely snow was falling—but then, one could not be 370 certain witness to anything: Miriam, so vividly there—and yet, where was she? Where? Where?

As though moving in a dream, she sank to a chair. The room was losing shape; it was dark and getting darker and there was nothing to be done about it; she could not lift her hand to light a lamp.

375 Suddenly, closing her eyes, she felt an upward surge, like a diver emerg-ing from some deeper, greener depth. In times of terror or immense dis-tress, there are moments when the mind waits, as though for a revelation, while a skein of calm is woven over thought; it is like a sleep, or a supernatural

Guided Questions

14. How does the inclusion of this reaction from the neighbors contribute to the plot?

15. How does this description contribute to the resolution of the story?

trance; and during this lull one is aware of a force of quiet reasoning: well,
380 what if she had never really known a girl named Miriam? That she had
been foolishly frightened on the street? In the end, like everything else, it
was of no importance. For the only thing she had lost to Miriam was her
identity, but now she knew she had found again the person who lived in
this room, who cooked her own meals, who owned a canary, who was
385 someone she could trust and believe in: Mrs. H. T. Miller.

Listening in contentment, she became aware of a double sound: a
bureau drawer opening and closing; she seemed to hear it long after completion—opening and closing. Then gradually, the harshness of it was
replaced by the murmur of a silk dress and this, delicately faint, was mov-
390 ing nearer and swelling in intensity till the walls trembled with the vibra-
tion and the room was caving under a wave of whispers. Mrs. Miller
stiffened and opened her eyes to a dull, direct stare.

"Hello," said Miriam.

Guided Questions

16. What is the
narrator revealing
in the last line of
dialogue? Why
does the narrator
end with this
greeting?

PRACTICE TEXT

The Minister's Black Veil: A Parable

Nathaniel Hawthorne

THE TEXT IN CONTEXT

Along with Edgar Allan Poe (1809–1849) and Herman Melville
(1819–1891), Nathaniel Hawthorne (1804–1864) wrote fiction
that expressed an American version of Dark Romanticism:
stories preoccupied with sin, madness, the supernatural, and
the grotesque. Hawthorne was born in Salem, Massachusetts,
and often set his stories in grim Puritan Massachusetts, two
hundred years before his own time. These settings — and their
attendant customs and values — do much more than give a backdrop to the characters
and plot. In "The Minister's Black Veil: A Parable" (1836), Hawthorne provides a good
illustration of the dark atmosphere that pervades his fiction. The story's subtitle, "A
Parable," is important, too: a parable is a highly symbolic story that teaches a moral or
religious lesson. Hawthorne's most well-known works include *Twice-Told Tales* (1837),
The Scarlet Letter (1850), and *The Blithedale Romance* (1852).

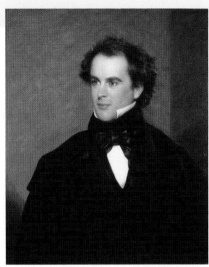

Nathaniel Hawthorne (1804–64) 1840 (oil on canvas)/Osgood, Charles
(1809–90)/©Peabody Essex Museum/Bridgeman Images

AP® SKILLS PRACTICE | NARRATION
Analyzing Narrative Reliability

As you read "The Minister's Black Veil: A Parable," identify the point of view. Then record details from the story that contribute to the narrative reliability. Finally, explain how these details, along with your understanding of the narrator, contribute to your interpretation of the story.

Analyzing Narrative Reliability		
Who is telling the story?		
What is the point of view?		
First Person	**Third Person (Limited)**	**Third Person (Omniscient)**
• What role does this character play in the story?	• How does the narrator's limited knowledge affect the story?	• Does this narrator know everything about all characters?
• What is this character's background?	• How does the inclusion or exclusion of details reveal the narrator's bias?	• How does the inclusion or exclusion of details reveal the narrator's bias?
• What is this character's relationship to other characters?	• What is the narrative distance?	• What is the narrative distance?
• Is there any reason not to trust this character?	• What is the effect of the limited information on the narrative?	• What is the effect of the comprehensive information on the narrative?
• What is the character's emotional or psychological state?		
Textual Details	**What the Details Reveal about the Narrator**	**Literary Effect**

The Minister's Black Veil: A Parable

The Sexton stood in the porch of Milford meeting-house, pulling busily at the bell-rope. The old people of the village came stooping along the street. Children, with
5 bright faces, tripped merrily beside their parents, or mimicked a graver gait, in the conscious dignity of their Sunday clothes. Spruce bachelors looked sidelong at the pretty maidens, and fancied that the Sabbath
10 sunshine made them prettier than on week days. When the throng had mostly streamed into the porch, the sexton began to toll the bell, keeping his eye on the Reverend Mr. Hooper's door. The first glimpse of the
15 clergyman's figure was the signal for the bell to cease its summons.

"But what has good Parson Hooper got upon his face?" cried the sexton in astonishment.

20 All within hearing immediately turned about, and beheld the semblance of Mr. Hooper, pacing slowly his meditative way towards the meeting-house. With one accord they started, expressing more wonder than if
25 some strange minister were coming to dust the cushions of Mr. Hooper's pulpit.

"Are you sure it is our parson?" inquired Goodman Gray of the sexton.

"Of a certainty it is good Mr. Hooper,"
30 replied the sexton. "He was to have exchanged pulpits with Parson Shute, of Westbury, but Parson Shute sent to excuse himself yesterday, being to preach a funeral sermon."

35 The cause of so much amazement may appear sufficiently slight. Mr. Hooper, a gentlemanly person, of about thirty, though still a bachelor, was dressed with due clerical neatness, as if a careful wife had starched
40 his band, and brushed the weekly dust from his Sunday's garb. There was but one thing remarkable in his appearance. Swathed about his forehead, and hanging down over his face, so low as to be shaken by his breath,
45 Mr. Hooper had on a black veil. On a nearer view it seemed to consist of two folds of crape, which entirely concealed his features, except the mouth and chin, but probably did not intercept his sight, further than to give a
50 darkened aspect to all living and inanimate things. With this gloomy shade before him, good Mr. Hooper walked onward, at a slow and quiet pace, stooping somewhat, and looking on the ground, as is customary with
55 abstracted men, yet nodding kindly to those of his parishioners who still waited on the meeting-house steps. But so wonder-struck were they that his greeting hardly met with a return.

60 "I can't really feel as if good Mr. Hooper's face was behind that piece of crape," said the sexton.

"I don't like it," muttered an old woman, as she hobbled into the meeting-house. "He
65 has changed himself into something awful, only by hiding his face."

"Our parson has gone mad!" cried Goodman Gray, following him across the threshold.

70 A rumor of some unaccountable phenomenon had preceded Mr. Hooper into the meeting-house, and set all the congregation astir. Few could refrain from twisting their heads towards the door; many stood upright,
75 and turned directly about; while several little boys clambered upon the seats, and came down again with a terrible racket. There was a general bustle, a rustling of the women's gowns and shuffling of the men's feet,
80 greatly at variance with that hushed repose which should attend the entrance of the minister. But Mr. Hooper appeared not to

notice the perturbation of his people. He entered with an almost noiseless step, bent
85 his head mildly to the pews on each side, and bowed as he passed his oldest parishioner, a white-haired great-grandsire, who occupied an arm-chair in the centre of the aisle. It was strange to observe how slowly
90 this venerable man became conscious of something singular in the appearance of his pastor. He seemed not fully to partake of the prevailing wonder, till Mr. Hooper had ascended the stairs, and showed himself in
95 the pulpit, face to face with his congregation, except for the black veil. That mysterious emblem was never once withdrawn. It shook with his measured breath, as he gave out the psalm; it threw its obscurity between him
100 and the holy page, as he read the Scriptures; and while he prayed, the veil lay heavily on his uplifted countenance. Did he seek to hide it from the dread Being whom he was addressing?
105 Such was the effect of this simple piece of crape, that more than one woman of delicate nerves was forced to leave the meetinghouse. Yet perhaps the pale-faced congregation was almost as fearful a sight to the
110 minister, as his black veil to them.

Mr. Hooper had the reputation of a good preacher, but not an energetic one: he strove to win his people heavenward by mild, persuasive influences, rather than to drive them
115 thither by the thunders of the Word. The sermon which he now delivered was marked by the same characteristics of style and manner as the general series of his pulpit oratory. But there was something, either in the sentiment
120 of the discourse itself, or in the imagination of the auditors, which made it greatly the most powerful effort that they had ever heard from their pastor's lips. It was tinged, rather more darkly than usual, with the gen-

125 tle gloom of Mr. Hooper's temperament. The subject had reference to secret sin, and those sad mysteries which we hide from our nearest and dearest, and would fain conceal from our own consciousness, even forgetting that
130 the Omniscient can detect them. A subtle power was breathed into his words. Each member of the congregation, the most innocent girl, and the man of hardened breast, felt as if the preacher had crept upon them,
135 behind his awful veil, and discovered their hoarded iniquity of deed or thought. Many spread their clasped hands on their bosoms. There was nothing terrible in what Mr. Hooper said, at least, no violence; and yet,
140 with every tremor of his melancholy voice, the hearers quaked. An unsought pathos came hand in hand with awe. So sensible were the audience of some unwonted attribute in their minister, that they longed for a
145 breath of wind to blow aside the veil, almost believing that a stranger's visage would be discovered, though the form, gesture, and voice were those of Mr. Hooper.

At the close of the services, the people
150 hurried out with indecorous confusion, eager to communicate their pent-up amazement, and conscious of lighter spirits the moment they lost sight of the black veil. Some gathered in little circles, huddled closely together,
155 with their mouths all whispering in the centre; some went homeward alone, wrapt in silent meditation; some talked loudly, and profaned the Sabbath day with ostentatious laughter. A few shook their sagacious heads,
160 intimating that they could penetrate the mystery; while one or two affirmed that there was no mystery at all, but only that Mr. Hooper's eyes were so weakened by the midnight lamp, as to require a shade. After a
165 brief interval, forth came good Mr. Hooper also, in the rear of his flock. Turning his

veiled face from one group to another, he paid due reverence to the hoary heads, saluted the middle aged with kind dignity as 170 their friend and spiritual guide, greeted the young with mingled authority and love, and laid his hands on the little children's heads to bless them. Such was always his custom on the Sabbath day. Strange and bewildered 175 looks repaid him for his courtesy. None, as on former occasions, aspired to the honor of walking by their pastor's side. Old Squire Saunders, doubtless by an accidental lapse of memory, neglected to invite Mr. Hooper to 180 his table, where the good clergyman had been wont to bless the food, almost every Sunday since his settlement. He returned, therefore, to the parsonage, and, at the moment of closing the door, was observed to 185 look back upon the people, all of whom had their eyes fixed upon the minister. A sad smile gleamed faintly from beneath the black veil, and flickered about his mouth, glimmering as he disappeared.

190   "How strange," said a lady, "that a simple black veil, such as any woman might wear on her bonnet, should become such a terrible thing on Mr. Hooper's face!"

    "Something must surely be amiss with 195 Mr. Hooper's intellects," observed her husband, the physician of the village. "But the strangest part of the affair is the effect of this vagary, even on a sober-minded man like myself. The black veil, though it covers 200 only our pastor's face, throws its influence over his whole person, and makes him ghostlike from head to foot. Do you not feel it so?"

    "Truly do I," replied the lady; "and I would 205 not be alone with him for the world. I wonder he is not afraid to be alone with himself!"

    "Men sometimes are so," said her husband.

The afternoon service was attended with 210 similar circumstances. At its conclusion the bell tolled for the funeral of a young lady. The relatives and friends were assembled in the house and the more distant acquaintances stood about the door, speaking of the 215 good qualities of the deceased, when their talk was interrupted by the appearance of Mr. Hooper, still covered with his black veil. It was now an appropriate emblem. The clergyman stepped into the room where the corpse 220 was laid, and bent over the coffin, to take a last farewell of his deceased parishioner. As he stooped, the veil hung straight down from his forehead, so that, if her eye-lids had not been closed forever, the dead maiden might 225 have seen his face. Could Mr. Hooper be fearful of her glance, that he so hastily caught back the black veil? A person who watched the interview between the dead and living, scrupled not to affirm, that, at the instant 230 when the clergyman's features were disclosed, the corpse had slightly shuddered, rustling the shroud and muslin cap, though the countenance retained the composure of death. A superstitious old woman was the 235 only witness of this prodigy. From the coffin Mr. Hooper passed into the chamber of the mourners, and thence to the head of the staircase, to make the funeral prayer. It was a tender and heart-dissolving prayer, full of 240 sorrow, yet so imbued with celestial hopes that the music of a heavenly harp swept by the fingers of the dead seemed faintly to be heard among the saddest accents of the minister. The people trembled, though they but 245 darkly understood him, when he prayed that they, and himself, and all of mortal race, might be ready, as he trusted this young maiden had been, for the dreadful hour that should snatch the veil from their faces. The 250 bearers went heavily forth, and the mourners followed, saddening all the street, with the dead before them, and Mr. Hooper in his black veil behind.

255 "Why do you look back?" said one in the procession to his partner.

I had a fancy," replied she, "that the minister and the maiden's spirit were walking hand in hand."

"And so had I, at the same moment," said 260 the other.

That night the handsomest couple in Milford village were to be joined in wedlock. Though reckoned a melancholy man, Mr. Hooper had a placid cheerfulness for 265 such occasions which often excited a sympathetic smile where livelier merriment would have been thrown away. There was no quality of his disposition which made him more beloved than this. The company at the wed- 270 ding awaited his arrival with impatience, trusting that the strange awe which had gathered over him throughout the day would now be dispelled. But such was not the result. When Mr. Hooper came, the first thing 275 that their eyes rested on was the same horrible black veil which had added deeper gloom to the funeral, and could portend nothing but evil to the wedding. Such was its immediate effect on the guests that a cloud 280 seemed to have rolled duskily from beneath the black crape, and dimmed the light of the candles. The bridal pair stood up before the minister, but the bride's cold fingers quivered in the tremulous hand of the bridegroom, 285 and her death-like paleness caused a whisper that the maiden who had been buried a few hours before was come from her grave to be married. If ever another wedding were so dismal, it was that famous one where they 290 tolled the wedding-knell.

After performing the ceremony Mr. Hooper raised a glass of wine to his lips,

wishing happiness to the new-married couple in a strain of mild pleasantry that ought 295 to have brightened the features of the guests like a cheerful gleam from the hearth. At that instant, catching a glimpse of his figure in the looking-glass, the black veil involved his own spirit in the horror with which it over- 300 whelmed all others. His frame shuddered, his lips grew white, he spilt the untasted wine upon the carpet and rushed forth into the darkness, for the Earth too had on her black veil.

305 The next day the whole village of Milford talked of little else than Parson Hooper's black veil. That, and the mystery concealed behind it, supplied a topic for discussion between acquaintances meeting in the street 310 and good women gossiping at their open windows. It was the first item of news that the tavernkeeper told to his guests. The children babbled of it on their way to school. One imitative little imp covered his face with an 315 old black handkerchief, thereby so affrighting his playmates that the panic seized himself and he well-nigh lost his wits by his own waggery.

It was remarkable that, of all the busybod- 320 ies and impertinent people in the parish, not one ventured to put the plain question to Mr. Hooper wherefore he did this thing. Hitherto, whenever there appeared the slightest call for such interference, he had never lacked 325 advisers nor shown himself adverse to be guided by their judgment. If he erred at all, it was by so painful a degree of self-distrust that even the mildest censure would lead him to consider an indifferent action as a 330 crime. Yet, though so well acquainted with this amiable weakness, no individual among his parishioners chose to make the black veil a subject of friendly remonstrance. There was a feeling of dread, neither plainly confessed nor carefully concealed, which caused each to shift the responsibility upon another, till at length it was found expedient to send a deputation of the church, in order to deal with Mr. Hooper about the mystery before it should grow into a scandal. Never did an embassy so ill discharge its duties. The minister received them with friendly courtesy, but became silent after they were seated, leaving to his visitors the whole burden of introducing their important business. The topic, it might be supposed, was obvious enough. There was the black veil swathed round Mr. Hooper's forehead and concealing every feature above his placid mouth, on which, at times, they could perceive the glimmering of a melancholy smile. But that piece of crape, to their imagination, seemed to hang down before his heart, the symbol of a fearful secret between him and them. Were the veil but cast aside, they might speak freely of it, but not till then. Thus they sat a considerable time, speechless, confused and shrinking uneasily from Mr. Hooper's eye, which they felt to be fixed upon them with an invisible glance. Finally, the deputies returned abashed to their constituents, pronouncing the matter too weighty to be handled except by a council of the churches, if, indeed, it might not require a General Synod.

But there was one person in the village unappalled by the awe with which the black veil had impressed all beside herself. When the deputies returned without an explanation, or even venturing to demand one, she, with the calm energy of her character, determined to chase away the strange cloud that appeared to be settling round Mr. Hooper, every moment more darkly than before. As his plighted wife it should be her privilege to know what the black veil concealed. At the minister's first visit, therefore, she entered upon the subject with a direct simplicity which made the task easier both for him and her. After he had seated himself she fixed her eyes steadfastly upon the veil, but could discern nothing of the dreadful gloom that had so overawed the multitude; it was but a double fold of crape hanging down from his forehead to his mouth, and slightly stirring with his breath.

"No," said she aloud, and smiling, "there is nothing terrible in this piece of crape, except that it hides a face which I am always glad to look upon. Come, good sir; let the sun shine from behind the cloud. First lay aside your black veil, then tell me why you put it on."

Mr. Hooper's smile glimmered faintly.

"There is an hour to come," said he, "when all of us shall cast aside our veils. Take it not amiss, beloved friend, if I wear this piece of crape till then."

"Your words are a mystery too," returned the young lady. "Take away the veil from them, at least."

"Elizabeth, I will," said he, "so far as my vow may suffer me. Know, then, this veil is a type and a symbol, and I am bound to wear it ever, both in light and darkness, in solitude and before the gaze of multitudes, and as with strangers, so with my familiar friends. No mortal eye will see it withdrawn. This dismal shade must separate me from the world; even you, Elizabeth, can never come behind it!"

"What grievous affliction hath befallen you," she earnestly inquired, "that you should thus darken your eyes forever?"

"If it be a sign of mourning," replied Mr. Hooper, "I, perhaps, like most other mortals, have sorrows dark enough to be typified by a black veil."

"But what if the world will not believe that it is the type of an innocent sorrow?"

urged Elizabeth. "Beloved and respected as
420 you are, there may be whispers that you hide
your face under the consciousness of secret
sin. For the sake of your holy office do away
this scandal."

The color rose into her cheeks as she inti-
425 mated the nature of the rumors that were
already abroad in the village. But Mr. Hooper's
mildness did not forsake him. He even
smiled again—that same sad smile which
always appeared like a faint glimmering of
430 light proceeding from the obscurity beneath
the veil.

"If I hide my face for sorrow, there is cause
enough," he merely replied; "and if I cover it
for secret sin, what mortal might not do the
435 same?"

And with this gentle but unconquerable
obstinacy did he resist all her entreaties. At
length Elizabeth sat silent. For a few moments
she appeared lost in thought, considering,
440 probably, what new methods might be tried
to withdraw her lover from so dark a fantasy,
which, if it had no other meaning, was perhaps a symptom of mental disease. Though
of a firmer character than his own, the tears
445 rolled down her cheeks. But in an instant, as
it were, a new feeling took the place of sorrow: her eyes were fixed insensibly on the
black veil, when like a sudden twilight in the
air, its terrors fell around her. She arose, and
450 stood trembling before him.

"And do you feel it then, at last?" said he,
mournfully.

She made no reply, but covered her eyes
with her hand and turned to leave the room.
455 He rushed forward and caught her arm.

"Have patience with me, Elizabeth!" cried
he, passionately. "Do not desert me though
this veil must be between us here on earth.
Be mine, and hereafter there shall be no veil
460 over my face, no darkness between our

souls! It is but a mortal veil; it is not for eternity! Oh, you know not how lonely I am, and
how frightened, to be alone behind my black
veil! Do not leave me in this miserable
465 obscurity for ever!"

"Lift the veil but once, and look me in the
face," said she.

"Never! It cannot be!" replied Mr. Hooper.

"Then farewell!" said Elizabeth.

470 She withdrew her arm from his grasp, and
slowly departed, pausing at the door to give
one long, shuddering gaze that seemed
almost to penetrate the mystery of the black
veil. But, even amid his grief Mr. Hooper
475 smiled to think that only a material emblem
had separated him from happiness, though
the horrors which it shadowed forth must be
drawn darkly between the fondest of lovers.

From that time no attempts were made to
480 remove Mr. Hooper's black veil or by a direct
appeal to discover the secret which it was
supposed to hide. By persons who claimed a
superiority to popular prejudice it was reckoned merely an eccentric whim, such as
485 often mingles with the sober actions of men
otherwise rational and tinges them all with
its own semblance of insanity. But with the
multitude good Mr. Hooper was irreparably a
bugbear. He could not walk the street with
490 any peace of mind, so conscious was he that
the gentle and timid would turn aside to
avoid him, and that others would make it a
point of hardihood to throw themselves in
his way. The impertinence of the latter class
495 compelled him to give up his customary
walk at sunset to the burial-ground; for
when he leaned pensively over the gate,
there would always be faces behind the
gravestones, peeping at his black veil. A fable
500 went the rounds that the stare of the dead
people drove him thence. It grieved him to
the very depth of his kind heart to observe

how the children fled from his approach, breaking up their merriest sports while his melancholy figure was yet afar off. Their instinctive dread caused him to feel more strongly than aught else that a preternatural horror was interwoven with the threads of the black crape. In truth, his own antipathy to the veil was known to be so great that he never willingly passed before a mirror, nor stooped to drink at a still fountain lest in its peaceful bosom he should be affrighted by himself. This was what gave plausibility to the whispers, that Mr. Hooper's conscience tortured him for some great crime too horrible to be entirely concealed or otherwise than so obscurely intimated. Thus from beneath the black veil there rolled a cloud into the sunshine, an ambiguity of sin or sorrow, which enveloped the poor minister, so that love or sympathy could never reach him. It was said that ghost and fiend consorted with him there. With self-shudderings and outward terrors he walked continually in its shadow, groping darkly within his own soul or gazing through a medium that saddened the whole world. Even the lawless wind, it was believed, respected his dreadful secret, and never blew aside the veil. But still good Mr. Hooper sadly smiled at the pale visages of the worldly throng as he passed by.

Among all its bad influences, the black veil had the one desirable effect of making its wearer a very efficient clergyman. By the aid of his mysterious emblem—for there was no other apparent cause—he became a man of awful power over souls that were in agony for sin. His converts always regarded him with a dread peculiar to themselves, affirming, though but figuratively, that, before he brought them to celestial light they had been with him behind the black veil. Its gloom, indeed, enabled him to sympathize with all dark affections. Dying sinners cried aloud for Mr. Hooper and would not yield their breath till he appeared, though ever, as he stooped to whisper consolation, they shuddered at the veiled face so near their own. Such were the terrors of the black veil even when Death had bared his visage. Strangers came long distances to attend service at his church with the mere idle purpose of gazing at his figure because it was forbidden them to behold his face. But many were made to quake ere they departed. Once, during Governor Belcher's administration, Mr. Hooper was appointed to preach the election sermon. Covered with his black veil, he stood before the chief magistrate, the council and the representatives, and wrought so deep an impression that the legislative measures of that year were characterized by all the gloom and piety of our earliest ancestral sway.

In this manner Mr. Hooper spent a long life, irreproachable in outward act, yet shrouded in dismal suspicions; kind and loving, though unloved, and dimly feared; a man apart from men, shunned in their health and joy, but ever summoned to their aid in mortal anguish. As years wore on, shedding their snows above his sable veil, he acquired a name throughout the New England churches, and they called him Father Hooper. Nearly all his parishioners who were of mature age when he was settled had been borne away by many a funeral: he had one congregation in the church and a more crowded one in the churchyard; and, having wrought so late into the evening and done his work so well, it was now good Father Hooper's turn to rest.

Several persons were visible by the shaded candlelight in the death-chamber of the old clergyman. Natural connections he had none. But there was the decorously grave though unmoved physician, seeking only to mitigate the last pangs of the patient 590 whom he could not save. There were the deacons and other eminently pious members of his church. There, also, was the Reverend Mr. Clark of Westbury, a young and zealous divine who had ridden in haste to 595 pray by the bedside of the expiring minister. There was the nurse—no hired handmaiden of Death, but one whose calm affection had endured thus long in secrecy, in solitude, amid the chill of age, and would not perish 600 even at the dying-hour. Who but Elizabeth! And there lay the hoary head of good Father Hooper upon the death-pillow with the black veil still swathed about his brow and reaching down over his face, so that each more 605 difficult gasp of his faint breath caused it to stir. All through life that piece of crape had hung between him and the world: it had separated him from cheerful brotherhood and woman's love and kept him in that sad- 610 dest of all prisons his own heart; and still it lay upon his face, as if to deepen the gloom of his darksome chamber and shade him from the sunshine of eternity.

For some time previous, his mind had 615 been confused, wavering doubtfully between the past and the present, and hovering forward, as it were, at intervals, into the indistinctness of the world to come. There had been feverish turns which tossed him from 620 side to side and wore away what little strength he had. But in his most convulsive struggles and in the wildest vagaries of his intellect, when no other thought retained its sober influence, he still showed an awful 625 solicitude lest the black veil should slip aside. Even if his bewildered soul could have forgotten, there was a faithful woman at his pillow who with averted eyes would have

covered that aged face which she had last 630 beheld in the comeliness of manhood.

At length the death-stricken old man lay quietly in the torpor of mental and bodily exhaustion, with an imperceptible pulse and breath that grew fainter and fainter except 635 when a long, deep and irregular inspiration seemed to prelude the flight of his spirit.

The minister of Westbury approached the bedside.

"Venerable Father Hooper," said he, "the 640 moment of your release is at hand. Are you ready for the lifting of the veil that shuts in time from eternity?"

Father Hooper at first replied merely by a feeble motion of his head; then—apprehensive, 645 perhaps, that his meaning might be doubtful—he exerted himself to speak.

"Yea," said he, in faint accents; "my soul hath a patient weariness until that veil be lifted."

650 "And is it fitting," resumed the Reverend Mr. Clark, "that a man so given to prayer, of such a blameless example, holy in deed and thought, so far as mortal judgment may pronounce,—is it fitting that a father in the 655 Church should leave a shadow on his memory that may seem to blacken a life so pure? I pray you, my venerable brother, let not this thing be! Suffer us to be gladdened by your triumphant aspect as you go to your reward. 660 Before the veil of eternity be lifted let me cast aside this black veil from your face;" and, thus speaking, the Reverend Mr. Clark bent forward to reveal the mystery of so many years.

665 But, exerting a sudden energy, that made all the beholders stand aghast, Father Hooper snatched both his hands from beneath the bedclothes and pressed them strongly on the black veil, resolute to struggle if the minister 670 of Westbury would contend with a dying man.

"Never!" cried the veiled clergyman. "On earth, never!"

"Dark old man!" exclaimed the affrighted minister, "with what horrible crime upon
675 your soul are you now passing to the judgment?"

Father Hooper's breath heaved; it rattled in his throat; but, with a mighty effort grasping forward with his hands, he caught hold
680 of life and held it back till he should speak. He even raised himself in bed, and there he sat shivering with the arms of Death around him, while the black veil hung down, awful at that last moment, in the gathered terrors
685 of a lifetime. And yet the faint, sad smile, so often there now seemed to glimmer from its obscurity and linger on Father Hooper's lips.

"Why do you tremble at me alone?" cried he, turning his veiled face round the circle of
690 pale spectators. "Tremble also at each other. Have men avoided me and women shown no pity and children screamed and fled only for my black veil? What but the mystery which it obscurely typifies has made this piece of
695 crape so awful? When the friend shows his inmost heart to his friend, the lover to his best-beloved; when man does not vainly shrink from the eye of his Creator, loathsomely treasuring up the secret of his
700 sin,—then deem me a monster for the symbol beneath which I have lived, and die. I look around me, and, lo! on every visage a black veil!"

While his auditors shrank from one
705 another in mutual affright, Father Hooper fell back upon his pillow, a veiled corpse, with a faint smile lingering on the lips. Still veiled, they laid him in his coffin, and a veiled corpse they bore him to the grave. The grass
710 of many years has sprung up and withered on that grave, the burial-stone is moss-grown, and good Mr. Hooper's face is dust; but awful is still the thought that it mouldered beneath the black veil!

715   NOTE. Another clergyman in New England, Mr. Joseph Moody, of York, Maine, who died about eighty years since, made himself remarkable by the same eccentricity that is here related of the Reverend Mr.
720 Hooper. In his case, however, the symbol had a different import. In early life he had accidentally killed a beloved friend; and from that day till the hour of his own death, he hid his face from men.

NARRATION

1. Who is the **narrator**? How does the story's **point of view** affect our sense of the narrator's **reliability**?

2. How does the narrator's inclusion of details affect the **reliability**?

3. Does the narrator reveal any **biases**? Can you identify and explain any cultural or community **biases** in the narrative? Find at least one example.

4. How do the descriptions of Mr. Hopper and the veil contribute to the **credibility** of the character and affect how the reader responds to his character?

5. Explain how we understand Mr. Hooper's **motivation**. What specifically does the **narrator** reveal about those motives through details that contribute to your interpretation of the text?

Symbolic Settings and Motifs

 Enduring Understanding (FIG-1)

Comparisons, representations, and associations shift meaning from the literal to the figurative and invite readers to interpret a text.

KEY POINT

Settings may be symbolic when their physical locations represent values and ideas that are associated with them.

Think about the decorations in your room at home—and what they might represent. You might have photos of your friends and loved ones, posters from your favorite movies, or pictures of your favorite musical artists and professional athletes. Or you might have flags, tapestries, and figurines that you like or trophies you have won. In other words, your room may be a place where you can express your identity.

As a result, the physical things associated with you can become symbolic as a representation of your values. In turn, a person who sees this real-life setting might infer aspects of your identity and develop expectations from interpreting your decor. The same process occurs with literary characters placed in specific settings.

For example, the setting could be a sunny beach, a dreary prison, a bustling marketplace, a dark forest, or a mysteriously sinister carnival. Each of these settings sets up an expectation for the readers. What do they expect to happen based on what that setting represents? What do you expect to happen?

Settings and Motifs Can Be Symbolic

Settings and **images** take on figurative meaning when they are not only *associated* with ideas and values but also come to *represent* a value or idea. Sometimes, a physical setting takes on a clear symbolic meaning—as when a prison represents confinement, for example. Or an author might create a **motif** by repeatedly presenting several related concrete objects that convey a figurative meaning—for example, when a character struggles with specific forces of nature, the motif may develop the theme of persistence and determination. In other words, settings and motifs become symbolic when they represent abstract ideas, ideologies, and beliefs.

Archetypal Settings

In earlier units, you learned that some settings may imply historical and cultural values. You've also learned that some settings are **archetypes** because the ideas traditionally associated with those settings cross different time periods and cultures. These familiar archetypal settings represent or **symbolize** particular concepts or ideas (see p. 455 for a list of some archetypal settings).

Changing and Contrasted Settings

Earlier in this unit, you learned that authors may set a story in multiple places. It's important to pay particular attention when the settings are in contrast or when they change. Authors contrast those settings to establish an evolution or tension of historical or cultural values that are *associated* with those settings. In the same way, an author may use contrasting or changing settings to highlight changing or contrasting values and ideas *represented* by those settings. Examining shifts and contrasts of the figurative meaning associated with physical settings — and the actions of characters within those settings — can contribute to a sophisticated interpretation of the literary work.

Motifs

While authors may use a motif to develop a setting, they can also use these related **images** more generally to create emotional associations with their readers and develop ideas in the narrative. Sometimes authors draw on a series of related images that are connected in some way. In the broadest sense, then, a **motif** is a concept, image, incident, or pattern that develops and expands throughout a literary work. Because **symbols** can contribute to imagery, they, too, can be part of a motif.

When a motif is used to represent an abstract idea or concept, it can take on symbolic meaning as well. Motifs may be colors, locations, senses, objects, or concepts.

SOME ADJECTIVES TO DESCRIBE MOTIFS		
Animalistic	Hopeful	Reflective
Associative	Idealistic	Regional
Biblical	Incongruous	Religious
Cautionary	Invitational	Revolutionary
Celebratory	Militaristic	Ritualistic
Comedic	Monetary	Romantic
Controlling	Mournful	Sacrificial
Culinary	Musical	Savagistic
Cyclical	Misogynistic	Scientific
Didactic	Mythological	Sensual
Economic	Naturalistic	Sentimental
Evolutionary	Nostalgic	Social
Exploratory	Occupational	Spiritual
Familial	Paradoxical	Suspenseful
Fantastical	Pastoral	Sympathetic
Geographic	Patriotic	Transformational
Gothic	Predatory	Whimsical
Heroic	Prophetic	Youthful
Hierarchical	Racial	

INSIDER AP® TIP

Patterns are important. A motif is a pattern of repeated and related images that an author draws upon to emphasize an idea or concept in an artistic work.

GUIDED READING

The Story of an Hour
Kate Chopin

THE TEXT IN CONTEXT

Often viewed as a precursor to modern feminist authors, novelist and short story writer Kate Chopin (1850–1904) wrote about themes related to gender and marriage: the constraints placed on wives, the illusions of respectability, the sexuality of women, and the amorality of infidelity. Chopin set most of her work in Louisiana, including two novels, *At-Fault* (1890) and *The Awakening* (1899), along with many of her short stories. "The Story of an Hour" takes place in a single house in an unnamed town or suburb, but Chopin captures a woman, a moment, and a marriage with startling insight. The story is also dense with irony, ambiguity, and symbolism.

Courtesy of the Missouri History Museum, St. Louis.

The Story of an Hour

Knowing that Mrs. Mallard was afflicted with a heart trouble, great care was taken to break to her as gently as possible the news of her husband's death.

It was her sister Josephine who told her, in broken sentences; veiled
5   hints that revealed in half concealing. Her husband's friend Richards was there, too, near her. It was he who had been in the newspaper office when intelligence of the railroad disaster was received, with Brently Mallard's name leading the list of "killed." He had only taken the time to assure himself of its truth by a second telegram, and had hastened to forestall
10 any less careful, less tender friend in bearing the sad message.

Guided Questions

1. What does Mrs. Mallard's ailment reveal about her? How does Mrs. Mallard's condition contribute to a motif?

She did not hear the story as many women have heard the same, with a paralyzed inability to accept its significance. She wept at once, with sudden, wild abandonment, in her sister's arms. When the storm of grief had spent itself she went away to her room alone. She would have no one

15 follow her.

There stood, facing the open window, a comfortable, roomy armchair. Into this she sank, pressed down by a physical exhaustion that haunted her body and seemed to reach into her soul.

She could see in the open square before her house the tops of trees

20 that were all aquiver with the new spring life. The delicious breath of rain was in the air. In the street below a peddler was crying his wares. The notes of a distant song which some one was singing reached her faintly, and countless sparrows were twittering in the eaves.

There were patches of blue sky showing here and there through the

25 clouds that had met and piled one above the other in the west facing her window.

She sat with her head thrown back upon the cushion of the chair, quite motionless, except when a sob came up into her throat and shook her, as a child who has cried itself to sleep continues to sob in its dreams.

30 She was young, with a fair, calm face, whose lines bespoke repression and even a certain strength. But now there was a dull stare in her eyes, whose gaze was fixed away off yonder on one of those patches of blue sky. It was not a glance of reflection, but rather indicated a suspension of intelligent thought.

35 There was something coming to her and she was waiting for it, fearfully. What was it? She did not know; it was too subtle and elusive to name. But she felt it, creeping out of the sky, reaching toward her through the sounds, the scents, the color that filled the air.

Now her bosom rose and fell tumultuously. She was beginning to

40 recognize this thing that was approaching to possess her, and she was striving to beat it back with her will—as powerless as her two white slender hands would have been. When she abandoned herself a little whispered word escaped her slightly parted lips. She said it over and over under the breath: "free, free, free!" The vacant stare and the look of terror

45 that had followed it went from her eyes. They stayed keen and bright. Her pulses beat fast, and the coursing blood warmed and relaxed every inch of her body.

She did not stop to ask if it were or were not a monstrous joy that held her. A clear and exalted perception enabled her to dismiss the suggestion

50 as trivial. She knew that she would weep again when she saw the kind, tender hands folded in death; the face that had never looked save with

Guided Questions

2. What associations can be made from the "open window"?

3. What associations can be made from "the new spring life"? What is significant about this contrast?

4. What does the imagery of the blue sky and its figurative associations suggest? How is the sky symbolic?

5. What is coming to Mrs. Mallard? What does this imagery reveal?

6. What is Mrs. Mallard "free" from?

love upon her, fixed and gray and dead. But she saw beyond that bitter moment a long procession of years to come that would belong to her absolutely. And she opened and spread her arms out to them in welcome.

55 There would be no one to live for during those coming years; she would live for herself. There would be no powerful will bending hers in that blind persistence with which men and women believe they have a right to impose a private will upon a fellow-creature. A kind intention or a cruel intention made the act seem no less a crime as she looked upon it in 60 that brief moment of illumination.

And yet she had loved him—sometimes. Often she had not. What did it matter! What could love, the unsolved mystery, count for in the face of this possession of self-assertion which she suddenly recognized as the strongest impulse of her being!

65 "Free! Body and soul free!" she kept whispering.

Josephine was kneeling before the closed door with her lips to the key-hold, imploring for admission. "Louise, open the door! I beg; open the door—you will make yourself ill. What are you doing, Louise? For heaven's sake open the door."

70 "Go away. I am not making myself ill." No; she was drinking in a very elixir of life through that open window.

Her fancy was running riot along those days ahead of her. Spring days, and summer days, and all sorts of days that would be her own. She breathed a quick prayer that life might be long. It was only yesterday she 75 had thought with a shudder that life might be long.

7. What does this contrast reveal about Mrs. Mallard?

She arose at length and opened the door to her sister's importunities. There was a feverish triumph in her eyes, and she carried herself unwittingly like a goddess of Victory. She clasped her sister's waist, and together they descended the stairs. Richards stood waiting for them at 80 the bottom.

Some one was opening the front door with a latchkey. It was Brently Mallard who entered, a little travel-stained, composedly carrying his grip-sack and umbrella. He had been far from the scene of the accident, and did not even know there had been one. He stood amazed at Josephine's 85 piercing cry; at Richards' quick motion to screen him from the view of his wife.

When the doctors came they said she had died of heart disease—of the joy that kills.

8. How does the final image within a motif contribute to an interpretation?

PRACTICE TEXT

The Yellow Wallpaper
Charlotte Perkins Gilman

Fotosearch/Archive Photos/Getty Images

THE TEXT IN CONTEXT

One of the early leaders of the feminist movement in the United States, American lecturer, writer, and publisher Charlotte Perkins Gilman (1860–1935) wrote about women's issues in her time. In May 1884, she married Charles W. Stetson. After a complete nervous postpartum collapse, she divorced her husband and moved to Pasadena, California, with her young daughter. In her autobiography, *The Living of Charlotte Perkins Gilman* (1935), she describes her experience with the "rest cure" prescribed to her following the birth of her child. Her most famous short story, "The Yellow Wallpaper" (1892), is that fictionalized account.

AP® SKILLS PRACTICE | **FIGURATIVE LANGUAGE**
Analyzing Motifs

As you read "The Yellow Wallpaper," record the specific details of images that establish a single motif. Then explain how each detail contributes to a specific idea within your interpretation.

Analyzing Motifs	
Pattern or Motif:	
Textual Detail (Specific images that contribute to a pattern or motif):	**Literary Effect** (How the particular detail contributes to the motif, revealing an insight about a single idea):

The Yellow Wallpaper

It is very seldom that mere ordinary people like John and myself secure ancestral halls for the summer.

A colonial mansion, a hereditary estate, I
5 would say a haunted house, and reach the height of romantic felicity—but that would be asking too much of fate!

Still I will proudly declare that there is something queer about it.

10 Else, why should it be let so cheaply? And why have stood so long untenanted?

John laughs at me, of course, but one expects that in marriage.

John is practical in the extreme. He has
15 no patience with faith, an intense horror of superstition, and he scoffs openly at any talk of things not to be felt and seen and put down in figures.

John is a physician, and *perhaps*—(I would
20 not say it to a living soul, of course, but this is dead paper and a great relief to my mind)—*perhaps* that is one reason I do not get well faster.

You see, he does not believe I am sick!
25 And what can one do?

If a physician of high standing, and one's own husband, assures friends and relatives that there is really nothing the matter with one but temporary nervous depression—a
30 slight hysterical tendency—what is one to do?

My brother is also a physician, and also of high standing, and he says the same thing.

So I take phosphates or phosphites— whichever it is, and tonics, and journeys, and
35 air, and exercise, and am absolutely forbidden to "work" until I am well again.

Personally, I disagree with their ideas.

Personally, I believe that congenial work, with excitement and change, would do me
40 good.

But what is one to do?

I did write for a while in spite of them; but it *does* exhaust me a good deal—having to be so sly about it, or else meet with heavy
45 opposition.

I sometimes fancy that in my condition if I had less opposition and more society and stimulus—but John says the very worst thing I can do is to think about my
50 condition, and I confess it always makes me feel bad.

So I will let it alone and talk about the house.

The most beautiful place! It is quite alone,
55 standing well back from the road, quite three miles from the village. It makes me think of English places that you read about, for there are hedges and walls and gates that lock, and lots of separate little houses for the
60 gardeners and people.

There is a *delicious* garden! I never saw such a garden—large and shady, full of box-bordered paths, and lined with long grape-covered arbors with seats under them.

65 There were greenhouses, too, but they are all broken now.

There was some legal trouble, I believe, something about the heirs and co-heirs; anyhow, the place has been empty for years.

70 That spoils my ghostliness, I am afraid; but I don't care—there is something strange about the house—I can feel it.

I even said so to John one moonlight evening, but he said what I felt was a *draught*,
75 and shut the window.

I get unreasonably angry with John sometimes. I'm sure I never used to be so sensitive. I think it is due to this nervous condition.

But John says if I feel so I shall neglect
80 proper self-control; so I take pains to control myself,—before him, at least,—and that makes me very tired.

I don't like our room a bit. I wanted one downstairs that opened on the piazza and had roses all over the window, and such pretty old-fashioned chintz hangings! but John would not hear of it.

He said there was only one window and not room for two beds, and no near room for him if he took another.

He is very careful and loving, and hardly lets me stir without special direction.

I have a schedule prescription for each hour in the day; he takes all care from me, and so I feel basely ungrateful not to value it more.

He said we came here solely on my account, that I was to have perfect rest and all the air I could get. "Your exercise depends on your strength, my dear," said he, "and your food somewhat on your appetite; but air you can absorb all the time." So we took the nursery, at the top of the house.

It is a big, airy room, the whole floor nearly, with windows that look all ways, and air and sunshine galore. It was nursery first and then playground and gymnasium, I should judge; for the windows are barred for little children, and there are rings and things in the walls.

The paint and paper look as if a boys' school had used it. It is stripped off—the paper—in great patches all around the head of my bed, about as far as I can reach, and in a great place on the other side of the room low down. I never saw a worse paper in my life.

One of those sprawling flamboyant patterns committing every artistic sin.

It is dull enough to confuse the eye in following, pronounced enough to constantly irritate, and provoke study, and when you follow the lame, uncertain curves for a little distance they suddenly commit suicide—plunge off at outrageous angles, destroy themselves in unheard-of contradictions.

The color is repellant, almost revolting; a smouldering, unclean yellow, strangely faded by the slow-turning sunlight.

It is a dull yet lurid orange in some places, a sickly sulphur tint in others.

No wonder the children hated it! I should hate it myself if I had to live in this room long.

There comes John, and I must put this away,—he hates to have me write a word.

• • •

We have been here two weeks, and I haven't felt like writing before, since that first day.

I am sitting by the window now, up in this atrocious nursery, and there is nothing to hinder my writing as much as I please, save lack of strength.

John is away all day, and even some nights when his cases are serious.

I am glad my case is not serious!

But these nervous troubles are dreadfully depressing.

John does not know how much I really suffer. He knows there is no *reason* to suffer, and that satisfies him.

Of course it is only nervousness. It does weigh on me so not to do my duty in any way!

I meant to be such a help to John, such a real rest and comfort, and here I am a comparative burden already!

Nobody would believe what an effort it is to do what little I am able—to dress and entertain, and order things.

It is fortunate Mary is so good with the baby. Such a dear baby!

And yet I *cannot* be with him, it makes me so nervous.

I suppose John never was nervous in his life. He laughs at me so about this wallpaper!

165 At first he meant to repaper the room, but afterwards he said that I was letting it get the better of me, and that nothing was worse for a nervous patient than to give way to such fancies.

170 He said that after the wallpaper was changed it would be the heavy bedstead, and then the barred windows, and then that gate at the head of the stairs, and so on.

"You know the place is doing you good," 175 he said, "and really, dear, I don't care to renovate the house just for a three months' rental."

"Then do let us go downstairs," I said, "there are such pretty rooms there."

180 Then he took me in his arms and called me a blessed little goose, and said he would go down cellar if I wished, and have it white-washed into the bargain.

But he is right enough about the beds and 185 windows and things.

It is as airy and comfortable a room as any one need wish, and, of course, I would not be so silly as to make him uncomfortable just for a whim.

190 I'm really getting quite fond of the big room, all but that horrid paper.

Out of one window I can see the garden, those mysterious deep-shaded arbors, the riotous old-fashioned flowers, and bushes 195 and gnarly trees.

Out of another I get a lovely view of the bay and a little private wharf belonging to the estate. There is a beautiful shaded lane that runs down there from the house. I 200 always fancy I see people walking in these numerous paths and arbors, but John has cautioned me not to give way to fancy in the least. He says that with my imaginative power and habit of story-making a nervous 205 weakness like mine is sure to lead to all manner of excited fancies, and that I ought

to use my will and good sense to check the tendency. So I try.

I think sometimes that if I were only well 210 enough to write a little it would relieve the press of ideas and rest me.

But I find I get pretty tired when I try.

It is so discouraging not to have any advice and companionship about my work. 215 When I get really well John says we will ask Cousin Henry and Julia down for a long visit; but he says he would as soon put fire-works in my pillow-case as to let me have those stimulating people about now.

220 I wish I could get well faster.

But I must not think about that. This paper looks to me as if it *knew* what a vicious influence it had!

There is a recurrent spot where the pat-225 tern lolls like a broken neck and two bulbous eyes stare at you upside-down.

I get positively angry with the imperti-nence of it and the everlastingness. Up and down and sideways they crawl, and those 230 absurd, unblinking eyes are everywhere. There is one place where two breadths didn't match, and the eyes go all up and down the line, one a little higher than the other.

I never saw so much expression in an inani-235 mate thing before, and we all know how much expression they have! I used to lie awake as a child and get more entertainment and terror out of blank walls and plain furniture than most children could find in a toy-store.

240 I remember what a kindly wink the knobs of our big old bureau used to have, and there was one chair that always seemed like a strong friend.

I used to feel that if any of the other 245 things looked too fierce I could always hop into that chair and be safe.

The furniture in this room is no worse than inharmonious, however, for we had to bring it all from downstairs. I suppose when this was used as a playroom they had to take the nursery things out, and no wonder! I never saw such ravages as the children have made here.

The wallpaper, as I said before, is torn off in spots, and it sticketh closer than a brother—they must have had perseverance as well as hatred.

Then the floor is scratched and gouged and splintered, the plaster itself is dug out here and there, and this great heavy bed, which is all we found in the room, looks as if it had been through the wars.

But I don't mind it a bit—only the paper.

There comes John's sister. Such a dear girl as she is, and so careful of me! I must not let her find me writing.

She is a perfect, and enthusiastic house-keeper, and hopes for no better profession. I verily believe she thinks it is the writing which made me sick!

But I can write when she is out, and see her a long way off from these windows.

There is one that commands the road, a lovely, shaded, winding road, and one that just looks off over the country. A lovely country, too, full of great elms and velvet meadows.

This wallpaper has a kind of sub-pattern in a different shade, a particularly irritating one, for you can only see it in certain lights, and not clearly then.

But in the places where it isn't faded, and where the sun is just so, I can see a strange, provoking, formless sort of figure, that seems to sulk about behind that silly and conspicu-ous front design.

There's sister on the stairs!

• • •

Well, the Fourth of July is over! The people are gone and I am tired out. John thought it might do me good to see a little company, so we just had mother and Nellie and the chil-dren down for a week.

Of course I didn't do a thing. Jennie sees to everything now.

But it tired me all the same.

John says if I don't pick up faster he shall send me to Weir Mitchell in the fall.

But I don't want to go there at all. I had a friend who was in his hands once, and she says he is just like John and my brother, only more so!

Besides, it is such an undertaking to go so far.

I don't feel as if it was worth while to turn my hand over for anything, and I'm getting dreadfully fretful and querulous.

I cry at nothing, and cry most of the time.

Of course I don't when John is here, or anybody else, but when I am alone.

And I am alone a good deal just now. John is kept in town very often by serious cases, and Jennie is good and lets me alone when I want her to.

So I walk a little in the garden or down that lovely lane, sit on the porch under the roses, and lie down up here a good deal.

I'm getting really fond of the room in spite of the wallpaper. Perhaps *because* of the wall-paper.

It dwells in my mind so!

I lie here on this great immovable bed—it is nailed down, I believe—and follow that pattern about by the hour. It is as good as gymnastics, I assure you. I start, we'll say, at the bottom, down in the corner over there where it has not been touched, and I deter-mine for the thousandth time that I *will* follow that pointless pattern to some sort of a conclusion.

I know a little of the principle of design, and I know this thing was not arranged on

any laws of radiation, or alternation, or
repetition, or symmetry, or anything else
that I ever heard of.

It is repeated, of course, by the breadths,
335 but not otherwise.

Looked at in one way each breadth stands
alone, the bloated curves and flourishes—a
kind of "debased Romanesque" with *delirium
tremens*—go waddling up and down in iso-
340 lated columns of fatuity.

But, on the other hand, they connect
diagonally, and the sprawling outlines run
off in great slanting waves of optic horror,
like a lot of wallowing seaweeds in full
345 chase.

The whole thing goes horizontally, too, at
least it seems so, and I exhaust myself in trying to distinguish the order of its going in
that direction.
350 They have used a horizontal breadth for
a frieze, and that adds wonderfully to the
confusion.

There is one end of the room where it is
almost intact, and there, when the cross-
355 lights fade and the low sun shines directly
upon it, I can almost fancy radiation after
all,—the interminable grotesques seem to
form around a common centre and rush off
in headlong plunges of equal distraction.
360 It makes me tired to follow it. I will take a
nap, I guess.

• • •

I don't know why I should write this.

I don't want to.

I don't feel able.
365 And I know John would think it absurd.
But I *must* say what I feel and think in some
way—it is such a relief!

But the effort is getting to be greater than
the relief.
370 Half the time now I am awfully lazy, and
lie down ever so much.

John says I musn't lose my strength, and
has me take cod-liver oil and lots of tonics
and things, to say nothing of ale and wine
375 and rare meat.

Dear John! He loves me very dearly, and
hates to have me sick. I tried to have a real
earnest reasonable talk with him the other
day, and tell him how I wish he would let me
380 go and make a visit to Cousin Henry and
Julia.

But he said I wasn't able to go, nor able to
stand it after I got there; and I did not make
out a very good case for myself, for I was cry-
385 ing before I had finished.

It is getting to be a great effort for me to
think straight. Just this nervous weakness, I
suppose.

And dear John gathered me up in his
390 arms, and just carried me upstairs and laid
me on the bed, and sat by me and read to me
till it tired my head.

He said I was his darling and his comfort
and all he had, and that I must take care of
395 myself for his sake, and keep well.

He says no one but myself can help me
out of it, that I must use my will and
self-control and not let any silly fancies
run away with me.
400 There's one comfort, the baby is well and
happy, and does not have to occupy this
nursery with the horrid wallpaper.

If we had not used it that blessed child
would have! What a fortunate escape! Why, I
405 wouldn't have a child of mine, an impres-
sionable little thing, live in such a room for
worlds.

I never thought of it before, but it is
lucky that John kept me here after all.
410 I can stand it so much easier than a baby,
you see.

Of course I never mention it to them any
more,—I am too wise,—but I keep watch of
it all the same.

415 There are things in that paper that nobody knows but me, or ever will.

Behind that outside pattern the dim shapes get clearer every day.

It is always the same shape, only very 420 numerous.

And it is like a woman stooping down and creeping about behind that pattern. I don't like it a bit. I wonder—I begin to think—I wish John would take me away from here!

• • •

425 It is so hard to talk with John about my case, because he is so wise, and because he loves me so.

But I tried it last night.

It was moonlight. The moon shines in all 430 around, just as the sun does.

I hate to see it sometimes, it creeps so slowly, and always comes in by one window or another.

John was asleep and I hated to waken 435 him, so I kept still and watched the moonlight on that undulating wallpaper till I felt creepy.

The faint figure behind seemed to shake the pattern, just as if she wanted to get out.

440 I got up softly and went to feel and see if the paper *did* move, and when I came back John was awake.

"What is it, little girl?" he said. "Don't go walking about like that—you'll get cold."

445 I thought it was a good time to talk, so I told him that I really was not gaining here, and that I wished he would take me away.

"Why darling!" said he, "our lease will be up in three weeks, and I can't see how to 450 leave before.

"The repairs are not done at home, and I cannot possibly leave town just now. Of course if you were in any danger I could and would, but you really are better, dear, 455 whether you can see it or not. I am a doctor,

dear, and I know. You are gaining flesh and color, your appetite is better. I feel really much easier about you."

"I don't weigh a bit more," said I, "nor as 460 much; and my appetite may be better in the evening, when you are here, but it is worse in the morning when you are away."

"Bless her little heart!" said he with a big hug; "she shall be as sick as she pleases! 465 But now let's improve the shining hours by going to sleep, and talk about it in the morning!"

"And you won't go away?" I asked gloomily.

"Why, how can I, dear? It is only three 470 weeks more and then we will take a nice little trip of a few days while Jennie is getting the house ready. Really, dear, you are better!"

"Better in body perhaps"—I began, and stopped short, for he sat up straight and 475 looked at me with such a stern, reproachful look that I could not say another word.

"My darling," said he, "I beg of you, for my sake and for our child's sake, as well as for your own, that you will never for one instant 480 let that idea enter your mind! There is nothing so dangerous, so fascinating, to a temperament like yours. It is a false and foolish fancy. Can you not trust me as a physician when I tell you so?"

485 So of course I said no more on that score, and we went to sleep before long. He thought I was asleep first, but I wasn't,—I lay there for hours trying to decide whether that front pattern and the back pattern really did move 490 together or separately.

On a pattern like this, by daylight, there is a lack of sequence, a defiance of law, that is a constant irritant to a normal mind.

The color is hideous enough, and unreli- 495 able enough, and infuriating enough, but the pattern is torturing.

You think you have mastered it, but just as you get well under way in following, it

turns a back somersault and there you are. It
500 slaps you in the face, knocks you down, and
tramples upon you. It is like a bad dream.

The outside pattern is a florid arabesque,
reminding one of a fungus. If you can imagine a toadstool in joints, an interminable
505 string of toadstools, budding and sprouting
in endless convolutions,—why, that is something like it.

That is, sometimes!

There is one marked peculiarity about
510 this paper, a thing nobody seems to notice
but myself, and that is that it changes as the
light changes.

When the sun shoots in through the east
window—I always watch for that first long,
515 straight ray—it changes so quickly that I
never can quite believe it.

That is why I watch it always.

By moonlight—the moon shines in all
night when there is a moon—I wouldn't
520 know it was the same paper.

At night in any kind of light, in twilight,
candlelight, lamplight, and worst of all by
moonlight, it becomes bars! The outside pattern I mean, and the woman behind it is as
525 plain as can be.

I didn't realize for a long time what the
thing was that showed behind,—that dim
sub-pattern,—but now I am quite sure it is a
woman.

530 By daylight she is subdued, quiet. I fancy
it is the pattern that keeps her so still. It is so
puzzling. It keeps me quiet by the hour.

I lie down ever so much now. John says it
is good for me, and to sleep all I can.

535 Indeed, he started the habit by making me
lie down for an hour after each meal.

It is a very bad habit, I am convinced, for,
you see, I don't sleep.

And that cultivates deceit, for I don't tell
540 them I'm awake,—oh, no!

The fact is, I am getting a little afraid of
John.

He seems very queer sometimes, and
even Jennie has an inexplicable look.
545 It strikes me occasionally, just as a scientific hypothesis, that perhaps it is the paper!

I have watched John when he did not
know I was looking, and come into the room
suddenly on the most innocent excuses, and
550 I've caught him several times *looking at the
paper!* And Jennie too. I caught Jennie with
her hand on it once.

She didn't know I was in the room, and
when I asked her in a quiet, a very quiet
555 voice, with the most restrained manner possible, what she was doing with the paper she
turned around as if she had been caught
stealing, and looked quite angry—asked me
why I should frighten her so!

560 Then she said that the paper stained
everything it touched, that she had found yellow smooches on all my clothes and John's,
and she wished we would be more careful!

Did not that sound innocent? But I know
565 she was studying that pattern, and I am determined that nobody shall find it out but myself!

• • •

Life is very much more exciting now than it
used to be. You see I have something more to
expect, to look forward to, to watch. I really
570 do eat better, and am more quiet than I was.

John is so pleased to see me improve! He
laughed a little the other day, and said I seemed
to be flourishing in spite of my wallpaper.

I turned it off with a laugh. I had no inten-
575 tion of telling him it was *because* of the wallpaper—he would make fun of me. He might
even want to take me away.

I don't want to leave now until I have
found it out. There is a week more, and I
580 think that will be enough.

• • •

I'm feeling ever so much better! I don't sleep much at night, for it is so interesting to watch developments; but I sleep a good deal in the daytime.

585   In the daytime it is tiresome and perplexing.

There are always new shoots on the fungus, and new shades of yellow all over it. I cannot keep count of them, though I have tried conscientiously.

590   It is the strangest yellow, that wallpaper! It makes me think of all the yellow things I ever saw—not beautiful ones like buttercups, but old foul, bad yellow things.

But there is something else about that
595 paper—the smell! I noticed it the moment we came into the room, but with so much air and sun it was not bad. Now we have had a week of fog and rain, and whether the windows are open or not, the smell is here.

600   It creeps all over the house.

I find it hovering in the dining-room, skulking in the parlor, hiding in the hall, lying in wait for me on the stairs.

It gets into my hair.

605   Even when I go to ride, if I turn my head suddenly and surprise it—there is that smell!

Such a peculiar odor, too! I have spent hours in trying to analyze it, to find what it
610 smelled like.

It is not bad—at first, and very gentle, but quite the subtlest, most enduring odor I ever met.

In this damp weather it is awful. I wake
615 up in the night and find it hanging over me.

It used to disturb me at first. I thought seriously of burning the house—to reach the smell.

But now I am used to it. The only thing I
620 can think of that it is like is the *color* of the paper! A yellow smell.

There is a very funny mark on this wall, low down, near the mopboard. A streak that runs round the room. It goes behind every piece of
625 furniture, except the bed, a long, straight, even *smooch*, as if it had been rubbed over and over.

I wonder how it was done and who did it, and what they did it for. Round and round and round—round and round and round—it
630 makes me dizzy!

• • •

I really have discovered something at last.

Through watching so much at night, when it changes so, I have finally found out.

The front pattern *does* move—and no
635 wonder! The woman behind shakes it!

Sometimes I think there are a great many women behind, and sometimes only one, and she crawls around fast, and her crawling shakes it all over.

640   Then in the very bright spots she keeps still, and in the very shady spots she just takes hold of the bars and shakes them hard.

And she is all the time trying to climb through. But nobody could climb through
645 that pattern—it strangles so; I think that is why it has so many heads.

They get through, and then the pattern strangles them off and turns them upside-down, and makes their eyes white!

650   If those heads were covered or taken off it would not be half so bad.

• • •

I think that woman gets out in the daytime!

And I'll tell you why—privately—I've seen her!

655   I can see her out of every one of my windows!

It is the same woman, I know, for she is always creeping, and most women do not creep by daylight.

660 I see her on that long shaded lane, creeping up and down. I see her in those dark grape arbors, creeping all around the garden.

I see her on that long road under the trees, creeping along, and when a carriage
665 comes she hides under the blackberry vines.

I don't blame her a bit. It must be very humiliating to be caught creeping by daylight!

I always lock the door when I creep by
670 daylight. I can't do it at night, for I know John would suspect something at once.

And John is so queer now, that I don't want to irritate him. I wish he would take another room! Besides, I don't want anybody
675 to get that woman out at night but myself.

I often wonder if I could see her out of all the windows at once.

But, turn as fast as I can, I can only see out of one at one time.
680 And though I always see her she *may* be able to creep faster than I can turn!

I have watched her sometimes away off in the open country, creeping as fast as a cloud shadow in a high wind.

• • •

685 If only that top pattern could be gotten off from the under one! I mean to try it, little by little.

I have found out another funny thing, but I shan't tell it this time! It does not do to
690 trust people too much.

There are only two more days to get this paper off, and I believe John is beginning to notice. I don't like the look in his eyes.

And I heard him ask Jennie a lot of profes-
695 sional questions about me. She had a very good report to give.

She said I slept a good deal in the day-time.

John knows I don't sleep very well at
700 night, for all I'm so quiet!

He asked me all sorts of questions, too, and pretended to be very loving and kind.

As if I couldn't see through him!

Still, I don't wonder he acts so, sleeping
705 under this paper for three months.

It only interests me, but I feel sure John and Jennie are secretly affected by it.

• • •

Hurrah! This is the last day, but it is enough. John is to stay in town over night, and won't
710 be out until this evening.

Jennie wanted to sleep with me—the sly thing! but I told her I should undoubtedly rest better for a night all alone.

That was clever, for really I wasn't alone a
715 bit! As soon as it was moonlight, and that poor thing began to crawl and shake the pattern, I got up and ran to help her.

I pulled and she shook, I shook and she pulled, and before morning we had peeled
720 off yards of that paper.

A strip about as high as my head and half around the room.

And then when the sun came and that awful pattern began to laugh at me I
725 declared I would finish it to-day!

We go away to-morrow, and they are moving all my furniture down again to leave things as they were before.

Jennie looked at the wall in amazement,
730 but I told her merrily that I did it out of pure spite at the vicious thing.

She laughed and said she wouldn't mind doing it herself, but I must not get tired.

How she betrayed herself that time!
735 But I am here, and no person touches this paper but me—not *alive*!

She tried to get me out of the room—it was too patent! But I said it was so quiet and empty and clean now that I believed I would lie down
740 again and sleep all I could; and not to wake me even for dinner—I would call when I woke.

So now she is gone, and the servants are gone, and the things are gone, and there is nothing left but that great bedstead nailed
745 down, with the canvas mattress we found on it.

We shall sleep downstairs to-night, and take the boat home to-morrow.

I quite enjoy the room, now it is bare
750 again.

How those children did tear about here!

This bedstead is fairly gnawed!

But I must get to work.

I have locked the door and thrown the key
755 down into the front path.

I don't want to go out, and I don't want to have anybody come in, till John comes.

I want to astonish him.

I've got a rope up here that even Jennie
760 did not find. If that woman does get out, and tries to get away, I can tie her!

But I forgot I could not reach far without anything to stand on!

This bed will *not* move!
765 I tried to lift and push it until I was lame, and then I got so angry I bit off a little piece at one corner—but it hurt my teeth.

Then I peeled off all the paper I could reach standing on the floor. It sticks horribly
770 and the pattern just enjoys it! All those strangled heads and bulbous eyes and waddling fungus growths just shriek with derision!

I am getting angry enough to do some-
775 thing desperate. To jump out of the window would be admirable exercise, but the bars are too strong even to try.

Besides I wouldn't do it. Of course not. I know well enough that a step like that is
780 improper and might be misconstrued.

I don't like to *look* out of the windows even—there are so many of those creeping women, and they creep so fast.

I wonder if they all come out of that wall-
785 paper as I did?

But I am securely fastened now by my well-hidden rope—you don't get *me* out in the road there!

I suppose I shall have to get back behind
790 the pattern when it comes night, and that is hard!

It is so pleasant to be out in this great room and creep around as I please!

I don't want to go outside. I won't, even if
795 Jennie asks me to.

For outside you have to creep on the ground, and everything is green instead of yellow.

But here I can creep smoothly on the floor,
800 and my shoulder just fits in that long smooch around the wall, so I cannot lose my way.

Why, there's John at the door!

It is no use, young man, you can't open it!
805 How he does call and pound!

Now he's crying for an axe.

It would be a shame to break down that beautiful door!

"John dear!" said I in the gentlest voice,
810 "the key is down by the front steps, under a plantain leaf!"

That silenced him for a few moments.

Then he said—very quietly indeed, "Open the door, my darling!"
815 "I can't," said I. "The key is down by the front door under a plantain leaf!"

And then I said it again, several times, very gently and slowly, and said it so often that he had to go and see, and he got it, of
820 course, and came in. He stopped short by the door.

"What is the matter?" he cried. "For God's sake, what are you doing!"

I kept on creeping just the same, but I
825 looked at him over my shoulder.

"I've got out at last," said I, "in spite of you and Jane! And I've pulled off most of the paper, so you can't put me back!"

830 Now why should that man have fainted? But he did, and right across my path by the wall, so that I had to creep over him every time!

FIGURATIVE LANGUAGE: Word Choice, Imagery, and Symbols

1. What does the narrator's ailment indicate about her? How does it contribute to a **motif**?

2. How do the details of the summer house reveal it as a **symbol**?

3. How does the **imagery** of the wallpaper — and its figurative associations — reveal it as a **symbol**?

4. What frightens the narrator? What is figuratively trapping the narrator?

5. At the climax of the story, what associations can be made from the **symbols** and the **motif**? How do these associations contribute to your interpretation?

FIGURATIVE LANGUAGE: Comparisons

Similes and Personification

AP® Enduring Understanding (FIG-1)

Comparisons, representations, and associations shift meaning from the literal to the figurative and invite readers to interpret a text.

Aesop's fable of the Tortoise and the Hare wouldn't be the same if the main characters were a cat and a dog or a frog and a minnow. Hypothetically, Aesop could have chosen any animals to be the main characters and still communicated the moral of the story. But the obvious associations of tortoises and hares reinforce their roles in the narrative.

Writers use figurative language — simile, metaphor, personification — to make important comparisons. If the reader doesn't understand why the comparison has been made, it won't achieve the author's intended effect. So, readers must ask, Why did the author make this comparison? What attributes are being compared? What is significant about those traits in the context of the comparison?

In this workshop, we'll look at similes and personification in particular. Then in the next unit, we'll explore metaphors in greater depth.

KEY POINT

Authors use similes and personification to make strategic and intentional figurative comparisons between characters and physical objects or physical objects and human characteristics. Meaning is based on an analysis of the particular traits of the comparison.

Figurative Comparisons Highlight Significant Attributes

When authors make comparisons between characters (or human characteristics) and physical objects, they choose the objects of comparison to emphasize specific traits and attributes. So, when you are analyzing similes and personification, examine the specific traits that are included as part of the comparison. This is true for any comparison involving **figurative language**, including metaphor and symbolism.

Similes

You've learned that a **simile** is a comparison that uses the words *like* or *as*. But when you identify the literal objects of comparison, you have only taken the first step in analyzing the simile. Next, you must consider why the author made this comparison and explain the particular traits detailed in the comparison.

In Rihanna's song "Diamonds," for example, she instructs her love to "shine bright like a diamond." By using a simile that compares her love to a diamond, the singer suggests the following shared characteristics: (1) as diamonds reflect brilliant light, people in love often have a glow about them; (2) diamonds are valuable, as is love; (3) diamonds are indestructible, which implies that the singer's love is resilient and strong.

Personification

In the same way that you've studied similes, you've likely encountered literary works that include **personification**. When authors use personification, they give human qualities, features, or emotions to objects, places, animals, and ideas. In doing so, the objects or animals not only take on human characteristics but also convey attitudes and perspectives about ideas and values.

In some stories, many or all the characters may be animals or inanimate objects. These tales, called fables, draw upon the interactions between multiple nonhuman "characters," each with personified traits of comparison to create a plot. Authors use personification in fables to create distance, as these stories use humor and satire to teach lessons, point out human foolishness, or convey serious ideas. This ironic distance allows readers to focus on the story's point instead of its realism, its real-life associations, or other unnecessary details.

Personification is like all other figurative language in that readers must consider why an author used this form of comparison by analyzing the particular traits detailed in the text. Additionally, readers must pay close attention to the attitude or tone of the personified "character."

Characters, Objects, and Animals

In some works, nonhuman objects take on human attributes, such as the ability to speak to other personified objects, animals, or human characters. This technique, **prosopopoeia**, operates much like personification. As these personified objects and animals are functioning as characters, it may be helpful to understand their point of view, as well as their characterization when developing an interpretation.

Inversely, some characters in stories speak to inanimate objects and animals, even if these nonhuman "characters" are not personified. In fact, we use this literary technique, called **apostrophe**, in our daily lives when we express anger at our cars or smartphones for not working, or even complain about bad weather as if meteorological conditions had human motives. Why do literary characters do this? Usually, they are creating an invocation, posing a rhetorical question, or offering insight. In Mary Shelley's *Frankenstein*, for example, Victor Frankenstein expresses his despair by exclaiming, "Oh! stars and clouds and winds, ye are all about to mock me."

INSIDER AP® TIP   **The specific traits of comparison reveal insights.** When developing an interpretation, you must do more than identify points of similarity in a literary comparison. You must also analyze and explain the significance of the particular aspects or traits that are being compared.

GUIDED READING

The Masque of the Red Death

Edgar Allan Poe

THE TEXT IN CONTEXT

Edgar Allan Poe (1809–1849) is mostly known for his tales and poems of the macabre, such as "The Tell-Tale Heart," "The Cask of Amontillado," and "The Raven." But he was also a versatile writer and critic who invented the detective story with "The Murders in the Rue Morgue" (1841). This form was later refined by countless mystery writers from Sir Arthur Conan Doyle, creator of Sherlock Holmes, to Rian Johnson, screenwriter and director of the 2019 whodunit film *Knives Out*. Poe pioneered science fiction as a genre as well. Still, he specialized in stories such as "The Masque of the Red Death" (1842): Gothic, morbid, allegorical, and highly symbolic, set in Europe at the time of the bubonic plague (also known as the Black Death). Note the double meaning of *masque/mask* in the title. A masque is a courtly entertainment performed by figures who wear face-covering masks.

Nastasic/Getty Images

The Masque of the Red Death

The "Red Death" had long devastated the country. No pestilence had been ever so fatal, or so hideous. Blood was its Avatar and its seal—the redness and the horror of blood. There were sharp pains, and sudden dizziness, and then profuse bleedings at the pores, with dissolution. The scarlet
5 stains upon the body and especially upon the face of the victim, were the pest ban which shut him out from the aid and from the sympathy of his fellow-men. And the whole seizure, progress and termination of the disease were the incidents of half an hour.

But the Prince Prospero was happy and dauntless and sagacious. When
10 his dominions were half depopulated, he summoned to his presence a thousand hale and light-hearted friends from among the knights and dames of his court, and with these retired to the deep seclusion of one of his castellated abbeys. This was an extensive and magnificent structure, the creation of the prince's own eccentric yet august taste. A strong and
15 lofty wall girdled it in. This wall had gates of iron. The courtiers, having entered, brought furnaces and massy hammers and welded the bolts.

Guided Questions

1. What is the Red Death?

They resolved to leave means neither of ingress or egress to the sudden
impulses of despair from without or of frenzy from within. The abbey was
amply provisioned. With such precautions the courtiers might bid defi-
20 ance to contagion. The external world could take care of itself. In the
meantime it was folly to grieve, or to think. The prince had provided all
the appliances of pleasure. There were buffoons, there were improvisatori,
there were ballet-dancers, there were musicians, there were cards, there
was Beauty, there was wine. All these and security were within. Without
25 was the "Red Death."

It was towards the close of the fifth or sixth month of his seclusion,
and while the pestilence raged most furiously abroad, that the Prince
Prospero entertained his thousand friends at a masked ball of the most
unusual magnificence.

30 It was a voluptuous scene that masquerade. But first let me tell of the
rooms in which it was held. There were seven—an imperial suite. In many
palaces, however, such suites form a long and straight vista, while the
folding doors slide back nearly to the walls on either hand, so that the
view of the whole extent is scarcely impeded. Here the case was very dif-
35 ferent, as might have been expected from the duke's love of the *bizarre*.
The apartments were so irregularly disposed that the vision embraced but
little more than one at a time. There was a sharp turn at every twenty or
thirty yards, and at each turn a novel effect. To the right and left, in the
middle of each wall, a tall and narrow Gothic window looked out upon a
40 closed corridor which pursued the windings of the suite. These windows
were of stained glass whose colour varied in accordance with the prevailing hue of the decorations of the chamber into which it opened. That at
the eastern extremity was hung, for example in blue—and vividly blue
were its windows. The second chamber was purple in its ornaments and
45 tapestries, and here the panes were purple. The third was green throughout, and so were the casements. The fourth was furnished and lighted
with orange—the fifth with white—the sixth with violet. The seventh
apartment was closely shrouded in black velvet tapestries that hung all
over the ceiling and down the walls, falling in heavy folds upon a carpet of
50 the same material and hue. But, in this chamber only, the colour of the
windows failed to correspond with the decorations. The panes here were
scarlet—a deep blood colour. Now in no one of the seven apartments was
there any lamp or candelabrum, amid the profusion of golden ornaments
that lay scattered to and fro or depended from the roof. There was no light
55 of any kind emanating from lamp or candle within the suite of chambers.
But in the corridors that followed the suite, there stood, opposite to each
window, a heavy tripod, bearing a brazier of fire that projected its rays
through the tinted glass and so glaringly illumined the room. And thus

Guided Questions

2. Consider the architecture of each room: What might one window suggest? How does the interior design contribute to the pattern of images in the story?

3. Consider the colors of the rooms: What associations can be made about each color and the patterns created when the colors are combined?

4. What associations can be made about light and dark image patterns in this description?

were produced a multitude of gaudy and fantastic appearances. But in the
western or black chamber the effect of the fire-light that streamed upon
the dark hangings through the blood-tinted panes, was ghastly in the
extreme, and produced so wild a look upon the countenances of those
who entered, that there were few of the company bold enough to set foot
within its precincts at all.

It was in this apartment, also, that there stood against the western
wall, a gigantic clock of ebony. Its pendulum swung to and fro with a dull,
heavy, monotonous clang; and when its minute-hand made the circuit of
the face, and the hour was to be stricken, there came forth from the bra-
zen lungs of the clock a sound which was clear and loud and deep and
exceedingly musical, but of so peculiar a note and emphasis that, at each
lapse of an hour, the musicians in the orchestra were constrained to
pause, momently, in their performance, to harken to the sound; and thus
the waltzers perforce ceased their evolutions; and there was a brief disconcert of the whole gay company; and, while the chimes of the clock yet
rang, it was observed that the giddiest grew pale, and that the more aged
and sedate passed their hands over their brows as if in confused reverie or
meditation. But when the echoes had fully ceased, a light laughter at once
pervaded the assembly; the musicians looked at each other and smiled as
if at their own nervousness and folly, and made whispering vows, each to
the other, that the next chiming of the clock should produce in them no
similar emotion; and then, after the lapse of sixty minutes, (which
embrace three thousand and six hundred seconds of the Time that flies,)
there came yet another chiming of the clock, and then were the same
disconcert and tremulousness and meditation as before.

But, in spite of these things, it was a gay and magnificent revel. The
tastes of the duke were peculiar. He had a fine eye for colours and effects.
He disregarded the *decora* of mere fashion. His plans were bold and fiery,
and his conceptions glowed with barbaric lustre. There are some who
would have thought him mad. His followers felt that he was not. It was
necessary to hear and see and touch him to be sure that he was not.

He had directed, in great part, the moveable embellishments of the
seven chambers, upon occasion of this great *fête*; and it was his own guiding taste which had given character to the costumes of the masqueraders.
Be sure they were grotesque. There were much glare and glitter and
piquancy and phantasm—much of what has been since seen in
"Hernani." There were arabesque figures with unsuited limbs and appoint-
ments. There were delirious fancies such as the madman fashions. There
was much of the beautiful, much of the wanton, much of the *bizarre*,
something of the terrible, and not a little of that which might have excited
disgust. To and fro in the seven chambers there stalked, in fact, a multitude

Guided Questions

5. What is personified
in this apartment?
Explain the
effect of this
personification.
Consider the
specific aspects
that are being
compared to
human traits.

6. What is the
effect of the
personification of
the clock?

7. How do these
contrasts reveal
a pattern and
contribute to the
story's tension?

of dreams. And these—the dreams—writhed in and about, taking hue from the rooms, and causing the wild music of the orchestra to seem as the echo of their steps. And, anon, there strikes the ebony clock which stands in the hall of the velvet. And then, for a moment, all is still, and all
105 is silent save the voice of the clock. The dreams are stiff-frozen as they stand. But the echoes of the chime die away—they have endured but an instant—and a light, half-subdued laughter floats after them as they depart. And now again the music swells, and the dreams live, and writhe to and fro more merrily than ever, taking hue from the many tinted win-
110 dows through which stream the rays from the tripods. But to the chamber which lies most westwardly of the seven, there are now none of the mask-ers who venture; for the night is waning away; and there flows a ruddier light through the blood-coloured panes; and the blackness of the sable drapery appals; and to him whose foot falls upon the sable carpet, there
115 comes from the near clock of ebony a muffled peal more solemnly emphatic than any which reaches *their* ears who indulge in the more remote gaieties of the other apartments.

      But these other apartments were densely crowded, and in them beat feverishly the heart of life. And the revel went whirlingly on, until at
120 length was sounded the twelfth hour upon the clock. And then the music ceased, as I have told; and the evolutions of the waltzers were quieted; and there was an uneasy cessation of all things as before. But now there were twelve strokes to be sounded by the bell of the clock; and thus it happened, perhaps, that more of thought crept, with more of time, into
125 the meditations of the thoughtful among those who revelled. And thus too, it happened, perhaps, that before the last echoes of the last chime had utterly sunk into silence, there were many individuals in the crowd who had found leisure to become aware of the presence of a masked figure which had arrested the attention of no single individual before.
130 And the rumour of this new presence having spread itself whisperingly around, there arose at length from the whole company a buzz, or murmur, expressive at first of disapprobation and surprise—then, finally, of terror, of horror, and of disgust.

      In an assembly of phantasms such as I have painted, it may well be
135 supposed that no ordinary appearance could have excited such sensation. In truth the masquerade license of the night was nearly unlimited; but the figure in question had out-Heroded Herod, and gone beyond the bounds of even the prince's indefinite decorum. There are chords in the hearts of the most reckless which cannot be touched without emotion.
140 Even with the utterly lost, to whom life and death are equally jests, there are matters of which no jest can be properly made. The whole company, indeed, seemed now deeply to feel that in the costume and bearing of the

8. What does this personification reveal?

9. Who or what is this masked figure? How does the description of the masked figure contribute to the suspense?

10. How does this biblical imagery contribute to the personification of death?

stranger neither wit nor propriety existed. The figure was tall and gaunt, and shrouded from head to foot in the habiliments of the grave. The mask
145 which concealed the visage was made so nearly to resemble the counte- nance of a stiffened corpse that the closest scrutiny must have had diffi- culty in detecting the cheat. And yet all this might have been endured, if not approved, by the mad revellers around. But the mummer had gone so far as to assume the type of the Red Death. His vesture was dabbled in
150 blood—and his broad brow, with all the features of the face, was besprin- kled with the scarlet horror.

When the eyes of the Prince Prospero fell upon this spectral image (which, with a slow and solemn movement, as if more fully to sustain its role, stalked to and fro among the waltzers) he was seen to be convulsed,
155 in the first moment, with a strong shudder either of terror or distaste; but, in the next, his brow reddened with rage.

"Who dares?"—he demanded hoarsely of the courtiers who stood next him, "who dares insult us with this blasphemous mockery? Seize him and unmask him—that we may know whom we have to hang, at sunrise,
160 from the battlements!"

It was in the eastern or blue chamber in which stood the Prince Prospero as he uttered these words. They rang throughout the seven rooms loudly and clearly, for the prince was a bold and robust man, and the music had become hushed at the waving of his hand.

165 It was in the blue room where stood the prince, with a group of pale courtiers by his side. At first, as he spoke, there was a slight rushing movement of this group in the direction of the intruder, who at the moment was also near at hand, and now, with deliberate and stately step, made closer approach to the speaker. But from a certain nameless awe
170 with which the mad assumptions of the mummer had inspired the whole party, there were found none who put forth hand to seize him; so that, unimpeded, he passed within a yard of the prince's person; and, while the vast assembly, as if with one impulse, shrank from the centres of the rooms to the walls, he made his way uninterruptedly, but with the same
175 solemn and measured step which had distinguished him from the first, through the blue chamber to the purple—through the purple to the green—through the green to the orange—through this again to the white—and even thence to the violet, ere a decided movement had been made to arrest him. It was then, however, that the Prince Prospero, mad-
180 dening with rage and the shame of his own momentary cowardice, rushed hurriedly through the six chambers, while none followed him on account of a deadly terror that had seized upon all. He bore aloft a drawn dagger, and had approached, in rapid impetuosity, to within three or four feet of the retreating figure, when the latter, having attained the extremity of the

Guided Questions

11. What is being personified? What are the specific traits of comparison?

12. Describe how the masked figure could be archetypal.

13. What associations can be made from the description of the prince?

14. What patterns emerge as the characters pass through the colored rooms?

185 velvet apartment, turned suddenly round and confronted his pursuer.
There was a sharp cry—and the dagger dropped gleaming upon the sable
carpet, upon which, instantly afterwards, fell prostrate in death the Prince
Prospero. Then, summoning the wild courage of despair, a throng of the
revellers at once threw themselves into the black apartment, and, seizing
190 the mummer, whose tall figure stood erect and motionless within the
shadow of the ebony clock, gasped in unutterable horror at finding the
grave cerements and corpse-like mask, which they handled with so
violent a rudeness, untenanted by any tangible form.

And now was acknowledged the presence of the Red Death. He had
195 come like a thief in the night. And one by one dropped the revellers in the
blood-bedewed halls of their revel, and died each in the despairing posture of his fall. And the life of the ebony clock went out with that of the
last of the gay. And the flames of the tripods expired. And Darkness and
Decay and the Red Death held illimitable dominion over all.

Guided Questions

15. What happens to
    Prince Prospero?

16. Explain the effect
    of the simile, "like a
    thief in the night."

17. Explain how
    this story is
    allegorical. What
    is the allegory?

PRACTICE TEXT

The Paper Menagerie
Ken Liu

John Tlumacki/Boston Globe/Getty Images

THE TEXT IN CONTEXT

Science fiction and fantasy writer Ken Liu was born in
1976 in Lanzhou, China. When he was eleven, his family emigrated to the United States and ultimately settled
in Waterford, Connecticut. Liu received his undergrad-
uate and law school degrees from Harvard University. After working as a corporate lawyer
and specialist in high-tech litigation, he turned his attention to writing speculative fiction. Liu
also focused on developing the *silkpunk* literary genre, which he describes as a "technology aesthetic based on a science fictional elaboration of traditions of engineering in East
Asia's classical antiquity." In "The Paper Menagerie," he uses techniques from fantasy fiction and magical realism to tell a profoundly emotional story about ethnic difference, assimilation, and child-parent relationships. Liu is the author of *The Grace of Kings* (2015), *Wall
of Storms* (2016), *The Veiled Throne* (2021), and *Speaking Bones* (2022), which together
comprise an epic fantasy series called The Dandelion Dynasty.

Note: This text includes anti-Chinese language, which we have chosen to reprint
in this textbook. We wish to accurately reflect both Liu's original intent as well as the
time period, culture, and racism depicted in the text, but we also recognize that this
language has a long history as disrespectful and deeply hurtful. Be mindful of context,
both Liu's and yours, as you read.

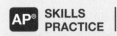

FIGURATIVE LANGUAGE
Analyzing Figurative Comparisons

As you read "The Paper Menagerie," record textual details that develop and explain how the origami animals take on figurative meaning by identifying the particular aspects of comparison.

Analyzing Figurative Comparisons		
Subject A — Literal:	Subject B — Figurative:	Idea:
Description: Aspects, Traits, or Characteristics	Description: Aspects, Traits, or Characteristics	Explanation: Significance of Comparison in Relation to Idea

The Paper Menagerie

One of my earliest memories starts with me sobbing. I refused to be soothed no matter what Mom and Dad tried.

Dad gave up and left the bedroom, but
5 Mom took me into the kitchen and sat me down at the breakfast table.

"*Kan, kan,*" she said, as she pulled a sheet of wrapping paper from on top of the fridge. For years, Mom carefully sliced open the
10 wrappings around Christmas gifts and saved them on top of the fridge in a thick stack.

She set the paper down, plain side facing up, and began to fold it. I stopped crying and watched her, curious. She turned the paper
15 over and folded it again. She pleated, packed, tucked, rolled, and twisted until the paper disappeared between her cupped hands. Then she lifted the folded-up paper packet to her mouth and blew into it, like a balloon.

20 "*Kan,*" she said. "*Laohu.*" She put her hands down on the table and let go. A little paper tiger stood on the table, the size of two fists placed together. The skin of the tiger was the pattern on the wrapping paper, white back-
25 ground with red candy canes and green Christmas trees.

I reached out to Mom's creation. Its tail twitched, and it pounced playfully at my finger. "*Rawrr-sa,*" it growled, the sound
30 somewhere between a cat and rustling newspapers.

I laughed, startled, and stroked its back with my index finger. The paper tiger vibrated under my finger, purring.

35 "*Zhe jiao zhezhi,*" Mom said. *This is called origami.*

I didn't know this at the time, but Mom's breath was special. She breathed into her

40 paper animals so that they shared her
breath, and thus moved with her life. This
was her magic.

• • •

Dad had picked Mom out of a catalog.

One time, when I was in high school, I
asked Dad about the details. He was trying to
45 get me to speak to Mom again. He had signed
up for the introduction service back in the
spring of 1973. Flipping through the pages
steadily, he had spent no more than a few
seconds on each page until he saw the pic-
50 ture of Mom.

I've never seen this picture. Dad described
it: Mom was sitting in a chair, her side to the
camera, wearing a tight green silk cheong-
sam. Her head was turned to the camera so
55 that her long black hair was draped artfully
over her chest and shoulder. She looked out
at him with the eyes of a calm child.

"That was the last page of the catalog I
saw," he said.

60 The catalog said she was eighteen, loved
to dance, and spoke good English because
she was from Hong Kong. None of these facts
turned out to be true. He wrote to her, and
the company passed their messages back
65 and forth. Finally, he flew to Hong Kong to
meet her. "The people at the company had
been writing her responses. She didn't know
any English other than 'hello' and 'good-
bye.'"

70 *What kind of woman puts herself into a cata-*
log so that she can be bought? The high school
me thought I knew so much about everything. Contempt felt good, like wine. Instead
of storming into the office to demand his
75 money back, he paid a waitress at the hotel
restaurant to translate for them.

"She would look at me, her eyes halfway
between scared and hopeful, while I spoke.

And when the girl began translating what I
80 said, she'd start to smile slowly."

He flew back to Connecticut and began to
apply for the papers for her to come to him. I
was born a year later, in the Year of the Tiger.

• • •

At my request, Mom also made a goat, a deer,
85 and a water buffalo out of wrapping paper.
They would run around the living room
while Laohu chased after them, growling.
When he caught them he would press down
until the air went out of them and they
90 became just flat, folded-up pieces of paper.
I would then have to blow into them to
re-inflate them so they could run around
some more.

Sometimes, the animals got into trouble.
95 Once, the water buffalo jumped into a dish of
soy sauce on the table at dinner. (He wanted
to wallow, like a real water buffalo.) I picked
him out quickly but the capillary action had
already pulled the dark liquid high up into
100 his legs. The sauce-softened legs would not
hold him up, and he collapsed onto the table.
I dried him out in the sun, but his legs
became crooked after that, and he ran around
with a limp. Mom eventually wrapped his
105 legs in saran wrap so that he could wallow to
his heart's content (just not in soy sauce).

Also, Laohu liked to pounce at sparrows
when he and I played in the backyard. But
one time, a cornered bird struck back in
110 desperation and tore his ear. He whimpered
and winced as I held him and Mom patched
his ear together with tape. He avoided birds
after that.

And then one day, I saw a TV documen-
115 tary about sharks and asked Mom for one of
my own. She made the shark, but he flapped
about on the table unhappily. I filled the sink
with water, and put him in. He swam around

and around happily. However, after a while he became soggy and translucent, and slowly sank to the bottom, the folds coming undone. I reached in to rescue him, and all I ended up with was a wet piece of paper.

Laohu put his front paws together at the edge of the sink and rested his head on them. Ears drooping, he made a low growl in his throat that made me feel guilty.

Mom made a new shark for me, this time out of tin foil. The shark lived happily in a large goldfish bowl. Laohu and I liked to sit next to the bowl to watch the tinfoil shark chasing the goldfish, Laohu sticking his face up against the bowl on the other side so that I saw his eyes, magnified to the size of coffee cups, staring at me from across the bowl.

• • •

When I was ten, we moved to a new house across town. Two of the women neighbors came by to welcome us. Dad served them drinks and then apologized for having to run off to the utility company to straighten out the prior owner's bills. "Make yourselves at home. My wife doesn't speak much English, so don't think she's being rude for not talking to you."

While I read in the dining room, Mom unpacked in the kitchen. The neighbors conversed in the living room, not trying to be particularly quiet.

"He seems like a normal enough man. Why did he do that?"

"Something about the mixing never seems right. The child looks unfinished. Slanty eyes, white face. A little monster."

"Do you think *he* can speak English?"

The women hushed. After a while they came into the dining room.

"Hello there! What's your name?"

"Jack," I said.

"That doesn't sound very Chinesey."

Mom came into the dining room then. She smiled at the women. The three of them stood in a triangle around me, smiling and nodding at each other, with nothing to say, until Dad came back.

• • •

Mark, one of the neighborhood boys, came over with his Star Wars action figures. Obi-Wan Kenobi's lightsaber lit up and he could swing his arms and say, in a tinny voice, "Use the Force!" I didn't think the figure looked much like the real Obi-Wan at all.

Together, we watched him repeat this performance five times on the coffee table. "Can he do anything else?" I asked.

Mark was annoyed by my question. "Look at all the details," he said.

I looked at the details. I wasn't sure what I was supposed to say.

Mark was disappointed by my response. "Show me your toys."

I didn't have any toys except my paper menagerie. I brought Laohu out from my bedroom. By then he was very worn, patched all over with tape and glue, evidence of the years of repairs Mom and I had done on him. He was no longer as nimble and sure-footed as before. I sat him down on the coffee table. I could hear the skittering steps of the other animals behind in the hallway, timidly peeking into the living room.

"*Xiao laohu*," I said, and stopped. I switched to English. "This is Tiger." Cautiously, Laohu strode up and purred at Mark, sniffing his hands.

Mark examined the Christmas-wrap pattern of Laohu's skin. "That doesn't look like a tiger at all. Your Mom makes toys for you from trash?"

I had never thought of Laohu as *trash*. But
200 looking at him now, he was really just a piece
of wrapping paper.

Mark pushed Obi-Wan's head again. The
lightsaber flashed; he moved his arms up
and down. "Use the Force!"

205 Laohu turned and pounced, knocking the
plastic figure off the table. It hit the floor and
broke and Obi-Wan's head rolled under the
couch. "*Rawwww*," Laohu laughed. I joined him.

Mark punched me, hard. "This was very
210 expensive! You can't even find it in the stores
now. It probably cost more than what your
dad paid for your mom!"

I stumbled and fell to the floor. Laohu
growled and leapt at Mark's face.

215 Mark screamed, more out of fear and surprise than pain. Laohu was only made of
paper, after all.

Mark grabbed Laohu and his snarl was
choked off as Mark crumpled him in his
220 hand and tore him in half. He balled up the
two pieces of paper and threw them at me.
"Here's your stupid cheap Chinese garbage."

After Mark left, I spent a long time trying,
without success, to tape together the pieces,
225 smooth out the paper, and follow the creases
to refold Laohu. Slowly, the other animals
came into the living room and gathered
around us, me and the torn wrapping paper
that used to be Laohu.

• • •

230 My fight with Mark didn't end there. Mark
was popular at school. I never want to think
again about the two weeks that followed.

I came home that Friday at the end of the
two weeks. "*Xuexiao hao ma?*" Mom asked. I said
235 nothing and went to the bathroom. I looked
into the mirror. *I look nothing like her, nothing.*

At dinner I asked Dad, "Do I have a chink
face?"

Dad put down his chopsticks. Even though
240 I had never told him what happened in
school, he seemed to understand. He closed
his eyes and rubbed the bridge of his nose.
"No. You don't."

Mom looked at Dad, not understanding.
245 She looked back at me. "*Sha jiao chink?*"

"English," I said. "Speak English."

She tried. "What happen?"

I pushed the chopsticks and the bowl
before me away: stir-fried green peppers
250 with five-spice beef. "We should eat American food."

Dad tried to reason. "A lot of families cook
Chinese sometimes."

"We are not other families." I looked at him.
255 *Other families don't have Moms who don't belong.*

He looked away. And then he put a hand
on Mom's shoulder. "I'll get you a cookbook."

Mom turned to me. "*Bu haochi?*"

"English," I said, raising my voice. "Speak
260 English."

Mom reached out to touch my forehead,
feeling for my temperature. "*Fashao la?*"

I brushed her hand away. "I'm fine. Speak
English!" I was shouting.

265 "Speak English to him," Dad said to Mom.
"You knew this was going to happen someday. What did you expect?"

Mom dropped her hands to her sides. She
sat, looking from Dad to me, and back to Dad
270 again. She tried to speak, stopped, and tried
again, and stopped again.

"You have to," Dad said. "I've been too
easy on you. Jack needs to fit in."

Mom looked at him. "If I say 'love,' I
275 feel here." She pointed to her lips. "If I say
'ai,' I feel here." She put her hand over
her heart.

Dad shook his head. "You are in America."

Mom hunched down in her seat, looking
280 like the water buffalo when Laohu used to

pounce on him and squeeze the air of life out of him.

"And I want some real toys."

• • •

Dad bought me a full set of Star Wars action
285 figures. I gave the Obi-Wan Kenobi to Mark.

I packed the paper menagerie in a large shoebox and put it under the bed.

The next morning, the animals had escaped and taken over their old favorite
290 spots in my room. I caught them all and put them back into the shoebox, taping the lid shut. But the animals made so much noise in the box that I finally shoved it into the corner of the attic as far away from my room as
295 possible.

If Mom spoke to me in Chinese, I refused to answer her. After a while, she tried to use more English. But her accent and broken sentences embarrassed me. I tried to correct
300 her. Eventually, she stopped speaking altogether if I was around.

Mom began to mime things if she needed to let me know something. She tried to hug me the way she saw American mothers do
305 on TV. I thought her movements exaggerated, uncertain, ridiculous, graceless. She saw that I was annoyed, and stopped.

"You shouldn't treat your mother that way," Dad said. But he couldn't look me in
310 the eyes as he said it. Deep in his heart, he must have realized that it was a mistake to have tried to take a Chinese peasant girl and expect her to fit in the suburbs of Connecticut.
315 Mom learned to cook American style. I played video games and studied French.

Every once in a while, I would see her at the kitchen table studying the plain side of a sheet of wrapping paper. Later a new paper
320 animal would appear on my nightstand

and try to cuddle up to me. I caught them, squeezed them until the air went out of them, and then stuffed them away in the box in the attic.
325 Mom finally stopped making the animals when I was in high school. By then her English was much better, but I was already at that age when I wasn't interested in what she had to say whatever language
330 she used.

Sometimes, when I came home and saw her tiny body busily moving about in the kitchen, singing a song in Chinese to herself, it was hard for me to believe that she gave
335 birth to me. We had nothing in common. She might as well be from the moon. I would hurry on to my room, where I could continue my all-American pursuit of happiness.

• • •

Dad and I stood, one on each side of Mom,
340 lying on the hospital bed. She was not yet even forty, but she looked much older.

For years she had refused to go to the doctor for the pain inside her that she said was no big deal. By the time an ambulance finally
345 carried her in, the cancer had spread far beyond the limits of surgery.

My mind was not in the room. It was the middle of the on-campus recruiting season, and I was focused on resumes, transcripts,
350 and strategically constructed interview schedules. I schemed about how to lie to the corporate recruiters most effectively so that they'd offer to buy me. I understood intellectually that it was terrible to think about this while
355 your mother lay dying. But that understanding didn't mean I could change how I felt.

She was conscious. Dad held her left hand with both of his own. He leaned down to kiss her forehead. He seemed weak and
360 old in a way that startled me. I realized that

I knew almost as little about Dad as I did about Mom.

Mom smiled at him. "I'm fine."

She turned to me, still smiling. "I know 365 you have to go back to school." Her voice was very weak and it was difficult to hear her over the hum of the machines hooked up to her. "Go. Don't worry about me. This is not a big deal. Just do well in school."

370 I reached out to touch her hand, because I thought that was what I was supposed to do. I was relieved. I was already thinking about the flight back, and the bright California sunshine.

375 She whispered something to Dad. He nodded and left the room.

"Jack, if—" she was caught up in a fit of coughing, and could not speak for some time. "If I don't make it, don't be too sad and 380 hurt your health. Focus on your life. Just keep that box you have in the attic with you, and every year, at *Qingming*, just take it out and think about me. I'll be with you always."

Qingming was the Chinese Festival for the 385 Dead. When I was very young, Mom used to write a letter on *Qingming* to her dead parents back in China, telling them the good news about the past year of her life in America. She would read the letter out loud to me, and if I 390 made a comment about something, she would write it down in the letter too. Then she would fold the letter into a paper crane, and release it, facing west. We would then watch, as the crane flapped its crisp wings on its long jour-395 ney west, towards the Pacific, towards China, towards the graves of Mom's family.

It had been many years since I last did that with her.

"I don't know anything about the Chinese 400 calendar," I said. "Just rest, Mom."

"Just keep the box with you and open it once in a while. Just open—" She began to cough again.

"It's okay, Mom." I stroked her arm 405 awkwardly.

"*Haizi, mama ai ni*—" Her cough took over again. An image from years ago flashed into my memory: Mom saying *ai* and then putting her hand over her heart.

410 "Alright, Mom. Stop talking."

Dad came back, and I said that I needed to get to the airport early because I didn't want to miss my flight.

She died when my plane was somewhere 415 over Nevada.

• • •

Dad aged rapidly after Mom died. The house was too big for him and had to be sold. My girlfriend Susan and I went to help him pack and clean the place. Susan found the 420 shoebox in the attic. The paper menagerie, hidden in the uninsulated darkness of the attic for so long, had become brittle and the bright wrapping paper patterns had faded.

"I've never seen origami like this," Susan 425 said. "Your Mom was an amazing artist."

The paper animals did not move. Perhaps whatever magic had animated them stopped when Mom died. Or perhaps I had only imagined that these paper constructions were 430 once alive. The memory of children could not be trusted.

• • •

It was the first weekend in April, two years after Mom's death. Susan was out of town on one of her endless trips as a Management 435 Consultant and I was home, lazily flipping through the TV channels.

I paused at a documentary about sharks. Suddenly I saw, in my mind, Mom's hands as they folded and refolded tinfoil to make a 440 shark for me, while Laohu and I watched.

A rustle. I looked up and saw that a ball of wrapping paper and torn tape was on the floor next to the bookshelf. I walked over to pick it up for the trash.

445 The ball of paper shifted, unfurled itself, and I saw that it was Laohu, who I hadn't thought about in a very long time. "*Rawrr-sa.*" Mom must have put him back together after I had given up.

450 He was smaller than I remembered. Or maybe it was just that back then my fists were smaller.

Susan had put the paper animals around our apartment as decoration. She probably
455 left Laohu in a hidden corner because he looked so shabby.

I sat down on the floor, and reached out a finger. Laohu's tail twitched, and he pounced playfully. I laughed, stroking his back. Laohu
460 purred under my hand.

"How've you been, old buddy?"

Laohu stopped playing. He got up, jumped with feline grace into my lap, and proceeded to unfold himself.

465 In my lap was a square of creased wrapping paper, the plain side up. It was filled with dense Chinese characters. I had never learned to read Chinese, but I knew the characters for *son*, and they were at the top, where you'd
470 expect them in a letter addressed to you, written in Mom's awkward, childish handwriting.

I went to the computer to check the Internet. Today was *Qingming*.

• • •

I took the letter with me downtown, where I
475 knew the Chinese tour buses stopped. I stopped every tourist, asking, "*Nin hui du zhongwen ma?*" Can you read Chinese? I hadn't spoken Chinese in so long that I wasn't sure if they understood.

480 A young woman agreed to help. We sat down on a bench together, and she read the letter to me aloud. The language that I had tried to forget for years came back, and I felt

the words sinking into me, through my skin,
485 through my bones, until they squeezed tight around my heart.

Son,

We haven't talked in a long time. You are so angry when I try to touch you that I'm afraid.
490 *And I think maybe this pain I feel all the time now is something serious.*

So I decided to write to you. I'm going to write in the paper animals I made for you that you used to like so much.

495 *The animals will stop moving when I stop breathing. But if I write to you with all my heart, I'll leave a little of myself behind on this paper, in these words. Then, if you think of me on Qingming, when the spirits of the departed are*
500 *allowed to visit their families, you'll make the parts of myself I leave behind come alive too. The creatures I made for you will again leap and run and pounce, and maybe you'll get to see these words then.*

505 *Because I have to write with all my heart, I need to write to you in Chinese.*

All this time I still haven't told you the story of my life. When you were little, I always thought I'd tell you the story when you were older, so you
510 *could understand. But somehow that chance never came up.*

I was born in 1957, in Sigulu Village, Hebei Province. Your grandparents were both from very poor peasant families with few relatives. Only a
515 *few years after I was born, the Great Famines struck China, during which thirty million people died. The first memory I have was waking up to see my mother eating dirt so that she could fill her belly and leave the last bit of flour for me.*

520 *Things got better after that. Sigulu is famous for its zhezhi papercraft, and my mother taught me how to make paper animals and give them life. This was practical magic in the life of the village. We made paper birds to chase grasshoppers*
525 *away from the fields, and paper tigers to keep away the mice. For Chinese New Year my friends*

and I made red paper dragons. I'll never forget the
sight of all those little dragons zooming across the
sky overhead, holding up strings of exploding
530 firecrackers to scare away all the bad memories of
the past year. You would have loved it.

Then came the Cultural Revolution in 1966.
Neighbor turned on neighbor, and brother against
brother. Someone remembered that my mother's
535 brother, my uncle, had left for Hong Kong back in
1946, and became a merchant there. Having a
relative in Hong Kong meant we were spies and
enemies of the people, and we had to be struggled
against in every way. Your poor grandmother—
540 she couldn't take the abuse and threw herself
down a well. Then some boys with hunting mus-
kets dragged your grandfather away one day into
the woods, and he never came back.

There I was, a ten-year-old orphan. The only
545 relative I had in the world was my uncle in Hong
Kong. I snuck away one night and climbed onto a
freight train going south.

Down in Guangdong Province a few days later,
some men caught me stealing food from a field.
550 When they heard that I was trying to get to
Hong Kong, they laughed. "It's your lucky day.
Our trade is to bring girls to Hong Kong."

They hid me in the bottom of a truck along
with other girls, and smuggled us across the
555 border.

We were taken to a basement and told to
stand up and look healthy and intelligent for the
buyers. Families paid the warehouse a fee and
came by to look us over and select one of us to
560 "adopt."

The Chin family picked me to take care of
their two boys. I got up every morning at four to
prepare breakfast. I fed and bathed the boys. I
shopped for food. I did the laundry and swept the
565 floors. I followed the boys around and did their
bidding. At night I was locked into a cupboard in
the kitchen to sleep. If I was slow or did anything
wrong I was beaten. If the boys did anything

wrong I was beaten. If I was caught trying to
570 learn English I was beaten.

"Why do you want to learn English?" Mr. Chin
asked. "You want to go to the police? We'll tell
the police that you are a mainlander illegally in
Hong Kong. They'd love to have you in their prison."

575 Six years I lived like this. One day, an old
woman who sold fish to me in the morning market pulled me aside.

"I know girls like you. How old are you now,
sixteen? One day, the man who owns you will get
580 drunk, and he'll look at you and pull you to him
and you can't stop him. The wife will find out,
and then you will think you really have gone to
hell. You have to get out of this life. I know someone who can help."

585 She told me about American men who wanted
Asian wives. If I can cook, clean, and take care of my
American husband, he'll give me a good life. It was
the only hope I had. And that was how I got into the
catalog with all those lies and met your father. It is
590 not a very romantic story, but it is my story.

In the suburbs of Connecticut, I was lonely.
Your father was kind and gentle with me, and I
was very grateful to him. But no one understood
me, and I understood nothing.

595 But then you were born! I was so happy when
I looked into your face and saw shades of my
mother, my father, and myself. I had lost my
entire family, all of Sigulu, everything I ever knew
and loved. But there you were, and your face was
600 proof that they were real. I hadn't made them up.

Now I had someone to talk to. I would teach
you my language, and we could together remake
a small piece of everything that I loved and lost.
When you said your first words to me, in Chinese
605 that had the same accent as my mother and me, I
cried for hours. When I made the first zhezhi
animals for you, and you laughed, I felt there
were no worries in the world.

You grew up a little, and now you could even
610 help your father and me talk to each other. I was

really at home now. I finally found a good life. I wished my parents could be here, so that I could cook for them, and give them a good life too. But my parents were no longer around. You know what the
615 Chinese think is the saddest feeling in the world? It's for a child to finally grow the desire to take care of his parents, only to realize that they were long gone.

Son, I know that you do not like your Chinese eyes, which are my eyes. I know that you do not
620 like your Chinese hair, which is my hair. But can you understand how much joy your very existence brought to me? And can you understand how it felt when you stopped talking to me and won't let me talk to you in Chinese?
625 I felt I was losing everything all over again.

Why won't you talk to me, son? The pain makes it hard to write.

• • •

The young woman handed the paper back to me. I could not bear to look into her face.
630   Without looking up, I asked for her help in tracing out the character for *ai* on the paper below Mom's letter. I wrote the character again and again on the paper, intertwining my pen strokes with her
635 words.

The young woman reached out and put a hand on my shoulder. Then she got up and left, leaving me alone with my mother.

Following the creases, I refolded the paper
640 back into Laohu. I cradled him in the crook of my arm, and as he purred, we began the walk home.

FIGURATIVE LANGUAGE: Comparisons

1. How do the characters' backgrounds establish values that contribute to the **comparisons**?

2. How does Jack's mother bring the origami animals to life? How are the animals **personified**?

3. Laohu is Jack's favorite. How does Laohu function as a **metaphor**? How does this idea contribute to the complexity of the text?

4. Explain how the Chinese language is important to "The Paper Menagerie." Consider how the author's use of **apostrophe** and **prosopopoeia** contribute to the complexity of the text.

IDEAS IN LITERATURE
Appearance and Reality

IDEA BANK

Anonymity

Appearance

Artificiality

Authenticity

Avant-Garde

Conformity

Connection

Consciousness

Deception

Endurance

Experimentation

Identity

Illusion

Impression

Infatuation

Influence

Innovation

Memory

Nationalism

Psychology

Reality

Relationships

The Victorian era in Britain witnessed the completion of the Industrial Revolution, groundbreaking discoveries in the sciences, social improvement at home, and colonial power abroad. The economy boomed; culture flourished. The British Empire reached the highest point of its power and prestige, even as it competed with other imperial powers like France, Belgium, and Germany for territories and resources. It was, in many ways, a period of optimism and faith in progress. With countries increasingly cooperative in their trade relations and increasingly connected through new technologies, a large-scale war seemed unthinkable. This perspective still persists today in the idea that increasing international commerce leads to stability and good relationships between countries. But beneath the appearance of stability, shifts were taking place: the reality of resurgent nationalism, colonial unrest, and a complex tangle of treaty arrangements.

Whatever the causes of World War I (1914–1918), its consequences were ruinous and profound. Britain and the Allies persevered, but the war devastated Europe, with the total number of civilian and military casualties estimated at around forty million. Moreover, many soldiers who returned from the war suffered from "shell shock," now understood as "post-traumatic stress disorder." The war had other effects as well. People witnessed the new technologies of the first

(*Left*) Pablo Picasso, *Girl before a Mirror*. Paris, Oil on Canvas, March 14, 1932. The Museum of Modern Art, New York, New York. (*Right*) *A Few Pounds* is a satirical work by Barry Kite. Kite creates a parody of Berthe Morisot's famous painting *The Psyche Mirror*.

Consider the two pieces of art, each from a different perspective. How does each of these images convey different perspectives about appearance and reality?

modern military conflict, including submarines, air attacks, tanks, and chemical weapons. This complicated the optimistic view that technological innovation leads to general progress — a tension that we still live with today. The war's horrors also created new attitudes, such as skepticism about lofty ideals and respectable appearances. After all, enlightened Christian nations had spent several years slaughtering each other. In a sense, World War I wiped away the past and created a new reality — one that reflected new perspectives and led to new forms of expression, ushering in the modern period.

Before the war, avant-garde artists had been experimenting with new techniques, such as cubism and expressionism. After the war, art became less focused on providing accurate representations of the world and more focused on opposing mainstream culture. For example, the Dadaists sought to resist authority, capitalism, and prevailing artistic conventions; the surrealists, seeking to reject rationality altogether, produced disturbing, dream-like images that combined incongruous elements.

Likewise, writers such Virginia Woolf (1882–1941) created new poetic and narrative strategies for expression. Woolf, in particular, developed a stream-of-consciousness style that takes the reader beneath the surface of her characters into the continuous flow of their thoughts, emotions, and perceptions.

In fact, part of the modernist movement was a rejection of accessibility, commercial popularity, and a broad reading public — all valued greatly by the Victorians. In the modernist view, the best and most authentic art was a difficult pleasure, to be appreciated by a cultured minority. This opposition between "good" art and the "popular" art persists in our culture with regard to film, books, music, painting, and other art forms. Modernist ideas about appearances and reality continue to resonate with contemporary audiences. For example, the popularity of reality TV — from *Big Brother* to *The Bachelor* to *Catfish* — brings questions about motivation and sincerity, as well as just what constitutes "reality."

◀ *Relativity* is a lithograph print by the Dutch artist M. C. Escher, first printed in December 1953.

The print depicts a world without color or gravity. Look closely at the stairwells, doorways, and windows. Look carefully at the people, their attire, and their direction. What does this print convey about humanity?

The New Dress
Virginia Woolf

THE TEXT IN CONTEXT

One of the major English novelists of the modernist period, Virginia Woolf (1882–1941) grew up in a wealthy, literary, and artistic family. She became a prolific and versatile author of plays, short stories, novels, biographies, and essays, as well as a progenitor of modern feminist criticism. But Woolf is best known for developing and refining stream-of-consciousness narration, along with James Joyce, William Faulkner, and other experimental writers. This technique not only lets her express her characters' seamless flow of thoughts and reveal their inner lives, beneath their appearances, but also allows her to contrast the narrator's subjective experience of time with the action of the story in "real time." "The New Dress," which was first published in 1927, offers an exemplary introduction to Woolf's style. The story includes characters that the author also portrayed in her novel *Mrs. Dalloway* (1925). Woolf's other major works include *To the Lighthouse* (1927), *Orlando: A Biography* (1928), and *A Room of One's Own* (1929).

Culture Club/Getty Images

The New Dress

Mabel had her first serious suspicion that something was wrong as she took her cloak off and Mrs. Barnet, while handing her the mirror and touching the brushes and thus
5 drawing her attention, perhaps rather markedly, to all the appliances for tidying and improving hair, complexion, clothes, which existed on the dressing table, confirmed the suspicion—that it was not right, not quite
10 right, which growing stronger as she went upstairs and springing at her, with conviction as she greeted Clarissa Dalloway, she went straight to the far end of the room, to a shaded corner where a looking-glass hung
15 and looked. No! It was not right. And at once the misery which she always tried to hide, the profound dissatisfaction—the sense she had had, ever since she was a child, of being inferior to other people—set upon her,
20 relentlessly, remorselessly, with an intensity which she could not beat off, as she would when she woke at night at home, by reading Borrow or Scott; for oh these men, oh these women, all were thinking—"What's Mabel
25 wearing? What a fright she looks! What a hideous new dress!"—their eyelids flickering as they came up and then their lids shutting rather tight. It was her own appalling inadequacy; her cowardice; her mean, water-
30 sprinkled blood that depressed her. And at once the whole of the room where, for ever so many hours, she had planned with the little dress-maker how it was to go, seemed sordid, repulsive; and her own drawing-room

so shabby, and herself, going out, puffed
up with vanity as she touched the letters on
the hall table and said: "How dull!" to show
off—all this now seemed unutterably silly,
paltry, and provincial. All this had been absolutely destroyed, shown up, exploded, the
moment she came into Mrs. Dalloway's
drawing-room.

What she had thought that evening when,
sitting over the teacups, Mrs. Dalloway's invitation came, was that, of course, she could
not be fashionable. It was absurd to pretend
it even—fashion meant cut, meant style,
meant thirty guineas at least—but why not
be original? Why not be herself, anyhow?
And, getting up, she had taken that old fashion book of her mother's, a Paris fashion
book of the time of the Empire, and had
thought how much prettier, more dignified,
and more womanly they were then, and so
set herself—oh, it was foolish—trying to
be like them, pluming herself in fact, upon
being modest and old-fashioned, and very
charming, giving herself up, no doubt about
it, to an orgy of self-love which deserved
to be chastised, and so rigged herself out
like this.

But she dared not look in the glass. She
could not face the whole horror—the pale
yellow, idiotically old-fashioned silk dress
with its long skirt and its high sleeves and
its waist and all the things that looked so
charming in the fashion book, but not on her,
not among all these ordinary people. She felt
like a dressmaker's dummy standing there,
for young people to stick pins into.

"But, my dear, it's perfectly charming!"
Rose Shaw said, looking her up and down
with that little satirical pucker of the lips
which she expected—Rose herself being
dressed in the height of the fashion, precisely like everybody else, always.

"We are all like flies trying to crawl over
the edge of the saucer," Mabel thought, and
repeated the phrase as if she were crossing
herself, as if she were trying to find some
spell to annul this pain, to make this agony
endurable. Tags of Shakespeare, lines from
books she had read ages ago, suddenly
came to her when she was in agony, and she
repeated them over and over again. "Flies
trying to crawl," she repeated. If she could
say that over often enough and make herself
see the flies, she would become numb, chill,
frozen, dumb. Now she could see flies crawling slowly out of a saucer of milk with their
wings stuck together; and she strained and
strained (standing in front of the looking-
glass, listening to Rose Shaw) to make herself see Rose Shaw and all the other people
there as flies, trying to hoist themselves out
of something, or into something, meagre,
insignificant, toiling flies. But she could not
see them like that, not other people. She saw
herself like that—she was a fly, but the
others were dragonflies, butterflies, beautiful
insects, dancing, fluttering, skimming, while
she alone dragged herself up out of the
saucer. (Envy and spite, the most detestable
of the vices, were her chief faults.)

"I feel like some dowdy, decrepit, horribly
dingy old fly," she said, making Robert
Haydon stop just to hear her say that, just
to reassure herself by furbishing up a poor
weak-kneed phrase and so showing how
detached she was, how witty, that she did
not feel in the least out of anything. And, of
course, Robert Haydon answered something,
quite polite, quite insincere, which she saw
through instantly, and said to herself,
directly he went (again from some book),
"Lies, lies, lies!" For a party makes things
either much more real, or much less real,
she thought; she saw in a flash to the

120 bottom of Robert Haydon's heart; she saw
through everything. She saw the truth. This
was true, this drawing-room, this self, and
the other false. Miss Milan's little work-
room was really terribly hot, stuffy, sordid. It
smelt of clothes and cabbage cooking; and
125 yet, when Miss Milan put the glass in her
hand, and she looked at herself with the
dress on, finished, an extraordinary bliss
shot through her heart. Suffused with light,
she sprang into existence. Rid of cares and
130 wrinkles, what she had dreamed of herself
was there—a beautiful woman. Just for a
second (she had not dared look longer, Miss
Milan wanted to know about the length of
the skirt), there looked at her, framed in the
135 scrolloping mahogany, a grey-white, mysteriously smiling, charming girl, the core of
herself, the soul of herself; and it was not
vanity only, not only self-love that made her
think it good, tender, and true. Miss Milan
140 said that the skirt could not well be longer;
if anything the skirt, said Miss Milan, puck-
ering her forehead, considering with all her
wits about her, must be shorter; and she
felt, suddenly, honestly, full of love for Miss
145 Milan, much, much fonder of Miss Milan
than of any one in the whole world, and
could have cried for pity that she should
be crawling on the floor with her mouth
full of pins, and her face red and her eyes
150 bulging—that one human being should be
doing this for another, and she saw them all
as human beings merely, and herself going
off to her party, and Miss Milan pulling the
cover over the canary's cage, or letting him
155 pick a hemp-seed from between her lips,
and the thought of it, of this side of human
nature and its patience and its endurance
and its being content with such miserable,
scanty, sordid, little pleasures filled her eyes
160 with tears. . . .

She faced herself straight in the glass; she
pecked at her left shoulder; she issued out
into the room, as if spears were thrown at
her yellow dress from all sides. But instead of
165 looking fierce or tragic, as Rose Shaw would
have done—Rose would have looked like
Boadicea—she looked foolish and self-
conscious, and simpered like a schoolgirl and
slouched across the room, positively slinking,
170 as if she were a beaten mongrel, and looked
at a picture, an engraving. As if one went to a
party to look at a picture! Everybody knew
why she did it—it was from shame, from
humiliation. . . .
175 But in her yellow dress tonight she could
not wring out one drop more; she wanted it
all, all for herself. She knew (she kept on
looking into the glass, dipping into that
dreadfully showing-up blue pool) that she
180 was condemned, despised, left like this in a
backwater, because of her being like this—a
feeble, vacillating creature; and it seemed to
her that the yellow dress was a penance
which she had deserved, and if she had been
185 dressed like Rose Shaw, in lovely, clinging
green with a ruffle of swansdown, she would
have deserved that; and she thought that
there was no escape for her—none whatever. But it was not her fault altogether, after
190 all. It was being one of a family of ten; never
having money enough, always skimping and
paring; and her mother carrying great cans,
and the linoleum worn on the stair edges,
and one sordid little domestic tragedy after
195 another—nothing catastrophic, the sheep
farm failing, but not utterly; her eldest
brother marrying beneath him but not
very much—there was no romance, nothing extreme about them all. They petered
200 out respectably in seaside resorts; every
watering-place had one of her aunts even
now asleep in some lodging with the front

windows not quite facing the sea. That was so like them—they had to squint at things

205 always. And she had done the same—she was just like her aunts. For all her dreams of living in India, married to some hero like Sir Henry Lawrence, some empire builder (still the sight of a native in a turban filled her

210 with romance), she had failed utterly. She had married Hubert, with his safe, permanent underling's job in the Law Courts, and they managed tolerably in a smallish house, without proper maids, and hash when she

215 was alone or just bread and butter, but now and then—Mrs. Holman was off, thinking her the most dried-up, unsympathetic twig she had ever met, absurdly dressed, too, and would tell every one about Mabel's fantastic

220 appearance—now and then, thought Mabel Waring, left alone on the blue sofa, punching the cushion in order to look occupied, for she would not join Charles Burt and Rose Shaw, chattering like magpies and perhaps laugh-

225 ing at her by the fireplace and then, there did come to her delicious moments, reading the other night in bed, for instance, or down by the sea on the sand in the sun, at Easter—let her recall it—a great tuft of pale sand-grass

230 standing all twisted like a shock of spears against the sky, which was blue like a smooth china egg, so firm, so hard, and then the melody of the waves—"Hush, hush," they said, and the children's shouts paddling—

235 yes, it was a divine moment, and there she lay, she felt, in the hand of the Goddess who was the world; rather a hard-hearted, but very beautiful Goddess, a little lamb laid on the altar (one did think these silly things,

240 and it didn't matter so long as one never said them). And also with Hubert sometimes she had quite unexpectedly—carving the mutton for Sunday lunch, for no reason, opening a letter, coming into a room—divine moments,

245 when she said to herself (for she would never say this to anybody else), "This is it. This has happened. This is it!" And the other way about it was equally surprising—that is, when everything was arranged—music,

250 weather, holidays, every reason for happiness was there—then nothing happened at all. One wasn't happy. It was flat, just flat, that was all.

Her wretched self again, no doubt! She

255 had always been a fretful, weak, unsatisfactory mother, a wobbly wife, lolling about in a kind of twilight existence with nothing very clear or very bold, or more one thing than another, like all her brothers and sisters,

260 except perhaps Herbert—they were all the same poor water-veined creatures who did nothing. Then in the midst of this creeping, crawling life, suddenly she was on the crest of a wave. That wretched fly—where had she

265 read the story that kept coming into her mind about the fly and the saucer?—struggled out. Yes, she had those moments. But now that she was forty, they might come more and more seldom. By degrees she

270 would cease to struggle any more. But that was deplorable! That was not to be endured! That made her feel ashamed of herself!

She would go to the London Library tomorrow. She would find some wonderful,

275 helpful, astonishing book, quite by chance, a book by a clergyman, by an American no one had ever heard of; or she would walk down the strand and drop, accidentally, into a hall where a miner was telling about the life in

280 the pit, and suddenly she would become a new Person. She would be absolutely transformed. She would wear a uniform; she would be called Sister Somebody; she would never give a thought to clothes again. And

285 forever after she would be perfectly clear about Charles Burt and Miss Milan and this

room and that room; and it would be always, day after day, as if she were lying in the sun or carving the mutton. It would be it!

290 So she got up from the blue sofa, and the yellow button in the looking-glass got up too, and she waved her hand to Charles and Rose to show them she did not depend on them one scrap, and the yellow button moved out 295 of the looking-glass, and all the spears were gathered into her breast as she walked towards Mrs. Dalloway and said, "Good night."

"But it's too early to go," said Mrs. Dalloway, who was always so charming.

300 "I'm afraid I must," said Mabel Waring. "But," she added in her weak, wobbly voice which only sounded ridiculous when she tried to strengthen it, "I have enjoyed myself enormously."

305 "I have enjoyed myself," she said to Mr. Dalloway, whom she met on the stairs.

"Lies, lies, lies!" she said to herself, going downstairs, and "Right in the saucer!" she said to herself as she thanked Mrs. Barnet for 310 helping her and wrapped herself, round and round and round, in the Chinese cloak she had worn these twenty years.

Noam Galai/Getty Images

▲

Fashion icon and designer Iris Apfel celebrated her one hundredth birthday on November 26, 2021. Apfel began her career in journalism and interior design. With her husband, Carl Apfel, she developed a famous clothing, fashion, and interior design business that, among other well-known patrons, served nine different U.S. presidents. In 2018, Mattel created the oldest Barbie in Apfel's image. In 2019, at the age of ninety-seven, she signed a modeling contract with global agency IMG.

What is "style"? How do individuals create or express style? What contributes to Apfel's style?

CHARACTER

1. How is Mabel Waring **characterized**, both physically and emotionally?

2. What do the contrasting traits of Mrs. Dalloway and Mabel reveal about the two characters, both individually and in their relationship with one another?

3. How does Mabel's relationship to the dress reveal conflicting values? How does the dress itself reflect these values? Is Mabel **static** or **dynamic**?

4. How does Mabel interact with other characters? What do these interactions indicate about her and also about the collective attitude of the characters toward Mabel?

5. How do Mabel's words and actions convey a particular **perspective** — one that creates ambiguity and reveals her complexity?

SETTING

6. What values are associated with the **setting**?

7. To what degree is Mabel accepted by her society?

8. How does Mabel behave within her surroundings? How does she describe them? Explain how her actions and descriptions reveal her attitude toward the setting.

STRUCTURE

9. How does the beginning sequence of events affect both the development of Mabel's character and a **conflict** in the story?

10. Explain how the **conflict** reveals opposing motivations or values.

11. What is the **narrative structure** of this story? Explain how the author's manipulation of the chronological narrative structure reveals **tensions** between characters.

NARRATION

12. What is the **point of view** in the story? What are the limitations of this point of view?

13. What do the details in the story reveal about the narrator's tone toward Mabel and the dress?

14. What is Mabel's psychological state? How does it contribute to your assessment of the narrator's **reliability**?

FIGURATIVE LANGUAGE: Word Choice, Imagery, and Symbols

15. How is the setting **symbolic**? What do you think the party represents? Explain.

16. What does the dress **symbolize**? Consider the details of the dress and then explain what these details may represent.

17. How might locations in the story take on **symbolic** meaning? For example, where does the party take place? What does that location suggest? Similarly, at the end of the story, Mabel goes downstairs. What idea does that location represent?

FIGURATIVE LANGUAGE: Comparisons

18. What **simile** does Mabel use to describe herself? Why does she make this comparison? What associations and connotations does the simile suggest?

19. Mabel also **compares** herself to other characters in the story. What images does she use in these comparisons?

IDEAS IN LITERATURE: Appearance and Reality

20. Appearances are essential in "The New Dress." Recall a time in your experience when you realized that appearances can be deceiving. For example, have you ever been fooled by the appearance of a person or place? How so? Alternatively, have you ever underestimated the importance of appearances? Explain.

PUTTING IT ALL TOGETHER

21. Consider how Woolf structures the story through complex syntax, point of view, pacing, and dialogue. Explain how these choices contribute to your interpretation of the text.

My Last Duchess
Robert Browning

DEA/A. DAGLI ORTI/DeAgostini/Getty Images

THE TEXT IN CONTEXT

English poet and playwright Robert Browning (1812–1889) remains one of the defining writers of the Victorian era. Like his contemporaries Alfred Tennyson (1809–1892) and Matthew Arnold (1822–1888), he was also perceived as a *sage* or public oracle of wisdom and insight. Browning is associated with a specific poetic form: the dramatic monologue. In these poems, an individual character gives a speech at a particular moment; in the process, the speaker unintentionally reveals different aspects of his or her character or ironically gives away "too much" information. Often, these monologues create tension between appearances and the incongruities that lie beneath those appearances. The following poem is one of Browning's most famous works. He based "My Last Duchess" (1842) loosely on a real-life historical incident: in 1561, the young wife of the Duke of Ferrara had died suspiciously.

My Last Duchess

That's my last Duchess painted on the wall,
Looking as if she were alive. I call
That piece a wonder, now; Fra Pandolf's hands
Worked busily a day, and there she stands.
5 Will't please you sit and look at her? I said
"Fra Pandolf" by design, for never read
Strangers like you that pictured countenance,
The depth and passion of its earnest glance,
But to myself they turned (since none puts by
10 The curtain I have drawn for you, but I)
And seemed as they would ask me, if they durst,
How such a glance came there; so, not the first
Are you to turn and ask thus. Sir, 'twas not
Her husband's presence only, called that spot
15 Of joy into the Duchess' cheek; perhaps
Fra Pandolf chanced to say, "Her mantle laps
Over my lady's wrist too much," or "Paint
Must never hope to reproduce the faint
Half-flush that dies along her throat." Such stuff
20 Was courtesy, she thought, and cause enough
For calling up that spot of joy. She had
A heart—how shall I say?—too soon made glad,
Too easily impressed; she liked whate'er
She looked on, and her looks went everywhere.
25 Sir, 'twas all one! My favour at her breast,
The dropping of the daylight in the West,
The bough of cherries some officious fool
Broke in the orchard for her, the white mule
She rode with round the terrace—all and each
30 Would draw from her alike the approving speech,
Or blush, at least. She thanked men—good! but thanked
Somehow—I know not how—as if she ranked
My gift of a nine-hundred-years-old name
With anybody's gift. Who'd stoop to blame
35 This sort of trifling? Even had you skill
In speech—which I have not—to make your will
Quite clear to such an one, and say, "Just this
Or that in you disgusts me; here you miss,
Or there exceed the mark"—and if she let
40 Herself be lessoned so, nor plainly set
Her wits to yours, forsooth, and made excuse—
E'en then would be some stooping; and I choose

Never to stoop. Oh, sir, she smiled, no doubt,
Whene'er I passed her; but who passed without
45 Much the same smile? This grew; I gave commands;
Then all smiles stopped together. There she stands
As if alive. Will't please you rise? We'll meet
The company below, then. I repeat,
The Count your master's known munificence
50 Is ample warrant that no just pretense
Of mine for dowry will be disallowed;
Though his fair daughter's self, as I avowed
At starting, is my object. Nay, we'll go
Together down, sir. Notice Neptune, though,
55 Taming a sea-horse, thought a rarity,
Which Claus of Innsbruck cast in bronze for me!

The painting depicts the duke looking at his last duchess.

Look carefully at the light and dark imagery in the painting. How do these contrasts reveal the relationship between the duke and his last duchess?

Robert Browning: My Last Duchess (colour litho)/Sullivan, Edmund Joseph (1869-1933)/
©Look and Learn/Bridgeman Images

CHARACTER

1. Who is speaking in the poem? What words, phrases, and details contribute to your understanding of the **speaker**?

2. What particular images, textual details, and passages in the speaker's **monologue** seem most relevant for revealing his relationship with his last duchess?

3. How do the speaker's contradictory or inconsistent traits contribute to his complexity as a character?

SETTING

4. What is the relationship between the speaker and the historical time period of the poem's **setting**?

5. Explain how the speaker behaves in his **setting**. How does this behavior reveal the duke's attitude about his surroundings and possessions?

6. At the end of the poem, how does the **setting** become symbolic?

STRUCTURE

7. What **contrasts** does the duke highlight in his description of the painting? How do they indicate a conflict of values? What ideas, traits, or values are emphasized in the contrasts?

8. How does a **flashback** interrupt the chronology of the poem's narrative? How does the information revealed in the flashback affect your interpretation of the poem?

9. "My Last Duchess" is a **dramatic monologue**: a poem in the form of a speech or first-person narrative, often in which the speaker inadvertently reveals aspects of his or her character. Does the speaker of this poem disclose anything about himself without intending to? Or does he seem self-aware in his speech? Explain.

10. Where in the poem does a noticeable **shift** occur with regard to the **pace** at which details are revealed? How does this abrupt change in tempo affect your interpretation of the poem?

NARRATION

11. Does the speaker seem trustworthy? Why or why not? How does his inclusion or exclusion of particular details — as well as his tone — affect your view of his **reliability**?

12. How do the details of the duke's description of the duchess convey his **perspective** and **tone** toward her?

13. How might the order in which information is revealed create a **cathartic** moment for the reader? What is your own emotional response? How does it affect your interpretation?

FIGURATIVE LANGUAGE: Word Choice, Imagery, and Symbols

14. Look carefully at how the speaker describes his last wife. What **connotations** suggest multiple meanings or ideas?

15. Choose a **symbolic** object or element in the poem. Explain the symbolism. How does the symbolism contribute to your interpretation of the poem?

16. The speaker makes many comparisons in his monologue. Choose one **simile** and explain the details and significance of the comparison in the context of the whole poem.

17. The final image in the poem is a bronze cast of the Greek god Neptune taming a seahorse. How does this **allusion** to Greek mythology contribute to your interpretation of the poem? Why do you think the poem ends with the image of another piece of art owned by the speaker?

18. The appearance of normality is important to the duke in this poem. How does the idea of "keeping up the appearance" remain today? Consider a time in your experience when keeping up an appearance disguised or obscured the reality of a situation.

19. The dramatic monologue reveals a shocking moment. Explain how the speaker's words and actions dramatically affect the pacing of the poem and foreshadow the revelation. How do these elements contribute to the complex perspective of the speaker?

Bloodchild
Octavia Butler

THE TEXT IN CONTEXT

Science fiction writer Octavia Butler (1947–2006) always suggested that being an African American woman working in a genre dominated by white men made her well suited to write about frightening dystopias and other hostile environments: "I'm black, I'm solitary, I've always been an outsider." Like many science fiction writers, she used her speculative stories to examine real-world themes: sex, gender, race, empathy, community, alienation, and hierarchies of power. Butler's "Bloodchild" (1984), the Hugo Award–winning story included here, highlights sex roles, immigration, and interdependence, among other ideas. Her books include *Patternmaster* (1976), *Dawn* (1987), and *Parable of the Sower* (1993). During her career, Butler won many awards, including a MacArthur Foundation "Genius Grant" in 1995.

Malcolm Ali/WireImage/Getty Images

Bloodchild

My last night of childhood began with a visit home. T'Gatoi's sister had given us two sterile eggs. T'Gatoi gave one to my mother, brother, and sisters. She insisted that I eat
5 the other one alone. It didn't matter. There was still enough to leave everyone feeling good. Almost everyone. My mother wouldn't take any. She sat, watching everyone drifting and dreaming without her. Most of the time
10 she watched me.

I lay against T'Gatoi's long, velvet underside, sipping from my egg now and then, wondering why my mother denied herself such a harmless pleasure. Less of her hair
15 would be gray if she indulged now and then. The eggs prolonged life, prolonged vigor. My father, who had never refused one in his life, had lived more than twice as long as he should have. And toward the end of his life,
20 when he should have been slowing down, he had married my mother and fathered four children.

But my mother seemed content to age before she had to. I saw her turn away as
25 several of T'Gatoi's limbs secured me closer. T'Gatoi liked our body heat and took advantage of it whenever she could. When I was little and at home more, my mother used to try to tell me how to behave with T'Gatoi—
30 how to be respectful and always obedient because T'Gatoi was the Tlic government official in charge of the Preserve, and thus the most important of her kind to deal directly with Terrans. It was an honor, my
35 mother said, that such a person had chosen to come into the family. My mother was at her most formal and severe when she was lying.

I had no idea why she was lying, or even
40 what she was lying about. It was an honor to have T'Gatoi in the family, but it was hardly a novelty. T'Gatoi and my mother had been friends all my mother's life, and T'Gatoi was not interested in being honored in the house
45 she considered her second home. She simply came in, climbed onto one of her special couches, and called me over to keep her warm. It was impossible to be formal with her while lying against her and hearing her
50 complain as usual that I was too skinny.

"You're better," she said this time, probing me with six or seven of her limbs. "You're gaining weight finally. Thinness is dangerous." The probing changed subtly, became a
55 series of caresses.

"He's still too thin," my mother said sharply.

T'Gatoi lifted her head and perhaps a meter of her body off the couch as though
60 she were sitting up. She looked at my mother, and my mother, her face lined and old looking, turned away.

"Lien, I would like you to have what's left of Gan's egg."
65 "The eggs are for the children," my mother said.

"They are for the family. Please take it."

Unwillingly obedient, my mother took it from me and put it to her mouth. There were
70 only a few drops left in the now-shrunken, elastic shell, but she squeezed them out, swallowed them, and after a few moments some of the lines of tension began to smooth from her face.
75 "It's good," she whispered. "Sometimes I forget how good it is."

"You should take more," T'Gatoi said. "Why are you in such a hurry to be old?"

My mother said nothing.
80 "I like being able to come here," T'Gatoi said. "This place is a refuge because of you, yet you won't take care of yourself."

T'Gatoi was hounded on the outside. Her people wanted more of us made available.
85 Only she and her political faction stood between us and the hordes who did not understand why there was a Preserve—why any Terran could not be courted, paid, drafted, in some way made available to
90 them. Or they did understand, but in their desperation, they did not care. She parceled us out to the desperate and sold us to the rich and powerful for their political support. Thus, we were necessities, status symbols,
95 and an independent people. She oversaw the joining of families, putting an end to the final remnants of the earlier system of breaking up Terran families to suit impatient Tlic. I had lived outside with her. I had seen
100 the desperate eagerness in the way some people looked at me. It was a little frightening to know that only she stood between us and that desperation that could so easily swallow us. My mother would look at her
105 sometimes and say to me, "Take care of her." And I would remember that she too had been outside, had seen.

Now T'Gatoi used four of her limbs to push me away from her onto the floor. "Go
110 on, Gan," she said. "Sit down there with your sisters and enjoy not being sober. You had most of the egg. Lien, come warm me."

"Nothing can buy him from me." Sober, she would not have permitted herself to
115 refer to such things.

"Nothing," T'Gatoi agreed, humoring her.

"Did you think I would sell him for eggs? For long life? My son?"

"Not for anything," T'Gatoi said, stroking
120 my mother's shoulders, toying with her long, graying hair.

I would like to have touched my mother, shared that moment with her. She would take my hand if I touched her now. Freed by

125 the egg and the sting, she would smile and perhaps say things long held in. But tomorrow, she would remember all this as a humiliation. I did not want to be part of a remembered humiliation. Best just be still
130 and know she loved me under all the duty and pride and pain.

"Xuan Hoa, take off her shoes," T'Gatoi said. "In a little while I'll sting her again and she can sleep."

135 My older sister obeyed, swaying drunkenly as she stood up. When she had finished, she sat down beside me and took my hand. We had always been a unit, she and I.

My mother put the back of her head
140 against T'Gatoi's underside and tried from that impossible angle to look up into the broad, round face. "You're going to sting me again?"

"Yes, Lien."

145 "I'll sleep until tomorrow noon."

"Good. You need it. When did you sleep last?"

My mother made a wordless sound of annoyance. "I should have stepped on you
150 when you were small enough," she muttered.

It was an old joke between them. They had grown up together, sort of, though T'Gatoi had not, in my mother's lifetime, been small enough for any Terran to step on. She was
155 nearly three times my mother's present age, yet would still be young when my mother died of age. But T'Gatoi and my mother had met as T'Gatoi was coming into a period of rapid development—a kind of Tlic adoles-
160 cence. My mother was only a child, but for a while they developed at the same rate and had no better friends than each other.

T'Gatoi had even introduced my mother to the man who became my father. My par-
165 ents, pleased with each other in spite of their different ages, married as T'Gatoi was going

into her family's business—politics. She and my mother saw each other less. But some-time before my older sister was born, my
170 mother promised T'Gatoi one of her children. She would have to give one of us to someone, and she preferred T'Gatoi to some stranger.

Years passed. T'Gatoi traveled and increased her influence. The Preserve was
175 hers by the time she came back to my mother to collect what she probably saw as her just reward for her hard work. My older sister took an instant liking to her and wanted to be chosen, but my mother was
180 just coming to term with me and T'Gatoi liked the idea of choosing an infant and watching and taking part in all the phases of development. I'm told I was first caged within T'Gatoi's many limbs only three min-
185 utes after my birth. A few days later, I was given my first taste of egg. I tell Terrans that when they ask whether I was ever afraid of her. And I tell it to Tlic when T'Gatoi suggests a young Terran child for them and they, anx-
190 ious and ignorant, demand an adolescent. Even my brother who had somehow grown up to fear and distrust the Tlic could proba-bly have gone smoothly into one of their families if he had been adopted early
195 enough. Sometimes, I think for his sake he should have been. I looked at him, stretched out on the floor across the room, his eyes open, but glazed as he dreamed his egg dream. No matter what he felt toward the
200 Tlic, he always demanded his share of egg.

"Lien, can you stand up?" T'Gatoi asked suddenly.

"Stand?" my mother said. "I thought I was going to sleep."

205 "Later. Something sounds wrong outside." The cage was abruptly gone.

"What?"

"Up, Lien!"

My mother recognized her tone and got
210 up just in time to avoid being dumped on the floor. T'Gatoi whipped her three meters of body off her couch, toward the door, and out at full speed. She had bones—ribs, a long spine, a skull, four sets of limb bones per
215 segment. But when she moved that way, twisting, hurling herself into controlled falls, landing running, she seemed not only bone-less, but aquatic—something swimming through the air as though it were water. I
220 loved watching her move.

I left my sister and started to follow her out the door, though I wasn't very steady on my own feet. It would have been better to sit and dream, better yet to find a girl and share
225 a waking dream with her. Back when the Tlic saw us as not much more than convenient, big, warm-blooded animals, they would pen several of us together, male and female, and feed us only eggs. That way they could be
230 sure of getting another generation of us no matter how we tried to hold out. We were lucky that didn't go on long. A few genera-tions of it and we would have been little more than convenient, big animals.

235 "Hold the door open, Gan," T'Gatoi said. "And tell the family to stay back."

"What is it?" I asked.

"N'Tlic."

I shrank back against the door. "Here?
240 Alone?"

"He was trying to reach a call box, I suppose." She carried the man past me, unconscious, folded like a coat over some of her limbs. He looked young—my brother's
245 age perhaps—and he was thinner than he should have been. What T'Gatoi would have called dangerously thin.

"Gan, go to the call box," she said. She put the man on the floor and began stripping off
250 his clothing.

I did not move.

After a moment, she looked up at me, her sudden stillness a sign of deep impatience.

"Send Qui," I told her. "I'll stay here. Maybe 255 I can help."

She let her limbs begin to move again, lifting the man and pulling his shirt over his head. "You don't want to see this," she said. "It will be hard. I can't help this man the way 260 his Tlic could."

"I know. But send Qui. He won't want to be of any help here. I'm at least willing to try."

She looked at my brother—older, bigger, stronger, certainly more able to help her 265 here. He was sitting up now, braced against the wall, staring at the man on the floor with undisguised fear and revulsion. Even she could see that he would be useless.

"Qui, go!" she said.

270 He didn't argue. He stood up, swayed briefly, then steadied, frightened sober.

"This man's name is Bram Lomas," she told him, reading from the man's armband. I fingered my own armband in sympathy. "He 275 needs T'Khotgif Teh. Do you hear?"

"Bram Lomas, T'Khotgif Teh," my brother said. "I'm going." He edged around Lomas and ran out the door.

Lomas began to regain consciousness. He 280 only moaned at first and clutched spasmodically at a pair of T'Gatoi's limbs. My younger sister, finally awake from her egg dream, came close to look at him, until my mother pulled her back.

285 T'Gatoi removed the man's shoes, then his pants, all the while leaving him two of her limbs to grip. Except for the final few, all her limbs were equally dexterous. "I want no argument from you this time, Gan," she said.

290 I straightened. "What shall I do?"

"Go out and slaughter an animal that is at least half your size."

"Slaughter? But I've never—"

She knocked me across the room. Her tail 295 was an efficient weapon whether she exposed the sting or not.

I got up, feeling stupid for having ignored her warning, and went into the kitchen. Maybe I could kill something with a knife or 300 an ax. My mother raised a few Terran animals for the table and several thousand local ones for their fur. T'Gatoi would probably prefer something local. An achti, perhaps. Some of those were the right size, though 305 they had about three times as many teeth as I did and a real love of using them. My mother, Hoa, and Qui could kill them with knives. I had never killed one at all, had never slaughtered any animal. I had spent 310 most of my time with T'Gatoi while my brother and sisters were learning the family business. T'Gatoi had been right. I should have been the one to go to the call box. At least I could do that.

315 I went to the corner cabinet where my mother kept her large house and garden tools. At the back of the cabinet there was a pipe that carried off waste water from the kitchen—except that it didn't anymore. My 320 father had rerouted the waste water below before I was born. Now the pipe could be turned so that one half slid around the other and a rifle could be stored inside. This wasn't our only gun, but it was our most easily 325 accessible one. I would have to use it to shoot one of the biggest of the achti. Then T'Gatoi would probably confiscate it. Firearms were illegal in the Preserve. There had been incidents right after the Preserve was 330 established—Terrans shooting Tlic, shooting N'Tlic. This was before the Joining of families began, before everyone had a personal stake in keeping the peace. No one had shot a Tlic in my lifetime or my mother's, but the law

335 still stood—for our protection, we were told. There were stories of whole Terran families wiped out in reprisal back during the assassinations.

I went out to the cages and shot the big-
340 gest achti I could find. It was a handsome breeding male, and my mother would not be pleased to see me bring it in. But it was the right size, and I was in a hurry.

I put the achti's long, warm body over my
345 shoulder—glad that some of the weight I'd gained was muscle—and took it to the kitchen. There, I put the gun back in its hiding place. If T'Gatoi noticed the achti's wounds and demanded the gun, I would
350 give it to her. Otherwise, let it stay where my father wanted it.

I turned to take the achti to her, then hesitated. For several seconds, I stood in front of the closed door wondering why I was sud-
355 denly afraid. I knew what was going to happen. I hadn't seen it before but T'Gatoi had shown me diagrams and drawings. She had made sure I knew the truth as soon as I was old enough to understand it.

360 Yet I did not want to go into that room. I wasted a little time choosing a knife from the carved, wooden box in which my mother kept them. T'Gatoi might want one, I told myself, for the tough, heavily furred hide of
365 the achti.

"Gan!" T'Gatoi called, her voice harsh with urgency.

I swallowed. I had not imagined a single moving of the feet could be so difficult. I
370 realized I was trembling and that shamed me. Shame impelled me through the door.

I put the achti down near T'Gatoi and saw that Lomas was unconscious again. She, Lomas, and I were alone in the room—my
375 mother and sisters probably sent out so they would not have to watch. I envied them.

But my mother came back into the room as T'Gatoi seized the achti. Ignoring the knife I offered her, she extended claws from sev-
380 eral of her limbs and slit the achti from throat to anus. She looked at me, her yellow eyes intent. "Hold this man's shoulders, Gan."

I stared at Lomas in panic, realizing that I did not want to touch him, let alone hold
385 him. This would not be like shooting an animal. Not as quick, not as merciful, and, I hoped, not as final, but there was nothing I wanted less than to be part of it.

My mother came forward. "Gan, you hold
390 his right side," she said. "I'll hold his left." And if he came to, he would throw her off without realizing he had done it. She was a tiny woman. She often wondered aloud how she had produced, as she said, such "huge"
395 children.

"Never mind," I told her, taking the man's shoulders. "I'll do it." She hovered nearby.

"Don't worry," I said. "I won't shame you. You don't have to stay and watch."

400 She looked at me uncertainly, then touched my face in a rare caress. Finally, she went back to her bedroom.

T'Gatoi lowered her head in relief. "Thank you, Gan," she said with courtesy more Ter-
405 ran than Tlic. "That one . . . she is always finding new ways for me to make her suffer."

Lomas began to groan and make choked sounds. I had hoped he would stay unconscious. T'Gatoi put her face near his so that
410 he focused on her.

"I've stung you as much as I dare for now," she told him. "When this is over, I'll sting you to sleep and you won't hurt anymore."

"Please," the man begged. "Wait . . ."

415 "There's no more time, Bram. I'll sting you as soon as it's over. When T'Khotgif arrives she'll give you eggs to help you heal. It will be over soon."

"T'Khotgif!" the man shouted, straining
420 against my hands.

"Soon, Bram." T'Gatoi glanced at me, then
placed a claw against his abdomen slightly to
the right of the middle, just below the left
rib. There was movement on the right side—
425 tiny, seemingly random pulsations moving
his brown flesh, creating a concavity here, a
convexity there, over and until I could see
the rhythm of it and knew where the next
pulse would be.

430 Lomas's entire body stiffened under
T'Gatoi's claw, though she merely rested it
against him as she wound the rear section of
her body around his legs. He might break my
grip, but he would not break hers. He wept
435 helplessly as she used his pants to tie his
hands, then pushed his hands above his
head so that I could kneel on the cloth
between them and pin them in place. She
rolled up his shirt and gave it to him to bite
440 down on.

And she opened him.

His body convulsed with the first cut. He
almost tore himself away from me. The
sound he made . . . I had never heard such
445 sounds come from anything human. T'Gatoi
seemed to pay no attention as she length-
ened and deepened the cut, now and then
pausing to lick away blood. His blood vessels
contracted, reacting to the chemistry of her
450 saliva, and the bleeding slowed.

I felt as though I were helping her torture
him, helping her consume him. I knew I
would vomit soon, didn't know why I hadn't
already. I couldn't possibly last until she was
455 finished.

She found the first grub. It was fat and
deep red with his blood—both inside and
out. It had already eaten its own egg case but
apparently had not yet begun to eat its host.
460 At this stage, it would eat any flesh except its

mother's. Let alone, it would have gone on
excreting the poisons that had both sickened
and alerted Lomas. Eventually it would have
begun to eat. By the time it ate its way out
465 of Lomas's flesh, Lomas would be dead or
dying—and unable to take revenge on the
thing that was killing him. There was always
a grace period between the time the host
sickened and the time the grubs began to
470 eat him.

T'Gatoi picked up the writhing grub carefully and looked at it, somehow ignoring the
terrible groans of the man.

Abruptly, the man lost consciousness.

475 "Good," T'Gatoi looked down at him. "I
wish you Terrans could do that at will." She
felt nothing. And the thing she held . . .

It was limbless and boneless at this stage,
perhaps fifteen centimeters long and two
480 thick, blind and slimy with blood. It was like
a large worm. T'Gatoi put it into the belly of
the achti, and it began at once to burrow. It
would stay there and eat as long as there
was anything to eat.

485 Probing through Lomas's flesh, she found
two more, one of them smaller and more vigorous. "A male!" she said happily. He would
be dead before I would. He would be through
his metamorphosis and screwing everything
490 that would hold still before his sisters even
had limbs. He was the only one to make a
serious effort to bite T'Gatoi as she placed
him in the achti.

Paler worms oozed to visibility in Lomas's
495 flesh. I closed my eyes. It was worse than
finding something dead, rotting, and filled
with tiny animal grubs. And it was far worse
than any drawing or diagram.

"Ah, there are more," T'Gatoi said, plucking
500 out two long, thick grubs. "You may have to
kill another animal, Gan. Everything lives
inside you Terrans."

I had been told all my life that this was a good and necessary thing Tlic and Terran did together—a kind of birth. I had believed it until now. I knew birth was painful and bloody, no matter what. But this was something else, something worse. And I wasn't ready to see it. Maybe I never would be. Yet I couldn't not see it. Closing my eyes didn't help.

T'Gatoi found a grub still eating its egg case. The remains of the case were still wired into a blood vessel by their own little tube or hook or whatever. That was the way the grubs were anchored and the way they fed. They took only blood until they were ready to emerge. Then they ate their stretched, elastic egg cases. Then they ate their hosts.

T'Gatoi bit away the egg case, licked away the blood. Did she like the taste? Did childhood habits die hard—or not die at all?

The whole procedure was wrong, alien. I wouldn't have thought anything about her could seem alien to me.

"One more, I think," she said. "Perhaps two. A good family. In a host animal these days, we would be happy to find one or two alive." She glanced at me. "Go outside, Gan, and empty your stomach. Go now while the man is unconscious."

I staggered out, barely made it. Beneath the tree just beyond the front door, I vomited until there was nothing left to bring up. Finally, I stood shaking, tears streaming down my face. I did not know why I was crying, but I could not stop. I went further from the house to avoid being seen. Every time I closed my eyes I saw red worms crawling over redder human flesh.

There was a car coming toward the house. Since Terrans were forbidden motorized vehicles except for certain farm equipment, I knew this must be Lomas's Tlic with Qui and

perhaps a Terran doctor. I wiped my face on my shirt, struggled for control.

"Gan," Qui called as the car stopped. "What happened?" He crawled out of the low, round, Tlic-convenient car door. Another Terran crawled out the other side and went into the house without speaking to me. The doctor. With his help and a few eggs, Lomas might make it.

"T'Khotgif Teh?" I said.

The Tlic driver surged out of her car, reared up half her length before me. She was paler and smaller than T'Gatoi—probably born from the body of an animal. Tlic from Terran bodies were always larger as well as more numerous.

"Six young," I told her. "Maybe seven, all alive. At least one male."

"Lomas?" she said harshly. I liked her for the question and the concern in her voice when she asked it. The last coherent thing he had said was her name.

"He's alive," I said.

She surged away to the house without another word.

"She's been sick," my brother said, watching her go. "When I called, I could hear people telling her she wasn't well enough to go out even for this."

I said nothing. I had extended courtesy to the Tlic. Now I didn't want to talk to anyone. I hoped he would go in—out of curiosity if nothing else.

"Finally found out more than you wanted to know, eh?"

I looked at him.

"Don't give me one of her looks," he said. "You're not her. You're just her property."

One of her looks. Had I picked up even an ability to imitate her expressions?

"What'd you do, puke?" He sniffed the air. "So now you know what you're in for."

I walked away from him. He and I had been close when we were kids. He would let me follow him around when I was home, and sometimes T'Gatoi would let me bring him along when she took me into the city. But something had happened when he reached adolescence. I never knew what. He began keeping out of T'Gatoi's way. Then he began running away—until he realized there was no "away." Not in the Preserve. Certainly not outside. After that he concentrated on getting his share of every egg that came into the house and on looking out for me in a way that made me all but hate him—a way that clearly said, as long as I was all right, he was safe from the Tlic.

"How was it, really?" he demanded, following me.

"I killed an achti. The young ate it."

"You didn't run out of the house and puke because they ate an achti."

"I had . . . never seen a person cut open before." That was true, and enough for him to know. I couldn't talk about the other. Not with him.

"Oh," he said. He glanced at me as though he wanted to say more, but he kept quiet.

We walked, not really headed anywhere. Toward the back, toward the cages, toward the fields.

"Did he say anything?" Qui asked. "Lomas, I mean."

"Who else would he mean?" He said T'Khotgif.'"

Qui shuddered. "If she had done that to me, she'd be the last person I'd call for."

"You'd call for her. Her sting would ease your pain without killing the grubs in you."

"You think I'd care if they died?"

No. Of course he wouldn't. Would I?

"Shit!" He drew a deep breath. "I've seen what they do. You think this thing with Lomas was bad? It was nothing."

I didn't argue. He didn't know what he was talking about.

"I saw them eat a man," he said.

I turned to face him. "You're lying!"

"I saw them eat a man." He paused. "It was when I was little. I had been to the Hartmund house and I was on my way home. Halfway here, I saw a man and a Tlic and the man was N'Tlic. The ground was hilly. I was able to hide from them and watch. The Tlic wouldn't open the man because she had nothing to feed the grubs. The man couldn't go any further and there were no houses around. He was in so much pain, he told her to kill him. He begged her to kill him. Finally, she did. She cut his throat. One swipe of one claw. I saw the grubs eat their way out, then burrow in again, still eating."

His words made me see Lomas's flesh again, parasitized, crawling. "Why didn't you tell me that?" I whispered.

He looked startled as though he'd forgotten I was listening. "I don't know."

"You started to run away not long after that, didn't you?"

"Yeah. Stupid. Running inside the Preserve. Running in a cage."

I shook my head, said what I should have said to him long ago. "She wouldn't take you, Qui. You don't have to worry."

"She would . . . if anything happened to you."

"No. She'd take Xuan Hoa. Hoa . . . wants it." She wouldn't if she had stayed to watch Lomas.

"They don't take women," he said with contempt.

"They do sometimes." I glanced at him. "Actually, they prefer women. You should be around them when they talk among themselves. They say women have more body fat to protect the grubs. But they usually take men to leave the women free to bear their own young."

675 "To provide the next generation of host animals," he said, switching from contempt to bitterness.

"It's more than that!" I countered. Was it?

"If it were going to happen to me, I'd want
680 to believe it was more, too."

"It is more!" I felt like a kid. Stupid argument.

"Did you think so while T'Gatoi was picking worms out of that guy's guts?"

685 "It's not supposed to happen that way."

"Sure it is. You weren't supposed to see it, that's all. And his Tlic was supposed to do it. She could sting him unconscious and the operation wouldn't have been as painful. But
690 she'd still open him, pick out the grubs, and if she missed even one, it would poison him and eat him from the inside out."

There was actually a time when my mother told me to show respect for Qui
695 because he was my older brother. I walked away, hating him. In his way, he was gloating. He was safe and I wasn't. I could have hit him, but I didn't think I would be able to stand it when he refused to hit back, when
700 he looked at me with contempt and pity.

He wouldn't let me get away. Longer legged, he swung ahead of me and made me feel as though I were following him.

"I'm sorry," he said.

705 I strode on, sick and furious.

"Look, it probably won't be that bad with you. T'Gatoi likes you. She'll be careful."

I turned back toward the house, almost running from him.

710 "Has she done it to you yet?" he asked, keeping up easily. "I mean, you're about the right age for implantation. Has she —"

I hit him. I didn't know I was going to do it, but I think I meant to kill him. If he hadn't
715 been bigger and stronger, I think I would have.

He tried to hold me off, but in the end, had to defend himself. He only hit me a couple of times. That was plenty. I don't
720 remember going down, but when I came to, he was gone. It was worth the pain to be rid of him.

I got up and walked slowly toward the house. The back was dark. No one was in the
725 kitchen. My mother and sisters were sleeping in their bedrooms—or pretending to.

Once I was in the kitchen, I could hear voices—Tlic and Terran from the next room. I couldn't make out what they were saying—
730 didn't want to make it out.

I sat down at my mother's table, waiting for quiet. The table was smooth and worn, heavy and well crafted. My father had made it for her just before he died. I remembered
735 hanging around underfoot when he built it. He didn't mind. Now I sat leaning on it, missing him. I could have talked to him. He had done it three times in his long life. Three clutches of eggs, three times being opened
740 up and sewed up. How had he done it? How did anyone do it?

I got up, took the rifle from its hiding place, and sat down again with it. It needed cleaning, oiling.

745 All I did was load it.

"Gan?"

She made a lot of little clicking sounds when she walked on bare floor, each limb clicking in succession as it touched down.
750 Waves of little clicks.

She came to the table, raised the front half of her body above it, and surged onto it. Sometimes she moved so smoothly she seemed to flow like water itself. She coiled
755 herself into a small hill in the middle of the table and looked at me.

"That was bad," she said softly. "You should not have seen it. It need not be that way."

"I know."

760 "T'Khotgif—Ch'Khotgif now—she will die of her disease. She will not live to raise her children. But her sister will provide for them, and for Bram Lomas." Sterile sister. One fertile female in every lot. One to keep the 765 family going. That sister owed Lomas more than she could ever repay.

"He'll live then?"

"Yes."

"I wonder if he would do it again."

770 "No one would ask him to do that again."

I looked into the yellow eyes, wondering how much I saw and understood there, and how much I only imagined. "No one ever asks us," I said. "You never asked me."

775 She moved her head slightly. "What's the matter with your face?"

"Nothing. Nothing important." Human eyes probably wouldn't have noticed the swelling in the darkness. The only light was 780 from one of the moons, shining through a window across the room.

"Did you use the rifle to shoot the achti?"

"Yes."

"And do you mean to use it to shoot me?"

785 I stared at her, outlined in the moonlight—coiled, graceful body. "What does Terran blood taste like to you?"

She said nothing.

"What are you?" I whispered. "What are 790 we to you?"

She lay still, rested her head on her topmost coil. "You know me as no other does," she said softly. "You must decide."

"That's what happened to my face," 795 I told her.

"What?"

"Qui goaded me into deciding to do something. It didn't turn out very well." I moved the gun slightly, brought the barrel up

800 diagonally under my own chin. "At least it was a decision I made."

"As this will be."

"Ask me, Gatoi."

"For my children's lives?"

805 She would say something like that. She knew how to manipulate people, Terran and Tlic. But not this time.

"I don't want to be a host animal," I said. "Not even yours."

810 It took her a long time to answer. "We use almost no host animals these days," she said. "You know that."

"You use us."

"We do. We wait long years for you and 815 teach you and join our families to yours." She moved restlessly. "You know you aren't animals to us."

I stared at her, saying nothing.

"The animals we once used began 820 killing most of our eggs after implantation long before your ancestors arrived," she said softly. "You know these things, Gan. Because your people arrived, we are relearning what it means to be a healthy, 825 thriving people. And your ancestors, fleeing from their homeworld, from their own kind who would have killed or enslaved them—they survived because of us. We saw them as people and gave them the 830 Preserve when they still tried to kill us as worms."

At the word "worms," I jumped. I couldn't help it, and she couldn't help noticing it.

"I see," she said quietly. "Would you really 835 rather die than bear my young, Gan?"

I didn't answer.

"Shall I go to Xuan Hoa?"

"Yes!" Hoa wanted it. Let her have it. She hadn't had to watch Lomas. She'd be proud.... 840 Not terrified.

T'Gatoi flowed off the table onto the floor, startling me almost too much.

"I'll sleep in Hoa's room tonight," she said. "And sometime tonight or in the morning, I'll tell her."

This was going too fast. My sister Hoa had had almost as much to do with raising me as my mother. I was still close to her—not like Qui. She could want T'Gatoi and still love me.

"Wait! Gatoi!"

She looked back, then raised nearly half her length off the floor and turned to face me. "These are adult things, Gan. This is my life, my family!"

"But she's . . . my sister."

"I have done what you demanded. I have asked you!"

"But—"

"It will be easier for Hoa. She has always expected to carry other lives inside her."

Human lives. Human young who should someday drink at her breasts, not at her veins.

I shook my head. "Don't do it to her, Gatoi." I was not Qui. It seemed I could become him, though, with no effort at all. I could make Xuan Hoa my shield. Would it be easier to know that red worms were growing in her flesh instead of mine?

"Don't do it to Hoa," I repeated.

She stared at me, utterly still.

I looked away, then back at her. "Do it to me."

I lowered the gun from my throat and she leaned forward to take it.

"No," I told her.

"It's the law," she said.

"Leave it for the family. One of them might use it to save my life someday."

She grasped the rifle barrel, but I wouldn't let go. I was pulled into a standing position over her.

"Leave it here!" I repeated. "If we're not your animals, if these are adult things, accept the risk. There is risk, Gatoi, in dealing with a partner."

It was clearly hard for her to let go of the rifle. A shudder went through her and she made a hissing sound of distress. It occurred to me that she was afraid. She was old enough to have seen what guns could do to people. Now her young and this gun would be together in the same house. She did not know about the other guns. In this dispute, they did not matter.

"I will implant the first egg tonight," she said as I put the gun away. "Do you hear, Gan?"

Why else had I been given a whole egg to eat while the rest of the family was left to share one? Why else had my mother kept looking at me as though I were going away from her, going where she could not follow? Did T'Gatoi imagine I hadn't known?

"I hear."

"Now!" I let her push me out of the kitchen, then walked ahead of her toward my bedroom. The sudden urgency in her voice sounded real. "You would have done it to Hoa tonight!" I accused.

"I must do it to someone tonight."

I stopped in spite of her urgency and stood in her way. "Don't you care who?"

She flowed around me and into my bedroom. I found her waiting on the couch we shared. There was nothing in Hoa's room that she could have used. She would have done it to Hoa on the floor. The thought of her doing it to Hoa at all disturbed me in a different way now, and I was suddenly angry.

Yet I undressed and lay down beside her. I knew what to do, what to expect. I had been told all my life. I felt the familiar sting, narcotic, mildly pleasant. Then the blind probing of her ovipositor. The puncture was painless, easy. So easy going in. She undulated slowly against me, her muscles forcing the egg from her body into mine. I held on to a pair of her limbs until I remembered Lomas holding her

that way. Then I let go, moved inadvertently,
930 and hurt her. She gave a low cry of pain and
I expected to be caged at once within her
limbs. When I wasn't, I held on to her again,
feeling oddly ashamed.

"I'm sorry," I whispered.

935 She rubbed my shoulders with four of her
limbs.

"Do you care?" I asked. "Do you care that
it's me?"

She did not answer for some time. Finally,
940 "You were the one making the choices
tonight, Gan. I made mine long ago."

"Would you have gone to Hoa?"

"Yes. How could I put my children into the
care of one who hates them?"

945 "It wasn't . . . hate."

"I know what it was."

"I was afraid."

Silence.

"I still am." I could admit it to her here,
950 now.

"But you came to me . . . to save Hoa."

"Yes." I leaned my forehead against her.
She was cool velvet, deceptively soft. "And to
keep you for myself," I said. It was so. I didn't
955 understand it, but it was so.

She made a soft hum of contentment. "I
couldn't believe I had made such a mistake
with you," she said. "I chose you. I believed
you had grown to choose me."

960 "I had, but . . ."

"Lomas."

"Yes."

"I had never known a Terran to see a
birth and take it well. Qui has seen one,
965 hasn't he?"

"Yes."

"Terrans should be protected from seeing."

I didn't like the sound of that—and I
doubted that it was possible. "Not protected,"

970 I said. "Shown. Shown when we're young
kids, and shown more than once. Gatoi, no
Terran ever sees a birth that goes right. All
we see is N'Tlic—pain and terror and maybe
death."

975 She looked down at me. "It is a private
thing. It has always been a private thing."

Her tone kept me from insisting—that
and the knowledge that if she changed her
mind, I might be the first public example.
980 But I had planted the thought in her mind.
Chances were it would grow, and eventually.
she would experiment.

"You won't see it again," she said. "I
don't want you thinking any more about
985 shooting me."

The small amount of fluid that came into
me with her egg relaxed me as completely
as a sterile egg would have, so that I could
remember the rifle in my hands and my
990 feelings of fear and revulsion, anger and
despair. I could remember the feelings without reviving them. I could talk about them.

"I wouldn't have shot you," I said. "Not
you." She had been taken from my father's
995 flesh when he was my age.

"You could have," she insisted.

"Not you." She stood between us and her
own people, protecting, interweaving.

"Would you have destroyed yourself?"

1000 I moved carefully, uncomfortable. "I could
have done that. I nearly did. That's Qui's
'away.' I wonder if he knows."

"What?"

I did not answer.

1005 "You will live now."

"Yes." *Take care of her*, my mother used to
say. Yes.

"I'm healthy and young," she said. "I won't
leave you as Lomas was left—alone, N'Tlic.
1010 I'll take care of you."

The 1950s popularized science fiction in film. The image shows a poster for the 1958 science fiction horror film *The Blob*.

Look closely at the poster's details. Why might audiences still find science fiction compelling? What accounts for the genre's enduring fascination for readers and viewers? Use the elements of the poster to support your response.

CHARACTER

1. How is Gan described both physically and emotionally? What **motivates** him to think and feel as he does?

2. How do Lien's personal characteristics reveal a **contrast**? What does this contrast reveal about Lien and Gan's relationship with the group?

3. In what ways do Gan's choices, actions, or speech seem contradictory or inconsistent?

4. When does Gan experience a realization? What is the **epiphany**? Describe Gan before and after this realization.

SETTING

5. What is the social and cultural **setting**? Describe the details in the text that convey one or more aspects of the story's setting.

6. What is the relationship between the society in the story's **setting** and the characters in the story? To what degree are each of the characters accepted by this society?

7. How does Gan interact with his surroundings? How do Gan's interactions reveal his attitude toward the **setting** and contribute to the development of his character?

STRUCTURE

8. How do the characters and events in the story's **exposition** represent competing value systems?

9. What is the **climax** of the story? Why is this event so significant in the context of Gan and his conflict?

10. How does the experience of Brad Lomas create important contrasts in "Bloodchild"? Do these **contrasts** add **ambiguity** or contradiction to the story? Explain.

11. Does the text have a clear **resolution**? In other words, is the story's **conflict** resolved, or does it still remain at the end of "Bloodchild"? How does the resolution (or lack of one) affect Gan and T'Gatoi?

NARRATION

12. Who is the **narrator** of "Bloodchild"? Which details from the text indicate the identity of the narrator?

13. How do the narrator's background and **perspective** shape his **tone** toward his experiences?

14. To what degree is the narrator aware of his own **biases**? Is the narrator reliable? How does the **narrator's reliability** (or unreliability) contribute to your interpretation of the text?

FIGURATIVE LANGUAGE: Word Choice, Imagery, and Symbols

15. The eggs become **symbolic** in the story. Explain the figurative associations of the eggs and how these associations contribute to your understanding of the text.

16. The narrator relies on parasitic **imagery** throughout the text. Choose two instances of this type of imagery and explain how they work together to develop an interpretation.

FIGURATIVE LANGUAGE: Comparisons

17. Butler sets the story in a family home within a dystopian society. Explain how this setting serves as a **metaphor** for domesticity and contributes to your interpretation of the story.

18. What human traits does Butler **personify** in the aliens? Explain the significance of Butler's having humans and aliens coexist.

19. In what sense is "Bloodchild" an **allegory**? How do its allegorical qualities contribute to your interpretation of the story?

IDEAS IN LITERATURE: Appearance and Reality

20. Science fiction and fantasy writers create alternative worlds where anything is possible. Oftentimes, when things are not possible in the real world, they are possible in the fantastical world. Think of an individual or group who may live in alternative realities. Is it possible for an individual or a group to function in both worlds simultaneously? Consider the implications and consequences as part of your response.

PUTTING IT ALL TOGETHER

21. "Bloodchild" is a *bildungsroman* or coming-of-age story. Choose a single pivotal moment in the psychological or moral development of Gan. Then explain how that single moment shapes your interpretation of the text.

IDEA BANK

Alienation

Anger

Apocalypse

Authority

Confusion

Critique

Depression

Despair

Despondency

Devastation

Dilemma

Disenchantment

Disillusionment

Disintegration

Distrust

Fragmentation

Frustration

Futility

Isolation

Loneliness

Loss

Vulnerability

Loss and Disillusionment

Modernist art and literature are often preoccupied with loss and disillusionment. In a literal sense, World War I had destroyed much of a continent — as well as much of a young European generation. But many of the war's survivors were lost too. The influential modernist writer and American expatriate Gertrude Stein (1874–1946) referred to those who came of age during the war as a "lost generation." The term came to connote not only a group of writers — Stein, Ernest Hemingway (1899–1961), F. Scott Fitzgerald (1896–1940), and John Dos Passos (1896–1970), among them — but also a set of themes: disillusionment, aimlessness, decadence, and the loss of meaning. That loss of meaning, in particular, preoccupied these authors.

The cynicism was widespread, underpinning both the aesthetics of the modernist movement and the hedonism and irreverence of the "Roaring Twenties." Fitzgerald captured this decadence in novels such as *The Great Gatsby* (1925), even if the glamorous pleasure-seeking always ends in tragedy. But decadence and escapism were only one response during the interwar period. Others sought new ways to recover lost meaning itself. For example, T. S. Eliot's landmark poem "The Waste Land" (1922) evokes a barren, contemporary postwar landscape, ruined both physically and spiritually.

Perhaps no modern novelist was more disillusioned by modernity than the English writer D. H. Lawrence (1885–1930). In his 1928 novel, *Lady Chatterley's*

The Son of Man is a 1964 work by Belgian surrealist painter René Magritte (1898–1967). At the most literal level, it depicts a man with an apple obstructing his face. But the painting has always inspired competing interpretations. Magritte's own explanation was cryptic, as he claimed that *The Son of Man* represents the "conflict . . . between the visible that is hidden and the visible that is present."

How does the painting suggest the disillusionment of individuals? Choose at least three specific elements of the painting and explain how these artistic choices contribute to your understanding of the painting.

Lover, the narrator says of the protagonist, "All the great words, it seemed to Connie, were canceled for her generation: love, joy, happiness, home." In his fiction, Lawrence often sought to counter modern alienation by recovering more primitive and authentic human connections, whether with each other or with nature. His explicit depictions of sexuality made him controversial in his time but also opened fiction to new modes of expression. In his 1926 story, "The Rocking-Horse Winner," Lawrence examines the antagonistic relationship between love and materialism — a conflict that we still struggle with today.

The modernist writers and artists continue to influence how we think about life, art, and humanity. As we do now, the people of that period dealt with a paradox: an era of information, progress, and technological sophistication that still felt chaotic, fragmented, and anxious. But they held out hope for humanity — and encourage us to investigate difficult truths and embrace the ambiguity of reality. At the same time, they held up art and literature as sources of both insight and escape, especially when they incorporated layers of significance from references to other works. If reality is complex, then art can reflect that complexity; if structure and meaning are difficult to find in the real world, then perhaps they can be found in aesthetically true and beautiful art. We can see a new iteration of this ideal in contemporary popular culture (among other places), whether in the moral ambiguity and narrative sophistication of prestige television such as *Stranger Things* and *Succession*, the appropriation of musical samples to create new songs and musical forms, or in the increasingly rich, complex world-building of contemporary video games.

Universal History Archive/UIG/Getty Images

◀ Edvard Munch's *The Scream* (1893) is one of five works in a series that creates a motif of existential loss and detachment.

How has the artist Edvard Munch conveyed modernist ideas in this work?

The Rocking-Horse Winner
D. H. Lawrence

THE TEXT IN CONTEXT

For many years, English writer, poet, and critic David Herbert Lawrence (1885–1930) was almost as well known for his work's supposed obscenity as for his work's literary merit. Lawrence grew up poor in a home filled with conflict between his parents. His early writing broke many literary conventions of the time, which often resulted in the censorship of his works. In fact, his most famous book, *Lady Chatterley's Lover* (1928), was banned in England until 1960. This novel explored themes that had preoccupied Lawrence's earlier fiction, as well: sexuality, vitality, industrialization, modernity, and the disillusionment caused by the devastation of World War I. The following tale, from his 1926 collection, *The Rocking-Horse Winner*, prompts readers to question whether money can buy happiness.

The Rocking-Horse Winner

There was a woman who was beautiful, who started with all the advantages, yet she had no luck. She married for love, and the love turned to dust. She had bonny children, yet
5   she felt they had been thrust upon her, and she could not love them. They looked at her coldly, as if they were finding fault with her. And hurriedly she felt she must cover up some fault in herself. Yet what it was that
10 she must cover up she never knew. Nevertheless, when her children were present, she always felt the centre of her heart go hard. This troubled her, and in her manner she was all the more gentle and anxious for her
15 children, as if she loved them very much. Only she herself knew that at the centre of her heart was a hard little place that could not feel love, no, not for anybody. Everybody else said of her: "She is such a good mother.
20 She adores her children." Only she herself, and her children themselves, knew it was not so. They read it in each other's eyes.

There were a boy and two little girls. They lived in a pleasant house, with a
25 garden, and they had discreet servants, and felt themselves superior to anyone in the neighbourhood.

Although they lived in style, they felt always an anxiety in the house. There was
30 never enough money. The mother had a small income, and the father had a small income, but not nearly enough for the social position which they had to keep up. The father went in to town to some office. But
35 though he had good prospects, these prospects never materialised. There was always the grinding sense of the shortage of money, though the style was always kept up.

At last the mother said, "I will see if I can't
40 make something." But she did not know where
to begin. She racked her brains, and tried this
thing and the other, but could not find anything successful. The failure made deep lines
come into her face. Her children were growing
45 up, they would have to go to school. There
must be more money, there must be more
money. The father, who was always very
handsome and expensive in his tastes,
seemed as if he never *would* be able to do any-
50 thing worth doing. And the mother, who had a
great belief in herself, did not succeed any better, and her tastes were just as expensive.

And so the house came to be haunted by
the unspoken phrase: *There must be more*
55 *money! There must be more money!* The children
could hear it all the time, though nobody
said it aloud. They heard it at Christmas,
when the expensive and splendid toys filled
the nursery. Behind the shining modern
60 rocking-horse, behind the smart doll's-house,
a voice would start whispering: "There *must*
be more money! There *must* be more money!"
And the children would stop playing, to listen for a moment. They would look into each
65 other's eyes, to see if they had all heard. And
each one saw in the eyes of the other two
that they too had heard. "There *must* be more
money! There *must* be more money!"

It came whispering from the springs of
70 the still-swaying rocking-horse, and even the
horse, bending his wooden, champing head,
heard it. The big doll, sitting so pink and
smirking in her new pram, could hear it
quite plainly, and seemed to be smirking all
75 the more self-consciously because of it. The
foolish puppy, too, that took the place of the
teddy-bear, he was looking so extraordinarily
foolish for no other reason but that he heard
the secret whisper all over the house: "There
80 *must* be more money."

Yet nobody ever said it aloud. The whisper
was everywhere, and therefore no one spoke
it. Just as no one ever says: "We are breathing!" in spite of the fact that breath is coming
85 and going all the time.

"Mother!" said the boy Paul one day. "Why
don't we keep a car of our own? Why do we
always use uncle's, or else a taxi?"

"Because we're the poor members of the
90 family," said the mother.

"But why *are* we, mother?"

"Well—I suppose," she said slowly and
bitterly, "it's because your father has no luck."

The boy was silent for some time.
95 "Is luck money, mother?" he asked, rather
timidly.

"No, Paul! Not quite. It's what causes you
to have money."

"Oh!" said Paul vaguely. "I thought when
100 Uncle Oscar said *filthy lucker*, it meant
money."

"*Filthy lucre* does mean money," said the
mother. "But it's lucre, not luck."

"Oh!" said the boy. "Then what is luck,
105 mother?"

"It's what causes you to have money. If
you're lucky you have money. That's why it's
better to be born lucky than rich. If you're
rich, you may lose your money. But if you're
110 lucky, you will always get more money."

"Oh! Will you! And is father not lucky?"

"Very unlucky, I should say," she said
bitterly.

The boy watched her with unsure eyes.
115 "Why?" he asked.

"I don't know. Nobody ever knows why
one person is lucky and another unlucky."

"Don't they? Nobody at all? Does *nobody*
know?"
120 "Perhaps God! But He never tells."

"He ought to, then. And aren't you lucky
either, mother?"

"I can't be, if I married an unlucky husband."

125   "But by yourself, aren't you?"

"I used to think I was, before I married. Now I think I am very unlucky indeed."

"Why?"

"Well—never mind! Perhaps I'm not

130   really," she said.

The child looked at her, to see if she meant it. But he saw, by the lines of her mouth, that she was only trying to hide something from him.

135   "Well, anyhow," he said stoutly, "I'm a lucky person."

"Why?" said his mother, with a sudden laugh.

He stared at her. He didn't even know why

140   he had said it.

"God told me," he asserted, brazening it out.

"I hope He did, dear!" she said, again with a laugh, but rather bitter.

145   "He did, mother!"

"Excellent!" said the mother, using one of her husband's exclamations.

The boy saw she did not believe him; or rather, that she paid no attention to his

150   assertion. This angered him somewhere, and made him want to compel her attention.

He went off by himself, vaguely, in a childish way, seeking for the clue to "luck." Absorbed, taking no heed of other people, he

155   went about with a sort of stealth, seeking inwardly for luck. He wanted luck, he wanted it, he wanted it. When the two girls were playing dolls, in the nursery, he would sit on his big rocking-horse, charging madly into

160   space, with a frenzy that made the little girls peer at him uneasily. Wildly the horse careered, the waving dark hair of the boy tossed, his eyes had a strange glare in them. The little girls dared not speak to him.

165   When he had ridden to the end of his mad little journey, he climbed down and stood in front of his rocking-horse, staring fixedly into its lowered face. Its red mouth was slightly open, its big eye was wide and

170   glassy bright.

"Now!" he would silently command the snorting steed. "Now take me to where there is luck! Now take me!"

And he would slash the horse on the neck

175   with the little whip he had asked Uncle Oscar for. He *knew* the horse could take him to where there was luck, if only he forced it. So he would mount again, and start on his furious ride, hoping at last to get there. He

180   knew he could get there.

"You'll break your horse, Paul!" said the nurse.

"He's always riding like that! I wish he'd leave off!" said his elder sister Joan.

185   But he only glared down on them in silence. Nurse gave him up. She could make nothing of him. Anyhow he was growing beyond her.

One day his mother and his Uncle Oscar came in when he was on one of his furious

190   rides. He did not speak to them.

"Hallo! you young jockey! Riding a winner?" said his uncle.

"Aren't you growing too big for a rocking-horse? You're not a very little boy any longer,

195   you know," said his mother.

But Paul only gave a blue glare from his big, rather close-set eyes. He would speak to nobody when he was in full tilt. His mother watched him with an anxious expression on

200   her face.

At last he suddenly stopped forcing his horse into the mechanical gallop, and slid down.

"Well, I got there!" he announced fiercely,

205   his blue eyes still flaring, and his sturdy long legs straddling apart.

"Where did you get to?" asked his mother.

"Where I wanted to go to," he flared back at her.

"That's right, son!" said Uncle Oscar. "Don't you stop till you get there. What's the horse's name?"

"He doesn't have a name," said the boy.

"Gets on without all right?" asked the uncle.

"Well, he has different names. He was called Sansovino last week."

"Sansovino, eh? Won the Ascot. How did you know his name?"

"He always talks about horse-races with Bassett," said Joan.

The uncle was delighted to find that his small nephew was posted with all the racing news. Bassett, the young gardener who had been wounded in the left foot in the war, and had got his present job through Oscar Cresswell, whose batman he had been, was a perfect blade of the "turf." He lived in the racing events, and the small boy lived with him.

Oscar Cresswell got it all from Bassett.

"Master Paul comes and asks me, so I can't do more than tell him, sir," said Bassett, his face terribly serious, as if he were speaking of religious matters.

"And does he ever put anything on a horse he fancies?"

"Well—I don't want to give him away—he's a young sport, a fine sport, sir. Would you mind asking him himself? He sort of takes a pleasure in it, and perhaps he'd feel I was giving him away, sir, if you don't mind."

Bassett was serious as a church.

The uncle went back to his nephew, and took him off for a ride in the car.

"Say, Paul, old man, do you ever put anything on a horse?" the uncle asked.

The boy watched the handsome man closely.

"Why, do you think I oughtn't to?" he parried.

"Not a bit of it! I thought perhaps you might give me a tip for the Lincoln."

The car sped on into the country, going down to Uncle Oscar's place in Hampshire.

"Honour bright?" said the nephew.

"Honour bright, son!" said the uncle.

"Well, then, Daffodil."

"Daffodil! I doubt it, sonny. What about Mirza?"

"I only know the winner," said the boy. "That's Daffodil!"

"Daffodil, eh?" There was a pause. Daffodil was an obscure horse comparatively.

"Uncle!"

"Yes, son?"

"You won't let it go any further, will you? I promised Bassett."

"Bassett be damned, old man! What's he got to do with it?"

"We're partners! We've been partners from the first! Uncle, he lent me my first five shillings, which I lost. I promised him, honour bright, it was only between me and him: only you gave me that ten-shilling note I started winning with, so I thought you were lucky. You won't let it go any further, will you?"

The boy gazed at his uncle from those big, hot, blue eyes, set rather close together. The uncle stirred and laughed uneasily.

"Right you are, son! I'll keep your tip private. Daffodil, eh! How much are you putting on him?"

"All except twenty pounds," said the boy. "I keep that in reserve."

The uncle thought it a good joke.

"You keep twenty pounds in reserve, do you, you young romancer? What are you betting, then?"

"I'm betting three hundred," said the boy gravely. "But it's between you and me, Uncle Oscar! Honour bright?"

The uncle burst into a roar of laughter.

295 "It's between you and me all right, you young Nat Gould," he said, laughing. "But where's your three hundred?"

"Bassett keeps it for me. We're partners."

"You are, are you! And what is Bassett
300 putting on Daffodil?"

"He won't go quite as high as I do, I expect. Perhaps he'll go a hundred and fifty."

"What, pennies?" laughed the uncle.

305 "Pounds," said the child, with a surprised look at his uncle. "Bassett keeps a bigger reserve than I do."

Between wonder and amusement, Uncle Oscar was silent. He pursued the matter no
310 further, but he determined to take his nephew with him to the Lincoln races.

"Now, son," he said, "I'm putting twenty on Mirza, and I'll put five for you on any horse you fancy. What's your pick?"

315 "Daffodil, uncle!"

"No, not the fiver on Daffodil!"

"I should if it was my own fiver," said the child.

"Good! Good! Right you are! A fiver for me
320 and a fiver for you on Daffodil."

The child had never been to a race-meeting before, and his eyes were blue fire. He pursed his mouth tight, and watched. A Frenchman just in front had put his money on Lancelot.
325 Wild with excitement, he flayed his arms up and down, yelling '*Lancelot! Lancelot!*' in his French accent.

Daffodil came in first, Lancelot second, Mirza third. The child, flushed and with eyes
330 blazing, was curiously serene. His uncle brought him five five-pound notes: four to one.

"What am I to do with these?" he cried, waving them before the boy's eyes.

335 "I suppose we'll talk to Bassett," said the boy. "I expect I have fifteen hundred now: and twenty in reserve: and this twenty."

His uncle studied him for some moments.

"Look here, son!" he said. "You're not seri-
340 ous about Bassett and that fifteen hundred, are you?"

"Yes, I am. But it's between you and me, uncle! Honour bright!"

"Honour bright all right, son! But I must
345 talk to Bassett."

"If you'd like to be a partner, uncle, with Bassett and me, we could all be partners. Only you'd have to promise, honour bright, uncle, not to let it go beyond us three. Bassett
350 and I are lucky, and you must be lucky, because it was your ten shillings I started winning with . . ."

Uncle Oscar took both Bassett and Paul into Richmond Park for an afternoon, and
355 there they talked.

"It's like this, you see, sir," Bassett said. "Master Paul would get me talking about racing events, spinning yarns, you know, sir. And he was always keen on knowing if I'd
360 made or if I'd lost. It's about a year since, now, that I put five shillings on Blush of Dawn for him: and we lost. Then the luck turned, with that ten shillings he had from you: that we put on Singhalese. And since
365 that time, it's been pretty steady, all things considering. What do you say, Master Paul?"

"We're all right when we're *sure*," said Paul. "It's when we're not quite sure that we go down."

370 "Oh, but we're careful then," said Bassett.

"But when are you *sure*?" smiled Uncle Oscar.

"It's Master Paul, sir," said Bassett, in a secret, religious voice. "It's as if he had it

375 from heaven. Like Daffodil now, for the Lincoln. That was as sure as eggs."

"Did you put anything on Daffodil?" asked Oscar Cresswell.

"Yes, sir. I made my bit."

380 "And my nephew?"

Bassett was obstinately silent, looking at Paul.

"I made twelve hundred, didn't I, Bassett? I told uncle I was putting three hundred on 385 Daffodil."

"That's right," said Bassett, nodding.

"But where's the money?" asked the uncle.

"I keep it safe locked up, sir. Master Paul, 390 he can have it any minute he likes to ask for it."

"What, fifteen hundred pounds?"

"And twenty! And *forty*, that is, with the twenty he made on the course."

395 "It's amazing!" said the uncle.

"If Master Paul offers you to be partners, sir, I would, if I were you: if you'll excuse me," said Bassett.

Oscar Cresswell thought about it.

400 "I'll see the money," he said.

They drove home again, and sure enough, Bassett came round to the garden-house with fifteen hundred pounds in notes. The twenty pounds reserve was left with Joe Glee, 405 in the Turf Commission deposit.

"You see, it's all right, uncle, when I'm *sure*! Then we go strong, for all we're worth. Don't we, Bassett?"

"We do that, Master Paul."

410 "And when are you sure?" said the uncle, laughing.

"Oh, well, sometimes I'm *absolutely* sure, like about Daffodil," said the boy; "and sometimes I have an idea; and sometimes I 415 haven't even an idea, have I, Bassett? Then we're careful, because we mostly go down."

"You do, do you! And when you're sure, like about Daffodil, what makes you sure, sonny?"

420 "Oh, well, I don't know," said the boy uneasily. "I'm sure, you know, uncle; that's all."

"It's as if he had it from heaven, sir," Bassett reiterated.

425 "I should say so!" said the uncle.

But he became a partner. And when the Leger was coming on, Paul was "sure" about Lively Spark, which was a quite inconsiderable horse. The boy insisted on putting a 430 thousand on the horse, Bassett went for five hundred, and Oscar Cresswell two hundred. Lively Spark came in first, and the betting had been ten to one against him. Paul had made ten thousand.

435 "You see," he said, "I was absolutely sure of him."

Even Oscar Cresswell had cleared two thousand.

"Look here, son," he said, "this sort of 440 thing makes me nervous."

"It needn't, uncle! Perhaps I shan't be sure again for a long time."

"But what are you going to do with your money?" asked the uncle.

445 "Of course," said the boy, "I started it for mother. She said she had no luck, because father is unlucky, so I thought if *I* was lucky, it might stop whispering."

"What might stop whispering?"

450 "Our house! I *hate* our house for whispering."

"What does it whisper?"

"Why—why"—the boy fidgeted—"why, I don't know! But it's always short of money, you know, uncle."

455 "I know it, son, I know it."

"You know people send mother writs, don't you, uncle?"

"I'm afraid I do," said the uncle.

"And then the house whispers like people
460 laughing at you behind your back. It's awful,
that is! I thought if I was lucky—"

"You might stop it," added the uncle.

The boy watched him with big blue eyes,
that had an uncanny cold fire in them, and
465 he said never a word.

"Well then!" said the uncle. "What are we
doing?"

"I shouldn't like mother to know I was
lucky," said the boy.

470   "Why not, son?"

"She'd stop me."

"I don't think she would."

"Oh!"—and the boy writhed in an odd
way—"I *don't* want her to know, uncle."

475   "All right, son! We'll manage it without
her knowing."

They managed it very easily. Paul, at the
other's suggestion, handed over five thousand pounds to his uncle, who deposited it
480 with the family lawyer, who was then to
inform Paul's mother that a relative had put
five thousand pounds into his hands, which
sum was to be paid out a thousand pounds
at a time, on the mother's birthday, for the
485 next five years.

"So she'll have a birthday present of a
thousand pounds for five successive years,"
said Uncle Oscar. "I hope it won't make it all
the harder for her later."

490   Paul's mother had her birthday in November. The house had been "whispering" worse
than ever lately, and even in spite of his luck,
Paul could not bear up against it. He was very
anxious to see the effect of the birthday let-
495 ter, telling his mother about the thousand
pounds.

When there were no visitors, Paul now
took his meals with his parents, as he was
beyond the nursery control. His mother went
500 into town nearly every day. She had discovered that she had an odd knack of sketching

furs and dress materials, so she worked
secretly in the studio of a friend who was the
chief "artist" for the leading drapers. She
505 drew the figures of ladies in furs and ladies
in silk and sequins for the newspaper advertisements. This young woman artist earned
several thousand pounds a year, but Paul's
mother only made several hundreds, and she
510 was again dissatisfied. She so wanted to be
first in something, and she did not succeed,
even in making sketches for drapery advertisements.

She was down to breakfast on the morn-
515 ing of her birthday. Paul watched her face as
she read her letters. He knew the lawyer's
letter. As his mother read it, her face hardened and became more expressionless. Then
a cold, determined look came on her mouth.
520 She hid the letter under the pile of others,
and said not a word about it.

"Didn't you have anything nice in the post
for your birthday, mother?" said Paul.

"Quite moderately nice," she said, her
525 voice cold and absent.

She went away to town without saying
more.

But in the afternoon Uncle Oscar
appeared. He said Paul's mother had had a
530 long interview with the lawyer, asking if the
whole five thousand could not be advanced
at once, as she was in debt.

"What do you think, uncle?" said the boy.

"I leave it to you, son."

535   "Oh, let her have it, then! We can get some
more with the other," said the boy.

"A bird in the hand is worth two in the
bush, laddie!" said Uncle Oscar.

"But I'm sure to *know* for the Grand
540 National; or the Lincolnshire; or else the
Derby. I'm sure to know for *one* of them,"
said Paul.

So Uncle Oscar signed the agreement,
and Paul's mother touched the whole five

545 thousand. Then something very curious happened. The voices in the house suddenly went mad, like a chorus of frogs on a spring evening. There were certain new furnishings, and Paul had a tutor. He was *really* going to Eton, his father's school, in the following autumn. There were flowers in the winter, and a blossoming of the luxury Paul's mother had been used to. And yet the voices in the house, behind the sprays of mimosa and almond-blossom, and from under the piles of iridescent cushions, simply trilled and screamed in a sort of ecstasy: "There *must* be more money! Oh-h-h! There *must* be more money! Oh, now, now-w! now-w-w—there *must* be more money!—more than ever! More than ever!"

It frightened Paul terribly. He studied away at his Latin and Greek with his tutors. But his intense hours were spent with Bassett. The Grand National had gone by: he had not "known," and had lost a hundred pounds. Summer was at hand. He was in agony for the Lincoln. But even for the Lincoln he didn't "know," and he lost fifty pounds. He became wild-eyed and strange, as if something were going to explode in him.

"Let it alone, son! Don't you bother about it!" urged Uncle Oscar. But it was as if the boy couldn't really hear what his uncle was saying.

"I've got to know for the Derby! I've *got* to know for the Derby!" the child reiterated, his big blue eyes blazing with a sort of madness.

His mother noticed how overwrought he was.

"You'd better go to the seaside. Wouldn't you like to go now to the seaside, instead of waiting? I think you'd better," she said, looking down at him anxiously, her heart curiously heavy because of him.

But the child lifted his uncanny blue eyes.

"I couldn't possibly go before the Derby, mother!" he said. "I couldn't possibly!"

"Why not?" she said, her voice becoming heavy when she was opposed. "Why not? You can still go from the seaside to see the Derby with your Uncle Oscar, if that's what you wish. No need for you to wait here. Besides, I think you care too much about these races. It's a bad sign. My family has been a gambling family, and you won't know till you grow up how much damage it has done. But it has done damage. I shall have to send Bassett away, and ask Uncle Oscar not to talk racing to you, unless you promise to be reasonable about it: go away to the seaside and forget it. You're all nerves!"

"I'll do what you like, mother, so long as you don't send me away till after the Derby," the boy said.

"Send you away from where? Just from this house?"

"Yes," he said, gazing at her.

"Why, you curious child, what makes you care about this house so much, suddenly? I never knew you loved it!"

He gazed at her without speaking. He had a secret within a secret, something he had not divulged, even to Bassett or to his Uncle Oscar.

But his mother, after standing undecided and a little bit sullen for some moments, said:

"Very well, then! Don't go to the seaside till after the Derby, if you don't wish it. But promise me you won't let your nerves go to pieces! Promise you won't think so much about horse-racing and *events,* as you call them!"

"Oh no!" said the boy, casually. "I won't think much about them, mother. You needn't worry. I wouldn't worry, mother, if I were you."

"If you were me and I were you," said his mother, "I wonder what we *should* do!"

"But you know you needn't worry, mother, don't you?" the boy repeated.

635 "I should be awfully glad to know it," she said wearily.

"Oh, well, you *can,* you know. I mean you *ought* to know you needn't worry!" he insisted.

640 "Ought I? Then I'll see about it," she said.

Paul's secret of secrets was his wooden horse, that which had no name. Since he was emancipated from a nurse and a nursery governess, he had had his rocking-horse 645 removed to his own bedroom at the top of the house.

"Surely you're too big for a rocking-horse!" his mother had remonstrated.

"Well, you see, mother, till I can have a *real* 650 horse, I like to have *some* sort of animal about," had been his quaint answer.

"Do you feel he keeps you company?" she laughed.

"Oh yes! He's very good, he always keeps 655 me company, when I'm there," said Paul.

So the horse, rather shabby, stood in an arrested prance in the boy's bedroom.

The Derby was drawing near, and the boy grew more and more tense. He hardly heard 660 what was spoken to him, he was very frail, and his eyes were really uncanny. His mother had sudden strange seizures of uneasiness about him. Sometimes, for half an hour, she would feel a sudden anxiety about him that 665 was almost anguish. She wanted to rush to him at once, and know he was safe.

Two nights before the Derby, she was at a big party in town, when one of her rushes of anxiety about her boy, her first-born, gripped 670 her heart till she could hardly speak. She fought with the feeling, might and main, for she believed in common-sense. But it was too strong. She had to leave the dance and go downstairs to telephone to the country. The 675 children's nursery governess was terribly surprised and startled at being rung up in the night.

"Are the children all right, Miss Wilmot?"

"Oh yes, they are quite all right."

680 "Master Paul? Is he all right?"

"He went to bed as right as a trivet. Shall I run up and look at him?"

"No!" said Paul's mother reluctantly. "No! Don't trouble. It's all right. Don't sit up. We 685 shall be home fairly soon." She did not want her son's privacy intruded upon.

"Very good," said the governess.

It was about one o'clock when Paul's mother and father drove up to their house. 690 All was still. Paul's mother went to her room and slipped off her white fur cloak. She had told her maid not to wait up for her. She heard her husband downstairs, mixing a whisky-and-soda.

695 And then, because of the strange anxiety at her heart, she stole upstairs to her son's room. Noiselessly she went along the upper corridor. Was there a faint noise? What was it?

She stood, with arrested muscles, outside 700 his door, listening. There was a strange, heavy, and yet not loud noise. Her heart stood still. It was a soundless noise, yet rush-ing and powerful. Something huge, in vio-lent, hushed motion. What was it? What in 705 God's Name was it? She ought to know. She felt that she *knew* the noise. She knew what it was.

Yet she could not place it. She couldn't say what it was. And on and on it went, like a 710 madness.

Softly, frozen with anxiety and fear, she turned the door-handle.

The room was dark. Yet in the space near the window, she heard and saw something 715 plunging to and fro. She gazed in fear and amazement.

Then suddenly she switched on the light, and saw her son, in his green pyjamas, madly surging on his rocking-horse. The blaze of light suddenly lit him up, as he urged the wooden horse, and lit her up, as she stood, blonde, in her dress of pale green and crystal, in the doorway.

"Paul!" she cried. "Whatever are you doing?"

"It's Malabar!" he screamed, in a powerful, strange voice. "It's Malabar!"

His eyes blazed at her for one strange and senseless second, as he ceased urging his wooden horse. Then he fell with a crash to the ground, and she, all her tormented motherhood flooding upon her, rushed to gather him up.

But he was unconscious, and unconscious he remained, with some brain-fever. He talked and tossed, and his mother sat stonily by his side.

"Malabar! It's Malabar! Bassett, Bassett, I *know*: it's Malabar!"

So the child cried, trying to get up and urge the rocking-horse that gave him his inspiration.

"What does he mean by Malabar?" asked the heart-frozen mother.

"I don't know," said the father, stonily.

"What does he mean by Malabar?" she asked her brother Oscar.

"It's one of the horses running for the Derby," was the answer.

And, in spite of himself, Oscar Cresswell spoke to Bassett, and himself put a thousand on Malabar: at fourteen to one.

The third day of the illness was critical: they were watching for a change. The boy, with his rather long, curly hair, was tossing ceaselessly on the pillow. He neither slept nor regained consciousness, and his eyes were like blue stones. His mother sat, feeling her heart had gone, turned actually into a stone.

In the evening, Oscar Cresswell did not come, but Bassett sent a message, saying could he come up for one moment, just one moment? Paul's mother was very angry at the intrusion, but on second thoughts she agreed. The boy was the same. Perhaps Bassett might bring him to consciousness.

The gardener, a shortish fellow with a little brown moustache and sharp little brown eyes, tiptoed into the room, touched his imaginary cap to Paul's mother, and stole to the bedside, staring with glittering, smallish eyes at the tossing, dying child.

"Master Paul!" he whispered. "Master Paul! Malabar came in first all right, a clean win. I did as you told me. You've made over seventy thousand pounds, you have; you've got over eighty thousand. Malabar came in all right, Master Paul."

"Malabar! Malabar! Did I say Malabar, mother? Did I say Malabar? Do you think I'm lucky, mother? I knew Malabar, didn't I? Over eighty thousand pounds! I call that lucky, don't you, mother? Over eighty thousand pounds! I knew, didn't I know I knew? Malabar came in all right. If I ride my horse till I'm sure, then I tell you, Basset, you can go as high as you like. Did you go for all you were worth, Bassett?"

"I went a thousand on it, Master Paul."

"I never told you, mother, that if I can ride my horse, and *get there*, then I'm absolutely sure—oh, absolutely! Mother, did I ever tell you? I *am* lucky!"

"No, you never did," said the mother.

But the boy died in the night.

And even as he lay dead, his mother heard her brother's voice saying to her: "My God, Hester, you're eighty-odd thousand to the good, and a poor devil of a son to the bad. But, poor devil, poor devil, he's best gone out of a life where he rides his rocking-horse to find a winner."

The Hobby Horse (oil on canvas) is an 1840 painting by American artist Robert Peckham.

What does the image suggest about the relationship between humans and nature? To what degree does this image reflect the themes of "The Rocking-Horse Winner"?

The Hobby Horse, c.1840 (oil on canvas)/North American, (19th century)/National Gallery of Art, Washington DC, USA/Bridgeman Images

CHARACTER

1. Which words, phrases, and details contribute to the **characterization** of the mother?

2. How are the children described in the story, both emotionally and psychologically?

3. In what way is Paul a **dynamic character**? Explain how Paul changes. What **circumstances** lead to these changes?

SETTING

4. What is the relationship between the society portrayed in the **setting** and the family in the story?

5. How does the description of the setting contribute to the **mood** of the story?

6. What values are revealed through the story's **setting**? How does Paul's behavior in the setting contribute to the development of his character and reveal a value?

STRUCTURE

7. How do Uncle Oscar and Paul differ in their attitudes about the rocking horse? How does this **contrast** create a tension in the text?

8. Why does Uncle Oscar partner with Paul in his gambling? What details about this partnership **foreshadow** Paul's fate?

9. Is the story ambiguous in its **resolution** and **conclusion**? How does the ending create **ambiguity**?

NARRATION

10. Who is the **narrator**? What is the point of view? How does the narrator's point of view affect the information and details presented to the reader?

11. What is the **tone** of the story? Choose specific words and phrases and explain how they reveal the tone.

12. What details and information can the narrator provide that other characters in the story cannot? How do these details contribute to your interpretation of the story?

FIGURATIVE LANGUAGE: Word Choice, Imagery, and Symbols

13. What does the rocking horse **symbolize**? How does this symbol contribute to your interpretation of the story?

14. How might the setting of the race track **symbolize** particular ideas and values? What are these ideas and values?

15. What **associations** does the author suggest with the description of Paul's eyes? How do these associations contribute to your understanding of Paul's character?

FIGURATIVE LANGUAGE: Comparisons

16. Choose a **simile** in the text and then explain how it contributes to your interpretation of the story.

17. The narrator uses **metaphor** to describe Hester's heart. What is the comparison in the metaphor? How does this comparison create figurative associations?

18. What are the voices that the narrator hears? When do they get louder? Explain the significance of this **personification** with evidence from the text.

IDEAS IN LITERATURE: Loss and Disillusionment

19. The story centers on luck. What role does luck play in opportunities for wealth and loss? How can success also lead to disillusionment?

PUTTING IT ALL TOGETHER

20. How do Paul's motivation and interactions with the minor characters contribute to the resolution and theme of the story?

A Hymn to Childhood
Li-Young Lee

©Blue Flower Arts, LLC

THE TEXT IN CONTEXT

Born in Jakarta, Indonesia, to Chinese parents, Li-Young Lee
(b. 1957) spent his early childhood in Hong Kong, Singapore,
and Japan before his family settled in western Pennsylvania in
1964. Much of Lee's work focuses on his family's experience
as political refugees, as well as his complex relationship with
his Chinese heritage. The following poem, or "hymn" (a spiritual
song of praise), is a reflection on childhood. It was published in
his 2008 collection *Behind My Eyes*, which captures some of
the pain, trauma, and grief that haunts his childhood memories.
Lee has published several collections of poetry, including *The
City in Which I Love You* (1990), *Book of My Nights* (2001), and
The Undressing (2018).

A Hymn to Childhood

Childhood? Which childhood?
The one that didn't last?
The one in which you learned to be afraid
of the boarded-up well in the backyard
5   and the ladder in the attic?

The one presided over by armed men
in ill-fitting uniforms
strolling the streets and alleys,
while loudspeakers declared a new era,
10   and the house around you grew bigger,
the rooms farther apart, with more and more
people missing?

The photographs whispered to each other
from their frames in the hallway.
15   The cooking pots said your name
each time you walked past the kitchen.

And you pretended to be dead with your sister
in games of rescue and abandonment.

You learned to lie still so long
20   the world seemed a play you viewed from the muffled
safety of a wing. Look! In
run the servants screaming, the soldiers shouting,
turning over the furniture,
smashing your mother's china.

25   Don't fall asleep.
Each act opens with your mother
reading a letter that makes her weep.
Each act closes with your father fallen
into the hands of Pharaoh.

30   Which childhood? The one that never ends? O you,
still a child, and slow to grow.
Still talking to God and thinking the snow
falling is the sound of God listening,
and winter is the high-ceilinged house
35   where God measures with one eye
an ocean wave in octaves and minutes,
and counts on many fingers
all the ways a child learns to say *Me*.

Which childhood?
40   The one from which you'll never escape? You,
so slow to know
what you know and don't know.
Still thinking you hear low song
in the wind in the eaves,
45   story in your breathing,
grief in the heard dove at evening,
and plentitude in the unseen bird
tolling at morning. Still slow to tell
memory from imagination, heaven
50   from here and now,
hell from here and now,
death from childhood, and both of them
from dreaming.

This photograph captures an adult standing in front of a larger image of her childhood self.

What does this image suggest about perceptions of memory? How does the photographer convey a perspective through this image?

Jonathan Kim/The Image Bank/Getty Images

CHARACTER

1. Who is the **speaker** and how does he interact with the other characters in the poem?

2. The **speaker** is reflecting on his childhood. How do his specific memories contribute to his **characterization**? How are the memories divided? In what ways do they represent a division in the speaker's identity?

3. What **epiphany** does the speaker experience at the end of the poem? Does this change his **perspective** on his childhood? Explain.

SETTING

4. How do the historical and cultural details at the beginning of "A Hymn to Childhood" convey one or more aspects of the poem's **setting**?

5. How does the **setting** change? Explain how this change suggests other movements, changes, or shifts in the poem.

6. How does the speaker interact with his surroundings? What do these interactions reveal about his home? How does this interaction contribute to the **mood** of the poem?

STRUCTURE

7. The speaker narrates specific events in the poem. Choose one and explain how it contributes to your interpretation of the text.

8. The poem includes many **contrasts**. Give an example and explain how this contrast contributes to the poem's complexity.

NARRATION

9. What aspects of the speaker's background contribute to his perceptions of the world?

10. How does the speaker's descriptive language convey his **narrative distance** from the events in the poem? Identify a specific example. How does this example affect your interpretation of the poem?

11. What is the speaker's **tone** toward childhood? Identify a specific example of diction, imagery, details, or other elements that contribute to that tone.

FIGURATIVE LANGUAGE: Word Choice, Imagery, and Symbols

12. The speaker's recollections reveal symbolic associations in the poem. Choose a **symbol** in the poem and explain its associations. How does it contribute to your understanding of the text?

13. Is the setting **symbolic**? Explain how the setting of the poem develops associations between a concept and a recognizable symbol for that concept.

14. What associations are implied by the **archetypal images** throughout stanza six? How do these associations contribute to your understanding of the poem?

FIGURATIVE LANGUAGE: Comparisons

15. Find an example of **personification** in "A Hymn to Childhood" and then explain the object of comparison and the human traits ascribed to that object. What is the effect of the personification? What does it contribute to your understanding of the text?

16. The last lines create a series of **comparisons**. How do the comparisons contribute to your interpretation of the poem?

IDEAS IN LITERATURE: Loss and Disillusionment

17. The poem expresses the speaker's sense of loss and disillusionment. Can you recall a time when you or another person experienced loss and disillusionment? How are the two concepts related? Can the loss of illusions be a good thing? Explain.

PUTTING IT ALL TOGETHER

18. Identify a juxtaposition or shift in the poem. Explain how this structural choice works with figurative elements to create a tension of values.

The Metamorphosis
Franz Kafka

THE TEXT IN CONTEXT

Perhaps no fiction writer has ever represented the absurdity, surrealism, and horror of modernity more vividly than Franz Kafka (1883–1924). The nightmarish quality of his work even spawned its own adjective: *Kafkaesque*, which denotes an atmosphere of anxiety, alienation, and powerlessness in the face of inscrutable authority. Born in Prague, now the capital of the Czech Republic, Kafka grew up in a German-speaking family and wrote all of his books in German. He practiced law and worked in business for much of his writing career; his legal training likely gave him insight into the bewildering intricacies of modern bureaucracy that suffuse his novels *The Trial* (1914) and *The Castle* (1926). In *The Metamorphosis* (1912), Kafka offers a macabre story that can be read allegorically or literally. He is also a progenitor of contemporary "body horror," a genre that emphasizes grotesque and horrific aspects of bodily transformation and decay.

The Metamorphosis

I

One morning, when Gregor Samsa woke from troubled dreams, he found himself transformed in his bed into a horrible ver-min. He lay on his armour-like back, and if
5 he lifted his head a little he could see his brown belly, slightly domed and divided by arches into stiff sections. The bedding was hardly able to cover it and seemed ready to slide off any moment. His many legs, pitifully
10 thin compared with the size of the rest of him, waved about helplessly as he looked.

"What's happened to me?" he thought. It wasn't a dream. His room, a proper human room although a little too small, lay peace-
15 fully between its four familiar walls. A collection of textile samples lay spread out on the table—Samsa was a travelling salesman—and above it there hung a picture that he had recently cut out of an illustrated
20 magazine and housed in a nice, gilded frame. It showed a lady fitted out with a fur hat and fur boa who sat upright, raising a heavy fur muff that covered the whole of her lower arm towards the viewer.

25   Gregor then turned to look out the win-dow at the dull weather. Drops of rain could be heard hitting the pane, which made him feel quite sad. "How about if I sleep a little bit longer and forget all this nonsense," he
30 thought, but that was something he was unable to do because he was used to sleep-ing on his right, and in his present state couldn't get into that position. However hard he threw himself onto his right, he always
35 rolled back to where he was. He must have

tried it a hundred times, shut his eyes so that
he wouldn't have to look at the floundering
legs, and only stopped when he began to feel
a mild, dull pain there that he had never felt
40 before.

"Oh, God," he thought, "what a strenuous
career it is that I've chosen! Travelling day in
and day out. Doing business like this takes
much more effort than doing your own busi-
45 ness at home, and on top of that there's the
curse of travelling, worries about making
train connections, bad and irregular food,
contact with different people all the time so
that you can never get to know anyone or
50 become friendly with them. It can all go to
Hell!" He felt a slight itch up on his belly;
pushed himself slowly up on his back
towards the headboard so that he could lift
his head better; found where the itch was,
55 and saw that it was covered with lots of little
white spots which he didn't know what to
make of; and when he tried to feel the place
with one of his legs he drew it quickly back
because as soon as he touched it he was
60 overcome by a cold shudder.

He slid back into his former position.
"Getting up early all the time," he thought, "it
makes you stupid. You've got to get enough
sleep. Other travelling salesmen live a life of
65 luxury. For instance, whenever I go back to
the guest house during the morning to copy
out the contract, these gentlemen are always
still sitting there eating their breakfasts. I
ought to just try that with my boss; I'd get
70 kicked out on the spot. But who knows,
maybe that would be the best thing for me. If
I didn't have my parents to think about I'd
have given in my notice a long time ago, I'd
have gone up to the boss and told him just
75 what I think, tell him everything I would, let
him know just what I feel. He'd fall right off
his desk! And it's a funny sort of business to

be sitting up there at your desk, talking down
at your subordinates from up there, espe-
80 cially when you have to go right up close
because the boss is hard of hearing. Well,
there's still some hope; once I've got the
money together to pay off my parents'
debt to him—another five or six years I
85 suppose—that's definitely what I'll do.
That's when I'll make the big change. First of
all though, I've got to get up, my train leaves
at five."

And he looked over at the alarm clock,
90 ticking on the chest of drawers. "God in
Heaven!" he thought. It was half past six and
the hands were quietly moving forwards, it
was even later than half past, more like
quarter to seven. Had the alarm clock not
95 rung? He could see from the bed that it had
been set for four o'clock as it should have
been; it certainly must have rung. Yes, but
was it possible to quietly sleep through that
furniture-rattling noise? True, he had not
100 slept peacefully, but probably all the more
deeply because of that. What should he do
now? The next train went at seven; if he
were to catch that he would have to rush like
mad and the collection of samples was still
105 not packed, and he did not at all feel particularly fresh and lively. And even if he did
catch the train he would not avoid his boss's
anger as the office assistant would have
been there to see the five o'clock train go, he
110 would have put in his report about Gregor's
not being there a long time ago. The office
assistant was the boss's man, spineless, and
with no understanding. What about if he
reported sick? But that would be extremely
115 strained and suspicious as in five years of
service Gregor had never once yet been ill.
His boss would certainly come round with
the doctor from the medical insurance
company, accuse his parents of having a lazy

120 son, and accept the doctor's recommendation not to make any claim as the doctor
believed that no-one was ever ill but that
many were workshy. And what's more, would
he have been entirely wrong in this case?

125 Gregor did in fact, apart from excessive
sleepiness after sleeping for so long, feel
completely well and even felt much hungrier
than usual.

He was still hurriedly thinking all this
130 through, unable to decide to get out of the
bed, when the clock struck quarter to seven.
There was a cautious knock at the door near
his head. "Gregor," somebody called—it was
his mother—"it's quarter to seven. Didn't
135 you want to go somewhere?" That gentle
voice! Gregor was shocked when he heard
his own voice answering, it could hardly be
recognised as the voice he had had before. As
if from deep inside him, there was a painful
140 and uncontrollable squeaking mixed in with
it, the words could be made out at first but
then there was a sort of echo which made
them unclear, leaving the hearer unsure
whether he had heard properly or not.
145 Gregor had wanted to give a full answer and
explain everything, but in the circumstances
contented himself with saying: "Yes, mother,
yes, thank-you, I'm getting up now." The
change in Gregor's voice probably could not
150 be noticed outside through the wooden door,
as his mother was satisfied with this explanation and shuffled away. But this short
conversation made the other members of
the family aware that Gregor, against their
155 expectations was still at home, and soon his
father came knocking at one of the side
doors, gently, but with his fist. "Gregor,
Gregor," he called, "what's wrong?" And
after a short while he called again with a
160 warning deepness in his voice: "Gregor!
Gregor!" At the other side door his sister

came plaintively: "Gregor? Aren't you well?
Do you need anything?" Gregor answered to
both sides: "I'm ready, now," making an effort
165 to remove all the strangeness from his voice
by enunciating very carefully and putting
long pauses between each, individual word.
His father went back to his breakfast, but his
sister whispered: "Gregor, open the door, I
170 beg of you." Gregor, however, had no thought
of opening the door, and instead congratu-
lated himself for his cautious habit, acquired
from his travelling, of locking all doors at
night even when he was at home.

175 The first thing he wanted to do was to get
up in peace without being disturbed, to get
dressed, and most of all to have his breakfast. Only then would he consider what to do
next, as he was well aware that he would not
180 bring his thoughts to any sensible conclusions by lying in bed. He remembered that he
had often felt a slight pain in bed, perhaps
caused by lying awkwardly, but that had
always turned out to be pure imagination
185 and he wondered how his imaginings would
slowly resolve themselves today. He did not
have the slightest doubt that the change in
his voice was nothing more than the first
sign of a serious cold, which was an occupa-
190 tional hazard for travelling salesmen.

It was a simple matter to throw off the
covers; he only had to blow himself up a little and they fell off by themselves. But it
became difficult after that, especially as he
195 was so exceptionally broad. He would have
used his arms and his hands to push himself
up; but instead of them he only had all those
little legs continuously moving in different
directions, and which he was moreover
200 unable to control. If he wanted to bend one
of them, then that was the first one that
would stretch itself out; and if he finally
managed to do what he wanted with that

leg, all the others seemed to be set free and would move about painfully. "This is something that can't be done in bed," Gregor said to himself, "so don't keep trying to do it."

The first thing he wanted to do was get the lower part of his body out of the bed, but he had never seen this lower part, and could not imagine what it looked like; it turned out to be too hard to move; it went so slowly; and finally, almost in a frenzy, when he carelessly shoved himself forwards with all the force he could gather, he chose the wrong direction, hit hard against the lower bedpost, and learned from the burning pain he felt that the lower part of his body might well, at present, be the most sensitive.

So then he tried to get the top part of his body out of the bed first, carefully turning his head to the side. This he managed quite easily, and despite its breadth and its weight, the bulk of his body eventually followed slowly in the direction of the head. But when he had at last got his head out of the bed and into the fresh air it occurred to him that if he let himself fall it would be a miracle if his head were not injured, so he became afraid to carry on pushing himself forward the same way. And he could not knock himself out now at any price; better to stay in bed than lose consciousness.

It took just as much effort to get back to where he had been earlier, but when he lay there sighing, and was once more watching his legs as they struggled against each other even harder than before, if that was possible, he could think of no way of bringing peace and order to this chaos. He told himself once more that it was not possible for him to stay in bed and that the most sensible thing to do would be to get free of it in whatever way he could at whatever sacrifice. At the same time, though, he did not forget to remind

himself that calm consideration was much better than rushing to desperate conclusions. At times like this he would direct his eyes to the window and look out as clearly as he could, but unfortunately, even the other side of the narrow street was enveloped in morning fog and the view had little confidence or cheer to offer him. "Seven o'clock, already," he said to himself when the clock struck again, "seven o'clock, and there's still a fog like this." And he lay there quietly a while longer, breathing lightly as if he perhaps expected the total stillness to bring things back to their real and natural state.

But then he said to himself: "Before it strikes quarter past seven I'll definitely have to have got properly out of bed. And by then somebody will have come round from work to ask what's happened to me as well, as they open up at work before seven o'clock." And so he set himself to the task of swinging the entire length of his body out of the bed all at the same time. If he succeeded in falling out of bed in this way and kept his head raised as he did so he could probably avoid injuring it. His back seemed to be quite hard, and probably nothing would happen to it falling onto the carpet. His main concern was for the loud noise he was bound to make, and which even through all the doors would probably raise concern if not alarm. But it was something that had to be risked.

When Gregor was already sticking half way out of the bed—the new method was more of a game than an effort, all he had to do was rock back and forth—it occurred to him how simple everything would be if somebody came to help him. Two strong people—he had his father and the maid in mind—would have been more than enough; they would only have to push their arms under the dome of his back, peel him away from the bed, bend down with the load and then be patient and careful as he swang over 290 onto the floor, where, hopefully, the little legs would find a use. Should he really call for help though, even apart from the fact that all the doors were locked? Despite all the difficulty he was in, he could not suppress a 295 smile at this thought.

After a while he had already moved so far across that it would have been hard for him to keep his balance if he rocked too hard. The time was now ten past seven and he would 300 have to make a final decision very soon. Then there was a ring at the door of the flat. "That'll be someone from work," he said to himself, and froze very still, although his little legs only became all the more lively as 305 they danced around. For a moment everything remained quiet. "They're not opening the door," Gregor said to himself, caught in some nonsensical hope. But then of course, the maid's firm steps went to the door as 310 ever and opened it. Gregor only needed to hear the visitor's first words of greeting and he knew who it was—the chief clerk himself. Why did Gregor have to be the only one condemned to work for a company where they 315 immediately became highly suspicious at the slightest shortcoming? Were all employees, every one of them, louts, was there not one of them who was faithful and devoted who would go so mad with pangs of conscience 320 that he couldn't get out of bed if he didn't spend at least a couple of hours in the morning on company business? Was it really not enough to let one of the trainees make enquiries—assuming enquiries were even 325 necessary—did the chief clerk have to come himself, and did they have to show the whole, innocent family that this was so suspicious that only the chief clerk could be trusted to have the wisdom to investigate it?

330 And more because these thoughts had made him upset than through any proper decision, he swang himself with all his force out of the bed. There was a loud thump, but it wasn't really a loud noise. His fall was softened a lit-335 tle by the carpet, and Gregor's back was also more elastic than he had thought, which made the sound muffled and not too noticeable. He had not held his head carefully enough, though, and hit it as he fell; annoyed 340 and in pain, he turned it and rubbed it against the carpet.

"Something's fallen down in there," said the chief clerk in the room on the left. Gregor tried to imagine whether something of the 345 sort that had happened to him today could ever happen to the chief clerk too; you had to concede that it was possible. But as if in gruff reply to this question, the chief clerk's firm footsteps in his highly polished boots could 350 now be heard in the adjoining room. From the room on his right, Gregor's sister whispered to him to let him know: "Gregor, the chief clerk is here." "Yes, I know," said Gregor to himself; but without daring to raise his 355 voice loud enough for his sister to hear him.

"Gregor," said his father now from the room to his left, "the chief clerk has come round and wants to know why you didn't leave on the early train. We don't know what 360 to say to him. And anyway, he wants to speak to you personally. So please open up this door. I'm sure he'll be good enough to forgive the untidiness of your room." Then the chief clerk called "Good morning, Mr. Samsa." "He 365 isn't well," said his mother to the chief clerk, while his father continued to speak through the door. "He isn't well, please believe me. Why else would Gregor have missed a train! The lad only ever thinks about the business. 370 It nearly makes me cross the way he never goes out in the evenings; he's been in town

for a week now but stayed home every evening. He sits with us in the kitchen and just
reads the paper or studies train timetables.
375 His idea of relaxation is working with his
fretsaw. He's made a little frame, for
instance, it only took him two or three evenings, you'll be amazed how nice it is; it's
hanging up in his room; you'll see it as soon
380 as Gregor opens the door. Anyway, I'm glad
you're here; we wouldn't have been able to
get Gregor to open the door by ourselves;
he's so stubborn; and I'm sure he isn't well,
he said this morning that he is, but he isn't."
385 "I'll be there in a moment," said Gregor
slowly and thoughtfully, but without moving
so that he would not miss any word of the
conversation. "Well I can't think of any other
way of explaining it, Mrs. Samsa," said the
390 chief clerk, "I hope it's nothing serious. But
on the other hand, I must say that if we people in commerce ever become slightly unwell
then, fortunately or unfortunately as you
like, we simply have to overcome it because
395 of business considerations." "Can the chief
clerk come in to see you now then?," asked
his father impatiently, knocking at the door
again. "No," said Gregor. In the room on his
right there followed a painful silence; in the
400 room on his left his sister began to cry.

So why did his sister not go and join the
others? She had probably only just got up
and had not even begun to get dressed. And
why was she crying? Was it because he had
405 not got up, and had not let the chief clerk in,
because he was in danger of losing his job
and if that happened his boss would once
more pursue their parents with the same
demands as before? There was no need to
410 worry about things like that yet. Gregor was
still there and had not the slightest intention
of abandoning his family. For the time being
he just lay there on the carpet, and no-one

who knew the condition he was in would
415 seriously have expected him to let the chief
clerk in. It was only a minor discourtesy, and
a suitable excuse could easily be found for it
later on, it was not something for which
Gregor could be sacked on the spot. And it
420 seemed to Gregor much more sensible to
leave him now in peace instead of disturbing
him with talking at him and crying. But the
others didn't know what was happening,
they were worried, that would excuse their
425 behaviour.

The chief clerk now raised his voice,
"Mr. Samsa," he called to him, "what is
wrong? You barricade yourself in your room,
give us no more than yes or no for an
430 answer, you are causing serious and unnecessary concern to your parents and you
fail—and I mention this just by the way—
you fail to carry out your business duties in a
way that is quite unheard of. I'm speaking
435 here on behalf of your parents and of your
employer, and really must request a clear
and immediate explanation. I am astonished,
quite astonished. I thought I knew you as a
calm and sensible person, and now you sud-
440 denly seem to be showing off with peculiar
whims. This morning, your employer did
suggest a possible reason for your failure to
appear, it's true—it had to do with the
money that was recently entrusted to
445 you—but I came near to giving him my word
of honour that that could not be the right
explanation. But now that I see your incomprehensible stubbornness I no longer feel
any wish whatsoever to intercede on your
450 behalf. And nor is your position all that
secure. I had originally intended to say all
this to you in private, but since you cause me
to waste my time here for no good reason I
don't see why your parents should not also
455 learn of it. Your turnover has been very

unsatisfactory of late; I grant you that it's not the time of year to do especially good business, we recognise that; but there simply is no time of year to do no business at all,
460 Mr. Samsa, we cannot allow there to be."

"But Sir," called Gregor, beside himself and forgetting all else in the excitement, "I'll open up immediately, just a moment. I'm slightly unwell, an attack of dizziness, I
465 haven't been able to get up. I'm still in bed now. I'm quite fresh again now, though. I'm just getting out of bed. Just a moment. Be patient! It's not quite as easy as I'd thought. I'm quite alright now, though. It's shocking,
470 what can suddenly happen to a person! I was quite alright last night, my parents know about it, perhaps better than me, I had a small symptom of it last night already. They must have noticed it. I don't know why I
475 didn't let you know at work! But you always think you can get over an illness without staying at home. Please, don't make my parents suffer! There's no basis for any of the accusations you're making; nobody's ever
480 said a word to me about any of these things. Maybe you haven't read the latest contracts I sent in. I'll set off with the eight o'clock train, as well, these few hours of rest have given me strength. You don't need to wait,
485 sir; I'll be in the office soon after you, and please be so good as to tell that to the boss and recommend me to him!"

And while Gregor gushed out these words, hardly knowing what he was saying, he
490 made his way over to the chest of drawers— this was easily done, probably because of the practise he had already had in bed—where he now tried to get himself upright. He really did want to open the door, really did want to
495 let them see him and to speak with the chief clerk; the others were being so insistent, and he was curious to learn what they would say

when they caught sight of him. If they were shocked then it would no longer be Gregor's
500 responsibility and he could rest. If, however, they took everything calmly he would still have no reason to be upset, and if he hurried he really could be at the station for eight o'clock. The first few times he tried to climb
505 up on the smooth chest of drawers he just slid down again, but he finally gave himself one last swing and stood there upright; the lower part of his body was in serious pain but he no longer gave any attention to it.
510 Now he let himself fall against the back of a nearby chair and held tightly to the edges of it with his little legs. By now he had also calmed down, and kept quiet so that he could listen to what the chief clerk was
515 saying.

"Did you understand a word of all that?" the chief clerk asked his parents, "surely he's not trying to make fools of us." "Oh, God!" called his mother, who was already
520 in tears, "he could be seriously ill and we're making him suffer. Grete! Grete!" she then cried. "Mother?" his sister called from the other side. They communicated across Gregor's room. "You'll have to go for the
525 doctor straight away. Gregor is ill. Quick, get the doctor. Did you hear the way Gregor spoke just now?" "That was the voice of an animal," said the chief clerk, with a calmness that was in contrast with his mother's
530 screams. "Anna! Anna!" his father called into the kitchen through the entrance hall, clapping his hands, "get a locksmith here, now!" And the two girls, their skirts swishing, immediately ran out through the hall,
535 wrenching open the front door of the flat as they went. How had his sister managed to get dressed so quickly? There was no sound of the door banging shut again; they must have left it open; people often do in

540 homes where something awful has happened.

Gregor, in contrast, had become much calmer. So they couldn't understand his words any more, although they seemed clear 545 enough to him, clearer than before—perhaps his ears had become used to the sound. They had realised, though, that there was some-thing wrong with him, and were ready to help. The first response to his situation had 550 been confident and wise, and that made him feel better. He felt that he had been drawn back in among people, and from the doctor and the locksmith he expected great and surprising achievements—although he did 555 not really distinguish one from the other. Whatever was said next would be crucial, so, in order to make his voice as clear as possi-ble, he coughed a little, but taking care to do this not too loudly as even this might well 560 sound different from the way that a human coughs and he was no longer sure he could judge this for himself. Meanwhile, it had become very quiet in the next room. Perhaps his parents were sat at the table whispering 565 with the chief clerk, or perhaps they were all pressed against the door and listening.

Gregor slowly pushed his way over to the door with the chair. Once there he let go of it and threw himself onto the door, holding 570 himself upright against it using the adhesive on the tips of his legs. He rested there a little while to recover from the effort involved and then set himself to the task of turning the key in the lock with his mouth. He seemed, 575 unfortunately, to have no proper teeth—how was he, then, to grasp the key?—but the lack of teeth was, of course, made up for with a very strong jaw; using the jaw, he really was able to start the key turning, ignoring the 580 fact that he must have been causing some kind of damage as a brown fluid came from his mouth, flowed over the key and dripped onto the floor. "Listen," said the chief clerk in the next room, "he's turning the key." Gregor 585 was greatly encouraged by this; but they all should have been calling to him, his father and his mother too: "Well done, Gregor," they should have cried, "keep at it, keep hold of the lock!" And with the idea that they were 590 all excitedly following his efforts, he bit on the key with all his strength, paying no attention to the pain he was causing himself. As the key turned round he turned around the lock with it, only holding himself upright 595 with his mouth, and hung onto the key or pushed it down again with the whole weight of his body as needed. The clear sound of the lock as it snapped back was Gregor's sign that he could break his concentration, and as 600 he regained his breath he said to himself: "So, I didn't need the locksmith after all." Then he lay his head on the handle of the door to open it completely.

Because he had to open the door in this 605 way, it was already wide open before he could be seen. He had first to slowly turn himself around one of the double doors, and he had to do it very carefully if he did not want to fall flat on his back before entering 610 the room. He was still occupied with this dif-ficult movement, unable to pay attention to anything else, when he heard the chief clerk exclaim a loud "Oh!," which sounded like the soughing of the wind. Now he also saw 615 him—he was the nearest to the door—his hand pressed against his open mouth and slowly retreating as if driven by a steady and invisible force. Gregor's mother, her hair still dishevelled from bed despite the chief clerk's 620 being there, looked at his father. Then she unfolded her arms, took two steps forward towards Gregor and sank down onto the floor into her skirts that spread themselves out

625 around her as her head disappeared down onto her breast. His father looked hostile, and clenched his fists as if wanting to knock Gregor back into his room. Then he looked uncertainly round the living room, covered his eyes with his hands and wept so that his

630 powerful chest shook.

So Gregor did not go into the room, but leant against the inside of the other door which was still held bolted in place. In this way only half of his body could be seen,

635 along with his head above it which he leant over to one side as he peered out at the others. Meanwhile the day had become much lighter; part of the endless, grey-black building on the other side of the street—which

640 was a hospital—could be seen quite clearly with the austere and regular line of windows piercing its façade; the rain was still falling, now throwing down large, individual droplets which hit the ground one at a time. The

645 washing up from breakfast lay on the table; there was so much of it because, for Gregor's father, breakfast was the most important meal of the day and he would stretch it out for several hours as he sat reading a number

650 of different newspapers. On the wall exactly opposite there was photograph of Gregor when he was a lieutenant in the army, his sword in his hand and a carefree smile on his face as he called forth respect for his uni-

655 form and bearing. The door to the entrance hall was open and as the front door of the flat was also open he could see onto the landing and the stairs where they began their way down below.

660 "Now, then," said Gregor, well aware that he was the only one to have kept calm, "I'll get dressed straight away now, pack up my samples and set off. Will you please just let me leave? You can see," he said to the chief

665 clerk, "that I'm not stubborn and I like to do my job; being a commercial traveller is arduous but without travelling I couldn't earn my living. So where are you going, in to the office? Yes? Will you report everything accu-

670 rately, then? It's quite possible for someone to be temporarily unable to work, but that's just the right time to remember what's been achieved in the past and consider that later on, once the difficulty has been removed, he

675 will certainly work with all the more diligence and concentration. You're well aware that I'm seriously in debt to our employer as well as having to look after my parents and my sister, so that I'm trapped in a difficult

680 situation, but I will work my way out of it again. Please don't make things any harder for me than they are already, and don't take sides against me at the office. I know that nobody likes the travellers. They think we

685 earn an enormous wage as well as having a soft time of it. That's just prejudice but they have no particular reason to think better of it. But you, sir, you have a better overview than the rest of the staff, in fact, if I can say

690 this in confidence, a better overview than the boss himself—it's very easy for a businessman like him to make mistakes about his employees and judge them more harshly than he should. And you're also well aware

695 that we travellers spend almost the whole year away from the office, so that we can very easily fall victim to gossip and chance and groundless complaints, and it's almost impossible to defend yourself from that sort

700 of thing, we don't usually even hear about them, or if at all it's when we arrive back home exhausted from a trip, and that's when we feel the harmful effects of what's been going on without even knowing what caused

705 them. Please, don't go away, at least first say something to show that you grant that I'm at least partly right!"

But the chief clerk had turned away as soon as Gregor had started to speak, and, with protruding lips, only stared back at him over his trembling shoulders as he left. He did not keep still for a moment while Gregor was speaking, but moved steadily towards the door without taking his eyes off him. He moved very gradually, as if there had been some secret prohibition on leaving the room. It was only when he had reached the entrance hall that he made a sudden movement, drew his foot from the living room, and rushed forward in a panic. In the hall, he stretched his right hand far out towards the stairway as if out there, there were some supernatural force waiting to save him.

Gregor realised that it was out of the question to let the chief clerk go away in this mood if his position in the firm was not to be put into extreme danger. That was something his parents did not understand very well; over the years, they had become convinced that this job would provide for Gregor for his entire life, and besides, they had so much to worry about at present that they had lost sight of any thought for the future. Gregor, though, did think about the future. The chief clerk had to be held back, calmed down, convinced and finally won over; the future of Gregor and his family depended on it! If only his sister were here! She was clever; she was already in tears while Gregor was still lying peacefully on his back. And the chief clerk was a lover of women, surely she could persuade him; she would close the front door in the entrance hall and talk him out of his shocked state. But his sister was not there, Gregor would have to do the job himself. And without considering that he still was not familiar with how well he could move about in his present state, or that his speech still might not—or probably would

not—be understood, he let go of the door; pushed himself through the opening; tried to reach the chief clerk on the landing who, ridiculously, was holding on to the banister with both hands; but Gregor fell immediately over and, with a little scream as he sought something to hold onto, landed on his numerous little legs. Hardly had that happened than, for the first time that day, he began to feel alright with his body; the little legs had the solid ground under them; to his pleasure, they did exactly as he told them; they were even making the effort to carry him where he wanted to go; and he was soon believing that all his sorrows would soon be finally at an end. He held back the urge to move but swayed from side to side as he crouched there on the floor. His mother was not far away in front of him and seemed, at first, quite engrossed in herself, but then she suddenly jumped up with her arms outstretched and her fingers spread shouting: "Help, for pity's sake, Help!" The way she held her head suggested she wanted to see Gregor better, but the unthinking way she was hurrying backwards showed that she did not; she had forgotten that the table was behind her with all the breakfast things on it; when she reached the table she sat quickly down on it without knowing what she was doing; without even seeming to notice that the coffee pot had been knocked over and a gush of coffee was pouring down onto the carpet.

"Mother, mother," said Gregor gently, looking up at her. He had completely forgotten the chief clerk for the moment, but could not help himself snapping in the air with his jaws at the sight of the flow of coffee. That set his mother screaming anew, she fled from the table and into the arms of his father as he rushed towards her. Gregor, though, had no time to spare for his parents now; the chief clerk had already reached the stairs; with his chin on the banister, he 795 looked back for the last time. Gregor made a run for him; he wanted to be sure of reaching him; the chief clerk must have expected something, as he leapt down several steps at once and disappeared; his shouts resounding 800 all around the staircase. The flight of the chief clerk seemed, unfortunately, to put Gregor's father into a panic as well. Until then he had been relatively self controlled, but now, instead of running after the chief 805 clerk himself, or at least not impeding Gregor as he ran after him, Gregor's father seized the chief clerk's stick in his right hand (the chief clerk had left it behind on a chair, along with his hat and overcoat), picked up a large 810 newspaper from the table with his left, and used them to drive Gregor back into his room, stamping his foot at him as he went. Gregor's appeals to his father were of no help, his appeals were simply not under- 815 stood, however much he humbly turned his head his father merely stamped his foot all the harder. Across the room, despite the chilly weather, Gregor's mother had pulled open a window, leant far out of it and 820 pressed her hands to her face. A strong draught of air flew in from the street towards the stairway, the curtains flew up, the news- papers on the table fluttered and some of them were blown onto the floor. Nothing 825 would stop Gregor's father as he drove him back, making hissing noises at him like a wild man. Gregor had never had any practice in moving backwards and was only able to go very slowly. If Gregor had only been allowed 830 to turn round he would have been back in his room straight away, but he was afraid that if he took the time to do that his father would become impatient, and there was the

threat of a lethal blow to his back or head 835 from the stick in his father's hand any moment. Eventually, though, Gregor realised that he had no choice as he saw, to his dis- gust, that he was quite incapable of going backwards in a straight line; so he began, as 840 quickly as possible and with frequent anx- ious glances at his father, to turn himself round. It went very slowly, but perhaps his father was able to see his good intentions as he did nothing to hinder him, in fact now 845 and then he used the tip of his stick to give directions from a distance as to which way to turn. If only his father would stop that unbearable hissing! It was making Gregor quite confused. When he had nearly finished 850 turning round, still listening to that hissing, he made a mistake and turned himself back a little the way he had just come. He was pleased when he finally had his head in front of the doorway, but then saw that it 855 was too narrow, and his body was too broad to get through it without further difficulty. In his present mood, it obviously did not occur to his father to open the other of the double doors so that Gregor would have enough 860 space to get through. He was merely fixed on the idea that Gregor should be got back into his room as quickly as possible. Nor would he ever have allowed Gregor the time to get himself upright as preparation for getting 865 through the doorway. What he did, making more noise than ever, was to drive Gregor forwards all the harder as if there had been nothing in the way; it sounded to Gregor as if there was now more than one father behind 870 him; it was not a pleasant experience, and Gregor pushed himself into the doorway without regard for what might happen. One side of his body lifted itself, he lay at an angle in the doorway, one flank scraped on 875 the white door and was painfully injured,

leaving vile brown flecks on it, soon he was stuck fast and would not have been able to move at all by himself, the little legs along one side hung quivering in the air while
880 those on the other side were pressed painfully against the ground. Then his father gave him a hefty shove from behind which released him from where he was held and sent him flying, and heavily bleeding, deep
885 into his room. The door was slammed shut with the stick, then, finally, all was quiet.

II

It was not until it was getting dark that evening that Gregor awoke from his deep and coma-like sleep. He would have woken soon
890 afterwards anyway even if he hadn't been disturbed, as he had had enough sleep and felt fully rested. But he had the impression that some hurried steps and the sound of the door leading into the front room being care-
895 fully shut had woken him. The light from the electric street lamps shone palely here and there onto the ceiling and tops of the furniture, but down below, where Gregor was, it was dark. He pushed himself over to the
900 door, feeling his way clumsily with his antennae—of which he was now beginning to learn the value—in order to see what had been happening there. The whole of his left side seemed like one, painfully stretched
905 scar, and he limped badly on his two rows of legs. One of the legs had been badly injured in the events of that morning—it was nearly a miracle that only one of them had been—and dragged along lifelessly.
910   It was only when he had reached the door that he realised what it actually was that had drawn him over to it; it was the smell of something to eat. By the door there was a dish filled with sweetened milk with little
915 pieces of white bread floating in it. He was so

pleased he almost laughed, as he was even hungrier than he had been that morning, and immediately dipped his head into the milk, nearly covering his eyes with it. But he
920 soon drew his head back again in disappointment; not only did the pain in his tender left side make it difficult to eat the food—he was only able to eat if his whole body worked together as a snuffling whole—but the milk
925 did not taste at all nice. Milk like this was normally his favourite drink, and his sister had certainly left it there for him because of that, but he turned, almost against his own will, away from the dish and crawled back
930 into the centre of the room.

    Through the crack in the door, Gregor could see that the gas had been lit in the living room. His father at this time would normally be sat with his evening paper, read-
935 ing it out in a loud voice to Gregor's mother, and sometimes to his sister, but there was now not a sound to be heard. Gregor's sister would often write and tell him about this reading, but maybe his father had lost the
940 habit in recent times. It was so quiet all around too, even though there must have been somebody in the flat. "What a quiet life it is the family lead," said Gregor to himself, and, gazing into the darkness, felt a great
945 pride that he was able to provide a life like that in such a nice home for his sister and parents. But what now, if all this peace and wealth and comfort should come to a horrible and frightening end? That was something
950 that Gregor did not want to think about too much, so he started to move about, crawling up and down the room.

    Once during that long evening, the door on one side of the room was opened very
955 slightly and hurriedly closed again; later on the door on the other side did the same; it seemed that someone needed to enter the

room but thought better of it. Gregor went
and waited immediately by the door,
960 resolved either to bring the timorous visitor
into the room in some way or at least to find
out who it was; but the door was opened no
more that night and Gregor waited in vain.
The previous morning while the doors were
965 locked everyone had wanted to get in there
to him, but now, now that he had opened up
one of the doors and the other had clearly
been unlocked some time during the day,
no-one came, and the keys were in the
970 other sides.

It was not until late at night that the
gaslight in the living room was put out, and
now it was easy to see that his parents and
sister had stayed awake all that time, as they
975 all could be distinctly heard as they went
away together on tip-toe. It was clear that
no-one would come into Gregor's room any
more until morning; that gave him plenty of
time to think undisturbed about how he
980 would have to re-arrange his life. For some
reason, the tall, empty room where he was
forced to remain made him feel uneasy as he
lay there flat on the floor, even though he
had been living in it for five years. Hardly
985 aware of what he was doing other than a
slight feeling of shame, he hurried under the
couch. It pressed down on his back a little,
and he was no longer able to lift his head,
but he nonetheless felt immediately at ease
990 and his only regret was that his body was too
broad to get it all underneath.

He spent the whole night there. Some of
the time he passed in a light sleep, although
he frequently woke from it in alarm because
995 of his hunger, and some of the time was
spent in worries and vague hopes which,
however, always led to the same conclusion:
for the time being he must remain calm,
he must show patience and the greatest

1000 consideration so that his family could bear
the unpleasantness that he, in his present
condition, was forced to impose on them.

Gregor soon had the opportunity to test
the strength of his decisions, as early the
1005 next morning, almost before the night had
ended, his sister, nearly fully dressed, opened
the door from the front room and looked
anxiously in. She did not see him straight
away, but when she did notice him under the
1010 couch—he had to be somewhere, for God's
sake, he couldn't have flown away—she was
so shocked that she lost control of herself
and slammed the door shut again from outside. But she seemed to regret her behaviour,
1015 as she opened the door again straight away
and came in on tip-toe as if entering the
room of someone seriously ill or even of a
stranger. Gregor had pushed his head forward, right to the edge of the couch, and
1020 watched her. Would she notice that he had
left the milk as it was, realise that it was not
from any lack of hunger and bring him in
some other food that was more suitable?
If she didn't do it herself he would rather
1025 go hungry than draw her attention to it,
although he did feel a terrible urge to rush
forward from under the couch, throw himself
at his sister's feet and beg her for something
good to eat. However, his sister noticed the
1030 full dish immediately and looked at it and
the few drops of milk splashed around it
with some surprise. She immediately picked
it up—using a rag, not her bare hands—and
carried it out. Gregor was extremely curious
1035 as to what she would bring in its place, imagining the wildest possibilities, but he never
could have guessed what his sister, in her
goodness, actually did bring. In order to test
his taste, she brought him a whole selection
1040 of things, all spread out on an old newspaper. There were old, half-rotten vegetables;

bones from the evening meal, covered in white sauce that had gone hard; a few raisins and almonds; some cheese that Gregor had declared inedible two days before; a dry roll and some bread spread with butter and salt. As well as all that she had poured some water into the dish, which had probably been permanently set aside for Gregor's use, and placed it beside them. Then, out of consideration for Gregor's feelings, as she knew that he would not eat in front of her, she hurried out again and even turned the key in the lock so that Gregor would know he could make things as comfortable for himself as he liked. Gregor's little legs whirred, at last he could eat. What's more, his injuries must already have completely healed as he found no difficulty in moving. This amazed him, as more than a month earlier he had cut his finger slightly with a knife, he thought of how his finger had still hurt the day before yesterday. "Am I less sensitive than I used to be, then?," he thought, and was already sucking greedily at the cheese which had immediately, almost compellingly, attracted him much more than the other foods on the newspaper. Quickly one after another, his eyes watering with pleasure, he consumed the cheese, the vegetables and the sauce; the fresh foods, on the other hand, he didn't like at all, and even dragged the things he did want to eat a little way away from them because he couldn't stand the smell. Long after he had finished eating and lay lethargic in the same place, his sister slowly turned the key in the lock as a sign to him that he should withdraw. He was immediately startled, although he had been half asleep, and he hurried back under the couch. But he needed great self-control to stay there even for the short time that his sister was in the room, as eating so much food had rounded out his body a little and he could hardly breathe in that narrow space. Half suffocating, he watched with bulging eyes as his sister unselfconsciously took a broom and swept up the left-overs, mixing them in with the food he had not even touched at all as if it could not be used any more. She quickly dropped it all into a bin, closed it with its wooden lid, and carried everything out. She had hardly turned her back before Gregor came out again from under the couch and stretched himself.

This was how Gregor received his food each day now, once in the morning while his parents and the maid were still asleep, and the second time after everyone had eaten their meal at midday as his parents would sleep for a little while then as well, and Gregor's sister would send the maid away on some errand. Gregor's father and mother certainly did not want him to starve either, but perhaps it would have been more than they could stand to have any more experience of his feeding than being told about it, and perhaps his sister wanted to spare them what distress she could as they were indeed suffering enough.

It was impossible for Gregor to find out what they had told the doctor and the locksmith that first morning to get them out of the flat. As nobody could understand him, nobody, not even his sister, thought that he could understand them, so he had to be content to hear his sister's sighs and appeals to the saints as she moved about his room. It was only later, when she had become a little more used to everything—there was, of course, no question of her ever becoming fully used to the situation—that Gregor would sometimes catch a friendly comment, or at least a comment that could be construed as friendly. "He's enjoyed his dinner today," she might say when he had diligently cleared away all the food left for him, or if he left most of it, which slowly became more and more frequent, she would often say, sadly, "now everything's just been left 1130 there again."

Although Gregor wasn't able to hear any news directly he did listen to much of what was said in the next rooms, and whenever he heard anyone speaking he would scurry 1135 straight to the appropriate door and press his whole body against it. There was seldom any conversation, especially at first, that was not about him in some way, even if only in secret. For two whole days, all the talk at 1140 every mealtime was about what they should do now; but even between meals they spoke about the same subject as there were always at least two members of the family at home—nobody wanted to be at home by 1145 themselves and it was out of the question to leave the flat entirely empty. And on the very first day the maid had fallen to her knees and begged Gregor's mother to let her go without delay. It was not very clear how 1150 much she knew of what had happened but she left within a quarter of an hour, tearfully thanking Gregor's mother for her dismissal as if she had done her an enormous service. She even swore emphatically not to tell any-1155 one the slightest about what had happened, even though no-one had asked that of her.

Now Gregor's sister also had to help his mother with the cooking; although that was not so much bother as no-one ate very much. 1160 Gregor often heard how one of them would unsuccessfully urge another to eat, and receive no more answer than "no thanks, I've had enough" or something similar. No-one drank very much either. His sister would 1165 sometimes ask his father whether he would like a beer, hoping for the chance to go and fetch it herself. When his father then said

nothing she would add, so that he would not feel selfish, that she could send the house-1170 keeper for it, but then his father would close the matter with a big, loud "No," and no more would be said.

Even before the first day had come to an end, his father had explained to Gregor's 1175 mother and sister what their finances and prospects were. Now and then he stood up from the table and took some receipt or doc-ument from the little cash box he had saved from his business when it had collapsed five 1180 years earlier. Gregor heard how he opened the complicated lock and then closed it again after he had taken the item he wanted. What he heard his father say was some of the first good news that Gregor heard since he had 1185 first been incarcerated in his room. He had thought that nothing at all remained from his father's business, at least he had never told him anything different, and Gregor had never asked him about it anyway. Their busi-1190 ness misfortune had reduced the family to a state of total despair, and Gregor's only con-cern at that time had been to arrange things so that they could all forget about it as quickly as possible. So then he started work-1195 ing especially hard, with a fiery vigour that raised him from a junior salesman to a trav-elling representative almost overnight, bring-ing with it the chance to earn money in quite different ways. Gregor converted his success 1200 at work straight into cash that he could lay on the table at home for the benefit of his astonished and delighted family. They had been good times and they had never come again, at least not with the same splendour, 1205 even though Gregor had later earned so much that he was in a position to bear the costs of the whole family, and did bear them. They had even got used to it, both Gregor and the family, they took the money with gratitude and he was glad to provide it, although there was no longer much warm affection given in return. Gregor only remained close to his sister now. Unlike him, she was very fond of music and a gifted and expressive violinist, it was his secret plan to send her to the conservatory next year even though it would cause great expense that would have to be made up for in some other way. During Gregor's short periods in town, conversation with his sister would often turn to the conservatory but it was only ever mentioned as a lovely dream that could never be realised. Their parents did not like to hear this innocent talk, but Gregor thought about it quite hard and decided he would let them know what he planned with a grand announcement of it on Christmas day.

That was the sort of totally pointless thing that went through his mind in his present state, pressed upright against the door and listening. There were times when he simply became too tired to continue listening, when his head would fall wearily against the door and he would pull it up again with a start, as even the slightest noise he caused would be heard next door and they would all go silent. "What's that he's doing now," his father would say after a while, clearly having gone over to the door, and only then would the interrupted conversation slowly be taken up again.

When explaining things, his father repeated himself several times, partly because it was a long time since he had been occupied with these matters himself and partly because Gregor's mother did not understand everything the first time. From these repeated explanations Gregor learned, to his pleasure, that despite all their misfortunes there was still some money available from the old days. It was not a lot, but it had not been touched in the meantime and some interest had accumulated. Besides that, they had not been using up all the money that Gregor had been bringing home every month, keeping only a little for himself, so that that, too, had been accumulating. Behind the door, Gregor nodded with enthusiasm in his pleasure at this unexpected thrift and caution. He could actually have used this surplus money to reduce his father's debt to his boss, and the day when he could have freed himself from that job would have come much closer, but now it was certainly better the way his father had done things.

This money, however, was certainly not enough to enable the family to live off the interest; it was enough to maintain them for, perhaps, one or two years, no more. That's to say, it was money that should not really be touched but set aside for emergencies; money to live on had to be earned. His father was healthy but old, and lacking in self confidence. During the five years that he had not been working—the first holiday in a life that had been full of strain and no success—he had put on a lot of weight and become very slow and clumsy. Would Gregor's elderly mother now have to go and earn money? She suffered from asthma and it was a strain for her just to move about the home, every other day would be spent struggling for breath on the sofa by the open window. Would his sister have to go and earn money? She was still a child of seventeen, her life up till then had been very enviable, consisting of wearing nice clothes, sleeping late, helping out in the business, joining in with a few modest pleasures and most of all playing the violin. Whenever they began to talk of the need to earn money, Gregor would always first let go of the door and then throw himself onto the

cool, leather sofa next to it, as he became
1295 quite hot with shame and regret.

He would often lie there the whole night
through, not sleeping a wink but scratching
at the leather for hours on end. Or he might
go to all the effort of pushing a chair to the
1300 window, climbing up onto the sill and,
propped up in the chair, leaning on the window to stare out of it. He had used to feel a
great sense of freedom from doing this, but
doing it now was obviously something more
1305 remembered than experienced, as what
he actually saw in this way was becoming
less distinct every day, even things that
were quite near; he had used to curse the
ever-present view of the hospital across
1310 the street, but now he could not see it at
all, and if he had not known that he lived in
Charlottenstrasse, which was a quiet street
despite being in the middle of the city, he
could have thought that he was looking out
1315 the window at a barren waste where the grey
sky and the grey earth mingled inseparably.
His observant sister only needed to notice
the chair twice before she would always
push it back to its exact position by the win-
1320 dow after she had tidied up the room, and
even left the inner pane of the window open
from then on.

If Gregor had only been able to speak to
his sister and thank her for all that she had
1325 to do for him it would have been easier for
him to bear it; but as it was it caused him
pain. His sister, naturally, tried as far as possible to pretend there was nothing burdensome about it, and the longer it went on, of
1330 course, the better she was able to do so, but
as time went by Gregor was also able to see
through it all so much better. It had even
become very unpleasant for him, now,
whenever she entered the room. No sooner
1335 had she come in than she would quickly

close the door as a precaution so that no-one
would have to suffer the view into Gregor's
room, then she would go straight to the window and pull it hurriedly open almost as if
1340 she were suffocating. Even if it was cold, she
would stay at the window breathing deeply
for a little while. She would alarm Gregor
twice a day with this running about and
noise making; he would stay under the
1345 couch shivering the whole while, knowing
full well that she would certainly have liked
to spare him this ordeal, but it was impossible for her to be in the same room with him
with the windows closed.

1350 One day, about a month after Gregor's
transformation when his sister no longer
had any particular reason to be shocked at
his appearance, she came into the room a
little earlier than usual and found him still
1355 staring out the window, motionless, and just
where he would be most horrible. In itself,
his sister's not coming into the room would
have been no surprise for Gregor as it would
have been difficult for her to immediately
1360 open the window while he was still there,
but not only did she not come in, she went
straight back and closed the door behind
her, a stranger would have thought he had
threatened her and tried to bite her. Gregor
1365 went straight to hide himself under the
couch, of course, but he had to wait until
midday before his sister came back and she
seemed much more uneasy than usual. It
made him realise that she still found his
1370 appearance unbearable and would continue
to do so, she probably even had to overcome
the urge to flee when she saw the little bit of
him that protruded from under the couch.
One day, in order to spare her even this sight,
1375 he spent four hours carrying the bedsheet
over to the couch on his back and arranged it
so that he was completely covered and his

sister would not be able to see him even if she bent down. If she did not think this sheet was necessary then all she had to do was take it off again, as it was clear enough that it was no pleasure for Gregor to cut himself off so completely. She left the sheet where it was. Gregor even thought he glimpsed a look of gratitude one time when he carefully looked out from under the sheet to see how his sister liked the new arrangement.

For the first fourteen days, Gregor's parents could not bring themselves to come into the room to see him. He would often hear them say how they appreciated all the new work his sister was doing even though, before, they had seen her as a girl who was somewhat useless and frequently been annoyed with her. But now the two of them, father and mother, would often both wait outside the door of Gregor's room while his sister tidied up in there, and as soon as she went out again she would have to tell them exactly how everything looked, what Gregor had eaten, how he had behaved this time and whether, perhaps, any slight improvement could be seen. His mother also wanted to go in and visit Gregor relatively soon but his father and sister at first persuaded her against it. Gregor listened very closely to all this, and approved fully. Later, though, she had to be held back by force, which made her call out: "Let me go and see Gregor, he is my unfortunate son! Can't you understand I have to see him?," and Gregor would think to himself that maybe it would be better if his mother came in, not every day of course, but one day a week, perhaps; she could understand everything much better than his sister who, for all her courage, was still just a child after all, and really might not have had an adult's appreciation of the burdensome job she had taken on.

Gregor's wish to see his mother was soon realised. Out of consideration for his parents, Gregor wanted to avoid being seen at the window during the day, the few square meters of the floor did not give him much room to crawl about, it was hard to just lie quietly through the night, his food soon stopped giving him any pleasure at all, and so, to entertain himself, he got into the habit of crawling up and down the walls and ceiling. He was especially fond of hanging from the ceiling; it was quite different from lying on the floor; he could breathe more freely; his body had a light swing to it; and up there, relaxed and almost happy, it might happen that he would surprise even himself by letting go of the ceiling and landing on the floor with a crash. But now, of course, he had far better control of his body than before and, even with a fall as great as that, caused himself no damage. Very soon his sister noticed Gregor's new way of entertaining himself— he had, after all, left traces of the adhesive from his feet as he crawled about—and got it into her head to make it as easy as possible for him by removing the furniture that got in his way, especially the chest of drawers and the desk. Now, this was not something that she would be able to do by herself; she did not dare to ask for help from her father; the sixteen year old maid had carried on bravely since the cook had left but she certainly would not have helped in this, she had even asked to be allowed to keep the kitchen locked at all times and never to have to open the door unless it was especially important; so his sister had no choice but to choose some time when Gregor's father was not there and fetch his mother to help her. As she approached the room, Gregor could hear his mother express her joy, but once at the door she went silent. First, of course, his

sister came in and looked round to see that everything in the room was alright; and only then did she let her mother enter. Gregor had
1465 hurriedly pulled the sheet down lower over the couch and put more folds into it so that everything really looked as if it had just been thrown down by chance. Gregor also refrained, this time, from spying out from
1470 under the sheet; he gave up the chance to see his mother until later and was simply glad that she had come. "You can come in, he can't be seen," said his sister, obviously leading her in by the hand. The old chest of
1475 drawers was too heavy for a pair of feeble women to be heaving about, but Gregor listened as they pushed it from its place, his sister always taking on the heaviest part of the work for herself and ignoring her moth-
1480 er's warnings that she would strain herself. This lasted a very long time. After labouring at it for fifteen minutes or more his mother said it would be better to leave the chest where it was, for one thing it was too heavy
1485 for them to get the job finished before Gregor's father got home and leaving it in the middle of the room it would be in his way even more, and for another thing it wasn't even sure that taking the furniture away
1490 would really be any help to him. She thought just the opposite; the sight of the bare walls saddened her right to her heart; and why wouldn't Gregor feel the same way about it, he'd been used to this furniture in his room
1495 for a long time and it would make him feel abandoned to be in an empty room like that. Then, quietly, almost whispering as if wanting Gregor (whose whereabouts she did not know) to hear not even the tone of her voice,
1500 as she was convinced that he did not understand her words, she added "and by taking the furniture away, won't it seem like we're showing that we've given up all hope of

improvement and we're abandoning him to
1505 cope for himself? I think it'd be best to leave the room exactly the way it was before so that when Gregor comes back to us again he'll find everything unchanged and he'll be able to forget the time in between all
1510 the easier."

Hearing these words from his mother made Gregor realise that the lack of any direct human communication, along with the monotonous life led by the family during
1515 these two months, must have made him confused—he could think of no other way of explaining to himself why he had seriously wanted his room emptied out. Had he really wanted to transform his room into a cave, a
1520 warm room fitted out with the nice furniture he had inherited? That would have let him crawl around unimpeded in any direction, but it would also have let him quickly forget his past when he had still been human. He
1525 had come very close to forgetting, and it had only been the voice of his mother, unheard for so long, that had shaken him out of it. Nothing should be removed; everything had to stay; he could not do without the good
1530 influence the furniture had on his condition; and if the furniture made it difficult for him to crawl about mindlessly that was not a loss but a great advantage.

His sister, unfortunately, did not agree;
1535 she had become used to the idea, not without reason, that she was Gregor's spokesman to his parents about the things that concerned him. This meant that his mother's advice now was sufficient reason for her to
1540 insist on removing not only the chest of drawers and the desk, as she had thought at first, but all the furniture apart from the all-important couch. It was more than childish perversity, of course, or the unexpected
1545 confidence she had recently acquired, that

made her insist; she had indeed noticed that Gregor needed a lot of room to crawl about in, whereas the furniture, as far as anyone could see, was of no use to him at all. Girls of that age, though, do become enthusiastic about things and feel they must get their way whenever they can. Perhaps this was what tempted Grete to make Gregor's situation seem even more shocking than it was so that she could do even more for him. Grete would probably be the only one who would dare enter a room dominated by Gregor crawling about the bare walls by himself.

So she refused to let her mother dissuade her. Gregor's mother already looked uneasy in his room, she soon stopped speaking and helped Gregor's sister to get the chest of drawers out with what strength she had. The chest of drawers was something that Gregor could do without if he had to, but the writing desk had to stay. Hardly had the two women pushed the chest of drawers, groaning, out of the room than Gregor poked his head out from under the couch to see what he could do about it. He meant to be as careful and considerate as he could, but, unfortunately, it was his mother who came back first while Grete in the next room had her arms round the chest, pushing and pulling at it from side to side by herself without, of course, moving it an inch. His mother was not used to the sight of Gregor, he might have made her ill, so Gregor hurried backwards to the far end of the couch. In his startlement, though, he was not able to prevent the sheet at its front from moving a little. It was enough to attract his mother's attention. She stood very still, remained there a moment, and then went back out to Grete.

Gregor kept trying to assure himself that nothing unusual was happening, it was just a few pieces of furniture being moved after all, but he soon had to admit that the women going to and fro, their little calls to each other, the scraping of the furniture on the floor, all these things made him feel as if he were being assailed from all sides. With his head and legs pulled in against him and his body pressed to the floor, he was forced to admit to himself that he could not stand all of this much longer. They were emptying his room out; taking away everything that was dear to him; they had already taken out the chest containing his fretsaw and other tools; now they threatened to remove the writing desk with its place clearly worn into the floor, the desk where he had done his homework as a business trainee, at high school, even while he had been at infant school— he really could not wait any longer to see whether the two women's intentions were good. He had nearly forgotten they were there anyway, as they were now too tired to say anything while they worked and he could only hear their feet as they stepped heavily on the floor.

So, while the women were leant against the desk in the other room catching their breath, he sallied out, changed direction four times not knowing what he should save first before his attention was suddenly caught by the picture on the wall—which was already denuded of everything else that had been on it—of the lady dressed in copious fur. He hurried up onto the picture and pressed himself against its glass, it held him firmly and felt good on his hot belly. This picture at least, now totally covered by Gregor, would certainly be taken away by no-one. He turned his head to face the door into the living room so that he could watch the women when they came back.

They had not allowed themselves a long rest and came back quite soon; Grete had put

1630 her arm around her mother and was nearly
carrying her. "What shall we take now,
then?," said Grete and looked around. Her
eyes met those of Gregor on the wall. Perhaps only because her mother was there, she
1635 remained calm, bent her face to her so that
she would not look round and said, albeit
hurriedly and with a tremor in her voice:
"Come on, let's go back in the living room for
a while?" Gregor could see what Grete had in
1640 mind, she wanted to take her mother somewhere safe and then chase him down from
the wall. Well, she could certainly try it! He
sat unyielding on his picture. He would
rather jump at Grete's face.

1645   But Grete's words had made her mother
quite worried, she stepped to one side, saw
the enormous brown patch against the
flowers of the wallpaper, and before she
even realised it was Gregor that she saw
1650 screamed: "Oh God, oh God!" Arms outstretched, she fell onto the couch as if she
had given up everything and stayed there
immobile. "Gregor!" shouted his sister, glow-
ering at him and shaking her fist. That was
1655 the first word she had spoken to him directly
since his transformation. She ran into the
other room to fetch some kind of smelling
salts to bring her mother out of her faint;
Gregor wanted to help too—he could save
1660 his picture later, although he stuck fast to
the glass and had to pull himself off by force;
then he, too, ran into the next room as if he
could advise his sister like in the old days;
but he had to just stand behind her doing
1665 nothing; she was looking into various bottles,
he startled her when she turned round; a
bottle fell to the ground and broke; a splinter
cut Gregor's face, some kind of caustic medicine splashed all over him; now, without
1670 delaying any longer, Grete took hold of all
the bottles she could and ran with them in to

her mother; she slammed the door shut with
her foot. So now Gregor was shut out from
his mother, who, because of him, might be
1675 near to death; he could not open the door
if he did not want to chase his sister away,
and she had to stay with his mother; there
was nothing for him to do but wait; and,
oppressed with anxiety and self-reproach, he
1680 began to crawl about, he crawled over everything, walls, furniture, ceiling, and finally in
his confusion as the whole room began to
spin around him he fell down into the middle of the dinner table.

1685   He lay there for a while, numb and immobile, all around him it was quiet, maybe that
was a good sign. Then there was someone at
the door. The maid, of course, had locked
herself in her kitchen so that Grete would
1690 have to go and answer it. His father had
arrived home. "What's happened?" were his
first words; Grete's appearance must have
made everything clear to him. She answered
him with subdued voice, and openly pressed
1695 her face into his chest: "Mother's fainted, but
she's better now. Gregor got out." "Just as I
expected," said his father, "just as I always
said, but you women wouldn't listen, would
you." It was clear to Gregor that Grete had
1700 not said enough and that his father took it to
mean that something bad had happened, that
he was responsible for some act of violence.
That meant Gregor would now have to try to
calm his father, as he did not have the time to
1705 explain things to him even if that had been
possible. So he fled to the door of his room
and pressed himself against it so that his
father, when he came in from the hall, could
see straight away that Gregor had the best
1710 intentions and would go back into his room
without delay, that it would not be necessary
to drive him back but that they had only to
open the door and he would disappear.

His father, though, was not in the mood to notice subtleties like that; "Ah!," he shouted as he came in, sounding as if he were both angry and glad at the same time. Gregor drew his head back from the door and lifted it towards his father. He really had not imagined his father the way he stood there now; of late, with his new habit of crawling about, he had neglected to pay attention to what was going on the rest of the flat the way he had done before. He really ought to have expected things to have changed, but still, still, was that really his father? The same tired man as used to be laying there entombed in his bed when Gregor came back from his business trips, who would receive him sitting in the armchair in his nightgown when he came back in the evenings; who was hardly even able to stand up but, as a sign of his pleasure, would just raise his arms and who, on the couple of times a year when they went for a walk together on a Sunday or public holiday wrapped up tightly in his overcoat between Gregor and his mother, would always labour his way forward a little more slowly than them, who were already walking slowly for his sake; who would place his stick down carefully and, if he wanted to say something would invariably stop and gather his companions around him. He was standing up straight enough now; dressed in a smart blue uniform with gold buttons, the sort worn by the employees at the banking institute; above the high, stiff collar of the coat his strong double-chin emerged; under the bushy eyebrows, his piercing, dark eyes looked out fresh and alert; his normally unkempt white hair was combed down painfully close to his scalp. He took his cap, with its gold monogram from, probably, some bank, and threw it in an arc right across the room onto the sofa, put his hands in his trouser pockets, pushing back the bottom of his long uniform coat, and, with look of determination, walked towards Gregor. He probably did not even know himself what he had in mind, but nonetheless lifted his feet unusually high. Gregor was amazed at the enormous size of the soles of his boots, but wasted no time with that—he knew full well, right from the first day of his new life, that his father thought it necessary to always be extremely strict with him. And so he ran up to his father, stopped when his father stopped, scurried forwards again when he moved, even slightly. In this way they went round the room several times without anything decisive happening, without even giving the impression of a chase as everything went so slowly. Gregor remained all this time on the floor, largely because he feared his father might see it as especially provoking if he fled onto the wall or ceiling. Whatever he did, Gregor had to admit that he certainly would not be able to keep up this running about for long, as for each step his father took he had to carry out countless movements. He became noticeably short of breath, even in his earlier life his lungs had not been very reliable. Now, as he lurched about in his efforts to muster all the strength he could for running he could hardly keep his eyes open; his thoughts became too slow for him to think of any other way of saving himself than running; he almost forgot that the walls were there for him to use although, here, they were concealed behind carefully carved furniture full of notches and protrusions— then, right beside him, lightly tossed, something flew down and rolled in front of him. It was an apple; then another one immediately flew at him; Gregor froze in shock; there was no longer any point in running as his father

had decided to bombard him. He had filled his pockets with fruit from the bowl on the
1800 sideboard and now, without even taking the time for careful aim, threw one apple after another. These little, red apples rolled about on the floor, knocking into each other as if they had electric motors. An apple thrown
1805 without much force glanced against Gregor's back and slid off without doing any harm. Another one however, immediately following it, hit squarely and lodged in his back; Gregor wanted to drag himself away, as if he could
1810 remove the surprising, the incredible pain by changing his position; but he felt as if nailed to the spot and spread himself out, all his senses in confusion. The last thing he saw was the door of his room being pulled open,
1815 his sister was screaming, his mother ran out in front of her in her blouse (as his sister had taken off some of her clothes after she had fainted to make it easier for her to breathe), she ran to his father, her skirts unfastened
1820 and sliding one after another to the ground, stumbling over the skirts she pushed herself to his father, her arms around him, uniting herself with him totally—now Gregor lost his ability to see anything—her hands
1825 behind his father's head begging him to spare Gregor's life.

III

No-one dared to remove the apple lodged in Gregor's flesh, so it remained there as a visible reminder of his injury. He had suffered it
1830 there for more than a month, and his condition seemed serious enough to remind even his father that Gregor, despite his current sad and revolting form, was a family member who could not be treated as an enemy. On
1835 the contrary, as a family there was a duty to swallow any revulsion for him and to be patient, just to be patient.

Because of his injuries, Gregor had lost much of his mobility—probably perma-
1840 nently. He had been reduced to the condition of an ancient invalid and it took him long, long minutes to crawl across his room— crawling over the ceiling was out of the question—but this deterioration in his con-
1845 dition was fully (in his opinion) made up for by the door to the living room being left open every evening. He got into the habit of closely watching it for one or two hours before it was opened and then, lying in the darkness
1850 of his room where he could not be seen from the living room, he could watch the family in the light of the dinner table and listen to their conversation—with everyone's permission, in a way, and thus quite differently
1855 from before.

They no longer held the lively conversations of earlier times, of course, the ones that Gregor always thought about with longing when he was tired and getting into the damp
1860 bed in some small hotel room. All of them were usually very quiet nowadays. Soon after dinner, his father would go to sleep in his chair; his mother and sister would urge each other to be quiet; his mother, bent deeply
1865 under the lamp, would sew fancy underwear for a fashion shop; his sister, who had taken a sales job, learned shorthand and French in the evenings so that she might be able to get a better position later on. Sometimes his
1870 father would wake up and say to Gregor's mother "you're doing so much sewing again today!," as if he did not know that he had been dozing—and then he would go back to sleep again while mother and sister would
1875 exchange a tired grin.

With a kind of stubbornness, Gregor's father refused to take his uniform off even at home; while his nightgown hung unused on its peg Gregor's father would slumber where he was, fully dressed, as if always ready to serve and expecting to hear the voice of his superior even here. The uniform had not been new to start with, but as a result of this it slowly became even shabbier despite the efforts of Gregor's mother and sister to look after it. Gregor would often spend the whole evening looking at all the stains on this coat, with its gold buttons always kept polished and shiny, while the old man in it would sleep, highly uncomfortable but peaceful.

As soon as it struck ten, Gregor's mother would speak gently to his father to wake him and try to persuade him to go to bed, as he couldn't sleep properly where he was and he really had to get his sleep if he was to be up at six to get to work. But since he had been in work he had become more obstinate and would always insist on staying longer at the table, even though he regularly fell asleep and it was then harder than ever to persuade him to exchange the chair for his bed. Then, however much mother and sister would importune him with little reproaches and warnings he would keep slowly shaking his head for a quarter of an hour with his eyes closed and refusing to get up. Gregor's mother would tug at his sleeve, whisper endearments into his ear, Gregor's sister would leave her work to help her mother, but nothing would have any effect on him. He would just sink deeper into his chair. Only when the two women took him under the arms he would abruptly open his eyes, look at them one after the other and say: "What a life! This is what peace I get in my old age!" And supported by the two women he would lift himself up carefully as if he were carrying the greatest load himself, let the women take him to the door, send them off and carry on by himself while Gregor's mother would throw down her needle and his sister

her pen so that they could run after his father and continue being of help to him.

Who, in this tired and overworked family, would have had time to give more attention to Gregor than was absolutely necessary? The household budget became even smaller; so now the maid was dismissed; an enormous, thick-boned charwoman with white hair that flapped around her head came every morning and evening to do the heaviest work; everything else was looked after by Gregor's mother on top of the large amount of sewing work she did. Gregor even learned, listening to the evening conversation about what price they had hoped for, that several items of jewellery belonging to the family had been sold, even though both mother and sister had been very fond of wearing them at functions and celebrations. But the loudest complaint was that although the flat was much too big for their present circumstances, they could not move out of it, there was no imaginable way of transferring Gregor to the new address. He could see quite well, though, that there were more reasons than consideration for him that made it difficult for them to move, it would have been quite easy to transport him in any suitable crate with a few air holes in it; the main thing holding the family back from their decision to move was much more to do with their total despair, and the thought that they had been struck with a misfortune unlike anything experienced by anyone else they knew or were related to. They carried out absolutely everything that the world expects from poor people, Gregor's father brought bank employees their breakfast, his mother sacrificed herself by washing clothes for strangers, his sister ran back and forth behind her desk at the behest of the customers, but they just did not have the strength to do any more. And the injury in Gregor's back 1965 began to hurt as much as when it was new. After they had come back from taking his father to bed Gregor's mother and sister would now leave their work where it was and sit close together, cheek to cheek; his 1970 mother would point to Gregor's room and say "Close that door, Grete," and then, when he was in the dark again, they would sit in the next room and their tears would mingle, or they would simply sit there staring dry-eyed 1975 at the table.

Gregor hardly slept at all, either night or day. Sometimes he would think of taking over the family's affairs, just like before, the next time the door was opened; he had long 1980 forgotten about his boss and the chief clerk, but they would appear again in his thoughts, the salesmen and the apprentices, that stupid teaboy, two or three friends from other businesses, one of the chambermaids from 1985 a provincial hotel, a tender memory that appeared and disappeared again, a cashier from a hat shop for whom his attention had been serious but too slow,—all of them appeared to him, mixed together with 1990 strangers and others he had forgotten, but instead of helping him and his family they were all of them inaccessible, and he was glad when they disappeared. Other times he was not at all in the mood to look after his 1995 family, he was filled with simple rage about the lack of attention he was shown, and although he could think of nothing he would have wanted, he made plans of how he could get into the pantry where he could take all 2000 the things he was entitled to, even if he was not hungry. Gregor's sister no longer thought about how she could please him but would hurriedly push some food or other into his room with her foot before she rushed out to 2005 work in the morning and at midday, and in

the evening she would sweep it away again with the broom, indifferent as to whether it had been eaten or—more often than not— had been left totally untouched. She still 2010 cleared up the room in the evening, but now she could not have been any quicker about it. Smears of dirt were left on the walls, here and there were little balls of dust and filth. At first, Gregor went into one of the worst of 2015 these places when his sister arrived as a reproach to her, but he could have stayed there for weeks without his sister doing anything about it; she could see the dirt as well as he could but she had simply decided to 2020 leave him to it. At the same time she became touchy in a way that was quite new for her and which everyone in the family understood—cleaning up Gregor's room was for her and her alone. Gregor's mother did once 2025 thoroughly clean his room, and needed to use several bucketfuls of water to do it— although that much dampness also made Gregor ill and he lay flat on the couch, bitter and immobile. But his mother was to be 2030 punished still more for what she had done, as hardly had his sister arrived home in the evening than she noticed the change in Gregor's room and, highly aggrieved, ran back into the living room where, despite her 2035 mothers raised and imploring hands, she broke into convulsive tears. Her father, of course, was startled out of his chair and the two parents looked on astonished and helpless; then they, too, became agitated; Gregor's 2040 father, standing to the right of his mother, accused her of not leaving the cleaning of Gregor's room to his sister; from her left, Gregor's sister screamed at her that she was never to clean Gregor's room again; while his 2045 mother tried to draw his father, who was beside himself with anger, into the bedroom; his sister, quaking with tears, thumped on the table with her small fists; and Gregor hissed in anger that no-one had even

2050 thought of closing the door to save him the sight of this and all its noise.

Gregor's sister was exhausted from going out to work, and looking after Gregor as she had done before was even more work for her,

2055 but even so his mother ought certainly not to have taken her place. Gregor, on the other hand, ought not to be neglected. Now, though, the charwoman was here. This elderly widow, with a robust bone structure

2060 that made her able to withstand the hardest of things in her long life, wasn't really repelled by Gregor. Just by chance one day, rather than any real curiosity, she opened the door to Gregor's room and found herself

2065 face to face with him. He was taken totally by surprise, no-one was chasing him but he began to rush to and fro while she just stood there in amazement with her hands crossed in front of her. From then on she never failed

2070 to open the door slightly every evening and morning and look briefly in on him. At first she would call to him as she did so with words that she probably considered friendly, such as "come on then, you old dung-

2075 beetle!," or "look at the old dung-beetle there!" Gregor never responded to being spoken to in that way, but just remained where he was without moving as if the door had never even been opened. If only they

2080 had told this charwoman to clean up his room every day instead of letting her disturb him for no reason whenever she felt like it! One day, early in the morning while a heavy rain struck the windowpanes, perhaps indi-

2085 cating that spring was coming, she began to speak to him in that way once again. Gregor was so resentful of it that he started to move toward her, he was slow and infirm, but it was like a kind of attack. Instead of being

2090 afraid, the charwoman just lifted up one of the chairs from near the door and stood there with her mouth open, clearly intending not to close her mouth until the chair in her hand had been slammed down into

2095 Gregor's back. "Aren't you coming any closer, then?," she asked when Gregor turned round again, and she calmly put the chair back in the corner.

Gregor had almost entirely stopped eat-
2100 ing. Only if he happened to find himself next to the food that had been prepared for him he might take some of it into his mouth to play with it, leave it there a few hours and then, more often than not, spit it out again.

2105 At first he thought it was distress at the state of his room that stopped him eating, but he had soon got used to the changes made there. They had got into the habit of putting things into this room that they had no room

2110 for anywhere else, and there were now many such things as one of the rooms in the flat had been rented out to three gentlemen. These earnest gentlemen—all three of them had full beards, as Gregor learned peering

2115 through the crack in the door one day—were painfully insistent on things' being tidy. This meant not only in their own room but, since they had taken a room in this establishment, in the entire flat and especially in the

2120 kitchen. Unnecessary clutter was something they could not tolerate, especially if it was dirty. They had moreover brought most of their own furnishings and equipment with them. For this reason, many things had

2125 become superfluous which, although they could not be sold, the family did not wish to discard. All these things found their way into Gregor's room. The dustbins from the kitchen found their way in there too. The charwoman

2130 was always in a hurry, and anything she couldn't use for the time being she would just chuck in there. He, fortunately, would usually see no more than the object and the hand that held it. The woman most likely meant to fetch the things back out again when she had time and the opportunity, or to throw everything out in one go, but what actually happened was that they were left where they landed when they had first been thrown unless Gregor made his way through the junk and moved it somewhere else. At first he moved it because, with no other room free where he could crawl about, he was forced to, but later on he came to enjoy it although moving about in that way left him sad and tired to death, and he would remain immobile for hours afterwards.

The gentlemen who rented the room would sometimes take their evening meal at home in the living room that was used by everyone, and so the door to this room was often kept closed in the evening. But Gregor found it easy to give up having the door open, he had, after all, often failed to make use of it when it was open and, without the family having noticed it, lain in his room in its darkest corner. One time, though, the charwoman left the door to the living room slightly open, and it remained open when the gentlemen who rented the room came in in the evening and the light was put on. They sat up at the table where, formerly, Gregor had taken his meals with his father and mother, they unfolded the serviettes and picked up their knives and forks. Gregor's mother immediately appeared in the doorway with a dish of meat and soon behind her came his sister with a dish piled high with potatoes. The food was steaming, and filled the room with its smell. The gentlemen bent over the dishes set in front of them as if they wanted to test the food before eating it, and the gentleman in the middle, who seemed to count as an authority for the other two, did indeed cut off a piece of meat while it was still in its dish, clearly wishing to establish whether it was sufficiently cooked or whether it should be sent back to the kitchen. It was to his satisfaction, and Gregor's mother and sister, who had been looking on anxiously, began to breathe again and smiled.

The family themselves ate in the kitchen. Nonetheless, Gregor's father came into the living room before he went into the kitchen, bowed once with his cap in his hand and did his round of the table. The gentlemen stood as one, and mumbled something into their beards. Then, once they were alone, they ate in near perfect silence. It seemed remarkable to Gregor that above all the various noises of eating their chewing teeth could still be heard, as if they had wanted to show Gregor that you need teeth in order to eat and it was not possible to perform anything with jaws that are toothless however nice they might be. "I'd like to eat something," said Gregor anxiously, "but not anything like they're eating. They do feed themselves. And here I am, dying!"

Throughout all this time, Gregor could not remember having heard the violin being played, but this evening it began to be heard from the kitchen. The three gentlemen had already finished their meal, the one in the middle had produced a newspaper, given a page to each of the others, and now they leant back in their chairs reading them and smoking. When the violin began playing they became attentive, stood up and went on tiptoe over to the door of the hallway where they stood pressed against each other. Someone must have heard them in the kitchen, as Gregor's father called out: "Is the playing perhaps unpleasant for the gentlemen? We can stop it straight away." "On the contrary," said the middle gentleman, "would the young lady not like to come in and play for us here in the room, where it is, after all, much more cosy and comfortable?" "Oh yes, we'd love to," called back Gregor's father as if he had been the violin player himself. The gentlemen stepped back into the room and waited. Gregor's father soon appeared with the music stand, his mother with the music and his sister with the violin. She calmly prepared everything for her to begin playing; his parents, who had never rented a room out before and therefore showed an exaggerated courtesy towards the three gentlemen, did not even dare to sit on their own chairs; his father leant against the door with his right hand pushed in between two buttons on his uniform coat; his mother, though, was offered a seat by one of the gentlemen and sat—leaving the chair where the gentleman happened to have placed it—out of the way in a corner.

His sister began to play; father and mother paid close attention, one on each side, to the movements of her hands. Drawn in by the playing, Gregor had dared to come forward a little and already had his head in the living room. Before, he had taken great pride in how considerate he was but now it hardly occurred to him that he had become so thoughtless about the others. What's more, there was now all the more reason to keep himself hidden as he was covered in the dust that lay everywhere in his room and flew up at the slightest movement; he carried threads, hairs, and remains of food about on his back and sides; he was much too indifferent to everything now to lay on his back and wipe himself on the carpet like he had used to do several times a day. And despite this condition, he was not too shy to move forward a little onto the immaculate floor of the living room.

No-one noticed him, though. The family was totally preoccupied with the violin playing; at first, the three gentlemen had put their hands in their pockets and come up far too close behind the music stand to look at all the notes being played, and they must have disturbed Gregor's sister, but soon, in contrast with the family, they withdrew back to the window with their heads sunk and talking to each other at half volume, and they stayed by the window while Gregor's father observed them anxiously. It really now seemed very obvious that they had expected to hear some beautiful or entertaining violin playing but had been disappointed, that they had had enough of the whole performance and it was only now out of politeness that they allowed their peace to be disturbed. It was especially unnerving, the way they all blew the smoke from their cigarettes upwards from their mouth and noses. Yet Gregor's sister was playing so beautifully. Her face was leant to one side, following the lines of music with a careful and melancholy expression. Gregor crawled a little further forward, keeping his head close to the ground so that he could meet her eyes if the chance came. Was he an animal if music could captivate him so? It seemed to him that he was being shown the way to the unknown nourishment he had been yearning for. He was determined to make his way forward to his sister and tug at her skirt to show her she might come into his room with her violin, as no-one appreciated her playing here as much as he would. He never wanted to let her out of his room, not while he lived, anyway; his shocking appearance should, for once, be of some use to him; he wanted to be at every door of his room at once to hiss and spit at the attackers; his sister should not be forced to stay with him, though, but stay of

2300 her own free will; she would sit beside him
on the couch with her ear bent down to
him while he told her how he had always
intended to send her to the conservatory,
how he would have told everyone about it
2305 last Christmas—had Christmas really come
and gone already?—if this misfortune hadn't
got in the way, and refuse to let anyone dissuade him from it. On hearing all this, his
sister would break out in tears of emotion,
2310 and Gregor would climb up to her shoulder
and kiss her neck, which, since she had been
going out to work, she had kept free without
any necklace or collar.

"Mr. Samsa!," shouted the middle gentle-
2315 man to Gregor's father, pointing, without
wasting any more words, with his forefinger
at Gregor as he slowly moved forward. The
violin went silent, the middle of the three
gentlemen first smiled at his two friends,
2320 shaking his head, and then looked back at
Gregor. His father seemed to think it more
important to calm the three gentlemen
before driving Gregor out, even though they
were not at all upset and seemed to think
2325 Gregor was more entertaining than the violin
playing had been. He rushed up to them with
his arms spread out and attempted to drive
them back into their room at the same time
as trying to block their view of Gregor with
2330 his body. Now they did become a little
annoyed, and it was not clear whether it was
his father's behaviour that annoyed them or
the dawning realisation that they had had a
neighbour like Gregor in the next room with-
2335 out knowing it. They asked Gregor's father
for explanations, raised their arms like he
had, tugged excitedly at their beards and
moved back towards their room only very
slowly. Meanwhile Gregor's sister had over-
2340 come the despair she had fallen into when
her playing was suddenly interrupted. She

had let her hands drop and let violin and
bow hang limply for a while but continued to
look at the music as if still playing, but then
2345 she suddenly pulled herself together, lay the
instrument on her mother's lap who still sat
laboriously struggling for breath where she
was, and ran into the next room which,
under pressure from her father, the three
2350 gentlemen were more quickly moving
toward. Under his sister's experienced hand,
the pillows and covers on the beds flew up
and were put into order and she had already
finished making the beds and slipped out
2355 again before the three gentlemen had
reached the room. Gregor's father seemed so
obsessed with what he was doing that he
forgot all the respect he owed to his tenants.
He urged them and pressed them until,
2360 when he was already at the door of the
room, the middle of the three gentlemen
shouted like thunder and stamped his foot
and thereby brought Gregor's father to a halt.
"I declare here and now," he said, raising his
2365 hand and glancing at Gregor's mother and
sister to gain their attention too, "that with
regard to the repugnant conditions that
prevail in this flat and with this family"—
here he looked briefly but decisively at the
2370 floor—"I give immediate notice on my room.
For the days that I have been living here I will,
of course, pay nothing at all, on the contrary I
will consider whether to proceed with some
kind of action for damages from you, and
2375 believe me it would be very easy to set out the
grounds for such an action." He was silent
and looked straight ahead as if waiting for
something. And indeed, his two friends joined
in with the words: "And we also give immedi-
2380 ate notice." With that, he took hold of the door
handle and slammed the door.

Gregor's father staggered back to his seat,
feeling his way with his hands, and fell into

it; it looked as if he was stretching himself out for his usual evening nap but from the uncontrolled way his head kept nodding it could be seen that he was not sleeping at all. Throughout all this, Gregor had lain still where the three gentlemen had first seen him. His disappointment at the failure of his plan, and perhaps also because he was weak from hunger, made it impossible for him to move. He was sure that everyone would turn on him any moment, and he waited. He was not even startled out of this state when the violin on his mother's lap fell from her trembling fingers and landed loudly on the floor.

"Father, Mother," said his sister, hitting the table with her hand as introduction, "we can't carry on like this. Maybe you can't see it, but I can. I don't want to call this monster my brother, all I can say is: we have to try and get rid of it. We've done all that's humanly possible to look after it and be patient, I don't think anyone could accuse us of doing anything wrong."

"She's absolutely right," said Gregor's father to himself. His mother, who still had not had time to catch her breath, began to cough dully, her hand held out in front of her and a deranged expression in her eyes.

Gregor's sister rushed to his mother and put her hand on her forehead. Her words seemed to give Gregor's father some more definite ideas. He sat upright, played with his uniform cap between the plates left by the three gentlemen after their meal, and occasionally looked down at Gregor as he lay there immobile.

"We have to try and get rid of it," said Gregor's sister, now speaking only to her father, as her mother was too occupied with coughing to listen, "it'll be the death of both of you, I can see it coming. We can't all work as hard as we have to and then come home

to be tortured like this, we can't endure it. I can't endure it any more." And she broke out so heavily in tears that they flowed down the face of her mother, and she wiped them away with mechanical hand movements.

"My child," said her father with sympathy and obvious understanding, "what are we to do?"

His sister just shrugged her shoulders as a sign of the helplessness and tears that had taken hold of her, displacing her earlier certainty.

"If he could just understand us," said his father almost as a question; his sister shook her hand vigorously through her tears as a sign that of that there was no question.

"If he could just understand us," repeated Gregor's father, closing his eyes in acceptance of his sister's certainty that that was quite impossible, "then perhaps we could come to some kind of arrangement with him. But as it is . . ."

"It's got to go," shouted his sister, "that's the only way, Father. You've got to get rid of the idea that that's Gregor. We've only harmed ourselves by believing it for so long. How can that be Gregor? If it were Gregor he would have seen long ago that it's not possible for human beings to live with an animal like that and he would have gone of his own free will. We wouldn't have a brother any more, then, but we could carry on with our lives and remember him with respect. As it is this animal is persecuting us, it's driven out our tenants, it obviously wants to take over the whole flat and force us to sleep on the streets. Father, look, just look," she suddenly screamed, "he's starting again!" In her alarm, which was totally beyond Gregor's comprehension, his sister even abandoned his mother as she pushed herself vigorously out of her chair as if more willing to sacrifice her own mother than stay anywhere near Gregor. She rushed over to behind her father, who 2470 had become excited merely because she was and stood up half raising his hands in front of Gregor's sister as if to protect her.

But Gregor had had no intention of frightening anyone, least of all his sister. All he 2475 had done was begin to turn round so that he could go back into his room, although that was in itself quite startling as his pain-wracked condition meant that turning round required a great deal of effort and he was 2480 using his head to help himself do it, repeatedly raising it and striking it against the floor. He stopped and looked round. They seemed to have realised his good intention and had only been alarmed briefly. Now 2485 they all looked at him in unhappy silence. His mother lay in her chair with her legs stretched out and pressed against each other, her eyes nearly closed with exhaustion; his sister sat next to his father with her 2490 arms around his neck.

"Maybe now they'll let me turn round," thought Gregor and went back to work. He could not help panting loudly with the effort and had sometimes to stop and take a rest. 2495 No-one was making him rush any more, everything was left up to him. As soon as he had finally finished turning round he began to move straight ahead. He was amazed at the great distance that separated him from 2500 his room, and could not understand how he had covered that distance in his weak state a little while before and almost without noticing it. He concentrated on crawling as fast as he could and hardly noticed that there was 2505 not a word, not any cry, from his family to distract him. He did not turn his head until he had reached the doorway. He did not turn it all the way round as he felt his neck becoming stiff, but it was nonetheless 2510 enough to see that nothing behind him had

changed, only his sister had stood up. With his last glance he saw that his mother had now fallen completely asleep.

He was hardly inside his room before the 2515 door was hurriedly shut, bolted and locked. The sudden noise behind Gregor so startled him that his little legs collapsed under him. It was his sister who had been in so much of a rush. She had been standing there waiting 2520 and sprung forward lightly, Gregor had not heard her coming at all, and as she turned the key in the lock she said loudly to her parents "At last!."

"What now, then?," Gregor asked himself 2525 as he looked round in the darkness. He soon made the discovery that he could no longer move at all. This was no surprise to him, it seemed rather that being able to actually move around on those spindly little legs until 2530 then was unnatural. He also felt relatively comfortable. It is true that his entire body was aching, but the pain seemed to be slowly getting weaker and weaker and would finally disappear altogether. He could already hardly 2535 feel the decayed apple in his back or the inflamed area around it, which was entirely covered in white dust. He thought back of his family with emotion and love. If it was possible, he felt that he must go away even more 2540 strongly than his sister. He remained in this state of empty and peaceful rumination until he heard the clock tower strike three in the morning. He watched as it slowly began to get light everywhere outside the window too. 2545 Then, without his willing it, his head sank down completely, and his last breath flowed weakly from his nostrils.

When the cleaner came in early in the morning—they'd often asked her not to keep 2550 slamming the doors but with her strength and in her hurry she still did, so that everyone in the flat knew when she'd arrived and from then on it was impossible to sleep in

peace—she made her usual brief look in on
2555 Gregor and at first found nothing special. She
thought he was laying there so still on purpose, playing the martyr; she attributed all
possible understanding to him. She happened to be holding the long broom in her
2560 hand, so she tried to tickle Gregor with it
from the doorway. When she had no success
with that she tried to make a nuisance of
herself and poked at him a little, and only
when she found she could shove him across
2565 the floor with no resistance at all did she
start to pay attention. She soon realised
what had really happened, opened her eyes
wide, whistled to herself, but did not waste
time to yank open the bedroom doors and
2570 shout loudly into the darkness of the bedrooms: "Come and 'ave a look at this, it's
dead, just lying there, stone dead!"

Mr. and Mrs. Samsa sat upright there in
their marriage bed and had to make an effort
2575 to get over the shock caused by the cleaner
before they could grasp what she was saying.
But then, each from his own side, they hurried out of bed. Mr. Samsa threw the blanket
over his shoulders, Mrs. Samsa just came out
2580 in her nightdress; and that is how they went
into Gregor's room. On the way they opened
the door to the living room where Grete had
been sleeping since the three gentlemen
had moved in; she was fully dressed as if she
2585 had never been asleep, and the paleness of
her face seemed to confirm this. "Dead?,"
asked Mrs. Samsa, looking at the charwoman
enquiringly, even though she could have
checked for herself and could have known
2590 it even without checking. "That's what I
said," replied the cleaner, and to prove it she
gave Gregor's body another shove with the
broom, sending it sideways across the floor.
Mrs. Samsa made a movement as if she
2595 wanted to hold back the broom, but did not
complete it. "Now then," said Mr. Samsa,

"let's give thanks to God for that." He crossed
himself, and the three women followed his
example. Grete, who had not taken her eyes
2600 from the corpse, said: "Just look how thin he
was. He didn't eat anything for so long. The
food came out again just the same as when
it went in." Gregor's body was indeed completely dried up and flat, they had not seen it
2605 until then, but now he was not lifted up on
his little legs, nor did he do anything to make
them look away.

"Grete, come with us in here for a little
while," said Mrs. Samsa with a pained smile,
2610 and Grete followed her parents into the
bedroom but not without looking back at the
body. The cleaner shut the door and opened
the window wide. Although it was still early
in the morning the fresh air had something
2615 of warmth mixed in with it. It was already
the end of March, after all.

The three gentlemen stepped out of their
room and looked round in amazement for
their breakfasts; they had been forgotten
2620 about. "Where is our breakfast?," the middle
gentleman asked the cleaner irritably. She
just put her finger on her lips and made a
quick and silent sign to the men that they
might like to come into Gregor's room. They
2625 did so, and stood around Gregor's corpse with
their hands in the pockets of their well-worn
coats. It was now quite light in the room.

Then the door of the bedroom opened and
Mr. Samsa appeared in his uniform with his
2630 wife on one arm and his daughter on the
other. All of them had been crying a little;
Grete now and then pressed her face against
her father's arm.

"Leave my home. Now!," said Mr. Samsa,
2635 indicating the door and without letting the
women from him. "What do you mean?,"
asked the middle of the three gentlemen
somewhat disconcerted, and he smiled
sweetly. The other two held their hands

2640 behind their backs and continually rubbed them together in gleeful anticipation of a loud quarrel which could only end in their favour. "I mean just what I said," answered Mr. Samsa, and, with his two companions, 2645 went in a straight line towards the man. At first, he stood there still, looking at the ground as if the contents of his head were rearranging themselves into new positions. "Alright, we'll go then," he said, and looked 2650 up at Mr. Samsa as if he had been suddenly overcome with humility and wanted permission again from Mr. Samsa for his decision. Mr. Samsa merely opened his eyes wide and briefly nodded to him several times. At that, 2655 and without delay, the man actually did take long strides into the front hallway; his two friends had stopped rubbing their hands some time before and had been listening to what was being said. Now they jumped off 2660 after their friend as if taken with a sudden fear that Mr. Samsa might go into the hallway in front of them and break the connection with their leader. Once there, all three took their hats from the stand, took their 2665 sticks from the holder, bowed without a word and left the premises. Mr. Samsa and the two women followed them out onto the landing; but they had had no reason to mistrust the men's intentions and as they leaned over the 2670 landing they saw how the three gentlemen made slow but steady progress down the many steps. As they turned the corner on each floor they disappeared and would reappear a few moments later; the further down 2675 they went, the more that the Samsa family lost interest in them; when a butcher's boy, proud of posture with his tray on his head, passed them on his way up and came nearer than they were, Mr. Samsa and the women 2680 came away from the landing and went, as if relieved, back into the flat.

They decided the best way to make use of that day was for relaxation and to go for a walk; not only had they earned a break from 2685 work but they were in serious need of it. So they sat at the table and wrote three letters of excusal, Mr. Samsa to his employers, Mrs. Samsa to her contractor and Grete to her principal. The cleaner came in while they 2690 were writing to tell them she was going, she'd finished her work for that morning. The three of them at first just nodded without looking up from what they were writing, and it was only when the cleaner still did not 2695 seem to want to leave that they looked up in irritation. "Well?," asked Mr. Samsa. The charwoman stood in the doorway with a smile on her face as if she had some tremendous good news to report, but would only do 2700 it if she was clearly asked to. The almost vertical little ostrich feather on her hat, which had been a source of irritation to Mr. Samsa all the time she had been working for them, swayed gently in all directions. 2705 "What is it you want then?," asked Mrs. Samsa, whom the cleaner had the most respect for. "Yes," she answered, and broke into a friendly laugh that made her unable to speak straight away, "well then, that thing in 2710 there, you needn't worry about how you're going to get rid of it. That's all been sorted out." Mrs. Samsa and Grete bent down over their letters as if intent on continuing with what they were writing; Mr. Samsa saw that 2715 the cleaner wanted to start describing everything in detail but, with outstretched hand, he made it quite clear that she was not to. So, as she was prevented from telling them all about it, she suddenly remembered what 2720 a hurry she was in and, clearly peeved, called out "Cheerio then, everyone," turned round sharply and left, slamming the door terribly as she went.

"Tonight she gets sacked," said Mr. Samsa, but he received no reply from either his wife or his daughter as the charwoman seemed to have destroyed the peace they had only just gained. They got up and went over to the window where they remained with their arms around each other. Mr. Samsa twisted round in his chair to look at them and sat there watching for a while. Then he called out: "Come here, then. Let's forget about all that old stuff, shall we. Come and give me a bit of attention." The two women immediately did as he said, hurrying over to him where they kissed him and hugged him and then they quickly finished their letters.

After that, the three of them left the flat together, which was something they had not done for months, and took the tram out to the open country outside the town. They had the tram, filled with warm sunshine, all to themselves. Leant back comfortably on their seats, they discussed their prospects and found that on closer examination they were not at all bad—until then they had never asked each other about their work but all three had jobs which were very good and held particularly good promise for the future. The greatest improvement for the time being, of course, would be achieved quite easily by moving house; what they needed now was a flat that was smaller and cheaper than the current one which had been chosen by Gregor, one that was in a better location and, most of all, more practical. All the time, Grete was becoming livelier. With all the worry they had been having of late her cheeks had become pale, but, while they were talking, Mr. and Mrs. Samsa were struck, almost simultaneously, with the thought of how their daughter was blossoming into a well built and beautiful young lady. They became quieter. Just from each other's glance and almost without knowing it they agreed that it would soon be time to find a good man for her. And, as if in confirmation of their new dreams and good intentions, as soon as they reached their destination Grete was the first to get up and stretch out her young body.

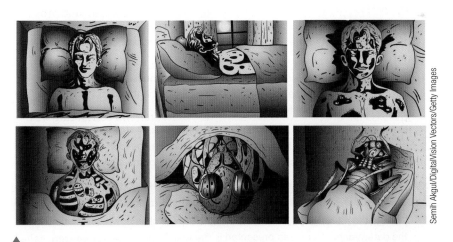

Semih Akgul/DigitalVision Vectors/Getty Images

▲

The digital images designed by Semih Akgul create frames of a storyboard of Kafka's *The Metamorphosis*.

How do the images depict Gregor's transformation? What does this storyboard suggest about modern individuals?

CHARACTER

1. Who or what are the story's **protagonist** and **antagonist**? What values does each represent?

2. How is Gregor **characterized**? Describe him physically, emotionally, and psychologically.

3. What is significant about Gregor's job and his role in the household? How does he get along with the other members of his family?

SETTING

4. Where is Gregor's room positioned within the Samsas's apartment? Why might this location be important? What is the significance of the locked door? Explain.

5. What are the **circumstances** surrounding Gregor's death? Consider the time of day and the time of year, for example. Choose two details and explain what they suggest about the meaning of his death.

6. Explain how the **setting** changes between the opening paragraphs and the conclusion of the story. What has changed?

7. What does the picture in Gregor's room reveal about both him and his relationship with others?

STRUCTURE

8. The text is divided into three sections. How are the events described in each section similar? How do these events create a relationship between the three sections?

9. What is the **climax** of *The Metamorphosis*? When is it revealed? How does this turning point in the story contribute to the structural complexity of the text?

10. How do the various changes in Gregor's **circumstances** lead to changes in Gregor himself? Choose two significant examples and then discuss how the circumstances contribute to the character's shift.

11. How does Kafka create **pacing** in *The Metamorphosis*? How does the arrangement of details, frequency of events, and the speed at which the narrative events occur contribute to the complexity of the story?

NARRATION

12. What is the narrative **point of view** in the story? Explain how this choice affects the details and information presented in the text.

13. How does the **narrator's distance** from the events of the story affect the details and information presented in the text?

FIGURATIVE LANGUAGE: Word Choice, Imagery, and Symbols

14. Is the setting **symbolic**? For example, how does Gregor's room contribute to and reveal his emotions, psychology, and beliefs?

15. Choose a **symbol** in the novella. Explain how these figurative associations contribute to the complexity of the text.

16. Explain how the mind and body function as **motifs** in the text. How do these motifs contribute to your understanding of the text?

FIGURATIVE LANGUAGE: Comparisons

17. Explain how Gregor's transformation is a **metaphorical** change. What is being compared in this metaphor?

18. How is Gregor's life as a vermin an **allegory**? Does viewing the story as an allegory contribute to your understanding of the text?

IDEAS IN LITERATURE: Loss and Disillusionment

19. In a sense, Gregor's disillusionment and loss reflect his alienation from his family, his coworkers, his society, and perhaps the modern world itself. What factors contribute to alienation in our own time? What makes people isolated, disengaged, and disconnected from each other and larger communities? How do people fight alienation?

PUTTING IT ALL TOGETHER

20. Explain the significance of the story's title, both literally and figuratively. Be sure to consider not only Gregor's transformation but also how it reflects a historical or cultural context.

Writing about Setting

 Enduring Understanding (LAN-1)

Readers establish and communicate their interpretations of literature through arguments supported by textual evidence.

KEY POINT

Writers use introductions to engage their readers and provide context that leads to a thesis that unifies their literary argument.

Writing Introductions

When we read, we can be transported to another time and place where we join the characters on their literal and psychological journeys. A story's **setting** may include places that are familiar and realistic—New York City, a farm in the South, a cubicle in an office building—or it may be completely imaginative—Hogwarts, Oz, Panem, or the Hundred Acre Wood. In most cases, the setting plays an important role in our understanding of the characters and their values.

When analyzing settings, careful readers should pay attention to more than literal details related to time and place. Setting also includes historical, social, and cultural contexts. Perceptive readers understand that these different aspects combine to create the characters' environment and surroundings.

They also pay close attention to the setting's **atmosphere**, which is created by details. For example, a dwelling may seem lavish and extravagant, but the author may reveal through subtle details and particular word choice a more ominous mood lurking behind the shiny exterior. Readers then detect the complexity of the characters and their conflicts within the story. Likewise, a scene in nature may appear to be primitive and harsh, yet still provide characters with freedom or present challenges necessary to the protagonist's development. Such incongruities and ironies often reveal tensions and conflicts that contribute to a reader's interpretation of the work.

In this composition workshop, you will learn to write a literary argument that analyzes how an author's use of setting contributes to your interpretation of the text. As you develop your literary argument, you will also focus on writing an introduction that hooks your reader, introduces your idea, provides useful narrative context, and conveys your thesis statement.

YOUR ASSIGNMENT

Choose a text from Unit 7 or one that your teacher has assigned. Then, write a literary argument that analyzes how one or more settings within the text contribute to an interpretation of the work. Support your thesis with evidence from the text.

Your argument should interpret a literary work and include the following:

- An introduction that hooks the reader; identifies the title, author, context, and setting; and explains the relevance of the idea

- A thesis statement with a claim that conveys an interpretation (a unifying idea + insight about that idea)
- A line of reasoning that justifies the interpretation in the claim
- Relevant and sufficient textual evidence that supports the line of reasoning
- Commentary that links the evidence to the unifying idea in the line of reasoning and claim
- Transitional elements that create coherence in the argument
- A conclusion that brings the literary argument to a unified end
- Syntactical choices that reveal associations and relationships within the argument

Potential Subjects

- How a setting (e.g., rural or urban) shapes or reveals a character's values
- How an unrealistic or completely imaginary setting reveals real-world values
- How setting details mirror human characteristics to reveal values
- How environment or surroundings reflect a character's traits and values
- How seasons or weather function to reveal an interpretation
- How a setting serves as a metaphor or symbol
- How contrasting settings reveal meaning through their different attributes
- How a change in setting creates or reveals a change in a character

Explaining Complexity

While you are exploring how the author's choice of setting impacts the details within a narrative, you should also consider how settings contribute to your understanding of the story's characters, the culture, and the society. Because authors create complex associations between characters and their surroundings, you should note the details included in the description of settings: each detail is a deliberate choice.

Authors often begin a work with a description of the physical details of a setting, and embedded within that precise description are details that may reveal information about the culture, the community, or the main characters. For example, an isolated rural setting may be preparing the readers to meet an innocent or naive character.

Characters may also move from one setting to another, or two settings may be juxtaposed to reveal changes or contrasts within the narrative. Readers should pay close attention to these shifts and contrasts to identify associations and implications of the details in the text.

Finally, readers should look for inconsistencies and incongruities within a story. If the physical surroundings would customarily suggest one atmosphere yet the events betray that expectation, then the reader should work to discover why the author created that inconsistency.

Here are some questions to help you dig a little deeper into the complexity of setting:

- How do the physical details of the setting reveal contrasts, tensions, or conflict within the story?
- How does a shift in setting reveal other important changes or shifts in the narrative?
- How do contrasts in settings reveal complexities in the characters and their values?
- How might the setting's details reveal irony through their incongruity with the story's events?
- How do setting details reveal an author's social criticism?

Set a Purpose for Reading

As you begin to analyze one or two settings from your selected text, identify a unifying idea to guide your annotations. Consider the following questions with your unifying idea in mind as you examine the details and function of one or more settings.

- What are the implications of the geographic location and the physical details of the setting?
- What are the implications of the historical era, time of year, or time of day?
- What kind of atmosphere or mood do the setting details create? How is this atmosphere established?
- How do the characters respond to their surroundings?
- What values are suggested by the setting's details?
- What abstract idea is associated with the setting?

AP® SKILLS PRACTICE | **LITERARY ARGUMENTATION**
Analyzing Setting

Review the text that you are analyzing for your literary argument. Record your unifying idea, as well as the topic and focus of your analysis. Then, use the graphic organizer to identify settings, record details from the text, and consider the implications or significance of these details as they relate to your unifying idea. (You may need to delete or add rows.)

Analyzing the Complexity of a Setting
Unifying idea:

Topic and focus of analysis:	
Setting	**Setting** (For contrasting or shifting settings)
Details from the text:	Details from the text:
Insights and connections to the unifying idea:	Insights and connections to the unifying idea:

Develop a Thesis

A thesis statement for an analysis of a setting, as in other literary arguments, requires a claim that includes your interpretation. In this essay, you will explain how the details of the setting contribute to this interpretation. You should identify the specific setting(s) and the specific focus of your analysis — along with your broader interpretation of the text — within your thesis statement.

As you develop your line of reasoning, consider the following aspects or functions of the setting:

- The physical, cultural, and historical details of the setting within the narrative that contribute to an interpretation
- The relationship between the literal and metaphorical details of a setting as they develop characters and contribute to an interpretation
- The contrasting or contradictory aspects within a single setting that contribute to an interpretation
- The contrasting details and atmosphere of two or more settings that convey tensions and conflicts within a narrative
- The shift that occurs when characters move from one setting to another and reveal character development in the process

WRITING A THESIS FOR ANALYSIS OF SETTING	
Template 1: The thesis identifies two or more aspects of the setting to establish a line of reasoning and connect to the idea.	In [title of work], [author], uses [identify setting] to reveal [unifying idea + insight] by highlighting [aspect 1], [aspect 2], and [aspect 3].
Template 2: The thesis identifies two or more aspects of the setting to explore contrasts, juxtaposition, or shifts and connects to the idea.	In [title of work], [author] • contrasts [aspect 1 of setting] with [aspect 2 of setting] • juxtaposes [aspect 1 of setting] and [aspect 2 of setting] • shifts from [aspect 1 of setting] to [aspect 2 of setting] to convey [unifying idea + insight].
Template 3: The thesis identifies the setting and connects to the idea as an open thesis that chooses not to preview the line of reasoning.	In [title of work], [author's] details of [setting] illustrate [unifying idea + insight].

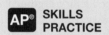 **SKILLS PRACTICE** | LITERARY ARGUMENTATION
Developing a Thesis Statement for Setting Analysis

Complete the following chart. In the left column, record the title, author, and aspect of the setting that you will explore. Next, record the unifying idea and insight that will convey your interpretation of your claim.

Developing a Defensible Thesis Statement for Setting Analysis		
Topic	**Claim**	
Title, Author, and Focus (aspect of setting)	Unifying Idea +	Insight

Organize a Line of Reasoning

Recall that you justify your interpretation through a line of reasoning that is revealed in your topic sentences. For a literary argument that analyzes setting, your line of reasoning focuses on specific aspects of the setting that relate back to the unifying idea in your claim.

The body of your analysis should be organized according to the line of reasoning that you used in crafting your thesis.

STRUCTURE OF AN ANALYSIS OF SETTING

Introduction

The **introduction** is an opportunity for the writer to establish the purpose of this literary argument and interest the audience in the literary work and the writer's interpretation of it. To achieve this goal, many literary arguments follow this structure:

- Engage the audience through an interesting hook
- Provide historical, cultural, or social context of a literary work
- Identify the title, author, genre (TAG)
- Introduce the setting(s) by
  - describing the importance of the setting(s) within the work; and
  - summarizing the work succinctly with details critical to the chosen setting(s)

The **thesis statement** presents a defensible interpretation that includes an idea and an insight about that idea.

Body

(Develops a line of reasoning with supporting evidence that justifies the thesis)

Topic Sentence 1	Topic Sentence 2	Topic Sentence 3
(Identify the first aspect of setting related to the unifying idea)	(Identify the second aspect of setting related to the unifying idea)	(Identify the third aspect of setting related to the unifying idea)
Textual Details	**Textual Details**	**Textual Details**
(Evidence of elements and techniques that contribute to setting development and complexity)	(Evidence of elements and techniques that contribute to setting development and complexity)	(Evidence of elements and techniques that contribute to setting development and complexity)
Commentary	**Commentary**	**Commentary**
(Link evidence by explaining its relevance to the line of reasoning and claim)	(Link evidence by explaining its relevance to the line of reasoning and claim)	(Link evidence by explaining its relevance to the line of reasoning and claim)

Conclusion

The **conclusion** should do more than restate the thesis; instead it should be a robust and important paragraph. It is the opportunity for the writer to establish literary work's relevance by explaining how the literary work stands the test of time and reflects the human experience. Writers further their idea and insight by:

- Discussing the significance or relevance of interpretation
- Relating the text to other relevant literary works
- Connecting the theme to their own experience
- Presenting alternate interpretations
- Explaining how the work explores complexities and tensions
- Situating the theme within a broader context

This table illustrates the general structure of a literary argument. It does not intend to imply that all literary arguments are five paragraphs. Writers should determine the number of reasons needed to justify their claim, as well as how much evidence is sufficient to support each of these reasons.

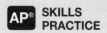 SKILLS PRACTICE | LITERARY ARGUMENTATION
Developing a Line of Reasoning

Review your thesis statement, which may or may not preview the line of reason-ing. Record the topic sentences to represent your line of reasoning and place them in a logical order. As you do this, consider the potential evidence from the text that helped you arrive at your line of reasoning. That textual evidence will serve as support for these reasons.

Organizing an Analysis of Setting		
Defensible Thesis Statement with Claim (idea + insight):		
Topic Sentence 1 (Identify the first aspect of the setting related to the unifying idea):	**Topic Sentence 2** (Identify the second aspect of the setting related to the unifying idea):	**Topic Sentence 3** (Identify the third aspect of the setting related to the unifying idea):

Select Relevant Evidence

In the writing workshops thus far, you examined how to select and introduce **relevant** and **sufficient evidence** from a text to support your line of reasoning. Recall that every reason must be accompanied by relevant supporting evidence. In other words, the evidence you select must relate directly to the purpose of that paragraph as defined by the topic sentence. Likewise, your evidence should be sufficient, meaning that it must include several details of the setting and support the setting's various functions and associations.

As you examine the setting and how it functions within the text, record specific details from the narrative accurately. If you misrepresent an aspect of the setting by using a detail out of context, your analysis could unravel. Remember to choose the best pieces of evidence and arrange them in the specific paragraphs where they provide the most apt support.

As you delve into the specific details of the setting, you may need to review and even revise your line of reasoning or your main idea and insight — especially if your evidence does not support your original interpretation. Remember that writ-ing a literary analysis requires you to examine and re-examine a text to make sure that your interpretation aligns with the details and evidence on the page.

Keeping your unifying idea in mind, you might incorporate evidence that illustrates, clarifies, exemplifies, associates, amplifies, or qualifies the following:

- Textual details that exemplify the physical qualities of a setting
- Textual details that reveal the time of day, season, weather, or general atmosphere of a setting

- Textual details that describe the historical, social, or cultural relevance of the setting
- Textual details that include multiple character reactions to or perspectives within a particular setting
- Textual details that demonstrate a contrast between two or more settings

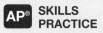 **SKILLS PRACTICE** | **LITERARY ARGUMENTATION**
Incorporating Relevant and Sufficient Evidence

Write your thesis statement and develop a logical line of reasoning to support your interpretation. Carefully organize your body paragraphs and arrange the evidence within them. Next, draft two or more body paragraphs that include evidence from the text to support each reason. Include transitions to link your reasons and evidence to your claim.

Incorporating Relevant and Sufficient Evidence		
Defensible Thesis Statement with Claim (idea + insight):		
Topic Sentence 1 (Identify the first aspect of the setting related to the unifying idea):	**Topic Sentence 2** (Identify the second aspect of the setting related to the unifying idea):	**Topic Sentence 3** (Identify the third aspect of the setting related to the unifying idea):
Textual Details (Relevant and sufficient evidence):	**Textual Details** (Relevant and sufficient evidence):	**Textual Details** (Relevant and sufficient evidence):

Write Insightful Commentary

In earlier units, you practiced writing commentary to achieve unity (connecting evidence to the idea) and coherence (connecting evidence to your reasons). Recall that your commentary is where your actual analysis takes place. When you analyze a setting in a work, therefore, you will still follow the basic pattern, identify-evidence-link, to write your complex argument. Effective commentary explains the function of the setting(s) and shows how setting contributes to your interpretation of the text.

In your analysis, you must not only identify the literal details but also explain their deeper implications for the meaning of the text. Your commentary links the specific setting detail to its function within the text and to the **unifying idea** and insight in your thesis.

EXPLAINING THE SIGNIFICANCE OF SETTING

Topics for Setting Analysis	Templates for Introducing Setting Details and Function of Details	Templates for Explaining Setting Details in Commentary
Geographical and Physical (topography, nature, weather, architecture, furnishings, living and working conditions)	The description of ____ as ____ • creates a sense of ____. • emphasizes ____. • reveals ____. • associates ____ with ____.	Through this choice, the author • explores the tension between ____ and ____. • develops the idea of ____. • implies that ____. • reveals the value of ____. • reveals the parallels between the values of ____ and ____.
Time (era, season, time of day)	By including the social convention of ____ indicative of this historical era, the author • characterizes ____ as ____. • criticizes the society that ____. • associates ____ with ____. Through the ____ detail of the time of year/season/time of day, the author emphasizes ____.	By including the detailed associations of time, the author • creates an atmosphere of ____ to amplify the idea that ____. • develops the idea of ____. • implies that ____. • represents the deeper observation that ____.
Historical (past, present, or future events in history that occurred at the time the story is set)	The historical backdrop of the narrative, specifically ____, • creates a tension between ____ and ____. • sheds light on the character's ____ [actions/thoughts].	The characters' interactions within the specific time period reveal the idea that ____.
Social (how people live, what people believe, traditions, rituals, customs) **Cultural** (urban, rural, popular interests, the arts, religion, folklore)	The author describes the tradition/culture/trend/ritual of ____ in order to • explore the implications that ____. • suggest the similarities between ____ and ____. • create a contrast between ____ and ____. • characterize the society as ____.	The author includes details of the character's/culture's/society's tradition of ____ to focus the attention on their ____ qualities/values/priorities and emphasize the idea that ____.
Atmosphere/Mood (words and images that convey feelings [e.g., joy, gloom, fear] in the reader)	The words/images of ____ convey the feelings of ____, creating a ____ atmosphere.	The ____ atmosphere created by the images/word choice contributes to the readers' understanding of ____.

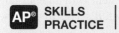 SKILLS PRACTICE | LITERARY ARGUMENTATION
Explaining the Significance of Setting

Build on your emerging literary argument by adding commentary to your relevant and sufficient evidence. Continue to incorporate transitions for coherence and craft your sentences to show balance and imbalance of ideas. Additionally, keep the focus on your unifying idea so that you may carry this idea throughout your argument in a unified way.

Explaining the Significance of Setting		
Defensible Thesis Statement with Claim (idea + insight):		
Topic Sentence 1 (Identify the first aspect of the setting related to the unifying idea):	**Topic Sentence 2** (Identify the second aspect of the setting related to the unifying idea):	**Topic Sentence 3** (Identify the third aspect of the setting related to the unifying idea):
Textual Details (Relevant and sufficient evidence):	**Textual Details** (Relevant and sufficient evidence):	**Textual Details** (Relevant and sufficient evidence):
Commentary (Link evidence to reason and idea)	**Commentary** (Link evidence to reason and idea)	**Commentary** (Link evidence to reason and idea)
Sentence stem and explanation of function of evidence:	Sentence stem and explanation of function of evidence:	Sentence stem and explanation of function of evidence:

Contextualize Your Argument

In prior workshops, you have written partial introductions that include narrative context, introduce the literary topic of discussion, identify the title and author, and funnel to the discussion of the unifying idea and insight in the thesis statement.

As you finish writing your analysis of setting, you will now add one more element to complete a full introduction. To engage your readers and invite them to explore your topic, you should begin your literary argument with an engaging **hook**. A hook is the first sentence or two in your argument; it serves to grab the attention of potential readers and encourage them to continue reading. Hooks are especially effective when they create a bookend for the argument that you completed in the conclusion. You will explore this strategy more in Unit 8 when you learn to write a formal conclusion.

One of the most difficult tasks for writers is to create a seamless journey from the hook, through the necessary context and introduction to the topic, and then finally to the thesis statement. You may need to use a transitional sentence, often called a bridge, so that your readers follow your train of thought.

ENGAGING HOOKS FOR LITERARY ARGUMENT

Type of Hook	Description	Example
Set up and pose a question	A rhetorical question that relates to the topic or unifying idea	*Almost everyone is familiar with Dorothy Gale's harrowing journey to return to Kansas after being flung into the Land of Oz. But after such an experience, can anyone ever really return home again?*
Quote from a literary text	A quotation from a literary work or author that relates to the topic or unifying idea	*James Baldwin once wrote, "You don't have a home until you leave it and then, when you have left it, you never can go back."*
Set a scene	A brief, detailed description that provides relevant context or sets up a contrast that relates to the unifying idea	*A cozy fire in the fireplace, a hot meal on the dining table, and the welcoming arms of beloved family members. For many, this is the meaning of home. But this scene may not be a reality for everyone.*
Share an insight about the idea	An observation or proverbial statement that relates to the unifying idea	*We never really appreciate our home until we have to leave it; then we learn too late that we should have treasured it all along.*
Create a comparison	A metaphor or simile that connects a topic that is familiar to the audience to the topic or unifying idea in the argument	*Like the baby bird who must be pushed out of her nest to learn to fly, people, too, must leave home to learn what they are truly capable of accomplishing.*

INSIDER AP TIP

Introductions engage readers and focus them on the rest of the argument. When you write a full introduction, you must both invite readers to read your analysis and preview the substance of your argument. Many writers finish writing the argument first and then add the introduction once they know how the argument will unfold. The most effective introductions contribute to the unity of the argument by connecting to a unifying idea.

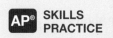 SKILLS PRACTICE | LITERARY ARGUMENTATION
Establishing Context and Explaining Relevance

In the following chart, record an idea for a hook to begin your argument. Next, record notes to help you communicate the context of your argument, introductory details about the setting, and introductory material that will funnel your ideas to your thesis statement. Then, record ideas to help you explain the relevance of your idea and insight in your concluding statement.

Establishing Context and Explaining Relevance	
Idea and insight	**Context for Introduction**
	Hook:
	Context:
	Significance of Idea in Conclusion

Revise Your Argument

When reviewing your analysis of setting, ask the following questions about the function and effect of the setting details. Revise your draft if your answer is "no" to any of the following questions.

- Have you established the associations, function, or purpose of the setting?
- Do your reasons in your line of reasoning refer to the function and relevance of the setting?
- Does your line of reasoning support your interpretation?
- Have you included textual evidence that directly exemplifies the relevance of the setting?
- Do you need to revise your thesis or line of reasoning based on the evidence that you have collected?
- Does your explanation of the evidence logically align with your interpretation of the work?
- Is your argument coherent, with a logical sequence of reasons and transitions to connect evidence, reasons, and claim?
- Does your commentary unify your argument by connecting your evidence and reasons to your unifying idea?
- Do you include effective transitional elements between and within your body paragraphs to create coherence?
- Does your introduction include a hook to engage your audience?

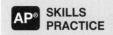

AP® SKILLS PRACTICE | LITERARY ARGUMENTATION
Revising and Editing an Analysis of Setting

After you have completed revising and editing your own argument, review another student's literary argument and provide helpful feedback.

Peer-Revision Checklist: Revising and Editing an Analysis of Setting		
Revising and Editing Checklist	**Unit 7 Focus Skills**	**Comment on the Effectiveness and/or Make a Suggestion**
Does the writer include an engaging hook, the narrative situation, title, and author of the literary text in the first paragraph?	Introductions for setting analysis	
Does the thesis statement convey an interpretation? Does the interpretation connect to an idea and an insight?	Defensible thesis	
Does the writer provide a logical sequence of reasons to support the idea and insight in the thesis? Are these reasons linked to the claim with transitions?	Line of reasoning: Unity	
Does the writer provide relevant and sufficient evidence to support the interpretation in the thesis? Is the evidence linked to the topic sentences with transitions?	Relevant and sufficient evidence: Coherence	
Does the writer explain how the evidence supports a reason and connects to the interpretation in the thesis? Does the commentary connect to the unifying idea?	Commentary: Unity and coherence	
Does the writer explain significance within a broader context?	Relevance	
Does the writer demonstrate control over the conventions of writing?	Conventions	

Student Model: Writing about Setting

Review the following student model that analyzes the setting in Margaret Atwood's *The Handmaid's Tale*. Observe how the thesis statement, line of reasoning, and evidence work together to convey an interpretation of the work.

A Cautionary Tale:
Culture as Setting in *The Handmaid's Tale*
Hannah Richards

Sometimes things are forcefully taken—fists clenching, teeth grinding, sweat burning the eyes. Margaret Atwood published her novel, *The Handmaid's Tale*, shortly after the election of Ronald Reagan. This novel, set in a dystopian future, acts to warn society of the recent sexual revolution being reversed. Though women spent decades attempting to fully exit the "private sphere," meaning to hold occupations and social lives outside of the home, the increase in religious conservatives in America posed a possible threat to existence in the "public sphere." Feminist activists at the time feared that their careers could be torn from their fingertips once again. Margaret Atwood sounds alarms through *The Handmaid's Tale* by utilizing separations in setting, which illustrate the consequences of tearing families and careers apart.

> thesis
> idea: separation
> insight: separation results in fractured relationships

One separation in setting would be the extreme differences between the immediate Pre-Gilead Age and the Rule of Gilead. Within the Rule of Gilead, mothers of lower-middle class were torn away from their children, adopting roles as Marthas, Handmaids, or being declared Unwoman. Their children were then sent away to the "colonies," where they were forced into either hard labor or groomed into Handmaids. The main character, Offred, was separated from her child as they both adopted their new roles in society. The Wife in charge of Offred, Serena Joy, did lessen this separation by at least a degree. Serena Joy was able to obtain a photograph of Offred's daughter. This photograph showed Offred's daughter adorned in a white dress, which acted as a symbol of innocence. Offred assumes that her daughter does not remember her, the white dress symbolizing her innocence and naivety to the heart wrenching separation she has endured. This separation affected Offred to such a degree that she felt it was easier to "think of her as dead," than revel in that loss. This heavy decision illustrates how separations in setting negatively affect those whose families have been torn apart with the Rule of Gilead. Additionally, women had their careers torn from them as a result of the Rule of Gilead as well. Offred recounts being fired from her job at the library and her money being transferred to her husband, Luke.

> topic sentence: identifies the first example of separation in the setting (time)

> evidence: Offred experiences separation from her daughter

> commentary: explains how difficult it was on Offred and other families to cope

> evidence: Gilead women were separated from their careers and money

This separation did not only affect Offred. It is soon revealed that every woman's money was transferred to either her husband or closest male kin. This is explained when Offred and the Commander venture into Jezebel's, where Offred states that the women there were once lawyers and in business, but that was "no longer." The separation between the Pre-Gilead Age and the Rule of Gilead illustrates the tearing of careers away from women as well, which is another way *The Handmaid's Tale* warns against the reversal of the sexual revolution. Through illustrating the negative effects of tearing women from their families and careers, Margaret Atwood effectively warns society against the possibilities the new rise in religious conservatives could mean.

> commentary: connects the characters' experiences to the author's contemporary context

Another instance of separation in setting is the two vastly different atmospheres during the birth of Janine's child. The novel utilizes the sounds of laughter and the tastes of rich foods to create imagery of the downstairs of the party. Downstairs the Wives mingle and enjoy conversation, while the upstairs is crowded in silence. As Janine births the child, the Handmaids stand surrounding the bed. The novel utilizes descriptions of breathing and silent communication to illustrate the tense atmosphere upstairs in comparison to the downstairs party. This separation in setting conveys the different roles of women in the Gilead society. Furthermore, Margaret Atwood reveals the pain of separating families once again as the Handmaids routinely step in front of Janine to hide the Wife naming and claiming the newborn as her own. This contrast in settings acts as another alarm to society that there could possibly be a transition from the lively "public sphere" existence of women back into the demeaning "private sphere." Margaret Atwood ultimately communicates that women could be reduced to having to "step aside," as they are taken advantage of as "vessels of life" solely.

> topic sentence: identifies the second separation in the setting (atmosphere)
>
> evidence: illustrates the contrast between those in power downstairs and the handmaids upstairs
>
> commentary: connects the downstairs and upstairs to the public and private spheres for women

The Handmaid's Tale acts as a warning to society, as Margaret Atwood along with other female activists feared that the new rise of religious conservatives could lead to the reversal of the sexual revolution. Through repeatedly illustrating the negative effects of tearing women from their prior empowered roles, Atwood is able to convey Feminist ideals to the audience. In present time, there is debate on whether *The Handmaid's Tale* is a Feminist or Anti-Feminist novel. This is largely because of the repeated illustration of women losing their identities; however, this acts as a cautionary tale rather than a manifestation. *The Handmaid's Tale* is a feminist novel that secures the roles of women in the "public sphere" for years to come.

> conclusion: explains the effects of the separation on the power afforded to women

Free-Response Question: Prose Fiction Analysis

AP® Enduring Understanding (LAN-1)

Readers establish and communicate their interpretations of literature through arguments supported by textual evidence.

Writing Introductions

Throughout the first six units, you have been learning to write effective literary arguments that address an assigned topic either for prose analysis, poetry analysis, or the open question. In this workshop, you will return to the prose fiction analysis question to continue developing your skills for the literary argument. Now you will turn your attention to making these arguments more complex and sophisticated by including helpful context before the thesis statement in your introduction.

Read the following practice prompt, which is a model of the type of prompt you may see on the AP® English Literature and Composition Exam.

Prompt:

The following passage is excerpted from the novel *Middlemarch* by George Eliot, the pen name of Mary Ann Evans (1819–1880). The passage reveals a conversation between now-widowed Dorothea Brooke and her late husband's cousin, Will Ladislaw. Dorothea must decide whether to give up her inheritance to marry Will, a man she loves, or refuse him and remain financially secure. Read the passage carefully.

Then, in a well-written essay, analyze how Eliot uses literary elements and techniques to portray the couple's complex psychological dilemma.

In your response, you should do the following:

- Respond to the prompt with a thesis that presents a defensible interpretation
- Select and use evidence to support your line of reasoning
- Explain how the evidence supports your line of reasoning
- Use appropriate grammar and punctuation in communicating your argument

Unifying Idea	*from* **Middlemarch** George Eliot	Effect of Literary Elements and Techniques
doubt doubt	They were wasting these last moments together in wretched silence. What could he say, since what had got obstinately uppermost in his mind was the passionate love for her which he 5 forbade himself to utter? What could she say, since she might offer him no help — since she was forced to keep the money that ought to have been his? — since to-day he seemed not to respond as he used to do to her thorough trust and liking? 10 But Will at last turned away from his portfolio and approached the window again.	word choices of "obstinately" and "forbade" reveal a tension leading to uncertainty both characters' doubtful thoughts and motivations are revealed through third-person, objective narrator
doubt	"I must go," he said, with that peculiar look of the eyes which sometimes accompanies bitter feeling, as if they had been tired and burned with 15 gazing too close at a light.	simile illustrates Will's resignation, suggesting his motive for denying his passion even in doubt
doubt	"What shall you do in life?" said Dorothea, timidly. "Have your intentions remained just the same as when we said good-by before?"	
doubt	"Yes," said Will, in a tone that seemed to waive 20 the subject as uninteresting. "I shall work away at the first thing that offers. I suppose one gets a habit of doing without happiness or hope."	the third-person narrator conveys an objective perspective of the internal conflicts of both characters
doubt	"Oh, what sad words!" said Dorothea, with a dangerous tendency to sob. Then trying to smile, 25 she added, "We used to agree that we were alike in speaking too strongly."	the word choice "dangerous" juxtaposed with "smile" sets up a contradiction
doubt	"I have not spoken too strongly now," said Will, leaning back against the angle of the wall. "There are certain things which a man can only 30 go through once in his life; and he must know some time or other that the best is over with him. This experience has happened to me while I am very young — that is all. What I care more for than I can ever care for anything else is abso- 35 lutely forbidden to me — I don't mean merely by being out of my reach, but forbidden me, even	Will's actions ("leaning back") and his speech ("the best is over . . . that is all") convey his epiphany that he cannot follow his passion

doubt

if it were within my reach, by my own pride and
honor — by everything I respect myself for. Of
course I shall go on living as a man might do who
40 had seen heaven in a trance."

Will reveals his uncertainty through a simile comparing himself to one in a trance

Will paused, imagining that it would be
impossible for Dorothea to misunderstand this;
indeed he felt that he was contradicting himself

doubt

and offending against his self-approval in speak-
45 ing to her so plainly; but still — it could not be
fairly called wooing a woman to tell her that he
would never woo her. It must be admitted to be a
ghostly kind of wooing.

Will admits the contradictory nature of his values, denying passion for logical reasons

But Dorothea's mind was rapidly going over
50 the past with quite another vision than his. The
thought that she herself might be what Will most
cared for did throb through her an instant, but
then came doubt. . . .

Dorothea's thoughts contrast Will's in that she reveals her doubt despite her own passion

→ ## Step One: Annotate the Passage Based on a Unifying Idea

In Unit 4, you practiced annotating a passage for specific details that reveal the important context, help you understand the central conflict, and lead you to your interpretation. These skills are a strong start to analyzing a passage, but you must also practice reading between the lines and considering the ideas beyond the immediate context of the passage.

For the final practice of the prose analysis question, you will focus your attention not only on the passage's characters, events, and details but also more specifically on the conflicts and tensions within the passage. Your goal is to identify and explain the **complexity** of the work within your argument. Something is complex when it explores a tension by analyzing different, yet connected parts.

In literature, complexity can emerge from any fictional elements, including characters, settings, narrators, images, symbols, and themes. As a result, careful readers do not merely examine the surface of a text but instead dive deeper to unearth the details that reveal conflicts and tensions. When you do this, you can understand and explain the complexity of a passage.

To guide your annotations, consider the following questions that will help you analyze complexity within the passage:

- Do the characters' thoughts, behaviors, and actions reveal contradictory traits? If so, what do these contradictions suggest?
- Is the central conflict in the passage internal, external, or both? If both, how are these conflicts related, and what do they reveal about the characters?

- Do the characters behave as expected for the era in which the passage is set? If not, how does this incongruity contribute to your understanding of the characters or to your interpretation?
- Is the narrator's perspective complex or nuanced? How do you know?
- What details and word choices within the passage are in contrast? What do these patterns or contrasts suggest?
- Is there a shift in the passage? Identify and describe the shift.
- What idea emerges from the details of the passage?
- What complex insight does the passage suggest about his idea?

For example, in the passage from *Middlemarch*, the author establishes a number of contrasts and incongruities. The tensions created by these incongruities reveal the complexity of the idea that when reason prevails over passion, a person will invariably doubt that choice. Here are a few of these incongruities:

- Though Will and Dorothea both feel helpless, his helplessness stems from suppressing his feelings, hers from knowing she has no options.
- Neither character is sure how the other feels about the relationship.
- Both characters' outward decisions and actions contrast their inner desires and thoughts.
- The couple's frankness in the moment contrasts the expectations of propriety.

Once you have detailed annotations, you are ready to express your interpretation of the passage with a thesis statement that addresses these complexities.

→ Step Two: Develop a Defensible Claim and a Unified Line of Reasoning

As you prepare to write more sophisticated literary arguments, you should include helpful and insightful context before your thesis statement. While you do not need a full introduction with an engaging hook (as in an untimed essay), you can still write a sentence or two before your thesis to help readers understand your interpretation (idea + insight).

To write this context, you can do any of the following:

- Provide background information about the historical or narrative context of the passage
- Introduce the central conflict or tension in the passage
- Introduce the unifying idea of the passage and explain its relevance within the narrative context of the passage
- Situate the characters, conflicts, or ideas within a larger context beyond the confines of the passage

Once you start looking at a passage more closely for the complexity within, you can develop a **thesis statement** to reflect that **complexity** and sophistication.

If you need help getting started, you may build from one of the following thesis templates or refer to the models that follows:

- In the passage from [title], [author] reveals [idea + insight] by contrasting [literary element 1] and [literary element 2].

- In the passage from [title], [author] reveals [idea + insight] by exploring the tension between [aspect 1] and [aspect 2].

- In the passage from [title], [author] reveals [idea + insight] by shifting from [aspect 1] to [aspect 2].

Review the following examples of thesis statements for prose fiction analysis.

Sample Thesis Statements	Notes on Effectiveness
In the passage from Middlemarch, *George Eliot explores the idea that when one chooses to abandon passion for reason, doubt will undoubtedly follow by contrasting the parting couple's affectionate thoughts with their pragmatic actions.*	Conveys the idea (doubt) and insight (abandoning passion for reason results in doubt). Previews a line of reasoning (contrast between Will and Dorothea's thoughts and actions).
In the passage from Middlemarch, *George Eliot explores the idea that when one chooses to abandon passion for reason, doubt will undoubtedly follow.*	Conveys the idea (doubt) and insight (abandoning passion for reason results in doubt). Chooses not to preview a line of reasoning.

Once you have a thesis statement that addresses the complexity of the passage, you can develop an effective argument by supporting your thesis with a logical line of reasoning that justifies your interpretation. The two sample thesis statements include the same claim, but the first thesis previews the line of reasoning. You do not need to include this part of the thesis. Instead, you may wait to reveal the line of reasoning in your topic sentences. Each reason within your line of reasoning will be a focus of each body paragraph of your essay. More importantly, these reasons serve to unify your essay so each reason must be related to the idea expressed in your thesis. Together, your reasons must justify your argument.

Review the following questions to determine the structure of your line of reasoning. They will help you write your topic sentences.

- Do the author's literary elements and techniques work together to present complexity in a character, a relationship, or a narrative perspective?

- Does the passage reveal a change in a character's traits, values, or perspectives that contributes to the complexity?

- Does the passage contrast two or more characters' traits, values, or perspectives that reveal a conflict or tension?

- Does the narrator's perspective or attitude change within the passage to reveal tension or conflict?

- Does the atmosphere or narrative tone change within the passage?

After considering these questions, you can determine a logical sequence for discussing your interpretation. Your topic sentences should include accurate and precise language that maintains the complexity established in your introduction; they should also relate directly to the single, unifying idea and insight in your thesis statement.

If you need help getting started, you may build from the following topic sentence templates or refer to the following models:

- [Author] includes [literary element] to reveal [connection to effect and unifying idea].

- [Transitional element] [author] includes [literary element] to further exemplify [connection to effect and unifying idea].

Review the following thesis statement and line of reasoning. Note that the unifying idea creates the connection between the claim in the thesis and the topic sentences that support the claim.

Sample Thesis Statement

In the passage from Middlemarch, *George Eliot explores the idea that when one chooses to abandon passion for reason, doubt will undoubtedly follow by contrasting the parting couple's affectionate thoughts with their pragmatic actions.*

Topic Sentence 1	Topic Sentence 2
In the passage, Eliot's use of an objective third-person narrator conveys both characters' internal thoughts, which reveal their conflict and the uncertainty that results from denying their passion.	*After establishing the internal conflict, Eliot contrasts the couple's thoughts with their external actions to reveal the self-doubt that results from the tension between their apparent passion and the duty each one feels to follow societal expectations.*

In this example, the first topic sentence focuses the paragraph on Eliot's use of the third-person objective narrator to convey the couple's internal struggles and doubts that cause a conflict and cause uncertainty. In the process, it establishes a context for exploring the tension that results from their difficult decisions.

The second topic sentence transitions from the first and shifts the focus from internal thoughts to external actions. The tension created by this contrast will lead to an analysis of the characters' individual values and motivations as revealed by their response to their uncertainty. This uncertainty results from their choice to do what is expected of them.

INSIDER AP® TIP

Introductions contribute to an argument's sophistication. One way to convey complexity in your introduction is to use subordinating conjunctions — *although, rather than, since, while* — before your insight about the idea. This can be done in the sentences preceding the thesis or within the thesis itself.

→ Step Three: Choose Relevant Evidence

Recall that when you choose **evidence** from the passage, it should be both relevant and sufficient. You should include one or more pieces of evidence from the text to support each reason in your line of reasoning. Make sure that this evidence is directly related to your topic sentence and your unifying idea. Also, include examples of multiple literary elements and techniques within your analysis.

You may paraphrase or quote directly from the passage when you include your evidence. If you are quoting directly, weave a few words of the text into your own sentences to maintain your own sentence fluency.

Topic Sentence 1	Topic Sentence 2
In the passage, Eliot's use of an objective third-person narrator conveys both characters' internal thoughts, which reveal their conflict and the uncertainty that results from denying their passion.	*After establishing the internal conflict, Eliot contrasts the couple's thoughts with their external actions to reveal the self-doubt that results from the tension between their apparent passion and the duty each one feels to follow societal expectations.*
Relevant and Sufficient Evidence	**Relevant and Sufficient Evidence**
Evidence 1:	Evidence 1:
". . . obstinately uppermost in his mind was the passionate love for her which he forbade himself to utter."	*"Of course I shall go on living as a man might do who had seen heaven in a trance."*
Evidence 2:	*"I suppose one gets a habit of doing without happiness or hope."*
". . . said Dorothea, with a dangerous tendency to sob."	Evidence 2:
"The thought that she herself might be what Will most cared for did throb through her an instant, but then came doubt. . . ."	*". . . she was forced to keep the money that ought to have been his . . ."*
	". . . trying to smile . . ."

→ Step Four: Develop Your Commentary

As you have learned in previous writing workshops, your **commentary** serves to link your evidence to your line of reasoning and to explain how that evidence relates to your idea and insight. Since you have been developing a complex thesis, establishing a line of reasoning, and choosing the most relevant evidence to support your interpretation, your commentary must also reflect the same level of complexity and sophistication.

You will now take the identify-evidence-link strategy to the next level by linking your evidence even more thoroughly and thoughtfully. For example, an author's use of a literary element or technique can serve multiple purposes within a text. A single metaphor can have more than one relevant association. A precise detail about a character or a setting may reveal more than one important quality about that character. After you determine a purpose or an association for an author's choice, then, ask yourself, "What else could this mean?"

When details within a passage contrast with each other, then they often reveal complexity. For example, a smile may simply reveal that a character is friendly, which would not be complex. But by reading the details carefully, you might determine that the character's smile is actually a mask concealing a more sinister intention. In this case, you get at the complexity by explaining both the appearance and the contradictory intent within your commentary. You also link these details to your idea and insight.

To help you add commentary that explains complexity within a passage, you might build from the following templates:

- By highlighting the tension between ___ and ___, the author suggests ___.
- The contrast between ___ and ___ portrays a deeper conflict between ___ and ___.
- ___ symbolizes ___ which serves not only to ___ but also to ___.
- By describing the character/setting as ___, the author emphasizes the complexity of ___.
- While the character appears ___, his/her ___ actions reveal the contrary in that ___.

Review the following example of commentary that addresses complexity by exploring the tension revealed by the third-person narrator who conveys the character's thoughts as two opposing forces that collide. The evidence and commentary explain the revelations from the narrator and also incorporate a discussion of the words Eliot chooses to describe these complex internal emotions. Finally, the commentary connects to both the topic sentence and the idea in the thesis.

Evidence	Commentary Connected to Idea
". . . obstinately uppermost in his mind was the passionate love for her which he forbade himself to utter."	The passage begins with a description of Will's internal thoughts during the "wretched silence" between the couple. The narrator describes his passionate love as "obstinately uppermost in his mind." The choice of the words "obstinately" and "uppermost" suggests that this passion may be too forceful for him to overcome. However, although this passion is strong, the narrator then reveals Will's equally stubborn nature that "forbade himself to utter" his true feelings. Eliot's use of the word "forbade" illustrates the intensity of Will's inner conflict and reveals the tension of the uncertainty that will follow him throughout the struggle to deny his love for Dorothea.

AP® EXAM PRACTICE

The following is an example of a prose fiction analysis free-response question. Practice the skills you have learned in this workshop to write an argument in response to the prompt. You may use the graphic organizer and templates to help you plan and write your analysis.

Remember to follow the four steps:

- Step One: Annotate the passage based on a **unifying idea**
- Step Two: Write a **defensible thesis statement**
- Step Three: Choose **relevant evidence**
- Step Four: Develop **insightful commentary**

Prompt:

The following excerpt is from *Native Son* by Richard Wright, published in 1940. In this passage from early in the novel, an African American youth named Bigger Thomas has just fought and killed an enormous rat in the tiny one-room apartment he shares with his mother and two siblings. Read the passage carefully.

Then, in a well-written essay, analyze how Wright uses literary elements and techniques to convey Bigger's complex attitude about his responsibility to his family.

In your response you should do the following:

- Respond to the prompt with a thesis that presents a defensible interpretation
- Select and use evidence to support your line of reasoning
- Explain how the evidence supports your line of reasoning
- Use appropriate grammar and punctuation in communicating your argument

Bigger walked across the floor and sat on the bed. His mother's eyes followed him.

"We wouldn't have to live in this garbage dump if you had any manhood in you," she
5 said.

"Aw, don't start that again."

"How you feel, Vera?" the mother asked.

Vera raised her head and looked about the room as though expecting to see
10 another rat.

"Oh, Mama!"

"You poor thing!"

"I couldn't help it. Bigger scared me."

"Did you hurt yourself?"
15 "I bumped my head."

"Here; take it easy. You'll be all right."

"How come' Bigger acts that way?" Vera asked, crying again.

"He's just crazy," the mother said. "Just
20 plain dumb black crazy."

"I'll be late for my sewing class at the Y.W.C.A.," Vera said.

"Here; stretch out on the bed. You'll feel better in a little while," the mother said.

25 She left Vera on the bed and turned a pair of cold eyes upon Bigger.

"Suppose you wake up some morning and find your sister dead? What would you think then?" she asked. "Suppose those rats 30 cut our veins at night when we sleep? Naw! Nothing like that ever bothers you! All you care about is your own pleasure! Even when the relief offers you a job you won't take it till they threaten to cut off your food and 35 starve you! Bigger, honest, you the most no-countest man I ever seen in all my life!"

"You done told me that a thousand times," he said, not looking round.

"Well, I'm telling you again. And mark 40 my word, some of these days you going to set down and *cry*. Some of these days you going to wish you had made something out of yourself, instead of just a tramp. But it'll be too late then."

45 "Stop prophesying about me," he said.

"I prophesy much as I please! And if you don't like it, you can get out. We can get along without you. We can live in one room just like we living now, even with you gone," she said.

50 "Aw, for chrissakes!" he said, his voice filled with nervous irritation.

"You'll regret how you living some day," she went on. "If you don't stop running with that gang of yours and do right you'll end 55 up where you never thought you would. You think I don't know what you boys is doing, but I do. And the gallows is at the end of the road you traveling, boy. Just remember that." She turned and looked at Buddy. "Throw 60 that box outside, Buddy."

"Yessum."

There was silence. Buddy took the box out. The mother went behind the curtain to the gas stove. Vera sat up in bed and swung 65 her feet to the floor.

"Lay back down, Vera," the mother said.

"I feel all right now, Ma. I got to go to my sewing class."

"Well, if you feel like it, set the table," the 70 mother said, going behind the curtain again. "Lord, I get so tired of this I don't know what to do," her voice floated plaintively from behind the curtain. "All I ever do is try to make a home for you children and you 75 don't care."

"Aw, Ma," Vera protested. "Don't say that."

"Vera sometimes I just want to lay down and quit."

"Ma, please don't say that."

80 "I can't last many more years, living like this."

"I'll be old enough to work soon, Ma."

"I reckon I'll be dead then. I reckon God'll call me home."

85 Vera went behind the curtain and Bigger heard her trying to comfort his mother. He shut their voices out of his mind. He hated his family because he knew that they were suffering and that he was powerless to 90 help them. He knew that the moment he allowed himself to feel to its fullness how they lived, the shame and misery of their lives, he would be swept out of himself with fear and despair. So he held toward 95 them an attitude of iron reserve; he lived with them, but behind a wall, a curtain. And toward himself he was even more exacting. He knew that the moment he allowed what his life meant to enter fully 100 into his consciousness, he would either kill himself or someone else. So he denied himself and acted tough.

ORGANIZING A PROSE FICTION ANALYSIS (III)

Introduction:

- Engage the audience through an interesting hook
- Provide historical, cultural, or social context of a literary work
- Identify the title, author, genre (TAG)
- Introduce the literary focus by
  - describing the importance of the (literary topic) within the work; and
  - summarizing the work succinctly with details critical to the chosen literary focus

Hook and context:

TAG:

Literary topic and concise summary:

Defensible Thesis Statement with Claim (idea + insight):

In [title], [his/her] [contextualize the work], [author] contrasts/explores the tension between [a and b] to reveal that [idea + insight].

Topic Sentence 1 (Identify the first aspect of the topic in relation to the unifying idea):	Topic Sentence 2 (Identify the second aspect of the topic, connect it to the first aspect in relation to the unifying idea):	Topic Sentence 3 (Identify the third aspect of the topic, connect it to the first and/ or second aspect in relation to the unifying idea):
To begin, [author] includes [technique/element 1] to [purpose connect to idea].	In contrast to [first aspect], [author] includes [technique/ element 2] to [purpose connect to idea].	Finally, [author] highlights the tension between [a and b] by including [technique/element 3] to [purpose connect to idea].
Textual Details (Relevant and sufficient evidence):	**Textual Details** (Relevant and sufficient evidence):	**Textual Details** (Relevant and sufficient evidence):
For example, the detail/image/ comparison [text evidence], used to describe [context], illustrates [link to topic sentence]. [Author] continues to explore [link to topic sentence] by including [detail/image/ comparison] which reveals [insight].	To illustrate, [author] compares/ contrasts [a and b] by describing [text evidence] to reveal [link to topic sentence]. Another point of comparison for [a and b] illustrated through [text evidence] reveals the [link to topic sentence].	As an example of [technique/ element], the author includes [text evidence] to explain [link to topic sentence]. To develop this idea further, [author] explores [link to topic sentence] through [technique/ element] in describing [text evidence].

(continued)

Commentary (Link evidence to reason and idea):	Commentary (Link evidence to reason and idea):	Commentary (Link evidence to reason and idea):
The association with [idea] reveals [idea and insight].	Through the similar/contrasting attributes, [author] develops [idea and insight].	By including this [element/ technique] the author suggests that [idea and insight].
Two to four sentences explaining how the evidence exemplifies the universal idea	*Two to four sentences explaining how the evidence exemplifies the universal idea*	*Two to four sentences explaining how the evidence exemplifies the universal idea*

Conclusion:

Further your idea and insight by

- discussing the significance or relevance of interpretation;
- relating the work to other relevant literary works;
- connecting the theme to your own experience;
- presenting alternate interpretations;
- explaining how the work explores complexities and tensions; or
- situating the theme within a broader context.

PREPARING FOR THE AP® EXAM

Multiple-Choice Questions: Prose

from A Tale of Two Cities
Charles Dickens

The following is an excerpt from a novel published in 1859.

Outside Tellson's[1] — never by any means in it, unless called in — was an odd-job-man, an occasional porter and messenger, who served as the live sign of the house.[2] He was never
5 absent during business hours, unless upon an errand, and then he was represented by his son: a grisly urchin[3] of twelve, who was his express image. People understood that Tellson's, in a stately way, tolerated the odd-job-man. The
10 house had always tolerated some person in that capacity, and time and tide had drifted this person to the post. His surname was Cruncher, and on the youthful occasion of his renouncing by proxy the works of darkness,[4] in the easterly
15 parish church of Hounsditch, he had received the added appellation of Jerry.

The scene was Mr. Cruncher's private lodging in Hanging-Sword-Alley, Whitefriars: the time, half-past seven of the clock on a windy
20 March morning, Anno Domini seventeen hundred and eighty. (Mr. Cruncher himself always spoke of the year of our Lord as Anna Dominoes: apparently under the impression that the Christian era dated from the invention of a
25 popular game, by a lady who had bestowed her name upon it.)

Mr. Cruncher's apartments were not in a savoury neighbourhood, and were but two in number, even if a closet with a single pane of
30 glass in it might be counted as one. But they were very decently kept. Early as it was, on the windy March morning, the room in which he lay abed was already scrubbed throughout; and between the cups and saucers arranged for
35 breakfast, and the lumbering deal table, a very clean white cloth was spread.

Mr. Cruncher reposed under a patchwork counterpane,[5] like a Harlequin[6] at home. At first, he slept heavily, but, by degrees, began to
40 roll and surge in bed, until he rose above the surface, with his spiky hair looking as if it must tear the sheets to ribbons. At which juncture, he exclaimed, in a voice of dire exasperation:

"Bust me, if she ain't at it agin!"

45 A woman of orderly and industrious appearance rose from her knees in a corner, with sufficient haste and trepidation to show that she was the person referred to.

"What!" said Mr. Cruncher, looking out of
50 bed for a boot. "You're at it agin, are you?"

After hailing the morn with this second salutation, he threw a boot at the woman as a third. It was a very muddy boot, and may introduce the odd circumstance connected with Mr.
55 Cruncher's domestic economy, that, whereas he often came home after banking hours with clean boots, he often got up next morning to find the same boots covered with clay.

"What," said Mr. Cruncher, varying his
60 apostrophe after missing his mark — "what are you up to, Aggerawayter[7]"?

"I was only saying my prayers."

---

[1] A bank in the novel.
[2] Business — the bank — in this case.
[3] A mischievous young child, especially one who is poorly or raggedly dressed.
[4] Reference to him having been christened with his name in a church during his youth, as most people were at the time.

[5] A bedspread.
[6] A silent and clownish character in traditional Italian theater.
[7] Mr. Cruncher's name for his wife, likely a mispronunciation of "Aggravator."

"Saying your prayers! You're a nice woman!
What do you mean by flopping yourself down
65 and praying agin me?"

"I was not praying against you; I was praying
for you."

"You weren't. And if you were, I won't be
took the liberty with. Here! your mother's a
70 nice woman, young Jerry, going a praying agin
your father's prosperity. You've got a dutiful
mother, you have, my son. You've got a religious mother, you have, my boy: going and
flopping herself down, and praying that the
75 bread-and-butter may be snatched out of the
mouth of her only child."

Master Cruncher (who was in his shirt) took
this very ill, and, turning to his mother, strongly
deprecated any praying away of his personal board.
80 "And what do you suppose, you conceited
female," said Mr. Cruncher, with unconscious
inconsistency, "that the worth of *your* prayers may
be? Name the price that you put *your* prayers at!"

"They only come from the heart, Jerry. They
85 are worth no more than that."

"Worth no more than that," repeated Mr.
Cruncher. "They ain't worth much, then.
Whether or no, I won't be prayed agin, I tell
you. I can't afford it. I'm not a going to be made
90 unlucky by *your* sneaking. If you must go
flopping yourself down, flop in favour of your
husband and child, and not in opposition to 'em.
If I had had any but a unnat'ral wife, and this
poor boy had had any but a unnat'ral mother, I
95 might have made some money last week instead
of being counter-prayed and countermined
and religiously circumwented into the worst of
luck. B-u-u-ust me!" said Mr. Cruncher, who
all this time had been putting on his clothes, "if
100 I ain't, what with piety and one blowed thing
and another, been choused[8] this last week into
as bad luck as ever a poor devil of a honest
tradesman met with! Young Jerry, dress yourself,
my boy, and while I clean my boots keep a eye
105 upon your mother now and then, and if you see
any signs of more flopping, give me a call. For, I
tell you," here he addressed his wife once more,

---

[8]To have been swindled or cheated.

"I won't be gone agin, in this manner. I am as
rickety as a hackney-coach, I'm as sleepy as lau-
110 danum,[9] my lines is strained to that degree that
I shouldn't know, if it wasn't for the pain in 'em,
which was me and which somebody else, yet
I'm none the better for it in pocket; and it's my
suspicion that you've been at it from morning
115 to night to prevent me from being the better for
it in pocket, and I won't put up with it, Aggerawayter, and what do you say now!"

1. The change in setting that happens
   between the first paragraph ("Outside . . .
   Jerry.") and the second paragraph ("The
   scene . . . upon it.)") illustrates a
   (A) juxtaposition of Mr. Cruncher and his
       son.
   (B) contrast between Mr. Cruncher and
       his wife.
   (C) shift in the narrative to focus on the
       Crunchers' home life.
   (D) significant passage of time in the
       chronology of the passage.
   (E) comparison between Mr. Cruncher
       and his son.

2. In the context of the passage, introducing
   Mr. Cruncher's job at the bank in lines
   1–16 ("Outside . . . Jerry.") before discuss-
   ing his apartment and family has which of
   the following effects on the narrative?
   (A) It allows for a comparison between
       the wealth of the bank and the
       poverty of his family circumstances.
   (B) It illustrates how his job relates to his
       family circumstances.
   (C) It creates a metaphor for better
       understanding his family circumstances.
   (D) It prevents the reader from making too
       many assumptions about the characters.
   (E) It details the relationship between
       Mr. Cruncher and his son.

---

[9]An alcoholic solution containing morphine, prepared from
opium and formerly used as a narcotic painkiller.

3. The description of the "apartments" given in lines 27–36 ("Mr. Cruncher's apartments . . . was spread.") suggests that the Crunchers
   (A) long for more spacious, more luxurious living.
   (B) take care of what little they have.
   (C) are content with what their lives have given them.
   (D) believe they deserve more.
   (E) feel bitter for the unfairness of life.

4. The description of Mr. Cruncher in his bed — lines 37–43 ("Mr. Cruncher reposed . . . dire exasperation.") — makes use of which of the following?
   (A) Extended metaphor
   (B) Motif
   (C) Symbol
   (D) Allusion
   (E) Epiphany

5. In the context of the passage, Mr. Cruncher's epiphany that his wife is praying for him — lines 42–44 ("At which . . . agin!'") — can best be described as
   (A) juxtaposed with how she feels about him.
   (B) central to the conflict between the two.
   (C) comparable to how their son reacts to his mother.
   (D) directly related to his job at the bank.
   (E) understandable given the circumstances.

6. Which of the following best describes something indicated about the wife based on the way she interacts with Mr. Cruncher?
   (A) She worries about him and is very patient with him.
   (B) She is concerned for his soul given all of the pain he has caused others.
   (C) She cannot accept their living situation.
   (D) She fears that her son will follow in his father's footsteps.
   (E) She loves him very much and accepts him for who he is.

7. In context, Mr. Cruncher's accusations and responses to his wife can best be said to
   (A) contrast with those of his son.
   (B) illustrate the problems that his work and his family life have created for him.
   (C) contradict the way his wife feels about him.
   (D) indicate his fear that she will leave him because of his inability to support their lifestyle.
   (E) demonstrate his frustration with his own recent performance and circumstances.

8. In the context of the passage as a whole, it can most reasonably be claimed that Mr. Cruncher and his wife
   (A) fail to understand one another enough to really care for their son and support the family.
   (B) display many more differences than similarities.
   (C) share a common concern about the well-being of the family despite their interpersonal conflict.
   (D) find themselves trapped in a loveless marriage only kept together by their commitment to their son.
   (E) long for more in their life despite the obvious inability of Mr. Cruncher to do more for the family.

Ozymandias
Percy Bysshe Shelley

I met a traveller from an antique land,
Who said — "Two vast and trunkless legs of stone
Stand in the desert. . . . Near them, on the sand,
Half sunk a shattered visage lies, whose frown,
5 And wrinkled lip, and sneer of cold command,
Tell that its sculptor well those passions read
Which yet survive, stamped on these lifeless things,
The hand that mocked them, and the heart that fed;
And on the pedestal, these words appear:
10 My name is Ozymandias, King of Kings;
Look on my Works, ye Mighty, and despair!
Nothing beside remains. Round the decay
Of that colossal, boundless and bare
The lone and level sands stretch far away."

1. Which of the following serves as the antecedent for the clause "the hand that mocked them" (line 8)?
   (A) "I" (line 1)
   (B) "traveller" (line 1)
   (C) "shattered visage" (line 4)
   (D) "sculptor" (line 6)
   (E) "Ozymandias" (line 10)

2. The shift that occurs at line 12 ("Nothing . . . decay") emphasizes which of the following?
   (A) The mocking voice developed by the words on the pedestal.
   (B) The emptiness despite the proclamations of the words on the pedestal in the preceding lines.
   (C) The grand nature of the statue remaining in the desert.
   (D) The failure of the speaker to really comprehend what the traveller has tried to describe to him.
   (E) The sadness displayed by the face sunk into the sand.

3. The function of the adjective "colossal" (line 13) is primarily to
   (A) ease Ozymandias's embarrassment and retain the glory of his works.
   (B) create an image of the greatness of Ozymandias and his legacy.
   (C) introduce Ozymandias's failure and reveal the speaker's attitude toward that failure.
   (D) further develop the comparison of Ozymandias's statue with the traveller's experience.
   (E) emphasize Ozymandias's failure and reveal the traveller's attitude toward that failure.

4. Contrasting the time setting of the traveller's tale with the time setting of the sculptor and the Ozymandias statue creates a contrast between the ideas of
   (A) immortality and power.
   (B) strength and legacy.
   (C) potential and failure.
   (D) power and ruin.
   (E) success and power.

5. Which of the following best describes the manipulation of time in the poem?
   (A) The speaker recalls having met a traveller who tells of the present state of the statue in the sand, of Ozymandias's past, and then returns to the present.
   (B) The speaker is the traveller in the present who tells of the past of Ozymandias's conquests but then returns to the present.
   (C) Ozymandias exists in both the present and the past and the speaker recalls his exploits and experiences.
   (D) Ozymandias persists across the present and the past of the poem and, by the end of the poem, will extend well into the future.
   (E) The traveller is the speaker of the present recalling his journeys and imagining an ancient legend that explains what he saw.

6. Which of the following best describes the traveller's perspective on the setting at the end of the poem?
   (A) The emptiness of the desert represents the emptiness of Ozymandias's power and promise.
   (B) The physical features of the desert emphasize what Ozymandias was able to overcome as he rose to power in his time.
   (C) The physical features of the desert and the wrecked statue represent the eventual fate of Ozymandias's legacy.
   (D) Ozymandias's legacy is as barren and empty as the sands of the desert.
   (E) Ozymandias is legendary, despite the wasteland of the desert around his statue.

7. By the end of the poem, it can most reasonably be claimed that the statue has come to symbolize
   (A) the fates of those who fail to protect their legacy.
   (B) the finite existence of people and their accomplishments.
   (C) the glory that will be the legacy of all great people.
   (D) how poets use language to manipulate people.
   (E) how artists determine how others see us.

UNIT

8

Analyzing Incongruities

UNIT GOALS

	Focus	Goals
Big Idea: Structure	**Irony and Paradox**	Explain how an author uses incongruities to emphasize and reveal an idea and insight about the human experience.
Big Idea: Figurative Language	**Ambiguity**	Explain the symbolic meaning of an object, character, or setting within its context.
Big Idea: Figurative Language	**Conceit and Allusion**	Explain how extended metaphors and allusions contribute to an interpretation.
Ideas in Literature	• **Alienation and Fragmentation** • **Identity and Identities**	Explain how the ideas of alienation, fragmentation, identity, and identities are reflected in classic and contemporary texts.
Big Idea: Literary Argumentation	**Writing about Structure and Irony**	Write a literary argument that analyzes how the author's use of irony contributes to an interpretation of a text.
Preparing for the AP® Exam	**Free-Response Question: Poetry Analysis** Writing Conclusions	Write a conclusion for a literary argument that explains the relevance of your idea.
	Multiple-Choice Questions: Prose	Analyze literary elements and techniques in classic and contemporary prose and poetry.
	Multiple-Choice Questions: Poetry	

Irony and Paradox

 Enduring Understanding (STR-1)

The arrangement of the parts and sections of a text, the relationship of the parts to each other, and the sequence in which the text reveals information are all structural choices made by a writer that contribute to the reader's interpretation of a text.

KEY POINT

Authors intentionally structure literary texts by establishing patterns, breaking patterns, and setting up incongruities through irony or juxtaposition that emphasize ideas and contribute to an interpretation.

If you've ever been in a situation where you felt two conflicting feelings, you know that two contradictory things can be true at once. The ability to have two conflicting feelings simultaneously is one aspect that makes humans complex. For example, when you graduate, you might be excited to leave behind your high school days for the next chapter of your life but still feel uncertain, anxious, or fearful about the future. While these two feelings can be in direct conflict, they can coexist and be equally true at the same time.

Just as there are incalculable kinds of experiences in life, there are just as many ways to represent the complex scope of that experience. So complexity is a critical element of literature's value. Life is often complex and incongruous. Writers who can capture those qualities give real insight into what it means to be human.

Authors Structure Literary Texts to Emphasize Ideas

Authors may establish a pivotal idea or image in one line or stanza and then develop it throughout the rest of the poem in greater depth.

Authors create **repetition** by using an idea or image multiple times to underscore its importance or value in interpreting the text as a whole. When a writer repeats an image or idea, the reader is more likely to remember it, notice its appearance later in the text, and consider its meaning. For example, think about which part of a song you memorize first: it's likely the **refrain** (or chorus), which repeats multiple times throughout the song. Likewise, poetry, too, can include refrains, which may either intentionally interrupt the structure of the poem or repeat within the poem's stanzas. Moreover, repetition of the same motifs throughout a text is yet another method authors use to stress critical concepts, insights, or images.

Just as authors carefully select the words, names, dialogue, and images in their texts, they also use punctuation with great care and precision. In earlier units, you learned to read a poem by its punctuation (as opposed to its line breaks). To get used to this strategy, some readers will retype a poem so that it looks like a piece of prose. Then, they'll read it again in this structure before returning to its original formatting.

Punctuation

Punctuation is a poem's traffic control: it signals where the reader should go, where to yield or pause, when to stop, and how other elements work in conjunction with one another. It also contributes to the poem's pace, rhythm, and mood. Even the *absence* of punctuation can indicate how the author wants the reader to experience the text. So when interpreting a poem, make sure to consider the punctuation: it is both easily identifiable and critical to the reader's experience.

Patterns and Interruptions

As a child, you learned to anticipate and replicate patterns in your everyday life. Consider the sequence: *square, circle, triangle; square, circle, triangle; square, circle, triangle.* You'd certainly be able to fill in the sequence yourself after several repetitions. However, if you saw this same pattern repeated hundreds of times but then suddenly one of the entries read *square, circle, octagon,* that sequence would stand out among the hundreds of others.

The same principle applies to poems, plays, and stories. When authors create structural patterns in a text, changes or interruptions in the pattern create emphasis. Recall that when writers compose a sonnet or some other **closed form**, they follow a prescribed pattern of rules known as **conventions**, such as a concluding couplet in an English sonnet or the required number of lines in a haiku. Alternatively, writers can intentionally break from structural conventions to innovate a new kind of structure. You've learned that in prose, writers can interrupt the chronology and narrative pacing of a text through flashbacks, foreshadowing, and antecedent action. These devices help vary the text's structure and call attention to meaningful details. Authors can do the same in poetry as well. Therefore, take special notice when patterns are broken within a text.

Incongruity

Authors also create emphasis and complexity in their texts by setting up **incongruities**. These incongruous elements highlight characters and circumstances that are inconsistent, incompatible, or otherwise inharmonious. Authors use **irony** and **juxtaposition** to set up incongruities and emphasize tensions.

Irony

Irony is a rhetorical technique that highlights the contrast between the expectations for a situation and the reality of the situation. In literature, the audience often participates in the irony along with the other characters. We can think of irony in terms of three different categories: dramatic, situational, and verbal.

You may recall **dramatic irony** from Unit 6. This type of irony emerges from the discrepancy between what characters know and what the audience knows. Dramatic irony can build suspense, highlight an idea, or reveal important aspects of a character. In the first three episodes of the *Star Wars* movies, for example, the viewer knows that Anakin Skywalker will become Darth Vader, but other characters do not. That irony shapes how we interpret the story and the characters.

Situational irony occurs when a developing character or narrative event is different from — or the opposite of — what the reader expects. For example, in the ancient Greek tragedy *Oedipus*, Oedipus tries desperately to avoid the prophecy that he will marry his own mother and kill his father. But every move and decision he makes in the play only brings him closer to his tragic fate.

Most of us engage in **verbal irony** in our daily lives, especially in the form of *sarcasm*: saying the opposite of what we mean. For example, if your car breaks down on the way to an important job interview, you might say to yourself, "Well, this is just *great*." But verbal irony can go well beyond sarcasm, as in the case of Jonathan Swift's *A Modest Proposal*: Swift's narrator provides a rational scheme based on the benefits of eating children. In the process, the author's sustained irony only underscores the cruelty of Britain's policies toward Ireland. Both exaggeration and understatement are forms of verbal irony as well.

Juxtaposition

Juxtaposition puts two situations, characters, or settings side by side to compare and contrast them. A contrast could add emphasis or reveal new information. A comparison could highlight a surprising similarity. Juxtapositions may even create or illustrate an **antithesis**, which sets up a stark contrast of exact opposites.

A **paradox** occurs when seemingly contradictory elements are juxtaposed, but the apparent contradiction — which may or may not be reconciled — allows the reader to discover a complex truth or insight. Paradox is a form of juxtaposition.

In his poem "My Heart Leaps Up," for example, William Wordsworth writes, "The child is the father of the man." On the surface, the statement is inverted and inaccurate: the man is the father of the child. But in a different sense, the assertion is true: childhood experiences precede our mature identities and continue to shape us long after they have occurred. Paradoxes can illuminate a complicated truth, encourage deeper thinking about a topic, or even suggest competing value systems.

An **oxymoron** is a type of paradox that combines contradictory words in a short phrase, such as *sweet sorrow*, *horribly good*, and *definitely maybe*. Oxymorons are often amusing and memorable, but they can also provide insight, as when the speaker in Robert Herrick's "Delight in Disorder" refers to the "wild civility" that women possess and use to their favor. The contradiction of their "neat" (civil) appearance creates an incongruity with their innate wildness.

INSIDER AP® TIP

Incongruity often signals complexity in a literary work. Authors use juxtaposition to create contrasts between situations, characters, or settings. These contrasts reveal a tension between the different values represented in the juxtaposition. Examining these tensions is an important part of the analysis that contributes to your interpretation.

TYPES OF INCONGRUITY		
Literary Technique	**Literary Element**	**Example**
Irony A literary technique that presents something different from an apparent truth or a reader's expectations	**Situational Irony** Occurs when what happens in a narrative is the opposite of what the reader expects to happen or what was supposed to happen	In *The Hunger Games*, Katniss Everdeen "saves" her sister Prim by taking her place in the Hunger Games, but Prim ends up being killed in a bombing.
	Verbal Irony Occurs when words mean the opposite of their denotation or mean something else entirely	In *Harry Potter and the Order of the Phoenix*, Harry says of Quirrel: "Yeah, Quirrell was a great teacher. There was just that minor drawback of him having Lord Voldemort sticking out of the back of his head!"
	Dramatic Irony Occurs when the audience has knowledge that a character does not	In *Beauty and the Beast*, the audience knows from the beginning that the beast is actually an attractive prince, but Belle does not.
Juxtaposition A literary technique that places two people, events, or places side by side for the purpose of comparing or contrasting them	**Paradox** Juxtaposing seemingly contradictory elements; however, upon closer examination the contradiction is actually true, revealing an insight	In *The Incredibles*, the villain Syndrome says, "With everyone super, no one will be."
	Antithesis Placing two ideas in stark opposition; the exact opposite	As he prepared to step on the surface of the moon, Neil Armstrong said, "That's one small step for a man, one giant leap for mankind."
	Oxymoron Placing two words that have opposite meanings side by side	The artist Andy Warhol once said, "I'm a deeply superficial person."

Cinderella
Anne Sexton

THE TEXT IN CONTEXT

Anne Sexton (1928–1974) is usually grouped with the "confessional poets" of the late 1950s and early 1960s. These
American writers, including Robert Lowell (1917–1977), Sylvia
Plath (1932–1963), and W. D. Snodgrass (1926–2009), explored
deeply personal problems and experiences: sexuality, depression, infidelity, trauma, suicide, and other then-taboo subjects.
Sexton herself began writing, in part, because her therapist
encouraged her to do so. The following poem is from her book
Transformations (1972), in which she parodies and revises several of Grimm's fairy tales.
While "Cinderella" is less overtly personal than much of Sexton's other poetry, it still
evokes the dark drama of a dysfunctional family. It also provides a cynical, allusive spin
on the idea of "happily ever after."

Cinderella

You always read about it:
The plumber with the twelve children
Who wins the Irish Sweepstakes;
From toilets to riches.
5 That story.

Or the nursemaid,
Some luscious sweet from Denmark
Who captures the oldest son's heart;
From diapers to Dior.
10 That story.

Or a milkman who serves the wealthy,
Eggs, cream, butter, yogurt, milk.
The white truck like an ambulance
Who goes into real estate
15 And makes a pile;
From homogenized to martinis at lunch.

Guided Questions

1. What is juxtaposed in the first stanza?

2. What is juxtaposed in the second stanza? How do these juxtapositions reveal an unexpected idea?

3. What images are inconsistent with the others in the stanza? How do these incongruities contribute to an idea?

Or the charwoman
Who is on the bus when it cracks up
And collects enough from the insurance;
20 From mops to Bonwit Teller.
That story.

Once
The wife of a rich man was on her deathbed
And she said to her daughter Cinderella:
25 Be devout. Be good. Then I will smile
Down from heaven in the seam of a cloud.
The man took another wife who had
Two daughters, pretty enough
But with hearts like blackjacks.
30 Cinderella was their maid.
She slept on the sooty hearth each night
And walked around looking like Al Jolson.
Her father brought presents home from town,
Jewels and gowns for the other women
35 But the twig of a tree for Cinderella.
She planted that twig on her mother's grave
And it grew to a tree where a white dove sat.
Whenever she wished for anything the dove
Would drop it like an egg upon the ground.
40 The bird is important, my dears, so heed him.

Next came the ball, as you all know.
It was a marriage market.
The prince was looking for a wife.
All but Cinderella were preparing
45 And gussying up for the event.
Cinderella begged to go, too.
Her stepmother threw a dish of lentils
Into the cinders and said: Pick them
Up in an hour and you shall go.
50 The white dove brought all his friends,
All the warm wings of the fatherland came
And picked up the lentils in a jiffy.
No, Cinderella, said the stepmother,
You have no clothes and cannot dance.
55 That's the way with stepmothers.

Guided Questions

4. What is the function of the repetition of "that story"? What is happening before and after each instance?

5. Give an example of how the gifts are contrasted and juxtaposed.

6. What unexpected help does Cinderella receive? What associations can be made from this?

Cinderella went to the tree at the grave
And cried forth like a gospel singer:
Mama! Mama! My turtledove,
Send me to the prince's ball!
60 The bird dropped down a golden dress
And delicate little slippers.
Rather a large package for a simple bird.
Her stepmother and sisters didn't
Recognize her without her cinder face
65 And the prince took her hand on the spot
And danced with no other the whole day.

As nightfall came, she thought she'd better
Get home. The prince walked her home
And she disappeared into the pigeon house
70 And although the prince took an axe and broke
It open, she was gone. Back to her cinders.
These events repeated themselves for three days.
However, on the third day the prince
Covered the palace steps with cobbler's wax
75 And Cinderella's gold shoe stuck upon it.
Now he would find whom the shoe fit
And find his strange dancing girl for keeps.
He went to their house and the two sisters
Were delighted because they had lovely feet.
80 The eldest went into a room to try the slipper on,
But her big toe got in the way so she simply
Sliced it off and put on the slipper.
The prince rode away with her until the white dove
Told him to look at the blood pouring forth.
85 That is the way with amputations.
They just don't heal up like a wish.
The other sister cut off her heel
But the blood told as blood will.
The prince was getting tired.
90 He began to feel like a shoe salesman.
But he gave it one last try.
This time Cinderella fit into the shoe
Like a love letter into its envelope.

7. What incongruity
   is created from
   the bird dropping
   the dress and the
   slippers?

8. What is ironic
   about the sisters'
   behavior?

At the wedding ceremony
95 The two sisters came to curry favor
And the white dove pecked their eyes out.
Two hollow spots were left
Like soup spoons.

Cinderella and the prince
100 Lived, they say, happily ever after.
Like two dolls in a museum case,
Never bothered by diapers or dust,
Never arguing over the timing of an egg,
Never telling the same story twice,
105 Never getting a middle-aged spread,
Their darling smiles pasted on for eternity.
Regular Bobbsey Twins,
That story.

Guided Questions

9. What is unexpected? How does this differ from the classic tale of Cinderella? Explain the irony.

10. How do these paradoxes reveal a hidden or unexpected idea?

PRACTICE TEXT

The Joy of Cooking
Elaine Magarrell

THE TEXT IN CONTEXT

Born in Clinton, Iowa, to immigrant Jewish parents, Elaine Magarrell (1928–2014) taught English in Iowa public schools, wrote for local newspapers, and then became a researcher for the *New York Times.* After she began publishing poems in her forties, she left her job at the *Times* to become a full-time writer. Her books include *On Hogback Mountain* (1985), *Blameless Lives* (1991), and the posthumous collection, *The Madness of Chefs* (2017). In "The Joy of Cooking," the speaker conveys a surprising attitude toward her siblings.

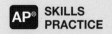 SKILLS PRACTICE | CHARACTER
Analyzing Incongruities

As you read "The Joy of Cooking," identify examples of irony or juxtaposition that create incongruities. Then describe the ideas being contrasted through each incongruity. Finally, explain the effect of that incongruity in relation to the work as a whole.

Analyzing Incongruities		
Authors use irony and juxtaposition to establish incongruities in literary texts. • Irony: Dramatic, Situational, Verbal • Juxtaposition: Paradox, Antithesis, Oxymoron		
Textual Evidence	**Idea Being Emphasized through the Incongruity**	**Type and Effect of Incongruity**

The Joy of Cooking

I have prepared my sister's tongue,
scrubbed and skinned it,
trimmed the roots, small bones, and gristle.
Carved through the hump it slices thin and neat.
5 Best with horseradish
and economical—it probably will grow back.
Next time perhaps a creole sauce
or mold of aspic?

I will have my brother's heart,
10 which is firm and rather dry,
slow cooked. It resembles muscle
more than organ meat

and needs an apple-onion stuffing
to make it interesting at all.
15 Although beef heart serves six
my brother's heart barely feeds two.
I could also have it braised
and served in sour sauce.

STRUCTURE

1. How do the **contrasting** images in the poem extend beyond the literal? Why does the speaker choose the sister's tongue and the brother's heart?

2. How are the ideas **juxtaposed**? How does this juxtaposition reveal an unexpected insight?

3. Explain how each stanza creates a **paradox**. What do these seemingly contradictory images reveal?

4. What makes this poem **ironic**? How do incongruous images reveal an idea?

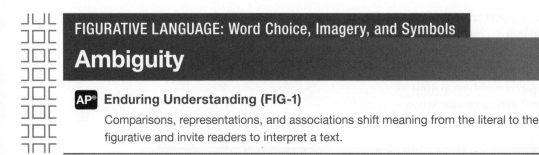

FIGURATIVE LANGUAGE: Word Choice, Imagery, and Symbols

Ambiguity

AP® **Enduring Understanding (FIG-1)**

Comparisons, representations, and associations shift meaning from the literal to the figurative and invite readers to interpret a text.

KEY POINT

An author may associate a symbol with a narrator, character, or speaker as a way of revealing a particular attitude, perspective, or tone.

Ambiguous images (or reversible images) are illusions that viewers can interpret as two or more distinct visual forms. For example, the "rabbit-duck" illusion is one of the most recognizable ambiguous images: it can be seen as either a rabbit or a duck, even as it is both in a literal sense.

You may also know another familiar example: the Rubin vase, in which the image appears to be both the shape of a vase and the shape of two faces looking directly at each other. These kinds of images create ambiguity and invite viewers to enjoy changing how they interpret a representation. Furthermore, some authors invite readers to step into ambiguous literary texts that can be interpreted in different ways.

Authors Use the Literal to Represent the Abstract

As you've learned in previous units, authors use literal objects, characters, and settings to represent abstract ideas and concepts. In this way, the object, character, or setting becomes symbolic. So authors expect readers to understand texts by interpreting how literal elements take on figurative meaning. This isn't always easy. Most authors avoid explaining their symbols, metaphors, and motifs. Instead, they create an **ambiguity** that requires readers to use the context and their prior knowledge to interpret concrete objects, characters, and settings. This process leads to a logical, evidence-based interpretation of the literary work. But it may not be the only logical interpretation; ambiguity allows for different readings of a text by different readers.

Readers must be able to support their interpretation based on textual evidence. And that requires looking at patterns like those you learned about in earlier units. You need enough evidence to justify your interpretation. In most cases, you will need more than one instance of an image or literary device to make your interpretation valid. So look for patterns of images and devices. Authors draw upon a variety of literary elements and techniques and combine them to reveal insights into the human experience.

Symbols and Tone

When an author uses a literal object, character, or setting in a symbolic way, it is important to consider how that **symbol** relates to the narrator or other characters. For example, a symbol may imply that a character has a particular attitude, perspective, or **tone**. You may find some symbolism obvious. In earlier units, you learned that many symbols are universal — so universal that they are easily recognizable **archetypes**. Because symbols represent ideas and concepts, an author may include them, associate them with a particular character or narrator, or have a narrator or character speak about them as a way of revealing a particular attitude, perspective, or tone.

Context

Symbols can be ambiguous. That is partly because we all bring our own backgrounds, experiences, and frames of reference when we read. Authors, however, often suggest symbolic meanings within the work's context, not the reader's. This means that we must be careful to interpret symbols as they relate to characters, settings, and objects in a text, not as they directly relate to our lives.

Take, for example, the apple. In literature and art, apples have become an archetype for sin: they allude to the Old Testament story in which Eve yields to temptation and eats forbidden fruit. But a contemporary play might use an apple as an allusion to Apple computers or the coming of autumn. So make sure to keep the symbol's immediate context in mind, including the work's time period, setting, and culture, along with the characters' occupations, interests, and activities, among other contextual factors. This information will help you infer the meaning of a symbol.

INSIDER AP® TIP

The meaning of a symbol may be contextual. Critical readers may consider three different contexts: when a literary work was written, when it is set, and when it is being read as they make their interpretation.

The Unknown Citizen
W. H. Auden

Jerry Cooke/Corbis Historical/Getty Images

THE TEXT IN CONTEXT

English poet, playwright, and critic Wystan Hugh Auden (1907–1973) was born in York, England, and educated at Oxford University. Influenced by writers like Robert Frost, Thomas Hardy, and Emily Dickinson, he began writing poetry at a young age and published his first collection, *Poems*, in 1930. In the decades that followed, Auden emerged as perhaps the era's most versatile and brilliant English poet, as well as a widely known public intellectual. His poetry explores politics, popular culture, art, love, philosophy, religion, science, meaning, and humanity in the modern world. He published many collections of poems and essays, such as *Another Time* (1940), *The Shield of Achilles* (1955), and *Secondary Worlds* (1968). His most well-known poems include "Stop All the Clocks" (1936), "Musée de Beaux Arts" (1938), "September 1, 1939" (1939), and "The Unknown Citizen" (1939), which is included here. This work looks at the effects of modern bureaucracy on individuality and humanity.

The Unknown Citizen

(To JS/07 M 378
This Marble Monument
Is Erected by the State)

He was found by the Bureau of Statistics to be
One against whom there was no official complaint,
And all the reports on his conduct agree
That, in the modern sense of an old-fashioned word, he was a saint,
5 For in everything he did he served the Greater Community.
Except for the War till the day he retired
He worked in a factory and never got fired,
But satisfied his employers, Fudge Motors Inc.
Yet he wasn't a scab or odd in his views,
10 For his Union reports that he paid his dues,
(Our report on his Union shows it was sound)
And our Social Psychology workers found
That he was popular with his mates and liked a drink.
The Press are convinced that he bought a paper every day
15 And that his reactions to advertisements were normal in every way.
Policies taken out in his name prove that he was fully insured,

Guided Questions

1. Why might it be significant that the citizen is "unknown"?

2. How does the parenthetical note create context for the poem?

3. What associations are created by the phrase "he was a saint"?

4. What associations does the company's name suggest?

And his Health-card shows he was once in hospital but left it cured.
Both Producers Research and High-Grade Living declare
He was fully sensible to the advantages of the Instalment Plan
20 And had everything necessary to the Modern Man,
A phonograph, a radio, a car and a frigidaire.
Our researchers into Public Opinion are content
That he held the proper opinions for the time of year;
When there was peace, he was for peace: when there was war, he went.
25 He was married and added five children to the population,
Which our Eugenist says was the right number for a parent of his generation.
And our teachers report that he never interfered with their education.
Was he free? Was he happy? The question is absurd:
Had anything been wrong, we should certainly have heard.

Guided Questions

5. How are these items representative of "modern" people?

6. How do the questions in line 28 create ambiguity? How do they reflect modernist ideas?

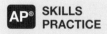

PRACTICE TEXT

Anecdote of the Jar
Wallace Stevens

THE TEXT IN CONTEXT

Wallace Stevens (1879–1955) stands with T. S. Eliot (1888–1965), Robert Frost (1874–1963), and Ezra Pound (1885–1972) as one of the major American modernist poets. In some ways, he also exemplified one type of "modern man": Stevens had a full career in the insurance industry and mostly lived a quiet family life in Hartford, Connecticut. But regardless of his unassuming appearance, his poetry is wildly strange and imaginative. It often focuses on the processes of creation and poetry, especially the interplay of perception, imagination, art, and reality. Like some of his other work, the 1918 poem "Anecdote of the Jar" (included here) is perceptive and evocative.

Bettmann/Getty Images

AP® SKILLS PRACTICE | **FIGURATIVE LANGUAGE**
Analyzing a Symbol in Context

As you read "Anecdote of the Jar," identify a symbol that is critical for interpreting the poem. Select details and evidence from the poem associated with the symbol. Then, explain the significance of your textual evidence based on both the context of the poem and the poem's unifying idea.

(continued)

Analyzing a Symbol in Context	
Symbol:	
Idea:	
Considerations: • How do symbolic objects, actions, events, characters, and settings contribute to a text's complexity and meaning as a whole? • Which symbol in a text do you recognize from other texts? • How is the symbol's meaning(s) in this text similar to or different from its meaning(s) in other texts?	
Textual Details	**Significance Based on Context**

Anecdote of the Jar

I placed a jar in Tennessee,
And round it was, upon a hill.
It made the slovenly wilderness
Surround that hill.

5   The wilderness rose up to it,
And sprawled around, no longer wild.
The jar was round upon the ground
And tall and of a port in air.

It took dominion everywhere.
10 The jar was gray and bare.
It did not give of bird or bush,
Like nothing else in Tennessee.

FIGURATIVE LANGUAGE: Word Choice, Imagery, and Symbols

1. What **associations** can be made about the power of the jar in Tennessee?

2. The images of the jar and the **images** of wilderness are juxtaposed. How does this **juxtaposition** create **ambiguity** and suggest an idea?

3. How do the **comparisons** in the third stanza contribute to the **ambiguous** connection between the jar and nature?

4. What does the jar **symbolize**? How does the symbol contribute to your interpretation of the poem?

FIGURATIVE LANGUAGE: Comparisons
Conceit and Allusion

AP® Enduring Understanding (FIG-1)

Comparisons, representations, and associations shift meaning from the literal to the figurative and invite readers to interpret a text.

KEY POINT

Extended metaphors allow for multiple attributes of comparison between the concrete object of comparison and a character, object, or circumstance. The particular aspects of comparison enable an author to emphasize and reveal important values and ideas.

Some stories and poems, such as Aesop's Fables, are *didactic* in that they offer ethical, moral, or religious insights or principles about life. Other stories — such as streaming a series or a movie in a trilogy — leave you hanging, desperate to find out what happens in the next episode. Still other stories are so intricate and complex you may be thinking about them for days, weeks, months, or years after you've read or watched them. Stories that linger with us long after we've read them do so because we actively engage with the ideas hidden within to make interpretations about them.

Comparisons and Incongruities Are Key to Interpretation

As you've already learned, **metaphors** and extended comparisons are important because they draw upon the comparison of a physical concrete object with the subject of a poem or other literary text to emphasize important specific and intentional attributes and characteristics of the subject of comparison. These comparisons also propose an **analogy** between the two subjects. This is achieved by ascribing qualities of the comparative object to the subject of the poem or literary work. Whether the comparison is obvious or surprising and incongruous, the author has carefully chosen it to reveal ideas, concepts, and values that convey some insight into the human experience.

Allegories

Allegories use symbols to establish two clear levels of meaning in a literary work: a literal one and a figurative one. While most writers use figurative language, allegories are unique in that the characters, settings, objects, *and* events take on a **symbolic** meaning. In some cases, authors want their ideas to be so obvious that they actually name their characters, settings, and objects after the value or idea. Allegories draw upon **personification**, too, as objects and settings take on human characteristics.

Allusions

Some allegories require historical, religious, or other contextual knowledge to fully understand them. Of course, the writer expects his or her intended audience to understand the **allusion**. While allusions may refer to **archetypes**, they are not themselves archetypes. You'll recall that archetypes are patterns (e.g., characters, settings, actions) that have been used so often across different cultures that we associate them with specific ideas or values. An allusion, on the other hand, is a specific reference to a literary, historical, religious, or cultural person, event, object, place, or text. Writers use them to evoke complex ideas, suggest comparisons, and create emotional associations for the reader.

Of course, if readers don't know the reference, they can only read the text literally. As a result, they will miss the author's intended effects and meaning. Many contemporary writers prefer symbolism over allegory, as symbols can remain open to interpretations, while allegories generally limit interpretations.

Controlling Metaphors

In some literary works, a comparison becomes even more significant because it runs throughout the text and forms an **extended comparison** or **controlling metaphor**. An author may signal a controlling metaphor by including it in the title of the work, as in George Orwell's *Animal Farm* (1945) and Maya Angelou's *I Know Why the Caged Bird Sings* (1969). On the other hand, a writer may draw upon multiple comparisons or combine different metaphors in complex ways. Whether an author uses one controlling metaphor or multiple related metaphors, you must carefully consider why the author chose these analogies and metaphors to reveal insight into the human experience.

Conceits

A **conceit** is a form of extended metaphor most often used in poetry. Conceits develop complex comparisons that present images, concepts, and associations in surprising or paradoxical ways. Conceits draw upon analogies that explain something unfamiliar by comparing it to something familiar.

Metaphysical Conceits

Metaphysical poetry originated in the seventeenth century from a small group of poets who broke away from the conventions of sixteenth-century Elizabethan verse. They wrote witty, punning, self-consciously intellectual poems, with deliberately strange images and unusual metaphors. Their poems often addressed religion, philosophy, and other metaphysical subjects — that is, ideas that transcended beyond human perception. The word *metaphysical* means "of or relating to the transcendent or to a reality beyond what is perceptible." Specifically, metaphysical poets explore human emotions, experiences, and ideas such as love, beauty, relationships, and religious faith. Their **metaphysical conceits** compare such human emotions to the objects and concepts of the natural, physical, scientific world. These comparisons can appear dissimilar or jarring, but their surprising strangeness and **incongruity** reveal truth and insight.

Comparisons reveal complexities. Identifying the points of comparison is not enough. Analysis requires explaining the comparisons function in the text, their meaning within the context, and their emotional impact on the reader.

COMPARISONS AND EXTENDED COMPARISONS

Literary Element	Description	Key Considerations
Simile	A comparison between two objects that explicitly states that one thing is "like" or "as" another	• What is significant about the selection of the objects being compared?
Metaphor	An implicit comparison between two unlike objects that draws upon specific points of comparison to suggest that one thing is like another	• What is significant about the selection of the objects being compared and their particular traits, qualities, or characteristics? • How does an extended metaphor continue a comparison in different parts of the text? • How might the figurative meaning of a metaphor depend on the context in which it is presented? • How does a metaphorical comparison contribute to the figurative meaning of a character, conflict, setting, theme, or other elements of the text?
Extended Metaphor	A metaphor that develops and continues the comparison throughout or over the course of a literary work	• How does an extended metaphor continue a comparison in different parts of the text? • How might the figurative meaning of a metaphor depend on the context in which it is presented? • How does a metaphorical comparison contribute to the figurative meaning of a character, conflict, setting, theme, or other elements of the text?
Conceit	An extended metaphor most often found in poetry that develops a complex comparison by presenting images, concepts, and associations in surprising or paradoxical ways	
Metaphysical Conceit	A form of conceit or extended metaphor that develops a complex comparison between the natural world and human experience	

(continued)

Literary Element	Description	Key Considerations
Personification	A type of comparison that assigns human traits or qualities to a nonhuman object, entity, or idea By making this specific comparison, the narrator or character communicates and emphasizes an attitude about that object, entity, or idea	• Which nonhuman entity is ascribed human traits? • What are the specific human traits? • How does the comparison characterize the nonhuman entity and convey meaning? • How does a narrator, speaker, or character convey an attitude toward a nonhuman entity by personifying it?
Allegory	A literary work that draws upon two levels of meaning: a literal one and a symbolic one	• How do characters or other literal objects take on symbolic significance in a unified way?
Allusion	A reference to another literary work, including myths and sacred texts; other works of art, including paintings and music; or people, places, or events outside of the text that the author expects the reader to know	• What are the points of comparison between the person, place, object, event, text, or idea in the reference and the primary text? • What is the background of the person, place, object, event, literary work, or idea referenced in the text? • How does an allusion affect a reader's experience of a text if he or she understands it? What aspects of meaning do readers miss if they fail to comprehend an allusion?

GUIDED READING

Upon a Spider Catching a Fly
Edward Taylor

THE TEXT IN CONTEXT

Edward Taylor (c. 1642–1729) was a colonial physician, poet, and Puritan minister of the Congregational Church in Westfield, Massachusetts. Born in England around 1642, he emigrated to the American colonies in 1668, seeking escape from the Church of England. In America, he graduated from Harvard and began a career in the ministry. But Taylor was also a remarkably prolific and original poet throughout his life. The roughness, cleverness, and intricacy of his style, as well as his transcendent subjects, are reminiscent of the seventeenth-century British metaphysical poets. For Taylor, poetry glorified God, celebrated the Christian experience, and illuminated biblical scripture as in the case of "Upon a Spider Catching a Fly" (1684; included here).

Classic Image/Alamy

Upon a Spider Catching a Fly

Thou sorrow, venom Elfe:
　　Is this thy play,
To spin a web out of thyselfe
　　To Catch a Fly?
5　　　　For Why?

I saw a pettish wasp
　　Fall foule therein:
Whom yet thy Whorle pins did not clasp
　　Lest he should fling
10　　　His sting.

But as affraid, remote
　　Didst stand hereat,
And with thy little fingers stroke
　　And gently tap
15　　　His back.

Thus gently him didst treate
　　Lest he should pet,
And in a froppish, aspish heate
　　Should greatly fret
20　　　Thy net.

Whereas the silly Fly,
　　Caught by its leg
Thou by the throate tookst hastily
　　And 'hinde the head
25　　　Bite Dead.

This goes to pot, that not
　　Nature doth call.
Strive not above what strength hath got,
　　Lest in the brawle
30　　　Thou fall.

This Frey seems thus to us.
　　Hells Spider gets
His intrails spun to whip Cords thus
　　And wove to nets
35　　　And sets.

Guided Questions

1. What is happening in the first stanza? Who are the two characters?

2. What is the relationship between the spider and the fly?

3. How are these actions personified, and what do they reflect about human actions?

4. What does the spider catch? What does he do with his prey?

5. In what ways might the fall be an archetype?

6. Who does the spider belong to?

7. What is the spider doing? Why?

To tangle Adams race
     In's stratigems
To their Destructions, spoil'd, made base
     By venom things,
40   Damn'd Sins.

But mighty, Gracious Lord
     Communicate
Thy Grace to breake the Cord, afford
     Us Glorys Gate
45   And State.

We'l Nightingaile sing like
     When pearcht on high
In Glories Cage, thy glory, bright,
     And thankfully,
50   For joy.

Guided Questions

8. How does the poem shift? What associations does the allusion suggest? What do they reveal about those caught in the spider's web?

9. What is the conceit? How does the metaphor of the spider create an unexpected message about nature and humanity?

PRACTICE TEXT

The Haunted Oak
Paul Laurence Dunbar

THE TEXT IN CONTEXT

One of the most influential African American poets and novelists of the nineteenth century, Paul Laurence Dunbar (1872–1906) was born in Dayton, Ohio, to formerly enslaved people. He began writing as a teenager and published his first collection of poetry, *Oak and Ivy*, in 1893. Soon, Dunbar's work caught the attention of the popular Ohio poet James Whitcomb Riley and influential novelist and editor William Dean Howells. Despite his short career, Dunbar was incredibly prolific, producing over twenty volumes of poetry, fiction, and essays. He also gained an international literary reputation. Dunbar is perhaps most famous for his "dialect" poems and stories, which deploy the stereotypical vernacular and slang of African Americans at the time. These stereotypes appealed to white readers and contributed to his popularity. But he also worked with more serious and conventional forms, as in the case of the following poem, "The Haunted Oak."

AP® SKILLS PRACTICE | FIGURATIVE LANGUAGE
Analyzing Extended Comparisons

As you read "The Haunted Oak," identify the multiple points of comparison. Then explain the significance of each aspect of comparison in relation to a unifying idea.

Analyzing Extended Comparisons		
Literal object of comparison:		
Unifying idea:		
Aspect of Comparison	**Evidence from the Text**	**Significance of the Aspect of Comparison**

The Haunted Oak

Pray why are you so bare, so bare,
    Oh, bough of the old oak-tree;
And why, when I go through the shade you throw,
    Runs a shudder over me?

5 My leaves were green as the best, I trow,
    And sap ran free in my veins,
But I saw in the moonlight dim and weird
    A guiltless victim's pains.

I bent me down to hear his sigh;
10   I shook with his gurgling moan,
And I trembled sore when they rode away,
    And left him here alone.

They'd charged him with the old, old crime,
    And set him fast in jail:
15 Oh, why does the dog howl all night long,
    And why does the night wind wail?

He prayed his prayer and he swore his oath,
    And he raised his hand to the sky;
But the beat of hoofs smote on his ear,
20   And the steady tread drew nigh.

Who is it rides by night, by night,
    Over the moonlit road?
And what is the spur that keeps the pace,
    What is the galling goad?

25 And now they beat at the prison door,
    "Ho, keeper, do not stay!
We are friends of him whom you hold within,
    And we fain would take him away

"From those who ride fast on our heels
30   With mind to do him wrong;
They have no care for his innocence,
    And the rope they bear is long."

They have fooled the jailer with lying words,
    They have fooled the man with lies;
35 The bolts unbar, the locks are drawn,
    And the great door open flies.

Now they have taken him from the jail,
    And hard and fast they ride,
And the leader laughs low down in his throat,
40   As they halt my trunk beside.

Oh, the judge, he wore a mask of black,
    And the doctor one of white,
And the minister, with his oldest son,
    Was curiously bedight.

45 Oh, foolish man, why weep you now?
    'Tis but a little space,
And the time will come when these shall dread
    The mem'ry of your face.

I feel the rope against my bark,
50   And the weight of him in my grain,
I feel in the throe of his final woe
    The touch of my own last pain.

And never more shall leaves come forth
   On the bough that bears the ban;
55 I am burned with dread, I am dried and dead,
   From the curse of a guiltless man.

And ever the judge rides by, rides by,
   And goes to hunt the deer,
And ever another rides his soul
60   In the guise of a mortal fear.

And ever the man he rides me hard,
   And never a night stays he;
For I feel his curse as a haunted bough,
   On the trunk of a haunted tree.

FIGURATIVE LANGUAGE: Comparisons

1. Who is the speaker of the poem? How does the **personification** of the speaker create an unexpected **comparison**? What is that comparison?

2. Explain the **metaphor** of the tree. What characteristics of the tree are compared in the metaphor, and how does this contribute to your understanding of the poem?

3. The rope is an extension of the tree. How does the relationship between the rope and the bough of the tree contribute to your understanding of the poem?

4. Give an example of a **paradox** in the poem. How does this paradox reveal an unexpected idea and contribute to your understanding of the poem?

Alienation and Fragmentation

IDEA BANK

Alienation

Authority

Communication

Confusion

Detachment

Devastation

Disconnection

Doubt

Eccentricity

Facade

Falsehood

Fragmentation

Illusion

Insecurity

Nostalgia

Obligation

Persona

Prejudice

Racism

Rejection

Suffering

Uncertainty

World War I (1914–1918) was the first modern, mechanized war, which included tanks, machine guns, airplanes, and chemical weapons. In a sense, all the expertise and technological progress of the Industrial Revolution had been turned to the purpose of death and destruction. But even in peacetime, modern urban society seemed increasingly materialistic, impersonal, and empty. For many, this led to *alienation* or a feeling of disconnection and isolation from family, community, religious authority, and society. Whether in Ernest Hemingway's (1899–1961) traumatized fictional veterans or the empty glamour of F. Scott Fitzgerald's (1896–1940) decadent jazz-age characters, this theme of isolation and disconnection animates nearly all modernist literature. Alienation had an internal component as well: the influential theories of Sigmund Freud (1856–1939) and other psychologists proposed that humans were alienated from their own unconsciousness and their inner drives. So modernist writers like Virginia Woolf (1882–1941) and William Faulkner (1897–1962) used stream-of-consciousness narratives to capture interior psychological and emotional states.

This alienation had far-reaching effects on culture. World War I not only destroyed most of Europe; it also led to a crisis in meaning. Many lost faith in civilization, industry, democracy, governments, churches, and other institutions that

The Old Guitarist is an oil painting by Pablo Picasso, which he created in late 1903 and early 1904.

Explain how the painting incorporates modern ideas through fragmented images and symbols. Explain how these fragmented images and symbols contribute to a message about the modern individual.

seemed hollow and ineffectual. For artists and writers, this condition led to new challenges. If the old forms and "truths" no longer applied, then they must find (in T. S. Eliot's words) a new way of "giving a shape and significance to the immense panorama of futility and anarchy which is contemporary history." If the old world had been shattered, then maybe meaning could be recovered by focusing on the fragments left behind. In fact, fragmentation emerges not only as a theme but also as a structural element in modernist texts. For example, in James Joyce's *Ulysses* (1921) or William Faulkner's *As I Lay Dying* (1930), a unifying first-person or omniscient narrator is replaced by multiple narrators or the subjective and eccentric perspective of stream-of-consciousness narration. Narrative "truth" becomes limited and provisional.

Perhaps no single work brings together modernist alienation and fragmentation as seamlessly as Eliot's "The Love Song of J. Alfred Prufrock" (1915). Prufrock's shattered and paralyzed psyche matches the fragmented and ironic structure of the poem. Indeed, even at the level of images and allusions, the text presents itself as a collection of fragments. Modernist literature can be demanding and obscure, but that's almost always by authorial choice. The old, familiar models of expression and representation no longer seemed relevant. Today, perhaps, as much as at any other time since, we can identify with a loss of faith in institutions and governments. Social media has become a primary medium for expressing personal and social alienation. But it also has a fragmenting function, whether it's dispersing our attention or spreading different versions of ourselves across different media platforms.

Nude Descending a Staircase (No. 2), 1912 (oil on canvas)/Duchamp, Marcel (1887–1968)/ © Philadelphia Museum of Art/The Louise and Walter Arensberg Collection, 1950/Bridgeman Images, © Association Marcel Duchamp/ADAGP, Paris/Artists Rights Society (ARS), New York 2022

◀ *Nude Descending a Staircase* is a 1912 painting by French-American artist Marcel Duchamp.

Explain how this painting depicts modern alienation. In a world surrounded by many, how can an individual be lonely?

The Love Song of J. Alfred Prufrock

T. S. Eliot

Bettmann/Getty Images

THE TEXT IN CONTEXT

Perhaps no single figure was more central to English poetry in the first half of the twentieth century than T. S. Eliot (1888–1965). Born into an upper-class family with Boston Brahmin roots, he spent most of his early life in St. Louis and then attended Harvard University. Eliot was not a prolific poet, playwright, or essayist, but the works that he did produce were groundbreaking and often controversial. Most of the techniques associated with modernism — mythic structures and allusions; fragmented narratives from multiple points of view; the emphasis on art as a way of making meaning in a fragmented world; the deliberately strange imagery and metaphors — are displayed in Eliot's works, especially "The Waste Land" (1922). This highly allusive text is an ironic retelling of the holy grail legend in post–World War I's alienated urban society. His other well-known poems include "The Hollow Men" (1925) along with the light verse collected in the book *Old Possum's Book of Practical Cats* (1939). The latter was made into the 1981 musical *Cats* by Andrew Lloyd Webber. Eliot first rattled the world of poetry in 1915 with the following dramatic monologue, "The Love Song of J. Alfred Prufrock." Spoken by the persona in the title, the poem remains startling in its imagery and haunting in its expression of modern alienation.

The Love Song of J. Alfred Prufrock

S'io credesse che mia risposta fosse
A persona che mai tornasse al mondo,
Questa fiamma staria senza piu scosse.
Ma percioche giammai di questo fondo
Non torno vivo alcun, s'i'odo il vero,
Senza tema d'infamia ti rispondo.

Let us go then, you and I,
When the evening is spread out against the sky
Like a patient etherized upon a table;
Let us go, through certain half-deserted streets,
5 The muttering retreats
Of restless nights in one-night cheap hotels
And sawdust restaurants with oyster-shells:
Streets that follow like a tedious argument

Of insidious intent
10 To lead you to an overwhelming question . . .
Oh, do not ask, "What is it?"
Let us go and make our visit.

In the room the women come and go
Talking of Michelangelo.

15 The yellow fog that rubs its back upon the window-panes,
The yellow smoke that rubs its muzzle on the window-panes,
Licked its tongue into the corners of the evening,
Lingered upon the pools that stand in drains,
Let fall upon its back the soot that falls from chimneys,
20 Slipped by the terrace, made a sudden leap,
And seeing that it was a soft October night,
Curled once about the house, and fell asleep.

And indeed there will be time
For the yellow smoke that slides along the street,
25 Rubbing its back upon the window-panes;
There will be time, there will be time
To prepare a face to meet the faces that you meet;
There will be time to murder and create,
And time for all the works and days of hands
30 That lift and drop a question on your plate;
Time for you and time for me,
And time yet for a hundred indecisions,
And for a hundred visions and revisions,
Before the taking of a toast and tea.

35 In the room the women come and go
Talking of Michelangelo.

And indeed there will be time
To wonder, "Do I dare?" and, "Do I dare?"
Time to turn back and descend the stair,
40 With a bald spot in the middle of my hair—
(They will say: "How his hair is growing thin!")
My morning coat, my collar mounting firmly to the chin,
My necktie rich and modest, but asserted by a simple pin—
(They will say: "But how his arms and legs are thin!")
45 Do I dare
Disturb the universe?
In a minute there is time
For decisions and revisions which a minute will reverse.

For I have known them all already, known them all:
50 Have known the evenings, mornings, afternoons,
I have measured out my life with coffee spoons;
I know the voices dying with a dying fall
Beneath the music from a farther room.
          So how should I presume?

55 And I have known the eyes already, known them all—
The eyes that fix you in a formulated phrase,
And when I am formulated, sprawling on a pin,
When I am pinned and wriggling on the wall,
Then how should I begin
60 To spit out all the butt-ends of my days and ways?
          And how should I presume?

And I have known the arms already, known them all—
Arms that are braceleted and white and bare
(But in the lamplight, downed with light brown hair!)
65 Is it perfume from a dress
That makes me so digress?
Arms that lie along a table, or wrap about a shawl.
          And should I then presume?
          And how should I begin?

70 Shall I say, I have gone at dusk through narrow streets
And watched the smoke that rises from the pipes
Of lonely men in shirt-sleeves, leaning out of windows? . . .

I should have been a pair of ragged claws
Scuttling across the floors of silent seas.

75 And the afternoon, the evening, sleeps so peacefully!
Smoothed by long fingers,
Asleep . . . tired . . . or it malingers,
Stretched on the floor, here beside you and me.
Should I, after tea and cakes and ices,
80 Have the strength to force the moment to its crisis?
But though I have wept and fasted, wept and prayed,
Though I have seen my head (grown slightly bald) brought in upon a platter,
I am no prophet—and here's no great matter;
I have seen the moment of my greatness flicker,
85 And I have seen the eternal Footman hold my coat, and snicker,
And in short, I was afraid.

And would it have been worth it, after all,
After the cups, the marmalade, the tea,

Among the porcelain, among some talk of you and me,
90 Would it have been worth while,
    To have bitten off the matter with a smile,
    To have squeezed the universe into a ball
    To roll it towards some overwhelming question,
    To say: "I am Lazarus, come from the dead,
95 Come back to tell you all, I shall tell you all"—
    If one, settling a pillow by her head
            Should say: "That is not what I meant at all;
            That is not it, at all."

    And would it have been worth it, after all,
100 Would it have been worth while,
    After the sunsets and the dooryards and the sprinkled streets,
    After the novels, after the teacups, after the skirts that trail along the floor—
    And this, and so much more?—
    It is impossible to say just what I mean!
105 But as if a magic lantern threw the nerves in patterns on a screen:
    Would it have been worth while
    If one, settling a pillow or throwing off a shawl,
    And turning toward the window, should say:
            "That is not it at all,
110   That is not what I meant, at all."

    No! I am not Prince Hamlet, nor was meant to be;
    Am an attendant lord, one that will do
    To swell a progress, start a scene or two,
    Advise the prince; no doubt, an easy tool,
115 Deferential, glad to be of use,
    Politic, cautious, and meticulous;
    Full of high sentence, but a bit obtuse;
    At times, indeed, almost ridiculous—
    Almost, at times, the Fool.

120 I grow old . . . I grow old . . .
    I shall wear the bottoms of my trousers rolled.

    Shall I part my hair behind? Do I dare to eat a peach?
    I shall wear white flannel trousers, and walk upon the beach.
    I have heard the mermaids singing, each to each.

125 I do not think that they will sing to me.

    I have seen them riding seaward on the waves
    Combing the white hair of the waves blown back
    When the wind blows the water white and black.

We have lingered in the chambers of the sea
130 By sea-girls wreathed with seaweed red and brown
Till human voices wake us, and we drown.

The painting titled *T. S. Eliot* (1949) is an oil on canvas by Patrick Heron.

The painting is of the author and poet T. S. Eliot. How does it express the author and poet? Why did the painter use fragmented images to depict Eliot? How does this contribute to your understanding of both T. S. Eliot and Prufrock?

STRUCTURE

1. Explain how the poem's introductory **images** create contrasts and contribute to your understanding of the poem.

2. Many images and ideas are **juxtaposed** in the text. Choose two instances of juxtaposition and explain how they contribute to the complexity of the poem.

3. **Paradox** often reveals an unexpected idea. Choose one paradox in the poem and explain what it reveals.

4. What is **ironic** in "The Love Song of J. Alfred Prufrock"? What events or situations contribute to this irony, and what do they reveal to the reader?

FIGURATIVE LANGUAGE: Word Choice, Imagery, and Symbols

5. There are many **symbols** in the poem. Explain how the streets and the rooms are symbolic. What figurative associations do they create?

6. How are Prufrock's questions **ambiguous**? Identify two ambiguous questions, and explain how their **imagery** contributes to their ambiguity.

7. What is the final **symbol** at the end of the poem? Explain how it reveals Prufrock's attitude and perspective.

FIGURATIVE LANGUAGE: Comparisons

8. What is the **conceit** in the first stanza? How do the images create complex, surprising, or **paradoxical** comparisons?

9. Explain the complex **comparisons** in the third and fourth stanzas. How does the speaker compare the natural world to a human individual?

10. The poem includes many **allusions** to texts, people, events, and other artifacts. Choose two allusions and then explain how each creates an emotional or intellectual effect. For example, do your examples suggest an irony?

IDEAS IN LITERATURE: Alienation and Fragmentation

11. The insecure, alienated Prufrock asks many questions. But he never specifies the "overwhelming question" in lines 10 and 93 of the poem. What do you think the question is? How might it reflect the speaker's alienation and fragmented self? How does it express a shared experience? Support your answer with textual and experiential evidence.

PUTTING IT ALL TOGETHER

12. How is the poem **paradoxical**? Explain how its complex **comparisons** and **ironic associations** contribute to your understanding of "The Love Song of J. Alfred Prufrock." For example, in what sense is this poem a "love song"?

I Invite My Parents to a Dinner Party

Chen Chen

©Jeff Gilbert

THE TEXT IN CONTEXT

Chinese American poet Chen Chen (b. 1989) was born in Xiamen, China, and grew up in Newton, Massachusetts. He attended Hampshire College, earned an MFA at Syracuse University, and a PhD at Texas Tech University. He is currently the Jacob Ziskind Poet-in-Residence at Brandeis University. Chen's first book of poetry, *When I Grow Up I Want to Be a List of Further Possibilities* (2017), focused on his often-strained relationship with his immigrant family and his perspective as a gay Asian American. The 2018 poem that follows investigates similar thematic territory and illustrates his wry sense of humor. Chen has published in many journals, such as *Drunken Boat*, *The Best American Poetry*, and *Poetry*. His first book of essays is titled *In Cahoots with the Rabbit God* (2023).

I Invite My Parents to a Dinner Party

In the invitation, I tell them for the seventeenth time
(the fourth in writing), that I am gay.

In the invitation, I include a picture of my boyfriend
& write, *You've met him two times. But this time,*

5 *you will ask him things other than can you pass the*
whatever. You will ask him

about him. You will enjoy dinner. You will be
enjoyable. Please RSVP.

They RSVP. They come.
10 They sit at the table & ask my boyfriend

the first of the conversation starters I slip them
upon arrival: *How is work going?*

I'm like the kid in *Home Alone*, orchestrating
every movement of a proper family, as if a pair

15 of scary yet deeply incompetent burglars
is watching from the outside.

My boyfriend responds in his chipper way.
I pass my father a bowl of fish ball soup—*So comforting,*

isn't it? My mother smiles her best
20 Sitting with Her Son's Boyfriend

Who Is a Boy Smile. I smile my Hurray for Doing
a Little Better Smile.

Everyone eats soup.
Then, my mother turns

25 to me, whispers in Mandarin, *Is he coming with you*
for Thanksgiving? My good friend is & she wouldn't like

this. I'm like the kid in *Home Alone*, pulling
on the string that makes my cardboard mother

more motherly, except she is
30 not cardboard, she is

already, exceedingly my mother. Waiting
for my answer.

While my father opens up
a *Boston Globe*, when the invitation

35 clearly stated: *No security*
blankets. I'm like the kid

in *Home Alone*, except the home
is my apartment, & I'm much older, & not alone,

& not the one who needs
40 to learn, has to—*Remind me*

what's in that recipe again, my boyfriend says
to my mother, as though they have always, easily

talked. As though no one has told him
many times, what a nonlinear slapstick meets

45 slasher flick meets psychological
pit he is now co-starring in.

Remind me, he says
to our family.

Luke Martineau is a London-based painter whose work encompasses portraiture, landscape, still life, and illustration.

The painting depicts a dinner party. How are the individuals presented? How are they contrasted? How do the images collectively convey an idea about human interaction?

STRUCTURE

1. What is being **contrasted** in the poem? How do these contrasts represent the conflict in the speaker's values and contribute to his perspective?

2. How does the speaker use line breaks and **repetition** to explore the ideas in the poem? How does this structure contribute to your interpretation?

3. The punctuation in the poem creates deliberate stops and starts. Choose a moment when punctuation stops the reader abruptly. How does it contribute to your understanding of the poem?

4. What is **ironic** about his mother's smile? What is the unexpected twist that breaks the tension of the poem? How does this moment reveal an insight or truth?

5. The poem ends with a **paradox**. What ideas seem contradictory when **juxtaposed** here? How does the paradox contribute to your interpretation of the poem?

FIGURATIVE LANGUAGE: Word Choice, Imagery, and Symbols

6. How are the words and phrases associated with the mother **ambiguous**? Find an example of this ambiguity. How does it reveal an idea about the human experience?

7. What is ambiguous about the reference to the *Boston Globe* as a "security blanket"? What **associations** does this term have? How do they apply to the father?

8. How does the phrase "remind me" at the end of the poem reveal insight into the human experience? How does it contribute to your interpretation of the poem?

FIGURATIVE LANGUAGE: Comparisons

9. How do the **allusions** to *Home Alone* create images and associations that go beyond the single moment in the text? Explain how the comparison contributes to the poem.

10. There are many **comparisons** in the text. Choose two and explain how they contribute to your understanding of the poem.

11. The speaker makes a comparison using film genres. What associations do these genres have? How does the reference convey insight into the human experience?

IDEAS IN LITERATURE: Alienation and Fragmentation

12. The family in the poem is fragmented. Consider a time when you or someone you know felt disconnected from a group or community. How did you (or others) find ways to connect? Did your connections include others who felt alienated?

PUTTING IT ALL TOGETHER

13. How does the poet use literary elements and techniques to convey the complexity of the speaker's experience at the dinner party?

How to Talk to Girls at Parties
Neil Gaiman

Jason LaVeris/FilmMagic/Getty Images

THE TEXT IN CONTEXT

Best-selling English writer Neil Gaiman (b. 1960) works in various media forms, including fiction, comics, audio drama, and film. He also writes across several different genres, such as fantasy, horror, and science fiction. But Gaiman blurs the distinctions between genres and categories too. As a character in his 2001 novel *American Gods* says, "I can believe things that are true and things that aren't true and I can believe things where nobody knows if they're true or not." In "How to Talk to Girls at Parties" (2006), Gaiman incorporates *magical realism*: a style that blends elements of the irrational, supernatural, or fantastic into realistic depictions of everyday life, ordinary characters, and familiar settings. As a result, the story's tension and plot largely emerge from the interplay between the "real" and the otherworldly.

How to Talk to Girls at Parties

"Come on," said Vic. "It'll be great."

"No, it won't," I said, although I'd lost this fight hours ago, and I knew it.

"It'll be brilliant," said Vic, for the hun-
5 dredth time. "Girls! Girls! Girls!" He grinned with white teeth.

We both attended an all-boys' school in south London. While it would be a lie to say that we had no experience with girls—Vic
10 seemed to have had many girlfriends, while I had kissed three of my sister's friends—it would, I think, be perfectly true to say that we both chiefly spoke to, interacted with, and only truly understood, other boys. Well, I
15 did, anyway. It's hard to speak for someone else, and I've not seen Vic for thirty years. I'm not sure that I would know what to say to him now if I did.

We were walking the backstreets that used
20 to twine in a grimy maze behind East Croydon station—a friend had told Vic about a party, and Vic was determined to go whether I liked it or not, and I didn't. But my parents were away that week at a conference, and I
25 was Vic's guest at his house, so I was trailing along beside him.

"It'll be the same as it always is," I said. "After an hour you'll be off somewhere snogging the prettiest girl at the party, and I'll
30 be in the kitchen listening to somebody's mum going on about politics or poetry or something."

"You just have to talk to them," he said. "I think it's probably that road at the end here."
35 He gestured cheerfully, swinging the bag with the bottle in it.

"Don't you know?"

"Alison gave me directions and I wrote them on a bit of paper, but I left it on the hall 40 table. S'okay. I can find it."

"How?" Hope welled slowly up inside me.

"We walk down the road," he said, as if speaking to an idiot child. "And we look for the party. Easy."

45   I looked, but saw no party: just narrow houses with rusting cars or bikes in their concreted front gardens; and the dusty glass fronts of newsagents, which smelled of alien spices and sold everything from birthday 50 cards and secondhand comics to the kind of magazines that were so pornographic that they were sold already sealed in plastic bags. I had been there when Vic had slipped one of those magazines beneath his sweater, but 55 the owner caught him on the pavement out-side and made him give it back.

We reached the end of the road and turned into a narrow street of terraced houses. Everything looked very still and empty in the 60 Summer's evening. "It's all right for you," I said. "They fancy you. You don't actually have to talk to them." It was true: one urchin grin from Vic and he could have his pick of the room.

65   "Nah. S'not like that. You've just got to talk."

The times I had kissed my sister's friends I had not spoken to them. They had been around while my sister was off doing some-70 thing elsewhere, and they had drifted into my orbit, and so I had kissed them. I do not remember any talking. I did not know what to say to girls, and I told him so.

They're just girls," said Vic. "They don't 75 come from another planet."

As we followed the curve of the road around, my hopes that the party would prove unfindable began to fade: a low pulsing

noise, music muffled by walls and doors, 80 could be heard from a house up ahead. It was eight in the evening, not that early if you aren't yet sixteen, and we weren't. Not quite.

I had parents who liked to know where I was, but I don't think Vic's parents cared that 85 much. He was the youngest of five boys. That in itself seemed magical to me: I merely had two sisters, both younger than I was, and I felt both unique and lonely. I had wanted a brother as far back as I could remember. 90 When I turned thirteen, I stopped wishing on falling stars or first stars, but back when I did, a brother was what I had wished for.

We went up the garden path, crazy paving leading us past a hedge and a solitary rose-95 bush to a pebble-dashed facade. We rang the doorbell, and the door was opened by a girl. I could not have told you how old she was, which was one of the things about girls I had begun to hate: when you start out as kids 100 you're just boys and girls, going through time at the same speed, and you're all five, or seven, or eleven, together. And then one day there's a lurch and the girls just sort of sprint off into the future ahead of you, and they 105 know all about everything, and they have periods and breasts and makeup and God-only-knew-what-else — for I certainly didn't. The diagrams in biology textbooks were no substitute for being, in a very real sense, 110 young adults. And the girls of our age were.

Vic and I weren't young adults, and I was beginning to suspect that even when I started needing to shave every day, instead of once every couple of weeks, I would still 115 be way behind.

The girl said, "Hello?"

Vic said, "We're friends of Alison's." We had met Alison, all freckles and orange hair and a wicked smile, in Hamburg, on a German 120 exchange. The exchange organizers had sent

some girls with us, from a local girls' school, to balance the sexes. The girls, our age, more or less, were raucous and funny, and had more or less adult boyfriends with cars and
125 jobs and motorbikes and—in the case of one girl with crooked teeth and a raccoon coat, who spoke to me about it sadly at the end of a party in Hamburg, in, of course, the kitchen—a wife and kids.

130   "She isn't here," said the girl at the door. "No Alison."

        "Not to worry," said Vic, with an easy grin. "I'm Vic. This is Enn." A beat, and then the girl smiled back at him. Vic had a bottle of
135 white wine in a plastic bag, removed from his parents' kitchen cabinet. "Where should I put this, then?"

        She stood out of the way, letting us enter. "There's a kitchen in the back," she said. "Put
140 it on the table there, with the other bottles." She had golden, wavy hair, and she was very beautiful. The hall was dim in the twilight, but I could see that she was beautiful.

        "What's your name, then?" said Vic.

145   She told him it was Stella, and he grinned his crooked white grin and told her that that had to be the prettiest name he had ever heard. Smooth bastard. And what was worse was that he said it like he meant it.

150   Vic headed back to drop off the wine in the kitchen, and I looked into the front room, where the music was coming from. There were people dancing in there. Stella walked in, and she started to dance, swaying to the
155 music all alone, and I watched her.

        This was during the early days of punk. On our own record players we would play the Adverts and the Jam, the Stranglers and the Clash and the Sex Pistols. At other people's
160 parties you'd hear ELO or 10cc or even Roxy Music. Maybe some Bowie, if you were lucky. During the German exchange, the only LP

that we had all been able to agree on was Neil Young's *Harvest*, and his song "Heart of
165 Gold" had threaded through the trip like a refrain: *I crossed the ocean for a heart of gold. . . .*

        The music playing in that front room wasn't anything I recognized.

        It sounded a bit like a German electronic
170 pop group called Kraftwerk, and a bit like an LP I'd been given for my last birthday, of strange sounds made by the BBC Radio-phonic Workshop. The music had a beat, though, and the half-dozen girls in that room
175 were moving gently to it, although I only looked at Stella. She shone.

        Vic pushed past me, into the room. He was holding a can of lager. "There's booze back in the kitchen," he told me. He wan-
180 dered over to Stella and he began to talk to her. I couldn't hear what they were saying over the music, but I knew that there was no room for me in that conversation.

        I didn't like beer, not back then. I went off
185 to see if there was something I wanted to drink. On the kitchen table stood a large bot-tle of Coca-Cola, and I poured myself a plas-tic tumblerful, and I didn't dare say anything to the pair of girls who were talking in the
190 underlit kitchen. They were animated and utterly lovely. Each of them had very black skin and glossy hair and movie star clothes, and their accents were foreign, and each of them was out of my league.

195   I wandered, Coke in hand.

        The house was deeper than it looked, larger and more complex than the two- up two-down model I had imagined. The rooms were underlit—I doubt there was a bulb of more
200 than 40 watts in the building—and each room I went into was inhabited: in my memory, inhabited only by girls. I did not go upstairs.

        A girl was the only occupant of the con-servatory. Her hair was so fair it was white,

205 and long, and straight, and she sat at the glass-topped table, her hands clasped together, staring at the garden outside, and the gathering dusk. She seemed wistful.

"Do you mind if I sit here?" I asked, ges-
210 turing with my cup. She shook her head, and then followed it up with a shrug, to indicate that it was all the same to her. I sat down.

Vic walked past the conservatory door. He was talking to Stella, but he looked in at me,
215 sitting at the table, wrapped in shyness and awkwardness, and he opened and closed his hand in a parody of a speaking mouth. Talk. Right.

"Are you from around here?" I asked the
220 girl.

She shook her head. She wore a low-cut silvery top, and I tried not to stare at the swell of her breasts.

I said, "What's your name? I'm Enn."
225   "Wain's Wain," she said, or something that sounded like it. "I'm a second."

"That's uh. That's a different name."

She fixed me with huge, liquid eyes. "It indicates that my progenitor was also Wain,
230 and that I am obliged to report back to her. I may not breed."

"Ah. Well. Bit early for that anyway, isn't it?"

She unclasped her hands, raised them above the table, spread her fingers. "You
235 see?" The little finger on her left hand was crooked, and it bifurcated at the top, splitting into two smaller fingertips. A minor deformity. "When I was finished a decision was needed. Would I be retained, or eliminated? I
240 was fortunate that the decision was with me. Now, I travel, while my more perfect sisters remain at home in stasis. They were firsts. I am a second.

Soon I must return to Wain, and tell her
245 all I have seen. All my impressions of this place of yours."

"I don't actually live in Croydon," I said. "I don't come from here." I wondered if she was American. I had no idea what she was
250 talking about.

"As you say," she agreed, "neither of us comes from here." She folded her six-fingered left hand beneath her right, as if tucking it out of sight. "I had expected it to be bigger,
255 and cleaner, and more colorful. But still, it is a jewel."

She yawned, covered her mouth with her right hand, only for a moment, before it was back on the table again. "I grow weary of the
260 journeying, and I wish sometimes that it would end. On a street in Rio at Carnival, I saw them on a bridge, golden and tall and insect-eyed and winged, and elated I almost ran to greet them, before I saw that they
265 were only people in costumes. I said to Hola Colt, 'Why do they try so hard to look like us?' and Hola Colt replied, 'Because they hate themselves, all shades of pink and brown, and so small.' It is what I experience, even
270 me, and I am not grown. It is like a world of children, or of elves." Then she smiled, and said, "It was a good thing they could not any of them see Hola Colt."

"Um," I said, "do you want to dance?"
275   She shook her head immediately. "It is not permitted," she said. "I can do nothing that might cause damage to property. I am Wain's."

"Would you like something to drink, then?"
280   "Water," she said.

I went back to the kitchen and poured myself another Coke, and filled a cup with water from the tap. From the kitchen back to the hall, and from there into the conserva-
285 tory, but now it was quite empty.

I wondered if the girl had gone to the toilet, and if she might change her mind about dancing later. I walked back to the front room

and stared in. The place was filling up. There
290 were more girls dancing, and several lads I
didn't know, who looked a few years older
than me and Vic. The lads and the girls all
kept their distance, but Vic was holding
Stella's hand as they danced, and when
295 the song ended he put an arm around her,
casually, almost proprietorially, to make sure
that nobody else cut in.

I wondered if the girl I had been talking to
in the conservatory was now upstairs, as she
300 did not appear to be on the ground floor.

I walked into the living room, which was
across the hall from the room where the
people were dancing, and I sat down on the
sofa. There was a girl sitting there already.
305 She had dark hair, cut short and spiky, and a
nervous manner.

Talk, I thought. "Um, this mug of water's
going spare," I told her, "if you want it?"

She nodded, and reached out her hand
310 and took the mug, extremely carefully, as
if she were unused to taking things, as if
she could trust neither her vision nor her
hands.

"I love being a tourist," she said, and
315 smiled hesitantly. She had a gap between her
two front teeth, and she sipped the tap water
as if she were an adult sipping a fine wine.
"The last tour, we went to sun, and we swam
in sunfire pools with the whales. We heard
320 their histories and we shivered in the chill of
the outer places, then we swam deepward
where the heat churned and comforted us.

I wanted to go back. This time, I wanted it.
There was so much I had not seen. Instead
325 we came to world. Do you like it?"

"Like what?"

She gestured vaguely to the room—the
sofa, the armchairs, the curtains, the unused
gas fire.
330   "It's all right, I suppose."

"I told them I did not wish to visit world,"
she said. "My parent-teacher was unim-
pressed. 'You will have much to learn,' it told
me. I said, 'I could learn more in sun, again.
335 Or in the deeps. Jessa spun webs between
galaxies. I want to do that.'

"But there was no reasoning with it, and I
came to world. Parent-teacher engulfed me,
and I was here, embodied in a decaying lump
340 of meat hanging on a frame of calcium. As I
incarnated I felt things deep inside me, fluttering and pumping and squishing. It was
my first experience with pushing air through
the mouth, vibrating the vocal cords on the
345 way, and I used it to tell parent-teacher that I
wished that I would die, which it acknowledged was the inevitable exit strategy from
world."

There were black worry beads wrapped
350 around her wrist, and she fiddled with them
as she spoke. "But knowledge is there, in the
meat," she said, "and I am resolved to learn
from it."

We were sitting close at the center of
355 the sofa now. I decided I should put an arm
around her, but casually. I would extend my
arm along the back of the sofa and eventually sort of creep it down, almost impercep-
tibly, until it was touching her. She said,
360 "The thing with the liquid in the eyes,
when the world blurs. Nobody told me, and
I still do not understand. I have touched
the folds of the Whisper and pulsed and
flown with the tachyon swans, and I still do
365 not understand."

She wasn't the prettiest girl there, but she
seemed nice enough, and she was a girl, anyway. I let my arm slide down a little, tenta-
tively, so that it made contact with her back,
370 and she did not tell me to take it away.

Vic called to me then, from the doorway.
He was standing with his arm around Stella,

protectively, waving at me. I tried to let him know, by shaking my head, that I was onto 375 something, but he called my name and, reluctantly, I got up from the sofa and walked over to the door. "What?"

"Er. Look. The party," said Vic, apologetically. "It's not the one I thought it was. I've 380 been talking to Stella and I figured it out. Well, she sort of explained it to me. We're at a different party."

"Christ. Are we in trouble? Do we have to go?"

385   Stella shook her head. He leaned down and kissed her, gently, on the lips. "You're just happy to have me here, aren't you darlin'?"

"You know I am," she told him.

390   He looked from her back to me, and he smiled his white smile: roguish, lovable, a little bit Artful Dodger, a little bit wide-boy Prince Charming. "Don't worry. They're all tourists here anyway. It's a foreign exchange 395 thing, innit? Like when we all went to Germany."

"It is?"

"Enn. You got to talk to them. And that means you got to listen to them, too. You 400 understand?"

"I did. I already talked to a couple of them."

"You getting anywhere?"

"I was till you called me over."

405   "Sorry about that. Look, I just wanted to fill you in. Right?"

And he patted my arm and he walked away with Stella. Then, together, the two of them went up the stairs.

410   Understand me, all the girls at that party, in the twilight, were lovely; they all had perfect faces but, more important than that, they had whatever strangeness of proportion, of oddness or humanity it is that makes

415 a beauty something more than a shop window dummy.

Stella was the most lovely of any of them, but she, of course, was Vic's, and they were going upstairs together, and that was just 420 how things would always be.

There were several people now sitting on the sofa, talking to the gap-toothed girl. Someone told a joke, and they all laughed. I would have had to push my way in there to 425 sit next to her again, and it didn't look like she was expecting me back, or cared that I had gone, so I wandered out into the hall. I glanced in at the dancers, and found myself wondering where the music was 430 coming from. I couldn't see a record player or speakers.

From the hall I walked back to the kitchen.

Kitchens are good at parties. You never 435 need an excuse to be there, and, on the good side, at this party I couldn't see any signs of someone's mum. I inspected the various bottles and cans on the kitchen table, then I poured a half an inch of Pernod into the bot- 440 tom of my plastic cup, which I filled to the top with Coke. I dropped in a couple of ice cubes and took a sip, relishing the sweet-shop tang of the drink.

"What's that you're drinking?" A girl's 445 voice.

"It's Pernod," I told her. "It tastes like ani-seed balls, only it's alcoholic." I didn't say that I only tried it because I'd heard someone in the crowd ask for a Pernod on a live Velvet 450 Underground LP.

"Can I have one?" I poured another Per-nod, topped it off with Coke, passed it to her. Her hair was a coppery auburn, and it tum-bled around her head in ringlets. It's not a 455 hair style you see much now, but you saw it a lot back then.

"What's your name?" I asked.

"Triolet," she said.

"Pretty name," I told her, although I wasn't
460 sure that it was. She was pretty, though.

"It's a verse form," she said, proudly. "Like
me."

"You're a poem?"

She smiled, and looked down and away,
465 perhaps bashfully. Her profile was almost
flat—a perfect Grecian nose that came down
from her forehead in a straight line. We did
Antigone in the school theater the previous
year. I was the messenger who brings Creon
470 the news of Antigone's death. We wore half-
masks that made us look like that. I thought
of that play, looking at her face, in the
kitchen, and I thought of Barry Smith's drawings of women in the Conan comics: five
475 years later I would have thought of the
Pre-Raphaelites, of Jane Morris and Lizzie
Siddall. But I was only fifteen then.

"You're a poem?" I repeated.

She chewed her lower lip. "If you want. I
480 am a poem, or I am a pattern, or a race of
people whose world was swallowed by the
sea."

"Isn't it hard to be three things at the
same time?"

485 "What's your name?"

"Enn."

"So you are Enn," she said. "And you are a
male. And you are a biped. Is it hard to be
three things at the same time?"

490 "But they aren't different things. I mean,
they aren't contradictory." It was a word I had
read many times but never said aloud before
that night, and I put the stresses in the wrong
places. *Contradictory.*

495 She wore a thin dress made of a white,
silky fabric. Her eyes were a pale green, a
color that would now make me think of
tinted contact lenses; but this was thirty

years ago; things were different then. I
500 remember wondering about Vic and Stella,
upstairs. By now, I was sure that they were
in one of the bedrooms, and I envied Vic so
much it almost hurt.

Still, I was talking to this girl, even if we
505 were talking nonsense, even if her name
wasn't really Triolet (my generation had not
been given hippie names: all the Rainbows
and the Sunshines and the Moons, they were
only six, seven, eight years old back then).

510 She said, "We knew that it would soon be
over, and so we put it all into a poem, to tell
the universe who we were, and why we were
here, and what we said and did and thought
and dreamed and yearned for. We wrapped
515 our dreams in words and patterned the
words so that they would live forever, unfor-
gettable. Then we sent the poem as a pattern
of flux, to wait in the heart of a star, beaming
out its message in pulses and bursts and
520 fuzzes across the electromagnetic spectrum,
until the time when, on worlds a thousand
sun systems distant, the pattern would be
decoded and read, and it would become a
poem once again."

525 "And then what happened?"

She looked at me with her green eyes, and
it was as if she stared out at me from her
own Antigone half-mask; but as if her pale
green eyes were just a different, deeper, part
530 of the mask. "You cannot hear a poem without it changing you," she told me. "They
heard it, and it colonized them. It inherited
them and it inhabited them, its rhythms
becoming part of the way that they thought;
535 its images permanently transmuting their
metaphors; its verses, its outlook, its aspirations becoming their lives. Within a generation their children would be born already
knowing the poem, and, sooner rather than
540 later, as these things go, there were no more

children born. There was no need for them, not any longer. There was only a poem, which took flesh and walked and spread itself across the vastness of the known."

545   I edged closer to her, so I could feel my leg pressing against hers.

She seemed to welcome it: she put her hand on my arm, affectionately, and I felt a smile spreading across my face.

550   "There are places that we are welcomed," said Triolet, "and places where we are regarded as a noxious weed, or as a disease, something immediately to be quarantined and eliminated. But where does contagion
555 end and art begin?"

"I don't know," I said, still smiling. I could hear the unfamiliar music as it pulsed and scattered and boomed in the front room.

She leaned into me then and—I suppose
560 it was a kiss. . . . I suppose. She pressed her lips to my lips, anyway, and then, satisfied, she pulled back, as if she had now marked me as her own.

"Would you like to hear it?" she asked,
565 and I nodded, unsure what she was offering me, but certain that I needed anything she was willing to give me.

She began to whisper something in my ear. It's the strangest thing about poetry—
570 you can tell it's poetry, even if you don't speak the language. You can hear Homer's Greek without understanding a word, and you still know it's poetry. I've heard Polish poetry, and Inuit poetry, and I knew what it
575 was without knowing. Her whisper was like that. I didn't know the language, but her words washed through me, perfect, and in my mind's eye I saw towers of glass and diamond; and people with eyes of the palest
580 green; and, unstoppable, beneath every syllable, I could feel the relentless advance of the ocean.

Perhaps I kissed her properly. I don't remember. I know I wanted to.

585   And then Vic was shaking me violently. "Come on!" he was shouting. "Quickly. Come on!"

In my head I began to come back from a thousand miles away.

590   "Idiot. Come on. Just get a move on," he said, and he swore at me. There was fury in his voice.

For the first time that evening I recognized one of the songs being played in the front
595 room. A sad saxophone wail followed by a cascade of liquid chords, a man's voice sing-ing cut-up lyrics about the sons of the silent age. I wanted to stay and hear the song.

She said, "I am not finished. There is yet
600 more of me."

"Sorry love," said Vic, but he wasn't smil-ing any longer. "There'll be another time," and he grabbed me by the elbow and he twisted and pulled, forcing me from the
605 room. I did not resist. I knew from experi-ence that Vic could beat the stuffing out me if he got it into his head to do so. He wouldn't do it unless he was upset or angry, but he was angry now.

610   Out into the front hall. As Vic pulled open the door, I looked back one last time, over my shoulder, hoping to see Triolet in the doorway to the kitchen, but she was not there. I saw Stella, though, at the top of the stairs. She was
615 staring down at Vic, and I saw her face.

This all happened thirty years ago. I have forgotten much, and I will forget more, and in the end I will forget everything; yet, if I have any certainty of life beyond death, it is
620 all wrapped up not in psalms or hymns, but in this one thing alone: I cannot believe that I will ever forget that moment, or forget the expression on Stella's face as she watched Vic hurrying away from her. Even in death I
625 shall remember that.

Her clothes were in disarray, and there was makeup smudged across her face, and her eyes—

You wouldn't want to make a universe
630 angry. I bet an angry universe would look at
you with eyes like that.

We ran then, me and Vic, away from the
party and the tourists and the twilight, ran
as if a lightning storm was on our heels, a
635 mad helter-skelter dash down the confusion
of streets, threading through the maze, and
we did not look back, and we did not stop
until we could not breathe; and then we
stopped and panted, unable to run any lon-
640 ger. We were in pain. I held on to a wall, and
Vic threw up, hard and long, into the gutter.

He wiped his mouth.

"She wasn't a—" He stopped.

He shook his head.

645 Then he said, "You know . . . I think there's
a thing. When you've gone as far as you dare.
And if you go any further, you wouldn't be
you anymore? You'd be the person who'd
done that? The places you just can't go. . . . I
650 think that happened to me tonight."

I thought I knew what he was saying.
"Screw her, you mean?" I said.

He rammed a knuckle hard against my
temple, and twisted it violently. I wondered
655 if I was going to have to fight him—and
lose—but after a moment he lowered his
hand and moved away from me, making a
low, gulping noise.

I looked at him curiously, and I realized
660 that he was crying: his face was scarlet; snot
and tears ran down his cheeks. Vic was sobbing in the street, as unselfconsciously and
heartbreakingly as a little boy.

He walked away from me then, shoulders
665 heaving, and he hurried down the road so he
was in front of me and I could no longer see
his face. I wondered what had occurred in
that upstairs room to make him behave like
that, to scare him so, and I could not even
670 begin to guess.

The streetlights came on, one by one; Vic
stumbled on ahead, while I trudged down
the street behind him in the dusk, my feet
treading out the measure of a poem that, try
675 as I might, I could not properly remember
and would never be able to repeat.

Norman Rockwell, Children Dancing at a Party, 1918

◀ *Children Dancing at a Party*, produced by Norman Rockwell, appeared on the cover of the January 26, 1918, issue of *The Saturday Evening Post*.

Look closely at the details in the painting. What does the image convey about young people and their interest in dancing at parties? Pay attention to all individuals in the painting. What does it communicate about their relationships?

STRUCTURE

1. Enn narrates the story thirty years after the events. What is the effect of this **flashback**? How does it contribute to the tension in the story?

2. Enn meets three girls at the party. How do the girls and the events in the story connect to create Enn's experience? Explain the **situational irony** of the party. What statements are inconsistent and contradictory? How do these inconsistencies reveal an unexpected idea?

3. Identify a **paradox** in the story. How are the details in a situation **juxtaposed** and what does this apparent contradiction reveal?

4. Explain other **situational ironies** in the text. What events are unexpected? How do they contribute to the complexity of the text?

FIGURATIVE LANGUAGE: Word Choice, Imagery, and Symbols

5. How do Enn's words and phrases contribute to the **ambiguity** between himself and the girls at the party? What words and phrases seem ambiguous?

6. The story includes several examples of **symbolism**. Choose two symbols and explain how their associations contribute to your understanding of the text.

7. At the end of "How to Talk to Girls at Parties," how do Vic's words and phrases contribute to the **inconsistencies** and ambiguities in the conclusion?

FIGURATIVE LANGUAGE: Comparisons

8. In the description of the party, what extended **comparisons** and associations combine to affect your understanding of the people present?

9. As Enn begins to talk to the girls, they make many references to unearthly or alien concepts. Give a specific example and then explain the associations of the reference.

IDEAS IN LITERATURE: Alienation and Fragmentation

10. How are Enn's memories of the party a reminder of the alienation he feels at the beginning and the end of the story? Explain how alienation affects humans differently at various times in their lives. Use your own experiences to support your response.

PUTTING IT ALL TOGETHER

11. What is the relationship between the narrator's reliability and the reader's understanding of the character's motivations? You should consider point of view, perspective, and narrative distance in your response.

IDEAS IN LITERATURE
Identity and Identities

The Great Depression and World War II profoundly changed the United States. But even before these two cataclysms, the country's identity was shifting. Between 1880 and 1920, more than twenty million immigrants arrived from all different parts of Europe, as well as Asia. Foreshadowing the conflicts we still see today, some Americans in the 1920s and 1930s feared that immigration threatened the country's ethnic, racial, religious, and cultural character. As a result, the government instituted stricter immigration laws, but the backlash did little to change America's status as a nation of immigrants. The Great Migration was well underway, too, as millions of African Americans were moving from the rural South to the urban Northeast and Midwest. This led to increased African American political activism: while Black people had more opportunities for education, employment, and political participation in cities like Philadelphia and Chicago, they still found prejudice and segregation. Even Franklin D. Roosevelt's New Deal—a series of federal programs, regulations, and reforms designed to help the economic recovery—excluded African Americans in various ways. These inequities, and many others, contributed to the early development of the modern civil rights movement.

While modernist literature reached its peak in the decade before World War II, many writers at the time were less interested in avant-garde experimentation and more interested in engaging with the social world around them. Some dramatized the effects of the Great Depression, like John Steinbeck (1902–1968) in novels such as *The Grapes of Wrath* (1939). Writers from the Harlem Renaissance expressed the realities of Black life in the United States. Richard Wright's (1908–1960) powerful autobiography *Black Boy* (1945) is a vivid, often horrifying narrative, as

IDEA BANK

Celebration
Community
Culture
Depravity
Devotion
Dignity
Expression
Facade
Family
Gender
Guilt
Heritage
History
Identities
Identity
Invisibility
Manipulation
Obligation
Persona
Power
Privilege
Race
Tradition
Truth

©Kafia Haile

Ceremony in Sisterhood is a painting by Kafia Haile (2012). The painting was created for the ten-year reunion of Spelman College's Class of 2002.

The painting depicts sisters looking at others from afar. How does the painting communicate contemporary ideas about individual and collective identities?

Wright seeks his identity as an individual, as part of a community, and as an artist in a racist society.

But African American writers were not alone in the struggle to share their identities. Other communities and cultures have used literature in the same way: to express shared customs, aspirations, traditions, and history. For example, Latinx, Chicano, and indigenous peoples express their cultural values through literature and art, as do those who identify as LGBTQ+, as part of a faith-based community, or as members of various cultures and ethnicities. At the same time, literature also allows us to transcend our own cultures and share the human experiences of people from other backgrounds and communities. By looking beyond the immediate context of the story, we can often reflect on our own assumptions, prejudices, and blind spots. Of course, contemporary authors such as Teri Foltz continue to explore identity from both a personal and a community perspective. In her one-act play *Manhunt* (p. 1195), the characters are forced to confront the truth about their own identities — a process that can be surprisingly difficult, both in literature and in life.

▲

Mattel redesigned Ken and Barbie dolls in 2020. The updated fashionista makeover was Mattel's "next step in the brand's evolution to offer more diverse products."

As you examine the redesigned dolls, notice the details that contribute to their diversity. How well did Mattel achieve its goal of accurately depicting identity and identities?

Manhunt
Teri Foltz

Teri Foltz

THE TEXT IN CONTEXT

Teri Foltz is a retired AP® English and drama teacher who started her career as a playwright and poet after she retired. From her home in Fort Thomas, Kentucky, she hosts a YouTube channel series, Teri's Playdate, where she provides an opportunity to watch her original one-act plays "read by her talented actor friends."

Manhunt

Cast of **Manhunt**:

TOM: *Male, 23, Robert's brother*

ROBERT: *Male, 22, Tom's brother*

MANHUNT: *A short play about the meaning of manhood*

Summary:

When Robert promises his father that he will teach Tom, his brother, to shoot a gun, they go hunting and find much more than they thought they would. Thinking that he already knows, Tom comes out to his brother. In an effort to help him overcome his fear of telling their dad, Robert convinces Tom to practice on him.

Both men enter the stage carrying rifles.

TOM   OK, Where's the target this time?

ROBERT   It's not called a target, pencil dick, it's a buck. A twelve point, hopefully.

TOM   Whoa, wait. I thought this was still
5   target practice. You want me to shoot a deer?

ROBERT   Yep. And then we're going to have it stuffed and hang it next to the flag in dad's barbershop. He'll love it.

10 **TOM**   Can't we just get him a pen and pencil set?

ROBERT   What? So he can put it next to all the other pen and pencil sets we have given him since we were ten? We talked about
15   this earlier. First, I was going to take you out and teach you to hit a target . . .

TOM   Yes, and that's where it ended. I could show dad that I could shoot a gun. He'd be proud and that would be gift enough. I
20   don't wanna kill a defenseless deer. So what?

ROBERT   Buck. My gift to dad is the knowledge that I finally made a man out of you. And your gift to him is that you let me.

25 **TOM**   What do you intend to do? Staple my balls to his wall? Would that make the pair of you happy?

ROBERT   Yeah, they'd look good under the clock. Or better yet, next to the flag where
30   our buck would have gone if you hadn't been such a coward.

TOM   I am not a coward. I am a man, just like you. Mom used to dress us alike in grade school and people couldn't tell us apart,
35   remember that? Well, we've grown up and we are not the same.

ROBERT   We are not that different. You learned how to shoot. You hit the target in practice

40 more often than I did. So what the hell's
the matter with you?

TOM   Nothing's the matter with me. It has
nothing to do with my being gay either, so
don't go there.

ROBERT   Gay?

45 **TOM**   Come on.

ROBERT   You're kidding . . . or you're lying.

TOM   Lying? Men lie about their golf score or
their military record. Not about being gay.

ROBERT   You're gay. You're gay. Really? You're
50 gay?

TOM   Yes.

ROBERT   How long have you felt gay?

TOM   How long have you felt straight? And I
don't feel gay. I am gay. It's not like feeling
55 sick.

ROBERT   I didn't say you were sick.

TOM   Well, good, because I feel fine.

ROBERT   So when did you discover you liked
guys?

60 **TOM**   When did you discover Elly Carver?

ROBERT   Shit, Elly Carver. I don't know . . . as
soon as she moved next door?

TOM   Well, that's when I noticed her brother.

ROBERT   You can't be gay.

65 **TOM**   I can't? Then you can't be straight.

ROBERT   We're brothers! Same gene pool!

TOM   Then why did you get As in high school
and I got Cs? How do you explain that?

ROBERT   Lack of focus on your part.

70 **TOM**   Well, I had a lot on my mind. High
school wasn't easy.

ROBERT   What do you mean? I played
football. You ran cross county. Everyone
knew us.

75 **TOM**   Everyone knew you. I am pretty sure no
one knew me.

ROBERT   So you were shy . . . so what?

TOM   It was always, "Hey, you know Robert,
right? And his brother . . . what's his
80 name?"

ROBERT   So I was a glory whore, and you
hated the limelight. You had tons of
friends, didn't you?

TOM   I had a few.

85 **ROBERT**   You went to the prom!

TOM   Yeah. So?

ROBERT   So you didn't have fun in high
school?

TOM   Sure, I did . . . some of the time. But not
90 the same easy way you did.

ROBERT   So, are they right when they say "it
gets better"?

TOM   You're quoting LGBT slogans now?

ROBERT   Shut up. Did it?

95 **TOM**   College was better. I hate to say it, but
that's because you were not there.

ROBERT   So that's why you didn't take the
scholarship to Indiana?

TOM   One of the reasons. I needed to grow up.
100 Not under the watchful eye of my brother.

ROBERT   So . . . was Joseph your. . . .

TOM   Roommate. He was my roommate.
That's all. Straight as you.

ROBERT   Did he know you were gay?

105 **TOM**   I assume he did. We didn't talk about it.

ROBERT   How can you not talk about it?

TOM   I don't talk about my sex life. I'm the
shy one, remember?

ROBERT   I don't talk about my sex life either.

110 **TOM**   So maybe we're not so different.

ROBERT   Seriously, when did you know?

TOM   When I was twelve.

ROBERT   Twelve?

TOM   Yeah. That's when Elly Carver's family
115 moved next door.

ROBERT   Oh . . . with her brother . . . what was
his name?

TOM   James.

ROBERT   THAT you remember, right? Was he
120 gay?

TOM   Hell no. That was the first of many
unrequited crushes I had.

ROBERT What about Jennie?

TOM I liked Jennie. If she thought I was gay,
125 she never mentioned it. I think she knew,
but she could tell I wasn't ready to talk
about it.

ROBERT Why couldn't you tell me?

TOM Secrets are heavy. I wasn't going to
130 burden you too.

ROBERT What about Mom and Dad?

TOM Mom knows.

ROBERT WHAT? No way.

TOM I told her when I was a sophomore in
135 college.

ROBERT And she didn't tell Dad?

TOM I asked her not to. That was something
I needed to do.

ROBERT And?

140 **TOM** That's too complicated. I can't do that
right now.

ROBERT So you were going to just let me
teach you how to shoot a gun so he would
think you were . . . I don't
145 know . . . manly?

TOM I am a man, and therefore, I am manly,
Robert. Just not the way he wants me to
be.

ROBERT Forget the buck on his wall. You need
150 to give him a better gift.

TOM No. Stop. I'm not coming out of the
closet to Dad. Forget it.

ROBERT Are you sorry you came out to me?

TOM I didn't know I was "coming out" to
155 you. I thought you knew!

ROBERT Tell you what. I'll stand right next to
you. We can dress identically if it helps.

TOM I'm not sure.

ROBERT Well, a man's gotta do what a man's
160 gotta do. Right?

TOM You're playing that card? You're gonna
tell him that you finally made a man out
of me?

ROBERT Exactly. Let's see how he takes it.

165 **TOM** You'd do that? Stand with me?

ROBERT Yeah . . . isn't this what they mean
when they say it gets better?

TOM Stop . . . it just doesn't sound right
coming out of your mouth!

170 **ROBERT** OK, if you weren't such a coward,
you'd tell Dad. Is that better? Grow some
balls.

TOM OK . . . but can I hold the gun and brag
about hitting the target more times than
175 you?

ROBERT Sure. By the way, how did Mom react
when you told her?

TOM She said, "Well, it's about time." I guess
you can fool some people, but never your
180 mom.

ROBERT I'm sorry.

TOM What are you sorry for?

ROBERT If Mom knew, I should have known.
Why didn't I know?

185 **TOM** Oh you probably did on some level. But I
worked hard to keep you from knowing.

ROBERT You couldn't trust my reaction? Was
it as hard as telling Dad?

TOM Well, we'll see. What do you think he'll
190 do?

ROBERT Truth? He'll tell you you're not gay.

TOM Yeah. I kinda think that too.

ROBERT It can't matter, you know.

TOM Easy for you to say.

195 **ROBERT** OK . . . then practice. Pretend I am
Dad and tell me.

TOM Quit. This isn't funny.

ROBERT I'm serious. I'll react every way he
might and you'll be prepared. Do it!

200 **TOM** (Taking a deep breath) Dad, I'm gay.

ROBERT No, you're not.

TOM Dad, I'm gay.

ROBERT If Rob's not gay, you're not gay.

TOM Dad, I'm gay.

205 **ROBERT** It's your mom's fault for coddling
you.

TOM Dad, I'm gay.

ROBERT You're not gay, you're a sissy. You'll grow out of it.

210 **TOM** I'll grow out of it? Shit . . . Rob, I'm twenty-three.

ROBERT Not to Dad. We're both twelve to him.

TOM Right.

ROBERT Go on.

215 **TOM** Dad, I'm gay.

ROBERT Get out.

TOM What?

ROBERT I said, "Get out and don't come back."

TOM Oh god.

220 **ROBERT** He might, you know.

TOM Hell yes, I know. This is my nightmare.

ROBERT And if he does, then what will you do?

TOM Get out, I guess.

225 **ROBERT** If you leave, I leave. Promise.

TOM And what about Mom?

ROBERT It'll take some time, but she'll bring him around. You'll have to be patient.

TOM And what do I do when and IF he

230 invites me back home?

ROBERT You go. He's your dad. You're his son.

TOM I won't go back home without you. Promise.

ROBERT I know that.

235 **TOM** So we wait . . .

ROBERT Yep . . . until "it gets better."

TOM You have to quit that. Really.

ROBERT Fine. Back to target practice.

TOM I think I'm going to get him a pen and

240 pencil set anyway. Just to be safe.

ROBERT I'm getting him something he wants, whether he likes it or not. I'm making a man out of you.

(**TOM** *punches him in the arm and they do the "slap the back" man hug.*)

The Broadway musical *Kinky Boots* was adapted from the film of the same name. The story focuses on the parallel lives of the main characters and highlights the theme of accepting people for who they are. In this 2017 production photo, the two main characters are played by Brendon Urie and J. Harrison Ghee.

———

The photo shows the curtain call of a production of *Kinky Boots*. Pay attention to the details of each character's costume. How might the costumes contribute to the theme of accepting people for who they are?

Andrew Toth/Getty Images

STRUCTURE

1. Explain the **ambiguities** in the dialogue as the reader is introduced to Robert and Tom.

2. How are the characters **juxtaposed**? Explain the contrast between them. How does it contribute to the ambiguity and complexity of the text?

3. The narrative projects the possibility of the future and the reaction of their father. How do these projections contribute to the **tension** between the characters?

FIGURATIVE LANGUAGE: Word Choice, Imagery, and Symbols

4. What **associations** do each of the brothers have regarding their respective childhoods? How do these associations contribute to the nuances and complexities of the characters?

5. How is the **motif** of hunting developed throughout the play? What associations does each of the associated **images** evoke?

6. What does high school **symbolize**? What does this symbol reveal for Tom? Explain Rob's reaction as he responds to Tom. How does that ambivalence create a complexity within the text?

FIGURATIVE LANGUAGE: Comparisons

7. In what way does "hunting" become an **extended metaphor**? What are the particular points of comparison and why are they significant?

8. The term *Manhunt* means an organized search of a person, especially a criminal. What does the title suggest? What emotional or intellectual associations does it imply?

IDEAS IN LITERATURE: Identity and Identities

9. The text communicates multiple tensions, including one brother not knowing his brother's sexuality. How does what we *don't* know in this text speak to broader tensions in the story's wider, cultural context? Reflect on tensions between individuals and groups in your own cultural surroundings. How might the lack of accurate information and knowledge lead to these tensions?

PUTTING IT ALL TOGETHER

10. How does Tom help illuminate Rob's experiences and memories? In what ways does this illumination reveal Rob's character? How does this revelation alter and affect the brothers' relationship?

Forgotten Portraits

Janine Solursh

THE TEXT IN CONTEXT

Although born in Toronto, poet Janine Solursh has lived in Georgia for most of her life. She currently works for Common Good Atlanta, an organization of professors, volunteers, and alumni who lead higher education programs in Georgia's prisons. In the following poem, she explores one of the most universal human questions — and perhaps even offers an answer.

Forgotten Portraits

Suddenly nobody knows where you are.
You're just a memory,
an echo,
an idea thin as smoke.
5 Your last text, call, letter, Facebook post—
only footprints in the surf.
Your edges blur and you become
a friend's story,
a lover's history.

10 Initially, you beat against the panes in set-aside frames
begging to be taken out
and rolled into motion once more.
But after a second winter,
then a third, and fourth,
15 there comes something serene and warm
behind the haze that smokes the broken hourglass.
Something new
and just for you.
This world belongs to you and yours
20 and when you glance back and recall your life's movement
with a sigh of days gone by,
you are irrevocably comforted
having become that final exhale
that hangs in the air after the passing.
25 You pose
and hold it.

We are all the dead.
I am not apart from you for long,
except for breath,
30 except for everything.

Mike Ford/Alamy

◀ The image depicts an extended family photo collage (canvas print).

___

How does this collage express ideas about identity? Look closely at the images and details throughout the collage. How do they combine to comment on the creator's perceptions of identity—and on the ways in which those identities are preserved?

STRUCTURE

1. Consider the **images** in the first **stanza**. How does this imagery extend beyond the first stanza and represent a larger **idea** in the poem?

2. How does the dash function in the first stanza? What is the relationship between the images before the dash and the images after the dash? How does this create **contrast** and contribute to your understanding of the poem?

3. Identify the **juxtaposition** in the second stanza and then explain how it reveals an unexpected idea.

FIGURATIVE LANGUAGE: Word Choice, Imagery, and Symbols

4. What **symbol** in the first stanza creates associations that reveal the speaker? What are the associations? How do they connect with the speaker?

5. What **associations** do the seasons suggest in the second stanza? How do those associations reveal a shared human experience?

6. How do the **words and phrases** at the end of the poem create **ambiguity**? How does the ambiguity contribute to your interpretation of the poem?

FIGURATIVE LANGUAGE: Comparisons

7. What is being **compared** in the first stanza? How does the **simile** evoke a shared human experience?

8. The second stanza begins with a **metaphor**. What is being compared? How does it contribute to your understanding of the poem?

9. How does the title of the poem establish an **extended metaphor**? What traits are being compared in the metaphor? What shared human experience does the poem evoke?

IDEAS IN LITERATURE: Identity and Identities

10. How does this contemporary poem speak to our current sense of identity? Is your sense of your identity and self separate from your image on social media? Explain.

PUTTING IT ALL TOGETHER

11. How does the poet use various poetic elements to convey the complex attitude of the speaker? What does the poem reveal about a shared human experience?

My Mother Pieced Quilts
Teresa Acosta

THE TEXT IN CONTEXT

Poet Teresa Acosta (b. 1949) was born in McGregor, Texas. Her parents migrated from Mexico to Texas during the Great Depression — a legacy that deeply informs her work. Acosta attended the University of Texas and earned an MS in journalism from Columbia University. Her poems have appeared in literary publications like *Tejidos*, *Riversedge*, and *Descant*. They have also been anthologized in collections such as *Infinite Divisions: An Anthology of Chicana Literature* (1993). In "My Mother Pieced Quilts" (1976), she writes about quilting both literally and metaphorically as she reflects on her family history.

Photo by Anna Munoz

My Mother Pieced Quilts

they were just meant as covers
in winters
as weapons
against pounding january winds

5 but it was just that every morning I awoke to these
october ripened canvases
passed my hand across their cloth faces
and began to wonder how you pieced
all these together
10 these strips of gentle communion cotton and flannel nightgowns
wedding organdies
dime store velvets

how you shaped patterns square and oblong and
round
15 positioned
balanced
then cemented them
with your thread
a steel needle
20 a thimble

how the thread darted in and out
galloping along the frayed edges, tucking them in
as you did us at night
oh how you stretched and turned and rearranged
25 your michigan spring faded curtain pieces
my father's santa fe work shirt
the summer denims, the tweeds of fall

in the evening you sat at your canvas
—our cracked linoleum floor the drawing board
30 me lounging on your arm
and you staking out the plan:

whether to put the lilac purple of easter against the red plaid of
    winter-going-into-
spring
whether to mix a yellow with blue and white and
35 paint the
corpus christi noon when my father held your hand

whether to shape a five-point star from the
somber black silk you wore to grandmother's funeral

you were the river current
40 carrying the roaring notes . . .
forming them into pictures of a little boy reclining
a swallow flying
you were the caravan master at the reins
driving your thread needle artillery across the mosaic
45 cloth bridges
delivering yourself in separate testimonies

oh mother you plunged me sobbing and laughing
into our past
into the river crossing at five
50 into the spinach fields
into the plainview cotton rows
into tuberculosis wards
into braids and muslin dresses
sewn hard and taut to withstand the thrashings of
55 twenty-five years

stretched out they lay
armed/ready/shouting/celebrating

knotted with love
the quilts sing on

The AIDS Memorial Quilt was conceived in November of 1985 by longtime San Francisco gay rights activist Cleve Jones. On October 11, 1987, the Quilt was displayed for the first time on the National Mall in Washington, D.C., during the National March on Washington for Lesbian and Gay Rights. The Quilt's inaugural display led to a four-month, twenty-city, national tour in the spring and summer of 1988. The tour raised nearly $500,000 for hundreds of AIDS service organizations.

The image shows the AIDS Memorial Quilt displayed on the National Mall in Washington, D.C. How might the Quilt impact the visitors, memorialize the victims, and chronicle history at the same time?

(Gerald) LEE SNIDER/Corbis Historical/Getty Images

STRUCTURE

1. How does the poem begin? How does this beginning **parallel** the quilt and the characters' lives?

2. What is the **juxtaposition** in the second stanza? What does the contrast reveal?

3. What is the poetic form of "My Mother Pieced Quilts"? How does this form contribute to the **rhythm** and **pacing** of the poem?

4. What does the phrase "the quilts sing on" imply?

FIGURATIVE LANGUAGE: Word Choice, Imagery, and Symbols

5. Choose two **images** that extend throughout the poem and then explain how they contribute to your understanding of the poem.

6. How do the **words and phrases** create ambiguity? Explain the ambiguity. What associations does it evoke?

7. How does the **symbolic** meaning of the quilt contribute to your interpretation of the poem?

FIGURATIVE LANGUAGE: Comparisons

8. How is sewing a **metaphor** in the poem? How does that metaphor contribute to your understanding of the text?

9. How does the speaker compare the mother to an artist? What characteristics are similar? How does the **comparison** reveal a shared human experience?

10. How do the comparisons change from the beginning to the end of the poem? How does the meaning of the quilt evolve?

IDEAS IN LITERATURE: Identity and Identities

11. This poem is about how quilts can detail our histories and reveal who we are. How do artifacts and material objects tell stories and preserve identities?

PUTTING IT ALL TOGETHER

12. How is the quilt a **motif** that expresses an idea and takes on figurative meaning? How does the motif contribute to the complexity of the poem?

Writing about Structure and Irony

 Enduring Understanding (LAN-1)

Readers establish and communicate their interpretations of literature through arguments supported by textual evidence.

KEY POINT

Writers use conclusions to explain the relevance of their idea and insight and to explore them within a larger context.

Writing Conclusions

Over many years of reading and experiencing stories, readers become adept at understanding how a story unfolds from "once upon a time" to "happily ever after." We grow to understand the progression of a narrative from beginning to middle to end; we learn to anticipate the final outcome as we go. In fact, you have likely read a story in the past and thought, *I knew that was going to happen.*

But you can probably recall a story or film that caught you off guard, as well. A writer may establish a pattern and then break it, create an incongruity, or thwart your expectations in any number of ways. As a result, you might even see things from a completely different perspective. When a story's events turn out differently than readers expect, the disparity between expectations and reality often creates **irony**. That irony adds a layer of complexity to the text.

In fact, the way an author structures a story creates this irony. Structure includes how a text is arranged, how time progresses in the narrative, and (sometimes) how the narrative perspective changes or evolves. To navigate poems, stories, novels, and plays effectively, pay close attention to how authors divide their texts structurally. Look for the author's strategic use of juxtaposition, contrasts, and shifts and consider the implications of these choices.

In this composition workshop, you will focus on writing a literary argument that analyzes how a text's structure reveals an irony that contributes to your interpretation. As you develop your literary argument, you will also focus on using the conclusion to emphasize the relevance of your idea within a larger context.

 YOUR ASSIGNMENT

Choose a text from Unit 8 or one that your teacher has assigned. Then, write a literary argument that analyzes how the author reveals irony through a text's structure in a way that contributes to an interpretation of the work. Support your thesis with evidence from the text.

Your argument should interpret a literary work and include the following:

- An introduction that identifies the title, author, context, and text structural choice and explains the relevance of the idea
- A thesis statement with a claim that conveys an interpretation (a unifying idea + insight about that idea)
- A line of reasoning that justifies the interpretation in the claim
- Relevant and sufficient textual evidence that supports the line of reasoning
- Commentary that links the evidence to the unifying idea in the line of reasoning and claim
- Transitional elements that create coherence in the argument
- A conclusion that explains the relevance of the idea and brings the literary argument to a unified end
- Syntactical choices that reveal associations and relationships within the argument

Potential Subjects

- How mystery or suspense shapes a narrative
- How an author manipulates time to develop a narrative
- How an action before the story's beginning affects the characters and the outcome of a narrative
- How a prophecy or an omen shapes a narrative
- How an author uses an ambiguous or unresolved ending to convey an interpretation
- How an author brings about catharsis in the reader
- How an author uses an accident or chance to shape a narrative
- How a character reveals an important secret to the reader or audience

Explaining Complexity

While you are exploring how an author's structural choices affect your interpretation of the text, you should also consider the irony that results from these choices. Look for unexpected outcomes, contrasting details, paradoxes, conflicts, and other incongruities created by the author's choices.

Here are some questions to help you dig a little deeper into the complexity of a text's structure:

- How do the shifts in time, place, or perspective reveal contrasts, tensions, or conflicts within a text?
- How does the author break established patterns within a text to create irony?
- How does a contrast or antithesis reveal competing values within a text?

- How does the conflict within the text represent cultural values?
- How does an ambiguous ending allow for multiple interpretations within the work?
- How do contrasting images within a poem reveal a speaker's complex attitude about a subject?
- How do multiple literary elements work together to reveal nuance within a literary work?

Set a Purpose for Reading

As you begin to analyze your selected text, identify a unifying idea to guide your annotations. First, consider how the text is divided and why the author made those structural choices. Works are often divided by stanzas, parts, or chapters based on the following factors:

- Events in the plot
- A shift in time, place, or perspective
- A shift from the literal to the abstract
- Comparisons or contrasts

Consider the following questions with your unifying idea in mind as you examine the author's structural choices.

- What is the significance of the order of the narrative events?
- What is the significance of the author's use of shifts or juxtaposition within the text?
- What is significant about the attributes of comparisons and contrasts within a text?
- What is the significance of the patterns within the text?
- What is emphasized and what are the implications when patterns are interrupted within a text?
- What is suggested when a text ends unexpectedly or ambiguously?

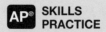 **SKILLS PRACTICE** | LITERARY ARGUMENTATION **Analyzing Structure and Irony**

Review the text that you are analyzing for your literary argument. In the graphic organizer, record your unifying idea, as well as the topic and focus of your analysis. Then, record the element of the text structure you will analyze, details from the text, and the implications or significance of these details as they relate to your unifying idea. (You may need to delete or add rows.)

Analyzing Structure and Irony		
Unifying idea:		
Topic and focus of analysis:		
Text Structure	Details from the Text	Insights and Connections to the Unifying Idea

Develop a Thesis

A thesis statement for an analysis of structure and irony, as in other literary arguments, requires a claim that includes your interpretation. In this essay, you will explain how the author's use of structure and irony contributes to this interpretation. You should identify the structural choice from the text and the specific focus of your analysis — along with your broader interpretation of the text — within your thesis statement.

When you develop and preview your line of reasoning, which will suggest how to organize your analysis, you may consider the following aspects of structure:

- The way two or more structural choices work to contribute to an interpretation of the work
- The way an author presents contrasts within a text to reveal contrasting values
- The juxtaposition of two opposing elements that amplify contrasts and reveal irony
- The way an author shifts from one setting, time, perspective, or attitude to reveal contrasts and tensions

WRITING A THESIS FOR ANALYSIS OF STRUCTURE AND IRONY	
Template 1: The thesis identifies two or more aspects of the structure to establish a line of reasoning and connect to the idea.	In [title of work], [author], uses [structural choice] to reveal [unifying idea + insight] by [aspect 1], [aspect 2], and [aspect 3].

(continued)

| Template 2:
The thesis identifies two or more aspects of structure to explore contrasts, juxtaposition, or shifts and connects to the idea. | In [title of work], [author]
• contrasts [aspect 1 of structure] with [aspect 2 of structure],
• juxtaposes [aspect 1 of structure] and [aspect 2 of structure], and
• shifts from [aspect 1 of structure] to [aspect 2 of structure] to convey [unifying idea + insight]. |
| Template 3:
The thesis identifies the structural choice and connects to the idea as an open thesis that does not preview the line of reasoning. | In [title of work], [author's] [choice of structure] reveals [unifying idea + insight]. |

AP® SKILLS PRACTICE | LITERARY ARGUMENTATION
Developing a Thesis Statement for Analysis of Structure and Irony

Complete the following chart. In the left column, record the title, author, and aspect of structure that you will explore. Next, record the unifying idea and insight that will convey your interpretation of your claim.

Developing a Defensible Thesis Statement for Analysis of Structure and Irony	
Topic	Claim
Title, Author, and Focus (aspect of structure)	Unifying Idea + Insight

Organize a Line of Reasoning

Recall that you justify your interpretation through a line of reasoning that is revealed in your topic sentences. For a literary argument that analyzes structure and irony, your line of reasoning focuses on specific aspects of the structure that relate to the unifying idea in your claim.

The body of your analysis should be organized according to the line of reasoning that you used in crafting your thesis. Since many of the choices for structure involve two elements informed by a contrast, shift, or juxtaposition, the two opposing forces can serve as the topics for each body paragraph. Alternatively, you might organize your paragraphs by the separate aspects of comparison and then discuss both opposing forces in each body paragraph.

STRUCTURE OF AN ANALYSIS OF STRUCTURE AND IRONY

Introduction

The **introduction** is an opportunity for the writer to establish the purpose of his or her literary argument and to invite and interest the audience in the literary work and the writer's interpretation of it. To achieve this goal, many literary arguments follow this structure:

- Engage the audience through an interesting hook
- Provide historical, cultural, or social context of a literary work
- Identify the title, author, genre (TAG)
- Introduce the structure and irony by
  - describing the importance of the structure within the work; and
  - summarizing the work succinctly with details critical to the structure and irony

The **thesis statement** presents a defensible interpretation that includes an idea and an insight into that idea.

Body

(Develops a line of reasoning with supporting evidence that justifies the thesis)

Topic Sentence 1 (Identify the first aspect of structure related to the unifying idea)	Topic Sentence 2 (Identify the second aspect of structure related to the unifying idea)	Topic Sentence 3 (Identify the third aspect of structure related to the unifying idea)
Textual Details (Evidence of elements and techniques that contribute to structure development and complexity)	Textual Details (Evidence of elements and techniques that contribute to structure development and complexity)	Textual Details (Evidence of elements and techniques that contribute to structure development and complexity)
Commentary (Link evidence by explaining its relevance to the line of reasoning and claim)	Commentary (Link evidence by explaining its relevance to the line of reasoning and claim)	Commentary (Link evidence by explaining its relevance to the line of reasoning and claim)

Conclusion

The **conclusion** should do more than restate the thesis; intstead, it should be a robust and important paragraph. It is the opportunity for the writer to demonstrate understanding of the literary work's relevance by explaining how the literary work stands the test of time and reflects the human experience. Writers further their idea and insight by:

- Discussing the significance or relevance of interpretation
- Relating the work to other relevant literary works
- Connecting the theme to their own experience
- Presenting alternate interpretations
- Explaining how the work explores complexities and tensions
- Situating the theme within a broader context

This table illustrates the general structure of a literary argument. It does not intend to imply that all literary arguments are five paragraphs. Writers should determine the number of reasons needed to justify their claim, as well as how much evidence is sufficient to support each of these reasons.

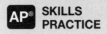 **SKILLS PRACTICE** | LITERARY ARGUMENTATION
Developing a Line of Reasoning

Review your thesis statement, which may or may not preview the line of reasoning. Record the topic sentences to represent your line of reasoning and place them in a logical order. As you do this, consider the potential evidence from the text that helped you arrive at your line of reasoning. That textual evidence will serve as support for these reasons.

Organizing an Analysis of Structure and Irony		
Defensible Thesis Statement with Claim (idea + insight):		
Topic Sentence 1 (Identify the first aspect of structure related to the unifying idea):	**Topic Sentence 2** (Identify the second aspect of structure related to the unifying idea):	**Topic Sentence 3** (Identify the third aspect of structure related to the unifying idea):

Select Relevant Evidence

As you search for relevant evidence to analyze structure in a text, make sure you are collecting textual support that demonstrates the author's choice directly, and not just summarizing the plot. Because you are exemplifying author techniques related to the plot, this may be tempting.

As you choose your evidence, you will be looking for examples of juxtaposition, shifts, and contrasts, among other things. Note that all of these author choices have two parts: two things are contrasted or juxtaposed, or one thing that shifts to another thing. So make sure that you include evidence for both parts. For example, if you are contrasting the attributes of two characters or the relevance of two scenes, you must include evidence from both and explain the relevance of both.

As you build the sophistication of your argument, your evidence must get more thorough and sophisticated as well. You should include multiple examples and arrange them so that you show how they work together to reveal your idea and insight.

Keeping your unifying idea in mind, you might incorporate evidence that illustrates, clarifies, exemplifies, associates, amplifies, or qualifies the following:

- Details that reveal shifts in time, place, or perspective within a text's structure
- Details that reveal patterns within a text
- Details that demonstrate contrasts within a text
- Details that reveal conflicts or tensions within a text

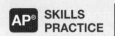 SKILLS PRACTICE

LITERARY ARGUMENTATION
Incorporating Relevant and Sufficient Evidence

Write your thesis statement and develop a logical line of reasoning to support your interpretation. Carefully organize your body paragraphs and arrange the evidence within them. Next, draft two or more body paragraphs that include evidence from the text to support each reason. Include transitions to link your reasons and evidence to your claim.

Incorporating Relevant and Sufficient Evidence		
Defensible Thesis Statement with Claim (idea + insight):		
Topic Sentence 1 (Identify the first aspect of structure related to the unifying idea):	**Topic Sentence 2** (Identify the second aspect of structure related to the unifying idea):	**Topic Sentence 3** (Identify the third aspect of structure related to the unifying idea):
Textual Details (Relevant and sufficient evidence):	**Textual Details** (Relevant and sufficient evidence):	**Textual Details** (Relevant and sufficient evidence):

Write Insightful Commentary

In the previous writing workshops, you have learned that your commentary serves the purpose of linking your carefully chosen evidence to your line of reasoning and the unifying idea in your thesis statement. In other words, after you *identify* the author's technique and provide *evidence* to exemplify it, your commentary then serves to *link* the evidence to your interpretation in the thesis.

Your commentary must accomplish some heavy lifting within a literary argument, such as explaining the purpose and effect of structure and irony within a text. But it is essential: your commentary reveals important details and nuances for the reader.

You will need multiple sentences to explain your evidence with helpful and illuminating context, and then link the evidence to your topic sentence and the unifying idea in your thesis. Review the following table that includes templates for introducing evidence and explaining the effects of the text's structure. You should explain until you believe that your readers have all the necessary information about each point you are making in your argument.

EXPLAINING THE SIGNIFICANCE OF STRUCTURE AND IRONY		
Techniques of Structure	**Templates for Introducing Structure Details and Function of Irony**	**Templates for Explaining the Effects of Structure Details in Commentary**
Chronology and Pacing	The author includes the scene of flashback when ____ in order to • explain the conflict between ____ and ____, • uncover the mystery of ____, or • develop the complexity of ____. The author speeds up/slows down the pace of the narrative by ____.	Through this structural choice, the author • explores the origin of the tension and suggests ____, • develops the idea of ____, • implies that ____, or • reveals the value of ____. By manipulating the pace of the story, the author • develops an atmosphere of ____, • creates suspense to lead the reader to understand ____, or • elicits the emotion of ____ in the reader to amplify the idea that ____.
Shifts and Juxtaposition	The shift from ____ to ____ within the text • suggests the contrast between ____ and ____, • reveals the development in ____ [character] ____, or • amplifies the change in attitude of ____. The juxtaposition of ____ and ____ amplifies the differences between them. One difference, ____, suggests ____. Another difference, ____, emphasizes ____.	This contrast/development/change reveals the complex nature of ____, suggesting not only ____ but also ____ and conveys the idea that ____. Thus, these contrasts reveal the larger tension between ____ and ____ and convey the idea that ____.
Irony	While the readers expected ____, the author instead • concludes the work by ____, • has the character choose to ____, or • sets the narrative in ____. The author includes the details of ____ in an aside to reveal the character's thoughts that ____.	This ironic choice contributes to the idea that ____. The insight the audience possesses about ____ amplifies the idea that ____.
Tension/Conflict	The author creates the tension/conflict between ____ and ____ by including the scene/details of ____.	This tension/conflict • emphasizes the idea that ____, or • suggests the complexity of the character's motives/values/perspectives that ____.

 **SKILLS PRACTICE** | LITERARY ARGUMENTATION
Explaining the Effect of Structural Choices

Build on your emerging literary argument by adding commentary to your relevant and sufficient evidence. Continue to incorporate transitions for coherence and craft your sentences to show the balance and imbalance of ideas. Additionally, keep the focus on your unifying idea so that you may sustain it throughout your argument in a unified way.

Explaining the Effect of Structural Choices		
Defensible Thesis Statement with Claim (idea + insight):		
Topic Sentence 1 (Identify the first aspect of structure related to the unifying idea):	**Topic Sentence 2** (Identify the second aspect of structure related to the unifying idea):	**Topic Sentence 3** (Identify the third aspect of structure related to the unifying idea):
Textual Details (Relevant and sufficient evidence):	**Textual Details** (Relevant and sufficient evidence):	**Textual Details** (Relevant and sufficient evidence):
Commentary (Link evidence to reason and idea):	**Commentary** (Link evidence to reason and idea):	**Commentary** (Link evidence to reason and idea):
Sentence stem and explanation of function of evidence:	Sentence stem and explanation of function of evidence:	Sentence stem and explanation of function of evidence:

Contextualize Your Argument

In earlier workshops, you have practiced writing introductions that include context and funnel to the idea and insight in your thesis. You have also written brief concluding statements that explain the relevance of your idea. You will now take a look at a more developed **conclusion** that adds to the level of sophistication in your literary analysis.

You can adequately analyze a literary text by discussing details within the immediate context of the literary work. If you wish to write a more comprehensive and sophisticated analysis, then you will situate your analysis of the work within a broader context. In other words, you are answering the "So what?" question for the final time. To make this more meaningful, you not only make observations about the characters' surroundings, perspectives, choices, conflicts, or qualities but also apply those observations to human nature, societal or cultural values, or social criticism in general.

You may also conclude your literary analysis by developing a relevant **analogy** for your reader to understand the idea and insight you have presented in your argument. Writers often introduce an analogy in the hook and develop it throughout the essay. In the final sentence, they return to their original analogy as a way of closing the argument. This method, called bookending, not only creates unity within the literary argument but also helps the reader grasp the writer's interpretation.

INSIDER **Conclusions create unity and demonstrate relevance.**
Because conclusions explore the relevance of the idea and insight from the introduction, they communicate the relevance of your interpretation and of the text as a whole. These final sentences finish your commentary as well, so stay focused on the idea and insight within a broader context.

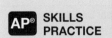 **SKILLS PRACTICE** | LITERARY ARGUMENTATION
Establishing Context and Explaining Relevance

In the following chart, record some notes to help you communicate the context of your argument, introductory details about the author's structural choices, and introductory material that will funnel your ideas to your thesis statement. Next, record ideas for your conclusion. Remember that it should explain the relevance of your idea and insight within a broader context.

Establishing Context and Explaining Relevance	
Idea and insight	Context for Introduction
	Hook:
	Context:
	Significance of Idea in Conclusion
	Broader Context for Conclusion:

Revise Your Argument

When reviewing your analysis of setting, ask the following questions related to your argument about the function and effect of the structural details. Revise your draft if your answer is "no" to any of the following questions.

- Have you identified one or more structural choices?
- Do your reasons in your line of reasoning refer to the function of the structure and irony, as well as their effects?
- Does your line of reasoning support your interpretation?
- Have you included textual evidence that exemplifies the structural choices?
- Does your explanation of the evidence reveal the irony and logically align with your interpretation of the work?
- Is your argument coherent with a logical sequence of reasons and transitions to connect evidence, reasons, and claims?
- Does your commentary unify your argument by connecting your evidence and reasons to your unifying idea?
- Do you include effective transitional elements between and within your body paragraphs to create coherence?

LITERARY ARGUMENTATION

AP® SKILLS PRACTICE | **Revising and Editing an Analysis of Structure and Irony**

After you have completed revising and editing your own argument, review another student's literary argument and provide helpful feedback.

Peer-Revision Checklist: Revising and Editing an Analysis of Structure and Irony		
Revising and Editing Checklist	Unit 8 Focus Skills	Comment on the Effectiveness and/or Make a Suggestion
Does the writer include an engaging hook, the narrative situation, title, and author of the literary text in the first paragraph?	Introductions for analysis of structure and irony	
Does the thesis statement convey an interpretation? Does the interpretation connect to an idea and an insight?	Defensible thesis	
Does the writer provide a logical sequence of reasons to support the idea and insight in the thesis? Are these reasons linked to the claim with transitions?	Line of reasoning: Unity	

(continued)

Revising and Editing Checklist	Unit 8 Focus Skills	Comment on the Effectiveness and/or Make a Suggestion
Does the writer provide relevant and sufficient evidence to support the interpretation in the thesis? Is the evidence linked to the topic sentences with transitions?	Relevant and sufficient evidence: Coherence	
Does the writer explain how the evidence supports a reason and connects to the interpretation in the thesis? Does the commentary connect to the unifying idea?	Commentary: Unity and Coherence	
Does the writer explain significance within a broader context?	Relevance and conclusion	
Does the writer demonstrate control over the conventions of writing?	Conventions	

Student Model: Writing about Structure and Irony

Review the following student model, which analyzes the structure of Franz Kafka's *The Metamorphosis*. Observe how the thesis statement, line of reasoning, and evidence work together to convey an interpretation of the work.

Kafka's Implausible Reality
Tim Mollette-Parks

Mexican poet Octavio Paz once said, "Reality is a staircase going neither up nor down . . ." However, on this staircase of reality, is there any room for a small number of implausible events? Perhaps this is a possibility that Franz Kafka was exploring with his novel *The Metamorphosis*. In this piece, the protagonist, Gregor Samsa, awakens one morning to find himself transformed into an insect, a truly unrealistic occurrence. As the plot progresses, Gregor's newly found form is met with a great deal of hostility from his family and ultimately leads to his death, which holds a slightly hidden allusion to real world problems that exist in many families today.

hook: Paz quotation
context: Gregor awakens as an insect, which causes hostility, then death

As a result of his incredible transformation, his outlandish persecution from family, and his quick, shocking death, Gregor's unrealistic character serves as an allegory for Kafka's more plausible theme regarding a family's inner workings.

thesis statement: connects unrealistic events to allegorical purpose

Gregor's stunning transfiguration is a vivid illustration of the manner in which family relationships can force an individual to be something that he or she does not want to be. In Gregor's case, he has been pushed into an occupation as a traveling salesman in order to repay several debts his father has acquired over the years. This position requires Gregor to be traveling at all times: a requirement that has tired and confused Gregor. Moments after Gregor's metamorphosis, Kafka states, "He had only his numerous little legs, which were in every different kind of perpetual motion and which, besides, he could not control." Gregor's uncontrollable human life is a result of his role as a family provider. In addition to this symbolism of the uncontrollable vermin legs, Gregor finds himself discovering certain pains that were before undetectable. Kafka's detail that Gregor "began to feel a slight, dull pain in his side, which he had never felt before" serves as an allegorical statement for the pains and problems that he experiences as his family's sole source of income that he did not feel before he realized exactly how crucial his role in the family was. Both the uncontrollability and pain imagery of Gregor's insect form symbolize the unavoidable, unwanted transformations that result from the pressure of poor family interactions.

idea + insight: unhealthy family interactions lead to individual destruction

topic sentence: transfiguration illustrates unhealthy expectations

evidence: transformation causes pain and lack of control

commentary: explains the allegory of the transformation

Along with pain, Gregor also experiences persecution and alienation from his pressure-packed relationship with his family members. The main source of this persecution is his father, who begins to feel more and more resentment for Gregor after his change in form prohibits him from continuing his all out support of his family. His father sees that he may be forced to return to work, a fact that distressed the father, and this distress is manifested through his mistreatment of Gregor. Gregor's first attempt to enter the living room of his family's apartment after his transmogrification is unsuccessful because of his father. Kafka details, "from behind his father gave him a hard shove . . . and . . . he flew far into his room. The door was slammed shut with the cane . . ." This type of scene re-occurs at the end of each of the three sections of the work, which symbolizes that an individual's family has a tendency to alienate a member who can no longer deal with his own burden, or in Gregor's case, the entire family's burdens. Gregor faces hostility not only from his father, but also from his sister, Grete, with whom he had been very close.

topic sentence: transformation results in alienation

evidence: transformation prompts the family to separate Gregor from them

commentary: explains that the effect of the transformation on the family serves as a symbol

Grete cries, "It has to go. That's the only answer, Father." With this excla-mation regarding her attitude toward Gregor, Grete functions as a sym-bol of a universal message that even the closest of family members can quickly begin to distance themselves from their kinship if they believe their sibling is no longer doing their part for the collective good of the family. Sadly, most family's execute this persecution without thinking of the other person's personal problems, which is also symbolized by Grete and the father. A further point about family alienation that Kafka devel-ops is that it is impossible to fully reverse or erase the pain. This idea is developed through the allegorical interpretation of the father's bombard-ment of Gregor with apples. One of the apples wounds Gregor. Kafka describes, "the apple remained embedded in his flesh as a visible sou-venir since no one dared to remove it." This immovable wound symbol-izes the impossibility of overcoming family persecution. Through this set of symbols, Kafka makes a statement about the cruelty and severity of being pushed out of a family.

Kafka's ideas of the internal interactions of families culminate through Gregor's sudden death. After a final struggle with trying to work his way back into his family's graces, Gregor returns to his room and "his head sank down to the floor, and from his nostrils streamed his last weak breath." This abrupt end to Gregor's life symbolizes the quick destructive nature of family difficulties. It is also through Gregor's ultimate downfall that Kafka portrays his final criticism of poor family relationships. After Gregor's demise, the father says to his wife and daughter, "Stop brooding over the past. And have a little consideration for me, too." This statement shows that Gregor's father symbolizes, not only an alienating father, but a father who does not care about the consequences of his actions. Also, with lack of remorse for his own dead son, a death for which he was at least partially at fault, completes Kafka's negative view of the inner work-ings of many families.

Thus, Gregor's unfathomable sufferings bring the reader to Kafka's theme that unhealthy inter-family relationships can bring destruction to the individual who suffers the burden of these interactions. The period of Gregor's life depicted in *The Metamorphosis* is a clear allegory for the development of this theme. Gregor's transformation, persecution, and sudden death add detail to this allegory. So then, is there room for unreal-istic occurrences on the staircase of reality? According to Kafka, not only is there room, but exempting these unreal events would leave the stair-case without a railing.

topic sentence:
transformation
ultimately leads to
death

evidence: Gregor's
death and his family's
dismissal exemplify the
loss of the relationship

commentary: connects
the transformation to
the destruction of the
family relationship

conclusion: links
implausible
transformation to the
human condition

analogy: concludes
with a reference to the
analogy established in
the introduction

Free-Response Question: Poetry Analysis

AP® **Enduring Understanding (LAN-1)**

Readers establish and communicate their interpretations of literature through arguments supported by textual evidence.

Writing Conclusions

For this final poetry analysis workshop, you will work on writing a literary argument that explores the complexity of the poem and conveys an interpretation of the work as a whole. In this workshop, you will continue developing your skills for the literary argument. Now you will turn your attention to making these arguments more complex and sophisticated by including helpful context before the thesis statement in your introduction and writing **conclusions** that explore your idea and insight within a broader context.

Read the following practice prompt, which is a model of the type of prompt you may see on the AP® English Literature and Composition Exam.

Prompt:

In the following poem, "Prayer of the Backhanded" by Jericho Brown (published in 2008), the speaker reflects on incidents from his childhood. Read the poem carefully.

Then, in a well-written essay, analyze how Brown uses poetic elements and techniques to convey the speaker's complex attitude toward his father.

In your response you should do the following:

- Respond to the prompt with a thesis that presents a defensible interpretation
- Select and use evidence to support your line of reasoning
- Explain how the evidence supports your line of reasoning
- Use appropriate grammar and punctuation in communicating your argument

Unifying Idea	Prayer of the Backhanded Jericho Brown	Effect of Literary Elements and Techniques
detachment	Not the palm, not the pear tree Switch, not the broomstick, Nor the closet extension Cord, not his braided belt, but God, 5 Bless the back of my daddy's hand Which, holding nothing tightly Against me and not wrapped In leather, eliminated the air Between itself and my cheek. 10 Make full this dimpled cheek Unworthy of its unfisted print And forgive my forgetting The love of a hand Hungry for reflex, a hand that took 15 No thought of its target Like hail from a blind sky, Involuntary, fast, but brutal In its bruising. Father, I bear the bridge Of what might have been 20 A broken nose. I lift to you What was a busted lip. Bless The boy who believes His best beatings lack Intention, the mark of the beast. 25 Bring back to life the son Who glories in the sin Of immediacy, calling it love. God, save the man whose arm Like an angel's invisible wing 30 May fly backward in fury Whether or not his son stands near. Help me hold in place my blazing jaw As I think to say, *excuse me.*	implements of punishment in contrast to the empty hand images of prayer and religion create irony and establish means of detachment personification suggests the hand had no intention simile compares hail to the hand and the blind sky to the detached father images of prayer contribute to the religious motif paradox "glories in sin" represents the boy's comfort in justifying abuse as impulse images of religion contribute to the religious motif abusive arm compared to an "angel's wing" reveals the irony of the speaker's perspective

→ Step One: Annotate the Passage Based on a Unifying Idea

In this final poetry analysis workshop, you will continue to explore complexity within a text. In addition to considering how an author's literary techniques and elements work together to convey an idea and insight, you should be ready to explore the details of a text beyond your initial impression.

Throughout the units, you have read poems on two levels — literal and figurative — and arrived at your interpretation based on the associations you make between the two. Once you understand how authors use patterns and comparisons, you can explore how these comparisons are often complex and nuanced to reveal deeper insight. It is not enough simply to identify objects of comparison or patterns of images and explain their associations.

When you annotate a poem, identify the narrative situation or context from beginning to middle to end. Note repetitions and shifts within the passage, and observe how an author creates patterns of comparisons or images throughout the entire work. As you follow the associations suggested by these patterns, pay close attention to how they change or evolve throughout the text. For example, comparisons carried over several lines or the entire poem often suggest multiple interpretations.

Poets may subvert your expectations by taking a familiar image and associating it with an idea that contradicts its qualities. For example, in "Prayer of the Backhanded," the poet, Jericho Brown, juxtaposes details of the father's harsh punishments with prayers and blessings. This contrast creates an irony: the reader must then determine whether the speaker's prayerful tone is genuine or sarcastic.

To guide your annotations, consider the following questions that will help you analyze the complexity within the passage:

- What idea emerges from the details of the passage?

- What details and word choices within the passage are juxtaposed or in contrast? What do these patterns or contrasts suggest?

- Are the details and images in the poem parallel or incongruous? Why did the poet make this choice?

- Is there a shift in the passage? Identify and describe the relationship between the details before and after the shift.

- Is the central conflict in the passage internal, external, or both? If both, how are these conflicts related, and what do they reveal about the speaker?

- Do the speaker's thoughts, behaviors, and attitudes reveal contradictory traits? If so, what do these contradictions suggest?

- Is the speaker's perspective complex or nuanced? How do the contrasts and tensions in the poem reveal this complexity?

- What complex insight does the passage suggest about the unifying idea?

→ ## Step Two: Develop a Defensible Claim and a Unified Line of Reasoning

As you continue to write more sophisticated literary arguments, don't forget to write a brief **introduction** that includes helpful and insightful **context** before your thesis statement. You can use the details in the prompt for necessary background information. You can also include a brief description of the narrative situation of the poem. For example, identify the speaker, the situation, and perhaps a brief reference to the figurative association.

While you don't need to write a full introduction with a hook, as would be expected for an untimed essay, you should still write a sentence or two before your thesis to deepen your readers' understanding of your interpretation (idea + insight).

When you are ready, write a thesis statement that identifies an author's technique and conveys your interpretation.

If you need help getting started, you may build from one of the following thesis templates or refer to the models that follow:

- In the poem, [title], [author] reveals [idea + insight] by contrasting/ juxtaposing [literary element 1] and [literary element 2].

- In the poem, [title], [author] reveals [idea + insight] by exploring the tension between [aspect 1] and [aspect 2].

- In the poem, [title], [author] reveals [idea + insight] by shifting from [aspect 1] to [aspect 2].

- In [title], a poem about [include brief context], [author] reveals [idea + insight].

Review the following examples of thesis statements for poetry analysis.

Sample Thesis Statements	Notes on Effectiveness
In the poem, "Prayer of the Backhanded," Jericho Brown reveals the irony that despite the speaker's best efforts to hide the emotional wounds of abuse, he cannot remain detached from his aggressive father by juxtaposing incongruous details of the violent acts with references to prayer and religion.	Conveys the idea (detachment) and insight (the abused may try but cannot truly remain detached). Previews a line of reasoning (the juxtaposition of violent acts and religious images that result in irony).
In "Prayer of the Backhanded," a poem about a young boy who attempts to cope with the actions of an abusive father, Jericho Brown suggests that while the abused may appear detached, ultimately they cannot escape the emotional wounds of abuse.	Conveys the idea (detachment) and insight (the abused may try but cannot truly remain detached). Includes genre and context. Chooses not to preview a line of reasoning.

The two sample thesis statements essentially include the same claim. The first thesis previews the line of reasoning by making reference to the author's technique of juxtaposition and identifying the irony of the conflicting images of religion and violence. You do not need to include this in your thesis if you wish to keep your thesis open.

Once you have a thesis statement that addresses the complexity of the passage, you can develop an effective argument by supporting your thesis with a logical line of reasoning that supports your interpretation.

Review the following questions to determine the structure of your line of reasoning. They will help you write your topic sentences.

- Do the author's literary elements and techniques work together to present complexity in the speaker's attitude, perspective, or situation?
- Do the images or details within the poem reveal an incongruity that contributes to your understanding of the text?
- Does the passage reveal a shift in the speaker's values or perspectives that contribute to the complexity?
- Does the passage contrast two or more values or perspectives that reveal a conflict, tension, meaning, or idea?

After considering these questions, you can determine a logical sequence for your argument's **line of reasoning**. Your topic sentences should include accurate, precise language that keeps the complexity established in your introduction; they should also relate directly to the single unifying idea and insight in your thesis statement.

If you need help getting started, you may build from the following topic sentence templates or refer to the models that follow:

- [Author] includes [literary element] to reveal [connection to effect and unifying idea].
- [Transitional element], [author] includes [literary element] to further exemplify [connection to effect and unifying idea].

Review the following thesis statement and line of reasoning. Note that the unifying idea creates the connection between the claim in the thesis and the topic sentences that support the claim.

Sample Thesis Statement

In the poem, "Prayer of the Backhanded," Jericho Brown reveals the irony that despite the speaker's best efforts to hide the emotional wounds of abuse, he cannot remain detached from his aggressive father by juxtaposing details of the violent acts with references to prayer and religion.

Topic Sentence 1	Topic Sentence 2
Brown ironically structures the poem as a prayer that includes details of cruelty and abuse to demonstrate the speaker's attempt to detach his abuser from intention and himself from reality.	*To develop the ironic associations further, Brown suggests that the speaker's ability to detach is futile, as his prayers continue to intertwine with violence and blessings, yet he experiences no resolution.*

In this example, the first topic sentence points out that the poem uses the structure of a prayer to reveal the speaker's attempt to detach from the reality of his circumstances.

The second topic sentence reveals that the speaker cannot detach and refers to additional associations between the juxtaposed images of violence and religion.

→ Step Three: Choose Relevant Evidence

Recall what you have learned in earlier units about selecting evidence that is both relevant and sufficient. In addition to quoting from the passage, you should also include helpful context along with your evidence. To do this, weave words and short phrases into your own sentence and paraphrase or explain additional context as needed.

You may also include examples from different parts of the poem that work as a pattern of images. Then, in your commentary, explain how these examples work together for the author's purpose.

More sophisticated literary arguments include evidence that clearly exemplifies contrasts, tensions, and incongruities when they are present in the work. Some poems appear to be straightforward based on a literal reading, but upon closer examination, readers find ironic or paradoxical meaning below the surface. Careful readers understand these nuances by exploring contrasts and patterns. You might think of your analysis as a coin. Your first impression is "heads," but what happens if you turn it over? When you consider the question, What else? You may discover what is on the other side of the coin.

If you need help introducing and contextualizing your evidence, you may build from the following templates:

- The [word/phrase], [text evidence], used to describe [context] conveys [emotion] because/in that [association/connotation].
- The image of [text evidence] depicts [picture/sense] because the reader [sees/connects/realizes].
- The subject [a] is compared to [b], which is fitting because they share these attributes [attribute 1], [attribute 2], [attribute 3].
- The poet includes a pattern of images related to [description of pattern] with the inclusion of [text evidence], [text evidence], and [text evidence] to reveal [association of the pattern].

Topic Sentence 1	Topic Sentence 2
Brown ironically structures the poem as a prayer that includes details of cruelty and abuse to demonstrate the speaker's attempt to detach his abuser from intention and himself from reality.	*To develop the ironic associations further, Brown suggests that the speaker's ability to detach is futile, as his prayers continue to intertwine with violence and blessings, yet he experiences no resolution.*

Relevant and Sufficient Evidence	Relevant and Sufficient Evidence
Evidence 1:	Evidence 1:
Title: "Prayer of the Backhanded" introduces the structure and contrast	*"brutal / In its bruising"*
	"broken nose . . . busted lip"
"God / Bless the back of my daddy's hand"	*"the son / Who glories in the sin / Of immediacy, calling it love"*
"Bless / The boy who believes . . ."	*"Like an angel's invisible wing / May fly backward in fury"*
Evidence 2:	
"not . . . the / Switch, not the broomstick, / Nor the closet extension / Cord"	Evidence 2:
	"God, save the man . . ."
"holding nothing"	*"Help me hold in place my blazing jaw . . . excuse me"*
"eliminated the air / Between itself and my cheek"	
"Like hail from a blind sky"	
"Involuntary"	

→ Step Four: Develop Your Commentary

Recall that your commentary serves to link your evidence to your line of reasoning and to explain how that evidence relates to your idea and insight. As you continue working on developing a complex thesis and line of reasoning and choosing the most relevant evidence to support your interpretation, your commentary must also reflect that level of complexity and sophistication.

You will now take the strategy, "identify — evidence — link," to the next level by linking your evidence even more thoroughly and thoughtfully. In Unit 7, you learned that an author's use of a literary element or technique can serve multiple purposes within a text. For example, a single metaphor can have more than one relevant association. As you explore this further and ponder what more an image might suggest, consider that a single image might have opposing associations. When this paradox happens within a text, the effect is usually ironic.

For example, in "Prayer of the Backhanded," the repeated references to prayer, blessings, and other religious allusions may lead a reader to believe that the speaker is relying on spiritual means to detach from the reality of his abuse. These images may appear comforting. However, as they are structured within the poem and juxtaposed with other images, the reader must also note that the prayer is meant as verbal irony. The image in the poem's final lines, "Help me hold in place my blazing jaw / As I think to say, *excuse me*," reveals verbal irony from the speaker, whose detachment is merely a means of survival.

To help you add commentary that explains complexity within a passage, you might build from the following templates:

- By highlighting the tension between _____ and _____, the poet suggests _____.
- The contrast between _____ and _____ portrays a deeper conflict between _____ and _____.
- _____ symbolizes _____, which serves not only to _____ but also to _____.
- While the speaker appears _____, his/her _____ images/details/tone reveal the contrary in that _____.

Review the following example of commentary that addresses complexity by exploring the related associations with several examples from the text. Also, notice how the commentary connects to both the topic sentence and the thesis.

Evidence	Commentary Connected to Idea
Evidence 1: "holding nothing" "eliminated the air / Between itself and my cheek" "Like hail from a blind sky" "Involuntary"	The speaker attempts to remain detached from the reality of his father's abuse by separating the father's hand from his father's intention. Unlike other implements of discipline — the switch, broomstick, or extension cord — his father's hand was "holding nothing" and "eliminated the air / Between itself and [the boy's] cheek." By characterizing the action with generic descriptions and passive language, Brown reveals the boy's fervent desire to detach both himself and his father from blame. The matter-of-fact language de-emphasizes the violence. Likewise, the simile comparing the movement of the hand to "hail from a blind sky" further emphasizes the speaker's prayer that the action is "Involuntary." Hail is a weather event that innocently falls rather than deliberately strikes. If the boy can think of the hand in such a context, perhaps there is no sinister intention, perhaps his father loves him despite the action of the hand.

Before you wrap up your literary analysis, you should write an effective **conclusion**. You have practiced explaining the relevance of your idea and insight in a concluding statement. You have also learned to avoid closing with a restatement of your thesis. A conclusion for a sophisticated argument should include several sentences that connect the idea and insight to a shared human experience, a social or cultural observation, or other relevant context beyond the pages of the text. In making these connections, you will not only convey the relevance of your interpretation but also of the work as a whole.

INSIDER **Conclusions reveal insight.** If you wish to write a
sophisticated argument, you should budget time and space
to develop a thoughtful conclusion that demonstrates your
understanding of the significance and relevance of the text.
Connecting the idea and insight within a broader context conveys the value
and complexity of the work.

AP® EXAM PRACTICE

The following is an example of a poetry analysis free-response question. Practice
the skills you have learned in this workshop to write an argument in response to
the prompt. You may use the graphic organizer and templates to help you plan and
write your analysis.

Remember to follow the four steps:

- Step One: Annotate the passage based on a **unifying idea**
- Step Two: Write a **defensible thesis statement**
- Step Three: Choose **relevant evidence**
- Step Four: Develop **insightful commentary**

Prompt:

In the following poem, "The Weary Blues" by Harlem Renaissance writer Langston Hughes (published in 1926), the speaker describes a musician he hears singing and playing in a nightclub. Read
the poem carefully. Then, in a well-written essay, analyze how Hughes uses poetic elements and
techniques to convey the speaker's complex perception of music.

In your response you should do the following:

- Respond to the prompt with a thesis that presents a defensible interpretation
- Select and use evidence to support your line of reasoning
- Explain how the evidence supports your line of reasoning
- Use appropriate grammar and punctuation in communicating your argument

> **The Weary Blues**
> Droning a drowsy syncopated tune,
> Rocking back and forth to a mellow croon,
>   I heard a Negro play.
> Down on Lenox Avenue the other night
> 5 By the pale dull pallor of an old gas light
>   He did a lazy sway . . .
>   He did a lazy sway . . .

To the tune o' those Weary Blues.
With his ebony hands on each ivory key
10   He made that poor piano moan with melody.
       O Blues!
Swaying to and fro on his rickety stool
He played that sad raggy tune like a musical fool.
       Sweet Blues!
15   Coming from a black man's soul.
       O Blues!
In a deep song voice with a melancholy tone
I heard that Negro sing, that old piano moan —
       "Ain't got nobody in all this world,
20   Ain't got nobody but ma self.
         I's gwine to quit ma frownin'
         And put ma troubles on the shelf."
Thump, thump, thump, went his foot on the floor.
He played a few chords then he sang some more —
25   "I got the Weary Blues
         And I can't be satisfied.
         Got the Weary Blues
         And can't be satisfied —
         I ain't happy no mo'
30   And I wish that I had died."
And far into the night he crooned that tune.
The stars went out and so did the moon.
The singer stopped playing and went to bed
While the Weary Blues echoed through his head.
35   He slept like a rock or a man that's dead.

ORGANIZING A POETRY ANALYSIS (III)

Introduction:

- Engage the audience through an interesting hook
- Provide historical, cultural, or social context of a literary work
- Identify the title, author, genre (TAG)
- Introduce the literary focus by
  - describing the importance of the topic within the work; and
  - summarizing the work succinctly with details critical to the chosen literary focus

Hook and context:

TAG:

Literary topic and concise summary:

Defensible Thesis Statement with Claim (idea + insight):

In [title], [contextualize the work], [poet] contrasts/explores the tension between [a and b] to reveal that [idea + insight].

Topic Sentence 1 (Identify the first aspect of the topic in relation to the unifying idea):	Topic Sentence 2 (Identify the second aspect of the topic; connect it to the first aspect in relation to the unifying idea):	Topic Sentence 3 (Identify the third aspect of the topic; connect it to the first and/ or second aspect in relation to the unifying idea):
To begin, [poet] includes [technique/element 1] to [purpose connect to idea].	In contrast to [first aspect], [poet] includes [technique/element 2] to [purpose connect to idea].	Finally, [poet] highlights the tension between [a and b] by including [technique/element 3] to [purpose connect to idea].
Textual Details (Relevant and sufficient evidence):	**Textual Details** (Relevant and sufficient evidence):	**Textual Details** (Relevant and sufficient evidence):
For example, the detail/image/ comparison [text evidence], used to describe [context] illustrates [link to topic sentence]. [Poet] continues to explore [link to topic sentence] by including [detail/image/comparison], which reveals [insight].	To illustrate, [poet] compares/ contrasts [a and b] by describing [text evidence] to emphasize [link to topic sentence]. Another point of comparison for [a and b] illustrated through [text evidence] reveals the [link to topic sentence].	As an example of [technique/ element], the poet includes [text evidence] to explain [link to topic sentence]. To develop this idea further, [poet] explores [link to topic sentence] through [technique/ element], in describing [text evidence].
Commentary (Link evidence to reason and idea):	**Commentary** (Link evidence to reason and idea):	**Commentary** (Link evidence to reason and idea):
The association with [idea] reveals [idea and insight]. *Two to four sentences explaining how the evidence exemplifies the universal idea*	Through this choice, [poet] develops [idea and insight]. *Two to four sentences explaining how the evidence exemplifies the universal idea*	By including this [element/ technique] the poet suggests that [idea and insight]. *Two to four sentences explaining how the evidence exemplifies the universal idea*

Conclusion:

Further your idea and insight by

- discussing the significance or relevance of interpretation;
- relating the work to other relevant literary works;
- connecting the theme to your own experience;
- presenting alternate interpretations;
- explaining how the work explores complexities and tensions; or
- situating the theme within a broader context.

from Roots

Alex Haley

The following is an excerpt from a novel published in 1976.

The rains came again the next night, and the
next — and the next — and only at night —
flooding the lowlands near the river, turning
their fields into a swamp and their village into
5 a mudhole. Yet each morning before breakfast,
all the farmers struggled through the mud to
Juffure's[1] little mosque and implored Allah to
send still *more* rain, for life itself depended
upon enough water to soak deeply into the
10 earth before the hot suns arrived, which would
wither those crops whose roots could not find
enough water to survive.

In the damp nursery hut, dimly lighted
and poorly heated by the burning dry sticks
15 and cattle-dung patties in the earthen floor's
shallow firehole, old Nyo Boto told Kunta
and the other children of the terrible time she
remembered when there were not enough big
rains. No matter how bad anything was, Nyo
20 Boto would always remember a time when it
was worse. After two days of big rain, she told
them, the burning suns had come. Although
the people prayed very hard to Allah, and
danced the ancestral rain dance, and sacrificed
25 two goats and a bullock every day, still everything growing in the ground began to parch
and die. Even the forest's waterholes dried up,
said Nyo Boto, and first wild fowl, and then
the forest's animals, sick from thirst, began to
30 appear at the village well. In crystal-clear skies
each night, thousands of bright stars shone,

and a cold wind blew, and more and more people grew ill. Clearly, evil spirits were abroad in
Juffure.
35 Those who were able continued their
prayers and their dances, and finally the
last goat and bullock had been sacrificed. It
was as if Allah had turned His back on Juffure. Some — the old and the weak and the
40 sick — began to die. Others left town, seeking
another village to beg someone who had food
to accept them as slaves, just to get something
into their bellies, and those who stayed behind
lost their spirit and lay down in their huts. It
45 was then, said Nyo Boto, that Allah had guided
the steps of marabout[2] Kairaba Kunta Kinte
into the starving village of Juffure. Seeing the
people's plight, he kneeled down and prayed to
Allah — almost without sleep and taking only a
50 few sips of water as nourishment — for the next
five days. And on the evening of the fifth day
came a great rain, which fell like a flood, and
saved Juffure.

When she finished her story, the other chil-
55 dren looked with new respect at Kunta, who
bore the name of that distinguished grandfather, husband of Kunta's Grandma Yaisa. Even
before now, Kunta had seen how the parents of
the other children acted toward Yaisa, and he
60 had sensed that she was an important woman,
just as old Nyo Boto surely was.

The big rains continued to fall every night
until Kunta and the other children began to
see grown-ups wading across the village in

---

[1] A village in west Africa located in what is today the Republic of the Gambia.

[2] A Muslim religious leader and teacher in west Africa who
is often a wandering and homeless hermit.

65 mud up to their ankles and even to their knees,
and even using canoes to paddle from place to
place. Kunta had heard Binta tell Omoro that
the rice fields were flooded in the bolong's high
waters. Cold and hungry, the children's fathers
70 sacrificed precious goats and bullocks to Allah
almost every day, patched leaking roofs, shored
up sagging huts — and prayed that their disappearing stock of rice and couscous would last
until the harvest.

75　　But Kunta and the others, being yet little
children, paid less attention to the hunger pangs
in their bellies than to playing in the mud,
wrestling each other and sliding on their naked
bottoms. Yet in their longing to see the sun
80 again, they would wave up at the slate-colored
sky and shout — as they had seen their parents
do — "Shine, sun, and I will kill you a goat!"

　　The rain had made every growing thing
fresh and luxuriant. Birds sang everywhere.
85 The trees and plants were explosions of fragrant blossoms. The reddish-brown, clinging
mud underfoot was newly carpeted each
morning, with the bright-colored petals and
green leaves beaten loose by the rain of the
90 night before. But amid all the lushness of
nature, sickness spread steadily among the
people of Juffure, for none of the richly growing
crops was ripe enough to eat. The adults and
children alike would stare hungrily at the
95 thousands of plump mangoes and monkey
apples hanging heavy on the trees, but the
green fruits were as hard as rocks, and those
who bit into them fell ill and vomited.

1. The behavior of the farmers in the first
paragraph (lines 1–12) indicates which of
the following about them and their rela-
tionship to the land?
   (A) They feel their faith has let them
       down and cannot understand how the
       land has not produced for them.
   (B) They are strong in their faith and have
       an understanding of the land that
       goes beyond their immediate wants
       and fears.
   (C) They rely on their faith to ensure
       success but have started to question
       the relationship between their
       religious faith and the productivity
       of the land.
   (D) Their faith is in the land, but they
       pray to Allah as a last resort.
   (E) Their understanding of the land relies
       on both the strength of their faith and
       their knowledge of the land and its
       history.

2. In the context of the passage, Nyo Boto's
recollection of the great drought in para-
graphs 2 and 3 ("In the damp . . . saved
Juffure.") can be best described as
   (A) confusing as it provides no useful
       information in the context of the
       passage.
   (B) ironic given the failure of the land to
       produce anything for the people of
       Juffure.
   (C) contradictory to the understanding
       of the land developed in the first
       paragraph.
   (D) juxtaposed to the scene of the big
       rains throughout the rest of the
       passage.
   (E) a cautionary tale about losing faith
       and not trusting your understanding.

3. The behaviors and interactions of Kunta and the children in paragraph 6 ("But Kunta . . . goat!") are significant because they
   (A) demonstrate that Kunta's relationship with the other children has not changed despite what they learned about him from Nyo Boto's story.
   (B) contradict what Nyo Boto implies about Kunta's place in the village and his relationship to village history.
   (C) support the suggestions that Kunta has a place above the other children in the village.
   (D) call to question the bias of Nyo Boto and the story she told about the drought and Kunta's ancestral connection to the village's history and mythology.
   (E) explain how the children of the village now view Kunta following the story told by Nyo Boto.

4. In the context of the passage as a whole, which of the following might be considered paradoxical based on how it is used in the passage?
   (A) ". . . before the hot suns arrived . . ." (line 10)
   (B) ". . . everything growing in the ground . . ." (lines 25–26)
   (C) ". . . almost without sleep . . ." (line 49)
   (D) ". . . hunger pangs in their bellies . . ." (lines 76–77)
   (E) ". . . growing thing fresh and luxuriant . . ." (lines 83–84)

5. Which of the following best describes the situational irony of the last sentence ("The adults . . . vomited.")?
   (A) The crops that might be expected to save the villagers from starvation, in fact, sicken them and make their situation worse.
   (B) The rain expected to save the people is actually killing them.
   (C) The prediction of drought offered by the trusted Nyo Boto has proven to be disastrously wrong.
   (D) The prayers of the farmers for more rain despite the already overwhelming rains they had experienced are actually proving more harmful than anyone expected.
   (E) The beauty of the village caused the people to expect safety from such disasters.

6. Imagery related to which of the following recurs most often throughout the passage?
   (A) Drought
   (B) Water
   (C) Fire
   (D) Dirt
   (E) Hunger

7. Which of the following best describes the narrator of the passage?
   (A) Biased against the farmers, implying their carelessness regarding the rains and the safety of the village
   (B) Biased against the position of Kunta and his relationship to the village's history and mythology
   (C) Biased against the circumstances of the village and the plight of the people and judgmental of their lack of faith
   (D) Biased toward Nyo Boto's perspective, especially in agreement with her perspective on Kunta's position above the other children
   (E) Biased toward the experiences of Kunta, as the narrator comes back to focus on Kunta at times, but does not seem to show favoritism

8. In the context of the passage as a whole, it can most reasonably be claimed that the people of the village are
   (A) failing to thrive despite their work and prayers.
   (B) more dependent on their faith than on their crops.
   (C) at the mercy of natural weather cycles.
   (D) continuing traditions that are thousands of years old.
   (E) being punished by Allah for some religious offense.

O Tobacco

Crystal Wilkinson

The following is a poem published in 2018.

You are a Kentucky tiller's[1] livelihood.
You were school clothes in August
the turkey at Thanksgiving
Christmas
5 with all the trimmings.

I close my eyes
see you tall
stately green
lined up in rows.
10 See sweat seeping
through Granddaddy's shirt
as he fathered you first.

You were protected by him
sometimes even more
15 than any other thing
that rooted in our earth.

Just like family you were
coddled
cuddled
20 coaxed
into making him proud.

Spread out for miles
you were the only
pretty thing
25 he knew.

When I think of you
at the edge of winter,
I see you, brown, wrinkled
just like Granddaddy's skin.

---

[1] One who works the land for farming crops; a farmer.

30 A ten-year old me
    plays in the shadows
    of the stripping² room
    the wood stove burns
    calloused hands twist
35 through the length
    of your leaves.
    Granddaddy smiles
    nods at me when he
    thinks I'm not looking.

40 You are pretty
    and braided³
    lined up in rows
    like a room full of
    brown girls
45 with skirts hooped⁴ out
    for dancing.

1. Which of the following best describes the
   relationship between the first line ("You . . .
   livelihood.") and the rest of the poem?
   (A) It creates irony by providing an
       expectation the poem never addresses.
   (B) It establishes the contrast that controls
       the rest of the poem.
   (C) It introduces the idea that the rest of the
       poem will develop.
   (D) It defines the relationship between the
       tiller and the speaker.
   (E) It explains the role of tobacco as a crop.

2. Which of the following best describes what is
   emphasized by the alliteration used in lines
   17–21 ("Just . . . proud.")?
   (A) That the speaker cannot understand the
       relationship between Granddaddy and
       tobacco.
   (B) That Granddaddy only cared for the
       tobacco because he could control it.
   (C) That the family was not as valuable to
       Granddaddy as the tobacco.
   (D) That Granddaddy cared for and
       controlled both the family and the
       tobacco.
   (E) That tobacco is more important to
       the family for what it provides than
       Granddaddy is.

²The removal of the dried/cured leaves from the main stalk of the plant—a regular part of processing tobacco.
³During the curing process, tobacco leaves were twisted into "pigtails" to dry faster; eventually, the term began to be used to describe hair braids that resembled those twisted tobacco leaves.
⁴Circular hoop frames sometimes worn under dresses and skirts to pull the material away from the legs for dancing, comfort, or general fashion.

3. In the context of the poem, the simile that likens tobacco to "Granddaddy's skin" (line 29) might be interpreted as all of the following EXCEPT
   (A) further illustrating the connection between Granddaddy and the tobacco.
   (B) connecting Granddaddy's aging to the time of year — his wrinkled skin related to him being "at the edge of winter" (line 27) of his life.
   (C) demonstrating how the speaker relies on both the tobacco and on their Granddaddy who farms it.
   (D) illustrating how both tobacco and Granddaddy are so important as to have a place in their thoughts and memories.
   (E) refusing to accept that neither tobacco nor Granddaddy is still a part of the speaker's life.

4. Which of the following words serves as an antecedent to the term "Granddaddy" as it is used throughout the poem?
   (A) "You" (line 1)
   (B) "tiller" (line 1)
   (C) "turkey" (line 3)
   (D) "trimmings" (line 5)
   (E) "I" (line 6)

5. Knowledge of which of the following would allow the reader to better understand allusions made throughout the poem?
   (A) The climatic and economic conditions of Kentucky.
   (B) The dynamics of the relationship between the speaker and Granddaddy.
   (C) The process of growing, harvesting, and preparing tobacco.
   (D) The race and class of the speaker.
   (E) The childhood history of the speaker and the family.

6. In the context of the poem, which of the following might be considered symbolic of how tobacco provides for the speaker's family?
   (A) ". . . school clothes in August . . ." (line 2)
   (B) ". . . sweat seeping / through Granddaddy's shirt . . ." (lines 10–11)
   (C) ". . . the edge of winter . . ." (line 27)
   (D) "calloused hands . . ." (line 34)
   (E) ". . . brown girls / with skirts hooped . . ." (lines 44–45)

7. Which of the following best describes how multiple comparisons, representations, or associations combine in the poem?
   (A) Multiple similes help to connect the speaker and Grandaddy to the actual nature of harvested tobacco, while imagery related to appearance and details related to what tobacco has provided all combine to develop the relationship between tobacco and the lives of the speaker and the speaker's family.
   (B) Several ironic statements develop the speaker's ambiguous perspective on tobacco and its role in providing for the speaker's family while details and imagery related to appearance and age further complicate that perspective.
   (C) Though details throughout the poem illustrate how the family was provided for through the cultivation of tobacco, the imagery associated with those details and the comparisons made through multiple similes introduce an uncertainty that develops into a complex perspective.
   (D) While the poem introduces a positive association with tobacco as providing for the livelihood of the speaker's family, the similes provided later in the poem — and the imagery associated with those similes — introduce an ambiguity that indicates a much more complex perspective.
   (E) The extended metaphor of the tobacco crop as the provider for the speaker's family is punctuated and explained through multiple similes that provide further imagery and details to create an association with diverse experiences.

Commercial Eye/The Image Bank/Getty Images

UNIT

9

Analyzing Complexities

UNIT GOALS

	Focus	Goals
Big Idea: Character	**Character Complexities**	Explain how a character's motivations, goals, and actions, both consistent and inconsistent, reveal complexities within that character.
Big Idea: Structure	**Significant Moments**	Explain how an author creates and weaves together moments within a narrative in a way that reveals insights into the human experience.
Big Idea: Narration	**Narrative Complexities**	Explain the significance of a narrative being told from multiple perspectives or points of view.
Ideas in Literature	**Power and Perception**	Explain how the ideas of power and perception are reflected in classic and contemporary texts.
Big Idea: Literary Argumentation	**Writing a Source-Based Literary Argument**	Write a literary argument that includes primary and secondary sources to convey an interpretation of a text.
Preparing for the AP® Exam	**Free-Response Question: Literary Argument** Considering Alternate Interpretations	Write a literary argument that explores alternative interpretations of a work of literature.
	Multiple-Choice Questions: Prose	Analyze literary elements and techniques in classic and contemporary prose and poetry.
	Multiple-Choice Questions: Poetry	

Character Inconsistencies

 Enduring Understanding

Characters in literature allow readers to study and explore a range of values, beliefs, assumptions, biases, and cultural norms represented by those characters.

KEY POINT

A character's choices, actions, and interactions with minor characters—especially when they are inconsistent with the character's primary values—add to the complexity of a text and should be considered when making an interpretation.

Are you the same person now that you were at the beginning of your freshman year? Do you study in the same way? Interact with your friends and family in the same way? Solve problems in the same way? While you may still be the same person at your core, your behaviors, perspectives, and values may change over time because of new experiences and new information.

Fictional characters may also experience drastic change throughout the course of a narrative. These changes and inconsistencies allow us as readers to understand more about the character, as well as that character's relationship with other characters and other narrative elements.

Characters in a Narrative Have a Goal

This is especially true of the story's protagonist. So as you read a narrative, try to identify the protagonist's goal and follow how the character goes about achieving it. In other words, what actions and choices does a character make to achieve that goal?

Character Change and Values

As you recall, **dynamic characters** evolve throughout the course of a narrative. This may happen slowly as a gradual effect, or it may happen in a split-second **epiphany**. Either way, as a result of their change, characters may adopt perspectives or values that differ from those they had earlier in the narrative.

In most stories, characters begin with a set of values and beliefs. But little do they know, they are actually on a collision course with other characters and conflicts in the narrative. Then, those characters must make choices within a dramatic narrative context. They must decide, act, or respond passively. Their choices and reactions to conflict reveal and shape their identities.

You can often tell whether a character has changed throughout the course of a narrative by examining the story's resolution. A character's decisions, words, and actions in response to the primary conflict convey their core values. Additionally, a character's understanding or insight may emerge after a narrative's climax, during the falling action, or as part of the resolution. This change in values is also a key factor when you are interpreting the text.

Character Inconsistencies

Characters become complex when they make choices that are inconsistent with their prior behavior or values. When characters act in contradictory or inconsistent ways, reader's may adjust their interpretation of any of the following:

- That character
- Other characters
- Events in the plot
- Conflicts
- The perspective of a character or the narrator/speaker
- The setting

A character's thoughts, words, or actions may become much different than those they demonstrated earlier in the narrative. These inconsistencies can reveal a shift in the character's perspective. They can also create **situational** and **dramatic ironies**, which readers should identify in their interpretations.

Just remember: a reader's interpretation takes into account a character's evolution (or lack thereof), as well as the consequences of those changes in relation to other characters and the narrative's resolution. If a character stays the same then he or she will maintain the exact system of values, beliefs, and perspectives through the story's resolution.

Empathy

Some readers may have had experiences similar to a character's, which may give them **empathy** for that character. An author may create empathetic characters as a way of making the narrative more relatable to readers.

Minor Characters

Recall that some characters do not change during the course of a narrative. These **static characters** may play only minor roles in the story, but they are still help to advance the plot or interact with major characters. Usually, **minor characters** contribute to the narrative in the following ways:

- Provide comic relief
- Provide details about other characters
- Serve as a foil to a major character
- Set a tone or mood for a scene
- Provide insight into the historical or cultural setting and related values

INSIDER AP TIP   **A character's behavior is key.** A character's goals, along with how the character goes about accomplishing them; how the character handles conflict; and how he or she changes over the course of a story reveal that character's values and contribute to an interpretation of a literary work.

CLASSIFICATION OF CHARACTERS

Classification	Description	Considerations for Effect on Narrative
Major and Minor Characters		
Protagonist	The main character or (in some cases) the hero in a narrative	• How do comparable traits of two or more characters contrast? • What do the differing traits between characters reveal about their individual qualities, their relationships with one another, and their relationships with other characters? • How does considering the significance of a contrast between characters contribute to meaning in the text?
Antagonist	A main character or force that opposes the protagonist	
Minor character	A character who has a minor, but potentially important, role in a narrative	• How does a character's changing or remaining unchanged affect other elements of the literary work and/or contribute to meaning of the work as a whole? • What role does a minor character play in relation to the narrative?
Changing and Unchanged Characters		
Static character	A character, most often a minor character, who does not change over the course of a narrative	• What provokes a character to change or remain unchanged? • What are the comparable traits of a character before and after he or she changes?
Dynamic character	A character who changes, often by coming to a new understanding or epiphany, as a result of choices, actions, and experiences over the course of a narrative	• To what degree does the text convey empathy for those characters who change or for those who remain unchanged? • To what degree does a character's change constitute progress or decline? • How does a character's changing or remaining unchanged affect other elements of the literary work and/or contribute to meaning of the work as a whole?
Other Classifications		
Invisible character	A character absent from a literary text whose influence is significant to the narrative	• How does a character who is not physically present in a narrative affect other characters or the plot of a narrative?
Foil character	A character who serves as a contrast to the protagonist or other major character to illuminate significant character traits or values	• What do the differing traits between characters reveal about them individually, their relationships with one another, and their relationships with other characters? • How does considering the significance of contrasts between characters contribute to meaning in the text?

Group character or chorus	Several people (e.g., group, team, community, organization, gang, entourage) who function collectively as one character	• Which particular images, character speech, and textual details are relevant for examining characters' relationships? • How do images, character speech, and other textual details reveal how characters interact? • Which words, phrases, and details contribute to a character's characterization? • How is a character described physically, emotionally, and/or psychologically? • How do diction and the details that a narrator or speaker offers (or does not offer) convey a particular perspective, ambiguity, and/or inconsistency and convey nuances and complexities in character relationships?
Stock character	An easily recognizable, conventional character type that most often serves as either a victim, villain, or vindicator within a narrative	
Archetypal character	A recurring character type that appears in literature and art across different times and cultures	

PRACTICE TEXT

from Geek Love (Chapter 1)
Katherine Dunn

Elisabetta Villa/Getty Images

THE TEXT IN CONTEXT

Kathleen Dunn (1945–2016) was a novelist, journalist, voice actor, poet, and sports writer. She attended Reed College without graduating and traveled widely before settling in Portland, Oregon. Dunn published two early novels, *Attic* (1970) and *Truck* (1971). She also became a prolific sports journalist, covering boxing for the *Willamette Week*, the *Oregonian*, and the *New York Times*. But she remains best known for her 1989 novel *Geek Love* (excerpted here): a dark, grotesquely funny family history of a traveling carnival. In addition to her vivid prose, Dunn manages to make a strange, seemingly unrelatable cast of characters sympathetic and human. Her other works include *One Ring Circus: Dispatches from the World of Boxing* (2009) and *Toad* (2009).

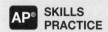 **SKILLS PRACTICE** | **CHARACTER**
Analyzing Minor Characters

As you read the excerpt from *Geek Love*, identify and describe the characters presented. Then, explain their function within the narrative in relation to a thematic idea.

Analyzing Minor Characters

Minor characters may function within a plot in a number of ways, such as the following:

- Provide comic relief
- Provide details about other characters
- Serve as a foil to major characters
- Set a tone or mood for a scene
- Provide insight into the historical or cultural setting and related values

Minor Characters	Description	Function in Relation to Thematic Idea

from Geek Love (Chapter 1)

The Nuclear Family: His Talk, Her Teeth

"When your mama was the geek, my dreamlets," Papa would say, "she made the nipping off of noggins such a crystal mystery that the hens themselves yearned toward her, waltz-
5 ing around her, hypnotized with longing. 'Spread your lips, sweet Lil,' they'd cluck, 'and show us your choppers!'"

This same Crystal Lil, our star-haired mama, sitting snug on the built-in sofa that
10 was Arty's bed at night, would chuckle at the sewing in her lap and shake her head. "Don't piffle to the children, Al. Those hens ran like whiteheads."

Nights on the road this would be, between
15 shows and towns in some campground or pull-off, with the other vans and trucks and trailers of Binewski's Carnival Fabulon ranged up around us, safe in our portable village.

After supper, sitting with full bellies in
20 the lamp glow, we Binewskis were supposed to read and study. But if it rained the story mood would sneak up on Papa. The hiss and tick on the metal of our big living van distracted him from his papers. Rain
25 on a show night was catastrophe. Rain on the road meant talk, which, for Papa, was pure pleasure.

"It's a shame and a pity, Lil," he'd say, "that these offspring of yours should only know
30 the slumming summer geeks from Yale."

"Princeton, dear," Mama would correct him mildly. "Randall will be a sophomore this fall. I believe he's our first Princeton boy."

We children would sense our story slip-
35 ping away to trivia. Arty would nudge me
and I'd pipe up with, "Tell about the time
when Mama was the geek!" and Arty and Elly
and Iphy and Chick would all slide into line
with me on the floor between Papa's chair
40 and Mama.

Mama would pretend to be fascinated by
her sewing and Papa would tweak his swoop-
ing mustache and vibrate his tangled eyebrows, pretending reluctance. "Welllll . . ."
45 he'd begin, "it was a long time ago . . ."

"Before we were born!"

"Before . . ." he'd proclaim, waving an arm
in his grandest ringmaster style, "before I
even dreamed you, my dreamlets!"

50 "I was still Lillian Hinchcliff in those
days," mused Mama. "And when your father
spoke to me, which was seldom and reluctantly, he called me 'Miss.'"

"Miss!" we would giggle. Papa would whis-
55 per to us loudly, as though Mama couldn't
hear, "Terrified! I was so smitten I'd stutter
when I tried to talk to her. 'M-M-M-Miss . . .'
I'd say."

We'd giggle helplessly at the idea of Papa,
60 the GREAT TALKER, so flummoxed.

"I, of course, addressed your father as
Mister Binewski."

"There I was," said Papa, "hosing the old
chicken blood and feathers out of the geek
65 pit on the morning of July 3rd and congratulating myself for having good geek posters,
telling myself I was going to sell tickets by
the bale because the weekend of the Fourth
is the hottest time for geeks and I had a fine,
70 brawny geek that year. Enthusiastic about
the work, he was. So I'm hosing away, feeling
very comfortable and proud of myself, when
up trips your mama, looking like angelfood,
and tells me my geek has done a flit in the
75 night, folded his rags as you might say, and
hailed a taxi for the airport. He leaves a note
claiming his pop is very sick and he, the

geek, must retire from the pit and take his
fangs home to Philadelphia to run the family
80 bank."

"Brokerage, dear," corrects Mama.

"And with your mama, Miss Hinchcliff,
standing there like three scoops of vanilla I
can't even cuss! What am I gonna do? The
85 geek posters are all over town!"

"It was during a war, darlings," explains
Mama. "I forget which one precisely. Your
father had difficulty getting help at that time
or he never would have hired me, even to
90 make costumes, as inexperienced as I was."

"So I'm standing there fuddled from
breathing Miss Hinchcliff's Midnight Marzi-
pan perfume and cross-eyed with figuring.
I couldn't climb into the pit myself because I
95 was doing twenty jobs already. I couldn't ask
Horst the Cat Man because he was a vegetarian to begin with, and his dentures would
disintegrate the first time he hit a chicken
neck anyhow. Suddenly your mama pops up
100 for all the world like she was offering me
sherry and biscuits. 'I'll do it, Mr. Binewski,'
she says, and I just about sent a present to
my laundryman."

Mama smiled sweetly into her sewing and
105 nodded. "I was anxious to prove myself useful to the show. I'd been with Binewski's Fabulon only two weeks at the time and I felt
very keenly that I was on trial."

"So I says," interrupts Papa, "'But, miss,
110 what about your teeth?' Meaning she might
break 'em or chip 'em, and she smiles wide,
just like she's smiling now, and says, 'They're
sharp enough, I think!'"

We looked at Mama and her teeth were
115 white and straight, but of course by that time
they were all false.

"I looked at her delicate little jaw and I
just groaned. 'No,' I says, 'I couldn't ask you
to . . .' but it did flash into my mind that a
120 blonde and lovely geek with legs—I mean
your mama has what we refer to in the trade

as LEGS—would do the business no real harm. I'd never heard of a girl geek before and the poster possibilities were glorious.

125 Then I thought again, No . . . she couldn't . . ."

"What your papa didn't know was that I'd watched the geek several times and of course I'd often helped Minna, our cook at home, when she slaughtered a fowl for the table. I had

130 him. He had no choice but to give me a try."

"Oh, but I was scared spitless when her first show came up that afternoon! Scared she'd be disgusted and go home to Boston. Scared she'd flub the deal and have the crowd

135 screaming for their money back. Scared she'd get hurt . . . A chicken could scratch her or peck an eye out quick as a blink."

"I was quite nervous myself," nodded Mama.

"The crowd was good. A hot Saturday that

140 was, and the Fourth of July was the Sunday. I was running like a geeked bird the whole day myself, and just had time to duck behind the pit for one second before I stood up front to lead in the mugs. There she was like a

145 butterfly . . ."

"I wore tatters really, white because it shows the blood so well even in the dark of the pit."

"But such artful tatters! Such low-necked,

150 slit-to-the-thigh, silky tatters! So I took a deep breath and went out to talk 'em in. And in they went. A lot of soldiers in the crowd. I was still selling tickets when the cheers and whistles started inside and the whooping

155 and stomping on those old wood bleachers drew even more people. I finally grabbed a popcorn kid to sell tickets and went inside to see for myself."

Papa grinned at Mama and twiddled his

160 mustache.

"I'll never forget," he chuckled.

"I couldn't growl, you see, or snarl convincingly So I sang," explained Mama.

"Happy little German songs! In a high,

165 thin voice!"

"Franz Schubert, my dears."

"She fluttered around like a dainty bird, and when she caught those ugly squawking hens you couldn't believe she'd actually do

170 anything. When she went right ahead and geeked 'em that whole larruping crowd went bonzo wild. There never was such a snap and twist of the wrist, such a vampire flick of the jaws over a neck or such a champagne

175 approach to the blood. She'd shake her star-white hair and the bitten-off chicken head would skew off into the corner while she dug her rosy little fingernails in and lifted the flopping, jittering carcass like a golden gob-

180 let, and sipped! Absolutely sipped at the wriggling guts! She was magnificent, a princess, a Cleopatra, an elfin queen! That was your mama in the geek pit.

"People swarmed her act. We built more

185 bleachers, moved her into the biggest top we had, eleven hundred capacity, and it was always jammed."

"It was fun." Lil nodded. "But I felt that it wasn't my true metier."

190 "Yeah." Papa would half frown, looking down at his hands, quieted suddenly.

Feeling the story mood evaporate, one of us children would coax, "What made you quit, Mama?"

195 She would sigh and look up from under her spun-glass eyebrows at Papa and then turn to where we were huddled on the floor in a heap and say softly, "I had always dreamed of flying. The Antifermos, the Ital-

200 ian trapeze clan, joined the show in Abilene and I begged them to teach me." Then she wasn't talking to us anymore but to Papa. "And, Al, you know you would never have got up the nerve to ask for my hand if I hadn't

205 fallen and got so bunged up. Where would we be now if I hadn't?"

Papa nodded, "Yes, yes, and I made you walk again just fine, didn't I?" But his face went flat and smileless and his eyes went to

210 the poster on the sliding door to their bedroom. It was old silvered paper, expensive,
with the lone lush figure of Mama in span-
gles and smile, high-stepping with arms
thrown up so her fingers, in red elbow-length
215 gloves, touched the starry letters arching
"CRYSTAL LIL" above her.

My father's name was Aloysius Binewski.
He was raised in a traveling carnival owned
by his father and called "Binewski's Fabulon."
220 Papa was twenty-four years old when Grandpa
died and the carnival fell into his hands. Al
carefully bolted the silver urn containing his
father's ashes to the hood of the generator
truck that powered the midway. The old man
225 had wandered with the show for so long that
his dust would have been miserable left
behind in some stationary vault.

Times were hard and, through no fault of
young Al's, business began to decline. Five
230 years after Grandpa died, the once flourishing carnival was fading.

The show was burdened with an aging
lion that repeatedly broke expensive dentures
by gnawing the bars of his cage; demands for
235 cost-of living increases from the fat lady,
whose food supply was written into her contract; and the midnight defection of an entire
family of animal eroticists, taking their donkey, goat, and Great Dane with them.
240 The fat lady eventually jumped ship to
become a model for a magazine called
Chubby Chaser. My father was left with a
cut-rate, diesel-fueled fire-eater and the
prospect of a very long stretch in a trailer
245 park outside of Fort Lauderdale.

Al was a standard-issue Yankee, set on
self-determination and independence, but in
that crisis his core of genius revealed itself.
He decided to breed his own freak show.
250 My mother, Lillian Hinchcliff, was a water-
cool aristocrat from the fastidious side of
Boston's Beacon Hill, who had abandoned
her heritage and joined the carnival to

become an aerialist. Nineteen is late to learn
255 to fly and Lillian fell, smashing her elegant
nose and her collarbones. She lost her nerve
but not her lust for sawdust and honky-tonk
lights. It was this passion that made her an
eager partner in Al's scheme. She was willing
260 to chip in on any effort to renew public
interest in the show. Then, too, the idea of
inherited security was ingrained from her
childhood. As she often said, "What greater
gift could you offer your children than an
265 inherent ability to earn a living just by being
themselves?"

The resourceful pair began experimenting
with illicit and prescription drugs, insecti-
cides, and eventually radioisotopes. My
270 mother developed a complex dependency on
various drugs during this process, but she
didn't mind. Relying on Papa's ingenuity to
keep her supplied, Lily seemed to view her
addiction as a minor by-product of their cre-
275 ative collaboration.

Their firstborn was my brother Arturo,
usually known as Aqua Boy. His hands
and feet were in the form of flippers that
sprouted directly from his torso without
280 intervening arms or legs. He was taught to
swim in infancy and was displayed nude in a
big clear-sided tank like an aquarium. His
favorite trick at the ages of three and four
was to put his face close to the glass, bulging
285 his eyes out at the audience, opening and
closing his mouth like a river bass, and then
to turn his back and paddle off, revealing the
turd trailing from his muscular little buttocks. Al and Lil laughed about it later, but at
290 the time it caused them great consternation
as well as the nuisance of sterilizing the tank
more often than usual. As the years passed,
Arty donned trunks and became more
sophisticated, but it's been said, with some
295 truth, that his attitude never really changed.

My sisters, Electra and Iphigenia, were born
when Arturo was two years old and starting to

haul in crowds. The girls were Siamese twins with perfect upper bodies joined at the waist
300 and sharing one set of hips and legs. They usually sat and walked and slept with their long arms around each other. They were, however, able to face directly forward by allowing the shoulder of one to overlap the other. They were
305 always beautiful, slim, and huge-eyed. They studied the piano and began performing piano duets at an early age. Their compositions for four hands were thought by some to have revolutionized the twelve-tone scale.

310   I was born three years after my sisters. My father spared no expense in these experiments. My mother had been liberally dosed with cocaine, amphetamines, and arsenic during her ovulation and throughout her
315 pregnancy with me. It was a disappointment when I emerged with such commonplace deformities. My albinism is the regular pink-eyed variety and my hump, though pronounced, is not remarkable in size or shape
320 as humps go. My situation was far too humdrum to be marketable on the same scale as my brother's and sisters'. Still, my parents noted that I had a strong voice and decided I might be an appropriate shill and talker
325 for the business. A bald albino hunchback

seemed the right enticement toward the esoteric talents of the rest of the family. The dwarfism, which was very apparent by my third birthday, came as a pleasant surprise
330 to the patient pair and increased my value. From the beginning I slept in the built-in cupboard beneath the sink in the family living van, and had a collection of exotic sunglasses to shield my sensitive eyes.

335   Despite the expensive radium treatments incorporated in his design, my younger brother, Fortunato, had a close call in being born to apparent normalcy. That drab state so depressed my enterprising parents that they
340 immediately prepared to abandon him on the doorstep of a closed service station as we passed through Green River, Wyoming, late one night. My father had actually parked the van for a quick getaway and had stepped
345 down to help my mother deposit the baby in the cardboard box on some safe part of the pavement. At that precise moment the two-week-old baby stared vaguely at my mother and in a matter of seconds revealed himself
350 as not a failure at all, but in fact my parents' masterwork. It was lucky, so they named him Fortunato. For one reason and another we always called him Chick.

CHARACTER

1. Describe some **inconsistencies** or unexpected developments in the character Lillian Hinchcliff. How do these inconsistencies affect your interpretation of the narrator and her mother?

2. How do the descriptions of the children as a group of characters provide insight into the values of Binewski's Fabulon?

3. Describe the choices that Lillian Hinchcliff and Aloysius Binewski make in response to a conflict. How do these choices reveal and shape who they are, as well as who they become?

4. The text ends with a description of the children. How do these **minor characters** interact with other characters and advance the plot?

5. As a reader, do you feel **empathy** for any of the characters? Explain the strategies and techniques Dunn uses to create connections — emotional and otherwise — with the reader.

AP® **Enduring Understanding (STR-1)**

The arrangement of the parts and sections of a text, the relationship of the parts to each other, and the sequence in which the text reveals information are all structural choices made by a writer that contribute to the reader's interpretation of a text.

As you think back on this school year, you may remember many events clearly. Some of those moments you may want to relive over and over; others, you may wish to forget. Nonetheless, those memorable events likely shaped you in some way: they taught you something; they caused you to reflect; they defined you.

The same is true for literary characters and narrators. As a reader, you live vicariously through fictional characters. When you experience literature, you want to think about which events are significant for each character or narrator — and why. For example, which specific experiences seem to provoke changes in the protagonist?

KEY POINT

Authors explore the complexity of the human experience by structuring and unifying important moments around a central conflict of competing values.

A Work of Literature Is Made Up of Significant Moments

Authors write literary texts as a way to reveal aspects of the human experience. They hope to connect with readers and share their perspectives. Sometimes a perspective resonates for you, especially if you identify with the characters, their world, and their struggles.

Significant **moments** — events, circumstances, interactions, situations, or outcomes — contribute to both the **narrative arc** of the plot and the progress of the story's **dramatic situation**, which develops a larger meaning in the work. The most significant moments often suggest figurative meaning by

- revealing a significant conflict or tension;
- showing how characters feel about each other; and
- causing a character to reflect.

Significant moments also contribute to the **unity** of the narrative. For example, an author may develop a conflict and explore it through multiple perspectives. Or the story may explore an idea across multiple settings and contexts, allowing a reader to consider it from several angles. By tracing a single idea, along with different characters' views of that idea, readers can understand its complexity.

Conflict and Tension

Significant moments set up and reveal competing value systems. Through these contrasts and **conflicts**, an author creates a **dramatic situation** within the narrative to explore **tensions** and complexities. In turn, these moments provoke questions for the reader about the human experience.

These unresolved questions and conflicts can hook readers, as the narrative's twists and turns create **suspense** and anticipation. In longer works of literature, an author may present multiple intersecting conflicts (often related to the same tension of ideas) that allow readers to view the competing value systems from multiple perspectives.

The suspenseful moments in the narrative build anticipation and create emotional connections with the audience. Readers may empathize, sympathize, or otherwise relate to the character and his or her circumstances. At the height of this **narrative arc**, some readers may experience a **catharsis**, or emotional release such as tears, laughter, or relief. Usually, the protagonist makes an important decision at this climactic moment, which becomes a turning point in the story.

Resolution

Often, a conflict's **resolution** will suggest something about the competing value systems in the narrative. For example, when a protagonist is involved in **external conflicts**, the ideas or values of the "winner" of the conflict may advance an idea and insight about a literary work's interpretation. But some authors intentionally leave narrative conflicts unresolved. While ambiguous endings can leave the audience unfulfilled or frustrated, they also allow readers to make up their own minds and bring their own value systems to their interpretations.

Seeing the Unseen

In the last unit, you learned how authors use irony and juxtaposition to create **incongruities** that emphasize contrasts in competing value systems. But other authorial choices can create incongruities that contribute to an interpretation as well, including anachronism, invisible characters, and antecedent actions.

An **anachronism** is an element or object that is historically out of place. And a character or narrator may make reference to **antecedent action** (a situation or event that occurred before the story begins). Similarly, the narrator or other characters may refer to an **invisible character**: or other figure who is not physically present in the narrative. Because authors make strategic and intentional choices when crafting their literary texts, it is important to ask why an author used the incongruity and what it emphasizes or reveals.

 **INSIDER AP® TIP**   **Conflict reveals thematic interpretation.** By developing a narrative that presents two competing values in conflict, that author invites a reader to consider these values. The way the author resolves the conflict presents thematic insight into those values.

PLOT DEVELOPMENT

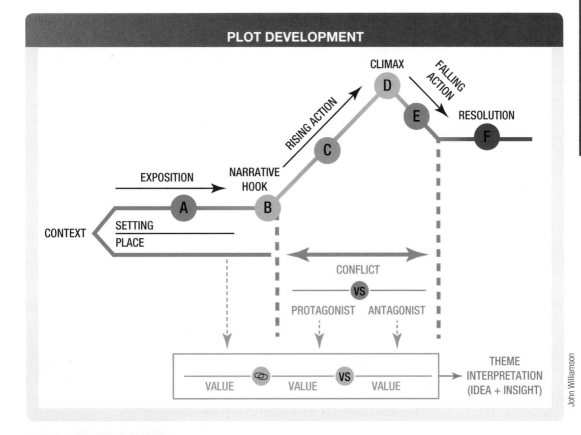

John Williamson

from Invisible Man (Chapter 10)
Ralph Ellison

The Estate of David Gahr/Premium Archive/
Getty Images

THE TEXT IN CONTEXT

While novelist and critic Ralph Ellison (1913–1994) published a relatively limited amount of fiction in his lifetime, his National Book Award–winning novel *Invisible Man* (1952) remains one of the most perceptive and powerful works of literature about being Black in America. Born in Oklahoma, Ellison attended the Tuskegee Institute, a distinguished historically Black university in Alabama. He moved to Harlem in New York City in 1936, which brought him into close contact with African American literary and intellectual life. In the following excerpt from *Invisible Man*, the nameless narrator of the novel describes his job at a paint factory in Long Island, New York.

Content Note: This story includes the N-word, which we have chosen to reprint in this textbook to accurately reflect Ellison's original intent as well as the culture depicted in the story. We recognize that this word has a long history as a disrespectful and deeply hurtful expression when used by white people toward Black people. Ellison's choice to use this word relates not only to that history but also to a larger cultural tradition in which the N-word can take on different meanings, emphasize shared experience, and be repurposed as a term of endearment within Black communities. While the use of that word in the context of this story might not be hurtful, the use of it in our current context very often is. Be mindful of context, both the author's and yours, as you read and discuss this chapter from *Invisible Man*.

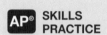 SKILLS PRACTICE | STRUCTURE **Analyzing Significant Moments of Plot**

As you read Chapter 10 of *Invisible Man*, identify significant moments in the excerpt's narrative arc. For each moment, find a relevant and meaningful quote. Then, describe how the moment fits into the narrative arc. Finally, explain the significance of the moment by considering how it contributes to the dramatic situation and reveals a thematic idea.

Analyzing Significant Moments of Plot		

Considerations

- Which event in a plot has a significant relationship to a character, conflict, another event, or thematic idea? What is the relationship?
- How does an event or related set of events cause, develop, or resolve a conflict?
- How can an event or related set of events represent competing value systems?
- How does the resolution or continuation of a conflict affect a character, plot, narrator, or speaker?
- How does an event or related set of events contribute to meaning in the whole work?
- How does a conflict contribute to meaning in the whole work?
- How does the resolution or continuation of a conflict affect a reader's experience with the text?

Moment and Important Textual Quote:	Component of the Plot or Excerpt and Its Function in Relation to Other Moments:	Significance in Relation to the Thematic Idea:

from **Invisible Man (Chapter 10)**

The plant was in Long Island, and I crossed a
bridge in the fog to get there and came down
in a stream of workers. Ahead of me a huge
electric sign announced its message through
5 the drifting strands of fog:

KEEP AMERICA PURE WITH LIBERTY PAINTS

Flags were fluttering in the breeze from
each of a maze of buildings below the sign,
and for a moment it was like watching some
10 vast patriotic ceremony from a distance. But
no shots were fired and no bugles sounded.
I hurried ahead with the others through
the fog.

I was worried, since I had used Emerson's
15 name without his permission, but when I
found my way to the personnel office it
worked like magic. I was interviewed by a little droopy-eyed man named Mr. MacDuffy
and sent to work for a Mr. Kimbro. An office
20 boy came along to direct me.

"If Kimbro needs him," MacDuffy told the
boy, "come back and have his name entered
on the shipping department's payroll."

"It's tremendous," I said as we left the
25 building. "It looks like a small city."

"It's big all right," he said. "We're one of
the biggest outfits in the business. Make a lot
of paint for the government."

We entered one of the buildings now and
30 started down a pure white hall.

"You better leave your things in the locker
room," he said, opening a door through
which I saw a room with low wooden benches
and rows of green lockers. There were keys
35 in several of the locks, and he selected one
for me. "Put your stuff in there and take
the key," he said. Dressing, I felt nervous.
He sprawled with one foot on a bench,
watching me closely as he chewed on a
40 match stem. Did he suspect that Emerson
hadn't sent me?

"They have a new racket around here," he
said, twirling the match between his finger
and thumb. There was a note of insinuation
45 in his voice, and I looked up from tying my
shoe, breathing with conscious evenness.

"What kind of racket?" I said.

"Oh, you know. The wise guys firing the
regular guys and putting on you colored col-
50 lege boys. Pretty smart," he said. "That way
they don't have to pay union wages."

"How did you know I went to college?" I
said.

"Oh, there's about six of you guys out
55 here already. Some up in the testing lab.
Everybody knows about that."

"But I had no idea that was why I was
hired," I said.

"Forget it, Mac," he said. "It's not your
60 fault. You new guys don't know the score.
Just like the union says, it's the wise guys in
the office. They're the ones who make scabs
out of you—Hey! we better hurry."

We entered a long, shed-like room in
65 which I saw a series of overhead doors along
one side and a row of small offices on the
other. I followed the boy down an aisle
between endless cans, buckets and drums
labeled with the company's trademark, a
70 screaming eagle. The paint was stacked in
neatly pyramided lots along the concrete
floor. Then, starting into one of the offices,
the boy stopped short and grinned.

"Listen to that!"

75 Someone inside the office was swearing
violently over a telephone. "Who's that?" I
asked.

He grinned. "Your boss, the terrible Mr.
Kimbro. We call him 'Colonel,' but don't let
80 him catch you."

I didn't like it. The voice was raving about
some failure of the laboratory and I felt a

swift uneasiness. I didn't like the idea of starting to work for a man who was in such a
85 nasty mood. Perhaps he was angry at one of the men from the school, and that wouldn't make him feel too friendly toward me.

"Let's go in," the boy said. "I've got to get back."

90 As we entered, the man slammed down the phone and picked up some papers.

"Mr. MacDuffy wants to know if you can use this new man," the boy said.

"You damn right I can use him and . . ."
95 the voice trailed off, the eyes above the stiff military mustache going hard.

"Well, can you use him?" the boy said. "I got to go make out his card."

"Okay," the man said finally. "I can use
100 him. I gotta. What's his name?"

The boy read my name off a card.

"All right," he said, "you go right to work. And you," he said to the boy, "get the hell out of here before I give you a chance to earn
105 some of the money wasted on you every payday!"

"Aw, gwan, you slave driver," the boy said, dashing from the room.

Reddening, Kimbro turned to me, "Come
110 along, let's get going."

I followed him into the long room where the lots of paint were stacked along the floor beneath numbered markers that hung from the ceiling. Toward the rear I could see two
115 men unloading heavy buckets from a truck, stacking them neatly on a low loading platform.

"Now get this straight," Kimbro said gruffly. "This is a busy department and I
120 don't have time to repeat things. You have to follow instructions and you're going to be doing things you don't understand, so get your orders the first time and get them right! I won't have time to stop and explain every-

125 thing. You have to catch on by doing exactly what I tell you. You got that?"

I nodded, noting that his voice became louder when the men across the floor stopped to listen.

130 "All right," he said, picking up several tools. "Now come over here."

"He's Kimbro," one of the men said.

I watched him kneel and open one of the buckets, stirring a milky brown substance. A
135 nauseating stench arose. I wanted to step away. But he stirred it vigorously until it became glossy white, holding the spatula like a delicate instrument and studying the paint as it laced off the blade, back into the
140 bucket. Kimbro frowned.

"Damn those laboratory blubberheads to hell! There's got to be dope put in every single sonofabitching bucket. And that's what you're going to do, and it's got to be put in so
145 it can be trucked out of here before 11:30." He handed me a white enamel graduate and what looked like a battery hydrometer.

"The idea is to open each bucket and put in ten drops of this stuff," he said. "Then you
150 stir it 'til it disappears. After it's mixed you take this brush and paint out a sample on one of these." He produced a number of small rectangular boards and a small brush from his jacket pocket. "You understand?"

155 "Yes, sir." But when I looked into the white graduate I hesitated; the liquid inside was dead black. Was he trying to kid me?

"What's wrong?"

"I don't know, sir . . . I mean. Well, I don't
160 want to start by asking a lot of stupid questions, but do you know what's in this graduate?"

His eyes snapped. "You damn right I know," he said. "You just do what you're
165 told!"

"I just wanted to make sure, sir," I said.

"Look," he said, drawing in his breath with an exaggerated show of patience. "Take the dropper and fill it full . . . Go on, do it!"

170   I filled it.

"Now measure ten drops into the paint . . . There, that's it, not too goddam fast. Now. You want no more than ten, and no less."

Slowly, I measured the glistening black
175 drops, seeing them settle upon the surface and become blacker still, spreading suddenly out to the edges.

"That's it. That's all you have to do," he said. "Never mind how it looks. That's my
180 worry. You just do what you're told and don't try to think about it. When you've done five or six buckets, come back and see if the samples are dry . . . And hurry, we've got to get this batch back off to Washington by
185 11:30 . . ."

I worked fast but carefully. With a man like this Kimbro the least thing done incorrectly would cause trouble. So I wasn't supposed to think! To hell with him. Just a flunkey, a
190 northern redneck, a Yankee cracker! I mixed the paint thoroughly, then brushed it smoothly on one of the pieces of board, careful that the brush strokes were uniform.

Struggling to remove an especially difficult
195 cover, I wondered if the same Liberty paint was used on the campus, or if this "Optic White" was something made exclusively for the government. Perhaps it was of a better quality, a special mix. And in my mind I could
200 see the brightly trimmed and freshly decorated campus buildings as they appeared on spring mornings—after the fall painting and the light winter snows, with a cloud riding over and a darting bird above—framed by the
205 trees and encircling vines. The buildings had always seemed more impressive because they were the only buildings to receive regular paintings; usually, the nearby houses and

cabins were left untouched to become the dull
210 grained gray of weathered wood. And I remembered how the splinters in some of the boards were raised from the grain by the wind, the sun and the rain until the clapboards shone with a satiny, silvery, silver-fish sheen.
215 Like Trueblood's cabin, or the Golden Day . . . The Golden Day had once been painted white; now its paint was flaking away with the years, the scratch of a finger being enough to send it showering down. Damn that Golden Day! But
220 it was strange how life connected up; because I had carried Mr. Norton to the old rundown building with rotting paint, I was here. If, I thought, one could slow down his heartbeats and memory to the tempo of the black drops
225 falling so slowly into the bucket yet reacting so swiftly, it would seem like a sequence in a feverish dream . . . I was so deep in reverie that I failed to hear Kimbro approach.

"How's it coming?" he said, standing with
230 hands on hips.

"All right, sir."

"Let's see," he said, selecting a sample and running his thumb across the board. "That's it, as white as George Washington's Sunday-
235 go-to-meetin' wig and as sound as the almighty dollar! That's paint!" he said proudly. "That's paint that'll cover just about anything!"

He looked as though I had expressed a
240 doubt and I hurried to say, "It's certainly white all right."

"White! It's the purest white that can be found. Nobody makes a paint any whiter. This batch right here is heading for a
245 national monument!"

"I see," I said, quite impressed.

He looked at his watch. "Just keep it up," he said. "If I don't hurry I'll be late for that production conference! Say, you're nearly out
250 of dope: you'd better go in the tank room and

refill it . . . And don't waste any time! I've got
to go."

He shot away without telling me where
the tank room was. It was easy to find, but I
255 wasn't prepared for so many tanks. There
were seven; each with a puzzling code sten-
ciled on it. It's just like Kimbro not to tell me,
I thought. You can't trust any of them. Well,
it doesn't matter, I'll pick the tank from the
260 contents of the drip cans hanging from the
spigots.

But while the first five tanks contained
clear liquids that smelled like turpentine, the
last two both contained something black like
265 the dope, but with different codes. So I had to
make a choice. Selecting the tank with the drip
can that smelled most like the dope, I filled the
graduate, congratulating myself for not having
to waste time until Kimbro returned.

270 The work went faster now, the mixing
easier. The pigment and heavy oils came free
of the bottom much quicker, and when
Kimbro returned I was going at top speed.
"How many have you finished?" he asked.
275 "About seventy-five, I think, sir. I lost
count."

"That's pretty good, but not fast enough.
They've been putting pressure on me to get
the stuff out. Here, I'll give you a hand."

280 They must have given him hell, I thought,
as he got grunting to his knees and began
removing covers from the buckets. But he
had hardly started when he was called away.

When he left I took a look at the last
285 bunch of samples and got a shock: Instead of
the smooth, hard surface of the first, they
were covered with a sticky goo through
which I could see the grain of the wood.
What on earth had happened? The paint was
290 not as white and glossy as before; it had a
gray tinge. I stirred it vigorously, then
grabbed a rag, wiping each of the boards

clean, then made a new sample of each
bucket. I grew panicky lest Kimbro return
295 before I finished. Working feverishly, I made
it, but since the paint required a few minutes
to dry I picked up two finished buckets and
started lugging them over to the loading
platform. I dropped them with a thump
300 as the voice rang out behind me. It was
Kimbro.

"What the hell!" he yelled, smearing his
finger over one of the samples. "This stuff's
still wet!"

305 I didn't know what to say. He snatched up
several of the later samples, smearing them,
and letting out a groan. "Of all the things to
happen to me. First they take all my good
men and then they send me you. What'd you
310 do to it?"

"Nothing, sir. I followed your directions," I
said defensively.

I watched him peer into the graduate, lifting the dropper and sniffing it, his face glow-
315 ing with exasperation.

"Who the hell gave you this?"

"No one . . ."

"Then where'd you get it?"

"From the tank room."

320 Suddenly he dashed for the tank room,
sloshing the liquid as he ran. I thought, Oh,
hell, and before I could follow, he burst out of
the door in a frenzy.

"You took the wrong tank," he shouted.
325 "What the hell, you trying to sabotage the
company? That stuff wouldn't work in a million years. It's remover, *concentrated* remover!
Don't you know the difference?"

"No, sir, I don't. It looked the same to me. I
330 didn't know what I was using and you didn't
tell me. I was trying to save time and took
what I thought was right."

"But why this one?"

"Because it smelled the same—" I began.

335 "*Smelled!*" he roared. "Goddamit, don't you
know you can't smell shit around all those
fumes? Come on to my office!"

I was torn between protesting and pleading for fairness. It was not all my fault and I
340 didn't want the blame, but I did wish to finish out the day. Throbbing with anger I followed, listening as he called personnel.

"Hello? Mac? Mac, this is Kimbro. It's
about this fellow you sent me this morning.
345 I'm sending him in to pick up his pay . . .
What did he do? He doesn't satisfy me, that's
what. I don't like his work . . . So the old man
has to have a report, so what? Make him one.
Tell him goddamit this fellow ruined a batch
350 of government stuff—Hey! No, don't tell him
that . . . Listen, Mac, you got anyone else out
there? . . . Okay, forget it."

He crashed down the phone and swung
toward me. "I swear I don't know why they
355 hire you fellows. You just don't belong in a
paint plant. Come on."

Bewildered, I followed him into the tank
room, yearning to quit and tell him to go
to hell. But I needed the money, and even
360 though this was the North I wasn't ready to
fight unless I had to. Here I'd be one against
how many?

I watched him empty the graduate back
into the tank and noted carefully when he
365 went to another marked SKA-3-69-T-Y and
refilled it. Next time I would know.

"Now, for God's sake," he said, handing me
the graduate, "be careful and try to do the job
right. And if you don't know what to do, ask
370 somebody. I'll be in my office."

I returned to the buckets, my emotions
whirling. Kimbro had forgotten to say what
was to be done with the spoiled paint. Seeing
it there I was suddenly seized by an angry
375 impulse, and, filling the dropper with fresh
dope, I stirred ten drops into each bucket and

pressed home the covers. Let the government worry about that, I thought, and started
to work on the unopened buckets. I stirred
380 until my arm ached and painted the samples
as smoothly as I could, becoming more skill-
ful as I went along.

When Kimbro came down the floor and
watched I glanced up silently and continued
385 stirring.

"How is it?" he said, frowning.

"I don't know," I said, picking up a sample
and hesitating.

"Well?"

390 "It's nothing . . . a speck of dirt," I said,
standing and holding out the sample, a tight-
ness growing within me.

Holding it close to his face, he ran his fingers over the surface and squinted at the
395 texture. "That's more like it," he said. "That's
the way it oughta be."

I watched with a sense of unbelief as he
rubbed his thumb over the sample, handed it
back and left without a further word.

400 I looked at the painted slab. It appeared
the same: a gray tinge glowed through the
whiteness, and Kimbro had failed to detect
it. I stared for about a minute, wondering if I
were seeing things, inspected another and
405 another. All were the same, a brilliant white
diffused with gray, I closed my eyes for a
moment and looked again and still no
change. Well, I thought, as long as he's
satisfied . . .

410 But I had a feeling that something had
gone wrong, something far more important
than the paint; that either I had played a
trick on Kimbro or he, like the trustees and
Bledsoe, was playing one on me . . .

415 When the truck backed up to the platform
I was pressing the cover on the last bucket—
and there stood Kimbro above me.

"Let's see your samples," he said.

I reached, trying to select the whitest, as
420 the blue-shirted truckmen climbed through
the loading door.

"How about it, Kimbro," one of them said,
"can we get started?"

"Just a minute, now," he said, studying the
425 sample, "just a minute . . ."

I watched him nervously, waiting for him
to throw a fit over the gray tinge and hating
myself for feeling nervous and afraid. What
would I say? But now he was turning to the
430 truckmen.

"All right, boys, get the hell out of here.

"And you," he said to me, "go see MacDuffy;
you're through."

I stood there, staring at the back of his
435 head, at the pink neck beneath the cloth cap
and the iron-gray hair. So he'd let me stay
only to finish the mixing. I turned away,
there was nothing that I could do. I cursed
him all the way to the personnel office.
440 Should I write the owners about what had
happened? Perhaps they didn't know that
Kimbro was having so much to do with the
quality of the paint. But upon reaching the
office I changed my mind. Perhaps that is
445 how things are done here, I thought, perhaps
the real quality of the paint is always determined by the man who ships it rather than
by those who mix it. To hell with the whole
thing . . . I'll find another job.
450 But I wasn't fired. MacDuffy sent me to
the basement of Building No. 2 on a new
assignment.

"When you get down there just tell Brockway that Mr. Sparland insists that he have an
455 assistant. You do whatever he tells you."

"What is that name again, sir?" I said.
"Lucius Brockway," he said. "He's in charge."

It was a deep basement. Three levels underground I pushed upon a heavy metal door

460 marked "Danger" and descended into a noisy,
dimly lit room. There was something familiar
about the fumes that filled the air and I had
just thought pine, when a high-pitched Negro
voice rang out above the machine sounds.
465 "Who you looking for down here?"

"I'm looking for the man in charge," I
called, straining to locate the voice.

"You talkin' to him. What you want?"

The man who moved out of the shadow
470 and looked at me sullenly was small, wiry
and very natty in his dirty overalls. And as I
approached him I saw his drawn face and
the cottony white hair showing beneath his
tight, striped engineer's cap. His manner
475 puzzled me. I couldn't tell whether he felt
guilty about something himself, or thought I
had committed some crime. I came closer,
staring. He was barely five feet tall, his overalls looking now as though he had been
480 dipped in pitch.

"All right," he said. "I'm a busy man. What
you want?"

"I'm looking for Lucius," I said.

He frowned. "That's me—and don't come
485 calling me by my first name. To you and all
like you I'm Mister Brockway . . ."

"You . . . ?" I began.

"Yeah, me! Who sent you down here anyway?"
490 "The personnel office," I said. "I was told
to tell you that Mr. Sparland said for you to
be given an assistant."

"Assistant!" he said. "I don't need no damn
assistant! Old Man Sparland must think I'm
495 getting old as him. Here I been running
things by myself all these years and now
they keep trying to send me some assistant.
You get on back up there and tell 'em that
when I want an assistant I'll ask for one!"
500 I was so disgusted to find such a man in
charge that I turned without a word and

started back up the stairs. First Kimbro, I thought, and now this old . . .

"Hey! wait a minute!"

505   I turned, seeing him beckon.

"Come on back here a minute," he called, his voice cutting sharply through the roar of the furnaces.

I went back, seeing him remove a white
510 cloth from his hip pocket and wipe the glass face of a pressure gauge, then bend close to squint at the position of the needle.

"Here," he said, straightening and handing me the cloth, "you can stay 'til I can get in
515 touch with the Old Man. These here have to be kept clean so's I can see how much pressure I'm getting."

I took the cloth without a word and began rubbing the glasses. He watched me critically.

520   "What's your name?" he said.

I told him, shouting it in the roar of the furnaces.

"Wait a minute," he called, going over and turning a valve in an intricate network of
525 pipes. I heard the noise rise to a higher, almost hysterical pitch, somehow making it possible to hear without yelling, our voices moving blurrily underneath.

Returning, he looked at me sharply, his
530 withered face an animated black walnut with shrewd, reddish eyes.

"This here's the first time they ever sent me anybody like you," he said as though puzzled. "That's how come I called you back.
535 Usually they sends down some young white fellow who thinks he's going to watch me a few days and ask me a heap of questions and then take over. Some folks is too damn simple to even talk about," he said, grimacing
540 and waving his hand in a violent gesture of dismissal. "You an engineer?" he said, looking quickly at me.

"An engineer?"

"Yeah, that's what I asked you," he said
545 challengingly.

"Why, no, sir, I'm no engineer."

"You sho?"

"Of course I'm sure. Why shouldn't I be?"

He seemed to relax. "That's all right then.
550 I have to watch them personnel fellows. One of them thinks he's going to git me out of here, when he ought to know by now he's wasting his time. Lucius Brockway not only intends to protect hisself, he knows how to
555 do it! Everybody knows I been here ever since there's been a here—even helped dig the first foundation. The Old Man hired me, nobody else; and, by God, it'll take the Old Man to fire me!"

I rubbed away at the gauges, wondering
560 what had brought on this outburst, and was somewhat relieved that he seemed to hold nothing against me personally.

"Where you go to school?" he said.

I told him.

565   "Is that so? What you learning down there?"

"Just general subjects, a regular college course," I said.

"Mechanics?"

570   "Oh no, nothing like that, just a liberal arts course. No trades."

"Is that so?" he said doubtfully. Then suddenly, "How much pressure I got on that gauge right there?"

575   "Which?"

"You see it," he pointed. "That one right there!"

I looked, calling off, "Forty-three and two-tenths pounds."

580   "Uh huh, uh huh, that's right." He squinted at the gauge and back at me. "Where you learn to read a gauge so good?"

"In my high-school physics class. It's like reading a clock."

585   "They teach you that in high school?"

"That's right."

"Well, that's going to be one of your jobs. These here gauges have to be checked every fifteen minutes. You ought to be able to do
590 that."

"I think I can," I said.

"Some kin, some caint. By the way, who hired you?"

"Mr. MacDuffy," I said, wondering why all
595 the questions.

"Yeah, then where you been all morning?"

"I was working over in Building No. 1."

"That there's a heap of building. Where 'bouts?"

600 "For Mr. Kimbro."

"I see, I see. I knowed they oughtn't to be hiring anybody this late in the day. What Kimbro have you doing?"

"Putting dope in some paint that went
605 bad," I said wearily, annoyed with all the questions.

His lips shot out belligerently. "What paint went bad?"

"I think it was some for the government . . ."

610 He cocked his head. "I wonder how come nobody said nothing to me about it," he said thoughtfully. "Was it in buckets or them little biddy cans?"

"Buckets."

615 "Oh, that ain't so bad, them little ones is a heap of work." He gave me a high dry laugh. "How you hear about this job?" he snapped suddenly, as though trying to catch me off guard.

620 "Look," I said slowly, "a man I know told me about the job; MacDuffy hired me; I worked this morning for Mr. Kimbro; and I was sent to you by Mr. MacDuffy."

His face tightened. "You friends to one of
625 those colored fellows?"

"Who?"

"Up in the lab?"

"No," I said. "Anything else you want to know?"

630 He gave me a long, suspicious look and spat upon a hot pipe, causing it to steam furiously. I watched him remove a heavy engineer's watch from his breast pocket and squint at the dial importantly, then turn to
635 check it with an electric clock that glowed from the wall. "You keep on wiping them gauges," he said. "I got to look at my soup. And look here." He pointed to one of the gauges. "I wants you to keep a 'specially sharp
640 eye on this here sonofabitch. The last couple of days he's 'veloped a habit of building up too fast. Causes me a heap of trouble. You see him gitting past 75, you yell, and yell loud!"

He went back into the shadows and I saw
645 a shaft of brightness mark the opening of a door.

Running the rag over a gauge I wondered how an apparently uneducated old man could gain such a responsible job. He cer-
650 tainly didn't sound like an engineer; yet he alone was on duty. And you could never be sure, for at home an old man employed as a janitor at the Water Works was the only one who knew the location of all of the water
655 mains. He had been employed at the beginning, before any records were kept, and actually functioned as an engineer though he drew a janitor's pay. Perhaps this old Brockway was protecting himself from something.
660 After all, there was antagonism to our being employed. Maybe he was dissimulating, like some of the teachers at the college, who, to avoid trouble when driving through the small surrounding towns, wore chauffeur
665 caps and pretended that their cars belonged to white men. But why was he pretending with me? And what was his job?

I looked around me. It was not just an engine room; I knew, for I had been in several,

670 the last at college. It was something more. For one thing, the furnaces were made differently and the flames that flared through the cracks of the fire chambers were too intense and too blue. And there were the odors. No, he was

675 making something down here, something that had to do with paint, and probably something too filthy and dangerous for white men to be willing to do even for money. It was not paint because I had been told that the paint was

680 made on the floors above, where, passing through, I had seen men in splattered aprons working over large vats filled with whirling pigment. One thing was certain: I had to be careful with this crazy Brockway; he didn't like

685 my being here . . . And there he was, entering the room now from the stairs.

"How's it going?" he asked.

"All right," I said. "Only it seems to have gotten louder."

690 "Oh, it gets pretty loud down here, all right; this here's the uproar department and I'm in charge . . . Did she go over the mark?"

"No, it's holding steady," I said.

"That's good. I been having plenty trouble

695 with it lately. Haveta bust it down and give it a good going over soon as I can get the tank clear."

Perhaps he is the engineer, I thought, watching him inspect the gauges and go to

700 another part of the room to adjust a series of valves. Then he went and said a few words into a wall phone and called me, pointing to the valves.

"I'm fixing to shoot it to 'em upstairs," he

705 said gravely. "When I give you the signal I want you to turn 'em wide open. 'N when I give you the second signal I want you to close 'em up again. Start with this here red one and work right straight across . . ."

710 I took my position and waited, as he took a stand near the gauge.

"Let her go," he called. I opened the valves, hearing the sound of liquids rushing through the huge pipes. At the sound of a buzzer I

715 looked up . . .

"Start closing," he yelled. "What you looking at? Close them valves!"

"What's wrong with you?" he asked when the last valve was closed.

720 "I expected you to call."

"I said I'd signal you. Caint you tell the difference between a signal and a call? Hell, I buzzed you. You don't want to do that no more. When I buzz you I want you to do

725 something and do it quick!"

"You're the boss," I said sarcastically.

"You mighty right, I'm the boss, and don't forget it. Now come on back here, we got work to do."

730 We came to a strange-looking machine consisting of a huge set of gears connecting a series of drum-like rollers. Brockway took a shovel and scooped up a load of brown crystals from a pile on the floor, pitching them

735 skillfully into a receptacle on top of the machine.

"Grab a scoop and let's git going," he ordered briskly. "You ever done this before?" he asked as I scooped into the pile.

740 "It's been a long time," I said. "What is this material?"

He stopped shoveling and gave me a long, black stare, then returned to the pile, his scoop ringing on the floor. You'll have to

745 remember not to ask this suspicious old bastard any questions, I thought, scooping into the brown pile.

Soon I was perspiring freely. My hands were sore and I began to tire. Brockway

750 watched me out of the corner of his eye, snickering noiselessly.

"You don't want to overwork yourself, young feller," he said blandly.

"I'll get used to it," I said, scooping up a
755 heavy load.

"Oh, sho, sho," he said. "Sho. But you better take a rest when you git tired."

I didn't stop. I piled on the material until
he said, "That there's the scoop we been
760 trying to find. That's what we want. You
better stand back a little, 'cause I'm fixing
to start her up."

I backed away, watching him go over and
push a switch. Shuddering into motion, the
765 machine gave a sudden scream like a circular saw, and sent a tattoo of sharp crystals
against my face. I moved clumsily away, seeing Brockway grin like a dried prune. Then
with the dying hum of the furiously whirling
770 drums, I heard the grains sifting lazily in the
sudden stillness, sliding sand-like down the
chute into the pot underneath.

I watched him go over and open a valve.
A sharp new smell of oil arose.
775 "Now she's all set to cook down; all we got
to do is put the fire to her," he said, pressing
a button on something that looked like the
burner of an oil furnace. There was an angry
hum, followed by a slight explosion that
780 caused something to rattle, and I could hear
a low roaring begin.

"Know what that's going to be when it's
cooked?"

"No, sir," I said.
785 "Well that's going to be the guts, what
they call the vee-hicle of the paint. Least it
will be by time I git through putting other
stuff with it."

"But I thought the paint was made
790 upstairs . . ."

"Naw, they just mixes in the color, make it
look pretty. Right down here is where the
real paint is made. Without what I do they
couldn't do nothing, they be making bricks
795 without straw. An' not only do I make up the

base, I fixes the varnishes and lots of the oils
too . . ."

"So that's it," I said. "I was wondering
what you did down here."
800 "A whole lots of folks wonders about that
without gitting anywhere. But as I was saying, caint a single doggone drop of paint
move out of the factory lessen it comes
through Lucius Brockway's hands."
805 "How long have you been doing this?"

"Long enough to know what I'm doing," he
said. "And I learned it without all that education that them what's been sent down here
is suppose to have. I learned it by doing it.
810 Them personnel fellows don't want to face
the facts, but Liberty Paints wouldn't be
worth a plugged nickel if they didn't have me
here to see that it got a good strong base. Old
Man Sparland know it though. I caint stop
815 laughing over the time when I was down
with a touch of pneumonia and they put
one of them so-called engineers to pooling
around down here. Why, they started to having so much paint go bad they didn't know
820 what to do. Paint was bleeding and wrin-
kling, wouldn't cover or nothing—you know,
a man could make hisself all kinds of money
if he found out what makes paint bleed. Anyway, everything was going bad. Then word
825 got to me that they done put that fellow in
my place and when I got well I wouldn't
come back. Here I been with 'em so long and
loyal and everything. Shucks, I just sent 'em
word that Lucius Brockway was retiring!
830 "Next thing you know here come the Old
Man. He so old hisself his chauffeur has to
help him up them steep stairs at my place.
Come in a-puffing and a-blowing, says,
'Lucius, what's this I hear 'bout you retiring?'
835 "'Well, sir, Mr. Sparland, sir,' I says, 'I been
pretty sick, as you well know, and I'm gitting
kinder along in my years, as you well know,

and I hear that this here Italian fellow you got in my place is doing so good I thought I'd

840 might as well take it easy round the house.'

"Why, you'd a-thought I'd done cursed him or something. 'What kind of talk is that from you, Lucius Brockway,' he said, 'taking it easy round the house when we need you out to the

845 plant? Don't you know the quickest way to die is to retire? Why, that fellow out at the plant don't know a thing about those furnaces. I'm so worried about what he's going to do, that he's liable to blow up the plant or something

850 that I took out some extra insurance. He can't do your job,' he said. 'He don't have the touch. We haven't put out a first-class batch of paint since you been gone.' Now that was the Old Man hisself!" Lucius Brockway said.

855 "So what happened?" I said.

"What you mean, what happened?" he said, looking as though it were the most unreasonable question in the world. "Shucks, a few days later the Old Man had me back

860 down here in full control. That engineer got so mad when he found out he had to take orders from me he quit the next day."

He spat on the floor and laughed. "Heh, heh, heh, he was a fool, that's what. A fool!

865 He wanted to boss me and I know more about this basement than anybody, boilers and everything. I helped lay the pipes and everything, and what I mean is I knows the location of each and every pipe and switch

870 and cable and wire and everything else—both in the floors and in the walls and out in the yard. Yes, sir! And what's more, I got it in my head so good I can trace it out on paper down to the last nut and bolt; and ain't never

875 been to nobody's engineering school neither, ain't even passed by one, as far as I know. Now what you think about that?"

"I think it's remarkable," I said, thinking, I don't like this old man.

880 "Oh, I wouldn't call it that," he said. "It's just that I been round here so long. I been studying this machinery for over twenty-five years. Sho, and that fellow thinking 'cause he been to some school and learned how to read

885 a blueprint and how to fire a boiler he knows more 'bout this plant than Lucius Brockway. That fool couldn't make no engineer 'cause he can't see what's staring him straight in the face . . . Say, you forgittin' to watch them

890 gauges."

I hurried over, finding all the needles steady.

"They're okay," I called.

"All right, but I'm warning you to keep

895 an eye on 'em. You caint forgit down here, 'cause if you do, you liable to blow up something. They got all this machinery, but that ain't everything; we are the machines inside the machine.

900 "You know the best selling paint we got, the one that made this here business?" he asked as I helped him fill a vat with a smelly substance.

"No, I don't."

905 "Our white, Optic White."

"Why the white rather than the others?"

" 'Cause we started stressing it from the first. We make the best white paint in the world, I don't give a damn what nobody says.

910 Our white is so white you can paint a chunka coal and you'd have to crack it open with a sledge hammer to prove it wasn't white clear through!"

His eyes glinted with humorless convic-

915 tion and I had to drop my head to hide my grin.

"You notice that sign on top of the building?"

"Oh, you can't miss that," I said.

920 "You read the slogan?"

"I don't remember, I was in such a hurry."

"Well, you might not believe it, but I helped the Old Man make up that slogan. 'If It's Optic White, It's the Right White,'" he
925 quoted with an upraised finger, like a preacher quoting holy writ. "I got me a three-hundred-dollar bonus for helping to think that up. These newfangled advertising folks is been tryin' to work up something
930 about the other colors, talking about rainbows or something, but hell, they caint get nowhere."

"'If It's Optic White, It's the Right White,'" I repeated and suddenly had to repress a
935 laugh as a childhood jingle rang through my mind: "'If you're white, you're right,'" I said.

"That's it," he said. "And that's another reason why the Old Man ain't goin' to let nobody come down here messing with me.
940 He knows what a lot of them new fellers don't; he knows that the reason our paint is so good is because of the way Lucius Brockway puts the pressure on them oils and resins before they even leaves the tanks." He
945 laughed maliciously. "They thinks 'cause everything down here is done by machinery, that's all there is to it. They crazy! Ain't a continental thing that happens down here that ain't as iffen I done put my black hands
950 into it! Them machines just do the cooking, these here hands right here do the sweeting. Yes, sir! Lucius Brockway hit it square on the head! I dips my fingers in and sweets it! Come on, let's eat . . ."

955 "But what about the gauges?" I said, seeing him go over and take a thermos bottle from a shelf near one of the furnaces.

"Oh, we'll be here close enough to keep an eye on 'em. Don't you worry 'bout that."

960 "But I left my lunch in the locker room over at Building No. 1."

"Go on and git it and come back here and eat. Down here we have to always be on the job. A man don't need no more'n fifteen min-
965 utes to eat no-how; then I say let him git on back on the job."

Upon opening the door I thought I had made a mistake. Men dressed in splattered painters' caps and overalls sat about on
970 benches, listening to a thin tubercular-looking man who was addressing them in a nasal voice. Everyone looked at me and I was starting out when the thin man called, "There's plenty of seats for late comers. Come in,
975 brother . . ."

Brother? Even after my weeks in the North this was surprising. "I was looking for the locker room," I spluttered.

"You're in it, brother. Weren't you told
980 about the meeting?"

"Meeting? Why, no, sir, I wasn't."

The chairman frowned. "You see, the bosses are not co-operating," he said to the others. "Brother, who's your foreman?"

985 "Mr. Brockway, sir," I said.

Suddenly the men began scraping their feet and cursing. I looked about me. What was wrong? Were they objecting to my referring to Brockway as Mister?

990 "Quiet, brothers," the chairman said, leaning across his table, his hand cupped to his ear. "Now what was that, brother; who is your foreman?"

"Lucius Brockway, sir," I said, dropping the
995 Mister.

But this seemed only to make them more hostile. "Get him the hell out of here," they shouted. I turned. A group on the far side of the room kicked over a bench, yelling,
1000 "Throw him out! Throw him out!"

I inched backwards, hearing the little man bang on the table for order. "Men, brothers! Give the brother a chance . . ."

"He looks like a dirty fink to me. A first-
1005 class enameled fink!"

The hoarsely voiced word grated my ears like "nigger" in an angry southern mouth . . .

"Brothers, please!" The chairman was waving his hands as I reached out behind me for the door and touched an arm, feeling it snatch violently away. I dropped my hand.

"Who sent this fink into the meeting, brother chairman? Ask him that!" a man demanded.

"No, wait," the chairman said. "Don't ride that word too hard . . ."

"Ask him, brother chairman!" another man said.

"Okay, but don't label a man a fink until you know for sure." The chairman turned to me. "How'd you happen in here, brother?" The men quieted, listening.

"I left my lunch in my locker," I said, my mouth dry.

"You weren't sent into the meeting?"

"No, sir, I didn't know about any meeting."

"The hell he says. None of these finks ever knows!"

"Throw the lousy bastard out!"

"Now, wait," I said.

They became louder, threatening. "Respect the chair!" the chairman shouted. "We're a democratic union here, following democratic—"

"Never mind, git rid of the fink!"

". . . procedures. It's our task to make friends with all the workers. And I mean all. That's how we build the union strong. Now let's hear what the brother's got to say. No more of that beefing and interrupting!"

I broke into a cold sweat, my eyes seeming to have become extremely sharp, causing each face to stand out vivid in its hostility.

I heard, "When were you hired, friend?"

"This morning," I said.

"See, brothers, he's a new man. We don't want to make the mistake of judging the worker by his foreman. Some of you also work for sonsabitches, remember?"

Suddenly the men began to laugh and curse. "Here's one right here," one of them yelled.

"Mine wants to marry the boss's daughter—a frigging eight-day wonder!"

This sudden change made me puzzled and angry, as though they were making me the butt of a joke.

"Order, brothers! Perhaps the brother would like to join the union. How about it, brother?"

"Sir . . . ?" I didn't know what to say. I knew very little about unions—but most of these men seemed hostile . . . And before I could answer a fat man with shaggy gray hair leaped to his feet, shouting angrily,

"I'm against it! Brothers, this fellow could be a fink, even if he was hired right this minute! Not that I aim to be unfair to anybody, either. Maybe he ain't a fink," he cried passionately, "but brothers, I want to remind you that nobody knows it; and it seems to me that anybody that would work under that sonofabitching, double-crossing Brockway for more than fifteen minutes is just as apt as not to be naturally fink-minded! Please, brothers!" he cried, waving his arms for quiet. "As some of you brothers have learned, to the sorrow of your wives and babies, a fink don't have to know about trade unionism to be a fink! Finkism? Hell, I've made a study of finkism! Finkism is born into some guys. It's born into some guys, just like a good eye for color is born into other guys. That's right, that's the honest, scientific truth! A fink don't even have to have heard of a union before," he cried in a frenzy of words. "All you have to do is bring him around the neighborhood of a union and next thing you know, why, zip! he's finking his finking ass off!"

1090 He was drowned out by shouts of approval. Men turned violently to look at me. I felt choked. I wanted to drop my head but faced them as though facing them was itself a denial of his statements. Another voice ripped

1095 out of the shouts of approval, spilling with great urgency from the lips of a little fellow with glasses who spoke with the index finger of one hand upraised and the thumb of the other crooked in the suspender of his overalls:

1100 "I want to put this brother's remarks in the form of a motion: I move that we determine through a thorough investigation whether the new worker is a fink or no; and if he is a fink, let us discover who he's fink-

1105 ing for! And this, brother members, would give the worker time, if he ain't a fink, to become acquainted with the work of the union and its aims. After all, brothers, we don't want to forget that workers like him

1110 aren't so highly developed as some of us who've been in the labor movement for a long time. So I says, let's give him time to see what we've done to improve the condition of the workers, and then, if he ain't a fink, we

1115 can decide in a democratic way whether we want to accept this brother into the union. Brother union members, I thank you!" He sat down with a bump.

The room roared. Biting anger grew inside
1120 me. So I was not so highly developed as they! What did he mean? Were they all Ph.D.'s? I couldn't move; too much was happening to me. It was as though by entering the room I had automatically applied for membership—

1125 even though I had no idea that a union existed, and had come up simply to get a cold pork chop sandwich. I stood trembling, afraid that they would ask me to join but angry that so many rejected me on sight.

1130 And worst of all, I knew they were forcing me to accept things on their own terms, and I was unable to leave.

"All right, brothers. We'll take a vote," the chairman shouted. "All in favor of the
1135 motion, signify by saying 'Aye' . . ."

The ayes drowned him out.

"The ayes carried it," the chairman announced as several men turned to stare at me. At last I could move. I started out, forget-
1140 ting why I had come.

"Come in, brother," the chairman called. "You can get your lunch now. Let him through, you brothers around the door!"

My face stung as though it had been
1145 slapped. They had made their decision without giving me a chance to speak for myself. I felt that every man present looked upon me with hostility; and though I had lived with hostility all my life, now for the first time it
1150 seemed to reach me, as though I had expected more of these men than of others—even though I had not known of their existence. Here in this room my defenses were negated, stripped away, checked at the door as the
1155 weapons, the knives and razors and owlhead pistols of the country boys were checked on Saturday night at the Golden Day. I kept my eyes lowered, mumbling "Pardon me, pardon me," all the way to the drab green locker,
1160 where I removed the sandwich, for which I no longer had an appetite, and stood fumbling with the bag, dreading to face the men on my way out. Then still hating myself for the apologies made coming over, I brushed
1165 past silently as I went back.

When I reached the door the chairman called, "Just a minute, brother, we want you to understand that this is nothing against you personally. What you see here is the results of
1170 certain conditions here at the plant. We want you to know that we are only trying to protect ourselves. Some day we hope to have you as a member in good standing."

From here and there came a half-hearted
1175 applause that quickly died. I swallowed and

stared unseeing, the words spurting to me from a red, misty distance.

"Okay, brothers," the voice said, "let him pass."

1180 I stumbled through the bright sunlight of the yard, past the office workers chatting on the grass, back to Building No. 2, to the basement. I stood on the stairs, feeling as though my bowels had been flooded with acid.

1185 Why hadn't I simply left, I thought with anguish. And since I had remained, why hadn't I said something, defended myself? Suddenly I snatched the wrapper off a sandwich and tore it violently with my teeth, hardly 1190 tasting the dry lumps that squeezed past my constricted throat when I swallowed. Dropping the remainder back into the bag, I held onto the handrail, my legs shaking as though I had just escaped a great danger. Finally, it went 1195 away and I pushed open the metal door.

"What kept you so long?" Brockway snapped from where he sat on a wheelbarrow. He had been drinking from a white mug now cupped in his grimy hands.

1200 I looked at him abstractedly, seeing how the light caught on his wrinkled forehead, his snowy hair. "I said, what kept you so long!" What had he to do with it, I thought, looking at him through a kind of mist, knowing that I 1205 disliked him and that I was very tired.

"I say . . ." he began, and I heard my voice come quiet from my tensed throat as I noticed by the clock that I had been gone only twenty minutes. "I ran into a union 1210 meeting—"

"Union!" I heard his white cup shatter against the floor as he uncrossed his legs, rising. "I knowed you belonged to that bunch of troublemaking foreigners! I knowed it! Git 1215 out!" he screamed. "Git out of my basement!"

He started toward me as in a dream, trembling like the needle of one of the gauges as he pointed toward the stairs, his voice shrieking. I stared; something seemed to 1220 have gone wrong, my reflexes were jammed.

"But what's the matter?" I stammered, my voice low and my mind understanding and yet failing exactly to understand. "What's wrong?"

1225 "You heard me. Git out!"

"But I don't understand . . ."

"Shut up and git!"

"But, Mr. Brockway," I cried, fighting to hold something that was giving way.

1230 "You two-bit, trouble-making union louse!"

"Look, man," I cried, urgently now, "I don't belong to any union."

"If you don't git outta here, you low-down skunk," he said, looking wildly about the 1235 floor, "I'm liable to kill you. The Lord being my witness, I'LL KILL YOU!"

It was incredible, things were speeding up. "You'll do what?" I stammered.

"I'LL KILL YOU, THAT'S WHAT!"

1240 He had said it again and something fell away from me, and I seemed to be telling myself in a rush: You were trained to accept the foolishness of such old men as this, even when you thought them clowns and fools; 1245 you were trained to pretend that you respected them and acknowledged in them the same quality of authority and power in your world as the whites before whom they bowed and scraped and feared and loved and imitated, 1250 and you were even trained to accept it when, angered or spiteful, or drunk with power, they came at you with a stick or strap or cane and you made no effort to strike back, but only to escape unmarked. But this was 1255 too much . . . he was not grandfather or uncle or father, nor preacher or teacher. Something uncoiled in my stomach and I was moving toward him, shouting, more at a black blur that irritated my eyes than at a clearly 1260 denned human face, "YOU'LL KILL WHO?"

"YOU, THAT'S WHO!"

"Listen here, you old fool, don't talk about killing me! Give me a chance to explain. I don't belong to anything—Go on, pick it up! Go on!" I yelled, seeing his eyes fasten upon a twisted iron bar. "You're old enough to be my grandfather, but if you touch that bar, I swear I'll make you eat it!"

"I done tole you, GIT OUTTA MY BASE-MENT! You impudent son'bitch," he screamed.

I moved forward, seeing him stoop and reach aside for the bar; and I was throwing myself forward, feeling him go over with a grunt, hard against the floor, rolling beneath the force of my lunge. It was as though I had landed upon a wiry rat. He scrambled beneath me, making angry sounds and striking my face as he tried to use the bar. I twisted it from his grasp, feeling a sharp pain stab through my shoulder. He's using a knife flashed through my mind and I slashed out with my elbow, sharp against his face, feeling it land solid and seeing his head fly backwards and up and back again as I struck again, hearing something fly free and skitter across the floor, thinking, It's gone, the knife is gone . . . and struck again as he tried to choke me, jabbing at his bobbing head, feeling the bar come free and bringing it down at his head, missing, the metal clinking against the floor, and bringing it up for a second try and him yelling, "No, no! You the best, you the best!"

"I'm going to beat your brains out!" I said, my throat dry, "stabbing me . . ."

"No," he panted. "I got enough. Ain't you heard me say I got enough?"

"So when you can't win you want to stop! Damn you, if you've cut me bad, I'll tear your head off!"

Watching him warily, I got to my feet. I dropped the bar, as a flash of heat swept over me: His face was caved in.

"What's wrong with you, old man?" I yelled nervously. "Don't you know better than to attack a man a third your age?"

He blanched at being called old, and I repeated it, adding insults I'd heard my grandfather use. "Why, you old-fashioned, slavery-time, mammy-made, handkerchief-headed bastard, you should know better! What made you think you could threaten my life? You meant nothing to me, I came down here because I was sent. I didn't know anything about you or the union either. Why'd you start riding me the minute I came in? Are you people crazy? Does this paint go to your head? Are you drinking it?"

He glared, panting tiredly. Great tucks showed in his overalls where the folds were stuck together by the goo with which he was covered, and I thought, Tar Baby, and wanted to blot him out of my sight. But now my anger was flowing fast from action to words.

"I go to get my lunch and they ask me who I work for and when I tell them, they call me a fink. A fink! You people must be out of your minds. No sooner do I get back down here than you start yelling that you're going to kill me! What's going on? What have you got against me? What did I do?"

He glowered at me silently, then pointed to the floor.

"Reach and draw back a nub," I warned.

"Caint a man even git his teeth?" he mumbled, his voice strange.

"TEETH?"

With a shamed frown, he opened his mouth. I saw a blue flash of shrunken gums. The thing that had skittered across the floor was not a knife, but a plate of false teeth. For a fraction of a second I was desperate, feeling some of my justification for wanting to kill him slipping away. My fingers leaped to my shoulder, finding wet cloth but no blood.

1345 The old fool had bitten me. A wild flash of laughter struggled to rise from beneath my anger. He had bitten me! I looked on the floor, seeing the smashed mug and the teeth glinting dully across the room.

1350 "Get them," I said, growing ashamed. Without his teeth, some of the hatefulness seemed to have gone out of him. But I stayed close as he got his teeth and went over to the tap and held them beneath a stream of 1355 water. A tooth fell away beneath the pressure of his thumb, and I heard him grumbling as he placed the plate in his mouth. Then, wiggling his chin, he became himself again.

"You was really trying to kill me," he said. 1360 He seemed unable to believe it.

"You started the killing. I don't go around fighting," I said. "Why didn't you let me explain? Is it against the law to belong to the union?"

1365 "That damn union," he cried, almost in tears. "That damn union! They after my job! I know they after my job! For one of us to join one of them damn unions is like we was to bite the hand of the man who teached us to 1370 bathe in a bathtub! I hates it, and I mean to keep on doing all I can to chase it outta the plant. They after my job, the chickenshit bastards!"

Spittle formed at the corners of his 1375 mouth; he seemed to boil with hatred.

"But what have I to do with that?" I said, feeling suddenly the older.

"'Cause them young colored fellers up in the lab is trying to join that outfit, that's what! 1380 Here the white man done give 'em jobs," he wheezed as though pleading a case. "He done give 'em good jobs too, and they so ungrateful they goes and joins up with that backbiting union! I never seen such a no-good ungrateful 1385 bunch. All they doing is making things bad for the rest of us!"

"Well, I'm sorry," I said, "I didn't know about all that. I came here to take a tempo- rary job and I certainly didn't intend to get 1390 mixed up in any quarrels. But as for us, I'm ready to forget our disagreement—if you are . . ." I held out my hand, causing my shoulder to pain.

He gave me a gruff look. "You ought to 1395 have more self-respect than to fight an old man," he said. "I got grown boys older than you."

"I thought you were trying to kill me," I said, my hand still extended. "I thought you 1400 had stabbed me."

"Well, I don't like a lot of bickering and confusion myself," he said, avoiding my eyes. And it was as though the closing of his sticky hand over mine was a signal. I heard a shrill 1405 hissing from the boilers behind me and turned, hearing Brockway yell, "I tole you to watch them gauges. Git over to the big valves, quick!"

I dashed for where a series of valve 1410 wheels projected from the wall near the crusher, seeing Brockway scrambling away in the other direction, thinking, Where's he going? as I reached the valves, and hearing him yell, "Turn it! Turn it!"

1415 "Which?" I yelled, reaching.

"The white one, fool, the white one!"

I jumped, catching it and pulling down with all my weight, feeling it give. But this only increased the noise and I seemed to 1420 hear Brockway laugh as I looked around to see him scrambling for the stairs, his hands clasping the back of his head, and his neck pulled in close, like a small boy who has thrown a brick into the air.

1425 "Hey you! Hey you!" I yelled. "Hey!" But it was too late. All my movements seemed too slow, ran together. I felt the wheel resisting and tried vainly to reverse it and tried to let

go, and it sticking to my palms and my fin-
1430 gers stiff and sticky, and I turned, running
now, seeing the needle on one of the gauges
swinging madly, like a beacon gone out of
control, and trying to think clearly, my eyes
darting here and there through the room of
1435 tanks and machines and up the stairs so far
away and hearing the clear new note arising
while I seemed to run swiftly up an incline
and shot forward with sudden acceleration
into a wet blast of black emptiness that was
1440 somehow a bath of whiteness.

It was a fall into space that seemed not a
fall but a suspension. Then a great weight
landed upon me and I seemed to sprawl in
an interval of clarity beneath a pile of bro-
1445 ken machinery, my head pressed back
against a huge wheel, my body splattered
with a stinking goo. Somewhere an engine
ground in furious futility, grating loudly

1450 until a pain shot around the curve of my
head and bounced me off into blackness for
a distance, only to strike another pain that
lobbed me back. And in that clear instant of
consciousness I opened my eyes to a
blinding flash.

1455 Holding on grimly, I could hear the sound
of someone wading, sloshing, nearby, and an
old man's garrulous voice saying, "I tole 'em
these here young Nineteen-Hundred boys
ain't no good for the job. They ain't got the
1460 nerves. Naw, sir, they just ain't got the
nerves."

I tried to speak, to answer, but something
heavy moved again, and I was understanding
something fully and trying again to answer
1465 but seemed to sink to the center of a lake of
heavy water and pause, transfixed and numb
with the sense that I had lost irrevocably an
important victory.

STRUCTURE

1. How does the labor union represent a competing value system illustrated by the **conflict** in the text?

2. The introduction of Mr. Kimbro is a significant **moment**. What is the narrator's attitude toward him? How does this relationship contribute to the **tension** between the two characters?

3. How does the narrator's decision in the tank contribute to the **suspense** of the narrative?

4. How does the relationship between Lucius Brockway and the narrator reveal **tensions**?

5. How does the **resolution** resolve the **conflict** of the narrative? What insight does the narrator discover? How does it contribute to your understanding of the text?

Narrative Complexities

 Enduring Understanding (NAR-1)

A narrator's or speaker's perspective controls the details and emphases that affect how readers experience and interpret a text.

Most of us have heard legends about *cryptids*: creatures whose existence is claimed, but not proven. But stories about creatures like the Loch Ness Monster, bigfoot, and Mothman gain their notoriety from the widespread variance of narratives about them. These tall tales are passed from individual to individual and community to community; they are told and retold by countless narrators, who can alter their accounts as they tell the story. For example, a grandmother may want her grandchildren to avoid going into the nearby woods. So she tells them that the forest is haunted by gruesome ghouls who like to eat people. In turn, the grandchildren might brag about their bravery by telling their friends that they explored the area, despite the tales about monsters. Different narrators (and their perspectives, points of view, motivations, and reliability) all add complexity to a story.

At the same time, we do not interpret literature in a vacuum. The act of interpretation includes what we bring to the story as readers, both personally and socially. In other words, your temperament, experiences, perspective, and background influence how you make meaning from a text. They play a role in what you pay attention to and how you interact with the narrative.

KEY POINT

When stories are told from multiple perspectives or points of view, readers must consider what the author is emphasizing through the shift, comparison, or contrast.

A Story's Point of View Reveals a Perspective

Whether prose, poetry, or drama, a literary text is like a block of clay molded and shaped intentionally (and unintentionally) by its author. The text's **narrator**(s) or speaker(s) often plays an important role in this process. Stories and poems may be told through a **persona**, an unnamed narrator, a **chorus**, individual characters, or a collection of multiple characters, all of whom make choices about how a reader experiences a narrative. A narrator's fingerprints mark each aspect of the story they tell. They filter *what* readers get to know, *when* they get to know it, and even *how* they get this information. As a result, your interpretation is directly influenced by the point of view and perspective of the narrator.

Shift in Perspective

Narrators or **speakers** may change over the course of a narrative as they reflect, speak, act, or interact with others. A narrator's **tone** will often reflect these shifts in values and **perspectives,** so pay close attention to it—especially if it changes. Readers can observe the narrative's tone on a particular subject to reveal the narrator's perspective. Noticing shifts in the narrator's tone allows a reader to interpret how that narrator's or speaker's values and perspectives have changed. Changes and inconsistencies in a narrator's perspective may also contribute to the text's overall **complexity** and **irony**.

Multiple Points of View

Some stories may be told from several **points of view**. For example, Mary Shelley's *Frankenstein* uses three distinct narrators, while William Faulkner's novel *As I Lay Dying* features fifteen. Similarly, Caryl Churchill's play *Top Girls* explores perspectives from a range of historical and contemporary women. Some narrators' accounts may be **juxtaposed** in order to reveal a contrast, similarity, or insight.

Multiple narrators make both the story and the ideas within it more complex. When a story is told by multiple storytellers, the narrative is complicated by different variations and perspectives (which may be in conflict with one another). That means the reader must reconcile each account in relation to the narrators' perspective, point-of-view, reliability, and motivations. In fact, the storyteller's motivations affect his or her credibility. Is the narrative an attempt to inform, confess, amuse, persuade, justify, or deceive? That goal will influence the details and information that the narrator chooses to share — or withhold.

 **INSIDER AP® TIP**

Why multiple perspectives? Multiple perspectives add complexity to narratives. When a story is told from multiple perspectives or points of view, readers must consider what ideas or values the author is emphasizing through the shift, comparison, or contrast.

PRACTICE TEXT

from All the Light We Cannot See (Chapters 3 and 4)
Anthony Doerr

Ulf Andersen/Getty Images

THE TEXT IN CONTEXT

Fiction writer, memoirist, and critic Anthony Doerr (b. 1973) is the author of *About Grace* (2004), *Four Seasons in Rome: On Twins, Insomnia, and the Biggest Funeral in the History of the World* (2007), *Memory Wall* (2010), and *Cloud Cuckoo Land* (2021), among other works. In his Pulitzer Prize–winning novel *All the Light We Cannot See* (2014; excerpted here), Doerr weaves together the intersecting stories of Marie, a blind girl living in occupied France during World War II, and Werner, a gifted German orphan living in Germany at the same time. Doerr has noted the appeal of writing about this historical period: "There's so much darkness that you really highlight the little flames of good and hope."

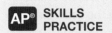 **SKILLS PRACTICE** | NARRATION
Analyzing Narrative Complexities

As you read the excerpt from *All the Light We Cannot See*, identify the multiple narrators. Describe each of their perspectives, and then explain how each contributes to an interpretation that reveals a thematic idea.

Analyzing Narrative Complexities

Considerations

- How does a narrator's or speaker's inclusion or exclusion of particular details affect their reliability?
- To what degree is the first-person narrator or speaker aware of their own biases?
- What is the relationship between a narrator's or speaker's reliability and a reader's understanding of a character's motivations?
- How might a change in tone toward a particular subject over the course of a text indicate a narrator's or speaker's change?
- How do the diction, imagery, details, and syntax in a text support multiple tones?

Narrator and Relevant Quotes:	Perspective and What It Reveals about Characters or Plot:	Significance of Perspective in Relation to a Thematic Idea:

from All the Light We Cannot See

The Girl

In a corner of the city, inside a tall, narrow house at Number 4 rue Vauborel, on the sixth and highest floor, a sightless sixteen-year-old named Marie-Laure LeBlanc kneels over a
5 low table covered entirely with a model. The model is a miniature of the city she kneels within, and contains scale replicas of the hundreds of houses and shops and hotels within its walls. There's the cathedral with
10 its perforated spire, and the bulky old Château

de Saint-Malo, and row after row of seaside mansions studded with chimneys. A slender wooden jetty arcs out from a beach called the Plage du Môle; a delicate, reticulated
15 atrium vaults over the seafood market; minute benches, the smallest no larger than apple seeds, dot the tiny public squares.

Marie-Laure runs her fingertips along the centimeter-wide parapet crowning the
20 ramparts, drawing an uneven star shape around the entire model. She finds the

opening atop the walls where four ceremonial cannons point to sea. "Bastion de la
Hollande," she whispers, and her fingers
25 walk down a little staircase. "Rue des
Cordiers. Rue Jacques Cartier."

In a corner of the room stand two galva-
nized buckets filled to the "with water. Fill
them up, her great-uncle has taught her,
30 whenever you can. The bathtub on the third
floor too. Who knows when the water will go
out again."

Her fingers travel back to the cathedral
spire. South to the Gate of Dinan. All evening
35 she has been marching her fingers around
the model, waiting for her great-uncle Etienne,
who owns this house, who went out the previous night while she slept, and who has not
returned. And now it is night again, another
40 revolution of the clock, and the whole block
is quiet, and she cannot sleep.

She can hear the bombers when they are
three miles away. A mounting static. The
hum inside a seashell.

45 When she opens the bedroom window,
the noise of the airplanes becomes louder.
Otherwise, the night is dreadfully silent: no
engines, no voices, no clatter. No sirens. No
footfalls on the cobbles. Not even gulls. Just
50 a high tide, one block away and six stories
below, lapping at the base of the city walls.

And something else.

Something rattling softly, very close. She
eases open the left-hand shutter and runs
55 her fingers up the slats of the right. A sheet
of paper has lodged there.

She holds it to her nose. It smells of fresh
ink. Gasoline, maybe. The paper is crisp; it
has not been outside long.

60 Marie-Laure hesitates at the window in
her stocking feet, her bedroom behind her,
seashells arranged along the top of the
armoire, pebbles along the baseboards. Her

cane stands in the corner; her big Braille
65 novel waits facedown on the bed. The drone
of the airplanes grows.

The Boy

Five streets to the north, a white-haired
eighteen-year-old German private named
Werner Pfennig wakes to a faint staccato
70 hum. Little more than a purr. Flies tapping at
a far-off windowpane.

Where is he? The sweet, slightly chemical
scent of gun oil; the raw wood of newly
constructed shell crates; the mothballed
75 odor of old bedspreads—he's in the hotel. Of
course. L'hôtel des Abeilles, the Hotel of Bees.

Still night. Still early.

From the direction of the sea come
whistles and booms; flak is going up.

80 An anti-air corporal hurries down the
corridor, heading for the stairwell. "Get to the
cellar," he calls over his shoulder, and Werner
switches on his field light, rolls his blanket
into his duffel, and starts down the hall.

85 Not so long ago, the Hotel of Bees was a
cheerful address, with bright blue shutters
on its facade and oysters on ice in its café
and Breton waiters in bow ties polishing
glasses behind its bar. It offered twenty-one
90 guest rooms, commanding sea views, and a
lobby fireplace as big as a truck. Parisians on
weekend holidays would drink aperitifs here,
and before them the occasional emissary
from the republic—ministers and vice
95 ministers and abbots and admirals—and in
the centuries before them, windburned
corsairs: killers, plunderers, raiders, seamen.

Before that, before it was ever a hotel at
all, five full centuries ago, it was the home of
100 a wealthy privateer who gave up raiding
ships to study bees in the pastures outside
Saint-Malo, scribbling in notebooks and
eating honey straight from combs. The crests

above the door lintels still have bumblebees
105 carved into the oak; the ivy-covered fountain
in the courtyard is shaped like a hive. Werner's
favorites are five faded frescoes on the ceil-
ings of the grandest upper rooms, where
bees as big as children float against blue
110 backdrops, big lazy drones and workers with
diaphanous wings—where, above a hexago-
nal bathtub, a single nine-foot-long queen,
with multiple eyes and a golden-furred
abdomen, curls across the ceiling.
115   Over the past four weeks, the hotel has
become something else: a fortress. A detachment of Austrian anti-airmen has boarded
up every window, overturned every bed.
They've reinforced the entrance, packed the
120 stairwells with crates of artillery shells. The
hotel's fourth floor, where garden rooms
with French balconies open directly onto the
ramparts, has become home to an aging high
velocity anti-air gun called an 88 that can
125 fire twenty-one-and-a-half-pound shells
nine miles.
    Her Majesty, the Austrians call their cannon,
and for the past week these men have tended
to it the way worker bees might tend to a
130 queen. They've fed her oils, repainted her barrels, lubricated her wheels; they've arranged
sandbags at her feet like offerings.

    The royal *acht acht*, a deathly monarch
meant to protect them all.
135   Werner is in the stairwell, halfway to the
ground floor, when the 88 fires twice in quick
succession. It's the first time he's heard the
gun at such close range, and it sounds as if
the top half of the hotel has torn off. He
140 stumbles and throws his arms over his ears.
The walls reverberate all the way down into
the foundation, then back up. Werner can
hear the Austrians two floors up scrambling,
reloading, and the receding screams of both
145 shells as they hurtle above the ocean, already
two or three miles away. One of the soldiers,
he realizes, is singing. Or maybe it is more
than one. Maybe they are all singing. Eight
Luftwaffe men, none of whom will survive
150 the hour, singing a love song to their queen.
    Werner chases the beam of his field light
through the lobby. The big gun detonates a
third time, and glass shatters somewhere
close by, and torrents of soot rattle down the
155 chimney, and the walls of the hotel toll like a
struck bell. Werner worries that the sound
will knock the teeth from his gums.
    He drags open the cellar door and pauses
a moment, vision swimming. "This is it?" he
160 asks. "They're really coming?"
    But who is there to answer?

NARRATION

1. From what **point of view** is the story told? What details from the text indicate the identity of the narrator?

2. In the section "The Girl," the narrative's **perspective** reveals information that Marie-Laure cannot process. What is that information? Why can't the narrator understand it?

3. In the section "The Boy," identify the shift in **perspective**. What does this shift reveal about the boy and his understanding of the world around him?

4. Explain what the contrast between the narrative **tones** in the two sections reveals about the characters.

5. What is the relationship between the **narrator's reliability** and the reader's understanding of both Marie-Laure and Werner?

IDEA BANK

Appearance

Celebration

Class

Confidence

Control

Dependency

Expression

Façade

Fluidity

Invisibility

Manipulation

Mendacity

Perception

Persona

Power

Presentation

Race

Reflection

Repression

Resilience

Subjugation

Submission

Transformation

Truth

The decades after World War II witnessed the Cold War, unprecedented prosperity; social and political turmoil; progress toward equality in race and gender; increasing disparities in wealth; revolutions in science, technology, and information; and intense political polarization. These historical currents have occurred in an era often given the label *postmodern* or *postmodernism*. While these terms are elusive, they denote both a condition (all of contemporary life) and a critical perspective that highlights certain ideas: "truth" is not universal but determined by social and cultural context; "science" and "reason" are social constructs, not a means for accessing objective truth; the "self" is also a fluid, performative construct, not a stable, unified entity. All grand historical or "master narratives" are suspect, including religion, Marxism, civilization, and human "progress." For postmodernists, "power" is ideological: it's embedded in language, everyday practices, countless social relationships, and fundamental assumptions that we no longer question. While Enlightenment writers, Romantics, and Modernists sought to uncover and express "depths" of meaning, postmodernists argue that "depth" and "meaning" are ultimately illusory. Meaning is on the surface. And in a fundamental sense, perception becomes reality.

Jeff Wall, After 'Invisible Man' by Ralph Ellison, the Prologue, 1999–2001, transparency in lightbox, 174.0 × 250.5 cm, Courtesy of the artist. Digital image ©The Museum of Modern Art/Licensed by SCALA / Art Resource, NY

▲

Jeff Wall's staged photograph *After "Invisible Man" by Ralph Ellison, the Prologue* (2000) is inspired by Ralph Ellison's 1952 novel. Wall refers to his method of photography as "cinematography."

Wall uses the term "cinematic" because his work requires elaborate sets and a cast of collaborators, much as movies do. Does *After "Invisible Man"* appear cinematic or filmlike in other ways? For example, does the image suggest a narrative? How do the specific elements of the image illustrate the artist's perception of the content?

We probably take many of these ideas for granted. For example, think about how our relationship with reality is usually mediated by technologies, institutions, and commercial transactions (as in the concept of "news" presented by the media). Or consider the ways in which social media disperses our identities through various avatars and images that, in turn, create different representations of—and narratives about—us. Many people make a distinction between "online" and "in real life," but from a postmodern perspective, that binary opposition is a fiction: neither sphere is more "real"—nor can they be separated. Likewise, our popular culture illustrates many postmodern impulses, from the paradox of "reality television," to shows about making television shows (*30 Rock*, *The Office*), and narrative-driven video games (*Bioshock Infinite*) that critique the conventions of video games. Note that postmodernism questions distinctions between "high culture" and "mass" or "popular" culture. For instance, Art Speigelman's *Maus* (1991) uses the comic or graphic novel form to tell his father's story of the Jewish Holocaust. Pop artist Andy Warhol toyed with this tension in much of his work. His famous painting *Campbell Soup Cans* (1962) turned banal, mass-produced images (labeled soup cans) into "original" art. If a thread runs through these postmodern tendencies, it's the notion that we should call attention to artifice rather than conceal it.

Many selections that you have encountered throughout this textbook were written in the late twentieth and early twenty-first centuries. During this time, literary voices from diverse cultures and communities have become less marginalized and more central. But these contemporary authors still explore broad questions of humanity, as well as themes important to them and more specific communities. For example, Caryl Churchill's *Top Girls* (p. 1278) dramatizes questions about female success, power, patriarchy, and perception. Ultimately, literature stands the test of time because—regardless of its cultural origins—it allows readers to explore what makes us human. We read and study literature because it allows us to go beyond our own perspectives and communities to understand our shared experiences and ideas.

Escapando de la crítica (Escaping Criticism) — Borrell del Caso, Pere (1835–1910) — Oil on canvas — 1874 trompe-l'oeil — Banco de Espana/Borell del Caso, Pere (1835–1910)/FINE ART IMAGES/Banco de España, Madrid, Spain/ Bridgeman Images

◀ Like much of Pere Borrell del Caso's work, his oil-on-canvas painting *Escaping Criticism* (1874) uses *trompe-l'œil*: a technique that creates the illusion of three dimensions.

What does the painting suggest about art, art criticism, and art critics? How does the painting's perspective shape your interpretation of the image?

Top Girls
Caryl Churchill

David Montgomery/Premium Archive/Getty Images

THE TEXT IN CONTEXT

British playwright Caryl Churchill (b. 1938) often writes about power, feminism, and sexual politics. With an all-female cast, her *Top Girls* (1982) explores gender roles in the context of Britain's right-wing turn under the leadership of Prime Minister Margaret Thatcher. In the play, a contemporary London businesswoman hosts a dinner party where the guests are women throughout history. The premise of *Top Girls* allows Churchill to explore the concept of female "success" from multiple points of view. But it does so with a nonlinear structure, intertextual references to myth and history, characters that decenter the protagonist, and overlapping dialogue that calls into question language's ability to communicate. The play's blend of fantasy and realism highlights the artifice of "realistic" drama. Churchill has written over fifty plays, including *Cloud 9* (1979), *Here We Go* (2015), *Bluebeard's Friends* (2019), and *What, If Only* (2021). She has also written many television and radio dramas.

Top Girls

Characters

MARLENE
WAITRESS/KIT/SHONA
ISABELLA BIRD/JOYCE/MRS. KIDD
LADY NIJO/WIN
DULL GRET/ANGIE
POPE JOAN/LOUISE
PATIENT GRISELDA/NELL/JEANINE

ACT I
Scene i: *A Restaurant.*
Scene ii: *Top Girls' Employment Agency, London.*
Scene iii: *Joyce's Backyard in Suffolk.*

ACT II
Scene i: *Top Girls' Employment Agency.*
Scene ii: *A Year Earlier. Joyce's kitchen.*
Production Note: *The seating order for Act I, Scene i in the original production at the Royal Court was (from right) Gret, Nijo, Marlene, Joan, Griselda, Isabella.*

The Characters

ISABELLA BIRD (B. 1831–1904): *Lived in Edinburgh, traveled extensively between the ages of forty and seventy.*

LADY NIJO (B. 1258): *Japanese, was an Emperor's courtesan and later a Buddhist nun who traveled on foot through Japan.*

DULL GRET: *Is the subject of the Brueghel painting* Dulle Griet, *in which a woman in an apron and armor leads a crowd of women charging through hell and fighting the devils.*

POPE JOAN: *Disguised as a man, is thought to have been pope between 854 and 856.*

PATIENT GRISELDA: *Is the obedient wife whose story is told by Chaucer in "The Clerk's Tale" of* The Canterbury Tales.

THE LAYOUT: *A speech usually follows the one immediately before it but: (1) When one character starts speaking before the other has finished, the point of interruption is marked/. E.g.,*

ISABELLA: This is the Emperor of Japan? / I once met the Emperor of Morocco.

NIJO: In fact he was the ex-Emperor.

(2) A character sometimes continues speaking right through another's speech. E.g.,

ISABELLA: When I was forty I thought my life was over. / Oh I was pitiful. I was

NIJO: I didn't say I felt it for twenty years. Not every minute.

ISABELLA: sent on a cruise for my health and felt even worse. Pains in my bones, pins and needles . . . etc.

(3) Sometimes a speech follows on from a speech earlier than the one immediately before it, and continuity is marked*. E.g.,

GRISELDA: I'd seen him riding by, we all had. And he'd seen me in the fields with the sheep.*

ISABELLA: I would have been well suited to minding sheep.

NIJO: And Mr. Nugent went riding by.

ISABELLA: Of course not, Nijo, I mean a healthy life in the open air.

JOAN: *He just rode up while you were minding the sheep and asked you to marry him?

where "in the fields with the sheep" is the cue to both "I would have been" and "He just rode up."

ACT I

SCENE i

(Restaurant. Saturday night. There is a table with a white cloth set for dinner with six places. The lights come up on Marlene and the Waitress.)

MARLENE: Excellent, yes, table for six. One of them's going to be late but we won't wait.

I'd like a bottle of Frascati straight away if you've got one really cold. *(The Waitress goes.*
5 *Isabella Bird arrives.)* Here we are. Isabella.

ISABELLA: Congratulations, my dear.

MARLENE: Well, it's a step. It makes for a party. I haven't time for a holiday. I'd like to go somewhere exotic like you but I

10   can't get away. I don't know how you
could bear to leave Hawaii. / I'd like to lie

ISABELLA: I did think of settling.

MARLENE: in the sun forever, except of
course I can't bear sitting still.

15 **ISABELLA:** I sent for my sister Hennie to
come and join me. I said, Hennie we'll
live here forever and help the natives.
You can buy two sirloins of beef for what
a pound of chops cost in Edinburgh. And

20   Hennie wrote back, the dear, that yes,
she would come to Hawaii if I wished,
but I said she had far better stay where
she was. Hennie was suited to life in
Tobermory.

25 **MARLENE:** Poor Hennie.

ISABELLA: Do you have a sister?

MARLENE: Yes in fact.

ISABELLA: Hennie was happy. She was good.
I did miss its face, my own pet. But I

30   couldn't stay in Scotland. I loathed the
constant murk. (*Lady Nijo arrives.*)

MARLENE (*seeing her*): Ah! Nijo! (*The Waitress
enters with the wine.*)

NIJO: Marlene! (*To Isabella.*) So excited when

35   Marlene told me / you were coming.

ISABELLA: I'm delighted / to meet you.

MARLENE: I think a drink while we wait for
the others. I think a drink anyway. What a
week. (*Marlene seats Nijo. The Waitress pours*

40   *the wine.*)

NIJO: It was always the men who used to get
so drunk I'd be one of the maidens, passing the sake.[1]

ISABELLA: I've had sake. Small hot drink.

45   Quite fortifying after a day in the wet.

NIJO: One night my father proposed three
rounds of three cups, which was normal,
and then the Emperor should have said
three rounds of three cups, but he said

---

[1]**43. sake:** Japanese rice wine.

---

50   three rounds of nine cups, so you can
imagine. Then the Emperor passed his
sake cup to my father and said, "Let the
wild goose come to me this spring."

MARLENE: Let the what?

55 **NIJO:** It's a literary allusion to a tenth-century
epic, / His Majesty was very cultured.

ISABELLA: This is the Emperor of Japan? / I
once met the Emperor of Morocco.

NIJO: In fact he was the ex-Emperor.

60 **MARLENE:** But he wasn't old? / Did you,
Isabella?

NIJO: Twenty-nine.

ISABELLA: Oh it's a long story.

MARLENE: Twenty-nine's an excellent age.

65 **NIJO:** Well I was only fourteen and I knew he
meant something but I didn't know what.
He sent me an eight-layered gown and I
sent it back. So when the time came I did
nothing but cry. My thin gowns were badly

70   ripped. But even that morning when he
left / he'd a green

MARLENE: Are you saying he raped you?

NIJO: robe with a scarlet lining and very
heavily embroidered trousers, I already

75   felt different about him. It made me
uneasy. No, of course not, Marlene, I
belonged to him, it was what I was
brought up for from a baby. I soon found I
was sad if he stayed away. It was depress-

80   ing day after day not knowing when he
would come. I never enjoyed taking other
women to him.

ISABELLA: I certainly never saw my father
drunk. He was a clergyman. / And I didn't

85   get married till I was fifty. (*The Waitress
brings the menus.*)

NIJO: Oh, my father was a very religious
man. Just before he died he said to me,
"Serve His Majesty, be respectful, if you

90   lose his favor enter holy orders."

MARLENE: But he meant stay in a convent,
not go wandering round the country.

NIJO: Priests were often vagrants, so why not a nun? You think I shouldn't? / I still did

95 what my father wanted.

MARLENE: No no, I think you should. / I think it was wonderful. (*Dull Gret arrives.*)

ISABELLA: I tried to do what my father wanted.

MARLENE: Gret, good. Nijo. Gret / I know

100 Griselda's going to be late, but should we wait for Joan? / Let's get you a drink.

ISABELLA: Hello, Gret! (*She continues to Nijo.*) I tried to be a clergyman's daughter. Needlework, music, charitable schemes.

105 I had a tumor removed from my spine and spent a great deal of time on the sofa. I studied the metaphysical poets and hymnology. / I thought I enjoyed intellectual pursuits.

110 NIJO: Ah, you like poetry. I come of a line of eight generations of poets. Father had a poem / in the anthology.

ISABELLA: My father taught me Latin although I was a girl. / But really I was

115 MARLENE: They didn't have Latin at my school.

ISABELLA: more suited to manual work. Cooking, washing, mending, riding horses. / Better than reading

120 NIJO: Oh but I'm sure you're very clever.

ISABELLA: books, eh Gret? A rough life in the open air.

NIJO: I can't say I enjoyed my rough life. What I enjoyed most was being the

125 Emperor's favorite / and wearing thin silk.

ISABELLA: Did you have any horses, Gret?

GRET: Pig. (*Pope Joan arrives.*)

MARLENE: Oh Joan, thank God, we can order.

130 Do you know everyone? We were just talking about learning Latin and being clever girls. Joan was by way of an infant prodigy. Of course you were. What excited you when you were ten?

135 JOAN: Because angels are without matter they are not individuals. Every angel is a species.

MARLENE: There you are. (*They laugh. They look at the menus.*)

140 ISABELLA: Yes, I forgot all my Latin. But my father was the mainspring of my life and when he died I was so grieved. I'll have the chicken, please, / and the soup.

NIJO: Of course you were grieved. My father

145 was saying his prayers and he dozed off in the sun. So I touched his knee to rouse him. "I wonder what will happen," he said, and then he was dead before he finished the sentence. / If he'd

150 MARLENE: What a shock.

NIJO: died saying his prayers he would have gone straight to heaven. / Waldorf salad.

JOAN: Death is the return of all creatures to God.

155 NIJO: I shouldn't have woken him.

JOAN: Damnation only means ignorance of the truth. I was always attracted by the teachings of John the Scot, though he was inclined to confuse / God and the world.

160 ISABELLA: Grief always overwhelmed me at the time.

MARLENE: What I fancy is a rare steak. Gret?

ISABELLA: I am of course a member of the / Church of England.

165 MARLENE: Gret?

GRET: Potatoes.

MARLENE: I haven't been to church for years. / I like Christmas carols.

ISABELLA: Good works matter more than

170 church attendance.

MARLENE: Make that two steaks and a lot of potatoes. Rare. But I don't do good works either.

JOAN: Canelloni, please, / and a salad.

175 ISABELLA: Well, I tried, but oh dear. Hennie did good works.

NIJO: The first half of my life was all sin and the second / all repentance.*

MARLENE: Oh what about starters?

180 GRET: Soup.

JOAN: *And which did you like best?

MARLENE: Were your travels just a penance? Avocado vinaigrette. Didn't you / enjoy yourself?

185 JOAN: Nothing to start with for me, thank you.

NIJO: Yes, but I was very unhappy. / It hurt to remember the past.

MARLENE: And the wine list.

190 NIJO: I think that was repentance.

MARLENE: Well I wonder.

NIJO: I might have just been homesick.

MARLENE: Or angry.

NIJO: Not angry, no, / why angry?

195 GRET: Can we have some more bread?

MARLENE: Don't you get angry? I get angry.

NIJO: But what about?

MARLENE: Yes let's have two more Frascati. And some more bread, please. (*The*
200 *Waitress exits.*)

ISABELLA: I tried to understand Buddhism when I was in Japan but all this birth and death succeeding each other through eternities just filled me with the most
205 profound melancholy. I do like something more active.

NIJO: You couldn't say I was inactive. I walked every day for twenty years.

ISABELLA: I don't mean walking. / I mean in
210 the head.

NIJO: I vowed to copy five Mahayana sutras. / Do you know how long they are?

MARLENE: I don't think religious beliefs are something we have in common. Activity
215 yes. (*Gret empties the bread basket into her apron.*)

NIJO: My head was active. / My head ached.

JOAN: It's no good being active in heresy.

ISABELLA: What heresy? She's calling the
220 Church of England / a heresy.

JOAN: There are some very attractive / heresies.

NIJO: I had never heard of Christianity. Never / heard of it. Barbarians.

225 MARLENE: Well I'm not a Christian. / And I'm not a Buddhist.

ISABELLA: You have heard of it?

MARLENE: We don't all have to believe the same.

230 ISABELLA: I knew coming to dinner with a Pope we should keep off religion.

JOAN: I always enjoy a theological argument. But I won't try to convert you, I'm not a missionary. Anyway I'm a heresy
235 myself.

ISABELLA: There are some barbaric practices in the east.

NIJO: Barbaric?

ISABELLA: Among the lower classes.

240 NIJO: I wouldn't know.

ISABELLA: Well theology always made my head ache.

MARLENE: Oh good, some food. (*The Waitress brings the first course, serves it during the*
245 *following, then exits.*)

NIJO: How else could I have left the court if I wasn't a nun? When father died I had only His Majesty. So when I fell out of favor I had nothing. Religion is a kind of
250 nothing / and I dedicated what was left of me to nothing.

ISABELLA: That's what I mean about Buddhism. It doesn't brace.

MARLENE: Come on, Nijo, have some wine.

255 NIJO: Haven't you ever felt like that? You've all felt / like that. Nothing will ever happen again. I am dead already.

ISABELLA: You thought your life was over but it wasn't.

260 JOAN: You wish it was over.

GRET: Sad.

MARLENE: Yes, when I first came to London I sometimes . . . and when I got back from America I did. But only for a few hours.
265 Not twenty years.

ISABELLA: When I was forty I thought my life was over. / Oh I was pitiful. I was sent

NIJO: I didn't say I felt it for twenty years. Not every minute.

270 ISABELLA: on a cruise for my health and I felt even worse. Pains in my bones, pins and needles in my hands, swelling behind the ears, and—oh, stupidity. I shook all over, indefinable terror. And Australia seemed
275 to me a hideous country, the acacias stank like drains. / I

NIJO: You were homesick. (Gret steals a bottle of wine.)

ISABELLA: had a photograph taken for
280 Hennie but I told her I wouldn't send it, my hair had fallen out and my clothes were crooked, I looked completely insane and suicidal.

NIJO: So did I, exactly, dressed as a nun. / I
285 was wearing walking shoes for the first time.

ISABELLA: I longed to go home, / but home to what? Houses are so perfectly dismal.*

NIJO: I longed to go back ten years.

290 MARLENE: *I thought traveling cheered you both up.

ISABELLA: Oh it did / of course. It was on

NIJO: I'm not a cheerful person, Marlene. I just laugh a lot.

295 ISABELLA: the trip from Australia to the Sandwich Isles, I fell in love with the sea. There were rats in the cabin and ants in the food but suddenly it was like a new world. I woke up every morning happy,
300 knowing there would be nothing to annoy me. No nervousness. No dressing.

NIJO: Don't you like getting dressed? I adored my clothes. / When I was chosen

MARLENE: You had prettier colors than
305 Isabella.

NIJO: to give sake to His Majesty's brother, the Emperor Kameyana, on his formal visit, I wore raw silk pleated trousers and a seven-layered gown in shades of red,
310 and two outer garments, / yellow lined with green

MARLENE: Yes, all that silk must have been very—(The Waitress enters, clears the first course and exits.)

315 JOAN: I dressed as a boy when I left home.*

NIJO: and a light green jacket. Lady Betto had a five-layered gown in shades of green and purple.

ISABELLA: *You dressed as a boy?

320 MARLENE: Of course, / for safety.

JOAN: It was easy, I was only twelve. / Also women weren't allowed in the library. We wanted to study in Athens.

MARLENE: You ran away alone?

325 JOAN: No, not alone, I went with my friend. / He was

NIJO: Ah, an elopement.

JOAN: sixteen but I thought I knew more science than he did and almost as much
330 philosophy.

ISABELLA: Well I always traveled as a lady and I repudiated strongly any suggestion in the press that I was other than feminine.

335 MARLENE: I don't wear trousers in the office. / I could but I don't.

ISABELLA: There was no great danger to a woman of my age and appearance.

MARLENE: And you got away with it, Joan?

340 JOAN: I did then. (The Waitress brings in the main course.)

MARLENE: And nobody noticed anything?

JOAN: They noticed I was a very clever boy. / And

345 MARLENE: I couldn't have kept pretending for so long.

JOAN: when I shared a bed with my friend, that was ordinary—two poor students in a lodging house. I think I forgot I was
350 pretending.

ISABELLA: Rocky Mountain Jim, Mr. Nugent, showed me no disrespect. He found it interesting, I think, that I could make scones and also lasso cattle. Indeed he
355 declared his love for me, which was most distressing.

NIJO: What did he say? / We always sent poems first.

MARLENE: What did you say?

360 ISABELLA: I urged him to give up whiskey, / but he said it was too late.

MARLENE: Oh Isabella.

ISABELLA: He had lived alone in the mountains for many years.

365 MARLENE: But did you—? (The Waitress goes.)

ISABELLA: Mr. Nugent was a man that any woman might love but none could marry. I came back to England.

NIJO: Did you write him a poem when you
370 left? / Snow on the mountains. My sleeves

MARLENE: Did you never see him again?

ISABELLA: No, never.

NIJO: are wet with tears. In England no tears, no snow.

375 ISABELLA: Well, I say never. One morning very early in Switzerland, it was a year later, I had a vision of him as I last saw him / in his trapper's clothes with his

NIJO: A ghost!

380 ISABELLA: hair round his face, and that was the day, / I learned later, he died with a

NIJO: Ah!

ISABELLA: bullet in his brain. / He just bowed to me and vanished.

385 MARLENE: Oh Isabella.

NIJO: When your lover dies—One of my lovers died. / The priest Ariake.

JOAN: My friend died. Have we all got dead lovers?

390 MARLENE: Not me, sorry.

NIJO (to Isabella): I wasn't a nun, I was still at court, but he was a priest, and when he came to me he dedicated his whole life to hell. / He knew that when he died he
395 would fall into one of the three lower realms. And he died, he did die.

JOAN (to Marlene): I'd quarreled with him over the teachings of John the Scot, who held that our ignorance of God is the
400 same as his ignorance of himself. He only knows what he creates because he creates everything he knows but he himself is above being—do you follow?

MARLENE: No, but go on.

405 NIJO: I couldn't bear to think / in what shape would he be reborn.*

JOAN: St. Augustine maintained that the Neo-Platonic Ideas are indivisible

ISABELLA: *Buddhism is really most uncom-
410 fortable.

JOAN: from God, but I agreed with John that the created world is essences derived from Ideas which derived from God. As Denys the Areopagite said—the
415 pseudo-Denys—first we give God a name, then deny it, / then reconcile the contradiction

NIJO: In what shape would he return?

JOAN: by looking beyond / those terms—

420 MARLENE: Sorry, what? Denys said what?

JOAN: Well we disagreed about it, we quarreled. And next day he was ill, / I was so annoyed with him

NIJO: Misery in this life and worse in the
425 next, all because of me.

JOAN: all the time I was nursing him I kept going over the arguments in my mind. Matter is not a means of knowing the essence. The source of the species is the
430 Idea. But then I realized he'd never understand my arguments again, and that night he died. John the Scot held that the

individual disintegrates / and there is no personal immortality.

435 ISABELLA: I wouldn't have you think I was in love with Jim Nugent. It was yearning to save him that I felt.

MARLENE (*to Joan*): So what did you do?

JOAN: First I decided to stay a man. I was

440 used to it. And I wanted to devote my life to learning. Do you know why I went to Rome? Italian men didn't have beards.

ISABELLA: The loves of my life were Hennie, my own pet, and my dear husband the

445 doctor, who nursed Hennie in her last illness. I knew it would be terrible when Hennie died but I didn't know how terrible. I felt half of myself had gone. How could I go on my travels without that

450 sweet soul waiting at home for my letters? It was Doctor Bishop's devotion to her in her last illness that made me decide to marry him. He and Hennie had the same sweet character. I had not.

455 NIJO: I thought His Majesty had sweet character because when he found out about Ariake he was so kind. But really it was because he no longer cared for me. One night he even sent me out to a man

460 who had been pursuing me. / He lay awake on the other side of the screens and listened.

ISABELLA: I did wish marriage had seemed more of a step. I tried very hard to cope

465 with the ordinary drudgery of life. I was ill again with carbuncles on the spine and nervous prostration. I ordered a tricycle, that was my idea of adventure then. And John himself fell ill, with erysipelas and

470 anemia. I began to love him with my whole heart but it was too late. He was a skeleton with transparent white hands. I wheeled him on various seafronts in a bathchair. And he faded and left me.

475 There was nothing in my life. The doctors said I had gout / and my heart was much affected.

NIJO: There was nothing in my life, nothing, without the Emperor's favor. The Empress

480 had always been my enemy, Marlene, she said I had no right to wear three-layered gowns. / But I was the adopted daughter of my grandfather the Prime Minister. I had been publicly granted permission to

485 wear thin silk.

JOAN: There was nothing in my life except my studies. I was obsessed with pursuit of the truth. I taught at the Greek School in Rome, which St. Augustine had made

490 famous. I was poor, I worked hard, I spoke apparently brilliantly, I was still very young, I was a stranger, suddenly I was quite famous, I was everyone's favorite. Huge crowds came to hear me. The day

495 after they made me cardinal I fell ill and lay two weeks without speaking, full of terror and regret. / But then I got up determined to

MARLENE: Yes, success is very . . .

500 JOAN: go on. I was seized again / with a desperate longing for the absolute.

ISABELLA: Yes, yes, to go on. I sat in Tobermory among Hennie's flowers and sewed a complete outfit in Jaeger flannel. /

505 I was fifty-six years old.

NIJO: Out of favor but I didn't die. I left on foot, nobody saw me go. For the next twenty years I walked through Japan.

GRET: Walking is good. (*Meanwhile, the*

510 *Waitress enters, pours lots of wine, then shows Marlene the empty bottle.*)

JOAN: Pope Leo died and I was chosen. All right then. I would be Pope. I would know God. I would know everything.

515 ISABELLA: I determined to leave my grief behind and set off for Tibet.

MARLENE: Magnificent all of you. We need some more wine, please, two bottles

I think, Griselda isn't even here yet, and I
520 want to drink a toast to you all. (*The
Waitress exits.*)

ISABELLA: To yourself surely, / we're here to
celebrate your success.

NIJO: Yes, Marlene.

525 JOAN: Yes, what is it exactly, Marlene?

MARLENE: Well it's not Pope but it is managing director.*

JOAN: And you find work for people.

MARLENE: Yes, an employment agency.

530 NIJO: *Over all the women you work with.
And the men.

ISABELLA: And very well deserved too. I'm
sure it's just the beginning of something
extraordinary.

535 MARLENE: Well it's worth a party.

ISABELLA: To Marlene.*

MARLENE: And all of us.

JOAN: *Marlene.

NIJO: Marlene.

540 GRET: Marlene.

MARLENE: We've all come a long way. To our
courage and the way we changed our lives
and our extraordinary achievements. (*They
laugh and drink a toast.*)

545 ISABELLA: Such adventures. We were crossing a mountain pass at seven thousand
feet, the cook was all to pieces, the mule-
teers suffered fever and snow blindness.
But even though my spine was agony I
550 managed very well.*

MARLENE: Wonderful.

NIJO: *Once I was ill for four months lying
alone at an inn. Nobody to offer a horse
to Buddha. I had to live for myself, and I
555 did live.

ISABELLA: Of course you did. It was far worse
returning to Tobermory. I always felt dull
when I was stationary. / That's why I could
never stay anywhere.

560 NIJO: Yes, that's it exactly. New sights. The
shrine by the beach, the moon shining on

the sea. The goddess had vowed to save
all living things. / She would even save the
fishes. I was full of hope.

565 JOAN: I had thought the Pope would know
everything. I thought God would speak to
me directly. But of course he knew I was a
woman.

MARLENE: But nobody else even suspected?

570 (*The Waitress brings more wine and then
exits.*)

JOAN: In the end I did take a lover again.*

ISABELLA: In the Vatican?

GRET: *Keep you warm.

575 NIJO: *Ah, lover.

MARLENE: *Good for you.

JOAN: He was one of my chamberlains.
There are such a lot of servants when
you're Pope. The food's very good. And I
580 realized I did know the truth. Because
whatever the Pope says, that's true.

NIJO: What was he like, the chamberlain?*

GRET: Big cock.

ISABELLA: Oh, Gret.

585 MARLENE: *Did he fancy you when he
thought you were a fella?

NIJO: What was he like?

JOAN: He could keep a secret.

MARLENE: So you did know everything.

590 JOAN: Yes, I enjoyed being Pope. I consecrated bishops and let people kiss my
feet. I received the King of England
when he came to submit to the church.
Unfortunately there were earthquakes,
595 and some village reported it had rained
blood, and in France there was a plague
of giant grasshoppers, but I don't think
that can have been my fault, do you?*
(*Laughter.*) The grasshoppers fell on the
600 English Channel / and were washed up
on shore.

NIJO: I once went to sea. It was very lonely.
I realized it made very little difference
where I went.

605 JOAN: and their bodies rotted and poisoned the air and everyone in those parts died. (*Laughter.*)

ISABELLA: *Such superstition! I was nearly murdered in China by a howling mob.

610 They thought the barbarians ate babies and put them under railway sleepers to make the tracks steady, and ground up their eyes to make the lenses of cameras. / So they were shouting,

615 MARLENE: And you had a camera!

ISABELLA: "Child-eater, child-eater." Some people tried to sell girl babies to Europeans for cameras or stew! (*Laughter.*)

MARLENE: So apart from the grasshoppers it

620 was a great success.

JOAN: Yes, if it hadn't been for the baby I expect I'd have lived to an old age like Theodora of Alexandria, who lived as a monk. She was accused by a girl / who fell

625 in love with her of being the father of her child and—

NIJO: But tell us what happened to your baby. I had some babies.

MARLENE: Didn't you think of getting rid of it?

630 JOAN: Wouldn't that be a worse sin than having it? / But a Pope with a child was about as bad as possible.

MARLENE: I don't know, you're the Pope.

JOAN: But I wouldn't have known how to get

635 rid of it.

MARLENE: Other Popes had children, surely.

JOAN: They didn't give birth to them.

NIJO: Well you were a woman.

JOAN: Exactly and I shouldn't have been a

640 woman. Women, children, and lunatics can't be Pope.

MARLENE: So the only thing to do / was to get rid of it somehow.

NIJO: You had to have it adopted secretly.

645 JOAN: But I didn't know what was happening. I thought I was getting fatter, but then I was eating more and sitting about, the

life of a Pope is quite luxurious. I don't think I'd spoken to a woman since I was

650 twelve. The chamberlain was the one who realized.

MARLENE: And by then it was too late.

JOAN: Oh I didn't want to pay attention. It was easier to do nothing.

655 NIJO: But you had to plan for having it. You had to say you were ill and go away.

JOAN: That's what I should have done I suppose.

MARLENE: Did you want them to find out?

660 NIJO: I too was often in embarrassing situations, there's no need for a scandal. My first child was His Majesty's, which unfortunately died, but my second was Akebono's. I was seventeen. He was in love with me

665 when I was thirteen, he was very upset when I had to go the Emperor, it was very romantic, a lot of poems. Now His Majesty hadn't been near me for two months so he thought I was four months pregnant

670 when I was really six, so when I reached the ninth month / I announced I was seriously ill,

JOAN: I never knew what month it was.

NIJO: and Akebono announced he had gone

675 on a religious retreat. He held me round the waist and lifted me up as the baby was born. He cut the cord with a short sword, wrapped the baby in white and took it away. It was only a girl but I was sorry to

680 lose it. Then I told the Emperor that the baby had miscarried because of my illness, and there you are. The danger was past.

JOAN: But, Nijo, I wasn't used to having a woman's body.

685 ISABELLA: So what happened?

JOAN: I didn't know of course that it was near the time. It was Rogation Day, there was always a procession. I was on the horse dressed in my robes and a cross

690 was carried in front of me, and all the

cardinals were following, and all the
clergy of Rome, and a huge crowd of
people. / We set off from St. Peter's to go

MARLENE: Total Pope. (*Gret pours the wine and*
695   *steals the bottle.*)

JOAN: to St. John's. I had felt a slight pain
earlier, I thought it was something I'd
eaten, and then it came back, and came
back more often. I thought when this is
700   over I'll go to bed. There were still long
gaps when I felt perfectly all right and I
didn't want to attract attention to myself
and spoil the ceremony. Then I suddenly
realized what it must be. I had to last out
705   till I could get home and hide. Then something changed, my breath started to catch,
I couldn't plan things properly anymore.
We were in a little street that goes between
St. Clement's and the Colosseum, and I
710   just had to get off the horse and sit down
for a minute. Great waves of pressure were
going through my body, I heard sounds
like a cow lowing, they came out of my
mouth. Far away I heard people scream-
715   ing, "The Pope is ill, the Pope is dying."
And the baby just slid out on to the road.*

MARLENE: The cardinals / won't have known
where to put themselves.

NIJO: Oh dear, Joan, what a thing to do! In
720   the street!

ISABELLA: *How embarrassing.

GRET: In a field, yah. (*They are laughing.*)

JOAN: One of the cardinals said, "The
Antichrist!" and fell over in a faint. (*They*
725   *all laugh.*)

MARLENE: So what did they do? They weren't
best pleased.

JOAN: They took me by the feet and dragged
me out of town and stoned me to death.
730   (*They stop laughing.*)

MARLENE: Joan, how horrible.

JOAN: I don't really remember.

NIJO: And the child died too?

JOAN: Oh yes, I think so, yes. (*The Waitress*
735   *enters to clear the plates. Pause. They start*
talking very quietly.)

ISABELLA (*to Joan*): I never had any children.
I was very fond of horses.

NIJO (*to Marlene*): I saw my daughter once.
740   She was three years old. She wore a plum-
red / small sleeved gown. Akebono's wife

ISABELLA: Birdie was my favorite. A little
Indian bay mare I rode in the Rocky
Mountains.

745 **NIJO:** had taken the child because her own
died. Everyone thought I was just a visitor.
She was being brought up carefully so she
could be sent to the palace like I was. (*Gret*
steals her empty plate.)

750 **ISABELLA:** Legs of iron and always cheerful,
and such a pretty face. If a stranger led
her she reared up like a bronco.

NIJO: I never saw my third child after he was
born, the son of Ariake the priest. Ariake
755   held him on his lap the day he was born
and talked to him as if he could understand, and cried. My fourth child was
Ariake's too. Ariake died before he was
born. I didn't want to see anyone, I stayed
760   alone in the hills. It was a boy again, my
third son. But oddly enough I felt nothing
for him.

MARLENE: How many children did you have,
Gret?

765 **GRET:** Ten.

ISABELLA: Whenever I came back to England
I felt I had so much to atone for. Hennie
and John were so good. I did no good in
my life. I spent years in self-gratification.
770   So I hurled myself into committees, I
nursed the people of Tobermory in the
epidemic of influenza, I lectured the
Young Women's Christian Association on
Thrift. I talked and talked explaining how

775 the East was corrupt and vicious. My travels must do good to someone besides myself. I wore myself out with good causes.

MARLENE (*pause*): Oh God, why are we all so
780 miserable?

JOAN (*pause*): The procession never went down that street again.

MARLENE: They rerouted it specially?

JOAN: Yes they had to go all round to avoid
785 it. And they introduced a pierced chair.

MARLENE: A pierced chair?

JOAN: Yes, a chair made out of solid marble with a hole in the seat / and it was

MARLENE: You're not serious.

790 JOAN: in the Chapel of the Savior, and after he was elected the Pope had to sit in it.

MARLENE: And someone looked up his skirts? / Not really!

ISABELLA: What an extraordinary thing.

795 JOAN: Two of the clergy / made sure he was a man.

NIJO: On their hands and knees!

MARLENE: A pierced chair!

GRET: Balls! (*Griselda arrives unnoticed.*)

800 NIJO: Why couldn't he just pull up his robe?

JOAN: He had to sit there and look dignified.

MARLENE: You could have made all your chamberlains sit in it.*

GRET: Big one. Small one.

805 NIJO: Very useful chair at court.

ISABELLA: *Or the Laird of Tobermory in his kilt. (*They are quite drunk. They get the giggles. Marlene notices Griselda and gets up to welcome her. The others go on talking and
810 laughing. Gret crosses to Joan and Isabella and pours them wine from her stolen bottles. The Waitress gives out the menus.*)

MARLENE: Griselda! / There you are. Do you want to eat?

815 GRISELDA: I'm sorry I'm so late. No, no, don't bother.

MARLENE: Of course it's no bother. / Have you eaten?

GRISELDA: No really, I'm not hungry.

820 MARLENE: Well have some pudding.

GRISELDA: I never eat pudding.

MARLENE: Griselda, I hope you're not anorexic. We're having pudding, I am, and getting nice and fat.

825 GRISELDA: Oh if everyone is. I don't mind.

MARLENE: Now who do you know? This is Joan who was Pope in the ninth century, and Isabella Bird, the Victorian traveler, and Lady Nijo from Japan, Emperor's
830 concubine and Buddhist nun, thirteenth century, nearer your own time, and Gret who was painted by Brueghel. Griselda's in Boccaccio and Petrarch and Chaucer because of her extraordinary marriage.
835 I'd like profiteroles because they're disgusting.

JOAN: Zabaglione, please.

ISABELLA: Apple pie / and cream.

NIJO: What's this?

840 MARLENE: Zabaglione, it's Italian, it's what Joan's having, / it's delicious.

NIJO: A Roman Catholic / dessert? Yes please.

MARLENE: Gret?

845 GRET: Cake.

GRISELDA: Just cheese and biscuits, thank you. (*The Waitress exits.*)

MARLENE: Yes, Griselda's life is like a fairy story, except it starts with marrying the
850 prince.

GRISELDA: He's only a marquis, Marlene.

MARLENE: Well everyone for miles around is his liege and he'd absolute lord of life and death and you were the poor but beautiful
855 peasant girl and he whisked you off. / Near enough a prince.

NIJO: How old were you?

GRISELDA: Fifteen.

NIJO: I was brought up in court circles and it
860   was still a shock. Had you ever seen him
before?

GRISELDA: I'd seen him riding by, we all had.
And he'd seen me in the fields with the
sheep.*

865 ISABELLA: I would have been well suited to
minding sheep.

NIJO: And Mr. Nugent riding by.

ISABELLA: Of course not, Nijo, I mean a
healthy life in the open air.

870 JOAN: *He just rode up while you were
minding the sheep and asked you to
marry him?

GRISELDA: No, no, it was on the wedding
day. I was waiting outside the door to
875   see the procession. Everyone wanted
him to get married so there'd be an heir
to look after us when he died, / and at
last he

MARLENE: I don't think Walter wanted to get
880   married. It is Walter? Yes.

GRISELDA: announced a day for the wedding
but nobody knew who the bride was, we
thought it must be a foreign princess, we
were longing to see her. Then the carriage
885   stopped outside our cottage and we
couldn't see the bride anywhere. And he
came and spoke to my father.

NIJO: And your father told you to serve the
Prince.

890 GRISELDA: My father could hardly speak. The
Marquis said it wasn't an order, I could
say no, but if I said yes I must always obey
him in everything.

MARLENE: That's when you should have
895   suspected.

GRISELDA: But of course a wife must obey
her husband. / And of course I must obey
the Marquis.*

ISABELLA: I swore to obey dear John, of
900   course, but it didn't seem to arise.

Naturally I wouldn't have wanted to go
abroad while I was married.

MARLENE: *Then why bother to mention it at
all? He'd got a thing about it, that's why.

905 GRISELDA: I'd rather obey the Marquis than a
boy from the village.

MARLENE: Yes, that's a point.

JOAN: I never obeyed anyone. They all
obeyed me.

910 NIJO: And what did you wear? He didn't
make you get married in your own
clothes? That would be perverse.*

MARLENE: Oh, you wait.

GRISELDA: *He had ladies with him who
915   undressed me and they had a white silk
dress and jewels for my hair.

MARLENE: And at first he seemed perfectly
normal?

GRISELDA: Marlene, you're always so critical
920   of him. / Of course he was normal, he was
very kind.

MARLENE: But, Griselda, come on, he took
your baby.

GRISELDA: Walter found it hard to believe I
925   loved him. He couldn't believe I would
always obey him. He had to prove it.

MARLENE: I don't think Walter likes women.

GRISELDA: I'm sure he loved me, Marlene, all
the time.

930 MARLENE: He just had a funny way / of
showing it.

GRISELDA: It was hard for him too.

JOAN: How do you mean he took away your
baby?

935 NIJO: Was it a boy?

GRISELDA: No, the first one was a girl.

NIJO: Even so it's hard when they take it
away. Did you see it at all?

GRISELDA: Oh yes, she was six weeks old.

940 NIJO: Much better to do it straight away.

ISABELLA: But why did your husband take
the child?

GRISELDA: He said all the people hated me because I was just one of them. And now I had a child they were restless. So he had to get rid of the child to keep them quiet. But he said he wouldn't snatch her, I had to agree and obey and give her up. So when I was feeding her a man came in and took her away. I thought he was going to kill her even before he was out of the room.

MARLENE: But you let him take her? You didn't struggle?

GRISELDA: I asked him to give her back so I could kiss her. And I asked him to bury her where no animals could dig her up. / It was Walter's child to do what he

ISABELLA: Oh, my dear.

GRISELDA: liked with.*

MARLENE: Walter was bonkers.

GRET: Bastard.

ISABELLA: *But surely, murder.

GRISELDA: I had promised.

MARLENE: I can't stand this. I'm going for a pee. (*Marlene goes out. The Waitress brings the dessert, serves it during the following, then exits.*)

NIJO: No, I understand. Of course you had to, he was your life. And were you in favor after that?

GRISELDA: Oh yes, we were very happy together. We never spoke about what had happened.

ISABELLA: I can see you were doing what you thought was your duty. But didn't it make you ill?

GRISELDA: No, I was very well, thank you.

NIJO: And you had another child?

GRISELDA: Not for four years, but then I did, yes, a boy.

NIJO: Ah a boy. / So it all ended happily.

GRISELDA: Yes he was pleased. I kept my son till he was two years old. A peasant's grandson. It made the people angry. Walter explained.

ISABELLA: But surely he wouldn't kill his children / just because—

GRISELDA: Oh it wasn't true. Walter would never give in to the people. He wanted to see if I loved him enough.

JOAN: He killed his children / to see if you loved him enough?

NIJO: Was it easier the second time or harder?

GRISELDA: It was always easy because I always knew I would do what he said. (*Pause. They start to eat.*)

ISABELLA: I hope you didn't have any more children.

GRISELDA: Oh no, no more. It was twelve years till he tested me again.

ISABELLA: So whatever did he do this time? / My poor John, I never loved him enough, and he would never have dreamt . . .

GRISELDA: He sent me away. He said the people wanted him to marry someone else who'd give him an heir and he'd got special permission from the Pope. So I said I'd go home to my father. I came with nothing / so I went with nothing. I took

NIJO: Better to leave if your master doesn't want you.

GRISELDA: off my clothes. He let me keep a slip so he wouldn't be shamed. And I walked home barefoot. My father came out in tears. Everyone was crying except me.

NIJO: At least your father wasn't dead. / I had nobody.

ISABELLA: Well it can be a relief to come home. I loved to see Hennie's sweet face again.

GRISELDA: Oh yes, I was perfectly content. And quite soon he sent for me again.

JOAN: I don't think I would have gone.

GRISELDA: But he told me to come. I had to obey him. He wanted me to help prepare his wedding. He was getting married to a

1030   young girl from France / and nobody except me knew how to arrange things the way he liked them.

NIJO: It's always hard taking him another woman. (*Marlene comes back.*)

1035   JOAN: I didn't live a woman's life. I don't understand it.

GRISELDA: The girl was sixteen and far more beautiful than me. I could see why he loved her. / She had her younger brother

1040   with her as a page. (*The Waitress enters.*)

MARLENE: Oh God, I can't bear it. I want some coffee. Six coffees. Six brandies. / Double brandies. Straightaway. (*The Waitress exits.*)

1045   GRISELDA: They all went into the feast I'd prepared. And he stayed behind and put his arms round me and kissed me. / I felt half asleep with the shock.

NIJO: Oh, like a dream.

1050   MARLENE: And he said, "This is your daughter and your son."

GRISELDA: Yes.

JOAN: What?

NIJO: Oh. Oh I see. You got them back.

1055   ISABELLA: I did think it was remarkably barbaric to kill them but you learn not to say anything. / So he had them brought up secretly I suppose.

MARLENE: Walter's a monster. Weren't you

1060   angry? What did you do?

GRISELDA: Well I fainted. Then I cried and kissed the children. / Everyone was making a fuss of me.

NIJO: But did you feel anything for them?

1065   GRISELDA: What?

NIJO: Did you feel anything for the children?

GRISELDA: Of course, I loved them.

JOAN: So you forgave him and lived with him?

GRISELDA: He suffered so much all those

1070   years.

ISABELLA: Hennie had the same sweet nature.

NIJO: So they dressed you again?

GRISELDA: Cloth of gold.

JOAN: I can't forgive anything.

1075   MARLENE: You really are exceptional, Griselda.

NIJO: Nobody gave me back my children. (*She cries.*) (*The Waitress brings the brandies and then exits. During the following, Joan goes to Nijo.*)

1080   ISABELLA: I can never be like Hennie. I was always so busy in England, a kind of business I detested. The very presence of people exhausted my emotional reserves. I could not be like Hennie however I tried.

1085   I tried and was as ill as could be. The doctor suggested a steel net to support my head, the weight of my own head was too much for my diseased spine. It is dangerous to put oneself in depressing

1090   circumstances. Why should I do it?

JOAN (*to Nijo*):   Don't cry.

NIJO: My father and the Emperor both died in the autumn. So much pain.

JOAN: Yes, but don't cry.

1095   NIJO: They wouldn't let me into the palace when he was dying. I hid in the room with his coffin, then I couldn't find where I'd left my shoes, I ran after the funeral procession in bare feet, I couldn't keep up.

1100   When I got there it was over, a few wisps of smoke in the sky, that's all that was left of him. What I want to know is, if I'd still been at court, would I have been allowed to wear full mourning?

1105   MARLENE: I'm sure you would.

NIJO: Why do you say that? You don't know anything about it. Would I have been allowed to wear full mourning?

ISABELLA: How can people live in this dim

1110   pale island and wear our hideous

clothes? I cannot and will not live the life of a lady.

NIJO: I'll tell you something that made me angry. I was eighteen, at the Full Moon Ceremony. They make a special rice gruel and stir it with their sticks, and then they beat their women across the loins so they'll have sons and not daughters. So the Emperor beat us all / very hard as

MARLENE: What a sod. (*The Waitress enters with the coffees.*)

NIJO: usual—that's not it, Marlene, that's normal, what made us angry he told his attendants they could beat us too. Well they had a wonderful time. / So Lady Genki and I made a plan, and the ladies

MARLENE: I'd like another brandy, please. Better make it six. (*The Waitress exits.*)

NIJO: all hid in his rooms, and Lady Mashimizu stood guard with a stick at the door, and when His Majesty came in Genki seized him and I beat him till he cried out and promised he would never order anyone to hit us again. Afterward there was a terrible fuss. The nobles were horrified. "We wouldn't even dream of stepping on Your Majesty's shadow." And I had hit him with a stick. Yes, I hit him with a stick. (*The Waitress brings the brandy bottle and tops up the glasses. Joan crosses in front of the table and back to her place while drunkenly reciting:*)

JOAN: Suave, mari magno turantibus aequora ventis, e terra magnum alterius spectare laborem; non quia vexari quemquamst iucunda voluptas, sed quibus ipse malis careas quia cernere suave est. Suave etiam belli certamina magna tueri per campos instructa tua sine parse pericli. Sed nil dulcius est, bene quam munita tenere edita doctrine sapientum temple serena, / despicere uncle queas alios passimque videre errare atque viam palantis quaerere vitae,

GRISELDA: I do think—I do wonder—it would have been nicer if Walter hadn't had to.

ISABELLA: Why should I? Why should I?

MARLENE: Of course not.

NIJO: I hit him with a stick.

JOAN: certare ingenio, contendere nobilitate, noctes atque dies niti praestante labore ad summas emergere opes rerumque potiri. O miseras hominum mentis, / o pectora caeca![2*]

ISABELLA: O miseras!

NIJO: *Pectora caeca!

JOAN: qualibus in tenebris vitae quantisque periclis degitur hoc aevi quodcumquest! / none videre nil aliud sibi naturam latrare, nisi utqui corpore seiunctus dolor absit, mente fruatur[3] . . . (*She subsides.*)

GRET: We come to hell through a big mouth. Hell's black and red. / It's

MARLENE (*to Joan*): Shut up, pet.

---

[2]**1144–1164. Suave, . . . o pectora caeca!:** Joan's speech is from the Second Book of *On the Nature of Things* by Titus Lucretius Carus (97?–54 B.C.), the Latin poet and philosopher. The following translation of the passage is by Cyril Bailey: Sweet it is, when on the great sea the winds are buffeting the waters, to gaze from the land on another's great struggles; not because it is pleasure or joy that any one should be distressed, but because it is sweet to perceive from what misfortune you yourself are free. Sweet is it too, to behold great contests of war in full array over the plains, when you have no part in the danger. But nothing is more gladdening than to dwell in the calm high places, firmly embattled on the heights by the teaching of the wise, whence you can look down on others, and see them wandering hither and thither, going astray as they seek the way of life, in strife matching their wits or rival claims of birth, struggling night and day by surpassing effort to rise up to the height of power and gain possession of the world. Ah! miserable minds of men, blind hearts!

[3]**1168–1172. qualibus . . . fruatur:** In what darkness of life, in what great dangers ye spend this little span of years! to think that ye should not see that nature cries aloud for nothing else but that pain may be kept far sundered from the body, and that, withdrawn from care and fear, she may enjoy in mind the sense of pleasure!

1175 GRISELDA: Hush, please.

ISABELLA: Listen, she's been to hell.

GRET: like the village where I come from. There's a river and a bridge and houses. There's places on fire like when the

1180 soldiers come. There's a big devil sat on a roof with a big hole in his arse and he's scooping stuff out of it with a big ladle and it's falling down on us, and it's money, so a lot of the women stop and get some.

1185 But most of us is fighting the devils. There's lots of little devils, our size, and we get them down all right and give them a beating. There's lots of funny creatures round your feet, you don't like to look, like

1190 rats and lizards, and nasty things, a bum with a face, and fish with legs, and faces on things that don't have faces on. But they don't hurt, you just keep going. Well we'd had worse, you see, we'd had the

1195 Spanish. We'd all had family killed. My big son die on a wheel. Birds eat him. My baby, a soldier run her through with a sword. I'd had enough, I was mad, I hate the bastards. I come out of my front door

1200 that morning and shout till my neighbors come out and I said, "Come on, we're going where the evil come from and pay the bastards out." And they all come out just as they was / from baking or

1205 NIJO: All the ladies come.

GRET: washing in their aprons, and we push down the street and the ground opens up and we go through a big mouth into a street just like ours but in hell. I've got a

1210 sword in my hand from somewhere and I fill a basket with gold cups they drink out of down there. You just keep running on and fighting, / you didn't stop for nothing. Oh we give them devils such

1215 a beating.*

NIJO: Take that, take that.

JOAN: *Something something something mortisque timores tum vacuum pectus[4]— damn. Quod si ridicula—something

1220 something on and on and on and something splendorem purpureai.

ISABELLA: I thought I would have a last jaunt up the west river in China. Why not? But the doctors were so very grave I just went

1225 to Morocco. The sea was so wild I had to be landed by ship's crane in a coal bucket. / My horse was a terror to me, a powerful black charger.

GRET: Coal bucket good.

1230 JOAN: nos in luce timemus
    something
    terrorem[5] (*Nijo is laughing and crying. Joan gets up and is sick. Griselda looks after her.*)

GRISELDA: Can I have some water, please?

1235 (*The Waitress exits.*)

ISABELLA: So off I went to visit the Berber sheikhs in full blue trousers and great brass spurs. I was the only European woman ever to have seen the Emperor of

1240 Morocco. I was (*the Waitress brings the water*) seventy years old. What lengths to go to for a last chance of joy. I knew my return of vigor was only temporary, but how marvelous while it lasted.

---

[4]**1217–1218. Something . . . pectus:** Fragments from Lucretius meaning "the dread of death leaves your heart empty . . ."
[5]**1219–1221, 1230–1231. Quod . . . purpureai. . . . nos in luce . . . terrorem:** Fragments from the following passage by Lucretius: But if we see that these thoughts are mere mirth and mockery, and in very truth the fears of men and the cares that dog them fear not the clash of arms nor the weapons of war, but pass boldly among kings and lords of the world, nor dread the glitter that comes from gold nor the bright sheen of the purple robe, can you doubt that all such power belongs to reason alone, above all when the whole of life is but a struggle in darkness? For even as children tremble and fear everything in blinding darkness, so we sometimes dread in the light things that are no whit more to be feared than what children shudder at in the dark.

SCENE ii

(*"Top Girls" Employment Agency. Monday morning. The lights come up on Marlene and Jeanine.*)

MARLENE: Right, Jeanine, you are Jeanine aren't you? Let's have a look. O's and A's.[1] / No A's, all those

JEANINE: Six O's.

5 MARLENE: O's you probably could have got an A. / Speeds, not brilliant, not too bad.

JEANINE: I wanted to go to work.

MARLENE: Well, Jeanine, what's your present job like?

10 JEANINE: I'm a secretary.

MARLENE: Secretary or typist?

JEANINE: I did start as a typist but the last six months I've been a secretary.

MARLENE: To?

15 JEANINE: To three of them, really, they share me. There's Mr. Ashford, he's the office manager, and Mr. Philly / is sales, and—

MARLENE: Quite a small place?

JEANINE: A bit small.

20 MARLENE: Friendly?

JEANINE: Oh it's friendly enough.

MARLENE: Prospects?

JEANINE: I don't think so, that's the trouble. Miss Lewis is secretary to the managing

25 director and she's been there forever, and Mrs. Bradford / is—

MARLENE: So you want a job with better prospects?

JEANINE: I want a change.

30 MARLENE: So you'll take anything comparable?

JEANINE: No, I do want prospects. I want more money.

MARLENE: You're getting—?

35 JEANINE: Hundred.

MARLENE: It's not bad you know. You're what? Twenty?

JEANINE: I'm saving to get married.

MARLENE: Does that mean you don't want a 40 long-term job, Jeanine?

JEANINE: I might do.

MARLENE: Because where do the prospects come in? No kids for a bit?

JEANINE: Oh no, not kids, not yet.

45 MARLENE: So you won't tell them you're getting married?

JEANINE: Had I better not?

MARLENE: It would probably help.

JEANINE: I'm not wearing a ring. We thought 50 we wouldn't spend on a ring.

MARLENE: Saves taking it off.

JEANINE: I wouldn't take it off.

MARLENE: There's no need to mention it when you go for an interview. / Now, 55 Jeanine, do you have a feel

JEANINE: But what if they ask?

MARLENE: for any particular kind of company?

JEANINE: I thought advertising.

60 MARLENE: People often do think advertising. I have got a few vacancies but I think they're looking for something glossier.

JEANINE: You mean how I dress? / I can

65 MARLENE: I mean experience.

JEANINE: dress different. I dress like this on purpose for where I am now.

MARLENE: I have a marketing department here of a knitwear manufacturer. / 70 Marketing is near enough

JEANINE: Knitwear?

MARLENE: advertising. Secretary to the marketing manager, he's thirty-five,

---

[1]**2. O's and A's:** O-level and A-level examinations in the British education system. An O-level is a public examination for secondary-school students testing basic knowledge in various subjects; it is required before advancement to more specialized courses of study. A-level exams require advanced knowledge in a subject and are taken at the end of secondary school, usually two years after O-levels.

married, I've sent him a girl before and
75 she was happy, left to have a baby, you
won't want to mention marriage there.
He's very fair I think, good at his job, you
won't have to nurse him along. Hundred
and ten, so that's better than you're doing
80 now.

JEANINE: I don't know.

MARLENE: I've a fairly small concern here,
father and two sons, you'd have more say
potentially, secretarial and reception
85 duties, only a hundred but the job's going
to grow with the concern and then you'll
be in at the top with new girls coming in
underneath you.

JEANINE: What is it they do?

90 **MARLENE:** Lampshades. / This would be my
first choice for you.

JEANINE: Just lampshades?

MARLENE: There's plenty of different kinds
of lampshade. So we'll send you there,
95 shall we, and the knitwear second choice.
Are you free to go for an interview any day
they call you?

JEANINE: I'd like to travel.

MARLENE: We don't have any foreign clients.
100 You'd have to go elsewhere.

JEANINE: Yes I know. I don't really . . . I just
mean . . .

MARLENE: Does your fiancé want to travel?

JEANINE: I'd like a job where I was here in
105 London and with him and everything but
now and then—I expect it's silly. Are there
jobs like that?

MARLENE: There's personal assistant to a
top executive in a multinational. If that's
110 the idea you need to be planning ahead.
Is that where you want to be in ten
years?

JEANINE: I might not be alive in ten years.

MARLENE: Yes but you will be. You'll have
115 children.

JEANINE: I can't think about ten years.

MARLENE: You haven't got the speeds
anyway. So I'll send you to these two
shall I? You haven't been to any other
120 agency? Just so we don't get crossed
wires. Now, Jeanine, I want you to get
one of these jobs, all right? If I send you
that means I'm putting myself on the
line for you. Your presentation's OK, you
125 look fine, just be confident and go in
there convinced that this is the best job
for you and you're the best person for
the job. If you don't believe it they won't
believe it.

130 **JEANINE:** Do you believe it?

MARLENE: I think you could make me believe
it if you put your mind to it.

JEANINE: Yes, all right.

SCENE iii

*(Joyce's backyard. Sunday afternoon. The house
with a back door is upstage. Downstage is a shelter made of junk, made by children. The lights
come up on two girls, Angie and Kit, who are
squashed together in the shelter. Angie is sixteen,
Kit is twelve. They cannot be seen from the
house.)*

JOYCE *(off, calling from the house):* Angie.
Angie, are you out there? *(Silence. They keep
still and wait. When nothing else happens
they relax.)*

5 **ANGIE:** Wish she was dead.

KIT: Wanna watch *The Exterminator?*

ANGIE: You're sitting on my leg.

KIT: There's nothing on telly. We can have
an ice cream. Angie?

10 **ANGIE:** Shall I tell you something?

KIT: Do you wanna watch *The Exterminator?*

ANGIE: It's X, innit?

KIT: I can get into Xs.

ANGIE: Shall I tell you something?

15 **KIT:** We'll go to something else. We'll go to
Ipswich. What's on the Odeon?

ANGIE: She won't let me, will she.

KIT: Don't tell her.

ANGIE: I've no money.

20 **KIT:** I'll pay.

ANGIE: She'll moan though, won't she.

KIT: I'll ask her for you if you like.

ANGIE: I've no money, I don't want you to pay.

KIT: I'll ask her.

25 **ANGIE:** She don't like you.

KIT: I still got three pounds birthday money. Did she say she don't like me? I'll go by myself then.

ANGIE: Your mum don't let you. I got to take

30 you.

KIT: She won't know.

ANGIE: You'd be scared who'd sit next to you.

KIT: No I wouldn't. She does like me anyway. Tell me then.

35 **ANGIE:** Tell you what?

KIT: It's you she doesn't like.

ANGIE: Well I don't like her so tough shit.

JOYCE (*off*): Angie. Angie. Angie. I know you're out there. I'm not coming out after

40 you. You come in here. (*Silence. Nothing happens.*)

ANGIE: Last night when I was in bed. I been thinking yesterday could I make things move. You know, make things move by

45 thinking about them without touching them. Last night I was in bed and suddenly a picture fell down off the wall.

KIT: What picture?

ANGIE: My gran, that picture. Not the poster.

50 The photograph in the frame.

KIT: Had you done something to make it fall down?

ANGIE: I must have done.

KIT: But were you thinking about it?

55 **ANGIE:** Not about it, but about something.

KIT: I don't think that's very good.

ANGIE: You know the kitten?

KIT: Which one?

ANGIE: There only is one. The dead one.

60 **KIT:** What about it?

ANGIE: I heard it last night.

KIT: Where?

ANGIE: Out here. In the dark. What if I left you here in the dark all night?

65 **KIT:** You couldn't. I'd go home.

ANGIE: You couldn't.

KIT: I'd / go home.

ANGIE: No you couldn't, not if I said.

KIT: I could.

70 **ANGIE:** Then you wouldn't see anything. You'd just be ignorant.

KIT: I can see in the daytime.

ANGIE: No you can't. You can't hear it in the daytime.

75 **KIT:** I don't want to hear it.

ANGIE: You're scared that's all.

KIT: I'm not scared of anything.

ANGIE: You're scared of blood.

KIT: It's not the same kitten anyway. You

80 just heard an old cat, / you just heard some old cat.

ANGIE: You don't know what I heard. Or what I saw. You don't know nothing because you're a baby.

85 **KIT:** You're sitting on me.

ANGIE: Mind my hair / you silly cunt°.

KIT: Stupid f***ing cow, I hate you.

ANGIE: I don't care if you do.

KIT: You're horrible.

90 **ANGIE:** I'm going to kill my mother and you're going to watch.

KIT: I'm not playing.

ANGIE: You're scared of blood. (*Kit puts her hand under dress, brings it out with blood on*

95 *her finger.*)

KIT: There, see, I got my own blood, so. (*Angie takes Kit's hand and licks her finger.*)

ANGIE: Now I'm a cannibal. I might turn into a vampire now.

°A misogynistic term that carries harsher connotations in the U.S. than in the U.K., where the play takes place.—Eds.

100   **KIT:** That picture wasn't nailed up right.

     ANGIE: You'll have to do that when I get mine.

     KIT: I don't have to.

     ANGIE: You're scared.

105   **KIT:** I'll do it, I might do it. I don't have to just because you say. I'll be sick on you.

     ANGIE: I don't care if you are sick on me, I don't mind sick. I don't mind blood. If I don't get away from here I'm going

110   to die.

     KIT: I'm going home.

     ANGIE: You can't go through the house. She'll see you.

     KIT: I won't tell her.

115   **ANGIE:** Oh great, fine.

     KIT: I'll say I was by myself. I'll tell her you're at my house and I'm going there to get you.

     ANGIE: She knows I'm here, stupid.

120   **KIT:** Then why can't I go through the house?

     ANGIE: Because I said not.

     KIT: My mum don't like you anyway.

     ANGIE: I don't want her to like me. She's

125   a slag.

     KIT: She is not.

     ANGIE: She does it with everyone.

     KIT: She does not.

     ANGIE: You don't even know what it is.

130   **KIT:** Yes I do.

     ANGIE: Tell me then.

     KIT: We get it all at school, cleverclogs. It's on television. You haven't done it.

     ANGIE: How do you know?

135   **KIT:** Because I know you haven't.

     ANGIE: You know wrong then because I have.

     KIT: Who with?

     ANGIE: I'm not telling you / who with.

140   **KIT:** You haven't anyway.

     ANGIE: How do you know?

     KIT: Who with?

     ANGIE: I'm not telling you.

     KIT: You said you told me everything.

145   **ANGIE:** I was lying wasn't I.

     KIT: Who with? You can't tell me who with because / you never—

     ANGIE: Sh. (*Joyce has come out of the house. She stops halfway across the yard and listens.*

150   *They listen.*)

     JOYCE: You there Angie? Kit? You there Kitty? Want a cup of tea? I've got some chocolate biscuits. Come on now I'll put the kettle on. Want a choccy biccy, Angie? (*They all*

155   *listen and wait.*) F***ing rotten little cunt. You can stay there and die. I'll lock the door. (*They all wait. Joyce goes back to the house. Angie and Kit sit in silence for a while.*)

160   **KIT:** When there's a war, where's the safest place?

     ANGIE: Nowhere.

     KIT: New Zealand is, my mum said. Your skin's burned right off. Shall we go to New

165   Zealand?

     ANGIE: I'm not staying here.

     KIT: Shall we go to New Zealand?

     ANGIE: You're not old enough.

     KIT: You're not old enough.

170   **ANGIE:** I'm old enough to get married.

     KIT: You don't want to get married.

     ANGIE: No but I'm old enough.

     KIT: I'd find out where they were going to drop it and stand right in the place.

175   **ANGIE:** You couldn't find out.

     KIT: Better than walking round with your skin dragging on the ground. Eugh. / Would you like walking round with your skin dragging on the ground?

180   **ANGIE:** You couldn't find out, stupid, it's a secret.

     KIT: Where are you going?

     ANGIE: I'm not telling you.

KIT: Why?

185 ANGIE: It's a secret.

KIT: But you tell me all your secrets.

ANGIE: Not the true secrets.

KIT: Yes you do.

ANGIE: No I don't.

190 KIT: I want to go somewhere away from the war.

ANGIE: Just forget the war.

KIT: I can't.

ANGIE: You have to. It's so boring.

195 KIT: I'll remember it at night.

ANGIE: I'm going to do something else anyway.

KIT: What? Angie, come on. Angie.

ANGIE: It's a true secret.

200 KIT: It can't be worse than the kitten. And killing your mother. And the war.

ANGIE: Well I'm not telling you so you can die for all I care.

KIT: My mother says there's something

205 wrong with you playing with someone my age. She says why haven't you got friends your own age. People your own age know there's something funny about you. She says you're a bad influence. She says she's

210 going to speak to your mother. (*Angie twists Kit's arm till she cries out.*)

ANGIE: Say you're a liar.

KIT: She said it not me.

ANGIE: Say you eat shit.

215 KIT: You can't make me. (*Angie lets go.*)

ANGIE: I don't care anyway. I'm leaving.

KIT: Go on then.

ANGIE: You'll all wake up one morning and find I've gone.

220 KIT: Go on then.

ANGIE: You'll wake up one morning and find I've gone.

KIT: Good.

ANGIE: I'm not telling you when.

225 KIT: Go on then.

ANGIE: I'm sorry I hurt you.

KIT: I'm tired.

ANGIE: Do you like me?

KIT: I don't know.

230 ANGIE: You do like me.

KIT: I'm going home. (*She gets up.*)

ANGIE: No you're not.

KIT: I'm tired.

ANGIE: She'll see you.

235 KIT: She'll give me a chocolate biscuit.

ANGIE: Kitty.

KIT: Tell me where you're going.

ANGIE: Sit down.

KIT (*sitting down again*): Go on then.

240 ANGIE: Swear?

KIT: Swear.

ANGIE: I'm going to London. To see my aunt.

KIT: And what?

ANGIE: That's it.

245 KIT: I see my aunt all the time.

ANGIE: I don't see my aunt.

KIT: What's so special?

ANGIE: It is special. She's special.

KIT: Why?

250 ANGIE: She is.

KIT: Why?

ANGIE: She is.

KIT: Why?

ANGIE: My mother hates her.

255 KIT: Why?

ANGIE: Because she does.

KIT: Perhaps she's not very nice.

ANGIE: She is nice.

KIT: How do you know?

260 ANGIE: Because I know her.

KIT: You said you never see her.

ANGIE: I saw her last year. You saw her.

KIT: Did I?

ANGIE: Never mind.

265 KIT: I remember her. That aunt. What's so special?

ANGIE: She gets people jobs.

KIT: What's so special?

ANGIE: I think I'm my aunt's child. I think
270   my mother's really my aunt.

KIT: Why?

ANGIE: Because she goes to America, now
shut up.

KIT: I've been to London.

275   ANGIE: Now give us a cuddle and shut up
because I'm sick.

KIT: You're sitting on my arm. (*They curl up
in each other's arms. Silence. Joyce comes out
of the house and comes up to them quietly.*)

280   JOYCE: Come on.

KIT: Oh hello.

JOYCE: Time you went home.

KIT: We want to go to the Odeon.

JOYCE: What time?

285   KIT: Don't know.

JOYCE: What's on?

KIT: Don't know.

JOYCE: Don't know much do you?

KIT: That all right then?

290   JOYCE: Angie's got to clean her room first.

ANGIE: No I don't.

JOYCE: Yes you do, it's a pigsty.

ANGIE: Well I'm not.

JOYCE: Then you're not going. I don't care.

295   ANGIE: Well I am going.

JOYCE: You've no money, have you?

ANGIE: Kit's paying anyway.

JOYCE: No she's not.

KIT: I'll help you with your room.

300   JOYCE: That's nice.

ANGIE: No you won't. You wait here.

KIT: Hurry then.

ANGIE: I'm not hurrying. You just wait.
(*Angie goes slowly into the house. Silence.*)

305   JOYCE: I don't know. (*Silence.*) How's school
then?

KIT: All right.

JOYCE: What are you now? Third year?

KIT: Second year.

310   JOYCE: Your mum says you're good at English.
(*Silence.*) Maybe Angie should've stayed on.

KIT: She didn't like it.

JOYCE: I didn't like it. And look at me. If your
face fits at school it's going to fit other
315   places too. It wouldn't make no difference
to Angie. She's not going to get a job when
jobs are hard to get. I'd be sorry for anyone
in charge of her. She'd better get married. I
don't know who'd have her, mind. She's
320   one of those girls might never leave home.
What do you want to be when you grow
up, Kit?

KIT: Physicist.

JOYCE: What?

325   KIT: Nuclear physicist.

JOYCE: Whatever for?

KIT: I could, I'm clever.

JOYCE: I know you're clever, pet. (*Silence.*) I'll
make a cup of tea. (*Silence.*) Looks like it's
330   going to rain. (*Silence.*) Don't you have
friends your own age?

KIT: Yes.

JOYCE: Well then.

KIT: I'm old for my age.

335   JOYCE: And Angie's simple is she? She's not
simple.

KIT: I love Angie.

JOYCE: She's clever in her own way.

KIT: You can't stop me.

340   JOYCE: I don't want to.

KIT: You can't, so.

JOYCE: Don't be cheeky, Kitty. She's always
kind to little children.

KIT: She's coming so you better leave me
345   alone. (*Angie comes out. She has changed into
an old best dress, slightly small for her.*)

JOYCE: What you put that on for? Have you
done your room? You can't clean your
room in that.

350   ANGIE: I looked in the cupboard and it was
there.

JOYCE: Of course it was there, it's meant to be there. Is that why it was a surprise, finding something in the right place? I

355   should think she's surprised, wouldn't you, Kit, to find something in her room in the right place.

ANGIE: I decided to wear it.

JOYCE: Not today, why? To clean your

360   room? You're not going to the pictures till you've done your room. You can put your dress on after if you like. (*Angie picks up a brick.*) Have you done your room? You're not getting out of it, you

365   know.

KIT: Angie, let's go.

JOYCE: She's not going till she's done her room.

KIT: It's starting to rain.

370   JOYCE: Come on, come on then. Hurry and do your room, Angie, and then you can go to the cinema with Kit. Oh it's wet, come on. We'll look up the time in the paper. Does your mother know, Kit, it's going to

375   be a late night for you, isn't it? Hurry up, Angie. You'll spoil your dress. You make me sick. (*Joyce and Kit run into the house. Angie stays where she is. There is the sound of rain. Kit comes out of the house.*)

380   KIT (*shouting*):   Angie. Angie, come on, you'll get wet. (*She comes back to Angie.*)

ANGIE: I put on this dress to kill my mother.

KIT: I suppose you thought you'd do it with a brick.

385   ANGIE: You can kill people with a brick. (*She puts the brick down.*)

KIT: Well you didn't, so.

Sara Krulwich/The New York Times/Redux Pictures

◀ Photograph of *Top Girls* playing at the Biltmore Theater in 2008, directed by James Macdonald.

How does the image of the dinner party illustrate the historical context and reflect the multiple perspectives of the play? Does it contribute to your understanding of the play? Explain.

CHARACTER

1. In Act I, what do the characters' backgrounds and speech reveal about their values?

2. How do Marlene's **diction** and the details she shares convey a particular perspective?

3. Give an example in which Marlene's values are revealed through a decision. How do inconsistencies in her perspective convey the complexities of her relationships?

4. How does the group of women at dinner function as a single character? How do these women interact as a group? How do their interactions highlight the **nuances** of each **character**?

STRUCTURE

5. How do the events at the restaurant affect the development of Marlene's character and contribute to her **conflicts** with other characters?

6. How do the interactions between Marlene and Jeannie reveal Marlene's perspective? How does their relationship contribute to your understanding of the text?

7. How does the relationship between Angie and Kit represent competing value systems?

8. The play has multiple threads (or plot lines) and **moments** significant to each of those threads. Choose two moments — that is, one moment from each plot line — and explain how it contributes to the plot.

NARRATION

9. How do Marlene's background and **perspective** shape her tone toward the subject of women and success? What is that **tone**?

10. Many women appear in Act I. How do they present multiple **points of view** and contrasting perspectives? Choose two **contrasting perspectives** and explain how they contribute to the complexity of the text.

11. At the end of Act I, how does Joyce's **monologue** about Angie evoke an emotional reaction? How does it reveal the true relationship between mother and daughter?

IDEAS IN LITERATURE: Power and Perception

12. How do insights from earlier generations — that is, insights that you have heard or read — shape your perceptions of important issues in your own life?

ACT II

SCENE i

(*"Top Girls" Employment Agency. Monday morning. There are three desks in the main office and a separate small interviewing area. The lights come up in the main office on Win and Nell who have just arrived for work.*)

NELL: Coffee coffee coffee coffee / coffee.

WIN: The roses were smashing. / Mermaid.

NELL: Ohhh.

WIN: Iceberg. He taught me all their names.

5 (*Nell has some coffee now.*)

NELL: Ah. Now then.

WIN: He has one of the finest rose gardens in West Sussex. He exhibits.

NELL: He what?

10 **WIN:** His wife was visiting her mother. It was like living together.

NELL: Crafty, you never said.

WIN: He rang on Saturday morning.

NELL: Lucky you were free.

15 **WIN:** That's what I told him.

NELL: Did you hell.

WIN: Have you ever seen a really beautiful rose garden?

NELL: I don't like flowers. / I like swimming

20 pools.

WIN: Marilyn. Esther's Baby. They're all called after birds.

NELL: Our friend's late. Celebrating all weekend I bet you.

25 **WIN:** I'd call a rose Elvis. Or John Conteh.

NELL: Is Howard in yet?

WIN: If he is he'll be bleeping us with a problem.

NELL: Howard can just hang on to himself.

30 **WIN:** Howard's really cut up.

NELL: Howard thinks because he's a fella the job was his as of right. Our Marlene's got far more balls than Howard and that's that.

WIN: Poor little bugger.

35 **NELL:** He'll live.

WIN: He'll move on.

NELL: I wouldn't mind a change of air myself.

WIN: Serious?

40 **NELL:** I've never been a staying-put lady. Pastures new.

WIN: So who's the pirate?

NELL: There's nothing definite.

WIN: Inquiries?

45 **NELL:** There's always inquiries. I'd think I'd got bad breath if there stopped being inquiries. Most of them can't afford me. Or you.

WIN: I'm all right for the time being. Unless

50 I go to Australia.

NELL: There's not a lot of room upward.

WIN: Marlene's filled it up.

NELL: Good luck to her. Unless there's some prospects moneywise.

55 **WIN:** You can but ask.

NELL: Can always but ask.

WIN: So what have we got? I've got a Mr. Holden I saw last week.

NELL: Any use?

60 **WIN:** Pushy. Bit of a cowboy.

NELL: Goodlooker?

WIN: Good dresser.

NELL: High flyer?

WIN: That's his general idea certainly but

65 I'm not sure he's got it up there.

NELL: Prestel wants six flyers and I've only seen two and a half.

WIN: He's making a bomb on the road but he thinks it's time for an office. I sent him

70 to IBM but he didn't get it.

NELL: Prestel's on the road.

WIN: He's not overbright.

NELL: Can he handle an office?

WIN: Provided his secretary can punctuate

75 he should go far.

NELL: Bear Prestel in mind then, I might put my head round the door. I've got that poor little nerd I should never had said I could help. Tender heart me.

80 **WIN:** Tender like old boots. How old?

NELL: Yes well forty-five.

WIN: Say no more.

NELL: He knows his place, he's not after calling himself a manager, he's just a poor

85 little bod wants a better commission and a bit of sunshine.

WIN: Don't we all.

NELL: He's just got to relocate. He's got a bungalow in Dymchurch.

90 **WIN:** And his wife says.

NELL: The lady wife wouldn't care to relocate. She's going through the change.

WIN: It's his funeral, don't waste your time.

NELL: I don't waste a lot.

95 **WIN:** Good weekend you?

NELL: You could say.

WIN: Which one?

NELL: One Friday, one Saturday.

WIN: Aye—aye.

100 **NELL:** Sunday night I watched telly.

WIN: Which of them do you like best really?

NELL: Sunday was best, I like the Ovaltine.

WIN: Holden, Barker, Gardner, Duke.

NELL: I've a lady here thinks she can sell.

105 **WIN:** Taking her on?

NELL: She's had some jobs.

WIN: Services?

NELL: No, quite heavy stuff, electric.

WIN: Tough bird like us.

110 **NELL:** We could do with a few more here.

WIN: There's nothing going here.

NELL: No but I always want the tough ones when I see them. Hang on to them.

WIN: I think we're plenty.

115 **NELL:** Derek asked me to marry him again.

WIN: He doesn't know when he's beaten.

NELL: I told him I'm not going to play house, not even in Ascot.

WIN: Mind you, you could play house.

120 **NELL:** If I chose to play house I would play house ace.

WIN: You could marry him and go on working.

NELL: I could go on working and not marry

125 him. (*Marlene arrives.*)

MARLENE: Morning ladies. (*Win and Nell cheer and whistle.*) Mind my head.

NELL: Coffee coffee coffee.

WIN: We're tactfully not mentioning you're

130 late.

MARLENE: F***ing tube.

WIN: We've heard that one.

NELL: We've used that one.

WIN: It's the top executive doesn't come in

135 as early as the poor working girl.

MARLENE: Pass the sugar and shut your face, pet.

WIN: Well I'm delighted.

NELL: Howard's looking sick.

140 **WIN:** Howard is sick. He's got ulcers and heart. He told me.

NELL: He'll have to stop then, won't he?

WIN: Stop what?

NELL: Smoking, drinking, shouting. Working.

145 **WIN:** Well, working.

NELL: We're just looking through the day.

MARLENE: I'm doing some of Pam's ladies. They've been piling up while she's away.

NELL: Half a dozen little girls and an arts

150 graduate who can't type.

WIN: I spent the whole weekend at his place in Sussex.

NELL: She fancies his rose garden.

WIN: I had to lie down in the back of the car

155 so the neighbors wouldn't see me go in.

NELL: You're kidding.

WIN: It was funny.

NELL: F*** that for a joke.

WIN: It was funny.

160 MARLENE: Anyway they'd see you in the garden.

WIN: The garden has extremely high walls.

NELL: I think I'll tell the wife.

WIN: Like hell.

165 NELL: She might leave him and you could have the rose garden.

WIN: The minute it's not a secret I'm out on my ear.

NELL: Don't know why you bother.

170 WIN: Bit of fun.

NELL: I think it's time you went to Australia.

WIN: I think it's pushy Mr. Holden time.

NELL: If you've any really pretty bastards, Marlene, I want some for Prestel.

175 MARLENE: I might have one this afternoon. This morning it's all Pam's secretarial.

NELL: Not long now and you'll be upstairs watching over us all.

MARLENE: Do you feel bad about it?

180 NELL: I don't like coming second.

MARLENE: Who does?

WIN: We'd rather it was you than Howard. We're glad for you, aren't we, Nell?

NELL: Oh yes. Aces. (*Louise enters the inter-*

185 *viewing area. The lights crossfade to Win and Louise in the interviewing area. Nell exits.*)

WIN: Now, Louise, hello, I have your details here. You've been very loyal to the one job I see.

190 LOUISE: Yes I have.

WIN: Twenty-one years is a long time in one place.

LOUISE: I feel it is. I feel it's time to move on.

WIN: And you are what age now?

195 LOUISE: I'm in my early forties.

WIN: Exactly?

LOUISE: Forty-six.

WIN: It's not necessarily a handicap, well it is of course we have to face that, but it's

200 not necessarily a disabling handicap, experience does count for something.

LOUISE: I hope so.

WIN: Now between ourselves is there any trouble, any reason why you're leaving

205 that wouldn't appear on the form?

LOUISE: Nothing like that.

WIN: Like what?

LOUISE: Nothing at all.

WIN: No long-term understandings come to

210 a sudden end, making for an insupportable atmosphere?

LOUISE: I've always completely avoided anything like that at all.

WIN: No personality clashes with your

215 immediate superiors or inferiors?

LOUISE: I've always taken care to get on very well with everyone.

WIN: I only ask because it can affect the reference and it also affects your motiva-

220 tion, I want to be quite clear why you're moving on. So I take it the job itself no longer satisfies you. Is it the money?

LOUISE: It's partly the money. It's not so much the money.

225 WIN: Nine thousand is very respectable. Have you dependents?

LOUISE: No, no dependents. My mother died.

WIN: So why are you making a change?

LOUISE: Other people make changes.

230 WIN: But why are you, now, after spending most of your life in the one place?

LOUISE: There you are, I've lived for that company, I've given my life really you could say because I haven't had a great

235 deal of social life, I've worked in the evenings. I haven't had office entanglements for the very reason you just mentioned and if you are committed to your work you don't move in many other

240 circles. I had management status from the age of twenty-seven and you'll appreciate

what that means. I've built up a department. And there it is, it works extremely
well, and I feel I'm stuck there. I've spent
245 twenty years in middle management. I've
seen young men who I trained go on, in
my own company or elsewhere, to higher
things. Nobody notices me, I don't expect
it, I don't attract attention by making
250 mistakes, everybody takes it for granted
that my work is perfect. They will notice
me when I go, they will be sorry I think to
lose me, they will offer me more money of
course, I will refuse. They will see when
255 I've gone what I was doing for them.

WIN: If they offer you more money you
won't stay?

LOUISE: No I won't.

WIN: Are you the only woman?

260 LOUISE: Apart from the girls of course, yes.
There was one, she was my assistant, it
was the only time I took on a young
woman assistant, I always had my doubts.
I don't care greatly for working with
265 women, I think I pass as a man at work.
But I did take on this young woman, her
qualifications were excellent, and she did
well, she got a department of her own,
and left the company for a competitor
270 where she's now on the board and good
luck to her. She has a different style, she's
a new kind of attractive well dressed—
I don't mean I don't dress properly. But
there is a kind of woman who is thirty
275 now who grew up in a different climate.
They are not so careful. They take themselves for granted. I have had to justify my
existence every minute, and I have done
so, I have proved—well.

280 WIN: Let's face it, vacancies are ones where
you'll be in competition with younger
men. And there are companies that will
value your experience enough that you'll

be in with a chance. There are also fields
285 that are easier for a woman, there is a
cosmetic company here where your experience might be relevant. It's eight and a
half, I don't know if that appeals.

LOUISE: I've proved I can earn money. It's
290 more important to get away. I feel it's now
or never. I sometimes / think—

WIN: You shouldn't talk too much at an
interview.

LOUISE: I don't. I don't normally talk about
295 myself. I know very well how to handle
myself in an office situation. I only talk to
you because it seems to me this is different, it's your job to understand me, surely.
You asked the questions.

300 WIN: I think I understand you sufficiently.

LOUISE: Well good, that's good.

WIN: Do you drink?

LOUISE: Certainly not. I'm not a teetotaler, I
think that's very suspect, it's seen as being
305 an alcoholic if you're teetotal. What do
you mean? I don't drink. Why?

WIN: I drink.

LOUISE: I don't.

WIN: Good for you. (*The lights crossfade to the
310 main office with Marlene sitting at her desk.
Win and Louise exit. Angie arrives in the main
office.*)

ANGIE: Hello.

MARLENE: Have you an appointment?

315 ANGIE: It's me. I've come.

MARLENE: What? It's not Angie?

ANGIE: It was hard to find this place. I got
lost.

MARLENE: How did you get past the recep-
320 tionist? The girl on the desk, didn't she try
to stop you?

ANGIE: What desk?

MARLENE: Never mind.

ANGIE: I just walked in. I was looking for
325 you.

MARLENE: Well you found me.

ANGIE: Yes.

MARLENE: So where's your mum? Are you up in town for the day?

330 ANGIE: Not really.

MARLENE: Sit down. Do you feel all right?

ANGIE: Yes thank you.

MARLENE: So where's Joyce?

ANGIE: She's at home.

335 MARLENE: Did you come up on a school trip then?

ANGIE: I've left school.

MARLENE: Did you come up with a friend?

ANGIE: No. There's just me.

340 MARLENE: You came up by yourself, that's fun. What have you been doing? Shopping? Tower of London?

ANGIE: No, I just come here. I come to you.

MARLENE: That's very nice of you to think of

345 paying your aunty a visit. There's not many nieces make that the first port of call. Would you like a cup of coffee?

ANGIE: No thank you.

MARLENE: Tea, orange?

350 ANGIE: No thank you.

MARLENE: Do you feel all right?

ANGIE: Yes thank you.

MARLENE: Are you tired from the journey?

ANGIE: Yes, I'm tired from the journey.

355 MARLENE: You sit there for a bit then. How's Joyce?

ANGIE: She's all right.

MARLENE: Same as ever.

ANGIE: Oh yes.

360 MARLENE: Unfortunately you've picked a day when I'm rather busy, if there's ever a day when I'm not, or I'd take you out to lunch and we'd go to Madame Tussaud's. We could go shopping. What time do you

365 have to be back? Have you got a day return?

ANGIE: No.

MARLENE: So what train are you going back on?

370 ANGIE: I came on the bus.

MARLENE: So what bus are you going back on? Are you staying the night?

ANGIE: Yes.

MARLENE: Who are you staying with? Do you

375 want me to put you up for the night, is that it?

ANGIE: Yes please.

MARLENE: I haven't got a spare bed.

ANGIE: I can sleep on the floor.

380 MARLENE: You can sleep on the sofa.

ANGIE: Yes please.

MARLENE: I do think Joyce might have phoned me. It's like her.

ANGIE: This is where you work is it?

385 MARLENE: It's where I have been working the last two years but I'm going to move into another office.

ANGIE: It's lovely.

MARLENE: My new office is nicer than this.

390 There's just the one big desk in it for me.

ANGIE: Can I see it?

MARLENE: Not now, no, there's someone else in it now. But he's leaving at the end of next week and I'm going to do his job.

395 ANGIE: Is that good?

MARLENE: Yes, it's very good.

ANGIE: Are you going to be in charge?

MARLENE: Yes I am.

ANGIE: I knew you would be.

400 MARLENE: How did you know?

ANGIE: I knew you'd be in charge of every-thing.

MARLENE: Not quite everything.

ANGIE: You will be.

405 MARLENE: Well we'll see.

ANGIE: Can I see it next week then?

MARLENE: Will you still be here next week?

ANGIE: Yes.

MARLENE: Don't you have to go home?

410 **ANGIE:** No.

MARLENE: Why not?

ANGIE: It's all right.

MARLENE: Is it all right?

ANGIE: Yes, don't worry about it.

415 **MARLENE:** Does Joyce know where you are?

ANGIE: Yes of course she does.

MARLENE: Well does she?

ANGIE: Don't worry about it.

MARLENE: How long are you planning to stay
420   with me then?

ANGIE: You know when you came to see us
last year?

MARLENE: Yes, that was nice wasn't it.

ANGIE: That was the best day of my whole
425   life.

MARLENE: So how long are you planning to
stay?

ANGIE: Don't you want me?

MARLENE: Yes yes, I just wondered.

430 **ANGIE:** I won't stay if you don't want me.

MARLENE: No, of course you can stay.

ANGIE: I'll sleep on the floor. I won't be any
bother.

MARLENE: Don't get upset.

435 **ANGIE:** I'm not, I'm not. Don't worry about it.
(*Mrs. Kidd comes in.*)

MRS. KIDD: Excuse me.

MARLENE: Yes.

MRS. KIDD: Excuse me.

440 **MARLENE:** Can I help you?

MRS. KIDD: Excuse me bursting in on you
like this but I have to talk to you.

MARLENE: I am engaged at the moment. / If
you could go to reception—

445 **MRS. KIDD:** I'm Rosemary Kidd, Howard's
wife, you don't recognize me but we did
meet, I remember you of course / but you
wouldn't—

MARLENE: Yes of course, Mrs. Kidd, I'm sorry,
450   we did meet. Howard's about somewhere I
expect, have you looked in his office?

MRS. KIDD: Howard's not about, no. I'm
afraid it's you I've come to see if I could
have a minute or two.

455 **MARLENE:** I do have an appointment in five
minutes.

MRS. KIDD: This won't take five minutes.
I'm very sorry. It is a matter of some
urgency.

460 **MARLENE:** Well of course. What can I do for
you?

MRS. KIDD: I just wanted a chat, an informal
chat. It's not something I can simply—I'm
sorry if I'm interrupting your work. I know
465   office work isn't like housework / which
is all interruptions.

MARLENE: No no, this is my niece. Angie.
Mrs. Kidd.

MRS. KIDD: Very pleased to meet you.

470 **ANGIE:** Very well thank you.

MRS. KIDD: Howard's not in today.

MARLENE: Isn't he?

MRS. KIDD: He's feeling poorly.

MARLENE: I didn't know. I'm sorry to hear
475   that.

MRS. KIDD: The fact is he's in a state of
shock. About what's happened.

MARLENE: What has happened?

MRS. KIDD: You should know if anyone. I'm
480   referring to you been appointed managing
director instead of Howard. He hasn't
been at all well all weekend. He hasn't
slept for three nights. I haven't slept.

MARLENE: I'm sorry to hear that, Mrs. Kidd.
485   Has he thought of taking sleeping pills?

MRS. KIDD: It's very hard when someone has
worked all these years.

MARLENE: Business life is full of little
setbacks. I'm sure Howard knows that.
490   He'll bounce back in a day or two. We all
bounce back.

MRS. KIDD: If you could see him you'd know
what I'm talking about. What's it going to

495 do to him working for a woman? I think if it was a man he'd get over it as something normal.

MARLENE: I think he's going to have to get over it.

500 MRS. KIDD: It's me that bears the brunt. I'm not the one that's been promoted. I put him first every inch of the way. And now what do I get? You women this, you women that. It's not my fault. You're going to have to be very careful how you handle 505 him. He's very hurt.

MARLENE: Naturally I'll be tactful and pleasant to him, you don't start pushing someone around. I'll consult him over any decisions affecting his department. But 510 that's no different, Mrs. Kidd, from any of my other colleagues.

MRS. KIDD: I think it is different, because he's a man.

MARLENE: I'm not quite sure why you came 515 to see me.

MRS. KIDD: I had to do something.

MARLENE: Well you've done it, you've seen me. I think that's probably all we've time for. I'm sorry he's been taking it out on 520 you. He really is a shit, Howard.

MRS. KIDD: But he's got a family to support. He's got three children. It's only fair.

MARLENE: Are you suggesting I give up the job to him then?

525 MRS. KIDD: It had crossed my mind if you were unavailable after all for some reason, he would be the natural second choice I think, don't you? I'm not asking.

MARLENE: Good.

530 MRS. KIDD: You mustn't tell him I came. He's very proud.

MARLENE: If he doesn't like what's happening here he can go and work somewhere else.

535 MRS. KIDD: Is that a threat?

MARLENE: I'm sorry but I do have some work to do.

MRS. KIDD: It's not that easy, a man of Howard's age. You don't care. I thought he 540 was going too far but he's right. You're one of these ballbreakers, / that's what you

MARLENE: I'm sorry but I do have some work to do.

MRS. KIDD: are. You'll end up miserable and 545 lonely. You're not natural.

MARLENE: Could you please piss off?

MRS. KIDD: I thought if I saw you at least I'd be doing something. (Mrs. Kidd goes.)

MARLENE: I've got to go and do some work 550 now. Will you come back later?

ANGIE: I think you were wonderful.

MARLENE: I've got to go and do some work now.

ANGIE: You told her to piss off.

555 MARLENE: Will you come back later?

ANGIE: Can't I stay here?

MARLENE: Don't you want to go sightseeing?

ANGIE: I'd rather stay here.

MARLENE: You can stay here I suppose, if it's 560 not boring.

ANGIE: It's where I most want to be in the world.

MARLENE: I'll see you later then. (Marlene goes. Shona and Nell enter the interviewing 565 area. Angie sits at Win's desk. The lights crossfade to Nell and Shona in the interviewing area.)

NELL: Is this right? You are Shona?

SHONA: Yeh.

570 NELL: It says here you're twenty-nine.

SHONA: Yeh.

NELL: Too many late nights, me. So you've been where you are for four years, Shona, you're earning six basic and three 575 commission. So what's the problem?

SHONA: No problem.

NELL: Why do you want a change?

SHONA: Just a change.

NELL: Change of product, change of area?

580 SHONA: Both.

NELL: But you're happy on the road?

SHONA: I like driving.

NELL: You're not after management status?

SHONA: I would like management status.

585 NELL: You'd be interested in titular management status but not come off the road?

SHONA: I want to be on the road, yeh.

NELL: So how many calls have you been
making a day?

590 SHONA: Six.

NELL: And what proportion of those are
successful?

SHONA: Six.

NELL: That's hard to believe.

595 SHONA: Four.

NELL: You find it easy to get the initial interest
do you?

SHONA: Oh yeh, I get plenty of initial interest.

NELL: And what about closing?

600 SHONA: I close, don't I?

NELL: Because that's what an employer is
going to have doubts about with a lady as
I needn't tell you, whether she's got the
guts to push through to a closing situa-

605   tion. They think we're too nice. They think
we listen to the buyer's doubts. They
think we consider his needs and his
feelings.

SHONA: I never consider people's feelings.

610 NELL: I was selling for six years, I can sell
anything, I've sold in three continents,
and I'm jolly as they come but I'm not
very nice.

SHONA: I'm not very nice.

615 NELL: What sort of time do you have on the
road with the other reps? Get on all right?
Handle the chat?

SHONA: I get on. Keep myself to myself.

NELL: Fairly much of a loner are you?

620 SHONA: Sometimes.

NELL: So what field are you interested in?

SHONA: Computers.

NELL: That's a top field as you know and
you'll be up against some very slick fellas

625   there, there's some very pretty boys in
computers, it's an American-style field.

SHONA: That's why I want to do it.

NELL: Video systems appeal? That's a highflying situation.

630 SHONA: Video systems appeal OK.

NELL: Because Prestel have half a dozen
vacancies I'm looking to fill at the
moment. We're talking in the area of ten
to fifteen thousand here and upwards.

635 SHONA: Sounds OK.

NELL: I've half a mind to go for it myself.
But it's good money here if you've got
the top clients. Could you fancy it do you
think?

640 SHONA: Work here?

NELL: I'm not in a position to offer, there's
nothing officially going just now, but we're
always on the lookout. There's not that
many of us. We could keep in touch.

645 SHONA: I like driving.

NELL: So the Prestel appeals.

SHONA: Yeh.

NELL: What about ties?

SHONA: No ties.

650 NELL: So relocation wouldn't be a problem.

SHONA: No problem.

NELL: So just fill me in a bit more could you
about what you've been doing.

SHONA: What I've been doing. It's all down

655   there.

NELL: The bare facts are down here but I've
got to present you to an employer.

SHONA: I'm twenty-nine years old.

NELL: So it says here.

660 SHONA: We look young. Youngness runs in
the family in our family.

NELL: So just describe your present job for me.

SHONA: My present job at present. I have a
665 car. I have a Porsche. I go up the M1 a lot. Burn up the M1 a lot. Straight up the M1 in the fast lane to where the clients are, Staffordshire, Yorkshire, I do a lot in Yorkshire. I'm selling electric things. Like
670 dishwashers, washing machines, stainless steel tubs are a feature and the reliability of the program. After sales service, we offer a very good after sales service, spare parts, plenty of spare parts. And fridges,
675 I sell a lot of fridges specially in the summer. People want to buy fridges in the summer because of the heat melting the butter and you get fed up standing the milk in a basin of cold water with a cloth
680 over, stands to reason people don't want to do that in this day and age. So I sell a lot of them. Big ones with big freezers. Big freezers. And I stay in hotels at night when I'm away from home. On my
685 expense account. I stay in various hotels. They know me, the ones I go to. I check in, have a bath, have a shower. Then I go down to the bar, have a gin and tonic, have a chat. Then I go into the dining
690 room and have dinner. I usually have fillet steak and mushrooms, I like mushrooms. I like smoked salmon very much. I like having a salad on the side. Green salad. I don't like tomatoes.

695 **NELL:** Christ what a waste of time.

SHONA: Beg your pardon?

NELL: Not a word of this is true, is it?

SHONA: How do you mean?

NELL: You just filled in the form with a pack
700 of lies.

SHONA: Not exactly.

NELL: How old are you?

SHONA: Twenty-nine.

NELL: Nineteen?

705 **SHONA:** Twenty-one.

NELL: And what jobs have you done? Have you done any?

SHONA: I could though, I bet you. (*The lights crossfade to the main office with Angie sitting*
710 *as before. Win comes in to the main office. Shona and Nell exit.*)

WIN: Who's sitting in my chair?

ANGIE: What? Sorry.

WIN: Who's been eating my porridge?

715 **ANGIE:** What?

WIN: It's all right, I saw Marlene. Angie, isn't it? I'm Win. And I'm not going out for lunch because I'm knackered. I'm going to set me down here and have a yogurt. Do
720 you like yogurt?

ANGIE: No.

WIN: That's good because I've only got one. Are you hungry?

ANGIE: No.

725 **WIN:** There's a café on the corner.

ANGIE: No thank you. Do you work here?

WIN: How did you guess?

ANGIE: Because you look as if you might work here and you're sitting at the desk.
730 Have you always worked here?

WIN: No I was headhunted. That means I was working for another outfit like this and this lot came and offered me more money. I broke my contract, there was a
735 hell of a stink. There's not many top ladies about. Your aunty's a smashing bird.

ANGIE: Yes I know.

MARLENE: Fan are you? Fan of your aunty's?

740 **ANGIE:** Do you think I could work here?

WIN: Not at the moment.

ANGIE: How do I start?

WIN: What can you do?

ANGIE: I don't know. Nothing.

745 **WIN:** Type?

ANGIE: Not very well. The letters jump up when I do capitals. I was going to do a CSE[1] in commerce but I didn't.

WIN: What have you got?

750 ANGIE: What?

WIN: CSE's, O's.

ANGIE: Nothing, none of that. Did you do all that?

WIN: Oh yes, all that, and a science degree

755 funnily enough. I started out doing medical research but there's no money in it. I thought I'd go abroad. Did you know they sell Coca Cola in Russia and Pepsi-Cola in China? You don't have to be qualified as

760 much as you might think. Men are awful bullshitters, they like to make out jobs are harder than they are. Any job I ever did I started doing it better than the rest of the crowd and they didn't like it. So I'd get

765 unpopular and I'd have a drink to cheer myself up. I lived with a fella and supported him for four years, he couldn't get work. After that I went to California. I like the sunshine. Americans know how to live. This

770 country's too slow. Then I went to Mexico, still in sales, but it's no country for a single lady. I came home, went bonkers for a bit, thought I was five different people, got over that all right, the psychiatrist said I was

775 perfectly sane and highly intelligent. Got married in a moment of weakness and he's inside now, he's been inside four years, and I've not been to see him too much this last year. I like this better than sales, I'm not

780 really that aggressive. I started thinking sales was a good job if you want to meet people, but you're meeting people that don't want to meet you. It's no good if you like being liked. Here your clients want to

785 meet you because you're the one doing

[1]749. CSE: Certificate of Secondary Education.

them some good. They hope. (*Angie has fallen asleep. Nell comes in.*)

NELL: You're talking to yourself, sunshine.

WIN: So what's new?

790 NELL: Who is this?

WIN: Marlene's little niece.

NELL: What's she got, brother, sister? She never talks about her family.

WIN: I was telling her my life story.

795 NELL: Violins?

WIN: No, success story.

NELL: You've heard Howard's had a heart attack?

WIN: No, when?

800 NELL: I heard just now. He hadn't come in, he was at home, he's gone to hospital. He's not dead. His wife was here, she rushed off in a cab.

WIN: Too much butter, too much smoke.

805 We must send him some flowers. (*Marlene comes in.*) You've heard about Howard?

MARLENE: Poor sod.

NELL: Lucky he didn't get the job if that's

810 what his health's like.

MARLENE: Is she asleep?

WIN: She wants to work here.

MARLENE: Packer in Tesco more like.

WIN: She's a nice kid. Isn't she?

815 MARLENE: She's a bit thick. She's a bit funny.

WIN: She thinks you're wonderful.

MARLENE: She's not going to make it.

SCENE ii

(*Joyce's kitchen. Sunday evening, a year earlier. The lights come up on Joyce, Angie, and Marlene. Marlene is taking presents out of bright carrier bag. Angie has already opened a box of chocolates.*)

MARLENE: Just a few little things. / I've

JOYCE: There's no need.

MARLENE: no memory for birthdays have I, and Christmas seems to slip by. So I think

5 I owe Angie a few presents.

JOYCE: What do you say?

ANGIE: Thank you very much. Thank you very much, Aunty Marlene. (*She opens a present. It is the dress from Act I, new.*) Oh

10 look, Mum, isn't it lovely?

MARLENE: I don't know if it's the right size. She's grown up since I saw her. / I knew she was always

ANGIE: Isn't it lovely?

15 MARLENE: tall for her age.

JOYCE: She's a big lump.

MARLENE: Hold it up, Angie, let's see.

ANGIE: I'll put it on, shall I?

MARLENE: Yes, try it on.

20 JOYCE: Go on to your room then, we don't want / a strip show thank you.

ANGIE: Of course I'm going to my room, what do you think. Look, Mum, here's something for you. Open it, go on. What is

25 it? Can I open it for you?

JOYCE: Yes, you open it, pet.

ANGIE: Don't you want to open it yourself? / Go on.

JOYCE: I don't mind, you can do it.

30 ANGIE: It's something hard. It's—what is it? A bottle. Drink is it? No, it's what? Perfume, look. What a lot. Open it, look, let's smell it. Oh it's strong. It's lovely. Put it on me. How do you do it? Put it on me.

35 JOYCE: You're too young.

ANGIE: I can play wearing it like dressing up.

JOYCE: And you're too old for that. Here, give it here, I'll do it, you'll tip the whole bottle over yourself / and we'll have you smell-

40 ing all summer.

ANGIE: Put it on you. Do I smell? Put it on Aunty too. Put it on Aunty too. Let's all smell.

MARLENE: I didn't know what you'd like.

45 JOYCE: There's no danger I'd have it already, / that's one thing.

ANGIE: Now we all smell the same.

MARLENE: It's a bit of nonsense.

JOYCE: It's very kind of you Marlene, you

50 shouldn't.

ANGIE: Now I'll put on the dress and then we'll see. (*Angie goes.*)

JOYCE: You've caught me on the hop with the place in the mess. / If you'd

55 let me

MARLENE: That doesn't matter.

JOYCE: know you was coming I'd have got something in to eat. We had our dinner dinnertime. We're just going to have a cup

60 of tea. You could have an egg.

MARLENE: No, I'm not hungry. Tea's fine.

JOYCE: I don't expect you take sugar.

MARLENE: Why not?

JOYCE: You take care of yourself.

65 MARLENE: How do you mean you didn't know I was coming?

JOYCE: You could have written. I know we're not on the phone but we're not completely in the dark ages, / we do have a postman.

70 MARLENE: But you asked me to come.

JOYCE: How did I ask you to come?

MARLENE: Angie said when she phoned up.

JOYCE: Angie phoned up, did she.

MARLENE: Was it just Angie's idea?

75 JOYCE: What did she say?

MARLENE: She said you wanted me to come and see you. / It was a couple of

JOYCE: Ha.

MARLENE: weeks ago. How was I to know

80 that's a ridiculous idea? My diary's always full a couple of weeks ahead so we fixed it for this weekend. I was meant to get here earlier but I was held up. She gave me messages from you.

85 JOYCE: Didn't you wonder why I didn't phone you myself?

MARLENE: She said you didn't like using the phone. You're shy on the phone and can't use it. I don't know what you're like, do I?

90 JOYCE: Are there people who can't use the phone?

MARLENE: I expect so.

JOYCE: I haven't met any.

MARLENE: Why should I think she was lying?

95 JOYCE: Because she's like what she's like.

MARLENE: How do I know / what she's like?

JOYCE: It's not my fault you don't know what she's like. You never come and see her.

MARLENE: Well I have now / and you don't
100   seem over the moon.*

JOYCE: Good. *Well I'd have got a cake if she'd told me. (*Pause.*)

MARLENE: I did wonder why you wanted to see me.

105 JOYCE: I didn't want to see you.

MARLENE: Yes, I know. Shall I go?

JOYCE: I don't mind seeing you.

MARLENE: Great, I feel really welcome.

JOYCE: You can come and see Angie any time
110   you like, I'm not stopping you. / You

MARLENE: Ta ever so.

JOYCE: know where we are. You're the one went away, not me. I'm right here where I was. And will be a few years yet I
115   shouldn't wonder.

MARLENE: All right. All right. (*Joyce gives Marlene a cup of tea.*)

JOYCE: Tea.

MARLENE: Sugar? (*Joyce passes Marlene the*
120   *sugar.*) It's very quiet down here.

JOYCE: I expect you'd notice it.

MARLENE: The air smells different too.

JOYCE: That's the scent.

MARLENE: No, I mean walking down the
125   lane.

JOYCE: What sort of air you get in London then? (*Angie comes in, wearing the dress. It fits.*)

MARLENE: Oh, very pretty. / You do look
130   pretty, Angie.

JOYCE: That fits all right.

MARLENE: Do you like the color?

ANGIE: Beautiful. Beautiful.

JOYCE: You better take it off, / you'll get it
135   dirty.

ANGIE: I want to wear it. I want to wear it.

MARLENE: It is for wearing after all. You can't just hang it up and look at it.

ANGIE: I love it.

140 JOYCE: Well if you must you must.

ANGIE: If someone asks me what's my favorite color I'll tell them it's this. Thank you very much Aunty Marlene.

MARLENE: You didn't tell your mum you
145   asked me down.

ANGIE: I wanted it to be a surprise.

JOYCE: I'll give you a surprise / one of these days.

ANGIE: I thought you'd like to see her. She
150   hasn't been here since I was nine. People do see their aunts.

MARLENE: Is it that long? Doesn't time fly.

ANGIE: I wanted to.

JOYCE: I'm not cross.

155 ANGIE: Are you glad?

JOYCE: I smell nicer anyhow, don't I? (*Kit comes in without saying anything, as if she lived there.*)

MARLENE: I think it was a good idea, Angie,
160   about time. We are sisters after all. It's a pity to let that go.

JOYCE: This is Kitty, / who lives up the road. This is Angie's Aunty Marlene.

KIT: What's that?

165 ANGIE: It's a present. Do you like it?

KIT: It's all right. / Are you coming out?*

MARLENE: Hello, Kitty.

ANGIE: *No.

KIT: What's that smell?

170 ANGIE: It's a present.

KIT: It's horrible. Come on.*

MARLENE: Have a chocolate.

ANGIE: *No, I'm busy.

KIT: Coming out later?

175 ANGIE: No.

KIT (to Marlene): Hello. (Kit goes without a chocolate.)

JOYCE: She's a little girl Angie sometimes plays with because she's the only child

180   lives really close. She's like a little sister to her really. Angie's good with little children.

MARLENE: Do you want to work with children, Angie? / Be a teacher or a nursery

185   nurse?

JOYCE: I don't think she's ever thought of it.

MARLENE: What do you want to do?

JOYCE: She hasn't an idea in her head what she wants to do. / Lucky to get anything.

190 MARLENE: Angie?

JOYCE: She's not clever like you. (Pause.)

MARLENE: I'm not clever, just pushy.

JOYCE: True enough. (Marlene takes a bottle of whiskey out of the bag.) I don't drink spirits.

195 ANGIE: You do at Christmas.

JOYCE: It's not Christmas, is it?

ANGIE: It's better than Christmas.

MARLENE: Glasses?

JOYCE: Just a small one then.

200 MARLENE: Do you want some, Angie?

ANGIE: I can't, can I?

JOYCE: Taste it if you want. You won't like it. (Angie tastes it.)

ANGIE: Mmm.

205 MARLENE: We got drunk together the night your grandfather died.

JOYCE: We did not get drunk.

MARLENE: I got drunk. You were just overcome with grief.

210 JOYCE: I still keep up the grave with flowers.

MARLENE: Do you really?

JOYCE: Why wouldn't I?

MARLENE: Have you seen Mother?

JOYCE: Of course I've seen Mother.

215 MARLENE: I mean lately.

JOYCE: Of course I've seen her lately, I go every Thursday.

MARLENE (to Angie): Do you remember your grandfather?

220 ANGIE: He got me out of the bath one night in a towel.

MARLENE: Did he? I don't think he ever gave me a bath. Did he give you a bath, Joyce? He probably got soft in his old age. Did

225   you like him?

ANGIE: Yes of course.

MARLENE: Why?

ANGIE: What?

MARLENE: So what's the news? How's Mrs.

230   Paisley? Still going crazily? / And Dorothy. What happened to Dorothy?*

ANGIE: Who's Mrs. Paisley?

JOYCE: *She went to Canada.

MARLENE: Did she? What to do?

235 JOYCE: I don't know. She just went to Canada.

MARLENE: Well / good for her.

ANGIE: Mr. Connolly killed his wife.

MARLENE: What, Connolly at Whitegates?

ANGIE: They found her body in the garden. /

240   Under the cabbages.

MARLENE: He was always so proper.

JOYCE: Stuck up git, Connolly. Best lawyer money could buy but he couldn't get out of it. She was carrying on with Matthew.

245 MARLENE: How old's Matthew then?

JOYCE: Twenty-one. / He's got a motorbike.

MARLENE: I think he's about six.

ANGIE: How can he be six? He's six years older than me. / If he was six I'd be noth-

250   ing, I'd be just born this minute.

JOYCE: Your aunty knows that, she's just being silly. She means it's so long since she's been here she's forgotten about Matthew.

255   **ANGIE:**   You were here for my birthday when I was nine. I had a pink cake. Kit was only five then, she was four, she hadn't started school yet. She could read already when she went to school. You remember my
260   birthday? / You remember me?

MARLENE: Yes, I remember the cake.

ANGIE: You remember me?

MARLENE: Yes, I remember you.

ANGIE: And Mum and Dad was there, and
265   Kit was.

MARLENE: Yes, how is your dad? Where is he tonight? Up the pub?

JOYCE: No, he's not here.

MARLENE: I can see he's not here.

270   **JOYCE:**   He moved out.

MARLENE: What? When did he? / Just recently?*

ANGIE: Didn't you know that? You don't know much.

275   **JOYCE:**   *No, it must be three years ago. Don't be rude, Angie.

ANGIE: I'm not, am I, Aunty? What else don't you know?

JOYCE: You was in America or somewhere.
280   You sent a postcard.

ANGIE: I've got that in my room. It's the Grand Canyon. Do you want to see it? Shall I get it? I can get it for you.

MARLENE: Yes, all right. (*Angie goes.*)

285   **JOYCE:**   You could be married with twins for all I know. You must have affairs and break up and I don't need to know about any of that so I don't see what the fuss is about.

290   **MARLENE:**   What fuss? (*Angie comes back with the postcard.*)

ANGIE: "Driving across the states for a new job in L.A. It's a long way but the car goes very fast. It's very hot. Wish you were
295   here. Love from Aunty Marlene."

JOYCE: Did you make a lot of money?

MARLENE: I spent a lot.

ANGIE: I want to go to America. Will you take me?

300   **JOYCE:**   She's not going to America, she's been to America, stupid.

ANGIE: She might go again, stupid. It's not something you do once. People who go keep going all the time, back and forth on
305   jets. They go on Concorde and Laker and get jet lag. Will you take me?

MARLENE: I'm not planning a trip.

ANGIE: Will you let me know?

JOYCE: Angie, / you're getting silly.

310   **ANGIE:**   I want to be American.

JOYCE: It's time you were in bed.

ANGIE: No it's not. / I don't have to go to bed at all tonight.

JOYCE: School in the morning.

315   **ANGIE:**   I'll wake up.

JOYCE: Come on now, you know how you get.

ANGIE: How do I get? / I don't get anyhow.*

JOYCE: Angie. *Are you staying the night?

MARLENE: Yes, if that's all right. / I'll see you
320   in the morning.

ANGIE: You can have my bed. I'll sleep on the sofa.

JOYCE: You will not, you'll sleep in your bed. / Think

325   **ANGIE:**   Mum.

JOYCE: I can't see through that? I can just see you going to sleep / with us talking.

ANGIE: I would, I would go to sleep, I'd love that.

330   **JOYCE:**   I'm going to get cross, Angie.

ANGIE: I want to show her something.

JOYCE: Then bed.

ANGIE: It's a secret.

JOYCE: Then I expect it's in your room so off
335   you go. Give us a shout when you're ready for bed and your aunty'll be up and see you.

ANGIE: Will you?

MARLENE: Yes of course. (*Angie goes. Silence.*)
340   It's cold tonight.

JOYCE: Will you be all right on the sofa? You can / have my bed.

MARLENE: The sofa's fine.

JOYCE: Yes the forecast said rain tonight but
345   it's held off.

MARLENE: I was going to walk down to the estuary but I've left it a bit late. Is it just the same?

JOYCE: They cut down the hedges a few
350   years back. Is that since you were here?

MARLENE: But it's not changed down the end, all the mud? And the reeds? We used to pick them up when they were bigger than us. Are there still lapwings?

355 JOYCE: You get strangers walking there on a Sunday. I expect they're looking at the mud and the lapwings, yes.

MARLENE: You could have left.

JOYCE: Who says I wanted to leave?

360 MARLENE: Stop getting at me then, you're really boring.

JOYCE: How could I have left?

MARLENE: Did you want to?

JOYCE: I said how, / how could I?

365 MARLENE: If you'd wanted to you'd have done it.

JOYCE: Christ.

MARLENE: Are we getting drunk?

JOYCE: Do you want something to eat?

370 MARLENE: No, I'm getting drunk.

JOYCE: Funny time to visit, Sunday evening.

MARLENE: I came this morning. I spent the day—

ANGIE (*off*): Aunty! Aunty Marlene!

375 MARLENE: I'd better go.

JOYCE: Go on then.

MARLENE: All right.

ANGIE (*off*): Aunty! Can you hear me? I'm ready. (*Marlene goes. Joyce goes on sitting,*
380   *clears up, sits again. Marlene comes back.*)

JOYCE: So what's the secret?

MARLENE: It's a secret.

JOYCE: I know what it is anyway.

MARLENE: I bet you don't. You always said
385   that.

JOYCE: It's her exercise book.

MARLENE: Yes, but you don't know what's in it.

JOYCE: It's some game, some secret society she has with Kit.

390 MARLENE: You don't know the password. You don't know the code.

JOYCE: You're really in it, aren't you. Can you do the handshake?

MARLENE: She didn't mention a handshake.

395 JOYCE: I thought they'd have a special handshake. She spends hours writing that but she's useless at school. She copies things out of books about black magic, and politicians out of the paper. It's a bit childish.

400 MARLENE: I think it's a plot to take over the world.

JOYCE: She's been in the remedial class the last two years.

MARLENE: I came up this morning and spent
405   the day in Ipswich. I went to see Mother.

JOYCE: Did she recognize you?

MARLENE: Are you trying to be funny?

JOYCE: No, she does wander.

MARLENE: She wasn't wandering at all, she
410   was very lucid thank you.

JOYCE: You were very lucky then.

MARLENE: F***ing awful life she's had.

JOYCE: Don't tell me.

MARLENE: F***ing waste.

415 JOYCE: Don't talk to me.

MARLENE: Why shouldn't I talk? Why shouldn't I talk to you? / Isn't she my mother too?

JOYCE: Look, you've left, you've gone away, /
420   we can do without you.

MARLENE: I left home, so what, I left home. People do leave home / it is normal.

JOYCE: We understand that, we can do without you.

425 MARLENE: We weren't happy. Were you
happy?

JOYCE: Don't come back.

MARLENE: So it's just your mother is it, your
child, you never wanted me round, / you
430 were jealous

JOYCE: Here we go.

MARLENE: of me because I was the little one
and I was clever.

JOYCE: I'm not clever enough for all this
435 psychology / if that's what it is.

MARLENE: Why can't I visit my own family /
without

JOYCE: Aah.

MARLENE: all this?

440 JOYCE: Just don't go on about Mum's life when
you haven't been to see her for how many
years. / I go

MARLENE: It's up to me.

JOYCE: and see her every week.

445 MARLENE: Then don't go and see her every
week.

JOYCE: Somebody has to.

MARLENE: No they don't. / Why do they?

JOYCE: How would I feel if I didn't go?

450 MARLENE: A lot better.

JOYCE: I hope you feel better.

MARLENE: It's up to me.

JOYCE: You couldn't get out of here fast
enough. (*Pause.*)

455 MARLENE: Of course I couldn't get out of
here fast enough. What was I going to do?
Marry a dairyman who'd come home
pissed? / Don't you f***ing this

JOYCE: Christ.

460 MARLENE: f***ing that f***ing bitch f***ing tell
me what to f***ing do f***ing.

JOYCE: I don't know how you could leave
your own child.

MARLENE: You were quick enough to take her.

465 JOYCE: What does that mean?

MARLENE: You were quick enough to take
her.

JOYCE: Or what? Have her put in a home?
Have some stranger / take her would you
470 rather?

MARLENE: You couldn't have one so you took
mine.

JOYCE: I didn't know that then.

MARLENE: Like hell, / married three years.

475 JOYCE: I didn't know that. Plenty of people /
take that long.

MARLENE: Well it turned out lucky for you,
didn't it?

JOYCE: Turned out all right for you by the
480 look of you. You'd be getting a few less
thousand a year.

MARLENE: Not necessarily.

JOYCE: You'd be stuck here / like you said.

MARLENE: I could have taken her with me.

485 JOYCE: You didn't want to take her with you.
It's no good coming back now, Marlene, /
and saying—

MARLENE: I know a managing director who's
got two children, she breastfeeds in the
490 board room, she pays a hundred pounds a
week on domestic help alone and she can
afford that because she's an extremely
high-powered lady earning a great deal of
money.

495 JOYCE: So what's that got to do with you at
the age of seventeen?

MARLENE: Just because you were married
and had somewhere to live—

JOYCE: You could have lived at home. / Or
500 live

MARLENE: Don't be stupid.

JOYCE: with me and Frank. / You

MARLENE: You never suggested.

JOYCE: said you weren't keeping it. You
505 shouldn't have had it / if you wasn't

MARLENE: Here we go.

JOYCE: going to keep it. You was the most
stupid, / for someone so clever you was
the most stupid, get yourself pregnant,
510 not go to the doctor, not tell.

MARLENE: You wanted it, you said you were
glad, I remember the day, you said I'm
glad you never got rid of it, I'll look after it,
you said that down by the river. So what
515 are you saying, sunshine, you don't want
her?

JOYCE: Course I'm not saying that.

MARLENE: Because I'll take her, / wake her
up and pack now.

520 JOYCE: You wouldn't know how to begin to
look after her.

MARLENE: Don't you want her?

JOYCE: Course I do, she's my child.

MARLENE: Then what are you going on
525 about / why did I have her?

JOYCE: You said I got her off you / when you
didn't—

MARLENE: I said you were lucky / the way it—

JOYCE: Have a child now if you want one.
530 You're not old.

MARLENE: I might do.

JOYCE: Good. (*Pause.*)

MARLENE: I've been on the pill so long / I'm
probably sterile.

535 JOYCE: Listen when Angie was six months
I did get pregnant and I lost it because
I was so tired looking after your f***ing
baby / because she cried so

MARLENE: You never told me.

540 JOYCE: much—yes I did tell you— / and the
doctor

MARLENE: Well I forgot.

JOYCE: said if I'd sat down all day with my
feet up I'd've kept it / and that's the only
545 chance I ever had because after that—

MARLENE: I've had two abortions, are you
interested? Shall I tell you about them?
Well I won't, it's boring, it wasn't a

problem. I don't like messy talk about
550 blood / and what a bad time we all had. I

JOYCE: If I hadn't had your baby. The doctor
said.

MARLENE: don't want a baby. I don't want to
talk about gynecology.

555 JOYCE: Then stop trying to get Angie off of
me.

MARLENE: I come down here after six years.
All night you've been saying I don't come
often enough. If I don't come for another
560 six years she'll be twenty-one, will that be
OK?

JOYCE: That'll be fine, yes, six years would
suit me fine. (*Pause.*)

MARLENE: I was afraid of this. I only came
565 because I thought you wanted . . . I just
want . . . (*She cries.*)

JOYCE: Don't grizzle, Marlene, for God's sake.
Marly? Come on, pet. Love you really.
F***ing stop it, will you? (*She goes to*
570 *Marlene.*)

MARLENE: No, let me cry. I like it. (*They laugh,*
Marlene begins to stop crying.) I knew I'd cry
if I wasn't careful.

JOYCE: Everyone's always crying in this
575 house. Nobody takes any notice.

MARLENE: You've been wonderful looking
after Angie.

JOYCE: Don't get carried away.

MARLENE: I can't write letters but I do think
580 of you.

JOYCE: You're getting drunk. I'm going to
make some tea.

MARLENE: Love you. (*Joyce goes to make tea.*)

JOYCE: I can see why you'd want to leave. It's
585 a dump here.

MARLENE: So what's this about you and Frank?

JOYCE: He was always carrying on, wasn't he.
And if I wanted to go out in the evening
he'd go mad, even if it was nothing, a class,
590 I was going to go to an evening class. So he

had this girlfriend, only twenty-two
poor cow, and I said go on, off you
go, hoppit. I don't think he even likes
her.

595 MARLENE: So what about money?

JOYCE: I've always said I don't want your
money.

MARLENE: No, does he send you money?

JOYCE: I've got four different cleaning jobs.

600   Adds up. There's not a lot round here.

MARLENE: Does Angie miss him?

JOYCE: She doesn't say.

MARLENE: Does she see him?

JOYCE: He was never that fond of her to be

605   honest.

MARLENE: He tried to kiss me once. When
you were engaged.

JOYCE: Did you fancy him?

MARLENE: No, he looked like a fish.

610 JOYCE: He was lovely then.

MARLENE: Ugh.

JOYCE: Well I fancied him. For about three
years.

MARLENE: Have you got someone else?

615 JOYCE: There's not a lot round here. Mind
you, the minute you're on your own, you'd
be amazed how your friends' husbands
drop by. I'd sooner do without.

MARLENE: I don't see why you couldn't take

620   my money.

JOYCE: I do, so don't bother about it.

MARLENE: Only got to ask.

JOYCE: So what about you? Good job?

MARLENE: Good for a laugh. / Got back

625 JOYCE: Good for more than a laugh I should
think.

MARLENE: from the US of A a bit wiped out
and slotted into this speedy employment
agency and still there.

630 JOYCE: You can always find yourself work
then?

MARLENE: That's right.

JOYCE: And men?

MARLENE: Oh there's always men.

635 JOYCE: No one special?

MARLENE: There's fellas who like to be seen
with a highflying lady. Shows they've got
something really good in their pants. But
they can't take the day to day. They're

640   waiting for me to turn into the little
woman. Or maybe I'm just horrible of
course.

JOYCE: Who needs them.

MARLENE: Who needs them. Well I do. But I

645   need adventures more. So on on into the
sunset. I think the eighties are going to be
stupendous.

JOYCE: Who for?

MARLENE: For me. / I think I'm going up up up.

650 JOYCE: Oh for you. Yes, I'm sure they will.

MARLENE: And for the country, come to that.
Get the economy back on its feet and
whoosh. She's a tough lady, Maggie. I'd
give her a job. / She just needs to hang

655 JOYCE: You voted for them, did you?

MARLENE: in there. This country needs to
stop whining. / Monetarism is not

JOYCE: Drink your tea and shut up, pet.

MARLENE: stupid. It takes time, determina-

660   tion. No more slop. / And

JOYCE: Well I think they're filthy bastards.

MARLENE: who's got to drive it on? First
woman prime minister. Terrifico. Aces.
Right on. / You must admit. Certainly gets

665   my vote.

JOYCE: What good's first woman if it's her? I
suppose you'd have liked Hitler if he was a
woman. Ms. Hitler. Got a lot done,
Hitlerina. / Great adventures.

670 MARLENE: Bosses still walking on the work-
er's faces? Still dadda's little parrot?
Haven't you learned to think for yourself?
I believe in the individual. Look at me.

JOYCE: I am looking at you.

675   **MARLENE:** Come on, Joyce, we're not going to quarrel over politics.

JOYCE: We are though.

MARLENE: Forget I mentioned it. Not a word about the slimy unions will cross my lips.

680   (*Pause.*)

JOYCE: You say Mother had a wasted life.

MARLENE: Yes I do. Married to that bastard.

JOYCE: What sort of life did he have? / Working in the fields like

685   **MARLENE:** Violent life?

JOYCE: an animal. / Why

MARLENE: Come off it.

JOYCE: wouldn't he want a drink? You want a drink. He couldn't afford whiskey.

690   **MARLENE:** I don't want to talk about him.

JOYCE: You started, I was talking about her. She had a rotten life because she had nothing. She went hungry.

MARLENE: She was hungry because he drank

695   the money. / He used to hit her.

JOYCE: It's not all down to him. / Their

MARLENE: She didn't hit him.

JOYCE: lives were rubbish. They were treated like rubbish. He's dead and she'll die soon

700   and what sort of life / did they have?

MARLENE: I saw him one night. I came down.

JOYCE: Do you think I didn't? / They

MARLENE: I still have dreams.

JOYCE: didn't get to America and drive across it

705   in a fast car. / Bad nights, they had bad days.

MARLENE: America, America, you're jealous. / I had to get out, I knew when I

JOYCE: Jealous?

MARLENE: was thirteen, out of their house,

710   out of them, never let that happen to me, / never let him, make my own way, out.

JOYCE: Jealous of what you've done, you'd be ashamed of me if I came to your office, your smart friends, wouldn't you, I'm

715   ashamed of you, think of nothing but yourself, you've got on, nothing's changed for most people, / has it?

MARLENE: I hate the working class / which is what

720   **JOYCE:** Yes you do.

MARLENE: you're going to go on about now, it doesn't exist any more, it means lazy and stupid. / I don't

JOYCE: Come on, now we're getting it.

725   **MARLENE:** like the way they talk. I don't like beer guts and football vomit and saucy tits / and brothers and sisters—

JOYCE: I spit when I see a Rolls Royce, scratch it with my ring / Mercedes it was.

730   **MARLENE:** Oh very mature—

JOYCE: I hate the cows I work for / and their dirty dishes with blanquette of f***ing veau.

MARLENE: and I will not be pulled down to

735   their level by a flying picket and I won't be sent to Siberia / or a loony bin just because I'm original. And I support

JOYCE: No, you'll be on a yacht, you'll be head of Coca Cola and you wait, the eight-

740   ies is going to be stupendous all right because we'll get you lot off our backs—

MARLENE: Reagan even if he is a lousy movie star because the reds are swarming up his map and I want to be free in a free

745   world—

JOYCE: What? / What?

MARLENE: I know what I mean / by that— not shut up here.

JOYCE: So don't be round here when it

750   happens because if someone's kicking you I'll just laugh. (*Silence.*)

MARLENE: I don't mean anything personal. I don't believe in class. Anyone can do anything if they've got what it takes.

755   **JOYCE:** And if they haven't?

MARLENE: If they're stupid or lazy or fright-ened, I'm not going to help them get a job, why should I?

JOYCE: What about Angie?

760   **MARLENE:** What about Angie?

JOYCE: She's stupid, lazy, and frightened, so what about her?

MARLENE: You run her down too much. She'll be all right.

765 JOYCE: I don't expect so, no. I expect her children will say what a wasted life she had. If she has children. Because nothing's changed and it won't with them in.

MARLENE: Them, them. / Us and them?

770 JOYCE: And you're one of them.

MARLENE: And you're us, wonderful us, and Angie's us / and Mum and Dad's us.

JOYCE: Yes, that's right, and you're them.

MARLENE: Come on, Joyce, what a night.

775 You've got what it takes.

JOYCE: I know I have.

MARLENE: I didn't really mean all that.

JOYCE: I did.

MARLENE: But we're friends anyway.

780 JOYCE: I don't think so, no.

MARLENE: Well it's lovely to be out in the country. I really must make the effort to come more often. I want to go to sleep. I want to go to sleep. (*Joyce gets blankets for the sofa.*)

785 JOYCE: Goodnight then. I hope you'll be warm enough.

MARLENE: Goodnight. Joyce—

JOYCE: No, pet. Sorry. (*Joyce goes. Marlene sits wrapped in a blanket and has another drink.*

790 *Angie comes in.*)

ANGIE: Mum?

MARLENE: Angie? What's the matter?

ANGIE: Mum?

MARLENE: No, she's gone to bed. It's Aunty

795 Marlene.

ANGIE: Frightening.

MARLENE: Did you have a bad dream? What happened in it? Well you're awake now, aren't you, pet?

800 ANGIE: Frightening.

Alexi Rosenfeld/Getty Images

▲

Fearless Girl is a 2017 bronze sculpture by Kristen Visbal. It depicts a young girl defiantly staring up at the New York Stock Exchange. On International Woman's Day in 2021, shattered glass was installed around the sculpture. Shattering the "glass ceiling," is a common metaphor for the invisible barriers that hinder women's professional success. The work was commissioned by the financial firm State Street Global Advisors.

———

Women have changed history and their power has been reflected in art and literature throughout the ages. But in many contexts, women have been treated as inferior or subordinate to men, especially in the workplace. What messages does this sculpture convey about "breaking the glass ceiling"?

CHARACTER

1. What **motivates** Joyce and Angie to think and feel the way that they do?

2. What do the **contrasting** traits of Joyce and Marlene reveal about them individually? What do these traits reveal about their relationships with one another and their relationships with other characters?

3. There are many unexpected developments throughout the play. Explain an inconsistency or unexpected development between Angie and Joyce. How does it affect Marlene's **perspective**?

4. What is Marlene's **epiphany**? What minor characters in the play help her achieve this insight? Choose two **minor characters** and explain how their interactions contribute to Marlene's epiphany.

STRUCTURE

5. How does the conversation between Winn and Nell reveal a **conflict** of values?

6. Angie and Marlene's conversation at the beginning of Act II creates verbal **irony**. Which statements in their interaction are inconsistent with the expectations of the audience? How would you explain the irony, using specific textual evidence?

7. How is the interaction between Marlene and Mrs. Kidd **paradoxical**? What contradictions does it reveal? How does the **flashback** in Act II, Scene ii reveal inconsistencies and create **tension** between Marlene and Angie?

8. The final scene is a long argument between Marlene and Joyce. How is this final scene **cathartic**? Explain the emotional release that this scene reveals.

9. How does the **unresolved ending** of the play contribute to the **complexity** of the play? How does it contribute to your understanding of *Top Girls*?

NARRATION

10. How does Marlene's **perspective** change throughout the play as a result of her interactions with Angie?

11. Describe the inconsistencies in Marlene's and Joyce's **perspectives**. Explain how these inconsistencies contribute to the irony of the text.

12. The multiple **points of view** play a significant part in this play. Explain how these perspectives affect Marlene and influence her story.

IDEAS IN LITERATURE: Power and Perception

13. The play explores the power of mothers and the perceptions of children. How does the mother-daughter relationship contribute to your perception of female success?

PUTTING IT ALL TOGETHER

14. How is the title *Top Girls* a metaphor? How do its associations and connotations contribute to the complexity and significance of the play's title?

Cat on a Hot Tin Roof
Tennessee Williams

Bettmann/Getty Images

THE TEXT IN CONTEXT

Playwright Tennessee Williams (1911–1983) was born
Thomas Lanier Williams III in Columbus, Missouri. Along
with Eugene O'Neill, Arthur Miller, and Edward Albee, he is
one of the major American playwrights of the twentieth century. Williams was a precocious writer, publishing articles in
national magazines as a high school student. After graduating from the University of Iowa in 1938, he traveled, worked
odd jobs, and struggled as a playwright. But in 1944, his
drama *The Glass Menagerie* became an enormous Broadway hit. This began a
series of successes, including *A Streetcar Named Desire* (1947) and *Cat on a Hot
Tin Roof* (1955) (excerpted here). Williams's plays are intense explorations of desire,
deception, isolation, sexual identity, and family drama set in the American South.
For example, *Cat on a Hot Tin Roof* takes place on a Mississippi family estate.
These settings — both literally and culturally — influence the themes, characters,
and language of his work.

   This story includes the N-word, which we have chosen not to reprint in full here. We wish
to accurately reflect both Williams's original intent as well as the racism of the time period,
but we also recognize that this word has a long history as a derogatory and deeply hurtful
expression when used by white people toward Black people, as it is in the context of this
story. We have replaced the term without hindering understanding of the work as a whole.
Be mindful of context, both Williams's and yours, as you read and discuss *Cat on a Hot
Tin Roof*.

Cat on a Hot Tin Roof

The set is the bed-sitting-room of a plantation home in the Mississippi Delta. It is along
an upstairs gallery which probably runs
around the entire house; it has two pairs of
5 very wide doors opening onto the gallery,
showing white balustrades against a fair
summer sky that fades into dusk and night
during the course of the play, which occupies
precisely the time of its performance,
10 excepting, of course, the fifteen minutes
of intermission.

Perhaps the style of the room is not what
you would expect in the home of the Delta's
biggest cotton-planter. It is Victorian with
15 a touch of the Far East. It hasn't changed
much since it was occupied by the original
owners of the place, Jack Straw and Peter
Ochello, a pair of old bachelors who shared
this room all their lives together. In other
20 words, the room must evoke some ghosts;
it is gently and poetically haunted by a
relationship that must have involved a

tenderness which was uncommon. This may be irrelevant or unnecessary, but I once
25 saw a reproduction of a faded photograph of the veranda of Robert Louis Stevenson's home on that Samoan Island where he spent his last years, and there was a quality of tender light on weathered wood, such
30 as porch furniture made of bamboo and wicker, exposed to tropical suns and tropical rains, which came to mind when I thought about the set for this play, bringing also to mind the grace and comfort of light,
35 the reassurance it gives, on a late and fair afternoon in summer, the way that no matter what, even dread of death, is gently touched and soothed by it. For the set is the background for a play that deals with
40 human extremities of emotion, and it needs that softness behind it.

The bathroom door, showing only pale-blue tile and silver towel racks, is in one side wall; the hall door in the opposite
45 wall. Two articles of furniture need mention: a big double bed which staging should make a functional part of the set as often as suitable, the surface of which should be slightly raked to make figures on it seen
50 more easily; and against the wall space between the two huge double doors upstage: a monumental monstrosity peculiar to our times, a huge console combination of radio-phonograph (Hi-Fi with three
55 speakers) TV set and liquor cabinet, bearing and containing many glasses and bottles, all in one piece, which is a composition of muted silver tones, and the opalescent tones of reflecting glass, a
60 chromatic link, this thing, between the sepia (tawny gold) tones of the interior and the cool (white and blue) tones of the gallery and sky. This piece of furniture (?!), this monument, is a very complete and
65 compact little shrine to virtually all the comforts and illusions behind which we hide from such things as the characters in the play are faced with. . . .

The set should be far less realistic than I
70 have so far implied in this description of it. I think the walls below the ceiling should dissolve mysteriously into air; the set should be roofed by the sky; stars and moon suggested by traces of milky pallor,
75 as if they were observed through a telescope lens out of focus.

Anything else I can think of? Oh, yes, fanlights (transoms shaped like an open glass fan) above all the doors in the set,
80 with panes of blue and amber, and above all, the designer should take as many pains to give the actors room to move about freely (to show their restlessness, their passion for breaking out) as if it were a set for
85 a ballet.

An evening in summer. The action is continuous, with two intermissions.

Main Characters

MARGARET

BRICK

MAE

GOOPER

BIG MAMA

BIG DADDY

REVEREND TOOKER

DOCTOR BAUGH

ACT I

At the rise of the curtain someone is taking a shower in the bathroom, the door of which is half open. A pretty young woman, with anxious lines in her face, enters the bedroom and crosses to the bathroom door.

MARGARET [*shouting above roar of water*]:
   One of those no-neck monsters hit me with a hot buttered biscuit so I havet' change!

5 [MARGARET'S *voice is both rapid and drawling. In her long speeches she has the vocal tricks of a priest delivering a liturgical chant, the lines are almost sung, always continuing a little beyond her breath so she has to gasp for*
10 *another. Sometimes she intersperses the lines with a little wordless singing, such as "Da-da-daaaa"* Water turns off and BRICK *calls out to her, but is still unseen. A tone of politely feigned interest, masking indifference, or*
15 *worse, is characteristic of his speech with* MARGARET.]

BRICK: Wha'd you say, Maggie? Water was on s' loud I couldn't hear ya. . . .

MARGARET: Well, I!—just remarked that!—
20 one of th' no-neck monsters messed up m' lovely lace dress so I got t' cha-a-ange. . . .

[*She opens and kicks shut drawers of the dresser.*]

BRICK: Why d'ya call Gooper's kiddies
25 no-neck monsters?

MARGARET: Because they've got no necks! Isn't that a good enough reason?

BRICK: Don't they have any necks?

MARGARET: None visible. Their fat little
30 heads are set on their fat little bodies without a bit of connexion.

BRICK: That's too bad.

MARGARET: Yes, it's too bad because you can't wring their necks if they've got no
35 necks to wring! Isn't that right, honey?

[*She steps out of her dress, stands in a slip of ivory satin and lace.*] Yep, they're no-neck monsters, monsters. . . . All no-neck people are monsters. . . .

40 [*Children shriek downstairs.*]

Hear them? Hear them screaming? I don't know where their voice-boxes are located since they don't have necks. I tell you I got so nervous at that table tonight I thought I
45 would throw back my head and utter a scream you could hear across the Arkansas border an' parts of Louisiana an' Tennessee. I said to your charming sister-in-law, Mae, honey, couldn't you feed
50 those precious little things at a separate table with an oilcloth cover? They make such a mess an' the lace cloth looks so pretty! She made enormous eyes at me and said, 'Ohhh, noooooo! On Big Daddy's
55 birthday? Why, he would never forgive me!' Well, I want you to know, Big Daddy hadn't been at the table two minutes with those five no-neck monsters slobbering and drooling over their food before he
60 threw down his fork an' shouted, 'Fo' God's sake, Gooper, why don't you put them pigs at a trough in th' kitchen?'— Well, I swear, I simply could have di-ieed!

   Think of it, Brick, they've got five of
65 them and number six is coming. They've brought the whole bunch down here like animals to display at a county fair. Why, they have those children doin' tricks all the time! 'Junior, show Big Daddy how you
70 do this, show Big Daddy how you do that, say your little piece fo' Big Daddy, Sister. Show your dimples, Sugar. Brother, show Big Daddy how you stand on your head!'— It goes on all the time, along with
75 constant little remarks and innuendoes about the fact that you and I have not

produced any children, are totally childless and therefore totally useless!—Of course it's comical but it's also disgusting
80 since it's so obvious what they're up to!

BRICK [*without interest*]: What are they up to, Maggie?

MARGARET: Why, you know what they're up to!

85 BRICK [*appearing*]: No, I don't know what they're up to.

[*He stands there in the bathroom doorway drying his hair with a towel and hanging on to the towel rack because one ankle is broken, plastered and*
90 *bound. He is still slim and firm as a boy.—His liquor hasn't started tearing him down outside. He has the additional charm of that cool air of detachment that people have who have given up the struggle. But now and then, when disturbed, some-*
95 *thing flashes behind it, like lightning in a fair sky, which shows that at some deeper level he is far from peaceful. Perhaps in a stronger light he would show some signs of deliquescence, but the fading, still warm, light from the gallery treats him gently.*]

100 MARGARET: I'll tell you what they're up to, boy of mine!—They're up to cutting you out of your father's estate, and—

[*She freezes momentarily before her next remark. Her voice drops as if it were somehow a person-*
105 *ally embarrassing admission.*]

—Now we know that Big Daddy's dyin' of—cancer. . . .

[*There are voices on the lawn below | long-drawn calls across distance.* MARGARET *raises her lovely*
110 *bare arms and powders her armpits with a light sigh. | She adjusts the angle of a magnifying mirror to straighten an eyelash, then rises fretfully saying:*]

There's so much light in the room it—

BRICK [*softly but sharply*]: Do we?

115 MARGARET: Do we what?

BRICK: Know Big Daddy's dyin' of cancer?

MARGARET: Got the report today.

BRICK: Oh . . .

MARGARET [*letting down bamboo blinds which*
120 *cast long, gold-fretted shadows over the room*]: Yep, got th' report just now . . . it didn't surprise me, Baby. . . .

[*Her voice has range, and music; sometimes it drops low as a boy's and you have a sudden*
125 *image of her playing boy's games as a child.*]

I recognized the symptoms soon's we got here last spring and I'm willin' to bet you that Brother Man and his wife were pretty sure of it, too. That more than likely
130 explains why their usual summer migration to the coolness of the Great Smokies was passed up this summer in favor of hustlin' down here ev'ry whipstitch with their whole screamin' tribe! And why so many
135 allusions have been made to Rainbow Hill lately. You know what Rainbow Hill is? Place that's famous for treatin' alcoholics an' dope fiends in the movies!

BRICK: I'm not in the movies.

140 MARGARET: No, and you don't take dope. Otherwise you're a perfect candidate for Rainbow Hill, Baby, and that's where they aim to ship you—over my dead body! Yep, over my dead body they'll ship you there,
145 but nothing would please them better. Then Brother Man could get a-hold of the purse strings and dole out remittances to us, maybe get power-of-attorney and sign checks for us and cut off our credit wher-
150 ever, whenever he wanted! Son-of-a-bitch!— How'd you like that, Baby?—Well, you've been doin' just about ev'rything in your power to bring it about, you've just been doin' ev'rything you can think of to aid
155 and abet them in this scheme of theirs! Quittin' work, devoting yourself to the occupation of drinkin'!—Breakin' your ankle last night on the high school athletic field—doin' what? Jumpin'
160 hurdles? At two or three in the morning?

Just fantastic! Got in the paper. Clarksdale Register carried a nice little item about it, human interest story about a well-known former athlete stagin' a one-man track
165 meet on the Glorious Hill High School athletic field last night, but was slightly out of condition and didn't clear the first hurdle! Brother Man Gooper claims he exercised his influence t' keep it
170 from goin' out over AP or UP or every goddam' P'.

But, Brick? You still have one big advantage!

[*During the above swift flood of words,* BRICK *has*
175 *reclined with contrapuntal leisure on the snowy surface of the bed and has rolled over carefully on his side or belly.*]

BRICK [*wryly*]: Did you say something, Maggie?

180 MARGARET: Big Daddy dotes on you, honey. And he can't stand Brother Man and Brother Man's wife, that monster of fertility, Mae; she's downright odious to him! Know how I know? By little expressions
185 that flicker over his face when that woman is holding fo'th on one of her choice topics such as—how she refused twilight sleep!—when the twins were delivered! Because she feels motherhood's
190 an experience that a woman ought to experience fully!—in order to fully appreciate the wonder and beauty of it! HAH!

[*This loud 'HAH!' is accompanied by a violent*
195 *action such as slamming a drawer shut.*]

—and how she made Brother Man come in an' stand beside her in the delivery room so he would not miss out on the 'wonder and beauty' of it either!—producin' those
200 no-neck monsters. . . .

[*A speech of this kind would be antipathetic from almost anybody but* MARGARET; *she makes it oddly funny, because her eyes constantly twinkle*
205 *and her voice shakes with laughter which is basically indulgent*]

—Big Daddy shares my attitude toward those two! As for me, well—I give him a laugh now and then and he tolerates me. In fact!—I sometimes suspect that Big
210 Daddy harbors a little unconscious 'lech' fo' me. . . .

BRICK: What makes you think that Big Daddy has a lech for you, Maggie?

MARGARET: Way he always drops his eyes
215 down my body when I'm talkin' to him, drops his eyes to my boobs an' licks his old chops! Ha ha!

BRICK: That kind of talk is disgusting.

MARGARET: Did anyone ever tell you that
220 you're an ass-aching Puritan, Brick? I think it's mighty fine that that ole fellow, on the doorstep of death, still takes in my shape with what I think is deserved appreciation! And you wanta know some-
225 thing else? Big Daddy didn't know how many little Maes and Goopers had been produced! 'How many kids have you got?' he asked at the table, just like Brother Man and his wife were new acquain-
230 tances to him! Big Mama said he was jokin', but that ole boy wasn't jokin', Lord, no! And when they infawmed him that they had five already and were turning out number six!—The news seemed to
235 come as a sort of unpleasant surprise. . . .

[*Children yell below.*]

Scream, monsters!

[*Turns to* BRICK *with a sudden, gay, charming smile which fades as she notices that he is not*
240 *looking at her but into fading gold space with a troubled expression. It is constant rejection that makes her humor 'bitchy'.*]

Yes, you should of been at that supper-table, Baby.

245 [*Whenever she calls him 'baby' the word is a soft caress . . .*]

Y'know, Big Daddy, bless his ole sweet soul, he's the dearest ole thing in the world, but he does hunch over his food as if he preferred not to notice anything else. Well, Mae an' Gooper were side by side at the table, direckly across from Big Daddy, watchin' his face like hawks while they jawed an' jabbered about the cuteness an' brilliance of th' no-neck monsters!

[*She giggles with a hand fluttering at her throat and her breast and her long throat arched. She comes downstage and recreates the scene with voice and gesture.*]

And the no-neck monsters were ranged around the table, some in high chairs and some on th' Books of Knowledge, all in fancy little paper caps in honour of Big Daddy's birthday, and all through dinner, well, I want you to know that Brother Man an' his partner never once, for one moment, stopped exchanging pokes an' pinches an' kicks an' signs an' signals I—Why, they were like a couple of cardsharps fleecing a sucker.—Even Big Mama, bless her ole sweet soul, she isn't th' quickest an' bright-est thing in the world, she finally noticed, at last, an' said to Gooper, 'Gooper, what are you an' Mae makin' all these signs at each other about?'—I swear t' goodness, I nearly choked on my chicken!

[MARGARET, *back at the dressing-table, still doesn't see* BRICK. | *He is watching her with a look that is not quite definable—Amused? shocked? contemptuous?—part of those and part of something else.*]

Y'know—your brother Gooper still cher-ishes the illusion he took a giant step up on the social ladder when he married Miss Mae Flynn of the Memphis Flynns.

[MARGARET *moves about the room as she talks, stops before the mirror, moves on.*]

But I have a piece of Spanish news for Gooper. The Flynns never had a thing in this world but money and they lost that, they were nothing at all but fairly successful climbers. Of course, Mae Flynn came out in Memphis eight years before I made my debut in Nashville, but I had friends at Ward-Belmont who came from Memphis and they used to come to see me and I used to go to see them for Christmas and spring vacations, and so I know who rates an' who doesn't rate in Memphis society. Why, y'know ole Papa Flynn, he barely escaped doing time in the Federal pen for shady manipulations on th' stock market when his chain stores crashed, and as for Mae having been a cotton carnival queen, as they remind us so often, lest we forget, well, that's one honour that I don't envy her for!—Sit on a brass throne on a tacky float an' ride down Main Street, smilin', bowin', and blowin' kisses to all the trash on the street—

[*She picks out a pair of jewelled sandals and rushes to the dressing-table.*]

Why, year before last, when Susan McPheeters was singled out fo' that honour, y'know what happened to her? Y'know what happened to poor little Susie McPheeters?

BRICK [*absently*]: No. What happened to little Susie McPheeters?

MARGARET: Somebody spit tobacco juice in her face.

BRICK [*dreamily*]: Somebody spit tobacco juice in her face?

MARGARET: That's right, some old drunk leaned out of a window in the Hotel Gayoso and yelled, 'Hey, Queen, hey, hey there, Queenie!' Poor Susie looked up and flashed him a radiant smile and he shot out a squirt of tobacco juice right in poor Susie's face.

BRICK: Well, what d'you know about that.

MARGARET [*gaily*]: What do I know about it? I was there, I saw it!

335 BRICK [*absently*]: Must have been kind of funny.

MARGARET: Susie didn't think so. Had hysterics. Screamed like a banshee. They had to stop th' parade an' remove her from her throne an' go on with—

340 [*She catches sight of him in the mirror, gasps slightly, wheels about to face him. Count ten.*]

Why are you looking at me like that?

BRICK [*whistling softly, now*]: Like what, Maggie?

345 MARGARET [*intensely, fearfully*]: The way y' were lookin' at me just now, befo' I caught your eye in the mirror and you started t' whistle! I don't know how t' describe it but it froze my blood!—I've caught you

350 lookin' at me like that so often lately. What are you thinkin' of when you look at me like that?

BRICK: I wasn't conscious of lookin' at you, Maggie.

355 MARGARET: Well, I was conscious of it! What were you thinkin'?

BRICK: I don't remember thinking of anything, Maggie.

MARGARET: Don't you think I know that—?

360 Don't you—?—Think I know that—?

BRICK [*coolly*]: Know what, Maggie?

MARGARET [*struggling for expression*]: That I've gone through this—hideous!— transformation, become—hard! Frantic!

365 [*Then she adds, almost tenderly:*]—cruel!! That's what you've been observing in me lately. How could y' help but observe it? That's all right. I'm not—thin-skinned any more, can't afford t' be thin-skinned

370 any more.

[*She is now recovering her power.*]

—But Brick? Brick?

BRICK: Did you say something?

MARGARET: I was goin' t' say something—

375 that I get—lonely.—Very!

BRICK: Ev'rybody gets that . . .

MARGARET: Living with someone you love can be lonelier—than living entirely alone!—if the one that y' love doesn't

380 love you. . . .

[*There is a pause.* BRICK *hobbles downstage and asks, without looking at her:*]

BRICK: Would you like to live alone, Maggie?

[*Another pause: then—after she has caught a*

385 *quick, hurt breath:*]

MARGARET: No!—God!—I wouldn't!

[*Another gasping breath. She forcibly controls what must have been an impulse to cry out. We see her deliberately, very forcibly going all the*

390 *way back to the world in which you can talk about ordinary matters.*]

Did you have a nice shower?

BRICK: Uh-huh.

MARGARET: Was the water cool?

395 BRICK: No.

MARGARET: But it made y' feel fresh, huh?

BRICK: Fresher. . . .

MARGARET: I know something would make y' feel much fresher!

400 BRICK: What?

MARGARET: An alcohol rub. Or cologne, a rub with cologne!

BRICK: That's good after a workout but I haven't been workin' out, Maggie.

405 MARGARET: You've kept in good shape, though.

BRICK [*indifferently*]: You think so, Maggie?

MARGARET: I always thought drinkin' men lost their looks, but I was plainly

410 mistaken.

BRICK [*wryly*]: Why, thanks, Maggie.

MARGARET: You're the only drinkin' man I know that it never seems t' put fat on.

BRICK: I'm gettin' softer, Maggie.

415 MARGARET: Well, sooner or later it's bound to soften you up. It was just beginning to soften up Skipper when—

[*She stops short.*]

I'm sorry. I never could keep my fingers
420   off a sore—I wish you would lose your
looks. If you did it would make the
martyrdom of Saint Maggie a little more
bearable. But no such goddam luck. I actually believe you've gotten better looking
425   since you've gone on the bottle. Yeah, a
person who didn't know you would think
you'd never had a tense nerve in your
body or a strained muscle.
[*There are sounds of croquet on the lawn below |*
430 *the click of mallets, light voices, near and distant.*]
Of course, you always had that
detached quality as if you were playing a
game without much concern over
whether you won or lost, and now that
435   you've lost the game, not lost but just quit
playing, you have that rare sort of charm
that usually only happens in very old or
hopelessly sick people, the charm of the
defeated.—You look so cool, so cool, so
440   enviably cool.
[*Music is heard.*]
They're playing croquet. The moon has
appeared and it's white, just beginning to
turn a little bit yellow. . . . You were a
445   wonderful lover. . . . Such a wonderful
person to go to bed with, and I think
mostly because you were really indifferent to it. Isn't that right? Never had any
anxiety about it, did it naturally, easily,
450   slowly, with absolute confidence and
perfect calm, more like opening a door for
a lady or seating her at a table than giving
expression to any longing for her. Your
indifference made you wonderful at love-
455   making—strange?—but true. . . . You
know, if I thought you would never, never,
never make love to me again—I would go
downstairs to the kitchen and pick out the
longest and sharpest knife I could find
460   and stick it straight into my heart, I swear
that I would!

But one thing I don't have is the charm
of the defeated, my hat is still in the ring,
and I am determined to win!
465 [*There is the sound of croquet mallets hitting*
croquet balls.]
—What is the victory of a cat on a hot tin
roof?—I wish I knew. . . . Just staying on it,
I guess, as long as she can. . . .
470 [*More croquet sounds.*]
Later tonight I'm going to tell you I love
you an' maybe by that time you'll be
drunk enough to believe me. Yes, they're
playing croquet. . . . Big Daddy is dying of
475   cancer. . . .
What were you thinking of when I
caught you looking at me like that? Were
you thinking of Skipper?
[**BRICK** *takes up his crutch, rises.*]
480   Oh, excuse me, forgive me, but laws of
silence don't work! No, laws of silence
don't work. . . .
[**BRICK** *crosses to the bar, takes a quick drink, and*
rubs his head with a towel.]
485   Laws of silence don't work. . . . When something is festering in your memory or
your imagination, laws of silence don't work,
it's just like shutting a door and locking it on
a house on fire in hope of forgetting that the
490   house is burning. But not facing a fire
doesn't put it out. Silence about a thing just
magnifies it. It grows and festers in silence,
becomes malignant. . . . Get dressed, Brick.
[*He drops his crutch.*]
495 **BRICK:** I've dropped my crutch.
[*He has stopped rubbing his hair dry but still*
stands hanging on to the towel rack in a white
towel-cloth robe.]
MARGARET: Lean on me.
500 **BRICK:** No, just give me my crutch.
MARGARET: Lean on my shoulder.
BRICK: I don't want to lean on your shoulder,
I want my crutch! [*This is spoken like*
sudden lightning.]

505 Are you going to give me my crutch or do I
have to get down on my knees on the
floor and—

MARGARET: Here, here, take it, take it!

[*She has thrust the crutch at him.*]

510 **BRICK** [*hobbling out*]: Thanks . . .

MARGARET: We mustn't scream at each other,
the walls in this house have ears. . . .

[*He hobbles directly to liquor cabinet to get a new
drink.*]

515 —but that's the first time I've heard you
raise your voice in a long time, Brick. A
crack in the wall?—Of composure?—I
think that's a good sign. . . . A sign of
nerves in a player on the defensive!

520 [**BRICK** *turns and smiles at her coolly over his
fresh drink.*]

BRICK: It just hasn't happened yet, Maggie.

MARGARET: What?

BRICK: The click I get in my head when I've

525 had enough of this stuff to make me
peaceful. . . . Will you do me a favor?

MARGARET: Maybe I will. What favor?

BRICK: Just, just keep your voice down!

MARGARET [*in a hoarse whisper*]: I'll do you

530 that favor, I'll speak in a whisper, if not
shut up completely, if you will do me a
favor and make that drink your last one
till after the party.

BRICK: What party?

535 **MARGARET:** Big Daddy's birthday party.

BRICK: Is this Big Daddy's birthday?

MARGARET: You know this is Big Daddy's
birthday!

BRICK: No, I don't, I forgot it.

540 **MARGARET:** Well, I remembered it for you. . . .

[*They are both speaking as breathlessly as a pair
of kids after a fight, drawing deep exhausted
breaths and looking at each other with faraway
eyes, shaking and panting together as if they had

545 broken apart from a violent struggle.*]

BRICK: Good for you, Maggie.

MARGARET: You just have to scribble a few
lines on this card.

BRICK: You scribble something, Maggie.

550 **MARGARET:** It's got to be your handwriting;
it's your present, I've given him my present; it's got to be your handwriting!

[*The tension between them is building again, the
voices becoming shrill once more.*]

555 **BRICK:** I didn't get him a present.

MARGARET: I got one for you.

BRICK: All right. You write the card, then.

MARGARET: And have him know you didn't
remember his birthday?

560 **BRICK:** I didn't remember his birthday.

MARGARET: You don't have to prove you
didn't!

BRICK: I don't want to fool him about it.

MARGARET: Just write 'Love, Brick!' for

565 God's—

BRICK: No.

MARGARET: You've got to!

BRICK: I don't have to do anything I don't
want to do. You keep forgetting the condi-

570 tions on which I agreed to stay on living
with you.

MARGARET [*out before she knows it*]: I'm not
living with you. We occupy the same cage.

BRICK: You've got to remember the condi-

575 tions agreed on.

MARGARET: They're impossible conditions!

BRICK: Then why don't you—?

MARGARET: HUSH! Who is out there? Is
somebody at the door?

580 [*There are footsteps in hall.*]

MAE [*outside*]: May I enter a moment?

MARGARET: Oh, you! Sure. Come in, Mae.

[**MAE** *enters bearing aloft the bow of a young
lady's archery set.*]

585 **MAE:** Brick, is this thing yours?

MARGARET: Why, Sister Woman—that's my
Diana Trophy. Won it at the intercollegiate
archery contest on the Ole Miss campus.

MAE: It's a mighty dangerous thing to leave
590   exposed round a house full of nawmal
       rid-blooded children attracted t'weapons.

MARGARET: 'Nawmal rid-blooded children
       attracted t'weapons' ought t'be taught to
       keep their hands off things that don't
595   belong to them.

MAE: Maggie, honey, if you had children of
       your own you'd know how funny that is.
       Will you please lock this up and put the
       key out of reach?

600 MARGARET: Sister Woman, nobody is plotting
       the destruction of your kiddies.—Brick
       and I still have our special archers'
       license. We're goin' deer-huntin' on Moon
       Lake as soon as the season starts. I love to
605   run with dogs through chilly woods, run,
       run, leap over obstructions—

[She goes into the closet carrying the bow.]

MAE: How's the injured ankle, Brick?

BRICK: Doesn't hurt. Just itches.

610 MAE: Oh, my! Brick—Brick, you should've
       been downstairs after supper! Kiddies
       put on a show. Polly played the piano,
       Buster an' Sonny drums, an' then they
       turned out the lights an' Dixie an' Trixie
615   puhfawmed a toe dance in fairy costume
       with spahkluhs! Big Daddy just beamed!
       He just beamed!

MARGARET [from the closet with a sharp laugh]:
       Oh, I bet. It breaks my heart that we
620   missed it!

[She re-enters.]
       But Mae? Why did y'give dawgs' names to
       all your kiddies?

MAE: Dogs' names?

625 [MARGARET has made this observation as she goes
to raise the bamboo blinds, since the sunset glare
has diminished. In crossing she winks at BRICK.]

MARGARET [sweetly]: Dixie, Trixie, Buster,
       Sonny, Polly!—Sounds like four dogs and
630   a parrot—animal act in a circus!

MAE: Maggie?

[MARGARET turns with a smile.]
       Why are you so catty?

MARGARET: 'Cause I'm a cat! But why can't
635   you take a joke, Sister Woman?

MAE: Nothin' pleases me more than a joke
       that's funny. You know the real names of
       our kiddies. Buster's real name is Robert.
       Sonny's real name is Saunders. Trixie's
640   real name is Marlene and Dixie's—

[Someone downstairs calls for her. 'Hey,
MAE!'—She rushes to door, saying:]
       Intermission is over!

MARGARET [as MAE closes door]: I wonder
645   what Dixie's real name is?

BRICK: Maggie, being catty doesn't help
       things any. . . .

MARGARET: I know! WHY!—am I so catty?—
       'Cause I'm consumed with envy an' eaten
650   up with longing?—Brick, I've laid out your
       beautiful Shantung silk suit from Rome
       and one of your monogrammed silk
       shirts. I'll put your cuff-links in it, those
       lovely star sapphires I get you to wear so
655   rarely. . . .

BRICK: I can't get trousers on over this
       plaster cast.

MARGARET: Yes, you can, I'll help you.

BRICK: I'm not going to get dressed, Maggie.

660 MARGARET: Will you just put on a pair of
       white silk pyjamas?

BRICK: Yes, I'll do that, Maggie.

MARGARET: Thank you, thank you so much!

BRICK: Don't mention it.

665 MARGARET: Oh, Brick! How long does it have
       t' go on? This punishment? Haven't I done
       time enough, haven't I served my term,
       can't I apply for a—pardon?

BRICK: Maggie, you're spoiling my liquor.
670   Lately your voice always sounds like you'd
       been running upstairs to warn somebody
       that the house was on fire!

MARGARET: Well, no wonder, no wonder. Y'know what I feel like, Brick?

675 [*Children's and grownups' voices are blended, below, in a loud but uncertain rendition of 'My Wild Irish Rose'.*]

I feel all the time like a cat on a hot tin roof!

680 BRICK: Then jump off the roof, jump off it, cats can jump off roofs and land on their four feet uninjured!

MARGARET: Oh, yes!

BRICK: Do it!—fo' God's sake, do it . . .

685 MARGARET: Do what?

BRICK: Take a lover!

MARGARET: I can't see a man but you! Even with my eyes closed, I just see you! Why don't you get ugly, Brick, why don't you

690 please get fat or ugly or something so I could stand it?

[*She rushes to hall door, opens it, listens.*]

The concert is still going on! Bravo, no-necks, bravo!

695 [*She slams and locks door fiercely.*]

BRICK: What did you lock the door for?

MARGARET: To give us a little privacy for a while.

BRICK: You know better, Maggie.

700 MARGARET: No, I don't know better. . . .

[*She rushes to gallery doors, draws the rose-silk drapes across them.*]

BRICK: Don't make a fool of yourself.

MARGARET: I don't mind makin' a fool of

705 myself over you!

BRICK: I mind, Maggie. I feel embarrassed for you.

MARGARET: Feel embarrassed! But don't continue my torture. I can't live on and on

710 under these circumstances.

BRICK: You agreed to—

MARGARET: I know but—

BRICK: —accept that condition!

MARGARET: I CAN'T! CAN'T! CAN'T!

715 [*She seizes his shoulder.*]

BRICK: Let go!

[*He breaks away from her and seizes the small boudoir chair and raises it like a lion-tamer facing a big circus cat. | Count five. She stares at him*

720 *with her fist pressed to her mouth, then bursts into shrill, almost hysterical laughter. | He remains grave for a moment, then grins and puts the chair down.* BIG MAMA *calls through closed door:*]

725 BIG MAMA: Son? Son? Son?

BRICK: What is it, Big Mama?

BIG MAMA [*outside*]: Oh, son! We got the most wonderful news about Big Daddy. I just had t' run up an' tell you right this—

730 [*She rattles the knob.*]

—What's this door doin', locked, faw? You all think there's robbers in the house?

MARGARET: Big Mama, Brick is dressin', he's not dressed yet.

735 BIG MAMA: That's all right, it won't be the first time I've seen Brick not dressed. Come on, open this door!

[MARGARET, *with a grimace, goes to unlock and open the hall door, as* BRICK *hobbles rapidly to the*

740 *bathroom and kicks the door shut.* BIG MAMA *has disappeared from the hall.*]

MARGARET: Big Mama?

[BIG MAMA *appears through the opposite gallery doors behind* MARGARET, *huffing and puffing like*

745 *an old bulldog. She is a short, stout woman; her sixty years and 170 pounds have left her some-what breathless most of the time; she's always tensed like a boxer, or rather, a Japanese wrestler. Her 'family' was maybe a little superior to* BIG

750 DADDY'S, *but not much. She wears a black or silver lace dress and at least half a million in flashy gems. She is very sincere.*]

BIG MAMA [*loudly, startling* MARGARET]: Here— I come through Gooper's and Mae's gall'ry

755 door. Where's Brick? Brick—Hurry on out of there, son. I just have a second and

want to give you the news about Big Daddy.—I hate locked doors in a house. . . .

MARGARET [*with affected lightness*]: I've noticed you do, Big Mama, but people have got to have some moments of privacy, don't they?

BIG MAMA: No, ma'am, not in my house. [*Without pause.*] Whacha took off you' dress faw? I thought that little lace dress was so sweet on yuh, honey.

MARGARET: I thought it looked sweet on me, too, but one of m' cute little table-partners used it for a napkin so!

BIG MAMA [*picking up stockings on floor*]: What?

MARGARET: You know, Big Mama, Mae and Gooper's so touchy about those children—thanks, Big Mama . . .

[BIG MAMA *has thrust the picked-up stockings in* MARGARET'S *hand with a grunt.*]
—that you just don't dare to suggest there's any room for improvement in their—

BIG MAMA: Brick, hurry out!—Shoot, Maggie, you just don't like children.

MARGARET: I do SO like children! Adore them!—well brought up!

BIG MAMA [*gentle—loving*]: Well, why don't you have some and bring them up well, then, instead of all the time pickin' on Gooper's an' Mae's?

GOOPER [*shouting up the stairs*]: Hey, hey, Big Mama, Betsy an' Hugh got to go, waitin' t' tell yuh g'by!

BIG MAMA: Tell 'em to hold their hawses, I'll be right down in a jiffy!

[*She turns to the bathroom door and calls out.*]
Son? Can you hear me in there?

[*There is a muffled answer.*]
We just got the full report from the laboratory at the Ochsner Clinic, completely negative, son, ev'rything negative, right on down the line! Nothin' a-tall's wrong with him but some little functional thing called a spastic colon. Can you hear me, son?

MARGARET: He can hear you, Big Mama.

BIG MAMA: Then why don't he say something? God Almighty, a piece of news like that should make him shout. It made me shout, I can tell you. I shouted and sobbed and fell right down on my knees!—Look!

[*She pulls up her skirt.*]
See the bruises where I hit my kneecaps? Took both doctors to haul me back on my feet!

[*She laughs—she always laughs like hell at herself.*]
BIG DADDY was furious with me! But ain't that wonderful news?

[*Facing bathroom again, she continues:*]
After all the anxiety we been through to git a report like that on Big Daddy's birthday? Big Daddy tried to hide how much of a load that news took off his mind, but didn't fool me. He was mighty close to crying about it himself!

[*Goodbyes are shouted downstairs, and she rushes to door.*]
Hold those people down there, don't let them go!—Now, git dressed, we're all comin' up to this room fo' Big Daddy's birthday party because of your ankle.—How's his ankle, Maggie?

MARGARET: Well, he broke it, Big Mama.

BIG MAMA: I know he broke it.

[*A phone is ringing in hall. A Negro voice answers: 'Mistuh Polly's res'dence.'*]
I mean does it hurt him much still.

MARGARET: I'm afraid I can't give you that information, Big Mama. You'll have to ask Brick if it hurts much still or not.

SOOKEY [*in the hall*]: It's Memphis, Mizz Polly, it's Miss Sally in Memphis.

BIG MAMA: Awright, Sookey.

[BIG MAMA *rushes into the hall and is heard shouting on the phone:*]

Hello, Miss Sally. How are you, Miss
Sally?—Yes, well, I was just gonna call
you about it. Shoot!—

[*She raises her voice to a bellow.*]

845   Miss Sally? Don't ever call me from the
Gayoso Lobby, too much talk goes on in
that hotel lobby, no wonder you can't
hear me! Now listen, Miss Sally. They's
nothin' serious wrong with Big Daddy. We
850   got the report just now, they's nothin'
wrong but a thing called a—spastic!
SPASTIC!—colon . . .

[*She appears at the hall door and calls to*
MARGARET.]

855   —Maggie, come out here and talk to
that fool on the phone. I'm shouted
breathless!

MARGARET [*goes out and is heard sweetly at
phone*]: Miss Sally? This is Brick's wife,
860   Maggie. So nice to hear your voice. Can
you hear mine? Well, good!—Big Mama
just wanted you to know that they've got
the report from the Ochsner Clinic and
what Big Daddy has is a spastic colon. Yes.
865   Spastic colon, Miss Sally. That's right,
spastic colon. G'bye Miss Sally, hope I'll
see you real soon!

[*Hangs up a little before Miss Sally was probably
ready to terminate the talk. She returns through*
870   *the hall door.*]

She heard me perfectly. I've discovered
with deaf people the thing to do is not
shout at them but just enunciate clearly.
My rich old Aunt Cornelia was deaf as the
875   dead but I could make her hear me just by
sayin' each word slowly, distinctly, close to
her ear. I read her the Commercial Appeal
ev'ry night, read her the classified ads in
it, even, she never missed a word of it. But
880   was she a mean ole thing! Know what I
got when she died? Her unexpired
subscriptions to five magazines and the
Book-of-the-Month Club and a LIBRARY

full of ev'ry dull book ever written! All else
885   went to her hellcat of a sister . . . meaner
than she was, even!

[BIG MAMA *has been straightening things up in
the room during this speech.*]

BIG MAMA [*closing closet door on discarded
890   clothes*]: Miss Sally sure is a case! Big
Daddy says she's always got her hand out
fo' something. He's not mistaken. That
poor ole thing always has her hand out fo'
somethin'. I don't think Big Daddy gives
895   her as much as he should.

[*Somebody shouts for her downstairs and she
shouts:*] I'm comin'!

[*She starts out. At the hall door, turns and jerks a
forefinger, first towards the bathroom door, then
900   towards the liquor cabinet, meaning: 'Has* BRICK
been drinking?' MARGARET *pretends not to understand, cocks her head and raises her brows as if
the pantomimic performance was completely
mystifying to her.* BIG MAMA *rushes back to*
905   MARGARET.]

Shoot! Stop playin' so dumb!—I mean has
he been drinkin' that stuff much yet?

MARGARET [*with a little laugh*]: Oh! I think he
had a highball after supper.

910   BIG MAMA: Don't laugh about it!—Some
single men stop drinkin' when they git
married and others start! Brick never
touched liquor before he—!

MARGARET [*crying out*]: THAT'S NOT FAIR!

915   BIG MAMA: Fair or not fair I want to ask you
a question, one question—D'you make
Brick happy in bed?

MARGARET: Why don't you ask if he makes
me happy in bed?

920   BIG MAMA: Because I know that—

MARGARET: It works both ways!

BIG MAMA: Something's not right! You're
childless and my son drinks!

[*Someone has called her downstairs and she has
925   rushed to the door on the line above. She turns at
the door and points at the bed.*]

—When a marriage goes on the rocks, the rocks are there, right there!

MARGARET: That's—

[BIG MAMA *has swept out of the room and*
930 *slammed the door.*]

—not-fair . . .

[MARGARET *is alone, completely alone, and she feels it. She draws in, hunches her shoulders, raises her arms with fists clenched, shuts her eyes*
935 *tight as a child about to be stabbed with a vaccination needle. When she opens her eyes again, what she sees is the long oval mirror and she rushes straight to it, stares into it with a grimace and says: 'Who are you?'—Then she crouches a*
940 *little and answers herself in a different voice which is high, thin, mocking: 'I am Maggie the Cat!'—Straightens quickly as bathroom door opens a little and* BRICK *calls out to her.*]

BRICK: Has Big Mama gone?

945 MARGARET: She's gone.

[He *opens the bathroom door and hobbles out, with his liquor glass now empty, straight to the liquor cabinet. He is whistling softly.* MARGARET'S *head pivots on her long, slender throat to watch*
950 *him. She raises a hand uncertainly to the base of her throat, as if it was difficult for her to swallow, before she speaks:*]

You know, our sex life didn't just peter out in the usual way, it was cut off short,
955 long before the natural time for it to, and it's going to revive again, just as sudden as that. I'm confident of it. That's what I'm keeping myself attractive for. For the time when you'll see me again like other
960 men see me. Yes, like other men see me. They still see me, Brick, and they like what they see. Uh-huh. Some of them would give their—Look, Brick!

[*She stands before the long oval mirror, touches her*
965 *breast and then her hips with her two hands.*]

How high my body stays on me!—Nothing has fallen on me—not a fraction—

[*Her voice is soft and trembling—a pleading*
970 *child's. At this moment as he turns to glance at her—a look which is like a player passing a ball to another player, third down and goal to go—she has to capture the audience in a grip so tight that she can hold it till the first intermission without*
975 *any lapse of attention.*]

Other men still want me. My face looks strained, sometimes, but I've kept my figure as well as you've kept yours, and men admire it. I still turn heads on the
980 street. Why, last week in Memphis everywhere that I went men's eyes burned holes in my clothes, at the country club and in restaurants and department stores, there wasn't a man I met or walked by
985 that didn't just eat me up with his eyes and turn around when I passed him and look back at me. Why, at Alice's party for her New York cousins, the best lookin' man in the crowd—followed me upstairs
990 and tried to force his way in the powder room with me, followed me to the door and tried to force his way in!

BRICK: Why didn't you let him, Maggie?

MARGARET: Because I'm not that common,
995 for one thing. Not that I wasn't almost tempted to. You like to know who it was? It was Sonny Boy Maxwell, that's who!

BRICK: Oh, yeah, Sonny Boy Maxwell, he was a good end-runner but had a little injury
1000 to his back and had to quit.

MARGARET: He has no injury now and has no wife and still has a lech for me!

BRICK: I see no reason to lock him out of a powder room in that case.

1005 MARGARET: And have someone catch me at it? I'm not that stupid. Oh, I might some time cheat on you with someone, since you're so insultingly eager to have me do it!—But if I do, you can be damned sure it
1010 will be in a place and a time where no one but me and the man could possibly know.

Because I'm not going to give you any
excuse to divorce me for being unfaithful
or anything else. . . .

1015 BRICK: Maggie, I wouldn't divorce you for
being unfaithful or anything else. Don't
you know that? Hell. I'd be relieved to
know that you'd found yourself a lover.

MARGARET: Well, I'm taking no chances. No,
1020 I'd rather stay on this hot tin roof.

BRICK: A hot tin roof's 'n uncomfo'table
place t' stay on. . . .

[*He starts to whistle softly.*]

MARGARET [*through his whistle*]: Yeah, but I
1025 can stay on it just as long as I have to.

BRICK: You could leave me, Maggie.

[*He resumes whistle. She wheels about to glare at
him.*]

MARGARET: Don't want to and will not!
1030 Besides if I did, you don't have a cent to
pay for it but what you get from Big Daddy
and he's dying of cancer!

[*For the first time a realisation of* BIG DADDY'S
doom seems to penetrate to BRICK'S *conscious-*
1035 *ness, visibly, and he looks at* MARGARET.]

BRICK: Big Mama just said he wasn't, that
the report was okay.

MARGARET: That's what she thinks because
she got the same story that they gave Big
1040 Daddy. And was just as taken in by it as
he was, poor ole things. . . . But tonight
they're going to tell her the truth about it.
When Big Daddy goes to bed, they're going
to tell her that he is dying of cancer.

1045 [*She slams the dresser drawer.*]
—It's malignant and it's terminal.

BRICK: Does Big Daddy know it?

MARGARET: Hell, do they ever know it?
Nobody says, 'You're dying.' You have to
1050 fool them. They have to fool themselves.

BRICK: Why?

MARGARET: Why? Because human beings
dream of life everlasting, that's the

reason! But most of them want it on earth
1055 and not in heaven.

[*He gives a short, hard laugh at her touch of
humor.*]

Well. . . . [*She touches up her mascara.*] That's
how it is, anyhow. . . . [*She looks about.*]
1060 Where did I put down my cigarette? Don't
want to burn up the home-place, at least
not with Mae and Gooper and their five
monsters in it!

[*She has found it and sucks at it greedily. Blows
1065 out smoke and continues:*]

So this is Big Daddy's last birthday. And
Mae and Gooper, they know it, oh, they
know it, all right. They got the first information from the Ochsner Clinic. That's
1070 why they rushed down here with their
no-neck monsters. Because. Do you know
something? Big Daddy's made no will? Big
Daddy's never made out any will in his
life, and so this campaign's afoot to
1075 impress him, forcibly as possible, with
the fact that you drink and I've borne no
children!

[*He continues to stare at her a moment, then
mutters something sharp but not audible and
1080 hobbles rather rapidly out on to the long gallery
in the fading, much faded, gold light.*]

MARGARET [*continuing her liturgical chant*]:
Y'know, I'm fond of Big Daddy, I am genuinely fond of that old man, I really am,
1085 you know—

BRICK [*faintly, vaguely*]: Yes, I know you are. . . .

MARGARET: I've always sort of admired him
in spite of his coarseness, his four-letter
words and so forth. Because Big Daddy is
1090 what he is, and he makes no bones about
it. He hasn't turned gentleman farmer,
he's still a Mississippi red neck, as much
of a red neck as he must have been when
he was just overseer here on the old Jack
1095 Straw and Peter Ochello place. But he got

hold of it an' built it into th' biggest an' finest plantation in the Delta.—I've always liked Big Daddy. . . .

[*She crosses to the proscenium*]

1100 Well, this is Big Daddy's last birthday. I'm sorry about it. But I'm facing the facts. It takes money to take care of a drinker and that's the office that I've been elected to lately.

1105 BRICK: You don't have to take care of me.

MARGARET: Yes, I do. Two people in the same boat have got to take care of each other. At least you want money to buy more Echo Spring when this supply

1110 is exhausted, or will you be satisfied with a ten-cent beer?—Mae an' Gooper are plannin' to freeze us out of Big Daddy's estate because you drink and I'm childless. But we can defeat that

1115 plan. We're going to defeat that plan!— Brick, y'know, I've been so God damn disgustingly poor all my life!—That's the truth, Brick!

BRICK: I'm not sayin' it isn't.

1120 MARGARET: Always had to suck up to people I couldn't stand because they had money and I was poor as Job's turkey. You don't know what that's like. Well, I'll tell you, it's like you would feel a thousand miles away

1125 from Echo Spring!—And had to get back to it on that broken ankle . . . without a crutch!

That's how it feels to be as poor as Job's turkey and have to suck up to relatives that

1130 you hated because they had money and all you had was a bunch of hand-me-down clothes and a few old mouldy three per cent government bonds. My daddy loved his liquor, he fell in love with his liquor

1135 the way you've fallen in love with Echo Spring!—And my poor Mama, having to maintain some semblance of social

position, to keep appearances up, on an income of one hundred and fifty dollars a

1140 month on those old government bonds!

When I came out, the year that I made my debut, I had just two evening dresses! One Mother made me from a pattern in Vogue, the other a hand-me-down from a

1145 snotty rich cousin I hated!

—The dress that I married you in was my grandmother's weddin' gown. . . . So that's why I'm like a cat on a hot tin roof!

[BRICK *is still on the gallery. Someone below calls*

1150 *up to him in a warm Negro voice,* 'Hiya, Mistah BRICK, how yuh feelin'?']

[BRICK *raises his liquor glass as if that answered the question.*]

MARGARET: You can be young without

1155 money but you can't be old without it. You've got to be old with money because to be old without it is just too awful, you've got to be one or the other, either young or with money, you can't be old and

1160 without it.—That's the truth, Brick. . . .

[BRICK *whistles softly, vaguely.*]

Well, now I'm dressed, I'm all dressed, there's nothing else for me to do.

[*Forlornly, almost fearfully.*]

1165 I'm dressed, all dressed, nothing else for me to do. . . .

[*She moves about restlessly, aimlessly, and speaks, as if to herself.*]

I know when I made my mistake.— What

1170 am I—? Oh!—my bracelets. . . .

[*She starts working a collection of bracelets over her hands on to her wrists, about six on each, as she talks.*]

I've thought a whole lot about it and now I

1175 know when I made my mistake. Yes, I made my mistake when I told you the truth about that thing with Skipper. Never should have confessed it, a fatal error, tellin' you about that thing with Skipper.

1180 **BRICK:** Maggie, shut up about Skipper. I mean it, Maggie; you got to shut up about Skipper.

MARGARET: You ought to understand that Skipper and I—

1185 **BRICK:** You don't think I'm serious, Maggie? You're fooled by the fact that I am saying this quiet? Look, Maggie. What you're doing is a dangerous thing to do. You're—you're—you're—foolin' 1190 with something that—nobody ought to fool with.

MARGARET: This time I'm going to finish what I have to say to you. Skipper and I made love, if love you could call it, 1195 because it made both of us feel a little bit closer to you. You see, you son of a bitch, you asked too much of people, of me, of him, of all the unlucky poor damned sons of bitches that happen to love you, and 1200 there was a whole pack of them, yes, there was a pack of them besides me and Skipper, you asked too goddam much of people that loved you, you—superior creature!—you godlike being!—And so 1205 we made love to each other to dream it was you, both of us! Yes, yes, yes! Truth, truth! What's so awful about it? I like it, I think the truth is—yeah! I shouldn't have told you. . . .

1210 **BRICK** [*holding his head unnaturally still and uptilted a bit*]: It was Skipper that told me about it. Not you, Maggie.

MARGARET: I told you!

BRICK: After he told me!

1215 **MARGARET:** What does it matter who—?
[**BRICK** *turns suddenly out upon the gallery and calls:*]

BRICK: Little girl! Hey, little girl!

GIRL [*at a distance*]: What, Uncle Brick?

1220 **BRICK:** Tell the folks to come up!—Bring everybody upstairs!

MARGARET: I can't stop myself! I'd go on telling you this in front of them all, if I had to!

1225 **BRICK:** Little girl! Go on, go on, will you? Do what I told you, call them!

MARGARET: Because it's got to be told and you, you!—you never let me!
[*She sobs, then controls herself, and continues* 1230 *almost calmly.*]

It was one of those beautiful, ideal things they tell about in the Greek legends, it couldn't be anything else, you being you, and that's what made it so sad, that's 1235 what made it so awful, because it was love that never could be carried through to anything satisfying or even talked about plainly. Brick, I tell you, you got to believe me, Brick, I do understand all 1240 about it! I—I think it was—noble! Can't you tell I'm sincere when I say I respect it? My only point, the only point that I'm making, is life has got to be allowed to continue even after the dream of life 1245 is—all—over. . . .
[**BRICK** *is without his crutch, leaning on furniture, he crosses to pick it up as she continues as if possessed by a will outside herself:*]

Why I remember when we double-dated 1250 at college, Gladys Fitzgerald and I and you and Skipper, it was more like a date between you and Skipper. Gladys and I were just sort of tagging along as if it was necessary to chaperone you!—to make a 1255 good public impression—

BRICK [*turns to face her, half lifting his crutch*]: Maggie, you want me to hit you with this crutch? Don't you know I could kill you with this crutch?

1260 **MARGARET:** Good Lord, man, d' you think I'd care if you did?

BRICK: One man has one great good true thing in his life. One great good thing

which is true!—I had friendship with
1265 Skipper.—You are naming it dirty!

MARGARET: I'm not naming it dirty! I am
naming it clean.

BRICK: Not love with you, Maggie, but friendship with Skipper was that one great true
1270 thing, and you are naming it dirty!

MARGARET: Then you haven't been listenin',
not understood what I'm saying! I'm
naming it so damn clean that it killed
poor Skipper!—You two had something
1275 that had to be kept on ice, yes, incorruptible, yes!—and death was the only icebox
where you could keep it. . . .

BRICK: I married you, Maggie. Why would I
marry you, Maggie, if I was—?

1280 MARGARET: Brick, don't brain me yet, let me
finish!—I know, believe me I know, that
it was only Skipper that harbored even
any unconscious desire for anything not
perfectly pure between you two!—Now
1285 let me skip a little. You married me early
that summer we graduated out of Ole
Miss, and we were happy, weren't we, we
were blissful, yes, hit heaven together
ev'ry time that we loved! But that fall
1290 you an' Skipper turned down wonderful
offers of jobs in order to keep on bein'
football heroes—pro-football heroes.
You organized the Dixie Stars that fall,
so you could keep on bein' team-mates
1295 for ever! But somethin' was not right with
it!—Me included!—between you. Skipper
began hittin' the bottle . . . you got a spinal
injury—couldn't play the Thanksgivin'
game in Chicago, watched it on TV from a
1300 traction bed in Toledo. I joined Skipper. The
Dixie Stars lost because poor Skipper was
drunk. We drank together that night all
night in the bar of the Blackstone and
when cold day was comin' up over the Lake
1305 an' we were comin' out drunk to take a

dizzy look at it, I said, 'SKIPPER! STOP
LOVIN' MY HUSBAND OR TELL HIM HE'S
GOT TO LET YOU ADMIT IT TO HIM!'—one
way or another!

1310 HE SLAPPED ME HARD ON THE
MOUTH!—then turned and ran without
stopping once, I am sure, all the way back
into his room at the Blackstone. . . .

—When I came to his room that night,
1315 with a little scratch like a shy little mouse
at his door, he made that pitiful, ineffectual little attempt to prove that what I had
said wasn't true—

[BRICK strikes at her with crutch, a blow that
1320 shatters the gemlike lamp on the table.]

—In this way, I destroyed him, by telling him truth that he and his world which
he was born and raised in, yours and his
world, had told him could not be told?
1325 —From then on Skipper was nothing at
all but a receptacle for liquor and drugs. . . .
—Who shot cock-robin? I with my—
[She throws back her head with tight shut
eyes.]—merciful arrow!

1330 [BRICK strikes at her; misses.]
Missed me!—Sorry,—I'm not tryin' to
whitewash my behaviour, Christ, no!
Brick, I'm not good. I don't know why
people have to pretend to be good,
1335 nobody's good. The rich or the well-to-do
can afford to respect moral patterns,
conventional moral patterns, but I could
never afford to, yeah, but—I'm honest!
Give me credit for just that, will you
1340 please?—Born poor, raised poor, expect to
die poor unless I manage to get us something out of what Big Daddy leaves when
he dies of cancer! But Brick?!—Skipper is
dead! I'm alive! Maggie the cat is—
1345 [BRICK hops awkwardly forward and strikes at
her again with his crutch.]—alive! I am
alive! I am . . .

[*He hurls the crutch at her, across the bed she took refuge behind, and pitches forward on the* 1350 *floor as she completes her speech.*]

—alive!

[*A little girl,* DIXIE, *bursts into the room, wearing an Indian war bonnet and firing a cap pistol at* MARGARET *and shouting: 'Bang, bang, bang!'* 1355 *Laughter downstairs floats through the open ball door.* | MARGARET *had crouched gasping to bed at child's entrance. She now rises and says with cool fury:*]

Little girl, your mother or someone should 1360 teach you—[*gasping*]—to knock at a door before you come into a room. Otherwise people might think that you—lack—good breeding. . . .

DIXIE: Yanh, yanh, yanh, what is Uncle Brick 1365 doin' on th' floor?

BRICK: I tried to kill your Aunt Maggie, but I failed—and I fell. Little girl, give me my crutch so I can get up off th' floor.

MARGARET: Yes, give your uncle his crutch, 1370 he's a cripple, honey, he broke his ankle last night jumping hurdles on the high school athletic field!

DIXIE: What were you jumping hurdles for, Uncle Brick?

1375 BRICK: Because I used to jump them, and people like to do what they used to do, even after they've stopped being able to do it. . . .

MARGARET: That's right, that's your answer, 1380 now go away, little girl. [DIXIE *fires cap pistol at* MARGARET *three times.*]

Stop, you stop that, monster! You little no-neck monster!

[*She seizes the cap pistol and hurls it through* 1385 *gallery doors.*]

DIXIE [*with a precocious instinct for the cruelest thing*]: You're jealous!—You're just jealous because you can't have babies!

[*She sticks out her tongue at* MARGARET *as she* 1390 *sashays past her with her stomach stuck out, to the gallery.* MARGARET *slams the gallery doors and leans panting against them. There is a pause.* BRICK *has replaced his spilt drink and sits, faraway, on the great four-poster bed.*]

1395 MARGARET: You see?—they gloat over us being childless, even in front of their five little no-neck monsters!

[*Pause. Voices approach on the stairs.*]

Brick?—I've been to a doctor in Memphis, 1400 a—a gynaecologist. . . . I've been completely examined, and there is no reason why we can't have a child whenever we want one. And this is my time by the calendar to conceive. Are you listening to me? Are you? 1405 Are you LISTENING TO ME!

BRICK: Yes. I hear you, Maggie.

[*His attention returns to her inflamed face.*]

—But how in hell on earth do you imagine—that you're going to have a 1410 child by a man that can't stand you?

MARGARET: That's a problem that I will have to work out.

[*She wheels about to face the hall door.*] Here they come! [*The lights dim.*]

CURTAIN

Sara Kruwich/The New York Times/Redux Pictures

◄ The image shows a 2013 production of Tennessee Williams's *Cat on a Hot Tin Roof* at the Richard Rodgers Theater in New York. The image conveys the distress between Brick (played by Benjamin Walker) and Maggie (played by Scarlett Johansson).

―――――

What details in the photograph both reveal Maggie's character and communicate the conflict between Brick and Maggie?

CHARACTER

1. Describe how the play characterizes Brick and Maggie, physically and emotionally. How does this characterization contribute to your understanding of their relationship?

2. At the end of Act I, what unexpected developments in Brick and Maggie's relationship contribute to their competing value systems and build **tension** in the play?

3. How does the animal imagery in Act I extend beyond a single occurrence and contribute to the **complexity** of Maggie's character?

STRUCTURE

4. How does the sequence of events in Act I affect the development of characters and **conflict**?

5. How does the **contrast** between Maggie and Gooper indicate a **conflict** of values?

6. The events and **pacing** in the first act develop quickly. How does the speed of events contribute to the play's conflict?

NARRATION

7. Act I reveals many **contrasting perspectives**. How do Maggie's speech and actions contribute to the **tension** between Maggie and Big Mama?

8. The information revealed in Act I primarily comes from Maggie and Brick's conversation in their bedroom. How do the interruptions in the conversation contribute to the play's suspense?

9. Big Daddy's wealth and the possibility of an inheritance motivate the characters in Act I. How do the power of money and the perception of wealth motivate you or people you know? In what ways can these motivations have positive effects? What debilitating effects might they have?

ACT II

There is no lapse of time. MARGARET *and* BRICK *are in the same positions they held at the end of Act I.*

MARGARET [*at door*]: Here they come!
[BIG DADDY *appears first, a tall man with a fierce, anxious look, moving carefully not to betray his weakness even, or especially, to*
5 *himself.*]
BIG DADDY: Well, Brick.
BRICK: Hello, Big Daddy.—Congratulations!
BIG DADDY: —Crap. . . .
[*Some of the people are approaching through the*
10 *hall, others along the gallery | voices from both directions.* GOOPER *and* REVEREND TOOKER *become visible outside gallery doors, and their voices come in clearly. They pause outside as* GOOPER *lights a cigar.*]
15 REVEREND TOOKER [*vivaciously*]: Oh, but St Paul's in Grenada has three memorial windows, and the latest one is a Tiffany stained-glass window that cost twenty-five hundred dollars, a picture of Christ
20 the Good Shepherd with a Lamb in His arms.
GOOPER: Who give that window, Preach?
REVEREND TOOKER: Clyde Fletcher's widow. Also presented St Paul's with a baptismal
25 font.
GOOPER: Y'know what somebody ought t' give your church is a coolin' system, Preach.
REVEREND TOOKER: Yes, siree, Bob! And
30 y'know what Gus Hamma's family gave

in his memory to the church at Two Rivers? A complete new stone parish-house with a basketball court in the basement and a—
BIG DADDY [*uttering a loud barking laugh which*
35 *is far from truly mirthful*]: Hey, Preach! What's all this talk about memorials, Preach? Y' think somebody's about t' kick off around here? 'S that it?
[*Startled by this interjection,* REVEREND TOOKER
40 *decides to laugh at the question almost as loud as he can. How he would answer the question we'll never know, as he's spared that embarrassment by the voice of* GOOPER'S *wife,* MAE, *rising high and clear as she appears with* DOC' BAUGH, *the*
45 *family doctor, through the hall door.*]
MAE [*almost religiously*]: —Let's see now, they've had their tyyy-phoid shots, and their tetanus shots, their diphtheria shots and their hepatitis shots and their polio
50 shots, they got those shots every month from May through September, and— Gooper? Hey! Gooper!—What all have the kiddies been shot faw?
MARGARET [*overlapping a bit*]: Turn on the
55 Hi-Fi, Brick! Let's have some music t' start off th' party with!
[*The talk becomes so general that the room sounds like a great aviary of chattering birds. Only* BRICK *remains unengaged, leaning upon*
60 *the liquor cabinet with his faraway smile, an ice cube in a paper napkin with which he now and then rubs his forehead. He doesn't respond to* MARGARET'S *command. She bounds forward*

and stoops over the instrument panel of the
65 *console.*]

GOOPER: We gave 'em that thing for a third
anniversary present, got three speakers
in it.

[*The room is suddenly blasted by the climax of a*
70 *Wagnerian opera or a Beethoven symphony.*]

BIG DADDY: Turn that damn thing off!

[*Almost instant silence, almost instantly broken
by the shouting charge of* **BIG MAMA**, *entering
through hall door like a charging rhino.*]

75 **BIG MAMA:** Wha's my Brick, wha's mah
precious baby!!

BIG DADDY: Sorry! Turn it back on!

[*Everyone laughs very loud.* **BIG DADDY** *is
famous for his jokes at* **BIG MAMA's** *expense,*
80 *and nobody laughs louder at these jokes than*
BIG MAMA *herself, though sometimes they're
pretty cruel and* **BIG MAMA** *has to pick up or
fuss with something to cover the hurt that the
loud laugh doesn't quite cover. On this occasion,*
85 *a happy occasion, because the dread in her heart
has also been lifted by the false report on* **BIG
DADDY's** *condition, she giggles, grotesquely,
coyly, in* **BIG DADDY's** *direction and bears down
upon* **BRICK**, *all very quick and alive.*]

90 **BIG MAMA:** Here he is, here's my precious
baby! What's that you've got in your
hand? You put that liquor down, son, your
hand was made fo' holdin' somethin'
better than that!

95 **GOOPER:** Look at Brick put it down!

[**BRICK** *has obeyed* **BIG MAMA** *by draining the
glass and handing it to her. Again everyone
laughs, some high, some low.*]

BIG MAMA: Oh, you bad boy, you, you're my
100 bad little boy. Give Big Mama a kiss, you
bad boy, you!—Look at him shy away, will
you? Brick never liked bein' kissed or
made a fuss over, I guess because he's
always had too much of it! Son, you turn
105 that thing off!

[**BRICK** *has switched on the TV set.*]

I can't stand TV, radio was bad enough
but TV has gone it one better, I mean—
[*Plops wheeling in chair*]—one worse, ha
110 ha! Now what'm I sittin' down here faw?
I want t' sit next to my sweetheart on the
sofa, hold hands with him and love him
up a little!

[**BIG MAMA** *has on a black and white figured*
115 *chiffon. The large irregular patterns, like the
markings of some massive animal, the luster of
her great diamonds and many pearls, the bril-
liants set in the silver frames of her glasses, her
riotous voice, booming laugh, have dominated*
120 *the room since she entered.* **BIG DADDY** *has been
regarding her with a steady grimace of chronic
annoyance.*]

BIG MAMA [*still louder*]: Preacher, Preacher,
hey, Preach! Give me you' hand an' help
125 me up from this chair!

REVEREND TOOKER: None of your tricks, Big
Mama!

BIG MAMA: What tricks? You give me you'
hand so I can get up an'—

130 [**REVEREND TOOKER** *extends her his hand. She
grabs it and pulls him into her lap with a shrill
laugh that spans an octave in two notes.*]

Ever seen a preacher in a fat lady's lap?
Hey, hey, folks! Ever seen a preacher in a
135 fat lady's lap?

[**BIG MAMA** *is notorious throughout the Delta for
this sort of inelegant horseplay.* **MARGARET** *looks
on with indulgent humor, sipping Dubonnet 'on the
rocks' and watching* **BRICK**, *but* **MAE** *and* **GOOPER**
140 *exchange signs of humorless anxiety over these
antics, the sort of behaviour which* **MAE** *thinks
may account for their failure to quite get in with
the smartest young married set in Memphis,
despite all. One of the Negroes, Lacy or Sookey,*
145 *peeks in, cackling. They are waiting for a sign to
bring in the cake and champagne. But* **BIG
DADDY's** *not amused. He doesn't understand why,*

in spite of the infinite mental relief he's received
from the doctor's report, he still has these same
150 old fox teeth in his guts. 'This spastic thing sure is
something?' he says to himself, but aloud he
roars at BIG MAMA:]

BIG DADDY: Big Mama, WILL YOU QUIT
HOR-SIN'?—You're too old an' too fat fo'
155 that sort of crazy kid stuff an' besides a
woman with your blood-pressure—she
had two hundred last spring!—is riskin'
a stroke when you mess around like
that....

160 BIG MAMA: Here comes Big Daddy's birthday!
[Negroes in white jackets enter with an enormous birthday cake ablaze with candles and
carrying buckets of champagne with satin
ribbons about the bottle necks. | MAE and
165 GOOPER strike up song, and everybody, including
the Negroes and children, joins in. Only BRICK
remains aloof.]

EVERYONE: Happy birthday to you. Happy
birthday to you. Happy birthday, Big
170 Daddy—[Some sing: 'Dear, BIG DADDY!']—
Happy birthday to you. [Some sing: 'How old
are you!']

[MAE has come down center and is organizing her
children like a chorus. She gives them a barely
175 audible: 'One, two, three!' and they are off in the
new tune.]

CHILDREN: Skinamarinka—dinka—
dink Skinamarinka—do We love
you. Skinamarinka—dinka—dink
180 Skinamarinka—do.
[All together, they turn to BIG DADDY.] Big
Daddy, you!
[They turn back front, like a musical comedy
chorus.]

185 We love you in the morning; We love you
in the night. We love you when we're
with you. And we love you out of
sight. Skinamarinka—dinka—dink
Skinamarinka—do.

190 [MAE turns to BIG MAMA.]
Big Mama, too!
[BIG MAMA bursts into tears. The Negroes leave.]

BIG DADDY: Now Ida, what the hell is the
matter with you?

195 MAE: She's just so happy.

BIG MAMA: I'm just so happy, Big Daddy, I
have to cry or something.
[Sudden and loud in the hush:]
Brick, do you know the wonderful news
200 that Doc Baugh got from the clinic about
Big Daddy? Big Daddy's one hundred per
cent!

MARGARET: Isn't that wonderful?

BIG MAMA: He's just one hundred per cent.
205 Passed the examination with flying colors.
Now that we know there's nothing wrong
with Big Daddy but a spastic colon, I can
tell you something. I was worried sick,
half out of my mind, for fear that Big
210 Daddy might have a thing like—
[MARGARET cuts through this speech, jumping up
and exclaiming shrilly:]

MARGARET: Brick, honey, aren't you going to
give Big Daddy his birthday present?
215 [Passing by him, she snatches his liquor glass
from him. She picks up a fancily wrapped package.]
Here it is, Big Daddy, this is from Brick!

BIG MAMA: This is the biggest birthday Big
220 Daddy's ever had, a hundred presents and
bushels of telegrams from—

MAE [at same time]: What is it, Brick?

GOOPER: I bet 500 to 50 that Brick don't know
what it is.

225 BIG MAMA: The fun of presents is not knowing what they are till you open the package. Open your present, Big Daddy.

BIG DADDY: Open it you'self. I want to ask
Brick somethin'! Come here, Brick.

230 MARGARET: Big Daddy's callin' you, Brick.
[She is opening the package.]

BRICK: Tell Big Daddy I'm crippled.

BIG DADDY: I see you're crippled. I want to know how you got crippled.

235 MARGARET [*making diversionary tactics*]: Oh, look, oh, look, why, it's a cashmere robe! [*She holds the robe up for all to see.*]

MAE: You sound surprised, Maggie.

MARGARET: I never saw one before.

240 MAE: That's funny.—Hah!

MARGARET [*turning on her fiercely, with a brilliant smile*]: Why is it funny? All my family ever had was family—and luxuries such as cashmere robes still surprise me!

245 BIG DADDY [*ominously*]: Quiet!

MAE [*heedless in her fury*]: I don't see how you could be so surprised when you bought it yourself at Loewenstein's in Memphis last Saturday. You know how I know?

250 BIG DADDY: I said, Quiet!

MAE: —I know because the salesgirl that sold it to you waited on me and said, Oh, Mrs Pollitt, your sister-in-law just bought a cashmere robe for your husband's
255 father!

MARGARET: Sister Woman! Your talents are wasted as a housewife and mother, you really ought to be with the FBI or—

BIG DADDY: QUIET!

260 [REVEREND TOOKER'S *reflexes are slower than the others'. He finishes a sentence after the bellow.*]

REVEREND TOOKER [*to* DOC BAUGH]: —the Stork and the Reaper are running neck
265 and neck!

[*He starts to laugh gaily when he notices the silence and* BIG DADDY'S *glare. His laugh dies falsely.*]

BIG DADDY: Preacher, I hope I'm not butting
270 in on more talk about memorial stained-glass windows, am I, Preacher?

[REVEREND TOOKER *laughs feebly, then coughs dryly in the embarrassed silence.*]

Preacher?

275 BIG MAMA: Now, Big Daddy, don't you pick on Preacher!

BIG DADDY [*raising his voice*]: You ever hear that expression all hawk and no spit? You bring that expression to mind with that
280 little dry cough of yours, all hawk an' no spit. . . .

[*The pause is broken only by a short startled laugh from* MARGARET, *the only one there who is conscious of and amused by the*
285 *grotesque.*]

MAE [*raising her arms and jangling her bracelets*]: I wonder if the mosquitoes are active tonight?

BIG DADDY: What's that, Little Mama? Did
290 you make some remark?

MAE: Yes, I said I wondered if the mosquitoes would eat us alive if we went out on the gallery for a while.

BIG DADDY: Well, if they do, I'll have your
295 bones pulverized for fertilizer!

BIG MAMA [*quickly*]: Last week we had an airplane spraying the place and I think it done some good, at least I haven't had a—

300 BIG DADDY [*cutting her speech*]: Brick, they tell me, if what they tell me is true, that you done some jumping last night on the high school athletic field?

BIG MAMA: Brick, Big Daddy is talking to
305 you, son.

BRICK [*smiling vaguely over his drink*]: What was that, Big Daddy?

BIG DADDY: They said you done some jumping on the high school track field
310 last night.

BRICK: That's what they told me, too.

BIG DADDY: Was it jumping or humping that you were doing out there? What were you doing out there at three a.m., layin' a
315 woman on that cinder track?

BIG MAMA: Big Daddy, you are off the sick-
list, now, and I'm not going to excuse you
for talkin' so—

BIG DADDY: Quiet!

320 BIG MAMA: —nasty in front of Preacher
and—

BIG DADDY: QUIET!—I ast you, Brick, if you
was cuttin' you'self a piece o' poon-tang
last night on that cinder track? I thought

325 maybe you were chasin' poon-tang on
that track an' tripped over something in
the heat of the chase—'s that it?

[GOOPER *laughs, loud and false, others nervously
following suit.* BIG MAMA *stamps her foot, and*

330 *purses her lips, crossing to* MAE *and whispering
something to her as* BRICK *meets his father's
hard, intent, grinning stare with a slow, vague
smile that he offers all situations from behind the
screen of his liquor.*]

335 BRICK: No, sir, I don't think so. . . .

MAE [*at the same time, sweetly*]:   Reverend
Tooker, let's you and I take a stroll on the
widow's walk.

[*She and the preacher go out on the gallery as* BIG

340 DADDY *says:*]

BIG DADDY: Then what the hell were you
doing out there at three o'clock in the
morning?

BRICK: Jumping the hurdles, Big Daddy,

345 runnin' and jumpin' the hurdles, but
those high hurdles have gotten too high
for me, now.

BIG DADDY: 'Cause you was drunk?

BRICK [*his vague smile fading a little*]:   Sober

350 I wouldn't have tried to jump the low
ones. . . .

BIG MAMA [*quickly*]:   Big Daddy, blow out the
candles on your birthday cake!

MARGARET [*at the same time*]:   I want to

355 propose a toast to Big Daddy Pollitt on his
sixty-fifth birthday, the biggest cotton-
planter in—

BIG DADDY [*bellowing with fury and disgust*]:   I
told you to stop it, now stop it, quit this—!

360 BIG MAMA [*coming in front of* BIG DADDY *with
the cake*]:   Big Daddy, I will not allow you
to talk that way, not even on your birthday, I—

BIG DADDY: I'll talk like I want to on my

365 birthday, Ida, or any other goddam day of
the year and anybody here that don't like
it knows what they can do!

BIG MAMA: You don't mean that!

BIG DADDY: What makes you think I don't

370 mean it?

[*Meanwhile various discreet signals have been
exchanged and* GOOPER *has also gone out on the
gallery.*]

BIG MAMA: I just know you don't mean it.

375 BIG DADDY: You don't know a goddam thing
and you never did!

BIG MAMA: Big Daddy, you don't mean that.

BIG DADDY: Oh, yes, I do, oh, yes, I do, I mean
it! I put up with a whole lot of crap around

380 here because I thought I was dying. And
you thought I was dying and you started
taking over, well, you can stop taking over
now, Ida, because I'm not gonna die, you
can just stop now this business of taking

385 over because you're not taking over
because I'm not dying, I went through the
laboratory and the goddam exploratory
operation and there's nothing wrong with
me but a spastic colon. And I'm not dying

390 of cancer which you thought I was dying
of. Ain't that so? Didn't you think that I
was dying of cancer, Ida?

[*Almost everybody is out on the gallery but the
two old people glaring at each other across the

395 flaming cake.* BIG MAMA'S *chest heaves and she
presses a fat fist to her mouth.* BIG DADDY *continues, hoarsely:*]

Ain't that so, Ida? Didn't you have an idea
I was dying of cancer and now you could

400 take control of this place and everything
on it? I got that impression, I seemed to
get that impression. Your loud voice
everywhere, your fat old body butting in
here and there!

405 BIG MAMA: Hush! The Preacher!

BIG DADDY: Rut the goddam preacher!

[BIG MAMA *gasps loudly and sits down on the
sofa which is almost too small for her.*]

Did you hear what I said? I said rut the

410 goddam preacher!

[*Somebody closes the gallery doors from outside
just as there is a burst of fireworks and excited
cries from the children.*]

BIG MAMA: I never seen you act like this

415 before and I can't think what's got in you!

BIG DADDY: I went through all that laboratory and operation and all just so I would
know if you or me was boss here! Well,
now it turns out that I am and you

420 ain't—and that's my birthday present—
and my cake and champagne!—because
for three years now you been gradually
taking over. Bossing. Talking. Sashaying
your fat old body around the place I made!

425 I made this place! I was overseer on it! I
was the overseer on the old Straw and
Ochello plantation. I quit school at ten! I
quit school at ten years old and went to
work like a n***** in the fields. And I rose

430 to be overseer of the Straw and Ochello
plantation. And old Straw died and I was
Ochello's partner and the place got bigger
and bigger and bigger and bigger and
bigger! I did all that myself with no

435 goddam help from you, and now you
think you're just about to take over. Well, I
am just about to tell you that you are not
just about to take over, you are not just
about to take over a God damn thing. Is

440 that clear to you, Ida? Is that very plain to
you, now? Is that understood completely?

I been through the laboratory from A to Z.
I've had the goddam exploratory operation, and nothing is wrong with me but a

445 spastic colon—made spastic, I guess, by
disgust! By all the goddam lies and liars
that I have had to put up with, and all
the goddam hypocrisy that I lived with
all these forty years that we been livin'

450 together!—Hey! Ida! Blow out the candles
on the birthday cake! Purse up your lips
and draw a deep breath and blow out the
goddam candles on the cake!

BIG MAMA: Oh, Big Daddy, oh, oh, oh, Big

455 Daddy!

BIG DADDY: What's the matter with you?

BIG MAMA: In all these years you never
believed that I loved you??

BIG DADDY: Huh?

460 BIG MAMA: And I did, I did so much, I did
love you!—I even loved your hate and
your hardness, Big Daddy! [*She sobs and
rushes awkwardly out on to the gallery.*]

BIG DADDY [*to himself*]: Wouldn't it be funny

465 if that was true—

[*A pause is followed by a burst of light in the sky
from the fireworks.*]

Brick! HEY, Brick!

[*He stands over his flaming birthday cake.* | *After

470 some moments,* BRICK *hobbles in on his crutch,
holding his glass.* MARGARET *follows him with a
bright, anxious smile.*]

I didn't call you, Maggie. I called Brick.

MARGARET: I'm just delivering him to you.

475 [*She kisses* BRICK *on the mouth which he immediately wipes with the back of his hand. She flies
girlishly back out.* BRICK *and his father are
alone.*]

BIG DADDY: Why did you do that?

480 BRICK: Do what, Big Daddy?

BIG DADDY: Wipe her kiss off your mouth
like she'd spit on you.

BRICK: I don't know. I wasn't conscious of it.

BIG DADDY: That woman of yours has a better shape on her than Gooper's but somehow or other they got the same look about them.

BRICK: What sort of look is that, Big Daddy?

BIG DADDY: I don't know how to describe it but it's the same look.

BRICK: They don't look peaceful, do they?

BIG DADDY: No, they sure in hell don't.

BRICK: They look nervous as cats?

BIG DADDY: That's right, they look nervous as cats.

BRICK: Nervous as a couple of cats on a hot tin roof?

BIG DADDY: That's right, boy, they look like a couple of cats on a hot tin roof. It's funny that you and Gooper being so different would pick out the same type of woman.

BRICK: Both of us married into society, Big Daddy.

BIG DADDY: Crap . . . I wonder what gives them both that look?

BRICK: Well. They're sittin' in the middle of a big piece of land, Big Daddy, twenty-eight thousand acres is a pretty big piece of land and so they're squaring off on it, each determined to knock off a bigger piece of it than the other whenever you let it go.

BIG DADDY: I got a surprise for those women. I'm not gonna let it go for a long time yet if that's what they're waiting for.

BRICK: That's right, Big Daddy. You just sit tight and let them scratch each other's eyes out. . . .

BIG DADDY: You bet your life I'm going to sit tight on it and let those sons of bitches scratch their eyes out, ha ha ha. . . . But Gooper's wife's a good breeder, you got to admit she's fertile. Hell, at supper tonight she had them all at the table and they had to put a couple of extra leafs in the table to

make room for them, she's got five head of them, now, and another one's comin'.

BRICK: Yep, number six is comin'. . . .

BIG DADDY: Brick, you know, I swear to God, I don't know the way it happens?

BRICK: The way what happens, Big Daddy?

BIG DADDY: You git you a piece of land, by hook or crook, an' things start growin' on it, things accumulate on it, and the first thing you know it's completely out of hand, completely out of hand!

BRICK: Well, they say nature hates a vacuum, Big Daddy.

BIG DADDY: That's what they say, but some-times I think that a vacuum is a hell of a lot better than some of the stuff that nature replaces it with. Is someone out there by that door?

BRICK: Yep.

BIG DADDY: Who?

[*He has lowered his voice.*]

BRICK: Someone int'rested in what we say to each other.

BIG DADDY: Gooper?—

GOOPER!

[*After a discreet pause,* MAE *appears in the gallery door.*]

MAE: Did you call Gooper, Big Daddy?

BIG DADDY: Aw, it was you.

MAE: Do you want Gooper, Big Daddy?

BIG DADDY: No, and I don't want you. I want some privacy here, while I'm having a confidential talk with my son Brick. Now it's too hot in here to close them doors, but if I have to close those rutten doors in order to have a private talk with my son Brick, just let me know and I'll close 'em. Because I hate eavesdroppers, I don't like any kind of sneakin' an' spyin'.

MAE: Why, Big Daddy—

BIG DADDY: You stood on the wrong side of the moon, it threw your shadow!

MAE: I was just—

BIG DADDY: You was just nothing but spyin'
570 an' you know it!

MAE [begins to sniff and sob]: Oh, Big Daddy,
you're so unkind for some reason to those
that really love you!

BIG DADDY: Shut up, shut up, shut up! I'm
575 going to move you and Gooper out of that
room next to this! It's none of your
goddam business what goes on in here at
night between Brick an' Maggie. You
listen at night like a couple of rutten
580 peek-hole spies and go and give a report
on what you hear to Big Mama an' she
comes to me and says they say such and
such and so and so about what they
heard goin' on between Brick an' Maggie,
585 and Jesus, it makes me sick. I'm goin' to
move you an' Gooper out of that room, I
can't stand sneakin' an' spyin', it makes
me sick. . . .

[MAE throws back her head and rolls her eyes
590 heavenward and extends her arms as if invoking
God's pity for this unjust martyrdom; then
she presses a handkerchief to her nose and
flies from the room with a loud swish of
skirts.]

595 BRICK [now at the liquor cabinet]: They listen,
do they?

BIG DADDY: Yeah. They listen and give
reports to Big Mama on what goes on in
here between you and Maggie. They say
600 that—

[He stops as if embarrassed.]

—You won't sleep with her, that you sleep
on the sofa. Is that true or not true? If you
don't like Maggie, get rid of
605 Maggie!—What are you doin' there now?

BRICK: Fresh'nin' up my drink.

BIG DADDY: Son, you know you got a real
liquor problem?

BRICK: Yes, sir, yes, I know.

610 BIG DADDY: Is that why you quit sports-
announcing, because of this liquor
problem?

BRICK: Yes, sir, yes, sir, I guess so.

[He smiles vaguely and amiably at his father
615 across his replenished drink.]

BIG DADDY: Son, don't guess about it, it's too
important.

BRICK [vaguely]: Yes, sir.

BIG DADDY: And listen to me, don't look at
620 the damn chandelier. . . . [Pause. BIG DADDY'S
voice is husky.]
—Somethin' else we picked up at th' big
fire sale in Europe. [Another pause.]
Life is important. There's nothing else to
625 hold on to. A man that drinks is throwing
his life away. Don't do it, hold on to your life.
There's nothing else to hold on to. . . . Sit
down over here so we don't have to raise
our voices, the walls have ears in this place.

630 BRICK [hobbling over to sit on the sofa beside
him]: All right, Big Daddy.

BIG DADDY: Quit!—how'd that come about?
Some disappointment?

BRICK: I don't know. Do you?

635 BIG DADDY: I'm askin' you, God damn it!
How in hell would I know if you don't?

BRICK: I just got out there and found that I
had a mouth full of cotton. I was always
two or three beats behind what was goin'
640 on on the field and so I—

BIG DADDY: Quit!

BRICK [amiably]: Yes, quit.

BIG DADDY: Son?

BRICK: Huh?

645 BIG DADDY [inhales loudly and deeply from his
cigar; then bends suddenly a little forward,
exhaling loudly and raising a hand to his fore-
head]: —Whew!—ha ha!—I took in too
much smoke, it made me a little light-
650 headed. . . .

[The mantel clock chimes.]

Why is it so damn hard for people to talk?

BRICK: Yeah. . . .

[*The clock goes on sweetly chiming till it has* completed *the stroke of ten.*]

—Nice peaceful-soundin' clock, I like to hear it all night. . . .

[*He slides low and comfortable on the sofa;* **BIG DADDY** *sits up straight and rigid with some unspoken anxiety. All his gestures are tense and jerky as he talks. He wheezes and pants and sniffs through his nervous speech, glancing quickly, shyly, from time to time, at his son.*]

BIG DADDY: We got that clock the summer we wint to Europe, me an' Big Mama on that damn Cook's Tour, never had such an awful time in my life, I'm tellin' you, son, those gooks over there, they gouge your eyeballs out in their grand hotels. And Big Mama bought more stuff than you could haul in a couple of boxcars, that's no crap. Everywhere she wint on this whirlwind tour, she bought, bought, bought. Why, half that stuff she bought is still crated up in the cellar, under water last spring!

[*He laughs.*]

That Europe is nothin' on earth but a great big auction, that's all it is, that bunch of old worn-out places, it's just a big fire-sale, the whole rutten thing, an' Big Mama wint wild in it, why, you couldn't hold that woman with a mule's harness! Bought, bought, bought!—lucky I'm a rich man, yes siree, Bob, an' half that stuff is mildewin' in th' basement. It's lucky I'm a rich man, it sure is lucky, well, I'm a rich man, Brick, yep, I'm a mighty rich man.

[*His eyes light up for a moment.*]

Y'know how much I'm worth? Guess, Brick! Guess how much I'm worth!

[**BRICK** *smiles vaguely over his drink.*]

Close on ten million in cash an' blue chip stocks, outside, mind you, of twenty-eight thousand acres of the richest land this side of the valley Nile!

[*A puff and crackle and the night sky blooms with an eerie greenish glow. Children shriek on the gallery.*]

But a man can't buy his life with it, he can't buy back his life with it when his life has been spent, that's one thing not offered in the Europe fire-sale or in the American markets or any markets on earth, a man can't buy his life with it, he can't buy back his life when his life is finished. . . . That's a sobering thought, a very sobering thought, and that's a thought that I was turning over in my head, over and over and over—until today. . . . I'm wiser and sadder, Brick, for this experience which I just gone through. They's one thing else that I remember in Europe.

BRICK: What is that, Big Daddy?

BIG DADDY: The hills around Barcelona in the country of Spain and the children running over those bare hills in their bare skins beggin' like starvin' dogs with howls and screeches, and how fat the priests are on the streets of Barcelona, so many of them and so fat and so pleasant, ha ha!—Y'know I could feed that country? I got money enough to feed that goddam country, but the human animal is a selfish beast and I don't reckon the money I passed out there to those howling children in the hills around Barcelona would more than upholster one of the chairs in this room, I mean pay to put a new cover on this chair! Hell, I threw them money like you'd scatter feed corn for chickens, I threw money at them just to get rid of them long enough to climb back into th' car and—drive away. . . .

And then in Morocco, them Arabs, why, prostitution begins at four or five, that's

no exaggeration, why, I remember one day
in Marrakech that old walled Arab city, I
set on a broken-down wall to have a cigar,
it was fearful hot there and this Arab
740 woman stood in the road and looked at
me till I was embarrassed, she stood stock
still in the dusty hot road and looked at
me till I was embarrassed. But listen to
this. She had a naked child with her, a
745 little naked girl with her, barely able to
toddle, and after a while she set this child
on the ground and give her a push and
whispered something to her. This child
come toward me, barely able t' walk, come
750 toddling up to me and—Jesus, it makes
you sick t' remember a thing like this! It
stuck out its hand and tried to unbutton
my trousers! That child was not yet five!
Can you believe me? Or do you think that
755 I am making this up? I wint back to the
hotel and said to Big Mama, Git packed!
We're clearing out of this country. . . .

BRICK: Big Daddy, you're on a talkin' jag
tonight.

760 BIG DADDY [ignoring this remark]: Yes, sir,
that's how it is, the human animal is a
beast that dies but the fact that he's dying
don't give him pity for others, no, sir, it—
Did you say something?

765 BRICK: Yes.

BIG DADDY: What?

BRICK: Hand me over that crutch so I can
get up.

BIG DADDY: Where you goin'?

770 BRICK: I'm takin' a little short trip to Echo
Spring.

BIG DADDY: To where?

BRICK: Liquor cabinet. . . .

BIG DADDY: Yes, sir, boy—

775 [He hands BRICK the crutch.]

—The human animal is a beast that dies
and if he's got money he buys and buys

and buys and I think the reason
he buys everything he can buy is that
780 in the back of his mind he has the crazy
hope that one of his purchases will be
life everlasting!—Which it never can
be—The human animal is a beast
that—

785 BRICK [at the liquor cabinet]: Big Daddy, you
sure are shootin' th' breeze here tonight.

[There is a pause and voices are heard outside.]

BIG DADDY: I been quiet here lately, spoke
not a word, just sat and stared into space.
790 I had something heavy weighing on my
mind but tonight that load was took off
me. That's why I'm talking.—The sky
looks diff'rent to me. . . .

BRICK: You know what I like to hear most?

795 BIG DADDY: What?

BRICK: Solid quiet. Perfect unbroken quiet.

BIG DADDY: Why?

BRICK: Because it's more peaceful.

BIG DADDY: Man, you'll hear a lot of that in
800 the grave.

[He chuckles agreeably.]

BRICK: Are you through talkin' to me?

BIG DADDY: Why are you so anxious to shut
me up?

805 BRICK: Well, sir, ever so often you say to
me, Brick, I want to have a talk with you,
but when we talk, it never materializes.
Nothing is said. You sit in a chair and gas
about this and that and I look like I listen.
810 I try to look like I listen, but I don't listen,
not much. Communication is—awful hard
between people an'—somehow between
you and me, it just don't—

BIG DADDY: Have you ever been scared? I
815 mean have you ever felt downright terror
of something?

[He gets up.]

Just one moment. I'm going to close these
doors. . . .

820 [*He closes doors on gallery as if he were going to tell an important szecret.*]

BRICK: What?

BIG DADDY: Brick?

BRICK: Huh?

825 **BIG DADDY:** Son, I thought I had it!

BRICK: Had what? Had what, Big Daddy?

BIG DADDY: Cancer!

BRICK: Oh . . .

BIG DADDY: I thought the old man made out
830 of bones had laid his cold and heavy hand on my shoulder!

BRICK: Well, Big Daddy, you kept a tight mouth about it.

BIG DADDY: A pig squeals. A man keeps a
835 tight mouth about it, in spite of a man not having a pig's advantage.

BRICK: What advantage is that?

BIG DADDY: Ignorance—of mortality—is a comfort. A man don't have that comfort,
840 he's the only living thing that conceives of death, that knows what it is. The others go without knowing, which is the way that anything living should go, go without knowing, without any knowledge of it,
845 and yet a pig squeals, but a man some-times, he can keep a tight mouth about it. Sometimes he—

[*There is a deep, smouldering ferocity in the old man.*]

850 —can keep a tight mouth about it. I wonder if—

BRICK: What, Big Daddy?

BIG DADDY: A whisky highball would injure this spastic condition?

855 **BRICK:** No, sir, it might do it good.

BIG DADDY [*grins suddenly, wolfishly*]:
Jesus, I can't tell you! The sky is open! Christ, it's open again! It's open, boy, it's open!

860 [**BRICK** *looks down at his drink.*]

BRICK: You feel better, Big Daddy?

BIG DADDY: Better? Hell! I can breathe!—All of my life I been like a doubled up fist. . . . [*He pours a drink.*] Poundin', smashin',
865 drivin' I—now I'm going to loosen these doubled up hands and touch things easy with them. . . .

[*He spreads his hands as if caressing the air.*]
You know what I'm contemplating?

870 **BRICK** [*vaguely*]: No, sir. What are you contemplating?

BIG DADDY: Ha ha!—Pleasure!—pleasure with women!

[**BRICK'S** *smile fades a little but lingers.*]

875 Brick, this stuff burns me!—Yes, boy. I'll tell you something that you might not guess. I still have desire for women and this is my sixty-fifth birthday.

BRICK: I think that's mighty remarkable, Big
880 Daddy.

BIG DADDY: Remarkable?

BRICK: Admirable, Big Daddy.

BIG DADDY: You're damn right it is, remark-able and admirable both. I realize now that
885 I never had me enough. I let many chances slip by because of scruples about it, scru-ples, convention—crap. . . . All that stuff is bull, bull, bull!—It took the shadow of death to make me see it. Now that shad-
890 ow's lifted, I'm going to cut loose and have, what is it they call it, have me a—ball!

BRICK: A ball, huh?

BIG DADDY: That's right, a ball, a ball! Hell!—I slept with Big Mama till, let's see, five years
895 ago, till I was sixty and she was fifty-eight, and never even liked her, never did!

[*The phone has been ringing down the hall.* **BIG MAMA** *enters, exclaiming:*]

BIG MAMA: Don't you men hear that phone
900 ring? I heard it way out on the gall'ry.

BIG DADDY: There's five rooms off this front gall'ry that you could go through. Why do you go through this one?

[BIG MAMA *makes a playful face as she bustles*
905 *out the hall door.*]

Huh!—Why, when Big Mama goes out of a
room, I can't remember what that woman
looks like, but when Big Mama comes
back into the room, boy, then I see what
910 she looks like, and I wish I didn't!

[*Bends over laughing at this joke till it hurts his
guts and he straightens with a grimace. The laugh
subsides to a chuckle as he puts the liquor glass a
little distrustfully down on the table.* | BRICK *has
915 risen and hobbled to the gallery doors.*]

Hey! Where you goin'?

BRICK: Out for a breather.

BIG DADDY: Not yet you ain't. Stay here till
this talk is finished, young fellow.

920 BRICK: I thought it was finished, Big Daddy.

BIG DADDY: It ain't even begun.

BRICK: My mistake. Excuse me. I just wanted
to feel that river breeze.

BIG DADDY: Turn on the ceiling fan and set
925 back down in that chair.

[BIG MAMA'S *voice rises, carrying down the hall.*]

BIG MAMA: Miss Sally, you're a case! You're a
caution, Miss Sally. Why didn't you give
me a chance to explain it to you?

930 BIG DADDY: Jesus, she's talking to my old
maid sister again.

BIG MAMA: Well, goodbye, now, Miss Sally.
You come down real soon, Big Daddy's
dying to see you! Yaisss, goodbye, Miss
935 Sally. . . .

[*She hangs up and bellows with mirth.* BIG
DADDY *groans and covers his ears as she
approaches. Bursting in:*]

Big Daddy, that was Miss Sally callin' from
940 Memphis again! You know what she done,
Big Daddy? She called her doctor in
Memphis to git him to tell her what that
spastic thing is!! Ha-HAAAA!—And called
back to tell me how relieved she was
945 that—Hey! Let me in!

[BIG DADDY *has been holding the door half closed
against her.*]

BIG DADDY: Naw I ain't. I told you not to
come and go through this room. You just
950 back out and go through those five other
rooms.

BIG MAMA: Big Daddy? Big Daddy? Oh, Big
Daddy!—You didn't mean those things
you said to me, did you?

955 [*He shuts door firmly against her but she still
calls.*]

Sweetheart? Sweetheart? Big Daddy? You
didn't mean those awful things you said to
me?—I know you didn't. I know you didn't
960 mean those things in your heart. . . .

[*The childlike voice fades with a sob and her
heavy footsteps retreat down the hall.* BRICK *has
risen once more on his crutch and starts for the
gallery again.*]

965 BIG DADDY: All I ask of that woman is that
she leave me alone. But she can't admit
to herself that she makes me sick. That
comes of having slept with her too many
years. Should of quit much sooner but
970 that old woman she never got enough of
it—and I was good in bed . . . I never
should of wasted so much of it on her. . . .
They say you got just so many and each
one is numbered. Well, I got a few left in
975 me, a few, and I'm going to pick me a good
one to spend 'em on! I'm going to pick me
a choice one, I don't care how much she
costs, I'll smother her in—minks! Ha ha!
I'll strip her naked and smother her in
980 minks and choke her with diamonds! Ha
ha! I'll strip her naked and choke her with
diamonds and smother her with minks
and hump her from hell to breakfast. Ha
ha ha ha ha!

985 MAE [*gaily at door*]:   Who's that laughin' in
there?

GOOPER: Is Big Daddy laughin' in there?

BIG DADDY: Crap!—them two—drips. . . .

[*He goes over and touches* BRICK'S *shoulder.*]

990 Yes, son. Brick, boy.—I'm—happy! I'm happy, son, I'm happy!

[*He chokes a little and bites his under lip, pressing his head quickly, shyly against his son's head and then, coughing with embarrassment, goes*

995 *uncertainly back to the table where he set down the glass. He drinks and makes a grimace as it burns his guts.* BRICK *sighs and rises with effort.*]

What makes you so restless? Have you got

1000 ants in your britches?

BRICK: Yes, sir . . .

BIG DADDY: Why?

BRICK: —Something—hasn't—happened. . . .

BIG DADDY: Yeah? What is that!

1005 BRICK [*sadly*]: —the click. . . .

BIG DADDY: Did you say click?

BRICK: Yes, click.

BIG DADDY: What click?

BRICK: A click that I get in my head that

1010 makes me peaceful.

BIG DADDY: I sure in hell don't know what you're talking about, but it disturbs me.

BRICK: It's just a mechanical thing.

BIG DADDY: What is a mechanical thing?

1015 BRICK: This click that I get in my head that makes me peaceful. I got to drink till I get it. It's just a mechanical thing, something like a—like a—like a—

BIG DADDY: Like a—

1020 BRICK: Switch clicking off in my head, turning the hot light off and the cool night on and—

[*He looks up, smiling sadly.*]—all of a sudden there's—peace!

1025 BIG DADDY [*whistles long and soft with astonishment; he goes back to* BRICK *and clasps his son's two shoulders*]: Jesus! I didn't know it had gotten that bad with you. Why, boy, you're—alcoholic!

1030 BRICK: That's the truth, Big Daddy. I'm alcoholic.

BIG DADDY: This shows how I—let things go!

BRICK: I have to hear that little click in my head that makes me peaceful. Usually

1035 I hear it sooner than this, sometimes as early as—noon, but—Today it's— dilatory. . . . I just haven't got the right level of alcohol in my bloodstream yet!

[*This last statement is made with energy as he*

1040 *freshens his drink.*]

BIG DADDY: Uh—huh. Expecting death made me blind. I didn't have no idea that a son of mine was turning into a drunkard under my nose.

1045 BRICK [*gently*]: Well, now you do, Big Daddy, the news has penetrated.

BIG DADDY: Uh-huh, yes, now I do, the news has—penetrated. . . .

BRICK: And so if you'll excuse me—

1050 BIG DADDY: No, I won't excuse you.

BRICK: —I'd better sit by myself till I hear that click in my head, it's just a mechanical thing but it don't happen except when I'm alone or talking to no one. . . .

1055 BIG DADDY: You got a long, long time to sit still, boy, and talk to no one, but now you're talkin' to me. At least I'm talking to you. And you set there and listen until I tell you the conversation is over!

1060 BRICK: But this talk is like all the others we've ever had together in our lives! It's nowhere, nowhere!—it's—it's painful, Big Daddy. . . .

BIG DADDY: All right, then let it be painful,

1065 but don't you move from that chair!—I'm going to remove that crutch. . . .

[*He seizes the crutch and tosses it across room.*]

BRICK: I can hop on one foot, and if I fall, I can crawl!

1070 BIG DADDY: If you ain't careful you're gonna crawl off this plantation and then, by

Jesus, you'll have to hustle your drinks along Skid Row!

BRICK: That'll come, Big Daddy.

1075 BIG DADDY: Naw, it won't. You're my son, and I'm going to straighten you out; now that I'm straightened out, I'm going to straighten you out!

BRICK: Yeah?

1080 BIG DADDY: Today the report come in from Ochsner Clinic. Y'know what they told me?

[*His face glows with triumph.*]

The only thing that they could detect with
1085 all the instruments of science in that great hospital is a little spastic condition of the colon! And nerves torn to pieces by all that worry about it.

[*A little girl bursts into room with a sparkler
1090 clutched in each fist, bops and shrieks like a monkey gone mad and rushes back out again as
BIG DADDY strikes at her. Silence. The two men stare at each other. A woman laughs gaily outside.*]

1095 I want you to know I breathed a sigh of relief almost as powerful as the Vicksburg tornado!

BRICK: You weren't ready to go?

BIG DADDY: GO WHERE?—crap....

1100 —When you are gone from here, boy, you are long gone and nowhere! The human machine is not so different from the animal machine or the fish machine or the bird machine or the reptile machine;
1105 or the insect machine! It's just a whole God damn lot more complicated and consequently more trouble to keep together. Yep. I thought I had it. The earth shook under my foot, the sky come down
1110 like the black lid of a kettle and I couldn't breathe!—Today!!—that lid was lifted, I drew my first free breath in—how many years?—God!—three....

[*There is laughter outside, running footsteps, the
1115 soft, plushy sound and light of exploding rockets.
BRICK stares at him soberly for a long moment;
then makes a sort of startled sound in his
nostrils and springs up on one foot and bops
across the room to grab his crutch, swinging on
1120 the furniture for support. He gets the crutch and
flees as if in horror for the gallery. His father
seizes him by the sleeve of his white silk
pyjamas.*]

Stay here, you son of a bitch!—till
1125 I say go!

BRICK: I can't.

BIG DADDY: You sure in hell will, God damn it.

BRICK: No, I can't. We talk, you talk, in—
1130 circles! We get nowhere, nowhere! It's always the same, you say you want to talk to me and don't have a ruttin' thing to say to me!

BIG DADDY: Nothin' to say when I'm tellin'
1135 you I'm going to live when I thought I was dying?!

BRICK: Oh—that!—Is that what you have to say to me?

BIG DADDY: Why, you son of a bitch! Ain't
1140 that, ain't that—important?!

BRICK: Well, you said that, that's said, and now I—

BIG DADDY: Now you set back down.

BRICK: You're all balled up, you—

1145 BIG DADDY: I ain't balled up!

BRICK: You are, you're all balled up!

BIG DADDY: Don't tell me what I am, you drunken whelp! I'm going to tear this coat sleeve off if you don't set down!

1150 BRICK: Big Daddy—

BIG DADDY: Do what I tell you! I'm the boss here, now! I want you to know I'm back in the driver's seat now!

[*BIG MAMA rushes in, clutching her great heaving
1155 bosom.*]

What in hell do you want in here, Big
Mama?

BIG MAMA: Oh, Big Daddy! Why are you
shouting like that? I just cain't

1160   stainnnnnnnd—it. . . .

BIG DADDY [*raising the back of his hand above
his head*]: GIT!—outa here.

[*She rushes back out, sobbing.*]

BRICK [*softly, sadly*]: Christ . . .

1165 **BIG DADDY** [*fiercely*]: Yeah! Christ!—is
right. . . .

[**BRICK** *breaks loose and hobbles toward the
gallery.* | **BIG DADDY** *jerks his crutch from under*
BRICK *so he steps with the injured ankle. He*

1170 *utters a hissing cry of anguish, clutches a chair
and pulls it over on top of him on the floor.*]

Son of a—tub of—hog fat. . . .

BRICK: Big Daddy! Give me my crutch.

[**BIG DADDY** *throws the crutch out of reach.*]

1175   Give me that crutch, Big Daddy.

BIG DADDY: Why do you drink?

BRICK: Don't know, give me my crutch!

BIG DADDY: You better think why you drink
or give up drinking!

1180 **BRICK:** Will you please give me my crutch so
I can get up off this floor?

BIG DADDY: First you answer my question.
Why do you drink? Why are you throwing
your life away, boy, like somethin' disgust-

1185   ing you picked up on the street?

BRICK [*getting on to his knees*]: Big Daddy, I'm
in pain, I stepped on that foot.

BIG DADDY: Good! I'm glad you're not too
numb with the liquor in you to feel some

1190   pain!

BRICK: You—spilled my—drink. . . .

BIG DADDY: I'll make a bargain with you. You
tell me why you drink and I'll hand you
one. I'll pour you the liquor myself and

1195   hand it to you.

BRICK: Why do I drink?

BIG DADDY: Yeah! Why?

BRICK: Give me a drink and I'll tell you.

BIG DADDY: Tell me first!

1200 **BRICK:** I'll tell you in one word.

BIG DADDY: What word?

BRICK: DISGUST!

[*The clock chimes softly, sweetly.* **BIG DADDY** *gives
it a short, outraged glance.*]

1205   Now how about that drink?

BIG DADDY: What are you disgusted with?
You got to tell me that, first. Otherwise
being disgusted don't make no sense!

BRICK: Give me my crutch.

1210 **BIG DADDY:** You heard me, you got to tell me
what I asked you first.

BRICK: I told you, I said to kill my disgust!

BIG DADDY: DISGUST WITH WHAT!

BRICK: You strike a hard bargain.

1215 **BIG DADDY:** What are you disgusted
with?—an' I'll pass you the liquor.

BRICK: I can hop on one foot, and if I fall, I
can crawl.

BIG DADDY: You want liquor that bad?

1220 **BRICK** [*dragging himself up, clinging to bedstead*]:
Yeah, I want it that bad.

BIG DADDY: If I give you a drink, will you
tell me what it is you're disgusted with,
Brick?

1225 **BRICK:** Yes, sir, I will try to.

[*The old man pours him a drink and solemnly
passes it to him. There is silence as* **BRICK** *drinks.*]
Have you ever heard the word
'mendacity'?

1230 **BIG DADDY:** Sure. Mendacity is one of them
five-dollar words that cheap politicians
throw back and forth at each other.

BRICK: You know what it means?

BIG DADDY: Don't it mean lying and liars?

1235 **BRICK:** Yes, sir, lying and liars.

BIG DADDY: Has someone been lying to you?

CHILDREN [*chanting in chorus offstage*]: We want
Big Dad-dee! We want Big Dad-dee!

[**GOOPER** *appears in the gallery door.*]

1240 **GOOPER:** Big Daddy, the kiddies are shouting
for you out there.

BIG DADDY [*fiercely*]: Keep out, Gooper!

GOOPER: 'Scuse me!

[**BIG DADDY** *slams the doors after* **GOOPER**.]

1245 **BIG DADDY:** Who's been lying to you, has Margaret been lying to you, has your wife been lying to you about something, Brick?

BRICK: Not her. That wouldn't matter.

BIG DADDY: Then who's been lying to you,
1250 and what about?

BRICK: No one single person and no one lie. . . .

BIG DADDY: Then what, what then, for Christ's sake?

1255 **BRICK:** —The whole, the whole—thing. . . .

BIG DADDY: Why are you rubbing your head? You got a headache?

BRICK: No, I'm tryin' to—

BIG DADDY: —Concentrate, but you can't
1260 because your brain's all soaked with liquor, is that the trouble? Wet brain!

[*He snatches the glass from* **BRICK'S** *hand*.]
 What do you know about this mendacity thing? Hell! I could write a book on it!
1265 Don't you know that? I could write a book on it and still not cover the subject? Well, I could, I could write a goddam book on it and still not cover the subject anywhere near enough!!—Think of all the lies I got
1270 to put up with!—Pretences! Ain't that mendacity? Having to pretend stuff you don't think or feel or have any idea of? Having for instance to act like I care for Big Mama!—I haven't been able to stand
1275 the sight, sound, or smell of that woman for forty years now!—even when I laid her!—regular as a piston. . . . Pretend to love that son of a bitch of a Gooper and his wife Mae and those five same screech-
1280 ers out there like parrots in a jungle? Jesus I Can't stand to look at 'em! Church!—it bores the Bejesus out of me but I go!— I go an' sit there and listen to the fool

preacher! Clubs!—Elks! Masons! Rotary!—
1285 crap!

[*A spasm of pain makes him clutch his belly. He sinks into a chair and his voice is softer and hoarser*.]
 You I do like for some reason, did always
1290 have some kind of real feeling for— affection—respect—yes, always. . . . You and being a success as a planter is all I ever had any devotion to in my whole life!—and that's the truth. . . . I don't
1295 know why, but it is! I've lived with mendacity!—Why can't you live with it? Hell, you got to live with it, there's nothing else to live with except mendacity, is there?

BRICK: Yes, sir. Yes, sir, there is something
1300 else that you can live with!

BIG DADDY: What?

BRICK [*lifting his glass*]: This!—Liquor . . .

BIG DADDY: That's not living, that's dodging away from life.

1305 **BRICK:** I want to dodge away from it.

BIG DADDY: Then why don't you kill yourself, man?

BRICK: I like to drink. . . .

BIG DADDY: Oh, God, I can't talk to you. . . .

1310 **BRICK:** I'm sorry, Big Daddy.

BIG DADDY: Not as sorry as I am. I'll tell you something. A little while back when I thought my number was up—

[*This speech should have torrential pace and*
1315 *fury*.]
 —before I found out it was just this— spastic—colon. I thought about you. Should I or should I not, if the jig was up, give you this place when I go—since I
1320 hate Gooper an' Mae an' know that they hate me, and since all five same monkeys are little Maes an' Goopers.—And I thought, No!—Then I thought, Yes!—I couldn't make up my mind. I hate Gooper
1325 and his five same monkeys and that bitch

Mae! Why should I turn over twenty-eight thousand acres of the richest land this side of the valley Nile to not my kind?— But why in hell, on the other hand, Brick—

1330 should I subsidize a goddam fool on the bottle?—Liked or not liked, well, maybe even—loved!—Why should I do that?— Subsidize worthless behaviour? Rot? Corruption?

1335 BRICK [*smiling*]: I understand.

BIG DADDY: Well, if you do, you're smarter than I am, God damn it, because I don't understand. And this I will tell you frankly. I didn't make up my mind at all

1340 on that question and still to this day I ain't made out no will!—Well, now I don't have to. The pressure is gone. I can just wait and see if you pull yourself together or if you don't.

1345 BRICK: That's right, Big Daddy.

BIG DADDY: You sound like you thought I was kidding.

BRICK [*rising*]: No, sir, I know you're not kidding.

1350 BIG DADDY: But you don't care—?

BRICK [*hobbling toward the gallery door*]: No, sir, I don't care. . . . Now how about taking a look at your birthday fireworks and getting some of that cool breeze off the

1355 river?

[*He stands in the gallery doorway as the night sky turns pink and green and gold with successive flashes of light.*]

BIG DADDY: WAIT!—Brick . . .

1360 [*His voice drops. Suddenly there is something shy, almost tender, in his restraining gesture.*]

Don't let's—leave it like this, like them other talks we've had, we've always— talked around things, we've—just talked

1365 around things for some rutten reason, I don't know what, it's always like something was left not spoken, something

avoided because neither of us was honest enough with the—other. . . .

1370 BRICK: I never lied to you, Big Daddy.

BIG DADDY: Did I ever to you?

BRICK: No, sir. . . .

BIG DADDY: Then there is at least two people that never lied to each other.

1375 BRICK: But we've never talked to each other.

BIG DADDY: We can now.

BRICK: Big Daddy, there don't seem to be anything much to say.

1380 BIG DADDY: You say that you drink to kill your disgust with lying.

BRICK: You said to give you a reason.

BIG DADDY: Is liquor the only thing that'll kill this disgust?

1385 BRICK: Now. Yes.

BIG DADDY: But not once, huh?

BRICK: Not when I was still young an' believing. A drinking man's someone who wants to forget he isn't still young an'

1390 believing.

BIG DADDY: Believing what?

BRICK: Believing. . . .

BIG DADDY: Believing what?

BRICK [*stubbornly evasive*]: Believing. . . .

1395 BIG DADDY: I don't know what the hell you mean by believing and I don't think you know what you mean by believing, but if you still got sports in your blood, go back to sports announcing and—

1400 BRICK: Sit in a glass box watching games I can't play? Describing what I can't do while players do it? Sweating out their disgust and confusion in contests I'm not fit for? Drinkin' a coke, half bourbon, so I

1405 can stand it? That's no goddam good any more, no help—time just outran me, Big Daddy—got there first . . .

BIG DADDY: I think you're passing the buck.

BRICK: You know many drinkin' men?

1410 BIG DADDY [*with a slight, charming smile*]: I have known a fair number of that species.

BRICK: Could any of them tell you why he drank?

BIG DADDY: Yep, you're passin' the buck to
1415 things like time and disgust with 'mendacity' and—crap!—if you got to use that kind of language about a thing, it's ninety-proof bull, and I'm not buying any.

BRICK: I had to give you a reason to get a
1420 drink!

BIG DADDY: You started drinkin' when your friend Skipper died.

[*Silence for five beats. Then* BRICK *makes a startled movement, reaching for his crutch.*]

1425 BRICK: What are you suggesting?

BIG DADDY: I'm suggesting nothing.

[*The shuffle and clop of* BRICK'S *rapid hobble away from his father's steady, grave attention.*]

—But Gooper an' Mae suggested that
1430 there was something not right exactly in your—

BRICK [*stopping short downstage as if backed to a wall*]: 'Not right'?

BIG DADDY: Not, well, exactly normal in your
1435 friendship with—

BRICK: They suggested that, too? I thought that was Maggie's suggestion.

[BRICK'S *detachment is at last broken through. His heart is accelerated; his forehead sweat-*
1440 *beaded; his breath becomes more rapid and his voice hoarse. The thing they're discussing, timidly and painfully on the side of* BIG DADDY, *fiercely, violently on* BRICK'S *side, is the inadmissible thing that Skipper died to disavow between them. The*
1445 *fact that if it existed it had to be disavowed to 'keep face' in the world they lived in, may be at the heart of the 'mendacity' that* BRICK *drinks to kill his disgust with. It may be the root of his collapse. Or maybe it is only a single manifesta-*
1450 *tion of it, not even the most important. The bird that I hope to catch in the net of this play is not*

the solution of one man's psychological problem. I'm trying to catch the true quality of experience in a group of people, that cloudy, flickering,
1455 evanescent—fiercely charged!—interplay of live human beings in the thundercloud of a common crisis. Some mystery should be left in the revelation of character in a play, just as a great deal of mystery is always left in the revelation of charac-
1460 ter in life, even in one's own character to himself. This does not absolve the playwright of his duty to observe and probe as clearly and deeply as he legitimately can—but it should steer him away from 'pat' conclusions, facile definitions which
1465 make a play just play, not a snare for the truth of human experience. | The following scene should be played with great concentration, with most of the power leashed but palpable in what is left unspoken.]

1470 Who else's suggestion is it, is it yours? How many others thought that Skipper and I were—

BIG DADDY [*gently*]: Now, hold on, hold on a minute, son.—I knocked around in my
1475 time.

BRICK: What's that got to do with—

BIG DADDY: I said 'Hold on!'—I bummed, I bummed this country till I was—

BRICK: Whose suggestion, who else's sugges-
1480 tion is it?

BIG DADDY: Slept in hobo jungles and railroad Y's and flophouses in all cities before I—

BRICK: Oh, you think so, too, you call me your son and a queer. Oh!! Maybe that's
1485 why you put Maggie and me in this room that was Jack Straw's and Peter Ochello's, in which that pair of old sisters slept in a double bed where both of 'em died!

BIG DADDY: Now just don't go throwing rocks
1490 at—

[*Suddenly* REVEREND TOOKER *appears in the gallery doors, his head slightly, playfully, fatuously cocked, with a practised clergyman's smile, sincere as a*

bird-call blown on a hunter's whistle, the living
1495 embodiment of the pious, conventional lie. | **BIG
DADDY** gasps a little at this perfectly timed, but
incongruous, apparition.]

 —What're you looking for, Preacher?

REVEREND TOOKER: The gentlemen's lavatory,
1500 ha ha!—heh, heh . . .

BIG DADDY [with strained courtesy]: —Go
 back out and walk down to the other end
 of the gallery, Reverend Tooker, and use
 the bathroom connected with my
1505 bedroom, and if you can't find it, ask
 them where it is!

REVEREND TOOKER: Ah, thanks.

[He goes out with a deprecatory chuckle.]

BIG DADDY: It's hard to talk in this place . . .

1510 **BRICK:** Son of a—!

BIG DADDY [leaving a lot unspoken]: —I seen
 all things and understood a lot of them,
 till 1910. Christ, the year that—I had worn
 my shoes through, hocked my—I hopped
1515 off a yellow dog freight car half a mile
 down the road, slept in a wagon of cotton
 outside the gin—Jack Straw an' Peter
 Ochello took me in. Hired me to manage
 this place which grew into this one.—
1520 When Jack Straw died—why, old Peter
 Ochello quit eatin' like a dog does when
 its master's dead, and died, too!

BRICK: Christ!

BIG DADDY: I'm just saying I understand
1525 such—

BRICK [violently]: Skipper is dead. I have not
 quit eating!

BIG DADDY: No, but you started drinking.

[**BRICK** wheels on his crutch and hurls his glass
1530 across the room shouting.]

BRICK: YOU THINK SO, TOO?

BIG DADDY: Shhh!

[Footsteps run on the gallery. There are women's
calls. **BIG DADDY** goes toward the door.]

1535 Go 'way!—Just broke a glass. . . .

[**BRICK** is transformed, as if a quiet mountain
blew suddenly up in volcanic flame.]

BRICK: You think so, too? You think so, too?
 You think me an' Skipper did, did, did!—
1540 sodomy!—together?

BIG DADDY: Hold—!

BRICK: That what you—

BIG DADDY: —ON—a minute!

BRICK: You think we did dirty things
1545 between us, Skipper an'—

BIG DADDY: Why are you shouting like that?
 Why are you—

BRICK: —Me, is that what you think of
 Skipper, is that—

1550 **BIG DADDY:** —so excited? I don't think nothing. I don't know nothing. I'm simply telling you what—

BRICK: You think that Skipper and me were a
 pair of dirty old men?

1555 **BIG DADDY:** Now that's—

BRICK: Straw? Ochello? A couple of—

BIG DADDY: Now just—

BRICK: —f***ing sissies? Queers? Is that what
 you—

1560 **BIG DADDY:** Shhh.

BRICK: —think?

[He loses his balance and pitches to his knees
without noticing the pain. He grabs the bed and
drags himself up.]

1565 **BIG DADDY:** Jesus!—Whew. . . . Grab my
 hand!

BRICK: Naw, I don't want your hand. . . .

BIG DADDY: Well, I want yours. Git up!

[He draws him up, keeps an arm about him
1570 with concern and affection.] You broken out
 in a sweat! You're panting like you'd run a
 race with—

BRICK [freeing himself from his father's hold]:
 Big Daddy, you shock me, Big Daddy, you,
1575 you—shock me! Talkin' so—

[He turns away from his father.]

 —casually!—about a—thing like that . . .

—Don't you know how people feel about things like that? How, how disgusted they are by things like that? Why, at Ole Miss when it was discovered a pledge to our fraternity, Skipper's and mine, did a, attempted to do a, unnatural thing with—We not only dropped him like a hot rock!—We told him to git off the campus, and he did, he got!—All the way to—

[*He halts, breathless.*]

BIG DADDY: —Where?

BRICK: —North Africa, last I heard!

BIG DADDY: Well, I have come back from further away than that, I have just now returned from the other side of the moon, death's country, son, and I'm not easy to shock by anything here.

[*He comes downstage and faces out.*]

Always, anyhow, lived with too much space around me to be infected by ideas of other people. One thing you can grow on a big place more important than cotton!—is tolerance!—I grown it.

[*He returns toward* BRICK.]

BRICK: Why can't exceptional friendship, real, real, deep, deep friendship! between two men be respected as something clean and decent without being thought of as—

BIG DADDY: It can, it is, for God's sake.

BRICK: —Fairies. . . .

[*In his utterance of this word, we gauge the wide and profound reach of the conventional mores he got from the world that crowned him with early laurel.*]

BIG DADDY: I told Mae an' Gooper—

BRICK: Frig Mae and Gooper, frig all dirty lies and liars!—Skipper and me had a clean, true thing between us!—had a clean friendship, practically all our lives, till Maggie got the idea you're talking about. Normal? No!—It was too rare to be normal, any true thing between two

people is too rare to be normal. Oh, once in a while he put his hand on my shoulder or I'd put mine on his, oh, maybe even, when we were touring the country in pro-football an' shared hotel-rooms we'd reach across the space between the two beds and shake hands to say goodnight, yeah, one or two times we—

BIG DADDY: Brick, nobody thinks that that's not normal!

BRICK: Well, they're mistaken, it was! It was a pure an' true thing an' that's not normal.

[*They both stare straight at each other for a long moment. The tension breaks and both turn away as if tired.*]

BIG DADDY: Yeah, it's—hard t'—talk. . . .

BRICK: All right, then, let's—let it go. . . .

BIG DADDY: Why did Skipper crack up? Why have you?

[BRICK *looks back at his father again. He has already decided, without knowing that he has made this decision, that he is going to tell his father that he is dying of cancer. Only this could even the score between them | one inadmissible thing in return for another.*]

BRICK [*ominously*]:   All right. You're asking for it, Big Daddy. We're finally going to have that real true talk you wanted. It's too late to stop it, now, we got to carry it through and cover every subject.

[*He hobbles back to the liquor cabinet.*]

Uh-huh.

[*He opens the ice bucket and picks up the silver tongs with slow admiration of their frosty brightness.*]

Maggie declares that Skipper and I went into pro-football after we left 'Ole Miss' because we were scared to grow up . . .

[*He moves downstage with the shuffle and clop of a cripple on a crutch. As* MARGARET *did when her speech became 'recitative,' he looks out into the*

house, commanding its attention by his direct,
concentrated gaze—a broken, 'tragically elegant'
figure telling simply as much as he knows of
1665 *'the Truth'.]*

—Wanted to—keep on tossing—those
long, long!—high, high!—passes that—
couldn't be intercepted except by time,
the aerial attack that made us famous!
1670 And so we did, we did, we kept it up for
one season, that aerial attack, we held it
high!—Yeah, but—that summer, Maggie,
she laid the law down to me, said, Now or
never, and so I married Maggie. . . .

1675 BIG DADDY: How was Maggie in bed?

BRICK [*wryly*]: Great! the greatest!

[BIG DADDY *nods as if be thought so.*]

She went on the road that fall with the
Dixie Stars. Oh, she made a great show of
1680 being the world's best sport. She wore
a—wore a—tall bearskin cap! A shako,
they call it, a dyed moleskin coat, a moleskin coat dyed red!—Cut up crazy! Rented
hotel ballrooms for victory celebrations,
1685 wouldn't cancel them when it—turned
out—defeat. . . . MAGGIE THE CAT! Ha ha!

[BIG DADDY *nods.*]

—But Skipper, he had some fever which
came back on him which doctors couldn't
1690 explain and I got that injury—turned
out to be just a shadow on the X-ray
plate—and a touch of bursitis. . . . I lay in
a hospital bed, watched our games on TV,
saw Maggie on the bench next to Skipper
1695 when he was hauled out of a game for
stumbles, fumbles!—Burned me up the
way she hung on his arm!—Y'know, I
think that Maggie had always felt sort of
left out because she and me never got
1700 any closer together than two people just
get in bed, which is not much closer than
two cats on a—fence humping. . . . So!
She took this time to work on poor dumb

Skipper. He was a less than average
1705 student at Ole Miss, you know that, don't
you?!—Poured in his mind the dirty, false
idea that what we were, him and me, was
a frustrated case of that ole pair of sisters
that lived in this room, Jack Straw and
1710 Peter Ochello!—He, poor Skipper, went to
bed with Maggie to prove it wasn't true,
and when it didn't work out, he thought it
was true!— Skipper broke in two like a
rotten stick— nobody ever turned so fast
1715 to a lush—or died of it so quick. . . .—Now
are you satisfied?

[BIG DADDY *has listened to this story, dividing the*
grain from the chaff. Now he looks at his son.]

BIG DADDY: Are you satisfied?

1720 BRICK: With what?

BIG DADDY: That half-ass story!

BRICK: What's half-ass about it?

BIG DADDY: Something's left out of that
story. What did you leave out?

1725 [*The phone has started ringing in the hall. As if it*
reminded him of something, BRICK *glances*
suddenly toward the sound and says:]

BRICK: Yes!—I left out a long-distance call
which I had from Skipper, in which he
1730 made a drunken confession to me and on
which I hung up!—last time we spoke to
each other in our lives. . . .

[*Muted ring stops as someone answers phone in a*
soft, indistinct voice in hall.]

1735 BIG DADDY: You hung up?

BRICK: Hung up. Jesus! Well—

BIG DADDY: Anyhow now!—we have tracked
down the lie with which you're disgusted
and which you are drinking to kill your
1740 disgust with, Brick. You been passing the
buck. This disgust with mendacity is
disgust with yourself.

You!—dug the grave of your friend and
kicked him in it!—before you'd face truth
1745 with him!

BRICK: His truth, not mine!

BIG DADDY: His truth, okay! But you wouldn't face it with him!

BRICK: Who can face truth? Can you?

1750 BIG DADDY: Now don't start passin' the rotten buck again, boy!

BRICK: How about these birthday congratulations, these many, many happy returns of the day, when ev'rybody but you knows

1755   there won't be any!

[*Whoever has answered the hall phone lets out a high, shrill laugh; the voice becomes audible saying: 'no, no, you got it all wrong! Upside down! Are you crazy?'* | BRICK *suddenly catches his*

1760 *breath as he realises that he has made a shocking disclosure. He hobbles a few paces, then freezes, and without looking at his father's shocked face, says:*]

Let's, let's—go out, now, and—

1765 [BIG DADDY *moves suddenly forward and grabs hold of the boy's crutch like it was a weapon for which they were fighting for possession.*]

BIG DADDY: Oh, no, no! No one's going out! What did you start to say?

1770 BRICK: I don't remember.

BIG DADDY: 'Many happy returns when they know there won't be any'?

BRICK: Aw, hell, Big Daddy, forget it. Come on out on the gallery and look at the fire-

1775   works they're shooting off for your birthday. . . .

BIG DADDY: First you finish that remark you were makin' before you cut off. 'Many happy returns when they know there

1780   won't be any'?—Ain't that what you just said?

BRICK: Look, now. I can get around without that crutch if I have to but it would be a lot easier on the furniture an' glassware

1785   if I didn' have to go swinging along like Tarzan of th'—

BIG DADDY: FINISH WHAT YOU WAS SAYIN'!

[*An eerie green glow shows in sky behind him.*]

BRICK [*sucking the ice in his glass, speech becom-*

1790   *ing thick*]:   Leave th' place to Gooper and Mae an' their five little same little monkeys. All I want is—

BIG DADDY: 'LEAVE TH' PLACE,' did you say?

BRICK [*vaguely*]:   All twenty-eight thousand

1795   acres of the richest land this side of the valley Nile.

BIG DADDY: Who said I was 'leaving the place' to Gooper or anybody? This is my sixty-fifth birthday! I got fifteen years or

1800   twenty years left in me! I'll outlive you! I'll bury you an' have to pay for your coffin!

BRICK: Sure. Many happy returns. Now let's go watch the fireworks, come on, let's—

BIG DADDY: Lying, have they been lying? About

1805   the report from th'—clinic? Did they, did they—find something?—Cancer. Maybe?

BRICK: Mendacity is a system that we live in. Liquor is one way out an' death's the other. . . .

1810 [*He takes the crutch from* BIG DADDY'S *loose grip and swings out on the gallery leaving the doors open. A song, 'Pick a Bale of Cotton', is heard.*]

MAE [*appearing in door*]:   Oh, Big Daddy, the field-hands are singin' fo' you!

1815 BIG DADDY [*shouting hoarsely*]:   Brick! Brick!

MAE: He's outside drinkin', Big Daddy.

BIG DADDY: Brick!

[MAE *retreats, awed by the passion of his voice. Children call* BRICK *in tones mocking* BIG DADDY.

1820 *His face crumbles like broken yellow plaster about to fall into dust.* | *There is a glow in the sky.* BRICK *swings back through the doors, slowly, gravely, quite soberly.*]

BRICK: I'm sorry, Big Daddy. My head don't

1825   work any more and it's hard for me to understand how anybody could care if he lived or died or was dying or cared about anything but whether or not there was liquor left in the bottle and so I said what I

1830 said without thinking. In some ways I'm no
better than the others, in some ways worse
because I'm less alive. Maybe it's being alive
that makes them lie, and being almost not
alive makes me sort of accidentally truthful
1835 —I don't know but—anyway—we've been
friends . . .—And being friends is telling
each other the truth. . . . [*There is a pause.*]
You told me! I told you!

[*A child rushes into the room and grabs a fistful*
1840 *of fire-crackers, and runs out again.*]

CHILD [*screaming*]:   Bang, bang, bang, bang,
bang, bang, bang, bang, bang!

BIG DADDY [*slowly and passionately*]:   CHRIST—
DAMN—ALL—LYING SONS OF—LYING
1845 BITCHES!

[*He straightens at last and crosses to the inside
door. At the door he turns and looks back as if he
had some desperate question he couldn't put into
words. Then he nods reflectively and says in a*
1850 *hoarse voice:*]

Yes, all liars, all liars, all lying dying
liars!

[*This is said slowly, slowly, with a fierce revulsion. He goes on out.*]

1855 —Lying! Dying! Liars!

[*His voice dies out. There is the sound of a child
being slapped. It rushes, hideously bawling,
through room and out the hall door.* BRICK
remains motionless as the lights dim out and the
1860 *curtain falls.*]

CURTAIN

Terrence Howard and James Earl Jones star in the 2008 Broadway revival of Tennessee Williams's *Cat on a Hot Tin Roof* at the Broadhurst Theater.

When *Cat on a Hot Tin Roof* was originally performed on Broadway in 1958, it featured an all-white cast. The 2008 revival, however, featured an all-black cast. Given the play's historical, cultural, and social settings, how might the casting choices affect its message?

CHARACTER

1. Reflect on the relationship between Big Daddy and Big Mama. How do their speech and their actions contribute to your understanding of their relationship?

2. Big Daddy speaks about his trip to Europe and his wealth. How does this speech reveal a change that emerges from a conflict of values in the play?

3. What effect does the **invisible character** Skipper have on the narrative? Explain how his inclusion advances the plot.

4. How does the conversation about Skipper reveal his relationship with Brick? How does it affect Brick's attitude toward society?

STRUCTURE

5. The events in Act II are centered on Big Daddy. Choose two interactions that illustrate competing value systems and contribute to a **conflict**. What are the value systems?

6. How do the stage directions create an **incongruity** for the characters? How does this incongruity contribute to the situational irony throughout the play?

7. The play's **climax** occurs at the end of Act II. What is the climax? Explain the **moment** of change for the protagonist.

NARRATION

8. The play reveals multiple perspectives and multiple **points of view**. How do Brick's and Big Daddy's speeches reveal **perspectives** that contribute to the complexity of their relationship?

9. How does Brick's change in tone at the end of Act II indicate a change in tone toward a particular subject? Explain.

10. In Act II, characters both tell the truth and lie. Choose one truth and one lie from Act II. Then explain whether the character(s) speaking are reliable.

IDEAS IN LITERATURE: Power and Perception

11. The play dramatizes the difficulty of communication. What makes communicating so difficult in the play? What factors contribute to the power and the effect of communication — in the play and in real life?

Tennessee Williams wrote two endings for Cat on a Hot Tin Roof. *The ending that follows is the original ending. The updated ending, adapted for the Broadway production, can be found on p. 1381.*

Note: *The following is the original third act of* Cat on a Hot Tin Roof.

ACT III (original)

There is no lapse of time.

[MAE *enters with* REVEREND TOOKER.]

MAE: Where is Big Daddy! Big Daddy?

BIG MAMA [*entering*]: Too much smell of burnt fireworks makes me feel a little bit sick at my stomach.—Where is Big
5   Daddy?

MAE: That's what I want to know, where has Big Daddy gone?

BIG MAMA: He must have turned in, I reckon he went to baid. . . .

10 [GOOPER *enters.*]

GOOPER: Where is Big Daddy?

MAE: We don't know where he is!

BIG MAMA: I reckon he's gone to baid.

GOOPER: Well, then, now we can talk.

15 BIG MAMA: What is this talk, what talk?

[MARGARET *appears on gallery, talking to* DR BAUGH.]

MARGARET [*musically*]: My family freed their slaves ten years before abolition, my
20 great-great-grandfather gave his slaves their freedom five years before the war between the States started!

MAE: Oh, for God's sake! Maggie's climbed back up in her family tree!

25 MARGARET [*sweetly*]: What, Mae?—Oh, where's Big Daddy?!

[*The pace must be very quick. Great Southern animation.*]

BIG MAMA [*addressing them all*]: I think Big
30 Daddy was just worn out. He loves his family, he loves to have them around him, but it's a strain on his nerves. He wasn't himself tonight, Big Daddy wasn't himself, I could tell he was all
35 worked up.

REVEREND TOOKER: I think he's remarkable.

BIG MAMA: Yaisss! Just remarkable. Did you all notice the food he ate at that table? Did you all notice the supper he put
40 away? Why, he ate like a hawss!

GOOPER: I hope he doesn't regret it.

BIG MAMA: Why, that man—ate a huge piece of cawn-bread with molasses on it! Helped himself twice to hoppin' john.

45 MARGARET: Big Daddy loves hoppin' john.—We had a real country dinner.

BIG MAMA [*overlapping* MARGARET]: Yais, he simply adores it! An' candied yams? That man put away enough food at that table
50 to stuffa field-hand!

GOOPER [*with grim relish*]: I hope he don't have to pay for it later on. . . .

BIG MAMA [*fiercely*]: What's that, Gooper?

MAE: Gooper says he hopes Big Daddy
55 doesn't suffer tonight.

BIG MAMA: Oh, shoot, Gooper says, Gooper says! Why should Big Daddy suffer for satisfying a normal appetite? There's nothin' wrong with that man but nerves,

60 he's sound as a dollar! And now he knows he is an' that's why he ate such a supper. He had a big load off his mind, knowin' he wasn't doomed t'—what he thought he was doomed to. . . .

65 MARGARET [*sadly and sweetly*]: Bless his old sweet soul. . . .

BIG MAMA [*vaguely*]: Yais, bless his heart, wher's Brick?

MAE: Outside.

70 GOOPER: —Drinkin' . . .

BIG MAMA: I know he's drinkin'. You all don't have to keep tellin' me Brick is drinkin'. Cain't I see he's drinkin' without you continually tellin' me that boy's drinkin'?

75 MARGARET: Good for you, Big Mama!

[*She applauds.*]

BIG MAMA: Other people drink and have drunk an' will drink, as long as they make that stuff an' put it in bottles.

80 MARGARET: That's the truth. I never trusted a man that didn't drink.

MAE: Gooper never drinks. Don't you trust Gooper?

MARGARET: Why, Gooper, don't you drink? If
85 I'd known you didn't drink, I wouldn't of made that remark—

BIG MAMA: Brick?

MARGARET: —at least, not in your presence.

[*She laughs sweetly.*]

90 BIG MAMA: Brick!

MARGARET: He's still on the gall'ry. I'll go bring him in so we can talk.

BIG MAMA [*worriedly*]: I don't know what this mysterious family conference is about.

95 [*Awkward silence.* BIG MAMA *looks from face to face, then belches slightly and mutters, 'Excuse me. . . .' She opens an ornamental fan suspended about her throat, a black lace fan to go with her black lace gown and fans her wilting corsage,*
100 *sniffing nervously and looking from face to face in the uncomfortable silence as* MARGARET *calls*

'BRICK?' *and* BRICK *sings to the moon on the gallery.*]

105 I don't know what's wrong here, you all have such long faces! Open that door on the hall and let some air circulate through here, will you please, Gooper?

MAE: I think we'd better leave that door closed, Big Mama, till after the talk.

110 BIG MAMA: Reveren' Tooker, will you please open that door?!

REVEREND TOOKER: I sure will, Big Mama.

MAE: I just didn't think we ought t' take any chance of Big Daddy hearin' a word of this

115 discussion.

BIG MAMA: I swan! Nothing's going to be said in Big Daddy's house that he cain't hear if he wants to!

GOOPER: Well, Big Mama, it's—

120 [MAE *gives him a quick, hard poke to shut him up. He glares at her fiercely as she circles before him like a burlesque ballerina, raising her skinny bare arms over her head, jangling her bracelets, exclaiming:*]

125 MAE: A breeze! A breeze!

REVEREND TOOKER: I think this house is the coolest house in the Delta.—Did you all know that Halsey Banks' widow put air-conditioning units in the church and

130 rectory at Friar's Point in memory of Halsey?

[*General conversation has resumed; everybody is chatting so that the stage sounds like a big bird-cage.*]

GOOPER: Too bad nobody cools your church

135 off for you. I bet you sweat in that pulpit these hot Sundays, Reverend Tooker.

REVEREND TOOKER: Yes, my vestments are drenched.

MAE [*at the same time to* DR BAUGH]: You think

140 those vitamin B12 injections are what they're cracked up t' be, Doc Baugh?

DOCTOR BAUGH: Well, if you want to be stuck with something I guess they're as good to be stuck with as anything else.

145 BIG MAMA [*at gallery door*]: Maggie, Maggie, aren't you comin' with Brick?

MAE [*suddenly and loudly, creating a silence*]: I have a strange feeling, I have a peculiar feeling!

150 BIG MAMA [*turning from gallery*]: What feeling?

MAE: That Brick said somethin' he shouldn't of said t' Big Daddy.

BIG MAMA: Now what on earth could Brick of

155 said t' Big Daddy that he shouldn't say?

GOOPER: Big Mama, there's somethin'—

MAE: NOW, WAIT!

[*She rushes up to* BIG MAMA *and gives her a quick hug and kiss.* BIG MAMA *pushes her impa-*

160 *tiently off as the* REVEREND TOOKER'S *voice rises serenely in a little pocket of silence:*]

REVEREND TOOKER: Yes, last Sunday the gold in my chasuble faded into th' purple. . . .

GOOPER: Reveren', you must of been

165 preachin' hell's fire last Sunday!

[*He guffaws at this witticism but the* REVEREND *is not sincerely amused. At the same time* BIG MAMA *has crossed over to* DR BAUGH *and is saying to him:*]

170 BIG MAMA [*her breathless voice rising high-pitched above the others*]: In my day they had what they call the Keeley cure for heavy drinkers. But now I understand they just take some kind of tablets, they

175 call them 'Annie Bust' tablets. But Brick don't need to take nothin'.

[BRICK *appears in gallery doors with* MARGARET *behind him.*]

BIG MAMA [*unaware of his presence behind her*]:

180 That boy is just broken up over Skipper's death. You know how poor Skipper died. They gave him a big, big dose of that sodium amytal stuff at his home and then they called the ambulance and give him

185 another big, big dose of it at the hospital and that and all of the alcohol in his system fo' months an months an' months

just proved too much for his heart. . . . I'm
scared of needles! I'm more scared of a
190 needle than the knife. . . . I think more
people have been needled out of this
world than-
[*She stops short and wheels about.*]
OH!—here's Brick! My precious baby—
195 [*She turns upon* BRICK *with short, fat arms
extended, at the same time uttering a loud, short
sob, which is both comic and touching.* | BRICK
*smiles and bows slightly, making a burlesque
gesture of gallantry for Maggie to pass before him
200 into the room. Then he hobbles on his crutch
directly to the liquor cabinet and there is absolute
silence, with everybody looking at* BRICK *as everybody has always looked at* BRICK *when he spoke
or moved or appeared. One by one he drops ice
205 cubes in his glass, then suddenly, but not quickly,
looks back over his shoulder with a wry, charming smile, and says:*]
BRICK: I'm sorry! Anyone else?
BIG MAMA [*sadly*]: No, son. I wish you
210   wouldn't!
BRICK: I wish I didn't have to, Big Mama, but
I'm still waiting for that click in my head
which makes it all smooth out!
BIG MAMA: Aw, Brick, you—BREAK MY
215   HEART!
MARGARET [*at the same time*]: Brick, go sit
with Big Mama!
BIG MAMA: I just cain't staiiiiiiiii-
nnnnnd—it. . . .
220 [*She sobs.*]
MAE: Now that we're all assembled—
GOOPER: We kin talk. . . .
BIG MAMA: Breaks my heart. . . .
MARGARET: Sit with Big Mama, Brick, and
225   hold her hand.
[BIG MAMA *sniffs very loudly three times, almost
like three drum beats in the pocket of silence.*]
BRICK: You do that, Maggie. I'm a restless
cripple. I got to stay on my crutch.

230 [BRICK *hobbles to the gallery door; leans there as
if waiting.* | MAE *sits beside* BIG MAMA, *while*
GOOPER *moves in front and sits on the end of the
couch, facing her.* REVEREND TOOKER *moves
nervously into the space between them; on the
235 other side,* DR BAUGH *stands looking at nothing in
particular and lights a cigar.* MARGARET *turns
away.*]
BIG MAMA: Why're you all surroundin'
me—like this? Why're you all starin' at
240   me like this an' makin' signs at each
other?
[REVEREND TOOKER *steps back startled.*]
MAE: Calm yourself, Big Mama.
BIG MAMA: Calm you'self, you'self, Sister
245   Woman. How could I calm myself with
everyone starin' at me as if big drops of
blood had broken out on m'face? What's
this all about, Annh! What?
[GOOPER *coughs and takes a center position.*]
250 GOOPER: Now, Doc Baugh.
MAE: Doc Baugh?
BRICK [*suddenly*]: SHHH-!
[*Then he grins and chuckles and shakes his head
regretfully.*]
255   —Naw!—that wasn't th' click.
GOOPER: Brick, shut up or stay out there on
the gallery with your liquor! We got to
talk about a serious matter. Big Mama
wants to know the complete truth about
260   the report we got today from the Ochsner
Clinic.
MAE [*eagerly*]: —on Big Daddy's condition!
GOOPER: Yais, on Big Daddy's condition, we
got to face it.
265 DOCTOR BAUGH: Well . . .
BIG MAMA [*terrified, rising*]: Is there?
Something? Something that I?
Don't—Know?
[*In these few words, this startled, very soft, ques-
270 tion,* BIG MAMA *reviews the history of her forty-
five years with* BIG DADDY, *her great, almost*

embarrassingly true-hearted and simple-minded
devotion to BIG DADDY, who must have had
something BRICK has, who made himself loved so
275 much by the 'simple expedient' of not loving
enough to disturb his charming detachment, also
once coupled, like BRICK'S, with virile beauty. BIG
MAMA has a dignity at this moment | she almost
stops being fat.]
280 DOCTOR BAUGH [after a pause, uncomfortably]:
Yes?—Well—
BIG MAMA: I!!!—want to—knowwwwwww....
[Immediately she thrusts her fist to her mouth as
if to deny that statement. Then, for some curious
285 reason, she snatches the withered corsage from
her breast and hurls it on the floor and steps on it
with her short, fat feet.]
—Somebody must be lyin'!—I want to
know!
290 MAE: Sit down, Big Mama, sit down on this
sofa.
MARGARET [quickly]: Brick, go sit with Big
Mama.
BIG MAMA: What is it, what is it?
295 DOCTOR BAUGH: I never have seen a more
thorough examination than Big Daddy
Pollitt was given in all my experience with
the Ochsner Clinic.
GOOPER: It's one of the best in the country.
300 MAE: It's THE best in the country—bar none!
[For some reason she gives GOOPER a violent
poke as she goes past him. He slaps at her hand
without removing his eyes from his mother's
face.]
305 DOCTOR BAUGH: Of course they were ninety-
nine and nine-tenths per cent sure before
they even started.
BIG MAMA: Sure of what, sure of what, sure
of—what?—what!
310 [She catches her breath in a startled sob. MAE
kisses her quickly. She thrusts MAE fiercely away
from her, staring at the doctor.]
MAE: Mommy, be a brave girl!

BRICK [in the doorway, softly]: 'By the light, by
315 the light, Of the sil-ve-ry mo-ooo-n'
GOOPER: Shut up!—Brick.
BRICK: —Sorry....
[He wanders out on the gallery.]
DOCTOR BAUGH: But now, you see, Big Mama,
320 they cut a piece off this growth, a speci-
men of the tissue and—
BIG MAMA: Growth? You told Big Daddy—
DOCTOR BAUGH: Now wait.
BIG MAMA [fiercely]: You told me and Big
325 Daddy there wasn't a thing wrong with
him but—
MAE: Big Mama, they always—
GOOPER: Let Doc Baugh talk, will yuh?
BIG MAMA: —little spastic condition of-
330 [Her breath gives out in a sob.]
DOCTOR BAUGH: Yes, that's what we told Big
Daddy. But we had this bit of tissue run
through the laboratory and I'm sorry to
say the test was positive on it. It's—
335 well—malignant.... [Pause.]
BIG MAMA: —Cancer?! Cancer?!
[DR BAUGH nods gravely. | BIG MAMA gives long
gasping cry.]
MAE and GOOPER: Now, now, now, Big Mama,
340 you had to know....
BIG MAMA: WHY DIDN'T THEY CUT IT OUT
OF HIM? HANH? HANH?
DOCTOR BAUGH: Involved too much, Big
Mama, too many organs affected.
345 MAE: Big Mama, the liver's affected and so's
the kidneys, both! It's gone way past what
they call a—
GOOPER: A surgical risk.
MAE: —Uh-huh....
350 [BIG MAMA draws a breath like a dying gasp.]
REVEREND TOOKER: Tch, tch, tch, tch, tch!
DOCTOR BAUGH: Yes, it's gone past the knife.
MAE: That's why he's turned yellow, Mommy!
BIG MAMA: Git away from me, git away from
355 me, Mae!

[*She rises abruptly.*]

I want Brick! Where's Brick? Where is my only son?

MAE: Mama! Did she say 'only son'?

360 **GOOPER:** What does that make me?

MAE: A sober responsible man with five precious children!—Six!

BIG MAMA: I want Brick to tell me! Brick! Brick!

365 **MARGARET** [*rising from her reflections in a corner*]: Brick was so upset he went back out.

BIG MAMA: Brick!

MARGARET: Mama, let me tell you!

370 **BIG MAMA:** No, no, leave me alone, you're not my blood!

GOOPER: Mama, I'm your son! Listen to me!

MAE: Gooper's your son, Mama, he's your first-born!

375 **BIG MAMA:** Gooper never liked Daddy.

MAE [*as if terribly shocked*]: That's not TRUE! [*There is a pause. The minister coughs and rises.*]

REVEREND TOOKER [*to* MAE]: I think I'd better slip away at this point.

380 **MAE** [*sweetly and sadly*]: Yes, Doctor Tooker, you go.

REVEREND TOOKER [*discreetly*]: Good night, good night, everybody, and God bless you all . . . on this place. . . . [*He slips out.*]

385 **DOCTOR BAUGH:** That man is a good man but lacking in tact. Talking about people giving memorial windows—if he mentioned one memorial window, he must have spoke of a dozen, and saying how awful it was 390 when somebody died intestate, the legal wrangles, and so forth. [MAE *coughs, and points at* BIG MAMA.]

DOCTOR BAUGH: Well, Big Mama. . . . [*He sighs.*]

BIG MAMA: It's all a mistake. I know it's just a 395 bad dream.

DOCTOR BAUGH: We're gonna keep Big Daddy as comfortable as we can.

BIG MAMA: Yes, it's just a bad dream, that's all it is, it's just an awful dream.

400 **GOOPER:** In my opinion Big Daddy is having some pain but won't admit that he has it.

BIG MAMA: Just a dream, a bad dream.

DOCTOR BAUGH: That's what lots of them do, they think if they don't admit they're 405 having the pain they can sort of escape the fact of it.

GOOPER [*with relish*]: Yes, they get sly about it, they get real sly about it.

MAE: Gooper and I think—

410 **GOOPER:** Shut up, Mae!—Big Daddy ought to be started on morphine.

BIG MAMA: Nobody's going to give Big Daddy morphine.

DOCTOR BAUGH: Now, Big Mama, when that 415 pain strikes it's going to strike mighty hard and Big Daddy's going to need the needle to bear it.

BIG MAMA: I tell you, nobody's going to give him morphine.

420 **MAE:** Big Mama, you don't want to see Big Daddy suffer, you know you—[GOOPER *standing beside her gives her a savage poke.*]

DOCTOR BAUGH [*placing a package on the table*]: I'm leaving this stuff here, so if there's a 425 sudden attack you all won't have to send out for it.

MAE: I know how to give a hypo.

GOOPER: Mae took a course in nursing during the war.

430 **MARGARET:** Somehow I don't think Big Daddy would want Mae to give him a hypo.

MAE: You think he'd want you to do it? [DR BAUGH *rises.*]

435 **GOOPER:** Doctor Baugh is goin'.

DOCTOR BAUGH: Yes, I got to be goin'. Well, keep your chin up, Big Mama.

GOOPER [*with jocularity*]: She's gonna keep both chins up, aren't you, Big Mama?

440 [BIG MAMA *sobs.*]

Now stop that, Big Mama.

MAE: Sit down with me, Big Mama.

GOOPER [*at door with* DR BAUGH]:   Well, Doc, we sure do appreciate all you done. I'm
445 telling you, we're surely obligated to you for—

[DR BAUGH *has gone out without a glance at him.*]

GOOPER: —I guess that doctor has got a lot on his mind but it wouldn't hurt him to
450 act a little more human. . . .

[BIG MAMA *sobs.*]

Now be a brave girl, Mommy.

BIG MAMA: It's not true, I know that it's just not true!

455 GOOPER: Mama, those tests are infallible!

BIG MAMA: Why are you so determined to see your father daid?

MAE: Big Mama!

MARGARET [*gently*]:   I know what Big Mama
460 means.

MAE [*fiercely*]:   Oh, do you?

MARGARET [*quietly and very sadly*]:   Yes, I think I do.

MAE: For a newcomer in the family you sure
465 do show a lot of understanding.

MARGARET: Understanding is needed on this place.

MAE: I guess you must have needed a lot of it in your family Maggie, with your father's
470 liquor problem and now you've got Brick with his!

MARGARET: Brick does not have a liquor problem at all. Brick is devoted to Big Daddy. This thing is a terrible strain on
475 him.

BIG MAMA: Brick is Big Daddy's boy, but he drinks too much and it worries me and Big Daddy, and, Margaret, you've got to cooperate with us, you've got to cooperate
480 with Big Daddy and me in getting Brick straightened out. Because it will break Big Daddy's heart if Brick don't pull himself together and take hold of things.

MAE: Take hold of what things, Big Mama?

485 BIG MAMA: The place.

[*There is a quick violent look between* MAE *and* GOOPER.]

GOOPER: Big Mama, you've had a shock.

MAE: Yais, we've all had a shock, but . . .

490 GOOPER: Let's be realistic—

MAE: —Big Daddy would never, would never, be foolish enough to—

GOOPER: —put this place in irresponsible hands!

495 BIG MAMA: Big Daddy ain't going to leave the place in anybody's hands; Big Daddy is not going to die. I want you to get that in your heads, all of you!

MAE: Mommy, Mommy, Big Mama, we're just
500 as hopeful an' optimistic as you are about Big Daddy's prospects, we have faith in prayer—but nevertheless there are certain matters that have to be discussed an' dealt with, because otherwise—

505 GOOPER: Eventualities have to be considered and now's the time. . . . Mae, will you please get my briefcase out of our room?

MAE: Yes, honey.

[*She rises and goes out through the hall door.*]

510 GOOPER [*standing over* BIG MAMA]:   Now, Big Mom. What you said just now was not at all true and you know it. I've always loved Big Daddy in my own quiet way. I never made a show of it, and I know that Big
515 Daddy has always been fond of me in a quiet way, too, and he never made a show of it neither.

[MAE *returns with* GOOPER's *briefcase.*]

MAE: Here's your briefcase, Gooper, honey.

520 GOOPER [*handing the briefcase back to her*]:   Thank you—Of cou'se, my relationship with Big Daddy is different from Brick's.

MAE: You're eight years older'n Brick an'
525 always had t' carry a bigger load of th'
responsibilities than Brick ever had t'
carry. He never carried a thing in his life
but a football or a highball.

GOOPER: Mae, will y' let me talk, please?

530 MAE: Yes, honey.

GOOPER: Now, a twenty-eight thousand acre
plantation's a mighty big thing t'run.

MAE: Almost singlehanded.

[MARGARET *has gone out on to the gallery, and*
535 *can be heard calling softly to* BRICK.]

BIG MAMA: You never had to run this place!
What are you talking about? As if Big
Daddy was dead and in his grave, you
had to run it? Why, you just helped him
540 out with a few business details and had
your law practice at the same time in
Memphis!

MAE: Oh, Mommy, Mommy, Big Mommy!
Let's be fair! Why, Gooper has given
545 himself body and soul to keeping this
place up for the past five years since Big
Daddy's health started failing. Gooper
won't say it, Gooper never thought of it as
a duty, he just did it. And what did Brick
550 do? Brick kept living in his past glory at
college! Still a football player at twenty-
seven!

MARGARET [*returning alone*]: Who are you
talking about, now? Brick? A football
555 player? He isn't a football player and you
know it. Brick is a sports announcer on TV
and one of the best-known ones in the
country!

MAE: I'm talking about what he was.

560 MARGARET: Well, I wish you would just stop
talking about my husband.

GOOPER: I've got a right to discuss my
brother with other members of MY OWN
family which don't include you. Why don't
565 you go out there and drink with Brick?

MARGARET: I've never seen such malice
toward a brother.

GOOPER: How about his for me? Why, he
can't stand to be in the same room with
570 me!

MARGARET: This is a deliberate campaign of
vilification for the most disgusting and
sordid reason on earth, and I know what it
is! It's avarice, avarice, greed, greed!

575 BIG MAMA: Oh, I'll scream! I will scream in a
moment unless this stops!

[GOOPER *has stalked up to* MARGARET *with
clenched fists at his sides as if he would strike
her.* MAE *distorts her face again into a hideous*
580 *grimace behind* MARGARET'S *back.*]

MARGARET: We only remain on the place
because of Big Mom and Big Daddy. If it is
true what they say about Big Daddy we
are going to leave here just as soon as it's
585 over. Not a moment later.

BIG MAMA [*sobs*]: Margaret. Child. Come here.
Sit next to Big Mama.

MARGARET: Precious Mommy. I'm sorry, I'm
so sorry, I—!

590 [*She bends her long graceful neck to press her
forehead to* BIG MAMA'S *bulging shoulder under
its black chiffon.*]

GOOPER: How beautiful, how touching, this
display of devotion!

595 MAE: Do you know why she's childless?
She's childless because that big beautiful
athlete husband of hers won't go to bed
with her!

GOOPER: You jest won't let me do this in a
600 nice way, will yah? Aw right—Mae and I
have five kids with another one coming! I
don't give a goddam if Big Daddy likes me
or don't like me or did or never did or will
or will never! I'm just appealing to a sense
605 of common decency and fair play. I'll tell
you the truth. I've resented Big Daddy's
partiality to Brick ever since Brick was

born, and the way I've been treated like I was just barely good enough to spit on

610 and sometimes not even good enough for that. Big Daddy is dying of cancer, and it's spread all through him and it's attacking all his vital organs including the kidneys and right now he is sinking into uremia,

615 and you all know what uremia is, it's poisoning of the whole system due to the failure of the body to eliminate its poisons.

MARGARET [to herself, downstage, hissingly]:

620 Poisons, poisons! Venomous thoughts and words! In hearts and minds!—That's poisons!

GOOPER [overlapping her]: I am asking for a square deal, and I expect to get one. But

625 if I don't get one, if there's any peculiar shenanigans going on around here behind my back, or before me, well, I'm not a corporation lawyer for nothing I know how to protect my own interests.—OH! A

630 late arrival!

[BRICK enters from the gallery with a tranquil, blurred smile, carrying an empty glass with him.]

MAE: Behold the conquering hero comes!

GOOPER: The fabulous Brick Pollitt!

635 Remember him?—Who could forget him!

MAE: He looks like he's been injured in a game!

GOOPER: Yep, I'm afraid you'll have to warm the bench at the Sugar Bowl this year,

640 Brick!

[MAE laughs shrilly.]

Or was it the Rose Bowl that he made that famous run in?

MAE: The punch bowl, honey. It was in the

645 punch bowl, the cut-glass punch bowl!

GOOPER: Oh, that's right, I'm getting the bowls mixed up!

MARGARET: Why don't you stop venting your malice and envy on a sick boy?

650 BIG MAMA: Now you two hush, I mean it, hush, all of you, hush!

GOOPER: All right, Big Mama. A family crisis brings out the best and the worst in every member of it.

655 MAE: That's the truth.

MARGARET: Amen!

BIG MAMA: I said, hush! I won't tolerate any more catty talk in my house.

[MAE gives GOOPER a sign indicating briefcase. |

660 BRICK'S smile has grown both brighter and vaguer. As he prepares a drink, he sings softly:]

BRICK: 'Show me the way to go home, I'm tired and I wanta go to bed, I had a little drink about an hour ago—'

665 GOOPER [at the same time]: Big Mama, you know it's necessary for me t'go back to Memphis in th' mornin' t' represent the Parker estate in a lawsuit.

[MAE sits on the bed and arranges papers she has

670 taken from the briefcase.]

BRICK [continuing the song]: 'Wherever I may roam, On land or sea or foam.'

BIG MAMA: Is it, Gooper?

MAE: Yaiss.

675 GOOPER: That's why I'm forced to—to bring up a problem that—

MAE: Somethin' that's too important t' be put off!

GOOPER: If Brick was sober, he ought to be in

680 on this.

MARGARET: Brick is present; we're here.

GOOPER: Well, good. I will now give you this outline my partner, Tom Bullitt, an' me have drawn up—a sort of dummy—

685 trusteeship.

MARGARET: Oh, that's it! You'll be in charge an' dole out remittances, will you?

GOOPER: This we did as soon as we got the report on Big Daddy from th' Ochsner

690 Laboratories. We did this thing, I mean we drew up this dummy outline with

the advice and assistance of the
Chairman of the Boa'd of Directors of
th' Southern Plantahs Bank and Trust
695   Company in Memphis, C. C. Bellowes,
a man who handles estates for all th'
prominent fam'lies in West Tennessee
and th' Delta.

BIG MAMA: Gooper?

700 **GOOPER** [*crouching in front of* **BIG MAMA**]: Now
this is not—not final, or anything like it.
This is just a preliminary outline. But it
does provide a basis—a design—a—
possible, feasible—plan!

705 **MARGARET:** Yes, I'll bet.

MAE: It's a plan to protect the biggest estate
in the Delta from irresponsibility an'—

BIG MAMA: Now you listen to me, all of you,
you listen here! They's not goin' to be any
710   more catty talk in my house! And Gooper,
you put that away before I grab it out of
your hand and tear it right up! I don't
know what the hell's in it, and I don't
want to know what the hell's in it. I'm
715   talkin' in Big Daddy's language now; I'm
his wife, not his widow, I'm still his wife!
And I'm talkin' to you in his language
an'—

GOOPER: Big Mama, what I have here is—

720 **MAE:** Gooper explained that it's just a plan....

BIG MAMA: I don't care what you got there.
Just put it back where it came from, an'
don't let me see it again, not even the
outside of the envelope of it! Is that
725   understood? Basis! Plan! Preliminary!
Design! I say—what is it Big Daddy always
says when he's disgusted?

BRICK [*from the bar*]: Big Daddy says 'crap'
when he's disgusted.

730 **BIG MAMA** [*rising*]: That's right—CRAP! I say
CRAP too, like Big Daddy!

MAE: Coarse language doesn't seem called
for in this—

GOOPER: Somethin' in me is deeply outraged
735   by hearin' you talk like this.

BIG MAMA: Nobody's goin' to take nothin'!—
till Big Daddy lets go of it, and maybe, just
possibly, not—not even then! No, not even
then!

740 **BRICK:** 'You can always hear me singin' this
song, Show me the way to go home.'

BIG MAMA: Tonight Brick looks like he used
to look when he was a little boy, just like
he did when he played wild games and
745   used to come home all sweaty and
pink-cheeked and sleepy, with his—red
curls shining. . . .

[*She comes over to him and runs her fat shaky
hand through his hair. He draws aside as he
750 does from all physical contact and continues
the song in a whisper, opening the ice bucket
and dropping in the ice cubes one by one as if
he were mixing some important chemical
formula.*]

755 **BIG MAMA** [*continuing*]: Time goes by so fast.
Nothin' can outrun it. Death commences
too early—almost before you're half-
acquainted with life—you meet with the
other . . . Oh, you know we just got to love
760   each other an' stay together, all of us, just
as close as we can, especially now that
such a black thing has come and moved
into this place without invitation.

[*Awkwardly embracing* **BRICK**, *she presses
765 her head to his shoulder.* | **GOOPER** *has been
returning papers to* **MAE** *who has restored them
to briefcase with an air of severely tried
patience.*]

GOOPER: Big Mama? Big Mama?

770 [*He stands behind her, tense with sibling
envy.*]

BIG MAMA [*oblivious of* **GOOPER**]: Brick, you
hear me, don't you?

MARGARET: Brick hears you, Big Mama, he
775   understands what you're saying.

BIG MAMA: Oh, Brick, son of Big Daddy! Big Daddy does so love you! Y'know what would be his fondest dream come true? If before he passed on, if Big Daddy has to pass on, you gave him a child of yours, a grandson as much like his son as his son is like Big Daddy!

MAE [*popping briefcase shut | an incongruous sound*]: Such a pity that Maggie an' Brick can't oblige!

MARGARET [*suddenly and quietly but forcefully*]: Everybody listen.

[*She crosses to the center of the room, holding her hands rigidly together.*]

MAE: Listen to what, Maggie?

MARGARET: I have an announcement to make.

GOOPER: A sports announcement, Maggie?

MARGARET: Brick and I are going to—have a child!

[BIG MAMA *catches her breath in a loud gasp. | Pause. |* BIG MAMA *rises.*]

BIG MAMA: Maggie! Brick! This is too good to believe!

MAE: That's right, too good to believe.

BIG MAMA: Oh, my, my! This is Big Daddy's dream, his dream come true! I'm going to tell him right now before he—

MARGARET: We'll tell him in the morning. Don't disturb him now.

BIG MAMA: I want to tell him before he goes to sleep, I'm going to tell him his dream's come true this minute! And Brick! A child will make you pull yourself together and quit this drinking!

[*She seizes the glass from his hand.*]

The responsibilities of a father will—

[*Her face contorts and she makes an excited gesture; bursting into sobs, she rushes out, crying.*]

I'm going to tell Big Daddy right this minute!

[*Her voice fades out down the hall. |* BRICK *shrugs slightly and drops an ice cube into another glass. |* MARGARET *crosses quickly to his side, saying something under her breath, and she pours the liquor for him, staring up almost fiercely into his face.*]

BRICK [*coolly*]: Thank you, Maggie, that's a nice big shot.

[MAE *has joined* GOOPER *and she gives him a fierce poke, making a low hissing sound and a grimace of fury.*]

GOOPER [*pushing her aside*]: Brick, could you possibly spare me one small shot of that liquor?

BRICK: Why, help yourself, Gooper boy.

GOOPER: I will.

MAE [*shrilly*]: Of course we know that this is—

GOOPER: Be still, Mae!

MAE: I won't be still! I know she's made this up!

GOOPER: God damn it, I said to shut up!

MARGARET: Gracious! I didn't know that my little announcement was going to provoke such a storm!

MAE: That woman, isn't pregnant!

GOOPER: Who said she was?

MAE: She did.

GOOPER: The doctor didn't. Doc Baugh didn't.

MARGARET: I haven't gone to Doc Baugh.

GOOPER: Then who'd you go to, Maggie?

MARGARET: One of the best gynaecologists in the South.

GOOPER: Uh huh, uh huh!—I see . . .

[*He takes out pencil and notebook.*]
—May we have his name, please?

MARGARET: No, you may not, Mister Prosecuting Attorney!

MAE: He doesn't have any name, he doesn't exist!

MARGARET: Oh, he exists all right, and so does my child, Brick's baby!

860 MAE: You can't conceive a child by a man that won't sleep with you unless you think you're—

[BRICK *has turned on the phonograph. A scat song cuts* MAE'S *speech.*]

865 GOOPER: Turn that off!

MAE: We know it's a lie because we hear you in here; he won't sleep with you, we hear you! So don't imagine you're going to put a trick over on us, to fool a dying man

870 with a—

[*A long drawn cry of agony and rage fills the house.* MARGARET *turns phonograph down to a whisper.* | *The cry is repeated.*]

MAE [*awed*]: Did you hear that, Gooper, did

875 you hear that?

GOOPER: Sounds like the pain has struck.

MAE: Go see, Gooper!

GOOPER: Come along and leave these love birds together in their nest!

880 [*He goes out first,* MAE *follows but turns at the door, contorting her face and hissing at* MARGARET.]

MAE: Liar!

[*She slams the door.* MARGARET *exhales with*

885 *relief and moves a little unsteadily to catch hold of* BRICK'S *arm.*]

MARGARET: Thank you for—keeping still....

BRICK: OK, Maggie.

MARGARET: It was gallant of you to save my

890 face!

BRICK: —It hasn't happened yet.

MARGARET: What?

BRICK: The click....

MARGARET: —the click in your head that

895 makes you peaceful, honey?

BRICK: Uh-huh. It hasn't happened.... I've got to make it happen before I can sleep....

MARGARET: —I—know what you—mean....

BRICK: Give me that pillow in the big chair,

900 Maggie.

MARGARET: I'll put it on the bed for you.

BRICK: No, put it on the sofa, where I sleep.

MARGARET: Not tonight, Brick.

BRICK: I want it on the sofa. That's where I

905 sleep.

[*He has hobbled to the liquor cabinet. He now pours down three shots in quick succession and stands waiting, silent. All at once he turns with a smile and says:*]

910 There!

MARGARET: What?

BRICK: The click....

[*His gratitude seems almost infinite as he hobbles out on the gallery with a drink. We*

915 *hear his crutch as he swings out of sight. Then, at some distance, he begins singing to himself a peaceful song.* | MARGARET *holds the big pillow forlornly as if it were her only companion, for a few moments, then throws it on the bed. She*

920 *rushes to the liquor cabinet, gathers all the bottles in her arms, turns about undecidedly, then runs out of the room with them, leaving the door ajar on the dim yellow hall.* BRICK *is heard hobbling back along the gallery, singing*

925 *his peaceful song. He comes back in, sees the pillow on the bed, laughs lightly, sadly, picks it up. He has it under his arm as* MARGARET *returns to the room.* MARGARET *softly shuts the door and leans against it, smiling softly at*

930 BRICK.]

MARGARET: Brick, I used to think that you were stronger than me and I didn't want to be overpowered by you. But now, since you've taken to liquor—you know

935 what?—I guess it's bad, but now I'm stronger than you and I can love you more truly! Don't move that pillow. I'll move it right back if you do!—Brick?

[*She turns out all the lamps but a single rose-silk-*

940 *shaded one by the bed.*]

I really have been to a doctor and I know what to do and—Brick?—this is my time by the calendar to conceive!

BRICK: Yes, I understand, Maggie. But how
945   are you going to conceive a child by a man
in love with his liquor?

MARGARET: By locking his liquor up and making
him satisfy my desire before I unlock it!

BRICK: Is that what you've done, Maggie?

950   MARGARET: Look and see. That cabinet's
mighty empty compared to before!

BRICK: Well, I'll be a son of a—

[*He reaches for his crutch but she beats him to it and
rushes out on the gallery, hurls the crutch over the*
955   *rail and comes back in, panting.* | *There are running
footsteps.* BIG MAMA *bursts into the room, her face
all awry, gasping, stammering.*]

BIG MAMA: Oh, my God, oh, my God, oh, my
God, where is it?

960   MARGARET: Is this what you want, Big Mama?

[MARGARET *hands her the package left by the doctor.*]

BIG MAMA: I can't bear it, oh! God! Oh, Brick!
Brick, baby!

[*She rushes at him. He averts his face from her*
965   *sobbing kisses.* | MARGARET *watches with a tight
smile.*]

My son, Big Daddy's boy! Little Father!

[*The groaning cry is heard again. She runs out,
sobbing.*]

970   MARGARET: And so tonight we're going to
make the lie true, and when that's done, I'll
bring the liquor back here and we'll get
drunk together, here, tonight, in this place
that death has come into. . . .—What do

975   you say?

BRICK: I don't say anything. I guess there's
nothing to say.

MARGARET: Oh, you weak people, you weak,
beautiful people!—who give up.—What

980   you want is someone to—

[*She turns out the rose-silk lamp.*]

—take hold of you.—Gently, gently, with
love! And—

[*The curtain begins to fall slowly.*] I do love
985   you, Brick, I do!

BRICK [*smiling with charming sadness*]:
Wouldn't it be funny if that was true?
    THE CURTAIN COMES DOWN
    THE END

◀ The image shows *Le Solitaire,* a 1976
oil-and-canvas painting by Tennessee
Williams.

———

How does the painting reflect a sense
of alienation and isolation? Does
the painting suggest a perspective
or message similar to that of *Cat on
a Hot Tin Roof*? Does the painting
give you insight into the play? Does
the play give you insight into the
painting? Explain.

CHARACTER

1. How do the changes in Big Mama's **circumstances** lead to a change in her character?

2. How does the exclusion of Brick at the beginning of Act III reveal the family's attitude toward him?

3. Maggie experiences an **epiphany**. What is this moment of insight? How does it change her relationship with Brick?

4. How are Brick's words and actions juxtaposed with the words and actions of Big Daddy? Does this add complexity to Brick's character? Explain.

5. Is Brick a **static** or **dynamic character**? Explain. What does this suggest about the values that he represents?

STRUCTURE

6. How does Act III reveal a collision of earlier events that result in a **climactic** moment for Maggie?

7. Consider the divisions in the play, as well as the presentation of events. How do the speed and the breaks contribute to the **narrative pacing**?

8. Are the **tensions** in the play ever **resolved**? Explain. How does the ending of the play contribute to your interpretation?

9. How does the order in which information is revealed affect the storyline and contribute to the **conflict** of the play?

NARRATION

10. How do Big Mama's and Maggie's **perspectives** change during the play as a result of actions and interactions with others?

11. At the end of the play, how have Brick's and Big Daddy's **inconsistencies** revealed a change in their relationship with others?

12. What is the significance of Maggie's final lines?

IDEAS IN LITERATURE: Power and Perception

13. *Cat on a Hot Tin Roof* revolves around truth and lies. Does the play support the adage that "the truth hurts"? How does it illustrate the saying? Can you recall a time in your life when lying was easier than telling the truth? How can the perceptions of others lead people to lie?

PUTTING IT ALL TOGETHER

14. How does the setting of the play (including the culture and physical surroundings) shape Brick's psychology and behavior? How does it affect his relationships with others? And how does that contribute to your interpretation of the play?

PERSON-TO-PERSON

Of course it is a pity that so much of all creative work is so closely related to the personality of the one who does it.

5 It is sad and embarrassing and unattractive that those emotions that stir him deeply enough to demand expression, and to charge their expression with some measure of light and power, are nearly all rooted, however changed in their surface, in the par-
10 ticular and sometimes peculiar concerns of the artist himself, that special world, the passions and images of it that each of us weaves about him from birth to death, a web of monstrous complexity, spun forth at a
15 speed that is incalculable to a length beyond measure, from the spider mouth of his own singular perceptions.

It is a lonely idea, a lonely condition, so terrifying to think of that we usually don't.
20 And so we talk to each other, write and wire each other, call each other short and long distance across land and sea, clasp hands with each other at meeting and at parting, fight each other and even destroy each other
25 because of this always somewhat thwarted effort to break through walls to each other. As a character in a play once said, 'We're all of us sentenced to solitary confinement inside our own skins.'
30 Personal lyricism is the outcry of prisoner to prisoner from the cell in solitary where each is confined for the duration of his life.

I once saw a group of little girls on a Mississippi sidewalk, all dolled up in their
35 mothers' and sisters' cast-off finery, old raggedy ball gowns and plumed hats and high-heeled slippers, enacting a meeting of ladies in a parlour with a perfect mimicry of polite Southern gush and simper. But one child was
40 not satisfied with the attention paid her

enraptured performance by the others, they were too involved in their own performances to suit her, so she stretched out her skinny arms and threw back her skinny neck and
45 shrieked to the deaf heavens and her equally oblivious playmates, 'Look at me, look at me, look at me!'

And then her mother's high-heeled slippers threw her off balance and she fell to the
50 sidewalk in a great howling tangle of soiled white satin and torn pink net, and still nobody looked at her.

I wonder if she is not, now, a Southern writer.
55 Of course it is not only Southern writers, of lyrical bent, who engage in such histrionics and shout, 'Look at me!' Perhaps it is a parable of all artists. And not always do we topple over and land in a tangle of trappings
60 that don't fit us. However, it is well to be aware of that peril, and not to content yourself with a demand for attention, to know that out of your personal lyricism, your sidewalk histrionics, something has to be created
65 that will not only attract observers but participants in the performance.

I try very hard to do that.

The fact that I want you to observe what I do for your possible pleasure and to give you
70 knowledge of things that I feel I may know better than you, because my world is different from yours, as different as every man's world is from the world of others, is not enough excuse for a personal lyricism that has not yet
75 mastered its necessary trick of rising above the singular to the plural concern, from personal to general import. But for years and years now, which may have passed like a dream because of this obsession, I have been
80 trying to learn how to perform this trick and make it truthful, and sometimes I feel that I

am able to do it. Sometimes, when the enraptured street-corner performer in me cries out
'Look at me!', I feel that my hazardous foot-
85 wear and fantastic regalia may not quite
throw me off balance. Then, suddenly, you
fellow-performers in the sidewalk show may
turn to give me your attention and allow me
to hold it, at least for the interval between
90 8:40 and 11 something p.m.

Eleven years ago this month of March, when
I was far closer than I knew, only nine months
away from that long-delayed, but always
expected, something that I lived for, the time
95 when I would first catch and hold an audience's attention, I wrote my first preface to a
long play. The final paragraph went like this:

'There is too much to say and not
enough time to say it. Nor is there power
100 enough. I am not a good writer. Sometimes
I am a very bad writer indeed. There is
hardly a successful writer in the field who
cannot write circles around me, but I think
of writing as something more organic than
105 words, something closer to being and
action. I want to work more and more with
a more plastic theatre than the one I have
(worked with) before. I have never for one
moment doubted that there are people—
110 millions!—to say things to. We come to
each other, gradually, but with love. It is the
short reach of my arms that hinders, not
the length and multiplicity of theirs. With
love and with honesty, the embrace is
115 inevitable.'

This characteristically emotional, if not
rhetorical, statement of mine at that time
seems to suggest that I thought of myself
as having a highly personal, even intimate
120 relationship with people who go to see
plays. I did and I still do. A morbid shyness
once prevented me from having much
direct communication with people, and
possibly that is why I began to write to

125 them plays and stories. But even now when
that tongue-locking, face-flushing, silent
and crouching timidity has worn off with
the passage of the troublesome youth
that it sprang from, I still find it somehow
130 easier to 'level with' crowds of strangers
in the hushed twilight of orchestra and
balcony sections of theatres than with
individuals across a table from me. Their
being strangers somehow makes them
135 more familiar and more approachable,
easier to talk to.

Of course I know that I have sometimes
presumed too much upon corresponding
sympathies and interest in those to whom I
140 talk boldly, and this has led to rejections that
were painful and costly enough to inspire
more prudence. But when I weigh one thing
against another, an easy liking against a hard
respect, the balance always tips the same way,
145 and whatever the risk of being turned a cold
shoulder, I still don't want to talk to people
only about the surface aspects of their lives,
the sort of things that acquaintances laugh
and chatter about on ordinary social occasions.
150 I feel that they get plenty of that, and
heaven knows so do I, before and after the
little interval of time in which I have their
attention and say what I have to say to them.
The discretion of social conversation, even
155 among friends, is exceeded only by the
discretion of 'the deep six', that grave
wherein nothing is mentioned at all.
Emily Dickinson, that lyrical spinster of
Amherst, Massachusetts, who wore a strict
160 and savage heart on a taffeta sleeve, commented wryly on that kind of posthumous
discourse among friends in these lines:

I died for beauty, but was scarce
Adjusted in the tomb,
165 When one who died for truth was lain
In an adjoining room.

He questioned softly why I failed?
'For beauty,' I replied.
'And I for truth,—the two are one,
170 We brethren are,' he said.

And so, as kinsmen met a night,
We talked between the rooms,
Until the moss had reached our lips,
And covered up our names.

175 Meanwhile!—I want to go on talking to
you as freely and intimately about what we
live and die for as if I knew you better than
anyone else whom you know.
TENNESSEE WILLIAMS

NOTE OF EXPLANATION

180 Some day when time permits I would like to
write a piece about the influence, its dangers
and its values, of a powerful and highly
imaginative director upon the development
of a play, before and during production. It
185 does have dangers, but it has them only if
the playwright is excessively malleable or
submissive, or the director is excessively
insistent on ideas or interpretations of his
own. Elia Kazan and I have enjoyed the
190 advantages and avoided the dangers of this
highly explosive relationship because of the
deepest mutual respect for each other's creative function: we have worked together
three times with a phenomenal absence of
195 friction between us and each occasion has
increased the trust.

If you don't want a director's influence on
your play, there are two ways to avoid it, and
neither is good. One way is to arrive at an
200 absolutely final draft of your play before you
let your director see it, then hand it to him
saying, Here it is, take it or leave it! The other
way is to select a director who is content to
put your play on the stage precisely as you
205 conceived it with no ideas of his own. I said

neither is a good way, and I meant it. No living playwright, that I can think of, hasn't
something valuable to learn about his own
work from a director so keenly perceptive as
210 Elia Kazan. It so happened that in the case of
Streetcar, Kazan was given a script that was
completely finished. In the case of Cat, he
was shown the first typed version of the play,
and he was excited by it, but he had definite
215 reservations about it which were concentrated in the third act. The gist of his reservations can be listed as three points: one, he
felt that Big Daddy was too vivid and important a character to disappear from the play
220 except as an offstage cry after the second act
curtain; two, he felt that the character of
Brick should undergo some apparent muta-
tion as a result of the virtual vivisection that
he undergoes in his interview with his father
225 in Act Two. Three, he felt that the character
of Margaret, while he understood that I sym-
pathized with her and liked her myself,
should be, if possible, more clearly sympathetic to an audience.

230 It was only the third of these suggestions
that I embraced wholeheartedly from the
outset, because it so happened that Maggie
the Cat had become steadily more charming
to me as I worked on her characterization. I
235 didn't want Big Daddy to reappear in Act
Three and I felt that the moral paralysis of
Brick was a root thing in his tragedy, and to
show a dramatic progression would obscure
the meaning of that tragedy in him and
240 because I don't believe that a conversation,
however revelatory, ever effects so immediate a change in the heart or even conduct of
a person in Brick's state of spiritual disrepair.

However, I wanted Kazan to direct the
245 play, and though these suggestions were not
made in the form of an ultimatum, I was
fearful that I would lose his interest if I
didn't re-examine the script from his point

of view. I did. And you will find included in
250 this published script the new third act that
resulted from his creative influence on the
play. The reception of the playing-script has
more than justified, in my opinion, the
adjustments made to that influence. A fail-
255 ure reaches fewer people, and touches fewer,
than does a play that succeeds.

It may be that Cat number one would
have done just as well, or nearly, as Cat

number two; it's an interesting question.
260 At any rate, with the publication of both
third acts in this volume, the reader can,
if he wishes, make up his own mind
about it.

TENNESSEE WILLIAMS

265 *Tennessee Williams wrote two endings for* Cat on a
Hot Tin Roof. *The ending that follows is the updated
ending adapted for the Broadway production.*

ACT III (updated — "Broadway Version")

*(With "Stage Management" and "Blocking
Notations")*

Proofer's note: This updated Act III contains a
significant number of "Stage Management" |
"Blocking Notations" (which is shorthand
used in the production book). Since this ver-
5 sion of the Act III is unmodified/unproofed, it
will also contain typos and OCR remnants that
the above updated Act III will not contain.

Here are a number of notations expanded
with their meanings. All will not be found in
10 the act (and some may be found that are not
indicated here). Look them up yourself.

Remember that directions are given from
the actor's perspective when looking at the
audience. Here are some useful shorthand
15 blocking abbreviations:

Areas of the Stage
SR = Stage Right
SL = Stage Left
CS = Center Stage

RC = Right of Center
20 LC = Left of Center
US = Upstage
DS = Downstage
DR = Down Right
DL = Down Left
25 UR = Up Right
UL = Up Left
UC = Up Center
DC = Down Center
PL = Plaster Line
30 QS = Quarter Stage

Other Useful Blocking Notation
X = Cross
ntr = Enter
Kn = Kneel
FZ = Freeze
35 / = Beat
w/ = With
CC = Countercross
BK = Break
@ = At

*(Retaining: "Stage Management" and "Blocking
Notations")*

AS PLAYED IN NEW YORK PRODUCTION

BIG DADDY *is seen leaving as at the end of Act II.*

BIG DADDY [*shouts, as be goes out DR on gallery*]:
ALL—LYIN'—DYIN'—LIARS! LIARS! LIARS!
[*After* **BIG DADDY** *has gone,* **MARGARET** *enters
from DR on gallery, into room through DS door.*
5 *She X to* **BRICK** *at LC*]

MARGARET: Brick, what in the name of God was goin' on in this room?

[DIXIE and TRIXIE *rush through the room from the hall, L to gallery R, brandishing cap pistols,*
10 *which they fire repeatedly, as they shout: 'Bang! Bang! Bang!'* — MAE *appears from DR gallery entrance, and turns the children back UL, along gallery. At the same moment,* GOOPER, REVEREND TOOKER *and* DR BAUGH *enter from L*
15 *in the hall.*]

MAE: Dixie! You quit that! Gooper, will y'please git these kiddies t'baid? Right now?

[GOOPER *and* REVEREND TOOKER *X along upper gallery,* DR BAUGH *holds, UC, near hall door.*
20 REVEREND TOOKER *X to* MAE *near section of gallery Just outside doors, R.*]

GOOPER [*urging the children along*]: Mae — you seen Big Mama?

MAE: Not yet.

25 [DIXIE *and* TRIXIE *vanish through hall, L.*]

REVEREND TOOKER [*to* MAE]: Those kiddies are so full of vitality. I think I'll have to be startin' back to town.

[MARGARET *turns to watch and listen.*]

30 MAE: Not yet, Preacher. You know we regard you as a member of this fam'ly, one of our closest an' dearest, so you just got t'be with us when Doc Baugh gives Big Mama th' actual truth about th' report from th'
35 clinic.

[*Calls through door:*]

Has Big Daddy gone to bed, Brick?

[GOOPER *has gone out DR at the beginning of the exchange between* MAE *and* REVEREND TOOKER.]
40 MARGARET [*replying to* MAE]: Yes, he's gone to bed. [*To* BRICK:]

Why'd Big Daddy shout 'liars'?

GOOPER [*off DR*]: Mae!

[MAE *exits D R.* REVEREND TOOKER *drifts along*
45 *upper gallery.*]

BRICK: I didn't lie to Big Daddy. I've lied to nobody, nobody but myself, just lied to

myself. The time has come to put me in Rainbow Hill, put me in Rainbow Hill,
50 Maggie, I ought to go there.

MARGARET: Over my dead body! [BRICK *starts R. She holds him.*] Where do you think you're goin'?

[MAE *enters from DR on gallery, X to* REVEREND
55 TOOKER, *who comes to meet her:*]

BRICK [*X below to C*]: Out for some air, I want air —

GOOPER [*entering from DR to* MAE, *on gallery*]: Now, where is that old lady?

60 MAE: Cantcha find her, Gooper?

[REVEREND TOOKER *goes out D R.*]

GOOPER [*X to Doc above hall door*]: She's avoidin' this talk.

MAE: I think she senses somethin'.

65 GOOPER [*calls off L.*]: Sookey! Go find Big Mama an' tell her Doc Baugh an' the Preacher've got to go soon.

MAE: Don't let Big Daddy hear yuh! [*Brings* DR BAUGH *to R on gallery.*]

70 REVEREND TOOKER [*off DR, calls*]: Big Mama.

SOOKEY *and* DAISY [*running from L to R in lawn, calling*]: Miss Ida! Miss Ida! [*They go out UR.*]

GOOPER [*calling off upper gallery*]: Lacey, you
75 look downstairs for Big Mama!

MARGARET: Brick, they're going to tell Big Mama the truth now, an' she needs you!

[REVEREND TOOKER *appears in lawn area, UR, X C*]

DOCTOR BAUGH [*to* MAE, *on R gallery*]: This is
80 going to be painful.

MAE: Painful things can't always be avoided.

DOCTOR BAUGH: That's what I've noticed about 'em, Sister Woman.

REVEREND TOOKER [*on lawn, points off R*]: I see
85 Big Mama! [*Hurries off L and reappears shortly in hall.*]

GOOPER [*hurrying into half*]: She's gone round the gall'ry to Big Daddy's room. Hey, Mama!

90 [*Off:*]

Hey, Big Mama! Come here!

MAE [*calls*]'. Hush, Gooper! Don't holler, go to
her!

[GOOPER *and* REVEREND TOOKER *now appear*
95 *together in hall.* BIG MAMA *runs in from
D R, carrying a glass of milk. She X past* DR
BAUGH *to* MAE, *on R gallery.* DR BAUGH *turns
away.*]

BIG MAMA: Here I am! What d'you all want
100 with me?

GOOPER [*steps toward* BIG MAMA]: Big Mama, I
told you we got to have this talk.

BIG MAMA: What talk you talkin' about? I
saw the light go on in Big Daddy's bedroom
105 an' took him his glass of milk, an' he just
shut the shutters right in my face.

[*Steps into room through R door.*]

When old couples have been together as
long as me an' Big Daddy, they, they get
110 irritable with each other just from too
much—devotion! Isn't that so?

[*X below wicker seat to R C area.*]

MARGARET [*X to* BIG MAMA, *embracing her*]:
Yes, of course it's so.

115 [BRICK *starts out UC through hall, but sees*
GOOPER *and* REVEREND TOOKER *entering, so he
hobbles through C out DS door and on to gallery.*]

BIG MAMA: I think Big Daddy was just worn
out. He loves his fam'ly. He loves to have
120 'em around him, but it's a strain on his
nerves. He wasn't himself tonight, Brick—
[*X C toward* BRICK, BRICK *passes her on his
way out, DS.*] Big Daddy wasn't himself, I
could tell he was all worked up.

125 REVEREND TOOKER [*USC*]: I think he's remarkable.

BIG MAMA: Yaiss! Just remarkable.

[*Faces US, turns, X to bar, puts down glass of
milk.*] Did you notice all the food he ate at
130 that table?

[*X R a bit.*] Why he ate like a hawss!

GOOPER [*USC*]: I hope he don't regret it.

BIG MAMA [*turns US toward* GOOPER]: What!
Why that man ate a huge piece of cawn
135 bread with molasses on it! Helped himself
twice to hoppin' john!

MARGARET [*X to* BIG MAMA]: Big Daddy loves
hoppin' john. We had a real country
dinner.

140 BIG MAMA: Yais, he simply adores it! An'
candied yams. Son—

[*X to DS door, looking out at* BRICK. MARGARET *X
above* BIG MAMA *to her L.*]

That man put away enough food at that
145 table to stuff a field-hand.

GOOPER: I hope he don't have to pay for it
later on.

BIG MAMA [*turns US*]: What's that, Gooper?

MAE: Gooper says he hopes Big Daddy
150 doesn't suffer tonight.

BIG MAMA [*turns to* MARGARET, *DC*]: Oh, shoot,
Gooper says, Gooper says! Why should Big
Daddy suffer for satisfyin' a nawmal
appetite? There's nothin' wrong with that
155 man but nerves; he's sound as a dollar!
An' now he knows he is, an' that's why he
ate such a supper. He had a big load off
his mind, knowin' he wasn't doomed
to—what—he thought he was—doomed
160 t'—[*She wavers.* MARGARET *puts her arms
around* BIG MAMA.]

GOOPER [*urging* MAE *forward*]: MAE!

[MAE *runs forward below wicker seat. She stands
below* BIG MAMA, MARGARET *above* BIG MAMA.
165 *They help her to the wicker seat.* BIG MAMA *sits.*
MARGARET *sits above her.* MAE *stands behind
her.*]

MARGARET: Bless his ole sweet soul.

BIG MAMA: Yes—bless his heart.

170 BRICK [*DS on gallery, looking out front*]: Hello,
moon, I envy you, you cool son of a
bitch.

BIG MAMA: I want Brick!

MARGARET: He just stepped out for some
175   fresh air.

BIG MAMA: Honey! I want Brick!

MAE: Bring li'l Brother in here so we cin
    talk.

[MARGARET *rises, X through DS door to* BRICK *on*
180 *gallery.*]

BRICK [*to the moon*]: I envy you—you cool son
    of a bitch.

MARGARET: Brick what're you doin' out here
    on the gall'ry baby?

185 BRICK: Admirin' an' complimentin' th' man
    in the moon.

[MAE *X to* DR BAUGH *on R gallery.* REVEREND
TOOKER *and* GOOPER *move R U C, looking at* BIG
MAMA.]

190 MARGARET [*to* BRICK]: Come in, baby. They're
    gettin' ready to tell Big Mama the truth.

BRICK: I can't witness that thing in there.

MAE: Doc Baugh, d'you think those vitamin
    BI2 injections are all they're cracked up t'be?

195 [*Enters room to upper side, behind wicker seat.*]

DOCTOR BAUGH [*X to below wicker seat*]: Well, I
    guess they're as good t'be stuck with as
    anything else.

[*Looks at watch; X through to LC*]

200 MARGARET [*to* BRICK]: Big Mama needs you!

BRICK: I can't witness that thing in there!

BIG MAMA: What's wrong here? You all have
    such long faces, you sit here waitin' for
    somethin' like a bomb—to go off.

205 GOOPER: We're waitin' for Brick an' Maggie to
    come in for this talk.

MARGARET [*X above* BRICK, *to his R*]: Brother
    Man an' Mae have got a trick up their
    sleeves, an' if you don't go in there t'help
210   Big Mama, y'know what I'm goin' to do—?

BIG MAMA: Talk. Whispers! Whispers! [*Looks
    out DR.*]
    Brick! . . .

MARGARET [*answering* BIG MAMA'S *call*]: Comin',
215   Big Mama! [*To* BRICK.] I'm goin' to take every

dam' bottle on this place an' pitch it off th'
    levee into th' river!

BIG MAMA: Never had this sort of atmo-
    sphere here before.

220 MAE [*sits above* BIG MAMA *on wicker seat*]:
    Before what, Big Mama?

BIG MAMA: This occasion. What's Brick an'
    Maggie doin' out there now?

GOOPER [*XD C, looks out*]: They seem to be
225   havin' some little altercation.

[BRICK *X toward DS step.* MAGGIE *moves R above
him to portal D R.* REVEREND TOOKER *joins* DR
BAUGH, *L C*]

BIG MAMA [*taking a pill from pill box on chain at
230   her wrist*]: Give me a little somethin' to
    wash this tablet down with. Smell of
    burnt fireworks always makes me sick.

[MAE *X to bar to pour glass of water.* DR BAUGH
joins her. GOOPER *X to* REVEREND TOOKER, *L C*]

235 BRICK [*to* MAGGIE]: You're a live cat, aren't you?

MARGARET: You're dam' right I am!

BIG MAMA: Gooper, will y'please open that
    hall door—an' let some air circulate in
    this stiflin' room? [GOOPER *starts US, but is
240   restrained by* MAE *who X through C with glass
    of water.* GOOPER *turns to men D L C*]

MAE [*X to* BIG MAMA *with water, sits above her*]:
    Big Mama, I think we ought to keep that
    door closed till after we talk.

245 BIG MAMA: I swan!

[*Drinks water. Washes down pill.*]

MAE: I just don't think we ought to take any
    chance of Big Daddy hearin' a word of this
    discussion.

250 BIG MAMA [*hands glass to* MAE]: What discus-
    sion of what? Maggie! Brick! Nothin' is
    goin' to be said in th' house of Big Daddy
    Pollitt that he can't hear if he wants to!

[MAE *rises, X to bar, puts down glass, joins
255 GOOPER *and the two men, LC*]

BRICK: How long are you goin' to stand
    behind me, Maggie?

MARGARET: Forever, if necessary. [BRICK *XUS to R gallery door.*]

260 BIG MAMA: Brick!

[MAE *rises, looks out D S, sits.*]

GOOPER: That boy's gone t'pieces—he's just gone t'pieces.

DOCTOR BAUGH: Y'know, in my day they used
265 to have somethin' they called the Keeley cure for drinkers.

BIG MAMA: Shoot!

DOCTOR BAUGH: But nowadays, I understand they take some kind of tablets that kill
270 their taste for the stuff.

GOOPER [*turns to* DR BAUGH]:   Call 'em anti-bust tablets.

BIG MAMA: Brick don't need to take nothin'.
That boy is just broken up over Skipper's
275 death. You know how poor Skipper died.
They gave him a big, big dose of that
sodium amytal stuff at his home an' then
they called the ambulance an' give him
another big, big dose of it at th' hospital
280 an' that an' all the alcohol in his system
fo' months an' months just proved too
much for his heart an' his heart quit
beatin'. I'm scared of needles! I'm more
scared of a needle than th' knife—

285 [BRICK *has entered the room to behind the wicker
seat. He rests his hand on* BIG MAMA'S *head.*
GOOPER *has moved a bit UK C, facing* BIG MAMA.]

BIG MAMA: Oh! Here's Brickl My precious baby!

[DR BAUGH *X to bar, puts down drink.* BRICK *X
290 below* BIG MAMA *through C to bar.*]

BRICK: Take it, Gooper!

MAE [*rising*]:   What?

BRICK: Gooper knows what. Take it, Gooper!

[MAE *turns to* GOOPER URC. DR BAUGH *X to
295* REVEREND TOOKER. MARGARET, *who has followed*
BRICK *US on R gallery before he entered the room,
now enters room, to behind wicker seat.*]

BIG MAMA [*to* BRICK]:   You just break my heart.

BRICK [*at bar*]:   Sorry—anyone else?

300 MARGARET: Brick, sit with Big Mama an' hold her hand while we talk.

BRICK: You do that, Maggie. I'm a restless cripple. I got to stay on my crutch.

[MAE *sits above* BIG MAMA, GOOPER *moves in
305 front, below, and sits on couch, facing* BIG MAMA.
REVEREND TOOKER *closes in to R C.* DR BAUGH
XD C, faces upstage, smoking cigar. MARGARET
turns away to R doors.]

BIG MAMA: Why're you all surroundin'
310 me?—like this? Why're you all starin' at me like this an' makin' signs at each other?

[BRICK *hobbles out hall door and X along R
gallery.*] I don't need nobody to hold my
315 hand. Are you all crazy? Since when did Big Daddy or me need anybody—?

[REVEREND TOOKER *moves behind wicker seat.*]

MAE: Calm yourself, Big Mama.

BIG MAMA: Calm you'self you'self, Sister
320 Woman! How could I calm myself with everyone starin' at me as if big drops of blood had broken out on m'face? What's this all about Annh! What?

GOOPER: Doc Baugh—

325 [MAE *rises.*] Sit down, Mae—

[MAE *sits.*]

—Big Mama wants to know the complete truth about th' report we got today from the Ochsner Clinic! [DR BAUGH *buttons his
330 coat, faces group at R C*]

BIG MAMA: Is there somethin'—somethin' that I don't know?

DOCTOR BAUGH: Yes—well . . .

BIG MAMA [*rises*]:   I—want to—knowwwww!
335 [*X to* DR BAUGH.] Somebody must be lyin'! I want to know!

[MAE, GOOPER, REVEREND TOOKER *surround* BIG
MAMA.]

MAE: Sit down, Big Mama, sit down on this
340 sofa! [BRICK *has passed* MARGARET *Xing DR
on gallery.*]

MARGARET: Brick! Brick!

BIG MAMA: What is it, what is it?

[BIG MAMA *drives* DR BAUGH *a bit DLC. Others*
345 *follow, surrounding* BIG MAMA.]

DOCTOR BAUGH: I never have seen a more
     thorough examination than Big Daddy
     Pollitt was given in all my experience at
     the Ochsner Clinic.

350 GOOPER: It's one of th' best in th' country.

MAE: It's THE best in th' country—bar none!

DOCTOR BAUGH: Of course they were ninety-
     nine and nine-tenths per cent certain
     before they even started.

355 BIG MAMA: Sure of what, sure of what, sure
     of what—what!?

MAE: Now, Mommy, be a brave girl!

BRICK [*on DR gallery, covers his ears, sings*]: 'By
     the light, by the light, of the silvery moon!'

360 GOOPER [*breaks DR. Calls out to* BRICK]: Shut
     up, Brick!

[*Returns to group LC*]

BRICK: Sorry . . .

[*Continues singing.*]

365 DOCTOR BAUGH: But now, you see, Big Mama,
     they cut a piece off this growth, a speci-
     men of the tissue, an'—

BIG MAMA: Growth? You told Big Daddy—

DOCTOR BAUGH: Now, wait—

370 BIG MAMA: You told me an' Big Daddy there
     wasn't a thing wrong with him but—

MAE: Big Mama, they always—

GOOPER: Let Doc Baugh talk, will yuh?

BIG MAMA: —little spastic condition of—

375 REVEREND TOOKER [*throughout all this*]: Shh!
     Shh! Shh!

[BIG MAMA *breaks UC, they all follow.*]

DOCTOR BAUGH: Yes, that's what we told Big
     Daddy. But we had this bit of tissue run
380   through the laboratory, an' I'm sorry t'say
     the test was positive on it. It's malignant.

[*Pause.*]

BIG MAMA: Cancer! Cancer!

MAE: Now now, Mommy—

385 GOOPER [*at the same time*]: You had to know,
     Big Mama.

BIG MAMA: Why didn't they cut it out of
     him? Hanh? Hannh?

DOCTOR BAUGH: Involved too much, Big
390   Mama, too many organs affected.

MAE: Big Mama, the liver's affected, an' so's
     the kidneys, both. It's gone way past what
     they call a—

GOOPER: —a surgical risk. [BIG MAMA *gasps.*]

395 REVEREND TOOKER: Teh, tch, tch.

DOCTOR BAUGH: Yes, it's gone past the
     knife.

MAE: That's why he's turned yellow!

[BRICK *stops singing, turns away UR on gallery.*]

400 BIG MAMA [*pushes* MAE *DS*]: Git away from
     me, git away from me, Mae! [*XDSR.*]
     I want Brick! Where's Brick I Where's my
     only son?

MAE [*a step after* BIG MAMA]: Mama! Did she
405   say 'only' son?

GOOPER [*following* BIG MAMA]: What does that
     make me?

MAE [*above* GOOPER]: A sober responsible
     man with five precious children—six!

410 BIG MAMA: I want Brick! Brick! Brick!

MARGARET [*a step to* BIG MAMA *above couch*]:
     Mama, let me tell you.

BIG MAMA [*pushing her aside*]: No, no, leave
     me alone, you're not my blood!

415 [*She rushes on to the D S gallery.*]

GOOPER [*X to* BIG MAMA *on gallery*]: Mama! I'm
     your son! Listen to me!

MAE: Gooper's your son, Mama, he's your
     first-born!

420 BIG MAMA: Gooper never liked Daddy!

MAE: That's not true!

REVEREND TOOKER [*UC*]: I think I'd better slip
     away at this point. Good night, good night
     everybody, and God bless you all—on this
425   place. [*Goes out through hall.*]

DOCTOR BAUGH [*XDR to above DS door*]: Well, Big Mama—

BIG MAMA [*leaning against* **GOOPER**, *on lower gallery*]: It's all a mistake, I know it's just 430 a bad dream.

DOCTOR BAUGH: We're gonna keep Big Daddy as comfortable as we can.

BIG MAMA: Yes, it's just a bad dream, that's all it is, it's just an awful dream.

435 **GOOPER:** In my opinion Big Daddy is havin' some pain but won't admit that he has it.

BIG MAMA: Just a dream, a bad dream.

DOCTOR BAUGH: That's what lots of 'em do, they think if they don't admit they're 440 havin' the pain they can sort of escape th' fact of it.

[**BRICK** *X US on R gallery.* **MARGARET** *watches him from R doors.*]

GOOPER: Yes, they get sly about it, get real sly 445 about it.

MAE [*X to R of* **DR BAUGH**]: Gooper an' I think—

GOOPER: Shut up, Mae!—Big Mama, I really do think Big Daddy should be started on 450 morphine.

BIG MAMA [*pulling away from* **GOOPER**]: Nobody's goin' to give Big Daddy morphine!

DOCTOR BAUGH: Now, Big Mama, when that pain strikes it's goin' to strike mighty hard 455 an' Big Daddy's goin' t'need the needle to bear it.

BIG MAMA [*X to* **DR BAUGH**]: I tell you, nobody's goin' to give him morphine!

MAE: Big Mama, you don't want to see Big 460 Daddy suffer, y'know y'—

DOCTOR BAUGH [*X to bar*]: Well, I'm leavin' this stuff here. [*Puts packet of morphine, etc., on bar.*] so if there's a sudden attack you won't have to send out for it.

465 [**BIG MAMA** *hurries to L side bar.*]

MAE [*XC, below* **DR BAUGH**]: I know how to give a hypo.

BIG MAMA: Nobody's goin' to give Big Daddy morphine!

470 **GOOPER** [*XC*]: Mae took a course in nursin' durin' th' war.

MARGARET: Somehow I don't think Big Daddy would want Mae t'give him a hypo.

MAE [*to* **MARGARET**]: You think he'd want you 475 to do it?

DOCTOR BAUGH: Well—

GOOPER: Well, Doc Baugh is goin'—

DOCTOR BAUGH: Yes, I got to be goin'. Well, keep your chin up, Big Mama.

480 [*X to hall.*]

GOOPER [*as he and* **MAE** *follow* **DR BAUGH** *into the hall*]: She's goin' to keep her ole chin up, aren't you, Big Mama?

[*They go out L.*]

485 Well, Doc, we sure do appreciate all you've done. I'm telling you, we're obligated—

BIG MAMA: Margaret!

[*XRC*]

490 **MARGARET** [*meeting* **BIG MAMA** *in front of wicker seat*]: I'm right here, Big Mama.

BIG MAMA: Margaret, you've got to cooperate with me an' Big Daddy to straighten Brick out now—

495 **GOOPER** [*off L, returning with* **MAE**]: I guess that Doctor has got a lot on his mind, but it wouldn't hurt him to act a little more human—

BIG MAMA: —because it'll break Big Daddy's 500 heart if Brick don't pull himself together an' take hold of things here.

[**BRICK** *XDSR on gallery.*]

MAE [*UC, overhearing*]: Take hold of what things, Big Mama?

505 **BIG MAMA** [*sits in wicker chair,* **MARGARET** *standing behind chair.*] The place.

GOOPER [*UC*]: Big Mama, you've had a shock.

MAE [*X with* **GOOPER** *to* **BIG MAMA**]: Yais, we've all had a shock, but—

510 GOOPER: Let's be realistic—

MAE: Big Daddy would not, would never, be foolish enough to—

GOOPER: —put this place in irresponsible hands!

515 BIG MAMA: Big Daddy ain't goin' t'put th' place in anybody's hands, Big Daddy is not goin' t'die! I want you to git that into your haids, all of you!

[MAE sits above BIG MAMA, MARGARET turns R to
520 door, GOOPER X LC a bit.]

MAE: Mommy, Mommy, Big Mama, we're just as hopeful an' optimistic as you are about Big Daddy's prospects, we have faith in prayer—but nevertheless there are
525 certain matters that have to be discussed an' dealt with, because otherwise—

GOOPER: Mae, will y'please get my briefcase out of our room?

MAE: Yes, honey.

530 [Rises, goes out through hall L.]

MARGARET [X to BRICK on DS gallery]: Hear them in there?

[X back to R gallery door.]

GOOPER [stands above BIG MAMA. Leaning over
535 her]: Big Mama, what you said just now was not at all true, an' you know it. I've always loved Big Daddy in my own quiet way. I never made a show of it. I know that Big Daddy has always been fond of
540 me in a quiet way, too.

[MARGARET drifts UR on gallery. MAE returns, X to GOOPER's L, with briefcase.]

MAE: Here's your briefcase, Gooper, honey. [Hands it to him.]

545 GOOPER [hands briefcase back to MAE]: Thank you. Of ca'use, my relationship with Big Daddy is different from Brick's.

MAE: You're eight years older'n Brick an' always had t' carry a bigger load of th'
550 responsibilities than Brick ever had t'carry; he never carried a thing in his life but a football or a highball.

GOOPER: Mae, will y'let me talk, please?

MAE: Yes, honey.

555 GOOPER: Now, a twenty-eight thousand acre plantation's a mighty big thing t'run.

MAE: Almost single-handed!

BIG MAMA: You never had t'run this place, Brother Man, what're you talkin' about, as
560 if Big Daddy was dead an' in his grave, you had to run it? Why, you just had t'help him out with a few business details an' had your law practice at the same time in Memphis.

565 MAE: Oh, Mommy, Mommy, Mommy! Let's be fair! Why, Gooper has given himself body an' soul t'keepin' this place up fo' the past five years since Big Daddy's health started fallin'. Gooper won't say it,
570 Gooper never thought of it as a duty, he just did it. An' what did Brick do? Brick kep' livin' in his past glory at college!

[GOOPER places a restraining hand on MAE'S leg; MARGARET drifts DS in gallery.]

575 GOOPER: Still a football player at twenty-seven!

MARGARET [bursts into UR door]: Who are you talkin' about now? Brick? A football player? He isn't a football player an' you know it!
580 Brick is a sports announcer on TV an' one of the best-known ones in the country!

MAE [breaks UC]: I'm talkin' about what he was!

MARGARET [X to above lower gallery door]:
585 Well, I wish you would just stop talkin' about my husband!

GOOPER [X to above MARGARET]: Listen, Margaret, I've got a right to discuss my own brother with other members of my
590 own fam'ly, which don't include you! [Pokes finger at her; she slaps his finger away.] Now, why don't you go on out there an' drink with Brick?

MARGARET: I've never seen such malice
595 toward a brother.

GOOPER: How about his for me? Why he can't stand to be in the same room with me!

BRICK [*on lower gallery*]: That's the truth!

600 **MARGARET:** This is a deliberate campaign of vilification for the most disgusting and sordid reason on earth, and I know what it is! It's avarice, avarice, greed, greed!

BIG MAMA: Oh, I'll scream, I will scream in a
605 moment unless this stops! Margaret, child, come here, sit next to Big Mama.

MARGARET [*X to* BIG MAMA, *sits above her*]: Precious Mommy.

[GOOPER *X to bar.*]

610 **MAE:** How beautiful, how touchin' this display of devotion! Do you know why she's childless? She's childless because that big, beautiful athlete husband of hers won't go to bed with her, that's why!

615 [*X to LC of bed, looks at* GOOPER.]

GOOPER: You jest won't let me do this the nice way, will yuh? Aw right—

[*X to above wicker seat.*]

I don't give a goddam if Big Daddy likes
620 me or don't like me or did or never did or will or will never! I'm just ap-pealin' to a sense of common decency an' fair play! I'm tellin' you th' truth—

[*X DS through lower door to* BRICK *on DR*
625 *gallery.*] I've resented Big Daddy's partiality to Brick ever since th' goddam day you were born, son, an' th' way I've been treated, like I was just barely good enough to spit on, an' sometimes not even good
630 enough for that.

[*X back through room to above wicker seat.*] Big Daddy is dyin' of cancer an' it's spread all through him an' it's attacked all his vital organs includin' the kidneys an' right
635 now he is sinkin' into uraemia, an' you all know what uraemia is, it's poisonin' of the whole system due to th' failure of th' body to eliminate its poisons.

MARGARET: Poisons, poisons, venomous
640 thoughts and words! In hearts and minds! That's poisons!

GOOPER: I'm askin' for a square deal an' by God I expect to get one. But if I don't get one, if there's any peculiar shenanigans
645 goin' on around here behind my back, well I'm not a corporation lawyer for nothin'!

[*X DS toward lower gallery door, on apex.*] I know how to protect my own interests.
650 [*Rumble of distant thunder.*]

BRICK [*entering the room through D S door*]: Storm comin' up.

GOOPER: Oh, a late arrival!

MAE [*X through C to below bar, LCO*]: Behold,
655 the conquerin' hero comes!

GOOPER [*X through C to bar, following* BRICK, *imitating his limp*]: The fabulous Brick Pollitt! Remember him? Who could forget him?

MAE: He looks like he's been injured in a
660 game!

GOOPER: Yep, I'm afraid you'll have to warm th' bench at the Sugar Bowl this year, Brick! Or was it the Rose Bowl that he made his famous run in.

665 [*Another rumble of thunder, sound of wind rising.*]

MAE [*X to L of* BRICK, *who has reached the bar*]: The punch bowl, honey, it was the punch bowl, the cut-glass punch bowl!

GOOPER: That's right! I'm always gettin'
670 the boy's bowls mixed up! [*Pats* BRICK *on the butt.*]

MARGARET [*rushes at* GOOPER, *striking him*]: Stop that! You stop that! [*Thunder.* MAE *X toward* MARGARET *from L of* GOOPER, *flails at*
675 MARGARET; GOOPER *keeps the women apart.* LACEY *runs through the US lawn area in a raincoat.*]

DAISY and **SOOKEY** [*off UL*]: Storm! Storm comin'! Storm! Storm!

680 **LACEY** [*running out UR*]: Brightie, close them shutters!

GOOPER [X on to R gallery, calls after LACEY]: Lacey, put the top up on my Cadillac, will yuh?

685 LACEY [off R]: Yes, sur, Mistah Pollitt!

GOOPER [X to above BIG MAMA]: Big Mama, you know it's goin' to be necessary for me t'go back to Memphis in th' mornin' t'represent the Parker estate in a lawsuit. [MAE sits on

690 L side bed, arranges papers she removes from briefcase.]

BIG MAMA: Is it, Gooper?

MAE: Yaiss.

GOOPER: That's why I'm forced to—to bring

695 up a problem that—

MAE: Somethin' that's too important t' be put off!

GOOPER: If Brick was sober, he ought to be in on this. I think he ought to be present

700 when I present this plan.

MARGARET [L/C]: Brick is present, we're present!

GOOPER: Well, good. I will now give you this outline my partner, Tom Bullitt, an' me

705 have drawn up—a sort of dummy— trusteeship!

MARGARET: Oh, that's it! You'll be in charge an' dole out remittances, will you?

GOOPER: This we did as soon as we got the

710 report on Big Daddy from th' Ochsner Laboratories. We did this thing, I mean we drew up this dummy outline with the advice and assistance of the Chairman of the Boa'd of Directors of th' Southern

715 Plantuhs Bank and Trust Company in Memphis, C. C. Bellowes, a man who handles estates for all th' prominent fam'lies in West Tennessee and th' Delta!

BIG MAMA: Gooper?

720 GOOPER [X behind seat to below BIG MAMA]: Now this is not—not final, or anything like it, this is just a preliminary outline. But it does provide a—basis—a design—

a—possible, feasible—plan! [He waves
725 papers MAE has thrust into his hand, US.]

MARGARET [XDL]: Yes, I'll bet it's a plan! [Thunder rolls. Interior lighting dims.]

MAE: It's a plan to protect the biggest estate in the Delta from irresponsibility an'—

730 BIG MAMA: Now you listen to me, all of you, you listen here! They's not goin' to be no more catty talk in my house! And Gooper, you put that away before I grab it out of your hand and tear it right up! I don't

735 know what the hell's in it, and I don't want to know what the hell's in it. I'm talkin' in Big Daddy's language now, I'm his wife, not his widow, I'm still his wife! And I'm talkin' to you in his language

740 an'—

GOOPER: Big Mama, what I have here is—

MAE: Gooper explained that it's just a plan . . .

BIG MAMA: I don't care what you got there, just put it back where it come from an'

745 don't let me see it again, not even the outside of the envelope of it! Is that understood? Basis! Plan! Preliminary! Design!—I say—what is it that Big Daddy always says when he's disgusted? [Storm

750 clouds race across sky.]

BRICK [from bar]: Big Daddy says 'crap' when he is disgusted.

BIG MAMA [rising]: That's right—CRAPPPP! I say CRAP too, like Big Daddy! [Thunder rolls.]

755 MAE: Coarse language don't seem called for in this—

GOOPER: Somethin' in me is deeply outraged by this.

BIG MAMA: Nobody's goin' to do nothin'!—

760 till Big Daddy lets go of it, and maybe just possibly not—not even then! No, not even then! [Thunder clap. Glass crash, off L. Off UR, children commence crying. Many storm sounds, L and R—barnyard animals in terror,

765 papers crackling, shutters rattling. SOOKEY and

DAISY *hurry from L to R in lawn area.*
Inexplicably, DAISY *hits together two leather*
pillows. They cry, 'Storm! Storm!' SOOKEY
waves a piece of wrapping paper to cover
770 *lawn furniture.* MAE *exits to hall and upper*
gallery. Strange man runs across lawn, R to L.
Thunder rolls repeatedly.]

MAE: Sookey, hurry up an' git that po'ch
fu'niture covahed; want th' paint to come
775 off? [*Starts DR on gallery.* GOOPER *runs*
through hall to R gallery.]

GOOPER [*yells to* LACEY, *who appears from R*]:
Lacey, put mah car away!

LACEY: Cain't, Mistah Pollitt, you got the keys!
780 [*Exit US.*]

GOOPER: Naw, you got 'em, man.
[*Exit D R. Reappears UR, calls to* MAE]
Where th' keys to th' car, honey?
[*Runs C*]

785 MAE [*DR on gallery*]: You got 'em in your pocket!
[*Exit DR* GOOPER *exits UR. Dog howls.* DAISY
and SOOKEY *sing off UR to comfort children.*
MAE *is heard placating the children. Storm*
fades away. During the storm, MARGARET *X*
790 *and sits on couch, DR.* BIG MAMA *X DC.*]

BIG MAMA: Brick! Come here, Brick, I need
you. [*Thunder distantly. Children whimper,*
off L. MAE *consoles them.* BRICK *X to R of* BIG
MAMA.]

795 BIG MAMA: Tonight Brick looks like he used
to look when he was a little boy just like
he did when he played wild games in the
orchard back of the house and used to
come home when I hollered myself
800 hoarse for him! all—sweaty—and
pink-cheeked—an' sleepy with his curls
shinin'—
[*Thunder distantly. Children whimper off L.*
MAE *consoles them. Dog howls, off.*] Time goes
805 by so fast. Nothin' can outrun it. Death
commences too early—almost before
you're half-acquainted with life—you

meet with the other. Oh, you know we just
got to love each other, an' stay together all
810 of us just as close as we can, specially now
that such a black thing has come and
moved into this place without invitation.
[*Dog howls, off.*]
Oh, Brick, son of Big Daddy, Big Daddy
815 does so love you. Y'know what would be
his fondest dream come true? If before he
passed on, if Big Daddy has to pass on . . .
[*Dog howls, off.*]
You give him a child of yours, a grandson
820 as much like his son as his son is like Big
Daddy. . . .

MARGARET: I know that's Big Daddy's dream.

BIG MAMA: That's his dream.

BIG DADDY [*off DR on gallery*]: Looks like the
825 wind was takin' liberties with this place.
[LACEY *appears UL, X to UC in lawn area;*
BRIGHTIE *and* SMALL *appear UR on lawn.* BIG
DADDY *X on to the UR gallery.*]

LACEY: Evenin', Mr Pollitt.

830 BRIGHTIE *and* SMALL: Evenin', Cap'n. Hello,
Cap'n.

MARGARET [*X to R door*]: Big Daddy's on the
gall'ry.

BIG DADDY: Stawm crossed th' river, Laeey?

835 LACEY: Gone to Arkansas, Cap'n.
[BIG MAMA *has turned toward the hall door at the*
sound of BIG DADDY'S *voice on the gallery. Now she*
X's DSR an out the DS door on to the gallery.]

BIG MAMA: I can't stay here. He'll see
840 somethin' in my eyes.

BIG DADDY [*on upper gallery, to the boys*]:
Stawm done any damage around here?

BRIGHTIE: Took the po'ch off ole Aunt
Crawley's house.

845 BIG DADDY: Ole Aunt Crawley should of been
settin' on it. It's time fo' th' wind to blow
that ole girl away! [*Field-hands laugh, exit,*
UR. BIG DADDY *enters room, UC, hall door.*]
Can I come in?

850 [*Puts his cigar in ash tray on bar.* **MAE** *and*
GOOPER *hurry along the upper gallery and stand
behind* **BIG DADDY** *in hall door.*]

MARGARET: Did the storm wake you up, Big
Daddy?

855 **BIG DADDY:** Which stawm are you talkin'
about—th' one outside or th' hullaballoo
in here? [**GOOPER** *squeezes past* **BIG DADDY.**]

GOOPER [*X toward bed, where legal papers are
strewn*]: 'Scuse me, sir . . .

860 [**MAE** *tries to squeeze past* **BIG DADDY** *to join*
GOOPER, *but* **BIG DADDY** *puts his arm firmly
around her.*]

BIG DADDY: I heard some mighty loud talk.
Sounded like somethin' important was
865 bein' discussed. What was the powwow
about?

MAE [*flustered*]: Why—nothin', Big Daddy . . .

BIG DADDY [*X DLC, taking* **MAE** *with him*]:
What is that pregnant-lookin' envelope
870 you're puttin' back in your briefcase,
Gooper?

GOOPER [*at foot of bed, caught, as he stuffs
papers into envelope*]: That? Nothin', suh—
nothin' much of anythin' at all . . .

875 **BIG DADDY:** Nothin'? It looks like a whole lot
of nothing!

[*Turns US to group:*]
You all know th' story about th' young
married couple—

880 **GOOPER:** Yes, sir!

BIG DADDY: Hello, Brick—

BRICK: Hello, Big Daddy.

[*The group is arranged in a semi-circle above*
BIG DADDY, **MARGARET** *at the extreme R, then*
885 **MAE** *and* **GOOPER,** *then* **BIG MAMA,** *with* **BRICK**
at L.]

BIG DADDY: Young married couple took
Junior out to th' zoo one Sunday,
inspected all of God's creatures in their
890 cages, with satisfaction.

GOOPER: Satisfaction.

BIG DADDY [*X USC, face front*]: This afternoon
was a warm afternoon in spring an' that
ole elephant had somethin' else on his
895 mind which was bigger'n peanuts. You
know this story, Brick?

[**GOOPER** *nods.*]

BRICK: No, sir, I don't know it.

BIG DADDY: Y'see, in th' cage adjoinin' they
900 was a young female elephant in heat!

BIG MAMA [*at* **BIG DADDY'S** *shoulder*]: Oh, Big
Daddy!

BIG DADDY: What's the matter, preacher's
gone, ain't he? All right. That female
905 elephant in the next cage was per-meatin'
the atmosphere about her with a powerful
and excitin' odour of female fertility!
Huh! Ain't that a nice way to put it,
Brick?

910 **BRICK:** Yes, sir, nothin' wrong with it.

BIG DADDY: Brick says the's nothin' wrong
with it!

BIG MAMA: Oh, Big Daddy!

BIG DADDY [*X DSC*]: So this ole bull elephant
915 still had a couple of fornications left in
him. He reared back his trunk an' got a
whiff of that elephant lady next door!—
began to paw at the dirt in his cage an'
butt his head against the separatin' parti-
920 tion and, first thing y'know, there was a
conspicuous change in his profile—very
conspicuous! Ain't I tellin' this story in
decent language, Brick?

BRICK: Yes, sir, too ruttin' decent!

925 **BIG DADDY:** So, the little boy pointed at it
and said, 'What's that?' His Mam said, 'Oh,
that's nothin'!'—His Papa said, 'She's
spoiled!'

[*Field-hands sing off R, featuring* **SOOKEY:** *'I Just
930 Can't Stay Here by Myself,' through following
scene.* **BIG DADDY** *X to* **BRICK** *at L.*]

BIG DADDY: You didn't laugh at that story,
Brick.

[**BIG MAMA** *X D R C crying.* **MARGARET** *goes to*
935   *her.* **MAE** *and* **GOOPER** *hold UR C.*]

    BRICK: No, sir, I didn't laugh at that story.
[*On the lower gallery,* **BIG MAMA** *sobs.* **BIG DADDY**
looks toward her.]

    BIG DADDY: What's wrong with that long,
940   thin woman over there, loaded with
       diamonds? Hey, what's-your-name, what's
       the matter with you?

    MARGARET [*X toward* **BIG DADDY**]:   She had a
       slight dizzy spell, Big Daddy.

945 **BIG DADDY** [*ULC*]:   You better watch that, Big
       Mama. A stroke is a bad way to go.

    MARGARET [*X to* **BIG DADDY** *at C*]:   Oh, Brick,
       Big Daddy has on your birthday present to
       him, Brick, he has on your cashmere robe,
950   the softest material I have ever felt.

    BIG DADDY: Yeah, this is my soft birthday,
       Maggie. . . . Not my gold or my silver
       birthday, but my soft birthday, every-
       thing's got to be soft for Big Daddy on this
955   soft birthday.

[**MAGGIE** *kneels before* **BIG DADDY** *C. As* **GOOPER**
and **MAE** *speak,* **BIG MAMA** *X USRC in front of*
them, bushing them with a gesture.]

    GOOPER: Maggie, I hate to make such a crude
960   observation, but there is somethin' a little
       indecent about your—

    MAE: Like a slow-motion football tackle—

    MARGARET: Big Daddy's got on his Chinese
       slippers that I gave him, Brick. Big Daddy,
965   I haven't given you my big present yet,
       but now I will, now's the time for me to
       present it to you! I have an announce-
       ment to make!

    MAE: What? What kind of announcement?

970 **GOOPER:**   A sports announcement, Maggie?

    MARGARET: Announcement of life beginning!
       A child is coming, sired by Brick, and out
       of Maggie the Cat! I have Brick's child in
       my body, an' that's my birthday present to
975   Big Daddy on this birthday!

[**BIG DADDY** *looks at* **BRICK** *who X behind* **BIG**
DADDY *to DS portal, L.*]

    BIG DADDY: Get up, girl, get up off your
       knees, girl.

980 [**BIG DADDY** *helps* **MARGARET** *rise. He X above*
her, to her R, bites off the end of a fresh cigar,
taken from his bathrobe pocket, as he studies
MARGARET.]

       Uh-huh, this girl has life in her body,
985   that's no lie!

    BIG MAMA: BIG DADDY'S DREAM COME TRUE!

    BRICK: JESUS!

    BIG DADDY [*X R below wicker seat*]:   Gooper, I
       want my lawyer in the mornin'.

990 **BRICK:**   Where are you goin', Big Daddy?

    BIG DADDY: Son, I'm goin' up on the roof to
       the belvedere on th' roof to look over my
       kingdom before I give up my kingdom—
       twenty-eight thousand acres of th' richest
995   land this side of the Valley Nile! [*Exit*
       through R doors, and DR on gallery.]

    BIG MAMA [*following*]:   Sweetheart, sweetheart,
       sweetheart—can I come with you? [*Exits*
       DR. **MARGARET** *is DSC in mirror area.*]

1000 **GOOPER** [*X to bar*]:   Brick, could you possibly
       spare me one small shot of that liquor?

    BRICK [*DLC*]:   Why, help yourself, Gooper boy.

    GOOPER: I will.

    MAE [*X forward*]:   Of course we know that this
1005   is a lie!

    GOOPER [*drinks*]:   Be still, Mae!

    MAE [*X to* **GOOPER** *at bar*]:   I won't be still! I
       know she's made this up!

    GOOPER: God damn it, I said to shut up!

1010 **MAE:**   That woman isn't pregnant!

    GOOPER: Who said she was?

    MAE: She did!

    GOOPER: The doctor didn't. Doc Baugh didn't.

    MARGARET [*XR to above couch*]:   I haven't gone
1015   to Doc Baugh.

    GOOPER [*X through to L of* **MARGARET**]:   Then
       who'd you go to, Maggie?

[*Offstage song finishes.*]

MARGARET: One of the best gynaecologists in
1020   the South.

GOOPER: Uh-huh, I see—

[*Foot on end of couch, trapping to* MARGARET]
    May we have his name please?

MARGARET: No, you may not, Mister—
1025   Prosecutin' Attorney!

MAE [*X to R of* MARGARET, *above*]: He doesn't
    have any name, he doesn't exist!

MARGARET: He does so exist, and so does my
    baby, Brick's baby!

1030 MAE: You can't conceive a child by a man
    that won't sleep with you unless you
    think you're—[*Forces* MARGARET *on to
    couch, turns away C.* BRICK *starts C for* MAE.]
    He drinks all the time to be able to toler-
1035   ate you! Sleeps on the sofa to keep out of
    contact with you!

GOOPER [*X above* MARGARET, *who lies face down
    on couch*]: Don't try to kid us, Margaret—

MAE [*X to bed, L side, rumpling pillows*]: How
1040   can you conceive a child by a man that
    won't sleep with you? How can you
    conceive? How can you? How can you!

GOOPER [*sharply*]: MAE!

BRICK [*X below* MAE *to her R, takes hold of her*]:
1045   Mae, Sister Woman, how d'you know that
    I don't sleep with Maggie?

MAE: We occupy the next room an' th' wall
    between isn't soundproof.

BRICK: Oh . . .

1050 MAE: We hear the nightly pleadin' and the
    nightly refusal. So don't imagine you're
    goin' t'put a trick over on us, to fool a
    dyin' man with—a—

BRICK: Mae, Sister Woman, not everybody
1055   makes much noise about love. Oh, I know
    some people are huffers an' puffers, but
    others are silent lovers.

GOOPER [*behind seat, R*]: This talk is pointless,
    completely.

1060 BRICK: How d'y'know that we're not silent
    lovers? Even if y'got a peep-hole drilled in
    the wall, how can y'tell if sometime when
    Gooper's got business in Memphis an'
    you're playin' scrabble at the country club
1065   with other ex-queens of cotton, Maggie
    and I don't come to some temporary
    agreement? How do you know that—?

[*He X above wicker seat to above R end
    couch.*]

1070 MAE: Brick, I never thought that you would
    stoop to her level, I just never dreamed
    that you would stoop to her level.

GOOPER: I don't think Brick will stoop to her
    level.

1075 BRICK [*sits R of* MARGARET *on couch*]: What is
    your level? Tell me your level so I can sink
    or rise to it.

[*Rises.*]
    You heard what Big Daddy said. This girl
1080   has life in her body.

MAE: That is a lie!

BRICK: No, truth is something desperate, an'
    she's got it. Believe me, it's somethin'
    desperate, an' she's got it.

1085 [*X below seat to below bar.*]
    An' now if you will stop actin' as if Brick
    Pollitt was dead an' buried, invisible, not
    heard, an' go on back to your peep-hole in
    the wall—I'm drunk, and sleepy—not as
1090   alive as Maggie, but still alive. . . . [*Pours
    drink, drinks.*]

GOOPER [*picks up brief case from R foot of bed*]:
    Come on, Mae. We'll leave these love birds
    together in their nest.

1095 MAE: Yeah, nest of lice! Liars!

GOOPER: Mae—Mae, you jes' go on back to
    our room—

MAE: Liars!

[*Exits through hall.*]

1100 GOOPER [*DR above* MARGARET]: We're jest
    goin' to wait an' see. Time will tell. [*X to R

of bar.] Yes, sir, little brother, we're just
   goin' to wait an' see!
[*Exit, hall. The clock strikes twelve. Maggie and*
1105 **BRICK** *exchange a look. He drinks deeply, puts his
   glass on the bar. Gradually, his expression changes.
   He utters a sharp exhalation. The exhalation is
   echoed by the singers, off UR, who commence
   vocalizing with 'Gimme a Cool Drink of Water Fo' I*
1110 *Die', and continue till end of act.*]
   MARGARET [*as she hears* **BRICK'S** *exhalation*]:
      The click?
   [**BRICK** *looks toward the singers, happily, almost
   gratefully. He XR to bed, picks up his pillow, and*
1115 *starts toward head of couch, DR, Xing above
   wicker seat.* **MARGARET** *seizes the pillow from his
   grasp, rises, stands facing C, holding the pillow
   close.* **BRICK** *watches her with growing admiration. She moves quickly USC, throwing pillow on*
1120 *to bed. She X to bar.* **BRICK** *counters below wicker
   seat, watching her.* **MARGARET** *grabs all the
   bottles from the bar. She goes into hall, pitches
   the bottles, one after the other, off the platform
   into the UL lawn area. Bottles break, off L.*
1125 **MARGARET** *re-enters the room, stands UC, facing*
   BRICK.]
      Echo Spring has gone dry, and no one but
      me could drive you to town for more.
   BRICK: Lacey will get me—

1130 **MARGARET:** Lacey's been told not to!
   BRICK: I could drive—
   MARGARET: And you lost your driver's
      licence! I'd phone ahead and have you
      stopped on the highway before you got
1135   halfway to Ruby Lightfoot's gin mill. I
      told a lie to Big Daddy, but we can make
      that lie come true. And then I'll bring you
      liquor, and we'll get drunk together, here,
      tonight, in this place that death has come
1140   into! What do you say? What do you say,
      baby?
   BRICK [*X to L side bed*]: I admire you, Maggie.
   [**BRICK** *sits on edge of bed. He looks up at the
   overhead light, then at* **MARGARET**. *She reaches*
1145 *for the light, turns it out; then she kneels quickly
   beside* **BRICK** *at foot of bed.*]
   MARGARET: Oh, you weak, beautiful people
      who give up with such grace. What you
      need is someone to take hold of you—
1150   gently, with love, and hand your life back
      to you, like something gold you let go
      of—and I can! I'm determined to do
      it—and nothing's more determined than
      a cat on a tin roof—is there? Is there,
1155   baby?
   [*She touches his cheek gently.*]
      CURTAIN

Writing a Source-Based Literary Argument

AP® **Enduring Understanding (LAN-1)**

Readers establish and communicate their interpretations of literature through arguments supported by textual evidence.

Using and Citing Secondary Sources

Until now, when you have written about a literary text, you have examined the work and perhaps the author's background or historical context to inform your analysis. If you wish to explore the work further and enhance your analysis, you may also research the following:

- The historical, social, political, or economic context of the era in which the work was written (or set)
- The author's life and body of work
- Other works of literature from the same era or genre
- Key allusions or archetypes within the work
- Scholarly and critical studies of the work

KEY POINT

Writers use (and attribute) evidence from both primary and secondary sources to examine a work through a particular critical lens or perspective.

Once you select a research question, you will begin to search for sources on the internet or in the library. A research argument should still largely be your own thoughts and observations with the work you are analyzing (the primary source) as your main focus. You will use the information from your research (secondary sources) to explore different approaches and deepen your readers' understanding of your analysis.

In this composition workshop, you will learn how to write a literary argument that cites the work or works being analyzed as primary source(s). You will also learn how to use secondary sources to develop an interpretation of the text. As you develop your argument, you can practice acknowledging evidence from these sources using attribution, citation, or reference.

✏️ YOUR ASSIGNMENT

Choose a text from Unit 9 or one that your teacher has assigned. Research the literary criticism that has been published in response to your text. Then, write a literary argument that analyzes the text by applying a critical lens. Support your thesis with evidence from the text (primary source) and from secondary sources from your research.

Your argument should interpret a literary work and include the following:

- An introduction that identifies the title, author, and context; and explains your critical lens (or focus) and the relevance of the idea
- A thesis statement with a claim that conveys an interpretation (a unifying idea + insight about that idea)
- A line of reasoning that justifies the interpretation in the claim
- Relevant and sufficient textual evidence from both the primary source and secondary sources that support the line of reasoning
- Commentary that links the evidence to the unifying idea in the line of reasoning and claim
- Transitional elements that create coherence in the argument
- A conclusion that explains the relevance of the idea and brings the literary argument to a unified end
- Syntactical choices that reveal associations and relationships within the argument
- Proper documentation of sources

Potential Critical Lenses

(See the following table for questions to help focus your analysis.)

- Formalism
- Traditional
- Cultural
- Psychological
- Materialism
- Gender Studies
- Mythological

Explaining Complexity

One way to understand the complexity of a work of literature is to explore alternative interpretations of the same text. Scholars usually use one or more of the critical approaches to literary analysis as a way to focus their analysis. These approaches, also called lenses, encourage readers to consider the settings, characters, structures, and details within a text from a focused perspective. For instance, a psychological approach investigates the characters' psyches, motivations, and identities within a text, while a biographical approach focuses on the life and times of the author.

As many critical approaches evolved over the last century, readers have many tools to deepen their understanding of a text. Of course, two readers approaching the same work through different critical lenses may arrive at different interpretations. Each will focus on and emphasize different elements of the text, as well as different specific evidence. Likewise, a reader who examines a text through multiple lenses may discover complexities that change or reinforce his or her interpretation.

A text may suggest several plausible interpretations. But to make an interpretation valid and persuasive, the reader must justify it with relevant and sufficient evidence.

Here are some questions to help you write a more sophisticated analysis:

- How do the events or characters challenge the values of the author, or the dominant values of author's background and biographical context?
- How does examining a text from different critical approaches reveal the complexity of the characters or the work as a whole?
- How does the work contradict previously established literary patterns or expectations?
- How do the conflicts and tensions within the work remain unresolved or (alternately) resolve themselves in surprising or ironic ways?
- How do minor characters, scenes, or details in a text work with (or against) the main idea of the narrative to create complexity?

Set a Purpose for Reading

Once you have read through your primary text and reviewed the literary techniques and elements, you should begin to develop a research question. The best research questions engage your own curiosity, so begin by thinking about what interests you most about the work, such as the characters, the conflict, an interesting symbol, or the cultural and historical setting.

Next, search the internet or the library for scholarly sources related to your interest in the text. In this process, you may discover new questions, connections, and ideas that help you develop your own argument.

Check your school or local public library for access to helpful databases such as the following:

- The author's official website
- EBSCO Literature PowerSearch
- Gale Literary Databases
- Gale Literature Criticism Online
- JSTOR
- Literary Reference Center
- Modern Language Association
- Project Muse

Keep in mind: sources such as Lit Charts, SparkNotes, and other study materials are meant to serve as reading guides but they are not acceptable scholarly sources.

When you have a sense of what information and criticism are available, you can narrow your focus by developing a specific question to guide your research. You should be able to adapt questions based on the critical lenses for your particular text. Each perspective offers multiple questions that will deepen your understanding and provide a framework for your interpretation.

When you have chosen your research question, record specific notes and textual evidence from your primary text related to the question. Then, compare your notes to the literary claims and evidence that you find in your critical research. You should begin to see patterns emerging that will help you later as you plan your line of reasoning and arrange your evidence.

The following chart identifies established critical lenses with brief descriptions and sample questions to help you get started. In your research, you may find that the approaches have slightly different names based on the source; however, the basic ideas remain the same. To deepen your understanding, read further explanations of the approaches or find an expanded list of questions to consider in Appendix C on p. A-14.

CRITICAL APPROACHES TO ANALYZING LITERATURE

Critical Approach	Description	Key Questions to Consider
Moral and Philosophical	Views literature as a medium for communicating moral and philosophical lessons Sees art and literature as a reflection of the human experience: they must be interpreted in the context of their relationship to objective reality	What philosophical or ethical issues and ideas does the text confront? How does the text conform or rebel against the morals of its historical context? What effect is the text likely to have on the thoughts and behaviors of the reader?
Biographical and Historical	Interprets the text through the perspective of the author's background, views, and life Looks at how biographical or historical events influenced the writing of a text	What biographical facts has the author used and how do they impact the characters, plot, theme, or other elements of the text? How do the historical events at the time of publication influence the text? What historical events are depicted in the text? How are they presented?
Formalist and New Critical	Emphasizes the text itself, rather than other factors like the author's intention Focuses on how the parts of the work relate to other parts and contribute to the whole of the work, as well as to universal meaning Explains how the form and structure of a poem, story, or play work to resolve its conflicts and tensions	How is the work's structure unified? How do various elements and patterns in the work reinforce its meaning? How do the various elements interact to suggest a universal meaning? How does the poem resolve its ironies, tensions, and paradoxes?
Psychological Psychoanalytic Freudian Jungian Lacanian	Reads the text from the perspective of the prevailing theories of human behavior, consciousness, and cognition Freudian: Focuses on desire, repression, and the unconscious	What is the nature of the internal conflicts within the characters of the text? How do family conflicts shape character, narrative, and perspective?

	Jungian: Analyzes archetypal patterns and images in literature which manifest in all humanity Lacanian: Sees the unconscious as a system structured like a language	How do desire and repression influence the text? In what ways do the structure and organization of the text connect to/express/reflect/analogize the operations of the mind?
Mythological and Archetypal	Examines how a work reiterates or defies common patterns literature, such as character types, settings, storylines, and motifs (see also Jungian criticism) May integrate approaches from anthropology, linguistics, folklore, and other disciplines	What universal themes, archetypal patterns, and experiences does the text represent? What aspects of the work evoke deep universal responses? How do stories from one culture correspond to those of another? How do the archetypes within the work reveal a universal truth?
Deconstruction and Post-Structuralism	Analyzes a text to show how its contradictions and irreconcilable elements undermine its meaning Focuses on the text, like formalism, but while formalist approaches find unity and meaning, deconstruction reveals the gaps between what a text claims to say and what it actually says (see Formalism) Asserts that there is no meaning prior to — or outside of — the text (and language itself)	How does the text express opposing and contradictory meanings? What do contradictory or irreconcilable meanings in the text reveal about the limits of language as a medium of communication? How does the text work against the apparent intention or purpose of the author? What does the text disguise or conceal? Where is the language of the text elusive and ambiguous?
Materialist Marxist Cultural Studies New Historicist	Interprets a text from a political or economic standpoint, one usually focused on class structure and power relationships Identifies the ideological function of a text — that is, its biases, assumptions, and role in reproducing a specific social order	How is material production or economic organization presented in the text? Who has political or economic power within the text? What voices or perspectives are marginalized in the text? Why? Does the balance of power shift within the narrative, or does the text reinforce existing power structures?
Gender Feminism LGBTQ	Analyzes texts for the ways they represent women, gender roles, and power relationships in the context of dominant patriarchal culture Views sexuality and gender as socially constructed rather than innate	How are women and gender roles portrayed? How do these portrayals relate to the gender norms and conflicts of the text's era? What elements in a text challenge women or feminine power? How are the gender identities revealed in the text?

Review the text that you are analyzing and your notes from your secondary research sources. Using the graphic organizer, record your unifying idea, as well as the topic and focus of your analysis. Then, identify your sources and record relevant details from the text, as well as the significance of these details to your unifying idea. (You may need to delete or add rows.)

Writing a Source-Based Literary Argument		
Unifying idea:		
Topic and focus of analysis:		
Literary Text (primary source)	**Relevant Details**	**Insights and Connections to the Unifying Idea**
Secondary Sources	**Relevant Information from the Source**	**Insights and Connections to the Unifying Idea**

Develop a Thesis

A **thesis statement** for a researched literary analysis, as in other literary arguments, requires a claim that includes your interpretation. In this essay, you will choose a literary focus and analyze how that literary focus contributes to an interpretation of the text. You should identify the specific focus of your analysis — along with your broader interpretation of the text — within your thesis statement.

When you develop and preview your **line of reasoning**, which will suggest how to organize your analysis, you may consider the following aspects for your literary focus based on the critical lens you chose:

- Historical: The way two or more biographical or historical facts related to the author's background influence a text

- Psychological: The way a character's choices explain a character's psyche, conflicts, values, or motivations

- Mythological: The way two or more archetypes create patterns in a text that reveal character motivations, conflicts, or tension
- Materialism or Gender Studies: The way specific aspects of conflict, tension, or imbalance between classes, genders, or other groups represent power struggles
- Formalism: The way specific attributes of juxtaposed images, characters, or other details reveal complexity in the text

WRITING A THESIS FOR A SOURCE-BASED LITERARY ARGUMENT	
Template 1: Thesis identifies the critical lens and previews a line of reasoning, and then connects to the idea and insight.	In [title of work], [author] [verb] [focus of critical lens] through [aspect 1], [aspect 2], and [aspect 3] in order to [reveal/illustrate/suggest] [unifying idea + insight].
Template 2: Thesis identifies the critical lens and connects to the idea and insight.	In [title of work], [author] [verb] [focus of critical lens] in order to [reveal/illustrate/suggest] [unifying idea + insight].

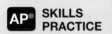 **SKILLS PRACTICE** | LITERARY ARGUMENTATION
Developing a Thesis Statement for a Source-Based Literary Argument

Complete the following chart. In the left column, record the title, author, and literary focus that you will explore. Next, record the unifying idea and insight that will convey your interpretation in your claim.

Developing a Defensible Thesis Statement for a Source-Based Literary Argument		
Topic	Claim	
Title, Author, and Focus (aspect of literary focus or critical lens)	Unifying Idea +	Insight

Organize a Line of Reasoning

A researched argument is usually longer than a typical literary analysis because you are synthesizing evidence from multiple sources. You may also wish to include more than three body paragraphs depending on what you discover from your research.

Organize your reasons in a way that logically brings a reader to your conclusion. Most often, your chosen **critical lens** will determine your **arrangement of reasons**. You must illustrate the connections between the reasons. Remember, each reason within your line of reason must justify your claim and unify your argument.

STRUCTURE OF A SOURCE-BASED LITERARY ARGUMENT

Introduction

The **introduction** is an opportunity for the writer to establish the purpose of his or her literary argument and to interest the audience in the literary work and the writer's interpretation of it. To achieve this goal, many literary arguments follow this structure:

- Engage the audience through an interesting hook
- Provide historical, cultural, or social context of a literary work
- Identify the title, author, genre (TAG)
- Introduce the critical lens by
  - describing the importance of the critical lens in relation to the work; and
  - summarizing the work succinctly with details critical to the focus

The **thesis statement** presents a defensible interpretation that includes an idea and insight into that idea.

Body

(Develops a line of reasoning with supporting evidence that justifies the thesis)

Topic Sentence 1 (Identify the first aspect of analysis related to the unifying idea)	Topic Sentence 2 (Identify the second aspect of analysis related to the unifying idea)	Topic Sentence 3 (Identify the third aspect of analysis related to the unifying idea)
Supporting Details (Evidence from the literary work that contributes to the focus of analysis) (Evidence from secondary sources that contributes to the focus of analysis)	Supporting Details (Evidence from the literary work that contributes to the focus of analysis) (Evidence from secondary sources that contributes to the focus of analysis)	Supporting Details (Evidence from the literary work that contributes to the focus of analysis) (Evidence from secondary sources that contributes to the focus of analysis)
Commentary (Link evidence by explaining its relevance to the line of reasoning and claim)	Commentary (Link evidence by explaining its relevance to the line of reasoning and claim)	Commentary (Link evidence by explaining its relevance to the line of reasoning and claim)

Conclusion

The **conclusion** should do more than restate the thesis; instead, it should be a robust and important paragraph. It is the opportunity for the writer to demonstrate understanding of the literary work's relevance by explaining how the literary work stands the test of time and reflects the human experience. Writers further their idea and insight by:

- Discussing the significance or relevance of interpretation
- Relating the work to other relevant literary works
- Connecting the theme to their own experience
- Presenting alternate interpretations
- Explaining how the work explores complexities and tensions
- Situating the theme within a broader context

This table illustrates the general structure of a literary argument. It does not intend to imply that all literary arguments are five paragraphs. Writers should determine the number of reasons needed to justify their claim, as well as how much evidence is sufficient to support each of these reasons.

AP® SKILLS PRACTICE | **LITERARY ARGUMENTATION**
Developing a Line of Reasoning

Review your thesis statement, which may or may not preview the line of reasoning. Record the topic sentences to represent your line of reasoning and place them in a logical order. As you do this, consider the potential evidence from both your literary text and secondary sources that helped you arrive at your line of reasoning. That textual evidence will serve as support for these reasons.

Organizing a Source-Based Literary Argument		
Defensible Thesis Statement with Claim (idea + insight):		
Topic Sentence 1 (Identify the first aspect of analysis related to the unifying idea):	**Topic Sentence 2** (Identify the second aspect of analysis related to the unifying idea):	**Topic Sentence 3** (Identify the third aspect of analysis related to the unifying idea):

Select Relevant Evidence

Throughout the previous writing workshops, you have learned to incorporate **relevant** and **sufficient evidence** from a literary text to support a literary argument. As you plan for your researched argument, you will continue this practice. You can quote directly or paraphrase from your text, but remember that textual evidence should be apt and specific. For example, instead of making an overly general reference to a character's attitude or behavior, refer to a specific moment in the narrative and include details and context. In other words, your evidence should exemplify the point you are trying to make in your argument.

Likewise, in a researched argument, you will include evidence from secondary sources to support your line of reasoning and deepen the reader's understanding of the text. But choose the evidence strategically: make sure it contributes directly to your reasoning, idea, and insight. To introduce this evidence, include a signal phrase or embed the evidence.

In your researched literary argument, you must properly cite any evidence that you include whether it is paraphrased or quoted directly. Add a parenthetical citation to the end of the clause that includes the quoted text, with the author's last name and page number (if available).

Here are a few templates to help you incorporate evidence from a secondary source:

- In the essay, [title], [author] contends, "[text evidence]" ([author] [page #]).
- According to literary critic [author], "[text evidence]" ([author] [page #]).
- [Author] explores [literary focus] by revealing that "[embedded text evidence]" ([author] [page #]).

Finally, you must include a Works Cited list as the final page of your literary argument. This formatted page provides bibliographical information for your primary source(s) and all your secondary sources cited within your essay. List each entry individually; alphabetize the entries on your page based on the first piece of information in the citation.

For more information about citing sources and assembling a Works Cited page, consult the MLA Guide that can be found in Appendix B on page A-7.

 **INSIDER AP® TIP**

Secondary sources give credibility to your argument. They can serve to corroborate and substantiate a claim that your claims. Your analysis of the text and evidence from your primary source should take the lead in a literary argument. Evidence from secondary sources serves to reinforce your unifying idea and insight rather than to dominate the essay.

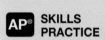 **AP® SKILLS PRACTICE**

LITERARY ARGUMENTATION
Incorporating Relevant and Sufficient Evidence from Primary and Secondary Sources

Write your thesis statement and develop a logical line of reasoning to support your interpretation. Carefully organize your body paragraphs and arrange evidence from your literary text and from secondary sources within them. Next, draft two or more body paragraphs that include evidence from the text and the secondary sources to support each reason. Include transitions to link your reasons and evidence to your claim, as well as citations for the textual evidence.

Incorporating Relevant and Sufficient Evidence from Primary and Secondary Sources
Defensible Thesis Statement with Claim (idea + insight):

Topic Sentence 1 (Identify the first aspect of analysis related to the unifying idea):	Topic Sentence 2 (Identify the second aspect of analysis related to the unifying idea):	Topic Sentence 3 (Identify the third aspect of analysis related to the unifying idea):
Supporting Details (Evidence from the literary work that contributes to the focus of analysis):	Supporting Details (Evidence from the literary work that contributes to the focus of analysis):	Supporting Details (Evidence from the literary work that contributes to the focus of analysis):
Supporting Details (Evidence from secondary sources that contributes to the focus of analysis):	Supporting Details (Evidence from secondary sources that contributes to the focus of analysis):	Supporting Details (Evidence from secondary sources that contributes to the focus of analysis):

Write Insightful Commentary

In Units 3–8, you learned to write insightful **commentary** that explains the effects of an author's choices within a text. Commentary also links to the idea and insight in your thesis statement. For your researched argument, this kind of commentary is still necessary for analyzing your literary text. But now your commentary must also explain the relevance of evidence from your secondary sources — for example, the significance of a particular event in the author's personal history as it connects to an element in one of their works.

Some writers mistakenly think that including literary criticism or historical context is enough — on its own — to explain the relevance. But evidence from your research does *not* do the job of commentary. So keep in mind that you are creating an original literary argument. You develop your commentary by connecting information from other sources to your analysis of the primary text and to the idea and insight in your thesis. You can often stay focused on your thesis by explaining the relevance of your evidence in relation to your claim's unifying idea.

WRITING COMMENTARY FOR SECONDARY SOURCES

Type of Evidence	Templates for Introducing Evidence	Templates for Explaining the Relevance of Evidence
Opinions from a literary critic	In the essay, [title], [author] contends "[text evidence]" ([author] [page #]). According to literary critic [author], "[text evidence]" ([author] [page #]). [Author] explores [literary focus] by revealing "[embedded text evidence]" ([author] [page #]).	Through this observation, [critic] • explores the origin of the conflict/tension and suggests _____. • develops the idea that _____. • implies that _____. • reveals the significance of _____. • sheds light on the fact that _____. • connects the [literary observation] to a deeper exploration of _____.
Historical, cultural, or personal events and experiences	During [historical era], [specific events, attitudes, laws, conflicts] can be seen in the character's actions/choices/relationships in that _____. It is important to note that in his/her life, [author] experienced [author detail] ([author] [page #]). [Author's] experience with [author detail] parallels [character's] situation within the narrative in that _____.	In examining the events/attitudes/conflicts that serve as a backdrop for the text, readers gain a deeper understanding of [aspect]. Because of [author's] experience with [author detail], the reader further understands [literary choice and effect] and concludes [idea and insight]. The connection between [author background] and [literary context] • reveals _____. • sheds light on _____. • leads to the ironic observation that _____. • allows the reader to see the complexity of [concept].
Theories and concepts	When readers examine [literary character(s)] according to [theory] which suggests that a person/community will [identify behavior/reaction] within [explain circumstance], they can better understand [values/motives/conflicts] ([author] [page #]).	These values/motives/conflicts • reveal _____. • develop the idea that _____. • sheds light on _____. • leads to the ironic observation that _____. • allow the reader to see the complexity of [theory].

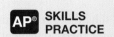 **SKILLS PRACTICE** | LITERARY ARGUMENTATION
Explaining Evidence from Primary and Secondary Sources

Build on your emerging literary argument by adding commentary to your relevant and sufficient evidence (for both primary and secondary sources). Continue to incorporate transitions for coherence, and craft your sentences to show the balance or imbalance of ideas. Additionally, keep focusing on your unifying idea so that you may sustain it throughout your argument in a unified way.

Explaining Evidence from Primary and Secondary Sources		
Defensible Thesis Statement with Claim (idea + insight):		
Topic Sentence 1 (Identify the first aspect of analysis related to the unifying idea):	**Topic Sentence 2** (Identify the second aspect of analysis related to the unifying idea):	**Topic Sentence 3** (Identify the third aspect of analysis related to the unifying idea):
Textual Details (Relevant and sufficient evidence from primary source):	**Textual Details** (Relevant and sufficient evidence from primary source):	**Textual Details** (Relevant and sufficient evidence from primary source):
Commentary (Link evidence to reason and idea):	**Commentary** (Link evidence to reason and idea):	**Commentary** (Link evidence to reason and idea):
Sentence stem and explanation of function of evidence:	Sentence stem and explanation of function of evidence:	Sentence stem and explanation of function of evidence:
Textual Details (Relevant and sufficient evidence from secondary source):	**Textual Details** (Relevant and sufficient evidence from secondary source):	**Textual Details** (Relevant and sufficient evidence from secondary source):
Commentary (Link evidence to reason and idea):	**Commentary** (Link evidence to reason and idea):	**Commentary** (Link evidence to reason and idea):
Sentence stem and explanation of function of evidence:	Sentence stem and explanation of function of evidence:	Sentence stem and explanation of function of evidence:

Contextualize Your Argument

As in other literary arguments, your researched argument should begin with an **introduction** that includes a hook, necessary context, and a thesis statement. Because you will be incorporating additional sources, you may need to provide even more background or context to help your reader understand the claim in your thesis.

If you have chosen to analyze the work through a particular critical lens, you should write several sentences that focus the reader on that particular perspective. In other words, depending on the chosen literary topic or critical lens, your introduction should provide relevant facts and essential background including the following:

- historical, political, economic or cultural events;
- author background;
- descriptions of conflict or tension;
- connections to patterns in literature;
- descriptions of psychological states;
- comparing and contrasting perspectives; and
- conventions or expectations of a genre.

Throughout your literary argument, you should continue to make relevant connections to the background established in your introduction. You can do this in your **commentary** so that each reason includes evidence from your primary (or secondary sources), which you then link to your unifying idea and insight.

In your **conclusion**, your reader should anticipate your final remarks about the relevance of your idea and insight because you have established this connection throughout the argument. Along with bringing your analysis to a unified conclusion, you should reiterate the relevance of your argument by including observations about human nature, social or cultural values, social criticism, or other relevant connections.

You can wrap up your final paragraph using any of the following methods:

- Refer back to an idea, quotation, or analogy established in the hook
- Connect the historical, political, and cultural context, or author's personal background to the contemporary reader
- Discuss the nature of the conflict or tension in a contemporary context
- Connect the characters' psychological state to basic human nature
- Reconcile the different perspectives on the text among readers, critics, or critical approaches

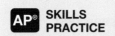 **SKILLS PRACTICE** | LITERARY ARGUMENTATION
Establishing Context and Explaining Relevance

In the following chart, record some notes to help you communicate the context of your argument, introductory details about the author's structural choices, and introductory material that will funnel your ideas to your thesis statement. Next, record ideas to help you explain the relevance of your idea and insight within a broader context in your conclusion.

Establishing Context and Explaining Relevance	
Idea and insight	**Context for Introduction**
	Hook:
	Context:
	Significance of Idea in Conclusion
	Broader context for conclusion:

Revise Your Argument

When reviewing your researched literary analysis, ask the following questions about the function and effect of the structural details. Revise your draft if your answer is "no" to any of these:

- Have you identified the focus of your research and literary analysis?
- Have you shaped your interpretation based on a critical lens?
- Do your reasons in your line of reasoning refer to different aspects of your analysis?
- Does your line of reasoning support your interpretation?
- Have you included textual evidence from both your literary text and secondary sources that directly exemplify the aspects of your analysis?
- Does your explanation reveal the purpose of your evidence and logically align with your interpretation of the work?
- Is your argument coherent with a logical sequence of reasons and transitions to connect evidence, reasons, and claims?
- Does your commentary unify your argument by connecting your evidence and reasons to your unifying idea?
- Do you include effective transitional elements between and within your body paragraphs to create coherence?
- Have you properly introduced and cited evidence from all sources?
- Have you included a Works Cited page to list all sources within your argument?

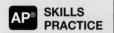 LITERARY ARGUMENTATION
Revising and Editing a Researched Literary Argument

After you have completed revising and editing your own argument, review another student's literary argument and provide helpful feedback.

Student Model: Writing a Source-Based Literary Argument		
Revising and Editing Checklist	**Unit 9 Focus Skills**	**Comment on the Effectiveness and/or Make a Suggestion**
Does the writer include an engaging hook, the focus based on the critical lens, title, and author of the literary text in the first paragraph?	Introductions for literary research	
Does the thesis statement convey an interpretation? Does the interpretation connect to an idea and an insight?	Defensible thesis	
Does the writer provide a logical sequence of reasons to support the idea and insight in the thesis? Are these reasons linked to the claim with transitions?	Line of reasoning	
Does the writer provide relevant and sufficient evidence from the literary text and from secondary sources to support the interpretation in the thesis? Is the evidence linked to the topic sentences with transitions?	Relevant and sufficient evidence: Coherence	
Does the writer explain how the evidence supports a reason and connects to the interpretation in the thesis? Does the commentary connect to the unifying idea?	Commentary: Unity and coherence	
Does the writer explain significance within a broader context, discuss alternative interpretations, or use relevant analogies?	Relevance and conclusion	
Does the writer properly document source information with parenthetical citation and a Works Cited page? Does the writer demonstrate control over the conventions of writing?	Conventions	

Student Model: Writing about Structure and Irony

Review the following student model that explores the concept of feminism in Charlotte Brontë's *Jane Eyre*. Observe how the thesis statement, line of reasoning, and evidence from primary and secondary sources work together to convey an interpretation of the work.

Jane Eyre and Feminism:
How Characterization Sparked
the Women's Movement
Katrina Ruiz

Charlotte Brontë's second novel continuously provokes debate within scholarly communities, even over one hundred and fifty years after its publication. Many see it as a simple love story; others, a complex societal message, speaking to feminism and women's empowerment; and some, a frustrating, anti-feminist depiction of acquiescence and toxicity. One thing is universally accepted, however: Brontë's masterful use of numerous literary devices is what truly makes the novel worth debate. Through careful examination and interpretation in historical context, it can be seen plainly throughout the novel that Brontë's use of characterization and character development serves to explore, reject, and encourage deviation from societal expectations for women, contributing greatly to the early feminist movement.

> **thesis statement:** connects character development to societal expectations
> **idea:** expectations
> **insight:** women should have the choice to deviate from societal expectations

Brontë relies on several different types of characterization throughout the novel, yet none are used more blatantly than extrinsic characterization. While characterization is often quite subtle within a text, it appears that Brontë purposefully emphasized the ways in which other characters contribute to Jane's characterization, likely to emphasize the societal effect of Victorian-era viewpoints upon women. Jane's struggle with social status and representation is exemplified by the characters surrounding her (Murphy); there is consistently a subtle contrast between Jane and the people around her—in mannerism, behavior, wealth, dress, and even speech. Each detail about a character seems to be enunciated simply to show the ways in which Jane differs from this "normal" behavior; some cases are subtle, like the contrasts drawn between Jane and her cousins, and some are so emphasized that it is obvious a message lies beneath the surface of the text—Blanche, the object of Rochester's affection prior to Jane, is drastically different in social status, dress, femininity, and overall

> **topic sentence:** identifies direct characterization through contrasts
> **evidence:** cites a source to explore the effect of character contrasts

mannerism. This contrast between Jane and the characters surrounding her establishes a severe difference in status and wealth, as well as behavior, that is utilized throughout the novel to discuss the effects of societal pressure upon women.

commentary: explores the pressure Jane feels based on the expectations of others

   In addition, internal characterization is commonly used in the text, setting a precedent for Jane's character growth and societal relationship throughout the novel. The expectations established for Jane through external influence play a significant role in Jane's response to the society around her, as well as her own perceptions of identity and women's roles. From the beginning of the novel, Jane's character is established to be quite rebellious in response to external management of her actions and thoughts, as exemplified in the very first scene of the novel (in which she flies into a fit of rage at her cousin in response to his belittling and bullying). Her internal monologue is complex, however: she longs to be accepted by those around her, yet she is obstinate and refuses to let herself conform to standards they hold for her. This is exemplified in her search to belong, to have a parental figure in her life: "After failed attempts at realizing mothers in Mrs. Reed, Miss Temple, and Helen Burns, Jane is eventually disenchanted with motherhood and subconsciously rejects it as a potential role for herself" (Lemaster). Her rejection of traditionally motherly, feminine roles, one of the few consistent character traits throughout the novel, speaks to the feminism and societal rejection Brontë had likely intended within *Jane Eyre* (Lemaster).

topic sentence: introduces the character's internal response to external factors

evidence: incorporates a source to exemplify a character choice

commentary: explains the character's decision to reject the social norms

paraphrases source to further explain significance of textual evidence

   The way in which Brontë approaches society's impact upon identity is seen more obviously within the character development throughout the story than in the frequent characterization. Jane's endeavor to convey her deep sense of injustice begins with the outrage she voices toward her aunt as a child, and develops throughout the novel as she pursues her voice and happiness (Mardorossian); this provides the framework for the rest of the development seen in her character. Jane's obstinance as a child was received by those around her in a way that indicated "she must become a tyrant figure herself" (Leggatt) in order to maintain her identity; essentially, the response of those around her to her behavior is what made Jane adhere to such rebellion, as she found it accomplished deviation from both her family and the societal expectations for a girl her age.

topic sentence: connects the character development to her search her identity as independent of societal pressure

evidence: incorporates source information to explain the character's rebellion

commentary: explains that her journey in rejecting expectations began when she was a girl

   However, as Jane ages, she begins to rely on validation from others to the extent that she loses that sense of self that she so desperately clung onto as a child. Her apparent lack of opposition in her early adulthood,

topic sentence: introduces the character's temporary adherence to expectations

however, "does not signify her acceptance of pathological conditions of domination . . . but her reliance on a type of 'oppositional power' that, although it derives from existing power structures and as such does not challenge them overtly, 'has the extremely tricky ability to erode insidiously and almost invisible, the very power from which it derives'" (Mardorossian); that is, her need for validation and acceptance overrule the stubborn tyranny she uses in her childhood to maintain her identity. This is a result of Jane's transition from childhood to adolescence, and speaks to the impact of societal standards upon young women. The brief time in which Jane is passively accepting of her situational oppression and opposition indicates the true extent of such strong societal pressure.

evidence: incorporates source evidence that explores her reasons for seeking validation

commentary: explores the character motivation and values in seeking acceptance in society

Jane's response to control throughout the story advances with her character, eventually creating a woman who has found that she can be strong without passively obeying or becoming a tyrant herself (Leggatt). Throughout her time as a governess within the Rochester household, Jane struggles to escape the bounds of her social status; it is only with her departure from her position and relationship with Rochester that she begins to realize the power she holds over her identity. Previously, it was expressed that Jane's staunch refusal to adhere to standards, then her severe adherence to the very societal bounds against which she previously rebelled, were a result of both a need for validation and a desire to deviate from her complex familial relationships. However, in her time away from Thornfield, she discovers that she has the ability and strength to take control of her identity and societal place without adhering to anyone's standards but her own, and it is with this discovery that her place in feminism is framed: Jane Eyre was one of the first female characters within literature that held this security and power in her femininity. She continues to explore this discovery in the remaining chapters of the novel, returning to Rochester after her rejection of St. John's proposal, and this security she holds in her power and identity is why her return to the very man who continuously pushed her to be someone she was not can't truly be framed as an anti-feminist; the character development to this point turned Jane into a woman who is self-aware and secure in her identity, and therefore makes the choice to return to one of her oppressors in full awareness of the possible repercussions.

topic sentence: introduces a character epiphany that she can balance strength and rebellion of expectations

evidence: provides paraphrased examples from the primary text to illustrate the character's actions

commentary: links the character's actions to the critical lens of feminism, exploring the impact of the character on future

The true impact of *Jane Eyre* upon femininity can be found, as Brontë intended, within the characterization and character development prevalent throughout the novel. The external characterization and oppression that Jane continuously faces serves as a consistent opposition, an enemy to conquer, and having this constant societal pressure and judgment is

topic sentence: explores the influence of the character's development through the feminist lens

what brings her to realize that her sense of self is independent of the idea of normality that everyone around her pushes. The societal manipulation of her self-image and identity accomplish the exact opposite of the intended repression of individuality: she learns to revel in her identity and power (Godfrey) in the very face of the pressure and manipulation intended to destroy that strength. This speaks to Victorian era society directly: the ways in which Jane's family and lover consistently try to change her eventually create the powerful woman she becomes, and this sends the message to women that they hold a similar "capacity to control [their] own story" (Murphy). Much of the effects of characterization upon Jane Eyre challenged traditional gender roles in more ways than simply the feminist interpretation as well: "Jane's strength of character and will along with her refusal to be forced into a submissive position seem very masculine" (Peters), and this new perception of gender and equality within the novel reinforced the ideas that it should be acceptable for women and men to hold traits considered previously un-masculine or feminine.

evidence: cites sources to illustrate how the character's strength contributes to feminist identity

commentary: explains how the characterization contributes to gender and equality issues

Character development plays a great role in the new feminist ideas ushered in by *Jane Eyre* as well; Jane's character development directly challenges gender roles and status constraints prevalent within Victorian society. Throughout the novel, Jane's character develops from the androgyny associated with the Victorian working class as she explores versions of femininity and eventually assumes a type of almost masculine femininity through her relationship with Rochester, both challenging and reinforcing gender roles (Godfrey). In addition, Jane constantly fights off social threats with self-representation, a character trait that distinguishes her from the array of other women throughout the book (Murphy). This new perception of the power one holds over their gender and status was highly uncommon in literature of this era; the ideas of power and identity held within *Jane Eyre* were largely developed through Jane's evolution as a woman and a member of society, and they challenged traditional expectations and roles for women in ways that were rarely seen previously.

topic sentence: introduces how the character development challenges gender roles

evidence: cites sources to illustrate the character's identity developed through challenging social expectations

commentary: explores the revolutionary nature of the character's power over expectations

However, much of Jane's choice to remain within the conventional standards for Victorian women results from her discovery that social customs aren't easily dissipated or avoided (Mardorossian), and this is what creates the strong messages of self-advocacy and liberation from class construct and gender roles; Brontë masterfully ended the novel in a way which provoked thought about the situations and expectations for women of that era, and in doing so encouraged deviation from societal normality. Jane's creation of her identity through self-representation introduced the idea that women hold power over their own identity, and the societal oppression they faced could be utilized to create a security and strength of self, rather than the formation of the societally acceptable woman. By having these ideas of power and identity masterfully created by characterization and character development, Brontë successfully left women with the idea that they had the power to control their narrative as Jane did; it was this idea that fueled the upcoming women's movement, and from there, changed the course of history forever.

conclusion: reiterates the thesis established in the introduction

broader context: explains the relevance of the idea that women and men have power over social expectations

Works Cited

documentation: lists citations of primary and secondary texts alphabetically based on the first piece of information in the citation

Godfrey, Esther. "*Jane Eyre,* from Governess to Girl Bride." *Nineteenth-Century Literature Criticism*, vol. 217, Gale, 2010. *Gale Literature Resource Center*, link.gale.com/apps/doc/H1420093650/GLS?u =j220907&sid=GLS&xid=d0b4a037. Accessed 6 Mar. 2021.

Leggatt, Judith, and Christopher Parkes. "From the red room to Rochester's haircut: mind control in *Jane Eyre*." *English Studies in Canada*, vol. 32, no. 4, 2006, p. 169+. *Gale Academic OneFile*, link.gale.com /apps/doc/A180271568/AONE?u=j220907&sid=AONE&xid=880c8559. Accessed 6 Mar. 2021.

Lemaster, Tracy. "M/Othering the children: pregnancy and motherhood as obstacle to self-actualization in *Jane Eyre*." *Genders*, no. 47, 2008. *Gale In Context: Opposing Viewpoints*, link.gale.com/apps/doc /A179660950/OVIC?u=j220907&sid=OVIC&xid=8d1c9edb. Accessed 6 Mar. 2021.

Mardorossian, Carine M. "Unsuspecting storyteller and suspect listener: a postcolonial reading of Charlotte Brontë's *Jane Eyre*." *ARIEL*, vol. 37, no. 2-3, 2006, p. 1+. *Gale Academic OneFile*, link.gale.com/apps/doc /A167378944/AONE?u=j220907&sid=AONE&xid=d65b3401. Accessed 6 Mar. 2021.

Murphy, Sara. "The Trials of Vision: Experience and Autobiography in Charlotte Brontë and Charlotte Tonna." *Nineteenth-Century Literature Criticism*, edited by Russel Whitaker, vol. 152, Gale, 2005. *Gale Literature Resource Center*, link.gale.com/apps/doc/H1420065099/GLS?u= j220907&sid=GLS&xid=9c9eb0c6. Accessed 6 Mar. 2021.

Peters, John G. "Inside and outside 'Jane Eyre' and marginalization through labeling." *Studies in the Novel*, vol. 28, no. 1, 1996, p. 57+. *Gale Academic OneFile*, link.gale.com/apps/doc/A18440991 /AONE?u=j220907&sid=AONE&xid=50650d48. Accessed 6 Mar. 2021.

JUL
JOC
JOC
JOC
JOC
JOC
JOC
JOC
JOC
JOC
JOC
JNr

Free-Response Question: Literary Argument

AP® **Enduring Understanding (LAN-1)**

Readers establish and communicate their interpretations of literature through arguments supported by textual evidence.

Considering Alternate Interpretations

For your final practice with the third free-response prompt on the AP® English Literature and Composition Exam, you will apply the skills you have learned throughout the book to write a sophisticated literary argument. In other words, you should now be able to demonstrate your understanding of a complex text through a nuanced and thoughtful literary analysis. In this workshop, you will practice contextualizing your argument and developing commentary that considers alternate interpretations and examines the work within a broader context.

Read the following practice prompt, which is a model of the type of prompt you may see on the AP® English Literature and Composition Exam.

Prompt:

Many works of literature include characters who, at a particular moment within a narrative, behave in a manner that contradicts the values and motives that readers have come to expect from that character within the story. The character's words, thoughts, and/or actions not only surprise the reader but also reveal complexity within the character and the work.

Either from your own reading or from the following list, choose a work of fiction in which a character's choice at a particular moment contradicts his or her earlier choices. Then, in a well-written essay, analyze how this surprising choice reveals the complexity of the character and contributes to an interpretation of the work as a whole. Do not merely summarize the plot.

In your response you should do the following:

- Respond to the prompt with a thesis that presents a defensible interpretation
- Select and use evidence to support your line of reasoning
- Explain how the evidence supports your line of reasoning
- Use appropriate grammar and punctuation in communicating your argument

The Awakening	*The Kite Runner*
Bless Me, Ultima	*The Leavers*
Bone: A Novel	*Master Harold and the Boys*
The Brief Wondrous Life of Oscar Wao	*The Metamorphosis*
Cat on a Hot Tin Roof	*Middlemarch*
Chronicle of a Death Foretold	*Mudbound*
Circe	*Never Let Me Go*
The Color Purple	*The Nickel Boys*
The Crucible	*Of Mice and Men*
Don Quixote	*Othello*
Fences	*The Picture of Dorian Gray*
Frankenstein	*The Poisonwood Bible*
Geek Love	*A Raisin in the Sun*
The Handmaid's Tale	*The Round House*
Homegoing	*The Scarlet Letter*
House Made of Dawn	*Sense and Sensibility*
The Inheritance of Loss	*Sing, Unburied Sing*
Invisible Man	*A Tale of Two Cities*
Jane Eyre	*Their Eyes Were Watching God*
The Joy Luck Club	*Top Girls*

→ Step One: Determine a Unifying Idea and Brainstorm Relevant Examples from a Text

Once you thoroughly examine the prompt and understand the nature of the question, you will need to choose a character within a work of fiction that you know well to analyze in conjunction with the literary question. Next, consider the abstract ideas associated with your choice of text and character. One of these ideas will serve as the unifying idea in your literary argument.

You will arrive at this idea once you narrow the focus of your argument. For example, in the model prompt, you are instructed to choose a character from a work of fiction whose words, thoughts, or actions contradict the values the author has developed within the work.

For instance, if you choose to write about *The Crucible*, Arthur Miller's play set during the Salem witch trials, you might analyze the character of Elizabeth Proctor, who is characterized as a "covenanted Christian" woman. Throughout the play, several characters testify that Elizabeth has never and would never lie under any circumstance. However, the audience is shocked when they see that the pressure of the public court forces Elizabeth to disregard her Puritan values and lie under oath to save her husband's life. In examining this scenario, you might notice several ideas emerging: *loyalty, honesty, sacrifice, humanity, love.*

Once you choose your specific character and moment within a work, you will then select the most fitting idea to explore in your argument. Remember that you can consider a body of evidence first to choose the idea, or you may choose the idea and brainstorm evidence that supports that idea. Once you have chosen your idea, you will develop a thesis statement that includes your interpretation (idea + insight) to unify your argument.

→ Step Two: Develop a Defensible Claim and a Unified Line of Reasoning

As you plan your literary argument, remember to include a sentence or two of helpful context before your thesis statement. You might introduce your unifying idea, consider the relevance of the work in a broader context, or introduce an analogy that will help unify your argument.

When you are ready, write a thesis statement that identifies the character's complexity and includes your interpretation (idea + insight).

If you need help getting started, you may build from one of the following thesis templates or refer to the following models:

- In [title], a novel/play about [narrative context], [author] suggests [idea + insight] by including the surprising actions of [character] who shifts from [character observation 1] and [character observation 2] to the contrasting [character observation 3].

- In [title], a novel/play about [narrative context], [author] reveals [idea + insight] through the surprising actions of [character].

Review the following examples of thesis statements for the literary argument.

Sample Thesis Statements	Notes on Effectiveness
In The Crucible, *a play about the devastating hysteria of the Salem witch trials, Arthur Miller suggests that humans are willing to sacrifice even their deepest beliefs for the ones they love by showing the surprising actions of Elizabeth Proctor, who shifts from being a devout though often judgmental Puritan to a sinner because of her fierce love for her husband and family.*	Conveys the idea (love) and insight (humans are willing to sacrifice their deepest beliefs for love). Includes the genre and brief context. Previews a line of reasoning by introducing the initial characteristics of Elizabeth and then shifting to the contradictory characteristic.
In The Crucible, *a play about the devastating hysteria of the Salem witch trials, Arthur Miller reveals that humans are willing to sacrifice even their deepest beliefs for the ones they love through the surprising actions of the seemingly devout and virtuous Elizabeth Proctor.*	Conveys the idea (love) and insight (humans are willing to sacrifice their deepest beliefs for love). Includes the genre and brief context. Chooses not to preview a line of reasoning.

Once you have written your thesis statement, you will begin developing your line of reasoning. When you are addressing character complexity, you might organize your reasons based on the following structures:

- The character's initial behavior, the contradictory behavior, and the implications of the contrast
- The contrast between the character's external actions and internal feelings
- The cause of the character's unexpected behavior; then the effects of the choice on the reader's understanding of the character's motives or values
- An analysis of the contrasting behavior, then two or more possible implications of the contrast

Consider the most effective order for your line of reasoning and make sure each reason connects directly to your thesis. Finally, choose helpful transitions to connect your reasons to each other and to the claim in the thesis.

If you need help getting started, you may build from the following topic sentence templates or refer to the models below:

- [Author] first includes [character observation] to reveal [values/motives] and associate it with [idea].
- [Transitional element to build on first reason] [author] continues the association from [first value/motive] to [second value/motive] to emphasize [insight about the idea].
- [Transitional element to indicate contrast] [author] shifts the association from [first and second values/motivations] to [third value/motive] to reveal the character's complexity and to emphasize [insight about the idea].

Review the following thesis statement and line of reasoning. Note that the unifying idea creates the connection between the claim in the thesis and the topic sentences that support the claim.

Thesis Statement

In The Crucible, *a play about the devastating hysteria of the Salem witch trials, Arthur Miller suggests that* humans are willing to sacrifice even their deepest beliefs for the ones they love by showing the surprising actions of Elizabeth Proctor, who shifts from being a devout though often judgmental Puritan to a sinner because of her fierce love for her husband and family.

Topic Sentence 1	Topic Sentence 2	Topic Sentence 3
Initially, Miller characterizes Elizabeth Proctor as a virtuous and humble Puritan woman who demonstrates her love for her family through her hard work and devotion to the covenant of the community.	*As the underlying conflict within the Proctor household surfaces, the audience begins to see that when her love is tested by John's infidelity, Elizabeth's virtue manifests in judgment.*	*In a pivotal moment during the trial, Elizabeth reveals her true value — her unconditional love for her husband and family — when she sacrifices her virtue and abandons her judgment to sacrifice herself and lie under oath.*

In this example, the first two paragraphs establish a pattern of behavior for Elizabeth. Paragraph 1 will provide evidence of her virtue, especially her truthfulness, and her devotion to her family. Paragraph 2 will build on Elizabeth's virtue by characterizing her as judgmental of others who commit sinful acts. Both of these paragraphs will establish the background that will amplify her choice in the trial. Paragraph 3 will establish the complexity of Elizabeth's choice by explaining not only the contradictory action of her lying under oath but also the ironic consequence that results from her decision. All three paragraphs are unified by the idea of love as a motivating factor for her actions.

→ Step Three: Choose Relevant Evidence

With your line of reasoning established, you can arrange your relevant and sufficient evidence in the proper body paragraph. For an analysis of character, you should first consider direct and indirect methods of characterization that contribute to your own expectations as a reader. Upon examining the moment(s) when the character defies these expectations, you should gather evidence that explains the character's motives and values.

For your evidence to be relevant, it should relate directly to the character's choice and to the unifying idea. For it to be sufficient, the evidence should represent the importance of the character's development throughout the beginning, middle, and end of the narrative but particularly focus on the moment(s) that reveal complexity.

Because you are writing about a longer work and will not be permitted to use a copy of the text, your evidence will be paraphrased from the narrative. Some students have found it helpful to memorize a few pertinent quotations related to the theme of the text that they can draw upon quickly as evidence. Evidence should be apt and specific, including enough details to support your reasons and your claim.

If you need help introducing and contextualizing your evidence, you may build from the following templates:

- By highlighting the tension between _____ and _____, the author suggests _____.
- The contrast between _____ and _____ portrays a deeper conflict between _____ and _____.
- The character's actions of _____ reveal _____, which serves not only to _____ but also to _____.
- By describing the character as _____, the author emphasizes the complexity of _____.
- While the character appears _____, his/her _____ actions reveal the contrary in that _____.
- Upon further examination of this action/detail, the reader might also conclude that _____.

Review the following notes for evidence to support the line of reasoning in the model prompt.

Topic Sentence 1	Topic Sentence 2	Topic Sentence 3
Initially, Miller characterizes Elizabeth Proctor as a virtuous and humble Puritan woman who demonstrates her love for her family through her hard work and devotion to the covenant of the community.	*As the underlying conflict within the Proctor household surfaces, the audience begins to see that when her love is tested by John's infidelity, Elizabeth's virtue manifests in judgment.*	*In a pivotal moment in the trial, Elizabeth reveals her true value — her unconditional love for her husband and family — when she sacrifices her virtue and abandons her judgment to sacrifice herself and lie under oath.*
Relevant and Sufficient Evidence	**Relevant and Sufficient Evidence**	**Relevant and Sufficient Evidence**
Elizabeth . . . *has the children in bed and dinner waiting for John;* *reads the Bible to her children;* *knows her Commandments;* *is known for never lying;* *is a faithful wife* *protects her family by dismissing Abigail Williams from their service yet keeping their secret*	*Elizabeth . . .* *insists she does not judge John, though he says her "justice would freeze beer";* *voices her suspicions that John still loves Abigail;* *acts defensive when her virtue is questioned by Reverend Hale and lashes out at Abigail*	*Elizabeth . . .* *tries to evade Governor Danforth's questions as long as she can;* *chooses to lie in the court to save her husband and her family only to find that she has condemned him;* *confesses her pride, veiled in virtue, and reconciles with John;* *sacrifices her life with John so that he may "have his goodness" in the end*

→ Step Four: Develop Your Commentary

As you have learned in prior units, commentary serves to link your evidence to your line of reasoning and to explain how that evidence relates to your idea and insight. As you practice developing a complex thesis, establishing a line of reasoning, and choosing the most relevant evidence to support your interpretation, your commentary should also reflect the highest level of complexity and sophistication.

You have considered how literary techniques and elements work together for effect. For example, in addition to the methods of characterization, an author may use narrative perspective, setting details, and plot structure together to reveal the values of the characters. Alternatively, a single detail from a text may elicit more than one insight within the context of the narrative. For example, a single action from a character may reveal more than one motive or value. Therefore, when you include specific evidence, your commentary should explore these nuances and possibilities.

To help you add commentary that explains complexity within a passage, you might build from the following templates:

- By contrasting _____ and _____, the author reveals _____. This tension may also suggest _____.
- The contradiction between the character's _____ and _____ develops the complexity of the character in that _____. Through this complexity, the author illustrates the human tendency to _____.
- The character's shift from _____ to _____ illustrates a change in values/motivation and suggests _____. By including this change, the author explores the universal dilemma/conflict that _____.

Review the following example of commentary that addresses complexity by suggesting more than one possible interpretation of the character's actions. Also, notice how the commentary connects to both the topic sentence and the thesis.

Evidence	Commentary Connected to Idea
In a shocking turn of events, Elizabeth Proctor, who was known in all of Salem for never telling a lie, swore under oath that John had not had an affair with Abigail Williams.	*In previous scenes, Miller establishes the gravity of Elizabeth's decision through the verbal threats of Governor Danforth who tells the witness they will "burn in hell" for perjury. Elizabeth knows her lie is a mortal sin, and she goes to great lengths to avoid it through her evasions; however, her love for her husband and her desire to protect her family prevails. Elizabeth abandons her lifelong code of behavior and the very human instinct to protect herself from what Puritans believed to be eternal separation from God. Because of her reputation and the close-knit Puritan community, some readers may also attribute her actions to personal pride and fear of alienation from her community. However, in presenting Elizabeth's desperate attempt to salvage her family from the corruption of the witch hunt, Miller ultimately reveals the lengths that people will go to protect their loved ones.*

Before you wrap up your literary analysis, you should provide a **conclusion**. You have practiced explaining the relevance of your idea and insight in a concluding statement. The conclusion of a complex and thoughtful literary argument should avoid simply restating the thesis. Instead, it should include several sentences that connect the idea and insight to a shared human experience, a social or cultural observation, or other relevant context beyond the pages of the text. In doing so, you will not only convey the relevance of your interpretation, but also of the work as a whole.

INSIDER AP® TIP

Your style reveals your understanding. The precision of your words and the sophistication of your language communicate the author's tone and attitude toward the subject of the work. Choosing the most precise language in your analysis illustrates your nuanced understanding of the literary work.

AP® EXAM PRACTICE

The following is an example of the literary argument free-response question. Practice the skills you have learned in this workshop to write an argument in response to the prompt. You may use the graphic organizer and templates to help you plan and write your analysis.

Remember to follow the four steps:

- Step One: Determine a **unifying idea** and brainstorm relevant examples from a text
- Step Two: Write a **defensible thesis statement**
- Step Three: Choose **relevant evidence**
- Step Four: Develop **insightful commentary**

Prompt:

Many works of literature incorporate multiple perspectives to tell the story. Novelists may use a single narrator whose perspective shifts or changes or even rotate two or more narrators with contrasting perspectives throughout the narrative. Playwrights reveal contrasting perspectives through the dialogue among the characters. Such shifts or contrasts in perspective contribute to the reader's understanding of the values of the characters and to the complexity of the work.

Either from your own reading or from the following list, choose a work of fiction that includes a complex narrative perspective. Then, in a well-written essay, analyze how the author's manipulation of perspective contributes to an interpretation of the work as a whole. Do not merely summarize the plot.

In your response you should do the following:

- Respond to the prompt with a thesis that presents a defensible interpretation
- Select and use evidence to support your line of reasoning
- Explain how the evidence supports your line of reasoning
- Use appropriate grammar and punctuation in communicating your argument

The Alchemist	*King Lear*
All the Light We Cannot See	*A Lesson Before Dying*
As I Lay Dying	*Mudbound*
Beloved	*Oedipus, the King*
The Brief Wondrous Life of Oscar Wao	*Olive Kitteridge*
Brown Girl, Brownstones	*The Poisonwood Bible*
Cat on a Hot Tin Roof	*Pride and Prejudice*
The Color Purple	*A Raisin in the Sun*
The Crucible	*The Rime of the Ancient Mariner*
Frankenstein	*The Round House*
A Gesture Life	*The Scarlet Letter*
Half of a Yellow Sun	*Sing, Unburied Sing*
The Handmaid's Tale	*The Song of Achilles*
Heart of Darkness	*The Strange Case of Dr. Jekyll and Mr. Hyde*
Homegoing	*Their Eyes Were Watching God*
House Made of Dawn	*There There*
The House on Mango Street	*Things Fall Apart*
In the Time of Butterflies	*A Thousand Splendid Suns*
Invisible Man	*Top Girls*
The Joy Luck Club	*Wuthering Heights*

ORGANIZING A LITERARY ARGUMENT (III)

Introduction

- Engage the audience through an interesting hook
- Provide historical, cultural, or social context of a literary work
- Identify the title, author, genre (TAG)
- Introduce the literary topic by
  - describing the importance of the literary topic within the work; and
  - summarizing the work succinctly with details critical to the literary topic

Hook and context:
TAG:
Literary topic and concise summary:

Defensible Thesis Statement with Claim (idea + insight):

In [title], his/her [contextualize the work], [author] contrasts/explores the tension between [a and b] to reveal that [idea + insight].

Topic Sentence 1 (Identify the first aspect of the topic in relation to the unifying idea):	Topic Sentence 2 (Identify the second aspect of the topic, connect it to the first aspect in relation to the unifying idea):	Topic Sentence 3 (Identify the third aspect of the topic, connect it to the first and/ or second aspect in relation to the unifying idea):
To begin, [author] includes [technique/element 1] to reveal [universal idea].	In contrast to [first aspect], [author] includes [technique/ element 2] to [purpose connect to idea].	Finally, [author] highlights the tension between [a and b] by including [technique/element 3] to [purpose connect to idea].
Textual Details (Relevant and sufficient evidence):	**Textual Details** (Relevant and sufficient evidence):	**Textual Details** (Relevant and sufficient evidence):
For example, by developing [technique] through [evidence in context], [author] illustrates [link to topic sentence].	To illustrate, [author] compares/ contrasts [a and b] by describing [evidence] to reveal [link to topic sentence].	To explore [link to topic sentence], [author] includes [evidence in context].
[Author] continues to explore [link to topic sentence] by including [evidence in context] which reveals [insight].	Another point of comparison for [a and b] illustrated by [evidence] reveals the [link to topic sentence].	On the other hand, the author creates irony by juxtaposing [a and b] in describing [text evidence].
Commentary (Link evidence to reason and idea):	**Commentary** (Link evidence to reason and idea):	**Commentary** (Link evidence to reason and idea):
The association with [idea] reveals [idea and insight].	Through the similar/contrasting attributes, [author] develops [idea and insight].	By exploring the tension between [a and b] the author emphasizes [idea and insight].
Two to four sentences explaining how the evidence exemplifies the universal idea	*Two to four sentences explaining how the evidence exemplifies the universal idea*	*Two to four sentences explaining how the evidence exemplifies the universal idea*

Conclusion:

Further your idea and insight by

- discussing the significance or relevance of interpretation;
- relating the work to other relevant literary works;
- connecting the theme to your own experience;
- presenting alternate interpretations;
- explaining how the work explores complexities and tensions; or
- situating the theme within a broader context.

Where Are You?

Joyce Carol Oates

The following is an entire short story published in 2018.

The husband had got into the habit of calling the wife from somewhere in the house — if she was upstairs, he was downstairs; if she was downstairs, he was upstairs — and when she
5 answered, "Yes? What?," he would continue to call her, as if he hadn't heard and with an air of strained patience: "Hello? Hello? Where are you?" And so she had no choice but to hurry to him, wherever he was, elsewhere in the house,
10 downstairs, upstairs, in the basement or outside on the deck, in the back yard or in the driveway. "Yes?" she called, trying to remain calm. "What is it?" And he would tell her — a complaint, a remark, an observation, a reminder,
15 a query — and then, later, she would hear him calling again with a new urgency, "Hello? Hello? Where are you?," and she would call back, "Yes? What is it?," trying to determine where he was. He would continue to call, not
20 hearing her, for he disliked wearing his hearing aid around the house, where there was only the wife to be heard. He complained that one of the little plastic devices in the shape of a snail hurt his ear, the tender inner ear was reddened and
25 had even bled, and so he would call, pettishly,[1] "Hello? Where are you?" — for the woman was always going off somewhere out of the range of his hearing, and he never knew where the hell she was or what she was doing; at times, her
30 very being exasperated[2] him — until finally she

gave in and ran breathless to search for him, and when he saw her he said reproachfully, "Where were you? I worry about you when you don't answer." And she said, laughing, trying
35 to laugh, though none of this was funny, "But I was here all along!" And he retorted, "No, you were not. You were not. I was here, and you were not here." And later that day, after his lunch and before his nap, unless it was before
40 his lunch and after his nap, the wife heard the husband calling to her, "Hello? Hello? Where are you?," and the thought came to her, "No. I will hide from him." But she would not do such a childish thing. Instead she stood on the stairs
45 and cupped her hands to her mouth and called to him, "I'm here. I'm always here. Where else would I be?" But the husband couldn't hear her and continued to call, "Hello? Hello? Where are you?," until at last she screamed, "What do you
50 want? I've told you, I'm here." But the husband couldn't hear and continued to call, "Hello? Where are you? Hello!," and finally the wife had no choice but to give in, for the husband was sounding vexed and angry and anxious.
55 Descending the stairs, she tripped and fell, fell hard, and her neck was broken in an instant, and she died at the foot of the stairs, while in one of the downstairs rooms, or perhaps in the cellar, or on the deck at the rear of the
60 house, the husband continued to call, with mounting urgency, "Hello? Hello? Where are you?"

---

[1] As one who is easily irritated or annoyed; childishly bad-tempered.

[2] Intensely irritated and frustrated; annoyed.

1. Which of the following best describes the effect of the statement "at times, her very being exasperated him" (lines 29–30) on the story?
   (A) It creates a contrast between how she claims to feel and how she actually feels about him on the inside.
   (B) It emphasizes how she cares very little for him, despite her seeming concern about his well emotional well-being.
   (C) It emphasizes how she becomes frustrated with him because of his unwillingness to wear his hearing aid, despite her caring for him.
   (D) It illustrates the fears that she has, which she cannot express to him because he is so frail that he is easily overwhelmed by his own fears.
   (E) It illustrates the sense of entrapment and isolation she feels as a result of her commitment to care for and comfort him in his own time of fear and confusion.

2. In context, the phrases "after his lunch and before his nap, unless it was before his lunch and after his nap" (lines 38–40) and their syntactical arrangement might be best described as
   (A) nonsensical to represent the constant confusion of the characters and even of the narrator as an observer trying to make sense of the scene.
   (B) paradoxical in the way they indicate that she never actually hid from him because the times mentioned cancel out one another.
   (C) contradicting one another to show the confusion and anxiety of both characters.
   (D) illustrating that events like these take place so often that it is difficult to say exactly when they occur.
   (E) confusing as it provides no useful information in the context of the passage.

3. Which of the following describes how the woman's thought "No. I will hide from him." (lines 42–43) contributes to irony in the story?
   (A) Her actually hiding from him may have meant that he would have died, and then she would no longer be frustrated by his calling for her and his fear that she would not respond.
   (B) Had she actually hidden from him, it is less likely that she would have fallen down the stairs and died; her commitment to comforting him with her presence brought about her death.
   (C) She would never hide from him because he was too fragile.
   (D) He would never have found her if she had hidden because he could not climb the stairs, and she could have simply avoided him the entire time by remaining upstairs.
   (E) The narrator sees this as childish, but the woman could have actually done this to avoid the man.

4. Which of the following best describes the role of the man in the situation of the narrative?
   (A) His values consistently and directly oppose those of the woman, creating the conflict around which the story develops.
   (B) He is the antagonist to the woman as he opposes her regularly abandoning him in the house.
   (C) He acts as a foil to the woman by showing what caring for someone is really like in contrast to her not truly caring for him.
   (D) He is the focus of the narrative and functions ironically as the cause of death for the woman.
   (E) He is an unchanging character whose actions move the plot forward.

5. Her tripping, falling, and dying on the stairs (lines 55–57) reveals what about values and conflict in the story?
   (A) A conflict must have some sort of action to develop the plot and the characters.
   (B) He valued having her near while she valued comforting him: illustrating the man as the more selfish of the two; her death came about as a result of those conflicting values being acted upon.
   (C) Conflict can only be resolved when those involved examine their values.
   (D) She and the man share a conflict with the values and perspective of the narrator.
   (E) She is so focused on not allowing the man to see her frustration that she compromises her values of honesty and compassion; in fact, not following her own plan to hide from him and dying as a result.

6. As provided in the last sentence, lines 55–62 ("Descending . . . 'Where are you?'"), the ending of the story can best be described as
   (A) contradictory to the man's established character.
   (B) providing catharsis.
   (C) lacking resolution.
   (D) creating suspense.
   (E) inconsistent with the rest of the story.

7. By the end of the story, it can be most reasonably argued that the stairs symbolize
   (A) a climb toward heaven or descent into the underworld.
   (B) a journey that the woman must undertake as the heroine of the story.
   (C) a boundary between the man and woman that should not be crossed.
   (D) the vow of commitment made between the two when they were married.
   (E) the increasing bitterness of the woman toward the man.

8. In the context of the story as a whole, all of the following could be reasonably argued as indirect causes for the woman's death EXCEPT
   (A) her commitment to the man.
   (B) his dislike for his hearing aid and his discomfort with it.
   (C) her emotional response to him.
   (D) his going to the deck at the rear of the house.
   (E) her decision not to hide from him.

Thanatopsis

William Cullen Bryant

The following poem was published in 1817.

> To him who in the love of Nature holds
> Communion[1] with her visible forms, she speaks
> A various language; for his gayer hours
> She has a voice of gladness, and a smile
> 5 And eloquence of beauty, and she glides
> Into his darker musings, with a mild
> And healing sympathy, that steals away
> Their sharpness, ere he is aware. When thoughts
> Of the last bitter hour come like a blight
> 10 Over thy spirit, and sad images
> Of the stern agony, and shroud, and pall,
> And breathless darkness, and the narrow house,
> Make thee to shudder, and grow sick at heart; —
> Go forth, under the open sky, and list
> 15 To Nature's teachings, while from all around —
> Earth and her waters, and the depths of air —
> Comes a still voice —
>   Yet a few days, and thee
> The all-beholding **sun** shall see no more
> 20 In all his course; nor yet in the cold ground,
> Where thy pale form was laid, with many tears,
> Nor in the embrace of ocean, shall exist
> Thy image. Earth, that nourished thee, shall claim
> Thy growth, to be resolved to earth again,
> 25 And, lost each human trace, surrendering up
> Thine individual being, shalt thou go
> To mix for ever with the elements,
> To be a brother to the insensible rock
> And to the sluggish clod,[2] which the rude swain

---

[1] The sharing or exchanging of intimate thoughts and feelings, especially when the exchange is on a mental or spiritual level.

[2] A lump of earth or clay.

30 Turns with his share, and treads upon. The oak
    Shall send his roots abroad, and pierce thy mould.[3]
       Yet not to thine eternal resting-place
    Shalt thou retire alone, nor couldst thou wish
    Couch[4] more magnificent. Thou shalt lie down
35 With patriarchs[5] of the infant world — with kings,
    The powerful of the earth — the wise, the good,
    Fair forms, and hoary[6] seers of ages past,
    All in one mighty sepulchre.[7] The hills
    Rock-ribbed and ancient as the sun, — the vales
40 Stretching in pensive quietness between;
    The venerable woods — rivers that move
    In majesty, and the complaining brooks
    That make the meadows green; and, poured round all,
    Old Ocean's gray and melancholy waste, —
45 Are but the solemn decorations all
    Of the great tomb of man. The golden sun,
    The planets, all the infinite hosts of heaven,
    Are shining on the sad abodes of death,
    Through the still lapse of ages. All that tread
50 The globe are but a handful to the tribes
    That slumber in its bosom. — Take the wings
    Of morning, pierce the Barcan wilderness,
    Or lose thyself in the continuous woods
    Where rolls the Oregon,[8] and hears no sound,
55 Save his own dashings — yet the dead are there:
    And millions in those solitudes, since first
    The flight of years began, have laid them down
    In their last sleep — the dead reign there alone.
    So shalt thou rest, and what if thou withdraw
60 In silence from the living, and no friend
    Take note of thy departure? All that breathe
    Will share thy destiny. The gay will laugh
    When thou art gone, the solemn brood of care
    Plod on, and each one as before will chase
65 His favorite phantom; yet all these shall leave
    Their mirth and their employments, and shall come
    And make their bed with thee. As the long train
    Of ages glide away, the sons of men,

---

[3] Coffin in that it is shaped (moulded) to fit a body.

[4] In this sense, to lie down.

[5] Any of those figures — often religious — regarded as fathers of the human race.

[6] Grayish white; relating to something elderly.

[7] A small room or monument, cut in rock or built of stone, in which a dead person is laid or buried.

[8] Meaning "great river of the west"; this was the original native name for the Columbia River in the northwestern United States.

The youth in life's green spring, and he who goes
In the full strength of years, matron and maid,
The speechless babe, and the gray-headed man —
Shall one by one be gathered to thy side,
By those, who in their turn shall follow them.
    So live, that when thy summons comes to join
The innumerable caravan, which moves
To that mysterious realm, where each shall take
His chamber in the silent halls of death,
Thou go not, like the quarry-slave at night,
Scourged to his dungeon, but, sustained and soothed
By an unfaltering trust, approach thy grave,
Like one who wraps the drapery of his couch
About him, and lies down to pleasant dreams.

1. The stanza break between lines 17 and 18
   ("Comes . . . and thee") is notable for all of the
   following reasons EXCEPT it
   (A) shifts to the speaker directly addressing
       someone.
   (B) is the only broken line in the entire poem.
   (C) breaks the line but completes the
       established metrical pattern of the lines
       across the two lines.
   (D) carries the sentence over from stanza one
       to stanza two while all other stanzas end
       at the end of a sentence.
   (E) connects the life in the first stanza to
       death in the second.

2. In the context of the poem, which of the fol-
   lowing is the most likely literal meaning of the
   sentence spanning lines 49–51 ("All that . . . its
   bosom.")?
   (A) Those who are still alive owe a great debt
       to those who lived and died before them.
   (B) Death is more like a peaceful sleep than a
       fearful curse.
   (C) The people who have traveled the globe
       will be those who find rest in death.
   (D) Only those who are members of certain
       tribes can find actual rest in their deaths.
   (E) Many more people have died than there
       are people living on the earth.

3. Which of the following best describes the
   conceit developed in lines 67–73 ("As the . . .
   follow them.")?
   (A) Those people who are not on the same
       philosophical train as the speaker will be
       left behind when their death comes.
   (B) The lives of all people of all ages and all
       backgrounds are connected like the cars
       of a train that continually moves and
       passes through time, life, and death.
   (C) The green spring of youth can drown
       those who do not follow the prescribed
       course for their lives and attempt to
       remain youthful.
   (D) It takes people of all ages and all
       backgrounds to make life experiences
       unique and meaningful.
   (E) The experiences of the young and the
       old are ultimately the same, like the
       connected cars of a train, with the only
       differences being the context of those
       experiences, represented by the train
       moving through time.

4. Which of the following lines suggests a shift
   toward a resolution for the poem?
   (A) "Yet not to thine . . ." (line 32)
   (B) "The golden sun . . ." (line 46)
   (C) "So shalt thou rest . . ." (line 59)
   (D) "So live . . ." (line 74)
   (E) "By an unfaltering trust . . ." (line 80)

5. In the context of the poem as a whole, the sun is most likely symbolic of BOTH
   (A) infinite time and the impermanence of life.
   (B) vast possibility and foolish immortality.
   (C) "embrace of ocean" (line 22) and "insensible rock" (line 28).
   (D) the "powerful of the earth" (line 36) and eventual death.
   (E) the "green spring" (line 69) of life and the inevitability of "gray-headed man" (line 71).

6. All of the following are personified in the poem EXCEPT
   (A) nature (lines 1 and 15).
   (B) the Earth (lines 16 and 23).
   (C) the sun (lines 19, 39, and 46).
   (D) the ocean (lines 22 and 44).
   (E) the couch (lines 34 and 81).

7. Which of the following is the most reasonable claim to be made about the poem as a whole?
   (A) Love makes life worth living and the only way to overcome death is to love and be loved in return; in doing so, we can expect death to be peaceful.
   (B) Death is to be feared because of the uncertainty it presents; in fact, the lack of control over when — and what happens to us when — we die means we should resist natural death as long as possible.
   (C) We should not worry about death because all people die and life goes on without them; instead, we should live our lives until the time comes for us to greet death and accept the peace and rest it offers.
   (D) Death is natural and cannot be resisted; however, that does not mean that we must accept the finality of death.
   (E) Only the gray-headed, elderly can rest peacefully in death, as they have traveled the world and truly lived; likewise, those who die young are doomed to restless deaths because of their unfinished lives.

Writing a College Application Essay

In the first few months of their senior year, many high school students begin the journey of applying to college. In addition to filling out an admission application, updating a résumé, and securing letters of recommendation, applicants are often required to write one or more essays to complete their application packet. This workshop will guide you through the process of writing an effective college application essay.

Preparing to Write Your College Application Essay

Your formal application shares important facts and statistics about you: your standardized test scores, grade point average, coursework, extracurricular activities, leadership positions, honors and awards, work experience, and community service. In short, these documents reveal *what you did* during your high school years.

In contrast, the essay allows you to show *who you are* as a person. By reading these essays during the application process, admissions committees can better differentiate between applicants who appear equally qualified based on their applications. Writing an essay for this purpose may seem daunting, but do not fret. Your job is to reveal your personality — and your voice — within the parameters of the essay prompt, and no one knows you better than you know yourself.

Like all the other essays you have written, your college application essay must focus on a **unifying idea.** Before you start to write, you may wish to take an inventory to help you brainstorm possible ideas and to focus on the personal values and traits you wish to highlight in your essay response. In other words, what would you like the admissions committee to understand about you?

Use the following questions to help you identify a unifying idea:

- How would your friends describe you?
- How would your teachers, your parents, or your siblings describe you?
- What is your greatest accomplishment?
- When have you changed your mind over an important issue — and why?
- What was your most embarrassing moment?
- How do you enjoy spending your time?

- What is your greatest fear or biggest regret?
- What is your greatest accomplishment or most surprising victory?
- What is your favorite subject? What do you love about it?
- What is your passion? What does it reveal about you?
- How do you spend your free time — and why?
- What are your values and beliefs? How do you show them in practice?
- What are your goals for the future?

Once you have done some reflection on the significance of your experiences, carefully review the essay prompts in the application. Make sure that you read each college's admission requirements carefully. For example, some colleges have open-ended and traditional topics (e.g., "Tell us about yourself."), while others may have more specific or even creative topics (e.g., "Kermit the Frog famously lamented, 'It's not easy being green.' Do you agree?"). Check to see if you have options from several prompts for the essay or if the college specifies the prompt that you must address. If you have a choice, select the prompt that will allow you to share your most important traits and values and focus on the idea you wish to convey. Remember that your goal is to allow the committee to get to know you better.

Common college application essay topics:

- An interest, identity, or talent that defines you
- A belief you hold or no longer hold to be true
- A lesson you learned through a challenge or failure
- A moment that you overcame an obstacle
- An accomplishment that demonstrates growth
- Something that brings you joy
- A place you would like to visit

Planning and Organizing Your College Application Essay

In most cases, your college application essay will be a personal narrative: an essay that tells a brief, focused personal story that reveals an insight that you have come to understand. As in all effective writing, your essay should include a **unifying idea**: an abstract noun that ties your story details to your **message** and purpose. Review the following partial list of ideas that you might use to unify your personal narrative.

Possible ideas for college essays:

• Balance	• Challenge	• Compassion	• Curiosity
• Belonging	• Community	• Courage	• Discipline

- Diversity
- Education
- Endurance
- Honesty
- Identity
- Imagination
- Inclusion
- Individualism
- Inspiration
- Loyalty
- Originality
- Passion
- Perseverance
- Resilience
- Wonder
- Work ethic

Before you begin you must know your insight and commit to it. Every detail of your essay must help reveal that insight.

As you introduce and develop your narrative, keep your unifying idea in focus. It is easy to get carried away with details, but you should include only those details relevant to your unifying idea and overall purpose. You may decide to narrate the story chronologically, begin *in medias res*, or explore other creative methods of development. The college essay offers opportunities for you to explore. No matter what approach you choose, your essay must have a narrative arc with a clear beginning, middle, and end.

Within your narrative, you should share an insight about that idea. This insight serves as the **thesis statement** for your personal narrative, which may be stated directly or revealed implicitly. While your story details may be entertaining or engaging to your readers, if you do not follow them with reflection on their deeper meaning or relevance to your own life and development, then your essay will be less likely to serve the purpose it is designed to accomplish. Review the following examples to see the difference between merely mentioning an idea and revealing a message that includes both an idea and insight.

Idea only: "I learned the importance of balance in my life."

Idea + insight: "Learning to balance my responsibilities and my free time became the key to improving my mental health and overall well-being."

Finally, most colleges will provide specific instructions for the length of your essay response (e.g., character, word, or page count). You must strictly adhere to the instructions for each prompt and for each application. Keep in mind that most admissions officials read thousands of essays a year and prefer concise narratives. Review the following chart for a suggested outline for your personal essay. Note that each section (beginning, middle, and end) may include more than one paragraph as needed.

A word of caution: You want to stand out from thousands of applicants. So as you consider your topic, you may want to avoid writing about experiences that are common to so many of your classmates, such as mission trips, band camp, babysitting, the pandemic, and team sports. However, if you do choose a topic that is commonly experienced, then focus on a nuanced aspect of it. Likewise, try to avoid ending your essay with a cliché, such as, "So I learned that every cloud has a silver lining," or, "Alas, there are plenty of fish in the sea." These phrases reduce your individual experience and insight to an impersonal generalization. Tell a story only *you* can tell, in your own words.

ORGANIZING A COLLEGE APPLICATION ESSAY

Unifying Idea: *Abstract idea that ties your narrative and your message together*

Message: *The purpose of your narrative that combines your idea plus your insight about the idea.*

Beginning (The Set-Up)	Middle (The Blow-Up)	End (The Wrap-Up)
• Includes an engaging hook • Establishes the situation in the narrative and sets up the conflict • May reveal or forecast the unifying idea	• Includes specific details to develop the story with the unifying idea in mind • Explores the conflict or the problem	• Resolves the conflict • Shares the deeper understanding of the story • Reveals the insight about the unifying idea

Writing with an Engaging and Personal Voice

College admissions counselors across the country all agree that the most effective essays are ones that not only relate a focused story with relevant details but also do so in an engaging and personal voice. Whether your tone is funny, quirky, introspective, or serious, the most convincing essays are authentic and real — not impersonal or detached, not forced or formulaic. In other words, do not rely on the academic voice of an expository essay for your English teacher. Your specific audience is a representative for a college you wish to attend — a representative who genuinely wants to get to know you better.

College admission officers urge applicants to do the following in their essays:

- Open with a creative hook
- Include specific details
- Choose original topics
- Write clearly and conversationally
- Write to show, not to tell
- Write in your own voice

Review the following chart that includes examples of common mistakes students make on college essays and solutions to eliminate those mistakes.

ENGAGING AN AUDIENCE IN A COLLEGE APPLICATION ESSAY

Common Mistakes in College Essays	Solutions for an Effective Essay
Repeating the prompt as the hook: *"There are many important lessons I have learned in my life."*	Be creative: *"A batch of brownies with no eggs in the mix will emerge from the oven as a warm, sloppy mess. I discovered this fact the hard way one winter afternoon. After that experience, I now take the time to read directions carefully."*
Using general and vague language: *"After months of practice, my hard work paid off."*	Be precise and specific: *"Dedicating 30 extra minutes of focused practice every afternoon gave me the confidence and muscle memory I needed to earn a spot in the all-state orchestra."*
Relying on clichés: *"My experience with my lab partner taught me that I should never judge a book by its cover."*	Be original: *"At first, I dreaded working with the girl in my science lab who frantically searched through her messy, overstuffed backpack for her wrinkled homework. But a few days after my misguided first impression, I discovered how brilliant she was and felt lucky to be her lab partner."*
Overusing a thesaurus: *"The ramifications of my misguided jaunt to see* The Avengers *proved to be both prodigious and calamitous for my athletic endeavors."*	Be clear and direct: *"My choice to skip soccer practice to see the new* Avengers *movie cost me my starting position for the next three games."*
Writing in passive voice; overusing "be verbs": *"I was given the opportunity to work with a professor who had been appointed as the manager of a research lab at the local university."*	Be engaging and active: *"I look forward to every Friday afternoon when I get the chance to work as a lab technician researching Time-Resolved Microscopy with Texas A&M University chemistry professor Dr. Beverly Williams."*
Writing in an impersonal academic tone: *"When one considers the important people in one's life, he or she naturally thinks of family members."*	Be personal and authentic: *"My dad, orphaned at birth and rescued from the streets when he was just a boy, worked two jobs most of his life so I would have the opportunity to go to college."*

Demonstrating Control over the Conventions of Writing

As the final step in writing your college application essay, you must revise and edit carefully and thoroughly. It is important that you not only share your personality but also that you demonstrate your skill as a writer. Your essay should be coherent and unified. You can achieve coherence by making sure that you organize your story details in a logical order and provide **transitions** to lead your reader. You can achieve unity by keeping your **unifying idea** in mind throughout the beginning, middle, and end of your essay. You should reinforce that unity by providing insight about the idea in your reflection throughout the narrative.

Once you have written your essay, it is a good idea to wait a day or so before you revise and edit. Get a little distance, and when you have fresh eyes, review your essay with the following questions in mind.

Questions to guide your revisions and edits:

- Does the essay connect my topic to an idea?
- Does my essay convey an insight about that idea?
- Are all of the details in my essay focused on an idea?
- Does my essay have a good balance between story and reflection?
- Does my essay include engaging details presented in a concise style?
- Is my tone personal, engaging, and appropriate for my audience?
- Is my writing fluent with a variety of sentence types and helpful transitions?
- Does my story reflect my unique voice and speak clearly to the reader?
- Is my essay free from spelling, punctuation, and other errors in writing conventions?

Finally, make sure you leave yourself time to have a trusted friend, teacher, counselor, or parent read your essay as well and offer you suggestions.

Additional questions for your peer editor:

- Can you identify the idea and message of my narrative?
- Were my story details clear, concise, and focused on my idea?
- Did I leave any unanswered questions?
- Did my story logically lead to the reflection and message?
- Does this essay sound like my voice?
- Do you feel like you know me a little better after reading my story?

If you are looking for additional information or would like to read sample essays, first visit your prospective college's website and read their advice and tips. Additionally, you may also visit some of the following helpful online sources:

- College Essay Guy
- Prep Scholar
- Khan Academy

MLA Documentation and Citation

Drawing upon the ideas and scholarship of others can often strengthen and give credibility to your argument. The purpose of citing and documenting sources is to provide thorough, accurate, and quick information about your sources when you incorporate ideas and words that are not your own.

While there are several styles for documentation, Modern Language Association (MLA) is most common in English classes. The MLA is one of many organizations that provide documentation and publication style guidelines for academic disciplines. Generally speaking, MLA is used when working in English, the arts, and the humanities.

MLA Style Guide

Generally, MLA in-text citations provide the name of the author and the page numbers of the publication where the source material first appeared. Note that different types of sources may require additional information in citations, such as the line numbers of a play or the name of a specific television episode.

MLA In-Text Citations

Prose (fewer than four lines)

You can include the author's name in the sentence itself or in parentheses following the quotation. For a subsequent citation to the same source within a paragraph, only use a page number (unless there's possible confusion with another text by the same author). The page number(s) must appear in the parentheses, not in the text of your sentence. For example:

> According to critic Stephen Knight, no figure in literature has a "stronger hold on the public imagination than Sherlock Holmes" (67).

> No literary character has a "stronger hold on the public imagination than Sherlock Holmes" (Knight 67).

Prose (more than four lines)

Begin the quotation on a separate line indented one inch from the left margin. Do not use quotation marks: the formatting indicates the passage is a quotation. Introduce the passage with a complete sentence followed by a colon. Use double spacing and place the period after the quotation, not the parenthetical citation.

The narrator reacts to Bartleby with fear, ambivalence, and paralysis:

> Again I sat ruminating what I should do. Mortified as I was at his behavior, and resolved as I had been to dismiss him when I entered my offices, nevertheless I strangely felt something superstitious knocking at my heart, and forbidding me to carry out my purpose, and denouncing me for a villain if I dared to breathe one bitter word against this forlornest of mankind. (Melville 137)

Poetry (three lines or fewer)

The first time you quote a poem, use the word "line" or "lines." For the citations that follow, only include the actual line numbers. If the poet or title is not mentioned in the sentence, include it in the parenthetical citation. For example:

> The poet begins "Ode on a Grecian Urn" with personification: "Thou still unravish'd bride of quietness, / Thou foster-child of silence and slow time . . ." (Keats lines 1–2)

> Keats begins the poem with personification: "Thou still unravish'd bride of quietness, / Thou foster-child of silence and slow time . . ." ("Ode on a Grecian Urn" 1–2).

Poetry (four lines or more)

For longer sections of poetry, follow rules similar to the guidelines for prose. Start a new line for every line break in the poem:

> In "Terence, This Is Stupid Stuff," the unnamed listener of *A Shropshire Lad* finally becomes frustrated with the speaker's melancholy, death-haunted poems:
>
> > Terence, this is stupid stuff:
> > You eat your victuals fast enough;
> > There can't be much amiss, 'tis clear,
> > To see the rate you drink your beer.
> > But oh, good Lord, the verse you make,
> > It gives a chap the belly-ache. (Housman 1–6)

All of these in-text citations should have corresponding entries on your works-cited page.

More Than One Text by the Same Author

Sometimes, you will be working with more than one text by the same author. To avoid confusion, you may identify the specific title and abbreviate it in the parenthetical citation. For example, in this passage, the writer cites two poems by John Keats: "Ode on a Grecian Urn" and "To Autumn."

> Keats begins the poem with personification: "Thou still unravish'd bride of quietness, / Thou foster-child of silence and slow time . . ." ("Grecian Urn" lines 1–2). This technique is familiar from his other odes in which the speaker personifies a

nightingale or even a season, as in this address to autumn: "Sometimes whoever seeks abroad may find / Thee sitting careless on a granary flood, / They hair soft-lifted by the winnowing wind" (Keats "To Autumn" lines 13–15)

Include a works cited page at the end of your paper. Here, you will provide a list of all the specific texts and sources referred to within your argument. Each entry will also include key bibliographical information.

Basic Style Guidelines for a List of Works Cited

- Begin the works cited list on a new page after the last page of your text.
- Begin each entry flush with the left-hand margin; indent subsequent lines one-half inch.
- List references alphabetically by the author's last name (or by the first major word of the title, if no author is identified).
- Double-space the list of entries.
- Every in-text citation must have a corresponding works cited entry (and vice versa).

Generally, each entry should include the author, the title of the source, the place of publication, the name of the publisher, and the date of publication. Depending on the type of source (e.g., essay in an edited anthology, a video on YouTube, an article in an online magazine), you may need to include additional or different information.

GUIDELINES FOR A LIST OF WORKS CITED

Books	Works Cited
Book by one author	Verma, Neil. *Theater of the Mind: Imagination, Aesthetics, and American Radio Drama.* University of Chicago Press, 2012.
Multiple selections from a single book	In the previous in-text citation examples, a writer quotes lines from John Keats's poem "Ode on a Grecian Urn" from the collection *Keats's Poetry and Prose*. This entry will appear on the works-cited page in this form: Keats, John. "Ode on a Grecian Urn." *Keats's Poetry and Prose*, edited by Jeffrey N. Cox, W. W. Norton, 2009, pp. 460–63. If you quote lines from different poems (stories, plays, or essays) in the same collection by a single author, then you can generally identify the individual work(s) in your essay work(s) and cite the collection as a whole in the works-cited entry.
Book by two authors	Gilbert, Sandra and Susan Gubar. *The Madwoman in the Attic: The Woman Writer and the Nineteenth-Century Literary Imagination.* Yale UP, 1979.
Book by three or more authors	Hand, Cynthia, et al. *My Lady Jane.* HarperTeen, 2017.
Edited book	Pollack, Harriet, editor. *New Essays on Eudora Welty, Class, and Race.* University Press of Mississippi, 2019.

(continued)

Books	Works Cited
Essay in an edited book or anthology	Chithm, Edward. "The Themes of *Wuthering Heights*." *Critical Essays on Emily Brontë*, edited by Thomas John Winnifirth, G. K. Hall & Co., 1997, 33–48.
Translation	Simenon, Georges. *Maigret in New York*. Translated by Linda Coverdale, Penguin, 2016.
Poem (in a book)	Oliver, Mary. "The Dog Has Run Off Again." *New and Selected Poems*, Beacon Press, 2005, p. 123.
Short story (in an anthology)	Minot, Susan. "Lust." *The Compact Bedford Introduction to Literature*, edited by Michael Meyer, Bedford/St. Martin's, 2012, pp. 279–86.

Periodicals	Works Cited
Article in a journal (print)	Landon, Philip J. "From Cowboy to Organization Man: The Hollywood War Hero, 1940–1955." *Studies in Popular Culture*, vol. 12, no. 1, 1989, pp. 28–41.
Article in a magazine (print)	Mallon, Thomas. "Weegee the Famous, the Voyeur and Exhibitionist," *The New Yorker*, 28 May 2018, pp. 64–70.
Article in a newspaper (print)	Shearer, Lloyd. "Crime Certainly Pays Onscreen." *The New York Times*, 5 Aug. 1945, p. 77.
Interview in a periodical (print)	Morrison, Toni. Interview with Cecil Brown. *The Massachusetts Review*, vol. 26, no. 3, 1995, pp. 455–73.
Anonymous articles (print)	"The Complex Legacy of Thomas Becket's Life and Death." *The Economist*, 15 May 2021, p. 34.

Internet Sources	Works Cited
Book on a website	Chesnutt, Charles W. *The Colonel's Dream*. Doubleday, Page, & Co., 1905. *The Literature Network*, http://www.online-literature.com/charles-chesnutt/colonels-dream.
E-book	Ruefle, Mary. *The Most of It*. E-book ed., Wave Books, 2008.
Website	"Writing Center Commitment to Antiracism, Inclusion, and Equity." The Writing Center at Franklin and Marshall College, https://www.fandm.edu/writing-center. Accessed 11 May 2021.
Article from an online database	Griffith, Robert. "The Selling of America: The Advertising Council and American Politics, 1942–1960." *The Business History Review*, vol. 57, no. 3, 1983, pp. 388–412. JSTOR, https://doi.org/10.2307/3114050.
Article in an online magazine	Epstein, David. "General Education Has a Bad Rap." *Slate*, 17 Apr. 2021, https://slate.com/human-interest/2021/04/vocational-training-general-education-debate-research-range-david-epstein.html.
Article in an online journal	Laine, Tarja. "Traumatic Horror Beyond the Edge: *It Follows* and *Get Out*." *Film-Philosophy*, vol. 22, no. 1, 2019, https://doi.org/10.3366/film.2019.0117.
Online interview	Browning, Sommer. Expanding Language with Sommer Browning. Peter McGraw, 26 Dec. 2018, https://petermcgraw.org/expanding-language-with-sommer-browning. Accessed 5 Jan. 2022.

Email	O'Brien, Kate. Email to Sam Hoffman. 1 Feb. 2021.
YouTube videos	"What Is Literature For?" YouTube, uploaded by The School of Life, 18 Sep. 2014, https://www.youtube.com/watch?v=4RCFLobfqcw.
Blog post	Mike H [Mike Howlett]. "Tried and True and Something New." *Hit Me With Your Nature Stick*, 24 Apr. 2021, https://hitmewithyournaturestick.blogspot.com/2021/04/tried-and-true-and-something-new-april.html.
Streaming television show (specific episode)	"Port in a Storm." Directed by Robert F. Colseberry. *The Wire*, Season 2, episode 12, HBO, 12 May 2021. *Netflix Video* app.
Painting (or other artwork) on the internet	Hassam, Childe. *At Dusk (Boston Common at Twilight)*. 1886. Boston Museum of Fine Arts. https://collections.mfa.org/objects/32415.
Photograph on the internet	Leifer, Neil. *Muhammad Ali vs. Sonny Liston*. 1965. "*Time* 100 Photos," http://100photos.time.com/photos/neil-leifer-muhammad-ali-sonny-liston.
Podcast	"When Brains Attack!" *Radiolab*, hosted by Jad Abumrad and Robert Krulwich, season 10, episode 9, 12 June 2012. https://www.wnycstudios.org/podcasts/radiolab/episodes/217555-when-brains-attack.

Critical Approaches to Literature

CRITICAL APPROACH			
Moral and Philosophical	**Biographical and Historical**	**Formalist and New Critical**	**Psychological** Psychoanalytic Freudian Jungian Lacanian
DESCRIPTION			
• Views literature as a medium for communicating moral and philosophical lessons • Sees art and literature as a reflection of the human experience: they must be interpreted in the context of their relationship to objective reality • Assumes that texts and ideas influence readers to think and behave in certain ways	• Interprets the text through the perspective of the author's background, views, and life • Looks at how biographical or historical events influenced the writing of the text • Investigates the specific "objective" historical events that are represented in the text • Sees art and literature as *mimetic*: they must be interpreted in the context of their relationship to objective reality	• Emphasizes the text itself rather than other factors like the author's intention • Focuses on how the parts of the work relate to other parts and contribute to the whole of the work, as well as to universal meaning • Explains how the form and structure of a poem, story, or play work to resolve its conflicts and tensions • Assumes the meaning exists in the text: the meaning cannot be fully summarized or paraphrased without the text	• Reads the text from the perspective of the prevailing theories of human behavior, consciousness, and cognition • Focuses on desire, repression, Oedipal conflict, and the "interpretation" of the unconscious (Freudian) • Analyzes the archetypal patterns and images in literature, which (for Jungians) manifest the primordial "collective unconscious" of all humanity (Jungian; see also archetypal criticism) • Sees the unconsciousness as structured like a language (a system of codes and meaning) (Lacanian)

CRITICAL APPROACH

Mythological and Archetypal	Deconstruction and Post-Structuralism	Materialist Marxist Cultural Studies New Historicist	Gender Feminist LGBTQ

DESCRIPTION

Mythological and Archetypal	Deconstruction and Post-Structuralism	Materialist	Gender
• Examines how a work reiterates or defies common patterns in literature, such as character types (e.g., the hero), settings (e.g., the innocent garden), story lines (e.g., the rite of passage), and motifs (e.g., water imagery for rebirth or fertility; see also Jungian criticism) • May integrate approaches from anthropology, linguistics, folklore, and other disciplines	• Analyzes a text to show how its contradictions and irreconcilable elements undermine its meaning • Focuses on the text, like formalism, but while formalist approaches find unity and meaning, deconstruction reveals the gap between what a text claims to say and what it actually says (see Formalism) • Asserts that there is no meaning prior to — or outside of — the text (and language itself) • Looks at how ostensibly "natural" binary oppositions (speech/writing, original/copy, presence/absence) collapse under close scrutiny	• Interprets a text from a political or economic standpoint, one usually focused on class structure and power relationships • Identifies the ideological function of a text — that is, its biases, assumptions, and role in reproducing a specific social order • Assumes the textuality of history, which means all texts — literary, historical, critical — are shaped by material and political circumstances by which to interpret texts (see also Deconstruction) • Remains skeptical of claims about "universal truth" • Challenges distinctions between "text" and "context," as well as "high" culture and "popular" culture: advertising, sports, social media memes — all are worthy of critical scrutiny	• Focuses on recuperating forgotten or marginalized texts by women writers • Analyzes texts for the ways they represent women, gender roles, and power relationships in the context of dominant patriarchal culture • Views sexuality and gender as socially constructed rather than innate • Challenges binary views of sex and gender (see also Deconstruction and Psychoanalytic Criticism)

Key Questions for Critical Approaches

CRITICAL APPROACH			
Moral and Philosophical	**Biographical and Historical**	**Formalist and New Critical**	**Psychological** Psychoanalytic Freudian Jungian Lacanian

KEY QUESTIONS			
• What philosophical or ethical issues and ideas does the text confront? • How does the text conform or rebel against the morals of its historical context? • What effect is the text likely to have on the thoughts and behaviors of the reader?	• What biographical facts has the author used in the text? • What events in the author's life impact the details of the text? • How do the historical events at the time of publication influence the text? • What historical events are depicted in the text? How are they presented?	• How is the work's structure unified? • How do various elements and patterns in the work reinforce its meaning? • How do the various elements interact to suggest a universal meaning? • How does the text resolve its ironies, tensions, and paradoxes?	• What is the nature of the internal conflicts within the characters of the text? • How do family conflicts shape character, narrative, and perspective? • How do desire and repression influence the text? • What are the recurring symbols and motifs of the text? • In what ways does the structure and organization of the text connect to (express, reflect, analogize) the operations of the mind?

CRITICAL APPROACH

Mythological and Archetypal	Deconstruction and Post-Structuralism	Materialist Marxist Cultural Studies New Historicist	Gender Feminist LGBTQ

KEY QUESTIONS

• What universal themes and experiences does the text represent? • Does the text suggest archetypal patterns? • What aspects of the work reflect myths? • How do stories from one culture correspond to those of another? • How do the archetypes within the work reveal a universal truth?	• How does the text express opposing and contradictory meanings? • What do contradictory or irreconcilable meanings in the text reveal about the limits of language as a medium of communication? • How does the text work against the apparent intention or purpose of the author? • What does the text disguise or conceal? • Where is the language of the text elusive and ambiguous?	• How is economic organization presented in the text? • Who has political or economic power within the text? • Does the balance of power shift within the narrative? Or does the text reinforce existing power structures? • What voices or perspectives are marginalized in the text? Why?	• How are women and gender roles portrayed? • How do these portrayals relate to the gender norms and conflicts of the text's era? • What elements in a text challenge women or feminine power? • Is a hierarchial society presented, and, if so, what is the significance? • How are the gender identities revealed in the text? • How does the text present sex and gender constructions?

Glossary of Literary Terms
Glosario de Términos Literarios

English	Español
A	
act A division of a play used to signal changes in time, setting, characters, mood, and other shifts during the course of a drama. *(p. 228)*	**acto** División de una obra teatral que se usa para señalar cambios de tiempo, ambientación, personajes, humor y otros cambios durante el curso del drama.
agency The autonomy given to literary characters that allows them to exert their will or make meaningful decisions in a play or story. *(p. 419)*	**albedrío** Autonomía que se da a los personajes literarios para que ejerzan su voluntad o tomen decisiones importantes en una obra teatral o historia.
allegory A story that uses a series of deliberately obvious symbols to represent abstract ideas and meanings. *(p. 711)*	**alegoría** Historia que contiene una serie de símbolos deliberadamente obvios para representar ideas y significados abstractos.
alliteration A repetition of consonant sounds at the beginning of consecutive or closely placed words in a text. *(p. 133)*	**aliteración** Repetición de sonidos consonantes al principio de palabras consecutivas o cercanas dentro de un texto.
allusion A reference to literature, culture, religion, or history that connects a writer's subject to a larger idea or broader context. *(p. 580)*	**alusión** Referencia literaria, cultural, religiosa o histórica que relaciona el tema del escritor con una idea más general o con un contexto más amplio.
ambiguity A word, phrase, action, or situation in a literary work that allows for two or more simultaneous interpretations supported by the text. *(p. 1158)*	**ambigüedad** Palabra, frase, acción o situación en una obra literaria que permite dos o más interpretaciones simultáneas apoyadas por el texto.
anachronism An object within a literary work that is out of place historically. *(p. 1250)*	**anacronismo** Un objeto de una obra literaria que está históricamente fuera de lugar.
analogy A comparison of two unrelated objects that reveals their shared qualities, often used to explain an unfamiliar subject or concept in terms that are more familiar to an audience. *(p. 1163)*	**analogía** Comparación de dos objetos no relacionados que revela sus cualidades comunes. Por lo general, se usa para explicar un tema o concepto poco conocido en términos que son más conocidos por la audiencia.
antagonist An individual or force that opposes the protagonist, represents contrasting values, and creates conflict in a story or drama; antagonists may be another character, a group, an internal struggle, or a force of nature. See PROTAGONIST. *(p. 419)*	**antagonista** Individuo o fuerza que se opone al protagonista, representa valores contrastantes y crea conflicto en un cuento o drama. El antagonista puede ser otro personaje, un grupo, una lucha interna o una fuerza de la naturaleza. Ver PROTAGONISTA.
antecedent action The events that have occurred prior to the beginning of a story or play. *(p. 133)*	**acción antecedente** Eventos que han ocurrido previamente desde el inicio de una historia u obra teatral.

antithesis The placement of two opposing ideas next to each other, often through parallel grammatical structure or other rhetorical techniques. See also JUXTAPOSITION. *(p. 1150)*

apostrophe A speech or passage in a literary work that's addressed either to an absent individual or to an inanimate object. *(p. 580)*

archetype A character, setting, object, theme, situation, or story line that occurs so frequently across cultures and time periods that it becomes a pattern and embodies a universal meaning. *(p. 452)*

aside A comment or speech uttered directly to the audience of a play, but unheard by other characters. *(p. 961)*

association A relationship between the reader and the text when the reader recognizes the connotations and implications of words or the figurative meaning of objects. *(p. 132)*

atmosphere A mood or emotional tone evoked by the description of the setting within a literary work. *(p. 437)*

attitude A narrator or speaker's feeling about a subject, character, setting, event, or other element within a literary work. See also TONE. *(p. 436)*

antítesis Colocación de dos ideas opuestas, una cerca de la otra, por lo general, mediante una estructura gramatical paralela u otra técnica retórica. Ver también YUXTAPOSICIÓN.

apóstrofe Discurso o pasaje de una obra literaria que se dirige a un individuo ausente o a un objeto inanimado.

arquetipo Personaje, escenario, objeto, tema, situación o trama que ocurre con tanta frecuencia en diversas culturas y períodos de tiempo que se convierte en patrón y adquiere un significado universal.

acotaciones Comentario o discurso expresado directamente a la audiencia de una obra teatral, pero que no escuchan los personajes.

asociación Relación entre el lector y el texto cuando el lector reconoce las connotaciones y las implicaciones de las palabras o el significado figurativo de los objetos.

atmósfera Tono humorístico o emotivo evocado por la descripción de una ambientación dentro de una obra literaria.

actitud Opinión que tiene el narrador o hablante sobre un tema, personaje, ambientación, evento u otro elemento dentro de una obra literaria. Ver también TONO.

B

bias The assumptions, attitudes, values, and other (often unexamined) factors that shape a character's perspective. *(p. 118)*

sesgo Supuestos, actitudes, valores y otros factores (por lo general, no examinados) que le dan forma a la perspectiva de un personaje.

C

caesura A rest or pause within a line of poetry, often marked by punctuation such as a comma or a dash. *(p. 567)*

catharsis The intense release of emotion (often pity or fear) evoked in the audience by a narrative or play. *(p. 692)*

character A person, group, or force that acts and speaks in a narrative or play; a character may also represent ideas, values, assumptions, and cultural norms. *(p. 4)*

characterization An author's use of speech, action, narrative, and description to establish a character's values, beliefs, and identity. *(p. 4)*

cesura Descanso o pausa en un verso poético, marcado por lo general con un signo de puntuación, como una coma o un guion.

catarsis Liberación intensa de emociones (por lo general, lástima o miedo) que produce en la audiencia una obra narrativa u de teatro.

personaje Persona, grupo o fuerza que actúa y habla en una obra narrativa o de teatro. El personaje también puede representar ideas, valores, supuestos y normas culturales.

caracterización Cuando un autor usa un discurso, acción, narración o descripción para establecer los valores, creencias e identidad de un personaje.

chorus A set of characters in a classical tragedy who comment on the action of the play and help the audience understand the characters and plot, as well as provide background on the play's wider moral and social context. *(p. 1271)*

coro Conjunto de personajes en una tragedia clásica, que comenta lo sucedido en la obra y ayuda a la audiencia a entender los personajes y la trama. Además, enmarca la obra en un contexto moral y social más amplio.

circumstance The cultural, historical, and social settings in which characters find themselves. *(p. 218)*

circunstancia La ambientación cultural, histórica y social en la cual se encuentran los personajes.

clause A group of words with a related subject and verb; the phrase may stand alone (as an *independent* clause), or it can establish a subordinate relationship in a complex sentence (*subordinate* or *dependent* clause). *(p. 702)*

cláusula Grupo de palabras con un sujeto y un verbo relacionados; puede ser una frase independiente (como una cláusula independiente) o puede establecer una relación subordinada en una oración compleja (cláusula subordinada o dependiente).

climax The section of a plot that produces the strongest emotional tension and serves as the main turning point in the story or play. *(p. 29)*

clímax Sección de una trama que produce la mayor tensión emocional y sirve como el principal punto de inflexión en la historia o la obra de teatro.

closed form A poetic structure that follows an established convention of lines, meter, rhymes, and stanzas (such as the sonnet, the villanelle, and the haiku). *(p. 567)*

forma cerrada Estructura poética que sigue una convención establecida de versos, métrica, rima y estrofas (como el soneto, el villanelle y el haiku).

comparison A literary and rhetorical device that uses similarities between people, places, things, and/or ideas to help the reader recognize figurative meaning or an abstract concept. See METAPHOR and SIMILE. *(p. 139)*

comparación Recurso literario o retórico que usa las similitudes entre personas, lugares, cosas y/o ideas para ayudar al lector a reconocer un significado figurativo o un concepto abstracto. Ver METÁFORA y SÍMIL.

complexity The ambiguous, inconsistent, or contradictory aspects of a character, theme, or other literary element that suggest layered meanings and multiple interpretations. *(p. 685)*

complejidad Aspectos ambiguos, inconsistentes o contradictorios de un personaje, tema u otro elemento literario que sugieren significados escondidos y múltiples interpretaciones.

conceit An extended metaphor that compares or contrasts images, concepts, and associations in surprising, elaborate, and paradoxical ways. *(p. 1164)*

alegoría Metáfora continuada que compara o contrasta imágenes, conceptos y asociaciones de maneras sorpresivas, elaboradas y paradójicas.

conflict The problem, question, opposition, or tension in a play or story that the protagonist faces. See also ANTAGONIST and PROTAGONIST. *(p. 228)*

conflicto Problema, pregunta, oposición o tensión en una obra teatral o historia que enfrenta el protagonista. Ver también ANTAGONISTA y PROTAGONISTA.

connotation The sensory, emotional, and cultural associations of a word that imply meanings beyond its literal definition. See DENOTATION. *(p. 573)*

connotación Asociaciones sensoriales, emocionales y culturales de una palabra, que implican significados más allá de su definición literal. Ver DENOTACIÓN.

context The social, historical, or cultural circumstances that shape a literary work's creation or provide background to the setting of a play or story. *(p. 218)*

contexto Circunstancias sociales, históricas o culturales que le dan forma a la creación de una obra literaria o que proveen los antecedentes de la ambientación de una obra teatral o historia.

contrast The opposition of two literary elements or events of plot, usually presented to highlight the differences between them. *(p. 567)*

contraste Oposición de dos elementos literarios o eventos de la trama, que generalmente se presentan para resaltar las diferencias entre ellos.

convention An element, aspect, or technique used so frequently that it becomes a defining and identifiable feature of the genre. *(p. 567)*

convención Elemento, aspecto o técnica que se usa con tal frecuencia que se convierte en un rasgo definitorio e identificable del género.

couplet Two successive lines (usually the same length) that rhyme in poetry. *(p. 567)*	**copla** Dos versos sucesivos (por lo general, de la misma longitud) que riman en poesía.
cultural context The artistic and popular interests, customs, of a story's setting. *(p. 218)*	**contexto cultural** Intereses y costumbres artísticos y populares de la ambientación de una historia.

D

denotation The dictionary definition or literal meaning of a word. See also CONNOTATION. *(p. 573)*	**denotación** Definición del diccionario o significado literal de una palabra. Ver también CONNOTACIÓN.
description The details and sensory language used to depict the writer's subject in the reader's mind. *(p. 5)*	**descripción** Detalles y lenguaje sensorial que se usa para describir el tema del escritor en la mente de lector.
detail A specific piece of information about a character, setting, plot, or narrator that provides insight into that element. *(p. 4)*	**detalle** Información específica que amplía el conocimiento de un personaje, ambiente, trama o narrador.
deus ex machina "God from the machine" (literally), an unexpected, unlikely, or implausible incident that resolves a story's conflict, often viewed as the sign of a poorly constructed plot. *(p. 961)*	**deus ex machina** "Dios a partir de una máquina" (literalmente), incidente inesperado o improbable que resuelve el conflicto de la historia. Por lo general, es visto como señal de una trama mal armada.
dialect The distinctive vocabulary, pronunciation, and speech patterns of a specific community, region, or other group.	**dialecto** Vocabulario, pronunciación y patrones del habla particulares de una comunidad, región o grupo específico.
dialogue Conversations between two or more characters in a play or narrative; these exchanges reveal how characters think, feel, and interact. *(p. 5)*	**diálogo** Conversaciones entre dos o más personajes en una obra teatral o narrativa. Estos intercambios revelan cómo piensan, sienten e interactúan los personajes.
diction The vocabulary and specific word choices of an author or poet. *(p. 701)*	**dicción** Vocabulario específico que escoge un autor o poeta.
dramatic irony A moment in a play or novel when the audience understands more about the characters' situations than the characters themselves. See IRONY. *(p. 685)*	**ironía dramática** Momento en una obra teatral o novela en la que la audiencia entiende más sobre la situación de los personajes que los mismos personajes. Ver IRONÍA.
dramatic situation The problem, conflict, or tension resulting from the arrangement of events in narrative. *(p. 29)*	**situación dramática** El problema, conflicto o tensión que resulta del orden de eventos en la narración.
dynamic character A character who develops or changes perspective over the course of a narrative or drama (see EPIPHANY). *(p. 211)*	**personaje dinámico** Personaje que se desarrolla o cambia de perspectiva a lo largo de la narración o drama (Ver EPIFANÍA).

E

empathy The reader's or audience's emotional identification with a character in a story. *(p. 1241)*	**empatía** Identificación emocional del lector o de la audiencia con un personaje de la historia.
epiphany A moment in a story or drama when a character receives sudden insight or clarity; this new realization often changes the meaning of the work or presents the work in a new light. *(p. 928)*	**epifanía** Momento en una historia o drama en el que un personaje se dé cuenta de algo repentinamente. Esta situación por lo general cambia el significado de la obra o la presenta bajo una nueva luz.

episode A brief event that is part of a larger sequence of scenes in a play or story. *(p. 228)*

episodio Breve evento que es parte de una secuencia más larga de escenas de la obra teatral o historia.

exaggeration A figurative overstatement, often to amplify or minimize. See HYPERBOLE. *(p. 574)*

exageración Magnificación figurativa, por lo general, para amplificar o minimizar. Ver HIPÉRBOLE.

exposition The part of narrative's plot when the characters and setting are introduced. *(p. 29)*

exposición La parte de la trama de una narración en la cual se presentan los personajes y el escenario.

extended metaphor A comparison of two unrelated things that focus on traits, qualities, or characteristics throughout a text. See CONCEIT and METAPHOR. *(p. 579)*

metáfora extendida Comparación de dos cosas sin relación, que se enfoca en rasgos, cualidades, y características a lo largo de un texto. Ver ALEGORÍA y METÁFORA.

external conflict The tensions between a literary character and another character, a group, or other outside force. See CONFLICT. *(p. 229)*

conflicto externo Tensiones entre un personaje literario y otro personaje, grupo o fuerza externa. Ver CONFLICTO.

F

falling action The section of a narrative or drama that occurs after the climax and leads to the resolution of the plot. *(p. 29)*

desenlace Sección de una narración o drama que ocurre después del clímax y que lleva a la resolución de la trama.

figurative language A comparison or association (e.g., analogy, symbol, metaphor, simile, personification) that draws upon concrete objects to represent abstract ideas. *(p. 132)*

lenguaje figurativo Comparación o asociación (p.ej., analogía, símbolo, metáfora, símil, personificación) que hace uso de los objetos concretos para representar ideas abstractas.

first-person point of view A technique in which the narrator uses "I" and presents the story from his or her perspective; these narrators only have knowledge from that subjective frame of reference. See POINT OF VIEW. *(p. 40)*

punto de vista de primera persona Técnica en la que el narrador usa "Yo" y presenta la historia desde su perspectiva. Estos narradores solo están conscientes de ese marco de referencia subjetivo. Ver PUNTO DE VISTA.

flashback A structural element of a narrative that interrupts linear chronological time to show readers events that happened in the past. *(p. 691)*

evocación Elemento estructural de una narración que interrumpe el tiempo cronológico lineal para mostrar a los lectores eventos que sucedieron en el pasado.

foil A character contrasts with another character (especially a protagonist) to highlight their opposing qualities and distinctions. *(p. 684)*

contraparte Personaje que se contrasta con otro personaje (sobre todo el protagonista) para poner de relieve sus diferencias o cualidades opuestas.

foreshadowing A narrative structure that provides hints and clues about events that are yet to occur in the story. *(p. 691)*

presagio Recurso narrativo que ofrece pistas sobre eventos que aún están por ocurrir en la historia.

form The shape, structure, and arrangement of a poem or other work. *(p. 567)*

forma Estructura y organización de un poema u otra obra.

frame story A narrative in which another narrative is embedded; the tale (or tales) within the wider story often highlight the act of storytelling itself, while the frame provides context or ironic distance. *(p. 961)*

historia marco Narración que contiene otra narración. El cuento (o cuentos) dentro de la historia más general suele poner de relieve el acto mismo de contar un cuento, mientras que el marco ofrece contexto o distancia irónica.

G

genre A type, classification, or category of literature, such as drama, fiction, and poetry.

género Tipo, clasificación o categoría de literatura, como drama, ficción y poesía.

goal A character's objective during the course of a narrative. *(p. 5)*

meta Objetivo del personaje durante el curso de la narración.

group character A collection of people who function as a single character within a narrative or drama (e.g., chorus, community, society, or organization). *(p. 1271)*

personaje grupal Conjunto de personas que se desempeñan como un solo personaje dentro de la narración o drama (p.ej., coro, comunidad, sociedad u organización).

H

hamartia A Greek term that refers to a tragic hero's blind spot, weakness, or error in judgment. See TRAGIC FLAW. *(p. 929)*

hamartia Término griego que se refiere al punto débil, debilidad o error de juicio del héroe trágico. Ver ERROR TRÁGICO.

historical context The circumstances specifically including the historical events and background occurring at the time a story is set. *(p. 218)*

contexto histórico Las circunstancias, que incluyen específicamente eventos históricos y contexto, en el momento en que se lleva a cabo una historia.

hyperbole An exaggerated comparison to emphasize the similarity or difference of a particular trait or aspect of what is being compared. See EXAGGERATION. *(p. 574)*

hipérbole Comparación exagerada para resaltar la similitud o diferencia de un rasgo particular de lo que se está comparando. Ver EXAGERACIÓN.

I

idea An abstract concept or thought that—in literature—often captures an aspect of the human experience. *(p. 4)*

idea Concepto o pensamiento abstracto que (en literatura) representa con frecuencia un aspecto de la vivencia humana.

image A literary device that appeals to the reader's senses and sensory experiences, especially the creation of visual pictures in the minds of the audience. See IMAGERY. *(p. 574)*

imagen Recurso literario que apela a los sentidos y a las experiencias sensoriales del lector, sobre todo al crear descripciones visuales en las mentes de quienes conforman la audiencia. Ver IMAGINERÍA.

imagery A collection of sensory images (e.g., visual images, sounds, tastes, smells, or tactile/touch images) in a literary work. See IMAGE. *(p. 574)*

imaginería Conjunto de imágenes sensoriales (p.ej., imágenes visuales, auditivas, de gusto, olfativas o táctiles) en una obra literaria. Ver IMAGEN.

in medias res A narrative structure that begins by placing the reader or audience in the middle of the story, rather than at the chronological beginning. *(p. 691)*

in medias res Estructura literaria que comienza colocando al lector o a la audiencia en medio de la historia y no en el inicio cronológico.

incongruity An often deliberate inconsistency in a literary work that juxtaposes unrelated ideas, events, or circumstances; they usually subvert, clash with, or otherwise unsettle the audience's expectations. See IRONY and JUXTAPOSITION. *(p. 1149)*

incongruencia Inconsistencia por lo general deliberada en una obra literaria que yuxtapone ideas, eventos o circunstancias no relacionadas. Por lo general, estas subvierten, chocan con o perturban las expectativas de la audiencia. Ver IRONÍA y YUXTAPOSICIÓN.

inconsistency A contradiction within the dramatic situation, such as irony or incongruity, that contributes to a tension or complexity. *(p. 229)*

inconsistencia Contradicción dentro de la situación dramática, como una ironía o incongruencia, que aporta una mayor tensión o complejidad.

internal conflict A literary character's struggle with psychological, emotional, moral, or other conflict within the character's mind. See CONFLICT. *(p. 229)*

conflicto interno Lucha psicológica, emocional, moral o de otro tipo dentro de la mente del personaje literario. Ver CONFLICTO.

intertextuality A relationship between texts, in which one text responds to another literary work. *(p. 580)*

intertextualidad Relación entre textos en la que un texto responde a otra obra literaria.

invisible character An unseen character who remains literally and physically absent from a literary text but whose influence is significant to the narrative. *(p. 1250)*

personaje invisible Personaje que no se ve y que permanece literal y físicamente ausente del texto literario, pero cuya influencia es importante en la narración.

irony A literary device in which a word, statement, or situation takes on a different meaning from its apparent meaning, or departs from expectations (often surprisingly). See also DRAMATIC IRONY, SITUATIONAL IRONY, and VERBAL IRONY. *(p. 1149)*

ironía Recurso literario en el que una palabra, enunciado o situación adquiere un significado diferente de su significado aparente; o que se aleja de las expectativas (por lo general, de manera sorpresiva). Ver también IRONÍA DRAMÁTICA, IRONÍA SITUACIONAL e IRONÍA VERBAL.

J

juxtaposition A literary technique that places two people, events, or places side by side to compare, contrast, or illuminate the relationship between them. *(p. 126)*

yuxtaposición Técnica literaria que pone dos personas, eventos o lugares uno junto al otro para comparar, contrastar o iluminar la relación entre ellos.

L

limited third-person point of view A narrative technique in which the narrator shares the perceptions, thoughts, and vantage point of one character, while the inner lives of other characters remain inaccessible. See POINT OF VIEW. *(p. 41)*

punto de vista de tercera persona limitada Técnica narrativa en la que el narrador comunica sus percepciones, pensamientos y el punto de vista ventajoso de un personaje, mientras que la vida interior de los demás personajes permanece inaccesible. Ver PUNTO DE VISTA.

literal The understanding of words, characters, and events in their most basic and denotative sense. See FIGURATIVE LANGUAGE. *(p. 4)*

literal Comprensión de palabras, personajes y eventos en su sentido más básico y denotativo. Ver LENGUAJE FIGURADO.

M

message An author's perspective about universal concepts, which create meaning in a narrative, play, or poem. See THEME. *(p. 28)*

mensaje Perspectiva del autor en cuanto a los conceptos universales, que le da sentido a la narración, obra teatral o poema. Ver también TEMA.

metaphor A comparison of two unrelated objects that assigns ideas to their points of comparison. *(p. 140)*

metáfora Comparación de dos objetos no relacionados que asigna ideas a sus puntos de comparación.

meter A rhythm that repeats in a pattern of verse based on the number of syllables and their emphasis within a line. *(p. 567)*

métrica Ritmo que se repite en el patrón de los versos según el número de sílabas y énfasis en un verso.

minor character A character who fulfills a supporting role within a narrative or drama; in many cases a *static* rather than *dynamic* character. *(p. 1240)*

personaje secundario Personaje que cumple un papel de apoyo en una narración o drama. En muchos casos, es más un personaje estático que dinámico.

moment A single, significant part of a narrative's plot that is important to the dramatic situation. *(p. 229)*	**momento** Una parte significante de una trama narrativa que es importante en la situación dramática.
mood The general feeling evoked in the reader by the word choice, descriptions, and other elements of a literary work. *(p. 437)*	**estado de ánimo** Sentimiento general evocado en el lector por selección de palabras, descripciones y otros elementos de una obra literaria.
motif A pattern of related images, metaphors, and objects that conveys a significant idea in a text. *(p. 574)*	**motivo** Patrón de imágenes, metáforas y objetos relacionados que transmite una idea significativa en un texto.
motivation The inner wants, needs, values, or other factors that drive the actions of characters within a narrative. *(p. 6)*	**motivación** Intereses, necesidades y otros factores internos que impulsan las acciones de los personajes en una narración.

N

narration A writer's way of telling a story to convey a message. *(p. 49)*	**narración** Manera en que el escritor cuenta una historia para expresar un mensaje.
narrative arc The structure of a narrative in which conflict creates a plot, leading to a climax and an ending with a resolution. *(p. 28)*	**arco narrativo** Estructura de una narración en la que el conflicto crea una trama y lleva al clímax y al final.
narrative distance The physical distance, chronological distance, relationships, or emotional investment of the narrator to the events or characters of the narrative. *(p. 473)*	**distancia narrativa** Distancia física, distancia cronológica, relaciones o nivel de inversión emocional del narrador en los eventos o personajes de la narrativa.
narrative hook The part of a narrative's plot when the problem or conflict begins. *(p. 29)*	**gancho narrativo** Punto de la trama de la narración donde comienza el problema o conflicto.
narrative pacing An author's choices of order and tempo to reveal the events of story's plot. *(p. 692)*	**ritmo narrativo** Las decisiones del autor respecto al orden y el ritmo según los cuales revelará los sucesos de la trama de la historia.
narrative perspective The lens through which a narrator perceives and presents the characters, setting, and events of a story, influenced by the narrator's background, experiences, values, attitudes, and narrative distance. *(p. 40)*	**perspectiva narrativa** Lente a través de la cual el narrador percibe y presenta los personajes, la ambientación y los eventos de una historia; influida por el contexto, las experiencias, los valores, las actitudes y la distancia narrativa del narrador.
narrative technique The devices, methods, and strategies used by an author to tell a story. *(p. 186)*	**técnica narrativa** Recursos, métodos y estrategias que usa el autor para contar una historia.
narrator A character or person who directly addresses readers and either recalls events or describes them as they occur, relates a story to the reader, and builds connections between the reader and the text. In poetry, the narrator is referred to as the speaker. *(p. 40)*	**narrador** Personaje o persona que se dirige a los lectores y recrea sucesos o los describe a medida que ocurren, relata una historia para el lector y hace conexiones entre el lector y el texto. En la poesía, el narrador se conoce como el hablante.
nonlinear structure A narrative, drama, or poem that does not follow a linear, chronological sequence; it may incorporate flashbacks, stream of consciousness, and other techniques to develop the story. *(p. 692)*	**estructura no lineal** Narración, drama o poema que no sigue una secuencia cronológica lineal; puede incluir evocaciones, flujos de conciencia y otras técnicas para desarrollar la historia.

O

omniscient narrator A narrative technique in which the narrator who is not bound by space and time relates the thoughts and experiences of all of the characters. *(p. 41)*

narrador omnisciente Técnica narrativa en la cual el narrador no está limitado por el tiempo o el espacio y relata los pensamientos y experiencias de todos los personajes.

onomatopoeia Words that sound like the object or action they denote, and reflect their own meaning.

onomatopeya Palabras que suenan como el objeto o la acción que denotan y que reflejan su propio significado.

open form A poem or verse that does not follow established patterns of lines, meter, rhyme, and stanzas (e.g., concrete poetry, free verse). *(p. 567)*

forma abierta Poema o verso que no sigue patrones establecidos de versos, métrica, rima y estrofas (p.ej., poesía concreta, verso libre).

oxymoron A figure of speech that combines contradictory, self-canceling elements to create emphasis, paradox, or complex meaning. *(p. 1150)*

contrasentido Figura del habla que combina elementos contradictorios que se contrapesan para hacer énfasis, generar paradojas o generar un significado más complejo.

P

pacing See NARRATIVE PACING. *(p. 961)*

ritmo Ver RITMO NARRATIVO.

paradox A seemingly contradictory statement that reveals complexity, insight, or a truth. *(p. 1151)*

paradoja Un enunciado aparentemente contradictorio que revela complejidad, un nuevo ángulo o una verdad.

pathetic fallacy A narrative technique that draws upon external events or circumstances to reflect the psychological state of a character. *(p. 436)*

falacia patética Técnica narrativa que recurre a circunstancias o eventos externos para reflejar el estado psicológico de un personaje.

pathos An audience's emotional response to a poem, story, or play that is elicited by the author's choices. *(p. 692)*

pathos Respuesta emocional de la audiencia ante un poema, historia u obra teatral, que es producida por las elecciones del autor.

persona An invented voice, perspective, or character that an author uses to narrate a story or poem. *(p. 976)*

persona Voz, perspectiva o personaje inventado que usa el autor para narrar una historia o poema.

personification Figurative device that gives human qualities to inanimate or nonhuman objects, places, and concepts. *(p. 580)*

personificación Recurso figurativo que atribuye cualidades humanas a objetos inanimados o no humanos, lugares y conceptos.

perspective The lens through which a person makes sense of their experiences and circumstances. *(p. 5)*

perspectiva Lente a través de la cual la persona le da sentido a sus experiencias y circunstancias.

phrase A group of words that function as a meaningful part of a sentence or clause. *(p. 702)*

frase Grupo de palabras que funcionan como una parte con sentido de una oración o cláusula.

plot The series of events in a narrative revolving around a conflict or dramatic situation. See NARRATIVE ARC. *(p. 28)*

trama Serie de eventos en una narración que giran alrededor de un conflicto o situación dramática. Ver ARCO NARRATIVO.

point of view The position from which the narrator or speaker relates the narrative; it refers to both who is telling the story and the narrator's degree of involvement in the story. See FIRST-PERSON POINT OF VIEW, THIRD-PERSON LIMITED OMNISCIENT, THIRD-PERSON OMNISCIENT, and SECOND-PERSON POINT OF VIEW. *(p. 40)*

punto de vista Posición desde la cual el narrador o hablante relata su narración. Se refiere tanto a quién cuenta la historia y el nivel de involucramiento del narrador en la historia. Ver también PRIMERA PERSONA, TERCERA PERSONA OMNISCIENTE LIMITADA, TERCERA PERSONA OMNISCIENTE y SEGUNDA PERSONA.

pronoun A word that replaces a previously identified noun, noun phrase, or pronoun within a sentence. *(p. 132)*

pronombre Palabra que reemplaza un sustantivo, una frase o un pronombre anteriormente identificado en una oración.

prosopopoeia A literary device that attributes speech and action to an animal, an abstraction, an imagined person, or an inanimate object. *(p. 1016)*

prosopopeya Recurso literario que le atribuye habla y acción a un animal, a una abstracción, a una persona imaginada o a un objeto inanimado.

protagonist The main character in a narrative (often the "hero") who may also represent a value or belief. *(p. 419)*

protagonista Persona principal de una narración (por lo general, el "héroe"), que también puede representar un valor o creencia.

pun Words that play on the similar (or identical) sounds of words with different meanings to create humor, ambiguity, and insight. *(p. 574)*

juego de palabras Figura del habla que consiste en usar palabras que suenan parecido (o igual) pero que tienen diferentes significados con el fin de crear humor, ambigüedad o explicar algo.

R

referent The person, place, thing, concept, or action that a word denotes or stands for. *(p. 132)*

referente Persona, lugar, cosa, concepto o acción denotada o representada por una palabra.

refrain A recurring or repeating words, sounds, phrases, clauses, or lines in texts to create emphasis or to suggest associations. *(p. 133)*

estribillo Palabras, sonidos, frases, cláusulas o líneas repetitivas o recurrentes en un texto con el fin de crear énfasis o sugerir asociaciones.

reliability The narrator's motives, credibility, and biases (or lack thereof) that readers use to determine the credibility and accuracy of a narrative. *(p. 702)*

confiabilidad Motivos, credibilidad y sesgos (o falta de sesgos) del narrador, que los lectores usan para determinar la credibilidad y precisión de una narración.

reliable narrator A credible, trustworthy, and consistent storyteller. *(p. 702)*

narrador confiable Contador de historias creíble, confiable y coherente.

repetition The deliberate and repeated use of a word, phrase, sentence, or other element to create emphasis or another effect. *(p. 133)*

repetición Uso repetido y deliberado de una palabra, frase, oración u otro elemento para hacer énfasis o crear otro efecto.

resolution The section of the plot where the conflict is solved and important questions are answered. *(p. 29)*

resolución Sección de la trama en la que se resuelve el conflicto y se despejan preguntas importantes.

rhyme A literary technique in which different words with identical or similar concluding syllable sounds are repeated, usually at the end of poetic lines. *(p. 567)*

rima Recurso literario en el que diferentes palabras con sonidos vocálicos finales idénticos o parecidos se repiten, por lo general, al final de los versos poéticos.

rhyme scheme The pattern or order in which end rhyming sounds occur in a poem, often determined by the poetic form. *(p. 567)*

esquema rítmico Patrón u orden en el que ocurren los sonidos que riman al final de un poema. Por lo general, vienen determinados por la forma poética.

rhythm A regular or repeated pattern of sound in poetry — especially regarding the sequence of stressed and unstressed syllables of words. *(p. 567)*

ritmo Patrón de sonido regular o repetido en la poesía, sobre todo en la secuencia de sílabas acentuadas y no acentuadas de las palabras.

rising action The section of a plot that builds suspense and leads to a climax. *(p. 29)*

tensión dramática creciente Sección de la trama que genera suspenso y lleva al clímax.

S

scene A section of an act in dramatic literature in which characters speak or perform an action. *(p. 228)*

escena Sección de un acto en la literatura dramática en la que los personajes hablan o realizan una acción.

second-person point of view A narrative technique in which the narrator addresses the audience as "you," and the reader becomes a character in the story. *(p. 41)*

punto de vista de segunda persona Técnica narrativa en la que el autor se dirige de "tú" a la audiencia y el lector se convierte en un personaje de la historia.

setting The time and place during which a story takes place, which includes historical, social, and cultural context. *(p. 16)*

ambientación Tiempo y lugar en el que sucede una historia; incluye el contexto histórico, social y cultural.

shift A change in character's thinking, insight, or another literary choice that creates an emphasis or reveals an insight. *(p. 125)*

cambio Cambio en el pensamiento, perspectiva u otra decisión literaria que enfatiza o revela una perspectiva.

simile A comparison that uses words such as "like" or "as" to make an explicit comparison between two objects or concepts. *(p. 140)*

símil Comparación que usa palabras como "como" o "cual" para explicitar una comparación entre dos objetos o conceptos.

situational irony A moment in a narrative or drama when events defy reader expectations or have the opposite of their intended effect. See IRONY. *(p. 1150)*

ironía situacional Momento en la narración o drama en el que los eventos desafían las expectativas del lector o tienen un efecto opuesto al esperado. Ver IRONÍA.

social context The circumstances including what people believe and how they live at the time the story is set. *(p. 218)*

contexto social Circunstancias, como lo que la gente cree y cómo vive, en el momento que se lleva a cabo la historia.

sound The aural quality of words, phrases, and pauses that allow readers to hear a text. *(p. 576)*

sonido Calidad auditiva de las palabras, frases y pauses que les permite a los lectores escuchar un texto.

speaker The voice that narrates a poem and builds connections between the reader and the text. *(p. 40)*

hablante Voz que narra un poema y genera conexiones entre el lector y el texto.

stage directions The playwright's guidelines for stage props, character movement, set design, sound effects, and other nonspoken information within a play.

instrucciones escénicas Instrucciones el dramaturgo relacionadas con la utilería, el movimiento del personaje, el diseño de la escenografía, los efectos de sonido y otra información no hablada dentro de la obra teatral.

stanza A group of lines in a poem set apart from other lines and groups by spacing or indentation. *(p. 125)*

estrofa Grupo de versos de un poema que se separan de otros versos y grupos con un espacio o sangría.

static character A character who remains unchanged within a narrative or drama. *(p. 211)*

personaje estático Personaje que no cambia dentro de la narración o drama.

stock character A standard character type that is easily recognizable to readers of a particular literary genre. *(p. 685)*

personaje estereotípico Tipo de personaje estándar que es fácil de reconocer por los lectores de un género literario en particular.

stream of consciousness A narrative technique that communicates a character's interior thoughts, feelings, sensations, and associations in a continuous flow without regard for logic or formal structure. *(p. 473)*

flujo de conciencia Técnica para contar historias que comunica los pensamientos, sentimientos, sensaciones y asociaciones del personaje como un flujo continuo sin tomar en cuenta la lógica o la estructura formal.

structure The author's basic organization of character, theme, plot, and narrative arc within a story or drama. *(p. 29)*

estructura Organización básica del autor en cuanto a personaje, tema, trama y arco narrativo dentro de la historia o drama.

suspense A feeling of tension and delayed expectation created in a reader by the events leading to a story's climax. *(p. 961)*

suspenso Sentimiento de tensión y expectativas retrasadas que crean en el lector los eventos que llevan al clímax de una historia.

suspension of disbelief The willingness of readers to suppress their critical or logical faculties and become emotionally engaged with fictional characters and situations. *(p. 692)*

suspensión de creencia Voluntad de los lectores de suprimir sus facultades críticas y lógicas y de involucrarse emocionalmente con personajes y situaciones ficticios.

symbol A concrete object in a text that represents a value, idea, or other abstract concept. *(p. 710)*

símbolo Objeto concreto en un texto, que representa un valor, una idea u otro concepto abstracto.

synonym A word or phrase that means exactly or nearly the same as another word or phrase. *(p. 133)*

sinónimo Palabra o frase que significa exactamente o casi lo mismo que otra palabra o frase.

syntax The arrangement of words, phrases, and clauses in a sentence. *(p. 702)*

sintaxis Organización de las palabras, las frases y las cláusulas de una oración.

T

tension A component of a dramatic situation that present a struggle or conflict of values or ideas resulting from a dilemma choice, or competing circumstances. *(p. 29)*

tensión Componente de una situación dramática que presenta una lucha o conflicto de valores o ideas que resultan de un dilema o de circunstancias en competencia.

theme An author's underlying idea and insight about the human condition revealed through a literary text, separate from "plot." *(p. 92)*

tema Idea de fondo o situación sobre la condición humana que el autor revela a través de un texto literario; no es lo mismo que la trama.

third-person point of view A narrative technique in which the narrator is an unknown voice outside the story rather than a character who participates in the story. See OMNISCIENT NARRATOR and POINT OF VIEW. *(p. 40)*

punto de vista de tercera persona Técnica narrativa en la que el narrador es una voz desconocida fuera de la historia en ves de un personaje que participa en la historia. Ver también NARRADOR OMNISCIENTE y PUNTO DE VISTA.

tone The attitude of the author, narrator, or speaker toward the subject, characters, or setting of a literary work, as revealed through diction, syntax, and other stylistic choices. *(p. 473)*

tono Actitud del autor, narrador o hablante hacia el tema, los personajes o la ambientación de una obra literaria. Esta se revela en la dicción, la sintaxis y otros elementos estilísticos.

tragic flaw A blind spot, weakness, or error in judgment that causes the downfall of a tragic hero. See HAMARTIA. *(p. 929)*

error trágico Punto ciego, debilidad o error de juicio que produce la caída del héroe dramático. Ver también HAMARTIA.

tragic hero A protagonist in a tragedy who brings about his or her own destruction (and the destruction of others) because of a personal weakness, blind spot, or error in judgment. *(p. 929)*

héroe trágico Protagonista de una tragedia, que produce su propia destrucción (y la destrucción de los demás) debido a una debilidad, un punto ciego o un error de juicio.

U

understatement A figure of speech that deliberately minimizes the importance, magnitude, or effect of something; the opposite of EXAGGERATION and HYPERBOLE. *(p. 575)*

subestimación Figura del habla que minimiza deliberadamente la importancia, la magnitud o el efecto de algo. Es lo opuesto de la EXAGERACIÓN y la HIPÉRBOLE.

unity The unifying or controlling idea that a text revolves around. *(p. 540)*

unidad Idea unificadora o controladora alrededor de la cual gira un texto.

unreliable narrator A storyteller who lacks credibility because of bias, deception, inexperience, cognitive impairment, lack of information, or other factor that undermines the accuracy of a narrative. *(p. 975)*

narrador no confiable Un contador de historias que carece de credibilidad debido a algún sesgo, decepción, inexperiencia, incapacidad cognitiva, falta de información u otro factor que socava la precisión de la narración.

unresolved ending A type of plot structure where the conflict is not solved, leaving the reader to determine the ending or allowing for the story to continue. *(p. 29)*

final sin resolución Tipo de estructura de trama donde el conflicto no se resuelve, de tal manera que el lector determina si es el final o si permite que la historia continúe.

V

values An idea, attitude, or belief about the human condition, often illustrated by a character or setting in a literary work. *(p. 4)*

valor Idea, actitud o creencia sobre la condición humana ilustrada por lo general por un personaje o ambientación de una obra literaria.

verbal irony A figure of speech in which a person says one thing but means another thing, or even communicates the opposite of the words' surface meaning. *(p. 150)*

ironía verbal Figura del habla en la que una persona dice una cosa, pero quiere decir otra, o que comunica el opuesto del significado superficial de las palabras.

verisimilitude The semblance of truth, reality, or authenticity of a literary work.

verosimilitud Autenticidad o parecido que tiene una obra literaria con la verdad o la realidad.

W

word choice The decisions an author makes when determining the language and usage of words. See DICTION. *(p. 132)*

elección de palabras Las decisiones que toma un autor al determinar el lenguaje y uso de palabras. Ver DICCIÓN.

Acknowledgments

Teresa Palomo Acosta, "My Mother Pieced Quilts." Copyright © 1976 by Teresa Palomo Acosta. Used with permission. All rights reserved.

Chimamanda Ngozi Adichie, "Cell One" from THE THING AROUND YOUR NECK by Chimamanda Ngozi Adichie, Copyright © 2009 Chimamanda Ngozi Adichie. Reprinted by permission of Vintage Canada/Alfred A. Knopf Canada, a division of Penguin Random House Canada Limited and by permission of The Wylie Agency LLC. All rights reserved.

W. H. Auden. "The Unknown Citizen" from *Collected Poems* by W. H. Auden. Copyright © 1940 and renewed 1968 by W. H. Auden. Used by permission of Random House, an imprint and division of Penguin Random House LLC and Curtis Brown, Ltd. All rights reserved.

Elizabeth Bowen, "The Demon Lover" from *The Demon Lover and Other Stories*, 1945. Reproduced with permission of Curtis Brown Group Ltd, London on behalf of the beneficiaries of the Estate of Elizabeth Bowen. Copyright © Elizabeth Bowen, 1945.

Jericho Brown, "Prayer for the Backhanded." From *Please* (New Issues Press, 2008). Reprinted from *Split This Rock's The Quarry: A Social Justice Poetry Database*. Copyright © 2008 by Jericho Brown. Used with permission.

Octavia E. Butler, "Bloodchild" from *Bloodchild and Other Stories*. Originally published in Isaac Asimov's *Science Fiction Magazine* (June 1984). Copyright © 1984, 2005 by Octavia E. Butler. Reprinted with the permission of The Permissions Company, LLC on behalf of Seven Stories Press, sevenstories.com.

Italo Calvino, "The Enchanted Garden: from DIFFICULT LOVES, translated by William Weaver. Copyright 1949 by Giulio Einaudi editore, Torino. Copyright © 1958 by Giulio Einaudi editore, s.p.a. Torino. English translation copyright © 1983, 1984 by Houghton Mifflin Harcourt Publishing Company. Reprinted by permission of Mariner Books, an imprint of HarperCollins Publishers. All rights reserved.

Truman Capote, "Miriam," copyright 1945, 1946, 1947, 1948, 1949 by Truman Capote, © renewed 1976 by Truman Capote. Originally published in "Mademoiselle"; from A TREE OF NIGHT AND OTHER STORIES by Truman Capote. Used by permission of Random House, an imprint and division of Penguin Random House LLC. All rights reserved.

Dorothy Chan, "Ode to Chinese Superstitions," from *Poetry Magazine*, Copyright © October 2020 by Dorothy Chan. Used with permission.

Chen Chen, "I Invite My Parents to a Dinner Party." Academy of American Poets. Originally published in *Poem-a-Day* on April 19, 2018, by the Academy of American Poets. Copyright © 2018 by Chen Chen. Used with permission.

Caryl Churchill, "Top Girls." Methuen Drama. Copyright © 2018 by Caryl Churchill. An imprint of Bloomsbury Publishing Plc. Used with permission.

Ciardi, John. "Suburban," from FOR INSTANCE by John Ciardi. Copyright © 1979 by John Ciardi. Used by permission of W. W. Norton & Company, Inc.

Billy Collins, "The Lanyard" from *The Trouble With Poetry: and Other Poems* by Billy Collins, copyright © 2005 by Billy Collins. Used by permission of Random House, an imprint and division of Penguin Random House LLC. All rights reserved.

Sharon E. Cooper, "Mistaken Identity." Copyright © 2021 by Sharon E. Cooper. Used by permission of the author. www.Sharonecooper.com

ee cummings, "she being Brand." Copyright 1926, 1954, © 1991 by the Trustees for the E. E. Cummings Trust. Copyright © 1985 by George James Firmage, from COMPLETE POEMS: 1904–1962 by E. E. Cummings, edited by George J. Firmage. Used by permission of Liveright Publishing Corporation.

Roald Dahl, "Landlady." © Roald Dahl. Reprinted by kind permission of David Higham Associates. 'The Landlady' first appeared in 'Kiss Kiss.'

Toi Derricotte, "Black Boys Play the Classics" from *Tender* ©1997. Reprinted by permission of University of Pittsburgh Press.

Erick Didricksen, "Sonnet XVIII" from *Pop Sonnets: Shakespearean Spins on Your Favorite Songs*. Copyright © 2015 by Erick Didricksen. Reprinted with permission from Quirk Books.

Anthony Doerr, Chapter 3 and Chapter 4 from ALL THE LIGHT WE CANNOT SEE. Copyright © 2014 by Anthony Doerr. Reprinted with the permission of Scribner, a division of Simon & Schuster, Inc. All rights reserved.

Katherine Dunn, "The Nuclear Family: His Talk, Her Teeth" from GEEK LOVE by Katherine Dunn, 1989 by Katherine Dunn. Used by permission of Alfred A. Knopf, an imprint of the Knopf Doubleday Publishing Group, a division of Penguin Random House LLC. All rights reserved.

Index

IDEA BANK

Abstraction
Achievement
Adventure
Aestheticism
Alienation
Altruism
Ambition
Anger
Anonymity
Apocalypse
Appearance
Art
Artificiality
Attraction
Authenticity
Authority
Avant-garde
Balance
Beauty
Betrayal
Carpe Diem
Celebration
Change
Character
Class
Comedy
Comfort
Communication
Community
Confidence
Conflict
Conformity
Confusion

Connection
Consciousness
Consequence
Continuity
Contradiction
Contrast
Control
Control
Convention
Conviction
Corruption
Courage
Creativity
Criticism
Critique
Culture
Curiosity
Deception
Dependency
Depravity
Depression
Desire
Despair
Despondency
Destiny
Detachment
Devastation
Development
Devotion
Didacticism
Dignity
Dilemma
Disconnection

Disenchantment
Disillusionment
Disintegration
Distortion
Distrust
Doubt
Eccentricity
Education
Egoism
Emotion
Empathy
Endurance
Environment
Ethnocentrism
Evil
Evolution
Exaggeration
Excess
Exotic (the)
Experience
Experimentation
Expression
Facade
Faith
Falsehood
Family
Fantasy
Fate
Faustian
Feelings
Fervor
Flaw
Fluidity

Forgiveness
Formality
Fortune
Fragmentation
Frivolity
Frustration
Futility
Gender
Good
Gothic (the)
Government
Greed
Guilt
Heritage
Heroism
History
Honesty
Honor
Hubris
Humanism
Humanity
Humor
Ideal
Idealism
Identities
Identity
Illusion
Imagination
Immortality
Imperialism
Impression
Impulse
Incongruity